21世紀世界人名典拠録 欧文名

3 索引

日外アソシエーツ

Noted Personalities of the World in the 21th-Century

Reference Guide with Japanese Readings of Each Personal Name

3 Index

Compiled by
Nichigai Associates, Inc.

本書はディジタルデータでご利用いただくことができます。詳細はお問い合わせください。

●編集スタッフ● 小川 修司／青木 竜馬／山本 幸子／岡田 真弓／村末 照代／成田 さくら子

凡　例

1. 索引見出し

1）本文に収録した人名の見出しの片仮名表記、およびすべての片仮名異表記の、主に姓の部分を見出しとした。

2）収録した片仮名表記は、61,700 件である。

2. 排　列

1）片仮名表記の五十音順に排列した。

2）排列上、濁音・半濁音は清音扱い、拗促音は直音扱いとし、長音符（ー）や中点（・）は無視した。またヱ→エ、ヲ→オとみなした。

3）姓が同一の場合は、原綴の ABC 順に排列した。

3. 所在指示

本文の原綴見出しとその掲載ページを示した。

【ア】

ア
A, Lai 1
アー
A, Lai 1
Awe, Micah 72
アアマラ
Aamara, Abdelkader 1
アイ
Ai, Wei-wei 21
アイアー
Iyer, Ananth V. 654
アイアコッカ
Iacocca, Lee A. 641
アイアコノ
Iacono, William G. 641
アイアトン
Ireton, William 649
アイアネッタ
Iannetta, Chris 642
アイアポーズ
Iapoce, Anthony 642
アイアランド
Ireland, Christopher 649
Ireland, David E. 649
Ireland, Liz 649
アイアンガー
Iyengar, B.K.S. 654
アイアンサイド
Ironside, J.W. 649
Ironside, Virginia 649
アイアンシティ
Iansiti, Marco 642
アイアンズ
Irons, Diane 649
Irons, Jeremy 649
アイヴァス
Ajvaz, Michal 23
アイヴァースン
Iverson, Cheryl 653
アイヴァーセン
Iversen, Leslie L. 653
アイヴァーソン
Iverson, Allen 653
アイヴァリー
Ivereigh, Austen 653
アイヴァリオティス
Aivaliotis, Dimitri 22
アイヴァン
Ivan, Liera Manuel 653
アイヴィデ・リンドクヴィスト
Ajvide Lindqvist, John 23
アイヴィミ
Ivimy, John 654
アイヴィンズ
Ivins, Molly 654
アイウォラー
Iworah, *Prince* Charles 654
アイヴォリー
Ivory, James 654
Ivory, Michael 654
アイヴォリィ
Ivory, James 654
アイヴス
Ives, Harris G. 653
Ives, Martine 653
Ives, Susanna 653
アイエ
Ahye, Michelle-Lee 21
Aie, Michele Delle 21
Aye, Fouad Ahmed 73
アイェウ
Ayew, Andre 73
アイエティ
Ajeti, Arlind 23
アイェド
Ayed, Jelloul 73
アイエバ
Ayéva, Zarifou 73
アイエロ
Aiello, Rita 22
アイエンガー
Iyengar, Sheena 654
アイオアディ
Ayoade, Richard 74
アイオスファ
Iosefa, Joey 648
アイオニディス
Ioannidis, Matthew 648
アイオミ
Iommi, Tony 648
アイガー
Iger, Robert Allen 643
アイカード
Ikard, Gabe 644
アイカーン
Icahn, Carl 643
Icahn, Gail 643
アイギ
Aigi, Gennadii 22
アイギュン
Aygun, Nafi 73
アイク
Icke, David 643
アイクス
Ickes, William John 643
アイグナー
Aigner, Hannes 22
Aigner, Ilse 22
Aigner, Martin 22
アイグナー・クラーク
Aigner-Clark, Julie 22
アイグラー
Eigler, Florian 394
アイグルハート
Iglehart, James Monroe 643
アイゲン
Eigen, Manfred 394
アイケングリーン
Eichengreen, Barry 393
アイケンバウム
Eichenbaum, Luise 393
アイケンベリー
Ikenberry, G.John 644
アイコエ
Ayikoe, Kossivi 73
アイコフ
Eickhoff, Jerad 394
アイサ
Aissa, Mohamed 22
al-Aissa, Shawqi 22
アイザクセン
Isaksen, Margaux 650
アイサコフ
Isacoff, Stuart 650
アイサタ
Aïssata, Amadou 22
アイザック
Isaak, Marcel 650
Issac, Mary 652
アイザックス
Isaacs, Cheryl Boone 650
Isaacs, David 650
Isaacs, Florence 650
Isaacs, Gregory 650
Isaacs, Susan 650
アイザックソン
Isaacson, Clifford E. 650
Isaacson, Rupert 650
Isaacson, Walter 650
アイザード
Isard, Walter 650
アイサノア・デルカルピオ
Ayzanoa del Carpio, Gerardo 74
アイザノフ
Isanove, Richard 650
アイザーマンズ
IJzermans, Theo 644
アイザルド
Isard, Peter 650
アイザワ
Aizawa, Hatsuro 22
アイジ
Ahizi, Aka Daniel 19
アイシャ
Aisha, Mohammed Mussa 22
アイシャム
Isham, C.J. 651
Isham, Mark 651
アイジョン
Ayllón, Cecilia 73
アイシンジュエルオ
Aixinjueluo, Xian-qi 22
アイス・サランユー
Ice Sarunyu 643
アイスター
Eyster, M.Elaine 414
アイスナー
Eisner, Michael Dammann 395
Eisner, Thomas 395
アイズナー
Eisner, Michael Dammann 395
Eisner, Will 395
アイスバーグ＝トホーフト
Eisberg-'t Hooft, Saskia 394
アイズピリ
Aizpili, Paul 22
アイズマン
Eiseman, Leatrice 394
Eisman, Kathryn 395
アイスラー
Eisler, Barry 394
Eisler, Riane Tennenhaus 394
アイズラー
Isler, Saul 651
アイスランド
Iceland, John 643
アイズリー
Eiseley, Loren C. 394
Eisley, Anthony 394
アイスレイン
Eiselein, Gregory 394
アイスワート
Eiswert, David 395
アイセイ
Isay, David 650
アイ・ゼット
I.Z. 654
アイゼレ
Eisele, Petra 394
アイゼン
Eisen, Cliff 394
Eisen, Jane L. 394
Eisen, Jonathan 394
Eisen, Peter J. 394
Eisen, Roland 394
アイセンアッカー
Eisenecker, Ulrich 394
アイゼンク
Eysenck, Michael W. 414
アイゼンシュタイン
Eisenstein, Bernice 394
アイゼンシュタット
Eisenstadt, Shmuel Noah 394
Eisenstat, Russell A. 394
アイゼンスタット
Eisenstadt, Shmuel Noah 394
Eisenstat, Russell A. 394
アイゼンステイン
Eisenstein, Elizabeth L. 394
Eisenstein, Zillah R. 394
アイゼンドラス
Eisendrath, Craig R. 394
アイゼンハウアー
Eisenhower, Dwight David 394
アイゼンバーグ
Eisenberg, Arlene 394
Eisenberg, David 394
Eisenberg, Jesse 394
Eisenberg, Laura Zittrain 394
Eisenberg, Melvin Aron 394
Isenberg, Barbara S. 651
Issenberg, Sasha 652
アイゼンハート
Eisenhardt, Kathleen M. 394
アイゼンバート
Eisenbarth, Pia 394
アイゼンハワー
Eisenhauer, Peggy 394
Eisenhower, Dwight David 394
Eisenhower, John 394
アイゼンブルガー
Eisenburger, Doris 394
アイゼンマン
Eisenman, Peter 394
アイソム
Isom, Lanier Scott 652
アイダック
Ayduk, Ozlem 73
アイタミ・アルティレス
Aythami Artiles 74
アイダム
Aïdam, Célestine Akouavi 21
Aïdam, Georges Kwawu 21
アイダラリエフ
Aydaraliev, Taalaybek 73
Aydaraliyev, Iskenderbek 73
アイダルス

al-Aidarous, Amir Salem 21
アイダルベコフ
Aidarbekov, Chingiz 21
アイチケエワ
Aitikeyeva, Toktobubu 22
アイチフェルド
Eichfeld, Casey 393
アイチモワ
Aitimova, Byrganym 22
アイテー
Ayitey, Hanny-Sherry 73
アイデ
Eide, Espen Barth 394
アイティ
Ayitey, Hanny-Sherry 73
アイディ
Aïdi, Saïd 21
Aydi, Said 73
アイディード
Aldeed, Hussein Mohamed Farah 27
アイテキン
Aytekin, Fevzi 74
アイデランド
Eydeland, Alexander 414
アイデル
Eydal, Guðný 414
アイデルバーグ
Eidelberg, J. 394
アイド
al-Ayed, Ali 73
アイド・アルマグロ
Aído Almagro, Bibiana 21
アイドゥン
Aydin, Mehmet 73
アイドガン
Aydogan, Can Luka 73
アイドグディエフ
Aidogdyev, Dortkuli 21
Aydogdyev, Durtguly 73
Aydogdyyev, Maksat 73
アイドグドイエフ
Aidogdyev, Dortkuli 21
Aidogdyev, Orazgeldy 21
アイトジャノワ
Aitzhanova, Zhanar 22
アイトデハーゲ
Uytdehaage, Jochem 1437
アイトバエフ
Aitbayev, Tashtemir 22
アイトマートフ
Aitmatov, Chingiz Torekulovich 22
アイトマトフ
Aitmatov, Askar 22
Aitmatov, Chingiz Torekulovich 22
アイトマン
Eiteman, David K. 395
アイトムルザエフ
Aytmurzayev, Nurlan 74
アイドル
Idle, Eric 643
アイトール・カンタラピエドラ
Aitor Cantalapiedra 22
アイドルソン
Eidelson, Meyer 394
アイトール・ブニュエル
Aitor Bunuel 22
アイトン
Ayton, Sarah 74
アイドン
Aydin, Koray 73
アイナ
Aina, Ola 22
アイニ
Aini, Martin 22
アイニーナ
Ainina, Hindou Mint 22
アイネス
Innes, John F. 647
アイノン
Einon, Dorothy 394
アイバー
Aybar, Erick 73
アイバジャン
Ayvazian, Vardan 74
アイバーセン
Iversen, Kristen 653
Iversen, Portia 653
アイバーソン
Iverson, Allen 653
Iverson, Ken 653
アイバーン
al-Aiban, Musaed bin Mohammed 21
アイバン
al-Aiban, Musaed bin Mohammed 21
アイバンス
Ivins, Bruce E. 654
アイビー
Ivey, Susan M. 653
アイビイ
Ivey, Allen E. 653
Ivey, Mary Bradford 653
アイヒヴァルト
Eichwald, Maria 394
アイヒェル
Eichel, Hans 393
アイヒナー
Aigner, Hannes 22
アイヒホルン
Eichhorn, Jan 393
アイヒラー
Eichler, Wolfgang 393
アイヒンガー
Aichinger, Ilse 21
Eichinger, Bernd 393
アイビンス
Ivins, Molly 654
アイビンズ
Ivins, Bruce E. 654
Ivins, Molly 654
アーイブ
al-Ayib, Abdulqadir Mohammad 73
アイブ
Ibe, Jordon 642
アイファート
Eifert, Georg H. 394
Eifert, Tyler 394
アイフェル
Eifel, Patricia J. 394
アイブス
Ives, Clay 653
アイフディ
Ifedi, Germain 643
Ifedi, Martin 643
アイ・ブニャミン
Ayik Bunyamin 73
アイブル・アイベスフェルト
Eibl-Eibesfeldt, Irenaus 393
アイヘル
Eichel, Hans 393
アイヘルブルク
Aichelburg, Peter C. 21
アイボリー
Ivory, Chris 654
Ivory, James 654
Ivory, Judith 654
Ivory, Lesley Anne 654
アイマール
Aimar, Pablo 22
アイモ
Aimo, Tony 22
アイヤー
Eyer, Diane E. 414
Eyre, Linda 414
Eyre, Richard M. 414
Iyer, Pico 654
アイヤーズ
Ayers, Akeem 73
Ayers, DeMarcus 73
Ayers, Robert 73
アイヤル
Aiyar, Mani Shankar 22
アイユー
IU 653
アイラ
Aira, César 22
アイラペティアン
Ayrapetyan, David 74
アイリッシュ
Irish, Jeffrey S. 649
Irish, Martin 649
アイリフ
Ayliffe, Alex 73
アイリョン・キスベルト
Ayllon Quisbert, Angela Karin 73
アイル
Ailu 22
アイルズ
Iles, Greg 644
アイルソン
Ireson, Judith 649
アイルランド
Ireland, Kathy 649
Ireland, Michael 649
Ireland, R.Duane 649
Ireland, Stephen 649
アイレス
Ayres, Honor 74
Ayres, J.G. 74
Ayres, John 74
アイレス・ペレイラ
Aires Pereira, Antonio Juracy 22
アイレルス
Eilers, Justin 394
アイワジアン
Aivazian, Artur 22
アイン
Anh, Chu Ngoc 49
Anh, Hoang Tuan 49
Anh, Le Hong 49
Anh, Tran Tuan 49
アインジガー
Einziger, Michael 394
アインスバーグ
Ainsberg, Arthur 22
アインテ
Aynte, Cabdirixman Yusuf Ali 74
Eynte, Abdirahman Yusuf Ali 414
アインホルン
Einhorn, Stefan 394
アインホーン
Einhorn, Amy 394
Einhorn, David 394
Einhorn, Eddie 394
アーヴ
Aav, Marianne 1
アウ
Au, Tsukutlane 68
Au, Wagner James 68
アウー
Haour, Georges 568
アウアー
Auer, Ken 69
Auer, Margit 69
Auer, Peter 69
Auer, Wolfgang M. 69
アーヴァイン
Irvine, Alexander C. 649
Irvine, William Braxton 649
アヴァッローネ
Avallone, Silvia 71
アヴァネシアン
Avanesyan, Hrachya 71
アウアバック
Auerbach, Red 69
アウアーバッハ
Auerbach, Red 69
アヴァンツィーニ
Avanzini, Lena 71
アヴィ
Avi 71
アヴィグドル
Avigdor, Barrett S. 71
アヴィーソン
Avieson, Bunty 71
アヴィーチー
Avicii 71
アーウィット
Erwitt, Elliott 408
アヴィル
Avril, Lynne 72
アーウィン
Erwin, Ellen 408
Erwin, Steve 408
Irwin, Alexander C. 650
Irwin, Bill 650
Irwin, David G. 650
Irwin, Manley R. 650
Irwin, Michael R. 650
Irwin, Neil 650
Irwin, Richard S. 650
Irwin, Steve 650
Irwin, Will 650
Irwin, William 650
Urwin, Cathy 1436
アーヴィン
Ervin, Anthony 407
Irvin, Candace 649
Irvin, Monte 649
Irvine, Alexander C. 649
アーヴィング
Irving, Clifford 649
Irving, John 649
Irving, Mark 649
アウヴェス
Alves, Daniel 38
アウヴェルター
Auwärter, Heinrich 71

アヴェイ
Avei, Ole 71
アウェケ
Ahoueke, Max 21
アウェサ
Awesa, Francis 72
アヴェディキアン
Avédikian, Serge 71
アヴェドン
Avedon, Richard 71
アヴェニ
Aveni, Anthony F. 71
アヴェラ
Avella, Natalie 71
アヴェラール
Avelar, Danilo 71
アヴェ＝ラルマン
Avé-Lallemant, Ursula 71
アヴェランジェ
Havelange, João 583
アウェリカ
Awerika, Tanieru 72
アヴェルバッハ
Averbakh, IUriĭ 71
アヴェルブフ
Averbukh, Ilia 71
アウォリ
Awori, Aggrey 72
Awori, Moody 72
アウガ
Auga, Augustine 69
アウク
Auch, Mary Jane 69
アウクシュタイン
Augstein, Rudolf 69
アウグシュタイン
Augstein, Rudolf 69
アウグスト
August, Bille 69
Augusto, Jessica 69
Augusto, Jose 69
アウグストゥソン
Agustsson, Gudni 19
アウグスト・フェルナンデス
Augusto Fernandez 69
アウクラン
Aukland, Anders 70
アウグリス
Augulis, Uldis 69
アウゲロ
Augello, Haley 69
アウケン
Auken, Ida 70
Auken, Svend 70
アウス
Ahoussou, Jeannot Kouadio 21
アウスゲイル・ジョウンソン
Ásgeir Jónsson 63
アウスト＝クラウス
Aust-Claus, Elisabeth 70
アウズルン
Ousland, Borge 1064
アウスロイグ・ヨーンスドッティル
Áslaug Jónsdóttir 65
アウセジョ
Ausejo, Lorena 70
アウゼル
Houzel, Didier 627
アウタガバイア
Autagavaia, Fa'atoina 71
アウタリッジ
Outteridge, Nathan 1064
アウッジャル
Aujjar, Mohammed 70
アウティ
Autti, Antti 71
アウディ
Audi, Raymond 69
Awodey, Steve 72
アウティオ
Autio, Jonas 71
アウディナ・チプタワン
Audina Tjiptawan, Mia 69
アヴディヤイ
Avdijaj, Donis 71
アヴデーエワ
Avdeeva, Yulianna 71
アウテマン
Altheman, Maria Suelen 37
アウデルス
Auders, Āris 69
アウテレロ
Outerelo, Luiz 1064
アウデロ
Audero, Emil 69
アウド
Aoudou, Joseph 52
アウドア
Audoa, Anthony 69
アウトゥオリ
Autuori, Paulo 71
アウトリム
Outtrim, Eliza 1064
アヴネル
Avenel, Antony 71
アウーノー
Awoonor, Kofi Nyidevu 72
アウノー
Awoonor, Kofi Nyidevu 72
アウバート
Aubart, Johann 68
アウファルト
Auffarth, Sandra 69
アウフガング
Aufgang, Joel 69
アウフデンブラッテン
Aufdenblatten, Fraenzi 69
アウベス
Alves, Daniel 38
Alves, Oswald 38
Alves, Wellinton 38
アウベリー
Aubeli, Otto 68
アウマン
Aumann, Robert John 70
アウミレル
Aumiller, Andrzej 70
アヴュツキー
Avioutskii, Viatcheslav 72
アウラキ
al-Awlaki, Anwar 72
al-Awlaqi, Nihal Ali 72
アウラキ師
al-Awlaki, Anwar 72
アウリ
Auri, Lucio 70
アウリカ
Aulika, Halani 70
アヴリッチ
Avrich, Paul 72
アウリッヒ
Aulich, Bruno 70
アヴリル
Avril, Francois 72
Avril, Philippe 72
アウール
Ahoure, Murielle 21
アウル
Auel, Jean M. 69
アウルダル
Aurdal, Aleksander 70
アウレスク
Aurescu, Bogdan 70
アウレスティア
Aulestia, Diego 70
アウレンティ
Aulenti, Gae 70
アヴロン
Avron, Philippe 72
アウワド
Aouad, Abderhamid 52
Awwad, Jawad 72
アウワーバッハー
Auerbacher, Inge 69
アウン
Aoun, Mario 52
Aoun, Michel 52
アウン・キン
Aung Khin 70
アウン・サン
Aung San 70
アウン・サン・スー・チー
Aung San Suu Kyi 70
アウン・ジー
Aung Gyi 70
アウン・ジイ
Aung Gyi 70
アウン・タウン
Aung Thaung 70
アウン・チー
Aung Kyi 70
アウン・トゥ
Aung Thu 70
アウン・ナイン
Aung Naing 70
アウン・ポウン
Aung Phone 70
アウン・ミン
Aung Min 70
アオヴィニ
Auvini, Kadresengane 71
アオキ
Aoki, Albert Masaji 52
Aoki, Naoka 52
Aoki, Steve 52
アオゴ
Aogo, Dennis 52
アオメイズニュ
Ahoomey-zunu, Kwesi Séléagodji 21
アオンドアカ
Aondoakaa, Mike 52
アーカー
Aaker, David A. 1
Aaker, Jennifer Lynn 1
アーガ
Agha, Irfan A. 17
アガ
al-Agha, Haifaa 17
Agha, Mohammed 17
Agha, Riyadh Nāsan 17
Agha, Sayd Ghiasuddin 17
Agha, Sayed Ekramuddin 17
アガー
Agur, Anne M.R. 19
アカアイジ
Akaahizi, Daniel 23
アカーエフ
Akayev, Askar Akayevich 23
アカエフ
Akayev, Askar Akayevich 23
Akkaev, Khadzhimurat 24
アガエフ
Aghayev, Rustam 17
アカガムバ
Akaga Mba, Christophe 23
アーガー・カーン
Aga Khan Ⅳ 17
アガ・カーン4世
Aga Khan Ⅳ 17
アガグ
Agagu, Olusegun 17
アカサキ
Akasaki, Isamu 23
アガザデ
Aqazadeh, Gholamreza 54
アガザリアン
Agazarian, Yvonne M. 17
アガサンスキー
Agacinski, Sylviane 16
アガシ
Agassi, Andre 17
Agassi, Joseph 17
Agazzi, Ernesto 17
アカス
Akass, Kim 23
アガスティア
Agasthiya, Sri 17
アガタ
Agatha Bednarczuk 17
アガダジ
Agadazi, Ouro Koura 17
アガツトン
Agatston, Arthur 17
アガーティ
Agati, Magdi el 17
アカディリ
Akadiri, Saliou 23
アガニ
Agani, Ferid 17
アーガー・ハーン
Aga Khan Ⅳ 17
アガ・ハーン
Aga Khan Ⅳ 17
アガビ
Agabi, Kanu Godwin 16
アカマツ
Akamatsu, Nelo 23
アガム
Agam, Yaacov 17
アガムイラドフ
Agamyradov, Purli 17
アカランガ
Akaranga, Moses 23
アカーランド
Akerlund, Jonas 23
アーカリ
Arcari, Jason 55
アガリ

Aghali, Mano 17
アガル・アヤル
Agar Ayar, Malik 17
アガルウォル
Agarwal, Sanjiv 17
アカルディ
Accardi, Luigi 10
アカルド
Accardo, Pasquale J. 10
アカロフ
Akerlof, George Arthur 23
アガーワル
Agarwal, Sunil 17
アガワル
Aggarwal, Vinod K. 17
アカン
Akunne, Derek 24
アガンガ
Aganga, Olusegun 17
アカンジ
Akanji, Manuel 23
アーカンド
Arcand, Kimberly K. 55
アカンバーク
Achenbach, Joel 10
アガンベン
Agamben, Giorgio 17
アカンポーラ
Acampora, Ralph 10
アギー
Agee, Tommie 17
アギアル
Aguiar, Mayra 18
アギアールブランコ
Aguiar-branco, José Pedro 18
アギアレイ
Aguirre, Ann 18
アギウス
Agius, Marcus Ambrose Paul 17
アキガ
Akiga, Steven 24
アギガ
Aguigah, Angèle 18
アキク
Achike, Onochie 10
アキシルロッド
Axilrod, S.H. 73
アキタ
Akita, George 24
アギトン
Aguiton, Christophe 19
アギナガ
Novoa Aguinaga, Juan Camilo 1035
アギニス
Aguinis, Marcos 18
アギニャガ
Aguiñaga, Marcela 18
アキーノ
Aquino, Aristides 54
Aquino, Jayson 54
アキノ
Aquino, Albert 54
Aquino, Benigno 54
Aquino, Corazón 54
Aquino, Joe 54
アキノ・アルベングリン
Aquino Albengrin, Alexis Paul 54
アキノ・ガルシア
Aquino García, Ramón 54
アキバ
Akiba 24
アーキブージ
Archibugi, Daniele 56
アキマシュカダリウ
Achimaş-cadariu, Patriciu 10
アキモフ
Akimov, Boris B. 24
アキモン
Atchimon, Charles 67
アキヤマ
Akiyama, Bruce 24
アギュイイロンシ
Aguiyi-ironsi, Thomas 19
アーギュラ
Argula, Anne 57
アキュンレル
Akunler, Nazan 24
アギョン
Aghion, Gaby 17
アギラ
Aguilar, Jesus 18
アギラシンセール
Aguilar Zinser, Adolfo Miguel 18
アギラール
Aguilar, José M. 18
Aguilar, Víctor 18
アギラル
Aguilar, Alvaro 18
Aguilar, Felipe 18
Aguilar, Pepe 18
Aguilar, Roberto 18
Aguilar, Sandra 18
Kaguilar Chacon, Karel 695
アギラル・ゴメス
Aguilar Gómez, Roberto Iván 18
アギラル・ピネダ
Aguilar Pineda, Carlos Roberto 18
アギラール・リベロ
Aguilar Rivero, Rosa 18
アキール
Aqeel, Moinuddin 54
アキル
Aqil, Aqil Husayn 54
アギーレ
Aguirre, Adalberto, Jr. 18
Aguirre, Damaris 18
Aguirre, Javier 18
Aguirre, Jeinkler 18
Aguirre, Jose Antonio 18
Aguirre, Mason 19
Aguirre, Vitaliano 19
アギレ
Aguirre, Francisco 18
Aguirre, Marcelo 19
アキレオス
Achilleos, Georgios 10
アギレサバラ
Aguirrezabala, Martín 19
アギレチェ
Agirretxe, Imanol 17
アギレ・マルティネス
Aguirre Martinez, Juan 19
アギレラ
Aguilera, Christina 18
Aguilera, Rodolfo 18
アギレラ・マリン
Aguilera Marin, Pablo Enrique 18
アキロフ
Akilov, Akil 24
アーキン
Arkin, Alan 58
Arkin, David 58
Arkin, William M. 58
アキン
Akin, Fatih 24
アキンデス・アデクペジュ
Akindes Adekpedjou, Sylvain 24
アキンデス・アデペジュ
Akindes Adekpedjou, Sylvain 24
アキンフェエフ
Akinfeev, Igor 24
アクア
Akua, Riddell 24
アクアー
Acquah, Afriyie 11
アグア
Aguad, Oscar 18
アグアヨ
Aguayo, Perro, Jr. 18
アクアララアティポー
Akouala Atipault, Alain 24
アクアララアティポール
Akouala Atipault, Alain 24
アグアラサヌ
Ag Alassane, Agathane 17
アグ・アラサネ
Ag Alassane, Agathane 17
アクィスタ
Acquista, Angelo 11
アクイスト
Acquisto, Charles J. 11
アクイラーニ
Aquilani, Alberto 54
アクイル
Acuil, Awut Deng 11
アグエイアス
Argüelles, José 57
アーグエイエス
Argüelles, José 57
Argüelles, Miriam 57
アグエイヨ
Aguayo, Roberto 18
アークェット
Arquette, Patricia 61
Arquette, Rosanna 61
アークエット
Arquette, Patricia 61
Arquette, Rosanna 61
アクエティ
Acouetey, Massan Loretta 11
アグエロ
Aguero, Matias 18
Agüero, Pablo 18
Aguero, Sergio 18
アグエロ・ララ
Agüero Lara, María Dolores 18
アクオゼル
Aközer, Emel 24
アクギュル
Akgul, Taha 23
アクク
Akuku, Ancentus 24
アクシット
Aksit, Güldal 24
アクシト
Aksit, Güldal 24
アクージャ
Agulla, Horacio 19
アクショーネンコ
Aksenenko, Nikolai Yemelyanovich 24
アクショネンコ
Aksenenko, Nikolai Yemelyanovich 24
アクショーノフ
Aksenoff, E. 24
Aksenov, Vasilii Pavlovich 24
Aksyonov, Sergei Valeryevich 24
アクショノフ
Aksenoff, E. 24
Aksyonov, Sergei Valeryevich 24
アクス
Aksu, Abdulkadir 24
Aksu, Sezen 24
アグス
Agus, Milena 19
アグスティアニ
Agustiani, Sri Wahyuni 19
アクスト
Akst, Daniel 24
Axt, Peter 73
アクスト＝ガーデルマン
Axt-Gadermann, Michaela 73
アグストッソン
Agustsson, Gudni 19
アグストーニ
Agustoni, Daniel 19
アクスライン
Axline, Virginia Mae 73
アクセノクス
Aksenoks, Aivars 24
アクセノフ
Aksenoff, E. 24
アクセル
Axel, Gabriel 72
Axel, Richard 72
アクゼル
Aczel, Amir D. 11
Aczel, Peter 11
アクセルセン
Akselsen, Olav 24
Axelsen, Viktor 72
アクセルソン
Axelson, Jan 73
Axelson, Peter 73
Axelsson, Carina 73
Axelsson, Per 73
アクセルロッド
Axelrod, Alan 72
Axelrod, Beth 72
Axelrod, Emily M. 72
Axelrod, George 72
Axelrod, Julius 72
Axelrod, Richard H. 72
Axelrod, Robert M. 72
アクセロス
Axelos, Kostas 72
アクタ
Acta, Manny 11
アクター
Achter, A.J. 10
Actor, Jeffrey K. 11

Akhtar, Ayad 23
アクダー
Akdağ, Recep 23
アグダシュルー
Aghdashloo, Shohreh 17
アクタル
Akhtar, Miriam 24
アクチオグル
Axchioglou, Efi 72
アクチャカヤ
Akcakaya, H.R. 23
アグテ
Agte, Patrick 18
アクティマイアー
Achtemeier, Paul J. 10
アクドアン
Akdoğan, Yalçin 23
アクナザロワ
Aknazarova, Roza 24
アクニイリ
Akunyili, Dora 24
アクニス
Akunis, Ofir 24
アクニャ
Acunña, Luis 11
アグニュー
Agnew, Eleanor 18
Agnew, Harold 18
Agnew, Thomas George Arnold 18
アクニリ
Akunyili, Dora 24
アクーニン
Akunin, Boris 24
アグネ
Agne, Abdourahim 17
アグネタ
Agnetha 18
アグネッタ
Agnetha 18
アクバー
Achbar, Mark 10
アグバ
Agba, Charles Condji 17
Agba, Kondi Charles 17
アークハート
Urquhart, Brian 1436
Urquhart, Ian Thomas 1436
アクバト
Akbat, Ahmed 23
アクハブ
Achab, Jaouad 10
アクハリ
al-Akhali, Ra'afat 23
アグバリ
al-Aghbari, Ghazi Shaif 17
アクバル
Akbar, Mohammad 23
Akbar, Rosy 23
アクバロワ
Akbarova, Farida 23
アクパン
Akpan, Rita 24
アクフォー
Addo-kufuor, Kwame 14
アクフォアド
Akufo-addo, Nana Addo Dankwa 24
アクプロガン
Akplogan, Fatiou 24
アグベトメイ
Agbetomey, Pius 17
アグベニエヌ
Agbegnenou, Clarisse 17
アグボ
Agbo, Joseph 17
Agbo, Uche 17
アグボス
Agbossou, Bernadette Sohoudji 17
アグボブリ
Agbobli, Edoh Kodjo 17
アクポム
Akpom, Chuba 24
アグボリ
Agboli, Hope 17
アグホロー
Agholor, Nelson 17
アクマタリエフ
Akmataliyev, Temirbek 24
アクマメドフ
Akmammedov, Myratgeldi 24
アグマン
Agman, Gilles 17
アクマンメドフ
Akmammedov, Seyitmammet 24
アグム
Agum, Gumelar 19
アクムイラドフ
Akmyradov, Makhtumkuli 24
アクムフィ
Akumfi, Christopher Ameyaw 24
アクムラドフ
Akmyradov, Makhtumkuli 24
アグヤポング
Agyapong, Felix Owusu 19
アグラシビリ
Agulashvili, Gigla 19
アクラム
Akram, Omar 24
Akram, Sheikh Waqas 24
アクラム・アフィフ
Akram Afif 24
アグラワール
Agrawal, Govind P. 18
アグラワル
Agrawal, Neeraj 18
アクリー
Ackley, Dustin 10
アグリ
Agre, Peter C. 18
アグリエッタ
Aglietta, Michel 17
アークル
Arkell, Vincent Thomas John 58
Arkle, Peter 58
アーグル
Eargle, John 387
アクル
Akour, Abdul Rahim 24
アグルカック
Aglukkaq, Leona 17
アグレ
Agre, Peter C. 18
アグレイ
Aggrey, Albert 17
アークレス
Arkless, Jan 58
アグレスタ
Agresta, Julie 18
アクレドロ
Acredolo, Linda P. 11
アグロ
Aglo, John Siabi Kwamé-Koma 17
アクロイド
Ackroyd, Peter 11
Aykroyd, Dan 73
アグロウ
Uglow, Jennifer S. 1432
アグロトゥ
Agroti, Androula 18
アクワ
al-Akwa'a, Abdulrahman 24
アクワア
al-Akwa'a, Abdullah 24
アークーン
Ah-Koon, Didier 19
アクンド
Akhund, Mohammad Isa 24
アグンドゥクア・ムビサ
Agoundoukoua Mbissa, Albertine 18
アグンロエ
Agunloye, Olu 19
アケ
Ake, Nathan 23
Aké, Natondé 23
アゲエフ
Ageeb, Aleksandr 17
アケソン
Akesson, Elizabeth J. 23
アケチェ
Aketxe, Ager 23
アケチーオクロ
Akech-okullo, Betty Grace 23
アゲナ
Agena, Craig John 17
アケリドウ
Akkelidou, Costandia 24
アケルマン
Akerman, Chantal 23
アゲレ
Aguerre, Tabaré 18
アケロイド
Akeroyd, Simon 23
アーゲン
Ergen, Charlie 406
アケンボ
Ake N'gbo, Gilbert Marie 23
アコイタイ
Akoitai, Sam 24
アーコウィッツ
Arkowitz, Hal 58
アゴシン
Agosín, Marjorie 18
アゴス
Agossou, Albert 18
アコスタ
Acosta, Alberto 11
Acosta, Alexander 11
Acosta, Allan James 11
Acosta, Carlos 11
Acosta, Mario Ernesto 11
Acosta, Patricio 11
Acosta Valdez, Luz Mercedes 11
アゴスタ
Agosta, William C. 18
アコスタ・サンタナ
Acosta Santana, Fernando 11
アコスタドゥアルテ
Acosta Duarte, Osmai 11
アコスタバルデス
Acosta Valdez, Luz Mercedes 11
アコスタ・モンタルバン
Acosta Montalván, Iván Adolfo 11
アゴスティ
Agosti, Silvano 18
アゴスティネリ
Agostinelli, Maria Enrica 18
アゴスト
Agosto, Benjamin 18
アコテ
Akotey, Mohamed 24
アコード
Acord, David 11
Acord, Lance 11
アゴバカ
Agovaka, Peter Shanel 18
アコビ
Akobi, Ahmed 24
アコビャン
Hakobyan, Hranush 556
アコピャン
Hakobyan, Hranush 556
アーコフ
Arkoff, Samuel Z. 58
アーゴフ
Argov, Sherry 57
アコフォジ
Akofodji, Grégoire 24
アーコム
Arkhom, Termpittayapaisith 58
アコル
Akol, Jacob J. 24
アコロ
Akolo, Lisiate Aloveita 24
アゴン
Agon, Jean-Paul 18
アコンド
Akhond, Abdol Razaq 23
Akhond, Mohammad Hasan 23
Akhond, Obaidollah 23
アーサ
Arthur, Beatrice 61
アーサー
Arthur, Beatrice 61
Arthur, Charles 61
Arthur, Darrell 61
Arthur, Elizabeth 61
Arthur, James 61
Arthur, James G. 61
Arthur, Jenny Lyvette 61
Arthur, Kay 61
Arthur, Linda B. 61
Arthur, Lisa 62
Arthur, M. 62
Arthur, Owen 62
Arthur, Paul 62
Arthur, Robert 62
Arthur, W.Brian 62
アサイ
Asai, Carrie 62

ア

アサイアス
Assayas, Michka 65
アザーイザ
Azaizeh, Wajih 74
アザイゼ
Azayzah, Wajih 74
アサイヤス
Assayas, Olivier 65
アザウィ
Azzaoui, Ismail 75
アサウォナク
Asayonak, Petr 62
アサガ
Asaga, Moses 62
アサカロフ
Assakalov, Rustam 65
アサガロフ
Asagaroff, Grischa 62
アサダウスカイテ
Asadauskaite, Laura 62
アザチャン
Azatyan, Karen 74
アサディ
al-Asadi, Adil 62
アーザード
Azād, Mahmūd 74
アサド
Asad, Talal 62
Assad, Bashar al 65
Assad, Thomas Joseph 65
Assado, Odair 65
Assado, Sergio 65
Azad, Bahman 74
アザド
Ajada, Humayuna 22
Azad, Abudus Samad 74
Azad, Abul Kalam 74
Azad, Ghulam Nabi 74
アサドフ
Asadov, Heydar 62
アサトリャン
Asatryan, Artem 62
アサートン
Atherton, Nancy 67
アザナイ
Azannaï, Candide 74
アサナウ
Asanau, Dzmitry 62
アザナヴィシウス
Hazanavicius, Michel 586
アザナビシウス
Hazanavicius, Michel 586
アサニゼ
Asanidze, Georgi 62
アーサノ
Ursano, Robert J. 1436
アサノ
Asano, David 62
Asano, Tadanobu 62
アサノビッチ
Asanovich, Mark 62
アザブ
al-Azab, Faleh Abdullah 74
アザマ
Azama, Michel 74
アサム
Assam, Mervyn 65
アーザム・ザンギャネー
Azam Zanganeh, Lila 74
アサモア
Asamoah, Kwadwo 62
アサヤス
Assayas, Olivier 65
アサラフ
Assaraf, John 65
アサリ
al-Asali, Saif Mahyub 62
アザリ
Azali, Assoumani 74
Azzali, Assumani 75
アザリアウンウイ
Azaria Hounhoui, Naomi 74
アザリナ
Azalina, Othman 74
アサール
Azar, Christian 74
アサル
Assar, Omar 65
アザール
Azhar, Mobeen 74
Hazard, Eden 586
Hazard, Thorgan 586
アザル
Azar, Wasif 74
アーザルギン
Azargin, Azuyuta 74
アザレロ
Azzarello, Brian 75
アザレンカ
Azarenka, Victoria 74
アサロ
Asaro, Catherine 62
アザロフ
Azarov, Mykola 74
アーサン
Ahsan, Mohammad 21
アサン
Asang, Laoly 62
アザン
Hazan, Éric 586
アサンジ
Assange, Julian 65
アサンジュ
Assange, Julian 65
アサンデ
Azandé, Placide 74
アサンバ
Assamba, Aloun 65
アーシ
Assi, Lamia Mari 66
アシ
Achi, Patrick 10
アジ
Adji, Mahamat Mamadou 15
アージア
Argea, Angelo 57
アシアスエ
Assi-assoue, Weiding 66
アシアータ
Asiata, Matt 64
アジェ
Atget, Eugene 67
アジエ
Aziez, Yasmina 75
アジェイ
Adjei, Oteng 15
アジェイダーコ
Adjeidarko, Kwadwo 15
アジェイネ
Alleyne, Camilo 34
アジェオダ
Adjeoda, Kokou Dzifa 15
アシエシヴィリ
Asieshvili, Kakha 64
アジェージュ
Hagège, Claude 554
アジェマン
Agyeman, Hackman Owusu 19
Agyemang, Jane Naana Opoku 19
アジエマン
Agyeman, Hackman Owusu 19
アジェマンメンサ
Agyemang-mensah, Kwaku 19
アーシェラ
Urshela, Giovanny 1436
アーシェル
Urschel, John 1436
アシエル・ガリターノ
Asier Garitano 64
アジェルサ
Ayerza, Marcos 73
アシエル・ベニート
Asier Benito 64
アジェンデ
Allende, Isabel 34
アージェンティ
Argenti, Paul A. 57
アシェンバーグ
Ashenburg, Katherine 63
アシオーン
Ascione, Frank R. 63
アージカ
Arzika, Mohammed 62
アシク
Asik, Omer 64
アシケナージ
Ashkenazy, Vladimir 64
アジジ
Azizi, Ebrahim 75
アジジ・ハジ・アブドゥラー
Azizi Haji Abdullah 75
アシシンヌ
Akhchichine, Ahmed 23
アジズ
Aziz, Abdul 75
Aziz, Rafidah 75
Aziz, Sartaj 75
Aziz, Shaukat 75
Aziz, Tariq Mikhail 75
Azizou, Issa 75
アジズホジャエフ
Azizkhodzhayev, Alisher 75
アジゾフ
Azizov, Mehman 75
アジゾワ
Azizova, Farida 75
アジソン
Addison, Paul S. 14
アジダルマ
Ajidarma, Seno Gumira 23
アジッチ
Adzic, Gojko 16
アシテリ
Acitelli, Linda K. 10
アシート
Acito, Marc 10
アジニ
Ajdini, Milaim 23
アシフ
Asif, Muhammad 64
アジベーコフ
Adibekov, Grant Mkrtychevich 14
アシマイドゥ
Assimaidou, Kossi 66
アシマン
Aciman, André 10
アジーマン
Azziman, Omar 75
アジマンメンサ
Agyemang-mensah, Kwaku 19
アジミ
Azimi, Nassrine 75
Azimi, Salamat 75
アジミナグロウ
Hadji-Minaglou, Francis 553
アーシム
Asim, Mohamed 64
アシモフ
Ashimov, Nurgali 63
アジモフ
Azimov, Rustam 75
アシャ
Asa 62
アジャ
Aja, David 22
アジャイ
Adjaye, David 15
アジャウィン
Ajawin, Lam Akhol 22
アジャグバ
Ajagba, Efe 22
アジャシャンティ
Adyashanti 16
アシャースミス
Asher-smith, Dina 63
アシャット
Axat, Federico 72
アジャーニ
Adjani, Isabelle 15
アジャニー
Ajani, Jaffer A. 22
アジャポング
Adjapong, Felix Owusu 15
Agyapong, Felix Owusu 19
アジャミー
Ajami, Fouad 22
アジャム
al-Ajam, Qasim Ahmad 22
アジャラ
Ayala, Daniel 73
アシャーリ
Achaari, Mohamed 10
アシャリ
Asyari, Mohammad Yusuf 66
アシャール
Achard, Guy 10
アジャール
Ajhar, Brian 23
アジャルメ
Ajarmah, Nofan 22
アジャレス
Ayares, Gustavo 73
アジャレス・エスナ
Ayales Esna, Édgar 73
アシャロン
Asheron, Sara 63

アーシャン
Ahsian, Naisha 21
アジャンサ
Ajinca, Alexis 23
アシャンティ
Ashanti 63
アシュ
Asch, Frank 62
Ash, Richard 63
アシュヴァル
Asvall, Jo Erik 66
アシュウィニ
Ashwini, Ponnappa 64
アシュウェル
Ashwell, Ken W.S. 64
Ashwell, Rachel 64
アシュウッド
Ashwood, Jessica 64
アシュカル
Achcar, Gilbert 10
アシュクロフト
Ashcroft, Bill 63
Ashcroft, John 63
Ashcroft, Neil W. 63
Ashcroft, Richard 63
アシュケナージ
Ashkenazy, Vladimir 64
Askenazy, Philippe 64
アシュケナス
Ashkenas, Ronald N. 64
アシュトン
Ashton, Anthony 64
Ashton, Catherine 64
Ashton, John 64
Ashton, Karen 64
Ashton, Kevin 64
Ashton, Rosemary 64
Ashton, Steven 64
Ashton, Toni 64
Aston, Guy 66
アジュバリス
Ažubalis, Andronius 75
アシュビー
Ashby, Harold Kenneth 63
Ashby, Madeline 63
アシュファク
Ashfaq, Qais 63
アシュフィールド
Ashfield, Keith 63
Ashfield, Stephen 63
アシュフォード
Ashford, Annaleigh 63
Ashford, Janet 63
Ashford, Mary-Wynne 63
Ashford, Nickolas 63
Ashford, Stephen 63
アシュブレス
Ashbless, Janine 63
アシュベ
Ashbé, Jeanne 63
アシュホフ
Aschhoff, Gunther 63
アジュマニ
Adjoumani, Kobenan Kouassi 15
アジュマルディ・アズラ
Azra, Azyumardi 75
アシュマン
Ashman, Linda 64
アシュミード
Ashmeade, Nickel 64
アシュモア
Ashmore, Sonia 64
アジュモゴビア
Ajumogobia, Henry Odein 23
アシュモワ
Ashumova, Irada 64
アシュラーウィ
Ashrawi, Hanan 64
アシュラウィ
Ashrawi, Hanan 64
アシュラフ
Ashraf, Javed 64
Ashraf, Raja Pervez 64
Ashraff, Ferial 64
アジュラミ
al-Ajrami, Ashraf 23
アシュリー
Ashley, Anne 64
Ashley, Bernard 64
Ashley, Jennifer 64
Ashley, Kristen 64
Ashley, Mike 64
Ashley, Robert 64
Ashley, Ted 64
Ashley, Tom 64
el-Ashry, Nahed 64
アシュリー＝クーパー
Ashley-cooper, Adam 64
アシュール
Ashur, Abdurakhim 64
アシュレー
Ashley, Ted 64
アシュレイ
Ashley, James 64
Ashley, Jo Ann 64
アシュロフ
Ashur, Abdurakhim 64
アージュロン
Ageron, Charles Robert 17
アジュロン
Ageron, Charles Robert 17
アシュワース
Ashworth, Frederick L. 64
Ashworth, Susie 64
アシュワデン
Aschwanden, Sergei 63
アシュワル
al-Ashwal, Abdul-Razzaq 64
アショク
Ashok, Aditi 64
アジョジャ
Ajodhia, Jules Rattankoemar 23
アショチャン
Ashotyan, Armen 64
アジョビ
Adjobi, Christine 15
Adjovi, Severin 15
アジリ
al-Ajili, Abd Diab 23
アージリス
Argyris, Chris 57
アシル
Acyl, Ahmat Mahamat 11
Ashiru, Olugbenga 64
アシルムハメドフ
Ashirmukhammedov, Geldymukhamed 63
アシルムラートワ
Asylmuratova, Altynai 66
アシレム
Assilem, Melissa Anana 66
アシン
Ashin 63
アシンガンビ
Assingambi, Zarambo 66
アシン・ターワラ
Ashin Htarwara 63
アース
Aas, Arto 1
アズー
Azou, Jeremie 75
アスアド
Assaad, bin Tariq al-Said 65
アスアヘ
Asuaje, Carlos 66
Azuaje, Olga 75
アズイランクロフ
Azyrankulov, Aybek 75
アスィルムラートワ
Asylmuratova, Altynai 66
アスエマンゲ
Asue Mangue, Reginaldo 66
アスエラ
Azuela, Arturo 75
アスカリ
Askari, Fred K. 64
アスカル
Askalu, Menkerios 64
アズカル
Azkalu, Menkerios 75
アスガロフ
Asgarov, Toghrul 63
アスキ
Haski, Pierre 579
アスキー
Askey, Dennis 64
アスキュー
Askew, Luke 64
Askew, Mike 64
Askew, Reubin O'Donovan 64
アースキン
Erskine, Kathryn 407
Erskine, Peter 407
アスキンズ
Askins, Robert A. 64
アスク
Ask, Beatrice 64
Ask, Sten 64
アスクイ
Azcuy, Filiberto 74
アスクエス
Ascues, Carlos 63
アスクゴー
Askgaard, Ejnar 64
アスグリムソン
Asgrimsson, Halldor 63
アスクレン
Askren, Ben 64
アスコー
Ascough, Richard S. 63
アスコエト
Hascoët, Guy 579
アースコット
Arscott, Noel 61
アスコナ
Azcona, Rafael 74
Azcona Hoyo, José 74
アスコナ・ボコック
Azcona Bocock, Lizzy 74
アスス
Assous, Eric 66
アスター
Aster, Jon C. 66
Aster, Misha 66
Astor, Brooke 66
アースタッド
Erstad, Ola 407
アスタファン
Astaphan, Dwyer 66
Astaphan, Jamie 66
アスターフィエフ
Astafiev, Viktor P. 66
アスタホフ
Astakhov, Anton 66
アスタポフ
Astapov, Valery P. 66
アスティエ
Astier, Pierre 66
アスティカ
Astica, Juan 66
アステミロワ
Astemirova, Eter 66
アステル
Astell, Chrissie 66
Astels, David 66
Aster, Mamo 66
アステルス
Astels, David 66
アストラ
Astra 66
アストーリ
Astori, Davide 66
アストリ
Astori, Danilo 66
アストリュック
Astruc, Alexandre 66
アストル
Astle, Jeff 66
アスドルバル
Asdrubal, Padron 63
アストルフォード
Astleford, Gary 66
アストン
Aston, Dianna Hutts 66
Aston, Ken 66
Aston, Maxine C. 66
アズナヴール
Aznavour, Charles 75
アズナヴール＝ガルヴァレンツ
Aznavour-Garvarentz, Aïda 75
アズナブール
Aznavour, Charles 75
アスナール
Aznar López, José María 75
アスナール・ロペス
Aznar López, José María 75
アスパー
Asper, Kathrin 65
アズバ
Azuba, Ntege 75
アスパーケル
Aspaker, Elizabeth 65
アスパケル
Aspaker, Elizabeth 65
アスバヒ
al-Asbahi, Eiz al-Din 62
アズハリ
Azahari 74
el-Azhary, Khaled Mahmoud 74

アスピナル
Aspinall, Neil 65
アスピリクエタ
Azpilicueta, Cesar 75
アスプ
Asp, Anette 65
アスファウ
Asfaw, Gashaw 63
アスフォ
Asfaw, Dingamo 63
アスプデン
Aspden, Kester 65
アスプランド
Asplund, Jim 65
Asplund, Lillian Gertrud 65
Asplundh, Kurt Horigan 65
アスプリー
Asprey, Dave 65
アスプリン
Asprin, Robert 65
アスフール
Asfour, Gaber 63
Asfour, Hassan 63
アスプルンド
Asplund, Lillian Gertrud 65
アスプロモンテ
Aspromonte, Valerio 65
アスペ
Aspect, Alain 65
アズヘッド
Adshead, Mark 16
アズベリー
Asbury, Kathryn 62
Asbury, Stephen 62
アスペリン
Aspelin, Simon 65
アスポール
Aspord, Ophelie 65
アスマ
Asmah, Gladys 65
Assémat, Isabelle 65
Assouma, Suzanne Aho 66
アスマット
Asmat, bin Kamaludin 65
アスマニ
Athoumani, Mohamed Ali 67
アズマル
Asmal, Kader 65
アスマン
Asman, Abnur 65
Asman, Bub 65
Assmann, Aleida 66
Assmann, Dirk 66
Assmann, Heinz-Dieter 66
アズミ
Azmi, Khalid 75
アスムアヘンサ
Asum-ahensah, Alexander 66
アスムス
Asmus, James 65
アスムセン
Asmussen, Eva 65
アスムムンムノス
Asumu Mum Munoz, Anastasio 66
アスメル
Asmer, Toivo 65
アスメロン
Asmerom, Yared 65
アスラ
Aslam, Mohamed 64
アスラー
Asrar, Mahmud 65
アズラ
Azra, Azyumardi 75
アズライ
Azoulay, David 75
アスラニ
Aslani, Marilyn 64
Asrani, Arjun G. 65
アスラノフ
Aslanov, Fuad 65
アスラマゾフ
Aslamazov, L.G. 64
アスラム
Aslam, Mohamed 64
アスラン
Aslan, Reza 64
アスリーヌ
Assouline, Pierre 66
アスリム
Assilem, Melissa Anana 66
アズリン
Azrin, Nathan 75
アスル
Assr, Muneer Ali 66
アズール
Azour, Jihad 75
アズレ
Azoulay, Audrey 75
アスレイナー
Uslaner, Eric M. 1436
アスレット
Aslett, Don 65
アスロフ
Aslov, Sirojidin 65
アスロリ
Asrori, Mirzoshokhrukh 65
アスロロフ
Asrori, Mirzoshokhrukh 65
アスワディ
al-Aswadi, Abdul-Raqib 66
アスワド
al-Aswad, Husam 66
アスン
Assoun, Paul-Laurent 66
アゼアリアン
Azarian, Mary 74
アセヴェド
Acevedo, César Augusto 10
アゼヴェド
Azevedo, Ana Francisca de 74
アセオ
Asséo, Henriette 65
アセート
Aceto, Chris 10
アセナティ
Asenathi, Jim 63
アセニャ
Aceña, María del Carmen 10
アセノフ
Asenov, Daniel 63
アセファ
Asefa, Kesito 63
Assefa, Sofia 65
アセベス
Acebes, Ángel 10
アセベス・パニアグア
Acebes Paniagua, Angel 10
アセベド
Acevedo, Euclides 10
アゼベド
Azevedo, Ramiro 74
Azevêdo, Roberto 74
アセマ
Assémat, Isabelle 65
アセマニ
Asemani, Raheleh 63
アセモグル
Acemoglu, Daron 10
アゼリア
Azalea, Iggy 74
アーセル
Arcel, Nikolaj 55
アセール
Assael, Shaun 65
アゼレードロペス
Azeredo Lopes, José Alberto 74
アセング
Aceng, Jane 10
アセンシ
Asensi, Matilde 63
アセンシオ
Asensio, Marco 63
Asensio, Nacho 63
アゼンバーグ
Azenberg, Emanuel 74
アソア
Assoa, Adou 66
アソウマナキ
Asoumanaki, Sofia 65
アソゾダ
Asozoda, Khayrullo 65
アソバ
Assogba, Françoise Abraoua 66
アゾパルディ
Azzopardi, Gilles 75
アソマネ
Assoumane, Issoufou 66
アソロ
Asoro, Joel 65
アーター
Arter, Harry 61
Oerter, Al 1045
アーダ
Ardagh, Philip 56
アーダー
Ardagh, John 56
Ardagh, Philip 56
アタ
Atta, Mohamed 68
アダ
Ada, Salissou 11
Ada, Serhan 11
Adda, Jacques 13
Adda, Kofi 13
アダウィ
el-Adawi, Adel 13
アダウト
Adauto, Anderson 13
アタウラ
Athaulla, A.L.M. 67
アタエフ
Ataev, Chary 66
Atayev, Amangeldy 67
Atayev, Gurbanmurat 67
Atayev, Redzhepdurdy 67
Atayev, Valery 67
アタエワ
Atayeva, Enebay 67
アタオチュー
Attaochu, Jeremiah 68
アタク
Atak, Hursit 66
アタグルイエフ
Atagulyyev, Nokerguly 66
アダジ
Haddad, Fernando 552
アタ・シダルタ
Atta Sidharta 68
アダーソン
Adderson, Caroline 13
アダダ
Adada, Rodolphe 11
アダチ
Adachi, Barbara 11
アダチア
Adatia, Rahim 13
アダット
Adatto, Kiku 13
アダデ
Adade, Koffi 11
アダートン
Adderton, Dennis 13
アタナシウ
Atanasiu, Teodor 66
アタナシオ
Attanasio, Mark 68
アタナソ
Attanasso, Marie Odile 68
アタナソバ
Atanasova, Desislava Valcheva 66
アタナソフ
Atanasof, Alfredo Néstor 66
Atanasov, Stanimir 66
Atanassov, Vladimir 66
アタナヤケ
Attanayake, Tissa 68
アダナン
Adanan, Yusof 13
アタハノフ
Atahanov, Shamil 66
アタマ
Atama, Crispin 66
アダマ
Adama, Haman 11
Adama, Sy 11
アタマタベ
Atama Tabe, Crispin 66
アタマニアック
Atamaniuk, Randal 66
アダマール
Hadamard, Jacques 552
アダミ
Adami, Edward Fenech 11
Adami, Mimi Rodriguez 11
アダミー
Adamy, David 13
アダミャク
Adamiak, Elżbieta 11
アダム
Adam 11
Adam, Birgit 11
Adam, Charlie 11
Adam, Christophe 11

Adam, Iruthisham 11
Adam, Jean-Paul 11
Adam, John A. 11
Adam, Otmar 11
Adam, Paul 11
Adamou, Moumouni Djermakoye 11
Adamu, Adamu 13
Adamu, Hassan 13
Adamu, Suleiman Hussain 13

アダムクス
Adamkus, Valdas 11

アタムクロフ
Atamkulov, Beibut 66

アダム公
Hans Adam II 567

アダムシャ
Adamchak, Raoul W. 11

アダムス
Adams, Amy 12
Adams, Andrew 12
Adams, Arthur 12
Adams, Audra 12
Adams, Austin 12
Adams, Brett 12
Adams, Bryan 12
Adams, Carol 12
Adams, C.B.T. 12
Adams, Chris 12
Adams, Davante 12
Adams, David 12
Adams, Don 12
Adams, Douglas Noel 12
Adams, Eddie 12
Adams, Elisa 12
Adams, Ernest W. 12
Adams, Francis Gerard 12
Adams, George 12
Adams, Guy 12
Adams, James L. 12
Adams, Jay 12
Adams, Jeff 12
Adams, Jerell 12
Adams, John 12
Adams, Jonathan 12
Adams, Kat 12
Adams, Linda 12
Adams, Lynn W. 12
Adams, Mareike 12
Adams, Marilee G. 12
Adams, Mark 12
Adams, Matt 12
Adams, Matthew 12
Adams, Michael A. 12
Adams, Mike 12
Adams, Neal 12
Adams, Nicky 12
Adams, Okere 13
Adams, Paul 13
Adams, Richard 13
Adams, Ricky 13
Adams, Scott 13
Adams, Steve 13
Adams, Tom 13
Adams, Tyrell 13
Adams, Valerie 13
Adams, Vincanne 13
Adams, Walter 13
Adams, Yolanda 13
Adamse, Michael 13

アダムズ
Adams, Adrienne 12
Adams, A.E. 12
Adams, Amy 12
Adams, Anna 12
Adams, Cammile 12
Adams, Cecil 12
Adams, Chris 12
Adams, Christine A. 12
Adams, Diane 12
Adams, Don 12
Adams, Eddie 12
Adams, Eleston 12
Adams, Emily E. 12
Adams, Fred C. 12
Adams, Gemini 12
Adams, George 12
Adams, Gerry 12
Adams, Guy 12
Adams, James L. 12
Adams, Jane 12
Adams, Jennie 12
Adams, John 12
Adams, John Luther 12
Adams, Jordan 12
Adams, Kevin 12
Adams, Luke 12
Adams, Lynn W. 12
Adams, Nel 12
Adams, Nicola 13
Adams, Precious 13
Adams, Reginald B., Jr. 13
Adams, Richard 13
Adams, Ron 13
Adams, Samuel Hopkins 13
Adams, Scott 13
Adams, Simon 13
Adams, Stephen J. 13
Adams, Steven 13
Adams, Tim 13
Adams, Valerie 13
Adams, Will 13

アダムスン
Adamson, Eve 13
Adamson, Isaac 13

アダムソン
Adamson, Alan H. 13
Adamson, Bob 13
Adamson, Brent 13
Adamson, Clement Nii 13
Adamson, Isaac 13
Adamson, Stuart 13

アダムチク
Adamczyk, Andrzej 11

アダムツィク
Adamzik, Kirsten 13

アタムバエフ
Atambayev, Almazbek 66

アタムラドフ
Atamuradov, Begench 66

アダメズ
Adames, Cristhian 11
Adames, Willy 11

アダメツ
Adamec, Ladislav 11

アダメック
Adamec, Christine A. 11

アダメッツ
Adamec, Ladislav 11

アダモ
Adamo, Salvatore 11
Adamou, Assoumane 11

アダモフ
Adamov, Yevgeny O. 12

アダモフスキ
Adamovsky, Ezequiel 12

アダモフスキー
Adamovsky, Ezequiel 12

アタラ
Attalah, Béatrice 68

アタライ
Atalay, Beşir 66

アダラビオヨ
Adarabioyo, Tosin 13

アタリ
Attali, Jacques 68

アダリー
Adderly, Brenda 13

アダリオ
Addario, Lynsey 13

アタリフォ
Atalifo, Lee-roy 66

アダル
Adar, Yasemin 13

アータレイ
Atalay, Bülent 66

アタン
Attin, Joseph 68

アダン
Adam, Jean-Michel 11
Adan, Antonio 13
Adan, Mahmud Said 13
Adán, Pedro 13
Adan, Umar Hashi 13

アタンガナクナ
Atangana Kouna, Basile 66

アタンガナ・メバラ
Atangana Mebara, Jean-Marie 67

アタンガナメバラ
Atangana Mebara, Jean-Marie 67

アダンキ
Addanki, Sumanth 13

アダン・ショーヒヨウ
Adan Shaahiyow, Mohamed Hassan 13

アダンマイ
Adanmayï, Justin 13

アーチー
Archie, Susan 56

アチェベ
Achebe, Chinua 10

アチェルビ
Acerbi, Francesco 10

アチク
Achikwe, Trema 10

アチソン
Acheson, D.J. 10

アーチディアコノ
Arcidiacono, Ryan 56

アーチディコン
Archdeacon, Thomas J. 55

アチポエ
Attipoé, Richard 68

アーチボルト
Archbold, Shane 55

アーチボルド
Archbold, Rick 55
Archibald, Jan 56

アーチャー
Archer, Amanda 55
Archer, Catherine 55
Archer, Chris 55
Archer, Connie 55
Archer, Dennis Wayne 55
Archer, Jeffrey Howard 55
Archer, Margaret Scotford 56
Archer, Scott E. 56
Archer, William 56

アチャーガ
Atxaga, Bernardo 68

アチャカ
Atchaka, Sibunruang 67

アチャコジョ・トラ
Achacollo Tola, Nemecia 10

アチャコリョ・トラ
Achacollo Tola, Nemecia 10

アチャバヒアン
Atchabahian, Arthur 67

アーチャー・マッケンジー
Archer-Mackenzie, Christine 56

アーチャー・ライト
Archer-Wright, Ian 56

アチャリア
Acharya, Viral V. 10

アチャリャ
Acharya, Mahesh 10
Acharya, Narhari 10

アチャリヤ
Acharya, Mahesh 10

アチャン・オグワロ
Achan Ogwaro, Betty 10

アチャンタ
Achanta, Sharath Kamal 10

アチュイル
Acuil, Awut Deng 11

アチュガリー
Atchugarry, Alejandro 67

アチュベ
Achebe, Chinua 10

アーチュル
Erchul, William P. 405

アチョー
Acho, Sam 10

アチョン
Achong, Lawrence 10

アチリー
Atchley, Robert C. 67

アーツ
Aerts, Mario 16
Aerts, Peter 16
Ertz, Zach 407

アツィリ
Atzili, Omer 68

アッカー
Acker, Kenneth 10

アッガー
Haggar, Sidick Abdelkerim 554

アッカス
al-Akkas, Abdulmohsin bin Abdulaziz 24

アッカド
Akkad, Moustapha 24

アッカーマン
Ackerman, Angela 10
Ackerman, Diane 10
Ackerman, Forrest J. 10
Ackerman, Jennifer 10
Ackerman, Karen 10
Ackerman, Kenneth B. 10
Ackerman, Larry 10
Ackerman, Laurence D. 10
Ackerman, Michael J. 10
Ackerman, Robert 10
Ackerman, Robert Allan 10
Ackerman, Will 10

ア

Ackermann, Abigail 10
Ackermann, Adrienne 10
Ackermann, Ronny 10
Akerman, Chantal 23

ア

アッカマン
Ackerman, Bruce A. 10
アッカンバウム
Achenbaum, W.Andrew 10
アックアフレスカ
Acquafresca, Roberto 11
アックス
Ax, Emanuel 72
アックスフォード
Axford, John 73
アックスロッド
Axelrod, Alan 72
アックマン
Ackman, Bill 10
Ackman, Karen 10
アッコラ
Accola, Paul 10
アツコラレ
Atukorala, Gamini 68
アッサ
Assa, Ariel 65
アッサード
Assaad, bin Tariq al-Said 65
アッサーフ
al-Assaf, Ibrahim bin Abdulaziz 65
Assaf, Waleed 65
アッザム
Azzam, Mansour 75
アッサール
Assar, Muhammad el 65
アッシ
Asche, Cody 62
Azzi, María Susana 75
アッジェイ・バリマー
Adjei-barimah, Jude 15
アッシャー
Ascher, David 63
Ascher, Susan M. 63
Ascher, Uri M. 63
Ascher, William 63
Asher, Alec 63
Asher, Bridget 63
Asher, Ellen 63
Asher, Jay 63
Asher, John 63
Asher, Marty 63
Asher, Neal 63
Asher, R.E. 63
Asher, William 63
Asscher, Lodewijk 65
Usher 1436
Usher, Carol 1436
Usher, Scott 1436
Usher, Shaun 1436
アッ・シャラ
al-Shara, Farouk 1282
アッシュ
Asch, Frank 62
Ash, Mary Kay 63
Ash, Ronnie 63
Ash, Roy Lawrence 63
Ash, Russell 63
Ash, Tracey 63
Ashe, Katharine 63
アッシュクロフト
Ashcroft, Bill 63
Ashcroft, Frances M. 63
アッシュクロフト＝ノーウィッキ
Ashcroft-Nowicki, Dolores 63
アッシュバーン
Ashburn, Boni 63
アッシュベッカー
Aschbacher, Michael 62
アッシュマン
Ashman, Sam 64
アッセ
Asset, Philippe 65
アッセルト
Asselt, Willem Jan van 65
アッセルボルン
Asselborn, Jean 65
アッセレ
Assele, Jean-Boniface 65
Assele, Nicole 65
アッセン
Assen, Klaas van 65
Assen, Marcel van 65
Assen, Ronald Richenel 65
アッゾパルディ
Azzopardi, Jason 75
アッダエフ
Atdayev, Batyr 67
アッターバック
Utterback, James M. 1437
アッタベリー
Attaberry, Elsie 68
アッタール
Attar, Abdelmadjid 68
アッタル
al-Attar, Najah 68
アッチェリー
Atchley, Robert C. 67
アッツォーニ
Azzoni, Silvia 75
アッツォパルディ
Azzopardi, Trezza 75
アッティヤ
Al-Attiyah, Nasser 68
アッティラ
Attila, Cseke 68
アッテファール
Attefall, Stefan 68
アッテンボロー
Attenborough, David Frederick 68
Attenborough, Richard 68
アットウッド
Attwood, Chris 68
Attwood, Janet Bray 68
アッバサドゥ
Aba Sadou 2
アッバサドゥ
Abba Sadou 2
アッバース
Abbas, Mahmoud 2
アッバス
Abbas, Baderaldien Mahmoud 2
Abbas, Mahmoud 2
Abbas, Mirza 2
Abbas, Mohamed-Cherif 2
Abbas, Mohamed El-Had 2
Abbas, Mohammed Abul 2
Abbas, Sadi Tuma 2
al-Abbas, Suleiman 2
Abbas, Youssouf Saleh 2
アッバディ
Abbadi, Abdul Salam 2
アッバード
Abbado, Claudio 2
アッピア
Appiah, Kwame Anthony 53
アッピアー
Appiah, Kwesi 53
アッピアオポン
Appiahoppiong, Marrieta Brew 53
アッピグナネッセイ
Appignanesi, Richard 53
アッフォルテル
Affolter, Christian 16
アップクラフト
Upcraft, M.Lee 1435
アップショー
Upshaw, Courtney 1435
Upshaw, Grace 1435
アップショウ
Upshaw, Dawn 1435
アップダイク
Updike, John 1435
アップデール
Updale, Eleanor 1435
アップトン
Upton, Justin 1435
Upton, Melvin 1435
Upton, Simon 1435
アップリチャード
Upritchard, Francis 1435
アップル
Apple, Eli 53
Apple, Fiona 53
Apple, Michael 53
Apple, Michael W. 53
Apple, Rima D. 53
Apple, R.W. 53
アップルゲイト
Applegate, Katherine 53
Applegate, Royce D. 53
アップルゲート
Applegate, Debby 53
Applegate, Katherine 53
Applegate, Royce D. 53
アップルトン
Appleton, Brad 53
アップルバウム
Applebaum, Julia 53
アップルビー
Appleby, Michael C. 53
Appleby, Stuart 53
アップルマン
Appleman, Daniel 53
アッベ
Abbe, Godwin 2
アッペル
Appel, Mark 53
アッペルト
Appelt, Kathi 53
アッペルバウム
Appelbaum, Eileen 53
アッペルボーム
Appelbaum, Paul S. 53
アッポルド
Appold, Kenneth G. 53
アツモン
Atzmon, Gilad 68
アッラグリエフ
Allaguliyev, Oraz 32
アッラルト
Allardt, Erik 32
アッレーグリ
Allegri, Renzo 33
アッレグリ
Allegri, Massimiliano 33
アッロ
Arro, Lena 61
アデ
Ade, Maren 14
アデア
Adair, Bill 11
Adair, Cherry 11
Adair, Christopher Smith 11
Adair, Gene 11
Adair, Gilbert 11
Adair, John Eric 11
Adair, Olivia 11
Adair, Paul Neal 11
アデアン
Adeang, David 14
アーディ
Ardai, Charles 56
Ardi, Dana 56
アディ
Addy, Axel 14
Adi, Ignatius 14
アディー
Addae, Jahleel 13
アティア
Atiyah, Michael Francis 67
アディアエノ
Adiahenot, Jacques 14
アティアス
Atias, Ariel 67
アディウ
Adihou, Alain 14
アデイェミ
Adeyemi, Kenton 14
アティエンザ
Atienza, Jose 67
アディカ
Addica, Milo 13
アディガ
Adiga, Aravind 14
アディカリ
Adhikari, Khagraj 14
アーティガン
Ertegun, Ahmet M. 407
アディキ
Adiki, Safi 14
アティク
Atik, Baris 67
アディサイ
Adisai, Bodharamik 14
アティサノエ
Atisanoe, Anoaro 67
アデイシビリ
Adeishvili, Zurab 14
アディシャクティ
Adishakti, Laretna 14
アディス
Addis, Michael E. 13
Addisu, Legesse 14
アーティス・ペイン
Artis-payne, Cameron 62
アディスン
Addison, Katherine 13
アーディゾーニ
Ardizzone, Aingelda 56
アディソン
Addison, Bralon 13
Addison, Brian 13

Addison, Josephine 13
Addison, Mario 13
アディーチェ
Adichie, Chimamanda Ngozi 14
アティヌーケ
Atinuke 67
アティフ
Atef, Muhammad 67
アディブ
al-Adib, Ali 14
アティボ
Ativor, Dzifa Aku 67
アティーヤ
Attiya, Ahmed 68
al-Attiyah, Abdullah bin Hamad 68
al-Attiyah, Khalid bin Mohammad 68
Al-Attiyah, Nasser 68
アティヤ
Atiyah, Michael Francis 67
Attiya, Tahani Abdalla 68
アティヤー
Atiyah, Michael Francis 67
アディヤサンブー
Adiyasambuu, Tsolmon 15
アティヤファ
Atiyafa, Robert 67
アーディラ
Ardila, Alfredo 56
アディリ
Adiri, Niv 14
アディル
Adili, Jumatuerdi 14
アディルベクウール
Adylbek Uulu, Erkin 16
アディレックス
Adirex, Paul 14
アディーン
Adhin, Ashwin 14
アーティンガー
Oetinger, Bolko von 1045
アディング
Ading, Jack 14
アデウォレ
Adewole, Isaac 14
アデオスン
Adeosun, Kemi 14
アデクロイエ
Adekuoroye, Odunayo Folasade 14
アデシナ
Adesina, Akinwunmi 14
アデシャン
Adesiyan, Abdul Jelili Oyewale 14
アデス
Adès, Thomas 14
アデトクンボ
Antetokounmpo, Giannis 51
アデナン
Adenan, Satem 14
アデニイ
Adeniyi, Aminat 14
アデニジ
Adeniji, Olu 14
Adeniji, Oluyemi 14
アデニラン
Adeniran, Tunde 14
アデバヨ
Adebayo, Cornelius 14
Adebayo, Edrice 14
アーテフ
Atef, Muhammad 67
アテフ
Atef, Muhammad 67
アデポジュ
Adepoju, Sikiru 14
アデミ
Ademi, Abdilaqim 14
Ademi, Arbr 14
アデム
Adem, Ibrahim 14
アデライン
Adeline, L.Marie 14
アデラジャ
Adelaja, Dupe 14
アーデリー
Adeli, Muhammad Hossein 14
アデリ
Adeli, Muhammad Hossein 14
アデリッツィ
Adelizzi, Beatrice 14
アデリノ
Ascenso, Adelino 62
アーテル
Ertel, Danny 407
アーデル
Áder, János 14
アデール
Adair, Beegie 11
Adair, Bill 11
アデル
Adel, Ibrahim 14
Adele 14
Adele, Deborah 14
アデルソン
Adelson, Edna 14
Adelson, Sheldon 14
アデルマン
Adelman, David 14
Adleman, Tim 15
アーデン
Alden, Jami 27
Arden, Andrea 56
Arden, Darlene 56
Arden, Harvey 56
Arden, John 56
Arden, John Boghosian 56
Arden, Paul 56
Arden, Ron 56
Henin, Justine 594
アデン
Aden, Aden Hassan 14
Aden, Ahmed Abdisalam 14
Aden, Fawzia Yusuf 14
アデン・ヒラレ
Aden Hirale, Barre Shire 14
アト
Atto, Ossman Hassan Ali 68
アド
Addo, Nana Akufo 14
アードイン
Ardoin, John 56
アドゥ
Adou, Assoa 15
アドゥー
Haddou, Marie 552
アドゥアヨム
Aduayom, Messan Adimado 16
アトウェル
Atwell, Debby 68
Atwell, James D. 68
アドウォク・ニャバ
Adwok Nyaba, Peter 16
アトウォル
Atwal, Anita 68
アトゥコララ
Athukorala, Thalatha 67
アトゥジュ
Atici, Sevil 67
アトゥツェルト
Atzert, Thomas 68
アトウッド
Attwood, Tony 68
Atwood, Christee Gabour 68
Atwood, Colleen 68
Atwood, Heather 68
Atwood, Margaret Eleanor 68
Atwood, Russell 68
アトゥボ
Atubo, Omara 68
アトゥマン
Attoumane, Sounhadji 68
アドゥーム
Addoum, Adnan 14
アドゥム
Adoum, Djimet 15
アドゥリス
Aduriz, Aritz 16
アドゥン
Adul, Saengsingkaew 16
アトエフ
Atoev, Abbos 68
アドガード・イヴァーセン
Odgård Iversen, Bo 1044
アトキソン
Atkisson, Alan 67
アトキン
Atkin, Jacqui 67
アトキンス
Atkins, Ace 67
Atkins, Alison 67
Atkins, Chet 67
Atkins, *Dame* Eileen 67
Atkins, Geno 67
Atkins, Lucy 67
Atkins, Peter William 67
Atkins, Robert C. 67
Atkins, Sue 67
アトキンズ
Atkins, Chet 67
Atkins, Dawn 67
Atkins, Jacqueline M. 67
Atkins, John L., Ⅲ 67
Atkins, Robert C. 67
Atkins, Steven C. 67
Atkins, Stuart 67
アドキンス
Adkins, David 15
アドキンズ
Adkins, Lesley 15
Adkins, Roy A. 15
アトキンスン
Atkinson, Mary 67
アトキンソン
Atkinson, Alia 67
Atkinson, Anthony Barnes 67
Atkinson, Bill 67
Atkinson, Dan 67
Atkinson, Erick John 67
Atkinson, George 67
Atkinson, Ian 67
Atkinson, Janette 67
Atkinson, Kate 67
Atkinson, Kenny 67
Atkinson, Richard C. 67
Atkinson, Rita L. 67
Atkinson, Robert 67
Atkinson, Rowan Sebastian 67
アドキンソン
Adkinson, Robert 15
アド・クフォー
Addo-kufuor, Kwame 14
アドケ
Adoke, Mohammed Bello 15
アドコック
Adcock, Chris 13
Adcock, Edward P. 13
Adcock, Gabrielle 13
アドコリ
Adkoli, Anand 15
アドシェイド
Adshade, Marina 16
アドシェッド
Adshed, Gwen 16
アードス
Erdoes, Mary Callahan 405
Erdoes, Richard 406
アートセン
Aartsen, Gerard 1
アドック
Adok, Peter 15
アドナ
Adna, Ismanto 15
アドナー
Adner, Ron 15
アドナン
Adnan, Ali 15
Adnan, Mansor 15
アドニー
Adoni, Hanna 15
アトニオ
Atonio, Uini 68
アドニス
Adonis 15
アドバニ
Advani, Lal Kishanchand 16
Advani, Lal Krishna 16
アトパレ
Atopare, Sailas 68
アドフォカート
Advocaat, Dick 16
アードボーゲ
Adbåge, Emma 13
アドマイト
Adomeit, Klaus 15
アドマティ
Admati, Anat R. 15
アトマール
Atmar, Mohamad Hanif 68
アードマン
Erdmann, Terry J. 405
アトーメン
Attoumane, Said 68
アドュンヤヌコソン
Adulyanukosol, Kanjana 16

アドラー
Adler, Alexandra 15
Adler, Bill 15
Adler, Bill, Jr. 15
Adler, Carlye 15
Adler, Charles L. 15
Adler, Gordon 15
Adler, Jerry 15
Adler, Joseph 15
Adler, Joseph Alan 15
Adler, Kathleen 15
Adler, Larry 15
Adler, Margot 15
Adler, Mortimer Jerome 15
Adler, Nancy J. 15
Adler, Nellie 15
Adler, Paul S. 15
Adler, Rene 15
Adler, Richard 15
Adler, Robert 15
Adler, Saul 15
Adler, Susan S. 15
Adler, Victoria 15
アトラシュ
al-Atrash, Hilal 68
アドラード
Adlard, Charles 15
アトラン
Atlan, Henri 67
アドラン
Adlan, Shambul 15
アドランティ
Adoranti, Frank 15
アトリ
Atli, Suleyman 68
アトリー
Utley, Chase 1437
アドリ
Adly, Habib Ibrahim El 15
アドリア
Adrià, Albert 15
Adrià, Ferran 15
アドリア・アコスタ
Adria Acosta, Ferran 15
アドリアーノ
Adriano 16
アドリアン
Adrian 15
Adrian, Gonzalez 16
Adrian, Lopez 16
アドリアンザ
Adrianza, Ehire 16
アドリァーンセンス
Adriaenssens, Peter 15
アドリアン・マリン
Adrian Marin 16
アドリエン・シルヴァ
Adrien Silva 16
アドリエンヌ
Adrienne, Carol 16
アードリック
Erdrich, Louise 406
アドリード
Aldrete, Mike 27
アドリン
Adlin, Tamara 15
アドリントン
Adlington, L.J. 15
Adlington, Rebecca 15
アドル
Adl, Shirin 15
アドルフ
Adolph, Gerald 15
アトルベイ
Athorbei, David Deng 67
アードレー
Ardley, Neil 56
アトレー
Attlee, Helena 68
アドレシチュ
Adlešič, Djurda 15
アートレス
Artress, Lauren 62
アトレーヤ
Atreya, Mohan 68
アードロン
Ardron, Tyler 56
アトワーン
Atwan, Abdel Bari 68
アトワン
Atwan, Robert 68
アドワン
Udwan, Atef 1432
アートン
Urton, Gary 1436
アナ
Anna, Dawn 50
アナキン
Annakin, Ken 50
アナグノストウ
Anagnostou, Evdokia 42
アナザリャン
Ahnazarian, Narek 21
アナス
Annas, George J. 50
Annas, Julia 50
Annas, Max 50
アナスタシ
Anastasi, Elizabeth 43
アナスタシアディス
Anastasiades, Nicos 43
アナスタシオ
Anastacio, Sabino 43
アナストポウロス
Anastopoulos, Arthur D. 43
アナセン
Andersen, Jens 43
アーナソン
Arnason, David 59
Arnason, Vincent 59
アナツイ
Anatsui, El 43
アナテ
Anaté, Kouméalo 43
アナディフ
Annadif, Mahamat Saleh 50
アナトリオス
Anatolios, Khaled 43
アナナソワ
Ananasova, Lolita 42
アナニ
Anani, Cassa Gustave 42
アナニアシヴィリ
Ananiashvili, Nina 42
アナニアシビリ
Ananiashvili, Nina 42
アナニアス
Ananias, Patrus 42
アナニチ
Ananich, Liliya S. 43
アナネ
Anane, Richard 42
アナパウラ
Connelly, Ana Paula 283
アナフィ
Annafi, Agnes 50
アナポール
Anapol, Deborah M. 43
アナマライ
Annamalai, E. 50
アナーリナ
Anarina, N. 43
アーナルデュル・インドリダソン
Arnaldur Indridason 59
アナワルト
Anawalt, Patricia Rieff 43
アナン
Anane, Richard 42
Annan, Kofi Atta 50
Annan, Nane 50
Annan, Noel Gilroy Annan 50
Hanin, Roger 566
アナングウェ
Anangwe, Amukowa 42
アナンサスワーミー
Ananthaswamy, Anil 43
アーナンダ・クマラセリ
Ananda Kumarasiri, G. K. 42
アナンダ・クリシュナン
Ananda Krishnan 42
アナンタポーン
Anantaporn, Kanjanarat 43
アーナンド
Anand, Mulk Raj 42
アナンド
Anand, Anita 42
Anand, Geeta 42
Anand, Mulk Raj 42
アナント・クマール
Ananthkumar 43
アナントクマール
Ananthkumar 43
アナンドラ
Anandra, Norbert 42
アナンノビー
Anunoby, O.G. 52
アーニ
Arni, Faiz 59
アニエスb
Agnès b. 18
アニエスベー
Agnès b. 18
アニェーゼ
Agnese, Giorgio 18
アニェッリ
Agnelli, Susanna 18
アニエッリ
Agnelli, Giovanni 18
Agnelli, Umberto 18
アニェリ
Agnelli, Giovanni 18
Agnelli, Susanna 18
Agnelli, Umberto 18
アニエリ
Agnelli, Giovanni 18
Agnelli, Umberto 18
アニエル
Agnel, Yannick 17
アニオロフスキ
Aniolowski, Scott David 50
アニオロフスキー
Aniolowski, Scott David 50
アニシナ
Anissina, Marina 50
Aniushina, Elena 50
アニシモフ
Anisimov, Leonid 50
アニシュチャンカ
Anishchanka, Aliaksandr 50
アニス
Anies, Baswedan 49
Annis, Barbara 50
アニストン
Aniston, Jennifer 50
アニチェベ
Anichebe, Victor 49
アニツ
Anic, Franka 49
アニババ
Anibaba, Obafemi 49
アニバリ
Annibali, Michele 50
アニファ
Anifah, Aman 49
アニー・ベイビー
Anny baby 50
アニマル・ウォリアー
Animal Warrior 50
アニマル・レスリー
Animal Lesley 49
アニミ
Animi, Ahamat Barkai 50
アニュ
Agne, Abdourahim 17
アニュプイェ
Agne-pouye, Aïcha 18
アニル
Anil, Mohamed 49
Anil, Robin 49
アヌ
Annou, Badamassi 50
アヌカン
Hennequin, Benjamin Didier 594
アヌス
Hanus, Michel 568
アヌディット
Anudit, Nakornthap 52
アヌノビー
Anunoby, Chigbo 52
アヌポン
Anupong, Paochinda 52
アヌラック
Anurak, Chureemas 52
アヌール
Annour, Samir Adam 50
アヌルッダ
Anuruddha 52
アヌンセン
Anundsen, Anders 52
アーネ
Ahrne, Goran 21
アーネイ
Aanei, Andreea 1
アネジ
Anesi, Matteo 48
アーネス
Arnes, James 59
アーネスト
Earnest, Peter 387
Ernest, Paul 407
アーネセン
Arnesen, Laura Kristine 59

アーネソン
Arneson, Steve 59
アネッダ
Anedda, Antonella 48
アーネット
Arnett, Peter Gregg 59
Arnett, Robert C. 59
アネット
Annett, Cora 50
アネニ
Anenih, Tony 48
アネニイ
Anenih, Iyom Josephine 48
アネファル
Anefal, Sebastian 48
アーネル
Arnell, Peter 59
アネルカ
Anelka, Nicolas 48
アネン
Annen, Blake 50
Annen, Jolanda 50
アネンバーグ
Annenberg, Walter H. 50
アノー
Annaud, Jean-Jacques 50
アノウシラバニハムラバド
Anoushiravani Hamlabad, Sajjad 50
アノシュキン
Anoshkin, Roman 50
アノーソフ
Anosov, Dmitrii Viktorovich 50
アーノット
Arnot, Madeleine 60
Arnott, Jake 60
Arnott, Robert D. 60
アノヒン
Anokhin, Vadim 50
アーノブ
Arnove, Anthony 60
Arnove, Robert F. 60
アノメリティス
Anomeritis, Georgios 50
アーノルディ
Arnoldi, Per 60
アーノルト
Arnault, Anne 59
Arnold, Frank 60
アーノルド
Arnold, Andrea 60
Arnold, Caroline 60
Arnold, Caroline L. 60
Arnold, Dana 60
Arnold, Dave 60
Arnold, Eddy 60
Arnold, Eve 60
Arnold, Glen 60
Arnold, Hans 60
Arnold, Johann Christoph 60
Arnold, John 60
Arnold, John D. 60
Arnold, Judith 60
Arnold, Ken 60
Arnold, Laura 60
Arnold, Louise 60
Arnold, Malcolm 60
Arnold, Marsha Diane 60
Arnold, Matthias 60
Arnold, Nick 60
Arnold, Susan E. 60
Arnold, Tedd 60
Arnold, Vladimir I. 60
Arnold, Vladimir Igorevich 60
アルノー
Arnault, Anne 59
アノンアディビメ
Anong Adibime, Pascal 50
アーノンクール
Harnoncourt, Nikolaus 572
アーバー
Arber, Werner 55
Arbour, Louise 55
アバアバ
Abah Abah, Polycarpe 1
アバイ
Abay, Tsehaye 2
アパイ
Apai, Chanthanajulaka 52
アーバイン
Irvine, Abby 649
Irvine, Alexander C. 649
アーバイン卿
Lord Irvine 649
アバエフ
Abayev, Bayar 2
Abayev, Dauren 2
アバガナ
Abba-Gana, Mohammed 2
アバカノヴィッチ
Abakanowicz, Magdalena 1
アバカノビッチ
Abakanowicz, Magdalena 1
アバカル
Abakar, Abdoulaye 1
Abakar, Siid Warsameh 1
アバカロワ
Abakarova, Patimat 1
アバギャン
Avagyan, Aram 71
アーバーグ
Aaberg, Everett 1
アパク
Apak, Esref 52
アバグネイル
Abagnale, Frank W. 1
アバクモワ
Abakumova, Maria 1
アーバクル
Arbuckle, Warren 55
アバークロンビー
Abercrombie, Ian 6
Abercrombie, Nicholas 6
アバコフ
Avakov, Arsen 71
アバーザ
Abaza, Amin 2
アバサドゥ
Aba Sadou 2
アバサラー
Abassalah, Youssouf 2
アバサラーラ
Avasarala, Govinda 71
アバサララ
Avasarala, Satya 71
アバシ
Abbasi, Fereydoon 2
Abbasi, Mohammad 2
Abbasi, Shahid Khaqan 2
アパ・シェルパ
Appa Sherpa 53
アバス
Abas, Stephen 2
Abbas, Attoumane Djaffar 2
Abbas, Mohammed Abul 2
アバスカル・カランサ
Abascal Carranza, Carlos María 2
アバソフ
Abasov, Ismet 2
Abbasov, Abbas A. 2
Abbasov, Ali 2
Abbasov, Ismet 2
Abbasov, Namik R. 2
アバソワ
Abassova, Tamilla 2
アバーソン
Aberson, Helen 6
アパタ
Apata, Joseph Lititiyo 52
アハターンブッシュ
Achternbusch, Herbert 10
アーバックル
Arbuckle, Brad B. 55
Arbuckle, Ruth 55
アバッサラー
Abassalah, Youssouf 2
アバッド
Abad, Fernando 1
アバッローネ
Avallone, Silvia 71
アバーテ
Abate, Carmine 2
Abate, Ignazio 2
アバテ
Abbate, Janet 2
アバデ
Abade, Ahmed Abdirahman 1
アハディ
Ahady, Anwar-Ul-Haq 19
アバーディ
Abbadi, Abdul Salam 2
アバディ
al-Abadi, Haider 1
Abbadi, Mamdouh 2
アハティサーリ
Ahtisaari, Martti 21
アバディーン
Aburdene, Patricia 9
アパデュライ
Appadurai, Arjun 53
アバード
Abbado, Claudio 2
アバド
Abad, Abdelhamid 1
Abad, Florencio 1
Abad, Julia Andrea 1
Abad, Xavier 1
Abbad, Gunvor Larsson 2
Abbado, Claudio 2
アバドゥラ
Abadula, Gemeda 1
アパドゥライ
Appadurai, Arjun 53
アハトワ
Akhatova, Albina 23
アハドワ
Akhadova, Svitlana 23
アバナ
Abana, Steve 1
アバナシー
Abernathy, Jerome D. 6
アバニ
Abani, Chris 2
アハヌッシュ
Akhannouch, Aziz 23
アバネイル
Abagnale, Frank W. 1
アバーバネル
Abarbanel, Andrew 2
アバビ
Ababii, Ion 1
アバホ
Abajo, Jose Luis 1
アハマディ
Ahamadi, Abdoulbastoi 19
Ahmadi, Elaheh 20
アハマディネジャド
Ahmadinejad, Mahmoud 20
アハマディプール
Ahmadipour, Zahra 20
アハマト
Ahmat, Haoua Agyl 20
アハマド
Ahamad, bin Naser al-Thani 19
Ahmad, Abdullah al-Ahmad al-Sabah 19
Ahmad, al-hamoud al-Sabah 19
Ahmad, Ali 19
al-Ahmad, Azam 19
Ahmad, bin Nasir al-Thani 19
Ahmad, Fahad al-Ahmad al-Sabah 19
Ahmad, Hafizuddin 19
al-Ahmad, Muhammad 19
Ahmad, Sheikh Rashid 20
al-Ahmad, Yusuf Sulayman 20
Ahmed, bin Jassim bin Mohamed al-Thani 20
Ahmed, Hany El Saed 20
アハマド・ハリド
Ahmad al-Khalid, al-Hamad al-Sabah 20
アハマドフ
Ahmadov, Emin 20
Ahmadov, Rashad 20
アハマド・フムード
Ahmad al-Humoud, al-Sabah 20
アハマル
al-Ahmar, Ali Mohsen 20
アハメド
Ahamed, Liaquat 19
Ahmed, Abdi Houssein 20
Ahmed, Abdullah Bos 20
Ahmed, Abdullah Mohamed Sid 20
Ahmed, Aboubekrine Ould 20
Ahmed, Abtew 20
Ahmed, Aneesa 20
Ahmed, Asim 20
Ahmed, Azleen 20
Ahmed, bin Mohammed al-Khalifa 20
Ahmed, Enas Mostafa Youssef 20
Ahmed, Esraa 20
Ahmed, Fakhruddin 20
Ahmed, Hafizuddin M. 20
Ahmed, Haji Ali 20
Ahmed, Iajuddin 20
Ahmed, Lemrabott Sidi Mahmoud Ould

ア

Cheikh 20
Ahmed, Majzoub al-Khalifa 20
Ahmed, Mohamed Ghaly Ould Chérif 20
Ahmed, Mohamed Jameel 20
Ahmed, Mohammed 20
Ahmed, Mohammed Nasir 20
Ahmed, Mona 20
Ahmed, Moudud 20
Ahmed, Moussa Mohamed 20
Ahmed, Nabil Mohamed 20
Ahmed, Ougoureh Kifleh 20
Ahmed, Qutbi al-Mahdi 20
Ahmed, Raees Muneer 20
Ahmed, Samia 20
Ahmed, Sara 20
Ahmed, Shafiq 20
Ahmed, Sheikh Sharif 20
Ahmed, Shide 20
Ahmed, Tofail 20
Ahmed, Zemzem 20
Ahmedou, Ahmedou Ould 21

アハメドゥ
Ahmedou, Ahmedou Ould 21
Ahmedou, Ely Ould 21
Ahmedou, Mehla Mint 21

アハメド・モハメド
Ahmed Mohamed 20

アハメド・ラズ
Ahmed Raju, Raziuddin 21

アバヤ
Abaya, Joseph Emilio 2

アバラミス
Avramis, Dimitrios 72

アハラヤ
Akhalaia, Bachana 23

アパリー
Apperley, Dawn 53

アパリシオ
Aparicio, Julio Villoria 52

アパリシオ・ペレス
Aparicio Pérez, Juan-Carlos 52

アーバル
Ağbal, Naci 17

アバル
Abal, Sam 1

アバルカ
Abarca, Ana del Socorro 2

アバルキン
Abalkin, Leonid Ivanovich 1

アハルハボ
Ahlhabo, Mahamat Ahamat 19

アバルメディナ
Abal Medina, Juan Manuel 1

アパロ
Aparo, Jim 52

アバロス
Avalos, Saul 71

アハロニ
Aharoni, Mati 19

アハロニー
Aharony, Amnon 19

アハロノビッチ
Aharonovitch, Yitzhak 19

アハロノビッツ
Aharonovitch, Yitzhak 19

アハワニー
el-Ahwany, Naglaa 21

アーバン
Urban, Brent 1435
Urban, Glen L. 1435
Urban, Hal 1435
Urban, Keith 1435
Urban, William L. 1435

アハーン
Ahearn, Frank M. 19
Ahearn, Luke 19
Ahern, Bertie 19
Ahern, Cecelia 19
Ahern, Dermot 19
Ahern, Kevin G. 19

アバンシーニ
Avancini, Henrique 71

アバンズ
Abanes, Richard 1

アバンダ
Abanda, Joseph Tsanga 1

アハンハンゾグレレ
Ahanhanzo Glele, Blaise 19

アービー
Erbey, William 405

アビ
Abi, Tchessa 7
Avi 71

アビー
Abbey, Edward 2
Abbey, Michael 2
Abiy, Ahmed 7
Ivy, Robert A. 654

アピアカブラン
Appiah Kabran, Aimé 53

アビーアッシ
Abi Assi, Pierre 7

アビアビテオボリコ
Abia Biteoborico, Miguel 7

アビアン
Abian, Pablo 7

アビエフ
Abiyev, Safar 7
Aviyev, Safar A. 72

アビオラ
Abiola, François Adéboyo 7

アービク
Urbik, Kraig 1435

アービクソー
Aaviksoo, Jaak 1

アピサック
Apisak, Tantivorawong 53

アピシット・ウェチャチワ
Abhisit Vejjajiva 7

アピシット・ウェーチャーチーワ
Abhisit Vejjajiva 7

アピシット・ウェチャチワ
Abhisit Vejjajiva 7

アヒース＝ビリャベルデ
Agís Villaverde, Marcelino 17

アビーソン
Avieson, Bunty 71

アビダル
Abidal, Eric 7

アピチャッポン・ウィーラセタクン
Apichatpong Weerasethakul 53

アビッシュ
Abish, Walter 7

アビティア
Avitia, Mariana 72

アビディン
Abidin, Hani 7
Abidine, Mohamed Zine 7
Mizan Zainal Abidin 958

アビド
Abid, Abdellatif 7

アビドフ
Abidov, Akiljon 7
Abidov, Akilzhan 7

アビトワ
Abitova, Inga Eduardovna 7

アピニャネジ
Appignanesi, Richard 53

アビハイル
Avichail, Rabbi Eliyahu 71

アビーハリル
Abi Khalil, Cesar 7

アビモラ
Abimbola, Babalola Jean-Michel Hérvé 7

アビヤンカー
Abhyankar, Shreeram S. 7

アビーラ
Avila, Al 71
Avila, Alex 71

アビラ
Avila, Artur 71
Ávila, Carlos 71
Avila, Ceiber David 71
Ávila, Felícito 71
Avila, J.J. 71
Ávila, María Luisa 71

アビラ・ゴンサレス
Ávila González, Luis Manuel 71

アビラシェド
Abirached, Zeina 7

アピラディー
Apiradi, Tantraporn 53

アビラン
Avilan, Luis 71

アビール
Abeel, Samantha 6

アビル
Abil, Iolu 7
Abil, Iolu Johnson 7

アビルアブデルラハマン
Abdelrahman, Abeer 3

アビルダエフ
Abildayev, Bolot 7

アヒーレ
Agirre, Naroa 17

アービン
Arbin, M.von 55
Ervin, Anthony 407
Ervin, Diane Lang 408
Ervin, Phillip 408
Ervin, Tyler 408
Irvin, Bruce 649
Irvin, Monte 649

アービング
Erving, Cameron 408
Irving, Arthur 649
Irving, David 649
Irving, Frazer 649
Irving, John 649
Irving, Kyrie 649
Irving, Mary B. 650
Irving, Nate 650
Irving, Zoe 650

アビング
Abbing, Hans 2

アビンク・スパインク
Abbink Spaink, Laurens 2

アピンサ
Apinsa, Richel 53

アーヒン・テンコラン
Arhin-Tenkorang, Dyna 57

アピントン
Upington, Marion 1435

アーブ
Aab, Jaak 1

アブ
Abbe, Cheikh Ould 2
Habou, Gambo 551

アブー
Abbou, Mohammed 2

アブアイシャ
Abu Eisheh, Samir 9

アブ・アサド
Abu Assad, Hany 9

アブー・アサド
Abu Assad, Hany 9

アファティア
Afatia, Viliamu 16

アファナーシェフ
Afanasiev, Valery 16

アファナシエフ
Afanasiev, Evgenii 16
Afanasiev, Valery 16

アファナーシェフ・エフゲニー
Afanasiev, Evgenii 16

アファナセワ
Afanasyeva, Ksenia 16

アファブレ
Afable, Silvestre, Jr. 16

アブアムル
Abu Amr, Ziad 9

アブアメル
Abuamer, Muhammad Zaki 9

アブアラファ
Abu Arafeh, Khaled 9

アファラ・マシエル
Afara Maciel, Juan Eudes 16

アブアリ
Abu Ali, Said 9

アブアルホムス
Abu-al-hommus, Naem 9

アファンクアシ
Aphing Kouassi, René 53

アフィ
Affi, N'guessan 16

アブイ
Avui, Ishmael 72

アブイゾフ
Abyzov, Mikhail A. 10

アブ・イータ
Abu-eitta, Mitri 9

アブイータ
Abu-eitta, Mitri 9

アブイトフ
Abytov, Almasbek 10

アフィバーンラト
Aphibarnrat, Kiradech 53

アフィーフ

Afeef, Hassan 16
アフィフィ
Afifi, Talaat 16
アーフィールド
Arfield, Scott 57
アフウォイ
Ahwoi, Kwesei 21
アフェマイ
Afemai, Vavao 16
アフェライ
Afellay, Ibrahim 16
アブエライシュ
Abuelaish, Izzeldin 9
アブ・エル＝アサール
Abu El-Assal, Riah 9
アブエルカセム
Abouelkassem, Alaaeldin 7
アブ・エル・ファドル
Abou El Fadl, Khaled 7
アフォ
Affo, Safiou Idrissou 16
アブオヌドリ
Abouo-n'dori, Raymond 7
アフォベ
Afobe, Benik 16
アフォラビ
Afolabi, S.M. 16
アフォラヤン
Afolayan, Kunle 16
アブカシャワ
Abu-kashawa, Somia 9
アブガシュ
Abughaush, Ahmad 9
アブガネム
Abu-ghanem, Fadhel 9
アフカミ
Afkhami, Mahnaz 16
アブカラキ
Abu-karaki, Riyad 9
アブガリャン
Abgaryan, Narek 7
アブカルダ
Abu-garda, Bahar Idris 9
アブガルダ
Abu-garda, Bahar Idris 9
アブク
Abuk, Christine 9
アブクラア
Abu Kraa, Umran Ibrahim 9
アブ・ゲイダ
Abu-gheida, Hosni 9
アブゲイダ
Abu-gheida, Hosni 9
アブサアド
Abusaad, Abdulsalam Mohammad 9
アブサウード
Abu Saud, Raed 10
アブサウド
Abu Saud, Raed 10
アブサハミーン
Abu Sahmain, Nouri 10
アブサーブ
Abu Saab, Elias 9
アブサフィーエ
Abu Safiyeh, Yusef 9
アフザリ
Afzali, Amina 16
アフザル
Afzal, Amir 16
アブサロム
Absalom, Stacy 8
アブサロン
Absalon, Julien 8
アプサロン
Absalon, Julien 8
アブシ
al-Abssi, Shaker 8
アブジ
Abse, Dannie 8
アブ・ジアド
Abu-ziad, Zeyad 10
アブシエ
Absieh, Abdi Ibrahim 8
アフージャ
Ahuja, Simone 21
アフジャ
Ahuja, Anjana 21
Ahuja, Maneet 21
アブシャイア
Abshire, David Manker 8
アブシャイアー
Abshire, David Manker 8
アブシャイヤー
Abshire, David Manker 8
アブシャナブ
Abu Shanab, Ismail 10
アブシャハラ
Abu Shahla, Ma'moun 10
アブ＝ジャマール
Abu-Jamal, Mumia 9
アブジャムラ
Abou Jamra, Issam 7
アブジュ
Avci, Nabi 71
アーブシュロー
Erbschloe, Michael 405
アフス
Hafs, Zahia 553
アプス
Aps, Soetkine 53
アプストン
Upston, Louise 1435
アブスネイネ
Abu-sneineh, Suleiman 10
アフズーリ
el-Akhzouri, Boubakeru 24
アブゼイド
Abou-zeid, Mahmoud 7
Abu-zeid, Mahmoud 10
アプター
Apter, David Ernest 54
アブダッカ
Abu Daqqa, Mashhour 9
Abu Daqqa, Tahani 9
アブダッラ
Abdallah, Mahamat Ali 3
アブタヒ
Abtahi, Mohammad Ali 8
アブダラ
Abdalla, Al-Hadi 3
Abdalla, Farah Mustafa 3
Abdallah, Abdelwahab 3
Abdallah, al-Fateh Taj al-Sir 3
Abdallah, Anna 3
Abdallah, Charif 3
Abdallah, Houssen 3
Abdallah, Mahamat Ali 3
Abdallah, Mohammed Yusuf 3
Abdullah, Sheik Ahmed 5
アブダラー
Abdallah, Houmadi 3
Abdallah, Nia 3
Abdullah, Ameer 5
アブダライ
Abdallahi, Sidi Mohamed Ould Cheikh 3
アブダラーナスール
Abdallah Nassour, Mahamat Ali 3
アブダラマン
Abd-al-Raman, Abd-al-Qadir Maalin 3
アブダリャン
Avdalyan, Nazik 71
アブダルハミード
Abdulhamid, Ammar 4
アブタン
Abtan, Abd al-Hussein 8
アブツ
Abts, Tomma 9
アプツィアウリ
Aptsiauri, Giorgi 54
アプテ
Apte, D.P. 53
アブディ
Abdi, Abdiirizak Ashkir 4
Abdi, Abdullahi Gaal 4
Abdi, Ali Ismail 4
Abdi, Hammoud Ould 4
Abdi, Zakariya Mahmud Haji 4
al-Abudi, Yarub 9
アブデイ
Abdi, Youcef 4
アフディアット・K.ミハルジャ
Kartamihardja, Achdiat 706
アブディカリコワ
Abdykalikova, Gulshara 6
アブディファラー
Abdi Farah, Ali 4
アブディヤーク
Abu Diyak, Ali 9
アブディラヒ
Abdillahi, Mohamed Barkat 4
アブディラヒミギル
Abdillahimiguil, Abdallah 4
アブディルダエフ
Abdyldaev, Erlan 6
アブディン
Abdin, Hosam Hussein Bakr 4
アブデーエフ
Avdeyev, Alexander A. 71
アブデスマッド
Abdesmad, Mehdi 4
アブデッサラーム
Abdessalem, Rafik 4
アプテッド
Apted, Michael 54
アブデッラ
Abdella, Ahmedou Ould 3
アブデッルウーフ
Abderraouf, Ahmed Salem Ould 4
アブデヌール
Abdennour, Aymen 4
アブデノフ
Abdenov, Serik 4
アブデーフ
Avdeev, Anton 71
アブデラ
Abdella, Ahmedou Ould 3
アブデラール
Abdelaal, Mohamed 3
アブデルアジズ
Abdel Aziz, Khaled 3
アブデルアーティ
Abdel Aati, Muhammad 3
アブデルアール
Abdel-aal, Khaled 3
アブデルガッバール
Abdel-Gabbar, Salma Sha'ban 3
アブデルカデル
Abdel-Kader, Isselmou Ould 3
Abdelkader, Kamougue Wadal 3
Abdelqader, Mustafa Muhammad 3
アブデルガファル
Abdel Ghafar, Magdi 3
アブデルガフル
Abdel-Ghafur, Humam Abdelkhaliq 3
アブデルケフィ
Abdelkefi, Fadhel 3
アブデルケリム
Abdelkerim, Nadjo 3
アブデルシャフィ
Abdel Shafi, Haidar 3
アブデルヌール
Abdel Nour, Mounir Fakhri 3
アブデルハディ
Abdel-Hady, Aisha 3
アブデルマクスード
Abdel Maqsood, Salah 3
アブデルマジェド
Abdel-Majed, Abdel-Basit 3
アブデル・マジド・アブドル・アジズ
Abdel Majid Abdel Aziz 3
アブデルマジド王子
Abdel Majid Abdel Aziz 3
アブデル・マジド・ビン・アブドル・アジズ
Abdel Majid Abdel Aziz 3
アブデルマリク
Abdel-Malek, Anouar I. 3
アブデル・マレク
Abdel-Malek, Anouar I. 3
アブデルマン
Abderemane, Salime Mohamed 4
アブデルムウミン
Abdel Mo'men, Muhammad Salah 3
アブデルムーメヌ
Abdelmoumene, Mohamed-Larbi 3
アブデル・メギド
Abdel-Meguid, Ahmed Esmat 3
アブデルモタレブ
Abdelmottaleb, Diaaeldin Kamal Gouda 3
アブデルラザク
Abdelrazzaq, Muhammad Zimam 3
アブデルラジム

ア

Abdelazim, Tarek 3
アブデルラスール
Abdel-Rasoul, Ali Mahmoud 3
アブデルラティフ
Abdel-Latif, Hatem 3
アブデルラーマン
Abdelrahman, Abdelrahman Saïd 3
アブデルワーヘド
Abdelwahed, Said I. 3
アブデレマン
Abderemane, Moussa 4
アブード
Abboud, Fadi 2
Aboud, Frances E. 7
アブト
Abt, Alexander 8
アブド
Abudo, Jose 9
アブドー
Abdou, Ahmed 4
アブドイラフマノフ
Abdyrakhmanov, Zhakyp 6
アブドゥ
Abdou, Amani 4
Abdou, Asmane 4
Abdou, Mahmoud Ahmed 4
Abdou, Mhoumadi 4
Abdou, Moustadroine 4
Abdou, Ousmane 4
Abdou, Yahaya Baaré Haoua 4
Aboudou, Assoumany 7
アブドゥッラ
Abdulla, Kamal 5
アブドゥハキモフ
Abdukhakimov, Aziz 4
アブドゥーラ
Abdula, Nazira Karimo Vali 4
アブドゥラ
Abdullah, Rayan 5
アブドゥライ
Abdoulahi, Mohamed 4
Abdoulaye, Kadi 4
アブドゥライェ
Abdoulaye, Mahamat 4
アブドゥライエ
Abdoulaye, Aissa Diallo 4
アブドゥラエ
Abdoulaye, Mahamat 4
アブドゥラエフ
Abdullaev, Fahtullah 5
Abdullaev, Muminjon 5
Abdullayev, Abdulkadir 5
アブドゥラハマン
Abdourahamane, Sani 4
アブドゥラヒ
Abdoulahi, Mohamed 4
Abdullahi, Abdi Hashi 5
Abdullahi, Bolaji 5
アブドゥラヒモフ
Abdurakhimov, Khairiddin 6
アブドゥラフマノワ
Abdurakhmanova, Rano 6
アブドゥラフモノフ
Abdurakhmonov, Bekzod 6
アブドゥラマン
Abdurahman, Sheikh Mohammed 6
アブドゥルアジズ
Abdulaziz, Mohammed 4
アブドゥルカダリ
Abdoulkadari, Tidjani Idrissa 4
アブドゥルガニ
Abdulgani, Ruslan 4
アブドゥル・カラム
Abdul Kalam, Avul Pakir Jainulabdeen 5
アブドゥルカリム
Abdoul Karim, Moussa Bako 4
アブドゥル－クッドゥス
Abdul-quddus, Isa 5
アブドゥル－ハミド
Abdul-Hamid, Walid 4
アブドゥルハミド
Abdoulhamid, Mohamed 4
Abdul-Hamid, Mustapha 4
Abudul-hamid, Mustapha 9
アブドゥルフェタ
Abdulfetah, Sheikh Abdulahi 4
アブドゥルヘキモフ
Abdylhekimov, Wepa 6
アブドゥルマリク
Abdel-Malek, Anouar I. 3
アブドゥルムネイム
Abdel Muneim, Yehia Mohamed 3
アブドゥル・ムヒト
Abdul Muhith, Abul Maal 5
アブドゥルラエワ
Abdullayeva, Uktomkhan 5
アブドゥル・ラーマン
Abdul Rahman, Dahlan 5
アブドゥレ
Abdulle, Abdiqadir Muhammad 5
アブドゥレイ
Abdoulaye, Aissa Diallo 4
アブドキリム
Abudogupur, Abudokirim 9
アブドサロモフ
Abdusalomov, Yusup 6
アブドッラー
Abdullah, Rania Al 5
アブドッラハマーン
Abd al-Rahman, A'ishah 3
アブドードッサル
Abdou Dossar, Mohamed Bacar 4
アブドバリ
Abdevali, Saeid 4
アブドラ
Abdulla, Ahmed 5
Abdulla, bin Khalid al-Khalifa 5
Abdulla, bin Salman al-Khalifa 5
Abdullah, Abdullah 5
Abdullah, Ahmad Hassan 5
Abdullah, Ahmed 5
al-Abdullah, Ali 5
Abdullah, Badawi 5
Abdullah, Bakar 5
Abdullah, bin Abdul-Aziz 5
Abdullah, bin Hamad al-Thani 5
Abdullah, bin Khalid al-Khalifa 5
Abdullah, bin Khalid al-Thani 5
Abdullah, bin Nasser bin Khalifa al-Thani 5
Abdullah, bin Salman al-Khalifa 5
Abdullah, Farooq 5
Abdullah, Ibn Abdul-Aziz 5
Abdullah, Jamal Mansour 5
al-Abdullah, Khalaf Sleiman 5
Abdullah, Mohammed bin Abdul-Gafar 5
Abdullah, Nasr al-Mabrouk 5
Abdullah, Riyadh 5
Abdullah, Salwa 5
Abdullah, Samir 5
Abdullah, Tarmugi 5
Abdullahi, Hassan 5
Abudulla, Ahmed 9
Abudulla, Hisham Sharaf 9
Abudullah, Ali Ajaj 9
Abudullah, bin Khalid al-Thani 9
Abudullah, bin Khalifa al-Thani 9
Abudullah, bin Zayed al-Nahyan 9
アブドライ
Abdallahi, Sidi Mohamed Ould Cheikh 3
アブドラ・イブン・アブドルアジズ
Abdullah bin Abdul Aziz 5
アブドラ・イブン・フセイン
Abdullah ibn al-Hussein 5
アブドラエフ
Abdullaev, Fahtullah 5
アブドラクマノフ
Abdrakhmanov, Berik 4
アブドーラ・ザ・ブッチャー
Abdullah The Butcher 5
アブドラジク
Abdelrazig, Suad 3
アブドラ・バダウィ
Abdullah Badawi 5
アブドラヒ
Abdallahi, Sidi Mohamed Ould Cheikh 3
アブドラヒ・モハメド
Abbullahi Mohamed, Mohamed 3
アブドラヒモフ
Abdurakhimov, Khairiddin 6
アブドラ・ビン・アブドル・アジズ
Abdullah bin Abdul Aziz 5
アブドラ・ビン・フセイン
Abdullah ibn al-Hussein 5
アブドラ・ファドル
Abdalla Fadl, Fadl 3
アブドラフマノフ
Abdrakhmanov, Kairat 4
アブドラボ
Abd Rabo, Noha 4
アブドラマン
Abderrahmane, Ba 4
アブドル
Abdul, Halim Muadzam Shah 4
アブドルアジズ
Abdelaziz, Mohamed Ould 3
Abdul-Aziz, bin Fahd bin Abdul-Aziz 4
Abdul-Aziz, bin Mohammed al-Fadhel 4
Abdulaziz, Mohammad Imhamid 4
Abdul Aziz, Shamsuddin 4
アブドルアジズ・アルナジム
Abdul-Aziz al-Nagem, Samil 4
アブドルアリザデ
Abdol-Alizadeh, Ali 4
アブドル・カディール
Abdul Qadir 5
アブドル・カディル
Abdul Qadir 5
アブドルカディル
Abdul Kadir, Sheikh Fadzir 4
アブドル・ガーニー
Abdulghani, Abdul-Aziz 4
アブドルガニ
Abdulghani, Abdul-Aziz 4
アブドールガフール
Abdoelgafoer, Faizal 4
アブドルガフール
Abdul-Gafoor, Ahmed Adeeb 4
アブドルサラーム
Abdulsalam, Muhammed Al-Farooq 6
アブドルジャリル
Abdeljalil, Mustafa Mohamed 3
Abduljaleel, Mostafa Mohamed 4
Abdul Jalil, Mustafa 4
アブドルスフニ
Abdul-sukhni, Adnan 6
アブドルハイ
Abdul-Hay, Murad 4
アブドルハディ
Abdel-Hady, Aisha 3
アブドルハフェズ
Abdelhafiz, Abdelrahim 3
アブドルハミド
Abdul-Hamid, Mustapha 4
アブドルハリク
Abdel Khalek, Sayed 3
アブドル・ハリム
Abdul Halim, Muadzam Shah 4
アブドルハーレク
Abdelkhaleq, Mahmoud 3
アブドルフセイン
Abdul-Hussain, bin Ali Mirza 4
アブドルマジド
Abdul-majid, Bassam 5
アブドルマジド・ビン・アブドルアジズ王子
Abdel Majid Abdel Aziz 3
アブドルマハディ
Abd Al-Mahdi, Adil 3
アブドルムーティ
Abdul-mouti, Nasser 5
アブドル・ムヒト
Abdul Muhith, Abul Maal 5
アブドルラジク
Abdul-raziq, Suad 6

アブドルラゼク
Abdul-razeq, Hisham 5
Abdul Razeq, Omar 6
アブドルラティフ
Abdul-Lateef, Layla 5
Abdul-Latif, Waal 5
アブドルラティフ・ビン・アブドルマリク・ビン・オマル・シェイフ
Abdullatif bin Abdulmalik bin Omar al-Sheikh 5
アブドルラハマン
Abdel-Rahman, Hassabo Mohammed 3
Abdul-rahman, Ahmad 5
Abdul-rahman, bin Khalifa bin Abdul-Aziz al-Thani 5
アブドルラヒーム
Abdul-raheem, Tayyeb 5
アブドルラヒム
Abdul-rahim, Kamal Abdul-Latif 5
アブドルラフマン
Abdel Rahman, Ahmad 3
Abdul-rahman, Farouk 5
Abdul-rahman, Mudathir Abdulghani 5
Abdulrahman, Sadiq Abdulkarim 5
アブドル・ラフマーン・フムード・アル・オタイビ
Abdul-Rahman Humood Al-Otaibi 5
アブドル・ラーマン
Abdul Rahman, Dahlan 5
アブドルラーマン
Abdul Rahman, Taib 5
アブドルワヒド
Abdelwahid, Yousuf Ibrahim 3
アブドレラ
Abdulelah, Ahmed Alderwish 4
アプトン
Upton, Eben 1435
Upton, Graham 1435
Upton, Kate 1435
Upton, Melvin 1435
Upton, Roy 1435
Upton, Simon 1435
アブナ
Abouna, Akia 7
アブナー
Avner, Amit 72
アブナスル
Abul Nasr, Mahmoud Muhammad 9
アブ・ニダル
Abu Nidal 9
アブー・ニダル
Abu Nidal 9
アフヌッシュ
Akhannouch, Aziz 23
アブネット
Abnett, Dan 7
Abnett, Kathryn 7
アブバ
Abouba, Albadé 7
アブバカル
Aboubacar, Yaya 7
Aboubakar, Abderassoul 7
Aboubakar, Vincent 7
Abu Bakar, Apong 9
Abubakar, Atiku 9
Abubakar, Muhammed 9
アブバクル
Abu-baker, Ali Omar 9
Abubaker, Fuad 9
Abubaker, Mohammad Hassan 9
アブバクル・バクダディ師
Abu Bakr al-Baghdadi 9
アブバケール
Aboubaker, Ali Guelleh 7
アブーバスツ
Abu Basutu, Titus Mehliswa Jonathan 9
アブハッサン
Abu Hassan, Reem 9
アブハディド
Abo-hadid, Ayman 7
アブハデイブ
Abu Hdeib, Shihadeh 9
アブハムール
Abu Hammour, Mohammad 9
アブハムル
Abu Hammour, Mohammad 9
アブハラフ
Abu Khalaf, Nayef 9
アブ・ハンナ
Abu Hanna, Joel 9
アブファウル
Abu Faour, Wael 9
アブフナス
Abufunas, Mustafa Mohammad 9
アブー・マーゼン
Abbas, Mahmoud 2
アフマダリエフ
Akhmadaliev, Murodjon 23
アフマディ
Ahmadi, Elaheh 20
アフマディーネジャード
Ahmadinejad, Mahmoud 20
アフマディネジャド
Ahmadinejad, Mahmoud 20
アフマド
al-Ahmad, Najm Hamad 19
Ahmad, Qazi Hussain 19
Ahmad, Shabery Cheek 19
Ahmad, Tontowi 20
Ahmed, Aftab 20
al-Hamad, Najm Hamad 560
アフマトゥーリナ
Akhmadulina, Bella 23
アフマドゥーリナ
Akhmadulina, Bella 23
アフマドゥリナ
Akhmadulina, Bella 23
アフマド・シャベリー
Ahmad Shabery, Cheek 20
アフマドシャベリー
Ahmad Shabery, Cheek 20
アフマードフ
Akhmadov, Musa 23
アフマドフ
Ahmadov, Rashad 20
Akhmadov, Alamkhon 23
アフマニ
Aghmani, Jamal 17
アブ・ミデン
Abu-meddain, Fraih 9
アフメイズヌ
Ahumey-zunu, Séléagodji 21
アフメタイ
Ahmetaj, Arben 21
アフメド
Ahmed, Aneesa 20
Ahmed, Hannah 20
Ahmed, Maryan Qasim 20
Ahmed, Mohamed Jameel 20
Ahmed, Moinafouraha 20
Ahmed, Sheikh Sharif 20
Ahmed, Tofail 20
アフメド・アリ
Ahmed Ali, Mahdi 20
アフメドバエ
Akhmedbaev, Adkham 23
アフメドバエフ
Akhmedbaev, Adkham 23
アフメトビッチ
Ahmetović, Sodik 21
アフメトフ
Ahmetov, Bakyt 21
Akhmetov, Danial 23
Akhmetov, Serik 23
Akhmetov, Ulan 23
アフメドフ
Akhmedov, Ali 23
Akhmedov, Bakhodir 23
Akhmedov, Bakhtiyar 23
Akhmedov, Kasimali 23
Akhmedov, Nadir A. 23
アブモグリ
Abu Moghli, Fathi 9
アフラ
Afrah, Abdullahi Ahmed 16
Afrah, Mohamed Qanyare 16
アブラアム
Abraham, Herard 8
アフラギ
Akhlaghi, Habibollah 23
アプラク
Apraku, Kofi Konadu 53
アブラシ
Abrashi, Amir 8
Abrashi, Arban 8
アブラシェフ
Abrashev, Bojidar 8
アブラシュ
Abrash, Ibrahim 8
アブラショフ
Abrashoff, D.Michael 8
アブラス
Abu-rass, Sadiq Ameen 9
アーブラスター
Arblaster, Anthony 55
アブラナス
Avranas, Alexandros 72
アブラハ
Abraha, Asfaha 7
Abraha, Petros 7
アブラハミアン
Abrahamian, Ara 8
アブラハミャン
Abrahamian, Hovik 8
Abrahamyan, Hovik 8
アブラハム
Abraham, Ajith 7
Abraham, Bérengère 7
Abraham, Charles 7
Abraham, Gloria 7
Abraham, Ken 8
Abraham, Tadesse 8
Abrahams, Ramon 8
Abrham, Tekeste 8
Avraham, Ruhama 72
アブラハムス
Abrahams, Peter Herbert 8
Abrahams, Ramon 8
アブラハムズ
Abrahams, Peter Herbert 8
アブラハムソン
Abrahamsson, Britt-Louise 8
アブラーム
Abraham, David 7
アブラムス
Abrams, Douglas Carlton 8
Abrams, Michael 8
アブラムソン
Abramson, Alan J. 8
Abramson, Ian 8
Abramson, Lauren 8
アブラムチュク
Abramchuk, Alena 8
アブラメンコ
Abramenko, Oleksandr 8
アブラモヴィッチ
Abramović, Marina 8
Abramovich, Roman Arkadyevich 8
Abramowicz, Janet 8
アブラモウィッツ
Abramowitz, Jonathan S. 8
Abramowitz, Morton I. 8
アブラモービッチ
Abramovich, Roman Arkadyevich 8
アブラモビッチ
Abramovich, Roman Arkadyevich 8
アブラモフ
Avramov, Lucien 72
アブラモプロス
Avramopoulos, Dimitris 72
アフラロ
Afflalo, Arron 16
Afflalo, Eli 16
アブラン
Ablan, Dan 7
アブリ
Abri, Julius 8
アフリイエ
Afriyie, Kuwaku 16
アフリエ
Afriyie, Kuwaku 16
アフリカーノ
Africano, Manuel António 16
アブリコソフ
Abrikosov, Alexei Alexeyevich 8
アフリディ
Afridi, Hameed Ullah Jan 16
Afridi, Nawabzada Fazal Karim 16
アフリディー
Afridi, Abbass Khan 16

ア

ア

アブリーデリス
Abbrederis, Jared 3
アブリネス
Abrines, Alex 8
アブリビダモン
Abli-bidamon, Dédériwé 7
アブリブダ
Abu Libda, Hassan 9
アブリャジン
Abliazin, Denis 7
Ablyazin, Denis 7
アプリーレ
Aprile, Pino 53
アプリン
Aplin, Andrew 53
アプリング
Appling, Dean Ramsay 53
アブル
Abul, Yasser Hassan 9
アブルカ
Avluca, Nazmi 72
アブルガジエフ
Abulgaziev, Mukhammetkaly 9
アブルゲイト
Abul Gheit, Ahmed Ali 9
アプルゲート
Applegate, Royce D. 53
アブー=ルゴド
Abu-Lughod, Janet L. 9
Abu-Lughod, Lila 9
アブルサミーン
Abulsamin, Mahil 9
アブルソン
Ableson, W.Frank 7
アプルトン
Appleton, Jay 53
アブルナガ
Abou El-naga, Fayza Muhammad 7
アプルバウム
Applbaum, Arthur Isak 53
Applebaum, Robert 53
アブルハサン
Abul Hassan, Muhammad Abdullah Abbas 9
アブルフムス
Abul-humus, Naim 9
アプルボーム
Applebaum, Anne 53
アブルホムス
Abu-al-hommos, Naeem 9
アブルレイル
Abul Leil, Mahmoud 9
アフレイテン
Afraitane, Kamaliddine 16
アブレイユ
Abreu, Jose 8
アブレウ
Abreu, Alcinda 8
Abreu, Kátia 8
Abreu, Sergio 8
アプレジャー
Upledger, John E. 1435
アフレック
Affleck, Ben 16
Affleck, Geoff 16
アブレット
Ablett, Barry 7
アブロウ
Ablow, Keith R. 7
アプロガンジボデ
Aplogan-djibode, Didier 53
アブロシモワ
Abrosimova, Anastasia 8
アフロジャック
Afrojack 16
アブロマビチュス
Abromavicius, Aivaras 8
アブロン
Ablon, J.Stuart 7
Ablon, Steven Luria 7
Avron, Philippe 72
アーベ
Ahbe, Kelsie 19
アベイ
Avei, Moi 71
アペイ・アワンジンメイ
Apei Awangjinmei 52
アベイドゥナ
Abeidna, Mohamed Ould Ismail Ould 6
アベイレゲッセ
Abeylegesse, Elvan 6
アベイワルダナ
Abeywardena, Mahinda Yapa 7
Abeywardena, Vajira 7
アベカシス
Abecassis, Eliette 6
アベカシス - フィリップス
Abecasis-Phillips, John Andrew Stephen 6
アベグレン
Abegglen, James C. 6
アベサラ
Abessallah, Youssouf 6
アベジャン
Abellán, Miquel 6
アベジョ・ビベス
Abello Vives, Natalia 6
アベス
Abbes, Djamel 2
Abbes, Mohamed Chérif 2
アペソス
Apesos, Anthony 53
アベソフマ
Abeso Fuma, Fausto 6
アベッツ
Abetz, Eric 6
アベッド
Abed, Fazle Hasan 6
アベディ
Abedi, Isabel 6
アベディニ
Abedini, Mojtaba 6
アベディン
Abedin, Zainul 6
アベド
Abed, Mohamed Ould 6
Abed, Sheila 6
アベドラボ
Abed-rabbo, Yasser 6
アベドン
Avedon, Richard 71
アベナ
Abena, Ange Antoine 6
Abena, Paul 6
アベナ・オンドゥア・オバマ
Abena Ondoua Obama, Marie Thérèse 6
アベナリウス
Avenarius, Hermann 71
アベニー
Abney, Mike 7
アベノンシ
Agbenonci, Aurélien 17
アベベ
Abebe, Daniel 6
アヘメトフ
Ahmetov, Bakyt 21
アベーラ
Abela, Carmelo 6
Abela, George 6
アベラ
Abela, Deborah 6
Abela, George 6
Abella, Alex 6
アベラルド
Aberaldo, Fernandez 6
アベランジェ
Havelange, João 583
アベリー
Avery, Sid 71
アペリ
Apperry, Yann 53
アベリカ
Awerika, Tebao 72
アベリヤ
Abella, Ernest 6
アーベリン
Abelin, Björn 6
アーペル
Apel, Friedmar 52
Apel, Karl-Otto 52
アベール
Abeele, Véronique van den 6
アベル
Abel, Bas van 6
Abel, Charles 6
Abel, Dominique 6
Abel, Heather 6
Abel, Jennifer 6
Abele, Anton 6
アペル
Apel, Katrin 53
Appel, Benjamin 53
Appel, Gerald 53
Appel, Jacob 53
Appel, Karel Christian 53
アベルカヌ
Aberkane, Abdelhamid 6
アペルクライン
Appelcline, Shannon 53
アベルサノ
Aversano, Nina 71
アーベル=シュトルート
Abel-Struth, Sigrid 6
アベルス
Abells, Chana Byers 6
アーベルスハウザー
Abelshauser, Werner 6
アーベルソン
Abelson, Philip Hauge 6
アベルト
Avelluto, Pablo 71
アペルト
Appelt, Christian W. 53
Appelt, Kathi 53
アペルバーム
Appelbaum, Eileen 53
アベルブフ
Averbukh, Alexander 71
Averbukh, Ilia 71
アペロ
Appelo, Tim 53
アペロー
Aperlo, Peter 53
アーベンハウス
Avenhaus, Rudolf 71
アホ
Aho, Ninos 21
'Aho, Siaosi Taimani 21
アポ・アワン・ジグメー
Apei Awangjinmei 52
アボイエ
Aboye, Mohamed Lemine Ould 7
アボイボ
Agboyibo, Yawovi Madji 17
アホウンディ
Akhoundi, Abbas 23
アボカ
Avoka, Cletus 72
アボゴヌコノ
Abogo Nkono, Louis Marie 7
アボコル
Abokor, Sayid Warsame 7
アボゴンコノ
Abogo Nkono, Louis Marie 7
アボーシ
Aboushi, Oday 7
アポストル
Apostol, Adrian 53
Apostol, Tom M. 53
Apostolou, Vangelis 53
アポストロ
Apostolo, Giorgio 53
アポストロス=カッパドナ
Apostolos-Cappadona, Diane 53
アポダカ
Apodaca, Anthony A. 53
Apodaca, Jennifer 53
Apodaca, Rose 53
アボット
Abbot, Judi 2
Abbot, Laura 2
Abbott, Andrew Delano 2
Abbott, Chris 2
Abbott, Elizabeth 2
Abbott, Geoffrey 2
Abbott, Jeff 2
Abbott, Jennifer 2
Abbott, Jeremy 2
Abbott, Kingsley 2
Abbott, Mara 2
Abbott, Megan E. 2
Abbott, Paul 2
Abbott, Raylene 2
Abbott, Tony 2
アホネン
Ahonen, Janne 21
アホラ
Ahola, Tapani 21
アボラ
Avola, Giorgio 72
アボルティニャ
Aboltina, Solvita 7
アボルハッサン
Abolhassan, Ferri 7
アーボレリウス
Arborelius, Lotta 55
アポロニア
Apolonia, Tiago 53

アーボン
Arbon, Jason 55
アマー
Ammar, Alain 41
アマウィ
Amawi, Ahmad Ahmad El 40
アマエチ
Amaechi, Rotimi 39
アマゴアリク
Amagoalik, John 39
アーマコスト
Armacost, Michael Hayden 58
アマコスト
Armacost, Michael Hayden 58
アマジョダ
Hamadjoda, Adjoudi 560
アマソン
Amason, Craig 39
アマダ
Amada, Gerald 39
アマダー
Amador, Xavier Francisco 39
アマダジ＝グッゾ
Amadasi-Guzzo, Maria Giulia 39
アーマッド
Ahmad 19
Ahmad, David R.Mirza 19
Ahmad, F. 19
Ahmad, Waqar 20
アマーティ
Amartey, Daniel 39
アマディ
Amadi, Elechi 39
Amady, Augustin 39
アマデイ
Amadei, Bernard 39
アマティア
Amatya, Deepak Chandra 40
アマディオ
Amadio, James 39
Amadio, Peter C. 39
アマティラ
Amathila, Libertina 39
アマティル
Armethil, Christine 58
アーマド
Ahmad, Jumat 19
Ahmad, Muhammad Ali 19
Tontowi Ahmad 1412
アマート
Amato, Giuliano 39
Amato, Mary 39
アマード
Amado, Jorge 39
Amado, Luís 39
Anado, Luis Filipe Margues 42
アマト
Amat, Jordi 39
Amato, Giuliano 39
Amato, Serena 39
アマド
Amado, Jorge 39
アマトイレオン・チャベス
Amaty Léon Chavez, Carlos 40
アマドゥ
Amadou, Baba 39
Amadou, Hama 39
Amadou, Marou 39
Hamadou, Baba 560
アマドゥジブリ
Amadoud Jibril, Fatouma 39
アマトゥーゾ
Amatuzio, Janis 40
アマトーリ
Amatori, Franco 40
アマトリアイン
Amatriain, Alicia 40
アマドルビカザコバ
Amador Bikkazakova, Andrey 39
アマトン
Amatong, Juanita 39
アマナアマナ
Amama Amama, Benjamin 39
アマナット
Amanat, Ebrahim 39
アマニ
Amani, Michel N'guessan 39
Amani, René 39
Hamani, Ahmed Mohamed Ag 560
アマニヌゲサン
Amani N'guessan, Michel 39
アマノ
Amano, Hiroshi 39
Amanor, Stephen Kwao 39
アマノフ
Amanov, Charymyrat 39
アマビール
Amabile, Teresa M. 38
アマフォ
Amafo, Alice 39
アマーブル
Amable, Bruno 39
アマラ
Amara, Abdelkader 39
Amara, Fadela 39
アマラウィーラ
Amaraweera, Mahinda 39
アマラトゥンガ
Amarathunga, John 39
アマラドス
Amaladoss, Michael 39
アマラル
Amaral, Francisco Xavier do 39
Amaral, Ovidio 39
Amaral, Roberto 39
アマランテ
Amarante, Jose Ajiu 39
アマランテバレ
Amarante Baret, Carlos 39
アマランテバレト
Amarante Baret, Carlos 39
アマリ
Amri, Marwa 42
アマリスタ
Amarista, Alexi 39
アマリーリォ
Amariglio, Jack 39
アマリン
Amarin, Vladimir V. 39
アマール
Amar, Corinne 39
Amar, Patrick 39
Amar, Sidy Mohamed Ould Taleb 39
アマルゴ
Amargo, Pablo 39
Amargo, Rafael 39
アマルリック
Amalric, Mathieu 39
アマレロウィリアムス
Amarello-williams, Joyce 39
アマロ
Amaro, Jace 39
Amaro, Ruben, Jr. 39
アーマン
Ehrman, Bart D. 393
Ehrman, Mark 393
Erman, Darren 407
Urman, Scott 1436
アマン
Aman, Acharya 39
Aman, Wahi 39
Amann, Hans 39
Amann, Martina 39
Ammann, Daniel 41
Ammann, Simon 41
Geleto, Mohammed Aman 487
Hamman, Adalbert-G. 563
アマンク
Amangku, Enoch 39
アマンスハウザー
Amanshauser, Martin 39
アマンダ
Amanda 39
アーマントラウト
Armantrout, Rae 58
アマンネペソフ
Amannepesov, Nurmuhammet 39
アマンプール
Amanpour, Christiane 39
アマンマルクサー
Amann-marxer, Marlies 39
アマンムイラドフ
Amanmyradov, Orazgeldy 39
アミ
Ami, Korren 41
アミアリュシク
Amialiusik, Alena 41
アミェ
Amiez, Sébastien 41
アミエイロ
Amieiro, Nuno 41
アミエル
Amiel, Jean-Claude 41
アミシア
Amichia, François Albert 41
アーミステッド
Armitstead, Elizabeth 58
アーミテイジ
Armitage, David 58
Armitage, Kenneth 58
アーミテージ
Armitage, Carol 58
Armitage, Gary C. 58
Armitage, John 58
Armitage, Kenneth 58
Armitage, Peter 58
Armitage, Richard Lee 58
Armitage, Simon 58
アーミテジ
Armitage, Kenneth 58
アーミテステッド
Armitstead, Elizabeth 58
アミドゥ
Amidu, Martin 41
アミナ
Amina, Nur Hussein 41
アミナシビリ
Aminashvili, Sandro 41
アミナバビ
Aminabhavi, Tejraj M. 41
アミニ
Amini, Hossein 41
アミヌ
Aminu, Al-Farouq 41
アミヌディン
Aminuddin, Usman 41
アミムール
Amimour, Mahieddine 41
アミリ
al-Amiri, Hadi 41
Amiri, Hossein Ali 41
Amiri, Nadiem 41
アミリャン
Amiryan, Armen 41
アーミル
Amil, Farukh 41
アミール
Amir, Lital 41
アミル
Amir, Syamsuddin 41
アミルタマセブ
Amir-tahmasseb, Babak 41
アミロフ
Amirov, Feodor 41
Amirov, Rajabmad 41
アミーン
Ameen, Afsarul 40
アミン
Ameen, Afsarul 40
Amiin, Muse Nur 41
amin 41
Amin, Abdulkadir 41
Amin, Adnan 41
Amin, Bakhityar 41
al-Amin, Habib Mohammad 41
Amin, Haron 41
Amin, Majid 41
Amin, Samir 41
Amin, Yusuf Maalin 41
Amin, Yusuf Moallim 41
Amin Dada, Idi 41
アミンザデ
Aminzadeh, Elham 41
アミン・ダダ
Amin Dada, Idi 41
アム
Amu, Amir Hossain 42
アムー
Amu, Amir Hossain 42
アムウィーロ
Amweelo, Moses 42
アムカマラ
Amukamara, Prince 42
アムクヤ
Hamukuya, Albertina Julia 564
アムゲムバ
Amoughe Mba, Pierre 42
アムザラグ
Amzalag, Michael 42

ア

アームシャー
Irmscher, Christoph 649
アームス
Armus, Adam 59
アームズ
Arms, Richard W., Jr. 58
アムス
Amoussou, Bruno 42
アムスー
Amoussou, Bruno 42
アムスガ
Amoussouga, Fullbert Géro 42
アムズジャケ
Amouzou-djake, Angèle 42
アムスタッツ
Amstutz, Mark R. 42
アムスター＝バートン
Amster-Burton, Matthew 42
アームステッド
Armstead, Arik 59
Armstead, Terron 59
アムスデン
Amsden, Alice Hoffenberg 42
アームストロング
Armstrong, Alan 59
Armstrong, Alan W. 59
Armstrong, Arthur 59
Armstrong, Billie Joe 59
Armstrong, Brad 59
Armstrong, C.Michael 59
Armstrong, Craig 59
Armstrong, Darrell 59
Armstrong, David Malet 59
Armstrong, Dylan 59
Armstrong, Felicity 59
Armstrong, Gary M. 59
Armstrong, Harvey 59
Armstrong, Helen 59
Armstrong, Hilary 59
Armstrong, Hilton 59
Armstrong, Howard 59
Armstrong, Jennifer 59
Armstrong, John 59
Armstrong, Karen 59
Armstrong, Kelley 59
Armstrong, Ken 59
Armstrong, Kristin 59
Armstrong, Lance 59
Armstrong, Lindsay 59
Armstrong, Louise 59
Armstrong, Mark Anthony 59
Armstrong, Matthew S. 59
Armstrong, Neil Alden 59
Armstrong, Nicky 59
Armstrong, Nigel 59
Armstrong, Ray-Ray 59
Armstrong, R.G. 59
Armstrong, Shawn 59
Armstrong, Shelagh 59
Armstrong, Sue 59
Armstrong, Terri 59
Armstrong, Thomas 59
Armstrong, Wally 59
アームソン
Urmson, J.O. 1436
アムダー
Amdur, Robert J. 40
アムダール
Amdahl, Gene 40
アムチャステギ
Amuchastegui, Cristian Emanuel 42
アムテ
Amte, Murlidhar Devidas 42
アムディ
al-Amudi, Umar Muhsin Abdul-Rahman 42
アムドゥ
Hamdou, Ykoubou Koumadjo 561
アムドポ
Amoudokpo, Komi Dotse 42
アムナ
Amna, Nur Hussein 41
アムナト
Ruenroeng, Amnat 1215
アムヌガマ
Amunugama, Sarath 42
アムバクシア
Ambachtsheer, Keith P. 40
アムバサラ
Amba Salla, Patrice 40
アームブリスター
Armbrister, Thurston 58
アムブロゼク
Ambrozek, Libor 40
アムラニ
al-Amrani, Ahmed Ali 42
アムラーネ
Amurane, Adelaide Anchia 42
アムラバト
Amrabat, Nordin 42
アムラム
Amram, Martha 42
アムラン
Amran, Sulaiman 42
Hamelin, Charles 561
Hamelin, Marc-André 561
アムリ
Amri, Marwa 42
アムリタスワルーパーナンダ
Amritaswarupananda, Swami 42
アムリターナンダマイー
Amritanandamayi, Mata 42
アムリターナンダマイー・デーヴィ
Amritanandamayi, Mata 42
アムリン
Ameline, Jean-Paul 40
アムール
Ameur, Mohammed 41
アムル
Amr, Muhammad Kamel 42
Amro, Nabil 42
アムンセン
Amundsen, Per-Willy 42
アムンドソン
Amundson, Lou (Louis) 42
Amundson, Norman E. 42
アーメイ
A-MEI 40
アメイ
A-MEI 40
アメカン
Amekan, Hassan 40
アメジョグベ
Amedjogbe, Henriette Kuevi 40
アメジョグベクエビ
Amedjogbekouevi, Henriette Olivia 40
アーメッド
Ahmed, Ajaz 20
Ahmed, Nick 20
アメット
Amette, Jacques-Pierre 41
アメッド
Ahmed, Mohi 20
アメティ
Ameti, Bashkim 41
アーメド
Āhameda, Humāyūna 19
Ahmed, Khawar Zaman 20
Ahmed, Mustapha 20
Ahmed, Shahabuddin 20
アメト
Amet, Arnold 41
アメド
Ahmed, Ettouhami Moulay 20
アーメド・ビン・サルマン・ビン・アブドルアジズ
Ahmed bin Salman bin Abdul-Aziz 20
アメナーバル
Amenábar, Alejandro 40
アメナバール
Amenábar, Alejandro 40
アメニオ
Amenyo, Afi Ntifa 40
アメラリ
Ameerali, Robert 40
アメリー
Amery, Colin 40
Amery, Heather 40
アメリアチ
Ameliach, Francisco José 40
アメリオ
Amelio, Gianni 40
Amelio, William J. 40
アメリカーナー
Amerikaner, Susan 40
アメリキン
Amel'kin, Vladimir Vasil'evich 40
アメリコ
Americo, Tiago 40
アメリス
Améris, Jean-Pierre 40
アメリーヌ
Ameline, Nicole 40
アメリヤノビチ
Ameliyanovich, Mikhail M. 40
アメリヤノビッチ
Amelianovich, Mikhail M. 40
アメリン
Ameline, Nicole 40
Hamelin, Charles 561
Hamelin, François 561
アメル
Amel, Arash 40
Amer, Musa 40
アメールディン
Ameeruddin, Syed 40
アメルハノフ
Amerkhanov, Ruslan 40
アメルング
Amelung, Knut 40
アメン
Ament, Jeff 40
アーメンターノ
Armentano, Paul 58
アメンドーラ
Amendola, Danny 40
アモース
Amorth, Gabriele 41
アモス
Amos, Hallam 42
Amos, Nijel 42
アモーソフ
Amosov, Nikolai Mikhailovich 42
アモソフ
Amosov, Nikolai Mikhailovich 42
アーモット
Aamodt, Sandra 1
アモテンスティーン
Amatenstein, Sherry 39
アモファ
Amofo, Alice 41
アモヤン
Amoyan, Roman 42
アモリム
Amorim, Celso 41
アモリン
Amorim, Celso 41
Amorín, José 41
アモール
Amor, Daniel 41
アモルーソ
Amoruso, Sophia 42
アモレ
Amore, Dom 41
アモレビエタ
Amorebieta, Fernando 41
アーモン
Almon, Clopper 35
Almon, Joan 35
アモン
Amon, Benoît 41
Hamon, Herve 564
アモンギ
Amongi, Betty 41
アモンズ
Ammons, A.R. 41
Ammons, Mark 41
アモン・タノ
Amon-tanoh, Marcel 41
アモンタノー
Amon-tanoh, Marcel 41
アーモンド
Almond, David 35
Almond, Gabriel Abraham 35
Almond, Mark 35
アヤ
Ahya, Shubhada N. 21
Hayat, Pierre 584
アヤコ
Ayacko, Ochillo 73
アヤゴン
Aillagon, Jean-Jacques 22
アヤシュ
Ayache, Alain 73
アヤソル
Ayassor, Adji Otèth 73
アヤット

Hayat, Candice 584
アヤディ
Ayadi, Kamel 73
アヤド
Ayad, Sara 73
アヤトラ・サデク・ハルハリ
Khalkhali, Mohammed Sadeq 725
アヤナ
Ayana, Almaz 73
アヤーラ
Ayala, Francisco 73
アヤラ
Ayala, Francisco 73
Ayala, Francisco Jose 73
Ayala, Jaime Augusto Zobel de 73
Ayala, Roselyne de 73
アヤラ・アルバレンガ
Ayala Alvarenga, Héctor Leonel 73
アヤリ
Ayari, Hela 73
アヤリガ
Ayariga, Mahama 73
アヤレウ
Ayalew, Hiwot 73
アユ
Ayu, Iyorchia Demenonyo 74
アユ・ウタミ
Utami, Ayu 1437
アユカル
Ayúcar, Enrique 74
アユカワ
Ayukawa, Michiko Midge 74
アユビ
al-Ayyubi, Muhammad Ziyad 74
Ayyubi, Muhammad Ziyadal 74
アユメ
Ayume, Francis 74
アヨジャ
Ajodhia, Jules Rattankoemar 23
アラ
Ala, Efkan 24
Allah, Rémi 32
アラー
Allah, Rémi 32
Aller, Susan Bivin 34
Alur, Deepak 37
アラアッサ
Alahassa, Damien 25
アライ
Arai, Fuyu 54
Arai, Munehito 54
アライアス
Alias, Don 31
アライエン
Arrien, Angeles 61
アライタ・アリ
Araïta Ali, Ahmed 54
アラウ
Alaw, Sufiyan 25
アラヴァムダン
Aravamudan, Gita 55
アラウィ
Allawi, Ayad 32
Allawi, Muhammed 32
アラウイ
Alaoui, Abderkebir M'daghri 25
Alaoui, Ismail 25
Allaoui, Darousse 32
アラウィ・ビン・アブドラ
Alawi bin Abdullah, Yousuf bin 25
アラウシシ
Allaouchiche, Abdelmoumene 32
アラウージョ
Araujo, Adriana 55
Araújo, Jorge Homero Tolentino 55
Araújo, Matilde Rosa 55
アラウジョ
Araujo, Adriana 55
Araújo, Bruno 55
Araujo, Marcio 55
Araujo, Maria Tome de 55
アラウス
Arauz, Andrés 55
Arauz, Luis Felipe 55
アラウズ
Araouzou, Kalliopi 54
アラウソ
Arauzo, Stella 55
アラウホ
Araújo, Consuelo 55
Araújo, Heriberto 55
Araújo, Maria Consuelo 55
Araujo, Roxana 55
Araujo, Sergio 55
アラウホ・カストロ
Araújo Castro, María Consuero 55
アラウヨ
Araujo, Rui 55
アラオス・フェルナンデス
Aráoz Fernández, Mercedes Rosalba 54
アラガ・ド・マレルブ
Arraga de Malherbe, Virginia 61
アラガン
Aragao, Manuel da Costa 54
アラギ
Allagui, Sami 32
アラキージャ
Alakija, Folorunsho 25
アラキジャ
Alakija, Folorunsho 25
Alakija, Polly 25
アラキ・ラッセル
Araki-Russell, Mie 54
アラギリ
Alagiri, M.K. 25
アラク
Alak, Julio 25
アラグエス
Aragüés, Ramón 54
アラクバロフ
Alakbarov, Vugar 25
アラケリャン
Aragelyan, Ignati 54
アラゴネス
Aragones, Luis 54
アラゴン
Aragon, Lorenzo 54
アラサニア
Alasania, Irakli 25
アラジ
Araj, Allaedin 54
al-Araj, Hussein 54
al-Araj, Khalid bin Abdullah 54
al-Araji, Baha 54
アラシェフスカ
Alaszewski, Andy 25
アラジディ
Aladjidi, Virginie 24
アラシャニ
al-Arashani, Murshed Ali 54
アラジン
Arasin, Peter 54
アラーズ
Allers, Roger 34
アラス
Arasse, Daniel 55
Arras, Davide 61
アラスコ
Alasko, Carl 25
アラゾフ
Arazov, Rezepbai 55
アラタス
Alatas, Ali 25
アラタニ
Aratani, George 55
アラティン
Halatine, Zakyatou Oualett 556
アラーナ
Arana, George W. 54
アラナ
Arana, Mariano 54
Arana, Mario 54
Araña Osorio, Carlos Manuel 54
アラナ・オソリオ
Araña Osorio, Carlos Manuel 54
アラナ・カステジョン
Arana Castellon, Saul 54
アラーニア
Araña Osorio, Carlos Manuel 54
アラーニア・オソリオ
Araña Osorio, Carlos Manuel 54
アラニッツ
Alaniz, Adam 25
アラーニャ
Alagna, Roberto 25
アラバ
Alaba, David 24
Álava, Alexandra 25
アラバウ
Alabau, Marina 24
アラバジオウル
Arabacioglu, Reyhan 54
アラバストロ
Alabastro, Estrella 24
アラハペルマ
Alahapperuma, Dullas 25
アラバール
Arrabal, Fernando 61
アラバル
Arrabal, Fernando 61
アラビ
Alabi, Solomon 24
Alavi, Mahmoud 25
el-Araby, Ashraf 54
Araby, Nabil el- 54
アラビー
Allaby, Michael 32
アラビゼ
Alavidze, Zurab 25
アラビヤト
Arabiyat, Wael 54
アーラブ
Arlove, Catherine 58
アラブ
Arab, Hussein 54
Arab, Muhammad Saber 54
Arab, Zahra Seyyed 54
アラプ
Arapu, Anatol 54
アラファト
Arafat, Fathi 54
Arafat, Raed 54
Arafat, Yasser 54
アラフィ
Arafi, Rababe 54
アラフィリップ
Alaphilippe, Julian 25
アラフーゾス
Alafouzos, Aristides 25
アラプタニー
Araptany, Jacob 54
アラベ・ポゴド
Allagbe Kpogodo, Yabavi 32
アラポビッチ
Arapovic, Marko 54
アラミ
al-Alami, Lamis 25
Alami, Mohamed Saad 25
Alami, Mohammed 25
Alami, Rachid Talbi 25
Alamy, Hafid 25
Allam-mi, Ahmad 32
アラミー
El Alami, Dawoud Sudqi 395
アラミシェル
Alamichel, Dominique 25
アラミヌ・ウスマヌ・メイ
Alamine Ousmane Mey 25
アラミャン
Aramyan, Vardan 54
アラミヤン
Alamiyan, Noshad 25
アラミラ
Alamilla, Lisel 25
アラミンウスマンメイ
Alamine Ousmane Mey 25
アラム
Allam, Roger 32
Allum, Marc 35
Aramu, Mattia 54
Arum, Bob 62
アラムギール
Alamgir, Mohiuddin Khan 25
アラムギル
Alamgir, Mohiuddin Khan 25
アラムナウ
Aramnau, Andrei 54
アラメル
Alamelu, K. 25
アラルコン
Alarcón, Daniel 25
Alarcón, Ricardo 25
アラルコン・オルティス
Alarcón Ortiz, Rodolfo 25
アラルサ

ア

Alarza, Fernando 25
アラレ
Arale, Abdalqadir Nur 54
アラン
Alain, Marie-Claire 25
Alan 25
Alan, Marjarie 25
Alan, Steven 25
Allan 32
Allan, Alasdair 32
Allan, Benny 32
Allan, Charlotte 32
Allan, C. William 32
Allan, Graham 32
Allan, Jay 32
Allan, Jeremy 32
Allan, John A.B. 32
Allan, Nicholas 32
Allan, Tommaso 32
Allan, Tony 32
Allan, Vicky 32
アランギス
Aranguiz, Charles 54
アラング
Alingue, Madeleine 32
アラングレン
Aranguren, Juan José 54
アランゴ
Alango, Mildred 25
Arango, Jorge 54
Arango, Sascha 54
アランダ
Aranda, Sanchia 54
Aranda, Vicente 54
アランデール
Arundale, G.S. 62
アーランドソン
Erlandson, Eddie 407
アーランハフト
Ehrenhaft, Daniel 393
アランブル
Aramburu, Juan Jose 54
アランベイエ
Allambeye, Maïdagi 32
アーリ
Urry, John 1436
アーリー
Earley, Dave 387
Earley, P.Christopher 387
アリ
Ali, Abdikarim Ahmed 30
Ali, Abdiweli Mohamed 30
Ali, Abdu 30
Ali, Abdullah 30
Ali, Abdurahaman Mohamud 30
Ali, Abul Hassan Mahmood 31
Ali, Ahmat Lamine 31
al-Ali, Ahmed Khaled 31
Ali, Ahmed Thasmeen 31
Ali, Aires Bonifácio 31
Ali, al-Jarrah al-Sabah 31
Ali, Amadou 31
Ali, Annabel Laure 31
Ali, Apong 31
Ali, Attoumani 31
Ali, Bachar 31
Ali, Belal Mansoor 31
Ali, bin Hamoud al-Busaidi 31
Ali, bin Khalifa al-Khalifa 31
Ali, bin Saleh al-Saleh 31
Ali, Dan 31
Ali, Faysal Mahmud 31
Ali, Garba Madaki 31
Ali, Hana 31
Ali, Irfaan 31
Ali, Jasim 31
Ali, Kamal Eddien Hassan 31
Ali, Kamal Mohamed 31
Ali, Khadra Bashir 31
Ali, Maha 31
Ali, Mahdi Muhammed 31
Ali, M.A.Yusuff 31
Ali, M'Madi 31
Ali, Mohammed Nesir Ahmad 31
Ali, Moses 31
Ali, Muhammad 31
Ali, Muhammad Ibrahim 31
Ali, Muhammad Warsameh 31
Ali, Naushad 31
Ali, Nia 31
Ali, Nujood 31
Ali, Said Abdella 31
Ali, Said Ali Boina 31
al-Ali, Salah bin Ghanem bin Nasser 31
al-Ali, Suhair 31
Ali, Syed Mohsin 31
Ali, Syed Z. 31
Ali, Tariq 31
Ali, Yaya Ag Mohamed 31
al-Ali, Yousef Mohammad Abdullah 31
Alli, Dele 34
Ally, Tony 35
Aly, Mohamed 38
アリー
Ali, Muhammad 31
Alley, R.W. 34
Ally, Amna 35
Aly, Götz 38
Aree, Wong-araya 56
Wiratthaworn, Aree 1517
アリア
Alia, Edgard Charlemagne 31
Alia, Ramiz 31
アリアーガ
Aliaga, Roberto 31
アリアガ
Arriaga, Guillermo 61
Arriaga, Ximena B. 61
アリアクバリ
Ali Akbari, Mohammad Javad 31
アリ・アクバル・カーン
Ali Akbar Khan 31
アリ・アクバル・ハーン
Ali Akbar Khan 31
アリアス
Arias, Emilio 57
Arias, José 57
Arias, Juan 57
Arias, Juan Bautista 57
Arias, Michael 57
Arias, Rodrigo 57
Arias, Santiago 57
Arias-Sánchez, Oscar 57
アリアス・カニェテ
Arias Cañete, Miguel 57
アリアスカニェテ
Arias Cañete, Miguel 57
アリアス・サンチェス
Arias-Sánchez, Oscar 57
アリアス・レイバ
Arias Leyva, Andrés 57
アリアナ
Ariana, I Ketut 57
アリアバディ
Ali Abadi, Mohammad 31
アリアハマディ
Ali-ahmadi, Ali-Reza 31
アリ・アブダラーナスール
Ali Abdallah Nassour, Mahamat 31
アリアンズ
Arians, Bruce 57
アリアンダ
Arianda, Nina 57
アリアンロッド
Arianrhod, Robyn 57
アリ・イドリス
Ali Idris, Alhaji Mustapha 32
アリウ
Aliu, Imer 32
アリウア
Alioua, Khalid 32
アリウンバートル・ガンバートル
Ariunbaatar Ganbaatar 58
アリエス
Ariès, Paul 57
Ariès, Philippe 57
アリエタ
Arrieta, Jake 61
Arrieta, Jesús 61
アリエティ
Arieti, Silvano 57
アリーエフ
Aliyev, Heydar 32
アリエフ
Aliyev, Farkhad 32
Aliyev, Geidar 32
Aliyev, Haji 32
Aliyev, Hasan 32
Aliyev, Heydar 32
Aliyev, Ilham 32
Aliyev, Irshad N. 32
Aliyev, Natig 32
アリエリー
Ariely, Dan 57
アリエル
Ariel, Uri 57
アリエロ
Aliero, Mohammed A. 31
アリエンティ
Arienti, Ermanno 57
アリ王子
Ali Bin Al Hussein 31
アリオーネ
Allione, Tsultrim 34
アリオマリ
Alliot-Marie, Michèle 34
アリオラ・イバニェス
Arriola Ibañez, María Elena 61
アリカット
Erekat, Saeb 406
Erekat, Saib 406
アリキ
Brandenberg, Aliki 176
アリギ
Arrighi, Giovanni 61
アリク
Alik, Alik 32
アリグザンダー
Alexander, Lloyd Chudley 29
アリグゾ
Ariguzo, Chi Chi 57
アリグッド
Alligood, Kathleen T. 34
アリクマー
Allikmaa, Margus 34
アリコック
Allicock, Clement Philip Ricardo 34
Allicock, Sydney 34
アリーザ
Ariza, Trevor 58
アリザデゼヌリン
Alizadeh Zenoorin, Kimia 32
アリサバラガ
Arrizabalaga, Heidi 61
Arrizabalaga, Kepa 61
アリシャウスカス
Alisauskas, Arvydas 32
アリジャベド
Alijawed, Sayed Mohammad 32
アーリス
Earith, Simon 387
アリス
Allis, David 34
Alÿs, Francis 38
al-Aris, Louei Hatim 57
Aris, Michael 57
アリス王女
Alice 31
アリスター
Allister, William 35
アリスティデス
Aristides, Juliette 57
アリスティド
Aristide, Jean-Bertrand 57
Aristidou, Aristos A. 57
アリスミ
Arisumi, Hiroshi 57
アリスメンディ
Arismendi, Marina 57
アリスメンディ・チュマセロ
Arismendi Chumacero, Elizabeth 57
アリスン
Allyson, June 35
アリソプ
Allisop, Andrique 35
アリソン
Alisson 32
Allison, Catherine 34
Allison, Christine 34
Allison, Damon 34
Allison, Geronimo 34
Allison, Graham T. 34
Allison, Herbert M. 34
Allison, Joe Marion 34
Allison, Mose 35
Allison, Sarah E. 35
Allison, Wade 35
Allyson, June 35
Arison, Micky 57
Arison, Shari 57
Arrison, Sonia 61
アリソン・マドゥエケ
Alison-madueke, Diezani 32
アリソンマドゥエケ
Alison-madueke, Diezani 32
Allison-madueke, Deziani 35
アリタ

Arita, Hissao 58
アリーチェ
Alice, Gianna 31
アーリック
Ehrlich, Robert 393
Erlich, Jonathan 407
アリックス
Alix, Jay 32
Allix, Dick 35
アーリッジ
Arledge, Roone Pinckney 58
アーリッヒ
Erlich, Gloria C. 407
アリップ
Alip, Jaime Aristotle B. 32
アリディ
al-Aridi, Ghazi 57
Aridi, Ghazi 57
アリディス
Aridjis, Homero 57
アリディヒス
Aridjis, Homero 57
アリート
Alito, Samuel Anthony, Jr. 32
アリトン
Ariton, Ion 58
アリーナ
Arena, Felice 56
アリバー
Alibar, Lucy 31
Aliber, Robert Z. 31
アリ・バグダディ
Ali Baghdadi, Abdulkadir Sheikh 31
アリーバス
Arribas, Alejandro 61
アリヒス
Aridjis, Homero 57
アリ・ビン・アル・フセイン
Ali Bin Al Hussein 31
アリフ
Arief, Yahya 57
Arif, Dayala 57
アリフィ
Arifi, Teuta 57
アリフィレンコ
Alifirenko, Sergey 32
アリフェイ
Alifei, Moustapha Ali 31
アリプガジエフ
Aripgadjiev, Magomed 57
アリ・フセイン王子
Ali Bin Al Hussein 31
アリベアイ
Alibeaj, Enkelejd 31
アリベゴビッチ
Alibegović, Dubravka Jurlina 31
アリベック
Alibek, Ken 31
アリベルティ
Aliberti, Lucia 31
アリボット
Aribot, Mariama 57
アリポフ
Alipov, Aleksey 32
Aripov, Abdulla 57
アリボーン
Allibone, Judith 34
アリマクトウム
Almaktoum, Saeed 35
アリマルドン
Alimardon, Murodali 32
アリーミ
al-Aleemi, Rashad 28
アリミ
Halimi, Besar 557
アリムサ
Ali Moussa, Mariam 32
アリムハヌリ
Alimkhanuly, Zhanibek 32
アリモハマディ
Ali-Mohammadi, Masoud 32
アリモハンマディ
Ali-Mohammadi, Masoud 32
アリモフ
Alimov, Anvar 32
アリーヤ
Aaliyah 1
アリヤラトネ
Ariyaratne, Ahangamage Tudor 58
Ariyaratne, Indrani 58
アリヤル
Aryal, Krishna Chandra 62
アリュー
Allieu, Yves 34
Allioux, Yves Marie 34
アリヨシ
Ariyoshi, George R. 58
Ariyoshi, Jean Miya 58
Ariyoshi, Rita 58
アリヨマリ
Alliot-Marie, Michèle 34
アーリン
Erlin, Robbie 407
アリン
Allin, Bud 34
Allyn, Doug 35
アリンガム
Allingham, Henry 34
Allingham, M.G. 34
アーリング
Erling, Elizabeth J. 407
アリンゲ
Alingue, Jean Bawoyen 32
アリンジャー
Alinger, Brandon 32
アーリンダー
Erlinder, C.Peter 407
アーリントン
Arrington, C.T. 61
Arrington, Kyle 61
アール
Earl, Robert 387
Earle, Jonathan Halperin 387
Earle, Martyn J. 387
Earle, Rebecca 387
Earle, Roger W. 387
Earle, Steve 387
Earle, Sylvia A. 387
Erle, Schuyler 407
Eyre, Richard 414
Hale, Nathan 557
アル
Aru, Fabio 62
アルー
Alou, Matty 36
アル・アウフィ
al-Aufi, Hamid bin Said 69
アル・アクワ
al-Akwa, Abd al-Rahman 24
al-Akwa'a, Abdulrahman 24
アル・アゲム
al-Agem, Kassem 17
アル・アザウイ
Al-Azzawi, Hikmat Mizban Ibrahim 75
アル‐アザウイ
al-Azzawi, Fadhil 75
アル・アサフ
al-Asaf, Ibrahim Abdel Aziz 62
アル・アジジ
al-Azizi, Abdulaziz bin Matar 75
アルアス
Aluas, Ioana Maria 37
アル・アスワド
al-Aswad, Husam 66
アル・アッタス
al-Attas, Alawi Hassan 68
アル・アッバール
al-Abbar, Abdel-Rahman Moussa 2
アルアティア
Al-Attiyah, Nasser 68
アル・アディリ
al-Adili, Farouk 14
アル・アデル
al-Adel, Saif 14
アルアトバ
Al-athba, Rashid 67
アル・アトラシュ
al-Atrash, Hilal 68
al-Atrash, Mohamad 68
al-Atrash, Taha 68
アル・アニ
al-Ani, Adnan Abdelmajid Jasim 49
アル・アニシ
al-Anisi, Ahmad Muhammad 50
アル・アハマディ
al-Ahmadi, Ali Hassan 20
アル・アハマド
al-Ahmad, Azam 19
al-Ahmad, Mahmoud Diyab 19
アル・アブドラ
al-Abdullah, Ahmad Yaqoub Baqer 5
アル・アブヤドハ
al-Abyadh, Yahya 10
アルアメリ
Alameri, Khaled Omran Sqait Sarhan 25
アル・アヤル
al-Ayar, Talal Mubarak 73
アル・アラウィ
al-Alawi, Khamis bin Mubarak bin Isa 25
al-Alawi, Majid bin Muhsen 25
al-Alawi, Muhammad bin Ali bin Nasir 25
アル・アラブ
al-Arab, Husayn Muhammad 54
アル・アリディ
al-Aridi, Ghazi 57
アル・アリーミ
al-Aleemi, Rashad 28
アルアル
Alualu, Tyson 37
アル・アワド
al-Awad, al-Hadi Abdalla Mohamed 72
アルアワド
Alawad, Sumaieh 25
アル・アワドヒ
al-Awadhi, Hussein Dhaif Allah 72
アル・イーサ
al-Eisa, Muhammad 394
アル・イブラヒム
al-Ibrahim, Youssef Hamad 643
アル・イマディ
al-Imadi, Muhammad 645
アルイムクロフ
Alymkulov, Aliasbek 38
アル・イリヤニ
al-Iryani, Abdul-Malik Abdul-Rahman 650
アルヴァイ
Arvay, Clemens G. 62
アルヴァレス
Álvares, José Marinho 37
Alvarez, Lorena 38
アルヴァレズ
Alvarez, Alfred 37
Alvarez, Anne 37
アルヴァレス＝ノヴォア
Alvarez-Novoa, Carlos 38
アルヴィー
Alavi, Muhammad Rais 25
アルー＝ヴィニョ
Arrou-Vignod, Jean-Philippe 61
アルウォード
Alward, Donna 38
アルヴォード
Alvord, Katharine T. 38
アルウコビチ
Arłukowicz, Bartosz 58
アル・ウスマン
al-Uthman, Abd al-Rahman Muhammad Ali 1437
アルヴテーゲン
Alvtegen, Karin 38
アルエゴ
Aruego, José 62
アル・オラエド
al-Orayed, Jawad bin Salem 1056
アル・オワイス
al-Owais, Humaid bin Nasir 1065
アルカイヤー
Alkyer, Frank 32
アル＝ガウル
al-Ghaul, Muhammad bn Shahāda 493
アールカーザー
Alcazar, Pedro 27
アルカサール
Alcazar, Pedro 27
アル・カシミ
al-Qasimi, Fahim bin Sultan 1142
アルカディ
Arcudi, John 56

ア

アルカティリ
Alkatiri, Mari 32
アルカード
Alucard, George 37
アル・ガドバーン
Al-Ghadhban, Thamir Abbas Ghadhban 492
アル・ガニム
al-Ghanim, Abdallah Ahmad 493
アル・カフド
al-Kafud, Muhammad Abdelrahim 695
アル・カマーリー
Al-Kamali, Abdullah Abdulghani Kassim 699
アル・カマル
al-Kamal, Yousef Hussein 698
アルガミッセン
Algermissen, Jo Ann 30
アルカラ
Alcala, Proceso 27
Arcara, Kristin M. 55
アルカライ
Alkalaj, Sven 32
アルカラス
Alcaraz, Frances 27
アル＝カリーリ
Al-Khalili, Jim 725
アルカン
Arcan, Nelly 55
Arcand, Denys 55
アルカンジョ
Arcanjo, Geisa 55
Arcanjo, Maria Manuela 55
アルカンターラ
Alcantara, Ricardo 27
アルカンタラ
Alcantara, Arismendy 27
Alcántara, Isabel 27
Alcantara, Pedro de 27
Alcantara, Raul 27
Alcantara, Tomas I. 27
Alcantara, Victor 27
アルガンディワル
Arghandiwal, Abdul Hadi 57
アルキブジ
Archibugi, Francesca 56
アル・キルビ
al-Kirbi, Abu-Baker Abdullah 740
アルク
Arık, Umut 57
アルグアシル
Alguacil, Jose 30
アールクイスト
Ahlquist, Diane 19
アルグエヨ
Argüello, Kiko 57
アル・クセイビ
al-Qusseibi, Khalid Bin Muhammad 1146
アル・クタビ
al-Qutaybi, Muhammad bin Ali 1146
アル・クドシ
al-Qudsi, Baria 1144
アル・クバティ
al-Kubati, Abdu Ali 770
アル・クマイム
al-Kumaim, Abdul-Aziz 772
アルクール
Harcourt, Bernard E. 569
アル・クルンズ
Al-kurunz, Sa'adi 775
アル・クワリ
al-Kuwari, Ali bin Saad 776
アルゲジョ
Arguello, Mariangeles 57
アルゲダス
Arguedas, José María 57
アルゲタ・デバリジャス
Argueta de Barillas, Marisol 57
アルゲリッチ
Argerich, Martha 57
アルゲリョ
Argüello, Alexis 57
Arguello, Betzabeth 57
アルゴ
Algoe, Sooresh 30
アルゴエ
Algoe, Sooresh 30
アルコス
Arcos, Gustavo 56
アルコック
Alcock, Alan 27
Alcock, Peter 27
アルゴットソンオスルト
Algotsson Ostholt, Sara 30
アルコデアス
Arkoudeas, Konstantinos 58
アルゴブ
Argov, Shlomo 57
アルコベフォン
Alcobé Font, Jordi 27
アルコーン
Alcorn, Nancy 27
Alcorn, Randy C. 27
アルコン
Alkon, Amy 32
アル・サイディ
al-Saidi, Mutahhar 1227
アル・サイフ
al-Sa'igh, Yousif 1227
アル・ザイーム
al-Zaeem, Issam 1545
アル・ザイム
al-Zaim, Issam 1545
アル・サエド
al-Sayyid, Mahmoud 1247
アルサダ
Alçada, Isabel 27
アルザック
Arzac, Enrique R. 62
アルサディール
Alsadir, Nuar 36
アル・サテリ
al-Sateri, Mohammed Ali bin al-Shaikh Mansoor 1244
アルサナ
Arsana, Lother 61
アル・サハフ
al-Sahhaf, Muhammad Saeed 1226
al-Sahhaf, Muhammad Said Kazim 1226
アル・サファディ
al-Safadi, Hussam 1225
アルザマソワ
Arzamasova, Marina 62
アルサモラ
Alzamora, Miquel 38
アル・サヤニ
al-Sayani, Abd al-Malik Ali 1247
アルサラ
Arsala, Hedayat Amin 61
アル・サラミ
al-Salami, Alawi Salah 1229
al-Sallami, Alawi Saleh 1231
アル・サリフ
al-Salih, Ali Salih Abdullah 1231
アルサール
Arusaar, Ardo 62
アル・サルサム
al-Sarsam, Maan Abdullah 1243
アル・サルミ
al-Salimi, Abdullah bin Mohammed 1231
アル・サルーム
al-Sallum, Naser Bin Muhammad 1232
アル・サレハ
al-Saleh, Abdullah Hamid Mahmoud 1230
al-Saleh, Ali bin Saleh 1230
al-Saleh, Muhammad Mahdi 1230
アルサン
Arsan, Emmanuelle 61
アルーシ
al-Arusi, Abdulbari 62
アルシア
Arcia, Dilio 56
Arcia, Orlando 56
Arcia, Oswaldo 56
アルシエ
Arcier, Agnès 56
アルジェンティ
Argenti, Paul A. 57
アルジェント
Argento, Dario 57
アル・ジスル
al-Jisr, Samir 674
アルジッリ
Argilli, Marcello 57
Arzilli, Marco 62
アルジナ
Alzina, Guida 38
アルシニェガス
Arciniegas, Fabio 56
アル・シニオラ
al-Siniora, Fuad 1307
アル・シビ
al-Shibi, Ahmad 1289
アルジャー
Alger, Amy 30
アル・ジャアファリー
al-Jaafari, Ibrahim 654
アル・シャイバニ
al-Shaibani, Nashir Muhammad 1279
アル・シャーウィ
al-Shawi, Mundhir Ibrahim 1284
アルジャウィ
Arjaoui, Mohammed 58
アルジャウイ
Arjaoui, Mohammed 58
アルジャコワ
Arzhakova, Elena 62
アル＝ジャザーイリー
Jazairi, Abu Bakr Jabir 667
アル・シャティ
al-Shatti, Iyad 1283
アル・ジャバリ
al-Jabali, Ahmed Salem 655
アル・ジャビ
al-Jabi, Ghada 655
アル・ジャブリ
al-Jabburi, Sultan Hashim Ahmad 655
アルシャマール
Alshammar, Therese 36
アル・シャミーリ
Al-Shamiri, Mansour Abdul-Ghani 1280
アル・シャメフ
al-Shamekh, Mubarak Abdullah 1280
アル・ジャラッラ
al-Jarallah, Muhammad Bin Ibrahim 665
アル・ジャラッラー
al-Jarallah, Muhammad Bin Ibrahim 665
アル・シャラフ
al-Sharaf, Ali Hamid 1282
al-Sharaf, Khaled 1282
アル・シャルハン
al-Sharhan, Abdul-Aziz 1282
アル・シュアイビ
al-Shuaibi, Yahya Mohammed 1294
アル・シュアラ
al-Shuala, Abd al-Nabi 1294
アル・ジュナイド
al-Junaid, Muhammad Ahmad 691
アルジュンワドカル
Arjunwadkar, Krishna S. 58
アル・ジョウダル
al-Jowdar, Fahmi bin Ali 689
アルジョゼリー
Al-jothery, Rahman Loan Muhsin 688
アル・ショラ
al-Shola, Abdul-Nabi bin Abdullah 1292
アルジール
Alzeer, Muhammad bn Hassan 38
アルジンバ
Ardzinba, Vladislav 56
アールズ
Earls, Keith 387
アルス
Arzu, Alvaro 62
アルスー
Arzu, Alvaro 62
アルスアガ
Arsuaga, Juan Luis de 61
アル・スウェイディ
Al Sowaidi, Nasser Ahmed Khalifa 36
アルスゴール
Alsgaard, Thomas 36

アールスト
Aalst, Mariska van 1
アルスト
Aelst, Marcel P.R.C. van 16
アルストランド
Ahlstrand, Bruce W. 19
アルストン
Alston, Richard 36
アルスニールセン
Als-Nielsen, Jens 36
アルスノー
Arsenault, Isabelle 61
アル・ズバイディ
al-Zubaydi, Muhammad Hamza 1558
アル・スファン
al-Suffan, Ahmad Muhammad Abdallah 1363
アル・スベイフ
al-Subeih, Adel Khaled 1362
アルスポー
Alspaugh, Blanton 36
アルズマン
Alzmann, Christian 38
アル・スーラニ
al-Sourani, Zuheir 1331
アルスラン
Arslan, Ahmet 61
Arslan, Antonia 61
Arslan, Talal 61
Arslan, Tolgay 61
Erslan, Talal 407
アルセ・カタコラ
Arce Catacora, Luis 55
アルセ・サパタ
Arce Zapata, Germán 55
アルセニシビリ
Arsenishvili, Giorgi 61
アルセニス
Arsenis, Gerasimos 61
アルゼノワ
Arsenova, Dolores 61
アル・セーフ
al-Seif, Abdullah Hassan 1270
アルセロ
Arcero, Patricia 55
アールセン
Aertssen, Kristien 16
アルソガライ
Alsogaray, Julio 36
アルソップ
Alsop, Jonathon 36
アルソビッチ
Arsovic, Andrea 61
アル・ゾベイル
al-Zobeir, Mohamed Kheir 1556
アルソン
Alson, Roy L. 36
アールダ
Alda, Arlene 27
アルター
Alter, Hobie 37
アルダ
Alda, Alan 27
Arda, Turan 56
アルダー
Alder, Harry 27
Alder, Roger W. 27
アル・タイブ
al-Tayib, Muhammad Muhammad 1384
アル・タウィル
al-Tawil, Samir 1384
アルタエフ
Artayev, Bakhtiyar 61
アル・タエル
al-Tayer, Ahmed Humaid 1384
al-Tayer, Matar Humayd 1384
アルタサ
Artaza, Osvaldo 61
アルダシン
Aldashin, Mikhail 27
アルダーソン
Alderson, Sandy 27
アルタッカー
Altucher, Claudia Azula 37
Altucher, James 37
アルタッチャー
Altucher, James 37
アルダートン
Alderton, David 27
アルダナザーロフ
Aldanazarov, Askanbek 27
アル・ダハル
al-Dahar, Munib Saim 312
アルタビラ
Altavilla, Dan 36
アル・タヒル
al-Tahir, al-Tigani Adam 1376
アルタフ
Altaf, M.Anjum 36
アル・ダファイ
al-Dafaee, Abdullah Hussein 312
アル・ダファイー
al-Dafaee, Abdullah Hussein 312
アルダベルゲノワ
Aldabergenova, Zhanbota 27
アルダマ
Aldama, Yamile 27
アルダラジー
Al-daradji, Mohamed 319
アルダラン
Ardalan, Hayde 56
アルタン
Altan, Francesco Tullio 36
アルダン
Ardant, Fanny 56
アルタンホヤグ
Altanhuyag, Ravsal 36
Altankhuyag, Norov 36
アルチャート
Alciato, Alessandro 27
アルチュコフ
Altukhov, Pavlo 37
アルチュザラ
Altuzarra, Joseph 37
アルチュニャン
Arutyunyan, Migran 62
Harutyunyan, Aram 578
アルチュホフ
Artyukhov, Vitaly G. 62
アルチョウロン
Alchouron, Guillermo E. 27
アルチラ
Archila, Érick Estuardo 56
Archila, Raúl 56
アルチロスリャン
Martirosyan, Tigran Gevorg 912
アルチンボルド
Arcimboldi, Giuseppe 56
アールツ
Aerts, Erik 16
Aerts, Jef 16
アルテ
Arte, Mohamed Omar 61
Carte, Mohammed Omar 231
Halter, Marek 560
Halter, Paul 560
アルテア
Altea, Rosemary 36
アルティ
Artis, Amélie 62
アルディ
Hardy, Adrien 570
Hardy, Françoise 570
アルディー
Ardee, Saylom 56
アルティエフ
Altyyev, Tekebay 37
アルディカ
Ardika, I Gde 56
アルティガス
Artigas, Mariano 62
アルティコフ
Artykov, Izzat 62
Artykov, Rustem 62
アルディッティ
Arditi, Pierre 56
Arditti, Paul 56
アルディティ
Arditi, Pierre 56
アルティドール
Altidore, Jozy 37
アルティメット・ウォリアー
Ultimate Warrior 1433
アル・ティリキ
al-Tiriki, Ali Abdel-Salam 1406
アルディレス
Ardiles, Osvaldo Cesar 56
アルティン
Artin, Michael 62
アルディーン
Aldean, Jason 27
アルティントップ
Altintop, Halil 37
アルデガーニ
Aldegani, Gabriele 27
アルテス
Altés, Marta 37
アルデハニ
Aldeehani, Fehaid 27
アルデブロン
Aldebron, Charlotte 27
アルテポスト
Altepost, Lutz 37
アルテミエヴァ
Artem'eva, Galina 61
アルテーミエフ
Artem'ev, A.R. 61
アルテメフ
Artemev, Alexander 61
アルテュス＝ベルトラン
Arthus-Bertrand, Yann 62
アルテュニャーン
Arutyunyan, Aleksandr Grigorievich 62
アルテュニャン
Arutyunyan, Aleksandr Grigorievich 62
アルテール
Alter, Anna 37
Altherr, Aaron 37
アルデルヴァイレルト
Alderweireld, Toby 27
アルデレーテ
Aldrete, Jorge Antonio 27
アルデレテ
Alderete, José Alberto 27
アルテンドルフ
Altendorf, Alan von 36
アルデンドルフ
Aldendorff, Johan 27
アルテンミュラー
Altenmüller, Eckart 36
アルト
Alt, Franz 36
Alt, Helene 36
Alt, Peter-André 36
Arlt, Tobias 58
アルトイコフ
Artykov, Myrat 62
アルトインバエフ
Altynbayev, Mukhtar 37
アルドヴィーニ
Aldovini, Giulia 27
アルトゥガマゲ
Aluthgamage, Mahindananda 37
Aluthugamage, Mahindananda 37
アルトゥチ
Artuc, Sedat 62
アルトゥニャン
Altunyan, Levon 37
アルトゥーベ
Altuve, Jose 37
アル・ドカイル
al-Du-qayr, Jalal Yousif Mohamed 383
アルトーグ
Hartog, François 578
アルトハウス
Althaus, Thomas 37
アルトバッカー
Altbacker, E.J. 36
アルトバック
Altbach, Philip G. 36
アールドフ
Ardov, Mikhail 56
アルトファーター
Altvater, Elmar 37
アルトフェスト
Altfest, Lewis J. 37
アルトーペ
Artopé, Alexander 62
アルトホーフ
Althoff, Gerd 37
アルトホフ
Althoff, Gerd 37
アルトマイヤー
Altmaier, Peter 37
アルトマン
Altheman, Maria Suelen 37
Altman, Daniel 37

Altman, Dennis 37
Altman, Douglas G. 37
Altman, Edward I. 37
Altman, Elizabeth J. 37
Altman, Robert 37
Altman, Roger 37
Altmann, Maria 37
Artmann, Benno 62

アルトラギレ
Altolaguirre, Manuel 37

アルトランド
Altland, Alexander 37

アルドリッジ
Aldredge, Theoni V. 27
Aldridge, Alan 28
Aldridge, Michelle 28
Aldridge, Richard J. 28

アルドリッチ
Aldrich, Daniel P. 27

アルドリッヒ
Aldrich, Knight 27

アルトン
Alton, Steve 37

アルナ
Arouna, Aboubakar 61
Aruna, Quadri 62

アルナウトヴィッチ
Arnautovic, Marko 59

アル・ナクシャバンディ
al-Naqshabandi, Mondhir Muhammed Asad 1005

アル・ナシャシビ
Al-nasha-shibi, Mohammad 1006

アル・ナシリ
al-Nasili, Obayd bin Saif 1006
al-Nassiri, Obeid bin Saif 1007

アルナソン
Arnason, Arni 59

アル・ナチェ
al-Natsheh, Rafiq 1008

アル・ナチェハ
al-Natsheh, Rafiq 1008

アルナドッティル
Arnadottir, Ragna 59
Árnadóttir, Ragnheiður 59

アル・ナムラ
al-Namla, Ali bin Ibrahim 1004

アルヌース
Arnous, Hussein 60

アルノ
Arno 60

アルノー
Arnaud, Noël 59
Arnault, Bernard 59
Arnaut, José Luís 59

アルノビッチ
Arunovic, Zorana 62

アルノルト
Arnold, Claus 60
Arnold, Dietmar 60
Arnold, Ingmar 60
Arnold, Johann Christoph 60
Arnold, Maximilian 60

アルノワ
Harnois, Marlene 572

アルノンクール
Harnoncourt, Nikolaus 572

アルバ
Alba, Elisabeth 25
Alba, Jessica 25

アルバー
Arber, Werner 55

アルパー
Alper, Basak 36
Alper, Joseph S. 36

アルバイラク
Albayrak, Berat 25

アルバカーキ
Albuquerque, Rafael Emerson 27 401

アルバカーキー
Alburquerque, Al 27

アールバーグ
Ahlberg, Allan 19

アルバーグ
Ahlberg, Allan 19
Ahlberg, Jessica 19

アル＝バグダーディー
al-Baghdadi, Abu Bakr 79

アルバクル
Arbuckle, Luk 55

アル・ハサン
al-Hasan, Hani 579

アルパジェス
Harpagès, Didier 572

アルバジーニ
Albasini, Michael 25

アル・バシャ
al-Basha, Sayed Abdel-Jaleel 102

アル・バシール
al-Bashir, Omar Hassan Ahmed 102

アル・バシル
al-Bashir, Isam Ahmed 102
al-Bashir, Omar Hassan Ahmed 102

アルバース
Albers, Brian 26
Albers, Susan 26

アルパーソン
Alperson, Ruth 36

アルバータイン
Albertine 26

アル・バタニ
al-Batani, Muhammad Abdallah 103

アルバーツ
Alberts, Bruce 26
Alberts, David Stephen 26
Alberts, Willem 26

アールバック
Erlbach, Arlene 407

アルハッサン
Alhassan, Malik Yakubu 30
Alhassane, Ahmadaye 30

アル・ハティーブ
Al Khatib, Fatima 32

アル・ハティブ
al-Khatib, Ghassan 727

アルハティム
al-Khatim, Abdel Rahman Sir 727

アル・ハティル
al-Khatir, Ali bin Muhammad 727

アルバート
Albert, Alexa 26
Albert, Branden 26
Albert, Eddie 26
Albert, Edward 26
Albert, Jim 26
Albert, Karsten 26
Albert, Michael H. 26
Albert, Roy E. 26
Albert, Stuart 26
Albert, Tim 26
Alberto, Paul 26

アルパート
Alpert, Herb 36
Alpert, Jon 36
Alpert, Jonathan Boyd 36
Alpert, Mark 36
Alpert, Michael 36
Alpert, Stephen M. 36

アルバートソン
Albertson, Joshua 26

アルバートフ
Arbatov, Georgii Arkadevich 55

アルバトフ
Arbatov, Aleksei Georgievich 55
Arbatov, Georgii Arkadevich 55

アル・バドリ
al-Badri, Abdulsalam 78

アルバニーズ
Albanese, Anthony 25
Albanese, Mark J. 25

アルバニトプロス
Arvanitopoulos, Konstantinos 62

アルバネーゼ
Albanese, Andrew 25
Albanese, Licia 25

アルバネル
Albanel, Christine 25

アルバーノ
Albano, Anne Marie 25

アルハビ
al-Arhabi, Abdul-Kareem 57

アル・ハマル
al-Hamar, Nabeel bin Yaqoob 561

アルバーラ
Albala, Ken 25

アル・ハラウィ
al-Hrawi, Khalil 629

アルバラシン
Albarracin, Matias 25

アルバラード
Alvarado, Anita 37
Alvarado, Jose 37

アルバラド
Alvarado, Carlos 37
Alvarado, Fausto 37
Alvarado, Guillermo 37
Alvarado, José Antonio 37
Alvarado, José Arturo 37
Alvarado, Vinicio 37

アルバラド・エスピネル
Alvarado Espinel, Vinicio 37

アル・ハリリ
al-Hariri, Rafik 571

アル・バルーチ
al-Baluchi, Ahmad bin Suwaydan 88

アル・ハルーン
al-Aroun, Mosaed Rashed 61
al-Haroun, Mosaed Rashed 572

アルバレス
Álvares, Agenor 37
Alvarez, Alberto 37
Álvarez, Antonio 37
Alvarez, Carlos 37
Alvarez, Cesar 37
Alvarez, Cindy 38
Alvarez, Dariel 38
Alvarez, Dario 38
Alvarez, David 38
Álvarez, Diana 38
Álvarez, Eduardo 38
Alvarez, Eduardo 38
Alvarez, Eliezer 38
Alvarez, Felix Perez 38
Álvarez, Gregorio 38
Alvarez, Jose 38
Alvarez, Juan José 38
Alvarez, Julia 38
Alvarez, Lazaro Jorge 38
Álvarez, Magdalena 38
Alvarez, Manny 38
Alvarez, Marcelo 38
Alvarez, Melissa 38
Álvarez, Nelson 38
Alvarez, Oscar 38
Alvarez, Pantaleon 38
Alvarez, Pedro 38
Alvarez, Ralph 38
Alvarez, Ricardo 38
Alvarez, Ricardo Antonio 38
Alvarez, Tomás 38
Alvarez Boulet, Sergio 38
Álvarez Estévez, Rolando 38
Alvarez Estrada, Lazaro 38

アルバレズ
Alvarez, Tony 38

アルバレス・カスコス・フェルナンデス
Álvarez-cascos Fernández, Francisco 38

アルバレスカスコス・フェルナンデス
Álvarez-cascos Fernández, Francisco 38

アルバレスコレア・グレン
Álvarez-correa Glen, Cecilia 38

アルバレス・ボガー
Alvarez Bogaert, Fernando 38

アルバレスマルファニ
Alvarezmarfany, Calres 38

アル・バレド
al-Bared, Osama Mae 93

アルバレンガ・デ・オルテガ
Alvarenga de Ortega, Hermelinda 37

アルバロ
Alvaro, Gonzalez 38
Alvaro, Vazquez 38

アルバロ・セフード
Alvaro Cejudo 38

アルバーン
Albarn, Damon 25

アルバン
Albán, Ana 25

アルビ
Alvi, Amir Faisal 38

アルピ
Arpi, Claude 61

アルヒア
Alhir, Sinan Si 30
アルビア
Arbia, Giuseppe 55
アルビエフ
Albiev, Islam 26
アルビオル
Albiol, Raul 26
アルビオン
Albion, Mark S. 26
Albion, Peter R. 26
アルビージャ
Arbilla, Anaitz 55
アル・ビシャリ
al-Bishari, Ahmad Ali 141
アルビーズ
Albies, Ozzie 26
アルビストン
Albiston, Mark 26
アル・ビタニ
al-Bitani, Mohammed Abdullah 142
アルビッソン
Albisson, Amandine 26
アル・ヒナイ
al-Hinai, Mohammed bin Abdullah 608
アルピノ
Arpino, Gerald 61
アルビハレ
Aluvihare, Alick 37
アルヒラゴス
Argilagos, Joahnys 57
アルヒラル
Alhilal, Hamdi 30
アルビン
Albin, Cecilia 26
Albin, Christian 26
Albin, Gennifer 26
Albin, Peter S. 26
Albin, Richard 26
Alvin, Jacklick 38
アルヒンマキ
Arhinmäki, Paavo 57
アルファー
Alpher, Ralph Asher 36
アル・ファイズ
al-Fayez, Trad 424
アルファイド
Al Fayed, Mohamed 30
アルファウイ
Arfaoui, Mohamed Salah 56
アル・ファドヘル
al-Fadhel, Abdulaziz 415
アルファノ
Alfano, Angelino 30
アル・ファルージ
al-Falouji, Imad 418
アルファロ
Alfaro, Gustavo 30
Alfaro, Jorge 30
Alfaro, Juan Francisco 30
アルファロ・サラス
Alfaro Salas, Sergio 30
アルファロールフィーヴァ
Alfaro-LeFevre, Rosalinda 30
アルファロ - ルフィーヴァ
Alfaro-LeFevre, Rosalinda 30
アルファンデリ
Alphandery, Edmond Gerard 36
アルフィエ
Alfie, Isaac 30
アルフィン
Alphin, Tom 36
アルフェーフスキー
Alfeevskii, V. 30
アルフェロフ
Alferov, Zhores Ivanovich 30
アルフォード
Alford, Alan F. 30
Alford, Anthony 30
Alford, Mario 30
Alford, Mimi 30
Alford, Robert 30
アルフォール
Alfort, Bérangère 30
アルフォンシ
Alfonsi, Alice 30
アルフォンシン
Alfonsín, Raúl 30
アルフォンソ
Alfonso, Vincent C. 30
アルブケルケ
Albuquerque, Maria Luís 27
アルフケン
Arfken, George Brown 57
アル・フサイン
al-Husayn, Ahmad Musaid 638
アル・フスニ
al-Husni, Amir bin Shuwayn 638
アルフセイニ
Alhousseini, Malick 30
アル・フセイン
al-Husayn, Muhammad 638
アルフセイン
al-Hussein, Ali bin 638
アルブゾフ
Arbuzov, Serhiy 55
アルブット
Aelvoet, Magda 16
アルフート
al-Hout, Shafig 627
アル・フムス
al-Hummus, Naim Abu 635
アルフォーロフ
Alferov, Zhores Ivanovich 30
アルフョロフ
Alferov, Zhores Ivanovich 30
アルブライト
Albright, Bryson 27
Albright, Matthew 27
アルブリットン
Albritton, Sarah C. 27
アルブール
Arbour, Louise 55
アルブルケルケ
Alburquerque, Rafael 27
アルブレッチェン
Albrechtsen, Nicky 26
アルフレッド
Alfred, Alfred 30
Alfred, Maynard 30
アルフレッドソン
Alfredson, Tomas 30
アルブレヒト
Albrecht, Daniel 26
Albrecht, Donald 26
Albrecht, Gerd 26
Albrecht, Karin 26
Albrecht, Karl, Jr. 26
Albrecht, Karl Hans 26
Albrecht, Kilian 26
Albrecht, Marc 26
Albrecht, Theo 26
アルベアル
Alvear, María Soledad 38
Alvear, Yuri 38
アルペイ
Alupei, Angela 37
アルベゴフ
Albegov, Ruslan 25
アルベス
Alves, Gil Da Costa 38
Alves, Henrique Eduardo 38
Alves, Maria Domingas Fernandes 38
アルベス・フィリョ
Alves Filho, Garibaldi 38
アルベッソン
Alvesson, Mats 38
アルヘニャル・サンドバル
Argeñal Sandoval, Juana 57
アルベラゼ
Arveladze, Georgi 62
アルベリーゴ
Alberigo, Giuseppe 26
アルヘリチ
Argerich, Martha 57
アルヘリッチ
Argerich, Martha 57
アルベール
Albert, Jimmy 26
Albert, Michel 26
Albert II 26
アルベル
Alves, Gil Da Costa 38
アルペル
Alper, Potuk 36
アルベール2世
Albert II 26
アルベルタッツィ
Albertazzi, Giorgio 26
アルベルチ
Alberti, Trude 26
アルベルツ
Albertz, Rainer 26
アルベルティ
Alberti, Mario 26
Alberti, Rafael 26
Alberti, Robert E. 26
アルベルト
Alberto, Hanser 26
アルベルト・ピレス・ゴメス
Alberto Pires Gomes, Carlos 26
アルベルト・マルティン
Alberto Martin 26
アルベルト・モレノ
Alberto Moreno 26
アルベレツ
Arbelaez, Ana Maria 55
アルベロア
Arbeloa, Alvaro 55
アルベローニ
Alberoni, Francesco 26
アルベローラ
Alberola, Jean-Michael 26
アルベロラ
Alberola, Jean-Michael 26
アルベントサ
Albentosa, Raul 26
アルボ
Arbo, John E. 55
アルポ
Alupo, Jessica 37
アル・ホスニ
al-Hosni, Amer bin Shuwain 625
アルボ・ソサ
Arbo Sosa, Antonio Heriberto 55
アルホーナ
Arjona 58
アルホビン・ガッサニ
Aljovín Gazzani, Cayetana 32
アルホフ
Erlhoff, Michael 407
アールボム
Ahlbom, Jens 19
アルボム
Albom, Mitch 26
アルボムッレ・スマナサーラ
Alubomulle Sumanasara 37
アルボリオ・メッラ・ディ・サンテリア
Arborio Mella Di Sant'Elia, Maria Teresa 55
アルボルク
Alborch, Bataller Carmen 26
アルボルタ
Alborta, Freddy 26
アルボルノス
Albornoz, Esteban 26
Albornoz, Laura 26
アルボレダ
Arboleda, Carlos 55
アルボレダ - フローレス
Arboleda-Flórez, Julio 55
アルボレート
Alboreto, Michele 26
アルボレヤ
Arboleya, Carlos 55
アルボーン
Albone, Eric 26
アルマー
Almaer, Dion 35
Ulmer, Sarah 1433
アル・マアマリ
al-Ma'amari, Malik bin Suleiman 858
アル・マイア
al-Mai'a, Fahd Dahisan Zein 885
アル・マーイタハ
al-Maaitah, Rowaida 857
アルマグロ
Almagro, Luis 35
Almagro, Nicolas 35
アル・マジド
al-Majid, Ali Hassan 887
アルマジド
al-Majid, Ali Hassan 887
アルマジドハブ
al-Majdhub, Mubarek

ア

Mohamed Ali 887
アルマシユ
Armashu, Octavian 58
アルマス・マルセロ
Armas Marcelo, J.J. 58
アル・マスリ
al-Masri, Maher 915
アルマスリ
Al-Masri, Abu Baseer 915
アルマダ
Almada, Anthony L. 35
Almada, Janira Isabel 35
アルマーダ・ロペス
Almada López, Carlos Fernando 35
アル・マッキ
al-Makki, Ahmad bin Abd al-Nabi 888
アル・マッリ
al-Marri, Ahmad bin Abdullah 905
アルマトフ
Almatov, Zakirzhon 35
アル・マドファ
al-Madfa, Hamad Abdul-Rahman 880
アル・マーニ
al-Maani, Walid 858
アルマーニ
Armani, Giorgio 58
アル・マハイニ
al-Mahayni, Khaled 884
アル・マハルース
al-Mahroos, Ali Ibrahim 885
アル・ママリ
al-Mamari, Ali bin Majid 892
al-Mamari, Malik bin Sulayman 892
アルマリオ
Almario, Virgilio S. 35
アルマン
Allemand, Sylvain 33
Arman 58
Ullman, Dana 1433
アル・マンシリ
al-Mantheri, Yahya bin Mahfoodh 897
アル・マンスーリ
al-Mansuri, Ahmad bin Khalifa Busherbak 897
アル・マンスール
al-Mansour, Haifaa 897
アル・マンセリ
al-Mantheri, Yahya bin Mahfoodh 897
アルミダ
Armida, Alisjahbana 58
アルミリアート
Armiliato, Fabio 58
アルミンク
Arming, Christian 58
アル・ムアラ
al-Mualla, Humaid bin Ahmed 985
アル・ムアリミ
al-Mualimi, Abdul-Malik 985
アル・ムサウィ
al-Musawi, Faysal Radhi 996
アルムザフ
Almudhaf, Khaled 35
アル・ムスラティ
al-Musrati, Muhammad Ali 997
アル・ムスラヒ
Al-muslahi, Khalid bin Hashil bin Mohammed 996
アルムダフ
Almudhaf, Khaled 35
アル・ムタワ
al-Mutawa, Mohammed bin Ibrahim 997
アル・ムナジェド
al-Mounajed, Bashir 982
アルムブルスター
Armbruster, Ludwíg 58
アルムブルステル・マイヤー
Armbruster-Mayer, Reinhold 58
アル・ムール
al-Murr, Elias 994
アルメイダ
Almeida, Abdurremane Lino de 35
Almeida, Francisca De Fátima Do Espírito Santo De Carvalho e 35
Almeida, Franklin 35
Almeida, José António 35
Almeida, José Antonio da Cruz 35
Almeida, Juan 35
Almeida, Kaio 35
Almeyda, Franklin 35
D'almeida, Damiao Vaz 314
アルメイダ・ボスケ
Almeida Bosque, Juan 35
アルメス
Almes, Rozy 35
アル・メッリ
al-Merri, Ahmad bin abdullah 936
アルメリャダ
Armellada, Cesareo de 58
アルメル
Armel, Aliette 58
Harmel, Roger Charles 572
アルメロ
Armero, Pablo 58
アルメンダリス
Armendariz, Pedro, Jr. 58
アルメンダリズ
Armendariz, Beatriz 58
アルメンテロス
Armenteros, Jose 58
アルメンドラス
Almendras, Jose Rene 35
アルモドヴァル
Almodóvar, Pedro 35
アルモドーバル
Almodóvar, Pedro 35
アルモドバル
Almodóvar, Pedro 35
アルモーラ
Almora, Albert, Jr. 35
アルモンテ
Almonte, Abraham 35
Almonte, Miguel 35
Almonte, Yency 35
アルヤヴィルタ
Arjavirta, Annukka 58
アル・ヤシン
al-Yassin, Salam 1536
アル・ユーセフィ
al-Yousefi, Mohsen 1542
アルユーニ
Arjouni, Jakob 58
アルラウィ
Al-rawi, Faris 1161
アル・ラウィハ
al-Rawih, Abd al-Wahhab 1161
アルラウスキス
Arlauskis, Giedrius 58
アル・ラカド
al-Rakad, Rakad bin Salem 1152
アル・ラカバニ
al-Raqabani, Said Muhammad 1158
アル・ラガバニ
al-Ragabani, Saeed Muhammad 1149
アル・ラゲブ
al-Ragheb, Ali Abu 1149
アル・ラシード
al-Rasheed, Muhammad bin Ahmad 1158
アル・ラシュディ
al-Rashdi, Hamad bin Mohammed 1158
アル・ラゼク
Al-razek, Hisham Abdel 1163
アル・ラワヒ
al-Rawahi, Ahmad bin Khalfan bin Muhammad 1161
アルランディ
Arlandi, Gian Franco 58
アル・リファイ
al-Rifai, Ghassam 1181
アルール
Arrour, Samir 61
アルル
Aloulou, Mohamed 36
アル・ルタイーフ
al-Lutayyif, Ammar Mabruk 854
アルルト
Arlt, Tobias 58
アルールプラガサム
Arulpragasam, A.R. (Rajpol) 62
アル・ルワス
al-Ruwas, Abd al-Aziz bin Mohammad 1220
アルレー
Arley, Catherine 58
アルレッド
Alred, Gerald J. 36
アルロー
Arlaud, Philippe 58
Arlaux-Maréchal, Christine 58
アル・ロウハニ
al-Rowhani, Abdul-Wahab 1211
アルワイス
Alweiss, Lilian 38
アル・ワジハ
al-Wajih, Muhammad al-Khadim 1468
アル・ワジル
al-Wazil, Intissar 1484
al-Wazir, Ismail Ahmad 1484
アルワース
Allworth, James 35
アル・ワセイラハ
al-Waseilah, al-Sammani al-Sheikh 1480
アルワタ
Alwata, Ichata Sahi 38
アルワリア
Ahluwalia, D.Pal S. 19
Ahluwalia, Montek Singh 19
アルワン
al-Alwan, Alaa-Adien 38
アルンスタッド
Arnstad, Marit 60
アルンス・ニウマン
Arns Neumann, Zilda 60
アルンチ
Arinç, Bülent 57
アールンド
Ahlund, Mikael 19
アルント
Arndt, Andreas 59
Arndt, Ingo 59
Arndt, Judith 59
アルンハイム
Arnheim, Rudolf 59
アーレ
Aleh, Jo 28
アーレー
Aleh, Jo 28
アレ
Allais, Maurice 32
Halley, Paul-Louis 559
Re, Maurizio 1163
アレー
Allais, Maurice 32
Alley, Vernon 34
Halley, Paul-Auguste 559
Halley, Paul-Louis 559
アレアサ
Arreaza, Jorge Alberto 61
アレアン
Alean, Jürg 28
アレィ
Allais, Maurice 32
アレイ
Alley, Richard B. 34
Arey, Janet 56
アレイクサンドレ
Aleixandre, Vicente 28
アレイクス・ビダル
Aleix Vidal 28
アレイショ・ダ・クルス
Aleixo da Cruz, Filomeno 28
アレイン
Alain, Patrick 25
アレイントピン
Alleyne-toppin, Vernella 34
アレウ
Aleu, Aleu Ayieny 28
アレオラ
Areola, Alphonse 56
Arreola, Juan José 61
アレガウィ
Aregawi, Abeba 56
アレキサンダー
Alexander, Caroline 29
Alexander, D.J. 29
Alexander, Dominique 29
Alexander, Kristen 29
Alexander, Kwon 29

Alexander, Lamer 29
Alexander, Leslie 29
Alexander, Lorenzo 29
Alexander, Mackensie 29
Alexander, Maurice 29
Alexander, Monty 29
Alexander, Noellie 29
Alexander, Rene 29
Alexander, R.G."Wick" 29
Alexander, Robert C. 29
Alexander, Robert McNeill 29
Alexander, Ronni 29
Alexander, Vadal 29
Lord Alexander of Weedon 30
アレキサンドリア
Alexandria, Lorez 30
アレキサンドレスク
Alexandrescu, Andrei 30
アレクサニャン
Aleksanyan, Artur 28
Aleksanyan, Ruben 28
アレクサンダー
Alexander, Amir R. 29
Alexander, Carrie 29
Alexander, Chester, Jr. 29
Alexander, Claire 29
Alexander, Cliff 29
Alexander, Douglas Garven 29
Alexander, Graham 29
Alexander, Ian 29
Alexander, Idith 29
Alexander, Jane 29
Alexander, Jason Shawn 29
Alexander, Jesse 29
Alexander, John 29
Alexander, Kathryn J. 29
Alexander, Kwame 29
Alexander, Lamer 29
Alexander, Lloyd Chudley 29
Alexander, Martha G. 29
Alexander, Meg 29
Alexander, Megan 29
Alexander, Michele 29
Alexander, Monty 29
Alexander, Pat 29
Alexander, Paul 29
Alexander, Peter-Jorg 29
Alexander, Robert McNeill 29
Alexander, Skye 29
Alexander, Susan 29
Alexander, Tasha 29
Alexander, Trisha 29
Alexander, Victoria 30
Lord Alexander of Weedon 30
アレクザンダー
Alexander, Lamer 29
Alexander, Scott 29
Alexander, T.Desmond 29
Lord Alexander of Weedon 30
アレグサンダー
Alexander, Catherine Austin 29
アレグザンダー
Alexander, Brian 29
Alexander, Caroline 29
Alexander, Chris 29
Alexander, Christine 29
Alexander, Christopher 29
Alexander, Danny 29
Alexander, David 29
Alexander, Douglas Garven 29
Alexander, Eben 29
Alexander, Frances 29
Alexander, Kathie 29
Alexander, Lamer 29
Alexander, Lloyd Chudley 29
Alexander, Michele 29
Alexander, Monty 29
Alexander, Pat 29
Alexander, Tasha 29
Alexander, William 30
Alexander, William Joseph 30
アレクサンダー・アーノルド
Alexander-arnold, Trent 30
アレクサンダー・オブ・ウィードン
Lord Alexander of Weedon 30
アレクサンダーソン
Alexandersson, Olof 30
アレクサンダル2世
Aleksandar II 28
アレクサンデル
Alexander, Héctor 29
アレクサンデルソン
Alexandersson, Runar 30
アレクサンドリアン
Alexandrian, Sarane 30
アレクサンドル
Alexandre, Boniface 30
Alexandru, Victoria-Violeta 30
アレクサンドレスク
Alexandrescu, Vlad 30
アレクサンドロヴァ
Aleksandrova, Galina Vladimirovna 28
アレクサンドロフ
Aleksandrov, Aleksandar 28
アレクサンドロワ
Alexandrova, Maria 30
アレクサンヤン
Aleksanyan, Artur 28
アレクシー
Alecxih, Chas 28
Aleksei II 28
Alexie, Sherman 30
アレクシー2世
Aleksei II 28
アレクシエーヴィチ
Aleksievich, Svetlana Aleksandrovna 28
アレクシエヴィチ
Aleksievich, Svetlana Aleksandrovna 28
アレクシエーヴィッチ
Aleksievich, Svetlana Aleksandrovna 28
アレクシエービチ
Aleksievich, Svetlana Aleksandrovna 28
アレクシェービッチ
Alexievich, Svetlana 30
アレクシエービッチ
Aleksievich, Svetlana Aleksandrovna 28
アレクシシビリ
Alexishvili, Alexi 30
アレクシス
Alexis, Jacques-Edouard 30
Alexis, Ruano 30
アレクシス・サンチェス
Alexis Sanchez 30
アレクシスバーナディン
Alexis-bernadine, Franca 30
アレクスク・チウラリウ
Alexuc-Ciurariu, Alin 30
アレクセイ
Aleksei II 28
アレクセイ2世
Aleksei II 28
アレクセイエフ
Alexeev, Alexei 30
アレクセーエフ
Alekseev, Vasily 28
アレクセブナ
Alekseevna, Yana 28
アレクナ
Alekna, Virgilijus 28
アレクペロフ
Alekperov, Fizuly 28
アレグリアペニャ
Alegria Pena, Jannet 28
アレーグル
Alègre, Jean-Paul 28
Allègre, Claude Jean 33
アレグレ
Allègre, Claude Jean 33
アレグレ・サシアイン
Alegre Sasiain, Pedro Efraín 28
アレグレッティ
Alegretti, Wagner 28
アレグロ
Allegro, John Marco 33
アレコ
Areco, Amelie 56
アレーサミ
Aleesami, Haitam 28
アレ・サレハ
al-Saleh, Abdullah Hamid Mahmoud 1230
アレジ
Alesi, Jean 28
アレシャンドレ
Alexandre, Waldemar Pires 30
アレーシン
Olesin, Mikhail 1049
アレタ
Aletter, Frank 28
アレックス
Alex, Lionel 28
Alex, L.M. 28
アレックス・アレグリーア
Alex Alegria 29
アレックス・サンドロ
Alex Sandro 30
アレックス・テレス
Alex Telles 30
アレックス・ベルガンティニョス
Alex Bergantinos 30
アレックス・マルティネス
Alex Martinez 30
アレックス・ミネイロ
Alex Mineiro 30
アレッサンドリーニ
Alessandrini, Gerard 28
Alessandrini, Jean 28
アレッシィ
Alessi, Alberto 28
アレッシュ
Alesch, Stephen 28
アレッター
Aletter, Frank 28
アレトラリス
Aletraris, Sophocles 28
アレドンド
Arredondo, Gonzalo 61
アレーナ
Arena, Marie 56
アレナス
Arenas, Alberto 56
Arenas, Amelia 56
Arenas, Javier 56
アレナード
Arenado, Nolan 56
アレニウス
Arenius, Päivi 56
アレノ
Alléno, Yannick 34
アレバロ
Arevalo, Eduardo Lacs 56
Arevalo, Samantha 56
アレフ
Alef, Bryson 28
Aref, Abdel Rahman Mohammed 56
Aref, Mohammad Reza 56
アレファイネ
Arefaine, Berhe 56
アレホス
Alejos, Luis 28
アレマイエ
Alemayehu, Tegenu 28
アレマーニャ
Alemagna, Béatrice 28
アレマノ
Alemanno, Giovanni 28
アレマン
Alemán, Álvaro 28
Aleman, Arnoldo 28
Alemán, Héctor 28
Alemán, José Miugel 28
アレマンノ
Alemanno, Gianni 28
Alemanno, Matias 28
アレム
Alem, Thaher 28
Alemu, Elfenesh 28
アレモン
Alemao 28
アレヤーノ
Arellano, Carlo 56
アレ・ラマ
AleLama 28
アレル
Harel, Barbara 570
アレルストルファー
Allerstorfer, Daniel 34
アレロ
Arero, Hassan 56
アレワ
Alewa, Abdullah Ali 28
Alewa, Kaba Ould 28
アーレン
Ahrens, C.Donald 21
Irlen, Helen 649
アレン
Alene, Margarita 28
Allen, Algernon 33

ア

Allen, Alpian 33
Allen, Antonio 33
Allen, Beau 33
Allen, Benny 33
Allen, Beverly 33
Allen, Brandon 33
Allen, Charles 33
Allen, Charlotte Vale 33
Allen, Christopher 33
Allen, Clifford 33
Allen, Cody 33
Allen, Constance 33
Allen, Corey 33
Allen, Cortez 33
Allen, Cory 33
Allen, David 33
Allen, Deborah E. 33
Allen, Dennis 33
Allen, Devon 33
Allen, Diane M. 33
Allen, Dwayne 33
Allen, Elizabeth K. 33
Allen, Emma 33
Allen, Franklin 33
Allen, Gary 33
Allen, Gary J. 33
Allen, Graham 33
Allen, Grayson 33
Allen, Harper 33
Allen, Heather L. 33
Allen, Hunter 33
Allen, Jack 33
Allen, James 33
Allen, Jarrett 33
Allen, Javorius 33
Allen, Jeff 33
Allen, Jerome 33
Allen, Joan 33
Allen, Joe 33
Allen, Jonathan 33
Allen, Jon G. 33
Allen, Joseph Patrick 33
Allen, Josh 33
Allen, Justin 33
Allen, Kate 33
Allen, Kathleen R. 33
Allen, Keenan 33
Allen, Kevin 33
Allen, Larry 33
Allen, Lavoy 33
Allen, Lily L. 33
Allen, Linda 33
Allen, Liz 33
Allen, Louise 33
Allen, Malik 33
Allen, Mark 33
Allen, MaryJean 33
Allen, Nate 33
Allen, Neil 33
Allen, Pamela 34
Allen, Patrick 34
Allen, Paul 34
Allen, RaShaun 34
Allen, Ray 34
Allen, Ricardo 34
Allen, Rick 34
Allen, Robbie 34
Allen, Robert 34
Allen, Robert C. 34
Allen, Robert G. 34
Allen, Roger E. 34
Allen, Ruth 34
Allen, Ryan 34
Allen, Sandy 34
Allen, Sarah Addison 34
Allen, Sharon 34
Allen, Stanley 34
Allen, Stephen D. 34
Allen, Stewart Lee 34
Allen, Terence David 34
Allen, Thomas B. 34
Allen, Thomas John 34
Allen, Timothy A. 34
Allen, Tom 34
Allen, Tony 34
Allen, Torrence 34
Allen, Tricia 34
Allen, William Clifford 34
Allen, Woody 34
Harent, Sophie 570

アレンカール
Alencar, Chico 28
Alencar, José 28

アレンカル
Alencar, José 28

アレン・コン
Allen-Conn, B.J. 34

アレンシビア
Arencibia, Yordanis 56

アーレンス
Ahrens, Hans-Jürgen 21
Ahrens, Ingo 21

アレンス
Ahrens, Thomas 21

アレンズ
Arends, Jacco 56

アーレンツ
Ahrendts, Angela 21

アレンツ
Aerents, Jasper 16

アーレンド
Ahrend, Susan 21

アーレント＝シュルテ
Ahrendt-Schulte, Ingrid 21

アレンビー
Allenby, Kate 34
Allenby, Sasha 34

アーレンフェルド
Ehrenfeld, Jesse M. 393

アレン＝ミアーズ
Allen-Meares, Paula 34

アロー
Alaux, François 25
Arrow, Kenneth Joseph 61

アロイア
Aloia, Mark 36

アロイアン
Aloian, Misha 36

アロイス
Alois 36

アロウェイ
Alloway, Ross G. 35
Alloway, Tracy Packiam 35

アロゴスクフィス
Alogoskoufis, Georgios 36

アロシュ
Haroche, Serge 572

アロージョ
Araujo, Edson 55

アローズ
Araoz, Gustavo 54

アロスカー
Aroskar, Mila Ann 60

アロステギ
Arostegui, Martin C. 60

アロステギ・サンチェス
Aróstegui Sánchez, Julio 60

アロースミス
Arrowsmith, Claire 61

アロセメナ
Arosemena, Augusto 60
Arosemena, Ramón 60
Arosemena, Rubén 60
Arosemena Monroy, Carlos Julio 60

アロチャ
Arrocha, Melitón 61

アロチャ・マシド
Arocha Masid, César Ignacio 60

アロット
Allott, Nicholas Elwyn 35
Allott, Philip 35

アロップ
Arop, Martin Malwal 60

アロニ
Aloni, Shulamit 36

アロニカ
Aronica, Lou 60

アーロノヴィッチ
Aaronovitch, Ben 1

アロノウィッツ
Aronowitz, Al 60

アーロノビッチ
Aaronovitch, Ben 1
Aaronovitch, David 1

アロノフ
Aronoff, Frances Webber 60

アロノフスキー
Aronofsky, Darren 60

アローマ
Aruoma, Okezie I. 62

アロマー
Alomar, Robert 36
Alomar, Sandy, Jr. 36

アロマリ
Alomari, Ahmed 36

アロム
Arom, Simha 60

アローヨ
Arroyo, Bronson 61
Arroyo, Luis 61
Arroyo, McWilliams 61

アロヨ
Arroyo, Gloria Macapagal 61
Arroyo, Luis 61

アロヨバルデス
Arroyo Valdez, Jorge David 61

アローラ
Arora, Nikesh 60

アロラ
Alora, Kirstie Elaine 36

アロレ
Arore, David 60

アーロン
Aaron 1
Aaron, Escandell 1
Aaron, Hank 1
Aaron, Henry Louis 1
Aaron, Jason 1
Aaron, Jonathan 1
Aaron, Marjorie Corman 1
Aaron, Martin 1
Aaron, Raymond 1
Aron, Elaine N. 60

アロン
Alon, Dalia 36
Aron, Arthur 60

アーロンズ
Aarons, Maureen 1
Ahrons, Constance R. 21

アロンソ
Alonso, Agustin 36
Alonso, Alberto 36
Alonso, Alfonso 36
Alonso, Alicia 36
Alonso, Alvaro 36
Alonso, Ana 36
Alonso, Damaso 36
Alonso, Fernando 36
Alonso, José Antonio 36
Alonso, Kiko 36

アロンゾ
Alonso, Alicia 36
Alonso, Yonder 36

アロンソ＝プッチ
Alonso Puig, Mario 36

アロンソ・マサリエゴス
Alonzo Mazariegos, Denis 36

アーロンソン
Aaronson, Deborah 1
Aaronson, Kathy 1
Aaronson, Philip Irving 1
Aronson, Virginia 60

アロンソン
Aronson, Andrew C. 60
Aronson, Bradley 60
Aronson, David R. 60
Aronson, Elliot 60

アワー
Auer, James E. 69

アワダラ
Awadallah, Bassem 72

アワダラハ
Awadallah, Bassem 72

アーワディ
Arwady, Meredith 62

アワド
Awad, Makkawi Mohammed 72
Awad, Mohamed 72
Awad, Mohammed Zayed 72

アワド＝ガイスラー
Awad-Geissler, Johanna 72

アワドヒ
al-Awadhi, Hussein Dhaif Allah 72

アワナ
Awana, Theyab 72

アワル
al-Awar, Najla bint Mohammed 72

アワルディン
Awaluddin, Hamid 72

アワレ
Awaleh, Mohamed Ahmed 72

アワン
Awan, Firdous Ashiq 72
Awan, Irung 72
Awan, Zaheeruddin Babar 72
Awang, Mohd Azizulhasni 72

アン
Ahn, Byong-man 21
Ahn, Byong-yub 21
Ahn, Ché 21
Ahn, Cheol-soo 21
Ahn, Choong-yong 21
Ahn, Jae-hwan 21
Ahn, Jung-hwahn 21
Ahn, Sang-soo 21

Ahn, Sang-young 21
Ahn, Sung-kee 21
Ahn, Viktor 21
An, Do-hyeon 42
An, Jong Do 42
An, Jong-su 42
An, Kum-ae 42
An, Tong-chun 42
An, Victor 42
An, Yong-hak 42
An, Yun-Jo 42
Ang Vong Vathana 49
Princess Anne 50
Anne, Venkat Sridhar 50
アンウィン
Unwin, Christina 1434
Unwin, David 1434
Unwin, Simon 1434
Unwin, Stanley 1434
アン王女
Princess Anne 50
アンカ
Anka, Darryl 50
アンガ
Unga, Uani' 1434
アンガー
Anger, Bryan 49
Anger, Kenneth 49
Anger, Norbert 49
Unger, Craig 1434
Unger, J.Marshall 1434
Unger, Lorin 1434
Unger, Max 1434
Unger, Rhoda Kesler 1434
アンカーセン
Ankersen, Rasmus 50
アンガー=ハミルトン
Unger-Hamilton, Clive 1434
アンガマル
Engammare, Max 402
アンガーミュラー
Angermüller, Rudolph 49
アンガラ
Angara, Edgardo J. 48
アンガラモ
Angaramo, Roberta 48
アンガリ
al-Angari, Khalid bin Muhammad 48
アンカーン・カンラヤーナポン
Angkhan Kanlayanaphong 49
アンギマテ
Anguimaté, Eloi 49
アンギャル
Angyal, Erica 49
アーンキル
Arnkil, Tom Erik 60
アング
Ang, Andrew 48
Ang, Tom 48
アングアン
Angouin, Michel Ange 49
アングウィン
Angwin, Julia 49
アングスト
Angst, Jules 49
アングバン
Angban, Victorien 48
アングラ
Angula, Helmut 49
Angula, Nahas 49
アングラオ
Ingrao, Christian 647
アングランド
Anglund, Joan Walsh 49
アングリス
Angliss, Sarah 49
アングリスト
Angrist, Joshua David 49
アンクリッチ
Unkrich, Lee 1434
アングリム
Anglim, Simon 49
アングル
Angle, Colin 49
Angle, Kurt 49
アングルバーガー
Angleberger, Tom 49
アングルベール
Englebert, Jean-Luc 403
アングレール
Englert, François 403
アングロシーノ
Angrosino, Michael V. 49
アングロ・パルド
Angulo Pardo, Jacinto 49
アンクワブ
Ankvab, Aleksandr Zolotinska-ipa 50
アンケファー
Unkefer, Robert F. 1434
アンゲラー
Angerer, Bernhard 49
Angerer, Tobias 49
Ungerer, Tomi 1434
アンゲルコバ
Angelkova, Nikolina 49
アンゲル・ジャティ・ウィジャヤ
Angger Jati Wijaya 49
アンゲロフ
Angelov, Anyu 49
Angelov, Ivo Serafimov 49
アンゲロプル
Angelopoulou, Vasiliki 49
アンゲロプロス
Angelopoulos, Théo 49
Angelopoulos, Thodoros 49
アンコーナ
Ancona, Deborah Gladstein 43
アンコナ
Ancona, Deborah Gladstein 43
アンコマ
Ankoma, Papa Owusu 50
アンサー
Ansah, Ezekiel 50
アンサラ
Ansara, Michael 50
アンサーリー
Ansary, Mir Tamim 50
アンサリ
Ansari, Aziz 50
Ansari, Chakir 50
Ansari, Jamshid 50
Ansari, Majid 50
Ansari, Mohammad Hamid 50
アンサール
Ansart, Pierre 50
アンサルディ
Ansaldi, Cristian 50
アンシ
al-Ansi, Ahmed Qassim 51
アンジアタビソン
Andriatavison, Bruno Ramaroson 48
アンジアナリスン
Andrianarison, Oliber Sahobisoa 48
アンジアマナリボ
Andriamanarivo, Mamy Lalatiana 48
アンジアマンジャト
Andriamanjato, Ny Hasina 48
アンジアモサリソア
Andriamosarisoa, Jean Anicet 48
アンジアンサジャチニウニ
Randriasandratriniony, Yvan 1156
アンジアンジャト・ラザフィンダンボ
Andrianjato Razafindambo, Vonison 48
アンジアンティアナ
Andriantiana, Jacques Ulrich 48
アンジアンパーラニ
Andriamparany, Benjamin 48
アンジアンパンザーバ
Andriampanjava, Jacob Felicien 48
アンジェ
Angier, Natalie 49
Angier, Roswell 49
Aunger, Robert 70
アンジェイエフスキー
Andrezejewski, Stanislaw 48
アンジェッラ
Angella, Gabriele 49
アンジェラ
Angela, Alberto 49
アンジェラー
Ungerer, Tomi 1434
アンジェラベイビー
Angelababy 49
アンジェリ
Angjeli, Anastas 49
アンジェリス
Angelis, Barbara De 49
アンジェリーノ
Angelino 49
アンジェリル
Angélil, René 49
アンジェル
Angel, Benjamin 48
アンジェルー
Angelou, Maya 49
アンジェルッチ
Angelucci, Enzo 49
アンジェレ
Engerer, Brigitte 403
アンジェロ
Angelo, Bonnie 49
Angelo, Jack 49
アンジェロウ
Angelou, Maya 49
アンジェロス
Angelos, Peter G. 49
アンシプ
Ansip, Andrus 51
アンジャー
Angier, Michael 49
アンジャンジェ
Enginger, Véronique 403
アンジュ
Ange, Daniel 48
アンシュッツ
Anschuetz Thoms, Daniela 51
Anschutz, Felix 51
Anschutz Thoms, Daniela 51
アンシュッツ・トームス
Anschutz Thoms, Daniela 51
アンシュッツ・トムス
Anschutz Thoms, Daniela 51
アーンショー
Earnshaw, Christopher 387
アンジョ
Andjo, Tchamdja 46
アンジョス
Anjos, Assunção Afonso Dos 50
アーンズ
Earns, Lane R. 387
アンスエト・ヒロン
Anzueto Girón, Ulises Noé 52
アンスコム
Anscombe, G.E.M. 51
アーンスタイン
Arnstein, Laura 60
アンスティ
Anstee, Margaret 51
アンステット
Anstett, Vincent 51
アンスデル
Ansdell, Gary 51
アンスネス
Andsnes, Leif Ove 48
アンスパック
Anspach, Mark Rogin 51
Anspach, Solveig 51
アンスバッハー
Ansbacher, Heinz 50
Ansbacher, Rowena 51
アンスリンガー
Anslinger, Patricia L. 51
アンスロー
Anslow, Philip 51
アンスロップ
Anthrop, Danny 51
アンスワース
Unsworth, Barry 1434
Unsworth, John 1434
アンズワース
Unsworth, Barry 1434
Unsworth, Cathi 1434
アンセ
Hanze, Roberto 568
アンセルド
Unseld, Wes, Jr. 1434
アンセルメ
Ansermet, François 51
アンセルモ
Anselmo, Mataix 51
アンセロ
Ansello, Edward F. 51
アンソニー
Anthony, Carmelo 51

Anthony, Frank 51
Anthony, Joel 51
Anthony, Kenny 51
Anthony, Lawrence 51
Anthony, Mark 51
Anthony, Robert 51
Anthony, Robert Newton 51
Anthony, Ronald 51
Anthony, Scott D. 51
Anthony, Stephone 51
Anthony, William Alan 51
アンソニイ
Anthony, Piers 51
アンゾフ
Ansoff, H.Igor 51
アンソレーナ
Anzorena, Jorge 52
アンソン
Anson, Mark J.P. 51
アンダ
Anda, Gunawan 43
アンダー
Ander, Willard N. 43
アンタイ
Hantai, Pierre 568
Hantaï, Simon 568
アンダーウッド
Underwood, Blair 1434
Underwood, Carrie 1434
Underwood, Cecil H. 1434
Underwood, Colton 1434
Underwood, Deb 1434
Underwood, Deborah 1434
Underwood, Duane, Jr. 1434
Underwood, Geoffrey D. M. 1434
Underwood, James Cressee Elphinstone 1434
Underwood, Laurie 1434
Underwood, LeBea 1434
Underwood, Liam 1434
Underwood, Lynn Gordon 1434
Underwood, Patricia 1434
Underwood, Peter 1434
アンダーシ
Andahazi, Federico 43
アンダース
Anders, Allison 43
Anders, George 43
Anders, Karen 43
アンダーズ
Anders, Maud 43
アンダースン
Andersen, Francis I. 43
Anderson, Brad 43
Anderson, Burton 43
Anderson, C.L. 44
Anderson, David 44
Anderson, James 44
Anderson, Jennifer 44
Anderson, Jon Lee 45
Anderson, Kent 45
Anderson, Kevin J. 45
Anderson, Peggy M. 45
Anderson, Poul William 45
Anderson, Wayne 46
Zettel, Sarah 1551
アンタゼ
Antadze, Merab 51
アンダーセン
Andersen, Chris 43
Andersen, Christopher P. 43
Andersen, Jodi 43
Andersen, Mark B. 43
Andersen, Susan 43
Andersen, Tom 43
Anderson, Christopher 44
アンダーソン
Anderson, Alan 43
Anderson, Allen 43
Anderson, Andy 43
Anderson, Ann 43
Anderson, AnnMarie 43
Anderson, Benedict 43
Anderson, Bernhard W. 43
Anderson, Betty Lise 43
Anderson, Bill 43
Anderson, Bob 43
Anderson, Brad 43
Anderson, Brent Eric 43
Anderson, Brett 43
Anderson, C.A. 43
Anderson, Carl 43
Anderson, Carol Boyles 43
Anderson, Caroline 43
Anderson, Carol M. 43
Anderson, Carol Shaffer 44
Anderson, Catherine 44
Anderson, Chase 44
Anderson, Chris 44
Anderson, C.J. 44
Anderson, Cody 44
Anderson, Colt 44
Anderson, Dave 44
Anderson, David 44
Anderson, David J. 44
Anderson, Debra Gay 44
Anderson, Demetris 44
Anderson, Derek 44
Anderson, Diane M. 44
Anderson, Douglas Allen 44
Anderson, Douglas R. 44
Anderson, Dres 44
Anderson, Drew 44
Anderson, Eli 44
Anderson, Elijah 44
Anderson, Elizabeth 44
Anderson, Elizabeth L. 44
Anderson, Elizabeth T. 44
Anderson, E.M. 44
Anderson, Eric 44
Anderson, Erin 44
Anderson, Ernestine 44
Anderson, Gail 44
Anderson, George 44
Anderson, Gerry 44
Anderson, Gillian 44
Anderson, Greg 44
Anderson, Haley 44
Anderson, Harlene 44
Anderson, Henry 44
Anderson, Henry Lee Norman 44
Anderson, Hugh 44
Anderson, Jack Northman 44
Anderson, James 44
Anderson, James C. 44
Anderson, Jamie 44
Anderson, Jan 44
Anderson, Janet 44
Anderson, Jasey-Jay 44
Anderson, Jenny 44
Anderson, Jill 44
Anderson, Jim 44
Anderson, Joan 44
Anderson, Jodi Lynn 44
Anderson, Johanna M. 44
Anderson, John 44
Anderson, John David, Jr. 44
Anderson, John J.B. 44
Anderson, John R. 44
Anderson, Jonathan 44
Anderson, Jonathan William 45
Anderson, Juel E. 45
Anderson, Julie 45
Anderson, Justin 45
Anderson, Kay J. 45
Anderson, Kevin 45
Anderson, Kristin 45
Anderson, Kyle 45
Anderson, Laurie 45
Anderson, Laurie Halse 45
Anderson, L.Desaix 45
Anderson, Linda C. 45
Anderson, Lynn 45
Anderson, Malcolm 45
Anderson, Mark 45
Anderson, Martin 45
Anderson, Mary B. 45
Anderson, Max 45
Anderson, Michael P. 45
Anderson, M.T. 45
Anderson, Natalie 45
Anderson, Paul Thomas 45
Anderson, Paul W.S. 45
Anderson, Perry 45
Anderson, Pete 45
Anderson, Peter W. 45
Anderson, Poul William 45
Anderson, Rachel 45
Anderson, Raffaela 45
Anderson, Ray C. 45
Anderson, Richard 45
Anderson, Richard H. 45
Anderson, Richard L. 45
Anderson, Rob 45
Anderson, Robby 45
Anderson, Robert 45
Anderson, Robert David 45
Anderson, Robert Woodruff 45
Anderson, Roger Charles 45
Anderson, Romola 45
Anderson, Rory 45
Anderson, Roy 45
Anderson, R.P. 45
Anderson, Ryan 45
Anderson, Sandra K. 45
Anderson, Sarah 45
Anderson, Scott 45
Anderson, Scott C. 45
Anderson, Scoular 45
Anderson, Sean 45
Anderson, Shannon 45
Anderson, Sparky 45
Anderson, Stephen 45
Anderson, Stephen A. 45
Anderson, Stephen Axel 45
Anderson, Steve 45
Anderson, Steven R. 45
Anderson, Susan 45
Anderson, Ted 45
Anderson, Terry 46
Anderson, Tim 46
Anderson, Timothy 46
Anderson, Tyler 46
Anderson, Vicki 46
Anderson, Virginia 46
Anderson, Warren M. 46
Anderson, Wayne 46
Anderson, Wes 46
Anderson, William Allen 46
Anderson, William Robert 46
Anderson, William S. 46
Anderson, William T. 46
Anderson, Zaire 46
Anderson-Allen, Moira 46
Andersson, Gerhard 46
Andersson, Kenneth 46
Andersson, Leif 46
Andersson, Max 46
Andersson, Ove 46
Andersson, Roy 46
アンダーソン＝アレン
Anderson-Allen, Moira 46
アンダーソン - インマン
Anderson-Inman, Lynne 46
アンダーソン・ヤング
Anderson Young, Shauna Christine 46
アンダーソン＝ロペス
Anderson-Lopez, Kristen 46
アンダートン
Anderton, Jim 46
アンダーヒル
Underhill, Brian O. 1434
Underhill, Paco 1434
アンダヤ
Andaya, Rolando 43
アンタル
Intallou, Nina Walett 648
アンチェロッティ
Ancelotti, Carlo 43
アンチオープ
Entiope, Gabriel 404
アンチッチ
Ancic, Mario 43
アンチャイルド
Annechild, Annette 50
アンチュライ
Antulay, A.R. 52
アン・チュリアン
Ang Choulean 48
アンチョルドギー
Anchordoguy, Marie 43
アーンツ
Arntz, Arnoud 60
Arntz, William 60
アンティ
Anti 51
Anti, Michael 51
アンテイ
Antei, Luca 51
アンディー
Andy 48
アンティ・アウル
Auntie Owl 70
アンティエ
Antier, Edwige 51
アンティオー
Antieau, Kim 51
アンティカロフ
Antikarov, Vladimir 51
アンティジョン
Antillón, Mayi 51
アンティッチ
Antić, Aleksandar 51
アンディノ
Andino, Francisco 46

アンティラ
Anttila, Sirkka-Liisa 52
アンティル
Antill, Peter 51
アンデェション
Anderson, Lena 45
アンデオル
Andeol, Emilie 43
アンテカスティージョ
Antes Castillo, Lissette Alexandra 51
アンテサナ・アラニバル
Antezana Aranibar, Fernando 51
アンデジェフスキー
Anderszewski, Piotr 46
アンデシェン
Andersen, Dag Terje 43
Andersen, Petter 43
アンデション
Andersson, Emil 46
Andersson, Lina 46
Andersson, Magdalena 46
Andersson, Stina 46
アンテス
Antes, Horst 51
Anthes, Emily 51
アンデュ
Undeux 1434
アンテュク
Antyukh, Natalya 52
アンデリン
Andelin, Helen B. 43
アンデル・エレーラ
Ander Herrera 43
アンデルコヴィッチ
Andelkovic, Sinisa 43
アンデルシェフスキ
Anderszewski, Piotr 46
アンデルセン
Á.andersen, Sigríður 1
Andersen, Anne 43
Andersen, Esben Sloth 43
Andersen, Hjalmar 43
Andersen, Kjel 43
Andersen, Tom 43
アンデルソン
Anderson 43
Andersonn, Margit 46
Andersson, Sten 46
Benny 123
アンデルマン
Andermann, Eva 43
アーント
Arndt, Michael 59
アンドゥ
Ando, Obadiah 46
アンドゥシチマクシモビッチ
Maksimovic Andusic, Ivana 888
アントゥネス
Antunes, Vitorino 52
アントゥノビッチ
Antunović, Željka 52
アンドゥーハー
Andujar, Joaquin 48
Andujar, Miguel 48
アンドゥハル
Andujar, Joaquin 48
アントゥライ
Antulay, Abdul Rehman 52
アンドゥルース
Andrus, Elvis 48
アンドゥン
Andung, Nitimiharja 48
アントザク
Antczak, Gina 51
Antczak, Stephen 51
アントシ
Antosii, Vladimir 52
アントソバ
Antosova, Lenka 52
アントッチャ
Antoccia, Luca 51
アントナッチ
Antonacci, Gary 51
アントニー
Anthony, Marc 51
Antony, A.K. 52
Antony, Martin M. 52
Antony, Steve 52
アントニイ
Antony, Peter 52
アントニウ
Antoniou, Grigoris 52
アントニオ
Antonio, Joseph 52
Antonio, Michail 52
アントニオズ
Anthonioz, Deborah 51
アントニオーニ
Antonioni, Michelangelo 52
アントニーニ
Antonini, Gabriele 52
アンドネ
Andone, Florin 46
アントネスク
Antonescu, Marius 52
アントネッティ
Antonetti, Chris 52
アントネッリ
Antonelli, Laura 52
Antonelli, Luca 52
Antonelli, Paola 52
アントネリ
Antonelli, Laura 52
アントネンコフ
Antonenkov, Evgenii 52
アントーノヴァ
Antonova, Irina Aleksandrovna 52
アントノフ
Antonov, Sergey 52
Antonov, Vladislav 52
アントノフスキー
Antonovsky, Aaron 52
アントノプロス
Antonopoulos, Andreas M. 52
アンドノール
Andnor, Berit 46
アントノワ
Antonova, Olena 52
アントユフ
Antyukh, Natalya 52
アンドラーシュ
András, Dániel 46
Andras, Szasz 46
アンドラス
Andrus, Mark 48
アンドラスキー
Andraski, Joseph 46
アンドラダ
Andrada, Celestino Da Graca 46
アンドラーデ
Andrade, Arnaldo 46
アンドラデ
Andrade, Efren 46
Andrade, Fernando Elíseo Leboucher de 46
Andrade, Osvaldo 46
Andrade, Trajano 46
アンドラデ・マルティネス
Andrade Martínez, Virgilio 46
アンドラド
Andrade, José Manuel 46
アンドリー
Andely, Roger Rigobert 43
アンドリ・S.マグナソン
Andri Snær Magnason 48
アンドリアセン
Andreasen, Nancy C. 47
アンドリアナイナリベロ
Andrianainarivelo, Hajo 48
アンドリアナサンドラトリニオニ
Andrianasandratriniony, Yvan 48
アンドリアナリブ
Andrianarivo, Tantely 48
アンドリアーニ
Andriani, Renee 48
アンドリアニリナ
Andrianirina, Fetison 48
アンドリアノフ
Andrianov, Nikolai 48
アンドリアノワ
Andrianova, Tatyana 48
アンドリアマハゾ
Andriamahazo, Nirhy Lanto 48
アンドリアマンジャート
Andriamanjato, Ny Hasina 48
アンドリアミセザ
Andriamiseza, Charles 48
アンドリアンパンジャバ
Andriampanjava, Jacob Felicien 48
アンドリオプロス
Andriopoulos, Thodoris 48
アンドリサーニ
Andrisani, John 48
アンドリザーニ
Andrisani, John 48
アンドリース
Andriese, Matt 48
アンドリーセン
Andreasen, Alan R. 47
Andreessen, Marc 47
アンドリツェフ
Andriitsev, Valerii 48
アンドリッチ
Andrić, Vojislav 48
アントリーニ
Antorini, Christine 52
アンドリノフ
Andrinof, Chaniago 48
アンドリュー
Prince Andrew 47
Andrew, James P. 47
Andrew, Marion I. 47
Andrieu, Philippe 48
アンドリュウカイティス
Andriukaitis, Vytenis Povilas 48
アンドリュース
Andrews, Antonio 47
Andrews, David 47
Andrews, Donald Arthur 47
Andrews, Gavin 47
Andrews, George E. 47
Andrews, Guy 47
Andrews, Heather A. 47
Andrews, Jean 47
Andrews, Josh 47
Andrews, Julie 47
Andrews, Kate 47
Andrews, Kevin 47
Andrews, Mark 47
Andrews, Neil H. 47
Andrews, Peter 48
Andrews, Phil 48
Andrews, Philip 48
Andrews, Shirley 48
アンドリューズ
Andrews, Andrew 47
Andrews, Andy 47
Andrews, Beth 47
Andrews, Donna 47
Andrews, Edna 47
Andrews, Julian E. 47
Andrews, Julie 47
Andrews, Lori B. 47
Andrews, Paul 47
Andrews, Sarah 48
Andrews, Ted 48
アンドル
Andre, Bella 46
アンドルー
Andrew, Sylvia 47
アンドルエット
Andruetto, Maria Teresa 48
アンドルー王子
Prince Andrew 47
アンドルース
Andrews, Julie 47
Andrews, Marc 47
Andrews, Mark 47
Andrews, Russell 48
アンドルーズ
Andrews, Amy 47
Andrews, Andy 47
Andrews, Ilona 47
Andrews, Julie 47
Andrews, Kevin 47
Andrews, Lori B. 47
Andrews, Mary Kay 47
Andrews, Paul 47
Andrews, Robert E. 48
アントルモン
Entremont, Philippe 404
アンドレ
Andre 46
André, Christophe 46
André, Ghislain 46
André, Helena 46
André, Jacques 46
Andre, Mary Lou 46
André, Maurice 46
アンドレア
Andrea, Yann 46
Andreae, Giles 46
アンドレアエ
Andreae, Simon 46
アンドレアス
Andreas, Connirae 46
Andreas, Erich 47

ア

Andreas, Irène Victoire 47
Andreas, Joel 47
Andreas, Steve 47
Andreas, Tamara 47
アンドレアス・ペレイラ
Andreas Pereira 47
アンドレーアセン
Andreassen, Bjarne 47
アンドレアソン
Andréasson, Claes 47
アンドレアッシ
Andreassi, John L. 47
アンドレ・アルメイダ
Andre Almeida 46
アンドレ・アンドレ
Andre Andre 46
アンドレイ
Andre, Bella 46
Andreae, Giles 46
アンドレイアセン
Andreasen, Dan 47
アンドレイエフ
Andreev, Aleksei V. 47
アンドレイカ
Andraka, Jack 46
アンドレイチク
Andrejczyk, Maria 47
アンドレウ
Andreu, Conrado López 47
アンドレウェルス
Andre Wells, Georges 47
アンドレーエフ
Andreyev, Vladimir 48
アンドレエフ
Andreev, Igor 47
アンドレエワ
Andreeva, Viktoriia 47
アンドレオッチ
Andreotti, Giulio 47
アンドレオッティ
Andreotti, Giulio 47
アンドレオッリ
Andreolli, Marco 47
アンドレオリ
Andreoli, Mystica 47
アンドレ・キム
Kim, Andre 732
アンドレ・キン
Kim, Andre 732
アンドレ・ゴメス
Andre Gomes 47
アンドレ＝サルヴィニ
André-Salvini, Béatrice 47
アンドレ・シルヴァ
Andre Silva 47
アンドレス
Andres, Cynthia 47
アンドレス・フェルナンデス
Andres Fernandez 47
アンドレス・プリエト
Andres Prieto 47
アンドレーセン
Andreessen, Marc 47
アンドレセン
Andresen, Astrid Haukland 47
Andresen, Frode 47
アンドレゼン
Andresen, Sophia de Mello Breyner 47
アンドレッタ
Andretta, Thierry 47
アンドレッティ
Andretti, Marco 47
アンドレード
Andrade, Demetrius 46
アンドロディア
Androdias, Matthieu 48
アンドロネスク
Andronescu, Ecaterina 48
アントワーヌ
Antoine, Ann David 51
Antoine, Santos 51
アントワーヌ・ダリオー
Antoine-Dariaux, Geneviève 51
アントワン
Antoine, Ancil 51
Antoine, Matthew 51
アントン
Anton, Apriyantono 51
Anton, Franz 51
Anton, Jon 51
Anton, Linda Hunt 51
Anton, Shari 51
Anton, Sinan 51
アンドン
Andon, Nick 46
アンナアマノフ
Annaamanov, Mukhammetgeldi 50
アンナバイラモフ
Annabayramov, Babageldy 50
アンナメレドフ
Annameredov, Bayram 50
アンニ・フリッド
Frida 462
アンニョリ
Agnoli, Antonella 18
アンヌッカ
Annukka, Sanna 50
アーンハイム
Arnheim, Rudolf 59
アンバチョ
Ambachew, Mekonnen 40
アーンハート
Earnhardt, Dale 387
Earnhart, Philip 387
アンバニ
Ambani, Anil D. 40
Ambani, Dhirubhai 40
Ambani, Mukesh D. 40
Ambani, Nita 40
アンプエロ
Ampuero, Roberto 42
アンフツェツェグ・ムンフジャンツァン
Ankhtsetseg Monkhjantsangiin 50
アンブラー
Ambler, Scott W. 40
Ambler, Tim 40
アンブライト
Umbreit, Alexa W. 1433
Umbreit, Mark S. 1433
アンブラス
Ambruas, Victor 40
アンブル
Umble, M.Michael 1433
アンブレイト
Umbreit, Mark 1433
アンフレッド
Umphred, Darcy Ann 1433
アンブロ
Ambro, Darrell 40
アンブロイセ
Ambroise, Mankenda 40
アンブロージ
Ambrosi, Olga 40
アンブロシアーニ
Ambrosiani, Björn 40
アンブロジェッティ
Ambrogetti, Francesca 40
アンブロース
Ambrose, Richard 40
アンブローズ
Ambrose, Alice 40
Ambrose, David 40
Ambrose, Gavin 40
Ambrose, Hugh 40
Ambrose, Rona 40
Ambrose, Starr 40
Ambrose, Stephen E. 40
Ambrose, Susan A. 40
Ambrose, Tom 40
アンブロス
Ambros, Victor R. 40
アンブンダ
Ambunda, Paulus 40
アンベッケン
Anbäcken, Els-Marie 43
アーンヘム
Ahnhem, Stefan 21
アンベール
Humbert, Jean-Baptiste 634
Humbert, Marc 634
Humbert, Vincent 634
アンベルト
Anvelt, Andres 52
アン・ホイ
Hui, Ann 634
アンポフォ
Ampofo, Ofosu 42
アンホールト
Anholt, Catherine 49
Anholt, Laurence 49
アンホルト
Anholt, Robert Rene Henri 49
アン・マーグレット
Ann-Margrett 50
アンマニーティ
Ammaniti, Niccolò 41
アンミラート
Ammirato, Piero 41
アンメホパ
Unmehopa, Musa 1434
アンユル
Anyuru, Andreas 52
アンライン
Unrein, Mitch 1434
アンリ
Henri, Adrian 595
Henry, Ariel 595
Henry, Guillaume 595
Henry, Michel 596
Henry, Thierry 596
アンリアンヌ
Anliane, Ahmed 50
アンリオ
Henriot, Christian 595
Henriot, Nicole 595
アンリグ
Anring, Claudia 50
アンリケ
Henriquez, Elsa 595
アンリコ
Enrico, Robert 404
アンリ大公
Henri, Grand Duc 595
アンリッシ
Umrysh, Cary E. 1433
アンルー
Unruh, Rebecca 1434
アーンルンド
Ahnlund, Knut 21
アンレザーク
Anlezark, Justin 50
アンロ
Henrot, Camille 595
アンワリ
Anwari, Hussein 52
Anwari, Jamahir 52
アンワル
Anwar, Abdul Basir 52
Anwar, Amer 52
Anwar, M.K. 52
Anwar, Muhammad 52
Anwar, Yusuf 52
アンワール・イブラヒム
Anwar Ibrahim 52
アンワル・イブラヒム
Anwar Ibrahim 52
アンワル・リドワン
Anwar Ridhwan 52

【イ】

イ
I, Man-gap 641
I, Yeong-ju 641
I, Yong-hui 641
Lee, Bu-jin 803
Lee, Byong-ho 803
Lee, Byung-hoon 803
Lee, Byung-hun 803
Lee, Byung Jik 803
Lee, Byung-kee 803
Lee, Chae-pil 803
Lee, Cham 803
Lee, Chang-dong 803
Lee, Chang-ho 803
Lee, Chang-jae 803
Lee, Chang-yul 803
Lee, Chi-beom 803
Lee, Chul-hwan 803
Lee, Chung-Yong 803
Lee, Dae-ho 803
Lee, Dal-gon 803
Lee, Dong-gun 804
Lee, Dong-phil 804
Lee, Dong-woon 804
Lee, Eun 804
Lee, Eun-joo 804
Lee, Hae-chan 804
Lee, Hae-jin 804
Lee, Han-dong 804
Lee, Hee-beom 804
Lee, Hee-ho 804
Lee, Ho-baek 804
Lee, Hoi-chang 804
Lee, Hong-koo 804
Lee, Ho-suk 804
Lee, Hun-jai 804
Lee, Hu-rak 804
Lee, Hyoung-sik 804
Lee, Hyun-ju 804
Lee, Hyun-seung 804
Lee, Jae-gyu 804

Lee, Jae-han 804
Lee, Jae-joung 804
Lee, Jae-oh 804
Lee, Jae-yong 804
Lee, Jang-ho 804
Lee, Jeong-beom 804
Lee, Jeonghee 804
Lee, Jong-seok 805
Lee, Jong-suk 805
Lee, Jong-wook 805
Lee, Joon-sik 805
Lee, Joung-binn 805
Lee, Ju-ho 805
Lee, Jun 805
Lee, Jung-hyang 805
Lee, Jung-jae 805
Lee, Jung-myung 805
Lee, Jung-soo 805
Lee, Jung-su 805
Lee, Jun-ik 805
Lee, Jun-ki 805
Lee, Kang-beak 805
Lee, Kang-ryol 805
Lee, Kang-seok 805
Lee, Keun-ho 805
Lee, Keunho 805
Lee, Keun-sik 805
Lee, Ki-kweon 805
Lee, Kun-hee 805
Lee, Kwi-nam 805
Lee, Kyou-hyuk 805
Lee, Maan-ee 805
Lee, Min-ho 805
Lee, Min-jung 805
Lee, Myung-bak 805
Lee, Nak-youn 805
Lee, Na-young 805
Lee, One-Koo 805
Lee, Sang-chul 806
Lee, Sang-deuk 806
Lee, Sang-hee 806
Lee, Sang-hwa 806
Lee, Sang-joo 806
Lee, Sang-soo 806
Lee, Seo-jin 806
Lee, Seong-kang 806
Lee, Seung-chul 806
Lee, Seung-gi 806
Lee, Seung-hoon 806
Lee, Seung-u 806
Lee, Seung-yun 806
Lee, Seung-yuop 806
Lee, Soo-man 806
Lee, Sung-Chan 806
Lee, Sung Dae 806
Lee, Sung-jae 806
Lee, Sung-jin 806
Lee, Sun-shine 806
Lee, Tae-sung 806
Lee, Wan-koo 806
Lee, Wong-gyon 806
Lee, Won Ja 806
Lee, Won-sook 806
Lee, Won-soon 806
Lee, Yong-dae 806
Lee, Yong-hoon 806
Lee, Yong-Ja 807
Lee, Yong-sup 807
Lee, Yoon Ah 807
Lee, Yoon-ki 807
Lee, Yoon-woo 807
Lee, Yoshik 807
Lee, Young-ae 807
Lee, Young-do 807
Lee, Young-hee 807
Lee, Youn-ho 807
Lee, Yo-won 807
Lee, Yura 807
Li, Du-Ik 823
Rhee, Chang-yong 1175
Ri, Yong-ho 1176
Ri, Yong-mu 1176
Yi, Chong-jun 1538
Yi, Ho-chol 1538
Yi, Min-u 1538

イー
Lee, Jong Kuk 805
Lim, Chang-yong 828
Yee, Wong Herbert 1537
Yi, Chong-jun 1538
Yi, Ho-chol 1538

イアウコイアリス
Iauko Iaris, Harry 642

イアガル
Iagar, Monica 641

イアキーニ
Iachini, Giuseppe 641

イアクシナ
Iakushina, Iaroslava 642

イアゴ・アスパス
Iago Aspas 641

イアコヴィーノ
Iacovino, Raffaele 641

イアゴ・エレリン
Iago Herrerin 641

イアコノ
Iakono, Sal 642

イアコビシビリ
Iakobishvili, Zurabi 642

イアゴ・ファルケ
Iago Falque 641

イアコブッチ
Iacobucci, Dawn 641

イアコボーニ
Iacoboni, Marco 641

イアシャイシュ
Iashaish, Hussein 642

イァーネス
Ianes, Alberto 642

イアハート
Earhart, Kristin 387

イアルチェフ
Iartcev, Denis 642

イアロッシ
Iarossi, Giuseppe 642

イアロムカ
Iaromka, Svitlana 642

イアン
Ian, Janis 642
Tsutsui, Ian 1424

イアンシティ
Iansiti, Marco 642

イアンチュク
Ianchuk, Dmytro 642

イアンヌ
Yanne, Jean 1535

イイノ
Iino, Thomas 644

イヴ
Eve 413

イヴァシキン
Ivashkin, Aleksandr 653
Ivashkin, Alexander 653

イーヴァニー
Yee vani, Chandra S. 1537

イヴァニッチ
Ivanić, Mladen 653

イヴァネク
Ivanek, Zeljko 653

イヴァノヴィッチ
Evanovich, Janet 411
Ivanovic, Ana 653
Ivanovic, Branislav 653

イヴァノフ
Ivanov, Bratislav Ionchev 653
Ivanov, Gjorge 653

イヴィングス
Ivings, Kristina 654

イヴェール
Iver, Bon 653

イヴェレット
Everret, Chad 413

イウォビ
Iwobi, Alex 654

イヴシック
Ivsic, Radovan 654

イーヴズ
Eaves, Morris 388

イウパティ
Iupati, Mike 653

イヴリー
Ivry, Benjamin 654

イェ
Yeh, Chris 1537

イェー
Yeh, Pochi 1537

イエ
Ye, Bin 1536
Ye, Bongnessan 1537
Ye, Lin-Sheng 1537

イェ・アウン
Ye Aung 1537

イェイツ
Yates, Judith 1536

イエイツ
Yates, Pamela M. 1536

イェーガー
Jaeger, Robert A. 658
Jäger, Jill 659
Jäger, Lorenz 659
Jäger, Willigis 659
Jäger, Wolfgang 659
Joerger, David 675
Yeager, Steve 1537
Yeager, Timothy J. 1537

イェガー
Yager, Jan 1532

イエーガー
Jaegar, Lars 658
Jaeger, Paul T. 658
Jaeger, Robert A. 658

イエガー
Jaeger, Anne-Celine 658
Jaeger, Connor 658
Jaeger, Mirjam 658

イェカブソンス
Jekabsons, Eriks 669

イエキニ
Yekini, Rashidi 1537

イエクティエル
Yekutiel, Gal 1537

イエゲヌドン
Eyeghe Ndong, Jean 414

イエゲル
Jaeger, Clarice 658

イエゴ
Yego, Alfred Kirwa 1537
Yego, Julius 1537

イエコワ
Jekova, Alexandra 669

イエーシ
Iehsi, Ieske 643

イェジェイチャク
Jedrzejczak, Otylia 668

イエジェク
Jezek, Stanislav 672

イェシェック
Jescheck, Hans-Heinrich 672

イェシェー・ドゥンデン
Yeshi Donen 1538

イエシエン
Jesien, Anna Olichwierczuk 672

イエシャネ
Yeshaneh, Ababel 1538

イェシュケ
Jaeschke, Rex 658
Jaeschke, Roman 658
Jaeschke, Walter 658
Jeschke, Mathias 672
Jeschke, Tanja 672

イェシュテット
Jestaedt, Matthias 672

イェスコム
Yescombe, Edward 1538

イエスパーセン
Jespersen, Karen 672

イエスパセン
Jespersen, Karen 672

イエスペシェン
Jespersen, Chris Andre 672

イェーツ
Yates, Brock 1536
Yates, Charles 1536
Yates, David 1536
Yates, Kirby 1536
Yates, Louise 1536
Yates, Ruth 1536

イエーツ
Yates, Brock 1536
Yates, Butler 1536
Yates, Charles 1536
Yates, Maisey 1536
Yates, Peter 1536
Yates, Philip 1536

イエッサー
Jesser, Eugen 672

イエッター
Jetter, Martin 672

イェッツ
Yates, Russel 1536

イエッツ
Yates, Russel 1536

イエッツイ
Yezzi, Katie 1538

イェッツォネン
Jetsonen, Jari 672
Jetsonen, Sirkkaliisa 672

イエットギリエス
Ietto-Gillies, Grazia 643

イェップ
Yep, Laurence 1537

イェップセン
Jepsen, Maria Kristina 671

イェ・トゥ
Ye Htut 1537

イェドヴァイ
Jedvaj, Tin 668

イェトマン
Yetman, Robert J. 1538

イェトミン
Yetming, Gerald 1538

イエーナ

イ

Jena, S. 669
イェニー
Yenny, Sharon 1537
イェーニッケ
Jänicke, Martin 663
イエーニッシュ
Jaenisch, Rudolf 658
イェニテルズィ
Yeniterzi, Emine 1537
イエノウ
Ieno, Elena N. 643
イエビッチ
Jevtic, Olivera 672
イェフェス
Yeffeth, Glenn 1537
イェフダ
Yahuda, Rachel 1532
イェブティッチ
Jevtić, Dalibor 672
イエブネ
Jevne, Erling 672
イェフリチュカ
Jehlicka, Václav 669
イェホシュア
Yehoshua, Abraham B. 1537
イェムティン
Jämtin, Carin 662
イエムレ
Gjoemle, Ella Berg 503
イェライ
Yeray, Alvarez 1537
イェラハウ
Yelahow, Musse Sudi 1537
イエリガドゥ
Yerrigadoo, Ravi 1538
イェリッチ
Yelich, Christian 1537
イェリネク
Jelinek, Elfriede 669
Jellinek, Joseph Stephan 669
イエリネク
Jelinek, Elfriede 669
イェリマピエール
Yerima Pierre, Patrick 1538
イエリヤツカヤ
Yeretskaya, Yevgeniya 1537
イェリル
Yerrill, Gail 1538
イェリン
Yellin, Frank 1537
Yellin, Jerry 1537
イエリン
Yellin, Jerry 1537
イエール
Yale, Pat 1533
イェルヴィ
Järvi, Neeme 665
イェルウェン
Jerven, Morten 672
イエルギュー
Yergeau, Robert 1537
イエルク
Joerg, Selina 675
イエルゲンセン
Jørgensen, Anker Henrik 687
イェルシチュ
Jelušič, Ljubica 669
イェルシャルミ
Yerushalmi, Yosef Hayim 1538
イェルチン
Yelchin, Anton 1537
Yelchin, Eugene 1537
イェルドン
Yeldon, T.J. 1537
イェルハルドセン
Gerhardsen, Carin 490
イェルヒェル
Jerchel, Michael 671
イェルベズ
Jelved, Marianne 669
イェルムバーレン
Hjelmwallén, Lena 610
イエルメセト
Hjelmeset, Odd Bjorn 610
イェルリカヤ
Yerlikaya, Hamza 1538
イェレイェレ
Yereyere, Paluku Kisaka 1537
イエレク
Jezek, Jaromir 672
Jezek, Stanislav 672
イエレミア
Ielemia, Apisai 643
イェレミアス
Jeremias, Jörg 671
イェレミース
Jeremies, Christian 671
Jeremies, Fabian 671
イェレミッチ
Jeremić, Vuk 671
イェレル
Gerell, Par 490
イェレン
Yellen, Janet Louise 1537
イエレン
Yellen, Janet Louise 1537
イエレンコヴィッチ
Jelenkovich, Barbara 669
イエレンコビッチ
Jelenkovich, Barbara 669
イェーレンステン
Gyllensten, Lars Johan Wictor 550
イェレンステン
Gyllensten, Lars Johan Wictor 550
イエロ
Hierro, Luis 604
イエロディアコヌ
Lassila, Lydia 793
イェロバシリ
Ierovasili, Olga 643
イェン
Yan, An-sheng 1534
Yan, Jerry 1534
Yan, Wen-jing 1534
Yen, Donnie 1537
Yeung, Craig Au 1538
Yien, Tut 1538
イエン
Hien, Fidele 604
Hien, Theodore Kilmite 604
Yan, Lian-ke 1534
イエンガー
Iyengar, Sridhar 654
イエンガネ
Yengane, Sixakeko 1537
イエン・サリ
Ieng Sary 643
イェンス
Jens, Inge 670
Jens, Walter 670
イエンスビュ
Jensby, Svend Aage 670
イェンセン
Jensen, Jens H. 671
Jensen, Kristian Ditlev 671
Jensen, Morgens 671
Jensen, Rolf 671
Jensen, Siv 671
イエンセン
Jensen, Frank 670
Jensen, Harald 670
Jensen, Kristian 671
Jensen, Virginia Allen 671
イェンソン
Jaensson, Håkan 658
Jonsson, Reidar 686
イエンソン
Joensson, Emil 675
イェンチ
Jentsch, Julia 671
イエンチャブレ
Yentchabré, Yandja 1537
イエン・チリト
Ieng Thirith 643
イェンツ
Jentz, Thomas L. 671
イエンハーゲル
Enhager, Kjell 403
イエンメッロ
Iemmello, Pietro 643
イオアニーディス
Ioannidis, Dimitris 648
イオアヌ
Ioannou, Kyriakos 648
イオアネ
Ioane, Mona 648
Ioane, TJ. 648
Ioane, Vaipava Nevo 648
イオシア
Iosia, Iosia 648
イォセリアーニ
Iosseliani, Otar 648
イオセリアーニ
Iosseliani, Otar 648
イオニタ
Ionita, Artur 648
Ionita, Florin 648
イオニツァ
Ionită, Andrei Ionut 648
イオーネ
Ione, Larissa 648
イオネスク
Ionescu, Alex 648
Ionescu, Ovidiu 648
イオネスコ
Ionesco, Eva 648
Ionesco, Irina 648
イオノフ
Ionov, Aleksei 648
イオバルディ
Eovaldi, Nathan 404
イオブ
Iovu, Cristina 648
Iovv, Vasile 648
イオルグレ
Iorgulescu, Adrian 648
イオルダケ
Iordache, Larisa Andreea 648
イーガー
Eager, Allen 387
イカウニエツェアドミジナ
Ikauniece-admidina, Laura 644
イカサ・ロメロ
Icaza Romero, José 643
イガシュ
Igas, Traian 643
イカスリアガ
Icazuriaga, Héctor 643
イーカーチ
Ekirch, A.Roger 395
イガリ
Igali, Daniel 643
Igaly, Diana 643
イカルディ
Icardi, Mauro 643
イガロ
Ighalo, Odion 643
イーガン
Eagan, Ed 387
Egan, Caroline LaVelle 392
Egan, Greg 392
Egan, Jennifer 392
Egan, Kate 392
Egan, Kenny 392
Egan, Kieran 392
Egan, Sean 392
Egan, Tim 392
Egan, Timothy 392
Egan, Vicky 392
イギデル
Iguider, Abdalaati 644
イギンラ
Iginla, Jarome 643
イーク
Yeack, William R. 1537
イグアイン
Higuain, Gonzalo 605
イグウェ
Igwe, Bekky 644
イクエベ
Ikouébé, Basile 644
イクェンシ
Ekwensi, Cyprian 395
イクゴポレング
Ikgopoleng, Khumiso 644
イグザム
Exum, Antone 414
イグセト
Yggeseth, Torbjøorn 1538
イクセンバーグ
Iksenburg, Raul 644
イグダーラ
Iguodala, Andre 644
イ・クトゥット
I Ketut, Surajaya 644
イグナシェヴィッチ
Ignashevich, Sergei 644
イグナチェフ
Ignatyev, Mikhail 644
イグナチエフ
Ignatiev, Sergei Mikhailovich 644
イグナチオ
Ignacio, Juan 644
イグナティエフ
Ignatieff, Michael 644

イグナテンコ
Ignatenko, Pablo 644
イグナトビッチ
Ignatovich, Vladimir Kazimirovich 644
イグナトフ
Ignatov, Sergei 644
イグナロ
Ignarro, Louis J. 644
イグニョフスキ
Ignjovski, Aleksandar 644
イグネイシアス
Ignatius, David 644
イグネーシアス
Ignatius, David 644
イグバーシュ
Ighbash, Saqr Ighbash Saeed 643
イクバール
Iqbal, Ahasan 649
イクバル
Iqbal, Muhammad 649
Iqbal, Rao Sikandar 649
Iqbal, Tahir 649
イクバル・ラウザー
Iqbal Rawther, Mohamed 649
イクラモフ
Ikramov, Adkham 644
Ikramov, Muzraf 644
イーグル
Eagle, Alan 387
Eagle, Jake 387
Eagle, Nathan 387
イーグルシャム
Eaglesham, Dale 387
イーグルズ
Eagles, Paul F.J. 387
イーグルストン
Eaglestone, Robert 387
イーグルトン
Eagleton, Terry 387
Eagleton, Thomas Francis 387
イーグルバーガー
Eagleburger, Lawrence Sidney 387
イーグルマン
Eagleman, David 387
Eagleman, David M. 387
イクレ
Iklé, Fred Charles 644
イグレシアス
Iglesias, Enrique V. 643
Iglesias, Joes 643
Iglesias, Julio 644
Iglesias, Karl 644
Iglesias, Leire 644
Iglesias, María Cristina 644
Iglesias, Raisel 644
Iglesias, Roniel 644
Yglesias, Rafael 1538
イゲ
Ige, Bola 643
Igue, John 644
イケダ
Ikeda, Kazuhiro 644
Ikeda, Sidney Kiyoshi 644
イーゲマン
Ygeman, Anders 1538
イゲロ
Higuero, Juan Carlos 605
イーゲン
Eeghen, Idzard van 392
イケンソン
Ikenson, Ben 644
イコイトンギイエ
Icoyitungiye, Juliette 643
イコシア
Ikosia, Kensely 644
イコネ
Ikone, Nanitamo 644
イーコブ
Ecob, Simon 389
イコリ・ムドンボ
Ikoli Ndombo, Michel Bongongo 644
イコンニコフ
Ikonnikov, Kirill 644
イーサ
al-Eisa, Muhammad 394
al-Essa, Khalid bin Abdulrahman 409
al-Issa, Abd 652
Issa, Ageela Saleh 652
al-Issa, Bader Hamad 652
イーザー
Iser, Wolfgang 651
イサ
al-Isa, Ahmed 650
Isa, Awang 650
Isa, bin Ali bin Hamad al-Khalifa 650
Isa, Facundo 650
Isa, Ibrahim 650
Isa, Mohamad 650
イサイア
Isaia, Pelenike 650
イサイアス・アフェウェルキ
Issaias Afewerki 652
イザイリ
Izairi, Nurhan 654
イーザウ
Isau, Ralf 650
イサウィ
al-Isawi, Ali Abdulaziz 650
al-Isawi, Rafie 650
al-Issawi, Nasir 652
イサウイ
al-Isawi, Rafie 650
イサエフ
Isaev, Mansur 650
Isaev, Radik 650
Isayev, Anatoly 650
イサカ
Issaka, Labo 652
イサガー
Isager, Ditte 650
Isager, Marianne 650
イサカーン
Isakhan, Benjamin 650
イサギレインサウスティ
Izaguirre Insausti, Jon 654
イサーク
Isaac, Mark 650
イザーク
Izák, Jaroslay 654
イサクセン
Isaksen, Margaux 650
Isaksen, Torbjørn Røe 650
イサクノワ
Isakunova, Taalaykul 650
イサコー
Isakow, Warren 650
イサコウィッツ
Isacowitz, Rael 650
イサコビッチ
Isakovic, Sara 650
イサコフ
Isakov, Erkin 650
Isakov, Ismail 650
Isakov, Miodrag 650
Isakov, Victor 650
Isakov, Vladimir 650
イサコンデ
Isa Conde, Antonio 650
イサチェンコ
Issachenko, Vladimir 652
イサード
Issa-ard, Kanchana 652
イザドーラ
Isadora, Rachel 650
イサヌブ
Isanove, Richard 650
イサノワ
Issanova, Gulzhan 652
イサベコフ
Isabekov, Azim 650
イーサム
Essam, bin Abdulla Khalaf 409
イサラ
Issara, Bodin 652
Izarra, Andrés 654
イサーリス
Isserlis, Steven 652
イーサリッジ
Etheridge, Alison 411
イサレスク
Isărescu, Mugur 650
イサンダル
Ysander, Bengt-Christer 1542
イザンバール
Izambard, Sebastien 654
イーシア
Ethier, Kay 411
イーシアー
Ethier, Andre 411
イシェ
Icher, François 643
イシェイ
Ishay, Micheline 651
イーシェンコ
Ishchenko, Natalia 651
イシカネ
Ishikane, Joh 651
イシカワ・コバヤシ
Ishikawa Kobayashi, Seiko Luis 651
イシキエル
Isikiel, Paul 651
イシグロ
Ishiguro, Kazuo 651
イジコフスキー
Idzikowski, Christopher 643
イジ・コラウォレ
Idji Kolawole, Antoine 643
イジードビヒ
Izidbih, Isselkou Ould Ahmed 654
イシハラ
Ishihara, Wayne Toshimi 651
イシマイラ
Issimaila, Mohamed 652
イシマツ
Ishimatsu, Haley 651
イシマ・ミラン
Isimat-mirin, Nicolas 651
イシムラトワ
Ishmouratova, Svetlana 651
イーシャ
Isha 651
イシャイ
Yishai, Eliyahu 1538
イシャーウッド
Isherwood, Christopher 651
イシャウッド
Isherwood, Baron 651
イシャエフ
Ishayev, Viktor I. 651
イシャグプール
Ishaghpour, Youssef 651
イジャズル・ハク
Ijaz-ul-haq, Muhammad 644
イジャネス
Illanes, Fernando 645
イジャラメンディ
Illarramendi, Asier 645
イシュ
Isch, Édgar 651
イーシュヴァラクリシュナ
Isvarakrsna 652
イシュメイル
Ishmael, Kemal 651
イーシュワラン
Easwaran, Eknath 388
イジョフォー
Ejiofor, Chiwetel 395
イシンバエワ
Isinbayeva, Yelena 651
イーズ
Eades, Keith M. 387
イズィドルチク
Izydorczyk, Jacek 654
イスカコフ
Iskakov, Bulat 651
Iskakov, Nurlan 651
イスカン
Iskan, Dahlan 651
イスカンダル
Iskander, Laila Rashid 651
Iskander, Nasry 651
イスカンデル
Iskander, Fazil' 651
イスキエルド
Izquierdo, Jose 654
イスキエルド・トレス
Izquierdo Torres, Gerardo José 654
イスキエルドメンデス
Izquierdo Mendez, Carlos Arturo 654
イスキエルド・ロドリゲス
Yzquierdo Rodríguez, Adel Onofre 1544
イスグローヴ
Isgrove, Lloyd 651
イスケ
Iske, Chad 651
イスコ
Isco 651
Izco, Mariano 654
イースター
Easter, Wayne 387

イ

イースタウェイ
Eastaway, Robert 387
イースターバイ＝スミス
Easterby-Smith, Mark 387
イースタム
Eastham, John H. 387
イースタリー
Easterly, William Russell 387
イースタリング
Easterling, Ed 387
イスティチョアイア・ブドゥラ
Isticioaia-Budura, Viorel 652
イスティチワヤ
Isticioaia-Budura, Viorel 652
イズデル
Isdell, Edward Neville 651
イースト
East, Andrew 387
East, Marjorie 387
East, Michael 387
イーストー
Eastoe, Madeleine 387
イーストウッド
Eastwood, Clint 387
Eastwood, Kyle 388
イストゥリス・アルメイダ
Istúriz Almeida, Aristóbulo 652
イーストコット
Eastcott, John 387
イーストマン
Eastman 387
Eastman, Ben 387
Eastman, Brian 387
Eastman, Kevin 387
イストミン
Istomin, Denis 652
Istomin, Eugène 652
Istomin, Sergey 652
イーストモンド
Eastmond, Lynette 387
Eastmond, Rawle 387
イストラーテ
Istrate, George Dan 652
イーストン
Easton, David 387
Easton, K. 387
Easton, Nick 387
Easton, Roger 387
イスナー
Isner, John 652
イズバサ
Izbasa, Sandra 654
イスビー
Isby, David C. 651
イズビン
Isbin, Sharon 650
イスフ
Issouf, Barkaï 652
Issoufou, Issaka 652
Issoufou, Mahamadou 652
イスブ
Isbouts, Jean-Pierre 651
イスフアルファガ
Issoufou Alfaga, Abdoulrazak 652
イスベル
Isber, Isber 650
イスマイール
Ismail, Farouk 651
イスマイル
Ismael, Ismael 651
Ismail, Abdullahi Sheikh 651
Ismail, Aishat 651
Ismail, Amat 651
Ismail, Amir Abdul-Jabal 651
Ismail, Damit 651
Ismail, Ismail Ahmed 651
Ismail, Koybasi 651
Ismail, Mustafa Osman 651
Ismail, Sabri Yaakob 651
Ismail, Salim 651
Ismail, Sherif 651
Ismail El Shamy, Ahmed 651
イスマイルザーデ
Ismayilzada, Gursel 652
イスマイル・ハーン
Ismail Khan, Mohammad 651
イスマイロフ
Ismailov, Abdulkhakim 651
Ismailov, Uktam 651
Ismayilov, Daniyar 652
イスマエルザーデ
Ismayilzada, Gursel 652
イスマト
Ismat, Abdel-Rahman 652
イスマ・ロペス
Isma Lopez 652
イズムハムベトフ
Izmukhambetov, Bakrykozha 654
イスモイロフ
Ismoilov, Sayfiddin 652
イスラ
Isla, Mauricio 651
Ysla, Luis 1542
イスライロフ
Israilov, Ulan 652
イスラエル
Israel, Laurie 652
Israel, Shel 652
イズラエル
Israël, Inge 652
Israel, Richard 652
イスラエルアチヴィリ
Israelachvili, Jacob Nissim 652
イスラミ
Islami, Kastriot 651
イスラム
Islam, Ashraful 651
İslam, Ayşenur 651
Islam, Nurul 651
Islam, Qamrul 651
Islam, Rafiqul 651
Islam, Shamusul 651
Islam, Syed Ashraful 651
Islam, Tariqul 651
イースリー
Easley, David 387
イーズリー
Easley, Dominique 387
Easley, Marcus 387
イズリアル
Israel, Betsy 652
イスリエタ
Izurieta, Raúl 654
イズリーヌ
Izrine, Agnès 654
イスレ
Isselé, Erik 652
イスレイフスドッティル
Isleifsdottir, Kristin 651
イスワラン
Iswaran, S. 652
イセケシェフ
Issekeshev, Asset 652
イーセスコーグ
Iseskog, Tommy 651
イゼディン
Izedin, Ali 654
イゼトベゴヴィチ
Izetbegović, Bakir 654
イゼトベゴヴィッチ
Izetbegović, Alija 654
Izetbegović, Bakir 654
イゼトベーゴビッチ
Izetbegović, Alija 654
イゼトベゴビッチ
Izetbegović, Alija 654
Izetbegović, Bakir 654
イセモト
Isemoto, Larry Shunji 651
イゼルビット
Yzerbyt, Vincent Y. 1544
イセーレス
Iserles, Inbali 651
イーゼンゼー
Isensee, Josef 651
イゾー
Izzo, John 654
イソイベカ
Issoibeka, Pacifique 652
イソウン
Isoun, Turner 652
イソコスキ
Isokoski, Soile 652
イソゼンゴンデ
Issozengondet, Emmanuel 652
イゾトフ
Izotov, Danila 654
イソラ
Isola, Maija 652
イゾリア
Izoria, Levan 654
イソール
Isol 652
イソン
Isong, Tuner 652
イダイス
Ideiss, Youssef 643
イタクラ
Itakura, Mitsuo 652
イーダスハイム
Edersheim, Elizabeth Haas 390
イタナ
Ithana, Pendukeni 652
イタニ
Itani, Frances 652
イタラ
Itälä, Ville 652
イタランタ
Itäranta, Emmi 652
イダルゴ
Hidalgo, Anne 604
Hidalgo, Giovanni 604
Hidalgo, Wilfredo 604
イタルマゾフ
Italmazov, Babaniyaz 652
イタレリ
Italeli, Iakoba Taeia 652
イチオカ
Ichioka, Yuji 643
イチンノロブ・ガンバートル
Ichinnorov Ganbaatar 643
イーツ
Yeats, Dorothy 1537
Yeats, Robert S. 1537
イツィック
Itzik, Dalia 653
イッガ
Igga, James Wani 643
イックス
Ickes, William John 643
イッサ
Issa, Assoumana Mallam 652
イッサラ
Issara, Somchai 652
イッサーリス
Isserlis, Steven 652
イッシドリデース
Issidorides, Diana 652
イッシンガー
Ischinger, Wolfgang 651
イッセルム
Isselmou, Moustaph Ould Sid'El 652
イッタ
Jitta, Ceseli Josephus 674
イッターハイム
Itterheim, Steffen 652
イッツォ
Izzo, Armando 654
Izzo, John Baptist 654
イット
Ith Sam Heng 652
イットリ
Yttri, Birgitte 1542
イットリング
Yttling, Björn 1542
イッパリート
Ippolito, Pauline M. 649
イップ
Ip, Greg 648
Ip, Regina 648
Yip, Daenie 1538
Yip, Virginia 1538
イッペン
Ippen, Chandra Ghosh 649
イーディー
Eadie, Jo 387
イディア
Iddir, Alexandre 643
イティマイ
Itimai, Francis 652
イディムアヌケ
Idi Muanuke, Xavier 643
イディングス
Iddings, Drew 643
イデム
Idem, Josefa 643
イーデルソン
Edelson, Edward 389
イーデルマン
Edelman, Ric 389
イーデン
Eden, Cynthia 390
Eden, Donna 390
Eden, Jeremy 390
イテンベルク

Itenberg, Il'ia Vladimirovich 652
イード
Eid, Said Hussein 394
イトウ
Ito, Mitsuru 652
Ito, Toyo 652
イドウ
Idowu, Phillips 643
イトゥア
Itoua, Bruno Jean Richard 652
イートウェル
Eatwell, John 388
イトゥノ
Itno, Daoussa Deby 652
イトゥラスペ
Iturraspe, Ander 653
イドゥリ
Iduri, Sam 643
イトゥリサ
Iturriza, Reinaldo 653
イドゥリス
Ahmad Izlan bin Idris, Dato' 20
イトゥルベ
Iturbe, Antonio G. 653
Iturbe, Juan 653
イードソン
Eidson, Tom 394
イドリス
Iddrisu, Betty Mould 643
Iddrisu, Haruna 643
Idris, Jusoh 643
Idris, Kamil E. 643
Idriss, Idriss Ahamat 643
イドリソフ
Idrissov, Erlan 643
イートン
Eaton, Adam 388
Eaton, Ashton 388
Eaton, C.B. 388
Eaton, Cliff van 388
Eaton, Jan 388
Eaton, Jason Carter 388
Eaton, Katherine Bliss 388
Eaton, Michael A. 388
Eaton, Nanette J. 388
Eyton, Wendy 414
イナ
Ina, Chaibou Dan 646
Ina, Kyoko 646
イナゴシ
Inagosi, Geneviève 646
イナム
Inam, Ahmet 646
イナモワ
Inamova, Svetlana 646
イナール
Hinard, François 608
イーナン
Yinan, Diao 1538
イニー
Iny, Alan 648
イニエスタ
Iniesta, Aǹdres 647
イニオンス
Inions, Cynthia 647
イニガー
Inniger, Heinz 647
イニゴ・マルティネス
Inigo Martinez 647
イニス
Innis, Chris 647
Inniss, Donville 647
イニャリトゥ
Iñárritu, Alejandro González 646
イニャンガ
Hygnanga, Francis Bernardin 641
イニュンバ
Inyumba, Aloysia 648
イヌ
Inu, Hasanul Haq 648
イヌヤマ
Inuyama, Shannon Ken 648
イネイチェン
Ineichen, Alexander M. 646
イーネグ
Ĭjneg, Ŏnihsoy 644
イネス
Innes, Christopher 647
イーノ
Eno, Brian 404
イノーア
Ynoa, Michael 1538
イノア
Ynoa, Gabriel 1538
イノウエ
Inoue, Shinya 648
Inouye, Daniel Ken 648
Inouye, Mamoru 648
イノセ
Inose, Kay Kayoko 648
イノゼンシオ
Inocencio, Matheus 647
イーノセンティ
Innocenti, Roberto 647
イーノック
Enoch, Suzanne 404
イノック
Enoch, Wesley 404
イノックス
Enochs, Susan 404
イノニ
Inoni, Ephraim 648
イノニュ
Inönü, Erdal 648
イノニュー
Inönü, Erdal 648
イノホサ
Hinojosa, Milton Claros 608
イノヤトフ
Inoyatov, Ulugbek 648
イノンゴ
Inongo, Dominique Sakombi 648
イハ
Iha, James Jonas 644
イバ
Iva, Kaia 653
イバイ・ゴメス
Ibai Gomez 642
イバーカ
Ibaka, Serge 642
イバッハ
Ibach, Harald 642
イーバート
Ebert, Alex 388
Ebert, Roger 388
イバトーリーン
Ibatoulline, Bagram 642
イバニェス
Ibañez, José María 642
イバニエス
Ibáñez, Antonio 642
イバニシェビッチ
Ivanišević, Miroslav 653
Ivanišević, Stjepan 653
イバニッチ
Ivanić, Mladen 653
イバネット
Evenett, Simon.J. 413
イバノビッチ
Evanovich, Janet 411
Ivanovic, Ana 653
Ivanović, Petar 653
Ivanović, Predrag 653
イバノフ
Ivanov, Georgi 653
Ivanov, Hristo 653
Ivanov, Ivaylo 653
Ivanov, Tikhomir 653
Ivanov, Vassil 653
イバノブ
Ivanov, Violeta 653
イバーラ
Ibarra, Herminia 642
イバラ
Ibarra, Ana 642
Ibarra, Andrés 642
Ivala, Clotaire Christian 653
イハライネン
Ihalainen, Lauri 644
イハラーナ
Ijalana, Ben 644
イバルグエン
Ibarguen, Caterine 642
イバルゲン
Ibarguen, Caterine 642
イバンガ
Ibanga, Esther Abimiku 642
イバン・ビジャール
Ivan Villar 653
イビ
Ibbi, Abdirahman Adan Ibrahim 642
イビシェヴィッチ
Ibisevic, Vedad 642
イビッチ
Ivić, Tomislav 654
イヒマエラ
Ihimaera, Witi Tame 644
イビラヒム
Ibrahim, Karam 642
イヒレ
Ihle, Andreas 644
イブ
Eve, Laverne 413
イファシ
al-Ifasi, Mohammad Mohsen 643
イフェロス
Hijuelos, Oscar 605
イフォト
Ifoto, Ingele 643
イプカー
Ipcar, Dahlov Zorach 649
イーブス
Eaves, Edward 388
イブセン
Ebsen, Buddy 388
Ibsen, Martin Kirketerp 643
イプセン
Ipsen, Kristian 649
イブヌ・ストゥォ
Ibunu Sutowo 643
イブヌ・ストオ
Ibunu Sutowo 643
イブライタナ
Iivula-ithana, Pendukeni 644
イブライマ
Ibrahima, Memounatou 643
イブライミ
Ibraimi, Bedredin 643
イブラギモヴァ
Ibragimova, Alina 642
イブラギモフ
Ibragimov, Gulomjon 642
Ibragimov, Magomed 642
Ibragimov, Mamed 642
イブラヒマ
Ibrahima, Memounatou 643
イブラヒミ
Ebrahimi, Kobra 388
イブラヒム
Anwar Ibrahim 52
Ebrahim, Karam Mohamed Gaber 388
Ibrahim, Abdel-Gasim Mohamed 642
al-Ibrahim, Abdulaziz Abdulatif 642
Ibrahim, Abdullah 642
Ibrahim, Ali Mariama Elhadji 642
Ibrahim, Amirul Hamizan 642
Ibrahim, Ari 642
Ibrahim, bin Khalifa al-Khalifa 642
Ibrahim, Faisal Hassan 642
Ibrahim, Farouk Walid 642
Ibrahim, Gasim 642
Ibrahim, Hamid Mohammed 642
Ibrahim, Hassan Ibrahim Madany 642
Ibrahim, Ilyas 642
Ibrahim, Mohamed Ali Ag 642
Ibrahim, Mohamed Mukhtar 642
Ibrahim, Mohamud Abdi 642
Ibrahim, Mourad Said 642
Ibrahim, Muhammad 642
Ibrahim, Muhiddin Mohamed Haji 642
Ibrahim, Nazim 642
Ibrahim, Thoriq 642
Ibrahim, Yaacob 642
Ibrahim, Yassine 642
Ibrahim, Yusuf Hassan 643
Ibrahim Gaber, Karam 643
イブラヒム・アル・シェイク
Ibrahim al-Sheikh, Abdullah Bin Muhammad Bin 643
イブラヒム・ファルゲティ
Ibrahim Fargeti, Mohamed Adan 643
イブラヒムフメド
Ibrahim Houmed, Ismäil 643
イブラヒモヴィッチ

Iburahimovic, Zlatan 643
イブラヒモビッチ
Iburahimovic, Zlatan 643
イブランド
Eveland, Dana 413
イフル
Yifru, Birhane 1538
イブロウ
Ibrow, Salim Aliyow 643
イブロヒム
Ibrohim, Azim 643
イブロヒモフ
Ibrohimov, Shavkatbek 643
イブンオウフ
Ibn-auf, Awad 642
イヘアナチョ
Iheanacho, Emmanuel 644
Iheanacho, Kelechi 644
イヘナーチョ
Ihenacho, Duke 644
イベリングス
Ibelings, Anne 642
イーペル
Epel, David 404
イベール
Hybert, Fabrice 640
イベルセン
Iversen, Trond 653
イボットソン
Ibbotson, Eva 642
Ibbotson, Toby 642
イボビ
Ibovi, François 642
イボーラ
Iborra, Vicente 642
イポリット
Hippolyte 609
Hyppolite, Jean 641
イポリト
Hypolito, Daniele 641
イボルド
Ibold, Mark 642
イーホルム
Egholm, Elsebeth 393
イボワ
Hybois, Arnaud 640
イボンボ
Ibombo, Léon Juste 642
イマーエワ
Imaeva, Zara 645
イマシェフ
Imashev, Berik 645
Imashev, Chorobek 645
イマダ
Imada, Andrew S. 645
イマナリエフ
Imanaliev, Muratbek 645
イマノル・ガルシア
Imanol Garcia 645
イマミ
Imami, Arben 645
イマーム
Imam, Ikram Abdulsalam 645
イマム
Emam, Ahmed 400
Imam, Haji 645
Imam, Nahrawi 645
イミンク
Immink, Gerrit 646
イム
Im, Chol-ung 645
Im, Heung-Soon 645
Im, Kwon-taek 645
Im, Sang-gyu 645
Im, Sang-soo 645
Im Chhun Lim 646
Imm, Pamela 646
Im Sethy 646
Lim, Chang-yong 828
Lim, Dong-hyek 828
Lim, Dong Min 828
Lim, Dong-won 828
Lim, Hyo-Sun 828
Lim, Hyung-joo 828
Lim, In-taik 828
Lim, Ji Young 828
Lim, Ju-hwan 828
Lim, Seu-long 828
Lim, Soo-jung 828
Rim, Che-min 1183
Yim, Sung-joon 1538
Yim, Tae-hee 1538
イームズ
Eames, Anne 387
イムホーフ
Imhoof, Markus 646
イムホフ
Imhof, Herwig 646
イムラノフ
Imranov, Shahin 646
イムラヒム
Ibrahim, Gasim 642
イムリー
Imrie, Celia 646
イムレ
Imre, Geza 646
イメルト
Immelt, Jeff 646
イメルマン
Immelman, Trevor 646
イメンドルフ
Immendorff, Jörg 646
イモケ
Imoke, Liyel 646
イモフ
Imhoff, Juan 646
イモンゴタタガニ
Immongault Tatagani, Régis 646
イヤーウッド
Yearwood, Guy 1537
Yearwood, Robin 1537
イヤコバキス
Iakovakis, Periklis 642
イヤス
Iyasu, Abrha 654
イヤドハウエデルニ
Iyadh Ouederni, Ahmed 654
イヤムレニュ
Iyamurenye, Augustin 654
イヤール
Eyal, Nir 414
イヤンボ
Iyambo, Abraham 654
Iyambo, Nickey 654
イラ
Illa, Mohamed Tahir 645
イライアス
Elias, Maurice J. 397
Elias, Thomas 397
イライソス
Iraizoz, Gorka 649
イラゴリ・バレンシア
Iragorri Valencia, Aurelio 649
イラーシック
Ellersick, Raymond 398
イラシュコ
Iraschko-stolz, Daniela 649
イラーチェ
Irace, Pina 649
イラード
Ilardo, Joseph A. 644
イラニ
Irani, Khalid 649
Irani, Romin 649
Irani, Smriti Zubin 649
イーラム
Elam, Jack 395
Elam, Kimberly 395
Elam, Matt 395
Elam, Richard M. 395
イラル
Iralu, Kaka Dierhekolie 649
イラワン
Irawan, Eko Yuli 649
イランアネス
Iranmanesh, Ali 649
イーランド
Eiland, Dave 394
イーリ
Ely, David 400
イーリー
Ealy, Kony 387
Earey, Mark 387
Ely, David 400
イリー
Illy, Andrea 645
イリアサ
Iliassa, Yahaya Mohamed 645
イリアス
Eliane 397
Iliassa, Yahaya Mohamed 645
イリアソフ
Ilyasov, Talgat 645
イリアディス
Iliadis, Ilias 644
イリアーヌ
Eliane 397
イリアルテ・ヒメネス
Iriarte Jiménez, Eduardo 649
イーリイ
Ely, David 400
イリイチ
Illich, Ivan 645
イリーイン
Ilyin, Vladimir 645
イリエ
Ilie, Aurel Constantin 645
イリエス
Illies, Florian 645
イリエスク
Iliescu, Ion 645
イリエンコ
Ilienko, Yurii 645
イリオパウロス
Eliopoulos, Charlotte 397
イリオポウロス
Iliopoulos, Constantin 645
イリゴエン
Hirigoyen, Marie-France 609
イリザリー
Irizarry, Aaron 649
Irizarry, Rafael A. 649
イリチ
Ilich, John 645
イリチェフ
Ilitchev, Alexander 645
イリチッチ
Ilicic, Josip 645
イリッグ
Illig, Randy 645
イリッチ
Ilic, Slobodan 645
Ilić, Velimir 645
Ilitch, Chris 645
Illich, Ivan 645
イリナ
Ilyina, Vera 645
イリニフ
Ilinykh, Elena 645
イリバギザ
Ilibagiza, Immaculée 645
イリバルネ
Iribarne, Alberto 649
イリハンヌクセラ
Yli-hannuksela, Marko 1538
イリメスク
Irimescu, Achim 649
イリヤソワ
Ilyasova, Ersan 645
イリヤーニ
al-Eryani, Muammar 408
イリヤニ
al-Iriyani, Abdul-Rahman 649
Iryani, Abd al-Karim 650
al-Iryani, Abdul-Malik Abdul-Rahman 650
al-Iryani, Mohammed Luft 650
イリュヒナ
Ilyukhina, Ekaterina 645
イリュミジノフ
Ilyumzhinov, Kirsan 645
イリュムジノフ
Ilyumzhinov, Kirsan 645
イリン
Ilin, Ilya 645
Ilyin, Ilya 645
イリンガー
Ihringer, Michael 644
イリンスキー
Iliinsky, Noah P.N. 645
イルヴァイン
Irvine, Alexander C. 649
イールヴァール
Irvall, Birgitta 649
イルガシェフ
Irgashev, Akmal 649
イルカジル
Ilkajir, Abdullahi Ahmed Jama Aka 645
イルカハナフ
Ilkahanaf, Aideed Abdullahi 645
イルガング
Irrgang, Bernhard 649
イルグロヴァ
Irglova, Marketa 649
イルゲン
Ilgen, Fre 644

イルゲンス
Irgens, Jacob 649
イルゴイエンヌ
Hirigoyen, Marie-France 609
イルサ・シグルザルドッティル
Yrsa Sigurðardóttir 1542
イルサン
Irsan, Abdul 649
イルサンカー
Ilsanker, Stefan 645
イルジェ
Iloudjè, Ebina Dorothée 645
イルシェダト
Irsheidat, Saleh 649
イルジーグラー
Irsigler, Franz 649
イルシング
Hirsching, Nicolas de 609
イールス
Eeles, Peter 392
イールズ
Eeles, Peter 392
イルス
Illes, Judika 645
イールズ＝ホワイト
Eales-White, Rupert 387
イルズリー
Ilsley, Blaise 645
イルチェンコ
Ilchenko, Larisa 644
イルデム
Ildem, Cenk 644
イルドス
Ildos, Angela S. 644
イルトン
Hilton, George 607
イルナム
Ilnam, Yavuz 645
イルハルト
Illhardt, Franz Josef 645
イルビング
Irving, Thomas Ballantine 650
イルブド
Ilboudo, Monique 644
イルベス
Ilves, Toomas Hendrik 645
イルマズ
Yilmaz, Hakan 1538
イルレタ
Irureta, Saúl 649
イルレタ・サラレギ
Irureta Saralegui, Saul 649
イルンガムブンドゥワビルバ
Ilunga Mbundo Wa Biluba, Pierre 645
イーレ
Ihle, Nico 644
イレス
Iles, Salim 644
Illes, Judy 645
イレッリ
Irelli, Giuseppina Cerulli 649
イレート
Ileto, Reynaldo Clemeña 644
イレト
Ileto, Rafael M. 644
イレバエフ
Ilebayev, Nurdin 644
イレール
Hilaire, Laurent 605
Hilaire, Sébastien 605
イロイロ
Iloilo, Josefa 645
イローカ
Iloka, George 645
イロネン
Ilonen, Mikko 645
イロリ
Ilori, Tiago 645
イロロフ
Ilolov, Mamadsho 645
イロン
Ilon, Epel 645
イワサキ
Iwasaki Cauti, Fernando 654
イワシェンコ
Ivashchenko, Elena 653
イワシシェンコ
Ivashchenko, Elena 653
イワシネフ
Ivashnev, Vitaliĭ 653
イワニエク
Iwaniec, Dorota 654
イワニーク
Iwaniec, Dorota 654
イワニシヴィリ
Ivanishvili, Bidzina 653
イワニシビリ
Ivanishvili, Bidzina 653
イワニセビッチ
Ivanišević, Miroslav 653
イワノヴィッチ
Ivanovic, Ana 653
イワノビッチ
Ivanovic, Ana 653
Ivanović, Predrag 653
イワノフ
Ivanoff, Nicolas 653
Ivanov, Aleksandr 653
Ivanov, Gjorge 653
Ivanov, Igor Sergeevich 653
Ivanov, Mikhail 653
Ivanov, Sergei Borisovich 653
Ivanov, Valery N. 653
Ivanov, Viktor 653
Ivanov, Vladimir 653
Ivanov, Yossif 653
イワノフスキ
Ivanovski, Ivo 653
イワノワ
Ivanova, Kira 653
Ivanova, Olimpiada 653
Ivanova, Tatiana 653
イワハシ
Iwahashi, Scott 654
イワハナ
Iwahana, Hiroyuki 654
イワブチ
Iwabuchi, Deborah 654
イワマ
Iwama, Michael K. 654
イーワルド
Ewald, Paul W. 414
イワルド
Ewald, Timothy 414
イーワン
Ewan, Chris 414
イワンコフ
Ivankov, Aleksandr I. 653
Ivankov, Ivan 653
イワンセビッチ
Ivancevich, John M. 653
イン
Ing Kuntha Phavi 647
Inn, Frank 647
Yin, Amorah Quan 1538
Yin, Elizabeth 1538
Yin, Qing-zhu 1538
Yin, Robert K. 1538
Yin, Yiqing 1538
Ying, Ruo-cheng 1538
Ying, Victoria 1538
Yun, Hak-jun 1543
インウッド
Inwood, Mathew 648
インカー
Inker, Ben 647
インガソル
Ingersoll, Robert Stephen 646
インガソル＝デイトン
Ingersoll-Dayton, Berit 646
インガーマン
Ingerman, Sandra 646
インガム
Ingham, Patricia 647
インガルス
Ingalls, Dan H.H. 646
インキネン
Inkinen, Pietari 647
Inkinen, Sami 647
インギビョルグ・シーグルザルドッティル
Ingibjörg Sigurdardóttir 647
インギレアリー
Inghilleri, Leonardo 647
イング
Ing, Todd S. 646
イングアンソ
Inguanzo, Ozzy 647
イングス
Ings, Danny 647
Ings, Simon 647
Ings, William 647
イングスタット
Ingstad, Helge Marcus 647
イングスタッド
Ingstad, Benedicte 647
インクスタト
Ingstad, Helge Marcus 647
イングドール
Engdahl, William 402
イングバー
Ingber, Donald E. 646
インクペン
Inkpen, Mick 647
イングペン
Ingpen, Robert 647
イングマン
Engman, Camilla 403
Ingman, Bruce 647
イングラオ
Ingrao, Pietro 647
イングラッシア
Ingrassia, Ciccio 647
イングラート
Englert, J.F. 403
イングラード
Englard, Baruch 403
イングラハム
Ingraham, Erick 647
Ingraham, Hubert Alexander 647
イングラム
Ingrahm, Pamela 647
Ingram, Brandon 647
Ingram, Catherine 647
Ingram, David 647
Ingram, Dexter 647
Ingram, Jay 647
Ingram, Kerry 647
Ingram, Luther 647
Ingram, Mark 647
Ingram, Melvin 647
Ingram, Zoë 647
イングランダー
Englander, Israel 403
Englander, Nathan 403
Englander, Otto 403
イングランド
England, Breck 403
イングリス
Inglis, Fiona 647
Inglis, Ian 647
Inglis, Kim 647
Inglis, T.J.J. 647
イングリッシュ
English, Bill 403
English, Christy 403
English, Deirdre 403
English, Manalani 403
English, Richard 403
English, T.J. 403
Ingrisch, Lotte 647
イングル
Engle, Ed 403
Engle, Ryan 403
イングルス
Ingles, Joe 647
イングルンド
Englund, Magnus 403
イングレイド
Englade, Ken 403
イングレス
Ingles, Elisabeth 647
イングレーゼ
Inglese, Roberto 647
イングレバート
Englebert, Clear 403
インゲソン
Ingesson, Magnus 646
インゲブリクトセン
Ingebrigtsen, Guri 646
Ingebrigtsen, Henrik 646
インゲマルスドッター
Ingemarsdotter, Ida 646
インゲマルスドッテル
Ingemarsdotter, Ida 646
インゲランド
Engelland, Chip 403
インケルス
Inkeles, Alex 647
インゲルマン＝スンドベリ
Ingelman-Sundberg, Catharina 646
インゴウルフソン
Ingólfsson, Viktor Arnar 647

インコニート
Incognito, Richie 646
インゴールド
Ingold, Tim 647
インゴルド
Ingold, Tim 647
インコルバイア
Incorvaia, Antonio 646
インコントレラ
Incontrera, Kate 646
インザーギ
Inzaghi, Filippo 648
Inzaghi, Simone 648
インザギ
Inzaghi, Filippo 648
インサナリ
Insanally, Samuel Rudolph 648
インサノフ
Insanov, Ali 648
インサム
Insam, Evelyn 648
インシアーテ
Inciarte, Ender 646
インシアラーノ
Inciarrano, Michelle 646
インシーニェ
Insigne, Lorenzo 648
Insigne, Roberto 648
インジャイ・フェルナンデス
Injai Fernandes, Aida 647
インジャナ
Ingianna, Yolanda 647
インジャンナシ
Injannasi 647
インス
Ince, Catherine 646
インスーア
Insua, Pablo 648
インスア
Insua, Martin 648
インスコア
Inscore, Jim 648
インズーディン
Inzouddine, Hodhoaer 648
インスドーフ
Insdorf, Annette 648
インストール
Install, Deborah 648
インスペテル
Hinzpeter, Rodrigo 609
インスルサ
Insulza, José Miguel 648
インタクン
Intakul, Sakul 648
インダージート
Inderjeet, Singh 646
インタノン
Intanon, Ratchanok 648
インダービネン
Inderbinen, Ulrich 646
インチーザ
Incisa, Nicolò 646
インチャウステギ・バルガス
Incháustegui Vargas, Juan 646
インディア・アリー
India.Arie 646
インティザール
Intizar, Husain 648
インディック
Indick, William 646
インテマ
Yntema, Sharon K. 1538
インテリゲーター
Intriligator, Michael David 648
インデルガンド
Indergand, Linda 646
インドゥリ
Iduri, Sam 643
インドラワティ
Indrawati, Sri Mulyani 646
インドリダソン
Indridason, Arnaldur 646
イントリリゲーター
Intriligator, Michael David 648
インドルフ
Indruch, Tomas 646
イントレイター
Intrater, Roberta Grobel 648
インドロヨノ
Indroyono, Soesilo 646
インナロ
Innaro, Marc 647
インネス
Innes, Anthea 647
インネルホファー
Innerhofer, Christof 647
インノチェンティ
Innocenti, Marco 647
Innocenti, Roberto 647
インバート
Imbert, Colm 645
インバリ
Imbali, Faustino Fudut 645
インバル
Inbal, Eliahu 646
インピ
Impey, Rose 646
インピー
Impey, Chris 646
Impey, Daryl 646
インビキ
Imbiky, Anaclet 645
インビュラ
Imbula, Giannelli 646
インファンテ
Infante, Omar 646
インフェルド
Infeld, Emily 646
インブルーリア
Imbruglia, Natalie Jane 645
インペラート
Imperato, Teresa 646
インペリオーリ
Imperioli, Michael 646
インボーデン
Imboden, Urs 645
インホフ
Imhoff, Daniel 646
インマゼール
Immerseel, Jos van 646
インマン
Inman, Dontrelle 647
Inman, Matthew 647
インメルト
Immelt, Jeff 646
インモース
Immoos, Thomas 646
インモネン
Immonen, Stuart 646
インモービレ
Immobile, Ciro 646
インモン
Inmon, William H. 647
インラック・シナワット
Yingluck Shinawatra 1538
インラック・チナワット
Yingluck Shinawatra 1538
インレル
Inler, Gokhan 647
インロガ
Inroga, Armando 648
インワーゲン
Inwagen, Peter van 648

【ウ】

ウ
Woo, Haram 1523
Woo, Suk-hoon 1523
Wu, Tian-ming 1529
Wu, Zu-guang 1529
Yu, Ruo-mu 1543
ウー
Ng, Franees 1019
Woo, Jacky 1523
Woo, John 1523
Woo, Mason 1523
Woo, Peter 1523
Wu, Alina 1529
Wu, Annie 1529
Wu, Bang-guo 1529
Wu, Daniel 1529
Wu, David Y.H. 1529
Wu, Da-wei 1529
Wu, Den-yih 1529
Wu, Fan 1529
Wu, Felipe Almeida 1529
Wu, Frank 1529
Wu, Frankie P. 1529
Wu, Gang 1529
Wu, Guan-zhong 1529
Wu, Haiyun 1529
Wu, Harry 1529
Wu, Jason 1529
Wu, Jian-min 1529
Wu, Jie-ping 1529
Wu, Jonathan 1529
Wu, Lawrence 1529
Wu, Leng-xi 1529
Wu, Melissa 1529
Wu, Ming 1529
Wu, Min-xia 1529
Wu, Poh-hsiung 1529
Wu, Rufina 1529
Wu, Ru-jun 1529
Wu, Shao-tsu 1529
Wu, Shu-chen 1529
Wu, Stephen 1529
Wu, Tian-ming 1529
Wu, Tiejian 1529
Wu, Tim 1529
Wu, Wen-ying 1529
Wu, Xue 1529
Wu, Xue-qian 1529
Wu, Yi 1529
Wu, Zu-guang 1529
Wuchun 1529
Wu Ma 1530
Wuu, Weiwei 1530
ヴー
Vũ, Thị Phụng 1465
ヴーア
Voors, William 1464
ヴァイ
Vai, Steve 1438
ヴァイエンマイヤー
Weihenmayer, Erik 1487
ヴァイオラ
Viola, Herman J. 1459
ヴァイカート
Weikath, Michael 1487
ヴァイグル
Weigl, Julian 1487
ヴァイグレ
Weigle, Sebastian 1487
ヴァイケニ
Vahekeni, João Miguel 1438
ヴァイザー
Weiser, Glade 1489
Weiser, Mitchell 1489
ヴァイス
Vise, David A. 1459
Weis, Karin 1489
Weiss, Anne 1489
Weiss, Clifford R. 1490
Weiss, David 1490
Weiß, Günter 1490
Weiss, Ulli 1490
Weisse, Joseph 1490
ヴァイスヴァイラー
Weissweiler, Eva 1490
ヴァイスコップ
Weisskopf, Victor Frederik 1490
ヴァイスコップフ
Weisskopf, Victor Frederik 1490
ヴァイスハウプト
Weishaupt, Luzie 1489
ヴァイスマン
Weissman, Elisabeth 1490
ヴァイセ
Weise, Dirk 1489
ヴァイセンシュタイナー
Weissensteiner, Friedrich 1490
ヴァイセンバッハー
Weissenbacher, Manfred 1490
ヴァイセンベルク
Weissenberg, Alexis 1490
ヴァイダヤ
Vaidya, Jaideep 1438
ヴァイツェホフスキー
Voitsekhovskii, Aleksandr 1462
ヴァイツクス
Vaitkus, Rimantas 1438
ヴァイツゼッカー
Weizsäcker, Carl-Friedrich von 1491
Weizsäcker, Richard von 1491
ヴァイディアナサン
Vaidhyanathan, Siva 1438
ヴァイテカンプ
Weitekamp, Michael R. 1490
ヴァイテルスハウゼン
Weitershausen, Philipp von 1490
ヴァイデンフェラー
Weidenfeller, Roman 1487
ヴァイデンフェルト

Weidenfeld, Nathalie 1487
ヴァイド
Vaid, Krishna Baldev 1438
ヴァイナー
Viner, Katharine 1458
Viner, Spencer W. 1458
Vyner, Tim 1466
ヴァイニーオ
Vainio, Pirkko 1438
ヴァイニコロ
Vainikolo, Fetu'u 1438
ヴァイニンガー
Weininger, Radhule 1488
ヴァイニング
Vining, Aidan R. 1458
Vining, Alex 1458
Vining, David 1458
ヴァイヤース
Weyers, Hans-Leo 1496
ヴァイラ
Vaira, Angelo 1438
ヴァイラー
Weiler, Klaus 1488
ヴァイラーティ
Vailati, Germano 1438
ヴァイラント
Vaillant, George E. 1438
ヴァイランド
Weiland, Johannes 1488
ウアイリ
Ouaili, Montassar 1063
ヴァイル
Weil, Bruno 1487
ヴァイルテルスハウゼン
Weitershausen, Philipp von 1490
ヴァイレッリ
Vairelli, Stefania 1438
ヴァイン
Vine, Barbara 1458
Vine, David 1458
Vine, F.J. 1458
ヴァインエック
Weineck, Jürgen 1488
ヴァインガルト
Weingart, Dieter 1488
ヴァインケ
Weinke, Annette 1488
ヴァインズ
Vines, David 1458
Vines, Lois 1458
ヴァインスハイマー
Weinsheimer, Rudolf 1489
ヴァインツィアル
Weinzierl, Markus 1489
ヴァインホルト
Weinhold, Angela 1488
ヴァインマイヤー
Weinmay, Elmar 1489
ヴァインリヒ
Weinrich, Harald 1489
ヴァヴァ
Vava 1448
ヴァヴェン
Verwaayen, Ben 1454
ヴァウェンサ
Walesa, Lech 1469
ヴァーガ
Virga, Vincent 1459
ヴァカン
Wacquant, Loïc J.D. 1466
ウアカンガ
Ouakanga, Albert Francis 1063
ヴァカンティ
Vacanti, Charles A. 1437
ウアキ
Ouaki, Fabien 1063
ヴァクス
Vachss, Andrew H. 1437
ヴァーグナー
Wagner, Gerhard 1467
Wagner, Katharina 1467
Wagner, Sandro 1467
Wagner, Wolfgang 1467
ヴァグナー
Wagner, Bernd C. 1467
ヴァグネル
Wagner, Charles 1467
Wagner, Ulla 1467
ヴァーグレン
Verguren, Enamel 1452
ヴァケ
Waquet, Françoise 1477
ヴァーゲンバッハ
Wagenbach, Klaus 1467
ヴァーゲンホーファー
Wagenhofer, Erwin 1467
ヴァサン
Vasan, Gandee 1447
ヴァジニ
Wazny, Lori D. 1484
ヴァーシューレン
Verschueren, Jef 1454
ヴァショー
Vachaud, Laurent 1437
ヴァション
Vachon, Christine 1437
ヴァジラーニ
Vazirani, Vijay V. 1449
ヴァシーリエフ
Vasiliev, Ivan 1447
Vasiliev, Vladimir Viktorovich 1447
ヴァシリエフ
Vasiliev, Vladimir 1447
ヴァシレ
Vasile, Radu 1447
ヴァジレ
Vasile, Radu 1447
ヴァシレヴスキ
Wasielewski, Krys 1480
ヴァシレフスキ
Wasilewski, Marcin 1480
ヴァシロフスキー
Wassilowsky, Günter 1481
ヴァース
Waas, Uli 1466
ヴァス
Wass, Daniel 1481
ヴァズ
Vaz, Mark Cotta 1449
ヴァスケ
Vaske, Hermann 1448
ヴァスケス
Vasquez, Greivis 1448
Vazquez, Liesl 1449
Vázquez, Tabaré 1449
ヴァスケス・モンタルバン
Vázquez Montalbán, Manuel 1449
ヴァスコ
Vasko, Anne 1448
ヴァースタイネン
Verstynen, Timothy 1454
ヴァスト
Vast, Emilie 1448
ヴァスール
Vasseur, veronique 1448
ヴァスレ
Wasle, Elmar 1480
ヴァセラ
Vasella, Daniel 1447
ヴァソヴィッチ
Vasovic, Velibor 1448
ウアタ
Uata, Uliti 1431
ウアダー
Ouaddar, Abdelkebir 1063
ヴァーダイン
Verduyn, Chrissie 1452
ヴァタネン
Vatanen, Ari Pieti Uolevi 1448
ウアダヒ
Ouadahi, Mohamed Amine 1063
ヴァーダマン
Vardaman, E.Jan 1446
ウアタラ
Ouattara, Bénoît 1063
ヴァーチュ
Virtue, Doreen L. 1459
ヴァーチュー
Virtue, Tessa 1459
ヴァッカー
Wacker, Albrecht 1466
Wacker, Sabine 1466
ヴァツケ
Watzke, Megan K. 1483
ヴァッサンジ
Vassanji, M.G. 1448
ヴァッシャー
Vasher, Roy 1447
ヴァッシーリ
Vassili, Amaury 1448
ヴァッシル
Vassil, Andrew D. 1448
ヴァッターニ
Vattani, Umberto 1448
ヴァッティモ
Vattimo, Gianni 1448
ヴァッリ
Valli, Alida 1440
ヴァツリーク
Vaclik, Tomas 1437
Vaculík, Ludvík 1437
ヴァーディ
Vardey, Lucinda 1446
Vardy, Jamie 1446
Vardy, Peter 1446
ヴァデーラ
Vadehra, Colonel Krishan Lal 1437
Vadehra, Sharad 1437
ヴァートシック
Vertosick, Frank T., Jr. 1454
ヴァートン
Verton, Dan 1454
ヴァーナー
Varner, Linda 1447
Varner, Mark 1447
ヴァナーケン
Vanaken, Hans 1441
ヴァナコア
Vanacore, Victor 1441
ヴァナス
Vanas, D.J. 1441
ヴァナック
Vanak, Bonnie 1441
ヴァーナー・ボンズ
Verner-Bonds, Lilian 1453
ヴァーナム・アットキン
Varnam-Atkin, Stuart 1447
ヴァニエ
Vanier, Alain 1444
Vanier, Nicolas 1444
ヴァーニカス
Vernikos, Joan 1453
ヴァヌチ
Vannucci, Marta 1445
ウアネ
Ouane, Moctar 1063
ヴァネステ
Vanneste, Sven 1444
ヴァネック
Vaneck, Pierre 1443
ヴァネッサ・メイ
Vanessa-Mae 1443
ヴァーノン
Vernon, Vaughn 1453
ヴァノンシニ
Vanoncini, André 1445
ヴァーバ
Verba, Sidney 1451
ヴァハテリスト
Vahteristo, Anna 1438
ヴァービンスキー
Verbinski, Gore 1452
ウアファ
Ouafa, Mohamed El 1063
ヴァブス
Wabbes, Marie 1466
ヴァプニャール
Vapnyar, Lara 1446
ヴァーホーヴェン
Verhoeven, Julie 1452
Verhoeven, Paul 1452
ヴァポリス
Vaporis, Constantine Nomikos 1446
ヴァーマ
Verma, Surendra 1453
ヴァーマス
Varmus, Harold Eliot 1447
ヴァーミューラン
Vermeulen, Frans 1453
ヴァーミューレン
Vermeulen, Freek 1453
ヴァーメット
Vermette, Margaret 1453
ヴァモシュ
Vamos, Miriam Feinberg 1441
ウァーモールド
Wormald, Jenny 1526
ヴァーモレル
Varmorel, Fred 1447
Vermorel, Judy 1453
ヴァラ
Valla, Kristin 1440
Vallat, Christelle 1440
Varra, Alethea A. 1447
ヴァラヴァニス
Valavanis, Alexandra 1438
ヴァーラステ

ウ

Vallaste, Heikki 1440
ヴァラダーン
Varadhan, Srinivasa S. R. 1446
ヴァラダン
Varadhan, Srinivasa S. R. 1446
ヴァラニ
Valani, Rahim 1438
ヴァラピラ
Valappila, Margaritha 1438
ウアラルー
Oualalou, Fathallah 1063
ヴァラン
Varane, Raphael 1446
ヴァランシ
Valensi, Lucette 1439
ヴァーランダー
Verlander, Justin 1453
ヴァランチュナス
Valanciunas, Jonas 1438
ヴァランドレイ
Valandrey, Charlotte 1438
ウアリ
Ouali, Abdelkader 1063
ヴァーリ
Valle, Angelo 1440
ヴァーリー
Varley, John 1447
ヴァリ
Valli, Alida 1440
ヴァリアン
Varian, Hal R. 1447
ヴァリアンテ
Valiante, Gio 1440
ヴァリアント
Valiant, Leslie 1440
ヴァーリィ
Varley, John 1447
ヴァリエ
Vargö, Lars 1447
ヴァリエー
Vargö, Lars 1447
ヴァリション
Varichon, Anne 1447
ヴァリッキオ
Varricchio, Eda 1447
ヴァリテック
Varitek, Jason 1447
ヴァリロン
Valiron, François 1440
ヴァリーン
Vereen, Bob 1452
Vereen, Diane 1452
ヴァール
Waal, Edmund de 1466
Waal, Frans B.M.de 1466
Wahl, Alfred 1468
Wahl, Hauke 1468
Wahl, Rainer 1468
ヴァルヴェルデ
Valverde, Ernesto 1441
ヴァルガ
Varga, Tibor 1446
ウーアルカイシ
Wuerkaixi 1529
ウーアルカイシー
Wuerkaixi 1529
ウアルカイシ
Wuerkaixi 1529
ヴァルガス
Vargas, Fred 1446
ヴァルカマ
Valkama, Samuli 1440
ヴァルクス
Valckx, Catharina 1438
ヴァルグレン
Vallgren, Carl-Johan 1440
ウァルザー
Walser, Martin 1473
ヴァルサー
Walser, Hans 1473
ヴァルザー
Walser, Martin 1473
ヴァルジッチ
Vargic, Ivan 1447
ヴァルジッツ
Warsitz, Lutz 1480
ヴァルシナー
Valsiner, Jaan 1440
ヴァルス
Valls, Manuel 1440
ヴァルスタ
Warsta, Elina 1480
ヴァルスツェック
Waluszek, Christian 1475
ヴァルター
Walter, Fritz 1473
Walter, Peter 1474
Walther, Ingo F. 1474
ヴァルダ
Varda, Agnès 1446
ヴァルダイ
Várdai, István 1446
ヴァルタニアン
Vartanian, Ivan 1447
ヴァルダーラマ
Valderrama, Rosario 1439
ヴァルダロス
Vardalos, Nia 1446
ヴァルタン
Vartan, Sylvie 1447
ヴァルチャノヴァ
Valtchanova, Maria 1440
ヴァルツ
Waltz, Christoph 1475
ヴァルツィコス
Varoutsikos, Yannis 1447
ヴァルデ
Verdet, Jean-Pierre 1452
ウアルディ
Ouardi, El Hossein El 1063
ヴァルディフィオーリ
Valdifiori, Mirko 1439
ヴァルデス
Valdés, Chucho 1439
Valdez, Lisa 1439
ヴァルデツキー
Wardetzki, Bärbel 1478
ヴァルテール
Walter, Henriette 1474
Walter, Philippe 1474
ヴァルデンフェルス
Waldenfels, Bernhard 1469
ヴァルデンベルガー
Waldenberger, Franz 1469
ヴァルト
Wald, Anton 1469
ヴァルドシュミット
Waldschmidt, Gian-Luca 1469
ヴァルトハイム
Waldheim, Kurt 1469
ヴァルドマン・ブルン
Waldmann-Brun, Sabine 1469
ヴァルナイ
Varnay, Astrid 1447
ヴァルバノフ
Varbanov, Valentin 1446
ヴァルブエナ
Valbuena, Mathieu 1438
ヴァルベリー
Wallberg, Harriet 1472
ヴァルベルデ
Valverde, Ernesto 1441
ヴァルマ
Varma, Pavan K. 1447
Verma, Harish 1453
ヴァルマス
Varmus, Harold Eliot 1447
ヴァルマン
Wallmann, Johannes 1473
ヴァルメル
Warmer, Jos B. 1479
ヴァルラモフ
Varlamov, A.A. 1447
ヴァルンケ
Warncke, Carsten-Peter 1479
Warnke, Martin 1479
ヴァーレ
Vahle, Fredrik 1438
ヴァレ
Vallee, Jacques 1440
Vallée, Sylvain 1440
Vallet, Odon 1440
ヴァレー
Vallée, Martine 1440
ヴァレア
Valeur, Erik 1440
ヴァーレイ
Varley, Susan 1447
ヴァレジャオ
Varejao, Anderson 1446
ヴァレジョン
Varejão, Adriana 1446
ヴァレラ
Varela, Francisco J. 1446
Varela, Silvestre 1446
Varella, Lelio 1446
ヴァレリ
Valeri, Stéphane 1440
ヴァレリー
Valéry, Philippe 1440
ヴァレーン
Wallen, Mosse 1472
ヴァレンシア
Valencia, Mark J. 1439
ヴァレンスタイン
Valenstein, Elliot S. 1439
ヴァレンタイン
Valentine, Gill 1439
Valentine, James 1439
Valentine, Jenny 1439
Valentine, Minette 1439
ヴァレンチ
Valenti, Jack 1439
ヴァレンツァ
Valenza, Giuseppe 1439
ヴァレンテ
Valente, Catherynne M. 1439
ヴァレンティ
Valenti, Jack 1439
ヴァレンティーニ
Valentini, Giacomo 1439
Valentini, Robert F. 1439
ヴァレンティーノ
Valentino, Crystalle 1439
ヴァレンティノ
Valentino 1439
ヴァレント
Valente, Tony 1439
ヴァロエフ
Valuev, Nikolay 1440
ヴァローネ
Vallone, Raf 1440
ヴァロー・ベルカセム
Vallaud-Belkacem, Najat 1440
ヴァロン
Vallon, Jacqueline 1440
ヴァン
Van, Gilles de 1441
Van, Marina de 1441
Vann, Lizzie 1444
ヴァン・アッシュ
Van Assche, Kris 1441
ヴァン・アレン
Van Allen, James Alfred 1441
ヴァンアンデル
Van Andel, Jay 1441
Van Andel, Steve 1441
ヴァンアントワーペン
VanAntwerpen, Jonathan 1441
ヴァン・イタリー
Van Itallie, Jean Claude 1444
ヴァン・ヴェルサ
Van Velsor, Ellen 1445
ヴァン・エカレン
Van Ekeren, Glenn 1443
ヴァン・エクセル
Van Exel, Nick 1443
ヴァン・オオステルチィ
Van Oosterzee, Penny 1445
ヴァンオーケン
VanAuken, Brad 1441
ヴァン・カーク
Van Kirk, Sylvia 1444
ヴァン・ガンディ
Van Gundy, Stan 1444
ヴァン・クー
Van Kooy, R.C. 1444
ヴァンク
Wank, Andreas 1477
ヴァング
Vangout, Cécile 1443
ヴァンクープス
Van Coops, Margaret Rogers 1441
ヴァンクラ
Vancura, Olaf 1441
ヴァンクリーヴ
Vancleave, Ted 1441
ヴァンクリーブ
VanCleave, Janice Pratt 1441
ヴァンクレー
Winckler, Martin 1515
ヴァンゲリス
Vangelis 1443

ヴァン・ゲルダー
Van Gelder, Gordon 1443
Van Gelder, Sarah 1443
ヴァンサン
Vincent, Bernard 1458
Vincent, Guillaume 1458
ヴァン・サント
Van Sant, Gus 1445
ヴァンザント
Vanzant, Iyanla 1446
ヴァンジ
Vangi, Giuliano 1443
ヴァンシタート
Vansittart, Peter 1445
ヴァンシッタート
Vansittart, Peter 1445
ヴァン・シル
Van Sijll, Jennifer 1445
ヴァンス
Vance, Connie 1441
Vance, Courtney B. 1441
Vance, Cyrus Roberts 1441
Vance, Ellie 1441
Vance, Jack 1441
Vance, Lee G. 1441
Vance, William A. 1441
ヴァンスカ
Vänskä, Osmo 1445
ヴァン・スカイバー
Van Sciver, Ethan 1445
ヴァン・スコット
Van Scott, Miriam 1445
ヴァン・スコヤック
Van Scoyck, Robert 1445
ヴァン・スティーンウィク
Van Steenwyk, Elizabeth 1445
ヴァン・ストラーテン
Van Straten, Michael 1445
ヴァン・ストーン
Van Stone, Mark 1445
ヴァンストーン
Vanstone, Hugh 1445
Vanstone, Philippa 1445
ヴァンスリック
Van Slyck, Abigail Ayres 1445
ヴァン・ゼブラン
Van Zeveren, Michel 1446
ヴァン・ダイクン
Van Dyken, Rachel 1443
ヴァン・ダイケン
Van Dyken, Rachel 1443
ヴァン・ダーヴァット
Van Der Vat, Dan 1442
ヴァンダーウェル
Vanderwell, Howard 1443
ヴァンダーヴェルド
Vandervelde, Maryanne 1442
ヴァンダーカム
VanderKam, James C. 1442
ヴァン・ダーハート
Hart, Onno van der 577
ヴァンダービルト
Vanderbilt, Tom 1442
ヴァンダープール
Vanderpool, Clare 1442
Vanterpool, David 1445
ヴァンダーポスト
Van der Post, Lucia 1442
ヴァンダーマーブ
Vandermerwe, Sandra 1442
ヴァンダーミーア
Vandermeer, John H. 1442
ヴァンダミア
VanderMeer, Ann 1442
VanderMeer, Jeff 1442
ヴァン・ダム
Van Damme, Jean-Claude 1441
ヴァン・ダー・リン
Van der Ryn, Ethan 1442
ヴァンダーリンデン
Vanderlinden, Barbara 1442
Vanderlinden, Kathy 1442
ヴァン・ダルケン
Van Dulken, Stephen 1443
ヴァンチーニ
Vancini, Florestano 1441
ヴァン・チャウ
Van Chau, Andre N. 1441
ヴァン・デァ・クレイ
Van der Kley, Martin 1442
ヴァン・デア・コーク
Van der Kolk, Bessel A. 1442
ヴァン・デア・ゼー
Van der Zee, Karen 1443
ヴァンディー
Vandehey, Tim 1442
ヴァン・ディーンデレン
Van Dienderen, An 1443
ヴァンデ・ヴェルデ
Vande Velde, Vivian 1443
ヴァンデヴォールデ
Vandevoorde, David 1443
ヴァン・デ・カー
Van De Car, Nikki 1441
ヴァン・デル・ウァルデン
Van Der Waerden, Bartel L. 1443
ヴァンデルカンプ
Van der Kemp, Gerald 1442
ヴァン・デル・クローン
van der Kroon, Coen 1442
ヴァン・デル・スツール
van der Stoel, Max 1442
ヴァン・デル・ハイデン
Van der Heijden, Kees 1442
ヴァンデルホフ
Van der Hoff Boersma, Francisco 1442
ヴァンデルメルシュ
Vandermersch, Bernard 1442
ヴァン・デン・アレンド
Van den Arend, Erwin 1442
ヴァンデン - オウェール
Vanden Auweele, Yves 1442
ヴァンデンブリンク
VandenBrink, Mark 1442
ヴァン・デン・ボイナンツ
Van den Boeynants, Paul 1442
ヴァンデンボス
VandenBos, Gary R. 1442
ヴァント
Wand, Günter 1475
Wandt, Manfred 1475
ヴァン・ド・ヴァイア
Van de Weyer, Robert 1443
ヴァンドヴィル
Vandewiele, Agnès 1443
ヴァンドゥワラ
Vande Walle, Willy 1443
ヴァン・ド・カステル・シュヴァイツァー
Van de Casteele-Schweitzer, Sylvie 1441
ヴァントリーズ
Vantrease, Brenda Rickman 1445
ヴァンドーレン
Vandoren, Stefan 1443
ヴァンドロス
Vandross, Luther Ronzoni 1443
ヴァンナー
Wanner, Gerhard 1477
ヴァン・ナッタ
Van Natta, Don, Jr. 1444
ヴァンニ
Vanni, Gian Berto 1444
ヴァンニーニ
Vannini, Vanio 1444
ヴァン・ノッテン
Van Noten, Dries 1444
ヴァン・パオ
Vang Pao 1444
ヴァンバーグ
Vernberg, F.John 1453
Vernberg, Winona B. 1453
ヴァン・ハース
Van Haas, Gary 1444
ヴァン・バスカーク
Van Buskirk, Richard L. 1441
ヴァン・パタン
Van Patten, Tim 1445
ヴァンパック
Wampach, Lydie Marie-Josee 1475
ヴァン・ハッセル
Van Hasselt, Vincent B. 1444
ヴァン・ハネハン
Van Haneghan, James P. 1444
ヴァン・ハル
Hul, Brian Van't 634
ヴァン・ビーマ
Van Biema, Michael 1441
ヴァンフーザー
Vanhoozer, Kevin J. 1444
ヴァン・フッフト
van Hooft, Stan 1444
ヴァン・フッレ
Van Hulle, Marc M. 1444
ヴァン・プラーグ
Van Praag, Menna 1445
ヴァン・プラグ
Van Praagh, James 1445
ヴァン・ブラフト
Van Bragt, Jan 1441
ヴァン・フリート
Van Fleet, Matthew 1443
ヴァン・ブリート
Captain Beefheart 223
ヴァンフリート
VanFleet, Risë 1443
ヴァンブリート
Vanvleet, Fred 1445
ヴァンプルー
Vamplew, Wray 1441
ヴァーンブロッド
Wänblad, Mats 1475
ヴァン・ヘイレン
Van Halen, Edward 1444
ヴァンヘック
Van Hecke, Madeleine L. 1444
ヴァンペレーラ
Vanpereira 1445
ヴァン・ホーヴェ
Van Hove, Ivo 1444
ヴァンホーナッカー
Vanhoenacker, Mark 1444
ヴァン・ホルダ
Van Holde, Kensal Edward 1444
ヴァン・ホーン
Van Horn, Patricia 1444
ヴァン・マーネン
Van Manen, Max 1444
ヴァン - マーネン
Van Maanen, John 1444
ヴァン＝マーネン
Van Maanen, John 1444
Van Manen, Max 1444
ヴァン・メーター
Van Meter, Jen 1444
ヴァン・モリヴァン
Vann Molyvann 1444
ヴァン・リー
Van Leer, Lia 1444
ヴァンリア
Van Lier, Leo 1444
ヴァンリアー
Van Liere, Donna 1444
ヴァン・リーケン
Van Reken, Ruth E. 1445
ヴァン・ルーン
Van Loon, Borin 1444
ヴァンレル
Vanrell, Luc 1445
ヴァン・レンテ
Van Lente, Fred 1444
ヴァン・ロイ
Van-Roy, Peter 1445
ヴァン・ロンク
Van Ronk, Dave 1445
ヴァン・ワイク
Van Wyk, Kenneth R. 1446
ウィ
Wee, Kim-wee 1486
ウィー
Oei, Tian Po 1044
Wee, Cho Yaw 1486
Wie, Michelle 1502
ウィーア
Weaire, Denis 1484
ウィア
Garvin, Johnny 482
Weir, Johnny 1489
Weir, Warren 1489
ウィアー
Weir, Andy 1489
Weir, Charles 1489
Weir, Doffy 1489
Weir, Duncan 1489
Weir, James 1489
Weir, Jamie 1489

ウ

Weir, Johnny 1489
Weir, Peter Lindsay 1489
ヴィアー
Vere, Ed 1452
ヴィアイ
V.I 1455
ヴィアガス
Viagas, Belinda Grant 1455
ウィアーズ
Wears, Robert L. 1484
ウィアーズマ
Wiersema, Fred D. 1502
ウィアセーマ
Wiersema, Fred D. 1502
ウィアゼムスキー
Wiazemsky, Anne 1501
ヴィアゼムスキー
Wiazemsky, Anne 1501
ウィアット
Wyatt, Rawdon 1530
ヴィアラ
Viala, Alain 1455
ヴィアリ
Vialli, Gianluca 1455
ヴィアール
Viard, Bruno 1455
ヴィアル
Vial, Jean 1455
Vial, Véronique 1455
ヴィアレク
Viereck, Peter 1456
ウィーヴァー
Weaver, Ashley 1484
Weaver, Dennis 1484
Weaver, Earl 1484
Weaver, Ingrid 1484
Weaver, Jacki 1484
Weaver, Sigourney 1484
Weaver, Stewart 1484
Weaver, William 1484
ウィヴァー
Wever, Merritt 1496
ヴィヴィアーニ
Viviani, Federico 1460
ヴィヴィアーノ
Viviano, Emiliano 1460
ヴィヴィアン
Viviant, Arnaud 1460
ヴィヴィエ
Viviers, Casper 1460
ヴィヴィオルカ
Wieviorka, Annette 1503
Wieviorka, Michel 1503
ウィーヴィング
Weaving, Andrew 1484
ヴィーヴェス
Vives, Carlos 1460
ヴィヴェス
Vivès, Bastien 1460
Vives, Giuseppe 1460
ウィヴェル
Wivel, Anders 1519
ヴィヴェル
Wivel, Marie Moesgaard 1519
ヴィヴレ
Viveret, Patrick 1460
ウイエ
Houllier, Gerard 626
ヴィエイラ
Vieira, João-Bernardo 1456
Vieira, Meredith Louise 1456
ヴィエイリーニャ
Vieirinha 1456
ヴィエガ
Viégas, Fernanda 1456
ウィエジュボウスカ
Wierzbowska, Anna 1502
Wierzbowska, Maria 1502
ヴィエタ
Vieta, Eduard 1456
ヴィエッツ
Viets, Elaine 1456
ウィエヘツキ
Wiechecki, Rafał 1502
ウィエラー
Wierer, Dorothea 1502
ヴィエルジュビツカ
Wierzbicka, Anna 1502
ヴィエルメッター
Vielmetter, Georg 1456
ヴィエロ
Viero, Gianni 1456
ヴィエン
Vienne, Véronique 1456
ウイェンガ
Ouyenga, Agouta 1064
ヴィエンヌ
Vienne, Véronique 1456
ヴィオースト
Viorst, Judith 1459
ヴィオッティ
Viotti, Marcello 1459
ヴィオラ
Viola, Al 1459
Viola, Alessandra 1459
Viola, Bill 1459
Viola, Tom 1459
ヴィオリ
Violi, Marcello 1459
ヴィオレ
Viollet, Fanny 1459
ヴィオレ＝ル＝デュック
Viollet-le-Duc, Eugene Emmanuel 1459
ウィーガー
Wiegers, Karl 1502
ヴィガー
Wigger, Lothar 1503
ウィーガーズ
Wiegers, Karl 1502
Wiegers, Karl Eugene 1502
ヴィカーズ
Vickers, Lucy 1455
ウィカム
Wicomb, Zoë 1501
ヴィカリー
Vickcry, Roy 1455
ウィカール
Wekerle, Christine 1491
ウィガル
Wigal, Donald 1503
ウイガル
Uygar, Mert Zeybek 1437
ヴィガル
Wigal, Donald 1503
ウィーガルツ
Wiegartz, Pamela S. 1502
ヴィガレロ
Vigarello, Georges 1456
ウィガン
Wiegand, Debra J.Lynn-McHale 1502
ヴィガン
Vigan, Delphine de 1456
ウィーガンド
Wiegand, Wayne A. 1502
ヴィギ
Vighi, Carlos 1456
ウィー・キムウィー
Wee, Kim-wee 1486
ヴィギュエリ
Viguerie, Patrick 1456
ウィギン
Wiggin, Addison 1503
ウィキングス
Wickings, Ruth 1501
ウィギンス
Wiggins, Bradley 1503
Wiggins, Kenny 1503
Wiggins, Richard H., Ⅲ 1503
ウィギンズ
Wiggins, Andrew 1503
Wiggins, Arthur W. 1503
Wiggins, Bradley 1503
Wiggins, David 1503
Wiggins, Grant P. 1503
Wiggins, Loudy 1503
Wiggins, Melanie 1503
ウィーク
Wieck, Stewart 1502
ヴィグ
Vig, Butch 1456
ウィークス
Weekes, Claire 1486
Weeks, Antonia 1486
Weeks, Jeffrey 1486
Weeks, Jemile 1486
Weeks, John 1486
Weeks, Jon 1486
Weeks, Kent R. 1486
Weeks, Lee 1486
Weeks, Louis 1486
Weeks, Marcus 1486
Weeks, Rickie, Jr. 1486
Weeks, Sarah 1487
ウイークス
Weeks, Stanley Byron 1487
ウィクストラム
Wikström, Per-Olof H. 1503
ウィクストロム
Wikström, Gabriel 1503
ウィクセル
Wicksell, Rikard K. 1501
ヴィグセル
Wigzell, Hans 1503
ヴィクター
Victor, Barbara 1455
ヴィクトリア
Beckham, Victoria 112
Victoria, Brian A. 1455
ヴィクトリア王女
Victoria, HRH Crown Princess 1455
ヴィクトリノ
Victorino, Shane 1455
ヴィクトル
Victor, Jean-Christophe 1455
ヴィクトローヴァ
Viktorova, Anna 1456
ウィグナル
Wignall, Maurice 1503
Wignall, Paul B. 1503
ウィグノール
Wignall, Kevin 1503
ウイグハム
Whigham, Julian 1497
ウィグモア
Wigmore, Richard 1503
ウィクラマシンゲ
Wickramasinghe, Nalin Chandra 1501
ウィクラマシンハ
Wickremasinghe, Ranil 1501
ウィクラマナヤケ
Wickramanayaka, Ratnasiri 1501
ウィグラム
Wigram, Tony 1503
ヴィークランド
Wikland, Ilon 1503
ウィークリー
Weekley, Boo 1486
ヴィグルー
Vigouroux, Mark 1456
ウィグルスワース
Wigglesworth, Richard 1503
ウィグレン
Wittgren, Nick 1519
ヴィクロム・クロマディット
Vikrom Kromadit 1456
ウィーケル
Weikel, Dana 1487
ウィケルグレン
Wickelgren, Wayne A. 1501
ヴィケン
Wikén, Emma 1503
ウィササ
Wisasa, Cheewan 1518
ウィザーズ
Withers, Harvey J.S. 1519
Withers, Robert T. 1519
ウィザースプーン
Witherspoon, Kimberly 1519
Witherspoon, Reese 1519
ヴィザード
Vizard, Michael 1460
ウィサヌ
Wissanu, Krua-Ngam 1518
ウィザム
Witham, Scott 1519
ウィザリー
Witherly, Jeffre L. 1519
ウィザリントン
Witherington, Ben, Ⅲ 1519
ウィージ
Wiese, Carl 1502
ヴィーシー
Veasey, Nick 1449
ウィジェシンハ
Wijesinghe, Chandrasena 1503
ウィジェセケラ
Wijesekera, Mahinda 1503
ウィジェトンガ
Wijetunga, Dingiri Banda 1503
ヴィシェール

Visscher, Charles de 1459
ウィジガー
Widiger, Thomas A. 1501
ウィシット・サーサナティアン
Wisit Sartsanatieng 1518
ウィシット・サーサナティヤン
Wisit Sartsanatieng 1518
ウィジナーマン
Wijnerman, Adeline 1503
ヴィジーニ
Vizzini, Ned 1460
ヴィシニョーワ
Vishneva, Diana 1459
ヴィシネーフスカヤ
Vishnevskaya, Galina Pavlovna 1459
ヴィシネフスカヤ
Vishnevskaya, Galina Pavlovna 1459
ヴィシネフスキー
Vishnevskii, Nikolai 1459
ウィジネン
Wijnen, Edo 1503
ウィジャー
Widger, Chuck 1501
ウィーシャウス
Wieschaus, Eric F. 1502
ウィシャウス
Wieschaus, Eric F. 1502
ヴィーシャウス
Wieschaus, Eric F. 1502
ウィシャート
Wishart, Adam 1518
Wishart, Trevor 1518
ヴィシャーノ
Visciano, Joe 1459
ウィジャヤナーヤカ
Wijayanayake, Sujeewa 1503
ウィジャン
Wijarn, Wirach 1503
ウィシュネフスキ
Wischnewski, Anke 1518
ヴィシュワナス
Vishwanath, Vijay 1459
ヴィシュワナータン
Viswanathan, Gauri 1460
ヴィシュワナンダ
Vishwananda, Sri Swami 1459
ウィジョヨ・ニチサストロ
Widjojo Nitisastro 1501
ウィジョヨ・ニティサストロ
Widjojo Nitisastro 1501
ウィション
Wishon, Tom W. 1518
ウィシン
Wisin 1518
ウィジンガー
Wiesinger, Johannes 1503
ウィス
Wyss, Hansjörg 1531
ヴィース
Wies, Ernst W. 1502
Wyss, Beat 1531
ヴィス
Visse, Dominique 1459
ヴィスヴァナタン
Visvanathan, R. 1460
ヴィスヴェー
Wisweh, Lutz 1518
ヴィスカス
Viescas, John 1456
ウィズ・カリファ
Wiz Khalifa 1519
ウィスケ
Wiske, Martha Stone 1518
ヴィスコヴォ
Viscovo, Aniello 1459
ウィズダム
Wisdom, Linda Randall 1518
Wisdom, Neville 1518
Wisdom, Stephen 1518
ウィスット・ポンニミット
Wisut Ponnmit 1518
ヴィステンドール
Hvistendahl, Mara 640
ウィースト
Wiest, Dianne 1503
ヴィストリヒ
Wistrich, Robert S. 1518
ウィースナー
Wiesner, William 1503
ウィーズナー
Wiesner, David 1503
ウィズナー
Wiesner, Dieter 1503
ウィスナム
Wisnom, David, Ⅲ 1518
ウィスニアウスカス
Vysniauskas, Ramunas 1466
ウィスニースキー
Wisniewski, Stefen 1518
ヴィスネポルスキー
Visnepolschi, Svetlana 1459
ウィスペルウェイ
Wispelwey, Pieter 1518
ヴィースホイ
Wiesheu, Gerhard 1503
ウィスマン
Wisman, Thomas 1518
ヴィズミアラ
Wyszumialal, Edward 1531
ヴィースミュラー
Wiesmüller, Dieter 1503
ヴィスメール
Wissmer, Jean-Michel 1518
ウィスラー
Wisler, Matt 1518
ウィズラー
Wiseler, Claude 1518
ヴィースランデル
Wieslander, Jujja 1503
ウィズロウ
Withrow, Chris 1519
ヴィスロフ
Wisloff, Carl Johan Fredrik 1518
ヴィゼナー
Vizenor, Gerald Robert 1460
ウィーゼル
Wiesel, Elie 1502
Wiesel, Torsten Nils 1502
ヴィーセル
Wiesel, Torsten Nils 1502
ヴィーゼル
Wiesel, Elie 1502
Wiesel, Eliezer 1502
Wiesel, Torsten Nils 1502
ウィーゼンタール
Wiesenthal, Simon 1503
ヴィーゼンタール
Wiesenthal, Simon 1503
ヴィセント
Vicente, Mark 1455
Vincent, Amy 1458
ウィーゼンハント
Whisenhunt, Ken 1497
ウィーセンフェルド
Wiesenfeld, David 1503
ヴィソルカス
Vithoulkas, George 1460
ウィーダー
Wieder, Joshua M. 1502
Wieder, Nicolas 1502
Wieder, Serena 1502
ヴィータ
Vita, Sharon De 1460
ヴィーダ
Vida, Vendela 1455
ヴィダ
Vida, Domagoj 1455
ウィタカ
Whitaker, Andrew C. 1497
ウィタカー
Whitaker, Robert 1497
Whittaker, Fozzy 1500
Whittaker, Jim 1500
ウィーターズ
Wieters, Matt 1503
ヴィタノフ
Vitanov, Milen 1460
ヴィーダーホルト
Wiederholt, Sven 1502
ウィタヤ
Witthaya, Kaewparadai 1519
ウィダヤティ
Widayati, Lies 1501
ウィタラナ
Vitarana, Tissa 1460
ヴィターリ
Vitale, Jennifer 1460
Vitali, Andrea 1460
ウィタル
Whittal, Yvonne 1500
ヴィタール
Vitale, Stefano 1460
ヴィダール
Vidal, Gore 1455
ヴィダル
Vidal, Catherine 1455
Vidal, Dominique 1455
Vidal, Gore 1455
Vidal, Séverine 1455
ヴィダル・ナケ
Vidal-Naquet, Pierre 1455
ヴィダル＝ナケ
Vidal-Naquet, Pierre 1455
ヴィターレ
Vitale, Joe 1460
Vitale, Joseph G. 1460
ヴィタレ
Vitale, Geoffrey 1460
Vitale, Graziano 1460
ヴィーチ
Veatch, Robert M. 1449
ウィチット
Wijit, Srisa-arn 1503
ウィチャー
Whicher, Olive 1497
ウィチョレクツォイル
Wieczorek-zeul, Heidemarie 1502
ヴィツェル
Witzel, Michael 1519
ウィッカー
Whicker, Alan 1497
Wicker, Ken 1501
Wicker, Tom 1501
ヴィッカーズ
Vickers, Andrew 1455
Vickers, Jon 1455
Vickers, Salley 1455
Vickers, Tanya M. 1455
ウィッカム
Wickham, Connor 1501
Wickham, Gary 1501
Wickham, Hadley 1501
ヴィッカリー
Vickery, Brian Campbell 1455
ウィツガル
Witzgall, Peter 1519
ウィッキービッツ
Witkiewitz, Katie 1519
ウィック
Wick, Cole 1501
Wick, Rowan 1501
Wick, Walter 1501
Wicke, Laura S. 1501
ヴィック
Vick, Michael 1455
ウィックス
Wicks, Andrew C. 1501
Wicks, Maris 1501
ウィッグス
Wiggs, Robert B. 1503
Wiggs, Susan 1503
ウィックマイヤー
Wickmayer, Yanina 1501
ウィックランド
Wickland, Carl August 1501
ウィッケンズ
Wickens, Thomas D. 1501
ウィッケンデン
Wickenden, Nadine 1501
ウィッケンハイザー
Wickenheiser, Hayley 1501
ウィッゲンホーン
Wiggenhorn, William 1503
ヴィッサー
Visser, Jan 1459
Wisser, Richard 1518
ウィッザム
Witham, Anna 1519
ヴィッシャー
Visher, Emily B. 1459
Visher, John S. 1459
ウィッスィー
Withey, Jeff 1519
ウィッタ
Whitta, Gary 1500
ウィッター
Witter, Bret 1519
ウィッタム
Whitham, Cynthia 1500
ウィッチェル
Witchel, Alex 1518
ウィッチャー

Whicher, Stephen E. 1497
Witcher, Moony 1518
ウィッツェル
Wetzel, Gary 1496
Witzel, Morgen 1519
ウィッツマン
Witzmann, Bryan 1519
ヴィッツマン
Wizmann, Reingard 1519
ウィッテ
Witte, John 1519
ウィッティ
Whitty, Geoff 1500
Witty, Christine 1519
Witty, Paul Andrew 1519
ウィッティー
Whitty, Geoff 1500
ヴィッティ
Vitti, Anthony 1460
ウィッテイカー
Whittaker, A.G. 1500
ウィッティング
Witting, Amy 1519
ウィッティンデール
Whittingdale, John 1500
ウィッティントン
Whittington, Geoffrey 1500
Whittington, Harry Blackmore 1500
Whittington, Lucy 1500
Whittington, Richard 1500
ウィッテキンド
Wittekind, Christian 1519
ウィッテッカー
Whitaker, Richard 1497
ウィッテル
Whittle, Richard 1500
ウィッテルン
Wittern, Christian 1519
ウィッテン
Whitten, Tara 1500
Witten, Edward 1519
Witten, Jason 1519
ウイッテン
Witten, Thomas A. 1519
ウイッテングトン
Whittington, Frank J. 1500
ヴィッテンゾン
Vittenzon, Janna Z. 1460
ウィッテンバーグ
Whittenburg, Karen Toller 1500
Wittenberg, Isca 1519
ウィッテンバーグ - ライルス
Wittenberg-Lyles, Elaine M. 1519
ウィット
Witt, Chad A. 1519
Witt, James Lee 1519
Witt, Jonathan 1519
Witt, Stephen 1519
ヴィット
Vit, Patricia 1460
Wit, Juliette de 1518
ウィットウェル
Whitwell, Mark 1500
ウィットゥロー
Whitlow, Steve 1500
ヴィットコップ
Wittkop-Ménardeau, Gabrielle 1519
ウィットコム
Whitcomb, Christopher 1497
Whitcomb, John E. 1497
ヴィツドス
Vizdos, Michael J. 1460
ウィットニー
Witney, William 1519
ウィットフィールド
Whitfield, John 1500
Whitfield, Susan 1500
ウィットフォード
Whitford, Brad 1500
Whitford, Bradley 1500
Whitford, Frank 1500
ウィットフト
Witthoft, Scott 1519
ウィットボーイ
Witbooi, Hendrik 1518
ウイットボーイ
Witbooi, Hendrik 1518
ウィットマン
Whitman, James Q. 1500
Whitman, Meg 1500
Wittman, Donald A. 1519
Wittman, Eric J. 1519
Wittman, Robert K. 1519
Wittman, William 1519
ウイットマン
Whitman, Meg 1500
ウィットモア
Whitmore, James 1500
Whitmore, John 1500
ウィットラッチ
Whitlatch, Terryl 1500
ウィットラム
Whitlam, Edward Gough 1500
ウィットリー
Whitley, Chase 1500
ヴィットーリ
Vittori, Nadia 1460
ヴィットリーニ
Vitturini, Davide 1460
ヴィットリンガー
Wittlinger, Andreas 1519
Wittlinger, Dieter 1519
Wittlinger, Heidi 1519
Wittlinger, Hildegard 1519
Wittlinger, M. 1519
ウィットロック
Whitlock, Max 1500
Whitlock, Nikita 1500
ウィットワー
Witwer, Michael 1519
ウィットワース
Whitworth, Andrew 1501
Whitworth, Anthony P. 1501
Whitworth, Laura 1501
Whitworth, Michael H. 1501
ウィッパーファース
Wipperfürth, Alex 1517
ヴィッパーマン
Wippermann, Wolfgang 1517
ウィップル
Whipple, Beverly 1497
ヴィッラリ
Villari, Rosario 1457
ウィディアント
Widianto, Nova 1501
ヴィティエッロ
Vitiello, Roberto 1460
ヴィティエール
Vitier, Cintio 1460
ヴィティエロ
Vitiello, Giuseppe 1460
ウィティカー
Whitacre, Edward, Jr. 1497
Whitaker, Forest 1497
Whitaker, Tu-Shonda L. 1497
Whitiker, Gail 1500
ウィテイカー
Whitaker, Andrew 1497
Whitaker, Forest 1497
ウィティッグ
Wittig, Monique 1519
ウィディックス
Wijdicks, Eelco F.M. 1503
ヴィディヤーランカール
Vidyalankar, Anil 1456
ヴィディヤランカール
Vidyalankar, Anil 1456
ウィティングトン
Whitington, John 1500
ウィーデーカー
Wiederkehr, Daniel 1502
ウィテカー
Whitacre, Eric 1497
Whitaker, Forest 1497
Whitaker, John 1497
Whitaker, Robert 1497
Whittaker, James A. 1500
ウィーデキング
Wiedeking, Wendelin 1502
ヴィーデキング
Wiedeking, Wendelin 1502
ウィテク
Witek, Elżbieta 1519
ヴィーテゲ
Wiethege, Katrin 1503
ウィテック
Wittek, Max 1519
ヴィデティック
Videtic, Gregory M. M. 1455
ヴィデベック
Videbeck, Sheila L. 1455
ウイテマ
Huitema, Christian 634
ウィテリック
Witterick, J.L. 1519
ウィーデン
Weeden, Brandon 1486
ウィート
Wheat, Carolyn 1496
Wheat, Ed 1496
Wheat, Gaye 1496
ウィード
Weed, Becky 1486
Weed, Susun S. 1486
Weide, Robert B. 1487
ヴィートー
Vietor, Richard H.K. 1456
ヴィト
Vit, Armin 1460
Wit, Antoni 1518
ヴィトー
Vitaux, Jean 1460
Vito, Victor 1460
ヴィド
Videau, Valérie 1455
ヴィートヴァルト
Wiedwald, Felix 1502
ヴィトヴィ - ヤコブセン
Hvitved-Jacobsen, Thorkild 640
ウィドウズ
Widdows, Nancy 1501
ウィドゥソン
Widdowson, H.G. 1501
ウィドウソン
Widdowson, Rosalind 1501
ウィドゥフィールド
Widdowfield, Rebekah 1501
ウイトゥメン・オルゴドル
Uitumen Orgodolyn 1432
ウィトゥラル
Witoelar, Rachmat 1519
ウィトゥーン
Witoon, Nambutr 1519
ウィトォー
Uitto, Juha I. 1432
ウィトカウアー
Wittkower, Rudolf 1519
ヴィトキーヌ
Vitkine, Antoine 1460
ウィトキン
Witkin, Georgia 1519
ウィートクロフツ
Wheatcroft, Andrew 1496
ヴィドゲン
Vidgen, Lucas 1455
ウィトコウスキー
Witkowski, Jan Anthony 1519
ウィトコップ
Witkop, Bernhard 1519
ヴィトコップ
Wittokop, Gabrièlle 1519
ウィトコフ
Wittkopf, Kevin 1519
ヴィトーセク
Vitousek, Peter M. 1460
ウィドーソン
Widdowson, Kay 1501
ウィドド
Widodo, Adi Sutjipto 1502
ヴィトネル
Wittner, Laurence 1519
ウィトフィールド
Whitfield, David 1500
Whitfield, Roy 1500
ウイドブロ
Huidobro, Eleuterio 634
ウィドマー
Widmer, Edward L. 1502
Widmer, Rolf 1502
Wiedemer, John David 1502
Wiedemer, Robert A. 1502
ヴィドマー
Vidmar, Neil 1456
Widmer, Silvan 1502
ウィドマーク
Widmark, Erik 1502
Widmark, Richard 1502
ヴィトマー・シュルンプフ
Widmer-schlumpf, Eveline 1502
ウィードマン
Wiedemann, Julius 1502
ヴィドラー

Vidler, Anthony 1456
ウィトラル
Witoelar, Erna 1519
ウィートリー
Wheatley, Andrew 1496
Wheatley, Margaret J. 1496
ウィドリグ
Widrig, Don 1502
ウィトルシー
Whittlesey, Saunders N. 1500
ヴィドロシェ
Widlöcher, Daniel 1502
ウィートン
Wheaton, Markus 1496
Wheaton, William C. 1496
ウィードン
Weedon, Bert 1486
ウィドン
Whiddon, Karen 1497
ウィーナー
Weiner, Allen 1488
Wiener, Charles M. 1502
Wiener, Jerry M. 1502
Wiener, Jon 1502
Wiener, Lori 1502
ウィナ
Wina, Inonge 1515
ウィナー
Winner, David 1516
Winner, Ellen 1516
Winner, Michael 1516
Winner, Michelle Garcia 1516
ヴィーナー
Wiener, Antje 1502
ヴィナヴェール
Vinaver, Michel 1458
ウィーナー＝クローニッシュ
Wiener-Kronish, Jeanine P. 1502
ウィナー・ミュラム
Winer-Muram, Helen T. 1515
ウィナレー
Whineray, Wilson 1497
ウィニー
Winnie, Robert 1516
Wynne, Jane M. 1531
ヴィニツカヤ
Vinnitskaya, Anna 1458
ウィニック
Winick, Judd 1516
ウィニフリス
Winnifrith, Tom 1516
ヴィニュロン
Vigneron, E. 1456
ヴィーニンガー
Wieninger, Peter R. 1502
ヴィネーカル
Vinekar, S.L. 1458
ヴィネン
Vinen, Richard 1458
ウィノグラッド
Winograd, Morley 1516
ウィノグラード
Winograd, Terry 1516
ヴィノグラードヴァ
Vinogradova, Luba 1458
ヴィノグラードフ
Vinogradov, V.K. 1458
ヴィノック
Winock, Michel 1516
ウィーバー
Weaver, Dennis 1484
Weaver, Earl 1484
Weaver, Gertrude 1484
Weaver, Jacki 1484
Weaver, Jason 1484
Weaver, Jered 1484
Weaver, Kaitlyn 1484
Weaver, Kevin 1484
Weaver, Luke 1484
Weaver, Richard G. 1484
Weaver, Sigourney 1484
Weaver, Sylvester L. 1484
Weaver, Will 1484
Weber, Aimee 1485
Weber, Michael W. 1486
Wieber, Jordyn Marie 1502
ウイパー
Wipha, Arawan 1517
ヴィハー
Vehar, Jonathan 1450
ウィーバー・ザーカー
Weaver-Zercher, David 1484
ウィバツカ
Łybacka, Krystyna 855
ウィーバリー
Wibberley, Cormac 1501
Wibberley, Marianne 1501
ウィバリー
Wibberley, Mary 1501
ウィハルジャ
Wiharja, Yati Maryati 1503
ウィービー
Wiebe, Erica Elizabeth 1502
ヴィーヒェルト
Wiechert, Christof 1502
ウィビソノ
Wibisono, Djoko 1501
ウィーブ
Wiebe, Trina 1502
ウィフテルレ
Wichterle, Otto 1501
ウィフラー
Wipfler, Patty 1517
ウィプラッド
Wiprud, Brian M. 1517
ウィーフリング
Wiefling, Kimberly 1502
ウィヘイ
Ujhelyi, Maria 1432
ウィベリー
Wiberg, Hakan 1501
ウイベリー
Wiberg, Hakan 1501
ウイベル
Uibel, Arvid 1432
ウィベン
Wuebben, Jon 1529
ウィホニー
Wihongi, Verina 1503
ヴィボニー
Vyborny, Lee 1466
ウイマー
Wimmer, Kurt 1515
ヴィマー
Wimmer, Kevin 1515
Wimmer, Wolfgang 1515
ウィームス
Weems, Darrion 1487
Weems, Eric 1487
ウィームズ
Weems, Sonny 1487
ウイメット
Ouimet, David 1064
ウィーモーツ
Weimorts, Albert L., Jr. 1488
ヴィユレ
Villeret, Jacques 1457
ヴィヨーム
Vuillaume, Jean-Pierre 1465
ウィーラ
Wheeler, C.Miki 1497
ウィーラー
Wheeler, Adam 1496
Wheeler, Claire Michaels 1497
Wheeler, Eliza 1497
Wheeler, Harvey, Jr. 1497
Wheeler, Jennifer G. 1497
Wheeler, Jody 1497
Wheeler, John Archibald 1497
Wheeler, Maria 1497
Wheeler, Michael 1497
Wheeler, Paul 1497
Wheeler, Philip 1497
Wheeler, Quentin D. 1497
Wheeler, Rebecca 1497
Wheeler, Stephanie 1497
Wheeler, Thomas 1497
Wheeler, Thomas Hutchin 1497
Wheeler, Tim 1497
Wheeler, Zack 1497
ウィラ
Veera, Rojpojanarat 1449
ヴィラ
Villa, Dana Richard 1457
ウィライワン
Vilayvanh, Phomkhe 1457
ヴィラ・ヴィセンシオ
Villa-Vicencio, Charles 1457
ウィーラクーン
Weerakoon, Batty 1487
Weerakoon, Gunaratne 1487
ウィーラコディ
Weerakkody, Chandima 1487
ウィラサクレック・ウォンパーサ
Weelasakreck Wongpaser 1487
ヴィラージェーシュワラ
Virajeshver 1459
ヴィラジョンガ
Vilallonga, Jose Luis de 1456
ウィラーズ
Willers, Michael 1506
ヴィラス・ボアス
Villas-Boas, Andre 1457
ヴィラータ
Virata, Cesar Enrique Aguinaldo 1459
ウィラチャイ
Virachai, Virameteekul 1459
ウィラツ
Wirathu 1517
ウィラード
Willard, Dallas 1506
Willard, Fred 1506
Willard, Huntington F. 1506
Willard, Nancy 1506
Willard, Sandra 1506
Willard, Terry 1506
ウィラトゥ
Wirathu 1517
ウィラトゥ師
Wirathu 1517
ヴィラーニ
Villani, Cédric 1457
ヴィラニ
Villani, Cédric 1457
ウィラハディクスマ
Umar Wirahadikusumah 1433
ウィラハン
Whelehan, Imelda 1497
ウィーラー＝ベネット
Wheeler-Bennett, John W. 1497
ウィーラマントリー
Weeramantry, Christopher G. 1487
ヴィラール
Vilar, Luc 1457
ヴィラロ
Vilaró, Ramón 1457
ヴィラロンガ
Vilallonga, Jose Luis de 1456
ウィーラワンサ
Weerawansa, Wimal 1487
ウィーラン
Wheelan, Charles J. 1496
Whelan, Glenn 1497
Whelan, Gloria 1497
Whelan, Richard 1497
ウィラン
Willain, Pascal 1506
ヴィランコート
Vaillancourt McGrath, Renée 1438
ウィランスキー
Wilansky, Ethan 1503
ウィーランド
Wieland, Bob 1502
Wieland, Carl 1502
ウィラント
Wiranto 1517
ウィーリー
Whealy, Chris 1496
ウィリー
Willey, David 1507
Willey, Liane Holliday 1507
Willie, Alphonse Morial 1511
ウィリアム王子
Prince William 1507
ウィリアム・カルヴァーリョ
William Carvalho 1507
ウィリアム卿
Lord William 1507
ウィリアム・ジャストセン
Williams-Justsen, Kim A. 1511
ウィリアムス
Williams, Andrew 1507
Williams, Andy 1507
Williams, Aurora 1507
Williams, Basil 1507

ウ

Williams, Bernie 1507
Williams, Cliff 1507
Williams, David R. 1507
Williams, Geoffrey 1508
Williams, Hayley 1508
Williams, Inaki 1508
Williams, Jenny 1508
Williams, John 1508
Williams, John McLaughlin 1508
Williams, Kim 1509
Williams, Kyle 1509
Williams, Lee 1509
Williams, Luke 1509
Williams, Nathan 1509
Williams, Noel H. 1509
Williams, Pharrell 1509
Williams, Robbie 1510
Williams, Robin 1510
Williams, Roger 1510
Williams, Scott 1510
Williams, Scott E. 1510
Williams, Serena Jameke 1510
Williams, Sheila 1510
Williams, Simon 1510
Williams, Steve 1510
Williams, Suzanne 1510
Williams, Ted 1510
Williams, Vanessa 1510
Williams, Venus 1510
Williams, W. 1510
Williams, Walt 1510
Williams, Walter Jon 1510
Williams, Wendy Melissa 1510

ウィリアムズ
Willams, Steve 1506
Willams, Trevor 1506
William, Serena 1507
Williams, Alan 1507
Williams, Amy 1507
Williams, Andy 1507
Williams, Anthony 1507
Williams, Anthony D. 1507
Williams, A.R. 1507
Williams, Art 1507
Williams, Ashley 1507
Williams, Bernard 1507
Williams, Bernard, Ⅲ 1507
Williams, Bernie 1507
Williams, Betty 1507
Williams, Bill 1507
Williams, Brian 1507
Williams, Brian James 1507
Williams, Bronwyn 1507
Williams, Camilla 1507
Williams, Caroline 1507
Williams, Caroline S. 1507
Williams, Cathy 1507
Williams, Charlie 1507
Williams, Chester 1507
Williams, China 1507
Williams, Chris 1507
Williams, Christania 1507
Williams, Christopher G. 1507
Williams, C.J. 1507
Williams, Cliff 1507
Williams, Clyde 1507
Williams, Corliss Elizabeth 1507
Williams, Craig 1507
Williams, Daniel 1507
Williams, Daniel Gwyn 1507
Williams, Darrent 1507
Williams, Daryl 1507
Williams, David 1507
Williams, David Glyndwr Tudor 1507
Williams, Dean 1507
Williams, Debbie 1507
Williams, Deron 1508
Williams, Derrick 1508
Williams, Dick 1508
Williams, Donna 1508
Williams, Earl 1508
Williams, Earl George 1508
Williams, Eliud 1508
Williams, Elizabeth 1508
Williams, Elizabeth Friar 1508
Williams, Elliot 1508
Williams, Emma 1508
Williams, Eric 1508
Williams, Esther 1508
Williams, Evan 1508
Williams, Evan B. 1508
Williams, Florence 1508
Williams, F.Mary 1508
Williams, Frank 1508
Williams, Freddie E., Ⅱ 1508
Williams, Gary A. 1508
Williams, Geoffrey 1508
Williams, George C. 1508
Williams, George Christopher 1508
Williams, Gianna 1508
Williams, Hank 1508
Williams, Harvey G. 1508
Williams, Heather Andrea 1508
Williams, Ian 1508
Williams, Jackson 1508
Williams, Janet B.W. 1508
Williams, Jason 1508
Williams, Jenny 1508
Williams, Jessica 1508
Williams, J.H., Ⅲ 1508
Williams, J.Mark G. 1508
Williams, Jody 1508
Williams, Joe 1508
Williams, John 1508
Williams, John-Paul 1508
Williams, John Tyerman 1508
Williams, Joseph M. 1508
Williams, Joss 1508
Williams, Joy 1508
Williams, Judith 1508
Williams, Judy 1508
Williams, Justin, Sr. 1509
Williams, Karen Lynn 1509
Williams, KaShamba 1509
Williams, Kevin 1509
Williams, Kimberly 1509
Williams, Kristjana S. 1509
Williams, Larry R. 1509
Williams, Laura 1509
Williams, Laura E. 1509
Williams, Laurie 1509
Williams, Lauryn 1509
Williams, Liam 1509
Williams, Lloyd 1509
Williams, Louis 1509
Williams, Maiya 1509
Williams, Mark 1509
Williams, Mark A. 1509
Williams, Mark London 1509
Williams, Marvin 1509
Williams, Mary Beth 1509
Williams, Mason 1509
Williams, Meg Harris 1509
Williams, Meredith 1509
Williams, Merryn 1509
Williams, Michael 1509
Williams, Michelle 1509
Williams, Mickey 1509
Williams, Nancy 1509
Williams, Niall 1509
Williams, Nick 1509
Williams, Nicola 1509
Williams, P. 1509
Williams, Pat 1509
Williams, Paul 1509
Williams, Penny 1509
Williams, Pete 1509
Williams, Philip 1509
Williams, Rachel 1509
Williams, Richard 1509
Williams, Rob 1509
Williams, Robert 1510
Williams, Robert Joseph Paton 1510
Williams, Robin 1510
Williams, Rodney 1510
Williams, Roger 1510
Williams, Rowan Douglas 1510
Williams, Roy H. 1510
Williams, Sam 1510
Williams, Scott 1510
Williams, Sean 1510
Williams, Serena Jameke 1510
Williams, Shericka 1510
Williams, Skip 1510
Williams, Sonia 1510
Williams, Sonny Bill 1510
Williams, Stanley 1510
Williams, Stephanie 1510
Williams, Stephen P. 1510
Williams, Susan 1510
Williams, Suzanne 1510
Williams, Tad 1510
Williams, Taylor 1510
Williams, Ted 1510
Williams, Terry Moses 1510
Williams, Tim 1510
Williams, Timothy 1510
Williams, Troy 1510
Williams, Ursula Moray 1510
Williams, V. 1510
Williams, Val 1510
Williams, Venus 1510
Williams, Vera B. 1510
Williams, Walter Jon 1510
Williams, Wesley M. 1510
Williams, William J. 1510
Williams, Winston 1510
Williams, W.Larry 1511
Williams-darling, Tonique 1511

ウイリアムス
Williams, Aaron 1507
Williams, Andre 1507
Williams, Antwione 1507
Williams, Brandon 1507
Williams, Bryce 1507
Williams, Damien 1507
Williams, Dan 1507
Williams, Darrell 1507
Williams, Daryl 1507
Williams, DeAngelo 1507
Williams, DeShawn 1508
Williams, Dom 1508
Williams, Dominique 1508
Williams, Donovan 1508
Williams, Duke 1508
Williams, Ed 1508
Williams, Frankie 1508
Williams, Garry 1508
Williams, Gregg 1508
Williams, Isaiah 1508
Williams, Ishaq 1508
Williams, Jonathan 1508
Williams, Kasen 1509
Williams, Kerwynn 1509
Williams, Kyle 1509
Williams, Leonard 1509
Williams, Marcus 1509
Williams, Mario 1509
Williams, Marquise 1509
Williams, Maxx 1509
Williams, Michael 1509
Williams, Mike 1509
Williams, P.J. 1509
Williams, Shawn 1510
Williams, Steve 1510
Williams, Sylvester 1510
Williams, Teddy 1510
Williams, Terrance 1510
Williams, Terry 1510
Williams, Tourek 1510
Williams, Tramon 1510
Williams, Trent 1510
Williams, Trevor 1510
Williams, Trey 1510
Williams, Tyrell 1510
Williams, Vanessa 1510
Williams, Vince 1510
Williams, Wendall 1510
Williams, Xavier 1511

ウイリアムズ
Williams, Anne Douglas 1507
Williams, Art 1507
Williams, Brian 1507
Williams, Hywel 1508
Williams, Kathryn 1509
Williams, Margaret 1509
Williams, Nancy Rothenberg 1509
Williams, Paul L. 1509
Williams, Peter 1509
Williams, Robert R. 1510

ウィリアムス・アガセ
Williams Agasse, Vicente 1511

ウィリアムズ＝ガルシア
Williams-Garcia, Rita 1511

ウィリアム・スタイグ
Steig, William 1345

ウィリアムズミルズ
Williams-mills, Novlene 1511

ウィリアムスン
Williamson, Jack 1511
Williamson, Sheri 1511

ウィリアムソン
Williamson, Alison 1511
Williamson, Casper 1511
Williamson, Corliss 1511
Williamson, Darold 1511
Williamson, David P. 1511
Williamson, Gordon 1511
Williamson, Gwyneth 1511
Williamson, Hugh Godfrey Maturin 1511

Williamson, Ian 1511
Williamson, Jack 1511
Williamson, Jeffrey G. 1511
Williamson, Jo 1511
Williamson, John 1511
Williamson, Karen 1511
Williamson, Lamar 1511
Williamson, Leslie Anne 1511
Williamson, Mac 1511
Williamson, Marianne 1511
Williamson, Melanie 1511
Williamson, Michael 1511
Williamson, Michael S. 1511
Williamson, Nicol 1511
Williamson, Oliver Eaton 1511
Williamson, Penelope 1511
Williamson, Peter J. 1511
Williamson, Peter S. 1511
Williamson, Piers R. 1511
Williamson, Stephen D. 1511

ウイリアムソン
Williamson, Andrew 1511
Williamson, Avery 1511
Williamson, Marianne 1511

ウィリアモン
Williamon, Aaron 1507

ウィリアン
Willian Jose 1511

ウィリアン・ジョゼ
Willian Jose 1511

ヴィリィ
Willi, Jürg 1507

ヴィリエ
Villiers, Gérard de 1458

ウィリグ
Willig, Lauren 1511

ウィリ・コロファイ
Uili Kolo'ofai 1432

ウィリス
Willis, Andrew 1511
Willis, Bruce 1511
Willis, Bryan 1511
Willis, Christine 1511
Willis, Christopher 1511
Willis, Clint 1511
Willis, Connie 1511
Willis, Ellen 1511
Willis, Ethan 1511
Willis, Gordon 1511
Willis, Jane 1511
Willis, Jeanne 1511
Willis, Jim 1511
Willis, Kimberly 1511
Willis, Lynn 1511
Willis, Mariaemma 1511
Willis, Nicholas 1511
Willis, Norman David 1512
Willis, Patty Christiena 1512
Willis, Paul 1512
Willis, Sarah 1512
Willis, Will 1512

ウイリス
Willis, Kathy 1511

ウィリッグ
Willing, Carla 1511

ヴィリナック
Vilinac, Doragana 1457

ウィリー"パイントップ"パーキンス
Willie "Pinetop" Perkins, Joe 1511

ウイリムス
Wilmoth, John R. 1512

ウィリモブスキー
Wilimovsky, Jordan 1505

ウィリモン
Willimon, William H. 1511

ヴィリリオ
Virilio, Paul 1459

ウィリン
Willin, Melvyn J. 1511

ヴィリーン
Verene, Donald Phillip 1452

ウィリンギ
Wiringi, Michael 1518

ウィーリング
Wierling, Damian 1502

ウィリング
Willing, R.Duane 1511

ウィリンスキー
Wilensky, Amy 1505

ウィール
Weal, John A. 1484
Weale, Anne 1484
Wiehl, Lis W. 1502

ウィル
Lipkind, William 833
Will 1506
Will, Frazer 1506
Will, George F. 1506

ヴィール
Veal, Michael E. 1449
Wiehle, Katrin 1502

ヴィル
Ville, Simon P. 1457

ウィル・アイ・アム
will.i.am 1507

ヴィルアルドゥワン
Villehardouin, Geoffroi de 1457

ウィルカースン
Wilkerson, Isabel 1505
Wilkerson, James A. 1505

ウィルカーソン
Wilkerson, Muhammad 1505

ウィルキー
Wilkie, William 1505

ウィルキン
Wilkin, Karen 1505
Wilkin, Sam 1505

ウィルキンス
Wilkens, Katy G. 1505
Wilkins, Ben 1505
Wilkins, Bill 1505
Wilkins, Esther M. 1505
Wilkins, Marne 1505
Wilkins, Maurice Hugh Frederick 1505
Wilkins, Mira 1505

ウィルキンズ
Wilkins, Celia 1505
Wilkins, Gina 1505
Wilkins, Maurice 1505
Wilkins, Maurice Hugh Frederick 1505
Wilkins, Richard 1506
Wilkins, W. 1506

ウィルキンソン
Wilkinson, Amy 1506
Wilkinson, Beth 1506
Wilkinson, Bruce 1506
Wilkinson, Carole 1506
Wilkinson, Christopher 1506
Wilkinson, Darlene 1506
Wilkinson, David M. 1506
Wilkinson, Grant R. 1506
Wilkinson, Greg 1506
Wilkinson, Jill 1506
Wilkinson, Jonny 1506
Wilkinson, Julia 1506
Wilkinson, Karen 1506
Wilkinson, Kate 1506
Wilkinson, Laura 1506
Wilkinson, Lee 1506
Wilkinson, Mark 1506
Wilkinson, Paul 1506
Wilkinson, Philip 1506
Wilkinson, Richard G. 1506
Wilkinson, Richard H. 1506
Wilkinson, Roy 1506
Wilkinson, Toby A.H. 1506
Wilkinson, Tom 1506
Wilkinson, Tony J. 1506

ウイルキンソン
Wilkinson, I.M.S. 1506
Wilkinson, Tracy 1506

ウィルク
Wilk, Adam 1505
Wilk, Brad 1505
Wilk, Kevin E. 1505

ウィルクス
Wilkes, Joseph E. 1505
Wilkes, Maria D. 1505
Wilkes, Maurice Vincent 1505
Wilkes, Paget 1505
Wilkes, Rich 1505
Wilks, Eileen 1506
Wilks, Mike 1506

ウィルクソン
Wilkeson, Leon 1505

ウィルケ
Wilke, Manfred 1505

ヴィルケ
Wilke, Anna 1505

ウィルケン
Wilken, Robert Louis 1505

ウィルケンズ
Wilkens, Todd 1505

ヴィルケンス
Wilckens, Ulrich 1504
Wilkens, Johannes 1505

ウィルコクス
Wilcox, Mark 1504

ウィルコック
Wilcock, Andrew 1504
Wilcock, David 1504
Willcock, David 1506

ウィルコックス
Wilcox, Annie Tremmel 1504
Wilcox, Bob 1504
Wilcox, Brett 1504
Wilcox, Charlotte 1504
Wilcox, C.J. 1504
Wilcox, J.J. 1504
Wilcox, Leigh Attaway 1504
Wilcox, Michael 1504
Wilcox, Peter 1504
Wilcox, Sherman 1504
Wilcox, Tina Marie 1504
Wilcox, Wes 1504
Willcocks, David James 1506
Willcox, Bradley J. 1506
Willcox, Daniel 1506
Willcox, D.Craig 1506

ウィルコブ
Wilcove, David S. 1504

ヴィルコン
Wilkón, Józef 1506

ヴィルコンドレ
Vircondelet, Alain 1459

ヴィルサック
Vilsack, Tom 1458

ヴィルサラーゼ
Virsaladze, Elisso 1459

ウィルシー
Wilsey, Sean 1512

ウィルジェン
Wildgen, Michelle 1504

ウィルシャー
Wilshere, Jack 1512

ウィルジャー
Wiltjer, Kyle 1515

ウィルス
Wilce, Ysabeau S. 1504
Willis, Carl 1511
Wills, Frank 1512
Wills, Garry 1512
Wills, Josh 1512
Wills, Margaret Sabo 1512

ウィルズ
Wills, Adrian 1512
Wills, Charles 1512
Wills, Christopher 1512
Wills, David 1512
Wills, Garry 1512
Wills, Howard 1512
Wills, John Elliot 1512

ウィルスドルフ
Wilsdorf, Anne 1512

ウィルスン
Wilson, Allister 1512
Wilson, Deirdre 1513
Wilson, F.Paul 1513
Wilson, John M. 1513
Wilson, Peter Hamish 1514
Wilson, Robert 1514
Wilson, Robert Anton 1514
Wilson, Robert Charles 1514

ヴィルセン
Wirsén, Carin 1518
Wirsén, Stina 1518

ウィルソン
Willson, C.Grant 1512
Willson, Chris 1512
Willson, Sarah 1512
Willson, Thomas 1512
Wilson, Al 1512
Wilson, Alex 1512
Wilson, Alexandra Wilkis 1512
Wilson, Amy Howard 1512
Wilson, A.N. 1512
Wilson, Andrew 1512
Wilson, Angus 1512
Wilson, Anthony 1512
Wilson, August 1512
Wilson, Barbara A. 1512
Wilson, Barbara Ker 1512
Wilson, Barrie A. 1512
Wilson, Bee 1512
Wilson, Bill 1512

Wilson, Brendan 1512
Wilson, Brent G. 1512
Wilson, Brian 1512
Wilson, Brian C. 1512
Wilson, Bryan R. 1512
Wilson, Bryon 1512
Wilson, Budge 1512
Wilson, Callum 1512
Wilson, Cassandra 1512
Wilson, Charles 1513
Wilson, Charlie 1513
Wilson, Christopher 1513
Wilson, C.J. 1513
Wilson, Colin 1513
Wilson, Damon 1513
Wilson, Dan 1513
Wilson, Daniel Howard 1513
Wilson, David 1513
Wilson, David Sloan 1513
Wilson, Don 1513
Wilson, Donald Alan 1513
Wilson, Don E. 1513
Wilson, Earl 1513
Wilson, Ed 1513
Wilson, Edward Osborne 1513
Wilson, Eliane 1513
Wilson, Elizabeth 1513
Wilson, Elwin 1513
Wilson, Frank R. 1513
Wilson, Fred 1513
Wilson, Gayle 1513
Wilson, Geoff J. 1513
Wilson, George Macklin 1513
Wilson, Georges 1513
Wilson, Gerald Stanley 1513
Wilson, Glenn Daniel 1513
Wilson, Graeme 1513
Wilson, Grant 1513
Wilson, Greg 1513
Wilson, Gretchen 1513
Wilson, G.Willow 1513
Wilson, Hannah 1513
Wilson, Helen 1513
Wilson, Henrike 1513
Wilson, H.James 1513
Wilson, Iain 1513
Wilson, Jacqueline 1513
Wilson, James E. 1513
Wilson, James L. 1513
Wilson, Jeni 1513
Wilson, Jeremy 1513
Wilson, Jim R. 1513
Wilson, John 1513
Wilson, Jonathan 1513
Wilson, Judith 1513
Wilson, Justin 1513
Wilson, Kane 1513
Wilson, Karma 1513
Wilson, Kelly G. 1513
Wilson, Kemmons 1513
Wilson, Kendra 1514
Wilson, Kenneth Geddes 1514
Wilson, Kevin 1514
Wilson, Lanford 1514
Wilson, Laura 1514
Wilson, Leanna 1514
Wilson, Lesley 1514
Wilson, Madison 1514
Wilson, Marc 1514
Wilson, Margaret 1514
Wilson, Margo 1514
Wilson, Marvin R. 1514
Wilson, Mary 1514
Wilson, Mary Anne 1514
Wilson, Mary Louise 1514
Wilson, Michael 1514
Wilson, Michael Henry 1514
Wilson, Nancy 1514
Wilson, Nancy Hope 1514
Wilson, Nancy J. 1514
Wilson, Nathan D. 1514
Wilson, Nile 1514
Wilson, Nona 1514
Wilson, Norman James 1514
Wilson, Opal V. 1514
Wilson, Owen 1514
Wilson, Patricia 1514
Wilson, Paul 1514
Wilson, Pelham Mark Hedley 1514
Wilson, Penelope 1514
Wilson, Peter 1514
Wilson, Peter Colin 1514
Wilson, Peter Lamborn 1514
Wilson, Phil 1514
Wilson, Pippa 1514
Wilson, Ralph F. 1514
Wilson, Robert Anton 1514
Wilson, Robert Charles 1514
Wilson, Robert J. 1514
Wilson, Robert M. 1514
Wilson, Robert Reid 1514
Wilson, Robin J. 1514
Wilson, Robley 1514
Wilson, Russell 1514
Wilson, Ruth 1514
Wilson, Ryan 1514
Wilson, Sally 1514
Wilson, Sandy 1514
Wilson, Sarah 1514
Wilson, Scarlet 1514
Wilson, Scott 1514
Wilson, Simon 1514
Wilson, Sloan 1514
Wilson, Steve 1514
Wilson, Ted N.C. 1514
Wilson, Timothy D. 1514
Wilson, Tony 1514, 1515
Wilson, Tyler 1515
Wilson, Valerie Plame 1515
Wilson, Ward 1515

ウイルソン
Willson, Albert 1512
Willson, C.Grant 1512
Willson, Luke 1512
Wilson, C.J. 1513
Wilson, Damien 1513
Wilson, David G., Ⅲ 1513
Wilson, Gahan 1513
Wilson, Glenn Daniel 1513
Wilson, Holly Skodol 1513
Wilson, Jarrod 1513
Wilson, Jimmy 1513
Wilson, Julian 1513
Wilson, Kyle 1514
Wilson, Kyrie 1514
Wilson, Mark 1514
Wilson, Marquess 1514
Wilson, Ramik 1514
Wilson, Russell 1514
Wilson, Tavon 1514
Wilson, Tracey 1515
Wilson, William Scott 1515

ウィルソン＝スミス
Wilson-Smith, Timothy 1515

ウイルソンドスーザ
Wilson De Souza, Leonardina Rita Doris 1515

ウイルソン＝ポウエルズ
Wilson-Pauwels, Linda 1515

ウィルソン・マックス
Wilson-Max, Ken 1515

ウィルソン＝リッチ
Wilson-Rich, Noah 1515

ウィルソンレイボールド
Wilson-raybould, Jody 1515

ウィルチェック
Wilczek, Frank 1504

ウィルチカム
Wilchcombe, Obediah 1504

ウィルチャ
Wilcha, Christopher 1504

ウィルチャク
Wilczak, Becky 1504

ウィルツ
Wiltse, David 1515
Wiltz, Chris 1515
Wirtz, James J. 1518
Wirtz, Jochen 1518

ウィルッカラ
Wirkkala, Teemu 1518

ウィルディング
Wilding, Mark 1504

ウィルデブール
Wildeboer Faber, Aschwin 1504

ウイルデンスタイン
Wildenstein, Daniel 1504

ウィルト
Wild, Kirsten 1504
Wilt, Val 1515

ヴィルト
Wild, Helmut 1504

ウィルトシャー
Wiltshire, Alex 1515
Wiltshire, Steve 1515

ヴィルトナー
Wildner, Martina 1504

ウィルトベルガー
Wildberger, Jacques 1504

ヴィルトベルガー
Wildberger, Jacques 1504

ウィルドルフ
Willdorf, Nina 1506

ウィールドン
Wheeldon, Christopher 1496

ウィルトン
Wilton, Penelope 1515

ヴィルヌーヴ
Villeneuve, Claude 1457
Villeneuve, Estelle 1457
Villeneuve, Jacques 1457

ヴィルノ
Virno, Paolo 1459

ウィルバー
Wilber, Ken 1503
Wilber, Kyle 1503
Wilbur, Richard 1503

ウィルハイド
Wilhide, Elizabeth 1505

ウィルバーカー
Weilbacher, Lukner 1488

ウィルパーズ
Wilpers, John, Jr. 1512

ウィルバーン
Wilburn, Teddy 1504

ウィルファート
Wilfert, Bryon 1505

ウィルフォーク
Wilfork, Vince 1505

ウィルフォード
Wilford, D.Sykes 1505
Wilford, John Noble 1505
Wilford, Michael 1505
Willeford, William 1506

ウィルフリィ
Wilfley, Denise E. 1505

ウィルフレッドマディウス
Wilfred Madius, Tangau 1505

ヴィルヘルミー＝ドリンガー
Wilhelmy-Dollinger, Petra 1505

ウィルヘルム
Wilhelm, Hoyt 1505
Wilhelm, Kati 1505
Wilhelm, Maria 1505
Wilhelm, Mike 1505
Wilhelm, Paul J. 1505
Wilhelm, Toni 1505

ウイルヘルム
Wilhelm, Kate 1505

ヴィルヘルム
Wilheim, Karin 1505
Wilhelm, Hans 1505

ウィルヘルムセン
Wilhelmsen, Tom 1505

ウィルヘルムソン
Vilhelmson-silfven, Tinne 1457

ウィルホイティー
Wilhoite, Michael 1505

ウィルポン
Wilpon, Fred 1512

ヴィルマー
Vilmur, Peter 1458

ウィルマット
Wilmut, Ian 1512

ウィルマン
Willemin, Véronique 1506
Willman, Paul 1512

ヴィルマン
Villemant, Claire 1457

ウィルムス
Wilms, Sven 1512

ウィルムスタッド
Willumstad, Robert B. 1512

ウィルメス
Wilmès, Sophie 1512

ウィルモア
Willmore, Joe 1512

ウイルモア
Willmore, Ben 1512

ウィルモッツ
Wilmots, Marc 1512

ヴィルモッツ
Wilmots, Marc 1512

ウィルモット
Willmott, Aimee 1512
Willmott, H.P. 1512
Willmott, Hugh 1512
Wilmot, Nathan 1512
Wilmot, William W. 1512

Wilmott, Paul 1512
ウィールライト
Wheelwright, Steven C. 1497
ヴィレガス
Villegas, Anna Tuttle 1457
ヴィーレック
Viereck, Peter 1456
ウィレッツ
Willetts, Lucy 1507
ウィレット
Ouellette, Raymond 1064
Willett, Albert V. 1506
Willett, Danny 1506
Willett, James 1506
Willett, John B. 1506
Willett, Walter C. 1506
ウィレドゥ
Wiredu, Kwadjo Baah 1517
ウィレム
Willem 1506
ウイレム
Wuilleme, Adeline 1530
ヴィレーム
Willaime, Jean-Paul 1506
ウィレム・アレキサンダー
Willem-Alexander, King 1506
ウィレム・アレクサンダー国王
Willem-Alexander, King 1506
ウィレム・アレクサンデル
Willem-Alexander, King 1506
ウィレムス
Willems, Jetro 1506
ウィレムズ
Willems, Mo 1506
ヴィレル
Villers, Jean-Pierre Andreoli de 1458
ウィレンズ
Wilens, Timote 1505
Wilens, Timothy E. 1505
ウィレンツ
Wilentz, Sean 1505
ヴィレンバッハー
Willenbacher, Matthias 1506
ウィレンブリンク
Willenbrink, Mark 1506
Willenbrink, Mary 1506
ヴィレンベルク
Willenberg, Samuel 1506
ウィーロック
Wheelock, Martha 1497
ヴィロティッチ
Vilotic, Milan 1458
ウィロビー
Willoughby, Bob 1512
Willoughby, Sam 1512
ヴィローリ
Viroli, Maurizio 1459
ヴィロル
Virole, Benoit 1459
ウィーン
Wheen, Francis 1497
ウィン
Winn, Billy 1516
Winn, George 1516
Winn, Steven 1516
Wyne, Ali 1531
Wynn, Adam 1531
Wynn, Charles M. 1531
Wynn, Dylan 1531
Wynn, Eric 1531
Wynn, Garrison 1531
Wynn, Kerry 1531
Wynn, Steve 1531
Wynne, Ian 1531
Wynne, Marcus 1531
Wynne, Patricia 1531
Wynne, Patricia J. 1531
ウイン
Winn, Bonnie K. 1516
Wynn, Shane 1531
Wynne, Frank 1531
ヴィーン
Veen, Jeffrey 1449
ウィン・アウン
Win Aung 1515
ウィンウッド
Winwood, Steve 1517
ウィンカー
Winker, Jesse 1516
Winkler, Daniel 1516
ウィンガー
Winger, Debra 1516
ウィン・カイン
Win Khaing 1516
ウィンガーター
Wingerter, Linda S. 1516
ウィンク
Wink, Walter 1516
ウィング
Wing, Brad 1515
Wing, Craig 1516
Wing, Lorna 1516
ウィング・ジャン
Wing Jan, Lesley 1516
ウィンクス
Winks, Harry 1516
ウィングフィールド
Wingfield, Gorge 1516
Wingfield, R.D. 1516
ウィンクラー
Winkler, Beate 1516
Winkler, Conrad 1516
Winkler, Donald 1516
Winkler, Gershon 1516
Winkler, Josef 1516
Winkler, Kathleen 1516
Winkler, Kati 1516
Winkler, Marion F. 1516
Winkler, Peter 1516
ヴィンクラー
Winkler, Franz 1516
Winkler, Heinrich August 1516
Winkler, Josef 1516
ウィンクルマン
Winkelmann, Kurt 1516
ウィンゲート
Wingate, John 1516
ウィンケルヘフェロヴァー
Winkelhoferova, Vlasta 1516
ウィンサー
Winser, Kim 1516
ウィンザー
Windsor, Alan 1515
Winser, Kim 1516
Winsor, Janice 1516
ウインザー
Winser, Kim 1516
ヴィンサー
Vincer, Carole 1458
ウインサビ
Ouinsavi, Christine 1064
ヴィンジ
Vinge, Vernor 1458
ウィン・シェイン
Win Shein 1516
ウィンジェル
Wingell, Richard 1516
ウィンシップ
Winship, Thomas 1516
ウィンシャーマン
Winschermann, Helmut 1516
ヴィンシャーマン
Winschermann, Helmut 1516
ヴィンシャマン
Winschermann, Helmut 1516
ヴィンジャムリ
Vinjamuri, David 1458
ヴィンシュルス
Winshluss 1516
ウィンス
Wyss, Hansjörg 1531
ヴィンス
Vince, Gaia 1458
ウィンストン
Whinston, Andrew B. 1497
Winston, Andrew S. 1516
Winston, Anne Marie 1516
Winston, Arnold 1516
Winston, David 1516
Winston, Eric 1516
Winston, Jameis 1517
Winston, Judith E. 1517
Winston, Lolly 1517
Winston, Mark L. 1517
Winston, Patrick Henry 1517
Winston, Robert M. L. 1517
Winston, Ronald 1517
Winston, Shirley Rabb 1517
Winston, Stan 1517
Winston, Stephanie 1517
ウインストン
Winston, Glenn 1516
ウィンスパー
Winspur, Ian 1516
ウィンスピア
Winspear, Jacqueline 1516
ウインスラー
Winsler, Adam 1516
ウィンズレイド
Winslade, John 1516
ウィンスレット
Winslet, Kate 1516
ウインスレット
Winslet, Kate 1516
ウィンズロー
Winslow, Emily R. 1516
Winslow, Justise 1516
ウインズロー
Winslow, Darcy 1516
ウィンスロゥ
Winslow, Valerie L. 1516
ウィンズロウ
Winslow, Don 1516
ウィンスロップ
Winthrop, Simon 1517
ウィン・セイン
Win Sein 1516
ヴィンセック
Wiencek, Henry 1502
ウィンセミウス
Winsemius, Pieter 1516
ヴィンセンツォーニ
Vincenzoni, Luciano 1458
ヴィンセンティ
Vincenti, Virginia Bramble 1458
ヴィンセンテリ
Vincentelli, Elisabeth 1458
ヴィンセント
Vicente, Mark 1455
Vincent, Andrew 1458
Vincent, Charles A. 1458
Vincent, David 1458
Vincent, Gina M. 1458
Vincent, Karyn D. 1458
Vincent, Lynn 1458
Vincent, Mary 1458
ヴィンソン
Vinson, Fred 1459
Vinson, James 1459
ウィンター
Winter, Ariel S. 1517
Winter, Douglas E. 1517
Winter, Harold 1517
Winter, Henry 1517
Winter, Jeanette 1517
Winter, Johnny 1517
Winter, Jonah 1517
Winter, Miriam Therese 1517
Winter, Paul 1517
Winter, Paul C. 1517
Winter, Ralph D. 1517
Winter, Scott A. 1517
Winter, Sidney G. 1517
Winter, Steve 1517
Winter, Susan 1517
Winter, Tex 1517
Wintour, Anna 1517
ウインター
Winter, Johnny 1517
Winter, Michael F. 1517
ヴィンター
Winter, Detlev G. 1517
Winter, Michael 1517
ヴィンターコルン
Winterkorn, Martin 1517
ヴィンターコーン
Winterkorn, Martin 1517
ウィンタース
Winters, Ben H. 1517
Winters, Brian 1517
Winters, Jonathan 1517
Winters, Nancy C. 1517
Winters, Rose 1517
Winters, Shelley 1517
ウィンターズ
Winters, Catherine 1517
Winters, Eden 1517
Winters, Jason 1517
Winters, Jonathan 1517
Winters, Nancy 1517
Winters, Shelley 1517
ウインターズ
Winters, Rebecca 1517
ウィンタースン
Winterson, Jeanette 1517
ウィンターソン
Winterson, Jeanette 1517

ウインタハ								
	Winterson, Julia	1517	ヴェアテマン			ウエイス		
ヴィンターハーガー				Werthemann, Helene	1494		Weiss, K.F.B.	1490
	Winterhager, Daniele	1517	ヴェアベック			ウェイズボード		
ヴィンターベア				Werbeck, Barbara	1493		Weisbord, Merrily	1489
	Vinterberg, Thomas	1459	ウェアラム			ウェイスマン		
ウィンターボトム				Wareham, John	1478		Wuissman, David	1530
	Winterbottom, Michael	1517	ウェアリン			ウェイゼス		
	Winterbottom, Walter	1517		Wearin, Otha Donner	1484		Weisaeth, Lars	1489
ウインターボトム			ウェアリング			ウェイターズ		
	Winterbottom, Walter	1517		Waring, Richard	1478		Waiters, Dion	1468
ヴィンターホフ				Wearing, Deborah	1484	ウェイツ		
	Winterhoff, Michael	1517	ヴェアンブローム				Waites, Junee	1468
ウィンダム				Wernbloom, Pontus	1493		Waits, Tom	1468
	Windham, Ryder	1515	ウェイ				Weitz, Chris	1490
	Wyndham, Jeremy	1531		Way, Daniel	1484		Weitz, Paul	1490
ウィンチ				Way, Gerard	1484	ウェイツキン		
	Winch, Donald	1515		Way, Griffith	1484		Waitzkin, Fred	1468
	Winch, Guy	1515		Way, Margaret	1484		Waitzkin, Josh	1468
	Winch, Peter	1515		Way, Tress	1484	ヴェイティーズワラン		
ヴィンチ				Wei, David	1487		Vaitheeswaran, Vijay V.	1438
	Vinci, Simona	1458		Wei, Fu-hai	1487			
ウィンチェスター				Wei, George	1487	ウェイト		
	Winchester, James	1515		Wei, Jianjun	1487		Wait, Lea	1468
	Winchester, Jim	1515		Wei, Jian-xing	1487		Waite, Polly	1468
	Winchester, Robert J.	1515		Wei, Jing-sheng	1487		Waite, Ric	1468
				Wei, Te-sheng	1487		Waite, Robert G.L.	1468
	Winchester, Simon	1515		Wei-hui	1487		Waite, Thomas J.	1468
ウインチェスター			ウェイ				Waite, Urban	1468
	Winchester, Kent	1515		Wei, Fu-hai	1487	ウェイド		
ウィンチェル			ウェイアンズ				Wade, Dwyane	1466
	Winchell, Paul	1515		Wayans, Marlon	1484		Wade, Kevin	1466
ヴィンチェンツォ				Wayans, Shawn	1484		Wade, Leroy G., Jr.	1466
	Vincenzo, Mark Di	1458	ウェイウェイオール				Wade, Mark	1466
ヴィンチェンツォーニ				Waiwaiole, Lono	1468		Wade, Nicholas	1466
	Vincenzoni, Luciano	1458	ヴェイエルガンス				Wade, Rosalyn	1466
ヴィンチェンティ				Weyergans, François	1496		Wade, Trevin	1466
	Vincenti, Antonio	1458	ウェイガー				Wade, Woody	1466
ウィンツ				Weiger, Wendy A.	1487		Waid, Mark	1468
	Wintz, Jack	1517	ヴェイガン			ウェイド＝マシューズ		
ウィン・ティン				Weygand, Zina	1496		Wade-Matthews, Max	1466
	Win Tin	1517	ウェイガント					
ヴィンディング				Weygant, Peter	1496	ウェイトマン		
	Winding, Thomas	1515	ウェイク				Weightman, Laura	1487
ウィント				Wake, Cameron	1468	ウェイドマン		
	Windt, Mike	1515		Wake, Marvalee H.	1469		Wademan, Daisy	1466
ウィンド				Wake, William C.	1469	ウェイトリー		
	Wind, Gary G.	1515		Weick, Karl E.	1487		Waitley, Denis	1468
	Wind, Yoram "Jerry"	1515	ウェイクセル				Whately, Alice	1496
ウィンド				Weixel, L.J.	1490	ヴェイドン		
	Wind, Herbert Warren	1515	ウェイクフィールド				Vadon, Mark	1438
				Wakefield, Darcy	1469	ウェイナー		
	Wind, Ruth	1515		Wakefield, Graham	1469		Wayner, Peter	1484
ウィンドウォーカー				Wakefield, Jerome C.	1469		Weiner, Eric J.	1488
	Windwalker, Stephen	1515		Wakefield, Michael	1469		Weiner, Jennifer	1488
ウィン・トゥン				Wakefield, Richard J.	1469		Weiner, Jessie Kanelos	1488
	Win Tun	1517	ウェイクフォード					
ヴィントガッセン				Wakeford, Tom	1469	ヴェイナチャック		
	Windgassen, Antje	1515	ウェイクリン				Vaynerchuk, Gary	1449
ヴィントフォルスト				Wakelin, Derek	1469	ウェイバー		
	Windhorst, Hans-Wilhelm	1515		Wakelin, Martyn Francis	1469		Waber, Ben	1466
						ウェイバーマン		
ウィンドリング			ウェイゲル				Waverman, Leonard	1483
	Windling, Terri	1515		Wagele, Elizabeth	1467	ウェイバリー		
ウィンドロウ				Weigel, Jonathan	1487		Waverly, Shannon	1483
	Windrow, Martin	1515	ウェイジャー			ウェイフェイ		
ウィントン				Wager, Walter W.	1467		Wei-hui	1487
	Winton, Mark A.	1517	ウェイジンガー			ウェイブレクト		
	Winton, Nicholas	1517		Weisinger, Hendrie	1489		Weibrecht, Andrew	1487
	Winton, Tim	1517	ウェイス			ウェイマン		
ウィンナー				Weiss, Glenn	1490		Weymann, Eduardo	1496
	Winner, Paul	1516		Weiss, Lizzy	1490	ヴェイユ		
				Weiss, Mitch	1490		Veil, Simone	1450
				Weiss, Ra'anan	1490		Weil, Sylvie	1488
							Weill, Alain	1488

ウィンバーグ
　Wijnberg, Jeffrey 1503
ウィンブラッド
　Winblad, Ann 1515
　Wiinblad, Bjorn 1503
ウィンフリー
　Winfrey, Oprah 1515
ウィン・ペリー
　Wynn Parry, Christopher B. 1531
ヴィンベルク
　Vinberg, Ernest Borisovich 1458
ヴィーンホヴェン
　Veenhoven, Ruut 1449
ウィンボーン
　Winborne, Hughes 1515
ウィン・ミャ・エー
　Win Myat Aye 1516
ウィン・ミン
　Win Myat Aye 1516
ヴィンヤード
　Vineyard, Ben S. 1458
　Vineyard, Jeremy 1458
ヴィンランド
　Windland, Ida Falk 1515
ヴィンルンド
　Winlund, Gunnel 1516
ウィンレンツェク
　Wylenzek, Tomasz 1530
ウヴァーロフ
　Uvarov, Andrei 1437
ウウィゼイエ
　Uwizeye, Judith 1437
ウ・ウィン・アウン
　Win Aung 1515
ウウナプー
　Õunapuu, Harri 1064
ウウナプー
　Õunapuu, Jaan 1064
ウヴネース・モーベリ
　Uvnäs-Moberg, Kerstin 1437
ウエ
　Heuet, Stéphane 602
　Huet, Nicolas 632
ウェーア
　Wehr, Demaris S. 1487
ウェア
　Ware, Alyn 1478
　Ware, Bronnie 1478
　Ware, Casper 1478
　Ware, Chris 1478
　Ware, Jim 1478
　Ware, Pamela 1478
　Weah, George 1484
　Wear, Travis 1484
　Weir, Johnny 1489
ウェアー
　Ware, DeMarcus 1478
　Ware, Spencer 1478
　Weir, Johnny 1489
ウエア
　Weah, George 1484
ヴェア
　Vare, Ethlie Ann 1446
ウェアアリー
　Uea-aree, Attapon 1432
ヴェアシュア
　Verschuer, Charlotte von 1454

ヴェイヨン
Veillon, Béatrice 1450
ウェイラー
Weyler, Javier 1496
ウェイラム
Whalum, Kirk 1496
ウェイラン
Whalen, Rob 1496
ウェイランド
Weiland, Matt 1488
ウェイリー
Whaley, Lindsay J. 1496
ウェイリッチ
Weyrich, Paul 1496
ヴェイリン
Valin, Jonathan 1440
ウェイル
Weil, Elizabeth Ann 1487
Weill, Peter 1488
ヴェイル
Vaile, Carilyn 1438
ウェイルベッカー
Weilbacher, Lukner 1488
ヴェイロン
Veyron, Martin 1454
ウェイン
Waine, Peter 1468
Wayne, Joanna 1484
Wayne, Lil 1484
Wayne, Michael 1484
Wein, Elizabeth 1488
Wein, Len 1488
Weyn, Suzanne 1496
ヴェイン
Vane, Howard R. 1443
Vane, John Robert 1443
ウェインガーテン
Weingarten, Gene 1488
ウェインズ
Waynes, Trae 1484
ウェインスタイン
Weinstein, Matt 1489
ウェインストック
Weinstock, Arnold 1489
ウェイントラウブ
Weintraub, Pamela 1489
ウェイントラーブ
Weintraub, Karen 1489
ウェインバーガー
Weinberger, Richard 1488
ウェインバーグ
Weinberg, George H. 1488
ウェインベルグ
Weinberg, Serge 1488
ウェインホールド
Weinhold, Kent J. 1488
ウェインライト
Wainwright, Adam 1468
Wainwright, Jen 1468
Wainwright, Loudon, Ⅲ 1468
Wainwright, Lucy 1468
Wainwright, Rufus 1468
Wainwright, Sally 1468
ウエインライト
Wainwright, Kevin 1468
ウェインラウブ
Weinraub, Judith 1489
ウエウチュゴフ
Ustiugov, Sergey 1437
ヴェガ
Vega, Louie 1449
ウェカール
Wekerle, Gerda R. 1491
ウェグジュツキ
Wegrzycki-szymczyk, Natan 1487
ウェクスナー
Wexner, Leslie 1496
ウェクスラー
Wexler, Alice 1496
Wexler, David B. 1496
Wexler, Haskel 1496
Wexler, Jerry 1496
Wexler, Lisa 1496
Wexler, Milton 1496
ウェグナー
Wegner, Fritz 1487
Wegner, Hans Jorgen 1487
Wegner, Isa 1487
Wegner, Judith Welch 1487
Wegner, Nina 1487
ヴェーグナー
Wegner, Stefanie 1487
ウェグハー
Wegher, Brandon 1487
ウェグマン
Wegman, William 1487
ヴェークラー
Wegler, Monika 1487
ウェケサ
Wekesa, Noah 1491
ヴェゲナー
Wegener, Paul 1487
Wegener, Ursula 1487
ヴェゲリウス
Wegelius, Jakob 1487
ヴェケルディ
Vekerdy, Tamás 1450
ウェザーオール
Weatherall, James Owen 1484
ウェザーズ
Weathers, Beck 1484
Weathers, Charles 1484
ウェザーストーン
Weatherstone, Dennis 1484
ウェザーストン
Weatherston, Deborah J. 1484
Weatherstone, Dennis 1484
ウェザースプーン
Weatherspoon, Sean 1484
ウェザビー
Wetherby, Amy M. 1496
ウェザーフォード
Weatherford, Carole Boston 1484
Weatherford, J. McIver 1484
ウェザフォード
Weatherford, Carole Boston 1484
ウェザーヘッド
Weatherhead, Marion 1484
ウェザリー
Weatherly, Stephen 1484
ウェザリル
Weatherill, Bernard 1484
ウエザロール
Wetherall, David J. 1496
ヴェジェスナ
Vegesna, Srinivas 1450
ヴェシエール
Vaissière, Jacqueline 1438
ヴェジビツカ
Wierzbicka, Anna 1502
ヴェシュチェク
Wieszczek-kordus, Agnieszka Jadwiga 1503
ウェシュラー
Weschler, Lawrence 1494
Weschler, Toni 1494
ヴェース
Vaes, Leon P.J. 1438
ヴェス
Vess, Charles 1454
Wess, Julius 1494
ヴェズィログル
Veziroglu, T.Nejat 1454
ウェスカー
Wesker, Arnold 1494
ヴェスカー
Wesker, Karl H. 1494
ヴェスコ
Vesco, Edi 1454
ウェスコット
Wescott, Seth 1494
ウェスター
Wester, Leonard 1495
Wester, Ture 1495
ウェスターウェレ
Westerwelle, Guido 1495
ウェスターガード
Westergaard, John 1495
ウェスタッド
Westad, Odd Arne 1495
ウエスターフェルド
Westerfeld, Scott 1495
ウェスターベルト
Westervelt, R.M. 1495
ウェスターマン
Westerman, Paul 1495
ウエスターマン
Westerman, Christian 1495
ヴェスターマン
Westerman, Frank 1495
Westermann, Heiko 1495
Westermann, Peter 1495
ウェスタン
Western, Colin 1495
ウェスティン
Westin, Boel 1495
ヴェスティング
Vesting, Thomas 1454
ウェステラ
Westera, Bette 1495
ヴェステルゴーア
Vestergaard, Jannik 1454
ウェステルヘイム
Westerheim, Malin 1495
ヴェステルマン
Westermann, Mariët 1495
ウェステン
Westen, Robin 1495
ヴェステンドルプ
Westendorp, Fiep 1495
ウェステンホファー
Westenhofer, Bill 1495
ウェスト
West, Annie 1494
West, Bing 1494
West, Cornel 1494
West, David 1494
West, Jessica Pallington 1494
West, John Burnard 1494
West, John Michael 1494
West, Kanye 1494
West, Lee 1494
West, Michael A. 1494
West, Michael Lee 1494
West, Nancy M. 1494
West, Richard 1494
West, Scott 1495
Weste, Neil H.E. 1495
ウエスト
West, Alex 1494
West, Annie 1494
West, Anthony R. 1494
West, Arch 1494
West, Beverly 1494
West, Cameron 1494
West, Charcandrick 1494
West, Christopher 1494
West, Darron L. 1494
West, David 1494
West, Janet 1494
West, Jarrod 1494
West, Jennifer 1494
West, John Burnard 1494
West, Keith R. 1494
West, Rosemary 1495
West, Sandy 1495
West, Terrance 1495
West, Tracey 1495
ヴェスト
Vest, Charles Marstiller 1454
West, Franz 1494
ウェストウッド
Westwood, J.N. 1495
Westwood, Lee 1495
Westwood, Vivienne 1495
ウエストウッド
Westwood, Lee 1495
Westwood, Vivienne 1495
ウェストコット
Westcott, Lisa 1495
Westcott, Nadine Bernard 1495
ウエストコット
Westcott, Helen L. 1495
ウエストソン
Westesson, Per-Lennart 1495
ウェストニー
Westney, D.Eleanor 1495
Westney, William 1495
ウエストニー
Westney, D.Eleanor 1495
ウェストハイマー
Westheimer, David 1495
ウェストバーグ
Westberg, Granger E. 1495
ウェストフォード
Westford, Jennifer 1495
ウェストフォール
Westfall, Emily 1495
ウェストブルック
Westbrook, Catherine 1495
Westbrook, Robert 1495
Westbrook, Russell 1495
ウエストブルック
Westbrook, David 1495
Westbrook, Robert 1495
Westbrook, Russell 1495
Westbrook, Tevin 1495

ウェストブルックス
Westbrooks, Ethan 1495
ウェストブロック
Westbroek, Eva-maria 1495
ウェストヘーゼン
Oosthuizen, Louis 1055
ウェストメイツェ
Westmijze, W.K. 1495
ウェストモア
Westmor, Monty 1495
Westmore, Ann 1495
ウェストモーランド
Westmoreland, William Childs 1495
ウェストランド
Westland, Pamela 1495
ウェストリー
Westley, Frances 1495
ウエストリー
Westleigh, Sarah 1495
ウェストレイク
Westlake, Abby 1495
Westlake, Donald Edwin 1495
ウェストレーク
Westlake, Donald Edwin 1495
ウエストレーク
Westlake, Donald Edwin 1495
ウェストン
Weston, Anthony 1495
Weston, Carrie 1495
Weston, Judith 1495
Weston, Martha 1495
Weston, Molly 1495
Weston, Stasia 1495
ウエストン
Weston, Anthony 1495
Weston, Sophie 1495
ヴェスペ
Wäspe, Roland 1481
ウェスラ
Westra, Henny A. 1495
ウエスラティ
Oueslati, Oussama 1064
ウェスリー
Wesley, De'Ondre 1494
ウェズリー
Wesley, Mary 1494
ウェズリイ
Wesley, Kathryn 1494
ウェスルマン
Wesselman, Henry Barnard 1494
ウエスルマン
Wesselman, Henry Barnard 1494
ウェズレー
Wesley, Mary 1494
ウェズレイ
Wesley 1494
ウェセッド
Westhead, David R. 1495
ヴェセット
Veysset, Frédérique 1454
ヴェセニナ
Vesenina, Antonina 1454
ウェセリー
Wessely, Simon 1494
ヴェセリ
Veseli, Frederic 1454
ヴェゼンコフ
Vezenkov, Aleksandar 1454
ウエダ
Ueda, Yoshihiko 1432
Uyeda, Laura 1437
Uyeda, Massami 1437
ヴェーダー
Weder, Hans 1486
ヴェダー
Vedder, Eddie 1449
ウェタングラ
Wetangula, Moses 1495
ヴェダンタム
Vedantam, Shankar 1449
ヴェツァーリ
Vezzali, Valentina 1454
ヴェッカー
Wecker, Konstantin 1486
ヴェック
Weck, Claudia de 1486
ウェッジ
Wedge, Chris 1486
Wedge, Eric 1486
ウェッシェ
Waesche, Horst 1467
ウェッセル
Wessel, David 1494
Wessel, John 1494
ウェッセルズ
Wessels, David 1494
ヴェッセル・テルホーン
Wessel-Therhorn, Oliver 1494
ウェッセルマン
Wesselmann, D V 1494
Wesselmann, Tom 1494
ウェッソン
Watson, Christine 1482
Wesson, John 1494
ウェッタシンハ
Weththasinghe, Dayananda 1496
Wettasinghe, Sybil 1496
ウェッツェル
Wetzel, John 1496
ヴェッツェル
Wetzell, Tupua Friedrich Wilhelm 1496
ヴェッツォシ
Vezzosi, Al'essandro 1454
ウエッツラー
Wetzler, Peter Michael 1496
ヴェッテ
Wette, Wolfram 1496
ウェッデル
Weddell, Doreen 1486
ウェットラウファー
Wetlaufer, Suzy 1496
ウェットローファー
Wetlaufer, Suzy 1496
ウェットン
Wetton, John 1496
ウェッバー
Webber, Christopher L. 1485
ウェッブ
Webb, Bernard Winston 1485
Webb, Brandon 1485
Webb, Caroline 1485
Webb, Charles Richard 1485
Webb, Debra 1485
Webb, Everette 1485
Webb, George 1485
Webb, Glenn Taylor 1485
Webb, Holly 1485
Webb, James Ⅲ 1485
Webb, Jarrett 1485
Webb, Jeremy 1485
Webb, Jim 1485
Webb, Kathleen 1485
Webb, Linda D. 1485
Webb, Marc 1485
Webb, Marcus A. 1485
Webb, Matt 1485
Webb, Peggy 1485
Webb, Rhys 1485
Webb, Ryan 1485
Webb, Stephen 1485
Webb, Tyler 1485
Webb, Wanda G. 1485
Webb, Wayne Richard 1485
ウエッブ
Webb, Jim 1485
ヴェディス・ヨンスドゥッター
Védís Jónsdóttir 1449
ウェディング
Wedding, Alex 1486
ヴェデニフスキー
Wedeniwski, Sebastian 1486
ウェテリンク
Wetering, Ernst van de 1496
ヴェーデル
Vedel, Ellen 1449
ウェデル＝ウェデルスボルグ
Wedell-Wedellsborg, Thomas 1486
ヴェテルリ
Vetterli, Martin 1454
ウェード
Wade, David 1466
ヴェトー
Vetö, Miklós 1454
ヴェトゥスン
Watson, Galadriel Findlay 1482
ヴェドハラ
Vedhara, Kav 1449
ウエドラオゴ
Ouedraogo, Albert 1063
Ouedraogo, Emile 1063
Ouedraogo, Gilbert 1063
Ouedraogo, Guédé Jacques 1063
Ouedraogo, Jacob 1063
Ouedraogo, Jacques Guédé 1063
Ouedraogo, Jean 1063
Ouedraogo, Jérémie 1063
Ouedraogo, Josephine 1063
Ouedraogo, Mahamoudou 1063
Ouedraogo, Mathieu R. 1063
Ouedraogo, Niouga Ambroise 1063
Ouedraogo, Ram 1063
Ouedraogo, Raymond Edouard 1064
Ouedraogo, Smaïla 1064
Ouedraogo, Yacouba 1064
Ouédraogo, Youssouf 1064
ウエドラオゴ・ボニ
Ouedraogo Boni, Bibiane 1064
ウエドラゴ
Ouedrago, Mahamoudou 1063
ウェートリー
Waitley, Dayna 1468
Waitley, Deborah 1468
ウェドル
Weddle, Erick 1486
ウェドン
Whedon, Joss 1496
ウェーナー
Wehner, E.A. 1487
ウェナー
Wenner, Jann 1493
ヴェナブルズ
Venables, Stephen 1451
Venables, William N. 1451
ウェナム
Wenham, Gordon J. 1493
ヴェニガー
Weniger, Matthias 1493
ウェニング
Wenning, Keith 1493
ヴェーヌ
Veyne, Paul 1454
ウェネズイ
Wenezoui, Sebastien 1493
ウエネズイ
Wénézoui, Charles Hervé 1493
ヴェネツィア
Venezia, Shlomo 1451
ヴェネマン
Veneman, Ann Margaret 1451
ウエノ
Ueno, Antônio 1432
ウェーバー
Waber, Bernard 1466
Webber, Christine 1485
Webber, Jim 1485
Webber, Mark 1485
Weber, Axel A. 1485
Weber, David 1485
Weber, Doron 1485
Weber, Franziska 1485
Weber, Fred 1485
Weber, Hans-Jurgen 1485
Weber, Ingo M. 1486
Weber, James 1486
Weber, Julian 1486
Weber, Karl 1486
Weber, Klaus G. 1486
Weber, Larry 1486
Weber, Samuel 1486
Weber, Wendell W. 1486
Weber, William 1486
Weber-gale, Garrett 1486
ウェバー
Webber, Alan 1485
Webber, Mark 1485
Webber, Meredith 1485
Webber, Rob 1485
Webber, Tim 1485
Weber, Briante 1485
Weber, David 1485
Weber, Dick 1485
Weber, Kenneth J. 1486
Weber, Kristine Kaoverii 1486
Weber, Mark 1486
Weber, Penny 1486
Weber, Phil 1486

Weber, Steve 1486
Wever, Chris 1496
ウエバー
Weber, Ken 1486
ヴェーバー
Weber, Gunthard 1485
Weber, Mathias 1486
Weber, Rudolf 1486
Weber, Theodor 1486
Weeber, Karl-Wilhelm 1486
ウエハシ
Uehashi, Nahoko 1432
ウエハラ
Uehara, Humberto 1432
ヴェヒター
Waechter, Friedrich Karl 1467
Waechter, Philip 1467
ウェブ
Webb, Allen P. 1484
Webb, Betty 1485
Webb, B.W. 1485
Webb, Elizabeth 1485
Webb, Frank J. 1485
Webb, James H.M. 1485
Webb, J'Marcus 1485
Webb, Joe 1485
Webb, John Graydon 1485
Webb, Joseph W. 1485
Webb, Kamál 1485
Webb, Karen 1485
Webb, Karrie 1485
Webb, Lardarius 1485
Webb, Marc 1485
Webb, Mark A. 1485
Webb, Michael 1485
Webb, Paul D. 1485
Webb, Ruth 1485
Webb, Sarah 1485
Webb, Susan 1485
ウエブ
Webb, Catherine 1485
ウェブスター
Webster, Adrian 1486
Webster, Allen 1486
Webster, Chris 1486
Webster, Frank 1486
Webster, Jason 1486
Webster, Jennifer 1486
Webster, John 1486
Webster, Kayvon 1486
Webster, Larry 1486
Webster, Leslie T., Jr. 1486
Webster, Mike 1486
Webster, Richard 1486
Webster, Sam 1486
Webster, Steve 1486
ウエブスター
Webster, Francis X. 1486
ウェブスター＝ストラットン
Webster-Stratton, Carolyn 1486
ウェペ
Huepe, Claudio 632
ウェベール
Weber, Henri 1485
ウエーベル
Weber, Edith 1485
ウエマツ
Uematsu, Kenji 1432
ウエムラ・ヨシモト
Huemura Yoshimoto, Luis Alfonso 632
ウェヤ
Weya, Jérôme Klôh 1496
ウェヤーズ
Weyers, Howard 1496
ヴェーユ
Veil, Simone 1450
ヴェーヨニス
Vējonis, Raimonds 1450
ウェーラー
Wehler, Hans-Ulrich 1487
ウェラー
Waehler, Charles A. 1467
Weller, Ana 1491
Weller, Anthony 1491
Weller, Duncan 1491
Weller, George 1491
Weller, Harry 1491
Weller, Patrick Moray 1491
Weller, Paul 1491
Weller, Sam 1491
Weller, Thomas Huckle 1491
Weller, Walter 1491
Woller, Steffen 1522
ヴェーラ
Vela, Carmen 1450
ヴェーラー
Wehler, Hans-Ulrich 1487
ヴェラー
Weller, Walter 1491
ヴェラスケス
Velasquez, Eric 1450
Velasquez, Mary Marden 1450
ヴェラセカ
Vilaseca, Estel 1457
ヴェーラック
Verlhac, Pierre-Henri 1453
ヴェラッティ
Verratti, Marco 1453
ヴェラマチャネニー
Veeramachaneni, Nirmal K. 1449
ウェーラン
Whelan, Richard 1497
ウェラン
Whelan, James P. 1497
Whelan, Jonathan 1497
Whelan, Richard 1497
Whelan, Susan 1497
ヴェラン
Veyrenc, Thomas 1454
ウェランド
Welland, Michael 1491
ウェリー
Werry, Chris 1494
ヴェリー
Véry, Pierre 1454
ウェリグトン
Weligton 1491
ヴェリコヴィッチ
Veljkovic, Milos 1450
ヴェリッシモ
Veríssimo, Luís Fernanndo 1453
ヴェリホフ
Velikhov, Evgenii Pavlovich 1450
ヴェリヤト
Veliath, Cyril 1450
ウェリンガー
Wellinger, Andreas 1491
ウェリングズ
Wellings, Eloise 1491
ウェリンズ
Wellins, Richard S. 1491
ウェリントン
Wellington, Monica 1491
ウェール
Weil, Prosper 1487
Werle, Loukie 1493
ウェル
Wel, Steven van 1491
ヴェール
Vale, Leah 1439
ヴェルー
Vellut, Natacha 1451
Verou, Lea 1453
ヴェルイーユ
Verhille, Alexandre 1452
ウェ・ルウィン
Wai Lwin 1468
ヴェルカー
Welker, Michael 1491
ウェルガマ
Welgama, Kumara 1491
ウェルカム
Welcome, John 1491
ヴェルサーチ
Versace, Donatella 1454
Versace, Vincent 1454
ウェルサム
Welsome, Eileen 1492
ウェルザー・メスト
Welser-Möst, Franz 1492
ヴェルザー・メスト
Welser-Möst, Franz 1492
ヴェルジェ
Verger, Jacques 1452
ヴェルジェス
Vergès, Françoise 1452
ヴェルシャヴ
Verschave, François-Xavier 1454
ウェルシュ
Welch, Bob 1491
Welch, Randy 1491
Welsch, Glenn A. 1492
Welsh, Betty L. 1492
Welsh, Brandon C. 1492
Welsh, Irvin 1492
Welsh, Jon 1492
Welsh, Louise 1492
Welsh, Matt 1492
Welsh, Pete 1492
Welsh, Thomas 1492
ヴェルシュ
Welsh, Renate 1492
ヴェルジュイス
Velthuijs, Max 1451
ウェルシュマン
Welshman, Malcolm D. 1492
ヴェルジュリ
Vergely, Bertrand 1452
ウェールズ
Wales, Jimmy 1469
ウェルス
Wells, Brad 1492
Wells, Robin 1492
Wels, Andreas 1492
ウェルズ
Welles, Orson 1491
Wells, Adrian 1491
Wells, Angela 1491
Wells, Anne Sharp 1492
Wells, Beau-James 1492
Wells, Cory 1492
Wells, David 1492
Wells, David G. 1492
Wells, Donna L. 1492
Wells, George Andre 1492
Wells, Jennifer Foehner 1492
Wells, John Christopher 1492
Wells, Joseph T. 1492
Wells, Josh 1492
Wells, Josiah 1492
Wells, Karen 1492
Wells, Kellie 1492
Wells, M. 1492
Wells, Malcolm 1492
Wells, Matt 1492
Wells, Mick 1492
Wells, Mike 1492
Wells, Pamela 1492
Wells, Rachel 1492
Wells, Rebecca 1492
Wells, Robert E. 1492
Wells, Robin 1492
Wells, Rosemary 1492
Wells, Scott 1492
Wells, Spencer 1492
Wells, Stanley W. 1492
Wells, Steve 1492
Wells, Zeb 1492
ウエールズ
Welles, G.W.H. 1491
ウエルズ
Wells, Jonathan 1492
ヴェルス
Werth, Dirk 1494
ウェルストン
Wellstone, Paul 1492
ウェルスマン
Welsman, Carol 1492
ヴェルダー
Werder, Peter R. 1493
ウェルタス
Huertas, Marcelo 632
ウエルタ・デ・ソト
Huerta de Soto, Jesús 632
ウェルチ
Welch, Bob 1491
Welch, Chris 1491
Welch, David A. 1491
Welch, Fern Stewart 1491
Welch, Florence 1491
Welch, Graham F. 1491
Welch, H.Gilbert 1491
Welch, Jack 1491
Welch, Jeanie M. 1491
Welch, Jessica 1491
Welch, John 1491
Welch, John Francis, Jr. 1491
Welch, R.Robinson 1491
Welch, Ruth 1491
Welch, Shawn 1491
Welch, Suzy 1491
ウェルチャー
Welcher, Rosalind 1491
ウェルツ
Weltz, Scott 1492
Woertz, Patricia A. 1520
ウェルッシュ
Welsh, Alex 1492
ヴェルテ
Welte, Miriam 1492

ヴェルデ
Velde, Beth P. 1450
Verde, Alegra 1452
Verde, Antonio 1452
ウェルティ
Welty, Eudora 1492
ヴェルディ
Verdi, Simone 1452
Verdy, Violette 1452
ヴェルディエ
Verdier, Fabienne 1452
ヴェルディエール
Verdier, Zoe Le 1452
ヴェルデュイス
Veldhuis, Johannes D. 1450
ウェルデリッヒ
Werderich, Donna E. 1493
ヴェルテン
Velten, Hannah 1451
ウェルデンケイル
Weldenkeil, Gebremariam 1491
ウェルト
Werth, Isabell 1494
ウェルド
Weld, Nicki 1491
ヴェルト
Werth, Nicolas 1494
ウェルトハイマー
Wertheimer, Andrew B. 1494
ウェールトマン
Weertman, Ferry 1487
ヴェルトマン
Veltman, Martinus 1451
ヴェルトローニ
Veltroni, Walter 1451
ウェルトン
Welton, Jude 1492
ウェルドン
Weldon, William C. 1491
Wheldon, Dan 1497
ヴェルドン
Verdon, Jean 1452
Verdon, René 1452
ヴェルトンゲン
Vertonghen, Jan 1454
ウェルナー
Werner, Carolina 1493
Werner, Helmut 1493
Werner, Joseph 1493
Werner, Pierre 1493
Werner, Wendelin 1493
Woellner, Joel 1520
ヴェルナー
Verner, Miroslav 1453
Werner, Alexander 1493
Werner, Florian 1493
Werner, Götz W. 1493
Werner, Helmut 1493
Werner, Herbert A. 1493
Werner, Monika 1493
Werner, Richard A. 1493
Werner, Timo 1493
ヴェルナー＝イェンセン
Werner-Jensen, Arnold 1493
ヴェルナン
Vernant, Jean-Pierre 1453
ヴェルニ
Verni, Ken A. 1453
ヴェルニケ
Wernicke, Herbert 1493
ヴェルニーノ
Vernino, Arthur R. 1453
ヴェルヌイユ
Verneuil, Henri 1453
ヴェルネ
Verney, Jean-Pierre 1453
ヴェルノア
Vernoit, Stephen 1453
ヴェルノン
Vernon, Richie 1453
ヴェル・バークモース
Ver Berkmoes, Ryan 1452
ヴェル・バークモーズ
Ver Berkmoes, Ryan 1452
ウェルファンダー
Welfonder, Sue-Ellen 1491
ヴェルフェル
Wolfel, Ursula 1521
ウェルフォード
Welford, Mary 1491
ヴェルフリ
Wolfli, Marco 1521
ウェルフレ
Woelfle, Gretchen 1520
ヴェルベーケ
Verbeke, Annelies 1452
ウェルベック
Welbeck, Danny 1491
ウエルベック
Houellebecq, Michel 625
ヴェルヘリング
Welchering, Björn 1491
ヴェルベール
Werber, Bernard 1493
ヴェールホフ
Werlhof, Claudia von 1493
ウェルボーン
Whelbourne, Jack 1497
ヴェルマー
Wellmer, Albrecht 1491
ヴェルマーレン
Vermaelen, Thomas 1453
ウェルマン
Wellman, W.A. 1491
Wellman, Wendell 1491
ヴェルマン
Vehlmann, Fabien 1450
ヴェルメシ
Vermes, Geza 1453
ヴェルメシュ
Vermes, Timur 1453
ヴェルメール
Vermeire, Kaatje 1453
ウェールリ
Wehrli, Ursus 1487
ヴェルレプト
Verrept, Paul 1453
ヴェルロークン
Verroken, Sarah 1454
ヴェルンリ
Wernly, Julia 1493
ヴェーレ
Verre, Valerio 1453
ヴェレア
Véléa, Dan 1450
ヴェレズ
Velez, Ray 1450
ウェレデ
Werede, Wold Wolde 1493
ウェレニケ
Wernicke, María 1493
ヴェレルスト
Verelst, Suana 1452
ウェレン
Wellen, Edward 1491
ヴェーレンシオル
Wereskiold, Erik 1493
ヴェーレンバーグ
Wehrenberg, Margaret 1487
ヴェレンホーファー
Wellenhofer-Klein, Marina 1491
ヴェレンロイター
Wellenreuther, Timon 1491
ヴェロ
Verrot, Pascal 1454
ヴェローゾ
Veloso, Miguel 1451
ヴェロネージ
Veronesi, Sandro 1453
ヴェロン
Veron, J.Michael 1453
Verón, Juan Sebastián 1453
ウェン
Hsu, Wen 630
Wen, Jia-bao 1492
Wen, Wanda 1492
ヴェーン
Vane, John Robert 1443
ウェンガー
Wenger, Etienne 1493
Wenger, Win 1493
ヴェンカタラマン
Venkataraman, Ramaswamy Iyer 1451
ヴェンカテッシュ
Venkatesh, Sudhir Alladi 1451
ヴェンカトラマン
Venkatraman, Padma 1451
ヴェンキャット
Vencat, Emily Flynn 1451
ウェンク
Wenk, Shari Lesser 1493
ウェングラー
Wengler, John 1493
ヴェンゲーロフ
Vengerov, Maxim 1451
ウェンジャー
Wenger, J.Michael 1493
ヴェンシュ
Wünsch, Wolfgang 1530
ウェンス
Wenth, Jennifer 1493
ウェンスタイン
Weinstein, Allison 1489
ウエンスタイン
Weinstein, Stan 1489
ウェーンストック
Weinstock, Arnold 1489
ウェンゼル
Wenzel, David 1493
Wenzel, Ty 1493
ウェン・セレイウット
Veng Sereyvuth 1451
ウェンダー
Wender, Paul H. 1492
ヴェンター
Venter, J.Craig 1451
ウェンダース
Wenders, Wim 1492
ヴェンダース
Wenders, Wim 1492
ヴェンチュラ
Ventura, Jesse 1451
Ventura, Robin Mark 1451
ウェンツ
Wentz, Carson 1493
ウェンツェル
Wenzel, Brendan 1493
Wenzel, Christine 1493
ヴェンツェル
Wenzel, Angela 1493
Wenzel, Jennifer 1493
ヴェンツーラ
Ventura, Antonio 1451
ヴェンテ
Wendte, Martin 1493
ウェンディグ
Wendig, Chuck 1492
ヴェンディッティ
Venditti, Giovanbattista 1451
ヴェンデブルク
Wendebourg, Dorothea 1492
ウェンデル
Wendell 1492
Wendell, Patrick 1492
ウェント
Wendt, Albert 1493
ヴェント
Wendt, Oscar 1493
ヴェントゥーリ
Venturi, Alessandro 1451
ヴェントゥリーニ・フェンディ
Venturini Fendi, Ilaria 1451
ヴェントカー
Wentker, Hermann 1493
ウェンドコス
Wendkos, Paul 1492
ウエンドコス
Wendkos, Paul 1492
ヴェントーラ
Ventola, Pamela E. 1451
ヴェンドラー
Vendler, Helen 1451
ヴェントリーニ・フェンディ
Venturini Fendi, Ilaria 1451
ウェンドル
Wendl, Tobias 1492
Wendle, Joey 1492
ヴェントレラ
Ventrella, Scott W. 1451
ウェントワース
Wentworth, Sally 1493
ヴェンベーリア
Wennberg, Birgitta 1493
ウォー
Wahl, Jan 1468
Waugh, Alexander 1483
Waugh, Anne 1483
Waugh, Hillary 1483
Waugh, Joanna 1483
Waugh, Jonathan B. 1483
Waugh, Kathy 1483
Waugh, Sylvia 1483
Woehr, William A. 1520
ヴォ

Vo, Trong Nghia 1461
ヴォ＝アン
Vo-Anh, Sandra 1461
ヴォイェヴォドゥスキー
Voevodsky, Vladimir 1461
ヴォイケ
Woicke, Peter L. 1520
ヴォイチェサック
Wojcieszak, Doug 1520
ヴォイチェホフスカ
Wojciechowska, Maia 1520
ウォイッキ
Wojcicki, Anne 1520
ヴォイテック
Voytek, Bradley 1464
ウォイト
Woit, Peter 1520
ヴォイト
Voight, Jon 1462
Voight, Mike 1462
Voigt, Cynthia 1462
Voigt, Deborah 1462
Voigt, Leigh 1462
ウォイナロフスカ
Wojnarowska, Ewelina 1520
ヴォイノフ
Voinov, Aleksandr 1462
ウォイボゴ
Woibogo, Issa Sokoye Esther 1520
ヴォイルズ
Voiels, Veronica 1462
ウォーウィック
Warwick, Ben 1480
ウォーウェライト
Wowereit, Klaus 1527
ヴォヴェル
Vovelle, Michel 1464
ウォッーパー
Whopper, Willie 1501
ウォエウォジン
Voyevodin, Aleksey 1464
ウォエウォダ
Voevoda, Alexey 1461
ヴォエヴォダ
Voevoda, Alexey 1461
ヴォエヴォドスキー
Voevodsky, Vladimir 1461
ウォーカー
Walker, Aidan 1470
Walker, Alan 1470
Walker, Alexander 1470
Walker, Alice Malsenior 1470
Walker, Alleyne 1470
Walker, Amy 1470
Walker, Andrew Kevin 1470
Walker, Anna 1470
Walker, Bernard 1470
Walker, Brad 1470
Walker, Brett L. 1470
Walker, Cami 1470
Walker, Carol L. 1470
Walker, Casey 1470
Walker, Catherine 1470
Walker, C.B.F. 1470
Walker, Christian 1470
Walker, David 1470
Walker, David Alan 1470
Walker, Decker F. 1470
Walker, Delanie 1470
Walker, Douglas M. 1470
Walker, E.Cardon 1470
Walker, Elaine F. 1470
Walker, Elizabeth 1470
Walker, Gabrielle 1470
Walker, Gordon A.H. 1470
Walker, Jamie 1470
Walker, J.C. 1470
Walker, Jearl 1470
Walker, Jeremy 1470
Walker, Jess 1470
Walker, Jesse 1470
Walker, Joan Hustace 1470
Walker, Joe 1470
Walker, John, Jr. 1470
Walker, John Albert 1470
Walker, John Ernest 1470
Walker, Josh 1470
Walker, J.Samuel 1470
Walker, Julie Ann 1470
Walker, Karen Thompson 1470
Walker, Kate 1470
Walker, Kemba 1470
Walker, Kent 1470
Walker, Kyle 1470
Walker, Landry Quinn 1470
Walker, Lester 1470
Walker, Mark H. 1470
Walker, Martin 1470
Walker, Melaine 1470
Walker, Michael Jon 1470
Walker, Mike 1470
Walker, Mort 1470
Walker, Morton 1470
Walker, Neil 1470
Walker, Nicola 1470
Walker, Nicola L. 1470
Walker, Paul 1470
Walker, Paul L. 1470
Walker, Pete 1470
Walker, Peter 1470
Walker, Peter W.L. 1471
Walker, R. 1471
Walker, Richard 1471
Walker, Richard F. 1471
Walker, Robert W. 1471
Walker, Rodger 1471
Walker, Sally M. 1471
Walker, Salvatore 1471
Walker, Sarah 1471
Walker, Saskia 1471
Walker, Scott Kevin 1471
Walker, Shiloh 1471
Walker, Stephen 1471
Walker, Susan 1471
Walker, Taijuan 1471
Walker, Tara 1471
Walker, Thomas Worth 1471
Walker, T.J. 1471
Walker, Trevor 1471
Walker, Tristan 1471
Walker, Tyrunn 1471
Walker, Vance 1471
Walker, William 1471
Walker, Wyatt Tee 1471
ウォーカス
Warchus, Matthew 1477
ウォーカップ
Walkup, Thomas 1471
ウォーカーヘボーン
Walker-hebborn, Chris 1471
ヴォーガン
Vorgan, Gigi 1464
ウォーキンショー
Walkinshaw, Tom 1471
ウォーク
Wolk, Harman S. 1522
Wolk, Harry I. 1522
ウォグ
Wogu, Chukwuemeka Ngozichineke 1520
Wogu, Emeka 1520
ヴォーク
Voake, Charlotte 1461
Voake, Steve 1461
ヴォー・グエン・ザップ
Vo Nguyen Giap 1463
ヴォークス
Vokes, Sam 1462
ウォークデン
Walkden, Bianca 1470
ヴォークト
Vogt, William 1462
ヴォグト
Vogt, Richard Carl 1462
ヴォークレール
Vauclair, Jacques 1448
ヴォーゲル
Vogel, Ezra Feivel 1461
Vogel, Frank 1461
Vogel, Gib 1461
Vogel, Harold L. 1461
Vogel, Joshua 1461
Vogel, Steven K. 1461
Vogel, Susan 1461
Vogels, Josey 1461
ウォーケン
Walken, Christopher 1470
ウォーケンティン
Warkentin, Mark 1479
ウォーコウィッツ
Walkowitz, Judith R. 1471
ヴォーコス
Voulkos, Peter 1464
ウォザースプーン
Wotherspoon, Jeremy Lee 1527
ウォーシー
Worthy, Chandler 1527
ウォーシェル
Warshel, Arieh 1480
ヴォージェル
Vogel, Louis 1461
ヴォジェル
Vogel, Nadine 1461
ウォジスキ
Wojcicki, Susan Diane 1520
ウォジスキー
Wojcicki, Susan Diane 1520
ウォシチェフスキー
Voschevskyi, Valerii 1464
ウォジニャク
Woźniak, Piotr 1527
ウォシャウスキー
Wachowski, Andy 1466
Wachowski, Lana 1466
Wachowski, Larry 1466
ウォーシャック
Warshak, Richard Ades 1480
ヴォジャンスキー
Wogenscky, André 1520
ウォーシュ
Warsh, Larry 1480
ヴォージュラード
Vaugelade, Anaïs 1448
ウォーショー
Warschauer, Mark 1480
ウォース
Warth, Keith 1480
ヴォース
Vause, Jordan 1448
Vose, David 1464
ヴォースー
Worsoe, Kirsten 1526
ヴォス
Vos, Catherine F. 1464
Voss, Jonathan D. 1464
Voss, Louise 1464
ヴォスクレセンスキー
Voskresensky, Mikhail S. 1464
ヴォス・サヴァント
Vos Savant, Marilyn 1464
ウォズニアク
Wozniak, Dagmara 1527
Woźniak, Jacek 1527
Wozniak, Steve 1527
ウォズニアッキ
Wozniacki, Caroline 1527
ウォズニアック
Wozniak, Steve 1527
ヴォズニツキ
Voznitski, Borys 1465
ウォズニャク
Voznyak, Anastasiya 1465
ウォズネセンスキー
Voznesenskii, Andrei 1464
ヴォズネセーンスキー
Voznesenskii, Andrei 1464
ヴォズネセンスキー
Voznesenskii, Andrei 1464
ウォーズマン
Wasmund, Sháá 1480
ヴォセン
Vossen, Jelle 1464
ウオソ
Ouosso, Emile 1064
ヴォーター
Vawter, Vince 1448
ウォータース
Waters, Alice 1481
Waters, Daryl 1481
Waters, Roger 1481
ウォーターズ
Walters, Patric 1474
Waters, Alice 1481
Waters, David 1481
Waters, Herb 1481
Waters, Jason T. 1481
Waters, John 1481
Waters, John M. 1481
Waters, Lesley 1481
Waters, Mark 1481
Waters, Michael R. 1481
Waters, Roger 1481
Waters, Sarah 1481
Watters, Derrin Harper 1483
Wauters, Ambika 1483
ウォータス
Wotus, Ron 1527
ヴォダック
Wodak, Ruth 1520
ウォーターハウス
Waterhouse, David Boyer 1481
Waterhouse, Jason 1481

ウ

Waterhouse, Jo 1481
Waterhouse, Stephen 1481
ウォーターバーグ
Waterberg, Celsius 1481
ウォーターフィールド
Waterfield, Peter 1481
ウォーターマン
Waterman, Fanny 1481
Waterman, Peter 1481
Waterman, Russell 1481
ウォータマン
Waterman, Robert H. 1481
ヴォーダマン
Vorderman, Carol 1464
ウォダルチク
Wlodarczyk, Anita 1519
ヴォーチェ
Voce, Lello 1461
ウォーチェスター
Worcester, Retta Scott 1526
ヴォー・チ・コン
Vo Chi Cong 1461
ヴォー・チー・コン
Vo Chi Cong 1461
ウォーツ
Woertz, Patricia A. 1520
ヴォツァーク
Wowzack, Violetta 1527
ヴォックス
Vox, Valentine 1464
ウォックナー
Workneh, Gebeyehu 1526
ウォッシュ
Wash, Todd 1480
ウォッシュバーン
Washburn, Livia J. 1480
ウォッターズ
Watters, Ethan 1483
ウォッチマン
Wichmann, Cody 1501
ウォッツ
Watts, André 1483
ウォッペル
Woeppel, Mark J. 1520
ウオッペル
Woeppel, Mark J. 1520
ウォディエ
Wodie, Victorine 1520
ウォディングトン
Waddington, Ivan 1466
ウォーテラ
Wartella, Ellen 1480
ウオーテラ
Wartella, Ellen 1480
ウォーデル
Waddell, Martin 1466
Wordell, Charles 1526
ウォーデン
Warden, Jack 1478
Worden, James William 1526
Worden, Jennifer 1526
ウォード
Ward, Allen C. 1477
Ward, Amanda Eyre 1477
Ward, Andre 1477
Ward, Andrew 1477
Ward, Beck 1477
Ward, Brian 1477
Ward, Brian R. 1477
Ward, Channing 1477
Ward, Christopher 1477
Ward, David 1477
Ward, G.Kingsley 1477
Ward, Helen 1477
Ward, Ian 1477
Ward, James 1477
Ward, Jamie 1477
Ward, Jane 1477
Ward, Jeremy P.T. 1478
Ward, Jihad 1478
Ward, Jimmie 1478
Ward, Joel 1478
Ward, John L. 1478
Ward, J.R. 1478
Ward, Laura 1478
Ward, Martin F. 1478
Ward, Pat 1478
Ward, Pendleton 1478
Ward, Peter Douglas 1478
Ward, Robert 1478
Ward, Sally 1478
Ward, Sarah F. 1478
Ward, Simon 1478
Ward, Stephen 1478
Ward, Terron 1478
Ward, T.J. 1478
Ward, Tony 1478
Ward, Turner 1478
Ward, Willa Parks 1478
Warde, Fran 1478
ヴォート
Voet, Donald 1461
Voet, Judith G. 1461
Vogt, Lisa 1462
ヴォートー
Votto, Joey 1464
ヴォド
Vodoz, Olivier 1461
ヴォトヴィッツ
Wojtowicz, Robert 1520
ウォトソン
Watson, James Dewey 1482
ウォード＝パーキンズ
Ward-Perkins, Bryan 1478
ウォード・プラウズ
Ward-prowse, James 1478
ウォドボデ
Wodobode, Jean Prosper 1520
ヴォートラン
Vautrin, Jean 1448
ウォードル
Wardle, Jane 1478
ウォートレイ
Wortley, Richard K. 1527
ヴォドワ
Vaudoit, Hervé 1448
ウォートン
Warton, Barbara 1480
Wharton, Thomas 1496
Wharton, Tim 1496
Worton, Dean 1527
ウォーナー
Warner, Alan 1479
Warner, Austin Jack 1479
Warner, Charles Dudley 1479
Warner, John W. 1479
Warner, Malcolm 1479
Warner, Marina 1479
Warner, Melanie 1479
Warner, Penny 1479
ヴォナ
Vona, Abigail 1463
ヴォネガット
Vonnegut, Kurt, Jr. 1463
Vonnegut, Norb 1463
ウォーノック
Warnock, Mary 1479
ヴォーハウス
Vorhaus, John 1464
ウォーバートン
Warburton, Nigel 1477
Warburton, Sam 1477
Warburton, Sarah 1477
ウォーフ
Wharfe, Ken 1496
ウォフ
Woff, Richard 1520
ウォーフィールド
Warfield, Terry D. 1478
ウォーフォード
Warford, Larry 1478
ウォフク
Vovk, Vitaly M. 1464
Vovk, Vladimir 1464
ウォフクン
Vovkun, Vasily 1464
ウォボルディング
Wubbolding, Robert E. 1529
ウォーマー
Wormer, Laura Van 1526
ウォーマーダム
Warmerdam, Cornelius Dutch 1479
ウォーマック
Warmack, Chance 1479
Womack, James P. 1522
ウォマック
Womack, Bobby 1522
Womack, James E. 1522
ウォーマルド
Wormald, Richard 1526
ウォームズ
Worms, Penny 1526
ウォームスリー
Warmsley, Julius 1479
ウォームズリー
Walmsley, Ann 1473
ウォーメル
Wormell, Chris 1526
Wormell, Christoper 1526
Wormell, Mary 1526
ウォヨンゴ
Woyongo, Mark Owen 1527
ウォーラー
Waller, Darren 1472
Waller, Gordon 1472
ウォラー
Waller, John H. 1472
Waller, Robert James 1472
ウォラギネ
Voragine, Jacobus de 1464
ウォラク
Wallach, Janet 1472
ウォーラス
Wallace, Aaron 1471
Wallace, Cleveland 1471
Wallace, Cody 1471
Wallace, Eric 1471
Wallace, Martin 1472
Wallace, Mike 1472
ウォラス
Wallace, Brett 1471
Wallace, Eric 1471
Wallace, Wendy 1472
ヴォラーズ
Vollers, Maryanne 1462
ウォラースタイン
Wallerstein, Judith S. 1472
ウォーラーステイン
Wallerstein, Immanuel Maurice 1472
ウォーラック
Wallach, Eli 1472
ウォラック
Wallach, Eli 1472
Wallach, Janet 1472
Wallach, Lise 1472
Wallach, Michael A. 1472
Wallach, Tim 1472
Wallach, Wendell 1472
Wallack, Roy M. 1472
Worrack, Trixi 1526
ウォラッシュ
Wallach, Van 1472
ウォラード
Wollard, Kathy 1522
ウォラナー
Wolaner, Robin 1520
ヴォーラペット
Vorapheth, Kham 1464
ウォラポート
Petchkoom, Worapoj 1101
Worapoj, Petchkoom 1526
ウォーラル
Worrall, Nick 1526
ウォラル
Worrall, Frank 1526
Worrall, Jennifer G. 1526
ウォラワット
Worawat, Ua-apinyakul 1526
ウォランスキ
Wolinski, Georges 1522
ウォーリー
Walley, Deborah 1472
Worley, Daryl 1526
Worley, Vance 1526
ウォリ
Wuori, Matti Ossian 1530
ウオリ
Wuori, G.K. 1530
ヴォリ
Vuori, Julia 1465
Vuori, Pekka 1465
ウォリアー
Warrier, Gopi 1480
Warrior, Padmasree 1480
ウォリアムズ
Walliams, David 1472
ヴオリオ
Vuorio, Maria 1465
ウォーリス
Wallis, Jamie 1472
Wallis, Velma 1472
ウォリス
Wallis, Brian 1472
Wallis, Jim 1472
Wallis, Michael 1472
Wallis, Pete 1472
Wallis, Sarah 1472
Wallis, Shannon 1472
ウォリスキー
Volskii, Arkadii Ivanovich 1463
ヴォリスキー
Volskii, Arkadii

Ivanovich 1463
ウォリック
Warrick, Joby 1480
Warrick, Ruth 1480
ウォリナー
Wariner, Jeremy 1478
Wariner, Steve 1478
ウォリニーク
Wolyniec, Krzysztof 1522
ウォリネツ
Volynets, Oleksandr 1463
ウォリロウ
Worrilow, Paul 1526
ウォーリン
Wallin, David J. 1472
Wallin, Nils Lennart 1472
Wolin, Richard 1522
Wolin, Sheldon S. 1522
Wolin, Steven J. 1522
Wolin, Sybil 1522
ウォリン
Wallin, Pauline 1472
Wolin, Sheldon S. 1522
ウォリンジャー
Wallinger, Mark 1472
ウォリントン
Wallington, Aury 1472
Wallington, Vivienne 1472
ウォール
Waal, Edmund de 1466
Wahl, Bobby 1468
Wahl, Erik 1468
Wahl, Jan 1468
Wahl, Mats 1468
Wahl, Phoebe 1468
Wall, Angus 1471
Wall, Art 1471
Wall, David 1471
Wall, Derek 1471
Wall, Dianne 1471
Wall, James Charles 1471
Wall, Jeff 1471
Wall, John 1471
Wall, Karen 1471
Wall, Larry 1471
Wall, Mick 1471
Wall, Patrick David 1471
Wohl, Dave 1520
Wohl, Ellen E. 1520
Woll, Jeff 1522
ウォル
Worou, Théophile 1526
ヴォール
Wahl, Asbjørn 1468
Wahl, Mats 1468
ヴォル
Volle, Danielle 1462
ウォルヴィン
Walvin, James 1475
ウォルウォル
Worwor, Raphael 1527
ウォルヴン
Wolven, Scott 1522
ヴォルカールト
Volckaert, Didier 1462
ヴォルカン
Volkan, Demirel 1462
Volkan, Sen 1462
ウォルキンスキー
Wallechinsky, David 1472
ウォルク
Wolke, Robert L. 1522
ヴォルク
Volk, Holger A. 1462
Volk, Tyler 1462
ヴォルクマー
Volkmar, Fred R. 1462
ヴォルクマン
Volkman, Ernest 1462
ヴォルケスト
Wahlquist, Håkan 1468
ヴォルゲマス
Wolgemuth, Bobbie 1522
ウォルケル
Warker, Ignacio 1479
ヴォールケル
Voelkel, James Robert 1461
ウォルコット
Walcott, Derek 1469
Walcott, Jerome 1469
Walcott, Keshorn 1469
Walcott, Theo 1469
Wolcott, David A. 1520
Wolcott, Robert C. 1520
Wolcott, William Linz 1520
ウオルコット
Wolcott, Gary 1520
ヴォルコフ
Volkov, Alexey 1462
Volkov, Solomon 1462
ウォルコワ
Volkova, Yekaterina 1462
ウォルサー
Walser, Robyn D. 1473
Walther, David S. 1474
Walther, George R. 1474
ヴォルシャイト
Wollscheid, Philipp 1522
ウォルシュ
Walsch, Neale Donald 1473
Walsh, Ann 1473
Walsh, Barent W. 1473
Walsh, Bill 1473
Walsh, Blair 1473
Walsh, Campbell 1473
Walsh, Carl E. 1473
Walsh, Ciaran 1473
Walsh, Clare Monica 1473
Walsh, Darren 1473
Walsh, David Allen 1473
Walsh, Dearbhla 1473
Walsh, Enda 1473
Walsh, Evan 1473
Walsh, Fran 1473
Walsh, G. 1473
Walsh, George 1473
Walsh, Joanna 1473
Walsh, Joe 1473
Walsh, Jordan 1473
Walsh, Julie 1473
Walsh, Kerri 1473
Walsh, Marcie 1473
Walsh, Melanie 1473
Walsh, Michael 1473
Walsh, Michael J. 1473
Walsh, Pat 1473
Walsh, Patrick C. 1473
Walsh, Peter 1473
Walsh, Ruby 1473
Walsh, Thommie 1473
Walsh, Tomas 1473
Walsh, Vivian 1473
Walsh, Walter 1473
Walsh, Willie M. 1473
Warsh, Sylvia Maultash 1480
ウォルシュ・ジェニングス
Walsh Jennings, Kerri 1473
ヴォルシュレガー
Wullschläger, Jackie 1530
ウォルシン
Vorsin, Yevgeny N. 1464
ウォールズ
Walls, Darrin 1473
Walls, Jeannette 1473
Walls, Ron M. 1473
ウォルスキー
Wolski, L.A. 1522
ウォールステッター
Wohlstetter, Roberta 1520
ウォルストン
Walston, Ray 1473
ウォールセン
Wohlsen, Marcus 1520
ウォルソール
Walthall, Anne 1474
ウォルター
Waltar, Alan Edward 1473
Walter, Catherine 1473
Walter, Chip 1473
Walter, Dawna 1473
Walter, Derek 1473
Walter, Ekaterina 1473
Walter, Elisse B. 1473
Walter, Garry 1473
Walter, Gilbert G. 1474
Walter, Ingo 1474
Walter, Isabel 1474
Walter, Jess 1474
Walter, John L. 1474
Walter, Magdalena 1474
Walter, Mark 1474
Walter, Matthew 1474
Walter, Nadine 1474
Walter, Stephen 1474
Walters, Martin 1474
Wolter, Michel 1522
ウォルダー
Waldherr, Kris 1469
ヴォルタ
Volta, Ornella 1463
ヴォルター
Wolter, Annette 1522
ウォルターズ
Walters, Alan Arthur 1474
Walters, Barbara 1474
Walters, Bryan 1474
Walters, Catherine 1474
Walters, David 1474
Walters, Derek 1474
Walters, D.Eric 1474
Walters, Eric 1474
Walters, Gale Climenson 1474
Walters, Guy 1474
Walters, Helen 1474
Walters, J.Donald 1474
Walters, Jonathan 1474
Walters, Julie 1474
Walters, Mark Jerome 1474
Walters, Matthew 1474
Walters, Michael 1474
Walters, Minette 1474
Walters, R.F.C. 1474
Walters, Robert 1474
Walters, Selmon 1474
Walters, Tony 1474
Walters, Vernon A. 1474
Walters, William 1474
Wolters, Nate 1522
Wolters, Syrt 1522
Wolters, Tony 1522
ウォルターストーフ
Wolterstorff, Nicholas 1522
ウォルチ
Wortche, Allison 1526
ウォルツ
Waltz, Kenneth 1475
Waltz, Mitzi 1475
Woertz, Patricia A. 1520
Woltz, Anna 1522
ヴォルツ
Voltz, Stephen 1463
ウォルツァー
Walzer, Michael 1475
ウォルデ
Wolde, Mamo 1520
Wolde, Michael Chemo 1520
ヴォルデ
Wolde, Gunilla 1520
ウォルデイ
Woldai, Futur 1520
ウォルデミカエル
Woldemichael, Abraha 1520
Woldemichael, Gebremariam 1520
Woldenkiel, Abraha 1520
ウォールデン
Walden, Mark 1469
ウォルデン
Walden, Erik 1469
Walden, Ian 1469
Warden, Jack 1478
ウォルデンキエル
Woldenkiel, Abraha 1520
ウォルト
Walt, Stephen M. 1473
ウォルド
Wald, Elijah 1469
Wald, Eric 1469
Waldo, Jim 1469
ウォルトキー
Waltke, Bruce K. 1474
ウォルトナー＝テーブズ
Waltner-Toews, David 1474
ウォルドハイム
Waldheim, Charles 1469
ウォルドバウアー
Waldbauer, Gilbert 1469
ウォルドフォーゲル
Waldfogel, Joel 1469
ウォルドホルツ
Waldholz, Michael 1469
ウォールドマン
Waldman, Anne 1469
Waldman, Irwin D. 1469
ウォルトマン
Waltman, Paul E. 1474
ウォルドマン
Waldman, Amy 1469
Waldman, Ayelet 1469
Waldman, Jonathan 1469
Waldman, Mark Robert 1469
Waldman, Murray 1469
ヴォルドマン
Voldman, Danièle 1462
ウォルドミカエル
Woldemichael, Gebremariam 1520

ウ

ウォルトル
Waltl, Herbert 1474
ウォルドループ
Waldroop, James 1469
ウォールドロップ
Waldrop, Keith 1469
ウォルドロン
Waldron, Arthur 1469
Waldron, Jeremy 1469
Waldron, Mal 1469
ウォールトン
Walton, Henry John 1474
ウォルトン
Walton, Alice 1474
Walton, Ashley 1474
Walton, Cedar 1474
Walton, Christy 1474
Walton, Henry John 1474
Walton, Jessica 1474
Walton, Jim 1474
Walton, Jo 1474
Walton, John T. 1474
Walton, Jonathan 1474
Walton, Ken 1474
Walton, Kendall L. 1474
Walton, L.T. 1474
Walton, Luke 1474
Walton, Roger 1474
Walton, Samuel Robson 1474
Walton, Sean 1475
Walton, Stephen 1475
Wolton, Dominique 1522
Wolton, Thierry 1522
ウォールナー
Wallner, John 1473
ウォルナー
Wallner, Kent 1473
ヴォルナー
Wollner, Fred 1522
ヴォルニー
Wollny, Peter 1522
ウォルパー
Wolper, David Lloyd 1522
ウォールバーグ
Wahlberg, Mark 1468
ウォルバーグ
Wahlberg, Mark 1468
ウォルパート
Wolpert, Jay 1522
Wolpert, Lewis 1522
ウォルビー
Walby, Sylvia 1469
ヴォルピ
Volpi, Mike 1463
Volpi, Vittorio 1463
ヴォルピー
Volpe, Joseph 1463
ウォルフ
Wolf, Alexander 1520
Wolf, Alex de 1520
Wolf, Christa 1520
Wolf, David W. 1520
Wolf, Edwin 1520
Wolf, Emil 1520
Wolf, Jenny 1520
Wolf, Markus 1521
Wolf, S. 1521
Wolfe, Brenda L. 1521
Wolfe, David 1521
Wolff, Edwin 1521
Wolff, Kurt 1521
Wolff, Milton 1521
Wolff, Patricia 1521
Wolff, Rene 1521
ヴォルフ
Wolf, Cendrine 1520
Wolf, Christa 1520
Wolf, Jochen 1520
Wolf, Karl-Jürgen 1521
Wolf, Klaus-Peter 1521
Wolf, Manfred 1521
Wolf, Markus 1521
Wolf, Norbert 1521
Wolf, Raphael 1521
Wolf, Ursula 1521
Wolff, Christoph 1521
Wolff, Johannes 1521
Wolf-sampath, Gita 1522
ヴォルファース
Wohlfarth, Alexander 1520
ウォルフィンガー
Wolfinger, Eric 1521
ウォルフェ
Wolfe, Pat 1521
ウォルフェンソン
Wolfensohn, James D. 1521
Wolfensohn, Sarah 1521
ウォルフォウィッツ
Wolfowitz, Paul Dundes 1521
ウォールフォース
Wohlforth, William C. 1520
ウォルフォード
Walford, Clive 1469
Walford, Geoffrey 1469
Walford, Jonathan 1469
Wolford, Wendy 1521
ウォルフォビッツ
Wolfowitz, Paul Dundes 1521
ウォルフソン
Wolfson, Evelyn 1522
Wolfson, Martin H. 1522
Wolfson, Richard 1522
ヴォルフ=ハイデッガー
Wolf-Heidegger, Gerhard 1521
ウォルフラム
Wolfram, Martin 1521
ウォルブリング
Wolbring, Gregor 1520
ヴォルフルム
Wolfrum, Edgar 1521
ウォルフレン
Wolferen, Karel G. Van 1521
ウォルブン
Wolven, Scott 1522
ヴォルペ
Volpe, Angelina 1463
ウォルポール
Walpole, Brenda 1473
ウォルマー
Wolmar, Christian 1522
ヴォルマー
Vollmer, Christopher 1462
ウォールマン
Wallman, Steven M. H. 1472
ウォルマン
Wolman, Benjamin B. 1522
Wolman, David 1522
ヴォルマン
Vollmann, William T. 1462
ヴォルム
Worm, Nicolai 1526
ウォルラス
Walrath, Kathy 1473
ヴォルリチェク
Worlitschek, Michael 1526
ウォルワード
Walvoord, Barbara E. Fassler 1475
ウォレイス
Wallace, Patti 1472
ウォレシュ
Walesh, Kimberly 1469
ウォーレス
Wallace, Chris 1471
Wallace, Claire 1471
Wallace, Daniel 1471
Wallace, David 1471
Wallace, George 1471
Wallace, John 1472
Wallace, Ken 1472
Wallace, Meredith 1472
Wallace, Mike 1472
Wallace, Nancy Elizabeth 1472
Wallace, Paul 1472
Wallace, Sandra Neil 1472
Wallace, Sean 1472
Wallace, Tyrone 1472
ウォレス
Wallace, Barbara 1471
Wallace, Benjamin 1471
Wallace, Dan 1471
Wallace, Daniel 1471
Wallace, Danny 1471
Wallace, Daphne 1471
Wallace, David Foster 1471
Wallace, David Rains 1471
Wallace, Doug 1471
Wallace, Harvey 1471
Wallace, Ian 1472
Wallace, James 1472
Wallace, Jane 1472
Wallace, John 1472
Wallace, Marcia 1472
Wallace, Mark 1472
Wallace, Patricia M. 1472
Wallace, Randall 1472
Wallace, Robert 1472
Wallace, Robert B. 1472
Wallace, Sandra Neil 1472
Wallace, Shawn P. 1472
Wallace, Terry C. 1472
Wallis, Quvenzhane 1472
ウォレス=マーフィー
Wallace-Murphy, Tim 1472
ウォーレック
Wollek, Bob 1522
ヴォレラン
Vaulerin, Arnaud 1448
ウォーレル
Worrell, Bernie 1526
Worrell, Bill 1526
ウォレル
Warrell, Margie 1479
ウォーレン
Warren, Adam 1479
Warren, Alison 1479
Warren, Andrea 1479
Warren, Butch 1479
Warren, David 1479
Warren, David Alexander 1479
Warren, Diane 1479
Warren, Earl 1479
Warren, Elizabeth 1479
Warren, Emma 1479
Warren, Greg 1479
Warren, Henry S., Jr. 1479
Warren, James 1479
Warren, John 1479
Warren, J.Robin 1479
Warren, Neil Clark 1479
Warren, Sharon A. 1480
Warren, Stuart G. 1480
Warren, T.J. 1480
Whalen, Edward 1496
Whalen, Paul J. 1496
ウォレン
Warren, David 1479
Warren, David Alexander 1479
Warren, Ethan 1479
Warren, Kay 1479
Warren, Linda 1479
Warren, Lissa 1479
Warren, Nancy 1479
Warren, Pat 1479
Warren, Rick 1479
Warren, Sally 1480
Warren, Tracy Anne 1480
Warren, Wendy 1480
ウォーレン・ジボン
Zevon, Warren William 1551
ウォーレンシュタイン
Wallenstein, Gene 1472
ヴオレンソラ
Vuorensola, Timo 1465
ウォロシン
Woloshin, Steve 1522
ウォロジン
Volodin, Vyacheslav V. 1462
ヴォロダースキー
Volodarsky, Mike 1462
ヴォロック
Volokh, Eugene 1462
ヴォロディーヌ
Volodine, Antoine 1462
ヴォロドス
Volodos, Arcadi 1462
ウォローニン
Voronin, Vladimir Nikoraevich 1464
ウォロニン
Voronin, Vladimir Nikoraevich 1464
ヴォローニン
Voronin, Vladimir Nikoraevich 1464
ヴォロニン
Voronin, Vladimir Nikoraevich 1464
ヴォーロノワ
Voronova, Beata Grigorievna 1464
ウォーロール
Worrall, Frank 1526
ウォロンツォーフ
Vorontsov, Yurii Mikhailovich 1464
ウォロンツォフ
Vorontsov, Alexei A. 1464
Vorontsov, Gennady N. 1464
Vorontsov, Nikolai Nikolaevich 1464
Vorontsov, Yurii Mikhailovich 1464

ヴォロンツォーフ
Vorontsov, Yurii Mikhailovich 1464
ヴォロンツォフ
Vorontsov, Nikolai Nikolaevich 1464
ヴォワイヨ
Voillot, Patrick 1462
ヴォワト
Voight, Gayle 1462
ウォーン
Woan, Graham 1520
ウォン
Uon, Yu-soon 1435
Won, Jae-Yeon 1522
Won, Jin Young 1522
Won, Ok Im 1522
Won, Sei-hoon 1522
Wong, Anthony 1522
Wong, Arthur 1522
Wong, Bill 1522
Wong, Cheryl M. 1522
Wong, Chi-huey 1522
Wong, David 1522
Wong, Dona M. 1522
Wong, Duncan 1522
Wong, Faye 1522
Wong, Glenn M. 1522
Wong, James 1522
Wong, John B. 1522
Wong, Kan Seng 1523
Wong, Kar-wai 1523
Wong, Ken 1523
Wong, Kent 1523
Wong, Kolten 1523
Wong, Kwok-shing Thomas 1523
Wong, Lawrence 1523
Wong, Mew Choo 1523
Wong, Ming 1523
Wong, Pansy 1523
Wong, Penny 1523
Wong, Ray 1523
Wong, Rich 1523
Wong, Ricky 1523
Wong, Stanford 1523
Wong, Stephen C.P. 1523
Wong, Victor 1523
Wong, Walden 1523
Woon, Khe Wei 1526
ヴォーン
Vaughan, Andrew 1448
Vaughan, Brian K. 1448
Vaughan, Christopher C. 1448
Vaughan, Elizabeth A. 1448
Vaughan, Gary V. 1448
Vaughan, Hal 1448
Vaughan, Jenny 1448
Vaughan, Margaret E. 1448
Vaughan, Robin Anthony 1448
Vaughn, Evelyn 1448
Vaughn, Jacque 1448
Vaughn, Lewis 1448
Vaughn, Matthew 1448
Vaughn, Rashad 1448
ウォンイェンチェオン
Wongyen Cheong, Marie Roland Alain 1523
ウォンウィパー・テーワハッサディン・ナ・アユッタヤー
Wongvipa Devahastin na Ayudhya 1523
ヴォンヴォラ
Volavola, Ben 1462
ウォーンキー
Warnke, Georgia 1479
ウォング
Wong, Junko 1523
Wong, Nicole E. 1523
Wong, Winnie Won Yin 1523
ウォンコムトン
Wongkhomthong, Som-Arch 1523
ヴォンサヴァン・ダムロンスク
Vongsavanh Damrongsouk 1463
ウォーンズ
Warnes, David 1479
ウォンズブラ
Wansbrough, Henry 1477
ウォント
Want, Lorna 1477
ウォンドレイ
Wandrei, Karin Evon 1475
ウォンパッタナキット
Wongpattanakit, Panipak 1523
ウォンビン
Wonbin 1522
ウォンプム
Wongpoom, Parkpoom 1523
ヴォンヘリクテン
Vongerichten, Jean-Georges 1463
ウォンボー
Wambaugh, Joseph 1475
ヴォンリー
Vonleh, Noah 1463
ウガス
Ugas, Yordenis 1432
ウガルテ・ウビジュス
Ugarte Ubillús, Óscal 1432
ウギェン・ドルジ
Yab Ugyen Dorji 1532
ヴクサヴィッチ
Vukcevich, Ray 1465
ヴクシク
Vukšić, V. 1465
ウグベシア
Ugbesia, Odion 1432
ウグル
Uguru, Usani Usani 1432
ウグルラ
Ugurla, Fatih 1432
ウクレバ
Ukleba, Mikheil 1432
ウクレヤ
Ukleja, Mick 1432
ヴケティツ
Wuketits, Franz M. 1530
ウケル・アバンゴ
Ukel Abango, Joseph 1432
ウーケン
Uken, Adriana 1432
ウゲン
Ugen, Lorraine 1432
ヴコヴィック
Vukovic, Laurel 1465
ウゴフスキ
Wugofski, Ted 1529
ウーゴ・マジョ
Hugo Mallo 633
ウコロワ
Ukolova, Evgenia 1432
ウサ
Usa, Guadalcanal Siriako 1436
Usa, Siriako 1436
ウサイミーン
Uthaymin, Muhammad Salih 1437
ウサキェヴィチ
Usakiewicz, Agnieszka 1436
Usakiewicz, Wojciech 1436
ウザクバエフ
Uzakbaev, Chyngysbek 1437
ウサトゥイ
Usatîi, Andrei 1436
ウサビアガ
Usabiaga, Javier 1436
ウサマテ
Usamate, Jone 1436
ウシ
Euchi, Hatem El 411
ウジー
Ousey, Byron 1064
ウジェ
Huget, Yoann 632
ウシェフ
Ushev, Theodore 1436
ウージェル
Heugel, Inès 602
ウシク
Usyk, Oleksandr 1437
ウジノフ
Uzhinov, Oleg 1437
ウジフサ
Ujifusa, Grant 1432
ウシャコフ
Ushakov, Dmitrii 1436
ウシャツカス
Ušackas, Vygaudas 1436
ウージャール
Oujar, Mohamed 1064
ウシュク
Işik, Fikri 651
Usyk, Oleksandr 1437
ウジョア
Ulloa, Leonardo 1433
ウジリ
Ujiri, Masai 1432
ウーズ
Woese, Carl R. 1520
ウス
Houssou, Dona Jean-Claude 626
ウスヴァイスカヤ
Usvayskaya, Tanya 1437
ウスココビッチ
Usković, Borislav 1436
Usković, Darko 1436
ウースター
Wooster, Steven 1526
Wurster, Thomas S. 1530
ウズダビニス
Uzdavinis, Arturo 1437
ウスタリス・アルセ
Ustariz Arze, Reginaldo 1436
ウスチノフ
Ustinov, Nikolai 1436
Ustinov, Vladimir V. 1437
ウスチュゴフ
Ustyugov, Evgeny 1437
ウスチュナー
Üstüner, Tuba 1437
ウスツン
Üstün, T.Bedirhan 1437
ウスティノフ
Oustinoff, Michaël 1064
ウスティノワ
Ustinova, Daria 1437
ウストイウゴフ
Ustyugov, Evgeny 1437
ウストゥーン
Üstün, T.Bedirhan 1437
ウーストハイゼン
Oosthuizen, Coenie 1055
Oosthuizen, Louis 1055
ウストピリョン
Ustopiriyon, Komronshokh 1437
ウースナー
Wuerthner, George 1529
ウスナウ
Wuthnow, Robert 1530
ウズニエ
Usunier, Jean-Claude 1437
ウスパスキフ
Uspaskich, Viktor 1436
ウスペンスキー
Uspenskii, Petr Dem'ianovich 1436
Uspensky, Eduard 1436
ウスボフ
Usubov, Ramil 1437
ウスマノフ
Usmanov, Alisher 1436
Usmanov, Mirabror 1436
ウスマン
Ousmane, Ba 1064
Ousmane, Mahamane Elhadji 1064
Usman, Abubakar Abdid 1436
Usman, Esther Nenadi 1436
Usman, Hussein Muhammad 1436
Usman, Mariam 1436
Usman, Samsudeen 1436
ウスモノフ
Usmanov, Mirabror 1436
ウスモンゾダ
Usmonzoda, Usmonali 1436
ウースラー
Uslar, Moritz von 1436
ウスラル・ピエトリ
Uslar-Pietri, Arturo 1436
ウースラント
Ousland, Borge 1064
ウーズン
Wuchun 1529
ウセイニ
Ousseini, Abdoulwahid Halimatou 1064
Ousseini, Mamadou 1064
ウセニ
Ousseni, Abdou 1064
ウセノフ
Usenov, Daniyar 1436
ウゼラツ
Uzelac, Slobodan 1437

ウ

ウセルバエフ
Usserbayev, Galymzhan 1436
ウーゼンクラフト
Wozencraft, Kim 1527
ウゾマー
Uzomah, C.J. 1437
ウター
Uther, Hans-Jörg 1437
ウダーア
Oudaa, Mohamed Abdallahi Ould 1063
ウダイ・フセイン
Hussein, Uday 638
ウダイ・プラカーシ
Udaya Prakāśa 1431
ウダエタ・ベラスケス
Udaeta Velásquez, Maria Esther 1431
ウダガワ
Udagawa, Anna 1431
ウダチン
Udachyn, Artem 1431
ウタマ
Oetama, Jacob 1045
ウタミ
Utami, Ayu 1437
ウタール
Houtart, François 627
ウダール
Houdart, Sophie 625
ウーダン
Houdin, Jean-Pierre 625
WuDunn, Sheryl 1529
ウダン
Oudin, Bernard 1063
ウチダ
Uchida, Mitsuko 1431
Uchida, Pamela 1431
ヴチッチ
Vučić, Aleksandar 1465
ウック
Huch, José María 631
Ouk Rabun 1064
ウッサン
Houssin, Xavier 626
ウッシリー
Ussilly, Lesly Novia Shila 1436
ウッジンヌ
Ouzzine, Mohamed 1064
ウッズ
Woods, Al 1525
Woods, Antwaun 1525
Woods, Bob 1525
Woods, Caspian 1525
Woods, Dan 1525
Woods, David 1525
Woods, Donald 1525
Woods, Donald R. 1525
Woods, Earl 1525
Woods, Emily 1525
Woods, Eoin 1525
Woods, Gordon 1525
Woods, James 1525
Woods, Michael 1525
Woods, Paula L. 1525
Woods, Pete 1525
Woods, Phil 1525
Woods, Robert 1525
Woods, Robert (Bob) T. 1525
Woods, Rosemary 1525
Woods, Rose Mary 1525
Woods, Samuel Kofi 1525
Woods, Sherryl 1525
Woods, Stuart 1525
Woods, Thomas E. 1525
Woods, Tiger 1525
Woods, Vanessa 1525
ウーツソーン
Utzon, Jørn 1437
ウツソン
Utzon, Jørn 1437
ウッダー
Oudaa, Mohamed Abdallahi Ould 1063
ウッダード
Woodard, Jonathan 1524
ウッタマ
Uttama, Savanayana 1437
ウッダル
Woodall, James 1524
ウッツ
Utz, Arthur Fridolin 1437
Utz, Peter 1437
ウッツォン
Utzon, Jørn 1437
ウッディウィス
Woodiwiss, Kathleen E. 1524
ウッディング
Wooding, Chris 1524
ウッテン
Wooten, Tom 1526
ウッデン
Wooden, John R. 1524
ウッデンベリ
Uddenberg, Nils 1431
ウッド
Wood, A.J. 1523
Wood, Alex 1523
Wood, Alison 1523
Wood, Andrea 1523
Wood, Andrew 1523
Wood, Anna Lomax 1523
Wood, Anthony 1523
Wood, Ashley 1523
Wood, Audrey 1523
Wood, Bernard 1523
Wood, Blake 1523
Wood, Bobby 1523
Wood, Carol 1523
Wood, Charles W. 1523
Wood, Chip 1523
Wood, Christian 1523
Wood, Christopher 1523
Wood, David 1523
Wood, Deborah 1523
Wood, Diana F. 1523
Wood, Don 1523
Wood, Dorothy 1523
Wood, Douglas 1523
Wood, Elijah 1523
Wood, Ellen Meiksins 1523
Wood, Eric 1523
Wood, Fiona 1523
Wood, Frances 1523
Wood, Gaby 1523
Wood, Gordon S. 1523
Wood, Hannah 1524
Wood, Hunter 1524
Wood, James B. 1524
Wood, James M. 1524
Wood, J.B. 1524
Wood, Jeffrey C. 1524
Wood, Joanne 1524
Wood, John 1524
Wood, Joyce 1524
Wood, Kay 1524
Wood, Lamont 1524
Wood, Leslie 1524
Wood, Marie E. 1524
Wood, Matthew 1524
Wood, Michael 1524
Wood, Monica 1524
Wood, Myron 1524
Wood, Nancy C. 1524
Wood, Oenone 1524
Wood, Patricia 1524
Wood, Philip R. 1524
Wood, Ralph C. 1524
Wood, Richard H. 1524
Wood, Robert Muir 1524
Wood, Ron 1524
Wood, Sara 1524
Wood, Scott 1524
Wood, Selina 1524
Wood, Tom 1524
Wood, Travis 1524
Wood, Trevor 1524
Wood, Vaughan 1524
Wood, Zach 1524
ウッドウォース
Woodworth, Michael 1525
ウッドウォード
Woodward, Debra 1525
ウッドオール
Woodall, Clive 1524
ウッド・キャタノ
Wood Catano, Janice 1524
ウッドコック
Woodcock, Jon 1524
Woodcock, Leonard 1524
ウッドサイド
Woodside, Alexander 1525
Woodside, Byran 1525
ウッドスモール
Woodsmall, Wyatt Lee 1525
ウッドソン
Woodson, Ali-Ollie 1525
Woodson, Jacqueline 1525
Woodson, Mike 1525
ウッドハウス
Woodhouse, Christopher Montague 1524
Woodhouse, Edward J. 1524
Woodhouse, Margaret 1524
Woodhouse, Michael 1524
Woodhouse, Tom 1524
ウッドハム
Woodhams, Jessica 1524
ウッドハル
Woodhull, Albert S. 1524
ウッドバーン
Woodburn, Woody 1524
ウッドフォード
Woodford, Chris 1524
Woodford, Michael 1524
Woodford, Susan 1524
ウッドヘッド
Woodhead, Danny 1524
Woodhead, Lindy 1524
ウッドホール
Woodhall, Maureen 1524
ウッドマン
Woodman, Conor 1525
Woodman, Josef 1525
Woodman, Natalie 1525
ウッドヤード
Woodyard, Wesley 1525
ウッドラフ
Woodruff, Tom, Jr. 1525
Woodruff, William 1525
ウッドランド
Woodland, Joseph 1525
ウッドレル
Woodrell, Daniel 1525
ウッドロウ
Woodrow, Patrick 1525
ウッドワース
Woodworth, Lynn 1525
Woodworth, Stephen 1525
ウッドワード
Woodward, Benjamin 1525
Woodward, Bob 1525
Woodward, Chris 1525
Woodward, Christopher 1525
Woodward, Diana 1525
Woodward, F.Ian 1525
Woodward, Harry 1525
Woodward, James 1525
Woodward, John 1525
Woodward, Kay 1525
Woodward, Kenneth L. 1525
Woodward, Patricia 1525
Woodward, Patrick M. 1525
Woodward, Peter 1525
Woodward, Shaun 1525
Woodward, Woody 1525
ウーデ
Houdé, Valentin 625
ウデ
Ude, Filip 1432
ウティット・ヘーマムーン
Uthit Hēmamūn 1437
ウティポフ
Latipov, Jasurbek 794
ウティーム
Uttem, Cassam 1437
ウディン
Oudine, Saleban Omar 1063
Oudine, Souleiman Omar 1063
Woodin, Karen E. 1524
Woodin, Michael 1524
ウーデゴーア
Odegaard, Martin 1043
ウテショフ
Uteshov, Almas 1437
ウテヒン
Utekhin, Ilya 1437
ウデル
Udell, Lawrence J. 1432
ウデルニ
Quederni, Ahmed Lyadh 1144
ウーデルホーヴェン
Udelhoven, Hermann-Josef 1432
ウーテン
Wooten, James A. 1526
Wooten, James T. 1526
ウデンワ
Udenwa, Achike 1432
ウート
Uth, Mark 1437
ウドー
Udoh, Blessed 1432
ウトイカマヌ
Utoikamanu, Siosiua 1437

ウドヴェンコ
Udovenko, Hennadii Yosipovich 1432
ウトゥカン
Utkan, Necati 1437
ウドゥラオゴ
Ouedraogo, Fulgence 1063
ウドゥン
Wooden, John R. 1524
ウドカ
Udoka, Ime 1432
ウドコック
Woodcock, Tony 1524
ウドビチッチ
Udovičić, Vanja 1432
ウドビチュキ
Udovički, Kori 1432
ウドビツキ
Udovički, Kori 1432
ウドベンコ
Udovenko, Hennadii Yosipovich 1432
ウドマ
Udoma, Udo Udo 1432
ウトマンジャメ
Outhmane Djame, Haoua 1064
ウドムルトワ
Udmurtova, Oksana 1432
ウドリー
Udry, Christopher 1432
ウトリオ
Utrio, Kaari 1437
ウードリック
Udorih, Beno 1432
ウードリング
Woodring, Jim 1525
ウドレー
Houdret, Jean-Claude 625
ウドレア
Udrea, Elena 1432
ウートン
Wooton, Rus 1526
ウドンポーン
Polsak, Udomporn 1122
ウナ
Una, Benjamin 1433
ウナイエス
Ouneies, Ahmed 1064
ウナイ・ガルシア
Unai Garcia 1434
ウナイ・ロペス
Unai Lopez 1434
ウナクタン
Unakitan, Kemal 1434
ウナサ
Unasa, Mesi Galo 1434
ウナル
Ünal, Mahir 1434
Unal, Mehmet Nadir 1434
ヴニーザ
Vunisa, Samuela 1465
ヴニポラ
Vunipola, Billy 1465
Vunipola, Mako 1465
ウヌテ
Ounouted, Raymond 1064
ウヌルバト・プレブジャブ
Onorbat Purevjavyn 1054
ウノ
Uno, Raymond S. 1434
ウノンペ・アティパ
Hounnonkpe Attikpa, Honorine 626
ウハイシ
al-Wuhayshi, Nasser 1530
ウバイド
Ubad, Hamoud 1431
Ubayd, Hamud Mohammed 1431
Ubayd, Makram 1431
ウーハガード
Övergaard, Gunnar 1065
ウパダヤ
Upadhyaya, Amod Prasad 1435
Upadhyaya, Shailendra Kumar 1435
ウパデアーエ
Upadhyay, Vibhav Kant 1435
ウバーリ
Oubaali, Nordine 1063
ウバルデ
Ubalde, Jonard 1431
ウビダ
Oubida, François 1063
ウーフダド
Hoefdraad, Gillmore 612
ウブティル
Oubtil, Mahjouba 1063
ウブナージ
Obonaji, Osama Abdul-Salam 1041
ウープラン
Houplain, Ludovic 626
ウフリアリク
Uhliarik, Ivan 1432
ウブルリ
Oubrerie, Clément 1063
ウベローデ
Ubbelohde, O. 1431
ウホフ
Ukhov, Ivan 1432
ウボン
Ubol, Renu 1431
Ubol, Thanarat 1431
ウー・マ
Wu Ma 1530
ウーマック
Womack, Bobby 1522
ウマニ
Oumani, Bety Aïchatou Habibou 1064
ウマラ
Humala, Ollanta 634
ウマリ
Umali, Rick 1433
ウマール
Umar, Idris 1433
ウマル
Omar, Muhammad 1052
Oumarou, Alma 1064
Oumarou, Ide 1064
Oumarou, Seyni 1064
Oumarou, Sidikou 1064
Umar, Mohammed 1433
Umar, Sadiq 1433
Umar Wirahadikusumah 1433
ウマル・ウィラハディクスマ
Umar Wirahadikusumah 1433
ウマル・カヤム
Umar Kayam 1433
ウマロゥ
Oumarou, Almou 1064
ウミア
Oumiha, Sofiane 1064
ウ・ミンジョー
Min Kyaw 953
ウム
Oum, Tae Hoon 1064
ウー・ムーイェ
Wu, Mu-Ye 1529
ウム・サンガレ
Oumou Sangare 1064
ウムベトフ
Umbetov, Serik 1433
ウメニオーラ
Umenyiora, Osi 1433
ウヤズドフスキ
Ujazdowski, Kazimierz 1432
ウーヤヒア
Ouyahia, Ahmed 1064
ウーヤヒヤ
Ouyahia, Ahmed 1064
ヴュストルツ
Wüstholz, Gisbert 1530
ヴュチェビッチ
Vucevic, Nikola 1465
ヴュートリッヒ
Wüthrich, Kurt 1530
ヴュートリヒ
Wüthrich, Kurt 1530
ヴュトリヒ
Wuthrich, Gregory 1530
ヴュルテンベルガー
Würtenberger, Thomas 1530
ウユンタナ
Wuyontana 1530
ウヨンタナ
Wuyontana 1530
ウーラ
Olah, Benedek 1048
ウライエ
Oulaye, Hubert 1064
ヴライク
Vlaicu, Florin 1461
ウライワン
Uraiwan, Thienthong 1435
ウラカン・ラミレス
Huracan Ramirez 637
ヴラシック
Vlasic, Bill 1461
ウラジーミル・マラーホフ
Malakhov, Vladimir 889
ウラジーモフ
Vladimov, Georgii Nikolaevich 1460
ヴラジーモフ
Vladimov, Georgii Nikolaevich 1460
ヴラスコ
Velasco, Jean-Jacques 1450
ヴラスコヴィッツ
Vlaskovits, Patrick 1461
ウラソフ
Vlasov, Fedor 1461
ヴラダー
Vladar, Stefan 1460
ヴラツァノス
Vratsanos, Dimos 1465
ウーラッハ
Urach, Hans 1435
ウラニ
Euranie, Annabelle 411
ウラノフ
Ulanov, Denis 1433
ヴラミス
Vlamis, Gregory 1461
ウラムス
Woollams, Stanley 1526
ウラムヌ
Ourahmoune, Sarah 1064
ウラーン
Ulaan, Chultem 1432
ウラン
Oran, Mouhammad 1056
Ulan, Helen 1433
ウランウラン
Uran Uran, Rigoberto 1435
ヴランチッチ
Vrancic, Mario 1465
ウランチメグ
Uranchimeg, Munkh-Erdene 1435
ウランツェツェグ・ムンフバット
Urantsetseg Monkhbatyn 1435
ウーリー
Oury, Gerard 1064
Wooley, Sheb 1526
ウリ
Oury, Jean 1064
ウリー
Woolley, Benjamin 1526
Wurie, Alpha 1530
ウリアス
Urias, Julio 1435
ヴリアミー
Vulliamy, Clara 1465
ウーリアムズ
Woolliams, Peter 1526
ウリアルテ
Uriarte, Felimon 1435
Uriarte, Sugoi 1435
ウリアルテ・ロドリゲス
Uriarte Rodríguez, Ana Lya 1435
ウリエ
Houllier, Gerard 626
ウリエット
Ullyett, Kevin 1433
ウリクト
Wright, Georg Henrik von 1528
ウリシェフ
Urishev, Anzor 1435
ウーリス
Woolis, Rebecca 1526
ヴリース
Vries, Hent de 1465
ウーリスクロフト
Woolliscroft, Tony 1526
ウリチャック
Urichuck, Bob 1435
ウリツカヤ
Ulitskaia, Liudmila 1433
ウーリッチ
Ulich, Michaela 1433
ウーリッヒ
Uhlig, Helmut 1432
ウリーナ

Urena, Jose 1435
Urena, Richard 1435
ヴリナ
Vrinat, Jean-Claude 1465
ウリノフ
Urinov, Alexander 1435
ウーリヒ
Uhlich, Gerald R. 1432
ウリーベ
Uribe Vélez, Álvaro 1435
ウリベ
Uribe, Kirmen 1435
Uribe, Mariajo 1435
Uribe, Nora 1435
Uribe, Veronica 1435
Uribe Escobar, Fernando 1435
Uribe Vélez, Álvaro 1435
ウリベ・エチェバリア
Uribe Echevarría, Jorge Alberto 1435
ウリベ・ベガララ
Uribe Vegalara, Juan Gabriel 1435
ウリベ・ベレス
Uribe Vélez, Álvaro 1435
ウリベ・ボテロ
Uribe Botero, Beatriz 1435
ウリャテ・ファボ
Ullate Fabo, José Antonio 1433
ウリヤーノフ
Ulyanov, Mikhail Aleksandrovich 1433
ウリヤノフ
Ulyanov, Mikhail Aleksandrovich 1433
ウリヤノワ
Ulyanova, Olga 1433
ウリュカエフ
Ulyukayev, Alexei V. 1433
ヴリーランド
Vreeland, Shannon 1465
Vreeland, Susan 1465
ウリーン
Ulin, Bengt 1433
ウール
Uhl, Axel 1432
Uhl, Matthias 1432
Wool, Robert 1525
ウル
Ulu, Vaomalo Kini 1433
Urru, Franco 1436
Wulu, Samuel 1530
ウー・ルイン
U Lwin 1433
ウールヴァートン
Woolverton, Linda 1526
ウルヴァートン
Wolverton, Lisa 1522
ウ・ルウィン
U Lwin 1433
ウールウェイ
Woolway, Erica 1526
ウルヴェーティ
Urveti, Ram Singh 1436
ウルヴェル
Ulver, Stanislav 1433
ウルガー
Woolger, Roger J. 1526
ウルカデ
Hourcade, Daniel 626
ウルカララ
Prince Ulukalala Lavaka-Ata 1433
ウルカララ・ラバカアタ王子
Prince Ulukalala Lavaka-Ata 1433
ウルキディ・バラウ
Urquidi Barrau, Jorge 1436
ウルク
Hulk 634
ウルクハート
Urquhart, Stephen 1436
ウルクメン
Ulkumen, Selahattin 1433
ウルケシ
Wuerkaixi 1529
ウルケシュ
Wuerkaixi 1529
ウルケル
Ülker, Murat 1433
ウルゴビッチ
Hrgovic, Filip 629
ウルサケ
Ursache, Andrei 1436
Ursache, Valentin 1436
ウルサノ
Ursano, Robert J. 1436
ヴルサリコ
Vrsaljko, Sime 1465
ウールジー
Woolsey, Lynn 1526
ウルジカ
Urzica, Marius Daniel 1436
ウルシーニ
Ursini, James 1436
ウルシニー
Ursiny, Timothy E. 1436
ウルシャゼ
Urushadze, Andria 1436
ウルス
Ulusu, Bülent 1433
Ursu, Vasile 1436
ウルスト
Wurst, Gregor 1530
ウルスリアック
Ursuliak, Wally 1436
ウルスル
Ulsrud, Thomas 1433
ウルセマル
Urusemal, Joseph 1436
ウルセル
Oursel, Luc 1064
ウルタド
Hurtado, Eliezer 637
ウルダバエワ
Urdabayeva, Marian 1435
ウルタン
Heurtin, Jean-Philippe 602
ウルチ
Uruci, Esmeralda 1436
ヴルチェク
Vlcek, Ernst 1461
Vltchek, Andre 1461
ウルツ
Ultz 1433
ヴルツ
Wurz, Alex 1530
ウルティア
Urrutia, Paulina 1436
Urrutia, Salvador 1436
ウルト
Würth, Reinhold 1530
ウルトー
Heurtaux, Thomas 602
ウルド・アッバス
Ould Abbas, Djamel 1064
ウルドアッバス
Ould Abbas, Djamel 1064
ウルドアベス
Ould Abbas, Djamel 1064
ウルドカブリア
Ould Kablia, Dahou 1064
ウルド・ブラーム
Ould Braham, Myriam 1064
ウールドリッジ
Wooldridge, Adrian 1526
Wooldridge, Doug 1526
Wooldridge, Michael 1526
ウルドリッチ
Uldrich, Jack 1433
ウルナール
Uchnár, Peter 1431
ウルバニ
Urbani, Giuliano 1435
ウルバネハ
Urbaneja, Mariá Lourdes 1435
ウルバーノデソウザ
Urbano De Sousa, Constança 1435
ウルバン
Urban, Knut 1435
Urban, Milan 1435
Urban, Simon 1435
ウルピライネン
Urpilainen, Jutta 1436
ウールフ
Woolfe, Angela 1526
ウルフ
Wolf, Anthony E. 1520
Wolf, Barbara 1520
Wolf, Diane Lauren 1520
Wolf, Dick 1520
Wolf, Edward L. 1520
Wolf, Ernest S. 1520
Wolf, Fred 1520
Wolf, Joan B. 1520
Wolf, Joan M. 1520
Wolf, Karen 1521
Wolf, Martin 1521
Wolf, Maryanne 1521
Wolf, Naomi 1521
Wolf, Steve 1521
Wolf, Susan 1521
Wolfe, Alan 1521
Wolfe, Burton H. 1521
Wolfe, Cary 1521
Wolfe, David 1521
Wolfe, David Allen 1521
Wolfe, Dennis 1521
Wolfe, Derek 1521
Wolfe, Gary K. 1521
Wolfe, Gene 1521
Wolfe, Inger Ash 1521
Wolfe, Julia 1521
Wolfe, Nathan 1521
Wolfe, Pamela S. 1521
Wolfe, Tom 1521
Wolfe, Walter Beran 1521
Wolff, Alan 1521
Wolff, Ashley 1521
Wolff, Daniel 1521
Wolff, David 1521
Wolff, Earl 1521
Wolff, Ferida 1521
Wolff, Janet 1521
Wolff, Jonathan 1521
Wolff, Siegfried 1521
Wolff, Steven B. 1521
Wolff, Tobias Jonathan Ansell 1521
Wolff, Tracy 1521
Wolff, Virginia Euwer 1521
Wolf-sampath, Gita 1522
Woolf, Brian P. 1526
Woolf, Karen 1526
Woolf, Stuart Joseph 1526
Wulf, Andrea 1530
Wulff, Christian 1530
Wulff, Mary L. 1530
ヴルフ
Wulf, Christoph 1530
Wulff, Christian 1530
Wulff, Hans E. 1530
ウルフィ
al-Urfi, Ahmed Ali 1435
ウルフェン
Wulfen, Gijs van 1530
ウルフォウィッツ
Wolfowitz, Paul 1521
Wolfowitz, Paul Dundes 1521
ウルブスコーグ
Ulvskog, Marita 1433
ウールフスン
Woolfson, Richard C. 1526
ウルフソン
Wolfson, Mike 1522
ウルフ - ティルフォード
Wulff-Tilford, Mary 1530
ウルフマン
Wolfman, Marv 1521
ウルブリヒト
Ulbricht, Catherine E. 1433
ヴルブレフスカ=ストラウス
Wróblewska-Straus, Hanna 1529
ウールベック
Houellebecq, Michel 625
ウルベルアーガ
Urberuaga, Emilio 1435
ウルボアス
Urvoas, Jean-Jacques 1436
ウールマー
Woolmer, Bob 1526
ウルマーナ
Urmana, Violeta 1436
ウールマン
Uhrmann, Michael 1432
Woolman, Matt 1526
ウルマン
Ullman, Ellen 1433
Ullman, Jeffery D. 1433
Ullman, Larry Edward 1433
Ullmann, Liv 1433
Ullmann, Michael 1433
Urman, Richard D. 1435
ウルミ
Ulumi, Noorul-Haq 1433
ウルムシュナイダー
Ulmschneider, Peter 1433
ウルライヒ
Ulreich, Sven 1433
ウールリッジ
Woolridge, Georgie 1526
ウルリッチ
Ulrich, David 1433

Ulrich, Deborah L. 1433
Ulrich, Jan 1433
Ulrich, Mike 1433
Ulrich, Wendy 1433
ウルリッヒ
Ullrich, Axel 1433
Ulrich, Lars 1433
Ulrich, Wolfgang 1433
ウルリヒ
Ullrich, Jan 1433
Ullrich, Wolfgang 1433
ウレア
Urrea, Luis Alberto 1436
ヴレイ
Vrij, Aldert 1465
ウレイカート
Wreikat, Abdul Latif 1527
ウレイカト
Wreikat, Rami 1527
ヴレーシューヴェル
Vleeschouwer, Olivier de 1461
ウレスティ・エレラ
Urresti Elera, Daniel 1436
ウーレット
Ouellette, Alicia 1064
Ouellette, Jennifer 1064
Ouellette, Robert J. 1064
ウーレン
Woollen, Rob 1526
ウーレンカム
Uhlenkamp, Jeannie 1432
ウレンハーグ
Ullenhag, Erik 1433
ウロコフ
Urokov, Bekmurod 1436
ウロシュチョフスカ
Wloszczowska, Maja 1520
ウロズボエフ
Urozboev, Diyorbek 1436
ウロト
Oulotto, Anne Désirée 1064
ウロベル
Wrobel, Agata 1529
ヴロンスキー
Vronsky, Peter 1465
ウワタラ
Ouattara, Tené Birahima 1063
ウワチュ
Uwacu, Julienne 1437
ウワンゼ
Nwanze, Kanayo F. 1038
ウン
Eun, Hee-kyung 411
Ng, Anthony T. 1019
Ng, Eng Hen 1019
Ng, Pak Tee 1019
Ng, Yan Yee 1019
Ng, Yen Yen 1019
ウンガー
Ungar, Michael 1434
Unger, Daniel 1434
Unger, Felix 1434
Unger, Lisa 1434
Unger, Tobias 1434
ウンガク
Kim, Un Guk 735
ウングソン
Ungson, Gerardo R. 1434
ウングバリ
Ungvari, Miklos 1434
ウンクペ
Hounkpè, Léa 626
ウングボ
Houngbo, Gilbert Fossoun 626
ウングリアヌ
Ungureanu, Monica 1434
ウングリック
Unglik, Georges 1434
ウンクルンジザ
Nkurunziza, Pierre 1029
ウングレアース
Ungureanu, Mihai-Razvan 1434
ウングレアーヌ
Ungureanu, Mihai-Razvan 1434
ウンゲラー
Ungerer, Tomi 1434
ウンジャン
Oundjian, Peter 1064
ウンシュ
Wunsch, Marjory 1530
ウンスエータ
Unzueta, Angel 1435
ウンゼルト
Unseld, Siegfried 1434
ウンダ
Unda, Hugo 1434
Unda, Maider 1434
ヴンダー
Wunder, Ingolf 1530
ウンターウルザッハー
Unterwurzacher, Kathrin 1434
ウンターベルグ
Unterberg, Bastian 1434
ウンタラー
Ounthala, Khambai 1064
ヴンダーリッヒ
Wunderlich, Paul 1530
ウンダーリヒ
Wunderlich, Paul 1530
ヴンダーリヒ
Wunderlich, Paul 1530
ウンツナー
Unzner-Fischer, Christa 1435
ウンデンゲ
Undenge, Samuel 1434
ウンドゥラガ
Undurraga, Alberto 1434
ヴントラム
Wundram, Manfred 1530
ウンブラル
Umbral, Francisco 1433
ウンペ
Hounkpe, Paul 626
ウンル
Unruh, Lisa 1434

【エ】

エア
Eyre, Lucy 414
Eyre, Richard 414
エアー
Ayer, David 73
Eyre, Richard 414
エアシポール・スリサワラック
Eathipol Srisawaluck 388
エアース
Airth, Rennie 22
エアーズ
Ayers, Kevin 73
Ayres, Charlie 74
Ayres, Chris 74
Ayres, David 74
Ayres, Ed 74
Ayres, Honor 74
Ayres, Ian 74
Ayres, Katherine 74
エアズ
Ayres, Virginia E. 74
エアテトミ
Ehate Tomi, Vicente 393
エアハート
Ehrhart, William Daniel 393
エーアハルト
Ehrhardt, Jana U. 393
エアハルト
Ehrhardt, Michael C. 393
Erhardt, Jean 406
エアリク
Ehrlich, Amy 393
エアリンガー
Erlinger, Rainer 407
エァルブルッフ
Erlbruch, Wolf 407
エイ
Aye, John 73
エイー
Eyih, Ghdafna Ould 414
エイヴァリー
Avery, Dennis T. 71
Avery, Gilliann 71
Avery, Ryan 71
エイヴィス
Avis, Ed 72
Avis, Paul D.L. 72
エイヴリー
Avery, Gilliann 71
Avery, James K. 71
エイヴリル
Averill, Thomas Fox 71
エイエイ
Rong Rong 1201
エイカー
Achor, Shawn 10
エイガー
Agar, John 17
エイカーズ
Akers, Kevin 23
Akers, William M. 23
エイガス
Agus, David 19
エイカーソン
Akerson, Alan 23
エイカフ
Acuff, Amy 11
エイカーリンド
Akerlind, Christopher 23
エイガンズ
Agans, David J. 17
エイキン
Aiken, Joan Delano 22
Akin, Fatih 24
Akin, Sylvia Seymour 24
エイキンス
Aikens, Walt 22
エイキンズ
Aikins, Dave 22
エイクボーン
Ayckbourn, Alan 73
エイグラン
Agran, Martin 18
エイクロイド
Aykroyd, Dan 73
エイゲル
Eygel, Pavel 414
エイケン
Aiken, Joan Delano 22
Aiken, Kamar 22
Aiken, Linda H. 22
Aitken, Kenneth 22
エイゲン
Aigen, Kenneth 22
エイコフ
Ackoff, Russell Lincoln 11
エイザー
Azar, Betty Schrampfer 74
エイサギレ
Eyzaguirre, Nicolás 414
エイサン
Athan, Mattie Sue 67
エイシ
Ayissi, Henri Eyebe 73
エイシー
Acy, Quincy 11
エイジー
Agee, Jon 17
Agee, Philip 17
エイジアス
Agius, Marcus Ambrose Paul 17
エイジェイ
A.J. 22
Ajayi, Jay 23
エイスナー
Eisner, Will 395
エイズベット
Aisbett, Bev 22
エイダ
Eide, Lita 394
エイタム
Eitam, Efraim 395
エイタン
Eitan, Michael 395
Eitan, Rafi 395
Eitan, Raphael 395
エイチソン
Aitchison, Jean 22
HDR
HDR, Daniel 586
エイック
Eick, Stephen G. 394
エイディ
Adie, Kate 14
エイディー
Adey, Robert 14
エイデルステイン
Eydelsteyn, Gustavo 414
エイデルマン
Adelman, Bob 14
Edelman, Gwen 389
Edelmann, Anton 389
Eidelman, Polina 394
エイデン
Aiden, Erez 21
エイデンハート
Adenhart, Nick 14
エイト

エ

Ayto, Russell 74
エイドガン
Aydogan, Oguzhan 73
エイトケン
Aitken, J.T. 22
エイドリアン
Adreon, Diane 15
Adrian, Lara 16
Adrian, Nathan 16
Yeo, Adrian 1537
エイドリゲビシウス
Eidrigevicius, Stasys 394
エイトール
Heitor, Manuel 590
エイナウディ
Einaudi, Ludovico 394
エイナル・ガリレア
Einar Galilea 394
エイノーディ
Einaudi, Jean-Luc 394
エイノン
Einon, Dorothy 394
エイバイズ
Avise, John C. 72
エイバソールド
Aebersold, JoAnn 16
エイバーハート
Eberhart, Richard Ghormley 388
エイバリー
Avery, Gilliann 71
エイハーン
Ahern, Patric V. 19
エイバン
al-E'ban, Musa'ed bin Muhammad 388
エイビス
Avis, Warren 72
Avise, John C. 72
エイブ
Abé, Shana 6
エイフェックス・ツイン
Twin, Aphex 1430
エイブナー
Eibner, Brett 393
エイフマン
Eifman, Boris Yakovlevich 394
エイブラー
Abelar, Taisha 6
エイブラハム
Abraham, Daniel 7
Abraham, Ivo Luc 8
Abraham, Jay 8
Abraham, Ralph 8
Abraham, William James 8
エイブラハムズ
Abrahams, Marc 8
Abrahams, Peter 8
エイブラハムソン
Abrahamson, Eric 8
Abrahamson, Peter 8
Abrahamson, Shaun 8
エイブラム
Abram, Jan 8
Abrams, Roger I. 8
エイブラムス
Abrams, Donald I. 8
Abrams, Douglas 8
Abrams, J.J. 8
Abrams, Rachel Carlton 8
エイブラムズ
Abrams, Rhonda M. 8
エイブラムソン
Abramson, Arnold 8
Abramson, Jill 8
エイブリー
Abley, Mark 7
Avery, Gilliann 71
Avery, Julius 71
Avery, Sid 71
エイブルソン
Abelson, Harold 6
Abelson, Philip Hauge 6
エイフレム
Eifrem, Emil 394
エイベアイシ
Eyebe Ayissi, Henri 414
Eyebe Ayssi, Henri 414
エイベル
Abel, David Oliver 6
Abell, Roger 6
Aibel, Jonathan 21
エイペル
Appel, Andrew W. 53
エイベルソン
Abelson, Philip Hauge 6
エイホ
Aho, Alfred V. 21
エイボン
Avorn, Jerry 72
エイマール - デュヴルネ
Eymard-Duvernay, François 414
エイマン
Heymann, Mathias 603
エイミーズ
Amies, Hardy 41
エイミス
Amies, Hardy 41
Amis, Kingsley 41
Amis, Martin Louis 41
エイミズ
Amies, Hardy 41
エイ・ミン
Aye Myint 73
エイ・ミン・チュー
Aye Myint Kyu 73
エイムス
Ames, Amethyst 41
Ames, Kenneth M. 41
エイムズ
Aames, Avery 1
エイメン
Amen, Daniel G. 40
エイメンソン
Amenson, Christopher S. 40
エイモーイ
Eymooy, Mohamed Omar 414
エイモイ
Eymoy, Mohamed Omar 414
エイモス
Amos, Adrian 42
Amos, Daniel Paul 42
Amos, Martyn 42
Amos, Paul 42
Amos, Robyn 42
Amos, Valerie 42
エイモリー
Amory, Jay 42
Amory, Vance 42
エイモン
Amon, Chris 41
エイヤーズ
Ayres, Robert L. 74
Ayres, Robert U. 74
エイユボフ
Eiyubov, Yagub 395
エイラーズ
Eilers, Joachim 394
エイラーツセン
Eilertsen, Trond 394
エイラト
Ehlert, Lois 393
エイリー
Airey, David 22
エイリアス
Aleas, Richard 28
エイルウィン
Aylwin, Mariana 73
Aylwin, Patricio 73
Aylwin Azocar, Patricio 73
エイルズ
Ales, Barney 28
エイルズワース
Aylesworth, Jim 73
エイレン
Heylen, Ilse 602
エーインガー
Ehinger, Parker 393
エインジ
Ainge, Danny 22
エインスコウ
Ainscow, Mel 22
エインズリー
Ainslie, Ben 22
Ainslie, George 22
エインズワース
Ainsworth, Sophie 22
エインビッケ
Eimbcke, Fernando 394
エインレイ
Ainlay, Chuck 22
エヴァーツ
Eversz, Robert M. 413
エヴァット
Evatt, Alison 413
エヴァート
Evert, Chris 413
エヴァニアー
Evanier, David 411
エヴァリー
Everly, George S., Jr 413
Everly, Phil 413
エヴァリット
Everitt, Anthony 413
エヴァレット
Everett, David 413
Everett, William 413
エヴァーロール
Everall, Nayera 413
エヴァン
Hévin, Jean-Paul 602
エヴァンゲリスタ
Evangelista, Lucas 411
エヴァンジェリスティ
Evangelisti, Giorgio 411
エヴァンス
Evans, Andy 411
Evans, Colin 412
Evans, Daniel 412
Evans, Dylan 412
Evans, Eric 412
Evans, Gareth 412
Evans, Gareth John 412
Evans, Gil 412
Evans, Ianto 412
Evans, Jason 412
Evans, J.M. 412
Evans, Jodie 412
Evans, Katarina 412
Evans, Lloyd T. 412
Evans, Lois K. 412
Evans, Mandy 412
Evans, Mark 412
Evans, Matt 412
Evans, Matthew 412
Evans, Michael 412
Evans, Nicholas 412
Evans, Nicola 412
Evans, Peter 412
Evans, Richard Mark 412
Evans, Ronald M. 413
Evans, Ruth Dudley 413
Evans, Shane W. 413
Evans, Susan Toby 413
Evans, Vaughan 413
エヴァンズ
Evans, Brent 411
Evans, Chris 411
Evans, Christopher 412
Evans, Dale 412
Evans, Douglas K. 412
Evans, Emma 412
Evans, F.J. 412
Evans, Gillian Rosemary 412
Evans, Glen 412
Evans, Jeff 412
Evans, John M. 412
Evans, Jon 412
Evans, Jonathan Duane 412
Evans, Jonny 412
Evans, Marsha J. 412
Evans, Michael 412
Evans, Mike 412
Evans, Ray 412
Evans, Richard 412
Evans, Richard Paul 413
Evans, Robert 413
Evans, Robert John Weston 413
Evans, Sara Margaret 413
Evans, Shane W. 413
Evans, Shelley 413
Evans, Siân 413
エヴァンズ＝プリチャード
Evans-Pritchard, Edward Evan 413
エヴァンソン
Evenson, Norma 413
エヴァンドロ
Evandro 411
Ewandro 414
エヴィット
Evitt, Gisela Cloos 413
エヴェラ
Van Evera, Stephen 1443
エヴェリット
Everitt, Brian S. 413
エーヴェルス
Ewers, H.G. 414
エーヴェルト
Ewert, Hansjörg 414
エヴェレスト
Everest, D.D. 413
エヴェレット
Everett, Daniel Leonard 413

Everett, Douglas Hugh 413
Everett, Jeffrey 413
Everret, Chad 413
エーヴェンス
Eeuwens, Adam 392
エヴェンス
Evens, Brecht 413
エヴェンソン
Evenson, B.K. 413
エウォボル
Ewovor, Kossi Messan 414
エヴォラ
Évora, Cesária 413
エウォルド
Ewald, Axel 414
エウォン
Ewon, Ebin 414
エウズ
Ehouzu, Jean-Marie 393
エウスク
Euske, Ken 411
エウゼビオ
Eusebio 411
Eusebio, Sacristan 411
エヴラ
Evra, Patrice 413
エヴラール
Evrard, Jacques 413
エヴレン
Evren, Kenan 413
エヴンソン
Evenson, Brian 413
エエトヴェシュ
Eötvös, Peter 404
エカウト
Eeckhout, Emmanuelle 392
Eekhout, Blanca 392
エカエテ
Ekaette, Ufot 395
エカ・クルニアワン
Eka Kurniawan 395
エガース
Eggers, Helga 393
エガーズ
Eggers, Dave 393
エガス
Egas, Eduardo 392
エカード
Echard, Clayton 389
エガート
Eggert, Paul 393
エカナヤケ
Ekanayake, T.B. 395
エガル
Egal, Mohamed Ibrahim 392
エカンガキ
Ekangaki, Nzo 395
エカンジョ
Ekandjo, Jerry 395
エキエル
Ekiel, Jan 395
エギエルスキー
Egielski, Richard 393
エギバル
Eguibar, Lucas 393
エキモフ
Ekimov, Leonid 395
Ekimov, Viatcheslav 395
エキンズ
Ekins, Bud 395
エーク
Ek, Lena 395
エク
Ek, Daniel 395
エグ
Egwu, Sam 393
エグアラス
Eguaras, Louis 393
エークヴィスト
Öquist, Gunnar 1055
エクウェンシ
Ekwensi, Cyprian 395
エクエ
Ekoué, Dédé Ahoéfa 395
エクェンシー
Ekwensi, Cyprian 395
エクエンシー
Ekwensi, Cyprian 395
エクサム
Exum, Dante 414
エグザルコプロス
Exarchopoulos, Adèle 414
エクサワン
Eksavang, Vongvichit 395
エクスタイン
Eckstein, Robert 389
Eckstein, Warren 389
エクスタインズ
Eksteins, Modris 395
エクスタット
Eckstut, Arielle 389
Eckstut, Joann 389
エクストラント
Ekstrand, Jan 395
エクストローム
Ekström, Mats 395
エクストロム
Ekström, Anna 395
エクスナー
Exner, John E. 414
エクスレイ
Exley, Helen 414
エグゼラー
Exeler, Steffen 414
エクセル
Axel, Richard 72
Eksell, Olle 395
エクソン
Exon, James, Jr. 414
エクダル
Ekdal, Albin 395
エークド
Aked, Susan 23
エクトル
Hector, Hernandez 588
エクトン
Eckton, Chip 389
エグノルフ
Egnolff, Sandra 393
エクバーグ
Ekberg, Anita 395
エクハルト
Eckhardt, Maik 389
エグベ
Elegbe, Amos 396
エグベアチュオ
Egbe Achuo, Hillman 392
エクベリ
Ekberg, Peo 395
Ekberg, Peter 395
エグベンダ
Egbenda, Pascal 392
エクポ
Ekpo, Felix 395
エグボ
Egbor, Gahoun 392
エクホフ
Eckhoff, Tiril 389
エクホルム
Ekholm, Matilda 395
Ekholm, Sven 395
エクマン
Ekman, Paul 395
エクムフィ
Akumfi, Christopher Ameyaw 24
エクランド
Ekeland, Ivar 395
エグリ
Egli, Diego 393
エグリッチ
Eggerichs, Emerson 392
エグリティス
Eglitis, Ivars 393
エクルスシェア
Eccleshare, Julia 388
エグルストン
Eggleston, William 393
エクルズヘア
Eccleshare, Julia 388
エグルトン
Eggleton, Arthur 393
エクレス
Eccles, Robert G. 388
エクレストン
Ecclestone, Bernie 389
エクレン
Ekren, Nazim 395
エグロフ
Egloff, Joël 393
エグワケ
Egwake, Omer 393
エグワケヤンゲベ
Egwake Yangembe, Omer 393
エケ
Eke, Aisake 395
Hecquet, Laura 588
エーゲラン
Egeland, Tom 392
エケル
Eker, Mehmet Mehdi 395
エーゲルディンゲル
Eigeldinger, Jean Jacques 394
エーゲルバーグ
Egelberg, Jan 392
エゲレエフ
Yegeleyev, Akmyrat 1537
エケング
Ekeng, Patrick 395
エーコ
Eco, Umberto 389
エコ
Eko, Putro Sandjoyo 395
エゴスキュー
Egoscue, Pete 393
エーコート
Eeckhout, Emmanuelle 392
エコ・ヌセ
Eko Nsue, Constantine 395
エコノミ
Ekonomi, Milva 395
エコノミー
Economy, Elizabeth 389
Economy, Peter 389
エゴヤン
Egoyan, Atom 393
エコユリ
Irawan, Eko Yuli 649
エゴリアン
Egorian, Yana 393
エコロ
Ecoro, Mari Carmen 389
Ekoro, Maria del Carmen 395
エゴロフ
Egorov, Vasilii 393
エゴロワ
Yegorova, Lyubov 1537
エコン・ヌセ
Ekong Nsue, Constantino 395
エゴン=ラミ
Aigon-Rami, Carole 22
エーサ
Ehsa, John 393
エーザー
Eser, Albin 408
Oeser, Jennifer 1045
エサウ
Esau, Bernhard 408
エサウィ
al-Essawi, Rafa 409
エザウイア
Ezzaouia, Khalil 414
エサオ
Esaw, Koffi 408
エサギ
Esagui, Veronica 408
エサバリ
Echavarri, Fernando 389
エサム
Essam, Jean Pierre Biyiti Bi 409
エザメル
Ezzamel, Mahmoud 414
エザラウイ
Ez Zahraoui, Zohra 414
エージー
Agee, Jon 17
エシー
Essy, Amara 410
エシェヴァリア
Echevarria, René 389
エジェヴィト
Ecevit, Bülent 389
エシェヴェヒア
Echeverria, Regina 389
エシェテ
Eshete, Shitaye 408
エジェビット
Ecevit, Bülent 389
エジェビト
Ecevit, Bülent 389
エージーエフデー
EJFD, Thomas 395
エジェリ
Yezhel, Mykhailo 1538
エジェル
Edgell, Stephen 390
エシエン
Essien, Michael 410
Essien, Nduese 410

エシッグ
Essig, Don 410
エジーヌ
Ezzine, Ali 414
Ezzine, Hamid 414
エジハスリンダ・ガー
Ezilhaslinda Ngah 414
エシマムベトフ
Yeshmambetov, Radbek 1538
エシミメンイ
Essimi Menye, Lazare 410
エシモフ
Esimov, Akhmetzhan 408
Yesimov, Akhmetzhan 1538
エシモワ
Eshimova, Zhuldyz 408
エシャー
Escher, Jean-Philippe 408
エジャートン
Edgerton, Leslie 390
エシャム
Esham, Barbara 408
エシュ
Esch, Jake 408
エシュノー
Echenoz, Jean Maurice Emmanuel 389
エシュノーズ
Echenoz, Jean Maurice Emmanuel 389
エシュバッハ
Eschbach, Andreas 408
エシュルマン
Eshleman, Clayton 408
エジーリ
Ezeli, Festus 414
エシリルマク
Yesilirmak, Elif Jale 1538
エジル
Özil, Mesut 1067
エジン
Edgin, Josh 390
エジントン
Edgington, David W. 390
Edginton, Ian 390
エジンバラ公
Edinburgh, The Duke of 390
エス
Ess, Margarete van 409
エズ
Ezz, Khaled el-Enany 414
エスエネ
Esuene, Helen 410
エスガイオ
Esgaio, Ricardo 408
エスカット
Escaith, Hubert 408
エスカーラ
Escarra, Consol 408
エスカランテ
Escalante, Amat 408
Escalante, Gonzalo 408
Escalante, Oscar 408
エスカロナ
Escalona, Arnulfo 408
エズカン
Ozcan, Ramazan 1066
Ozcan, Salih 1066
エスキス
Esquith, Rafe 409
エスキベル・モラ
Esquivel Mora, Laura Maria 409
エスキャンダリ
Eskandari, Mohammad Reza 408
エスクデロ
Escudero, Sergio 408
エスクリッジ
Eskridge, Durell 408
エスクリット
Escritt, Stephen 408
エスクリバーノ
Escribano, Francesc 408
エスクレド
Escuredo, Jose Antonio 408
エスケルダ・ビフェト
Esquerda Bifet, Juan 409
エスコット
Escot, Pozzi 408
Escott, Colin 408
エスコット - スタンプ
Escott-Stump, Sylvia 408
エスコト
Escoto, Marlon 408
エスコバー
Escobar, Alcides 408
Escobar, Eduardo 408
Escobar, Gavin 408
Escobar, Yunel 408
エスコバル
Escobar, Arturo 408
Escobar, Flora Marina 408
Escobar, Leonardo 408
Escobar, Mario 408
Escobar, Sergi 408
Escobar Guerrero, Maria Alexandra 408
エスコバルゲレロ
Escobar Guerrero, Maria Alexandra 408
エスコバル・プリエト
Escobar Prieto, Abelardo 408
エスコフィエ
Escoffier, Jean-Yves 408
Escoffier, Michaël 408
エスター
Ester, Ralf Martin 410
Oester, Marlies 1045
エスターハス
Eszterhas, Suzi 410
エスタブレ
Establet, Roger 410
エスタンゲ
Estanguet, Tony 410
エスチューリン
Estulin, Daniel 410
エスティ
Esty, Daniel C. 410
エスティビル
Estivill, Eduard 410
エスティファノス・アフォワキ・ハイレ
Estifanos Afeworki Haile 410
エスティブ・コール
Esteve-Coll, Elizabeth Anne Loosemore 410
エスティル
Estil, Frode 410
エステーヴ
Estève, Maurice 410
エステヴェス
Estevez, Emilio 410
エステス
Estes, Billie Sol 410
Estes, Evgenia 410
Estes, Kenneth W. 410
エステバ
Esteva, Gustavo 410
エステバン
Esteban, Ángel 410
Esteban, Claude 410
エステーブ
Estève, Maurice 410
エステファノス
Estefanos, Habte 410
エステファン
Estephane, Edmund 410
エステベス
Estéves, Carlos 410
Estévez, Ángel 410
Estevez, Carlos 410
Estevez, Emilio 410
Estevez, Reyes 410
エステミロワ
Estemirova, Natalia 410
エステル
Estelle 410
エステルハージ
Esterházy, Péter 410
エステロン
Estellon, Pascale 410
エステンヌ
Estenne, Luc 410
エストウィック
Estwick, David 410
エズトゥナリ
Oztunali, Levin 1067
エストゥルース
Eschtruth, Andrew D. 408
エストベルグ
Oestberg, Ingvild Flugstad 1045
Østberg, Ingvild 1061
エストラーダ
Estrada, Joseph 410
Estrada, Julio 410
Estrada, Marco 410
Estrada, Pau 410
Estrada, Rita Clay 410
エストラダ
Estrada, Jason 410
Estrada, Joseph 410
Estrada, Julio Héctor 410
エストラダファルコン
Estrada Falcon, Yunior 410
エストロジ
Estrosi, Christian 410
エストロス
Östros, Thomas 1061
エスパイジャット
Espaillat, Rhina P. 409
エスパーセン
Espersen, Lene 409
エスパセン
Espersen, Lene 409
エスパーダ
Espada, Joe 409
エスパダ
Espada, Rafael 409
エスパト
Espat, Jorge 409
Espat, Mark 409
Espat, Michael 409
エスパルザ
Esparza, Marlen 409
エスビー
Espy, Duane 409
エスピー
Espie, Colin A. 409
Espie, Linda 409
エスピナル
Espinal, Jaime 409
Espinal, José 409
エスピネリ
Espineli, Gilbert C. 409
エスピネル
Espinel, Ramón 409
エスピノーザ
Espinosa, Albert 409
Espinosa, Danny 409
エスピノサ
Espinosa, Alberto Garzón 409
Espinosa, Augusto Xavier 409
Espinosa, Elena 409
Espinosa, Geovanni 409
Espinosa, María Fernanda 409
Espinosa, Maricet 409
Espinosa, Oscar 409
Espinosa, Paola 409
Espinosa, Richard 409
Espinosa, Yaniuska 409
Espinoza, Cristian 409
Espinoza, Maria 409
エスピノザ
Espinoza, Maurice H. 409
エスピノサ・カンテジャノ
Espinosa Cantellano, Patricia 409
エスピノサ・クルス
Espinoza Cruz, Marisol 409
エスピン
Espin, Salva 409
エスピン＝アンデルセン
Esping-Andersen, Gøsta 409
エスピン・トバル
Espín Tobar, Augusto 409
エスペホ
Espejo, Sergio 409
エスペランサ
Esperanza 409
エスペランド
Espeland, Pamela 409
エスポシト
Esposito, Dino 409
エスポジト
Esposito, Chloe 409
Esposito, Elena 409
Esposito, John L. 409
Esposito, Max 409
Esposito, Roberto 409
エスポットサモーラ
Espot Zamora, Xavier 409
エスポンダ
Esponda, Hector 409
エスマイルプルジュイバリ
Esmaeilpoorjouybari, Masoud 408
エスマハン
Esmahan, Ricardo 408

エスマン
Esman, Aaron H. 409
エズラ
Ezra, Gideon 414
エーズラ・オールスン
Adler-Olsen, Jussi 15
エスリッジ
Etheridge, Melissa 411
Ethridge, Shannon 411
エスリンガー
Esslinger, Hartmut 410
エスルマン
Estleman, Loren D. 410
Estleman, Loren Daniel 410
エセキア
Esekia, Teagi 408
エゼクウェシリ
Ezekwesili, Obiageli 414
エセックス
Essex, Elizabeth 410
Essex, Karen 410
Essex, Nathan L. 410
Essex, Susie 410
エセナマノフ
Esenamanov, Zamirbek 408
エセブア
Esebua, Kristine 408
エセル
Aïssel, Selim 22
Eselu, O'brian 408
Hessel, Stéphane 601
Hessel, Stéphane F. 601
エゼル
Ezer, Sini 414
エゼルスキス
Ezerskis, Mindaugas 414
エセルスティン
Esselstyn, Caldwell B., Jr. 409
エセンバエフ
Yesenbayev, Mazhit 1538
エセンベル
Esenbel, Ayse Selcuk 408
Esenbel, Selcuk 408
エソ
Esso, Laurent 410
Esso, Solitoki Magnim 410
エソー
Esaw, Kofi 408
エソネ・メンゲ
Essono Mengue, Vincent 410
エソノアバ
Esono Ava, Tomas 409
エソノエジョ
Esono Edjo, Melchor 409
エソノエヨン
Esono Eyang, Faustino Ndong 409
エソノオウォロヌフォノ
Esono Oworonfono, Baltasar 409
エゾール
Ezor, Jonathan 414
エソン
Esson, Louis 410
エソンベティアコ
Essombe Tiako, Joseph Emilienne 410
エーダー
Eder, Klaus 390
エタ
Etah, Jerome 410
エダー
Eder, Simon 390
エダラ
Eddalia, Ghania 389
エダール
Ederle, Gertrude 390
エチアンブル
Etiemble, René 411
エチェイタ
Etxeita, Xabier 411
エチェパレ
Etxepare, Bernat 411
エチェビット
Ecevit, Bülent 389
エチェベリ
Etcheberry, Javier 410
Etcheverry, Jeronimo 411
エチェベリ・ガルソン
Echeverry Garzón, Juan Carlos 389
エチェレク
Etchelecu, Mario 411
エチエンヌ
Etienne, Bruno 411
エチオーニ
Etzioni, Amitai 411
エチクソン
Echikson, William 389
エチゴ
Echigo, Sergio 389
エチメンディ
Etchemendy, John 411
Etchemendy, Nancy 411
エチャス
Echazú, Luis Alberto 389
エチャバリ
Echavarri, Luis 389
エチャバリア
Hechavarria, Adeiny 588
エチャリ
Etxarri, Mikel 411
エチヤンブル
Etiemble, René 411
エツィオーニ
Etzioni, Amitai 411
エッカー
Ecker, Daniel 389
Eker, T.Harv 395
Ekker, Ernst A. 395
エッガー
Egger, Max 392
Egger, Norbert 392
Egger, Reinhard 392
エッガース
Eggers, William D. 393
エッカースレイ
Eckersley, Robyn 389
エッカート
Eckardt, Ralph 389
Eckert, Carter J. 389
Eckert, Rinde 389
Eckert, Robert A. 389
エッカードシュタイン
Eckardstein, Severin von 389
エッガーマン
Eggermann, Vera 393
エッカルト
Eckart, Wolfgang Uwe 389
エック
Eck, Diana L. 389
Eck, John E. 389
Eck, Thomas 389
Ek, Mats 395
エックシュラーガー
Eckschlager, Karel 389
エックス
X 1531
エックハルト
Eckhardt, Maik 389
エックホフ
Eckhoff, Tiril 389
エッゲシュタイン
Eggestein, Maximilian 393
エッケス
Eckes, George 389
エッゲブレヒト
Eggebrecht, Harald 392
エッケル
Eckel, Sara 389
エッケルト
Eckert, Michael 389
エッゲルト
Eggert, Toni 393
エツコウィッツ
Etzkowitz, Henry 411
エッサー
Aissah, Irene Ashira 22
Esser, Caietanus 409
Esser, Michael 410
Esser, Otto 410
エッサース
Essers, Volkmar 410
エッジ
Edge 390
エッジウッド
Edgewood, Paula 390
エッシェー
Escher, Katalin 408
エッシェン
Essien, Michael 410
エッシェンバッハ
Eschenbach, Christoph 408
エッシェンバハ
Eschenbach, Christoph 408
エッシグ
Essig, Terry Parent 410
エッジソン
Edgson, Alison 390
エッジマン - レヴィタン
Edgman-Levitan, Susan 390
エッシャー
Escher, Jean-Philippe 408
Escher, Peter 408
Escher, Sandra 408
エッシンガー
Essinger, James 410
エッスヴァイン
Esswein, Alexander 410
エッセル
Hessel, Stéphane F. 601
エッセルボルン=クレムビーゲル
Esselborn-Krumbiegel, Helga 409
エッセン
Essen, Laura 409
Essene, Virginia 409
エッソ
Esso, Laurent 410
エッター
Etter, D.M. 411
エッチェン
Etgen, Fernand 411
エッツ
Heitz, Bruno 590
エッディーン
El Din, Hamza 396
エッティンガー
Ettinger, Dan 411
Ettinger, Robert 411
Ettinger, Susan 411
エッティンゲン
Oettingen, Gabriele 1045
エッテンバーグ
Ettenberg, Elliott 411
エッピンガー
Eppinger, Steven D. 405
エッピング
Epping, Charles 405
Epping, Duncan 405
Epping, Randy Charles 405
エッピンジャー
Eppinger, Steven D. 405
エップ
Ebb, Fred 388
エップス
Epps, Aaron 405
エツベス
Etzebeth, Eben 411
エッレゴード
Ellegård, Kajsa 397
エテ
Ete, Douglas 411
エディ
Eddie, Jarell 389
Eddy, J.Mark 389
Eddy, John A. 389
Eddy, Paul 389
Edye, Dave 392
エディー
Eddy, Celia 389
エティエーヌ
Etienne, Marie 411
エティエンヌ
Etienne, Ophelie-Cyrielle 411
エディソン
Edison, Cornelius 390
エーディナウ
Eidinow, John 394
エディマ
Edima, Ferdinand Koungou 390
エティヤンブル
Etiemble, René 411
エディンガー
Edinger, Jack D. 390
エディングス
Eddings, David 389
Eddings, Leigh 389
エディントン
Eddington, Roderick 389
エディンバラ公
Edinburgh, The Duke of 390
エテギー
Ettedgui, Edouard 411
エテックス
Étaix, Pierre 410
エデニウソン
Edenilson 390

エ

エデバリ
Edebali, Kasim 389
エデバーン
Edeburn, Carl 389
エテム
Etem, Emel 411
エデム
Edem, Offiong 390
エデュヌドン
Edu Ndong, Eugenio 391
エデリー
Eddery, Pat 389
Edery, Jacob 390
エデル
Eder 390
エーデルウィッチ
Edelwich, Jerry 390
エーデルシュタイン
Edelstein, Yuli 390
エデルシュタイン
Edelstein, Michael Royce 390
エデルスタイン
Edelstein, David 390
エデルソン
Edelson, Burton I. 389
Ederson 390
エーデルマン
Adelman, Kenneth L. 14
Adelman, Kim 14
Edelman, Gerald Maurice 389
Edelman, Murray Jacob 389
Edelmann, Friedrich 389
Edelmann, Otto Karl 389
Edelmann, Sergei 389
エデルマン
Edelman, Julian 389
Edelman, Marek 389
Edelmann, Sergei 389
エデレイン
Ederaine, Ejiro 390
エデン
Eden, Patrick 390
Eden, Paul E. 390
エデンス
Edens, John F. 390
Edens, Wesley 390
エデンズ
Edens, Cooper 390
Edens, Eleana 390
エトー
Eto, Ken 411
Eto'o, Samuel 411
エドー
Edoh, Antoine Agbéwanou 390
エドアード
Edouard, Alidina 390
エトウ
Eto, Kinbo Ishii 411
エドゥ
Edou, Raphaël 390
Eydoux, Anne 414
エドゥアルド
Eduardo 390
エートヴェーシュ
Eötvös, Peter 404
エトヴェシュ
Eötvös, Peter 404
エトゥス
Ettus, Samantha 411
エドゥワルド
Eduardo, Leigh 391
エトゥンディヌゴア
Etoundi Ngoa, Laurent 411
Etoundi Ngoa, Laurent Serge 411
エトゥンディンゴア
Etoundi Ngoa, Laurent Serge 411
エトオ
Eto'o, Samuel 411
エドガー
Edgar, Andrew 390
Edgar, Blake 390
Edgar, Frank 390
Edgar, James Jennings 390
Edgar, Ross 390
エドガア
Edgar, Morton 390
エドガル・メンデス
Edgar Mendez 390
エドキンズ
Edkins, Diana 390
エドシーク
Heidsieck, Eric 589
エトシュゴワン
Etchegoin, Marie-France 410
エドジョア
Edjoa, Augustin 390
エドゼル
Edsel, Robert M. 390
エドゾア
Edzoa, Augustin 392
エドソン
Edson, Margaret 390
Edson, Russell 390
エドニー
Edney, Samuel 390
エドバーグ
Edberg, Stefan 389
エトベシュ
Eötvös, Peter 404
エドベリ
Edberg, Stefan 389
エドマイヤー
Edmaier, Bernhard 390
エドマンス
Edmans, Judi 390
エドマンズ
Edmunds, Francis 390
エドムンド
Edmund, Kyle 390
エドモンズ
Edmonds, David 390
Edmonds, Genevieve 390
エドモンド
Edmonds, Genevieve 390
Edmonds, M.E. 390
エドモンドソン
Edmondson, Amy C. 390
Edmondson, Annette 390
Edmondson, Ray 390
エドランド
Edlund, Matthew 390
Edlund, Richard 390
エードリアン
Adrian, Nathan 16
エドリス
Edlis, Stefan T. 390
Edris, Muktar 390
エトロ
Etro, Gimmo 411
エドワーズ
Edward, Wade 391
Edwards, Amelia B. 391
Edwards, Andrea 391
Edwards, Andrew 391
Edwards, Anne 391
Edwards, Anthony 391
Edwards, Ben 391
Edwards, Betty 391
Edwards, Blake 391
Edwards, Bradley C. 391
Edwards, Bruce L. 391
Edwards, Carl, Jr. 391
Edwards, Carolyn McVickar 391
Edwards, Carolyn P. 391
Edwards, Chris 391
Edwards, Clive 391
Edwards, David "Honeyboy" 391
Edwards, Dorothy 391
Edwards, Elizabeth 391
Edwards, Elwyn Hartley 391
Edwards, Frank John 391
Edwards, Gareth 391
Edwards, Gareth Owen 391
Edwards, Gene 391
Edwards, George 391
Edwards, Gunvor 391
Edwards, Harold M. 391
Edwards, Hugh 391
Edwards, Jahwan 391
Edwards, Jane 391
Edwards, Jeffery S. 391
Edwards, Jon 391
Edwards, Jorge 391
Edwards, Judith 391
Edwards, Kadeem 391
Edwards, Kim 391
Edwards, Lac 391
Edwards, Lavar 391
Edwards, Lee 391
Edwards, Leigh 391
Edwards, Leonard John 391
Edwards, Linda 391
Edwards, Lynn 391
Edwards, Margaret J. A. 391
Edwards, Marilyn 391
Edwards, Mario 391
Edwards, Mark 391
Edwards, Martin 391
Edwards, Michael 391
Edwards, Michelle 391
Edwards, Michelle Claire 391
Edwards, Mike 391
Edwards, Nicola 391
Edwards, Nina 391
Edwards, Nokie 391
Edwards, Owen Dudley 391
Edwards, Paul 391
Edwards, Paul N. 392
Edwards, Penny 392
Edwards, Perrie 392
Edwards, Pete 392
Edwards, Peter 392
Edwards, Richard 392
Edwards, Robert 392
Edwards, Roberta 392
Edwards, Robert Geoffrey 392
Edwards, Russell 392
Edwards, Ruth 392
Edwards, SaQwan 392
Edwards, Sarah A. 392
Edwards, Steve 392
Edwards, Susan S.M. 392
Edwards, Teddy 392
Edwards, Teresa 392
Edwards, Todd M. 392
Edwards, tommy Lee 392
Edwards, Torri 392
Edwards, Vincent 392
Edwards, Wallace 392
Edwards, William Clive 392
エドワーズ-ジョーンズ
Edwards-Jones, Imogen 392
エドワード
Edward, Alonso 391
Edward, John J. 391
Edward, Julia 391
Edward, Mark 391
Edward, Shawn 391
Edwards, Laura Jane 391
エドワード王子
Prince Edward 391
エナウイ
Ennaoui, Sofia 404
エナオ
Henao Cardona, Luis Felipe 593
エナオ・カルドナ
Henao Cardona, Luis Felipe 593
エナオモントジャ
Henao Montoya, Sergio Luis 593
エナーセン
Enersen, Adele 402
エナムウェイ
Enunwa, Quincy 404
エナメ
Ename, Samson Ename 402
エナール
Énard, Mathias 402
Hénart, Laurent 593
エナン
Henin, Justine 594
エニグ
Hennig, Jean Luc 595
エニコシェプジェス
Hennicot-schoepges, Elna 595
エニス
Ennis, Garth 404
Ennis, James 404
Ennis, Jessica 404
Ennis, Susan 404
Ennis, Tyler 404
エニスヒル
Ennis-hill, Jessica 404
エニック
Heinich, Nathalie 590
エニュレ
Haigneré, Claudie 555
エニル
Enill, Conrad 403
エヌゼル
Hennezel, Marie de 595
エヌデュルー
Ndulue, Chuka 1011
エーネス

Ehnes, James 393
エネスタム
Enestam, Jan-Erik 402
エネビシ
Enebish, Lhamsurengiin 402
エネラマウ
Enelamah, Okechukwu 402
エネル
Haenel, Adèle 553
Haenel, Yannick 553
エネルンガ
Enerunga, Anselme 402
エネンパリ
Enemkpali, IK 402
エノキャン
Yenokyan, Harutyun 1537
エノク
Enoch, Dayang Menwa 404
エーノクセン
Enoksen, Lars Magnar 404
Enoksen, Odd Roger 404
エノン
Hénon, Daniel 595
エパイェ
Epaye, Emilie Béatrice 404
エパイエ
Epaye, Emilie Béatrice 404
エバウェイン
Eberwein, Jane Donahue 388
エバーショフ
Ebershoff, David 388
エバース
Evers, Adalbert 413
Evers-swindell, Caroline 413
Evers-swindell, Georgina 413
エバーズ
Evers, Lucas 413
Evers-swindell, Caroline 413
Evers-swindell, Georgina 413
エバースタット
Eberstadt, Nicholas 388
エバスティ
Ervasti, Jenni 407
エバーソール
Ebersole, Christine 388
Ebersole, Priscilla 388
エパーソン
Epperson, Tom 405
エバーツ
Eberts, Jake 388
Eversz, Robert M. 413
エバット
Ebbutt, Blanche 388
Ebbutt, Sheila 388
エバディ
Ebadi, Shirin 388
エバート
Ebert, Gabriel 388
Ebert, Roger 388
Evert, Chris 413
エハヌロフ
Yekhanurov, Yuriy 1537
エバーハート
Everhart, Emerald 413
エバハート
Eberhart, Mark E. 388
Eberhart, Richard Ghormley 388
エパムビリベ
Epam Biribe, María Leonor 404
エーバーライン
Eberlein, Johann Konrad 388
エバラガンサ
e Braganca, Joao Maria de Orleans 388
エバリー
Everly, Phil 413
エパリー
Epperly, Elizabeth R. 405
エバルト
Ewald, Manfred 414
エバン
Eban, Abba 388
エパンゲ
Epangue, Gwladys 404
エバンゲラトス
Evanghelatos, Kostas 411
エバンゲリスタ
Evangelista, Mauro 411
エバンス
Evans 411
Evans, Cadel 411
Evans, Christopher 412
Evans, Dale 412
Evans, David E. 412
Evans, Douglas 412
Evans, Freddie 412
Evans, Gail 412
Evans, Gareth 412
Evans, Gareth John 412
Evans, Huw 412
Evans, Isabel 412
Evans, Jahri 412
Evans, Jeremy 412
Evans, Josh 412
Evans, Josh Ryan 412
Evans, Kyle 412
Evans, Martin John 412
Evans, Marwin 412
Evans, M.G. 412
Evans, Michael 412
Evans, Michele M. 412
Evans, Mike 412
Evans, Nicholas 412
Evans, Patricia 412
Evans, Paul M. 412
Evans, Phil 412
Evans, Phillip 412
Evans, Randall 412
Evans, Richard Mark 412
Evans, Shaq 413
Evans, Suzanne 413
Evans, Tyreke 413
Evans, Vaughan 413
エバンズ
Evans, Cambria 411
Evans, Chris 411, 412
Evans, Dale 412
Evans, Don 412
Evans, Douglas 412
Evans, Gareth John 412
Evans, Jon 412
Evans, Katie 412
Evans, Martin John 412
Evans, Michael 412
Evans, Ray 412
Evans, Rebecca 412
Evans, Richard W. 413
Evans, Scott 413
Evans, Vyvyan 413
Evans, William E. 413
エパンニャ
Epanya, Christian 404
エバーンハム
Evernham, Ray 413
エビアカムエテ
Ebiaka Muete, Aniceto 388
エビアカモホテ
Ebiaka Mohote, Aniceto 388
エヒン
Ehin, Andres 393
エビングハウス
Ebbinghaus, Heinz-Dieter 388
エビンジャー
Ebinger, Charles 388
エブ
Ebb, Fred 388
エファ・アサンゴノ
Efua Asangono, Teresa 392
エフィーモフ
Efimov, Boris 392
エフィモワ
Efimova, Yulia 392
エフィンジャー
Effinger, George Alec 392
エフェンディ
Effendi, Norwawi 392
Effendi, Taufiq 392
エフェンディエフ
Efendiyev, Elchin 392
エフォード
Efford, Ruben John 392
エフォレ
Efole, Hubert 392
エブカババカス
Ebouka Babakas, Ingrid Olga 388
エブケ
Ebke, Werner F. 388
エフシミウ
Efthymiou, Efthymios 392
Ephthimiou, Petros 405
エフシュキナ
Evstyukhina, Nadezda 413
エプシュタイン
Epstein, Gerald A. 405
Epstein, Israel 405
エプスタイン
Eppstein, Chris 405
Epstein, Adam Jay 405
Epstein, Barbara 405
Epstein, Brian 405
Epstein, David J. 405
Epstein, Edward Jay 405
Epstein, Eugene 405
Epstein, Fred 405
Epstein, Hans G. 405
Epstein, Israel 405
Epstein, Jason 405
Epstein, Joseph 405
Epstein, Lawrence L.J. 405
Epstein, Marc J. 405
Epstein, Mark 405
Epstein, Richard A. 405
Epstein, Samuel S. 405
Epstein, Steven 405
Epstein, Theo 405
エプスティーン
Epstein, Samuel S. 405
Epstein, Theo 405
エプステイン
Epstein, Donny 405
エプストン
Epston, David 405
エブセン
Ebsen, Buddy 388
エフダーエフ
Evdaev, Nobert 413
エブダネ
Ebdane, Hermogenes 388
エブティカール
Ebtekar, Masoumeh 388
エプティング
Epting, Steve 405
エブテカー
Ebtekar, Masoumeh 388
エブテカール
Ebtekar, Masomeh 388
Ebtekar, Masoumeh 388
Ebtekar, Masumeh 388
エフドキモヴァ
Evdokimova, Eva 413
エフドキモバ
Evdokimova, Eva 413
エフドキモワ
Evdokimova, Eva 413
Yevdokimova, Natalya 1538
エブナー
Ebner, Nate 388
エブナ・オウォノ・アサンゴノ
Evuna Owono Asangono, Alejandro 414
エブナオウォノアサンゴノ
Evuna Owono Asangono, Alejandro 414
エブラ
Evra, Patrice 413
エプラー
Eppler, Billy 405
Eppler, Mark 405
エーブラハム
Abraham, Spencer 8
エブラハムズ
Abrahams, David 8
エブラーヒーミー
Ebrahimi, Ja'afar 388
エブラヒミ
Ebrahimi Farbod Kamachali, Asghar 388
エブラヒム
Ebrahim, Zak 388
エフラム
Ephram, Georges 405
エーブラムソン
Abramson, Jill 8
エブラール
Evrard, Jane 413
エフランド
Efland, Arthur D. 392
エーブリー
Avery, Gilliann 71
エプリー
Epley, Nicholas 405
エプリ・オロム
Ekpre-olomu, Ifo 395
エプリッジ
Eppridge, Bill 405
エフリム
Efrim, Oleg 392
エブリル
Avril, Cliff 72
エフリン

Eflin, Zach 392
エーブルソン
Abelson, Mike 6
エフレモフ
Efremov, Ivan 392
エフレモワ
Vaygina-efremova, Lilia 1448
エブレン
Evren, Kenan 413
エフロン
Efron, Zac 392
Ephron, Nora 405
エブロン
Ebron, Eric 388
エプワース
Epworth, Paul 405
エブンソン
Evenson, Brian 413
エペス
Yépez, Mauricio 1537
エベノイス
Ebenois, William 388
エベリング
Ebeling, Bob 388
エーベル
Abel, Andrew B. 6
Abell, Derek F. 6
エベール
Hebert, Anne 587
Hebert, Eric 587
エベル
Ebel, Dino 388
Ebell, Mark H. 388
エペル
Epel, Naomi 405
エーベルソン
Abelson, Philip Hauge 6
エベルト
Evert, Lori 413
エベルトフト
Ebeltoft, Paul 388
エベルハルター
Eberharter, Stephan 388
エーベルラン
Haeberlin, Paul 553
エーベルレ
Eberle, Henrik 388
エベレット
Everett, Antoine 413
Everett, Craig A. 413
Everett, Deshazor 413
Everett, Douglas Hugh 413
Everette, Mikell 413
Everret, Chad 413
エーベンシュタイン
Ebenstein, Alan O. 388
Ebenstein, Lanny 388
エボック
Eboch, Douglas J. 388
エボラ
Évora, Cesária 413
Evora, Nelson 413
エボンザ
Ebondza, Cathérine 388
エーマー
Ehmer, Josef 393
エマ
Emma 401
エマーソン
Amerson, David 40
Emerson, Carolyn J. 401
Emerson, Claudia 401
Emerson, Craig 401
Emerson, David 401
Emerson, Keith 401
Emerson, Ken 401
Emerson, Michael 401
Emerson, Sandra L. 401
Emerson, Scott 401
エマディ
al-Emadi, Ali Sherif 400
エマニュエル
Emanuel, Kyle 401
Emanuel, Louise 401
Emanuel, Rahm 401
エマヌ
Emane, Gevrise 401
エマヌエリ
Emmanuelli, Xavier 401
エマヌエル
Emmanuel, Clive 401
エマヌエーレ
Emanuele, Pietro 401
エマミ
Emami, Houman 400
エマリー
Emerlye, Cynthia 401
エマリング
Emmerling, Leonhard 402
エマール
Aimard, Pierre-Laurent 22
Aymard, Maurice 74
Aymard, Pierre 74
Emard, Jeanne 401
Emerle, Henry F. 401
エマン
Emam, Khaled El 400
エミソン
Emison, Patricia A. 401
エミッサーアーサー
Amissah-arthur, Kwesi Bekoe 41
エミネム
Eminem 401
エミリア
Emilia, Reggio 401
エミリアニドゥ
Emilianidou, Georgia 401
エミリオ
Emílio, Paulo 401
エミルソン
Emilson, Peje 401
エミン
Emin, Tracey 401
エミンズ
Emmins, Alan 402
エムアイエイ
M.I.A. 941
エームケ
Ehmcke, Franziska 393
エムシュウィラー
Emshwiller, Carol 402
エームズ
Ames, David 41
エムズ
Emms, Gail 402
エムズリー
Emsley, John 402
エムセレム
Emsellem, Helene A. 402
エムディ
Emde, Robert N. 401
エムナー
Emunah, Renée 402
エムバイェ
Mbaye, Ibrahima 927
エムバロ
Embalo, António Sirifo 401
Embalo, Umaro Sissoco 401
エムメロバー
Emmerová, Milada 402
エムラー
Emler, Nicolas 401
エムリヒ
Emmrich, Peter 402
エムレ・チョラク
Emre Colak 402
エムレン
Emlen, Douglas John 401
エーメ
Aimée, Anouk 22
エメ
Aimée, Louis Hervé 22
エメシオール
Emesiochel, Masa-Aki 401
エメツ
Yemets, Illia 1537
エメット
Emmett, Jonathan 402
Emmett, Rita 402
エメニケ
Emenike, Emmanuel 401
エメノー
Emeneau, Murray Barnson 401
エメリ
Emery, Unai 401
エメリー
Emery, Andrew 401
Emery, James 401
Emery, Stewart 401
エメリィ
Emery, Gary 401
エメリック
Emerick, Geoff 401
Emmerich, Michael 402
エメリッヒ
Emmerich, Lothar 401
Emmerich, Roland 402
エメール
Haemers, Guy 553
エメル
Omer, Sismanoglu 1052
エメルソン
Emerson 401
エメルソン・パソス
Emerson 401
エメルソン・パッソス
Emerson 401
エメルソン・パッソフ
Emerson 401
エモット
Emmott, Bill 402
Emmott, Shelagh D. 402
Emmott, Stephen 402
Emmott, William John 402
エーモン
Amon, Chris 41
エモンシュ
Emmons, Katerina 402
エモンズ
Emmons, Matthew 402
Emmons, Michael L. 402
Emmons, Robert A. 402
Emmons, Shirlee 402
Emmons, Willis 402
エヤオロモ
Eya Olomo, Vicente 414
エヤケニィ
Eyakenyi, Akon 414
エヤデマ
Eyadéma, Gnassingbe 414
エラー
Eller, Helmut 398
Eller, Walton Glenn 398
エライク
Elhaïk, Serge 396
エライネ
Elaine Teo 395
エラオヤナ
Ela Oyana, Jose 396
エラオヤマ
Ela Oyana, Jose 396
エラギン
Yelagin, Vladimir V. 1537
エーラース
Ehlers, Dirk 393
Ehlers, John F. 393
エーラーズ
Ehlers, Anke 393
エラーズ
Ellers, Kevin L. 398
エラス
Heras, Chema 596
エラスリス
Errázuriz, Pedro 407
エラソ
Eraso, Javier 405
エラソ・ラトレ
Erazo Latorre, Álvaro 405
エラート
Aehlert, Barbara 16
エラード
Ellard, Colin 397
Ellard, Kristen K. 397
Erard, Robert E. 405
エラド
Elad, Michael 395
エラーニ
Errani, Sara 407
エラニ
Errani, Sara 407
エラヌツグヌザ
Ela Ntugu Nsa, Atanasio 396
エラヌドング
Ela Ndong, Jaime 395
エラービー
Ellerbe, Dannell 398
エラヒ
Ellahi, Pervez 397
エラビッチ
Jelavić, Ante 669
エラーブ
Ellerbe, Helen 398
エラ・マング
Ela Mangue, Julio Ndong 395
エラミヌ
Elamine, Soeuf Mohamed 395
エラミフム
Ela Mifumu, Hermes 395
エラム
Elam, Jack 395
エラーモ
Eramo, Mirko 405
エラリアン

El-Erian, Mohamed A. 406
エラリエフ
Eraliev, Arsen 405
Yeraliyev, Kairat 1537
エラール
Hélard, André 591
エラワン・ウイパー
Arawan Wipha 55
エラン
Elan, Maika 395
Héran Hean, François 596
エーランソン
Erlandsson, Eskil 407
エランド
Errando, Tono 407
エリ
Eli, Ilana 397
Ely, Cheyakh Ould 400
エリー
Eley, Jon 396
Elie, Daniel 397
Ely, Hacenna Ould 400
Ely, Jack 400
Ely, Lesley 400
Ely, Rodrigo 400
エリア
Elias, F. 397
エリアキム
Eliakim, Philippe 397
エリアシェフ
Eliacheff, Caroline 397
エリアス
Elias 397
Elias, Buddy 397
Elias, Cassius 397
Elias, Gastao 397
Elias, Jamal J. 397
Elias, Roenis 397
エリアソン
Eliasson, Olafur 397
エリアーデス
Eliades, Demetris 397
エリアドール
Héliadore 591
エリアン
Erian, Alicia 406
エリウド・キプチョゲ
Rotich, Eliud Kipchoge 1210
エリオ
Héliot, Eric 591
エリオット
Eliot, George Fielding 397
Eliot, Lise 397
Eliot, Marc 397
Eliot, Peter B. 397
Elliot, Adam 398
Elliot, Bob 398
Elliot, David 398
Elliot, Jay 398
Elliott, Anthony 398
Elliott, Bill 398
Elliott, Bronwen 398
Elliott, Cara 398
Elliott, Carl 398
Elliott, Clark Davidson 398
Elliott, David 398
Elliott, DeAndre 398
Elliott, Donald R. 398
Elliott, Ezekiel 398
Elliott, Gail Pursell 398
Elliott, Geroge 398
Elliott, James 398
Elliott, Jane 398
Elliott, Javien 398
Elliott, Jay 398
Elliott, Jennifer A. 398
Elliott, Joe 398
Elliott, John Huxtable 398
Elliott, Larry 398
Elliott, Lorraine M. 398
Elliott, Marianne 398
Elliott, Mark W. 398
Elliott, Missy 398
Elliott, Peter 398
Elliott, Ralph Warren Victor 398
Elliott, Ramblin' Jack 398
Elliott, Rebecca 398
Elliott, Robert 398
Elliott, Sam 398
Elliott, Sara 398
Elliott, Ted 398
Elliott, William I. 398
エリオプロス
Eliopoulos, Chris 397
エリクスン
Erikson, Steven 406
エーリクセン
Eriksen, Odd 406
エリクセン
Erichsen, Fie Udby 406
Eriksen, Christian 406
Eriksen, Jens 406
Eriksen, John 406
Eriksen, Michael P. 406
Eriksen, Rolf 406
Eriksen, Thomas Hylland 406
エリクセン・スールアイデ
Eriksen Søreide, Ine 406
エリクソン
Erickson, Alex 406
Erickson, Betty Alice 406
Erickson, Carolly 406
Erickson, Chris 406
Erickson, Gary 406
Erickson, Jim 406
Erickson, Jon Mark 406
Erickson, Millard J. 406
Erickson, Richard B. 406
Erickson, Russell E. 406
Erickson, Sheryl 406
Erickson, Steve 406
Erickson, Tamara J. 406
Erickson, Thomas D. 406
Ericson, Lisa 406
Ericsson, Ingvar 406
Ericsson, Karl Anders 406
Ericsson, Kent 406
Ericsson, Maria 406
Erikkson, John 406
Erikson, Duke 406
Erikson, Joan Mowat 406
Erikson, Kai 406
Erikson, Robert 406
Eriksson, Bengt G. 406
Eriksson, Christina Wyss 406
Eriksson, Eva 406
Eriksson, Hans-Erik 406
Eriksson, Kimmo 406
Eriksson, Per 406
Eriksson, Peter 406
Eriksson, Robert 406
Eriksson, Sven Goran 406
エリクソン - クライン
Erickson-Klein, Roxanna 406
エリーゴ
Errigo, Arianna 407
エリゴ
Errigo, Arianna 407
エリコニン
El'konin, Daniil Borisovich 397
エリザベス2世
Elizabeth Ⅱ 397
エリザベス皇太后
Elizabeth, the Queen Mother 397
エリザベス女王
Elizabeth Ⅱ 397
エリザベト（ボヘミア王女）
Elisabeth 397
エリサルデ
Elizalde, Álvaro 397
エリザーロフ
Elizarov, Mikhail 397
エリシュカ
Eliška, Radomil 397
エリス
Ellis, A.J. 398
Ellis, Albert 398
Ellis, Alex 398
Ellis, Bret Easton 398
Ellis, Carson 398
Ellis, Charles D. 398
Ellis, Cliff 398
Ellis, Craig 398
Ellis, Dana 398
Ellis, David 398
Ellis, Deborah 398
Ellis, Gail 398
Ellis, Geoffrey James 398
Ellis, Harold 398
Ellis, Janice Rider 398
Ellis, John 399
Ellis, Jonathan 399
Ellis, Joseph H. 399
Ellis, Joyce M. 399
Ellis, Justin 399
Ellis, K.C. 399
Ellis, Keith 399
Ellis, Kenrick 399
Ellis, Lauren 399
Ellis, Libby 399
Ellis, Lucy 399
Ellis, Lyn 399
Ellis, Marcus 399
Ellis, Monta 399
Ellis, Neenah 399
Ellis, Perry 399
Ellis, Robert 399
Ellis, Rod 399
Ellis, Shaun 399
Ellis, Susan J. 399
Ellis, Thomas E. 399
Ellis, Warren 399
Ellys, Indirayanthi 399
エリスドッティル
Elisdottir, Thorey Edda 397
エリストン
Elliston, Ben 399
エリスマン
Erisman, Porter 407
エリスン
Ellison, Harlan 399
エリセ
Erice, Victor 406
エリセイエワ
Yelisseyeva, Margarita 1537
エリゼウ
Eliseu 397
エリセーエフ
Elisseeff, Danielle 397
Elisseeff, Vadime 397
エリソン
Elison, Jennifer 397
Ellison, Brady 399
Ellison, Brooke 399
Ellison, James M. 399
Ellison, James W. 399
Ellison, Jean 399
Ellison, J.T. 399
Ellison, Katherine 399
Ellison, Larry 399
Ellison, Rhett 399
Ellison, Sarah 399
Ellison, Sheila 399
エリソンド・トレス
Elizondo Torres, Rodolfo 397
エリソンド・バラガン
Elizondo Barragán, Fernando 397
エリタシュ
Elitaş, Mustafa 397
エリチエ
Héritier, Françoise 597
エリチャン
Yeritsian, Sergo 1538
エリツィン
Yeltsin, Boris Nikolaevich 1537
エリッカー
Elicker, Brett M. 397
エーリック
Ehrlich, Anne H. 393
Ehrlich, Paul R. 393
エリック
Eric 406
エリック・ダイアー
Eric Dier 406
エリッソン
Hérisson, Pierre 597
エリツャン
Yeritzyan, Armen 1538
Yeritzyan, Nerces 1538
エリツヤン
Yeritzyan, Armen 1538
エーリヒ
Ehrich, Dieter 393
エリボン
Eribon, Didier 406
エリミ
Elimi, Ousmane Mahamat Nour 397
エリムベトフ
Yerimbetov, Yernar 1538
エリャソフ
Elyasov, Gurbanmammet 400
エリヤベツ
Erjavec, Karl 407
エリーン
Ehrlin, Carl-Johan 393
エリング
Elling, Kurt 398
Ering, Timothy B. 406
エリングウッド
Ellingwood, Ken 398
エリンダー
Elinder, Carl-Gustaf 397
エリントン
Ellington, Andre 398

Ellington, Brian 398
Ellington, Bruce 398
Ellington, Wayne 398
エール
Ehle, Jennifer 393
Erre, Jean-Marcel 407
エル
Elle 397
L 779
エルアイ
Eluay, Theys Huyo 400
エルアイサミ
El Aissami, Tareck 395
エル‐アグラ
El-Agraa, Ali M. 18
エルアザリィ
Elazary, Yuval 396
エルアトフィ
El-atfy, Hussein 67
エルウィス
Elwes, Richard 400
エルウィン
Elwyn, Glyn 400
Erwin, Alec 408
Erwin, Alexander 408
エルヴィン
Elvin, Mark 400
エルウィング
Elwing, Jill E. 400
エルヴェディ
Elvedi, Nico 400
エルヴェホイ
Elvehøi, Ole-Martin 400
エルウッド
Ellwood, Wayne 399
Elwood, Ann 400
Elwood, Christopher 400
エール‐エバンス
Hale-Evans, Ron 557
エルオフ
Yeleuov, Serik 1537
エルカー
Elcar, Dana 396
Oelker, Petra 1044
エルガー
Elgar, Rebecca 396
Elger, Dietmar 396
エルカインド
Elkind, David 397
エル・ガジ
El Ghazi, Anwar 396
エル・カドゥーリ
El Kaddouri, Omar 397
エルガルヒ
Elgarhi, Amr 396
エルカン
Elkann, John 397
エルギュン
Ergün, Nihat 406
エルキン
Elkin, Zeev 397
Erkin, Mukrem 407
エルギン
Elgin, Catherine Z. 396
Ergian, Sadullah 406
エルキンス
Elkins, Caroline 397
Elkins, Debra 397
エルキンズ
Elkins, Aaron J. 397
Elkins, Charlotte 397
エルキントン
Elkington, John 397
エルク
Elk, Black 397
エルクジャー
Elkjer, Thom 397
エルゲゼン
Ergezen, Zeki 406
エルケーニュ
Örkény, István 1057
エルゲラ
Helguera, Pablo 591
エルゲルージ
El Guerrouj, Hicham 396
エルゲルト
Elgert, Norbert 396
エルコック
Elcock, W.D. 396
エルコムリ
El Khomri, Myriam 397
エルコリーニ
Ercolini, David 405
エルサ
Elsa, María 400
エルサエディ
El-saeidi, Ami Fahmy Ibrahim 1225
エルサエド
Elsayed, Mohamed 400
エル・ザール
El Zhar, Nabil 400
エルサワリ
Elsawalhy, Seham 400
エルザン
Erzan, Ayşe 408
エルジー
Elsey, Dave 400
エルシェハビ
El Shehaby, Islam 400
エルシェリフ
Elsherif, Mahmud Ahmad 400
エル・シャーラウィ
El Shaarawy, Stephan 400
エルシュテイン
Elshtain, Jean Bethke 400
エルシュメル
Ersumer, Mustafa Cumfur 407
エールシュレーガー
Oehlschlaeger, Fritz 1044
エルジンガ
Elzinga, Kenneth G. 400
エルジンチリオール
Erzinçlioglu, Zakaria 408
エルス
Els, Ernie 400
Else, David 400
エルスウィット
Elswit, Robert 400
エルスコヴィシ
Herscovici, Armand 600
エルスター
Elster, Allen D. 400
Elster, Jon 400
エルスデール
Elsdale, Bob 400
エルストン
Ellston, Peter 399
Elston, Trae 400
エルストンド
Elustondo, Aritz 400
Elustondo, Gorka 400
エルズバーグ
Ellsberg, Daniel 399
エルズバリー
Ellsbury, Jacoby 399
エルズビエタ
Elzbieta 400
エルズブリー
Ellsbury, Jacoby 399
エルスベリー
Ellsbury, Jacoby 399
エルズベリー
Ellsbury, Jacoby 399
エルスベルグ
Elsberg, Marc 400
エルスワース
Ellsworth, Loretta 399
エル・ゼイニ
El Zeini, Hanny 400
エルセイフィ
Elseify, Ashraf Amgad 400
エルセギ
Elosegi, Ander 400
エルセサー
Elsaesser, Thomas 400
エルゼサー
Elsässer, Jürgen 400
エルゼン
Erzen, Jale 408
エルゾーグ
Herzog, Maurice 600
エルゾグ
Herzog, Maurice 600
エルソン
Elson, Diane 400
Elson, Richard 400
エルダー
Elder, Alexander 396
Elder, Glen H., Jr. 396
Elder, Linda 396
Elder, R.A. 396
エルダーキン
Elderkin, Susan 396
エルタザロフ
Eltazarov, Juliboy 400
エルダラトリー
El-Dawlatly, Nadeen 328
エルダン
Erdan, Gilad 405
エルチャニノフ
Eltchaninoff, Michel 400
エルツ
Hertz, Robert 600
エルツォーグ
Herzog, Lise 600
エルデ
Elde, Anna-Karin 396
エルデーイ
Erdély, Gábor 405
エルティス
Eltis, David 400
エルディーン
El Din, Hamza 396
エルデスーキ
El-desouki, Nagwa 346
エルデネ
Erdene, Sodnomzundui 405
エルデネバト
Erdenebat, Badarchiin 405
Erdenebat, Dondogdorj 405
Erdenebat, Jargaltulgyin 405
エルデネバトツェンバータル
Erdenebat, Tsendbaatar 405
エルデネバートル
Erdenebaator, Ichinhorloogiin 405
Erudenebaatar, Ichinhorloogiin 407
エル・テハノ
El Texano 400
エルデル・ロペス
Helder Lopes 591
エルデンチュルーン
Erdenechuluun, Luvsangiin 405
エルド
Held, Riccardo 591
エルドアン
Erdogan, Recep Tayyip 406
エルトイスバエフ
Yertysbaev, Yermukhamet 1538
エルトゥール
Ertur, Omer S. 407
エルトゥル
Ertl, Gerhard 407
エルトゥルディ
El Troudi, Haiman 400
エルトゥールル
Ertuğrul, İlter 407
Ertugrul, Taskiran 407
エルドス
Erdos, Thomas 406
エルドニエフ
Erdniev, B.P. 405
Erdniev, P.M. 405
エルドバーグ
Erdberg, Philip 405
エルドマン
Erdmann, Mojca 405
エルドリッジ
Eldredge, John 396
Eldredge, Niles 396
Eldredge, Todd 396
Eldridge, Barbara 396
Eldridge, Kiki 396
Eldridge, Robert D. 396
エルトル
Ertl, Gerhard 407
Ertl-renz, Martina 407
エルトル＝ヴァグナー
Ertl-Wagner, Birgit 407
エルトロウディ
El Troudi, Haiman 400
エルトン
Elton, Chester 400
エルナー
Hoerner, Jean-Michel 613
エルナーニ
Ernani, Francesco 407
エルナニ・メロニ
Hernani Meloni, Remigio 599
エルナネス
Hernanes 598
エルナン
Hernan, Santana 598
エルナンゴメス
Hernangomez, Juan 598
Hernangomez, Willy 598
エルナンス

Hernanz, Samuel 599
エルナンスアゲリア
Hernanz Agueira, Javier 599
エルナンデス
Hernandes, Motesinos Manuel 598
Hernandez, Abel 598
Hernandez, Anaysi 598
Hernandez, Angel 598
Hernandez, Cruz 598
Hernandez, Felix 598
Hernández, Gabriel 598
Hernandez, Genaro 598
Hernandez, Glenhis 598
Hernández, Hilda 598
Hernandez, Javier 598
Hernandez, Juan Martin 598
Hernández, Juan Orlando 598
Hernández, María Pilar 598
Hernández, Maritza 598
Hernandez, Melba 598
Hernández, Roberto 598
Hernández, Socorro 598
Hernandez, Stefany 598
Hernandez, Vicente 598
Hernandez, Yagnier 598
Hernandez, Yohandrys 598
Hernandez G, Yampier 598
Pereira Hernández, Carlos Miguel 1097
Shorey Hernandez, Pablo Enrique 1293
エルナンデスアルセロ
Hernández Alcerro, Jorge Ramón 598
エルナンデス・アルバラド
Hernández Alvarado, Juan Orlando 598
エルナンデスウスカンガ
Hernandez Uscanga, Ismael Marcelo 598
エルナンデス・カルデロン
Heenández Calderón, José Manuel 588
エルナンデス - サラサール
Hernández-Salazar, Daniel 598
エルナンデス・シマル
Hernandez Simal, Lander 598
エルナンデスパウミエル
Hernandez Paumier, Yoelmis 598
エルナンデスマック
Hernández Mack, Lucrecia 598
エルナンデスリオス
Hernandez Rios, Yurisandy 598
エルナンデス・ルイペレス
Hernández Ruipérez, Daniel 598
エルナン・ペレス
Hernan Perez 599
エルニ
Erni, Hans 407
エルニー
Erni, Hans 407
エルニュ
Hernu, Laurent 599
エルネ
Erne, Andrea 407
エルネストゥス
Ernestus, Horst 407
エルネニー
Elneny, Mohamed 400
エルノー
Ernault, Romuald 407
Ernaux, Annie 407
エルバ
Elba, Idris 396
エル＝ハイ
El-Hai, Jack 555
エルバカリ
Elbakkali, Soufiane 396
エルバカン
Erbakan, Necmettin 405
エルバキ
Abdel Baki, Mohamed 3
エルハジ・ムサ
Elhadi Moussa, Maty 396
エル・バシャ
El Bacha, Abdel Rahman 396
エルバース
Elberse, Anita 396
エルバス
Elbaz, Alber 396
エルバズ
Elbaz, Alber 396
エルバート
Elbert, Thomas 396
エルハドハド
Elhodhod, Afaf 396
エルバノバ
Erbanova, Marcela 405
エルバフ
Elbakh, Fares Ibrahim E. H. 396
エルバーフェルト
Elberfeld, Rolf 396
エルハム
Elham, Gholamhossein 396
エルバラダイ
El-baradei, Fathy 91
ElBaradei, Mohamed 396
Elbaradei, Muhammad Mostafa 396
エル・ハリファ
El-khalifa, Mohamed 725
エルバリング
Elberling, Claus 396
エルバン
Elvan, Lütfi 400
エルビィ
Elby, Andrew 396
エル・ヒガンテ
El Gigante 396
エル・ヒヤリ
El-khyari, Thamil 729
エルビラ・ケサダ
Elvira Quesada, Juan Rafael 400
エルファーズ
Elffers, Joost 396
エルファディング
Elfferding, Susanne 396
エル・フィスゴン
El Fisgón 396
エルフィック
Elphick, Jonathan 400
エルフェンバイン
Elfenbein, Stefan W. 396
エルフォント
Elfont, Edna A. 396
エルフグリエン
Elfgren, Sara Bergmark 396
エルフサイニ
Al-husseiny, Abdallah 639
エルフチナ
Elfutina, Stefaniya 396
エルフマン
Elfman, Danny 396
エルフリ
Eljuri, Gladys 397
エルブリング
Elbling, Peter 396
エル・フルータス
El Frutas 396
エルベ
Elbe, Frank 396
エルベグドルジ
Elbegdorj, Tsakhiagiin 396
エルベック
Herbecq, Jean-Martin 596
エールベルガー
Öhlberger, Camillo 1046
Ohlberger, Karl 1046
エルベンスポーク
Elwenspoek, Miko 400
エルペンベック
Erpenbeck, Jenny 407
エルボー
Hellebaut, Tia 591
Herbauts, Anne 596
エルボウ
Elbow, Gary S. 396
エルマー
Elmer, Ruth M. 399
エルマコワ
Yermakova, Anastasiya 1538
エル - マラーク
El-Mallakh, Rif S. 890
エールマン
Oehlman, Damon 1044
エルマン
Elleman, Barbara 397
Ellman, Ira Mark 399
Elman, Benjamin A. 399
Elman, Colin 399
Elman, Miriam Fendius 399
Elman, R.Amy 399
Erman, Mateja Vraničar 407
Erman, Suparno 407
エルマンジャ
Elmandjra, Mahdi 399
エルマンジュラ
Elmandjra, Mahdi 399
エルミガー
Elmiger, Jean 399
エルミタ
Ermita, Eduardo 407
エルミダ
Hermida Ramos, Jose Antonio 598
エルミダラモス
Hermida Ramos, Jose Antonio 598
エル・ミドウイ
El-mideoui, Ahmed 944
エルミニ
Herminie, William 598
エルミブー
Elmi Bouh, Yacin 399
エルミロフ
Yermilov, Serhiy 1538
エルムウッド
Elmwood, Emelia 399
エルムグリーン
Elmgreen, Michael 399
エルムスタフ
Elmoustaphe, Yahya Ould Sid 399
エルムスリー
Elmslie, Brittany 399
エルムズリー
Elmslie, Brittany 399
エルムセーテルスベード
Elmsätersvärd, Catharina 399
エルムハースト
Elmhirst, Tom 399
エル・ムヘナウイ
El Mhenaoui, Hamadi 399
エルムレル
Ermler, Mark 407
エルメ
Hermé, Pierre 598
エルメクバエフ
Yermekbayev, Nurlan 1538
エルメラドゥカガ
Ermela Doukaga, Destinée 407
エルモア
Elmore, Richard F. 399
Elmore, Tim 399
エル・モクタール
El Moctar, Mohamed 399
エルモクタル
El Moctar, Mohamed 399
エルモサ・サガス
Hermoza Sagaz, Victor Manuel 598
エルモシン
Yermoshin, Vladimir V. 1538
エルモスニーノ
Elmosnino, Eric 399
エルモハマディ
Elmohamady, Ahmed 399
エルモレンコ
Ermolenko, Boris 407
エルモント
Elmont, Dex 399
Elmont, Guillaume 399
エルヤニ
al-Eryani, Muammar 408
エルユヌシ
Elyounoussi, Mohamed 400
エルラー
Erler, Michael 407
エルラフ
Erlaf, Mohamed Ag 407
エルランド＝ブランダンブルグ
Erlande-Brandenburg, Alain 407
エルランビエケカタイ
Yeerlanbieke Katai 1537
エルリ
Erlih, Devy 407
エルリー
Erlih, Devy 407
エルリッチ
Ehrlich, Ricardo 393
Erlich, Jonathan 407

エルリッヒ
Eelich, Leandro 392
エールリヒ
Ehrlich, Fred 393
エルリファイ
El-rifai, Mustafa Mohammed Osman 1181
エールリンク
Ehrling, Sixten 393
エールリング
Ehrling, Sixten 393
エルリンソン
Erlingsson, Ulf 407
エルリントン
Elrington, Wilfred 400
エルロイ
Ellroy, James 399
エルワイ
Eluay, Theys Huyo 400
エルワージー
Elworthy, Scilla 400
エルンスト
Ernst, Bruno 407
Ernst, Edzard 407
Ernst, Gerhard 407
Ernst, Lisa Campbell 407
Ernst, Richard Robert 407
エレ
Hélé, Pierre 591
エレアタイシ
Ereateiti, Temate 406
エレウシノフ
Yeleussinov, Daniyar 1537
エレガント
Elegant, Linda 396
エレクトラ
Electra, Carmen 396
エレショフ
Eresov, Batyr 406
エレズィ
Elezi, Shurete 396
エレット
Ellet, William 398
エレディア・ミランダ
Heredia Miranda, Nila 597
エレート
Eröd, Adrian 407
エレナ
Ellena, Jean-Claude 397
エレフソン
Ellefson, Dave 397
エレフトエリウ
Eleftheriou, Andri 396
エレマン
Ellemann, Karen 397
エレミア
Eremia, Alexandra 406
エレミャン
Yeremyan, Arman 1537
エレム
Erem, Suzan 406
エレメンコ
Eremenko, Roman 406
エレーラ
Herrera, Hector 599
Herrera, Paloma 599
Herrera, Ramiro 599
エレラ
Herrera, Balbina 599
Herrera, Fausto 599
Herrera, Hernando 599
Herrera, Lorena Enriqueta 599
Herrera, Mauricio 599
Herrera, Nelson 599
Herrera, Pablo 599
Herrera, Paloma 599
エレラ・カンピンス
Herrera Campins, Luis 599
エレラ・テジョ
Herrera Tello, María Teresa 599
エレラ・デスカルシ
Herrera Descalzi, Carlos 599
エレル
Erelle, Anna 406
エレルス
Ehlers, Freddy 393
エーレルテ
Ēlerte, Sarmīte 396
エレロ
Herrero, Fernando 599
エレワ
Elewa, Kaba Ould 396
エレン
Ellen, Richard P. 397
エレンゲ・オコンゴ
Elengue-okongo, Marc 396
エレンショウ
Ellenshaw, Peter 398
エレンソン
Ellenson, Henry 398
エレンバ
Elemba, Franck 396
Elemba, Michel Lokola 396
エレンバーグ
Ellenberg, Jordan 397
エーレンハフト
Ehrenhaft, Daniel 393
エーレンハルト
Ehrenhalt, Alan 393
エレンビー
Ellenby, John 398
エレンベッカー
Ellenbecker, Todd S. 397
エーレンベルク
Ehrenberg, John 393
エーレンライク
Ehrenreich, Barbara 393
エロー
Ayrault, Jean-Marc 74
エロウル
Eroglu, Seref 407
Eroğlu, Veysel 407
エロヌドングヌセフム
Elo Ndong Nsefumu, Demetrio 400
エロヒン
Erokhin, Igor 407
エロフソン
Elofsson, Per 400
エロリー
Ellory, Roger Jon 399
エロール
Eroğlu, Dervis 407
Eroğlu, Veysel 407
エロン
Elon, Amos 400
Eronn, Gisela 407
エワ
Ewa, Ita Okon Bassey 414
エンヴェゾー
Enwezor, Okwui 404
エンガー
Enger, Leif 403
エンカーナシオン
Encarnacion, Edwin 402
エンクイスト
Enquist, Per Olov 404
エーンクヴィスト
Enquist, Per Olov 404
エンクウィスト
Engquist, Bjorn 403
エンクヴィスト
Enquist, Per Olov 404
エングクビスト
Engqvist, Lars 403
エングストローム
Engström, Hillevi 403
エンクドゥ
Nkoudou, Georges-Kevin 1029
エングハグ
Enghag, Per 403
エンクバット
Enkhbat, Badar-Uugan 403
エングバンダ
Engbanda, Joseph 402
エングラー
Engler, Henry 403
Engler, Wolfgang 403
エングラート
Englert, Berthold-Georg 403
エングリッヒ
Englich, Mirko 403
エングル
Engle, Margarita 403
Engle, Patricia M. 403
Engle, Robert F. 403
エングルマイアー
Englmaier, Tobias 403
エングレーダー
Engleder, Barbara 403
エングレダー
Engleder, Barbara 403
エンケ
Enke, Robert 403
エンゲストローム
Engeström, Yrjö 403
エンゲハム
Engeham, Vicki 402
エンゲハルト
Eugelhardt, Dietrich von 411
エンゲラー
Engerer, Brigitte 403
エンゲラウ
Engellau, Elisabet 403
エンゲル
Engel, Adam 402
Engel, Beverly 402
Engel, Elliot 402
Engel, Friedrich 402
Engel, Gerhard 402
Engel, Howard 402
Engel, Joel 402
Engel, Joyce 402
Engel, Jules 402
Engel, Richard 402
Enger, Thomas 403
Engle, Robert F. 403
エンゲルキング
Engelking, Barbara 403
エンゲルシャル
Engelschall, Ralf S. 403
エンゲルス
Engels, Bjorn 403
Engels, Gert 403
Engels, Mary-Louise 403
エンゲルスマン
Engelsman, Michelle 403
エンゲルバーグ
Engelberg, Morris 402
Engelberg, Stephen 402
Engelberg, Tom 402
エンゲルハート
Engelhardt, Lisa O. 403
エンゲルバート
Engelbart, Douglas Carl 402
エンゲルハルト
Engelhardt, Dietrich von 403
エンゲルブレヒト
Engelbrecht, Benny 403
エンゲルベルク
Engelberg, Ernst 402
エンケルマン
Enkelmann, Nikolaus B. 403
エンゲルマン
Engelman, Peter G. 403
Engelmann, Ines 403
Engelmann, Kai 403
エンゲン
Engen, Alexandra 403
Engin, A.Ege 403
エンコ
Enhco, Thomas 403
エンゴイ
Ngoy, Julien 1020
エンゴンガ・エジョ
Engonga Edjo, Baltasar 403
エンゴンガエジョ
Engonga Edjo, Baltasar 403
エンゴンガオビアンエヨン
Engonga Obiang Eyang, Miguel 403
エンゴンガ・ヌゲマ・オンゲネ
Engonga Nguema Onguene, Clemente 403
エンゴンガヌゲマオンゲネ
Engonga Nguema Onguene, Clemente 403
エンゴンガヌドン
Engonga Ndong, Jesus 403
エンジェシス
Engeseth, Stefan 403
エンジェル
Angel, Dave 48
Angel, Edward 49
Angel, Heather 49
Angel, Jan V. 49
Angel, Karen 49
Angell, Jeannette 49
Angell, Marcia 49
Angell, Tony 49
Engel, Cindy 402
エンジェルハート
Engelhardt, Lisa O. 403
エンジオ
Enzio, Mario Bellio 404
エンジカット
Ensikat, Klaus 404
エンジカート

Ensikat, Klaus 404
エンス
Enns, Dietrich 404
エンスエ
Nsue, Emilio 1036
エンストローム
Enström, Karin 404
エンスラー
Ensler, Eve 404
エンスール
Ensour, Abdullah 404
Ensour, Fahd Abul-Athem 404
エンゼオカ
Nzeocha, Mark 1039
エンソゾンジ
N'zonzi, Steven 1039
エンソ・ペレス
Enzo Perez 404
エンタイン
Entine, Jon 404
エンダコット
Endacott, Jan 402
エンダース
Enders, Giulia 402
Enders, Jill 402
エンダーズ
Enders, Walter 402
エンダースビィ
Endersby, Frank 402
エンダラ
Endara, Guillermo 402
Endara, Mirei 402
エンダン
Endang, Rahayu Sedyaningsih 402
エンチャ・エビア
Entcha-ebia, Gabriel 404
エンチャエビア
Entcha-ebia, Gabriel 404
エンツィンガー
Enzinger, Gerald 404
エンツェンスベルガー
Enzensberger, Hans Magnus 404
Enzensberger, Ulrich 404
エンツェンベルガー
Enzensberger, Hans Magnus 404
エンディ
Ndi, Dani 1010
エンディアイェ
Ndiaye, Alfred 1010
エンディコット
Endicott, Josephine Ann 402
エンデリカ・サルガド
Enderica Salgado, Xavier 402
エントウィスル
Entwistle, Joanne 404
Entwistle, Noel James 404
エントウィッスル
Entwistle, Basil 404
Entwistle, John 404
エンドラー
Endler, Franz 402
エンドレクソン
Endrekson, Tonu 402
エンドレス
Endres, Albert 402
エンドング
N'dong, Didier 1011
エンドン・マフムード
Endon Mahmood 402
エンドン・マムード
Endon Mahmood 402
エンナブ
Ennab, Lina 404
エンヌカン
Hennequin, Benjamin Didier 594
エン・ネシリ
En-nesyri, Yousef 404
エンバス
Embas, Douglas Uggah 401
エンバッハ
Embach, Carsten 401
エンバッハー
Embacher, Michael 401
エンバートン
Emberton, David J. 401
エンバリー
Emberley, Barbara 401
Emberley, Ed 401
Emberley, Michael 401
エンバリン
Emberlin, Randy 401
エンバレシュ
Embaresh, El Mahdie Moftah 401
エンバロ
Embalo, António Sirifo 401
Embalo, Braima 401
Embalo, Carlos 401
Embalo, Daniel Suleimane 401
Embalo, Helena Nosolini 401
Embalo, Serifo Antonio 401
エンビード
Embiid, Joel 401
エンフィールド
Enfield, Nicholas James 402
エンフェルト
Garbrecht-enfeldt, Monique 477
エンフサイハン
Enkhsaihan, Mendsaihany 404
エンフジャルガル
Enkhjargal, Tsogtbazaryn 404
エンフトブシン
Enkhtuvshin, Ulziisaihany 404
Enkntuvshin, Olziisaihany 404
エンフバヤル
Enkhbayar, Nambaryn 403
エンフボルド
Enkhbold, Miegombyn 404
Enkhbold, Nyamaagiin 404
エンブリー
Embree, Lester E. 401
エンブリッチ
Embrich, Irina 401
エンブルトン
Embleton, Chris 401
Embleton, Gerry A. 401
エンブレイ
Embrey, Sue Kunitomi 401
エンベル
Embel, Philemon 401
エンヘルス
Engels, Jaco 403
エンボベラ
Envo Bela, Eulalia 404
エンボロ
Embolo, Breel 401
エンメルカンプ
Emmelkamp, Paul M. G. 401
エンヤ
Enya 404
エンライト
Enright, Amanda 404
Enright, Anne 404
Enright, Dennis Joseph 404
Enright, Dominique 404
Enright, Robert D. 404
エンリケ
Enrique, Luis 404
Henrique, Bruno 595
エンリケス
Enriquez, Barbara 404
Henríquez, Milton 595
Henríquez, Roberto 595
Henriquez, Yadira 595
エンリケ・マルティン
Enrique Martin 404
エンロー
Enloe, Cynthia H. 404

【オ】

オ
O, Jong Ae 1039
O, Song-nam 1039
O, Su-yong 1039
O, Tar-su 1040
Oh, Dae-Soo 1046
Oh, Eun-sun 1046
Oh, Jae-shik 1046
Oh, Ji-ho 1046
Oh, Jin-hyek 1046
Oh, Joung-wan 1046
Oh, Keo-don 1046
Oh, Myung 1046
Oh, Se-hoon 1046
Oh, Seung-hwan 1046
Oh, Seung Hwan 1046
Oh, Tae-seok 1046
Oh, Young-doo 1046
Oh, Young-kyo 1046
オー
Ko, Chun-hsiung 749
Oh, Michael 1046
Oh, Sandra 1046
Orr, Gordon 1058
Orr, Mary 1058
オーア
Oher, Michael 1046
Orr, Leon 1058
Orr, Zach 1058
オァー
Orr, Leonard 1058
オア
Orr, Anne Murray 1058
Orr, Mary 1058
オアー
Oher, Michael 1046
オーアーバック
Auerbach, Dan 69
オアロ
Hoarau, Guillaume 611
オーイ
Ohi, Debbie Ridpath 1046
オイェイェミ
Oyeyemi, Helen 1066
オイェタデ
Oyètádé, Benjamin Akintúndé 1066
オイエムバ
Oyé Mba, Casimir 1066
オイエル
Oier, Olazabal 1047
Oier, Sanjurjo 1047
オイエンバ
Oyé Mba, Casimir 1066
オイコノム
Oikonomou, Marios 1047
オイストハイセン
Oosthuizen, Louis 1055
オイティシカ
Oiticica, Christina 1047
オイヌ
Ohin, Eliott 1046
オイハ
Ojha, Siddaraj 1047
オイバ
Oyiba, Jean-Pierre 1066
オイピタン
Oyepitan, Abiodun 1066
オイヤー
Oyer, John S. 1066
Oyer, Paul Edward 1066
オイルシュレーガー
Olschleger, Hans-Dieter 1051
オイレン
Euren, Johan 411
オイロー
Oilouch, Raynold 1047
オウ
Wang, Wayne 1476
Wong, Kar-wai 1523
オーヴァーストリート
Overstreet, Nash 1065
オーヴァソン
Ovason, David 1064
オウアタ
Ouatah, Newfel 1063
オヴァートン
Overton, Tina 1065
オーヴァーバイ
Overbye, Dennis 1065
オーヴァバイ
Overbye, Dennis 1065
オーヴァーマイヤー
Overmyer, Eric 1065
オーヴァーマン
Overman, Howard 1065
オヴァリー
Ovary, Zoltan 1064
オーウィグ
Orwig, Sara 1059
オーウィングス
Owings, Chris 1066
オウヴァリー
Overy, R.J. 1065
オウヴェハンド
Ouwehand, André 1064
オウェイス
al-Oweis, Abdul-Rahman Mohammed 1065

Oweis, Wajih 1065
オウェゾフ
Ovezov, Bayramgeldi 1065
オーウェン
Owen, Bruce M. 1065
Owen, Charlie 1065
Owen, Clive 1065
Owen, David 1065
Owen, Gareth 1065
Owen, Geoffrey 1065
Owen, James A. 1065
Owen, James P. 1065
Owen, Mark 1065
Owen, Michael 1065
Owen, Roger 1065
Owen, Sarah 1065
Owen, Sean 1065
Owen, Thomas 1065
オウエン
Owen, Charlotte 1065
オーウェンス
Owens, David 1065
Owens, Eric 1066
Owens, Henry 1066
Owens, Terrell 1066
オーウェンズ
Owens, J.F. 1066
Owens, Ken 1066
Owens, Patricia 1066
Owens, Terrell 1066
オウエンス
Owens, Solomon 1066
オウエンズ
Owens, Buck 1065
オウェンズ＝リード
Owens-Reid, Dannielle 1066
オウオシ
Ohouochi, Clotilde 1047
オウオチ
Ohouochi, Clotilde 1047
オウォナ
Owona, Grégoire 1066
Owona, Joseph 1066
オウォノ
Owono, François Engonga 1066
オウォノ・アサンゴノ
Owono Asangono, Alejandro Evuna 1066
オウォノ・エソノ
Owono Essono, Fabian 1066
オウォノエドゥ
Owono Edu, Marcelino 1066
オウカシャ
Oukacha, Larification 1064
オウジェドニーク
Ouredník, Patrik 1064
オウジェリー
Augeri, Steve 69
オウジャン
Ozhan, Najibullah 1067
オウスアギマン
Owusuagyeman, Hackman 1066
オウスアンコマ
Owusuaankoma, Paapa 1066
Owusuankomah, Papa 1066
オウズハン
Oguzhan, Ozyakup 1046
オウスラント
Ousland, Borge 1064
オウダ
Ouda, Bassem 1063
オウト
Haut, Elliott R. 582
オウトリー
Oatley, Kristy 1040
ヲゥーパー
Whopper, Willie 1501
オウハドフ
Aukhadov, Apti 70
オヴルツキー
Ovrutsky, Mikhail 1065
オウルドマン
Oldman, Gary 1049
オウロフィーノ
Orofino, Francisco 1058
オウン
Aun Porn Moniroth 70
Own, Ahmed Abdel Karim Salem 1066
オーエル
Howell, Catherine Herbert 628
オーエン
Owen, Clive 1065
Owen, Dave 1065
Owen, Harrison 1065
Owen, Jean 1065
Owen, Jo 1065
Owen, Mark 1065
Owen, Michael 1065
Owen, Sean 1065
Owen, Thomas 1065
オーエンジョーンズ
Owen-Jones, Lindsay 1065
オーエンス
Owens, Terrell 1066
オーエンズ
Owens, Allan 1065
Owens, Buck 1065
Owens, Diana L. 1065
Owens, Elizabeth 1066
Owens, Jerry M. 1066
Owens, Laura 1066
Owens, Simon 1066
Owens, Trevor 1066
オオイワ
Oiwa, Oscar 1047
オオクボ
Okubo, Mine 1048
オオシロ
Oshiro, Robert C. 1060
オオタ
Ohta, Herb 1047
Ohta, Tomoko 1047
Ota, Henry Yasushi 1062
オオタハラ
Ohtahara, Shunsuke 1047
オオツカ
Otsuka, Julie 1062
Otsuka, Ronald Yetsuo 1062
オオナリ
Onari, Benedicto Zulita 1053
オオニシ
Ohnishi, S.Tsuyoshi 1046
オオヌキ
Ohnuki, Mari 1046
オオヌキ・ティアニー
Ohnuki-Tierney, Emiko 1047
オオハラ
Ohara, Tuyoci 1046
オーカー
Auker, Eldon LeRoy 70
オガー
Ogar, Jolanta 1045
オカイン
Okine, Earl 1048
オカカ
Okaka, Stefano 1047
オカグバレ
Okagbare, Blessing 1047
オカザキ
Okazaki, Krystyna 1047
Okazaki, Steven 1047
オガサビア
Oghassabian, Jean 1045
オカシオロドリゲス
Ocasio Rodriguez, Asuncion 1042
オカーシャ
Okasha, Samir 1047
オカシャ
Okasha, A. 1047
オーガス
Ogas, Ogi 1045
オーガスチン
Augustine, Norman R. 69
オーガスティン
Augustin, D.J. 69
Augustine, Jonathan M. 69
Augustine, Liz 69
Augustine, Sue 69
オーガスト
August, Elizabeth 69
August, John 69
Auguste, Zach 69
オーカソン
Aakeson, Kim Fupz 1
オカダ
Okada, Pamela J. 1047
Okada, Victor N. 1047
オガタ
Ogata, Ken 1045
オーガード
Augarde, Steve 69
オカート
Okert, Steven 1047
オカニャ
Ocaña, Graciela 1042
オカノ
Okano, Kenneth Takashi 1047
オカフォー
Okafor, Alex 1047
Okafor, Franky 1047
Okafor, Jahlil 1047
オカーマ
Okarma, Thomas B. 1047
オガーマン
Ogerman, Claus 1045
オカムラ
Okamura, Frank Masao 1047
Okamura, Tomio 1047
オカモト
Okamoto, Tetsuo 1047
Okamoto, Toshikazu 1047
オガワ
Ogawa, Dennis Masaaki 1045
Ogawa, Masako 1045
Ogawa, Yoshikazu 1045
オーガン
Organ, Dennis W. 1057
オカング
Okung, Russell 1048
オガンダガ
Ogandaga, Jean-Marie 1045
オカンテ・ダシルバ
Ocante Da Silva, Aristides 1042
オカンテダシルバ
Ocante Da Silva, Aristides 1042
オガンド
Ogando, Nefi 1045
オガンネシャン
Hovhannisyan, Arpine 627
オカンポ
Ocampo, Jahir 1042
Ocampo, José Antonio 1042
オカンポス
Ocampos, Lucas 1042
オカンラ
Okanla, Moussa 1047
オーキー
Okey, Robin 1047
オキエ
Okieh, Djama Elmi 1047
オキエミ
Okiemy, Bienvenu 1047
オギオ
Ogio, Michael 1045
オーキーズ
Okies, Leigh 1047
オキツンドゥ
Okitundu, She 1048
オキトゥンドゥ
Okitundu, Léonard She 1048
オキーフ
O'Keefe, Arthur Joseph, Ⅳ 1047
O'Keefe, Catherine 1047
O'Keefe, John 1047
O'keefe, Julie 1047
O'Keefe, Mark 1047
O'keeffe, Batt 1047
O'Keeffe, Jac 1047
O'Keeffe, Katherine O'Brien 1047
O'Keeffe, Niamh 1047
オギーフィールド
Ogiefield, Mike L. 1045
オキモト
Okimoto, Daniel I. 1047
Okimoto, Jean Davies 1048
Okimoto, Poliana 1048
オキャラハン
O'Callaghan, Maxine 1042
オキャロル
O'Carroll, Brendan 1042
オギュスタン
Augustin, Jean Kevin 69
オーギュスト
Auguste, Marie Carmelle Rose-Ann 69
Auguste, Robert 69
オギルヴィー
Ogilvie, Sara 1045
オーキン
Okin, Susan Moller 1048

オーキンクロース
Auchincloss, Louis Stanton 69
オーキンクロス
Auchincloss, Louis Stanton 69
オーク
Oke, Alan 1047
Oke, Janette 1047
オーグ
Hoog, Emmanuel 621
オクィーブ
Ó'cuív, Éamon 1043
オークイン
O'Quinn, Ken 1055
オクィン
O'Quinn, Terry 1055
オクイン
O'quinn, Kyle 1055
オグウ
Oguwu, Joy 1046
オクウィリ
Okwiri, Rayton Nduku 1048
オクウィル
Okwir, Betty 1048
オグウチェ
Oguwuche, Grace 1046
オクエフナ
Okuefuna, David 1048
オクサネン
Oksanen, Sofi 1048
Oksanen, Tuula 1048
オクサラ
Oksala, Johanna 1048
オークショット
Oakeshott, Isabel 1040
オークス
Aakhus, Mark A. 1
Oakes, John Bertram 1040
Oaks, Scott 1040
オクス
Ochs, Michael 1043
Ochs, Philipp 1043
オクスズ
Oksuz, Enis 1048
オグスティニアック
Augustyniak, Mathias 69
オクスナム
Oxnam, Robert B. 1066
オクスレー
Oxley, Philip 1066
オクスレイ
Oxley, Mat 1066
オクセンベリー
Oxenbury, Helen 1066
オグソー
Augusseau, Stéphanie 69
オクダ
Okouda, Martin 1048
Okuda, D. 1048
Okuda, Junji 1048
Okuda, Michael 1048
オグデン
Ogden, Jonathan 1045
Ogden, Joseph P. 1045
Ogden, Michael 1045
Ogden, Pat 1045
Ogden, Thomas H. 1045
Ogden, Timothy N. 1045
オグニ
Oguni, Hirokazu 1046
オグバ
Ogbah, Emmanuel 1045
オクパラーゴ
Okpalaugo, Tristan 1048
オグバン
Ogburn, Jacqueline K. 1045
オグビー
Ogilvy, Ian 1045
オク・ビトン
Uk Vithun 1432
オグブエウ
Ogbuewu, Franklin 1045
オグベウ
Ogbeh, Andu Innocent 1045
オグボーン
Ogborn, Jon 1045
オグボンナ
Ogbonna, Angelo 1045
オクマン
Ockman, Joan 1043
オグム
Ogoum, Ahmat Abdoulaye 1046
オクムラ
Okumura, Akihisa 1048
オークメイド
Alkemade, Kim van 32
Alkemade, Len 32
オクヤン
Okuyan, Yasar 1048
オクラ
Okura, Patrick 1048
オークラニア
Orkrania, Alexia 1057
オクラポ
Orakpo, Brian 1055
オクラン
Ockrent, Christine 1043
オークランド
Oakland, Thomas 1040
Okrand, Fred 1048
オークリー
Oakley, Barbara A. 1040
Oakley, Graham 1040
Oakley, Natasha 1040
オクリ
Okri, Ben 1048
オグリスコ
Ohryzko, Volodimir 1047
オクリックズ
Okulicz, Karen 1048
オクリーン
O'Crean, Maureen 1043
オクル
Okell, Sam 1047
オグル
Ogle, James L. 1045
オクルアシビ
Okruashvili, Irakli 1048
オクルアシビリ
Okruashvili, Adam 1048
オグルヴィ
Ogilvy, Guy 1045
オグルヴィー
Ogilvie, Gregory K. 1045
オクルカンチャティ
Okoulou-kantchati, Issifou 1048
オクルト
Okurut, Mary 1048
オークレイ
Oakley, Barbara A. 1040
Oakley, Francis 1040
Oakley, Ros 1040
オグレイディ
O'Grady, Stuart 1046
O'Grady, William 1046
オクレグラク
Okreglak, Maciej 1048
オグレディ
O'Grady, Stuart 1046
オグレトリー
Ogletree, Alec 1045
オークレー・ブラウン
Oakley-Browne, Mark A. 1040
オクレヤク
Oklejak, Marianna 1048
オクレリー
O'Clery, Conor 1043
オグワ
Oguéwa, Célestine 1046
オクワチ
Okwachi, Rebecca Joshua 1048
オクワラ
Okwara, Romeo 1048
オグワンガウォレ
Ogouwalangaawore, Lucienne 1046
オークン
Okun, Michael S. 1048
オグンケル
Ogunkelu, Bimbola 1046
オクンコフ
Okounkov, Andrei 1048
オグンレウェ
Ogunlewe, Adeseye 1046
オケ
Oke, Tosin 1047
オーケソン
Aakeson, Kim Fupz 1
オケソン
Okeson, Jeffrey P. 1047
オケタ
Oketa, Gazmend 1047
オーゲ・ボーア
Bohr, Aage Niels 155
オケモ
Okemo, Chrisanthus 1047
オケリー
O'Kelly, Eugene 1047
オーゲル
Hauguel, Claire 582
Orgel, Doris 1057
オケロ
Okelo, Joseph 1047
オケンド
Oquendo Zabala, Carlos Mario 1055
オケンドサバラ
Oquendo Zabala, Carlos Mario 1055
オケンベヌドホ
Okenve Ndoho, Conrado 1047
オコイエ
Okoye, Lawrence 1048
オゴケ
Ogoke, Edith 1045
オゴゴ
Ogogo, Anthony 1045
オコチャ
Okotcha, Bennett 1048
オーコット
Aucott, Karen 69
オコティ
Okotie, Elleen 1048
オコーナー
O'Connor, Barbara 1043
O'Connor, Cian 1043
O'Connor, Michael J. 1043
O'Connor, Philip F. 1043
O'Connor, Siobhan-Marie 1043
O'connor, Susan 1043
O'Conor, John 1043
オコナー
O'Conner, Carroll 1043
O'Connor, Barbara 1043
O'connor, Brendan 1043
O'Connor, Cian 1043
O'connor, Damien 1043
O'Connor, David 1043
O'Connor, Denis 1043
O'Connor, Donald 1043
O'Connor, Francis G. 1043
O'Connor, Gordon 1043
O'Connor, Joseph 1043
O'Connor, Kaori 1043
O'Connor, Kelley 1043
O'connor, Mary Mitchell 1043
O'Connor, Michael 1043
O'Connor, Robert 1043
O'Connor, Sandra Webb 1043
O'Connor, Ulick 1043
O'Connor, Varley 1043
O'Connor, Victoria 1043
O'Conor, John 1043
O'Cooner, Patricia T. 1043
オコナー・フォン
O'Conner-Von, Susan 1043
オコネド
Okonedo, Sophie 1048
オコネル
O'Connell, Fergus 1043
O'Connell, Jack 1043
オゴーマン
O'Gorman, Jim 1045
オコリー
Okolie, Lawrence 1048
オコルフォア
Okorafor, Nnedi 1048
オコルミ
Okormi, Mahamat Bechir 1048
オコロ
Okolo, Courtney 1048
オコンコフ
Okounkov, Andrei 1048
オコンジョ・イウェアラ
Okonjo-iweala, Ngozi 1048
オコンジョイウェアラ
Okonjo-iweala, Ngozi 1048
オコンナー
O'Connor, Paul 1043
オコンネル
O'Connell, Carol 1043
O'Connell, Jennifer L. 1043
O'connell, Paul 1043
O'Connell, Stephen A. 1043
オコンビ・サリサ
Okombi Salissa, André 1048

オコンビサリサ
Okombi Salissa, André 1048
オーサー
Orser, Brian 1058
オザイナ
al-Uthayna, Salem 1437
オサイミーン
al-Othaimeen, Yusuf bin Ahmad 1062
オサオサエコロ
Osa Osa Ekoro, Jeronimo 1059
オサギー
Osagie, Andrew 1059
オザク
Özak, Faruk Nafiz 1066
オザクマン
Özakman, Turgut 1066
オザースキー
Ozersky, Josh 1067
オサッチー
Osadchil, A. 1059
オサナ
Ossana, Diana 1061
オサフォマルフォ
Osafo-marfo, Yaw 1059
オサフマルフォ
Osafo-marfo, Yaw 1059
オサマン
Othaman, Rizafizah Binti 1062
オサリヴァン
O'Sullivan, Anne 1061
O'Sullivan, Kate 1061
O'Sullivan, Shane 1061
オサリバン
O'Sullivan, Brian 1061
O'Sullivan, Catherine 1061
O'sullivan, Jan 1061
O'Sullivan, Patrick 1061
O'Sullivan, Shane 1061
O'Sullivan, Susan B. 1061
オーザリー - ルートン
Auzary-Luton, Sylvie 71
オザリー＝ルトン
Auzary-Luton, Sylvie 71
オサール
Ossard, Claudie 1061
オザル
Ozal, Mehmet 1066
オザルプ
Ozalp, Ayse 1066
オザワ
Ozawa, Luke H. 1066
Ozawa, Seiji 1066
オザーン
Ozanne, Robert W. 1066
オザン
Ozan, Tufan 1066
オザング
Osang, Alexander 1059
オザンヌ
Ozanne, Marie-Angélique 1066
オーシー
Oshea, Glenn 1060
オシー
O'Shea, Mark 1060
オシア
O'Shea, Donal 1060
オージエ
Auxier, Jonathan 71
オシエー
O'Shea, John 1060
オジェ
Augé, Marc 69
オーシェイ
O'Shea, Michael 1060
O'Shei, Tim 1060
オシェイ
Oshea, Glenn 1060
O'shea, John 1060
O'Shea, Mick 1060
オジェック
Osieck, Holger 1060
オージェロ
Augello, Terri 69
オシェロフ
Osheroff, Douglas Dean 1060
オシオ・アクニャ
Ossio Acuña, Juan 1061
オジシャリア
Odisharia, Guram 1044
オジズ
Augis, Axel 69
オージック
Ozick, Cynthia 1067
オシック
Osich, Josh 1060
オシネエ
Oshineye, Adewale 1060
オシノフスキー
Ossinovski, Jevgeni 1061
オシペンコ
Osypenko, Inna 1062
オシペンコロドムスカ
Osipenko-rodomska, Inna 1060
オシポワ
Osipova, Natalia 1060
オシム
Osim, Ivica 1060
オジムダイア
Ojemudia, Mario 1047
オジャ
Ojha, Devi Prasad 1047
オシャネシー
Shan, Darren 1280
オジャラン
Öcalan, Abdullah 1042
オーシャン
Ocean, Frank 1042
オジャンドル
Augendre, Jacques 69
オージュ
Auge, Laura 69
オジュク
Ojukwu, Chukwuemeka Odumegwu 1047
オーシュコルヌ
Hauchecorne, Bertrand 581
オシュマン
Oschman, James L. 1059
オシュリン
Oshrin, Andy 1060
オショ
Osho, Pierre 1060
オジョ
Ojo, Bayo 1047
Ojo, Matthews A. 1047
Ojo, Sheyi 1047
オショティメイン
Osotimehin, Babatunde 1060
オショーネシー
O'shaughnessy, James 1060
O'Shaughnessy, James P. 1060
O'Shaughnessy, Perri 1060
オー・シール
O Siadhail, Micheal 1060
オジル
Özil, Mesut 1067
オージルヴィー＝ヘラルド
Ogilvie-Herald, Chris 1045
オーシロ
Orsillo, Susan M. 1058
オシンスキー
Oshinsky, David M. 1060
オシンバジョ
Osinbajyo, Yemi 1060
オース
Auth, Tony 71
オス
Os, Erik van 1059
Os, H.W.van 1059
オズ
Oz, Amos 1066
Oz, Mehmet C. 1066
Oz, Tony 1066
Ozu, Nikola 1067
オスイペンコ
Osypenko, Inna 1062
オズィルハン
Ozilhan, Tuncay 1067
オズウィック
Oswick, Cliff 1062
オズウェイラー
Osweiler, Brock 1062
オーズウォルト
Oswalt, Roy 1062
オスカー
Oscar, Amy 1059
オスカニアン
Oscanyan, Frederick S. 1059
オスカニャン
Oskanian, Vardan 1060
オズガービー
Osgerby, Bill 1059
オスカ・ラポンダ
Ossoucah Raponda, Christiane Rose 1061
オスカル
Osacar 1059
Oscar 1059
オスカルション
Oscarsson, Markus 1059
Oscarsson, Per 1059
オスカルソン
Oscarsson, Markus 1059
Oscarsson, Per 1059
オスカル・ドゥアルテ
Oscar Duarte 1059
オズカン
Ozkan, Husamettin 1067
Özkan, Serdar 1067
Ozkan, Sibel 1067
Özkan, Suha 1067
オスキー
Oski, Frank A. 1060
オズギュル
Ozgur, Gozde 1067
オズグッド
Osgood, Peter 1060
オスジ
Osuji, Fabian Ngozi Chinedum 1061
オースター
Auster, Paul Benjamin 70
オスタ
Osta, Clairemarie 1061
オスター
Oster, Emily 1061
Oster, Gerald D. 1061
Oster, Sharon M. 1061
オスターヴァルダー
Osterwalder, Konrad 1061
オスターウォルド
Osterwald, Bibi 1061
オスターヴォルト
Osterwold, Tilman 1061
オスタゴー
Østergaard, Morten 1061
オスタチャー
Ostacher, Michael J. 1061
オースタッド
Austad, Steven N. 70
オスターハウス
Osterhaus, Frank 1061
オースタハメル
Osterhammel, Jürgen 1061
オスターバルダー
Osterwalder, Konrad 1061
オスターバルト
Oosterveld, Jan P. 1055
オスタプチュク
Ostapchuk, Nadzeya 1061
Ostapchuk, Yuliya 1061
オスターブロック
Osterbrock, Donald E. 1061
オスターヘーベン
Osterhaven, M. Eugene 1061
オスターベリ
Österberg, Sven-Erik 1061
オスターマイヤー
Ostermayer, Josef 1061
オスターマン
Osterman, Paul 1061
オスターワルダー
Osterwalder, Alexander 1061
オースチン
Austin, David J.C. 70
Austin, Mike 70
Austin, Robert D. 70
Austin, Stone Cold Steve 70
オースティン
Astin, Barrett 66
Austen, Alfred Walter 70
Austin, Charlie 70
Austin, Christopher 70
Austin, David J.C. 70
Austin, James 70
Austin, John 70
Austin, Karin A. 70
Austin, Neil 70
Austin, Patti 70
Austin, Peter 70
Austin, Robert D. 70
Austin, Robert Daniel 70
Austin, Tavon 70
Austin, Teryl 70
Austin, Thomas 70

Austin, Tyler 70
Austin, Valerie 70
Austin, Wendy 71
Osteen, Joel 1061
オスティーン
Osteen, Joel 1061
オスデビラ・キロガ
Hoz De Vila Quiroga, Tito 629
オズデミル
Ozdemir, Ali 1066
オステール
Oster, Christian 1061
オステル
Oster, Grigoriy 1061
オステル・ススエフ
Oster Soussouev, Pierre 1061
オステルメイエ
Ostermeyer, Micheline 1061
オーステルリンク
Oosterlinck, André 1055
オステロート
Osterroth, Jochen von 1061
オステロフ
Osterloh, Margit 1061
オーステロム
Oosterom, Arne van 1055
オステン
Osten, Manfred 1061
オステンソン
Östensson, Pia 1061
オスト
Ost, Daniel 1061
オストイッチ
Ostojić, Ranko 1061
Ostojić, Veljko 1061
オストゥニ
Ostuni, Elizabeth 1061
オストライカー
Ostriker, Jeremiah P. 1061
オーストリー
Austrie, Reginald 71
オストルツィル
Ostrcil, Marian 1061
オストルツォレク
Ostrzolek, Matthias 1061
オストロー
Ostrow, Kim 1061
オストロウスキー
Ostrowski, Helen 1061
オストロゴルスキー
Ostrogorski, Georgije 1061
オストローフ
Ostrov, Svetozar Aleksandrovich 1061
オストロム
Ostrom, Elinor 1061
Ostrom, Hans A. 1061
オスーナ
Osuna, Jose 1061
Osuna, Roberto 1061
オスナ
Osuna, Rosa 1061
オズーナ
Ozuna, Marcell 1067
オスネイ
Osnei 1060
オズノス
Osnos, Evan 1060
オズハセキ
Ozhaseki, Mehmet 1067
オスピナ
Ospina, Bernardo 1060
Ospina, David 1061
オズビリス
Ozbiliz, Aras 1066
オズビレン
Ozbilen, Ilham Tanui 1066
オズーフ
Ozouf, Mona 1067
オスファテール
Hausfater, Rachel 582
オースベル
Ausubel, Ramona 71
オズボーン
Ausbourne, Robert 70
Osborn, Anne G. 1059
Osborn, Claudia L. 1059
Osborn, Cynthia J. 1059
Osborn, Rick 1059
Osborn, Tommy Lee 1059
Osborne, Carl A. 1059
Osborne, Carol 1059
Osborne, Charles 1059
Osborne, David E. 1059
Osborne, Elsie 1059
Osborne, Frances 1059
Osborne, George 1059
Osborne, Jason 1059
Osborne, Kenan B. 1059
Osborne, Marie 1059
Osborne, Mark 1059
Osborne, Mary Pope 1059
Osborne, Richard 1059
Osborne, Roger 1059
Osborne, Will 1059
Osbourne, Dale 1059
Osbourne, Ozzy 1059
オズボン
Osborne, Robin 1059
オスマー
Othmer, Donald Frederick 1062
オースマス
Ausmus, Brad 70
オスマーニ
Osmani, Addy 1060
オスマニ
Osmani, Ali Ahmad 1060
Osmani, Bujar 1060
Osmani, Faiz Mohammad 1060
オスマノビッチ
Osmanović, Adil 1060
オスマーン
Osman, Tarek 1060
オスマン
Adem, Abrar Osman 14
Osman, Abdelwahab Mohamed 1060
Osman, Abdirahman Abdi 1060
Osman, Abdul-Wahab Mohamed 1060
Osman, Aden Abdulla 1060
Osman, Ahmatjan 1060
Osman, Ahmed Bilal 1060
Osman, Ali Hassan 1060
Osman, Chris 1060
Osman, Kassim Issak 1060
Osman, Osman Muhammad 1060
Osman, Saleh 1060
Osman, Yeafesh 1060
Othman, Abdul-Rahman Mohammed Ali 1062
Othman, Arwaa 1062
Othman, Mamo Farhad 1062
Othman, Muhammad 1062
Othman, Narmin 1062
オスマン・ムセ
Osman Muse, Saleh Sheikh 1060
オスミッチ
Osmić, Zekerijah 1060
オズメント
Ozment, Steven E. 1067
オスモノフ
Osmonov, Kyrmanbek 1060
オスラー
Osler, Audrey 1060
オースラン
Aasland, Tora 1
オスランス
Oslance, Jeff 1060
オズリー
Oslie, Pamala 1060
Ozley, Lee 1067
オズリュ
Ozlu, Faruk 1067
オズル
Ozlu, Bekir 1067
オースルード
Aasrud, Rigmor 1
オスレンダー
Oslender, Ulrich 1060
オスロ
Ocelot, Michel 1042
オズワルト
Oswalt, Roy 1062
オズワルド
Oswald, Gerhard 1061
Oswald, Yvonne 1061
Ozsvald, Ian 1067
オーゼ
Aase, Jannike 1
オセアリー
Oseary, Guy 1059
オセイ
Osseyi, Rodolphe Kossivi 1061
オゼキ
Ozeki, Ruth L. 1067
オセトゥンバ
Ossetoumba, Lekoundzou Itihi 1061
オセビ
Ossébi, Henri 1061
オーセフ
Ouseph, Rajiv 1064
オセメリー
Osemele, Kelechi 1059
オーセル
Woeser, Tsering 1520
オーセルー
Aaserud, Finn 1
オーゼル
Orzel, Chad 1059
オゼル
Ozer, Tiki 1067
オゼレツ
Ozerets, Alexander V. 1067
オゾキ
Odzoki, Serge Michel 1044
オソキンス
Osokins, Andrejs 1060
オソティメイン
Osotimehin, Babatunde 1060
オゾノフ
Ozonoff, Sally 1067
オソモ
Osomo, Mobolaji 1060
オソリオ
Osorio, Ana 1060
Osorio, Carlos 1060
Osorio, Elsa 1060
Osorio, Félix 1060
Osorio, Marta 1060
Osorio, Óscar Armando 1060
Osorio, Víctor 1060
オソリオ・チョン
Osorio Chong, Miguel Ángel 1060
オゾン
Ozon, François 1067
オーター
Oerter, Al 1045
オダ
Oda, Beverly 1043
オタイ
Otai, Mana 1062
オタヴィオ
Otavio 1062
オタウェイ
Ottaway, Peter Berry 1062
オダジュ
Odagiu, Stefan 1043
オダースキー
Odersky, Martin 1044
オタゾ
Otazo, Karen L. 1062
オダネル
O'Donnell, Joe 1044
オタフィーレ
Otafiire, Kahinda 1062
オタフィレ
Otafiire, Kahinda 1062
オタホノフ
Otakhonov, Foziljon 1062
オーダム
Odam, George 1043
Odum, Eugene Pleasants 1044
オダム
Odum, Eugene Pleasants 1044
オタメンディ
Otamendi, Nicolas 1062
オタリ
al-Otari, Muhammad Naji 1062
オタルスルタノフ
Otarsultanov, Dzhamal 1062
オタロラ
Otárola, Fredy 1062
オータン
Autain, Clémentine 71
オダン
Odent, Michel 1044
オーチー
Orci, Roberto 1056
オチ
Ochi, Victor 1042
オチェフ

オ

Ochefu, Daniel 1042
オチェペ
Ochekpe, Sarah Reng 1042
オチオグロッソ
Occhiogrosso, Peter 1042
オチガヴァ
Ochigava, Zurab 1042
オチガワ
Ochigava, Sofya 1042
オチコ
Oczko, Aleksander 1043
オチチ
Ochichi, Isabella 1042
オーチャード
Orchard, Grant 1056
Orchard, Nate 1056
オチャラハン
O'Callaghan, Gemma 1042
オチュペ
Ochekpe, Sarah Reng 1042
オチョア
Ochoa, Francisco Fernandez 1042
Ochoa, Guillermo 1042
Ochoa, Isis 1042
Ochoa, Lorena 1042
Ochoa, Paquito 1042
オチョア・キンテロス
Ochoa Quinteros, Pablo Alcides 1042
オチルバティーン・ダシバルバル
Ochirbatyn Dashbalbar 1042
オチルバト
Ochirbat, Burmaa 1042
Ochirbat, P. 1042
オチルフー
Ochirkhuu, Tuvdengiin 1042
オーチンクロス
Auchincloss, Louis Stanton 69
オーツ
Oates, Colin 1040
Oates, Joan 1040
Oates, John 1040
Oates, John A. 1040
Oates, John F. 1040
Oates, Jonny Lane 1040
Oates, Joyce Carol 1040
Oates, R.Kim 1040
オツィプカ
Oczipka, Bastian 1043
オーツカ
Otsuka, Julie 1062
オッカー
Ocker, J.W. 1043
Okker, Patricia 1048
オッカーマン
Öckerman, Per-Arne 1043
オッキウツィ
Occhiuzzi, Diego 1042
オッグ
Ogg, Gabi M. 1045
Ogg, James George 1045
オックスフォード
Oxford, Reece 1066
オックスレイド・チェンバレン
Oxlade-chamberlain, Alex 1066
オックスレード
Oxlade, Chris 1066
オックマン
Hochmann, Jacques 612
オックラン
Ockrent, Christine 1043
オックルフォード
Ockleford, Elizabeth M. 1043
オッシ
Hossi, Victorino Domingos 625
Occhi, Gilberto 1042
オッジ
Ozzie, Ray 1067
オーツセン
Ortzen, Tony 1059
オッター
Otter, Anne Sophie von 1063
オッタヴィアニ
Ottaviani, Jim 1062
オッタビーノ
Ottavino, Adam 1062
オッタンジェ
Ottinger, Didier 1063
オッティ
Ottey, Merlene 1063
オッテセン
Ottesen, Jeanette 1063
オッテリアッド
Otryad, Gundegmaa 1062
オッテリーニ
Otellini, Paul S. 1062
オッテン
Otten, Jürgen 1063
オット
Ott, Alexander 1062
Ott, Alice Sara 1062
Ott, Carole 1062
Ott, Hermann E. 1062
Ott, John 1062
Ott, Jordan 1062
Ott, Jurg 1062
Ott, Konrad 1062
Otto, Paul 1063
オットー
Ott, Henry W. 1062
Ott, Tyler 1062
Otto, Bjorn 1063
Otto, Christie 1063
Otto, Eckart 1063
Otto, Frei 1063
Otto, Michael 1063
Otto, Michael W. 1063
Otto, Svend 1063
Otto, Sylke 1063
Otto, Thomas 1063
オッド
Oddo, Massimo 1043
オットソン
Ottosson, Anna 1063
Ottosson, Christina 1063
Ottosson, Paul N.J. 1063
オッドソン
Oddsson, David 1043
オットーネ
Ottone, Ernesto 1063
オットレー
Otley, David 1062
オッフェ
Offe, Claus 1045
オッフェンバック
Offenbach, Jacques 1045
オッペル
Oppel, Kenneth 1055
オッペンハイマー
Oppenheimer, Andres 1055
Oppenheimer, Catherine 1055
Oppenheimer, Helen 1055
Oppenheimer, Jerry 1055
Oppenheimer, Joshua 1055
Oppenheimer, Michael 1055
Oppenheimer, Stephen 1055
オッペンハイム
Oppenheim, David 1055
Oppenheim, Dennis 1055
Oppenheim, Joanne 1055
オッリ
Olli, Petra 1051
オデ
Odeh, Abeer 1043
Odeh, Ayman 1043
Odeh, John 1043
オデー
Oudeh, Mohammad 1063
オーディ
Audi, Paul 69
オティ
Oti, Patterson 1062
オディ
O'day, Darren 1043
O'dea, Willie 1043
Odey, John Ogar 1044
Ody, Penelope 1044
オデイ
O'Day, Anita 1043
O'day, Gail R. 1043
オディアイズワ
Odighizuwa, Owa 1044
オーディアール
Audiard, Jaques 69
オディアール
Audiard, Jaques 69
オディアンボー
Odhiambo, Rees 1044
オディウェン
Odewahn, Andrew 1044
オティエノ
Otieno, Tabitha 1062
Otieno, Wambui Waiyaki 1062
オーティエール
Hautière, Régis 582
オディオ
Odio, Elizabeth 1044
オディカゼ
Odikadze, Elizbar 1044
オーティス
Otis, John D. 1062
Otis, Johnny 1062
オティーズ
Ortiz, David 1058
Ortiz, Hector 1058
オディノ
Odinot, Jan Hendrik 1044
オディフレッディ
Odifreddi, Piergiorgio 1044
オディベール
Audibert, Catherine 69
オディンガ
Odinga, Raila 1044
オーデカーク
Oedekerk, Steve 1044
オテギ
Otegui, Antonio 1062
オデコン
Odekon, Mehmet 1043
オデッタ
Odetta 1044
オーデット
Audet, Richard 69
オデット
O'Dette, Paul 1044
オデッロ
Odello, Luigi 1043
オテテオマンガ
Otete Omanga, Laurent-Charles 1062
オテプカ
Otepka, Hannah 1062
オデムウィンギ
Odemwingie, Peter 1044
オデムウィンギー
Odemwingie, Peter 1044
オーデュス
Audus, Hilary 69
オーデル
O'Dell, Chris 1043
Odell, Mats 1043
オデール
O'Dell, Charles Robert 1043
Odell, Tom 1043
オデル
Odell, Jay Scott 1043
オテロ
Otero, Dan 1062
オーデン
Oden, Tinsley 1044
Orden, David 1056
Uden, Grant 1432
オーデンタール
Odenthal, Marc 1044
オーデンベリ
Odenberg, Mikael 1044
オート
Oud, Sam 1063
オード
Ord, Timothy 1056
オドーア
Odor, Rougned 1044
オドゥー
Odoux, Eric 1044
オドゥアオギエンウォニ
Oduahogiemwonyi, Stella 1044
オドゥアール
Audouard, Antoine 69
オートゥイユ
Auteuil, Daniel 71
オトゥェー
Otway, Helen 1063
オトウェイ
Otway, Helen 1063
オトゥオマ
Otuoma, Paul 1063
オドゥバジョ
Odubajo, Moses 1044
オドゥモス
Odumosu, Muizat Ajoke 1044
オトゥール
O'Toole, Brian 1062
O'Toole, Dan 1062

O'toole, Erin 1062
O'Toole, Jim 1062
O'Toole, Mary Ellen 1062
O'Toole, Mary Louise 1062
O'Toole, Peter 1062
オドゥワン＝マミコニアン
Audouin-Mamikonian, Sophie 69
オトゥンガオシバジョ
Otounga Ossibadjouo, Mathias 1062
オトゥンバエワ
Otunbayeva, Roza Isakovna 1063
オードギー
Audeguy, Stéphane 69
オトゴンツェツェグ・ガルバドラフ
Otgontsetseg Galbadrakhyn 1062
オトゴンバートル
Otgonbaatar, Uuganbaatar 1062
オトゴンバヤル
Otgonbayar, Sainbuyangiin 1062
Otgonbayar, Yondongiin 1062
オートシ
Otoshi, Kathryn 1062
オートナー
Ortner, Nick 1059
オドナー
Odhner, John L. 1044
オドナヒュー
O'Donohue, William T. 1044
オトニエル
Othoniel, Jean-Michel 1062
オドーネ
Odone, Lorenzo 1044
オドネル
O'Donnell, Adam J. 1044
O'donnell, Chris 1044
O'Donnell, E.B. 1044
O'Donnell, Jodi 1044
O'Donnell, Mark 1044
O'donnell, Pat 1044
O'donnell, Phil 1044
O'Donnell, Rosie 1044
O'donnell, Tela 1044
O'Donnell, Timothy 1044
オドノヴァン
O'Donovan, Gene 1044
オドノヒュー
O'donoghue, John 1044
O'Donohue, William T. 1044
オドノフー
O'donoghue, John 1044
オートバーグ
Ortberg, John 1058
オドバヤル
Odbayar, Dorjiin 1043
オドバル
Udval, Natsag 1432
オードヒューム
Ord-Hume, Arthur W.J. G. 1056
オートフイユ
Hautefeuille, Michel 582
オトマニ
Othmani, Saad-Eddine El 1062
オドム
Odom, John C. 1044
Odom, Lamar 1044
Odom, Mel 1044
Odom, Wendell 1044
オドラム
Odlum, George 1044
オートリー
Autry, Denico 71
Oatley, Keith 1040
オードリー
Awdry, Christopher 72
Haudry, Jean 581
オドリオゾーラ
Odriozola, Elena 1044
オドリスコル
O'Driscoll, Brian 1044
O'Driscoll, Michael P. 1044
オドリック
Odrick, Jared 1044
オドリッジ
Odorizzi, Jake 1044
オトリャド
Otryad, Gundegmaa 1062
オトルバエフ
Otorbayev, Joomalt 1062
オドルリ
Audrerie, Dominique 69
オドレール
Haudrère, Philippe 581
オドロバ
Odorova, Eva 1044
オドワイヤー
O'dwyer, Kelly 1044
オートン
Orton, Bob 1059
Orton, Randy 1059
オドンゴ
Odongo, Jeje 1044
オドンチメド
Odonchimed, Luvsangiin 1044
オドンネル
O'Donnell, Donat 1044
O'Donnell, John R. 1044
O'Donnell, Shannon 1044
オナ
Ona, Enrique 1053
オナイアンズ
Onians, John 1054
オナオノ
Ona Ono, Daniel 1053
オナオンド
Ona Ondo, Daniel 1053
オナナ
Onana, Andre 1053
オニェフル
Onyefulu, Ifeoma 1054
オニェマー
Onyemah, Vincent 1054
オニエマータ
Onyemata, David 1054
オニオンズ
Onions, Oliver 1054
オニカ
Onika, Joseph 1054
オニシウォ
Onisiwo, Karim 1054
オニシコ
Onyshko, Isabela 1054
オニシチェンコ
Onyschenko, Hanna 1054
オニシチュク
Onishchuk, Mykola 1054
オーニッシュ
Ornish, Dean 1057
オニファデババムッサ
Onifade Babamoussa, Sofiatou 1054
オニャ
Oña, Iván 1053
オニール
O'neal, Cedric 1053
O'Neal, Katherine 1053
O'Neal, Shaquille 1053
O'Neal, Stanley 1053
OŃeal, Synthia 1053
O'Neal, Tatum 1053
O'Neal, Ted 1053
O'Neil, Buck 1053
O'Neil, Cathy 1053
O'Neil, Dennis 1053
O'Neil, Denny 1053
O'Neil, Di 1053
O'Neil, James M. 1053
O'neil, Jim 1053
O'Neil, John R. 1053
O'Neil, Joseph 1053
O'Neil, Louisa Peat 1053
O'neil, Peter 1053
O'Neil, William J. 1053
O'neill, Aiden 1053
O'Neill, Barrett 1053
O'Neill, Gerard 1053
O'Neill, Hannah 1053
O'Neill, Jason 1053
O'Neill, Jim 1053
O'Neill, John 1053
O'Neill, Joseph 1053
O'Neill, Kevin 1053
O'Neill, Luke A.J. 1053
O'Neill, Matthew 1053
O'Neill, Michael E. 1054
O'Neill, Onora 1054
O'Neill, Patrick 1054
O'neill, Paul 1054
O'Neill, Paul 1054
O'Neill, Peter 1054
O'Neill, Robert E. 1054
O'Neill, Robert V. 1054
O'Neill, Susan 1054
O'Neill, Susan A. 1054
O'Neill, Thomas J. 1054
O'Neill, Timothy R. 1054
O'neill, Tyler 1054
オヌ
Onu, Ogbonnaya 1054
オヌア
Onneua, Phommachanh 1054
オヌアク
Onuaku, Arinze 1054
Onuaku, Chinanu 1054
オヌオラ
Onuora, Anyika 1054
オヌザー
Onwuasor, Patrick 1054
オヌビエ
Onouviet, Richard Auguste 1054
オネー
Oney, Walter 1054
オネイ
Oney, Steve 1054
オネーク
Onek, Joseph 1054
オネク
Onec, Omnec 1053
Onek, Hilary 1054
オーノ
Ohno, Apolo Anton 1046
オノ
Ono, hana 1054
Ono, Kentaro 1054
オノズカ・デ・ゴメス - モラン
Onozuka de Gómez-Morán, Chiho 1054
オノ・ナカムラ
Ono Nakamura, Armando 1054
オノマー
Onomah, Josh 1054
オノ・ヨーコ
Ono, Yoko 1054
オノリオ
Onorio, Teima 1054
オノルド
Honnold, Alex 620
オノレ
Honoré 620
Honoré, Jean-Paul 620
オノレイ
Honoré, Carl 620
オノレメメン
Onolememen, Mike 1054
オノン
Onon, Urgungge 1054
オーバー
Ober, Clinton 1040
Ober, Lisa 1040
オハー
Oher, James M. 1046
オバ
Oba, Pierre 1040
オバイド
Obaid, Ali Muftah 1040
Obaid, Obaidullah 1040
オパウスキ
Opawski, Krzysztof 1055
オバーグ
Oberg, Dianne 1040
Oberg, Scott 1040
オバサンジョ
Obasanjo, Olusegun 1040
オバジェ・カブレラ
Ovalle Cabrera, Ludwig Werner 1064
オバースキ
Obarski, Tom 1040
オーバーストリート
Overstreet, Nash 1065
オバダ
Obada, Efe 1040
オパチッチ
Opačić, Milanka 1055
オーバック
Auerbach, Red 69
Ohrbach, Barbara Milo 1047
Orbach, Susie 1056
Orback, Jens 1056
オーバーテュアー
Oberthur, Sebastian 1041
オーバードーファー
Oberdorfer, Don 1040
オーバードルファー
Oberdorfer, Bernd 1040

オーバートン
Overton, Dillon 1065
Overton, Matt 1065
オバートン
Overton, Richard E. 1065
オハナ
Ohana, Asher 1046
オバナン
O'Bannon, Frank Lewis 1040
オハニャン
Ohanyan, Seyran 1046
オバーノン
O'Bannon, Frank Lewis 1040
オバノン
O'Bannon, Dan 1040
オーバーハウザー
Oberhauser, Sabine 1040
オーバービー
Overby, Charles M. 1065
Overby, Jason Scott 1065
オーバビー
Overby, Charles M. 1065
オーバービーク
Overbeek, Edzard J. C. 1065
オーバーヒューマ
Oberhuemer, Pamela 1041
オーバーベック
Overbeck, Lndger 1065
オーバーボー
Overbaugh, Jeff 1065
オバーホルツァー
Oberholtzer, Brett 1041
オーバーホルト
Overholt, Emily 1065
オバマ
Obama, Barack 1040
Obama, Michelle 1040
オバマアスエ
Obama Asue, Francisco Pascual 1040
オーバーマイヤー
Obermaier, Frederik 1041
Obermayer, Bastian 1041
Obermeier, Siegfried 1041
Overmier, J.Bruce 1065
オーバマーズ
Overmars, Mark 1065
オバマヌスエ
Obama Nsue, Francisco-Pascual 1040
オバマヌチャマ
Obama Nchama, Nicolas 1040
オバマヌベ
Obama Nve, Justino 1040
オバーマン
Oberman, Michelle 1041
オバム
Obame, Anthony 1040
オーバメヤン
Aubameyang, Pierre-Emerick 68
オハラ
O'Hara, Daniel T. 1046
O'Hara, Elizabeth 1046
O'Hara, John 1046
O'Hara, Karen 1046
O'Hara, Kelli 1046
O'Hara, Maureen 1046
オパラ
Opala, Grzegorz 1055
オーバーランド
Overland, Amanda 1065
オーバリー
Overly, Michael R. 1065
オハーリー
O'Herlihy, Dan 1046
オバリー
O'Barry, Richard 1040
オパル
Opal, Charlotte 1055
オパルカ
Opałka, Roman 1055
オバルク
Obalk, Hector 1040
オパレ
Opare, Daniel 1055
オパレフ
Opalev, Maksim 1055
オハロー
O'Harrow, Robert 1046
オーバーワーター
Overwater, Georgien 1065
オーバーン
Auburn, David 69
オーバン
Aubin, Henri-Jean 68
オバーン
O'Byrne, Patrick 1042
オハンロン
O'Hanlon, Bill 1046
O'Hanlon, Michael E. 1046
O'Hanlon, Pete 1046
O'Hanlon, Redmond 1046
O'Hanlon, William Hudson 1046
オーピー
Opie, Julian 1055
オビ
Obi, Joel 1041
オビー
Obee, Patricia 1040
オピー
Opie, Julian 1055
Opie, Lionel H. 1055
オビアン
Obiang, Eugenio Nze 1041
Obichang, Charles 1041
オビアング
Obiang, Pedro 1041
オービエ
Aubier, Eric 68
オビエド
Oviedo, Bryan 1065
Oviedo, Francisco 1065
オピオ
Opio, Gabriel 1055
オビオーハ
Obioha, Julien 1041
オビオラ
Obiora, Leslie 1041
オビーガドゥー
Obeegadoo, Louis Steven 1040
オヒギンズ
O'Higgins, Michael 1046
オビクウェル
Obikwelu, Francis 1041
オピッツ
Oppitz, Gerhard 1055
オビドフ
Obidov, Okiljon 1041
オビリ
Obiri, Hellen Onsando 1041
オビール
Oviir, Liisa 1065
Oviir, Siiri 1065
オービン
Aubin, Paul F. 68
オーヒンク
Oogink, Reshmie 1055
オビンナ
Obinna, Victor 1041
オピンバ
Opimbat, Léon Alfred 1055
オフ
Off, Carol 1045
Off, Frank 1045
オファーマン
Offermann, Lynn R. 1045
オファムボ
Ofa Mbo, Fortunato 1045
オーファラ
Orfalea, Paul 1057
オ・ファリル
O'Farrill, Arturo 1045
オファリル
O'Farrill, Chico 1045
オファレ
O'Farrell, Brigid 1045
オファーレル
O'Farrell, John 1045
O'Farrell, Maggie 1045
オファレル
O'Farrell, John 1045
オフィサー
Officer, Alana 1045
オフィット
Offit, Paul A. 1045
オフィリ
Ofili, Cindy 1045
オフィル
Offill, Jenny 1045
オブウェイヒ
Ogbuehi, Cedric 1045
オフェイロン
O'Faolain, Julia 1045
O'Faolain, Nuala 1045
オフェール・アルマダ
Hopffer Almada, Janira Isabel 621
オフェールアルマダ
Hopffer Almada, Janira Isabel 621
オフォスアジェレ
Ofosu-adjare, Elizabeth 1045
オフォスアジャレ
Ofosu-adjare, Elizabeth 1045
オブオチャ
Obwocha, Henry 1042
オプゲノールト
Opgenoorth, Winfried 1055
オブシェブー
Obsieh Bouh, Elmi 1042
オブシェワイス
Obsieh Waiss, Elmi 1042
オブシエーワイス
Obsieh Waiss, Elmi 1042
オプスヴィック
Opsvik, Peter 1055
オプステルテン
Opstelten, Ivo 1055
オブズフェルド
Obstfeld, Maurice 1042
オフチニコフ
Ovchinnikov, Serguey 1064
オフチャロフ
Ovcharov, Rumen 1064
Ovtcharov, Dimitrij 1065
オフチンニコフ
Ovchinnikov, Vsevolod Vladimirovich 1064
オフト
Ooft, Hans 1054
オプトウ
Opotow, Susan 1055
オフナー
Ofner, Katrin 1045
オプーナ
Opeña, Jerome 1055
オブホルツァー
Obholzer, Anton 1041
オブホルツァー
Obholzer, Karin 1041
オブマシック
Obmascik, Mark 1041
オフマン
Offmann, Karl 1045
オフュルス
Ophüls, Marcel 1055
オブラー
Obler, Loraine K. 1041
Obler, Martin 1041
オブライアン
O'Brian, Hugh 1041
O'Brien, Charles 1041
O'Brien, Jeffrey M. 1041
O'Brien, Niall 1042
O'Brien, William B. 1042
オブライアント
O'bryant, Johnny 1042
オブライエン
O'Brian, Hugh 1041
O'Brien, Anne 1041
O'Brien, Anthony Patrick 1041
O'brien, Bill 1041
O'Brien, Brendan 1041
Obrien, Brittany 1041
O'Brien, Conor Cruise 1041
O'Brien, Cormac 1041
O'Brien, Daniel 1041
O'Brien, Dominic 1041
O'Brien, Ed 1041
O'Brien, Edna 1041
O'Brien, Glenn 1041
O'Brien, Greg 1041
O'Brien, Jack 1041
O'Brien, James 1041
O'brien, Jim 1041
O'brien, J.J. 1042
O'Brien, John 1042
O'Brien, Justine 1042
Obrien, Kate 1042
O'Brien, Kathleen 1042
O'Brien, Kevin 1042
O'brien, Kitt 1042
O'Brien, Larry 1042
O'Brien, Lucy 1042
O'Brien, Mary Barmeyer 1042
O'brien, Meg 1042
O'Brien, Michael Vincent 1042
O'Brien, Parry 1042

O'brien, Peter 1042
O'Brien, Sally 1042
O'Brien, S.C. 1042
O'brien, Seán 1042
O'Brien, Stacey 1042
O'Brien, Terry 1042
O'Brien, Tim 1042
O'Brien, Timothy M. 1042
O'Brien, Virginia 1042

オブラク
Oblak, Jan 1041

オブラスツォヴァ
Obraztsova, Elena Vasilievna 1041

オブラスツォバ
Obraztsova, Elena Vasilievna 1041

オブラズツォフ
Obraztsov, Youri 1041

オブラスツォーワ
Obraztsova, Yevgenia 1041

オブラスツォワ
Obraztsova, Elena Vasilievna 1041

オブラック
Aubrac, Lucie 68

オブラドヴィッチ
Obradovic, Zivota 1041

オブラドビッチ
Obradović, Žarko 1041

オフラナガン
O'Flanagan, Sheila 1045

オフラハティ
O'flaherty, Eric 1045

オーフリ
Ofri, Danielle 1045

オーブリ
Aubry, Cécile 69

オーブリー
Aubry, Cécile 69
Awbrey, Brian J. 72

オブリ
Aubry, Cécile 69
Aubry, Isabelle 69
Aubry, Martine Louise Marie 69

オブリェンコルジネク
Obuljen Koržinek, Nina 1042

オブリスト
Obrist, Hans-Ulrich 1042
Obrist, Jürg 1042

オブリンガー
Oblinger, Helmut 1041

オブリンガー・ペータース
Oblinger-peters, Violetta 1041

オーブル
Houbre, Gilbert 625
Oubre, Carroll L. 1063

オブル
Obure, Chris 1042

オフルオグ
Ohuruogu, Christine 1047

オーブレー
Aubrey, Robert 68

オフレ
Auffret, Benjamin 69
Auffret, Dominique 69

オブレ
Obure, Chris 1042

オプレ
Ople, Blas F. 1055

オプレア
Oprea, Gabriel 1055
Oprea, Marian 1055

オーブレイ
Oubre, Kelly 1063

オーフレイム
Overeem, Alistair 1065

オブレゴン
Obregón, Manuel 1041

オブレノ
Obreno, Hannes 1041

オブレヒト
Obrecht, Jas 1041
Obreht, Téa 1041

オプレヒト
Obrecht, Bettina 1041

オブロブスキー
Obrowsky, Walter 1042

オープンショー
Openshaw, Peter J. M. 1055

オーブンデン
Ovenden, Mark 1065

オヘア
O'Hare, Mick 1046

オヘイガン
O'Hagan, Andrew 1046

オベイダト
Obeidat, Mohammad 1040

オベイディ
al-Obaidi, Abdul-Qadir Jashim 1040
al-Obaidi, Ali Saad 1040
al-Obeidi, Abdul-Fittah Younis 1040
al-Obeidi, Khalid 1040

オベイド
Obaid, Samira 1040
Obaid, Thoraya Ahmed 1040
Obeid, Abdullah bin Salih 1040
Obeid, Atef Muhammad Muhammad 1040
Obeid, Kamal Mohamed 1040
Obeid, Mokarram 1040

オベイド・チノイ
Obaid-Chinoy, Sharmeen 1040

オベクサー
Obexer, Linus 1041

オベーセーカラ
Obeyesekere, Gananath 1041

オベゾフ
Ovezov, Bayramgeldi 1065

オベチキン
Ovechkin, Alexander 1064

オベツェビランプティ
Obetsebi-lamptey, Jake 1041

オベッド
Obed, Ellen Bryan 1040

オペラ
Oprea, Laura 1055

オベラル
Ovelar, Blanca 1065
Ovelar, Silvio 1065

オベラル・デ・ドゥアルテ
Obelar de Duarte, Blanca 1040

オーベリー
Åberg, Jessica 6
Aubery, Patty 68

オベール
Aubert, Brigitte 68
Aubert, Sandrine 68

オーベルィ
Åberg, Berit 6

オーベルクフェル
Obergfoll, Christina 1040

オーベルシュトルツ
Oberstolz, Christian 1041

オーベルソン
Oberson, Swann 1041

オベルタス
Obertas, Julia 1041

オペルティ
Opertti, Didier 1055

オベルホファー
Oberhofer, Karin 1040

オベロイ
Oberoi, Mohan Singh 1041

オペロゲ
Opeloge, Ele 1055

オベン
Oben, Tanyi Mbianyor 1040

オポーク
Opoku, Andrew 1055

オポチェンスキー
Opocensky, Milan 1055

オボテ
Obote, Apollo Milton 1041

オボノエンゴノ
Obono Engono, Jesusa 1041

オボルドゥドゥ
Oborududu, Blessing 1041

オーボーン
Oborne, Martine 1041

オポンフォス
Oppong-fosu, Akwasi 1055

オマー
Omer, Haim 1052

オマーティアン
Omartian, Stormie 1052

オマトゥク
Omatuku, Philomène 1052

オマホニー
O'mahony, Peter 1052

オマモ
Omamo, Raychelle 1052

オマランガ
Omalanga, Lambert Mende 1052

オマリー
O'Malley, Bryan Lee 1052
O'Malley, Kevin 1052
O'Malley, Martin Joseph 1052
O'Malley, Michael 1052
O'Malley, Peter 1052
O'malley, Ryan 1052
O'malley, Shawn 1052

オマール
Omaar, Mohamed Abdullahi 1052
Omar, Dullah 1052
Omar, Julian 1052
Omar, Muhammad 1052
Omarr, Sydney 1052

オマル
Omar, Abdul 1052
Omar, Abdusalam Hadlie 1052
Omar, Mohamed Ben 1052
Omar, Muhammad 1052
Omar, Muneer Ali 1052
Omar, Rashad 1052
Omer, Ahmed Sa'ad 1052
Omer, Ibrahim Ahmad 1052

オマロフ
Omarov, Magomed 1052

オマロワ
Omarova, Anna 1052

オーマン
Aumann, Robert John 70
Oermann, Marilyn H. 1045
Oman, Jason 1052
Orman, Suze 1057

オマーン
Oman, Kathleen S. 1052

オマン
Osman, Monique 1060

オミシュル
Omischl, Steve 1053

オミディア
Omidyar, Pierre M. 1052

オミナミ
Ominami Pascual, Carlos Ⅲ 1052

オーミラー
Aumiller, Gary S. 70

オミラノフスカ
Omilanowska, Małgorzata 1052

オーム
Ohm, Jeanne 1046

オム
Om, Yun-chol 1052
Uhm, Tae-woong 1432

オムシュ
Omoush, Ibrahim 1053

オムシン
Ormsin, Chivapruck 1057

オームス
Ooms, Herman 1055

オムス
Homs, José 619

オームステッド
Olmstead, Marvin L. 1051

オムラリエフ
Omuraliyev, Taalaibek 1053
Omuraliyev, Tolobek 1053

オムラン
Omran, Adnan 1053
Omran, Al-Mabrouk Gharaira 1053

オームロッド
Ormerod, Paul 1057

オーメイメー
Omameh, Patrick 1052

オメーラ
O'Meara, Mark 1052

オメリャン
Omelyan, Volodymyr 1052

オメール
al-Omair, Ali Saleh 1052

オメル
Omer, Devorah 1052
Omer Cubukcu 1052

オメルチュク
Omelchuk, Oleh 1052

オーメロッド
Ormerod, Jan 1057

オメン

オ

オ

Ommen, Erik van 1053
Ommen, Sylvia Van 1053
オモイル
Omoile, Oni 1053
オーモット
Aamodt, Kjetil André 1
オモトバ
Omotoba, Babatunde 1053
オーモン
Aumont, Jean-Pierre 70
Haumont, Raphaël 582
オモンテ・ドゥランド
Omonte Durand, Carmen 1053
オーモンド
Ormond, Julia 1057
オヤ
Oja, Erkki 1047
オヤルサバル
Oyarzabal, Mikel 1066
オーヤング
O'Young, Bryan 1066
オユビ
Oyoubi, Luc 1066
オユランド
Ojuland, Kristiina 1047
オユンホロル
Oyunhorol, Dulamsurengiin 1066
オヨエブル
Oyoebule, Evangelina Filomena 1066
オヨエブレ
Oyo Ebule, Evangelina 1066
オヨノ
Oyono, Ferdinand Léopold 1066
オヨノニュトゥム
Oyono Nyutumu, Marcelino 1066
オヨーン
Oyun, Sanjaasuren 1066
オヨーンゲレル
Oyungerel, Tsedevdamba 1066
オヨーンバータル
Oyunbaatar, Tserendash 1066
オヨーンホロル
Oyunhorol, Dulamsurengiin 1066
オーラ
Ola, Michael 1048
オーラー
Ohler, Norbert 1046
オラ
Ola, Sis Ram 1048
Ora, Rita 1055
オラー
Olah, George Andrew 1048
Oller, Erika 1051
Oller, Olga Brody 1051
オライアン
Olayan, Lubna S. 1049
O'Ryan, Ellie 1059
オライソラ
Olaizola, José Luis 1048
オライノコフ
Oleinokov, Igor 1049
オライリー
O'Reilly, Barry 1056
O'Reilly, Bill 1056
O'Reilly, Charles A. 1056
O'Reilly, Dave 1056
O'Reilly, David 1056
O'Reilly, Emily 1056
O'Reilly, Evelyn M. 1056
O'Reilly, Kathleen 1056
O'Reilly, Michael 1056
O'Reilly, Tim 1056
オーライン
Oualline, Steve 1063
オラウエ
Olavae, Trevor 1048
オラウソン - セル
Olausson-Säll, Katarina 1048
オラサバル
Olazábal, José María 1049
オラズグルイエフ
Orazguliyev, Yarmuhammed 1056
オラズゲルディエフ
Orazgeldiev, Esenmyrat 1056
オラズバコフ
Orazbakov, Galym 1056
オラズムイラドフ
Orazmyradov, Dovran 1056
Orazmyradov, Saparmyrat 1056
オラスンカンミ
Olasunkanmi, Akinlabi 1048
オラゾフ
Orazov, Deryageldi 1056
オラタンジ
Olatunji, Bunmi O. 1048
オラディポ
Oladipo, Victor 1048
オラトイ
Olatoye, Deji 1048
オラトラ
Ortola, Adrian 1059
オラバエ
Olavae, Trevor 1048
オラハリー
Ó Raghallaigh, Colmán 1055
オラビデ
Olavide, Miguel 1048
オラフ・オラフソン
Olafsson, Olaf 1048
オラフスドッティル
Ólafsdóttir, Björt 1048
オラフセン
Olafsen, Helene 1048
オラフソン
Olafsson, Olaf 1048
オラフリン
O'Laughlin, Michael 1048
O'Loughlin, James 1051
オラベリアドロンソロ
Olaberria Dorronsoro, Leire 1048
オラマス
Oramas, Faustino 1055
オーラム
Oram, Gayle 1055
オラム
Oram, Andrew 1055
Oram, Christopher 1055
Oram, Hiawyn 1055
Oram, Jual 1055
オラムス
Orams, Mark 1056
オラモ
Oramo, Sakari 1056
オラヤグティエレス
Olaya Gutierrez, Andrea Carolina 1048
オラヤン
Olayan, Lubna 1049
Olayan, Lubna S. 1049
オラーリン
O'Laughlin, Michael 1048
オラル
Oral, Feridun 1055
Oral, Sumer 1055
Oral, Yilmaz 1055
オラワリー
Olawale, Jamize 1048
オラーン
Ulaan, Chultem 1432
オラン
Olin, Nelly 1049
オランゲナ・アウォノ
Olanguenaawono, Urbain 1048
オランゲナアウォノ
Olanguenaawono, Urbain 1048
オーランズ
Orlans, Michael 1057
オーランダー
Olander, Stefan 1048
オーランディ
Orlandi, Claudia Waller 1057
オランデール＝ラフォン
Hollander-Lafon, Magda 616
オーランド
Orland, Ted 1057
Orlando, Paulo 1057
オランド
Hollande, François 616
オリ
Oli, K.P. Sharma 1049
オリー
Olley, Greg 1051
オリアリー
O'leary, Nick 1049
O'Leary, Patrick 1049
オーリアン
Orlean, Susan 1057
オリアンズ
Orians, Gordon H. 1057
オリアンスキー
Oliansky, Joel 1049
オリーヴ
Olive, David I. 1050
オリウ
Oliu, Walter E. 1049
オリヴァー
Oliver, Clayton 1050
Oliver, Jamie 1050
Oliver, Lauren 1050
Oliver, Paul 1050
Oliver, Roland Anthony 1050
Oliver, Steve 1050
オリヴァー＝スミス
Oliver-Smith, Anthony 1050
オリヴァンヌ
Olivennes, Francois 1050
オリヴィエ
Olivier, Christiane 1050
Olivier, Suzannah 1050
Ollivier, Bernard 1051
Ollivier, Jean-Yves 1051
Ollivier, Jonathan 1051
オリヴィエリ
Olivieri, Aldo 1050
オリヴェイラ
Oliveira, Álamo 1050
Oliveira, Ana Rodrigues 1050
Oliveira, Bruno 1050
Oliveira, Carmen L. 1050
Oliveira, Manoel de 1050
Oliveira, Odecil Costa 1050
Oliveira, Oswaldo 1050
オリヴェイラ・イ・コスタ
Oliveira e Costa, João Paulo 1050
オリヴェイラ - ソーザ
Oliveira-Souza, Ricardo de 1050
オリウエラ
Orihuela, Nuris 1057
オリヴェリ
Oliveri, Fabio 1050
オリヴェリオ
Oliverio, Alberto 1050
オリヴェリオ・フェッラーリス
Oliverio Ferraris, Anna 1050
オリヴェーロ
Olivero, Magda 1050
オリヴェロス
Oliveros, Pauline 1050
オリヴェンシュタイン
Oliwenstein, Lori 1050
オーリエ
Aurier, Serge 70
オリエ
Hollier, Denis 617
オリエント
Orient, Jane M. 1057
オリオーダン
O'Riordan, Dolores 1057
O'Riordan, Kate 1057
オリオール・リエラ
Oriol Riera 1057
オリガ
Origa 1057
オリガス
Origas, Jean-Jacques 1057
オリーガン
O'Regan, Hannah 1056
オーリコフスキー
Orlikowski, Wanda J. 1057
オリジ
Origi, Divock 1057
オリシヴァング
Ol'shvang, V. 1051
オリシエ
Olicier, Pieriche 1049
オリツィオ
Orizio, Riccardo 1057
オーリック
Orlick, Sheila 1057
Orlick, Terry 1057
オーリッグ
Ohlig, Stefanie 1046
オリーニク

Oliinyk, Denys 1049
オリニク
Olijnik, Andrej 1049
Olynyk, Kelly 1052
オリバー
Olivar, Celia Bocobo 1049
Oliver, Anne 1050
Oliver, Branden 1050
Oliver, Cameron 1050
Oliver, Chad 1050
Oliver, Clare 1050
Oliver, David 1050
Oliver, Elizabeth Anne 1050
Oliver, Frank 1050
Oliver, Jamie 1050
Oliver, Joan Duncan 1050
Oliver, Joe 1050
Oliver, Lauren 1050
Oliver, Lloyd 1050
Oliver, Mark 1050
Oliver, Martin 1050
Oliver, Michael 1050
Oliver, Paul 1050
Oliver, Richard W. 1050
Oliver, Roland Anthony 1050
Oliver, Willard Varnell 1050
オリビエ
Olivé, Eva 1050
Olivier, Marc-Antoine 1050
Ollivier, Jean-Yves 1051
Ollivier, Jonathan 1051
オリビエリ
Olivieri, Aldo 1050
オリビエール
Olivierre, Nicole 1050
オリーブ
Olivé, Sylvie 1050
オリファント
Oliphant, Mildred 1049
オリフェ
Olliffe, Patrick 1051
オリベイラ
Oliveira, Anderson 1050
Oliveira, Dyogo 1050
Oliveira, Eunício 1050
Oliveira, Flavia 1050
Oliveira, Ingrid 1050
Oliveira, Lorrane 1050
Oliveira, Manoel de 1050
Oliveira, Oswaldo 1050
Oliveira, Pamella 1050
Santos Simoes Oliveira, Nelson Filipe 1240
オリベッティ
Olivetti, Ariel 1050
オリベーラ
Olivera, Maximiliano 1050
オリベラボロプ
Oliveraboropu, Antoino Pedro 1050
オリベル
Oliver, Torres 1050
オリベーロ
Olivero, Magda 1050
オリベロ
Olivero, Magda 1050
オリベロス
Oliveros, Pauline 1050
オリボ
Olivo, Karen 1050
オリポフ
Oripov, Abdulla 1057
オリモフ
Olimov, Karomatullo 1049
オリヤヘイル
Oryakhil, Nasreen 1059
オリヤルス
Olijars, Stanislavs 1049
オリューニン
Olyunin, Nikolay 1052
オリーリ
O'Leary, Charles J. 1049
オリーリー
O'Leary, John 1049
オーリン
Olin, Mary 1049
オリン
Olin, Chuck 1049
Oline, Lena 1049
オーリンジャー
Ollinger, Michael 1051
オリンジャー
Orringer, Julie 1058
オリンズ
Olins, Wally 1049
オリンバエフ
Orynbayev, Yerbol 1059
オリンピオ
Olympio, Harry Octavianus 1052
オリンピオ・ストック
Olimpio Stock, Carlos 1049
オリンピオストック
Olimpio Stock, Carlos 1049
オール
Orr, David 1058
Orr, Gordon 1058
Orr, Zelma 1058
Wall, Kurt 1471
オル
Orou, Sakinatou Abdou Alfa 1058
Orr, Alberta L. 1058
Orr, Richard 1058
Oru, Stephen Orise 1059
オルー
Orou, Jean Bio Tchabi 1058
Orr, Wendy 1058
オルインバエフ
Orynbayev, Yerbol 1059
オルヴ
Olve, Nils-Göran 1052
オルヴァー
Olver, Elizabeth 1052
オールウィン
Allwine, Wayne 35
オルヴェウス
Olweus, Dan 1052
オルヴォラ
Orvola, Mirja 1059
オルガッド
Orgad, Dorit 1057
オルギン・クエジャル
Holguín Cuéllar, María Ángela 616
オルギン・サルディ
Holguín Sardi, Carlos 616
オールグー
Ohuruogu, Christine 1047
オルーク
O'Rourke, Jim 1058
O'Rourke, Joseph 1058
O'rourke, Mary 1058
O'rourke, Ryan 1058
オルグネル
Olguner, Fahrettin 1049
オルケシ
Wuerkaixi 1529
オルコック
Alcock, John 27
Alcock, Lindsay 27
オルコット
Olcott, George 1049
オルコフスキ
Olkowski, Pawel 1051
オルサー
Ölçer, Ramazan 1049
オルサグ
Orsag, Jiri 1058
オールザック
Oorzhak, Lorisa 1055
オルサッグ
Orsag, Jiri 1058
オルジ
Orji, Keturah 1057
オルシェイ
Olshey, Neil 1051
オルシェイカー
Olshaker, Mark 1051
オルジャイ
Olcay, Sahan 1049
オルジャティ
Olgiati, Valerio 1049
オルシャンスキー
Olshansky, Stuart Jay 1051
オルジョイ
Orujov, Rustam 1059
オルジラ
Oljira, Beleynesh 1050
オルジンミ
Olujinmi, Akinlolu 1052
オールズ
Olds, Sharon 1049
Olds, Shelley 1049
オルスキー
Olski, Patrick 1051
オールストン
Allston, Aaron 35
オールズバーグ
Allsburg, Chris Van 35
オルスポー
Allspaw, John 35
オルスン
Olson, Neil 1051
オルゼック
Orzeck, Pam 1059
オルセナ
Orsenna, Erik 1058
オルセニウス
Olsenius, Richard 1051
オールセン
Ohlsen, Becky 1046
Olsen, Rolf Bang 1051
Olsen, Timothy 1051
オルセン
Olesen, Thorbjorn 1049
Olsen, Corey 1051
Olsen, David 1051
Olsen, Frances E. 1051
Olsen, Greg 1051
Olsen, Ib Spang 1051
Olsen, Joachim Broechner 1051
Olsen, Justin 1051
Olsen, Kenneth Harry 1051
Olsen, Larry Dean 1051
Olsen, Morten 1051
Olsen, Rikke 1051
Olsen, Russ 1051
Olsen, Scott Anthony 1051
Olsen, Shallon 1051
Olsen, Vivian Zarl 1051
Olsen, Winifred I. 1051
Olssen, Mark 1052
オールソップ
Allsop, Ryan 35
Allsopp, Nigel 35
Allsopp, Sophie 35
Alsop, Marin 36
オルソップ
Alsop, Marin 36
Alsop, Ronald 36
オルソラ
Olusola, Kevin 1052
オールソン
Ohlsson, Esbjørn 1046
Ohlsson, Garrick 1046
オルソン
Ohlsson, Birgitta 1046
Ohlsson, Kristina 1046
Olsen, Andy 1051
Olson, Barbara 1051
Olson, Carl 1051
Olson, Cheryl K. 1051
Olson, Danel 1051
Olson, Greg 1051
Olson, Jeff A. 1051
Olson, Matt 1051
Olson, Matthew S. 1051
Olson, Parmy 1051
Olson, Roberta K. 1051
Olson, Russell L. 1052
Olson, S. 1052
Olson, Shannon 1052
Olson, Steve 1052
Olson, Steven Douglas 1052
Olsson, Anna 1052
Olsson, Christian 1052
Olsson, Fredrik T. 1052
Olsson, Gunnar L. 1052
Olsson, Johan 1052
Olsson, Jonas 1052
Olsson, Josefin 1052
Olsson, Linda 1052
オルソン＝ホート
Olson-Hort, Sven E. 1052
オールター
Alter, Anna 37
オールダー
Alder, Ken 27
オルタ
Horta, Andre 624
オルター
Alter, Adam L. 37
Alter, Michael J. 37
オルタク
Ortag, Christian 1058
オルダージー
Aldersey, Olympia 27
オルダシ
Olldashi, Sokol 1051
オールダシー＝ウィリアムズ
Aldersey-Williams, Hugh 27
オールダーショー

オ

Oldershaw, Mark 1049
オールダス
Aldous, Joan M. 27
オルダースハウゼン
Oldershausen, Karin von 1049
オルダーソン
Alderson, Brian 27
Alderson, J.Charles 27
オール・ダーティー・バスタード
Ol'Dirty Bastard 1049
オルダートン
Alderton, David 27
オールダム
Oldham, Andrew Loog 1049
Oldham, John M. 1049
オルダム
Oldham, Keith B. 1049
オルタロ＝マーニェ
Ortalo-Magné, François 1058
オルテ
Ortet, Eva Verona Teixeira 1058
オルデー
Holder, David 615
オールディス
Aldiss, Brian Wilson 27
オルティーズ
Ortiz, Christina 1058
オルティス
Ortiz, Christina 1058
Ortiz, Cristóbal Francisco 1058
Ortiz, David 1058
Ortiz, Ernesto 1058
Ortiz, Idalys 1058
Ortiz, José 1058
Ortiz, Patricio 1059
Ortiz, Rosa María 1059
Ortiz, Tatiana 1059
オルティス・アセンシオ
Ortiz Ascencio, Óscar Samuel 1059
オルティス・ヌエボ
Ortiz Nuevo, José Luis 1059
オルティス・ペラエス
Oritiz Peláez, Luis Romero 1057
オルティス・ボッシュ
Ortiz Bosch, Milagros Maria 1059
オルディネ
Ordine, Nuccio 1056
オルテガ
Ortega, Amancio 1058
Ortega, Ariel 1058
Ortega, Daniel 1058
Ortega, Dionisio 1058
Ortega, Flora Pérez 1058
Ortega, Kenny 1058
Ortega, Orlando 1058
Ortega, Rafael 1058
Ortega, Victor 1058
Ortega, Yuvirí 1058
オルテガ・サアベドラ
Ortega Saavedra, José Daniel 1058
オルテガ・サーベドラ
Ortega, Daniel 1058
Ortega Saavedra, José Daniel 1058
オルテガ・ディアス
Ortega Díaz, Humberto 1058
オルテガ・デシオ
Ortega Desio, Javier 1058
オルテガ・ナバレテ
Ortega Navarete, Luis 1058
オルテガ・パチェコ
Ortega Pacheco, Daniel 1058
オルテガ・バレド
Ortega Barredo, Mary Blanca 1058
オルテス・アンドラデ
Ortez Andrade, Orestes Fredesman 1058
オルテン
Alten, Steve 36
オルデンバーグ
Oldenburg, Ray 1049
オルデンブルク
Oldenburg, Brandon 1049
オールト
Ault, Sandi 70
オールド
Auld, William 70
Old, Hughes Oliphant 1049
Old, Marnie 1049
オルト
Ault, Doug 70
オルドウェイ
Ordway, Jerry 1056
オールトカーム
Altkorn, Diane 37
オルドクロフト
Aldcroft, Derek Howard 27
オルドニェス
Ordóñez, Roberto 1056
Ordóñez, Sara 1056
オルトハイル
Ortheil, Hanns-Josef 1058
オルトフー
Hortefeux, Brice 624
オールドフィールド
Oldfield, Amelia 1049
Oldfield, Elizabeth 1049
Oldfield, Jenny 1049
オールトマン
Altman, John 37
オールドマン
Oldman, Gary 1049
Oldman, Mark 1049
オルトマン
Altman, Robert 37
Ortmann, Andreas 1059
オルトラーニ
Ortolani, Riz 1059
オルトラニ
Ortolani, Riz 1059
オールドランド
Oldland, Nicholas 1049
オルトリ
Ortoli, François-Xavier 1059
オールドリッジ
Aldridge, Robert 28
Aldridge, Susan 28
オルドリッジ
Aldridge, Blake 28
Aldridge, LaMarcus 28
Oldridge, Darren 1049
オールドリッチ
Aldredge, Theoni V. 27
Aldrich, Robert 28
オルドリッチ
Aldrich, Cole 27
Aldrich, Howard 27
Aldrich, Richard 28
Aldrich, Richard James 28
Aldrich, Sandra Picklesimer 28
オールドリン
Aldrin, Buzz 28
オルドリン
Aldrin, Buzz 28
オールトン
Oulton, Will 1064
オルナ
Orna, Elizabeth 1057
オルナギ
Ornaghi, Lorenzo 1057
オルニッツ
Ornitz, Edward M. 1057
オールネス
Allness, Deborah J. 35
オルネック
Olnek, Madeleine 1051
オルネラス
Ornellas, Waldeck 1057
オルバフ
Orbach, Uri 1056
オールバラ
Alborough, Jez 26
オルバリー
Albury, Charles 27
オルバーン
Orbán, Viktor 1056
オルバン
Orban, Leonard 1056
Orban, Lukas 1056
Orbán, Viktor 1056
Orban, Willi 1056
オールビー
Albee, Edward 25
オルピーニャス
Orpinas, Jean-Paul 1058
オルピン
Olpin, Michael 1051
オルファート
Olfert, Ernest D. 1049
オルブソラ
Olubusola, Omobola Johnson 1052
オルブライト
Albright, Kathie J. 27
Albright, Madeleine 27
オルブライトン
Albrighton, Marc 27
オルブリフスキ
Olbrychski, Daniel 1049
オルブロウ
Albrow, Martin 27
オールヘイム
Orheim, Karita Bekkemellem 1057
オルベベ
Orubebe, Peter Godsday 1059
オルベーンズ
Orbanes, Philip E. 1056
オルポ
Orpo, Petteri 1058
オルボラデ
Olubolade, Caleb 1052
オルホン・プレブドルジ
Orkhon Purevdorjiin 1057
オルマエチェア
Ormaechea, Agustin 1057
オールマン
Alleman, James H. 33
Allman, Eric 35
Allman, Gregg 35
Allman, Keith G. 35
Allman, Vandana 35
Alman, Carol 35
Oermann, Marilyn H. 1045
オルミ
Olmi, Ermanno 1051
オルミゴ
Hormigo, Ana 623
オルームーガピュッテン
Auroomooga Putten, Prithviraj 70
オルムス
Oremus, Stephen 1056
オルムステッド
Olmstead, Evan 1051
Olmsted, Frederick Law 1051
オルムベクゾダ
Orumbekzoda, Shamsiddin 1059
オルムリッド
Holmlid, Stefan 618
オルメルト
Olmert, Ehud 1051
オールライト
Allwright, Deborah 35
オルランド
Orlando, Andrea 1057
Orlando, Silvio 1057
オルリス
Olris, Vibeke 1051
オルリッチ
Olrich, Tomas Ingi 1051
オルリンスカ
Orlińska, Wanda 1057
オルリンスキ
Orliński, Bogusław 1057
オルレアン
Orléan, André 1057
オルレッド
Allred, Katherine 35
Allred, Keith G. 35
オルレブ
Orlev, Uri 1057
オルロフ
Orloff, Judith 1057
Orloff, Judith Handler 1057
Orlov, Dmitry 1057
オルロワ
Orlova, Anna 1057
Orlova, Maria 1057
オルワン
Alwang, Jeffrey R. 38
オルン
Orhun, Emre 1057
オルンシテイン
Ornstein, Leo 1057
オルンスタイン
Ornstein, Leo 1057
オルンステッド
Ornstedt, Louise 1057
オレ
Ore, Djimon 1056

オレアリ
O'Leary, Brian Francis 1049
オレアリー
O'Leary, Hal 1049
オレイ
Orey, Cal 1057
オレイジ
Oreiji, Rony 1056
オレイニク
Oleinic, Sergiu 1049
オレイニコフ
Oleynikov, Igor 1049
オレイニチャク
Olejniczak, Wojciech 1049
オレイビ
Oraybi, Muhammad 1056
オレイリー
O'Reilly, Arthur 1056
O'Reilly, Mark F. 1056
O'Reilly, Sonnie 1056
オレイン
Euren, Johan 411
オレエイリ
O'Reilly, John Boyle 1056
オレカス
Olekas, Juozas 1049
オレガリオ
Olegario, Rowena 1049
オレクシ
Oleksy, Józef 1049
オレクシアク
Oleksiak, Carol 1049
Oleksiak, Penny 1049
オレゴ
Orrego, Claudio 1058
オレシ
Oresi, Peter 1057
オレシキン
Oreshkin, Maksim S. 1057
オレジャーナ
Orellana, Fabian 1056
オレジャナ
Orellana, Gabriel 1056
Orellana, René Gonzalo 1056
オレジャナ・メルカド
Orellana Mercado, Ángel Edmundo 1056
オレシャルスキ
Oresharski, Plamen 1057
オレシュコビッチ
Orešković, Tihomir 1057
オレスケス
Oreskes, Naomi 1057
オレスケル
Olesker, Daniel 1049
オーレスン
Olesen, Peter 1049
オレッサバサン
Olezza Bazan, Facundo 1049
オーレッタ
Auletta, Ken 70
オーレット
Aulet, Bill 70
オレッリ
Orelli, Carlo 1056
オレピッチ
Orepić, Vlaho 1057
オレブ
Oreb, Tom 1056
オーレベーク
Oorebeek, André 1055
オレホワ
Orekhova, Natalia 1056
オレム
Orem, Dorothea Elizabeth 1056
オーレル
Aurelle 70
Orrell, Martin 1058
オレル
Orrell, David 1058
オーレン
Oren, Daniel 1056
Oren, Tim 1056
オレン
Oren, Daniel 1056
Oren, Eitan 1056
Oren, Ido 1056
Oren, Michael B. 1056
オレングハンコイ
Olenghankoy, Joseph 1049
オレンゴ
Orengo, James 1056
オレンジ
Orange, Jason 1056
オレンシュタイン
Orenstein, Arbie 1056
オレンスタイン
Orenstein, Julian 1057
Orenstein, Peggy 1057
オレンスティーン
Orenstein, Catherine 1057
オレンダー
Olender, Piotr 1049
オロズ
Orosz, Joel J. 1058
オロスコ
Orozco, Alejandra 1058
Orozco, Gabriel 1058
Orozco, John 1058
オーロット
Ohlott, Patricia J. 1046
オロパデ
Olopade, Dayo 1051
オーロフ
Orlov, Melissa 1057
オロフ
Orloff, Greg 1057
オーロフスキー
Orlovsky, Dan 1057
オロフソン
Olofsson, Anna carin 1051
Olofsson, Maud 1051
Olofsson-zidek, Anna Carin 1051
オロペサ
Oropeza, José 1058
オロペン
Olopeng, Thapelo 1051
オローリン
O'Loughlin, Gerald Stuart 1051
オワナ
Owona, Grégoire 1066
Owona, Joseph 1066
オン
Ong, Carah 1054
Ong, Jason C. 1054
Ong, Ka Chuan 1054
Ong, Ka Ting 1054
Ong, Keng-sen 1054
Ong, Keng-yong 1054
Ong, Tee Keat 1054
Ong, Teng-cheong 1054
オン・ウィン
Ohn Win 1047
オンエアマ
Onyeama, Geoffrey 1054
オンカリンクス
Onkelinx, Laurette 1054
オング
Ong, Aihwa 1054
Ong, Andrew Chester 1054
Ong, Wilson 1054
オンゲリ
Ongeri, Sam 1054
Ongeri, Samson 1054
オンケン
Oncken, William, Jr. 1053
オン・ケン・セン
Ong, Keng-sen 1054
オン・ケンセン
Ong, Keng-sen 1054
オンジェンダ
Ongenda, Hervin 1054
オンス
Hense, Nathalie 596
オーンスタイン
Ornstein, Leo 1057
Ornstein, Paul H. 1057
Ornstein, Robert Evan 1058
オンスワース
Ounsworth, Alec 1064
オンズンガ
Ondzounga, Ruffin Pacome 1053
オンソエソノ
Onso Esono, Anselmo 1054
オンダーチェ
Ondaatje, Michael 1053
オンチャン
Onechanh, Thammavong 1053
オンティベロス
Ontiveros, Javier 1054
オンデカネ
Ondekane, Jean-Pierre 1053
オン・テンチョン
Ong, Teng-cheong 1054
オンド
Ondo, Estelle 1053
オンドア
Ondoa, Christine 1053
オンドゥア
Ondoua, Pius 1053
Ondoua, Sylvestre Naah 1053
オンドオッサ
Ondo Ossa, Albert 1053
オンドサバル
Ondosabar, Carmen 1053
オンドジーチェク
Ondříček, Miroslav 1053
オンドヌクム
Ondo Nkumu, Salvador 1053
オンドヌゲマ
Ondo Nguema, Pedro 1053
オンドヌザン
Ondo Nzang, Consuelo 1053
オンドビレ
Ondo Bile, Pastor Micha 1053
オンドメトゴ
Ondo Methogo, Emmanuel 1053
オンドリチェク
Ondříček, Miroslav 1053
オンドルセック
Ondrusek, Logan 1053
オンドレイカ
Ondrejka, Cory 1053
オンドンゴ
Ondongo, Gilbert 1053
オンニス
Onnis, Maurizio 1054
オンバビオンゴロ
Omba Biongolo, Paul 1052
オンフレ
Onfray, Michel 1054
オンベル
Ombel, Constant 1052
オンポカ
Ompoka, Jean-Pierre Bokole 1053
オン・マウン
Ohn Maung 1046
オン・ミン
Ohn Myint 1046
オンヤンゴ
Onyango, Zeituni 1054

【カ】

カ
Ka, Djibo Leyti 693
Kâ, jibo Leïty 693
カー
Carr, Albert H. Zolatkoff 228
Carr, Alistair 228
Carr, Allen 228
Carr, Amanda 228
Carr, Bob 228
Carr, Brandon 228
Carr, Caleb 228
Carr, Caroline 228
Carr, Charmian 228
Carr, Derek 228
Carr, Deveron 228
Carr, G.Lloyd 228
Carr, Glyn 228
Carr, Gwendolyn C. 228
Carr, Henry 228
Carr, James 228
Carr, James E. 228
Carr, James Gordon 228
Carr, Johnnie 228
Carr, Kim 228
Carr, Kris 228
Carr, Lucien 228
Carr, Margaret 228
Carr, Nicholas G. 228
Carr, Norman 228
Carr, Paul 228
Carr, Robert K. 228
Carr, Sally 228
Carr, Sasha 229
Carr, Sean D. 229
Carr, Shelly Dickson 229
Carr, Susanna 229
Carr, Thomas K. 229
Carr, Tony 229
Carr, Viola 229

Ker, Ian Turnbull 721
Ker, Madeleine 721
Kerr, Alex 721
Kerr, Baine 721
Kerr, Cristie 721
Kerr, Deborah 721
Kerr, D.P. 721
Kerr, E.Bartlett 721
Kerr, Errol 721
Kerr, Fergus 722
Kerr, George 722
Kerr, John 722
Kerr, Judith 722
Kerr, Ken P. 722
Kerr, Michael E. 722
Kerr, Miranda 722
Kerr, Philip Ballantyne 722
Kerr, Steve 722
Kerr, Steven 722
Kerr, Zach 722
Kha, Yusupha 724
ガー
Gaa, James C. 469
カアビー
al-Ka'abi, Ali bin Abdullah 693
カアマーニョ・ドミンゲス
Caamaño Domínguez, Francisco 211
カイ
Cai, June 213
Cai, Yun 213
Chuth, Khay 263
Kay, Cristobal 711
Key, Paul 723
Khai, Nghiem Vu 724
Khai, Phan Van 724
ガイ
Gai, Mass Axi 471
Gai, Sofia 471
Guy, Billy 549
Guy, Bradley 549
Guy, Buddy 549
Guy, Geoffrey 549
Guy, James 549
Guy, John Alexander 549
Guy, Lawrence 549
Guy, Nathan 549
Guy, Richard K. 549
Guy, Robert Lincoln 549
Guy, Romain 549
Guy, Rosa Cuthbert 549
Guy, Winston 549
Gye, Mass Axi 550
ガイア
Gire, Ken 502
ガイアット
Guyatt, Nicholas 549
ガイイ
Gailly, Christian 471
Gailly, Pierre Antoine 471
カイウ
Qaiouh, Abdessamad 1142
カイヴォラ
Kaivola, Taina 696
カイウビー
Caiuby 214
カイエ
Caillé, Alain 214
カイエア
Kaiea, Manraoi 696
カイエターナ
Cayetana 238
カイエタノ・トエリダ
Cayetano Toherida, Ernesto Maria 238
ガイェック
Gajek, Bernhard 472
カイエド
Kayed, Mahmoud 712
カイエール
Cahierre, Armel 213
カイオ
Caio, Henrique 214
カイオ・ジュニオール
Caio Júnior 214
ガイオソ
Gayoso, Romulo Werran 485
カイオーリ
Caioli, Luca 214
ガイオン
Guion, Letroy 545
カイガー
Kyger, Joanne 778
ガイガー
Geiger, Arno 487
Geiger, Dennis 487
Geiger, John 487
Geiger, Reinold 487
カイカイ
Kaikai, Maya 696
Kaikai, Moijueh 696
Kaikai, Septimus 696
ガイギャクス
Gygax, Gary 550
カイケル
Keuchel, Dallas 723
ガイゲル
Geigel, Bob 487
カイコー
Kaige, Chen 696
カイザー
Kaiser, Dominik 696
Kaiser, George 696
Kaiser, Gert 696
Kaiser, Götz Peter 696
Kaiser, Joachim 696
Kayser, Benjamin 712
Kayser, Éric 712
Keiser, Paige 715
Keiser, Thomas C. 715
Keizer, Garret 715
Keizer, Joost M. 715
Kiser, Roger Dean 742
ガイサー
Gaisah, Ignisious 471
ガイサート
Geisert, Arthur 487
Geisert, Bonnie 487
カイサラ
Caicara, Junior 214
カイザーリンク
Keyserlingk, Linde von 724
カイシ
al-Qaissi, Daoud 1142
カイシー
Khaisri, Sri-aroon 724
カイシエポ
Kaisiepo, Manuel 696
ガイジュセク
Gajdusek, Daniel Carleton 471
ガイス
al-Gaith, Saif Khalfan 471
Geis, Georgia 487
Geis, Johannes 487
Geiss, Peter 487
Guice, Butch 544
ガイズ
Geis, Oliver 487
ガイスト
Geisst, Charles R. 487
Geist, Richard A. 487
ガイスバース
Gysbers, Norman C. 550
ガイスマン
Geissmann, Thomas 487
ガイスラー
Geisler, Bruce 487
Geisler, Dagmar 487
Geissler, Uwe 487
ガイスライター
Geisreiter, Moritz 487
ガイズワイト
Guisewite, Cathy 545
カイセド
Caicedo, Felipe 214
Caicedo Piedrahita, Andres Mauricio 214
カイゼール
Kaiser, Adeline 696
ガイゼルマン
Geiselman, R.Edward 487
ガイゼン
Geisen, Cynthia 487
ガイゼンベルガー
Geisenberger, Natalie 487
カイター
Keiter, Eric 715
ガイダ
Guida, Dean 544
カイタニ
Kaitani, Simione 696
ガイダール
Gaidar, Egor Timurovich 471
ガイダル
Gaidar, Egor Timurovich 471
ガイダルスキ
Gaydarski, Radoslav 485
ガイダルベコフ
Gaydarbekov, Gaydarbek 485
カイダロフ
Khaidarov, Timur 724
ガイダロフ
Gaidarov, Murad 471
ガイタン
Gaitan, Nicolas 471
ガイチュク
Gaiciuc, Victor 471
カイツ
Keitz, Christine 715
カイッコネン
Kaikkonen, Markku 696
ガイッチ
Gajic, Milan 472
カイテシ
Kayitesi, Odette 712
Kayitesi, Sylvie Zayinabu 712
カイテジ
Kayitesi, Annick 712
カイテル
Keitel, Harvey 715
カイト
Kite, Rebecca 742
Kuyt, Dirk 776
カイトゥウ
Kaitu'u, Tautai Agikimua 696
カイドエセブシ
Caid Essebsi, Béji 214
ガイドク
Haiduk, Vitaliy 555
ガイドシュ
Gajdoš, Peter 471
カイドセブシ
Caid Essebsi, Béji 214
ガイトナー
Geithner, Carole 487
Geithner, Timothy 487
カイトリー
Kightly, Michael 731
ガイトン
Guyton, Arthur C. 549
カイナー
Kiner, Ralph 737
ガイナ
Gaina, Tino 471
カイナク
Kaynak, Veysi 712
カイナード
Kynard, Erik 778
カイナル
Kaynar, Alican 712
ガイナン
Guinan, John 544
ガイネル
Gynell, Donna 550
カイネロ
Cainero, Chiara 214
カイノ
Kaino, Jerome 696
ガイバ
Gaiba, Francesca 471
カイパース
Kuipers, Alice 772
Kuipers, Elizabeth 772
カイバード
Kiberd, Declan 730
カイバール
Kibar, Osman 729
ガイブナザロフ
Gaibnazarov, Fazliddin 471
カイプル
Kiple, Kenneth F. 739
ガイフロー
Gayflor, Vada 485
カイペルス
Kuipers, Simon 772
カイポフ
Kaiypov, Marat 696
ガイポフ
Gaipov, Batyr 471
カイマー
Kaymer, Martin 712
カイミ
Caymmi, Dorival 238
ガイム
Geim, Andre 487
カイメニ
Kaimenyi, Jacob 696
ガイヤー
Guyer, Brandon 549
カイヤカ
Kaijaka, Diāna 696

ガイヤルデ
Gaillardet, Frédéric 471
ガイヤン
Gayan, Anil Kumarsingh 485
カイユ
Caillou, Pierre 214
ガイユマン
Gaillemin, Jean-Louis 471
カイユム
Khaiyum, Aiyza Sayed 724
ガイ・ヨア
Gai Yoah, John 471
カイラ
Kaila, Juha 696
Kaira, Qamar Zaman 696
カイラー
Cuyler, Margery 310
ガイラー
Gayler, Winnie 485
カイラット
Khairat, Ismail 724
カイリー
Khairy, Jamaluddin 724
カイル
Kile, Darryl 731
Kyle, Chris 778
Kyle, Christopher 778
Kyle, David 778
ガイル
Gahiru, Rose 471
Guile, David 544
Guile, Gill 544
カイルキ
Kairuki, Angela 696
ガイルズ
Giles, Howard 498
カイルベコワ
Kairbekova, Salidat 696
カイルリーナ
Hairullina, Roza 555
カイン
Kain, Z.N. 696
Khine, Myint Swe 728
Kyne, Dennis J. 778
Kyne, Peter B. 778
カイング
Kaingu, Michael 696
ガインコブ
Geingob, Hage 487
ガインゴブ
Geingob, Hage 487
カインジャ
Kainja, Kate 696
カインツ
Kainz, Florian 696
カインミ
Caimmi, Luca 214
ガーヴ
Garve, Andrew 482
ガウ
Gaou, Djimnaye 477
Gau, John 484
Gow, Ian 522
Gow, Melanie 522
Gow, Michael 522
カーヴァ
Kava, Alex 710
カーヴァー
Carver, Dante 232
Carver, Terrell 232
カウア
Kaua, Toswell 710
Khaoua, Tahar 726
ガウアー
Gower, Teri 522
カヴァコス
Kavakos, Leonidas 710
ガヴァシ
Gervasi, Sacha 492
ガウアーズ
Gowers, Timothy 522
カヴァッラーロ
Cavallaro, Brittany 238
カヴァナ
Cavanna, Francois 238
Kavanagh, Kathryn Hopkins 711
カヴァナッハ
Kavanagh, John J. 711
カヴァリ
Cavalli, Roberto 238
カヴァリア
Cavaglià, Gianfranco 238
カヴァリエ
Cavalier, Philippe 238
カヴァリエリ
Cavalieri, Paola 238
ガヴァリエリ
Cavalieri, Paola 238
カヴァルカンテ
Cavalcante, Wilson 238
ガヴァルダ
Gavalda, Anna 484
カヴァーロ・ヒーロス
Cavallo Jhlos, Maurizio 238
ガヴァンデル
Gavander, Kerstin 484
カウイー
Cowie, A.P. 297
カヴィエゼル
Caviezel, Giovanni 238
カヴィーゼル
Caviezel, Jim 238
カヴィッキャ
Cavicchia, Daniele 238
カヴィリカシヴィリ
Kvirikashvili, Merab 777
カーウィン
Karwin, Bill 706
Kerwin, Robert 722
ガーウィン
Garwin, Laura 482
ガヴィン
Gavin, Jamila 484
ガーヴェイ
Garvey, Amy 482
Garvey, James 482
ガーウェイン
Gawain, Shakti 485
カヴェーリウス
Cavelius, Alexandra 238
カヴェリン
Kavelin, John 711
カーヴェル
Carvel, Bertie 232
カウェル
Cowell, Simon 297
カヴェル
Cavell, Stanley 238
カヴェロ
Cavero, Arturo 238
カーウェン
Curwen, Bernie 309
カーヴェン
Kerven, Rosalind 722
カウエン
Cowen, Brian 297
カヴェンディッシュ
Cavendish, Mark 238
カヴォヴィット
Kavovit, Barbara 711
カーウォウスキー
Karwowski, Waldemar 706
ガウク
Gauck, Joachim 484
カウサー
Cowser, James 297
カウジェル
Kauzer, Peter 710
カウージャ
Kałuza, Roman 698
カウシャンスキー
Kaushansky, Kenneth 710
カウシル
Cowsill, Alan 297
ガウス
Gaus, Valerie L. 484
ガウスタッド
Gaustad, Edwin Scott 484
カウズマン
Kauzmann, Walter Joseph 710
カウゼル
Kauzer, Peter 710
カウソーン
Cawthorne, Nigel 238
カウダー
Kauder, Volker 710
ガウダー
Gauder, Áron 484
Gauder, Hartwig 484
カウチ
Couch, Dick 294
Couch, Greg 294
Couch, Tonia 294
ガウチ
Gautschi, Peter 484
ガウチャー
Goucher, Adam 521
カウチンスキ
Kauczinski, Markus 710
ガーウッド
Garwood, Dave 482
Garwood, Duncan 482
Garwood, Julie 482
カウット-コイブラ
Kautto-Koivula, Kaisa 710
ガウディ
Gowdy, Barbara 522
ガウディー
Gowdy, Barbara 522
ガウディアーノ
Gaudiano, Stefano 484
ガウディアノ
Gaudiano, Emanuele 484
ガウディオージ
Gaudiosi, Gaetano 484
ガウデシ
Gaudesi, Andrea Ricciardi di 484
カウデリー
Cowdery, William 297
カヴート
Cavuto, Neil 238
ガウード
Gaood, Abdul Majeed 477
カウナ
Cauna, Aleksandr 237
カウパース
Kuipers, Ben 772
カウピネン
Kauppinen, Liisa 710
カウフ
Knauf, Charles 747
Knauf, Daniel 747
カウファー
Kaufer, Katrin 710
Kaufer, Steve 710
カウフマン
Kauffman, Donna 710
Kauffman, Stuart A. 710
Kauffmann, Jean-Paul 710
Kaufman, Alan S. 710
Kaufman, Andrew 710
Kaufman, Bel 710
Kaufman, Ben 710
Kaufman, Charlie 710
Kaufman, Daniel 710
Kaufman, David A. 710
Kaufman, Ed 710
Kaufman, Edy 710
Kaufman, Francine Ratner 710
Kaufman, Gershen 710
Kaufman, Henry 710
Kaufman, Herbert 710
Kaufman, Josh 710
Kaufman, Kenneth 710
Kaufman, Lar 710
Kaufman, Marc 710
Kaufman, Michael T. 710
Kaufman, Nadeen L. 710
Kaufman, Philip 710
Kaufman, Richard 710
Kaufman, Stephen P. 710
Kaufmann, Angelika 710
Kaufmann, Arthur 710
Kaufmann, Carol 710
Kaufmann, Daniel 710
Kaufmann, Franz-Xaver 710
Kaufmann, H.W. 710
Kaufmann, J.E. 710
Kaufmann, Jonas 710
Kaufmann, Thomas 710
Kaufmann, Tohko 710
ガウラー
Gowler, David B. 522
カヴラク
Kavlak, Veli 711
ガヴラス
Gavras, Romain 484
カウリー
Cowley, Joy 297
ガウリ
Ghauri, Babar Khan 493
ガウリスー
Gowreesoo, Mahendra 522
カウリスマキ
Kaurismäki, Aki 710
Kaurismäki, Mika 710
ガヴリリュク
Gavrylyuk, Alexander 485
カウル
Kaul, Inge 710
ガウル

カ

Gaul, Hans Friedhelm 484
ガウルド
Gould, Georgia 521
カウン
Cowne, Elizabeth A. 297
Kahoun, Joseph 696
ガウン
Gaun, Albert 484
カウンスル
Counsel, June 295
カウンセル
Counsell, Craig 295
カウンター
Counter, Ben 295
カウンダ
Kaunda, Vuwa 710
カウンテス
Countess, Blake 295
カウント
Caunt, John 237
カエ
Kahe, Eric 695
カエウ・プットリャスメイ
Keo Puthreasmey 720
カエタノ
Caetano, Pedrito 213
Caetano, Trisha 213
カエナ
Kayena, Laure-Marie Kawanda 712
カエール
Caer, Jean-Claude 213
カエン
Cahen, Corinne 213
カーオ
Kragh, Helge 763
カオ
Cao, Lan 222
Kao, Charles Kuen 702
ガオ
Gao, Isabelle 477
Gao, Ning 477
Gao, Sabiou Dadi 477
Gao, Xing-jian 477
ガオジア
Gaojia, Stephen 477
カオジェ
Kaoje, Bala 702
カオ・ダイ・レ
Cao Dai Le 222
ガオムバレ
Gaombalet, Célestin 477
カカ
Kaká 696
Kaka, N'gade Nana Hadiza Noma 696
カカー
Kaká 696
カーカーヴァンド
Kakavand, Kambiz 696
ガガウゾフ
Gagauzov, Assen 471
カカエフ
Kakayev, Yagshygeldy 696
カガシェキ
Kagasheki, Khamis Sued 695
カーカップ
Kirkup, James 741
ガガニャン
Geghamyan, Levon 486
カカバエフ
Kakabayev, Annaberdy 696
カカバゼ
Kakabadze, Malkhaz 696
カガメ
Kagame, Paul 695
カガヨ
Kagayo, Jeanne d'Arc 695
カカリエフ
Kakalyev, Yazguly 696
ガガリマブ
Gagarimabu, Gabia 471
カカル
Kakar, Rehmatullah 696
カガワ
Kagawa, Julie 695
カガン
Kagan, Henri B. 695
カキ
Kaki, Abubaker 696
カギアリス
Kagialis, Pavlos 695
カキムジャノフ
Kakimzhanov, Zeinulla 696
カーギル
Cargill, Peter 225
Cargill, Thomas F. 225
ガーキン
Gerkin, Charles V. 490
カギンビ
Kagimbi, Dieudonné Upira Sunguma 695
カーク
Kirk, Beverly 740
Kirk, Bradford C. 740
Kirk, Connie Ann 740
Kirk, Daniel 740
Kirk, David 740
Kirk, Douglas 740
Kirk, E.J. 741
Kirk, Frank 741
Kirk, Geoffrey Stephen 741
Kirk, Jacqueline 741
Kirk, Joan 741
Kirk, John Thomas Osmond 741
Kirk, Raymond Maurice 741
Kirk, Shannon 741
Kirk, Steve 741
Kirk, Stuart A. 741
Kirk, Tara 741
Kirke, Simon 741
Kuć, Rafal 770
Kurke, Lance B. 774
カク
Kakou, Roger 696
Kaku, Michio 696
Kwak, Jae-young 777
Kwak, Ji-gyoon 777
Kwak, Tae-hwi 777
ガーク
Girke, Nikola 502
Guhrke, Laura Lee 544
ガーグ
Gaag, Nikki van der 469
Garg, Gaurav 480
ガク
Gakou, El Hadji Malick 472
Gakou, Salimata Fofana 472
カグイオア
Caguioa, Alfredo 213
カグウェ
Kagwe, Mutahi 695
カークウッド
Kirkwood, T.B.L. 741
カクオル
Kacuol, Moses Macal 694
カクジ
Kakudji, Gaetan 696
カクシュカ
Kakuska, Thomas 696
カークセイ
Kirksey, Chris 741
カクタ
Kakuta, Gaël 696
カクチ
Kakuchi, Suvendrini 696
カークパトリック
Kirkpatrick, Betty 741
Kirkpatrick, David 741
Kirkpatrick, Dre 741
Kirkpatrick, Jeane Duane Jordan 741
Kirkpatrick, Rob 741
Kirkpatrick, Sidney 741
カークハム
Kirkham, Tyler 741
カークビー
Kirkby, Emma 741
カーク=プリンツ
Kirch-Prinz, Ulla 740
ガクペ
Gakpe, Serge 472
カーグボ
Kargbo, Alex 705
カグボ
Kargbo, Momodu 705
カークホフス
Kerkhofs, Jan 721
カクマレック
Kacmarek, Robert M. 694
カークマン
Kirkman, Alfred John 741
Kirkman, Robert 741
カーグマン
Kargman, Jill 705
カクラマナキス
Kaklamanakis, Nikolaos 696
カクラマニス
Kaklamanis, Nikitas 696
カグラム
Khagram, Sanjeev 724
カクラン
Coughlan, Mary 295
カークランド
Kirkland, Anna Rutherford 741
Kirkland, Denver 741
Kirkland, Douglas 741
Kirkland, Hal 741
Kirkland, Jane 741
カグリアータ
Quagliata, Emanuela 1143
ガグリアーノ
Gagliano, Alfonso 471
カー=グレッグ
Carr-Gregg, Michel 229
ガクワヤ
Gakwaya, Theobold Lwaka 472
カケトラ
Khaketla, Mamphono 724
カーケリング
Kerkeling, Hape 721
カーゲル
Kágel, Mauricio Raúl 695
ガーケン
Gerken, Till 490
ガーゲン
Gergen, David 490
Gergen, Kenneth J. 490
カーケンダル
Kirkendall, Donald T. 741
カーケンドール
Kirkendall, Donald T. 741
ガゴ
Gago, José Mariano 471
Gago, Mariano 471
ガーコウ
Ngakoue, Yannick 1019
ガゴシゼ
Gagoshidze, Iulon 471
ガコソ
Gakosso, Jean-Claude 472
カゴネラ
Kagonyera, Mondo 695
カー=ゴム
Carr-Gomm, Philip 229
Carr-Gomm, Sarah 229
カコヤニス
Cacoyannis, Michael 212
カーコリアン
Kerkorian, Kirk 721
カコリアン
Kerkorian, Kirk 721
カゴール
Cagol, Andrea 213
カコロア
Kakoroa, Moteti 696
ガーコン
Garcon, Pierre 479
カーサ
Kassa, Tekeleberhan 707
Katia, Pinto 708
カーザー
Kaser, Karl 707
カサ
Kasa, Jožef 707
Kassa, Barthélémy 707
カサー
Cassar, Jon 234
カザ
Kasza, Gregory J. 708
Kasza, Keiko 708
Kaza, Abdou 712
ガーザ
Garza, David Lee 482
Garza, Matt 482
カサイ
Kassaï, Moussa Saïbou 707
カサイジャ
Kasaijia, Matia 707
カサイラ
Kasaila, Francis Lazalo 707
ガザウィ
Ghezawi, Ali 493
カサウス
Casaus, Victor 233
カザウレ
Kazaure, A. 712
カサエワ
Kasaeva, Zarema 707
カサキナ
Kasatkina, Daria 707

カザク
Kazak, Mikalai 712
カザクバエフ
Kazakbayev, Ruslan 712
カザケーヴィチ
Kazakevich, Vecheslav 712
カザケビッツ
Kazakevic, Aleksandr 712
カザコフ
Kazakov, Sergey 712
Kazakov, Tugelbay 712
カザーコワ
Kazakova, Vesela 712
カザジャン
Kazazyan, Haik 712
カサス
Casas, Julio 233
Casas, Kevin 233
Casas, Lola 233
カサスベ
Kasasbeh, Hamad 707
カサス・レゲイロ
Casas Regueiro, Julio 233
カザーダ
Quesada, Joe 1144
カサディ
Cassaday, John 234
カザーティ
Casati, Giulio 233
カサーディオ
Casadio, Mariuccia 233
カサード・カニェーケ
Casado Cañeque, Fernando 233
カサナス
Casanas, Frank 233
ガザニガ
Gazzaniga, Michael S. 485
カサニャス
Casanas, Frank 233
カザノヴァ
Casanova, Pascale 233
カザノウスキー
Kazanowski, Mary K. 712
カサノバ
Casanova, Sarah 233
カサビ
Kasabi, Yahia 707
al-Qasaibi, Majid bin Abdullah 1142
カサピ
Kasapi, Vasiliki 707
カサビエフ
Kasabiev, Arsen 707
カサブ
Kassab, Gilberto 707
カサフン
Kasahun, Ayele 707
カサマ
Cassama, Cipriano 234
ガサマ
Gassama, Alhaji Yankuba 482
Gassama, Sadio 482
ガサマディア
Gassama Dia, Yaye Kene 483
カサマユウ
Casamayou, Maureen Hogan 233
カサマヨル
Casamayor, Joel 233
カザマヨール
Casamayor, Pierre 233
カザミアス
Kazamias, Kyriakos 712
カサミケラ
Casamiquela, Carlos 233
ガザーラ
Gazzara, Ben 485
カサリ
Casali, Curt 233
ガザリャン
Ghazaryan, Armen 493
Ghazaryan, Gabriel 493
ガザル
Gazard, Akoko Kinde 485
Ghazal, Muhammad Walid 493
カザルス
Cazals, Jean 239
カサーレ
Casale, Giovanni Nicola 233
ガザーレ
Gazale, Alberto 485
ガザレ
Gazalé, Midhat J. 485
ガザレク
Gazarek, Sara 485
カサレッジョ
Casaleggio, Gianroberto 233
カザレッジョ
Casaleggio, Gianroberto 233
カサレット
Casarett, David J. 233
カサローヴァ
Kasarova, Vesselina 707
カサロヴァ
Kasarova, Vesselina 707
カサローザ
Casarosa, Enrico 233
カサローバ
Kasarova, Vesselina 707
カサロバ
Kasarova, Vesselina 707
カザン
Cazan, Gheorghe Romeo Leonard 239
Kazan, Elia 712
カザンアレン
Kazan-Allen, Laurie 712
カサンガ
Kasanga, Kasim 707
カザンチウク
Cazanciuc, Robert 239
カザンツィス
Kazantzis, Nikolaos 712
カサンドラ
Casandra, Cristina 233
カサンバラ
Kasambara, Ralph 707
ガザンファリ
Ghazanfari, Mehdi 493
ガザンファル
Ghazanfar, Husn Banu 493
カーシー
Keirsey, David 715
Kersey, Cynthia 722
カシ
Kasi, Abdul Malik 707
カジ
Qazzi, Sejaan 1142
カジー
Kazee, Steve 712
ガーシ
Gashi, Alush 482
ガシ
Gashi, Dardan 482
ガジ
Ghazi, Mahmood Ahmad 493
Ghazi, Mohamed el 493
Ghazi, Polly 493
ガジー
Guzy, Carol 550
カジェ
Cagé, Julia 213
Calle, Maria Luisa 216
ガシェ
Gachet, Sophie 470
Gasché, Rodolphe 482
ガジェゴ・エナオ
Gallego Henao, Andrés Uriel 473
ガジェゴ・ガルシア
Gallego García, Laura 473
カージェス
Kersjes, Michael E. 722
ガジエフ
Gadzhiev, Rizvan 470
Gajiyev, Danyal 472
カジェホン
Callejon, Jose 216
カシエラ
Cassierra, Mateo 234
カージェール
Kargere, Audrey 705
カー＝シェルマン
Carr-Chellman, Alison A. 229
ガーシェンソン
Gershenson, David Marc 491
カーシェンバウム
Kirschenbaum, Howard 741
Kirshenbaum, Richard 741
Kirshenbaum, Sheril 741
ガーシェンフェルド
Gershenfeld, Neil A. 491
カーシェンマン
Kirschenmann, Fred 741
カシオ
Cascio, Frank 233
カシオポ
Cacioppo, John T. 212
カシオーリ
Cascioli, Gianluca 233
ガシオロウィッツ
Gasiorowicz, Stephen 482
カシージャス
Casillas, Iker 234
カシジャス
Casillas, Iker 234
カジシュキー
Kasischke, Laura 707
カシシュケ
Kasischke, Laura 707
カシス
Qassis, Nabil 1142
ガジズリン
Gazizullin, Farit R. 485
カシタ
Kasitah, Gaddam 707
カシタティ
Kasitati, Nila 707
カシツキー
Kašick'y, František 707
ガジック
Gadzik, Jonathan P. 470
ガシッチ
Gašić, Bratislav 482
ガジッチ
Gadzić, Mila 470
ガシット
Kasit, Piromya 707
カシディー
Cassidy, John 234
カシーニ
Casini, Barbara Palmer 234
カシネッリ
Cassinelli, Juan Carlos 234
カジブウェ
Kazibwe, Speciosa Wandira 712
ガジマ
Gwajima, Josephat 550
カシミ
al-Qasimi, Fahim bin Sultan 1142
Qasimi, Sheikha Lubna bint Khalid Al 1142
カジミール
Casimir, Richard 234
Kažimír, Peter 712
カーシム
Qāsim, Na'im 1142
カシーム
Kassim, Siti 708
カシム
Kacem, Rafik Belhaj 694
Kassim, Siti 708
Khassimou, Oumar 727
Qasim, Guled Hussein 1142
Qasim, Maryan 1142
カシモフ
Kasimov, Gurban 707
Kasymov, Rustam 708
ガシモフ
Gasimov, Elmar 482
カシーヤ
Casilla, Santiago 234
カシャ
Kasha, Abdel-Hamid Musa 707
カジャ
Calla, Ricardo 216
ガジャ
Gajda, Wlodzimierz 471
カジャイア
Kajaia, Iakob 696
ガシャイナ
Gashyna, Kevin 482
カシヤス
Casillas, Jonathan 234
カシャップ
Kashyap, Anil K. 707
ガジャディーラ
Gajadeera, Chandrasiri 471
ガーシャニー
Gershuny, Grace 491
カシャノフ
Kasyanov, Oleksiy 708
カシヤーノフ

Kasyanov, Mikhail Mikhailovich 708
カシヤノフ
Kasyanov, Mikhail M. 708
Kasyanov, Mikhail Mikhailovich 708
カシャミラ
Kachamila, John 694
カジャラミ
Kadjallami, Oumar Boukar 694
ガジャルド
Gallardo, Jorge 473
Gallardo, Juan Ignacio 473
Gallardo, Leonor 473
Gallardo, Roberto Javier 473
ガジャルド・ク
Gallardo Ku, José 473
ガジャルド・クー
Gallardo Ku, José 473
カジャルド・ヌニェス
Gallardo Núñez, Roberto 473
カシャワバキンジ
Kashawa Bakinzi, Benjamin 707
カシャン
Cachin, Françoise 212
Kasyan, Anna 708
ガジャン
Gajan, Olivier 471
カジャンダー
Kajander, Rebecca 696
カーシュ
Karsh, Yousuf 706
Kirsch, Irving 741
Kirsch, Jonathan 741
ガーシュ
Gershe, Leonard 491
ガーシュウィン
Gershwin, M.Eric 491
カーシュヴィンク
Kirschvink, Joseph L. 741
カシュカシーアン
Kashkashian, Kim 707
カシュカシャン
Kashkashian, Kim 707
カシュダン
Kashdan, Todd B. 707
カーシュナー
Kershner, Irvin 722
Kirchner, Zane 740
Kirschner, Marc 741
Kirschner, Rick 741
Kirschner, Robert H. 741
Kirshner, Robert P. 741
カシュナー
Kushner, Ellen 776
ガシュパル
Gaspar, Acsinte 482
ガシュパロヴィッチ
Gašparovič, Ivan 482
ガシュパロビッチ
Gašparovič, Ivan 482
ガシユブウェンゲ
Gaciyubwenge, Pontien 470
ガシュペルシッチ
Gašperšič, Peter 482
カシュモア
Cashmore, Ellis 234
ガジュモフ
Gazyumov, Khetag 485
カジュラ
Kajura, Henry 696
Kajura, Muganwa 696
カシュラル
Caslaru, Beatrice 234
ガジュレル
Gajurel, Haribol Prasad 472
ガシュンバ
Gashumba, Diane 482
カーショー
Kershaw, Clayton 722
Kershaw, Devon 722
Kershaw, Ian 722
カショア
Cashore, Kristin 234
カーショウ
Kershaw, Alex 722
Kershaw, Clayton 722
カショヌグウェ
Kashongwe, Zacharie 707
カショーリ
Cascioli, Riccardo 233
ガーション
Gershon, David 491
Gershon, Freddie 491
カシラー
Kassirer, Jerome P. 708
カシラギ
Casiraghi, Andrea 234
Casiraghi, Tatiana 234
ガジラジ
Gajraj, Ronald 472
カシリエ
Kasirye, Ruth 707
カシリナ
Kashirina, Tatiana 707
カシリャス
Casillas, Iker 234
カーシル
Kerschl, Karl 722
カシール
Kassir, Samir 708
カシレクマコエ
Kassirecoumakoye, Nouradine Delwa 708
カシワギ
Kashiwagi, Hiroshi 707
カシーン
Karsin, Asa 706
カシン
Cassin, Riccardo 234
ガシンジグワ
Gasinzigwa, Oda 482
カシンジャ
Kassindja, Fauziya 708
カジンスキー
Kazinski, A.J. 712
カース
Kearse, Frank 713
Kearse, Jayron 713
Kearse, Jermaine 713
カス
Kas, Christopher 706
Kass, Danny 707
Kass, Leon 707
Kassu, Ilala 708
カズ
Cases, Zoé de Las 233
ガース
Gerth, Hans Heinrich 491
Gerth, Jeff 491
Gerth, Melanie 491
カズアザマ
Kaz'azama, Khakez Ekir 712
カスイマリエフ
Kasymaliev, Adylbek 708
カスイムベク
Kassymbek, Zhenis 708
カスイモフ
Kassymov, Kalmukhanbet 708
Kasymov, Bakhadyr 708
Kasymov, Kalmukhanbet 708
Kasymov, Rustam 708
カーズィン
Kerzin, Barry 722
カスウェシ
Kasweshi, Fridolin 708
カスウェシ・ムソカ
Kasweshi Musoka, Fridolin 708
カズウェル
Caswell, Julie A. 237
カスウェル - チェン
Caswell-Chen, Edward P. 237
カスカート
Cathcart, Thomas 237
カスキー
Caskie, Kathryn 234
カスキン
Kuskin, Karla 776
ガスキン
Gaskin, Dominic 482
Gaskin, Ina May 482
ガスキンズ
Gaskins, Kendall 482
ガースク
Garske, John P. 481
カスクウェレ
Kasukuwere, Sevior 708
ガスケ
Gasquet, Bernadette de 482
Gasquet, Richard 482
カスケイ
Caskey, John 234
カスケイド
Kaskade 707
カスケード
Kaskade 707
ガスコイン
Gascoigne, Marc 482
Gascoigne, Paul 482
カズシオナク
Kazusenok, Andrei 712
カースター
Koster, Amy Sky 759
カスター
Kastor, Deena 708
ガスター
Gaster, Moses 483
カスタイニョス
Castaignos, Luc 235
ガスタヴァス・ジョーンズ
Gustavus Jones, Sarah 548
ガースタッド
Gerstad, Harry W., II 491
カスタートン
Casterton, Peter 235
カスタニェーダ
Castaneda, Jorge 235
カスタニェダ
Castañeda, Jorge 235
カスタニェット
Castagnetto, Jesus M. 235
カスタニディス
Kastanidis, Haris 708
カスターニャ
Castagna, Vanessa J. 235
ガスタニャガ
Gaztanaga, Jon 485
カスタニョ
Castaño, Crescencio Tamarite 235
カスターノ
Castano, Rose-Marie 235
ガスタフェロー
Guastaferro, John 541
ガスタフソン
Gustafson, Christine 548
Gustafson, David L. 548
カスターマン
Casterman, Geneviève 235
ガスタルディ
Gastaldi, Silvia 483
ガスタルデッロ
Gastaldello, Daniele 483
カスタルド
Castaldo, Meg 235
カスタ＝ローザ
Casta-Rosaz, Fabienne 235
カスダン
Kasdan, Lawrence 707
カスチーロ
Castillo, Valdemar 236
ガステ
Gasté, Éric 483
カスティ
Casty, Gian 237
ガスディア
Gasdia, Cecilia 482
カスティオーニ
Castioni, Nicole 236
カスティグリオニ
Castiglioni, Luis 235
カスティジャ・ルビオ
Castilla Rubio, Luis Miguel 235
カスティージョ
Castillo, Carolina 235
Castillo Huerta, Yahel 236
Renteria Castillo, Jackeline 1172
カスティジョ
Castillo, Arnaldo 235
Castillo, Carmen 235
Castillo, Eduardo 235
Castillo, Gonzalo 235
Castillo, José Enrique 235
Castillo, Pelegrín 236
カスティジョ・クエスタ
Castillo Cuesta, Barbara 236
カスティジョ・クルス
Castillo Cruz, Bosco Martín 236
カスティジョ・ルアノ
Castillo Ruano, Guillermo 236
カースティッチ
Krstić, Ivan 768
カスティーヤ
Castilla, Emilio J. 235

カスティーヨ
Castillo, Lauren 235
Castillo, Luis 235
Castillo, Michel del 236
Castillo, Rusney 236
Castillo, Welington 236
カスティヨン
Castillon, Claire 236
カスティーラ
Castilla, Denise de 235
カスティリオーニ
Castiglioni, Achille 235
Castiglioni, Consuelo 235
カスティリオニ
Castiglioni, Arianna 235
カスティーリョ
Castillo, Yahel 236
Castillo, Yalennis 236
Castillo Huerta, Yahel 236
カスティリョーニ
Castiglioni, Achille 235
カスティリョ・ベラ
Castillo Vera, Pilar del 236
ガスティル
Gastil, John 483
カスティーロ
Castillo, Linda 235
カスティロ
Castillo, David Diaz 235
Castillo, Linda 235
Castillo, Randy 236
Castillo, Santiago 236
Castillo, Valdemar 236
ガースティン
Gerstein, David 491
Gerstein, Mordicai 491
カステジャノス
Castellanos, Edwin J. 235
Castellanos, María 235
Castellanos, Plutarco 235
カステジャーノス・モヤ
Castellanos Moya, Horacio 235
カステヤノス
Castellanos, Nick 235
カステラ
Castella, Pierre 235
カステラ＝イ＝プジョルス
Castellà i Pujols, Maria Betlem 235
カステラーニ
Castellani, Enrico 235
カステラーノ
Castellano, Philippe 235
カステリ
Castelli, Roberto 235
カステリーニ
Castellini, Jean 235
Castellini, Robert H. 235
カステリャノス
Castellanos, Rosario 235
カステル
Castel, Alexianne 235
Castel, Anissa 235
Castel, Robert 235
Castell, Dianne 235
Castells, Manuel 235
ガステル
Gastel, Barbara 483
カステールス
Casteels, Koen 235
カステルーチ
Castellucci, Cecil 235
カステルッチ
Castellucci, Cecil 235
カステルバジャック
Castelbajac, Jean-Charles de 235
カステレン
Castelen, Guno Henry George 235
カステロ・コルテス
Castello-Cortes, Ian 235
カステロ・ダビッド
Castelo David, Adelino 235
カステロダビッド
Castelo David, Adelino 235
カステロン
Castellon, Fernando 235
ガーステン
Gersten, Bernard 491
カーステンス
Carstens, E. 231
カステンス
Kastēns, Oskars 708
カステンズ
Kastēns, Oskars 708
カステンバウム
Kastenbaum, Robert 708
カースト
Karst, M. 706
Kast, Verena 708
カスト
Kast, Felipe 708
ガスト
Gast, Matthew 483
Gastaut, Charlotte 483
カスト・ツァーン
Kast-Zahn, Annette 708
カストナー
Kastner, Jeffrey 708
カストリニャーノ
Castrignano, Daniela 236
カストリン
Castlin, Kristi 236
ガーストル
Gerstle, C.Andrew 491
Gerstle, Gary 491
カストロ
Castro, Adam-Troy 236
Castro, Angela 236
Castro, B.Rey De 236
Castro, Carlos 236
Castro, Cesar 236
Castro, Dana 236
Castro, Edmond 236
Castro, Eduardo Batalha Viveiros de 236
Castro, Elizabeth 236
Castro, Elliot 236
Castro, Eve de 236
Castro, Fidel 236
Castro, Gonzalo 236
Castro, Jason 236
Castro, Jose 236
Castro, Julián 236
Castro, Lucas 236
Castro, Luis Joel 236
Castro, Marcelo 236
Castro, Mariela 236
Castro, Miguel 236
Castro, Miranda 236
Castro, Ramón 236
Castro, Raúl 236
Castro, René 236
Castro, Ruy 236
Castro, Starlin 236
Castro, Wilmar 236
Castro Ruz, Juanita 236
カストロ・ゴンサレス
Castro González, Sonia 236
カストロジョヴァンニ
Castrogiovanni, Martin 236
カストロ・ソテルド
Castro Soteldo, Willmar 236
カストロネヴェス
Castro-Neves, Helio 236
カストロ・ネベス
Castro-Neves, Helio 236
カストロネベス
Castro-Neves, Helio 236
カストロノヴァ
Castronova, Edward 236
Castronovo, Deen 236
カストロノバ
Castronovo, Deen 236
カストロビエホ
Castroviejo Nicolas, Jonathan 236
カストロ・フェルナンデス
Castro Fernández, Pedro 236
カストロ・フォンセカ
Castro Fonseca, Rodrigo 236
カストロメンデス
Castro Mendes, Luís 236
カストロ・ロチャ
Castro Rocha, Joao Cezar de 236
カーストン
Carston, Robyn 231
ガストン
Gasston, Peter 483
Gaston, Bruce 483
Gaston, Diane 483
ガストン・シルバ
Gaston Silva 483
カーズナー
Kerzner, Harold 722
Kirzner, Israel M. 741
ガースナー
Gerstner, Louis, Jr. 491
カズナザニ
al-Kasnazani, Milas 707
カズニック
Kuznick, Peter J. 777
カズヌーヴ
Cazeneuve, Jean 239
カズヌーブ
Cazeneuve, Bernard 239
カズネスキ
Kuzneski, Chris 776
カスノーカ
Casnocha, Ben 234
カスパー
Kasper (Agent) 707
Kasper, Dennis L. 707
Kasper, Klaus Peter 707
Kasper, Siegfried 707
カスパー捜査官
Kasper (Agent) 707
カスパーソン
Kasperson, James 707
カスバート
Cuthbert, Cheslor 310
ガスパード
Gaspard, John 482
カスパーリ
Caspari, John A. 234
Caspari, Pamela 234
ガスパリ
Gaspari, Antonio 482
Gaspari, Mitja 482
Gasparri, Maurizio 482
ガスパリーノ
Gasparino, Charles 482
ガスパリン
Gasparin, Elisa 482
Gasparin, Selina 482
カスパル
Kaspar, Jonas 707
ガスパール
Gaspar, Vítor 482
ガスパル
Gaspar, Acsinte 482
ガスパレット
Gasparetto, Zibia 482
ガスパロヴィッチ
Gašparovič, Ivan 482
カスパロビッチ
Kaspiarovich, Dzmitry 707
ガスパロビッチ
Gašparovič, Ivan 482
カスパーロフ
Kasparov, Garri Kimovich 707
カスパロフ
Kasparov, Garri Kimovich 707
カスピ
Casspi, Omri 235
カスプリスキ
Kaspriske, Ron 707
カスペ
Caspe, David 234
ガスペリーニ
Gasperini, Gian Piero 482
カスペルスキー
Kaspersky, Yevgeny 707
ガーズマ
Gerzema, John 492
カズマレック
Ksczmarek, Tom 770
ガスマン
Gassmann, Oliver 483
ガズマン
Guzman, Joel 549
カズミ
Kazmi, Syed Hamid Saeed 712
カズミアー
Kazmir, Scott 712
ガズミン
Gazmin, Voltaire 485
カスム
Kassoum, Moctar 708
カズラウスカス
Kazlauskas, Gediminas 712
カースリー
Kearsley, Greg 713
カスリ
Kasuri, Khursheed Mehmood 708
カズリ
Khazri, Wahbi 727

ガスリ
Guthrie, Donald 548
ガスリー
Guthrie, Belinda 548
Guthrie, Donald 548
Guthrie, Jeremy 548
Guthrie, Nora 548
Guthrie, Shirley C. 548
Guthrie, Stewart 548
カスーリス
Kasulis, Thomas P. 708
カスリス
Kasulis, Thomas P. 708
ガスリッジ
Guthridge, Liz 548
カスリーディス
Kasoulides, Ioannis 707
カスリデス
Kasoulides, Ioannis 707
カスリルス
Kasrils, Ronnie 707
カースル
Castle, Barbara Anne 236
カスール
Kasule, Samuel 708
カスルー
Khasru, Abdul Matin 727
カースルズ
Castles, Stephen 236
カズロウ
Kazlou, Uladzimir 712
カーズワイル
Kurzweil, Allen 775
カースン
Carson, Paul 231
カズン
Cousin, Ertharin 296
Kazdin, Alan E. 712
カズング
Kazungu, Dan 712
カズンズ
Cousins, A.D. 296
Cousins, DeMarcus 296
Cousins, Isaiah 296
Cousins, Kirk 296
Cousins, Lucy 296
Cozens, Dylan 298
Cozens, Simon 298
Cozzens, James Gould 298
ガーセ
Gahse, Frank 471
ガセ
Gassée, Jean-Louis 483
カセカンプ
Kasekamp, Andres 707
カセスニエミ
Kasesniemi, Eija-Liisa 707
ガゼッタ
Guzzetta, Cathie E. 550
カセッリ
Caselli, Stefano 233
カセートシリ
Charnvit Kasetsiri 248
カセナリ
Kasenally, Abu Twalib 707
カゼナンボ
Kazenambo, Kazenambo 712
カセミ
Qasemi, Enayatullah 1142
カゼミ
Kazemi, Mustafa 712
ガセミ
Ghasemi, Komeil Nemat 493
Ghasemi, Rostam 493
カゼミーロ
Casemiro 233
カーゼム
Kurzem, Mark 775
カセーム
Kasem, Sanitwong 707
カセム
Cassim, Ahmed Mumtaz Masoon 234
Cassim, Julia 234
Kasem, Watanachai 707
カセーラ
Casella, George 233
カセル
Cassel, Guilherme 234
カセレス
Caceres, Carlos 212
Caceres, Juan Ignacio 212
Caceres, Lucio 212
カセレス・チャベス
Cáceres Chávez, Juan Carlos 212
Cáceres Chávez, Juan Ramón Carlos Enrique 212
カーセン
Karssen, Gien 706
ガーゼン
Goerzen, John 508
カゼンベ
Kazembe, Eunice 712
カゾアール
Casoar, Phil 234
ガソイ
Gasoi, Jennifer 482
カソヴィッツ
Kassovitz, Mathieu 708
カソナ
Casona, Alejandro 234
カソビッツ
Kassovitz, Mathieu 708
カソマ
Kassoma, António Paulo 708
カゾール
Cazor, Anne 239
ガソル
Gasol, Marc 482
Gasol, Pau 482
カソルラ
Cazorla, Santi 239
カーソーン
Cawthorn, Rachel 238
カーソン
Carson, Ben 230
Carson, Ciaran 230
Carson, Clayborne 230
Carson, David 230
Carson, Iain 231
Carson, Johnny 231
Carson, Lillian 231
Carson, Mary Kay 231
Carson, Mike 231
Carson, Rae 231
Carson, Ron 231
Carson, Tra 231
Carson, Wayne 231
Casson, Sophie 235
Kurson, Robert 775
カソン
Casson, Mark 235
ガーソン
Gerson, Carole 491
Gerson, Daniel 491
Gerson, Joseph 491
Gerson, Randy 491
ガーゾーン
Girzone, Joseph F. 502
ガーゾン
Gerzon, Mark 492
カソンガ
Katsonga, Davis 709
カソンゴ
Kasongo, Emile 707
カゾンダ
Kazonda, Eustarckio 712
カソンデ
Kasonde, Emmanuel 707
Kasonde, Joseph 707
カーター
Carter, Aimée 231
Carter, Alex 231
Carter, Ally 231
Carter, Ashton B. 231
Carter, Benny 231
Carter, Breck 231
Carter, Bruce 231
Carter, Chris 231
Carter, Cris 231
Carter, Dan 231
Carter, David 231
Carter, David A. 231
Carter, David E. 231
Carter, David M. 231
Carter, DeAndre 231
Carter, Dean Vincent 231
Carter, Don 231
Carter, Earl 231
Carter, Elliott 231
Carter, Gary Edmund 231
Carter, George 231
Carter, Gerald 231
Carter, Hamish 231
Carter, Harriet H. 231
Carter, Howard 231
Carter, James 231
Carter, Janette 231
Carter, Janice 231
Carter, Jimmy 231
Carter, John 231
Carter, John F. 231
Carter, Josh 231
Carter, Kyle 231
Carter, Matt 231
Carter, Michelle 231
Carter, Miranda 231
Carter, Nell 231
Carter, Nesta 231
Carter, Noëlle 231
Carter, Philip 231
Carter, Philip J. 231
Carter, Rachel 232
Carter, Rick 232
Carter, Rita 232
Carter, Rob 232
Carter, Robert Edgar 232
Carter, Ron 232
Carter, Rosemary 232
Carter, Ruben 232
Carter, Rubin 232
Carter, Sandy 232
Carter, Stephen L. 232
Carter, Steven 232
Carter, Tom 232
Carter, Tony 232
Carter, Vince 232
Cater, Douglass 237
Cater, Gordon R. 237
Cater, Jay 237
Kater, Fritz 708
カーダー
Cader, A.R.M. 213
Carder, Tank 224
ガダ
Gada, Bello 470
Gada, Hemal 470
カタイ
Katai, Aleksandar 708
ガータイス
Gerteis, Margaret 491
カタイネン
Katainen, Jyrki 708
カーター・ヴィッカース
Carter-vickers, Cameron 232
カーター・ウィリアムズ
Carter-williams, Michael 232
カダガ
Kadaga, Rebecca 694
カーダシアン
Kardashian, Kim 704
カーター＝スコット
Carter-Scott, Chérie 232
カタソノワ
Katasonova, Elena Leont'evna 708
ガタチュ
Getachew, Belay 492
カタトニ
al-Katatni, Saad 708
カターニア
Catania, Enzo 237
Catania, Mario 237
カタネオ
Cattaneo, Hernan 237
カダノフ
Kadanoff, Leo P. 694
ガダノフ
Gadanov, Alim 470
ガダバゼ
Gadabadze, Shalva 470
カタパーノ
Catapano, Mike 237
カタビ
al-Qatabi, Mohammed 1142
カダフィ
Qaddafi, Khamis 1142
al-Qaddafi, Muammar 1142
Qaddafi, Saif Al-Arab 1142
al-Qaddafi, Saif al-Islam 1142
カタフィアツ
Katafiasz, Karen 708
ガーダマー
Gadamer, Hans Georg 470
ガダマー
Gadamer, Hans Georg 470
カタミ
al-Qatami, Humaid Mohammed Obaid 1142
カタミーゼ
Katamidze, Viacheslav Ivanovich 708
カタミン
Qatamine, Nidal al 1142
カダム
Kadam, Moussa 694

ガダム
Gaddam, Sai 470
カタラ
Catalá, Rafael 237
ガダラ
Gadalla, Ulaya 470
カタラーノ
Catalano, Nick 237
カタラノ
Catalano, Ellen Mohr 237
カタリ
Cuttaree, Jaya Krishna 310
Katali, Isak 708
カダリ
Kadali, Krishna 694
ガタリ
Gattelli, Christopher 483
カタルディ
Cataldi, Danilo 237
カタルネ
Qatarneh, Fares 1142
カダレ
Kadaré, Ismaïl 694
ガタレ
Gatare, Francis 483
カータン
Curtan, Patricia 309
カタンザロ
Catanzaro, Chandler 237
カタンツァロ
Catanzaro, Michele 237
カタンボ
Katambo, Michael 708
カチアク
Katsiak, Maryia 709
ガチェチラゼ
Gachechiladze, Georgi 470
カチェレ
Kachere, Reen 694
ガチカー
Gachkar, Andrew 470
カチカデーリス
Katsikadelis, John T. 709
カチク
Kachikwu, Emmanuel Ibe 694
カチコ
Kachiko, Anna 694
カーチス
Curtis, Gerald L. 309
Curtis, Richard 309
Curtis, Tony 309
ガチーナ
Gacina, Andrej 470
ガチノヴィッチ
Gacinovic, Mijat 470
カチマレク
Kaczmarek, Janusz 694
カーチマン
Kirchman, David L. 740
カチャック
Tkachuk, Douglas C. 1407
カチャノフ
Kachanoff, Kim 694
カチャラヴァ
Kacharava, Davit 694
カチャリ
Kachali, Khumbo 694
カチャル
Kacar, Gojko 694
カチャルスキー
Katchalsky, Aharon 708
カチャン
Kachan, Oleg L. 694
カチュニッヒ
Katschnig, Heinz 709
カチュマレク
Kaczmarek, Jan A.P. 694
カチュルー
Kachru, Yamuna 694
カチョ・トカ
Cacho Toca, Roberto 212
カチョマレク
Kaczmarek, Pawel 694
カチョル
Kaczor, Tomasz 694
カチル
Katzir, Ephraim 710
カチロー
Cutchlow, Tracy 310
ガチンジ
Gatsinzi, Marcel 483
カチンス
Kutchins, Herb 776
カチンスキ
Kaczyński, Jarosław Aleksander 694
Kaczyński, Lech Aleksander 694
カーツ
Katz, Eugenii 709
Katz, M. 709
Kurtz, Howard 775
Kurtz, John William 775
Kurtz, Lisa A. 775
Kurtz, Sylvie 775
Kurtz, Thomas E. 775
Kurz, John 775
ガーツ
Goertz, Gary 508
カーツァー
Kertzer, David I. 722
カツァブ
Katsav, Moshe 709
カツァラポフ
Katsalapov, Nikita 709
カツァリス
Katsaris, Cyprien 709
ガツァロフ
Gatsalov, Khadjimourat 483
ガツィエフ
Gattsiev, Soslan 483
カツィール
Katzir, Ephraim 710
カツェネルソン
Katsenelson, Vitaliy N. 709
カツェリ
Katseli, Louka 709
カツォンガ
Katsonga, Davis 709
カツク
Katuku, Mutua 709
カックス
Cox, Stella M. 298
Kucks, Johnny 771
カックル
Cockle, George Maralious 273
カッサー
Cassar, Joe 234
カツサ
Katusa, Marin 709
カッサーノ
Cassano, Antonio 234
Cassano, Franco 234
Cassano, Silvano 234
カッサノ
Cassano, Antonio 234
カッサーラ
Cassara, Andrea 234
カッサル
Kassar, Adnan 708
カッサル - ミクラ
Kassal-Mikula, Renata 708
カッシオーラ
Kassiola, Joel Jay 708
カッジオラト
Cazziolato, Flavia 239
カッシーナ
Cassina, Igor 234
カッシーニ
Cassini, Oleg 234
カッシネリ
Cassinelli, Attilio 234
カッシーノ
Cassino, Mark 235
ガッシュ
Gasch, Robert 482
Gush, Cathy 548
カッシュケー
Katsheke, Judy 709
カッシーリ
Casilli, Antonio A. 234
カッシンガム
Cassingham, Randy C. 234
カッシング
Cushing, Steven 310
カッスラー
Cussler, Clive Eric 310
Cussler, Dirk 310
カッセ
Casse, Pierre 234
カッセーゼ
Cassese, Antonio 234
カッセム
Kassem, Nicholas 708
カッセル
Cassel, Frédéric 234
Cassel, Jean-Pierre 234
Cassel, Vincent 234
Kassel, Jon 708
Kassell, Nicole 708
Kasser, Rodolphe 708
カッセルズ
Cassels, Alan 234
ガッセン
Gessen, Masha 492
カッソン
Casson, Lionel 235
Casson, Mark 235
ガッソン
Gasson, Sam 483
カッタ
Catta, Hervé-Marie 237
カッター
Cutter, Nick 310
カッターネオ
Cattaneo, Marco 237
カッターミ
al-Qatami, Humaid Mohammed Obaid 1142
カッターモール
Cattermole, Peter John 237
カッチャー
Katchor, Ben 708
Kutcher, Ashton 776
ガッチャダール
Gachchhadar, Bijaya Kumar 470
Gachhedar, Bijaya Kumar 470
ガッチャダル
Gachchhadar, Bijaya Kumar 470
カッチャトーレ
Cacciatore, Fabrizio 212
カッチャプオティ
Cacciapuoti, Castrese 212
カッチャーリ
Cacciari, Massimo 212
ガッチョーネ
Gaccione, Angelo 470
カッツ
Cutts, Dominique C. 310
Katz, Bernard 709
Katz, Charles, Jr. 709
Katz, Craig L. 709
Katz, David 709
Katz, Eliakim 709
Katz, Elihu 709
Katz, Elliott 709
Katz, Eran 709
Katz, Haim 709
Katz, Israel 709
Katz, James Everett 709
Katz, Jon 709
Katz, Joshua 709
Katz, Karen 709
Katz, Lilian 709
Katz, Mabel 709
Katz, Marcus 709
Katz, Martin 709
Katz, Mitchell H. 709
Katz, Natasha 709
Katz, Nathan 709
Katz, Ralph 709
Katz, Raul Luciano 709
Katz, Richard 709
Katz, Samuel M. 709
Katz, Sheldon H. 709
Katz, Stephen Ira 709
Katz, Victor J. 709
Katz, Yehuda 709
Katz, Yisrael 709
ガッツ
Gatz, Jean 484
カッツァーブ
Katsav, Moshe 709
ガッツィ
Gazzi, Alessandro 485
カッツィン
Katzin, Lee H. 710
カッツェンスタイン
Katzenstein, Peter J. 710
カッツェンバーグ
Katzenberg, Jeffrey 710
カッツェンバック
Katzenbach, John 710
Katzenbach, Jon R. 710
ガッツォーラ
Gazzola, Marcello 485
カッツング
Katzung, Bertram G. 710
ガッティ
Gatti, Arturo 483
Gatti, Daniele 483
Gatti, Francesco 483

カ

ガッティカー
Gattiker, Urs E. 483
ガッティング
Gutting, Gary 549
ガッテーニョ
Gattegno, Jean-Pierre 483
ガット
Gat, Azar 483
Gatt, Austin 483
Gatto, John Taylor 483
Gatto, Lorenzo 483
ガッド
Gadd, Ben 470
Gadd, Carl-Johan 470
Gadd, Steve 470
カットウフンド
Katn'fund, Bijou 709
カッドゥール
Qaddour, Nasser 1142
ガットゥング
Gattung, Theresa 484
ガットステイン
Gutstein, Steven E. 549
ガットソン
Gatson, Frank, Jr. 483
カットバートソン
Cuthbertson, Keith 310
カットホール
Cutshall, Susanne M. 310
ガットマン
Gutman, Amy 549
Gutman, Dan 549
Gutmann, Amy 549
Gutmann, Michelle 549
Guttman, Michael 549
Guttman, Peter 549
ガッドール
Gaddor, Abdul-Latif 470
カットン
Catton, Eleanor 237
ガッパ
Gappah, Petina 477
カッパイ
Cappai, Manuel 223
カッパーチェク
Kacperczyk, Marcin 694
ガッバーナ
Gabbana, Stefano 469
カッバニ
Qabbani, Khaled 1142
カッパーフィールド
Copperfield, David 289
カッバーラ
Kabbara, Mohammed 693
カッパロフ
Kapparov, Nurlan 703
ガッバーン
al-Ghabban, Muhammad 492
カッピー
Cuppy, Will 308
ガッビアディーニ
Gabbiadini, Manolo 469
カッブ
Cobb, Alex 272
Cobb, David 272
Cobb, Randall 272
Cobb, Vicki 272
カップ
Kopp, Rochelle 756
カッファレッリ
Caffarelli, Luis 213
カップダビラ
Capdevila, Carles 222
Capdevila i Valls, Roser 222
カッペッリ
Cappelli, Gari 223
カッペリーニ
Cappellini, Anna 223
カッペリーノ
Cappellino, Neal 223
カッポリーノ
Capolino, Filippo 223
カーツマン
Kertzman, Mitchell 722
Kurtzman, Alex 775
カツミレク
Kazmirek, Kai 712
カツヤマ
Katsuyama, Hideaki 709
カッラ
Kalla, Charlotte 698
カッラーダ
Carrada, Giovanni 229
カッラリーニ
Carrarini, Rose 229
カッリオマキ
Kalliomäki, Antti 698
カッリージ
Carrisi, Donato 230
ガッルイエフ
Garryyev, Myrat 481
カッレル
Carrer, Chiara 229
カッレントフト
Kallentoft, Mons 698
ガッロ
Gallo, Lucio 474
カッロッツォ
Carrozzo, Mario 230
ガッローネ
Garrone, Riccardo 481
カーツワイル
Kurzweil, Ray 775
カーテ
Cate, Marijke ten 237
カテ
Kate, Sabaï 708
カデ
Cadet, Yves 213
ガデア
Gadea, Kevin 470
カーティ
Kurtti, Jeff 775
カーティー
Carty, Nigel 232
カーディ
Qadi, Yasser el 1142
カティ
Catty, Suzanne 237
Kgathi, Shaw 724
カディ
Cuddy, Amy Joy Casselberry 306
Cuddy, Robin 306
Cudi, Kid 306
Kadi, Abdelkader 694
al-Qadi, Abdulsalam 1142
ガーティ
Ghartey, Joe 493
ガディ
Gaddy, Clifford G. 470
ガティウス
Gatius, Alfredo 483
カディオ
Cadiot, Olivier 213
ガディオ
Gadio, Cheikh Tidiane 470
カティグバック - シリック
Katigbak-Sillick, Marie Clare 709
カーティス
Curtis, Alan 309
Curtis, Anthony James 309
Curtis, Ben 309
Curtis, Bill 309
Curtis, Chris 309
Curtis, Christopher Paul 309
Curtis, Deborah 309
Curtis, Gerald L. 309
Curtis, Hillman 309
Curtis, Jamie Lee 309
Curtis, Keene 309
Curtis, Keith E. 309
Curtis, Mark 309
Curtis, Neil 309
Curtis, Richard 309
Curtis, Susan 309
Curtis, Tony 309
Curtis, Vesta Sarkhosh 309
Curtis, Zac 309
Curtiss, Kendra 309
Kertesz, Andrew 722
カディス
Kadis, Asya L. 694
Kadis, Costas 694
カディック
Caddick, David 212
カーディッシュ
Kardish, Laurence 704
ガディッシュ
Gadiesh, Orit 470
カティッチ
Katič, Andreja 708
カティティマ
Katitima, Norbert Basengezi 709
ガーディナー
Gardiner, B.G. 479
Gardiner, Deirdre 479
Gardiner, John Eliot 479
Gardiner, John Reynolds 479
Gardiner, Lindsey 479
Gardiner, Lizzy 479
Gardiner, Meg 479
Gardiner, Robin 479
カーディナル
Cardinal, Catherine 224
Cardinal, Louis 224
ガティニ
Gattini, Jorge 483
カーディネル
Cardinell, Cassandra 224
カディヒー
Cuddihy, Tim 306
カーディフ
Cardiff, Jack 224
Cardiff, Janet 224
カティブ
Khatibu, Mohamed Seif 727
カディマ＝ンジュジ
Kadima-Nzuji, Mukala 694
カティヤ・サワディポン
Khattiya Sawasdipol 727
カティーラ
Katila, Riitta 709
カディリ
al-Qadiri, Rima 1142
カディリアン
Ghadirian, Abdu'l-Missagh 492
カーディル
Kadeer, Rabiya 694
カディルガマル
Kadirgamar, Lakshman 694
ガディルガマル
Kadirgamar, Lakshman 694
カディロフ
Kadyrov, Akhmed 695
Kadyrov, Ramzan Akhmadovich 695
カーティン
Curtin, Philip D. 309
Curtin, Thomas G. 309
カティン
Katin, Peter Roy 709
カテガヤ
Kategaya, Eriya 708
カデゲ
Kadege, Alphonse Marie 694
カデジャーベク
Kaderabek, Pavel 694
ガデス
Gades, Antonio 470
ガーデック
Gardeck, Ian 479
カデット
Cadet, Travaris 213
ガテテ
Gatete, Claver 483
ガーデ・ドゥエ
Garde Due, Ulrik 479
カデナ
Cadena, Raul Almeida 213
ガーデナ
Gardiner, Michael 479
カデナ・モスケラ
Cadena Mosquera, José Medardo 213
カテフォレス
Catephores, George 237
カテマ
Katema, Joseph 708
カデム
Khadem, Riaz 724
カデューシン
Kadushin, Alfred 694
カテラン
Cattelan, Maurizio 237
カデリ
Qaderi, Habibullah 1142
ガテリ
Gattelli, Daniela 483
カテリアノ・ベジド
Cateriano Bellido, Pedro 237
カテリニッチ
Katerinich, Dmitry S. 708
カーデル
Kader, Linda 694
カデール
Kader, Obaidul 694
カデル
Quader, Ghulam

Muhammed 1143
Quader, Golam Mohammad 1143
Quader, Obaidul 1143
ガテル・アリモント
Gatell Arimont, Cristina 483
ガテルス
Gaters, Ivars 483
カーデルバッハ
Kadelbach, Gerd 694
Kadelbach, Stefan 694
カデロ
Cadelo, Manlio 213
カーテン
Karten, Naomi 706
カデン
Kadden, Ronald M. 694
ガーテン
Garten, Jeffrey E. 482
ガーデン
Garden, Jo 479
Garden, Timothy 479
ガテン
Gathen, Joachim von zur 483
カテンデ
Katende, Kennedy 708
ガーデンハイア
Gardenhire, Ron 479
ガーデンハイアー
Gardenhire, Ron 479
ガーデンハイヤー
Gardenhire, Ron 479
カード
Card, Andrew 224
Card, Gary 224
Card, Melanie 224
Card, Orson Scott 224
カト
Cat, Carlos 237
Kato, Issiah Ag 709
カトー
Kato, J.L. 709
カド
Cadot, Jeremy 213
ガド
Gado, Foumakoye 470
カトィヤー
Catoir, Barbara 237
カドイロフ
Kadyrov, Akhmed 695
Kadyrov, Ramzan Akhmadovich 695
カトウ
Kato, Mikio 709
Kato, Shizuru 709
Kato, Takafumi 709
Kato, Tomonari 709
カドウ
Cadow, Kenneth M. 213
カードウェル
Cardwell, Don 225
Cardwell, Nancy 225
カドゥカ
Khadka, Khum Bahadur 724
カトゥーシャ
Katoucha 709
カドゥシン
Kadushin, Charles 695
ガトゥーソ
Gattuso, Joan M. 484
カドゥソン
Kaduson, Heidi 695
カドウミ
Kaddoumi, Farouk 694
カドゥーリー
Kadoorie, Michael 694
カトゥリーベ
Katureebe, Bart 709
ガトゥルアク
Gatluak, Kuong Danhier 483
カトゥルガロス
Katrougalos, Giorgos 709
カトゥン
Khatun, Shahara 727
カドカ
Khadka, Narayan 724
ガドカリ
Gadkari, Nitin Jairam 470
カドグチ
Kadoguchi, Shizuko 694
カトサン
Katosang, Mario 709
ガドジン
Gudgin, Martin 542
カドス＝アーヴィン
Chodos-Irvine, Margaret 258
カトチ
Katoch, Chandresh K. 709
カードナ
Cardona, Joe 224
カトナ
Katona, Cornelius L. E. 709
カトナー
Kutner, Joe 776
Kutner, Lawrence 776
ガートナー
Gaertner, Wulf 470
Gartner, Alan 482
Gartner, Leslie P. 482
Gartner, Richard B. 482
Gertner, Jon 491
ガードナー
Gardener, Hilary 479
Gardener, Jason 479
Gardner, Andrew 479
Gardner, Ben 479
Gardner, Bill 479
Gardner, Brett 479
Gardner, Brian 479
Gardner, Chris P. 479
Gardner, Craig 479
Gardner, Craig Shaw 479
Gardner, Dan 479
Gardner, David 479
Gardner, Dede 479
Gardner, Edward 479
Gardner, Ella 479
Gardner, English 479
Gardner, Floyd Martin 479
Gardner, Gary 479
Gardner, Hayley 479
Gardner, Howard 479
Gardner, James Alan 479
Gardner, James C. 479
Gardner, James N. 479
Gardner, John N. 479
Gardner, John William 479
Gardner, Karen M. 479
Gardner, Katy 479
Gardner, Laurence 479
Gardner, Lisa 479
Gardner, Lloyd C. 479
Gardner, Mark 479
Gardner, Martin 479
Gardner, Nicole 480
Gardner, Nuala 480
Gardner, Pierce 480
Gardner, R.H. 480
Gardner, Richard A. 480
Gardner, R.L. 480
Gardner, Roy S. 480
Gardner, Rulon 480
Gardner, Sally 480
Gardner, Steve 480
Gardner, W.Booth 480
Gardner, Zoë E. 480
ガトニー
Gwatney, Bill 550
カトニッチ
Katnić, Milorad 709
カドニヤン
Guidanian, Avedis 544
カドハタ
Kadohata, Cynthia 694
カドバニー
Kadvany, John David 695
ガドバン
Al-Ghadhban, Thamir Abbas Ghadhban 492
カドビナ
Kadobina, Maria 694
ガトマイタン
Gatmaitan, Luis P. 483
カートメル
Cartmel, Fred 232
カドモア
Cudmore, Jamie 306
カドモン
Kadmon, Cristina 694
Kadmon, Naftali 694
カトラー
Cutler, Alan 310
Cutler, Brian L. 310
Cutler, Chris 310
Cutler, Jane 310
Cutler, Jay 310
Cutler, Judy Goffman 310
Cutler, Laurence S. 310
Cutler, Lloyd 310
Cutler, Paul 310
Cutler, Ronald 310
Cutler, Sam 310
Cutler, Tony 310
Cuttler, Ian 310
カドラ
Khadra, Yasmina 724
カートライト
Cartwright, John 232
Cartwright, Kivon 232
Cartwright, Lawrence 232
Cartwright, Peter 232
Cartwright, Silvia 232
Cartwright, Stephen 232
Cartwright, Sue 232
Cartwright, Thomas C. 232
Cartwright, Thomas Campbell 232
カトラン
Cathelin, Bernard 237
カートランド
Cartland, Barbara 232
ガートランド
Gehtland, Justin 486
ガトランド
Gatland, Warren 483
カトリ
Khatri, Ravinder 727
カドリ
Kadri, Shahid 694
al-Qadri, Ahmad 1142
カトリカラ
Catricalà, Antonio 237
カートリッジ
Cartledge, Paul 232
Cartlidge, Katrin 232
Cartlidge, Michelle 232
カトリップ
Cutlip, Scott M. 310
カトリニチ
Catrinici, Larisa 237
ガトリフ
Gatlif, Tony 483
カトリン
Catlin, Katherine 237
Catlin, Pamela A. 237
ガトリン
Gatlin, Justin 483
カトル
Cattell, Roderic Geoffrey Galton 237
ガドール
Gadour, Ali 470
カドレ
Kadre, Abdalla 694
ガードレー
Girdley, Michael 502
カドレツ
Kadlec, Milan 694
カトレット
Catret, Juan 237
ガトロー
Gautreaux, Tim 484
ガトロアイファアナ
Gatoloaifaana, Amataga Alesana Gidlow 483
ガドロス
Quadros, Ketleyn 1143
カート・ワークマン
Kurt Workman 775
ガトワール
Ghatowar, Paban Singh 493
カートン
Carton, Rick 232
Kirton, John 741
Kirton, Wayne Harold 741
ガートン
Garton, Alison 482
Garton, Ray 482
Garton, Ryan 482
ガードン
Gurdon, John Bertrand 547
ガートン・アッシュ
Garton-Ash, Timothy 482
カトンバ
Katomba, Germain Kambinga 709
カーナー
Koerner, Robert M. 751
カナ
Khanna, Tarun 726
カナー
Kanner, Bernice 702
Kanner, Leo 702
ガーナー

Garner, Alan 481
Garner, David M. 481
Garner, Helen 481
Garner, James 481
Garner, Jennifer 481
Garner, Judith 481
Garner, Manasseh 481
Garner, Margaret 481
Garner, Montell 481
Garner, Perci 481
Garner, Philippe 481

ガナ
Gana, Jerry 475

カナヴェイル
Cannavale, Bobby 221

カナエワ
Kanayeva, Yevgenia 700

カナザワ
Kanazawa, Satoshi 700

カナジ
Kanazi, George J. 700

カナシロ・デ・レオン
Kanashiro de León, Dora 700

カーナゼス
Karnazes, Dean 705

カナーダ
Kanād 700

ガナッシ
Ganassi, Sonia 475

カナデイ
Canaday, Kameron 220

カナバン
Canavan, Matt 221

カナビリャス
Canavilhas, Gabriela 221

カナヘレ
Kanahele, Pua Kanaka'ole 700

カナマ
Kamana, Vénant 699

カナム
Canham, Stefan 221

カナリ
Canale, S.Terry 220

カナリー
Cunnally, John 308

カーナル
Kanar, Stephen 700

カナル
Canal, Gustavo 220
Khanal, Jhala Nath 726

カナルス
Canals, Caca 221

カナレス
Canales, Juan Díaz 220
Canales, Kaleb 220
Canales, Sergio 220

カナレス・クラリオン
Canales Clariond, Fernando 221

カナワアティ
Canahuati, Mario 220

カーナン
Kernan, Alvin B. 721

カナーン
Canaan, Isaiah 220
Kanaan, Ghazi 700

カナン
Cannan, Richard 221
Kanaan, Ghazi 700
Kan'an, Ghazi 700
Kanan, Sean 700

カーニー
Carney, Art 227
Carney, Elizabeth 227
Carney, John 227
Carney, Mark 227
Carney, Michael 227
Carney, Rodney 227
Carney, Scott 227
Kearney, A.T. 713
Kearney, Christopher A. 713
Kearney, David 713
Kearney, Hannah 713
Kearney, Michael 713
Kearney, Rob 713
Kearney, Susan 713

カニ
Cani, Shkëlqim 221
Kani, Mathieu Martial 701

カニー
Kany, Roland 702

ガーニー
Garney, Ron 481
Gurney, A.R. 547
Gurney, James 547
Gurney, Stella 547

ガニ
Ghani, Ashraf 493

カニア
Kania, Paula 701

ガーニアー
Guarnier, Megan 541

ガニア
Gagne, Verne 471

カーニィ
Carney, Colleen 227

ガーニィ
Gurney, Jud W. 547

ガニェ
Gagné, David 471
Gagné, Robert Mills 471

ガニエ
Gagné, Lori Saint-Martin Paul 471
Gagne, Philippe 471
Gagne, Raphael 471

ガニエフ
Ganiev, Eler 476
Ganiev, Elyor 476
Ganiyev, Elyor 476

ガニェール
Ggagnaire, Pierre 492

カニェンキコ
Kanyenkiko, Anatole 702

ガニオ
Ganio, Mathieu 476

ガニオン
Gagnon, Claude 471

カニーク
Kaník, Ľudovít 701

カニグズバーグ
Konigsburg, E.L. 755

カニーゲル
Kanigel, Robert 701

カニゲル
Kanigel, Robert 701

カニサレス
Cañizales, Miguel Angel 221
Cañizares, Juan Manuel 221

カニス
Kanis, Pavol 701
Kanis, Willy 701

ガニス
Ganis, Giorgio 476

カニスキナ
Kaniskina, Olga 701

カーニック
Curnick, Pippa 309
Kernick, Simon 721

カーニハン
Kernighan, Brian W. 721

ガーニム
Ghanem, Ali 493
Ghanim, Faraj Said bin 493

カニャッツォ
Cagnazzo, Alvise 213

カニャナ
Kanyana, Aimée Laurentine 702

ガニユイ
Ganiyu, Muideen 476

カニュイック
Kaniuk, Jeanne 701

ガニュパン
Gagnepain, Bernard 471

カニュンバ
Kanyumba, Grandson 702

カニョット
Cagnotto, Tania 213

ガニョン
Gagnon, Alain-G. 471
Gagnon, Claude 471
Gagnon, Marc 471
Gagnon, Marc-Antoine 471

ガニヨン
Gagnon, Claude 471

ガニラウ
Ganilau, Epeli 476

カニンガム
Coningham, Robin 282
Cunningham, Bill 308
Cunningham, Charles E. 308
Cunningham, Elaine 308
Cunningham, Floyd Timothy 308
Cunningham, Frank 308
Cunningham, Hugh 308
Cunningham, Jack 308
Cunningham, Janet 308
Cunningham, Laura Shaine 308
Cunningham, Lawrence 308
Cunningham, Lawrence A. 308
Cunningham, Merce 308
Cunningham, Michael 308
Cunningham, Michael J. 308
Cunningham, Peter 308
Cunningham, Stace 308
Cunningham, Stuart 308
Cunningham, Vashti 308

ガニング
Gunning, Jennifer 546
Gunning, Stephanie 546

カニングハム
Cunningham, Alison J. 308
Cunningham, Benny 308
Cunningham, Chet 308
Cunningham, Dante 308
Cunningham, Jerome 308
Cunningham, Justice 308
Cunningham, Mark 308
Cunningham, Merce 308
Cunningham, Michael 308
Cunningham, Todd 308

カニンバ
Kanimba, François 701

カニンハム
Cunningham, Suki 308

カヌ
Kane, Amadou 701
Kanu, Alpha 702

ガヌー
Ganoo, Alan 476

カヌウ
Canu, Ivan 222

カヌースター
Knoester, Bob 748

カヌート
Qanout, Maha 1142

カヌニ
Qanuni, Yunus 1142

カーネ
Kane, Herbert Kawainui 701

カネ
Canet, Guillaume 221
Kanneh, Vamba 702

ガネ
Gane, Laurent 476

ガーネイ
Gurney, Gene 547

カネヴァ
Kaneva, Daniela Danailova 701
Kaneva, Liliana 701

カネコ
Kaneko, Kalani 701

カネサ
Canessa, Mario 221

ガネーサン
Ganesan, Sivaji 476

ガネサン
Ganesan, Mano 476

カネージャ
Canella, Roberto 221

ガネーシャン
Ganesan, Sivaji 476

カネッティー
Canete, Eric 221

ガーネット
Gârnet, Ilian 481
Garnett, John 481
Garnett, Joshua 481
Garnett, Kevin 481
Garnett, Marlon 481

ガネット
Gannett, Ruth Stiles 476

カネーテ
Canete, Eric 221

カネハラ
Kanehara, Rina 701

ガネーフ
Ganeyev, Renal 476

ガネフ
Ganev, Mihail 476
Ganev, Stoyan 476

カーネマン
Kahneman, Daniel 696

ガネム
Ghanem, Abdullah Ahmed 493
al-Ghanem, Hassan bin Abdullah 493
Ghanem, Shukri 493
Ghanem, Shukuri

Muhammad 493
Ghanim, Faraj Said bin 493
カネモト
Kanemoto, Kousuke 701
カネラキス
Canellakis, Evangelos S. 221
ガネリ
Ganeri, Anita 476
カネール
Kanner, Patrick 702
カネル
Caneele, Severine 221
Cannell, Jon 221
ガネル
Gunnell, John G. 546
カネロン
Canelon, Hersony 221
カノ
Cano, Alfonso 222
Canó, Robinson 222
Cano, Victor 222
カノー
Canó, Robinson 222
カーノイ
Carnoy, Martin 227
カノウ
Khanou, Ahmed 726
ガーノウ
Garneau, Dustin 481
カノヴァン
Canovan, Margaret 222
カノコギ
Kanokogi, Rena Rusty 702
Kanokogi, Rusty 702
カノーザ
Canosa, Hans 222
カノ・サンス
Cano Sanz, Carlos Gustavo 222
カノス
Chanos, James S. 246
カノディア
Kanodia, Chandra 702
カノネロ
Canonero, Milena 222
カノ・モレノ
Cano Moreno, Oscar Pedro 222
ガノール
Ganor, Solly 476
ガノンゴ
Ganongo, Calixte 476
カーバー
Carver, Robert 232
Kerber, Linda K. 721
カーパー
Carper, Jean 228
カバ
Cava, Roberta 238
Kaba, Brahima 693
Kaba, Camara Sanaba 693
Kaba, Malado 693
Kaba, Mamadi 693
Kaba, Mory 693
Kaba, Nialé 693
Kaba, Sideiki 693
Kaba, Sidibe Fatoumata 693
Kabbah, Ahmad Tejan 693
Kabua, David 694
カバー
Kabbah, Afsatu 693
Kabbah, Ahmad Tejan 693
カパ
Capa, Ander 222
カパー
Copper, Basil 289
ガーバー
Garber, Joseph R. 477
Garber, Roland 477
Garver, Mitch 482
Gerber, Craig 490
Gerber, David 490
Gerber, Michael 490
Gerber, Michael E. 490
ガバイ
Gabai, Avi 469
Gabaix, Xavier 469
カバイェーロ
Caballero, Eugenio 211
カバイジャ
Kabaija, Ephraim 693
ガパイヤール
Gapaillard, Laurent 477
カバウ
Kabaou, Mahamane 693
ガーバー＝エッカード
Gerber-Eckard, Lisa N. 490
カバエバ
Kabaeva, Alina 693
カバエワ
Kabaeva, Alina 693
カーバーガー
Kirberger, Kimbery 740
カバーガ
Cabarga, Leslie 212
カバカ
Kabaka, Gaudentia Mugosi 693
カバクレ
Kavakure, Laurent 711
ガハクワ
Gahakwa, Daphrose 471
カバコ・シルバ
Cavaco-Silva, Anibal 238
カバコシルバ
Cavaco-Silva, Anibal 238
カバコス
Kavakos, Leonidas 710
カバコーフ
Kabakov, Emilia 693
Kabakov, Ilya Iosifovich 693
カバコフ
Kabakov, Emilia 693
Kabakov, Ilya Iosifovich 693
カパーサ
Capasa, Ennio 222
カパサ
Capasa, Ennio 222
カハサイ
Kahsai, Gabrehiwet 696
カバザンジャン
Kavazanjian, Edward, Jr. 711
カバシ
Kabashi, Mohammed al-Amin Issa 693
カパシ
Kapashi, Neha 702
ガバシ
Gervasi, Sacha 492
カバジェロ
Caballero, Carlos 211
Caballero, Gradis 211
Caballero, Willy 211
カバジェロス
Caballeros, Harold 211
カバジェロス・オテロ
Caballeros Otero, Rómulo 211
カバジェロ・ベニテス
Caballero Benítez, Carmelo José 211
カバジェロ・ボナルド
Caballero Bonald, José Manuel 211
ガバジオ
Gavaggio, Enak 484
ガバシビリ
Gabashvili, Georgi 469
カパシュ
Kapas, Boglarka 702
ガバス
Gabas, Carlos Eduardo 469
カバズッティ
Cavazzuti, Cinzia 238
カバセレ
Kabasele, Christian 693
カパタ
Kapata, Jean 702
カパタナ
Capatana, Eugen 222
カハタニ
al-Qahtani, Abdullah bin Khalid 1142
カハタン
Qahtan, Abdul-Qader 1142
カパチンスカヤ
Kapachinskaya, Anastasia 702
カバッサ
Cavazza, José Luis 238
ガバッチア
Gabaccia, Donna R. 469
カパッティ
Capatti, Alberto 222
Capatti, Bérénice 222
カバットジン
Kabat-Zinn, Jon 693
カバディ
Kabadi, Haroun 693
ガーバーディング
Gerberding, Julie Louise 490
ガバーディング
Gerberding, Julie Louise 490
カーハート
Carhart, Thaddeus 225
カーバート
Cuthbert, Alex 310
ガーバート
Gerbert, Philipp 490
ガバート
Gabhart, Kyle 469
カパトスト
Capatosto, Terri 222
カハナー
Kahaner, Larry 695
カバナ
Cavanagh, John 238
カバナー
Cavanagh, Roland R. 238
カバーニ
Cavani, Edinson 238
カバニリャス・アロンソ
Cabanillas Alonso, Pio 211
カハノフ
Kahanoff, Ruth 695
カバハ
Qabha, Wasfi 1142
カバヒジャ
Kabaija, Ephraim 693
カパーフィールド
Copperfield, David 289
カハマ
Kahama, George 695
ガバマン
Guberman, Nancy 542
カハラニ
al-Kahlani, Ahmed Mohammed Yahya Hasan 695
ガバリ
El-gabaly, Hatem Mostafa 469
Al-gabaly, Hatem Mostafa 469
ガハリア
Gakharia, Giorgi 472
カバリェロ
Caballero, Denia 211
カバリェロ・フラド
Caballero Jurado, Carlos 211
カバリク
Kavaliku, Langi 711
カバリッチ
Kavarić, Vladimir 711
カバリノ
Cavallino, Paola 238
カバルス
Cabarrús, Carlos Rafael 212
ガバルドン
Gabaldon, Diana 469
Gabaldon, Guy 469
カバレベ
Kabarebe, James 693
カハレワイ
Kahalewai, Nancy S. 695
カー＝バーロー
Kerr-barlow, Tawera 722
カハロフ
Kahharov, Abdurahim 695
カハロン
Kahlon, Moshe 695
カバン
Cabane, Olivia Fox 211
Kaban, M.S. 693
Kavan, Jan 711
ガバン
al-Ghaban, Ali Faik 492
カバンガ
Kabanga, Célestin Mbuyu 693
カパンギ
Khapangi, Gore Bahadur 726
カバンゲ・ヌンビ
Kabange Numbi, Félix 693
カバンシ
Kabanshi, Emerine 693
カパンジー
Kapandji, Adalbert I. 702
カパンジ・カララ

Kapanji Kalala, Bruno 702
カパンジカララ
Kapanji Kalala, Bruno 702
カバンダ
Kabanda, Celestin 693
カパンダ
Kaapanda, Joel 693
カパンディ
Kapandji, Ibrahim Adalbert 702
カバントゥ
Cabantous, Alain 212
カバンヌ
Cabanne, Pierre 212
カービ
Kaabi, Abdallah 693
al-Ka'abi, Juma Ahmed 693
Kirby, Bruno 740
カービー
Kirby, Bruno 740
Kirby, David 740
Kirby, David G. 740
Kirby, F.E. 740
Kirby, Jack 740
Kirby, Jill 740
Kirby, Julia 740
Kirby, Juvaun J. 740
Kirby, Matthew J. 740
Kirby, Michael 740
Kirby, Wayne 740
カビ
Cabi, Dionisio 212
Kabi, Martinho 693
カピー
Capie, David H. 223
ガビ
Gabi 469
カビア
Kabia, Soccoh 693
カービィ
Kirby, Brian E. 740
Kirby, Jessi 740
Kirby, John R. 740
Kirby, Linda K. 740
ガビエ
Gabier, Shane 469
カビエゼル
Caviezel, Giovanni 238
カピエルスキー
Kapielski, Thomas 702
カービエルヤクローツ
Caabi El-yachroutu, Mohammed 211
カピシク
Capicik, Andy 223
カヒシビリ
Kakhishvili, Kakha 696
カピジンパンガ
Kapijimpanga, Judith 702
カヒゼ
Kakhidze, Aslan 696
カビーゼル
Caviezel, Jim 238
カピタ
Kapita, Ben 702
カピタニオ
Capitanio, Antonella 223
カピタニッチ
Capitanich, Jorge 223
カピターニョヴァー
Kapitáňova, Daniela 702
カピッキオーニ
Capicchinoni, Gian Carlo 223
カビッチ
Cavic, Milorad 238
ガービッチ
Grbich, Carol 528
カピッツァ
Kapitza, P. 702
カビッボ
Cabibbo, Nicola 212
カピトニェンコ
Kapitonenko, Aleksandr Maksimovich 702
カービ・ネジャディヤン
Kaabi-nejadian, Abdolrazzagh 693
カビュ
Cabu 212
カピュ
Capus, Alex 224
ガビュス
Gabus, Pierre 470
カピュタ
Kaputa, Catherine 703
カビラ
Kabila, Joseph 693
Kabila, Laurent Désiré 693
カピラ
Kapila, Monisha 702
ガビラコリャド
Gavira Collado, Adrian 484
ガビリア
Gaviria, Herman 484
Gaviria, Simon Muñoz 484
ガビリア・ウリベ
Gaviria Uribe, Alejandro 484
ガビリアレンドン
Gaviria Rendon, Fernando 484
カー＝ヒル
Carr-Hill, Micah 229
カービール
Qabil, Tareq 1142
カヒル
Cahill, David 213
カビール
Kabeer, Naila 693
Kabir 693
Kabir, Mohammed J. 693
カビル
Kabil, Nihat 693
Kabir, Abdol 693
カビロフ
Kabirov, Shodi 693
ガビロンド・プジョル
Gabilondo Pujol, Ángel 469
カヒン
Kahin, Brian 695
ガービン
Garvin, David A. 482
Garvin, Terence 482
カビンデレ
Kavindele, Enock 711
カビンバ
Kabimba, Wynter 693
カーフ
Karhu, Clifton 705
カープ
Karp, Alexander 706
Karp, Cary 706
Karp, David 706
Karp, Gerald C. 706
Karp, Harvey 706
Karp, Jason 706
Karpf, Anne 706
Kirp, David 741
カフ
Kahu, Moses 696
カブ
Cobb, John B., Jr. 272
カプ
Kapu, Moses 703
カプー
Capoue, Etienne 223
ガーブ
Garb, Howard N. 477
Garb, Tamar 477
Garbe, Suzanne 477
Garve, Andrew 482
ガフ
Gough, Alex 521
Gough, Alfred 521
Gough, Michael 521
カプーア
Kapoor, Anish 703
ガファ
Gafa, Ioelu Elisara 470
カファーイン
Kefayen, Fahad Salem 714
ガーファイン
Garfein, Herschel 480
カファティ
Kafati, Oscar 695
カプアーナ
Capuana, Luigi 224
カプアーノ
Capuano, Marco 224
カファレラ
Caffarella, Rosemary Shelly 213
カファレル
Caffarel, Henri 213
カファロ
Cafaro, Debra 213
ガーファンクル
Garfunkel, Art 480
カファンド
Kafando, Michel 695
Kafando, Patiendé 695
カフィ
Cufí, Carles 307
Kafi, Ali 695
カフィー
Cuffie, Maxie 307
カブイ
Kabui, Frank 694
ガフィス
al-Ghafis, Ali bin Nasser 492
ガーフィールド
Garfield, Andrew 480
Garfield, Bob 480
Garfield, Patricia L. 480
Garfield, Simon 480
ガーフィンケル
Garfinkel, Harold 480
Garfinkel, Paul E. 480
Garfinkel, Simson 480
カブウェルル
Kabwelulu, Martin 694
カブウェルル・ラビロ
Kabwelulu Labilo, Martin 694
ガブエニ王子
Prince Gabheni 469
カブエ・ムエウ・ロンゴ
Kabwe Mwewu Longo, Isidore 694
カフォーリオ
Caforio, Maria P. 213
カブキ
Kabuki, Sawako 694
カブキアン
Cavoukian, Ann 238
カフキワ
Kahukiwa, Robin 696
ガブーザ
Gabuza, Joel 470
ガブサー
Gubser, Steven Scott 542
カプシチンスキ
Kapuściński, Ryszard 703
カプシチンスキー
Kapuściński, Ryszard 703
カブシュ
Kabush, Geoff 694
カーブース・イブン・サイード
Qaboos bin Said 1142
カブスギル
Cavusgil, S.Tamer 238
カプストカ
Kapustka, Bartosz 703
カブース・ビン・サイド
Qaboos bin Said 1142
カプーゾ
Capuzzo, Michael 224
カプソン
Capuçon, Gautier 224
Capuçon, Renaud 224
ガフター
Gafter, Neal 471
カブタラゼ
Kavtaradze, Georgi 711
カプタリ
Captari, Dumitru 224
カプチャク
Kaptchuk, Ted 703
カプチャック
Kupchak, Mitch 774
カプチャン
Kupchan, Charles A. 774
カプチュフ
Kaptyukh, Vasiliy 703
カプチーリ
Capucilli, Alyssa Satin 224
ガーフット
Garfoot, Katrin 480
ガプティル
Guptill, Arthur Leighton 547
カプティン
Kaputin, John 703
カプデビラ
Capdevila i Valls, Roser 222
カプート
Caputo, John D. 224
Caputo, Mike 224
Caputo, Robert 224
カプトゥ
Kaput, Victor Makwenge 703
カプトゥム
Kaptoum, Wilfrid 703

カプナー
Kapner, Arne 703
Kapner, Mitchell 703
ガフナー
Gafner, George 471
カブバティ
Cavubati, Tevita 238
カプフェレ
Kapferer, Jean-Noël 702
カフムカチェ
Kafumukache, Patrick 695
カプヤ
Kapuya, Juma 703
カブラ
Cabra, Raul 212
カプラ
Capra, Fritjof 223
Capra, Greg 223
Capra, Nick 223
カプラー
Kappler, Chris 703
Kappler, John 703
ガーブラー
Gabler, Hans Walter 469
カプライ
Caprai, Luca 223
カープラス
Karplus, Martin 706
カプラノス
Kapranos, Alex 703
カプラノワ
Kapranova, Olga 703
カプラーリ
Caprari, Gianluca 223
カブラル
Cabral, Donald 212
Cabral, Esperanza 212
Cabral, Gustavo 212
Cabral, Johnathan 212
Cabral, Marcelino Simaõ Lopes 212
Cabral, Maria da Conceicao Nobre 212
Cabral, Sérgio 212
カプラロフ
Kapralov, Andrey 703
カプラン
Caplan, Bryan Douglas 223
Caplan, Jeremy B. 223
Caplan, Louis R. 223
Caplan, Mariana 223
Caplan, Paula J. 223
Caplan, Richard 223
Caplan, Stephen 223
Kaplan, Amy 702
Kaplan, Avi 702
Kaplan, Bruce Eric 702
Kaplan, Candia P. 702
Kaplan, Caren 702
Kaplan, David E. 703
Kaplan, Ellen 703
Kaplan, Eugene H. 703
Kaplan, Frédéric 703
Kaplan, Helmut Friedrich 703
Kaplan, Hester 703
Kaplan, James 703
Kaplan, Jerry 703
Kaplan, Jonathan 703
Kaplan, Lawrence F. 703
Kaplan, Lisa 703
Kaplan, Martin M. 703
Kaplan, Matthew S. 703
Kaplan, Mehmet 703
Kaplan, Michael 703
Kaplan, Michael B. 703
Kaplan, Mitchell 703
Kaplan, Paul E. 703
Kaplan, Rachel 703
Kaplan, Robert 703
Kaplan, Robert D. 703
Kaplan, Robert Steven 703
Kaplan, Sarah 703
Kaplan, Soren 703
Kaplan, Stanley H. 703
Kaplan, Stephen 703
Kaplan, Steve 703
Kaplan, Steven L. 703
Kaplan, Temma 703
Kaplan, Wendy 703
Kaplan, William 703
カプランオール
Kaplanoglu, Semih 703
カブリ
Kavli, Fred 711
ガフリ
al-Ghafri, Muhammad 492
カプリアティ
Capriati, Jennifer 223
カプリイオリウ
Caprioriu, Corina 223
ガブリエ
Gabilliet, Jean-Paul 469
ガブリエウ
Gabriel 470
Gabriel, Barbosa 470
Gabriel, Silva 470
ガブリエッラ
Mészáros, Gabriella 939
ガブリエリ
Gabrielli, Gabrielle K. 470
ガブリエリャン
Gabrielyan, Vache 470
ガブリエル
Gabriel, Eberhard 470
Gabriel, Jacques 470
Gabriel, J.C. 470
Gabriel, Jon 470
Gabriel, Kristin 470
Gabriel, Markus 470
Gabriel, Mike 470
Gabriel, Peter 470
Gabriel, Sigmar 470
Gabriel, Wenyen 470
Gabriels, Jaak 470
ガブリエルセン
Gabrielsen, Ansgar 470
ガブリエルソン
Gabrielsson, Alf 470
Gabrielsson, Eva 470
カプリオ
Caprio, Mark 223
カプリオリウ
Caprioriu, Corina 223
カプリオーロ
Capriolo, Edward 223
カブリサス・ルイス
Cabrisas Ruiz, Ricardo 212
カプリス
Kapris, Gabriel 703
カブリタ
Cabrita, Eduardo 212
ガブリリディス
Gavriilidis, Ioannis 484
ガブリリュク
Gavriljuk, Nina 484
Gavrylyuk, Alexander 485
ガブリレスク
Gavrilescu, Graţiela 484
ガブリロワ
Gavrilova, Daria 485
カプリン
Caplin, Andrew 223
カブール
Kaboul, Younes 694
カプール
Kapoor, Anish 703
Kapur, Shekhar 703
ガフール
Ghafoor, Ahmed Adheeb Abdul 492
カプルス
Couples, Fred 295
カプルズ
Couples, Fred 295
カプルソ
Capurso, Marta 224
カブレ
Kabre, David 694
カプレッツ
Caprez, Andrea 223
カプレッティ
Capretti, Elena 223
カプレット
Couplet, English 295
カプレニク
Kaplanek, Beth A. 703
カブレラ
Cabrera, Alfredo 212
Cabrera, Angel 212
Cabrera, Asdrubal 212
Cabrera, Everth 212
Cabrera, Francisco 212
Cabrera, Jane 212
Cabrera, José Alfonso 212
Cabrera, Juan Carlos 212
Cabrera, Luis 212
Cabrera, Mauricio 212
Cabrera, Melky 212
Cabrera, Mercedes 212
Cabrera, Miguel 212
Cabrera, Noel 212
Cabrera, Ramon 212
カブレラ・インファンテ
Cabrera Infante, Guillermo 212
カブレラ・ダルケア
Cabrera Darquea, Javier 212
カブレラ・フランコ
Cabrera Franco, Jafeth Ernesto 212
カブレラベロ
Cabrera Bello, Rafa 212
カプロ
Capullo, Greg 224
カプロー
Kapleau, Philip 703
Kaprow, Allan 703
カプロウィッツ
Kaplowitz, Robert 703
ガブログル
Gacroglou, Konstantinos 470
ガブロン
Gavron, Robert 485
カブワジエレ
Kabwegyere, Tarsis 694
カフーン
Cahoon, Heather 213
Colquhoun, Ian 280
ガフング
Gahungu, Athanase 471
カフンブ
Kahumbu, Paula 696
ガフンホルト
Gavnholt, Kristina 484
カベ
Cavet, Benjamin 238
ガーベ
Gervais, Cedric 492
ガペエフ
Gapeev, Vasily I. 477
カベゲ
Kavégué, Dovi 711
カベサス
Cabezas, Bryan 212
Cabezas, Rodrigo 212
Cavezas, Hugo 238
カベシナ
Cabecinha, Ana 212
カペジャ
Capella, Roger 222
カベージョ
Cabello, José David 212
カベジョ
Cabello, Diosdado 212
Cabello, José David 212
カベスード
Cabezudo, Alicia 212
ガベソウ
Gavezou, Artemi 484
カペタノヴィッチ
Kapetanovic, Vlado 702
カベツキ
Kawecki, Radoslaw 711
カペッキ
Capecchi, Mario Renato 222
カーベック
Carbeck, Hank 224
ガベッタ
Gabetta, Sol 469
カペッツィ
Capezzi, Leonardo 223
ガーベット
Garbett, Lee 477
カペッリ
Cappelli, Peter 223
カペッロ
Capello, Fabio 223
カヘーテ
Cajete, Gregory 214
カヘーニ
Kahaney, Amelia 695
カペラ
Capela, Clint 222
Capella, Anthony 222
Cappella, Joseph N. 223
ガーベラ
Garbera, Katherine 477
カベリ
Kabeli, Cheryl 693
カペリ
Capelli, Vincenzo 223
カーヘル
Kágel, Mauricio Raúl 695
カーベル
Carvell, Kermit J. 232
カベル
Cabel, Eitan 212
カペール
Cappaert, Jeroen 223

カ

カペル
Kappl, Michael 703
ガベル
Gaber, Omar 469
Gaber, Slavko 469
カベルカ
Kaberuka, Donald 693
カペレ
Capelle, Donald 222
カペレッティ
Capelletti, Franco 222
カベロ
Cavero, Arturo 238
カペーロ
Cappello, Dominic 223
カペロ
Capello, Fabio 223
Cappello, Frank 223
カヘン
Kahane, Adam 695
ガーベン
Garben, Cord 477
カーペンター
Carpenter, Aaron 228
Carpenter, Amanda 228
Carpenter, Cameron 228
Carpenter, Chris 228
Carpenter, Christopher R. 228
Carpenter, Dan 228
Carpenter, David 228
Carpenter, Dona Rinaldi 228
Carpenter, Edmund Snow 228
Carpenter, Gregory S. 228
Carpenter, Humphrey 228
Carpenter, James 228
Carpenter, James Wyman 228
Carpenter, Jennifer N. 228
Carpenter, John 228
Carpenter, John T. 228
Carpenter, Judith M. 228
Carpenter, Kenneth John 228
Carpenter, Kim 228
Carpenter, Kip 228
Carpenter, Krickitt 228
Carpenter, Lea 228
Carpenter, Matt 228
Carpenter, Murray 228
Carpenter, Nancy 228
Carpenter, Phil 228
Carpenter, Richard 228
Carpenter, Scott 228
Carpenter, Stephanie L. 228
Carpenter, Ted Galen 228
Carpenter, Teresa 228
Carpenter, Thomas H. 228
カベンディッシュ
Cavendish, Mark 238
カーボ
Karbo, Karen 704
Kargbo, Franklyn 705
Kargbo, Ibrahim Ben 705
カーボー
Carbaugh, John E., Jr. 224
カボ
Cavo, Arlina 238
カボー
Cabaud, Jacques 212
ガボー
Gabor, Don 469
ガーボーア
Gabor, Zsa Zsa 469
カポウラス・サントス
Capoulas Santos, Luís 223
カポウラスサントス
Capoulas Santos, Luís 223
カボキサ
Kavokisa, Matuka 711
ガボサボ
Gabo Sabo, Maman Sani 469
カポダイ
Capodagli, Bill 223
カポダグリ
Capodagli, Bill 223
カポニーロ
Caponigro, Andrew 223
カボネカ
Kaboneka, Francis 693
ガポネンコ
Gaponenko, Konstantin 477
カポフィ
Kapofi, Frans 703
ガボーベ
Gabobe, Ahmed Hassan 469
ガボベ
Gabobe, Ahmed Hassan 469
カポラレ
Caporale, Antonieta 223
ガボリ
Gaborit-Chopin, Danielle 469
ガボリオ
Gaboriau, Linda 469
ガボリ＝ショパン
Gaborit-Chopin, Danielle 469
カポール
Kapor, Mitchell 703
ガボール
Gabor, Zsa Zsa 469
カポルーポ
Capolupo, Angela 223
カボレ
Kabore, Nayabtigungu Congo 693
Kabore, Noel 694
Kabore, Rene Emile 694
Kaboré, Roch 694
Kabore, Salif 694
Kaboré, Seydou 694
カボロ
Caboclo, Bruno 212
ガボワ
Gabova, Elena 470
カーボーン
Carbone, Elisa Lynn 224
カーマ
Khama, Ian 725
Khama, Seretse Khama Ian 725
Khama, Tshekedi 725
カマ
Kama, Rosalie 698
Kama, Steven 698
Kamah, Philip 698
カマー
Comer, Douglas E. 281
ガマ
Gama, Jaime 474
カーマイケル
Carmichael, Alistair 227
Carmichael, Chris 227
Carmichael, Emily 227
Carmichael, Jesse 227
Carmichael, John 227
Carmichael, Liz 227
Carmichael, Pete 227
Carmichael, Rachel 227
カマウ
Kamau, Jamleck 699
Kamau, Michael 699
ガマエル
Gemayel, Pierre 488
カマーク
Kamarck, Elaine Ciulla 699
ガマゲ
Gamage, Daya 474
Gamage, Piyasena 474
ガマゲー
Gamage, David Thenuwara 474
カマーゴ
Camargo, Johan 218
ガマーシー
al-Gamassi, Mohamed Abdul Ghani 475
ガマシ
al-Gamassi, Mohamed Abdul Ghani 475
ガマシー
al-Gamassi, Mohamed Abdul Ghani 475
ガーマス
Garmus, David 481
カマーチョ
Camacho, Ignacio 217
Camacho, José Antonio 217
カマチョ
Camacho, Hector 217
Camacho, José Antonio 217
Camacho, Jose Isidro 217
Camacho, Keith Lujan 217
ガマティー
Gamatié, Ali Badjo 475
ガマティエ
Gamatié, Ali Badjo 475
カマト
Kamath, Kundapur Vaman 699
カマナ
Kamana, Jean 699
Kamana, Vénant 699
カマーニ
Camagni, Jacopo 217
カマニ
Kamani, Bayano 699
Kamani, Titus 699
ガーマニー
Garmany, Tami Hutton 480
カマニアマユア
Kama-niamayoua, Rosalie 699
カマニョ
Camaño, Graciela 217
カマネティ
Caminiti, Ken 218
カマラ
Camara, Abdoul Kabélé 217
Camara, Abou 217
Camara, Aboubacar Titi 217
Camara, Albert Damantang 217
Camara, Alpha Kabine 217
Camara, Amedi 217
Camara, Baba 217
Camara, Chad 217
Camara, Cheick Amadou 217
Camara, Damantang Albert 217
Camara, Djene Saran 217
Camara, Eugene 217
Cámara, Eva Minguet 217
Camara, Fatou Sike 217
Cámara, Javier 217
Camara, Kandia 217
Camara, Loucény 217
Camara, Lousény 217
Camara, Madikaba 217
Camara, Mady Kaba 217
Camara, Makalé 217
Camara, Mamadouba Toto 217
Camara, Mamadou Toto 217
Camara, Morikè Damaro 217
Camara, Moussa Dadis 217
Camara, Oumou 217
Camara, Sekou Decazie 218
Camara, Sheik Amadou 218
Camara, Yamoussa 218
Kamala, Diodorus Buberwa 698
Kamara, Alimamy 699
Kamara, Boimah 699
Kamara, Dauda Sulaiman 699
Kamara, Joseph 699
Kamara, Lamine 699
Kamara, Losseni 699
Kamara, Mariatu 699
Kamara, Marjon 699
Kamara, Paul 699
Kamara, Samura 699
Kamara, Victoria Saidu 699
ガマラ
Gamarra, Carlos 475
カマラサ
Camarasa, Victor 218
カマラス
Kamaras, Mate 699
カマリ
Kamali, Hosein 699
カマリロ
Camarillo, Gonzalo 218
カマル
Kamal, Abubaker Ali 698
Kamal, Muhammad 698
Kamal, Mustafa 698
Kamal, Osama 698
Kamal, Yousef Hussain 698
Kamal, Zahiera 698
Kamalu, Ufomba 699
Kamar, Ahmed 699
Kamarou, Fassassi 699
Qamar, Naveed 1142
Qamar, Syed Naveed 1142
ガマル
Al-gamal, Yousry Sabry 474

カマルゴ
Camargo, Daniel 218
Camargo, Milton 218
カマールディーン
Kamaaludeen, Abdulla 698
Kamaludeen, Abdulla 699
カマルディーン
Kamaluddeen, Abdulla 699
ガマワン
Gamawan, Fauzi 475
カーマン
Carman, Patrick 227
Kerman, Joseph 721
Kurman, Melba 775
カマンジ
Kamanzi, Pauni 699
Kamanzi, Stanislas 699
カマンダ
Kamanda, Gérard 699
Kamanda, Kama Sywor 699
Kamanda, Maina 699
カーミ
Carmi, Tali 227
カミー
Kammie, George 700
ガミー
Ghaemi, S.Nassir 492
カミイ
Kamii, Constance 699
カミオ
Kamio, Mayuko 700
カミオンコウスキー
Kamionkowski, Marc 700
カミサ
Khamisa, Bob 725
カミース
Khamis, Samir Mohamed 725
カミソコカマラ
Kamissoko Camara, Kandia 700
カミータ
Kameeta, Zephania 699
カミタツ・エツ
Kamitatu Etsu, Olivier 700
カミタツエツ
Kamitatu Etsu, Olivier 700
カーミッシェル
Carmichael, Clay 227
カミッレーリ
Camilleri, Andrea 218
カミナ
Kamina, Pierre 699
カミナー
Kaminer, Debra B. 699
ガミナラ
Gaminara, Juan Manuel 475
カミニティ
Caminiti, Ken 218
カミニティー
Caminiti, Ken 218
カミノフ
Kaminoff, Leslie 699
カミュ
Camus, Philippe 220
カミラ
Camilla 218
カミラ・ハニファ
Kamilah Hanifah 699
カミラ夫人
Camilla 218
カミリエリ
Camillieri, Martine 218
カミリオネア
Chamillionaire 243
カミール
Camille, Michael 218
カミル
Kamil, Mohammed Abdullahi 699
Khamil, Mohamed Ali 725
カミルモハメド
Kamil Mohamed, Abdoulkader 699
カミレーリ
Camilleri, Joseph A. 218
カミレリ
Camilleri, Louis C. 218
カミロ
Camillo, Chris 218
Camilo, Jeannet 218
Camilo, Michel 218
Camilo, Tiago 218
カミロフ
Kamilov, Abdulaziz 699
カーミン
Karmin, Craig 705
カミング
Cumming, Andrew 307
Cumming, Catherine 307
Cumming, Charles 307
Cumming, Hannah 307
Cumming, Heather 307
Cumming, Robert 307
カミングス
Cumings, Bruce 307
Cummings, Constance 307
Cummings, E.Mark 307
Cummings, John Hedley 307
Cummings, Lindsay 307
Cummings, Phil 307
Cummings, Rhoda Woods 307
Cummings, Steven R. 307
カミングズ
Cummings, Joe 307
Cummings, Priscilla 307
カミンズ
Comins, Neil F. 281
Cummins, Jim 307
カミンスキ
Kamiński, Mariusz 699
Kaminski, Mateusz 699
Kaminski, Michael D. 699
Kaminski, Patricia 700
Kaminsky, Philip 700
カミンスキー
Kaminski, Anneliese 699
Kaminski, Janusz 699
Kaminsky, Dan"Effugas" 700
Kaminsky, Frank 700
Kaminsky, Howard 700
Kaminsky, Peter 700
Kaminsky, Philip 700
Kaminsky, Stuart 700
カーム
Calm, Bill 216
カム
Cam, Nguyen Manh 217
Kam, Okko 698
Kam, Peter 698
Kam, Woo-sung 698
ガム
Gamm, Annett 475
カムイ
Kamwi, Richard 700
カムウアン
Khamouan, Boupha 725
カムキ
Kumkee, Waysang 773
ガムクレリゼ
Gamkrelidze, Amiran 475
カムクワンバ
Kamkwamba, William 700
カムゲ
Kamougue, Wadal Abdelkader 700
ガムザートフ
Gamzatov, Rasul Gamzatovich 475
ガムザトフ
Gamzatov, Rasul Gamzatovich 475
カムタイ
Khamtay, Siphandone 725
カム・チョン
Cam Trong 220
カムデン
Comden, Betty 281
カムドゥシュ
Camdessus, Michel Jean 218
カムドシュ
Camdessus, Michel Jean 218
カム・パカー
Lakkhanā Panwichai 783
ガムビーニ
Gambini, Rodolfo 475
カムベロバ
Kamberova, Reneta 699
カムマン
Cammann, Hans-Hermann 218
Khammanh, Sounvileuth 725
ガムラリ
Gamurari, Boris 475
カムリー
Comley, Nancy R. 281
ガムリエル
Gamliel, Gila 475
カムリン
Kamrin, Janice 700
カムロート
Khamlouad, Sitlakone 725
カムン
Kamoun, Mahamat 700
カムンコリ
Camuncoli, Giuseppe 220
カムントゥ
Kamuntu, Ephraim 700
ガメイロ
Gameiro, Kevin 475
ガメゼ
Gamedze, Christopher 475
ガメッゼ
Gamedze, Mgwagwa 475
カメニ
Kameni, Carlos 699
Kameni, Idriss 699
カメネッツ
Kamenetz, Anya 699
カメノス
Kammenos, Panos 700
カメホ
Arroyo Camejo, Silvia 61
Camejo, Ibrahim 218
カメラー
Kammerer, Doro 700
ガメラシュムイルコ
Gamera-shmyrko, Tetyana 475
カメリーノ
Camerino, Giuliana Coen 218
カメル
Kamal, Ibrahim 698
Kamel, Mohammed Ibrahim 699
Kamel, Tarek 699
Kamel, Yusuf Saad 699
ガメル
Gammel, Irene 475
ガメルトフト
Gammeltoft, Lone 475
カメレル
Knapek, Edina 747
カメロン
Cameron, Deborah 218
カーメン
Kamen, Dean 699
Kamen, Gary 699
Kamen, Gloria 699
Kamen, Martin David 699
Kamen, Paula 699
Kammen, Daniel M. 700
カメンスキー
Kamenskiy, Sergey 699
ガーメント
Garment, Leonard 480
ガモス
Gamos, Albert E. 475
カモソ
Kamotho, Joseph 700
カーモディー
Carmody, Isobelle 227
カーモード
Kermode, Frank 721
Kermode, Mark 721
カーモド
Kermode, Frank 721
カモード
Kermode, Frank 721
ガモネダ
Gamoneda, Antonio 475
カモレッティ
Camoletti, Marc 218
カモワン
Camoin, Philippe 218
カヤ
Kaya, Fatma Betul Sayan 711
ガヤ
Gaya, Jose Luis 485
カヤアルプ
Kayaalp, Riza 711
ガヤード
Gallardo, Yovani 473
カヤム
Kayam, Umar 711
カヤ・モヨ
Khaya Moyo, Simon 727
カヤリ
Kayali, Ahmad Qusay 711

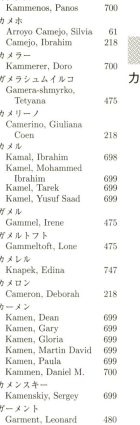

カヤルプ
Kayaalp, Riza 711
カヤン
Kayan, Cruetong 711
カヤンジャ
Kayanja, Robert 711
ガユーム
Gayoom, Maumoon Abdul 485
カヨデ
Kayode, Adetokunbo 712
Kayode, A.I. 712
カーラ
Kaarla, Riina 693
Kaarla, Sami 693
カーラー
Koehler, Lora 751
カラ
Calla, Davide 216
Kalla, Jusuf 698
Kalla, Yusuf 698
Kara, Mohamed Seghir 703
カラー
Culler, Jonathan 307
al-Qalaa, Sádallah Agha 1142
ガラ
Gala, Antonio 472
Gara, Larry 477
Gara, Lenna Mae 477
カーライ
Kállay, Dušan 698
ガライ
Galai, Dan 472
Garai, Romola 477
Garay, Ezequiel 477
Garay, Ricardo 477
カーライオン
Carlyon, Julian 227
ガライサバル
Garaizabal, Cristina 477
カライツァ
Kalaica, Branimir 697
ガライド
Galaid, Ali Khalif 472
カーライナー
Carliner, Saul 226
ガライラ
Gharaira, Al-Mabrouk 493
カーライル
Carlisle, Bill 226
Carlisle, James B. 226
Carlisle, Kate 226
Carlisle, Liz 226
Carlisle, Rick 226
Carlyle, Liz 227
Carlyle, Marie-Claire 227
Carlyle, Robert 227
Carlyle, Warren 227
カライル
Kallayil, Gopi 698
カラウ
Karau, Holden 704
カラヴァン
Karavan, Dani 704
ガラヴォッリャ
Garavoglia, Rosa Anna 477
カラエフ
Garayev, Abulfaz 477
ガラエワ
Garayeva, Aliya 477
カラオグル
Karaoglou, Theodoros 704
カラオスマオール
Karaosmanoğlu, Attila 704
カラオスマンオル
Karaosmanoğlu, Attila 704
カラオラノ
Calahorrano, Miguel 214
カラカシュ
Karakas, Hedvig 704
カラカス
Karakas, Hedvig 704
カラカセビッチ
Karakasevic, Aleksandar 704
カラキ
Karaki, Khaled 704
カラグソワ
Karagusova, Gulzhana 704
カラケ
Qaraqa, Isa 1142
カラゴズ
Karagoz, Nurdan 704
カラコチ
Karakoc, Nur 704
カラザス
Karatzas, Ioannis 704
カラシェフ
Karashev, Aaly 704
ガラジオラ
Garagiola, Joe 477
カラーシク
Karasik, Yulii 704
カラシク
Karasik, Yulii 704
カラシック
Karasik, Judy 704
Karasik, Paul 704
カラジッチ
Karadžić, Radovan 704
カラシニコフ
Kalashnikov, Mikhail Timofeevich 697
ガラジャエフ
Garajayev, Annageldi 477
カラジョバ
Karadjova, Nona 703
カラショフ
Karasyov, Carrie Doyle 704
カラジョワ
Karadjova, Nona 703
カラシン
Karasin, Grigory 704
カラジンスカヤ
Kaladzinskaya, Vanesa 697
カラス
Kallas, Siim 698
Karas, G.Brian 704
Karas, Joža 704
Karras, Alex 706
Karras, Ted 706
Kharas, Homi J. 726
ガラス
Galas, Judith C. 472
カラスカラオ
Carascalão, Manuel Viegas 224
ガーラスキ
Garlaschi, Giacomo 480
カラスキジャ・バレラ
Carrasquilla Barrera, Alberto 229
カラスケル
Carrasquel, Chico 229
カラスコ
Carrasco, Carlos 229
Carrasco, Carlos Marx 229
Carrasco, Jesús 229
Carrasco, Marta 229
Carrasco, Yannick Ferreira 229
カラスコサ
Carrascosa, Ana 229
カラゼ
Kaladze, Kakha 697
ガラセ
Qarase, Laisenia 1142
カラソ
Carazo, Rodrigo 224
カラゾ
Carazo, Rodrigo 224
カラタ
Kalata, Anna 697
Kalata, Kurt 697
カラタイウド
Calatayud, Zulia 214
カラーチー
Corace, Jen 289
ガラチ
Galati, Simon Bulupiy 472
カラツォリス
Karatsolis, Loukas 704
カラックス
Carax, Leos 224
カラッソ
Calasso, Roberto 214
ガラッソー
Galasso, Francis S. 472
カラット
Carlat, Daniel J. 225
Currutt, Brian 309
ガラット
Garratt, James 481
カラティギナ
Karatygina, Margarita Ivanovna 704
カラティーニ
Caratini, Victor 224
カラディマ
Caladima, Ousmane 214
カラード
Calado, Carlos 214
ガラード
Garard, Charles 477
Garrard, Judith 481
ガラトプーロス
Galatopoulos, Stelios 472
カラトラバ
Calatrava, Santiago 214
ガラーナ
Garana, Zoheir 477
カラニシ
Kalanithi, Paul 697
ガラニチェフ
Garanichev, Evgeniy 477
カラニック
Kalanick, Travis 697
ガラーノ
Garano, Lorna 477
ガラノ
Garano, Lorna 477
カラノビッチ
Kalanović, Verica 697
カラノベ
Caranobe, Benoit 224
カラバ
Calaba, Jeannine Lemare 214
Kalaba, Harry 697
ガラハー
Gallagher, Thomas P. 473
カラバエワ
Karavaeva, Irina 704
カラバーシュ
Karabash, Mohamed Ahmed 703
カラバジョカブレラ
Caraballo Cabrera, Erwin Jose 224
ガラバノ
Garavano, Germán 477
カラハン
Callahan, Daniel 216
Callahan, David 216
Callahan, Kevin R. 216
カラバン
Karavan, Dani 704
カラビオット
Craviotto Rivero, Saul 300
カラビシ
Kalabish, Mohammed al-Tahir Abu 697
カラファティス
Kalafatis, Stavros 697
カラフェテアヌ
Calafeteanu, Valentin 214
カラブリア
Calabria, Davide 214
Calabria, Michael D. 214
カラプリス
Calaprice, Alice 214
カラブレイジ
Calabresi, Paul 214
カラブレシ
Calabresi, Linda 214
カラブレーセ
Calabrese, Lucas 214
カラブレーゼ
Calabrese, Omar 214
カラブレセ
Calabrese, Veronica 214
カラペチャン
Karapetyan, Karen 704
Karapetyan, Sergo 704
カラペティヤン
Karapetyan, Andranik 704
ガラーポ
Galapo, Ronit 472
ガラボス
Galambos, George 472
ガラポン
Garapon, Antoine 477
カラマ
Carama, Amedi 224
カラマギ
Karamagi, Nazir 704
カラマトフ
Karamatov, Hamidulla 704
カラマフォニ
Kalamafoni, Sione 697
ガラマラ
Gallamallah, Bouabdellah 473
Ghalamallah, Bouabdellah 492
カラマルコ

Karamarko, Tomislav 704
カラマンリス
Karamanlis, Konstantinos Alexandrou 704
Karamanlis, Kostas 704
カラーミ
Karami, Omar 704
カラーミー
Karami, Omar 704
カラミ
Karami, Ahmad 704
Karami, Faisal 704
Karami, Omar 704
Karami, Yousef 704
カラミアン
Kalamian, Rex 697
カラミトル
Caramitru, Ion 224
カラム
Cullum, Jamie 307
Kalam, Abdul 697
Karam, Antoine 704
Karam, Karam 704
Karam, Pete 704
Karam, Salim 704
カラムジーン
Karamzin, N.M. 704
カラムチャコワ
Karamchakova, Lidiya 704
カラムペロビッチ
Kalamperović, Jusuf 697
カラモイエツ
Kalamoyets, Siarhei 697
カラヤー
Kalaya, Sophonpanich 697
ガラヤニ・ワッタナ
Galyani Vadhana 474
ガラヤニ・ワッタナー
Galyani Vadhana 474
カラヤノプルー
Karagiannopoulou, Maria 704
カラヤン
Karajan, Eliette von 704
Karajan, Herbert Von 704
Karayan, Suren 704
カラーラ
Carrara, Vera 229
カララ
Kalala, Marie-Madeleine 697
カラリ
al-Qalallie, Abdul-Salam 1142
カラリヤダ
Karalliyadda, Tissa 704
カラリヤッダ
Karalliyadda, Tissa 704
ガラルサ
Galarza, Mariano 472
ガラルサ・コントレラス
Galarza Contreras, Elsa Patricia 472
カラルス
Karalus, Paul 704
カラルデ
Kalaldeh, Khaled al 697
Kalaldeh, Mohammad 697
ガラワンジ
Ghalawanji, Omar Ibahim 493
カーラン
Karlan, Dean S. 705
カラン
Calan, Ronan de 214
Calin, Rodolphe 215
Curran, Bob 309
Curran, Charles E. 309
Curran, Colleen 309
Curran, James 309
Curran, Jim 309
Curran, John 309
Curran, Paul 309
Curran, Peter Ferguson 309
Curran, Robert 309
Curran, Tina 309
Karan, Pradyumna Prasad 704
ガラン
Galan, Giancarlo 472
Galán, Rafael 472
Galant, Jacqueline 472
Garang, John 477
カランカ
Karanka, Aitor 704
カランサ
Carranza, Andreu 229
Carranza, Jorge 229
Carranza, Victor 229
カランザ
Carranza, Fermin A. 229
カランサ・ウガルテ
Carranza Ugarte, Luis 229
カランザサロリ
Carranza Saroli, Cecilia 229
カラン・シン
Karan Singh 704
カーランスキー
Kurlansky, Mark 775
ガランダロフ
Galandarov, Bashimklych 472
ガランチャ
Garanča, Elina 477
カランツィス
Kalantzis, George 697
Kalantzis, Georgios 697
カランデ
Karande, Mohnaz Ashish 704
ガランテ
Galante, Cecilia 472
カーランド
Kurland, Lynn 775
ガーランド
Garland, Alex 480
Garland, Ben 480
Garland, Brent 480
Garland, Caroline 480
Garland, David 480
Garland, Hank 480
Garland, Michael 480
Garland, Robert 480
Garland, Sarah 480
Gerland, Gunilla 490
ガラント
Galant, Yoav 472
ガランド
Galland, Richard Wolfrik 473
ガラントリー
Gallantree, Rebecca 473
カランドレリ
Calandrelli, Jorge 214
カランバル
Karambal, Ahmat Mahamat 704
カランブララウリク
Carambula Raurich, Adrian Ignacio 224
カランペロビッチ
Kalamperović, Jusuf 697
カーリー
Carey, Andy 225
Carley, Kathleen M. 226
Cary, Phoebe 232
Curlee, Pamela 308
Curley, Christopher 308
Curley, Marianne 308
Curley, Steven A. 308
Curley, Thomas 309
Curley, Tom 309
Currie, Lauren 309
Kerley, Jeremy 721
カリ
Calì, Davide 215
カリー
Carey, Vincent J. 225
Carrie, Allan 229
Currey, Anna 309
Currey, Mason 309
Currie, Justin 309
Currie, Ron, Jr. 309
Curry, Adam 309
Curry, Constance 309
Curry, Jay 309
Curry, Jeffrey E. 309
Curry, Seth 309
Curry, Stephen 309
Curry, Vinny 309
Kalinin, Anatoly N. 697
Kállay, Dušan 698
ガーリ
Ghali, Nadia Youssef 493
ガーリー
Ghali, Amin 493
Gurley, Bill 547
Gurley, James 547
Gurley, Nan 547
Gurley, Todd 547
ガリ
Galli, Mauro 473
Gary, Roba 482
Ghali, Boutros Boutros 493
Ghali, Youssef Boutros 493
ガリー
Galli, Richard 473
Golley, Gregory 512
Gulli, Andrew F. 545
Gulli, Lamia 545
カリア
Calia, Charles Laird 215
Karia, Akash 705
Karia, Jayantilal M. 705
カリアー
Kallir, Jane 698
Karier, Thomas Mark 705
ガリア
Galea, Censu 472
Galea, Louis 472
Garia, Adrian 480
カーリアイネン
Kääriäinen, Seppo 693
カーリアス
Callias, Maria 216
カリアス
Callias, Aurore 216
Carías, Durval 225
Carias, Euda 225
ガリアッツォ
Galiazzo, Marco 472
カリアティ
Kaliati, Patricia Anne 697
ガリアーノ
Galliano, John 473
ガリアルド
Gagliardo, Antonio 471
カリアンプル
Kallianpur, Amy 698
カーリイ
Kerley, Jack 721
カリウ
Cariou, A. 225
Cariou, Marie 225
カリヴァン
Currivan, Jude 309
カリウキ
Kariuki, Sicily 705
カリウス
Carius, Otto 225
Karius, Loris 705
カリエ
Carrié, Jean 229
ガリエ
Garrier, Gilbert 481
カリエール
Carrière, Beate 229
Carrière, Jean-Claude 229
カリエル
Kaliel, Mohammadu Bello 697
カリエワ
Kaliyeva, Sholpan 698
ガリエンヌ
Gallienne, Guillaume 474
カリオーティ
Caglioti, Giuseppe 213
カリオラート
Cariolato, Alfonso 225
カリオン
Carion, Christian 225
Carrión, Raúl 230
カリガリス
Calligaris, Contardo 216
ガリキオ
Gallicchio, Marc S. 474
カリキス
Karikis, Mikhail 705
ガリク
Gallik, Andy 474
ガリグ
Garrigue, Anne 481
カリクス・フィゲロア
Calix Figueroa, Ramon 215
カリクルブ
Karikurubu, Charles 705
カリサレス
Carrizales, Ramon Alonzo 230
カリサレス・レンヒフォ
Carrizales Rengifo, Ramón 230
カリシェイン
Calishain, Tara 215
ガリシェワ
Galysheva, Yulia 474
カリシュ
Kalisz, Ryszard 697
カリジューリ
Caligiuri, Daniel 215

カリージョ
Carrillo, Andre 229
Carrillo, Edna 229
Carrillo, Guido 230
カリジョ
Carrillo, Federico 229
カリジョ・フロレス
Carrillo Flórez, Fernando 230
カーリス
Carlis, Zamir 226
カリス
Kaliss, Jeff 697
Kallis, Aristotle A. 698
カリスカ
Kaliska, Elena 697
カリスカン
Caliskan, Tuncay 215
カリス・スズキ
Cullis-Suzuki, Severn 307
カリス＝スズキ
Cullis-Suzuki, Severn 307
カリスト
Calixte, Pierre-Claude 216
Callisto, Nicole 216
カリズナー
Karizna, Ivan 705
カーリスリー
Carlisle, Amir 226
カリーゼ
Calise, Mauro 215
カリーソ
Carrico, Daniel 229
Carrizo, Juan Pablo 230
ガリソ
Gallissot, Romain 474
カリソン
Callison, Johnny 216
ガリソン
Garrison, Barbara 481
ガリターノ
Garitano, Gaizka 480
ガリチェンコ
Gal'chenko, Ekaterina Mikhailovna 472
カリチューン
Callichurn, Soodesh Satkam 216
ガリツィン
Galitzine, Irene 473
ガリツカヤ
Galitskaya, Elena 473
カリック
Calic, Edouard 215
ガーリック
Garlick, Mark Antony 480
カリッシュ
Kalich, Richard 697
Kalich, Robert Allen 697
カリッチマン
Kalichman, Seth C. 697
カーリッツ
Karlitz, Gail 705
ガリッツ
Galitz, Cathleen 473
ガリット
Galite, John La 473
ガリッリ
Garilli, Alessia 480
カリテ
Kalite, Joseph 697
カリディ
Qaridi, Abdiaziz Mukhtar 1142
カリティディ
Kharitidi, Olga 727
ガリード
Garrido, Paulo Ivo 481
ガリドレカ
Garrido Lecca, Hernán 481
カリーナ
Karina, Anna 705
カリナ
Kalina, Yuliya 697
ガリナリ
Gallinari, Danilo 474
カリーニ
Carini, Patricia F. 225
カリニコス
Callinicos, Alex 216
カリニッチ
Kalinic, Nikola 697
カリーニナ
Kalinina, Valentina Aleksandrovna 697
カリニャーク
Kaliňák, Robert 697
カリニャーニ
Carignani, Paolo 225
ガリーノ
Garino, Patricio 480
カリノフスキ
Kalinowski, Jarosław 697
カリバー
Culliver, Chris 307
ガリバー
Gulliver, Amanda 545
ガリバシビリ
Garibashvili, Irakli 480
カリバタ
Kalibata, Agnes 697
ガリバラ
Garibay, Victor Manuel Estrada 480
ガリーブ
Gharib, Riyad 493
ガリブ
Ghalib, Habibullah 493
Gharib, Jaouad 493
カリファ
Kalifa, Dominique 697
Khalifa, M'hamed 725
カリフィア
Califia, Pat 215
カリプソ
Calypso, Gnobo A. 217
ガーリー・ブラウン
Gurley Brown, Helen 547
カリフングワ
Kalifungwa, Patrick 697
カリポット
Karippot, Anoop 705
ガリボフ
Garibov, Emin 480
カリマ
Kalima, Victoria 697
カリミ
Karimi, Rahim 705
カリミマチアニ
Karimimachiani, Alireza Mohammad 705
カリム
Karim, Fazal 705
Karim, Rafiatou 705
カリムジャノフ
Karimzhanov, Nurzhan 705
カリムメッカスア
Meckassoua, Abdou Karim 928
カリムルー
Karimloo, Ramin 705
カリモフ
Karimov, Islam Abduganievich 705
Karimov, Majid 705
Karimov, Tarlan 705
ガリヤ
Ghaliyah, bint Muhammad al-Thani 493
ガリャイ
Gallay, Ana 473
カリャーキン
Kariakin, Iurii 705
カリャーギン
Kalyagin, Aleksandr Aleksandrovich 698
カリヤーギン
Kalyagin, Aleksandr Aleksandrovich 698
ガリャルディーニ
Gagliardini, Roberto 471
ガリャルドン
Gallardón, Alberto Ruiz 473
カリヤワサム
Kariyawasam, Akila Viraj 705
カリユステ
Kaljuste, Tõnu 698
カリユライド
Kaljulaid, Kersti 698
カリユランド
Kaljurand, Marina 698
カリラーニ
Kalilani, Jean 697
Kalilani, Jean Alfazema Nachika 697
カリーリョ
Carrillo, Santiago 230
カリリョ
Carrillo, Santiago 230
カリル
Abir Abdelrahman, Khalil Mahmoud K 7
Caryl, Christian 232
Käläntär, Kälil 697
Kalil, Matt 697
Kalil, Ryan 697
Khalil, Yaacob 725
ガリレア
Galilea, José Antonio 472
Galilea, Thomás Mecheba Fernández 472
カリロフ
Kalilov, Zhamshitbek 697
カーリーン
Carleen, Sally 226
カーリン
Carlin, George 226
Carlin, Jazz 226
Carlin, John 226
Carlin, John W. 226
Carlin, Laura 226
Carlin, Peter Ames 226
Carlin, Robert 226
Carline, Jan D. 226
Kerlin, Michael 721
カリン
Cullen, Dave 307
Cullin, Mitch 307
ガーリン
Galin, Alexander 472
カリンガム
Callingham, Glyn 216
カリンジアン
Kalindjian, Claudia 697
カリンシュ
Karinš, Krišjanis 705
カーリンズ
Karlins, Marvin 705
カーリンスキー
Karlinsky, Simon 705
ガリンスキー
Galinsky, Ellen 473
カリンチ
Karinch, Maryann 705
カリンデ
Kalinde, Anita 697
ガリンド
Galindo, José Antonio 472
Galindo, Regina José 473
カリントン
Carrington, Leonora 230
ガリン・ヌグロホ
Garin Nugroho 480
ガリンベルティ
Galimberti, Gabriele 472
Galimberti, Umberto 472
カール
Carl, Joanna 225
Carl, Klaus H. 225
Carl, William J., Jr. 225
Carle, Eric 226
Carle, Shane 226
Curl, R.F. 308
Kahl, Virginia 695
Kahle, Dave 695
Kahle, Werner 695
Karl, Beatrix 705
Karl, Benjamin 705
Karl, Wilhelm 705
Karle, Jerome 705
Kuhl, Patricia Katherine 771
Kurrle, Susan 775
カル
Cal, David 214
Calle, Carlos I. 216
Calle, Sophie 216
Cull, Brian 307
Karr, Jean-Alphonse 706
Khar, Hina Rabbani 726
カルー
Carew, David 225
Carew, Francis M. 225
Kalou, Salomon 698
ガール
Garr, Sherry B. 481
ガル
Gal, Csaba 472
Gal, Robert 472
Gal, Sandra 472
Gal, Uziel 472
Gall, Michel 473
Garu, Moses 482
カール16世
Carl XVI 225
カルア
Karua, Martha 706
ガルア

Garoua, Adoum 481
カルアナ
Caruana, Wally 232
カルイエフ
Kalyev, Bakytbek 698
ガルイナンディ
Galuinadi, Jonetani 474
ガルウ
Galloux, Patrick 474
カルヴァート
Kalvert, Scott 698
カルヴァーリョ
Carvalho, Bernardo 232
ガルヴァン
Galvin, Matthew 474
カルヴィン
Calvin, William H. 217
ガルヴィン
Galvin, Robert William 474
カルヴェ
Calvet, Corinne 217
Calvet, Louis Jean 217
ガルウェイ
Gallwey, W.Timothy 474
カルウェオ
Kalweo, Jackson 698
カルヴェッティ
Calvetti, Leonello 217
Calvetti, Paola 217
カルウェル
Culwell, Christopher 307
カルヴェン
Carven, Marie-Louise 232
Karven, Ursula 706
カルヴォコレッシ
Calvocoressi, Peter 217
Calvocoressi, Richard 217
カルヴォコレッシー
Calvocoressi, Peter 217
カルヴォネン
Karvonen, Inkeri 706
ガルガーウィ
al-Gergawi, Mohammed Abdullah 490
ガルガウシャヌ
Gargaud Chanut, Denis 480
カルカサスカロシル
Carcasses Kalosil, Moana 224
ガルガーシュ
Gargash, Anwar Mohammed 480
カルカセス
Carcasses Kalosil, Moana 224
カルカテラ
Carcaterra, Lorenzo 224
カールガード
Karlgaard, Richard 705
カルカノ
Carcano, Luana 224
ガルガノ
Gargano, Reynaldo 480
カルガラマ
Karugarama, Tharcisse 706
カルガル
Kargar, Shaker 705
カルキ
Karki, Surendra Kumar 705
ガルキナ
Galkina, Gulnara 473
Galkina, Lioubov 473
カルキン
Qarqeen, Noor Mohammad 1142
カルキンズ
Calkins, Lucy 216
カルク
Kuyk, Jef J.van 776
ガルグ
Garg, Mridula 480
Garg, Vijay Kumar 480
ガルグム
Gargoum, Adoum 480
カールグレン
Carlgren, Andreas 226
カルゲ
Kharge, Mallikarjun 727
ガルコ
Galko, L'ubomír 473
ガルコーマ
Galkoma, Haider 473
カルサ
Khalsa, Shakta Kaur 725
Khalsa, Soram 725
カルサー
Khalsa, Mahan 725
ガルザー
Gulzar 545
カルザイ
Karzai, Ahmed Wali 706
Karzai, Hamid 706
カルサカウ
Kalsakau, Joshua 698
Kalsakau, Steven 698
カルサーダ
Calzada Mangues, Esteve 217
カルサダ・ロビロサ
Calzada Rovirosa, José Eduardo 217
カルサディジャ
Calzadilla, Pedro 217
カルザン
Carzan, Carlo 233
ガルサン
Garcin, Jérôme 479
ガルシーア
Garcia, Keith S. 478
Garcia, Rudi 478
ガルシア
Garcea, Nicky 477
Garcia, Adonis 477
Garcia, Alejandro L. 477
Garcia, Alejandro Ramirez 477
García, Alvaro 477
Garcia, Andy 477
Garcia, Anier 477
Garcia, Anthony 477, 478
Garcia, Avisail 478
Garcia, Caroline 478
Garcia, Catherine 478
Garcia, Cesar 478
Garcia, Charles Patrick 478
Garcia, Clóvis 478
García, Cristina 478
Garcia, Dave 478
Garcia, Dolores Balderamos 478
Garcia, Elniery 478
Garcia, Eric 478
García, Francisco Javier 478
García, Fravía 478
García, Genaro 478
Garcia, Gonzalo 478
Garcia, Greg 478
Garcia, Hanser 478
Garcia, Jaime 478
Garcia, Jarlin 478
Garcia, Jason 478
Garcia, Jon 478
García, Jorge 478
Garcia, Kami 478
García, Laura Gallego 478
Garcia, Leury 478
Garcia, Lucas 478
Garcia, Luis 478
Garcia, Manuel 478
Garcia, Marc 478
Garcia, Marci Frohock 478
Garcia, Marcilina S. 478
García, Marco Tulio 478
Garcia, Max 478
Garcia, Nina 478
García, Norman 478
Garcia, Paulina 478
García, Pedro 478
Garcia, Rodorigo 478
Garcia, Rudi 478
Garcia, Samuel Ruiz 478
Garcia, Santiago 478
Garcia, Sergio 478
Garcia, Ulisses 478
Garcia, Willy 478
Garcia, Yimi 478
Garcia Bragado, Jesus Angel 478
Garcia Hemme, Nicolas 478
Garcia Navarro, Ivan 479
García Pérez, Alan Gabriel 479
García Puigcerver, Héctor 479
ガルシア＝アコスタ
Garcia-Acosta, Virginia 478
ガルシア・コチャグネ
Garcia Cochagne, Manuela Esperanza 478
ガルシアコレイア
Garcia Correia, Olavo Avelino 478
ガルシアサヤン
García Sayán, Diego 479
ガルシア・セデニョ
García Cedeño, Walter 478
ガルシア・セバスティアン
García Sebastián, M. 479
ガルシア・デ・アルノルド
García de Arnold, María Liz 478
ガルシア・テヘリーナ
García Tejerina, Isabel 479
ガルシアテヘリーナ
García Tejerina, Isabel 479
ガルシア・デ・ラ・クルス
Garcia de la Cruz, Berenice 478
ガルシア・トゥサン
García Toussaintt, Juan 479
ガルシア・トオマ
García Toma, Víctor Oscar Shiyin 479
ガルシア・フォレス
Garcia Forés, David 478
ガルシア・フネグラ
García Funegra, Patricia 478
ガルシアブリト
Garcia Brito, Luis Alberto 478
ガルシア・ベラ
García Vera, Yadira 479
ガルシア・ベラウンデ
García Belaúnde, José Antonio 478
ガルシア・ベルランガ
García-Berlanga, Luis 478
ガルシア・ペレス
García Pérez, Alan Gabriel 479
ガルシア・マーチン
García-Martín, Miguel A. 478
ガルシア - マーチン
García-Martín, Miguel A. 478
ガルシアマルガリョ
García-margallo, José Manuel 478
ガルシア・マルケス
García Márquez, Gabriel 478
ガルシアメンドーサ
Garcia Mendoza, Alex Maxell 478
ガルシア・モラレス
García Morales, Adelaida 479
García Morales, Aldo Estuardo 479
ガルシア・ラミレス
García Ramírez, Orlando Celso 479
ガルシア・リネラ
García Linera, Álvaro Marcelo 478
ガルシア・レガス・ポンセ
García-Legaz Ponce, Jaime 478
ガルシェ
Garesché, Juliette 480
カルシェッド
Kalsched, Donald 698
カルシガ
Quarshigah, Courage 1143
ガルシカ
Galushka, Alexander S. 474
ガルジャーニ
Gargiani, Roberto 480
カルシュ
Karsch, Monika 706
カールション
Karlsson, Kristian 705
カールズ
Karls, James M. 705
カルース
Carruth, Hayden 230
Caruth, Cathy 232
ガルスチャン
Galstyan, Arsen 474
Galstyan, Vaghinak 474
Galustyan, Karen 474
ガルステア
Garştea, Mihail 482
ガルスティアン
Galustian, Alfred 474
カールステン
Karsten, Gunther 706

カルステン
Karsten, Ekaterina 706
Karsten, Uwe 706
カルステンス
Carstens, Agustin 231
Carstens Salceda, Carolena 231
Karstens, Anke 706
カルステンス・カルステンス
Carstens Carstens, Agustín 231
ガルストヤン
Galstyan, Arsen 474
カールストロム
Carlstrom, Nancy White 226
ガルセス・コルドバ
Garcés Córdoba, Mariana 477
ガルセス・ダシルバ
Garcés Da Silva, Francisco 477
カルセラ・ゴンサレス
Carcela-gonsalez, Mehdi 224
カルセル
Carcelle, Yves 224
カールセン
Carlsen, Magnus 226
カールセン・ブラッカー
Callsen-bracker, Jan-Ingwer 216
カルーソ
Caruso, Anthony 232
Caruso, David R. 232
カルソ
Caruso, Alex 232
カルソープ
Calthorpe, Peter 217
カールソン
Carleson, J.C. 226
Carlson, Barbara Z. 226
Carlson, Bruce M. 226
Carlson, Curtis Ray 226
Carlson, David A. 226
Carlson, Ed 226
Carlson, Jeff 226
Carlson, Jon 226
Carlson, Karen K. 226
Carlson, Kristine 226
Carlson, Lucas 226
Carlson, Matthew 226
Carlson, Melody 226
Carlson, Nancy L. 226
Carlson, Natalie Savage 226
Carlson, Neil R. 226
Carlson, Nicholas 226
Carlson, Richard 226
Carlson, Sam 226
Carlson, Stephan C. 226
Carlson, Timothy H. 226
Carlsson, Arvid 226
Carlsson, Gunilla 226
Carlsson, Gunnar E. 226
Karlsson, Björn 705
Karlsson, Ewert 705
Karlsson, Gunnar 705
Karlsson, Hans 705
Karlsson, Ida-Theres 705
Karlsson, Jan Ch. 705
Karlsson, Jan o 705
Karlsson, Mats Arne 705
Karlzon, Hanna 705
ガルソン
Garzón, Angelino 482
Garzon, Geandry 482
Garzón, Luis Eduardo 482
カルタ
Carta, Fabio 231
カルター
Coulter, Daniel 295
Cutler, Joel 310
カルダー
Calder, Alexander 215
Calder, Bobby J. 215
Calder, Ian R. 215
Calder, Kent E. 215
カルタジャヤ
Kartajaya, Hermawan 706
カルタショワ
Kartashova, Alena 706
カルダス
Caldas, Julio Castro 214
カルダノフ
Kardanov, Amiran 704
カルダヒ
Kordahi, Jean-Louis 757
カルタホワ
Kartashova, Alena 706
カルダマ
Cardama, María Placer 224
カルタミハルジャ
Kartamihardja, Achdiat 706
ガルダメス
Galdámez, José Antonio 472
カルダラ
Caldara, Mattia 214
ガルタル
Gantar, Tomáž 476
カルタレスク
Cărtărescu, Mircea 231
カルダレリ
Caldarelli, Guido 214
カルダン
Cardin, Pierre 224
カルタンマルク
Kaltenmark, Max 698
カルチェ
Calce, Antonio 214
カルチェフ
Kalchev, Dimitar 697
ガルチエリ
Galtieri, Leopoldo Fortunato 474
カルチェンコ
Karyuchenko, Dmytro 706
カルチコフ
Kartikov, Doszhan 706
カルツ
Karz, Devery 706
カルツァ
Calza, Gian Carlo 217
ガルッサリ
Ghaesalli, Mohamed Najem 492
ガルッツィ
Galluzzi, Paolo 474
カルティ
Karti, Ali Ahmed 706
Kurti, Richard 775
カルティエ・ブレッソン
Cartier-Bresson, Henri 232
ガルティエリ
Galtieri, Leopoldo Fortunato 474
カルディコット
Caldicott, Helen 215
カルディナーレ
Cardinale, Claudia 224
カルディナレ
Cardinale, Salvatore 224
ガルディーニ
Gardini, Ubaldo 479
Gardini, Walter 479
カルデイラカブラル
Caldeira Cabral, Manuel 215
カルディロ
Cardillo, Joseph 224
Cardillo, Linda 224
カルディローラ
Caldirola, Luca 215
カルテス・ハラ
Cartes Jara, Horacio Manuel 232
カルデナス
Cárdenas, Mauricio 224
Cardenas, Miguel 224
カルデナス・サンタ・マリア
Cárdenas Santa María, Mauricio 224
カルデナス・サンタマリア
Cárdenas Santa María, Mauricio 224
カルデナス・ヒメネス
Cárdenas Jiménez, Alberto 224
カルデナル
Cardenal, Juan Pablo 224
Cardenal, Luis 224
ガルデフ
Gardev, Javor 479
カルデラ
Caldera, Jesús 215
Caldera, Norman 215
Caldera, Rafael 215
ガルデラ
Gardella, André Antoine 479
Gardella, Danny 479
カルデラノ
Calderano, Hugo 215
カルデロリ
Calderoli, Roberto 215
カルデロン
Calderón, Felipe 215
Calderón, Gloria 215
Calderon, Jose 215
Calderón, Leonor 215
Calderon, Rafael 215
カルデロン・イノホサ
Calderón Hinojasa, Felipe de Jesús 215
カルテン
Karten, Toby J. 706
カルテンブラナー
Kaltenbrunner, Gabriele 698
カルデン・ローゼンフェルト
Kalden-Rosenfeld, Iris 697
カルドー
Kaldor, Mary 697
カルドウェル
Caldwell, Hilary 215
ガルトゥング
Galtung, Johan 474
カルトジア
Kartozia, Alexandre 706
ガルドシュ
Gardos, Florin 480
ガルドス
Gardos, Robert 480
カルドーゾ
Cardoso, Fernando Henrique 225
カルドソ
Cardoso, Boaventura 225
Cardoso, Higino 225
カルドゾ
Cardoso, Alberto 225
Cardoso, Fernando Henrique 225
Cardoso, Ruth 225
Cardoso, Santina 225
Cardozo, José Eduardo 225
カルドソ・ヒメネス
Cardozo Jiménez, Enzo 225
カルドーナ
Cardona, Christian 224
Cardona, Jose 224
カルドナ
Cardona, Manuel 224
Cardona, Marcel 224
Cardona, Maria Celeste 224
Cardona, Phillipe 225
Cardona, Ricardo 225
カルドナ・グティエレス
Cardona Gutiérrez, Germán 225
ガルドリシ
Galdorisi, George 472
カールトン
Carlton, Larry 227
Carlton, Vanessa 227
カルドン
Cardon, Dominique 224
Cardon, Laurent 224
ガルドン
Gordon, Grigoriĭ Borisovich 518
カルトンガ
Kaltongga, Bakoa 698
カルナー
Karner, Regina 706
カルナカラ
Karunakara, Unni 706
カルナップ
Carnap, Rudolf 227
カルナティラカ
Karunathilaka, Gayantha 706
カルナナヤケ
Karunanayake, Ravi 706
カルナラトナ
Karunaratne, Kusuma 706
カルナン
Culnan, Mary J. 307
ガルニエ
Garnier, Laurent 481
Garnier, Marie Josée 481
Garnier, Red 481
カルニエテ
Kalniete, Sandra 698
ガルニエリ
Guarnieri, Albina 541
ガルニエル
Garnier, Leonardo 481
カルニシュ
Kalnysh, Nataliya 698

Kalnysh, Natallia 698
カルニセロ
Carnicero, Susan 227
ガルニド
Guarnido, Juanjo 541
カルヌサムディ
Karnou-samedi, Nicaise 706
カルネイロ
Carneiro, Francisco Higino Lopes 227
カルネエフ
Karneyeu, Siarhei 706
カルネシ
Carnesi, Mônica 227
カルネジス
Karnezis, Orestis 706
Karnezis, Panos 706
ガルネリ
Guarneri, Mimi 541
カルーネン
Karhunen, Juha 705
カルノー
Carnot, Nicolas Leonard Sadi 227
ガルノー
Garneau, Marc 481
カルバー
Culver, Bruce 307
Culver, Gary 307
ガルバ
Garba, Almoustapha 477
Garba, Joseph Nanven 477
Garba, Salibou 477
カルパク
Karpak, Deniss 706
ガルバジャフンパ
Garba-jahumpa, Bala 477
カルバジョ
Carballo, María Elena 224
カルバス
Carbasse, Jean-Marie 224
ガルバーズ
Garbarz, Elie 477
Garbarz, Moshè 477
カルバスチ
Karbaschi, Gholamhossein 704
カルバーソン
Culberson, Charlie 307
カルパッチョ
Carpaccio, Federico 228
カルバート
Culbert, Timothy 307
Kalvert, Scott 698
カルパナ・スワミナタン
Kalpana Swaminathan 698
カルバーニ
al-Kalbani, Mohammed bin Said bin Saif 697
カルバハル
Carvajal, Daniel 232
Carvajal, Hugo 232
Carvajal, Paola 232
Carvajal, Víctor Hugo 232
カルバヨ
Calvalho, Arlindo de Ceita 217
ガルバリーノ
Garbarino, James 477
カルバリョ
Carvalho, Arlindo de 232
Carvalho, Celestino de 232
Carvalho, Ernesto 232
Carvalho, Evaristo 232
Carvalho, Maria da Graça 232
Carvalho, Maria de Cristo da Costa 232
Carvalho, Paulo 232
ガルバレク
Garbarek, Jan 477
カルバン
Carven, Marie-Louise 232
ガルバン
Galbán, Manuel 472
Galván, Guillermo 474
カルバントナ - ヴェルニッケ
Kalbantner-Wernicke, Karin 697
カルヒ
Karch, Steffen 704
カルビ
Karubi, Kikaya Bin 706
カルピ
Carpi, Lúcia 228
ガルビ
al-Gharbi, Abdullah 493
Gharbi, Jameleddine 493
ガルビス
Gulbis, Natalie 545
カルビティス
Kalvitis, Aigars 698
カルビモンテス
Calvimontes, Juan Carlos 217
カルピン
Culpin, Christopher 307
ガルビン
Galvin, Robert William 474
Garvin, Elaine 482
カルピンスキ
Karpiński, Włodzimierz 706
カルブ
Kalb, Marvin 697
カルプ
Culp, Andrew 307
Culp, Christopher L. 307
Culp, Robert 307
Karp, Sergueï IA. 706
ガルファ
Garfa, Mahamat 480
カルブアディ
Kalbuady, Francisco 697
カルファーニャ
Carfagna, Mara 225
カルファンタン
Carfantan, Jean Yves 225
ガルフィアス
Garfias, Robert 480
カルフィン
Kalfin, Ivailo 697
ガルフェッティ
Galfetti, Gustau Gili 472
ガルフォード
Galford, Robert 472
Galford, Robert M. 472
カルフーニ
Khalfouni, Dominique 724
ガルブル
Galbur, Andrei 472
ガルブレイス
Galbraith, Benjamin Layne 472
Galbraith, James K. 472
Galbraith, Jay R. 472
Galbraith, John Kenneth 472
Galbraith, Judy 472
Galbraith, Robert 472
Galbraith, Stuart, Ⅳ 472
ガルブレース
Galbraith, John Kenneth 472
カルフーン
Calhoun, Anne 215
Calhoun, Kole 215
Calhoun, Ward 215
カルベ
Calvet, Corinne 217
ガルベス
Galvez, Alejandro 474
Galvez, Fatima 474
Galvez, Felicity 474
Galvez, Isaac 474
ガルベス・タロンシェール
Gálvez-taroncher, Miguel 474
ガルベス・ママニ
Galvez Mamani, Santiago Alex 474
カルペッパー
Culpepper, R.Alan 307
カルペニート
Carpenito-Moyet, Lynda Juall 228
カルペニート＝モイエ
Carpenito-Moyet, Lynda Juall 228
カルペパー
Culpepper, R.Alan 307
カルペラ
Karpela, Tanja 706
カルペラン
Carpelan, Bo Gustaf Bertelsson 228
ガルペリン
Galperin, Gleb 474
カルペンコ
Karpenko, Igor V. 706
カルボ
Calvo, Carmen 217
Calvo, Giselle Goyenaga 217
カルポ
Carpo, Daniel 228
Carpo, Mario 228
カルボアメンゴル
Calvó Armengol, Silvia 217
カルポカス
Kalpokas, Donald 698
カルボゴメス
Calvo Gomez, Eva 217
カルボコレッシ
Calvocoressi, Peter 217
Calvocoressi, Richard 217
カルボコレッシー
Calvocoressi, Peter 217
カルボ・ソテロ
Calvo-Sotelo, Leopoldo 217
カルボネ
Carbone, Fernando 224
カルボネル
Carbonell, Ona 224
カルボネーロ
Carbonero, Carios 224
カルポフ
Carpov, Eugen 228
Karpov, Dmitriy 706
Karpov, R.S. 706
Karpov, Viktor 706
カルボモレノ
Calvo Moreno, Jossimar Orlando 217
カルホーン
Calhoun, Mary 215
Calhoun, Shilique 215
Calhoun, Taveze 215
カルマカル
Karmakar, Dipa 705
Karmakar, Joydeep 705
ガルマシュ
Garmash, Denys 480
カルマシン
Karmasin, Sophie 705
カルマ・チョペル
Karma Chophel 705
カルマパ
Karmapa ⅩⅦ 705
カルマパ17世
Karmapa ⅩⅦ 705
カルマヘリゼ
Kalmakhelidze, Khatuna 698
カルマムベトフ
Kalmambetov, Avtandil 698
ガルマリーニ
Galmarini, Nevin 474
カルマール
Kalmar, Zsolt 698
カルマン
Kalman, Maira 698
Karman, Tawakel 705
Karman, Tawakkol 705
カルマンチ
Karumanchi, Narasimha 706
カルミ
Carmi, Daniella 227
Carmi, Eugenio 227
カルミナーティ
Carminati, Marco 227
カルミナーティモリーナ
Carminati Molina, Emanuele 227
カルミニョーラ
Carmignola, Giuliano 227
カルミー＝レイ
Calmy-Rey, Micheline 217
カルミレイ
Calmy-Rey, Micheline 217
カルムイク
Calmac, Octavian 216
カルムス
Calmes, Mary 217
カルメ
Karume, Amani Abeid 706
Karume, Ngenga 706
カルメタ
Kalmeta, Božidar 698
カルメット
Kalmet, Norris 698
カルメヌンビ
Kalume Numbi, Gal Denis 698
カルメル
Calmel, Mireille 216
カルメルス

カ

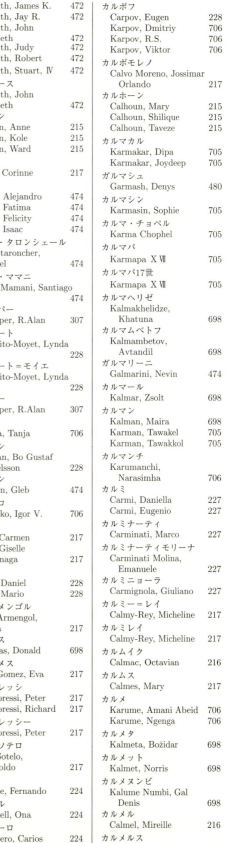

Carmel Sou, Ngarbatina 227
カルメンソン
Calmenson, Stephanie 216
ガルメンディア・メンディサバル
Garmendia Mendizábel, Christina 480
カルモー
Kalmoe, Megan 698
カルモイ
Kalmoy, Muhyadin Mohamed 698
カルモナ
Carmona, Adriana 227
Carmona, Anthony 227
Carmona, Carlos 227
カルモナエレディア
Carmona Heredia, Samuel 227
カルヤ
Calja, Briken 216
カルヤライネン
Karjalainen, Elina 705
Karjalainen, Olli-Pekka 705
Karjalainen, Tuula 705
カルランド
Kalleland, Alf Magne 698
ガルリツキ
Garlicki, Andrzej 480
カルル
Kalulu, Aldo 698
ガルルイエフ
Garryyev, Myrat 481
カルレス
Carles, Eduardo Enrique 226
Carles, Luis Ernesto 226
カルレス・ヒル
Carles Gil 226
カルレソン
Carleson, Lennart 226
カルレッティ
Carletti, Luigi 226
カルレバーロ
Carlevaro, Abel 226
カルロス
Carlos, Bun E. 226
Carlos, Roberto 226
カルロス・ウーゴ公
Carlos Hugo, Duke of Perma and Piacenza 226
カルロス・サンチェス
Carlos Sanchez 226
カルロス・ソレール
Carlos Soler 226
カルロス・フェルナンデス
Carlos Fernandez 226
カルロス・マルティネス
Carlos Martinez 226
カルロット
Carlot, Alfred 226
ガルワ
Galwak, Deng 474
カルワス
Kalwas, Andrzej 698
カルワリョ
Carvalho, Joao de 232
カルン
Karun, K. 706
ガルン
Garun, Abdullahi Abdi 482
カルンバ
Kalumba, Katele 698
カルンバ・ムワナ・ヌゴンゴ
Kalumba Mwana Ngongo, Justin 698
カルンビ
Kalumbi, Ferdinand Kambere 698
カレ
Carre, Cyrille 229
Carré, Guillaume 229
Carré, Isabelle 229
カレー
Calley, John 216
ガレ
Garré, Nilda 481
ガレア
Gallea, Anthony 473
ガレアーノ
Galeano, Eduardo 472
ガレアノ
Galeano, Eduardo 472
ガレアノ・ペロネ
Galeano Perrone, Horacio 472
ガレイ
Galley, François Agbéviadé 473
カレイワ
Kareiva, Natallia 704
カレウィリアムズ
Calle Williams, Maria Luisa 216
カレガ
Karega, Vincent 704
カレガリ
Callegari, Lorenzo 216
ガレゴ
Gallego, Fernando 473
ガレゴス
Gallegos, Giovanny 473
カレサース
Carrethers, Ryan 229
カレジェッスキー
Kolodzieski, Edward 753
カレージェルマン
Calais-Germain, Blandine 214
カレシュワール
Kaleshwar, Swami 697
カレスニコ
Kalesniko, Michael 697
ガレスピー
Gillaspie, Casey 498
Gillaspie, Conor 498
Gillespie, S.H. 499
Gillispie, Kay J. 499
カレスワール
Kaleshwar 697
カレソ
Kaleso, Peter 697
カレッジ
Courage, Katherine Harmon 295
ガレッジ
Gulledge, Thomas R. 545
ガレッティ
Galletti, Gianluca 473
Galletti, Marina 473
ガレティ
Garety, Philippa A. 480
カレド
Khaled, Nordin 724
カレーニョ
Carreño, José Manuel 229
カレニョ
Carreño, Pedro 229
カレニョ＝キング
Carreno King, Tania 229
カレフ
Calef, Noël 215
カレベ
Kalebe, Ted 697
カレーム
Carême, Maurice 225
カレムファリデ・アチャチ
Karem Faride Achach Ramirez 704
カレヤ
Calleja, Joseph 216
カレーラ
Carrera, Ezequiel 229
カレラ
Carrera, Pablo 229
カレーラス
Carreras, Genís 229
Carreras, José 229
カレラス
Carreras, José 229
カレーリ
Calleri, Jonathan 216
カレリン
Karelin, Aleksandr 704
カレール
Carrère, Emmanuel 229
カレル
Carell, Steve 225
Carrere, Tia 229
Currell, Christopher 309
Kallel, Abdallah 698
Kharel, Agni Prasad 727
ガーレル
Gerrell, Spike 491
ガレル
Garrel, Philippe 481
カレルズ
Karels, Michael J. 704
カレール・ダンコース
Carrère d'Encausse, Hélène 229
カレレカビラ
Kalele Kabila, Mathieu 697
カレロ
Calero, Dennis 215
ガレロン
Galeron, Henri 472
カーレン
Carlen, John 226
カレン
Callen, Gayle 216
Cullen, Cheryl Dangel 307
Cullen, Francis T. 307
Cullen, Heidi 307
Cullen, Julie 307
Cullen, Lizzie Mary 307
Cullen, Mathew 307
Cullen, Michael 307
Cullen, Robert 307
ガレン
Galen, Shana 472
Gallen, Ron 473
Garin, Eugenio 480
カレンガ
Kalenga, Ilunga 697
Karenga, Ramadhani 704
ガレンカンプ
Gallenkamp, Charles 473
カレンダ
Calenda, Carlo 215
カレンダー
Callender, Jane 216
Callender, Stanford 216
カレンチエワ
Kalentyeva, Irina 697
ガレンテ
Guarente, Leonard 541
カレンバ
Kalemba, Stanisław 697
カレンバーグ
Calenberg, Tom 215
Cullenberg, Stephen 307
カーロ
Carlo, George Louis 226
Caro, Anthony 227
Caro, Isabelle 227
Caro, Robert A. 227
カーロー
Carroo, Leonte 230
カロ
Caro, Anthony 227
Caro, Dan 227
Caro, Isabelle 227
Kalo, Toara Daniel 698
ガーロ
Garro, Elena 481
ガロ
Gallo, Carmine 474
Gallo, David 474
Gallo, Ernest 474
Gallo, Joseph J. 474
Gallo, Max Louis 474
ガロー
Gallo, Ernest 474
カロ・イノホサ
Caro Hinojosa, Elba Viviana 227
カーロウ
Carlow, Emma 226
Kerlow, Isaac Victor 721
カロウ
Callow, John 216
Carrau, Bob 229
カーロヴィッツ
Carlowicz, Michael J. 226
カロウセク
Kalousek, Miroslav 698
カログリディス
Kalogridis, Laeta 698
カロセリ
Caroselli, Marlene 227
カーロック
Carlock, Randel S. 226
ガロッタ
Gallotta, Jean-Claude 474
ガロッツォ
Garozzo, Daniele 481
Garozzo, Enrico 481
ガロディ
Garaudy, Roger Jean Charles 477
カロニウス
Calonius, Erik 217
ガローネ
Garrone, Matteo 481
Garrone, Riccardo 481
カロネン
Karonen, Lassi 706
カロビッチ

Karlovic, Ivo 705
カロフ
Calof, Olga 217
ガロファロ
Garofalo, Gianluca 481
カロフィーリオ
Carofiglio, Gianrico 227
ガロフェ
Garrofé, Josep M. 481
ガロフォリ
Garófoli, Viviana 481
ガロポロ
Gareppolo, Jimmy 480
ガロヤン
Galoyan, Mane 474
カロライン
Caroline, Hau 227
カローリ
Karori, Ahmed Mohammed Sadig 706
al-Karouri, Sadiq Ahmed 706
カロリス
Carolis, Patrick de 227
カロレワ
Koroleva, Olga 757
ガロワ
Gallois, Louis 474
Gallois, Patrick 474
Gallois, Pierre 474
カーロン
Carlon, Patricia 226
Caron, Samuel R. 227
カロン
Calonne, David Stephen 217
Karon, Jan 706
カロンジ
Kalongi, Atis Kabongo 698
カロンダヤ
Kalondaya, Jean Amisi 698
カワ
Kawah, Lamie 711
ガワー
Gawer, Annabelle 485
Gower, Eric 522
ガワイン
Gawain, Shakti 485
カワカミ
Kawakami, Tomoko 711
カワグチ
Kawaguchi, Sanae 711
カワサキ
Kawasaki, Guy 711
カワジー
Kahwajy, Jean L. 696
ガワーズ
Gowers, Andrew 522
Gowers, Simon G. 522
Gowers, Timothy 522
カワスミ
Kawasmi, Ali 711
Qawasmeh, Khaled 1142
カワセ
Kawase, Naomi 711
カワタ
Kawata, Nobuyuki 711
カワダ
Kawada, Tetsuo 711
カワチ
Kawachi, Ichiro 711
カーワーディン
Carwardine, Mark 232
カーワディン
Carwardine, Mark 232
カワード
Coward, Noel 297
カワナ
Kawana, Albert 711
カワベ・タモリ
Kawabe Tamori, Shiguenori 711
カワリ
al-Kawari, Hamad bin Abdul al-Aziz 711
al-Kuwari, Hamad bin Abdul Aziz 776
カワレロウィッチ
Kawalerowicz, Jerzy 711
カーワン
Kirwan, John 741
Kirwan, Larry 741
ガワンデ
Gawande, Atul 485
カワンバ
Kawambwa, Shukuru 711
カワンブワ
Kawambwa, Shukuru 711
カーン
Cahn, Edgar S. 213
Cahn, John Werner 213
Cahn, Miriam 213
Cahn, Robert W. 213
Calne, Roy Yorke 217
Kahan, Ernesto 695
Kahn, Ashley 695
Kahn, Axel 695
Kahn, C.Ronald 695
Kahn, Cynthia M. 695
Kahn, James 695
Kahn, Joseph 695
Kahn, Judd 695
Kahn, Lloyd 695
Kahn, Michal 695
Kahn, Oliver 695
Kahn, Paul 695
Kahn, Richard 695
Kahn, Robert 695
Kahn, Timothy J. 696
Kahng, Kim 696
Kane, Ariel 701
Kane, Shya 701
Karn, Mick 705
Kern, Brett 721
Kern, Georges 721
Kern, Morton J. 721
Kern, Noris 721
Kern, Peter 721
Kern, Richard 721
Kern, Stephen 721
Khan, Aamir 725
Khan, Abbas Sarfraz 725
Khan, Abdul Moyeen 725
Khan, Abdul Qadeer 725
Khan, Akram 726
Khan, Amir 726
Khan, Arbab Alamgir 726
Khan, Asaduzzaman 726
Khan, Bismillah 726
Khan, Chaka 726
Khan, Chaudhry Nauraiz Shakoor 726
Khan, Farah 726
Khan, Faruk 726
Khan, Franklin 726
Khan, Fuad 726
Khan, Ghulam Ishaq 726
Khan, Ghulam Sarwar 726
Khan, Humayoon Akhtar 726
Khan, Idris 726
Khan, Imran 726
Khan, Irene Zubaida 726
Khan, José Salamat 726
Khan, Karen 726
Khan, Karim 726
Khan, Khurram Dastgir 726
Khan, K. Rahman 726
Khan, M.I.Gabriel 726
Khan, Morshed 726
Khan, Moyeen 726
Khan, Muhammad Ajmal 726
Khan, Muhammad Asim 726
Khan, Muhammad Faruk 726
Khan, Muhammad Nasir 726
Khan, Mushtaq Husain 726
Khan, Nadia 726
Khan, Najamuddin 726
Khan, Nisar Ali 726
Khan, Omar Asghar 726
Khan, Rana Farooq Saeed 726
Khan, Riz 726
Khan, Rukhsana 726
Khan, Sadruddin Aga 726
Khan, Salim Saifullah 726
Khan, Salman 726
Khan, Sarah 726
Khan, Shah Rukh 726
Khan, Shajahan 726
Khan, Waqar Ahmed 726
Kirn, Walter 741
カン
Gang, Dong-won 476
Gang, Hae-jeong 476
Kamg, Ho-in 699
Kan, Gene 700
Kan, Mark 700
Kan, Young-sook 700
Kane, Mansour Elimane 701
Kane, Souleymane 701
Kane, Yaya Abdoul 701
Kang, Clara Jumi 701
Kang, Dong-suk 701
Kang, Eun-hee 701
Kang, Ha-guk 701
Kang, Hildi 701
Kang, Hyeong-cheol 701
Kang, In-duk 701
Kang, Jae Eup 701
Kang, Jae-sup 701
Kang, Je-gyu 701
kang, Ji-hwan 701
Kang, Jong-gwan 701
Kang, Jung Ho 701
Kang, Min-chol 701
Kang, Nam-chu 701
Kang, Nung-su 701
Kang, Seung Min 701
Kang, Seung-yoon 701
Kang, Shin-ho 701
Kang, Sok-ju 701
Kang, Sue-jin 701
Kang, Woo-suk 701
Kang, Yong-chol 701
Kang, Yong-su 701
Kang, Yun Mi 701
Kann 702
Kann, Hans 702
Khan, Mairaj Ahmad 726
Khan, Zia 726
Quint, Michel 1145
ガーン
Garn, Randy 481
ガン
Gan, Kim Yong 475
Gann, Alexander 476
Gann, David 476
Gunn, Angus 546
Gunn, Anna 546
Gunn, Douglas 546
Gunn, Eileen 546
Gunn, Erik 546
Gunn, James 546
Gunn, James E. 546
Gunn, Nathan 546
Gunn, Thom 546
Gunn, Tim 546
Ngan, Nguyen Thi Kim 1019
カンウェア
Kahnweah, Harrison 696
カーンウェイラー
Kahnweiler, Jennifer B. 696
カンガ
Canga, Afonso Pedro 221
ガンガジ
Gangaji 476
カンガス
Kangas, Kirsi-Klaudia 701
ガンガラム・パンデイ
Gangarampanday, Geetapersad 476
ガンガラムパンデイ
Gangarampanday, Geetapersad 476
カンガルー
Kangaloo, Christine 701
ガンク
Gankou, Jean-Marie 476
ガングレール
Gangler, Bernard 476
ガンケル
Gunkel, Joe 546
ガンコス
Gancos, James 475
カンザー
Kanzer, Mark 702
ガンサ
Gansa, Alex 476
ガンサー
Gunther, Robert E. 547
カンサス
Kansas, Dave 702
カンジ
Kanji, Gopal K. 701
ガンジー
Gandhi, Manek Sanjay 475
Gandhi, Rahul 475
Gandhi, Ramchandra 475
Gandhi, Sonia 475
Gangjee, Dev 476
Ghandhi, Maneka Sanjay 493
カンジェ
Kanje, Mohamed Ali Saleh 701
カンシオ
Câncio, João 221
カンジグ
Kunzig, Robert 774

カンシーノ
Cansino, Eliacer 222
カンジムランギ
Kandjii-murangi, Itah 700
ガンジャルゾダ
Ganjalzoda, Sherali 476
ガンシュ
Gansch, Christian 476
カンジョ
Kanjou, Youssef 702
カンジョゼ
Kandjoze, Obeth 700
カーンズ
Carnes, Bruce A. 227
Carnes, Patrick 227
Karns, Nathan 706
Kearns, Antony 713
Kearns, Brad 713
Kearns, Devon 713
Kerns, Lawrence L. 721
ガーンス
Gaens, Bart 470
ガンズ
Gans, Christophe 476
Gans, Danny 476
Gans, Herbert J. 476
Gans, Joshua 476
Gans, Roma 476
ガンスキー
Gansky, Alton 476
Gansky, Lisa 476
ガンスフ
Gansukh, Amarjargal 476
Gansukh, Luimediin 476
ガンスラー
Gansler, Laura Leedy 476
カンセコ
Canseco, José 222
カンセララ
Cancellara, Fabian 221
カンゼル
Kunzel, Erich 774
カンセロ
Cancelo, Joao 221
カン・ゾー
Kan Zaw 702
カンソ
Kanso, Ali 702
Kanso, Assem 702
Qanso, Ali 1142
ガンソ
Ganso 476
ガンゾリグ
Ganzorig, Chimiddorjiin 477
ガンゾリグマンダフナラン
Ganzorigiin Mandakhnaran 477
ガンソン
Gunson, Dave 546
カンタ
Cantat, Isabelle 222
Kantha, K.D. Lal 702
カンター
Canter, Marc 222
Cantor, Murray 222
Cantor, Norman F. 222
Kanter, Hal 702
Kanter, Jonathan 702
Kanter, Rosabeth Moss 702
Kantor, Edward M. 702
Kantor, Jean-Michel 702
Kantor, Mickey 702
カンダ
Canda, Edward R. 221
ガンター
Gunter, Barrie 546
Gunter, LaDarius 546
Gunter, Rodney 546
Gunter, Susan E. 546
カンダイ
Kandhai, Ganeshkoemar 700
カンダカイ
Kandakai, Evelyn 700
カンダケル
Khandaker, A K 726
ガンダーセン
Gundersen, Arnie 546
ガンダーソン
Gunderson, John G. 546
ガンダートン
Ganderton, Lucinda 475
カンタニェデ
Cantanhede, Francisco 222
カンタニス
Kantanis, Tanya 702
カン・ダパー
Kandapaah, Albert 700
カンダパー
Kandapaah, Albert 700
カンタメッサ
Cantamessa, Gene S. 222
Cantamessa, Steve 222
ガンダラ
Gándara, Salvador 475
カンタラメッサ
Cantalamessa, Raniero 222
カンダリ
al-Kandari, Eissa Ahmad 700
カンダル
Cundall, Arthur Ernest 307
ガンタル
Gantar, Pavel 476
カンタルポ
Cantalupo, Jim 222
カンタレヴィック
Kantarevic, Mirna 702
ガンダロビッチ
Gandalovic, Petr 475
カンタン
Cantin, Marie-Anne 222
Quintin, Michel 1145
カンチェスカ・ミレフスカ
Kancheska-Milevska, Elizabeta 700
ガンチェフ
Gantschev, Ivan 476
カンチェラーラ
Cancellara, Fabian 221
カンチェーリ
Kancheli, Giya 700
カンチェリエリ
Cancellieri, Anna Maria 221
カンチャー
Kanchier, Carole 700
カンチュガ
Kanchuga, Aleksandr Aleksandrovich 700
ガンツ
Gandt, Robert L. 476
Gants, David 476
Ganz, Bruno 477
Ganz, Nicholas 477
Gunts, Bucky 547
カンツィアン
Khantzian, Edward J. 726
カンツォーク
Kanzog, Klaus 702
カンテ
Cantet, Laurent 222
Kante, N'Golo 702
カンデ
Cande, Botche 221
カンディ
Candi, Néstor 221
Cundey, Angus 307
Kandeh, Musu 700
ガンディ
Gandi, Togsjargalyn 475
Gandy, Ellen 476
ガンディー
Gandhi, Manek Sanjay 475
Gandhi, Sameer 475
Gandhi, Sonia 475
カンディア
Candia, Miguel 221
カンディエ
Kandie, Phyllis 700
カンディスノン
Kandissounon, Céline 700
カンティック
Quantick, David 1143
ガンディーニ
Gandini, Lella 475
ガンディヨ
Gandillot, Clémence 475
カンディール
Candaele, Casey 221
Qandil, Hisham Muhammad 1142
カーン＝ディン
Khan-Din, Ayub 726
カンデラ・ガルシア
Candela Garcia, Maria del Carmen 221
カンテル
Kanter, Gerd 702
カンデル
Kandel, Eric Richard 700
Kandel, Johannes 700
Kandel, Joseph 700
Kandel, Susan 700
ガンデル
Gandel, Pauline 475
カンテロン
Cantelon, Mike 222
カント
Canto, Flavio 222
Kant, Krishan 702
Kanto, Erik 702
Kanto, Ilona 702
カンド
Khand, Bal Krishna 726
ガンド
Gando, Alphonse 475
ガンドイモフ
Gandymov, Seitbay 476
カントゥ
Cantù, Marco 222
カンドゥ
Candu, Adrian 221
カントウェル
Cantwell, Dennis P. 222
カンドゥッチ
Canducci, Mario T. 221
カンドゥノ
Kandouno, Joseph 700
ガントゥムル
Gantumur, Luvsannyam 477
ガントゥモル
Gantumur, Luvsannyam 477
カンドゥリ
Khanduri, Kamini 726
ガンドゥール
Ghandour, Ibrahim 493
カンドシュ
Camdessus, Michel Jean 218
カンドド
Kandodo, Ken 700
カントナ
Cantona, Eric 222
カントナー
Kantner, Paul 702
Kantner, Rob 702
カントーネ
Cantone, Anna-Laura 222
カーン・トーバ
Cahn-Tober, Theresa 213
ガントマン
Gantman, Marcelo 476
カントラ
Kantra, Virginia 702
ガンドラック
Gundlach, Jeffrey 546
ガンドラム
Gandulam, U. 476
Temuuzhin, B. 1390
カンドリアン
Candrian, Sina 221
カントール
Kantor, Israel 702
カントル
Kantor, Piotr 702
ガンドルフィ
Gandolfi, Giorgio 475
Gandolfi, Silvana 476
ガンドルフィーニ
Gandolfini, James 476
カンドレーヴァ
Candreva, Antonio 221
カントレス
Camp Torres, Francesc 220
カントレル
Cantrell, Rebecca 222
カントロフ
Kantorow, Jean-Jacques 702
カントン
Canton, Henry 222
Canton, Maria P. 222
ガントン
Gunton, Colin E. 547
カンナ
Canna, Carlo 221
Khanna, Parag 726
カンナヴァーロ
Cannavaro, Fabio 221
Cannavaro, Paolo 221
カンナヴァロ
Cannavaro, Fabio 221
カンナバーレ
Cannavale, Enzo 221
カンナバーロ

Cannavaro, Fabio 221
カンナバロ
Cannavaro, Fabio 221
ガンニング
Gunning, Brett 546
ガンヌーシ
Ghannouchi, Mohamed 493
カンハ
Canha, Mark 221
ガンバー
Ganbar, Ron 475
カーンバーグ
Kernberg, Otto F. 721
Kernberg, Paulina F. 721
カンバーグ
Kamberg, Mary-Lane 699
カンパス
Kampas, Paul J. 700
ガンパーズ
Gumperz, John Joseph 546
ガンバータル
Ganbaatar, Odbayar 475
ガンバッチーニ
Gambaccini, Sciascia 475
ガンバット
Ganbat, D. 475
ガンバト
Ganbat, Dangaagiin 475
ガンバートル
Ganbaatar, Ichinnorov 475
カンパナ
Campana, Fernando 219
Campana, Humberto 219
カンパナーリ
Campanari, José 219
カーン＝パニ
Khan-Panni, Phillip 726
カンパニー
Campany, David 219
カンパニャーロ
Campagnaro, Hugo 219
Campagnaro, Michele 219
カンパネラ
Campanella, Thomas J. 219
カンバーバッチ
Cumberbatch, Benedict 307
カンパーヨ
Campayo, Ramón 219
カンバーランド
Cumberland, Jeff 307
ガンバリ
Gambari, Ibrahim Agboola 475
ガンバリーニ
Gambarini, Roberta 475
カンバル
Cambar Rodriguez, Ivan 218
カンパルス
Kampars, Artis 700
カンバルロドリゲス
Cambar Rodriguez, Ivan 218
カンパン
Khampane, Philavong 725
カンビ
Kambi, Kazungu 699
ガンビ
Gambi, Antoine 475
カンビアッソ
Cambiasso, Esteban 218
カンピオーネ
Campione, Mary 220
カンピオン
Campion, Anna 220
Campion, Jane 220
ガンビーノ
Gambino, Christopher J. 475
カンピョンゴ
Kampyongo, Stephen 700
カンピラパーブ・スネート
Kampeeraparb Sunate 700
カンビル
Kambile, Sansan 699
カンブ
Kamb, John 699
カンプ
Kamp, Henk 700
ガンフー
Gankhuu, Purevjavyin 476
ガンプ
Gampp, Josua Leander 475
カンブアヤ
Kambuaya, Balthazar 699
カンブウィリ
Kambwili, Chishimba 699
カーン・フェルナンデス
Khan Fernández, José 726
カンフォート
Comfort, Alex 281
ガンフォード
Ganfoud, Badi Ould 476
カンブシュネ
Kambouchner, Denis 699
カンプス
Kamps, John 700
ガンフード
Ganfoud, Badi Ould 476
カンプトン
Cumpton, Brandon 307
カンブフォール
Cambefort, Yves 218
カンプマン＝カロッサ
Kampmann-Carossa, Eva 700
ガンフヤグ
Gankhuyag, Gan-Erdene 476
カンブラス
Cambras, Josep 218
カンプラード
Kamprad, Ingvar 700
カンフラ・リナレス
Canjura Linares, Carlos Mauricio 221
ガンブラン
Gamblin, Jacques 475
カンプリアーニ
Campriani, Niccoló 220
カンプル
Kampl, Kevin 700
カンプルビ
Camprubi, Krystal 220
カンブルラン
Cambreling, Sylvain 218
ガンブレル
Gambrelle, Fabienne 475
ガンベリーニ
Gamberini, Alessandro 475
ガンペル
Gumpel, Glenn 546
カンペルマン
Kampelman, Max M. 700
カンペロ
Campello, Tereza 220
カンペロ・ナバ
Campero Nava, Ariana 220
カンペーン
Khampheng, Xaysompheng 725
カンポ
Campo, Eva 220
ガンボ
Gangbo, Flore 476
ガンボア
Gamboa, Celso 475
Gamboa, Jaime 475
Gamboa, Yuriorkis 475
カンポ・サアベドラ
Campo Saavedra, María Fernanda 220
カンポ・サーベドラ
Campo Saavedra, María Fernanda 220
カンポス
Campos, Eduardo 220
Campos, Esperanza 220
Campos, Irene 220
Campos, Jaime 220
Campos, Paulo 220
Campos, Ruben 220
Campos, Vicente 220
カンポスフェルナンデス
Campos Fernandes, Adalberto 220
カンポス・ロドリゲス
Campos Rodrigues, Augusto Jorge 220
ガンボーデラ
Gambordella, Theodore L. 475
ガンポート
Gumport, Patricia J. 546
カンボニ
Camboni, Mattia 218
ガンボーニ
Gamboni, Dario 475
カンポ・バエザ
Campo Baeza, Alberto 220
ガンホヤグ
Gankhuyag, Davaajav 476
ガンホヤッグ
Gankhuyag, Davaajav 476
ガンボルド
Ganbold, Sh. 475
カンポン・トーンブンヌム
Kampol Thongbunnum 700
ガンマ
Gamma, Erich 475
カンマニ
Khammani, Inthilath 725
カンマレリ
Cammarelle, Roberto 218
カンラス
Canlas, Dante 221
カンリフ
Cunliffe, Bill 308
Cunliffe, David 308
ガンワール
Ganwar, Santosh Kumar 477

【キ】

キ
Ki, Bo-bae 729
Ki, Kwang-ho 729
Ki, Sung-yueng 729
キー
Kee, Leslie 713
Kee, Tris 713
Key, John 723
Key, Joshua 723
Key, Stephen 723
Key, Watt 723
ギ
Nghi, Pham Quang 1020
ギー
Guy, Rosa Cuthbert 549
キア
Kier, Udo 730
ギア
Gear, Felice D. 485
Gere, Richard 490
Gier, Kerstin 496
Nghia, Truong Quang 1020
ギアーツ
Geertz, Clifford James 486
ギアツ
Geertz, Clifford James 486
ギアーティ
Gearty, Eugene 486
キアナン
Kiernan, Caitlín R. 730
キアマイアー
Kiermaier, Kevin 730
キアラビーニ
Chiarabini, Andrea 254
キアリ
Khiari, Sadri 728
ギアリ
Geary, Patrick J. 486
Geary, Valerie 486
ギアリー
Geary, Brent B. 486
Geary, David C. 486
Geary, David M. 486
Geary, Patricia 486
キアリーニ
Chiarini, Marco 254
ギアリン
Gearrin, Cory 486
ギアリン‐トッシュ
Gearin-Tosh, Michael 486
キアレッリ
Chiarelli, Cosimo 254
キアロスタミ
Kiarostami, Abbas 729
キアンプツ
Kiamputu, Simon Mboso 729
キアンプール
Kianpour, Fredun 729
ギアンマルヴォ
Giammalvo, Paul 494
キーイ
Keay, John 713
キイス
Keyes, Daniel 723
Keyes, J.Gregory 723
ギィユー

Guillou, Jan 544
キヴィ
Kivi, Mirja 742
キヴィニエミ
Kiviniemi, Mari 742
キーヴィル
Keevil, Susan 714
キヴェル
Kivel, Beth 742
キヴォーキアン
Kevorkian, Jack 723
キウザーノ
Chiusano, Paul 257
キーヴス
Kiwus, Karin 742
キウーラ
Ciulla, Joanne B. 265
キウル
Kiuru, Krista 742
キウレヤン
Kiouregkian, Artiom 739
キウロ
Ciullo, Peter A. 265
ギヴン
Given, Shay 503
キウンジュリ
Kiunjuri, Mwangi 742
ギヴンズ
Givens, David B. 503
ギエ
Guillet, Jacques 544
キエーザ
Chiesa, Federico 255
キエザ
Chiesa, Bruno della 255
キェシロフスキ
Kieślowski, Krzysztof 731
キエスウェテル
Kieswetter, Emilio 731
キエスーラ
Chiesura, Fabrizio 255
キエソ
Kieso, Donald E. 731
キエット
Keat Chhon 713
キエット・チョン
Keat Chhon 713
キエッリーニ
Chiellini, Giorgio 255
キエデゴー
Kjaedegaard, Lars 743
キエフ
Kiev, Ari 731
キエム
Khiem, Pham Gia 728
Kiem, Nguyen Manh 730
ギエム
Guillem, Sylvie 544
ギェラルップ
Gjellerup, Pia 503
キェル
Kyelu, Athenase 778
キエル
Kyelu, Athanase Matenda 778
キェルガード
Kjelgaard, Jim 743
ギエルシュ
Giersz, Adam 496
ギエルティフ
Giertych, Roman 496
ギェレク
Gierek, Edward 496
ギエレク
Gierek, Edward 496
キェレマンテン
Kyeremanten, Alan 778
キエレマンテン
Kyeremanten, Alan 778
ギーエン
Guillen, Ozzie 544
ギェンゲダル
Gjengedal, Eva 503
キエントガ
Kientga, Fidele 730
キーオ
Kehoe, John 714
Keogh, Barbara K. 720
Keogh, Pamela Clarke 720
Keough, Donald R. 720
ギオ
Guihot, Hervé 544
Guyot, Sarah 549
ギオウラ
Gioura, Derog 501
キオタ
Kiota, Kutumisa 739
ギオニス
Gionis, Panagiotis 501
ギオネ
Guionet, Emmanuel 545
ギオマール
Guiomar, Julien 545
ギオルカゼ
Giorgadze, Muraz 501
ギオルガゼ
Giorgadze, Mikheil 501
ギオルギス
Giorgis, Teklemikael 501
キオロ
Chioro, Arthur 256
キーオン
Keown, Dale 720
Keown, Damien 720
ギーガー
Giger, H.R. 497
ギカウ
Gikow, Louise 497
キガナヘ
Kiganahe, Didace 731
キカハ
Kikaha, Hau'oli 731
ギガバ
Gigaba, Malusi 497
キーガン
Keegan, Claire 713
Keegan, E.Mary 713
Keegan, John 713
Keegan, Lynn 714
Keegan, Rebecca 714
Kegan, Robert 714
ギガンテス
Gigantes 497
キカンポワ
Quiquampoix, Jean 1145
ギキエヴィッツ
Gikiewicz, Rafal 497
キキニウ
Kikiniou, Aliaksandr 731
キーグ
Keig, Larry 715
ギグー
Guigou, Élisabeth Alexandrine Marie 544
キクウェテ
Kikwete, Jakaya Mrisho 731
キクク
Kikuku, Nkulu 731
ギグス
Giggs, Ryan 497
ギクヌリ
Gjiknuri, Damian 503
ギグマ
Guigma, Gisèle 544
キクムラ・ヤノ
Kikumura Yano, Akemi 731
ギグリエリ
Ghiglieri, Michael Patrick 493
キクルヴィッチ
Kiklevich, J.Veronika 731
ギグレ
Giguére, Eric 497
キグレイ
Quigley, Sebastian 1144
キケ・ガルシア
Kike Garcia 731
キケ・セティエン
Quique Setien 1145
キケ・フローレス
Quique Flores 1145
ギーゲリッヒ
Giegerich, Wolfgang 496
ギーゲレンツァァー
Gigerenzer, Gerd 497
キコ・カシージャ
Kiko Casilla 731
キゴダ
Kigoda, Abdallah 731
ギゴフ
Gigov, Nikola 497
キコ・フェメニア
Kiko Femenia 731
ギコロ
Gikoro, Emmanuel 497
キーザーズ
Keysers, Christian 724
ギーサーズ
Geathers, Clayton 486
キーサノスキー
Kiesanowski, Joanne 731
キザール
Kizart, Takesha Meshé 743
ギザン
Gisin, Dominique 502
キサンガ
Kisanga, Jean-Pierre 741
キージー
Kesey, Ken Elton 722
ギジ
Gygi, Kathleen 550
ギジェンデボグラン
Guillén De Bográn, María Antonieta 544
ギシオラ
Githiora, Chege J. 502
ギジス
Guirgis, Stephen Adly 545
キシテイニー
Kishtainy, Niall 742
キジバエフ
Kidibayev, Mustafa 730
キシバシ
Kishi Bashi 742
キシモト
Kishimoto, Tadamitsu 742
ギジャ
Ghiggia, Alcides 493
ギシャール
Guichard, Joëlle 544
Guichard, Olivier Marie Maurice 544
キシュ
Kis, Gergo 741
Kiss, Péter 742
ギシュー
Gouichoux, René 521
キシュカ
Kischka, Udo 742
キシュシュ
Kiss, Gergely 742
キシュナ
Kishna, Ricardo 742
ギシュメール
Guichemerre, Roger 544
ギシュラー
Gischler, Victor 502
キショー
Kishor, Nalin 742
キジョ
Kidjo, Angélique 730
キジョー
Kidjo, Angélique 730
ギジョ
Guillot, Olga 544
ギショネ
Guichonnet, Paul 544
キション
Kishon, Ephraim 742
キシル
Kisil, Yuri 742
キシロフ
Kicillof, Axel 730
キーシン
Kissin, Evgenii 742
キース
Keith, Clinton 715
Keith, Doug 715
Keith, Erick 715
Keith, Eros 715
Keith, John 715
Keith, Kent M. 715
Keith, Lois 715
Keith, Robert L. 715
Keith, Toby 715
Kerth, Norm 722
Keyes, Evelyn 723
Keyes, J.Gregory 723
Keyes, Ralph 723
Kiisel, Karolyn 731
キーズ
Keyes, Evelyn 723
Keyes, Marian 723
Keyes, Ralph 723
Keys, Alicia 724
Keys, Ancel 724
Keys, Bobby 724
Keys, Madison 724
ギース
Gies, Frances 496
Gies, Jean-Pierre 496
Gies, Joseph 496
キスカ
Kiska, Andrej 742
キースキネン
Kiiskinen, Jyrki 731

ギスケ
Giske, Trond 502
キース・ソーヤー
Sawyer, Robert Keith 1246
キスチオン
Kistion, Volodymyr 742
キースト
Keast, Karen 713
ギースト
Geest, Yuri van 486
ギスト
Gist, Richard 502
キストラー
Kistler, Julie 742
キストリーニ
Chistolini, Dario 257
キーストン
Keystone, J.S. 724
キスナー
Kisner, Carolyn 742
ギースブレヒト
Giesbrecht, Gordon G. 496
キースラー
Kiessler, Richard E. 731
キースリー
Keighley, Tom 715
ギースリン
Geeslin, Campbell 486
キースリンク
Kiessling, Stefan 731
キースリング
Keesling, Barbara 714
Kiesling, Stephen 731
Kiessling, Ann A. 731
キースレル
Kiisler, Siim-Valmar 731
キセイン
Kissane, David William 742
キーゼヴェター
Kiesewetter, Hubert 731
ギセック
Giesecke, Johan 496
ギーゼブレヒト
Giesbrecht, Martin Gerhard 496
キーゼル
Kiesel, Helmuth 731
ギゼレフ
Ghuiselev, Iassen 494
ギゼンガ
Gizenga, Antoine 503
ギーソン
Giesen, Jonathan Van 496
キーダ
Kida, Thomas Edward 730
キタ
Kita, Joe 742
Kita, Kihatiro 742
キダ
Kida, Mateus 730
キダー
Kidder, David S. 730
Kidder, Rushworth M. 730
Kidder, Tracy 730
ギタ
Gita, Irawan Wirjawan 502
ギター
Guitar, Barry 545
キタイ
Kitai, Adrian 742
ギタウ
Giteau, Matt 502
ギタエ
Githae, Njeru 502
ギダスポフ
Gidaspov, Boris Veniaminovich 496
キタダイ
Kitadai, Felipe 742
キダネ
Kidane, Werknesh 730
キタノ
Kitano, Takeshi 742
キダンビ
Kidambi, Srikanth 730
キー・タン・リム
Khy Taing Lim 729
キー・タンリム
Khy Taing Lim 729
ギーチ
Geach, James 485
Geach, Peter Thomas 485
ギチェット
Guichet, Yvel 544
キーチェル
Kiechel, Walter, Ⅲ 730
キチナー
Kijiner, Tom D. 731
ギチノフ
Gitinov, Arsen 502
キーツ
Keats, John 713
ギーツィー
Ghyczy, Tiha von 494
キツォイユ
Chitoiu, Daniel 257
キック
Kick, Russell 730
ギッグス
Giggs, Ryan 497
キッザ
Kizza, Joseph Migga 743
キッシュ
Kish, Matt 742
Kiss, Elemér 742
Kiss, Péter 742
キッジンガー
Kitzinger, Sheila 742
ギッシング
Gissing, Vera 502
キッシンジャー
Kissinger, Henry Alfred 742
キッセル
Kissel, Howard 742
キッソン
Kitson, Clare 742
キツソン
Kitson, Michael 742
ギッターマン
Gitterman, Alex 502
キッチェル
Kitchel, JoAnn E. 742
キッチナー
Kitchener, Betty 742
キッチン
Kitchen, Ishmaáily 742
キッツ
Kitz, Volker 742
キッツィンガー
Kitzinger, Sheila 742
キッツィング
Kitzing, Constanze V. 742
キッツホフ
Kitshoff, Rohan 742
キッティ
Chitty, Alison 257
ギッティング
Gittings, John 502
ギッティンズ
Gittins, Ian 502
キッテル
Kittel, Charles 742
Kittel, Sonny 742
ギッテル
Gittell, Jody Hoffer 502
ギッテンズ
Gittens, Tessa 502
キット
Kitt, Eartha 742
Kitt, Tom 742
キッド
Kidd, Chip 730
Kidd, Jason 730
Kidd, Michael 730
Kidd, Paul 730
Kidd, Richard 730
Kidd, Rob 730
Kidd, Sue Monk 730
ギット
Gitt, Werner 502
キッド・ギルクリスト
Kidd-gilchrist, Michael 730
キットソン
Kitson, Barry 742
キッドソン
Kidston, Cath 730
キッドマン
Kidman, Matthew J. 730
Kidman, Nicole 730
キットラー
Kittler, Friedrich A. 742
ギッパー
Gipper, Helmut 501
ギッフェン
Giffen, Keith 496
キップス
Kipps, Thomas J. 739
ギップス
Gipps, C.V. 501
キッペス
Kippes, Waldemar 739
キッペンハーン
Kippenhahn, Rudolf 739
キッペンベルク
Kippenberg, Hans Gehard 739
キッポラ
Kippola, Tom 739
キーツマン
Keatman, Martin 713
ギーテ
Geete, Anant 486
Gheete, Anant G. 493
ギデア
Guidea, Ivan 544
キテイ
Kittay, Eva Feder 742
キディ
Keady, John 712
ギディウス
Gidius, Joe 496
キーディス
Kiedis, Anthony 730
キティッキクアンバ
Kiticki-kouamba, Joseph 742
キティラット・ナラノン
Kittirat Na Ranong 742
キーティング
Keating, H.R.F. 713
Keating, Kathleen 713
Keating, Paul 713
ギティンズ
Gittines, Roger 502
Gittins, Ian 502
ギデオン
Gideon, Melanie 496
ギテラス
Guiteras, Wálter 545
ギデール
Guidère, Mathieu 544
ギテルジ
Giteruji, Dieudonné 502
ギテルマン
Gitelman, Zvi Y. 502
ギテレーツ
Gutierrez, Alejandro 548
ギデンス
Giddens, Anthony 496
ギデンズ
Giddens, Anthony 496
キテンボ
Kitembo, Gertrude 742
キート
Keet, Louise 714
Keet, Michael 714
キド
Kido, Markis 730
ギド
Guido, Guilherme 544
キトゥ
Chitu, Andreea 257
キドゥ
Kidu, *Dame* Carol 730
ギドゥー
Guidoux, Valerie 544
キトゥイ
Kituyi, Mukhisa 742
キトゥム
Kitum, Timothy 742
ギドゥーム
Guiddoum, Yahia 544
ギトゥン
Guitoune, Sofiane 545
ギトゥンズ
Gittens, Tessa 502
キドナー
Kidner, Derek 730
Kidner, Lisa 730
ギトマー
Gitomer, Jeffrey H. 502
キドランド
Kydland, Finn K. 778
キトリッジ
Kittredge, William 742
ギトリン
Gitlin, Todd 502
キトル
Kittle, Katrina 742
ギトルマン
Gittleman, Ann Louise 502
キドロン
Kidron, Peretz 730

キ

キトワンガ
Kitwanga, Charles 742
キートン
Keaton, Derek 713
Keaton, Diane 713
Keaton, Michael 713
Keeton, Bryson 714
ギトン
Guitton, René 545
キーナー
Keener, James P. 714
キナセ
Kinase, Ito 736
キーナート
Kuehnert, Martin P. 771
Kuehnert, Marty 771
キナード
Kynard, Erik 778
キナフ
Kinakh, Anatoly 736
キナマン
Kinnaman, Laura 739
キーナム
Keenum, Case 714
ギナルディ
Ginaldi, Lia 500
キーナン
Keenan, Daniel 714
Keenan, Jack 714
Keenan, Julian Paul 714
Keenan, Michael 714
Keenan, Paul 714
Kiernan, Kevin 730
ギナンジャール
Ginandjar Kartasasmita 500
ギナンジャール・カルタサスミタ
Ginandjar Kartasasmita 500
キーニー
Keeney, Bradford P. 714
Keeney, Maddison 714
Keeney, Ralph L. 714
キニ
Kinni, Donna 739
Kinni, Theodore B. 739
キニー
Kinney, Jeff 739
Kinney, Steven 739
ギニー
Guiney, Eamonn 545
キニア
Kinnear, Jim 739
Kinnear, Rory 739
キーニィ
Keeney, Mark H. 714
キニキニラウ
Kinikinilau, Paula 739
キニスキー
Kiniski, Gene 739
キニャール
Quignard, Pascal Charles Edmond 1144
キニョネス
Quinones, Victor 1145
Quinonez, Alex 1145
Quinonez, Jackson 1145
キーネ
Kiene, H. 730
ギネス
Gunes, Tata 546
キネル
Kinnell, Galway 739
キネーン
Kinnane, Adrian 739
キノ
Quino 1145
ギノー
Guineau, Bernard 545
キノシタ
Kinoshita, Robert 739
ギノット
Ginott, Alice 500
キノドス
Quinodoz, Jean-Michel 1145
キノネス
Quinones, C.Kenneth 1145
キノン
Quinon, Pierre 1145
キーバ
Kiver, Christopher 742
ギバ
Gibba, Momodou Lamin 495
キバキ
Kibaki, Mwai 729
キパシビリ
Kipashvili, Vladimir 739
ギバーソン
Guiberson, Brenda Z. 544
キハダ
Quijada, Flavio 1144
ギバート
Gibert, Teresa 495
キハノ
Quijano, Ricardo 1144
キーバーベック
Kieber-beck, Rita 730
キバラ
Kibala, Jean-Claude 729
ギバン
Givhan, Robin 503
キハンドリア
Quijandría, Alvaro 1144
キハンドリア・サルモン
Qui-jandría Salmón, Alvaro Enrique 1144
Quijandría Salmón, Jaime 1144
キビ
Kivi, Signe 742
ギビー
Gibbie, Mike 495
キピアニ
Kipiani, Levan 739
キビウォト
Kibiwot, Viola Jelagat 730
キピエゴ
Kipyego, Sally Jepkosgei 740
キビカイ
Kibikai, Paul 730
キビニエミ
Kiviniemi, Mari 742
キビマキ
Kivimäki, Mika 742
ギビリスコ
Gibilisco, Stan 495
キーピング
Keeping, Charles 714
ギビンズ
Gibbins, David 495
キーフ
Keefe, Brian 713
Keefe, Patrick Radden 713
キーブ
al-Keib, Abdurrahim 715
ギフ
Giff, Patricia Reilly 496
ギブ
Gibb, Andrea 495
Gibb, Camilla 495
Gibb, Fiona 495
Gibb, Jakob 495
Gibb, Maurice 495
Gibb, Mike 495
Gibb, Robin 495
Gibb, Sarah 495
キーファー
Kiefer, Anselm 730
Kiefer, Charles F. 730
Kiefer, Christie W. 730
Kiefer, David 730
Kiefer, Lee 730
Kiefer, Meghan M. 730
Kiefer, Nicolas 730
ギーファー
Giefer, Fabian 496
Giefer, Rena 496
Giefer, Thomas 496
キブイェン
Quibuyen, Floro C. 1144
ギフィン
Giffin, Emily 496
ギフォーズ
Giffords, Gabrielle 497
ギフォート
Giffort, Daniel W. 497
ギフォード
Gifford, Barry 496
Gifford, Clive 496
Gifford, Elizabeth V. 496
Gifford, Ernest M. 496
Gifford, Jane 496
Gifford, Robert 497
キプケテル
Kipketer, Alfred 739
Kipketer, Wilson 739
キプサング
Kiprotich, Wilson Kipsang 740
Kipsang, Wilson 740
キプシロ
Kipsiro, Moses Ndiema 740
ギブス
Gibbes, E.B. 495
Gibbs, Andy 495
Gibbs, Edward 495
Gibbs, Georgia 495
Gibbs, Kieran 495
Gibbs, Lois Marie 495
Gibbs, May 495
Gibbs, Megan 495
Gibbs, Nancy 495
Gibbs, Nick 495
Gibbs, Stuart 495
Gibbs, Terri 495
Gibbs, Tony 495
ギブズ
Gibbs, Raymond W., Jr. 495
ギブスン
Gibson, Mel 496
Gibson, William 496
ギブソン
Gibson, Althea 495
Gibson, Ben 495
Gibson, Charles 495
Gibson, Clare K. 495
Gibson, Darron 495
Gibson, Deonte 495
Gibson, Don 495
Gibson, Duff 495
Gibson, Eleanor Jack 495
Gibson, Faith 495
Gibson, Grant 495
Gibson, Hugh 496
Gibson, Ian 496
Gibson, James 496
Gibson, J.N.Alastair 496
Gibson, Johnny Anthony 496
Gibson, Jonathan 496
Gibson, Joyce Taylor 496
Gibson, Katherine 496
Gibson, Kirk 496
Gibson, Kyle 496
Gibson, Laurence 496
Gibson, Laurieann 496
Gibson, L.James 496
Gibson, Mathu 496
Gibson, Mel 496
Gibson, Phillip 496
Gibson, Rachel 496
Gibson, Rich 496
Gibson, Rosemary 496
Gibson, Shane 496
Gibson, Taj 496
Gibson, Warwick 496
Gibson, William 496
ギプソン
Gipson, Tashaun 501
キプタヌイ
Kiptanui, Timothy 740
キプチョゲ
Kipchoge Rotich, Eliud 739
Rotich, Eliud Kipchoge 1210
ギフト
Gift, Knowlson 497
ギブニー
Gibney, Frank Bray 495
キプニス
Kipnis, Igor 739
Kipnis, Jason 739
キープニュース
Keepnews, Orrin 714
キープニューズ
Keepnews, Orrin 714
キプファー
Kipfer, Barbara Ann 739
キーブーム
Kieboom, Spencer 730
キブラー
Kibbler, Donald 730
キプラガド
Kiplagat, Lornah 739
キプラガト
Kiplagat, Lornah 739
Kiplagat, Silas 739
キブリア
Kibria, Shah A.M.S. 730
キプリアヌ
Kyprianou, Markos 778
Kyprianou, Spyros 778
ギブリン
Giblin, Les 495
キーブル
Keeble, Emma J. 713
キブルツ

Kyburz, Josef A. 778
キプルト
Kipruto, Brimin Kiprop 740
Kipruto, Conseslus 740
Kipruto, Vincent 740
キプロップ
Kiprop, Asbel 739
Kiprop, Asbel Kipruto 739
キプロティク
Kiprotich, Stephen 740
キプロプ
Kiprop Toroitich, Boniface 740
キブワナ
Kibwana, Kivutha 730
ギブンス
Givens, Mychal 503
ギブンズ
Givens, Chris 503
キベジンジャ
Kivejinja, Kirunda 742
キベト
Kibet, Sylvia Jebiwott 730
キベヤ
Kibeya, Saidi 730
ギベール
Guibert, Emmanuel 544
Guibert, Françoise de 544
キベルラン
Kiberlain, Sandrine 730
キベンジンジャ
Kivenjinja, Kirunda 742
キボウェン
Kibowen, John 730
キボキアン
Kevorkian, Jack 723
キボピラタシ
Quipo Pilataxi, Carlos Eduardo 1145
ギホン
Gichon, Mordechai 496
ギボン
Gibbon, David 495
Gibbon, Miriam 495
Gibbon, Piers 495
ギボンス
Gibbons, John 495
ギボンズ
Gibbons, Alan 495
Gibbons, Andrew S. 495
Gibbons, Ann 495
Gibbons, Barry J. 495
Gibbons, Dave 495
Gibbons, Eugenia 495
Gibbons, Gemma 495
Gibbons, James F. 495
Gibbons, John 495
Gibbons, Kaye 495
Gibbons, Tony 495
キマニ・マルゲ
Kimani Nganga Maruge 736
ギ・マニュエル
Guy-Manuel 549
キマニ・ンガンガ・マルゲ
Kimani Nganga Maruge 736
キマネン
Kimanen, Seppo 736
キマラー
Kimmerer, Robin Wall 736
キマーリング
Kimmerling, Baruch 736
ギマール
Guimard, Paul 544
ギマレス
Guimarães, Helder 544
キ・マンタプ・スダルソノ
Ki Manteb Soedharsono 736
キ・マントゥブ・スダルソノ
Ki Manteb Soedharsono 736
キミコ
Kimiko 736
KIMIKO 736
キミソパ
Kimisopa, Bire 736
キミッヒ
Kimmich, Joshua 736
キム
Kim, Ae-ran 732
Kim, A-jung 732
Kim, A-lang 732
Kim, Amy Jo 732
Kim, Andre 732
Kim, Bo-kyung 732
Kim, Bom 732
Kim, Bomsori 732
Kim, Boom Soo 732
Kim, Bum 732
Kim, Byoul A 732
Kim, Byung-hyun 732
Kim, Byung-il 732
Kim, Chaelee 732
Kim, Chai-ho 732
Kim, Chang-ryong 732
Kim, Chang-sik 732
Kim, Chang-su 732
Kim, Chol Jin 732
Kim, Chon-gyun 732
Kim, Choon-mie 732
Kim, Dae-hwan 732
Kim, Dae-jung 732
Kim, Dami 732
Kim, Daniel 732
Kim, Daniel H. 732
Kim, Da Sol 732
Kim, Daul 732
Kim, Dong-hoon 732
Kim, Dong-jin 732
Kim, Dong-jo 732
Kim, Dong-joo 732
Kim, Dong-Kyoon 732
Kim, Dong-tae 732
Kim, Dong-wan 732
Kim, Dong-wook 732
Kim, Doo-gwan 732
Kim, Duk-soo 732
Kim, Du-nam 732
Kim, Elaine H. 732
Kim, Elizabeth 732
Kim, Eul-dong 732
Kim, Eunjung 732
Kim, Gene 732
Kim, Georgy 732
Kim, Geun-hong 732
Kim, Geun-tae 732
Kim, Gin-pyo 732
Kim, Guk-tae 732
Kim, Gyok-sik 733
Kim, Ha-neul 733
Kim, Han-gil 733
Kim, Hee-jung 733
Kim, Hee-seon 733
Kim, Ho-jin 733
Kim, Hoon 733
Kim, Ho-shik 733
Kim, Hui-yong 733
Kim, Hwang-sik 733
Kim, Hyang Mi 733
Kim, Hye-Gyong 733
Kim, Hye-ja 733
Kim, Hyeon-woo 733
Kim, Hye-Song 733
Kim, Hye-soo 733
Kim, Hyo-Jung 733
Kim, Hyong-sik 733
Kim, Hyon-gyong 733
Kim, Hyon-hui 733
Kim, Hyon Ung 733
Kim, Hyun-chong 733
Kim, Hyung-joong 733
Kim, Hyun Soo 733
Kim, Hyun-woong 733
Kim, Il-chol 733
Kim, Il-guk 733
Kim, In-sik 733
Kim, In-Young 733
Kim, Jacqueline 733
Kim, Jae-bum 733
Kim, Jaegwon 733
Kim, Jae-Hong 733
Kim, Jae-song 733
Kim, Jae-soo 733
Kim, Jae-won 733
Kim, Jai-ok 733
Kim, Jang-mi 733
Kim, Jang-soo 733
Kim, Jeong-hak 733
Kim, Ji-ha 733
Kim, Ji-hoo 733
Kim, Jim Yong 733
Kim, Jin-kyu 733
Kim, Jin-kyung 733
Kim, Jin-pyo 733
Kim, Jin-Su 733
Kim, Jin-woo 733
Kim, Ji-u 733
Kim, Ji-woon 733
Kim, Ji Yeon 733
Kim, Ji-yeon 733
Kim, Jong-chul 733
Kim, Jong-deok 733
Kim, Jong-gak 733
Kim, Jong-hoon 733
Kim, Jong-il 733
Kim, Jong-nam 733
Kim, Jong-pil 733
Kim, Jong Su 733
Kim, Jong-un 733
Kim, Jung-eun 733
Kim, Junghum 733
Kim, Jung-hyuk 733
Kim, Jung-kil 734
Kim, Jung-rin 734
Kim, Jun-Hee 734
Kim, Kap-soo 734
Kim, Kenneth A. 734
Kim, Ki-choon 734
Kim, Ki-duk 734
Kim, Kuk-hyang 734
Kim, Kum-lae 734
Kim, Kwang-chol 734
Kim, Kwang-hyun 734
Kim, Kwang-rin 734
Kim, Kwang-soo 734
Kim, Kwang-ung 734
Kim, Kwang-yong 734
Kim, Kwan-jin 734
Kim, Kye-gwan 734
Kim, Kyok-sik 734
Kim, Kyong-hui 734
Kim, Kyong-jun 734
Kim, Kyong-nam 734
Kim, Kyoung hee 734
Kim, Kyung-han 734
Kim, Kyung-Hee 734
Kim, Kyu-ri 734
Kim, Larry 734
Kim, Man-bok 734
Kim, Man-su 734
Kim, Mea-ja 734
Kim, Min-joon 734
Kim, Min-woo 734
Kim, Mi-rae 734
Kim, Myong Hyok 734
Kim, Myung-gon 734
Kim, Myung-ja 734
Kim, Myung-min 734
Kim, Nam-gil 734
Kim, Nam-il 734
Kim, Peter 734
Kim, Pong-chol 734
Kim, Rae-won 734
Kim, Rak-hui 734
Kim, Rang 734
Kim, Richard E. 734
Kim, Ri-hye 734
Kim, Ryon-mi 734
Kim, Sang-kyung 734
Kim, Sang-man 734
Kim, Sang-su 734
Kim, Scott 734
Kim, Seong Ju 734
Kim, Seong-min 734
Kim, Seung Beom 734
Kim, Seung-kew 734
Kim, Seung-woo 734
Kim, Seung-youn 734
Kim, Seung-yul 734
Kim, Shin Dong 734
Kim, Shin-il 734
Kim, Sinclair 734
Kim, Sol-mi 734
Kim, Song Guk 734
Kim, Song I 734
Kim, Soo-hyun 735
Kim, Soo-ja 735
Kim, Sou-hwan 735
Kim, So-yeon 735
Kim, Suck Won 735
Kim, Su-hak 735
Kim, Suki 735
Kim, Suk-jun 735
Kim, Suk-soo 735
Kim, Sung 735
Kim, Sung-du 735
Kim, Sung-ho 735
Kim, Sung-hwan 735
Kim, Sung-hyon 735
Kim, Sung-jae 735
Kim, Sung-jin 735
Kim, Sung-jong 735
Kim, Sung-keun 735
Kim, Sung Tai 735
Kim, Sung Teack 735
Kim, Su-ro 735
Kim, Suyoen 735
Kim, Tae-chang 735
Kim, Tae-hee 735
Kim, Tae-ho 735
Kim, Tae-Hyung 735
Kim, Tae-kyun 735
Kim, Tae Whan 735
Kim, Tae-young 735
Kim, Tag-hwan 735
Kim, Thae-bong 735
Kim, Thae-yong 735
Kim, Tok-hun 735
Kim, Ui-sun 735
Kim, Ung-gwan 735
Kim, Un-guk 735
Kim, Un Hyang 735
Kim, Un-su 735

Kim, Wan-su 735
Kim, W.Chan 735
Kim, Won-hong 735
Kim, Woo-sik 735
Kim, Yang 735
Kim, Yang-gon 735
Kim, Yeong-ae 735
Kim, Yeon-koung 735
Kim, Yeon-su 735
Kim, Yong-chun 735
Kim, Yong-gwang 735
Kim, Yong-ho 735
Kim, Yong-hun 735
Kim, Yong-il 735
Kim, Yong-jae 735
Kim, Yong-jin 735
Kim, Yong-ju 735
Kim, Yong-nam 735
Kim, Yong-sam 735
Kim, Yong-shun 735
Kim, Yong-sun 735
Kim, Yong-woon 735
Kim, Yon-ja 735
Kim, Yoon 736
Kim, Yoon-ki 736
Kim, Yoon-whan 736
Kim, Youg-suk 736
Kim, Young 736
Kim, Young-Chan 736
Kim, Young-gwon 736
Kim, Young-ha 736
Kim, Young-hwan 736
Kim, Young-ju 736
Kim, Young-sam 736
Kim, Yu Jin 736
Kim, Yu-na 736
Kim, Yun-jin 736
Kim, Yun-seok 736
Kim Hyon Hui 736

キムジーハウス
Kimsey-House, Henry 736
Kimsey-House, Karen 736

キムト
Kimto, Fatime 736

キムニャ
Kimnya, Amos 736
Kimunya, Amos 736

キムニヤ
Kimunya, Amos 736

キム・マーフィ
Kim, Murphy 734

キムマン
Kimmann, Niek 736

キム・モダン
Mordaunt, Kim 973

キム・ヨンジャ
Kim, Yon-ja 735

キムラ
Kimura, Doreen 736
Kimura, Kathleen 736
Kimura, Taky 736

キムリ
Kimuli, Michael 736

キムリッカ
Kymlicka, Will 778

キームル
Kiemle, David J. 730

キメット
Kimetto, Dennis 736

ギメネス
Gimenez, Carlos 500

キメル
Kimmel, Elizabeth Cody 736
Kimmel, Eric A. 736

キメルマン
Kimmelman, Michael 736

キモ・スタンボイル
Kimo Stamboel 736

キャー
Kjaer, Henriette 743

ギャイエ
Galliez, Roxane Marie 474

キャヴァナー
Cavanagh, Steve 238

キャヴァラーロ
Cavallaro, Gina 238

キャヴァリア
Cavalier, Stephen 238

キャヴァリ＝スフォルツァ
Cavalli-Sforza, Luigi Luca 238

キャヴィネス
Caviness, Madeline Harrison 238

ギャウロフ
Ghiaurov, Nicolai 493

ギャガン
Gaghan, Stephen 471

キャサーウッド
Catherwood, Frederick 237

ギャザコール
Gathercole, Susan E. 483

ギャザーズ
Gathers, Rico 483

キャサデイ
Cassaday, John 234

ギャザラ
Gazzara, Ben 485

キャサリー
Casserly, Michael 234
Casserly, Peter 234

キャサリン妃
Catherine 237

キャシー
Casey, Meghan 233
Cathey, Jack M. 237
Cathy, Dan 237

キャシディ
Cassidy, Anne 234
Cassidy, Carla Bracale 234
Cassidy, Cathy 234
Cassidy, Dawn 234
Cassidy, Laura 234
Cassidy, Virginia R. 234
Cassidy, Wanda 234

キャシディー
Cassidy, Cathy 234
Cassidy, J.J. 234

キャシュフォード
Cashford, Jules 233

キャシン＝スコット
Cassin-Scott, Jack 235

キャス
Cass, Kiera 234

キャスカート
Cathcart, Craig 237

ギャスキル
Gaskill, William 482

キャスター
Castor, Harriet 236

キャスティ
Casti, John L. 235

キャスティール
Casteel, Seth 235

ギャスティル
Gastil, John 483

キャステリー
Castelly, Asnage 235

キャスト
Cast, Kristin 235
Cast, P.C. 235

キャストナー
Castner, Brian 236

キャストラ
Castera, Georges 235

キャストンゾ
Castonzo, Anthony 236

キャスパー
Casper, Billy 234
Casper, Drew 234

ギャスマン
Gassman, Julie 483

キャズミアー
Kazmir, Scott 712

キャスリオーネ
Caslione, John A. 234

キャスリルズ
Kasrils, Ronald 707
Kasrils, Ronnie 707

キャセッセ
Casssese, Silvia Fano 235

キャセール
Cassell, Sam 234

ギヤソフ
Giyasov, Shakhram 503

キャタモール
Cattermole, Lee 237

キャッシュ
Cars, Jane 230
Cash, Jeremy 233
Cash, Johnny 233
Cash, Kevin 233
Cash, Michaelia 233
Cash, Rosanne 233
Cash, Wiley 233
Cash, William 233

キャッシュダン
Cashdan, Sheldon 233

キャッシュナー
Cashner, Andrew 234

キャッシュマン
Cashman, Brian 234
Cashman, Kevin 234

キャッシン
Cashin, Cheryl 234

キャッスル
Castle, Caroline 236
Castle, Frances 236
Castle, Jayne 236
Castle, J.R. 236
Castle, Lana R. 236
Castle, Richard 236

キャッセル
Cassel, Matt 234
Cassell, Eric J. 234

キャッソス
Catsos, Patsy 237

キャッチ
Katsh, Abraham Isaac 709

キャッチプール
Catchpool, Michael 237

キャッチャー
Kacher, Chris 694
Katcher, Aaron Hanori 708
Katcher, Philip R.N. 708

キャッチングス
Catchings, Tamika 237

キャッツ
Catz, Safra 237
Katz, Sandor Ellix 709

キャッツク
Katschke, Judy 709

ギャッド
Gad, Josh 470

キャットフォード
Catford, John Cunnison 237

キャットムル
Catmull, Ed 237

ギャツビードリー
Gasdby-dolly, Nyan 482

キャップ
Kapp, Joseph 703

キャップス
Capps, Carter 223
Capps, Ronald Everett 223

キャップリン
Caplin, Robert 223

ギャテ
Gates, Bryan 483

キャディ
Caddy, Alice 213
Caddy, Eileen 213
Khady 724

キャディガン
Cadigan, Pat 213

ギャティス
Gattis, Evan 483

ギャディス
Gaddis, John Lewis 470

キャトー
Catto, Henry Edward 237

キャドウォーラダー
Cadwallader, Allen Clayton 213

キャドバリー
Cadbury, Adrian 212

キャドベリー
Cadbury, Adrian 212
Cadbury, Deborah 212

キャトラル
Cattrall, Kim 237

キャドリー
Kadrey, Richard 694

キャトリン
Catlin, George 237

キャトロウ
Catrow, David 237

キャドワラダー
Cadwallader, Mike 213

ギャナス
Ganus, Jake 477

キャナダイン
Cannadine, David 221

キャナディー
Canady, Maurice 220

キャナン
Canan, Penelope 221

キャニオン
Canyon, Christopher 222

ギャニオン
Gagnon, Elisa 471
Gagnon, George W. 471

キャニング
Canning, John 221

キャネル
Cannell, Stephen 221

ギャネンドラ・ビル・ビクラム・シャー・デブ
Gyanendra Bir Bikram

Shah Dev 550
ギャネンドラ・ビル・ビクラム・シャハ・デブ
Gyanendra Bir Bikram Shah Dev 550
ギャノ
Gano, Graham 476
キャノン
Cannon, Barbara 221
Cannon, Christopher P. 221
Cannon, Curt 221
Cannon, Dee 221
Cannon, Dolores 221
Cannon, Jeff 221
Cannon, Jon 221
Cannon, Joseph G. 221
Cannon, Lawrence 221
Cannon, Marcia G. 221
Cannon, Marcus 221
Cannon, Nick 221
Cannon, Zander 222
Kanon, Joseph 702
ギャノン
Gannon, Jack R. 476
Gannon, Michael 476
Ganong, Travis 476
ギャノング
Ganong, William F. 476
キャノン・ブルックス
Cannon-brookes, Mike 222
キャパ
Capa, Cornell 222
キャバイェ
Cabaye, Yohan 212
キャパス
Kappas, John G. 703
ギャバート
Gabbert, Blaine 469
ギャバード
Gabbard, Glen O. 469
キャバナー
Cavanagh, Steve 238
キャパニック
Kaepernick, Colin 695
キャバニュー
Cavagnoud, Regine 238
キャハラン
Cahalan, Susannah 213
キャパルディ
Capaldi, Jim 222
キャパレル
Capparell, Stephanie 223
キャバン
Cabban, Vanessa 212
キャピ
Capi, Nordly 223
キャピー
Capie, Forrest 223
キャピー原田
Cappy Harada 223
キャビラ
Chavira, Denise A. 250
ギャビン
Gavin, Francesca 484
Gavin, James 484
キャファティ
Cafferty, Thomas P. 213
キャプタン
Captan, Monie 223
キャプテン・ビーフハート
Captain Beefheart 223
ギャフニー
Gaffney, Tyler 470
キャプラン
Caplan, Elinor 223
Caplan, Neil 223
Kaplan, Wendy 703
ギャブリー
Gabree, Jon 470
キャプリエイアン
Kaprielian, James 703
キャプリン
Caplin, Adam 223
キャプリンスキー
Caplivski, Daniel 223
キャプロー
Kaplow, Louis 703
ギャベイ
Gabbay, Tom 469
キャペリ
Cappelli, Peter 223
キャベンディッシュ
Cavendish, Lucy 238
キャボット
Cabot, Meg 212
Cabot, Tracy 212
キャマコサ
Kyamakosa, Mutombo 778
キャム
Cam, Philip 217
キャムセル
Camsell, Don 220
ギャムツォ
Gyamtsho, Pema 550
Gyamtsho, Thinley 550
ギャメル
Gamel, Ben 475
キャメロン
Cameron, David 218
Cameron, DeAnna 218
Cameron, Debra 218
Cameron, Geoff 218
Cameron, Graeme 218
Cameron, James 218
Cameron, Jordan 218
Cameron, Julia 218
Cameron, Kenneth 218
Cameron, Kim S. 218
Cameron, Kirk 218
Cameron, Marc 218
Cameron, Michael J. 218
Cameron, Miriam E. 218
Cameron, Peter 218
Cameron, Rebecca P. 218
Cameron, Rondo E. 218
Cameron, Stella 218
Cameron, Susan M. 218
Cameron, W.Bruce 218
キャメロン・ワット
Cameron Watt, Donald 218
キャモン
Camon, Alessandro 218
ギャモン
Gamon, David 475
ギャラ
Garat, Anne-Marie 477
キャラウェイ
Callaway, Barbara J. 216
Callaway, Mickey 216
Callaway, Phillip R. 216
ギャラウェイ
Galloway, Matt 474
ギャラガー
Gallagher, Ann 473
Gallagher, Cam 473
Gallagher, Christopher 473
Gallagher, Fred 473
Gallagher, Hugh 473
Gallagher, James P. 473
Gallagher, John, Jr. 473
Gallagher, Liam 473
Gallagher, Margie Lee 473
Gallagher, Noel 473
Gallagher, Paul Richard 473
Gallagher, Shaun 473
Gallagher, Tess 473
Gallagher, Thomas H. 473
Gallagher, Vincent A. 473
Gallagher Hateley, Barbara J. 473
ギャラガー＝マンディー
Gallagher-Mundy, Chrissie 473
ギャラクシー
Galaxy, Jackson 472
キャラス
Karras, Alex 706
キャラダイン
Carradine, David 229
ギャラット
Garratt, Chris 481
Garratt, John 481
ギャラップ
Gallup, Gordon G., Jr. 474
キャラディン
Carradine, David 229
Carradine, Tank 229
キャラナン
Callanan, Liam 216
Callanan, Patrick 216
Callanan, Tom 216
ギャラニヨン
Garagnon, Françoise 477
ギャラハグ
Gallehugh, Allen 473
Gallehugh, D.Sue 473
キャラハン
Callaghan, Garth 216
Callaghan, Glenn M. 216
Callaghan, James 216
Callahan, Bryce 216
Callahan, Gene 216
Callahan, James J. 216
Callahan, Joanne M. 216
Callahan, Joe 216
Callahan, Lisa P. 216
Callahan, Maureen 216
Callahan, Raymond E. 216
Callahan, Roger 216
キャラビン
Carabin, Ioana G. 224
ギャラファー
Gallagher, Margaret 473
ギャラベ
Garrabé, Jean 481
キャラン
Callan, Jamie Cat 216
Karan, Donna 704
ギャラント
Gallant, David 473
Gallant, Janet 473
ギャランド
Galland, Jonathan 473
Galland, Leo 473
キャリー
Calley, John 216
Carey, Benedict 225
Carey, David Leonard 225
Carey, Don 225
Carey, Ka'Deem 225
Carey, Mariah 225
Carey, Nessa 225
Carey, Pat 225
Carey, Thomas J. 225
Carrey, Jim 229
Carrie, T.J. 229
Carry, David 230
ギャリ
Gally 474
キャリア
Carrier, Chubby 229
Carrier, James 229
キャリアー
Carrier, Derek 229
Carrier, L.Mark 229
キャリィ
Carey, Lois J. 225
キャリガー
Carriger, Gail 229
キャリガン
Carrigan, Sara 229
キャリクスティ
Calixte, Orland 216
キャリコット
Callicott, J.Baird 216
キャリーズ
Callies, David L. 216
キャリスター
Callister, William D. 216
ギャリスン
Garrison, Paul 481
キャリソン
Carrison, Dan 230
ギャリソン
Galison, Peter 473
Garrison, Susan J. 481
キャリック
Carrick, Michael 229
ギャリックス
Garrix, Martin 481
ギャリック＝スティール
Garrick-Steele, Rodger 481
ギャリフ
Gariff, David 480
キャリル
Carril, Pete 229
キャリン
Carrin, Charles 230
キャリングトン
Carrington, Lloyd 230
キャリントン
Carrington, Leonora 230
Carrington, Lisa 230
Carrington, Lucinda 230
Carrington, Patricia 230
Carrington, Terri Lyne 230
Carrington, Tori 230
ギヤール
Guyart, Astrid 549
Guyart, Brice 549
キャルコート
Calcote, Aaron S. 214
キャルシディス
Calcidise, Kathleen 214
ギャルツェン
Gyaltshen, Dawa 550
ギャルトン
Galton, Jeremy 474
キャルナン
Calnan, James 217

ギャルネール
Gerner, Jochen 491
ギャルビス
Galvis, Freddy 474
ギャルフォード
Galford, Robert 472
キャルホーン
Calhoun, Craig 215
キャレイ
Caillat, Colbie 214
Carey, James R. 225
Carey, Suzanne 225
ギャレイズ
Gallays, Jillian Alice 473
ギャレスピー＝セルズ
Gillespie-Sells, Kath 499
ギャレット
Garrett, Amir 481
Garrett, Betty 481
Garrett, Brad 481
Garrett, Bradley L. 481
Garrett, Brandon 481
Garrett, David 481
Garrett, Diante 481
Garrett, Jason 481
Garrett, Keyarris 481
Garrett, Laurie 481
Garrett, Mary Ann 481
Garrett, Peter 481
Garrett, Siedah 481
Garrett, William E., Jr. 481
Garrett, Zach 481
ギャレリ
Garelli, Cristina 480
キャレール
Carrère, Emmanuel 229
キャレル
Carrell, Jennifer Lee 229
ギャレル
Garel, Béatrice 480
ギャレン
Gallen, Joses 473
ギャレンバーガー
Gallenberger, Joseph 473
キャレンバッハ
Callenbach, Ernest 216
キャロ
Carrot, Béatrice 230
ギャロ
Gallo, David A. 474
Gallo, Ernest 474
Gallo, Irene 474
Gallo, Joey 474
Gallo, Vincent 474
ギャロウェー
Galloway, Jackie 474
キャロウェイ
Callaway, Ely R. 216
Calloway, Cassidy 216
ギャロウェイ
Galloway, Brendan 474
Galloway, Jeff 474
Galloway, Joseph L. 474
Galloway, Langston 474
Galloway, Ruth 474
Galloway, Steven 474
キャロザース
Carothers, Merlin R. 227
キャロット
Keret, Etgar 721
Kerrett, Etgar 722
キャロニタ
Calonita, Jen 217
キャロライズ
Karolides, Nicholas J. 706
キャロリン・イヴ・カンジュウロウ
Carolyn Eve Kanjuro 227
キャロル
Carrol, Aileen 230
Carrol, Eugene J. 230
Carrol, John 230
Carroll, Aaron E. 230
Carroll, Alice 230
Carroll, Amber 230
Carroll, Andy 230
Carroll, Bernadette 230
Carroll, Cynthia 230
Carroll, Deborah 230
Carroll, DeMarre 230
Carroll, Don 230
Carroll, Douglas 230
Carroll, Heidi 230
Carroll, James 230
Carroll, Jenny 230
Carroll, Jim 230
Carroll, John 230
Carroll, John D. 230
Carroll, John Millar 230
Carroll, Jonathan 230
Carroll, Judy 230
Carroll, Kathleen M. 230
Carroll, Kevin 230
Carroll, Lara 230
Carroll, Lee 230
Carroll, Marisa 230
Carroll, Michael 230
Carroll, Nancy 230
Carroll, Nolan 230
Carroll, Paul B. 230
Carroll, Pete 230
Carroll, Peter James 230
Carroll, Robert G. 230
Carroll, Robert Todd 230
Carroll, Rory 230
Carroll, Sean B. 230
Carroll, Sean M. 230
Carroll, Susan 230
Carroll, Tom 230
キャローロ
Carollo, Jeff 227
キャロン
Caron, Ann F. 227
Caron, Gérard 227
Caron, Joseph 227
Caron, Leslie 227
Caron, Romi 227
ギャワリ
Gyawali, Deepak 550
Gyawali, Radha Kumari 550
キャン
Cain, Matt 214
Can, Yasemin 220
Cann, A.J. 221
ギャングウィッシュ
Gangwish, Jack 476
ギャングロフ
Gangloff, Mark 476
キャンザス
Kansas, Dave 702
ギャンジー
Ganji, Pariyoush 476
キャンシラ
Cancilla, Dorothy Rose 221
キャンター
Cantor, Norman F. 222
Kanter, Enes 702
Kantor, Michael 702
キャンタメッサ
Cantamessa, Gene S. 222
キャンタローン
Cantillon, Eli Aleksandersen 222
キャンティ
Canty, Morton John 222
キャンティン
Cantin, Candis 222
キャンデラリオ
Candelario, Jeimer 221
キャント
Canto, Victor A. 222
ギャント
Gant, John 476
キャントウェル
Cantwell, Christian 222
Cantwell, Hendrika B. 222
ギャントス
Gantos, Jack 476
キャンドランド
Candland, Paul 221
ギャンドルフィーニ
Gandolfini, James 476
キャントレル
Cantrell, Kat 222
Cantrell, Rebecca 222
キャンドロット
Kandrot, Edward 700
キャントン
Canton, James 222
キャンパナロ
Campanaro, Michael 219
ギャンバレ
Gambale, Frank 475
キャンビアス
Cambias, James L. 218
キャンピオン
Campion, Alexander 220
Campion, Nicholas 220
キャンピス
Campisi, Judith 220
ギャンビニ
Gambini, Cécile 475
キャンプ
Camp, Brandon 218
Camp, Candace 218
Camp, Garrett 218
Camp, Jim 218
Camp, Joe 218
Camp, John McK. 219
キャンフィールド
Canfield, Jack 221
キャンプベル
Campbell, Ian 219
キャンプリン
Camplin, Alisa 220
ギャンブリング
Gambling, John Alfred 475
キャンブル
Campbell, Ramsey 220
ギャンブル
Gamble, Andrew 475
Gamble, Clive 475
Gamble, Kim 475
Gamble, William 475
キャンブロン＝マッケイブ
Cambron-McCabe, Nelda H. 218
キャンベル
Cambell, William 218
Campbell, Alan 219
Campbell, Alastair 219
Campbell, Alastair V. 219
Campbell, Amber 219
Campbell, Andrew 219
Campbell, Anna 219
Campbell, Barbara W. 219
Campbell, Bebe Moore 219
Campbell, Ben Nighthorse 219
Campbell, Bethany 219
Campbell, Bronte 219
Campbell, Calais 219
Campbell, Cate 219
Campbell, Chad 219
Campbell, Chellie 219
Campbell, Darren 219
Campbell, David 219
Campbell, David P. 219
Campbell, De'Vondre 219
Campbell, DiAndre 219
Campbell, Donald Wilfred 219
Campbell, Don G. 219
Campbell, Duncan 219
Campbell, Eddie 219
Campbell, Elizabeth A. 219
Campbell, Erica 219
Campbell, Fiona 219
Campbell, Fraizer 219
Campbell, Gaylon S. 219
Campbell, Gaylon Sanford 219
Campbell, Glen 219
Campbell, G.Michael 219
Campbell, Gordon 219
Campbell, Iain 219
Campbell, Ian 219
Campbell, Ibraheim 219
Campbell, Jack 219
Campbell, James W.P. 219
Campbell, Jane 219
Campbell, Jean 219
Campbell, Jeff 219
Campbell, Jennifer P. L. 219
Campbell, Joel 219
Campbell, John Creighton 219
Campbell, John Dixon 219
Campbell, John E. 219
Campbell, John Y. 219
Campbell, Keith 219
Campbell, Keith Gordon 219
Campbell, Kurt M. 219
Campbell, Laurie 219
Campbell, Luke 219
Campbell, Magda 219
Campbell, Martin 219
Campbell, Mary K. 220
Campbell, Milton 220
Campbell, Nancy Marie 220
Campbell, Naomi 220
Campbell, Neil 220
Campbell, Peter Nelson 220
Campbell, Ramsey 220
Campbell, Rod 220
Campbell, Ross 220
Campbell, Ruth 220
Campbell, Scott 220
Campbell, Shawna 220
Campbell, Stan 220

Campbell, Stephen John 220
Campbell, Stuart 220
Campbell, Susan B. 220
Campbell, T.Colin 220
Campbell, Terry W. 220
Campbell, Thomas Lothrop 220
Campbell, Thomas M. 220
Campbell, Vera Leona 220
Campbell, Verity 220
Campbell, Veronica 220
Campbell, William 220
Campbell, William C. 220
Campbell, W.Keith 220

キャンベル・ブラウン
Campbell-Brown, Veronica 220

キャンペン
Kampen, Thomas 700

キュー
Kew, Yvonne 723
Khieu Kanharith 728
Kiew, Ruth 731

キュアロン
Cuarón, Alfonso Orozco 306
Cuarón, Jonás 306

ギュイヨン
Guyon, Maxime 549

キュヴェリエ
Cuvellier, Vincent 310

キューウェル
Kewell, Harry 723

キュヴリエ
Cuverlier, Jean 310

キューエル
Kewell, Harry 723

キュー・カナリット
Khieu Kanharith 728

キューグラー
Kuegler, Sabine 771

キュークリー
Kuechly, Luke 771

キューサック
Cusack, Joan 309
Cusack, John 309

キューザック
Cusack, Joan 309
Cusack, John 309

キュー・サムファン
Khieu Samphan 728

キュザン
Cuzin, Jean-Pierre 310

キュー・サンパン
Khieu Samphan 728

キュー・サンファン
Khieu Samphan 728

キュシェラ
Cucherat, Yann 306

キュシュ
Cuche, Didier 306

ギュスターブ
Gustave, Faubert 548

キュステンマッハー
Küstenmacher, Marion 776
Küstenmacher, Werner Tiki 776

キュセ
Cusset, François 310

キューゼンベリー
Quesenbery, Whitney 1144

キューダー
Kuder, Tyler 771

キュタリー
Cuttaree, Jaya 310

ギュチュリュ
Güçlü, Sami 542

キュック
Cuq, Henri 308

キュッセ
Cusset, Catherine 310

キュッテル
Kuettel, Andreas 771

キュット
Kütt, Helmen 776

キュッヒェル
Küchl, Rainer 770

キュッヒル
Küchl, Rainer 770

ギュッマン
Gutman, Claude 549

キュッロネン
Kyllönen, Merja 778

ギュティエレズ
Gutierrez, Ernesto 548

Q－ティップ
Q-Tip 1143

ギューティング
Güting, Eberhard W. 549

キュトゥックチュオウル・メフメット
Kütükçüoğlu Mehmet 776

ギュナイ
Günay, Ertuğrul 546

キュナスト
Künast, Renate 773

キューヌル
Kühnl, Karel 771

ギュネシュ
Gunes, Senol 546

キューネン
Kunen, Kenneth 773

キューパック
Cupach, William R. 308

キューバート
Kubert, Adam 770
Kubert, Andy 770
Kubert, Joe 770

キューバン
Cuban, Larry 306
Cuban, Mark 306

キュービック
Kubick, Dana 770
Kubik, Jeff 770

キュービット
Cubitt, Allan 306

キューピット
Cupitt, Don 308

キュービー＝マクダウェル
Kube-McDowell, Michael P. 770

キューブラ
Kuebler, Kim K. 771

キューブラー
Kubler, Roland 770

キュブラー
Kubler, Lukas 770

キューブラー・ロス
Kübler-Ross, Elisabeth 770

キュプリアヌ
Kyprianou, Michael 778

キューブリック
Kubrick, Christiane 770

キュベルベック
Kuebelbeck, Julie 771

ギュミノ
Guilleminot, Marie-Ange 544

キュメナル
Cumenal, Frédéric 307

キューメロウ
Kumerow, Jake 773

ギュラルニック
Guralnick, Peter 547

ギュラルプ
Guralp, Inci 547

キュリー
Curie, Eve 308
Cury, Philippe 309

ギュリ
Gyu-ri 550

キュリアス
Curíace, Gísmonde 308

キュリアン
Curien, Hubert 308

ギュリヴェール
Gulliver, Lili 545

ギュリブ・ファキム
Gurib-fakim, Bibi Ameenah Firdaus 547

キュリレンコ
Kurylenko, Olga 775

キュール
Kühl, Johannes 771

ギュル
Gül, Abdullah 545

ギュルトラー
Gurtler, Helga 548

キュールブス
Kuelbs, Jasmin 771

ギュルベヤズ
Gülbeyaz, Abdurrahman 545

ギュルメン
Gürmen, Osman Necmi 547

ギュルルジェ
Güllüce, İdris 545

ギュレ
Guillerey, Aurélie 544

ギュレット
Guerette, Michelle 542

キュレリ
Curelli, Augusta 308

ギュレル
Güler, Mehmet Hilmi 545

キューレン
Keulen, Mensje van 723

ギュレン
Gülen, Fethullah 545

ギュロウスキ
Gyurovszky, László 550

キューン
Kuehn, Eileen 771
Kühn, Johannes 771
Kün, Mathias 773

ギュン
Gun, Bediha 546

キュング
Küng, Hans 773
Küng, Thomas 773

ギュンター
Guenther, Doris 542
Gunter, Christian 546
Günter, Ingo 546

キュンツェル
Künzel-nystad, Claudia 774

ギュンドアン
Gundogan, Ilkay 546

ギュンベル
Gumbel, Dietrich 546

キュンメル
Kümmel, Friedrich 773

キーヨ
Keogh, Barbara K. 720

キョ
Koh, Sekai 751

ギヨ
Guyot, Celine 549

ギヨー
Guillaud, Jean Louis 544

キョウ
Jiang, Jian-hua 673
Jiang, Wen 673
Qiao, Pei-xin 1143

キヨオカ
Kiyooka, Roy 742

ギョカルプ
Gokalp, Hunus Yusuf 508

ギョクハン
Gokhan, Gonul 508

ギョクハン・トレ
Gokhan Tore 508

ギョクベルク
Gokberk, Koray 508

キヨサキ
Kiyosaki, Emi 743
Kiyosaki, Kim 743
Kiyosaki, Robert 743

ギョニュル
Gönül, Vecdi 514

キョプルル
Koprulu, Emine 756

ギョールコー
Gyoerkoe, Kevin L. 550

ギョルチェフ
Gjorcev, Marjan 503

キヨンガ
Kiyonga, Crispus 742

ギョンベール
Gyomber, Norbert 550

キーラー
Keeler, O.B. 714

ギラー
Giller, Esther 498
Giller, Pinchas 498

キライ
Kiraj, Stefan 740
Kiraly, Karch 740

ギラヴォギ
Guilavogui, Josuha 544

ギラウリ
Gilauri, Nika 497
Gilauri, Nikoloz 497

キラカ
Kilaka, John 731

キラ・クーチ
Quiller-Couch, *Sir* Arthur Thomas 1144

キラー・コワルスキー
Killer Kowalski 731

ギラシ
Guirassy, Moustapha 545
Guirassy, Sehrou 545

キラス
Kiras, James 740

キラタ

キ

キ

Kirata, Natanaera 740
ギーラック
Gierach, John 496
ギラッド
Gilad, Benjamin 497
ギラード
Gillard, Julia 498
Girard, Christine 501
ギラド
Guirado, Guilhem 545
キラー・トーア・カマタ
Killer Tor Kamata 731
ギラニ
Gilani, Syed Yousuf Raza 497
Gillani, Pir Aftab Hussain Shah 498
Gillani, Syed Mumtaz Alam 498
ギラボキ
Guilavogui, Oyé 544
ギラボギ
Guilavogui, Galema 544
Guilavogui, Oyé 544
ギラム
Gillam, Frederick 498
キラール
Kilar, Wojciech 731
キラル
Kilar, Wojciech 731
ギラルディーニ
Ghiraldini, Leonardo 493
ギラン
Gielan, Michelle 496
Gillan, Ian 498
Guilland, Josiane 544
ギランダース
Gillanders, Ann 498
キランティ
Kiranti, Gopal 740
キーリ
Kiely, Sophia 730
キーリー
Keeley, Brian 714
Keeley, Jackie 714
Keeley, Larry 714
Keeley, Stuart M. 714
Keely, Jack 714
Kiley, David 731
Kiley, Kevin F. 731
キリ
Killi, Anita 731
ギリ
Gilley, Bruce 499
Giri, Deepak 502
ギリー
Gilley, Sheridan 499
キリアコ
Chiriaco, Sonia 256
キリアコフ
Kiriakov, Tanyu 740
キリアシス
Kiriasis, Sandra 740
キリアム
Quilliam, Susan 1144
ギリアム
Gilliam, Garry 499
Gilliam, Terry 499
Gilliam, Walter S. 499
キリアーン
Kylián, Jiří 778
キリアン
Killian, Diana 731
Kylián, Jiří 778
ギリエウル
Guirieoulou, Emile 545
ギリェム
Guillem Primo, Vicent 544
キリエラ
Kiriella, Lakshman 740
ギリェルメ
Guilherme 544
ギリェン
Guillen, Ozzie 544
キリエンカ
Kiryienka, Vasili 741
ギリオーニ
Ghiglione, Michael 493
キリオン
Killion, Ann 731
Killion, Kimberly 731
Killion, Redley 732
ギリオン
Gillion, Colin 499
ギリガシビリ
Giligashvili, Roland 498
ギリガン
Gilligan, James 499
Gilligan, Stephen 499
キリク
Kilic, Yakup 731
キリケシュ
Chiriches, Vlad 256
ギーリシュ
Gierisch, Kristin 496
キーリス
Ķīlis, Roberts 731
ギリース
Gillies, Donald 499
ギリス
Gillis, Alec 499
Gillis, Deborah 499
Gillis, Eric 499
Gillis, Jennifer 499
Gillis, John R. 499
Gillis, Tracy Knippenburg 499
ギリスピー
Gillispie, Charles Coulston 499
ギリソン
Gillison, Karen 499
キリチェンコ
Kirichenko, Alekseĭ Alekseevich 740
キリツォフ
Kiritzov, Stefan 740
ギリック
Gillick, Pat 499
キリッチ
Kilicci, Adem 731
キリトフスカ
Kalitovska, Lesya 697
キリバルダ
Kilibarda, Vesna 731
キリフィ
Kilifi, Olive 731
キリモ
Kilimo, Linah Jebii 731
ギリヤ
Giria, Evgeniĭ IUr'evich 502
ギリランド
Gilliland, Ben 499
キリル
Kill 731
キリレンコ
Kirilenko, Maria 740
Kirilenko, Vyacheslav 740
Kyrylenko, Ivan 778
キリロフ
Kirillov, Aleksandr Aleksandrovich 740
キリーン
Killeen, Liam 731
キリン
Kirin, Ivica 740
ギリンガム
Gillingham, Sara 499
キーリング
Keeling, Charles David 714
Keeling, J.B.M. 714
Keeling, Shaun 714
ギリングス
Gillings, Bev 499
Gillings, Zoe 499
キリンチュク
Chirinciuc, Iurie 256
キール
Keel, Howard 714
Keel, John A. 714
Keel, Philipp 714
Kiel, Fred 730
Kiel, Richard 730
Kiir, Salva 731
キル
Quill, John 1144
ギル
Gil, Eliana 497
Gill, Andy 498
Gill, Bates 498
Gill, Bob 498
Gill, Denis 498
Gill, Frank B. 498
Gill, Graeme J. 498
Gill, Jerry H. 498
Gill, Margery 498
Gill, Mel 498
Gill, Michael Gates 498
Gill, M.S. 498
Gill, Nathan 498
Gill, Simryn 498
Gill, Tom 498
Gill, Vince 498
キルイ
Kirui, Abel 741
ギルエイロ
Guilheiro, Leandro 544
キルカー
Kilcarr, Patrick J. 731
キルガー
Kilgour, David 731
キルキー
Kilkey, Majella 731
ギルキー
Gilkey, Garrett 498
ギルギノフ
Girginov, Vassil 502
キルキラス
Kirkilas, Gediminas 741
キルクシュタイン
Kirchstein, Olaf 740
ギルクライスト
Gilchrist, Don 498
ギルクリスト
Gilchrist, Gary 498
Gilchrist, Iain D. 498
Gilchrist, Marcus 498
キルゴ
Kilgo, Darius 731
キルゴーア
Kilgore, Daniel 731
ギルシェ
Guilcher, Jean-Michel 544
キルジャプキナ
Kirdyapkina, Anisya 740
キルジャプキン
Kirdyapkin, Sergey 740
キルシュ
Kirsch, Beatrice 741
Kirsch, Hans-Jurgen 741
Kirsch, Sarah 741
キルシュナー
Kirschner, Josef 741
Kirshner, Robert P. 741
キルステン
Kirsten, Wolfgang 741
ギルストラップ
Gilstrap, John 500
ギルソン
Gilson, Stuart C. 500
ギルダー
Gilder, Anne-Lee 498
Gilder, George F. 498
Gilder, Joshua 498
Gilder, Louisa 498
キルチェフ
Kirchev, Miroslav 740
キルチネル
Fernández de Kirchner, Cristina Elisabet 430
Kirchner, Alicia 740
Kirchner, Néstor Carlos 740
キルツ
Kilts, James M. 732
キルティ
Kilty, Richard 732
キルト
Quilt, Linda 1144
キルドー
Kildow (vonn), Lindsey 731
ギルド
Guild, Tricia 544
キルドウ
Kildow, Betty A. 731
ギルトブルグ
Giltburg, Boris 500
ギルトロウ
Giltrow, Helen 500
ギルドン
Guiraudon, Virginie 545
キールナン
Kiernan, Denise 730
キルネチル
Kirchner, Alicia 740
キルパ
Kirpa, Georgiy 741
キールバーガー
Kielburger, Craig 730
Kielburger, Marc 730
キルバーグ
Kilburg, Richard R. 731
ギルバーグ
Gillberg, Christopher 498
ギルバース
Gilbers, Harald 497
ギルバート
Gelabert, Jorge 487

Gilbert, Adrian Geoffrey 497
Gilbert, Alan 497
Gilbert, Alyce 497
Gilbert, Anne Yvonne 497
Gilbert, Avery N. 497
Gilbert, Bobby 497
Gilbert, Brad 497
Gilbert, Dan 497
Gilbert, Daniel Todd 497
Gilbert, David 497
Gilbert, Elizabeth 497
Gilbert, Elizabeth Steep 497
Gilbert, Elizabeth T. 497
Gilbert, G.Nigel 497
Gilbert, Helen 497
Gilbert, Ian 497
Gilbert, Jacqueline 497
Gilbert, James L. 497
Gilbert, John K. 497
Gilbert, Joseph 497
Gilbert, Justin 497
Gilbert, Kei 497
Gilbert, Keon 497
Gilbert, Lucia Albino 497
Gilbert, Marcus 497
Gilbert, Martin 497
Gilbert, Melissa 497
Gilbert, Michael Francis 497
Gilbert, Paul 497
Gilbert, Reggie 497
Gilbert, Sandra 498
Gilbert, Scott F. 498
Gilbert, Shirli 498
Gilbert, Susan 498
Gilbert, Walter 498

ギルバートソン
Gilbertson, Ashley 498

ギルバドッティ
Gylfadóttir, Þórdís Kolbrún Reykfjörð 550

キルパトリック
Kilpatrick, Sean 732

キルヒ
Kirch, Leo 740

キルビ
al-Kirbi, Abu-Baker Abdullah 740
al-Qirbi, Abu-Bakur 1143

キルビー
Kilby, Clyde S. 731
Kilby, Jack St.Clair 731
Kilby, Janice Eaton 731
Kilby, Joan 731

キルヒアイゼン
Kircheisen, Bjoern 740

キルヒガサー
Kirchgasser, Michaela 740

キルヒシュラーガー
Kirchschlager, Angelika 740

キルヒシュレーガー
Kirchschlager, Angelika 740

キルヒヘル
Kirchherr, Astrid 740

キルヒホッフ
Kirchhoff, Gerd Ferdinand 740

キルヒホフ
Kirchhoff, Jan 740

キルヒマー
Kirchmer, Mathias 740

キルヒマン
Kirchmann, Leah 740

ギルビン
Gilpin, Daniel 500

ギルピン
Gilpin, A.M. 500
Gilpin, Daniel 500
Gilpin, Robert 500

キルプ
Kirpu, Erika 741

ギルフォイル
Guilfoile, Kevin 544

キルブリュー
Killebrew, Harmon 731
Killebrew, Miles 731

キルブルー
Killebrew, Harmon 731

ギルヘイロ
Guilheiro, Leandro 544

ギルベリー
Gilberry, Wallace 497

キルヘン
Kirchen, Kim 740

キルペンシュタイン
Kirpensteijn, Jolle 741

ギルボー
Guillebaud, John 544

ギルボア
Gilboa, Amos 498
Gilboa, Itzhak 498

ギルボア＝シェヒトマン
Gilboa-Schechtman, Eva 498

ギルボーイ
Gilboy, George 498

キールホフナー
Kielhofner, Gary 730

キルボーン
Kilborn, Jack 731
Kilbourne, Susan 731

ギルボーン
Gillborn, David 498

キルマー
Kilmer, James V. 732
Kilmer, Jason R. 732
Kilmer, Val 732

ギルマ
Girma, Amante 502
Girma, Birru 502

ギルマー
Gilmer, Maureen 499

キールマイヤー
Kiermayer, Susanne 730

ギルマ・ウォルドギオルギス
Girma Woldegiorgis 502

ギルマーティン
Gilmartin, Rene 499
Gilmartin, Sean 499

キルマン
Kilman, Scott 732

ギルマン
Gillman, Peter 499
Gillman, Sid 499
Gillman, Steve 499
Gilman, Alfred Goodman 499
Gilman, Alfred Zack 499
Gilman, Cheryl 499
Gilman, Dorothy 499
Gilman, Richard 499
Gilman, Susan Jane 499

キルマント
Kirmanto, Joko 741

キルマン・リブトゥンバヌ
Kilman Livtuvanu, Meltek Sato 732

キルミスター
Kilmister, Lemmy 732

ギルメット
Guilmette, Jonathan 544

ギルモア
Gillmor, Dan 499
Gillmore, Crockett 499
Gilmore, Alec 499
Gilmore, Eamon 499
Gilmore, James H. 499
Gilmore, Jennifer 499
Gilmore, Jessica 499
Gilmore, Jim 499
Gilmore, Michael T. 499
Gilmore, Norbert 499
Gilmore, Robert 499
Gilmore, Stephan 499
Gilmour, Dave 499
Gilmour, David 499
Gilmour, H.B. 499
Gilmour, Ian 500
Gilmour, Kyle 500

ギルラス
Gilruth, Susan 500

キルリーヴィ
Killeavy, Maureen 731

ギルレー
Guillerey, Aurélie 544

ギルロー
Gillow, John 499

キルロイ
Kilroy, Phil 732

ギルロイ
Gilroy, Anne M. 500
Gilroy, Dan 500
Gilroy, Frank D. 500
Gilroy, Paul 500
Gilroy, Tony 500

キルワ
Kirwa, Eunice Jepkirui 741
Kirwa, Kipruto Arap 741

キルワース
Kilworth, Garry 732

キルワリゼ
Kirvalidze, David 741

キーレ
Kyireh, Yieleh 778

キレ
Kile, Nelson 731

ギレス
Gilles, Peter 498

ギレスピー
Gillespie, Angus K. 499
Gillespie, Gilbert W., Jr. 499
Gillespie, Ian 499
Gillespie, John Kinsey 499
Gillespie, Lisa Jane 499

ギレーヌ
Guilaine, Jean 544

ギレボー
Guillebeau, Chris 544

キーレン
Kierein, Tom 730

キレーン
Killeen, Richard 731

ギレン
Gillen, Kieron 498

ギレンホール
Gyllenhaal, Jake 550
Gyllenhaal, Maggie 550

キロ
Cheiro 251

ギロ
Ghiro, Alfred 493

ギロー
Guiraud, Charles 545
Guiraud, Florence 545

ギロウ
Gillow, John 499

ギロヴィッチ
Gilovich, Thomas 500

キロガ
Quiroga, María Soledad 1145

キロガ・ラミレス
Quiroga Ramírez, Jorge 1145

キロショ
Kilosho, Jean-Marie Bulambo 732

キロス
Quiros, José Angel 1145
Quiroz, Ulises Granados 1145

ギロフスカ
Gilowska, Zyta 500

ギロペ
Guilloppé, Antoine 544

ギロリー
Guillory, John 544

キロンゾ
Kilonzo, Mutula 732

キワヌーカ
Kiwanuka, Michael 742

キワヌカ
Kiwanuka, Maria 742

キーン
Kean, Alasdair 713
Kean, Sam 713
Kean, Simon 713
Keane, Bryan 713
Keane, John 713
Keane, Marc Peter 713
Keane, Michael 713
Keane, Michael S. 713
Keane, Patrick 713
Keane, Robbie 713
Keane, Roy 713
Keane, Terence Martin 713
Keane, Will 713
Keen, Andrew 714
Keen, Linda 714
Keen, Peter G.W. 714
Keene, Bruce W. 714
Keene, Carolyn 714
Keene, Daniel 714
Keene, Dennis 714
Keene, Donald 714
Keene, Ellin Oliver 714
Keene, M.Lamar 714
Kiehn, Jesper 730

キン
Kim, Dong-jo 732
Kim, Duk-soo 732
Kim, Seung-woo 734
Kim, Yu-na 736
Kinne, Susan Clare 739
Qin, Esther 1143

ギン
Ginn, Ted 500

キン・アウン・ミン
Khin Aung Myint 728

キン・イー
Khin Yi 728

キ

キン・オーンマー
Khin Ohmar 728
キンガム
Kingham, Nick 738
ギンガリッチ
Gingerich, Owen 500
Gingerich, Susan 500
キ
キンキ
Kinkiey, Tryphon 739
キンギ
Kingi, Amason 738
キンキエイ・ムルンバ
Kin-kiey Mulumba, Triphon 739
キンキエイムルンバ
Kin-kiey Mulumba, Triphon 739
キンキエイ・ワ・ムルンバ
Kinkiey Wa Mulumba, Tryphon 739
キンキントゥー
Khin Khin Htoo 728
キング
King, Akeem 737
King, Alan 737
King, Allan 737
King, Alois 737
King, Andrew 737
King, Andy 737
King, Angela E.V. 737
King, Annette 737
King, Audrey J. 737
King, Barbara J. 737
King, Ben E. 737
King, Billie Jean 737
King, Brad 737
King, Brandon 737
King, Brett 737
King, Brian 737
King, Cammie 737
King, Carole 737
King, Cheryl A. Polewach 737
King, Chidi 737
King, Chris 737
King, Christopher Peter 737
King, Claude V. 737
King, Clive 737
King, Colin 737
King, Coretta Scott 737
King, Daren 737
King, Darian 737
King, David 737
King, David C. 737
King, Deborah 737
King, Deon 737
King, Don 737
King, Don Roy 737
King, Earl 737
King, Edmund 737
King, Edward 737
King, Francis Henry 737
King, Gary 737
King, Gary M. 737
King, Gavin 737
King, Gilbert 737
King, Isaac 737
King, Jack Leon 737
King, James 737
King, Jannet 737
King, Jason Gregory 737
King, Jeff 737
King, Jennifer 738
King, John 738
King, John Edward 738
King, John Leonard 738
King, John Paul 738
King, John Robert 738
King, Jonathan 738
King, Jonathon 738
King, Joshua 738
King, Karen L. 738
King, Kitty 738
King, Larry 738
King, Larry W. 738
King, Laurie R. 738
King, Lilly 738
King, Mark 738
King, Marquette 738
King, Martin 738
King, Mary 738
King, Mary C. 738
King, M.C. 738
King, Mervyn Allister 738
King, Michael Patrick 738
King, Morghan Whitney 738
King, Nancy M.P. 738
King, Patricia A. 738
King, Richard 738
King, Robert 738
King, Rodney G. 738
King, Ross 738
King, Russell 738
King, Serge 738
King, Sorrel 738
King, Stephen 738
King, Stephen Michael 738
King, Stephenson 738
King, Susan 738
King, Tavarres 738
King, Thomas A. 738
King, Tom 738
King, Yolanda Denise 738
King, Zalman 738
Kynge, James 778
Yeoh, Michelle 1537
キングアケレレ
King-akerele, Bankie 738
キングシアーズ
King-Sears, Margaret E. 738
キングストン
Kingston, Denise 739
Kingston, Jeff 739
Kingston, Karen 739
Kingston, Katherine 739
Kingston, Maxine Hong 739
Kingston, Paul 739
Kingston, Steve 739
キングスノース
Kingsnorth, Paul 738
キングズバリ
Kingsbury, Noël 738
キングズバリー
Kingsbury, Kate 738
キングズベリー
Kingsbury, Karen 738
Kingsbury, Mikael 738
Kingsbury, Noël 738
キング・スミス
King-Smith, Dick 738
キングスリー
Kingsley, Moses 738
Kingsley, Stephen 738
キングズリー
Kingsley, Ben 738
Kingsley, Kaza 738
キングスレー
Kingsley, Ben 738
Kingsley, Kaza 738
キングズレー
Kingsley, Patrick 738
キングスレイ
Kingsley, Kaza 738
キングソルヴァー
Kingsolver, Barbara 738
キング・ダンラップ
King Dunlap 738
キングドン
Kingdon, David G. 738
キングフィッシャー
Kingfisher, Rupert 738
キング夫人
King, Billie Jean 737
キングホーン
Kinghorn, Kenneth C. 738
キングマ
Kingma, Daphne Rose 738
Kingma, Mireille 738
キングマタム
Kingue Matam, Bernardin Ledoux 739
キングマン
Kingman, Lee 738
ギングラス
Gingras, Sandy 500
ギングリッチ
Gingrich, Newt 500
キンケイド
Kincaid, Nanci 736
Kinkade, Kathleen 739
Kinkade, Thomas 739
キンケード
Kinkade, Thomas 739
キンケル
Kinkel, Tanja 739
キンケレ
Kinkele, Thomas 739
ギンゴナ
Guingona, Teofisto 545
キンザー
Kinzer, Stephen 739
キン・サン・イー
Khin San Yee 728
キンジー
Kinsey, Marie 739
キンジェルスカ
Kindzerska, Iryna 737
キンジェルスキ
Kindzierski, Lovern 737
キンジー‐ワーノック
Kinsey-Warnock, Natalie 739
ギンジン
Gindin, Alexander 500
ギンズ
Gins, Madeline H. 500
キンスキー
Kinski, Nastassja 739
キーンズ・ダグラス
Keens-Douglas, Paul 714
キンステッド
Kindstedt, Paul S. 737
ギンズバーグ
Ginsberg, Debra 500
Ginsberg, Lionel 500
Ginsberg, Robert J. 500
Ginsberg, Steven H. 500
Ginsburg, Dan 500
Ginsburg, David 500
Ginsburg, Jane 500
Ginsburg, Mirra 500
Ginsburg, Ruth Jone Bader 500
Ginzburg, Lev R. 501
Ginzburg, Vitalii Lazarevich 501
ギンスバッハ
Ginsbach, Julia 500
ギーンズブルク
Ginzburg, Vitalii Lazarevich 501
ギンズブルク
Ginzburg, Aleksandr Ilich 501
ギンズブルグ
Ginzburg, Aleksandr Ilich 501
Ginzburg, Carlo 501
Ginzburg, Vitalii Lazarevich 501
キンズラー
Kinsler, Ian 739
キンズレー
Kinsley, Michael E. 739
キンズロー
Kinslow, Frank J. 739
キンゼイ
Quinsey, Vernon L. 1145
キンセイル
Kinsale, Laura 739
キンセラ
Kinsella, David Todd 739
Kinsella, Sharon 739
Kinsella, Sophie 739
Kinsella, William Patrick 739
Kinsella, W.P. 739
キンダー
Kinder, Donald R. 736
Kinder, George 736
Kinder, Richard 737
ギンター
Ginter, Matthias 501
ギンタス
Gintis, Herbert 501
キンターナ
Quintana, Jose 1145
キンタナ
Quintana, José M. 1145
Quintana, Juan Ramón 1145
Quintana, Yandro Miguel 1145
キンタナ・タボルガ
Quintana Taborga, Juan Ramón 1145
キンタナ・メレンデス
Quintana Meléndez, Paula 1145
キンタナル
Quintanal, Maria 1145
キンタニジャ
Quintanilla, Carlos 1145
キンダーマン
Kindermann, Barbara 737
Kindermann, Wilfried 737
キンタン
Quintão, Geraldo Magela 1145
キンチェガシビリ
Khinchegashvili, Vladimer 728
キンチェガシュビリ
Khinchegashvili, Vladimer 728

キンツ
Kinz, Wieland 739
キンツィンガー
Kintzinger, Martin 739
ギンツブルク
Ginzburg, Vitalii Lazarevich 501
ギンツブルグ
Ginzburg, Carlo 501
キンツラー
Kintzler, Brandon 739
キンディ
al-Kindi, Muhammad Saeed 737
ギンディ
Guindi, Amina Hamza Muhammad El 545
キンディア
Kyndiah, P.R. 778
ギンディン
Gindin, Alexander 500
Gindin, Sam 500
キンテラ
Quintella, Maurício 1145
キンデラン
Kindelan, Mario 736
キンデリス
Kinderis, Justinas 737
キンテロ
Quintero, Rafael 1145
キンテロス・アギラル
Quinteros Aguilar, Manuel Orlando 1145
ギンド
Guindo, Housseïni Amion 545
キントナー
Kintner, Jill 739
キンドラー
Kindler, Jeffrey B. 737
キンドルバーガー
Kindleberger, Charles Poor 737
キンドル・ホドソン
Kindle Hodson, Victoria 737
キンドレッド
Kindred, Derrick 737
キンドロン
Kindlon, Daniel James 737
キン・ニュン
Khin Nyunt 728
キンヌネン
Kinnunen, Tommi 739
Kinnunen, Ulla 739
キンバー
Kinber, Efim 736
キンバーリー
Kimberly, John R. 736
キンバリー
Kimberly, Alice 736
Kimberly, John R. 736
ギンバリソン
Gimbergsson, Sara 500
キンプトン
Kimpton, Diana 736
キンブラ
Kimbra 736
キンブレル
Kimbrel, Craig 736
Kimbrell, Andrew 736
Kimbrell, Grady 736
キンブロ
Kimbro, Dennis Paul 736
キンブロー
Kimbrough, R.Keller 736
キンベル
Kimbell, Lucy 736
ギンベル
Gimbel, Theo 500
ギンペル
Gimpel, Erich 500
ギンベルナート＝オルダイク
Gimbernat Ordeig, Enrique 500
キンペンベ
Kimpembe, Presnel 736
キンポミ
Kimpomi, Zacharie 736
キンボール
Kimball, Kristin 736
Kimball, Ward 736
キン・マウン・ギイ
Khin-Maung-Gyi, Felix A. 728
キン・マウン・ソー
Khin Maung Soe 728
キン・マウン・チョー
Khin Maung Cho 728
キン・マウン・テイン
Khin Maung Thein 728
キン・マウン・ミン
Khin Maung Myint 728
キンメル
Kimmel, Bruce L. 736
Kimmel, Douglas C. 736
Kimmel, Marek 736
キーンリーサイド
Keenlyside, Simon 714
キーンリサイド
Keenlyside, Simon 714
ギンリック
Gingrich, Newt 500
キーンレ
Kienle, G.S. 730
キンレアンドロ
Quinn-leandro, Jacqui 1145
キンレイ・ドルジ
Kinley Dorji 739
キンロー
Kinlaw, Dennis F. 739

【ク】

ク
Koo, Bon-moo 756
Koo, Ja-Cheol 756
Ku, Ok-hee 770
クー
Gu, Chang-wei 541
Gu, Yue 541
Khoo, Hoo-neng 728
Khoo, Rachel 728
Khoo, Swee-chiow 728
Ko, Chun-hsiung 749
Koo, Hagen 756
Koo, Kien Keat 756
Koo, Louis 756
Koo, Richard 756
Ku, Chen-fu 770
グ
Koo, Bon-moo 756
グー
Goux, Jean-Joseph 522
Gu, Chao-hao 541
Gu, Mu 541
Gu, Qing 541
Gueu, Michel 543
Ku, Chen-fu 770
Ku, Lien-sung 770
クア
Koua, Mahamat Hamid 760
Kua, Kerenga 770
Kua, Patrick 770
クアイ
Quay, Stephen 1143
グアイ
Guay, Erik 541
クアイソン
Quaison, Robin 1143
グアイタ
Guaita, Ovidio 541
クアイティ
al-Quaiti, Munasser 1143
グアイラ
Guaila, Abdulsalam Abdullah 541
クァク
Kwak, Jae-young 777
Kwak, Ji-gyoon 777
Kwak, Kyul-ho 777
Kwak, Kyung-taek 777
Kwak, Pom-gi 777
クアク
Kouakou, Amédée Koffi 760
Kouakou, Gervais Jean-Baptiste 760
Kouakou, Pascal Abinan 760
クアシ
Kouassi, Jean-Claude 760
Kouassi, Moise Lida 760
Kuassi, Gérard 770
クアシガ
Quashigah, Courage 1143
グアーダッド
Guardado, Eddie 541
グアダルーピ
Guadalupi, Gianni 541
クアッケンブッシュ
Quackenbush, Kevin 1143
クアディオ
Kouadio, Komoé Augustin 760
Kouadio, Rémi Allah 760
クアデラー
Quaderer, Hugo 1143
クアドラード
Cuadrado, Juan 306
クアトラロ
Quatraro, Matt 1143
クァードリ
Quadri, Argeo 1143
クァドリ
Quadri, Argeo 1143
クアトロッチ
Quattrocchi, Vito 1143
グアハルド・ビジャレアル
Guajardo Villarreal, Ildefonso 541
クアメン
Quammen, David 1143
グァラ
Guala, Francesco 541
グアラ
Guara, Ig 541
クアリャレッラ
Quagliarella, Fabio 1143
グアル
Gual, Roger 541
グアルダード
Guardado, Andres 541
クアルティー
Kuartei, Billy 770
クアルテイ
Kuartei, Billy 770
Kuartei, Stevenson 770
グアルディオーラ
Guardiola, Josep 541
グアルディオラ
Guardiola, Josep 541
クアルテローニ
Quarteroni, Alfio 1143
グアルドゥッチ
Guarducci, Ilaria 541
グアルナッチャ
Guarnaccia, Steven 541
クアーレス
Quarles, Kelcy 1143
Quarless, Andrew 1143
クアレスマ
Quaresma, Ricardo 1143
クアレズマ・ドス・サントス・アフォンソ・フェルナンデス
Quaresma Dos Santos Afonso Fernandes, Agostinho 1143
クアロン
Cuarón, Alfonso Orozco 306
クァン
Kwan, Stanley 777
クアン
Quan, Nguyen 1143
Quan, Nguyen Hong 1143
Quang, Tran Dai 1143
グァン
Guan, Tian-lang 541
グアン
Quang, Nguyen Minh 1143
グアンジカ
Gouandjika, Fidèle 521
グアンジャ
Gouandja, Claude Richard 521
クアン・マチャド
Cuan Machado, Juana Maritza 306
クーイ
Kooi, Barteld Pieter 756
グイ
Guey, Lun-mei 543
Gui, Lin 544
Gui, Shi-yong 544
クイアコスキー
Kwiatkoski, Nick 777
クイギン
Quiggin, John 1144
クィグリー
Quigley, James H. 1144
クイグリー
Quigley, Claire 1144
Quigley, Colleen 1144
Quigley, Ryan 1144
クイケン
Kuijken, Barthold 772

Kuijken, Sigiswald 772
Kuijken, Wieland 772
Kuyken, Willem 776
グイシュー
Gouichoux, René 521
クイスト
Quist, Rasmus 1146
クイック
Crick, Thomas K. 302
Quick, Amanda 1144
Quick, Brian 1144
Quick, Jeff 1144
Quick, Matthew 1144
Quick, William Thomas 1144
クイットニー
Kwitney, Alisa 777
グイディ
Guidi, Federica 544
Guidi, Guido 544
グイデッティ
Guidetti, John 544
クイート
Cuito, Aurora 307
クイトゥネン
Kuitunen, Virpi 772
グイドーニ
Guidoni, Enrico 544
グイドリン
Guidolin, Francesco 544
クイナ
Quina, Domingos 1144
グイネス
Gunes, Tata 546
クイネット
Quinnett, Paul G. 1145
クィネル
Quinnell, A.J. 1145
クイビダ
Kuybida, Vasily 776
グィヤール
Guyard, Virginie 549
グイヤール
Gouillart, Francis J. 521
グィリー
Guiley, Rosemary 544
Guilly, Rosemary Ellen 544
クィレン
Quillen, Daniel G. 1144
クィーン
Queen, Carol 1144
クィン
Quin, Glover 1144
Quinn, Bill 1145
Quinn, Dan 1145
Quinn, Eric 1145
Quinn, Molly Jane 1145
Quinn, Robert 1145
クイーン
Queen, Ben 1144
Queen, Mel 1144
クイン
Quinn, Aidan 1145
Quinn, Anthony 1145
Quinn, Brian 1145
Quinn, Brian, C.S.W. 1145
Quinn, Chris 1145
Quinn, Erin 1145
Quinn, Feargal 1145
Quinn, Francesco 1145
Quinn, Gary 1145
Quinn, Glenn 1145
Quinn, Helen R. 1145
Quinn, James E. 1145
Quinn, Joanna 1145
Quinn, Julia 1145
Quinn, Kelly 1145
Quinn, Patricia O. 1145
Quinn, Paula 1145
Quinn, Robert E. 1145
Quinn, Roman 1145
Quinn, Ruairí 1145
Quinn, Spencer 1145
Quinn, Tara Taylor 1145
Quinn, Tom 1145
グイン
Guinn, Matthew 545
Gwyn, Richard 550
クインシー
Quincy, Diana 1144
クインタヴァレ
Quintavalle, Giulia 1145
クインタバレ
Quintavalle, Giulia 1145
グインディ
Guindi, Amina Hamza Muhammad El 545
クインテロ
Quintero, Josephine 1145
グインド
Guindo, Diabate Fatoumata 545
クィンドレン
Quindlen, Anna 1144
クィントン
Quinton, John Grand 1145
クイントン
Quinton, Anthony 1145
クィンラン
Quinlan, David 1144
クインラン
Quinlan, Joseph P. 1144
Quinlan, Michael Edward 1145
Quinlan, Susan E. 1145
クウ
Ku, Chen-fu 770
クーヴァー
Coover, Robert 288
クヴァストホフ
Quasthoff, Thomas 1143
クヴァスナースキー
Kvasnosky, Laura McGee 777
クヴァーニス
Kvarnes, Robert G. 777
クヴァーミー
Kvamme, E.Floyd 777
グヴァラ
Guwara, Leon 549
クヴァール
Kvale, Steinar 777
クヴァル
Kvale, Steinar 777
クゥアレーロ
Quarello, Maurizio A. C. 1143
クーヴァン
Couvin, Yann 296
クヴァンテ
Quante, Michael 1143
クヴァント
Quandt, Johanna 1143
Quandt, Stefan 1143
クウィアトコフスキ
Kwiatkowski, Michal 777
グウィヴナ
Dhuibhne, Éilis Ní 349
クヴィエチェン
Kwiechen, Mariusz 777
グヴィシアニ
Gvishiani, Jermen Mikhailovich 550
クヴィツィンスキー
Kvitsinskii, Yurii Aleksandrovich 777
クウィック
Kwiek, Kian Gie 777
クヴィーデラン
Kvideland, Reimund 777
グウィリム
Gwillim, Linda 550
クウィーン
Queen, William 1144
クウィン
Quinn, Anthony 1145
グウィン
Gwynn, M.I. 550
Gwynn, Tony 550
Gwynne, Samuel C. 550
グウイン
Gwynn, Tony 550
グウィン - ブレット
Gwynn-Brett, Kathryn A. 550
クウェイ
Kwei, Zita Okai 777
クウェイド
Quaid, Dennis 1143
クウェク
Kwaku, Edward Osei 777
クウェック
Quek, Leng Chan 1144
クウェティ
Kwetey, Fifi 777
グウェニゲイル
Gwenigale, Walter 550
グウェブ
Gwebu-dlamini, Lindiwe 550
グウェブドラミニ
Gwebu-dlamini, Lindiwe 550
クヴェラゼ
Kveladze, Karlo 777
クウェラホベ
Kwelagobe, Daniel 777
グウェル
Ghwell, Khalifa 494
クウェルチ
Quelch, John A. 1144
クウェレ
Cwele, Siyabonga 310
Cwele, Siyabonga Cyprian 310
グウェンド
Gwend, Edwige 550
クウォーツ
Quartz, Steven 1143
グウォルトニー
Gwaltney, Chad 550
クウゴンゲルワ
Kuugongelwa-amadhila, Saara 776
クエ
Kuye, Jibril Martins 776
クエイ
Quay, Emma 1143
クエイケン
Kuijken, Susan 772
クェイド
Quaid, Dennis 1143
クエイト
Cueto, Johnny 306
クエイド
Quaid, Dennis 1143
クエジャル
Cuellar, Ivan 306
Cuéllar, Rigoberto 306
クエスタ
Cuesta Rubio, Miguel 306
クエスト
Quest, Paul 1144
クエチェン
Kuechen, Roman 771
クエチェン修道士
Kuechen, Roman 771
クェック・レンベン
Kwek Leng Beng 777
グエッラ
Guerra, Simona 543
Guerra, Tonino 543
グエデス
Guedes, Goncalo 542
Guedes, Luís Castro 542
クエバス
Cuevas, Marcio 306
Cuevas, Pablo 306
クエフ
Cueff, Virginie 306
グエラ
Guerra, Jose 543
Guerra Oliva, Jose Antonio 543
グエラロドリゲス
Guerra Rodriguez, Lisandra 543
グエル
Guell, Fernando 542
クエルテン
Kuerten, Gustavo 771
クエルボ・デハラミジョ
Cuervo De Jaramillo, Elvira 306
クエルマルツ
Quellmalz, Edys 1144
クェルレ
Köhle, Anne-Bärbel 751
クエレネイア
Cuereneia, Aiuba 306
クエーン
Kuhn, Enrico 771
グェン
Nguyen, Duc 1021
Nguyen, Phanxicô Xaviê Văn Thuan 1021
Nguyen, Thi Dinh 1021
グエン
Nguyen, Bac Son 1021
Nguyêñ, Duc Kiên 1021
Nguyen, Dustin 1021
Nguyen, Eric 1021
Nguyen, Frank 1021
Nguyen, Hong Thai 1021
Nguyen, Hung Quoc 1021
Nguyen, Kien 1021
Nguyen, Le Nhung 1021
Nguyen, Mai Hoa 1021
Nguyen, Ngọc Thuan 1021
Nguyen, Nhât Ánh 1021
Nguyen, Peter 1021

Nguyen, Pham Khoi 1021
Nguyen, Quang Thieu 1021
Nguyen, Quang Trung Tien 1021
Nguyen, Quoc Cuong 1021
Nguyen, Quoc Huan 1021
Nguyen, The Sang 1021
Nguyen, Thi Binh 1021
Nguyen, Thi Lua 1021
Nguyen, Thi Phuong Thao 1021
Nguyen, Tien Minh 1021
Nguyen, Tri Dung 1021
Nguyen, Tri Huan 1021
Nguyen, Văn Hàm 1021
Nguyen, Van-Thuan 1021
Nguyen, Xuan Oanh 1021

グエン・ヴァン・ティユウ
Nguyen Van Thieu 1021

クエンカ
Cuenca, Isaac 306

グエン・カイン
Nguyen Khanh 1021

グエン・カオ・キ
Nguyen Cao Ky 1021

グエン・カオ・キイ
Nguyen Cao Ky 1021

グエン・カーン
Nguyen Khanh 1021

クエンク
Quenk, Naomi L. 1144

グエンサー
Guenther, Paul 542

グエン・スアン・オアイン
Nguyen Xuan Oanh 1021

クエンタス
Cuentas, Guillermo 306

グエン・タン・ズン
Nguyen Tan Dung 1021

グエン・ティ・クック
Nguyen Thi Cuc 1021

クエンティン
Quentin, Carlos 1144

グェン・ディン・ティ
Nguyên Dinh Thi 1021

グエン・ディン・ティ
Nguyên Dinh Thi 1021

グエン・ドク
Nguyen, Duc 1021
Nguyen Duc 1021

グエン＝ハツシバ
Nguyen-Hatsushiba, Jun 1021

グエン・バン・チュー
Nguyen Van Thieu 1021

グエン・バン・ティエウ
Nguyen Van Thieu 1021

グエン・バン・トゥアン
Nguyen Van Thuan 1021

グエン・フー・チョン
Nguyen Phu Trong 1021

グエン・ベト
Nguyen Viet 1021

グエン・ミン・チェット
Nguyen Minh Triet 1021

グエン・ラン・フン
Nguyen Lan Phuong 1021

クォ
Guo, Pei 547

クォー
Kwoh, Christopher 777
Quow, Renny 1146

クオ
Gou, Tai-ming 521
Guo, Jing-ming 547
Kuo, Julia 774
Kuo, Pao Kun 774

クオー
Guo, Pei 547

グォ
Guo, Jing-ming 547

グオ
Gou, Terry 521
Guo, Feng 547
Guo, Guangchang 547
Guo, Jing-jing 547
Guo, Pei 547
Guo, Xiao-lu 547
Guo, Yue 547

クオーギ
Cuoghi, Roberto 308

クオコ
Cuoco, Kaley 308

クォーターマン
Quarterman, John S. 1143
Quarterman, Tim 1143

グオ・チョンウー
Guo, Chengwu 547

クォック
Kwok, Aaron 777
Kwok, Audrey Nanette 777
Kwok, Derek 777

クオック
Kwok, Raymond 777
Kwok, Robert 777
Kwok, Thomas 777
Kwok, Walter 778

クォート
Quart, Alissa 1143

クォートン
Quarton, Marjorie 1143

クオメニ
Koumegni, Augustin Kontchou 760

クォメン
Quammen, David 1143

クオーモ
Cuomo, Giuseppe 308
Cuomo, Mario Matthew 308

クオモ
Cuomo, Mario Matthew 308
Cuomo, Rivers 308

クオラティエロ
Quaratiello, Arlene Rodda 1143

クォリントン
Quarrington, Paul 1143

クオルズ
Qualls, Chad 1143

クォールズ＝コルベット
Qualls-Corbett, Nancy 1143

クォルマン
Qualman, Erik 1143

クオレク
Kwolek, Stephanie 778

クォレス
Quarless, Sylvester 1143

クォロバ
Kgoroba, George 724

クォン
Kwon, Chol-hyun 778
Kwon, Dae Woong 778
Kwon, Do-youp 778
Kwon, Heon-jung 778
Kwon, Hyukbin 778
Kwon, Jae-jin 778
Kwon, O-gi 778
Kwon, Okyu 778
Kwon, Sang-woo 778
Kwon, Song-ho 778
Kwon, Un Sil 778
Kwon, Yong Gwang 778
Kwong, Tiarite 778

クオン
Cuong, Ha Hung 308
Cuong, Nguyen Xuan 308

グォン
Kwon, Sang-woo 778

クガー
Koger, Freya 751

クーカーズ
Kukors, Ariana 772

グガニック
Gugganig, Martin 543

クカーリ
Cucari, Attilio 306

クーガン
Coogan, Steve 285

クカン
Kukan, Eduard 772

クキエ
Cukier, Kenneth 307

グキオカス
Gkiokas, Thanasis 503

クキノ・ガリド
Kukino Garrido, Gladys 772

グギ・ワ・ジオンゴ
Ngugi Wa Thiong'o 1020

クーク
Cooke, Tim 286

クク
Cucu, Andrei 306
Kuku, John Deau 772

ククセンコフ
Kuksenkov, Mykola 772
Kuksenkov, Nikolai 772

グクナ
Gukuna, Seth 545

クークラ
Kukla, André 772

クーグラー
Coogler, Ryan 285
Kugler, Walter 771

クグラー
Kugler, Robert 771

ググリアータ
Gugliotta, Gianluca 544

ククーリッチ
Cuculich, Phillip S. 306

クークリン
Kuklin, Susan 772

ククリンスキ
Kuklinski, Courtesy Ryszard 772
Kuklinski, Richard 772

クーグル
Koogle, Tim 756

ククル
Cucullu, Santiago 306

ククレワ
Koukleva, Galina 760

クコッチ
Kucoc, Yerko 771

クコリ
Kukolj, Aleksandar 772

クーゴンゲルワアマディラ
Kuugongelwa-amadhila, Saara 776

クーサ
Kousa, Mousa 760
Koussa, Moussa 760

クーサー
Koussa, Moussa 760

クーザー
Kooser, Ted 756

クサイノフ
Kusainov, Abelgazy 775

クサイビ
Khusaibi, Said bin Nasser bin Mansoor Al 729

クサイ・フセイン
Fussein, Qusay 469

グザヴィエ
Xavier, Clément 1531

グザーノフ
Guzanov, Vitaliy 549

グザノフ
Guzanov, Vitaliy 549

クサバ
Xaba, Bennedict 1531

クサマ
Kusama, Yayoi 775

クサリリラ
Kusari-lila, Mimoza 775

グサロフ
Gusarov, Eevgenii 548

クーザン
Cousin, Pierre Jean 296

クザン
Cousin, Mathias 296

グザン
Guzan, Brad 549

クサンソス
Xanthos, Andreas 1531

クザンデ
Kouzande, Delphine Oloronto 761

グサン・マルトハルトノ
Gesang Martohartono 492

クシ
Cusi, Alfonso 310

グージ
Goudge, Eileen 521

グジ
Gudz, Boris 542

グジー
Gudzy, Nataliya 542

クシアノビッチ
Cussiánovich, Alejandro 310

グーシェ
Gusheh, Maryam 548

グシェーヴァ
Guseva, Elena 548

クジェシェフスキ
Krzeszewski, Tomasz 770

クジエフ
Kuziev, Tursunali 776

クシェラ
Kuschela, Kurt 775

クシェルバエフ
Kusherbaev, Krymbek 775

グシオネ
Guccione, Chris 542

クシキヤン

Kushkyan, Harutyun 775
グジコウスキ
Guzikowski, Aaron 549
クシシュ
Kchich, Mohamed Rachid 712
クーシス
Koosis, Donald J. 756
グシチナ
Gushchina, Yulia 548
グシチンスキ
Gushchinskiy, Viktor 548
クジック
Cusick, Richie Tankersley 310
クシニエレウィッチ
Kusznierewicz, Mateusz 776
クシニッチ
Kucinich, Dennis 770
クシニル
Kushnir, Anton 776
グジネビチウテ
Gudzineviciute, Daina 542
クジノー
Cousineau, Julien 296
グジボフスカ
Grzybowska-franc, Katarzyna 541
クシモビッチ
Joksimović, Jadranka 681
クーシャン
Kušan, Ivan 775
クーシュ
Kush, Eric 775
グジュ
Guedj, Nicole 542
クシュチェビッチ
Kuščević, Lovro 775
クジュティナ
Kuziutina, Natalia 776
クシュナー
Kushner, Barak 776
Kushner, Harold S. 776
Kushner, Joshua 776
Kushner, Marc 776
Kushner, Tony 776
クシュニール
Kushnir, Anton 776
クシュニル
Kushnir, Anton 776
クシュネール
Kouchner, Bernard 760
クシュネル
Kouchner, Bernard 760
クジュバルト
Kužvart, Miloš 777
クシュパン
Couchepin, Pascal 294
クシュマン
Cushman, Doug 310
Cushman, Karen 310
グジュラール
Gujral, Inder Kumar 545
グジュラル
Gujral, Inder Kumar 545
クシュリド
Kechrid, Ridha 713
グシュワンドトナー
Gschwandtner, Selina 541
クジョー
Cudjo, Jermelle 306
Cudjoe, Shamfa 306
クシラム
Khushiram, Khushhal Chand 729
クジロフ
Kuzilov, Albert 776
クジン
Kuzin, Denis 776
Kuzin, Valery 776
クーシンズ
Cousins, Farquharson 296
Kushins, Josh 775
クシンスキー
Kucinski, Bernardo 770
グース
Geus, Arie P.de 492
Gousse, Bernard 522
グズィ
Gusy, Christoph 548
クスガック
Kusugak, Michael 776
クスケ
Kuske, Kevin 776
グスタヴスン
Gustafsson, Lars 548
グスタヴソン
Gustafsson, Lars 548
グスタス
Gustas, Evaldas 548
グスタフスドティル
Gustafsdottir, Eyglo Osk 548
グスタフセン
Gustavsen, Terje Moe 548
グスタフソン
Gustafson, Samuel 548
Gustafson, Sophie 548
Gustafsson, Anders 548
Gustafsson, Jukka 548
Gustafsson, Lars 548
Gustavsson, Anders 548
Gustavsson, Ane 548
Gustavsson, Per 548
グスターベ
Gustave, Jandel 548
グスティ
Gusti 548
Rosemffet, Gustavo 1203
クストゥリツァ
Kusturica, Emir 776
グストーフ
Gustorf, Oliver Koerner von 548
クストリツァ
Kusturica, Emir 776
クストリッツァ
Kusturica, Emir 776
グーズナー
Goozner, Merrill 517
グズナク
Guznac, Valentin 550
クスニエキ
Kuzniecky, Dany 777
クズネツォフ
Kuznetsov, Andrey 776
Kuznetsov, Evgenii 776
Kuznetsov, Lev V. 776
Kuznetsov, Mikhail 777
Kuznetsov, Sergei Il'ich 777
グズネツォフ
Kuznyetsov, Viktor 777
クズネツォワ
Kuznetsova, Svetlana 777
グズフィンソン
Gudfinnsson, Einar Kristinn 542
クズマ
Kuzma, Janina 776
グスマオ
Gusmão, Xanana 548
クスマノ
Cusumano, Michael A. 310
クズマノヴィッチ
Kuzmanovic, Zdravko 776
クスーマブング
Coussoud-mavoungou, Martin Parfait Aimé 296
クスマヤント
Kusmayanto, Kadiman 776
グーズマン
Guzman, Ronald 549
グスマン
Gusmão, Xanana 548
Guzmán, Altagracia 549
Guzmán, Marta 549
Guzmán, Patricio 549
グズマン
Guzman, Leonardo 549
クズミナ
Kuzmina, Anastazia 776
クズミンスカス
Kuzminskas, Mindaugas 776
クスムア
Kussumua, João Baptista 776
クズムク
Kuzmuk, Oleksandr I. 776
クス・ムルティア・パク・ブウォノ
Koes Murtiyah Paku Buwono 751
グズムンドソン
Gudmundsson, Johann Berg 542
クズワヨ
Kuzwayo, Royce Bongizizwe 777
クーゼ
Kuhse, Helga 772
クゼ
Kuze, Josip 776
グセ
Gousset, Marie-Therese 522
グゼジャニ
Gujejiani, Lasha 545
クーゼス
Kouzes, James M. 761
クセック
Kusek, David 775
クセナキス
Xenakis, Iannis 1531
グゼニナ・リカルドソン
Guzenina-richardson, Maria 549
グセフ
Gusev, Oleg 548
クーセラ
Kuusela, Kari 776
クセラ
Ksera, Spiro 770
Kucera, Maria 770
グゼリミアン
Guzelimian, Ara 549
クセルク
Kyselka, Will 778
グセルマン
Gsellman, Robert 541
クゼンコワ
Kuzenkova, Olga 776
グーゼンバウアー
Guzenbauer, Alfred 549
クーゼンベルク
Kusenberg, Kurt 775
グソー
Gusau, Aliyu 548
グゾウスキ
Guzowski, Mary 550
グゾウスキー
Guzauski, Mick 549
クソス
Qussos, Zeid 1146
クーター
Cooter, Jim Bob 288
クーダー
Cooder, Ry 285
クダイベルジエワ
Kudayberdieva, Gulmira 771
クダイベルディエフ
Kudaiberdiev, Abibilla 771
クダイベルディエワ
Kudayberdieva, Gulmira 771
グタス
Gutas, Dimitri 548
クタテラゼ
Kutateladze, Vakhtang 776
クダト
Qudah, Yarub 1144
クタバ
Koutaba, Justin 761
クダブクス
Khudabux, Mohamed Rakieb 729
グーダル
Godal, Bjorn Tore 506
グダルジ
Goudarzi, Mahmoud 521
Goudarzi, Sadegh Saeed 521
クタンセ
Coutansais, Cyrille P. 296
クーチ
Couch, Tonia 294
クチ
Kuchi, Driton 770
Kuçi, Hajredin 770
クヂ
Kudsi, Mark 771
グーチ
Gooch, Lynden 515
クチェ
Koutche, Komi 761
クチェラ＝モーリン
Kuchera-Morin, JoAnn 770
グチエレス
Gutierrez, Sebastian 549
グチェレツ
Gutiérrez, José María 549
クチェレンコ
Kucherenko, Oleksy 770
クチシュヴィリ

Khutsishvili, Vazha 729
クチネッリ
Cucinelli, Brunello 306
クチネリ
Cucinelli, Brunello 306
クチマ
Kuchma, Leonid D. 770
クーチャー
Kuchar, Matt 770
クチャク
Kuciak, Dusan 770
クーチャン
Kučan, Milan 770
クー・チャンウェイ
Gu, Changwei 541
クーチン
Kutin, Joe 776
クチンスカス
Kuchinskas, Susan 770
クチンスキ
Kuczynski, Pedro-Pablo 771
クチンスキー
Kuczynski, Alex 771
Kuczynski, Pedro-Pablo 771
クーツ
Coutts, Alicia 296
Coutu, Diane L. 296
グツ
Gutu, Ion 549
Gutu, Lidia 549
クツィウパス
Koutsioumpas, Georgios 761
Koutsioumpas, Xenofon 761
クツィシビリ
Khutsishvili, Davit 729
クツィンスキス
Kucinskis, Maris 771
クツェー
Coetzee, J.M. 274
クツォペトル
Koutsopetrou, Sotiria 761
クツカ
Kucka, Juraj 771
クッキー
Cooke, Pauline 286
クッキング
Cooking, Rodney R. 286
クック
Cook, Aaron 285
Cook, Bernadine 285
Cook, Bruce 285
Cook, Christopher 285
Cook, Christopher D. 285
Cook, Claire 285
Cook, Connor 285
Cook, Curtis R. 285
Cook, Dane 285
Cook, Douglas S. 285
Cook, Elgin 285
Cook, Emily 285
Cook, Frank D. 285
Cook, Gareth 285
Cook, Guy W.D. 285
Cook, James R. 285
Cook, Jared 285
Cook, Jonathan 285
Cook, Kassidy 285
Cook, Katherine Tapscott 285
Cook, Katie 285
Cook, Kenny 285
Cook, Kerry 285
Cook, Kristina 285
Cook, Lee 285
Cook, Lewis 285
Cook, Linda Zarda 285
Cook, Luis 285
Cook, M.A. 285
Cook, Malcolm 286
Cook, Marion Belden 286
Cook, Michael 286
Cook, Monte 286
Cook, Natalie 286
Cook, Quinn 286
Cook, Randy 286
Cook, Richard 286
Cook, Richard W. 286
Cook, Rick 286
Cook, Robin 286
Cook, Scott D. 286
Cook, Steve 286
Cook, Tamsin 286
Cook, Terry 286
Cook, Thomas H. 286
Cook, Tim 286
Cook, Troy 286
Cook, Vivian James 286
Cook, William H. 286
Cook, William J. 286
Cook, Yvonne 286
Cooke, Alistair 286
Cooke, Anne 286
Cooke, Charlie 286
Cooke, Claire 286
Cooke, C.W. 286
Cooke, Darwyn 286
Cooke, Derek, Jr. 286
Cooke, Dominic 286
Cooke, Fred 286
Cooke, Howard 286
Cooke, Jamie 286
Cooke, Nicole 286
Cooke, Rebecca 286
Cooke, Robin A. 286
Cooke, Roger M. 286
Cooke, Sasha 286
Cooke, Stephanie 286
Koch, Sam 750
Kuck, Jonathan 771
クック＝グロイター
Cook-Greuter, Susanne 286
クックス
Cooks, Brandin 286
クックソン・スミス
Cookson Smith, Peter 286
グッケンハイマー
Guckenheimer, Sam 542
グッゲンハイム
Guggenheim, Bill 543
Guggenheim, Charles 543
Guggenheim, Judy 544
Guggenheim, Marc 544
グッゲンビヒラー
Guggenbichler, S. 543
グッゲンビュール
Guggenbühl, Allan 543
グッゲンビュール＝クレイグ
Guggenbühl-Craig, Adolf 543
グッゲンベルガー
Guggenberger, Matthias 543
クッシング
Cushing, Brian 309
Cushing, Lincoln 309
グッセンベルク
Gussenberg, Oliver 548
グッタ
Gutta, Jwala 549
グッターグ
Guttag, John V. 549
グッダン
Guduan, Reymin 542
クッチ
Cucci, Mary 306
グッチ
Gucci, Patrizia 542
グッチオーネ
Guccione, Bob 542
クッチャー
Kutscher, Marco 776
Kutscher, Volker 776
グッチョウ
Gutschow, Niels 549
グッチョーネ
Guccione, Bob 542
クッツ
Kutz, Arie 776
クッツェー
Coetzee, Aranos 274
Coetzee, J.M. 274
グッツォーニ
Guzzoni, Ute 550
グッツオーニ
Guzzoni, Alfredo 550
グッディ
Goody, Jack 517
Goody, Jade 517
Goody, Nick 517
グッティエレス
Gutierrez, Carlos M. 548
グッディル
Goodill, Sherry 515
グッデイル
Goodale, Melvyn A. 515
Goodale, Ralph 515
グッディング
Gooding, Cuba Jr. 516
グッデン
Gooden, Philip 515
Gooden, Zaviar 515
グッテンベルク
Guttenberg, Karl-Theodor zu 549
グッド
Good, Byron 515
Good, David C. 515
Good, Denzelle 515
Good, Lynn 515
Good, Marion 515
Good, Nancy 515
Good, Nancy J. 515
Goode, Alex 515
Goode, David 515
Goode, Diane 515
Goode, Greg 515
Goode, Jamie 515
Goode, Najee 515
グッドイヴ
Goodeve, Thyrza Nichols 515
グッドイナフ
Goodenough, John 515
Goodenough, Ward Hunt 515
グッドウィル
Goodwill, James 516
グッドウィン
Goodwin, Archie 516
Goodwin, Brian 516
Goodwin, Bridget 516
Goodwin, C.J. 516
Goodwin, Clive 516
Goodwin, Donald W. 516
Goodwin, Doris Kearns 516
Goodwin, Frederick K. 516
Goodwin, Gordon L. 516
Goodwin, Harold 517
Goodwin, Harry 517
Goodwin, Jason 517
Goodwin, John B.L. 517
Goodwin, Marquise 517
Goodwin, Prue 517
Goodwin, Ron 517
Goodwin, Rosie 517
Goodwin, Tali 517
Goodwin, Tom 517
Goodwyn, Susan 517
グッドエーカー
Goodacre, Charles J. 515
グッドカインド
Goodkind, Elisa 516
Goodkind, Terry 516
グッドキー
Goodkey, Rich 516
グッドシップ
Goodship, Judith 516
グッドスタイン
Goodstein, Phyllis Kaufman 516
グッドセル
Goodsell, Dan 516
Goodsell, David S. 516
グッドソン
Goodson, B.J. 516
Goodson, Demetri 516
Goodson, Ivor 516
Goodson, Larry P. 516
Goodson, Scott 516
グッドナイト
Goodnight, Jim 516
Goodnight, Linda 516
グッドナウ
Goodenow, Melia 515
グッドハート
Goodhart, Charles Albert Erie 515
Goodhart, Frances 515
Goodhart, Philip 515
Goodhart, Pippa 515
グッドヒュー
Goodhew, Jo 515
グッドフェロー
Goodfellow, Daniel 515
Goodfellow, Rob 515
グッドフュー
Goodhew, Jo 515
グッドフレンド
Goodfriend, Marvin 515
グットマン
Goodman, Danny 516
Goodman, Steven R. 516
Gutman, Anne 549
Gutman, Natalia 549
Guttman, Michael 549
グッドマン
Goodman, Alison 516
Goodman, Allegra 516
Goodman, Amy 516
Goodman, Barak 516
Goodman, Carol 516
Goodman, Danny 516

ク

ク

Goodman, David 516
Goodman, David C. 516
Goodman, David Gordon 516
Goodman, Jeremy 516
Goodman, Joel B. 516
Goodman, John 516
Goodman, John A. 516
Goodman, Jordan Elliot 516
Goodman, Joseph W. 516
Goodman, Kenneth W. 516
Goodman, Lawrence Roger 516
Goodman, Lion 516
Goodman, Lizzy 516
Goodman, Malliciah 516
Goodman, Marc 516
Goodman, Martin 516
Goodman, Matthew 516
Goodman, Richard E. 516
Goodman, Robert 516
Goodman, Robert G. 516
Goodman, Roger 516
Goodman, Shdema 516
Goodman, Victor 516
Goodman, Wayne K. 516

グッドラッド
Goodlad, John I. 516

グッドランド
Goodland, Robert 516

グッドリー
Goodley, Antwan 516

グッドリック
Goodrick, Mick 516

グッドリッジ
Goodridge, Reginald 516

グッドリッチ
Goodrich, Joseph 516

グッドリフ
Goodliffe, Pete 516

グッドール
Goodall, Howard 515
Goodall, Jane 515
Goodall, Nigel 515

クットルフ
Kuttruff, Heinrich 776

グッドレム
Goodrem, Delta 516

クッファー
Kupfer, David J. 774

クーデア
Coudert, Jo 295

クーディー
Coudy, René 295

クティ
Kuti, Mohamed 776
Kuti, Seun 776

グディ
Goodey, Jo 515
Goody, Jack 517
Goody, Peter Charles 517

グティエレス
Gutierrez, Carlos 548
Gutierrez, Carlos M. 548
Gutierrez, Cesar Dario 548
Gutierrez, Claudio 548
Gutiérrez, David 548
Gutiérrez, Edgar 548
Gutiérrez, Elsa 548
Gutierrez, Franklin 548
Gutiérrez, Gladis 548
Gutierrez, Gonzalo 548
Gutiérrez, Gustavo 548
Gutierrez, Jorge 549
Gutiérrez, Lucio 549
Gutiérrez, Luis 549

グティエレス・オルティス
Gutiérrez Ortìz, Fernando 549

グティエーレス・モリーナ
Gutiérrez Molina, José Luis 549

グティエレス・ロンゴ
Gutiérrez Longo, Víctor Manuel 549

クテイシャト
Qteishat, Khaldoun 1143

グディス
Gudis, Catherine 542

グディソン
Goodison, Paul 516

グーディッシュ
Goodish, Barbara 516

グディム
Gudym, Valeriia 542

クディラ
Kurdyla, Francis J. 774

グーテイル
Gutheil, Thomas G. 548

グディングス
Goodings, Christina 516

クテサ
Kutesa, Dereck 776
Kutesa, Sam Kahamba 776

クー・テック・プアット
Khoo Teck Puat 728

クーテニコフ
Kootnikoff, David 756

クデュホフ
Kudukhov, Besik 771

クーテュール
Couture, Amélie 296

グデュル
Gudule 542

クデヨワ
Kudejova, Katerina 771

グデリ
Gudelj, Nemanja 542

クデリスキー
Kudel'skii, Anatolii Viktorovich 771

クデール
Coudert, Stephanie 295

グーデル
Gudele, Ina 542

グテル
Guterl, Fred 548

クーデルカ
Koudelka, Josef 760

クデルカ
kudelka, marty 771

グデルツォ
Guderzo, Tatiana 542

グテーレス
Guterres, Antonio 548

グテレス
Guterres, Antonio 548
Guterres, Isabel 548
Guterres, José Luís Lú Olo 853

クーデンホーフ・カレルギー
Coudenhove-Kalergi, Michael 294

グーテンマッヘル
Gutenmacher, Victor L'vovich 548

クドー
Kudo, Miteki 771

グート
Gut, Lara 548
Guth, Claus 548

グード
Goode, Richard 515
Goude, Jean-Paul 521

クトゥ
Koutou, Somanogo 761

クートゥア
Couture, Randy 296

グドゥコフィ
Goudou Coffie, Raymonde 521

グドゥザ王子
Prince Guduza 542

グドゥジ
Gudz, Boris 542

クトゥジス
Koutouzis, Michel 761

クドゥナリス
Koudounaris, Paul 760

クドゥホフ
Kudukhov, Besik 771

クドゥリャフツェワ
Kudryavtseva, Yana 771

クドゥングエレ
Koudounguéré, Rosalie 760

グドジウス
Gudzius, Andrius 542

グドナソン
Gudnason, Laurie 542

クトビイ
Kutovyi, Taras 776

グドーフ
Gudorf, Christine E. 542

グートマン
Gootman, Marilyn E. 517
Gutman, Natalia 549

グードヨンス
Gudjons, Herbert 542

クドラ
Kudla, Denis 771
Kudla, Michal 771

クドランスキ
Kudranski, Szymon 771

クドランスキー
Kudranski, Szymon 771

クドリツカ
Kudlicka, Jan 771
Kudrycka, Barbara 771

クドリャフツェフ
Kudryavtsev, Nikolai 771

クドリン
Kudrin, Aleksei Leonidovich 771

グドール
Goodall, Jane 515

クドルスキー
Kdolsky, Andrea 712

クードレイ
Coudray, Jean-Luc 295
Coudray, Philippe 295

クードレット
Couldrette 295

クトロ
Coutrot, Thomas 296

クーナ
Khouna, Cheikh El Afia Ould Mohamed 728

クーナー
Kooner, Andrew 756

クナ
Cunha, Ana Marcela 307

クナイフェル
Kneifel, Hans 747

クナウアー
Knauer, Sebastian 747

クナウスゴール
Knausgård, Karl Ove 747

クナウゼ
Krause, Gesa Felicitas 764

グナガ
Gungah, Ashit Kumar 546

クナコフ
Kunakov, Yuriy 773

クナジュコ
Knažko, Milan 747

クナーゼ
Kunadze, Georgii Fridrikhovich 773

グナセカラ
Gunasekara, D.E.W. 546

グナセケラ
Goonesekere, Savitri 517

グナッシア
Ghnassia, Virginia Jill Dix 493

クナッゼ
Kunadze, Georgii Fridrikhovich 773

クナッツ
Knatz, Birgit 747

クナッパー
Knäpper, Gerd 747

クナッパート
Knappert, Jan 747

クナップ
Knapp, Karin 747
Knapp, M. 747
Knapp, Robert C. 747

クナプコヴァ
Knapková, Miroslava 747

クナプコバ
Knapkova, Mirka 747
Knapková, Miroslava 747

クーナラキス
Kounalakis, Markos 760

グナラタナ
Gunaratana, Bhante Henepola 546

グナラトゥナ
Gooneratne, Sylvester Merrick 517

グナワルダ
Gunawardane, Bandula 546

グナワルダナ
Gunawardane, Bandula 546
Gunawardane, Leslie 546
Gunawardene, M.K.A.D. S. 546

グナワルデナ
Gunawardena, Dinesh 546
Gunawardena, Indika 546

グナワン
Gunawan, Tony 546

クーナン
Coonan, Helen 287

グーナン
Goonan, Michael 517

クーニー

Cooney, Caroline B. 287
Cooney, Eleanor 287
Cooney, Ned L. 287
Cooney, Ray 287
Cooney, Tim 287
グニア
Genia, Mahdi al-Taher 488
クニアフスキー
Kuniavsky, Mike 774
クニイ
Kunii, Patama Udomprasert 774
クニス
Kunis, Mila 774
クニスター
Knister 748
グニーセン
Gnessen, Simonne 506
クニーツィア
Knizia, Reiner 748
クニツィア
Knizia, Reiner 748
クニッシュ
Knysh, Mary E. 749
グニデンコ
Gnidenko, Ekaterina 506
クニバーグ
Kniberg, Henrik 747
クーニヒ
Kunig, Philip 774
クニフケ
Kniffke, Sophie 747
クニーベル
Knievel, Evel 747
クニベルティ
Cuniberti, Pier Achille 308
クーニャ
Cunha, Ana Marcela 307
Cunha, Arlind 308
Cunha, Pedro 308
クニャジェワ
Knyazyeva, Hanna 749
クニャジェワミネンコ
Knyazyeva-minenko, Hanna 749
クニャゼビッチ
Knyazevich, Vasily 749
クニャーゼフ
Kniazev, Alexander 747
クニャル
Cunhal, Alvaro 308
クニーリム
Knierim, Rolf P. 747
グニルカ
Gnilka, Joachim 506
クーニン
Kunin, Iosif Filippovich 774
クニン
Cunin, Olivier 308
クヌー
Cneut, Carll 272
グヌ
Gounou, Idrissou Sina Bio 522
クヌース
Knuth, Donald E. 749
クヌストン
Knutson, Kraig 749
クヌースン
Knudsen, Jim 749
クヌーセン
Knudsen, Jim 749
クヌッドストープ
Knudstorp, Jørgen Vig 749
クヌッドソン
Knudson, Alfred George, Jr. 749
クヌート
Cneut, Carll 272
クヌートセン
Knudsen, Grete 749
クヌートソン
Knutsson, Helene 749
クヌードソン
Knudson, Mary 749
クヌドソン
Knudson, Alfred George, Jr. 749
グネ
Guenée, Bernard 542
グネイム
Ghneim, Maher 493
クネイン
Cunnane, Kelly 308
クネジェビッチ
Knežević, Gašo 747
Knežević, Goran 747
グネジェンコ
Gnedenko, B.V. 506
クネーゼ
Kneese, Allen V. 747
クネッケ
Könnecke, Ole 755
クネーネ
Kunene, Mazisi 773
クネバ
Kuneva, Maglena 773
グネバナ
Gounebana, Nathalie Constance 522
クネヒト
Knecht, Peter 747
クネフ
Knef, Hildegard 747
クネフト
Knegt, Sjinkie 747
クネーブル
Knebl, Helmut 747
クネベル
Knebel, Arthur 747
グネル
Gounelle, Laurent 522
クネーレ
Kneale, Tim 747
クーネン
Coenen, Harry 273
クネン
Kunen, James Simon 773
クネンシルト
Knoernschild, Kirk 748
クノ
Cuno, Sabine 308
Kuno, Kanako 774
クノー
Cuno, James 308
Cuno, James B. 308
グノイス
Gneuss, Helmut 506
グノコ
Gounokou, Haounaye 522
グノスペリウス
Gnosspelius, Staffan 506
クノッパース
Knoppers, Bartha Maria 748
クノップ
Knopf, Chris 748
Knopp, Guido 748
クノッヘ
Knoche, Robin 748
クノート
Knauth, Lothar 747
クノーブラウフ
Knoblauch, Jörg 748
クノブロッホ
Knobloch, Susann 748
クーハー
Kuhar, Michael J. 771
クーバー
Kubr, Milan 770
クーパー
Cooper, Abraham 287
Cooper, Adam 287
Cooper, Al 287
Cooper, Alan 287
Cooper, Alex 287
Cooper, Alice 287
Cooper, Alison 287
Cooper, Amari 287
Cooper, Ann Nixon 287
Cooper, Arnold M. 287
Cooper, Artemis 287
Cooper, Barbara 287
Cooper, Barry 287
Cooper, Barry J. 287
Cooper, Besse 287
Cooper, Bradley 287
Cooper, Brant 287
Cooper, Cary L. 287
Cooper, Chris 287
Cooper, Christopher 287
Cooper, Claudia 287
Cooper, Dan 287
Cooper, Daniel 287
Cooper, Daniel H. 287
Cooper, David Edward 287
Cooper, David K.C. 287
Cooper, Diana 287
Cooper, Don 287
Cooper, Elisha 287
Cooper, Emmanuel 287
Cooper, Fahn 287
Cooper, Floyd 287
Cooper, George 287
Cooper, Glenn 287
Cooper, Gordon 287
Cooper, Grosvenor W. 287
Cooper, Gwen 287
Cooper, Helen F. 287
Cooper, Ian 287
Cooper, Jack R. 287
Cooper, Jacqui 287
Cooper, James William 287
Cooper, Jeane 287
Cooper, John Frederick 287
Cooper, John O. 287
Cooper, Jonathan 287
Cooper, Judy 287
Cooper, Laura 287
Cooper, Leon N. 287
Cooper, Marcus 287
Cooper, Mariel 287
Cooper, Mark 287
Cooper, M.Bixby 287
Cooper, Merian C. 287
Cooper, Michael 287
Cooper, Mick 288
Cooper, Mimi 288
Cooper, Musleng 288
Cooper, Pharoh 288
Cooper, Quade 288
Cooper, Rachel Valerie 288
Cooper, Richard Newell 288
Cooper, Robert 288
Cooper, Robert Gravlin 288
Cooper, Rose 288
Cooper, Sally 288
Cooper, Sarah 288
Cooper, Scot J. 288
Cooper, Scott 288
Cooper, Sharon W. 288
Cooper, Simon 288
Cooper, Stephanie 288
Cooper, Stephen Andrew 288
Cooper, Susan 288
Cooper, Suzanne Fagence 288
Cooper, Thea 288
Cooper, Tom 288
Cooper, Xavier 288
Cooper, Yvette 288
Cooper, Zafra 288
Couper, Heather 295
Kooper, Al 756
Kuper, Simon 774
クバ
Kuba, Martin 770
クパー
Kupper, Martin 774
グーバー
Guber, Peter 542
グーパー
Gubar, Susan 542
グハ
Guha, Ramachandra 544
グバ
Guba, Lawan Gana 541
クバイン
Qubain, Karim Elias Wadie 1143
クパキ
Koukpaki, Pascal Irénée 760
Koupaki, Pascal Irénée 760
グバグ
Gubag, Mathew 542
グバグビ
Gbagbi, Ruth Marie Christelle 485
グハザリャン
Ghazaryan, Eduard 493
クバシャ
Kvasha, Illya 777
グバーシュ
Ghubash, Saqr Ghubash Saeed 494
クーパーシュミット
Kupersmidt, Janis B. 774
クバソフ
Kubasov, Valery 770
クパチ
Cupac, Petar 308
クバーティ
Qubati, Mohammaed 1143
クバティ
al-Kubati, Abdu Ali 770
クパブレシリ
Kpabre-sylli, Batienne 762
クーパー・ポージー
Cooper-Posey, Tracy 288

グバミン
Gbamin, Jean-Philippe 485
クバラ
Kubala, Ladislao 770
クーパーライダー
Cooperrider, David L. 288
クハリ
al-Quhali, Mujahid 1144
クハルスキ
Kucharski, Tomasz 770
グーバレフ
Gubarev, Vladimir 542
クービアク
Kubiak, Gary 770
クビカ
Kubica, Mary 770
Kubica, Robert 770
クビサ
Kubica, Robert 770
グビシアニ
Gvishiani, Jermen Mikhailovich 550
クビシュ
Kubiš, Ján 770
クビタシビリ
Kvitashvili, Alexander 777
Kvitashvili, Sandro 777
クビチンスキー
Kvitsinskii, Yurii Aleksandrovich 777
クビツァ
Kubica, Robert 770
クビツィンスキー
Kvitsinskii, Yurii Aleksandrovich 777
クビツェ
Kubice, Jan 770
クビト
Kvit, Serhii 777
クピード
Cupido, Alberto 308
クビトバ
Kvitova, Petra 777
グビニアシビリ
Gviniashvili, Beka 550
クビフ
Kubiv, Stepan 770
クビリウス
Kubilius, Andrius 770
クビリカシビリ
Kvirikashvili, Giorgi 777
グビン
Gubbin, Barbara 542
クープ
Koop, C.Everett 756
クフ
Kuf, Jan 771
クブアボラ
Kubuabola, Inoke 770
Kubuabola, Jone 770
クーフィ
Koofi, Fawzia 756
クフィアトコフスキ
Kwiatkowski, Krzysztof 777
グフェラー
Gfeller, Kate E. 492
クフォー
Kuffuor, John 771
Kuffuor, Kwame Addo 771
Kufuor, John
Agyekum 771
クブシノブ
Kuvshinov, Ilya 776
グブジャマ
Gbujama, Shirley 485
クフタ
Kuchta, Kenny 770
Kukhta, Tatsiana 772
グプタ
Gupta, Anil K. 547
Gupta, Desh Bandhu 547
Gupta, Jay Prakash Prasad 547
Gupta, Parmeshwari Lal 547
Gupta, Prem Chand 547
Gupta, Ruchir 547
Gupta, Sanjay 547
Gupta, Sunil 547
Gupta, Suranjit Sen 547
Gupta, Udayan 547
Gupta, Yash 547
グプテ
Gupte, Amole 547
Gupte, Partho 547
グプティル
Guptill, Amy E. 547
グープトゥ
Gooptu, Sudarshan 517
クフトバー
Kuchtová, Dana 770
クプファー
Kupfer, Harry 774
クープマン
Koopman, Siem Jan 756
Koopmans, Loek 756
クーブラー
Kubler, Alison 770
クブラ
Koubra, Sani Hadiza 760
クープラン
Couplan, François 295
クープランド
Coupland, Douglas 295
Coupland, Ken 295
クブリアシヴィリ
Kubriashvili, Davit 770
グブリアム
Gubrium, Jaber F. 542
クプレナス
Kuprenas, John 774
クブロビッチ
Kubrović, Nela 770
クーベ
Kube 770
クーペ
Khupe, Thokozani 729
クペイジック
Kupesic, Rajka 774
クベイル
Qvale, Brent 1146
クベイロ
Cubeiro, Juan Carlos 306
グベゼラブリア
Gbezera-bria, Michel 485
クベゼレリ
Kvezereli, Bakur 777
クペッツ
Kupets, Courtney 774
クベッリ
Cubelli, Tomas 306
グベリナ
Guberina, Petar 542
クーペル
Cúper, Héctor 308
Kooper, Gisella 756
グベール
Goubert, Pierre 521
グベル
Goubel, Mathieu 521
クーペルス
Cuperus, René 308
クベロス
Cubelos Sanchez, Francisco 306
グーベン
Guven, Egemen 549
グボジディク
Gvozdyk, Oleksandr 550
グボズデノビッチ
Gvozdenović, Branimir 550
クボタ
Kubota, Hiroshi 770
Kubota, Shigeko 770
クボット
Kubot, Lukasz 770
クポツラ
Kpotsra, Yao Roland 762
クーマー
Kumar, Vijay 773
クマ
Kuma, Demeksa 772
クマー
Kumar, Martha Joynt 773
Kumar, Nirmalya 773
Kumar, Sadish 773
Kumar, Sudhir 773
Kummer, Benno 773
クマイム
al-Kumaim, Abdul-Aziz 772
クマサカ
Kumasaka, Izuru 773
クマハラ
Kumahara, Caroline 772
クマラスワミ
Coomaraswamy, Radhika 286
クマラトゥンガ
Kumaratunga, Chandrika Bandaranaike 773
クマラナトゥンガ
Kumaranatunga, Jeewan 773
クマラナヤケ
Kumaranayake, Lilani 773
クマリ
Kumari, Deepika 773
クマリタシビリ
Kumaritashvili, Nodar 773
クマール
Kumar, Akhil 772
Kumar, Archana 772
Kumar, Ashwani 772
Kumar, Jitender 773
kumar, Leela Raj 773
Kumar, Manjit 773
Kumar, Nitish 773
Kumar, Parveen 773
Kumar, Pradeep 773
Kumar, Ravindra 773
Kumar, Sajeesh 773
Kumar, Sameet M. 773
Kumar, Satish 773
Kumar, Shanta 773
Kumar, Somesh 773
Kumar, Sushil 773
Kumar, Vijay 773
Kumar (singh), Vijender 773
クマル
Kumar, Jainend 773
Kumar, Meira 773
クマール・ナス
Kumar Nath, Deb 773
クマレ
Koumaré, Abdoulaye 760
Koumaré, Mamadou Hachim 760
クマロ
Khumalo, Vukile 729
クーマン
Koeman, Ronald 751
クマン
Kemen, Olivier 718
Kuman, Nick 772
クーミン
Kumin, Maxine 773
クミン
Cumine, Val 307
Kumin, Libby 773
クムサップ
Khumsap, Chatchai 729
クムシシビリ
Kumsishvili, Dimitri 773
クームズ
Coombs, Kate 286
Coombs, Mark 286
Cooms, Rod 286
クムス
Kums, Sven 773
グムチジャン
Gumuchdjian, Philip 546
クムバコル
Kumbakor, Andrew 773
クムパルメ
Kumpalume, Peter 773
クムバロ
Kumbaro, Mirela 773
クムリク
Chmelik, Stefan 257
グメソン
Gummesson, Evert 546
クメラ
Chmela, Kristin 257
グメリン
Gmelin, Jeannine 506
グメルス
Gummels, Antje 546
クメロウ
Kummerow, Jean M. 773
クーメン
Koomen, Pete 756
クメント
Kmentt, Waldemar 747
グモ
Gumo, Fredrick 546
クヤテ
Kouyate, Cheikhou 761
Kouyate, Oumar 761
Kouyate, Sotigui 761
クヤリス
Kouyialis, Nicos 761
グュエン
Nguyen, Van Chuyen 1021
グユーシ
Geyoushi, Saad el 492
クユンジッチ

Kujundžić, Milan 772
クーラ
Cura, José 308
クーラー
Köhler, Ulrich 752
クライ
Klaï, Haj 743
グライ
Glei, Jocelyn Kendall 504
クライアン
Cryan, Dan 306
クライガーシュタイン
Kriegerstein, Steffi 766
クライゲル
Kraigher, Sergej 763
クライシュ
al-Quraish, Al Samawaal Khakafalla 1146
クライシュテルス
Clijsters, Kim 271
Clijsters, Leo 271
クライス
Kleis, Constanze 745
Klise, Kate 746
Klise, M.Sarah 746
Kreis, Levi 765
グライス
Greis, Michael 533
クライスターリー
Kleisterlee, Gerard Johannes 745
グライスティーン
Gleysteen, William H., Jr. 505
クライスト
Christe, Ian 260
Kleist, Reinhard 745
クライスマン
Kreisman, Jerold Jay 765
クライスラー
Kleissler, Thomas A. 745
クライソン・チャンシリ
Chansiri, Kraisorn 246
クライター
Kreiter, Casey 765
クライダー
Crider, Bill 302
Kreider, Robert Standford 765
Kryder, Cynthia L. 769
グライダー
Greider, Carol W. 533
クライダラス
Clidaras, Jimmy 271
クライツァー
Critser, Greg 302
Kreitzer, Mary Jo 765
クライツィグ
Kreyszig, Erwin 766
クライツェル
Krajcer, Daniel 763
クライツマン
Kreitzman, Leon 765
グライツマン
Gleitzman, Morris 504
クライデル
Kridel, Donald J. 766
クライト
Kreit, John W. 765
グライド
Glied, Sherry 505
クライトル
Kraitor, Andrey 763
クライトン
Claiton 266
Creighton, Christopher 301
Crichton, Michael 301
Crichton, Robert R. 301
クライナー
Kleiner, Art 744
Kleiner, Israel 744
Kreiner, Josef 765
Kreiner, Marion 765
グライナー
Greiner, Johannes 533
Greiner, Walter 533
クライニク
Krainik, Andrew J. 763
クライネルト
Kleinert, Annemarie 744
Kleinert-schmitt, Nadine 744
クライネルメルン
Kleinelümern, Ute 744
クライネンバーグ
Klinenberg, Eric 745
クライバー
Klaiber, Walter 743
Kleiber, Carlos 744
グライバー
Greiber, Peter 533
クライバーン
Cliburn, Van 271
Clyburn, Danny, Jr. 272
クライバン
Cliburn, Van 271
グライヒ
Gleich, Jacky 504
クライフ
Clive, Eric M. 271
Cruyff, Johan 305
クライブ
Clive, Eric M. 271
グライフ
Greif, Avner 533
Greif, R. 533
グライブ
al-Glaib, Mustafa 503
グライフ・ニール
Greif-Neill, Cole Marsden 533
クライブリンク
Kleibrink, Benjamin 744
クライベル
Kleiber, Michał 744
クライボーケル
Kleibeuker, Carien 744
クライマー
Clymer, Eleanor Lowenton 272
クライマイアー
Kreimeier, Klaus 765
グライムス
Grimes, William W. 536
グライムズ
Grimes, Andrew J. 536
Grimes, Brent 536
Grimes, Jonathan 536
Grimes, Martha 536
Grimes, Nikki 536
Grimes, William W. 536
Grymes, Aaron 541
Grymes, James A. 541
クライヤー
Cryer, Jon 306
Cryer, Robert 306
グライユ
Graille, Patrick 524
クライル
Crile, George Ⅲ 302
クライルガート
Kreilgaard, Peter 765
クライン
Cline, Elizabeth L. 271
Cline, Ernest 271
Cline, Foster 271
Clyne, Nathaniel 272
Clyne, T.W. 272
Klein, Aaron J. 744
Klein, A.J. 744
Klein, Alec 744
Klein, Allen 744
Klein, Arnold 744
Klein, Calvin 744
Klein, Charles 744
Klein, Daniel M. 744
Klein, David R. 744
Klein, Edward 744
Klein, Freada Kapor 744
Klein, Gary A. 744
Klein, George 744
Klein, Gillian 744
Klein, Herbert S. 744
Klein, James D. 744
Klein, Janet 744
Klein, Jean-Pierre 744
Klein, John P. 744
Klein, Leonore 744
Klein, Marc 744
Klein, Matthew 744
Klein, Maury 744
Klein, Michael 744
Klein, Naomi 744
Klein, Nicholas 744
Klein, Ralph Phillip 744
Klein, Rebekka A. 744
Klein, Richard 744
Klein, Richard G. 744
Klein, Sascha 744
Klein, Stefan 744
Klein, Steve 744
Klein, T.E.D. 744
Klein, Tobias 744
Klein, Tom 744
Klein, Volker 744
Klin, Ami 745
Kline, Carol 745
Kline, Christina Baker 745
Kline, David 745
Kline, Josh 745
Kline, Karen 745
Kline, Kevin 745
Kline, Maggie 745
Kline, Michael P. 745
Kline, Nancy 745
Kline, Peter 745
Kline, Thomas L. 745
クラインシュミット
Kleinschmidt, Harald 745
クラインツ
Krajnc, Luca 763
クラインハイスラー
Kleinheisler, Laszlo 744
クラインハインツ
Kleinheinz, Markus 744
クラインバーグ
Kleinberg, Jon 744
クラインフェルト
Kleinfeld, Klaus 744
クラインマン
Kleinman, Arthur 745
Kleinman, Joan 745
Kleinman, Sherryl 745
クライン＝ルブール
Klein-Rebour, F. 745
クラインロック
Kleinrock, Leonard 745
クラウ
Krag, Astrid 763
グラウ
Grau, Lester W. 527
Grau, Philippe 527
グラウアー
Grauer, Ken 527
Grauer, Peter T. 527
グラヴァー
Glover, Jane 505
Glover, Jonathan 505
クラヴァン
Klavan, Andrew 743
Klavan, Ragnar 743
グラヴィエ
Gravier, Anne 527
クラウイェリス
Kraujelis, Jeronimas 764
クラヴィッツ
Kravitz, Lee 765
Kravitz, Lenny 765
グラー＝ヴィティッヒ
Grah-Wittich, Claudia 524
グラヴィニチ
Glavinic, Thomas 504
クラヴィン
Clavin, Thomas 269
グラヴィン
Glavine, Tom 504
グラウウェ
Grauwe, Paul de 527
クラヴェー
Clavé, Antoni 269
グラウエ
Grauwe, Paul de 527
クラヴェツ
Kravets, Artem 765
グラヴェット
Gravett, Christopher 527
Gravett, Emily 527
グラウエルト
Grauert, Hans 527
クラーヴェン
Craven, John 300
クラウク
Klauck, Hans-Josef 743
クラウサー
Crowther, Robert 305
クラウザー
Clauser, John F. 269
Crowther, Peter 305
Crowther, Yasmin 305
Klauser, Henriette Anne 743
グラウザー
Glauser, Fred 504
クラウジミール
Claudemir 269
クラウシャー
Kraushaar, Judah S. 765
クラウス
Claus, Hugo Maurice Julien 269
Klaus, Josef 743
Klaus, Marshall H. 743
Klaus, Peggy 743
Klaus, Phyllis H. 743

ク

ク

Klaus, Václav 743
Klause, Annette Curtis 743
Klauss, Gauthier 743
Klauss, Jochen 743
Kraus, Alanna 764
Kraus, Marinus 764
Kraus, Michael 764
Kraus, Nicola 764
Kraus, Robert 764
Krause, Bernard L. 764
Krause, Jerry 764
Krause, Jim 764
Krause, Jonathan 764
Krause, Loretta 764
Krause, Martin 764
Krause, Shari Stamford 765
Krauss, Alejandra 765
Krauss, Alison 765
Krauss, Ellis S. 765
Krauss, Lawrence Maxwell 765
Krauss, Nicole 765
Krauss, Robert M. 765
Krauss, Rosalind E. 765
Krauss, Trisha 765
Krausz, Robert 765
Krouse, Erika 768

クラウズ
Krausz, Erwin 765

クラウス殿下
Prince Claus 269

クラウス・バジェ
Krauss Valle, Alejandra 765

クラウスハール
Kraushaar, Silke 765

グラウスベック
Grousbeck, Wyc 539

クラウスマイヤー
Klausmeier, Jesse 743

クラウズリー・トンプソン
Cloudsley-Thompson, John Leonard 272

クラウセ
Krause, Tom 765
Krauze, Enrique 765

クラウゼ
Krause, Egon 764
Krause, Jerry 764
Krause, Richard M. 764
Krause, Tom 765
Krause, Ute 765
Krauze, Krzysztof 765

クラウセン
Claussen, Claus 269
Claussen, Johann Hinrich 269

クラウダー
Clouder, Christopher 272
Crowder, Carolyn Zoe 304
Crowder, Robert 304

クラウチ
Crouch, Adele 304
Crouch, Blake 304
Crouch, Cathy 304
Crouch, Colin 304
Crouch, Peter 304

クラウチク
Krawczyk, Katarzyna 765

クラウチャンカ
Krauchanka, Andrei 764

クラウディ
Crowdy, Terry 304

クラウティア
Cloutier, Marissa 272

クラウディオ
Claudio, Alex 269

クラウド
Cloud, Henry 272

グラウト
Grout, Pam 539

クラウバー
Klauber, Trudy 743

グラウバー
Glauber, Robert R. 504
Glauber, Roy J. 504

グラウバック
Glaubach, Jay 504

グラウプ
Graupp, Patrick 527

クラウリー
Crowley, David 304
Crowley, John F. 304

クラヴリ
Claverie, Élisabeth 269

クラヴルー
Claveloux, Nicole 269

クラウンズ
Crowns, Casting 304

グラウンド
Ground, Ian 539

クラーエ
Krahé, Barbara 763

グラエギン
Graegin, Stephanie 523

グラエル
Grael, Martine 523
Grael, Torben 523

グラエンボル
Groenvold, Audun 538

クラカワー
Krakauer, Jon 763

クラガン
Cragun, Richard 299

クラーク
Clark, Andy 266
Clark, Angus 266
Clark, Anne K. 266
Clark, Aoife 266
Clark, Bob 266
Clark, Bruce 266
Clark, Burton R. 266
Clark, Carol Higgins 266
Clark, Chris 266
Clark, Colin 266
Clark, Dave 266
Clark, David 266
Clark, David A. 266
Clark, David H. 266
Clark, David Hazell 266
Clark, David M. 267
Clark, David P. 267
Clark, Dick 267
Clark, Donavon 267
Clark, E.Gillian 267
Clark, Emma Chichester 267
Clark, Eric 267
Clark, Frank 267
Clark, Gary 267
Clark, Gary, Jr. 267
Clark, Gillian 267
Clark, Greg 267
Clark, Gregory 267
Clark, Guy 267
Clark, Helen 267
Clark, Howard, Sr. 267
Clark, Ian 267
Clark, James J.J. 267
Clark, Jan 267
Clark, Jane Osborn 267
Clark, Jeffrey 267
Clark, Jim 267
Clark, John 267
Clark, John Earl 267
Clark, John F.M. 267
Clark, John Owen Edward 267
Clark, Josh 267
Clark, Judith Freeman 267
Clark, Julie 267
Clark, Katie 267
Clark, Kelly 267
Clark, Kenny 267
Clark, Kim B. 267
Clark, Laurel 267
Clark, Laurel Blair Salton 267
Clark, Le'Raven 267
Clark, Linda 267
Clark, Linda A. 267
Clark, Lynn 267
Clark, Margery 267
Clark, Mark 267
Clark, Martin 267
Clark, Mary Higgins 267
Clark, Mary Jane Behrends 267
Clark, Mary Jo Dummer 267
Clark, M.Carolyn 267
Clark, Michael 267
Clark, Mike 267
Clark, Myrtle 267
Clark, Neil 267
Clark, Paul 267
Clark, Ramsey 267
Clark, Richard 267
Clark, Richard E. 267
Clark, Richard K. 267
Clark, Robert 267
Clark, Robin E. 267
Clark, Ron 267
Clark, Ruth Colvin 267
Clark, Saskia 267
Clark, Scott 267
Clark, Simon 267
Clark, Stephen P.H. 268
Clark, Stephen R.L. 268
Clark, Steven 268
Clark, Stuart G. 268
Clark, Taylor 268
Clark, Terry N. 268
Clark, Tim 268
Clark, Timothy 268
Clark, Tom 268
Clark, Tony 268
Clark, Victoria 268
Clark, Willard G. 268
Clark, William 268
Clark, William, Jr. 268
Clark, William C. 268
Clark, William P. 268
Clark, William R. 268
Clarke, Ali 268
Clarke, Alicia 268
Clarke, Andy 268
Clarke, Ardy S. 268
Clarke, Arthur Charles 268
Clarke, Boyd 268
Clarke, Bryan R. 268
Clarke, Charles 268
Clarke, Darren 268
Clarke, Davian 268
Clarke, Ellis Emmanuel Innocent 268
Clarke, Finn 268
Clarke, Gill 268
Clarke, Gillian 268
Clarke, Gline 268
Clarke, Graham 268
Clarke, Gregory 268
Clarke, Gus 268
Clarke, Helen 268
Clarke, Hugh Denis Blake 268
Clarke, Isabel 268
Clarke, Jane 268
Clarke, Jason 268
Clarke, Joseph 268
Clarke, Juanne Nancarrow 268
Clarke, Judith 268
Clarke, Kenneth 268
Clarke, Lauren Nancarrow 268
Clarke, Lawrence 268
Clarke, Michaela 268
Clarke, Miranda 268
Clarke, Neil 268
Clarke, Peter Hugh 268
Clarke, Peter T. 268
Clarke, P.F. 268
Clarke, Phil 268
Clarke, Pippa 268
Clarke, Richard A. 268
Clarke, Robert W. 268
Clarke, Robin 268
Clarke, Roger 268
Clarke, Ron 268
Clarke, Ronald V. 269
Clarke, Sean 269
Clarke, Sharon D. 269
Clarke, Shirley 269
Clarke, Stanley 269
Clarke, Stephen 269
Clarke, Sue 269
Clarke, Susanna 269
Clarke, Thurston 269
Clarke, Tony 269
Clarke, Will 269
Clerk, Christian 271
Golding-clarke, Lacena 510
Krag, Werner 763
Miles Clark, Jearl 946
Scott-Clark, Cathy 1265

クラク
Kulak, Daryl 772

クラークケイテルデイク
Kraag-keteldijk, Lygia 762

クラクストン
Claxton, William 269

クラークスン
Clarkson, Michael 269

クラークソン
Clarkson, Adrienne 269
Clarkson, Janet 269
Clarkson, Jordan 269
Clarkson, Kelly 269
Clarkson, Mark Alan 269
Clarkson, Wensley 269

クラークマン
Kraakman, Reinier H. 762

クラグマン
Klugman, Jack 746

クラーケ
Klaetke, Fritz 743

クラーゲス
Klages, Ellen 743

クラゴー
Cragoe, Carol

Davidson 299
グラゴウ
Glagow (beck),
Martina 503
クラコウスキー
Krakowski, Jane 763
グラコウスキー
Gradkowski, Bruce 523
Gradkowski, Gino 523
クラコベツキー
Krakovetskii, Iurii 763
クラコーラ
Krakora, Joseph J. 763
グラゴレヴァ
Glagoleva, Elena
Georgievna 503
クラザー
Crother, Cyndi 304
グラーザー
Glaser, Christian 503
Glaser, Hermann 503
Glaser, Pernilla 503
グラサ
Glasa, Josef 503
Graça, Job 523
グラサー
Glasser, Brian 504
グラサウア
Glasauer, Willi 503
クラーシ
Clasie, Jordy 269
グラジア
Grazia, Florence 528
グラシアガルシア
Gracia Garcia,
Fernando 523
グラジアノ
Graziano, Dan 528
グラジアノ・ダ・シルバ
Graziano da Silva,
José 528
クラジェ
Kragelj, Ursa 763
グラジエ
Glazier, Sidney 504
クラシェフスキ
Kraszewski, Andrzej 764
グラジオラ
Garagiola, Joe 477
グラシッチ
Grasic, Andreja 526
グラシメニャ
Gerasimenya,
Aleksandra 490
クラシュ
Kulash, Damian, Jr. 772
クラジュ
Curaj, Adrian 308
グラシュー
Glasziou, Paul P. 504
クラシュウィッツ
Kruschwitz, Nina 769
クラジュキ
Krasucki, Henri 764
クラシルニコフ
Krasilnikov, Gennadiy 764
Krasilnikov,
Viacheslav 764
クラシロフスキー
Krasilovsky, Phyllis 764
クラース
Klaas, Kathrin 743
Klass, David 743
クラス
Klass, David 743
Klassou, Komi Sélom 743
Kras, Reyer 764
Kruse, Richard 769
グラース
Glass, David J. 504
Glass, Stephen 504
Grasse, Marie-
Christine 526
グラス
Glas, Jorge 503
Glass, Adam 503
Glass, Calliope 504
Glass, Cathy 504
Glass, David 504
Glass, Graham 504
Glass, Ira 504
Glass, Julia 504
Glass, Leslie 504
Glass, Lillian 504
Glass, Philip 504
Glass, Robert L. 504
Glass, Suzanne 504
Grass, Günter
Wilhelm 526
Grasu, Nicoleta 527
グラスキン
Glaskin, Max 503
クラスク
Klask, Charles 743
グラスゴー
Glasgow, Russell E. 503
Glasgow, Sean C. 503
グラスゴウ
Glasgow, Graham 503
グラズコワ
Glazkov, Vyacheslav 504
クラステ
Craste, Marc 300
クラストリン
Klastorin, Michael 743
グラスドルフ
Grasdorff, Gilles van 526
グラスナー
Glassner, Barry 504
クラスナホルカイ
Krasznahorkai, László 764
クラスニチ
Krasniqi, Jakup 764
Krasniqi, Memli 764
クラスニヒ
Krassnig, Dieter 764
クラスニフ
Krasnykh, Aleksandr 764
クラスノー
Krasnow, Iris 764
グラスノー
Glasnow, Tyler 503
クラスノウ
Krasnow, Iris 764
クラスノシュタン
Krasnostein, Alisa 764
グラスノビッチ
Glasnovic, Josip 503
Glasnovic, Nikita 503
グラスパー
Glasper, Robert 503
グラスビー
Grassby, Albert Jaime 526
グラスベルガー
Grassberger, Martin 526
グラスホフ
Grasshoff, Alex 527
グラスマン - ディール
Glasman-Deal, Hilary 503
グラスユー
Grasu, Hroniss 527
クラーゼ
Krase, Andreas 764
クラセー
Krasae, Chanawongse 764
クラーセン
Klaassen, Curtis D. 743
Klaassen, Davy 743
Klaassen, Pieter 743
Klaassen, Roel 743
クラソフスカヤ
Krasovska, Olena 764
クラーソン
Claeson, Bonnie 266
Claesson, Stig 266
グラタウス
Grothaus, Heather 539
クラダップ
Crudup, Billy 305
グラーチ
Gulacsi, Peter 545
グラチョフ
Grachev, Pavel
Sergeevich 523
クラーツ
Kraatz, Victor 762
クラツ
Craats, Rennay 298
クラッグ
Cragg, Amy 299
Cragg, Dan 299
Cragg, Tony 299
Klug, Karl 746
グラック
Glattke, Theodore J. 504
Gluck, Carol 505
Gluck, Cellin 505
Gluck, Frederick W. 505
Gracq, Julien 523
グラッグ
Gragg, Chris 523
クラックストーン
Clackstone, Josh 266
クラックストン
Claxton, Sarah 269
グラックスマン
Glucksmann, Miriam 505
クラッグマン
Krugman, Michael 769
クラッコー
Krackow, Elisa 762
クラッコフ
Krakoff, Reed 763
グラッサー
Glasser, Carleen 504
Glasser, William 504
Grasser, Karl-Heinz 526
グラッシ
Grassi, Alberto 527
Grassi, Mitch 527
グラッシー
Glassie, Nandi 504
Grassi, Walter 527
クラッシャー・バンバン・ビガロ
Crasher Bam Bam
Bigelow 300
クラッシュ
Clash, Kevin 269
グラッスル
Grassle, John
Frederick 527
グラッセ
Grasset, Jules 526
グラッセッリ
Grasselli, Fabrizio 526
クラッセン
Classen, Catherine 269
Klassen, Cindy 743
Klassen, Jon 743
Klassen, William 743
グラッソ
Grasso, Patricia 527
Grasso, Santiago'Bou' 527
クラッター
Kratter, Giacomo 764
グラッタウアー
Glattauer, Daniel 504
グラッタン
Grattan, Nick 527
グラッタン・ギネス
Grattan-Guinness, Ivor
Owen 527
クラッチ
Klutch, M.S. 747
クラッチフィールド
Crutchfield, Leslie R. 305
Crutchfield, Stephen 305
クラッチャー
Crutcher, Chris 305
クラッツ
Klatz, Ronald 743
Kratz, Erik 764
グラッツ
Gratz, Dwayne 527
Gratz, Kim L. 527
グラッツァー
Glatzer, Richard 504
Glatzer, Robert 504
グラッツァーニ
Grazzani, Roberta 528
クラッテン
Klatten, Susanne 743
クラッテンデン
Cruttenden, Pete 305
グラット
Glatt, John 504
グラッド
Grad, Marcela 523
Grad, Marcia 523
グラッドウィン
Gladwin, Mark 503
グラッドウェル
Gladwell, Malcolm 503
グラットザー
Gratzer, Walter Bruno 527
グラッドシュタイン
Gradstein, Felix M. 523
グラッドスター
Gladstar, Rosemary 503
グラッドストーン
Gladstone, William 503
グラッドストン
Gladstone, Eve 503
グラッドマン
Gladman, Dafna D. 503
クラットワージー
Clatworthy, Simon 269
グラットン
Gratton, Lynda 527

ク

クラットン＝ブロック
Clutton-Brock, Juliet 272
クラッパー
Klapper, Joseph T. 743
クラッパート
Klappert, Bertold 743
クラッパム
Clapham, Michael John Sinclair 266
クラップ
Clapp, Jennifer 266
Clapp, Nicholas 266
Krupp, Fred 769
グラッブ
Grubb, Davis 540
Grubb, Thomas C., Jr. 540
クラッファム
Clapham, Caroline 266
グラッブス
Grubbs, Robert H. 540
クラッベ
Krabbé, Jeroen 762
グラッベ
Grabbe, Christian Dietrich 522
クラッペンバッハ
Klappenbach, Nicolas 743
グラテイ
Gulati, Om P. 545
クラティシュ
Kratysh, Ilana 764
クラティラカ
Kulatilaka, Nalin 772
Kulatilake, Gilbert 772
グラデル
Gradel, Max 523
グラテロル
Graterol, Juan 527
クラート
Crato, Nuno 300
グーラート
Goulart, Ron 521
グラート
Graat, Junko 522
グラド
Grad, Aleksander 523
クラドゥマジ
Kladoumadji, Nojitolbaye 743
グラドゥム
Grodum, Oystein 538
グラドキー
Gladky, Olexander 503
クラトスカ
Kratoska, Paul H. 764
グラドス・カラロ
Grados Carraro, Alfonso Fernando 523
クラドストラップ
Kladstrup, Don 743
Kladstrup, Petie 743
クラドック
Craddock, Fred B. 298
Cradock, Percy 298
Cradock, Steve 298
グラドビチ
Gladovic, Dragana 503
グラトン
Gratton, Lynda 527
クラーナ
Khurana, Rakesh 729
クラナ
Khurana, Rakesh 729
グラナイト
Granite, Zach 525
グラナダ
Granada, Julieta 525
Granada, Luis de 525
グラナード
Granado, Alberto 525
グラナド
Granado, Alberto 525
グラナドス
Granados, Stefan 525
クラニー
Kuranyi, Kevin 774
グラニア
Glania, Jan-Philip 503
クラニェツ
Kranjec, Robert 764
グラニエドフェール
Granier-Deferre, Pierre 525
クラニク
Kranich, Heiki 764
クラニチャール
Kranjčar, Niko 764
Kranjčar, Zlatko 764
クラニチャル
Kranjčar, Niko 764
Kranjčar, Zlatko 764
クラニツァール
Kranjčar, Niko 764
クラニッシュ
Kranish, Michael 764
グラニッチ
Granić, Goran 525
クラニッツ
Kranitz, Rick 764
グラニンガー
Graninger, Göran 525
グラネ
Granet, Danièle 525
クラネビッテル
Kranevitter, Matias 764
グラネル
Granel, Gérard 525
クラーネルト
Krahnert, Sebastian 763
グラネロ
Granero, Esteban 525
クラーネンドンク
Kranendonk, Anke 764
グラノウ
Graneau, Ashton 525
Graneau, Kelly 525
クラノウィッツ
Kranowitz, Carol Stock 764
グラノヴェッター
Granovetter, Ellen 525
Granovetter, Mark 525
グラノット
Granot, Hayim 525
グラノフ
Granov, Adi 525
グラバー
Glover, Helen 505
Glover, Koda 505
Glover, Robert A. 505
Graber, James M. 522
Gruber, Marcia 540
グラバーズ
Grabarz, Robert 522
クラハト
Kracht, Klaus 762
グラバニ
Glavany, Jean 504
グラバーマン
Glaberman, Martin 503
グラハム
Graham, Anne 524
Graham, Bill 524
Graham, Billy 524
Graham, Brandon 524
Graham, Carol 524
Graham, Corey 524
Graham, David 524
Graham, Dorothy 524
Graham, Garrett 524
Graham, Heather 524
Graham, Helen 524
Graham, Ian 524
Graham, James 524
Graham, Jay 524
Graham, Jeffrey A. 524
Graham, Jimmy 524
Graham, John L. 524
Graham, Karen 524
Graham, Katherine Meyer 524
Graham, Lisa 524
Graham, Matt 524
Graham, Mike 524
Graham, Oakley 524
Graham, Otto 524
Graham, Robert 524
Graham, Ron 524
Graham, Shayne 524
Graham, Stephen R. 524
Graham, Susan 524
Graham, T.J. 524
Graham, Tony 524
Graham, Treveon 524
Graham, William 524
グラハム＝キャンベル
Graham-Campbell, James 524
グラハム＝ジョンストン
Grahame-Johnstone, Anne 524
Grahame-Johnstone, Janet 524
グラハム・スミス
Grahame-Smith, Seth 524
グラハムダグラス
Grahm-douglass, Tonye 524
グラバルキタロヴィッチ
Grabar-Kitarović, Kolinda 522
グラバルキタロビッチ
Grabar-Kitarović, Kolinda 522
グラバルチク
Grabarczyk, Cezary 522
グラハレス
Grajales, Crisanto 525
クラハン
Krahn, Betina M. 763
クラバン
Klavan, Andrew 743
クラパン
Clapin, Jérémy 266
グラバン
Glavan, Ruxanda 504
Grabban, Lewis 522
グラビアス
Grabias, Bernadetta 522
クラビエ
Clavier, Jerome 269
クラビオット
Craviotto, Saúl 300
クラビオトリベロ
Craviotto, Saúl 300
Craviotto Rivero, Saul 300
グラピオン
Glapion, Jonathan 503
クラピカス
Krapikas, Titas 764
グラビス
Kravis, Henry 765
クラピッシュ
Klapisch, Cédric 743
クラピッチ
Krapič, Milan 764
クラビッツ
Kravitz, Lenny 765
クラビド
Cravid, Raul Antonio da Costa 300
グラビナー
Grabinar, John 523
クラピビナ
Krapyvina, Anastasiya 764
グラビン
Glavine, Tom 504
クラフ
Clough, Nick 272
Keraf, Sonny 721
Klaff, Oren 743
クラブ
Clubb, Barbara 272
Crabb, Jason 298
Crabb, Lawrence J. 298
Crabb, Stephen 298
Crabbe, Allen 298
グラーフ
Graf, Bernhard 523
Graf, Friedrich Wilhelm 523
Gráf, József 523
グラーブ
Grube, Chris 540
グラフ
Graf, Bernadette 523
Graf, David 523
Graf, Friedrich Wilhelm 523
Graf, Karlheinz 523
Graf, Olga 523
Graf, Steffi 523
Graff, Cyril 523
Graff, Laurent 523
Graff, Lisa Colleen 523
Graff, Mark G. 523
Graffe, Anne-Caroline 523
グラブ
Grab, Michael 522
Grabb, Gwen Schubert 522
Grubb, Jeff 540
グラフィン
Graffin, Greg 523
グラーフェ
Grafe, Ogar 523
グラフェン
Grafen, Alan 523
グラフォフ
Grafov, Boris Vasilyevich 523
クラフォルツ
Klapholz, Richard 743

クラフキー
Klafki, Wolfgang 743
グラブシュ
Grabsch, Bert 523
クラフス
Krafth, Emil 763
グラブス
Grubbs, David 540
Grubbs, Robert H. 540
クラフチェンコ
Kravchenko, Yury 765
クラフチク
Krawczyk, Robert 765
クラプチチ
Clapcich, Francesca 266
クラフチュク
Kravchuk, Stanislav 765
クラフツィック
Krafzig, Dirk 763
クラフツェヴィチ
Kravtsevich, Andrei Ivanovich 765
クラブツリー
Crabtree, Sally 298
クラフティ
Crafti, Stephen 299
クラーフト
Kraft, Victor 763
クラフト
Craft, Anna 298
Craft, Kathryn A. 298
Craft, Kinuko Y. 298
Craft, Melanie 298
Craft, Melissa 298
Craft, Morgan 298
Craft, Shanice 298
Krafft, Martin F. 763
Kraft, Heinrich 763
Kraft, Heinz 763
Kraft, Herbert R. 763
Kraft, Ivonne 763
Kraft, Kraig 763
Kraft, Noah 763
Kraft, Rahasya Fritjof 763
Kraft, Robert 763
Kraft, Thomas 763
クラブトゥリー
Crabtree, Caroline 298
Crabtree, Margo 298
Crabtree, Michael 298
クラフトン
Crafton, Donald 299
クラプトン
Clapton, Eric 266
グラフトン
Grafton, Anthony 523
Grafton, David 523
Grafton, Sue 523
グラブナー
Grabner, Siegfried 523
グラブホーン
Grabhorn, Lynn 522
クラフラ
Krahula, Beckah 763
クラベ
Clavé, Antoni 269
クラベー
Krabbe, Tim 762
グラベンスタイン
Grabenstein, Chris 522
グラポ
Grappo, Gary Joseph 526
グラボウスキー
Grabowski, Richard 523
クラポビッチ
Krapović, Slobodan 764
グラボフスキ
Grabowski, Maciej 523
グラボベツカヤ
Grabovetskaya, Mariya 523
クラーマー
Cramer, Dettmar 299
Cramer, Jacqueline 299
Cramer, Konrad 299
Kramer, IJsbrand M. 763
クラマー
Clammer, J.R. 266
Cramer, Dettmar 299
Cramer, Friedrich 299
Klamer, Arjo 743
Klamer, Rachel 743
Kramer, Christoph 763
Kramer, Jack 763
Kramer, Lotte 763
Kramer, Roderick M. 764
Kramer, Steven J. 764
Kramer, Sven 764
Kramer, Ulrich 764
グラマー
Grammer, Kelsey 525
グラマグリア
Gramaglia, Marie-Pierre 525
クラマゴメドフ
Kuramagomedov, Kuramagomed 774
Kuramagomedov, Zaur 774
クラマラー
Koulamallah, Ibrahim 760
グラマラ
Ghlamallah, Bouabdellah 493
クラマリッチ
Kramaric, Andrej 763
クラマレンコ
Kramarenko, Ekaterina 763
Kramarenko, Grigoriĭ Amosovits 763
Kramarenko, Zhorzh 763
クラーマン
Klarman, Alex 743
クラマン
Claman, Liz 266
クラム
Clum, Gerard W. 272
Cram, Donald James 299
Cramm, Dagmar von 299
Crum, Dan 305
Crum, Gert 305
Crum, Steven James 305
Crumb, Robert 305
Klum, Heidi 747
Kram, Kathy E. 763
Krum, Sharon 769
Krumm, Kathie L. 769
グラム
Ghoulam, Faouzi 494
Graham, Lindsay O. 524
Gram, Dewey 525
Gram, Eduard 525
グラムス
Grams, Rod 525
グラムズ
Grams, Rod 525
クラムパッカー
Crumpacker, Bunny 305
クラムリー
Crumley, James 305
グラムリヒ＝オカ
Gramlich-Oka, Bettina 525
グラメット
Grummett, Tom 541
グラメーニャ
Gramegna, Pierre 525
クラメール
Cramér, Ivo 299
クラメル
Cramér, Ivo 299
クラーモント
Clermont, Kevin M. 271
グララ
Gralla, Preston 525
クララトナ
Kularatne, Ananda 772
クラーリ
Clari, Anna 266
クラリー
Clary, Tyler 269
クラリエビッチ
Kraljević, Hrvoje 763
クラリク
Kralik, John 763
クラリッジ
Claridge, Timothy D. W. 266
クラーリングボールド
Claringbould, Michael John 266
クラール
Klaar, J.Margus 743
Král, Petr 763
Krall, Diana 763
グーラール
Goulard, François 521
グラール
Goulard, François 521
クラルスフェルド
Klarsfeld, André 743
グラルニック
Guralnick, Peter 547
クラレ
Claret, Jacques 266
クラレッティ
Claretti, Clarissa 266
クラレフ
Kralev, Krasen 763
Kralev, Pance 763
クラーン
Kraan, Hanna 762
クラン
Chlan, Linda L. 257
Cran, William 299
Klein, Jean-Pierre 744
Klein, Michel 744
グラン
Gran, Sara 525
Grand, Emmanuel 525
Grann, David 525
グランヴィル
Glanville, Brian 503
Grainville, Patrick 525
Granville, Gillian 526
クラングル
Crangle, Maeve Byrne 299
グランコフスカヤ
Grankovskaya, Svetlana 525
グランサム
Grantham, Charles E. 526
クランシー
Clancy, Deirdre 266
Clancy, Ed 266
Clancy, Edward 266
Clancy, Eva 266
Clancy, John 266
Clancy, Susan A. 266
Clancy, Taliqua 266
Clancy, Tom 266
グランシー
Glancey, Jonathan 503
グランジ
Grange, John M. 525
Grange, Olivia 525
グランジェ
Grangé, Jean-Christophe 525
グランジャン
Grandjean, Etienne 525
Grandjean, Philippe 525
グランジュ
Granju, Katie Allison 525
グランジョルジュ
Grandgeorge, Didier 525
グランストローム
Granström, Brita 525
クランストン
Cranston, Bryan 299
Cranston, Edwin A. 300
クーランダー
Courlander, Harold 295
グランダーソン
Granderson, Curtis 525
グランダッジ
Grandazzi, Alexandre 525
クランダル
Crandall, Susan 299
グランダル
Grandal, Yasmani 525
クランチィ
Clanchy, Kate 266
グランチャロワ
Grancharova, Gergana 525
クランツ
Cranz, Christl 300
Krantz, Judith 764
Krantz, Patricia J. 764
Krantz, Steven George 764
Krnac, Jozef 767
グランツ
Glantz, David M. 503
Granz, Norman 526
クランテ
Clante, Iben 266
グランデ
Grande, Ariana 525
グランディ
Grundy, Peter 541
クランディニン
Clandinin, D.Jean 266
グランディン
Grandin, Greg 525
Grandin, Temple 525
グランデージ
Grandage, Michael 525
クーランド
Kurland, Michael 775
クラント
Klandt, Patric 743
グラント

ク

Grant, Adam M. 525
Grant, Adrian 525
Grant, Alan 525
Grant, Alexander 525
Grant, Allan 526
Grant, Allison Wynn 526
Grant, Amy 526
Grant, Anthony 526
Grant, Anthony M. 526
Grant, Antwane 526
Grant, Avram 526
Grant, Barbara Rosemary 526
Grant, Barry Keith 526
Grant, Carl A. 526
Grant, Charles Benedict 526
Grant, Charles L. 526
Grant, Corey 526
Grant, Curtis 526
Grant, Cynthia D. 526
Grant, Donald 526
Grant, Doran 526
Grant, Edward 526
Grant, Edward A. 526
Grant, Emmanuel 526
Grant, Frances 526
Grant, Gavin J. 526
Grant, George, Jr. 526
Grant, Heather McLeod 526
Grant, Hugh 526
Grant, Jakeem 526
Grant, Jerami 526
Grant, Jerian 526
Grant, Jessica C.H. 526
Grant, Joan 526
Grant, Joe 526
Grant, Johny 526
Grant, Jon E. 526
Grant, Joy 526
Grant, Kenneth L. 526
Grant, Kim 526
Grant, Lee 526
Grant, Lindsay 526
Grant, Marcus 526
Grant, Mary 526
Grant, Melissa Gira 526
Grant, Michael 526
Grant, Neko 526
Grant, Peter Raymond 526
Grant, Reg 526
Grant, R.G. 526
Grant, Robert M. 526
Grant, Ryan 526
Grant, Steven 526
Grant, Suzi 526

グランド
Grand, David 525
Grand, Joseph“Kingpin” 525
Grand, Steve 525

グラント＝ウィリアムズ
Grant-Williams, Renee 526

クランドール
Crandall, Robert W. 299

クラントン
Clinton, Harry 271
Cranton, Elmer M. 300
Cranton, Patricia 300
Kranton, Rachel E. 764

グラントン
Glanton, Adarius 503

グランナー
Granner, Daryl K. 525

グランネマン
Granneman, Scott 525

グランバック
Grumbach, Didier 541

グランバッシ
Granbassi, Margherita 525

グランバム
Grunbaum, Mara 541

クランプ
Cramp, Bradley 299
Crump, John 305
Crump, Martha L. 305
Klump, Valdean 747

クランフィールド
Cranfield, Bill 299
Cranfield, Charles Ernest Burland 299

グランフェルド
Grunfeld, Ernie 541

クランプトン
Crampton, Alexandra Lee 299
Crampton, David S. 299
Crampton, R.J. 299

グランプレ
GrandPré, Mary 525

グランベール
Grimbert, Philippe 536

クランボルツ
Krumboltz, John D. 769

クランマー
Cranmer, Kathryn 299

グランモン
Grandmont, Jean-Michel 525

グラーンラーソネン
Grahn-laasonen, Sanni 524

グランラーソネン
Grahn-laasonen, Sanni 524

グランルンド
Granlund, Paul 525

グランワルド
Grunwald, Henry Anatole 541

クーリー
Cooley, John K. 286
Cooley, Thomas F. 286
Khoury, Raymond 729

クリ
Cury, Augusto 309
Cury, Augusto Jorge 309

クリー
Cree, Ann Elizabeth 301

グーリー
Gooley, Tristan 517

グリ
Gries, Patrick 535
Guri, Elis 547

クーリア
Coulier, Mark 295

クリア
Clear, Jacob 269

グリーア
Greer, Cassandra 532
Greer, Jane 532
Greer, Mary Katherine 532
Gurria, José Angel 547

グリア
Greer, Germaine 532
Greer, John Michael 532
Greer, Steven 532
Greer, Steven M. 532
Grier, Pam 534
Gurria, José Angel 547

グリアー
Greer, Andy 532
Grier, Francis 534
Grier, Pam 534

グリーアドル
Gleadle, Jonathan 504

クリアーヌ＝ペトレスク
Culianu-Petrescu, Tereza 307

クリアリー
Cleary, Anna 269
Cleary, Beverly 269
Cleary, Emmett 269
Cleary, Jon 269
Cleary, Noelle 269

クリアレーゼ
Crialese, Emanuele 301

グリアン
Gulian, Constantin Ionescu 545
Gurian, Michael 547

クリアンサク・チャマナン
Kriangsak Chamanand 766

クリアンサック
Kriangsak Chamanand 766

クリアンスキー
Kuriansky, Judith 774

クリーヴ
Cleave, Chris 270
Cleave, Paul 270

グリーヴ
Greive, Bradley Trevor 533

グリーヴァー
Greever, Tom 532

クリヴィツキー
Krivitsky, Walter G. 767

クリヴィヌ
Krivine, Emmanuel 767

クリヴィン
Krivine, Emmanuel 767

クリウコフ
Kriukov, Nikita 767

クリーヴス
Cleeves, Ann 270

クーリエ
Courier, Robert 295

グリエフ
Guliyev, Ramil 545
Guliyev, Vilayat 545

グリエリ
Guerrieri, Taylor 543

クリエル
Kriel, Jesse 766

グリエル
Gourriel, Yuliesky 522
Gurriel, Lourdes 547
Gurriel, Yulieski 547

グリエルモ
Guglielmo, Anthony 544

グリオッタ
Gugliotta, Guy 544

グリオリ
Gliori, Debi 505

クリオン
Klion, Mark 746

クリーガー
Kreger, Randi 765
Krieger, David 766
Krieger, Dolores 766
Krieger, Henry 766
Krieger, Pascal 766

クリーガーコブル
Krieger Coble, Henry 766

グリガル
Grigar, Jakub 536

クリキ
Kuriki, Massao 774

グリク
Glik, Kamil 505

グリグスビー
Grigsby, Nicholas 536

グリクスン
Gulliksen, Øyvind Tveitereid 545

クリグマン
Kligman, Albert 745

クリグラー
Crigler, Ann N. 302

クリーゲスコルテ
Kriegeskorte, Werner 766

クリーゲル
Kregel, Jan Allen 765
Kriegel, Gail 766
Kriegel, Volker 766

クリーゲンブルク
Kriegenburg, Andreas 766

クリコーカ
Krykorka, Vladyana 769

クリコフ
Kulikov, Boris 772
Kulikov, Viktor Georgievich 772

グリゴラシ
Grigoras, Stela 536

グリゴーリエバ
Grigorieva, Tatiana Petrovna 536

グリゴリエフ
Grigorev, Vladimir 536
Grigoriev, Dmitry 536

グリゴリエワ
Grigorjeva, Anastasija 536
Grigoryeva, Lidiya 536

グリゴリク
Grigorik, Ilya 536

グリゴリッチ
Gligorić, Tihomir 505

グリゴリャン
Grigoryan, Armen 536
Grigoryan, Artur 536
Grigoryan, Kirill 536

グリゴレスク
Grigorescu, Victor Vlad 536

グリゴーロ
Grigòlo, Vittorio 536

グリゴローヴィチ
Grigorovich, Yurii Nikolaevich 536

グリゴロービチ
Grigorovich, Yurii Nikolaevich 536

グリゴロフ
Gligorov, Kiro 505
Grigorov, Aleksandr V. 536

グリーザー
Grieser, Dietmer 535

クリサダー・ウィサワティーラノン
Krisada Visavateeranon 766

クリサダー・ヴィサワティーラノン
Krisada Visavateeranon 766

クリサダー・ビサワティーラ

ノン
Krisada Visavateeranon 766
クリサフリ
Crisafulli, Patricia 302
クリサン
Crisan, Marian 302
クリザン
Crisan, Adrian 302
クリシー
Clichy, Gael 271
グリーシー
Griesy, Paul V. 535
クリシェック
Krischek, Manfred Gerhard 767
グリシェンコ
Grishchenko, Boris 537
Hryschenko, Kostyantyn 629
クリシカス
Chryssicas, Mary Kaye 262
クリシス
Chrissis, Mary Beth 260
グリシッチ
Glisic, Nenad 505
クリシナ
Klishina, Darya 746
グリジニック
Grichnik, Kaj 534
クリシバエフ
Kurishbayev, Akylbek 774
クリシャー
Krisher, Trudy 767
クリジャニチュ
Križanič, Franc 767
クリジャーノフ
Kulidzhanov, Lev Aleksandrovich 772
グリシャム
Grisham, John 537
クリシャン
Crisan, Adrian 302
クリシュ
Kulish, Kiril 772
Kulish, Serhiy 772
クリシュナ
Krishna, Aradhna 767
Krishna, Golden 767
Krishna, S.M. 767
Krishna, Upadhyaya Karinje 767
Krṣṇa 768
クリシュナスワミ
Krishnaswamy, Suj 767
クリシュナナンダ
Krishnananda 767
クリシュナ・マーン・ムルガ
Krishna maan Muruga 767
クリシュナムルティ
Krishnamurthi, Lakshman 767
Krishnamurthy, Balachander 767
クリシュナラジュ
Krishnaraju, Alluri V. 767
クリシュナン
Krishnan, Mayuram S. 767
Krishnan, Sriram 767
グリジョ
Grillo, Emiliano 536
グリシン
Grishin, Alexei 537
クリース
Crease, Robert P. 301
クリーズ
Cleese, John 270
クリス
Chris, Salim 260
Chriss, Marquese 260
Klys (pilocik), Katarzyna 747
グリース
Gries, David 535
Gries, Paul 535
グリーズ
Griez, Eric 535
グリス
Grice, Charlie 534
Griss, Martin 537
グリスウォルド
Griswold, Jerome 537
グリズウォルド
Griswold, Eliza 537
クリスクオーロ
Criscuolo, C.Clark 302
グリスケヴィシウス
Griskevicius, Vladas 537
クリスゴー
Christgau, Robert 261
グリスコニス
Griskonis, Mindaugas 537
クリスター
Christer, Sam 261
クリスタキス
Christakis, Nicholas A. 260
クリスタス
Cristas, Assunção 302
クリスターソン
Christerson, Magnus 261
Christersson, Gunilla 261
Kristersson, Ulf 767
クリスタラン
Cristalin, Yves 302
クリスタル
Chrystal, K.Alec 262
Crystal, Billy 306
Crystal, David 306
Crystal, Shawn 306
Krystal, Henry 769
Krystal, Phyllis 769
クリスタン
Christin, Anne Marie 261
クリスタンテ
Cristante, Bryan 302
クリスチアナ
Christiana, David 261
クリスチアーノ
Cristiano Ronaldo 302
クリスチャーノ・ロナウド
Cristiano Ronaldo 302
クリスチャン
Christian, Brian 261
Christian, Cindy W. 261
Christian, David 261
Christian, Gerald 261
Christian, Linda 261
Christian, Marqui 261
Christian, Mary Blount 261
Christian, Mike 261
Christian, Peter 261
Christian, Shannon L. O'Connor 261
クリスチャンセン
Christensen, Dana N. 260
Christensen, Max 261
Christiansen, Henrik 261
Christiansen, Tom 261
Kristiansen, Kjeld Kirk 767
クリスチャンソン
Kristiansson, Leif 767
クリステア
Cristea, Valerian 302
クリスティ
Christie, Bunny 261
Christie, Chris 261
Christie, Elise 261
Christie, Gregory 261
Christie, Ian 261
Christie, Julie 261
Christie, Nils 261
Christie, Perry Gladstone 261
Christie, R.Gregory 261
Christie, William Lincorn 261
Christy, Jana 262
Christy, Martha M. 262
Christy, Robert 262
クリスティー
Christie, Gregory 261
Christie, Julie 261
クリスティアニーニ
Cristianini, Nello 302
クリスティアーノ・ロナウド
Cristiano Ronaldo 302
クリスティアーノ・ロナルド
Cristiano Ronaldo 302
クリスティアン
Christian, Debbie 261
Christian, Nick 261
Christian, Tom 261
クリスティアンゼン
Christiansen, Max 261
クリスティアンソン
Christianson, Gale E. 261
クリスティーエ
Christie, Nils 261
クリスティナ
Cristina, Dolores 302
クリスティナティス
Kristinatis, Kestutis 767
クリスティーヌ
Christine, Mari 261
クリスティン
Cristin, Renato 302
クリステヴァ
Kristeva, Julia 767
クリステバ
Kristeva, Julia 767
クリステル
Kristel, Sylvia 767
クリステン
Christen, Lesley 260
Christen, Nina 260
クリステンセン
Chrilstensen, Clyde 260
Christensen, Andreas 260
Christensen, Bente Lis 260
Christensen, Bonnie 260
Christensen, Carina 260
Christensen, Carl Roland 260
Christensen, Clayton M. 260
Christensen, Doris 260
Christensen, Hayden 260
Christensen, Inger 261
Christensen, John 261
Christensen, John Asmus 261
Christensen, John F. 261
Christensen, Joss 261
Christensen, Loren W. 261
Christensen, Pernille Fischer 261
Christensen, Peter 261
Christensen, Ralph 261
Christensen, Richard M. 261
Christensen, Simone 261
Kristensen, Henrik 767
Kristensen, Kai 767
Kristensen, Tom 767
クリステンソン
Christenson, Amy Beth 261
クリスト
Christ, Renate 260
Christ, Wolfram 260
Christo 261
Crist, Michael K. 302
Crist, Steven G. 302
グリースト
Greist, John H. 533
クリストウ
Christou, Ioannis 262
クリストウスキス
Kristovskis, Ģirts Valdis 767
グリストウッド
Gristwood, Sarah 537
クリストッフェション
Christoffersson, Britt-Marie 261
Kristoffersson, Sara 767
クリストドゥラキス
Christodoulakis, Nikolaos 261
クリストドゥリディス
Christodoulidis, Emilios A. 261
クリストドゥル
Christodoulou, Chiristodoulos 261
クリストバン
Cristóvão, Cirilo 302
クリストフ
Christoph, Jamey 261
Christoph, Vanessa 261
Kristóf, Ágota 767
Kristof, Aziz 767
Kristof, Nicholas D. 767
Kristoff, Alexander 767
Kristoff, Jay 767
Krystof, Doris 769
クリストファー
Christopher, Elphis 261
Christopher, John 261
Christopher, Michael S. 261
Christopher, Warren Minor 262
クリストファーセン
Christophersen, Alf 262
クリストファーソン
Kristofferson, Kris 767
クリストファロ
Cristofaro, Rob 302
クリストフェシェン
Kristoffersen, Henrik 767
クリストフォロ
Cristoforo, Sebastian 302
クリストフォロウ
Christoforou,

ク

Christina 261
クリスト・ブストス
Cristo Bustos, Juan Fernando 302
クリストヤンソン
Kristjansson, Jon 767
クリストル
Cristol, Steven M. 302
Kristol, Irving 767
Kristol, William 767
クリストワ
Christova, Christina 262
クリストン
Christon, Semaj 261
クリスピン
Crispin, A.C. 302
Crispin, Lisa 302
クリスプ
Chrisp, Peter 260
Crisp, Coco 302
Crisp, Dan 302
Crisp, Jessica 302
Crisp, Rob 302
Crisp, Roger 302
クリスフラ
Crisfulla, Karen 302
グリズブルック
Grisbrooke, William Jardine 537
クリスマス
Christmas, Bobbie 261
Christmas, Rakeem 261
クリスマニッチ
Crismanich, Sebastián 302
グリーズマン
Griezmann, Antoine 535
グリスマン
Griessman, Annette 535
クリスマンスキ
Krysmanski, Hans Jürgen 769
クリスマンソン
Kristmundsson, Thor 767
グリズリー・スミス
Grizzly Smith 537
クリス＝レッテンベック
Kriss-Rettenbeck, Lenz 767
グリズロフ
Gryzlov, Bolis Vyacheslavovich 541
クリスンベリ
Christenberry, Judy 260
グリーゼ
Griese, Dietmar 535
Griese, Peter 535
クリセティグ
Crisetig, Lorenzo 302
グリセンディ
Grisendi, Adele 537
グリゾニ
Grisoni, Michel 537
クリソホイディス
Chrysochoidis, Michalis 262
クリソルド
Clissold, Tim 271
グリゾルド
Grizold, Anton 537
グリーソン
Gleason, Colleen 504
Gleason, Patrick 504
Gleason, Ralph 504
Gleeson, Brendan 504
Gleeson, Kerry 504
Gleeson, Libby 504
グリーソン・ホワイト
Gleeson-White, Jane 504
クリダ
Clidat, France 271
グリダソワ
Gridasova, Oleksandra 534
クリーチ
Creach, Jerome Frederick Davis 301
Creech, Sharon 301
クリチコ
Klitchko, Vladimir 746
Klitschko, Vitali 746
クリチコフ
Kulichkov, Aleksandr N. 772
グリチック
Grichuk, Randal 534
クリチトゥン
Crichton, Margaret 301
クリチトン
Crichton, Scott 301
クリチマン
Krichman, Mikhail 766
グリツェンコ
Gritsenko, Anatoly 537
Hrytsenko, Anatoliy 629
クーリック
Kulick, Don 772
クリック
Crick, Bernard 301
Crick, Debbie 301
Crick, Francis Harry Compton 301
Crick, Jared 301
Crick, Kyle 302
グリック
Gleick, James 504
Glick, Marion E. 505
グリッグ
Grigg, David B. 536
クリックス
Kuritzkes, Daniel R. 774
グリックマン
Glickman, Dan 505
Glickman, Marty 505
Glickman, Michael 505
Glickman, Rosalene 505
クリックロウコックバーン
Crichlowcockburen, Cherrie-Ann 301
クリッサ
Chryssa 262
グリッサン
Glissant, Édouard 505
クリッシェ
Kliche, Martin 745
クリッジャーノフ
Kulidzhanov, Lev Aleksandrovich 772
グリッソ
Grisso, Thomas 537
グリッソム
Grissom, David 537
Grissom, Geneo 537
クリッチェル
Critchell, Mary King 302
クリッチェルズ
Krichels, Jennifer 766
グリッチカ
Glitschka, Von 505
クリッチリー
Critchley, Simon 302
グリッツ
Gritz, Larry 537
クリッツァー
Kritzer, Basil 767
クリッツマン
Klitzman, Robert 746
Kritzman, Mark P. 767
グリッツマン
Gritzmann, Peter 537
グリッデン
Glidden, David 505
グーリット
Gullit, Ruud 545
グリット
Gullit, Ruud 545
クリッパ
Crippa, Luca 302
Crippa, Maria Antonietta 302
クリッパー
Klipper, Miriam Z. 746
クリッパード
Clippard, Tyler 271
グリッパンド
Grippando, James 537
クリッヒ
Krich, Rochelle 766
クリッピンガー
Clippinger, Karen S. 271
クリッブ
Cribb, Reg 301
グリッフィ
Griffi, Giuseppe Patroni 535
グリップ・ジャンソン
Grip-Jansson, Patrik 537
クリップス
Cripps, Peter 302
クリッペン
Crippen, Fran 302
クリッペンドルフ
Krippendorff, Kaihan 766
グリッポ
Grippo, Daniel 537
グリッランディ
Grillandi, Massimo 536
グリッロ
Grillo, Beppe 536
クリート
Cliett, Reshard 271
クリード
Creed, John 301
Creed, Michael 301
グリード
Guled, Muhammad Mahumud 545
クリトル
Crittle, Simon 302
クリドル
Criddle, Craig 302
クリートン
Cleeton, David L. 270
クリトンドン
Crittendon, Robert 302
クリーナ
Klena, Mattehew 745
グリーナウェイ
Greenaway, Kate 530
Greenaway, Peter 530
クリニ
Clini, Corrado 271
グリーニ
Gulini, Faye 545
グリーニー
Greaney, Mark 529
クリニチ
Kulinich, Mykola 772
グリーニッジ
Greenidge, Carl 532
グリニッジ
Greenidge, Rudolph 532
クリニッツ
Krinitz, Esther Nisenthal 766
クリニャク
Kulynyak, Mykhailo 772
グリーニング
Greening, Justine 532
クリネラ
Crinella, Francis M. 302
クリーノ
Crino, Rocco 302
クリノワ
Klinova, Inna 746
クリーバー
Kleiber, Douglas A. 744
グリバウスカイテ
Grybauskaitė, Dalia 541
クリバノフ
Klibanoff, Hank 745
グリバノフ
Gribanov, Denis 534
クリバリ
Coulibaly, Abdou Latif 295
Coulibaly, Aboubacary 295
Coulibaly, Alizatou Rosine 295
Coulibaly, Ally 295
Coulibaly, Gnénéma Mamadou 295
Coulibaly, Ismael 295
Coulibaly, Issa 295
Coulibaly, Jean-Martin 295
Coulibaly, Malick 295
Coulibaly, Mamadou Sangafowa 295
Coulibaly, Moussa Sinko 295
Coulibaly, N'diaye Fatoumata 295
Coulibaly, Pascal Daba 295
Coulibaly, Samadou 295
Coulibaly, Tiéman Hubert 295
Coulibaly, Tiénan 295
Koulibaly, Kalidou 760
Koulibaly, Leonie 760
Koulibaly, Mamadou 760
グリパリ
Gripari, Pierre 537
グリービー
Greavey, Nathan 529
グリビ
Ghribi, Habiba 494
クリビヌ
Krivine, Emmanuel 767
クリビン
Krivine, Emmanuel 767
グリビン
Gribbin, John R. 534
Gribbin, Mary 534

クリーブ
Cleave, Chris 270
Cleave, Maureen 270
Cleave, Paul 270
クリフ
Cliff, Jimmy 271
Cliff, Nigel 271
Cliff, Stafford 271
Cliffe, Sarah 271
Klich, Bogdan 745
クリブ
Cribb, Joe 301
Cribb, Julian 301
グリーブ
Graeve, Stan 523
グリファル
Griffall, Preston 535
グリフィー
Griffey, Anthony Dean 535
Griffey, Harriet 535
Griffey, Ken, Jr. 535
グリフィス
Griffith, Andy 535
Griffith, Charles B. 535
Griffith, Clare 535
Griffith, Colin 535
Griffith, Erskine 535
Griffith, Gary 535
Griffith, Helen V. 535
Griffith, Jerome 535
Griffith, Johnny 535
Griffith, John W. 535
Griffith, Mari 535
Griffith, Melanie 535
Griffith, Rupert 535
Griffith, Sam 535
Griffith, Vicoria 535
Griffiths, Andy 536
Griffiths, Antony 536
Griffith's, Bill 536
Griffiths, Chris 536
Griffiths, David 536
Griffiths, Dawn 536
Griffiths, Elly 536
Griffiths, Eric 536
Griffiths, Gareth 536
Griffiths, Ian 536
Griffiths, Jay 536
Griffiths, Matt 536
Griffiths, Paul 536
Griffiths, Paul E. 536
Griffiths, Peter 536
Griffiths, Philip Jones 536
Griffiths, Phillip A. 536
Griffiths, Ralph Alan 536
Griffiths, Richard 536
Griffiths, Sam 536
Griffiths, Simon 536
グリフィス・ジョーンズ
Griffith-Jones, Stephany 536
グリフィン
Griffin, Abbie 535
Griffin, Adrian 535
Griffin, A.J. 535
Griffin, Alfredo 535
Griffin, Allan 535
Griffin, Blake 535
Griffin, Dale 535
Griffin, David 535
Griffin, David Ray 535
Griffin, Eddie 535
Griffin, Garrett 535
Griffin, G.Edward 535
Griffin, Helen 535
Griffin, Jacqui 535
Griffin, James 535
Griffin, John 535
Griffin, Johnny 535
Griffin, Kathy 535
Griffin, Kenneth C. 535
Griffin, Laura 535
Griffin, Melanie 535
Griffin, Merv 535
Griffin, Michael 535
Griffin, Michael D. 535
Griffin, Natalie Shope 535
Griffin, Nicholas 535
Griffin, Patrick E. 535
Griffin, Patty 535
Griffin, Paul 535
Griffin, Phil 535
Griffin, Randall C. 535
Griffin, Robert, Ⅲ 535
Griffin, Robert D. 535
Griffin, Ryan 535
Griffin, Thomas 535
Griffin, Trenholme J. 535
Griffyn, Sally 536
クリーフェルド
Kleefeld, Carolyn Mary 744
グリフェン
Griffen, Everson 535
グリフォ
Grifo, Vincenzo 536
クリフォード
Clifford, Herbert John 271
Clifford, Jackie 271
Clifford, James 271
Clifford, McCarthy 271
Clifford, Richard M. 271
Clifford, Sandy 271
Clifford, Steve 271
グリフォル
Grifol, Pedro 536
クリプキ
Kripke, Eric 766
クリーブス
Cleeves, Ann 270
グリーブス
Greaves, Damian 529
Greaves, Melvyn F. 529
クリフト
Clift, Simon 271
クリフトン
Clifton, Christopher W. 271
Clifton, Claire 271
Clifton, Donald O. 271
Clifton, Lucille 271
Clifton, Mark 271
クリフトンーブラウン
Clifton-Brown, Holly 271
クリフトン・モグ
Clifton-Mogg, Caroline 271
グリブ・ファキム
Gurib-fakim, Bibi Ameenah Firdaus 547
クリーブランド
Cleveland, Asante 271
Cleveland, Ashley 271
Cleveland, Brad 271
グリブル
Gribble, Kate 534
グリーペ
Gripe, Maria 537
クリベラ
Crivella, Marcelo 302
クリベリョワ
Krivelyova, Svetlana 767
クリベルド
Kreveld, Marc van 766
クリーベンステイン
Kliebenstein, James B. 745
クリホヴィアク
Krychowiak, Grzegorz 769
クリボシャプカ
Krivoshapka, Antonina 767
クリーマ
Clima, Gabriele 271
Klíma, Ivan 745
クリーマー
Creamer, Mark 301
Creamer, Paula 301
クリマ
Klíma, Ivan 745
グリマルディ
Grimaldi, Martina 536
グリマルド
Grimaldo, Alejandro 536
クリーマン
Kleeman, Terry F. 744
クリマン
Kliman, Anton 745
グリミー
Grimmie, Christina 537
グリミネッリ
Griminelli, Andrea 536
グリミンガー
Grimminger, Kris 537
クリミンス
Crimmins, C.E. 302
グリム
Grim, Pamela 536
Grimm, Alexander 536
Grimm, Hans-Ulrich 536
Grimm, Justin 537
Grimm, Laurence G. 537
Grimm, Peter 537
Grimm, Peter D. 537
グリムウッド
Grimwood, Jon Courtenay 537
Grimwood, Ken 537
クリムキン
Klimkin, Pavlo 745
クリムケ
Klimke, Ingrid 745
グリムジー
Grimsey, Tom 537
グリムシャー
Glimcher, Paul W. 505
グリムショー
Grimshaw, Charlotte 537
グリムス
Grimes, Richard 536
グリムズ
Grimes, Nikki 536
クリムスキー
Krimsky, Sheldon 766
グリムズリ
Grimsley, Ronald 537
グリムズリー
Grimsley, Jim 537
グリムソン
Grimsson, Olafur Ragnar 537
クリムバーグ
Klimberg, V.Suzanne 745
クリムプシュツィンツァゼ
Klympushtsintsadze, Ivanna 747
クリームラー
Kriemler, Albert 766
クリムリス
Crimlis, Roger 302
グリメ
Grimme, Karin H. 537
クリメッツ
Krimets, Konstantin D. 766
グリメット
Grimmette, Mark 537
グリメル
Grimmel, Torben 537
クリメンコ
Klymenko, Oleksander 747
クリモ
Climo, Liz 271
グリモー
Grimaud, Hélène 536
クリモウスキー
Klimowski, Andrzej 745
クリモフ
Klimov, Alexei 745
Klimov, Fedor 745
グリャコ
Gulyako, Leonid P. 545
クリャコビッチ
Kljakovic Gaspic, Ivan 746
クリャシュトルヌイ
Klyashtornui, Sergei Grigor'evich 747
グリャック
Gulyak, Sofya 545
クリヤナンダ
Kriyananda, Sarawati 767
グリャモフ
Gulyamov, Kadir 545
Gulyamov, Ravshan 545
Gulyamov, Saidakhror 545
グリャモワ
Gulyamova, Dilbar 545
クリュエフ
Klyuev, Andriy 747
グリュオー
Gruault, Jean 540
クリューガ
Krueger, Robert F. 768
クリューガー
Krüger, Christa 769
Krüger, Harald 769
Kruger, John M. 769
Krüger, Manfred 769
Kruger, Stephan 769
クリュカ
Klyuka, Svetlana 747
クリュクルンド
Kyrklund, Kyra 778
クリューゲ
Kluge, Roger 746
クリュゲール
Kruger, Josiane 769
グリューゲル
Grugel, Jean 540
クリュコフ
Kriukov, Nikita 767
Kryukov, Nikolay 769
クリュゼ
Cluzet, Francois 272
クリュチコフ

Kryuchkov, Vladimir A. 769
クリュッグ
Krug, Olivier 768
クリュックシャンク
Cruickshank, Dan 305
グリュックスマン
Glucksmann, André 505
クリュックマン
Krukmann, Peter O. 769
グリュツナー
Gruetzner, Howard 540
クリューツフェルト
Kreutzfeldt, Daniel 766
グリュデ
Grudet, Claude 540
グリューナー
Gruener, Lukas 540
グリューネ
Gruhne, Hans 540
グリュネカー
Gruenecker, Michael 540
グリューネンベルク
Grunenberg, Christoph 541
クリューバー
Kluver, Cayla 747
クリュフト
Kluft, Carolina 746
グリューベル
Grübel, Oswald J. 540
グリュミエ
Grumier, Gauthier 541
グリューン
Gruen, Arno 540
Grün, Anselm 541
グリュン
Grun, Max 541
グリューンバイン
Grünbein, Durs 541
クリュンパーヴェストカンプ
Klümper-Westkamp, Heinrich 747
グリューンベルク
Grünberg, Peter 541
グリュンベルク
Grünberg, Peter 541
クリュンメル
Krummel, Debra A. 769
グリラ
Grira, Ridha 537
グリラブ
Gurirab, Theo-Ben 547
クリーランド
Cleland, Jane K. 270
クリーリー
Creeley, Robert White 301
クリリー
Crilly, A.J. 302
グリーリー
Greeley, Andrew 529
グリリ
Grilli, Jason 536
Grilli, Vittorio 536
グリリッチュ
Grillitsch, Florian 536
クリール
Creel, Gavin 301
グリール
Griehl, Manfred 534
グリル
Grill, William 536
クリルクベリア
Kvirkelia, Manuchar 777
グリルス
Grylls, Bear 541
グリロ
Grillo, Ioan 536
クリーン
Crean, Simon 301
クリン
Klin, Ami 745
グリーン
Glean, Carlyle 504
Green, Aaron 529
Green, Abby 529
Green, Adolph 529
Green, A.J. 529
Green, Al 529
Green, Amy Boothe 529
Green, André 529
Green, Andy 529
Green, Ann E. 529
Green, Barry 529
Green, Bill 529
Green, Billie 529
Green, Brad 529
Green, Carolyn W. 529
Green, Cecil Howard 529
Green, Cee Lo 529
Green, Chad 529
Green, Charles H. 529
Green, Chaz 529
Green, Christina 529
Green, Christine 529
Green, Crystal 529
Green, Cynthia R. 529
Green, Dale 529
Green, Damian 529
Green, Dan 529
Green, Danny 529
Green, David 529
Green, David Geoffrey 529
Green, David Gordon 529
Green, Deborah M. 529
Green, Douglas R. 529
Green, Draymond 529
Green, Eileen 529
Green, Eleanor 529
Green, Elizabeth Salter 530
Green, Fern 530
Green, Florence 530
Green, Georgia M. 530
Green, Gerald 530
Green, Glenda 530
Green, Gopa Bhattacharyya 530
Green, Grace 530
Green, Guy 530
Green, Holly G. 530
Green, Howard E. 530
Green, Ilya 530
Green, James R. 530
Green, JaMychal 530
Green, Jane 530
Green, Jeff 530
Green, Jen 530
Green, Jesse 530
Green, Joel B. 530
Green, Joey 530
Green, John 530
Green, Jonathon 530
Green, Julian 530
Green, Keith Evan 530
Green, Ladarius 530
Green, Laura 530
Green, Laurie 530
Green, Lawrence W. 530
Green, Leford 530
Green, Louise 530
Green, Luis 530
Green, Lynne 530
Green, Martin Burgess 530
Green, Michael 530
Green, Michael J. 530
Green, Mim 530
Green, Miranda J. 530
Green, Naomi 530
Green, Phil 530
Green, Philip 530
Green, Reg 530
Green, Risa 530
Green, Robert D. 530
Green, Rod 530
Green, Roger 530
Green, Roger Lancelyn 530
Green, S. 530
Green, Sally 530
Green, Scott 530
Green, Stephen 530
Green, Stephen A. 530
Green, Stephen Keith 530
Green, Susan Eikov 530
Green, Susan M.E. 530
Green, Tami 530
Green, Thomas Henry 530
Green, Tim 530
Green, Timothy, II 530
Green, T.J. 530
Green, Toby 530
Green, Virgil 530
Green, Winifred 530
Greene, Anthony F. 531
Greene, Bob 531
Greene, Brian 531
Greene, Carolyn 531
Greene, Charles S. 531
Greene, Chet 531
Greene, Darrell 531
Greene, David 531
Greene, Dennis 531
Greene, Diane 531
Greene, Don 531
Greene, Ellin 531
Greene, Eric 531
Greene, Jack P. 531
Greene, Jennifer 531
Greene, Joshua David 531
Greene, Kate 531
Greene, Khaseem 531
Greene, Liz 531
Greene, Maurice 531
Greene, Melissa Fay 531
Greene, Molly 531
Greene, Paul 531
Greene, Rashad 531
Greene, Robert 531
Greene, Roberta Rubin 531
Greene, Robert William 531
Greene, Ross W. 531
Greene, Shane 531
Greene, St.John 531
Grene, David 534
グリン
Glyn, Andrew 506
Glynn, Alan 506
Glynn, Gene 506
Glynn, Jay 506
Glynn, Paul 506
Glynne, Andy 506
Glynne, Jess 506
Grine, Hamid 537
グリーンウェイ
Greenway, Chad 532
グリーンウェル
Greenwell, Bonnie 532
グリーンウォルド
Greenwald, Bruce 532
Greenwald, Glenn 532
Greenwald, Ken 532
Greenwald, Rachel 532
Greenwald, Sheila 532
Greenwald, Tommy 532
グリーンウッド
Greenwood, Brian 532
Greenwood, Colin Charles 532
Greenwood, Derek A. 532
Greenwood, Ed 532
Greenwood, Jane 532
Greenwood, Jonny 532
Greenwood, L.B. 532
Greenwood, Leigh 532
Greenwood, Marie 532
Greenwood, Rees 532
Greenwood, Ron 532
Greenwood, Susan 532
クリンガ
Klinga, Hanna 745
クリンガー
Klinger, Leslie S. 746
グリンカー
Grinker, Roy Richard 537
グリーンガード
Greengard, Paul 532
グリンキー
Greinke, Zack 533
クーリング
Cooling, J.E. 286
Cooling, Wendy 286
Coulling, Anna 295
クリンク
Clink, Tony 271
Klink, Ab 746
クリング
Kling, John 745
Kling, Rob 745
Kling, Tammy 745
Kring, Ann M. 766
Kring, Tim 766
クリングヴァル
Klingvall, Lena Maria 746
クリングス
Krings, Antoon 766
クリンクゾール＝ルロワ
Klingsöhr-Leroy, Cathrin 746
クリングバーグ
Klingberg, Haddon, Jr. 745
Klingberg, Torkel 746
クリングバル
Klingvall, Maj-Inger 746
クリングマン
Clingman, Stephen 271
グリーングラス
Greengrass, Mark 532
Greengrass, Paul 532
グリーングロス
Greengross, Wendy 532
クリンゲ
Klinge, Gunther 746
クリンケサスメリェ
Krinke-susmelj, Marcela 766
クリンケン
Klinken, Jaap van 746

クリンゲンベルク
Klingenberg, Georg 746
クリンケンボルグ
Klinkenborg, Verlyn 746
グリンゴルツ
Gringolts, Ilya 537
グリーンサル
Greenthal, Jill 532
クリンジェン
Merry, Clingen 937
グリン＝ジョーンズ
Glynne-Jones, Tim 506
クリンジリー
Cringely, Robert X. 302
グリンスキ
Gliński, Piotr 505
グリーンスタイン
Greenstein, Ben 532
Greenstein, Elaine 532
Greenstein, George 532
グリーンスパン
Greenspan, Alan 532
Greenspan, Bud 532
Greenspan, Deborah 532
Greenspan, Jacob 532
Greenspan, John S. 532
Greenspan, Karen 532
Greenspan, Nancy Thorndike 532
Greenspan, Stanley I. 532
クリンスマン
Klinsmann, Jürgen 746
グリンタ
Glinta, Robert 505
グリンダ
Grindea, Carola 537
グリンダー
Grinder, John 537
グリンツ
Glinz, Hans 505
グリンデ
Grinde, Donald A., Jr. 537
グリンデアーヌ
Grindeanu, Sorin 537
クリンティング
Klinting, Lars 746
グリント
Grint, Rupert 537
クリントマルム
Klintmalm, Goran B. 746
クリンドラニ
Kuridrani, Tevita 774
グリンドリー
Grindley, Sally 537
グリンドル
Grindle, Lucretia W. 537
Grindle, Merilee S. 537
グリンドレー
Grindley, Sally 537
クリントン
Clinton, Bill 271
Clinton, George 271
Clinton, Hillary 271
クリントン・ディックス
Clinton-dix, Ha Ha 271
グリーン・トンプソン
Green-thompson, Shaq 532
グリーンナウェイ
Greenaway, David 530
グリンネル
Grinnell, Frederick 537
グリーンハウス
Greenhouse, Steven 532
グリーンバウム
Greenbaum, David 530
グリーンバーガー
Greenberger, Dennis 531
Greenberger, Robert 531
グリーンバーグ
Greenberg, Andrew 531
Greenberg, Arthur 531
Greenberg, Benjamin D. 531
Greenberg, Cathy L. 531
Greenberg, Daniel Asher 531
Greenberg, David H. 531
Greenberg, David T. 531
Greenberg, Gary 531
Greenberg, Jay R. 531
Greenberg, Jeffrey Alan 531
Greenberg, Jerrold S. 531
Greenberg, Joseph Harold 531
Greenberg, Keith Elliot 531
Greenberg, Leslie S. 531
Greenberg, Margaret 531
Greenberg, Mark S. 531
Greenberg, Martin 531
Greenberg, Martin H. 531
Greenberg, Paul 531
Greenberg, Peter 531
Greenberg, Polly 531
Greenberg, Ray S. 531
Greenberg, Stanley R. 531
Greenberg, Valerie D. 531
Greenburg, Dan 531
Greenburg, Zack O'Malley 531
グリーンハーフ
Greenhalgh, Trisha 532
クリーンバリ
Cronberg, Tarja 303
グリーンハルシュ
Greenhalgh, Ailsa 532
グリーンハルジュ
Greenhalgh, Chris 532
グリーンフィールド
Greenfield, Amy Butler 531
Greenfield, Bruce 532
Greenfield, David 532
Greenfield, Jack 532
Greenfield, Kent 532
Greenfield, Robert 532
Greenfield, Susan 532
グリンフィールド
Greenfield, Beth 532
グリーンフェルド
Greenfeld, Karl Taro 531
グリーンブラット
Greenblat, Rodney Alan 531
Greenblatt, Alan 531
Greenblatt, Bruce 531
Greenblatt, James 531
Greenblatt, Joel 531
Greenblatt, Stephen J. 531
グリンブル
Grimble, Xavier 536
グリーン・ベッカム
Green-beckham, Dorial 531
グリーンマン
Greenman, Ben 532
グリーンリーフ
Greenleaf, Stephen 532
グリーンロウ
Greenlaw, Linda 532
グリーンワルド
Greenwald, Anthony G. 532
グリンワルド
Greenwald, Gerald 532
クール
Cool, Tracy Britt 286
Cool, Tre 286
Kuhl, Chad 771
Kuhl, David 771
Kuhl, David E. 771
クルー
Crewe, Bob 301
グール
Ghoul, Amar 494
Ghoul, Omar 494
Ghoul, Tamam 494
グル
Gul, Hamid 545
Gul, Sherali 545
グルー
Groult, Benoîte 539
Groult, Flora 539
Groux, Dominique 539
クルーイ
Crouhy, Michel 304
クルイス
Kruis, George 769
グルィズロフ
Gryzlov, Bolis Vyacheslavovich 541
グルイッチ
Grujic, Marko 541
Grujic, Nebojsa 541
Grujic, Slobodan 541
クルーヴァー
Kluver, Billy 747
グルーウェル
Gruwell, Erin 541
クルエ
Cluett, Elizabeth R. 272
グルエフスキ
Gruevski, Nikola 540
グルーエン
Gruen, Bob 540
Gruen, Lori 540
Gruen, Sara 540
グルーエンスタイン
Gruenstein, John M.L. 540
グルエンフェルド
Gruenfeld, Lee 540
クルーガー
Kroeger, Chad 767
Kroeger, Mike 767
Kroger, Fritz 767
Krueger, Alan Bennett 768
Krueger, Ann O. 768
Krueger, David 768
Krueger, Elizabeth 768
Krueger, Jim 768
Krueger, Myron W. 768
Krueger, Roice N. 768
Krueger, Tira 768
Krueger, William Kent 768
Kruger, Barbara 768
Kruger, Diane 769
Kruger, Ehren 769
Kruger, Frantz 769
Kruger, Niku 769
Kruger, Paul 769
クルカ
Kulka, János 772
Kulka, John 772
Kulka, Otto Dov 772
クルーカス
Clucas, Sam 272
クルカス
Kurucs, Rodions 775
グルーカット
Groucutt, Kelly 539
クルガップキナ
Kurgapkina, Ninel 774
クルカーニ
Kulkarni, Devadatta 772
グルガラエフ
Gulgarayev, Ashirgeldi 545
クルカルニ
Kulkarni, Sanjeev 772
Kulkarni, Shrikrishna G. 772
クルーギ
Kluge, John 746
クルキ
Kurki, Anja 775
グルキ
Ghurki, Samina Khalid 494
グルギーア・ヒル
Grugier-hill, Kamu 540
グルギッチ
Grgic, Filip 534
クルキッチ・ペレス
Bojan, Krkić 155
クルキナ
Kurkina, Larisa 775
グルキュフ
Gourcuff, Yoann 522
クールクー
Courcoult, Jean-Luc 295
クルーク
Crook, Thomas 303
Crooke, Pamela 303
Klug, Gerald 746
Kruuk, Hans 769
クルーグ
Klug, Aaron 746
Klug, Chris 746
Krug, Cassidy 768
Krug, Steve 768
クルグ
Klug, Georgina 746
グルグ
Görög, Júlia 519
クルークシャンク
Cruikshank, Jeffrey L. 305
クルクシャンク
Cruikshank, Jeffrey L. 305
クルーグマン
Krugman, Paul Robin 769
Krugman, Richard D. 769
クルクライ
Krirkkrai, Jirapaet 766
クルグラーク
Kruglak, Haym 769
クルグロフ
Kruglov, Serguei 769
クルーゲ
Kluge, Heidelore 746
Kluge, John 746
クルコウェル
Krukower, Daniela 769
クルコバビッチ
Krkobabić, Jovan 767

グルゴビッチ
Grgovic, Rade 534
クルコフ
Kurkov, Andrei 775
クルコフスキー
Krukovsky, Nikolai A. 769
クルーサ
Kurusa 775
クルーザー
Crouser, Ryan 304
グルザデ
Guluzade, Ramin 545
クルサート
Coulthart, John 295
クルザニッチ
Krzanich, Brian 769
クルサーノフ
Krusanova, Andreia 769
グルザマガギ
Gourouza Magagi, Djibo Salamatou 522
クルザワ
Kurzama, Layvin 775
クルージ
Kluge, John 746
クルージー
Crusie, Jennifer 305
クルーシアス
Crusius, Timothy W. 305
クルジェ
Kluger, Catherine 746
クールシェッド
Coulshed, Veronica 295
クルジクロストコフスカ
Kluzikrostkowska, Joanna 747
クルシード
Khurshid, Salman 729
グルシナ
Grushina, Elena 541
クルシャミ
al-Kurshami, Umar Abdullah 775
al-Kurshumi, Omar 775
クルーシュテン
Kruchten, Philippe 768
クルジョン
Courgeon, Rémi 295
グルジョン
Grullón, Sergio 541
クルシンスキー
Kruszynski, Anette 769
グルジンスキ
Grudziński, Albert 540
Grudziński, Antoni 540
クールス
Cools, Dion 286
クールズ
Cools, Sammy 286
クルース
Cruz, Celia 305
Cruz, Jose 305
Kroes, Neelie 767
Krooth, Richard 768
Kruis, John G. 769
Kruse, Richard 769
Kruth, John 769
クルーズ
Crews, Caitlin 301
Crews, John E. 301
Cruess, Richard L. 305
Cruess, Sylvia R. 305
Cruess, Sylvia Robinson 305
Cruise, Robin 305
Cruise, Tom 305
Cruse, Alan 305
Cruz, A.J. 305
Cruz, Francisco Gaspar 305
Cruz, Isabel de la 305
Cruz, Nelson 305
Cruz, Roger 305
Cruz, Ted 305
Cruz, Victor 305
Kreuz, Tamara 766
Kruse, Colin G. 769
Kruse, Robbie 769
Kruse, Robert Leroy 769
クルス
Cruz, Avelino 305
Cruz, Benjamin Vera 305
Cruz, Carlos 305
Cruz, Claudina Augusto 305
Cruz, Gaspar da 305
Cruz, Ilidio Alexandre 305
Cruz, Lidio Alexandre 305
Cruz, Nelson 305
Cruz, Penélope 305
Cruz, Zoe 305
De La Cruz, Eglys Yahima 335
Kluth, Paula 747
Kroes, Neelie 767
Krzus, Michael P. 770
Kurth, Steve 775
グルース
Gruss, Peter 541
クルースヴァル
Kruusval, Catarina 769
グルスカ
Gruska, Jozef 541
クルスカル
Kruskal, Martin 769
グルスキー
Gursky, Andreas 548
クルスコケ
Cruz-coke, Luciano 306
クルースター
Klooster, Fred H. 746
クルスチェン
Kruschen, Jack 769
クルスティチェビッチ
Krstičević, Damir 768
クルスティチッチ
Krsticic, Nenad 768
クルステフスキ
Krstevski, Zoran 768
グールストン
Goulston, Mark 521
グールスビー
Goolsbee, Austan 517
クルス・モリナ
Cruz Molina, Alejandro 306
クルーセ
Kruuse, Urmas 769
クルーゼ
Kruse, Johannes 769
Kruse, Max 769
クルーゾ
Clouzot, Marianne 272
グルソープ
Goulthorpe, Mark 521
クールソン
Coulson, Arlene 295
クルソン
Culson, Javier 307
クルーター
Crouter, Richard 304
クルター
Coulter, Jacqueline 295
クルタニゼ
Kurtanidze, Eldar 775
クルターマン
Kultermann, Udo 772
クールタン
Courtin, Thierry 296
クルタン
Courtin, Jean 296
Courtin, Sophie 296
Courtin, Thierry 296
Cretin, Thierry 301
クルチ
Curci, Gianluca 308
Curti, Anna 309
Kiliç, Akif Çağatay 731
Kiliç, Suat 731
クルチェツキ
Kulczycki, Chris 772
クルチェト
Curuchet, Juan 309
グルチェンコ
Gurchenko, Lyudmila 547
グルチッチ
Grčić, Branko 528
クルチナ
Klučina, Petr 746
クルチュク
Kurczuk, Grzegorz 774
クルーツ
Kreutz, Olin 766
クルツ
Cruz, Ray 305
Kurtz, Ron 775
Kurz, Heinz-Dieter 775
Kurz, Joachim 775
Kurz, Robert 775
Kurz, Sebastian 775
クルツァー
Kurzer, Manfred 775
クルツィウス
Curtius, Ernst Robert 309
クルック
Crook, Christina 303
Crook, Colin 303
Crook, G.T. 303
クルックシャンク
Cruickshank, Allan 305
Cruickshank, Paul 305
Cruikshank, Jeffrey L. 305
グルックリッチ
Glucklich, Ariel 505
クルッケンバーグ
Kruckenberg, Kory 768
クルッツェ
Kloutsé, Daniel 746
クルッツェン
Crutzen, Paul Josef 305
クルツナリック
Krznaric, Roman 770
クルツバン
Kurzban, Robert 775
クルツマン
Kurtzman, Joel 775
クルツレル
Krutzler, Eszter 769
クルーテ
Cloete, Hestrie 271
グルデ
Gulde, Manuel 545
クルティ
Curti, Anna 309
クルディアティ
Couldiaty, Jean 295
グルディアン
Gurdián, Virgilio 547
クルティエル
Cloutier, Claude 272
クルティシェフ
Kultishev, Miroslav 772
クルティッチ
Kurtic, Jasmin 775
グルディーナ
Grudina, Paola Bertolini 540
クルティーヌ
Courtine, Jean-Jacques 296
クルティーヌ＝ドゥナミ
Courtine-Denamy, Sylvie 296
グルディン
Grudin, Jonathan 540
グールディング
Goulding, Marrack 521
Goulding, Matt 521
Goulding, Michael 521
グルーデム
Grudem, Wayne A. 540
クルデリ
Crudelli, Chris 305
グルーデン
Gruden, Jon 540
クルート
Clute, John 272
クルト
Curto, Rosa Maria 309
Kurt, Sinan 775
クルド
Kurd, Humayun Aziz 774
グールド
Goold, Rupert 517
Gould, Anthony 521
Gould, Eliga H. 521
Gould, Elliott 521
Gould, George M. 521
Gould, Georgia 521
Gould, Jay Martin 521
Gould, K.Lance 521
Gould, Peter R. 521
Gould, Robert 521
Gould, Stephen 521
Gould, Stephen Jay 521
Gould, Steven 521
Gould, Tony 521
グルート
Glut, Donald F. 506
グルド
Gould, Karina 521
Guled, Abdikarim Hussein 545
Guled, Muhammad Mahumud 545
クールドイアン
Khourdoïan, Saténik 729
クルトゥア
Courtois, Gaston 296
グルトヴォイ
Gurtovoy, Aleksey 548
クルトゥルム

Kurtulmus, Numan 775
クルトゥルムシュ
Kurtulmus, Numan 775
クルトゥワ
Courtois, Thibaut 296
クルトビッチ
Kurtović, Mirsad 775
グールドモンターニュ
Gourdault-Montagne, Maurice 522
グルドーモンターニュ
Gourdault-Montagne, Maurice 522
クルトワ
Courtois, Stéphane 296
Courtois, Thibaut 296
グルーナー
Gruner, Jessica 541
Gruner, Wolf D. 541
グルナザコ
Gourna Zacko, Justin 522
クルナス
Clunas, Craig 272
クルナレトネ
Karunaratne, Niluka 706
クルーナン
Cloonan, Becky 271
Cloonan, Paula 271
クルーニー
Clooney, George 271
Clooney, Rosemary 271
クルニアワン
Kurniawan, Eka 775
グルニエ
Grenier, Catherine 534
Grenier, Christian 534
Grenier, Clement 534
Grenier, Roger 534
クルニッチ
Krunic, Rade 769
グルーニング
Greuning, Hennie van 534
グルネー
Gournay, Chantal De 522
グルーネウド
Groenewoud, Rosalind 538
クルネリ
Kuruneri, Christopher 775
グルーノー
Grunow, Richard 541
クルノゴラッチ
Crnogorac, Jovana 302
クルノワイエ
Cournoyer, Charle 295
クルーバー
Cruver, Brian 305
Cruver, Daniel 305
Kluber, Corey 746
グルーバー
Gruber, Andreas 540
Gruber, Bernhard 540
Gruber, Beth 540
Gruber, Christoph 540
Gruber, David F. 540
Gruber, Michael 540
Gruber, Patrick 540
クルハヴィ
Kulhavý, Jaroslav 772
グルーバーガー
Gruberger, Risa Munitz 540
クルバージュ
Courbage, Youssef 295
クールハース
Koolhaas, Rem 756
グルバーチ
Glváč, Martin 506
グルバチュ
Grubač, Momčilo 540
クルバノフ
Kurbanov, Dzhakhon 774
Kurbanov, Kurban 774
グルバノフ
Gurbanov, Kakageldi 547
クルハビ
Kulhavý, Jaroslav 772
グルハラ
Gruchala, Sylwia 540
グルバルチク
Gróbarczyk, Marek 537
クルパレク
Krpalek, Lukas 768
グルバンドルディエフ
Gurbandurdyev, Mele 547
グルバンナザロフ
Gurbannazarov, Orazmyrat 547
グルバンマメドフ
Gurbanmammedov, Tacmammet 547
グルバンムラドフ
Gurbanmuradov, Yolly 547
クルーピ
Crupi, John 305
クルピ
Culpi, Levir 307
グルビス
Gulbis, Māris 545
Gulbis, Natalie 545
クールビル・アンデルセン
Colville-Andersen, Mikael 280
クルヒン
Krhin, Rene 766
クルピンスキ
Krupinski, Loretta 769
クルピンスキー
Krupinski, Elizabeth A. 769
Krupinski, Eve 769
グルブイェシッチ
Grubješić, Suzana 540
クルプコ
Krupko, Petro 769
クルフト
Kruft, Hanno-Walter 768
クルプフル
Klüpfel, Volker 747
グループマン
Groopman, Jerome 538
クルブリス
Kouroumplis, Panagiotis 760
グルーベ
Grube, Nikolai 540
グルーペ
Grupe, Ommo 541
クールベ＝ヴィロン
Courbet-Viron, Lionelle 295
クルペクカイテ
Krupeckaite, Simona 769
グルベシャ
Grubeša, Josip 540
クルベリ
Kullberg, Mirkku 772
Kullberg, Tove 772
クルベル
Clouvel, Elodie 272
グルーベル
Grübel, Oswald J. 540
グルベール
Gruber, Alain Charles 540
グルベローヴァ
Gruberová, Edita 540
グルベローバ
Gruberová, Edita 540
グルーペン
Grupen, Claus 541
クールボー
Coolbaugh, Mike 286
Coolbaugh, Scott 286
クルボニヨン
Qurboniyon, Abdusalom 1146
クルボノフ
Kurbonov, Rustam 774
Qurbonov, Abdusalom 1146
Qurbonov, Bahrom 1146
クルボノワ
Kurbonova, Rukiya 774
グルホフスキー
Glukhovsky, Dmitry 505
クルマ
Kourouma, Ahmadou 760
Kourouma, Elhadj Papa Koly 760
Kourouma, Ibrahima 760
Kourouma, Papa Koly 760
Kourouma, Sékou 760
クルマイヒ
Krumeich, Gerd 769
クルマス
Coulmas, Florian 295
クールマン
Kuhlmann, Torben 771
クルマン
Kullman, Ellen J. 772
Kullmann, Katja 772
グールマン
Gurman, Stephen 547
クールマン＝ホディック
Kuhlmann-Hodick, Petra 771
クルミー
Crumey, Andrew 305
クルーミニャ
Krumina, Brigita Baiba 769
クルミンシ
Kruminš, Janis 769
クルーム
Crume, Eric 305
Crume, Jeff 305
クルム
Klum, Heidi 747
Krumm, Michael 769
クルムハメド
Kul-mukhammed, Mukhtar 772
クルユ
Kulju, Mika 772
グルラグチャー
Gurragchaa, Jugderdemidiin 547
クルリ
Koulouri, Christina 760
グルーリー
Gruley, Bryan 541
クルリック
Krulik, Nancy E. 769
グルリット
Gurlitt, Cornelius 547
クルール
Krul, J.T. 769
クルル
Krul, Tim 769
Krull, Kathleen 769
クルーロー
Clewlow, Les 271
クルーン
Kluun 747
Krohn, Leena 768
Kroon, Hans de 768
グルーン
Gruhn, Wilfried 540
グルン
Gurung, Dev Prasad 548
Gurung, Kiran 548
Gurung, Palten 548
Gurung, Prabal 548
Gurung, Suryaman 548
グルンウォールド
Grunwald, Henry Anatole 541
クルンゴルカス
Krungolcas, Edvinas 769
クルンズ
al-Krunz, Saadi 769
グールンス
Goerens, Charles 508
グルンスタイン
Grunstein, Michael 541
グルンステン
Groensteen, Thierry 538
クルンター
Klunter, Lukas 747
グルンド
Grund, Jens 541
クルンドゥ
Kulundu, Newton 772
クルンフレ
Qurunfleh, Mustafa 1146
グルンルース
Grönroos, Christian 538
グルンワルド
Grunwald, Peter 541
クレー
Klee, Ernst 744
Kraeh, Mareen 763
グーレ
Goulet, Robert Gerard 521
グレ
Grée, Alain 529
グレー
Gray, Adeline Maria 527
Gray, Dolores 528
Gray, Patrick 528
Gray, Pete 528
Gray, Warren C. 528
クレア
Clair, Alicia Ann 266
Clair, Daphne 266
Claire, Elizabeth 266
Claire, Hirary 266
Clare, Cassandra 266
Clare, John 266
Clare, Pamela 266
Clare, Peter 266
Clare, Tiffany 266

Cryer, Debby 306
Klare, Jean 743
Klare, Michael T. 743
Klehr, Harvey 744
クレアー
Clair, Merven 266
グレアー
Glar, Jinny 503
グレアソン
Gleason, Andrew M. 504
グレアム
Graham, Amanda 523
Graham, Billy 524
Graham, Bob 524
Graham, Brian J. 524
Graham, Caroline 524
Graham, Colin 524
Graham, Dan 524
Graham, Donald 524
Graham, Dorie 524
Graham, Elizabeth 524
Graham, Heather 524
Graham, Joan Bransfield 524
Graham, Katherine Meyer 524
Graham, Loren 524
Graham, Lynne 524
Graham, Margaret Bloy 524
Graham, Mark 524
Graham, Matt 524
Graham, Matthew 524
Graham, Paul 524
Graham, Rob 524
Graham, Steve 524
グレアム・スミス
Grahame-Smith, Seth 524
グレアム＝ディクソン
Graham-Dixon, Andrew 524
クレアモント
Claremont, Chris 266
Claremont, Máire 266
クレアリー
Crary, Elizabeth 300
クーレイ
Cooray, Anton 288
Cooray, Reginold 288
クレイ
Clay, Bryan 269
Clay, Charles 269
Clay, Kaelin 269
Claye, Will 269
Cooray, Dulanya 288
Cray, David 300
Cray, Jordan 300
Klay, Phil 744
Qrei, Ahmed 1143
グレイ
Du Plessix Gray, Francine 382
Gray, Alasdair James 527
Gray, Alexandra 527
Gray, Alfred 527
Gray, Andre 527
Gray, Andrew 527
Gray, Carol 527
Gray, Christopher 527
Gray, Colin S. 527
Gray, Cyrus 527
Gray, Dave 527
Gray, David 527
Gray, David Winchester 527
Gray, Demarai 527
Gray, Denis Pereira 528
Gray, Dolores 528
Gray, Edwyn 528
Gray, Elizabeth 528
Gray, Françoise 528
Gray, Ginna 528
Gray, Gwen 528
Gray, Harry B. 528
Gray, Herbert 528
Gray, Jamie Lynn 528
Gray, Jeffrey A. 528
Gray, Jeffrey Alan 528
Gray, Jeremy J. 528
Gray, Jim 528
Gray, Joanna 528
Gray, John 528
Gray, John Armstrong Muir 528
Gray, Jon 528
Gray, Jonathan 528
Gray, Jonny 528
Gray, Juliana 528
Gray, Keith 528
Gray, Kes 528
Gray, Kris 528
Gray, Leon 528
Gray, Marcy 528
Gray, MarQueis 528
Gray, Martin 528
Gray, Michael 528
Gray, Michael D. 528
Gray, Patrick 528
Gray, Paul R. 528
Gray, Pete 528
Gray, Richie 528
Gray, Rob 528
Gray, Scott 528
Gray, Scott Fitzgerald 528
Gray, Shelley Shepard 528
Gray, S.J. 528
Gray, Sonny 528
Gray, Spalding 528
Gray, Theodore W. 528
Gray, Thomas Cecil 528
Gray, Todd 528
Gray, Tyler 528
Gray, Virginia 528
Gray, W.Blake 528
Grey, Alex 534
Grey, Alfred 534
Grey, Amelia 534
Grey, Andrew 534
Grey, George 534
Grey, India 534
Grey, Jacob 534
Grey, Jake 534
Grey, Mini 534
Grey, Peter 534
Grey, Stephen 534
Grey, Tony 534
Grey, Vergeneas Alfred 534
クレイア
Claire, Roger W. 266
グレイアム
Graham, Billy 524
Graham, Carolyn 524
Graham, Ian 524
クレイヴァー
Craver, William 300
グレイヴァー
Graver, Lawrence 527
グレィヴズ
Graves, Lucia 527
Graves, Stephen C. 527
グレイヴス
Graves, Christopher 527
Graves, Jaya 527
Graves, Michael 527
Graves, Peter 527
グレイヴズ
Graves, Gregory 527
Graves, Tom 527
クレイヴン
Craven, Sara 300
Craven, Wes 300
グレイカス
Greicus, M.S. 533
クレイガン
Cragun, Richard 299
Kragen, Kyle 763
クレイギ
Craigie, Peter C. 299
クレイグ
Craig, Albert M. 299
Craig, Allen 299
Craig, Cameron 299
Craig, Catherine L. 299
Craig, Daniel 299
Craig, David 299
Craig, Emily A. 299
Craig, Gary 299
Craig, Gordon Alexander 299
Craig, Helen 299
Craig, J.Marshall 299
Craig, John William 299
Craig, Peter 299
Kraig, Donaid Michael 763
グレイク
Gleick, Beth Youman 504
グレイグ
Greig, Martin 533
Greig, Tamsin 533
グレイケン
Grayken, John 528
クレイザー
Glaser, Donald Arthur 503
グレイサー
Glaser, Byron 503
Glaser, Danya 503
グレイザー
Glaeser, Edward Ludwig 503
Glaser, Linda 503
Glaser, Milton 503
Glazer, Jonathan 504
Glazer, Mitch 504
Glazer, Mitchell 504
Grazer, Brian 528
Grazer, Gigi Levangie 528
クレイシ
Kureishi, Hanif 774
グレイシー
Gracie, Anne 523
Gracie, Hélio 523
Gracie, Renzo 523
Gracie, Rickson 523
Gracie, Roger 523
Gracie, Royce 523
Gracie, Royler 523
Gracie, Ryan 523
グレイシカルンス
Greiskalns, Karlis 533
クレイジー・ボーン
Krayzie Bone 765
クレイショーズ
Krashos, George 764
クレイス
Crace, Jim 298
Crais, Robert 299
クレイズ
Claeys, Gregory 266
Craze, Richard 301
グレイス
Grace, Carol 523
Grace, Jaclyn 523
Grace, Matt 523
グレイスティーン
Gleysteen, William H., Jr. 505
グレイスミス
Graysmith, Robert 528
クレイソン
Clayson, Alan 269
グレイソン
Grayson, Andrew 528
Grayson, Garrett 528
Grayson, Kristine 528
クレイダー
Kreider, Richard B. 765
クレイダーマン
Clayderman, Richard 269
クレイチー
Krejci, Ladislav 765
クレイディー
Clady, Ryan 266
グレイディ
Grady, James 523
Grady, Robyn 523
グレイデン
Gladen, Steve 503
グレイトハウス
Greathouse, William M. 529
クレイドマン
Kreidman, Ellen 765
クレイトモア
Creightmore, Richard 301
クレイドラー
Kreidler, William J. 765
クレイトン
Clayton, Adam 269
Clayton, Adam Charles 269
Clayton, Custio 269
Clayton, Donna 269
Clayton, Gary E. 269
Clayton, John 269
Clayton, Martin 269
Clayton, Max 269
Clayton, Paul 269
Clayton, Vicki 269
Crayton, Carolyn 300
Crayton, Gary E. 301
Creighton, Kathleen 301
Creighton, Thomas E. 301
グレイドン
Graydon, Michael 528
クレイナー
Crainer, Stuart 299
Kleiner, Brian M. 744
Kreiner, David 765
クレイナウ
Kleinow, Pete 745
グレイニエツ
Grejniec, Michael 534
クレイノヴァ
Kleinová, Pavla 745
クレイノフスカ
Klejnowska-krzywanska, Aleksandra J 745
クレイノフスカクルジワニスカ
Klejnowska-krzywanska, Aleksandra J 745

クレイバー
Klaver, M.Nora 743
クレイバーグ
Clayburgh, Jill 269
クレイパス
Kleypas, Lisa 745
グレイバーズ
Grevers, Matt 534
Grevers, Matthew 534
クレイビー
Cravy, Tyler 300
クレイビース
Kreivys, Dainius 765
クレイビル
Kraybill, Donald B. 765
グレイブ
Greive, Duncan 533
グレイブス
Graves, Bonnie 527
Graves, Michael 527
Graves, Peter 527
グレイブズ
Graves, Ryan 527
Graves, Samantha 527
グレイブマン
Graveman, Kendall 527
クレイブン
Craven, Wes 300
クレイブンス
Cravens, Jesse 300
クレイベンズ
Cravens, Su'a 300
クレイボーン
Claiborne, Liz 266
Claiborne, Morris 266
Clayborn, Adrian 269
Claybourne, Anna 269
クレイマー
Cramer, Jim 299
Kramer, Ann 763
Kramer, Billy J. 763
Kramer, Christine L. 763
Kramer, Don 763
Kramer, Edith 763
Kramer, Jack 763
Kramer, Joey 763
Kramer, Kieran 763
Kramer, Larry 763
Kramer, Maeona K. 764
Kramer, Matt 764
Kramer, Stanley 764
Kramer, Stephen P. 764
Kramer, Steven J. 764
クレイマン
Kleiman, Naum 744
グレイマン
Glayman, Claude 504
Greiman, Lois 533
クレイムズ
Krames, Jeffrey A. 764
クレイメルマン
Kreimerman, Roberto 765
グレイリング
Grayling, A.C. 528
Grayling, Chris 528
クレイン
Crain, Brooke 299
Crain, S.R. 299
Craine, Debra 299
Craine, Leslie E. 299
Crane, Anna 299
Crane, Caprice 299
Crane, Greg 299
Crane, Hart 299
Crane, Jim 299
Crane, Nicholas 299
Crane, Peter Robert 299
Crane, Stephen 299
Crane, Susan A. 299
Crane, Tim 299
Klein, Marty 744
Klein, Ralph Phillip 744
グレインキー
Greinke, Zack 533
グレインジャー
Grainger, Katherine 524
Grainger, Sally 525
Grainger, Teresa 525
クレインス
Cryns, Frederik 306
クレインスミス
Kleinsmith, Lewis J. 745
クレインベルジェ
Kleinberger, Laurence 744
クレインロック
Kleinrock, Leonard 745
クレヴァリー
Cleverley, Tom 271
グレーヴィチ
Gurevich, Aron Yakovlevich 547
クレヴェン
Kleven, Elisa 745
グレヴェン
Greven, John 534
クレヴェンジャー
Clevenger, Craig 271
グレーヴス
Graves, Don 527
グレーヴズ
Graves, Jane 527
グレーヴリー
Gravlee, Glenn P. 527
クレーヴン
Craven, Wes 300
グレーエ
Gröhe, Hermann 538
クレオン
Kleon, Austin 745
クレーガー
Kleiger, James H. 744
Kröger, Teppo 767
グレーガー
Groger, Helmut 538
グレガーセン
Gregersen, Hal B. 533
Gregersen, Peter K. 533
グレガーソン
Gregerson, Luke 533
グレギーナ
Guleghina, Maria 545
グレキン
Grekin, Linda Zitomer 534
クレグ
Clegg, Stewart 270
グレク
Greku, Borana 534
グレグ
Gregg, Jamie 533
Gregg, Jessica 533
グレグソン
Gregson, Jessica 533
Gregson, Olga 533
Gregson, Ryan 533
グレーグッセン
Gregussen, Otto 533
クレーグヘッド
Craighead, Christopher W. 299
グレグル
Grégr, Miroslav 533
クレケエフ
Kulekeyev, Zhaksybek 772
クレゲナウ
Kregenow, Julia 765
クレーゲル
Kregel, Jan Allen 765
グレコ
Greco, Daniele 529
Greco, Francesca 529
Greco, John 529
Gréco, Juliette 529
Greco, Laurie A. 529
Greco, Thomas H. 529
グレゴリ
Gregori, Giuliana 533
Gregori, Jose 533
グレゴリー
Gregory, Alex 533
Gregory, David 533
Gregory, Deborah 533
Gregory, James 533
Gregory, Janet 533
Gregory, Jason 533
Gregory, Jonathan Thorp 533
Gregory, Julie 533
Gregory, Morna E. 533
Gregory, Nan 533
Gregory, P. 533
Gregory, Paul R. 533
Gregory, Peter 533
Gregory, Peter H. 533
Gregory, Philippa 533
Gregory, Richard Langton 533
Gregory, Sandra 533
Gregory, Valiska 533
グレゴリアス
Gregorius, Didi 533
グレゴリオ
Gregorio, Jadel 533
Gregorio, Joan 533
Gregorio, Michael 533
Gregorio, Rossella 533
グレゴリ・スミス
Gregor-Smith, Bernard 533
グレゴリチュ
Gregoritsch, Michael 533
グレゴリン
Gregorin, Teja 533
グレゴール
Gregor, Erika 533
Gregor, Ulrich 533
グレゴロビッチ
Grigorovich, Yurii Nikolaevich 536
グレーコワ
Grekova, Irina Nikolaevna 534
グレーサー
Glaesser, Dirk 503
Glaesser, Jasmin 503
グレーザー
Glaser, Connie Brown 503
Glaser, Donald Arthur 503
Glaser, Milton 503
Glazer, Amihai 504
Glazer, Malcolm 504
グレーザーズフェルド
Glasersfeld, Ernst von 503
クレサル
Kresal, Katarina 766
クレシ
Qureshi, Mehmood 1146
グレージア
Glazier, Sidney 504
グレシアン
Grecian, Alex 529
クレシェンツィ
Crescenzi, Alessandro 301
クレシェンツォ
Creschenzo, Luciano De 301
クレシャ
Kulesha, Iryna 772
グレシャート
Greschat, Martin 534
グレシャト
Greschat, Martin 534
グレジャーマン
Gregerman, Alan S. 533
グレシャム
Gresham, Jermaine 534
Gresham, Stephen D. 534
クレージュ
Courrèges, André 295
グレーシュ
Greisch, Jean 533
クレシュチ
Kleszcz, Grzegorz 745
グレシュベック
Gresbeck, Heinrich 534
クレショフ
Kuleshov, Anatoly N. 772
グレシンジャー
Grössinger, Christa 539
クレス
Kress, Bodo 766
Kress, Nancy 766
Kress, W.John 766
グレース
Grace, Catherine O'neill 523
Grace, Cathy 523
Grace, James 523
Grace, Jarrett 523
Grace, Kate 523
Grace, Maria 523
Grace, Nader Halim Kaldas 523
Grace, N.B. 523
グレス
Gress, Daryl R. 534
Gress, Michael A. 534
クレスウェル
Cresswell, Aaron 301
Cresswell, Helen 301
Cresswell, Jasmine 301
Creswell, John W. 301
グレスコー
Grescoe, Taras 534
クレスタン＝ビエ
Crestin-Billet, Frédérique 301
グレステ
Greste, Peter 534
クレスティ
Cresti, Carlo 301
Cresti, Renzo 301
クレスティル
Klestil, Thomas 745
クレストマン

ク

Chrestman, Kelly R. 260
クレスパン
Crespin, Régine 301
クレスピ
Crespi, Francesca 301
Crespy, Michel 301
グレース・フー
Fu Hai Yien, Grace 466
クレスポ
Crespo, Hernan 301
Crespo, Manuel 301
クレスポ・ビジャテ
Crespo Villate, Mercedes Tania 301
クレスマン
Klessmann, Christoph 745
グレスリン
Grasslin, Jurgen 527
クレゼール
Kreutzer, Bruce 766
クレーゼルバーグ
Krayzelburg, Lenny 765
グレーダー
Greder, Armin 529
クレチ
Krech, Roman 765
グレチアニ
Greciani, Zinaida 529
グレチヒナ
Grechykhina, Olena 529
グレチャヌイ
Greceanii, Zinaida 529
グレチン
Grechin, Andrey 529
グレーツ
Grätz, Ina 527
グレーツァー
Glaetzer, Matthew 503
グレツィンゲル
Gretzyngier, Robert 534
クレッカー
Klöcker, Michael 746
グレツキ
Górecki, Henryk Mikołaj 519
Gorecki, Ryszard Jozef 519
グレツキー
Gretzky, Wayne 534
クレック
Kreck, Walter 765
クレッグ
Clegg, Brian 270
Clegg, Nick 270
グレック
Grech, Louis 529
グレッグ
Gregg, Donald 533
Gregg, Eric 533
Gregg, Jennifer 533
Gregg, L.B. 533
Gregg, Susan 533
Greig, Geordie 533
グレッグソン
Gregson, Susan R. 533
グレックラー
Glöckler, Michaela 505
クレッケ
Krecke, Jeannot 765
グレッサー
Gressor, Megan 534
グレッジ
Gulledge, Thomas R. 545
グレッジオ
Greggio, Luciano 533
グレッシュ
Gresh, Alain 534
Gresh, Lois H. 534
クレッスマン
Klessmann, Edda 745
クレッセ
Kresse, John 766
クレッチマー
Krätschmer, Marion 764
Kretschmer, Hildegard 766
Kretschmer, Peter 766
クレッチマン
Kretschmann, Hans-Joachim 766
クレッチュマン
Kretschmann, Winfried 766
クレッツ
Kletz, Trevor 745
Kroetz, Franz Xaver 767
クレッパ
Kleppa, Magnhild Meltveit 745
クレッヒェル
Krechel, Ursula 765
クレップナー
Kleppner, Daniel 745
クレッペ
Kleppe, Anneke G. 745
クレツリ
Kloetzli, Randy 746
クレツレスコ
Kretzulesco, Ottomar Rodolphe Vlad Dracula Prince 766
クレディ
Cready, Gwyn 301
クレティアン
Chretien, Margaux 260
クレティエ
Cretier, Claude 301
クレティエン
Chrétien, Jean 260
クレティッチ
Kuretich, Michael 774
グレディッチュ
Gleditsch, J. 504
グレテン
Grethen, Henri 534
クレト
Kuret, Karlo 774
グレド
Gouled Aptidon, Hassan 521
グレド・アプティドン
Gouled Aptidon, Hassan 521
グレート・アントニオ
Great Antonio 529
グレドラー
Gredler, Ludwig 529
グレニー
Glennie, Evelyn 505
Glenny, Misha 505
Grenny, Joseph 534
グレニーアス
Greanias, Thomas 529
グレニンガー
Greninger, Richard 534
グレーニング
Gröning, Philip 538
グレニング
Grenning, James W. 534
クレノー
Clenow, Andreas F. 270
グレノット
Grenot Martinez, Libania 534
クレノフ
Krenov, James 766
グレノン
Glennon, Dennis C. 505
Glennon, Michael 505
Glennon, Mike 505
クレバー
Kleber, Marc S. 744
グレーバー
Graeber, David 523
Greber, Christian 529
クレパクス
Crepax, Guido 301
クレパツカ
Klepacka, Zofia 745
クレバノフ
Klebanov, Ilya Iosifovich 744
クレパルディ
Crepaldi, Gabriele 301
グレバン
Gréban, Quentin 529
Gréban, Tanguy 529
クレービ
Creevy, Agustin 301
クレピネヴィッチ
Krepinevich, Andrew F. 766
クレピヒ
Kleppich, Lars 745
クレービール
Krehbiel, Henry E. 765
クレビール
Krehbiel, Timothy C. 765
クレビンジャー
Clevinger, Mike 271
クレビン・ベイリー
Crebbin-Bailey, Jane 301
グレープ
Grape, Jan 526
グレフ
Gref, Herman Oskarovich 533
Greffe, Xavier 533
クレーファー
Klever, Ulrich 745
クレフェルト
Creveld, Martin van 301
クレブス
Krebs, Edwin Gerhard 765
Krebs, John Richard 765
Krebs, Valdis 765
クレプス
Krebs, Angelika 765
Kreps, David M. 766
グレーブス
Graves, Jared 527
Graves, Laura 527
Graves, Michael 527
Graves, Morris 527
Graves, Peter 527
Graves, Teresa 527
グレープス
Grapes, Ken 526
クレフスン
Krevsun, Yuliya 766
クレプファー
Kloepfer, Michael 746
クレフマン
Kleffmann, Tom 744
グレブル
Gröbl, Petra 537
クレーブン
Craven, Philip 300
Craven, Wes 300
グレーベ
Grebe, Camilla 529
グレベ
Grebe, Horst 529
クレーベル
Cleber 270
クレーベルガー
Kleberger, Ilse 744
グレーベン
Greven, Alec 534
グレベンカ
Grebenka, Evgenii Pavlovich 529
クレベンジャー
Clevenger, Craig 271
クレヘンビュール
Krähenbühl, Pierre 763
クレポン
Crépon, Marc 301
クレーマー
Kraemer, William J. 763
Kraemer, Wolfgang 763
Krämer, Dietmer 763
Kramer, Edith 763
Krämer, Eva-Maria 763
Krämer, Hans Joachim 763
Kramer, Jack 763
Kramer, Joey 763
Kramer, Robert J. 764
Kramer, Stanley 764
Krämer, Sybille 764
Krammer, Ralph M. 764
Kremer, Detlef 766
Kroemer, Herbert 767
クレマ
Crema, Katya 301
クレマー
Clemmer, Jim 270
Kramer, David 763
Kremer, Anja 766
Kremer, Chuck 766
Kremmer, Christopher 766
クレマン
Clement, Arnaud 270
Clément, Bruno 270
Clément, Catherine 270
Clément, Claire 270
Clément, Gilles 270
Clément, Jérôme 270
Clément, Pascal 270
Clément, Philippe 270
クレマンソー
Clémenceau, Jean-Pierre 270
グレミヨン
Grémillon, Hélène 534
グレミリオン
Gremillion, Lee Louis 534
クレミングス
Clemmings, T.J. 270
クレミンソン
Cleminson, Katie 270
クレーム
Creme, Benjamin 301

クレメット
Clemet, Kristin 270
クレメトセン
Klemetsen, Håvard 745
クレメニュク
Kremenyuk, Victor 766
クレーメル
Kremer, Gidon 766
クレメール
Crémer, Bruno 301
クレメル
Crémer, Bruno 301
Kremer, Gidon 766
クレメロヴァー
Kraemerova, Alice 763
クレメン
Kremen, Vasyl 765
クレメンス
Clemence, Christianna 270
Clemens, Christian 270
Clemens, Helmut 270
Clemens, Kellen 270
Clemens, Paul 270
Clemens, Roger 270
Klemens, Letícia Deusina da Silva 745
クレメンチッチ
Klemenčič, Goran 745
クレメンツ
Clements, Alan 270
Clements, Andrew 270
Clements, David Mark 270
Clements, Kevin P. 270
Clements, M.Susan 270
Clements, Ron 270
Clements, Ronald Ernest 270
Clements, Rory 270
Clements, Stewart R. 270
Clements, Vassar 270
クレメンテ
Clemente, Francesco 270
クレメンティ
Clementi, David Cecil 270
Clementi, Gian Luca 270
クレメント
Clement, Hal 270
Clément, Jérôme 270
Clement, Kerron 270
Clement, Peter 270
Clement, Stephanie Jean 270
Clement, Tony 270
Clement, Wolfgang 270
Klement, Philipp 745
クレメント＝デイヴィーズ
Clement-Davies, David 270
クレモネージ
Cremonesi, Alessandro 301
クレモンス
Clemons, Steven 270
クレモンズ
Clemons, Chris 270
Clemons, Clarence 270
Clemons, Steven 270
クレモンティーヌ
Clémentine 270
グレーラー
Grealer, Louis 529
グレラ
Grella, George, Jr. 534
クレランド
Cleland, John G.F. 270
クレーリー
Crary, Jonathan 300
クレリ
Cleri, Valerio 270
クレリスメ
Clerisme, Jean Reynald 271
クレリチ
Clerici, Umberto 270
クレリデス
Clerides, Glafcos 270
Clerides, Takis 270
グレーリング
Greyling, JC. 534
クレリンステン
Crelinsten, Gordon L. 301
クレール
Clair, Jean 266
Clair, Sandie 266
Clerc, Olivier 270
クレルク
Clerc, Carlos 270
クレルグ
Clergue, Lucien 270
グレルシェン
Gloeersen, Anders 505
クレルジョウ
Clergeaud, Chantal 270
Clergeaud, Lionel 270
クレール・ミランダ
Creel Miranda, Santiago 301
クーレン
Keulen, Isabelle van 723
クレーン
Crane, Alberto 299
Crane, Peter Robert 299
Crane, Rebecca 299
Crane, Stephen W. 299
クレン
Cullen, Martin 307
グレン
Glen, Sally 504
Glenn, Alan 504
Glenn, Andrea L. 504
Glenn, Cordy 504
Glenn, Jacoby 504
Glenn, John 505
Glenn, Jules 505
Glenn, Terri M. 505
Glenn, Thomas 505
Glenn, Victoria 505
Glenn, Walter J. 505
グレンヴィル
Grenville, Bruce 534
Grenville, Kate 534
グレンジャー
Grainger, Eve 524
Granger, Bill 525
Granger, Clive W.J. 525
Granger, David 525
Granger, Katherine 525
Granger, Russell H. 525
クレンシャウ
Crenshaw, Russell Sydnor 301
クレンショー
Crenshaw, Charles A. 301
クレンズ
Krens, Thomas 766
クレンスキー
Krensky, Stephen 766
グレンチ
Grench, Eileen 534
クレンツ
Krantz, Les 764
Krentz, Jayne Ann 766
Krenz, Egon 766
グレンツ
Grenz, Dagmar 534
Gurrentz, Sheryl 547
クレンツァー
Krenzer, Rolf 766
グレンディ
Glenday, Craig 504
クレンデノン
Clendenon, Donn Alvin 270
グレントレガロ
Green Tregaro, Emma 532
グレンドン
Glendon, Kellie J. 504
クレンナ
Crenna, Richard 301
クレンニエミ
Kurenniemi, Marjatta 774
クレンネル
Crennel, Romeo 301
グレンビル
Glenville, Marilyn 505
グレンプ
Glemp, Józef 504
グレンライト
Glenwright, Jerry 505
クロ
Queloz, Didier 1144
クロー
Clot, Andre 272
Crow, Ben 304
Crow, Kim 304
Krog, Inge 767
Krogh, Anders 768
Krogh, Georg Von 768
グロ
Gros, Frédéric 538
グロー
Grau, Andrée 527
Grau, François-Marie 527
Groh, Michael 538
クロアビエ
Croibier, Alain 303
クロアレク
Cloarec, Françoise 271
クローアンズ
Klawans, Harold L. 743
クロイ
Croy, Anita 305
Croy, Elden 305
グロイ
Groy, Ryan 540
グロイエル
Greuel, Gert-Martin 534
グロイス
Grois, Boris 538
Groys, Boris 540
グロイスバーグ
Groysberg, Boris 540
グロイスマン
Groysman, Volodymyr 540
クロイター
Croiter, Jeff 303
Kreuter, Marshall W. 766
クロイツァー
Kreutzer, Hans Joachim 766
クロイツベルガー
Kreutzberger, Stefan 766
クロイトル
Croitoru, Tal 303
グロイブ
Graeub, Ralph 523
クロイヤー
Kroijer, Lars 768
クロイワ・ホリウチ
Kuroiwa Horiuchi, Julio 775
クーロウ
Kwok, Blondi 777
クロウ
Clough, Roger 272
Clow, Barbara Hand 272
Crow, Bill 304
Crow, Sheryl 304
Crowe, Cameron 304
Crowe, Jeanne P. 304
Crowe, Judith 304
Crowe, Lauren Goldstein 304
Crowe, Michael J. 304
Crowe, Russell 304
Crowe, William James, Jr. 304
グローヴ
Grove, Andy 540
Grove, Hannah Shaw 540
Grove, S.E. 540
グロウ
Groe, Diana 538
Groe, Gerald M. 538
クローヴァー
Clover, Charles 272
Glover, Savion 505
グローヴァー
Glover, Danny 505
Glover, Savion 505
グロウアー
Grauer, Lally 527
クローウィッツ
Krawitz, Roy 765
グロウィンスキー
Glowinski, Mark 505
グロヴィンスキ
Glovinsky, Paul B. 505
グロゥヴ
Grove, Eric 540
クローウェ
Crowe, David 304
グローヴェ
Grove, Bernd 540
クローウェル
Craughwell, Thomas J. 300
Crowell, Isaiah 304
Crowell, Rodney 304
クロウェル
Crowell, Beverly 304
クロウエル
Crouwel, Wim 304
グロウクス
Groux, Pablo 539
グロウクス・カネド
Groux Canedo, Pablo 539
クロウザー
Klauser, Henriette Anne 743
クロウス
Kloos, Marko 746
クロウズ
Clowes, Daniel 272

ク

ク

グローヴス
Groves, Judy 540
Groves, Richard F. 540
グローヴズ
Groves, Sarah 540
クロヴスキー
Kurowski, Franz 775
グロウズベック
Grousbeck, Wyc 539
クロウソン
Crowson, Andrew 304
クロウダー
Crowder, Jae 304
Crowder, Jamison 304
クロウチ
Kroetsch, Robert 767
クロウチェック
Krawcheck, Sallie L. 765
クロウト
Kroto, H.W. 768
クロウトヴォル
Kroutvor, Josef 768
クロウニー
Clowney, Jadeveon 272
クロウビ
Crowby, Patrick 304
グロウブナー
Grosvenor, Gerald Cavendish 539
クロウリー
Crawley, Ken 300
Crowley, Chris 304
Crowley, John 304
クロウンフェルド
Kronfeld, Josh 768
クロエス
Kroes, Neelie 767
グロエッチュ
Groetsch, C.W. 538
クローカー
Kroker, Arthur 768
クロガー
Kroger, Jane 767
クロカワ
Kurokawa, Ryoichi 775
グローガン
Grogan, Jeff 538
Grogan, John 538
クロキ
Kuroki, Ben 775
Kuroki, Haru 775
クローグ
Krog, Magnus 767
クログ
Krog, Magnus 767
クログスガード
Krogsgaard, Jan 768
クロケ
Cloquet, Louis 271
クロケット
Crocket, Kathie 302
Crockett, Aldene “Scruffie” 302
Crockett, Andrew Duncan 302
Crockett, Barbara A. 302
Crockett, John 302
Crockett, Kyle 302
Crockett, William R. 303
Crockett, Wyatt 303
クロゲラス
Krogerus, Mikael 768
グロコット卿
Lord Grocott 538
クロコフ
Klokov, Dmitriy 746
クローサー
Crowther, Kiesha 305
クローザー
Crowther, Kitty 305
Crowther, Nicky 305
クロザ
Crausaz, Anne 300
グローサー
Glocer, Tom 505
Groser, Tim 538
クロザウスカ
Krosoczka, Jarrett 768
クロザック
Krozak, Joseph 768
クロサワ
Kurosawa, Kiyoshi 775
グローサン
Grosan, Crina 538
クロシ
Klosi, Blendi 746
クロジア
Crozier, Lesley 305
クロジエ
Crozier, Michel 305
クローシェイ
Crawshay, David 300
グロジェバ
Grozdeva, Maria 540
グローシェル
Groeschel, Craig 538
グロシチ
Grosics, Gyula 538
クロジック
Crossick, Matt 304
グロジャン
Grosjean, Jean 538
Grosjean, Nelly 538
Grosjean, Sebastien 538
グロシュ
Glocheux, Dominique 505
グロシュー
Glocheux, Dominique 505
クローショー
Crawshaw, Alwyn 300
Crawshaw, June 300
クロシンガム
Crossingham, Adam 304
クロース
Close, Frank E. 271
Close, Glenn 272
Kloos, Anne D. 746
Kroos, Toni 768
クローズ
Close, Frank E. 271
Close, Glenn 272
Close, Marvin 272
クロス
Clos, Joan 271
Closs, David J. 272
Closs, S.José 272
Cros, Charles 303
Cross, Alan 303
Cross, Amanda 303
Cross, Caroline 303
Cross, Charles R. 304
Cross, Daphne 304
Cross, David 304
Cross, Donna Woolfolk 304
Cross, Ethan 304
Cross, Gillian 304
Cross, Ian 304
Cross, John 304
Cross, Kady 304
Cross, Kathryn Patricia 304
Cross, Neil 304
Cross, Neville 304
Cross, Nigel 304
Cross, Rodney 304
Cross, Tom 304
Kloss, Berthold 746
Kross, Jaan 768
グロース
Grose, Lynda 538
Grose, Peter 538
Grose, Timothy J. 538
Groß, Benedikt 538
Gross, Gunter F. 539
Grothe, Mardy 539
グロス
Glos, Michael 505
Gross, Andrew 538
Groß, Benedikt 538
Gross, Bill 538
Gross, Cynthia R. 538
Gross, Daniel 538
Gross, David 538
Gross, Heinrich 539
Gross, Jan Tomasz 539
Gross, John 539
Gross, Jürgen H. 539
Gross, Ken 539
Gross, Leonard 539
Gross, Marcus 539
Gross, Michael 539
Gross, Miriam 539
Gross, Pascal 539
Gross, Raphael 539
Groß, Ricco 539
Gross, Richard 539
Gross, Ronald 539
Gross, Stanislav 539
Gross, Stefano 539
Groß, Stephanie 539
Gross, Steven E. 539
Gross, T.Scott 539
Grosz, Stephen 539
Groth, Gary 539
クロスウェル
Crosswell, Kathy 304
グロスクラウス
Grossklaus, Ciril 539
クロスコ
Klosko, Janet S. 746
グロスター公
Gloucester 505
クロスターマン＝ケテルス
Klostermann-Ketels, Joan 746
クロステルマン
Klostermann, Lukas 746
グロズニック
Grosenick, Uta 538
グロスバーグ
Grosberg, A.IU. 538
Grossberg, George T. 539
Grossberg, Jack 539
Grossberg, Lawrence 539
グロスバード
Grosbard, Ulu 538
クロスビー
Crosby, Alfred W. 303
Crosby, Daniel 303
Crosby, Ian 303
Crosby, Lori E. 303
Crosby, Robbin 303
Crosby, Robert Clifton 303
Crosby, Sidney Patrick 303
Crosby, Susan 303
クロズビー
Crosby, Mason 303
Crosby, Philip 303
クロスフィールド
Crossfield, Scott 304
グロスフェルト
Grossfeld, Bernhard 539
グロスブラット
Grossblatt, Ben 539
クロスマン
Crossman, A.R. 304
グロスマン
Grossman, Bill 539
Grossman, Dave 539
Grossman, David 539
Grossman, Debbie 539
Grossman, Jerome H. 539
Grossman, Ken 539
Grossman, Lev 539
Grossman, Marc 539
Grossman, Mary 539
Grossman, Mendel 539
Grossman, Robbie 539
Grossman, Valerie G. A. 539
Grossman, William 539
Grossmann, Ben 539
グロスマン・ヘンゼル
Grossmann-Hensel, Katharina 539
クロスランド
Crosland, Margaret 303
Crossland, Jonathan 304
Crossland, Ron 304
クロスリー
Crossley, Michele L. 304
Crossley, Nick 304
Crossley, Pamela Kyle 304
Crossley, Paul 304
クロスリー＝ホランド
Crossley-Holland, Kevin 304
グロス＝ロー
Gross-Loh, Christine 539
グロスロー
Gross-Loh, Christine 539
クロースン
Clawson, Calvin C. 269
クローゼ
Klose, Miroslav 746
クロセ
Kurose, James F. 775
クロセッティ
Crosetti, Frank 303
グロゼニック
Grosenick, Uta 538
クローゼル
Clausell, Blaine 269
クローセン
Clausen, Alden Winship 269
Clausen, John A. 269
クロソウスカ・ド・ローラ
Klossowska de Rola, Harumi 746
クロソウスカドローラ
Klossowska de Rola, Harumi 746
クロソウスキー
Klossowski, Pierre 746
クロソウスキ・ド・ローラ

Klossowski de Rola, Stanislas 746
クロソフスキ
Klossowski, Pierre 746
クロソフスキー・ド・ローラ
Klossowski de Rola, Stanislas 746
クロゾン
Crozon, Alain 305
グローダヴァ
Gulordava, Marika 545
グロタンディエク
Grothendiek, Alexander 539
グロタンディーク
Grothendieck, Alexandre 539
Grothendiek, Alexander 539
グロタンディク
Grothendiek, Alexander 539
クローチェ
Croce, Augusto 302
Croce, Daniele 302
クローチェク
Krawczyk, Sabine 765
クローチェック
Krawcheck, Sallie L. 765
クロチェッティ
Crocetti, Venanzo 302
クロチェット
Crocetto, Leah 302
クロチキン
Kurochkin, Gennady F. 775
クロチコ
Kloczko, Edouard 746
クロチコワ
Klochkova, Yana 746
クロツォバ
Klocova, Lucia 746
クロッカー
Crocker, Ian 302
Crocker, Richard L. 302
クロッカリス
Klokkaris, Phivos 746
クロッグ
Clogg, Richard 271
グロック
Glock, Hans-Johann 505
クロッグマン
Krogman, Dane 768
グロッサー
Grosser, Manfred 539
グロッサルト＝マティチェク
Grossarth-Maticek, Ronald 539
クロッサン
Crossan, John Dominic 304
グロッショルツ
Grosholz, Emily 538
グロッズィンスキー
Grodzinsky, Yosef 538
グロッスマン
Grossman, Marc 539
グロッソ
Grosso, Giuseppe 539
Grosso, Ramón Moreno 539
グロッタ
Gulotta, Loreta 545
クロッツ
Klotz, Claude 746
Klotz, Irving Myron 746
グロッツ
Glotz, Peter 505
クロット
Clottes, Jean 272
Krott, Rob 768
クロッパー
Cropper, Maureen L. 303
Cropper, William H. 303
グロッピ
Groppi, Susan Marie 538
クロップ
Cropp, Robert 303
Klopp, Jürgen 746
グロップ
Gropp, William 538
クロッペンバーグ
Kloppenberg, James T. 746
クロッペンボルグ
Kloppenborg, Timothy J. 746
クロッホ
Krog, Antjie 767
グロテア
Grotheer, Jan 539
クロティ
Crotty, David A. 304
クロディー
Croddy, Eric 303
グロテリューシェン
Groteluschen, Simon 539
クローデル
Claudel, Philippe 269
グローデル
Glodell, Evan 505
クロート
Kroth, Thomas 768
Kroto, Harold Walter 768
Kulot-Frisch, Daniela 772
クロトー
Kroto, David 768
Kroto, Harold Walter 768
Kroto, Harry 768
グロート
Groat, Diane de 537
Groht, Mildred A. 538
Groth, Jonathan 539
グロード
Glaudes, Pierre 504
Gourraud, Philippe Hubert Marie 522
Gourraund, Philippe 522
クロドゥマー
Clodumar, Kinza 271
クロトワ
Courtois, Thibaut 296
クローニー
Cloney, William T. 271
グロニツキ
Gronicki, Mirosław 538
クローニン
Cronin, Doreen 303
Cronin, Helena 303
Cronin, James 303
Cronin, Michael 303
Cronin, Patricia 303
Cronin, Patrick M. 303
Cronyn, Hume 303
クロニン
Cronin, Sean 303
クローネ
Krone, Fabian 768
グローネフェルト
Gronefeld, Anna-Lena 538
グローネマイヤー
Gronemeyer, Andrea 538
クローネン
Croenen, Louis 303
Krohnen, Michael 768
クローネンバーグ
Cronenberg, David 303
クロネンバーグ
Cronenberg, David 303
クロノン
Cronon, William 303
クローバー
Clover, Charles 272
グローバ
Glover, Antonio 505
グローバー
Glover, Andrew 505
Glover, Danny 505
Glover, Helen 505
Glover, Lucas 505
Glover, Savion 505
Grover, Tim S. 540
グロバー
Glover, Shelly 505
グローバク
Graabak, Jørgen 522
グロバーグ
Groberg, D. 537
グロバク
Glovak, Sandra 505
クロパチェフ
Kropachev, Nikolay Mikhaylovich 768
クローハートマン
Kroah-Hartman, Greg 767
グローバーマン
Glouberman, Dina 505
グローバー・ライト
Glover-wright, Tay 505
クロバリ
Koulobaly, Aboubacar Sidikhi 760
グローバン
Groban, Josh 537
クロバンド
Kroband, Eran 767
クロピブニツキ
Kropiwnicki, Jerzy 768
クロフ
Kropf, Nancy P. 768
グローブ
Grobe, Deana 537
Grobe, Fritz 537
Grove, Andrew S. 540
Grove, Andy 540
Grove, Linda 540
Grove, Stephen John 540
Grove, Suzan K. 540
グロフ
Groff, Sarah 538
Gulov, Alisher 545
Gulov, Sherali 545
クローフォード
Crawford, Bryce Low, Jr. 300
Crawford, Dorothy H. 300
Crawford, Jeremy 300
Crawford, T.S. 300
クロフォード
Crafford, Danielle 298
Crawford, Andy 300
Crawford, Brandon 300
Crawford, Bryce Low, Jr. 300
Crawford, Carl 300
Crawford, Chandra 300
Crawford, Chris 300
Crawford, Cindy 300
Crawford, Corey 300
Crawford, Drew 300
Crawford, Frederick A. 300
Crawford, Holly 300
Crawford, Jack 300
Crawford, Jamal 300
Crawford, John Fort 300
Crawford, J.P. 300
Crawford, Michael 300
Crawford, Michael A. 300
Crawford, Peter Alan 300
Crawford, Randy 300
Crawford, Richard 300
Crawford, Roger 300
Crawford, Saffi 300
Crawford, Sharon 300
Crawford, Shawn 300
Crawford, Steve 300
Crawford, Ted 300
Crawford, Tony 300
Crawford, Tyrone 300
Crawford, William 300
Crawford, Yunaika 300
グローブス
Groves, Kristina 540
Groves, Madeline 540
Groves, Nicola 540
グロブダル
Grovdal, Karoline Bjerkeli 539
クロフト
Croft, James 303
Croft, John J., Ⅳ 303
Croft, Sydney 303
Kroft, Tyler 767
グローブマン
Glaubman, Richard 504
グロブラー
Grobler, Ursula 538
クロベット
Crovetto, Francisca 304
クロベト
Crovetto, Francisca 304
グローベル
Grobel, Lawrence 537
グロベルト
Grobert, Helen 537
クロボー
Kloborg, Sebastian 746
クロマティ
Cromatie, Antonio 303
クロマティー
Cromartie, Marcus 303
グロマラ
Gromala, Diane 538
グローマン
Grauman, Walter E. 527
クローミー
Cromey, Felix 303
グロミス・ディ・トラナ
Gromis di Trana, Caterina 538
クロム
Crom, J.Oliver 303
Crom, Michael A. 303
グロム

ク

Grom, Federico 538
クロムウェル
Cromwell, James 303
Cromwell, Peter R. 303
クロムス
Krommes, Beth 768
クロムハウト
Kromhout, Rindert 768
クロモスト
Kromosoeto, Ginmardo 768
クロモビジョヨ
Kromowidjojo, Ranomi 768
グロモフ
Gromov, Aleksei Alekseyevich 538
Gromov, Artem 538
Gromov, Mikhael Leonidovich 538
Gulomov, Asadullo 545
クローラー
Kröller, Eva-Marie 768
グロラ
Gurrola Ortiz, Eva Alicia 547
グロランベール
Groslambert, Louis 538
クローリー
Crawley, Talitiga 300
Crowley, Kieran 304
クロール
Croll, Alistair 303
Krol, Ian 768
Kroll, Eric 768
Kroll, Per 768
クロル
Kroll, Danielle 768
Kroll, Frank-Lothar 768
Kroll, Jeri 768
グロール
Grohl, Dave 538
グロル
Grol, Rik van 538
グロルマン
Grollman, Earl A. 538
Grollman, Sharon Hya 538
グロールマンド
Grolemund, Garrett 538
グロレ
Grolee, Antoine de 538
クローレイ
Crowley, Bob 304
グロワ
Gurova, Viktoriya 547
クロワビエ
Croibier, Alain 303
クーロン
Kuroń, Jacek Jan 775
クローン
Crone, Deanne A. 303
Crone, Rainer 303
Kron, Lisa 768
クロン
Cron, C.J. 303
Cron, Lisa 303
クロンカイト
Cronkhite, Cathy 303
Cronkite, Walter, Jr. 303
クロンキ
Kroenke, Enos Stanley 767
グロンコウスキー
Gronkowski, Glenn 538
Gronkowski, Rob 538
クローンズ
Krones, C.A. 768
クロンス
Cronce, Jessica M. 303
クロンゼック
Kronzek, Allan Zola 768
Kronzek, Elizabeth 768
クロンゾン
Kronzon, Itzhak 768
グロンダン
Grondin, Jean 538
クロンツ
Klontz, Brad 746
Klontz, Ted 746
クローン・デリ
Krohn Dehli, Michael 768
グロンドーナ
Grondona, Julio 538
クロンバック
Crombac, Gérard 303
クロンビー
Crombie, David 303
Crombie, Deborah 303
Crombie, I.K. 303
クロンベ
Crombé, Véronique 303
グロンホルツ
Grønholdt, Lars 538
クワ
Kwa, Geok-choo 777
クワイ
Kwai, Terence H. 777
クワイトリー
Quitely, Frank 1146
クワーク
Quirk, Matthew 1145
クワコウ
Coicaud, Jean-Marc 276
クワジェ・ラスバ
Kwaje Lasuba, Agnes 777
クワシニエフスキ
Kwaśniewski, Aleksander 777
クワジマ
Kuwajima, Kunihiro 776
クワシャ
Kvasha, Alona 777
グワダベ
Gwadabe, Musa 550
クワチー
Kwakye, Jeanette 777
グワチャム
Gwacham, Obum 550
クワック
Kwak, James 777
Kwak, Mary 777
Kwak, Sang Hee 777
クワッグ
Kwak, Mary 777
グワトニー
Gwatney, Bill 550
クワードブリット
Quaadvliet, Hendrikus 1143
クワドリ
Quadri, Argeo 1143
クワヤマ
Kuwayama, Patricia Hagan 776
クワユレ
Kwahulé, Koffi 777
グワラミア
Gvaramia, Nika 550
クワーリ
al-Kuwari, Hanan Mohamed 776
クワリ
al-Kuwari, Ghaith bin Mubarak Ali Omran 776
クワル
Kuwal, Maniang Ajok 776
クワルトロー
Qualtrough, Carla 1143
クヮン
Kwun, Hyuk-joo 778
クワン
K'wan 777
Kwan, Kevin 777
Kwan, Michelle 777
Kwan, Moon 777
Kwan, Stanley 777
Quan, Tracy 1143
クワン・ウイリアムス
K'waun Williams 777
クワンクワソ
Kwankwaso, Mohammed Rabiu 777
クヮント
Quant, Mary 1143
クーン
Koon, Jeff 756
Kuehne, Valerie 771
Kuhn, Andy 771
Kuhn, Annette 771
Kuhn, Bowie 771
Kuhn, Brett R. 771
Kuhn, Daniel 771
Kuhn, Gabriel 771
Kuhn, Hans 771
Kuhn, Harold William 771
Kuhn, Maggie 771
Kuhn, Markus 771
Kuhn, Robert Lawrence 771
クン
Khun Haing 729
Kun, Roland 773
Kung, Candie 773
グン
Gun, Nirmalendu 546
グンアージャビン・アヨルザナ
Gunaazhavyn Aiuurzana 546
クンアビシケ
Koung Bissike, À Jacqueline 760
グンガ
Gungah, Ashit Kumar 546
クンクーユ
Kunkuyu, Moses 774
クンケ
Kuhnke, Alice 771
クンケル
Kunkel, Dennis 774
クンコロ
Kuncoro, Sony Dwi 773
クン・サ
Khun Sa 729
クン・サー
Khun Sa 729
クンサン・ゲルツェン
Kun-bzan-rgyal-mtshan 773
クンサン・チョデン
Kunzang choden 774
クンジグ
Kunzig, Robert 774
クンジャラニ
Kunjarani, Namecrakpam 774
クンジュー
Koonjoo, Premdut 756
クーンジョー
Koonjoo, Premdut 756
クーンズ
Coons, Travis 287
Koons, Jeff 756
Koonz, Claudia 756
クンズル
Kunzru, Hari 774
クンゼ
Kunze, Kahena 774
クンゼル
Kuntzel, Olivier 774
クンダ
Kunda, George 773
Kunda, Gideon 773
Kundah, Khames Kajo 773
グンダナ
Gundana, Feliciano Salomao 546
グンダライ
Gundalai, Lamjavyn 546
クンタラフ
Kuntaraf, Kathleen Kiem Hoa Oey 774
クンタルソ
Koentarso, Poedji 751
クンチク
Kuntschik, Sebastian 774
クンチョック・シタル
Kunchok Sithar 773
クーンツ
Coonts, Deborah 287
Coonts, Stephen 287
Coontz, Stephanie 287
Koontz, Christie 756
Koontz, Dean Ray 756
Koontz, Trixie 756
Kuntz, Rusty 774
クンツ
Kundtz, David 773
Kunz, Barbara 774
Kunz, Kevin 774
Kunz, Samuel 774
グンツ
Göncz, Árpád 513
クンツェ
Kunze, Johannes Maximilian 774
Kunze, Michael 774
Kunze, Reiner 774
Kunze, Yvonne 774
クンツエ
Kunze, Reiner 774
クンツリ
Künzli, Otto 774
クンデ
Kunde, Gregory 773
グンディル
Gundill, Michael 546
グンデクマー・オッテリアッド
Gundegmaa Otryadyn 546
クンデラ
Kundera, Milan 773
クーンデルス
Koenders, Bert 751

クンドゥ
Kundu, Anupam 773
グンドグディエフ
Gundogdyev, Begench 546
グンドグドイエフ
Gundogdyev, Begench 546
クンドラ
Kountoura, Elena 760
クンドロタス
Kundrotas, Ar-unas 773
グンナション
Gunnarsson, Torsten 546
クンナス
Kunnas, Mauri 774
グンナルスドッティ
Gunnarsdóttir, Þorgerður Katrín 546
グンナルスドッティル
Gunnarsdottir, Thora Jenny 546
グンナルソン
Gunnarson, Jón 546
Gunnarsson, Haukur 546
Gunnarsson, Illugi 546
グンネリウソン・ヴィストマン
Gunnerriusson, Wistman, Christina 546
クーンバー
Coomber, Alex 286
クンバ
Cumba, Yumileidi 307
Koumba, Bounandele 760
Kumba, Jemma Nunu 773
グンバ
Goumba, Abel 522
クンバコル
Kumbakor, Andrew 773
クンハート
Kunhardt, Edith 774
クン・ハン
Khun Haing 729
クンブアンボラ
Kubuabola, Ratu Inoke 770
Kubuabola, Ratu Jone 770
グンブレヒト
Gumbrecht, Hans Ulrich 546
クンペアーヌ
Cîmpeanu, Sorin 264
クンペアヌ
Câmpeanu, Mariana 220
グンペルト
Gumpert, Clara Hellner 546
クンボー
Bewa-Nyong Kunbuor, Benjamin 134
グンボ
Gumbo, Joram 546
Gumbo, Rugare 546
クンマー
Kummer, Patrizia 773
グンラウグソン
Gunnlaugsson, Sigmundur 546
クーンラット
Coonradt, Charles A. 287
クンリューサー
Kunreuther, Howard 774
クンルーサー
Kunreuther, Howard 774
クーンレ
Kuhnle, Corinna 771
グンロイグソン
Gunnlaugsson, Sigmundur 546

【ケ】

ケ
Ke Kim Yan 715
ケー
K 693
Kye, Sun-hi 778
ゲ
Gay, Gabriel 485
Gay, Michel 485
Gay, Richard 485
Gué, Joanas 542
ケーア
Kehr, Karoline 714
ケア
Care, Danny 225
Care, Esther 225
Kerr, George 722
Kerr, John 722
Kerr, Sinead 722
Kjaer, Simon 743
ケアー
Kiaer, Benedikte 729
ゲーア
Goehr, Lydia 507
ゲアスコウ
Gjerskov, Mette 503
ケアスティング
Kersting, Wolfgang 722
ケアディアン
Kherdian, David 727
ケアード
Caird, George Bradford 214
Caird, John 214
ケアニー
Cairney, John 214
ゲーアマン
Gehrmann, Katja 486
ゲアマン
Gehrman, Philip R. 486
ケアリー
Carey, Dennis C. 225
Carey, Diane 225
Carey, Edward 225
Carey, Frances 225
Carey, Harry, Jr. 225
Carey, Hugh 225
Carey, Jacqueline 225
Carey, James O. 225
Carey, James W. 225
Carey, Janet Lee 225
Carey, Lou 225
Carey, Maggie 225
Carey, Mariah 225
Carey, M.R. 225
Carey, Peter Philip 225
Carey Ernestine, Gilbreth 225
Cary, Frank T. 232
Kealy, J.Kevin 713
Kerley, Barbara 721
Kerley, Jack 721
ゲアリー
Geary, P.T. 486
ケアリキ
Keariki, Teambo 713
ケアルス
Carelse, Bernadette 225
ケアレ
Keale, Moe 712
ケアロハ・ヤマムロ
Kealoha Yamamuro, Chii 713
ケアンズ
Cairns, Alun 214
Cairns, Geroge 214
Cairns, Kathleen A. 214
ケイ
K 693
Kay, Alan 711
Kay, Andrew 711
Kay, Ann 711
Kay, Carl 711
Kay, Carol McGinnis 711
Kay, Elizabeth 711
Kay, Guy Gavriel 711
Kay, Helen 711
Kay, Ira 711
Kay, Jack 711
Kay, Jackie 711
Kay, Janet 711
Kay, Jay 711
Kay, Jim 711
Kay, John Anderson 711
Kay, Joyce 711
Kay, Katty 711
Kay, Melvyn 711
Kay, Michael 711
Kay, Patricia 711
Kay, Paul 711
Kay, Richard 711
Kay, Robert S. 711
Kay, Rosemary 711
Kay, Stephen 711
Kay, Terry 711
Kaye, Alan David 711
Kaye, Beverly 711
Kaye, Buddy 712
Kaye, David 712
Kaye, David H. 712
Kaye, Doug 712
Kaye, Erin 712
Kaye, Jezra 712
Kaye, Judy 712
Kaye, Laura 712
Kaye, Marguerite 712
Kaye, Marilyn 712
Kaye, Marvin 712
Kaye, Nikki 712
Kaye, Robin 712
Kaye, Sharon M. 712
Kaye, Tony 712
Kye, Ung-tae 778
ゲイ
Gay, Jordan 485
Gay, Marie-Louise 485
Gay, Michel 485
Gay, Peter 485
Gay, Rudy 485
Gay, Tyson 485
Gay, William 485
Gaye, Abu Bakarr 485
Gaye, Fatou Ndeye 485
Guay, Jean-Pierre 541
Guei, Robert 542
Gueye, Khadim 543
Gueye, Oumar 543
Gueye, Ousseynou 543
ゲイアー
Gair, Angela 471
ケイヴ
Cave, Lucie 238
Cave, Patrick 238
Cave, Roderick 238
Cave, Susan 238
ゲイヴィンス
Gavins, Joanna 484
ゲイェ
Gueye, Idrissa 543
ケイエス
Keyes, Josh 723
ゲイエリン
Geyelin, Philip L. 492
ケイエワ
Keyewa, Oulegoh 723
ケイガル
Koegel, Timothy J. 751
ケイガン
Cagan, Andrea 213
Kagan, Annie 695
Kagan, Elena 695
Kagan, Jeremy Paul 695
ケイギル
Caygill, Howard 238
Caygill, Marjorie 238
ゲイグ
Geig, Mike 487
ケイグル
Cagle, Eric 213
ケイサー
Cassar, May 234
Kacer, Kathy 694
Kaser, Drew 707
ケイザー・ボイド
Kaser-Boyd, Nancy 707
ケイサム
Kasem, Casey 707
ケイシー
Casey, Aggie 233
Casey, Andrew 233
Casey, Dwane 233
Casey, Jo 233
Casey, Joan Frances 233
Casey, Joe 233
Casey, John 233
Casey, Kochmer 233
ケイジ
Cage, Nicolas 213
ゲイジ
Gage, Christos N. 471
ゲイジャー
Gager, John G. 471
ゲイシャイトー
Gershator, Phillis 491
ケイジャスト
Cajuste, Devon 214
ケイス
Case, George 233
Case, Mary 233
ケイスネス
Caithness, Betty 214
ケイスパー
Keijsper, Gerard 715
ゲイズラー
Geisler, Donald 487
ゲイセック
Gueye Seck, Oumou Khaïry 543
ケイセン
Kaysen, Carl 712
Kaysen, Susanna 712
ゲイソッチ
Gacioch, Rose M. 470

ケ

ケイタ
Keita, Abdoulaye 715
Keita, Aïda M'bo 715
Keita, Ba Hawa 715
Keita, Balde Diao 715
Keita, Daba Modibo 715
Keita, Ibrahim 715
Keita, Mamadou 715
Keïta, Mamadou Frankaly 715
Keita, Mamadou Lamine 715
Keïta, Modibo 715
Keita, Naby 715
Keïta, Naman 715
Kéita, Nancouma 715
Keita, Nankoman 715
Queita, Adelino Mano 1144
ケイター
Kater, Michael H. 708
ゲイター
Gaiter, Dorothy J. 471
Gater, Will 483
ケイタニー
Keitany, Mary Jepkosgei 715
ケイツ
Cates, Bailey 237
ケイツー
K2 693
ゲイツ
Gates, Antonio 483
Gates, Bill 483
Gates, Evalyn 483
Gates, Henry Louis, Jr. 483
Gates, Melinda 483
Gates, Olivia 483
Gates, Robert Michael 483
Gates, Sterling 483
Gates, William H. 483
ケイティ
Katie, Byron 708
ケイディーズ
Cadiz, Stephen 213
ケイト
Cate, Annette 237
Kate, Lauren 708
ケイトー
Cato, Ken 237
ケイド
Cade, Lance 213
Cade, Mark 213
ケイドー
Kador, John 694
ゲイトウッド
Gatewood, Warren 483
ゲイドス
Gaydos, Michael 485
ゲイドマン
Geidman, Boris Petrovich 486
ゲイトリー
Gately, Stephen 483
ケイトン
Caton, Helen 237
Caton, Thomas 237
ケイトン・ジョーンズ
Caton-Jones, Michael 237
ケイナー
Cainer, Jonathan 214
Kaner, Simon 701
ゲイナー
Gaynor, Mitchell L. 485
ケイナーン
K'naan 747
ケイニー
Kahney, Leander 696
ケイニン
Canin, Ethan 221
ゲイネム
Ganem, Lawrence 476
ケイネン
Kainen, Dan 696
ケイノ
Keino, Kipchoge A. 715
ケイパー
Caper, Robert 223
ゲイバー
Gaber, Susan 469
ケイパーズ
Capers, Avius 223
Capers, Dom 223
ゲイバーソン
Gaberson, Kathleen B. 469
ケイヒル
Cahill, Thomas 213
Cahill, Tim 213
Cahill, Trevor 213
ケイブ
Cave, Darren 238
ケイブズ
Caves, Richard E. 238
ゲイブラー
Gabler, Milt 469
Gabler, Neal 469
ゲイブリエル
Gabriel, Taylor 470
ケイプリング・アラキジャ
Capeling-Alakija, Sharon 222
ケイプル
Caple, Laurie A. 223
ゲイフロー
Gayflor, Varbah 485
ケイマン
Camann, William 217
ゲイマン
Gaiman, Neil 471
ケイム
Keim, Samuel M. 715
ゲイムス
Games, Alexander 475
ケイメン
Kamen, Henry 699
Kamen, Martin David 699
Kamen, Michael 699
Kamen, Robert Mark 699
ケイメンモウミン
Kamen, Michael 699
ケイラ
Keira, Alpha Ibrahima 715
ゲイラー
Gayler, Paul 485
ケイランス
Keirans, James E. 715
ケイランヌ
Queyranne, Jean-Jack 1144
ケイリー
Cayley, David 238
ゲイリー
Gailey, Chan 471
Gary, Roberta 482
ケイリシュ
Kalisz, Chase 697
ゲイリン
Gaylin, Alison 485
Gaylin, Willard 485
Geyelin, Philip L. 492
ケイル
Cale, J.J. 215
Kael, Pauline 695
ゲイル
Gale, Bob 472
Gale, Catharine R. 472
Gale, Cathy 472
Gale, Karen Buhler 472
Gale, Robert L. 472
Gale, Robert Peter 472
Gayle, Jackie 485
Gayle, Losksley Beanny 485
Gayle, Mike 485
ゲイレル
Gueiler, Lidia 542
ゲイロー
Gayraud, Jean-François 485
ケイロス
Queirós, Bartolomeu Campos 1144
Queirós, Manuel Francisco 1144
Queiroz, Agnelo 1144
Queiroz, Carlos 1144
ケイロスドスサントス
Queiroz Dos Santos, Isaquias 1144
ケイロル・ナバス
Keylor Navas 723
ケイン
Cain, Chelsea 214
Cain, Herman 214
Cain, James Hallie 214
Cain, Janan 214
Cain, Jonathan 214
Cain, Lorenzo 214
Cain, Madelyn 214
Cain, Matt 214
Cain, Michael Lee 214
Cain, Susan 214
Cain, Tom 214
Caine, Geoffrey 214
Caine, Michael 214
Caine, Peter 214
Caine, Renate Nummela 214
Cane, Sam 221
Kain, Andrew 696
Kane, Alex 701
Kane, Andrea 701
Kane, Barbara 701
Kane, Charles 701
Kane, G.L. 701
Kane, Harry 701
Kane, Larry 701
Kane, Mary Kay 701
Kane, Rosalie A. 701
Kane, Sunanda V. 701
Kane, Tim 701
ゲインゴブ
Geingob, Hage 487
ケインス
Cairns, Bryan 214
ケインズ
Cairns, Bryan 214
Keynes, Randal 723
ゲインズ
Gaines, Alice 471
Gaines, Boyd 471
Gaines, Charles 471
Gaines, E.J. 471
Gaines, James R. 471
Gaines, Phillip 471
Gaines, Rohan 471
Gaines, Stanley O., Jr. 471
ゲインズ＝ロス
Gaines-Ross, Leslie 471
ケインメーカー
Canemaker, John 221
ケインリー
Kahnle, Tommy 696
ケヴァル
Queval, Michel 1144
ゲヴィンソン
Gevinson, Tavi 492
ケヴェール
Kövér, György 761
ゲウォルギャン
Gevorgyan, Zaven 492
ケエンジャ
Keenja, Charles 714
ゲーオ
Pongprayoon, Kaeo 1123
ゲオクレノバ
Geoklenova, Jemal 489
ゲオルガコプロス
Georgakopoulos, Harry 489
ゲオルガリス
Geogaris, Dean 489
ゲオルギウ
Gheorghiu, Angela 493
Gheorghiu, Constantin Virgil 493
ゲオルギエフ
Georgiev, Boris 490
Georgiev, Georgi 490
Georgiev, Maksim 490
Gergov, Nikolay 490
ゲオルギエフスキ
Georgievski, Ljupco 490
ゲオルギュ
Gheorghiu, Angela 493
ゲオルギュー
Gheorghiu, Angela 493
ゲオルグシェリング
Georgschelling, Johann 490
ゲオルゲ
Gheorghe, Ionut 493
ケーガン
Cagan, Jonathan 213
Cagan, Leslie 213
Kagan, Robert 695
ゲーガン
Geoghegan, Michael F. 489
ゲガーン
Guéguen, Yves 542
ケキ
Chechi, Yuri 250
ケギー
Keaggy, Ian 712
ゲキエア
Gekiere, Madeleine 487
ゲキチ
Gekić, Kemal 487
ケクラン
Koechlin, Stéphane 751
ケーグル
Cagle, Kurt 213
Kagle, Jill Doner 695
ゲーグル

ケ

Goergl, Elisabeth 508
ケケ
Keke, Kieren 715
ケケィト
Checchetto, Marco 250
ゲゲシゼ
Gegeshidze, Vladimer 486
ケーケーニー
Kökény, Roland 752
ケケーニ
Kökény, Roland 752
ケケニ
Kökény, Roland 752
ケーゲル
Kaergel, Julia 695
Kegel, Bernhard 714
Kegel, Gerd 714
Koegel, Lynn Kern 751
Koegel, Robert L. 751
ケコ
Keko 715
ゲコスキー
Gekoski, R.A. 487
ケーザー
Kaser, Michael Charles 707
ケサヴァン
Kesavan, Kuunnavakkam Vinjamur 722
ケサダ
Quesada, Yoelvis 1144
ケサダ・トルーニョ
Quezada Toruno, Rodolfo 1144
ケサバン
Kesavan, Kuunnavakkam Vinjamur 722
ケーサム
Kasem, Casey 707
ゲザル
Ghezzal, Rachid 493
ケーサン
Kesan, Jay P. 722
ケーシー
Casey, Albert V. 233
Casey, Dwane 233
Casey, Edward S. 233
Casey, Jane 233
Casey, Jurrell 233
Casey, Neil 233
Casey, Richard Conway 233
ケージ
Cage, Nicolas 213
ケージー
Casey, Patricia 233
ケシ
Keshi, Stephen 722
ケシー
Kessy, Jennifer 723
ゲージ
Gage, Christos N. 471
ゲジ
Gezi, Border 492
Guedj, Denis 542
ケシェ
Kessie, Franck 723
ゲシェ・ケルサン・ギャッツオ
Kelsang Gyatso 717
ゲージェン
Gaetjen, Scott 470
ゲシキ
Geschke, Charles M. 492
ケシーシュ
Kechiche, Abdellatif 713
ケシシュ
Kechiche, Abdellatif 713
ゲジス
Guedes, Luís Carlos 542
ケジチ
Kezich, Tullio 724
ケーシック
Kasich, John Richard 707
ケシャ
KE$HA 722
ゲシャイダー
Gescheider, George A. 492
ケーシャブ
Keshav, Satish 722
ゲージュ
Guedj, Denis 542
ゲシュケ
Geschke, Charles M. 492
Geschke, Simon 492
ゲシュベルト
Gesbert, Stephane 492
ケジリワル
Kejriwal, Arvind 715
ケジルスカ
Kedzierska, Karolina 713
ケース
Case, Andy 233
Case, Dan 233
Case, David E. 233
Case, Frances 233
Case, John 233
Case, Richard 233
Case, Steve 233
Keisse, Iljo 715
ゲース
Gase, Adam 482
Gees, Michael 486
ゲズ
Ghez, Didier 493
ケスキネン
Keskinen, Kalevi 722
Keskinen, Soili 722
ケスス
Kessous, Mustapha 723
ケスター
Coester, Michael 273
Kester, Mark 723
Koester, Helmut 751
ケスター＝ヴァルチェン
Coester-Waltjen, Dagmar 273
ゲスタコフスキ
Gestakovski, Aleksandar 492
ケスター＝レッツェ
Koster-Losche, Kari 759
ケスティング
Kesting, Jürgen 723
ケステリッチ
Koesterich, Russ 751
ゲスト
Gest, Thomas R. 492
Guest, Ann Hutchinson 543
Guest, Ivor Farbes 543
Guest, Mike 543
Guest, Robert 543
Guest, Tim 543
Guest, Val 543
ケストナー
Kastner, Joerg 708
ゲストナー
Gerstner, Louis, Jr. 491
ケストラー
Kestler, Bernd 723
ケストレル
Kestrel, Gwendolyn F. M. 723
ケスナー
Kesner, Idalene F. 722
ケスパー
Kesper, Ingrid 722
ケースマイケル
Keersmaeker, Anne Teresa De 714
ケースマン
Kässmann, Margot 708
ケースメント
Casement, Ann 233
Casement, Patrick 233
ケスラー
Käsler, Dirk 707
Kesseler, Rob 723
Kessler, Andy 723
Kessler, Cody 723
Kessler, David 723
Kessler, David A. 723
Kessler, Leonard 723
Kessler, Liz 723
Kessler, Matthias 723
Kessler, Robert R. 723
Kessler, Ronald 723
Kessler, Thomas 723
ゲスラー
Gessler, Tatjana 492
ケスラー・ハイデ
Käsler-Heide, Helga 707
ケースリン
Kaslin, Ariella 707
ケスレル
Kessler, German 723
ケー・スンヒ
Kye, Sun-hi 778
ケ・セイン
Ket Sein 723
ケセテベルハン
Kesete Berhan, Admasu 722
ケゼマ
Kezema, Conan 724
ケゼラシビリ
Kezerashvili, David 724
ケセル
Kesel, Barbara Randall 722
ゲーセル
Gössel, Peter 520
ケセルヴァニ
Keservani, Raj K. 722
ケセルマン
Keselman, Gabriela 722
Kesselman, Jeff 723
ゲソー
Gayssot, Jean-Claude 485
ケータ
Keita, Naman 715
ケーター
Keter, Charles 723
ケダー
Kedar, Ido 713
ケタイ
Ketai, Loren 723
ゲタキ
Qetaki, Alipate 1142
ケダシェ
Kedache, Zohir 713
ゲタチョウ
Getachew, Ambaye 492
ゲタフン
Getahun, Mukuria 492
ゲータルス
Goethals, Raymond 508
ケターレ
Ketterle, Wolfgang 723
ゲターロワ
Getalova, Olga 492
ゲチエ
Guettier, Bénédicte 543
ケチチアン
Kechichián, Liliam 713
ゲーチル
Götschl, Renate 520
ケーツ
Kates, Andrew M. 708
ゲーツ
Gates, Bill 483
Gates, Melinda 483
Gates, Robert Michael 483
Goetz, Brian 508
ケツォ
Ketso, Leketekete 723
ケック
Keck, Leander E. 713
ゲック
Geck, Martin 486
ケッサ
Chessa, Francesca 253
ゲッシ
Ghezzi, Piero 493
ゲッジ
Guedj, Nathalie 542
ゲッシン
Gethin, Amorey 492
ゲッズ
Ghez, Andrea 493
ケッセル
Kessel, Barney 722
Kessel, John 722
Kessel, Joseph 722
Kessel, Neil 723
ゲッセル
Geossel, Peter 490
ケッセルシュレーガー
Kesselschlager, Sonja 723
ケッセルスクライマー
Kesselskramer 723
ケッセル・マルティネス
Kessel Martínez, Georgina 723
ゲッセン
Gessen, Masha 492
ゲッタ
Guetta, David 543
ケッタレ
Ketterle, Wolfgang 723
ケッチャム
Ketcham, Hank 723
Ketcham, Katherine 723
Ketchum, Jack 723
ケッツ
Kötz, Hein 760
ゲッツ
Getz, David 492
Getz, Gary 492
Goetz, Hans-Werner 508

Goetz, Jim 508
Goetz, Rainald 508
Goetz, Rainer H. 508
Gotz, Ashton 521
ゲッツェ
Gotze, Mario 521
ゲッツェル
Goetzel, Sascha 508
ケッツ・デ・ブリース
Kets de Vries, Manfred F. R. 723
ケッツ・ド・ブリース
Kets de Vries, Manfred F. R. 723
ゲッツ・ノイマン
Götz-Neumann, Kirsten 521
ゲッティ
Getty, Gordon 492
Getty, John Arch 492
ゲッデス
Geddes, Barbara Bel 486
Geddes, Keith 486
Geddes, Linda 486
ゲッデス‐ワード
Geddes-Ward, Alicen 486
ゲッテル
Guettel, Adam 543
ケットナー
Ketner, Joseph D., Ⅱ 723
ゲットランド
Gehtland, Justin 486
ケッピー
Keppie, L.J.F. 721
ゲッフェン
Geffen, David 486
ゲッフェンブラード
Geffenblad, Lotta 486
ゲッペールト
Goeppert, Alain 508
ゲッペルト
Geppert, Denis 490
Geppert, T. 490
ケッペン
Koeppen, Peter 751
ケツン・サンポ
Khetsun Sangpo Rinbochay 727
ゲーデ
Gade, Søren 470
Gaede, Daniel 470
ゲデ
Guede, Karim 542
ケディ
Kedi, Kenneth 713
ゲティ
Getty, Estelle 492
ゲティー
Getty, Donald 492
ゲディ
Gedi, Ali Mohamed 486
ゲディウラ
Guedioura, Adlene 542
ゲティエ
Guettier, Bénédicte 543
ゲディギアン
Guédiguian, Robert 542
ゲディギャン
Guédiguian, Robert 542
ケディキルウェ
Kedikilwe, Ponatshego Honorius Kefhaeng 713
ゲティス
Gettis, Adam 492
ゲディマン
Gediman, Corinne L. 486
ケディラ
Khedira, Rani 727
Khedira, Sami 727
ゲディラ
Ghedira, Anis 493
ケーティン
Katin, Peter Roy 709
ゲティング
Getting, Ivan A. 492
ゲデス
Geddes, Barbara Bel 486
Geddes, John 486
ケテラー
Ketelaar, James Edward 723
ケテラール
Ketelaar, Eric 723
ケテル
Quétel, Claude 1144
ケード
Cade, J.Robert 213
ゲート
Gate 483
Gate, Aaron 483
ゲード
Gade, Peter 470
ゲド
Guedon, Désiré 542
ゲドゥエフ
Geduev, Aniuar 486
ケトエフ
Ketoev, Georgy 723
ケトビ
Ketbi, Si Mohamed 723
ゲートマン＝ジーフェルト
Gethmmann-Siefert, Annemarie 492
ケトラ
Ketola, Outi 723
ケトリー
Ketley, Barry 723
ゲートリー
Gately, Iain 483
ケトリ・チェトリ
Khatri Chetri, Arjun Narsingh 727
ケトル
Kettl, Donald F. 723
ケトルウェル
Kettlewell, Caroline 723
ゲドン
Guedon, Désiré 542
ケーナー
Kaner, Simon 701
Koerner, Joseph Leo 751
ケナー
Kenner, Corrine 719
Kenner, Hugh 719
Kenner, Julie 720
Kenner, Laurel 720
ゲーナー
Göhner, Ulrich 508
ゲナイジア
Guenaizia, Abdelmalek 542
ケナウェイ
Kennaway, Adrienne 719
ゲナツィーノ
Genazino, Wilhelm 488
ケナード
Kennard, Devon 719
Kennard, Sean 719
ケナーリー
Kennerley, Mike 720
ケナリー
Kennerley, Helen 720
ゲナール
Guénard, Tim 542
ケナン
Kennan, George Frost 719
ケナン・コドロ
Kenan Kodro 718
ケニー
Kenney, Jason 720
Kenney, Linda 720
Kenney, Martin 720
Kenny, Anthony John Patrick 720
Kenny, Barry J. 720
Kenny, Carolyn 720
Kenny, Charles 720
Kenny, David 720
Kenny, Enda 720
Kenny, Janette 720
Kenny, Jason 720
Kenny, Michael 720
ゲニア
Genia, Kilroy 488
Genia, Will 488
ゲニエヴァ
Genieva, Ekaterina Yurievna 488
ケニオン
Kenyon, Tom 720
ゲニス
Genis, Aleksandr 488
ケニソン
Kenison, Katrina 719
Kennison, Kathryn 720
ケーニッヒ
König, Hans-Peter 755
ケーニッヒ・アーキブージ
Koenig-Archibugi, Mathias 751
ケーニヒ
Koenig, Jason 751
Konig, Eberhard 755
Konig, Rene 755
ゲニャツ
Genjac, Halid 488
ケニヤッタ
Kenyatta, Uhuru Muigai 720
ゲニューシャス
Geniušas, Lukas 488
ケニョン
Kenyon, J.N. 720
Kenyon, Richard Walton 720
ケニヨン
Kenyon, Andrea 720
Kenyon, Nicholas 720
Kenyon, Peter 720
Kenyon, Sherrilyn 720
Kenyon, Tony 720
ケニョン・ルヴィネ
Kenyon-Rouvinez, Denise 720
ケニーリー
Kennealy, Jerry 719
ケニロレア
Kenilorea, Peter 719
ケニン
Kanin, Fay 701
ケネソン
Kenneson, Claude 720
ケネッケ
Könnecke, Ole 755
ケネット
Kennett, Dylan 720
ケネディ
Kenedy 719
Kennedy, Allan A. 719
Kennedy, Betsy 719
Kennedy, Bruce P. 719
Kennedy, Burt 719
Kennedy, Caroline Bouvier 719
Kennedy, Charles 719
Kennedy, Dan 719
Kennedy, Dane Keith 719
Kennedy, David 719
Kennedy, Dennis 719
Kennedy, Diane M. 719
Kennedy, D.J. 719
Kennedy, Donald 719
Kennedy, Douglas 719
Kennedy, Edward 719
Kennedy, Erica 719
Kennedy, Gavin 719
Kennedy, George 719
Kennedy, George D. 719
Kennedy, Gerry 719
Kennedy, Ian 719
Kennedy, Joe 719
Kennedy, Joshua 719
Kennedy, Kara 719
Kennedy, Karen L. 719
Kennedy, Kathryne 719
Kennedy, Ludovic 719
Kennedy, Marc 719
Kennedy, Mary Richardson 719
Kennedy, Maxwell Taylor 719
Kennedy, Nell L. 719
Kennedy, Nigel 719
Kennedy, Paul Michael 719
Kennedy, Richard 719
Kennedy, Robert H. 719
Kennedy, Rosemary 719
Kennedy, Stanislaus 719
Kennedy, Steve Canyon 719
Kennedy, Susan 719
Kennedy, Thomas L. 719
Kennedy, X.J. 719
ケネディー
Kennedy, Joe 719
ゲネト
Genet, Zewdie 488
ケネードラー
Knoedler, William H. 748
ケネバン
Kenilorea, Peter 719
ケネフィック
Kennefick, Daniel 719
ケネリー
Kennealy, Molly 719
ケネル
Kennell, John H. 719
ケネン
Kennen, Ally 719
ゲーノ
Guéhenno, Jean-Marie 542
ゲノ

Guéno, Jean-Pierre 542
Guenot, Steeve François Fabien 542
ケパ
Kepa, Ro Teimumu Vuikaba 720
ゲーパー
Goepper, Nicholas 507
ケバゴ
Kovago, Zoltan 761
ゲバス
Gebas, Vitezslav 486
ゲバラ
Guevara, Aleida 543
Guevara, Ana 543
Guevara, Ana Rossana 543
Guevara, Margarita 543
Guevara March, Aleida 543
ゲバラ・オブレゴン
Guevara Obregón, Alberto José 543
ゲバラ・ペレス
Guevara Pérez, Sandra Edibel 543
ゲバラ・マンソ
Guevara Manzo, Gloria 543
ケバル
Queval, Michel 1144
ゲーパルト
Gebhardt, Lisette 486
ゲバールト
Gevaert, Kim 492
ゲビア
Gebbia, Joe 486
ケビサス
Kevisas, Gintautas 723
ケビスパエフ
Kebispayev, Almat 713
ケヒリー
Kehily, Mary Jane 714
ケーヒル
Cahill, Gary 213
Cahill, Tim 213
ケービル
Keevill, Elizabeth 714
ケピロ
Képíró, Sándor 721
ケビン
Kevin 723
ケフ
Quej, Haroldo 1144
ケプ
Kepu, Sekope 721
ケファス
Kephas, Kalwin 721
ゲプアルト
Gebhardt, Steffen 486
ケファロヤニ
Kefalogianni, Olga 714
ケファロヤニス
Kefaloyannis, Manolis 714
ケフィ
Kefi, Faiza 714
ゲフィン
Geffin, David 486
ゲフェナス
Gefenas, Eugenijus 486
ケフェレック
Queffélec, Anne 1144
ゲフェン
Geffen, Shira 486
ケフォード
Kefford, Naomi 714
ケプケ
Koepke, Hermann 751
ゲブーザ
Guebuza, Armando Emílio 542
ゲブザ
Guebuza, Armando Emílio 542
ケブザボ
Kebzabo, Saleh 713
ケプセル
Koepsell, David R. 751
ケプネス
Kepnes, Caroline 721
ゲプハルト
Gebhardt, Steffen 486
ケブヒシビリ
Kevkhishvili, David 723
ケブモ
Keb'Mo' 713
ケプラー
Kaeppler, Adrienne Lois 695
Kepler, Max 721
ケブリ
Khebri, Salah 727
ケーブル
Cable, Vince 212
ケープル
Caple, Jim 223
ゲーブル
Goebel, Timothy 507
ゲブルヒウェト
Gebrhiwet, Hagos 486
ゲブレアブ
Gebreab, Newayechristos 486
ケフレジギ
Keflezighi, Mebrahtom 714
ゲブレシラシエ
Gebrselassie, Haile 486
ゲブレスラシエ
Ghebreslassie, Ghirmay 493
ゲブレ・セラシェ
Gebre Selassie, Theodor 486
ゲブレセラシエ
Gebreselassie, Yoseph 486
Gebrselassie, Haile 486
ゲブレマリアム
Gebremariam, Gebregziabher 486
ゲブレメスケル
Gebremeskel, Dejen 486
ゲブレメディン
Wolegiorgis, Mekonnen gebremedhin 1520
ケプレル
Kepler, Lars 721
ケベ
Kébé, Awa Guèye 713
ゲヘーガン
Geoghegan, John J. 489
ケベデ
Kebede, Chane 713
Kebede, Tadesse 713
Kebede, Tsegaye 713
ケベド
Quevedo, Manuel 1144
ケベド・フロレス
Quevedo Flores, Rafael 1144
ケベヤ
Kebeya, Saidi 713
ケベル
Keber, Dušan 713
ケペル
Kepel, Gilles 721
ゲーベル
Gebel, Reinhard 486
Goebel, Wolfgang 507
ケボ
Kebo, Mirsad 713
ケホエ
Kehoe, Sally 714
ケボーキアン
Kevorkian, Jack 723
ケ・ポク
Keo Pok 720
ケボナン
Kebonang, Sadique 713
ケボルギャン
Gevorgyan, Arayik 492
ゲボルギャン
Gevorgyan, Armen 492
ケマー
Kemmer, Heike 718
ケマケザ
Kemakeza, Allan 717
Kemakeza, Mark Roboliu 718
ゲマール
Gaymard, Hervé 485
ゲマワット
Ghemawat, Pankaj 493
ゲーマン
Gehman, Richard 486
ケミル
Khémir, Nacer 727
ケーム
Kehm, Sabine 714
ゲムス
Guemessou, Adoum 542
ケムニー
Kemeny, John 718
ケムボ
Khembo, Clement 727
ケメテー
Kemmeter, Philippe de 718
ゲメド
Gemedo, Dale 488
ケメニー
Kemeny, Jim 718
Kemeny, John 718
ゲメル
Gemmell, Jim 488
ケメルマン
Kemelman, Harry 718
ケーメン
Kamen, Dean 699
Kamen, Martin David 699
Kamen, Michael 699
ケモイ
Kwemoi, Ronald 777
ケーラ
Khera, Shiv 727
ケーラー
Kaehler, Adrian 695
Kaehler, Ted 695
Kehrer, Thilo 715
Keller, Eric 716
Köhler, Horst 752
Köhler, Joachim 752
Köhler, Lotte 752
Köhler, Rolf 752
Köhler, Wolfgang R. 752
ケラ
Kela, Keone 715
ケラー
Keller, Bill 715
Keller, Colleen 716
Keller, Ed 716
Keller, Emil G. 716
Keller, Eric 716
Keller, Evelyn Fox 716
Keller, Gary 716
Keller, George 716
Keller, Gottfried 716
Keller, Holly 716
Keller, Horst 716
Keller, Jeff 716
Keller, John B. 716
Keller, John M. 716
Keller, Kalyn 716
Keller, Kathy Louise 716
Keller, Kevin Lane 716
Keller, Klete 716
Keller, Laurie 716
Keller, Markus 716
Keller, Maryann N. 716
Keller, Thomas A. 716
Keller, Timothy J. 716
Keller, Ursula 716
Keller, Wendy 716
ゲーラ
Guerra, Juan Luis 543
ゲーラー
Gehrer, Elisabeth 486
ゲラ
Guerra, Deolis 543
Guerra, Javier 543
Guerra, José Adán 543
Guerra, Juan Luis 543
Guerra, Junior 543
Guerra, Pia 543
Guerra de Hoyos, J.A. 543
ゲラー
Galler, Edward 473
Gellar, Sarah Michelle 487
Geller, Dmitry 487
Geller, Evelyn 487
Geller, Margaret J. 487
Geller, Paul Edward 487
Geller, Tamar 487
Geller, Uri 487
ゲラ・アブド
Guerra Abud, Juan José 543
ケラヴァ
Kelava, Ivan 715
ケラ＝ヴィレジェ
Quella-Villéger, Alain 1144
ゲラゴス
Geragos, Mark 490
ゲラシチェンコ
Herashchenko, Iryna 596
ケラス
Callus, Ashley 216
Queyras, Jean-Guihen 1144
ケラスコエット
Kerascoët 721
ゲラセヴァ
Gueraseva, Stacy 542
ケラソテ
Kerasote, Ted 721

ケ

ゲラ・デラエスプリエジャ
Guerra de la Espriella, María del Rosario 543
ケラート
Kellert, Stephen R. 716
ゲラトゥリ
Gellatly, Angus 487
ゲラナ
Gelana, Tiki 487
ケラハー
Kelleher, Linda O. 715
Kelleher, Victor 715
ゲラブ
Ghellab, Karim 493
ケラブノス
Keravnos, Iacovos 721
ケラペス
Kelepecz, Dolly 715
ゲラベルファブレガ
Gelabert Fàbrega, Olga 487
ケラーマン
Kellerman, Barbara 716
Kellerman, Faye 716
Kellerman, Jesse 716
Kellerman, John 716
Kellerman, Jonathan 716
Kellerman, Wouter 716
ケーラム
Kellam, Theresa 715
ゲラルド
Gerrard, Nicci 491
ケラルト・デル・イエロ
Queralt, María Pilar 1144
ゲラン
Guérin, Isabelle 543
Guerlain, Jean-Paul 543
Guerrand, Roger-Henri 543
ゲラン・ダッレ・メーゼ
Guérin-Dalle Mese, Jeannine 543
ゲラント
Gelant, Elroy 487
ケーリ
Cary, Otis 232
ケーリー
Carey, Harry, Jr. 225
Carey, Hugh 225
Cary, Otis 232
Kealy, J.Kevin 713
ケリー
Carey, Harry, Jr. 225
Cary, Otis 232
Keli, Tynisha 715
Kelley, Al 716
Kelley, Charles 716
Kelley, Christie 716
Kelley, David 716
Kelley, David E. 716
Kelley, James 716
Kelley, Johnny 716
Kelley, Karen 716
Kelley, Kitty 716
Kelley, Mike 716
Kelley, Rob 716
Kelley, Robin D.G. 716
Kelley, Shawn 716
Kelley, Tom 716
Kelley, True 716
Kelly, Alan 716
Kelly, Alison 716
Kelly, Allan 716
Kelly, Bill 716
Kelly, Brendan 716
Kelly, Carla 716
Kelly, Carson 716
Kelly, Cathy 716
Kelly, Charles 716
Kelly, Chip 716
Kelly, Christopher 716
Kelly, Colin 716
Kelly, Craig 716
Kelly, Daniel 716
Kelly, David Christopher 716
Kelly, Dennis 716, 717
Kelly, Donna Meeks 717
Kelly, Ellsworth 717
Kelly, Erin 717
Kelly, Fergus 717
Kelly, Freda 717
Kelly, Ian 717
Kelly, Jack 717
Kelly, Jacqueline 717
Kelly, James A. 717
Kelly, James M. 717
Kelly, James Patrick 717
Kelly, Jamill 717
Kelly, Jason 717
Kelly, Jim 717
Kelly, Joe 717
Kelly, John 717
Kelly, John Edward, Ⅲ 717
Kelly, John Norman Davidson 717
Kelly, Karen 717
Kelly, Kay 717
Kelly, Kevin 717
Kelly, Laura Michelle 717
Kelly, Lauren 717
Kelly, Leslie 717
Kelly, Liz 717
Kelly, Luke 717
Kelly, Lynne 717
Kelly, Martin 717
Kelly, Matthew 717
Kelly, Michael J. 717
Kelly, Mij 717
Kelly, Paul 717
Kelly, Paul Joseph 717
Kelly, R. 717
Kelly, Richard 717
Kelly, Robert J. 717
Kelly, Ruth 717
Kelly, Ryan 717
Kelly, Seamus 717
Kelly, Sean 717
Kelly, Shane 717
Kelly, Stuart 717
Kelly, Susan 717
Kelly, Tracey 717
Kelly, Ty 717
Kelly, William Wright 717
Kerry, John 722
Kery, Beth 722
ゲーリー
Gary, Shamiel 482
Geary, David 486
Geary, David M. 486
Gehry, Frank Owen 486
ゲリー
Guery, Jerome 543
ケリア
Kellier, Derrick 716
ゲリエー
Guerrier, Marc 543
ケリーエブスキー
Kerievsky, Joshua 721
ゲリオス
Gelios, Ioannis 487
ケリガン
Kerrigan, Gene 722
Kerrigan, Michael 722
Kerrigan, Ryan 722
Kerrigan, Seanna 722
ケリスク
Kerrisk, Michael 722
ケリー・チャン
Chang, Kelly 245
ゲリツァー
Geritzer, Andreas 490
ケリッジ
Kerridge, Joe 722
ゲリッセン
Gelissen, Rena Kornreich 487
ゲリッツ
Gerrits, Travis 491
ゲリットソン
Gerritsen, Annette 491
ゲーリッヒ＝バーギン
Gierlich-Burgin, Marisa 496
ゲリフ
Guérif, François 542
ゲリファンド
Gelfand, Izrail Moiseevich 487
ゲリマ
Gerima, Haile 490
ケリム
Kerim, Srgjan 721
ケリムクロフ
Kerimkulov, Medetbek 721
ケリムスキ
Chelimsky, David 251
ケリムベトフ
Kelimbetov, Kairat 715
Kelīmbetov, N. 715
ケリモフ
Kerimov, Medzhid 721
ケリン
Kerin, Zac 721
ゲリン
Guerín, José Luis 543
ゲリンガス
Geringas, David 490
ケリング
Kelling, George L. 716
ゲーリング
Gehring, Walter J. 486
Gehring, Walter Jakob 486
Goering, Richard V. 508
ゲリンジャー
Geringer, Laura 490
ケール
Cale, J.J. 215
Kael, Pauline 695
Keel, Othmar 714
Kehl, Medard 714
Kehl, Sebastian 714
ケル
Kell, George 715
ゲール
Gale, Harold 472
Gale, Tristan 472
Gehl, Jan 486
Guell, Fernando 542
ゲルー
Gerou, Tom 491
ゲルヴァルト
Gerwarth, Robert 492
ゲルガー
Görger, Kurt 519
ゲルギエフ
Gergiev, Valery Abesalovich 490
ゲルク
Gerg, Annemarie 490
Gerg, Hilde 490
ゲルゲイ
Görgey, Gábor 519
ゲルゲル
Gherghel, Ioan 493
ゲルゴヴァ
Gergova, Diana 490
ケルサン・ギャッツォ
Kelsang Gyatso 717
ケルシー
Kelsey, Dick 717
Kelsey, Frances 717
Kelsey, Jane 717
Kelsey, Morton T. 717
Kelsey, Seth 717
ケルシズ
Quercize, Stanislas de 1144
ケルシュ
Kersch, Dan 722
Koelsch, Stefan 751
ケルス
Kelce, Jason 715
Kelce, Travis 715
ケルスショット
Kersschot, Jan 722
ケルステン
Kersten, Holger 722
Kersten, Wolfgang 722
ゲルストナー
Gerstner, Karl 491
ゲルズマヴァ
Gerzmava, Khibla 492
ゲルズマバ
Gerzmava, Khibla 492
ゲルズマーワ
Gerzmava, Khibla 492
ゲルズマワ
Gerzmava, Khibla 492
ゲルソン
Gerson, Charlotte 491
ケルダー
Kelder, Peter 715
ゲルダ
Guerdat, Steve 542
ゲルダー
Gelder, Michael 487
ゲルダート
Geldart, William 487
ゲルタン
Guertin, Ghyslaine 543
ゲルダン
Guerdan, René 542
ケルタンギ
Kertanguy, Inès de 722
ケルツ
Kelts, Roland 717
ゲルツ
Gerz, Ferdinand 492
ゲルツェフ
Gertsev, Alexandr Victorovich 492
ゲルーデ
Geroudet, Tiffany 491
ゲルディオ
Gueludio, Kamara Ali 542

ゲルディムイラドフ
Geldimyradov, Khodzhamyrat 487
ケルテース
Kertész, Imre 722
ゲルテマーカー
Görtemaker, Heike B. 519
Görtemaker, Manfred 519
ケルデラン
Kerdellant, Christine 721
ゲルデンフイス
Geldenhuys, Quintin 487
ケルドセン
Kjeldsen, Soren 743
ケルトナー
Körtner, Ulrich H.J. 758
ゲルトナー
Geltner, David 488
ゲルドフ
Geldof, Bob 487
Geldof, Peaches 487
ゲルドム
Gerdom, Susanne 490
ケルトン
Kelton, W.David 717
ケルナー
Kellner, Robert A. 716
Kerner, Hans-Jürgen 721
Kerner, Max 721
Korner, Thomas William 757
ゲルーナス
Gelūnas, Arūnas 488
ゲルネ
Goerne, Matthias 508
ケルネッキー
Chernecky, Cynthia C. 253
ケルネン
Kernen, Bruno 721
ケルバー
Kerber, Angelique 721
Korber, Nils 757
ゲルバー
Gelber, Bruno-Leonardo 487
Gerber, Hans U. 490
ケルバーケル
Kerbaker, Andrea 721
ゲルバート
Gelbart, Larry 487
Gelbert, Marsh 487
ゲルハーヘル
Gerhaher, Christian 490
ゲルハルツ
Gerhards, Kaspars 490
ゲルハルト
Gerhard, Jürgen 490
Gerhardt, Yannick 490
Gerhart, John 490
ゲルハルドス
Gerhards, Kaspars 490
ケルビー
Kelby, Scott 715
ケルビン
Calvin 217
ケールブ
Calve, Caroline 217
ゲルブ
Gelb, Michael 487
Gelb, Peter 487
ゲルファント
Gelfand, Izrail Moiseevich 487
Gelfant, Blanche Housman 487
ゲルファンド
Gelfand, Izrail Moiseevich 487
ゲルフィ
Ghelfi, Brent 493
ケルブレ
Kaelble, Hartmut 695
ゲルマニカ
Germanika, Valeriya Gai 491
ゲルマノビッチ
Germanovich, Svetlana 491
ケールマン
Kehlmann, Daniel 714
ケルマン
Kellman, Denis 716
Kelman, Jerson 717
Kelman, Judith 717
Kelman, Marcy 717
ゲールマン
Guerman, Mikhail 543
ゲル・マン
Gell-Mann, Murray 488
ゲルマン
Gellman, Barton 488
Gellman, Marc 488
Gell-Mann, Murray 488
Gelman, Alexander 488
Gelman, Debra Levin 488
Gelman, Sheldon 488
German, Aleksei 491
German, Aleksei, Jr. 491
German, Arkadii Adol'fovich 491
Gherman, Andrei 493
Gherman, Natalia 493
Gherman, Simona 493
ゲルム
Gerum, Philippe 492
ケルメンディ
Kelmendi, Majlinda 717
Kelmendi, Nekibe 717
ゲルモン
Gelmon, Sherril B. 488
ケルラー
Kerler, Rolf 721
ゲルラク
Guerlac, Suzanne 543
ゲルラノス
Geroulanos, Pavlos 491
ゲルリッヒ
Gellrich, Martin 488
ゲルリヒ
Görlich, Ernst Joseph 519
ゲルレ
Guerlais, Gerald 543
ケルロック
Kerloc'h, Jean Pierre 721
ケルン
Kern, Christian 721
Kern, Étienne 721
Kern, Ludwik Jerzy 721
Kern, Peter 721
ゲルント
Gerndt, Alexander 491
ゲルンハルト
Gernhardt, Robert 491
ケレ
Quéré, David 1144
ゲレ
Gelle, Peter 487
Guelleh, Ismaïl Omar 542
ゲレイロ
Guerreiro, Raphael 543
ケレキ
Kereki, Federico 721
ケレク
Kérékou, Mathieu 721
Kerekou, Modeste 721
ケレクー
Kérékou, Mathieu 721
ケレシドゥ
Kelesidou, Anastasia 715
ゲレス
Gelles, David 488
Gelles, Richard J. 488
ケレダ
Quereda, Alejandra 1144
ゲレーター
Gelehrter, Thomas D. 487
ケレツ
Kerez, Christian 721
ゲレツガイアー
Gerezgiher, Joel 490
ゲレック
Gerek, William M. 490
Guelec, Tahir 542
ケレット
Kehret, Peg 715
Keret, Etgar 721
Kerrett, Etgar 722
ゲレトシュレーガー
Geretschläger, Robert 490
ケレマニ
Skelemani, Phandu 1309
ゲレメク
Geremek, Bronisław 490
ケレメティー
Kelemete, Senio 715
ケレメン
Kelemen, Pavel 715
ゲレル
Gerrell, Spike 491
ゲレーロ
Guerrero, Giancarlo 543
Guerrero, Miguel Angel 543
Guerrero, Tayron 543
Guerrero, Vladimir 543
ゲレロ
Guerrero, Belem 543
Guerrero, Carlos 543
Guerrero, Donald 543
Guerrero, Eddy 543
Guerrero, Vladimir 543
ゲレロ・ルイス
Guerrero Ruiz, Jaime 543
ゲレン
Geren, Bob 490
ケレンバーガー
Kellenberger, Jakob 715
ケーロ
Chelo, Alessandro 251
ゲロ＝ジャラベール
Guerreau-Jalabert, Anita 543
ケロッグ
Kellogg, Steven 716
ケロッド
Kerrod, Robin 722
ゲロート
Gehlot, Thaawar Chand 486
ケロフ
Kelov, Baimukhammet 717
ケーロール
Cayrol, Jean 238
ケロール
Cayrol, Jean 238
ゲロルド
Gerold, Ulrike 491
ケーン
Cain, Matt 214
Kahane, Tony 695
Kane, Gareth 701
Kane, Theresa E. 701
Kehn, Dan 714
Koehn, Daryl 751
Koehn, Nancy Fowler 751
ケン
Ken, Don 718
Ken, Ton 718
Ken, Ton Steven 718
ゲンキン
Genkin, Sergei Aleksandrovich 488
ゲング
Gäng, Marianne 476
ケン・グルフィー・ジュニア
Griffey, Ken, Jr. 535
ケンケット
Kien Keat, Koo 730
ケンケル
Kenkel, John 719
ゲンジ
Genge, Ngaire 488
ケンジェハヌリー
Kenzhekhanuly, Rauan 720
ケンジサリエフ
Kenzhisariev, Marat 720
ゲンシツカ
Gęsicka, Grażyna 492
ケンジャ
Kennja, Charles 720
ゲンシャー
Genscher, Hans-Dietrich 488
ケンジントン
Kensington, Ella 720
ゲンズ
Gens, Véronique 488
ゲンス＝カタニャン
Gens, I.IU. 488
ゲンズブール
Gainsbourg, Charlotte 471
ゲンスラー
Gaensler, Bryan M. 470
Gensler, Lianne S. 488
ゲンゼル
Genzel, Reinhard 489
ケンダール
Kendall, Barbara 718
Kendall, Gavin 718
ケンダル
Kendall, Beverley 718
Kendall, Florence Peterson 718
Kendall, Jackie 718
Kendall, R.T. 718
ケンタレ
Kenatale, Nemia 718
ゲンツ
Göncz, Árpád 513
Göncz, Kinga 513

ケンディ
Chendi, Patricia 252
ケンディッグ
Kendig, Bobbi 718
ケンデレシ
Kenderesi, Tamas 718
ケント
Kent, Alexander 720
Kent, Alison 720
Kent, Christopher 720
Kent, Derrin 720
Kent, George Cantine 720
Kent, Hannah 720
Kent, Jennifer 720
Kent, Jonathan 720
Kent, Julie 720
Kent, Margaret 720
Kent, Matt 720
Kent, Meg 720
Kent, Pauline 720
Kent, Peter 720
Kent, Steven L. 720
Kent, Stuart 720
ケンドー
Kendor, Losay 718
ケントリー
Kentley, Eric 720
ケンドリクス
Kendricks, Sam 719
ケンドリック
Kendrick, Alex 718
Kendrick, Anna 718
Kendrick, Howie 718
Kendrick, Ken 718
Kendrick, Kyle 718
Kendrick, Sharon 719
Kendrick, Stephen 719
ケンドリックス
Kendricks, Eric 719
Kendricks, Lance 719
Kendricks, Mychal 719
ケントリッジ
Kentridge, William 720
ケンドール
Kendall, Barbara 718
Kendall, Elisa F. 718
Kendall, Gerald I. 718
Kendall, Gideon 718
Kendall, John S. 718
Kendall, Stephen 718
Kendall, Wilfred 718
ケンドルー
Kendrew, J.C. 718
ケンナ
Kenna, Michael 719
ゲンヌ
Guène, Faïza 542
ケンバー
Kember, Jane 718
Kember, Peter 718
ケンパ
Kempa, Beata 718
ケンパー
Kemper, Hunter 718
Kemper, Steve 718
Kemper, Thomas 718
ケンパイネン
Kemppainen, Antti-Jussi 718
Kemppainen, Marko 718
ゲンバーグ
Genberg, Ira 488
ケンプ
Kemp, Anna 718
Kemp, Anthony E. 718
Kemp, Bryan J. 718
Kemp, David 718
Kemp, Gillian 718
Kemp, Hans 718
Kemp, Hugh P. 718
Kemp, Jack F. 718
Kemp, Kenny 718
Kemp, Martin 718
Kemp, Matt 718
Kemp, Moira 718
Kemp, Paul Stuart 718
Kemp, Peter 718
Kemp, Tony 718
Kemp, Will 718
Kemp, Wolfgang 718
Kempe, Frederick 718
Kempe, Ruth S. 718
Kempf, Freddy 718
Kempf, Hervé 718
Kempff, Frida 718
Kempff, Manfred 718
ケンプケン
Kämpken, Nicole 700
ケンプソーン
Kempthorne, Dirk 718
ケンプソン
Kempson, Rachel 718
ゲンプト
Gempt, Volker 488
ケンプトン
Kempton, Linda 718
ケンプナー
Kempner, Nan 718
ケンプフ
Kempf, Marc Oliver 718
ゲンブリス
Gembris, Heiner 488
ケンプレコス
Kemprecos, Paul 718
ケンペラー
Klemperer, David 745
ケンボイ
Kemboi, Ezekiel 718
ケンマニ
Khemmani, Pholsena 727
ゲンメル
Gemmel, Paul 488
Gemmel, Stefan 488
ケンリック
Kenrick, Andrew 720
Kenrick, Douglas T. 720
ケンワーシー
Kenworthy, Christopher 720
ケンワージー
Kenworthy, Gus 720

【コ】

コ
Go, So-young 506
Ko, Gon 749
Ko, Hye Jung 749
Ko, Jung-wook 749
Ko, Lydia 749
Ko, Soo 749
Ko, Un 749
Ko, Young-koo 749
Koh, Song Koo 751
コー
Caux, Jacqueline 238
Coe, Michael D. 273
Coe, Peter N. 273
Coe, Rodney 273
Coe, Sebastian 273
Corr, Christopher 291
Corr, O.Casey 291
Ge, Zhao-guang 485
Hsu, Shih-kai 630
Ke, Zai-shuo 712
Keo, Shiloh 720
Khaw, Boon Wan 727
Kho, Alvin T. 728
Ko, Chun-hsiung 749
Ko, Cindy 749
Ko, Giddens 749
Ko, Lydia 749
Koh, Tommy Thong Bee 751
Kohe, Jack Martin 751
ゴ
Ngo, Le Huy 1020
ゴー
Ge, Zhao-guang 485
Go, Frank M. 506
Goh, Cheng Liang 508
Goh, Chok Tong 508
Goh, Keng Swee 508
Goh, Liu Ying 508
Goh, V Shem 508
Gokongwei, John 508
Gove, Michael 522
コーア
Core, Cody 290
コア
Coerr, Eleanor 273
Cohat, Elisabeth 274
コアー
Corr, Andrea 291
Corr, Caroline 291
Corr, Jim 291
Corr, Sharon 291
Kohr, Knud 752
ゴーア
Gore, Frank 518
Gore, Lesley 518
ゴア
Gore, Albert, Jr. 518
Gore, Amanda 518
Gore, Delilah 518
Gore, Kristin 518
Gore, Leonid 518
Gore, Rick 519
Gore, Terrance 519
ゴアシリューター
Gorschluter, Jutta 519
ゴアズ
Gores, Joe 519
Gores, Tom 519
コアテス
Coates, Sebastian 272
コアラ
Koala, Aline 749
ゴアリク
Gorelick, Micha 519
コーアン
Cowan, Debra 297
コアン
Khoan, Vu 728
ゴアン
Goan, Annabel A. 506
コアンジオ
Kouandjio, Arie 760
Kouandjio, Cyrus 760
コアント
Cointot, Jean-Philippe 276
コーイ
Kooij, Rachel van 756
コイ
Nkoy, Boongo 1029
ゴーイー
Goewey, Don Joseph 508
コイヴ
Koivu, Saku 752
コイエ
Coye, José 298
コイケ
Koike, Masaki 752
ゴイコヴィッチ
Gojkovic, Jovan 508
ゴイコビッチ
Gojkovic, Jovan 508
コイシェ
Coixet, Isabel 276
コイジャイガノフ
Koizhaiganov, Nurlan 752
ゴイス
Geuss, Raymond 492
コイタ
Koita, Abdoulaye 752
Koïta, Amadou 752
ゴイティア・カバジェロ
Goitia Caballero, Javier Torres 508
ゴイティソーロ
Goytisolo, Juan 522
ゴイティソロ
Goytisolo, Juan 522
コイト
Koyt, Michel 762
ゴイトケ
Goydke, Tim 522
コイパー
Kuyper, Sjoerd 776
コイブ
Koivu, Saku 752
コイプ
Keup, Erwin J. 723
コイブランタ
Koivuranta, Anssi 752
コイムドドフ
Koimdodov, Kizidavlat 752
コイヤー
Kuijer, Guus 772
コイララ
Koirala, Girija Prasad 752
Koirala, Prakash 752
Koirala, Sushil 752
コイリー
Coiley, John 276
コイル
Coyle, Andrew 298
Coyle, Brian 298
Coyle, Brock 298
Coyle, Cleo 298
Coyle, Daniel 298
Coyle, Diane 298
Coyle, Frank P. 298
Coyle, Natalya 298
ゴイレン
Geulen, Eva 492
コイン
Coyne, Jerry A. 298
Coyne, Kevin P. 298
Coyne, Lisa W. 298

Coyne, Shawn T. 298
ゴーイング
Going, K.L. 508
ゴインズ
Goins, Ryan 508
コウ
Coe, Jeffrey T. 273
Ko, Dorothy 749
Koh, Hesung Chun 751
Kou, Lei 760
ゴウ
Gou, Terry 521
コヴァーチ
Kovács, Péter 761
コヴァチ
Kováč, Michal 761
Kovac, Niko 761
コヴァチェヴィク
Kovacevic, Jelena 761
コヴァチッチ
Kovacic, Mateo 761
コヴァーチュ
Kovács, Katalin 761
コヴァック
Kovac, Jeffrey 761
コヴァックス
Kovacs, Laszlo 761
Kovacs, Mark 761
コヴァッチ
Kovach, Bill 761
コヴァート
Covert, Jack 296
コヴァライネン
Kovalainen, Ritva 761
コヴァリョフ
Kovalyov, Igor 761
コヴァル
Koval, Kenneth J. 761
Koval, Maksym 761
Koval, Robin 761
コヴァルスキー
Kowalski, Jochen 762
Kowalski, Oldrich 762
コヴァルチク
Kowalczyk, August 762
コヴァレンコ
Kovalenko, Dima 761
コーヴァン
Cauvin, Patrick 238
コヴァン
Kovan, Dawne 761
コーヴィー
Covey, Stephen R. 296
コウイー
Cowie, Helen 297
コヴィー
Covey, Sean 296
Covey, Stephen M.R. 296
Covey, Stephen R. 296
ゴヴィエ
Govier, Katherine 522
コーヴィル
Coville, Andrea 296
Coville, Bruce 296
コーウィン
Corwin, Norman 293
Corwin, Tom 293
ゴウィン
Gowin, Jarosław 522
ゴーヴィンダン
Govindan, Ramaswamy 522
コヴィントン
Covington, Joey 296
コウヴィル
Coville, Bruce 296
コーウェル
Cowell, Cresida 297
Cowell, Simon 297
コヴェル
Kovel, Joel 761
ゴウェロ
Gowelo, Trasizio Thom 522
コーウェン
Cowens, Al 297
Keohane, Nannerl Overholser 720
コウエン
Cowen, Elle 297
コヴェンチューク
Kovenchuk, Georgiĭ Vasil'evich 761
コウォトコ
Kołodko, Grzegorz 753
コウカ
Coca, Imogene 273
コウカル
Koukal, Martin 760
Koukal, Petr 760
コウスリー
Causley, Charles 238
ゴウダ
Gowda, Sadananda 522
コウチ
Couch, Sue 294
コウチーニョ
Coutinho, Philippe 296
Coutinho, S.C. 296
コウチヤマ
Kochiyama, Yuri 750
コウティーノ
Coutinho, Alex G. 296
ゴウディン
Godin, Seth 507
コウト
Couto, Pedro Conceição 296
Kout, Jiří 760
コヴネイ
Coveney, James 296
コウノ
Kono, Mai 755
コウバーン
Cockburn, Cynthia 273
コウフォス
Koufos, Kosta 760
コウム
Koum, Jan 760
ゴウラー
Gawler, Ian 485
コーヴラール
Cauwelaert, Didier van 238
コヴラルト
Cauwelaert, Didier van 238
ゴウランエンリケ
Goulao-henrique, Raiza 521
コウリー
Corey, Gerald 290
Corey, Marianne Schneider 290
Cowley, Stewart 297
ゴウルストン
Goulston, Mark 521
コウルディ
Kourdi, Jeremy 760
ゴウルド
Gould, Patricia 521
ゴウルナー
Gollner, Adam 512
コウレス
Cowles, Libby 297
ゴウレット
Goullet, Tim 521
コウロスキー
Kowroski, Maria 762
コエ
Cauuet, Paul 238
コエチ
Koech, Haron 750
Koech, Isiah Kiplangat 750
Koech, Paul Kipsiele 750
コエナリエフ
Koyenaliyev, Turuspek 762
コエーリョ
Coelho, Luis Pedro 273
Coelho, Paulo 273
Coelho, Pedro Passos 273
コエリョ
Coelho, Hernâni 273
Coelho, Jorge 273
Coelho, Pedro Passos 273
コエリョ・フィリョ
Coelho Filho, Fernando 273
ゴエル
Goel, Vijay 507
コーエン
Coen, Ethan 273
Coen, Joel 273
Cohen, Aaron 274
Cohen, Abby Joseph 274
Cohen, Abraham E. 274
Cohen, Akiba 274
Cohen, Alan 274
Cohen, Albert Diamond 274
Cohen, Alex 274
Cohen, Alexandra 274
Cohen, Allan R. 274
Cohen, Andrew 274
Cohen, Andrew D. 274
Cohen, Andy 274
Cohen, Annabel J. 274
Cohen, Anthony Paul 274
Cohen, Ari Seth 274
Cohen, Barbara 274
Cohen, Barry M. 274
Cohen, Ben R. 274
Cohen, Betsy 274
Cohen, Calvin J. 274
Cohen, Carl M. 274
Cohen, Cathi 274
Cohen, Claudine 274
Cohen, Daniel 274
Cohen, David 274
Cohen, David S. 274
Cohen, Dean S. 274
Cohen, Don 274
Cohen, Donald 274
Cohen, Dov 274
Cohen, Edward M. 274
Cohen, Edward S. 274
Cohen, Eliot A. 274
Cohen, Frederick 274
Cohen, Gabriel 274
Cohen, Gene D. 274
Cohen, Gerald Allan 275
Cohen, Harold 275
Cohen, Herb 275
Cohen, I.Bernard 275
Cohen, Isaac 275
Cohen, Jared 275
Cohen, Jean-Louis 275
Cohen, Jon 275
Cohen, Judith A. 275
Cohen, Julie 275
Cohen, Juliet 275
Cohen, Larry 275
Cohen, Lawrence J. 275
Cohen, Leonard 275
Cohen, Martin 275
Cohen, Michael D. 275
Cohen, Mikal R. 275
Cohen, Mitch 275
Cohen, Morris 275
Cohen, Nathan 275
Cohen, Norman A. 275
Cohen, Oded 275
Cohen, Paula 275
Cohen, Paul Joseph 275
Cohen, Pete 275
Cohen, Randy 275
Cohen, Rob 275
Cohen, Robin 275
Cohen, Ronald D. 275
Cohen, Sacha Baron 275
Cohen, Samuel 275
Cohen, Sasha 275
Cohen, Sheldon 275
Cohen, Shoshanah 275
Cohen, Stanley 275
Cohen, Stephen P. 275
Cohen, Stephen Philip 275
Cohen, Stephen S. 275
Cohen, Steve 275
Cohen, Steven 275
Cohen, Susan Simon 275
Cohen, Suzanne Liberman 275
Cohen, Warren I. 275
Cohen, William A. 275
Cohen, William S. 275
Cowen, Tyler 297
Koehn, Daryl 751
コーエン・アダ
Cohen-Addad, S. 275
コーエン - グリーン
Cohen Greene, Cheryl T. 275
コーエン=ジャンカ
Cohen-Janca, Irène 275
コーエン=ソラル
Cohen-Solal, Annie 275
コーエンタヌージ
Cohen-Tannoudji, Claude Nessim 275
コーエンタヌジ
Cohen-Tannoudji, Claude Nessim 275
コーエンタノージュ
Cohen-Tannoudji, Claude Nessim 275
コエントラン
Coentrao, Fabio 273
コーエン・ポージー
Cohen-Posey, Kate 275
コーカ
Kóka, János 752
コーカー
Coker, Newton J. 276
コカ
Coca, Óscar 273
Khoka, Sadeq Hossain 728
Koka, Lefter 752

コカー
Coker, Jake 276
コカ・アンテサナ
Coca Antezana, Óscar 273
コカウリ
Kokauri, Ushangi 752
ゴーガティ
Gogarty, Jim 508
Gogarty, Paul 508
コカラニス
Kokkalanis, Vyron 752
コカリコ・ヤナ
Cocarico Yana, César 273
コカール
Coquart, Julie 289
コカル
Coquard, Bryan 289
コガワ
Kogawa, Joy 751
Kogawa, Joy Nozomi 751
コーガン
Cogan, Jim 274
Cogan, Robert 274
Coggan, Andrew 274
Corgan, Billy 290
Kogan, Judith 751
Kogan, Marcos 751
Kogan, Natasha 751
コガン
Coggan, Philip 274
ゴーガン
Gaughan, Richard 484
コーギー
Kogge, Michael 751
コギヌドゥロ
Kogui N'douro, Issifou 751
ゴギベリゼ
Gogiberidze, Sesili 508
コーキン
Corkin, Suzanne 291
コーキンス
Cokins, Gary 276
コーク
Cooke, David J. 286
Cork, Jack 291
Cork, John 291
Corke, Estelle 291
Koch, Bill 750
Koch, Charles 750
Koch, David 750
Koch, Edward 750
Koch, Jim 750
Koke, Stephen 752
コク
Cocu, Phillip 273
Kok, Riek Gai 752
Kokou, Lucien 752
Kwok, Aaron 777
コクー
Cocu, Phillip 273
ゴーク
Goeke, Reginald W. 507
ゴク
Ngoc, Ta Quang 1020
コグアシビリ
Koguashvili, Gogi 751
コグイ・ヌドゥロ
Kogui N'douro, Issifou 751
コクジ
Koczi, Flavius 750
ゴグシェリジェ
Gogshelidze, George 508
ゴグシェリゼ
Gogshelidze, George 508
コグズウェル
Cogswell, David 274
Cogswell, Jeff 274
Cogswell, Theodore R. 274
コクセター
Coxeter, Harold Scott Macdonald 298
コクソン
Coxon, Graham 298
コグデル
Cogdell, Corey 274
コクバーン
Cockburn, Karen 273
コークホーン
Colquhoun, Arjen 280
コクラン
Cochran, David Lee 273
Cochran, Gregory 273
Cochran, Johnnie L., Jr. 273
Cochran, Larry 273
Cochran, Robert 273
Cochrane, Jenny 273
Cochrane, Ryan 273
Coquelin, Francis 289
Koechlin, Lionel 750
Koechlin, Philippe 751
コグラン
Coghlan, Chris 274
Coughlan, Anne T. 295
コークリー
Coakley, Jay J. 272
コグリアニーズ
Coglianese, Cary 274
コーグリン
Coughlin, Natalie 295
コクリン
Coughlin, Con 295
コグリン
Coughlin, Jack 295
Coughlin, Natalie 295
Coughlin, Patricia 295
ゴクール
Gokhool, Dharambeer 508
ゴグル
Gógl, Árpád 508
ゴクレール
Gauckler, Geneviève 484
コクレーン
Cochrane, Ryan 273
コグレンボ
Kogréngbo, Gilbert 751
コケ
Coke 276
Koke 752
Koke, Tatjana 752
コケニ
Kökény, Roland 752
コケル
Cockell, Charles 273
コー・コー
Ko Ko 752
ココ
Koko, Abderaman 752
Koko, Georgette 752
コゴ
Kogo, Micah 751
コー・コー・ウー
Ko Ko Oo 752
ココシュ
Cocos, Roxana Daniela 273
ココス
Cocos, Roxana Daniela 273
ココスコフ
Kokoskov, Igor 752
ココット
Kockott, Rory 750
ココディス
Kokkodis, Ioannis 752
ゴコマ王子
Prince Gcokoma 485
ゴゴラゼ
Gogoladze, Khatuna 508
コーコラン
Corcoran, Barbara Ann 289
Corcoran, Judy 289
Corcoran, Kevin J. 289
Corcoran, Louise 290
Corcoran, Neil 290
ココルウェ
Kokorwe, Gladys 752
ココレフ
Kokorev, Boris 752
Kokorev, Valery I. 752
コーゴン
Kogon, Kory 751
ココンヤンギ
Kokonyangi, Joseph 752
コーサー
Kosar, Scott 758
コーザ
Khoza, Arthur 729
コザー
Kosar, Kevin R. 758
ゴサイビ
al-Gosaibi, Ghazi bin Abdulrahman 520
al-Gosaibi, Khalid bin Muhammad 520
コーザイン
Corzine, Jon Stevens 293
コザク
Kozák, Danuta 762
Kozak, Dmitry N. 762
Kozak, Volodymyr 762
コザクーマルクリ
Kozakou Markoullis, Erato 762
コサチュク
Kozaczuk, Malgorzata 762
コザック
Kozák, Danuta 762
Kozak, Harley Jane 762
Kulczak, Theresa Ann 772
コザート
Cosart, Jarred 293
Cozart, Zack 298
コザド
Cozad, Amy 298
ゴーサナンダ
Ghosananda 494
コサラ
Kosara, Robert 758
ゴーサール
Goossaert, Vincent 517
コサルチウク
Cosarciuc, Valeriu 293
ゴザン
Gozan, Kokou 522
ゴーサンス
Goossens, Philippe 517
コージー
Causey, Jennifer 238
コシ
Kossi, Etienne 759
コジアス
Kotzias, Nikos 760
コジアヌ
Cogianu, Roxana 274
コシアン
Kocian, Madison 750
コシウスコモリゼ
Kosciuskomorizet, Nathalie 758
ゴーシェ
Gauchet, Marcel 484
ゴジェク
Gozgec, Batuhan 522
コジェナー
Kožená, Magdalena 762
コシエニウスキー
Kocieniewski, David 750
コジェニョフスキ
Korzeniowski, Pawel 758
Korzeniowski, Robert 758
ゴシェハ
Ghosheh, Samir 494
ゴーシェ・ヒル
Gausche-Hill, Marianne 484
ゴシェフ
Gošev, Petar 520
ゴシエフスキ
Gosiewski, Przemysław 520
コシェルニー
Koscielny, Laurent 758
コジェンコワ
Kozhenkova, Anastasiya 762
コジオル・マックレーン
Koziol-McLain, Jane 762
コシガ
Cossiga, Francesco 293
コーシキン
Koshkin, Anatolii 758
コシク
Kosik, Kenneth S. 758
コジク
Kozik, Leonid P. 762
コシス
Koshis, Nicos 758
コジチ
Kozich, Alina 762
コーシック
Kaushik, Avinash 710
Koushik, Srinivas 760
コシッチ
Cosic, Uros 293
コシット
Kosit, Panpiemras 758
コーシーニ
Corsini, Raymond J. 292
コシニァクカミシュ
Kosiniak-kamysz, Władysław 758
コシニアクカミシュ
Kosiniak-kamysz, Władysław 758
コシネツ
Kosinets, Aleksandr N. 758
コジネッツ

Kozinets, Robert V. 762
コシバ
Koshiba, Fritz 758
コシベラ
Kossi-bella, Denis 759
コジマ
Kojima, Yuzuru 752
コシモフ
Kosimov, Kosim 758
ゴジャシビリ
Gogiashvili, Mirian 508
コジャソ
Collazo, William 278
コジャナ
Kodiyana, Amina 750
コシャバ
Khoshaba, Deborah M. 728
ゴーシャミ
Goswami, Joy 520
コジャラ
Kozhara, Leonid 762
ゴシャール
Ghoshal, Sumantra 494
ゴーシュ
Ghosh, Amitav 494
Ghosh, Debasish 494
Ghosh, Dilip 494
Ghosh, Sankha 494
Ghosh, Soumyajit 494
Gosche, Mark 520
コジュヴァル
Cogeval, Guy 274
コジュキン
Kozhukhin, Denis 762
ゴシュケ
Goschke, Julia 520
コシュトゥニツァ
Koštunica, Vojislav 759
コシュトゥニッツァ
Koštunica, Vojislav 759
ゴシュトニ
Gosztonyi, Alexsander 520
ゴシュトニー
Gosztony, Peter 520
コシュトニツァ
Koštunica, Vojislav 759
コシュトニツア
Koštunica, Vojislav 759
コジュバル
Cogeval, Guy 274
コシュマン
Koschmann, J.Victor 758
ゴーシュロン
Gaucheron, Jacques H. 484
コジョ
Codjo, Dossou Simplice 273
Kodjo, Agbeyome 750
コジョカル
Cojocaru, Alina 276
コジョシェフ
Kozhoshev, Arzybek 762
コーション
Cauchon, Rose 237
コション
Cauchon, Martin 237
ゴーション
Gauchon, Pascal 484
コシール
Kosir, Dejan 758
Kosir, Zan 758
コジレフ＝ルファー
Kozyreff-Rouffart, Chantal 762
コジロフ
Kodirov, Abdurakhmon 750
コージン
Corzine, Jon Stevens 293
ゴーシン
Gorshin, Frank 519
コシンズ
Cossins, Peter 293
コシンスキー
Kosinski, Joseph 758
Kosynskyy, Dmytro 759
コース
Causse, Jean-Gabriel 238
Coase, Ronald 272
Kors, Michael 758
Korth, Hank 758
コーズ
Coase, Ronald 272
コス
Cosse, Emmanuelle 293
Koss, Johann Olav 759
Koss, Marry P. 759
Koss, Robert S. 759
ゴース
Gause, Quentin 484
ゴーズ
Gause, F.Gregory, Ⅲ 484
Godes, David 507
Gose, Anthony 520
ゴス
Goss, Porter J. 520
Goss, Theodora 520
ゴズィー
Gauzy, Simon 484
コズィン
Kozinn, Allan 762
ゴーズウィッシュ
Gosewisch, Tuffy 520
コースガード
Korsgaard, Christine Marion 758
コスキ
Koski, Markku 758
コスキネン
Koskinen, Jari 758
Koskinen, Johannes 758
コスキパー
Koskipää, Ritva 758
コスグレーヴ
Cosgrave, Bronwyn 293
コスグレーブ
Cosgrave, Bronwyn 293
コスグロー
Kosglow, Lisa 758
コスグローヴ
Cosgrove, Denis E. 293
コスグロウ
Cosgrow, Wallace 293
コスグローブ
Cosgrov, Brian 293
Cosgrove, Clayton 293
Cosgrove, Denis E. 293
Cosgrove, Peter 293
コズグローブ
Cosgrove, Ellen Mary 293
コスゲイ
Kosgey, Felix 758
Kosgey, Henry 758
Kosgey, Sally 758
コースゴー
Korsgaard, Ove 758
ゴスコウスキー
Gostkowski, Stephen 520
コスース
Kosuth, Joseph 759
コスス
Kosuth, Joseph 759
コスタ
Costa, Alberto 293
Costa, Andrea 293
Costa, António 293
Costa, Brenda 293
Costa, Carlos 293
Costa, Desidério da Graça Veríssimo da 293
Costa, Diego 293
Costa, Eduardo 293
Costa, Eduardo Moreira da 293
Costa, Enrico 293
Costa, Filippo 293
Costa, Francesco 293
Costa, Gal 293
Costa, Gino 293
Costa, Hélio 293
Costa, Humberto 293
Costa, Januaria Tavares Silva Moreira 293
Costa, J.M. 293
Costa, João 293
Costa, Jose 293
Costa, Marianne 293
Costa, Monte 293
Costa, Nicoletta 293
Costa, Pedro 293
Costa, Rebecca D. 293
Costa, Susana 293
Costa, Thomas 293
コスター
Koster, Joyce 759
Koster, Raph 759
コスタ・ガヴラス
Costa-Gavras, Constantin 293
コスタ・ガブラス
Costa-Gavras, Constantin 293
コスタッツァ
Costazza, Chiara 294
コスタデカルバリョ
Costa De Carvalho, Maria de Cristo Hilario Dos Santos Raposo 293
コスタデボアエスペランサ
Costa De Boa Esperanca, Deolindo 293
コスタビ
Kostabi, Mark 759
コスタリッチ
Kostelić, Ivica 759
コースター・ルーカス
Coster-Lucas, Jacqueline 294
コスタンザ
Costanza, Stephen 294
コスタンゾ
Costanzo, Charlene 294
Costanzo, Linda S. 294
コスタンティーニ
Costantini, Costanzo 294
ゴスチャ
Goscha, Richard Joseph 520
コスチュク
Kostyuk, Aleksandr 759
コスチュチェンコ
Kostyuchenko, Leonid 759
コスチン
Kostin, Igor F. 759
コステ
Coste, Joanne Koenig 294
コステア
Costea, Claudia-Ana 294
コスティ
Kosti, Manibe 759
コスティウチャク
Kostiuczyk, Nadiezda 759
コスティジェン
Kostigen, Thomas 759
ゴスティック
Gostick, Adrian Robert 520
コスティッチ
Kostic, Filip 759
コスティン
Costin, Carolyn 294
コステキ＝ショー
Kostecki-Shaw, Jenny Sue 759
コステスク
Costescu, Dan Marian 294
コステツキー
Kostecký, Lubomír 759
コステビッチ
Kostevych, Olena 759
コステュック
Kostyuk, Lena 759
コステリッチ
Kostelić, Ivica 759
Kostelić, Janica 759
コステリッツ
Kostelić, Ivica 759
Kostelić, Janica 759
コステル
Coster, Theo 294
コステールス
Costales, Bryan 294
コステレツキー
Kostelecky, David 759
コステロ
Costello, Elvis 294
Costello, Joan 294
Costello, Matt 294
Costello, Peter 294
Costello, Sarah 294
Costello, Tim 294
Costelloe, Marina 294
ゴスデン
Gosden, Roger 520
コステンコ
Kostenko, Yurii 759
コスト
Coste, Daniel 294
ゴースト
Gorst, Martin 519
コストヴァ
Kostova, Elizabeth 759
コストゥマル
Costemalle, Bruno 294
コストナー
Kostner, Carolina 759
Kostner, Isolde 759
コストバ
Kostova, Elizabeth 759
コストフ
Kostov, Borislav 759

Kostov, Hari 759
Kostov, Ivan 759
Kostov, Pavle 759
コストマロフ
Kostomarov, Pavel 759
Kostomarov, Roman 759
コストリーホワイト
Costley-white, Roberto 294
コストロ
Costolo, Dick 294
コストロフ
Kostrov, P.I. 759
コストワ
Kostova, Boyanka 759
コスナー
Costner, Kevin 294
コズニック
Kosnik, Clare Madott 758
コスノー
Cosneau, Olivia 293
コスパー
Cosper, Darcy 293
ゴスパー
Gosper, Kevan 520
コスバエフ
Kosubayev, Yesetzhan 759
コスビー
Cosby, Bill 293
コズマ
Cosma, Viorel 293
Cozma, Artur 298
Kozma, Bob 762
コースマイヤー
Korsmeyer, Carolyn 758
コズマトカ
Kosmatka, Ted 758
コスマトス
Cosmatos, George Pan 293
コズマン
Cosman, Madeleine Pelner 293
ゴースマン
Gausman, Kevin 484
ゴスマン
Gosman, Fred G. 520
コスムー
Kosmo, Jorgen 758
コズムス
Kozmus, Primož 762
コズムンカ
Cozmâncă, Octav 298
コスモスキー
Kosmoski, Jon 758
コースラ
Khosla, Vinod 728
コズラ
Khosla, Romi 728
ゴズラン
Ghozland, F. 494
Ghozland, Freddy 494
コーズリー
Causley, Charles Stanley 238
コスリー
Cossery, Albert 293
コズリコバ
Kozlikova, Lada 762
コスリナ
Kosulina, Liudmila Gennad'evna 759
コスリン
Kosslyn, Stephen Michael 759
ゴスリン
Gosling, James 520
Gosselin, Phil 520
ゴスリング
Gosling, Dan 520
Gosling, John 520
Gosling, Jonathan 520
Gosling, Patricia 520
ゴズリング
Gosling, Paula 520
Gosling, Sam 520
Gosling, Sharon 520
コースレイ
Cawthray, Richard 238
コズロウスキス
Kozlovskis, Rihards 762
コスロカヴァール
Khosrokhavar, Farhad 728
コズロバ
Kozlova, Anna 762
コズロフ
Kozlov, Andrei A. 762
Kozlov, Petr A. 762
コズロフスキス
Kozlovskis, Rihards 762
コースロン
Corthron, Kia 293
コスロン
Cosseron, Serge 293
ゴーズワース
Gawesworth, Simon 485
ゴスワミ
Goswami, Amit 520
Goswami, Usha 520
コズン
Kozun, Wayne 762
ゴスン
Ghosn, Fayez 494
コセ
Coce, María Victoria 273
ゴセージ
Gossage, Rich 520
ゴーゼラニー
Gorzelanny, Tom 520
コセリウ
Coseriu, Eugenio 293
ゴーセール
Goossaert, Vincent 517
コゼルスカフェンクロバ
Kozelska Fenclova, Veronika 762
ゴーセルフ
Gothelf, Jeff 520
ゴーセン
Goossens, Dennis 517
コセンサ・ヒメネス
Cosenza Jiménez, Luis 293
コーゼンズ
Cozens, Sheila 298
コゼンティーノ
Cosentino, Marc 293
コーソ
Corso, Gregory Nunzio 292
コソウスキー
Kosowsky, Joshua M. 758
コーゾック
Kosog, Simone 758
コソフ
Kossoff, David 759
コソラーポフ
Kosolapov, Richard Ivanovich 758
コソラポフ
Kosolapov, Richard Ivanovich 758
コゾリーノ
Cozolino, Louis 298
コソル
Kosor, Jadranka 758
コーソーン
Cawthorn, Rachel 238
コーソン
Cawson, Pat 238
ゴソン
Gozun, Elisea 522
コーター
Koetter, Dirk 751
コーダ
Coda, Andrea 273
コーダー
Corder, Zizou 290
ゴーダ
Gowda, Vikas 522
コタイエ
Kotaye, Moïse 759
ゴタス
Gotaas, Thor 520
コタゾ
Kotazo, André Toby 759
コタック
Kotak, Uday 759
コータッツィ
Cortazzi, Hugh 292
コータッド
Courtad, Jeanette Flannery 296
ゴータット
Gortat, Marcin 519
ゴダッド
Goddard, J. 507
ゴダート
Goddard, H.Wallace 506
Goddart, Michael 507
ゴダード
Goddard, Clive 506
Goddard, Hester 506
Goddard, Oliver 507
Goddard, Phillip 507
Goddard, Robert 507
ゴダナ
Godana, Bonaya 506
コタニスキ
Kotański, Wiesław Roman 759
コダバクシ
Khodabakhshi, Mahdi 728
コダマ
Kodama, María 750
ゴータム
Gautam, Bamdev 484
ゴダラ
Godara, Hemant 506
ゴダール
Godard, Alain 506
Godard, Jean-Luc 506
Goddar, Heinz 506
Goddard, Andrew W. 506
コタン
Cotan, Antonio 294
ゴーダン
Gaudin, Christian 484
Gaudin, Claire 484
Gordhan, Pravin Jamnadas 517
ゴダン
Godin, Nicolas 507
コタンスキ
Kotański, Wiesław Roman 759
コーチ
Couch, Greg 294
Koech, John 750
コチ
Koci, Marta 750
Koci, Vladan 750
ゴーチ
Gauch, Patricia Lee 484
ゴーチエ
Gauthier, Alain 484
Gauthier, Xavière 484
ゴチェ
Goche, Nicholas 506
コチェツコヴァ
Kochetkova, Alla A. 750
ゴチエフ
Gochyev, Taganmyrat 506
ゴチェフスキ
Gottschewski, Hermann 521
ゴーチェル
Gorchels, Linda 517
コチシュ
Kocsis, Károly 750
Kocsis, Zoltán 750
コチネフ
Kochnev, Gerasim 750
コチャクチンスキー
Kozaczynski, Wojtek 762
ゴチャシビリ
Gochashvili, Besarion 506
コチャノワ
Kochanova, Natalia I. 750
コーチヤマ
Kochiyama, Yuri 750
コチヤマ
Kochiyama, Yuri 750
コチャリヤン
Kocharian, Robert 750
コチャール
Kochhar, Chanda 750
コーチャン
Kochan, Stephen G. 750
Kotchian, Archibold Carl 759
コチュ
Koç, Atilla 750
ゴチュイエフ
Gochyev, Annamuhammet 506
コチュガ
Kotyuga, Anzhelika 760
ゴー・チョクトン
Goh, Chok Tong 508
コーツ
Coates, Dorothy Love 272
Coates, John 272
Coates, Sammie 272
コーツィー
Coetzee, Felix 274
コツィ
Coetzee, J.M. 274
コツィアン
Kotzian, Ditte 760
ゴツィック
Godzik, Maren 507

コツウィンクル
Kotzwinkle, William 760
コーツェ
Coetzee, J.M. 274
コツォウレク
Kocourek, Martin 750
コッカ
Kocka, Jürgen 750
コッカー
Cocker, James Cecil 273
Cocker, Joe 273
コッカレル
Cockerell, Lee 273
コッキナキ
Kokkinaki, Flora 752
コッキナキス
Kokkinakis, Thanasi 752
コック
Cook, Minnie 286
Cook, Susan 286
Koch, Andrew K. 750
Koch, Antonio 750
Koch, julia 750
Kok, Wim 752
Kwok, Aaron 777
コッグ
Kogge, Michael 751
コッククロフト
Cockcroft, Jason 273
コックス
Cox, Alan J. 297
Cox, Archibald 297
Cox, Barbara 297
Cox, Bobby 297
Cox, Brad J. 297
Cox, Brian 297
Cox, Britteny 297
Cox, Charlie 297
Cox, Christopher 297
Cox, C.Jay 297
Cox, Danny 297
Cox, David 297
Cox, David A. 297
Cox, Eleanor Worthington 297
Cox, Fletcher 297
Cox, Greg 297
Cox, Harvey 297
Cox, Howard 297
Cox, J'den 297
Cox, Jeff 297
Cox, Jennifer 297
Cox, Jill 297
Cox, Jo 297
Cox, John 297
Cox, John D. 297
Cox, Lionel 297
Cox, Lynne 297
Cox, Maggie 297
Cox, Michael 297
Cox, Michael M. 297
Cox, Michele 297
Cox, Morgan 297
Cox, Neil 297
Cox, P.A. 297
Cox, Paul 297, 298
Cox, Paul Alan 298
Cox, Perrish 298
Cox, Peter 298
Cox, Quinn 298
Cox, Rakim 298
Cox, Robert 298
Cox, Rosamund Kidman 298
Cox, Simon 298
Cox, Steve 298
Cox, Sue 298
Cox, Tom 298
Cox, Tracey 298
Cox, Trevor J. 298
Coxe, Paula Peisner 298
Kox, Killer Karl 762
コッグス
Kogge, Michael 751
コック・スターキー
Cock-Starkey, Claire 273
コッグヒル
Coghill, Roger 274
コッククラル＝キング
Cockrall-King, Jennifer 273
コックラン
Cockran, Theiren 273
コックリル
Cockrill, Pauline 273
コックレル
Cockrell, Alan 273
Cockrell, Ross 273
コック・ロナ
Kok Rona, James 752
コッケルハム
Cockerham, William C. 273
コッコ
Cocco, Gaetano 273
Kokko, Yrjo 752
コッサード
Caussade, Jean-Pierre de 238
コッシ
Kossi, Etienne 759
ゴッジ
Goggi, Gianluigi 508
ゴッシフ
Godsiff, Roger Duncan 507
コッシュ
Khosh, Mary 728
ゴッシュ
Gosch, Florian 520
ゴッス
Goss, Mimi 520
コッセ
Cosse, Carolina 293
ゴッセージ
Gossage, Rich 520
コッセンス
Kossens, Michael 759
コッソン
Kosson, David S. 759
コッタ
Cotta, Elena 294
コッター
Cotter, Kevin 294
Cotter, Vern 294
Koetter, Fred 751
Kotter, John P. 760
コッタス
Kottas, Dimitris 760
ゴッダード
Goddard, Angela 506
Goddard, Drew 506
Goddard, James 507
コッタリル
Cotterill, Colin 294
コッチ
Koch, Edward Irving 750
Koch, Matt 750
Koch, Richard 750
Koch, Roberto 750
ゴッチ
Gotch, Karl 520
ゴッチャーク
Gottschalk, Ben 520
コッツ
Cotts, David G. 294
ゴッツ
Götz, Veruschka 521
コッツァ
Cotza, Elio 294
コッツィ
Cozzi, Luigi 298
コッツウィンクル
Kotzwinkle, William 760
コッツェ
Kotze, Hildegard von 760
Kotzé, Theuns 760
コッツェイ
Kotsay, Mark 760
ゴッツェン
Gotzen, Frank 521
コッツェンバーグ
Kotsenburg, Sage 760
コッツォリーノ
Cozzolino, Angelo 298
Cozzolino, Carmine 298
ゴッツフレッセン
Godtfredsen, Nuka K. 507
ゴッティ
Gotti, John 520
コッティンガム
Cottingham, W.Noel 294
ゴッテスディーナー
Gottesdiener, Ellen 520
ゴッテスフェルド
Gottesfeld, Jeff 520
ゴッテスマン
Gottesman, David 520
Gottesman, Irving 520
ゴッデル
Goeddel, Erik 507
Goeddel, Tyler 507
コット
Cott, Jonathan 294
Cotte, Olivier 294
Cotte, Pascal 294
Kot, Maciej 759
Kott, Jan 760
ゴット
Got, Yves 520
Gott, Barry 520
Gott, J.Richard 520
Gott, Trevor 520
ゴットヴァルト
Gottwald, Felix 521
コットグローヴ
Cotgrove, Mark'Snowboy' 294
ゴットシス
Gotsis, Adam 520
ゴットシャル
Gottschall, Jonathan 520
Gottschall, Karin 521
ゴッドセイ
Godsey, George 507
ゴッドソン
Godson, Dale L. 507
ゴッドバー
Godber, Tim 506
ゴッドバーセン
Godbersen, Anna 506
ゴットバルト
Gottwald, Peter 521
ゴッドフリー
Godfrey, Bob 507
Godfrey, Jason 507
ゴッドフリィ
Godfrey, A.Blanton 507
ゴットフリート
Gottfried, Heidi 520
ゴッドフレイ
Godfrey, Jan 507
Godfrey, Jason 507
ゴットフレッドセン
Godtfredsen, John 507
ゴットフレッドソン
Gottfredson, Floyd 520
ゴッドマニス
Godmanis, Ivars 507
コットマン
Kottman, Michal 760
ゴットマン
Gottman, John Mordechai 520
ゴッドマン
Godman, David 507
コットム
Cottom, Brandon 294
ゴットリー
Gottry, Steven R. 520
ゴッドリー
Godley, Zack 507
ゴットリーブ
Gottlieb, Annie 520
Gottlieb, Benjamin H. 520
Gottlieb, Daniel 520
Gottlieb, Laurie N. 520
Gottlieb, Michael A. 520
Gottlieb, William 520
ゴットリーブ＝ウォーカー
Gottlieb-Walker, Kim 520
コットリル
Cottrill, Torah 294
コットレ
Cottret, Bernard 294
コットレル
Cotterell, Arthur 294
Cottrell, David 294
Cottrell, William 294
Piller Cottrer, Pietro 1112
コットレル・ボイス
Cottrell Boyce, Frank 294
ゴッドロビッチ
Godlovitch, Glenys 507
ゴットワルト
Gottwald, Felix 521
ゴットワルド
Gottwald, Felix 521
コットン
Cotton, Charlotte 294
Cotton, C.M. 294
Cotton, Jharel 294
Cotton, Katie 294
Cotton, Ronald 294
コッハー
Kocher, Ethel 750
コッパー
Copper, Basil 289
Kopper, Lisa 756
コッパーマン
Copperman, E.J. 289
ゴッビ
Gobbi, Massimo 506
コッヒル

Coghill, Roger 274
コッピング
Copping, Peter 289
コッピンジャー
Coppinger, Raymond 289
コッブ
Cobb, Grace 272
Cobb, James Henry 272
Cobb, Nancy 272
Cobb, Rebecca 272
コップ
Copp, Martha A. 289
Kopp, P.E. 756
Kopp, Wendy 756
ゴッフェン
Goffen, Rona 508
コップス
Copps, Sheila 289
Kobs, Karsten 750
コップランド
Copeland, Mary Ellen 288
コップリッチ
Coprich, Marshaun 289
コッペ
Coppee, Francois Ferdinand Joacim 289
Koppe, Susanne 756
コッペル
Koeppel, Dan 751
ゴッベル
Gobbell, John J. 506
コッペルマン
Koppelman, Joel M. 756
コッペン
Koppens, Judith 756
コッホ
Koch, Christof 750
Koch, Ebba 750
Koch, Edward Irving 750
Koch, Hans-Joachim 750
Koch, Herman 750
Koch, Klaus 750
Koch, Marco 750
Koch, Marianne 750
Koch, Martin 750
Koch, Matthias 750
ゴッホ
Gogh, Theo Van 508
ゴッボ
Ngcobo, Lauretta 1020
コッポラ
Coppola, Eleanor 289
Coppola, Francis Ford 289
Coppola, Sofia 289
コッポリーノ
Coppolino, Andrea 289
コッラ
Colla, Enrico 278
コッリーナ
Collina, Pierluigi 278
コーテ
Cote, Kaizon 294
Kothe, Hans W. 759
コテ
Côté, Geneviève 294
Kote, Zakalia 759
コテー
Kauter, Fabian 710
ゴーテ
Gothe, Alexander 520
ゴデ
Gaude, Laurent 484
Godet, Damien 507
コーディ
Coady, Margaret 272
Cordy, Michael 290
コティ
Koty, Lambert 760
コディ
Cody, Diabro 273
ゴーティ
Gauthier, Marie Bénédicte 484
ゴーディ
Godey, John 507
Gordy, Graham 518
Gordy, Terry 518
ゴディ
Gordy, Terry 518
ゴーティエ
Gauthier, Ursula 484
ゴティエ
Gauthier, Jacques 484
Gotye 521
Gouthier, Leslie 522
ゴディオ
Goddio, Franck 507
コーディナ
Cordina, Joseph 290
ゴーディマ
Gordimer, Nadine 517
ゴーディマー
Gordimer, Nadine 517
コティヤール
Cotillard, Marion 294
ゴーディン
Godin, Seth 507
Gordin, Michael D. 517
ゴディン
Godin, Diego 507
Godin, Nicolas 507
Godin, Seth 507
ゴーディング
Gauding, Madonna 484
コディントン
Coddington, Grace 273
コーテス
Coates, Timothy J. 272
コーデス
Cordes, Joseph J. 290
コーデスタニ
Kordestani, Omid 757
コーデスマン
Cordesman, Anthony H. 290
ゴデツ・シュミット
Godec-Schmidt, Jelka 507
コーテナール
Kortenaar, Neil Ten 758
コーデュロイ
Corderoy, Tracey 290
コデリ
Kodheli, Mimi 750
ゴデリス
Goddeeris, John H. 507
コーデル
Cordell, Bruce R. 290
Cordell, Larry 290
Cordell, Matthew 290
Cordell, Ryan 290
コデール
Coderre, Denis 273
コデル
Codell, Esmé Raji 273
ゴデール
Godel, Armen 507
ゴデル
Godel, Armen 507
コデルク
Coderch, Anna Maria 273
コーデロ
Cordero, Franchy 290
Cordero, Jimmy 290
ゴーデロック
Goudelock, Andrew 521
コーテン
Korten, David 758
Korten, David C. 758
コーデン
Corden, James 290
コート
Coat, Janik 272
Cort, Ben 292
Cort, Errol 292
Cort, John 292
Cort, Margaret 292
Côté, Denis 294
Cote, François 294
Court, Hazel 295
Court, Richard Fairfax 296
Court, Sibella 296
Couto, C.Guillermo 296
Koht, Lars 752
コト
Coto, Rodolfo 294
Koto, Bernard 759
Koto, Sunia 760
ゴトー
Goto, Hiromi 520
ゴド
Godo, Anila 507
ゴドー
Godeau, Eric 507
Godeau, Vincent 507
Godeaux, Jean 507
ゴドイ
Godoy, Rody Adán 507
Godoy, Salvador 507
Godoy, Victor Hugo 507
ゴドイ・デ・ルビン
Godoy de Rubin, Gloria Beatriz 507
ゴトウ
Goto, Kelly 520
コトヴァル
Kotval, Jeroo 760
コトヴィチ
Kotovich, Tat'iana V. 760
ゴドゥイユ
Gaudeuille, Isabelle 484
ゴドウィン
Godwin, Gail 507
Godwin, Jack 507
Godwin, Jane 507
Godwin, Joscelyn 507
Godwin, Laura 507
Godwin, Malcolm 507
Godwin, Marshall 507
コードウェル
Caudwell, Sarah 237
コードゥライ
Courdray, Marlene 295
ゴドゥンコ
Godunko, Natalia 507
コトキン
Kotkin, Joel 759
コートショー
Kotrschal, Kurt 760
コトチュウォー
Kotschwar, Barbara 760
コードック
Cordock, Richard Parkes 290
コドック
Kodock, Augustin-Frédérick 750
コートナー
Cortner, Hanna 293
コトナー
Cotoner, Kate 294
コートナル
Courtnall, Roy 296
コートニー
Courtenay, Molly 296
Courtenay, Tom 296
Courtney, Dave 296
Courtney, Hugh G. 296
Courtney, Mark E. 296
Courtney, Michael 296
コートニー＝クラーク
Courtney-Clarke, Margaret 296
コートニー・ティックル
Courtney-Tickle, Jessica 296
コトネー
Courtenay, Eamon 296
コートネイ
Courtenay, Eamon 296
Courtenay, Tom 296
コードバ
Cordoba, Allen 290
コートバウアー
Kothbauer, Max 759
ゴードハマー
Gordhamer, Soren 517
ゴトビ
Ghotbi, Afshin 494
ゴドフリー
Godfrey, Bob 507
Godfrey, Laurence 507
Godfrey, Tony 507
ゴドフレイ
Godfrey, Jayne Maree 507
ゴドフロイ
Godefroy, Cristian 507
ゴドフロワ
Godefroid, Sebastien 507
Godefroy, Regine 507
ゴドマニス
Godmanis, Ivars 507
コトラー
Cotler, Amy 294
Cotler, Emily 294
Cotler, Irwin 294
Kotler, Milton 759
Kotler, Neil G. 759
Kotler, Philip 759
Kotler, Steven 759
Kottler, Jeffrey A. 760
ゴドラ
Gaudrat, Marie-Agnès 484
コートライト
Courtwright, David T. 296
コトラージョヴァー
Kotlarova, Hana 759
ゴートラン
Gautrand, Jean-Claude 484
ゴドリエ
Godelier, Maurice 507

コトリコフ
Kotlikoff, Laurence J. 759
コドルコフスキー
Khodorkovskii, Mikhail Borisovich 728
コートールド
Courtauld, Sarah 296
コードレイ
Cordray, Terrie L. 290
ゴドレジ
Godrej, Adi 507
ゴドレージュ
Godrej, Dinyar 507
コトレル
Cottrell, Sue 294
Cottrell, William 294
ゴドロ
Gaudreault, Noella Marie 484
コトロネーオ
Cotroneo, Roberto 294
コトロマノビッチ
Kotromanović, Ante 760
コトワ
Kotova, Tatyana 760
ゴートン
Gorton, Gary 519
Gorton, John Grey 519
Gorton, Julia 519
ゴードン
Gordon, Aaron 517
Gordon, Abigail 517
Gordon, Alastair 517
Gordon, Alex 517
Gordon, Andrew D. 517
Gordon, Beate Sirota 517
Gordon, Bernard 517
Gordon, Cambria 517
Gordon, Carl 517, 518
Gordon, David 518
Gordon, David George 518
Gordon, Deborah M. 518
Gordon, Deborah R. 518
Gordon, Dee 518
Gordon, Dillon 518
Gordon, Eric 518
Gordon, Ernest 518
Gordon, Fiona 518
Gordon, Gary F. 518
Gordon, Howard 518
Gordon, Ilene 518
Gordon, Jack 518
Gordon, Jaimy 518
Gordon, Jeff 518
Gordon, Jehue 518
Gordon, Joanne 518
Gordon, Jon 518
Gordon, Josh 518
Gordon, June A. 518
Gordon, Kim 518
Gordon, Lalonde 518
Gordon, Lorraine 518
Gordon, Lucy 518
Gordon, Maggi McCormick 518
Gordon, Marjory 518
Gordon, Mary 518
Gordon, Matthew 518
Gordon, Mel 518
Gordon, Melvin 518
Gordon, Michael W. 518
Gordon, Mike 518
Gordon, Neil 518
Gordon, Nick 518
Gordon, Noah 518
Gordon, Pamela 518
Gordon, Paul 518
Gordon, Phil 518
Gordon, Philip H. 518
Gordon, Richard 518
Gordon, Robert 518
Gordon, Roderick 518
Gordon, Sarah 518
Gordon, Suzanne 518
Gordon, Thomas 518
Gordon, Tony 518
Gordon, Tuula 518
Gordon, Winston 518
Gordon, W.Terrence 518
Gordon, Yefim 518
ゴドン
Godon, Ingrid 507
ゴードン・リード
Gordon-Reed, Annette 518
ゴードン・レヴィット
Gordon-Levitt, Joseph 518
ゴードン・レビット
Gordon-Levitt, Joseph 518
コーナー
Corner, Donald 291
Koerner, Brendan I. 751
Koerner, Kelly 751
Körner, Ann M. 757
コナー
Conner, Amanda 283
Conner, Kavell 283
Conner, Marcia L. 283
Connor, Adam 283
Connor, Chris 283
Connor, Daniel F. 283
Connor, F.R. 283
Connor, Ian 283
Connor, Leslie 283
Connor, Richard A. 283
Connor, Tim 283
コナウェイ
Conaway, James 282
コナーズ
Conners, C.Keith 283
Connors, Gerard Joseph 283
Connors, Jimmy 283
Connors, Laurence A. 283
Connors, Roger 283
Connors, Rose 283
コナテ
Konaté, Abdel Karim 754
Konate, Gnissa 754
Konaté, Hamadou 754
Konaté, Mamadou Ismaël 754
Konate, Sekouba 754
Konate, Sidiki 754
Konaté, Tiefing 754
Konate, Tiémoko 754
コナーティ
Conati, Marcello 282
コナティ
Conaty, Bill 282
コナトン
Connerton, Paul 283
コナハン
Conaghan, Dan 282
コナブル
Conable, Barbara 282
Conable, Barbar B., Jr. 282
コナリー
Connally, Nellie 283
Connelly, Michael 283
Connolly, John 283
Connolly, Sara 283
コーナル
Cornall, Catherine 291
ゴナール
Gonnard, Henri 514
コナレ
Konaré, Alpha Oumar 754
ゴナロン
Gonalons, Maxime 513
コナン
Conant, Douglas R. 282
Konan, Sebastien 754
コナンナ
Konamna, Lala 754
コニー
Conee, Earl Brink 282
コーニイ
Coney, Michael 282
コニイ
Coney, Michael 282
コニェビッチ
Konjević, Raško 755
コニオルドゥ
Koniordou, Lidia 755
ゴニ・カラスコ
Goñi Carrasco, José 514
コーニグ
Koenig, Andrew 751
コニコヴァ
Konnikova, Maria 755
コニツァー
Konizer, Robert 755
コーニック
Cornick, Nicola 291
Koenig, Harold George 751
コニック
Connick, Harry, Jr. 283
Konik, Michael 755
ゴニック
Gonick, Larry 514
コーニッシュ
Cornish 291
Cornish, Jody 291
Cornish, Joe 291
コニッツ
Konitz, Lee 755
コニフ
Conniff, Ray 283
Conniff, Richard 283
コニャノフスキ
Konjanovski, Zoran 755
コニュ
Konjuh, Ana 755
コニョレ
Konjore, Willem 755
コニン
Coninx, Dorian 282
Konin, Jeff G. 755
コーヌ
Caune, Jean 237
コヌノーヴァ
Conunova, Alexandra 285
コネ
Kone, Adama 754
Kone, Amadou 754
Kone, Amadou Adrien 754
Kone, Arouna 754
Kone, Bacary 754
Kone, Bakary 754
Kone, Bruno Nabagné 754
Kone, Gilbert 754
Kone, Kafougouna 754
Kone, Lamine 754
Kone, Léonce 754
Kone, Mamadou 754
Koné, Mamadou 754
Kone, Mariatou 755
Kone, Messamba 755
Koné, Ousmane 755
Kone, Panagiotis 755
コネー
Konneh, Amara 755
コーネイ
Cooney, Doug 287
ゴネイム
Ghoneim, Ibrahim Ahmed 494
コネサ
Conesa, Pierre 282
コネス
Kones, Kipkalya 755
コーネツキー
Kornetsky, L.A. 757
コネフスカトライコフスカ
Konevska-trajkovska, Gabriela 755
コネラン
Connellan, Thomas K. 283
コネリー
Conneeley, Serene 283
Connelly, Cara 283
Connelly, Jennifer 283
Connelly, Kevin 283
Connelly, Tim 283
Connery, Sean 283
Konnelly, Joe 755
コーネリアス
Cornelius, Don 291
Konelios, Michael 755
コネリオス
Konelios, Michael 755
コーネル
Connell, Jo 283
Cornell, Ann Weiser 291
Cornell, Chris 291
Cornell, Drucilla 291
Cornell, Eric Allin 291
Cornell, Gary 291
Cornell, Joseph Bharat 291
Cornell, Laura 291
Cornell, Tim 291
コネル
Connell, Andrew 283
Connell, Evan S. 283
Connell, Jo 283
Connell, Tom 283
コーネル＝アヴェンダーノ
Cornel-Avendano, Beverly 291
コーネル‐アベンダーニョ
Cornel-Avendano, Beverly 291
コーネン
Cohnen, Mathias 276
コノヴァー
Conover, Chris 283
コノーズ
Connors, Barry W. 283
コノートン
Connaughton, James L. 283
Connaughton, Pat 283
コーノノフ
Kononov, Nikolai 755
コノパセク

Konopasek, Roger 755
コノプカ
Konopka, Dan 755
コノプリャンカ
Konoplyanka, Yevhen 755
コノマニ
Konomanyi, Finda Diana 755
コノマニー
Konomanyi, Finda Diana 755
コノリー
Connolly, Billy 283
Connolly, Derek 283
Connolly, Fergal 283
Connolly, J.J. 283
Connolly, John 283
Connolly, Kieron 283
Connolly, Marie 283
Connolly, Mickey 283
Connolly, Peter 283
Connolly, Ray 283
Connolly, Sean 283
Connolly, Suzanne M. 283
Connolly, William E. 283
コノール
Conort, Benoît 283
コノワロフ
Konovalov, Alexander V. 755
コノワロワ
Konovalova, Maria 755
コノン
Connon, Derek F. 283
コーバー
Kober, James Jeff 749
Korver, Kyle 758
コハ
Koha, Rebeka 751
コハー
Kocher, Martina 750
コバー
Kober, Amelie 749
コパー
Copper, Basil 289
ゴーバー
Govar, Daniel Mikah 522
コーバイン
Corbijn, Anton 289
ゴ・バオ・チャウ
Châu, Ngô Bào 249
コパオル
Kopaol, Robert 756
コバコ
Kobako, Gaspard 749
コバゴ
Kovago, Zoltan 761
コパ・コンドリ
Copa Condori, Nilda 288
コバ・サトウ
Koba Sato, Katsuko Tereza 749
コーハシ
Kokhas, Konstantin Petrovich 752
コバシェビッチ
Kovašević, Bozo 761
コバシッチ
Kovacich, Gerald L. 761
コバスト
Cobast, Éric 272
コバーチ
Kováč, Michal 761
Kováč, Roman 761
Kovács, Kálmán 761
Kovács, László 761
コバチ
Kováč, Michal 761
Kovač, Zdenka 761
Kovacs, Agnes 761
Kovács, Katalin 761
Kovacs, Sarolta 761
Kovacs, Zsofia 761
コパチ
Kopač, Janez 756
Kopacz, Ewa 756
コバチェバ
Kovatcheva, Diana 761
コバチェビッチ
Kovačević, Božo 761
Kovačević, Zorica 761
コバチェフ
Kovachev, Milko 761
コバチッチ
Kovačić, Ivan 761
コバーチュ
Kovács, György 761
コバチュ
Kovač, Miodrag 761
Kovač, Miro 761
Kovač, Slobodan 761
コパチンスカヤ
Kopatchinskaja, Patricia 756
コパツ
Kopac, Jiri 756
コーバック
Kovach, Robert 761
コバックス
Kovacs, Diane 761
Kovacs, Joe 761
Kovacs, Jordan 761
Kovacs, Laszlo 761
ゴパッラワ
Gopallawa, Monti 517
ゴバディ
Ghobadi, Bahman 493
コバート
Covert, Abby 296
Covert, Brian 296
Kobart, Ruth 749
コハネ
Kohane, Isaac S. 751
コバヒゼ
Kobakhidze, Maĭia 749
コバブール
Kaaberbol, Lene 693
コーバベル
Kaaberbol, Lene 693
ゴーハム
Gorham, Ursula 519
コバヤシ
Kobayashi, Ann H. 749
Kobayashi, Makoto 749
Kobayashi, Martin Blake 749
Kobayashi, Paulo 749
ゴパラクリシュナン
Gopalakrishnan, Kris 517
Gopalkrishnan, Senapathy 517
コバリア
Kobalia, Vera 749
コバリウ
Covaliu, Mihai 296
コバリエル
Kåberger, Tomas 693
コーバリス
Corballis, Michael C. 289
コバル
Koval, Anastasiia 761
Kowal, Yoann 762
コバルス
Kovals, Ainars 761
コバルチュク
Kovalchuk, Yury 761
コバレフ
Kovalev, Gennady 761
コバレブスキー
Kowalewski, Bettina 762
コバレンコ
Kovalenko, Sergey 761
コーハン
Cohan, Malcolm 274
コーバーン
Cockburn, Alistair 273
コーバン
Cauvin, Patrick 238
コバーン
Coburn, Ann 273
Coburn, Broughton 273
Coburn, Emma 273
Coburn, James 273
Cockburn, Andrew 273
Cockburn, Patrick 273
コパン
Coppens, Yves 289
ゴバーン
Gauvin, Bernard 484
コパンス
Coppens, Yves 289
ゴ・バン・ロング
Ngo Van Long 1020
コーヒー
Coffee, Peter 274
コービー
Corby, Brian 289
Covey, Stephen R. 296
コビ
Cobbi, Jane 272
コビー
Cobbi, Jane 272
Covey, Dylan 296
Covey, Stephen R. 296
ゴビ
Gobi, Salou 506
コピエテルス
Coppieters, Bernice 289
コビシー
Covici, Ann 296
ゴピーシン
Gopeesingh, Tim 517
ゴピスクーン
Gopee-scoon, Paula 517
コビニッチ
Kovinic, Danka 761
コビャコフ
Kobyakov, Andrey V. 750
コービル
Coville, Bruce 296
コビルカ
Kobilka, Brian 749
コビルスキ
Kobiljski, Aleksandra Majstorac 749
コービン
Corbin, Juliet M. 289
Corbin, Patrick 289
Corbin, Tyrone 289
Corbyn, Jeremy Bernard 289
Korbin, Jill E. 757
ゴビン
Gowin, Jarosław 522
コビング
Cobbing, Andrew 272
ゴビンダラジャン
Govindarajan, Vijay 522
コビントン
Covington, Christian 296
Covington, Joey 296
Covington, Robert 297
コープ
Cope, Andrew 288
Cope, David 288
Cope, Denys 288
Cope, Haley 288
Cope, Julian 288
Cope, Lewis 288
Cope, Wendy 288
Koepp, David 751
Koop, Volker 756
コブ
Cobb, Carlene 272
Cobb, Cathy 272
Cobb, Linda 272
Cobb, Vicki 272
Kob, Tetyana 749
コプ
Kopp, Pavol 756
Kopu, Dudley 756
ゴーブ
Gove, John 522
ゴフ
Goff, Beth 508
Goff, Christine 508
Goff, Jared 508
Goff, Madison Lee 508
Goff, Phil 508
Gough, Alex 521
Gough, Amy 521
Gough, Clare 521
Gough, Ian 521
Gough, Julian 521
Gough, Michael 521
コファレンコフ
Kovalenkov, Sergey 761
ゴファン
Goffin, Josse 508
コファンコ
Cojuangco, Eduardo, Jr. 276
コーフィー
Coffey, Lucy 274
コフィ
Coffie, Raymonde 274
Cofie, Isaac 274
Koffi, Paul Koffi 751
コフィー
Coffey, Lisa Marie 274
Coffey, Wayne R. 274
ゴーフィー
Goffee, Rob 508
Goffee, Robert 508
ゴフィ
Goffee, Robert 508
コフィゴー
Koffigoh, Kokou Joseph 751
コフィファ
Khofifah, Indar Parawansa 728

Kofifah, Indar Parawangsa 751
コフィ・ヤオ
Koffi Yao, Eloge 751
コーフィールド
Cockfield, Francis Arthur 273
Corfield, David 290
Corfield, Richard M. 290
Corfield, Robin Bell 290
コフィールド
Cofield, Takoby 274
コフィン
Coffin, William Sloane 274
ゴーフィン
Goffin, Josse 508
ゴフィン
Goffin, Gerry 508
Goffin, Josse 508
ゴフェット
Goffette, Guy 508
コープカン
Kobkarn, Wattanavrangkul 750
コプサック
Korbsak, Sabhavasu 757
コーフシ
Kaufusi, Bronson 710
コブス
Cobbs, Tasha 272
コフスタ
Kofstad, Espen 751
ゴフスタイン
Goffstein, Marilyn Brooke 508
コプチェク
Copjec, Joan 288
コプツィク
Koptsik, Vladimir A. 756
コプティ
Copti, Scandar 289
コフート
Kohut, Matthew 752
ゴプニク
Gopnik, Adam 517
Gopnik, Myrna 517
ゴプニック
Gopnik, Alison 517
コブネイ
Coveney, James 296
コプフ
Kopf, Gereon 756
コフフト
Kovkhuto, Andrei M. 762
コーフマン
Kaufman, Natalie Hevener 710
コープマン
Koopman, Amerentske 756
Koopman, Ton 756
Koopmans, Loek 756
コフマン
Coffman, Chase 274
Coffman, Curt 274
Coffman, Elaine 274
Kaufmann, Jean Claude 710
Kofman, Fred 751
Kofman, Sarah 751
ゴフマン
Gofman, Alex 508
Gofman, John W. 508
コープマンス
Koopmans, Luuk 756
コブヨル
Kobjoll, Klaus 750
コフラー
Kofler, Andreas 751
コブラー
Kobler, Flip 750
コプラン
Coplan, Jeremy D. 288
Coplan, Robert J. 288
コプランス
Coplans, John 289
コープランド
Copeland, B.Jack 288
Copeland, Brandon 288
Copeland, Chris 288
Copeland, Cynthia L. 288
Copeland, Cyrus M. 288
Copeland, David 288
Copeland, Edna D. 288
Copeland, Edwin Luther 288
Copeland, E.Luther 288
Copeland, Katherine 288
Copeland, Lee 288
Copeland, Misty 288
Copeland, Peter 288
Copeland, Peter F. 288
Copeland, Thomas E. 288
コプリー
Copley, Sharlto 289
コブリアシビリ
Kobliashvili, Roberti 750
コプリウニカル
Koprivnikar, Boris 756
コプリエン
Coplien, James O. 289
Coplien, Jim 289
コブリック
Kobrick, Frederick R. 750
コブリッシュ
Koblish, Scott 750
コブリッツ
Koblitz, Neal 750
コフリン
Coughlin, Jack 295
Coughlin, Natalie 295
コブリン
Koblin, Aaron 750
Kobrin, Alexander 750
コブル
Kobr, Michael 750
ゴーブル
Goble, Paul 506
コプルズ
Coples, Quinton 289
コプルトン
Copelton, Denise A. 288
コプレウィッツ
Koplewicz, Harold S. 756
コブロワゾロボワ
Koblova Zholobova, Valeria Sergeyevna 750
コフーン
Colquhoun, Margaret 280
コペ
Copé, Jean-François 288
ゴーベ
Gobé, Marc 506
ゴベ
Gobe, Siaka 506
コヘーア・ド・ラーゴ
Corrêa do Lago, André 292
コーヘイン
Keohane, Robert Owen 720
コヘイン
Keohane, Robert Owen 720
コペエフ
Kopeyev, Mukhambet 756
コーペック
Kopech, Michael 756
コペッコヴァ
Kopečková, Veronika 756
コーベット
Corbett, Brad 289
Corbett, David 289
Corbett, Sara 289
Corbett, Thomas 289
Corbett, William 289
コベナン
Kobenan, Anaky 749
コベニー
Coveney, Simon 296
ゴベービル
Goberville, Celine 506
コペリョ
Copello, Alexis 288
Copello, Yasmani 288
コーベル
Korbel, Kathleen 757
コベール
Kober, Marc 749
コベル
Covel, Michael 296
Kobel, Gregor 749
Kobel, Stefan 749
Kober, Noemie 749
コペル
Koppel, Tom 756
ゴーベル
Gobel, Rachmat 506
ゴベール
Gobert, Rudy 506
コペルニクス
Copernicus, Nicolaus 288
ゴベルビユ
Goberville, Celine 506
コペルマン
Kopelman, Jay 756
Kopelman, Josh 756
Kopelman, Richard I. 756
コーヘン
Cohen, Almog 274
Cohen, Eli 274
Cohen, Gili 275
Cohen, Michele Andree 275
Cohen, Solomon Ibrahim 275
コーベン
Coben, Harlan 272
Corben, Richard 289
コヘン
Cohen, Adam 274
コペンズ
Coppens, Patrick 289
ゴベンス・ボーテルダール
Gobbens-Boterdael, Paule 506
コヘンチ
Corrente, Trio 292
コベントリー
Coventry, Kirsty 296
コーペンヘイヴァー
Copenhaver, Brian P. 288
コボ
Cobo, Yohana 272
コボス
Cobos, Julio César Cleto 272
コポス
Copos, Gheorghe 289
コホネン
Kohonen, Teuvo 752
コポマー
Kopomaa, Timo 756
ゴポール
Gopaul, Nanda 517
コーボールド
Corbould, Chris 289
Corbould, Neil 289
コボルド
Cobbold, Richard 272
コホロバ
Kohlova, Martina 752
ゴボロフ
Govorov, Andrii 522
コーホン
Cohon, Rhody 276
ゴマー
Gomaa, Muhammad Mokhtar 512
コマイユ
Commaille, Jacques 281
コマキ
Komaki, Ritsuko 754
コマストリ＝モンタナーリ
Comastri Montanari, Danila 281
ゴマソール
Gomersall, Stephen John 512
コーマック
Cormack, Peter 291
Cormack, Ronald Sidney 291
コマネスク
Comănescu, Lazăr 281
コマネチ
Comăneci, Nadia 281
コマーフォード
Commerford, Tim 281
コマフォード・リンチ
Comaford-Lynch, Christine 281
コマラ
Komara, Kabine 754
コマリンスキ
Komarinski, Mark F. 754
コマーロヴァ
Komarova, Natalia L. 754
コマロフスキー
Komarovskii, George E. 754
コマロワ
Komarova, Stanislava 754
コーマン
Corman, Avery 291
Corman, Roger William 291
Koman, Aleta 754
Korman, Gordon 757
Korman, Harvey 757
Korman, Susan 757
コマーン
Comment, Bernard 281
コマン

コ

Coman, Dragos 281
Coman, Kingsley 281
ゴーマン
Gorman, Cliff 519
Gorman, Dave 519
Gorman, Edward 519
Gorman, Jack M. 519
Gorman, James 519
Gorman, James P. 519
Gorman, Joseph Tolle 519
Gorman, Leon 519
Gorman, Lou 519
Gorman, Mary 519
Gorman, Mary Alice 519
Gorman, Michael 519
Gorman, R.C. 519
Gorman, Robert 519
Gorman, Siobhan 519
コマンダー
Commandeur, Jacques J. F. 281
コマンヤーカ
Komunyakaa, Yusef 754
コミー
Comey, James Brien, Jr. 281
コーミア
Cormier, Robert 291
コーミアー
Cormier, Daniel 291
コミサー
Komisar, Randy 754
コミサリュック
Komisaruk, Barry R. 754
コミサロフ
Komissarov, Sergei 754
ゴミス
Gomis, Alfred 513
Gomis, Kafetien 513
ゴミズ
Gomis, Anna 513
コミスキー
Comiskey, Eugene E. 281
コミン・コミン
Comín Comín, Francisco 281
コム
Comm, Joel 281
Komu, Martha 754
コムシッチ
Komšić, Željko 754
コームズ
Combs, Dennis R. 281
ゴームズ
Gomes, Yan 512
コムストック
Comstock, Beth 282
コムデン
Comden, Betty 281
コムトア
Comtois, Philippe 282
コムドン
Comden, Betty 281
ゴムブリッチ
Gombrich, Ernst Hans Josef 512
ゴムボッチ
Gomboc, Adrian 512
コームリー
Combley, Margaret 281
コムリ
Khomri, Abdelkader 728
コムリー
Comrie, Bernard 282
ゴームリー
Gormley, Antony 519
Gormley, Beatrice 519
Gormley, John 519
Gormly, Peter 519
ゴーメ
Gorme, Eydie 519
コメイ
Comay, Joan 281
ゴメス
Gomes, Antonieta Roa 512
Gomes, Aristides 512
Gomes, Carlos 512
Gomes, Carolyn 512
Gomes, Cid 512
Gomes, Ciro 512
Gomes, Daniel 512
Gomes, Fernando 512
Gomes, Francisco Da Costa 512
Gomes, Heurelho 512
Gomes, Joao, Jr. 512
Gómes, José 512
Gomes, Marcelo 512
Gomes, Miguel 512
Gomes, Namuano Dias 512
Gomes, Nilma Lino 512
Gomes, Renato 512
Gomez, Alejandro 512
Gomez, Alseny René 512
Gomez, Ana M. 512
Gomez, Carlos 512
Gomez, Edward 512
Gomez, Elena 512
Gomez, E.T. 512
Gomez, Fabian 512
Gomez, Gustavo 512
Gomez, Javier 512
Gomez, Jeanmar 512
Gomez, Joan 512
Gomez, Joe 513
Gómez, José Antonio 513
Gómez, Juan Carlos 513
Gomez, Laura 513
Gomez, Mario 513
Gomez, Miguel 513
Gomez, Perry 513
Gomez, Preston 513
Gomez, Selena 513
Gomez, Sheriff 513
Gomez, Silvia 513
Gómez, Sonia 513
Gomez, Vinicio 513
ゴメス・イ・オリヴェル
Gómez i Oliver, Valentí 513
ゴメス・グティエレス
Gómez Gutiérrez, Luis Ignacio 513
ゴメス・ゴンサレス
Gómez González, Arely 513
ゴメス・サンチェス
Gómez Sánchez, Valeriano 513
ゴメス・ジュニオル
Gomes Junior, Carlos 512
ゴメス・シルヴァン
Gómez Silván, Sergio 513
ゴメス＝セルダ
Gómez Cerdá, Alfredo 513
ゴメス＝パラシオ
Gomez-Palacio, Bryony 513
ゴメスペレイラ
Gomes Pereira, Victor 512
ゴメスマトス
Gomez Matos, Franklin 513
ゴメス・モラン
Onozuka de Gómez-Morán, Chiho 1054
ゴメスモント・ウルエタ
Gómezmont Urueta, Fernando Francisco 513
コメスロボ
Gómez-lobo, Andrés 513
ゴメスロボ
Gómez-lobo, Andrés 513
コメッティ
Cometti, Gilles 281
ゴメラ
Gomella, Leonard G. 512
コメリーニ
Comellini, Franca 281
コメール
Commère, Hervé 281
ゴメル
Gomel, Bob 512
コメンチーニ
Comencini, Luigi 281
コモ
Comeau, Mehdi 281
Como, Perry 281
コモー
Comeaux, Zachary 281
コモウォフスキ
Komołowski, Longin 754
コモナー
Commoner, Barry 281
コモリ・デル・ビジャル
Komori del Villar, Carlos Hugo 754
コモロフスキ
Komorowski, Bronisław 754
コモワ
Komova, Viktoria Aleksandrovna 754
コモン
Common 281
ゴモン
Gomon, Yevgeniya 513
コモンズ
Commons, Anne 281
コヤ
Koya, Faiyaz 762
コヤサンビア
Koyassambia, Jean-Baptiste 762
コヤック
Koyack, Ben 762
コヤディノビッチ
Kojadinović, Dragan 752
コヤマ
Koyama, Micael S. 762
Koyama-Richard, Brigitte 762
コヤメネ
Koyamene, Pascal 762
コヤラ
Koyara, Marie Noëlle 762
ゴヤル
Goyal, Piyush 522
ゴヤン
Gojan, Veaceslav 508
コヤンブヌ
Koyambonou, Gabriel Jean Edouard 762
コヨイ・エチェベリア
Coyoy Echeverría, Erick Haroldo 298
コーラ
Cora, Alex 289
Cora, Joey 289
コーラー
Cohler, Matt 275
Koehler, Tom 751
Kohler, Chris 752
Kohler, Irene 752
Kohler, Sarah 752
Kohler, Sheila 752
Kohlert, Mats 752
Kolar, Bob 753
コラ
Colas, Guilbaut 276
コラー
Kolar, Brad 753
Koller, Hans 753
Koller, Tim 753
ゴーラー
Gowler, Kerri 522
ゴラー
Goller, Sara 511
ゴライエブ
Ghorayeb, Antoine 494
コラカキ
Korakaki, Anna 757
コラク
Kolak, Sara 753
ゴラコチ
Golakoti, Trimurtulu 508
コラザキ
Kora Zaki, Maïmouna 757
ゴラジ
Gorage, Sardar Al-Haaj Mohammad Umar 517
コラジオ
Coraggio, Peter 289
コラシナチ
Kolasinac, Asmir 753
コラシナツ
Kolasinac, Sead 753
コラス
Colasse, Bernard 276
Collasse, Richard 278
ゴラス
Golas, Katharine C. 508
コラスオンノ
Colasuonno, Francesco 276
コラータ
Kolata, Gina Bari 753
コラチ
Korać, Žarko 757
コラチェ
Colacce, Carlos 276
コラチェク
Kolaczek, Marie 752
コラッサ
Kolassa, E.M. “Mick” 753
コラッジオ
Coraggio, José Luis 289
Coraggio, Peter 289
コラティ
Colati, Isei 276
コラード
Collard, Anna 278
Collard, Patrizia 278
ゴラード
Gorard, S. 517

コラード・バルデス
Corado Valdez, Victor Enrique 289
コラーナ
Khorana, Har Gobind 728
コラナ
Khorana, Har Gobind 728
コラニ
Kolani, Gourdigou 753
コラニ・イェンチャレ
Kolani Yentchare, Tchabinandi 753
ゴラノ
Goranov, Vladislav 517
コラノヴィッチ
Kolanovič, Dubravka 753
ゴラノビッチ
Goranović, Pavle 517
ゴラノフ
Goranov, Vladislav 517
コラピント
Colapinto, John 276
ゴーラブ
Golub, Leon 512
ゴラブ
Gollub, Matthew 512
Golub, Leon 512
コラベロ
Colabello, Chris 276
コラマルコ
Colamarco, Benjamín 276
コラリーツィ
Colarizi, Simona 276
コーラル
Chorale, Phoenix 259
コラール
Collard, Franck 278
Collard, Jean-Philippe 278
コラル
Corral, Alejo 292
コラールシュ
Kolar, Josef 753
コラルスカボビンスカ
Kolarska-bobińska, Lena 753
コラルバロン
Corral Barron, Daniel 292
コラーレス
Corrales, Maria Mercedes M. 292
コラレス
Corrales, Arturo Geraldo 292
Corrales, Cesar 292
Corrales, William 292
コラレス・アルバレス
Corrales Álvarez, Arturo 292
コラレス・ディアス
Corrales Díaz, Daisy 292
コラ＝ロカテリ
Cora-Locatelli, Gabriela 289
コラロフ
Kolarov, Aleksandar 753
コラン
Colin, Daniel 278
Collin, Françise 278
Coran, Pierre 289
ゴーラン
Golan, David E. 508
Golan, Menahem 508
ゴラン
Golan, Galia 508
Goran, Vasilii Pavlovich 517
コランジェロ
Colangelo, Bryan 276
コランダー
Colander, LaTasha 276
コランタン
Corentin 290
Corentin, Philippe 290
コラント
Chourraut, Maialen 260
ゴラント
Golant, Mitch 508
Golant, Susan K. 508
コーリ
Coley, Noel 278
Corey, Elias James 290
Cori, Patricia 290
コーリー
Corey, Elias James 290
Corey, Jeff 290
Corey, Michael J. 290
Corley, Theresa 291
Corrie, Marcus 292
コリ
Cori, Jasmin Lee 290
Cori, Patricia 290
Koli, Johnson 753
コリー
Coley, Trevon 278
Colley, Angela 278
Colley, Jan 278
Colley, Linda 278
Colli, Andrea 278
Collie, Craig 278
Corey, Ryanne 290
Corrie, Heather 292
Kolley, Abdou 753
ゴーリ
Ghauri, Babar Khan 493
Ghori, Babar Khan 494
Gori, Edoardo 519
ゴーリー
Gorry, Conner 519
ゴリ
Gori, Severino 519
コリア
Collier, Aine 278
Corea, Chick 290
Correa, Charles M. 292
コリアー
Collier, Bruce 278
Collier, Bryan 278
Collier, David 278
Collier, Paul 278
Collier, Simon 278
コリアト
Coriat, Laurence 290
コーリィ
Corey, Gerald 290
Corey, James S.A. 290
Corey, Marianne Schneider 290
コーリイ
Corey, James S.A. 290
コリエ
Kolie, Frederic 753
コリエネック
Korienek, Gene 757
ゴリオルグラン
Golliot-legrand, Lise 512
コリガン
Corrigan, Dorothy D. 292
Corrigan, Gerald 292
Corrigan, Gina 292
Corrigan, Patrick B. 292
Corrigan, Patrick W. 292
コリガン・マグアイア
Corrigan-Maguire, Mairead 292
コリガン・マグワイア
Corrigan-Maguire, Mairead 292
コリガン・マグワイアー
Corrigan-Maguire, Mairead 292
コリグリアーノ
Corigliano, John 290
ゴリコワ
Golikova, Tatyana A. 511
ゴリサーノ
Golisano, Tom 511
コリシ
Kolisi, Siya 753
ゴリジョフ
Golijov, Osvaldo 511
コリス
Collis, David J. 279
ゴリス
Goris, Richard C. 519
コーリー・スタイン
Cauley-stein, Willie 237
コリソン
Collison, Darren 279
Collison, John 280
Collison, Nick 280
Collison, Patrick 280
コリータ
Koryta, Michael 758
ゴリチェワ
Goricheva, Karina 519
ゴリツェン
Golitzen, Alexander 511
コーリック
Couric, Katie 295
コリック
Colick, Lewis 278
ゴリッツェン
Golitzen, Alexander 511
コリドン
Corydon, Bjarne 293
コリーニ
Collini, Stefan 278
コリネ
Colllinet, Clementine 280
コリーノ
Corino, Karl 291
コリーモァ
Collymore, Peter 280
コリモア
Collymore, Clinton 280
コリモン・フェティエール
Colimon-féthière, Josseline 278
コリヤー
Collier, Richard 278
コリリン
Kolirin, Eran 753
コリリンテターケ
Koririntetaake, Toakai 757
コリル
Korir, John Cheruiyot 757
コーリン
Collin, Catherine 278
Coughlin, Bruce 295
コリン
Collen, Alanna 278
Collen, Phil 278
Collin, Renaud 278
Korine, Harmony 757
ゴリン
Gorin, Natalio 519
コリンガム
Collingham, Elizabeth M. 278
コーリング
Cowling, Graham 297
コリングス
Collings, Timothy 278
ゴリンコフ
Golinkoff, Roberta M. 511
コリンジ
Collinge, William 278
コリンジャー
Collinger, Tom 278
コリンズ
Colins, Phil 278
Collins, Alex 278
Collins, Allan 278
Collins, Andrew 278
Collins, Andy 278
Collins, Art 278
Collins, Ashlinn 278
Collins, Billy 278
Collins, Carolyn Strom 278
Collins, Catherine 278
Collins, Charlie E. 278
Collins, Christopher Herbert 278
Collins, Colleen 278
Collins, Dani 279
Collins, Daniel Joseph 279
Collins, Daryl 279
Collins, David 279
Collins, Dobson 279
Collins, Doris 279
Collins, Edwyn 279
Collins, Eileen Marie 279
Collins, Evangeline 279
Collins, Francis S. 279
Collins, Fred 279
Collins, Harry M. 279
Collins, Hugh 279
Collins, Jackie 279
Collins, Jalen 279
Collins, James 279
Collins, James Charles 279
Collins, Jamie 279
Collins, Jannette 279
Collins, Jarron 279
Collins, Jeff 279
Collins, Jerry 279
Collins, Joan 279
Collins, John 279
Collins, John Elbert 279
Collins, Josephine 279
Collins, Judith 279
Collins, Kim 279
Collins, La'el 279
Collins, Landon 279
Collins, Larry 279
Collins, Lily 279
Collins, Lynn 279
Collins, Maliek 279
Collins, Manda 279
Collins, María Antonieta 279
Collins, Max Allan 279
Collins, Michael 279
Collins, Michael

Patrick 279
Collins, Mike 279
Collins, Nancy A. 279
Collins, Nicolas 279
Collins, Paul 279
Collins, Philip 279
Collins, R.A. 279
Collins, Randall 279
Collins, R.Douglas 279
Collins, Rebecca Grace 279
Collins, R.Lorraine 279
Collins, Sophie 279
Collins, Susan 279
Collins, Suzanne 279
Collins, Tantum 279
Collins, Terry 279
Collins, Terry Lee 279
Collins, Timothy Clark 279
Collins, Toni 279
Collins, Tyler 279
Kolins, Scott 753

コリンス・サスマン
Collins-Sussman, Ben 279

コリンズワース
Collinsworth, Kyle 279

コリンソン
Collinson, Gill 279
Collinson, Patrick 279

コリンバ
Kolingba, Desiré 753

コール
Call, Ken 216
Call, Max 216
Call, Naomi 216
Coar, Ken A.L. 272
Cole, Adrian 276
Cole, A.J. 276
Cole, Ashley 276
Cole, Audie 276
Cole, August 276
Cole, Babette 276
Cole, Briony 276
Cole, Brock 276
Cole, Cheryl 276
Cole, Chloe 276
Cole, Dan 276
Cole, Emily 276
Cole, Freddie 276
Cole, George 276
Cole, Gerrit 276
Cole, Henry 276
Cole, Holly 276
Cole, Ian 276
Cole, Joanna 276
Cole, Joe 276
Cole, Jonathan 276
Cole, K.C. 276
Cole, Kresley 276
Cole, Lily 276
Cole, Martina 277
Cole, Michael 277
Cole, Michael Wayne 277
Cole, Natalie 277
Cole, Neil 277
Cole, R.Alan 277
Cole, Robert E. 277
Cole, Roger 277
Cole, Stephen 277
Cole, Stu 277
Cole, Tom Clohosy 277
Cole, Trent 277
Cole, Trevor 277
Coll, Elizabeth 278
Coll, Steve 278
Kohl, Helmut 751
Kohl, Richard 751
Kohr, Dominik 752
Korr, Charles P. 758

コル
Coll, Steve 278
Colle, Eric Benjamin 278
Kold, Christen 753
Kol Pheng 754

ゴール
Gall, Chris 473
Gorr, Rita 519

コルヴァン
Colvin, Geoffrey 281

ゴルヴィツァー
Gollwitzer, Heinz 512
Gollwitzer, Helmut 512

コール・ウィッタカー
Cole-Whittaker, Terry 278

ゴルヴィッチ
Gourevitch, Peter Alexis 522

コルヴィッツ
Kollwitz, Käthe (Shmidt) 753

コルヴィン
Colvin, Richard Lee 281

ゴールウェイ
Galway, James 474

コールウェル
Colwell, Rita Rossi 281

コルウェル
Colwell, Eileen 281
Colwell, Rita 281
Colwell, Rita Rossi 281
Colwill, Chris 281

コルヴェローニ
Corveloni, Sandra 293

ゴルカ
Gorka, Benjamin 519

コルカット
Collcutt, Martin 278

コルカバ
Kolcaba, Katharine 753

コルガン
Colgan, Jenny 278

コルキット
Colquitt, Britton 280
Colquitt, Dustin 280

ゴルギトアイア
Gheorghitoaia, Catalina 493

コルキュフ
Corcuff, Stéphane 290

コルク
Cork, Adam 291

コルクマン
Kolkman, P.A. 753

コルグレイザー
Colglazier, Elmer William, Jr. 278

コールグローブ
Colegrove, Clare Lee 277

ゴルケ
Gorke, Martin 519

コルケアオヤ
Korkeaoja, Juha 757

ゴルゲイジ
Gorgeij, Sardar Al-Haj Mohammad Umar 519

コルコ
Kolko, Gabriel 753
Kolko, Jon 753

ゴルゴゼ
Gorgodze, Mamuka 519

コルコット
Callcott, Pauline 216

ゴルサ
Gorsa, Petar 519

コルサールツ
Colsaerts, Nicolas 280

コルシ
Corsi, Cristiana 292
Corsi, Giancarlo 292

コルシア
Korcia, Laurent 757

コルジア
Corgiat, Sylviane 290

コルジェ
Kordjé, Bedoumra 757

ゴルジェル
Gourgel, Abraão Pio Dos Santos 522

ゴルシコボゾフ
Gorshkovozov, Oleksandr 519
Horshkovozov, Oleksandr 624

コルジツ
Korzits, Lee 758

コルシーニ
Corsini, Claudia 292

コルシニ
Corsini, Raymond J. 292

コルシュ
Korsch, Dietrich 758

ゴルジュ
Gorgé, Annie 519

コルシュノフ
Korshunow, Irina 758

コルシュノワ
Korshunova, Ekaterina 758
Korshunova, Ruslana 758

コールシュライバー
Kohlschreiber, Philipp 752

ゴルジュラン
Gorgelin, Mathieu 519

コルジョワ
Korzhoya, Natalya 758

コールス
Kohls, Florian 752

コールズ
Coles, Alex 277
Coles, B.H. 277
Coles, Catherine M. 277
Coles, Dane 277
Coles, Darnell 277
Coles, Meredith E. 277

コルスキー
Kolsky, Richard I. 754

ゴルスキ
Gorski, Kazimierz 519

コルスタッド
Kolstad, Charles D. 754

コルストン
Colston, Valerie 280

ゴールストン
Gholston, William 494
Goulston, Mark 521

ゴルストン
Golston, Kedric 512

ゴールズマン
Goldsman, Akiva 510

ゴールズワーシー
Goldsworthy, Adrian Keith 511

コルズン
Korzun, Nikita 758

コルスンスカヤ
Korsunskaia, Ella Arkadevna 758

コルセク
Coll-seck, Awa Marie 280

コール・セック
Coll-seck, Awa Marie 280

コルゼニオフスキ
Korzeniowski, Pawel 758

コルソ
Corso, Gregory Nunzio 292

ゴルゾウスキー
Goleszowski, Richard 511

コルソン
Colson, Aurélien 280
Colson, Charles 280
Colson, Mary 280
Colson, Rob 280

ゴルソン
Golson, Senquez 512

コールター
Colter, Cara 280
Coulter, Ann H. 295
Coulter, Catherine 295
Coulter, James 295
Coulter, Mary K. 295

コールダー
Calder, Nigel 215
Calder, Yoshiko 215

コルター
Colter, Kain 280
Coulter, Kevin 295
Kolter, Roberto 754

コルダ
Korda, Alberto 757

ゴールダー
Golder, Ben 510
Golder, Peter N. 510

コルダツ
Cordaz, Alex 290

コルタッサ
Cortassa, Nadia 292

コルタート
Coltart, David 280

ゴルダニーガ
Goldaniga, Edoardo 509

コールダーバンク
Calderbank, Robert 215

コルダヒ
Kordahi, Jean-Louis 757

コルタロロ
Quartarolo, Jennifer 1143

コルダン
Kordan, Ali 757

ゴルダン
Gordin, Jean 517

ゴルチエ
Gaultier, Jean-Paul 484

ゴルチェル
Gólcher, Olga 509

コルチノイ
Korchnoi, Viktor 757

コルチャノワ
Kolchanova, Lyudmila 753

コルチュ
Korzh, Viktor 758

コルチュノワ
Koltunova, Yulia 754

コルツ
Koltz, Tony 754

ゴルツ
Golts, Natalia 512
Gorz, André 520
コルツァーニ
Colzani, Anselmo 281
コルツノワ
Koltunova, Yulia 754
コルテ
Korte, Andreas 758
Korte, Bernhard H. 758
コルティ
Corti, Eugenio 293
ゴールディ
Goldie, Daniel C. 510
ゴルディ
Goldie, Mark 510
ゴルディアン
Gordian, Robert 517
コルディエ
Cordier, Severine 290
Kordjé, Bedoumra 757
コルディコット
Caldicott, Helen 215
ゴルディス
Gordis, Leon 517
コルティソ
Cortizo, Laurentino 293
ゴルディチューク
Gordiychuk, Valentin 517
コルディッツ
Kolditz, Thomas A. 753
コルティナラセラ
Cortina Lacerra, Javier 293
コルディムスキー
Kordemskii, B.A. 757
コルデイロ
Cordeiro, Paula A. 290
ゴールディン
Goldin, Nan 510
コルティング
Colting, Fredrik 280
ゴールディング
Golding, Anders 510
Golding, Bruce 510
Golding, Julia 510
Golding, Mark 510
Golding, Matthew 510
Goulding, June 521
ゴルデーエフ
Gordeyev, Aleksei Vassilyevich 517
コールデコット
Caldecott, Randolph 215
コルテジアーニ
Corteggiani, Jean Pierre 292
コルテス
Cortés, Alma 292
Cortés, Carlos E. 292
Cortés, Joaquín 292
Cortes, Mario 292
Cortes, Ricardo 292
Cortez, Donn 292
コルデス
Cordes, Kevin 290
Cordes, Ron 290
コルテス・デルガド
Cortés Delgado, José Luis 292
ゴルデーヌ
Goldaine, Louis 509
コルデムスキー
Kordemskii, B.A. 757
コルテリアル
Corte-real, Rosaria 292
ゴルデル
Gaarder, Jostein 469
コルデロ
Cordero, Fernando 290
Cordero, Hernesto 290
Cordero, Santiago 290
コルデロ・アロジョ
Cordero Arroyo, Ernesto 290
ゴールデン
Gaulden, Albert Clayton 484
Gaulden, Ray 484
Golden, Arthur 509
Golden, Brittan 509
Golden, Christie 509
Golden, Christopher 509
Golden, Eve 509
Golden, Gale 509
Golden, Jamal 509
Golden, Markus 509
Golden, Michael 509
Golden, Renny 509
Golden, Robert 509
Goulden, Gavin 521
コルテンカンプ
Kortenkamp, Ulrich H. 758
コルテンス
Cortens, Theolyn 292
ゴールデン・トゥミー
Golden Twomey, Emily 510
ゴールデンバーグ
Goldenberg, Jacob 510
Goldenberg, Michael 510
Goldenberg, William 510
コルト
Kolt, Gregory S. 754
Korto, Joseph 758
コルドー
Cordeo, Mikaelah 290
ゴールド
Gauld, Alan 484
Gauld, Tom 484
Gold, Andrew 509
Gold, Anne 509
Gold, Charles H. 509
Gold, Christina A. 509
Gold, Gina 509
Gold, Glen David 509
Gold, Gracie 509
Gold, Hal 509
Gold, Jeffrey 509
Gold, Jonathan 509
Gold, Julie 509
Gold, Kristi 509
Gold, Reggie 509
Gold, Sam 509
Gold, Stuart Avery 509
Gold, Thomas 509
Gold, Todd 509
Gould, Robbie 521
Gould, Robert Jay 521
コルドヴァ・アグィラー
Córdova Aguilar, Hildegardo 290
ゴールドヴァッサー
Goldwasser, Shafi 511
ゴールドウィン
Goldwyn, Samuel, Jr. 511
コールドウェル
Caldwell, Andre 215
Caldwell, Bobby 215
Caldwell, Gail 215
Caldwell, Graham E. 215
Caldwell, Harry M. 215
Caldwell, Ian 215
Caldwell, James Hugh 215
Caldwell, Jim 215
Caldwell, J.S. 215
Caldwell, Laura 215
Caldwell, Leigh 215
Caldwell, Robert R. 215
Caldwell, Sally 215
Caldwell, Sarah 215
Caldwell, Sophie 215
Caldwell, Thomas 215
Caldwell, Trey 215
コールドウエル
Caldwell, Richard S. 215
コルドウェル
Caldwell, Philip 215
Coldwell, Pedro Joaquín 276
コールドウェル・ポープ
Caldwell-pope, Kentavious 215
ゴールドエイカー
Goldacre, Ben 509
ゴールドサック
Goldsack, Gaby 510
ゴールドシャー
Goldsher, Alan 510
ゴールドシュタイン
Goldstein, Barbara 511
Goldstein, Eda 511
Goldstein, Janet 511
Goldstein, Joseph Leonard 511
Goldstein, Kurt Julius 511
ゴルドシュタイン
Goldshtein, Sasha 510
ゴールドシュナイダー
Goldschneider, Gary 510
ゴールドシュミット
Goldschmidt, Anthony 510
Goldschmidt, Ernst Philip 510
Goldschmidt, Judy 510
Goldschmidt, Paul 510
ゴルトシュミット
Goldschmidt, Bjorn 510
ゴールドスウェイト
Goldthwait, John 511
ゴールドスタイン
Goldstein, Donald M. 511
Goldstein, Gil 511
Goldstein, Herbert 511
Goldstein, Inge F. 511
Goldstein, Jan 511
Goldstein, Jess 511
Goldstein, Joseph Leonard 511
Goldstein, Martin 511
Goldstein, Melissa M. 511
Goldstein, Melvyn C. 511
Goldstein, Michael 511
Goldstein, Noah J. 511
Goldstein, Rebecca 511
Goldstein, Sam 511
Goldstine, Herman Heine 511
ゴールドスチン
Goldstein, Donald M. 511
ゴールドスティーン
Goldstein, Robert Justin 511
Goldstein, Sam 511
ゴールドステイン
Goldstein, David B. 511
Goldstein, Elisha 511
Goldstein, Harvey 511
Goldstein, Tina R. 511
ゴールドステン
Goldstein, Joseph Leonard 511
ゴールドストーン
Goldstone, Bruce 511
Goldstone, Lawrence 511
Goldstone, Nancy Bazelon 511
ゴールドスミス
Goldsmith, Andrea 511
Goldsmith, Andrew Feyk 511
Goldsmith, Barbara 511
Goldsmith, Barton 511
Goldsmith, Bruce 511
Goldsmith, Donald 511
Goldsmith, Douglas F. 511
Goldsmith, Edward 511
Goldsmith, James J. 511
Goldsmith, Jerry 511
Goldsmith, Joel 511
Goldsmith, John 511
Goldsmith, Josh 511
Goldsmith, Joy V. 511
Goldsmith, Malcolm 511
Goldsmith, Marshall 511
Goldsmith, Martin 511
Goldsmith, Mike 511
Goldsmith, Olivia 511
Goldsmith, Paul 511
Goldsmith, Stephen 511
ゴールドソン
Goldson, Edward 511
コルドバ
Cordoba, Jhon 290
Cordoba, Marlene Yadira 290
Cořdova, Marlene Yadira 290
Córdova, Yadira 290
コルトバウィ
Qortbawi, Shakib 1143
コルドバ・ウンダ
Córdova Unda, Javier 290
ゴールドバーガー
Goldberger, Arthur Stanley 509
Goldberger, Marvin Leonard 509
ゴールドバーク
Goldberg, David P. 509
Goldberg, Stephen 509
ゴールドバーグ
Goldberg, Adele E. 509
Goldberg, Alan S. 509
Goldberg, Alicia 509
Goldberg, Bill 509
Goldberg, Billy 509
Goldberg, Brad 509
Goldberg, Bruce 509
Goldberg, Carey 509
Goldberg, Dave 509
Goldberg, David 509
Goldberg, Elkhonon 509
Goldberg, Eric 509
Goldberg, Harold 509
Goldberg, Herb 509
Goldberg, Lee 509
Goldberg, Michael L. 509
Goldberg, Myla 509

Goldberg, Natalie 509
Goldberg, Philip 509
Goldberg, Richard S. 509
Goldberg, Sheryl 509
Goldberg, Stephen B. 509
Goldberg, Whoopi 509
ゴールドハーゲン
Goldhagen, Daniel Jonah 510
コルドバ・ゴンサレス
Córdova González, Boris Sebastián 290
ゴールドバッカー
Goldbacher, Sandra 509
ゴールドハーバー
Goldhaber, Maurice 510
コルドバ・ビジャロボス
Córdova Villalobos, José Ángel 290
コルトハーヘン
Korthagen, F.A.J. 758
ゴルトハマー
Goldhammer, Klaus 510
コルトハルス
Korthals, Benk 758
コルトビッチ
Koltovich, Vladimir V. 754
ゴルドビナ
Goldobina, Tatiana 510
ゴールドファーブ
Goldfarb, Alexander 510
Goldfarb, Daniel A. 510
Goldfarb, Robert W. 510
Goldfarb, Sylvia 510
ゴールドフェダー
Goldfedder, Brandon 510
Goldfeder, Steven 510
ゴールドブラット
Goldblatt, David S. 509
ゴールドブラム
Goldblum, Jeff 509
ゴールドフリード
Goldfried, Marvin R. 510
ゴールドブルム
Goldblum, Jeff 509
ゴールドベリ
Goldberg, Daniel 509
ゴールドベルグ
Goldberg, Joachim 509
ゴールドホーク
Goldhawk, Emma 510
コルトマン
Coltman, Leycester 280
ゴールドマン
Goldman, Aaron 510
Goldman, Benjamin A. 510
Goldman, Bob 510
Goldman, Burt 510
Goldman, Caren 510
Goldman, Eddie 510
Goldman, Edward 510
Goldman, Elaine Eller 510
Goldman, Howard 510
Goldman, Jay R. 510
Goldman, Jim 510
Goldman, Joel 510
Goldman, Jonathan 510
Goldman, Leslie 510
Goldman, Linda 510
Goldman, Lynda 510
Goldman, Marshall I. 510
Goldman, Michael 510
Goldman, Richard 510
Goldman, Seth 510
Goldman, Stuart Douglas 510
Goldman, Tamara Jaffe 510
Goldman, William 510
Goldmann, David R. 510
ゴルドマン
Goldmann, Pater Gereon 510
ゴールトライヒ
Goldreich, Oded 510
ゴールドラット
Goldratt, Eliyahu M. 510
Goldratt, Rami 510
ゴールドリック
Goldrick, Emma 510
ゴールドリング
Goldring, Ellen Borish 510
ゴルドール
Goldhor, Susan 510
コルトルティ
Coltorti, Fabio 280
コルトレイン
Coltrane, Alice 280
コルトレーン
Coltrane, Alice 280
Coltrane, John 280
Coltrane, Robbie 280
ゴールドワグ
Goldwag, Arthur 511
コールトン
Colton, David 280
コルトン
Colton, M.J. 280
コルドン
Cordon, Kevin 290
Kordon, Klaus 757
コルーナ
Koruna, Stefan 758
コルナイ
Kornai, János 757
コルナイユ
Cornaille, Alain 291
ゴルニック
Gaulunic, D.Charles 484
コルヌコフ
Kornukov, Anatolii Mikhailovich 757
コールネー
Koloniar, Thomas 754
コルネ
Cornet, Alize 291
Cornet, Maxwel 291
コルネイユ
Corneille 291
コルネット
Collenette, David 278
コルネホ
Cornejo, Francis 291
Cornejo, René 291
コルネホ・ラミレス
Cornejo Ramírez, Enrique 291
コルネリウス
Kornelius, Martin 757
コルネリセン
Cornelissen, Adelinde 291
コルノー
Corneau, Alain 291
コールハウゼン
Kohlhaussen, Martin 752
コールバーグ
Kohlberg, Jerome, Jr. 751
コルバーグ
Colberg, Sheri R. 276
コルパコワ
Kolpakova, Irina 754
コールハース
Koolhaas, Charlie 756
Koolhaas, Rem 756
コールハーゼ
Kohlhaase, Wolfgang 752
ゴルバーチ
Gorbach, Vitalii 517
ゴルバチョーヴァ
Gorbacheva, V.V. 517
コルバチョ・チャベス
Corbacho Chaves, Celestino 289
ゴルバチョフ
Gorbachev, Mikhail Sergeevich 517
Gorbachev, Valeri 517
コルバット
Corbat, Michael L. 289
コルバート
Colbert, Curt 276
Colbert, David 276
Colbert, Don 276
Colbert, Edwin Harris 276
Colbert, Stephen 276
Kolbert, Elizabeth 753
ゴルバハ
Gorbach, Hubert 517
コルバルト
Korvald, Lars 758
ゴルバルネジャド
Golbarnezhad, Bahman 508
コルバン
Corbin, Alain 289
Corbin, Hubert 289
コルビ
Korbi, Sadok 757
コルビー
Colby, Lynn Allen 276
Colby, Mark A. 276
Colby, William H. 276
コルピ
Colpi, Henri 280
コルビィ
Colby, Anne 276
コルビオ
Corbiau, Andree 289
Corbiau, Gerard 289
ゴルビツキー
Golubitsky, Martin 512
ゴルビツスキ
Golubytskyi, Carolin 512
コルビニエル
Corbiniere, Victor 289
コルビン
Colvin, Aaron 281
Colvin, Zach 281
コルフ
Kolff, Willem Johan 753
Korf, Benedikt 757
Korf, Bruce R. 757
コルブ
Kolb, Bonita M. 753
Kolb, Deborah M. 753
Kolb, Edward"Rocky" 753
Korb, Mihhail 757
コルプ
Korb, Julian 757
ゴルブ
Golub, Bennett W. 512
コルファー
Colfer, Chris 278
Colfer, Eoin 278
コールフィールド
Caulfield, Patrick Joseph 237
Caulfield, Tom 237
コルフェライ
Colferai, Luca 278
ゴルブチコワ
Golubchikova, Yuliya 512
コルブト
Korbut, Nikolai P. 757
ゴルブノーフ
Gorbunov, S.V. 517
ゴルブノフス
Gorbunovs, Anatolijs 517
コールブルック
Colebrook, Claire 277
コルベ
Kolbe, Uwe 753
コルペ
Corpet, Olivier 291
コルベット
Corbet, Jonathan 289
Corbett, Jennifer Marjorie 289
コルベリーニ
Corbellini, Erica 289
コルベール
Colbert, Gregory 276
コルベル
Kolber, István 753
コルベロ
Corberó, Ana 289
コル・ペン
Kol Pheng 754
コルボ
Corboz, Michel 289
コルホネン
Korhonen, Martti 757
コールホフ
Kohlhoff, Paul 752
ゴルボルネ
Golborne, Laurence 508
コルボーン
Colborn, Theo 276
Colborn, Theodora E. 276
コールマン
Calleman, Carl Johan 216
Calman, Claire 216
Coleman, Benjamin John 277
Coleman, Bill 277
Coleman, Brandon 277
Coleman, Brian 277
Coleman, Brian D. 277
Coleman, Cedric 277
Coleman, Charlotte 277
Coleman, Corey 277
Coleman, Cy 277
Coleman, David 277
Coleman, Davon 277
Coleman, Deandre 277
Coleman, Douglas 277
Coleman, Emily 277
Coleman, Gary 277
Coleman, Irwin 277
Coleman, Janet 277
Coleman, Jerry 277
Coleman, John 277

Coleman, John C. 277
Coleman, Jonathan 277
Coleman, Justin 277
Coleman, Kurt 277
Coleman, Kyle 277
Coleman, Lori 277
Coleman, Louis 277
Coleman, Lucien E., Jr. 277
Coleman, Mary 277
Coleman, Michelle 277
Coleman, Ornette 277
Coleman, Paul 277
Coleman, Peter 277
Coleman, Peter T. 277
Coleman, Reed Farrel 277
Coleman, Robert Emerson 277
Coleman, Samuel 277
Coleman, Seamus 277
Coleman, Shon 277
Coleman, Stuart Holmes 277
Coleman, Tevin 277
Coleman, Vernon 277
Colman, Alan 280
Colman, Audrey 280
Colman, Carol 280
Colman, Neil 280
Colman, Peter 280
Cormann, Mathias 291
Coulman, Valerie 295
Kollmann, Dana 753
Koolman, Jan 756

コルマン
Cormann, Enzo 291
Korman, Maxime Carlot 757
Korman, Susan 757

ゴールマン
Goleman, Daniel 511

コルミエ
Cormier, Jean 291

コルム
Kolm, John 753

コルメナレス・アランディ
Colmenares Arandi, Rodolfo 280

コルメン
Cormen, Thomas H. 291

コールメンター
Collmenter, Josh 280

コルラツェアン
Corlatean, Titus 291

ゴルラッチ
Gorlatch, Alexej 519

コールリッジ
Coleridge, Sara 277

コルンビス
Couloumbis, Audrey 295

コルンフーバー
Kornhuber, Hans Helmut 757

コーレ
Koole, Boudewijn 756
Koolen, Maayken 756

コーレー
Coley, Stephen 278

コレア
Correa, Angel 292
Correa, Arnaldo 292
Correa, Carlos 292
Correa, Carlos M. 292
Correa, Charles 292
Correa, Charles M. 292
Correa, Javier 292
Correa, Joaquin 292
Correa, Kamalei 292
Correa, Rafael 292

コレア・デルガド
Correa Delgado, Rafael Vicente 292

コレアバエアウ
Correa Bayeaux, Emilio 292

コレア・パラシオ
Correa Palacio, Ruth Stella 292

コーレイ
Corey, Gerald 290

コレイ
Collay, Michelle 278

コレイア
Correia, Carlos 292
Correia, Celso Ismael 292
Correia, Clara Pinto 292
Correia, Jorge Salgado 292
Correia, José Carlos Lopes 292
Correia, Julio 292

コレイアイシルバ
Correia E Silva, Antònio Leão 292
Correia E Silva, José Ulisses de Pina 292

コレイア・カンポス
Correia Campos, António 292

ゴーレイヴィッチ
Gourevitch, Philip 522

コレイラ
Correira, Telmo 292

コレイロプレカ
Coleiro Preca, Marie-Louise 277

コレイン
Colijn, Helen 278

コレエダ
Koreeda, Hirokazu 757

コレク
Kollek, Theodor 753

ゴレグリャード
Goregliad, Vladislav Nikanorovich 519

コレサー
Kowlessar, Saisnarine 762

コレサル
Kowlessar, Saisnarine 762

コレスニコヴァ
Kolesnikova, Irina 753

コレスニコフ
Kolesnikov, Borys 753

コレスニコワ
Kolesnikova, Irina 753

コレスニチェンコ
Kolesnichenko, Svetlana 753

コレチキー
Kolecki, Szymon 753

ゴレツカ
Goretzka, Leon 519

コーレック
Kollek, Theodor 753

コレック
Kollek, Theodor 753

コレッティ
Colletti, Jerome A. 278

コーレット
Corlett, Richard T. 291

コレット
Collett, Cary 278
Collett, Peter 278
Collette, Sandrine 278
Collette, Toni 278

コレッリ
Corelli, Franco 290

コレティ
Coleite, Aron Eli 277

ゴレトニジガマ
Gorethnizigama, Marie 519

コレドール・シエラ
Corredor Sierra, Beatriz 292

ゴレナック
Gorenak, Vinko 519

ゴレニシチエフ=クツゾフ
Golenishchev-Kutuzov, Arsenii Arkadievich 511

コレフ
Kollef, Marin H. 753

コレブネフ
Kolobnev, Alexandr 753

コレマツ
Korematsu, Fred 757

コレマンズ
Coremans, Danny 290

ゴレムビオフスキー
Golembiovskii, Igor Nesterovich 511

コレーラ
Corella, Angel 290
Corera, Gordon 290

コレラ
Kolelas, Euloge Landry 753
Kolélas, Guy Brice Parfait 753

コレリ
Corelli, Franco 290

コレリッチュ
Kolleritsch, Alfred 753

コーレル
Correll, Gemma 292

コレール
Coriell, Shelley 290

コレル
Correll, Gemma 292

コレルシヴィリ
Kolelishvili, Viktor 753

コレルリ
Corelli, Franco 290

コレロワ
Korelova, Alexandra 757

コーレン
Coren, Michael 290
Koren, Leonard 757
Koren, Steve 757
Koren, Ziv 757

コレン
Coren, Stanley 290
Koren, Steve 757

コレンク
Koreng, Eric 757

コレンコ
Kolenko, Eva 753

コレンダベルー
Collendavelloo, Ivan Leslie 278

コーレンバーグ
Kahlenberg, Mary Hunt 695
Kohlenberg, Robert J. 751

ゴレンビオフスキー
Golembiovskii, Igor Nesterovich 511

コロ
Colony, The Lost 280
Kollo, René 753

コロー
Kollo, René 753

コロイタマナ
Koroitamana, Jone 757

コロイラベソウ
Koroilavesau, Semi 757

ゴロウィン
Golowin, Sergius 512

ゴロヴィン
Golovin, Aleksandr 512
Golowin, Erik 512

コログナ
Cologna, Dario 280

コロコバ
Kolocova, Kristyna 753

コロコリツェフ
Kolokoltsev, Vladimir A. 753

コロコルツェフ
Kolokoltsev, Oleksiy 753

コロジェチャク
Kolodziejczak, Timothee 753

コロシモ
Colosimo, Jennifer 280

ゴロショーキン
Goloschekin, David Semyonovich 512

コロシンスカ
Kolosinska, Kinga 754

コロジンスキ
Kolodzinski, Pawel 753

コロスティロフ
Korostylov, Pavlo 757

コロスト
Chorost, Michael 259

コロチシュキン
Korotyshkin, Evgeny 758

ゴロチュツコフ
Golotsutskov, Anton 512

コーローディ
Kóródi, Mária 757

コロディエチュック
Kolodiejchuk, Brian 753

ゴロディッシャー
Gorodischer, Angélica 519

コロテエワ
Koroteyeva, Mariya 757

ゴロデツ
Golodets, Olga Y. 512

ゴロデンコ
Gorodenco, Anatolie 519

コロドコ
Kolodko, Evgeniia 753

コロトコフ
Korotkov, Egor 757
Korotkov, Ilya 758

コロトフ
Korotov, Konstantin 758

コロナ
Colonna, Catherine 280
Corona, Jesus 291

コロニア
Colonia, Nestor 280

コロニチ
Kolonics, György 754

コローニャ
Cologna, Dario 280
コロニャ
Cologna, Dario 280
コロネル・キンロック
Coronel Kinloch, María Amelia 291
コロバ
Kgoroba, George 724
ゴロビチュ
Golobič, Gregor 512
ゴロビナ
Golovina, Luba 512
コロブカ
Korobka, Olha 757
ゴロフキン
Golovkin, Gennady 512
コロブコフ
Kolobkov, Pavel A. 753
コロプコフ
Kolobkov, Pavel A. 753
コロブンラブラ
Korovulavula, Manu 758
コロボフ
Kolobov, Evgenii 753
Kolobov, Yuriy 753
コロボワ
Kolobova, Violetta 753
コロマ
Koroma, Abu Aya 757
Koroma, Alimamy 757
Koroma, Balogun 757
Koroma, Ernest Bai 757
Koroma, Momodu 757
コロマニコラス
Coloma Nicolas, Carlos 280
コロミーエツ
Kolomiets, Maksim 753
コローム
Coulombe, Daniel 295
コロム
Colom, Francesc 280
ゴロム
Golom, Routouang Yoma 512
Golomb, Solomon Wolf 512
ゴロムシトク
Golomshtok, Igor 512
コロメ
Colome, Alex 280
Colome, Delfin 280
コロメ・イバラ
Colomé Ibarra, Abelardo 280
コロレツ
Korolec, Marcin 757
コロレフスカ
Korolevska, Natalia 757
コロローソ
Coloroso, Barbara 280
ゴロワノフ
Golovanov, Viktor G. 512
コーロン
Choron, Sandra 259
コローン
Colon, Bartolo 280
Colon, Christian 280
Colon, Joseph 280
Colón, Raúl 280
コロン
Colom, Álvaro 280
Colom, Francesc 280
Colon, Bartolo 280
Colón, Ernie 280
ゴロン
Golon, Anne 512
コロンネ
Colonne, Guido delle 280
コロンバス
Columbus, Chris 280
コロンバーニ
Colombani, Jean-Marie 280
コロンバニ
Colombani, Jean-Marie 280
Colombani, Marie-Françoise 280
Colombani, Pascal 280
コロンビエ
Colombier, Michel 280
コロンビル
Collonville, Marie 280
コロンブ
Colomb, Gregory G. 280
コロンボ
Colombo, Chrystian 280
Colombo, Emilio 280
Colombo, Luann 280
Colombo, Roberto 280
コワコシー
Kovacocy, Marian 761
コワコフスキ
Kołakowski, Leszek 753
ゴワーズ
Gowers, Bruce 522
コワッチ
Kowatch, Robert A. 762
コワート
Cowart, Kaleb 297
コワペル
Coipel, Olivier 276
ゴワラン
Goiran, Claude 508
コワリ
Koval, George 761
コワリック
Kowalik, Trent 762
コワリョフ
Kovalyov, Anton 761
コワル
Kowal, Mary Robinette 762
コワルジック
Kowalczyk, Martin 762
コワルスキ
Kowalski, Robin M. 762
コワルスキー
Kowalski, Jochen 762
Kowalski, Michael J. 762
Kowalski, Piotr 762
コワルチク
Kowalczyk, Henryk 762
Kowalczyk, Justyna 762
コワレーニン
Kovalenin, Dmitrii 761
コワレフ
Kovalev, Gennady 761
Kovalev, Nikolay 761
コワレンコ
Kovalenko, Ivan Ivanovich 761
コワロー
Coirault, Christine 276
コーワン
Cowan, Carolyn Pape 297
Cowan, Catherine 297
Cowan, Charlotte 297
Cowan, Denys 297
Cowan, Douglas E. 297
Cowan, George 297
Cowan, Judith 297
Cowan, Philip A. 297
Cowan, Ruth Schwartz 297
コーン
Cohn, Jonathan 275
Cohn, Lee Michael 275
Cohn, Nik 275
Cohn, Norman 275
Cohn, Norman Rufus Colin 275
Cohn, Robin 275
Cohn, Ronald H. 275
Cone, James H. 282
Cone, Steve 282
Conn, David K. 283
Corn, Laura 291
Corne, David 291
Cornes, Ollie 291
Coyne, Kevin P. 298
Koehn, Marshall 751
Kohn, Alfie 752
Kohn, Eduardo 752
Kohn, George C. 752
Kohn, Jerome 752
Kohn, John 752
Kohn, Walter 752
コン
Conn, Charles 283
Conn, Peter J. 283
Gong, Ji-young 513
Gong, Li 513
Gong, Yoo 513
Kong, Bill 755
Kong, Cho Ha 755
Kong, Vorn 755
Kong Cho Ha 755
ゴーン
Ghosn, Carlos 494
Ghosn, Rita 494
Gorn, Michael H. 519
Kon, Dabbaransi 754
Korn, Chatikavanij 757
ゴン
Gon, Taikichi 513
Gong, Hongjia 513
コンヴィチュニー
Konwitschny, Peter 756
コンヴィツキ
Konwicki, Tadeusz 755
コンウィンスキ
Konwinski, Andy 755
コンウェー
Conway, Sally 285
コンウェイ
Conway, Anthony 285
Conway, Damian 285
Conway, David 285
Conway, Drew 285
Conway, Erik M. 285
Conway, Flo 285
Conway, Gerry 285
Conway, Hugh Graham 285
Conway, Joe 285
Conway, John Horton 285
Conway, Martha 285
Conway, Peter 285
Conway, Ron 285
Conway, Simon 285
Conway, Susan 285
Conway, William 285
コンウェイ=モリス
Conway Morris, Simon 285
コーンウェル
Cornwell, Bernard 291
Cornwell, Jessica 291
Cornwell, John 291
Cornwell, Nicki 291
Cornwell, Patricia Daniels 291
Cornwell, Ross 291
コンウェル
Conwell, Charles Albert Shone 285
コーンウォール
Cornwall, John 291
Cornwall, Lecia 291
コン・ウォン
Con Wong, Gil Reinaldo 285
コンカ
Konkka, U.S. 755
コンガ
Konga, Kenneth 755
コンガー
Conger, Jay A. 282
ゴンガー
Gongar, Othello 513
ゴンガラ
Gongarad, Celestin Nkoua 513
コンガンチエフ
Kongantiyev, Moldomusa 755
コンキャノン
Concannon, Jack 282
コング
Congue, Constantino 282
コンクェスト
Conquest, Robert 283
コンクエスト
Conquest, Robert 283
コングスバック
Kongsbak, Kirja 755
コング・ニュオン
Kong Nyuon, John 755
ゴンクリバリ
Gon-coulibaly, Amadou 513
コンクリン
Conklin, Bob 282
Conklin, Jack 282
Conklin, Robert 282
コンクル
Conkle, Gina 282
コングルトン
Congleton, Roger D. 282
コングレトン
Congleton, Roger D. 282
コンケスト
Conquest, Robert 283
コンコ
Konko, Abdoulay 755
コンゴドゥドゥ
Kongo Doudou, Toussaint 755
ゴンゴーラ
Gongora, Carlos 514
コンゴロ
Kongolo, Mwenze 755
ゴンサルヴェス
Gonsalves, Ralph E. 514

Gonsalves, Rob 514
ゴンサルベス
Goncalves, Antonio 513
Gonçalves, Davi 513
Gonçalves, João 513
Gonçalves, José da Silva 513
Gonsalves, Camillo 514
Gonsalves, Ralph E. 514
Gonsalves, Stephen 514
Gonsalves, Theresa J. 514
ゴンサーレス
Gonzalez Moreno, M. J. 515
ゴンサレス
Gonzales, Laurence 514
Gonzales, Manuel G. 514
Gonzalez, Adrian 514
Gonzalez, Alcides Lorenzo Rial 514
González, Anabel 514
Gonzalez, Asley 514
González, Carlos 514
Gonzalez, Derlis 514
Gonzalez, Driulys 514
Gonzalez, Fernando 514
Gonzalez, Giancarlo 514
González, Ginés 514
Gonzalez, Gio 514
Gonzalez, Gonzalo 514
González, José Luis 514
González, Justo L. 514
González, Karla 514
González, Manuel 514
Gonzalez, Maria Guadalupe 514
Gonzalez, Maximo 514
Gonzalez, Misleydis 514
Gonzalez, Pablo 514
González, Ramiro 514
González, Roberto 514
Gonzalez, Rodrigo 514
Gonzalez, Roman 514
Gonzalez, Romulo 514
Gonzalez, Rubén 514
Gonzalez, Santiago 514
González, Santiago Guillén 514
Gonzalez, Sergio 514
González, Tulio Mariano 514
Gonzalez Bonilla, Joel 515
González Ferreras, Julia 515
ゴンザレス
Gonzales, Alberto 514
Gonzales, Manuel 514
Gonzales, Marco 514
Gonzales, Norberto 514
Gonzales, Raul 514
Gonzalez, Adrian 514
Gonzalez, Alfredo 514
Gonzalez, Carlos 514
Gonzalez, ChiChi 514
Gonzalez, Erik 514
Gonzalez, Fredi 514
Gonzalez, Geremi 514
Gonzalez, Gio 514
Gonzalez, Gonzalo 514
González, Juan 514
Gonzalez, Marwin 514
Gonzalez, Miguel 514
Gonzalez, Rayan 514
Gonzalez, Richard 514
Gonzalez, Rubén 514
Gonzalez, Rudy 514
Gonzalez, Severino 514
Gonzalez, Tomas 514
Gonzalez, Tony 514
González, Virginia 515
ゴンサレス・アモロジーノ
Gonzalez Amorosino, Lucas 515
ゴンサレス・イグレシアス
Gonzalez Iglesias, Santiago 515
ゴンザレス・ウィプラー
González-Wippler, Migene 515
ゴンサレス・エストラダ
González Estrada, Tomás 515
ゴンサレス・ゴンサレス
González González, Guillermo José 515
ゴンサーレス・サインス
González Sainz, César 515
ゴンサレスシンデ・レイグ
González-sinde Reig, Ángels 515
ゴンサレスセプルベダ
Gonzalez Sepulveda, Enrique Tomas 515
ゴンサレス・トゥルモ
González Turmo, Isabel 515
ゴンサレス・トゥロヤーノ
González Troyano, Alberto 515
ゴンサレス・トレド
González Toledo, Julián 515
ゴンサレス・フェルナンデス
González Fernández, Margarita 515
ゴンサレス・プラナス
González Planas, Roberto Ignacio 515
ゴンサレスペレス
Gonzalez Perez, Yoanka 515
ゴンサレス・ポサダ
Gonzales Posada, Luis Javier Eyzaguirre 514
ゴンサレスボニリャ
Gonzalez Bonilla, Joel 515
ゴンサレス・マキ
González Macchi, Luis 515
ゴンザレス - メーナ
Gonzalez-Mena, Janet 515
ゴンザレス＝モリーナ
González Molina, Gabriel 515
ゴンサレス・ラライン
González Larraín, Santiago 515
ゴンザレス・ルッシ
González-Crussi, F. 515
ゴンサレス・ロペス
González López, Gustavo Enrique 515
ゴンサロ・カストロ
Gonzalo Castro 515
ゴンサロ・ロドリゲス
Gonzalo Rodriguez 515
ゴンジ
Gonzi, Lawrence 515
コーン・シェルボク
Cohn-Sherbok, Lavinia 276
ゴンシオア
Gonschior, Thomas 514
コーン＝シャーボク
Cohn-Sherbok, Dan 276
コンシャーボク
Cohn-Sherbok, Dan 276
ゴンジュウ
Gondjout, Laure Olga 513
コンシーリ
Consigli, Andrea 284
コーンスウェイト
Cornthwaite, Julie 291
コンスタブル
Constable, Giles 284
Constable, Kate 284
Constable, Nick 284
Constable, Patrick 284
Constable, Paule 284
Constable, Simon 284
Constable, Trevor J. 284
コーンスタム
Kohnstamm, Geldolph Adriaan 752
コンスタム
Konstam, Angus 755
ゴンスターラ
Gonstalla, Esther 514
コンスタン
Constans, Claire 284
Constant, Horace 284
Constant, Paule 284
コンスタンス
Constance, Debrah 284
コンスタンチノス2世
Constantinos II 284
コンスタンチン
Constantine, Larry 284
Constantine, Peter 284
コンスタンティニデス
Constantinides, Anthony 284
コンスタンティーヌ
Constantine, Barbara 284
コンスタンティノ
Constantino, Fiel Domingos 284
コンスタンティノス
Constantinos II 284
コンスタンディノス
Constantinos II 284
コンスタンティノフ
Konstantinov, Roman 755
Konstantinov, Stefan 755
コンスタンティノフスキー
Konstantinovsky, Vadim 755
コンスタンティン
Constantin, Daniel 284
コンスタント
Constant, Jules 284
コンスタントプーロス
Konstantopoulos, Dimitrios 755
コンセイサン
Conceição, Albino José Da 282
Conceicao, Robson 282
コンセイソン
Conceição, Pedro 282
Conceicao, Rosangela 282
コンセイユ
Conseil, Dominique 284
コンセディーン
Consedine, Jim 284
コンセプシオン・ゴンサレス
Concepción González, María del Carmen 282
コンゼンツィウス
Consentius, Ernst 284
コンタ
Konta, Johanna 755
コンダー
Conder, Michelle 282
Conder, Shane 282
ゴンタ
Gonta, Geshe Sonam Gyaltsen 514
ゴンダ
Gonda, Cyriaque 513
Gonda, Ivett 513
コンダウーロワ
Kondaurova, Yekaterina 754
コンタサル・サンス
Cortázar Sanz, René 292
コンタドール
Contador, Alberto 284
コンタミーヌ
Contamine, Philippe 284
ゴンダル
Gondal, Nazar Muhammad 513
コンチー
Conchie, Barry 282
コンチアス
Kontzias, Bill 755
コンチェラ
Konchelah, Gideon 754
コンチャ
Vinet, Sebastian Concha 1458
ゴンチャール
Gonchar, Andrei Aleksandrovich 513
ゴンチャレンコ
Goncharenko, Vladimir I. 513
ゴンチャロフ
Goncharov, Andrei 513
Goncharov, Ruslan 513
Goncharov, Valeri 513
Goncharov, Vladimir 513
Goncharova, Natalia 513
コンチャロフスキー
Koncalovskij, Andrej 754
ゴンチャン
Gongchan 513
ゴンチュク
Gontiuk, Roman 514
ゴンツィ
Gonci, Jozef 513
コンツェビッチ
Kontsevich, Maxim 755
コンツォシュ
Koncoš, Pavel 754
コンテ
Conte, Antonio 284
Conte, Chris 284
Conté, Lansana 284
Conte, Nicola 284
Conte, Patrizia 284
Conteh, Alfred Palo 284
Conteh, Paolo 284
Conteh, Richard 284
コンデ
Condé, Alhassane 282
Conde, Allou 282
Condé, Alpha 282
Conde, Amara 282

Condé, Boureima 282
Conde, H.Victor 282
Conde, Mamady 282
Condé, Maryse 282
Condé, Moussa 282
コンティ
Conti, Andrea 284
Conti, Beppe 284
Conti, Giulia 284
Conti, Joe Bova 284
コンディ
Condie, Ally 282
コンディット
Condit, Phil 282
コンティデス
Kontides, Pavlos 755
コンティン
Contin, Alexis 284
ゴンディン
Gondín, Carlos Fernández 513
コンテッサ
Contessa, Fabrizio 284
コンデプディ
Kondepudi, Dilip 754
ゴンテュク
Gontiuk, Roman 514
コンテルノ・マルティネリ
Conterno Martinelli, Elena 284
コント
Comte, Fernand 282
Cont, Jacques Lu 284
Conte, Arthur 284
コンドー
Condo, Jon 282
Condor, Sam 282
ゴンドー
Gondo, Glen Yoshiaki 513
ゴンドウェ
Gondwe, Goodall 513
Gondwe, Goodall Edward 513
コントゥラ
Kontula, Osmo 755
コンドグビア
Kondogbia, Geoffrey 754
コントス
Kontos, George 755
コント・スポンヴィル
Comte-Sponville, André 282
ゴントナー
Gauntner, John 484
コンドニス
Kontonis, Stavros 755
コンドラ
Kondra, Boka 754
コンドラッツ
Kondrats, Sandis 754
コントラレス
Contreras, Carlos Francisco 284
コンドリー
Condry, Ian 282
ゴンドリー
Gondry, Michel 513
Gondry, Olivier "Twist" 513
ゴンドール
Gondor, Emory 513
Gondor, Lillian 513
ゴンドルフ
Gondorf, Jerome 513
コントレーラス
Contreras, Loren 285
コントレラス
Contreras, Bret 284
Contreras, Carlos Francisco 284
Contreras, Dalia 284
Contreras, Edgar 285
Contreras, Erwin 285
Contreras, Manuel 285
Contreras, Marleny 285
Contreras, Rina 285
Contreras, William Antonio 285
Contreras, Willson 285
Contreras, Yuderqui Maridalia 285
Contreras Reyes, Nancy 285
Rienda Contreras, María José 1181
コンドレリ
Condorelli, Santo 282
コンドロコウキス
Chondrokoukis, Dimitrios 259
コンドン
Condon, Bill 282
Condon, Judith 282
Congdon, Lisa 282
コンヌ
Connes, Alain 283
コンネル
Connell, R.W. 283
コンノ・サトウ
Konno Sato, Victor 755
コンパー
Compper, Marvin 281
ゴンバ
Gomba, Alexis 512
コンパイ
Compay Segundo 281
コンパイ・セグンド
Compay Segundo 281
コンパオレ
Compaore, Benjamin 281
Compaoré, Blaise 281
Compaoré, Jean Baptiste 281
Compaore, Simon 281
コーンバーグ
Kornberg, Arthur 757
Kornberg, Roger D. 757
コンバース
Converse, Philip E. 285
ゴンパース
Gompers, Paul Alan 513
ゴンパーツ
Gomperts, Bastien D. 513
コンバニ
Kombani, Celina Ompeshi 754
コンパニ
Kompany, Vincent 754
コンパニョン
Compagnon, Antoine Marcel Thomas 281
コンバーバッハ
Comberbach, Stuart Harold 281
ゴンバラ
Gonbala, Laurent 513
コンビ
Comby, Bruno 281
コンビエヌ
Kombienou, Pocoun Damè 754
コンビチュニー
Konwitschny, Peter 756
コンビツキ
Konwicki, Tadeusz 755
コンビラ
Kombila, Pierre André 754
コンファロニエリ
Confalonieri, Diego 282
コンフィアン
Confiant, Raphael 282
コーンフィールド
Kornfield, Jack 757
コンフェンテ
Confente, Alessandro 282
コーンフォース
Cornforth, John Warcup 291
コーンフォード
Cornford, James 291
コンフォート
Comfort, Louise 281
Conforto, Michael 282
コンフォード
Conford, Ellen 282
コンプトン
Compton, Anne 281
Compton, Erik 281
Compton, John 281
Compton, John George Melvin 281
Compton, Petros 281
Compton, Petrus 281
Compton, Tom 281
Compton, Will 282
コンフリー
Conefrey, Mick 282
コンプリ
Compri, Gaetano 281
ゴンブリック
Gombrich, Ernst Hans Josef 512
ゴンブリッチ
Gombrich, Ernst Hans Josef 512
Gombrich, Richard Francis 512
コーンブリート
Cornbleet, Jennifer 291
コーンブルム
Kornblum, William 757
コンベット
Combet, Greg 281
コンペール
Compère, Daniel 281
コンボ
Combot, Sebastien 281
Kombo, Musikari 754
Kombo, Musikari Nazi 754
コンボー
Combeau, Yvan 281
コンボニ・サリナス
Comboni Salinas, Javier 281
コンボ・ヤヤ
Kombo Yaya, Dieudonné 754
ゴンボリ
Gomboli, Mario 512
コンポワン
Compoint, Stéphane 281
コン・ボーン
Kong Vorn 755
コーンマン
Kornman, Kenneth S. 757
コンメンツ
Commentz, Carlos Encina 281
コンヤノフスキ
Konjanovski, Zoran 755
コンヨン
Conyon, Martin 285
コーンライヒ
Kornreich, Gabriel 757
コンラーズ
Coenraads, Robert Raymond 273
コンラス
Konrath, Joe 755
コンラッド
Conrad, Barnaby, Ⅲ 284
Conrad, Heinrich 284
Conrad, Hy 284
Conrad, Jon M. 284
Conrad, Lauren 284
Conrad, Linda 284
Conrad, Pam 284
Conrad, Parker 284
Conrad, Paul 284
Conrad, Peter 284
Conrad, Sheree D. 284
Conrad, Susan 284
コンラーディ
Conrady, Karl Otto 284
コンラディ
Conradi, Peter 284
コンラディー
Conradie, Wian 284
コンラド
Konrad, Mike 755
コンラン
Conlan, Michael John 282
Conlan, Thomas D. 282
Conran, Shirley 284
Conran, Terence Orby 284
コン・リー
Gong, Li 513
コンリー
Conlee, Robert S. 282
Conley, Adam 282
Conley, Amy 282
Conley, Chip 282
Conley, Chris 282
Conley, Mike 282
Conly, Jane Leslie 283
コンリック
Conrick, John 284
コンリン
Conlin, Jonathan 283
コン・レ
Kong Le 755
コン・レー
Kong Le 755
コンロイ
Conroy, Frank 284
Conroy, Pat 284
Conroy, Stephen 284
コンロテ
Konrote, Jioji 755
コンロン
Conlon, Christopher 283
Conlon, Edward 283
Conlon, James 283
コンワタナクン

コ

Kongvattanakul, Somphon 755

【サ】

サ
Sa, Andre 1222
Sa, Jose 1222
サー
Sa, Ding-ding 1222
Sah, Ganesh 1226
Ser, Xiang Wei Jasmine 1274
Suhr, Jennifer 1363
ザー
Gia, Tran Xuan 494
サアカシビリ
Saakashvili, Mikheil 1222
サアカシュヴィリ
Saakashvili, Mikheil 1222
サアカシュビリ
Saakashvili, Mikheil 1222
サアキャン
Sahakian, Bako S. 1226
ザアズーア
Zaazou, Hisham 1544
ザアゾウ
Zaazou, Hisham 1544
サアット
Sa'at, Alfian 1222
サアディ
al-Sa'adi, Sa'ad bin Mohammed bin Said al-Mardhouf 1222
サアド・アブドラ・サレム・サバハ
Saad al-Abdullah al-Salem al-Sabah 1222
サアド・アル・アブドラ・アル・サレム・アル・サバハ
Saad al-Abdullah al-Salem al-Sabah 1222
サアベドラ
Saavedra, Jaime 1222
サアベドラ・チャンドゥビ
Saavedra Chanduví, Jaime 1222
サイ
Cui, Yang-uang 307
PSY 1138
Say, Fazil 1247
Say Samal 1247
Sy, Ousmane 1373
Tsai, Kun-Tsan 1423
Tsai, Mavis 1423
ザイア
Zaia, Luca 1545
ザイアンツ
Zajonc, Arthur G. 1545
ザイヴァート
Seiwert, Lothar 1270
サイェ
Sayeh, Antoinette 1247
サイエディ
Saiedi, Ali El 1227
サイエド
Syed, Hassina 1373
サイエドホセン
Sayed-hossen, Cader 1247
ザイエン
Zeien, Alfred M. 1549
ザイエンガ
Zaayenga, Karyn 1544
サイェンコ
Saienko, Olexandr 1227
サイカー
Siker, Jeffrey S. 1298
ザイガー
Zeiger, Eduardo 1549
Zeiger, Mimi 1549
サイキ
Saiki, Kenneth Takao 1227
サーイグ
al-Sayegh, Salim 1247
サイク
Saich, Tony 1227
Zajc, Hanna 1545
ザイク
Zeig, Jeffrey K. 1549
ザイグ
Zeig, Jeffrey K. 1549
サイクス
Sikes, Patricia J. 1298
Sykes, Brian 1373
Sykes, Charles J. 1373
Sykes, Christopher 1373
Sykes, Julie 1373
Sykes, Karen 1373
Sykes, Plum 1373
サイクロン・ネグロ
Cyclone Negro 310
サイゲルマン
Sigelman, Lee 1298
ザイコフ
Zaikov, Lev Nikolaevich 1545
ザイザイ
Zayzay, Augustine 1549
サイシ
Xaysi, Santivong 1531
サイシー
Xaysi, Santivong 1531
サイス
Saeijs, Frederieke 1225
Sáiz, Agustín 1228
Saiz, Jesus 1228
Theis, Samuel 1395
サイズ
Sides, Hampton 1296
Sze, David 1374
ザイスマン
Zysman, John 1560
サイズモア
Sisemore, Timothy A. 1308
Sizemore, Grady 1309
Sizemore, Susan 1309
ザイゼル
Zeizel, Jared 1550
サイセンリー
Saysengly, Tengbliachue 1247
Xaysenglee, Tengbliavue 1531
サイダー
Sider, Ronald J. 1296
Sider, Theodore 1296
Sydor, Alison 1373
サイダウ
Saidau, Ibrahim 1227
サイダコワ
Saidakova, Nadia 1227
サイダム
Saydam, Sabri 1247
ザイタムル
Zeithaml, Valarie A. 1549
ザイダン
al-Zaidan, Falah 1545
Zeidan, Abdul Rahman 1549
サイチ
Saich, Tony 1227
ザイチェンコ
Zaichenko, Nikolai P. 1545
ザイチコフ
Zaichikov, Alexandr 1545
サイチンガ
Na Sainchogt 1006
サイツ
Seitz, Frederic 1270
Seitz, Frederick 1270
Seitz, Justin 1270
Sites, Elizabeth 1308
ザイツ
Seitz, Elisabeth 1270
Seitz, Franz 1270
Seitz, Frederick 1270
Seitz, Manfred 1270
サイツァー
Seitzer, Kevin 1270
ザイツェワ
Zaitseva, Olga 1545
サーイディ
al-Saaidi, Abdullah 1222
サイーディ
al-Saeedi, Ahmed bin Mohammed bin Obaid 1225
al-Saidi, Abdullah bin Mohammed bin Said 1227
サイティ
Saiti, Dzemali 1228
サイディ
Saïdi, Mahieddine 1227
Saidy, Isatou Njie 1227
Sidey, Hugh 1296
ザイディ
Zaidi, Nadeem 1545
サイティエフ
Saytiev, Buvaysa 1247
サイーディキア
Saeedikia, Mohammad 1225
サイデマン
Suryohadiprojo, Sayidiman 1368
サイデマン・スリヨハディプロジョ
Suryohadiprojo, Sayidiman 1368
サイテル
Seitel, Fraser P. 1270
サイデル
Seidel, Robert W. 1269
ザイデル
Seidel, Christian 1269
Zaidel, Dahlia W. 1545
ザイデルフェルト
Zijderveld, Anton C. 1554
ザイデルヘルム
Seyderhelm, Bettina 1277
サイデンステッカー
Seidensticker, Edward George 1269
サイード
Saeed, Fathimath Dhiyana 1225
Saeed, Fouzia 1225
Saeed, Mohamed 1225
Saeed, Mohamed Shaheem Ali 1225
Saeed, Nadia 1225
Sa'eed, Reda 1225
Said 1227
Said, Abdelmonem 1227
Said, Abdelrahman 1227
Said, Chris 1227
Said, Edward Wadi 1227
Said, Essam bin Saad bin 1227
Said, Kurban 1227
Said, Mahmoud Ibrahim 1227
Said, S.F. 1227
al-Sayed, Muhammad aAbdul-Sattar 1247
Sayeed, Abu 1247
Sayeed, P.M. 1247
al-Sayyid, Mahmoud 1247
al-Sayyid, Muhammad Turki 1247
サイト
Sait, Sadiq M. 1228
Sayit, Kayra 1247
サイド
Said, Aqiel Munawar 1227
Said, Davlatali 1227
Said, Galal 1227
Said, Mohamed 1227
Said, Mohammed Kabir 1227
Said, Nuriddin 1227
Sayed, Sadoddin 1247
Syed, Matthew 1373
ザイド
Zeid, Hikmat 1549
サイドイブラヒム
Said Ibrahim, Fahmi 1227
サイトウ
Saïto, Christine 1228
Saito, Hiroshi 1228
Saito, Juniti 1228
Saito, Kazuya 1228
サイドゥ
Saidou, Oua 1227
Saïdou, Saley 1227
サイトウィック
Cytowic, Richard E. 310
サイード・カイユム
Sayed Khaiyum, Aiyaz 1247
サイドゲルニ
Said Guerni, Djabir 1227
サイドシラジュディン・サイドプトラ・ジャマルライル
Syed Sirajuddin Syed Putra Jamalullail 1373
サイトチ
Saitoti, George Kinuthia 1228
サイトティ
Saitoti, George Kinuthia 1228
サイド・バカル
Said Bakar, Abdourahim 1227
サイドバカル
Said Bakar, Abdourahim 1227
サイードハッサン
Said Hassane, Elarif 1227
サイドハミド
Syed Hamid, Albar 1373

サ

サイードパンギンジ
Said-panguindji, Dominique 1227
ザイド・ビン・スルタン・アル・ナハヤン
Zayed bin Sultan al-Nahyan 1549
ザイド・ビン・スルタン・ナハヤン
Zayed bin Sultan al-Nahyan 1549
サイトフ
Saitov, Oleg 1228
サイドフ
Saidov, Nuriddin 1227
Saidov, Renat 1227
Saidov, Zaid 1227
ザーイド・ブン・スルターン・ナヒーヤーン
Zayed bin Sultan al-Nahyan 1549
サイドボサム
Sidebotham, Thomas Hurst 1296
サイード・ボーシュ
Seid Bauche, Abdelkerim 1269
サイドボトム
Sidebottom, Harry 1296
サイドラー
Seidler, David 1269
Seidler, Robert 1269
ザイトラー
Zeitler, Kevin 1549
ザイトリン
Zeitlin, Benh 1549
サイドルー
Saeed Lou, Ali 1225
ザイトル
Seidl, Sebastian 1269
ザイドル
Seidl, Claudius 1269
Seidl, Ulrich 1269
ザイドルマイヤー
Seidlmeier, Heinrich 1269
サイドワ
Saidova, Galina 1227
サイナ
Cyna, Allan M. 310
Saina, Betsy 1227
サイナイ
Sinai, Allen 1305
ザイナル
Zainal, Abdullah bin 1545
ザイナル・アリレザ
Zainal Alireza, Abdullah bin Ahmed 1545
サイニ
Saini, Atul 1227
ザイヌディン
Zainuddin, Maidin 1545
サイネス
Saynez, Mariano 1247
Synez, Mariano 1374
サイパート
Cypert, Samuel A. 310
サイバートソン
Sivertson, Chris 1309
サイババ
Sai Baba, Sathya 1226
サイハンビレグ
Saikhanbileg, Chimed 1227
ザイヒト
Seicht, Gerhard 1269
サイフ
Saif, Abdullah bin Hassan 1227
Saif, bin Hamad al-Busaidi 1227
Saif, bin Zayed al-Nahyan 1227
Saif, Ibrahim 1227
Saif, Linda J. 1227
サイブ
Saibou, Ali 1227
サイプ
Sipe, Ken 1307
ザイプ
Seip, Stefan 1270
Seipp, Walter 1270
サイファー
Sypher, Wylie 1374
サイファース
Cyphers, Christopher J. 310
サイファーズ
Cyphers, Eric 310
ザイファート
Ziefert, Harriet 1554
サイフィ
Saïfi, Tokia 1227
サイフェ
Seife, Charles 1270
ザイフェルト
Seifert, Christian 1270
Seifert, Gero 1270
Seifert, Werner G. 1270
Seifert, Wolfgang 1270
Seiffert, Peter 1270
サイフジン
Saifuding 1227
ザイプス
Zipes, Jack 1556
サイフディン
Saifuding 1227
ザイフマン
Zeifman, Debra 1549
サイフラ
Syaifullah, Yusuf 1373
ザイフリート
Seifried, Dieter 1270
サイプリーン
Cyprien, Johnathan 310
サイフレス
Scifres, Mike 1263
サイフワンダ
Sayifwanda, Sarah 1247
サイベル
Seibel, Peter 1269
ザイベルト
Seibert, Dieter 1269
サイ・マウ・カン
Sai Mauk Kham 1227
サイ・マー・ラクシュミ・デヴィ
Sai Maa Lakshmi Devi 1227
ザイマン
Ziman, John Michael 1554
サイム
Sime, Ruth Lewin 1301
サイムス
Symes, Peter D. 1373
サイムズ
Symes, Ruth 1373
サイメル
Simel, David L. 1301
サイモン
Saimon, Esmon 1227
Simon, Alan R. 1302
Simon, Anne 1302
Simon, Annette Dauphin 1302
Simon, Bebe 1302
Simon, Bryant 1302
Simon, Carly 1302
Simon, Daniel 1303
Simon, Danny 1303
Simon, David 1303
Simon, Deon 1303
Simon, Eric J. 1303
Simon, Georg 1303
Simon, George K. 1303
Simon, Herb 1303
Simon, Herbert Alexander 1303
Simon, Hermann 1303
Simon, Ilanah 1303
Simon, Jack 1303
Simon, Joanna 1303
Simon, John 1303
Simon, Justin 1303
Simon, Mark 1303
Simon, Michael 1303
Simon, Neil 1303
Simon, Paul 1303
Simon, Rachel 1303
Simon, Sam 1303
Simon, Tami 1303
Simon, Tharold 1303
Simon, William L. 1303
サイモンズ
Simmons, Ed 1302
Simonds, John Ormsbee 1303
Simons, Benjamin D. 1303
Simons, Robert 1304
Symonds, Terry 1373
Symons, Donald 1374
Symons, Terrie 1374
サイモンソン
Simonson, Itamar 1304
サイモンタッチ
Simontacchi, Carol N. 1304
サイモント
Simont, Marc 1304
ザイヤーニ
al-Zayani, Zaid bin Rashid 1548
サイヨンマー
Saijonmaa, Arja 1227
サイラー
Seiler, Thomas 1270
Siler, Jenny 1299
ザイラー
Sailer, Anton Engelbert 1227
Seiler, Roland 1270
サイラス
Cyrus, Billy Ray 310
Cyrus, Miley 310
Silas, Stephen 1298
ザイラッハー
Seilacher, Adolf 1270
サイラフィザデー
Sayrafiezadeh, Said 1247
ザイリアン
Zaillian, Steven 1545
サイル
al-Sayer, Hilal Musaed 1247
ザイル
Zijl, Ida van 1554
ザイルストラ
Zijlstra, Jelle 1554
サイレン
Silen, William 1299
ザイロフ
Zairov, Intigam 1545
サイロン
Syron, Richard 1374
ザイン
Zain, Mohamed 1545
サインジャルガル
Sainjargal, Nyam-Ochir 1227
サインフェルド
Seinfeld, Jerry 1270
サインマロ
Saint Malo, Isabel 1228
サウ
Sau, Male 1244
Sau, Marco 1244
Sau, Phan Van 1244
ザウ
Giau, Nguyen Van 495
Zaü 1548
サウアー
Sauer, Tim 1244
ザヴァツキ
Zawadzki, Hubert 1548
サヴァリ
Savary, Jérôme 1245
サヴァリシュ
Sawallisch, Wolfgang 1246
サヴァリッシュ
Sawallisch, Wolfgang 1246
ザヴァリッシュ
Sawallisch, Wolfgang 1246
ザヴィアチッチ
Zaviačič, Milan 1548
サヴィアーノ
Saviano, Roberto 1245
サヴィオラ
Saviola, Javier 1246
サヴィオロ
Saviolo, Stefania 1246
サーヴィス
Service, Robert 1275
ザヴィストースキー
Zawistowski, Jerzy 1548
サヴィチェヴィッチ
Savićević, Dejan 1245
サウィツキ
Sawicki, Marek 1246
Sawicki, Mirosław 1246
サヴィッチ
Savic, Dragan 1245
Savic, Stefan 1245
サヴィッツ
Savitz, Harriet May 1246
サヴィデス
Savvides, Irini 1246
サーヴィナ
Savvina, Iya 1246
サヴィーナ
Savvina, Iya 1246
サヴィニャック
Savignac, Raymond Pierre Guillaume 1245
サヴィニョン
Savignon, Jéromine 1245
Savignon, Sandra J. 1245

サヴィノワ
Savinova, Mariya 1246
サヴィル
Savile, Jimmy 1245
サヴィン
Savin, Anatolii Pavlovich 1246
サヴィンビ
Savimbi, Jonas Malheiro 1246
サウヴォ
Sauvo, Tini 1245
サヴェア
Savea, Julian 1245
サーウェイ
Serway, Raymond A. 1275
サヴェージ
Savage, Dan 1245
Savage, Tom 1245
サウェタブット
Sawettabut, Suthasini 1246
サヴェッジ
Savage, Stephen 1245
サヴェリー
Savery, John R. 1245
サヴェーリエヴァ
Savel'eva, Elena Ivanovna 1245
ザウエルブライ
Sauerbreij, Nicolien 1244
サヴォイ
Savoy, Nick 1246
ザヴォス
Zavos, Panos 1548
ザヴォドニー
Zawodny, Janusz Kazimierz 1548
サヴォライネン
Savolainen, Salla 1246
ザウォロトニク
Zawrotniak, Radoslaw 1548
ザヴォロンコフ
Zhavoronkov, Alex 1552
ザウザー
Sauser, Christoph 1245
ザウザウ
Caucau, Asenaca 237
サウザム
Southam, Phil 1331
サウス
South, Leonard J. 1331
South, Stephanie 1331
サウスウィック
Southwick, Jack 1331
Southwick, Jessica 1331
Southwick, Steven M. 1331
Southwick, Teresa 1331
サウスウッド
Southwood, Peter 1331
Southwood, Richard 1331
サウスオール
Southall, Ivan 1331
サウスソール
Southall, Ivan 1331
サウス・ポール
South-Paul, Jeannette E. 1331
サウスワース
Southworth, Ian 1331
Southworth, Jo 1331
Southworth, John 1331
Southworth, Lucinda 1331
サウスワート
Southwart, Erizabeth 1331
サウスワード
Southward, Dezmen 1331
サウセダ
Sauceda, Sunny 1244
サウセ・ナバロ
Sauce Navarro, Luis Alfredo 1244
サウソール
Southall, Brian 1331
Southall, Humphrey 1331
ザウター
Sauter, Gerhard 1245
サウダバエフ
Saudabayev, Kanat 1244
サウティン
Sautin, Dmitri 1245
サウデン
Sowden, Linda A. 1332
サウード
Saud al-Faisal 1244
サウド
Saud, bin Hilal bin Hamad al-Busaidi 1244
Saud, bin Ibrahim al-Busaidi 1244
Saud, bin Ibrahim bin Saud al-Busaidi 1244
Saud, Narayan Prakash 1244
サウド・アル・ファイサル
Saud al-Faisal 1244
ザウドニ
Zawodny, Jeremy D. 1548
サウド・ファイサル
Saud al-Faisal 1244
サウナワーラ
Saunavaara, Juha 1244
ザウバー
Sauber, Tim 1244
サウマ
Saouma, Edouard 1241
サウマトゥア
Saumatua, Samuela 1244
サウミナデン
Sawmynaden, Yogida 1246
ザウム
Saum, Pater Kilian 1244
サウラ
Saura, Carlos 1245
サウララ
Saulala, Sione Sangster 1244
サウール
Saul, Niguez 1244
サウロ
Saulo, Manasa 1244
ザウワー
Sauer, Jürgen 1244
サウンダース
Saunders, Cicely 1244
Saunders, George 1244
Saunders, John 1245
Saunders, Raven 1245
サエイ
Saei, Hadi 1225
サエイボネコハル
Saei, Hadi 1225
サエス・マルチネス
Sáez-Martinez, Francisco J. 1225
ザエツ
Zayets, Ivan 1549
サエール
Saer, Juan José 1225
サエンコ
Saenko, Svetlana 1225
サエンス
Saénz, Guido 1225
Saénz, María del Rocío 1225
サエンスデサンタマリア
Sáenz De Santamaría Antón, Soraya 1225
サエンスデサンタマリア・アントン
Sáenz De Santamaría Antón, Soraya 1225
ザオ
Giao, Doan Manh 494
Zao, Wou-ki 1547
Zhao, Qi-zheng 1552
Zhao, Xian-shun 1552
Zhao, Zi-yang 1552
ザオ・ウー・キー
Zao, Wou-ki 1547
ザオバー
Sauber, Tim 1244
サオム
Som Kimsour 1327
ザオラー
Saurer, Helmut 1245
ザオラーレク
Zaorálek, Lubomír 1547
サーカー
Sarkar, Shrii Prabhat Ranjan 1242
サカ
Saca, Antonio 1223
Saka, Manolya 1228
サカイ
Sakai, Kenji 1228
サカイオ
Sakaio, Vete 1228
サカイダ
Sakaida, Henry 1228
ザカエフ
Zakayev, Akhmed 1546
サカサ
Sacasa, Noel 1223
サーカシヴィリ
Saakashvili, Mikheil 1222
サガジエフ
Sagadiyev, Yerlan 1226
サーカシビリ
Saakashvili, Mikheil 1222
ザカス
Zakas, Nicholas C. 1546
サガスティ
Sagasti, Raúl 1226
サガストゥメ
Sagastume, Gabriel 1226
サカタ
Sakata, Thomas S. 1228
Sakata, Tojuro 1228
サガード
Thagard, Paul 1393
サカニイ
Sakanyi, Henry Mova 1228
サガニック
Saganich, Al., Jr. 1226
サカフ
al-Sakaf, Nadia 1228
サカフィ
Sakafi, Khadijeh 1228
ザガミ
Zagami, Leo 1545
サカモト
Sakamoto, Kerri 1228
サガラ
Sagara, David 1226
ザカラキス
Zacharakis, Andrew 1544
ザカラス
Zachras, Mattlan 1544
ザカリ
Zacharie, Felicien Chabi 1544
Zakari, Aziz 1546
ザカリー
Zachary, G.Pascal 1544
ザカリア
Zakaria, Denis 1546
Zakaria, Fareed 1546
Zakaria, Haikal 1546
Zakaria, Sulaiman 1546
ザカリーアス
Zacarias, Felicio 1544
ザカリアス
Zacarias, Felicio 1544
サガリオ
Sagario, Mario 1226
サカリン
Sacharin, Ken 1223
ザカレイシビリ
Zakareishvili, Paata 1546
ザガレンスキー
Zagarenski, Pamela 1545
サカロプロ
Psacharopulo, Alessandra 1138
サガン
Sagan, Françoise 1226
Sagan, Iwona 1226
サーキ
Sarchie, Ralph 1241
ザキ
Zaki, Aminath Zenysha Shaheed 1546
Zaki, Ibrahim Hussain 1546
ザキオス
Zackios, Gerald 1544
サーキス
Sarkis, Stephanie 1242
Serkis, Andy 1275
サキック
Sakic, Joe 1229
サキネ
Sakine, Ahmat Awad 1229
サキム
Sakim, Maria 1229
ザキラス
Zackhras, Mattlan 1544
Zackhras, Ruben 1544
サギリ
Saghiri, Mahmud Ibrahim 1226
サギル
Saghir, Shaif Ezi 1226
Sagir, Taner 1226
ザキロフ
Zakirov, Batir 1546
サーキン
Serkin, Peter 1275
Sirkin, Harold L. 1308

サ

サギンタエフ
Sagintayev, Bakytzhan 1226
サギンバエワ
Sagymbaeva, Dinara 1226
サーク
Saq, Mohammed bin Faisal Abu 1241
サグ
Sag, Ivan A. 1226
ザク
Zaku, A.B. 1546
ザクァワ
Zakhour, Sharon 1546
ザクーク
Zakok, Ali Abu 1546
ザクシェフスキ
Zakrzewski, Andrzej 1546
サクス
Saks, Gidon 1229
Saks, Katrin 1229
ザクズーク
Zaqzouk, Mahmoud Hamdy 1547
サクスコブルクゴツキ
Saxe-coburg Gotha, Simeon 1247
サグスタッド
Sagstad, Egil 1226
サクストン
Saxton, Barefoot Ken Bob 1247
Saxton, Ben 1247
Saxton, Curtis 1247
Saxton, James W. 1247
Saxton, John 1247
Saxton, Wes 1247
Thaxton, David 1394
Thaxton, Giles 1394
サクセス
Success, Isaac 1362
サクセニアン
Saxenian, AnnaLee 1247
サクソン
Saxon, Victoria 1247
ザクチェフ
Zaczek, Iain 1544
サグデン
Sugden, Robert 1363
ザグニス
Zagunis, Mariel 1545
サグノ
Sagno, Christine 1226
Sagno, Niankoye 1226
サクマ
Sakuma, Tadanobu 1229
サグマイスター
Sagmeister, Stefan 1226
サグマン
Sagman, Stephen W. 1226
ザクマン
Sakmann, Bert 1229
ザグラ
Zagula, John 1545
Zagula, Matt 1545
サクライ・ナカガワ
Sakurai Nakagawa, María Guadalupe Eiko 1229
ザ・グラジエーター
The Gladiator 1395
ザクラス
Zackhras, Mattlan 1544
サクラモーン
Sacramone, Alicia 1224
サグルー
Sugrue, James 1363
ザグルール
Zaghloul, Mohamad Bahaa El-Din 1545
サクレ
Sacré, Marie José 1224
Sacre, Robert 1224
ザグロウ
Mohamed, Mohamed Aly Zaghloul 961
ザグロドニク
Zagrodnik, Pawel 1545
サクロフスキー
Saklofske, Donald H. 1229
サグン
Sagun, Miroslawa 1226
サゲイト
Suggate, Alan M. 1363
サケニ
Sakeni, Kennedy 1228
ザケリ
Zakelj, Tanja 1546
サーケンフェルド
Sakenfeld, Katharine Doob 1228
サコ
Sakho, Moussa 1229
Sako, Bakary 1229
Sako, Cheick 1229
Sako, Jean Willybiro 1229
サコー
Sakho, Diafra 1229
Sakho, Mamadou 1229
ザコーアー
Zakour, John 1546
ザゴエフ
Dzagoev, Alan 386
ザゴスキン
Zagoskin, Alexandre M. 1545
サコダ
Sakoda, Robin H. 1229
Sakota, Jimmy Takashi 1229
サコップ
Succop, Ryan 1362
サゴナ
Sagona, Marina 1226
ザゴリア
Zagoria, Donald S. 1545
ザゴルスカ
Zagorska, Dorota 1545
サコロウ
Sokolow, Fred 1324
ザザ
Thatha, Ziad 1394
Zaza, Simone 1549
ササキ
Sasaki, Mariko 1243
Sasaki, Marumo 1243
Sasaki, Tazue Kiyono 1243
サザートン
Sotherton, Kelly 1330
サザナベト
Sazanavets, Dzina 1247
サザーランド
Sutherland, Adam 1368
Sutherland, Amy 1368
Sutherland, Darren John 1368
Sutherland, Dean F. 1368
Sutherland, Donald 1368
Sutherland, Ivan Edward 1368
Sutherland, Jeffrey Victor 1368
Sutherland, Joan 1368
Sutherland, Kari 1368
Sutherland, Kiefer 1368
Sutherland, Louis 1368
Sutherland, Peter Denis 1368
Sutherland, T.T. 1368
Sutherland, Valerie J. 1368
サザランド
Sutherland, Ivan Edward 1368
Sutherland, James Runcieman 1368
Sutherland, Joan 1368
Sutherland, Peg 1368
サザーン
Sothern, Ann 1330
Southern, Richard William 1331
サザン
Southon, Mike 1331
サージー
Sirgy, M.Joseph 1307
サシ
Sasi, Kimmo 1243
Sassi, Hayet 1243
サジェス
Saggese, Jaclyn 1226
サジェット
Suggett, Martin 1363
サージェント
Sargeant, Malcolm 1242
Sargeant, Winthrop 1242
Sargent, Alvin 1242
Sargent, Carl 1242
Sargent, Emma 1242
Sargent, Inge 1242
Sargent, Joseph 1242
Sargent, Thomas John 1242
Seargeant, Philip 1266
ザジック
Zaczyk, Christian 1544
サジデュコフ
Sagindykov, Adilkhan 1226
サジドフ
Sazhidov, Sazhid 1247
サージャ
Czaja, Sara J. 310
サジャヤ
Sajaya, Nugzar 1228
サージャン
Sajjan, Harjit Singh 1228
サジュワーニ
al-Sajwani, Fuad bin Jaffar bin Mohammed 1228
サシングブ
Sahinguvu, Yves 1226
サス
Sass, Neil 1243
Saz, Eva Garcia del 1247
Szasz, Emese 1374
ザース
Sass, Katrin 1243
ザーズ
ZAZ 1549
サスカインド
Susskind, Lawrence 1368
サスキー
Suskie, Linda A. 1368
サスキンド
Suskind, Ron 1368
Susskind, Lawrence 1368
Susskind, Leonard 1368
サースク
Thirsk, Joan 1396
サステレン
Susteren, Greta Van 1368
ザストリズニー
Zastryzny, Rob 1548
サストレ
Sastre, Lluis 1243
サストロレジョ
Sastroredjo, Martinus 1243
サーストン
Thurston, Mark 1403
Thurston, William 1403
サス・ヌゲソ
Sassou-Nguesso, Denis 1243
サスー・ヌゲソ
Sassou-Nguesso, Denis 1243
サスヌゲソ
Sassou-Nguesso, Denis 1243
サスポルテス
Sasportes, Jose 1243
サスマン
Sussman, Allen E. 1368
Sussman, David 1368
Sussman, Deborah 1368
Sussman, Gerald Jay 1368
Sussman, Julie 1368
Sussman, Lyle 1368
Sussman, Norman 1368
Sussman, Paul 1368
Sussman, Robert W. 1368
ザスマンスハウゼン
Sassmannshausen, Wolfgang 1243
ザスラウ
Zaslaw, Neal 1548
ザスラーフスカヤ
Zaslavskaya, Tatiyana Ivanovna 1548
ザスラフスカヤ
Zaslavskaya, Tatiyana Ivanovna 1548
ザスラフスキー
Zaslavsky, Claudia 1548
Zaslavsky, Victor 1548
ザスロー
Zaslaw, Neal 1548
Zaslow, Jeffrey 1548
ザスロフ
Zasloff, Michael 1548
サースン
Sarson, Peter 1243
サスーン
Sassoon, Vidal 1243
サゼック
Sadzeck, Connor 1225
サーゾ
Sarzo, Rudy 1243
ザゾヴ
Zazove, Philip 1549
サゾノフ
Sazonov, Aleksandr Y. 1247
サソン
Sasson, Or 1243

サタ
Sata, Michael Chilufya 1243
サター
Sutter, Andrew J. 1369
Sutter, Robert G. 1369
サダ
Sada, Mohammed bin Saleh 1224
Sada, Muhammad 1224
Sad'aa, Musa Mohammed 1224
サダヴァ
Sadava, David 1224
サーダウィ
Saadawi, Nawal El- 1222
サーダウイ
Saadaoui, Mohamed 1222
サダカバツ
Sadakabatu, Connelly 1224
サダース
Sudderth, David B. 1363
サタスウェイト
Satterthwait, Walter 1244
サダト
Sadat, Mandana 1224
サターナ
Satana, Tura 1243
サターホワイト
Satterwhite, Robb 1244
サダム
Saddam, Abdellatif 1224
サダラージ
Sadalage, Pramod J. 1224
サタリー
Satterly, Faye 1244
サタリーノ
Satalino, Giacomo 1243
サタリファル
Satari-far, Mohammad 1243
サダン
Sadang, Elbuchel 1224
サチ
Thaçi, Hashim 1393
ザチオルスキー
Zatsiorsky, Vladimir M. 1548
ザ・チョジェ・リンポチェ
Za Choeje Rinpoche 1544
サッカ
Sacca, Chris 1223
Sadka, Dewey 1224
al-Saqqa, Saleem 1241
サッカー
Sachar, Louis 1223
Thacker, Cathy Gillen 1393
Thacker, Robert 1393
ザッカー
Zacker, Craig 1544
Zucker, Donald 1558
ザッカーバーグ
Zuckerberg, Mark Elliot 1558
ザッカーマン
Zuckerman, Gregory 1558
Zuckerman, Joseph David 1558
Zuckerman, Larry 1558
Zuckerman, Michael W. 1558
サッキ
Sacchi, Arrigo 1223
サック
Sack, John 1224
Sack, Richard 1224
Sak, Taras 1228
ザック
Zack, Devora 1544
Zak, Paul J. 1545
Zak, Victoria 1545
サックヴィル
Sackville, Tom 1224
サックス
Sachs, Angeli 1223
Sachs, Brad 1224
Sachs, Harvey 1224
Sachs, Jeffrey David 1224
Sachs, Jonah 1224
Sachs, Judith 1224
Sachs, Mendel 1224
Sacks, Leo 1224
Sacks, Lisbeth 1224
Sacks, Marcy Goldberg 1224
Sacks, Oliver Wolf 1224
Sacks, Steven 1224
Saks, Gene 1229
Sax, Boria 1246
Sax, Doug 1246
Sax, Joseph Lawrence 1246
Sax, Leonard 1246
Sax, Paul E. 1246
サッグス
Suggs, Terrell 1363
ザックス
Sachs, Hans 1224
Sachs, Wolfgang 1224
Zacks, Mitchell 1544
ザックナー
Zechner, Mario 1549
サックハイム
Sackheim, William 1224
サッケーリ
Saccheri, David 1223
ザッケローニ
Zaccheroni, Alberto 1544
サッコ
Sacco, Joe 1223
サッコニ
Sacconi, Maurizio 1223
ザッコーニ
Zacconi, Riccardo 1544
サッサー
Sasser, W.Earl 1243
サッサネッリ
Sassanelli, Paolo 1243
サッセン
Sassen, Saskia 1243
サッター
Sutter, Herb 1369
Sutter, Joseph F. 1369
ザッタ
Zatta, Christopher 1548
サッターステン
Sattersten, Todd 1244
サッタリ
Sattari, Sorena 1244
サッタル
Sattar, Abdus 1244
Sattar, Anbaree Abdul 1244
Sattar, Muhammad Farooq 1244
サッチ
Thach, Liz 1393
サッチャ
Zetsche, Frank 1551
サッチャー
Thatcher, David 1394
Thatcher, Denis 1394
Thatcher, Margaret Hilda 1394
サッドフェルド
Sudfeld, Nate 1363
Sudfeld, Zach 1363
サットフェン
Sutphen, Molly 1369
サットマリ
Szatmari, Peter 1374
サットン
Sutton, Adrian 1369
Sutton, Andrew 1369
Sutton, Antony 1369
Sutton, Bob 1369
Sutton, Bryan 1369
Sutton, Charmaine Vercimak 1369
Sutton, Christine 1369
Sutton, Daud 1369
Sutton, Dave 1369
Sutton, David 1369
Sutton, Emily 1369
Sutton, Jim 1369
Sutton, John 1369
Sutton, Margaret 1369
Sutton, Robert I. 1369
Sutton, Sally 1369
Sutton, Tina 1369
Sutton, Will 1369
ザッパコスタ
Zappacosta, Davide 1547
ザッハシュナイダー
Schachtschneider, Boris 1248
サッバティーニ
Sabbatini, Giuseppe 1223
ザッピー
Zappy, Erica 1547
サップ
Sapp, Warren 1241
ザップ
Zapf, Wolfgang 1547
ザッフェラーニ
Zafferani, Andrea 1545
ザッペリ
Zapperi, Roberto 1547
ザッヘンバッハー
Sachenbacher-Stehle, Evi 1223
ザッヘンバッハー・シュテレ
Sachenbacher-Stehle, Evi 1223
ザッヘンバハー
Sachenbacher-Stehle, Evi 1223
サッポ
Sapo, Sergio 1241
サッラーフ
al-Sarraf, Yaacoub 1243
サッリ
Sarri, Maurizio 1243
サツーロ
Satullo, Jane A.W. 1244
サーディ
al-Sa'adi, Mohammed 1222
Saadi, Salim 1222
al-Sa'di, Muhannad 1224
サディ
Saddy, Pierre 1224
Sadi, René Emmanuel 1224
サティアルティ
Satyarthi, Kailash 1244
サディク
Saddique, Boniface 1224
al-Sadig, Gazi 1224
Sadik, Nafis 1224
サディコフ
Sadykov, Kanat 1225
サーティース
Surtees, Bruce 1367
サーティーズ
Surtees, Bruce 1367
サディス
Sadissou, Yahouza 1224
サディック
Sadik, Nafis 1224
サーディナス
Sardinas, Luis 1242
サティバエフ
Sattibayev, Olzhas 1244
サティバルディエフ
Satybaldiev, Zhantoro 1244
サティヤティ
Satyarthi, Kailash 1244
サティヤナンド
Satyanand, Anand 1244
サティヤルティ
Satyarthi, Kailash 1244
サディリン
Sadirin, Pavel 1224
サーティン
Sartin, Laurence 1243
サー・ディンディン
Sa, Ding-ding 1222
サーデク
Sadegh, Ismael Ould 1224
サデク
Sadeq, Mirwais 1224
Sadeque, A.S.H.K. 1224
サデクボナブ
Sadeqbonab, Ahmad 1224
ザ・デストロイヤー
The Destroyer 1395
サデッキー
Sadecki, Ray 1224
ザデック
Zadek, Simon 1545
サーデッロ
Sardello, Robert J. 1242
サデム
Saddam, Abdellatif 1224
サテラ
Sater, Steven 1244
サテル
Satel, Sally L. 1243
サデル
Sader, Eugenia 1224
Sader, Talal 1224
サデレー
Sadelher, Malick 1224
サード
Saad, Ahmed 1222
Saad, Ahmed Mohamed Ibrahim 1222
Saad, bin Ibrahim al-Mahmoud 1222
Saad, John 1222
Sa'ad, Rafe'a Abu 1222
Sa'd, Ali 1224

サ

サド
Sado, Besu 1224
サドイコフ
Sadykov, Dovletgeldi 1225
サトウ
Sato, Esther Masako Tateishi 1244
Sato, Futaro 1244
Sato, Gary 1244
Sato, Gayle K. 1244
Sato, Mikio 1244
Sato, Sabrina 1244
サドゥ
Sadou, Ibrahim Issifi 1224
サートウェル
Sartwell, Matthew 1243
サドゥギ
Sadouqi, Mohammad Ali 1224
サドウスキー
Sadowski, Deborah A. 1224
Sadowski, Randall P. 1225
サトゥッフ
Sattouf, Riad 1244
サドーヴニチ
Sadovnichy, Victor Antonovich 1224
サドーヴニチィ
Sadovnichy, Victor Antonovich 1224
サドゥラエフ
Sadulaev, Abdulrashid 1225
サドゥラエワ
Sadulayeva, Zarema 1225
サトゥリス
Sahtouris, Elisabet 1226
サドゥルスカ
Sadurska, Kateryna 1225
サドゥルスキス
Šadurskis, Kārlis 1225
ザトゥロフスカヤ
Zatulovskaia, Irina 1548
サドゥン
Sadun, Erica 1225
サトクリフ
Sutcliffe, Jane 1368
Sutcliffe, Jenny 1368
Sutcliffe, Katherine 1368
Sutcliffe, Kathleen M. 1368
Sutcliffe, Mandy 1368
Sutcliffe, Phil 1368
Sutcliffe, William 1368
ザトコウスキ
Satkowski, Leon George 1244
サドック
Sadock, Benjamin J. 1224
Sadock, Virginia A. 1224
ザドネプロフスキス
Zadneprovskis, Andrejus 1545
サトパティ
Satopaty, Rajine 1244
サドビッチ
Sadović, Tarik 1224
サドービニチ
Sadovnichy, Victor Antonovich 1224
サドフニコフ
Sadovnikov, Aleksandr 1224
サドーブニチ
Sadovnichy, Victor Antonovich 1224
サートホフ
Saathoff, Adam 1222
サトマーリ
Szathmary, Eors 1374
サトヤルティ
Satyarthi, Kailash 1244
ザドヤン
Zadoyan, Davit 1545
サドラー
Saddler, Sandy 1224
Sadler, Barry 1224
Sadler, Christopher 1224
Sadler, Thomas W. 1224
サドラースミス
Sadler-Smith, Eugene 1224
サトラーニョ
Satragno, Luigi 1244
サトラピ
Satrapi, Marjane 1244
サトラム
Satrom, Brandon 1244
サトラン
Satran, Pamela Redmond 1244
サトランスキー
Satoransky, Tomas 1244
サドリ - タファゾリ
Sadri-Tafazoli, Faranak 1225
サドル
al-Sadr, Muqtada 1225
サトルイコフ
Satlykov, Satlyk 1244
Satylykov, Satlyk 1244
サドル師
al-Sadr, Muqtada 1225
サトレ
Sætre, Lasse 1225
サートレイ
Sartore, Joel 1243
ザトレルス
Zatlers, Valdis 1548
ザドロズナヤ
Zadorozhnaya, Yelena 1545
サドワ
Sadova, Natalya 1224
サナ
Sana, Aminata 1235
Sanna, Paul J. 1239
ザーナ
Zana, Leyla 1547
ザーナー
Saner, Hans 1238
サナア
al-Sanaa, Yaacoub Abdulmihsen 1235
サーナウ
Surnow, Joel 1367
サナゴ
Sanago, Salikou 1235
ザナック
Zanuck, Richard Darryl 1547
サーナット
Sarnat, Joan E. 1242
Sarnat, Marjorie 1242
サナデル
Sanader, Ivo 1235
サナト
Sanat, Aryel 1235
サナビー
Suneby, Elizabeth 1366
サナブリア
Sanabria, Antonio 1235
Sanabria, José 1235
サナーヘーエ
Sanderhage, Per 1237
ザナリーニ
Zanarini, Mary C. 1547
ザナルディ
Zanardi, Alex 1547
サナン
Sanan, Kachornprasat 1235
サーニ
Saarni, Carolyn 1222
サニー
Thuney, Joe 1402
ザーニアル
Zernial, Gus 1551
サニイ
Saniee, Parinoush 1238
サニエ
Sagnier, Ludivine 1226
サニキゼ
Sanikidze, Tamar 1238
ザニノビチ
Zaninovic, Ana 1547
Zaninovic, Lucija 1547
ザニノビッチ
Zaninovic, Lucija 1547
ザニマッキア
Zanimacchia, Luca 1547
サーニャ
Sanha, Issufo 1238
Sanhá, Malam Bacai 1238
サニャ
Sagna, Bacary 1226
Sagnia, Burama Keba 1226
Sanha, Eduardo Costa 1238
Sanhá, Malam Bacai 1238
Sanha, Rui 1238
サニヤル
Sanyal, Steve 1240
サニャング
Sanyang, Kebba 1241
サニョ
Sagno, Niankoye 1226
サヌ
Sanou, Mamadou 1239
Sanou, Stéphane 1239
Sanou, Wilfried 1239
サヌー
Sanou, Wilfried 1239
Sanu, Mohamed 1240
サヌイエ
Sanouillet, Michel 1239
サヌーシ
al-Sanousi, Al-Taher 1239
ザヌーシ
Zanussi, Krzysztof 1547
ザヌッシ
Zanussi, Krzysztof 1547
ザヌネ
Zannouneh, Zuhair 1547
ザヌン
Za'anoon, Riyad 1544
サネ
Sane, Lamine 1238
Sane, Malal 1238
Sané, Pierre Gabriel Michel 1238
Sanneh, Edward Saja 1239
Sanneh, Kanja 1239
ザネ
Sane, Leroy 1238
サネス
Sannes, Amy 1239
ザネタキス
Tzannetakis, Tzannis 1431
サネッティ
Zanetti, Javier 1547
ザネッティ
Zanetti, Arthur 1547
Zanetti, Michele 1547
サーネット
Sernett, Matthew 1275
サネッロ
Sanello, Frank 1238
サーノ
Sarno, John E. 1242
サノ
Sano, Koutoubou Moustapha 1239
Sano, Moustapha Koutoubou 1239
Sano, Takaya 1239
Sanoh, Abdouramane 1239
サノー
Sannoh, Benedict 1239
Sano, Miguel 1239
サノコ
Sanoko, Ousmane 1239
サノゴ
Sanogo, Mamadou 1239
Sanogo, Sekou 1239
Sanogo, Yaya 1239
ザノッティ
Zanotti, Guerrino 1547
ザノリーニ
Zanolini, Bruno 1547
サノン
Sanon, Jean Gustave 1239
Sanon, Jean Renel 1239
ザノン
Zanon, Edoardo 1547
サーバー
Sarver, Robert 1243
サハ
Saha, Amit 1226
Saha, Gopal B. 1226
Saha, Mark 1226
サバ
Saba, Daud Shah 1222
Saba, Elias 1222
Sabbah, Messod 1223
Sabbah, Roger 1223
サバー
Sabbagh, Karl 1223
サパー
Saper, Clifford B. 1241
ザハ
Zaha, Wilfried 1545
サバア
Saba, Elias 1222
サハイ
Sahay, Subodh Kant 1226
サーバイス
Servais, Scott 1275
サパイラ
Sapira, Joseph D. 1241
ザハヴィ

サ

Zahavi, Amots 1545
Zahavi, Avishag 1545
Zahavi, Dan 1545
サハキャン
Sahakian, Bako S. 1226
サバシア
Sabathia, CC 1222
サバス
Savas, Georgia Routsis 1245
サバダ
Sabada, Oleksandra 1222
サパタ
Zapata, Christian 1547
Zapata, Duvan 1547
サーバッジュー
Sarvatjoo, Saeed 1243
サバティア
Sabathia, CC 1222
サバティエ
Sabatier, Robert 1222
Sabatier, Roland 1222
サバティン
Sabatine, Marc S. 1222
サパディン
Sapadin, Linda 1241
サハデオ
Sahadeo, Christine 1226
サパテロ
Zapatero, José Luis Rodríguez 1547
サバード
Savard, Katerine 1245
サバト
Sábato, Ernesto 1222
Sabato, Larry J. 1223
サバドゴ
Savadogo, Lassané 1245
サハナイ
Sahanaye, Maina Touka 1226
サハニ
Sakhan, Ivan Y. 1228
サバネ
Savane, Landing 1245
サバハ
Sabah 1222
Sabah al-Ahmad al-Jabir al-Sabah 1222
Sabeh, Atallah 1223
サバハ・アル・アハマド・アル・ジャビル・アル・サバハ
Sabah al-Ahmad al-Jabir al-Sabah 1222
サバハ・ハリド
Sabah al-Khalid, al-Hamad al-Sabah 1222
サハビ
Sahabi, Ezzatollah 1226
Sahabi, Haleh 1226
サバフ
Sabbagh, Rana 1223
ザハフ
Zahaf, Cheik Ahmed Ould 1545
ザバフスカ
Zabawska (danilczyk), Krystyna 1544
サバラ
Zavala, Diego 1548
ザバラウィ
Zábalawi, Isam 1544
サバラ・コスタ
Zavala Costa, Jaime 1548
サバラ・バリャダレス
Zavala Valladares, María 1548
サバラ・ペニチェ
Zavala Peniche, Beatriz 1548
サバラ・ロンバルディ
Zavala Lombardi, Fernando 1548
Zavala Lombardi, Verónica 1548
サハリ
Sakhri, Ammar 1229
サバリ
Savary, Jérôme 1245
ザハリ
Zakhari, Nadia 1546
ザハリア
Zaharia, Matei 1545
ザハリエバ
Zaharieva, Ekaterina 1545
サバリッシュ
Sawallisch, Wolfgang 1246
ザバリッシュ
Sawallisch, Wolfgang 1246
ザハリャン
Zakharian, Yervand 1546
Zakharyan, Yervand 1546
サバリン
Savarin, Charles 1245
サバール
Savall, Jordi 1245
サバル
Saball, Paulina 1222
ザハル
Zahar, Mahmoud 1545
ザハルク
Zakharuk, Oleksandr 1546
ザハルチェンコ
Zakharchenko, Vitaliy 1546
サパルドゥルドィエフ
Sapardurdyyev, Nursahet 1241
サパルバエフ
Saparbayev, Berdibek 1241
サパルリエフ
Saparliyev, Hydyr 1241
サパルルイエフ
Saparliyev, Hydyr 1241
Saparlyyev, Khadyr 1241
サバレーゼ
Savarese, Daniel F. 1245
サバレタ
Zabaleta, Pablo 1544
サバローチ
Sabaroche, Herbert 1222
サハロフ
Sacharow, Anya 1223
Sakharov, Vsevolod Ivanovich 1228
サパロフ
Saparov, Redzhep 1241
ザハロフ
Zakharov, Anton 1546
Zakharov, Artyom 1546
Zakharov, Ilya 1546
Zakharov, Ruslan 1546
ザハーロワ
Zakharova, Svetlana 1546
ザハロワ
Zakharova, Svetlana 1546
サバン
Sabban, Françoise 1223
Savane, Landing 1245
サパン
Sapin, Michel 1241
サバンジャン
Sabounjian, Vrej 1223
サバンジュ
Sabancı, Güler 1222
サビアーノ
Saviano, Roberto 1245
サビアロワ
Savialova, Olga 1245
ザビエ
Saviye, David 1246
サピエフ
Sapiyev, Serik 1241
ザビエル
Xavier, Anthony 1531
Xavier, Grace 1531
サビオラ
Saviola, Javier 1246
サビカス
Savickas, Mark 1245
Savikas, Andrew 1245
サビサール
Savisaar, Edgar 1246
サビチェビッチ
Savićević, Dejan 1245
サビツァー
Sabitzer, Marcel 1223
サビツカヤ
Savitskaya, Kristina 1246
サビツキ
Sawicki, Marek 1246
サビッツ
Savitz, Andrew W. 1246
サビデス
Savvides, Frixos 1246
ザヒド
Zahed, Ramin 1545
ザヒド・ハミディ
Zahid Hamidi, Ahmad 1545
サビトフ
Sabitov, I.Kh. 1223
サービナ
Savvina, Iya 1246
サビニャック
Savignac, Raymond Pierre Guillaume 1245
ザビヌル
Zawinul, Joe 1548
サビネ
Savigne, Yargelis 1245
サビノ
Sabino, Mariano Assanami 1223
Savino, Irene 1246
サビノワ
Savinova, Mariya 1246
ザビヒ
Zabihi, Karina 1544
サビーフ
al-Subaih, Hind Subaih 1362
サヒリ
Sahili, Talal 1226
サビル
Savile, Jimmy 1245
Saville, Jane 1246
ザヒル
Zahir, Ahmed 1545
Zahir, Umar 1545
ザーヒル・シャー
Zahir Shah, Mohammed 1545
ザヒル・シャー
Zahir Shah, Mohammed 1545
ザビル・シャー
Zahir Shah, Mohammed 1545
ザヒルワル
Zakhilwal, Omar 1546
サピーロ
Shapiro, David A. 1281
サビロフ
Sabirov, Shakhzodbek 1223
サーピロム
Xaphilom, Bounmy 1531
ザビロワ
Zabirova, Zulfiya 1544
サヒン
Sahin, Ramazan 1226
サビーン
Sabine, Elizabeth 1223
サビンビ
Savimbi, Jonas Malheiro 1246
サビン・メリノ
Sabin Merino 1223
サーフ
Cerf, Vinton Gray 240
Saaf, Abdallah 1222
Saaf, Donald 1222
サープ
Tharp, Twyla 1394
Tharpe, Anne Marie 1394
ザーブ
Zarb, Frank Gustav 1547
Zarb, George A. 1547
Zarb, Mike 1548
サファ
Safa, Ali Mansur Mohammed bin 1225
サファー
Safar, Peter 1225
Saffer, Dan 1225
サファイア
Safire, William L. 1225
Sapphire 1241
サファエフ
Safayev, Sodik 1225
ザファーズ
Zaferes, Katie 1545
サファーストーン
Safferstone, Todd 1225
サーファティ
Sarfati, Jonathan D. 1242
サーファティー
Serfaty, Simon 1274
サファディ
Safadi, Ayman 1225
al-Safadi, Mohammad 1225
Safadi, Mohammed 1225
サファリ
Saffary, Sohrab Ali 1225
サファリャン
Safaryan, David 1225
Safaryan, Devid 1225
サファル
Safar, Adel Ahmed 1225

サ

サ

Safar, Fadhil Safar Ali 1225
ザファル
Zafar, Muhammad Wasi 1545
サファルハランディ
Saffar Harandi, Hossein 1225
サファロバ
Safarova, Lucie 1225
サファロフ
Safarov, Orkhan 1225
ザファロン
Zaffalon, Lorena 1545
サーファン
Saafan, Muhammad 1222
サフィ
al-Safi, Safa al-din 1225
Sufi, Amir 1363
サフィア
Safia, Youssef Abu 1225
ザフィア
Safier, David 1225
サフィエ
Safiye, Hassan 1225
サフィトリ
Safitri, Dewi 1225
サフィナ
Safina, Carl 1225
Safina, Dinara 1225
ザフィライ
Zafilahy, Ying Vah 1545
ザフィラザ
Zafilaza 1545
サフィル
Safir, Adil 1225
ザフィール
al-Zafir, Ali 1545
サフィン
Safin, Marat 1225
Safin, Timur 1225
サフェルクルス
Savelkouls, Tessie 1245
サフォシュキン
Safoshkin, Alexander 1225
サフォルド
Saffold, Rodger 1225
サーフコ
Safko, John L. 1225
サプコタ
Sapkota, Agni Prasad 1241
サプコフスキ
Sapkowski, Andrzej 1241
サプシリー
Sapsiree, Taerattanachai 1241
サブセク
Savsek, Benjamin 1246
サブダ
Sabuda, Robert 1223
サブダラト
Sabdarat, Abdel Basit Saleh 1223
サブチェンコ
Savchenko, Aliona 1245
サフチュク
Savchuk, Anastasiya 1245
サブティ
al-Sabti, Khalid bin Abdullah 1223
サブティー
Sabti, Qasim 1223
サフトラス
Saftlas, Zev 1226
サブナー
Savner, Jennifer L. 1246
ザブナー
Dzubnar, Nick 386
サフナウィ
Sehnawi, Nicolas 1269
サブニ
Sabbouni, Imad Abdul-Ghani 1223
Sabuni, Nyamko 1223
サフネイツウガ
Safuneituuga, Paaga Neri 1226
サフノフスキー
Sakhnovski, Sergei 1229
サブハン
ai-Sabhan, Thamer bin Ali 22
ザフファトビッチ・ヴァイダ
Zachwatowicz-Wajda, Krystyna 1544
サフラ
Safra, Joseph 1225
サブラ
Sabra, George 1223
サプラナ
Zaplana, Eduardo 1547
サブラマニアム
Subramaniam, Som 1362
サブラマニャム
Subrahmanyam, Allamaraju 1362
Subrahmanyam, Marti G. 1362
サブラル
Sabral, Jody 1223
サフラン
Safran, Samuel A. 1225
サブーラン
Sabourin, Eric 1223
ザフランスキー
Safranski, Rüdiger 1225
サブリ
Sabri, Naji 1223
Sabri, Nur Dhabitah 1223
Sabri, Wael 1223
サプリー
Supree, Burton 1367
ザフーリ
Zaafouri, Béchir 1544
サーブリーコヴァー
Sáblíková, Martina 1223
サブリコヴァ
Sáblíková, Martina 1223
サブリコバ
Sáblíková, Martina 1223
サブリコワ
Sáblíková, Martina 1223
サプリチ
Sapurić, Zoran 1241
サブリノビッチ
Sawrymowicz, Mateusz 1246
サフリュー
Safrew, Ethan 1226
ザブルディナ
Zabludina, Irina 1544
サブレ
Sabouret, Jean-François 1223
ザブレル
Zavřel, Stěpán 1548
サフレン
Safren, Steven A. 1226
サブロー
Sabouraud, Frédéric 1223
サブローサ
Sabrosa, Simão 1223
サブローザ
Sabrosa, Simão 1223
サブロサ
Sabrosa, Simão 1223
サブロー＝セガン
Sabouraud-Séguin, Aurore 1223
ザブロッキー
Zablocki, Courtney 1544
サプロネンコ
Sapronenko, Evgeni 1241
ザフロブスカ
Strachova, Sarka 1356
サブロン
Thubron, Colin 1402
ザフロン
Zaffron, Steve 1545
サフワヌッラー
Safwanullah, Syed 1226
サプーン
Sapoen, Raymond 1241
サーペイ
Sapey, Bob 1241
サベイジ
Savage, Tom 1245
サペギン
Sapegin, Pjotr 1241
サベージ
Savage, David 1245
Savage, Jon 1245
Savage, Randy 1245
サベジャ
Sabella, Alejandro 1223
サベッジ
Savage, Stephen 1245
ザペッリ
Zapelli, Monica 1547
ザーヘディ
Zahedi, Morteza 1545
ザヘド
Zahed, Hamdollah 1545
サーベドラ
Saavedra, Jaime 1222
サーベドラ・ソト
Saavedra Soto, Rubén 1222
サーベドラ・ブルノ
Saavedra Bruno, Carlos 1222
サーヘニー
Sahni, Bhisham 1226
サベーラ
Sabella, Alejandro 1223
サベラ
Sabella, Alejandro 1223
サベラバスケス
Zavala Vazquez, Alejandra 1548
サベリ
Saberi, Helen 1223
Saberi, Roxana 1223
サベリエフ
Savelyev, Oleg G. 1245
サベリエワ
Savelyeva, Elena 1245
サベリン
Saverin, Eduardo 1245
ザベーリン
Zabelin, Viktor Nikitovich 1544
ザベリンスカヤ
Zabelinskaya, Olga 1544
サーペル
Serpell, James 1275
サヘル
Sahel, El Mustapha 1226
サベル
Saber, Mahfouz 1223
ザーベル
Zurbel, Victor 1559
サーベロ
Cervero, Fernando 241
サーベンカ
Cervenka, Hunter 240
サーボー
Sarbaugh, Mike 1241
サホ
Sakho, Moussa 1229
サボ
Sabo, Josaph 1223
Sabo, Nassirou 1223
Sabot, Hamilton 1223
Szabo, Gabriela 1374
サボー
Szabo, Gabriella 1374
Szabó, Imre 1374
Szabo, Istvan 1374
Szabó, János 1374
Szabó, Magda 1374
Szabo, Matyas 1374
Szabó, Miklós 1374
ザボ
Szabó, Peter 1374
サボイ
Savoie, Matthew 1246
Savoy, Wilson 1246
サボジ
Saboji, Mohan 1223
サーボス
Servos, John William 1275
ザボス
Zavos, Panos 1548
サポート
Saport, Linda 1241
サポナーラ
Saponara, Riccardo 1241
サボニス
Sabonis, Domantas 1223
サボー・マグダ
Szabó, Magda 1374
サボヤスンエ
Saboya Sunyé, Gilbert 1223
サポリ
Sapori, Michelle 1241
サボリオ
Saborío, Lineth 1223
サボリト
Saborit, Enric 1223
サボリド・ロイディ
Saborido Loidi, José 1223
サポルスキー
Sapolsky, Fabrice 1241
Sapolsky, Robert M. 1241
サーポルド
Saupold, Warwick 1245
サボロ
Sabolo, Monica 1223

ザボロトナヤ
Zabolotnaya, Natalia 1544
サボン
Savon, Amarilis 1246
Savon, Erislandy 1246
サポーン
Sapone, Marcela 1241
ザポン
Zappone, Katherine 1547
サマ
Sama, Armand 1233
Sama, Koffi 1233
サマー
Sammer, Eric 1234
Summer, Donna 1365
Summer, Lauralee 1365
ザマ
Zama, Francis 1546
サマーイ
Samaai, Rushwal 1233
サマヴィル
Somervill, Margaret 1327
サマケ
Samaké, Sada 1233
サマコワ
Samakova, Aitkul 1233
サマージャ
Samardzija, Jeff 1233
サマーズ
Sommers, Sam 1327
Summers, Andy 1366
Summers, Anthony 1366
Summers, Ashley 1366
Summers, Cara 1366
Summers, Essie 1366
Summers, Harry G., Jr. 1366
Summers, Hilary 1366
Summers, Judith 1366
Summers, Lawrence Henry 1366
Summers, Muriel 1366
Summers, Rowan 1366
Summers, Vanessa 1366
サマースケイル
Summerscale, Kate 1366
サマーズ - ブレムナー
Summers-Bremner, Eluned 1366
サマタール
Samatar, Sofia 1233
サマタル
Samatar, Sahra Mohamed Ali 1233
サマック・スンタラウェット
Samak Sundaravej 1233
サマック・スンタラウェート
Samak Sundaravej 1233
サマック・スントラウェート
Samak Sundaravej 1233
サマド・アブドラ
Samad Abdulla, Abdul 1233
サマーニ
al-Samaani, Walid bin Mohammad 1233
ザマノフ
Zamanov, Asyrgeldy 1546
サマービル
Somerville, Richard 1327
Sommerville, Charles John 1327
サマビル
Somerville, Christopher 1327
サマーフィールド
Summerfield, Mark 1365
サマーヘイズ
Summerhayes, Katie 1366
サマラ
Samara, Elizabeta 1233
Samara, Timothy 1233
Samara, Tony 1233
サマライ
al-Samarray, Ayham 1233
al-Sammarai, Abd al-Karim 1234
サマラウィクラマ
Samarawickrama, Malik 1233
サマラウィーラ
Samaravīra, Piyal Udaya 1233
Samaraweera, Mangala 1233
サマラーキス
Samarakês, Antônês 1233
サマラキス
Samarakês, Antônês 1233
サマラシンハ
Samarasinghe, Mahinda 1233
サマラス
Samaras, Antonis C. 1233
サマランチ
Samaranch, Juan Antonio 1233
Samaranch, Juan Antonio, Jr. 1233
サマリス
Samaris, Andreas 1233
サマリターニ
Samaritani, Riccardo 1233
サマル
Samar, Sima 1233
サマルジッチマルコビッチ
Samardžić-marković, Snežana 1233
サマーレイン
Summer Rain, Mary 1366
サーマン
Surman, Andrew 1367
Surman, Craig 1367
Thurman, Dennis 1402
Thurman, Rob 1402
Thurman, Robert A. F. 1402
Thurman, Trip 1402
Thurman, Uma 1402
ザマン
Zaman, Zarida 1546
サーマンソン
Salmansohn, Karen 1232
サマンソン
Salmansohn, Karen 1232
ザマンドゥリディス
Zamanduridis, Jannis 1546
サミ
SAMi 1234
サミー
Samy, Vellu 1235
Summey, Mike 1366
ザミウカ
Zamylka, Hanna 1546
サミット
Summit, Steve 1366
ザミット
Zammit, Ninu 1546
サミトワ
Samitova-galkina, Gulnara 1234
サミトワガルキナ
Samitova-galkina, Gulnara 1234
サミュエル
Samuel, Charlesworth 1234
Samuel, Claude 1234
Samuel, Janet 1235
Samuel, Juan 1235
Samuel, Philip 1235
Samuel, Pierre 1235
Samuel, Rodger 1235
Samuel, Walter 1235
Samuell, Yann 1235
サミュエルズ
Samuels, Andrew 1235
Samuels, Barbara 1235
Samuels, Charlie 1235
Samuels, Dani 1235
Samuels, Martin A. 1235
Samuels, Maxwell 1235
Samuels, Richard J. 1235
Samuels, Robert 1235
サミュエルソン
Samuelson, Paul Anthony 1235
Samuelsson, Bengt Ingemar 1235
Samuelsson, Hakan 1235
サミューダ
Samuda, Karl 1234
サミーラ
Sameera, bint Ibrahim Rajab 1234
ザミリ
al-Zamili, Haider 1546
サミール
Samir 1234
ザミール
Zameer, Moosa 1546
ザミル
Zamir, Assadullah 1546
サミーン
Sameen, Mohamed Isfahani 1234
サム
Sam, Bob 1233
Sam, Sydney 1233
Samb, Issa Mbaye 1233
Shum, Lydia 1294
ザムウォルト
Zumwalt, Jordan 1559
サムエル
Samuel, Walter 1235
サムエルス・ウィルソン
Samuels Wilson, Sydney Alexander 1235
サムエルソン
Samuelson, Paul Anthony 1235
Samuelsson, Bengt Ingemar 1235
Samuelsson, Emma 1235
Samuelsson, Jimmy 1235
サムカイ
Samukai, Brownie 1235
サム・カスティジェホ
Samu Castillejo 1234
サムコヴァ
Samková, Eva 1234
サムコバ
Samková, Eva 1234
ザムコボイ
Zamkovoy, Andrey 1546
サムス
Sams, Crawford F. 1234
サムズ
Sams, Aaron 1234
Sams, Jamie 1234
サムスマナ
Sam-sumana, Sahr 1234
Sam-sumana, Samuel 1234
サムスン
Samson, Jim 1234
Samson, Mallory 1234
サムセビッチ
Samusevich-prokopenko, Anastasiya 1235
サムソノフ
Samsonov, Vladimir 1234
サムソン
Samson, Samsen 1234
サムソン・トー・ブアマッド
Samson Tow Buamaddo 1234
サムダ
Samuda, Karl 1234
サムデレリ
Samdereli, Yasemin 1234
サムドン・リンポチェ
Samdhong Rinpoche 1234
サムナー
Sumner, Adrian Thomas 1366
Sumner, Bernard 1366
Sumner, Edmond 1366
サムニー
Samnee, Chris 1234
サムバーグ
Samberg, Andy 1233
サムブルック
Sambrook, Clare 1233
サムボッデン
Sam-Bodden, Brian 1233
サム・ランシー
Sam Rainsy 1234
サムリ
Samli, A.Coskun 1234
サムリエ
Samrieh, Hassan Idriss 1234
サム・リャンシー
Sam Rainsy 1234
サムール
Samour, Saéed 1234
サムルガチェフ
Samurgashev, Varteres 1235
サム・レンシー
Sam Rainsy 1234
ザメル
Zamel, Mohamed El Moctar Ould 1546
サメルソン
Samelson, Nancy Morse 1234
サメレ
Samere, Russom 1234
ザメロフ
Sameroff, Arnold J. 1234
ザモイスキ
Zamoyski, Adam 1546
サモイロフス
Samoilovs, Aleksandrs 1234

サモイロワ
Samoilova, Tatyana 1234
サモイロワツベタノワ
Samoilovacvetanova, Ganka 1234
サモウラ
Zamora, Jorge 1546
サモウラガシェフ
Samurgashev, Varteres 1235
サモス
Samos, Daniel 1234
ザモート
Zamort, Ronald 1546
サモ・ハン・キンポー
Samo Hung Kimbo 1234
サモラ
Zamora, Mario 1546
サモラ・グティエレス
Zamora Gutiérrez, José 1546
サモラゴルディリョ
Zamora Gordillo, Elizabeth 1546
ザモロドチコワ
Zamolodchikova, Elena 1546
サーモン
Salmon, Catherine 1232
Salmon, Deborah 1232
Salmon, Laurie 1232
Salmon, Paul M. 1232
サモン
Salmon, Walter J. 1232
Sammon, Paul M. 1234
サモンズ
Sammons, Brian A. 1234
Sammons, Mary F. 1234
サーモンスン
Salmonson, Jessica Amanda 1232
サーモンド
Thurmond, Strom 1402
サモンド
Salmond, Alex 1232
サヤー
Saillard, Remi 1227
サヤグ
Sayag, Allain 1247
サヤーダ
Sayahda 1247
ザヤツ
Zajac, Rudolf 1545
Zayats, Leonid K. 1549
サヤドー
Sayādaw, Mahāsi 1247
サヤペット
Sayaphet, Ketkesone 1247
サヤン
Sayan, Nejat Bora 1247
サユン
Sayin, Nevzat 1247
サヨ
Sayo, Bernadette 1247
サーラ
Sala, Jacopo 1229
サーラー
Thaler, Mike 1394
サラ
Sala, Fata Pinati 1229
Sala, Marius 1229
Sala, Renzo 1229
Sala, Sharon 1229
Salah, Abdul Fattah 1229
Salah, Mahamat Abba Ali 1229
Sallah, Alhaji Hassan 1231
Sallah, Mamadou 1231
Sallah, Michael 1231
Sarah 1241
Surla, Branka 1367
サラー
Salah, Mohamed 1229
Sallah, Abderaman 1231
Sallah, Mahamat Abba Ali 1231
ザラ
Sala, Oskar 1229
Zare, Richard N. 1548
ザラー
Zahler, S.Craig 1545
Zahler, Thomas 1545
サライ
Sallai, Roland 1231
Sarai, Lisabet 1241
Szalai, Adam 1374
サライーヴァ
Saraiva, José H. 1241
サライバ
Reis, Fernando Saraiva 1170
サラ‐イ‐マーティン
Sala-i-Martin, Xavier 1229
サラヴィザ
Salaviza, Joao 1229
サラヴィッツ
Szalavitz, Maia 1374
サラオ
Salao, Idris 1229
サラオー
Sarao, Anthony 1241
サラオラビアブデルガウワド
Salah Orabi Abdelgawwad, Abdelrahman 1229
サラギ
Saragih, Bungaran 1241
サラグ
Sarrag, Nigel 1243
ザラコヴィッツ
Zarachowicz, Weronika 1547
サラゴサ
Zaragoza, Juan R. 1547
サラゴス
Saragosse, Marie-Christine 1241
サラザー
Salazar, Danny 1230
Salazar, Jeff 1230
Salazar, Michael 1230
サラサール
Salazar, Pamela 1230
Salazar Quintero, Diego 1230
Uran Salazar, Juan 1435
サラサル
Salazar, Iridia 1230
Salazar, Jesús 1230
Salazar, Jorge 1230
Salazar, Oscar 1230
Salazar, Viviana Martin 1230
サラザール
Salazar, Ken 1230
サラサル・アダメ
Salazar Adame, Florencio 1230
サラサル・ガルシア
Salazar García, Juan José 1230
サラサル・コル
Salazar Coll, César 1230
サラサル・ツェツァグイ
Salazar Tetzaguic, Manuel 1230
サラサル・テザウィック
Salazar Tetzaguic, Manuel 1230
サラサル・ニコラウ
Salazar Nicolau, Guillermo 1230
ザラシーヴィッチ
Zalasiewicz, Jan A. 1546
サラス
Salas, Eduardo 1229
Salas, Greg 1229
Salas, Patricia 1229
サラスキナ
Saraskina, Ludmila 1241
サラステ
Saraste, Jukka-Pekka 1241
サラスバシー
Sarasvathy, Saras D. 1241
サラスペレス
Salas Perez, Reineris 1229
サラス・ロドリゲス
Salas Rodriguez, Luis Alberto 1229
サラソーン
Sarasohn, Eileen Sunada 1241
サラダン‐グリジバツ
Saladin-Grizivatz, Catherine 1229
サラチニ
Saraqini, Valon 1241
サラチョ
Saracho, Olivia N. 1241
サラテ
Zarate, Mauro 1547
サラーテイ
Zarate, Oscar 1547
サラディーノ
Saladino, Tyler 1229
サラディノ
Saladino, Irving 1229
サラティン
Salatin, Joel 1229
サラドゥハ
Saladukha, Olga 1229
サラニエ
Salanié, Bernard 1229
サラーノ
Salerno, Shane 1230
サラハ
Salah, Abdul Fattah 1229
Salah, Munther 1229
Salah, Noureddine 1229
サラハディン
Salahddin, Ghazi 1229
サラビ
Sarabi, Habiba 1241
サラビア
Sarabia, Pablo 1241
サラファーノフ
Sarafanov, Leonid 1241
サラフィアン
Sarafian, Richard C. 1241
サラフディン・アブドル・アジズ・シャー
Salahuddin Abdul Aziz Shah 1229
ザラ・ブバカール
Zara Boubacar, Sabo Fatouma 1547
サラベリア
Salaverría, Mario 1229
サラホフ
Salakhov, Evgeny 1229
サラーマ
Salama, Amr 1229
サラマーゴ
Saramago, José 1241
サラマット
Salamat, Hashim 1229
サラミ
al-Sallami, Alawi Saleh 1231
サラミン
Salamín, Edwin 1229
サラーム
Salam, Tammam 1229
サラム
Sallam, Ismail 1231
Sallam, Qasim 1231
サラメ
Salameh, Ghassan 1229
Salameh, Youssef 1229
サラメハ
Salameh, Ghassan 1229
サラモニー
Salamony, Sandra 1229
サラ‐モランス
Sala-Molins, Louis 1229
サラモン
Salamon, Bartosz 1229
Salamon, Julie 1229
Salamon, Lester M. 1229
Sarramon, Christian 1243
サラリー
Saralee, Thungthongkam 1241
サラリマ
Salalima, Rodolfo 1229
ザラル
Zalar, Aleš 1546
サランジ
Sarandji, Simplice Mathieu 1241
ザランス
Zalans, Edgars 1546
サランディ
Salandy, Giselle 1229
サランドン
Sarandon, Susan 1241
サリ
al-Sari, Hassan 1242
Ssali, Bidandi 1338
サリー
Sally, David 1232
サリア・マーラ
Mara, Thalia 898
サリヴァン
Sullivan, Andrew 1364
Sullivan, Anita 1364
Sullivan, Dan 1364
Sullivan, Elizabeth A. 1364
Sullivan, E.Mary 1364
Sullivan, Ernest W. 1364
Sullivan, Geraldine 1364
Sullivan, Jane 1364
Sullivan, Jean 1364

Sullivan, Joyce 1364
Sullivan, Karen 1364
Sullivan, Lawrence Eugene 1364
Sullivan, Mark T. 1364
Sullivan, Michael 1365
Sullivan, Michael J. 1365
Sullivan, Patrick H. 1365
Sullivan, Patrick J. 1365
Sullivan, Paul 1365
Sullivan, Stephen D. 1365
Sullivan, Tim 1365
Sullivan, Wendy 1365
Sullivan, William M. 1365

サリエフ
Sariev, Temir 1242

サリエワ
Sarieva, Elvira 1242

サリオラ
Sariola, Petteri 1242

サリグ
Sarig, Oded H. 1242

サリス
Salissou, Habi Mahamadou 1231
Sallis, James 1232
Sallis, John 1232
Sarris, Greg 1243
Sarris, Michalis 1243
Surris, Andrew 1367

サリスバリー
Salisbury, Mark 1231

サリスベリ
Salisbury, Bill 1231

サリック
Saric, Lazar 1242

サリッチ
Saric, Dario 1242

サリット
Salit, Cathy Rose 1231

サリー・デ・ルケ
Sully de Luque, Mary F. 1365

サリトフ
Saritov, Albert 1242

サリドフ
Sayidov, Ramziddin 1247

サーリネン
Saarinen, Aino-Kaisa 1222

サリネン
Saarinen, Aino-Kaisa 1222

サリノグ
Salinog, Tomasa Dioso 1231

サリハ
Salih, Bakri Hassan 1231
Salih, Salah Ahmed Mohamed 1231

サリハノフ
Saryhanov, Mammetdurdy 1243

ザリバファン
Zaribafan, Masoud 1548

サリバン
Sullivan, Amanda 1364
Sullivan, Daniel 1364
Sullivan, Eamon 1364
Sullivan, Ed 1364
Sullivan, James 1364
Sullivan, Jean 1364
Sullivan, J.Michael 1364
Sullivan, John 1364
Sullivan, Joseph 1364
Sullivan, Karen 1364
Sullivan, Kathleen 1364
Sullivan, Laura 1364
Sullivan, Margaret 1364
Sullivan, Martin J. 1364
Sullivan, Maxine 1365
Sullivan, Michael 1365
Sullivan, Michael J. 1365
Sullivan, Mike 1365
Sullivan, Monique 1365
Sullivan, Nicholas P. 1365
Sullivan, Patrick 1365
Sullivan, Rodney N. 1365
Sullivan, Stephen D. 1365
Sullivan, Stephen M. 1365
Sullivan, Tim 1365
Sullivan, William 1365
Sullivan, William C. 1365
Sullivan, William M. 1365

サーリーフ
Sirleaf, Ellen 1308

サーリフ
Sālih, al-Tayyib 1231

サリフ
Salifou, Barmou 1231
Salih, Ucan 1231

ザリフ
Zarif, Jorge 1548
Zarif, Mohammad Javad 1548

ザリフィ
Zarifi, Hamrokhon 1548

サリフォ
Salifou, Amadou Elhadj 1231

ザリポフ
Zaripov, Khamrokhon 1548

ザリポワ
Zaripova, Yuliya 1548

サリマヌ
Salimane, Karimou 1231

サリーマン
Sulleyman, Sadat 1364

サリミ
al-Salimi, Abdullah bin Mohammed 1231
Salimikordasiabi, Behdad 1231

サリミコルダシアビ
Salimikordasiabi, Behdad 1231

サリーム
Saleem, Jennifer 1230
Saleem, Mohamed Adil 1230

サリム
Salem, Omar 1230
Salim, Anthoni 1231
Salim, Emil 1231
Salim, Frank 1231
Salim, Salim Ahmed 1231
Salim, Segaf Aljufri 1231
Salim, Sudono 1231

サリムゾダ
Salimzoda, Nusratullo 1231

サリモフ
Salimov, Abdudzhalol 1231
Salimov, Nusratullo 1231

ザリュスキ
Zalewski, Michal 1546

サーリョ
Säljö, Roger 1231

ザリール
Zareer, Zaahiya 1548

サーリン
Sahlin, Mona 1226

サリーン
Sahlin, Mona 1226
Sareen, Manu 1242

ザリーン
Salin, Edgar 1231

ザリン
Zarin, Jill 1548

サリンジポフ
Sarinzhipov, Aslan 1242

サリンジャー
Salinger, Jerome David 1231
Salinger, M.A. 1231
Salinger, Pierre Emil George 1231
Sullinger, Jared 1364

サーリンズ
Sahlins, Marshall David 1226

サリンズ
Sullins, Benjamin G. 1364

ザリンス
Zarins, Uldis 1548

サール
Sa'ar, Gideon 1222
Saar, Indrek 1222
Sall, Djibrine 1231
Sarr, Jean-paul 1243
Sarr, Mariama 1243
Sarr, Mouhamadou 1243
Sarr, Oumar 1243
Sarr, Samuel Améte 1243
Searle, Ann 1266
Searle, John R. 1266
Searle, Ronald 1266
Searle, Sally 1266

サル
Sall, Adama 1231
Sall, Hamath 1231
Sall, Macky 1231
Sall, Seydou Sy 1231
Sall, Thierno Alassane 1231
Sari, Fatma Güldemet 1242
Sar Kheng 1242
Sarr, Abdoulaye Diouf 1243
Sarr, Alioune 1243
Sarr, Diène Farba 1243
Sarr, Mariama 1243
Sarr, Oumar 1243
Sull, Donald Norman 1364

ザール
Zarr, Sara 1548

サルイ
Al-sarroi, Khalifa Mesbah 1243

サルイエフ
Saryyev, Geldi 1243

サルヴァトア
Salvatore, R.A. 1232

サルヴァドール
Salvador, Amos 1232
Salvador, Henri 1232

サルヴァトーレ
Salvatore, R.A. 1232

サルヴィ
Salvi, Manuela 1232

サルウェー
Salway, J.G. 1233

サルウェイ
Salway, Peter 1233

サルウォノ
Sarwono, Kusumaatmadja 1243

サールウォール
Thirlwall, A.P. 1396
Thirlwall, Jade 1396

サルカ
Salka, John 1231

ザルカウィ
al-Zarqawi, Abu Musab 1548

ザルカシ
Zarkasih, Noer 1548

ザルカダキス
Zarkadakēs, Giōrgos 1548

サルガド
Salgado, Elena 1231
Salgado, Sebastião 1231

サルガド・メンデス
Salgado Méndez, Elena 1231

サルガニク
Salganik, Laura Hersh 1231

サルカム
Sarkam, Siswoto 1242

サルカール・アラニ
Sarkar Arani, Mohammad Reza 1242

サルキ
Saarki, Aboubakary 1222
Sarki, Aboubakary 1242

サルキシャン
Sargsyan, Gurgen 1242
Sargsyan, Narek 1242
Sargsyan, Serzh 1242
Sargsyan, Tigran 1242
Sargsyan, Vigen 1242

サルキス
Sarkis, Joseph 1242
Sarkis, Nazira Farah 1242

サルキソフ
Sarkisov, K.O. 1242

ザルーク
Zarrouk, Ahmed 1548
Zarrouk, Neziha 1548

サルクワゼ
Salukvadze, Nino 1232

サルゲイロ
Salgueiro, Tiago 1231

サル・ケン
Sar Kheng 1242

ザルコウワー
Zarkower, Jonathan 1548

サルコジ
Sarkozy, Nicolas 1242

サルコーネ
Sarcone, Gianni A. 1241

サルコビッチ
Sulkowicz, Kerry J. 1364

サルコフスキス
Salkovskis, Paul M. 1231

サルコマー
Sarkomaa, Sari 1242

ザルコンヌ
Zarcone, Thierry 1548

サルザーアザロフ
Sulzer-Azaroff, Beth 1365

サルシセイ
Sarr-ceesay, Mariama 1243

サルジャエフ
Sarzhayev, Batyr 1243

サ

サルジュ
Sardjoe, Ramdien 1242
サールズ
Searles, Harold F. 1266
Searles, John 1266
Searls, Doc 1266
サルズ
Salz, Jonah 1233
サルストン
Sulston, John 1365
Sulston, John Edward 1365
サルスバーグ
Salsberg, Jon 1232
サルセクバエフ
Sarsekbayev, Bakhyt 1243
サルセド
Salcedo, Carlos 1230
Salcedo, Doris 1230
サルセド＝バスタルド
Salcedo-Bastardo, José Luis 1230
サルセンバエフ
Sarsenbayev, Altynbek 1243
サルダー
Sardar, Ziauddin 1242
サルダーニャ
Saldanha, Eugenia 1230
Saldanha, Gabriela 1230
サルタラマッキア
Saltalamacchia, Jarrod 1232
ザルダリ
Zardari, Asif Ali 1548
サルダ・リコ
Sardà Rico, Esther 1242
サルダール
Sardar, Zahid 1241
サルタレス
Saltares, Javier 1232
サルタレロ
Saltarello, Andrea 1232
サルツァーノ
Salzano, Aniello 1233
サルツァ・プリーナ・リコッティ
Salza Prina Ricotti, Eugenia 1233
ザルツゲベー
Salzgeber, Ulla 1233
サルツバーガー
Sulzberger, Arthur 1365
Sulzberger, Arthur Ochs 1365
ザルツバーガー
Sulzberger, Arthur Ochs 1365
ザルツバーガー - ウィッテンバーグ
Salzberger-Wittenberg, Isca 1233
サルツバーグ
Salzberg, Matt 1233
Salzberg, Sharon 1233
サルツブルグ
Salsburg, David 1232
サルツマン
Saltzman, Joel 1232
Salzman, Mark 1233
サルデ
Sardet, Christian 1242
サルディ
Sardi, Vincent 1242
サルティテ
Saltyte, Lina 1232
サルディバー
Saldivar, John 1230
サルデーニャ
Sardegna, Jill 1242
サルデンベルグ
Sardenberg, Ronaldo 1242
サルト
Sarto, Leonardo 1243
Sarto, Montserrat 1243
サルド
Sarde, Michèle 1242
Sardo, Gennaro 1242
サルドゥ
Sardou, Romain 1242
サルドゥア
Zaldua, Joseba 1546
サルトゥー＝ラジュ
Sarthou-Lajus, Nathalie 1243
サルドマン
Saldmann, Frédéric 1230
ザルトマン
Zaltman, Gerald 1546
サルトーリ
Sartori, Giovanni 1243
サルトリウス
Sartorius, Ghester 1243
Sartorius, N. 1243
サルトル
Sartore, Joel 1243
ザルトル
Sartor, Diana 1243
Sartor, Klaus 1243
サルナーヴ
Sallenave, Danièle 1231
サルナツキ
Sarnacki, Maciej 1242
サルナック
Sarnak, Peter 1242
サルネイ・フィリョ
Sarney Filho, José 1242
ザルバー
Salber, Linde 1230
サルバエフ
Sarbayev, Kadyrbek 1241
サルパシェフ
Sarpashev, Taiyrbek 1243
サルパシェフ
Sarpashev, Taiyrbek 1243
サルバ・セビージャ
Salva Sevilla 1232
サルバチ
Salvatti, Ideli 1232
サルバティエラ・グティエレス
Salvatierra Gutiérrez, Hugo 1232
サルバトア
Salvatore, R.A. 1232
サルバドール
Salvador, Henri 1232
サルバドル
Salvador, María Isabel 1232
サルバドール・ドス・ラモス
Salvador Dosramos, Manuel 1232
サルバドルドスラモス
Salvador Dosramos, Manuel 1232
サルバトーレ
Salvatore, R.A. 1232
Salvatore Rinella 1232
サルパネヴァ
Sarpaneva, Timo 1243
サルパネバ
Sarpaneva, Timo 1243
サルバ・ルイス
Salva Ruiz 1232
サルヒー
Salhi, Zahia Smail 1231
サルビ
Salvi, Cesare 1232
サルビオ
Salvio, Eduardo 1232
ザルービン
Zarubin, S.F. 1548
サルーフ
Salloukh, Fawzi 1232
ザルフェルナー
Salfellnera, Haralda 1231
サルボ
Salvo, Lucía 1233
サルマ
Salma, Hassen 1232
Sarouma, Abdallah Said 1243
サールマセン
Sahl-madsen, Charlotte 1226
サールマン
Saalman, Howard 1222
サルマン
Salman, al-Hamoud al-Sabah 1232
Salman, Ashraf 1232
Salman, bin Hamad al-Khalifa 1232
Salmane, Mohamed 1232
サルマン国王
Salman bin Abdul-Aziz 1232
サルマンズ
Salmans, Sandra 1232
サルマン・ビン・アブドルアジズ
Salman bin Abdul-Aziz 1232
サルマーン・ビン・ハマド・アール・ハリーファ
Shaikh Salman bin Hamad al-Khalifa 1279
サルミ
al-Salimi, Abdullah bin Mohammed 1231
Sarumi, Dapo 1243
サルミエント
Sarmiento, Mauro 1242
Sarmiento, Senen 1242
Sarmiento, Valeria 1242
サルミエントス
Sarmientos, Jorge 1242
サルミエントス・デ・レオン
Sarmientos De León, Jorge Alvaro 1242
サルミエント・ソト
Sarmiento Soto, Juan 1242
サルミネン
Salminen, Max 1232
サルム
Salum, Saada Mkuya 1232
ザルム
Salm, Frieder 1232
Zalm, Gerrit 1546
サルムサイ
Saleumxay, Khommasith 1231
ザルムーフ
Zarmuh, Ramadan Ali Mansour 1548
サルメント
Sarmento, Domingos 1242
Sarmento, Nuno Morais 1242
サルモン
Salmon, Dimitri 1232
Salmon, John 1232
サルヤネン
Sarjanen, Petri 1242
サルワイ
Salwai, Charlot 1233
サルンギ
Sarungi, Philemon 1243
サレ
Salé, Charles 1230
Saleh, Meki 1230
Sallé, Michel 1231
サレー
Sale, Jamie 1230
Saleh, Aziz Mahamat 1230
Saleh, Bahaa E.A. 1230
Saleh, Kimiya 1230
Saleh, Mina 1230
Salleh, Keruak 1231
サレス
Sales, Gemma 1230
Salles, Walter 1231
ザレスキ＝ザメンホフ
Zaleski-Zamenhof, L. C. 1546
ザレスン
Zalesne, E.Kinney 1546
ザレツキー
Zaretsky, Eli 1548
サレット
Surrette, Mark James 1367
ザレット
Zaret, Hy 1548
サレハ
Saleh, Abdelmunim Ahmad 1230
al-Saleh, Abdul-Hadi Abdul-Hamid 1230
Saleh, Ali Abdullah 1230
al-Saleh, Anas Khaled 1230
Saleh, Barham 1230
al-Saleh, Faiqa bint Saeed 1230
Saleh, Hatem 1230
Saleh, Idris Kekia 1230
Saleh, Mariam 1230
Saleh, Osama 1230
Saleh, Rachid Ould 1230
Salih, Bakri Hassan 1231
サレヒ
Salehi, Ali Akbar 1230
サレヒアミリ
Shlehi Amiri, Reza 1292
サレフ
Saleh, Husin 1230
ザレフスカ
Zalewska, Anna 1546
ザレフスキー
Zalewski, Zbigniev 1546
サレホフ
Salekhov, Makhmadnazar 1230

サーレム
Salem, Sidi Ould 1230
Salem, Zeinabou Mint Ely 1230
サレーム
Saleem, Hiner 1230
サレム
Salem, Bassem 1230
Salem, Ezedin Tlish 1230
サーレラ
Saarela, Tanja 1222
サレリ
Saleri, Fausto 1230
サーレル
Surrell, Jason 1367
サーレルズ
Sirles, Jeremiah 1308
サレルノ
Salerno, Shane 1230
サレルノ・ソネンバーグ
Salerno-Sonnenberg, Nadja 1230
サレン
Salen, Katie 1230
サレンバーガー
Sullenberger, Chesley B. Ⅲ 1364
サーロー
Thurlow, Setsuko 1402
サロー
Thurow, Lester C. 1403
Thurow, Roger 1403
サローア
Saloor, Harry 1232
サロイヤン
Saroyan, Aram 1243
ザロガ
Zaloga, Steve 1546
ザ・ロック
Rock 1193
The Rock 1395
サローナー
Saloner, Garth 1232
サロネン
Salonen, Esa-Pekka 1232
サロベイ
Salovey, Peter 1232
サロマン
Salomão, Tomas 1232
サロメ
Salomé, Jacques 1232
Salomé, Jean-Paul 1232
サロモン
Salomon, David 1232
サロワ
Sallois, Jacques 1232
サワ
Sawa, George Dimitri 1246
Sawa, Massoud Ahmed Belqasem 1246
Sawa, Maureen 1246
ザワ
Zawa, Ambroise 1548
ザワダ
Zawada, Craig C. 1548
ザワッキ
Zawacki, Tina M. 1548
サワド
Sawad, Ahmed Ali 1246
サワドゴ
Sawadogo, Clement 1246
Sawadogo, Filiga Michel 1246
Sawadogo, Filippe 1246
Sawadogo, Laya 1246
Sawadogo, Pengwindé Clément 1246
Sawadogo, Salamata 1246
Sawadogo, Salifou 1246
サワドゴタプソバ
Sawadogotapsoba, Salamah 1246
サワビー
Sawaby, Abdul Naser 1246
ザワーヒリー
Zawahiri, Ayman 1548
ザワヒリ
Zawahiri, Ayman 1548
ザワブリ
Zawabri, Antar 1548
ザワルジナ
Zavarzina, Alena 1548
サン
Sand, Ilse 1236
Sann, Jim 1239
Sun, Weizhong 1366
ザーン
Zahn, Timothy 1545
ザン
Chang, Ben-hang 245
Chang, Hsueh-liang 245
Chang, Jung 245
Chang, Yung-fa 246
Zan, Koethi 1547
Zhang, Ai-ping 1551
Zhang, Caroline 1551
Zhang, Cheng-zhi 1551
Zhang, Chun-qiao 1551
Zhang, De-jiang 1551
Zhang, Gao-li 1551
Zhang, Guang-nian 1551
Zhang, Jie 1552
Zhang, Li-chang 1552
Zhang, Rui-fang 1552
Zhang, Ting-fa 1552
Zhang, Wan-nian 1552
Zhang, Wan-xin 1552
Zhang, Xiang-shan 1552
Zhang, Yao-ci 1552
Zhang, Yi-mou 1552
Zhang, Yitang 1552
ザン・イェレム
Zan Yelemou, Nicole Angeline 1547
サンヴィターレ
Sanvitale, Francesco 1240
サン・ヴィンセンテ
San Vincente, Patxi del Campo 1240
サンヴォワザン
Sanvoisin, Éric 1240
サン＝エロワ
Saint Eloi, Rodney 1228
サンカ
Sanca, Doménico Oliveira 1235
Sanca, Luis de Oliveira 1235
サンカー
Sancar, Aziz 1235
サンガ
Sanga, Joses 1238
Sangha, Balvinder S. 1238
サンガー
Sanger, David E. 1238
Sanger, Frederick 1238
Sanger, James 1238
Sanger, Mark 1238
ザンカー
Zanker, Bill 1547
サンガイ
Sangay, Lobsang 1238
ザンガコリンバ
Zanga-kolingba, Desiré 1547
サンガッリ
Sangalli, Arturo 1238
サンガーニ
Sanghani, Radhika 1238
サンガラ
Sangala, Aaron 1238
サンガリ
Sangalli, Jeff 1238
サンガレ
Sangare, Abdul Kader 1238
Sangaré, Aboudramane 1238
Sangare, Nestrine 1238
Sangaré, Tiémoko 1238
サンキー
Sankey, Bishop 1239
Sankey, Darnell 1239
サンギ
Sangi, Vladimir Mikhaĭlovich 1238
サンギネッティ
Sanguinetti, Mateo 1238
ザンギャネ
Zangeneh, Bijan 1547
サンキン
Sonkin, Miles 1328
サンギン
Sangin, Amirzai 1238
サンク
Sanku, Rani 1239
ザング
Zang, Dieudonn Ambassa 1547
サンクイスト
Sunquist, Fiona 1367
Sunquist, Melvin E. 1367
サングィネーティ
Sanguineti, Edoardo 1238
サングイネーティ
Sanguineti, Edoardo 1238
サングカワン
Sungkawan, Decha 1366
サングスター
Sangster, Jim 1238
Sangster, Jimmy 1238
サングビ
Shanghvi, Dilip 1280
サングラ
Sangra Gibert, Jordi 1238
ザングル
Zangle, Fabrice 1547
サンクロワ
Ste-Croix, Gilles 1343
ザンケッタ
Zanchetta, Pietro 1547
サンゲーラー
Sanghera, Jasvinder 1238
ザンケル
Zankel, Arthur 1547
サンゲレ
St-gelais, Marianne 1351
サンコー
Sankoh, Foday 1239
サンゴ
Sango, Bernard Biando 1238
Sango, Damisi 1238
ザンコ
Zanco, Federica 1547
サンゴール
Senghor, Farba 1273
Senghor, Léopold Sédar 1273
Senghore, Aboubacar 1273
サンコン
Sankhon, Ousmane Youla 1239
サンザ
Sanza, André Moke 1241
サンサニー
Sansanee, Nakpong 1239
サンジェ
Sengers, Luuk 1273
サンシェス
Sanches, Daniel 1235
Sanchez, Clara 1235
サンジェレ
St-gelais, Marianne 1351
サンジミャタブ
Sanjmyatav, Yadamsuren 1239
サンシャー
Sancar, Aziz 1235
サンシャイン
Sunshine, Glenn S. 1367
Sunshine, Linda 1367
サンジャル
Sancar, Aziz 1235
サンス
Sanz, Rodolfo 1241
サンズ
Sands, Charlene 1238
Sands, Deanna J. 1238
Sands, Jerry 1238
Sands, Leevan 1238
Sands, Lynsay 1238
Sands, Matthew Linzee 1238
Sands, Stark 1238
Sanz, Alejandro 1241
Sons 1328
ザンス
Zinsou, Lionel 1556
ザンズ
Zanes, Daniel 1547
Zunz, Olivier 1559
サンスイート
Sansweet, Stephen J. 1239
サンスティーン
Sunstein, Cass R. 1367
サンセグンド
San Segundo, María Jesús 1239
サンセリ
Sunseri, Vinnie 1367
ザンゾット
Zanzotto, Andrea 1547
サンソーネ
Sansone, Nicola 1239
サンソム
Sansom, C.J. 1239
Sansom, Ian 1239
Sansom, William 1239
サンソン
Sanson, Yvonne 1239
サンダ
Sanda, Mounkaila 1236

Sanda, Soumana 1236
サンダー
Sander, Helge 1236
Sander, Ian 1236
Sander, Jil 1236
Sander, Peter J. 1237
ザンダー
Sander, Jil 1236
Sander, Otto 1236
Zander, Benjamin 1547
Zander, Edward J. 1547
Zander, Robin 1547
Zander, Rosamund Stone 1547
サンタヴィ
Saint-Avit, Gilles de 1228
サンタオラヤ
Santaolalla, Gustavo 1239
サンタガティ
Santagati, Steve 1239
サンタカナ・イ・トーラス
Santacana, Carles 1239
サンタ・クルス
Santa Cruz, Roque 1239
サンタジャ・トレス
Santalla Tórrez, Daniel 1239
サーンダース
Saunders, Kevin D. 1245
サンダース
Sanders, Allan 1237
Sanders, Barry 1237
Sanders, Ben 1237
Sanders, Bernie 1237
Sanders, Betsy A. 1237
Sanders, Chris 1237
Sanders, Corrie 1237
Sanders, Debra F. 1237
Sanders, Deion 1237
Sanders, Ed 1237
Sanders, Ella Frances 1237
Sanders, Emmanuel 1237
Sanders, E.P. 1237
Sanders, Jason 1237
Sanders, Kenneth 1237
Sanders, Leah 1237
Sanders, Lisa 1237
Sanders, Lori M. 1237
Sanders, Martin 1237
Sanders, Matthew R. 1237
Sanders, Nicholas M. 1237
Sanders, Pete 1237
Sanders, Peter 1237
Sanders, Rupert 1237
Sanders, Thomas 1237
Sanders, Tim 1237
Saunders, Anthony 1244
Saunders, Bernard 1244
Saunders, Catherine 1244
Saunders, David M. 1244
Saunders, George 1244
Saunders, John 1245
Saunders, Ryan 1245
Saunders, Sue 1245
Saunders, Zina 1245
サンダーズ
Sanders, Allan 1237
Sanders, Andrew 1237
Sanders, Catherine M. 1237
Sanders, Glenda 1237
Sanders, Leonard 1237
サンダスキ
Sanduski, Steve 1238
サンダース・ブラームス
Sanders-Brahms, Helma 1237
サンダースン
Sanderson, Brandon 1237
Sanderson, Henry 1237
Sanderson, Peter 1237
サンダーソン
Sanderson, Brandon 1237
Sanderson, Cael 1237
Sanderson, Dan 1237
Sanderson, Keith 1237
Sanderson, Mark Winfierd 1237
Sanderson, Michael 1237
Sanderson, Nicole 1237
Sanderson, William C. 1237
サンタット
Santat, Dan 1240
サンターナ
Santana, Telê 1239
サンタナ
Santana, Carlos 1239
Santana, Danny 1239
Santana, Domingo 1239
Santana, Ervin 1239
Santana, Isidoro 1239
Santana, Johan 1239
Santana, Juan Carlos 1239
Santana, Luz 1239
サンタナロペス
Santana Lopes, Pedro 1239
サンタマリア
Santamaria, Josefina O. 1239
Santamaria, Mongo 1239
サンタマリア・サラマンカ
Santamaría Salamanca, Mauricio 1239
サンダーランド
Sunderland, John 1366
Sunderland, Margot 1366
ザンタリウス
Santarius, Tilman 1239
サンダーリング
Sanderling, Kurt 1237
サンダール
Sandahl, Phillip 1236
サンダルソラ
Sunndalsøra, Thor 1367
サンタンジェロ
Santangelo, Elena 1239
ザンダンシャタル
Zandanshatar, Gombojavyn 1547
サンタンジュ
St.Ange, Alain 1227
サンタンデール
Santander, Anthony 1239
サンタンドレ
Saint Andre, Philippe 1227
サンチ
Santschi, David 1240
サンチアゴ
Santiago, Alvaro 1240
サンチェス
Sanchez, Aaron 1235
Sanchez, Agapito 1235
Sanchez, Alejandro 1235
Sánchez, Ana María 1235
Sanchez, Anibal 1235
Sanchez, Bo 1235
Sanchez, Davinson 1235
Sanchez, Eder 1235
Sanchez, Etel 1235
Sánchez, Félix 1235
Sánchez, Fidel 1235
Sánchez, Francisco 1235
Sanchez, Gary 1235
Sanchez, German 1235
Sanchéz, Glodomiro 1235
Sanchez, Hector 1235
Sánchez, Jeannette 1235
Sanchez, Julian 1236
Sanchez, Julio 1236
Sanchez, Laura 1236
Sánchez, Manuel Fernández 1236
Sanchez, Mark 1236
Sanchez, Natalia 1236
Sanchez, Nicolas 1236
Sánchez, Olga Marta 1236
Sanchez, Patti 1236
Sánchez, Reinaldo Antonio 1236
Sanchez, Robert 1236
Sánchez, Samuel 1236
Sanchez, Sofia 1236
Sanchez, Tania 1236
Sánchez, Victor 1236
Sánchez, Vladimir 1236
Sanchez, Yolmer 1236
Sanchez, Zack 1236
Sánchez Ferlosio, Rafael 1236
Sánchez Mora, Jonathan 1236
Sanchez Soto, Laura 1236
サンチェズ
Sanchez, Fabien 1235
サンチェス - ウクレス
Sanchez-Hucles, Janis 1236
サンチェス・エルナンデス
Sánchez, Fidel 1235
サンチェス・ガマラ
Sánchez Gamarra, Pedro 1236
サンチェス・セレン
Sánchez Cerén, Salvador 1236
サンチェス・デ・レブエルタ
Sánchez de Revuelta, Inés 1236
サンチェスデ・ロサダ
Sánches De Lozada, Gonzalo 1235
サンチェス・ピニョル
Sánchez Pinol, Albert 1236
サンチェス・フェルナンデス
Sánchez Fernández, Luis Alberto 1236
サンチェス・フェルロシオ
Sánchez Ferlosio, Rafael 1236
サンチェスブラスケス
Sanchez-Blazquez, Salustiano 1236
サンチェスベロン
Sanchez Beron, Vanina Paola 1236
サンチェス - ベントゥーラ・イ・パスクアル
Sánchez-Ventura y Pascual, Francisco 1236
サンチェス - ライリー
Sanchez-Reilly, Sandra 1236
サンチェスリベロ
Sanchez Rivero, Junior Antonio 1236
サンチェスロペス
Sanchez Lopez, David 1236
サンチェス・ロメロ
Sánchez Romero, Cecilia 1236
サンツォ
Sanzo, Salvatore 1241
サンツランツ
Sanz Lanz, Mateo 1241
サンデ
Sande, Mamadou 1236
Sande, Merle A. 1236
サンデー
Sandé, Emeli 1236
サンティ
Santee, Robert G. 1240
Santi, Franco 1240
Santi, Nello 1240
Santi, Promphat 1240
Santy, Christiana Soenarno 1240
サンディ
Sandi, Denis 1237
サンディー
Sandy, John Edmund 1238
ザンディ
Zandi, Mark 1547
サンティアゴ
Santiago, Angela Viegas 1240
Santiago, Carlos Manuel 1240
Santiago, Hector 1240
Santiago, Luis 1240
Santiago, Mikel 1240
サンティス
Santis, Pablo de 1240
サンディッジ
Sandage, Allan Rex 1236
サンティッチ
Santich, Barbara 1240
サンティーニ
Santini, Bertrand 1240
サンティ・ミナ
Santi Mina 1240
サン＝ティレール
St.-Hilaire, W. 1228
サンディーン
Sundeen, Mark 1366
サンディン
Sundin, Mats 1366
サン・テグジュペリ
Saint-Exupery, Arnaud de 1228
サンデージ
Sandage, Allan Rex 1236
Sandage, Scott A. 1236
サンデノ
Sandeno, Kaitlin 1236
サンデム
Sundem, Garth 1366
Sundem, Gary L. 1366
サンデモーセ
Sandemose, Iben 1236
サンテリ
Santelli, Robert 1240
サンデリック
Sunderic, Dejan 1366
サンテール
Santer, Jacques 1240
サンテル
Suntele, Inkululeko 1367
サンデール

Sanders, Alex 1237

サンデル

Sandel, Michael J. 1236
Sandell, Dennis 1236
Sandell, Scott 1236
Zander, Birgitta 1547
Zander, Joakim 1547

ザンデル

Zander, Pietro 1547

ザンデルリンク

Sanderling, Kurt 1237
Sanderling, Thomas 1237

ザンデルリング

Sanderling, Kurt 1237
Sanderling, Thomas 1237

サンデロウスキー

Sandelowski, Margarete 1236

サント

Santo, Branca Manuel da Costa Neto do Espírito 1240
Santo, Ron 1240
Santos, Demóstenes Vasconcelos Pires Dos 1240

サンド

Sand, Barbara Lourie 1236
Sand, Jordan 1236
Sand, Shlomo 1236

サントウ

Santow, Leonard Jay 1240

サンドゥ

Sandhu, Manavjit Singh 1237
Sandhu, Sukhdev 1237
Sandu, Gabriel 1238
Sandu, Maia 1238
Sindeu, Jean-Bernard 1305

サンドウ

Sandoe, James 1237

サンドヴァル

Sandoval, Arturo 1238

サンドゥル

Sandeul 1237

サントキ

Santokhi, Chandrikapersad 1240

ザントキューラー

Sandkühler, Hans-Jörg 1237

サンドクイスト

Sundquist, Eric J. 1366

サントス

Giovani 501
Santos, Aderlian 1240
Santos, Anne Marie 1240
Santos, Cairo 1240
Santos, Christian 1240
Santos, Eduardo 1240
Santos, Francisco San Emeterio 1240
Santos, Gustavo 1240
Santos, Joel Rufino dos 1240
Santos, Jordan 1240
Santos, Juan Manuel 1240
Santos, Luguelin 1240
Santos, Marcelo 1240
Santos, Marisa de los 1240
Santos, Migel Angel 1240
Santos, Rebeca 1240
Santos, Ricardo 1240
Santos, Vítor Pavao dos 1240

サントス・オルドニェス

Santos Ordóñez, Elvin Ernesto 1240

サントス・カルデロン

Santos Calderón, Francisco 1240
Santos Calderón, Juan Manuel 1240

サンドスキ

Sandoski, Aaron 1238

サントス・シルバ

Santos Silva, Augusto 1240

サントスシルバ

Santos Silva, Augusto 1240

サントスペレイラ

Santos Pereira, Álvaro 1240

サントス・ボレ

Santos Borre 1240

サントスレイエス

Santos Reyes, Arturo 1240

サントスレリス

Santos Lélis, Janine Tatiana 1240

サントス・ロペス

Santos López, Samuel 1240

サントトマス

Santo Tomas, Patricia 1240

サン＝ドニ

Saint-Denis, Alain 1228

サントニ

Santoni, François 1240

サンドバーグ

Sandberg, Ryne Dee 1236
Sandberg, Sheryl 1236
Sandburg, Carl 1236
Sundberg, Nick 1366

サンドバック

Sandbach, John 1236

サンドバル

Sandoval, Jonathan 1238
Sandoval, Lynda 1238
Sandoval, Manuela Ines 1238
Sandoval, Pablo 1238
Sandoval, Rafa 1238

サンドバル・ビジェダ

Sandoval Villeda, Leopoldo 1238

サントピエトロ

Santopietro, Tom 1240

サンドフォード

Sandford, Gina 1237
Sandford, John 1237

サンドベリ

Sandberg, Inger 1236
Sandberg, Lasse 1236

サンドマン＝リリウス

Sandman Lilius, Irmelin 1237

サントーラ

Santora, Nick 1240

サンドラー

Sandler, Adam 1237
Sandler, Corey 1237
Sandler, Joseph 1237
Sandler, Martin W. 1237
Sandler, Robert 1237

サントラウコ

Santolouco, Mateus 1240

サントラム

Santorum, Rick 1240

サンドラム

Sundaram, Rangarajan K. 1366
Sundram, Steve 1366

サンドランド

Sandland, Beau 1237

サントリ

Santry, Sean E. 1240

ザンドリ

Zandri, Jason 1547
Zandri, Vincent 1547

サンドリマン

Sandriman, Walter 1238

サンドール

Sandall, Robert 1236

サンドレイ

Sendrey, Gérard 1273

サンドレッリ

Sandrelli, Stefania 1238

サントロ

Santoro, Fabrice 1240

サンドロ

Sandro, Ramirez 1238

サントロファー

Santlofer, Jonathan 1240

サンドロリーニ

Sandrolini, John 1238

サントン

Santon, Davide 1240

サンナ

Sanna, Mario 1239

サンナー

Sander, Helge 1236

サンニー

Sanneh, Sidi Moro 1239

ザンニ

Zanni, Alessandro 1547

サンニア

Sannia, Alessandro 1239

サンネル

Sanner, Jan 1239

サンハ

Sanha, Antonio Artur 1238
Sanhá, Malam Bacai 1238

サンバ

Samba, Sidi Ould 1233
Samba, Sulayman 1233

サンバー

Sanbar, Elias 1235

サンパ

Sampa, Chitalu 1234

ザンパ

Zampa, Adam 1546

サンパイオ

Sampaio, Jorge 1234

サン・バオ

San Bao 1235

サンパオリ

Sampaoli, Jorge 1234

ザンパーノ

Zampano, Francesco 1546

サンバパンザ

Samba-Panza, Catherine 1233
Samba-panza, Cyriaque 1233

サンバ・マリアボ

Samba Maliavo, Marguérite 1233

サンバマリアボ

Samba Maliavo, Marguérite 1233

サンパール

Sampar 1234

サンパン

Samphan, Boonyanan 1234

サンビ

Sambi, Ahmed Abdallah Mohamed 1233

サンビア

Sambia, Chrysostome 1233

サンピエール

St.Pierre, Kennedy 1228

サンピエロ

Sampiero, Dominique 1234

サンヒネス

Sanjinés, Jorge 1238

サンビリ

Sambili, Helen 1233

サンピリージ

Sampirisi, Mario 1234

サンピル

Sampil, Moussa 1234

サンブ

Sambou, Benoît 1233
Sambou, Isabelle 1233
Sambou, Ismaila 1233
Sambu, Soares 1233

サンブー

Sambou, Isabelle 1233

サンファール

Saint-Phalle, Niki de 1228

サンファル

Saint-Phalle, Niki de 1228

サンフィリッポ

Sanfilippo, Simona 1238

サンフィリポ

Sanfilippo, Joseph S. 1238

サンフォード

Sandford, John Loren 1237
Sandford, Paula 1237
Sanford, Christopher 1238
Sanford, Isabel 1238
Sanford, Jamarca 1238
Sanford, John A. 1238

サンプソン

Sampson, Anthony Terrell Seward 1234
Sampson, Catherine 1234
Sampson, Dorothy Madway 1234
Sampson, Fred 1234
Sampson, JaKarr 1234
Sampson, Michael R. 1234
Sampson, Robert J. 1234

サンブチーノ

Sambuchino, Chuck 1234

サンブラ

Zambra, Alejandro 1546

サンプラス

Sampras, Pete 1234

サンフラテロ

Sanfratello, Ippolito 1238

ザンブラーノ

Zambrano, Gregory 1546

サン＝ブランカ

Saint-Blanquat, Henri de 1228

ザンブランネン

Zumbrunnen, Eric 1559

サンプル

Sample, Clinton Kennedy, Ⅲ 1234
Sample, Ian 1234
Sample, James 1234
Sample, Joe 1234

サンプルークラーン
Saint-Preux Craan, Eudes 1228
サン・フルラン
Saint Fleurant, Louisiane 1228
サンブレイロ
Sambrailo, Ty 1233
ザンブロッタ
Zambrotta, Gianluca 1546
サンペ
Sempé 1272
サンベク
Sandbech, Staale 1236
ザンペース
Zampese, Ken 1546
ザンベッリ
Zambelli, Marco 1546
サンペドロ
Sampedro, José Luis 1234
サンベーヌ
Sembène, Ousmane 1272
サンヘラ
Sanghera, Paul 1238
サンベラク
Sumberac, Manuel 1365
サンペリ
Samperi, Salvatore 1234
ザンベリ
Zambelli, Raymond 1546
ザンペリーニ
Zamperini, Louis 1546
サンペール
Simpère, Françoise 1304
サンペル
Samper, Sergi 1234
サンベルグ
Sandberg, Per 1236
サンボ
Sambo, Luís Gomes 1233
Sambo, Namadi 1233
Sambo, Youba 1233
サン・ホセ
San Jose, Mikel 1239
サンボッティ
Zambotti, Vanessa Martina 1546
ザンボーニ
Zamboni, Doriana 1546
サンボラ
Sambora, Richie 1233
サンボーン
Sanborn, David William 1235
Sanborn, Eunice 1235
Sanborn, Garrison 1235
Sanborn, Mark 1235
サン＝マルク
Saint-Marc, Laure 1228
サンミゲル
San Miguel, Esther 1239
Sanmiguel, Ines 1239
サンミゲル・ロドリゲス
Sanmiguel Rodríguez, Walker 1239
サンヤ・タマサク
Sanya Thammasak 1241
サンヤ・ダルマサクティ
Sanya Thammasak 1241
サンヤ・タンマサック
Sanya Thammasak 1241
サンヤー・タンマサック
Sanya Thammasak 1241
サンヤン
Sanyang, Ismaila 1241
サンラヴィル
Sanlaville, Mickaël 1239
サンリ
Sanli, Uno 1239
サン＝ルウ
Saint-Loup, Margot 1228
サンロ
Saint-Lot, Danielle 1228
サン・ローラン
Saint-Laurent, Yves 1228
サンローラン
Saint-Laurent, Yves 1228

【シ】

シ
Shi, Jay 1289
Shi, Zheng-rong 1289
Sy, Cheikh Tidiane 1373
Sy, Habib 1373
シー
See, Carolyn 1267
See, Lisa 1268
See, Prudence 1268
Shea, Andrew 1285
Shi, Shu-qing 1289
Shi, Wen-long 1289
Shi, Zhan-chun 1289
Shi, Zheng-rong 1289
Shih, Chen-jung 1290
Shih, Choon-fong 1290
Shih, Kien 1290
Shin, Fu-Jin 1290
Shin, Shaw-Niw 1291
Sy, Amadou Baba 1373
Sy, Cheikh Tidiane 1373
Sy, Habib 1373
Sy, Henry Sr. 1373
Sy, Monsour 1373
Sy, Omar 1373
Sy, Seydou 1373
Sze, Jackson 1374
Thie, John 1396
Thie, Matthew 1396
Xi, Jin-ping 1531
Xi, Zhong-xun 1531
ジ
Chi, Myong-kwan 254
Ji, Steven 673
ジー
Gee, Alonzo 486
Gee, Dillon 486
Gee, Henry 486
Ji, Xian-lin 673
Sze, David 1374
Zee, Ruth Vander 1549
シーア
Seah, M.P. 1266
Shea, William R. 1285
Sia 1295
シァ
Xia, Qingsu 1531
シア
Shea, Richard 1285
Shea, Shawn Christopher 1285
ジーア
Zeer, Darrin 1549
ジア
Zia, Ehsan 1553
Zia, Khaleda 1553
シアオシ・アホ
Siaosi 'Aho, Taimani 1295
シアカム
Siakam, Pascal 1295
ジアコミニ
Giacomini, Breno 494
シーアシー
Searcy, Da'Norris 1266
シアーズ
Sears, Alfred 1266
Sears, Barry 1266
Sears, James M. 1266
Sears, Martha 1266
Sears, Michael 1266
Sears, Robert 1266
Sears, Ted 1266
Sears, William 1266
Shears, Paul 1285
シアス
Theus, John 1395
ジアス
Dias, Manoel 351
シアーズ＝デュリュ
Sears-duru, Djustice 1266
シアソン
Siazon, Domingo L. 1295
シアゾン
Siazon, Domingo L. 1295
ジアダ
Ziada, Abdul-Raouf 1553
Ziada, Mohamad 1553
ジアダト
Ziadat, Ahmad 1553
ジアッキノ
Giacchino, Michael 494
ジァッコーニ
Giacconi, Ricardo 494
ジアデ
Ziadé, Tarek 1553
シアード
Sheard Michael 1285
ジアニーニ
Giannini, John 494
ジアネッティ
Giannetti, Eduardo 494
Giannetti, Louis D. 494
シアマー
Shearmur, Jeremy 1285
ジアマッティ
Giamatti, Paul 494
シアマン
Shearman, John K.G. 1285
シアミオナウ
Siamionau, Mikhail 1295
シアム
Siam, Said 1295
Thiam, Mahmoud 1395
Thiam, Ousmane 1395
シアムネ
Siamune, Richwell 1295
シアラ
Ciara 264
Sciarra, Paul 1263
シアラー
Schaerer, Peter 1249
Shearer, Alex 1285
Shearer, Moira 1285
ジアラ
Diarra, Mamadou 351
Diarra, Mamadou Gaoussou 351
Diarra, Mamadou Igor 351
シアラス
Tsiaras, Alexander 1424
ジアラワノン
Chearavanont, Dhanin 250
シアリー
Shirley, Josh 1291
ジアリ
Ziari, Abdelaziz 1553
シアリング
Shearing, George Albert 1285
ジアール
Djiar, Hachemi 359
Giard, Agnès 494
シアルディ
Ciardi, Michel 264
シアルリス
Siarlis, Vasos 1295
ジァン
Jahng, Doosub 659
ジアン
Jiang, Jia 673
Jiang, Yanmei 673
シアンシオ
Ciancio, Oscar 264
ジ・アンダーテイカー
The Undertaker 1395
ジアンビ
Giambi, Jason 494
ジアンビー
Giambi, Jason 494
ジアンフォルテ
Gianforte, Greg 494
シアンフランス
Cianfrance, Derek 264
シイ
Xu, Jing-lei 1532
ジィ
Ji, Haru 673
ジィー
Sze, S.M. 1374
ジィベリィ
Gyberg, Bo-Erik 550
ジィンドゥル
Zyndul, Jolanta 1560
シーヴァ
Shiva, Vandana 1292
シーヴァー
Siever, Larry J. 1297
シヴァ
Shiva, Vandana 1292
シーヴァス
Shivas, Mark 1292
シヴァーズ
Chivers, Natasha 257
Shivers, John 1292
ジーヴァース
Sievers, Eberhard 1297
ジヴァノヴィッツ
Siwanowicz, Igor 1309
ジヴァンシー
Givency, Hubert de 503
シヴィー
Schiwy Sj, Günther 1253
シウヴァ
Silva, Gilberto 1299
シヴェター
Siveter, David J. 1309
Siveter, Derek J. 1309
シーウェル
Sewell, Rufus 1277
Sewell, Tom 1277

シヴェル
Sivell, Vaughan 1309
シヴェルブシュ
Schivelbusch, Wolfgang 1253
シヴェルミュラ
Sivell-Muller, Marcus 1309
ジヴォン
Zevon, Warren William 1551
ジヴコヴィッチ
Zivkovic, Andrija 1556
Živković, Zoran 1556
シウコサーリ
Siukosaari, Jukka 1308
ジウチャロエミット
Jiewchaloemmit, Sutiya 673
シウネ
Siune, Mathew 1308
シウネビッチ
Shunevich, Igor A. 1294
シウバ
Silva, Ana Beatriz Barbosa 1299
Silva, Gilberto 1299
Silva, Wanderle 1300
ジウフ
Diouf, Abdou 357
シウファス
Sioufas, Dimitris 1307
ジウフラ・モンテベルデ
Giuffra Monteverde, Bruno 502
ジウベルトシウバ
Silva, Gilberto 1299
シウマロ
Seumalo, Isaac 1276
ジヴリスキー
Divulsky, Vasily Fyodoruvich 359
シウロ
Ciullo, Jeremy R. 265
Ciullo, Jerome V. 265
シエ
Hsieh, Chang-ting 629
Hsieh, Tung-min 630
Xie, Jin 1531
Xie, Tian 1531
シエー
Cseh, László 306
Shea, Gail 1285
Shieh, Jennifer C. 1289
シエ
Sie, Trish 1296
Sieh, Cletus 1297
Xie, Jin 1531
ジエー
Jay, Vincent 667
シエーア
Scheer, Hermann 1250
シエア
Schar, Fabian 1249
Scher, Paula 1251
Shea, Mark 1285
Shea, Victoria 1285
Sher, Barbara 1288
シエアー
Scheer, August-Wilhelm 1250
シエアード
Sheard, Jabaal 1285
Sheard, Karen Clark 1285
Sheard, Kierra "KiKi" 1285
Sheard, Paul 1285
Sheard Michael 1285
シエアマン
Shearman, Robert 1285
シエアリング
Scheuring, Paul T. 1251
シエイ
Hsieh, Tony 630
Shay, Bee 1284
Shay, Kathryn 1284
Shay, Ryan 1284
Shea, Ammon 1285
Shea, Chris 1285
Shea, Frank 1285
Shea, Jack 1285
Shea, Jamie Patrick 1285
Shea, Jim 1285
Shea, John 1285
Shea, Michael 1285
Shea, Therese 1285
Xu, Jing-lei 1532
ジエイ
Jay, Alison 667
Jay, Antony 667
Jay, Emma 667
Jay, Jon 667
Jay, Martin 667
Jay, Meg 667
Jay, Ros 667
Jay, Vincent 667
Jaye, Myles 667
ジエイ・Z
Jay-Z 667
ジエイZ
Jay-Z 667
シエイウィッツ
Shaywitz, Sally E. 1285
シエイヴルスン
Shavelson, Melville 1284
シエイカー
Shakar, Alex 1279
Shakir, Susie 1279
ジエイガー
Jager, Eric 659
ジエイ卿
Jay, Baroness 667
シエイキン
Sheinkin, Rachel 1286
シエイク
Cheikh, Moumin Ahmed 251
Shaikh, Abdul Hafeez 1279
Shaikh, Abdul Salam 1279
Sheikh, Anees A. 1286
ジエイク
Jaech, John L. 658
シエイクアキラフ
Cheikhachiraf, Abdourahamane Ben 251
シエイク・サルマン・ビン・エブラヒム・アル・ハリファ
Shaikh Salman bin Ebrahim Al Khalifa 1279
シエイク・サルマン・ビン・ハマド・アール・ハリーファ
Shaikh Salman bin Hamad al-Khalifa 1279
シエイク・サルマン・ビン・ハマド・アル・ハリファ
Shaikh Salman bin Hamad al-Khalifa 1279
ジエイクス
Jacques, Brian 658
Jacques, Martin 658
Jakes, John 660
Jakes, S.E. 660
シエイクスピア
Shakespeare, Robbie 1279
Shakespeare, Tom 1279
ジエイクマン
Jakeman, Jane 660
シエイク・ムデイ
Sheikh Mudey, Abdiweli Ibrahim 1286
シエイクリー
Shakely, Jamil 1279
ジエイコブ
Jacob, Adam 657
Jacob, Christian 657
Jacob, Daniel J. 657
Jacob, Dee 657
Jacob, Maurice 657
Jacob, Rhonda F. 657
Jacobs, Douglas 657
ジエイコブス
Jacobs, Barry J. 657
Jacobs, Ben 657
Jacobs, Brandon 657
Jacobs, Chuck 657
Jacobs, David Michael 657
Jacobs, Gregg D. 657
Jacobs, Irwin 657
Jacobs, James 657
Jacobs, Julian 657
Jacobs, Kate 657
Jacobs, Marc 657
Jacobs, Nic 657
Jacobs, Paul 657
Jacobs, Phil 657
Jacobs, Ron 657
Jacobs, Scott 657
Jacobs, Steven L. 657
Jacobs, Theodore J. 657
Jacobs, Tramain 657
ジエイコブズ
Jacobs, A.J. 657
Jacobs, Brandon 657
Jacobs, David 657
Jacobs, D.Lea 657
Jacobs, George M. 657
Jacobs, Harvey 657
Jacobs, Holly 657
Jacobs, Jay S. 657
Jacobs, John W. 657
Jacobs, Mara 657
Jacobs, Marc 657
Jacobs, Michael 657
Jacobs, Paul E. 657
Jacobs, Raymond 657
Jacobs, Robert A. 657
Jacobs, Robert Horace 657
Jacobs, Robert W. 657
Jacobs, Wilbur R. 658
ジエイコブスン
Jacobson, Andrew 658
Jacobson, Mark 658
ジエイコブセン
Jacobsen, Annie 658
Jacobsen, Rowan 658
ジエイコブソン
Jacobson, Andrew 658
Jacobson, Dan 658
Jacobson, Denise Sherer 658
Jacobson, Howard 658
Jacobson, Jennifer Richard 658
Jacobson, Leonard 658
Jacobson, Nina 658
Jacobson, Reed 658
Jacobson, Sid 658
Jacobson, Troy 658
ジエイジエイ
Jayjay, Roosevelt 667
ジエイソ
Jaso, John 666
シエイソン
Cheysson, Claude 254
ジエイソン
Jaison, Bala 659
Jayson, Malcolm I.V. 667
シエイト
Scheidt, Gintare Volungeviciute 1250
シエイド
Scheidt, Robert 1250
ジエイナル
Janal, Daniel S. 662
ジエイニチエンカ
Dzeinichenka, Tsimafei 386
シエイハ
al-Sheikha, Kamal 1286
シエイバー
Shavor, Sherry 1284
シエイピン
Shapin, Steven 1281
シエイフ
al-Asshaikh, Abdullatif bin Abdulmalik bin Omar 65
Cheikh, Mohamed Lemine Ould 251
Schaef, Anne Wilson 1248
al-Sheikh, Abdullah bin Muhammad bin Ibrahim 1286
al-Sheikh, Mohammed bin Adbulmalik 1286
Sheikh, Muhammad Ali el 1286
al-Sheikh, Saleh bin Abdulaziz 1286
シエイファー
Schaefer, Charles E. 1248
Schaefer, Mark W. 1248
Schafer, Logan 1249
Schafer, William K. 1249
Schaffer, Jane 1249
Schaffer, Ronald 1249
Shafer, Glenn 1278
Shafer, Jeffery S. 1278
Shaffer, Anthony 1278
Shaffer, Howard J. 1278
Shaffer, Mary Ann 1278
Shaffer, Peter Levin 1278
シエイフルーフー
Cheïkhrouhou, Héla 251
シエイベルソン
Shavelson, Melville 1284
シエイホルエスラミ
Sheikholeslami, Abdulreza 1286
シエイボン
Chabon, Michael 241
シエイマス
Schamus, James 1249
ジエイミスン
Jameson, Hanna 662
ジエイミソン

シ

Jamieson, Kathleen Hall 662
Jamison, R.N. 662
Jamison, Steve 662
シェイムズ
Shames, Laurence 1280
ジェイムス
James, Etta 661
James, Ian 661
James, Jasón 661
ジェイムズ
James, Arlene 661
James, Bethan 661
James, Bill 661
James, B.J. 661
James, E.L. 661
James, Elizabeth 661
James, Etta 661
James, Geraldine 661
James, Harold 661
James, Ioan Mackenzie 661
James, Jamie 661
James, Jason 661
James, John W. 661
James, José 661
James, Judi 661
James, Judith 661
James, Julia 661
James, Kristin 661
James, Melissa 661
James, Michael 661
James, P.D. 661
James, Peter 661
James, Peter J. 661
James, Richard D. 662
James, Samantha 662
James, Sammy, Jr. 662
James, Simon 662
James, Steve 662
James, Susanne 662
James, Tad 662
James, William E. 662
ジェイムス・グレイソン
Trulove, James Grayson 1422
ジェイムスン
Jameson, Bronwyn 662
ジェイムソン
Jameson, Claudia 662
Jameson, Cynthia 662
Jameson, Fredric R. 662
Jameson, Sam 662
ジェイラン
Ceylan, Nuri Bilge 241
シェイル
Scheil, Dennis 1250
シェイレブ
Shalev, Zahavit 1279
シェイン
Shain, Edith 1279
Shayne, Cameron 1285
Shayne, Maggie 1285
Shein, Ali Mohamed 1286
ジェイン
Jain, Anshu 659
Jain, Bijoy 659
Jain, Dipak 659
Jain, Purnendra 659
Jain, S.Lochlann 659
ジェインウェイ
Janeway, Charles A., Jr. 662
Janeway, Judith 663
シェインコフ
Scheinkopf, Lisa J. 1250
シェインズ
Shanes, Eric 1280
ジェインズ
Janes, Joseph Robert 662
シェインドリン
Scheindlin, Raymond P. 1250
シェインバーグ
Shainberg, Catherine 1279
シェインリー
Shanley, William 1281
シェヴィ
Chauvy, Michel 249
ジェウィルス
Gewirtz, Russell 492
シェヴィンスカ
Szewinska, Irena 1374
シェヴェレヴァ
Sheveleva, Svetlana A. 1289
シェーヴェン
Schaewen, Deidi von 1249
ジェヴティック
Jevtic, Zoran 672
シェウリング
Shewring, Leslie 1289
ジエエフ
Ziyeyev, Mirzo 1556
ジェエンベコフ
Jeenbekov, Sooronbay 668
シェカラウ
Shekarau, Ibrahim 1286
シェカラビ
Shekarabi, Ardalan 1286
シェカリッチ
Sekaric, Jasna 1270
シェカール
Shekhar, Chandra 1286
ジェーガン
Jagan, Janet 659
ジエギス
Diegues, Carlos 353
ジェクシェンクロフ
Dzhekshenkulov, Alikbek 386
シェクスナイダー
Schexnayder, Cliff J. 1251
シェークスピア
Shakespeare, Robbie 1279
シェクター
Schechter, Harriet 1250
Schecter, Darrow 1250
Shechter, Hofesh 1285
Shecter, Ben 1285
シェクマン
Schekman, Randy W. 1250
シェクリー
Sheckley, Robert 1285
シェクリイ
Sheckley, Robert 1285
シェグルト
Šegrt, Budimir 1269
シェグロフ
Schegloff, Emanuel A. 1250
シェケイ
Siekei, Jefferson 1297
シェケリンスカ
Šekerinska, Radmila 1270
シェケルベコワ
Shekerbekova, Zhaina 1286
ジェコ
Džeko, Edin 386
ジエゴ・アウヴェス
Diego Alves 353
ジェーコブ
Jacob, Christian 657
ジェーコブス
Jacobs, Marc 657
ジェーコブズ
Jacobs, Jane 657
Jacobs, Paul E. 657
ジェーコブセン
Jacobsen, Rowan 658
ジェーコブソン
Jacobson, Dan 658
Jacobson, Nina 658
Jacobson, Sada 658
ジェサー
Jesser, Jody Duncan 672
ジェザー
Jezer, Marty 672
ジェサップ
Jessup, Diane 672
ジェシー
Jessie 672
ジェシー・J
Jessie J 672
ジェジェ
Djedje, Alcide Irahiri 359
ジェジェラワ
Jejelava, Aleksandre 669
ジェジュン
Jejung 669
シェス
Sheth, Anish 1289
Sheth, Brian 1289
ジェス
Jesse, Jonathan 672
Jesse, Nico 672
ジエス
Giès, Jacques 496
シェスカ
Scieszka, Jon 1263
ジェスク
Geske, Mary 492
ジェズス
Jesus, Jorge 672
Jesus, Jorge Lopes Bom 672
ジェズズ
Jesus, Jorge Lopes Bom 672
シェスターク
Seszták, Miklós 1276
シェスタク
Sestak, Marija 1276
シェスタコフ
Shestakov, Vasily B. 1289
シェスタコワ
Shestakova, Oksana 1289
ジェスダーソン
Jesudason, James Vijayaseelan 672
ジェスティス
Jestice, Phyllis G. 672
Jsetice, Phyllis G. 689
ジェスト
Gest, Thomas R. 492
シェーストランド
Sjöstrand, Fritiof Stig 1309
シェストランド
Sjöstrand, Fritiof Stig 1309
シェスネ
Chesnais, Francois 253
ジェゼケル
Jezequel, Jean-Marc 672
Jézéquel, Patrick 672
ジェソップ
Jessop, Bob 672
シェーダー
Scheeder, Bettina 1250
シェダー
Scheder, Sophie 1250
ジェーダ
Geda, Fabio 486
ジェタ
Jethá, Cacilda 672
ジェター
Jeter, Michael 672
シェック
Scheck, Barry 1250
Scheck, Frank Rainer 1250
ジェック
Jeck, Mohamed Ould Ahmed Ould 668
シェックリー
Sheckley, Barry G. 1285
ジ・エッジ
Edge 390
シェッソウ
Schössow, Peter 1258
シェッター
Schejter, Amit 1250
ジェッター
Jetter, Dieter 672
シェッツィング
Schätzing, Frank 1249
ジェッツェン
Gietzen, Jean 496
ジェット
Jet 672
Jett, Juliet L. 672
Jett, Tish 672
Jette, Randall 672
ジェットゥ
Jettou, Driss 672
シェットラー
Schottler, Peter 1258
シェップ
Schepp, Emelie 1251
Schöpf, Alfred 1258
シェッファー
Schaffer, Heinz 1249
シェッフェル
Scheffel, Michael 1250
シェツレ
Schatzle, Anita 1250
ジェツン・ペマ王妃
Jetsun Pema 672
シェティ
Shetty, Devi Prasad 1289
Shetty, Salil 1289
シェディド
Chedid, Andrée 250
ジェド
Lledo, Pierre-Marie 836
ジェトゥー
Jettou, Driss 672
シェトキナ
Shchetkina, Marianna A. 1285
ジェドス
Gedoz, Felipe 486
シェトラー
Schettler, Ted 1251

Shetler, Joanne 1289
シェートリヒ
Schädlich, Hans Joachim 1248
シェトルズ
Shettles, Landrum B. 1289
シェトレ
Schöttle, Rupert 1258
シェドロフ
Shedroff, Nathan 1285
ジェナ
Jena, Srikant K. 669
ジェナリッチ
Jennerich, Lindsay 670
ジェニ
Jenni, Alexis 670
ジェニー
Jeanne, Jonathan 668
Jenny, Carole 670
Jenny, Peter 670
シェニウー＝ジャンドロン
Chénieux-Gendron, Jacqueline 252
ジェニエ
Geniet, Rémi 488
ジェニキー
Jaenicke, Chris 658
ジェニス
Geniesse, Jane Fletcher 488
ジェニセック
Jenicek, Milos 669
ジェニチェンカ
Dzeinichenka, Tsimafei 386
シエニチキン
Sienichkin, Andriy 1297
ジェニー・チャン
Chang, Jenny 245
ジェニック
Gennick, Jonathan 488
ジェニュワイン
Jenuwein, Thomas 671
シェーニン
Shenin, Oleg Semyonovich 1287
シェニン
Shenin, Oleg Semyonovich 1287
ジェニーン
Geneen, Harold Sydney 488
ジェニングス
Jennings, Andrew 670
Jennings, Brandon 670
Jennings, Dan 670
Jennings, Dana Andrew 670
Jennings, Darius 670
Jennings, David Harry 670
Jennings, Desmond 670
Jennings, Jason 670
Jennings, Karen 670
Jennings, Linda 670
Jennings, Marianne 670
Jennings, Peter Charles 670
Jennings, Rashad 670
Jennings, Roger 670
Jennings, Simon 670
Jennings, Terrence 670
Jennings, Vernon 670
Jennings, Waylon 670
ジェニングズ
Jennings, Andrew 670
Jennings, Ann 670
Jennings, Elizabeth 670
Jennings, Peter Charles 670
ジェヌイン
Genuin, Magda 489
シェヌーダ
Shenouda Ⅲ 1287
シェヌーダ3世
Shenouda Ⅲ 1287
シェーネ
Schöne, Albrecht 1257
Schone, Lasse 1257
シェネエフィールド
Shenefield, John H. 1287
ジェネシェイ
Gyenesei, István 550
ジェネシオ
Genesio, Bruno 488
ジェーネシキナ
Denezhkina, Irina 341
ジェネシス
Genesis, Mercy 488
ジェネット
Genett, Donna M. 488
Gennett, Scooter 488
ジェネリン
Genelin, Michael 488
シェネル
Chénel, Pascale 252
Che'nelle 252
Şener, Abdullatif 1273
Sener, Ozbayrakli 1273
ジェネンダ
Geneder, Jeff M. 488
シェノイ
Shenoy, Suchitra 1287
ジェノヴァ
Genova, Lisa 488
Goneva, Vereniki 513
ジェノウェイズ
Genoways, Ted 488
ジェノンタンアゴス
Djenontin-agossou, Valentin 359
シェバ
Sabee, David 1223
ジェバ
Zieba, Nadiezda 1554
シェハイブ
Shehayeb, Akram 1286
シェバウスキ
Szczerbowski, Maciek 1374
シェパーズ
Scheppers, Tanner 1251
シェハデ
Shehadeh, Ramsey D. 1286
シェパード
Shepard, Aaron 1287
Shepard, Andrea 1287
Shepard, Jim 1287
Shepard, Kris 1287
Shepard, Larry 1287
Shepard, Lucius 1287
Shepard, Martin 1287
Shepard, Richard 1287
Shepard, Russell 1287
Shepard, Sam 1287
Shepard, Sara 1287
Shepard, Sonny 1287
Shepard, Sterling 1287
Shephard, Roy J. 1287
Shephard, Sue 1287
Shepherd, David G. 1287
Shepherd, Elizabeth J. 1287
Shepherd, George 1287
Shepherd, Jack R. 1287
Shepherd, Jean 1287
Shepherd, Jodie 1287
Shepherd, John 1287
Shepherd, John Scott 1287
Shepherd, John Thompson 1288
Shepherd, Kandy 1288
Shepherd, Lloyd 1288
Shepherd, Mike 1288
Shepherd, Neil 1288
Shepherd, Samuel M. 1288
Shepherd, Sherry Renmu 1288
Shepherd, William G. 1288
Sheppard, Bob 1288
Sheppard, Kelvin 1288
Sheppard, Lowell 1288
Sheppard, Philip 1288
Sheppard, Rob 1288
Sheppard, Steve 1288
シェバートン
Cheverton, Peter 254
シェバノワ
Shebanova, Tatiana 1285
ジェバリ
Jebali, Hamadi 668
ジェバール
Djebar, Assia 359
シェパンスキー
Szczepanski, Anders 1374
シェビ
Chebbi, Ahmed Nejib 250
Chebbi, Lazhar Karoui 250
シェピ
Siepi, Cesare 1297
シエーピ
Siepi, Cesare 1297
シエピ
Siepi, Cesare 1297
ジェビーチェク
Rebícek, Aleš 1164
シェヒトマン
Shechtman, Daniel 1285
シェヒビ
Chehibi, Mouhssin 251
シェフ
Sheff, David 1286
シェブ
Chaïbou, Laouali 242
シェーファー
Schaefer, Carol 1248
Schaefer, Charles E. 1248
Schaefer, Jenni 1248
Schaefer, Lola M. 1248
Schaefer, Peter 1249
Schaefer, Richard T. 1249
Schaefer, Scott J. 1249
Schaefer, William Donald 1249
Schäfer, Bodo 1249
Schafer, Carolin 1249
Schäfer, Christine 1249
Schafer, Jack 1249
Schafer, Jordan 1249
Schäfer, Jürgen 1249
Schafer, Marcel 1249
Schäfer, Michael 1249
Schäfer, Peter 1249
Schafer, R.Murray 1249
Schafer, Roy 1249
Shafer, Andrew Clay 1278
Shafer, Doug 1278
Shaffer, Anthony 1278
Shaffer, Peter Levin 1278
シェファー
Schaefer, Carole Lexa 1248
Schafer, Pauline 1249
Scheffer, Mechthild 1250
Shaffer, Marjorie 1278
Shaffer, Peter Levin 1278
Shepher, Joseph 1287
ジェファ
Jeffah, Amason 668
ジェファース
Jeffers, Jim 668
ジェファーズ
Jeffers, Harry Paul 668
Jeffers, Oliver 668
Jeffers, Sharon 668
Jeffers, Susan 668
Jeffers, Susan J. 668
ジェファーソン
Jefarson, Elen 668
Jefferson, Al 668
Jefferson, Cameron 668
Jefferson, Cory 668
Jefferson, Denise 668
Jefferson, Jon 668
Jefferson, Quinton 668
Jefferson, Richard 668
Jefferson, Tony 668
Jefferson, Willie 668
ジェファソン
Jefferson, Gail 668
シェファード
Shephard, Ben 1287
Shephard, Roy J. 1287
Shepherd, Austin 1287
Shepherd, Gordon M. 1287
Shepherd, JaCorey 1287
ジェファリス
Jefferis, David 668
シェフィー
Sheffi, Yosef 1286
ジェフィ
Jaffe, Harold 659
シェフィールド
Sheffield, Brian 1286
Sheffield, Charles 1286
Sheffield, Justus 1286
Sheffield, Rob 1286
ジェフェリー
Jeffery, Keith 668
シェフェール
Schefer, Jean-Louis 1250
ジェフェルソン
Jefferson 668
ジェフォーズ
Jeffords, James 668
ジェフォード
Jefford, Darren 668
シェーフォルト
Schefold, Dian 1250
Schefold, Karl 1250
シェプキン
Schepkin, Sergei 1251
ジェプケモイ
Jepkemoi, Hyvin Kiyeng 671
シェフコムード
Shevkomud, Igor IAkovlevich 1289
ジェプコリル

シ

Jepkorir, Eunice 671
シェプス
Schoeps, Julius Hans 1257
ジェフス
Jeffes, Arthur 668
シェフストフ
Shevtsov, Aleksey 1289
ジェプセン
Jepsen, Carly Rae 671
Jepsen, Kevin 671
Jepsen, Thomas C. 671
ジェプソン
Jeppson, Morris Richard 671
Jepson, Brian 671
Jepson, Jeff 671
シェフター
Schefter, Karla 1250
シェフチェンコ
Shevchenko, Andriy 1289
Shevchenko, Ihor 1289
Shevchenko, Valentina 1289
Shevchenko, Yuri L. 1289
ジェフチャルク＝マイ
Dziechciaruk-Maj, Bogna Barbara 386
シェフチュク
Shevchuk, Vasyl 1289
ジェプトゥー
Jeptoo, Priscah 671
シェフトリス
Cheptoris, Sam 252
シェプフ
Schopf, Alessandro 1258
シェフーフォルト
Schefold, Karl 1250
シェフラー
Schaeffler, Georg F. W. 1249
Schaeffler, Jimmy 1249
Scheffler, Axel 1250
Scheffler, Israel 1250
Shefler, Yuri 1286
シェブラー
Schebler, Scott 1250
シェフラン
Scheffran, Jürgen 1250
シェブリ
al-Shebli, Hashim 1285
ジェフリー
Jeffery, Alshon 668
Jeffery, Arthur B. 668
Jeffery, Keith 668
Jeffery, Michael 668
Jeffery, Richard 668
Jeffrey, Craig 668
Jeffrey, Francis 668
Jeffrey, Henry 668
Jeffrey, Ian 668
Jeffrey, R.Brooke 668
ジェフリオン
Geoffrion, Bernie 489
ジェフリーズ
Jefferies, Cindy 668
Jefferies, Michelle 668
Jeffreys, Garland 668
Jeffries, Dennis 668
Jeffries, Harb 668
Jeffries, Lionel 669
Jeffries, Ron 669
Jeffries, Sabrina 669
Jeffries, Tony 669
ジェフリス
Jefferis, David 668
ジェフリーズ＝ジョーンズ
Jeffreys-Jones, Rhodri 668
シェフリン
Shefrin, Hersh 1286
シェブルレ
Šebrle, Roman 1267
ジェフレス
Jeffress, Jeremy 668
ジェフロワ
Geoffroy, Richard 489
シェーベ
Sebe, Emil 1267
シェベシュチェン
Sebestyen, Julia 1267
ジェベト
Jebet, Ruth 668
シェベル
Chebel, Malek 250
シェペル
Shepel, Dmitry 1287
シェベンダーク
Schebendach, Janet E. 1250
シェーボン
Chabon, Michael 241
ジェボンズ
Jevons, Marshall 672
シェマー
Shemer, Naomi 1287
ジェマイエル
Gemayel, Pierre 488
ジェマイリ
Dzemaili, Blerim 386
ジェマエワ
Jemayeva, Yelena 669
シェママ
Chemama, Roland 251
ジェマル
Jemal, Ahmedin 669
シェマロフ
Shemarov, Aleksandr 1287
Shemarov, Aleksei 1287
シェーマン
Schoeman, Henri 1257
Sjöman, Vilgot 1309
ジェミオラ
Jemiola, Zach 669
ジェミシン
Jemisin, N.K. 669
ジェーミソン
Jamieson, Michael 662
ジェミソン
Jemison, Mae G. 669
ジェミベウォン
Jemibewon, David 669
シェミャキナ
Shemyakina, Yana 1287
ジェミリ
Gemili, Adam 488
ジェミレフ
Dzhemilev, Mustafa 386
シェミン
Shemin, Robert 1287
ジエミンスキ
Zieminski, Kacper 1554
シェーム
Schoem, Alan H. 1257
ジェム
Cem, Ismail 240
Gemme, Kathryn 488
シェムイエーン
Semjén, Zsolt 1272
ジェームス
James, Alex 661
James, Bob 661
James, Charles 661
James, Cory 661
James, D.Clayton 661
James, Etta 661
James, Jason 661
James, Ja'Wuan 661
James, Jesse 661
James, Kirani 661
James, Mike 661
James, Richard 662
James, Rick 662
James, Simon 662
ジェームズ
James, Alexander 661
James, Allyson 661
James, Ann 661
James, Arsene 661
James, Bertram 661
James, Bethan 661
James, Beverly 661
James, Brian 661
James, Brian R. 661
James, David 661
James, E.L. 661
James, Eloisa 661
James, Etta 661
James, Gregory 661
James, Harold 661
James, Ian Andrew 661
James, Janice Sue 661
James, Jason 661
James, Jennifer 661
James, John W. 661
James, José 661
James, Julie 661
James, Kelly 661
James, Kirani 661
James, LeBron 661
James, Lily 661
James, Matty 661
James, Nikki M. 661
James, Patricia 661
James, Paul 661
James, P.D. 661
James, Peter J. 661
James, Rebecca 662
James, Renée J. 662
James, Richard D. 662
James, Rick 662
James, Sarah 662
James, Sian 662
James, Simon 662
ジェームソン
Jameson, Fredric R. 662
Jameson, Sam 662
シェム・トヴ
Shem-Tov, Tami 1287
シェム・トブ
Shem-Tov, Tami 1287
シェムラ
Schemla, Elisabeth 1251
シェメタ
Šemeta, Algirdas 1272
シェメトフ
Chemetoff, André 251
シェメル
Shemer, Naomi 1287
ジェメルソン
Jemerson 669
シェモニアク
Siemoniak, Tomasz 1297
シェモニヤク
Siemoniak, Tomasz 1297
シェーラー
Schärer, Kathrin 1249
Scherer, Hermann 1251
シェラー
Scheller, Christian Vibe 1251
Scherer, Sarah 1251
Shaler, Rhoberta 1279
シエラ
Sierra, Hector 1297
Sierra, Javier 1297
Sierra, Judy 1297
Sierra, Kathy 1297
Sierra, Magneuris 1297
シエラ・イ・ファブラ
Sierra i Fabra, Jordi 1297
シエラ・クルス
Sierra Cruz, Jorge Luis 1297
ジェラシー
Djerassi, Carl 359
ジェラス
Geras, Adèle 490
シェラツキ
Sieradzki, Sarah 1297
ジェラッシ
Djerassi, Carl 359
シェラット
Sherratt, Yvonne 1288
シエラ・デ・ラ・カジェ
Sierra de la Calle, Blas 1297
ジェラテリー
Gellately, Robert 487
シェラード
Shellard, Dominic 1286
ジェラード
Gerard, Cindy 490
Gerrard, Juliet A. 491
Gerrard, Mike 491
Gerrard, Steven 491
Gerrard, Tandi 491
Jerrard, Jane 672
ジェラトリー
Gellately, Robert 487
シェラハ
Shelah, Saharon 1286
ジェラブ
Djellab, Mohamed 359
ジェラベールファブレガ
Gelabert Fàbrega, Olga 487
ジェラーム
Jeram, Anita 671
シェラリエーヴァ
Sheralieva, Iuliia Rashidovna 1288
ジェラール
Gaillard, Jean Marc 471
Gérard, Jean-Pierre 490
Gerard, Moreno 490
Gérard, Valérie 490
ジェラルディ
Gelardi, Thom 487
Gherardi, Sylvianne 493
ジェラルド
Gerard, Robert Vincent 490
シェラン
Sheran, Ashtar 1288

ジェラン
Gélin, Daniel 487
Gjelland, Egil 503
Jerent, Daniel 671
シェリー
Scerri, Eric R. 1248
Shelley, John 1287
Shelley, Julia 1287
Shelley, Steve 1287
Shelley, Toby 1287
Shelley, Violet 1287
Shelly, Judith Allen 1287
Shelly, Susan 1287
Sherry, John F., Jr. 1288
Sherry, Kevin 1288
Sherry, Larry 1288
ジェリー
Gerry, Christopher C. 491
Jelley, Craig 669
Jerry, John 672
ジェリシオ
Gelisio, Deborah 487
ジェリソン
Jerison, Harry 671
シェリダン
Sheridan, Jim 1288
Sheridan, Karen 1288
Sheridan, Kirsten 1288
Sheridan, Naomi 1288
Sheridan, Richard 1288
Sheridan, Sam 1288
Sheridan, Tye 1288
シェリック
Scherick, Edgar J. 1251
ジェリッチ
Djelić, Božidar 359
ジェリッツェン
Gerritsen, Tess 491
ジェリネ
Gélinet, Patrice 487
ジェリビ
Jeribi, Ghazi 671
Jeribi, Jalloul 671
シェリフ
Cherif, Mustapha 253
Chérif, Nanténin 253
Cherif, Walid 253
Sherif, Muhammad Safwat El 1288
Sherif, Shamsur Rahmah 1288
Sherif, Yousef Mohammad 1288
シェリフアッバス
Cherif-abbas, Mohamed 253
シェリベリ
Kärrberg, Patrik 706
シェリポフ
Sheripov, Yldash 1288
ジェリホフスキ
Żelichowski, Stanisław 1550
ジェリモ
Jelimo, Pamela 669
ジェリヤウ
Žerjav, Radovan 1551
シェリル
Sherrill, Martha 1288
Sherrill, Steven 1288
ジェリル
Jelil, Dah Ould Abdel 669
シェリン
Kjellin, Sara 743
シェリング
Schelling, Thomas Crombie 1251
ジェリンスキ
Zielinski, Damian 1554
ジエリンスキ
Zieliński, Adrian Edward 1554
Zielinski, Piotr 1554
シェール
Cher 252
Scheel, Walter 1250
Scheer, James F. 1250
Shale, Erin 1279
Sher, Barbara 1288
Sher, Bartlett 1288
Sherr, Lynn 1288
シェル
Schell, David W. 1250
Schell, James M. 1251
Schell, Jonathan 1251
Schell, Jozef Stephaan 1251
Schell, Karl-Heinz 1251
Schell, Maria 1251
Schell, Maximilian 1251
Schell, Orville 1251
Shell, Brandon 1286
Shell, Ellen Ruppel 1286
Shell, G.Richard 1286
Shell, Marc 1286
シェルー
Chéroux, Clément 253
ジェルヴァシオ
Gervasio, Paola 492
ジェルヴァーゾ
Gervaso, Roberto 492
ジェルヴァル
Gerval, Olivier 492
シェルヴァン
Schelvan, Ronda L. 1251
ジェルヴェ
Gervais, Bernadette 492
シェルカウィ
Cherkaoui, Moulay Tayeb 253
シェルカウイ
Cherkaoui, Sidi Larbi 253
ジェルキル
Djelkhir, Khedafi 359
ジェルゲン
Görgens, Manfred 519
シェルシェーヴ
Cherchève, Perrine 252
シェルシャン
Shershan, Dzmitry 1288
シェルスキー
Shelsky, Rob 1287
ジェルスビック
Gjelsvik, Bente E. Bassøe 503
ジェルソン
Gerson 491
ジェルソン・マルティンス
Gelson Martins 488
シェルダ
Bede, Shelda 113
シェルダル
Skjeldal, Kristen 1310
シェルダン
Shelden, Lee 1286
Sheldon, Mary 1286
Sheldon, Sidney 1286
シェルチャン
Sherchan, Amik 1288
シェルツ
Sheltz, Matthew 1287
シェルツァー
Scherzer, Alfred L. 1251
シェルドリック
Sheldrick, Daphne 1286
シェルドレイク
Sheldrake, Philip 1286
Sheldrake, Rupert 1286
シェルトン
Shelton, Barrie 1287
Shelton, Danny 1287
Shelton, Derek 1287
Shelton, Helen 1287
Shelton, Ken 1287
Shelton, Robert D. 1287
Shelton, Ron 1287
シェルドン
Sheldon, Bill 1286
Sheldon, Rose Mary 1286
Sheldon, Sidney 1286
ジェルネール
Gerner, Jochen 491
シェルパオ
Sherpao, Aftab Ahmed Khan 1288
シェルビ
Chelbi, Afif 251
Chelbi, Mohamed Afif 251
シェルビー
Shelby, Amanda M. 1286
Shelby, Derrick 1286
Shelby, Philip 1286
ジェルビ
Gerbi, Yarden 490
シエルピナ
Sierpina, Victor S. 1297
シェルビーニ
Sherbini, El Helali el 1288
シェルフ
Cherif, Slaheddine 253
シェルフィー
Sherfy, Jimmie 1288
シェルブレット
Skjelbred, Per 1310
シェルベリ
Kjellberg, Anders 743
ジェルボ
Gerbod, Paul 490
シェルホルン
Scherhorn, Gerhard 1251
ジェルマイアー
Jermier, John M. 671
ジェルマーノ
Germano, Elio 491
シェルマルケ
Sharmarke, Omar Abdirashid Ali 1283
シェルマン
Schellmann, Jorg 1251
Shelman, Mary 1287
ジェルマン
Germain, Anne 491
Germain, Gérald 491
Germain, Jean-Marie Claude 491
Germain, Pierrette 491
Germain, Sylvie 491
Germain, Valere 491
シェルマンコワ
Shkermankova, Maryna 1292
ジェルミア
Jermia, Joseph 671
ジェルミニ
Gelmini, Mariastella 488
ジェルメッティ
Gelmetti, Gianluigi 488
ジェルメニ
Gjermeni, Eglantina 503
シェルレ
Scherle, Max 1251
シエレ
Siele, Peter 1297
ジェレ
Géré, François 490
ジェレア
Gerea, Andrei 490
ジェレヴィーニ
Gerevini, Alessandro G. 490
シェレシュ
Şereş, Codruţ 1274
シェレズ
Sherez, Stav 1288
シェレスタ
Shrestha, Durga 1294
シェレスチュク
Shelestyuk, Taras 1286
ジェレット
Jerrett, Grant 672
ジェレビーニ
Gerevini, Alessandro G. 490
ジェレフ
Zhelev, Evgenii 1552
Zhelev, Zhelyu Mitev 1552
ジェレブコ
Jerebko, Jonas 671
ジェレミア
Jeremiah, Dogabe 671
シェレメイ
Shelemay, Kay Kaufman 1286
シェレール
Scherer, Rene 1251
シェレル
Scherrer, Jean-Louis 1251
シェレルズ
Sherels, Marcus 1288
シェレン
Cheren, Mel 253
シェレンバーガー
Shellenbarger, Sue 1287
Shellenberger, Sylvia 1287
シェレンベルガー
Schellenberger, Hansjörg 1251
シェレンベルク
Schellenberg, Tobias 1251
シェロー
Chéreau, Patrice 253
ジェロー
Gerow, Aaron Andrew 491
ジェロウル
Jelloul, Néji 669
ジェロッド・エディー
Jerod-eddie, Tony 671
シエロフィリョ
Cielo Filho, Cesar 264
ジェローム
Jerome, Fred 671
Jerome, Jerry 672
ジェロン

シ

Geron, Scott 491
シェワルドナゼ
Shevardnadze, Eduard Amvrosievich 1289
シェワルナゼ
Shevardnadze, Eduard Amvrosievich 1289
Shevardnadze, Nanuli 1289
シェーン
Schoen, Carl Fredrik Stefan 1257
Shane, Scott Andrew 1280
シェン
Shen, Neil 1287
Shen, Yanfei 1287
Shin, Xue 1291
シエン
Siane, Saphangthong 1295
Siene, Saphangthong 1297
ジェン
Dieng, Gorgui 353
Jen, Frank C. 669
シェーンヴァルド
Schonwald, Josh 1258
ジェーンウェー
Janeway, Elizabeth Hall 662
ジェーンウェイ
Janeway, Elizabeth Hall 662
シェーンヴェルダー
Schönwälder, Stephan 1258
シェーンウォルフ
Schoenwolf, Gary C. 1257
シェンカー
Schenker, Michael 1251
Shenkar, Oded 1287
Shenkir, William G. 1287
ジェンキン
Jenkin, Charles Patrick Fleeming 669
ジェンキンス
Jenkins, Alan 669
Jenkins, A.M. 669
Jenkins, Charles Robert 669
Jenkins, Daniel P. 669
Jenkins, Davis 669
Jenkins, Emily 669
Jenkins, Emyl 669
Jenkins, George 669
Jenkins, Helen 669
Jenkins, Herman A. 669
Jenkins, Ian 669
Jenkins, Jane 669
Jenkins, Janoris 669
Jenkins, Jarvis 669
Jenkins, Jean F. 669
Jenkins, Jelani 669
Jenkins, John 669
Jenkins, Jordan 669
Jenkins, Karl 669
Jenkins, Katherine 669
Jenkins, Mack 670
Jenkins, Mackey 670
Jenkins, Malcolm 670
Jenkins, Marcelo 670
Jenkins, Mark 670
Jenkins, Mark Collins 670
Jenkins, Martin 670
Jenkins, Michael B. 670
Jenkins, Mike 670
Jenkins, Paul 670
Jenkins, Richard 670
Jenkins, Roy Harris 670
Jenkins, Sally 670
Jenkins, Shaneil 670
Jenkins, Susan M. 670
Jenkins, Taylor 670
Jenkins, Tyrell 670
ジェンキンズ
Jenkins, Amy 669
Jenkins, Gareth 669
Jenkins, Garry 669
Jenkins, Gethin 669
Jenkins, Jerry B. 669
Jenkins, Keith 669
Jenkins, Lucien 670
Jenkins, Mark 670
Jenkins, Martin 670
Jenkins, Paul F. 670
Jenkins, Robert L. 670
Jenkins, Roy Harris 670
Jenkins, Steve 670
Jenkins, Susan C. 670
Jenkins, T.M. 670
ジェンキンソン
Jenkinson, Carl 670
Jenkinson, Ceci 670
シェンク
Schenck, Kenneth 1251
Shenk, David 1287
Shenk, Joshua Wolf 1287
ジェンク
Cenk, Tosun 240
ジェンクス
Jencks, Charles 669
Jenks, Bruce 670
Jenks, R.Stephen 670
シェンクマン
Shenkman, Richard 1287
ジェンゲリ
Jengeli, Ali Ahmed Jama 669
シェンケル
Schenkel, Andrea Maria 1251
シェンゴールド
Shengold, Leonard 1287
シェンシン
Ciencin, Scott 264
シエンシン
Ciencin, Scott 264
ジェーンズ
Janes, Diane 662
ジェンス
Jenns, Karen 670
ジェンセン
Jensen, Alex 670
Jensen, Bernard 670
Jensen, Derrick 670
Jensen, Frances E. 670
Jensen, Iain 671
Jensen, James C. 671
Jensen, Kathryn 671
Jensen, Larsen 671
Jensen, Leyah 671
Jensen, Liz 671
Jensen, Marcel 671
Jensen, Marcus 671
Jensen, Peter 671
Jensen, Ryan 671
Jensen, Sharon 671
Jenssen, Hans 671
ジェンソン
Jenson, Peter 671
Jenson, Robert W. 671
シェンターク
Schentag, Jerome J. 1251
ジェンティローニ
Gentiloni, Paolo 489
シェンデルフェール
Schoendoerffer, Pierre 1257
シェンデルフェル
Schoendoerffer, Pierre 1257
ジェントリー
Gentry, Alvin 489
Gentry, Marshall Bruce 489
Gentry, Matthew Judah 489
ジェンドリージク
Jendrzejczyk, Mike 669
ジェンドリック
Jendrick, Megan 669
ジェントル
Gentle, Ashleigh 489
ジェントルマン
Gentleman, Robert 489
ジェンドロック
Jendrock, Eric 669
シェントン
Shenton, Oliver 1287
ジェンナ
Genna, Giuseppe 488
ジェンナー
Jenner, Rosalind 670
Jenner, W.J.F. 670
シェンナッハ
Schennach, Stefan 1251
シェンニコフ
Schennikov, Georgi 1251
シェーンハルス
Schoenhals, Michael 1257
シェンプ
Schempp, Simon 1251
シエンフエゴス・ゴリアラン
Cienfuegos Gorriarán, Osmany 264
シエンフエゴス・セペダ
Cienfuegos Zepeda, Salvador 264
シェーンフェルダー
Schoenfelder, Olivier 1257
Schoenfelder, Rainer 1257
ジェーンフェルダー
Schoenfelder, Olivier 1257
シェーンブッハー
Schönbucher, Philipp J. 1257
シェンブリー - ブラック
Schnebly-Black, Julia 1255
シェーンブルク
Schönburg, Alexander von 1257
ジエンベコフ
Dzhienbekov, Sadriddin 386
シェーンベルガー
Schönberger, Christoph 1257
シェーンベルク
Schönberg, Claude-Michel 1257
シェーンベルグ
Schönberg, Claude-Michel 1257
シェーンベルナー
Schoenberner, Gerhard 1257
シェンマー
Schemmer, Kenneth E. 1251
ジェンマ
Gemma, Giuliano 488
ジェンリェン
Jianlian, Yi 673
シェーンリッヒ
Schönrich, Gerhard 1258
ジェンロ
Genro, Tarso 488
シオ
Sio, Scott 1307
ジォ
Cho, Suck-rai 258
ジオウラ
Gioura, Derog 501
シオカ
Sioka, Doreen 1307
ジオバニ
Giovani 501
ジオフレット
Giaufret, Benedetta 495
ジオボテラ
Giavotella, Johnny 495
ジオムビー
Giambi, Jason 494
シオラー
Schiøler, Ebbe 1253
シオリ
Scioli, Daniel 1263
ジオリト
Giolito, Lucas 501
ジオルコフスキ
Ziolkowski, Szymon 1556
ジオルジ
Giorgi, Amedeo 501
ジオルダン
Giordan, Andre 501
シオン
Chion, Michel 256
Sion, Judi 1307
Sión, Verónica 1307
Xiong, Victor C. 1531
ジオンビ
Giambi, Jason 494
ジオンビー
Giambi, Jason 494
シーカ
Sica, Maria 1295
シーカー
Siecker, Bruce 1296
シーガー
Seager, Corey 1266
Seager, Joni 1266
Seager, Kyle 1266
Seeger, Elizabeth 1268
Seeger, Laura Vaccaro 1268
Seeger, Pete 1268
Seger, Linda 1268
Seger, Maura 1268
Sieger, Robin 1297
シカ
Sika, Semisi 1298
シガ
Shiga, Daniela 1290
ジーカー
Zircher, Patrick 1556
ジガ
Žiga, Peter 1554
シカウ
Sigcau, Stella 1298
ジガウ

シ

Jigau, Adrian Ioan 673
シカタナ
Sikatana, Mundia 1298
シカタニ
Shikatani, Gerry Osamu 1290
シガニー
Sigourney, Brita 1298
シガノス
Siganos, André 1298
シガフース
Sigafoose, James 1298
シガフーズ
Sigafoos, Jeff 1298
シカプワシャ
Shikapwasha, Ronald 1290
Shikapwasha, Ronnie 1290
ジカーマン
Zichermann, Gabe 1554
ジガーミ
Zigarmi, Drea 1554
Zigarmi, Patricia 1554
シーカム
Secombe, Harry 1267
シガーラー
Segaller, Stephen 1268
シーガル
Seagull, Elizabeth A. W. 1266
Segal, Charles 1268
Segal, Erich 1268
Segal, Peter 1268
Segal, Ronald 1268
Segal, Zindel V. 1268
Segall, Ken 1268
Siegal, Justine 1297
Siegal, Michael 1297
Siegel, Jan 1297
Sigar, Maaike 1298
シガール
Segal, Anna 1268
Segal, Inna 1268
シカルディ
Siccardi, Artie 1295
シガンダ
Ciganda, Carlota 264
ジガンテ
Gigante, Vincent 497
ジギスムンド
Sigismund, Charles G. 1298
シキチェンコ
Shkidchenko, Volodymyr 1292
シキッチ
Šikić, Nada 1298
ジキーナ
Zykina, Ludmila 1560
シーク
Sheik, Duncan 1286
シーグ
Sieg, Clara 1297
ジク
Zych, Tony 1560
シクア
Sikua, Derek 1298
シグアン
Siguán, Miquel 1298
ジグジッド
Jigjid, Rentsendoo 673
ジグジド
Jigjid, Byambyn 673
シクス
Sics, Andris 1295
Sics, Juris 1295
シクスー
Cixous, Hélène 265
シクスス
Cixous, Hélène 265
シグステッド
Sigstedt, Cyriel Odhner 1298
ジークナー
Siegner, Ingo 1297
ジーグナー
Ziegner, Kurd Albrecht von 1554
ジークハルト
Sieghart, Martin 1297
シーグバーン
Siegbahn, Kai 1297
ジーグバーン
Siegbahn, Kai 1297
シグフスソン
Sigfusson, Steingrimur 1298
シグフソン
Sigfusson, Ingimundur 1298
シーグフリード
Siegfried, Tom 1297
ジーグフリード
Siegfried, Tom 1297
シグペン
Thigpen, Lynne 1396
シグムント
Siegemund, Laura 1297
Sigmund, Karl 1298
ジークムント
Sigmund, Anna Maria 1298
ジグメ
Jigs-med 673
シグラ
Schygulla, Hanna 1263
シグラー
Sigler, DeVaunte 1298
Sigler, Scott 1298
ジーグラー
Ziegler, Brad 1554
Ziegler, Jean 1554
Ziegler, Robert 1554
Ziegler, Robert Loren 1554
Ziegler, Ronald Louis 1554
Ziegler, Shirley Melat 1554
ジグラー
Ziglar, Zig 1554
Zigler, Edward 1554
Zigler, Scott 1554
シーグラム
Seagram, Barbara 1266
ジグリ
Zygouri, Stavroula 1560
ジグリー
Zicree, Marc Scott 1554
シーグリスト
Siegrist, Kevin 1297
ジーグリスト
Siegrist, Johannes 1297
シクリャル
Shkliar, Vasyl' 1292
シクリャローフ
Shklyarov, Vladimir 1292
シーグル
Schiegl, Markus 1252
Schiegl, Tobias 1252
シグルザルドッティル
Sigurðardóttir, H. Sigurveig 1298
Sigurdardóttir, Jóhanna 1298
Sigurdardóttir, Yrsa 1298
シグルスソン
Sigurdsson, Jon 1298
シグルズソン
Sigurdsson, Gylfi 1298
シクルーナ
Scicluna, Edward 1263
シグレイン
Siglain, Michael 1298
シーグレーヴ
Seagrave, Peggy 1266
Seagrave, Sterling 1266
シークレスト
Seacrest, Ryan 1266
シーグレーブ
Seagrave, Sterling 1266
シーグレル
Ziegler, Pablo 1554
シグロウ
Siggelkow, Bill 1298
シグワース
Sigworth, Fred J. 1298
ジゲ
Jiguet, Frédéric 673
シケイラ
Siqueira, Guilherme 1307
Siqueira, Maicon 1307
Siqueira, Paulo 1307
シゲオ
Singeo, Isao Peter 1305
シゲタ
Shigeta, James 1290
シケット
Chiquet, Maureen 256
ジゲムデ
Djiguemde, Amedee Prosper 359
シーゲル
Segel, Rick 1268
Segell, Michael 1268
Seigel, Michael 1270
Siegel, Alice 1297
Siegel, Allen M. 1297
Siegel, Barry 1297
Siegel, Bernie S. 1297
Siegel, Daniel J. 1297
Siegel, Eric 1297
Siegel, James 1297
Siegel, Janis 1297
Siegel, Jeremy J. 1297
Siegel, Joel 1297
Siegel, Joel G. 1297
Siegel, Mark 1297
Siegel, Mo 1297
Siegel, Ronald K. 1297
Siegel, Seth M. 1297
Siegel, Sheldon M. 1297
Sighel, Roberto 1298
ジーゲル
Siegel, Mary E. 1297
ジゲール
Giguère, Sylvain 497
シーゲルマン
Siegelman, Jim 1297
ジーゲルミューラー
Ziegelmueller, George W. 1554
ジゲレ
Ziguele, Martin 1554
ジーゲンターラー
Siegenthaler, Maja 1297
ジーコ
Zico 1554
ジコ
Dicko, Moustapha 353
シコウリ
Sicouri, Silvia 1295
シーコソン
Sy-Coson, Teresita T. 1373
シコッティ
Ciccotti, Serge 264
シコティ
Chicoti, Georges Rebelo Pinto 255
シーコード
Seacord, Robert C. 1266
シコード
Secord, James A. 1267
シゴト
Sigoto, Charles 1298
シーコフ
Sekoff, Roy 1270
シーコム
Secombe, Harry 1267
シコラ
Sikora, Tomasz 1298
シコリナ
Shkolina, Svetlana 1292
シコリニク
Shkolnik, Vladimir 1292
シコルスキ
Sikorski, Radosław 1298
シコルスキー
Skulski, Janusz 1311
シコルニク
Shkolnik, Vladimir 1292
シコロバ
Sykorova, Adela 1373
ジゴン
Gigon, Marie-Laure 497
シーサ
Caesar, Ed 213
シーザー
Caesar, Saboto 213
Caeser, Sid 213
Ceaser, James W. 239
Szczur, Matt 1374
シザ
Ciza, Virginie 266
Siza, Álvaro 1309
シサコ
Sissako, Abderrahmane 1308
シサノ
Chissano, Joaquim Alberto 257
シサバネ
Sy Savané, Ibrahim 1374
シーサラー
Seethaler, Sherry 1268
シサワット
Sisavath, Keobounphanh 1308
シーシ
el-Sisi, Abdel Fattah Said 1308
シシ
el-Sisi, Abdel Fattah Said 1308

ジジ
Didi 353
ジジアルスキー
Zdziarski, Jonathan A. 1549
ジジェク
Zižek, Slavoj 1556
シーシェック
Cishek, Steve 265
シーシェル
Jirschele, Mike 674
ジーシェルト
Siechert, Carl 1296
ジジェンティ
Girgenti, Richard H. 502
シーシキン
Shishkin, Mikhail 1292
Shishkin, Sergei Nikolaevich 1292
シシコフ
Shishkoff, Eitan 1292
シジコワ
Syzdykova, Elmira 1374
ジジッチ
Zižić, Zoran 1556
シシップ
SyCip, Washington Z. 1373
シジモア
Sidgmore, John W. 1296
ジージャー
Jija 673
シシャドリ
Seshadri, Sridhar 1276
シシャバ
Chichava, Jose 255
シシャン
Chichin, Fred 255
シジャンスキー
Sidjanski, Brigitte 1296
Sidjanski-Hanhart, Brigitte 1296
シシュキナ
Shishkina, Alla 1292
シシュキン
Shishikin, V.A. 1292
シシュコ
Szyszko, Jan 1375
シシュコフ
Shishkov, Artiom 1292
シシル
Sicille 1295
シジンスキー
Csizinszky, A.A. 306
シース
Sheth, Jagdish 1289
シーズ
Sease, Catherine 1266
Sease, Virginia 1266
シス
Cisse, Abdoulaye Abdoulkader 265
Sis, Peter 1308
ジス
Gyss, Caroline 550
ジスカール・デスタン
Giscard d'Estaing, Valéry 502
ジスカールデスタン
Giscard d'Estaing, Valéry 502
ジスキン
Ziskin, Laura 1556
シスキンド
Siskind, Barry 1308
シスク
Sisk, Michael 1308
シスコ
Sisco, Chance 1308
Sisco, Joseph John 1308
Sisco, Lisa A. 1308
シスター・エマニュエル
Sister Emmanuelle 1308
シスターニ
al-Sistani, Ali 1308
シスターニシ
al-Sistani, Ali 1308
シスターニルマーラ
Nirmala 1027
ジズダン
Jizdan, Alexandru 674
シスト
Sisto, Pione 1308
シーストランク
Seastrunk, Lache 1266
シストロム
Systrom, Kevin 1374
シスナ
Cissna, Kenneth N. 265
シズニー
Cisney, Jennifer S. 265
シスネロス
Cisneros, Gustavo A. 265
Cisneros, Henry G. 265
Cisneros, Jesús 265
ジズベール
Giesbert, Franz-Olivier 496
シスーマ
Cissouma, Mamadou 265
シスマ
Cissouma, Mamadou 265
シズマー
Cizmar, Paula 266
シスマン
Sisman, Robyn 1308
ジーズマン
Ziessman, Harvey A. 1554
シスラー
Sisler, George, Jr. 1308
シースラート
Sisoulath, Bouakham 1308
シスル
Sisulu, Albertina 1308
Sisulu, Lindiwe 1308
Sisulu, Walter 1308
ジースロフト
Zeisloft, Nick 1549
シセ
Cisse, Abdoudrahmane 265
Cisse, Abdoulaye Abdoulkader 265
Cissé, Ahmed Tidiane 265
Cisse, Amara 265
Cissé, Boubou 265
Cisse, Cheick Sallah, Jr. 265
Cissé, Djibril 265
Cisse, Ibrahim 265
Cissé, Mahmoud 265
Cisse, Mamadaou 265
Cissé, Mouramani 265
Cissé, Souleymane 265
Cisse, Soumaila 265
シセイ
Ceesay, Sulayman 239
シセカ
Shiceka, Sicelo 1289
シセバコンゴ
Cisse Bacongo, Ibrahima 265
シセリ
Ceceri, Kathy 239
シーセル
Cecil, Brett 239
ジゼル
Gisele 502
シソーエフ
Sysoev, Vsevolod Petrovich 1374
シソコ
Cissokho, Issa 265
Cissokho, Souleymane Diop 265
Cissoko, Diango 265
Sissoko, Baba 1308
Sissoko, Bouare Fily 1308
Sissoko, Cheick Oumar 1308
Sissoko, Makan Moussa 1308
Sissoko, Moussa 1308
シソディア
Sisodia, Rajendra S. 1308
シソール
Sithole, Majozi 1308
シゾーワ
Sizova, Alla 1309
シソン
Sisson, Stéphanie Roth 1308
シーダ
Seedat, Soraya 1268
シーダー
Cedar, Howard 239
Cedar, Sally 239
Sedar, Ed 1267
シダー
Cedar, Joseph 239
ジータ
Jeetah, Rajeshwar 668
ジーター
Jeter, Carmelita 672
Jeter, Derek 672
Jeter, Michael 672
ジダ
Dida 353
Zida, Isaac 1554
シタウラ
Sitaula, Krishna Prasad 1308
シタネン
Sithanen, Rama Krishna 1308
ジダーノフ
Zhdanov, Ihor 1552
Zhdanov, Ivan 1552
シダハメド
Sidahmed, Ahmed Ould 1296
Sidahmed, Cheikh Ahmed Ould 1296
シタヘン
Sitaheng, Latsaphone 1308
シータラーマン
Seetharaman, Seshadri 1268
シタラマン
Sitharaman, Nirmala 1308
シータラム
Seetaram, Jangbahadoorsing Iswurdeo Mola Roopchand 1268
シタルディン
Sitaldin, Shirley 1308
ジダーン
Zedan, Ali 1549
ジダン
Zeidan, Ali 1549
Židan, Dejan 1554
Zidan, Mohamed Ali 1554
Zidane, Zinedine 1554
シタンダ
Shitanda, Peter 1292
Shitanda, Soita 1292
シチ
Sycz, Robert 1373
シチェトキナ
Shchetkina, Marianna A. 1285
シチェドリーン
Shchedrin, Rodion 1285
シチェドリン
Shchedrin, Rodion 1285
シチェルバ
Shcherba, L.V. 1285
シチェルボ
Shcherbo, Ivan I. 1285
シチェンコ
Shichenko, Anatoly Nikolaevich 1289
ジーチェンコ
Dyachenko, Alexander 385
シチャルウェ
Sichalwe, Lawrence 1295
シチル
Shtyl, Ivan 1294
シチンガ
Shicinga, Robert 1289
シーツ
Sheets, Dutch 1286
ジツェン・ペマ
Jetsun Pema 672
シッカーディ
Siccardi, Yann 1295
ジッキ
Gick, Paulo Warth 496
シック
Chic, Suzy 255
Schic, Anna Stella 1251
Schich, Maximilian 1251
Schick, Adina R. 1251
Schick, Patrik 1251
Schick, Thorsten 1251
Shick, Theorore, Jr. 1289
Thicke, Robin 1396
シッグ
Sigg, Pablo 1298
シックス
Sixx, Nikki 1309
シックススミス
Sixsmith, Martin 1309
ジッグマン
Zigman, Laura 1554
シックラー
Schickler, David 1251
シッケル
Schickel, Richard 1251
ジッケルズ
Jickells, Tim D. 673
ジッコ
Zico 1554

シッサウリ
Sissaouri, Guivi 1308
シッジモア
Sidgmore, John W. 1296
シッシュ
Chiche, Alain 255
シッセ
Cissé, Amadou Boubacar 265
Cisse, Ousmane 265
シッソン
Sisson, Natalie 1308
シッタ
Sitta, Margaret 1308
Sitta, Samuel John 1308
シッダール
Siddall, Mark Edward 1296
シッチン
Sitchin, Zecharia 1308
シッツァー
Sittser, Gerald Lawson 1308
シッド
al-Sid, Azhari al-Tigani Awad 1295
シットイサク
Suphalak, Sitthisak 1367
シットウェル
Sitwell, William Ronald Sacheverell 1308
ジットレイン
Zittrain, Jonathan L. 1556
シットン
Sitton, Josh 1308
シッパー
Schipper, Dörte 1253
Schipper, Jessicah 1253
Schipper, Mineke 1253
シッパーゲス
Schipperges, Heinrich 1253
シッピー
Shippey, T.A. 1291
ジッヒャー
Sicher, Harry 1295
Sicher, Lydia 1295
シッフ
Schiff, Joel Linn 1252
シップ
Sipp, Tony 1307
シップサイド
Shipside, Steve 1291
ジップス
Zipes, Jack 1556
シップトン
Shipton, Paul 1291
シップマン
Shipman, Claire 1291
Shipman, James T. 1291
Shipman, Mark 1291
Shipman, Pat 1291
シップリー
Shipley, Andrew H. 1291
シップロック
Schipplock, Sven 1253
ジッペル
Sippel, Tobias 1307
シッペルゲス
Schipperges, Heinrich 1253
シッペン
Shippen, Brandon 1291
シッラーニ
Sillani, Febe 1299
ジッリ
Gilli, Éric 499
シーディ
Sheedy, Edna C. 1285
Sheedy Kurcinka, Mary 1285
シティ
City, Elizabeth A. 265
Siti, Nurbaya 1308
シディ
Sidi, Baba Ould 1296
Sidi, Péter 1296
Sidi, Sakinatou Abdou Alfa Orou 1296
シディキ
Siddique, Abdul Latif 1296
Siddiqui, Haroon 1296
Siddiqui, L.K. 1296
Siddiqui, Muhammad Shamim 1296
シディク
al-Sidig, al-Samih 1296
シティザハラ
Siti Zaharah, Sulaiman 1308
シティチャイ
Sitthichai, Pokai-udom 1308
シディッキ
Siddiqui, Jeanne 1296
シディナ
Sidina, Sidi Mohamed Ould 1296
シディベ
Sidibe, Bana 1296
Sidibe, Djibril 1296
Sidibe, Konimba 1296
Sidibé, Malick 1296
Sidibe, Mamadou 1296
Sidibé, Mamadou 1296
Sidibe, Mande 1296
Sidibe, Mansa Moussa 1296
Sidibe, Modibo 1296
Sidibé, Saidou 1296
Sidibé, Souleymane 1296
Sidibe, Soumare Aminata 1296
シディメ
Sidime, Lamine 1296
シディヤ
Sidiya, Ismail Ould Bedde Ould Cheikh 1296
Sidya, Abdellahi Ould Souleimane Ould Cheikh 1296
シテーガ
Steger, Brigitte 1344
ジデク
Zidek, Radoslav 1554
シデュ
Sidhu, Gursharan 1296
シーデル
Seidel, Wolfgang 1269
シデーン
Sidén, Karin 1296
シーデントップ
Siedentop, Daryl 1297
Siedentop, Larry 1297
シード
Seed, Janet 1268
Shead, DeShawn 1285
Sheed, Wilfrid 1285
シト
Tito, Teburoro 1406
シド
Cid, Almudena 264
Essid, Habib 410
Siddo, Amadou Aissa 1296
シドー
Sydow, Björn Von 1373
Sydow, Max von 1373
シドアハメド
Sidahmed, Ahmed Ould 1296
シトゥ
Shittu, Adebayo 1292
Shittu, Aziz 1292
シドゥ
Sidhu, Heena 1296
シドウ
Sydow, Marianne 1373
シトーウィック
Cytowic, Richard E. 310
ジトウィッツ
Zitowitz, Philip 1556
シドゥウォ
Szydło, Beata 1375
シドウェル
Sidwell, Steve 1296
シドウェルズ
Sidwells, Chris 1296
シドウォ
Szydło, Beata 1375
ジトゥニ
Zitouni, Tayeb 1556
シドキー
Sedki, Atef Mohamed Naguib 1267
ジトケエフ
Zhitkeyev, Askhat 1552
シドコ
Sidko, Alena 1296
シトコヴェツキー
Sitkovetskii, Dmitrii 1308
シトコベツキー
Sitkovetskii, Dmitrii 1308
シドソン
Sidison, Joseph 1296
シドーティ
Sidoti, Beniamino 1296
シドニー
Sidney, George 1296
ジトニャンスカ
Žitňanská, Lucia 1556
ジトニャンスカー
Žitňanská, Lucia 1556
シドネイ
Sidnei 1296
シードマン
Seidman, Daniel F. 1269
Seidman, Dov 1269
Seidman, Laurence S. 1269
Seidman, Lewis William 1269
シドマン
Sidman, Joyce 1296
ジードラゴン
G-DRAGON 485
シドリ
Sidoli, Mara 1296
シトリート
Sheetrit, Meir 1286
シトリン
Citrin, James M. 265
Citrin, M. 265
シドル
Siddle, Ronald 1296
シドルスキー
Sidorsky, Sergei Syarheyovich 1296
シドルチュク
Sydorchuk, Serhiy 1373
シトレ
Sithole, Majozi 1308
シドレンコ
Sydorenko, Kseniya 1373
シトロン
Citron, Lana 265
シートン
Seaton, Ryan 1266
Seaton, Samuel 1266
Seton, Susannah 1276
ジトンゴ
Zitongo, Odile 1556
シドンズ
Siddons, Suzy 1296
シナ
Sina, Bio Gounou Idrissou 1305
シナー
Cinar, Yildiray 264
ジナ
Djina, Abdoulaye 359
ジナー
Zinnah, Moses 1555
Zinner, Peter 1556
シナイ
Sinai, Yakov G. 1305
ジナウイ
Jhinaoui, Khamaïyes 673
シナグラ
Sinagra, Laura 1305
シナジ
Schinazi, Rinaldo B. 1252
シナタンブー
Sinatambou, Marie Joseph NoëlEtienne Ghislain 1305
シナトラ
Sinatra, Stephen T. 1305
シナメニエ
Sinamenye, Mathias 1305
シナリエフ
Shynaliyev, Yerkebulan 1295
シナル
Cinar, Ates 264
Cinar, Deniz 264
シナンクワ
Sinankwa, Donise 1305
ジーニ
Zini, Mara 1555
ジニ
Gini, Gianluca 500
シニア
Senior, Donald 1273
Senior, Jennifer 1273
Senior, Tom 1273
シニアック
Siniac, Pierre 1307
シニオア
Senior, Clarence 1273
シニオラ
Siniora, Fouad 1307
シニガリア
Sinigaglia, Corrado 1307
シニサロ
Sinisalo, Johanna 1307

シ

シニシン
Synyshyn, Nataliya 1374
シニスカルコ
Siniscalco, Domenico 1307
シニバルディ
Sinibaldi, Alejandro Jorge 1307
シニュングルザ
Sinunguruza, Thérence 1307
シニョリーニ
Signorini, Gianluca 1298
シニョーレ
Signore, Marco 1298
ジニョン
Jinyoung 674
シニング
Sinning, Wayne E. 1307
シヌゥ
Cnu 272
シネ
Siene, Oulai 1297
シネク
Synek, Ondrej 1374
ジネスト
Gineste, Yves 500
シネター
Sinetar, Marsha 1305
シネック
Sinek, Simon 1305
シネルニコフ
Sinel'nikov, Mikhail Isaakovich 1305
シネルバッハー
Schnellbacher, Uwe 1256
ジーノ
Gino, Alex 500
Gino, Francesca 500
ジノヴァツ
Sinowatz, Fred 1307
ジノヴィエフ
Zinoviev, Aleksandr Aleksandrovich 1556
シノウェイ
Sinoway, Eric C. 1307
シノダ
Shinoda, Mike 1291
シノッティ
Cinotti, Eric 265
ジノティウェイ
Dzinotyiwei, Heneri 386
シノディノス
Sinodinos, Arthur 1307
ジノバツ
Sinowatz, Fred 1307
シノハラ
Shinohara, Yukito 1291
ジノビエフ
Zinoviev, Aleksandr Aleksandrovich 1556
ジノビリ
Ginobili, Manu (Emanuel) 500
シノフスキー
Sinofsky, Bruce 1307
ジノフスキー
Zinovsky, Vladimir I. 1556
シノーポリ
Sinopoli, Giuseppe 1307
シノポリ
Sinopoli, Giuseppe 1307
ジノマン
Zinoman, Peter 1556
シノワツ
Sinowatz, Fred 1307
ジノワツ
Sinowatz, Fred 1307
ジノワッツ
Sinowatz, Fred 1307
シノン
Shenon, Philip 1287
Sinon, Peter 1307
シーバ
Shiva, Vandana 1292
シーバー
Schieber, Julian 1252
Seaver, Charles 1266
Shever, David 1289
Sieber, Paul 1296
シバ
Shiba, Paul Kunio 1289
Shiva, Vandana 1292
ジーハ
Jeeha, Deelchand 668
ジーバ
Zieba, Nadiezda 1554
ジーバー
Sieber, Michael 1296
ジハ
Giha, Yaneth 497
シパイ
Sipahi, Kenan 1307
シバエフ
Shibaev, Alexander 1289
シーバーグ
Seaberg, Maureen 1266
シパコヴァトゥィー
Shpakovatyĭ, Mykola 1293
シーハサック
Sihasak Phuangketkeow 1298
シハサック・プアンゲッゲオ
Sihasak Phuangketkeow 1298
シーパサードベイチャン
Seepersad-bachan, Carolyn 1268
シーハサ・プワンゲーギャオ
Sihasak Phuangketkeow 1298
シーバース
Siebers, Tobin 1296
シーバス
Cibas, Edmund S. 264
Shivas, Mark 1292
シバスブラマニアン
Sivasubramanian, Balaji 1309
ジーバーツ
Sieverts, Thomas 1297
シーバッグ＝モンティフィオーリ
Sebag-Montefiore, Hugh 1266
ジハーディ・ジョン
Jihadi John 673
シーバート
Sebert, John A. 1267
Siebert, Al 1296
ジハド
Jihad, Abdulla 673
ジーバニッヒ
Sievernich, Gereon 1297
シハビ
al-Shehabi, Sadiq bin Abdul-Karim 1286
シハブ
Shehab, Mofid Mahmoud 1286
Shihab, Alwi 1290
シハム
Shiham, Aishath 1290
シハモニ
Sihamoni, Norodom 1298
シハモニ国王
Sihamoni, Norodom 1298
シハモニ殿下
Sihamoni, Norodom 1298
ジバラ
Gibara, Samir G. 495
ジバリ
al-Zibari, Hoshiyar 1553
Zibari, Hoshiyar 1554
シハリザダ
Shikhalizada, Nijat 1290
ジバリチ
Zwarycz, Krzysztof Maciej 1560
シバリンガム
Sivalingam, Muttu 1309
シバル
Sibal, Kapil 1295
シパル
Sipal, Onur 1307
ジバルディ
Gibaldi, Joseph 495
シハルリゼ
Shikharulidze, David 1290
Sikharulidze, Anton 1298
シーハン
Sheehan, Aaron 1285
Sheehan, Carly 1285
Sheehan, Cindy 1285
Sheehan, Frederick 1285
Sheehan, Michael 1285
Sheehan, Richard 1285
シーバン
Seebun, Idranee 1268
Sheban, Chris 1285
ジバンシー
Givency, Hubert de 503
ジバンシィ
Givency, Hubert de 503
シバンゼ
Sibandze, Macford 1295
シバンダ
Sibanda, Karabo 1295
シーヒー
Sheehy, Kate 1286
Sheehy, Sterling 1286
シヒ
Shihi, Ashraf 1290
シビ
Siby, Félix 1295
Siby, Ginette Bellegarde 1295
シーヒィ
Sheehy, Shawn 1286
ジビコフスキ
Zbikowski, Andrzej 1549
シビック
Sibbick, John 1295
シヒテル
Schiechtl, Hugo Meinhard 1252
シヒネ
Sihine, Sileshi 1298
ジヒョン
Jihyun 673
シピラ
Sipilä, Helvi 1307
Sipilä, Jorma 1307
Sipilä, Juha 1307
ジビリスコ
Gibilisco, Giuseppe 495
シビル
Sibille, Roselyne 1295
シビン
Sevene, Mario 1276
シービンガー
Schiebinger, Londa L. 1252
シーフー
Cifu, Adam S. 264
シープ
Sheep, Aria 1286
シフ
Schiff, András 1252
Schiff, Andrew J. 1252
Schiff, Heinrich 1252
Schiff, Nancy Rica 1252
Schiff, Nicholas D. 1252
Schiff, Peter D. 1252
Schiff, Stacy 1252
Shiff, Richard 1290
Siff, Lowell A. 1298
ジーフ
Zieff, Howard 1554
ジープ
Siep, Ludwig 1297
ジフ
Ziff, Michael F. 1554
Ziff, Sam 1554
Ziv, Edward 1556
シーファー
Schieffer, Thomas 1252
Seiffert, Rachel 1270
Sifa 1297
シファキス
Sifakis, Carl 1298
ジーファース
Sievers, Knut 1297
ジファード
Giffard, Charles Sydney Rycroft 496
シブイトコイ
Shvydkoi, Mikhail Y. 1295
シフィレ
Cifire, Angela 264
シフェタ
Shifeta, Pohamba 1290
シフェラー
Schifferer, Andreas 1252
シフェラウ
Shiferaw, Jarso 1290
Shiferaw, Shigute 1290
Shiferaw, Tekelemariam 1290
シフェール
Sieffert, René 1297
ジーフェルス
Sievers, Eric J. 1297
シフエンテ
Cifuentes, Vincete 264
シフォード
Sifford, Charlie 1298
シフーコ
Syjuco, Miguel 1373
ジブコヴィッチ
Živković, Zoran 1556

ジブコビッチ
Živković, Zoran 1556
シプサ
Sipser, Michael 1307
ジプサー
Zipser, Paul 1556
ジプシー・ジョー
Gypsy Joe 550
ジーブス
Jeeves, Malcolm A. 668
ジブソン
Gipson, Ken 501
シフチェンコ
Shevchenko, Irina 1289
シフツェフ
Sivtsev, Nikolai 1309
シプティ
Siptey, Kanda 1307
シプテイ
Siptey, Kanda 1307
シプトン
Shipton, Paul 1291
シフナキス
Sifounakis, Nikolaos 1298
シープバウアー
Scheepbouwer, Martin 1250
シーフマン
Seifman, Jonathan 1270
シフマン
Schiffman, Eric 1252
Schiffman, Mike 1252
Schiffman, Richard 1252
Schiffman, Stephan 1252
Schiffman, Suzanne 1252
Shiffman, Daniel 1290
Shiffman, John 1290
Shiffman, Saul 1290
シーブラ
Seabra, Verissimo Correira 1266
シーブラー
Schiebler, Ralf 1252
シフラ
Sychra, Jan 1373
シプラー
Shipler, David K. 1291
シーブライト
Seabright, Paul 1266
シブラル
Shibulal, S.D. 1289
シフリー
Sifry, David L. 1298
Sifry, Micah L. 1298
シブリー
Sibley, Brian 1295
Sibley, David 1295
Sibley, Veronica 1295
シプリー
Shipley, A.Q. 1291
Shipley, Braden 1291
Shipley, Jaxon 1291
Shipley, Mike 1291
ジブリ
al-Jibory, Mohammed 673
シプリアーノ
Cipriano, Joseph J. 265
ジブリール
Jibril, Muhammad Jihad 673
ジブリル
Djibril, Ibrahim Idriss 359
Jibril, Mahmoud 673
Jibril, Muhammad Jihad 673
シフリン
Schifrin, Matthew 1252
Shiffrin, Mikaela 1290
シブリン
Siblin, Eric 1295
シプリン
Shipulin, Anton 1291
シブール
Ciboul, Adèle 264
シブル
Ciboul, Adèle 264
シーブルック
Seabrook, Jeremy 1266
Seabrook, Sue 1266
シフレット
Shiflett, Chris 1290
シフレン
Schiffrin, André 1252
ジベ
Zibe, Sasa 1554
シベット
Sibbet, David 1295
シペリ
Sipeli, Pokotoa 1307
シーベル
Seibel, Scott 1269
ジーベル
Zibbell, Robert A. 1554
シベルツェン
Sivertzen, Stian 1309
ジーベルト
Siebert, Horst 1296
ジベルナウ
Gibernau, Santiago 495
ジーベンロック
Siebenrock, Roman A. 1296
シボー
Thiboldeaux, Kim 1396
ジボ
Djibo, Abdoulaye 359
Djibo, Salou 359
ジボツキ
Zsivoczky, Attila 1558
ジボツキファルカシュ
Zsivoczky-farkas, Gyorgyi 1558
シーボーム
Seebohm, Emily 1268
シーボム
Seebohm, Emily 1268
シボリ
Sivori, Enrique Omar 1309
シーボルト
Sebold, Alice 1267
Seybold, Patricia B. 1277
シーボルド
Sebold, Alice 1267
Sebold, John 1267
Seibold, J.Otto 1269
Siebold, Steve 1296
シホワ
Shikhova, Yekaterina 1290
ジボン
Zevon, Warren William 1551
シーマ
Seema, Patil 1268
シーマー
Siemer, Deanne C. 1297
シマ
Shima, Terry T. 1290
Sima, Gheorghe 1301
シマー
Simard, Jean-Jacques 1301
ジマ
Dzhyma, Juliya 386
Zima, Lukas 1554
ジマー
Zimmer, Bradley 1555
Zimmer, Don 1555
Zimmer, Hans 1555
Zimmer, Justin 1555
Zimmer, Kyle 1555
Zimmer, Marc 1555
Zimmer, Mike 1555
Zimmer, Oliver 1555
シマギナ
Simagina, Irina 1301
シマコヴァ
Chmakova, Svetlana 257
シマザキ
Shimazaki, Aki 1290
シマーシュス
Šimašius, Remigijus 1301
シマズ
Shimazu, Akihito 1290
ジマーソン
Jimerson, Shane R. 674
シマトカ
Shmatko, Nataliya Dmitrievna 1292
シマトコ
Shmatko, Sergei I. 1292
シマニスキ
Szymanski, Oliver 1375
シマノスフキ
Szymanowski, Alexander 1375
シマブク・アサト
Shimabuku Azato, Roberto Luis 1290
シマブクロ
Shimabukuro, Denise 1290
Shimabukuro, Jake 1290
ジマーマン
Zimmerman, Barry J. 1555
Zimmerman, Doris P. 1555
Zimmerman, Eric 1555
Zimmerman, Joann 1555
Zimmerman, John 1555
Zimmerman, Leigh 1555
Zimmerman, Marcia 1555
Zimmerman, Ryan 1555
Zimmerman, Stephen 1555
Zimmerman, Tyrequek 1555
Zimmerman, William 1555
Zimmermann, Claire 1555
Zimmermann, Jordan 1555
Zimmermann, Polly Gerber 1555
ジマーム
Zemam, Mohammed 1550
シーマリ
Simari, Maria Matilde 1301
シマリ
al-Shemali, Mustafa Jassem 1287
シマール
Simard, Genevieve 1301
シマル
Simart, Thomas 1301
シーマン
Schiemann, Gottfried 1252
Seaman, Carolyn 1266
Seaman, Donald 1266
Seaman, Julian 1266
Seeman, Neil 1268
Seeman, Philip 1268
Seemann, Glenn 1268
シマン
Simão, Leonardo 1301
Simão, Mpinda 1301
Simão, Valdir 1301
ジーマン
Ríman, Martin 1183
Zeeman, Carling 1549
Zyman, Sergio 1560
シマンガ
Simanga, Augustin 1301
シマンク
Schimank, Uwe 1252
シマンゴ
Simango, David 1301
シマンスキー
Szymanski, Jeff 1375
Szymanski, Stefan 1375
シマンセク
Simancek, Jeffrey A. 1301
シミー
Simy 1305
ジミー
Jimmy 674
シーミアン
Siemian, Trevor 1297
シミエン
Simien, Terrance 1302
シミオナート
Simionato, Chiara 1302
Simionato, Giulietta 1302
シミオン
Simion, Viorel 1302
シミタブ
Simitab, Jim 1302
シミチコー
Simicskó, István 1302
シミック
Simic, Charles 1302
シミティ
Simiti, Bernard 1302
シミティス
Simitis, Konstantinos 1302
シミネラ
Ciminera, Siobhan 264
シミノヴィッチ
Siminovich, Lorena 1302
シミントン
Symington, Joan 1373
Symington, Neville 1373
シム
Shim, Eduard Yu 1290
Shim, Hyung-rae 1290
Shim, Jae K. 1290
Shim, Man-sup 1290
Shim, Suk-hee 1290
Shim, Sung-bo 1290
Sim, Andrew 1301
Sim, Chol-ho 1301
Sim, David 1301
Sim, Eun-kyeong 1301
Sim, Jack 1301
Sim, Kihwan 1301
Sim, Sang-myoung 1301
Sim, Stuart 1301
Sim, Victor 1301

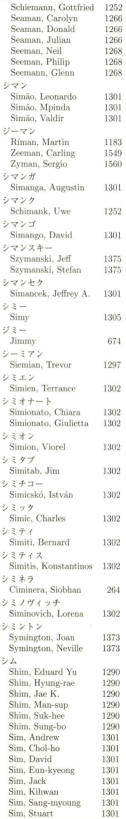

Simu, Sun-hyon 1305
ジム
Yim Chhay Ly 1538
シムキン
Simkin, Daniel 1302
Simkin, Daniil 1302
Simkin, Daren 1302
シムクーテ
Šimkutė, Lidija 1302
シムケ
Schimke, R.Neil 1252
シムコ
Šimko, Ivan 1302
シムコビアク
Szymkowiak, Kerstin 1375
シムサ
Simsa, Marko 1304
Simsa, Pavel 1304
シムシェキ
Şimşek, Mehmet 1304
シムシオン
Simsion, Graeme 1305
シームズ
Siems, Larry 1297
シムス
Sims, Chris 1304
Symes, R.F. 1373
シムズ
Simms, Andrew 1302
Simms, Chris 1302
Simms, Matt 1302
Sims, A.C.P. 1304
Sims, Charles 1304
Sims, Chris 1304
Sims, Christopher A. 1304
Sims, Dion 1304
Sims, Eugene 1304
Sims, Henry 1304
Sims, Josh 1304
Sims, LeShaun 1304
Sims, Lucas 1304
Sims, Oliver 1304
Sims, Pat 1304
Sims, Peter 1304
Sims, Richard 1304
Sims, Sean 1304
シームスター
Seamster, Sammy 1266
シムセク
Simsek, Sibel 1304
シムソン
Simson, Kadri 1305
シムッカ
Simukka, Salla 1305
ジムニー
Zimny, George H. 1555
Zimny, Thom 1555
シムバ
Simba, Iddi 1301
シムホン
Simhon, Shalom 1301
シムラー
Schimler, Amy 1252
ジムラー
Zimler, Richard 1555
シムレール
Simler, Isabelle 1302
シームンガル
Seemungal, Jairam 1268
シムーンズ
Simoons, Frederick J. 1304
シメオナ
Simeona, Mornnah Nalamaku 1301
シメオニデス
Symeonides, Nicos 1373
シメオネ
Simeone, Diego 1301
Simeone, Giovanni 1301
シメオノフ
Simeonov, Teodosii 1301
シメオン
Simeon, Yvon 1301
Timeon, Taberannang 1405
シメオン・ネグリン
Simeón Negrín, Rosa Elena 1301
ジメク
Ziemek, Zach 1554
シーメス
Siimes, Suvi-Anne 1298
シメチコ
Shymechko, Ihor 1295
ジメネス
Gimenez, Chris 500
ジメネッツ
Jimenez, Felix 673
シメラネ
Simelane, Constance 1301
Simelane, Maweni 1301
Simelane, Sibongile 1301
シメラメ
Simelane, Constance 1301
シメリョーフ
Shmelyov, Nikolai Petrovich 1292
シメール
Schimmel, Schim 1252
シメル
Schiemel, Andrew W. 1252
Schimel, Lawrence 1252
Schimmel, David 1252
ジーメル
Zemel, Eitan 1550
シメルム
Simelum, Maki 1301
シメン
Simmen, Hélène 1302
シメント
Ciment, Jill 264
シモ
Shimo, Cedrick M. 1290
シーモア
Seymour, Ana 1277
Seymour, Gerald 1277
Seymour, Miranda 1277
Seymour, Pedrya 1277
Seymour, Tommy 1277
Seymour, Tres 1277
シモセ
Shimose, Pedro 1290
シモナイズ
Simonise, Rashaun 1303
シモニス
Simonis, Damien 1303
ジモーニス
Simonis, Heide 1303
シモニッチ
Simonić, Ante 1303
ジモニッチ
Zimonjic, Nenad 1555
シモニテ
Šimonytė, Ingrida 1304
シモニティ
Simoniti, Vasko 1303
シモニデス
Symonides, Janusz 1373
シモネ
Simonnet, Dominique 1303
シモネッタ
Simonetta, Marcello 1303
シモネッティ
Simonetti, Jack L. 1303
シモネット
Symonette, Brent 1373
シモノー
Simoneau, Jacqueline 1303
Simoneau, Léopold 1303
シモノビッチ
Šimonović, Ivan 1303
シーモノフ
Simonov, Konstantin Mikhailovich 1303
シモノフスキー
Šimonovský, Milan 1303
シモハラ
Shimohara, Katsunori 1290
シモビッチ
Simović, Milutin 1304
シモフ
Shimov, Vladimir N. 1290
シモムラ
Shimomura, Osamu 1290
シモモト
Shimomoto, Hatiro 1290
シモリ
Cimoli, Gino 264
シモーン
Simone, Susan Suchman 1303
シモン
Simmons, Craig 1302
Simon, Anne 1302
Simon, Claude 1303
Simon, Dominique 1303
Simon, François 1303
Simon, Georg 1303
Simon, Lidia 1303
Simón, María 1303
Simon, Serge 1303
Simon, Simone 1303
Simon, Yoane 1303
Simon, Zsolt 1303
Simone, Gail 1303
Simone, Nina 1303
ジーモン
Simon, Erika 1303
Simon, Helmut 1303
Simon, Henrik 1303
ジモン
Simon, Winfried 1303
シモン・イサイアス
Simon Isaias, Jaime Roberto 1303
シモン=オイカワ
Simon-Oikawa, Marianne 1303
シモン=及川
Simon-Oikawa, Marianne 1303
ジーモン=シェーファー
Simon-Schaefer, Roland 1304
シーモンズ
Seamands, David A. 1266
シモンス
Simmonds, Elizabeth 1302
Simons, Timmy 1304
シモンズ
Simens, Dov S.-S. 1301
Simmonds, Elizabeth 1302
Simmonds, Jackie 1302
Simmonds, Posy 1302
Simmons, Alex 1302
Simmons, Andrelton 1302
Simmons, Annette 1302
Simmons, Ben 1302
Simmons, Cindy 1302
Simmons, Craig 1302
Simmons, Dan 1302
Simmons, David 1302
Simmons, Deborah 1302
Simmons, Delvon 1302
Simmons, Ed 1302
Simmons, Gene 1302
Simmons, Hardwick 1302
Simmons, Jalen 1302
Simmons, Jane 1302
Simmons, Jean 1302
Simmons, J.K. 1302
Simmons, Jo 1302
Simmons, John 1302
Simmons, Jonathon 1302
Simmons, Jumpin' Gene 1302
Simmons, Justin 1302
Simmons, Kim 1302
Simmons, Kimora Lee 1302
Simmons, Matthew R. 1302
Simmons, Patrick 1302
Simmons, Rachel 1302
Simmons, Rob 1302
Simmons, Robert 1302
Simmons, Robert., Jr. 1302
Simmons, Russell 1302
Simmons, Shae 1302
Simmons, Simone 1302
Simmons, Sylvie 1302
Simmons, Wayne 1302
Simons, Daniel J. 1303
Simons, James 1303
Simons, Judy 1303
Simons, Marilyn 1303
Simons, Moya 1303
Simons, Paullina 1304
Symmonds, Nick 1373
Symmons, Sarah 1373
Symonds, Craig L. 1373
Symons, Mitch 1374
シモンセン
Simonsen, Thorkild 1304
シモンソン
Simonson, Scott 1304
シモンチェリ
Simoncelli, Marco 1303
シモンチッチ
Simoncic, Vlastja 1303
シーモント
Simont, Marc 1304
シモン・ムナロ
Simon Munaro, Yehude 1303
シャ
Hsieh, Sheng-Chan 630
シャー
Hsia, R.Po-chia 629
Scher, Murray 1251
Scher, Stephen 1251
Shah, Anita 1278
Shah, Anup 1278

Shah, Kaushal 1278
Shah, Narendra Bikram 1278
Shah, Nilesh 1278
Shah, Rupesh 1278
Shah, Sneh 1278
Shah, Sonia 1278
Shah, Syed Khursheed Ahmed 1278
Shah, Syed Nadeem Alam 1278
Shah, Tanvi 1278
Shear, M.Katherine 1285
Sher, Brian 1288

ジャ
Djá, Baciro 359
Dja, Blé Joseph 359
Jha, Anil Kumar 672
Jha, Radhika 673
Jha, Ram Chandra 673
Jha, Yudu Bansha 673
Jia, Ping-wa 673
Jia, Qing-lin 673
Jia, Zhang-ke 673

ジャー
Jaa, Tony 654
Jah, S.U.M. 659
Jha, Alok 672
Jha, Rambharos 673
Jia, Yueting 673

シャア
Shah, Dharmesh 1278
Xia, Da 1531

ジャアファリ
al-Jaafari, Ibrahim 654

シャアール
al-Sha'ar, Muhammad Ibahim 1277

シャイ
Shy, Oz 1295

シャイー
Chailly, Riccardo 242

ジャイ
Diay, Mokhtar Ould 351

シャイア
Shire, Billy 1291

シャイアー
Scheier, Jacob 1250

シャイアズ
Shiers, David 1290

シャイアマン
Scheirman, Ben 1250

ジャイアント
Giant, Nikki 494

シャイエ
Chaillet, Jilles 242
Schaie, Klaus Warner 1249

ジャイエ
Jayer, Henri 667

シャイカ
Chaica, Alberto 242

シャイク
Shaikh, Anwar 1279
Shaikh, Nermeen 1279

シャイジアー
Shazier, Ryan 1285

シャイスマトフ
Shaismatov, Ergash 1279

ジャイスワル
Jaiswal, Sriprakash 659

シャイダ
Skeide, Andreas 1309

シャイダー
Schider, Brian 1251
Schider, Crystal 1251

ジャイテ
Jaiteh, Teneng Mba 660

ジャイディ
Jaidee, Thongchai 659

シャイト
Scheidt, Gintare 1250

シャイド
Scheid, Rickne C. 1250

ジャイトリー
Jaitley, Arun 660

シャイナ
Szajna, Józef 1374

シャイナー
Scheiner, David K. 1250
Scheiner, Elliot 1250
Shiner, Lewis 1291

シャイニー
Shainee, Mohamed 1279

シャイノワ
Shainova, Marina 1279

シャイバー
Scheiber, Mario 1250

シャイビ
al-Shaibi, Yahya Mohammed 1279

シャイフ
Chaifou, Ada 242
Shaykh, Khalid Rajih 1284
Shaykh, Mawlana 1285

シャイブ
Chaibou, Yahaya 242
Scheib, Walter 1250

シャイブナー
Scheibner, Herbert 1250

シャイブリ
Shively, Donald Howard 1292

シャイブリー
Shively, Donald Howard 1292

シャイプル
Scheipl, Josef 1250

ジャイプロン
Giai Pron, Cristina 494

ジャイボ a.k.a モンク
Jaybo A.K.A Monk 667

ジャイメ
Jaime, Aguinaldo 659

シャイモフ
Shimoff, Marci 1290

シャイヤブ
Sheyab, Mahmoud 1289

ジャイラウオフ
Zhailauov, Gani 1551

ジャイラニ
al-Jailani, Abdul-Bagi 659

シャーイル
al-Shaer, Ibrahim 1278

ジャイルズ
Giles, Bridget 498
Giles, Harry 498
Giles, Jeff 498
Giles, Jennifer St. 498
Giles, Ken 498
Giles, Stephen 498

シャイン
Schein, Edgar H. 1250
Schein, Elyse 1250
Schein, Phillip G. 1250
Shine, Betty 1291

ジャイン
Jain, Naresh 659

シャインバーグ
Shainberg, Lawrence 1279

シャインフェルド
Scheinfeld, Robert 1250

シャインベルガー
Scheinberger, Felix 1250

シャウ
Shaw, William T. 1284

シャウアー
Schauer, Frederick 1250
Schauer, Maggie 1250
Schauer, Martin 1250

ジャヴァーズ
Javers, Eamon 666

シャヴァニュー
Chavagneux, Christian 249

シャヴァル
Chabal, Sébastien 241
Chavel, Marie-Pierre 250

ジャウアル
Yahuar, Norberto 1532

ジャヴァン
Djavann, Chahdortt 359

ジャウイ
Jaoui, Agnès 664
Jaoui, Laurent 664

シャヴィエル
Xavier, Marcelo 1531

シャヴィエル・エステヴェス
Xavier Esteves, Francisco 1531

ジャーウィス
Jervis, Robert 672

ジャーヴィス
Jarvis, Aaron 665
Jarvis, Carolyn 665
Jarvis, James 666
Jarvis, Matt 666
Jarvis, Patricia 666
Jarvis, Peter 666
Jarvis, Robin 666
Jarvis, Steve 666
Jervis, Robert 672

ジャヴィダン
Javidan, Mansour 666

シャヴィット
Shavit, David 1284

ジャウイット
Jowett, Simon 689

ジャウィド
Jawid, Nehmatullah Ehsan 667

シャヴィロ
Shaviro, Steven 1284

シャーウィン
Sherwin, Bob 1289
Sherwin, Hiroko 1289
Sherwin, Martin J. 1289

シャーヴィントン
Shirvington, Jessica 1292

シャーウィン裕子
Sherwin, Hiroko 1289

シャヴエ
Chavouet, Florent 250

ジャーヴェイス
Gervais, Ricky 492

シャウエシュ
Chaouech, Ezzedine Bach 246

ジャウェーシュ
Jaweesh, Faysal 667

シャウェス
Shaweys, Rowsch 1284

ジャヴェル
Javelle, Pierre 666

ジャウエン
Jaouen, Hervé 664

ジャヴォイ
Javoy, Marie-Claire 667

ジャウォースキー
Jaworski, Joseph 667

ジャウォルスキー
Jaworski, Bernard J. 667

シャウカット
Shaukat, Sidra 1284

シャウーケ・オリベイラ
Chaúque Oliveria, Cidália Manuel 249

シャウジー
Shaugee, Mahmood 1283

シャウシュ
Chaouch, Ali 246

シャウツ
Schautz, Irmela 1250

シャーウッド
Sherwood, Ben 1289
Sherwood, Pamela 1289

ジャウデル
al-Jowder, Hisham bin Mohammed 689

シャウピブーンキット
Siawpiboonkit, Narin 1295

ジャウフィ
al-Jawfi, Abdul-Salam Mohammed Hizam 667

シャウフェリ
Schaufeli, Wilmar B. 1250

シャウフラー
Schaufler, Wolfgang 1250

ジャウメ・コスタ
Jaume Costa 666

ジャウラ
Jaura, Malam 666

シャエブ
Shayeb, Hamdy Abdel-Salam El 1284

シャエル
Shaer, Nasser 1278

シャオ
Hsiao, Aron 629
Hsiao, Wan-chang 629
Hsiao, William C. 629
Shao, Andrew 1281
Xiao, Xiang-qian 1531

ジャオ
Diaw, Diakaria 351
Jiao, Ben 673
Zhao, Qiguang 1552
Zhao, Yujia 1552

ジャオニナ
Jaonina, Mamitiana Juscelyno 664

シャオ・ユー
Shao, Yu 1281

ジャーガ
Jurga, Robert M. 692

ジャカ
Xhaka, Granit 1531
Xhaka, Taulant 1531

ジャガー
Jager, Evan 659
Jagger, Mick 659

ジャカイティエーネ
Žakaitienė, Roma 1545

シャーカフスキー
Szarkowski, John 1374

シャカム
Shuqum, Nabih 1294
シャガリ
Shagari, Muktari 1278
ジャカール
Jacquard, Roland 658
Jacquart, Danielle 658
シャカルチ
Shakarchi, Rami 1279
シャガン
Shagan, Ofer 1278
ジャーガン
Jagan, Janet 659
ジャカン
Jacquin, Philippe 658
シャーキー
Sharkey, John 1282
Sharkey, Niamh 1282
Shirky, Clay 1291
シャキエフ
Shakiyev, Nurlanbek 1279
ジャギエルカ
Jagielka, Phil 659
シャキブ
Shakib, Siba 1279
ジャキポフ
Zhakypov, Birzhan 1551
シャギマラトーワ
Shagimuratova, Albina 1278
シャキモワ
Shakimova, Dariga 1279
シャーキャ
Shakya, Ajaya Kranti 1279
シャキャ
Shakya, Asta Laxmi 1279
Shakya, Gopal 1279
シャキヤ
Shakya, Keshav Man 1279
シャキーラ
Shakeela, Mariyam 1279
Shakira 1279
シャキリ
Shaqiri, Xherdan 1282
シャキル
Shaker, Muhammad 1279
ジャキール
Çakir, Asli 214
Cakir Alptekin, Asli 214
シャキロワ
Shikarova, Albina 1290
ジャーキンス
Jerkins, Grant 671
ジャキント
Giaquinto, Marcus 494
シャーク
Shirk, David 1291
Shirk, Susan L. 1291
ジャーク
Jacques, Catherine 658
ジャクイス
Jaquith, Priscilla 665
ジャクスイベコフ
Dzhaksybekov, Adilbek 386
ジャクスン
Jackson, Andrew Jonathan 655
Jackson, James H. 656
Jackson, Julian 656
シャクソン
Shaxson, Nicholas 1284
ジャクソン
Jackson, Adam J. 655
Jackson, Alan 655
Jackson, Albert 655
Jackson, Alphonso 655
Jackson, Andrew 655
Jackson, Andrew Grant 655
Jackson, Asa 655
Jackson, Barbara 655
Jackson, Bennett 655
Jackson, Bershawn 655
Jackson, Branden 655
Jackson, Brenda 655
Jackson, Charles L. 655
Jackson, Chris 655
Jackson, Chris B. 655
Jackson, Daniel 655
Jackson, Darius 656
Jackson, Dave 656
Jackson, David Paul 656
Jackson, Demetrius 656
Jackson, DeSean 656
Jackson, D'Qwell 656
Jackson, Edwin 656
Jackson, Elaine 656
Jackson, Emma 656
Jackson, Gabe 656
Jackson, Glenda 656
Jackson, H. 656
Jackson, Henry J. 656
Jackson, Howard 656
Jackson, Howell E. 656
Jackson, Hue 656
Jackson, Ian 656
Jackson, Janet 656
Jackson, Janine 656
Jackson, Jeremy 656
Jackson, Jesse Louis 656
Jackson, Joanne 656
Jackson, John David 656
Jackson, John Harold 656
Jackson, Johnny 656
Jackson, Joseph Walter 656
Jackson, Josh 656
Jackson, Julie 656
Jackson, Justin 656
Jackson, Kareem 656
Jackson, Katherine 656
Jackson, Kathy Merlock 656
Jackson, Kevin 656
Jackson, Lee 656
Jackson, Leslie 656
Jackson, Lisa 656
Jackson, Luke 656
Jackson, Lynn 656
Jackson, M.A. 656
Jackson, Malcolm 656
Jackson, Malik 656
Jackson, Marguerite McMillan 656
Jackson, Mary 656
Jackson, Michael 656
Jackson, Michelle C. 656
Jackson, Mick 656
Jackson, Neta 656
Jackson, Paddy 656
Jackson, Paul 656
Jackson, Peter 656
Jackson, Phil 656
Jackson, Reggie 656
Jackson, Robert 656
Jackson, Roger 656
Jackson, Russell 656
Jackson, Ryan 656
Jackson, S. 656
Jackson, Samuel L. 656
Jackson, Shericka 656
Jackson, Simonette 656
Jackson, Stan 656
Jackson, Steve 656
Jackson, Steven 656
Jackson, Susan A. 656
Jackson, Tanard 657
Jackson, Tim 657
Jackson, Tom 657
Jackson, Tony 657
Jackson, T.R. 657
Jackson, Tre 657
Jackson, Tyson 657
Jackson, Vina 657
Jackson, Vincent 657
Jackson, William 657
Jacksone, Thérèese 657
ジャクソン・メイン
Jackson-Main, Peter 657
シャクター
Schachter, Steven 1248
Schacter, Daniel L. 1248
シャグダイン・ツェンドアヨーシ
Shagdain Tsend-Ayuush 1278
ジャグティアニ
Jagtiani, Micky 659
ジャグデオ
Jagdeo, Bharrat 659
シャクト
Schacht, Henry Brewer 1248
ジャクベック
Jakubec, David France 660
ジャクボウスキー
Jakubowski, Maxim 660
ジャグモハン
Jagmohan 659
シャクラ
Shaqra, Fahd Salim 1282
ジャクラニ
Jakhrani, Mir Aijaz Hussain 660
シャクリー
Shakely, Amanj 1279
Shaklee, Beverly D. 1279
ジャクリク
Jacklick, Alvin 655
ジャクリック
Jacklick, Alvin 655
シャークリフ
Shurcliff, William 1295
シャクール
Shakooru, Aishath Azima 1279
Shakur, Tupac 1279
シャグルイエフ
Shaguliyev, Nazarguly 1278
シャクルトン
Shackleton, Emma 1277
Shackleton, Nicholas John 1277
シャクンタラ・デビ
Shakuntara Davi 1279
シャーケ
Schaake, Erich 1248
ジャケ
Jacquet, Luc 658
Jaquet, Chantal 664
Jaquet, Gilles 664
Jaquet, Luc 664
ジャケー
Jacquet, Illinois 658
ジャケット
Jacket, Snakeskin 655
シャケド
Shaked, Ayelet 1279
シャケル
Chaker, Slim 242
Shaker, Zaid ibn 1279
シャケルフォード
Shackelford, Jole 1277
ジャーゲンス
Jergens, Adele 671
Jurgens, Dan 692
ジャコ
Jacquot, Benoit 658
Jacquot, Delphine 658
ジャコー
Jacquot, Benoit 658
ジャコッベ
Giacobbe, Giulio Cesare 494
ジャコテ
Jaccottet, Philippe 655
ジャコーニ
Giacconi, Ricardo 494
ジャコーバス
Jacobus, Mary 658
ジャコバッツィ
Giacobazzi, Leonardo 494
ジャコビ
Jacobi, Derek 657
ジャコビー
Jacoby, Brook 658
Jacoby, Henry 658
Jakoby, Don 660
ジャコービィ
Jacoby, Sanford M. 658
シヤコビッチ
Šijaković, Bogoljub 1298
ジャコブ
Jacob, Christian 657
Jacob, François 657
Jacob, Jean 657
Jacobs, Rémi 657
Yacob, Claudio 1532
ジャコベリス
Jacobellis, Lindsey 657
ジャコムッシ
Yacomuzzi, Paula 1532
ジャコメッティ
Giacometti, Eric 494
ジャコラ
Giancola, Donato 494
シャコン
Chacon, Coralie 241
シャコンボ
Shakombo, Suleiman 1279
シャーザー
Scherzer, Max 1251
ジャザイリ
al-Jazairee, Mufeed 667
ジャザエリ
al-Jazaeri, Humam 667
ジャサノフ
Jasanoff, Sheila 666
シャザル
Chazal, Martine 250
ジャサール
al-Jassar, Ahmad Khaled Ahmad 666
ジャザル

Ghazal, Majd Eddin 493
ジャージ
al-Jazi, Al-Kilani Abdulkareem 667
ジャジ
Jazi, Dali 667
ジャジー
Jazi, Dali 667
ジャ・ジェジェ
Dja Djedje, Brice 359
シャシェフスキー
Krzyzewski, Mike 770
シャシキン
Shashkin, Dimitri 1283
シャーシッヒ
Scharsig, Marc 1249
シャジマン
Shaziman, Abu Mansor 1285
ジャシム
Jasim, bin Hamad bin Khalifa al-Thani 666
Jassim, bin Abdul Aziz bin Jassim bin Hamad al-Thani 666
シャシャ
Shasha, Dennis Elliott 1283
ジャジュ
Jaju, Faris 660
シャジュス
Šadžius, Rimantas 1225
シャーシュミット
Scharschmidt, Sherry 1249
ジャジリ
Jaziri, Malek 667
ジャシール
Jacir, Emily 655
ジャシント
Jacinto, Kim 655
シャース
Shaath, Nabil 1277
ジャズ
al-Jaz, Awad Ahmed 667
シャスイユ
Chasseuil, Michel-Jack 249
ジャスカ
Juska, Jane 692
ジャスザコフ
Zhasuzakov, Saken 1552
シャスター
Schuster, D.J. 1261
ジャスター
Juster, Norton 692
シャスターマン
Shusterman, Neal 1295
シャスタマン
Shusterman, Neal 1295
ジャスティス
Justice, Bill 692
Justiss, Julia 693
シャスティン
Sastin, Marianna 1243
ジャスティン
Justine, Jane 692
シャステル
Chastel, Olivier 249
ジャスト
Just, Marion R. 692
ジャーストマン
Gerstman, Bradley 491
シャスネ
Chastanet, Allen 249
ジャスパー
Jasper, James M. 666
Jasper, Melanie 666
ジャスバーン
Jassburn, Hugh 666
ジャースマン
Hjersman, Peter 610
ジャスマン
Jasmin, Joseph 666
ジャスムヒーン
Jasmuheen 666
ジャスライ
Jasrai, Puntsagiin 666
シャズリ
Shazli, Kamal Muhammad El 1285
シャゼル
Chazelle, Celia Martin 250
ジャーセル
al-Jasser, Muhammad bin Sulaiman 666
シャタ
Chatat, Clobert 249
Shata, Mohammed 1283
Tchatat, Clobert 1387
ジャタ
Diatta, Christhian Sina 351
Jatta, Baboucarr 666
シャタック
Shattuck, Cybelle 1283
Shattuck, Roger 1283
シャタハ
Shatah, Mohammed 1283
ジャダラ
Djadallah, Bichara Issa 359
ジャーチェク
Zácek, Jirí 1544
ジヤチェンコ
Dyachenko, Alexander 385
シャチリ
Shaqiri, Xherdan 1282
ジャツウスキ
Jazdzewski, Chuck 667
シャツカー
Schatzker, Mark 1250
ジャッカ
Jacka, J.Mike 655
ジャッカル
Jacquart, Alain 658
ジャッキー
Jacquit, Simon 658
シャック
Shuck, J.B. 1294
ジャック
Jack, Albert 655
Jack, Boma Brimilo 655
Jack, David 655
Jack, Jarrett 655
Jack, Kristin 655
Jack, Marstella 655
Jack, Myles 655
Jack, Terry 655
Jackou, Kaffa Rékiatou Christelle 655
Jacq, Christian 658
Jacques, Thomas 658
Jak, Sable 660
ジャック・エラム
Elam, Jack 395
ジャックス
Jaques, Faith 664
シャックマン
Shackman, Mark 1278
ジャックマン
Jackman, Hugh 655
ジャックリト
Panichpatikum, Jakkrit 1075
シャックルトン
Shackleton, Nicholas John 1277
ジャッケッティ
Giacchetti, Igino 494
ジャッケリーニ
Giaccherini, Emanuele 494
ジャッケンドフ
Jackendoff, Ray 655
ジャッコーニ
Giacconi, Ricardo 494
ジャッシー
Jassi, Amita 666
ジャッジ
Judge, Aaron 690
Judge, Barbara 690
シャッター
Shatter, Alan 1283
ジャッタ
Jatta, Bakery 666
Jatta, Famara 666
シャッツ
Schatz, Albert 1249
Schatz, Dennis 1249
ジャッツォン
Giazzon, Davide 495
シャッツバーグ
Schatzberg, Alan F. 1249
シャッツマン
Schatzman, Evry Léon 1250
シャッティ
al-Shatti, Ismail Khudher 1283
シャット
Schutt, Rachel 1261
Shutt, Christopher 1295
ジャット
Judt, Tony 690
ジャッド
Judd, Ashley 690
Judd, Denis 690
Judd, Donald 690
シャットマン
Shachtman, Tom 1277
シャツバーグ
Schatzberg, Alan F. 1249
ジャップ
Japp, Andréa H. 664
シャッファー
Schaffer, Simon 1249
ジャッファ
Jaffa, Rick 659
ジャッフェ
Jaffe, Peter G. 659
Jaffe, Sam 659
Jaffe, William L. 659
シャッペル
Schappell, Elissa 1249
ジャッボリ
Jabbori, Marhabo 655
シャツマン
Schatzman, Evry Léon 1250
ジャッラーハ
al-Jarrah, Jamal 665
ジャッラーヤ
Jarraya, Sarra 665
ジャッリーニ
Giallini, Lio 494
シャツレ
Schaetzle, Anita 1249
シャテー
Shatté, Andrew 1283
ジャーディ
Jerde, Jon 671
ジャーディー
Jerde, Jon 671
シャディエフ
Shadiyev, Askarbek 1278
シャディク
Shadick, Bibi 1278
シャディッド
Shadid, Anthony 1278
シャディド
Shadid, Anthony 1278
ジャティヤ
Jatiya, Satya Narayan 666
シャティロフ
Shatilov, Alexander 1283
ジャーディン
Jardine, Al 665
Jardine, Michael 665
シャテル
Chatel, Luc 249
シャート
Schaadt, Renate-Maria 1248
Schad, Martha 1248
ジャード
Jerde, Jon 671
ジャド
Jade, Claude 658
Judd, Ashley 690
ジヤド
Ziyad, Ahmed 1556
ジャドアーン
al-Jada'an, Mohammed bin Abdullah 658
ジャトイ
Jatoi, Ghulam Murtaza Khan 666
Jatoi, Ghulam Mustafa 666
Jatoi, Liaqat Ali 666
シャドウ
Shadow, Nick 1278
シャドウィック
Shadwick, Keith 1278
ジャドゥール
Jadoul, Emile 658
ジャドゥーン
Jadoon, Amanullah Khan 658
ジャドキンス
Judkins, Rod 690
ジャドソン
Judson, Bruce 690
Judson, Olivia 690
シャトナー
Shatner, William 1283
ジャドービン
Zhadobin, Yuri V. 1551
シャドボルト
Shadbolt, Maurice 1278
シャドヤック
Shadyac, Tom 1278
シャドラー
Schadler, Ted 1248

シャトラン
Chatelin, Francoise 249
シャトリー
Shatley, Tyler 1283
シャドリ
Chadli, Bendjedid 241
Chadli, Nacer 241
シャドリー
Chadli, Bendjedid 241
シャトリエ
Chatelier, Denis 249
シャトリュス
Chatelus, Gautier 249
シャドリン
Shadrin, Valery Ivanovich 1278
シャートル
Schertle, Alice 1251
シャトルワース
Shuttleworth, Sally 1295
シャトレ
Châtelet, Noëlle 249
シャトーレイノ
Chatauraynaud, Francis 249
シャトローフ
Shatróv, Mikhail 1283
シャトロフ
Shatróv, Mikhail 1283
シャーナー
Shaner, Timothy 1280
ジャナ
Gjana, Jemin 503
シャナエワ
Shanaeva, Aida 1280
ジャナート
Janert, Philipp K. 662
シャーナバズ
Shahnavaz, Houshang 1279
シャナハン
Shanahan, Kyle 1280
Shanahan, Murray 1280
ジャナビ
al-Janabi, Adnan 662
al-Janabi, Hasan 662
シャーニ
Shani, Yaron 1280
ジャーニ
Jany, Andrea 664
ジャーニー
Jurney, Russell 692
ジャニ
Rzany, Andrzej 1222
Xhani, Mustafa 1531
シャニアル
Channial, Phillippe 246
ジャニエトフ
Janjetov, Zoran 663
ジャニオ
Jeanniot, Pierre Jean 668
ジャーニガン
Jernigan, Timmy 671
ジャニク
Janik, Allan 663
Janik, Erika 663
Janyk, Britt 664
ジャニクリ
Canikli, Nurettin 221
ジャニコウスキー
Janikowski, Sebastian 663
ジャニス
Janis, Jeff 663
Junis, Jake 692
シャニュー
Chagnoux, Herve 242
ジャニュ
Jagne, Baboucarr-Blaise 659
ジャニング
Janning, Stephen W. 663
シャニングワ
Shaningwa, Sophia 1280
ジャヌネー
Jeanneney, Jean-Noël 668
ジャネ
Janneh, Kabineh 663
Jeannet, Fabrice 668
ジャネイ
Janney, Allison 663
Janney, Rachel 663
ジャネス
Janes, Karen Hosack 662
ジャネタシオ
Giannetasio, Graciela 494
ジャネッタ
Jannetta, Ann Bowman 663
シャネマン
Shaneman, Jhampa 1280
ジャネリゼ
Janelidze, Mikheil 662
Janelidze, Mindia 662
シャネル
Che'nelle 252
Shanel, Peter 1280
ジャネル
Caner, Erkin 221
Janelle, Christopher M. 662
シャノー
Schano, Michael 1249
ジャノ
Janot, Francis 663
ジャノッティ
Gianotti, Fabiola 494
ジャノフ
Janoff, Sandra 663
ジャノ・ラモス
Llano Ramos, Blas Antonio 836
ジャノリ
Giannoli, Xavier 494
シャノン
Shannon, Claude Elwood 1281
Shannon, David 1281
Shannon, Eugene 1281
Shannon, Frank 1281
Shannon, George 1281
Shannon, Jeanne 1281
Shannon, Jennifer 1281
Shannon, Lauren McLernan 1281
Shannon, Lisa J. 1281
Shannon, Michael J. 1281
Shannon, Ray 1281
シャーバー
Schaber, Irme 1248
シャーパー
Schaper, Heinz-Christian 1249
シャバ
Xaba, Bennedict 1531
ジャバー
Jabeur, Ons 655
ジャバアービン
Javaherbin, Mina 666
シャパイロ
Shapiro, Mark A. 1281
Shapiro, Ronald M. 1281
シャハサバリ
Shahsavari, Neda 1279
シャバス
Schabas, William 1248
シャバズ
Shabazz, Al-Hajj 1277
ジャバーズ
Javers, Eamon 666
シャハタ
Shehata, Abdul Rahim 1286
シャハダ
Shehada, Salah 1286
ジャバテ
Diabate, Mamadou 349
Diabaté, Toumani 349
ジャバディ
Javadi, Fatemeh 666
ジャバデカル
Javadekar, Prakash 666
シャバート
Shabert, Judith K. 1277
ジャーハート
Gerhart, Garth 490
シャバニ
Shabani, Lirim 1277
ジャハニ
Jahani, Abdul Bari 659
シャーバヌ
Chaabane, Sadok 241
シャハブディーン
Shahabuddin, Makhdoom 1278
シャハム
Shaham, Gil 1278
ジャバラ
Jaballah, Faicel 655
シャハラニ
Shahrani, Nehmatullah 1279
シャハリ
Chakhari, Mohamed Lamine 242
ジャバーリ
Jabari, Abdul-Aziz 655
ジャバリ
Jabari, Issa 655
シャハリアリ
Shahriari, Majid 1279
シャハリスタニ
al-Shahristani, Hussein 1279
Shahristani, Hussein 1279
ジャバリニ
Giavarini, Adalberto Rodoríguez 495
シャハリン
Shakhlin, Boris 1279
シャバリン
Shabalin, Maxim 1277
シャバル
Chabal, Sébastien 241
ジャバール
Jabar, Cynthia 655
ジャパルクル
Zhapparkul, Zhazira 1552
シャハレビッチ
Shafarevich, Igor' Rotislavovich 1278
ジャバロフ
Jabbarov, Mikail 655
ジャパロフ
Dzhaparov, Akylbek 386
Japarov, Tuvakmammet 664
シャーバーン
Sha'ban, Mervet Akram 1277
シャーバン
Chaabane, Sadok 241
Shaaban, Bouthaynah 1277
シャバン
Schavan, Annette 1250
Shaban, Naomi 1277
ジャハンギリ
Jahangiri, Eshaq 659
シャバング
Shabangu, Albert 1277
Shabangu, Susan 1277
シャバンス
Chavance, Bernard 249
シャバンバイ
Shabanbay, Daulet 1277
ジャハーン＝フォルーズ
Jahanforuz, Rita 659
シャハンベ
Shakhanbeh, Sharari 1279
シャーヒー
Shahi, Jeevan Bahadur 1278
シャヒ
Shahi, Dan Bahadur 1278
シャビ
Xavi 1531
シャビ・アロンソ
Xabi Alonso 1531
ジャービス
Jarvis, Jeff 666
Jarvis, Peter 666
シャビッチ
Šabić, Rodoljuv 1223
シャヒデ
Shahidi, Mohammad Ali 1278
シャヒディ
Shahidi, Mohammad Ali 1278
ジャビディ
Javidi, Mitch 666
シャヒード
Shaheed, Ahmed 1278
シャヒド
Shaheed, Enamul Hoque Mostafa 1278
Shahid, Enamul Haq Mostafa 1278
ジャーヒド
Jahid, Taj Mohammad 659
ジャビド
Javid, Sajid 666
シャビ・トーレス
Xavi Torres 1531
シャビビ
al-Shabibi, Saif bin Mohammed 1277
シャビーブ
Shbeeb, Lina 1285
シャビ・プリエト
Xabi Prieto 1531
シャピュイ
Chapuis, Jean-Frédéric 247
シャーヒヨウ

Shaahiyow, Mohamed Hassan Aden 1277
シャピラ
Shapira, Naomi 1281
ジャビル
Jabir, Baqir 655
Jabir, Bayan 655
Jabir al-Ahmad al-Sabah 655
ジャービル・アッ・サバーハ
Jabir al-Ahmad al-Sabah 655
ジャビル・アル・アハマド・アル・サバハ
Jabir al-Ahmad al-Sabah 655
ジャービル・サバーハ
Jabir al-Ahmad al-Sabah 655
ジャビル・サバハ
Jabir al-Ahmad al-Sabah 655
ジャビル・ムバラク・ハマド・サバハ
Jabir Mubarak al-Hamad al-Sabah 655
シャピーロ
Shapiro, Joan 1281
シャピロ
Shapiro, Aaron 1281
Shapiro, A.K. 1281
Shapiro, Alan C. 1281
Shapiro, Anna D. 1281
Shapiro, Barbara J. 1281
Shapiro, Beth Alison 1281
Shapiro, Carl 1281
Shapiro, Cynthia 1281
Shapiro, Daniel 1281
Shapiro, David 1281
Shapiro, Francine 1281
Shapiro, Gary 1281
Shapiro, Gary R. 1281
Shapiro, Ian 1281
Shapiro, Isaac 1281
Shapiro, Lawrence A. 1281
Shapiro, Lawrence E. 1281
Shapiro, Marc 1281
Shapiro, Mary 1281
Shapiro, Matthew 1281
Shapiro, Matthias 1281
Shapiro, Michael 1281
Shapiro, Mo 1281
Shapiro, Robert J. 1281
Shapiro, Robin 1281
Shapiro, Semen 1281
Shapiro, Stewart 1281
Shapiro, Susan 1282
Shapiro, Theodore 1282
Shapiro, Vivian 1282
シャヒーン
Chahine, Youssef 242
Shaheen, Faiza 1278
Shaheen, Jamal Shaaban 1278
シャヒン
Şahin, Fatma 1226
Sahin, Hafize 1226
Şahin, İdris Naim 1226
Şahin, Mehmet Ali 1226
Sahin, Nuri 1226
Sahin, Ramazan 1226
Shahin, Abdul-Aziz 1278
シャーピング
Scharping, Rudolf 1249
ジャビンズ
Javins, Marie 666
シャービントン
Shirvington, Jessica 1292
シャーフ
Scharf, Caleb A. 1249
Scharf, Walter 1249
Scherff, Brandon 1251
シャーブ
Schab, Lisa M. 1248
シャープ
Sharp, Alena 1283
Sharp, Alex 1283
Sharp, Anne 1283
Sharp, Ann Margaret 1283
Sharp, Deborah 1283
Sharp, Evan 1283
Sharp, Gene 1283
Sharp, Hunter 1283
Sharp, Isadore 1283
Sharp, Ken 1283
Sharp, Kerri 1283
Sharp, Kevin 1283
Sharp, Lynsey 1283
Sharp, Pam 1283
Sharp, Peter 1283
Sharp, Phillip Allen 1283
Sharp, Remy 1283
Sharp, Timothy J. 1283
Sharpe, Alice 1283
Sharpe, Isabel 1283
Sharpe, Kenneth Evan 1283
Sharpe, Michael 1283
Sharpe, Shannon 1283
Sharpe, Tajae 1283
Sharpe, Tom 1283
Sharpe, William Forsyth 1283
シャフ
Schaff, Adam 1249
Shaff, Valerie 1278
Syaf, Ardian 1373
シャブ
Shiyab, Mahmoud 1292
ジャフ
Jaffe, Dennis T. 659
Jaffe, Seymour 659
シャファー
Schaffer, H.Rudolph 1249
Shaffer, Peter Levin 1278
ジャファ
Jafa, Manorama 658
Xhafa, Fatmir 1531
ジャファリ
al-Jaafari, Ibrahim 654
al-Jafari, Ibrahim 659
ジャファリ・ウシェイケル
Jafari al-Usheiker, Ibrahim 659
ジャーファル
Jaafar, Mohamed Mahmoud Ould 654
ジャファール
Djaffar, Ahmed Ben Said 359
ジャファル
Jaffar, Jasim 659
ジャファール・アブドル・ラーマン
Jaafar Rahman 655
ジャファール・ラーマン
Jaafar Rahman 655
シャファレヴィッチ
Shafarevich, Igor' Rotislavovich 1278
シャフィ
Shafie, Ghazali 1278
シャフィー
Shafie, Apdal 1278
Shafie, Salleh 1278
ジャフィ
Jaffe, Azriela 659
Jaffe, Joseph 659
ジャフィー
Jaffee, Dwight 659
シャフィイ
Shafii, Abdullah 1278
シャフィーウ
Shafeeu, Ahmed 1278
シャフィク
Shafik, Ahmed Muhammad 1278
Shafik, Nemat Minouche 1278
Shafiq, Ahmad 1278
シャフィーユ
Shafeeu, Ismail 1278
シャフィール
Shafir, Eldar 1278
ジャーブヴァーラー
Jhabvala, Ruth Prawer 673
ジャブヴァーラ
Jhabvala, Ruth Prawer 673
シャフェ
Schaffer, Herbert 1249
ジャフェ
Jaffe, Janet 659
Jaffe, Laura 659
Jaffe, Marie S. 659
Jaffé, Sophia 659
シャフェイ
Shafii, Abdullah 1278
ジャフェリ
Dzaferi, Valdet 386
Xhaferri, Ferdinand 1531
Xhaferri, Musa 1531
シャブガ
Savga, Larisa 1245
シャプコット
Shapcott, Richard 1281
シャプサル
Chapsal, Madeleine 247
シャフシール
Shakhshir, Khawla 1279
Shakhshir, Taher al 1279
シャフシル
Shakhshir, Taher al 1279
シャフスベルリ
Shakhsuvarly, Kamran 1279
シャフダトゥアシビリ
Shavdatuashvili, Lasha 1284
シャブダトゥアシビリ
Shavdatuashvili, Lasha 1284
シャフタミ
Chaktami, Hassen 242
シャブテ
Chabouté, Christophe 241
シャブティニ
Shabtini, Alice 1277
シャフナー
Shaffner, George 1278
シャフナザーロフ
Shakhnazarov, Georgii Khosroevich 1279
Shakhnazarov, Karen 1279
シャフナザロフ
Shakhnazarov, Georgii Khosroevich 1279
ジャーブーブ
Djaaboub, Hachemi 359
シャフラニ
Shahrani, Waheedullar 1279
シャフラン
Shafran, Andy 1278
ジャブランヌ
Jabrane, Touriya 655
シャープリー
Sharpley, Richard 1283
シャプリー
Shapley, Lloyd 1282
ジャフリ
al-Jafri, Adnan Umar Mohammed 659
ジャフリー
Jafri, Ehsan 659
ジャブリ
al-Jabri, Kamal Hussein 655
ジャブリー
al-Jabrii, Mohammad Nasser 655
シャブリアシビリ
Shavliashvili, Davit 1284
ジャプリゾ
Japrisot, Sébastien 664
シャフリール
Shahrir, Samad 1279
ジャブール
Jabbour, Eddie 655
シャープレー
Shapley, Lloyd 1282
シャプレ
Chaplet, Anne 246
シャプレー
Shapley, Lloyd 1282
シャープレス
Sharpless, Barry 1283
シャプレン
Shaplen, Jason T. 1282
ジャブロー
Jablow, Renée 655
ジャフロミ
Jahromi, Mohammad 659
シャブロール
Chabrol, Claude 241
シャブロル
Chabrol, Claude 241
ジャブロンスキー
Jablonski, Richard 655
ジャフンパ
Jahumpa, Bala Garba 659
シャヘ
Schache, Ruediger 1248
シャーベイ
Charvet, Shelle Rose 248
シャベコフ
Shabecoff, Philip 1277
シャヘシュヘ
Chahechouhe, Aatif 242
シャベス
Chaves, Henrique 250
シャベス・デ・メンドンサ
Chaves de Mendonça, Antônio Aureliano 250
ジャーベットソン
Jurvetson, Steve 692

シャヘド
Chahed, Youssef 242
シャベト
Thabet, Jawharah Hamoud 1393
シャヘラニ
Shahrani, Waheedullar 1279
シャベール
Chabbert, Sabine 241
Chabert, Alexis 241
Chabert, Catherine 241
シャベル
Shavell, Steven 1284
ジャベル
Jaber, Yassin 655
シャペレ
Chappelet, Jean-Loup 247
シャペロ
Chiapello, Ève 254
シャボ
Chabot, Jean-Phillipe 241
シャボー
Chabot, Steve 241
シャポシニク
Shaposhnyk, Oleksandr 1282
ジャボチンスキー
Zhabotinsky, Leonid 1551
シャポトゥーレ
Shapo Toure, Fode 1282
シャーボネ
Charbonnet, Gabrielle 247
シャボフスキー
Schabowski, Günter 1248
シャボロトフ
Shabolotov, Tajimamat 1277
シャーマ
Schama, Simon 1249
Sharma, Anand 1282
Sharma, Anil K. 1282
Sharma, Chandresh 1282
Sharma, Robin Shilp 1283
シャーマー
Scharmer, Claus Otto 1249
Shermer, Michael 1288
ジャーマー
Germer, L.H. 491
ジャマ
Djama, Osman Idriss 359
Jama, Abdulkareem Hassan 660
Jama, Mahmud Abdullahi 660
Jama, Uthman 660
ジャマイル
Jamail, Dahr 660
ジャマ・イルカジル
Jama Ilkajir, Abdullahi Ahmed 660
ジャマ・シーファー
Jama Siffir, Mohamud Abdullahi 661
ジャマ・ジャンガリ
Jama Jangali, Ali Ahmed 660
シャーマズ
Charmaz, Kathy 248
シャマス
Shamas, Suhail bin Mustahil 1280
Shammas, Hassib Elias 1280
シャーマット
Sharmat, Craig 1283
Sharmat, Marjorie Weinman 1283
シャマト
al-Shammat, Kinda 1280
ジャマーノ
Germano, William P. 491
シャマラン
Night Shyamalan, M. 1025
Shyamalan, M.Night 1295
ジャマーリ
Jamali, Mir Changez Khan 660
ジャマリ
Jamali, Zafarullah Khan 660
ジャマール
Jamal 660
Jamall, Maurice 660
Jamar, Herve 661
ジャマル
Djamal, Jusman Syafii 359
Jamal, Maryam Yusuf 660
Jamal, Mohamed Maleeh 660
Jamal, Muhammad Maher Hosni 660
Jamal, Syed Ghazi Gulab 660
ジャマルディノフ
Zhamaldinov, Ziyadin 1551
ジャマルディン
Jamaluddin, Jarjis 660
シャマルパ・リンポチェ
Kunzig Shamarpa Rinpoche 774
ジャマルル・キラム3世
Jamalul Kiram Ⅲ 661
シャマロフ
Shamalov, Kirill 1280
ジャマロフ
Jamalov, Yaver 660
シャーマン
Schuurman, Donna 1261
Sharman, Bill 1283
Sherman, Anthony 1288
Sherman, Bill 1288
Sherman, David 1288
Sherman, Delia 1288
Sherman, Eric 1288
Sherman, Judith 1288
Sherman, Lawrence W. 1288
Sherman, Richard 1288
Sherman, Robert B. 1288
Sherman, Ronald 1288
Sherman, Sallie 1288
Sherman, Vincent 1288
Sherman, Wendy 1288
Shireman, William K. 1291
ジャーマン
German, J.Bruce 491
German, Lindsey 491
Jarman, Derek 665
Jarman, Julia 665
ジャマン
Jamin, Jean 662
シャーマン＝ジョーンズ
Sherman-Jones, Carol 1288
シャマンスカ
Shaimardanova, Victorij 1279
シャーマン＝バーク
Sharman-Burke, Juliet 1283
シャーミ
al-Shami, Ali 1280
シャーミー
Shaami, Ahmed 1277
シャミ
Chami, Ahmed 243
Šami, Zoran 1234
Schami, Rafik 1249
Shami, Nailah 1280
Shami, Naser Al 1280
ジャミオロスキー
Jamiolkowski, Raymond M. 662
ジャミシェフ
Zhamishev, Bolat 1551
ジャーミソン
Jamieson, Ian 662
ジャミソン
Jamison, Kay R. 662
シャミフ
al-Shamekh, Embarak Abdallah 1280
シャミール
Shamir, Yitzhak 1280
シャミル
Shamil Aliev 1280
Shamir, Shimon 1280
Shamir, Yair 1280
Shamir, Yitzhak 1280
ジャミール
Jameel, Abdulla 661
Jameel, Aminath 661
Jameel, Fathulla 661
Jameel, Mohamed Mauroof 661
Jameel, Shahida 661
ジャミル
Jamil, Qadri 662
シャーム
Shyam, Bhajju 1295
シャム
Schum, Jacob 1260
Shamu, Webster Kotiwani 1280
シャムー
Chamoux, François 243
Shamoo, Adil E. 1280
シヤム
Siyam, Mohamed Abdellahi Ould 1309
シャムイラドフ
Shamyradov, Bekmyrat 1280
シャムウェー
Shumway, Norman Edward 1294
シャムウェイ
Shumway, Norman Edward 1294
シャムコ
Shamko, Alexander I. 1280
シャムザイ
Shamzai, Nizamuddin 1280
シャムサン
Shamsan, Nabil 1280
シヤムシウェ
Siyam Siewe, Alphonse 1309
シャムシディン
Chamsidine, Anissi 244
シャムジャエ
Syamujaye, Syamkayumbu 1373
シャムス
Shams, Mohammad Jalil 1280
シャムスカ
Chamusca, Pericles 244
シャムスッディーン
Shams al-Din, Muhammad Mahdi 1280
シャムダサーニ
Shamdasani, Sonu 1280
ジャームッシュ
Jarmusch, Jim 665
シャムハニ
Shamkhani, Ali 1280
シャムヒード
Shamheed, Ahmed 1280
ジャム・マスターJ
Jam Master Jay 662
ジャム・マスター・ジェイ
Jam Master Jay 662
ジャムヤン
Jamyang, Norbu 662
シャムラン
Shamlan, Mohammed Saleh 1280
ジャムリン・テンジン・ノルゲイ
Jamling Tenzing Norgay 662
シャムレイ
Shamlaye, Bernard 1280
ジャメ
Jammeh, Alieu 662
Jammeh, Ousman 662
Jammeh, Yahya 662
ジャーメイ
Jarmey, Chris 665
シャメンダ
Shamenda, Fackson 1280
シャモ
Chamo 243
ジャモドゥ
Jamodu, Kolawole 662
シャモニ
Schamoni, Wolfgang 1249
シャモワゾー
Chamoiseau, Patrick 243
ジャーモン
Germon, Jennifer 491
ジャヤクマル
Jayakumar, S. 667
ジャヤシンゲ
Jayasinghe, Migel 667
ジャヤスーリヤ
Jayasuriya, Karu 667
ジャヤスンダラ
Jayasundara, Vimukthi 667
ジャヤセカラ
Jayasekara, Dayasiri 667
ジャヤセナ
Jayasena, Sumedha 667
ジャヤソーリア
Jayasooria, Denison 667
ジャヤパル
Jayapal, Pramila 667
ジャヤラトナ
Jayaratne, D.M. 667
Jayaratne, Priyankara 667

ジャヤラトナム
Jeyaretnam, J.B. 672
ジャヤラリタ
Jayalalitha, Jayaram 667
ジャヤワルダナ
Jayawardhana, Ray 667
ジャヤワルダネ
Jayawardena, Kumari 667
シャーラー
Schaller, Lyle E. 1249
Scharrer, Hans-Eckart 1249
シャラ
Sciarra, Paul 1263
Shala, Ahmet 1279
Shala, Kujtim 1279
al-Shara, Farouk 1282
Shara, Munther 1282
シャラー
Schaller, Christian Tal 1249
Schaller, Marcus 1249
Schaller, Michael 1249
Scherer, Frances E. 1251
シヤラ
Siala, Osama Abdurauf 1295
ジャラ
Jallah, Peter 660
シャライデ
Sharideh, Khalid 1282
シャラコワ
Sharakova, Tatsiana 1282
シャラシェビチュウテ
Šalaševičiūtė, Rimantė 1229
ジャラツ
Žalac, Gabrijela 1546
シャラット
Sharratt, Aaron 1283
Sharratt, Nick 1283
ジャラッラ
al-Jarrallah, Muhammad Ahmad 665
ジャラートリ
Jaraatli, Ghayath 665
ジャラトリ
Jaratli, Ghayath 665
シャラビ
Shallabi, Fawziya 1280
シャラフ
Sharaf, Essam 1282
Sharaf, Hisham 1282
Sharaf, Ibrahim Al Saeed 1282
ジャラフマ
al-Jalahma, Yusuf bin Ahmed bin Hussain 660
シャラポア
Sharapova, Maria Yuryevna 1282
シャラポワ
Sharapova, Maria Yuryevna 1282
Sharapova, Suzan 1282
ジャラリ
Jalali, Ali-Ahmad 660
al-Jalali, Muhammmad Ghazi 660
シャラル
Salaru, Anatolie 1229
Salaru, Gheorghe 1229
Sharar, Muhammad Deifallah 1282
ジャラール
Jalal, Sheikh Ahmed 660
ジャラル
Jalal, Masooda 660
Jalal, Zobaida 660
シャラン
Shaalan, Hazim 1277
Sharan, Shlomo 1282
Sharan, Yael 1282
シャランスキー
Schalansky, Judith 1249
Sharansky, Natan 1282
シャーリ
Shaali, Muhammad Hussein al 1277
シャーリー
Shirley, James Paul 1291
Shirley, John 1291
シャリー
Sharry, John 1283
シャリアティ
Shariati, Sabah 1282
シャリアトマダリ
Shariatmadari, Mohammad 1282
シャーリエ
al-Shaaerie, Ali Morsie 1277
シャリエ
Chalier, Catherine 242
シャーリー・カーク
Shirley-Quirk, John 1291
シャリカシュヴィリ
Shalikashvili, John 1279
シャリカシュビリ
Shalikashvili, John 1279
シャリカゼ
Sharikadze, Merab 1282
シャリギナ
Shalygina, Yelena 1280
シャーリー・クアーク
Shirley-Quirk, John 1291
シャリザット
Shahrizat, Abdul Jalil 1279
ジャリージュ
Jarrige, Jean Francois 665
シャリース
Charice 247
Charisse, Cyd 247
シャリス
Sharis, Peter J. 1282
シャリタ
Shalita, Zamir P. 1280
シャリッチ
Saric, Sandra 1242
シャリット
Shalit, Wendy 1279
Sharit, Joseph 1282
シャーリップ
Charlip, Remy 248
シャリーフ
Shareef, Adam 1282
Shareef, Mohamed Hussain 1282
al-Sharif, Ibrahim al-Zarouq 1282
al-Sharif, Saif 1282
Sherif, Ibrahim al-Zarug 1288
シャリフ
Charif, Maoulana 247
al-Sharif, Ali Hussein 1282
Sharif, Muhammad Safwat 1282
Sharif, Nawaz 1282
Sharif, Omar 1282
al-Sharif, Osman Omer 1282
シャリファ
Sharifa, bint Khalfan bin Nasser al-Yahya 1282
シャリフィ
Sharifi, Rashid 1282
al-Sharifi, Sawsan 1282
シャリフォフ
Sharifov, Abid 1282
Sharifov, Samir 1282
Sharifov, Sharif 1282
シャリフザデガン
Sharifzadegan, Mohammad Hossein 1282
シャリホフ
Sharifov, Abid 1282
Sharifov, Sharif 1282
シャリポフ
Sharipov, Khomidin 1282
Sharipov, Mirali 1282
ジャリム
Djalim, Ahmed Ali 359
ジャリリ
Jalili, Abolfazl 660
ジャリール
Jaleel, Mohamed 660
ジャリル
Jalil, Abdul 660
Jalil, Iskandar 660
シャーリーン
Charlene 247
シャリーン
Chaline, Eric 242
シャール
Shaar, Bashar 1277
シャル
Shull, Clifford Glenwood 1294
ジャール
Jarre, Maurice-Alexis 665
シャルヴィス
Shalvis, Jill 1280
シャルカウィ
el-Sharkawy, Ashraf 1282
シャルガフ
Chargaff, Erwin 247
シャルガム
Chelghoum, Abdesslam 251
Shalgam, Abdulrahman Mohamed 1279
ジャルガルサイハン
Jargalsaihan, Bazarsadyn 665
Jargalsaikhan, Chuluunbat 665
ジャルク
Zharku, Lutfi 1552
ジャルコ
Zharko, Vasily I. 1552
シャルシェケエワ
Sharshekeeva, Kamila 1283
シャールシッヒ
Scharsig, Marc 1249
シャルジュ
Salci, Nuray 1230
ジャルジュ
Jarju, Pa Ousman 665
ジャルジン
Jardim, Filipe 665
ジャルスキー
Jaroussky, Philippe 665
ジャルソ
Jarso, Yakob 665
シャルダン
Chardin, Germain 247
シャルチエ
Chartier, Roger 248
シャルチェビッチ
Šarčević, Mladen 1241
ジャルティ
Dzharty, Vasyl 386
シャルティエ
Chartier, Roger 248
ジャルディーノ
Giardino, Angelo P. 495
Giardino, Eileen R. 495
ジャルディム
Jardim, Leonardo 665
ジャルディン
Jardim, Maria De Fátima Domingos Monteiro 665
Jardim, Torquato 665
ジャルデウ
Jardel 665
シャルテガー
Schaltegger, Stefan 1249
シャルテッガー
Schaltegger, Stefan 1249
シーヤールトー
Szijjártó, Péter 1374
シャルトラン
Chartrand, Lili 248
シャルニ
Cherni, Majdouline 253
ジャルニッチ
Žarnić, Roko 1548
ジャルバウィ
Jarbawi, Ali 665
シャルパク
Charpak, Georges 248
シャルパック
Charpak, Georges 248
Charpak, Nathalie 248
シャルバン
Charbin, Alice 247
シャルピー
Charpy, Elisabeth 248
ジャルビス
Jarvis, Korey 666
シャルーブ
Shalhoub, Tony 1279
シャルブ
Charbe 247
シャルフィ
Charfi, Mohamed 247
シャルフ＝クニーマイヤー
Scharff-Kniemeyer, Marlis 1249
シャルベイ
Shalvey, Declan 1280
シャルベル
Charbel, Marwan 247
シャルボニエ
Charbonier, Jean-Jacques 247
ジャルポン
Jarupong, Ruangsuwan 665
シャルマ
Sarma, M.K. 1242

シ

Sharma, Anand 1282
Sharma, Dinanath 1282
Sharma, Ishwar Chandra 1282
Sharma, Janardan 1282
Sharma, Kuber Prasad 1282
Sharma, Mahesh 1282
Sharma, Neil 1282
Sharma, Rahul 1282
Sharma, Rekha 1283
Sharma, Ruchir 1283
Sharma, Vijay Kumar 1283
Sharma, Yubraj 1283

シャルマソン
Charmasson, Thérèse 248

シャルミラ
Sharmila, Irom 1283

シャルメッツ
Charmatz, Bill 248

シャルリー
Charly, Isabelle 248

シャルリエ
Charlier, Jean-Michel 248
Charlier, Philippe 248

シャルル
Charle, Christophe 247
Charles, Benoît 247

ジャ・ルール
Ja Rule 665

シャルル・ルー
Charles-Roux, Edmonde 248

シャルレス
Charles 247

シャルレーヌ
Charlene 247

シャルレーン公妃
Charlene 247

シャレ
Charest, Isabelle 247

ジャレ
Jallet, Christophe 660

シャレイラ
Shalala, Donna Edna 1279

シャレヴ
Shalev, Tseruyah 1279

ジャレオンセッタシン
Jareonsettasin, Teerakiat 665

シャレック
Shalleck, David 1280

ジャレット
Jarrett, Charles E. 665
Jarrett, Christian 665
Jarrett, Grady 665
Jarrett, Keith 665
Jarrett, Liz 665
Jarrett, Miranda 665

シャレーラ
Shalala, Donna Edna 1279

ジャレリ
Jalleli, Mokhtar 660

ジャレル
Jarrell, Randall 665

シャーレンベルク
Scharenberg, Lucy 1249

シャーロー
Sherrow, Victoria 1288

ジャロ
Diallo, Abdoulaye Daouda 350
Diallo, Ahmed el Madani 350
Diallo, N'Diaye Ramatoulaye 350
Diallo, Sambel Bana 350
Diallo, Tierno Amadou Omar Hass 350
Djalo, Tcherno 359
Jalloh, Abubakarr 660
Jalloh, Chernor 660

ジャロー
Jarrow, Gail 665

ジャロウ
Jallow, Lamin 660
Jallow, Sarjo 660
Jarreau, Al 665

シャロウェイ
Shalloway, Alan 1280

ジャロエンラタナタラコン
Jaroenrattanatarakoon, Prapawadee 665

シャーロック
Sherlock, Glenn 1288
Sherlock, Patti 1288
Sherlock, Sheila 1288

シャロック
Schalock, Robert L. 1249

シャーロット
Sharot, Tali 1283

ジャロット
Jarrott, Charles 665

ジャローテ
Jalote, P. 660

ジャロート
Jalote, P. 660

ジャロ・ナンディーニャ
Djaló Nandigna, Adiatu 359

シャロビッチ
Šarović, Mirko 1243

シャロフ
Shalof, Tilda 1280

シャロポワ
Sharopova, Nigina 1283

シャローム
Shalom, Silvan 1280
Sharom, Silvan 1283

シャロヤン
Sharoyan, Roland 1283

ジャロロフ
Jalolov, Bakhodir 660

シャーロン
Qiu, Xiaolong 1143

シャロン
Chaloner, John 243
Charon, Rita 248
Sharon, Ariel 1283
Sharon, Nathan 1283
Sharon, Rona 1283
Sharon, Thomas A. 1283

シャワ
Shawa, Abbie 1284

シャワーズ
Showers, Jameill 1293
Showers, Valdez 1293

ジャワド
Jawad, Salem al-Urayed 667

ジャワヒシビリ
Javakhishvili, Nodar 666

シャワマハ
Szałamacha, Paweł 1374

ジャワラ
Diawara, Cheickna Seydi Ahamady 351

シャン
Chang, Manuel 245
Shan, Darren 1280
Shan, Sa 1280

ジャン
Can, Emre 220
Chang, Dae-whan 245
Chang, Do-yeong 245
Chang, Song-taek 245
Chang, Ung 246
Chiang, Ping-kun 254
Djang, Sam 359
Jane, Ali 662
Jang, Kerry Leslie 663
Jean 667
Jean, Aurore 667
Jean, Corentin 667
Jean, Michaëlle 667
Jean, Olivier 667
Jean, Raymond 667
Jiang, Dao-ding 673
Jiang, Jason 673
Jiang, Jian-hua 673
Jiang, Qin-min 673
Jiang, Rong 673
Jiang, Shan Shan 673
Jiang, Ze-min 673
Zhang, Caroline 1551
Zhang, Cheng-zhi 1551
Zhang, Dan 1551
Zhang, Hao 1552
Zhang, Jing-chu 1552
Zhang, Lily 1552
Zhang, Wei-qing 1552
Zhang, Xin 1552

シャンカー
Shanker, Wendy 1281

ジャンガー
Janger, Edward J. 663

ジャンガバエフ
Djangabaev, Rustam 359

シャンガラ
Shanghala, Sacky 1280

シャンカリ
Shankari 1281

ジャンガリ
Jangali, Ali Ahmad Jama 663

シャンカール
Shankar, Anoushka 1280
Shankar, Ravi 1281

シャンカル
Shankar, Anoushka 1280
Shankar, Pandrangi 1280
Shankar, Ravi 1281

シャンキン
Sheinkin, Steve 1286

シャンク
Schank, Marco 1249
Schank, Roger C. 1249
Schank, Stefan 1249
Schunk, Dale H. 1261
Shank, Sam 1280

シャング
Shang, William 1280

シャンクス
Shanks, Alison 1281
Shanks, Hershel 1281
Shanks, John 1281

シャンクマン
Shankman, Adam 1281
Shankman, Peter 1281

シャンクラン
Shanklin, J.D. 1281

シャンクル
Shankle, William Rodman 1281

ジャングレコ
Giangreco, D.M. 494

ジャンクロー
Janklow, William John 663

シャンゲ
Change, Manuel 246

ジャン公
Jean, Duke of Nassau 667

ジャンコヴィック
Jankovic, J. 663

ジャンコウスキー
Jankowski, Jordan 663
Jankowski, Mark A. 663
Jankowski, Travis 663

ジャンコフ
Djankov, Simeon 359

ジャンコラ
Jeancolas, Claude 667

ジャンサンティ
Giansanti, Gianni 494

シャンシー
Chancy, Adeline Magloire 244

ジャンジェ
Jenger, Jean 669

ジャンジャック
Jean-jacques, Charles 667

シャンジュー
Changeux, Jean-Pierre 246

ジャンジュリアン
Jean-julien, Olsen 667

ジャンス
Jance, Judith A. 662

ジャンズ
Jans, Nick 664

ジャンスズ
Cansiz, Deniz 222

ジャンセン
Jansen, J.J. 664
Jansen, Kenley 664
Jansen, Larry 664
Jansen, Patti 664
Jansen, Steve 664
Janssen, Victoria 664
Janzen, Tara 664
Jensen, Muriel 671

ジャンゼン
Janzen, Daniel Hunt 664

ジャンセンス
Janssens, Jeroen 664

ジャンソン
Janson, Anthony F. 664
Janson, Horst Woldemar 664
Janson, Michael 664
Jeanson, Francis 668

ジャンソン‐ベルクリー
Janson-Bjerklie, Susan 664

ジャンダー
Jander, Mary 662

ジャン大公
Jean, Duke of Nassau 667

ジャン・チャールズ
Jean-charles, Livio 667

シャンツ
Schanz, Waldemar 1249

ジャンツ
Jantz, Caroline 664
Jantz, Gregory L. 664

ジャンツァン

Jantsan, Gantugs 664
ジャンツァンノロブ
Jantsannorov, Natsag 664
シャンデ
Chande, Isac 244
ジャンテ
Jeantet, Claude 668
Jeantet, Pierre 668
Jeantet, Thierry 668
ジャンティ
Gentil, Pascal 488
Genty, Philippe 489
Jeanty, Georges 668
シャンデルナゴール
Chandernagor, Françoise 244
シャントー
Shanteau, Eric 1281
シャンド
Shand, Bruce 1280
Shand, Hope 1280
ジャンドゥビ
Jendoubi, Kamel 669
シャンド・キッド
Shand Kydd, Frances 1280
シャンドキッド
Shand Kydd, Frances 1280
ジャンドソフ
Zhandosov, Uraz 1551
シャンドラ
Shandra, Volodimir 1280
シャンドール
Sándor, György 1237
ジャンナティ
Jannati, Ali 663
ジャンナン
Jeannin, Pierre 668
ジャンニーニ
Giannini, Frida 494
Giannini, Stefania 494
Jannini, Emmanuele A. 663
ジャンヌ・クロード
Jeanne-Claude 668
ジャンヌネー
Jeanneney, Jean-Noël 668
ジャンヌロー
Jeannerod, Marc 668
ジャンネッティ
Giannetti, Niccolo 494
シャンパ
Jampa, Lobsang 662
ジャンパオロ
Giampaolo, Marco 494
ジャンバキエフ
Zhambakiyev, Aziz 1551
シャンバーグ
Schanberg, Sydney 1249
ジャンパグリア
Giampaglia, Corinne 494
シャンパート
Shumpert, Iman 1294
シャンパーニュ
Champagne, François-Philippe 243
Champagne, Patrick 243
シャンバラピティヤ
Siyambalapitya, Ranjith 1309
ジャンバルドルジ
Zhambaldorzh, S. 1551
シャンパン
Champagne, Keith 243
ジャンバンコ
Giambanco, V.M. 494
ジャンピエトリ
Giampietri, Luis Alejandro Rojas 494
ジャンピエトリ・ロハス
Giampietri, Luis Alejandro Rojas 494
ジャンピエール
Jean-pierre, Joël Desrosiers 668
ジャンピノ
Giampino, Sylviane 494
ジャンビーン・ダシドンドグ
Jambyn Dashdondog 661
ジャンプ
Jump, Shirley 691
シャンペーン
Champagne, Delight 243
シャンボー
Shambaugh, David L. 1280
ジャーンボキ
Zsámboki, Károlyné 1558
シャンボス
Shambos, Alecos 1280
ジャンボゾルグ
Jambozorg, Mahlagha 661
ジャンポルスキー
Jampolsky, Gerald G. 662
ジャンホン
Jianghong, Chen 673
シャンマリ
al-Shammari, Ali 1280
al-Shammari, Hasan 1280
al-Shammari, Muhsin 1280
ジャンマリ
Jean-marie, Marie-Carmel 668
シャンムガム
Shanmugam, K. 1281
シャンムガラトナム
Shanmugaratnam, Tharman 1281
ジャンメール
Jeanmaire, Zizi 667
シャンリー
Shanley, Andrew 1281
Shanley, John Patrick 1281
Shanley, Mark T. 1281
シャンリィ
Shanley, Eamon 1281
Shanley, John Patrick 1281
シャンリイ
Shanley, John Patrick 1281
ジャンルイ
Jean-louis, Jean Fritz 667
Jean Louis, Robinson 667
シュ
Zhu, Xiao-mei 1553
シュー
Chew, Hélène 254
Choo, Leanne 259
Choux, Nathalie 260
Hsü, Kenneth Jinghwa 630
Hsu, Martha Russell 630
Hsu, S.T. 630
Scheu, Steven 1251
Schu, Rick 1259
Schuh, Angela 1259
Schuh, Berengere 1259
Shu, Howard 1294
Shue, Elizabeth 1294
Su, Bu-qing 1361
Xu, Chuanhua 1532
Xu, Huaiwen 1532
Xu, Jiayin 1532
Xu, Jing-lei 1532
Xu, Shihui 1532
Xu, Zhi-yong 1532
シユ
Xu, Hui-zhi 1532
ジュ
Zhu, Rong-ji 1553
Zhu, Yu-ling 1553
シューア
Schuur, Jeremiah 1261
シュア
Suhr, Jennifer 1363
シュアー
Shure, Myrna B. 1295
シュアティル
Shatil, Sharron 1283
ジュアノ
Jouanno, Chantal 688
ジュアリ
Jury, David 692
ジュアロー
Gjerlow, Kris 503
シュイ
Hsu, Shih-kai 630
Hsu, Shui-teh 630
Shuy, Tanya 1295
Xu, Chai-hou 1532
Xu, Cheng-gang 1532
Xu, Hui-zi 1532
Xu, Jia-tun 1532
Xu, Ke 1532
Xu, Si-min 1532
Xu, Xin 1532
Xu, Zhan-tang 1532
ジュイス・ロペス
Lluis Lopez 837
シュイーツ
Scheetz, Linda Jean 1250
シュイナード
Chouinard, Yvon 260
ジュイニ
Jouini, Mohamed Nouri 689
シュイル
Schuil, Rich 1259
シュウ
Schuh, Angela 1259
Zhou, Dong-yu 1553
ジュウ
Ju, Ming 689
シュヴァイガー
Schweiger, Til 1263
シュヴァイケルト
Schweikert, Ulrike 1263
シュヴァイスグート
Schweisgut, Hans Dietmar 1263
シュヴァイツァー
Schweitzer, Friedrich 1263
Schweitzer, Louis 1263
Schweizer, Christel 1263
Schweizer, Eduard 1263
Schweizer, Peter 1263
Schweizer, Rolf 1263
シュヴァイド
Schweid, Richard 1263
シュヴァイドラー
Schweidler, Walter 1263
シュヴァインシュタイガー
Schweinsteiger, Bastian 1263
シュヴァニツ
Schwanitz, Dietrich 1261
シュヴァーブ
Schwaab, Daniel 1261
シュヴァーベ
Schwabe, Christoph 1261
シュヴァラ
Chevallaz, Georges-Andre 254
シュヴァリエ
Chevalier, Jean-Marie 254
Chevalier, Louis 254
Chevalier, Tracy 254
Chevallier, Marielle 254
Chevallier, Raymond 254
シューヴァル
Sjöwall, Maj 1309
シュヴァルツ
Schwartz, Laurent 1262
Schwartz, Richard Evan 1262
Schwarz, Britta 1262
Schwarz, Friedhelm 1262
Schwarz, Karl M. 1262
Schwarz, Rudolf 1262
シュヴァルツェンバッハ
Schwarzenbach, Regula 1262
シュヴァルツェンベルク
Schwarzenberg, Karel 1262
シュヴァルツコップ
Schwarzkopf, Elisabeth 1262
Schwarzkopf, H. Norman 1262
シュヴァルツコップフ
Schwarzkopf, Elisabeth 1262
シュヴァルツコプ
Schwarzkopf, Elisabeth 1262
シュヴァルツコプフ
Schwarzkopf, Elisabeth 1262
シュヴァルベ
Schwalbé, Michel 1261
シュヴァンクマイエル
Švankmajer, Jan 1369
Švankmajerová, Eva 1369
シュヴァンドネル
Schwandner, Johann Georg von 1261
シュヴィエジ
Swierzy, Waldemar 1372
シュウィーゲル
Schwegel, Theresa 1263
シュヴィーゲル
Schwegel, Theresa 1263
シュヴィツゲベル
Schwizgebel, Georges 1263
シュヴィンニング
Schwinning 1263
シュウェイカ
Shweikeh, Majd 1295
シュヴェクラー
Schwegler, Pirmin 1263
シュウェーズィヒ
Schwesig, Manuela 1263
ジュウェット
Jewett, D.L. 672
シュヴェッペ
Schweppe, Ronald P. 1263

シ

シュヴェート
Schwedt, Elke 1263
Schwedt, Herbert 1263
シュウェドワ
Shvedova, Yaroslava 1295
シュヴェヌマン
Chevénement, Jean-Pierre 254
シュウェブリン
Schweblin, Samanta 1263
シュウェーベル
Schwoebel, François 1263
シュヴェルマー
Schwermer, Heidemarie 1263
シュウェンク
Schwenke, Brian 1263
シュヴェンクメッツガー
Schwenkmezger, Peter 1263
シュウェンゲル
Schwengel, Deborah 1263
シュヴェントカー
Schwentker, Wolfgang 1263
シュウォーツ
Schwarcz, Steven L. 1261
Schwartz, Anna Jacobson 1261
Schwartz, Jeffrey M. 1262
Schwartz, Leslie 1262
Schwartz, Marilyn 1262
Schwartz, Oded 1262
Schwartz, Tony 1262
Schwarz, Patrick 1262
シュウォルツ
Schwartz, Barry 1261
シュヴォロウ
Schwolow, Alexander 1263
シュヴレル
Chevrel, Yves 254
シュヴロー＝カンデル
Chevreau-Kandel, Clotilde 254
シュエ
Xue, Mu-qiao 1532
シュエイバー
Schwaber, Ken 1261
シュエット
Schuette, Sarah L. 1259
シュエブカ
Schwebke, Shobhana 1263
シュエ・マン
Shwe Mann 1295
シューエル
Sewell, Elizabeth 1276
ジューエル
Jewell, Malcolm Edwin 672
ジュエル
Jewell, Lisa 672
Jewell, Richard 672
Jewell, Sally 672
Jewell, Tyler 672
シュエンツェル
Schwentzel, Christian-Georges 1263
ジュオー
Jouhaud, Christian 689
シュオバー
Schober, Florian 1256
ジュガシヴィリ
Dzhugashvili, Galina 386
ジュガシビリ
Dzhugashvili, Galina 386
ジュガード
Sjuggerud, Steve 1309
ジュカトバ
Dukatova, Jana 379
ジュカノヴィチ
Djukanović, Milo 360
ジュカノヴィッチ
Djukanović, Milo 360
ジュカノビッチ
Djukanović, Milo 360
ĐUkanović, Milo 379
ジュガーノフ
Zyuganov, Gennadii Andreevich 1560
ジュガノフ
Zyuganov, Gennadii Andreevich 1560
シュガーマン
Sugarman, Joseph 1363
ジュガム
Jegham, Mohamed 669
シュガルト
Shughart, William F., Ⅱ 1294
シュカレオジュボルト
Škare Ožbolt, Vesna 1309
シュキイス
Šukys, Raimondas 1364
シュキス
Šukys, Raimondas 1364
ジュキッチ
Jukic, Dinko 690
Jukic, Mirna 690
ジュギッチ
Žugić, Radoje 1558
ジューキッチ・デヤノビッチ
Đukić-Dejanović, Slavica 379
シュー＝キャロル
Chu-Carroll, Mark C. 262
シューク
Chouk, Houcine 260
Shook, E.Victoria 1293
シュク
Choukou, Mahamat Ahmat 260
シュグ
Schug, John A. 1259
シュークヴィスト
Sjöqvist, Suzanne 1309
シュクヴォレツキー
Škvorecký, Josef 1311
ジュグノース
Jugnauth, Anerood 690
ジュグノート
Jugnauth, Anerood 690
Jugnauth, Ashock Kumar 690
Jugnauth, Pravind Kumar 690
Jungnauth, Anerood 691
シュクプトフ
Shukputov, Andar 1294
シュクボレツキー
Škvorecký, Josef 1311
シュクママトフ
Shykmamatov, Almambet 1295
シュクム
Shuqum, Nabih 1294
Shuqum, Said 1294
ジュグラリス
Giuglaris, Marcel 502
シュクリ
Shoukry, Sameh Hassan 1293
al-Shukri, Ali 1294
シュクリニアル
Skriniar, Milan 1311
シュクリン
Shuklin, Jevgenij 1294
シュクルテル
Skrtel, Martin 1311
シュクレティッチ
Škuletić, Sreten 1311
シュクロマハ
Škromach, Zdeněk 1311
シュクンドリッチ
Škundrić, Petar 1311
ジュゲ
Juguet, Eugene 690
シュケエフ
Shukeev, Umirzak 1294
シュケット
Chouket, Khaled 260
シューゲル
Schugel, A.J. 1259
シュケル
Suker, Davor 1363
Šuker, Ivan 1363
ジュコウスキー
Zhukouski, Aliaksandr 1553
ジューコフ
Jukov, Boris 690
Zhukov, Aleksandr Dmitreyevich 1553
ジュコフスキ
Ziolkowski, Szymon 1556
ジュコワ
Zhukova, Inna 1553
Zhukova, Natalia 1553
ジュサブ
Djoussab, Abba Koi 360
ジューシー・J
Juicy J 690
ジュジアーノ
Giusiano, Philippe 502
ジュジアノ
Giusiano, Philippe 502
シュシケヴィッチ
Shushkewich, Val 1295
シュシャコフ
Shushakov, Konstantin 1295
ジュジャルディン
Dujardin, Charlotte 379
シュシャン
Chouchan, Lionel 260
シュシュコフ
Chushcoff, Jennifer Preston 263
シュシュタリ
Shoushtari, Mohammad Esmail 1293
シュシュテルシッチ
Šušteršič, Janez 1368
ジュジュル
Žužul, Miomir 1559
シュジンスキー
Chudzinski, Daniela 262
ジュース
Gius, Nicole 502
Suss, Esther 1368
ジュースキント
Suskind, Patrick 1368
シュスター
Schuster, Dirk 1261
Schuster, Julian 1261
Schuster, Marco 1261
Schuster, Robert 1261
シュスターマン
Schusterman, Lynn 1261
Shusterman, Richard 1295
シュスタル
Šustar, Predrag 1368
ジュスチノ
Justino, David 693
シュステル
Schuster, Rudolf 1261
ジューステン
Joosten, Kathryn 686
ジュスポフ
Zhussupov, Ablaikhan 1553
シュスラー
Schuessler, Deane L. 1259
Schüssler, Werner 1261
ジュスリン
Juslin, Patrik N. 692
ジュソ
Jousso, Théodore 689
ジューダ
Judah, Tim 690
シュタイア
Shteir, Rachel 1294
シュタイアー
Staier, Andreas 1339
シュタイガー
Steiger, Brad 1345
Steiger, Lothar 1345
Steiger, Otto 1345
Steiger, Sherry Hansen 1345
シュタイナー
Steiner, Bradley J. 1346
Steiner, Donald 1346
Steiner, Gerhard 1346
Steiner, John 1346
Steiner, Jörg 1346
Steiner, Matthias 1346
Steiner, Reinhard A. 1346
Steinherr, Marlene 1346
シュタイナッハー
Steinacher, Hans Peter 1345
シュタイナート
Steinert, Yvonne 1346
シュタイニッツ
Steinitz, Yuval 1346
シュタイネケ
Steineke, Inge 1346
シュタイン
Stein, Clifford 1345
Stein, David Ezra 1345
Stein, Dietrich 1345
Stein, Horst 1345
Stein, Ingeborg 1345
Stein, Peter 1345
Stein, Wolfram 1345
シュタインガート
Shteyngart, Gary 1294
シュタインガルト
Steingart, Andrea 1346

シュタインカンプ
Steinkamp, Norbert 1346
シュタイングルーバー
Steingruber, Giulia 1346
シュタイングレス
Steingress, Gerhard 1346
シュタインドルフ
Steindorf, Eberhard 1346
シュタインバッハー
Steinbacher, Arabella Miho 1345
シュタインブリュック
Steinbrück, Peer 1346
シュタインヘーフェル
Steinhöfel, Andreas 1346
シュタインホフ
Steinhoff, Janusz 1346
シュタインマイヤー
Steinmeier, Frank-Walter 1346
シュタインマン
Steinmann, Brigitte 1346
Steinmann, Lothar 1346
シュタインミューラー
Steinmüller, Angela 1346
Steinmüller, Karlheinz 1346
シュタインメッツ
Steinmetz, Ina 1346
Steinmetz, Karl-Heinz 1346
シュタヴィンスキー
Stawinski, Gregor 1343
シュタウダー
Stauder, Thomas 1343
シュタウダッハー
Staudacher, Patrick 1343
シュタウダハー
Staudacher, Patrick 1343
シュタゥディンガー
Staudinger, Eduard 1343
シュタウファー
Staufer, Marijan von 1343
シュタウフェンベルク
Stauffenberg, Nina von 1343
シュターク
Stark, Niklas 1342
シュタグーン
Staguhn, Gerhard 1339
シュターケ
Starke, Tom 1342
シュターツ
Staats, Imke 1338
シュタットフェルト
Stadtfeld, Martin 1339
シュタドラー
Stadler, Franz 1338
Stadler, Rosemarie 1339
ジュタヌガーン
Jutanugarn, Ariya 693
シュタノバツ
Šutanovac, Dragan 1368
シュタヘリ
Staeheli, Erwin 1339
シュタム
Stamm, Peter 1340
シュタール
Ståhl, Ingolf 1339
Stahl, Linda 1339
シュタルク
Stark, Holger 1341
シュタルケ
Starke, Andrasch 1342
シュタルケル
Starker, János 1342
ジュタン
Jetin, Bruno 672
シュタンツェライト
Stanzeleit, Barbara 1341
シュタンツェル
Stanzel, Volker 1341
シュタンツロヴァー
Štanclová, Kamila 1340
シュタンブク
Stambuk, Drago 1340
シュチェスニー
Szczesny, Wojciech 1374
シュチェパンスキ
Szczepanski, Piotr 1374
シュチェルバツェビッチ
Shcherbatsevich, Yury 1285
シュチグウォ
Szczygło, Aleksander 1374
シュチャルバチェニナ
Shcharbachenia, Stanislau 1285
シュチュレク
Szczurek, Mateusz 1374
シューツ
Shutes, Jeanne 1295
シュック
Shook, John 1293
Shook, Robert L. 1293
ジュック
Manyang Juuk, Kuol 898
シュッサー
Schusser, Adelbelt 1261
ジュッサーニ
Giussani, Luigi 502
シュッセル
Schüssel, Wolfgang 1261
シュッツ
Schutz, Bernard F. 1261
Schütz, Karl 1261
Schütz, Klaus 1261
Schutz, Sue 1261
Schutz, Susan Polis 1261
Schütz, Violaine 1261
Schutz, Will 1261
シュッツェ
Schütze, Sebastian 1261
シュッテ
Schütte, Thomas 1261
シュッティング
Schutting, Jutta (Julian) 1261
シュットペーダセン
Schjøtt-pedersen, Karl Eirik 1253
シュットラー
Schuttler, Rainer 1261
ジュッペ
Juppé, Alain Marie 692
ジュッポーニ
Giupponi, Matteo 502
ジュデ
Jude, Radu 690
Judeh, Nasser 690
シュテア
Stoehr, Hans-Joachim Alois 1353
ジュディ
Djoudi, Karim 360
Jeudy, Henri-Pierre 672
ジユーディ
al-Zeyoudi, Thani bin Ahamed 1551
シュティーガー
Stieger, Roland 1351
シュティガー
Styger, Nadia 1361
シュティーグラー
Stiegler, Bernd 1352
シュティーケル
Stiekel, Bettina 1352
ジューディージェイ
Giudice, Christian 502
ジュディース
Giudice, Maria 502
ジュディチェ
Giudice, Gaspare 502
シュティッヒ
Stich, Otto 1351
シュティバル
Stybar, Zdenek 1361
シュティヒテノス
Stichtenoth, Henning 1351
シュデイファト
Shdeifat, Omar 1285
シュティメツ
Stimec, Spomenka 1352
シュティーメルト
Stiemert, Elisabeth 1352
シュティンドル
Stindl, Lars 1352
ジュデオン
Gedeon, Mickaëlle Amëdée 486
シュテーガー
Steger, Jim 1344
Stöger, Alios 1353
Stoger, Peter 1353
シュデク
Siudek, Mariusz 1308
シュテークマン
Steegmann, Monica 1343
Stegmann, Matthias von 1344
シュテーゲマン
Stegemann, Michael 1344
シュテッカー
Stöcker, Horst 1353
シュテック
Steck, Brigitte 1343
シュテッフェン
Steffen, Renato 1344
シュテッフゲン
Steffgen, Georges 1344
シュテナー
Stenner, Chris 1347
シュテヒャー
Stecher, Mario 1343
シュテフェリング
Steveling, Angelika 1349
シュテフェン
Steffen, Benjamin 1344
Steffen, Britta 1344
シュテーブナー
Stewner, Tanya 1351
シュテープラー
Staebler, Gabriela 1339
シュテプラー
Staebler, Frank 1339
シュテブラー
Stabler, Frank 1338
シュテュルマー
Stuermer, Michael 1361
シュテーリ
Staehli, Gregor 1339
シュテーリク
Stehlik, Henrik 1344
シュテール
Stier, Davor Ivo 1352
シュテルク
Sterk, Wolfgang 1348
シュテルバ
Sterba, Jan 1348
シュテルマー
Störmer, Horst Ludwig 1355
シュテルン
Stern, Carola 1348
Stern, Klaus 1348
シュテルンベルク
Sternberg, Janek 1349
Sternberg, Thomas 1349
シュテンガー
Stenger, Christiane 1347
シュテンツェル
Stenzel, Pascal 1347
シュテンデラ
Stendera, Marc 1347
シュテンベルガー
Stemberger, Günter 1347
シュテンメ
Stemme, Nina 1347
シュート
Sciutto, Jim 1263
Shute, Chris 1295
Shute, Nancy 1295
Shute, Valerie J. 1295
シュト
Schut, Henk 1261
ジュート
Jute, Andre 693
シュトイアナーゲル
Steuernagel, Ulla 1349
シュトイケンス
Teunckens, Jens 1393
シュトイデ
Steude, Volkhard 1349
シュトゥーアマン
Stuhrmann, Jochen 1361
シュトゥッキ
Stucki, Alfred 1361
シュトゥッツァー
Stutzer, Beat 1361
シュトゥッツマン
Stutzmann, Nathalie 1361
シュトゥッピー
Stuppy, Wolfgang 1361
シュトゥデント
Student, Johann-Christoph 1361
シュトゥムペ
Stumpe, Jens 1361
シュトゥラドゥヴィク
Strudwick, Leslie 1360
シュトゥラノビッチ
Štranović, Željko 1357
シュトゥルツィナ
Struzyna, Peter 1360
シュトゥルーベ
Strube, Jürgen Friedrich 1360

シュトゥールマッハー
Stuhlmacher, Peter 1361
シュトゥルム
Šturm, Lovro 1361
シュトゥンプ
Stumpf, Axel 1361
Stumpf, Cordula 1361
シュトカロフ
Shtokalov, Ilia 1294
シュトーケンベルグズ
Štokenbergs, Aigars 1353
シュトケンベルクス
Štokenbergs, Aigars 1353
シュトッカー
Stocker, Valentin 1353
シュトックシュトルム
Stockstrom, Christoph 1353
シュトックハウゼン
Stockhausen, Karlheinz 1353
シュトッドダルト
Stoddart, Greg L. 1353
シュトッヒャー
Stocher, Franz 1352
シュドネス
Sydnes, Anne Kristin 1373
シュトライヒ
Streich, Christian 1358
シュトラインツ
Streinz, Rudolf 1358
シュトラウス
Strauss, Botho 1357
Strauss, David 1357
Strauss, Robert Schwarz 1357
シュトラウプ
Straub, Eberhard 1357
シュトラスナー
Straszner, Erich 1357
シュトラッサー
Strasser, Ernst 1357
Strasser, Johano 1357
シュトラノヴィッチ
Šturanović, Željko 1361
シュトラノビッチ
Šturanović, Željko 1361
シュトラール
Zdral, Wolfgang 1549
シュトリーディンガー
Striedinger, Otmar 1358
シュトール
Storl, David 1355
シュトルジック
Struzik, Edward 1360
シュトルツ
Stolz, Alexander 1354
Strutz, Martina 1360
シュトルック
Struck, Peter 1360
シュトルテンベルク
Stoltenberg, Gerhard 1354
Stoltenberg, Jens 1354
Stoltenberg, Thorvald 1354
シュトルテンベルグ
Stoltenberg, Jens 1354
Stoltenberg, Thorvald 1354
シュトルーベ
Strube, Jürgen Friedrich 1360
シュトルベ
Strube, Jürgen Friedrich 1360
シュトルペ
Stolpe, Manfred 1354
シュトルベック
Storbeck, Olaf 1355
シュトルム
Sturm, Erdmann 1361
Sturm, Pater Georg 1361
シュトルル
Storl, Wolf-Dieter 1355
シュトレイス
Stolleis, Michael 1354
シュトレーク
Streeck, Wolfgang 1357
シュトレビンガー
Strobinger, Rudolf 1359
シュトレープ
Straeb, Hermann 1356
Streb, Jochen 1357
シュトレーベ
Stroebe, Margaret S. 1359
Stroebe, Wolfgang 1359
シュトレールヴィッツ
Streeruwitz, Marlene 1357
シュトレルケ
Strehlke, Bernt 1358
シュトレーロフ
Strehlow, Wighard 1358
シュトロー・エンゲル
Stroh-engel, Dominik 1359
シュトロシェンルーサー
Strössenreuther, Roman H.K. 1359
シュトロッカ
Strocka, Volker Michael 1359
シュトロハイム
Stroheim, Josef von 1359
シュトロバッハ
Strobach, Susanne 1359
シュトローブル
Strobl, Tobias 1359
シュトロブル
Strobl, Fritz 1359
シュトローベル
Strobel, Margaret 1359
シュトローム
Strohm, Christoph 1359
シュトワ
Shutova, Lyubov 1295
ジュードン
Judon, Matt 690
シュトンプフ
Stumpf, István 1361
ジュナー
Junor, Amy 692
シュナイアー
Schneier, Bruce 1256
Schneier, Franklin R. 1256
シュナイアソン
Shnayerson, Michael 1292
シュナイウィンド
Schneewind, Jerome B. 1255
シュナイダー
Schneider, Anton 1256
Schneider, Arthur S. 1256
Schneider, Brian 1256
Schneider, Catherine Chemin 1256
Schneider, Christine 1256
Schneider, David 1256
Schneider, Dieter 1256
Schneider, Dirk 1256
Schneider, Dorothee 1256
Schneider, Elaine Ernst 1256
Schneider, Étienne 1256
Schneider, Fred 1256
Schneider, Fred B. 1256
Schneider, F.Wesley 1256
Schneider, Gregor 1256
Schneider, Hans 1256
Schneider, Helga 1256
Schneider, Jakob 1256
Schneider, Jeremy 1256
Schneider, John 1256
Schneider, John C. 1256
Schneider, Joseph W. 1256
Schneider, Konstantin 1256
Schneider, Manfred 1256
Schneider, Maria 1256
Schneider, Markus 1256
Schneider, Marv 1256
Schneider, Norbert 1256
Schneider, Othmar 1256
Schneider, Peter 1256
Schneider, Reinhard 1256
Schneider, Reto U. 1256
Schneider, Richard Harold 1256
Schneider, Rob 1256
Schneider, Robert 1256
Schneider, Rolf 1256
Schneider, Romain 1256
Schneider, Sherrie 1256
Schneider, Stephan 1256
Schneider, Stephen Henry 1256
Schneider, Steven Jay 1256
Schneider, Wolf 1256
Schneider, Wolfgang 1256
Snider, Stacey 1321
Snyder, Carolyn 1322
Snyder, Chris 1322
Snyder, Garth 1322
Snyder, Gary Sherman 1322
シュナイダーアマン
Schneider-ammann, Johann 1256
シュナイダース
Schneiders, Werner 1256
シュナイダーハインツェ
Schneiderheinze, Anja 1256
シュナイダーハーン
Schneiderhan, Wolfgang 1256
シュナイダーハン
Schneiderhan, Wolfgang 1256
シュナイダーマン
Schnaeiderman, Jill 1255
Shneiderman, Ben 1292
シュナイダーワイン
Snyderwine, Elizabeth G. 1322
シュナイデルラン
Schneiderlin, Morgan 1256
シュナイト
Schneidt, Hans-Martin 1256
シュナイドマン
Shneidman, Edwin S. 1292
シュナイユ
Chenaille, Louis 252
シュナウベルト
Schnaubelt, Kurt 1255
シュナーズ
Schnaars, Steven P. 1255
ジュナス
Duenas, Crispin 378
シュナーチ
Schnarch, David Morris 1255
シュナブル
Schnabl, Philipp 1255
シュナーベル
Schnabel, Julian 1255
シュナペール
Schnapper, Dominique 1255
シュナル
Chenal, Joel 252
シュニー
Schnee, Samantha 1255
ジュニ
Juni, Fuád Issa 691
ジュニア
Junior, Larry S. 692
ジュニオール
Junior, Fernando 692
Junior, Josh 692
Junior, Justin Morel 692
Júnior, Manuel Nunes 692
Neymar 1019
ジュニダル
Žnidar, Vesna Györkös 1556
ジュニッチ
Zunic, Stipe 1559
シュニッペンケッター
Schnippenkoetter, Beatrix 1256
ジュニーニョ・ペルナンブカノ
Juninho Pernambucano 692
ジュヌ
Geneus, Jean 488
シュヌーアバイン
Schnurbein, Stefanie V. 1256
ジュヌソフ
Junusov, Beyshenbay 692
Zhunusov, Ibragim 1553
ジュヌフォール
Genefort, Laurent 488
シュヌール
Schnur, Leslie 1256
シュヌレ
Schnurre, Wolfdietrich 1256
ジュネ
Jeunet, Jean-Pierre 672
シュネイダー
Schneider, Antoon 1256
シュネーヴァイス
Schneeweiss, Suzan 1255
ジュネジョ
Junejo, Khair Muhammad 691
ジュネット
Genette, Gérard 488
ジュネディン
Junedin, Sado 691
シュネデール
Schneider, Michel 1256

シ

シュネーデルバッハ
Schnädelbach, Herbert 1255
シュネビッチ
Shunevich, Igor A. 1294
シュネーベルガー
Schneeberger, Guido 1255
シューネマン
Schünemann, Bernd 1261
ジュネユス
Geneus, Jean 488
ジュネル
Jounel, Pierre 689
ジューノ
Junor, Penny 692
ジュノー
Junor, John 692
Junor, Penny 692
シューノーヴァー
Schoonover, Carl E. 1258
ジュバイエアバゼヌ
Djoubaye Abazène, Arnaud 360
シュハイエブ
Shuhayeb, Akram 1294
シュバイガー
Schwaiger, Doris 1261
Schwaiger, Stefanie 1261
Schweiger, Til 1263
シュパイザー
Speiser, David 1334
シュハイゼ
Chkhaidze, Giorgi 257
シュバイツァー
Schweitzer, Louis 1263
Schweizer, Andreas 1263
シュバイツェル
Schweitzer, Louis 1263
シュパイデル
Speidel, Manfred 1334
ジュハイミ
al-Juhaimi, Al-Tahir al-Hadi 690
シュバインシュタイガー
Schweinsteiger, Bastian 1263
ジュハス
Juhasz, Antonia 690
シュバーツァー
Schwazer, Alex 1263
シューバック
Shuback, Alan 1294
シューハート
Schuchardt, Erika 1259
シューバート
Schubert, Karl D. 1259
Schubert, Stephen 1259
シュハード
Schuchard, Ronald 1259
シュバート
Schubert, Karsten 1259
シュパード
Shepherd, Rebecca M. 1288
ジュバニッチ
Zbanic, Jasmila 1549
Žuvanić, Roland 1559
シュバラ
Chevallaz, Georges-Andre 254
ジュバラ
Jbara, Gregory 667
シュバリエ
Chevalier, Roger 254
Chevalier, Tracy 254
ジュパリッチ
Zuparic, Dario 1559
ジュハル・スタント
Djuhar Sutanto 360
シュバルツァンベルグ
Schwartzenberg, Roger-Gérard 1262
シューハルト
Schuchardt, Erika 1259
シュパルン
Sparn, Walter 1333
シュパン
Spang, Stefan 1333
シュパンク
Spank, Raul-Roland 1333
シュバンクマイエル
Švankmajer, Jan 1369
シュパングラー
Spangler, David 1333
ジュパンチッチ
Zupancic, Alenka 1559
シュパンバウアー
Spannbauer, Christa 1333
シュヒー
al-Shuhi, Ahmed bin Abdullah bin Mohammed 1294
シュービガー
Schubiger, Jürg 1259
シュピーグラー
Spiegler, Julie 1335
シュピーゲル
Spiegel, David A. 1335
Spiegel, Dixie Lee 1335
Spiegel, Evan 1335
Spiegel, Raphael 1335
シュピーゲルブルク
Spiegelburg, Silke 1335
シュピッツ
Spitz, Sabine 1336
シュピッツァー
Spitzer, Manfred 1336
シュピッツバート
Spitzbart, Michael 1336
シュビトコイ
Shvydkoi, Mikhail Y. 1295
シュピドラ
Spidla, Vladimír 1335
シュピネン
Spinnen, Burkhard 1336
シュピヒティク
Spichtig, Lou 1335
ジュヒリ
Jughli, Ahed 690
シュピリッチ
Špirić, Nikola 1336
シュピールベルガー
Spielberger, Walter J. 1336
シュピールベルク
Spielberg, Christoph 1335
シュピールマン
Spielmann, Yvonne 1336
シュピーレ
Broring-sprehe, Kristina 187
シュービン
Shubin, Mikhail Aleksandrovich 1294
Shubin, Neil 1294
シュピンデルエッガー
Spindelegger, Michael 1336
シュビーンバッハー
Schwienbacher, Freddy 1263
シュビンバハー
Schwienbacher, Freddy 1263
シューブ
Schupp, Werner 1261
Shupe, Joanna 1294
シュフ
Shuff, Jeremiah 1294
ジューブ
Dziub, Ivan 386
Dzyub, Ivan 386
ジュブ
Jouve, Sebastien 689
ジュファ
Jouffa, Susie 688
ジュファン
Gefen, Gérard 486
シューフェルト
Shewfelt, Kyle 1289
ジュフュレ
Zufferey, Daniel 1558
シュプーラー
Spuhler, Gregor 1337
ジュフリー
Giuffre, Jimmy 502
ジュブリ
al-Jubouri, Qutaibah 690
ジュフリダ
Giuffrida, Odette 502
シュフリッチ
Shufrych, Nestor 1294
シュプリンガー
Springer, Peter 1337
シュプルギ - ガンテルト
Spirgi-Gantert, Irene 1336
シュプルリェ
Šprlje, Ante 1337
シュプレー
Sprehe, Kristina 1337
シュプレンガー
Sprenger, Peter 1337
シュプレンガルト
Sprengard, Karl Anton 1337
ジュフロタン
Geffrotin, Thierry 486
ジュペ
Juppé, Alain Marie 692
シュペーア
Speer, Albert 1334
ジュベイル
Jubeir, Adel 690
シュベゼール
Schweitzer, Louis 1263
シュベーヌマン
Chevénement, Jean-Pierre 254
シュベヌマン
Chevénement, Jean-Pierre 254
シュペヒト
Specht, Theresa 1333
シュペーマン
Spaemann, Robert 1332
ジュベリ
Xhuveli, Lufter 1531
ジュベール
Joubert, Beverly 688
Joubert, Brian 688
Joubert, Dereck 688
シュペルツ
Speltz, Alexander 1334
シューベルト
Schobert, Joe 1256
Schubert, Andre 1259
Schubert, Dieter 1259
Schubert, E.Fred 1259
Schubert, Ernst 1259
Schubert, Ingrid 1259
Schubert, Klaus 1259
Schubert, Margaret 1259
Schubert, Pit 1259
シュペルバー
Sperber, Manès 1335
シュベンク
Schwenk, Theodor 1263
ジュボガール
Žbogar, Samuel 1549
シュポタコヴァ
Spotakova, Barbora 1337
シュポタコバ
Spotakova, Barbora 1337
シュポラル
Sporar, Andraz 1337
シュポンホルツ
Sponholz, Volker 1337
シューマー
Schumer, Chuck 1261
ジュマ
Juma, Abdalla Tiya 691
Juma, Marwan 691
Juma, Omar Ali 691
ジュマー
al-Jumaa, Jumaa bin Ali 691
シュマイケル
Schmeichel, Kasper 1254
シュマイジンスキ
Szmajdziński, Jerzy 1374
シュマイドラー
Schmeidler, David 1254
ジュマイリ
Jumaili, Rassim 691
al-Jumaili, Salman 691
al-Jumayli, Abdul-Karim 691
ジュマウツ
Žmavc, Gorazd 1556
ジュマガリエフ
Zhumagaliev, Askar 1553
ジュマグルイエフ
Jumaguliev, Ovliyaguly 691
ジュマグロフ
Zhumagulov, Bakytzhan 1553
シューマッカー
Schumacher, Joel 1260
Schumacher, Thomas 1260
シュマッカー
Schumacher, Joel 1260
シュマッチャー
Schumacher, Joel 1260
シューマッハ
Schumacher, Michael 1260
シューマッハー
Schumacher, Lori 1260
Schumacher, Michael 1260
ジュマベコフ
Zhumabekov, Onalsyn 1553

シ

Zhumabekov, Sabyr 1553
シュマラツ
Šumarac, Dragoslav 1365
ジュマリエフ
Zhumaliyev, Kubanychbek 1553
シュマルツ
Schmalz, Klaus 1254
シュマルフス
Schmalfuss, Conny 1254
シューマン
Schouman, Michel 1258
Schuman, Michael 1260
Schuman, Michael H. 1260
Schuman, Scott 1260
Schumann, Charles 1260
Schumann, Erik 1260
Schumann, Peter B. 1260
Schumann, Ralf 1261
Shuman, Carol 1294
Shuman, George D. 1294
Shuman, Michael 1294
Szuchman, Paula 1375
シュマン
Schumann, Sascha 1261
ジュマン
Geman, Hélyette 488
シュマン=アンテルム
Schumann-Antelme, Ruth 1261
シュマント
Schmandt, Chris 1254
シュマント=ベッセラ
Schmandt-Besserat, Denise 1254
シュミッツ
Schmitz, Anthony 1255
Schmitz, Benno 1255
Schmitz, Helene 1255
Schmitz, Jerry 1255
Schmitz, Martin 1255
Schmitz, Thomas J. 1255
シュミット
Schaudt, Martin 1250
Schmid, Andre 1254
Schmid, Daniel 1254
Schmid, Gary Bruno 1254
Schmid, Hanspeter 1254
Schmid, Helmut 1254
Schmid, Matthias 1254
Schmid, Michael 1254
Schmid, Samuel 1254
Schmid, Sil 1254
Schmid, Thamas 1254
Schmid, Wilfried 1254
Schmidt, Alfred 1254
Schmidt, André 1254
Schmidt, Andy 1254
Schmidt, Brian P. 1254
Schmidt, Bruno 1254
Schmidt, Carolina 1254
Schmidt, Chris 1254
Schmidt, Christian 1254
Schmidt, Christophe 1254
Schmidt, Chrystina 1254
Schmidt, Colton 1254
Schmidt, David 1254
Schmidt, Douglas C. 1254
Schmidt, Dylan 1254
Schmidt, Eric E. 1254
Schmidt, Eric von 1254
Schmidt, Gary D. 1254
Schmidt, Hans 1254
Schmidt, Hans Christian 1254
Schmidt, Harvey 1254
Schmidt, Helmut 1254
Schmidt, Jean 1254
Schmidt, Jeff von der 1254
Schmidt, J.Eric 1254
Schmidt, Joe 1254
Schmidt, Kim 1254
Schmidt, Louis A. 1254
Schmidt, M. 1255
Schmidt, Martin 1255
Schmidt, Michael 1255
Schmidt, Otto 1255
Schmidt, Peter 1255
Schmidt, Rainer 1255
Schmidt, Renate 1255
Schmidt, Richard 1255
Schmidt, Robert F. 1255
Schmidt, Roger 1255
Schmidt, Romy 1255
Schmidt, Stanley 1255
Schmidt, Suzanne 1255
Schmidt, Thomas 1255
Schmidt, Ulla 1255
Schmidt, Ulrike 1255
Schmidt, Warren H. 1255
Schmidt, Wendy 1255
Schmidt, Werner H. 1255
Schmit, Nicolas 1255
Schmitt, Al 1255
Schmitt, Allison 1255
Schmitt, Bernd 1255
Schmitt, Betsy 1255
Schmitt, Charles B. 1255
Schmitt, Christopher 1255
Schmitt, C.W. 1255
Schmitt, Donald R. 1255
Schmitt, Eric-Emmanuel 1255
Schmitt, Jean Claude 1255
Schmitt, Martin 1255
Schmitt, Pál 1255
Smidt, Sandra 1314
Smit, Heinrich 1314
Smit, Henk 1314
シュミッド
Schmid, Bernhard M. 1254
Schmid, Jonathan 1254
Schmid, Paul 1254
シュミット - アスマン
Schmidt-Assmann, Eberhard 1255
シュミット・ニールセン
Schmidt-Nielsen, Knut 1255
シュミットハイニー
Schmidheiny, Stephan 1254
シュミット=パンテル
Schmitt-Pantel, Pauline 1255
シュミット=ブレーク
Schmidt-Bleek, F. 1255
シュミット - レーガー
Schmidt-Röger, Heike 1255
シュミーデル
Schmidl, Peter 1254
シュミート
Schmid, Konrad 1254
Schmied, Claudia 1255
Schmied, Wieland 1255
シュミード
Schmied, Claudia 1255
シュミド
Schmid, Samuel 1254
シュミドバ
Smidova, Lenka 1314
シュミードル
Schmidl, Peter 1254
シュミラス
Szumilas, Krystyna 1375
シュミール
Schmirl, Alexander 1255
シュミル
Smil, Vaclav 1314
シュミンケ
Schmincke, Hans-Ulrich 1255
シューム
Schumm, Bruce A. 1261
シュムスキー
Shumsky, Susan G. 1294
シュムラー
Schmuller, Joseph 1255
シュムル
Shmull, Temmy 1292
ジュムール
Dzumhur, Damir 386
シューメイカー
Shoemaker, Matt 1292
Shoemaker, Willie 1292
シュメイカー
Schumaker, Ward 1260
シュメイユ
Schemeil, Yves 1251
シューメーカー
Schoemaker, Paul J. H. 1257
Shoemaker, Willie 1292
Shumaker, Millard 1294
シューメーク
Shewmake, Carrol Johnson 1289
シュメクネロバ
Schmögnerová, Brigita 1255
シュメーケル
Schmoeckel, Mathias 1255
シュメチョ
Shymechko, Ihor 1295
シュメディンシュ
Smedins, Janis 1314
シュメリング
Schmeling, Max 1254
シュメルツァー
Schmelzer, Marcel 1254
シュモー
Schmoe, Floyd 1255
ジュモー
Jumeau, Ronald 691
Jumeau, Ronny 691
シュモイシュ
Shmoys, David Bernard 1292
シュモウスカ
Szumowska, Małgorzata 1375
ジュモー=ラフォン
Jumeau-Lafond, Jean-David 691
シュモルト
Schmoldt, Hans 1255
シューラ
Shula, Mike 1294
シューラー
Schuerer, Doris 1259
Schüler, Bernhard 1259
Schuler, Candace 1260
Schüler, Jörg 1260
Schuller, Gunther 1260
シュラー
Schüler, Chris 1260
Schuller, Florian 1260
Schuller, Gunther 1260
Schuller, Robert Harold 1260
Shuler, Miles 1294
ジュライ
Gyulai, Istvan 550
July, Miranda 691
July, William 691
シュライアー
Schreyer, Paul 1259
Schrier, Robert W. 1259
シュライヴァー
Schrijvers, Joep P.M. 1259
Shriver, Lionel 1294
Shriver, Robert, Jr. 1294
シュライエック
Schreijäck, Thomas 1258
シュライナー
Schreiner, Andrea Streit 1259
Schreiner, Emily 1259
Schreiner, Klaus 1259
Schreiner, Peter 1259
Shreiner, Dave 1294
シュライバー
Schreiber, Ellen 1258
Schreiber, Georg 1258
Schreiber, Hermann 1258
Schreiber, Joe 1258
Schreiber, Liev 1258
Shriver, Duward F. 1294
Shriver, Eunice Kennedy 1294
Shriver, Robert, Jr. 1294
シュライヒ
Schlaich, Jörg 1253
Schlaich, Mike 1253
シュライヒャー
Schlegelmilch, Rainer W. 1253
Schleicher, Andreas 1253
シュライファー
Shleifer, Scott 1292
シュライフォーゲル
Schraivogel, Ralph 1258
シュライム
Shlaim, Avi 1292
Shuraim, Eizi 1294
シュライヤー
Schreyer, William Allen 1259
シュラウザー
Schrauzer, Gerhard N. 1258
ジュラヴリョフ
Zhuravlev, Andrey Yu 1553
ジュラエフ
Dzhurayev, Turobzhon 386
Juraev, Sherali 692
Juraev, Turobjon 692
Jurayev, Hairulla 692
Jurayev, Risboy 692
シュラカ
Sraka, Rasa 1338
シュラキ
Chouraqui, André 260
シュラーゲ
Schrage, Wolfgang 1258
シュラーゲンハイム
Schragenheim, Eli 1258
シューラー=シュプリンゴ

ルム
Schüler-Springorum, Horst 1260
シュラーズ
Schreurs, Miranda Alice 1259
シュラッツ
Schratz, Paul R. 1258
シュラットー
Suratteau, Daniel 1367
シュラッファー
Schlaffer, Heinz 1253
シュラーノワ
Shuranova, Antonina 1294
シュラノワ
Shuranova, Antonina 1294
シュラハ
Shlah, Miyassar Rijab 1292
ジュラフコフ
Zhuravkov, Mihail A. 1553
ジュラフスキー
Jurafsky, Dan 692
シュラーペ
Schrape, Klaus 1258
シュラミアク
Szramiak, Krzysztof 1375
シューラム
Schramm, Tex 1258
シュラム
Schlamme, Thomas 1253
Schram, Martin 1258
Schram, Stuart R. 1258
Schramm, Carl 1258
Schramm, Carl J. 1258
Schramm, Tex 1258
Schramm, Wilbur 1258
Shrum, Sandy 1294
Shulam, Joseph 1294
ジュラン
Jeuland, Pascale 672
シュランガー
Schlanger, Karin 1253
Schlanger, Melanie 1253
シュランク
Schlank, Anita 1253
シュラングセンピ王子
Prince Hlangusemphi 610
シュランメ
Schramme, Thomas 1258
シュリ
Chouly, Damien 260
シュリー
Schley, Sara 1253
Schlie, Tania 1253
ジュリー
Julie, Bruno 690
Jury, William A. 692
ジュリアス
Julius, Henri 690
Julius, Jessica 691
ジュリアーニ
Giuliani, Alfredo 502
Giuliani, Jean-Dominique 502
Giuliani, Rudolph W. 502
Giuliani, Sante L. 502
ジュリアーノ
Giuliano, Geoffrey 502
Giuliano, Simone 502
Guiliano, Mireille 544
シューリアン
Schurian, Walter 1261
ジュリアン
Julien, Jennifer 690
Julien, Maude 690
Julien, Patrice 690
Julien, Philippe 690
Julien, Yuri 690
Jullian, Philippe 691
Julliand, Anne-Dauphine 691
Jullien, Francois 691
Jullien, Jean 691
ジュリアンタラ
Juliantara, Dadang 690
シュリーヴ
Shreeve, James 1293
Shreve, Anita 1294
Shreve, Steven E. 1294
ジュリエ
Juliet, Charles 690
シュリエデ
Shriedeh, Nasser 1294
ジュリオ・セーザル
Julio Cesar 690
シュリカ
Shulika, Lyubov 1294
シューリギン
Shul'gin, Dmitriĭ Iosifovich 1294
シュリクティング
Schlichting, Mark 1253
ジュリチッチ
Djuricic, Filip 360
シュリッケンリーダー
Schlickenrieder, Peter 1253
シュリッター
Schlittler, Joao 1253
Schlütter, Andreas 1254
ジュリッチ
Julich, Bobby 690
ジュリッチマルコビッチ
Dulić-marković, Ivana 379
シュリッツ
Schlitz, Laura Amy 1253
シュリーデーヴィ
Sridevi 1338
シュリデヴィ
Sridevi 1338
ジュリーニ
Giulini, Carlo Maria 502
シュリパイリ
Shrepaili, Daljit 1294
シュリーブ
Shreeve, Jamie 1293
Shreve, Chasen 1294
シュリーファー
Schrieffer, John Robert 1259
シュリメ
Schlime, Francesco Tristano 1253
シュリャフティツキ
Sleahtitchi, Mihai 1312
シュリューター
Schlüter, Andreas 1254
シュリーレンツァウアー
Schlierenzauer, Gregor 1253
シュリンク
Schlink, Basilea 1253
Schlink, Bernhard 1253
シュリング
Schling, Jaromír 1253
シュリンゲンジーフ
Schlingensief, Christoph 1253
シュリンゲンズィーフ
Schlingensief, Christoph 1253
ジュリンスキー
Zhulinsky, Mykola 1553
ジュリンダ
Dzurinda, Mikuláš 386
シュール
Cyr, Donald 310
Schuhl, Jean-Jacques 1259
シュル
Schuhl, Jean-Jacques 1259
ジュール
Joule, Robert 689
Juhl, Peter 690
Jules, Edouard 690
Juul, Arne 693
Zuur, Alain F. 1559
ジュル
Jull, Gwendolen A. 691
ジュルー
Djourou, Johan 360
シュルイツァー
Sluizer, Georges 1313
シュルヴィッツ
Shulevitz, Uri 1294
シュルーカ
Chrougha, Nani Ould 262
シュルキン
Schulkin, Jay 1260
Shulkin, David 1294
シュルコバ
Slukova, Marketa 1313
ジュルシェ
Zurcher, Bernard 1559
ジュルジェヴィッチ
Djurdjevic, Marko 360
シュルシン
Shurshin, Nikita 1295
ジュールズ・エンゲル
Engel, Jules 402
シュルーズベリー
Shrewsberry, Micah 1294
シュルスワスキー
Szulczewski, Peter 1375
シュルゼ
Christophersen, Claudia 262
シュルーター
Schluter, Dolph 1254
シュルター
Schurter, Nino 1261
ジュルタ
Gyurta, Dániel 550
ジュールダン
Jourdan, Louis 689
ジュルチャーニ
Gyurcsány, Ferenc 550
シュルツ
Scholz, Tom 1257
Schultz, Bo 1260
Schultz, Don E. 1260
Schultz, Hans Jürgen 1260
Schultz, Heidi F. 1260
Schultz, Heiko 1260
Schultz, Helmut 1260
Schultz, Howard 1260
Schultz, Jaime 1260
Schultz, Judith M. 1260
Schultz, Majken 1260
Schultz, Pamela D. 1260
Schultz, Patricia 1260
Schultz, Philip 1260
Schultze, Norbert 1260
Schulz, Eric 1260
Schulz, Helga 1260
Schulz, Hermann 1260
Schulz, Kathryn 1260
Schulz, Linda 1260
Schulz, Marianne 1260
Schulz, Marvin 1260
Schulz, Mona Lisa 1260
Schulz, Nico 1260
Schulz, Wolfgang 1260
Schulze, Franz 1260
Schulze, Katja 1260
Shultz, George Pratt 1294
シュルツェ
Schulze, Dallas 1260
Schulze, Hans-Joachim 1260
Schulze, Hans Kurt 1260
Schulze, Ingo 1260
Schulze, Sabine 1260
Schulze, Sharon 1260
Schulze, Thomas 1260
シュルツェ＝マルメリンク
Schulze-Marmeling, Dietrich 1260
シュルック
Schleck, Andy 1253
シュルツ＝ジョーンズ
Schultz-Jones, Barbara 1260
シュルット
Šrut, Pavel 1338
シュルツ＝トルナウ
Schultz-Tornau, Joachim 1260
シュルツ‐ピーブルス
Schulte-Peevers, Andrea 1260
シュルップ
Schlupp, Jeff 1254
シュルテ
Schulte, Barbara 1260
Schulte, Günter 1260
ジュルディ
Jourdy, Camille 689
シュルテス
Schultes, Richard Evans 1260
シュルテ‐ネルケ
Schulte-Nölke, Hans 1260
シュルテ‐ピーバーズ
Schulte-Peevers, Andrea 1260
シュルト
Schilt, Semmy 1252
ジュルヌ
Journe, François-Paul 689
シュールバーグ
Schulberg, Budd 1259
シュルバーグ
Schulberg, Budd 1259
シュールハンマー
Schurhammer, George 1261
シュルプ
Schlumpf, Fabienne 1254
ジュルファラキャン
Julfalakyan, Arsen 690
ジュルフィ
Györffy, Anna F. 550
シュルフター

Schluchter, Wolfgang 1254
ジュルブヌ
Jelvoune, Ahmedou Ould Hademine Ould 669
ジュルベンコ
Zhurubenko, I.G. 1553
シュールマイヤー
Schulmeyer, Heribert 1260
シュールマン
Shulman, Lee S. 1294
シュルマン
Schulman, Donniel S. 1260
Schulman, Helen 1260
Schulman, Sam 1260
Shulman, Seth 1294
シュルムベルガー
Schlumberger, Andreas 1254
シュールレ
Schurrle, Andre 1261
ジュレ
Syré, Ludger 1374
シュレーア
Schlör, Joachim 1253
シュレイアン
al-Shuraiaan, Bader Shebib 1294
シュレイガー
Schrager, Adam 1258
シュレイキ
Shureiqi, Yousef 1295
シュレイク
Shrake, Edwin 1293
ジュレイサティ
Jreisati, Salim 689
シュレイダー
Schrader, Leonard 1258
Schrader, Paul 1258
Schraeder, Ryan 1258
Schroeder, Karl 1259
シュレイデ
Shreideh, Adel 1294
シュレイバー
Schreiber, Brad 1258
シュレイファー
Shleifer, Andrei 1292
シュレイヘル
Shleikher, Nikita 1292
シュレイン
Shlain, Leonard 1292
シュレーガー
Schrager, Ian 1258
ジュレク
Jurek, Scott 692
シュレーゲル
Schlegel, Stuart A. 1253
シュレゲルミルヒ
Schlegelmilch, Rainer W. 1253
シュレージンガー
Schlesinger, Arthur Meier, Jr. 1253
Schlesinger, John 1253
シュレシンガー
Schlesinger, Alice 1253
Schlesinger, John 1253
シュレジンガー
Schlesinger, Alice 1253
Schlesinger, Arthur Meier, Jr. 1253
Schlesinger, John 1253
Schlesinger, Sarah 1253
シュレシンジャー
Schlesinger, Arthur Meier, Jr. 1253
Schlesinger, Dan 1253
Schlesinger, James Rodney 1253
Schlesinger, John 1253
Schlesinger, Leonard A. 1253
シュレジンジャー
Schlesinger, Arthur Meier, Jr. 1253
Schlesinger, James Rodney 1253
Schlesinger, John 1253
シュレーズ
Shlaes, Amity 1292
シュレスタ
Shrestha, Badri Prasad 1294
Shrestha, Marich Man Singh 1294
Shrestha, Narayan Kaji 1294
Shrestha, Omkar Prasad 1294
Śreshtha, Durgalālā 1338
シュレセルス
Šlesers, Ainārs 1312
シュレーター
Schroeter, Werner 1259
Schröter, Michael 1259
シュレーダー
Schrader, Leonard 1258
Schrader, Paul 1258
Schreuder, Hinkelien 1259
Schröder, Gerhard 1259
Schröder, Jaap 1259
Schroder, Kate 1259
Schröder, Kristina 1259
Schroeder, Binette 1259
Schroeder, Hans-Werner 1259
Schroeder, Manfred Robert 1259
Schroeder, Roger G. 1259
シュレーダー＝フレチェット
Shrader-Frechette, K. 1293
シュレック
Schleck, Frank 1253
Schreck, Sam 1258
ジュレック
Jurek, Richard 692
シュレッセルス
Šlesers, Ainārs 1312
シュレット
Charrette, Mark N. 248
シュレットアウネ
Sletaune, Pal 1312
シュレットウエイン
Schlettwein, Calle 1253
シュレヒトリーム
Schlechtriem, Peter 1253
シュレーフ
Schleef, Einar 1253
シュレーファー
Schrefer, Eliot 1258
シュレファー
Schrepfer, Robert 1259
シュレフトバー
Šlechtová, Karla 1312
シュレベール
Schreiber, David Servan 1258
シュレーマン
Schloemann, Martin 1253
シュレーラ
Schlereth, Daniel 1253
シュレワ
Shouleva, Lydia 1293
シュレンク
Schrenk, Johann 1259
シュレンジャー
Schlenger, Sunny 1253
シュレンダー
Schlender, Brent 1253
シュレーンドルフ
Schlöndorff, Volker 1253
シュレンドルフ
Schlöndorff, Volker 1253
シューレンバーグ
Schulenberg, David 1259
シュレンプ
Schrempp, Juergen 1259
シュロー
Sureau, Claude 1367
シュロアエ
Hloaele, Mokoto 610
シュロイ
Schleu, Annika 1253
ジュロヴァ
Djourova, Axinia D. 360
シュロゥダー
Schroder, Dieter K. 1259
シュローサー
Schlosser, Eric 1254
シュロスバーグ
Schlosberg, Suzanne 1253
Schlossberg, Ari 1254
Schlossberg, Boris 1254
Schlossberg, David 1254
Schlossberg, Margaret C. 1254
シュローダー
Schroder, Carla 1259
Schroder, Dennis 1259
Schroder, Gerco 1259
Schroeder, Alice 1259
Schroeder, Russell K. 1259
Schroeder, Ted 1259
Schroeder, Will 1259
Shroder, Tom 1294
シュローダーズ
Schreuders, Piet 1259
シュロチキナ
Shurochkina, Mariia 1295
シュロック
Schrock, Richard Royce 1259
シュロット
Schrott, Beate 1259
Schrott, Erwin 1259
シュロットマン
Schlottmann, Antje 1254
ジュロビッチ
Djurović, Dragan 360
Djurović, Gordana 360
シュロフ
Schroff, Laura 1259
ジュロワ
Zhurova, Svetlana 1553
シュワイカー
Schweiker, Richard 1263
シュワイガー
Schweiger, Til 1263
シュワイツァー
Schweitzer, Wes 1263
シュワイル
Shuwail, Ashour 1295
シュワス
Schwass, Joachim 1263
シュワーツ
Schwartz, Geoff 1262
Schwartz, Jim 1262
Schwartz, Mitchell 1262
Schwarz, Roger M. 1262
シュワーツェル
Schwartzel, Charl 1262
シュワッガー
Schwager, Jack D. 1261
シュワッブ
Schwab, Charles 1261
Schwab, Francoise 1261
シュワード
Seward, Ingrid 1276
シュワニツ
Schwanitz, Christina 1261
シュワーバー
Schwarber, Kyle 1261
シュワーブ
Shwalb, Barbara J. 1295
Shwalb, David W. 1295
シュワブ
Schwab, Klaus 1261
Schwab, Susan Carroll 1261
ジュワフスキ
Żuławski, Andrzej 1559
シュワーベ
Schwabe, Caspar 1261
シュワルツ
Schwarcz, Joe 1261
Schwartz, Antoine 1261
Schwartz, Arthur P. 1261
Schwartz, Baron 1261
Schwartz, Barry 1262
Schwartz, Betty Ann 1262
Schwartz, Beverly 1262
Schwartz, Bob 1262
Schwartz, Cheryl M. 1262
Schwartz, David G. 1262
Schwartz, David Joseph 1262
Schwartz, David M. 1262
Schwartz, Ellen 1262
Schwartz, Eric J. 1262
Schwartz, Evan I. 1262
Schwartz, Herman M. 1262
Schwartz, Jacob Theodore 1262
Schwartz, Jeffrey H. 1262
Schwartz, John Burnham 1262
Schwartz, Joyce R. 1262
Schwartz, Lisa M. 1262
Schwartz, Maxime 1262
Schwartz, Melvin 1262
Schwartz, Nan 1262
Schwartz, Pepper 1262
Schwartz, Randal L. 1262
Schwartz, Richard 1262
Schwartz, Richard Evan 1262
Schwartz, Robert 1262
Schwartz, Roslyn 1262
Schwartz, Ruth Distler 1262
Schwartz, Stephanie 1262
Schwartz, Stephen 1262
Schwartz, Steven 1262
Schwartz, Tony 1262
Schwartz, William B. 1262
Schwarz, Bluma 1262

Schwarz, Christina 1262
Schwarz, Dieter 1262
Schwarz, Helene 1262
Schwarz, Norbert 1262
Schwarz, Samuel 1262
Schwarz, Shaul 1262
Schwarz, Viviane 1262
Swartz, Conrad M. 1371
Swartz, Mimi 1371
シュワルツェネガー
Schwarzenegger, Arnold 1262
シュワルツェネッガー
Schwarzenegger, Arnold 1262
シュワルツェンベルク
Schwarzenberg, Karel 1262
シュワルツェンベルグ
Schwarzenberg, Karel 1262
シュワルツコップ
Schwarzkopf, Elisabeth 1262
シュワルツコフ
Schwarzkopf, H. Norman 1262
シュワルツコプ
Schwarzkopf, Elisabeth 1262
シュワルツコプフ
Schwarzkopf, Lilli 1262
シュワルツ＝ノーベル
Schwartz-Nobel, Loretta 1262
シュワルツマン
Schwarzman, Stephen A. 1263
Shvartsman, Leonid 1295
シュワルト
Schwardt, Sara 1261
シュワルビ
Schwalbe, Will 1261
シュワルブ
Schwalb, Robert J. 1261
Schwalbe, Kathy 1261
シュワルベ
Schwalbé, Michel 1261
シュワロフ
Shuvalov, Igor I. 1295
シュワンクマイエル
Švankmajer, Jan 1369
シュワント
Schwandt, Thomas A. 1261
シュン
Xun, Zhou 1532
ジューン
Juhn, Peter 690
ジュンガー
Jungr, Barb 691
シュンク
Schunk, Rick 1261
ジュング
Jung, Andrea 691
ジュンクビスト
Ljungqvist, Alexander 836
ジュングマン
Jungmann, Raul 691
シュンケ
Schünke, Michael 1261
ジュンケイラ
Junqueira, Flavio 692
Junqueira, Luiz Carlos Uchôa 692
ジュンジュンワラ
Jhunjhunwala, Amitabh 673
ジュンス
Junsu 692
ジュン－タイ
Jun-Tai, Norma 692
ジュンベ
Jumbe, Friday 691
ジュンホン
Jun Hoong, Cheong 691
ショ
Chaud, Benjamin 249
ショー
Chaud, Benjamin 249
Chhor, Heang 254
Shaw, Artie 1284
Shaw, Audley 1284
Shaw, Bryony 1284
Shaw, Caroline 1284
Shaw, Chantelle 1284
Shaw, Charles G. 1284
Shaw, Christine 1284
Shaw, Connor 1284
Shaw, Donald L. 1284
Shaw, Fiona 1284
Shaw, Francesca 1284
Shaw, Garry J. 1284
Shaw, Graham 1284
Shaw, Greg 1284
Shaw, Hannah 1284
Shaw, Ian 1284
Shaw, Ida A. 1284
Shaw, Johnny 1284
Shaw, Josh 1284
Shaw, Leslie M. 1284
Shaw, Luke 1284
Shaw, Peter 1284
Shaw, Scott Richard 1284
Shaw, Stephen 1284
Shaw, Vernon Lorden 1284
Shaw, Victoria Felice 1284
Shaw, William 1284
Shorr, Karly 1293
ジョ
Cho, Chang-in 257
Cho, Choong-hoon 257
Cho, Kyung-hwan 257
Cho, Myong-chol 257
Cho, Se-hyung 257
Cho, Suck-rai 258
Cho, Sung-min 258
Cho, Yang-ho 258
Cho, Yong-pil 258
Chou, Kap-che 260
Jo, Myong-rok 674
ジョー
Jaud, Jean-Paul 666
Jo, Sumi 674
Joh, Howard 675
ショア
Schor, Juliet B. 1258
Shore, Edwina 1293
Shore, Howard 1293
Shore, Sidney X. 1293
Shore, Stephen 1293
Shore, Stephen M. 1293
Shorr, Gadiel 1293
ショアー
Schor, Juliet B. 1258
Schore, Neil Eric 1258
Shore, Cecilia M. 1293
Shore, Stephen 1293
Shores, Elizabeth F. 1293
ジョアジル
Joazil, Jean Rodolphe 674
ショアーズ
Shores, Christopher F. 1293
ジョアナ
Geoana, Mircea Dan 489
ジョアン
João, Armando Artur 674
ジョアン・コスタ
Joao Costa 674
ジョアン・テイシェイラ
Joao Teixeira 674
ジョアン・ペドロ
Joao Pedro 674
ジョアン・ペレイラ
Joao Pereira 674
ジョアン・マリオ
Joao Mario 674
ジョアン・モウティーニョ
Joao Moutinho 674
ジョイ
Joy 689
Joy, Bill 689
Joy, Dara 689
Joy, Nicki 689
Joy, Peter A. 689
Joye, Dan 689
ショイアーブフルク
Scheuerpflug, Andreas 1251
ショイイング
Scheuing, Dieter H. 1251
ショイグ
Shoigu, Sergei Kuzhugetovich 1292
ジョイス
Joyce 689
Joyce, Anna 689
Joyce, Barnaby 689
Joyce, Brenda 689
Joyce, Colin 689
Joyce, Graham 689
Joyce, Jerry 689
Joyce, Joe 689
Joyce, Kara Lynn 689
Joyce, Lydia 689
Joyce, Matt 689
Joyce, Nancy Eleanor 689
Joyce, Rachel 689
Joyce, Steven 689
Joyce, William 689
Joyce, William F. 689
Joyes, Claire 689
ジョイナー
Joyner, David 689
Joyner, Jerry 689
Joyner, Lamarcus 689
Joyner, Mark 689
Joyner, Rick 689
ジョイナー・ベイ
Joiner-Bey, Herb 681
ショイヒャー
Scheucher, Alois 1251
ショイフェレ
Schäuffele, Jörg 1250
ショイブレ
Schäuble, Wolfgang 1250
Scheuble, Bernhard 1251
ショイモシュ
Solymos, László 1326
ショインカ
Soyinka, Wole 1332
ジョインズ
Joines, Vann 681
ジョインソン
Joinson, Adam N. 681
Joinson, Suzanne 681
ショーヴ
Shove, Gary 1293
ショウ
Shaw, Artie 1284
Shaw, Arvell 1284
Shaw, Audley 1284
Shaw, Bob 1284
Shaw, Brian 1284
Shaw, Brian F. 1284
Shaw, Bryan 1284
Shaw, Ian 1284
Shaw, Julia 1284
Shaw, Kiran Mazumdar 1284
Shaw, Luke 1284
Shaw, Mary 1284
Shaw, Melvin 1284
Shaw, Phil 1284
Shaw, Rajib 1284
Shaw, Robert 1284
Shaw, Tara 1284
Shaw, Travis 1284
Shaw, Tucker 1284
SHOW 1293
ジョウ
Jow, Satang 689
Zhou, Kui 1553
Zhou, Long 1553
Zhou, Quan 1553
Zhou, Qunfei 1553
Zhou, Xun 1553
Zhou, Yang 1553
ジョヴァノヴィック
Jovanovic, Rob 689
ジョヴァノヴィッチ
Jovanovic, Rob 689
ショーヴァン
Chauvin, Yves 249
ショヴァン
Chauvin, Yves 249
ジョヴァンカ
Giovanca 501
ジョヴァンニ
Giovanni, José 501
Giovanni, Nikki 501
ショヴィレ
Chauviré, Yvette 249
ジョウェル
Jowell, Tessa 689
ジョヴォヴィッチ
Jovovich, Milla 689
ショーウォーター
Showalter, Dennis E. 1293
ジョウォルスキー
Jaworski, Jamie 667
ショーウォルター
Showalter, Buck 1293
ショウォルター
Showalter, Buck 1293
Showalter, Dennis E. 1293
Showalter, Gena 1293
ショウガー
Shauger, Daniel 1284
ショウクロス
Shawcross, Ryan 1284
ジョウコウ
Joko, Alice Tamie 681
ジョウゼフ
Joseph, Sandra 688
ショウダ
Shoda, Yuichi 1292
ジョウダ
Jowda, Hacen Ould

Limam Ould Amar 689
ショウドリー
Choudhry, Moorad 260
ジョウフラス
Jouflas, Leslie 689
ショウマロフ
Shoumarov, Gayrat 1293
ショウミエール
Chaumiere, Jean François 249
ショウリー
Shourie, Arun 1293
ジョウンズ
Jones, David P.H. 683
Jones, Kathleen 684
ショエット
Shohet, Robin 1292
ジヨエフ
Ziyeyev, Mirzo 1556
ショエル
Choeël, Raphaëlle 258
ジョエル
Joel, Billy 675
Joel, Mitch 675
Yoel, Rodriguez 1539
ショーエンヘール
Schoenherr, John 1257
ショーカー
Sarkar, Deepayan 1242
ショーカットゥラー
Shaukatullah 1284
ショーカトゥラー
Shaukatullah 1284
ショカヤ
Sokaya, Thabita 1324
ジョカル
Jokar, Masuod 681
ジョーギャリス
Georgaris, Dean 489
ショキロフ
Shokirov, Usmonkul 1292
ショキン
Shokin, Dmitriy 1292
ジョクス
Joxe, Alain 689
ジョクテング
Yockteng, Rafael 1539
ジョクノ
Diokno, Benjamin 357
ショーグレン
Shogren, Jason F. 1292
Sjögren, Anita Viola 1309
ショグレン
Shogren, Jason F. 1292
ショケ
Choquet, Maria 259
ショケット
Choquette, Sonia 259
ジョーケル
Joeckel, Luke 675
ジョーゲンセン
Jorgensen, Gwen 687
Jorgensen, Richard 687
ジョーコ
Gyorko, Jedd 550
ジョコヴィッチ
Djokovic, Novak 360
ジョコ・ウィドド
Joko Widodo 681
ジョコビッチ
Djokovic, Novak 360
Dokovic, Novak 363
ショゴレフ
Shchegolev, Igor O. 1285
ショーザー
Schoser, Benedikt 1258
ジョーシ
Joshi, Manoj 688
ジョージ
George, Adrian 489
George, Alexander L. 489
George, Ambrose 489
George, Anju Bobby 489
George, Anne 489
George, Bill 489
George, Calixte 489
George, Catherine 489
George, Demetra 489
George, Donny 489
George, Edward Alan John 489
George, Elizabeth 489
George, Emmanuel 489
George, Jamie 489
George, Jean Craighead 489
George, Jeremiah 489
George, Julia B. 489
George, Karen 489
George, Kathleen 489
George, Kristine O'Connell 489
George, Lars 489
George, Melanie 489
George, Nelson 489
George, Nic 489
George, Paul 489
George, Phylicia 489
George, Phyllis 489
George, Pullattu Abraham 489
George, Robert Lloyd 489
George, Roger 489
George, Rose 489
George, Sheba Mariam 489
George, Susan 489
George, Timothy S. 489
George, William 489
George, William H. 489
George, William W. 489
George, Wilma B. 489
George, Yosiwo 489
ジョシ
Joshi, Chandra Dev 688
Joshi, C.P. 688
Joshi, Jayadev 688
Joshi, Manohar 688
Joshi, Murli Manohar 688
Joshi, Nabindra Raj 688
Joshi, Shivaraj 688
Joshi, S.T. 688
ジョシー
Joshi, Jagdish 688
Joshi, Nivedita 688
ジョージァイ
Georgi, Howard 490
ジョージアン
Georgian, Linda M. 490
ジョージ・ウォーレン
George-Warren, Holly 490
ジョージェスク
Georgescu, Peter 489
ジョージェスク＝レーゲン
Georgescu-Roegen, Nicholas 489
ジョージズ
Georges, Michel A.J. 489
ジョージズ・ハント
Georges-hunt, Marcus 489
ジョシネ
Jossinet, Frederique 688
ショーシャ
Chauchard, Claude 249
ジョシャ
Gjosha, Klajda 503
ショジャイイ
Shojaee, Seyed Mahdi 1292
ショシャーナ
Shoshanna, Brenda 1293
ショジャニア
Shojania, Kaveh G. 1292
ジョシュ
Yoss 1540
ジョシュア
Joshua 688
Joshua, Anthony 688
ジョス
Joss, Morag 688
ジョスウ
Djossou, Mamatou 360
ジョスクン
Coşkun, Ali 293
ジョスコー
Joskow, Andrew S. 688
ジョスコヴィッツ
Joskowicz, Routie 688
ショスタク
Szostak, Jack William 1374
ショスタコーヴィチ
Shostakovich, Galina 1293
Shostakovich, Maksim Dmitrievich 1293
ショスタック
Szostak, Piotr 1374
ジョーステ
Jooste, Leon 686
ジョスティス
Josuttis, Nicolai M. 688
ジョスト
Jost, Allen 688
Jost, H.Peter 688
Jost, Jacques 688
ショーストロム
Sjostrom, Sarah 1309
ジョスパン
Jospin, Lionel Robert 688
ジョスラン
Jausserand, Corinne 666
Josselin, Charles 688
ジョスリン
Jocelyn, Marthe 674
Joslin, Mary 688
Joslin, Sesyle 688
Josling, Timothy Edward 688
ジョスリング
Josling, Timothy Edward 688
ジョゼ
José, Diakumpuna Sita 687
ジョセップ
Joseph, Louis Harold 688
ジョセフ
Joseph, Betty 687
Joseph, Caleb 687
Joseph, Claudia 687
Joseph, Cory 687
Joseph, Daniel 687
Joseph, David I. 687
Joseph, Ezechiel 687
Joseph, Frank 687
Joseph, Guy 687
Joseph, Johnathan 687
Joseph, Jonathan 687
Joseph, Karl 688
Joseph, Ken, Jr. 688
Joseph, Ken, Sr. 688
Joseph, Lawrence 688
Joseph, Lawrence E. 688
Joseph, Linval 688
Joseph, Martin 688
Joseph, Nadine 688
Joseph, Oliver 688
Joseph, Tommy 688
Joseph, Yance 688
ジョゼフ
Joseph, Bertrand 687
Joseph, Carl 687
Joseph, Celia 687
Joseph, Fred 687
Joseph, Molwyn 688
Joseph, Robert 688
Joseph, Robert L. 688
Joseph, Stephen 688
Joseph, Yolande Bain 688
Joseph, Yves Germain 688
ジョーゼフィ
Gioseffi, Claudia 501
ジョゼフィーヌ・シャルロット
Joséphine-Charlotte 688
ジョセフォウィッツ
Josefowicz, Leila 687
ジョセフソン
Josephson, Brian David 688
Josephson, Erland 688
ジョゼフソン
Josephson, Brian David 688
ジョセラン
Josserand, Marion 688
ショソン
Chausson, Anne-Caroline 249
ショーター
Shorter, Edward 1293
Shorter, Frank 1293
Shorter, Wayne 1293
ジョーダノヴァ
Jordanova, L.J. 687
ジョーダン
Jordan, Aggie 686
Jordan, Bella Bychkova 686
Jordan, Bertrand 686
Jordan, Brigitte 686
Jordan, Cameron 686
Jordan, David 686
Jordan, DeAndre 686
Jordan, Deloris 686
Jordan, Dion 686
Jordan, Duke 686
Jordan, Hamilton 686
Jordan, Ian 686
Jordan, Jeff 686
Jordan, Jennifer 686
Jordan, Jill 686
Jordan, Jon 686
Jordan, Kathleen 686
Jordan, Majid 686
Jordan, Michael 686
Jordan, Michael Hugh 686
Jordan, Neil 686
Jordan, Nicole 687

シ

Jordan, Penny 687
Jordan, Praveen 687
Jordan, Robert 687
Jordan, Roslyn 687
Jordan, Ruth 687
Jordan, Sophie 687
Jordan, William Chester 687
Jordan, Winston 687
Jordan, Zweledinga Pallo 687
ジョーダン＝エバンズ
Jordan-Evans, Sharon 687
ジョーダン＝ビチコフ
Jordan-Bychkov, Terry G. 687
ショーツ
Shorts, Cecil 1293
ショック
Schoch, Robert M. 1257
ジョック
Jock 674
ショック・スミス
Schock-Smith, Angyne J. 1257
ショックニー
Shockney, Lillie D. 1292
ショッケン
Schocken, Shimon 1257
ジョッシ
Joshi, Krishnakant Nathalal 688
ショッター
Schotter, Roni 1258
ジョッタ
Jota, Diogo 688
ショッテン
Shotten, Marc 1293
ショット
Schodt, Frederik L. 1257
Schott, Ben 1258
Schott, Hanna 1258
Schott, Jeffrey J. 1258
Schott, Marge 1258
ショットウェル
Shotwell, Gwynne 1293
ショットペーダシェン
Schjøtt-pedersen, Karl Eirik 1253
ショットロフ
Schottroff, Luise 1258
ショッパ
Schoppa, Leonard 1258
ジョップ
Diop, Abdoulaye 357
Diop, Traoré Seynabou 357
ショッホ
Schoch, Philipp 1256
Schoch, Simon 1257
ジョーティカ
Jotika, U. 688
ジョティサリコーン
Jotisalikorn, Chami 688
ジョティシュキー
Jotischky, Andrew 688
ジョディディオ
Jodidio, Philip 675
ショー・テイラー
Shawe-Taylor, John 1284
ジョテフ
Zhotev, Petar 1553
ジョーデン
Jorden, Eleanor Harz 687
ショート
Short, Christopher 1293
Short, Clare 1293
Short, Dan 1293
Short, John Rennie 1293
Short, Julian 1293
Short, Kawann 1293
Short, Keith 1293
Short, Kevin 1293
Short, Mick 1293
Short, Philip 1293
Short, Robert L. 1293
Short, Scott 1293
Shorto, Russell 1293
Shortt, Jim 1293
ジョード
Jode, Frédérique de 675
ジョトゥディ
Jaotody, Noeline 664
ジョトディア
Djotodia, Michel 360
ショートニ
Sotonyi, Peter 1330
ショドフ
Chodoff, Paul 258
ショートマー
Schoettmer, Jeff 1257
ショトレフ
Shurtleff, Michael 1295
ショードロン
Chaudron, Craig 249
ショートン
Scholten, Jan 1257
Shorten, Bill 1293
ジョナ
Djona, Avocksouma 360
Jonah, James O.C. 681
ジョナー
Jonah, Kathleen 681
ジョナイド
Djoenaid, Denny A. 359
ジョナサン
Jonathan, Goodluck Ebele 682
ジョーナス
Jonas, Alicia 681
ジョナス
Jonas 681
Jonas, Joe 681
Jonas, Kevin 681
Jonas, Natasha 681
Jonas, Nick 681
Jonath, Leslie 681
ジョナス・マルタン
Jonas Martin 681
ジョナセン
Jonassen, David 681
ジョナタン・ドス・サントス
Jonathan Dos Santos 682
ジョナタン・ビエラ
Jonathan Viera 682
ジョナン
Jonan, Ignasius 681
ジョニ
Gjoni, Ilir 503
Joni, Saj-nicole A. 686
ジョニエ
Jonnier, Emmanuel 686
ショニバー
Shoniber, Casiano 1293
ジョニ・ベコバ
Djoni Becoba, Vidal 360
ショーニュ
Chaunu, Pierre 249
ショーニュー
Chaunu, Pierre 249
ジョーヌ
Djhone, Leslie 359
ショーネシ
Shaughnessy, Pat 1284
ショーネシー
Shaughnessy, Adrian 1284
Shaughnessy, Matt 1284
ショーネボルン
Schoneborn, Lena 1257
ジョノジドゥ
Djonodjidou-ahabo, Gontran 360
ジョノジドゥアアボ
Djonodjidou-ahabo, Gontran 360
ショーバー
Schover, Leslie R. 1258
ショバ
Sova, Vasile 1332
ショバキ
Shobaki, Jamal 1292
ジョバナルディ
Giovanardi, Carlo 501
ショハミー
Shohamy, Elana Goldberg 1292
ジョハル
Djohar, Said Mohamed 360
ジョバルテ
Jobarteh, Justice Lamin 674
ショーバン
Chauvin, Yves 249
ショバン
Chauvin, Yves 249
ショパン
Choppin, Gregory R. 259
ジョバン
Jobin, Paul 674
ジョバンカ
Giovanca 501
ジョハンズ
Johanns, Mike 675
ジョハンセン
Johansen, Bruce Elliott 675
Johansen, Erika 675
Johansen, Iris 675
Johansen, Roy 675
ジョハンソン
Johanson, Anna-Lisa 675
Johanson, Donald C. 675
Johanson, Gary A. 675
Johansson, Scarlett 675
ジョバンニ
Giovanni, José 501
Giovannini, Carlotta 501
ジョバンニーニ
Giovannini, Enrico 501
ジョバンノーリ
Giovannoli, Jean-Louis 501
ジョビー
Giobbi, Robert 501
ショビレ
Chauviré, Yvette 249
ジョビン
Jobim, Nelson Azevedo 674
ジョビンコ
Giovinco, Sebastian 501
ショーブ
Schaub, Matt 1250
ジョーブ
Jobe, Frank Wilson 674
Jobe, Momodou Lamin Sedat 674
ジョフィ
Joffe, Charles H. 675
Joffe, Roland 675
ジョフェ
Joffe, Roland 675
ショフェル
Schoeffel, John 1257
ショフコフスキー
Shovkovskiy, Oleksandr 1293
ショブス
Shoobs, Nahum E. 1293
ジョブス
Jobs, Steve 674
ジョブズ
Jobs, Steve 674
ジョブソン
Jobson, Robert 674
ショブホワ
Shobukhova, Liliya 1292
ショフムロド
Shohmurod, Rustam 1292
ショプラー
Schopler, Eric 1258
ジョフラン
Joffrin, Laurent 675
ショーフリ
Chaudhuri, Kiran 249
ジョフリン
Joflin, Jones 675
ジョフレダ
Yoffreda, Giuseppe 1539
ジョブロ
Ziobro, Zbigniew 1556
ジョフロン
Geoffron, Patrice 489
ジョベ
Jobe, Abdou 674
ジョベコマス
Jover Comas, Eric 689
ジョベヌ
Djogbenou, Joseph 359
ジョベヌジャイ
Jobe-njie, Fatou Mas 674
ショーベリ
Sjoberg, Jalmar 1309
ショーベル
Schawbel, Dan 1250
ジョベール
Jobert, Michel 674
ショボクシ
Shobokshi, Osma Bin Abdul-Majid 1292
ジョボドワナ
Jobodwana, Anaso 674
ジョボビッチ
Jovovich, Milla 689
ショホーン
Ciochon, Russell L. 265
ジョマア
Jomaa, Mehdi 681
ショマーズ
Chaumaz, Benjamin 249
ジョーマットピターソン
Joematpettersson, Tina 675

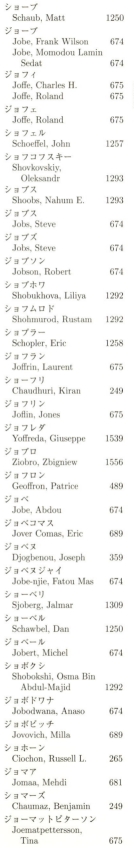

シヨーマッハー
Schomacher, Jochen 1257
シヨーマン
Shoman, Assad 1292
ジヨミ
Jomy, Alain 681
ジヨミニ
Jomini, Henri 681
シヨミン
Shomin, Valeriy 1292
ジヨーム
Jorm, Anthony F. 687
シヨムロン
Shomron, Dan 1292
シヨメ
Chomet, S. 259
シヨーメーカー
Schoemaker, Paul J. H. 1257
シヨメラ
Chomera, Lucas 259
ジヨモ・K.サンダラム
Jomo Kwame Sundaram 681
シヨモジ
Somogyi, Ferenc 1327
ジヨモジヤロ
Jomo-jalloh, A.B.S. 681
ジヨヤ
Joya, Malalai 689
シヨヤマン
Scheuermann, Hans-Dieter 1251
シヨーヨム
Sólyom, László 1326
シヨヨム
Sólyom, László 1326
シヨーラー
Schorer, Suki 1258
ジヨラス
Jolas, Betsy 681
ジヨラセウヌンドゥン
Joellasewnundun, Urmila 675
シヨーラック
Cholak, Moose 259
シヨーランデル
Sjölander, Sverre 1309
ジヨリ
Jolis, Alan 681
Joly, Alain 681
Joly, Damien 681
ジヨリー
Jolie, Angelina 681
Joly, Elena 681
Joly, Mélanie 681
Joly, Nicolas 681
ジヨリアン
Jollien, Alexandre 681
ジヨリヴェ
Jolivet, Joëlle 681
Jolivet, Muriel 681
ジヨリオン
Jorion, Philippe 687
Jorion, Thomas 687
ジヨリス
Joris, André 687
Tziolis, Fotios 1431
ジヨリッシュ
Joris, André 687
シヨール
Scholl, William 1257
Sholl, David S. 1292
シヨル
Scholl, Andreas 1257
ジヨルカ
Llorca, Fernando 837
シヨルカル
Sarkar, Saral K. 1242
ジヨルゲンソン
Jorgenson, Dale W. 687
シヨルコビー
Szolkowy, Robin 1374
ジヨルジ
Giorgi, Débora 501
Jorge, Miguel 687
ジヨルジアンニ
Giorgianni, Massimo 501
ジヨルジエ
Georger, Lucie 489
Jorge, Ana 687
ジヨルジエヴィッチ
Djordjevic, Filip 360
ジヨルジエスク
Georgescu, Florin 489
ジヨルジエッリ
Giorgelli, Pablo 501
ジヨルジエビッチ
Djordjević, Zoran 360
ジヨルジース
Jerjes, Khalid 671
ジヨルジーニョ
Jorginho 687
ジヨルジーニョ・ド・パンデイロ
Jorginho do Pandeiro 687
ジヨルジヤン
Georgen, Alec 489
ジヨルジユ
George, Maged 489
Gyorgy, Marx 550
ジヨルジヨリアニ
Zhorzholiani, Levan 1553
シヨールズ
Scholes, Myron S. 1257
Shaules, Joseph 1284
シヨールダイス
Shouldice, Warren 1293
シヨルダガー
Schjoldager, Mette 1253
ジヨルダーナ
Giordana, Marco Tullio 501
ジヨルダニ
Giordani, Jorge 501
ジヨルダーノ
Giordano, Maria 501
Giordano, Paolo 501
Giordano, Philip 501
Giordano, Ralph 501
ジヨルダノ
Giordano, Giuseppe 501
Giordano, Raphaëlle 501
ジヨルダン
Jordan, Armin 686
Jordan, Bertrand 686
Jordan, Philippe 687
シヨルツ
Scholtz, Gunter 1257
Scholtz, Jean 1257
Scholz, Christoph 1257
Scholz, Christopher H. 1257
Scholz, Dieter David 1257
Scholz, Olaf 1257
Scholz, Tom 1257
Scholz, Torsten 1257
Scholz, Uwe 1257
ジヨルディ・アルバ
Jordi Alba 687
シヨルテス
Soltesz, Stefan 1326
ジヨルニル
Žolnir, Urška 1557
シヨールハマー
Schollhammer, Hans 1257
ジヨルフィ
Gyorffy, Maria 550
ジヨルベナゼ
Jorbenadze, Avtandil 686
シヨルンベルク
Schornberg, Jasmin 1258
シヨレゲン
Schöllgen, Gregor 1257
ジヨレス
Joerres, Jeffrey A. 675
ジヨレダ
Lloreda, Francisco José 837
シヨレツ
Shorets, Andrei V. 1293
シヨーレット
Chaurette, Normand 249
シヨレット
Shorett, Peter 1293
ジヨレンス
Llorens Sabaté, Pedro 837
ジヨレンテ
Llorente, Diego 837
Llorente, Fernando 837
ジヨレンティ
Llorenti, Sacha Sergio 837
ジヨロボワ
Zholobova, Valeriia 1553
シヨワー
Scheuer, Michael 1251
ジヨワイヨン
Joyon, Francis 689
シヨーン
Schoen, Allen M. 1257
Schon, Mila 1257
Schon, Neal 1257
Schone, Mark 1257
Schone, Robin 1257
Schorn, Joel 1258
Shone, Richard 1292
ジヨン
Chon, Wol-son 259
Chon, Yo-ok 259
Chong, Hyon-suk 259
Chong, Jun-gi 259
Chun, Doo-hwan 262
Chung, Chung-kil 263
Chung, Dong-young 263
Chung, Jae-jeong 263
Chung, Ju-yong 263
Chung, Ku-chong 263
Chung, Kyung-wha 263
Chung, Mong-hun 263
Chung, Mong-joon 263
Chung, Mong-koo 263
Chung, Myung-whun 263
Chung, Se-Yung 263
Chung, Won-shik 263
Jean, Wyclef 667
Jeon, In-teak 671
Jeon, Min-hee 671
John, Augustine 675
John, Carlos 676
John, Cyril 676
John, David 676
John, Elton Hercules 676
John, Jeffrey 676
John, Joby 676
John, Jory 676
John, Karl-Heinz 676
John, Kose 676
John, Mark St. 676
John, Theophilus 676
John, Ulrick 676
John, Velon 676
Jon, Lil 681
Jong, Ho-seung 686
Jong, Lisa De 686
Joshi, Govindaraji 688
Joun, Young Soun 689
Jung, Byeong-ho 691
St.John, Richard 1228
Zheng, Hong-sheng 1552
ジヨン
Ji-young 674
ジヨンアプ
Jong-up 686
ジヨンク
Jonke, Tim 686
ジヨング
Jong, Erica 686
Jonge, Peter De 686
シヨングウェ
Shongwe, Elijah 1293
Shongwe, Nelisiwe 1293
Shongwe, Sibusiso 1293
Shongwe, Sipho 1293
Shongwe, Thandie 1293
ジヨンクール
Joncour, Serge 682
ジヨンケ
Jonquet, Thierry 686
ジヨン・コプランス
Coplans, John 289
ジヨンジグヨン
Janjigian, Vahan 663
ジヨン ジヨーゲンソン
Jorgenson, John 687
ジヨーンズ
Johns, Geoff 676
Johns, Jasper 676
Jones, Abigail 682
Jones, Abry 682
Jones, Adam 682
Jones, Alan 682
Jones, Alex S. 682
Jones, Allan Frewin 682
Jones, Alun Wyn 682
Jones, Andrea 682
Jones, Andrew 682
Jones, Andrew R. 682
Jones, Andruw 682
Jones, Andy 682
Jones, Anne 682
Jones, Anne Hudson 682
Jones, Annette 682
Jones, Aphrodite 682
Jones, Arthur 682
Jones, Aurelia Louise 682
Jones, B. 682
Jones, Barbara M. 682
Jones, Barrett 682
Jones, Ben 682
Jones, Beth Felker 682
Jones, Bill T. 682
Jones, Billy 682
Jones, BlackWolf 682
Jones, Bob 682
Jones, Booker T. 682

Jones, Brett 682
Jones, Brian K. 682
Jones, Bruce D. 682
Jones, Bryony 682
Jones, Byron 682
Jones, Cameron 682
Jones, Capers 682
Jones, Cardale 682
Jones, Cayleb 682
Jones, Chandler 682
Jones, Charles Edward 682
Jones, Charles Irving 682
Jones, Cherry 682
Jones, Chipper 682
Jones, Chris 682
Jones, Christian 682
Jones, Christianne C. 682
Jones, Christina 682
Jones, Christine 682
Jones, Christopher 682
Jones, Chuck 682
Jones, Colin 682
Jones, Colin P.A. 682
Jones, Cullen 682
Jones, Cyrus 682
Jones, Dahntay 682
Jones, Damian 682
Jones, Damon 682
Jones, Daniel T. 683
Jones, DaQuan 683
Jones, Datone 683
Jones, David 683
Jones, David Albert 683
Jones, David James 683
Jones, David L. 683
Jones, David Michael 683
Jones, David N. 683
Jones, David P.H. 683
Jones, David R. 683
Jones, David Wyn 683
Jones, Davy 683
Jones, Dean 683
Jones, Debby 683
Jones, Deion 683
Jones, Derrick 683
Jones, Diana Wynne 683
Jones, Dominique 683
Jones, Don 683
Jones, Donnie 683
Jones, Dorothy 683
Jones, Doug 683
Jones, Douglas B. 683
Jones, Duncan 683
Jones, E.C.B. 683
Jones, Eddie 683
Jones, Edward P. 683
Jones, Edwin 683
Jones, Elizabeth Orton 683
Jones, Elizabeth W. 683
Jones, Elvin Ray 683
Jones, Enrico E. 683
Jones, Eric L. 683
Jones, Ernest 683
Jones, Etta 683
Jones, Frederic Hicks 683
Jones, Gareth 683
Jones, Gareth A. 683
Jones, Gareth Stedman 683
Jones, Gary 683
Jones, Gemma 683
Jones, Geoffrey Gareth 683
Jones, George 683
Jones, Gerald E. 683
Jones, Gill 683
Jones, Gina 683
Jones, Glenys 683
Jones, Hamlyn Gordon 683
Jones, Hank 683
Jones, Harry 683
Jones, Hettie 683
Jones, Howard 683
Jones, Hugh 683
Jones, Ivan 683
Jones, Jack 683
Jones, JaCoby 683
Jones, Jacque 683
Jones, Jade 683
Jones, Jalen 683
Jones, James 683
Jones, James Earl 683
Jones, James L. 683
Jones, James Larkin 683
Jones, Janice 683
Jones, Jasmine 684
Jones, Jason 684
Jones, J.B. 684
Jones, Jeff 684
Jones, Jennifer 684
Jones, Jenny 684
Jones, J.G. 684
Jones, John D. 684
Jones, John Mesach 684
Jones, Jon 684
Jones, Jonathan 684
Jones, Josephine Mary 684
Jones, J.P. 684
Jones, Julian 684
Jones, Julio 684
Jones, Kathleen W. 684
Jones, K.C. 684
Jones, Kelly 684
Jones, Ken P. 684
Jones, Kristina 684
Jones, Landry 684
Jones, Lara 684
Jones, Laura 684
Jones, Laurie Beth 684
Jones, Leanne 684
Jones, Leisel 684
Jones, Lenny 684
Jones, LeRoi 684
Jones, Leslie 684
Jones, Leslie Ann 684
Jones, Lewis 684
Jones, Linda 684
Jones, Linda Winstead 684
Jones, Lloyd 684
Jones, Lolo 684
Jones, Luuka 684
Jones, Lyndon Hamer 684
Jones, Maggie 684
Jones, Maitland, Jr. 684
Jones, Marcel 684
Jones, Marcia Thornton 684
Jones, Marie D. 684
Jones, Marion 684
Jones, Marjorie G. 684
Jones, Mark 684
Jones, Mark A. 684
Jones, Martin 684
Jones, Marvin 684
Jones, Mary Doody 684
Jones, Matt 684
Jones, Megan 684
Jones, Michael 684
Jones, Michael K. 684
Jones, Miranda 684
Jones, Nate 684
Jones, Norah 684
Jones, Noreen 684
Jones, P. 684
Jones, Patricia 684
Jones, Patrick Monty 684
Jones, Perry 684
Jones, Pete 684
Jones, Peter H. 684
Jones, Peter J. 685
Jones, Peter Malcom 685
Jones, Phil 685
Jones, Popeye 685
Jones, Prudence 685
Jones, Quincy 685
Jones, Randall Sidney 685
Jones, Rashida 685
Jones, Rebecca K. 685
Jones, Reshad 685
Jones, Richard 685
Jones, Rob 685
Jones, Robert 685
Jones, Robert Earl 685
Jones, Rob Lloyd 685
Jones, Roderick 685
Jones, Ronald 685
Jones, Ronald Winthrop 685
Jones, Roy, Jr. 685
Jones, Salena 685
Jones, Sally Lloyd 685
Jones, Sarah 685
Jones, Seantavius 685
Jones, Shirley R. 685
Jones, Simon 685
Jones, Simon Peyton 685
Jones, Stephanie M. 685
Jones, Stephen 685
Jones, Stephen Lloyd 685
Jones, Steve 685
Jones, Steven 685
Jones, Steven H. 685
Jones, Susanna 685
Jones, Susannah 685
Jones, Taiwan 685
Jones, Terrence 685
Jones, Terry 685
Jones, Tevin 685
Jones, Thom 685
Jones, Thomas 685
Jones, Thomas O. 685
Jones, Timothy K. 685
Jones, T.J. 685
Jones, Tom 685
Jones, Tommy Lee 685
Jones, Tony 685
Jones, Travis 685
Jones, Trent 685
Jones, Tyler 685
Jones, Tyus 685
Jones, Ursula 685
Jones, Van 685
Jones, V.M. 685
Jones, Walter 685
Jones, Will 685
Jonze, Spike 686

ジョンズ
Johns, Brian 676
Johns, Chris 676
Johns, Geoff 676
Johns, Glyn 676
Johns, Linda 676
Jones, Tristan 685

ジョーンズ・クアーティー
Jones-quartey, Harold 685

ジョンスタッド
Johnstad, Kurt 680

ジョンストーン
Johnstone, Sam 681

ジョンストン
Johnston, Abigail 680
Johnston, Alan B. 680
Johnston, Andrew Kenneth 680
Johnston, Anita A. 680
Johnston, Antony 680
Johnston, Bruce 680
Johnston, David 680
Johnston, Dileri Borunda 680
Johnston, Jacob 680
Johnston, Jane 680
Johnston, Joan 680
Johnston, Joe 680
Johnston, Joni E. 680
Johnston, Joseph A. 680
Johnston, Linda O. 680
Johnston, Norma 680
Johnston, Norman Bruce 680
Johnston, Ollie 680
Johnston, Paul 680
Johnston, Ron 680
Johnston, Ronald John 681
Johnston, Sarah 681
Johnston, Summerfield 681
Johnston, Thomas Robert Roy 681
Johnston, Tim 681
Johnston, T.W. 681
Johnston, Victor S. 681
Johnston, William 681
Johnstone, Ainsley 681
Johnstone, Bob 681
Johnstone, Chris 681
Johnstone, Clarke 681
Johnstone, David 681
Johnstone, Gerry 681
Johnstone, Keith 681
Johnstone, Matthew 681
Johnstone, Megan-Jane 681
Johnstone, Nick 681
Johnstone, Tyler 681

ジョーンズモーガン
Jones-morgan, Judith 685

ジョンスン
Johnson, Denis 677
Johnson, Kij 678
Johnson, Rheta Grimsley 679
Johnson, Terry 680

ジョンセン
Jonsen, Albert R. 686

ジョンソン
Johnson, Abigail Pierrepont 676
Johnson, Adam 676
Johnson, Adrian 676
Johnson, Alan 676
Johnson, Aldene 676
Johnson, Alex 676
Johnson, Alexander 676
Johnson, Alissa 676
Johnson, Ambullai 676
Johnson, Amir 676
Johnson, Andre 676
Johnson, André 676
Johnson, Angela 676
Johnson, Anna 676
Johnson, Anne M. 676
Johnson, Anthony 676
Johnson, Anthony Godby 676
Johnson, Austin 676
Johnson, Avery 676
Johnson, Barbara 676
Johnson, Bea 676

Johnson, Ben 676
Johnson, Beni 676
Johnson, Bill 676
Johnson, Bob 676
Johnson, Boris 676
Johnson, Brian 676
Johnson, Brian David 676
Johnson, Brice 676
Johnson, Bruce 676
Johnson, Bryan P. 676
Johnson, Cam 676
Johnson, Catherine 677
Johnson, Chad 677
Johnson, Chalmers 677
Johnson, Charles 677
Johnson, Charles Richard 677
Johnson, Chase 677
Johnson, Chris 677
Johnson, Claudia 677
Johnson, Cory 677
Johnson, Craig Hella 677
Johnson, Craig W. 677
Johnson, C.Ray 677
Johnson, Crispin Grey 677
Johnson, Curtis W. 677
Johnson, Dale H. 677
Johnson, Dane 677
Johnson, Dani 677
Johnson, Daniel 677
Johnson, Dave 677
Johnson, Davey 677
Johnson, David 677
Johnson, David Leslie 677
Johnson, David T. 677
Johnson, David W. 677
Johnson, D.B. 677
Johnson, Denis 677
Johnson, Denise J. 677
Johnson, Derek 677
Johnson, Derrick 677
Johnson, Devon 677
Johnson, Devonte 677
Johnson, Diane 677
Johnson, Diane Clark 677
Johnson, Dontae 677
Johnson, Dorothea 677
Johnson, Douglas 677
Johnson, Douglas William John 677
Johnson, Duke 677
Johnson, Dustin 677
Johnson, Dwayne 677
Johnson, Earvin 677
Johnson, Eddie 677
Johnson, Elizabeth 677
Johnson, Elizabeth S. 677
Johnson, Erik 677
Johnson, Fabian 677
Johnson, Fran 677
Johnson, G. 677
Johnson, Gary Earl 677
Johnson, Gary V. 677
Johnson, Genevieve Fuji 677
Johnson, George 677
Johnson, George Brooks 677
Johnson, George Clayton 677
Johnson, Gerry 677
Johnson, Gillian 677
Johnson, Glen 677
Johnson, Gordon 678
Johnson, Gus 678
Johnson, Howard W. 678
Johnson, H.Thomas 678
Johnson, Hugh 678
Johnson, Ian 678
Johnson, Isaiah 678
Johnson, Jade 678
Johnson, Jamel 678
Johnson, James 678
Johnson, James-Michael 678
Johnson, Jane 678
Johnson, Janice Kay 678
Johnson, Jeff 678
Johnson, Jeff A. 678
Johnson, Jeh 678
Johnson, Jennifer 678
Johnson, Jeron 678
Johnson, Jerrod 678
Johnson, Jerry L. 678
Johnson, Jessica K. 678
Johnson, Jill 678
Johnson, Jim 678
Johnson, Jinny 678
Johnson, J.J. 678
Johnson, J.Karl 678
Johnson, Joe 678
Johnson, John H. 678
Johnson, Johnnie 678
Johnson, Josh 678
Johnson, Joy 678
Johnson, Judith A. 678
Johnson, June 678
Johnson, Kaleb 678
Johnson, Kamal 678
Johnson, Keith O. 678
Johnson, Kelby 678
Johnson, Kelley 678
Johnson, Ken 678
Johnson, Kenneth 678
Johnson, Kevin 678
Johnson, Kim K.P. 678
Johnson, Kristine 678
Johnson, Kurt W. 678
Johnson, Lane 678
Johnson, Larry 678
Johnson, Lauren 678
Johnson, Laveli Korboi 678
Johnson, Le'Andria 678
Johnson, Leavander 678
Johnson, Leonard 678
Johnson, Lisa 678
Johnson, Louise C. 678
Johnson, Luke 678
Johnson, Lynelle R. 678
Johnson, Magic 678
Johnson, Malcolm 678
Johnson, Manuel H.Jr. 678
Johnson, Marcus 678
Johnson, Marie 678
Johnson, Marion 678
Johnson, Mark 678, 679
Johnson, Mark Henry 679
Johnson, Mark Steven 679
Johnson, Mark W. 679
Johnson, Mary Ann 679
Johnson, Mary L. 679
Johnson, Micah 679
Johnson, Michael 679
Johnson, Michael David 679
Johnson, Michael L. 679
Johnson, Michel J. 679
Johnson, Mike 679
Johnson, Nanci W. 679
Johnson, Neil F. 679
Johnson, Nelson 679
Johnson, Nick 679
Johnson, Nicole 679
Johnson, Nkosi 679
Johnson, Norman 679
Johnson, Norris L., Jr. 679
Johnson, Omobola Olubusola 679
Johnson, Orlando 679
Johnson, Paul 679
Johnson, Penny 679
Johnson, Perry Lawrence 679
Johnson, Pete 679
Johnson, Phil 679
Johnson, Philip Cortelyou 679
Johnson, Pierce 679
Johnson, Rachel K. 679
Johnson, Ralph 679
Johnson, Randell 679
Johnson, Randy 679
Johnson, Rashad 679
Johnson, R.Burke 679
Johnson, Rebecca 679
Johnson, Rebecca L. 679
Johnson, Richard 679
Johnson, Richard Allen 679
Johnson, Rita Marie 679
Johnson, Robb 679
Johnson, Robert L. 679
Johnson, Robert Underwood 679
Johnson, Rod 679
Johnson, Roger T. 679
Johnson, Rufus 679
Johnson, Russell 679
Johnson, Ryan 679
Johnson, Sam 679
Johnson, Sandra L. 679
Johnson, Scott 679
Johnson, Shawn 679
Johnson (Tosta), Sheena 679
Johnson, Simon 679
Johnson, Spencer 679
Johnson, Stanley 680
Johnson, Staz 680
Johnson, Steele 680
Johnson, Stephen 680
Johnson, Stephen T. 680
Johnson, Sterling 680
Johnson, Steve 680
Johnson, Steven 680
Johnson, Storm 680
Johnson, Sue 680
Johnson, Susan 680
Johnson, Susan M. 680
Johnson, Susanne 680
Johnson, Suzanne M. Nora 680
Johnson, Terry 680
Johnson, Tim 680
Johnson, T.J. 680
Johnson, Toby 680
Johnson, Tom 680
Johnson, Tommy 680
Johnson, Tory 680
Johnson, Toureano 680
Johnson, Trumaine 680
Johnson, Tyler 680
Johnson, Van 680
Johnson, Vic 680
Johnson, Virginia E. 680
Johnson, Wesley 680
Johnson, Wilko 680
Johnson, Will 680
Johnson, William G. 680
Johnson, Zach 680
Johnson-Bennett, Pam 680
Jonson, Keith L. 686
Jonson, Roger T. 686
Jonsson, Patrik 686

ジョンソン＝シェルトン
Johnson-Shelton, Nils 680

ジョンソンスミス
Johnson-smith, Kamina 680

ジョンソン－デイヴィーズ
Johnson-Davies, Denys 680

ジョンソントンプソン
Johnson-thompson, Katarina 680

ジョンソンモリス
Johnsonmorris, Frances 680

ジョンソンモンタノ
Johnson Montano, Alysia 680

ションタワッ
Chomtawet, Chiedchai 259

ジョン・トラル
Jon Toral 686

ショーンバーグ
Schoenberg, Loren 1257
Schonberg, Harold C. 1257

ションバーグ
Schonberg, Alan R. 1257

ショーンフェルド
Schoenfeld, Steven A. 1257
Schonfeld, David J. 1258

ジョンフン
John-hoon 676

ジョンボ
Djombo, Henri 360

ショーンボーン
Schönborn, Richard 1257

ションラウ
Schonlau, Julia 1258

ジョン・リッター
Ritter, John 1185

ジョン・ルック
John Luk, Jok 676

シーラ
Sylla, Fanta 1373
Sylla, Modibo 1373

シラ
Sylla, Abdourhamane 1373
Sylla, Cheick Taliby 1373
Sylla, Hajda Makoura 1373
Sylla, Jacques 1373
Sylla, Mamadou 1373
Sylla, Ousmane 1373
Sylla, Senkoun 1373

シラー
Schiller, Alex 1252
Schiller, Bernt 1252
Schiller, Bradley R. 1252
Schiller, Carol 1252
Schiller, David 1252
Schiller, Lori 1252
Schiller, Pamela Byrne 1252
Schirra, Walter Marty, Jr. 1253
Shiller, Robert J. 1290
Shirar, Lynda 1291
Sillah, Jato 1299
Sillah, Musa 1299

ジラ
Gira, Dennis 501

ジラー
Ziller, Amanda 1554

シーラ・E.

Sheila· E. 1286
シライシ
Shiraishi, Kazoshi 1291
シライジッチ
Silajdžić, Haris 1298
ジラウド
Giroud, J.P. 502
ジラカシヴィリ
Zirakashvili, Davit 1556
シラカワ
Shirakawa, Sam H. 1291
シラーギ
Szilágyi, Áron 1374
シラギ
Silaghi, Ovidiu Ioan 1298
Szilagyi, Peter G. 1374
シラク
Chirac, Bernadette Chodron de Courcel 256
Chirac, Jacques René 256
Sirak, Ron 1307
シラグーザ
Siragusa, Antonino 1307
シラージ
Siraj, Iram 1307
シラジ
Shirazi, Jack 1291
Siraj, Fegessa 1307
Siraj, Shajahan 1307
シラジー
Szilagyi, Peter G. 1374
シラジェ
Siraj, Fegessa 1307
シラジッチ
Silajdžić, Haris 1298
シラ・ツアラウレレイ
Sila-tualaulelei, Faalavaau Perina Jacqueline 1298
シーラッハ
Schirach, Ferdinand von 1253
ジラーディ
Girardi, Joe 501
ジラード
Girard, Greg 501
Girard, Joe 501
シラトール
Silatolu, Amini 1298
シラニディス
Siranidis, Nikolaos 1307
シラネ
Shirane, Haruo 1291
シラパアチャ
Silpa Archa, Nakorn 1299
ジラユ
Jirayu, James 674
シーララ
Siirala, Antti 1298
シラリエフ
Shiraliyev, Ogtay 1291
ジラール
Girard, Bernard 501
Girard, Christine 501
Girard, François 501
Girard, Frédéric 501
Girard, René 501
Girard, René Noël 501
Girard, Serge 501
ジラルダン
Girardin, Annick 501
Girardin, Brigitte 501
ジラルデ
Girardet, Fredy 501
Girardet, Raoul 501
シラルディ
Schiraldi, Glenn R. 1253
ジラールディ
Girardi, Joe 501
ジラルディ
Girardi, Joe 501
ジラルディーノ
Gilardino, Alberto 497
ジラルディノ
Gilardino, Alberto 497
ジラルド
Girard, Judith L. 501
Girardot, Annie 501
Ziraldo 1556
シーラン
Sheeran, Ed 1286
Sheeran, Josette 1286
ジラン
Gillain, Anne 498
Gillan, Cheryl 498
シランスキ
Shelanski, Howard A. 1286
ジランド
Gilland, Joseph 498
シーリ
Thile, Chris 1396
シーリー
Scheele, Paul R. 1250
Sealy, Richard 1266
Seeley, Thomas D. 1268
Seeley, Tim 1268
Seely, Hart 1268
Seely, Ron 1268
Shealy, Daniel 1285
Sheely, Rachelle K. 1286
Shiely, John S. 1289
シリー
Schily, Otto 1252
ジリ
Giry, Annick de 502
ジリー
Gilly, Cécile 499
シリアズコ
Shliazhko, Tanya 1292
ジリアンゲ
Tjiriange, Ngarikutuke 1407
シーリィ
Scheele, Paul R. 1250
シリカ
Sirika, Hadi 1307
シリガ
Siliga, Sealver 1299
シリキオティス
Silikiotis, Neoklis 1299
シーリグ
Seelig, Tina 1268
シリグ
Sirigu, Salvatore 1307
Sirigu, Sandro 1307
シリクン・ニパットヨティン
Sirikul Nipatyothin 1308
シリケーオ
Sirikaew, Pimsiri 1307
シリーズ
Series, Caroline 1275
ジリスリー
Gillislee, Mike 499
シリセナ
Sirisena, Maithripala 1308
シリチャイ
Sirichai, Distakul 1307
シリット
Schilit, Howard Mark 1252
シリトー
Sillitoe, Alan 1299
シリニャ
Silina, Mara 1299
シリネッリ
Sirinelli, Jean-François 1308
シリノフ
Shirinov, Temir 1291
ジリノフスキー
Zhirinovskii, Vladimir Volfovich 1552
シリビモン
Pramongkhol, Sirivimon 1131
シリブット
Sirivudh, Norodom 1308
ジリボン
Giribone, Jean-Luc 502
シリマラ・スワンポキン
Sirimala Suwannapokin 1308
シリモンコン・シンワンチャー
Sirimongkol Singmanassuk 1308
シリヤ
Siliya, Dora 1299
シリュルニク
Cyrulnik, Boris 310
シリュルニック
Cyrulnik, Boris 310
シリラ
Shirilla, Joan J. 1291
シリラット
Serirath, Sisowath 1275
シリル
Syril, Binnie 1374
シリーロ
Crillo, Patrick 302
シリワタナパクディ
Sirivadhanabhakdi, Charoen 1308
シリン
Shīrīn, Nuzhat 1291
シーリング
Schilling, Govert 1252
シリング
Schilling, Dale 1252
シリングスバーグ
Shillingsburg, Peter L. 1290
シリングフォード
Shillingford, Gloria 1290
Shillingford, Ron 1290
シリンシォーネ
Cirincione, Diane V. 265
シリンシオーネ
Cirincione, Diane V. 265
シリンス
Silins, Egils 1299
シリントン
Sirindhorn, Maha Chakri 1308
シリントン王女
Sirindhorn, Maha Chakri 1308
シリンビンビ
Xirimbimbi, Salomão José Luheto 1531
シール
Seal 1266
Sire, Agnès 1307
シル
Shill, Steve 1290
Sill, Cathryn P. 1299
Sill, John 1299
al-Sir, al-Fatih Taj 1307
ジール
Giele, Janet Zollinger 496
Zihl, Josef 1554
ジル
Gil, Gilberto 497
Gil, Paulo Roberto Do Nascimento 497
Gile, Daniel 498
Gill, Bates 498
Gill, Bob 498
Gill, Jacko 498
Gill, Paramjit 498
Gill, Tom 498
Gilles, Baillet 498
ジルー
Giroud, Françoise 502
Giroud, Olivier 502
Giroux, Henry A. 502
シールア
Sileua, Bounkham 1299
シルアノフ
Siluanov, Anton G. 1299
シルヴァ
Silva, Adhonay 1299
Silva, Daniel 1299
Silva, Irlan 1299
Silva, Lisa De 1299
Silva, Marry Cipriano 1300
Silver, Julie K. 1300
Silver, Ron 1300
シルヴァー
Silver, Alain 1300
Silver, Amanda 1300
Silver, Elizabeth L. 1300
Silver, Eric 1300
Silver, Eve 1300
Silver, Horace Ward Martin Tauares 1300
Silver, Joel 1300
Silver, Lee M. 1300
Silver, Mitch 1300
Silver, Ron 1300
シルヴァーズ
Chilvers, Ian 256
Silvers, Michael 1300
シルヴァースタイン
Silverstein, Jacob 1300
Silverstein, Steven M. 1301
シルヴァーステイ
Silverstein, Craig 1300
シルヴァーストーン
Silverstone, Alicia 1301
シルヴァーノ
Silvano, Richard 1300
Silvano, Susan 1300
シルヴァノ
Silvano, Renu Rita 1300
シルヴァーバーグ
Silverberg, Robert 1300
シルヴァーマン
Silverman, Ellyn 1300
Silverman, Joseph H. 1300
Silverman, Kenneth 1300
シルヴァン
Sirven, Alfred 1308
Sylvain, Dominique 1373

シ

シルヴァンデール
Sylvander, Matthieu 1373
シルヴィア
Silvia 1301
Silvia, Paul J. 1301
シルヴィアンヌ
Sylviane, Jouenne 1373
シルヴェスター
Silvester, Christopher 1301
Silvester, Hans Walter 1301
Sylvester, David 1373
シルヴェストリ
Silvestri, Alan 1301
シルヴェストル
Silvestre, Mickael 1301
シルヴェストレ
Silvestre, Mickael 1301
シルキア
Sirchia, Girolamo 1307
シルク
Silk, Angèle M.J. 1299
Silk, Joan B. 1299
Silk, John 1299
Silk, Kenneth R. 1299
ジルクリスト
Gilchrist, Cherry 498
Gil Christ, Grant 498
シルコフスキー
Shilkofski, Nicole 1290
シルジェン
Schildgen, Robert 1252
シルシャブ
al-Shirshab, Adil Fahid 1292
シルジュ
Schildge, Sylvia 1252
シールズ
Sheils, William J. 1286
Shields, Andrew 1289
Shields, Brooke 1289
Shields, Carol Ann 1289
Shields, Carol Diggory 1289
Shields, Charles J. 1289
Shields, Claressa 1289
Shields, David 1289
Shields, Erin 1289
Shields, Gillian 1289
Shields, James 1289
Shields, Jody 1289
Shields, Martha 1289
Shields, Michael P. 1289
Shields, Sam 1289
Shields, Sarah D. 1289
Shields, Scott 1289
Shields, Tom 1289
Shields, Will 1289
シルズ
Sills, Beverly 1299
Sills, Charlotte 1299
Sills, David L. 1299
ジルセウ
Dirceu, José 357
ジルソン
Gilson, Patrick 500
Jillson, Joyce 673
シルタラ=ケイナネン
Siltala-Keinänen, Päivi 1299
ジルチ
Jirsch, Anne 674
シルツ
Schildt, Göran 1252
Schiltz, Jean-Louis 1252
Shilts, Donna 1290
シルツァ
Širca, Majda 1307
シールド
Schield, Cat 1252
シルト
Schild, Marlies 1252
Schild, Martina 1252
Schildt, Herbert 1252
シルドン
Shirdon, Abdi Farah 1291
シルノフ
Silnov, Andrey 1299
シールバー
Thielbar, Caleb 1396
シルバ
Silva, Alvaro 1299
Silva, António Burity da 1299
Silva, Armando Ramos da 1299
Silva, Artur 1299
Silva, Augusto Santos 1299
Silva, Cândida Celeste da 1299
Silva, Daniel 1299
Silva, David 1299
Silva, Diogo 1299
Silva, Edinanci 1299
Silva, Emanuel 1299
Silva, Eunice Andrade da 1299
Silva, Filomena Maria Delgado 1299
Silva, Gabriella 1299
Silva, Helder 1299
Silva, Jaime 1299
Silva, Joao 1299
Silva, João Pereira 1299
Silva, José António Da Conceição e 1299
Silva, José Ulysses Correia 1299
Silva, Loreto 1299
Silva, Magali 1299
Silva, Mariana 1299
Silva, Marina 1299
Silva, Mervyn 1300
Silva, Natalia Falavigna da 1300
Silva, Orlando 1300
Silva, Phil A. 1300
Silva, Rafael 1300
Silva, R.B. 1300
Silva, Rodrigo 1300
Silva, Rosa Maria Martins Da Cruz e 1300
Silva, Rui 1300
Silva, Vladimir 1300
Silva, Wanderle 1300
Silva, Washington 1300
Silva, Yadira 1300
Silva, Yarisley 1300
Sylva, Douglas A. 1373
シルバー
Silber, John 1298
Silber, Kevin 1298
Silber, Lee T. 1298
Silber, Nina 1298
Silber, William L. 1298
Silver, Amy 1300
Silver, Andrew 1300
Silver, Elizabeth L. 1300
Silver, Harold 1300
Silver, Horace Ward Martin Tauares 1300
Silver, Jago 1300
Silver, Joel 1300
Silver, Lee M. 1300
Silver, Lynne 1300
Silver, Margery Hutter 1300
Silver, Mitch 1300
Silver, Nan 1300
Silver, Nate 1300
Silver, Pete 1300
Silver, Ron 1300
Silver, Tosha 1300
Silver, Yanik 1300
シルパ
Silupa, Yawa 1299
シルバーウッド
Silverwood, Jane 1301
シルバ・エ・ソウザ・ダイオ
Silva E Sousa Daio, Olinto 1300
シルバーガー
Silberger, Eric 1298
シルバーグ
Silberg, Jackie 1298
シルバーシ
Szilvásy, György 1374
シルバーシャッツ
Silberschatz, Avi 1299
シルバーシュタイン
Silberstein, Stephen D. 1299
Silverstein, Robert Milton 1300
シルバースタイン
Silverstein, David 1300
Silverstein, Luise B. 1300
Silverstein, Michael J. 1300
シルバーストーン
Silverstone, Alicia 1301
Silverstone, Roger 1301
シルバーストン
Silverstone, Barbara 1301
シルバーソーン
Silverthorne, Judith 1301
シルバータウン
Silvertown, Jonathan W. 1301
シルバ・チャル
Sylva Charvet, Érika 1373
シルバ・チャルベ
Sylva Charvet, Érika 1373
シルバッハ
Schilbach, Erich 1252
シルバート
Sylbert, Richard 1373
シルバートン
Silverton, Nancy 1301
シルバーナグル
Silbernagl, Stefan 1299
シルバーブラット
Silverblatt, Art 1300
Silverblatt, Irene Marsha 1300
シルバ・ペレイラ
Silva Pereira, Pedro 1300
シルバ・マルティノト
Silva Martinot, José Luis 1300
シルバーマン
Silberman, Charles E. 1298
Silberman, Ian 1298
Silberman, Neil Asher 1298
Silberman, Steve 1298
Silbermann, Ben 1298
Silverman, Barry 1300
Silverman, David Kaye 1300
Silverman, Erica 1300
Silverman, Jay G. 1300
Silverman, Mark P. 1300
Silverman, Matt 1300
Silverman, Matthew 1300
Silverman, Richard E. 1300
シルバ・ルエテ
Silva Ruete, Jabier 1300
シルバン
Sirven, Alfred 1308
ジルバン・カートライト
Gilvan-Cartwright, Chris 500
シルビア王妃
Silvia 1301
シルビジャー
Silbiger, Steven Alan 1299
シルヒトマン
Schlichtmann, Klaus 1253
シルフ
Silf, Margaret 1299
シルフィ
Sirfi, Ali 1307
シルベスター
Silvester, Marc 1301
Sylvester, James T. 1373
Sylvestre, Junior 1373
シルベストリ
Silvestri, Enzo 1301
シルベストル
Silvestre, Mickael 1301
シルベストレ
Silvestre, Matias 1301
Silvestre, Mickael 1301
シルヘル
Schilcher, Heinz 1252
ジルベール
Gilbert, Dorothée 497
Gilbert, François 497
Gilbert, Gérard 497
Gilbert, Philippe 497
ジルベルシュタイン
Zilberstein, Lilya 1554
ジルベルシュテイン
Zilberstein, Lilya 1554
ジルベルト
Gilberto, João 498
ジルベルト・ジル
Gil, Gilberto 497
シルベルマン
Silberman, Serge 1298
シルマ
Sirma, Musa 1308
シルマー
Schirmer, Ulf 1253
シルマッハー
Schirrmacher, Frank 1253
ジルマール
Gylmar 550
ジールマン
Sielmann, Heinz 1297
シールマンス
Thielemans, Toots 1396
シルール
Shirur, Suma 1292
シルワ

Shirwa, Abdullahi Muhammad 1292
シルワンバ
Silwamba, Eric 1301
シーレ
Shire, Barre Adan 1291
Shire, Said Hassan 1291
ジレ
Gille, Christian 498
Zīle, Roberts 1554
シーレイ
Sealey, Peter 1266
シレイ
Sileye, Gandega 1299
ジレイ
Jiley, Muhammad Nur 673
シーレイジ
Searage, Ray 1266
ジレイジ
Jreij, Ramzi 689
シレオニ
Sileoni, Alberto 1299
シーレグダンバ
Shiilegdamba, Gankhuyag 1290
シレシ
Shileshi, Bekele 1290
Sileshi, Getahun 1299
シレス・デルバジェ
Siles del Valle, Juan Ignacio 1299
シレス・デルプラド
Siles del Prado, Hugo José 1299
ジレスピー
Gillespie, Jacquelyn 499
シレック
Sileck, Asseid Gamar 1299
シレッセン
Cillessen, Jasper 264
シレット
Sirett, Dawn 1307
ジレット
Gillet, Raphael 499
Gillett, Charlie 499
Gillette, Lindsay 499
シレドゥンブヤ
Siredoumbouya, Mamadou 1307
シレム
Chilemme, Guillaume 255
ジレール
Girerd, Jacques-Rémy 502
シーレン
Thielen, Adam 1396
Thielen, David 1396
シレーン
Sirén, Heikki 1307
シレン
Sirén, Heikki 1307
ジーレンジガー
Zielenziger, Michael 1554
シレント
Cilento, Diane 264
ジレンハマー
Gyllenhammar, Pehr Gustaf 550
シロ
Sireau, Kevin 1307
シロー
Shiloh, Michael 1290
ジロ
Gilot, Fabien 500
Giro, Bernard 502
Girod, Francis 502
ジロー
Gillot, Dominique 499
Gillot, Laurence 499
Gilot, Françoise 500
Girard, Anne-Sophie 501
Girard, Marie-Aldine 501
Giraud, Claude 501
Giraud, Yvette 501
Girault, Jacques 501
Giroux, Mathieu 502
ジロイェビッチ
Zirojević, Mladen 1556
ジロイエビッチ
Zirojević, Mladen 1556
シロウィッツ
Sirowitz, Hal 1308
シロカー
Siroker, Dan 1308
シロカプーラ
Shiroka-pula, Justina 1291
シロタ
Sirota, David 1308
ジロドー
Giraudeau, Bernard 501
ジロドゥ
Giraudeau, Bernard 501
シロニー
Shillony, Ben-Ami 1290
シーロフ
Shilov, Lev Alekseevich 1290
ジロボジ
Djilobodji, Papy 359
シロマ
Ciroma, Adamu 265
Ciroma, Maryan 265
シロマニー
Shiromany, A.A. 1291
ジロメン
Gilomen, Heinz 500
ジローラミ
Girolami, Adriana 502
ジロラーミ
De Girolami, Umberto 333
ジーロルド
Zierold, Norman J. 1554
ジロロモーニ
Girolomoni, Gino 502
ジロン
Dillon, C.Douglas 355
シロンディニ
Cirendini, Olivier 265
ジーワー
Jeewah, Ahmad Sulliman 668
シワク
Sivak, Anatoly A. 1308
シワコフ
Sivakov, Yury L. 1308
ジワニア
Zhvania, Lasha 1553
Zhvania, Zurab Vissarionovich 1553
ジワニードワ
Divanidova, Elizaveta Petrovna 358
ジワニヤ
Zhvaniya, Dabid 1553
ジワネフスカヤ
Zhivanevskaya, Nina 1552
シーン
Sheehan, Billy 1285
Sheen, Barry 1286
Sheen, Charlie 1286
Sheen, Martin 1286
シン
Shin, Chungha 1290
Shin, Gak-su 1290
Shin, Gyon-suk 1290
Shin, Ha-gyun 1290
Shin, Hyon-hwak 1290
Shin, Hyung-keun 1290
Shin, Hyun-joon 1290
Shin, Hyun Song 1290
Shin, Hyun-su 1291
Shin, Ji-yai 1291
Shin, Jong-kyun 1291
Shin, Kook-hwan 1291
Shin, Kuhn 1291
Shin, Min-ah 1291
Shin, Sang-okk 1291
Shin, Seung-hun 1291
Shin, Woon-hak 1291
Shing, Emmanuel Leung 1291
Shing, Fui-on 1291
Shingh, Ganga 1291
Shinn, James 1291
Shinn, Sharon 1291
Sin, Il-nam 1305
Sin, Jaime L. 1305
Sin, Thae-rok 1305
Singh, Ajit 1306
Singh, Anant 1306
Singh, Arjun 1306
Singh, Arjun J. 1306
Singh, Ashni 1306
Singh, Bhawani 1306
Singh, Chain 1306
Singh, Chaudhary Birender 1306
Singh, Doodnauth 1306
Singh, Douglas 1306
Singh, Ganga 1306
Singh, Gurpreet 1306
Singh, Harbir 1306
Singh, Janardan Prasad 1306
Singh, Jaswant 1306
Singh, Jerry 1306
Singh, Jitendra 1306
Singh, Khushwant 1306
Singh, K.Natwar 1306
Singh, Manmohan 1306
Singh, Mansher 1306
Singh, Nalini 1306
Singh, Nand Kishore 1306
Singh, Prakash Man 1306
Singh, Radha Mohan 1306
Singh, Raghuvansh Prasad 1306
Singh, Raj Nath 1306
Singh, Ram Narayan 1306
Singh, Renuka 1306
Singh, Sarina 1306
Singh, Simon 1306
Singh, Vijay 1306
Singh, Virbhadra 1306
Singh, Vishwanath Pratap 1306
Singh, V.K. 1306
ジーン
Jean, Ignatius 667
Jean, James 667
Jean, Olivier 667
ジン
Ginn, Drew 500
Ginn, Jay 500
Ginn, Robert Jay, Jr. 500
Jin, Ha 674
Jin, JadeNabi 674
Jin, Ren-qing 674
Jin, S.-B. 674
Zinn, Howard 1555
シンイ
Singhi, Abheek 1306
シンガ
Tinga, Beniamina 1405
シンガー
Singer, Barry 1305
Singer, Blair 1305
Singer, Bryan 1305
Singer, Cindy 1305
Singer, Ellen 1305
Singer, Eric 1305
Singer, Ernest 1305
Singer, Ilana 1305
Singer, Judith D. 1305
Singer, Marc 1305
Singer, Margaret Thaler 1305
Singer, Marilyn 1306
Singer, Marshall 1306
Singer, Mel 1306
Singer, Meriamne B. 1306
Singer, Michael A. 1306
Singer, Nicky 1306
Singer, Paul 1306
Singer, Peter Albert David 1306
Singer, Peter Warren 1306
Singer, Robert N. 1306
Singer, Siegfried Fred 1306
Singer, Susan R. 1306
ジンガイ
Dzingai, Brian 386
ジンガス
Zingas, Aurélien Simplice 1555
シンガーテ
Singhateh, Mama Fatima 1306
シンガテ
Singhatey, Edward 1306
シンカマテオス
Cinca Mateos, Jordi 264
シンカマナン
Singkhamanan, Somboon 1306
シンガーマン
Singerman, Brian 1306
シン・カラ
Sin Cara 1305
ジンガラシュ
Gingăraş, Georgiu 500
シンガル
Singhal, Arvind 1306
ジンガレス
Zingales, Luigi 1555
ジンガロ
Zingaro, Linde 1555
ジンキ
Zinke, Ryan 1555
シンギュラー
Singular, Stephen 1306
シンク
Cink, Stewart 265
シング
Sing, Lama 1305
Sing, Ronald F. 1305
Singh, Khushwant 1306
Singh, Sarina 1306
Singh, Vishwanath

シ

Pratap 1306
ジンク
Zinck, Kenneth 1555
シンクフィールド
Sinkfield, Terrell 1307
シンクフラーフェン
Sinkgraven, Daley 1307
シンクラー
Sinckler, Christopher 1305
シングラー
Shingler, Jo 1291
Shingler, Martin 1291
Singler, E.J. 1306
Singler, Kyle 1306
シングラニ
Cingrani, Tony 264
シングル
Singul, Francisco 1306
シングルトン
Singleton, Ann 1306
Singleton, Doris 1306
Singleton, Georgina 1306
Singleton, Jon 1306
Singleton, Mark 1306
シンクレア
Sinclair, Andrew 1305
Sinclair, Celia Brewer 1305
Sinclair, Charlotte 1305
Sinclair, Dani 1305
Sinclair, David 1305
Sinclair, David Cecil 1305
Sinclair, Hugh 1305
Sinclair, James 1305
Sinclair, Jebb 1305
Sinclair, Jerome 1305
Sinclair, Kenia 1305
Sinclair, Margaret 1305
Sinclair, Mark 1305
Sinclair, Mima 1305
Sinclair, M.Thea 1305
Sinclair, Tracy 1305
Sinclair, Vonda 1305
Sinclare, John 1305
シンクレアー
Sinclair, Gannon 1305
シンクレアン
Sincraian, Gabriel 1305
ジングローン
Zingrone, Frank 1555
シングワナ
Xingwana, Lulu 1531
ジングワナ
Xingwana, Lulama 1531
シンゲ
Singye, Jigme 1306
シンゲイ
Singay, Jigme 1305
シンケビチュス
Sinkevičius, Rimantas 1307
シンケビッチ
Sienkiewicz, Bill 1297
シンゲル
Singer, Saul 1306
シンコビッチ
Sinkovic, Martin 1307
Sinkovic, Valent 1307
ジンサー
Zinsser, William Knowlton 1556
ジンジッチ
Dindjić, Zoran 356
Djindjić, Zoran 359
ジンジャー
Ginger, Serge 500
ジンジャラス
Gingeras, Alison M. 500
ジンジャーリッチ
Gingerich, Wallace J. 500
ジーンズ
Jeans, Peter D. 668
シンセキ
Shinseki, Eric Ken 1291
シン・ソン
Sin Song 1307
シンソン
Singson, Regelio 1306
シンダー
Shinder, Debra Littlejohn 1291
Shinder, Thomas W. 1291
ジンター
Zinter, Alan 1556
シンダーガード
Syndergaard, Noah 1374
シンダビゼラ
Sindabizera, Genevieve 1305
ジンダル
Jindal, Bobby 674
ジンチェンコ
Zinchenko, Oleksandr 1555
Zinczenko, David 1555
シンデ
Shinde, Sushil Kumar 1291
シンデー
Shinde, Gauri 1291
シンディア
Scindia, J.M. 1263
シンディムオ
Sindimwo, Gaston 1305
ジンティリディス
Zintiridis, Revazi 1556
シンデーエット
Schindehette, Susan 1252
シンデル
Sindell, Milo 1305
Sindell, Thuy 1305
ジンデル
Zindell, David 1555
シンデン
Sinden, Donald 1305
Sinden, Pete 1305
ジンテンポ
Gentempo, Patrick 488
シンドゥ
Sindeu, Jean-Bernard 1305
シントゥーラ
Cintura, Iolanda 265
シントラー
Schindler, Regine 1253
シンドラー
Schindler, Ana Von 1252
Schindler, Emilie 1252
Schindler, Nina 1252
Schindler, S.D. 1253
Shindler, Kelley L. 1291
Sindler, Marek 1305
シントラ・フリアス
Cintra Frías, Leopoldo 265
シントロン
Cintron Ocasio, Jeyvier 265
シンニ
Thinni, Abdullah 1396
シンネマキ
Sinnemäki, Anni 1307
シンハ
Sinha, Indra 1306
Sinha, Janmejaya Kumar 1307
Sinha, Manoj 1307
Sinha, Prabhakant 1307
Sinha, Shatrughan 1307
Sinha, Yashwant 1307
シンバ
Simba, Charles Mwando 1301
Simba, Sophia 1301
Simba, Sophia Mnyambi 1301
ジンバ
Zimba, Newstead 1554
Zimba, Yeshey 1554
シンバオ
Simbao, Kapembwa 1301
シンバチャウェネ
Simbachawene, George 1301
ジーン・バプティステ
Jean-baptiste, Stanley 667
シンハマット
Singhamat, Nitas 1306
シンバラ
Cymbala, Jim 310
ジンバリスト
Zimbalist, Andrew 1554
Zimbalist, Efrem, Jr. 1554
ジンバルド
Zimbardo, Philip G. 1554
ジンバルドー
Zimbardo, Philip G. 1554
ジーンピエール
Jeanpierre, Lemuel 668
シンビネ
Simbine, Akani 1301
ジン・ピン
Jin Pyn 674
シンフ
Schimpf, Ryan 1252
シンブ
Simbu, Alphonce Felix 1301
シンフィールド
Sinfield, Joseph V. 1305
シンプスン
Simpson, Marcia 1304
シンプソン
Simpson, Adam 1304
Simpson, Alistair 1304
Simpson, Andrew 1304
Simpson, Anne 1304
Simpson, Brandon 1304
Simpson, Carolyn 1304
Simpson, Cornell 1304
Simpson, Danny 1304
Simpson, David 1304
Simpson, Donna 1304
Simpson, Dwain 1304
Simpson, Edwin L. 1304
Simpson, Gerry J. 1304
Simpson, Ian 1304
Simpson, James R. 1304
Simpson, Jeffry A. 1304
Simpson, Jennifer 1304
Simpson, Jerome 1304
Simpson, Kyle 1304
Simpson, Liz 1304
Simpson, Louis Aston Marantz 1304
Simpson, Margaret 1304
Simpson, Marita 1304
Simpson, Michael 1304
Simpson, Michael K. 1304
Simpson, Michael T. 1304
Simpson, N.F. 1304
Simpson, Ralph David 1304
Simpson, Savitri 1304
Simpson, Sherone 1304
Simpson, Sophie 1304
Simpson, Stephen 1304
Simpson, Webb 1304
シンプソン・ミラー
Simpson-Miller, Portia Lucretia 1304
シンブヤクラ
Simbyakula, Ngosa 1301
シンブラン
Simbulan, Roland G. 1301
シンプロット
Simplot, John Richard 1304
シンペット・クルアイトン
Sinphet Kruaithong 1307
ジンポー
Ching Po, Wong 256
シンボルスカ
Szymborska, Wisława 1375
シンマ
Simma, Maria 1302
ジンマー
Zimmer, Carl 1555
ジンマーマン
Zimmermann, Marie-Claire 1555
Zimmermann, Michel 1555
Zimmermann, Polly Gerber 1555
ジンマン
Zinman, David 1555
シンメル
Schimmel, Annemarie 1252
ジンメル
Simmel, Derry 1302
Simmel, Johannes Mario 1302
シンメルプフェニヒ
Schimmelpfennig, Roland 1252
シンメルペンニンク＝ファン＝デル＝オイェ
Schimmelpenninck van der Oye, David 1252
シンヤシキ
Shinyashiki, Roberto Tadeu 1291
シンラウォン
Sinlavong, Khoutphaythoune 1307
ジンランガーダドナジ
Djimrangar Dadnadji, Joseph 359
シンレイチ
Sinnreich, Richard Hart 1307
シンワリ
Shinwari, Faisal Ahmad 1291

【ス】

スー
Hsu, Jason C. 630
Hsu, Vivian 630
Seau, Ian 1266
Shi, Zhan-chun 1289
Shih, Chen-jung 1290
Shu, Qi 1294
Sou, Ngarbatina Carmel, Ⅳ 1330
Su, Chao-pin 1361
Sū, Tóng 1362
Su, Yuyan 1362
Suh, Elly 1363
Suh, H.Anna 1363
Suh, Nam Pyo 1363
Suh, Ndamukong 1363
Thu, Kendall 1402
ズー
Zhu, Michael 1553
ズアイタル
Zeaiter, Ghazi 1549
ズアイテル
Zoayter, Ghazi 1556
Zouaiter, Ghazi 1557
スアウ
Suau, Anthony 1362
スアクリ
Souakri, Salima 1330
スアゲル
Suagher, Emanuele 1362
スアーソ
Suazo, David 1362
スアソ
Suazo, David 1362
スアード
Seward, Desmond 1276
スアド
Souad 1330
ズーアリ
Zouari, Abderrahim 1557
スアリキ
Sualiki, Namoliki 1362
スアレ
Souare, Ahmed Tidiane 1330
Souare, Pape 1330
ズアーレイン
Zuerlein, Greg 1558
スアレース
Suarez, Daniel 1362
スアレス
Suárez, Adolfo 1362
Suarez, Albert 1362
Suarez, Andrew 1362
Suarez, Charly Coronel 1362
Suarez, Eugenio 1362
Suárez, Federico 1362
Suárez, Jesús 1362
Suarez, Leonel 1362
Suarez, Luis 1362
Suarez, Paola 1362
Suarez Fernandez, Miguel 1362
スアレズ＝オロズコ
Suarez-Orozco, Carola 1362
スアレスナバロ
Suarez Navarro, Carla 1362
スアレス・ハポン
Suárez Japón, Juan Manuel 1362
スアレス・ペレス
Suárez Pérez, Sandra 1362
スアレス・ロサーダ
Suárez Losada, Juan José 1362
スアン・トゥアン
Xuan Thuan, Trinh 1532
スイ
Sui, Anna 1363
Sui, Lu 1363
Suy Sem 1369
スィーアウォール
Thirlwall, Jade 1396
ズイキナ
Zykina, Ludmila 1560
ズィクリ
Zikri, Ali Yusif 1554
スィシェル
Sichère, Bernard 1295
スイス
Swiss, James Edwin 1372
Swiss, Jamy Ian 1372
スイ・セム
Suy Sem 1369
スイッシャー
Swisher, Joel N. 1372
スィッディーキー
Siddīqī, Shaukat 1296
スィート
Sweet, David 1371
スイート
Sweet, J.H. 1371
Sweet, Melissa 1372
スイトナー
Suitner, Otmar 1363
スイートランド
Sweetland, Ben 1372
ズィトリン
Zitrin, Richard A. 1556
スイニー
Sweeney, Matthew 1371
ズィーバー
Sieber, Ulrich 1296
スイフト
Swift, Taylor 1372
スィーボード
Thiebaud, Twinka 1396
スィーミーン・ダーネシュヴァル
Sīmīn Dāneshvar 1302
スィムンズソン
Simundsson, Elva 1305
スィユタ
Cieutat, Michel 264
スイリ
Souyri, Pierre 1332
スィール
Thiel, Pieter Gustav 1396
スィロミャートニコフ
Syromiatnikov, Nikolai Aleksandrovich 1374
スィン
Singh, Khushwant 1306
スィング
Singh, Khushwant 1306
ズィンク
Zink, Rui 1555
スウ
Hsu, Hwei P. 630
ズウ
Zhu, Xu 1553
スヴァア
Svarre, Birgitte 1370
スヴァーイ
Swaaij, Louise van 1370
スヴァイストロップ
Sveistrup, Søren 1370
ズヴァイヤー
Zwier, Lawrence J. 1560
スヴァーテングレン
Svartengren, Magnus 1370
スヴァルダル
Svardal, Geir 1369
スヴァン
Swann, Leonie 1371
スヴァンベリ
Swanberg, Lena Katarina 1371
スウィアジンスキー
Swierczynski, Duane 1372
スウィアテク
Swiatek, Frank 1372
スヴィエラーク
Svěrák, Jan 1370
Sverak, Zdenek 1370
スヴィオクラ
Sviokla, John 1370
スウィーガー
Swiger, Kristopher J. 1372
スウィサ
Suissa, Eliyahu 1363
スウィージー
Sweezy, J.R. 1372
Sweezy, Paul Marlor 1372
Swezey, Annette M. 1372
Swezey, Robert L. 1372
スウィズ・ビーツ
Swizz Beatz 1373
ズウィック
Zwick, Edward 1560
スウィッシャー
Swisher, Nick 1372
スウィッツァー
Switzer, Janet 1372
ズヴィッツアー
Zwitzer, H.L. 1560
スウィット
Suvit, Maesincee 1369
Suvit, Yodmani 1369
Suwit, Khunkitti 1369
スウィツラー
Switzler, Al 1372
スウィーティング
Sweeting, Paul 1372
スウィーテク
Switek, Brian 1372
スウィーテン
Sweeten, Sami 1372
スウィート
Sweet, Fay 1371
Sweet, Kelly 1371
Sweet, Melissa 1372
Sweet, Michael 1372
Sweet, Victoria 1372
スウィード
Swede, Shirley 1371
スウイトカウスキー
Switkowski, Ziggy 1372
スウィトコウスキー
Switkowski, Ziggy 1372
スウィトナー
Suitner, Otmar 1363
スウィートマン
Sweetman, Bill 1372
Sweetman, Paul 1372
スウィドラー
Swidler, Ann 1372
スウィーナ
Soueinae, Vatma Vall Mint 1330
スウィーニー
Sweeney, Anne Mary 1371
Sweeney, Charles W. 1371
Sweeney, Emma 1371
Sweeney, John 1371
Sweeney, Leann 1371
Sweeney, Matthew 1371
Sweeney, Michael S. 1371
Sweeney, Ryan 1371
Sweeney, Sean 1371
Sweeny, Frank 1371
Sweeny, John 1371
スウィーニィ
Sweeney, Michael S. 1371
スウィフト
Swift, Adam 1372
Swift, David 1372
Swift, Graham 1372
Swift, Michael 1372
Swift, Richard 1372
Swift, Ronald S. 1372
Swift, Sally 1372
Swift, Sue 1372
Swift, Taylor 1372
スウイフト
Swift, David 1372
スウィム
Swimme, Brian 1372
スヴィリドフ
Sviridov, Evgeny 1370
スウィング
Swing, Randy L. 1372
スウィングス
Swings, Bart 1372
ズウィングル
Zwingle, Erla 1560
スウィンソン
Swinson, Tim 1372
スヴィンダール
Svindal, Aksel Lund 1370
スヴィンダル
Svindal, Aksel Lund 1370
スウィンディン
Swindin, George Hedley 1372
スウィンデルズ
Swindells, Robert 1372
スウィンドル
Swindle, Howard 1372
Swindle, Jordan 1372
Swindoll, Charles R. 1372
スウィントン
Swinton, Tilda 1372
スウィンバーン
Swinburne, Richard 1372
スウィンバンク
Swinbank, Alan 1372
スウィンボーン
Swinbourne, Helen 1372
スウェアリンジャー
Swearinger, D.J. 1371
スウェイジ
Swayze, Patrick 1371

スウェイズ
Swayze, Patrick 1371
スウェイツ
Thwaites, Ronald 1403
スウェイツァー
Sweitzer, BobbieJean 1372
スウェイド
Suwayd, Joseph 1369
Suwayd, Yusuf 1369
スヴェイネ
Svane, Freddy 1369
スウェイ・ファイロ
Su'a-filo, Xavier 1362
スウェイム
Sveum, Dale 1370
Swaim, Geoff 1370
スウェイル
al-Suwaiyel, Mohammed Ibn Ibrahim 1369
ズウェイル
Zewail, Ahmed 1551
スウェイルズ
Swales, Michaela A. 1370
スウェイン
Swain, Chris 1370
Swain, Donald C. 1370
Swain, Frank 1370
Swain, Holly 1370
Swain, James 1370
Swain, John 1370
Swain, Monte 1370
スヴェインソン
Sveinsson, Kjartan 1370
スウェターリッチ
Sweterlitsch, Thomas 1372
スウェット
Sweat, Brooke 1371
Sweat, Matthew H. 1371
Sweat, Roy W. 1371
スウェッド
Szwed, John F. 1375
ズヴェーデン
Zweden, Jaap van 1560
スウェド
Szwed, John F. 1375
スヴェードボリ
Swedberg, Richard 1371
スヴェトラーナ
Svetlana, Chezhina 1370
スヴェトラーノフ
Svetlanov, Evgenii Fedorovich 1370
スウェドロー
Swedroe, Larry E. 1371
スウェプストン
Swepston, Lee 1372
スヴェラーク
Svěrák, Jan 1370
スウェーリング
Swerling, Lisa 1372
スウェル
Sewell, Bill 1276
Sewell, Carl 1276
Sewell, Laura M. 1277
Sewell, Marc T. 1277
ズウェル
Zwell, Michael 1560
スウェンセン
Swensen, David F. 1372
スヴェンセン
Svendsen, Emil Hegle 1370
Svendsen, Lars Fr.H. 1370
スウェンソン
Swenson, Jamie 1372
スヴェンソン
Svensson, Börje 1370
Svensson, Lars E.O. 1370
スウェンデン
Swenden, Wilfried 1372
スウェンドソン
Swendson, Shanna 1372
スウォーザック
Swarzak, Anthony 1371
スウォーツ
Swartz, Teresa A. 1371
スウォープ
Swope, Sam 1373
スヴォボーダ
Svoboda, Helmut 1370
スヴォボダ
Svoboda, Josef 1370
Svoboda, Peter 1370
Svoboda, Terese 1370
スウード
Suood, Husnu 1367
ズウビ
Zu'bi, Akef al 1558
スウープ
Swoope, Erik 1373
スヴャトコフスカ
Swiatkowska, Gabi 1372
スヴューム
Sveum, Sue 1370
スエ
Jooae 686
スエイシ
Suyeishi, Kazuye 1369
スエニョ
Sueño, Ismael 1363
ズエフ
Zuyev, Viktar 1559
ズエワ
Zueva, Anastasia 1558
スェン
Suen, Anastasia 1363
スエーン
Swain, Ben 1370
スエンセン
Swensen, David F. 1372
スオー
Suau, Anthony 1362
スオウ
Suau, Anthony 1362
スオフォード
Swofford, Anthony 1373
スオメラ
Suomela, Jukka Tapani 1367
ズオン・トゥー・フオン
Duong Thu Huong 382
ズオン・バン・ミン
Duong Van Minh 382
スカ
Ska, Jean Louis 1309
スカー
Scarre, Christopher 1248
スカイ
Sky, Rick 1311
Sukhai, Pauline 1363
スガイ
Sugai, Madoka 1363
スカイァミー
Skyrme, David J. 1311
スカイエレーズ
Scailliérez, Cécile 1247
スカイオーラ
Scajola, Claudio 1247
スカイフ
Scaife, Richard Mellon 1247
スカウ
Schou, Ingjerd 1258
Schow, David J. 1258
スカーヴィック
Skarvik, Roger 1309
ズカウスカス
Zukauskas, Henrikas 1558
スカウソン
Skousen, Mark 1310
スカウン
Scown, Rebecca 1265
スカクーン
Skakoon, James G. 1309
スカクン
Skakun, Nataliya 1309
スカージ
Scaasi, Arnold 1247
スカジンスキ
Skurzyinski, Gloria 1311
スカタ
Skuta, Dan 1311
スカーダマリア
Scardamalia, Marlene 1248
スカッツ
Scutts, Jerry 1266
スカッド
Scud 1265
スカッフ
Skaff, Elias 1309
スカティ
Sukati, Dumsile 1363
スカーディナ
Scardina, Mark 1248
スカーディーノ
Scardino, Marjorie Morris 1248
スカナイバル
Sukanaivalu, Netani 1363
スカナインバル
Sukanaivalu, Netani 1363
ズカノヴィッチ
Zukanovic, Ervin 1558
スガハラ
Sugahara, Akira 1363
スカフ
Skaff, Elias 1309
ズーカフ
Zukav, Gary 1558
スカープマン
Schaapman, Karina 1248
スカーボロー
Scarborough, Adrian 1248
ズーカーマン
Zukerman, Pinchas 1558
スカムポン
Sukumpol, Suwanatat 1364
スカヨラ
Scajola, Claudio 1247
スカラ
Scala, Delia 1247
Scala, James 1247
Scala, Simona 1247
スカラー
Sklar, Bernard 1310
スカラヴェリ
Scaravelli, Vanda 1248
スカラピーノ
Scalapino, Robert Anthony 1247
スカランティノ
Scarantino, Mirco 1248
スカリ
Scali, Massimo 1248
Skalli, Nouzha 1309
Skari-martinsen, Bente 1309
スカリー
Sculley, John 1265
Scully, Blaine 1265
Scully, Claire 1265
Scully, Matthew 1265
Scully, Vin 1265
スカリア
Scalia, Antonin 1248
スカリオン
Scullion, Nigel 1265
スカーリット
Skerrit, Roosevelt 1310
スカリーニ
Scalini, Mario 1248
スカール
Scarre, Geoffrey 1248
スカル
Scull, Christina 1265
ズカル
Zukal, Anna 1558
スカルスガルド
Skarsgård, J.Stellan 1309
スカルスゲールド
Skarsgård, J.Stellan 1309
スカルソープ
Sculthorp, Frederick C. 1265
Sculthorpe, Peter Joshua 1266
スカルタン
Skultans, Vieda 1311
スガルダン
Zgardan, Vasile 1551
ズガルダン
Zgardan, Vasile 1551
スカルタンス
Skultans, Vieda 1311
スカルディーノ
Scardino, Marjorie Morris 1248
Scardino, Peter T. 1248
スカルディノ
Scardino, Marjorie Morris 1248
Skardino, Nadezhda 1309
スガルドリ
Sgardoli, Guido 1277
スカルノ
Hartini 577
スカルパ
Scarpa, David 1248
Scarpa, Tiziano 1248
スカルファロ
Scalfaro, Oscar Luigi 1248
スカルプノルド
Skarpnord, Marianne 1309
スカルプヘイジンソン
Skarphedinsson, Ossur 1309
スカルペッタ
Scarpetta, Guy 1248

スカルペッリ
Scarpelli, Furio 1248
スカルメタ
Skármeta, Antonio 1309
スカレ
Sukale, Nyavu 1363
スカレーラ
Scalera, Darlene 1248
スカーレン
Skalén, Per 1309
スカロウ
Scarrow, Alex 1248
スカーロック
Scurlock, James D. 1266
スーカロバ
Soukalova, Gabriela 1330
スガン
Séguin, Benoît 1269
ズガンク
Zgank, Mihael 1551
スカンダリディス
Skandalidis, Konstantinos 1309
Skandalidis, Kostas 1309
スカンタル
Skantar, Ladislav 1309
Skantar, Peter 1309
スカンプ
Schamp, Tom 1249
スガン＝フォント
Séguin-Fontes, Marthe 1269
スカンラン
Scanlan, Laetisha 1248
スキアー
Squier, Harriet 1338
スキーアビ
Schiavi, Raul C. 1251
スキアフィーノ
Schiaffino, Juan Alberto 1251
スキアボーネ
Schiavone, Francesca 1251
スギアルト
Sugiarto, Tommy 1363
スキット
Skitt, Carolyn 1310
スキッドモア
Skidmore, Frank M. 1310
Skidmore, Steve 1310
スキッパーズ
Schippers, Dafne 1253
スキップ
Skipp, John 1310
スキッロ
Schillo, Keith K. 1252
スキティ
Schiti, Valerio 1253
スキデルスキー
Skidelsky, Edward 1310
Skidelsky, Robert 1310
スキーナ
Skiena, Steven S. 1310
スキナー
Skinner, Andrew Stewart 1310
Skinner, Callum 1310
Skinner, Catherine 1310
Skinner, Dave 1310
Skinner, Deontae 1310
Skinner, James 1310
Skinner, Jimmy 1310
Skinner, Kerry 1310
Skinner, Morgan 1310
Skinner, Quentin 1310
Skinner, Scott 1310
Skinner, Stephen 1310
Skinner, Todd 1310
スキナ・ビンティ・ペンギラン・ダト・パドゥカ・ハジ・ヒィドゥップ
Sukinah Binti Pg Dato Paduka Haji Hidup, Pg 1364
スキパース
Schippers, Lies 1253
スギハルト
Sugiharto 1363
スギマチ
Sugimachi, Mahau 1363
スキーム
Skeem, Jennifer L. 1309
スギモト
Sugimoto, Hiroshi 1363
スキャヴェリ
Schiavelli, Vincent Andrew 1251
スキャゲル
Scagell, Robin 1247
スキャゼロ
Scazzero, Peter 1248
スキャッグス
Scaggs, Boz 1247
Skaggs, Ricky 1309
Skaggs, Tyler 1309
スキャッデン
Scadden, Lawrence 1247
スキャブランド
Skabelund, Aaron Herald 1309
スキャベリ
Schiavelli, Vincent Andrew 1251
スキャメル＝カッツ
Scamell-Katz, Siemon 1248
スキャリー
Scarry, Huck 1248
Scarry, Patricia M. 1248
スキャロン
Scanlon, Tara 1248
スキャンドリック
Scandrick, Orlando 1248
スキャンロン
Scanlo, Brian L. 1248
Scanlon, Bill 1248
Scanlon, Dan 1248
Scanlon, Elizabeth Garton 1248
Scanlon, Kathleen M. 1248
Scanlon, Paul 1248
スキラング・テメンギル
Skilang Temengil, Florian 1310
スキランダ
Zuquilanda, Patricio 1559
スキリング
Skilling, April Dawn 1310
Skilling, Vita Akapito 1310
スキール
Skeel, Roland T. 1309
スキルダ
Skyrda, Liudmyla M. 1311
スキルダム＝レイド
Skildum-Reid, Kim 1310
スギルタラージャ
Sugirtharajah, Rasiah S. 1363
スキレ
Skille, Olav 1310
スキレッピ
Scindia, J.M. 1263
ズーキン
Zukin, Sharon 1559
スキンナリ
Skinnari, Jouko 1310
スーク
Sook, Ryan 1328
Suk, Josef 1363
ズーク
Zook, Ben 1557
スクイテ
Skujyte, Austra 1311
スクイテン
Schuiten, François 1259
スクウェアー
Square, Damion 1338
スクウェイヤ
Skweyiya, Zola 1311
スクウォルツォフ
Skvortsov, Nikolay 1311
スクウォルトフ
Scvortov, Victor 1266
スクーズ
Skues, Richard A. 1311
スクーセン
Skousen, Willard Cleon 1310
スクソ・イトゥリ
Suxo Iturry, Nardi 1369
スクッテン
Schutten, Jan Paul 1261
スクデフ
Sukhdev, Pavan 1364
スクナージ
Skenazy, Lenore 1310
スクナーフ
Schnarf, Johanna 1255
スクバルネリス
Skvernelis, Saulius 1311
スクビシェフスキ
Skubiszewski, Krzysztof Jan 1311
スクーピン
Skupin, Brian 1311
スクフェット
Scuffet, Simone 1265
スクボルツォワ
Skvortsova, Veronika I. 1311
スクーマン
Schoeman, Roland 1257
スクーラ
Skura, Matt 1311
スクーラー
Schooler, Lynn 1258
スクラー
Sclar, David Alexander 1263
Sklar, David 1310
Sklar, Holly 1310
Sklar, Marty 1310
ズクーラ
Zucula, Paulo 1558
スクライン
Skrine, Buster 1311
スクラッグス
Scruggs, Earl 1265
Scruggs, Greg 1265
Scruggs, Louise 1265
Scruggs, Randy 1265
スクラッチ
Scratchy, Lili 1265
スクラントン
Scranton, Philip 1265
Scranton, William Warren 1265
スクリーチ
Screech, Michael Andrew 1265
Screech, Timon 1265
スクリデ
Skride, Baiba 1311
スクリパック
Skrypuch, Marsha Forchuk 1311
スクリバーノ
Scribano, Philip V. 1265
スクリブナー
Scribner, Belding H. 1265
Scribner, Evan 1265
Scribner, Kenn 1265
Scrivner, Jane 1265
スクリプニク
Skripnik, Viktor 1311
Skrypnik, Darya 1311
スクリムガー
Scrimger, Rob 1265
スクリムショウ
Scrimshaw, Nevin Stewart 1265
スクリャロフ
Sklyarov, Ivan 1310
スクリレックス
Skrillex 1311
スクーリング
Schooling, Joseph 1258
スクリンニク
Skrynnik, Yelena B. 1311
スグルー
Sugrue, Thomas J. 1363
スクルーダー
Schreuder, H. 1259
スクルート
Skloot, Rebecca 1310
スクルートン
Scruton, Roger 1265
スクルレティス
Skourletis, Panos 1310
スグレッチャ
Sgreccia, Elio 1277
スクレナカ
Sklenicka, Carol 1310
スグロ
Sgro, Judy 1277
スクロヴァチェフスキ
Skrowaczewski, Stanisław 1311
スクロッシュナグル
Schlossnagle, Theo 1254
スクロバチェフスキ
Skrowaczewski, Stanisław 1311
ズグロフスキー
Zgurovsky, Mykhailo Zakharovych 1551
スクワィアー
Squire, Deborah L. 1338
スクワイア
Squire, Chris 1338
Squire, Larry R. 1338
Squire, Michael 1338
スクワイアウェル

Squirewell, Alstevis 1338
スクワイアーズ
Squires, Sally 1338
スクワイアズ
Squiers, Carol 1338
スクワイヤ
Squire, Jason E. 1338
Squires, Susan E. 1338
スクワイヤーズ
Squyres, Steve W. 1338
スクーンメイカー
Schoonmaker, Thelma 1258
スゲ
Sougueh, Abdi Youssouf 1330
スケア
Skea, Ralph 1309
スケイキン
Skakun, Michael 1309
スケイト
Skate, William Jack 1309
スケイヒル
Scahill, Jeremy 1247
Scahill, Lawrence 1247
Scahill, Rob 1247
スケイルズ
Scales, Patrick 1248
スケジャ・セラノ
Squella Serrano, Pablo 1338
スケース
Scase, Richard 1248
スケート
Skate, William Jack 1309
スケラス
Skerath, Chiara 1310
スケリット
Skerrit, Roosevelt 1310
Skerritt, Richard 1310
Skerritt, Ricky 1310
スーケル
Suker, Davor 1363
スケル
Skel, Steffen 1309
Suker, Davor 1363
スケールズ
Scales, Helen 1248
Scales, Pat 1248
スケルト
Scheld, W.Michael 1250
スケルトン
Skelton, Carol 1309
Skelton, Matthew 1309
Skelton, Nick 1309
Skelton, Will 1309
スケレット
Skerrett, Patrick J. 1310
スケレマニ
Skelemani, Phandu 1309
スケロット
Schelotto, Gianna 1251
スコ
Skog, Karolina 1310
スコー
Skou, Jens Christian 1310
スコア
Score, Herb 1263
スコウ
Schow, David J. 1258
Skou, Jens Christian 1310
スコウクロフト
Scowcroft, Brent 1265
ズコウスキ
Zukowski, John 1559
スコウフス
Skovhus, Bo 1311
スコウルズ
Scholes, Katherine 1257
スコウロン
Skowron, Moose 1311
スコヴロン
Skowron, Zbigniew 1311
スコーグ
Skoog, Sofie 1310
スコグ
Skog, Berit 1310
スコグスホルム
Skogsholm, Torild 1310
スコグランド
Skoglund, Eric 1310
スコグルンド
Skoglund, Kim 1310
スココワ
Skokova, Yuliya 1310
スコサナ
Skosana, Ben 1310
スコセッシ
Scorsese, Martin 1264
スコツォリ
Scozzoli, Fabio 1265
スコッチポル
Skocpol, Theda 1310
スコッチマー
Scotchmer, Suzanne 1264
スコッティ
Scotty, Charmaine 1265
Scotty, Ludwig Derangadage 1265
スコット
Scott, Adam 1264
Scott, Alicia 1264
Scott, Allen John 1264
Scott, Amber E. 1264
Scott, Andrew 1264
Scott, Andy 1264
Scott, Art 1264
Scott, Barbara Ann 1264
Scott, Beckie 1264
Scott, Carole 1264
Scott, Charles R. 1264
Scott, Chris 1264
Scott, Christian 1264
Scott, Christine 1264
Scott, Christopher Thomas 1264
Scott, Coleman 1264
Scott, Cynthia D. 1264
Scott, Damion 1264
Scott, David Meerman 1264
Scott, David Randolph 1264
Scott, Dick 1264
Scott, Doug 1264
Scott, Duncan 1264
Scott, Emily 1264
Scott, Erin L. 1264
Scott, Frederick 1264
Scott, Giles 1264
Scott, Gini Graham 1264
Scott, Gordon 1264
Scott, Guy 1264
Scott, Harold Lee, Jr. 1264
Scott, Helen 1264
Scott, Hillary 1264
Scott, James C. 1264
Scott, James F. 1264
Scott, Jasper T. 1264
Scott, Jay M. 1264
Scott, Jennifer Lynn 1264
Scott, Jeremiah 1264
Scott, Jessica 1264
Scott, Jill 1264
Scott, Jimmy 1264
Scott, J.Julius, Jr. 1264
Scott, J.M. 1264
Scott, Joan Wallach 1264
Scott, John 1264
Scott, Josey 1264
Scott, Justin 1264
Scott, Katie 1264
Scott, Kendall 1264
Scott, Larry 1264
Scott, Leslie Ann 1264
Scott, Lisa A. 1264
Scott, Liz 1264
Scott, Manda 1264
Scott, Martha 1264
Scott, Martin 1264
Scott, Martin J. 1264
Scott, Marylin 1264
Scott, Matt 1264
Scott, Michael 1264
Scott, Michele 1265
Scott, Mike 1265
Scott, Nathan Kumar 1265
Scott, P.Anne 1265
Scott, Peter 1265
Scott, Peter David 1265
Scott, Peter R. 1265
Scott, P.F. 1265
Scott, Philippa 1265
Scott, Rashawn 1265
Scott, Ridley 1265
Scott, Robby 1265
Scott, Stanley 1265
Scott, Stephen 1265
Scott, Steve 1265
Scott, Steven 1265
Scott, Susan 1265
Scott, Tim 1265
Scott, Tony 1265
Scott, Traer 1265
Scott, Trevor 1265
Scott, Vaughn 1265
Scott, Walter, Jr. 1265
Scott, William Robert 1265
Seebass, Scott 1268
スコット・RS・ホム
Scott, Judith 1264
スコット＝ストークス
Scott-Stokes, Henry 1265
スコットソン
Scotson, John L. 1264
スコット・トーマス
Scott-Thomas, Kristin Ann 1265
スコット・ヘロン
Scott-Heron, Gil 1265
スコット・モーガン
Scott-Morgan, Peter 1265
スコットライン
Scottoline, Lisa 1265
スコットン
Scotton, Rob 1265
スコッファム
Scoffham, Stephen 1263
スコティ
Scotty, Ludwig Derangadage 1265
スコーテン
Scouten, Rex 1265
スコト
Scott, Gordon 1264
スコトリ
al-Scotri, Awad Saad 1264
al-Socatri, Awadh Saad 1323
スコドール
Skodol, Andrew E. 1310
スコドルスキー
Sukhodolsky, Denis G. 1364
スコナード
Skonnard, Aaron 1310
ズゴバ
Zgoba, Dariya 1551
スコビィ
Scobie, Lorna 1263
スコープ
Schoop, Jonathan 1258
スコブ
Skov, Shayne 1311
ズーコフ
Zuckoff, Mitchell 1558
スコフィールド
Schofield, Deniece 1257
Schofield, Malcolm 1257
Schofield, Michael 1257
Schofield, Philip 1257
Schofield, S. 1257
Scofield, John 1263
Scofield, Paul 1263
スコフテルード
Skofterud, Vibeke W. 1310
スコーブル
Scoble, Robert 1263
スコブレフ
Skobrev, Ivan 1310
スコーベル
Scobell, Andrew 1263
スコベル
Scobell, Andrew 1263
スコーペン
Skorpen, Liesel Moak 1310
スコマル
Skomal, Marty 1310
スコーラ
Scola, Ettore 1263
スコラ
Scola, Ettore 1263
Scola, Luis 1263
スコラー
Schorer, Mark 1258
スコラーリ
Scolari, Luiz Felipe 1263
スコラリ
Scolari, Luiz Felipe 1263
スコーリー
Scholey, Robert 1257
スコーリオ
Scoglio, Franco 1263
スコリモウスキー
Skolimowski, Jerzy 1310
スコリモフスカ
Skolimowska, Kamila 1310
スコリモフスキ
Skolimowski, Jerzy 1310
スコーリンズ
Scollins, Richard 1263
スコール
Skole, Matt 1310
Skoll, Jeffrey 1310
スコルカ

Skorka, Abraham 1310
スコルジー
Scalzi, John 1248
スコールズ
Scholes, Edwin 1257
Scholes, Ken 1257
Scholes, Robert E. 1257
スコルプスキ
Skorupski, Lukasz 1310
スコーレー
Scholey, Robert 1257
スコロ
Scollo, Chris 1263
スコーロン
Scollon, Bill 1263
Skowron, Moose 1311
スコロン
Scollon, Bill 1263
スコーンオーヘ
Schoonooghe, Tom 1258
スコーンズ
Scoones, Ian 1263
スコンドゥムノン
Sukkhongdumnoen, Nootcharin 1364
スコンペル
Schomper, Pans 1257
スーザ
Sousa, Manuel Inocêncio 1331
Souza, Steven, Jr. 1332
スザー
Szur, Rolene 1375
スサイア
Susaia, Akillino 1368
スサエタ
Susaeta, Markel 1368
スーザック
Susac, Andrew 1368
ズーサック
Zusak, Markus 1559
スザニ
Suzani, Yusoff 1369
スサヌ
Susanu, Viorica 1368
スザルゼウスキ
Szarzewski, Dimitri 1374
スーザン
Susan, Eyemazing 1368
スサント
Susanto, Debby 1368
スシ
Susi, Pudjiastuti 1368
スシエ
Souchier, Raphaël 1330
スーシコフ
Sushkov, Boris Filippovich 1368
スージック
Sudjic, Deyan 1363
スジック
Sudjic, Deyan 1363
スジュディ
Sujudi, Ahmad 1363
スジョ
Sujo, Aly 1363
スジョストランド
Sjöstrand, Anna 1309
スジョストローム
Sjostrom, Lisa 1309
スショット
Szot, Paulo 1375
スジル
Sghyr, Ismail 1277
スシロ
Susilo, Ronald 1368
スーズ
Suse 1368
ススウォノ
Suswono 1368
スズキ
Suzuki, Akira 1369
Suzuki, Bob H. 1369
Suzuki, David 1369
Suzuki, Edward 1369
Suzuki, Kurt 1369
Suzuki, Masako Martha 1369
スズマン
Suzman, Helen 1369
スズラックマン
Szlakmann, Charles 1374
ススワ
al-Suswah, Amat al-Alim 1368
スーゼ
Souzay, Gérald 1332
スゼー
Souzay, Gérald 1332
スゼッタ
Suzetta, Paskah 1369
スソ
Suso 1368
スゾスタック
Szostak, Phil 1374
スーター
Souter, David H. 1331
Souter, Gerry 1331
Souter, Janet 1331
Suter, Brent 1368
スター
Star, Fleur 1341
Star, Midia 1341
Star, Nancy 1341
Starr, Chauncey 1342
Starr, Douglas 1342
Starr, Edwin 1342
Starr, Harvey 1342
Starr, Jason 1342
Starr, Kevin 1342
Starr, Leon 1342
Starr, Randy 1342
Starr, Ringo 1342
Starr, Tyler 1342
Sturr, Jimmy 1361
Suter, Fabienne 1368
ズーター
Suter, Martin 1368
ズタ
Zouta, Gertrude 1558
スタイエル
Steuer, Christin 1349
スタイガー
Steiger, Paul E. 1345
Steiger, Rod 1345
スタイグ
Steig, Jeremy 1345
Steig, William 1345
スタイコス
Staikos, Andreas 1339
スタイツ
Steitz, Thomas Arthur 1346
スタイナー
Steiner, Andy 1346
Steiner, Bob 1346
Steiner, Christopher 1346
Steiner, Claude 1346
Steiner, George 1346
Steiner, Hillel 1346
Steiner, Joan Catherine 1346
Steiner, Miriam 1346
Steiner, Rick 1346
Steiner, Therese 1346
Steiner Bennett, April 1346
Stiner, Carl 1352
スタイニッツ
Steinitz, Carl 1346
スタイネム
Steinem, Gloria 1346
スタイバー
Stiber, Alex 1351
Stiver, Mark C. 1352
スタイバル
Stibal, Guy 1351
Stibal, Vianna 1351
スタイプ
Stipe, Margo 1352
Stipe, Michael 1352
スタイリング
Styling, Mark 1361
スタイルズ
Stiles, Julia 1352
Stiles, Tara 1352
Stiles, T.J. 1352
Styles, Harry 1361
Styles, Morag 1361
スタイルマン
Stileman, Kali 1352
スタイロン
Styron, William 1361
スタイン
Stein, Abby 1345
Stein, Alexandra 1345
Stein, Benjamin 1345
Stein, Dan J. 1345
Stein, Diane 1345
Stein, Edward R. 1345
Stein, Elias M. 1345
Stein, Garth 1345
Stein, James D. 1345
Stein, Jeff 1345
Stein, Jon 1345
Stein, Joseph 1345
Stein, Lincoln D. 1345
Stein, Mike 1345
Stein, Murray B. 1345
Stein, Nan D. 1345
Stein, Peter 1345
Stein, Richard S. 1345
Stein, Sherman K. 1345
Stine, Jean 1352
Stine, Jesse C. 1352
Stine, Kate 1352
Stine, R.L. 1352
スタインガーテン
Steingarten, Jeffrey 1346
スタインハウアー
Steinhauer, Olen 1346
Steinhauer, Sherri 1346
スタインバーグ
Steinberg, Avi 1345
Steinberg, Daniel Howard 1345
Steinberg, Danny D. 1345
Steinberg, David 1345
Steinberg, Derek 1345
Steinberg, Hank 1345
Steinberg, James B. 1345
Steinberg, Janice 1345
Steinberg, Jonathan 1345
Steinberg, Jonathan S. 1345
Steinberg, Laurence D. 1345
Steinberg, Marc 1345
Steinberg, Mark I. 1345
Steinberg, Richard 1345
スタインハート
Steinhardt, Bernice 1346
Steinhardt, Paul J. 1346
スタインハルト
Steinhardt, Michael 1346
Steinhardt, Simon 1346
スタインフェルド
Steinfeld, Edward S. 1346
Steinfeld, Hailee 1346
スタインブレナー
Steinbrenner, George 1345
Steinbrenner, Hal 1346
Steinbrenner, Hank 1346
スタインベック
Steinbeck, Elaine 1345
スタインホフ
Steinhoff, Patricia G. 1346
スタインマン
Steinman, David 1346
Steinman, Ralph Marvin 1346
スタインメッツ・ロス
Steinmetz, Eulalie 1346
スタヴィスキー
Staviskii, B.Ya. 1343
スタウス
Stauss, Bernd 1343
スタウスカス
Stauskas, Nik 1343
ズタウタス
Zustautas, Henrikas 1559
スタウダマイアー
Stoudemire, Amare 1356
スタウト
Stout, Martha 1356
スタウトナー
Stautner, Ernie 1343
スタウドマイアー
Stoudemire, Amare 1356
スタウファー
Stauffer, David 1343
Stauffer, Dietrich 1343
Stouffer, Hannah 1356
スタヴラカキス
Stavrakakis, Yannis 1343
スタウントン
Staunton, Imelda 1343
スタカート
Stuckart, Diane A.S. 1360
スターキー
Starkey, David 1342
Starkey, Hugh 1342
スターク
Starc, Brandon 1341
Stark, David 1341
Stark, Ed 1341
Stark, Jonathan 1341
Stark, Peter 1342
Stark, Ray 1342
Stark, Richard 1342
Stark, Rodney 1342
Stark, Steven 1342
Stark, Steven D. 1342
Starke, Barry W. 1342
Starke, John 1342

ス

スタークス
Starks, James 1342
スタークマン
Starkman, Glenn D. 1342
スタクラ
Stakula 1339
スタークロフ
Starkloff, Friederike 1342
スタケ
Stake, Dagnija 1339
スターケン
Sturken, Marita 1361
スタサキス
Stathakis, Giorgos 1342
スタージェス
Sturgess, Jim 1361
スタシェフ
Stasheff, James D. 1342
スタージェル
Stargell, Willie 1341
スタシェロネク
Staszulonek, Ewelina 1342
スタージス
Sturges, Philemon 1361
Sturgis, Alexander 1361
Sturgis, Caleb 1361
Sturgis, Matthew 1361
スタシノポウロス
Stasinopoulos, Peter 1342
スタージャー
Stanger, James 1340
スタシャワー
Stashower, Daniel 1342
スタージョン
Sturgeon, Nicola 1361
スタースキー
Starsky, Stella 1342
スターズク
Stasyuk, Max 1342
スターズル
Starzl, Thomas Earl 1342
スターソフ
Stasov, Aleksandr Danilovich 1342
スタソプロス
Stathopoulos, Michalis 1342
スタタゲン
Stadthagen, Roberto 1339
スタチェル
Stachel, John J. 1338
スターツ
Staatz, Gundula 1338
Stertz, Bradley A. 1349
Sturz, James 1361
スタッキー
Stuckey, Darrell 1360
Stuckey, John 1360
Stuckey, Rodney 1360
Stuckey, Roy T. 1360
Stuckey, Scott S. 1360
Stucky, Steven 1361
スタック
Staake, Bob 1338
Stack, Charles 1338
Stack, George J. 1338
Stack, Jack 1338
Stack, Laura 1338
Stack, Robert 1338
スダック
Sudak, Donna M. 1362
スタッグス
Staggs, Chris 1339
スタックハウス
Stackhouse, Max L. 1338
スタックポール
Stackpole, Cynthia Snyder 1338
スタックラー
Stuckler, David 1361
スタッシ
Stassi, Max 1342
スタッダード
Stoddard, Frederick J., Jr. 1353
スタッダマイアー
Stoudemire, Amare 1356
スタッツ
Stutz, David 1361
Stutz, Phil 1361
スタッツァー
Stutzer, Alois 1361
スタッテン
Staten, Jimmy 1342
スタッドウェル
Studwell, Joe 1361
スタットラー
Statler, Oliver 1342
スタッドラー
Stadler, Alexander 1338
スタッドン
Staddon, J.E.R. 1338
スタップ
Stap, Sophie van der 1341
スタッフォード
Stafford, Daimion 1339
Stafford, Edward P. 1339
Stafford, Matthew 1339
Stafford, Tom 1339
スタッブス
Stubbs, David 1360
Stubbs, Levi 1360
スタッブズ
Stubbs, Michael 1360
Stubbs, Ray 1360
スタップルズ
Stupples, Karen 1361
スタッブルバイン
Stubblebine, Tony 1360
スターツル
Starzl, Thomas Earl 1342
スターデ
Stade, Ronald 1338
スタティック・メジャー
Static Major 1342
スターテヴァント
Sturtevant 1361
スタート
Sturt, David 1361
スタドニク
Stadnik, Andriy 1339
Stadnik, Mariya 1339
Stadnyk, Alina 1339
スタトラー
Statler, Oliver 1342
スタドラー
Stadler, Craig 1338
Stadler, Matthew 1338
Stadler, Michael A. 1339
スタドレン
Stadlen, Naomi 1338
スターナー
Sterner, Thomas M. 1349
スタナウェイ
Stanaway, John 1340
スタナード
Stannard, Daphne 1341
Stannard, Russell 1341
スタニー
Stanny, Barbara 1341
スダニ
al-Sudani, Abdul-Falah 1362
al-Sudani, Muhammad 1362
スタニウタ
Staniouta, Melitina 1340
スタニオニス
Stanionis, Eimantas 1340
スタニク
Stanik, Syuzanna R. 1340
スタニシェフ
Stanishev, Sergei 1340
スタニシチ
Stanišić, Saša 1340
スタニショアラ
Stănişoară, Mihai 1340
スタニスラス
Stanislas, Junior 1340
スタニスロー
Stanislaw, Joseph 1340
スタニャーラ
Stagnara, Denise 1339
スタニュラ
Stanjura, Zbyněk 1340
スタニョ・ウガルテ
Stagno Ugarte, Bruno 1339
スタニング
Stanning, Heather 1341
スタヌフ
Stanuch, Agnieszka 1341
スタネクザイ
Stanekzai, Masoom 1340
スタネスク
Stanescu, Robert 1340
スタネック
Stanek, Ryne 1340
Stanek, William R. 1340
スタノイウ
Stănoiu, Rodica Mihaela 1341
スタノイロヴィッチ
Stanoylovitch, Biliana 1341
スタノヴィッチ
Stanovich, Keith E. 1341
スタパー
Stupar, Nate 1361
スタバッド
Stavad, Ole 1343
スターバード
Starbird, Margaret 1341
Starbird, Michael 1341
スタバーマン
Staverman, Larry 1343
スタバンラート
Stabenrath, Bruno de 1338
スタビスキー
Staviski, Maxim 1343
スタビツキー
Stavytskyi, Eduard 1343
スタビレチ
Stavileci, Blerand 1343
スタビンス
Stubbins, Hugh 1360
スタビンスキー
Stabinsky, Doreen 1338
スタブ
Stabb, Ingrid 1338
スタフィリディス
Stafylidis, Konstantinos 1339
スタフォード
Stafford, Barbara Maria 1339
Stafford, Greg 1339
Stafford, Jo 1339
スタブス
Stubbs, Rennae 1360
Stubbs, Stephen 1360
スタブラー
Stabler, Mike 1338
スタブラキス
Stavrakis, Charilaos 1343
スタブラキス
Stavrakis, Charilaos 1343
スタブリエビッチルカビナ
Stavljevićrukavina, Maja 1343
スタブリック
Stablick, Elizabeth 1338
スタブルフィールド
Stubblefield, Harold W. 1360
Stubblefield, Mike 1360
スタブレスキ
Stavreski, Zoran 1343
スタブレフスキ
Stavreski, Zoran 1343
スタベノー
Stabenow, Cornelia 1338
スタペルツ
Stapert, Marta 1341
スターベンズ
Sterbenz, Carol Endler 1348
Sterbenz, Genevieve A. 1348
スターマー
Starmer, Anna 1342
スダマ
Sudama, Trevor 1362
スタマーズ
Stammers, Alfred H. 1340
スタマテアス
Stamateas, Bernardo 1339
スタマティー
Stamaty, Mark Alan 1339
スターマン
Sterman, John 1348
スターミー
Sturmey, Peter 1361
スターム
Sturm, Jake 1361
Sturm, Rick 1361
スタム
Stam, Robert 1339
Stamm, B.Hudnall 1340
Stamm, Jill 1340
Sutham, Saengprathum 1368
スターラー
Stahler, Wendy 1339
スタラク
Starak, Yaro 1341
スタラーチェ
Starace, Giorgio 1341
スダラット
Sudarat, Keyuraphan 1362

スタラード
Stallard, Paul 1339
スターリ
Steuerle, C.Eugene 1349
スターリー
Starry, Ace 1342
スターリッジ
Sturridge, Charles 1361
スタリッジ
Sturridge, Daniel 1361
スターリン
Starlin, Jim 1342
Starlin, Richard 1342
スターリング
Starling, Boris 1342
Starling, Bubba 1342
Starling, Simon 1342
Sterling, A.Justin 1348
Sterling, Bruce 1348
Sterling, Claire 1348
Sterling, Donald J. 1348
Sterling, Donna 1348
Sterling, Fred 1348
Sterling, Jan 1348
Sterling, Michael Bruce 1348
Sterling, Neal 1348
Sterling, Raheem 1348
Sterling, Thomas Lawrence 1348
Stirling, John D. 1352
Stirling, S.M. 1352
スターリングス
Stallings, Barbara 1339
Stallings, Jack 1339
Stallings, William 1339
スタール
Stahl, Betsy 1339
Stahl, Bob 1339
Starr, Nick 1342
スタル
Stull, Donald D. 1361
Stull, William J. 1361
スタルク
Starck, Philippe 1341
Stark, Ulf 1342
スタルケビチュス
Starkevičius, Kazimieras 1342
スダルソノ
Sudarsono, Juwono 1363
スタルチェビッチ
Starcevic, Bozo 1341
スタルヒン
Starffin, Natasha 1341
スタールフェルト
Stalfelt, Pernilla 1339
スタールブラス
Stallebrass, Pam 1339
スダルモノ
Sudharmono 1363
スターレット
Starrett, Paul 1342
スタロヴェイスキ
Starowieyski, Franciszek 1342
スタロスタ
Starosta, Paul 1342
スタロセーリスカヤ
Starosel'skaia, Natal'ia 1342
スタロック
Sturrock, David T. 1361
Sturrock, Ian 1361
スタロドゥブツェフ
Starodubtsev, Dmitry 1342
スタロドゥブツェフ
Starodubtsev, Vasilii Areksandrovich 1342
スタロドブツェフ
Starodubtsev, Dmitry 1342
スタロドブツェフ
Starodubtsev, Vasilii Areksandrovich 1342
スタローネ
Starone, Gilberto 1342
スタロバンスキー
Starobinski, Jean 1342
スタロビッチ
Starovic, Milica 1342
スタロビネツ
Starobinets, Anna 1342
スタロビン
Starobin, Michael 1342
Starobin, Paul 1342
スタローン
Stallone, Sylvester 1339
スタロン
Staron, Wojciech 1342
スタワルク
Stawaruk, Caitlin 1343
スーダン
Soodhun, Showkutally 1328
Soudant, Hubert 1330
スターン
Stearn, Jess 1343
Stein, Christina Tracy 1345
Stern, Arnold 1348
Stern, Bret 1348
Stern, Daniel 1348
Stern, Daniel N. 1348
Stern, David 1348
Stern, David Thomas 1348
Stern, Donnel B. 1348
Stern, Eric J. 1348
Stern, Hadley 1348
Stern, Hans 1348
Stern, Hellmut 1348
Stern, Howard Allan 1348
Stern, Isaac 1348
Stern, Jessica 1348
Stern, Joel M. 1348
Stern, Judith M. 1348
Stern, Louis W. 1348
Stern, Max 1348
Stern, Michael G. 1349
Stern, Mike 1349
Stern, Neil Z. 1349
Stern, Nicholas Herbert 1349
Stern, Paul C. 1349
Stern, Richard Martin 1349
Stern, Roger 1349
Stern, Ronald J. 1349
Stern, Sam 1349
Stern, Scott D.C. 1349
Stern, Stewart 1349
Stern, Theodore A. 1349
Sterne, Jim 1349
Sterne, Jonathan 1349
スタン
Stan, Alexandra 1340
Stang, Dorothy, Sr. 1340
スタン!
Stan! 1340
スダーン
Soudant, Hubert 1330
スタンウェイ
Stanway, Penny 1341
スタンウッド
Stanwood, Donald A. 1341
スタンカ
Stanca, Lucio 1340
スタンガー
Stanger, Ted 1340
スタング
Stang, Alan 1340
スターンクィスト
Sternquist, Brenda 1349
スタンクビー
Stangby, Joshua 1340
スターングラス
Sternglass, Ernest J. 1349
スタンコ
Stanko, Elizabeth A. 1340
スタンコヴィッチ
Stankovic, Dejan 1340
スタンコビッチ
Stankovic, Dejan 1340
スタンコフ
Stankov, Anton 1340
スターンサル
Sternthal, Brian 1349
スタンサル
Stansal, Léa 1341
スタンジェ
Stengers, Jean 1347
スタンジェール
Stengers, Isabelle 1347
スタンジェル
Stengel, Kilien 1347
スターンズ
Stearns, Beth 1343
Stearns, David 1343
スタンズベリー
Stansberry, Domenic 1341
スターンソル
Sternthal, Brian 1349
スタンダー
Stander, Burry 1340
スタンチェフ
Stanchev, Nikola Nikolov 1340
スタンデイジ
Standage, Simon 1340
スタンディッシュ
Standish, Paul 1340
スタンディフォード
Standiford, Natalie 1340
スタンディング
Standing, Guy 1340
スタンデージ
Standage, Tom 1340
スタンデファー
Standefer, Robin 1340
スタンドホルツ
Sandholtz, Kurt 1237
スタントン
Stanton, Andrew 1341
Stanton, Brian 1341
Stanton, Doug 1341
Stanton, Drew 1341
Stanton, Frank 1341
Stanton, Fredrik 1341
Stanton, Giancarlo 1341
Stanton, John 1341
Stanton, Katie Jacobs 1341
Stanton, Nadine 1341
Stanton, Neville Anthony 1341
Stanton, Phil 1341
Stanton, Richard 1341
Stanton, Warren R. 1341
スタンパー
Stamper, Martin 1340
スターンバーグ
Sternberg, Esther M. 1349
Sternberg, Janine 1349
Sternberg, Stuart 1349
Sternbergh, Adam 1349
スタンバーグ
Sternberg, Eliezer J. 1349
Sternberg, Robert J. 1349
スターンバック
Sternbach, Leo Henryk 1349
Sternback, Rick 1349
スタンフ
Stumpf, Daniel 1361
Stumpf, Doug 1361
Stumpf, John G. 1361
スタンプ
Stamp, Jonathan 1340
Stamp, Terence 1340
Stump, Bob 1361
スタンフィル
Stanfill, Louis 1340
スタンフィールド
Stanfield, James L. 1340
Stanfield, Lesley 1340
Stanfield, Maggie 1340
Stanfield, Robert Lorne 1340
スタンフォード
Stamford, Bryant A. 1340
Stanford, Craig Britton 1340
Stanford, Julian 1340
Stanford, Non 1340
Stanford, Sondra 1340
スタンプス
Stamps, Jeffrey 1340
Stamps, Timothy 1340
スタンプフリ
Stampfli, Joseph Gail 1340
スタンブラー
Stambler, Lyndon 1340
スタンブリ
Stambouli, Benjamin 1340
Stambuli, Clement 1340
スタンプルスキー
Stempleski, Susan 1347
スタンモア
Stanmore, Tia 1341
スタンリー
Stanley, Andy 1340
Stanley, J.B. 1340
Stanley, Jo 1340
Stanley, Kim 1340
Stanley, Mike 1340
Stanley, Paul 1341
Stanley, Ralph 1341
Stanley, Ronnie 1341
Stanley, Thomas J. 1341
Stanley, Tim 1341
Stanley, Vincent 1341
スタンリス
Stanlis, Peter James 1341
スタンリー・スミス
Stanley-Smith,

Venetia 1341
スタンルーム
Stangroom, Jeremy 1340
スタンレー
Stanley, Ann Marie 1340
Stanley, Barbara 1340
Stanley, Paul 1341
Stanley, Ralph 1341
スタンレイ
Stanley, Corolina 1340
Stanley, Mandy 1340
スタンロー
Stanlaw, James 1340
スー・チー
Shu, Qi 1294
スーチ
Szucs, Erika 1375
スチウ
Suciu, Ioan Silviu 1362
スチェパーシン
Stepashin, Sergey Vadimovich 1347
スチェパニアク
Szczepaniak, Yannick 1374
スチェパノビッチ
Stjepanovic, Velimir 1352
スチェルバティス
Scerbatihs, Viktors 1248
スチェロット
Schelotto, Ezequiel 1251
スチオピナ
Styopina, Vita 1361
スチーブンソン
Stevenson, William 1350
スチャート
Suchart, Jaovisidha 1362
スチュー
Stew 1350
スチュアート
Stewart, Alana 1350
Stewart, Amber 1350
Stewart, Cameron 1350
Stewart, Chris 1350
Stewart, Corki 1350
Stewart, Dave 1350
Stewart, David 1350
Stewart, Ellen 1350
Stewart, Glenford 1350
Stewart, Henry 1351
Stewart, Ian 1351
Stewart, Jeffrey 1351
Stewart, John 1351
Stewart, Jude 1351
Stewart, Katie 1351
Stewart, Kristen 1351
Stewart, Larry 1351
Stewart, Mariah 1351
Stewart, Mary 1351
Stewart, Matthew 1351
Stewart, Michael 1351
Stewart, Mike 1351
Stewart, Milton 1351
Stewart, Pamera Brown 1351
Stewart, Patrick 1351
Stewart, Paul 1351
Stewart, Rod 1351
Stewart, Susan 1351
Stewart, Thomas 1351
Stewart, Tricia 1351
Stuart, Anne Kristine 1360
Stuart, Dick 1360
Stuart, Freundel 1360
Stuart, Gail Wiscarz 1360
Stuart, George E. 1360
Stuart, Gloria 1360
Stuart, Greg 1360
Stuart, Heather L. 1360
Stuart, John 1360
Stuart, Lucia 1360
Stuart, Mary 1360
Stuart, Mel 1360
Stuart, Robert C. 1360
Stuart, Roy 1360
Stuart, Tristram 1360
スチュアート‐フォックス
Stuart-Fox, Martin 1360
スチューファマン
Stuvermann, Ralf 1361
スチュワート
Steuart, Cgris 1349
Stewart, Amy 1350
Stewart, Brock 1350
Stewart, Cameron 1350
Stewart, Chris 1350
Stewart, Courtenay 1350
Stewart, Darian 1350
Stewart, Dave 1350
Stewart, David Alan 1350
Stewart, Deborah C. 1350
Stewart, Dez 1350
Stewart, Elizabeth 1350
Stewart, Ellen 1350
Stewart, Gary L. 1350
Stewart, G.Bennett, Ⅲ 1350
Stewart, James B. 1351
Stewart, Jane 1351
Stewart, Joel 1351
Stewart, John 1351
Stewart, Jon 1351
Stewart, Jonathan 1351
Stewart, Kathryn 1351
Stewart, Katie 1351
Stewart, Kerron 1351
Stewart, Kevin 1351
Stewart, Kristen 1351
Stewart, Larry 1351
Stewart, Martha 1351
Stewart, Matthew 1351
Stewart, Michael 1351
Stewart, Moira 1351
Stewart, Murray 1351
Stewart, Pamela J. 1351
Stewart, Patricia A. 1351
Stewart, Patrick 1351
Stewart, Paul 1351
Stewart, Robert K. 1351
Stewart, Rod 1351
Stewart, Rory 1351
Stewart, Sarah 1351
Stewart, Sean 1351
Stewart, Sonja M. 1351
Stewart, Stanley 1351
Stewart, Thomas 1351
Stewart, Thomas A. 1351
Stewart, Tracey 1351
Stewart, Trenton Lee 1351
Stuart, Douglas K. 1360
Stuart, Freundel 1360
スチュワード
Steward, Emanuel 1350
Steward, Sid 1350
スチュワードソン
Stewardson, Dawn 1350
スチュワート＝フォックス
Stuart-Fox, Martin 1360
スーツ
Suits, Bernard Herbert 1363
ズッカ
Zucca, Pierre 1558
ズッカー
Zucker, Kenneth J. 1558
Zucker, Martin 1558
ズッカート
Zuccato, Edoardo 1558
ズッカーマン
Zuckerman, Daniel M. 1558
Zukerman, Pinchas 1558
ズッカーレ
Suckale, Robert 1362
ズック
Zook, Chris 1557
Zuk, Marlene 1558
ズックマン
Zucman, Gabriel 1558
スツケヴェル
Sutzkever, Abraham 1369
ズッケリ
Zuccheri, Laura 1558
スッコ
Sykkö, Sami 1373
ズッター
Sutter, Scott 1369
Zuttah, Jeremy 1559
ズッチ
Succi, Giancarlo 1362
スッチャイ
Soutchay, Thammasith 1331
スットケート
Sudket, Prapakamol 1363
ズットナー
Suttner, Markus 1369
スッバ
Subba, Ram Kumar 1362
ズッフィ
Zuffi, Luca 1558
Zuffi, Stefano 1558
ズッペー
Suppé, Barbara 1367
ステア
Stair, Nadine 1339
Stehr, Gerald 1345
ステアーズ
Stairs, Matt 1339
ステアール
Steyaert, Sarah 1351
ステイ
Sutej, Tina 1368
スディ
Sudi, Silalahi 1363
スティア
Setia, Putu 1276
スティアー
Stier, Ken 1352
スティアシヴィリ
Sutiashvili, Shalva 1369
スティアーズ
Stears, Marc 1343
Steers, Burr 1344
Steers, Richard M. 1344
スティアール
Stierle, Cynthia 1352
スティイェポビッチ
Stijepović, Slavoljub 1352
スティーヴンス
Stephens, Sharon 1348
Stephens, Susan 1348
Stevens, Alan 1349
Stevens, Amanda 1349
Stevens, Chevy 1349
Stevens, Damian 1349
Stevens, Dana 1349
Stevens, David L. 1349
Stevens, Lynsey 1350
Stevens, Mark 1350
Stevens, R.Paul 1350
Stevens, Taylor 1350
Stevens, Ted 1350
Stevens, W.Richard 1350
スティーヴンズ
Stephens, Richard 1348
Stevens, Anthony 1349
Stevens, Brooke 1349
Stevens, Gordon 1349
Stevens, Marcus 1350
Stevens, Ted 1350
スティーヴンスン
Stephenson, Neal 1348
Stevenson, Andrew 1350
スティーヴンソン
Steavenson, Wendell 1343
Stephenson, Charles 1348
Stevenson, Bryan 1350
Stevenson, Ian 1350
Stevenson, Jo 1350
Stevenson, N.J. 1350
Stevenson, Steve 1350
Stevenson, Victor 1350
スティエポビッチ
Stijepović, Slavoljub 1352
スティエンス
Stiens, Steven A. 1352
スティーガー
Steger, Manfred B. 1344
スティグウッド
Stigwood, Robert 1352
スティグラー
Stigler, James W. 1352
スティグリッツ
Steiglitz, Kenneth 1345
Stiglitz, Joseph Eugene 1352
スティグレール
Stiegler, Bernard 1351
スティーゲ
Stige, Brynjulf 1352
スティケティー
Steketee, Gail 1346
ステイサム
Statham, Jason 1342
ステイシー
Stacey, Jenny 1338
Stacey, Sarah 1338
ステイジ
Stage, Sarah 1339
スティーズ
Steeds, Will 1343
ステイス
Stace, Wesley 1338
スティックドーン
Stickdorn, Marc 1351
スティックベリー
Stichbury, Jo 1351
スティックランド
Stickland, Henrietta 1351
Stickland, Paul 1351
スティッケルズ
Stickels, Terry H. 1351
スティッチ
Stich, Francesca 1351
Stich, Stephen P. 1351
スティット

Stitt, Bill 1352
スティッド
Stead, Christopher 1343
スティッブ
Stibbe, Hugo L.P. 1351
スティップ
Stipp, David 1352
ステイテン
Staten, Joseph 1342
スティード
Steede, Kevin 1343
ステイドル
Steidl, Scott M. 1345
ステイトン
Staton, Dakota 1342
ステイニー
Steiny, Richard 1346
スティネット
Stinnett, Robert B. 1352
スティーバー
Steber, Rick 1343
スティーバーソン
Steverson, Todd 1350
スティバーソン
Stiverson, Boston 1352
スティパノビッチ
Stipanovic, Tonci 1352
スティバンヌ
Stibane 1351
ステイブ
Stave, Joel 1343
ステイプ
Stape, John Henry 1341
スティファニー
Stefani, Gwen 1344
スティーフェル
Stiefel, Ethan 1351
スティフェルマン
Stiffelman, Susan 1352
スティーフベーター
Stiefvater, Maggie 1351
スディブヨ
Sudibyo, Bambang 1363
ステイプルズ
Staples, Cleotha 1341
Staples, Fiona 1341
Staples, Justin 1341
Staples, Mavis 1341
スティプルトン
Stapleton, Maureen 1341
ステイプルトン
Stapleton, Jane 1341
Stapleton, Jean 1341
Stapleton, Maureen 1341
Stapleton, Paul 1341
スティブルフォード
Stableford, Brian M. 1338
ステイブルフォード
Stableford, Brian M. 1338
スティーブン
Stephen, Marcus 1347
Stephen, Mark 1347
Stephen, Shamar 1347
Stephens, Maria 1347
Steven, Davis 1349
Steven, Kenneth C. 1349
Steven, Mokin 1349
スティーブンス
Stephens, Ann 1347
Stephens, D.J. 1347
Stephens, Helen 1347
Stephens, Jackson 1347
Stephens, John 1347
Stephens, Owen K.C. 1348
Stephens, Rebecca 1348
Stephens, Robert S. 1348
Stephens, Sloane 1348
Stephens, Suzanne 1348
Stevens, Art 1349
Stevens, Brad 1349
Stevens, Chevy 1349
Stevens, Christopher 1349
Stevens, Craig 1349
Stevens, Dannelle D. 1349
Stevens, George, Jr. 1349
Stevens, John Paul 1350
Stevens, José 1350
Stevens, Juan Carlos 1350
Stevens, Karl 1350
Stevens, Leonard A. 1350
Stevens, Morkin 1350
Stevens, Peggy A. 1350
Stevens, Shelli 1350
Stevens, Taylor 1350
Stevens, Ted 1350
Stevens, Travis 1350
Stevens, W.Richard 1350
スティーブンズ
Stephens, Bret 1347
Stephens, Jack 1347
Stevens, Andrew 1349
Stevens, Anthony 1349
Stevens, Carla 1349
Stevens, Christopher 1349
Stevens, Deajah 1349
Stevens, John 1350
Stevens, Kathleen R. 1350
Stevens, Mark 1350
Stevens, Ted 1350
Stevens, Travis 1350
スティブンス
Stephens, Roberta L. 1348
スティーブンズイアティカ
Steavens Iatika, Morkin 1343
スティーブンスン
Stevenson, Neil 1350
スティーブンソン
Stephenson, Anne 1348
Stephenson, Donald 1348
Stephenson, Frederick 1348
Stephenson, Keith 1348
Stephenson, Lance 1348
Stephenson, Randall L. 1348
Stephenson, Robert 1348
Stephenson, Sean 1348
Stevenson, Gill 1350
Stevenson, Harold W. 1350
Stevenson, James 1350
Stevenson, Richard J. 1350
Stevenson, Sarah 1350
Stevenson, Shakur 1350
Stevenson, Toby 1350
スティベル
Stibel, Jeffrey M. 1351
スティームズマ
Stiemsma, Greg 1352
スティムソン
Stimson, Gerry Vivian 1352
スティラー
Stiller, Ben 1352
ステイラ
Steira, Kristin 1346
ステイリー
Staley, Joe 1339
Staley, Kathryn F. 1339
Staley, Layne Thomas 1339
スティリアニディス
Stilianidis, Evripidis 1352
スティリングス
Stillings, Marianne 1352
スティール
Steel, Danielle 1343
Steel, James 1343
Steel, Piers 1343
Steele, Allen M. 1343
Steele, Brandt F. 1343
Steele, David Ramsay 1343
Steele, G.R. 1343
Steele, Graig 1343
Steele, Guy L., Jr. 1343
Steele, Jackie F. 1343
Steele, James 1343
Steele, Jessica 1344
Steele, Julie 1344
Steele, Kathy 1344
Steele, Lockhart 1344
Steele, Michael Anthony 1344
Steele, Michael S. 1344
Steele, Miriam 1344
Steele, Nickolas 1344
Steele, Philip 1344
Steele, Robert 1344
Steele, Shelby 1344
Steer, Dugald A. 1344
Steil, Benn 1345
スティル
Still, Devon 1352
Still, Ray 1352
Stille, Mark 1352
ステイル
Steil, Benn 1345
スティルウェル
Stillwell, John 1352
Stilwell, Alexander 1352
スティルガー
Stilger, Bob 1352
スティール若希
Steele, Jackie F. 1343
スティルス
Stills, Kenny 1352
スティルソン
Stilson, Harold 1352
スティルトン
Stilton, Geronimo 1352
スティール＝パーキンス
Steele-Perkins, Chris 1344
スディルマン
Sudirman, Said 1363
スティー＝モーガン
Steele-Morgan, Alexandra 1344
スティルラン
Stierlin, Henri 1352
スティルリング
Stirling, Guillermo 1352
スティレットー
Stiletto 1352
スティロー
Stielow, Frederick J. 1352
スティワード
Steward, Tony 1350
スーティン
Sutin, Lawrence 1369
スティーン
Steen, Anthony 1344
Steen, Gerard 1344
Steen, Maarten van 1344
Steen, Sandra 1344
Steen, Sandy 1344
Steen, Susan 1344
スティン
Stein, George H. 1345
ステイン
Stein, Billy Jay 1345
Stein, Dave 1345
Stein, Eduardo 1345
Stein, Mathilde 1345
Steyn, Morné 1351
スティング
Sting 1352
スティングル
Stingl, Miloslav 1352
スティンジリー
Stingily, Byron 1352
Stingily, Cameron 1352
ステインズ
Staines, David 1339
スティンスン
Stinson, Kathy 1352
スティンソン
Stinson, Burke 1352
Stinson, Craig 1352
Stinson, Ed 1352
スティントソン
Stinson, Burke 1352
ステイントン
Stainton, Sue 1339
スティーンバーガー
Steenbarger, Brett N. 1344
スティンバーガー
Steenbarger, Brett N. 1344
スティーンバーグ
Steenbergh, Timothy A. 1344
スティーンマン
Steenman, Mitchel 1344
ステインメイヤー
Steinmeyer, Jim 1346
ステヴァンス
Stevens, Bernard 1349
ステェインズ
Staines, Anthony 1339
ステェーク
Steuck, Kyle 1349
スデ・オー
Sde-Or, Imi 1266
ステグマン
Stegman, Ryan 1344
ステケレンブルフ
Stekelenburg, Maarten 1346
ステゴール
Steggall, Susan 1344
ステージャ
Stager, Curt 1339
ステージャー
Stager, Gary 1339
ステシンジャー
Stoessinger, Caroline 1353
ステツ
Stets, Yurii 1349
ステッカー
Stecker, Robert 1343
ステッケル
Steckel, Janice A. 1343
ステッケンライダー
Steckenrider, Drew 1343
ステッツ

ス

Stets, Jan E. 1349
ステッド
Stead, Christian Karlson 1343
Stead, Emily 1343
Stead, Erin E. 1343
Stead, Jean Garner 1343
Stead, Philip Christian 1343
Stead, Rebecca 1343
Stead, W.Edward 1343
ステッドオール
Stedall, Jacqueline A. 1343
ステットナー
Stettner, Irving 1349
Stettner, Morey 1349
ステッドマン
Steadman, Henry J. 1343
Steadman, Philip 1343
Stedman, M.L. 1343
ステッビンス
Stebbings, Geoff 1343
ステッフィ
Steffy, Brian D. 1344
ステッフェンド
Steffend, Joan 1344
ステーディル
Stadil, Christian 1338
ステナック
Stenack, Richard J. 1347
ステニング
Stenning, Derek 1347
Stenning, Paul 1347
ステーヌー
Steenhout, Ivan 1344
ステーネシェン
Stenersen, Øivind 1347
ステネック
Steneck, Nicholas H. 1347
ステネール
Steiner, Philippe 1346
ステネルセン
Stenersen, Sverre 1347
ステパーシン
Stepashin, Sergey Vadimovich 1347
ステパシン
Stepashin, Sergey Vadimovich 1347
ステパッチャー
Steppacher, Rolf 1348
ステパニュク
Stepaniuc, Victor 1347
ステパネク
Stepanek, Mattie Joseph Thaddeus 1347
Stepanek, Radek 1347
ステパネンコ
Stepanenko, Galina 1347
ステパノフ
Stépanoff, Charles 1347
Stepanov, Alexander A. 1347
ステパノワ
Stepanova, Inna 1347
ステパン
Stepan, Alfred C. 1347
ステープ
Suthep, Thaugsuban 1368
ステファナー
Stefaner, Moritz 1344
ステファニ
Stefani, Helmut 1344
ステファニー
Stefani, Gwen 1344
ステファニス
Stefanis, Konstantinos 1344
ステファニディ
Stefanidi, Ekaterini 1344
ステファニデス
Stephanides, Myrsini 1347
ステファヌ
Stéphane, Bernard 1347
ステファネク
Stefanek, Davor 1344
ステファネス
Stephanes, Reinhold 1347
ステファネリ
Stefanelli, Lorella 1344
ステーファノ
Di Stefano, Giuseppe 358
ステファーノ
Di Stefano, Giuseppe 358
ステファノ
Stefano, Joseph 1344
ステファノバ
Stefanova, Kalina 1344
ステファノビッチ
Stefanovic, Milutin 1344
Stefanović, Nebojša 1344
ステファノフ
Stefanov, Stoyan 1344
ステファノフスキ
Stefanovski, Blagoj 1344
ステファノプロス
Stephanopoulos, Constantinos 1347
Stephanopoulos, George Robert 1347
ステファノポーラス
Stephanopoulos, G. 1347
ステファノポロス
Stephanopoulos, George Robert 1347
ステファン
Stefan, Gheorghita 1344
Steffen, Sandra 1344
Stephan, Kristina 1347
Stephan, Paula E. 1347
Stephens, Matt 1348
ステファンズ
Stephens, Daniel 1347
Stephens, Don 1347
Stephens, D.Ryan 1347
Stephens, Jeanne 1347
Stephens, John 1347
Stephens, Robert 1348
Stephens, Sam 1348
ステファンスキー
Stefanski, Daniel 1344
ステファン・スズキ
Stefan Suzuki, Kenji 1344
ステファンソン
Stefánsson, Magnús 1344
Stephansson, Ove 1347
Stephenson, Kristina 1348
ステフィック
Stefik, Barbara 1344
Stefik, Mark 1344
ステフェン
Steffen, Monika 1344
Stephens, Trent 1348
ステフォフ
Stefoff, Rebecca 1344
ステプコ
Stepko, Oleg 1348
ステフリーコバー
Stehlíková, Damila 1345
ステフリック
Steflik, Dick 1344
ステープルズ
Staples, Adrienne Lee 1341
Staples, Suzanne Fisher 1341
ステープルトン
Stapleton, Maureen 1341
ステベン
Stebben, Gregg 1343
ステベンソン
Stevenson, Teófilo 1350
Stevenson, Zoe 1350
ステポナビチュス
Steponavičius, Gintaras 1348
ステーム
Steem, Bjorm 1344
ステュアート
Stewart, Brian 1350
Stewart, Rod 1351
Stuart, Colin 1360
Stuart, Mel 1360
ステュエン
Stuen, Cynthia 1361
ステューダー
Studer, Quint 1361
ステューピカ
Stupica, Marlenka 1361
ステュールミラー
Stuhlmiller, Cynthia M. 1361
ステュワーカ
Stwertka, Albert 1361
ステュワート
Stewart, Ellen 1350
ステュワード
Steward, Oswald 1350
ステラ
Stella, Frank Philip 1346
ステラップ
Sterup, Zach 1349
ステール
Stehr, Frédéric 1345
Stehr, Gerald 1345
ステルター
Stelter, Daniel 1346
Stelter, Gordon Lee 1346
ステルツァー
Stelzer, Irwin M. 1347
ステルディニアック
Sterdyniak, Henri 1348
ステルベト
Sterbet, Valeria 1348
ステルペローネ
Sterpellone, Luciano 1349
ステルマック
Stelmach, Orest 1346
ステルン
Stern, Catherine 1348
ステルンバーグ
Sternberg, Hal 1349
ステレルニー
Sterelny, Kim 1348
ステン
Sten, Viveca 1347
ステンゲル
Stengel, Jim 1347
Stengel, Richard 1347
ステンシルス
Stensils, Linnea 1347
ステーンストロプ
Steenstrup, Kristian 1344
ステーンスネス
Steensnaes, Einar 1344
ステンソン
Stenson, Dernell 1347
Stenson, Henrik 1347
ステンダルド
Stendardo, Guglielmo 1347
ステンツ
Stentz, Zack 1347
ステンツェル
Stenzel, Anabel 1347
Stenzel Byrnes, Isabel 1347
ステント
Stent, Gunther Siegmund 1347
ズデンドルフ
Suddendorf, Thomas 1363
ステーン＝ノクレベルグ
Steen-Nøkleberg, Einar 1344
ステンプ
Stemp, Richard 1347
ステンペル
Stempel, Robert Carl 1347
ステンマン
Stenman, Kari 1347
ステンメ
Stemme, Nina 1347
ステンメッツ
Steinmetz, Jean-Luc 1346
ストー
Storr, Anthony 1355
Storr, Catherine 1355
Stowe, Madeleine 1356
ズート
Zoet, Jeroen 1557
ストア
Store, Signe Marie Fidge 1355
ストイアン
Stoian, Adrian 1353
ストイキツァ
Stoichita, Victor Ieronim 1353
ストイコ
Stojko, Elvis 1353
ストイコヴィッチ
Stojkovic, Dragan 1353
ストイコビッチ
Stojkovic, Dragan 1353
Stojković, Zoran 1353
ストイチェスク
Stoicescu, Nicolae 1353
ストイチェフ
Stoychev, Petar 1356
ストイツォフ
Stoitsov, Ivan 1353
ストイッチュ
Stojic, Manya 1353
ストイベア
Støjberg, Inger 1353
ストイベアー
Støjberg, Inger 1353
ストイヤン
Stoian, Petre 1353
ストイリュコヴィッチ
Stojiljkovic, Vlajko 1353

ストイリュコビッチ
Stojiljkovic, Vlajko 1353
ストイルコビッチ
Stojiljkovic, Vlajko 1353
スートゥー
Szeto, Wah 1374
ストウ
Stow, Dorrik A.V. 1356
Stowe, Madeleine 1356
ストーヴァー
Stover, Matthew Woodring 1356
ストゥアーニ
Stuani, Cristhian 1360
ストーヴァル
Stovall, Jim 1356
スドウィカトモノ
Sudwikatmono 1363
ストーウェル
Stowell, Baroness Tina 1356
Stowell, Belinda 1356
Stowell, Louie 1356
Stowell, Robin 1356
ストウェル
Stowell, Charlotte 1356
Stowell, Gordon 1356
ストゥカラワ
Stukalava, Tatsiana 1361
ストウシンガー
Stoessinger, John George 1353
ストゥブ
Stubb, Alexander 1360
ストゥプカ
Stupka, Bohdan 1361
ストゥーブハウグ
Stubhaug, Arild 1360
ストゥーボ
Stubo, Kirsti 1360
ストゥラーロ
Sturaro, Stefano 1361
ストゥリーニ
Strini, Giuliano 1358
ストゥリュオウル
Sutluoglu, Imdat 1369
ストゥルヴァルク
Sztulwark, Diego 1375
ストゥルーザン
Struzan, Drew 1360
Struzan, Dylan 1360
ストゥルナラス
Stournaras, Yannis 1356
ストウレイ
Storey, Reed K. 1355
ストゥレジンスカ
Strezyńska, Anna 1358
ストエネスク
Stoenescu, Dan 1353
ストエフ
Stoev, Borislav 1353
ストエレ
Støre, Jonas Gahr 1355
ストーカー
Stalker, John 1339
Stalker, Nancy K. 1339
Stalker, Peter 1339
Stalker, Thomas 1339
Stoker, Dacre 1353
Stoker, Gerry 1353
ストーク
Stalk, George 1339
Stork, Bryan 1355
Stork, David G. 1355
Stork, Francisco X. 1355
Stork, Royden 1355
ストークス
Scott-Stokes, Henry 1265
Stokes, Allison 1353
Stokes, Beverly 1353
Stokes, Bruce 1353
Stokes, Donald Gresham 1353
Stokes, Jarnell 1353
Stokes, John Whitley 1353
Stokes, Nelson Christian 1353
Stokes, Shirlee Ann 1354
Stokes, William S. 1354
ストクデック
Stokdyk, Scott 1353
ストケット
Stockett, Kathryn 1353
スドゴ
Sédogo, Laurent 1267
ストーサー
Stosur, Samantha 1355
ストダート
Stoddart, Ashley 1353
ストーダーマイアー
Stoudermire, Troy 1356
ストッカー
Stocker, Luke 1353
Stocker, Stefan 1353
ストック
Stock, Dennis 1352
Stock, Gregory 1352
Stock, James H. 1353
Stock, Jon 1353
ストックウィン
Stockwin, James Arthur 1353
Stockwin, Julian 1353
ストックウェル
Stockwell, Guy 1353
Stockwell, John 1353
Stockwell, Peter 1353
Stockwell, Stephen 1353
ストックデール
Stockdale, James 1353
ストックトン
Stockstrom, Christoph 1353
Stockton, Dave 1353
Stockton, Frank 1353
Stockton, Philip 1353
ストックハウゼン
Stockhausen, Adam 1353
ストックマン
Stockman, Steve 1353
ストックム
Van Stockum, Hilda 1445
ストックル
Stoeckle, John D. 1353
ストックルマイヤー
Stocklmayer, Susan 1353
ストックロッサ
Stoklossa, Uwe 1354
ストッケ
Stokke, Linn 1354
ストッケル
Stoeckel, Hayden 1353
ストッダード
Stoddard, Alexandra 1353
ストッツ
Stotts, Terry 1355
ストット
Stott, Ann 1355
Stott, Carole 1355
Stott, Etienne 1355
Stott, John R.W. 1355
Stott, Kathryn 1355
Stott, Ken 1355
Stott, Peter E. 1355
ストットラー
Stotlar, David Kent 1355
ストットルマイヤー
Stottlemyre, Mel 1355
ストッパード
Stoppard, Miriam 1355
Stoppard, Tom 1355
ストッパーニ
Stoppani, Angelo 1355
ストッフ
Stoch, Kamil 1352
ストッフェルス
Stoffels, Karlijn 1353
ストップフォード
Stopford, Martin 1355
ストップラー
Stopler, Tracy 1355
ストーナー
Stohner, Anu 1353
Stoner, Gary D. 1355
Stoner, Jesse 1355
Stoner, Susan A. 1355
ストニック
Stonich, Susan C. 1355
ストーバー
Stauber, John 1343
スドバ
Sudova, Nikola 1363
ストバート
Stobart, Simon 1352
スードフ
Südhof, Thomas Christian 1363
ストーブ
Staub, Wendy Corsi 1343
ストフ
Stoch, Kamil 1352
Stoch, Miroslav 1352
ストフィル
Stofile, Makhenkesi 1353
ストフィーレ
Stofile, Makhenkesi 1353
ストーベル
Stovel, Herb 1356
ズートホーフ
Südhof, Thomas Christian 1363
ストーマー
Stormer, Chris 1355
ストーム
Storm, Hyemeyohsts 1355
Storm, Morten 1355
Storm, Stella 1355
ストムビー
Stormby, Nils Gunnar Inge 1355
スドモ
Soedomo 1323
ストーモント
Stormont, Melissa 1355
ストヤコヴィッチ
Stojaković, Jadranka 1353
ストヤコビッチ
Stojaković, Jadranka 1353
Stojaković, Zoran 1353
ストヤノヴァ
Stoyanova, Krassimira 1356
ストヤノビッチ
Stojanović, Branimir 1353
ストヤノフ
Stoyanov, Nikolai 1356
Stoyanov, Petar 1356
Stoyanov, Yuri 1356
ストヤノフスキ
Stojanovski, Pero 1353
ストーラー
Stoler, Ann Laura 1354
Stoller, David W. 1354
ストラ
Stora, Benjamin 1355
ストライカー
Striker, Eric 1358
Stryker, Jon 1360
Stryker, Perrin 1360
ストライサンド
Streisand, Barbra 1358
ストライザンド
Streisand, Barbra 1358
Stresand, Barbra 1358
ストライスグス
Streissguth, Tom 1358
ストライナー
Streiner, David L. 1358
ストライブ
Streib, Tysen 1358
ストライヤー
Stryer, Lubert 1360
ストラヴィウス
Stravius, Jérémy 1357
ストラウス
Straus, David 1357
Straus, Hal 1357
Straus, Ulrich 1357
Strauss, Adriaan 1357
Strauss, Claudia J. 1357
Strauss, Darin 1357
Strauss, Esther 1357
Strauss, Gwen 1357
Strauss, Joseph B. 1357
Strauss, Josh 1357
Strauss, Neil 1357
Strauss, Richardt 1357
Strauss, Robert Schwarz 1357
Strauss, Rochelle 1357
Strauss, Steven D. 1357
Strouse, Charles 1359
Strouse, Daniel S. 1359
Strouse, Douglas A. 1359
ストラウストラップ
Stroustrup, Bjarne 1359
ストラウト
Strout, Elizabeth 1359
ストラウド
Stroud, Barry 1359
Stroud, Carsten 1359
Stroud, Jonathan 1359
ストラウブ
Straub, Peter 1357
ストラウユマ
Straujuma, Laimdota 1357
ストラク
Stollak, Mary Alice 1354
ストラコシャ
Strakosha, Thomas 1356
ストラザーズ
Struthers, Jane 1360

ス

ストラサーン
Strathern, Andrew 1357
ストラザーン
Strathairn, David 1357
Strathern, Marilyn 1357
Strathern, Paul 1357
ストラジェフ
Strazhev, Vasily I. 1357
ストラジンスキー
Straczynski, J. Michael 1356
ストラスカーン
Strauss-Kahn, Dominique 1357
ストラスキ
Stolarski, Richard S. 1354
ストラスクライド卿
Lord Strathclyde 1357
ストラスバーグ
Strasburg, Stephen 1357
ストラダ
Strada, Gino 1356
ストラタン
Stratan, Andrei 1357
Stratan, Cosmina 1357
ストラチャン
Strachan, Hope 1356
ストラックマン
Strachman, Daniel A. 1356
ストラッサー
Strasser, Susan 1357
ストラッチャン
Strachan, Tom 1356
ストラット
Strutt, Christina 1360
ストラットフォード
Stratford, Elaine 1357
ストラットン
Stratton, Allan 1357
Stratton, Brooke 1357
Stratton, Chris 1357
Stratton, Joanna L. 1357
Stratton, Sharleen 1357
ストラップ
Strupp, Peter 1360
ストラディ
Strady, Sophie 1356
ストラティラ
Stratila, Sabin 1357
ストラーテン
Straaten, Harmen van 1356
Straten, Roelof van 1357
ストラトフォード
Stratford, Patrick Walter 1357
ストラドリング
Stradling, R.A. 1356
ストラトン
Stratton, William O. 1357
ストラナハン
Stranahan, Susan Q. 1356
ストラニ
Storani, Federico 1355
ストラネオ
Straneo, Valeria 1356
ストラハン
Strahan, Jonathan 1356
ストラビウス
Stravius, Jérémy 1357
ストラマー
Strummer, Joe 1360
ストラーム
Strahm, Matt 1356
ストラム
Stram, Hank 1356
ストラーリ
Storari, Marco 1355
ストラルザー
Stralser, Steven 1356
ストラルストウ
Straltsou, Vadzim 1356
ストラーロ
Storaro, Vittorio 1355
ストラング
Strang, Debbie 1356
Strang, Gilbert 1356
Strang, John 1356
Strang, William R. 1356
ストランゲル
Stranger, Simon 1357
ストランド
Strand, Clark 1356
Strand, Jeff 1356
Strand, Mark 1356
Strand, Philip 1356
Strand, Ray D. 1356
ストランドベリ
Strandberg, Mats 1356
ストランドヘル
Strandhäll, Annika 1356
ストランドリ
Strandli, Are 1356
ストランフ
Strumpf, Casey 1360
ストランベリ
Strandberg, Carlos 1356
ストーリー
Storey, D.J. 1355
Storey, Sally 1355
Storry, Mike 1355
Story, Laura 1355
Story, Trevor 1355
ストリアウカス
Striaukas, Gintaras 1358
ストリイェク
Stryjek, Max 1360
ストリカーズ
Stricherz, Gregory 1358
ストリーク
Streeck, Wolfgang 1357
ストリクランド
Strickland, Shirley 1358
ストリグル
Strigl, Denny F. 1358
ストリゲル
Strige, Daniel 1358
ストリコバ
Zahlavova Strycova, Barbora 1545
ストリズマン
Stridsman, Thomas 1358
ストリーター
Streater, Rod 1357
Streeter, Elaine 1358
Streeter, Kristina 1358
Streeter, Michael 1358
ストリッカー
Stricker, Gabriel 1358
Stricker, Steve 1358
Strycker, Noah K. 1360
ストリックランド
Strickland, Bill 1358
Strickland, Chris 1358
Strickland, Hunter 1358
Strickland, Ora 1358
Strickland, Shadra 1358
ストリッチ
Stritch, Elaine 1359
ストリッド
Strid, Jakob Martin 1358
Strid, Steve 1358
ストリッフラー
Striffler, Steve 1358
ストリップリング
Stripling, Ross 1359
ストリート
Street, Devin 1357
Street, Huston 1358
Street, Richard 1358
ストリート・ハウ
Street Howe, Zöe 1358
ストリートン
Streeten, Roz 1358
ストリナチ
Strinati, Dominic 1358
ストリニッチ
Strinic, Ivan 1359
ストリノ
Storino, Sara 1355
ストリーバー
Strieber, Whitley 1358
ストリーフ
Strief, Zach 1358
ストリープ
Streep, Meryl 1357
Streep, Peg 1357
ストリーブンズ=マルゾー
Strevens-Marzo, Bridget 1358
ストリャロワ
Stolyarova, Ekaterina 1354
ストリューヴ=ドゥボー
Struve-Debeaux, Anne 1360
ストリル=ルヴェ
Stril-Rever, Sofia 1358
ストリンガー
Stringer, Chris 1358
Stringer, Ernest T. 1358
Stringer, Howard 1358
Stringer, Jan 1358
Stringer, Korey 1358
Stringer, Lauren 1358
Stringer, Lee 1358
Stringer, Mel 1358
Stringer, Vickie M. 1358
ストーリングス
Stallings, Fran 1339
ストーリングズ
Stallings, Barbara 1339
ストリングフィールド
Stringfield, Sam 1358
ストリングフェロー
Stringfellow, Jude 1358
ストール
Stahl, Rachel K. 1339
Stahl, Stephen M. 1339
Stall, Sam 1339
Stall, William R. 1339
Stohl, Margaret 1353
Stoll, Clifford 1354
Stoll, S.G. 1354
スドル
Sudol, Grzegorz 1363
ストールヴィーク
Storvik, Kjell Ove 1355
ストルヴィッチ
Stolovitch, Harold D. 1354
ストルガツキー
Strugatskii, Boris N. 1360
ストルガツキイ
Strugatskii, Boris N. 1360
ストルガル
Strugar, Branislav 1360
Strugar, Vladimir 1360
Strugar, Vlatka Rubinjoni 1360
ストルーザン
Struzan, Drew 1360
ストルーストラップ
Stroustrup, Bjarne 1359
ストルチコーワ
Struchkova, Raissa Stepanovna 1360
ストルチコワ
Struchkova, Raissa Stepanovna 1360
ストルチャエワ
Struchayeva, Yelena 1360
ストルツ
Stoltz, Paul Gordon 1354
ストルツフス
Stoltzfus, Matthew W. 1354
ストルツマン
Stoltzman, Richard 1354
ストールティ
Stoeltie, Barbara 1353
Stoeltie, René 1353
ストルテンバーグ
Stoltenberg, John 1354
ストルテンベルグ
Stoltenberg, Harald 1354
Stoltenberg, Jens 1354
Stoltenberg, Thorvald 1354
ストルヘイム
Stalheim, Jesper 1339
ストールベリ
Stålberg, Carl Eric 1339
ストールベルゲ
Storberget, Knut 1355
ストルボワ
Stolbova, Ksenia 1354
ストールマン
Stallman, Richard M. 1339
ストルム
Storm, Nikola 1355
ストルムエーリックセン
Strøm-erichsen, Anne-Grete 1359
ストレルキー
Strelecky, John P. 1358
ストルレッキー
Strelecky, John P. 1358
ストーレ
Støre, Jonas Gahr 1355
ストレイ
Stray, Geoff 1357
ストレイカー
Straker, David 1356
Straker, Jane K. 1356
ストレイト
Strait, George 1356
ストレイド
Strayed, Cheryl 1357
ストレイナー
Streiner, David L. 1358
ストレイハン

Strahan, Michael 1356
ストレイヤー
Strayer, W.Timothy 1357
ストレイリー
Straily, Dan 1356
ストレーカー
Straker, Louis 1356
ストレカロフ
Strekalov, Gennady 1358
ストレッサー
Strasser, Dale C. 1357
ストレッジ
Strege, Karen 1358
ストレッチャー
Strecher, Victor J. 1357
ストレート
Straight, Beatrice 1356
Straight, Susan 1356
Strete, Craig 1358
ストレトビッチ
Stretovich, Ivan 1358
ストレトン
Stretton, Ross 1358
ストレフ
Streff, Jean 1358
ストレブ
Strebe, Matthew 1357
ストレムビツキー
Strembitsky, Igor 1358
ストーレリ
Storelid, Kjell 1355
ストレリツォフ
Strel'tsov, Dmitriĭ Viktorovich 1358
ストレルコースカス
Strelkauskas, Anthony J. 1358
Strelkauskas, Jennifer 1358
ストレーレ
Strehle, Gabriele 1358
ストーレン
Storen, Drew 1355
ストレンジ
Strange, Marc 1356
Strange, Nicholas 1356
Strange, Phillip 1356
Strange, Tracey 1357
ストロー
Straw, Jack 1357
Stroh, Linda K. 1359
Stroh, Suzanne 1359
ズドロイェフスキ
Zdrojewski, Bogdan 1549
ストロイヤー
Stroyer, Torben 1359
ストロエスネル
Stroessner, Alfredo 1359
ストロエフ
Stroev, Egor S. 1359
ズドロエフスキ
Zdrojewski, Bogdan 1549
ストロガッツ
Strogatz, Steven Henry 1359
ストロコッシュ
Strokosch, Alasdair 1359
ストローザー
Strozer, Judith R. 1359
ストロサー
Strother, Jane 1359
ストローサル
Strosahl, Kirk 1359
ストロジャー
Strozier, Charles B. 1359
ストロース
Strauss, Frédéric 1357
ストロス
Stross, Charles 1359
Stross, Randall E. 1359
ストロスカーン
Strauss-Kahn, Dominique 1357
ストローソン
Strawson, Peter Frederick 1357
ストローチ
Strauch, Barbara 1357
ストロッズ
Strods, Jurijs 1359
ストロッセン
Strossen, Nadine 1359
ストロップ
Strop, Pedro 1359
ストロード
Strode, Lester 1359
ストロートマン
Strootman, Kevin 1359
ストロバー
Strober, Myra H. 1359
ストローブ
Straub, Jean-Marie 1357
Straub, Joseph T. 1357
ストロプニツキー
Stropnický, Martin 1359
ストローブル
Strobl, Gert R. 1359
ストロベリーズ
Strawberries, James 1357
ストローベル
Strobel, Ray G. 1359
Strobel, Tammy 1359
ストロベル
Strobel, Lee 1359
ストロマイヤー
Strohmeyer, Sarah 1359
ストローマン
Stroman, Marcus 1359
ストローム
Strom, Brent 1359
Strom, James 1359
ストロム
Strom, Georg 1359
ストロール
Strahl, Chuck 1356
ストロロウ
Stolorow, Robert D. 1354
ストローン
Strahan, David 1356
ストロンキスト
Stromquist, Nelly P. 1359
ストロング
Strong, Jaelen 1359
Strong, Jeremy 1359
Strong, Mark 1359
Strong, Maurice Frederick 1359
Strong, Roy 1359
Strong, Sanford 1359
Strong, Tony 1359
Stronge, Charles 1359
ストロングマン
Strongman, Jay 1359
Strongman, Phil 1359
ストロンバーグ
Stromberg, Robert 1359
ストロンベック
Strombeck, Donald R. 1359
ストロンベルグス
Strombergs, Maris 1359
ストーワー
Stower, Adam 1356
ストーン
Stern, Hal 1348
Stone 1354
Stone, Alex 1354
Stone, Andrew 1354
Stone, Biz 1354
Stone, Bob 1354
Stone, Brad 1354
Stone, Carolyn B. 1354
Stone, Dan 1354
Stone, David Lee 1354
Stone, Diamond 1354
Stone, Douglas 1354
Stone, Elaine Murray 1354
Stone, Elizabeth 1354
Stone, Emma 1354
Stone, Gene 1354
Stone, Genevra 1354
Stone, Harold J. 1354
Stone, Jasmine 1354
Stone, Jean 1354
Stone, Jeff 1354
Stone, Joan Wilkins 1354
Stone, Joshua David 1354
Stone, Joss 1354
Stone, Julyan 1354
Stone, Kazuko G. 1354
Stone, Lila Devi 1354
Stone, Linda 1354
Stone, Lyn 1354
Stone, Matt 1354
Stone, Matthew L. 1354
Stone, Michael 1354
Stone, Michael H. 1354
Stone, Nick 1354
Stone, Oliver 1354
Stone, Peter 1354
Stone, Rex 1354
Stone, Richard M. 1354
Stone, Robert 1354
Stone, Ronald H. 1355
Stone, Sandy 1355
Stone, Sharon 1355
Stone, Sly 1355
Stone, Victoria Jordan 1355
Stone, W.Clement 1355
ストーンズ
Stones, John 1355
Stones, Richard 1355
Stones, Rosemary 1355
ストーンストリート
Stonestreet, Eric 1355
ストーントン
Staunton, Mike 1343
ストーンハウス
Stonehouse, Bernard 1355
Stonehouse, Juria 1355
ストーンバーナー
Stoneburner, Jake 1355
ストーンヒル
Stonehill, Arthur I. 1355
ストーンマン
Stoneman, Jack 1355
スナイダー
Sneijder, Wesley 1321
Snider, Duke 1321
Snider, Stacey 1321
Snyder, Blake 1322
Snyder, Bob 1322
Snyder, Brandon 1322
Snyder, Christopher Allen 1322
Snyder, Cynthia Stackpole 1322
Snyder, Garth 1322
Snyder, Gary Sherman 1322
Snyder, Ilana 1322
Snyder, Kevin 1322
Snyder, Kyle 1322
Snyder, Laurel 1322
Snyder, Mariah 1322
Snyder, Maria V. 1322
Snyder, Marlene 1322
Snyder, Mary Gail 1322
Snyder, Midori 1322
Snyder, Mike 1322
Snyder, Quin 1322
Snyder, Rachel Louise 1322
Snyder, Scott 1322
Snyder, Scott A. 1322
Snyder, Steven 1322
Snyder, Timothy 1322
Snyder, Tom 1322
Snyder, William M. 1322
Snyder, Window 1322
Snyder, Zack 1322
Znaider, Nikolaj 1556
ズナイダー
Znaider, Nikolaj 1556
スナイダー＝マクラー
Snyder-Mackler, Lynn 1322
スナイディ
Sunaidy, Ali bin Masoud bin Ali Al 1366
スナイデル
Sneijder, Wesley 1321
スナイプス
Snips, Wesley 1321
スナッデン
Snadden, Russ 1321
スナルディアン
Sunardian 1366
スナルト
Sunarto, Sunarto 1366
スナルモ
Soenarmo 1323
スニウラ
Suniula, Andrew 1367
Suniula, Shalom 1367
スニガ
Zuniga, Enrique 1559
Zúñiga, Guillermo 1559
Zuniga, Juan Camilo 1559
スニガ・ロチャ
Zúñiga Rocha, Ledy 1559
スニケット
Snicket, Lemony 1321
スニサー・ウィッタヤーパンヤーノン
Sunisa Wittayapanyanon 1366
スニス
Smith, Justin 1321
スニチェンバウマー
Schnitzenbaumer, Sebastian 1256
スニッカー
Snitker, Brian 1321
スニード
Snead, G.Lynne 1321

ス

Snead, Sam 1321
Snead, Willie 1321
スニトウ
Snitow, Ann Barr 1321
ズニネド
Znined, Abdeslam 1556
ズニーノ
Zunino, Mike 1559
スニヤエフ
Sunyaev, Rashid 1367
Sunyayev, Rashid Aliyevich 1367
スヌ
Sunu, Ibrahim 1367
スヌープ・ドッグ
Snoop Dogg 1321
スネア
Snair, Scott 1321
スネイス
Snaith, John G. 1321
ズネイバート
Thneibat, Mohammad 1396
スネイプ
Snape, Steven R. 1321
スネージュ
Snaije, Olivia 1321
スネソン
Suneson, Carl 1366
Suneson, Karl 1366
スネーダー
Snader, Jon C. 1321
スネトセラール
Snetselaar, Linda G. 1321
スネドン
Sneddon, Tom 1321
スネル
Snel, Eline 1321
Snell, BJ. 1321
Snell, Blake 1321
Snell, Bradford C. 1321
Snell, Kate 1321
Snell, Martha E. 1321
Snell, Richard S. 1321
Snell, Tony 1321
スネルグローヴ
Snellgrove, David L. 1321
スノー
Snow, Dennis 1321
Snow, Jack 1321
Snow, John 1321
Snow, John W. 1321
Snow, Nancy 1321
Snow, Stephanie J. 1321
Snow, Tony 1321
スノウ
Snow, Alan 1321
Snow, Clyde 1321
Snow, Dean R. 1321
Snow, Heather 1321
Snow, Phoebe 1321
Snow, Shane 1321
スノウドン
Snowdon, David 1322
スノウリング
Snowling, Margaret J. 1322
スノエレン
Snoeren, Rolf 1321
スノーシル
Snowsill, Emma 1322
スノッドグラス
Snodgrass, Robert 1321
Snodgrass, W.D. 1321
スノッドグレス
Snodgress, Carrie 1321
スノティエ
Senotier, Danièle 1274
スノーデン
Snowden, Edward 1321
スノードン
Snowden, Paul 1322
Snowdon, Brian 1322
スノハラ
Sunohara, Vicky 1367
スノーハンセン
Snow-hansen, Paul 1322
スノプコフ
Snopkov, Nikolai G. 1321
スノーフラワー
Snowflower, Banbis 1322
スノラン
Snoeren, Rolf 1321
スノレール
Snollaerts, Claire Durand-Ruel 1321
ズーノン
Zunon, Elizabeth 1559
スーバー
Suber, Howard 1362
Suber, Melissa 1362
スーパー
Super, Carol 1367
スパー
Spar, Debora 1333
Spurr, Pam 1338
ズーバー
Zuber, Catherine 1558
ズバイ
Sbai, Abderrahmane 1247
スパイアー
Speier, Chris 1334
スパイアーズ
Spires, Elizabeth 1336
スパイヴィー
Spivey, Nigel Jonathan 1337
スパイクス
Spikes, Brandon 1336
スパイサー
Spicer, Mark 1335
Spicer, Michael 1335
ズバイディ
al-Zubaidi, Baqir 1558
スパイト
Speight, Henry 1334
ズバイドフ
Zuvaidov, Said 1559
スハイビ
al-Suhaibi, Numan Saleh 1363
スパイラ
Spira, Rupert 1336
ズハイラート
Thuheirat, Nader 1402
スハイル
Souhail, Abdelouahed 1330
Suhail, Mohammed al-Mazrouei 1363
スパイロ
Spiro, Samantha 1336
スハウテン
Schouten, Dirk 1258
Schouten, Ronald 1258
スパーク
Spark, Muriel Sarah 1333
Sparke, Penny 1333
スパク
Spac, Alexandr 1332
ズバク
Zubak, Krešimir 1558
スパークス
Sparkes, Ali 1333
Sparks, Colin 1333
Sparks, Greg 1333
Sparks, Kerrelyn 1333
Sparks, Leigh 1333
Sparks, Nicholas 1333
スパークマン
Sparkman, Glenn 1333
スパーゲル
Spergel, David N. 1335
スパーゴ
Spargo, Tamsin 1333
スパージェン
Spurgeon, Charles E. 1338
スバシッチ
Subasic, Danijel 1362
スパシブーホフ
Spasibukhov, IUrii 1333
スパジラクル
Supajirakul, Puttita 1367
スパージン
Spurgin, Anthony J. 1338
スパス
Spath, Patrice L. 1333
ズーパースベルゲン
Supersbergen, Nikolaus 1367
スパセノスキ
Spasenoski, Aco 1333
スパセノフスキ
Spasenoski, Aco 1333
スパソフ
Spasoff, Robert A. 1333
Spasov, Dime 1333
スパソフスキ
Spasovski, Oliver 1333
スパダ
Spada, Nina Margaret 1332
スパダヴェッキア
Spadavecchia, Fiorella 1332
スパダフォラ
Spadafora, Winston 1332
スパーダフォリ
Spadafori, Gina 1332
スパタロ
Spataro, Sandra 1333
スパチャイ・パニチャパク
Supachai Panitchpakdi 1367
スパチャイ・パニチャパック
Supachai Panitchpakdi 1367
スパーツ
Spartz, Emerson 1333
スパツィアニ
Spaziani, Beatrice 1333
ズーバッチ
Zubac, Ivica 1558
スパッドヴィラス
Spudvilas, Anne 1337
スパッフォード
Spafford, George 1332
Spafford, Suzy 1332
スパッレッティ
Spalletti, Luciano 1332
スパトゥリサノ
Spatrisano, Amy 1333
スパトラ
Spatola, Jamie K. 1333
スパドーラ
Spadola, Ryan 1332
スーパーナウ
Supernaw, Phillip 1367
スパニョーリ
Spagnoli, Cathy 1332
スパニョール
Spanogle, John A. 1333
Spanyol, Jessica 1333
スパニール
Spanier, Jerome 1333
スパヌオーロ
Spagnuolo, Steve 1332
スバネリッド
Svanelid, Göran 1369
スパーノ
Spano, Robert 1333
スパノス
Spanos, N. 1333
スパノビッチ
Spanovic, Ivana 1333
スハノフ
Sukhanov, Boris P. 1363
Sukhanov, Vladimir Vladimirovich 1363
スバノフ
Subanov, Bakhtiyar 1362
スパーバー
Sparber, Al 1333
Sperber, Jonathan 1335
Sperber, Wendie Jo 1335
スババルスドッティル
Svavarsdottir, Svandis 1370
スパヒジャ
Spahija, Neven 1332
スパヒッチ
Spahic, Emir 1332
スバブ
Svab, Filip 1369
スパフォード
Spafford, Gene 1332
スパポドック
Supapodok, Charles 1367
スパマス・トリウィサワウェー
Supamas Trivisvavet 1367
スーハミ
Souhami, Diana 1330
スバラクシュミ
Subbulakshmi, M.S. 1362
スパラコ
Sparaco, Simona 1333
スバリ
Subari, Sozar 1362
スパリ
Supari, Fadilah 1367
ズバリ
Zubari, Shahar 1558
スパーリング
Sparing, Chris 1333
Sparling, Nancy 1333
Sperling, Daniel 1335
Sperling, Gene B. 1335
Sperling, Ted 1335

Spurling, Hilary 1338
Spurring, Quentin 1338
スパルヴィス
Spalvis, Lukas 1332
スパールガレン
Spaargaren, O.C. 1332
スハルク
Schalk, Chaim 1249
スパルタス
Spartas, Dale C. 1333
スハルト
Suharto 1363
スパレッティ
Spalletti, Luciano 1332
スパロー
Sparrow, Giles 1333
Sparrow, Sara S. 1333
Sparrow, William Anthony 1333
スパロウ
Sparrow, Thomas 1333
スパロウダンサー
Sparrowdancer, Mary 1333
スパーロック
Spurlock, Morgan 1338
スバーン
Severn, Dan 1276
スバン
Soubanh, Srithirath 1330
スパーン
Spahn, Warren Edward 1332
スパン
Souphanh, Keomixay 1331
Span, Denard 1332
Spann, Scott 1333
ズーパン
Zupan, Janet 1559
ズバン
Zvan, Barbara 1559
ズパン
Zupan, Jure 1559
スパング
Spang, Markus 1332
Spang, Rebecca L. 1333
スパンジェンバーグ
Spangenberg, Cory 1333
スパーンス
Spaans, Yolande 1332
スパンタ
Spanta, Rangin Dadfar 1333
ズパンチッチ
Zupancic, Kelita 1559
スバンディー
Subandhi, Jamie 1362
スパント
Spunt, Georges 1337
スバンドリオ
Subandrio 1362
スバンベコフ
Subanbekov, Bakirdin 1362
スヒー
Suchy, Marek 1362
ズービ
Zube, Ervin H. 1558
ズビ
Zou'bi, Khalid Samara 1557
Zou'bi, Sharif 1558
Zubi, Fawwaz 1558
スピーア
Speer, Kevin P. 1334
スピア
Spear, Boonnie A. 1333
Spear, Burning 1333
Spear, Mónica 1333
Spier, Guy 1336
Spier, Jonathan 1336
Spier, Peter 1336
スピアー
Speer, James 1334
Speer, Phil 1334
スピアーズ
Spears, Britney 1333
Spears, Richard A. 1333
Spears, Russell 1333
Spears, William O., Jr. 1333
Speirs, Jack 1334
Spiers, Edward M. 1336
スピアモン
Spearmon, Wallace 1333
スヒィッフマッグァー
Schiffmacher, Henk 1252
スピヴァク
Spivak, Gayatri Chakravorty 1336
スピヴァコフ
Spivakov, Vladimir 1336
スピヴァック
Spivak, Gayatri Chakravorty 1336
Spivak, Michael 1336
スピオガーブラ
Spio-garbrah, Ekow 1336
スビオクラ
Sviokla, John 1370
スピーカー・ユアン
Speaker-Yuan, Margaret 1333
スピーク
Speak, Karl D. 1333
スピークス
Speakes, Larry Melvin 1333
Speaks, Charles E. 1333
スピークマン
Speakman, James 1333
スピーグル
Spiegl, Fritz 1335
スピケ
Spycket, Jérôme 1338
スピーゲル
Spiegel, David 1335
Spiegel, David A. 1335
Spiegel, Eric 1335
Spiegel, Evan 1335
Spiegel, H. 1335
スピーゲルマン
Spiegelman, Art 1335
Spiegelman, Peter 1335
スピサック
Spisak, Pawel 1336
ズビザリタ
Zubizarreta, Rosa 1558
スビス
Svith, Flemming Tait 1370
スピース
Spies, Heinz-Joachim 1336
Spieth, Jordan 1336
ズビズディッチ
Zvizdić, Denis 1559
スピッカー
Spicker, Paul 1335
スピックス
Spix, Joe 1337
スピッツ
Spitz, Ellen Handler 1336
スピッツァー
Spitzer, Alan R. 1336
Spitzer, Cindy S. 1336
Spitzer, Eliot 1336
Spitzer, Robert L. 1336
スピッツナー
Spitzner, Lance 1336
スピッツナーゲル
Spitznagel, Mark 1336
スピッツバーグ
Spitzberg, Brian H. 1336
スピッツマン
Spizman, Robyn Freedman 1337
スヒッペルス
Schippers, Edith 1253
ズビディ
Zbidi, Abdelkrim 1549
スピード
Speed, Gary 1334
Speed, Toby 1334
スビトリナ
Svitolina, Elina 1370
スピナッツォーラ
Spinazzola, Leonardo 1336
スビナロフ
Svinarov, Nikolay 1370
スピーニ
Spini, Giorgio 1336
スピニー
Spinney, Caroll 1336
スピネッリ
Spinelli, Jerry 1336
スピネリ
Spinelli, Eileen 1336
スピネロ
Spinello, Richard A. 1336
スピノーサ
Soinosa, Charles 1324
スピノジ
Spinosi, Jean-Christophe 1336
スビノニシビリ
Svinonishvili, Mikheil 1370
スピノーラ
Spinola, Luigi 1336
スピバク
Spivak, Gayatri Chakravorty 1336
スピバコフ
Spivakov, Vladimir 1336
スビヒ
Sbihi, Mohamed Amine 1247
ズビャギンツェフ
Zvyagintsev, Andrei 1560
ズビャダウリ
Zviadauri, Zurab 1559
ズピラ
Zpira, Lukas 1558
スピラー
Spiller, C.J. 1336
Spiller, Jan 1336
Spiller, Michael Alan 1336
スビラ・イ・クラウス
Subira i Claus, Antoni 1362
スビラナ
Subirana, Juan 1362
スビラノビッチ
Svilanović, Goran 1370
スピリー
Spilly, Alphonse P. 1336
スピリウス
Spillius, Elizabeth Bott 1336
スピリオトプロス
Spiliotopoulos, Aris 1336
Spiliotopoulos, Evan 1336
Spiliotopoulos, Spilios 1336
スピリク
Spirig, Nicola 1336
スピリッチ
Sprich, Susan 1337
スピリドノフ
Spiridonov, Leonid 1336
スピリドノワ
Spiridonova, Daria 1336
スビリドフ
Sviridov, Sergey 1370
スピリン
Spirin, Gennadij 1336
Spirin, Ilya 1336
スヒリング
Schilling, Govert 1252
スピルジス
Spirtzis, Christos 1336
スピルスバリー
Spilsbury, Ariel 1336
スピルズベリー
Spilsbury, Louise 1336
スヒルトイス
Schilthuis, Willy 1252
スヒルトハウゼン
Schilthuizen, Menno 1252
スピールバーグ
Spielberg, Steven 1335
スピルバーグ
Spielberg, Steven 1335
スピールマン
Spealman, Jill 1333
Spielman, Andrew 1336
Spielman, Arthur J. 1336
スピレイン
Spillane, Mickey 1336
スピレーン
Spillane, Johnny 1336
Spillane, Mickey 1336
スピーロ
Szpiro, George G. 1375
スピロ
Szpiro, George G. 1375
スピワコフ
Spivakov, Vladimir 1336
スピンク
Spink, Kathryn 1336
スピンクス
Spinks, Lee 1336
Spinks, W.A. 1336
スビンダル
Svindal, Aksel Lund 1370
スピンデル
Spindel, Carrie B. 1336
スピンドラー
Spindler, Erica 1336
スーフ
Souef, Mohamed Elamine 1330
スプアー

Spoor, Ryk E. 1337
スファキアヌ
Sfakianou, Florentia 1277
スファール
Sfar, Joann 1277
スフィ
Soufi, Ali 1330
al-Sufi, Hamud Khalid Naji 1363
スフィアン
Sufian, Ahmed 1363
スフィッリ
Sfilli, Claudia 1277
スプウッド
Supuwood, Laveli 1367
スフォーザ
Sforza, Michell 1277
ズブコ
Zubko, Hennadii 1558
ズプコ
Zubcu, Victor 1558
Zubko, Hennadii 1558
ズブコフ
Zubkov, Alexander 1558
Zubkov, Viktor Alekseevich 1558
ズブコーフ
Zubkov, Viktor Alekseevich 1558
ズプコフ
Zubkov, Viktor Alekseevich 1558
スブシンスキー
Subschinski, Nora 1362
スプーナー
Spooner, John D. 1337
スブビッチ
Zubcic, Martina 1558
スプラウル
Spraul, V.Anton 1337
スプラギンズ
Spragins, Ellyn 1337
スブラクシュミ
Subbulakshmi, M.S. 1362
ズブラシング
Zublasing, Petra 1558
スプラッグ
Spragg, Mark 1337
スプラット
Spratt, Greville Douglas 1337
スプラッドリー
Spradley, James P. 1337
スプラディン
Spradlin, Dwayne 1337
スプラドリン
Spradlin, Scott E. 1337
スブラフマニヤム
Subrahmanyam, Sanjay 1362
スブラマニアム
Subramaniam, S. 1362
Subramaniam, Venkat 1362
スブラマニアン
Subramaniam, Venkat 1362
Subramanian, S.V. 1362
スフリアス
Souflias, Georgios 1330
スブリエール
Soublière, Marion 1330
スプリギングズ
Sprigings, David C. 1337
スプリグマン
Sprigman, Christopher 1337
スプリシ
Suplicy, Marta 1367
ズブリック
Zubrick, James W. 1558
スプリッグス
Spriggs, Jason 1337
スプリッター
Splitter, Tiago 1337
スプリットオフ
Splittorff, Paul 1337
スプリットーフ
Splittorff, Paul 1337
ズブリロワ
Zubrilova, Olena 1558
スプリーン
Spreen, Otfried 1337
スプリンガー
Springer, George 1337
Springer, Jane 1337
Springer, Kristina 1337
Springer, Nancy 1337
Springer, Timothy A. 1337
スプリング
Spring, Amy 1337
Spring, Chris 1337
Spring, Janis Abrahms 1337
Spring, Michael 1337
スプリングスティーン
Springsteen, Bruce 1337
Springsteen, Kay 1337
スプリングマン
Springman, I.C. 1337
スプリンケル
Sprinkel, Beryl Wayne 1337
スプール
Spool, Jared M. 1337
ズフール
Zuhoor, Ahmed 1558
スプルージュス
Sprūdžs, Edmunds 1337
スプルジンシュ
Spurdziņš, Oskars 1337
スプルース
Spruce, Nelson 1337
スプルン
Suprun, Uliana Nadia 1367
スプレイグ
Sprague, David 1337
スプレーグ
Sprague, Susan 1337
スープレナント
Surprenant, Aimée M. 1367
スプレンガー
Sprenger, Christian 1337
Sprenger, Reinhard K. 1337
スプロケイ
Sprokay, Susan 1337
スプロース
Sprouse, Chris 1337
ズフロフ
Zuhurov, Saidamir 1558
Zukhurov, Saidamir 1558
Zukhurov, Shukurjon 1559
スプロール
Spraul, V.Anton 1337
Sproul, Robert Charles 1337
スプロールズ
Sproles, Darren 1337
スプロンデル
Sprondel, Walter Michael 1337
スプーン
Spoon, Lex 1337
スペー
Spee, Gitte 1334
スペアリング
Sperring, Mark 1335
スペイ
Speh, Thomas W. 1334
スヘイエン
Scheijen, Sjeng 1250
スペイシー
Spacey, Kevin 1332
Spacey, Siân D. 1332
スペイシク
Spacek, Sissy 1332
スペイセク
Spacek, Sissy 1332
スペイダー
Spader, James 1332
スペイツ
Speights, Marreese 1334
ズベイディ
Zubeidi, Zakaria 1558
スペイト
Spaight, Martrell 1332
Speight, Bev 1334
Speight, Stephen 1334
スベイヒ
al-Subaihy, Mahmoud 1362
ズベイル
Zewail, Ahmed 1551
スペイン
Spain, Quinton 1332
スベインソン
Sveinsson, Gunnar 1370
Sveinsson, Kjartan 1370
スペイン・ロドリゲス
Spain Rodriguez 1332
スペクター
Specter, Arlen 1333
Specter, Michael 1334
Spector, Aimee 1334
Spector, Craig 1334
Spector, Jon 1334
Spector, Nancy 1334
Spector, Phil 1334
Spector, Rebecca 1334
Spector, Robert 1334
Spector, Susan 1334
Spector, Timothy David 1334
スペザーノ
Spezzano, Chuck 1335
Spezzano, Lency 1335
スペーシー
Spacey, Kevin 1332
スペーシク
Spacek, Sissy 1332
スペス
Speth, James Gustave 1335
スペーゼ=リネハン
Speese-Linehan, D. 1334
スペーダー
Spader, James 1332
スベツ
Švec, Marek 1370
スペック
Speck, Katie 1333
Speck, William Arthur 1333
スペッツィ
Spezi, Mario 1335
スヘップ
Schep, Peter 1251
スヘティナ
Schetyna, Grzegorz 1251
スペディング
Spedding, David Rolland 1334
Spedding, Scott 1334
スペード
Spade, David 1332
Spade, Kate 1332
スベトラーナ
Svetlana, Chezhina 1370
スベトラーノフ
Svetlanov, Evgenii Fedorovich 1370
スベトラノフ
Svetlanov, Evgenii Fedorovich 1370
スベトリク
Svetlik, Ivan 1370
スベトロフ
Sveltov, Boris V. 1370
スベーフ
al-Subeeh, Nouriya Subeeh Barrak 1362
スペランス
Sperans, Felix 1335
スペランデオ
Sperandeo, Victor 1335
スペリ
Sperry, Joseph 1335
スペリー
Sperry, Dan 1335
Sperry, Len 1335
スベリアニ
Subeliani, Koba 1362
スベリスドッティル
Sverrisdottir, Valgerdur 1370
スペリング
Spelling, Aaron 1334
Spellings, Margaret La Montagne 1334
Sperring, Mark 1335
スペリングス
Spellings, Margaret La Montagne 1334
スペリングズ
Spellings, Margaret La Montagne 1334
ズベール
Zewail, Ahmed 1551
ズベル
Zver, Milan 1559
スベルビ・ボニジャ
Subervi Bonilla, Rafael 1362
スペルベル
Sperber, Dan 1335
スペルマン
Spellman, Cathy Cash 1334
Spelman, Caroline 1334
Spelman, Cornelia Maude 1334

Spelman, Lucy H. 1334
スベルリスドッティル
Sverrisdottir, Valgerdur 1370
スペレーゲン
Speregen, Devra N. 1335
ズベレワ
Zvereva, Ellina 1559
スベロ
Subero, Carlos 1362
スペロ
Spero, Nancy 1335
スペローニ
Speroni, Julian 1335
スペンサー
Spencer, A.Jeffrey 1334
Spencer, Anthony James Merrill 1334
Spencer, Ashley 1334
Spencer, Baldwin 1334
Spencer, Beth 1334
Spencer, Britt 1334
Spencer, Catherine 1334
Spencer, Damion O. 1334
Spencer, Evan 1334
Spencer, James Nelson 1334
Spencer, John 1334
Spencer, Judith 1334
Spencer, Julius 1334
Spencer, Kaliese 1334
Spencer, LaVyrle 1334
Spencer, Levern 1335
Spencer, Liv 1335
Spencer, Lyle M. 1335
Spencer, Margaret Meek 1335
Spencer, Mary 1335
Spencer, Maureen 1335
Spencer, Mimi 1335
Spencer, Neal 1335
Spencer, Nick 1335
Spencer, Nigel 1335
Spencer, Octavia 1335
Spencer, Patricia Elizabeth 1335
Spencer, Paul 1335
Spencer, Paul Francis 1335
Spencer, Rudyard 1335
Spencer, Signe M. 1335
Spencer, Wen 1335
Spencer, William Browning 1335
Spenser, Emma Jane 1335
Spenser, Jay P. 1335
スペンサー＝ウェンデル
Spencer-Wendel, Susan 1335
スペンサー＝オーティー
Spencer-Oatey, Helen 1335
スペンス
Spence, Akeem 1334
Spence, A.Michael 1334
Spence, Errol 1334
Spence, Floyd 1334
Spence, Gerry 1334
Spence, Godfrey 1334
Spence, Graham 1334
Spence, Jon 1334
Spence, Jonathan D. 1334
Spence, Michael 1334
Spence, Noah 1334
Spence, Sean 1334
Spence, Simon 1334
スペンス・アルマゲヤー
Spence-Almaguer, Emily 1334
スベンスマルク
Svensmark, Henrik 1370
スペンスリー
Spensley, Sheila 1335
スベンセン
Svendsen, Emil Hegle 1370
スベンソン
Svenson, James 1370
Svensson, Frida 1370
Svensson, Lars 1370
Svensson, Lars E.O. 1370
Svensson, Marcus 1370
スペンダー
Spender, J.C. 1335
Spender, Stephen 1335
スベンヌン
Svennung, Anna Malvina 1370
スホイル
Schuil, Rich 1259
スボエ
Svae, Christoffer 1369
ズボガル
Zbogar, Vasilij 1549
スボータ
Subota, Lena 1362
スポタコバ
Spotakova, Barbora 1337
スポータック
Sportack, Mark A. 1337
スホツカ
Suchocka, Hanna 1362
スホッツ
Schots, Mik 1258
スポッツウッド
Spotswood, Jessica 1337
スポッリ
Spolli, Nicolas 1337
スボティッチ
Subotic, Neven 1362
スポデック
Spodek, Bernard 1337
ズボナレワ
Zvonareva, Vera 1559
スホフ
Sukhov, Pavel 1364
スポフォース
Spofforth, Gemma 1337
スボボダ
Svoboda, Cyril 1370
Svoboda, David 1370
Svoboda, Josef 1370
スポール
Spall, Timothy 1332
スホルコフ
Sukhorukov, Alexander 1364
Sukhorukov, Yuriy 1364
スポールストラ
Spoelstra, Erik 1337
Spoelstra, Jon 1337
スポルティエッロ
Sportiello, Marco 1337
スポールディング
Spaulding, David 1333
スポルディング
Spalding, Bob 1332
Spalding, Esperanza 1332
Spalding, Neil 1332
Spaulding, William Delbert 1333
スポルテス
Sportès, Morgan 1337
ズボレンスカ
Zvolenská, Zuzana 1559
ズボロウスキー
Zborowsky, Terri 1549
スポーン
Spohn, William C. 1337
スポング
Spong, John Shelby 1337
スポーンハイム
Sponheim, Lars 1337
スマ
Soumah, Alpha Mady 1331
Soumah, Fode 1331
Soumah, Ibrahima 1331
ズマ
Zouma, Kurt 1558
Zuma, Jacob 1559
Zuma, Nkosazana Dlamini 1559
スマイ
Smy, Pam 1321
Sumai, Saleh Hasan 1365
スマイエ
Sumaye, Frederick Tluway 1365
スマイス
Smythe, Helen 1321
スマイト
Smight, Jack 1314
スマイラ
Smaila, Mahaman 1313
Soumaila, Saddi 1331
スマイリー
Smiley, Ben 1314
Smiley, Jane 1314
Smillie, Ian 1314
Smylie, James Hutchinson 1321
Smyly, Drew 1321
スマイルズ
Smiles, Sam 1314
ズマイロビッチ
Zmajlović, Mihael 1556
スマウト
Smout, T. Christopher 1321
スマエ
Sumaye, Frederick Tluway 1365
スマオロ
Soumahoro, Amadou 1331
Soumahoro, Youssouf 1331
スマグロフ
Smagulov, Zhansay 1313
スマジャ
Smadja, Éric 1313
Smadja, Isabelle 1313
スマッジャ
Smadja, Brigitte 1313
スマディ
Smadi, Tayseer 1313
スマート
Smart, Andrew 1314
Smart, Jacob E. 1314
Smart, Jean 1314
Smart, John Ferguson 1314
Smart, Keeth 1314
Smart, Keith 1314
Smart, Marcus 1314
Smart, Michelle 1314
Smart, Nigel Paul 1314
Smart, Ninian 1314
Smart, Peter 1314
ズマトリーコバー
Zmatlíková, Helena 1556
スマナサーラ
Sumanasara, Alubomulle 1365
スマニ
Sumani, Alice 1365
スマヌ
Soumanou, Alassane 1331
Soumanou, Moudjaîdou Issifou 1331
スマヌウ
Soumanou, Djimba 1331
ズマヤフロレス
Zumaya Flores, Goretti Alejandra 1559
ズマラ
Zoumara, Ĉome 1558
スマリヤン
Smullyan, Raymond M. 1321
スマル
Soumare, Cheikh Hadjibou 1331
Sumar, Konstantin A. 1365
スマルジャン
Soemardjan, Selo 1323
スマルディノ
Smaldino, Sharon E. 1313
スマレ
Soumare, Cheikh Hadjibou 1331
Soumare, Myriam 1331
ズマン
Sumann, Christoph 1365
スミー
Smee, Nicola 1314
Smee, Sebastian 1314
スミアー
Smear, Pat 1314
ズミエフスキ
Zmievski, Andrei 1556
スミグン
Smigun, Kristina 1314
スミザー
Smither, Paul 1320
スミシー
Smithee, Alan 1320
スミシーズ
Smithies, Oliver 1320
スミジズ
Smithies, Oliver 1320
スミシリャエフ
Smyshlyaev, Alexandr 1321
スミース
Smeeth, Liam 1314
スミス
Smith, Aaron 1314
Smith, Adam 1315
Smith, Alan 1315
Smith, Alastair 1315
Smith, Aldon 1315
Smith, Alex 1315
Smith, Alexander McCall 1315
Smith, Ali 1315
Smith, Anabelle 1315
Smith, Andre 1315
Smith, Andrea Claire

ス

Harte 1315
Smith, Andrew 1315
Smith, Andrew F. 1315
Smith, Andy 1315
Smith, Anna Nicole 1315
Smith, Anne 1315
Smith, Anne Fielding 1315
Smith, Ann W. 1315
Smith, Anthony D. 1315
Smith, Anthony Donald 1315
Smith, Antone 1315
Smith, A.Robert 1315
Smith, Arthur Henderson 1315
Smith, Audrey B. 1315
Smith, Ben 1315
Smith, Benson 1315
Smith, Bill 1315
Smith, Bison 1315
Smith, Bob 1315
Smith, Bobbie 1315
Smith, Brad 1315
Smith, Brad J. 1315
Smith, Brendan 1315
Smith, Bryan 1315
Smith, Bubba 1315
Smith, Caleb 1315
Smith, Carl 1315
Smith, Carl H. 1315
Smith, Carol J. 1315
Smith, Carolyn S. 1315
Smith, Carrie 1315
Smith, Carson 1315
Smith, Chad 1315
Smith, Cheryl Ann 1315
Smith, Chris 1315
Smith, Chuck 1315
Smith, C.J. 1315
Smith, Claydes 1315
Smith, Conrad 1315
Smith, Cornelius Alvin 1315
Smith, Cynthia E. 1315
Smith, Cynthia J. 1315
Smith, Dan 1315
Smith, Daniel 1315
Smith, Danna 1315
Smith, Darryl 1315
Smith, Daryl 1315
Smith, Dave 1316
Smith, David 1316
Smith, David Alexander 1316
Smith, David Julian 1316
Smith, David Livingston 1316
Smith, Dean 1316
Smith, Dean Wesley 1316
Smith, Debbi 1316
Smith, Deborah 1316
Smith, Deborah Takiff 1316
Smith, Dennis 1316
Smith, Dennis L. 1316
Smith, Derek Alan 1316
Smith, Derrick 1316
Smith, Derron 1316
Smith, Devin 1316
Smith, Diane Shader 1316
Smith, Dick 1316
Smith, D.James 1316
Smith, D'Joun 1316
Smith, Dominic 1316
Smith, Donald E.P. 1316
Smith, Donovan 1316
Smith, Douglas K. 1316
Smith, Dreamius 1316
Smith, Duncan 1316
Smith, Dwight, Jr. 1316
Smith, Dwight Moody 1316
Smith, Edward E. 1316
Smith, Elaine C. 1316
Smith, Elizabeth A. T. 1316
Smith, Elliott 1316
Smith, Emily 1316
Smith, Emily T. 1316
Smith, Emmitt 1316
Smith, Eric 1316
Smith, Evan 1316
Smith, Evelyn E. 1316
Smith, Fanny 1316
Smith, Felipe 1316
Smith, Fenella 1316
Smith, Fiona 1316
Smith, Frank 1316
Smith, Frederick E. 1316
Smith, Garrison 1316
Smith, Gary 1316
Smith, Gavin D. 1316
Smith, Gavin G. 1316
Smith, Geno 1316
Smith, George Davey 1316
Smith, George David 1316
Smith, George Elwood 1316
Smith, George Oliver 1316
Smith, Giles 1316
Smith, Godfrey 1316
Smith, Gordon 1316
Smith, Graeme 1316
Smith, Graham 1316
Smith, Gráinne 1316
Smith, Greg 1316
Smith, Gregory White 1316
Smith, Guy N. 1317
Smith, Hal L. 1317
Smith, Hamilton Othanel 1317
Smith, Harrison 1317
Smith, Hayden 1317
Smith, Hedrick 1317
Smith, Helen Dunstan 1317
Smith, Henrik 1317
Smith, Howard K. 1317
Smith, Howard S. 1317
Smith, Huston 1317
Smith, Hyrum W. 1317
Smith, Ian 1317
Smith, Ian Douglas 1317
Smith, Ish 1317
Smith, Jacqui 1317
Smith, Jacquies 1317
Smith, Jaden 1317
Smith, James 1317
Smith, James Bryan 1317
Smith, Jane 1317
Smith, Jane Ellen 1317
Smith, Janet Kiholm 1317
Smith, Janice Gorzynski 1317
Smith, Jared 1317
Smith, Jason 1317
Smith, Jason McColm 1317
Smith, Jaylon 1317
Smith, J.David 1317
Smith, Jean 1317
Smith, Jeff 1317
Smith, Jeffrey 1317
Smith, Jeffrey M. 1317
Smith, Jerry 1317
Smith, Jerry E. 1317
Smith, Jessica 1317
Smith, J.H. 1317
Smith, Jim B. 1317
Smith, Jimmy 1317
Smith, Jiromi 1317
Smith, Jo 1317
Smith, Joanne Huist 1317
Smith, Joe 1317
Smith, John 1317
Smith, John Boulton 1317
Smith, John G. 1317
Smith, John Henry 1317
Smith, John L. 1317
Smith, Joseph 1317
Smith, Joseph Anthony 1317
Smith, Josh 1317
Smith, J.R. 1317
Smith, Judy 1317
Smith, Julie 1317
Smith, Justine 1317
Smith, Karen Rose 1317
Smith, Karl A. 1317
Smith, Katherine Allen 1317
Smith, Kathryn 1317
Smith, Kathy 1317
Smith, Kay Nolte 1317
Smith, Keith 1317
Smith, Keith Cameron 1317
Smith, Ken 1317
Smith, Kennon M. 1317
Smith, Kevin 1318
Smith, Kierra 1318
Smith, Kurt W. 1318
Smith, Lamar C. 1318
Smith, Lane 1318
Smith, Larry E. 1318
Smith, Lauren 1318
Smith, Laurence C. 1318
Smith, Leah 1318
Smith, Lee 1318
Smith, Lisa J. 1318
Smith, Louis 1318
Smith, Maggie 1318
Smith, Malcolm 1318
Smith, Mallex 1318
Smith, Manuel J. 1318
Smith, Marc 1318
Smith, Marcus 1318
Smith, Mari 1318
Smith, Mark 1318
Smith, Mark A. 1318
Smith, Mark Allen 1318
Smith, Mark Eddy 1318
Smith, Martin Cruz 1318
Smith, Martin J. 1318
Smith, Mary-Ann Tirone 1318
Smith, Mel 1318
Smith, Melanie K. 1318
Smith, Michael 1318
Smith, Michael A. 1318
Smith, Michael B. 1318
Smith, Michael D. 1318
Smith, Michael H. 1318
Smith, Michael J. 1318
Smith, Michael Marshall 1318
Smith, Mickey C. 1318
Smith, Mike 1318
Smith, Miranda 1318
Smith, Mitchell Oakley 1318
Smith, Monica L. 1318
Smith, Moyra 1318
Smith, Murray 1318
Smith, Murray Charles Maurice 1318
Smith, Nate 1318
Smith, Neil 1318
Smith, Neilson Voyne 1318
Smith, Nick 1318
Smith, Nicky 1318
Smith, Nigel J.H. 1318
Smith, Patricia 1318
Smith, Patrick 1318
Smith, Patti 1318
Smith, Paul 1318, 1319
Smith, Penelope 1319
Smith, Penny 1319
Smith, Pete 1319
Smith, Peter B. 1319
Smith, Peter Bevington 1319
Smith, Peter Charles 1319
Smith, Peter Daniel 1319
Smith, Peter K. 1319
Smith, Peter Moore 1319
Smith, Philip J. 1319
Smith, Preston 1319
Smith, Preston G. 1319
Smith, Quanterus 1319
Smith, Rae 1319
Smith, Ralph F. 1319
Smith, Ray 1319
Smith, Richard 1319
Smith, Richard Lester 1319
Smith, Rick 1319
Smith, Robert 1319
Smith, Robert C. 1319
Smith, Robert D. 1319
Smith, Robert Dean 1319
Smith, Robert Kimmel 1319
Smith, Robert Rowland 1319
Smith, Robert William 1319
Smith, Rod 1319
Smith, Rod A. 1319
Smith, Rodney 1319
Smith, Roger 1319
Smith, Roger Bonham 1319
Smith, Roland 1319
Smith, Ron 1319
Smith, Ronald Austin 1319
Smith, Ronald Edward 1319
Smith, Roy C. 1319
Smith, Rupert 1319
Smith, Rusty 1319
Smith, Rutger 1319
Smith, Ruth 1319
Smith, Ryan 1319
Smith, Sam 1319
Smith, Sandra Fucci 1319
Smith, Santee 1319
Smith, Scott 1319
Smith, Sean 1319
Smith, Seth 1319
Smith, Shaun 1319
Smith, Sheila A. 1319
Smith, Shelley 1319
Smith, Sheridan 1319
Smith, Shirley Ann 1319
Smith, Sid 1319
Smith, Sidney J. 1319
Smith, Smutty 1319
Smith, Spencer 1319
Smith, Stephen 1319
Smith, Stephen C. 1319

Smith, Steve 1319
Smith, Steven M. 1319
Smith, Steven R. 1320
Smith, Suzi 1320
Smith, Sydney 1320
Smith, Sylvia 1320
Smith, Taylor 1320
Smith, Telvin 1320
Smith, Terrance 1320
Smith, Terry E. 1320
Smith, Tevaun 1320
Smith, Thomas A. 1320
Smith, Thomas C. 1320
Smith, Thomas E. 1320
Smith, Thomas J. 1320
Smith, Toby 1320
Smith, Tom Rob 1320
Smith, Torrey 1320
Smith, Tracy K. 1320
Smith, Trecia 1320
Smith, Tye 1320
Smith, Tyron 1320
Smith, Valerie 1320
Smith, Venetia Stanley 1320
Smith, Vernon L. 1320
Smith, Vince 1320
Smith, Virginia Sarah 1320
Smith, Webb 1320
Smith, Wendy 1320
Smith, Wilbur A. 1320
Smith, Wilbur L. 1320
Smith, Will 1320
Smith, Willie 1320
Smith, W.Leon 1320
Smith, Za'Darius 1320
Smith, Zadie 1320
Smyth, Iain 1321
Smyth, Joshua M. 1321
Smyth, Paul 1321
Smyth, Seamus 1321

スミス‐セラフィン
Smith-Serafin, Xanthe 1320

スミスデービス
Smythe-davis, Nekoda 1321

スミスバトル
Smith Battle, Lee 1320

スミス・リベラ
Smith-rivera, D'Vauntes 1320

スミース・レディ
Sumeeth Reddy 1365

スミチ・レビ
Simchi-Levi, David 1301
Simchi-Levi, Edith 1301

スミチ＝レビ
Simchi-Levi, David 1301
Simchi-Levi, Edith 1301

スミック
Smick, David M. 1314

スミッツ
Smits, Gregory James 1320
Smitz, Paul 1320

スミッテン
Smitten, Richard 1320

スミット
Smit, Barbara 1314
Smit, Gretha 1314
Smit, John 1314
Smit, Noëlle 1314
Smit, Sven 1314

スミティーズ
Smithies, Oliver 1320

スミド
Smidt, N. 1314

スミトロ・ジョヨハディクスモ
Sumitro Joyohadikusumo 1365

スミヤ・エルデネチメグ
Sumiyaa Erdenechimegiin 1365

スミヨン
Soumillon, Christophe 1331

スミル
Smil, Vaclav 1314

スミルノヴァ
Smirnova, Elena A. 1314
Smirnova, Sveta 1314

スミルノーフ
Smirnov, A. 1314

スミルノフ
Smirnov, Alexander 1314
Smirnov, Alexey 1314
Smirnov, Sergei Georgievich 1314
Smirnov, Stanislav 1314
Smirnov, Vitalii 1314
Smirnov, Yuriy 1314

スミルノルフ
Smirnov, Alexander 1314

スミルノワ
Smirnova, Olga 1314

スムイン
Smuin, Michael 1321

スムクラー
Szmukler, George 1374

スムゴング
Sumgong, Jemima Jelagat 1365

スムート
Smoot, George Fitzgerald Ⅲ 1320
Smoot, Kendra 1320
Smoot, Seth 1320

スムバナ
Sumbana, Fernando 1365

スムルデルス
Smulders, Laura 1321

スメイシム
Sumaysim, Liwa 1365

スメイス
Smythe, Elizabeth 1321

スメイスタース
Smeijsters, Henk 1314

スメイヤー
Smeyers, Paul 1314

スメイヤーズ
Smeijers, Fred 1314

スメイル
Smale, Stephen 1313

スメーケンス
Smeekens, Jan 1314

スメサースト
Smethurst, Mae J. 1314
Smethurst, Richard J. 1314

スメタナ
Smetana, Gerald W. 1314

スメーツ
Smeets, Marie-Luise 1314

スメット
Smet, Kathleen 1314
Smet, Marian De 1314

スメディンス
Smedins, Janis 1314

スメトフ
Smetov, Yeldos 1314

スメドリー
Smedley, Jenny 1314

スメラク
Sumerak, Marc 1365

スメリャンスキー
Smelianskiĭ, Anatoliĭ M. 1314

スメール
Smale, John G. 1313
Smale, Stephen 1313

スメルコル
Smerkolj, Alenka 1314

スメルサー
Smelser, Neil J. 1314

スメルター
Smelter, DeAndre 1314

スメルチェック
Smercek, Boris von 1314

スメンジャンカ
Smendzianka, Regina 1314

スモーカー
Smoker, Josh 1320

スモキン
Smochin, Afanasie 1320

スモーク
Smoak, Justin 1320

スモテク
Smotek, Connie 1320

スモラー
Smoller, Jordan W. 1320

スモーリー
Smalley, Art 1313
Smalley, Gary 1313
Smalley, R.E. 1313
Smalley, Richard Errett 1313

スモリガ
Smoliga, Olivia 1320

スモリック
Smolik, Kenneth F. 1320

スモリャコフ
Smolyakov, Sergey Vladimirovich 1320

スモーリン
Smallin, Donna 1313
Smolin, Ann 1320
Smolin, Lee 1320

スモーリング
Smalling, Chris 1313

スモリンスキー
Smolinski, Jake 1320

スモール
Small, Andrew B. 1313
Small, Christopher 1313
Small, David 1313
Small, Gary W. 1313
Small, Hugh 1313
Small, Ian 1313
Small, Jim 1313
Small, Lass 1313
Smoll, Frank L. 1320

スモールウッド
Smallwood, John 1313
Smallwood, K.Shawn 1313
Smallwood, Vicki 1314
Smallwood, Wendell 1314
Smallwood, W. Norman 1314

スモルツ
Smoltz, John 1320

スモールボン
Smallbone, Stephen W. 1313

スモールマン
Smallman, Steve 1313

スモレン
Smolen, Michal 1320

スモレンスキー
Smolensky, Michael 1320
Smolensky, Paul 1320

スモワ
Soumois, Frederic 1331

スヤディ
Suyadi 1369

スヤント
Suyanto, Djoko 1369

ズュベール
Zuber, Roger 1558

スヨイ
Suyoi, Osman 1369

スヨルジュ
Suyolcu, Orhan 1369

スライウォツキー
Slywotzky, Adrian J. 1313

スライウム
Slaium 1311

スライセリ
al-Suraiseri, Jubarah bin Eid 1367

ズライダー・イブラヒム
Zuraidah Ibrahim 1559

スライティ
al-Sulaiti, Jassim Seif Ahmed 1364

スライマノフ
Sulaymanov, Nurlan 1364
Suraimanov, Nurlan 1367

スライマン
Sulaiman, Jose 1364

スライマンクロフ
Sulaimankulov, Arzymat 1364

スライミ
al-Sulaimi, Yahya bin Saud 1364

スライモン
Sulaimon, Rasheed 1364

スライワ
Sulaywah, Sargon 1364

スラウィ
Slaoui, Younes 1311

スラヴィクシェク
Slavicsek, Bill 1312

スラヴィンスキー
Slavinskii, Boris N. 1312
Slavinskii, D.B. 1312

スラウェンスキー
Slawenski, Kenneth 1312

スラヴォヴァ
Slavova, Angela 1312

ズラウスキ
Żuławski, Andrzej 1559

ズラウスキー
Żuławski, Andrzej 1559

スラキアット・サティヤンタイ
Surakiart Sathirathai 1367

スラキアート
Surakiart Sathirathai 1367

スラキアト・サティエンタイ
Surakiart Sathirathai 1367

スラクテリス
Slakteris, Atis 1311

ス

スラクトリス
Slakteris, Atis 1311
スラサック
Surasak, Karnjanarat 1367
スーラージュ
Soulages, Pierre 1331
スラース
Thrasou, Haris 1402
スラタリー
Slattery, Mary 1312
ズラタル
Zlatar, Andrea 1556
ズラタルビオリッチ
Zlatar Violić, Andrea 1556
ズラタン
Zlatan 1556
スラッキン
Sluckin, Timothy J. 1313
スラック
Slack, Jonathan Michael Wyndham 1311
Slack, Paul 1311
スラック・シワラック
Sulak Sivaraksa 1364
スラッシャー
Thrasher, Virginia 1402
スラッシュ
Slash 1311
Thrash, Agatha M. 1402
Thrash, Calvin L. 1402
スラッター
Slatter, Jean 1312
Slatter, Stuart St.P. 1312
スラットキン
Slatkin, Brett 1312
Slatkin, Leonard 1312
ズラティッチ
Zlatic, Andrija 1556
ズラテバ
Zlateva, Stanka 1556
ズラテバフリストバ
Hristova, Stanka Zlateva 629
スラトキン
Slatkin, Leonard 1312
スラニア
Slania, Dan 1311
スラヒ
Slahi, Mohamedou Ould 1311
スラビカ
Slavica, Nik 1312
ズラビシビリ
Zurabishvili, Salomé 1559
ズラビシュヴィリ
Zurabishvili, Salomé 1559
ズラビシュビリ
Zurabishvili, Salomé 1559
スラビンスキ
Slavinski, Antoni 1312
スラビンスキー
Slavinskii, Boris N. 1312
スラフノフ
Slavnov, Sergei 1312
スラベスキ
Slaveski, Trajko 1312
スラベフスキ
Slaveski, Trajko 1312
ズラボフ
Zurabov, Mikhail Y. 1559
スラポン
Surapong, Suebwonglee 1367
Surapong, Tovijakchaikul 1367
スラマ
Slama, Dirk 1311
Soulama, Souleymane 1331
スラユット・ジュラノン
Surayud Chulanont 1367
スラユット・チュラーノン
Surayud Chulanont 1367
スラユット・チュラノン
Surayud Chulanont 1367
スラン
Sourang, Moustapha 1331
Thrun, Sebastian 1402
スラング
Slung, Michele 1313
スランヌディル
Sourang Ndir, Maïmouna 1331
スーリ
Suri, Jane Fulton 1367
スーリー
Suri, Manil 1367
スリ
Seli, Mbogo Ngabo 1271
Souli, Nanthavong 1331
Sri, Edward 1338
Suri, Gaurav 1367
スリー
Slee, Nicola M. 1312
スリーヴァ
Sliwa, Bob 1312
スリウォン
Soulivong, Daravong 1331
スリエマン
Sulieman, Muhammad Ibrahim 1364
スリカンス
Srikanth, Mokshagundam L. 1338
スリジエ
Cerisier, Alban 240
スリジェフスキー
Slizhevsky, Oleg L. 1312
スリスラット
Srisurat, Sukanya 1338
スリーター
Sleator, William 1312
スリダラン
Sreedharan, Elattuvalapil 1338
スリック
Sulic, Luka 1364
スリッパー
Slipper, James 1312
スリティ
Sliti, Youssef 1312
ズリティニ
Zlitini, Abdelhafidh 1556
al-Zlitni, Abdul-Hafeed 1556
スリドハルン
Sridharan, Prashant 1338
スリバス
Sorribas, Sebastià 1329
スリバン
Sullibvan, Drew 1364
Sullivan, Ben 1364
ズリービー
Zribi, Lamia 1558
スリフト
Thrift, N.J. 1402
スリベツ
Slivets, Oly 1312
スリベンコ
Slivenko, Oxana 1312
スリペンチュック
Slipenchuk, Viktor 1312
スリマニ
Slimani, Islam 1312
Slimani, Rabah 1312
スリム
Slim, Carlos 1312
Slym, Karl 1313
スリム・サグ
Slim Thug 1312
スリヤ
Suriya, Jungrungreangkit 1367
Suriya, Prasathinphimai 1367
スリヤー・ラタナクン
Suriyā Rattanakun 1367
スーリヤン
Soryan, Hamid 1329
スリュニャエフ
Slunyayev, Igor N. 1313
スリヨハディプロジョ
Suryohadiprojo, Sayidiman 1368
スリランガン
Srirangan 1338
スリンカチュ
Slinkachu 1312
スリング
Sulling, Anne 1364
スリングスタッド
Slyngstad, Yngve 1313
スリングスビー
Slingsby, Tom 1312
ズリンダ
Dzurinda, Mikuláš 386
スリン・ピスワン
Surin Pitsuwan 1367
スリン・ピッスワン
Surin Pitsuwan 1367
スール
Suhl, Sebastian 1363
スル
Sulu, Aytac 1365
ズールー
Zulu, Lindiwe 1559
ズル
Zull, James E. 1559
スルアガ
Zuluaga, Oscar Iván 1559
ズルーアリ
Zerouali, Najib 1551
スルイユス
Sluijs, Hans 1313
ズルカルナイン
Zulkarnain, Hanafi 1559
ズルカルニナ
Zulkarnina, Julia 1559
スルギア
Sourghia, Mamadou 1331
ズルキフリ
Zulkifli, Hasan 1559
スルーキン
Sluckin, Alice 1313
スルグラーゼ
Surguladze, Nino 1367
スルグラゼ
Surguladze, Kote 1367
スルコバ
Slukova, Marketa 1313
スルコフ
Surkov, Vladislav Y. 1367
スルサレワ
Slyusareva, Olga 1313
スルジュ
Surugiu, Florin 1368
スルジュキッチ
Sljukic, Andrija 1312
スルタノフ
Sultanov, Alexei 1365
Sultanov, Bakhyt 1365
Sultanov, Jalil 1365
Sultanov, Kalykbek 1365
Sultanov, Kylychbek 1365
Sultanov, Marat 1365
Sultanov, Utkir 1365
スルターン
Sultan bin Abdul-Aziz 1365
スルタン
Soultan, Hamoud Abdi 1331
Sultan, Abdul-Samad Rahman 1365
Sultan, bin Zayed al-Nahyan 1365
Sultan, Jean Claude 1365
Sultan, Maqbul bin Ali bin 1365
Sultan, Sufian 1365
Sultant, Jacqueline 1365
Sultant, Jakeline 1365
スルタン・イブン・アブドル・アジズ
Sultan bin Abdul-Aziz 1365
スルタン皇太子
Sultan bin Abdul-Aziz 1365
スルタン・ビン・アブドル・アジズ
Sultan bin Abdul-Aziz 1365
スルタンベコワ
Sultanbekova, Cholpon 1365
スルツカヤ
Slutskaya, Irina 1313
スルツキー
Slutskiy, Leonid 1313
Slutsky, Jeff 1313
スルティ
Surty, Mohamed Enver 1367
ズルーディ
Zouroudi, Anne 1558
スルトゥサ
Zurutuza, David 1559
スールニア
Sournia, Jean-Charles 1331
ズルハスナン
Zulhasnan, Rafique 1559
ズルバレフ
Zurbalev, Dima 1559
スルーフ
Sroufe, L.Alan 1338
スルブ
Sârbu, Ilie 1241
Sârbu, Marian 1241
ズルファ
Zulfa, Mariyam 1559
ズルファァカル

Zulfacar, Maliha 1559
ズルフィカルパシッチ
Zulfikarpasic, Bojan 1559
スルフ・ハッサン
Suluhu Hassan, Samia 1365
スルマ
Suruma, Ezra 1368
スルーマン
Sluman, Jeff 1313
ズルマン
Szulman, Julien 1375
スルヤジャヤ
Soerydjaya, William 1323
スールヤ・ダス
Surya Das 1368
スルヤダルマ
Suryadharma, Ali 1368
スルヤディ
Surjadi, Soedirdja 1367
ズルリ
Zrouri, Abdelkader 1558
スルール
Sorour, Gamal 1329
スルンテ
Sulunteh, Jeremiah 1365
スーレ
Soulé, Ba Bocar 1331
ズーレ
Sule, Niklas 1364
スーレイ
Souleye, Saade 1331
スレイ
Slay, Darius 1312
Souley, Hassane 1331
スレイヴィン
Slavin, Bill 1312
Slavin, Jim 1312
スレイヴス
Thraves, Jamie 1402
スレイター
Slater, Christian 1311
Slater, David H. 1311
Slater, Glenn 1311
Slater, Kim 1311
Slater, Lauren 1311
Slater, Matthew 1311
Slater, Michael 1311
Slater, Pearce 1311
Slater, Tracy 1312
スレイト
Slate, Jeremy 1311
Slate, Joe H. 1311
Sleit, Azzam 1312
スレイド
Slade, Chad 1311
Slade, Colin 1311
Slade, Henry 1311
Slade, Michael 1311
Slade, Robert 1311
スレイビッド
Slavid, Ruth 1312
スレイマニ
Sulejmani, Miralem 1364
Sulejmani, Rizvan 1364
スレイマン
Sleiman, Michel 1312
Souleiman, Ayanleh 1331
Souleymane, Bachar Ali 1331
Sulaiman, Abubakar 1364
Sulaiman, Jose 1364
Sulaiman, S.H. 1364
Suleiman, C.A. 1364
Suleiman, Ibrahim 1364
Suleiman, Michel 1364
Suleiman, Mohammad Ibrahim 1364
Suleiman, Omar 1364
Suleiman, Yusuf 1364
Suleyman, Mahamud Hassan 1364
スレイメノフ
Suleimenov, Kairbek 1364
Suleimenov, Timur 1364
スレザーク
Szlezak, Thomas Alexander 1374
スレサレンコ
Slesarenko, Yelena Vladimirovna 1312
スレーター
Slater, Allana 1311
Slater, Anthony 1311
Slater, Christian 1311
Slater, Daniel 1311
Slater, Douglas 1311
Slater, Evan 1311
Slater, Jenny 1311
Slater, Kelly 1311
Slater, Peter James Bramwell 1311
Slater, Robert 1311
スレチュコビッチ
Srećković, Srdjan 1338
スレッサー
Slesar, Henry 1312
Slessor, Catherine 1312
スレッジ
Sledge, Eugene Bondurant 1312
Sledge, Percy 1312
スレッシュ
Suresh, Subra 1367
スレッテン
Sletten, Brian 1312
スレート
Slate, Jeremy 1311
スレプツォワ
Sleptsova, Svetlana 1312
スレブロ
Srebro, Maciej 1338
スレブロドリスキー
Srebrodol'skii, Boris Ivanovich 1338
スレーヘルス
Slegers, Liesbet 1312
スレベンス
Slavens, Elaine 1312
スレマナ
Sulemana, Amin Amidu 1364
スレルフォール
Threlfall, Terry 1402
スレーワーゲン
Sleeuwagen, Gunther 1312
スレーン
Cyrén, Karin 310
スレン
Suren, Dolgor 1367
ズレンコ
Zlenko, Anatoliy 1556
ズレンシック
Zduriencik, Jack 1549
スレンツカ
Slenczka, Notger 1312
スーレン - フランセン
Souren-Franssen, Liduïn 1331
ズロ
Zullo, Germano 1559
スロイェギン
Surojegin, Nora 1367
Surojegin, Pirkko-Liisa 1367
スロウ
Thurow, Shari 1403
スロウィッキー
Surowiecki, James 1367
スロヴィック
Slovic, Scott 1313
スロウカ
Slouka, Mark 1313
ズロウザウワー
Zlozower, Neil 1556
ズロウリ
Zrouri, Abdelkader 1558
スロウル
Srour, Saad 1338
スローカム
Slocum, Jerry 1313
スロス
Sloss, Dakin 1313
Sloss, Marielle 1313
スロスビー
Throsby, C.D. 1402
Throsby, David 1402
スロソル
Throssell, Brianna 1402
スローソン
Slauson, Matt 1312
スローター
Slaughter, Anne-Marie 1312
Slaughter, Enos Bradsher 1312
Slaughter, Joseph 1312
Slaughter, Karin 1312
Slaughter, Sheila 1312
Slaughter, Tom 1312
スローターダイク
Sloterdijk, Peter 1313
ズロチェフスキー
Zlochevskiy, Mykola 1556
スロット
Slott, Dan 1313
スロードノフ
Sludnov, Roman 1313
スローニム
Slonim, Eva 1313
スロビック
Slovic, Scott 1313
ズーロフ
Durov, Sergei Fedorovich 384
スロボダ
Sloboda, John A. 1313
スロボドキーナ
Slobodkina, Esphyr 1313
スローマン
Sloman, Larry 1313
スロワー
Thrower, Norman Joseph William 1402
スローン
Sloan, Alfred Pritchard, Jr. 1312
Sloan, Annie 1312
Sloan, Donald 1312
Sloan, Douglas 1312
Sloan, Elinor Camille 1312
Sloan, Geoffrey R. 1312
Sloan, Holly Goldberg 1312
Sloan, Jacob 1313
Sloan, Jerry 1313
Sloan, John P. 1313
Sloan, Kim 1313
Sloan, Mark 1313
Sloan, Rebecca S. 1313
Sloan, Richard G. 1313
Sloan, Robin 1313
Sloane, Charles 1313
Sloane, Paul 1313
スロンチェフスキ
Slonczewski, Joan 1313
スワイウェリ
al-Suwaiyel, Mohammed Ibn Ibrahim 1369
スワイダスキー
Swiderski, Frank 1372
スワイツァー
Sweitzer, Letitia 1372
スワイド
Suwayd, Hassan Umar Mohammed 1369
Suwayd, Yusuf 1369
Sweid, Joseph 1372
スワイニ
Thuwainy, bin Shihab al-Said 1403
スワイハート
Swihart, Blake 1372
スワイン
Swain, Paul 1370
ズワオ
Zhuwao, Patric 1553
スワジンスキ
Swierczynski, Duane 1372
スワースキー
Swirsky, Rachel 1372
スワーツ
Swartz, Aaron 1371
スワット
Suwat, Liptapanlop 1369
スワップ
Swap, Walter C. 1371
スワディ
Swadi, Rasoul Abdul-Hussein 1370
スワートロー
Swertlow, Frank 1372
スワードロー
Swerdlow, Stewart A. 1372
スワドロン
Swadron, Stuart P. 1370
スワトン
Swatoń, Jerzy 1371
スワーナー
Swarner, Kristina 1371
スワナリエフ
Suvanaliyev, Omurbek 1369
スワニック
Swanwick, Keith 1371
ズワネ
Zwane, Mosebenji Joseph 1560
スワパン
Suwapan, Tanyuvardhana 1369
スワミダス
Swamidass, Paul M. 1370
スワミナサン

ス

セ

Swaminathan, Madhavan 1370
Swaminathan, Monkombu Sambasivan 1370
スワミナタン
Swaminathan, D.M. 1370
Swaminathan, Monkombu Sambasivan 1370
スワミナダン
Swaminathan, D.M. 1370
スワミ・ラムデブ
Swami Ramdev 1370
スワラジ
Swaraj, Sushma 1371
スワラットシン
Swaratsingh, Kennedy 1371
スワラップ
Swarup, Vikas 1371
ズワリチ
Zvarich, Roman 1559
スワリム
Sualim, Mohammad Fitouri 1362
スワーリング
Swerling, Beverly 1372
スワル
Siwar, Haj Magid 1309
スワルツ
Swartz, Clifford E. 1371
Swartz, Johnnie 1371
Swartz, Mark H. 1371
ズワルト
Zwart, Ron 1560
スワループ
Swarup, Vikas 1371
スワロウ
Swallow, James 1370
スワロフスキー
Svárovský, Leoš 1369
スワン
Swan, Annalyn 1370
Swan, Christopher A. 1370
Swan, Curt 1370
Swan, Harold Jeremy C. 1371
Swan, Isabel 1371
Swan, Michael 1371
Swan, Owen 1371
Swan, Robbyn 1371
Swan, Russ 1371
Swan, Teal 1371
Swan, Thomas 1371
Swan, Wayne 1371
Swann, Alan C. 1371
Swann, Damian 1371
Swann, E.L. 1371
Swann, Leda 1371
Swann, Mandy 1371
ズワン
Zhuang, Ze-dong 1553
スワンウィック
Swanwick, Michael 1371
スワンク
Swank, Hilary 1371
スワンストン
Swanston, Alexander 1371
Swanston, Malcolm 1371
スワンソン
Swanson, Dansby 1371
Swanson, Dax 1371
Swanson, Doug J. 1371
Swanson, Elizabeth 1371
Swanson, Garrett 1371
Swanson, James L. 1371
Swanson, Kara L. 1371
Swanson, Larry W. 1371
Swanson, Peter 1371
Swanson, Susan Marie 1371
Swanson, Travis 1371
スワンダ
Suwanda, Sandi 1369
スン
Seung, Sebastian 1276
Seung, Woo Back 1276
Sun, Dao-lin 1366
Sun, Ge 1366
Sun, Guangxin 1366
Sun, Jia-zheng 1366
Sun, Yang 1366
Sun, Yun-hsuan 1366
Sun, Zheng-cai 1366
Sun Chanthol 1366
Sung, Vo Van 1366
ズーン
Zone, Jacques 1557
ズン
Chung, Ching-wen 263
Dung, Dao Ngoc 381
Dung, Dinh Tien 381
Dung, Ho Nghia 381
Dung, Mai Tien 381
Dung, Nguyen Chi 381
Dung, Trinh Dinh 381
Zeng, Pei-yan 1550
Zeng, Qing-hong 1550
Zeng, Shu-sheng 1550
Zheng, bi-jian 1552
Zheng, Li-zhi 1552
ズンカンカッセル
Duncan-cassell, Julia 381
スンキ
al-Sunki, Omar 1367
スーンズ
Sounes, Howard 1331
スンタイエフ
Sntayehu, Weldemikael 1322
スンダーラー
Sundara, Viroth 1366
ズンダール
Zumdahl, Steven S. 1559
スン・チャントル
Sun Chanthol 1366
スンディン
Sundin, Mats 1366
スンド
Sundh, Kerstin 1366
ズントー
Zumthor, Peter 1559
ズントゥム
Suntum, Ulrich van 1367
スンドビー
Sundby, Siren 1366
スントフト
Sundtoft, Tine 1366
スンドベリ
Sundberg, Johan 1366
スントホルム
Sundholm, Goran 1366
スンドララジャン
Sundararajan, Arun 1366
スントン
Sounton, Martial 1331
スンナノー
Sunnaná, Lars Sigurd 1367
スンニョギイ
Szunyoghy, András 1375
ズンネガルド
Sunnegårdh, Erika 1367
ズンバド
Zumbado, Fernando 1559
スンバナ
Sumbana, António Correia 1365
Sumbana, Fernando 1365
スンビ
Sundby, Martin Johnsrud 1366
スーンピート
Soentpiet, Chris K. 1323
スンプラディット
Sumpradit, Sarat 1366
スンヨン
Seung-yeon 1276

【セ】

セア
Zea, Leopoldo 1549
セアー
Thayer, Patricia 1394
Thayer, Reginald 1394
ゼーア
Zehr, E.Paul 1549
ゼア
Zehr, Howard 1549
セアウ
Seau, Junior 1266
セアコシン
Seakgosing, John 1266
セアフォス
Searfoss, D.Gerald 1266
セアブラ
Seabra, Maria do Carmo 1266
セイ
Say, Allen 1247
Say, Rick 1247
Say, Rosa P. 1247
Sey, Omar 1277
セイアー
Thayer, Elizabeth S. 1394
セイイトクルイエフ
Seyitkulyev, Rozymyrat 1277
セイエルスタッド
Seierstad, Åsne 1269
セイエルステ
Sejersted, Lotte Smiseth 1270
セイカー
Thakor, Anjan V. 1393
セイガル
Sagal, Katey 1226
セイキー
Sakey, Marcus 1228
セイクス
Saeks, Diane Dorrans 1225
セイジ
Sage, Angie 1226
Sage, Lorna 1226
セイジャー
Sager, Mike 1226
セイス
Saith, Lenny 1228
セイセイ
Seisay, Mohammed 1270
セイタバチスタ
Ceita Batista, Maria 239
ゼイダン
Zeidan, Ali 1549
ゼイツ
Zeits, Andrey 1550
セイックラ
Seikkula, Jaakko 1270
セイデ
Seide, Cadi 1269
セイディ
Sadie, Stanley 1224
Seidi, Lassana 1269
セイディウ
Sejdiu, Fatmir 1270
ゼイテル
Zeaiter, Ghazi 1549
セイデン
Seiden, Allan 1269
Seiden, Art 1269
Seiden, Josh 1269
セイデンスティッカー
Seidensticker, John 1269
セイド
Seid, Brahim 1269
Seide, Ron 1269
ゼイド
Zeid, Hikmat 1549
セイドゥ
Saïdou, Saley 1227
Seïdou, Alassane 1269
Seydou, Abdourahamane 1277
Seydou, Sadou 1277
Seydoux, Léa 1277
セイドラー
Seidler, Tor 1269
ゼイニ
Zeini, Ali Mahaman Lmine 1549
セイニオ
Sainio, Caitlin 1227
ゼイハン
Zeihan, Peter 1549
セイビアン
Sabean, Brian R. 1223
セイブ
Saibou, Ali 1227
セイファー
Safer, Jeanne 1225
Safer, Morley 1225
セイフエルナスル
Seif El Nasr, Farouk Mahmoud 1270
セイフター
Seifter, Harvey 1270
セイフルアデル
al-Adel, Saif 14
ゼイベクジ
Zeybekci, Nihat 1551
ゼイベクチ
Zeybekci, Nihat 1551
セイボム
Sabom, Michael B. 1223
ゼイマリ
Zeimal', T.I. 1549
セイム
Seim, Mart 1270
セイムナウ
Samenow, Stanton E. 1234
セイメック
Samek, Toni 1234

セイモア
Seymour, John 1277
セイモアー
Seymour, Kevon 1277
Seymour, Ryan 1277
セイモア＝スミス
Seymour-Smith, Martin 1277
セイヤー
Sayer, Chloë 1247
Sayre, April Pulley 1247
Sayre, Jeff 1247
Sayre, Kate 1247
Thayer, Carlyle A. 1394
Thayer, James Stewart 1394
Thayer, Nathaniel Bowman 1394
ゼイヤー・ウィン
Zayar Win 1549
セイヤーズ
Sayers, Goldie 1247
セイヤック
Sayuk, Gregory S. 1247
セイヨム
Seyaum, Dawit 1277
セイヨム・メスフィン
Seyoum Mesfin 1277
セイラー
Saylor, David 1247
Thaler, Linda Kaplan 1394
Thaler, Richard H. 1394
セイラニャン
Seiranyan, Spartak 1270
セイラム
Salem, Lionel 1230
セイル
Sale, Kirkpatrick 1230
Sale, Tim 1230
セイルズ
Sayles, John Thomas 1247
セイレ
Seile, Mārīte 1270
セイン
Thain, John A. 1393
Thane, Pat 1394
Thayne, David A. 1394
Thayne, RaeAnne 1394
ゼイン
Zane, Carolyn 1547
Zane, J.Peder 1547
Zeine, Sidi Ould 1549
セイン・ウィン
Sein Win 1270
セインズブリー
Sainsbury, Richard Mark 1227
セインズベリー
Sainsbury, David 1227
Sainsbury, Lisa Ingeborg 1227
Sainsbury, Malcolm 1227
ゼインツ
Zaentz, Saul 1545
セイント
Saint, Harry F. 1227
Saint, Sanjay 1227
セイント・ヴィンセント
St.Vincent 1228
セイント・オールバンズ
St.Albans, David T. 1227
セイン・トワー
Sein Htwa 1270
セイン・フトゥワ
Sein Htwa 1270
セイン・ルイン
Sein Lwin 1270
セーヴァ
Seva, Bhakti 1276
ゼーヴァルト
Seewald, Peter 1268
Sewald, Wolfgang 1276
ゼーヴィ
Zevi, Fausto 1551
セヴィニー
Sevigny, Chloë 1276
ゼヴィン
Zevin, Gabrielle 1551
セウエト
Sehoueto, Lazare 1269
セウェリンスキ
Seweryński, Michał 1277
セウマヌ
Seumanu, Aita Ah Wa 1276
ゼエビ
Ze'evi, Ariel 1549
Zeevi, Rechavam 1549
セオ
Seo, Kay Kyeongju 1274
セオヴィク
Seović, Aleksandar 1274
セオ＝チョウ
Seo-cho, Joan M. 1274
セオドア
Théodore, José 1395
Theodore, Wayne 1395
セオトキ-アテシュリ
Theotoki-Atteshli, Panayiota 1395
セオドサキス
Theodosakis, Jason 1395
セオドロウ
Theodorou, Doros 1395
ゼーガー
Seeger, Melanie 1268
セガストローム
Segerstrom, Suzanne C. 1268
セカチョワ
Sekachova, Iryna 1270
セカトレ
Sekatle, Matumelo 1270
Sekatle, Pontšo 1270
Sekatle, Semano 1270
Sekatle, Suzan 1270
セカマネ
Sekhamane, Tlohang 1270
セガラン
Segaran, Toby 1268
セカリッチ
Sekaric, Jasna 1270
セーガル
Seagal, Steven 1266
Sehgal, Tino 1269
セカール
Sekal, Zbynek 1270
セガール
Seagal, Steven 1266
Sehgal, Kabir 1269
セカルディ
Ceccaldi, Hubert Jean 239
セーガン
Sagan, Drion 1226
Sagan, Paul 1226
セガン
Séguin, Onésime-Édouard 1269
Séguin, Philippe Daniel Alain 1269
セカンダ
Sekunda, Nick 1270
セカンディ
Ssekandi, Edward 1338
ゼキ
Zeki, Semir 1550
セキザワ
Sekizawa, Akihiko 1270
セギズバエフ
Segizbaev, Abdil 1269
セキボ
Sekibo, Abiye 1270
セキモト
Sekimoto, Shohei 1270
セキヤ
Sekiya, T.Raymond 1270
セギン
Seguin, Paul 1269
セク
Seck, Idrissa 1267
Seck, Mamadou 1267
Seck, Oumou Khairy Guèye 1267
セグア
Segua, Derek 1269
セグ・イ・マルティン
Segú y Martín, Fernando 1269
セクエイラ
Sequeira, Jack 1274
セクストン
Sexton, John 1277
Sexton, Jonathan 1277
Sexton, Katy 1277
Sexton, Marie 1277
Sexton, Mark 1277
セクスミス
Sexsmith, Giselle 1277
Sexsmith, John 1277
ゼクスル
Sexl, Roman U. 1277
セクソン
Sexson, Lynda 1277
セクター
Secter, Irving I. 1267
セグニット
Segnit, Niki 1269
セグニーニ
Segnini, Carlos 1269
セクヒー
Nsekhe, Ty 1035
セグベフィア
Segbefia, Alex 1268
ゼグベルム
Zegbelemou, Kemo 1549
セクモカス
Sekmokas, Arvydas 1270
セグーラ
Segura, Jean 1269
セグラ・バシ
Segura Vasi, Alonso 1269
セグラ・ボニージャ
Segura Bonilla, Olman 1269
セクリ
Sekkouri, Lahcen 1270
セクリスト
Sechrist, Elsie 1267
セクリッチ
Sekulić, Predrag 1270
セクリン
Seculin, Andrea 1267
セグリン
Seglin, Jeffrey L. 1269
Segrin, Chris 1269
セグリンシ
Segliņš, Mareks 1269
セグリンシュ
Segliņš, Mareks 1269
セグレ
Segre, Cesare 1269
Segre, Emanuele 1269
Segrè, Gino 1269
セグレスト
Segrest, James 1269
セクワレ
Sexwale, Tokyo 1277
セーケイ
Székely, Gábor J. 1374
Székely, Tamás 1374
セゲディ
Szegedi, Katalin 1374
セゲディン
Segedin, Rob 1268
セゲフ
Segev, Tom 1268
ゼーゲブレヒト
Sägebrecht, Marianne 1226
セゲラ
Séguéla, Philippe 1269
セケラマイ
Sekeramayi, Sydney 1270
セケリンスカ
Šekerinska, Radmila 1270
セーゲルスタム
Segerstam, Leif 1268
セゲルスタム
Segerstam, Leif 1268
セーゲルストレーム
Segelström, Fabian 1268
セーゲルストローレ
Segerstråle, Ullica Christina Olofsdotter 1268
セケレシュ
Szekeres, Imre 1374
ゼコ
Džeko, Edin 386
セゴヴィア
Segovia, Carmen 1269
セコスキ
Secoske, Matt 1267
セゴビア
Segovia, María Lorena 1269
Segovia, Stephen 1269
セコポ
Sekgopo, Motsereganye 1270
セコリ
Ceccoli, Nicoletta 239
セサイ
Sesay, Alfred Bobson 1275
Sesay, Kadi 1275
セサティ
Cesati, Marco 241
セザール
Cesar, Menothy 241
セージ
Sage, Hayley 1226
Sage, Peter 1226

Sage, Rosemary 1226
セシ
Ceci, Stephen J. 239
セシア
Sesia, Davide 1276
セシィ
Sethi, Ravi 1276
セジウィック
Sedgewick, Robert 1267
Sedgwick, David 1267
Sedgwick, Eve Kosofsky 1267
Sedgwick, Kyra 1267
Sedgwick, Marcus 1267
Sedgwick, Mitchel 1267
Sedgwick, Modwena 1267
Sedgwick, Peter R. 1267
Sedgwick, Toby 1267
セシェ
Séché, Andreas 1267
セシジャー
Thesiger, Wilfred 1395
セジベラ
Sezibera, Richard 1277
セジマ
Sejima, Kazuyo 1270
セシャドリ
Seshadri, Shyam 1276
セジャニ
Sejani, Ackson 1270
セシュエー
Sechehaye, M.-A. 1267
セジュード
Cejudo, Henry 239
セシリアーニ
Ceciliani, Darrell 239
セシル
Cecil, Ben 239
Cecil, Laura 239
Cecil, Randy 239
セスク
Cesc 241
セスク・ファブレガス
Cesc 241
Cesc Fabregas 241
セステル
Sester, Sven 1276
セスト
Sesto, Francisco 1276
セスブーエ
Sesboüé, Bernard 1276
セスペデス
Céspedes, Derlis 241
Céspedes, Luis Felipe 241
Cespedes, Yoenis 241
セスマ
Sessouma, Tioudoun 1276
セセ
Sese, Jacques 1276
セセイ
Sesay, Alfred Bobson 1275
Sesay, Ibrahim Kemoh 1275
Sesay, Kadi 1275
Sesay, Kemoh 1276
Sesay, Sam 1276
Sesay, Shekou 1276
セセヌ
Sessenou, Fiatuwo Kwadjo 1276
セゼール
Césaire, Aimé Fernand 241
セゼル
Sezer, Ahmet Necdet 1277
セダー
Ceder, Naomi 239
Seder, Rufus Butler 1267
ゼーダー
Soeder, Christiane 1323
ゼタ・ジョーンズ
Zeta-Jones, Catherine 1551
セダミヌ
Sedaminou, Afognon Kouakou 1267
セダーリス
Sedaris, David 1267
セダリス
Sedaris, David 1267
セタリン
Setharin, Penn 1276
ゼタールンド
Zetterlund, Monica 1551
セダン
Seddon, Tony 1267
セーチン
Sechin, Igor 1267
セチン
Sechin, Igor 1267
セツ
Shih, Kien 1290
ゼッカー
Säcker, Horst 1224
セック
Seck, Louis 1267
Seck, Maimouna Ndoye 1267
Seck, Oumou Khairy Guèye 1267
Seck, Papa Abdoulaye 1267
Seck, Pap Cheyassin 1267
Seck, Pathé 1267
ゼックハウザー
Zeckhauser, Bryn 1549
セッケル
Seckel, Al 1267
セッサ
Cessa, Luis 241
Sessa, Carlos 1276
セッションズ
Sessions, Jeff 1276
Sessions, Ramon 1276
セッシル
Sessle, Barry J. 1276
ゼッダ
Zedda, Alberto 1549
セッターフィールド
Setterfield, Diane 1276
セッチフィールド
Setchfield, Neil 1276
セッツァー
Setzer, Brian 1276
ゼッツェ
Zetsche, Dieter 1551
セッテ
Sette, Antonello 1276
セッティス
Settis, Salvatore 1276
ゼッテコルン
Settekorn, Marion 1276
セッテホルム
Zetterholm, Finn 1551
ゼッテル
Zettel, Anthony 1551
Zettel, Sarah 1551
セッテルンド
Zetterlund, Monica 1551
セッド
Said, S.F. 1227
ゼッド
Zedd 1549
セッパ
Sceppa, David 1248
セッパラ
Seppala, Hanna-Maria 1274
セッピ
Seppi, Andreas 1274
セッピク
Seppik, Ain 1274
ゼップ
Zep 1551
Zepp, George B. 1551
ゼッフィレッリ
Zeffirelli, Franco 1549
セッポ
Seppo, Sanni 1274
セーディ
Sadie, Stanley John 1224
セティ
Sethi, Anil K. 1276
Sethi, Arjun 1276
セディア
Sedia, Ekaterina 1267
ゼティ・アクタル・アジズ
Zeti Akhtar Aziz 1551
セティアディ
Setiadi, Jadi 1276
セティアワン
Setiawan, Hendra 1276
Setiawan, Iwan 1276
セディキ
Seddiki, Abdesslam 1267
セディク
Seddik, Saâd 1267
Sediq, Mir Mohammad 1267
Sediq, Sohaila 1267
セディジョ
Zedillo, Ernesto 1549
セディッキ
Seddiqui, Daniel 1267
セティパ
Setipa, Joshua 1276
セデゴ
Sedego, Laurent 1267
セーデシュトレム
Söderström, Elisabeth Anna 1323
セデス
Coedes, George 273
セデニオ
Cedenio, Machel 239
セデーニョ
Cedeno, Xavier 239
セデニョ
Cedeño, Cesar 239
Cedeno, Yudel Jhonson 239
セデニョ・デ・フェルナンデス
Cedeño de Fernández, Margarita 239
セデバカ
C'de Baca, Janet 239
セーデル
Seeder, Helir-Valdor 1268
セデルキスト
Söderqvist, Thomas 1323
セデルグレン
Södergren, Anders 1323
Soedergren, Anders 1323
セーデルシュトレーム
Söderström, Elisabeth Anna 1323
セーデルストレーム
Söderström, Elisabeth Anna 1323
セーデルバウム
Söderbaum, Peter 1323
セーデルベリ
Söderberg, Alexander 1323
セーデルボリ
Cederborg, Ann-Christin 239
セート
Seth, Aftab 1276
セト
Seto, Michael C. 1276
セートゥ
Seetoo, Da-Hong 1268
セドゥ
Seydoux, Léa 1277
セドゥー
Seydoux, Léa 1277
セドキ
Sedki, Atef Mohamed Naguib 1267
ゼドケア
Zedkaia, Jurelang 1549
セドゴ
Sédogo, Laurent 1267
セドフ
Sedov, Vladimir 1267
ゼドラ
Zadra, Dan 1545
セドラチェク
Sedláček, Tomáš 1267
セドリス
Scdoris, Rachael 1248
セドリック
Cedric 239
ゼドリック
Zedric, Lance Q. 1549
セトル
Settle, Jane T. 1276
Settle, Paul Gunter 1276
セドール
Sedor, John R. 1267
セードルフ
Seedorf, Clarence 1268
セドレー
Sedley, D.N. 1267
セトロウィジョジョ
Setrowidjojo, Hendrik 1276
セドワ
Sedova, Yana 1267
セドン
Seddon, Diane 1267
Seddon, John 1267
セナ
Sénat, David 1273
Senna, Marcos 1273
ゼナイディ
Zenaidi, Mondher 1550
セナイト
Senait, Meshesha 1273
セナウィラトナ

Senaviratne, Athauda 1273
Senaviratne, John 1273
ゼナギ
Zenagui, Yassir 1550
セナック
Cenac, Wyatt 240
ゼナッティ
Zenatti, Valérie 1550
セナトーレ
Senatore, Leonardo 1273
セナナヤケ
Senanayake, Rukman 1273
Senanayake, Sanjaya 1273
ゼナブ
Zeinabou, Elback Adam 1549
セナラトネ
Senaratne, Rajitha 1273
ゼニア
Zegna, Ermenegildo 1549
セニェ
Sene, Josep 1273
セニエ
Seigner, Emmanuelle 1270
ゼニオス
Zenios, Stefanos A. 1550
セーニー・サオワポン
Seni Sauvapong 1273
ゼーニナ
Zenina, Lyubov 1550
セニョーラ
Siniora, Fouad 1307
セニョレ
Seignoret, Clarence 1270
セニランガカリ
Senilagakali, Jona 1273
セニロイ
Seniloli, Henry 1273
セーヌファーダ
Saine-firdaus, Marie 1227
ゼネ
Zene, Ahmat Mahamat 1550
ゼネーヴィチ
Zenevich, Larisa 1550
セネウィラトナ
Senevirathna, John 1273
Seneviratne, Athauda 1273
Seneviratne, John 1273
Senewiratne, Lakshman 1273
セネシャル
Senechal, Marjorie 1273
セネット
Sennett, Richard 1273
ゼネビッチ
Zenevitch, Joe 1550
セネビラトナ
Seneviratne, W.D.J. 1273
セネビラトネ
Seneviratne, W.D.J. 1273
ゼネブ
Zenebu, Tadesse 1550
セーノ
Seno, Ethel 1273
ゼノヴィッチ
Zenovich, Marina 1551
セノフ
Sennov, Anni 1273
Sennov, Carsten 1273
セノール
Senor, Dan 1273
セバ
Sebba, Anne 1266
Scbba, Mark 1267
セバー
Sebbah, François-David 1267
セバジョス
Cevallos, José Francisco 241
セバージョスフエンテス
Ceballos Fuentes, Pedro Francisco 239
セバスチャオ
Sebastião, Francisco 1266
セバスチャン
Sebastian, Cuthbert 1266
Sebástian, Joan 1266
セバスティアン・ガスコン
Sebastián Gascón, Miguel 1266
セバーソン
Severson, Kimberly 1276
セバッグ
Sebbag, Georges 1267
セバート
Sebaht, Efrem 1266
セハナウィ
Sehnawi, Maurice 1269
セパバンド
Sepahvandi, Morteza 1274
セパーヒ
Sepaahi, Jamshid 1274
ゼハリ
Zehri, Mir Israrullah 1549
セバーリョス・デ・ラ・プエンテ
Zevallos de la Puente, Andrés 1551
セバリングハウス
Severinghaus, John Wendell 1276
ゼーバルト
Sebald, W.G. 1266
セバレンジ
Sebarenzi, Joseph 1266
ゼービ
Zeevi, Rechavam 1549
ゼビガー
Sebiger, Heinz 1267
ゼビディ
Zebidi, Abdelkarim 1549
セビリャ
Sevilla, Jordi 1276
セービン
Sabin, Caroline 1223
Sabin, James E. 1223
ゼビン
Zevin, Gabrielle 1551
セフ
Seff, Nancy R. 1268
Seff, Philip 1268
セブ
Saibou, Ali 1227
ゼフ
Zeff, Robbin 1549
Zeff, Ted 1549
ゼファニア
Zephaniah, Benjamin 1551
ゼフィー
Zéphir, Thierry 1551
ゼフィラン
Zephirin, Ardouin 1551
ゼフィレリ
Zeffirelli, Franco 1549
セフェリ
Seferi, Taulant 1268
セフェリアン・ジェンキンス
Seferian-jenkins, Austin 1268
ゼーフェルト
Seefeldt, Jürgen 1268
セフェロヴィッチ
Seferovic, Haris 1268
セフェンジャー
Seffinger, Michael A. 1268
セフォー
Sefo, Ray 1268
Sefor, Lynn 1268
セフォローシャ
Sefolosha, Thabo 1268
セフォン
Sefon, Jordan 1268
セブダンディ
Sebudandi, Venetia 1267
ゼプチンスキー
Rzepczynski, Marc 1222
セフディモフ
Sevdimov, Namig 1276
セブハト
Sebhat, Ephrem 1267
セブラン
Sevrin, Francois 1276
セーブル
Sabel, Charles Frederick 1223
セプルベダ
Sepúlveda, Luis 1274
Sepulveda, M.A. 1274
セブルレ
Sebrle, Roman 1267
ゼブロフスキ
Zebrowski, Gary 1549
セブン
SE7EN 1276
Seven, Doug 1276
セペ
Sepe, Luigi 1274
セベスキー
Sebesky, Don 1267
セベスチェン
Sebestyen, Victor 1267
セヘステッド
Sehested, Ove H. 1269
セペダ
Cepeda, Frederich 240
Cepeda, María Cristina García 240
Cepeda, Orlando 240
Zepeda, Omar 1551
ゼペダ
Zepeda, Lydia 1551
セペティス
Sepetys, Ruta 1274
セペデロイグ
Cepede Royg, Veronica 240
セベトレラ
Sebetlela, Boyce 1267
セベニウス
Sebenius, James K. 1267
セベネ
Sevene, Mario 1276
ゼーヘラール
Zeegelaar, Marvin 1549
セベリ
Cervelli, Francisco 240
セベリアノ・テイシェイラ
Severiano Teixeira, Nuno 1276
セベリウス
Sebelius, Kathleen 1267
セベリーノ
Severino, Luis 1276
Severino, Pedro 1276
セベリノ
Severino, Paola 1276
セベリン
Severin, Glenn A. 1276
セヘル
Sehar, Sardar Bahadur Khan 1269
セベレ
Sevele, Feleti 1276
セベロバン
Severovan, Mihai 1276
セペング
Sepeng, Hezekiel 1274
ゼボ
Zebo, Simon 1549
ゼーホーファー
Seehofer, Horst 1268
セマシコ
Semashko, Pyotr M. 1272
Semashko, Vladimir I. 1272
セマシュコ
Semashko, Pyotr M. 1272
Semashko, Vladimir I. 1272
セマニック
Semanick, Michael 1272
ゼーマン
Szeemann, Harald 1374
Zeman, Ludmila 1550
Zeman, Zbyněk 1550
Zeman, Zdenek 1550
ゼマン
Zeman, Eduard 1550
Zeman, Miloš 1550
セミエン
Semien, Marcus 1272
セミオノワ
Semionova, Polina 1272
ゼミギロ
Zemigiro, Ashrozo 1550
セミシュ
Semisch, Tim 1272
セミチャストヌイ
Semichastny, Vladimir Y. 1272
セミチャスヌイ
Semichastny, Vladimir Y. 1272
セミナラ
Seminara, George 1272
セミョーノヴァ
Semyonova, Marina 1272
セミョノフ
Semenov, A.A. 1272
セミョーノワ
Semyonova, Marina 1272
セミョノワ
Semyonova, Marina 1272
ゼミン
Zeming, Mao 1550
ゼム
Zem, Roschdy 1550
セムコフ

セ

セ

Semkov, Jerzy 1272
セームスドルフ
Sehmsdorf, Henning K. 1269
ゼムノビッチ
Zemunović, Zdravko 1550
セムラー
Semler, Ricardo 1272
ゼムラ
Zemla-krajewska, Anna 1550
ゼムラー
Semmler, Willi 1272
セムラン
Semelin, Jacques 1272
セムリ
Semri, Ben 1272
ゼムリャク
Zemlyak, Olha 1550
ゼムリン
Zemlin, Willard R. 1550
ゼムール
Zemmour, Éric 1550
セメイスム
Semeysum, Liwa 1272
セメガ
Semega, Hamed Diane 1272
ゼメカ
Zé Meka, Rémy 1550
ゼメキス
Zemeckis, Robert L. 1550
セメディ
Szemerédi, Endre 1374
セメド
Semedo, Bawa 1272
Semedo, Maria Helena 1272
Semedo, Odete 1272
Semedo, Rui Mendes 1272
セメニーク
Semenuik, Nathalie 1272
セメニャーカ
Semenyaka, Lyudmila 1272
セメニヤカ
Semenyaka, Lyudmila 1272
セメネンコ
Semenenko, Oleksii 1272
Semenennko, Ysvgeny 1272
セメノフ
Semenov, Konstantin 1272
Semenov, Mingiyan 1272
Semenov, Sergey 1272
セメノワ
Semenova, Ksenia 1272
セメラク
Semerak, Ostap 1272
セメル
Semel, Terry 1272
セメルジエフ
Semerdjiev, Ilko 1272
セメルロース
Semmelroth, Carl 1272
セメレ
Semere, Russom 1272
セメレンコ
Semerenko, Valj 1272
Semerenko, Vita 1272
セメンヤ
Semenya, Caster 1272
ゼモゴ
Zemogo, Fofana 1550
セモジ
Semodji, Mawussi Djossou 1272
セモソ
Semoso, Fidelis 1272
ゼーヤー・アウン
Zayar Aung 1548
セヨウム・メスフィン
Seyoum Mesfin 1277
セーラ
Cela, Camilo José 239
セラ
Cela, Camilo José 239
Sela, Dudi 1270
Sela, Jonathan 1270
Serra, Angelo 1275
Serra, Joãn 1275
Serra, José 1275
Serra, Richard 1275
セラー
Sellar, Polly 1271
Sellar, Wanda 1271
ゼラー
Zeller, Cody 1550
Zeller, Tyler 1550
セラヴェッツァ
Serravezza, Giuseppe 1275
セラコビッチ
Selaković, Nikola 1270
セラシーニ
Cerasini, Marc A. 240
セラーズ
Sellers, Alexandra 1271
ゼラズニー
Zelazny, Gene 1550
セラソリ
Cerasoli, Pasquale 240
セラッチ
Ceratti, Miriam Kaipper 240
セラデュライ
Selladurai, Ben 1271
セラト
Cerato, Mattia 240
Cerrat, Hector 240
Cerrato, Wilfredo 240
Cerrato, Wilfredo Rafael 240
セラト・バジャダレス
Cerrato Valladares, Fredis Alonso 240
セラーニ
Selänne, Teemu 1271
セラニ
Selänne, Teemu 1271
セラーノ
Serrano, Roberto 1275
セラノ
Serrano, António 1275
Serrano, Claudia 1275
Serrano, Jesus 1275
Serrano, José 1275
Serrano, Juan Rene 1275
セラノ・スニェル
Serrano Suñer, Ramón 1275
セーラ妃
Ferguson, Sarah 429
セラピナイテ
Serapinaite, Ieva 1274
セラファン
Seraphin, Kevin 1274
セラフィン
Serafin, Xanthe Smith 1274
セラヤ
Zelaya, José Francisco 1550
Zelaya, José Manuel 1550
Zelaya, Karen 1550
セラヤンディア・シスネロス
Zelayandía Cisneros, Gregorio Ernesto 1550
Zelayandia Cisneros, Martha Lidia 1550
セラリーニ
Séralini, Gilles-Eric 1274
セラル
Sellal, Abdelmalek 1271
セラロン
Selarón, Jorge 1271
セラン
Serran, Geris A. 1275
セランテス
Serantes, Jon 1274
ゼランド
Zeland, Vadim 1550
セリエ
Scellier, François 1248
Sellier, Marie 1271
Sellier, Philippe 1271
セリエール
Seillière, Ernest-Antoine 1270
セリガー
Seliger, Herbert W. 1271
セリカワ
Serikawa, Garrett Kazuhiro 1275
セリグ
Selig, Bud 1271
セリグソン
Seligson, Susan 1271
セリグマン
Seligman, B.Z. 1271
Seligman, Joel 1271
Seligman, Martin E. P. 1271
Seligman, Patricia 1271
Seligmann, Matthew S. 1271
セリーケマル
Serry-kemal, Abdul 1275
ゼリコウ
Zelikow, Philip 1550
セリス
Celis, Guillermo 239
ゼリーズ
Zerries, A.J. 1551
セリソラ
Cerisola, Pedro 240
セリソラ・ウェベル
Cerisola Weber, Pedro 240
セリチェ・ドゥガン
Seriche Dugan, Angel Serafin 1275
セリック
Selic, Bran 1271
Selick, Henry 1271
ゼーリック
Zoellick, Robert Bruce 1556
ゼリック
Zoellick, Robert Bruce 1556
セリヌス
Selinus, Olle 1271
セリフォヴィック
Šerifović, Nermin 1275
セリム
Selim, Fazlul Karim 1271
セリモフ
Selimov, Albert 1271
セリュラス
Sérullaz, Maurice 1275
セリン
Selin, Yevhen 1271
Serrin, James Burton 1275
ゼーリンガー
Selinger, Peter F. 1271
ゼリンカ
Zelinka, Jessica 1550
セリンジャー
Sellinger, Arie 1271
ゼリンスキー
Zelinski, Ernie John 1550
セール
Sale, Chris 1230
Sale, Colin 1230
Sales, Gemma 1230
Sère, Bénédicte 1274
Serres, Alain 1275
Serres, Michel 1275
セル
Sell, Colleen 1271
Sell, Yvonne 1271
セルー
Theroux, Paul 1395
ゼール
Seel, Martin 1268
ゼルーアリ
Zerouali, Najib 1551
セルイラト
Seruiratu, Inia Batikoto 1275
セルイラトゥ
Seruiratu, Inia Batikoto 1275
セルヴァ
Selva, T. 1272
セルヴァン
Servant, Jean-Charles 1275
セルヴァン＝シュレイベール
Servan-Schreiber, Perla 1275
セルヴァン・シュレベール
Servan-Schreiber, Jean-Jacques 1275
ゼルウィガー
Zellweger, Renée 1550
セールウィクズ
Salewicz, Chris 1231
セルヴィン
Selvin, Joel 1272
セルヴェ
Servais, Guy 1275
セルウェイ
Selway, Phil 1272
セルヴェリス
Cerveris, Michael 241
セルヴェンティ
Serventi, Silvano 1275
セルカ
Seluka, Alesana 1272
セルカス
Cercas, Javier 240
セルガス
Sergas, Giulia 1274

セルキン
Salekin, Randall T. 1230
ゼルキン
Serkin, Peter 1275
セルク
Selk, Jason 1271
ゼルケ
Selke, Davie 1271
セルゲイ
Sergay, Jane 1274
セルゲイェンコ
Sergeenko, David 1274
Sergeyenko, David 1274
セルケイラ
Cerqueira, Carolina 240
セルゲーエフ
Sergeev, Igor Dmitrievich 1274
Sergeev, Viktor 1274
Sergeyev, Igor D. 1274
セルゲエフ
Sergeev, Igor Dmitrievich 1274
セルゲエワ
Sergeyeva, Natalya 1274
セルゲレン
Sergelen, Pureviin 1274
セルコ
Celko, Joe 239
セルゴ
Csergo, Julia 306
Serugo, Ronald 1275
セルコワ
Selkow, Stanley 1271
セルーシ
Seroussi, Karyn 1275
セルージ
Ceruzzi, Paul E. 240
セルシェル
Söllscher, Göran 1325
セルジ・エンリク
Sergi Enrich 1274
セルジオ・オリヴェイラ
Sergio Oliveira 1275
セルジ・グアルティオラ
Sergi Guardiola 1275
セルジ・ゴメス
Sergi Gomez 1274
セルジノフ
Serdinov, Andriy 1274
セルジャ
Selja, Kumari 1271
セルジュコフ
Serdyukov, Anatolii 1274
セルジュリ
Sergerie, Karine 1274
セルジ・ロベルト
Sergi Roberto 1275
セールズ
Sales, Jane 1230
Sales, Nancy Jo 1231
セルス
Cels, Johan 240
セルズ
Sells, Chris 1271
セルスキー
Celski, J.R. 240
Selsky, Steve 1271
セルズニック
Selznick, Brian 1272
Selznick, Philip 1272
セルダーヘイス
Selderhuis, Herman J. 1271
セルダル
Serdar, Suat 1274
セルダロフ
Serdarov, Ata 1274
セルチャン
Seeruttun, Mahen Kumar 1268
セルツァー
Seltzer, David 1272
セルッティ
Cerutti, Alison 240
セルディス
Seldes, Marian 1271
Seldes, Rich 1271
セルティッチ
Sertić, Željko 1275
セルディン
Seldin, Peter 1271
セルデス
Seldes, Marian 1271
セルデン
Selden, Wayne 1271
ゼルテン
Selten, Reinhard 1271
セルート
Cerruto, Oscar 240
セルトマン
Seltman, Kent D. 1272
ゼルドマン
Zeldman, Jeffrey 1550
セルドン
Seldon, Anthony 1271
セルナ
Serna, Víctor de la 1275
ゼルナー
Zellner, William W. 1550
ゼルーニ
Zerhouni, Noureddine 1551
Zerhouni, Nouria Yasmina 1551
セルヌダ
Cernuda, Luis 240
セルノヴィッツ
Sernovitz, Andy 1275
セルバ
Selva, Stefano 1272
セルバー
Selver, Charlotte 1272
セルバーグ
Selberg, Atle 1271
セルバン
Serban, Florin 1274
セルバン・シュレベール
Servan-Schreiber, Jean-Jacques 1275
セルバンテス・アンドラデ
Cervantes Andrade, Raúl 240
セルビ
Cervi, Franco 241
セルビー
Selby, Andrew 1271
Selby, Anna 1271
Selby, David 1271
Selby, Hubert, Jr. 1271
Selby, John 1271
Selby, Philip 1271
Selby, Todd 1271
セルヒオ
Sergio, Alvarez 1275
セルヒオ・アセンホ
Sergio Asenjo 1275
セルヒオ・アルバレス
Sergio Alvarez 1275
セルヒオ・ジャマス
Sergio Llamas 1275
セルヒオ・ラモス
Sergio Ramos 1275
セルヒオ・リコ
Sergio Rico 1275
セルヒオ・レオン
Segio Leon 1269
セルビノ
Zerbino, Jorge 1551
セルフ
Self, David 1271
Self, Sharmistha 1271
Self, Will 1271
Selfe, Daphne 1271
セルプ
Serup, Linda Melanie Villumsen 1275
セルフォン
Cerfon, Osman 240
セルフリ
Serufuli, Eugène 1275
セルフリムガヤバセカ
Serufuli, Eugène 1275
セールベリ
Sehlberg, Dan T. 1269
セルマ
Selman, Eduardo 1271
セルマー
Celmer, Michelle 239
セルマイアー
Selmaier, Maria 1271
ゼルマイヤー
Sellmair, Nikola 1271
セルマーニ
Selmani, Massinissa 1271
セルマニ
Selmani, Imer 1271
Selmani, Rexhep 1271
セルマン
Selman, Martin J. 1271
Selmane, Mohamed Lemine Ould 1271
セルムス
Selms, Adrianus van 1271
セルメニョ
Cermeño, Antonio 240
セール＝モンテーユ
Serre-Monteil, Claudine 1275
セルワ
Serwa, Kelsey 1275
ゼレ
Sölle, Dorothee 1325
セレウカイテ
Sereikaite, Vilija 1274
セレク
Celek, Brent 239
Celek, Garrett 239
セレジー
Therezie, Robenson 1395
セレシュ
Seles, Monica 1271
セレス
Seles, Monica 1271
セレスコヴィッチ
Seleskovitch, Danica 1271
セレスティン
Celestin, Ray 239
セレスナ
Ceresna, Jake 240
ゼレズニー
Zelezny, Jan 1550
セレズニョフ
Seleznyov, Aleksandr I. 1271
セレーゾ
Cerezo, Toninho 240
セレソ
Cerezo, Celso David 240
セレツェ
Serertse, Vicente 1274
Seretse, Dikgakgamatso 1274
Seretse, Ramadeluka 1274
Seretse, Tebelelo 1274
Seretse, Vincent 1274
セレニー
Sereny, Gitta 1274
セレブロフ
Serebrov, Alexandre 1274
セレマイア
Seremaia, Matai 1274
セレル
Serrell, Allison 1275
Serrell, Mathilde 1275
セーレン
Ceelen, Vicky 239
セレン
Sellen, Abigail J. 1271
Seren, Leo 1274
ゼレンケビッチ
Zelenkevich, Igor B. 1550
セレンザ
Celenza, Anna Harwell 239
ゼレーンスキー
Zelenskii, Igor 1550
ゼレンスキー
Zelenskii, Igor 1550
セレンテ
Celente, Gerald 239
セーロ
Cerro, Manuel Del 240
セロー
Serrault, Michel 1275
Serreau, Coline 1275
Theroux, Louis 1395
Theroux, Marcel 1395
Theroux, Paul 1395
Theroux, Phyllis 1395
ゼロ
Zelo 1550
セロス
Seros, Alexandra 1275
セロータ
Serota, Nicholas Andrew 1275
セロチンスキ
Szello, Imre 1374
セロッシ
Seroussi, Gadiel 1275
セロフ
Serov, Alexander 1275
セロフィッリ
Serofilli, Loretta 1275
セロワ
Serova, V.V. 1275
Serroy, Jean 1275
セロン
Theron, Charlize 1395

セ

ゼワイル
Zewail, Ahmed 1551
セン
Sen, Amartya Kumar 1272
Sen, Chandan K. 1272
Sen, Colleen Taylor 1272
Sen, Jai 1272
Sen, Mala 1273
Sen, Ramesh Chandra 1273
Sen, Robi 1273
Sen, Romesh Chandra 1273
Sen, Sunanda 1273
Sene, Diégane 1273
Senn, Stephen 1273
Shing, Fui-on 1291
ゼーン
Zane, Richard D. 1547
Zane, Sig 1547
センウタイ
SengOuthai, Onesy 1273
センカー
Senker, Cath 1273
センガ
Senga, Valentin 1273
ゼンガー
Saenger, Ingo 1225
Zenger, John H. 1550
センカット
Senkut, Aydin 1273
センクット
Senkut, Aydin 1273
センクネシュ
Senknesh, Ejigu 1273
ゼンクハース
Senghaas, Dieter 1273
セングープタ
Sengoopta, Chandak 1273
セングプタ
Sengupta, Krishanu 1273
Sengupta, Preety 1273
センゲ
Sangay, Lobsang 1238
Senge, Peter M. 1273
ゼンケ
Zemke, Ron 1550
センゲバウ
Sengebau, Umiich 1273
センゲル
Senger, Harro von 1273
ゼンコ
Zenko, Micah 1551
センサー
Senser, Robert A. 1274
センザテラ
Senzatela, Antonio 1274
センシ
Sensi, Stefano 1274
センシア
Sensier, Collette 1274
ゼンシニ
Sensini, Alessandra 1274
センジャン
Saint-Jean, Petter 1228
センセイボー
Sensabaugh, Coty 1274
センセンブレナー
Sensenbrenner, Frank James 1274
センソン
Senson, Pat 1274
センター
Center, Allen H. 240
センダー
Sender, Ramón 1273
センダウラ
Sendawula, Gerald 1273
センダーク
Sendak, Maurice 1273
センダク
Sendak, Maurice 1273
センダジラサ
Sendazirasa, Annonciata 1273
センダース
Senders, Jacques 1273
センダック
Sendak, Jack 1273
Sendak, Maurice 1273
センチュリー
Century, Douglas 240
センツナー
Centner, James L. 240
センディック
Sendic, Raúl 1273
センテーノ
Centeno, Juan 240
Centeno, Mário 240
センテノ
Centeno, Pavel 240
センテノ・ガデア
Centeno Gadea, Edward Francisco 240
センテノ・ナハロ
Centeno Najarro, Humberto 240
センテ・バレラ・イ・タコナーゾ
Chente Barrera y Taconazo 252
センデーホ
Sendejo, Andrew 1273
センデロス
Senderos, Phillippe 1273
センデロール
Søndrål, Ådne 1327
ゼンデン
Senden, Marius von 1273
センテンス
Sentance, Bryan 1274
ゼンド
Zend, Ahmed al 1550
セント・アンドレ
St.Andre, Ken 1227
センドゥ
Saendou, Djazila 1225
センドゥアン
Sengdeuane, Lachathaboune 1273
セントゥンブウェ
Sentumbwe, Nayinda 1274
セントオンジ
St.Onge, Ryan 1228
センドカー
Sendker, Jan-Philipp 1273
セント・クレア
St.Claire, Erin 1228
St.Claire, Olivia 1228
セントクレア
St.Claire, Roxanne 1228
セント・ジェイムズ
St.James, Lyn 1228
セントジェームズ
St.James, Elaine 1228
St.James, Simone 1228
セントジャイルズ
St.Giles, Jennifer 1228
セント・ジョン
St.John, Cheryl 1228
St.John, Noah 1228
St.John, Susan 1228
St.John, Warren 1228
セントジョン
St.John, Lauren 1228
セントバーナード
St.Bernard, Andrea 1228
セントピエール
St.Pierre, Michael 1228
セント・ミッチェル
St.Michael, Mick 1228
センドラー
Sendlerowa, Irena 1273
センドリューテ
Sendriute, Zinaida 1273
セントルイス
St.Louis, Martin 1228
セントルース
St.luce, John 1228
センドロ
Sendolo, Patrick 1273
セントロウィッツ
Centrowitz, Matthew 240
セントロウィッツ
Centrowitz, Matthew 240
セントローレント
St.Laurent, Simon 1228
ゼンナー
Zenner, Zach 1551
センヌアン
Sengnouan, Xayalath 1273
ゼンバッハ
Sembach, Klaus-Jürgen 1272
センフ
Sempf, Bill 1272
センプリチーニ
Semplicini, Andrea 1272
センプリーニ
Semprini, Andrea 1272
センプル
Semple, Stuart 1272
センプルーン
Semprún, Jorge 1272
センプルン
Semprún, Jorge 1272
センベーヌ
Sembène, Ousmane 1272
センメルハック
Semmelhack, Peter 1272

【ソ】

ソ
Seo, Hee 1274
Seo, In-guk 1274
Seo, Jung-uck 1274
Seo, Seongjo 1274
Seo, Sun Young 1274
Seo, Young-Jae 1274
So, Ji-sub 1322
So, Man-sul 1322
Sot, Michel 1330
Su, Bu-qing 1361
Suh, Kyung-bae 1363
Suh, Kyu-yong 1363
Suh, Seoung-hwan 1363
Suh, Young-hoon 1363
ソー
Sawh, Satyadeow 1246
So, Augusto Ussumane 1322
So, Marie 1322
So, Meilo 1322
So Khun 1324
Sou, Ngarbatina Carmel, Ⅳ 1330
Thau, Dave 1394
Thaw, John 1394
Thor, Brad 1401
ゾー
Zoe, Rachel 1556
ゾア
Zoah, Michel 1556
ソアラオイ
Soalaoi, Clay Forau 1322
ソアラブライ
Soalablai, Sinton 1322
ソアレス
Soares, Bruno 1322
Soares, Claudio 1322
Soares, Dionisio Babo 1322
Soares, João 1322
Soares, Paul, Jr. 1322
Soares, Rinaldo Campos 1322
Soares, Rui Figueiredo 1322
Soares, Thiago 1322
ソアレスマルケス
Soares Marques, Antonio 1322
ゾアン
Doan, Nguyen Thi 360
ソーイ
Sawi, Beth 1246
ソイ
Soi, Edwin Cheruiyot 1324
ゾーイ
Zaoui, Myriam 1547
ソイエ＝フールネル
Sohier-Fournel, Anne 1324
ソイエ＝フルネル
Sohier-Fournel, Anne 1324
ソイサ
Zoysa, Vijith Wijayamuni 1558
ソイド・アルバレス
Zoido Álvarez, Juan Ignacio 1557
ソイニ
Soini, Timo 1324
ゾイフェルド
Zoehfeld, Kathleen Weidner 1556
ソイリー
Soailihi, Mohamed Ali 1322
ソイリヒ
Soilihi, Mohamed Ali 1324
Soilihi, Said Abdallah Cheikh 1324
ソイル
Soylu, Süleyman 1332
ゾイロフ
Zoirov, Shakhobidin 1557
ソインカ
Soyinka, Wole 1332
ソウ

Sow, Abdou Aziz 1332
Sow, Aliou 1332
Sow, Amadou 1332
Sow, Christian 1332
Sow, Daouda 1332
Sow, Dauda 1332
Sow, Djibril 1332
Sow, Mamadou Abdoulaye 1332
Sow, Moussa 1332
Sow, Sanoussy Bantama 1332
Thaw, John 1394
Tseng, Yani 1423

ゾゥ
Zhou, Duo 1553
Zhou, Er-fu 1553
Zhou, Gan-zhi 1553
Zhou, Guan-wu 1553
Zhou, Hai-ying 1553
Zhou, Qi-ren 1553
Zhou, Wei-zhi 1553

ゾウ
Zou, Kai 1557
Zou, Shi-ming 1557

ソーヴァ
Sova, Dawn B. 1332

ゾーヴァ
Sowa, Michael 1332

ソヴァニャルグ
Sauvagnargues, Jean Victor 1245

ソヴァーン
Sovern, Michael Ira 1332

ソー・ウィン
Soe Win 1323

ソーウィン
Sawin, Martica 1246

ソウエ
Sowe, Allieu Pat 1332

ソーウェル
Sowell, Thomas 1332

ソウェル
Sowell, Bradley 1332

ソウェルウイン
Sowerwine, Van 1332

ソウクプ
Soukup, Christoph 1330
Soukup, Jaroslav 1331

ソウザ
De Sousa, Mauricio 346
Sosa, Ernest 1330
Sousa, Mária Lúcio 1331
Sousa, Mario Cristina de 1331
Sousa, Óscar Aguiar Sacramento e 1331
Souza 1332
Souza, Paulo Renato 1332
Souza, Robert 1332

ソウチュコバー
Součková, Marie 1330

ソウト・デ・モウラ
Mouro, Eduardo Souto de 983

ゾウビ
al-Zoubi, Omran Ahed 1557
Zubi, Ghalib 1558

ソウマ
Souma, Ibrahima 1331

ゾウ・ミン
Zaw Min 1548

ソウヤー
Sawyer, Diane 1246
Sawyer, Robert J. 1246

ソウリアン
Soryan, Hamid 1329

ソウル
Saule, Beatrix 1244
Soule, Barbara M. 1331
Soule, Jeremy 1331

ソウルゼンバーグ
Stolzenburg, William 1354

ソウンダース
Saunders, George 1244

ソウンダール
Søvndal, Villy 1332

ソヴンダル
Sovndal, Shannon 1332

ソウンデルパンディアン
Sounderpandian, Jayavel 1331

ソウンルー
Sohounhloue, Dominique 1324

ソエサストロ
Soesastro, Hadi 1323

ソェダーマン
Söderman, Sten 1323

ソエトマン
Soeteman, Gerard 1323

ソエルド
Sõerd, Aivar 1323

ソガード
Sogard, Eric 1324

ゾカナシンガ
Cokanasiga, Joketani 276

ソガバレ
Sogavare, Manasseh 1324

ソーカル
Sokal, Alan D. 1324

ソーガンツィ
Soganci, Selda Marlin 1324

ソカンビ
Sokambi, Aristide 1324

ソギャル・リンポチェ
Sogyal Rinpoche 1324

ソキルスキー
Sokyrskiyy, Olexiy 1324

ゾキルゾダ
Zokirzoda, Mahmadtoir 1557

ソーキン
Sokin, Aaron 1324
Sorkin, Andrew Ross 1329
Sorkin, Michael 1329

ソク
Seuk, Joon Ho 1276
Sok An 1324

ゾーグ
Zogu, Leka 1557

ゾグ
Zogu, Leka 1557

ソク・アン
Sok An 1324

ソクラテス
Sócrates 1323
Sócrates, José 1323

ゾグリオ
Zoglio, Suzanne Willis 1557

ソーグリムセン
Thorgrimsen, Lene 1401

ソグロ
Soglo, Galiou 1324

ソクーロフ
Sokurov, Alexander 1324

ゾクワナ
Zokwana, Senzeni 1557

ソー・クン
So Khun 1324

ソケタ
Soqeta, Nemia 1329

ソコリ
Sokoli, Kristjan 1324

ソコル
Sokol, Julia 1324
Sokol, Kathy Arlyn 1324

ソコロヴァ＝デリューシナ・リヴォヴナ
Sokolova-Delusina Lvovna, Tatiana 1324

ソコロビッチ
Socolovich, Miguel 1323

ソコロフ
Sokolov, Aleksandr Rostislavovich 1324
Sokolov, Alexander Sergeevich 1324
Sokolov, Grigorii 1324
Sokolov, Maxim Y. 1324
Sokolov, Sasha 1324
Sokolov, Vladimir Alekseevich 1324

ソコロフスキー
Sokolovskyy, Andriy 1324

ソコロワ
Sokolova, Elena 1324
Sokolova, Ol'ga Ivanovna 1324

ソーサ
Sosa, Edmundo 1330
Sosa, Mercedes Haydée 1330
Sosa, Omar 1330
Sosa, Sammy 1330
Sousa, Ryan 1331

ソーザ
Sousa, Óscar Aguiar Sacramento e 1331

ソサ
Sosa, Guillermo 1330
Sosa, Jose 1330
Sosa, Juan José 1330
Sosa, Marco Tulio 1330
Sossa, Dorothée 1330

ソザ
Sousa, Candace A. 1331

ソサ・ルナ
Sosa Luna, Celinda 1330

ソーシア
Scioscia, Mike 1263

ソシアリー
Sotheary, Prak 1330

ソシーノ
Socino, Juan Pablo 1323

ソジャ
Soja 1324
Soja, Edward W. 1324

ソジョマン
Sjöman, Anders 1309

ソシーンスキー
Sosienski, Shanti 1330

ソーズ
Soz, Saifuddin 1332

ソス
Sossou, Marie-Laurence Sranon 1330

ゾス
Zossou, Gaston 1557

ゾスー
Zossou, Gaston 1557

ソスウント
Sossouhounto, Christian 1330

ソスキス
Soskice, David 1330

ソスキン
Soskin, Julie 1330

ソズノウスキ
Sosnowski, David 1330

ソスノフスキー
Sosnovsky, Aleksandr V. 1330
Sosnovsky, Vladimir G. 1330

ソーズバーグ
Salsberg, Brian 1232

ソーズビー
Soesbee, Ree 1323

ゾズリャ
Zozulya, Roman 1558

ソゾノフ
Sozonov, Ivan 1332

ソソホント
Sossouhounto, Evelyne 1330

ソーソン
Thorson, Anna 1402

ソー・タ
Soe Tha 1323

ソーター
Sautter, Elizabeth A. 1245
Sorter, Dorienne 1329

ソタ
Sota, Javier 1330

ソーダガラン
Saudagaran, Shahrokh M. 1244

ソーダクィスト
Soderquist, Don 1323

ソーダバーグ
Soderbergh, Steven 1323

ソダーバーグ
Soderbergh, Steven 1323

ソタマー
Sotamaa, Yrjö 1330

ソーチック
Sawchik, Travis 1246

ソーチャー
Sorcher, Melvin 1329

ソック
Sock, Jack 1323

ソック・デン
Thok Deng, Gabriel 1396

ソッザーニ
Sozzani, Franca 1332

ソッシイ
Sossi, Sergio 1330

ソッシイー
Sossi, Sergio 1330

ソッツァーニ
Sozzani, Franca 1332

ソットサス
Sottsass, Ettore, Jr. 1330

ゾッリ
Zolli, Andrew 1557

ソーテ
Sautai, Raoul 1245

ソテアラ・チョブ
Sotheara Chov 1330

ソティー

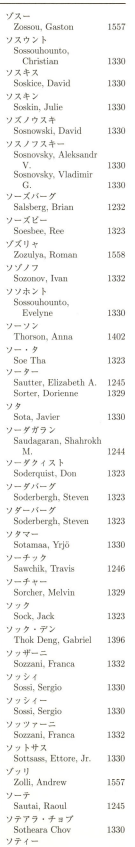

ソ

Sotir, Jake 1330
ソー・テイン
Soe Thein 1323
ソーデリンド
Søderlind, Didrik 1323
ソーテール
Sautter, Christian 1245
ソテール
Sautter, Christian 1245
ソーデルバリ
Soderberg, David 1323
ソテロ
Sotero, Alice 1330
ソーデン
Soden, Jack 1323
ソート
Soto, Geovany 1330
ソト
Soto, Catriel Andres 1330
Soto, Gary 1330
Soto, Geovany 1330
Soto, Giovanni 1330
Soto, Héctor 1330
Soto, Jésus-Raphaël 1330
Soto, Oscar 1330
Soto, Rafael 1330
ソトー
Soto, Gary 1330
ソドー
Sodeau, Michael 1323
ソドウ
Sodeau, Michael 1323
ソー・トゥン
Saw Tun 1246
ソト・エスティガリビア
Soto Estigarribia, Bernardino 1330
ソードセン
Thordsen, Isabella 1401
Thordsen, Pia 1401
ソトニコワ
Sotnikova, Adelina 1330
ソドノム
Sodnom, Dumaagiin 1323
ソト・ヒメネス
Soto Jiménez, José Miguel 1330
ゾートフ
Zotov, Nikolai Mikhailovich 1557
ソトマイヨール
Sotomayor, Sonia 1330
ソトマヨル
Sotomayor Collazo, Lorenzo 1330
ソー・ナイン
Soe Naing 1323
ソナベンド
Sonnabend, Yolanda 1328
ソーニー
Sawhney, Mohanbir 1246
ソニ
Soni, Ambika 1328
Soni, Rebecca 1328
ゾニアバ
Zoniaba, Serge Blaise 1557
ソニエ
Saunier, Matthieu 1245
Saunier, Nadine 1245
Sonnier, Jo-El 1328
ソーニクロフト
Thornicroft, Graham 1401
ソニス
Sonis, Stephen T. 1328
ゾニス
Zonis, Marvin 1557
ソネット
Sornette, D. 1329
ソネマン
Sonneman, Milly R. 1328
ソネンシュミット
Sonnenschmidt, Frederic H. 1328
ソネンバーグ
Sonenberg, Nahum 1327
Sonnenberg, Shirley 1328
Sonnenburg, Erica 1328
Sonnenburg, Justin 1328
ソネンフェルド
Sonnenfeld, Barry 1328
Sonnenfeld, Jeffrey 1328
ゾネンフェルド
Sonnenfeld, Barry 1328
ソーネンブリック
Sonnenblick, Jordan 1328
ソノダ
Sonoda, Toyooki 1328
ソノムピリ
Sonompil, Mishigiin 1328
ソノワール
Sonowal, Sarbananda 1328
ソノン
Sonon, Gustave Dépo 1328
ソノンピル
Sonompil, Mishig 1328
ソーバー
Sober, Elliott 1323
ソーパー
Soper, John 1328
ソハ
Socha, Aleksandra 1323
Socha, Jacek 1323
ソバ
Sova, Vasile 1332
ゾーハー
Zohar, Danah 1557
ゾバイ
Zawbai, Salam 1548
ソーハインド
Sorhaindo, Crispin Anselm 1329
ソパゲ
Sopage, Martin 1328
ソバージュ
Sauvage, Jeanne 1245
ソー・バ・ティン
Saw Ba Thin Sein 1246
ソーバート
Saubert, Jean 1244
ソーバニャルグ
Sauvagnargues, Jean Victor 1245
ソバニャルグ
Sauvagnargues, Jean Victor 1245
ソバレニ
Sovaleni, Siaosi 1332
ソーバーン
Thorburn, Christine 1401
ソバーン
Sovern, Michael Ira 1332
ソバンドラ王子
Prince Sobandla 1322
ソーヒ
Sohi, Amarjeet 1324
ゾービ
Zobi, Fawwaz 1556
ソビアック
Sobiech, Laura Ann 1323
ソヒエフ
Sokhiev, Tugan 1324
ソービクネス
Søviknes, Terje 1332
ソービノ
Sorvino, Mira 1329
ソヒマト
Suheimat, Tareq 1363
ソビャーニン
Sobyanin, Sergei 1323
ソビャニン
Sobyanin, Sergei 1323
ソビル
Sobir, Hassan 1323
ソビロフ
Sobirov, Rishod 1323
ソープ
Thorp, Darrell 1402
Thorp, Edward O. 1402
Thorp, Jer 1402
Thorpe, Chris 1402
Thorpe, Ian James 1402
Thorpe, I.J. 1402
Thorpe, Jeremy 1402
Thorpe, John A. 1402
Thorpe, Kay 1402
Thorpe, Kiki 1402
Thorpe, Mackenzie 1402
Thorpe, Neiko 1402
Thorpe, Richard 1402
Thorpe, Sara 1402
Thorpe, Scott 1402
Thorpe, T.J. 1402
Thorpe, Tony 1402
ソフ
Sofu, Stanley Festus 1324
ソファン
al-Sofan, Ahmed Mohammed 1323
ソフィアン
Sofian, Ahmed 1323
Sofjan, Wanandi 1324
Sofyan, Djalil 1324
ソプイエフ
Sopyyev, Byashim 1329
ソフィー妃
Sophie 1328
ソフィラス
Sofilas, Mark 1323
ソフィン
Sof'in, Pavel 1323
ソフェル
Soffer, Gilad 1323
ソフォクレウス
Sophocleous, Sophocles 1328
ゾフグン
Dovgun, Olga 371
ソプコ
Sopko, Eugen 1328
ソフスキー
Sofsky, Wolfgang 1324
ソブヒ
Sobhi, Ramadan 1323
Sobhi, Sedki 1323
ソブラト
Sobrato, Jamie 1323
Sobrato, John A. 1323
ソブラル
Sobral, Patrick 1323
ゾブリスト
Zobrist, Ben 1556
ソブリチャ
Sobritchea, Carolyn Israel 1323
ソブリーノ
Sobrino, Javier 1323
ソブリノ
Sobrino, Javier 1323
ソフロニネ
Sofronie, Nicoleta Daniela 1324
ソーベ
Saltveit, M.E. 1232
ソペ
Sope, Barak 1328
ソベック
Sobek, Durward K. 1322
ソベネス
Sobenes, Marcia Roxana 1322
ソベプラン
Sauveplane, Valerian 1245
ソーベル
Sobel, Andrew Carl 1322
Sobel, David Stuart 1322
Sobel, Robert 1322
ソベール
Sobel, David 1322
ソベル
Sobel, Dava 1322
Sobel, David 1322
Sobel, Paul J. 1322
ゾーベルノーラン
Zobel-Nolan, Allia 1556
ソベロン・サンス
Soberón Sanz, Vidal Francisco 1323
ソポアンガ
Sopoaga, Enele 1328
Sopoanga, Saufatu 1328
ソホ・ガルサアルダペ
Sojo Garza-Aldape, Eduardo 1324
ソボシ
Sogbossi, Michel 1324
ソボシボッコ
Sogbossi Bocco, Bernard 1324
ソボスライ
Szoboszlai, Mihaly 1374
ゾボタ
Sobota, Heinz 1323
ソボッカ
Sobotka, Dirk 1323
ソボトカ
Sobotka, Bohuslav 1323
Sobotka, Wolfgang 1323
ゾーボリ
Zoboli, Giovanna 1556
ソボル
Sobol, Donald J. 1323
Sobol, Gordana 1323
ソボレフ
Sobolev, Sergey 1323
ソーポン
Sophon, Sarum 1328
Sopon, Sarum 1329
ソーマ
Thoma, Godfrey 1396
ゾマー
Sommer, Yann 1327

ゾマヴィラ
Somavilla, Ilse 1326
ソー・マウン
Soe Maung 1323
ソマーズ
Sommers, Joe 1327
ソーマデーヴァ
Somadeva Bhatta 1326
ソマート
Sommad, Pholsena 1327
ソマビア
Somavia, Juan O. 1326
ゾマー・ボーデンブルク
Sommer-Bodenburg, Angela 1327
ゾマホン
Zomahoun Rufin 1557
ゾマホン・ルフィン
Zomahoun Rufin 1557
ソマリバ
Somarriba Arrola, Joane 1326
ソマルガ
Sommaruga, Simonetta 1327
ソマレ
Somare, Michael 1326
Somare, Michael Thomas 1326
ゾーマン
Zorman, Itamar 1557
ソミン
Somin, Ilya 1327
ソムキット・チャトゥシピタク
Somkid Jatusripitak 1327
ソムケオ
Somkeo, Silavong 1327
ソムコット
Somkot, Mangnormek 1327
ソムサク
Somsak, Thepsutin 1327
ソムサワット
Somsavat, Lengsavad 1327
ソムジット
Jongjohor, Somjit 686
ソームズ
Soames, Mary 1322
Solms, Mark 1326
ソムダ
Somda, Jean Emile 1327
ソムチャーイ
Somchai Wongsawat 1327
ソムチャイ・ウォンサワット
Somchai Wongsawat 1327
ソムディ
Somdy, Douangdy 1327
ソムディー
Somdy, Douangdy 1327
ソムトウ
Somtow, S.P. 1327
ソムバット・ソムポーン
Sombath Somphone 1327
ソムポン
Somphong, Mongkhonvilay 1327
ソムラール
Sommerard, Jean-Charles 1327
ソメタニ
Sometani, Shôta 1327
ソメル
Zomer, Clara 1557
ソモザ
Somoza, José Carlos 1327
ソモージャイ
Somorjai, Gabor Arpad 1327
ソモハルジョ
Somohardjo, Paul 1327
ソモライ
Somorjai, Gabor Arpad 1327
ソモルジャイ
Somorjai, Gabor Arpad 1327
ソモレンスカ＝ジェリンスカ
Smolenska, Barbara 1320
ソーモワ
Somova, Alina 1327
ソーヤー
Sawyer, Amos 1246
Sawyer, Charles 1246
Sawyer, Corinne Holt 1246
Sawyer, Diane 1246
Sawyer, Robert Keith 1246
Sawyer, Walter Warwick 1246
ソーヤーズ
Sawyers, Jazmin 1246
ソラ
Sora, Steven 1329
ゾラー
Zurer, Ayelet 1559
ソラアット
Soraat, Klinpratoom 1329
ソラアト
Soraat, Klinpratoom 1329
ソライヤー
Bakhtiari, Soraya Esfandiari 84
ソラコフ
Solakov, Nedko 1324
ソラーズ
Solarz, Stephen Joshua 1325
ソラス
Solás, Humberto 1325
ゾラーズ
Zollars, Jean Anne 1557
ソラースキ
Solarski, Chris 1325
ゾラック
Zorach, Rebecca 1557
ソラーテ
Solarte, Yangervis 1325
ゾラディ
Zoradi, Mark 1557
ソラーナ
Solana, Javier 1324
ソラナ
Solana, Javier 1324
ソラーノ
Solano, Donovan 1324
ソラノ
Solano, Elhadj Moussa 1324
Solano, Moussa 1324
ソラビ
Sorabi, Habiba 1329
ソラヤ王女
Bakhtiari, Soraya Esfandiari 84
ソラリ
Solari, Ricardo 1325
ソラリ・デラフエンテ
Solari de la Fuente, Luis 1325
ソランキ
Solanki, Bharatsinh 1324
ソランケ
Solanke, Dominic 1324
ソランタウス
Solantaus, Tytti 1325
ソラント
Solanto, Mary V. 1325
ソリア
Soria, Bernat 1329
Soria, Cherie 1329
Soria, Joakim 1329
Soria, José Manuel 1329
ソリアイ
Soliai, Paul 1325
ソリアコムア
Soriacomua, Freda Tuki 1329
ソリアック
Solliec, Michel 1325
ソリアーノ
Soriano, Alfonso 1329
Soriano, Ferran 1329
Soriano, Roberto 1329
ソリアノ
Soriano, Alfonso 1329
ソリアン
Sourian, Hamid 1331
ソリヴェン
Soliven, Maximo 1325
ソリエフ
Soliyev, Khakim 1325
ゾリグト
Zorigt, Dashdorjiin 1557
Zorigt, Dashzeveg 1557
Zorigt, Munkhchuluun 1557
ソリケス
Soriquez, Florante 1329
ソリース
Solís, Mireya 1325
Solis, Sammy 1325
ソリス
Solis, Brian 1325
Solís, Doris 1325
Solís, Edín 1325
Solis, Hilda 1325
Solís, Isidro 1325
Solis, Julia 1325
Solis, Leonard 1325
Solis, Leydi 1325
Solís, Luis 1325
Solís, Manuel 1325
Solis, Odlanier 1325
Solís, Walter 1325
Soliz, Doris 1325
ソリスティ
Solisti, Kate 1325
ソリス・リベラ
Solis Rivera, Luis Guillermo 1325
ゾリッチ
Zordan, Giovanna 1557
Zoric, Milenko 1557
Zoritch, George 1557
ソリディアロ
Sorry Diallo, Mahamane 1329
ソリト
Solito, Enrico 1325
ソリトキ
Solitoki, Esso 1325
ソリナス・ドンギ
Solinas Donghi, Beatrice 1325
ソリベン
Soliven, Maximo 1325
ソリマン
Soliman, Corazon 1325
ソーリャ
Soorya, Latha V. 1328
ソリーリョ
Sorrillo, Rondel 1329
ソーリン
Solin, Daniel 1325
ゾリン
Zorin, Valentin P. 1557
ゾーリンジャー
Zollinger, Adam 1557
ゾリンジャー
Zollinger, Robert M., Jr. 1557
ソール
Saul, John 1244
Sohl, Jerry 1324
Soll, Jacob 1325
Soru, Renato 1329
Soule, Chris 1331
ソル
Seol, Ki-hyeon 1274
SOL 1324
Sol, Kyong 1324
Sol, Kyung-gu 1324
ソールイェル
Solhjell, Bard Vegar 1325
ソー・ルイン
Saw Lwin 1246
ソルヴィーノ
Sorvino, Mira 1329
ソルヴィノ
Sorvino, Mira 1329
ソー・ルウィン
Saw Lwin 1246
ソルウェー
Solway, Andrew 1326
ソールウェイ
Solway, Andrew 1326
ソールエル
Solhjell, Bard Vegar 1325
ゾールカヤ
Zorkaia, Neia Markovna 1557
ソルクモ
Sorkmo, Maj Helen 1329
ゾルコビー
Szolkowy, Robin 1374
ソルサ
Sorsa, Heikki 1329
Sorsa, Kalevi 1329
ゾルジ
Zolzi, Alvise 1557
Zorzi, Cristian 1557
ソルジェニーツィン
Solzhenitsin, Aleksandr Isaevich 1326
ゾルズースキー
Szulczewski, Peter 1375
ソールスター
Solstad, Dag 1326
ソールズバーリー
Salisbury, Mark 1231
ソールズベリー
Salisbury, Dallas L. 1231
Salisbury, Dereck 1231

ソ

Salisbury, Gay 1231
Salisbury, Janet 1231
Salisbury, Laney 1231
Salisbury, Mark 1231
ソールセン
Thorsén, Lotta 1402
ソルター
Salter, Ammon J. 1232
Salter, Anna C. 1232
Salter, Colin 1232
Salter, James 1232
Salter, John 1232
Solter, Davor 1326
ソルダー
Solder, Nate 1325
Solder, Scott 1325
ソルダード
Soldado, Roberto 1325
ソルタニ
Soltani, Bouguerra 1326
ソルタニファル
Soltanifar, Masoud 1326
ソルタン
Soltan, Usama 1326
ゾルタン
Zoltan, Barbara 1557
ゾルダン
Zordan, Giovanna 1557
ソルタンハ
Soltankhah, Nasrin 1326
ゾルツィ
Zorzi, William F. 1557
ソルツマン
Salzman, Karen L. 1233
ソルディ
Sordi, Alberto 1329
ソルティス
Soltis, Jonas F. 1326
ゾルテス
Soltesz, Stefan 1326
ソルデン
Solden, Sari 1325
ソルト
Solt, George 1326
Solt, John 1326
ゾルトナース
Zoltners, Andris A. 1557
ゾルトナーズ
Zoltners, Andris A. 1557
ソールトノフ
Sultonov, Bahodirjon 1365
ソルトバーグ
Saltzberg, Barney 1232
ソルナード
Solnado, Alexandra 1326
ソールニア
Saulnier, Celine A. 1244
ソルニエ
Saulnier, Daniel 1244
ソルニット
Solnit, Rebecca 1326
ソルハ
Solh, Leila 1325
ゾルバ
Zorba, Furkan 1557
ソールハイム
Solheim, Erik 1325
Solheim, Jan 1325
ソルハイム
Solheim, Nina 1325
ソルバーグ
Solberg, Monte 1325
ソルバッケン
Solbakken, Bjarne 1325
ソルビアン
Sorbjan, Zbigniew 1329
ソルビク・オルセン
Solvik-olsen, Ketil 1326
ソルビーノ
Sorvino, Mira 1329
ソルビノ
Sorvino, Mira 1329
ゾルフォ
Zolfo, Victor J. 1557
ソルフォロジ
Solforosi, Franck 1325
ソルヘイム
Solheim, James 1325
Solheim, Nina 1325
ソルベス
Solbes, Pedro 1325
ゾルベルガー
Sollberger, Arthur 1325
ソルベルグ
Solberg, Erna 1325
Solberg, Petter 1325
Solberg Salgado, Pedro 1325
ゾルベルク
Sohlberg, Ragnhild 1324
ソルマン
Sorman, Guy 1329
ソルミニアク
Solminihac, Hernán de 1325
ソルミニャク
Solminihac, Hernán de 1325
ソルヤ
Solja, Petrissa 1325
ソルヤン
Soryan, Hamid 1329
ソレ
Solé, Jacques 1325
ソレーア
Soler, Jorge 1325
ソレッタ
Soletta, Luigi 1325
ソーレプー
Saarepuu, Anti 1222
ソレーマニ
Soleymani, Mohammad 1325
ソレム
Solem, Jan Erik 1325
ソレーリ
Soleri, Paolo 1325
ソレリ
Soleri, Paolo 1325
ソレール
Soler, André 1325
ソレル
Saurel, Étienne 1245
Saurel, Myrtho Célestin 1245
Soler, Juli 1325
Soler, Rafael 1325
Soler, Tomás 1325
Sorel, Edward 1329
Sorel, Reynal 1329
Sorrell, Jeanne M. 1329
Sorrell, Katherine 1329
Sorrell, Martin Stuart 1329
Sorrell, Roger Darrell 1329
Sorrell, Thomas N. 1329
ソレルス
Sollers, Philippe 1325
ソレン
Soren, Daniel 1329
Soren, Jack 1329
Soren, Shibu 1329
ソレンスタム
Sorenstam, Annika 1329
ソーレンセン
Soerensen, Frode 1323
Sorensen, Frederik 1329
ソレンセン
Sorensen, Brad 1329
Sorensen, Daniel 1329
Sørensen, Henrik 1329
Sorensen, Herb 1329
Sorensen, Joseph T. 1329
Sorensen, Lone 1329
Sørensen, Peter Birch 1329
Sorensen, Theodore 1329
ソレンソン
Sorensen, Marilyn J. 1329
Sorenson, Jim 1329
ソレンティーノ
Sorrentino, Paolo 1329
Sorrentino, Stefano 1329
ソレンティノ
Sorrentino, Richard M. 1329
ソレント
Sorrento, Paul 1329
ソロ
Solo, Hope 1326
Soro, Guillaume 1329
ソロー
Solow, Robert Merton 1326
ゾロ
Zollo, Anthony J., Jr. 1557
Zollo, Maurizio 1557
Zollo, Paul 1557
ソロイスツ
Soloists, Moscow 1326
ソローヴ
Solove, Daniel J. 1326
ソロウェイ
Soloway, Jeff 1326
ソローキナ
Sorokina, V.V. 1329
ソロキナ
Sorokina, Valeria 1329
ソローキン
Sorokin, Vladimir Georgevich 1329
ソログッド
Thorogood, Nicki 1402
ソロス
Soros, George 1329
ゾロタス
Zolotas, Xenophon 1557
ソロタレフ
Solotareff, Grégoire 1326
ゾロタロワ
Zolotarova, Olha 1557
ゾロトウ
Zolotow, Charlotte 1557
ソロビエフ
Soloviev, Dmitri 1326
ソロフ
Soloff, Paul H. 1326
ソロベイ
Solovay, Sondra 1326
ソロポギ
Soropogui, Yazora 1329
ソローミン
Solomin, Yury 1326
ソロム
Solomou, Despoina 1326
ソロモン
Salomon, Gavriel 1232
Salomon, William 1232
Solomon, Andrew 1326
Solomon, Annie 1326
Solomon, Barbara Stauffacher 1326
Solomon, Brian 1326
Solomon, Charles 1326
Solomon, David A. 1326
Solomon, Deborah 1326
Solomon, Diare 1326
Solomon, Duane 1326
Solomon, Hester 1326
Solomon, Ira 1326
Solomon, Jack 1326
Solomon, Jeffrey A. 1326
Solomon, Marion Fried 1326
Solomon, Maynard 1326
Solomon, Micah 1326
Solomon, Michael G. 1326
Solomon, Michael R. 1326
Solomon, Norman 1326
Solomon, Richard 1326
Solomon, Robert C. 1326
Solomon, Sheldon 1326
Solomon, Steven 1326
Solomons, T.W. Graham 1326
ソロルサノ
Solórzano, Pedro 1326
ソロルサノ・デルガディジョ
Solórzano Delgadillo, Orlando Salvador 1326
ソロンズ
Solondz, Todd 1326
ソロンゾンボルド
Soronzonbold, Battsetseg 1329
ソワリ
Soilihi, Mohamed Ali 1324
ソーン
Sohn, Amy 1324
Sohn, Anne-Marie 1324
Thorn, George R. 1401
Thorn, Victor 1401
Thorne, Brian 1401
Thorne, Claire 1401
Thorne, Jack 1401
Thorne, Ken 1401
Thorne, Peter S. 1401
ソン
Sohn, Hak-kyu 1324
Sohn, Ki-Sam 1324
Sohn, Kyung Shik 1324
Son, Chang-sop 1327
Son, Diana 1327
Son, Eun-Hye 1327
Son, Heung-Min 1327
Son, Jin-du 1327
Son, Jong-ho 1327
Son, Ki-jong 1327
Son, Nguyen Bac 1327
Son, Tae-young 1327
Son, Ye-jin 1327
Son, Yeol Eum 1327
Song, Dae-nam 1327
Song, Daria 1327
Song, De-fu 1327

Song, Gang-ho 1327
Song, Hae-seong 1327
Song, Hye-gyo 1327
Song, Hye-rim 1327
Song, Il-ho 1327
Song, Il-kook 1328
Song, Ir-kon 1328
Song, Ja-rip 1328
Song, Jian 1328
Song, Ji-na 1328
Song, Joong-ki 1328
Song, Ki-suk 1328
Song, Miho 1328
Song, Min-ho 1328
Song, Min-soon 1328
Song, Ren-qiong 1328
Song, Seung-heon 1328
Song, Siheng 1328
Song, Soo-keon 1328
Song, Soon Sup 1328
Song, Yoon-a 1328
Song, Young-sun 1328
Song, Zhi-guang 1328
Sun, Dong-yeol 1366
Sun, Ta-Shan 1366
Sung, Chu-yu 1366
Sung, Mei-ling 1366

ゾン
Zhong, Shi-tong 1553
Zong, Qinghou 1557

ソンガネ
Songane, Francisco 1328

ソンキン
Sonkin, Daniel Jay 1328
Sonkin, Paul 1328

ソング
Song, Allen W. 1327
Song, Yeoungsuk 1328
Thong, Roseanne 1401

ソンコ
Sonko, Ousman 1328

ゾンゴ
Zongo, Laure 1557
Zongo, Tertius 1557

ソンサイ
Sonexay, Siphandone 1327

ソンジカ
Sonjica, Buyelwa Patience 1328

ソーンズ
Sones, Bill 1327
Sones, Rich 1327

ソーンダイク
Thorndike, William, Jr. 1401

ソンダイマー
Sondheimer, Adrian 1327

ソンタグ
Sontag, Susan 1328

ソンダシ
Sondashi, Ludwig 1327

ソーンダース
Saunders, Jason 1245
Saunders, Michael 1245

ソーンダーズ
Saunders, George 1244
Saunders, Rebecca M. 1245

ソーンダス
Saunders, Kate 1245

ソンダース
Saunders, Cicely 1244

ソンタヤ
Sontaya, Kunplome 1328

ソンタヤー
Sontaya, Kunplome 1328

ゾンダーランド
Zonderland, Epke 1557

ソンディック
Sonduck, Michael 1327

ソンティ・ブンヤラガリン
Sonthi Boonyaratglin 1328

ソンドハイム
Sondheim, Stephen Joshua 1327

ソーントン
Thornton, Billy Bob 1401
Thornton, Bob 1401
Thornton, Cedric 1401
Thornton, Elizabeth 1401
Thornton, George C., Ⅲ 1401
Thornton, Hugh 1401
Thornton, Joe 1401
Thornton, Khyri 1401
Thornton, Kim Campbell 1401
Thornton, Laura 1401
Thornton, Lawrence 1401
Thornton, Marcus 1401
Thornton, Melanie 1401
Thornton, Robert Kelsey Rought 1401
Thornton, Sarah 1402
Thornton, Stephen J. 1402
Thornton, Warwick 1402

ソンニーノ
Sonnino, Roberta 1328

ゾンネ
Sonne, D.Christian 1328

ゾンネマン
Sonneman, Toby F. 1328

ゾンネンシャイン
Sonnenschein, David 1328

ゾンネンシュミット
Sonnenschmidt, Rosina 1328

ソンパー
Somper, Justin 1327

ソンハイム
Sonheim, Carla 1328

ソーンバーグ
Thornburg, Tyler 1401

ソンバット
Sambath, Oum 1233

ソンパワン
Somphavan, Inthavong 1327

ソンパン
Somphanh, Phengkhammy 1327

ゾンビ
Zombie, Rob 1557

ソーンヒル
Thornhill, Christopher J. 1401
Thornhill, Jan 1401
Thornhill, Randy 1401
Thornhill, Wallace 1401

ソンプソン
Thompson, Neil 1400

ゾンボ
Zombo, Frank 1557

ソンボ・ディベル
Sombo Dibele, Arlette 1327

ゾンマー
Sommer, Theo 1327

ソンマイ
Sommai, Phasee 1327

ゾンマー・ボーデンブルク
Sommer-Bodenburg, Angela 1327

ソーンミラー
Thorne-Miller, Boyce 1401

ソンミン
Sungmin 1366

ソンメズ
Sonmez, John Z. 1328

ソンメスタード
Sommestad, Lena 1327

ゾンメルラード
Sommerlad, Peter 1327

ソーンリー
Thornley, Victoria 1401

ソーンリィ
Thornley, Rebecca Gundersen 1401

【タ】

タ
Ta, Do Trung 1375

ター
Tah, Christiana 1376
Tah, Jonathan 1376
Tah, Sidi Ould 1376
Tarr, Babs 1382

ダー
Darr, Matt 320
Darr, Mike 320

ダア
Da, Tou-chun 311

ダアナア
Daanaa, Henry Seidu 311

ダアン
Daan, Sarge 311
Dahan, Olivier 312

タイ
Dai, Ai-lian 313
Dai, Bing-guo 313
Dai, Xiang-long 313
Thai, Nguyen Danh 1393
Thay, António 1394
Trye, Hindolo Sumanguru 1423
Tye, Joe 1430
Tye, Larry 1430
Tye, Will 1430

ダイ
Dai, Bing-guo 313
Dai, Sijie 313
Dai, Tobias 313
Dai, Weili 313
Dai, Xiang-long 313
Digh, Patricia 354
Dye, Dan 385
Dye, Donteea 385

ダイアー
Dyer, Chris 386
Dyer, Davis 386
Dyer, Hadley 386
Dyer, Heather 386
Dyer, Jeffrey M. 386
Dyer, Lois Faye 386
Dyer, Marcelene 386
Dyer, Nathan 386
Dyer, Richard 386
Dyer, Russell J.T. 386
Dyer, Sarah 386
Dyer, Serena J. 386
Dyer, Wayne W. 386

ダイアコニス
Diaconis, Persi 350

タイアーズ
Tyers, Jenny 1430
Tyers, Kathy 1430

ダイアズ
Diaz, Francesca 351

ダイアス・アベイシンハ
Dias Abeysinghe, Ian 351

タイアナ
Taiana, Jorge 1377

ダイアモンド
Diamand, Emily 350
Diamond, Cora 350
Diamond, David 350
Diamond, David J. 350
Diamond, Diana 350
Diamond, Hanna 350
Diamond, Harvey 350
Diamond, Ian 350
Diamond, Jacqueline 350
Diamond, Jared 350
Diamond, Jed 350
Diamond, Larry Jay 351
Diamond, Marilyn 351
Diamond, Martha Ourieff 351
Diamond, Michael 351
Diamond, Peter A. 351
Diamond, Ronald J. 351
Diamond, Stuart 351
Diamond, Susan 351
Diamond, Timothy 351

ダイアン
Dayan, Daniel 329

タイウィア
Taiwia, Nato 1377

ダイウト
D'Aiuto, Giuliano 313

タイエブ
Ettaieb, Samir 411
Tayeb, Mohammed Amine 1384

タイエブニア
Tayebnia, Ali 1384

ターイェルプール
Taherpour, Fereshteh 1376

ダイオ
Daio, Olinto Da Silva E Sousa 313

タイオネ
Taione, Elvis 1377

タイオン
Taillon, Jameson 1377

タイガ
Taiga 1377

タイガー
Tiger, Caroline 1404
Tyger, Rory 1430

タイガー・ジェット・シン
Tiger Jeet Singh 1404

ダイク
Dijk, Geke van 354
Dyck, Bevery 385
Dyk, Walter 386
Dyke, Greg 386

ダイクス
Dijks, Mitchell 354
Diks, Kevin 355

ダイクストラ
Dijkstra, Edsger W. 354

タ

タ

Dijkstra, Lida 354
Dijkstra, Peter 355
Dijkstra, Pieternel 355
Dykstra, John 386
ダイクスマ
Dijksma, Sharon 354
ダイグナン
Deignan, Alice 334
Duignan, Rene 379
タイクマン
Teichmann, Iris 1388
タイグル
Teigl, Georg 1389
タイザック
Tyzack, Margaret 1431
ダイサート
Dysart, Joshua 386
Dysart, Richard 386
Dysert, Zac 386
ダイサラ
Daïssala, Dakolé 313
ダイジ
Daij, bin Khalifa al-Khalifa 313
タイス
Tice, Louis E. 1403
ダイス
Deiss, Joseph 334
タイスン
Tyson, Donald 1431
ダイセルブルーム
Dijsselbloem, Jeroen 355
タイセン
Theiszen, Gerd 1395
タイセンイートン
Theisen Eaton, Brianne 1395
タイソ
Taisso, Mackaye Hassane 1377
タイソン
Tyson, Andrew 1431
Tyson, Cicely 1431
Tyson, DeAngelo 1431
Tyson, Iman 1431
Tyson, Mike 1431
Tyson, Neil De Grasse 1431
Tyson, Phyllis 1431
Tyson, Robert L. 1431
ダイソン
Dyson, Freeman J. 386
Dyson, George 386
Dyson, James 386
Dyson, Jarrod 386
Dyson, Michael Eric 386
Dyson, Ruth 386
Dyson, Sam 386
タイタス
Titus, Eve 1407
ダイチェ
Dyche, Sean 385
ダイチマン
Daichman, Lia Susana 313
タイデル
Taider, Saphir 1377
ダイテル
Deitel, Abbey 334
Deitel, Harvey M. 334
Deitel, Paul J. 334
タイテルト
Tuitert, Mark 1426
タイテルバウム
Teitelbaum, Michael 1389
タイト
Tait, Noel 1377
タイドマン
Tiedemann, Andrew 1404
Tydeman, Naomi 1430
ダイトワルド
Dychtwald, Maddy 385
ダイトン
Dighton, John 354
タイナ
Taina, Hannu 1377
タイナー
Tyner, McCoy 1431
タイナン
Tynan, Katharine 1431
Tynan, Kenneth 1431
Tynan, Ronan 1431
タイニー
Tinney, Stuart 1406
ダイネッリ
Dainelli, Dario 313
タイノン
Tynion, James, Ⅳ 1431
タイバー
Tiber, Elliot 1403
ダイバート
Deibert, Richard I. 334
タイバルザリ
Taivalsaari, Antero 1377
タイパレ
Taipale, Ilkka 1377
タイヒ
Teich, Malvin Carl 1388
タイヒマン
Teichmann, Axel 1388
ダイヒャー
Deicher, Susanne 334
タイヒラー
Teichler, Ulrich 1388
タイブ
Taib, Saad al-Din Ali bin 1377
ダイブラー
Deibler, Markus 334
Deibler, Steffen 334
ダイベック
Dybek, Nick 385
Dybek, Stuart 385
タイベルト
Tajbert, Vitali 1377
タイボ
Taibo, Carlos 1377
Taibo, Paco Ignacio, Ⅱ 1377
タイボー
Tybout, Alice M. 1430
タイポ
Taipo, Maria Helena 1377
タイマゾフ
Taymazov, Artur 1387
タイマン
Tieman, Robert 1404
ダイマン
Deimann, Markus 334
タイマンス
Tuymans, Luc 1430
タイミナ
Taimina, Daina 1377
ダイム
Daim, Zainuddin 313
ダイムバッグ・ダレル
Dimebag Darrell 356
ダイムラー
Deimler, Michael S. 334
ダイムリング
Deimling, Barbara 334
タイモスー
Taimsoo, Kaspar 1377
タイモン
Tymon, Josh 1431
ダイモン
Dimon, James 356
Dimon, Jamie 356
ダイモンド
Dimond, Bridgit 356
ダイヤー
Dyer, Alan 386
Dyer, Christopher L. 386
Dyer, Davis 386
Dyer, Geoff 386
Dyer, Gwynne 386
Dyer, Heather 386
Dyer, Henry 386
Dyer, Jane 386
Dyer, Kathleen 386
Dyer, Sarah 386
タイヤック
Tyack, David B. 1430
ダイヤモンド
Diamond, David 350
Diamond, Jessica Z. 351
Diamond, Louise 351
Diamond, Michael 351
Diamond, Peter A. 351
ダイユ
Daille, Etienne 313
タイラー
Taylor, Ceci 1385
Taylor, Jeremy 1386
Taylor, Scott 1387
Tiler, Rebekah 1404
Tyler, Andrea 1430
Tyler, Anne 1430
Tyler, Gillian 1430
Tyler, Jenny 1430
Tyler, Kermit 1430
Tyler, Liv 1430
Tyler, Steven 1430
Tyler, Val 1430
Tyler, Zan 1430
Tyrer, Peter J. 1431
タイラー・ザ・クリエイター
Tyler The Creator 1431
タイラビア
Tialavea, D.J. 1403
ダイラミ
Dailami, Mansoor 313
タイラン
Taylan, Nurcan 1384
タイリー
Tylee, Andre 1430
Tyree, Melvin T. 1431
ダーイリ
al-Dairi, Mohamed 313
ダイリ
al-Dairi, Mohamed 313
ダイリット
Dayrit, Manuel 329
ダイル
Dahir, Savid Ahmad Sheikh 312
タイルズ
Tiles, Mary 1404
タイローン
Taijeron, Travis 1377
タイロン
Tyronne, del Pino 1431
タイン
Thanh, Phung Quang 1394
Thanh, Quach Le 1394
Thanh, Ta Huu 1394
Thanh, Tin 1394
ダイン
Dine, Jim 356
タインガポロコ
Taïnga Poloko, Alfred 1377
タインシュ
Tainsh, Robert 1377
ダウ
Dah, Hyppolite 312
Dau, Stephen Dhieu 321
Dow, David R. 371
Dow, Kirstin 371
Dow, Patsy Busby 371
Dow, Unity 371
ダヴ
Dove, Rita 371
タウア
Taua, Tavaga Kitiona Seuala 1383
Taur, Yuan 1384
ダウアー
Dauer, Rich 322
タヴァレス
Tavares, Matt 1384
Tavarez, Shannon 1384
ダヴァンツォ＝ポーリ
Davanzo Poli, Doretta 322
タヴィアーニ
Taviani, Paolo 1384
Taviani, Vittorio 1384
ダヴィシャ
Dawisha, Adeed 328
ダヴィソン
Davison, John 327
ダヴィッチ
Davich, Victor N. 322
ダーヴィッツ
Davids, Edgar 323
ダヴィッディ
Daviddi, Evelyn 323
ダヴィッド
Davidts, Jean-Pierre 324
Davoud, Mokhtari 327
ダヴィド
David, Olivier 323
ダヴィドヴィッツ
Davidovits, Paul 323
ダヴィドソン
Davidson, Basil Risbridger 323
ダヴィド＝メナール
David-Ménard, Monique 323
ダヴィド・ルイス
David Luiz 323
ダヴィニヨン
Davignon, Etienne 325
ターウィリガー
Terwilliger, Terra 1392
タウィール
al-Taweel, Abdullah Abdul-Rahman 1384
ダーウィン
Darwin, Ian F. 320
Darwin, Leah Marasigan 320
タウエマ

Tawéma, Daniel 1384
ダウエル
Dawel, Akoli 328
Dowell, Anthony 371
Dowell, Kieran 371
タヴェルニエ
Tavernier, Bertrand 1384
Tavernier, Nils 1384
Tavernier, Sarah 1384
Tavernier, Tiffany 1384
ダーウェント
Derwent, Henry 345
ダヴェンポート
Davenport, Guy 322
Davenport, Jim 322
Davenport, Kiana 322
Davenport, Nigel 322
ダヴォドー
Davodeau, Étienne 327
ダウク
Daouk, Walid 319
ダウサ
Daoussa, Bichara Cherif 319
タウシ
Tausi, Otinielu 1384
タウシグ
Taussig, Michael T. 1384
タウシンガ
Tausinga, Job Dundley 1384
Tausinga, Silas 1384
ダウズ
Dawes, Chip 328
ダウスウェイト
Douthwaite, R.J. 371
ダウズウェル
Dowswell, Paul 372
タウスボールスタッド
Taus-Bolstad, Stacy 1384
ダウセ
Dausset, Jean 322
ダウゼンベルヒ
Duisenberg, Wim 379
ダウダ
Daouda, Abdou 319
Daouda, Idriss 319
Dauda, Collins 322
Dauda, Joseph 322
タウツ
Tautz, Jürgen 1384
ダウティー
Doughty, Andrew 370
ダウディ
Daoudi, Lahcen 319
ダウデン
Dowden, Joe 371
タウト
Thaut, Michael H. 1394
ダウード
Dawood, Hayel 328
Dawood, Qasim 328
ダウド
Daoud, Ahmed Ould Ahil 319
Daoud, Ali Mohamed 319
Daud, Aden Haji Ibrahim 322
Daud, Razzaq 322
Dowd, Dara 371
Dowd, John 371
Dowd, Siobhan 371
Dowd, Tom 371
ダウドゥ
Daoudou, Mohamed 319
ダウトオール
Davutoğlu, Ahmet 327
タウナー
Towner, Elizabeth 1415
タヴナー
Tavener, John 1384
ダウナー
Downer, Alexander 371
Downer, Lesley 371
ダウニー
Downey, Allen B. 371
Downey, Robert, Jr. 371
Downey, Roger 371
Downie, Elissa 371
Downie, Rebecca 371
ダウニィ
Downey, Roger 371
ダウニング
Downing, Carolyn 371
Downing, David C. 371
Downing, Stewart 371
Downing, Thomas E. 371
タウネンド
Townend, Tom 1415
タウバー
Tauber, Martin 1384
タウビー
Taube, Henry 1383
タウブ
Taube, Henry 1383
Taube, Herman 1384
タウフィク
Taufiq Kiemas 1384
タウフィック・キマス
Taufiq Kiemas 1384
タウフェウルンガキ
Taufe'ulungaki, Ana Maui 1384
タウフェテー
Taufete'e, Joseph 1384
タウベ
Taube, Henry 1383
ダウマ
Douma, S.W. 370
タウマロロ
Taumalolo, Sona (Alisona) 1384
タウモエペアウ
Taumoepeau, Aisea 1384
Taumoepeau, Malia Viviena 'Alisi 1384
ダウラ
Daura, Alhaji Sani Zango 322
ダウラハ
al-Dawlah, Izz al-Din 328
タウラフォ
Taulafo, Sakaria (Zak) 1384
ダウリー
Dowley, Tim 371
タウリ・コルプス
Tauli-Corpuz, Victoria 1384
タヴリス
Tavris, Carol 1384
ダヴリン
Davlin, Bennett Joshua 327
ダウリング
Dowling, Cindy 371
Dowling, Faye 371
Dowling, John E. 371
Dowling, Jonathan 371
Dowling, Mike C. 371
Dowling, Peter A. 371
ダウルディング
Dowlding, William J. 371
ダウルト
Dault, Adhyaksa 322
ダウレエアウー
Daureeawoo, Fazila 322
タウレル
Tauler, Antonio 1384
ダウロフ
Daurov, Soslan 322
タウワ
Tahuwa, Kelsang 1377
ダウワー
Dower, Laura 371
タウン
Thaung 1394
Town, Phil 1415
Towne, Roger 1415
タウンズ
Townes, Charles Hard 1415
Towns, Karl-Anthony 1416
ダウンズ
Downes, Alice 371
Downes, Belinda 371
Downes, John 371
Downes, Larry 371
Downs, Alan 371
Downs, Bernard W. 372
Downs, Chuck 372
Downs, Julie Suzanne 372
Downs, Lila 372
Downs, Michael 372
Downs, Timothy Edward 372
タウンズエンド
Townsend, Sam 1416
ダウンスコウ
Ravnskov, Uffe 1161
タウンゼント
Townsend, Andros 1416
Townsend, Darian 1416
Townsend, Elizabeth A. 1416
Townsend, Greg 1416
Townsend, John Sims 1416
Townsend, Peter David 1416
Townsend, Richard F. 1416
Townshend, Pete 1416
タウンゼンド
Townsend, Colin R. 1416
Townsend, Heather 1416
Townsend, Henry James 1416
Townsend, John 1416
Townsend, John Rowe 1416
Townsend, Kevin 1416
Townsend, Lindsay 1416
Townsend, Patricia K. 1416
Townsend, Sue 1416
Townshend, Charles 1416
Townshend, Pete 1416
Townshend, Steve 1416
ダウンハム
Downham, Jenny 371
ダヴンポート
Davenport, Willie 322
タウンリー
Townley, Gemma 1416
Townley, Rod 1416
タエ
Taye, Patricia 1384
タエー
Taher, Mahamat Allahou 1376
タエキス
Taekiti, Tiim 1376
タオ
Tao, Li 1381
Tao, Terence 1381
ダオ
Dao, Kathryn H. 319
タオカ
Taoka, Isao 1381
タオフ
Taov, Khasanbi 1381
タオム
Taom, James 1381
タオン
Thong Khon 1401
タガー
Tager, Mark J. 1376
ダーカー
Dierker, Joachim 354
ダカ
Daka, Peter 313
タカウ
Takau, Talifolau 1377
タカエズ
Takaezu, Toshiko 1377
タカオ
Takao, Yssamu 1377
タカキ
Takaki, Ronald 1377
タカギ
Takagi, Tammy 1377
タカキ・ヤスナガ
Takaki Yasunaga, Kuniyoshi 1377
タカサキ
Takasaki, Luiz Antonio 1377
タカシマ
Takashima, Bobbie 1377
ダガシュ
Daggash, Sanusi 312
タカスギ
Takasugi, Robert 1377
タカダ
Takada, Akane 1377
Takada, Tatsuki 1377
ダガタ
Agata, Antoine d' 17
ダーガダス
Daugirdas, John T. 322
タカーチ
Takacs, David 1377
ダーガッツ
Dargatz, Jan Lynette 319
ターカニス
Turkanis, Jonathan 1427
タガノフ
Taganov, Babamyrat 1376
Taganov, Palvan 1376
Taganov, Seyitmyrat 1376
タカノ・モロン
Takano Morón, Juan 1377
タカハシ
Takahashi, Dean 1377

Takahashi, Kazutoshi 1377
Takahashi, Takeo 1377
Takahashi, Tomoye 1377
タカハシ・ヌニェス
Takahashi Nuñez, Luis Abelardo 1377
タガビ
Taghavi, Nayyereh 1376
タガミ
Tagami, Kan 1376
タカムネ・ミシェル
Takamouné Michel, Marie José 1377
タカムラ
Takamura, Jeanette 1377
タカモト
Takamoto, Iwao 1377
タカヤマ
Takayama, Shuichi 1377
タカリ
Takkari, Bechir 1377
Thakali, Krishna Lal 1393
Thakali, Romi Gauchan 1393
ダカール
Dakar, Djiri 313
ダカル
Dhakal, Ek Nath 349
Dhakal, Tanka 349
タガロア
Tagaloa, Sale Tagaloa 1376
ダガン
Dagan, Avicdor 312
Dugan, Robert E. 378
Duggan, Christopher 378
Duggan, Gerry 378
Duggan, William R. 379
タキ
Theodoracopulos, Taki 1395
ダーギー
Doerge, Rebecca W. 362
タギエフ
Tagyyev, Tachberdy 1376
タキグチ
Takiguchi, Masako 1377
タキザワ
Takizawa, Bonnie 1377
ダギース
Dagys, Rimantas Jonas 312
タギプール
Taghipour, Reza 1376
ダギリ
D'Aquili, Eugene G. 319
タギワロ
Taguiwalo, Judy 1376
ダーキン
Durkin, James F. 384
ターキングトン
Turkington, Douglas 1427
ダーキンズ
Darkins, Ellie 319
ターキントン
Turkington, Carol 1427
ターク
Tuerk, Max 1425
Turk, Cynthia L. 1427
Turk, James 1427
Turk, Jonathan 1427
ダーク
D'Arc, Joan 319
Dark, Alvin Ralph 319
Dark, K. 319
タグーアン
Taghouane, Bouamour 1376
タグイエフ
Tagyyev, Tachberdy 1376
タクシン・シナワット
Thaksin Shinawatra 1393
タクシン・シンナワット
Thaksin Shinawatra 1393
タクシン・チナワット
Thaksin Shinawatra 1393
ダークス
Dirkes, Lisa Mann 358
ダクスベリー
Duxbury, Joy 385
ダークセン
Derksen, Rob 344
ダグダル
Dugdall, Ruth 378
タクツェル・リンポチェ
Taktser Rinpoche 1378
タクディ
Teguedi, Ahmed Ould 1388
タクナ
Takna, Sayed Yousif Suliman 1378
タクナル
Takna, Sayed Yousif Suliman 1378
ダグニーズ
D'Agnese, Joseph 312
ダグニーノ
Dagnino, Fernando 312
タクパラ
Takpara, Issifou 1378
ダグバンゾンビデ
Dagban-zonvide, Patricia 312
タクブンジャ
Stag-vbum-rgyal 1339
タクマキス
Tsakmakis, Christos 1423
ダグマン
Dagman, Nurideen Abdulhamid 312
ダグモア
Dugmore, Jenny 379
ダグラス
Dauglas, Jamil 322
Douglas 370
Douglas, Alan 370
Douglas, Alfred 370
Douglas, Barry 370
Douglas, Buck 370
Douglas, Carole Nelson 370
Douglas, Claire 370
Douglas, David 370
Douglas, Denzil Llewellyn 370
Douglas, Diana 370
Douglas, Donna 370
Douglas, Emory 370
Douglas, Eric 370
Douglas, Gabrielle 370
Douglas, Harry 370
Douglas, Ian 370
Douglas, Jerry 370
Douglas, Jo 370
Douglas, John E. 370
Douglas, Kane 370
Douglas, Kevin S. 370
Douglas, Kirk 370
Douglas, Kym 370
Douglas, Lincoln 370
Douglas, Mark J. 370
Douglas, Mary 370
Douglas, Michael 370
Douglas, Michelle 370
Douglas, Mike 370
Douglas, Scott 370
Douglas, Tom 370
Douglass, Bruce Powel 370
Douglass, Donna N. 370
Douglass, James W. 370
Douglass, Keith 370
Douglass, Merrill E. 370
ダグリ
Daghr, Ahmed Obaid bin 312
ダグリーシュ
Dagleish, John 312
ダクリタブレ
Dakoury-tabley, André 313
ダグリタブレ
Dakoury-tabley, André 313
ダグリディアバテ
Dagridiabate, Henriette 312
タークル
Thakur, Rajeev 1393
Turkle, Brinton 1427
タクール
Thakur, Mahanta 1393
タクル
Thakur, C.P. 1393
Thakur, Mahanta 1393
タクルア
Takulua, Sonatane 1378
ダクルス
Da Cruz, António Martins 311
Da Cruz, Arlindo Rangel 311
ダグレニアー
Dugrenier, Martine 379
タグロ
Tagro, Assegnini Désiré 1376
Tagro, Désiré 1376
ダークワ
Darkwa, Orleans 319
タケイ
Takei, Goerge 1377
Takei, Henry H. 1377
Takei, Noriyoshi 1377
タゲセ
Tagesse, Chafo 1376
タケダ
Takeda, Kenny 1377
Takeda, Yuko 1377
タゲッディン
Taggeddin, Muhammad Awad 1376
ターゲット
Targett, Matt 1382
タケット
Tuckett, Will 1425
ダーゲフェアデ
Dageförde, Klaus 312
タケモリ
Takemori, James H. 1377
ターケル
Terkel, Larry 1391
Terkel, Studs 1391
Terkel, Susan Neiburg 1392
ダーゴ
Dirgo, Craig 357
ダコ
Dako, Nestor 313
タゴイゾダ
Taghoizoda, Sumangul 1376
ターコウスキー
Tarkowski, James 1382
ダ・コスタ
Da Costa, Angelo 311
DaCosta, Barbara 311
Da Costa, Danny 311
Da Costa, Manuel Pinto 311
Da Costa, Portia 311
ダコスタ
Da Coasta, Manuel Pinto 311
Da Costa, Celia Maria 311
Da Costa, Desiderio da Graca Verissimo 311
Da Costa, Edeltrudes Maurício Fernandes Gaspar 311
Da Costa, Gabriel Arcanjo Ferreira 311
Da Costa, Manuel Pinto 311
Da Costa, Maria do Céu Pina 311
Da Costa, Peregrino 311
Da Costa, Zacarias 311
ダコスタテブストレス
Da Costa Tebus Torres, Maria dos Santos Lima 311
ダコスタ・ピナ
Dacosta Pina, Maria do Céu 311
ダゴスティーノ
D'Agostino, Gregory 312
D'Agostino, Maria-Antonietta 312
Dagostino, Mark 312
ダゴスティノ
Dagostino, Abbey 312
ダコ・タマダオ
Dako Tamadaho, Nadine 313
ダゴニェ
Dagognet, Françis 312
ダゴール
Dougall, Alastair 370
ダコレ
Dakole, Daissala 313
ダコンセイサオ
Da Conceição, António 311
ダコンセイサンイシルバ
Da Conceição E Silva, José António 311
ダコンセイソン
Da Conceição, António 311
ダコンセイソン・ピント
Da Conceição Pinto, Constâncio 311
ダコンタ
Daconta, Michael C. 311
ダサナイカ
Dassanayake, D.M. 321
タザフィ
Tazafy, Armand 1387
タシー
Tassie, Gregor 1383

ダーシー
Darcey, Lauren 319
Darcy, Emma 319
Darcy, Lilian 319
ダージ
Derge, Gillmer J. 344
ダシー
Dachy, Marc 311
Duthie, Torquil 384
タシアディス
Tasiadis, Sideris 1383
タジアディス
Tasiadis, Sideris 1383
ダーシィ
D'Arcy, Yvonne M. 319
タシウ
Tassiou, Aminou 1383
タシエス
Tàssies, José Antonio 1383
タジェディニ
Tajeddini, Mohammad-Reza 1377
タシエフ
Tashiyev, Kamchybek 1383
タシク
Tkacik, John J., Jr. 1407
タジク
Tajik, Hadia 1377
ダシグリ
Dassigli, Barnabé 321
タシジアン
Tashjian, Armen H. 1383
ターシス
Tarshis, Lauren 1382
ダシゼベギーン・バンズラグチ
Dashzevegiin Banzragch 321
タシック
Tkacik, John J., Jr. 1407
ダシドルジ
Dashdorj, Tsedeviin 321
ダシドルジーン・ナツァグドルジ
Dashdorjiin Natsagdorj 321
ダシドンドク
Dasidongdog, Jambaa iin 321
ダシドンドグ
Dasidongdog, Jambaa iin 321
タシナリ
Tassinari, Renato 1383
タシバエフ
Tashbayev, Uchkunbek 1383
タシパエワ
Tashpayeva, Nazgul 1383
ダシプルブ
Dashpurėv, Danzankhorloogiĭn 321
ダジャンス
Dagens, Bruno 312
ダーシュ
Das, Jibanananda 320
ダージュ
D'Arge, Ralph C. 319
ダシュ
Dash, Shobha Rani 321
ダーシュウィッツ
Dershwitz, Eli 344
ダシュクス
Dushkes, Laura S. 384
ダシュティ
Dashti, Rola Abdullah 321
ダシュドング・ゲレルマ
Dashdondog Gerelmaa 321
タシュナー
Taschner, Rudolf Josef 1383
ダシュナー
Dashner, James 321
ダシュル
Daschle, Thomas Andrew 320
タシュロー
Taschereau, Ghislain 1383
ダーショウィッツ
Dershowitz, Alan M. 344
タージョン
Turgeon, Alfred J. 1427
Turgeon, Mélanie 1427
ダジョン
Dudgeon, Gus 377
タージリ
Turzilli, Andrew 1429
ダシルヴァ
DeSilva, Bruce 345
ダ・シルバ
Da Silva, Bernarda Gonçalves Martins Henriques 321
ダ＝シルバ
Da Silva, Wellington L. S. 321
ダシルバ
da Silva, Adhemar 321
Da Silva, Altobeli 321
Da Silva, António Heriques 321
Da Silva, Arcanjo 321
Da Silva, Bernarda Gonçalves Martins Henriques 321
Da Silva, Cândida Celeste 321
Da Silva, Estanislau 321
Da Silva, Geoffrey 321
Da Silva, Joice Souza 321
Da Silva, Julio Lopes Lima 321
Da Silva, Luís Filipe 321
Da Silva, Mauro Vinicius 321
Da Silva, Pedro 321
da Silva, Rui Gomes 321
Da Silva, Thiago Braz 321
DeSilva, Bruce 345
ダシルバフェレイラ
Da Silva Ferreira, Aline 321
タシーロ
Tuccillo, Liz 1425
タージン
Tashjian, Jake 1383
Tashjian, Janet 1383
タジン
Tazhin, Marat 1387
ダーシン
Dassin, Jules 321
ダージン
Durgin, Doranna 383
ダシンスキー
Dashinski, Dmitri 321
タース
Turse, Nick 1429
タス
Tuss, David J. 1429
ダース
Dars, Jean François 320
Das, Gurcharan 320
ダス
Das, Amitava 320
Das, Ashok 320
Das, Jagannath Prasad 320
Das, Mouma 320
Das, Satyajit 320
Das, Veena 320
Dass, Veena 321
タスア
Tassoua, Jean-Marie 1383
タースィム
Tarsem 1382
タスカ
Tasca, Cathrine 1383
Tasker, Peter 1383
タスカー
Tasker, Peter 1383
ダスカレスク
Dascalescu, Constantin 320
ダスカロス
Daskalos 321
ダスキエ
Dasquié, Guillaume 321
ダスク
Dusk, Matt 384
タスクディス
Taskoudis, Apostolos 1383
ダースグプタ
Dasgupta, Ajit Kumar 321
ダスグプタ
Dasgupta, Partha Sarathi 321
Dasgupta, Rana 321
Dasgupta, Sunil 321
ダスティー
Dusty, Slim 384
ダスティス・ケセド
Dastis Quecedo, Alfonso María 321
ダスティン
Dustin, Elfriede 384
ダステュール
Dastur, Françoise 321
ダスデレン
Dasdelen, Aylin 320
ダスネベス
Das Neves, Delfim Santiago 321
Das Neves, Maria 321
タスファイエ
Tesfaye, Gelaye 1392
タスマガムベトフ
Tasmagambetov, Imangali 1383
タスマン
Tasman, Allan 1383
タスムラドフ
Tasmuradov, Elmurat 1383
ダスムンシ
Dasmunsi, Priyaranjan 321
ダスワーニ
Daswani, Kavita 321
タゼギュル
Tazegül, Servet 1387
ターセム
Tarsem 1382
ダゾ
Dazo, Bong 329
タソバッツ
Tasovac, Ivan 1383
ダソバッツ
Tasovac, Ivan 1383
タータ―
Tata, Ratan N. 1383
タタ
Tata, Ratan N. 1383
タダ
Tada, Joni Eareckson 1376
ダダ
Dada, Héctor Miguel Antonio 311
ダダエ
Dadae, Bob 312
タターソル
Tattersall, Ian 1383
タタソール
Tattersall, Graham 1383
ダダバエフ
Dadabaev, Timur 312
ダダモ
D'Adamo, Francesco 312
D'Adamo, Peter J. 312
タータ―リャ
Tartaglia, Louis A. 1382
タタル
Tatar, Nur 1383
タタルシャヌ
Tatarusanu, Ciprian 1383
タタルニコフ
Tatarnikov, Mikhail 1383
タタレワ
Tatareva, Anastasiia 1383
タタロウル
Tataroglu, Selim 1383
ダータン
Datan, Merav 321
タチ
Thaçi, Hashim 1393
ダチ
Dati, Rachida 321
ターチェウスキー
Tarczewski, Kaleb 1382
タチェバ
Tatcheva, Eva 1383
タチェワ
Tacheva, Miglena 1376
ダチッチ
Dačić, Ivica 311
タチュ
Thach, Kim Tuan 1393
タチルタール
Tati Loutard, Jean-Baptiste 1383
ターチン
Turchin, Peter 1427
ターツ
Turtu, Tony 1429
ターツァキアン
Tertzakian, Peter 1392
ダツィエーリ
Dazieri, Sandrone 329
タッカー
Thacker, Ed 1393
Thakkar, Meghraj 1393
Tucker, Beverley D. 1425
Tucker, Bruce 1425
Tucker, Chris 1425
Tucker, Cory 1425

Tucker, Cynthia DeLores 1425
Tucker, Harry 1425
Tucker, Holly 1425
Tucker, Jim B. 1425
Tucker, Jonathan B. 1425
Tucker, Justin 1425
Tucker, K.A. 1425
Tucker, Linda 1425
Tucker, Marcus 1425
Tucker, Mark 1425
Tucker, Mary Evelyn 1425
Tucker, Matthew 1425
Tucker, Mike 1425
Tucker, P.J. 1425
Tucker, Preston 1425

タッカレー
Thackeray, Bal 1393

ダッガン
Duggan, Hoyt N. 379

タッキーニ
Tacchini, Carlo 1376

タッキーノ
Tacchino, Gabriel 1376

タック
Tak, Peter J.P. 1377
Tuck, Lily 1425
Tuck, Richard 1425

タッグ
Tagg, Christine 1376

ダック
Duck, Jeanie Daniel 377
Duck, Steve 377

タックシン・チンナワット
Thaksin Shinawatra 1393

ダックスフィールド
Duxfield, Stephen 385

タックマン
Tuckman, Bruce 1425

タッグル
Tuggle, Justin 1426

ダックワース
Duckworth, Angela 377
Duckworth, Bruce 377
Duckworth, Katie 377
Duckworth, Ruth 377

タッゲディン
Taggeddin, Muhammad Awad 1376

タッケライ
Thackeray, Bal 1393

ダッコ
Dacko, Bruno 311
Dacko, David 311

タッコーネ
Taccone, Sergio 1376

ダッサン
Dessain, Vincent 346

タッジ
Tudge, Colin 1425

ダッジ
Dodge, Kenneth A. 362

タッシェン
Taschen, Angelika 1383
Taschen, Benedikt 1383

ダッシュ
Dash, Mike 321
Dash, Phil 321

ダッシュル
Daschle, Thomas Andrew 320

ダッシン
Dassin, Jules 321

ダッタ
Datta, Bidhan 321
Datta, E.Kyle 321
Datta, Sanjay 321
Datta, Saugato 321

ダッダ
Daddah, Brahim Ould 312
Daddah, Mokhtar Ould 312

タッターソール
Tattersall, Kirsty 1383

タッターソル
Tattersall, Ian 1383

ダッタトレーヤ
Dattatreya, Ravi E. 321

ダッタトレヤ
Dattatreya, Bandaru 321

タッチェル
Tatchell, Terri 1383

ダッチ・サベージ
Dutch Savage 384

ダッチャー
Dacher, Elliott S. 311
Dutcher, Jamie 384
Dutcher, Jim 384

タッデーイ
Taddei, Giuseppe 1376

タッデイ
Taddei, Giuseppe 1376
Taddei, Mario 1376

タッデイ
Taddei, Giuseppe 1376

ダッティリオ
Dattilio, Frank M. 321

ダッデン
Dudden, Faye E. 377

ダット
Dutt, Sunil 384

ダッド
Daddo, Andrew 312

ダッドソン
Dodson, James 362

ダットフィールド
Dutfield, Graham 384

タッドマン
Tadman, David 1376

ダットリ
Dattoli, Michael 321

ダッドリー
Dudley, Robert 377
Dudley, Underwood 377

タットン
Tutton, Chloe 1429

ダットン
Dutton, Garrett 385
Dutton, Janis 385
Dutton, Judy 385
Dutton, June 385
Dutton, Kevin 385
Dutton, Peter 385
Dutton, Phillip 385
Dutton, William H. 385

ダツナシビリ
Datunashvili, Zurabi 321

タツノ
Tatsuno, Dave 1383

タッパー
Tapper, Charles 1381
Tapper, Harold 1381
Tapper, Melissa 1381

ダッバス
Dabbas, Osama 311
Dabbas, Rabehah 311

タッパート
Tappert, Horst 1381

タップ
Ntap, Innocence 1036
Tapp, Darryl 1381
Tapp, Ian 1381

タッペ
Tappe, Horst 1381

タツミ
Tatsumi, Jo 1383
Tatsumi, Yukio 1383

タッラーウィ
Tallawy, Mervat 1378

ダッラージ
al-Daraji, Muhammed Sahib 319

ダッリ
Dalli, Helena 314

ターツロー
Turturro, John 1429

ダデ
Dade, Arta 312

ダティ
Dati, Rachida 321

タディエ
Tadie, Jean-Yves 1376

ダティス
Datis, Tony "Truand" 321

タディチ
Tadić, Dušan 1376

タディッチ
Tadić, Boris 1376
Tadic, Dusan 1376
Tadic, Tonci 1376

タティ・ルタール
Tati Loutard, Jean-Baptiste 1383

タティルータール
Tati Loutard, Jean-Baptiste 1383

タデセ
Tadese, Zersenay 1376

タデッセ
Tadese, Zersenay 1376

タデボシャン
Tadevosyan, Samvel 1376

ダーデン
Durden, Kenneth 383

タート
Tart, Charles T. 1382
Tartt, Donna 1383
Tartt, Jaquiski 1383

ダート
Dart, Jocelyn 320
Dart, Justin 320
Dart, Raymond A. 320

ダートゥゾス
Dertouzos, Michael L. 344

ダートウゾス
Dertouzos, Michael L. 344

ダトゥナシヴィリ
Datunashvili, Levan 321

ダトゥナシビリ
Datunashvili, Zurabi 321

ダトゥマノン
Datumanong, Simeon 321

タトゥーロ
Turturro, John 1429

ダトカ
Dutka, Jacques 384

ダドソン
Dodson, Terry 362

ダトナウ
Datnow, Amanda 321

ダドナジ
Dadnadji, Djimrangar 312

ダドニー
Dudney, Bill 377

ダートネル
Dartnell, Julie 320
Dartnell, Lewis 320

ダドファル
Dadfar, Ahzam 312
Dadfar, Mohammad Azam 312

ダトマノン
Datumanong, Simeon 321

ダドマン
Dadman, Rahman 312

タトラ
Tatola, Benaindo 1383

ダドリー
Dudley, George Austin 377
Dudley, Jared 377
Dudley, Michael Kioni 377
Dudley, Robert Warren 377
Dudley, William C. 377

タトル
Tuttle, Cameron 1429
Tuttle, Lisa 1429
Tuttle, William 1429

ダドル
Duddle, Jonny 377

タドルース
Tadrous, Mamdouh Riyad 1376

タートルトーブ
Turteltaub, Jon 1429

タートルトブ
Turteltaub, Saul 1429

タトルベン
Totleben, John 1414

タトロー
Tatlow, Ruth 1383

ダトロウ
Datlow, Ellen 321

タートン
Turton, Nigel D. 1429

ターナー
Tanner, Renée 1381
Tannor, David Joshua 1381
Turner, Adair 1428
Turner, Alice K. 1428
Turner, Alwyn W. 1428
Turner, Anthea 1428
Turner, Billy 1428
Turner, Bryan M. 1428
Turner, Bryan S. 1428
Turner, Colin 1428
Turner, Dale 1428
Turner, David 1428
Turner, Deborah 1428
Turner, Dennis C. 1428
Turner, Dona 1428
Turner, Elston 1428
Turner, Evan 1428
Turner, Fred L. 1428
Turner, Graeme 1428
Turner, Graham 1428
Turner, Henry Ashby, Jr. 1428
Turner, Howard R. 1428
Turner, Ike 1428
Turner, J.A. 1428
Turner, Jacob 1428

タ

Turner, James 1428
Turner, Jarvis 1428
Turner, Jason 1428
Turner, Jerome 1428
Turner, Joe Lynn 1428
Turner, John 1428
Turner, Jonathan H. 1428
Turner, Jon "Pearljammer" 1428
Turner, J.Scott 1428
Turner, Justin 1428
Turner, Kate 1428
Turner, Katharine 1428
Turner, Kathleen 1428
Turner, Kelly A. 1428
Turner, Landon 1428
Turner, Lewis 1428
Turner, Linda 1428
Turner, Lyndsey 1428
Turner, Marcia Layton 1428
Turner, Martha A. 1428
Turner, Matt 1428
Turner, Megan Whalen 1428
Turner, Michael 1428
Turner, Michael S. 1428
Turner, Monica Goigel 1428
Turner, Myles 1428
Turner, Norv 1428
Turner, Pamela S. 1428
Turner, Paul 1429
Turner, Philip 1429
Turner, Philip C. 1429
Turner, Piers Norris 1429
Turner, Richard 1429
Turner, R.Kerry 1429
Turner, Sandy 1429
Turner, Sarah E. 1429
Turner, Sheldon 1429
Turner, Steve 1429
Turner, Stuart 1429
Turner, Ted 1429
Turner, Toni 1429
Turner, Tracey 1429
Turner, Trai 1429
Turner, Trea 1429
Turner, Trevor 1429
Turner, V.J. 1429

タナ
Tana 1380

タナー
Tanner, Christine A. 1381
Tanner, Chuck 1381
Tanner, Julia 1381
Tanner, Lindsay 1381
Tanner, Norman P. 1381
Tanner, Rob 1381

ダナ
Dana, Barbara 316
Dana, Paul 316
Dana, Thierry 316
Danna, Mychael 318

ダナー
Danner, Blythe 318

ダナイロフ
Danailov, Stefan 316

ダナウェイ
Dunaway, Faye 380
Dunaway, Michele 380

タナウス
Tanous, Peter J. 1381

タナエフ
Tanayev, Nikolai 1380

タナカ
Tanaka, Emilia 1380
Tanaka, John 1380
Tanaka, Kenneth Ken'ichi 1380
Tanaka, Rodney Shinichi 1380
Tanaka, Shelly 1380
Tanaka, Wayne Norio 1380

ダナゴゴ
Danagogo, Tamuno 316

タナサック
Tanasak, Patimapragorn 1380

タナサン
Tanasan, Sopita 1380

ダナシュタイン
Dennerstein, Lorraine 342

タナズ
Tanase, Virgil 1380

タナセ
Tanase, Alexandru 1380

タナセスク
Tănăsescu, Mihai Nicolae 1380

タナタロフ
Tanatarov, Akzhurek 1380

タナット
Thanat Khoman 1394

タナット・コーマン
Thanat Khoman 1394

タナニヤアナン
Thanya-anan, Andrew V. 1394

ダナハー
Danaher, Simon 316

ダナヒー
Donaghy, Marie 365

タナヒル
Tannahill, Reay 1380

タナベ
Tanabe, Georg J., Jr. 1380
Tanabe, Koji 1380

ダナーマーク
Danermark, Berth 316

ダナム
Dunham, Lena 381
Dunham, Mikel 381

ダナリス
Danalis, John 316
Danalis, Stella 316

ダナン
Dhennin, Didier 349

タナンガダ
Tanangada, Jimson Fiau 1380

ターニー
Turney, Alan J. 1429
Turney, Chris 1429

タニ
Thani, Hridaya Ram 1394
Al-thani, Sheikh Ali 1394

タニー
Tanney, Alex 1381
Tunney, Stephen 1427

ダニー
Danny, Budiman Widjaja 318

ダニ・イグレシアス
Dani Iglesias 318

ダニエウ・アウヴェス
Daniel Alves 317

ダニエリアン
Danielyan, Edgar 318

ダニエリャン
Danielyan, Gevorg 318

ダニエル
Daniel, Amas 317
Daniel, Antoine B. 317
Daniel, Antonio Salvador 317
Daniel, Catherine 317
Daniel, Chase 317
Daniel, David Edwin 317
Daniel, Fielding 317
Daniel, Jean 317
Daniel, Jennifer 317
Daniel, John Morgan 317
Daniel, Matt "Boom" 317
Daniel, Montgomery 317
Daniel, Patricia 317
Daniel, Pete 317
Daniel, Robertson 317
Daniel, Roh 317
Daniel, Thomas 317
Daniel, Timothy P. 317
Daniel, Toara 317
Daniel, Werner G. 317
Daniel, Willmoth 317
Daniell, David 317
Daniell, John 317
Daniels, Maygene 317

ダニエルー
Daniélou, Alain 317

ダニエルス
Daniels, Christian 317
Daniels, Martha Catalina 317
Daniels, Michael 317

ダニエルズ
Daniels, Andrew 317
Daniels, B.J. 317
Daniels, Charlie 317
Daniels, Elle 317
Daniels, Gordon 317
Daniels, Harry 317
Daniels, Jack 317
Daniels, Jeff 317
Daniels, Jill 317
Daniels, John 317
Daniels, Joleen 317
Daniels, Jon 317
Daniels, Ken 317
Daniels, Lee 317
Daniels, Lucy 317
Daniels, Mike 317
Daniels, Mitchell E. 317
Daniels, Neil Andrew 317
Daniels, Norman 317
Daniels, Ray 317
Daniels, Rebecca 317
Daniels, Robert Vincent 317
Daniels, Stephen 317
Daniels, Steven 317
Daniels, Troy 317
Daniels, Val 317

ダニエルズ＝モーリング
Daniels-Mohring, Debbie 317

ダニエルソン
Danielson, Dennis Richard 318
Danielsson, Maria 318

ダニエル・タベット
Daniel Tabet, Joumana 318

ダニエル・トーレス
Daniel Torres 318

ダニエルマイヤー
Danielmeyer, Hans Gunter 317

ダニエル・ルシュール
Daniel-Lesur, J.Y. 317

ダニエル・レイビー
Daniel Raby, Lucy 317

ダニエーレ
Daniele, Pino 317

ダニエレブスキー
Danielewski, Mark Z. 317

ダニエロ
D'aniello, Francesco 317

ダニオス
Danioth, David 318

ダニオッティ
Daniotti, Tiziano 318

ダニ・カステジャーノ
Dani Castellano 317

ダニ・ガルシア
Dani Garcia 318

タニガワ
Tanigawa, Katsuki 1380
Tanigawa, Nobuhiko 1380

タニグチ
Taniguchi, José Kiyoshi 1380
Taniguchi, Yoshio 1380

タニクリフ
Tunnicliffe, Anna 1427

ダニシュ
Danish, Mohammad Sarwar 318
Danish, Sarwar 318

ダニス
Danis, Daniel 318

ダニ・セバージョス
Dani Ceballos 317

ダニチェー
Dunnichay, Mary Beth 382

ダニーノ
Dagnino, Fernando 312

ダニノス
Daninos, Pierre 318

ダニ・ヒメネス
Dani Gimenez 318

ダニリシン
Danilishin, Bohdan 318

ダニーリャン
Danielyan, Edgar 318

ダニリュク
Danyliuk, Olexandr 318

ダニリン
Danilin, Igor Mikhailovich 318

ダニーロ
Danilo 318
Danilo, Barbosa 318
Danilo, Pereira 318

ダニーロ・シウヴァ
Danilo Silva 318

ダニロフ
Danilov, Aleksandr Anatol'evich 318

ダニロフスキ
Danilovski, Dragan 318

ダニロワ
Danilova, Olga 318

ダーニング
Durning, Charles 384
Durning, Steven J. 384

ダニング
Dunning, Donna 382
Dunning, Eric 382
Dunning, John 382
Dunning, Ted 382

タ

タヌイ
Tanui, Paul Kipngetich 1381
タヌカレ
Tanukale, Taom 1381
ダヌレ
Danulle, Ahmad Muhammad 318
ターネイ
Tierney, Michael 1404
タネコ
Taneko, Augustine 1380
ダネージ
Danesi, Marcel 316
タネジャ
Taneja, Nawal K. 1380
ダネシュアシティアニ
Danesh Ashtiani, Fakhroddinn 316
ダネシュジャファリ
Danesh Jafari, Davoud 316
ダネシュジュー
Daneshjoo, Kamran 316
タネバ
Taneva, Desislava 1380
タネヒル
Tannehill, Ryan 1380
タネフ
Tanev, Todor 1380
ダネリー
Dannelley, Richard 318
ダネリア
Danelia, Otar 316
ターネル
Turnell, Andrew 1428
タネル
Tanel, Franco 1380
Tunnell, Lee 1427
ダーネル
Darnell, James E. 320
ダーネル・ステンソン
Stenson, Dernell 1347
ダネレク
Danelek, J.Allan 316
タネン
Tannen, Deborah 1380
タネンハウス
Tanenhaus, David Spinoza 1380
タネンバウム
Tanenbaum, Andrew S. 1380
Tanenbaum, Susie J. 1380
ダネンバーグ
Danenberg, Anne 316
タネンボーム
Tanenbaum, Robert K. 1380
タノ
Tano 1381
タノー
Tanoh, Thierry 1381
ダノ
Dano, Paul 318
Dano, Sébastien 318
ダーノウ
D'amaud, Travis 315
D'arnaud, Chase 320
タノヴィッチ
Tanović, Danis 1381
ダノウスキ
Danowski, Sonja 318
ダノ・ジェジェ
Dano Djédjé, Sébastien 318
ダノジェジェ
Dano Djédjé, Sébastien 318
ダーノシュ
Dános, Judit 318
タノック
Tannock, Ian 1381
Tannock, Stuart 1381
タノビッチ
Tanović, Danis 1381
ダーノフスキー
Darnovsky, Marcy 320
タノム・キッティカチョーン
Thanom Kittikachorn 1394
タノム・キッティカチョン
Thanom Kittikachorn 1394
タノム・キティカチョーン
Thanom Kittikachorn 1394
タノム・キティカチョン
Thanom Kittikachorn 1394
ダノンコート
d'Harnoncourt, Anne 349
ダノン＝ボワロー
Danon-Boileau, Laurent 318
ターバー
Tabár, László 1375
タハ
Tah, Sidi Ould 1376
Taha, Ali Osman Mohammed 1376
Taha, al-Zubeir Bashir 1376
タパ
Thapa, Dharma Bahadur 1394
Thapa, Gagan Kumar 1394
Thapa, Kamal 1394
Thapa, Manjushree 1394
Thapa, Ram Bahadur 1394
Thapa, Shiva 1394
Thapa, Surya Bahadur 1394
ダーバー
Durber, Matt 383
ダバー
Davaa, Byambasuren 322
タハ・アウディ
Taha Audi, Abir 1376
ダバァーギーン・バトバヤル
Davaagiin Batbayar 322
タバカ
Tabaka, Arta 1375
タバク
Tabak, John 1375
ダ・バーグ
De Burgh, Jane 331
ダハク
Dahak, Driss 312
タバコフ
Tabakov, Oleg Pavlovich 1375
タバコリ
Tavakoli, Janet M. 1384
ダバシ
Dabashi, Hamid 311
ダーバス
Darvas, Nicolas 320
ダバ・スミス
Dabba Smith, Frank 311
タバータバーイー
Tabatabaei, Mohammad Mahdi 1375
al-Tabātabā'ī, Muhammad Husayn 1375
ダバタビィ
Tabatabaee, Ali 1375
タバチニク
Tabachnik, Dmytro 1375
Tabachnyk, Dmytro 1375
タバチニコフ
Tabachnikov, Serge 1375
タバック
Taback, Simms 1375
ダハティ
Doherty, Fraser 363
ダバーディ
Davoudi, Parviz 327
ダバディー
Dabadie, Florent 311
タバヌ
Tabanou, Franck 1375
タハネ
Thahane, Timothy 1393
タバネ
Tabane, Titabu 1375
Thabane, Motsoahae Thomas 1393
ダハバ
Dahaba, Abubacar Demba 312
ダバー・バトバヤル
Davaagiin Batbayar 322
ダハビ
Dahabi, Nader al 312
タバーフ
Tabakh, Ekaterina 1375
タパホンソ
Tapahonso, Luci 1381
タハミ
Tahmi, Mohamed 1377
ダバヤティアンチュ
Dabaya Tientcheu, Vencelas 311
ダバヤティエンチェ
Dabaya Tientcheu, Vencelas 311
タバラ
Tabără, Valeriu 1375
タバル
Tabar, Malakai 1375
ダハル
Dahal, Pushpa Kamal 312
al-Dahar, Munib Saim 312
ダバル
Tabar, Malakai 1375
タバルジエフ
Tabaldiev, Busurmankul 1375
タバレス
Tabárez, Óscar 1375
Tavares, Ângelo De Barros Veiga 1384
Tavares, Carlos 1384
Tavares, Helder Magno Proenca Mendes 1384
Tavares, Luís Filipe Lopes 1384
Tavares, Martus 1384
Tavares, Octavio 1384
Tavares, Walter 1384
Tavarez, Aneury 1384
Tavarez, Shannon 1384
Tavarres, Myke 1384
タバレスベイガ
Tavares Veiga, Justino 1384
タバレフ
Tabarev, Andrei 1375
ダハロ
Dahalob, Hamid Mahamat 312
ダハロップ
Dahalob, Hamid Mahamat 312
ターバン
Terban, Marvin 1391
ダーハン
Dahan, André 312
Dahan, Udi 312
ダハン
Dahan, Nissim 312
ダバンガ
Dabanga, Theodore 311
タパンガラルア
Tapangararua, Willy Jimmy 1381
タバン・デン
Taban Deng, Gai 1375
タービー
Turvey, Nicholas 1429
タビ
Tabi, Banabas 1375
Tavai, J.R. 1384
ダーヒー
Dahy, Hany 313
ダービー
Darby, Alden 319
Darby, Ronald 319
Darby, Sabrina 319
Derby, A.J. 344
Derby, Susan 344
タヒア
Tahir, Sabaa 1376
タピア
Tapia, Bill 1381
Tapia, Johnny 1381
Tapia, Lorena 1381
Tapia, Raimel 1381
Tapia, Ramiro 1381
ダヒア
Dahir, C.A. 312
タピアス
Tapias, Alcides 1381
タビアーニ
Taviani, Paolo 1384
Taviani, Vittorio 1384
ダビエ
Dabie, Ali Souleymane 311
タピエス
Tàpies, Antoni 1381
タピコフ
Tupicoff, Dennis 1427
ダービーシャー
Darbyshire, Carolyn 319
Derbyshire, John 344
ダビジャン
Davidian, Norair 323
タビストック
Tavistock, Aaron 1384
ダビタイア
Davitaia, Mirza 327
ダビタシビリ
Davitashvili, Levan 327
ダービック
Darvic, Stevie Creo 320

ダービッツ
Davids, Edgar 323
ダビッツ
Davids, Edgar 323
ダビッド
David, Joaquim Duarte Da Costa 322
ダビッドソン
Davidson, Basil Risbridger 323
Davidson, Carli 323
Davidson, Jeffrey P. 323
ダビデンコ
Davydenko, Nikolay 327
ダビド
David, Houdeingar 322
Dávid, Ibolya 322
David, James Burty 322
David, Ophelie 323
ダビドウ
Davidow, William H. 323
タヒトゥア
Tahitu'a, Viliami 1376
ダビド・ガルシア
David Garcia 323
ダビド・コスタス
David Costas 323
ダビド・コンチャ
David Concha 323
ダビド・シモン
David Simon 323
ダビド・ソリア
David Soria 323
ダビドソン
Davidson, H.Christian 323
ダビド・ビージャ
David Villa 324
ダビド・ビジャ
David Villa 324
ダビドビッチ
Davidovich, Maayan 323
Dawidowicz, Aleksandra 328
ダビドフ
Davidoff, Jules 323
ダビド・ラミレス
David Ramirez 323
ダビド・ロペス
David Lopez 323
ダビドワ
Davydova, Anastasia 327
Davydova, Natalya 328
ターピニアン
Tarpinian, Steve 1382
ダビニッチ
Davinić, Prvoslav 325
ダビ・ビリヤ
David Villa 324
タヒミック
Tahimik, Kidlat 1376
タヒム
Thahim, Abdul Razzaq 1393
タヒューヒュー
Te Heuheu, Georgina 1388
ダビラ
Dávila, Amanda 325
Dávila, Claudia 325
Dávila, Luis 325
Davila, Tony 325
タヒリ
Tahiri, Edita 1376
Tahiri, Saimir 1376
ダーヒリ
al-Dhaheri, Hadef bin Jawa'an 349
al-Dhahiri, Muhammad Nukhaira 349
ダヒリ
al-Dakhil, Azzam bin Mohammed 313
ターヒル
Tahir, Muhammad Barjees 1376
タヒル
al-Tahir, al-Tigani Adam 1376
Tahir, Marie 1376
ダービル
Darville, Michael 320
ダヒール
Dekhil, Rafaa 335
ダヒル
Dahir, Fahad Yasin Haji 312
Dakhil, Rafaâ 313
ダビルグ
Dabilougou, Vincent T. 311
タービン
Turbin, Cassidy 1427
Turbin, Robert 1427
ターピン
Turpin, Ian 1429
ダービン
Durbin, Deanna 383
Durbin, James 383
Durbin, Richard 383
ダビン
Dubbin, William 376
タープ
Tharp, Van K. 1394
タフ
Tough, Paul 1414
タブ
Tubb, E.C. 1425
Tubb, Jonathan N. 1425
ダフ
Duff, Annis 378
Duff, Jeremy 378
Duff, Jim 378
Duff, Russell Gordon 378
ダブ
Dab, Moukhtar Wawa 311
Dabu, Anna 311
Dove, Anthea 371
Dove, Roja 371
タファイ
Tafaj, Myqerem 1376
ダファイー
al-Dafaee, Abdullah Hussein 312
ダーフィ
Durphy, Michael 384
ダーフィー
Durfee, Michael 383
ダフィ
Duffy, Carol Ann 378
Duffy, David 378
Duffy, Peter 378
Duffy, Stella 378
ダフィー
Duffey, Tyler 378
Duffie, Darrell 378
Duffy 378
Duffy, Danny 378
Duffy, Flora 378
Duffy, James D. 378
Duffy, Kate 378
Duffy, Margaret Gooch 378
Duffy, Mary Grace 378
Duffy, Matt 378
Duffy, Michael 378
Duffy, Patricia Lynne 378
ダブイドフ
Dabydov, Ilyas 311
タブイルジエフ
Tabyldiyev, Tynychbek 1376
ダブウィド
Dabwido, Sprent 311
タブエナ
Tabuena, Miguel Luis 1375
ターフェル
Terfel, Bryn 1391
ダフォー
Dafoe, Willem 312
ダフォフスカ
Dafovska, Ekaterina 312
ダ・フォンセカ
Da Fonseca, Fernando Alberto Soares 312
ダフォンセカ
Da Fonseca, Fernando Alberto Soares 312
タブキ
Tabke, Karin 1375
タプグン
Tapgun, Fidelis 1381
タフコ
Tahko, Tuomas E. 1376
ダブコフスキー
Dubcovsky, Jorge 376
ダブス
Dabbs, James McBride 311
Dabbs, Mary Godwin 311
ダブス＝オルソップ
Dobbs-Allsopp, F.W. 361
タプスコット
Tapscott, Alex 1381
Tapscott, Don 1381
タプソバ
Tapsoba, Achille 1381
ダプソバ
Tapsoba, Pierre Joseph Emmanuel 1381
タフタジャン
Takhtajan, Leon A. 1377
タブタバイ
al-Tabtabai, Adel Taleb 1375
ダフチャン
Davtyan, Gevorg 327
Davtyan, Hovhannes 327
ダブチャン
Davtyan, Tigran 327
タフツィディス
Tachtsidis, Panagiotis 1376
タブッキ
Tabucchi, Antonio 1375
タフト
Taft, Bob 1376
Tuft, Svein 1425
ダフード
Dahoud, Mahmoud 313
ダフト
Daft, Richard L. 312
ダブドフ
Davudov, Yusup 327
タフトン
Tufton, Christopher 1425
ダフトン
Dufton, Jennifer 378
タブナ
Tabuna, Dominic 1376
タブナー
Tavener, John 1384
ダブナー
Dabner, David 311
Dubner, Ronald 376
Dubner, Stephen J. 376
ダブニー
Dabney, Alan 311
ダーフホス
Dagevos, J.C. 312
タフマセビ
Tahmasbi, Alireza 1376
ダフヤン
Davtyan, Hovhannes 327
ダブラトフ
Davlatov, Matlubkhon 327
ダフララ
Dakhlallah, Mahdi 313
ダブラル
Du Brul, Jack B. 377
タフーリ
Tafuri, Manfredo 1376
タフリ
Tafuri, Nancy 1376
タプリー
Tapley, Rebecca 1381
タブリアン
Taborian, Alain 1375
ダブリエ
Davrieux, Ariel 327
タブリージ
Tabrizi, Behnam N. 1375
タブリズリ
Tabrizli, Sirus 1375
ダブリュー
W., Bill 1466
タプリン
Taplin, Bralon 1381
Taplin, Sam 1381
ダブルデイ
Doubleday, Nelson, Jr. 369
Doubleday, Simon R. 369
ダフルビル
Dafreville, Yves-Matthieu 312
タープレイ
Tarpley, Webster Griffin 1382
タフレイト
Tafrate, Raymond Chip 1376
ダブレオ
D'abreu, Osvaldo Cravid Viegas 311
タフレシ
Tafreshi, Babak A. 1376
ダブロー
Dubrow, Kevin 377
ダブロウスキー
Dabrowski, Gabriela 311
ダブロースキー
Dubrawsky, Ido 377
ダブロック
DuBrock, A. 377
ターペ
Tarpeh, Etomonia 1382

タ

タペ
Tarpeh, Etomonia 1382
ダベ
Dave, Anil Madhav 322
ダベイガ
Da Veiga, Pimenta 322
タベッキオ
Tavecchio, Giorgio 1384
ターベット
Tarbett, Debbie 1382
ダベニー
D'Aveni, Richard A. 322
ダベラクルス
Da Veracruz, Tome Soares 322
タベラス
Taveras, Oscar 1384
ターヘル
al-Taher, Abdulrahman 1376
ターベル
Tarbell, Alan 1382
タヘル
Taher, Issa Ali 1376
ダヘル
Daher, Ibrahim 312
タベルニエ
Tavernier, Alexandra 1384
Tavernier, Bertrand 1384
Tavernier, Jef 1384
Tavernier, Nils 1384
ダベンポート
Davenport, Deborah J. 322
Davenport, Fionn 322
Davenport, Jim 322
Davenport, John 322
Davenport, Lindsay 322
Davenport, Liz 322
Davenport, Nigel 322
Davenport, Noa 322
Davenport, Thomas H. 322
Davenport, Willie 322
タボ
Tavo, Vangjel 1384
タポ
Tapo, Abdoulaye Garba 1381
ダーボ
D'Abo, Christine 311
ダボウブ
Daboub, Juan José 311
タボエ
Taboye, Ahamat 1375
タボガ
Taboga, Giorgio 1375
ターボックス
Tarbox, Katherine 1382
タボーネ
Tabone, Vincent 1375
タボネ
Tabone, Vincent 1375
ダホメス
Dajomes, Neisi 313
タポヨ
Tapoyo, Alexandre 1381
タボラ
Tavola, Kaliopate 1384
タボーリ
Tabori, George 1375
タボリ
Tabori, George 1375
タボリヤン
Taborian, Alain 1375
ダーポン
Dapong, Ratanasuwan 319
ダポン
Dapong, Ratanasuwan 319
ダボンヌ
Dabonne, Zoulehia Abzetta 311
タマキ
Tamaki, Jullian 1379
Tamaki, Mariko 1379
Tamaki, Tadashi 1379
ダマシオ
Damasio, Antonio R. 315
ダマージュ
Damaj, Marwan Ahmed 315
タマシュ・ソモラツ
Tamas Somoracz 1379
タマセビ
Tahmasebi, Sha 1376
ダマティ
el-Damaty, Mamdouh 315
al-Damaty, Mamduh 315
ダマディアン
Damadian, Raymond V. 315
ダマディンスレン
Damdinsuren, Nyamkhuu 315
ダマート
D'Amato, Barbara 315
タマナハ
Tamanaha, Brian Z. 1379
タマーニ
Tamagni, Daniele 1379
ダマーニ
Damani, Nizam N. 315
ダーマニン
Darmanin, Lisa 320
ダマノスキ
Dumanoski, Dianne 380
タマヨ・フロレス
Tamayo Flores, Gonzalo Francisco 1379
タマラウ
Tamarau, Soso 1379
ターマリ
Taamari, Salah 1375
タマリッツ
Tamariz, Juan 1379
ダマルージ
al-Damalooji, Omar 315
タマーロ
Tamaro, Susanna 1379
ターマン
Tirman, Phillip F.J. 1406
Turman, John 1428
ダーマン
Darman, Richard Gordon 320
Derman, Emanuel 344
ターマンセン
Termansen, Jacob 1392
タミー
Tamme, Jacob 1379
ダミ
Dhami, Narinder 349
ダミアーニ
Damiani, Damiano 315
Damiani, Ludovica 316
Damiani, Salvatore 316
ダミアーノ
Damiano, Cesare 316
Damiano, Gerard 316
ダミアノ
Damiano, Gerard 316
ダミアン
Damian, Anca 315
Damian, Georgeta 315
Damian, Kate 315
Damian, Peter 315
ダミコ
D'Amico, Carmela 316
D'Amico, Steven 316
ダミッシュ
Damisch, Hubert 316
ダミトゥ
Demitu, Hambissa 340
タミニ
Tamini, Pascaline 1379
タミヌビウン
Tamini, Pascaline 1379
タミヘレ
Tamihere, John 1379
タミム
Tamim, Muhammad 1379
タミム・ビン・ハマド・サーニ
Tamim bin Hamad bin Khalifa al-Thani 1379
タミム・ビン・ハマド・ビン・ハリファ・アル・サーニ
Tamim bin Hamad bin Khalifa al-Thani 1379
ダミャノフ
Damyanov, Igor 316
タミール
Tamir, Yael 1379
Tamir, Yuli 1379
タミル
Tamir, Pinchas 1379
タミルセルバン
Thamilchelvan, S.P. 1394
タームー
Ta'amu, Alameda 1375
タム
Taam, Heidi 1375
Tam, Alan 1379
Tam, Marilyn 1379
Tamm, James W. 1379
ダム
Dam, Julie 315
Dam, Vu Duc 315
Damm, Antje 316
Damm, Sigrid 316
Damme, Dirk Van 316
タムキビ
Tamkivi, Jaanus 1379
ダムス
Daems, Rik 312
ダムスゴー
Damsgård, Puk 316
タム・ニュック・ティン
Tham Nyuk Tin, Peter 1394
タムパネ
Tampane, Likeleli 1379
タムラ
Tamura, Hibiki 1379
ダムラウ
Damrau, Diana 316
タムラカール
Tamrakar, Ramkrishna 1379
タムリンソン
Tumlinson, James H. 1426
タムル
Tammur, Patrick 1379
ダムール
D'Amour, Denis 316
ダムロッシュ
Damrosch, David 316
Damrosch, Leopold 316
ダメアン
Damehane, Yark 315
タメス・ゲラ
Tamez Guerra, Reyes 1379
タメスティ
Tamestit, Antoine 1379
タメット
Tammet, Daniel 1379
ダメット
Dummett, Michael Anthony Eardley 380
ダメルバル
Damerval, Jaime 315
ダーメンス
Damens, Leneve 315
タ・モク
Ta Mok 1379
ダモダラン
Damodaran, Aswath 316
ダーモディ
Dermody, Brenda 344
Dermody, Matt 344
タヤ
Taya, Maaouiya Ould Sidi Ahmed 1384
ダヤニタ・シン
Dayanita Sing 329
タヤラ
Tayyarah, Ghassan 1387
ダヤラトナ
Dayaratna, P. 329
ダヤル
Dayal, Jayeshwur Raj 329
Dayal, Suren 329
ダヤン
Dayan, Assi 329
Dayan, Max 329
タラ
Tala, Diarra Raky 1378
Talla, Mamadou 1378
Tarah, Abdi Mohamed 1382
ダラ
Dala, Nanyak 313
タライ
Talai, Boudjema 1378
Talay, Mustafa Istemihan 1378
ダライ・ラマ14世
Dalai Lama XIV 313
ダラ・ヴェッキア
Dalla Vecchia, Fabio Marco 314
タラウネ
Tarawneh, Suleiman 1382
ダラガン
Daragan, Oleksandr 319
ダラクリエフ
Dalakliev, Detelin 313
ダラ・コスタ
Dalla Costa, Mariarosa 314
ダラゴン
Darragon, Roddy 320
ダラジ

al-Daraji, Muhammed Sahib 319
Darragi, Kais 320
タラジッチ
Talajic, Dalibor 1378
タラシャイ
Tarashaj, Shani 1382
タラシュク
Tarasyuk, Boris 1382
ダラ・シン
Dara Singh 319
タラス
Talass, Mustafa 1378
Taras, Peter 1382
タラスキン
Taruskin, Richard 1383
ダラス＝コンテ
Dallas-Conte, Juliet 314
タラーソフ
Tarasov, Vladimir 1382
タラソワ
Tarasova, Irina 1382
Tarasova, Tatiana 1382
タラソン
Tarazón, Andreína 1382
タラダッシュ
Taradash, Daniel 1382
タラック
Tallach, John 1378
Tallack, Peter 1378
タラッセル
Troyat, Henri 1422
ダラッペ
Dallape, Francesca 314
タラト
Talat, Mehmet Ali 1378
ダラナ
Ndalana, René 1010
タラハゼ
Talakhadze, Lasha 1378
タラバーニ
Talabani, Jalal 1378
タラバニ
Talabani, Jalal 1378
ダラビ
Dalabih, Yousef 313
タラビーニ
Tarabini, Gianpaolo 1382
Tarabini, Patricia 1382
ダラフベリゼ
Darakhvelidze, David 319
タラブラ
Tarabra, Daniela 1382
ダラボシュ
Darabos, Norbert 319
ダラボス
Darabos, Norbert 319
タラボレッリ
Taraborrelli, J.Randy 1382
ダラボン
Darabont, Frank 319
ターラマエ
Taaramae, Rein 1375
ダラミー
Daramy, Mohamed 319
ダラム
Durham, Laura 383
Durham, Michael Schelling 383
タララ
Tarara, Stefan 1382
ダラーラ
Dallara, Charles H. 314
タラリコ
Talarico, Lita 1378
タラール
Talal, Al-Walid bin 1378
タラル
Tarar, Mohammed Rafiq 1382
ダラル
Dalal, A.Kamala 313
Dalal, Anita 313
タラワリ
Tarawally, Musa 1382
タラン
Talan, Jamie 1378
Taran, Lev Nikolaevich 1382
タランギ
Talagi, Billy 1378
Talagi, Toke Tufukia 1378
タランキン
Talankin, Igor 1378
ダランセ
D'Allancé, Mireille 314
タランチェフスキ
Taranczewski, Detlev 1382
タランティーノ
Tarantino, Jevon 1382
Tarantino, Luigi 1382
Tarantino, Quentin 1382
タラント
Tarrant, Mark 1382
ターリー
Turley, James S. 1427
タリ
Tahri, Bouabdellah 1377
タリー
Talley, Jeralean 1378
Talley, Marcia Dutton 1378
Tally, Ted 1378
Tulley, Gever 1426
ダーリー
al-Dalee, Abdelmonem Abdullah Mansur 314
Darley, Andrew 319
ダリ
Dali, Amira 314
Dalli, John 314
Dary, Mario 320
ダリー
Dalley, Horace 314
Dalley, Stephanie Mary 314
Daly, Joe 315
Daly, Jude 315
Daly, Niki 315
Daly-Weir, Catherine 315
Dully, Howard 379
ダリアス
Dareus, Marcell 319
タリアフェッリ
Tagliaferri, Mariarosari 1376
タリアフェロー
Taliaferro, Lorenzo 1378
タリアローリ
Tagliariol, Matteo 1376
ダリアン
Dorrian, Michael 368
ダリアン＝スミス
Darian-Smith, Kate 319
タリエシン
Taliesin 1378
タリエワ
Talieva, Kamila 1378
ダリオ
Dalio, Ray 314
Dario, Ruben 319
ダリガ
Daligga, Bonnie 314
ダリクワ
Darikwa, Tendayi 319
ダリーゴ
D'Arrigo, Angelo 320
タリーズ
Talese, Gay 1378
タリス
Tallis, Frank 1378
ダリス
Daris, Ahmed Abdullah 319
タリスカ
Talisca, Anderson 1378
タリタ
Talita Antunes 1378
ダリダ
Darida, Vladimir 319
タリチェアヌ
Tăriceanu, Călin Popescu 1382
タリチャーヌ
Tăriceanu, Călin Popescu 1382
ダリッチ
Dalić, Martina 314
タリブ
Talib, Aqib 1378
タリフィ
Tarifi, Jamil 1382
ダリュセック
Darrieussecq, Marie 320
ダリル
Dalil, Suraya 314
ダリワル
Dhaliwal, Herb 349
タリーン
Tareen, Jehangir Khan 1382
ダーリン
Darling, Andrew 319
Darling, Angela 319
Darling, Peter 320
ターリング
Tarling, Christine 1382
Tarling, Moyra 1382
ダーリング
Darling, Alistair 319
Darling, David 319
Darling, David J. 320
Darling, Kathy 320
Darling, Louis 320
Darling, Patrick 320
ダーリングーハモンド
Darling-Hammond, Linda 320
ダーリング＝ハモンド
Darling-Hammond, Linda 320
ターリントン
Turlington, Christy 1428
ダーリントン
Darlington, Steve 320
ダリンプル
Dalrymple, Jane 314
Dalrymple, Mark 314
タール
Tarr, Donald Arthur 1382
Tarr, Edward H. 1382
Tarr, Hope 1382
Thal, Lilli 1393
Tull, Davis 1426
タル
Tal, Hisham 1378
Tall, Aminata 1378
Tall, Mohamed 1378
Tall, Mountaga 1378
Tarr, Juraj 1382
タルー
Ta Lou, Marie-Josee 1378
ダール
Dahl, Anders 312
Dahl, Arne 312
Dahl, David 312
Dahl, Erling 312
Dahl, Felicity 312
Dahl, Hans Normann 312
Dahl, JoAnne 312
Dahl, Joe 312
Dahl, Robert Alan 312
Dahl, Shawn 313
Dahl, Sophie 313
Dahl, Victoria 313
Dar, Muhammad Ishaq 319
Darr, Mike 320
D'Heur, Valérie 349
ダル
Dalle, Béatrice 314
Dalle, Francois 314
Dhar, Mainak 349
ダルー
Darroux, Cassius 320
Darroux, Kelvar 320
Darroux, Kenneth 320
ダルイシュ
Derouiche, Nejib 344
ダルヴァス
Darvas, Gyorgy 320
ダルウィーシュ
Darwish, Ahmed 320
Darwish, bin Ismail al-Balushi 320
Darwīsh, Mahmūd 320
Derouiche, Nejib 344
ダルヴィッグ
Dahlvig, Anders 313
タルヴィティエ
Talvitie, Virpi 1379
ダルウィン
Darwin, Saleh 320
タルガマゼ
Targamadze, Kakha 1382
タルガム
Talgam, Itay 1378
タルガン
Tulgan, Bruce 1426
ダルカン
Dulcan, Mina K. 379
ダルカンジェロ
D'Arcangelo, Ildebrando 319
タルク
Taruc, Luis 1383
ダルグスト
Darguste, Josette 319
ダルグリッシュ
Dalglish, Kenny 314
ダルクール
D'Harcourt, Claire 349

タ

ダールグレン
Dahlgren, Lars Owe 313
ダールケ
Dahlke, Ruediger 313
ダルゲリ
Dargel', Olga B. 319
ダル・コ
Dal Co, Francesco 314
ダルコ
Darko, Kwadjo Adjei 319
ダルコー
Darkoh, Ernest 319
ダル・コォ
Dal Co, Francesco 314
ダルコス
Darcos, Xavier 319
タルコット
Talcott, DeAnna 1378
Turcotte, Élise 1427
タルジ
Tarzi, Zemaryalai 1383
タルジェ
Target, Mary 1382
ダルージオ
D'Aluisio, Faith 315
ダルジシュタ
Dardhishta, Ismail 319
ダルジーニオ
D'Argenio, David Z. 319
ダルシバ・アウアント
Da Silva Ahouanto, Evelyne 321
タルジャマン
Tourjman, Muhammad Ramez 1415
ダルシュ
Darch, Ahmed Mahrous 319
ダルジール
Dalziel, Lianne 315
Dalziel, Paul 315
Dalziel, Trina 315
ダルジル
Dalziel, Lianne 315
タルス
Tallus, Jaakko 1378
Tarus, Alexandru 1383
Tarus, Bogdan 1383
ダルスィ
al-Dersi, Mustafa Muftah Belied 344
ダールストレム
Dahlstrom, Emma 313
タルスマ
Talsma, Kelly 1379
Talsma, Nynke Mare 1379
ダルゼル
Dalzell, Frederick 315
ダルゼルジョブ
Dalzel-Job, Patrick 315
ダルソン
Dalson, Harold 314
ダールダー
Daalder, Hans 311
ダルダイ
Dardai, Pal 319
タルタコフスキー
Tartakovsky, Genndy 1382
ダルダリ
al-Dardari, Abdullah 319
タルタリーニ
Tartaglini, Flavia 1382
ダルタン
D'Altan, Paolo 314
タルディ
Tardi, Jacques 1382
タルディッツ
Tardits, Manuel 1382
タルディフ
Tardiff, Timothy J. 1382
タルデュー
Tardieu, Laurence 1382
Tardieu, Michel 1382
ダルデル
Darder, Sergi 319
ダールデン
Daerden, Michel 312
ダルデンヌ
Dardenne, Jean-Pierre 319
Dardenne, Luc 319
Dardenne, Sabine 319
タルトゥーフェリ
Tartuferi, Angelo 1383
ダルトリー
Daltrey, Roger 315
ダルドリー
Daldry, Stephen 314
ダールトン
Darlton, Clark 320
ダルトン
Dalton, Andy 315
Dalton, Annie 315
Dalton, Burt 315
Dalton, Cindy 315
Dalton, Jacob 315
Dalton, James H. 315
Dalton, Katharina 315
Dalton, Lily 315
Dalton, Margot 315
Dalton, Maxine A. 315
Dalton, Ray 315
Dalton, Richard 315
Dalton, Timothy Peter 315
Dalton, Tony 315
タルナイ
Tarnai, Tibor 1382
ダルニル
Darnil, Sylvain 320
タルノフ
Tarnoff, Terry 1382
タルノブスキ
Tarnovschi, Oleg 1382
Tarnovschi, Serghei 1382
ダルノフスキー
Darnovsky, Marcy 320
ダルハウサー
Dalhausser, Phil 314
ダールハウゼン
Daalhuizen, Jaap 311
タルバート
Talbert, Montae 1378
ダルバルコン
Dal Balcon, Isabella 313
タルハン
Tarhan, Ihsan Yildirim 1382
ダールビー
Dahlby, Hakan 313
ダルビー
Dalby, C.Reginald 313
Dalby, Liza Crihfield 314
Dalby, Richard 314
ダルビシャー
Darbyshiere, Philip 319
ダルビッシュ
Darwish, Ramadan 320
ダルファー
Dulfer, Candy 379
タルフーニ
Talhouni, Bassam al 1378
ダルベッコ
Dulbecco, Renato 379
タルベリ
Tallberg, Peter 1378
ダールベリ
Dahlberg, Anna 313
Dahlberg, Anton 313
ダルベルト
Dalberto, Michel 313
ダルベレ
Darbelet, Benjamin 319
ダルボ
Dal Bo, Daniel 313
タルボット
Talbot, Lisa 1378
Talbot, Rob 1378
Talbott, David N. 1378
Talbott, Hudson 1378
Talbott, Jenna 1378
Talbott, John R. 1378
Talbott, Strobe 1378
ダルマイヤー
Dallmayr, Fred Reinhard 314
タールマン
Taalman, Laura 1375
Thalmann, Rolf 1394
タルマン
Thalmann, Rita 1394
ダルミア
Dalmia, Aryaman 314
ダルミアン
Darmian, Matteo 320
タルムム
Tarmum, Abdul-Rahman Mohammed 1382
ダルメ
Dalmais, Irénée Henri 314
ダルメイダ
D'almeida, Damiao Vaz 314
D'almeida, Hélio Silva Vaz 314
d'Almeida, Komlangan Mawutoé 314
Dalmeida, Michael 314
タルモン
Talmon, Moshe 1378
ダルモン
Dalemont, Etienne 314
Darmon, Jean-Charles 320
Darmon, Pierre 320
タルヤト
Taljat, Saso 1378
タルラップ
Tarlap, Tiit 1382
ダルリュ
Darlu, Pierre 320
タルルス
Tallus, Jaakko 1378
タルレ
Tharlet, Eve 1394
ダルレ
Darley, Emmanuel 319
タルレフ
Tarlev, Vasile 1382
ダルワース
Dulworth, Mike 379
ダルワゼ
Darwazeh, Said 320
ターレ
Tále, Samko 1378
Talle, Aud 1378
ダーレ
Dahle, Gro 313
Dahle-Flesjå, Gunn-Rita 313
Dale, Jon Georg 314
ダレ
Darret, Mathieu Babaud 320
タレイ
Talay, Ufuk 1378
Talei, Netani 1378
ダーレオーエン
Dale Oen, Alexander 314
ダレク
Dallek, Robert 314
ダレサンドロ
D'Alessandro, Jacquie 314
ダレーシー
D'Lacey, Chris 360
ダレシュワー
Dhareshwar, Ashok 349
タレス
Tales, Rémi 1378
タレック
Tallec, Olivier 1378
ダレッサンドロ
D'Alessandro, David F. 314
D'Alessandro, Jacquie 314
Dalessandro, James 314
D'alessandro, Marco 314
タレブ
Taleb, Nassim Nicholas 1378
Taleb, Noureddine 1378
タレブラ
Talebula, Metuisela 1378
ダーレ・フレショ
Dahle-Flesjå, Gunn-Rita 313
ダレーマ
D'alema, Massimo 314
タレマエ
Taremae, Hypolite 1382
ダレヤー
Dalager, Stig 313
タレル
Turrell, James 1429
ダレール
Dallaire, Roméo 314
Roméo Dallaire, Lt.-Gen. 1200
ダーレン
Daalen, Gelske van 311
Dahlén, Torbjörn 313
ダレンセ
Dalence, José Guillermo 314
タレント
Tallent, Jared 1378
ダーレンドルフ
Dahrendorf, Ralf Gustav 313
タロ
Taro, Mathias 1382
タロー
Tarrow, Sidney G. 1382
Tharaud, Alexandre 1394
Turow, Scott F. 1429

ダロー
Daro, Deborah 320
ダロザ
Da Rosa, Mário Lopes 320
ダ・ロシャ
Da Rocha, Paulo Mendes 320
ダロシャ
Da Rocha, José de Carvalho 320
ダローズ
Dalloz, Danielle 314
タロック
Tulloch, Jonathan 1426
Tulloch, Mitch 1426
Tulloch, W.W. 1426
Tullock, Gordon 1426
タロッコ
Tarocco, Francesca 1382
ダ・ロッシャ・カマルゴ
da Rocha Camargo, Paulo 320
ダロッチオ
Dallocchio, Federico 314
タロッツィ
Tarozzi, Massimiliano 1382
タロン
Tallon, Ben 1378
Talon, Patrice Athanase Guillaume 1378
ダロン
Dalong, Solomon 314
タロン=ユゴン
Talon-Hugon, Carole 1378
タワー
Tower, Joan 1415
Tower, S.D. 1415
Tower, Wells 1415
ダワー
Dower, John W. 371
タワサ
Tawatha, Taleb 1384
タワーズ
Towers, Harry Alan 1415
ダワ・タシ
Zla-ba-bkra-sis 1556
ダワドルジ
Davaadorj, Tumurkhuleg 322
ダワニ
Dawani, Nadin 328
ダワラブ
al-Dawalab, Mashaer Mohammed al-Amin 328
ダワレ
Dawaleh, Ilyas Moussa 328
タワン・ダッチャニー
Thawan Duchanee 1394
タワン・ドゥチャネー
Thawan Duchanee 1394
タン
Dang, Ye-seo 316
Tan, Amy 1379
Tan, Billy 1379
Tan, Boon Heong 1379
Tan, Chade-Meng 1379
Tan, Chunan-Jing 1379
Tan, Dun 1379
Tan, Fiona 1379
Tan, Hock Beng 1379
Tan, Le Vinh 1379
Tan, Lucio 1379
Tan, Melvyn 1379
Tan, Neivelle 1379
Tan, Ngo Chew 1379
Tan, Nguyen Cong 1379
Tan, Philip 1379
Tan, Rui Wu 1379
Tan, Shaun 1379
Tan, Suyin G.M. 1379
Tan, Tony 1379
Tan, Wee Kiong 1379
Tan, Yuan-yuan 1379
Tan, Yuhan 1380
Tan, Zaldy Sy 1380
Tang, Alan 1380
Tang, Jia-xuan 1380
Tang, Wei 1380
Thang, Dinh La 1394
Thang, Leng Leng 1394
Tin, Louis-Georges 1405
Tonge, gary 1412
Tung, Anthony M. 1426
Tung, Hans 1426
ダーン
Dahn, Bernice 313
Dern, Bruce 344
Dern, Laura 344
ダン
Dan, Matei Agathon 316
Dang, Thuy Hien 316
Dann, Colin 318
Dann, Penny 318
Dann, Scott 318
Dun, David 380
Dunn, Albert H., Ⅲ 381
Dunn, Beverley 381
Dunn, Brandon 382
Dunn, Christopher 382
Dunn, Donald Duck 382
Dunn, Elizabeth 382
Dunn, Hank 382
Dunn, James D.G. 382
Dunn, Jancee 382
Dunn, Kris 382
Dunn, Michael 382
Dunn, Mike 382
Dunn, Opal 382
Dunn, Opal Lydia 382
Dunn, Peter F. 382
Dunn, Rae 382
Dunn, Rob R. 382
Dunn, Ryan 382
Dunn, Sarah 382
Dunn, Shannon 382
Dunn, T.R. 382
Dunn, Walter S., Jr. 382
Dunne, Anthony 382
Dunne, John Gregory 382
Dunne, Paul 382
Dunne, Timothy 382
タン・アウン
Than Aung 1394
タンイェリ
Tanyeli, Uğur 1381
ダンヴァーズ
Danvers, Dennis 318
タン・ウェイ
Tang, Wei 1380
タンカ
Tankha, Brij Mohan 1380
ダンカー
Danker, Uwe 318
タンガズ
Tangaz, Tomris 1380
ダンカース
Dankers, Arne 318
タンガラ
Tangara, Djibril 1380
Tangara, Mamadou 1380
タンカレー
Tanqueray, Rebecca 1381
ダンカン
Duncan, Alfred 380
Duncan, Andy 380
Duncan, Arne 380
Duncan, Barry L. 380
Duncan, Carol 381
Duncan, Dan 381
Duncan, Daniel Kablan 381
Duncan, David Douglas 381
Duncan, John 381
Duncan, Judith 381
Duncan, Kevin 381
Duncan, Kieren 381
Duncan, Kirsty 381
Duncan, Lois 381
Duncan, Michael Clarke 381
Duncan, Ray 381
Duncan, Richard 381
Duncan, Robert 381
Duncan, Stuart 381
Duncan, Susan K. 381
Duncan, Sylvia 381
Duncan, Tim 381
Duncan, Tina 381
Duncan, Todd 381
ダンカンキャッセル
Duncan-cassell, Julia 381
ダンカン=ジョーンズ
Duncan-Jones, Katherine 381
ダンカン・スミス
Duncan Smith, Iain 381
ダンカンスミス
Duncan Smith, Iain 381
タンギ
Tangi, Villiami 1380
タンク
Tank, Patrick W. 1380
Tincq, Henri 1405
ダンク
Dâncu, Vasile 316
ダンクア
Danqua, Fernando 318
タングェイ
Tanguay, Bridget 1380
ターンクエスト
Turnquest, Orville 1429
Turnquest, Tommy 1429
タンクス
Tunks, Benita 1426
ダンクス
Danks, Denise 318
Danks, John 318
Danks, Rabindra 318
タンクスレイ
Tanksley, Steven D. 1380
タングリエフ
Tangriev, Abdullo 1380
ダングルジャン
d'Anglejan, Geoffroy 316
タンクレディ
Tancredi, Laurence R. 1380
タンゲート
Tungate, Mark 1426
タンゲランギ
Tagelagi, Dalton 1376
ダンケル
Dunckel, Jean Benoit 381
Dunkel, Arthur 381
ダンケルマン
Dunkelman, Celia 381
タン・ケン・ヤム
Tan, Tony 1379
タンゴー
Tanggaard, Lene 1380
Tingaud, Jean-Luc 1405
ダンコ
Danko, Taras 318
Danko, William D. 318
タンコアノ
Tankoano, Joachim 1380
タンコック
Tancock, Liam 1380
ダンゴテ
Dangote, Aliko 317
ダンゴート
Dangote, Aliko 317
タンサー
Tancer, Bill 1380
Tancer, Manuel E. 1380
ダンサ
Danza, Andrés 318
ダンサー
Dancer, Faye 316
Dancer, Rex 316
タンサマイ
Thansamay, Khommasith 1394
ダンサンブール
d'Ansembourg, Thomas 318
タンジ
Tanzi, Rudolph E. 1381
ダンシー
Dancey, Charlie 316
Dancy, Rahima Baldwin 316
ダンジェル
Dangel, Jacqueline 316
ダンジェロ
D'angelo, Adam 316
ダンジガー
Danziger, Kurt 319
Danziger, Lucy S. 319
Danziger, Paula 319
ダンジヌ
Dandjinou, Rémis Fulgance 316
タンジャ
Tandia, Hawa 1380
Tandja, Mamadou 1380
ダンジュー
D'Anjou, Jim 318
タン・シュエ
Than Shwe 1394
ダンジュマ
Danjuma, Yakubu 318
タンジュン
Tanjung, Chairul 1380
Tanjung, Feisal 1380
タンシル
Tunsil, Laremy 1427
ダンシング
Duensing, Brian 378
ダンス
Dance, S.Peter 316
Dansou, Felix Essou 318
Dansou, Jean 318
ダンスア
Dansua, Akua 318

タン・ズィン・マウン
Thant Sin Maung 1394
ダンスター
Dunster, Bill 382
ダンスタン
Dunstan, Marcus 382
ダンスト
Dunst, Kirsten 382
タンストール
Tunstall, KT 1427
Tunstall, Tricia 1427
ダンズビー
Dansby, Karlos 318
タンズリー
Tansley, David 1381
ダンセイ
Dancey, Ryan S. 316
タンセラ
Tansella, Michele 1381
タンゼン・ルンドゥプ
Tanzen Lhundrup 1381
ダンソ
Dansou, Gnimbere 318
ダンソコ
Dansokho, Amath 318
ダンダ
Danda, Mahamadou 316
Dan Dah, Mahaman Laouali 316
ダン・タイ・ソン
Dang Thai Son 317
タンタウィ
Tantawi, Mohamed Said 1381
Tantawi, Muhammad Hussein 1381
タンタウィ師
Tantawi, Mohamed Said 1381
タンタウィ大導師
Tantawi, Mohamed Said 1381
タンタパニチャクン
Tanthapanichakoon, Wiwut 1381
タンタン
Tantan, Sadettin 1381
ダンチェフ
Danchev, Alex 316
タンチッチ
Tancsics, Laszlo 1380
タンチョス
Tanczos, Nandor 1380
ダンツァー
Danzer, Klaus 319
ダンツィガー
Danziger, Paula 319
ダンツィヒ
Dantzig, Rudi van 318
タンデ
Tande, Petter L. 1380
タン・テイ
Than Htay 1394
タンディー
Tandy, Bradley Edward 1380
Tandy, Keith 1380
ダンディー
Dundee, Angelo 381
ダンティカ
Danticat, Edwidge 318
ダンテス
Dantes, Edmond 318
ダンデス
Dundes, Alan 381
ダンテック
Dantec, Maurice G. 318
ダーント
Dirnt, Mike 358
ダント
Danto, Arthur C. 318
ダンドー
Dando, Malcolm 316
ダントナ
D'Antona, Rosanna 318
ダントーニ
D'antoni, Mike 318
ダントーニオ
D'Antonio, Michael 318
ダンドビ
Dandobi, Maïkibi Kadidiatou 316
ダンドロー
d'Andlau, Guillaume 316
ダーントン
Darnton, John 320
Darnton, Robert 320
ダントン
Denton, David 343
ダントン＝ダウナー
Dunton-Downer, Leslie 382
タンニネン
Tanninen, Oili 1381
タンネ
Tanne, Janice Hopkins 1380
タンネル
Tunnell, Michael O. 1427
タンネンバウム
Tannenbaum, Robert 1380
タンバ
Tamba, Pierre Biram 1379
Tamba-Mecz, Irène 1379
タンバー
Tambor, Jeffrey 1379
ダンバ
Damba, Maiga Sina 315
ダンバー
Dunbar, Anthony P. 380
Dunbar, Christopher, Jr. 380
Dunbar, Fiona 380
Dunbar, Geoff 380
Dunbar, Ian 380
Dunbar, Jenkins 380
Dunbar, Joyce 380
Dunbar, Lance 380
Dunbar, Nicholas 380
Dunbar, Polly 380
Dunbar, Quinton 380
Dunbar, Robin Ian MacDonald 380
Dunbar, Sly 380
ダンハイサー
Dannheisser, Ilana 318
タンパコス
Tampakos, Dimosthenis 1379
ダンバザウ
Dambazzau, Abdularahman Bello 315
ダンバーズスミス
Danvers-smith, Natasha 318
ダンハム
Dunham, Katherine 381
Dunham, M.L. 381
Dunham, William 381
ダンピェール
Dampier, Phil 316
ダンピエール
Dampierre, Florence de 316
ダンビル
Dumbill, Edd 380
ダンビーン・トゥルバト
Dambyn Törbat 315
ダンファ
Danfa, Wasna Papai 316
ダンフィー
Dunfee, Evan 381
タンブウェ
Thambwe Mwamba, Alexis 1394
タンブエ・ムワンバ
Thambwe Mwamba, Alexis 1394
タンブエムワンバ
Thambwe Mwamba, Alexis 1394
ダンフォード
Danford, Haward S. 316
Danford, Natalie 316
Dunford, Jason 381
Dunford, Michael 381
タンフック
Tan Fook, Choong 1380
タンブラ
Tamboura, Ascofare Ouleymatou 1379
タンブリン
Tamblin, Louise 1379
タンプリン
Tamplin, Arthur R. 1379
ターンブル
Turnbull, Ann 1428
Turnbull, Jessie 1428
Turnbull, Malcolm 1428
Turnbull, Oliver 1428
Turnbull, Peter 1428
Turnbull, Stephanie 1428
Turnbull, Walter J. 1428
ダンブレ
Dembelé, Dramane 340
ダンブロージオ
D'ambrosio, Danilo 315
ダンベリ
Damberg, Mikael 315
ダンベレ
Dembele, Nango 340
Dembele, Salifou 340
ダンベンゼ
Dambendzet, Jeanne 315
Dambenzet, Jeanne 315
タンポボロン
Tampubolon, Gindo 1379
ダンマー
Dunmur, David 381
タンマチャヨー
Thammachayō, Phikkhu 1394
ダンマナンダ
Dhammananda, K.Sri 349
タンマラク
Thammarak, Israngkulnaayuthaya 1394
タンミネン
Tamminen, Tuula 1379
ダンミピ
Dammipi, Noupokou 316
タン・ミン
Than Myint 1394
タン・ミン・ウー
Thant Myint-U 1394
タンミンウー
Thant Myint-U 1394
タンメルト
Tammert, Aleksander 1379
ダンモア
Dunmore, Helen 381
ダンラップ
Dunlap, Carlos 381
Dunlap, Glen 381
Dunlap, Julie 381
Dunlap, Richard A. 381
Dunlap, Susanne Emily 381
ダンリー
Donley, Richard 366
Dunrea, Olivier 382
タンリクル
Tanrikulu, Ahmet Kenan 1381
Tanrikulu, Azize 1381
Tanrikulu, Bahri 1381
ダンリービー
Dunleavy, Mike 381
ダンリービィー
Dunleavey, M.P. 381
ダンレイ
Dunrea, Olivier 382
ダンロスキー
Dunlosky, John 381
ダンロップ
Dunlop, Andy 381
Dunlop, Barbara 381
Dunlop, Fiona 381
Dunlop, Margaret J. 381
Dunlop, Storm 381
ダンワース
Dungworth, Richard 381
タンワーヒン
Tang Wah Hing, Sylvio Hock Sheen 1380

【チ】

チ
Chi, Chang-hoon 254
Chi, Myong-kwan 254
Ji, Dong-Won 673
Ji, Jin-hee 673
Ji, Soo-hyun 673
Ji, So-yun 673
Ji, Yeonho 673
Qi, Zhong-yi 1142
チー
Chee, Alexander 250
Chi, Po-lin 254
Qi, Gong 1142
チア
Chea, Chan Nakry 250
Chea, Kimtha 250
Chea, Sim 250
Chea Sophara 250
Chia, Siow Yue 254
Jia, Ping-wa 673
Jia, Qing-lin 673
チー・アウン
Kyi Aung 778

チアオ
Jiao, Tong 673
Qiao, Shi 1143
チアゴ
Thiago 1395
チアゴ・シウヴァ
Thiago Silva 1395
チア・サボン
Chea Savoeun 250
チア・シム
Chea Sim 250
チア・ソン
Chhea Song 254
チアナ
Tchiana, Omar Hamidou 1387
チアブラ
Chiabra, Robert 254
チアラビグリオ
Chiaraviglio, German 254
チアン
Chang, Jung 245
Chiang, Renee 254
Jiang, Fang-zhou 673
Jiang, Lei 673
Jiang, Qin-min 673
Jiang, Wen 673
Thiam, Nafissatou 1395
チィ
Chhi, Khiam-sin 254
チウ
Chiu, Lisa Seachrist 257
チヴァルディ
Civardi, Giovanni 265
チウェ
Chwe, Michael Suk-Young 264
チウォイジンスカ
Gawlikowska, Sylwia 485
チウッチ
Ciucci, Giorgio 265
チウミア
Chiumia, Grace Obama 257
チウメ
Chiume, Ephraim Mganda 257
チウレイ
Ciulei, Liviu 265
チェ
Chae, Dong-ha 242
Chae, Yung-bok 242
Che, Chew Chan 250
Chey, Tae-won 254
Choe, Chang-sik 258
Choe, Gyu-ha 258
Choe, Hyo Sim 258
Choe, Ik-gyu 258
Choe, Il-ryong 258
Choe, Jae-chun 258
Choe, Jong-gon 258
Choe, Jon Wi 258
Choe, Kum-Hui 258
Choe, Kwang-jin 258
Choe, Kwang-rae 258
Choe, Kwang-shik 258
Choe, Nam-gyong 258
Choe, Nam-gyun 258
Choe, Pu-il 258
Choe, Ryong-hae 258
Choe, Sang-gon 258
Choe, Sung-ho 258
Choe, Thae-bok 258
Choe, Un Sim 258
Choe, U-ram 258
Choe, Wan-gyu 258
Choe, Yong-gon 258
Choe, Yong-rim 258
Choi, Chang-kwon 258
Choi, Dong-hun 258
Choi, Hong-hi 258
Choi, Hong-man 258
Choi, In-ho 258
Choi, In-kee 258
Choi, Ji-Man 258
Choi, Jin-hyuk 258
Choi, Jin-sil 258
Choi, Ji-woo 258
Choi, Joong-kyung 258
Choi, Kyoung-hwan 258
Choi, Kyung-ju 258
Choi, Kyung-nok 258
Choi, Min-ho 258
Choi, Min-kyong 258
Choi, Min-sik 258
Choi, Min-soo 259
Choi, Na-yeon 259
Choi, Sang-yong 259
Choi, Sook Ja 259
Choi, Sung-bong 259
Choi, Sung-hong 259
Choi, Sun-jung 259
Choi, Won-shik 259
Choi, Yang-hee 259
Choi, Yo-sam 259
チェー
Cseh, László 306
チェア
Chea, Daniel 250
チェアウルエラ
Chea Urruela, José Luis 250
チェイカ
Cejka, Alex 239
Cheika, Michael 251
チェイキン
Chaykin, Howard 250
チェイシンズ
Chasins, Abram 249
チェイス
Chase, Adam W. 248
Chase, Clifford 248
Chase, David 249
Chase, Emma 249
Chase, Heather 249
Chase, Jamie 249
Chase, Katíe 249
Chase, Loretta 249
Chase, Marilyn 249
チェイスモア
Chasemore, Richard 249
チェイス・リボウ
Chase-Riboud, Barbara 249
チェイズン
Chazin, Suzanne 250
チェイニー
Chaney, Lisa 245
Cheney, Annie 252
Cheney, Dick 252
Cheney, Elizabeth Lynne 252
Cheney, Richard B. 252
Cheney, Tom 252
チェイピン
Chapin, Miles 246
チェイフィー
Chafee, Lincoln 242
Chaffee, Todd 242
チェイフィッツ
Cheyfitz, Kirk 254
チェイフィン
Chafin, Andrew 242
チェイワ
Cheywa, Milcah Chemos 254
チェインバーズ
Chambers, Aidan 243
チエウ
Trieu, Nguyen Quoc 1420
チェカノフ
Chekanov, Valentin S. 251
チェカレリ
Ceccarelli, Daniela 239
チェキーニ
Cecchini, Garin 239
Cecchini, Gavin 239
チェク
Çeku, Agim 239
チェクワ
Chekwa, Chimdi 251
チェケッツ
Checketts, Darby 250
チェコ
Ceco, Makbule 239
チェザーナ
Cesana, Andreas 241
チェザリニ
Cesarini, Claudia 241
チェサル
Cesar, Bostjan 241
チェシャー
Cheshire, Gerard 253
チエシュコ
Ciesko, Martin 264
チェース
Chase, Richard X. 249
Chasse, Betsy 249
チェスキー
Chesky, Brian 253
チェスター
Chester, Andrew 253
Chester, Chris 253
Chester, Darren 253
Chester, Jonathan 253
チェスタフィールド
Chesterfield, Sadie 253
チェスターリ
Cestari, Matteo 241
チェスチン
Czeschin, Tommy 311
チェストコフ
Zhestkov, Oleg 1552
チェストナット
Chestnut, Terrell 253
チェスナ
Česna, Petras 241
チェスニー
Chesney, Denise 253
チェズニー
Chesney, Kenny 253
チェスブロ
Chesbro, George C. 253
チェスブロウ
Chesbrough, Henry William 253
チェスマン
Chessman, Harriet Scott 253
チェスラ
Chesla, Catherine A. 253
チェスラー
Chesler, Ellen 253
チェスワーズ
Chesworth, Niki 253
チェゼラーニ
Ceserani, Gian Paolo 241
チェゾイ
Chedzoy, Sue 250
チェッキ
Cecchi d'Amico, Suso 239
チェッキ・ダミーコ
Cecchi d'Amico, Suso 239
チェッキーニ
Cecchini, Elena 239
チェック
Cech, Thomas Robert 239
チェックランド
Checkland, Olive 250
チェッケリーニ
Ceccherini, Federico 239
チェッコリ
Ceccoli, Nicoletta 239
チェット
Triet, Nguyen Minh 1420
チェッピィ
Ceppi, Carlo 240
チェッピテッリ
Ceppitelli, Luca 240
チェッリ
Celli, Simone 239
チェトゥーチ
Chetcuti, William 253
チェトクチ
Chetcuti, William 253
チェートフ
Chertoff, Michael 253
チェトリ
Chhetri, Neelam Khadka 254
チェニーリョ
Chenillo, Mariana 252
チェノウェス
Chenoweth, Emily 252
Chenoweth, Florence 252
Chenoweth, Kristin 252
チェノウエス
Chenoweth, Florence 252
チェノットゥ
Chennoth, Joseph 252
チェパイティス
Čepaitis, Virgilijus Juozas 240
チェハーク
Csehák, Judit 306
チェバート
Chabert, Antoine 241
チェハノバ
Ciechanover, Aaron 264
チェパロワ
Chepalova, Yuliya Anatolyevna 252
チェバン
Cheban, Iurii 250
Cheban, Yuri 250
チェビ
Cebi, Selcuk 239
チェピコフ
Tchepikov, Sergei 1387
チェフ
Cech, Petr 239
チェファーズ
Cheffers, Mark 251

チ

チェプクルイ
C'kurui, James Kwalia 266
チェプコエチ
Chepkoech, Beatrice 252
チェプチュゴフ
Chepchugov, Sergei 252
チェプツォフ
Teptsov, N.V. 1391
チェプテゲイ
Cheptegei, Joshua Kiprui 252
チェプラク
Ceplak, Jolanda 240
チェフロウウ
Cheikh Rouhou, Nihel 251
チェボタリ
Cebotari, Vladimir 239
チェポッラーロ
Cepollaro, Biagio 240
チェヨ
Cheyo, Gideon 254
チェラゾーリ
Cerasoli, Anna 240
チェラーミ
Cerami, Vincenzo 240
チェラリオ
Cellario, Patrice 239
チェラル
Chelaru, Marius 251
チェランド
Kjelland, James M. 743
チェリ
Celi, Lia 239
チェリー
Cherry, Brittainy C. 253
Cherry, Damu 253
Cherry, Demetrius 253
Cherry, Don 253
Cherry, Edith 253
Cherry, Georgia 253
Cherry, Neil James 253
チェリキ
Çelik, Faruk 239
Çelik, Hüseyin 239
Celik, Omer 239
チエリギーニ
Chierighini, Marcelo 255
チェリシェフ
Cheryshev, Denis 253
チェリス
Chellis, James 251
チェリーナ
Tcherina, Ludmilla 1387
チェリモ
Chelimo, Paul Kipkemoi 251
Chelimo, Rose 251
チェリラス
Cherilus, Gosder 253
チェル
Cherue, Frederick 253
チェルイヨット
Cheruiyot, Vivian Jepkemoi 253
チェルヴィ
Cervi, Antonio 241
チェルヴェッラーティ
Cervellati, Pier Luigi 240
チェルカソワ
Cherkasova, Alla 253
チェルカッスキー
Cherkasskiĭ, Sergeĭ 253
チェルコス
Cherkos, Abreham 253
チェルコフスキス
Cerkovskis, Deniss 240
チェルシー
Chelsea, David 251
チェールスタ
Kjolstad, Johan 743
チェルチ
Cerci, Alessio 240
チェルッティ
Cerruti, Linda 240
チェルディヴァラエサヌ
Cherdivara-esanu, Mariana 253
チェルトク
Chertok, Boris 253
チェルトコフ
Tchertkoff, Wladimir 1387
チェルトック
Chertok, Boris 253
チェルトフ
Chertoff, Michael 253
チェルナー
Czerner, Thomas B. 310
チェルナチ
Černač, Zvonko 240
チェルニー
Cerny, Vaclav 240
チェルニアク
Czerniak, Konrad 310
チェルニシュ
Chernysh, Vadym 253
チェルニー・ステファンスカ
Czerny-Stefanska, Halina 311
チェルニャク
Cherniak, Maryna 253
チェルヌイ
Cherny, Anatoly B. 253
チェルネッキー
Chernecky, Cynthia C. 253
チェルネツキー
Chernetskyi, Oleksandr 253
チェルノウソフ
Chernousov, Ilia 253
チェルノゴラズ
Cernogoraz, Giovanni 240
チェルノビチュキー
Csérnoviczki, Eva 306
チェルノフ
Chernov, Alexei 253
チェルノマズ
Cernomaz, Nikolae 240
チェルノムイルジン
Chernomyrdin, Viktor Stepanovich 253
チェルノワ
Chernova, Natalia 253
Chernova, Tatyana 253
チェルビ
Cervi, Antonio 241
チェルボネンコ
Chervonenko, Yevgen 253
チェルマク
Csérmák, József 306
チェルモシャンスカヤ
Chermoshanskaya, Yuliya 253
チェレゾフ
Tcherezov, Ivan 1387
チェレッティ
Celletti, Rodolfo 239
チェレパノフ
Cherepanov, Alexei 253
チェレビ
Celebi, Muge 239
チェレミシノフ
Cheremisinov, Alexey 253
チェロノ
Cherono, Mercy 253
チェーン
Chain, B.M. 242
チェン
Chan, Jackie 244
Chan, Koon-chung 244
Chang, Sylvia 245
Chen, Anthony 251
Chen, Arvin 251
Chen, Bo-lin 251
Chen, Cheer 251
Chen, Ding 251
Chen, Eva 251
Chen, Herbert 251
Chen, Ivy 251
Chen, Jie 251
Chen, Joan 251
Chen, Kai-ge 251
Chen, Kevin 251
Chen, Kuei-Min 251
Chen, Kun 251
Chen, Li-fu 251
Chen, Pauline W. 251
Chen, Qian-wu 251
Chen, Ran 251
Chen, Ray 251
Chen, Sean 251
Chen, Shiatzy 251
Chen, Shui-bian 251
Chen, Stephen T. 251
Chen, Wei-huan 251
Chen, Wei-Yin 251
Chen, Yi-bing 251
Chen, Yi-zi 251
Chen, Yuan 252
Chen, Yu-hsun 252
Chen, Zhen 252
Chen, Zhong-shi 252
Chen, Zi-ming 252
Chen, Zu-de 252
Cheng, Adam 252
Cheng, Chung-kuan 252
Cheng, Chu Sian 252
Cheng, Ekin 252
Cheng, Eugenia 252
Cheng, François 252
Cheng, Gloria 252
Cheng, Hsiao 252
Cheng, Joseph 252
Cheng, Patrick S. 252
Cheng, Ron 252
Cheng, Victor 252
Cheng, Yu-chieh 252
Cheng, Yu-tung 252
Chenn, Eric 252
Cheung, Jim 254
Cheung, Leslie 254
Cheung, Lilian W.Y. 254
Cheung, Maggie 254
Chieng, André 255
Qian, Jia-ju 1142
Qian, Qi-chen 1142
Qian, Wei-zhang 1142
Qian, Xue-sen 1143
Tseng, Yu-Chien 1423
Tsien, Roger 1424
Zheng, Li-zhi 1552
チエン
Chien, Catia 255
Chien, Do Van 255
Chien, Tran Thi Trung 255
Chieng, André 255
チェンゲ
Chenge, Andrew 252
チェンダ
Chenda, Emmanuel 252
チェントファンティ
Centofanti, Martina 240
チェンドロフスキー
Cendrowski, Harry 240
チェンバース
Chambers, Calum 243
Chambers, Deborah 243
Chambers, John 243
Chambers, John T. 243
Chambers, Marilyn 243
Chambers, Nicky 243
Chambers, Richard 243
Chambers, Robert 243
チェンバーズ
Chambers, Aidan 243
Chambers, Anna 243
Chambers, Anne Cox 243
Chambers, Harry E. 243
Chambers, John B. 243
Chambers, John M. 243
Chambers, John T. 243
Chambers, Mark 243
Chambers, Paul 243
Chambers, William Nisbet 243
チェンバリン
Chamberlin, J.Edward 243
チェンバレン
Chamberlain, Benedicta 243
Chamberlain, David Barnes 243
Chamberlain, Diane 243
Chamberlain, Joba 243
Chamberlain, John Angus 243
Chamberlain, Margaret 243
Chamberlain, Owen 243
Chamberlain, Trevor 243
Chamberlin, J.Edward 243
Chamberlin, Jimmy 243
チエンベケザ
Chiyembekeza, Allan 257
チェンボ
Tshempo, Ngeema Sangay 1423
チェンポ
Tshempo, Ngeema Sangay 1423
チェン・ユンジェ
Chen, Yunjie 252
チォドス・アーヴァイン
Chodos-Irvine, Margaret 258
チオボー
Ciobo, Steven 265
チオラ
Chiola, Martin 256
チオンカン
Cioncan, Maria 265
チオング・グティエレス
Chiong Gutiérrez, María Auxiliadora 256
チオンゴ
Tshiongo, Gilbert 1424

チ

チオンピ
Ciompi, Luc 265
チカイゼ
Tchikaidze, Aleksandre 1387
チカウェ
Chikawe, Mathias 255
Chikawe, Mathias Meinrad 255
チカオンダ
Chikaonda, Mathews 255
チカノーバー
Ciechanover, Aaron 264
チカノバー
Ciechanover, Aaron 264
チガリーニ
Cigarini, Luca 264
チカレッリ
Chiccarelli, Joseph 255
チギシェフ
Tchiguichev, Evgueni 1387
チギプコ
Tigipko, Sergiy 1404
チギレワ
Chigireva, Vlada 255
チキロ
Chickillo, Anthony 255
チキンデレアヌ
Tichindeleanu, Eugen 1403
チーク
Cheek, Bryce 250
Cheek, Joey 250
Cheek, Joseph 250
チクウィニャ
Chikwinya, Nyasha 255
チクウェ
Chikwe, Kema 255
チグウェデレ
Chigwedere, Aeneas 255
チークス
Cheeks, Maurice 250
チクセントミハイ
Csikszentmihalyi, Mihaly 306
チグノンパ
Tignonkpa, Ayaovi Demba 1404
チクリ
Cikuli, Maksim 264
チクリス
Chiklis, Michael 255
チグリッチ
Ciglic, Boris 264
チクワニネ
Chikwanine, Michel 255
チクワンダ
Chikwanda, Alexander 255
チケル
Chikelu, Chukwuemeka 255
Cikel, Lubos 264
チコイン
Chicoine, Brian 255
チコティッチ
Cikotić, Selmo 264
チコーネ
Ciccone, Christopher 264
チコネ
Ciccone, Angelo 264
チコラリ
Cicolari, Greta 264
チザ
Chiza, Christopher 257
チーサム
Cheatham, Jimmy 250
チーザム
Cheatham, Lillian 250
チザム
Chisholm, Alastair 257
Chisholm, Daniel 257
Chisholm, Penny 257
Chisholm, Roderick M. 257
Chisholm, Shirley 257
チサレ
Chisale, Benard 257
チシコフ
Tishkov, Leonid 1406
チシマリチャン
Chshmaritian, Karen 262
チジャニ
Tidjani, Assani 1403
チショーム
Chisholm, Marie-Helene 257
チズナール
Chisnall, David 257
チスホルム
Chisholm, Wendy 257
チスマール
Csizmár, Gábor 306
チーズマン
Cheesman, John 251
チスラーク
Čislák, Viliam 265
チゼンホール
Chisenhall, Lonnie 257
チゾム
Chisholm, Shirley 257
チソン
Ji-sung 674
チゾン
Tison, Annette 1406
チタク
Çitaku, Vlora 265
チダクワ
Chidhakwa, Walter 255
チータム
Cheatham, Jimmy 250
Cheetham, Craig 251
Cheetham, Dominic John 251
Cheetham, Nicolas 251
チタム
Chitham, Edward 257
チダムバラム
Chidambaram, P. 255
Chidambaram, Palaniappan 255
チダムバラル
Chidambaram, P. 255
チタレンコ
Titarenko, M.L. 1406
チチェキ
Çiçek, Cemil 264
チチェスター・クラーク
Chichester Clark, Emma 255
チチェロワ
Chicherova, Anna 255
チチップ
Cicip, Sharif Sutardjo 264
チチャ
Chicha, Marie-Thérèse 255
チチャバ
Chichava, Jose 255
チチョリーナ
Cicciolina 264
チチリナ
Tsitsilina, Arina 1424
チチル
Cechir, Serghei 239
チチンガル
Titingar, Mouadjidibaye 1406
チック
Chick, Jonathan 255
Chick, Victoria 255
Csik, Michaela 306
チックス
Chicks, Dixie 255
チッコリーニ
Ciccolini, Aldo 264
チッタディーニ
Cittadini, Lorenzo 265
チッチョリーナ
Cicciolina 264
チッティ
Citti, Sergio 265
チッパーフィールド
Chipperfield, David 256
チップチェイス
Chipchase, Jan 256
チップマン - エヴァンズ
Chipman-Evans, Carolyn 256
チッラグ
Csillag, István 306
チデスター
Chidester, David 255
チテンゲ
Tshitenge, Simon 1424
チート
Chaet, Mike 242
チトゥウォ
Chituwo, Brian 257
チトゥヴルテック
Ctvrtek, Vaclav 306
チドカ
Chidoka, Ositadinma 255
チドジー
Chidozie 255
チトチア
Chitchian, Hamid 257
チトチアン
Chitchian, Hamid 257
チトテラ
Chitotela, Ronald 257
チドラー
Chidler, Sue 255
チトラ・サウンダー
Chitra Soundar 257
チトラ・バハドゥル・K.C.
Chitra Bahadur K.C. 257
チトリツキ
Cytrycki, Sławomir 310
チードル
Cheadle, Don 250
チナウォン
Chinnaworn, Boonyakiat 256
チナマサ
Chinamasa, Patric 256
チーニー
Cheney, Sally 252
チニジ
Çinici, Can 264
チニンガ
Chininga, Edward Chindori 256
チネッリ
Cinelli, Amanda 264
チネリー
Chinnery, Patrick 256
チネン
Chinen, Allan B. 256
チノイ
Chinoy, Mike 256
Chinoy, Sujan R. 256
チーバー
Cheever, Nancy A. 251
チパシビリ
Chipashvili, Vladimir 256
チハナ
Chihana, Enoch Chakufwa 255
チバナ
Chibana, Charles 254
チハルティシビリ
Chkhartishvili, Ivane 257
チバンダ
Tshibanda, Raymond 1424
チバンダ・ヌトゥンガムロンゴ
Tshibanda N'tungammulongo, Raymond 1424
チバンベレラ
Tchibambéléla, Bernard 1387
チビソワ
Chibisova, Ksenia 255
チピリカ
Tjipilica, Paulo 1407
チビング
Chibingu, Paul 254
チフィエルトカ
Cwiertka, Katarzyna J. 310
チブス
Thibus, Ysaora 1396
チプラス
Tsipras, Alexis 1424
チプリ
Ciprì, Daniele 265
チプリッチ
Ćiplić, Svetozar 265
チフリノビッチ
Tsifrinovich, Vladimir I. 1424
チプング
Chipungu, Kenneth 256
チヘイーゼ
Chkheidze, Rezo 257
チペス
Csipes, Tamara 306
チベッツ
Tibbets, Paul 1403
チヘンケリ
Chkhenkeli, Merab 257
チボー
Thibaud, Laure 1395
Thibault, Guy 1395
Thibault, Robert 1395
チホツキ
Cichocki, Jacek 264
チポッラ
Cipolla, Carlo M. 265

チホノフ
Tikhonov, Alexei 1404
Tikhonov, Viktor 1404
チホバゼ
Chkhobadze, Nino 257
チホミロフ
Tikhomirov, Vladimir Mikhăilovich 1404
チホン
Tsikhan, Ivan 1424
チーマ
Cheema, Anwar Ali 251
Cheema, Mushtaq Ali 251
チー・マウン
Kyi Maung 778
チマガッリ
Cimagalli, Cristina 264
チミーノ
Cimmino, Marco Amedeo 264
チミノ
Cimino, Michael 264
チム・シエク・レン
Chhim Seak Leng 254
チムチュク
Timciuc, Iacob 1405
チムニク
Zimnik, Reiner 1555
チメグバータル
Chimegbaatar, Ch. 256
チモシェビッチ
Cimoszewicz, Włodzimierz 264
チモシェンコ
Tymoshenko, Yulia 1431
チモフチ
Timofti, Nicolae Vasilyevich 1405
チモンボ
Chimombo, Chapola 256
チャ
Ca, Agostinho 211
Cha, Kum Chol 241
Cha, Sung Sook 241
Cha, Sung-won 241
Cha, Tae-hyun 241
Cha, Victor D. 241
Chan, In-pyo 244
Chia, Maneewan 254
チャー
Cheah, Pheng 250
Tra, Pham Van 1416
チヤ
Cha, Tae-hyun 241
チャイ
Chai, R.Makana Risser 242
Chhay Than 254
Tsai, Ming-liang 1423
チャイウット
Chaiwuti, Bannawat 242
チャイカ
Chaika, Viktoria 242
Chaika, Yuri Y. 242
チャイゼ
Chkhaidze, Gennady 257
チャイ・タン
Chhay Than 254
チャイティン
Chaitin, Gregory J. 242
チャイデス
Chaidez, Natalie 242
チャイト
Chait, Galit 242
Chait, Norman 242
チャイトー
Chaitow, Leon 242
チャイハン
Chayhane, Said Ali 250
チャイポン・ポンパニッチ
Chaipong Pongpanich 242
チャイヤロット
Chaiyarose, Sunee 242
チャイヤワン
Chaiyawan, Vanich 242
チャイラスミサック
Chairasmisak, Korsak 242
チャイルズ
Childs, Billy 255
Childs, Karen 255
Childs, Laura 255
Childs, Marshall R. 255
Childs, Peter 255
Chiles, James R. 255
Chiles, John 255
チャイルド
Child, Greg 255
Child, John 255
Child, Julia 255
Child, Lauren 255
Child, Lee 255
Child, Lincoln 255
Child, Maureen 255
チャイン
Tranh, Huynh Phong 1417
チャウ
Chau, Solina 249
Chow, Sing-chi 260
Chyau, Carol 264
Tchao, Padumhèkou 1387
チャヴァリア
Chavarría, Daniel 249
チャヴァロ
Chavarro, Jorge 250
チャヴィ
Xavi 1531
チャヴィアノ
Chaviano, Daina 250
チャウシッチ
Causic, Goran 238
チャウ・シンチー
Chow, Sing-chi 260
チャウラ
Chawla, Kalpana 250
Chawla, Navin 250
Chawla, Neharika 250
チャウン
Chown, Marcus 260
チャオ
Chao, David 246
Chao, Elaine L. 246
Chao, Mark 246
Chao, Ramón 246
Chao, Ronald Kee Young 246
Qiao, Shi 1143
Tchao, Padumhèkou 1387
Zhao, Vicki 1552
チャーカ
Chayka, Doug 250
チャガー
Chagger, Bardish 242
チャカチャカ
Chaka Chaka, Yvonne 242
チャーカム
Charkham, Jonathan P. 247
チャカモン
Chakramon, Phasukavanich 242
チャカロトス
Tsakalotos, Euclides 1423
チャカロフ
Chakarov, Dzhevdet 242
チャーキ
Csáky, Pál 306
チャクベタゼ
Chakvetadze, Davit 242
チャクペレ
Tchakpele, Komi Paalamwé 1387
チャクマ
Chakma, Kalpa Ranjan 242
チャクマクオール
Cakmakoglu, Sabahattin 214
チャクラバーティ
Chakrabarti, Nina 242
チャクラバルティ
Chakrabarti, Rajesh 242
チャクラポン
Chakrapong, Norodom 242
チャクラポン殿下
Chakrapong, Norodom 242
チャグラル
Caglar, Soyuncu 213
チャクルースキー
Czuchlewski, David 311
チャケラ
Chakela, Ts'ele 242
チャーゴイス
Chargois, J.T. 247
チャーコーバー
Chercover, Sean 252
チャコーン
Chacon, Michael 241
チャコン
Chacon, Gloria 241
Chacón, Jesse 241
チャコン・エチェベリア
Chacón Echeverría, Ana Helena 241
チャコン・ピケラス
Chacón Piqueras, Carme 241
チャシエモフ
Chashemov, Mansurbek 249
チャシナ
Tchachina, Irina 1387
チャシーン
Chacin, Jhoulys 241
チャジンスキー
Chudzinski, Rob 262
チャスカルソン
Chaskalson, Michael 249
チャスキーニ
Ciaschini, Giorgio 264
チャステイン
Chastain, Jessica 249
チャースト
Chast, Roz 249
チャスラフスカ
Čáslavská, Věra 234
チャセク
Chasek, Pamela 249
チャーダ
Chadha, Gurinder 241
チャダ
Chadda, Sarwat 241
Chaddha, Navin 241
チャタジー
Chatterjee, Partha 249
Chatterjee, Pria 249
Chatterji, Somnath 249
Chatterji, Susanta Kumar 249
チャーターズ
Charters, Samuel 248
チャタトゥ
Tchatat, Clobert 1387
チャタリ
Csatary, Laszlo 306
チャータリス
Charteris, Luke 248
チャーチ
Church, Barry 263
Church, Brian T. 263
Church, Caroline 263
Church, Caroline Jayne 263
Church, Charlotte 263
Church, David B. 263
Church, James 263
Church, Mark 263
Church, Thomas Haden 263
Church, W.H. 263
チャチェフ
Chachev, Evgeni 241
チャチッチ
Čačić, Radimir 212
チャチャイ・チョムタワット
Chiedchai Chomtawat 255
チャチャート
Chadchart, Sittipunt 241
チャチュク
Cacuk, Sudarijanto 212
チャーチランド
Churchland, Patricia Smith 263
Churchland, Paul M. 263
チャーチル
Churchill, Don W. 263
Churchill, Elmer Richard 263
Churchill, Jill 263
Churchill, Rob 263
チャック
Chuck, Delroy 262
チャッコ
Chacko, George 241
チャッタワーラック
Jattawaalak 666
チャッチャイ
Chatchai, Sarikulya 249
チャットウッド
Chatwood, Tyler 249
チャッパローニ・ラ・ロッカ
Ciapparoni La Rocca, Teresa 264
チャップ
Chupp, Sam 263
チャップマン
Chapman, Alexander Lawrence 246
Chapman, Allan 246
Chapman, Anna 246
Chapman, Aroldis 246
Chapman, Aroldis Albertin 246
Chapman, Brenda 246
Chapman, Charles C. 246

Chapman, Chris 246
Chapman, Christopher S. 247
Chapman, Davis Howard 247
Chapman, Drew 247
Chapman, Gary D. 247
Chapman, Herb 247
Chapman, Jane 247
Chapman, Jason 247
Chapman, Jenny 247
Chapman, Judi 247
Chapman, Kevin 247
Chapman, Laura-Kate 247
Chapman, Linda 247
Chapman, Lynne 247
Chapman, Marina 247
Chapman, Mark David 247
Chapman, Matt 247
Chapman, Merrill R. 247
Chapman, Robert G. 247
Chapman, S.Michael 247
Chapman, Steven Curtis 247
Chapman, Ysanne 247
チャップリン
Chaplin, Geraldine 246
Chaplin, Sarah 246
Chaplin, Sydney 246
チャップロー
Chappelow, Craig 247
チャディ
Chadi, Abdelkader 241
チャデルトン
Chaderton, Roy 241
チャート
Chart, David 248
Chat, Kobjitti 249
チャード
Chard, Sylvia C. 247
チャトー
Chatto, Beth 249
チャドウィック
Chadwick, Alice 241
Chadwick, Andrés 241
Chadwick, Henry 241
Chadwick, Lynn 241
Chadwick, Owen 241
Chadwick, Paul D. 242
チャトゥパム
Chinnawong, Chatuphum 256
チャトゥロン
Chaturon, Chaisang 249
Jaturon, Chaisaeng 666
チャトゥン
Chatten, Cathy 249
チャート・ソンスィー
Cherd Songsri 253
チャード・ソンスィー
Cherd Songsri 253
チャートフ
Chartoff, Robert 248
Chertoff, Michael 253
チャドボーン
Chadbourn, Mark 241
チャドラーバリーン・ロドイダンバ
Chadraabalyn Lodoidamba 241
チャートランド
Chartrand, Gary 248
チャーナウ
Chernow, Ron 253
チャナティップ
Sonkham, Chanatip 1328
チャナラソポン
Chanaratsopon, Charlie 244
チャーニー
Charney, Dennis S. 248
Charney, Noah 248
チャーニアク
Cherniak, Christopher 253
チャーニイ
Charney, Noah 248
チャニャヴァナクル
Chanjavanakul, Natpat 246
チャーニン
Churnin, Nancy 263
チャニング
Channing, Stockard 246
チャヌヌガンバム
Chanu Ngangbam, Soniya 246
チャネ
Tchane, Abdoulaye Bio 1387
チャーネイク
Chernaik, Judith 253
チャーネス
Charness, Neil 248
チャノン
Channon, John 246
Channon, Paul Guinness 246
チャバック
Chubbuck, Ivana 262
チャバネ
Chabane, Collins 241
Chabane, Ohm Collins 241
チャバララ
Tshabalala, Siphiwe 1423
チャバララムシマング
Msimang, Mantombazana Tshabalala- 985
チャハル
Chahar, Digambar 242
チャビ
Xavi 1531
チャヒオ
Tjahjo, Kumolo 1407
チャビス
Chavis, Melody Ermachild 250
チャピン
Chapin, Rosemary Kennedy 246
Chapin, Tom 246
チャブ
Chubb, Kit 262
チャフィー
Chaffee, Todd 242
チャフケフ
Chakhkiev, Rakhim 242
チャブシオール
Çavuşoğlu, Mevlüt 238
チャプマン
Chapman, Anna 246
Chapman, Aroldis Albertin 246
Chapman, Bill G. 246
Chapman, David W., Jr. 247
Chapman, Simon 247
チャフヤディ
Cahyadi, Rusli 213
チャブラ
Chhabra, Anikar Bobby 254
チャプリカス
Čapilikas, Algis 223
チャブリス
Chabris, Christopher F. 241
チャプリン
Chaplin, L.Tarin 246
Chaplin, Sydney 246
チャプロビチ
Čaplovič, Dušan 223
チャプロビッチ
Čaplovič, Dušan 223
チャベス
Cháves, Javier 250
Chávez, Adán 250
Chávez, Asdrúbal 250
Chávez, Hernán Humberto Rosa 250
Chávez, Hugo 250
Chavez, Jesse 250
Chavez, Julio 250
Chavez, Julio Cesar 250
チャベス・ゴメス
Chávez Gómez, Jeannette 250
チャペス・ゴメス
Chávez Gómez, Jeannette 250
チャベス・ゴンサレス
Chaves González, Manuel 250
チャベス・チャベス
Chávez Chávez, Arturo 250
チャベス・ビエティ
Chavez Bietti, Ángela María de Lourdes 250
チャベス・フリアス
Chávez Frías, Adan 250
チャペック
Capek, Michael 222
チャペラー
Tschäppeler, Roman 1423
チャベリ
Chaverri, Danilo 250
チャペル
Chappel, Tim 247
Chappell, A.Paul 247
Chappell, David A. 247
Chappell, David W. 247
Chappell, J. 247
チャペロウ
Chappelhow, Mary 247
チャポー
Chapo, El 247
チャポンダ
Chaponda, George 247
Chaponda, George Thapatula 247
チャマ
Chama, Davis 243
チャマイエフ
Chermayeff, Ivan 253
チャーマーズ
Chalmers, David John 242
チャミ
Chami, Cyril Agust 243
チャミサ
Chamisa, Nelson 243
チャミゾマルケス
Chamizo Marquez, Frank 243
チャミン
Chamine, Shirzad 243
チャム
Cham, Alhaji Abdoulie 243
Cham, Momodou Kotu 243
Cham, Ugala Uriat 243
Cham Prasidh 244
Thiam, Serigne Mbaye 1395
チャーメル
Charmel, Patrick A. 248
チャモヴィッツ
Chamovitz, Daniel 243
チャモロ‐プリミュージク
Chamorro-Premuzic, Tomas 243
チャラ
Tchala, Kessile 1387
Tchalla, Pitang 1387
チャラビ
Chalabi, Ahmad Abdel Hadi 242
チャラビエフ
Chalabiyev, Javid 242
チャーラヤン
Çağlayan, Mehmet Zafer 213
チャラヤン
Chalayan, Hussein 242
チャラン
Charan, Ram 247
チャリアオ・ユーウィッタヤー
Chaleo Yoovidhya 242
チャリコフ
Sharikov, Sergey 1282
チャリシー
Charisse, Cyd 247
チャリース
Charisse, Cyd 247
チャーリッシュ
Charlish, Anne 248
チャリナー
Challinor, Joan R. 242
チャリハ
Chaliha, Jaya 242
チャリム
Tchalim, Tcitchao 1387
チャリンダ
Charinda, Mohamed 247
チャルアン
Chaleun, Yapaoher 242
チャルイエフ
Charyyev, Begench 248
チャルイフ
Chalykh, Elena 243
チャルカ
Charuca 248
チャルカシナ
Charkashyna, Liubou 247
チャルーシナ
Charyshina-Kapystina, Natalia 248
チャルーシン
Charushin, Nikita 248
チャールズ
Prince Charles 247
Charles, Claris 247
Charles, C.Leslie 247
Charles, Daniel 248

チ

Charles, Edward 248
Charles, Jamaal 248
Charles, Julia 248
Charles, Justina 248
Charles, Kate 248
Charles, Mary Eugenia 248
Charles, Maxwell 248
Charles, Nicola 248
Charles, Orson 248
Charles, Pearnel 248
Charles, Pierre 248
Charles, Ray 248
Charles, Stefan 248
Charles, Victoria 248
チャールズ＝エドワーズ
Charles-Edwards, T. M. 248
チャールズ皇太子
Prince Charles 247
チャールストン
Charlton, Bobby 248
チャールズワース
Charlesworth, Brian 248
Charlesworth, Chris 248
Charlesworth, Deborah 248
Charlesworth, James H. 248
チャルセン
Chalsen, Christopher E. 243
チャールソン
Charleson, Susannah 248
チャルディーニ
Cialdini, Robert B. 264
チャルトラン
Chartrand, Judy 248
チャールトン
Charlton, Andrew Henry George 248
Charlton, Ann 248
Charlton, Bobby 248
Charlton, James I. 248
チャールトン・ジョーンズ
Charlton-Jones, Richard 248
チャルネッキ
Czarnecki, Krzysztof 310
チャルノグルスキー
Čarnogurský, Ján 227
チャルハイカ
Charheika, Illia 247
チャルパコーン
Charupakorn, Joe 248
チャルハノール
Calhanoglu, Hakan 215
チャルフィー
Chalfie, Martin 242
チャルマース
Chalmers, Keryn 243
チャルマーズ
Chalmers, A.F. 242
Chalmers, Emily 243
Chalmers, Kyle 243
Chalmers, Mary 243
チャルーム
Chalerm, Ubumrung 242
チャルームチャイ
Chalermchai, Sri-on 242
チャルルイエフ
Charlyyev, Charygeldi 248
チャルーン
Chaleun, Yapaoher 242
チャレ
Kya leh 778
チャレフ
Chaleff, Ira 242
チャレロ
Chiarello, Michael 254
チャレンジャー
Challenger, James E. 242
チャレンダー
Challender, Jeff 242
チャロッキ
Ciarrochi, Joseph 264
チャロナー
Challoner, Jack 242
チャロバー
Chalobah, Nathaniel 243
チャワラット
Chavarat, Charnvirakul 249
チャワリット
Chavalit, Yongchaiyudh 249
チャーン
Cagan, Ibrahim Nami 213
Chern, Shiing-shen 253
Chern, Wen S. 253
チャン
Chan, Alan 244
Chan, Anita 244
Chan, Benny 244
Chan, Byron 244
Chan, Christine 244
Chan, Chun Sing 244
Chan, Francis 244
Chan, Fred 244
Chan, Fruit 244
Chan, Ka Wah 244
Chan, Kong Choy 244
Chan, Kylie 244
Chan, Laiwa 244
Chan, Laurie 244
Chan, Margaret 244
Chan, Norma P. 244
Chan, Otto 244
Chan, Patrick 244
Chan, Peng Soon 244
Chan, Peter 244
Chan, Priscilla 244
Chan, Ronald W. 244
Chan, Sucheng 244
Chan, Teddy 244
Chan, Tommy Koh 244
Chan, Victor 244
Chan, Vincent W.S. 244
Chan, Vivien 244
Chang, Angelin 245
Chang, Ben 245
Chang, Ben-hang 245
Chang, Bernard 245
Chang, Byoung-wan 245
Chang, Caroline 245
Chang, Chen 245
Chang, Dae-whan 245
Chang, Dong-Hwa 245
Chang, Do-yeong 245
Chang, Eileen 245
Chang, Gordon G. 245
Chang, Gordon H. 245
Chang, Ha-Joon 245
Chang, Hanna 245
Chang, Horace 245
Chang, Hsueh-liang 245
Chang, Iris 245
Chang, Jeff 245
Chang, Je-kuk 245
Chang, Jennifer 245
Chang, Jenny 245
Chang, Jin 245
Chang, Jung 245
Chang, Jung-chi 245
Chang, Kelly 245
Chang, Kenneth 245
Chang, Ken T. 245
Chang, Kwang-chih 245
Chang, Kyung Suk 245
Chang, Leonard 245
Chang, Leslie T. 245
Chang, Michael 245
Chang, Morris 245
Chang, Norman H. 245
Chang, Raymond 245
Chang, Richard Y. 245
Chang, Rigoberto 245
Chang, Sarah 245
Chang, Seung-woo 245
Chang, Shin-feng 245
Chang, Song-taek 245
Chang, Steve 245
Chang, Steven C. 245
Chang, Sylvia 245
Chang, Tae-pyong 245
Chang, Terence 246
Chang, Tso-chi 246
Chang, Winston 246
Chang, Yung-fa 246
Chang Hao 246
Chan Sarun 246
Chen, Yuan 252
Cheng, Anne 252
Cheung, Aaron 254
Cheung, Adora 254
Cheung, Cecilia 254
Cheung, Corjena K. 254
Cheung, Jim 254
Cheung, Ka Wai 254
Cheung, King-Kok 254
Cheung, Leslie 254
Cheung, Maggie 254
Cheung, Rickey 254
Chiang, Alpha C. 254
Chiang, Cliff 254
Chiang, Doug 254
Chiang, Ted 254
Chuang, Isaac L. 262
Chun, Clarissa Kyoko Mei Ling 262
Chung, Doo-ri 263
Chung, Erin Aeran 263
Chung, Patrick 263
Francis-Cheung, Theresa 455
Jang, Chol 663
Jang, Dong-gun 663
Jang, Ha-jin 663
Jang, Hyok 663
Jang, Hyuk 663
Jang, Il-son 663
Jang, Ja-yeon 663
Jang, Jin-young 663
Jang, Jong-nam 663
Jang, Keun-suk 663
Jang, Siyoung 663
Jang, Yoon-jeong 663
Jing, Junhong 674
Tran, Thùy Mai 1417
Vu, Thi Trang 1465
Zhang, Ai-ping 1551
Zhang, Bangxin 1551
Zhang, Cang-cang 1551
Zhang, Cuo 1551
Zhang, De-jiang 1551
Zhang, Gao-li 1551
Zhang, Han-yu 1552
Zhang, Hong 1552
Zhang, Ji-ke 1552
Zhang, Jindong 1552
Zhang, Jing-chu 1552
Zhang, Jinhao 1552
Zhang, Kitty 1552
Zhang, Leping 1552
Zhang, Li-chang 1552
Zhang, Mo 1552
Zhang, Ping 1552
Zhang, Rui-min 1552
Zhang, Yang 1552
Zhang, Yijing 1552
Zhang, Yi-mou 1552
Zhang, Yitang 1552
Zhang, Yue-ran 1552
Zhang, Yun-ling 1552
Zhang, Zhidong 1552
Zhang, Zhiyao 1552
Zhang, Ziyi 1552
Zhang, Z.John 1552
チャン・ヴァン
Tran Văn 1417
チャン・ヴァン・ザウ
Tran Van Giau 1417
チャーンウィット・カセートシリ
Charnvit Kasetsiri 248
チャン・エスクデロ
Chang Escobedo, José Antonio 246
チャン・エスコベド
Chang Escobedo, José Antonio 246
チャンギージー
Changizi, Mark A. 246
チャング
Chung, Ook 263
チャンクラチャンウォン
Chankrachangwong, Sathinee 246
チャンゴ
Tchango, Gabriel 1387
チャンサモーン
Chansamone, Chanyalath 246
チャン・サルン
Chan Sarun 246
チャンシ
Chansy, Phosikham 246
チャンシリ
Chansiri, Kraisorn 246
Chansiri, Thiraphong 246
チャンス
Chance, Britton 244
Chance, Jane 244
Chance, Jeremy 244
チャン・スアン・バク
Tran Xuan Bach 1417
チャン・ズアン・バク
Tran Xuan Bach 1417
チャンスラー
Chancellor, Kam 244
チャンセラー
Chancellor, Henry 244
チャンソン
Chanson, Hubert 246
チャンソン・チャン
Changson Chang, Gabriel 246
チャンター
Chanter, Catherine 246
チャンダ
Chanda, Nayan 244
チャンタソン・インタヴォン
Chanthasone

Inthavong 246
チャンダラ
Chandara, Boualy 244
チャンダルパル
Chandarpal, Indranie 244
Chandarpal, Navin 244
チャンチェン
Changchien, Louis Ozawa 246
チャンチオロ
Cianciolo, Susan 264
チャーンチャイ
Charnchai, Chairoongruang 248
Charnchai, Likhitjittha 248
チャンディオ
Chandio, Moula Bakhsh 244
チャン・ディン・ホアン
Chan Dinh Hoang 244
チャンデラ
Chandela, Apurvi 244
チャンド
Chand, Lokendra Bahadur 244
チャン・ドゥク・ルオン
Tran Duc Luong 1417
チャン・ドゥック・ルオン
Tran Duc Luong 1417
チャンドゥナ
Chandna, Asheem 245
チャントゥリア
Tchanturia, Romani 1387
チャン・ドク・ルオン
Tran Duc Luong 1417
チャントラー
Chantler, Marcia L. 246
チャンドラ
Chandra, Bipan 245
Chandra, Lokesh 245
Chandra, Ramesh 245
Chandra, Sheila 245
Chandra, Vikram A. 245
チャンドラー
Chandler, Adam 244
Chandler, Alfred Dupont, Jr. 244
Chandler, Charlotte 244
Chandler, Clay 244
Chandler, David 244
Chandler, David G. 244
Chandler, David P. 244
Chandler, Gary G. 244
Chandler, Karen 244
Chandler, Kyle 244
Chandler, Murray 244
Chandler, Otis 244
Chandler, P.J. 244
Chandler, Steve 244
Chandler, Timothy 245
Chandler, Tyson 245
Chandler, Wilson 245
チャンドラセカラン
Chandrasekaran, Rajiv 245
チャンドラセナ
Chandrasena, S.M. 245
チャンドラソニック
Chandrasonic 245
チャンドラ・ムザファ
Chandra Muzaffar 245
チャントレル
Chantrell, Glynnis 246
チャン・ナバロ
Chang Navarro, Luis Alfonso 246
チャン・ニェイン
Chan Nyein 246
チャン・ニン
Chan Nyein 246
チャンネッラ
Ciannella, Giuliano 264
チャンネル
Channell, Carolyn E. 246
チャンパイ
Csampai, Attila 306
チャンバース
Chambers, S.J. 243
チャンバーズ
Chambers, Catherine 243
チャンバッテ
Kyambadde, Amelia 778
チャンバッデ
Kyambadde, Amelia 778
チャンバーランド
Chamberland, Marc 243
チャン・バン・ザウ
Tran Van Giau 1417
チャンピ
Ciampi, Carlo Azeglio 264
チャンピー
Champy, James 244
チャンピオン
Champion, David 243
Champion, Janice 243
Champion, Will 243
チャンプ
Champ, Heather 243
Champ, Janet 243
チャンブリス
Chambliss, Daniel F. 243
Chambliss, Maxie 243
チャンベシ
Chambeshi, Abel 243
チャンミン
Changmin 246
チャンムガム
Chanmugam, Arjun S. 246
チャン・レ・スアン
Tran Le Xuan 1417
チュ
Chu, Tien-hsin 262
Chu, Tien-wen 262
Joo, Hyung-hwan 686
Joo, Jin-mo 686
Ju, Ji-hoon 689
Ju, Sang-song 689
Ju, Tong-il 689
チュー
Chew, Phillip 254
Chew, Tai Soo 254
Choo, Jimmy 259
Choo, Shin-soo 259
Chu, Dang Vu 262
Chu, Ernest D. 262
Chu, Pollyanna 262
Chu, Steven 262
Chu, Tien-hsin 262
Chu, Tien-wen 262
Chugh, Dolly 262
Zhu, Guang-ya 1553
Zhu, Hou-ze 1553
Zhu, Liming 1553
Zhu, Rong-ji 1553
Zhu, Shao-wen 1553
チュア
Chua, Amy 262
Chua, Jui Meng 262
Chua, Mui Hoong 262
Chua, Nam-hai 262
Chua, Soi Lek 262
チュアイフェット・チェモル
Chuayffet Chemor, Emilio 262
チュアン
Cheuang, Sombounkhanh 254
Zhuang, Ze-dong 1553
チュアン・アロン
Chuang Aloung, Gier 262
チュアンアン
Quan'an, Wang 1143
チュアンテ
Tchuinté, Madeleine 1388
チュイ
Thúy, Kim 1403
チュウ
Chew, Alex L. 254
Chew, Choon Seng 254
Chew, Ruth 254
Choo, Jimmy 259
Choo, Shin-soo 259
Zhu, Xu 1553
チュウイ
Chui, Glennda 262
チュウ・シー・チェ
Triêu Thi Choí 1420
チュウプリック
Cheplick, Gregory Paul 252
チュエカ
Chueca, Pilar 262
チュエン
Chuyen, Pham Thi Hai 264
Truyen, Tran Van 1423
チュエンテ
Tchuente, Maurice 1388
Tchuinté, Madeleine 1388
チュエンルディーモル
Chuenrudeemol, Chatpong 262
チュオン
Truong, Minh Dục 1422
チュオン・ザー・ビン
Truong Gia Binh 1422
チュオン・タン・サン
Truong Tan Sang 1422
チューキアット・サックウィーラクン
Chookiat Sakveerakul 259
チュク
Chuku, Christiam 262
Chukwu, Onyebuchi 262
チュクメリジェ
Chukwumerije, Chika Yagazie 262
チュクリエール
Tchoukriel, Emmanuelle 1387
チュゴシュビリ
Chugoshvili, Ioseb 262
チュー・サン
Kyaw Hsan 778
チュジノフ
Chudinov, Igor V. 262
Chudinov, Sergei 262
チュージン
Chudin, Semyon 262
チュース
Kjus, Lasse 743
チュソヴィチナ
Chusovitina, Oksana 263
チュソビチナ
Chusovitina, Oksana 263
チューター
Chuter, David 263
チューダー
Tudor, Keith 1425
Tudor, Tasha 1425
チュダコフ
Chudacoff, Howard P. 262
チューダー=サンダール
Tudor-Sandahl, Patricia 1425
チュチープ
Chucheep, Hansawat 262
チュチャー
Tschütscher, Klaus 1423
チューチャイ・チョムタワット
Chiedchai Chomtawat 255
チュチャワル
Chutchawal Khawlaor 263
チュチュノフ
Tyutyunov, Anatoly D. 1431
チュック
Truc, Mai Ai 1422
チュッチャー
Tschütscher, Klaus 1423
チューディー
Tschudy, Megan M. 1423
チュティ
Chuti, Krairiksh 264
チューディン
Tschudin, Verena 1423
チュードゥン
Chödrön, Pema 258
チュート・ソンスイー
Cherd Songsri 253
チュナエフ
Chunayev, Rasul 263
チュニシ
al-Tunisi, Abdul-Latif 849
チュニス
Tunis, Sidi Yahya 1426
Tuniz, Claudio 1426
チュネク
Cunek, Jirí 307
チュバイス
Chubais, Anatolii Borisovich 262
チュバキン
Chuvakin, Anton 264
チュパック
Chupack, Cindy 263
チュバン
Ceban, Nicolae 239
チュピチ
Čupić, Simona 308
チュブ
Chubb, Brandon 262
チュフォレッティ
Ciuffoletti, Luca 265
チュブクチュ
Çubukçu, Nimet 306
チュプコフ
Chupkov, Anton 263
チュフライ
Chukhrai, Grigorii Naumovich 262
チュポ・モティング

Choupo-moting, Eric Maxim 260
チユマ
Czuma, Andrzej 311
チユマク
Chumak, Dmytro 262
チユマコフ
Chumakov, Aleksandr P. 262
チユマチェンコ
Chumachenko, Ana 262
チユマルト
Cumart, Eray 307
チユミ
Tschumi, Bernard 1423
チユムポン
Chumpol, Silpa-archa 262
チユメオ
Tcheumeo, Audrey 1387
チユラポウスキー
Chrapkowski, Edward 260
チユラポーン王女
Princess Chulabhorn 262
チユリコワ
Churikova, Inna 263
チユーリナ
Tiourina, Svetlana 1406
チユーリン
Thulin, Inge G. 1402
Thulin, Ingrid 1402
チユリン
Jurin, Laksanawisit 692
チユールテミン
Tsultemin, Munkhjin 1424
チユルンバト・ジャルガルサイハン
Chuluunbat Jargalsaikhany 262
チユレイ
Ciulei, Liviu 265
チユーン
Cheung, Vincent 254
Choong, Joseph 259
Tune, Tommy 1426
チユン
Cheung, Jacky 254
Chun, Kam Fong 262
Chun, Shu 263
Chung, Angela E. 263
Chung, Chien-peng 263
Trung, Do Quang 1422
チユン・タン・サン
Truong Tan Sang 1422
チユンハ
Ryang, Chun Hwa 1221
チユンマリ
Choummaly Sayasone 260
チユンマリ・サイニャソーン
Choummaly Sayasone 260
チヨ
Cho, Chang-in 257
Cho, Choong-hoon 257
Cho, Dong-il 257
Cho, Eun-Hwa 257
Cho, Ha-ri 257
Cho, Hyun 257
Cho, hyun-jae 257
Cho, Jea-hyun 257
Cho, Kyeung-kyu 257
Cho, Kyung-hwan 257
Cho, Mahama 257
Cho, Myong-chol 257
Cho, Nam-chul 257
Cho, Se-hyung 257
Cho, Seong Jin 258
Cho, Seung-woo 258
Cho, Seung-Yeon 258
Cho, Suck-rai 258
Cho, Sung-min 258
Cho, Sung-tae 258
Cho, Yang-ho 258
Cho, Yong-pil 258
Cho, Yoon-Ho 258
Chou, Kap-che 260
Jo, Chang-dok 674
Jo, Myong-rok 674
Jo, Pyong-ju 674
Jo, Yong-chol 674
Jo, Yong Suk 674
Jo, Yun-hui 674
Joh, Ui-seok 675
Zo, In-sung 1556
チヨー
Cho, Alan 257
Cho, Esther Yoona 257
Cho, Lee-jay 257
Cho, Linda 257
Cho, Rich 257
Cho, Suck-rai 258
Cho, Sung-min 258
Cho, Yong-pil 258
Choo, Hyunjoo 259
Choo, Leanne 259
Chor, Chee Heung 259
Chou, Kap-che 260
チヨイ
Choi, Hyun-myung 258
Choi, Pat Tai 259
チヨイジリーン・チミド
Choijiliin Chinid 259
チヨイジルスレン
Choijilsuren, Battogtohyin 259
チヨウ
Cheung, William 254
Cho, Choong-hoon 257
Cho, Frank 257
Cho, Lee-jay 257
Cho, Tat-wah 258
Cho, Yong-pil 258
Chou, Jay 260
Chou, Joey 260
Chou, Kap-che 260
Chow, Yuen-fat 260
Zhang, Yang 1552
Zhang, Yun-ling 1552
Zhao, Jing 1552
Zhou, Dong-yu 1553
Zhou, Er-fu 1553
Zhou, Hai-ying 1553
Zhou, Jianping 1553
Zhou, Patricia 1553
Zhou, Qunfei 1553
Zhou, Yahui 1553
Zhou, Yong-kang 1553
チヨヴィッチ
Ković, Dragan 296
チヨー・ウィン
Kyaw Win 778
チヨウチン
Zhao, Jing 1552
チヨウドリ
Choudhury, Humayun Rashid 260
Chowdhury, Anwarul Karim 260
Chowdhury, Subir 260
チヨウドリー
Chowdhury, Naren 260
チヨウ・ユンファ
Chow, Yuen-fat 260
チヨウラガイン
Chaulagain, Kamal Prasad 249
チヨエツカ
Chojecka, Lidia 259
チヨーカー
Chalker, Jack Bridger 242
チヨーク
Chalk, Gary 242
Chalk, Rosemary A. 242
Ťok, Dan 1409
チヨク
Čok, Lucija 276
Ťok, Dan 1409
チヨクシー
Choksy, K.N. 259
チヨクニャイ
Csoknyai, Laszlo 306
チヨケワンカ・セスペデス
Choquehuanca Céspedes, David 259
チヨサック
Chosak, Anne 259
チヨー・サン
Kyaw Hsan 778
Kyaw San 778
チヨーシッチ
Ćosić, Dobrica 293
チヨシッチ
Ćosić, Dobrica 293
チヨー・スエ
Kyaw Swe 778
チヨスドスキー
Chossudovsky, Michel 259
チヨーダリ
Chaudhari, Ram Janam 249
チヨーダリー
Chaudhari, Gauri Shankar 249
チヨチェフ
Chochev, Ivaylo 258
チヨチノフ
Chochinov, Harvey Max 258
チヨチュア
Chochua, Irakli 258
チヨチヨシヴィリ
Chochoshvili, Shota Samsonovich 258
チヨチヨシビリ
Chochoshvili, Shota Samsonovich 258
チヨック
Chock, Madison 258
チヨッケ
Zschocke, Johannes 1558
Zschokke, Matthias 1558
チヨー・ティン・スエ
Kyaw Tint Swe 778
チヨデン
Choden, Dorji 258
Choden, Kunzang 258
チヨート
Choate, Pat 258
チヨードゥリー
Chowdhury, Bernie 260
チヨードリ
Choudhury, Surendra Prasad 260
Chowdhury, Abdul Matin 260
Chowdhury, Altaf Hossain 260
Chowdhury, Anwarul Karim 260
Chowdhury, Begum Matia 260
Chowdhury, Mahmud 260
Chowdhury, Syeda Sajeda 260
チヨードリー
Chaudhry, Mahendra 249
Chaudhuri, Arjun 249
Choudhury, Bikram 260
Choudhury, Zubayer Pasha 260
Chowdhry, Anwar 260
Chowdhury, Matia 260
チヨドリ
Chowdhury, Iftekhar Uddin 260
チヨドロ
Teodoro, Gilberto 1391
チヨドロン
Chödrön, Pema 258
チヨナイ
Tchonai, Hassan 1387
チヨーニー
Choonee, Mookhesswur 259
チヨネク
Cionek, Thiago 265
チヨバヌ
Cebanu, Ion 239
Ciobanu, Gennadie 265
チヨバンコビッチ
Čobanković, Petar 272
チヨピアク
Chopyak, Christine 259
チヨビッチ
Ković, Dragan 296
Covic, Nebojsa 296
チヨプ
Cop, Duje 288
チヨーフィ
Ciofi, Patrizia 265
チヨプラ
Chopra, Deepak 259
Chopra, Gotham 259
Chopra, Yash 259
チヨペ・ペルジョル・ツェリン
Chope Paljor Tsering 259
チヨボウスキー
Chbosky, Stephen 250
チヨボスキー
Chbosky, Stephen 250
チヨマ
Csoma, Gergely 306
チヨー・ミン
Kyaw Myint 778
チヨムスキー
Chomsky, Noam 259
チヨムタワット
Chomtawet, Chiedchai 259
チヨムボ
Chombo, Ignatius 259
チヨヤス
Tjoyas, Alexios 1407
チヨラク
Colak, Antonio 276
Çollaku, Bekim 278
チヨラコフ
Cholakov, Velichko 259

チョーラック
Čolak, Bariša 276
チョリエフ
Choriev, Dilshod 259
チョリエワ
Chorieva, Mavzuna 259
チョリッチ
Ćorić, Tomislav 290
チョー・ルウィン
Kyaw Lwin 778
チョルカス
Tsiolkas, Christos 1424
チョールズ
Choules, Claude 260
チョールデンコウ
Choldenko, Gennifer 259
チョルネ
Tschorne, Sonia 1423
チョルネイ
Ciornei, Silvia 265
チョロシュ
Cioloş, Dacian 265
チョロデンコ
Cholodenko, Lisa 259
チョロマ
Choroma, Aboubakar Assidik 259
チョワン
Zhuang, Ze-dong 1553
チョン
Cheng, Wei 252
Cheng, Yong-hua 252
Cheong, Jun Hoong 252
Cheong, Otfried 252
Cheung, Jacky 254
Cheung, Maggie 254
Cheung, William 254
Chon, Wol-son 259
Chon, Yo-ok 259
Chong, Curtis R. 259
Chong, Denise 259
Chong, Hyon-suk 259
Chong, Jong-sup 259
Chong, Jun-gi 259
Chong, Leighton K. 259
Chong, Te-se 259
Chong, Vincent 259
Choung, Byoung-guk 260
Chun, Doo-hwan 262
Chun, Hanbong 262
Chun, Jeong-myoung 262
Chun, Kwang-young 262
Chun, Woo-hee 263
Chun, Yung-woo 263
Chung, Ching-wen 263
Chung, Chin-youb 263
Chung, Chung-kil 263
Chung, Dong-chea 263
Chung, Dong-young 263
Chung, Hong-won 263
Chung, Jae-jeong 263
Chung, Jong-hwan 263
Chung, Joon-yang 263
Chung, Ju-yong 263
Chung, Ku-chong 263
Chung, Kyung-wha 263
Chung, Mong-hun 263
Chung, Mong-joon 263
Chung, Mong-koo 263
Chung, Myung-whun 263
Chung, Se-rang 263
Chung, Se-Yung 263
Chung, Sye-kyun 263
Chung, Ui-Hwa 263
Chung, Un-chan 263
Chung, Won-shik 263
Jeon, Ari 671
Jeon, Do-youn 671
Jeon, In-teak 671
Jeon, Jae-hee 671
Jeon, Ji-hyun 671
Jeon, Kyung-rin 671
Jeon, Min-hee 671
Jeon, Minje 671
Jeon, Yun-churl 671
Jeong, Ji-a 671
Jeong, Se-hyun 671
Jeong, Stephanie 671
Jhung, Myong-suk 673
Jon, Ha-chol 681
Jon, Kil-su 681
Jon, Sung-hun 681
Jong, Chun Mi 686
Jong, Mun-san 686
Jong, Myong-suk 686
Jong, Yong-su 686
Juhn, Jai-hong 690
Jung, Byeong-ho 691
Jung, Da-bin 691
Jung, Da-Yon 691
Jung, Ji-hyun 691
Jung, Jin-young 691
Jung, July 691
Jung, Jun-ho 691
Jung, Woo-sung 691
Jung, Wun Chul 691
Jung, Yi-hyun 691
Trong, Truong Vinh 1421
チョン・ウォン
Chong Wong, William 259
チョンカ
Csonka, Zsofia 306
チョング
Cheong, Robin 252
チョンコ
Chonko, Jon 259
チョーンシー
Chauncey, George 249
チョンシー
Chauncey, Dan 249
チョンジン
Junjin 692
チョン・チン・ユ
Tjon Tjin Joe, Jacques 1407
チョンチンユ
Tjon Tjin Joe, Jacques 1407
チョンテイ
Chontey, Arli 259
チョン・ドヨン
Do-yeon, Jeon 372
チョンビ
Tchombi, Fatime 1387
チョンボ
Chombo, Ignatius 259
チラオロ
Ciraolo, Simona 265
チラーズィ
Chirazi, Steffan 256
チラチャヴァ
Chilachava, Levan 255
チラナナ
Tsiranana, Ruffine 1424
チラベルト
Chilavert, Jose Luis 255
チランジービ
Chiranjeevi, K. 256
チリアンゲ
Tjiriange, Ngarikutuke 1407
チリィーダ
Chillida, Eduardo 255
チリガティ
Chiligati, John 255
チリキシビリ
Tchrikishvili, Avtandili 1388
チリク
Ciricu, Anatolie 265
チリーダ
Chillida, Eduardo 255
チリッチ
Cilic, Marin 264
チリーノ
Chirino, Willy 256
チリノス
Chirinos, Robinson 257
チリフ
Chirif, Micaela 256
チリベジャ
Chirivella, Pedro 257
チリボガ
Chriboga, David 260
チリマ
Chilima, Saulos Klaus 255
チリモコス
Tsirimokos, Yannis 1424
チール
Cheal, David J. 250
Chiel, Deborah 255
Thiel, Richard 1396
チル
Chill, Julia 255
Cyl, Agnieszka 310
チルヴァース
Chilvers, Ian 256
チルウェル
Chilwell, Ben 256
チルキー
Tschirky, Hugo 1423
チルチル
Chirchir, Davis 256
チルツェネ
Circene, Ingrīda 265
チルドレス
Childress, Brad 255
Childress, James F. 255
チルトン
Chilton, David 256
チルバ
Chiluba, Frederick 256
チルフヤ
Chilufya, Chitaru 256
チル＝ボルド
Tillous-borde, Sébastien 1405
チルマシェフ
Chyrmashyev, Satybaldy 264
チルマノフ
Chilmanov, Arman 256
チルワ
Chirwa, Khumbo 257
チルンパ
Chilumpha, Cassim 256
チルンファ
Chilumpha, Cassim 256
チレー
Chireh, Yile 256
チレキゼ
Tsirekidze, Irakli 1424
チロマバカリ
Tchiroma Bakary, Issa 1387
チワヤ
Chiwaya, Clement 257
チン
Chang, Kelly 245
Chen, Ehan 251
Chen, Kai-ge 251
Chen, Li-fu 251
Chen, Tyen-Po 251
Chin, Curtis S. 256
Chin, Dae-je 256
Chin, Elias 256
Chin, Hsiao-i 256
Chin, Jason 256
Chin, Peter 256
Chin, Siat Yoon 256
Chin, Soo-hee 256
Chin, Steven A. 256
Chin, Yam Chin 256
Ching, Julia 256
Ching, Siu-tung 256
Chinn, Menzie D. 256
Chinn, Peggy L. 256
Cin, Luigi Dal 264
Jin, Fei 674
Jin, Jong-oh 674
Jin, Nyum 674
Jin, Yao-ru 674
Qin, Chuan 1143
Quin, Hai-lu 1144
Shim, Man-sup 1290
チンクエッティ
Cinquetti, Nicola 265
チングンジ
Chingunji, Eduardo Jonatão 256
チン・コン・ソン
Trinh Cong Son 1420
チンシャン
Chinshanlo, Zulfiya 256
チンシャンロ
Chinshanlo, Zulfiya 256
チンゾリグ
Chinzorig, Sodonom 256
チン・タン
Ching, Tang 256
チンチジャ
Chinchilla, Laura 256
チンチジャ・ミランダ
Chinchilla Miranda, Laura 256
チンテーザ
Cinteză, Mircea 265
チンデマン
Tindemans, Leo 1405
チンデマンス
Tindemans, Leo 1405
チンナウォン
Chinnawong, Chatuphum 256
チンハイ
Ching Hai 256
チン・ペン
Chin Peng 256
チンベン
Chin Beng, Lim 256
チンマン
Chinman, Matthew 256
チンモイ
Chinmoy, Sri 256

チンモイシ
Chinmoy, Sri 256
チンリー
Chin Lee, Haward 256

【ツ】

ツァイ
Cai, Guo-qiang 213
Cai, Wu 213
Cai, Xiao Ru 213
Cai, Zhen-hua 213
Tsai, Eng-Meng 1423
Tsai, Ing-wen 1423
Tsai, Joseph 1423
Tsai, Ming-liang 1423
ツアイ
Cai, Guo-qiang 213
Chai, Ling 242
ツァイ・シャンチュン
Cai, Shangjun 213
ツァイツ
Zeitz, Paul 1550
ツァイツェフ
Zaitsev, Peter 1545
ツァイリンガー
Zeilinger, Anton 1549
Zeilinger, Gabriel 1549
ツァウネルト
Zaunert, Paul 1548
ツァオ
Cao, Shun-li 222
Chao, Chi 246
Tsao, Chin-hui 1423
Zhao, Hong-bo 1552
ツァガーン
Tsagaan, Puntsagiin 1423
ツァガンバータル
Tsagaanbaatar, Khashbaataryn 1423
ツァキ
Csáky, Pál 306
ツァグロセク
Zagrosek, Lothar 1545
ツァグロゼク
Zagrosek, Lothar 1545
ツァコス
Tsakos, Panagiotis 1423
ツァツィオニス
Tsatsionis, Nikos 1423
ツァネタキス
Tzannetakis, Tzannis 1431
ツァノレッティ
Zanoletti, Costanza 1547
ツァハー
Zacher, Hans Friedrich 1544
ツア・ハウゼン
Zur Hausen, Harald 1559
ツアハウゼン
Zur Hausen, Harald 1559
ツァハリーアス
Zacharias, Helmut 1544
ツァハリアス
Zacharias, Christian 1544
Zacharias, Helmut 1544
ツァパリニ
Capalini, Libor 222
ツァバル
Tzabar, Shimon 1431
ツァピシ
Ţapiş, Valentina 1381
ツァピンスキ
Capiński, Marek 223
ツアフクナ
Tsahkna, Margus 1423
ツァフタリス
Tsaftaris, Athanasios 1423
ツァベル
Zabel, Erik 1544
ツァヘルト
Zachert, Susanna 1544
ツアホルスト
Zurhorst, Eva-Maria 1559
ツァラ
Czarra, Fred Raymon 310
ツアラ
Tuala, Ainiu Iusitino 1425
Tuala, Sale Tagaloa 1425
ツァラナジ
Tsaranazy, Jean Emile 1423
ツァルグシュ
Tsargush, Denis 1423
ツァルケーワ
Tsarukaeva, Svetlana 1423
ツァルコ
Tsalko, Vladimir G. 1423
ツァルコフ
Tsarkov, Oleh 1423
ツァレフ
Tsarev, Ruslan 1423
ツァン
Tsang, Eric 1423
ツアン
Chang, Xiang-yu 246
Chang Hao 246
ツァンカル
Cankar, Stanka Setnikar 221
ツァンギライ
Tsvangirai, Morgan 1424
ツァンジド
Tsanjid, Ayurzanyn 1423
ツァンシュエ
Canxue 222
ツァンジーレ王女
Princess Tsandzile 1423
ツァンジレ王女
Princess Tsandzile 1423
ツァン・ツォ
Zhang, Zuo 1552
ツァンデル
Tsander, Olga Mikhaylovna 1423
ツーイ
Tsui, Daniel Chee 1424
ツイ
Cui, Tian-kai 307
Cui, Yang-uang 307
Tsui, Daniel Chee 1424
Tsui, Hark 1424
ツイアツア・ツプア・タマセセ・エフィ
Tuiatua Tupua Tamasese Efi 1426
ツィアンドピ
Tsiandopy, Jacky Mahafaly 1424
ツィエク
Ziyech, Hakim 1556
ツィギー
Twiggy 1430
ツイグ
Twigg, Emma 1430
ツィーグラー
Ziegler, Cornelia 1554
Ziegler, Günter M. 1554
Ziegler, Yvonne 1554
ツィクラウリ
Tsiklauri, Beka 1424
ツィーゲレ
Ziegele, Robin 1554
ツィスカリシビリ
Tsiskarishvili, Petre 1424
ツィスカリーゼ
Tsiskaridze, Nikolai 1424
ツイスガレタウア
Tuisugaletaua, Sofara Aveau 1426
ツイセセ
Tuisese, Ilaitia 1426
ツイタマ
Tuitama, Talalelei Tuitama 1426
ツイッギー
Twiggy 1430
ツィットラウ
Zittlau, Jörg 1556
ツィッパート
Zippert, Hans 1556
ツィトゥリディス
Tsitouridis, Savvas 1424
ツイドラキ
Tuidraki, Patiliai 1426
ツィバ
Tsiba, Florent 1424
ツィバコフ
Tsybakow, Véra 1425
ツィーハマ
Tsheehama, Peter 1423
ツィピナレ
Tshipinare, Michaele 1424
ツィプラス
Tsipras, Alexis 1424
ツィプリース
Zypries, Brigitte 1560
ツィヘラシビリ
Tsikhelashvili, Ketevan 1424
ツィマーマン
Zimerman, Krystian 1555
Zimmerman, Tabea 1555
Zimmermann, Frank Peter 1555
ツィムバリュク
Tsymbalyuk, Alexander 1425
ツィメルマン
Zimerman, Krystian 1555
ツィーメン
Zimen, Erik 1555
ツィーラー
Zieler, Ron-Robert 1554
ツイラエパ
Tuilaepa Sailele Malielegaoi 1426
ツィリエニチュ
Cirjenics, Miklos 265
ツイリム
Tuilimu, Lagitupu 1426
ツイリンスカヤ
Tsylinskaya, Natallia 1425
ツィルク
Zilk, Helmut 1554
ツィルヒャー
Zircher, Patrick 1556
ツィーレップ
Zierep, J. 1554
ツイロマ
Tuiloma, Pule Lameko 1426
ツィンカーナーゲル
Zinkernagel, Rolf Martin 1555
ツィンク
Cink, Ondrej 264
Zing, Jorg 1555
Zink, Jörg 1555
Zink, Klaus J. 1555
ツィンコウタ
Czinkota, Michael R. 311
ツインズ・セヴン・セヴン
Twins Seven Seven 1430
ツィンツァゼ
Tsintsadze, Levan 1424
ツイントゥリーズ
Twintreess, Marilyn 1430
Twintreess, T. 1430
ツィンナー
Zinner, Peter 1556
ツィンマー
Zimmer, Katharina 1555
ツィンマーマン
Zimerman, Krystian 1555
Zimmerman, Brenda 1555
Zimmerman, Jeffrey 1555
Zimmermann, Eliane 1555
Zimmermann, Frank Peter 1555
Zimmermann, Hans Dieter 1555
Zimmermann, Jörg 1555
Zimmermann, Manfred 1555
Zimmermann, Markus 1555
Zimmermann, Martin H. 1555
Zimmermann, Michael 1555
Zimmermann, Reinhard 1555
ツィンママン
Zimmerman, Keith 1555
Zimmerman, Kent 1555
ツヴァイク
Zweig, Stefanie 1560
ツヴァイグ
Zweig, Ronald W. 1560
ツヴァイフェル
Zweifel, George S. 1560
ヅヴァイヤー
Zwier, Lawrence J. 1560
ツゥイ
Cui, Yang-uang 307
ツヴィテシッチ
Cvitešić, Zrinka 310
ツヴィーバッハ
Zwiebach, Barton 1560
ツウィーフェルホーファー
Zwiefelhofer, Thomas 1560
ツウィンゲンバーガー
Zwingenberger, Allison L. 1560
ツヴィンゲンベルガー
Zwingenberger, Jeanette 1560
ツウウ
Tuuu, Anasii Leota 1429

ツウェテ
Tshwete, Steve Vukile 1424
ツヴェトコヴァ
Tsvetkova, Nina Yurievna 1425
ツヴェトコビッチ
Cvetkovikj, Andrijana 310
ツヴェトコフ
Tsvetkov, Valentin Ivanovich 1424
ツヴェルガー
Zwerger, Lisbeth 1560
ツヴェーレンツ
Zwerenz, Gerhard 1560
ツヴェレンツ
Zwerenz, Gerhard 1560
ツヴォリンスキー
Zwoliński, Mark 1560
ツゥラッハ
Tulach, Jaroslav 1426
ツェ
Tse, David K. 1423
Tse, Edward 1423
Tse, Su-mei 1423
ツェー
Zeh, Juli 1549
ツェーエトマイア
Zehetmair, Thomas 1549
ツェガエ
Tsegaye, Tirfi 1423
ツェゲラー
Zoeggeler, Armin 1556
ツェコア
Tsekoa, Mohlabi 1423
ツェッチェ
Zetsche, Dieter 1551
ツェッテル
Zettel, Kathrin 1551
ツェットナー
Zetner, Karl 1551
ツェデブ
TSedev, Dojoogiin 1423
ツェデブスレン
Tsedevsuren, Munkhzaya 1423
ツェデンバルジル
Tsedenbalzhir, M. 1423
ツェートマイアー
Zehetmair, Thomas 1549
ツェトマイヤー
Zehetmair, Thomas 1549
ツェトル
Zettle, Robert D. 1551
ツェフ
Cech, Petr 239
ツェーフェルト
Zeevaert, Sigrid 1549
ツェベクマ
Tsebegmaa, Baldangiin 1423
ツェヘトマイヤー
Zehetmair, Thomas 1549
ツェベリス
Tsebelis, George 1423
ツェマック
Zemach, Kaethe 1550
ツェラー
Zeller, Andreas 1550
Zeller, Kurt-Alexander 1550
Zöller, Elisabeth 1557
Zöller, Günter 1557
Zoller, Peter 1557
ツェラル
Cerar, Miro 240
ツェラルツ
Celarc, Marija Milojka Kolar 239
ツェリッチ
Ceric, Larisa 240
ツェリン
Tshering, Ugyen 1423
ツエル
Zell, Robert 1550
ツェルガー
Zelger, Franz 1550
ツェルディック
Zerdick, Axel 1551
ツェルナー
Zöllner, Frank 1557
Zöllner, Markus 1557
Zöllner, Reinhard 1557
ツェルニー・ステファンスカ
Czerny-Stefanska, Halina 311
ツェルノゴラズ
Cernogoraz, Giovanni 240
ツェルマン
Zelman, Walter A. 1550
ツェロフスキ
Cerovski, Valentin 240
Tserovski, Velantin 1423
ツェン
Tseng, Yani 1423
ツェンカー
Zenker, Helmut 1550
ツェンケ
Zencke, Peter 1550
ツェンゲル
Tsengel, Tsegmidiin 1423
ツェンツキェヴィッチ
Cenckiewicz, Sławomir 240
ツェンディーン・ダムディンスレン
Tsendiin Damdinsüren 1423
ツォイ
Choi, Francis 258
ツオイ
Chui, Sai-on 262
ツォイテン
Zeuthen, Frederik 1551
ツォイナー
Zeuner, Albrecht 1551
ツォク
Zogg, Julie 1557
ツォグツェツェグ
Tsogtsetseg, Ayushiin 1424
ツォグトバータル
Tsogtbaatar, Damdin 1424
ツォグバドラフ
Tsogbadrakh, Munkhzul 1424
ツォーデラー
Zoderer, Joseph 1556
ツォードリーン・ホラン
Tsoodolyn Khulan 1424
ツォニス
Tzonis, Alexander 1431
ツォネフ
Tsonev, Nikolai 1424
ツォハツプロス
Tsokhatzopoulos, Apostolos 1424
ツォフワネ
Tsogwane, Slumber 1424
ツォーベル
Zobel, Günter 1556
ツォラー
Zoller, Simon 1557
ツォーラス
Tsouras, Peter G. 1424
ツォルナー
Zöllner, Frank 1557
ツォルモン
Tsolmon, Tserendash 1424
ツォロ
Tsolo, Temeki Phoenix 1424
ツォン
Jiang, Ze-min 673
Tsang, Yam-kuen 1423
Zeng, Jian 1550
ツォンガ
Tsonga, Jo-Wilfried 1424
ツカダ
Tsukada, Nituo 1424
ツカモト
Tsukamoto, Mary 1424
ツガワ・マーダン
Tsugawa-Madden, Eriko 1424
ツキヤマ
Tsukiyama, Yoshihiro 1424
ツギレイエズ
Tugireyezu, Venantia 1426
ツグウェル
Tugwell, Finn 1426
ツケシェラシビリ
Tkeshelashvili, Davit 1407
ツーゲヘア
Zugehör, Rainer 1558
ツジゲシェワ
Tudegesheva, Ekaterina 1425
ツシパサ
Tshipasa, Venant 1424
ツジュ
Tuju, Raphael 1426
ツシュコ
Tsushko, Vasyl 1424
ツジンスキー
Tuzinsky, Juraj 1430
ツズキ
Tsuzuki, Seigo 1424
ツスソウバ
Tousouzova, Anna 1415
ツスト
Züst, Rainer 1559
ツター
Zuther, Joachim E. 1559
ツチ
Çuçi, Bledi 306
ツチガネ
Tsuchigane, Robert 1424
ツツ
Tutu, Desmond Mpilo 1429
ツツイ
Tsutsui, Ian 1424
Tsutsui, William M. 1424
ツッソーバ
Tousouzova, Anna 1415
ツナ
Tuna, Cari 1426
ツニャカオ
Tuñacao, Malcolm 1426
ツバー
Zuber, Steven 1558
ツバイク
Zweig, Jason 1560
Zweig, Martin E. 1560
Zweig, Pablo 1560
ツバイブラー
Zwiebler, Marc 1560
ツバカ
Tshubaka, Bishikwabo 1424
ツハコ・オシロ
Tsuhako Oshiro, Catalina 1424
ツハダイア
Tskhadaia, Manuchar 1424
ツバリ
Tsabary, Shefali 1423
ツーパンク
Zupanc, Günther Karl-Heinz 1559
ツブシンバヤル
Tuvshinbayar, Naidan 1429
ツヘイゼ
Chkheidze, Giorgi 257
ツベタノフ
Tsvetanov, Tsvetan 1424
Tsvetanov, Valeri 1424
ツベトコヴィッチ
Cvetković, Mirko 310
ツベトコビッチ
Cvetković, Mirko 310
ツベトコフ
Cvetkov, Mihail 310
Tsvetkov, Aleksandar 1424
Tsvetkov, Valentin Ivanovich 1424
ツペル
Tsuper, Alla 1424
ツベルガー
Zwerger, Lisbeth 1560
ツベレンツ
Zwerenz, Gerhard 1560
ツポー
Tupou Ⅳ 1427
Tupou Ⅴ 1427
ツボイ
Tsuboi, Gustavo 1424
ツポウ
Tupou, Fetu'utolu 1427
Tupou, Sonatane Taumoepeau 1427
Tupou, Tevita 1427
Tupou Ⅳ 1427
ツポウ4世
Tupou Ⅳ 1427
ツポウ5世
Tupou Ⅴ 1427
ツポウ6世
Tupou Ⅵ 1427
ツポウトア・ウルカララ
Tupouto'a Ulukalala 1427
ツボタ
Tsubota, Yuki 1424
ツポレフ
Tupolev, Aleksei Andreievich 1427
ツーマ

Tůma, Tomáš 1426
ツムケール
Zumkehr, Nadine 1559
ツムティ
Mucheru, Boniface 985
ツメレカ
Tsoumeleka, Athanasia 1424
ツヤ
Tuya, Jez 1429
ツラフカ
Zurawka, Thomas 1559
ツール
Tsur, Reuven 1424
ツル
Tulu, Derartu 1426
ツルカン
Turcan, Vladimir 1427
ツルキアニ
Tsulukiani, Tea 1424
ツルクベナツ
Crkvenac, Mato 302
ツルジエフ
Turdiev, Dilshodjon 1427
ツルツミア
Tsurtsumia, Georgiy 1424
ツルティム・ケサン
Tshul khrims skal bzan 1424
ツルナダク
Crnadak, Igor 302
ツルノヤ
Crnoja, Mijo 302
ツルパン
Turpin, Dominique 1429
ツルファ
Tsoulfa, Aimilia 1424
ツルブリッゲン
Zurbriggen, Silvan 1559
ツルベンコフスキ
Crvenkovski, Branko 306
ツルマキ
Tsurumaki, Marc 1424
ヅーロフ
Durov, Sergei Fedorovich 384
ツロワ
Turova, Margarita 1429
ツワイク
Zweig, Stefanie 1560
ツワルスキー
Twerski, Abraham J. 1430
ツン
Chen, Hao-su 251
Chen, Jin-hua 251
Chen, Jun-sheng 251
Chen, Kai-ge 251
Chen, Li-fu 251
Chen, Mu-hua 251
Chen, Qian-wu 251
Chen, Xi-tong 251
Chen, Yi-zi 251
Chen, Yuan 252
Chen, Yun-lin 252
Chen, Zhen 252
Chen, Zhi-li 252
Chen, Zhong-wei 252
Chen, Zu-de 252
Cheng, Si-yuan 252
Cheng, Wei-gao 252

【テ】

テ
Té, Baptista 1388
Tea, Jin-ah 1388
Thae, Hyong-chol 1393
Thae, Jong-su 1393
テー
Teh, Hong Piow 1388
The, Tjong Khing 1394
デ
De, Claude Issac 329
Dé, Yéro 329
Deh, Yéro 334
デー
Day, Christopher 328
テア
Terr, Lenore 1392
デア
Dare, Christopher 319
Dare, Tessa 319
Dea, Racheal 329
Derr, Mark 344
デアクバルドシュ
Deak-bardos, Mihaly 329
テア・シュテーゲン
Ter Stegen, Marc-Andre 1392
デアスンカオカルバリョ
De Assuncao Carvalho, Arlindo Vicente 330
テ・アタイランギカーフ
Te Atairangikaahu 1388
デアデリック
Deaderick, Brandon 329
テアノ
Theano, Ralph Ricardo 1395
デアビレス
Deavilés, Victoria Marina Velásquez 330
デアブレウ
De Abreu, Alcinda António 329
テアボ
Teabo, Alexander 1388
デアラウジョ
De Araújo, Fernando La Sama 330
De Araújo, Rui Maria 330
デアリエンディ
De Allende, Damian 329
テ・アリキヌイ・デーム・テ・アタイランギカーフ
Te Atairangikaahu 1388
テアル
Teale, Mehdi 1388
デ・アルウィス
De Alwis, Chandra Lal 329
デ・アンジェリス
De Angelis, Therese 330
デ・アンジェロ
De Angelo, Terri 330
デアンドリア
DeAndrea, William L. 330
デ・アンブロジオ
D'Ambrosio, Marcellino 315
テアンボ
Teambo, Mathew 1388
ティ
Teii, Tavau 1389
ティー
Tea, Michelle 1388
Tee, Jing Yi 1388
Thy, Lennart 1403
Ty, George 1430
テイ
Tay, Lee Yong 1384
Tei, Masahide 1388
Tei, Poasi 1388
Teii, Tavau 1389
ディ
De, Sankar 329
ディー
Dee, Bonnie 332
Dee, Dave 332
Dee, Frances 332
Dee, Jess 332
Dee, Jonathan 332
Dee, Ruby 332
Dee, Sandra 332
デイ
Day, Christopher E.I. 328
Day, David 328
Day, Dillon 328
Day, Dominic 328
Day, Doris 328
Day, George S. 328
Day, Hervey 328
Day, Jeni Pollack 328
Day, John Michael 328
Day, Jonathan D. 328
Day, Laraine 328
Day, Laura 328
Day, Malcolm 328
Day, Marele 328
Day, Mary 328
Day, Michael 328
Day, Mike 328
Day, Richard Hollis 328
Day, Richard Jasper 328
Day, Richard R. 329
Day, Robert A. 329
Day, Sheldon 329
Day, Stockwell 329
Day, Sylvia 329
Day, Terry Jean 329
Day, Third 329
Day, Thomas 329
Day, Trevor 329
Dei, George Jerry Sefa 334
ティア
Teare, Diane 1388
Tia, John Akologo 1403
Tiah, Hui Leng 1403
ティアー
Tier, Mark 1404
ディア
Dear, John 330
Dear, Peter 330
Dhir, Krishna S. 349
Dia, Bacar 349
Dia, Haoua 349
Dia, Oumar Khassimou 349
Diatta, Faustin 351
テイアウ
Teiaua, Kirabuke 1388
テイアウア
Teiaua, Kirabuke 1388
テイ・アウン
Htay Aung 630
ティアオ
Tiao, Luc Adolphe 1403
ディアオ
Diao, Yi-nan 351
ディアキテ
Diakité, Hadja Diaka 350
Diakite, Issa 350
Diakite, Koumba 350
Diakité, Modibo 350
Diakite, Moussa Balla 350
Diakite, Sékou 350
Diakite, Souleymane 350
Diakite, Sylla Koumba 350
ディアク
Diacu, Florin 350
ディアクテ
Diakite, Naby 350
ティアゴ
Tiago, Mendes 1403
ディアコヌ
Diaconu, Eusebiu Iancu 350
ディアコヌス
Diaconus, Paulus 350
ディアコネスク
Diaconescu, Cristian 350
ディアザ
Deaza, Alejandro 330
ディアシュ
Dias, António Álvaro Da Graça 351
ディアス
Dias, Celio 351
Dias, Cristina 351
Dias, Orlando 351
Diaz, Cameron 351
Díaz, Danilo 351
Diaz, David 351
Diaz, Felipe 351
Diaz, Felix 351
Diaz, Gabriela Maria 351
Diaz, Hidilyn 351
Diaz, Ineabelle 351
Diaz, James 351
Díaz, Javier Antonio 351
Díaz, José 351
Diaz, Junot 351
Diaz, Lena 351
Díaz, Marcelo 351
Diaz, Matias 351
Díaz, Miguel Ángel 351
Diaz, Nivaldo 352
Díaz, Simón 352
ディアズ
Diaz, Aledmys 351
Diaz, Edwin 351
Diaz, Einar 351
Diaz, Elias 351
Diaz, Jairo 351
Diaz, Jumbo 351
Diaz, J.W. 351
Diaz, Miguel 351
Diaz, Ruben 352
Diaz, Tony 352
ディアス・アバヤ
Diaz-Abaya, Marilou 352
ディアスアバヤ
Diaz-Abaya, Marilou 352
ディアズ・アバヤ
Diaz-Abaya, Marilou 352
ディアス＝オーティス
Díaz-Ortiz, Claire 352
ディアスカネル・ベルムデス
Días-canel Bermúdez, Miguel 351
Díazcanel Bermúdez,

Miguel 352
ディアスグラナドス・ギダ
Díaz Granados Guida, Sergio 352
ディアス・ゴメス
Diaz Gomez, Ritter Nobel 352
ディアス・ジュニオル
Dias Júnior, Manuel Hélder Vieira 351
ディアス・スアレス
Diaz Suarez, Adolfo 352
ディアス・ソトロンゴ
Díaz Sotolongo, Roberto 352
ディアスバラールト
Diaz-Balart, Fidel Castro 352
ディアス・ルア
Díaz Rúa, Víctor 352
ディアスロベルディ
Diaz Robertti, Jose Daniel 352
ディアス・ロボ
Díaz Lobo, Alberto 352
ディアセニ
Diasseny, Dorank Assifat 351
ディアタ
Diatta, Adama 351
ディアダン
Dearden, James S. 330
ディアチェンコ
Dyachenko, Alexander 385
ディアツ
Diaz, Antonello Madau 351
ディアデュ
Jarju, Malafi 665
ティアニー
Tierney, Alison J. 1404
Tierney, Elizabeth P. 1404
Tierney, John Marion 1404
Tierney, Lawrence 1404
Tierney, Lawrence M. 1404
Tierney, Therese 1404
Tierney, Thomas J. 1404
ディアニェ
Diagne, Fallou 350
ティアニー・ジョーンズ
Tierney-Jones, Adrian 1404
ディアーニュ
Diagne, Modou Fada 350
ディアニュ
Diagne, Assne 350
Diagne, Moussa 350
ディアネ
Diané, Mariam Koné 351
Diane, Mohamed 351
ディアバテ
Diabate, Fatoumata Guindo 349
ティア・バン
Tea Banh 1388
ディアビ
Diaby, Abdoulay 349
Diaby, Abdoulaye Cherif 349
Diaby, Kalifa Gassama 349
ディアビー
Diaby, Moustapha Mamy 349
ディアブ
Dhiabu, Tarek 349
Diab, Assad 349
Diab, Hassan 349
Diab, Rabiha 349
ディアボーン
Dearborn, Mary V. 330
ディアマイアー
Diermeier, Daniel 354
ディアマン
Dearmun, Nettie 330
ディアマンティ
Diamanti, Alessandro 350
Diamanti, Paula Ann 350
ディアマンディス
Diamandis, Peter 350
ディアマンティディス
Diamantidis, Yannis 350
ディアマント
Diamant, Anita 350
ディアマントプル
Diamantopoulou, Anna 350
ティアム
Thiam, Abdel Aziz 1395
Thiam, Khouraïchi 1395
Thiam, Ousmane 1395
Thiam, Safiatou 1395
ティアムソン
Tiamson-Kassab, Maria L.A. 1403
ディアラ
Diarra, Bocar Moussa 351
Diarra, Mamadou Igor 351
Diarra, Mamdou 351
Diarra, Mariam Flantié Diallo 351
Diarra, Marimantia 351
Diarra, Seydou 351
ティアラス
Tziallas, Georgios 1431
ディアラスバ
Diarrassouba, Souleymane 351
ディアラブ
Dearlove, Des 330
ディアリ
Deary, Ian J. 330
ディアリー
Deary, Vincent 330
ティアリンク
Teerlink, Rich 1388
ディアリング
Dearing, Ronda L. 330
ディアル
Dial, Quinton 350
Diar, Adoum 351
ディアレ
Diare, Mohamed 351
ディアロ
Diallo, Abdou 350
Diallo, Abdourahmane 350
Diallo, Ahmadou Abdoulaye 350
Diallo, Aisattou Bella 350
Diallo, Aliou 350
Diallo, Alpha 350
Diallo, Alpha Ousmane 350
Diallo, Anthony 350
Diallo, Bailo Téliwel 350
Diallo, Boubacar Yacine 350
Diallo, Cellou Dalein 350
Diallo, Cheick 350
Diallo, Dédia Mahamane Kattra 350
Diallo, Diarra Mariam Flantié 350
Diallo, Dioubate Binta 350
Diallo, Fatoumata Binta 350
Diallo, Kalidou 350
Diallo, Kanny 350
Diallo, Korka 350
Diallo, Madeleine Ba 350
Diallo, Mamadou Cellou 350
Diallo, Mamadou Korka 350
Diallo, Mamadou Saliou 350
Diallo, Mamadou Youba 350
Diallo, Salif 350
Diallo, Sidibe Aminata 350
Diallo, Téliwel Bailo 350
Diallo, Thierno Habib 350
Diallo, Thierno Ousmane 350
Diallo, Yaia 350
ディアワラ
Diawara, Amadou 351
ディアンガナ
Diangana, Grady 351
ティアンジェック・ムット
Tiangjiek Mut, Michael 1403
ディアンス
Dyens, Dominique 386
ティアンド
Tiando, Emmanuel 1403
ティアンポ
Tiampo, Ming 1403
ディーヴァー
Deaver, Jeffery 330
Deaver, Julie Reece 330
ディ・ヴァイオ
Di Vaio, Marco 358
ディヴァイン
Devine, Angela 348
Devine, Carol 348
Devine, Elizabeth 348
Devine, Thea 348
Devine, Tony 348
Divine, Mark 358
ディヴァーカルニ
Divakaruni, Chitra Banerjee 358
ディヴァカルニー
Divakaruni, Chitra Banerjee 358
ディーヴァス
Divas, Mariachi 358
ディヴィー
Davey, Andrew Paul 322
デイヴィ
Davey, Steve 322
デイヴィー
Davey, Miyoko 322
Davie, Helen 324
ディヴィス
Davies, Tom 325
Davis, Kyle 326
Davis, Martin 326
デイヴィース
Davies, Colin 324
Davies, Roy 325
デイヴィーズ
Davies, David Stuart 324
Davies, Jacqueline 324
Davies, Kevin 324
Davies, Patrick 324
Davies, Peter Ho 324
Davies, Philippa 324
Davies, Stephen 325
Davies, Steven Paul 325
デイヴィス
Davice, Valentine 322
Davies, Andrew 324
Davies, Barry 324
Davies, Ben 324
Davies, Benji 324
Davies, Clarice Stella Spencer 324
Davies, Curtis 324
Davies, Dan 324
Davies, Dominic 324
Davies, Douglas James 324
Davies, Gill 324
Davies, H.T.O. 324
Davies, Hunter 324
Davies, Hywel 324
Davies, Ian 324
Davies, Jane Carola 324
Davies, John H. 324
Davies, Kate 324
Davies, Matt 324
Davies, Murray 324
Davies, Neal 324
Davies, Nicholas B. 324
Davies, Nicolas Jack 324
Davies, Norman 324
Davies, Paul C.W. 324
Davies, Pete 324
Davies, Peter Maxwell 324
Davies, Philip John 324
Davies, Philip R. 324
Davies, Ray 324
Davies, Robertson 325
Davies, Wendy 325
Davis, Andrew 325
Davis, Angela Yvonne 325
Davis, Ann 325
Davis, Anna 325
Davis, Ann B. 325
Davis, Carol Anne 325
Davis, Caroline 325
Davis, Colin 325
Davis, David Brion 325
Davis, Dennis Russell 325
Davis, Devra Lee 325
Davis, Don 325
Davis, Donald A. 325
Davis, Ellen F. 325
Davis, Erik 325
Davis, Geena 326
Davis, Harry 326
Davis, Hope 326
Davis, James Cushman 326
Davis, J.E. 326
Davis, Jeff 326
Davis, Jill 326
Davis, Josh 326
Davis, Judy 326
Davis, Kate 326
Davis, Keith 326
Davis, Krista 326
Davis, Kristin 326
Davis, Kyra 326
Davis, Laura 326
Davis, Lenard J. 326
Davis, Lindsey 326
Davis, Lydia 326
Davis, Mark William 326
Davis, Martin 326
Davis, Marvin 326
Davis, Meryl 326
Davis, Mike 326

Davis, Myrna 326
Davis, Ossie 326
Davis, Patti 326
Davis, Pauline 326
Davis, Philip J. 326
Davis, Philip Maurice 326
Davis, Phyllis K. 326
Davis, Rankin 326
Davis, Rayford Lee 327
Davis, Robert 327
Davis, Robert Charles 327
Davis, R.W. 327
Davis, Sammy, Jr. 327
Davis, Skeeter 327
Davis, Stephen T. 327
Davis, Steven 327
Davis, Susan 327
Davis, Viola 327
Davis, Wade 327
Davis, Willie 327
デイヴィズ
Davies, Merryl Wyn 324
デイヴィソン
Davison, C. 327
Davison, Peter Hobley 327
デイヴィッド
David, Ann Rosalie 322
David, Craig 322
David, Evelyn 322
David, Hal 322
David, James F. 322
David, Joshua 323
David, Kay 323
David, Laurie 323
David, Lawrence 323
David, Leonard 323
David, Stuart 323
デイヴィッドソン
Davidson, Art 323
Davidson, Craig 323
Davidson, Cynthia C. 323
Davidson, Jane W. 323
Davidson, Robert 323
Davidson, Susanna 323
ディ・ヴィト
Di Vito, Andrea 358
デイヴィドソン
Davidson, Donald Herbert 323
Davidson, Howard A. 323
Davidson, Stephanie Goddard 323
デイヴィー美代子
Davey, Miyoko 322
ディ・ヴィンチェンティス
De Vincentiis, Fiammetta Positano 348
デイヴェルソン
Deyverson 349
デイウォルト
Daywalt, Drew 329
ティウォン
Tiwon, Sylvia 1407
ディウセ
Diousse, Assane 357
デイヴソン
Davison, Lang 327
ディウフ
Diouf, Abdou 357
Diouf, Bouna Semou 357
Diouf, El Hadj 357
Diouf, Jacques 357
Diouf, Madieyna 357
Diouf, Madior 357
Diouf, Mame Biram 357
Diouf, Mame Birame 357
Diouf, Pape 357
Diouf, Sylviane Anna 357
Joof, Joseph 686
ティウメンバエフ
Tiumenbaev, Ruslan 1407
ティエ
Tie, Ning 1404
ディエ
Die, Serey 353
ディエイ
Dièye, Cheikh Mamadou Abiboulaye 354
ディエウ
Dhieu Dau, Stephen 349
ディエウ・ダウ
Dhieu Dau, Stephen 349
ディエウ・マソック
Dhieu Mathok, Diing 349
ディエギス
Diegues, Carlos 353
ディエゴ
Diego, Gerardo 353
ディエゴ・リコ
Diego Rico 353
ディエゴ・レジェス
Diego Reyes 353
ディエゴ・ロペス
Diego Lopez 353
ティエス
Thiesse, Anne-Marie 1396
ディエス
Diez, Gabriel 354
Diez, Manuel 354
ディエス・カンセコ・テリ
Diez Canseco Terry, Raúl 354
ティエスト
Tiësto 1404
ディエス＝ホフライトネル
Díez Hochleitner, Ricardo 354
ディエテルレ
Dieterlé, Nathalie 354
ディエトリッチ
Dietrich, Guillermo 354
ティエバ
Thieba, Paul Kaba 1396
ティエボー
Thiébaut, Philippe 1396
ディエム
Diem, Nguyen Khoa 353
ティエラ
Tierra, Lesley 1404
Tierra, Michael 1404
ティエリー
Thierry, Raphaël 1396
ディエル
Diehl, Larry 353
ティエレ
Thiele, Annekatrin 1396
Thiele, Kerstin 1396
ティエロ
Thiero, Diarra Affoussatou 1396
ティエン
Tian, Cong-ming 1403
Tian, Zhuang-zhuang 1403
ティエン
Thien, Nguyen Ngoc 1396
Tian, Yuan 1403
Tian, Zhuang-zhuang 1403
Tien, Nguyen Thi Kim 1404
ティエンステン
Tiensten, Paul 1404
ティエンポ
Tiempo, Sergio Daniel 1404
テイオ
Te'o, Manti 1391
ディオ
Dio, Ronnie James 356
ディーオウ
Diaw, Boris 351
ディオゴ
Diogo, Bornito De Sousa Baltazar 357
Diogo, Luisa 357
Diogo, Vitória 357
Diogo, Vitoria Dias 357
ディオス
Dios, Olga de 357
ディオスダド
Diosdado Garcia, Nuria Lidon 357
ディオダート
Diodato, Virgil Pasquale 357
ディオニシ
Dionisi, David J. 357
ディオプ
Diop, Abdoulaye 357
Diop, Abdou Malal 357
Diop, Awa Fall 357
Diop, Bécaye 357
Diop, Fatou 357
Diop, Khadim 357
Diop, Mamadou 357
Diop, Moctar 357
Diop, Ndèye Khady 357
Diop, Pape Kouly 357
Diop, Safiétou Ndiaye 357
Diop, Serigne 357
Diop, Thérèse Coumba 357
ティオフィロ
Teofilo, Vi 1391
ディオマ
Dioma, Jean-Claude 357
ディオマンデ
Diomande, Adama 357
ディオム
Diome, Fatou 357
ディオムバール
Diombar, Thiam 357
ディオン
Dion, Céline 357
Dion, Dan 357
Dion, Franck 357
Dion, Leo 357
Dion, Roger 357
Dion, Stéphane 357
Dionne, Deidra 357
ディオンヌ
Dionne, Mohammed Boun Abdallah 357
ティオンビアノ
Thiombiano, Justin Tiéba 1396
ティーガー
Tieger, Paul D. 1404
ディカー
Dekker, Thomas 335
ディガー
Digard, Nicolas 354
ディカウ
Dikau, Richard 355
ティーガーデン
Teegarden, Bobbin 1388
ティガニ
Tigani, Jordan 1404
ディカプリオ
DiCaprio, Leonardo 352
ディカミロ
DiCamillo, Kate 352
ディカム
Dicum, Gregory 353
ディガール
Digard, Didier 354
ディカルリ
Di Carli, Marco 352
ディーガン
Deegan, Marilyn 333
Deegan, Mildred 333
ディカン
Dikan, Edgar 355
ディガンバラム
Digambaram, Palani 354
ディキアニ
Dicciani, Nance K. 352
ティギエフ
Tigiev, Soslan 1404
Tigiyev, Taimuraz 1404
ディキシット
Dixit, Avinash K. 359
Dixit, Jyotindra Nath 359
ディキスト
Dixit, Avinash K. 359
ディキチャン
Dikiciyan, Aram 355
ディーキン
Deakin, Frederick William 329
Deakin, Roger 329
デイキン
Dakin, Glenn 313
ディキンズ
Dickins, Rosie 352
ディギンズ
Diggins, Christopher 354
Diggins, Jessica 354
ディキンスン
Dickinson, H.T. 352
Dickinson, Peter 353
ディキンソン
Dickinson, Frederick R. 352
Dickinson, Ian 352
Dickinson, Matt 353
Dickinson, Peter 353
Dickinson, Terence 353
Dickinson, Trevor 353
ディギンバイエ
Diguimbaye, Christian Georges 354
ティーグ
Teague, Jeff 1388
Teague, Mark 1388
ディーク
Dieck, Martin tom 353
デイク
Deiq, Ismail 334
ティクヴァ
Tykwer, Tom 1430
ティクサ
Tixa, Serge 1407
ディクシット
Dikshit, Sudhakar S. 355
デイクシロス

Dijk-silos, Jeniffer 354
ディークス
Deakes, Nathan 329
デイクストラ
Dijkstra, M. 355
ディクスン
Dickson, Gordon Rupert 353
Dixon, C.Scott 359
Dixon, Larry 359
テイクセイラ
Teixeira, Gail 1389
ディクソン
Dickson, Anne 353
Dickson, Ed 353
Dickson, Gary W. 353
Dickson, Gordon Rupert 353
Dickson, Helen 353
Dickson, Louise 353
Dickson, Paul 353
Dickson, S.A. 353
Dixon, Anna 359
Dixon, Bill 359
Dixon, Brandon 359
Dixon, Brian 359
Dixon, Chuck 359
Dixon, Dougal 359
Dixon, E. 359
Dixon, Ellen B. 359
Dixon, Gail 359
Dixon, Gerald 359
Dixon, Kenneth 359
Dixon, Leslie 359
Dixon, Matthew 359
Dixon, Nancy M. 359
Dixon, Philip 359
Dixon, Riley 359
Dixon, Robert M.W. 359
Dixon, Thomas 359
Dixon, Thomas, Jr. 359
Dixon, Travell 359
ディクソン＝クーパー
Dixon-Cooper, Hazel 359
ディクソンバーンズ
Dixon-barnes, Wheatonia 359
ティクナー
Ticknor, Duane 1403
ティク・ナット・ハン
Thich Nhat Hanh 1396
ディグナン
Deignan, Charles Francis 334
ティクバ
Tykwer, Tom 1430
ディグビー
Digby, Anne 354
Digby, Marena 354
Digby, Marie 354
ティグペン
Thigpen, Paul 1396
ディークマイアー
Diekmeier, Dennis 353
ディークマン
Dieckmann, Christoph 353
Dieckmann, Maijaliisa 353
Diekman, Jake 353
ディーグマン
Digman, Kristina 354
ディクメ
Dikme, Mehmed 355
ディクリスティナ
Dichristina, Mariette 352
ティーグリーン
Tiegreen, Alan 1404
ディグル
Diggle, Andy 354
ディクレメンテ
DiClemente, Carlo C. 353
ディケーター
Dikötter, Frank 355
ディケチュ
Dikec, Yusuf 355
ディケナ
Dekena, Lucas Dava 335
ティゲラー
Tiggelaar, Ben 1404
ディケール
Dicker, Joël 352
ティーゲルカンプ
Tiegelkamp, Michael 1404
ディーケルマン
Diekelmann, Nancy L. 353
ディーケン
Dieken, Connie 353
ディケン
Dicken, Leslie 352
ディケンス
Dickens, Peggy 352
ディケンズ
Dickens, Chris 352
Dickens, Little Jimmy 352
ディケンソン
Dickenson, Donna 352
ディコ
Diko, Linus 355
デイコ
Deiko, Anna K. 334
ティコイロトゥマ
Tikoirotuma, Asaeli 1404
ディコルテ
De Corte, Erik 332
ディーコン
Deacon, Alexis 329
Deacon, John 329
ディコンシーリョ
DiConsiglio, John 353
ティコンドゥアンドゥア
Tikoduadua, Pio 1404
ディサイア
DiSaia, Vince 358
ディサシーナ
Disarcina, Gary 358
ディザージョ
DiZazzo, Raymond 359
ティザック
Tezak, Edward J. 1393
ディサーナーヤカ
Disanayake, Dhammika Ganganath 358
ディサナヤケ
Dissanayake, Anura Kumara 358
Dissanayake, D.M.S.B. 358
Dissanayake, Duminda 358
Dissanayake, Navin 358
Dissanayake, Salinda 358
Dissanayake, S.B. 358
テイサム
Tatham, Betty 1383
Tatham, Peter E.R. 1383
ティザリントン
Titherington, Arthur 1406
ディサルボ
Disalvo, Ryan 358
ディ・サント
Di Santo, Franco 358
ディサント
Di Santo, Michael 358
ティシー
Tichy, Noel M. 1403
ディシィ
Dichy, Albert 352
ティシエ
Tissier, Henry 1406
ディーシェ
Dische, Irene 358
DJスネイク
DJ Snake 360
テイシェイラ
Teieira, Nuno Severiano 1389
Teixeira, Antonia Mendes 1389
Teixeira, Dionatan 1389
Teixeira, Gail 1389
Teixeira, Izabella 1389
Teixeira, Jose 1389
Teixeira, Manuel 1389
Teixeira, Maria Cândida Pereira 1389
Teixeira, Miro 1389
ティシェイラダクルス
Teixeira Da Cruz, Paula 1389
テイシェイラダクルス
Teixeira Da Cruz, Paula 1389
テイシェイラ・ダ・シルヴァ
Teixeira da Silva, Yolanda Maria Alves Pimenta de Moura 1389
テイシェイラ・ドスサントス
Teixeira Dos Santos, Fernando 1389
ディ・ジェンナーロ
Di Gennaro, Davide 354
ディシコ
DiCicco, Sue 352
ディジック
Dijck, Peter Van 354
ディジバリス
Didzbalis, Aurimas 353
ティジャニ
al-Tijani, Saleh Fideil 1404
ティシャラ
Tesheira, Karen 1392
デ・イシュター
De Ishtar, Zohl 334
ティシュチェンコ
Tishchenko, Evgeny 1406
ディシュブール
Dieschbourg, Carole 354
ティシュラー
Tischler, Linda 1406
ディジョージオ
DiGeorgio, Carmen R. 354
ディジョネット
De Johnette, Jack 335
ティース
Teece, David J. 1388
Thies, Joyce 1396
Thies, Michael F. 1396
Thies, Sven Ingmar 1396
ティーズ
Teays, Terry 1388
ティス
This, Hervé 1396
Thys, Guy 1403
ディース
Deess, Perry 333
Diethe, Carol 354
ディーズ
Dees, Bowen Causey 333
Dees, Catherine 333
Dees, Cindy 333
Diez, Thomas 354
ティスカ
Tyszka, Alberto Barrera 1431
ディスキー
Diski, Jenny 358
ティスケンス
Theyskens, Olivier 1395
ティーズディル
Teasdill, Wendy 1388
ディ・ステーファノ
Di Stefano, Giuseppe 358
ディ・ステファノ
Di Stéfano, Alfredo 358
Di Stefano, Giuseppe 358
ディステファーノ
DeStefano, Anthony 346
ディステファノ
Di Stéfano, Alfredo 358
ティーズデール
Teasdale, John D. 1388
ティスデル
Tisdell, Clement Allan 1406
ティズデール
Tisdale, Jane 1406
ディステル
Distel, Sacha 358
ティステル・チカヤ
Thystere Tshicaya, Jean-Marc 1403
ティステルチカヤ
Thystere Tshicaya, Jean-Marc 1403
ディーストビール
Dienstbier, Jiři 353
ディスナダ・ディッサクン
Disnadda Diskul 358
ディズニー
Disney, Richard 358
Disney, Roy Edward 358
テイスバーグ
Teisberg, Elizabeth Olmstead 1389
ティスハースト
Ticehurst, Janie 1403
ディスパティエ
Despatie, Alexandre 346
ディスピニョ
Di Spigno, Daniele 358
ディス・プラン
Dith Pran 358
ディースブロック
Diesbrock, Tom 354
ディスペンザ
Dispenza, Joe 358
ディスポ
Dispot, Laurent 358
ディスミュークス
Dismukes, Reese 358
ティースラー
Thiesler, Sabine 1396
ディスラム
Dislam, Wiam 358
ティスランド
Tisserand, Robert 1406

テイズリー
Teasley, Sarah 1388
ディスル
Disl, Uschi 358
ティスロン
Tisseron, Serge 1406
テイセイラ・デ・メロ
Teixeira de Melo, Fabio 1389
ディ・セイント・ジョア
De St.Jorre, John 346
ディセティ
Decety, Jean 331
テイセードル
Teyssèdre, Fabienne 1393
テイセドル
Teyssèdre, Fabienne 1393
ティゼバ
Tizeba, Charles 1407
ディセポロ
Discepolo, Thierry 358
ティセラン
Tisserand, Marcel 1406
ディーゼル
Diesel, Vin 354
デイゼル
Deysel, Johan 349
ティゾン
Tison, Annette 1406
ティーター
Teetor, Paul 1388
ティター
Teter, Hannah 1393
ディーダ
Deida, David 334
ディダヴィ
Didavi, Daniel 353
ディータ・ヴォン・ティース
Dita von Teese 358
ティダ・タウォンセート
Tida Tawornseth 1403
ディダート
Didato, Salvatore V. 353
ディタ・フォン・ティース
Dita von Teese 358
ディタマソ
DiTomasso, Robert A. 358
テイタム
Tatham, Caroline 1383
Tatum, Jayson 1383
ディーチ
Deech, Ruth 332
Dietsch, Jean-Claude 354
ティチアーティ
Ticciati, Robin 1403
ディチェンゾ
DeCenzo, David A. 331
ディ・チェンタ
Di Centa, Giorgio 352
ディチコ
Dychko, Ivan 385
ディーチュ
Dietzsch, Steffen 354
ディチロ
Dicillo, Tom 352
ティーツ
Tietz, Jeff 1404
テイツ
Taiz, Lincoln 1377
ディーツ
Deetz, Stanley 333
Dietz, Adolf 354
Dietz, Steven 354
Dietz, Thomas 354
Dietz, William C. 354
ディッカー
Dicker, Katie 352
ディッカーズ
Dikkers, Scott 355
ディッカーソン
Dickerson, Alex 352
Dickerson, Bobby 352
Dickerson, Chris 352
Dickerson, Corey 352
ディッキー
Dicke, Thomas S. 352
Dickey, Clyde 352
Dickey, Eric Jerome 352
Dickey, Jean L. 352
Dickey, Lisa 352
Dickey, R.A. 352
Dickie, Iain 352
Dickie, Jim 352
ディッキンソン
Dickinson, Alasdair 352
Dickinson, Bruce 352
Dickinson, Ian 352
Dickinson, Peter 353
ティック
Tick, Judith 1403
ティッグ
Tigg, Jason 1404
ディック
Dick, Jonathan 352
Dick, Walter 352
ディックス
Dicks, Andrew 353
Dicks, Matthew 353
Dicks, Terrance 353
Dix, Alan 359
Dix, Isabel 359
Dix, Shane 359
Dix, Walter 359
ディッグス
Diggs, Quandre 354
Diggs, Reggie 354
Diggs, Stefon 354
ティックナー
Tickner, J.Ann 1403
ディックハイザー
Dickheiser, Michael 352
ディックフォード
Dick-forde, Emily 352
ティックル
Tickle, Cheryll 1403
Tickle, Jack 1403
Tickle, Phyllis A. 1403
ティッケル
Tickell, *Sir* Clispin 1403
ディッケル
Dickel, Hans 352
ディッケルマン
Diekelmann, Nancy L. 353
ディッケン
Dicken, Peter 352
ディッコ
Dicko, Oumar Hamadoun 353
Ditko, Steve 358
ディッサ
Dissa, Alpha Omar 358
ティッサラ
Thissera, Dayasritha 1396
ティッシャー
Teicher, Jonathan 1388
ティッシュ
Tisch, Robert 1406
ディッシュ
Disch, Thomas Michael 358
ティッセ
Tysse, Erik 1431
ティッセン
Thijssen, Jos M. 1396
Thyssen-Bornemisza de Kaszon, Hans Heinrich 1403
Tissen, Rene Johannes 1406
ティッセン・ボルネミッサ
Thyssen-Bornemisza de Kaszon, Hans Heinrich 1403
デイッダ
Deidda, Francesca 334
ディッチバーン
Ditchburn, Ted 358
ティッツ
Tits, Jacques 1406
ディッツェ
Dietze, Tina 354
ティッテル
Tittel, Ed 1406
ティッド
Tidd, Joseph 1403
ディット・プラン
Dith Pran 358
ディットマー
Dittmer, Janet 358
ティットムス
Titmuss, Christopher 1406
ティットモア
Tittemore, Brian D. 1406
ディッパー
Dipper, Frances 357
ティッピング
Tipping, Colin C. 1406
ティップス
Tips, Walter E.J. 1406
ディツラー
Ditzler, Jinny S. 358
ディーディ
Deedy, Carmen Agra 332
ディディ
Diddy 353
Didi 353
Didi, Ibrahim 353
Didi, Sidi Ould 353
ディディオン
Didion, Joan 353
ティディクサー
Tideiksaar, Rein 1403
ディディサ
Didiza, Angela Thoko 353
ティティピナ
Titikpina, Atcha Mohamed 1406
ディディ＝ユベルマン
Didi-Huberman, Georges 353
ディ・ティロ
Tiro, Hasan Muhammad di 1406
ティテニス
Titenis, Giedrius 1406
ディテラ
Di Tella, Guido 358
ディデリクセン
Dideriksen, Amalie 353
ティテル
Tittel, Ed 1406
Tittel, Joseph 1406
ティデル
Thydell, Johanna 1403
テイテル
Teitel, Lee 1389
テイテルバウム
Teitelbaum, Osnat 1389
Teitelbaum, Philip 1389
テイテルボイム
Teytelboym, Oleg M. 1393
ディーテルムジャーバー
Diethelm Gerber, Heidi 354
ディテルリッジ
DiTerlizzi, Tony 358
ディーデレン
Diederen, Suzanne 353
ティーテン
Tidten, Markus 1403
ティード
Tead, Ordway 1388
Teed, Elizabeth Lee 1388
ティト
Tito 1406
テイト
Tait, Gregor 1377
Tait, Kimberly Terri 1377
Tait, Vanessa 1377
Tate, Brandon 1383
Tate, Bruce A. 1383
Tate, Buddy 1383
Tate, Carson 1383
Tate, Golden 1383
Tate, Jeffrey 1383
Tate, John Torrence 1383
Tate, Ryan 1383
Thate, Bob 1394
デイト
Date, C.J. 321
ティドウェル
Tidwell, Jenifer 1403
Tidwell, John 1404
テイドウェル
Tidwell, Jenifer 1403
ティードゥス
Tiidus, Urve 1404
ティトゲンス
Tietgens, Hans 1404
ディドナート
DiDonato, Joyce 353
ティドハー
Tidhar, Lavie 1403
ディートハルト
Diethart, Thomas 354
ディト・プラン
Dith Pran 358
ティドボール
Tidball, Jeff 1403
ティードホルム
Tidholm, Anna Clara 1403
ディトマー
Ditmar, Mark F. 358
Dittmer, Andreas 358
ティートマイアー
Tietmeyer, Hans 1404
ティートマイヤー
Tietmeyer, Hans 1404
ディトマーシュ
Ditmarsch, Hans van 358
ディ・ドメニコ

テ

Di Doménico, Cristina 353
ディ・トラナ
Di Trana, Caterina Gromis 358
テイトリー
Tately, Chuck 1383
ディトリ
D'Itri, Frank M. 358
D'Itri, Patricia Ward 358
ディドリクソン
Didrickson, Betsy 353
ディートリック
Detrick, Bruce 347
Dietrich, Derek 354
ディートリッヒ
Dietrich, William 354
ディードリッヒ
Diedrich, Monica 353
ディトリッヒ
Dittrich, Boris 358
ディートリヒ
Diedrich, Karen K. 353
Dietrich, William 354
ディートル
Dietl, Helmut Max 354
ティトン
Tyton, Przemyslaw 1431
ディートン
Deaton, Angus 330
Deaton, Wendy 330
デイトン
Dayton, Gail 329
Dayton, Grant 329
Dayton, Linnea 329
Deighton, John 334
Drayton, Spencer 373
ディードンク
Dierdonck, Roland Van 353
ディ・ドンナ
di Donna, Annie 353
ディーナー
Diener, Alexander C. 353
Diener, Christian 353
Diener, Joan 353
ディナポリ
DiNapoli, Joe 356
ティナリエフ
Tinaliyev, Nurmakhan 1405
ディナレロ
Dinarello, Charles 356
ディナロ
Dinallo, Gregory S. 356
ティニ
Tiny, Carlos Alberto Pires 1406
ディーニ
Dini, Lamberto 356
ディーニー
Deeney, Troy 333
ディニ
Dini, Abdulkadir Sheikh Ali 356
Dini, Houmed Mohamed 356
Dini, Paul 356
Diniz, Yohann 356
ディニー
Dinnie, Keith 356
ディニシュ
Diniz, Luciana 356
ディーニハン
Deenihan, Jimmy 333
ティニベコワ
Tynybekova, Aisuluu 1431
ディニュ
Digne, Lucas 354
ティニュス
Tignous 1404
ディニーン
Dineen, Tom 356
ディヌディング
Di Ndinge, Didjob Divungi 356
ディネラリス
Dinelaris, Alexander, Jr. 356
ディーネル
Dienel, Peter C. 353
デイノー
Daigneau, Robert 313
ディノーヴィ
Denove, Chris 342
ディノシャ
Dinoša, Ferhat 356
ディノス
Denos, Julia 342
ディノスキー
DeNosky, Kathie 342
ディノト
DiNoto, Andrea 356
テイバー
Taber, George M. 1375
Tabor, James D. 1375
Tabor, James M. 1375
ディーバー
Deaver, Braxton 330
Deaver, Jeffery 330
Deaver, Michael Keith 330
ディバイオ
Di Vaio, Marco 358
ティバイジュカ
Tibaijuka, Anna 1403
ティバウト
Tybout, Arice 1430
ディパオラ
Di Paola, Giampaolo 357
ティバシマ
Tibasima, John 1403
ディーバス
Devers, Rafael 347
ディパスカ
DiPasqua, Lila 357
ディパスクェル
DiPasquale, Denise 357
ティハ・トゥラ・ティン・アウン・ミン・ウー
Thiha Thura Tin Aung Myint Oo 1396
ディーハニ
Aldeehani, Fehaid 27
ディハニ
Aldeehani, Fehaid 27
ディババ
Dibaba, Genzebe 352
Dibaba, Mare 352
Dibaba, Tirunesh 352
ディバラ
Dybala, Paulo 385
ディバルトロメオ
Di Bartolomeo, Mars 352
ディバルブ
Devalve, Seth 347
ティパワディ
Thipawadee, Meksawan 1396
ティーハン
Teehan, John 1388
ティビ
Tibi, Jawad 1403
ディビ
Diby, Charles Koffi 352
デイビー
Deybe, Daniel 349
DBCピエール
DBC Pierre 329
ディピエトロ
Di Pietro, Antonio 357
DiPietro, Joe 357
DiPietro, Michele 357
ディビズ
Davies, Rhona 325
デイビース
Davies, Craig 324
デイビーズ
Davies, Owen 324
デイビス
Davies, Anthea 324
Davies, Carl A. 324
Davies, Christie 324
Davies, Howard John 324
Davies, Hunter 324
Davies, John 324
Davies, Nicola 324
Davies, Paul Lyndon 324
Davies, Peter Maxwell 324
Davies, Stephen G. 325
Davies, Steve 325
Davies, Valerie 325
Davis, Alan 325
Davis, Alison Bonnie 325
Davis, Anne 325
Davis, Anthony 325
Davis, Barbara Gross 325
Davis, Barbee 325
Davis, Clive 325
Davis, Colin 325
Davis, Denise 325
Davis, Dennis K. 325
Davis, Deyonta 325
Davis, Ed 325
Davis, Geena 326
Davis, Glenn 326
Davis, Glenn D. 326
Davis, Graeme 326
Davis, Greg 326
Davis, Howard 326
Davis, Jim 326
Davis, Joshua 326
Davis, Judy 326
Davis, Justine 326
Davis, K.E. 326
Davis, Kristin 326
Davis, Lori J. 326
Davis, Monte 326
Davis, Nancy 326
Davis, Ossie 326
Davis, Robin 327
Davis, Ronald Dell 327
Davis, Sarah 327
Davis, Scott 327
Davis, Scott M. 327
Davis, Shane 327
Davis, Stan 327
Davis, Stephen M. 327
Davis, Tom 327
Davis, Viola 327
Davis, William 327
Davis, William Barron 327
ティヒッチ
Tihić, Sulejman 1404
デイビッド
David, Erica 322
David, Fred R. 322
David, Juliet 323
David, Matthew 323
David, Peter 323
デイビッドソン
Davidson, Andrew 323
Davidson, Carolyn 323
Davidson, Jonathan 323
Davidson, Jonathan R. T. 323
Davidson, Matthew 323
ディヒテル
Dichter, Avi 352
ディビドソン
Davidson, Alan 323
ディビニ
Divinyi, Joyce E. 358
ティヒー・ルーガー
Tichy-Luger, Ingeborg 1403
ティビロフ
Tibilov, Georgii 1403
ティピンズ
Tippins, Steven C. 1406
ティフ
Tych, Feliks 1430
ディープ
Deep, Samuel D. 333
デイブ
Dave, Subodh 322
ティファトゥル
Tifatul, Sembiring 1404
ティファニー
Tiffany, John 1404
ディ・フィオリ
Di Fiori, Lawrence 354
ディ・フィリポ
Di Filippo, Paul 354
ティフィン
Tiffin, Chris 1404
Tiffin, Helen 1404
ディフェイス
Deffeyes, Kenneth S. 333
ティーフェンゼー
Tiefensee, Wolfgang 1404
ディフェンソール
Defensor, Michael 333
ディフェンディ
Defendi, Claudia 333
ディフェンバー
Diffenbaugh, Vanessa 354
ディフォ
Difo, Wilmer 354
ディフォンツォ
DiFonzo, Nicholas 354
ディプキオ
DiPucchio, Kelly 357
ティプサレビッチ
Tipsarevic, Janko 1406
ティブシラニ
Tibshirani, Robert 1403
ティブッス
Tibbs, Margaret Anne 1403
ディプッチオ
DiPucchio, Kelly 357
ディブディン
Dibdin, Michael John 352
ティプトン

テ

Tipton, David 1406
Tipton, Scott 1406
Tipton, Steven M. 1406
ディプモニ
Dipu Moni 357
ディフランンチェスカ
Di Francisca, Elisa 354
ディ・フランチェスコ
Di Francesco, Eusebio 354
Di Francesco, Federico 354
ディフランンチスカ
Di Francisca, Elisa 354
ティプリック
Tipuric, Justin 1406
ディ・プリマ
Di Prima, Diane 357
ディブル
Dibble, Peter 352
デイブル
Dable, Anthony 311
ディ・フルヴィオ
Di Fulvio, Luca 354
T−ペイン
T-Pain 1416
ディベカール
Divekar, Rameshchandra Raghunath 358
デイベス
D'eibes, Khouloud 334
ティベッツ
Tibbets, Paul 1403
Tibbetts, Nate 1403
ティベディ
Thibedi, Patrick 1395
ティーベリ
Tiberg, Joar 1403
ティヘリノ・パチェコ
Tijerino Pacheco, José María 1404
ディベン
Dibben, Damian 352
Dibben, Nicola 352
ディペンドラ皇太子
Dipendra Bir Bikram 357
ディペンドラ・ビル・ビクラム
Dipendra Bir Bikram 357
ティーボー
Tebow, Tim 1388
ティボー
Thibault, Scott 1395
ティーボウ
Tebow, Tim 1388
ディボウスキ
Dibowski, Andreas 352
ディボース
Debose, Andre 331
ディポーター
DePorter, Vince 343
ティボット
Tibbott, Julie 1403
ティボーデ
Thibaudet, Jean-Yves 1395
ティポテ
Tipote, Filomena Mascarenhas 1406
ティボドー
Thibodeau, Tom 1395
ディボード
Debord, Clay 331
ディポート
Dipoto, Jerry 357
ティボネ
Tibone, Mbiganyi 1403
ティホノフ
Tykhonov, Viktor 1430
デイホフ
Dayhoff, Judith E. 329
ティボル
Frank, Tibor 456
ディ・ポール
De Paul, Lynsey 343
ディーボールド
Deibold, Alex 334
ティーポレ
T-pole, Hale 1416
ディーマー
Deamer, Bill 329
ディマジオ
DiMarzio, J.F. 355
ティマース
Timmers, Leo 1405
ディーマス
Demus, Lashinda 341
ディマス
Dimas, Pyrros 355
Dimas, Stavros 355
ディマーゾ
DeMarzo, Peter M. 339
ディマティア
DiMattia, Dominic J. 356
ディマティーニ
Demartini, John F. 339
ディマバカナ
Dwima-bakana, Fulgence 385
ティマーマン
Timmerman, Charles 1405
Timmermans, H.J.P. 1405
ディ・マリア
Di Maria, Angel 355
ディマルコ
Dimarco, Federico 355
Dimarco, Patrick 355
ティーマン
Tieman, Robert 1404
Tiemann, Michael 1404
ディマンチ
Dimanche, Jayson 355
ディミーザス
Dimizas, Constantine 356
ディミジアン
Dimidjian, Sona 356
ディミトリ
Dimitri, Simona 356
ディミトリアス
Dimitrius, Jo-Ellan 356
ディミトリアディス
Demetriades, Marios 340
Dimitriadis, Greg 356
ディミトリイェビッチ
Dimitrijević, Bojan 356
ディミトリウ
Demetriou, Andreas 340
ディミトリエフ
Dimitriev, Emil 356
ディミトローヴァ
Dimitrova, Ghena 356
ディミトローバ
Dimitrova, Ghena 356
ディミトロフ
Dimitrov, Dimiter 356
Dimitrov, Grigor 356
Dimitrov, Petar 356
ティミュ
Timu, John 1405
ディミュリアス
De Murias, Ramon 341
ティミラス
Timiras, Mary Letitia 1405
Timiras, Paola S. 1405
ティミンスカ
Tyminska, Karolina 1431
ティム
Timm, Bruce 1405
Timm, Carl 1405
Timm, Uwe 1405
ディム
Dym, Barry 386
ティムス
Timms, Stephen 1405
ディムスキ
Dymski, Gary 386
ディムスキー
Dymski, Gary 386
ディムソン
Dimson, Elroy 356
ティムチェンコ
Timchenko, Dimitriy 1405
Timchenko, Gennady 1405
Timchenko, Olga I. 1405
ティムパーレーク
Timperlake, Edward 1405
テイムーリヤーン
Taymourian, Anahita 1387
テイムリヤン
Taymourian, Anahita 1387
ティムリン
Timlin, Mark 1405
ティーメ
Thieme, Horst R. 1396
ディメク
Dimech, Francis Zammit 356
デイメク
Dejmek, Kazimierz 335
ディメフ
Dimeff, Linda A. 356
ティメル
Timel, Sam 1405
Timmer, Marianne 1405
ティメルス
Timmers, Pieter 1405
ティメルマン
Timerman, Hećtor 1405
ティメルマンス
Timmermans, Frans 1405
テイモア
Taymor, Julie 1387
ディモウスキ
Dimovski, Vlado 356
ディモク
Dimock, Wai-chee 356
ティモシー
Timothy, Julius 1405
ティモーシェンコ
Tymoshenko, Yulia 1431
ティモシェンコ
Tymoshenko, Yulia 1431
ティモ・ジャヤント
Timo Tjahjanto 1405
ティモシュチェンコ
Tymoshchenko, Pavlo 1431
ディモック
Dimock, Wai-chee 356
ティモネン
Timonen, Senni 1405
ディモフ
Dimov, Vladimir 356
ティモフェーエワ
Timofeeva, Irina 1405
ディモフスカ
Dimovska, Dosta 356
ディモフスキ
Dimovski, Ljupcho 356
ティモフティ
Timofti, Nicolae Vasilyevich 1405
ティモール
Timor, David 1405
デイモン
Damon, Johnny 316
Damon, Matt 316
Damon, William 316
ティモンズ
Timmons, Lawrence 1405
Timmons, Michael J. 1405
デイヤコノフ
D'yakonov, Igor'Mikhailovich 385
ディヤス
Dyjas, Jakub 386
ディヤチェンコ
Dyachenko, Alexander 385
Dyachenko, Ekaterina 385
ディヤチン
Dyatchin, Vladimir 385
ディヤング
De Jong, Peter 335
ディユー
Dewe, Philip 348
ディヨ
Deyo, Richard A. 349
ティヨン
Tillion, Germaine 1404
ディーヨン
Deayon, Donte 330
ティーラ
Teera, Slukpetch 1388
Theera, Wongsamut 1395
Thira, Haocharoen 1396
Thira, Sutabutra 1396
ティラー
Tiller, Andrew 1404
テイラー
Taylor, Abra 1385
Taylor, Alan 1385
Taylor, Alice 1385
Taylor, Alistair 1385
Taylor, Andrew 1385
Taylor, Angelo 1385
Taylor, Anthony James 1385
Taylor, Barbara 1385
Taylor, Barbara Brown 1385
Taylor, Billy 1385
Taylor, C.Barr 1385
Taylor, Cecil 1385
Taylor, Charles 1385
Taylor, Chris 1385
Taylor, Christian 1385
Taylor, Codie 1385
Taylor, Cooper 1385
Taylor, Cora 1385
Taylor, Daniel 1385
Taylor, Daniel J. 1385
Taylor, Dave 1385
Taylor, David 1385

テ

Taylor, David S. 1385
Taylor, Derek 1385
Taylor, Devin 1385
Taylor, Don 1385
Taylor, Donald M. 1385
Taylor, Edwin F. 1385
Taylor, Eleanor 1385
Taylor, Elizabeth 1385
Taylor, Elizabeth Johnston 1385
Taylor, Emma 1385
Taylor, Eric A. 1385
Taylor, George Douglass 1385
Taylor, George Howard 1385
Taylor, Geraldine 1385
Taylor, Gilbert 1385
Taylor, Glen 1385
Taylor, Gordon Rattray 1385
Taylor, G.P. 1385
Taylor, Greg 1385
Taylor, Harry 1385
Taylor, Ian 1385
Taylor, Ian Lance 1385
Taylor, Isaiah 1385
Taylor, Jamar 1385
Taylor, James 1385
Taylor, Jason deCaires 1385
Taylor, Jean 1385
Taylor, Jeanette 1385
Taylor, Jennifer 1386
Taylor, Jeremy 1386
Taylor, Jill 1386
Taylor, Jim 1386
Taylor, John 1386
Taylor, John B. 1386
Taylor, John F. 1386
Taylor, John R. 1386
Taylor, Jordan 1386
Taylor, Joseph Hooton, Jr. 1386
Taylor, Judy 1386
Taylor, Kathleen Eleanor 1386
Taylor, Kathrine Kressmann 1386
Taylor, Katie 1386
Taylor, Kelvin 1386
Taylor, Ken 1386
Taylor, Kerry 1386
Taylor, Kevin 1386
Taylor, Kevin J. 1386
Taylor, Koko 1386
Taylor, Laini 1386
Taylor, Lance 1386
Taylor, Lane 1386
Taylor, Leon 1386
Taylor, Lesley 1386
Taylor, Lester D. 1386
Taylor, Madisyn 1386
Taylor, Maria 1386
Taylor, Marianne 1386
Taylor, Mark C. 1386
Taylor, Martin 1386
Taylor, Matt 1386
Taylor, Matthew 1386
Taylor, Matthew J. 1386
Taylor, Maye 1386
Taylor, Michael 1386
Taylor, Myke 1386
Taylor, Neil 1386
Taylor, Palmer 1386
Taylor, Pat 1386
Taylor, Patricia A. 1386
Taylor, Paul Belville 1386
Taylor, Paul D. 1386
Taylor, Peter 1386
Taylor, Phil 1386
Taylor, Rachael 1386
Taylor, Richard 1386, 1387
Taylor, Richard Edward 1387
Taylor, Robert 1387
Taylor, Robert B. 1387
Taylor, Robert L. 1387
Taylor, Rod 1387
Taylor, Rodger 1387
Taylor, Roger 1387
Taylor, Ron 1387
Taylor, Sandra Anne 1387
Taylor, Sarah Stewart 1387
Taylor, Sean 1387
Taylor, Shelley E. 1387
Taylor, Shirley 1387
Taylor, Stepfan 1387
Taylor, Stephen 1387
Taylor, Steve 1387
Taylor, Stuart 1387
Taylor, Sylvester 1387
Taylor, Talus 1387
Taylor, Terry 1387
Taylor, Thom 1387
Taylor, Thomas 1387
Taylor, Timothy 1387
Taylor, Truda 1387
Taylor, Tyrod 1387
Taylor, Ward 1387
Taylor, William 1387

ディラー
Dillah, Lucienne 355
Diller, Barry 355
Diller, Phyllis 355

ディライト
D-LITE 360

ティラキアット
Teerakiat, Jaroensettasin 1388

テイラー・スミス
Taylor-Smith, Claire 1387

ティラーソン
Tillerson, Rex W. 1404

ティラッソー
Tiratsoo, Nick 1406

ティラート
Tirath, Krishna 1406

ティラード
Tirado, Alberto 1406

ディラード
Dillard, Annie 355
Dillard, Jeanne M. 355
Dillard, Sarah 355
Dillard, Sherrie 355
Dillard, William T. 355

ディラド
Dirado, Madeline 357

ティラドス
Tirados, Paola 1406

ティラパット
Thirapat, Serirangsan 1396

ディラボー
Dillabough, Jo-Anne 355

ティラポン・チャンシリ
Chansiri, Thiraphong 246

ティラマニ
Tiramani, Jenny 1406

ディラル
Dirar, Nabil 357

テイラー=ルイス
Tyler-Lewis, Kelly 1431

テイラールイス
Taylor-lewis, Agnes 1387

ディラロ
DiLallo, Richard 355

ティラン
Tiran, Denise 1406

ディラン
Dillon, Thomas 355
Dylan, Bob 386

ティリー
Tilley, Scott 1404
Tilly 1405

ディリ
Dill, Valery 355
Dilli, Ahmad 355

ディリー
Dirie, Waris 357

デイリー
Dailey, Janet 313
Daily, Gretchen 313
Daily, Gretchen C. 313
Daily, LaVerl 313
Daley, Dennis C. 314
Daley, Jennifer 314
Daley, Tom 314
Daley, William M. 314
Dalley, Arthur F. 314
Daly, Babara 315
Daly, Glyn 315
Daly, Herman E. 315
Daly, John 315
Daly, Martin 315
Daly, Mary 315
Daly, Peter Maurice 315
Daly, Tyne 315

デイリィ
Daly, Herman E. 315

ティリエ
Thilliez, Franck 1396
Thiriez, Régine 1396

ディリエ
Diriye, Khadijo Mohamed 358

ティリエッテ
Tilliette, Xavier 1404

ティリオン
Thirion, Samuel 1396

ティーリカイネン
Tiilikainen, Kimmo 1404

ディリシー
DeLisi, Peter S. 337

ティリス
Tsilis, Ioannis 1424

ディリバ
Diriba, Kuma 357

ディリバルヌ
d'Iribarne, Philippe 357

ディリベルト
Diliberto, Oliviero 355

ディリング
Dilling, H. 355

ディリンジャー
Diringer, Michael N. 357

ティール
Thiel, Peter 1396
Thiel, Phil 1396
Thiel, Winfried 1396

ティル
Tyl, Noel 1430

ディール
Deal, Richard A. 329
Diehl, Digby 353
Diehl, Kay 353

デイル
Dale, Angela 314
Dale, Anna 314
Dale, Rodney 314
Dale, Ruth Jean 314

デイ・ルイス
Day-Lewis, Daniel Michael Blake 329

ディルクセン
Dirksen, Jos 358

ディールケン
Dierken, Jörg 354

ティルコート
Tylecote, Andrew 1430

ディルズ
Dills, Ralph C. 355

デイルズ
Dales, Douglas J. 314

ティルストン
Tilston, John 1405

ティルズリー
Tyldesley, Joyce A. 1430

ディールセン
Dierssen, Andreas 354

ティルソン
Tilson, Charlie 1405

ティルソン・トーマス
Tilson-Thomas, Michael 1405

ティルソン・トマス
Tilson-Thomas, Michael 1405

ティルタ
Tirta, Iwan 1406

ディルダ
Dirda, Michael 357

ディルダベコフ
Dildabekov, Mukhtarkhan 355

ディルツ
Dilts, Robert 355
Diltz, Henry 355

ディ・ルッソ
Di Russo, Marisa 358

ディルディ
Dilday, Thaddeus 355

ディールティエンス
Dieltiens, Kristien 353

ティルディスレイ
Tyldesley, Joyce A. 1430

ティルトン
Tilton, Martha 1405

ティルニー
Tilney, Tony 1405

ディルノット
Dilnot, Andrew 355

ディールハンティー
Delehanty, Hugh 337

ティルビー
Tilby, Wendy 1404

ティルフォード
Tilford, Gregory L. 1404

ディ・ルポ
Di Rupo, Elio 358

ティールホフ
Tielhof, Milja van 1404

ティルマン
Tillman, Barrett 1404
Tillman, Chris 1404
Tillman, Lynne 1404
Tillman, Nancy 1405

Tillman, Pat 1405
Tillman, Peggy 1405
Tilman, Leo M. 1405
ディルマン
Dillman, Erika 355
ティルマンス
Tillmans, Wolfgang 1405
ティルマンズ
Tillmans, Wolfgang 1405
ティルワース
Tillworth, Mary 1405
ディルワース
Dilworth, Lee 355
ティーレ
Thiele, Stefan 1396
ティレ
Thillay, Alain 1396
ディレー
Delay, Dorothy 337
ディレイ
Delay, Dorothy 337
ディレイタ
Dileita, Dileita Mohamed 355
ディレイニー
Delany, Pat 336
ディレイニー
Delaney, Damien 336
Delaney, Joseph 336
Delaney, Malcolm 336
Delaney, Matthew B.J. 336
Delaney, Shelagh 336
Delany, Samuel R. 336
Delany, Samuel Ray 336
ディ・レオ
Di Leo, Joseph H. 355
ディレオ
Dileo, Cheryl 355
ティレット
Tillett, Barbara B. 1404
ディレーニー
Delaney, Joseph 336
Delaney, Shelagh 336
Delany, Samuel Ray 336
ティーレマン
Thielemann, Christian 1396
ティレマン
Tilemann, Walter 1404
ティレル
Tyrrell, Ian R. 1431
Tyrrell, James 1431
Tyrrell, Ken 1431
Tyrrell, Patricia 1431
Tyrrell, Susan 1431
ディレル
Dirrell, Andre 358
ディレロ
Dilello, Richard 355
ディレンバーガー
Dillenburger, Karola 355
ティーロ
Thilo, Karen 1396
ティロ
Thilo 1396
Tiro, Hasan Muhammad di 1406
ティロー
Thirault, Philippe 1396
ディロ
Dillo, Yaya 355
Dir, Etenesh 357
Diro, Etenesh 358
ディロウ
Dilou, Samir 355
ディロージャ
DeLozier, Judith 338
ディロッコ
Di Rocco, Michele 358
ティロド
Tirode, Stephanie 1406
ディ・ロビラント
Di Robilant, Andrea 358
ディローリオ
Dilorio, Colleen 355
ティロール
Tirole, Jean 1406
ティロルーイグナシオ
Tirol-ignacio, Marian Jocelyn R. 1406
ディロン
DeLong, Candice 338
Dillon, Brian 355
Dillon, C.Douglas 355
Dillon, Danny 355
Dillon, Diane 355
Dillon, Edmund 355
Dillon, Glyn 355
Dillon, Jo C. 355
Dillon, Karen 355
Dillon, Katherine V. 355
Dillon, K.J. 355
Dillon, Leo 355
Dillon, Matt 355
Dillon, Michelle 355
Dillon, Patricia 355
Dillon, Roxy 355
Dillon, Stephanie W. 355
ティワリ
Tewari, Manish 1393
Tiwari, Maya 1407
Tiwari, Shashank 1407
ティワリー
Tiwary, Vivek J. 1407
ディワン
Diwan, Audrey 359
ティン
Ding, Guan-gen 356
Thinh, Dang Thi Ngoc 1396
Tin, Christopher 1405
Tine, Augustin 1405
Ting, Samuel Chao Chung 1405
Ting, Wan-Qi 1405
テイン
Taine, John 1377
ディーン
Dean, Alyssa 329
Dean, Anthony 329
Dean, Bradley P. 329
Dean, Carolyn 329
Dean, Catherine 329
Dean, David 329
Dean, Debra 329
Dean, Geoff 329
Dean, Hartley 329
Dean, Howard 329
Dean, Ian 329
Dean, Jacqui 329
Dean, James 329
Dean, Jenny 329
Dean, Jeremy 329
Dean, Jimmy 329
Dean, John C. 329
Dean, Johnny 329
Dean, Ken 329
Dean, Liz 330
Dean, Lorraine 330
Dean, Melanie A. 330
Dean, Millvina 330
Dean, Peter B. 330
Dean, Roger 330
Dean, Sarah 330
Dean, Susan 330
Dean, Winton 330
Dean, Zoey 330
Deane, Bonnie St.John 330
Deane, Seamus 330
Deane, Seamus Francis 330
Deane, William 330
Deen, Alhaji Mohamed Swarray 333
Deen, Mohamed Waheed 333
ディン
Ding, Bing 356
Ding, Guan-gen 356
Ding, Ning 356
Ding, William 356
Dinh, Linh 356
Sharaf al-Din, Hasan Ahmed 1282
デイン
Dain, Phyllis 313
Dane, Jordan 316
Dane, Lance 316
Dane, Lauren 316
ティン・アウン
Htin Aung 630
テイン・アウン
Thein Aung 1395
ディン・アクオン
Diing Akuong, Garang 354
ティン・ウ
Tin Oo 1406
ティンウ
Tin Oo 1406
ティンウー
Tin Oo 1406
ディンウィディ
Dinwiddie, Robert 356
Dinwiddie, Spencer 356
ディンウィディー
Dinwiddie, Robert 356
ティン・ウィン
Tin Win 1406
ティン・エイ
Tin Aye 1405
ティンカー
Tinker, Carson 1406
ディンカ
Dinka, Tesfaye 356
ディンガ
Dinga, Ene 356
ディンガー
Dinger, Klaus 356
ディンガジョンド
Dinga Djondo, Antoinette 356
ディンガス
Dingus, Lowell 356
ティンカム
Tinkham, Michael 1406
ディンキッチ
Dinkić, Mlađan 356
ディンキン
Dynkin, Lev 386
ディンク
Dink, Hrant 356
ティン・グエ
Tin Ngwe 1406
ティンクラー
Tinkler, Amy 1406
ティングリー
Tingley, Suzanne Capek 1405
ディングリー
Dingley, Oliver 356
ディングル
Dingle, Adrian 356
ディンクレイジ
Dinklage, Peter 356
ティン・サン
Tint Hsan 1406
テイン・シュエ
Thein Swe 1395
ディンシン
Dincin, Jerry 356
ディーンズ
Deans, Graeme K. 330
Deans, Robbie 330
ディンズ
Danes, Claire 316
デインズ
Danes, Claire 316
Daynes, Katie 329
テイン・スエ
Thein Swe 1395
ディーンストビーア
Dienstbier, Jiří 353
ディーンストビール
Dienstbier, Jiří 353
ディンストビール
Dienstbier, Jiří 353
ディーンストフライ
Dienstfrey, H. 353
ディーンスビーア
Dienstbier, Jiří 353
ディンスモア
Dinsmore, Paul C. 356
ティンスリー
Tinsley, Vicky 1406
ティンズリー
Tinsley, Michael 1406
テイン・セイン
Thein Sein 1395
テイン・ゾウ
Thein Zaw 1395
ティンダール
Tindall, Carol 1405
ティンダル
Tindal, Corey 1405
Tindall, John 1405
Tyndall, John 1431
ディンチェフ
Dinchev, Kaloyan 356
ディンチェル
Dinçer, Ömer 356
ティン・チョー
Htin Kyaw 630
ディンツィス
Dintzis, H.M. 356
ディンツェルバッハー
Dinzelbacher, Peter 356
デインティス
Daintith, John 313
ティンデイル
Tyndale, Anne 1431
ティンデマンス
Tindemans, Leo 1405
ディンド
Dindo, Lilian 356
ティン・トゥ

テ

Tin Htut 1406
ティン・トゥン
Tin Tun 1406
ディンドサ
Dhindsa, Sukhdev Singh 349
ティンドール
Tindall, Blair 1405
ティンドル
Tyndall, John 1431
ティン・ナイン・テイン
Tin Naing Thein 1406
テイン・ニュン
Thein Nyunt 1395
ティンバース
Timbers, Sylvia 1405
ティンバランド
Timbaland 1405
ティンパーレー
Timperley, John 1405
ティンバーレイク
Timberlake, Amy 1405
Timberlake, Justin 1405
Timberlake, Karen C. 1405
Timberlake, William E. 1405
ティン・フトゥ
Tin Htut 1406
ティン・フラ
Tin Hla 1406
ティン・フライン
Tin Hlaing 1406
ティンボ
Timbo, Alpha 1405
ティンレイ
Thinley, Jigme 1396
テー・ウ
Htay Oo 630
テウア
Téhoua, Marie 1388
デーヴァ
Deva, Bigamudre Chaitanya 347
デ・ヴァール
de Waal, Frans B.M. 348
デ・ヴァールト
De Waart, Edo 348
デヴァン・ナイア
Devan Nair, Chengara Veetil 347
デヴァン・ネア
Devan Nair, Chengara Veetil 347
デーヴィ
Davey, Patrick 322
デヴィ
Devi, Phoolan 347
デーヴィス
Davies, Bradley 324
Davies, Brenda 324
Davies, Gareth 324
Davies, Mike 324
Davies, Phil 324
Davis, Alison T. 325
Davis, Anne J. 325
Davis, Colin 325
Davis, Jonathan 326
Davis, Nancy Yaw 326
Davis, Natalie Zemon 326
Davis, Patricia 326
Davis, Richard Franklin 327
Davis, Viola 327
デウィス
Dewis, Glyn 349
デ・ヴィータ
De Vita, Sharon 348
デヴィータ
DeVita, Vincent T., Jr. 348
デーヴィッズ
Davids, Kenneth 323
デ・ウィット
DeWitt, Dave 349
デーヴィッド
David, Paul A. 323
デウィット
Dewit, Andrew 349
Dewitt, Lincoln 349
deWitt, Patrick 349
Dewitt, William O., Jr. 349
デヴィッドスン
Davidson, Lionel 323
Davidson, MaryJanice 323
デヴィッドソン
Davidson, Ann 323
Davidson, Diane Mott 323
Davidson, Jane W. 323
Davidson, Jeffrey P. 323
Davidson, Kate M. 323
Davidson, Paul 323
デヴィート
DeVito, Basil V., Jr. 348
DeVito, Chris 348
DeVito, Danny 348
デーヴィドソン
Davidson, Basil Risbridger 323
デヴィドソン
Davidson, R. 323
デヴィリアス
De Villiers, Jean 348
テヴィンケル
Tewinkel, Christiane 1393
デヴィンセンティス
Devincentis, D.V. 348
デ・ヴェッキ
De Vecchi, Pierluigi 347
デ・ヴェック
de Weck, Olivier L. 348
テーヴェライト
Theweleit, Klaus 1395
テウェルデ
Tewelde, Kelati 1393
デウェールト
Weerd, Piet de 1487
デヴェレル
Deverell, Doré 347
デヴェンター
Deventer, Donald R. van 347
デヴォー
Désveaux, Benoît 346
デヴォス
Devos, Richard 348
デヴォート
DeVoto, Mark 348
テウォドロス
Tewodros, Adhanom 1393
デーヴォル
Devold, Simon Flem 348
デウォルト
DeWalt, Benjamin 348
デヴォールト
DeVault, Christine 347
デ・ウォルフ
de Wolfe, Patricia 349
デゥース
Duus, Peter 385
デウッチマン
Deutschman, Alan 347
テヴノー
Thévenot, Laurent 1395
デヴリーガー
Devlieger, Patrick 348
デヴリース
DeVries, Kelly 348
デヴリン
Devlin, Dean 348
Devlin, Es 348
Devlin, John 348
デヴロー
Deveraux, Jude 347
デウロフェウ
Deulofeu, Gerard 347
デエ
Deshayes, Laurent 345
デエスコバル
De Escobar, Ana Vilma 333
デエフスキー
Dejevsky, Nikolai J. 335
デェミードヴァ
Demidova, Nataliia 340
テオ
Teo, Chee Hean 1391
Teo, Samuelu 1391
Teo, Shun Xie 1391
Teo, Wanda Corazon 1391
Theo 1395
デオ
Deo, Kishore 343
テオ・エルナンデス
Theo Hernandez 1395
テオカラキス
Theocharakis, Basil 1395
デ・オーサ
De Osa, Veronica 343
デオジー
Deossie, Zak 343
デオダート
Deodato, Mike 343
テオドッシュウ
Theodossiou, Dimitra 1395
テオドビッチ・オルティス
Teodovich Ortiz, Freddy 1391
テオドラコプロス
Theodoracopulos, Taki 1395
テオドレスク
Theodorescu, Răzvan 1395
テオドロビッチ
Teodorovici, Eugen 1391
テオハロヴァ
Teokharova, Tatiana Vladimirovna 1391
テオフィルス
Theophilus, Lorne 1395
デオラ
Deora, Murli 343
デオランダ
De Hollanda, Anna Maria Buarque 334
デオリベイラ
De Oliveira, Gilda Maria 343
De Oliveira, Luís Valente 343
デオリベイララモス
De Oliveira Ramos, Américo 343
テオリン
Theorin, Iréne 1395
Theorin, Johan 1395
デオン
Déon, Michel 343
デガ
Deygas, Florence 349
テカアネネ
Tekanene, Maere 1389
テカイアラ
Tekaiara, Ruateki 1389
デ・カイザー
De Keijzer, Arne J. 335
デガイル
al-Degair, Jalal Yousif 333
テカウ
Tecau, Horia 1388
デカスティジャ・ウルビナ
De Castilla Urbina, Miguel 331
デカストロ
Decastro, David 331
De Castro, Luciano Andre 331
De Castro, Noli 331
De Castro, Paolo 331
デカタンザロ
DeCatanzaro, Denys 331
テ・カナワ
Te Kanawa, Kiri 1389
デガビディア
De Gavidia, Yolanda Mayora 333
デカポビジャ
de Capovilla, Maria Esther 331
テカリ
Tekkari, Béchir 1389
デ・カール
Des Cars, Jean 345
Des Cars, Laurence 345
デ・カルロ
De Carlo, Yvonne 331
デ・カーロ
De Carlo, Yvonne 331
De Caro, Stefano 331
デカーロ
DeCarlo, Neil 331
デカンヴィル
d'Équainville, David 343
デカンディード
DeCandido, Keith R. A. 331
デカンポス
De Campos, Teodorico 331
テキア
Tekia, Tangariki 1389
テキシエ
Texier, Catherine 1393
デキロン
Desquiron, Lilas 346
テキン
Tekin, Latife 1389
デーキン
Dakin, Glenn 313
デ・キンデル
De Kinder, Jan 335
デギンドス
De Guindos Jurado,

テ

Luis 334
デギンドス・フラード
De Guindos Jurado, Luis 334
デグアラ
Deguara, Louis 334
デ・クエアル
De Cuéllar, Javier Pérez 332
デクエヤル
De Cuéllar, Javier Pérez 332
デ・クエルク
De Clercq, Willy 332
テクシエ
Texier, Ophélie 1393
デクスター
Dexter, Brad 349
Dexter, Colin 349
Dexter, Pete 349
デ・グズマン
De Guzman, Jonathan 334
テクパー
Tekper, Seth Emmanuel 1389
Terkper, Seth Emmanuel 1392
デグベ
Degbe, Jocelyn 333
テクペティ
Tekpetey, Bernard 1389
テグマーク
Tegmark, Max 1388
デグラ
Degla, Benoît Assounan 334
デ・クラーク
De Klerk, AJ 335
デクラーク
Declerck, Gilbert 332
De Klerk, Frederik Willem 335
デクラーク・ルビン
De Klerk-Rubin, Vicki 335
デグラス
Degras, Jane 334
デグラッセ
De Grasse, Andre 334
デ・グラーフ
De Graaf, John 334
デグラーフ
De Graaf, Christian 334
De Graaff, Christian 334
デクランガ
De Kerangat, Mathilde 335
デクルー
Descouleurs, Bernard 345
デ・クルイヴァー
De Kluyver, Cornelis A. 335
デ・グルーチー
De Gruchy, John W. 334
デクレア
DeClaire, Joan 332
デグレイ
De Grey, Aubrey D.N. J. 334
デグレゴリオ
De Gregorio, José 334
デ・クレシェンツォ
Creschenzo, Luciano De 301
De Crescenzo, Luciano 332
De Crescenzo, Renato 332
デクレム
De Crem, Pieter 332
デクレルク
De Clerck, Stefaan 332
デクロー
De Croo, Alexander 332
デグロウ
DeGraw, Gavin 334
デグロフ
DeGroff, Dale 334
デグロム
Degrom, Jacob 334
テーゲ
Teege, Jennifer 1388
テケ
Tekee, Kataotika 1389
デーケ
Deecke, Lüder 332
デケトレ
De Ketele, Kenny 335
テケリ
Tekeli, Ilhan 1389
デゲリング
Degering, Etta B. 333
デゲール
Degale, James 333
デ・ゲレツ
De Gerez, Toni 333
デーケン
Deeken, Alfons 333
Deeken, Anneliese 333
デーゲン
Degen, Michael 333
Degen, Rolf 333
デ・ケンプ・エーヴェルツ
de Kemp-Everts, Christa 335
デコ
Deco 332
デゴ
Dego, Francesca 334
デコス
Décosse, Lucie 332
デコステ
DeCoste, Barbara 332
デコスペダル・ガルシア
De Cospedal García, María Dolores 332
デコック
De Cock, Michael 332
デコニンク
De Coninck, Monica 332
Dekoninck, Dieter 335
デコニング
De Koning, Coen 335
テコリ
Tekori, Joe 1389
テサー
Tesar, George 1392
デサイ
Desai, Anil 345
Desai, Anita 345
Desai, Kiran 345
Desai, Meghnad Jagdishchandra 345
Desai, Pooran 345
Desai, Priya Giri 345
Desai, Suresh 345
デザイナー エックス
Designer X. 345
デ・ザーコ
De Zurko, Edward Robert 349
デザーモ
Desormeaux, Kent 346
デザリック
Desserich, Brooke 346
Desserich, Keith 346
デ・サール
De Sart, Julien 345
デーサル
DeSalle, Robert 345
デサール
DeSalle, Robert 345
デサルボ
DeSalvo, Debra 345
デ・サンクティス
De Sanctis, Morgan 345
デサンクティス
DeSanctis, Gerardine 345
デサンジョ
Ndesandjo, Mark Obama 1010
デ・サンティアゴ・エルナンデス
de Santiago Hernandez, Santiago 345
デサント
DeSanto, F.J. 345
デシアー
Desir, Pierre 345
テシィケ
Teschke, Benno 1392
デジェ
Dégé, Guillaume 333
テシェイラ
Teixeira, Elisio Osvaldo Do Espirito Santo D'alva 1389
Teixeira, Lara 1389
Teixeira, Mark 1389
テジェス・クエンツレ
Téllez Kuenzler, Luís 1389
テジェス・クエンツレル
Téllez Kuenzler, Luís 1389
デ・ジェズス
De Jesus, Maria 335
デジェズス
De Jesus, Maria 335
デ・ジェズス・トロボアダ・ドス・サントス
De Jesus Trovoada Dos Santos, Maria 335
デジェネレス
DeGeneres, Ellen 333
テシェーラ
Teixeira, Mark 1389
デ・シェン
De Chene, Brent Eugene 332
デジェンナーロ
De Gennaro, Giovanni 333
デジオ
Desio, Ardito 345
デジサッピ
DiGiuseppe, Raymond 354
テシナ
Tessina, Tina B. 1392
デ・シニョリブス
De Signoribus, Eugenio 345
デジミニ
Desimini, Lisa 345
デーシャ
Desha, Cheryl 345
テシャエフ
Teshayev, Shukhrat 1392
テジャサーナンダ
Tejasānanda, Swami 1389
デシャネル
Deschanel, Zooey 345
デシャノン
Deshannon, Jackie 345
デ・ジャルダン
DesJardins, Joseph R. 345
デジャルダン
DesJardins, Joseph R. 345
デシャルヌ
Descharnes, Robert 345
デシャン
Descamps, Remy 345
Deschamps, Didier 345
テジャンジャロ
Tejan-jalloh, Ibrahim 1389
デシュパンデ
Deshpande, Niyanta 345
Deshpande, Salil 345
Deshpande, Vijay M. 345
デシュムーク
Deshmukh, Hanumant 345
デシュムク
Deshmukh, Vilasrao 345
デ・シュリーファー
De Schrijver, Jelle 345
テージョ
Tello, Andres 1389
Tello, Cristian 1389
テジョ
Tedjo, Edhi Purdijatno 1388
デジョイア
DeGioia, John J. 333
デ・ジョネット
De Johnette, Jack 335
テショメ
Teshome, Toga 1392
デ・ジョルジョ
De Giorgio, Pietro 333
デ・シリオ
De Sciglio, Mattia 345
デジール
Désir, Harlem 345
デ・シルヴェストリ
De Silvestri, Lorenzo 345
デ・ジルコフ
De Zirkoff, Boris 349
デシールズ
Deshields, Delino 345
デシルバ
De Silva, Amilra Prasanna 345
De Silva, Nimal Siripala 345
デジーン・ジョーンズ
Dejean-Jones, Bryce 335
テーズ
Thase, Michael E. 1394
Thesz, Lou 1395
デース
Dehs, Volker 334
デスアール
Dessuart, Annick 346
Dessuart, Joseph 346
デスカタ
D'Escatha, Yannick 345

デスカルソ
Descalso, Daniel 345
デスクラファニ
Desclafani, Anthony 345
テスケンズ
Theyskens, Olivier 1395
デスコト
D'Escoto 345
テスコニ
Tesconi, Luca 1392
デスコラ
Descola, Philippe 345
デスーザ
D'Souza, Steven 376
テスタ
Testa, Fulvio 1392
Testa, Irma 1392
テスター
Tester, Keith 1392
Tester, Maurice H. 1392
デスタ
Desta, Amare 346
テスタール
Testart, Jacques 1392
テスチュ
Testud, Sandrine 1392
デステ
D'Este, Carlo 346
デステノ
DeSteno, David 346
デ・ステファニ
De Stefani, Renzo 346
テステュ
Testu, Bernard 1392
テステュー
Testud, Sylvie 1392
テスト
Test, Zack 1392
デストロ
Destro, Mattia 346
デスノエス
Desnoes, Edmundo 346
デスパイグネ
Despaigne, Robelis 346
デスパイネ
Despaigne, Odrisamer 346
Despaigne, Yordanis 346
テスファイ
Tesfai, Gebreselassie 1392
テスファセラシエ
Tesfasellassie, Berhane 1392
デスプラ
Desplat, Alexandre 346
デスペルダー
DeSpelder, Lynne Ann 346
デスポトヴィッチ
Despotovic, Ranko 346
デスポトビッチ
Despotovic, Ranko 346
デスポプロス
Despopoulos, Agamemnon 346
デスモワノー
Desmoinaux, Christel 346
デズモンド
Desmond, Adrian J. 346
Desmond, Ian 346
Desmond, Jenni 346
デズモンド・ヘルマン
Desmond-Hellmann, Susan 346
デスルス
Dessources, Anthony 346
テセ
Tesser, Neil 1392
デセイ
DeSaix, Debbi Durland 345
Dessay, Natalie 346
デゼイ
Dezei, Bayan 349
デセイン
DeSain, Carol 345
デセティ
Decety, Jean 331
デセナ
De Sena, Erica 345
テセンガ
Thesenga, Susan 1395
デ・ソイザ
de Zoysa, Tilak 349
デ・ソウザ
De Sousa, Mauricio 346
デソウサ
De Sousa, Gregorio 346
De Souza, Vibert 346
デソウザ
De Sousa, Gastão 346
デソーサ
de Sosa, Eugenio 346
デソーザ
De Sousa, Rui Dia 346
デソーザアルメイダ
De Sousa Almeida, Maria de Fatima Leite 346
テソリ
Tesori, Jeanine 1392
テソリン
Tesolin, Arupa 1392
デソルニエ
Desaulniers, Robert 345
デ・ソーレス
De Saulles, Tony 345
テーター
Tatroe, Kevin 1383
デ・ダイン
De Deyn, P.P. 332
テタウア
Tetaua, Kobebe 1393
テタス・チャパロ
Tetaz Chaparro, Nahuel 1393
テタベア
Tetabea, Teiraoi 1392
テタマシムバ
Tetamashimba, Ben 1393
デタラモン
De Taramond, Guy 346
テタール
Teétart, Frank 1388
テダルディ
Tedaldi, Dylan 1388
テタンコ
Tetangco, Amando M., Jr. 1393
テタンジェ
Taittinger, Jean 1377
デチ
Decsi, Tamas 332
デ・チェザリス
De Cesaris, Andrea 331
デチャウ
Dechow, Doug 332
テー・チョンキン
The Tjong Khing 1395
テチントン
Techintong, Okada 1388
デッカー
Decker, Charles R. 332
Decker, Eric 332
Decker, Jesse 332
Decker, Kerstin 332
Decker, Rainer 332
Decker, Ray Thomas 332
Decker, Steve 332
Decker, Steven 332
Decker, Taylor 332
Deckker, Zilah 332
Dekker, Desmond 335
Dekker, Inge 335
Dekker, Paul 335
Dekker, Rudolf M. 335
Dekker, Sam 335
Dekker, Sidney 335
Dekker, Sybilla 335
Dekker, Ted 335
Dekker, Wisse 335
デッカース
Deckers, J.A. 332
デッカーズ
Deckers, Erik 332
デッカート
Deckert, Torsten 332
デッカー＝フォイクト
Decker-Voigt, Hans-Helmut 332
テック
Tec, Nechama 1388
デック
Dijk, Willibrord Chr. van 354
デックス
Daix, Pierre 313
デッケ
Dettke, Bodo 347
テッケントラップ
Teckentrup, Britta 1388
Teckentrupp, Britta 1388
テッケントラプ
Teckentrup, Britta 1388
テッサマンガル
Tessa Mangal, Charlotte 1392
デッサルト
Dessart, Francis 346
テッサロ
Tessaro, Kathleen 1392
デッサンツ
Dessants, Betty Abrahamsen 346
デッシー
Dessi, Daniela 346
テッシーナ
Tessina, Tina B. 1392
デッセ
Desse, Dalke 346
デッセーナ
Dessena, Daniele 346
テッセブロー
Tossebro, Jan 1414
デッセン
Dessen, Sarah 346
テッター
Tetter, Jan 1393
テッツェリ
Tetzeli, Rick 1393
テッツラフ
Tetzlaff, Christian 1393
デッティ
Detti, Gabriele 347
テット
Tett, Gillian 1393
デットヴィラー
Dettwiler, Fritz 347
テットーニ
Tettoni, Luca Invernizzi 1393
デットマー
Dettmer, H.William 347
デッドマウス
Deadmaus 329
デッドモン
Dedmon, Dewayne 332
テッドリー
Teddlie, Charles 1388
デットーリ
Dettori, Lanfranco 347
テットロウ
Tetlow, Adam 1393
テッパー
Tepper, David 1391
Tepper, Jonathan 1391
デップ
Depp, Daniel 343
Depp, Johnny 343
デッラ・ヴァッレ
Della Valle, Diego 338
Della Valle, Valeria 338
デッラ・カーサ
Della Casa, Lisa 338
テッラノーヴァ
Terranova, Emanuele 1392
テツラフ
Tetzlaff, Christian 1393
デッロルコ
Dell'orco, Cristian 338
デッロ・ルッソ
Dello Russo, Anna 338
テテ
Tete, Kenny 1393
Tetteh, Hannah 1393
デデ
Dede, Daniel Emery 332
デディアン
Dedeyan, Abraham 332
デデイン
Deyne, Wim de 349
デデウスリマ
Deus Lima, Manuel De 347
テテエニョ
Teteh-enyo, Alex 1393
テデエフ
Tedeyev, Elbrus 1388
デデ・コルクト
Dede Korkut 332
テデスコ
Tedesco, Juan Carlos 1388
デデヤン
Dedeyan, Claire 332
デデュー
Dedieu, Thierry 332
デデラ
Dedera, Don 332
テーテンバウム
Tetenbaum, Samara Pulver 1393
テート
Tate, Buddy 1383

Tate, Jeffrey 1383
Tödt, Heinz Eduard 1408
デート
Dej, Boonlong 335
デドー
Dedeaux, Raoul Martial 332
デトゥーシュ
Destouches, Lucette 346
デトゥワ
Déthoua, Janette 346
デトコフ
Detkov, Stanislav 347
デトマー
Dettmer, H.William 347
テトリー
Tetley, Glen 1393
デトーレス
De Torres, Pablo 347
デトレフゼン
Dethlefsen, Thorwald 346
テドロー
Tedlow, Richard S. 1388
テドロス
Tedros, Adhanom 1388
テトロック
Tetlock, Philip Eyrikson 1393
デトワイラー
Detwiler, Ross 347
テナー
Tener, Robert L. 1390
デナイヤー
Denayer, Jason 341
テ・ナイン・ウィン
Thet Naing Win 1395
テナウア
Tenaua, Kautu 1390
テナクーン
Tennekoon, Janaka Bandara 1391
デナード
Dennard, Darqueze 342
Dennard, Robert Heath 342
デナム
Denham, John 342
Denham, Robert D. 342
Denham, Sam 342
デナール
Denard, Bob 341
デナルディス
DeNardis, Laura 341
デナンクス
Daeninckx, Didier 312
テナント
Tennant, Alan 1391
Tennant, Don 1391
Tennant, Emma 1391
テニー
Tenney, Lester 1391
Tenney, Tom Fred 1391
Tenney, Tommy 1391
デニー
Denney, John 342
Denny, Mark W. 342
テニエウ
Tenieu, Teaiwa 1390
デニグリス
de Nigris, Antonio 342
デニケン
Däniken, Erich von 318
デニコロ
De Nicolo, Marco 342
デニシェフ
Denisyev, Alexandr 342
デニス
Denis, Gaëlle 342
Denise, Christopher 342
Dennis, Craig 342
Dennis, Daniel 342
Dennis, Don 342
Dennis, Everette E. 342
Dennis, Kane 342
Dennis, Marie 342
Dennis, Matt 342
Dennis, Melvin B., Jr. 342
Dennis, Pascal 342
Dennis, Rohan 342
Dennis, Steve 342
Dennis, Zach 342
デニス・サンチェス
Denis Sánchez, Amancio Óscar 342
デニス・スアレス
Denis Suarez 342
テニスバエフ
Tengizbayev, Nurbakyt 1390
デニセンコ
Denisenko, Alexey 342
デニソフ
Denisov, Kirill 342
Denisov, Valeriĭ Iosifovich 342
Denisov, Vitaly 342
デニソワ
Denisova, Lyudmila 342
デニソン
Denison, Edward 342
Denison, Janelle 342
Dennison, Rich 342
デニッシュ
Danish, Steven 318
Danish, Tyler 318
テーニッセ
Theunissen, Nickie 1395
デニッソン
Dennison, Gail E. 342
Dennison, Paul Ehrlich 342
デ・ニーロ
De Niro, Robert 342
デニーロ
De Niro, Robert 342
デニーン
Deneen, Patrick 341
デニング
Denning, Dorothy Elizabeth Robling 342
Denning, Stephen 342
Denning, Troy 342
デーネカンプ
Denekamp, Nienke 341
テネケチェジウ
Teneqexhiu, Gjergj 1390
デーネシュ
Denes, Nagy 341
テーネス
Thoenes, Christoph 1396
テネット
Tenet, George J. 1390
デネット
Dennett, Daniel Clement 342
デネヒー
Dennehy, Brian 342
テネフ
Tenev, Vlad 1390
デネロフ
Deneroff, Harvey 341
テネンバウム
Tenenbaum, G.David 1390
デノーイ
de Nooy, Wouter 342
デノエット
Desnoëttes, Caroline 346
デーノス
Denos, Julia 342
デノーフィア
Denorfia, Chris 342
デノーム
DeNomme, Donna 342
テノリオ
Tenorio, Otilino 1391
デノン
Denon, Kassoum 342
テーバー
Tabor, Amy 1375
Tabor, David 1375
Tabor, James M. 1375
デハ
Dekha, Iryna 335
デバ
Débat, Aurélien 330
デバイ
Debye, Kristina E. 331
デパイ
Depay, Memphis 343
デバイン
Devine, Dan 348
デパウリ
DePauli-Schimanovich, Werner 343
デ・パウル
De Paul, Rodrigo 343
デ・パオラ
de Paola, Tomie 343
デパオラ
Depaola, Andrew 343
デパオリ
Depaoli, Fabio 343
デバガ
Debagha, Slim Tahar 330
デバスク
DeBusk, Ruth M. 331
デバスコンセロス
De Vasconcelos, José Maria Botelho 347
テハーダ
Tejada, Ruben 1389
テハダ
Tejada, Alba 1389
デバッジオ
DeBaggio, Thomas 330
デバッシャー
DeBusschere, Dave 331
デパット
De Padt, Guido 343
デハート
DeHart, Robyn 334
デ・パドヴァ
de Padova, Thomas 343
デバニー
Devaney, Adam 347
Devaney, Robert L. 347
デハーネ
Dehaene, Jean-Luc 334
デハビッチ・ロスピグリオシ
De Habich Rospigliosi, Midori 334
デ・パーマ
De Palma, Brian 343
デパラシオ
De Palacio, Ana 343
デバリエ
Devalier, Warren J. 347
テバル
Tebar, Karen 1388
デバルガス
De Vargas, Francisco 347
デバルグ
Debargue, Lucas 330
テバルディ
Tebaldi, Renata 1388
デパルデュー
Depardieu, Gérard 343
デハルトグ
de Hartog, Jan 334
デパルドン
Depardon, Raymond 343
デ・パルフォード
De Pulford, Nicola 343
デ・パルマ
De Palma, Brian 343
デパルマ
Depalma, John 343
DePalma, Mary Newell 343
デバレラ
De Valera, Sile 347
デバレル
Deverell, Julian 347
Deverell, Richard 347
デパロー
DePalo, Anna 343
デバロス
De Barros, Bruno 330
De Barros, Carlos Alberto Kenedy 330
デ・ハーン
De Haan, Michelle 334
デパンディ
DePandi, Giuliana 343
デバン・ナイア
Devan Nair, Chengara Veetil 347
デバン・ネア
Devan Nair, Chengara Veetil 347
デパンフィリス
DePanfilis, Diane 343
デ・ビー
de Bie, Erik Scott 330
デービー
Davey, Edward 322
Davie, Alan 324
Davie, Daniel 324
デビ
Déby, Idriss 331
Devi, Indra 347
Devi, Phoolan 347
デビー
Déby, Idriss 331
Devey, Jordan 347
デ・ビア
De Beer, Hans 330
デビアトフスキ
Devyatovskiy, Maxim 348
デピエレフ
De Pierrefeu, Thierry 343

テ

デービース
Davies, Glyn 324
Davies, Laura 324
デービーズ
Davies, Glyn 324
Davies, Jacqueline 324
Davies, Laura 324
デービス
Davies, Benjamin 324
Davies, Cath 324
Davies, David 324
Davies, Emma 324
Davies, Georgia 324
Davies, Howard John 324
Davies, Laura 324
Davies, Merryl Wyn 324
Davies, Murray 324
Davies, Nicola 324
Davies, Omar 324
Davies, Patricia M. 324
Davies, Peter Maxwell 324
Davies, R.L. 325
Davies, Rob 325
Davis, Al 325
Davis, Alan Michael 325
Davis, Andre 325
Davis, Ann B. 325
Davis, Anne J. 325
Davis, Anthony 325
Davis, Austin 325
Davis, Bart 325
Davis, Bret W. 325
Davis, Carl 325
Davis, Chili 325
Davis, Chris 325
Davis, Clive 325
Davis, Cody 325
Davis, Colin 325
Davis, Daglas 325
Davis, David 325
Davis, Demario 325
Davis, Dennis Russell 325
Davis, Dominique 325
Davis, Edmond 325
Davis, Francis 326
Davis, Geena 326
Davis, Geremy 326
Davis, Greg 326
Davis, Ike 326
Davis, James-Andrew 326
Davis, J.D. 326
Davis, Jesse 326
Davis, Joann 326
Davis, Judy 326
Davis, Julie L. 326
Davis, Kellen 326
Davis, Kendall B. 326
Davis, Khris 326
Davis, Knile 326
Davis, Kristin 326
Davis, Kyra 326
Davis, Lindsey 326
Davis, Lydia 326
Davis, Marvin 326
Davis, Meryl 326
Davis, Michael H. 326
Davis, Mike 326
Davis, Ossie 326
Davis, Philip E. Brave 326
Davis, Quinshad 326
Davis, Rajai 326
Davis, Ray C. 327
Davis, Raymond, Jr. 327
Davis, Richard A. 327
Davis, Rookie 327
Davis, Ryan 327
Davis, Sean 327
Davis, Shani 327
Davis, Shiro 327
Davis, Skeeter 327
Davis, Thomas 327
Davis, Thomas E. 327
Davis, Titus 327
Davis, Todd 327
Davis, Trevor 327
Davis, Vernon 327
Davis, Viola 327
Davis, Vontae 327
Davis, Wade 327
Davis, Will 327
Davis, Willie 327
デビース
Davies, Jacqueline 324
Davies, Zack 325
デービス・フロイド
Davis-Floid, Robbie 327
デービスラッセル
Davis-russell, Elizabeth 327
デービソン
Davison, Bryce 327
Davison, Lea 327
Davison, Tyeler 327
デビソン
Davison, Gerald C. 327
デビータ
DeVita, Carol J. 348
デービッド
David, Craig 322
David, Hal 322
David, Joaquim Duarte Da Costa 322
David, Juliet 323
David, Lavonte 323
David, Peter 323
David, Russ 323
デビッド
David, David Mathayo 322
David, Hal 322
David, Peter 323
デービッドソン
Davidson, Andrew 323
Davidson, Basil Risbridger 323
デビッドソン
Davidson, Alexander 323
Davidson, Basil Risbridger 323
Davidson, Craig 323
Davidson, Diane Mott 323
Davidson, Donald Herbert 323
Davidson, James Duncan 323
Davidson, MaryJanice 323
Davidson, Matt 323
Davidson, Ogunlade 323
Davidson, Richard J. 323
テヒテール
Töchterle, Karlheinz 1408
デ・ビート
DeVito, Danny 348
デビド
De Vido, Julio 348
デビドフ
Davidoff, Jules 323
デピナ
De-pina, Jose 343
デ・ビーバー
de Bever, Leo 330
デヒャオ
Dechau, Wilfried 331
デビャトフスキー
Devyatovskiy, Vadim 348
デピュー
Depue, Roger L. 343
デビュイスト
De Buyst, Jasper 331
デビュース
Dubus, Andre, Ⅲ 377
デヒョン
Dae-hyun 312
デビリヤ
De Villa, Renato 348
デビンチェンティ
De Vincenti, Claudio 348
デビント
De Windt, Reginald 349
デブ
Dev, Sontosh Mohan 347
デ・ファー
De Fer, Thomas M. 333
デファー
Defar, Meseret 333
デファゴ
Défago, Didier 333
デファッラ
Defallah, Khayar Oumar 333
デファル
Defar, Meseret 333
デファルコ
DeFalco, Tom 333
デフィリッピス
de Filippis, Maria Teresa 333
デフィリッポ
D'Efilippo, Valentina 333
テフェラ
Tefera, Deribew 1388
Tefera, Walwa 1388
テフェリ
Teferi, Senbere 1388
デフェリス
DeFelice, Jim 333
デフェル
Deferr, Gervasio 333
デフェンソール
Defensor, Michael 333
デフォー
Dafoe, Willem 312
Defoe, Jermain 333
デフォルジュ
Deforges, Régine 333
デフォンスカ
Defonseca, Misha 333
デフガン
Dehqan, Hossein 334
デプケン
Depken, Kristen L. 343
デブコタ
Devkota, Upendra 348
テブザゼ
Tevzadze, David 1393
デフジャティアロフ
Devjatiarov, Mickail Jun. 348
テーブス
Toews, Vic 1408
テブス
Tebbs, Victoria 1388
デーブス
Debus, Michael 331
デブッシャー
DeBusschere, Dave 331
テブヌ
Tebboune, Abdelmadjid 1388
テプファー
Töpfer, Klaus 1412
デフフト
De Gucht, Karel 334
デブラ
Debrah, Julius 331
デブラー
Debrah, Ernest 331
デ・フライ
De Vrij, Stefan 348
デ・ブライネ
De Bruyne, Kevin 331
デ・ブラージ
De Blasi, Marlena 331
デブラシオ
DeBlasio, Allison 331
Deblasio, Bill 331
デ・ブラシス
De Blasis, Pablo 331
デ・ブラバンダー
De Brabander, Ellen 331
デフラーフ
De Graaf, Thom 334
デフラーフェ
De Grave, Frank 334
デフランコ
DeFranco, Anthony L. 333
DeFranco, Buddy 333
De Franco, Mario 333
De Franco, Silvio 333
デフランス
Defrance, Helene 333
デフランツ
Defrantz, Anita L. 333
デブリー
DeVrye, Catherine 348
デプリー
De Pree, Max 343
デ・フリース
de Vries, Sophia 348
デフリース
De Vries, Klaas 348
デプリースト
De Preist, James 343
テプリッツ
Teplitz, Jerry V. 1391
デブリッヒ
Dobrich, Anette 361
デブリュー
Debreu, Gerard 331
デブリン
Devlin, Delilah 348
Devlin, Keith J. 348
Devlin, Thomas M. 348
デブリンジャー
Deblinger, Esther 331
デプリンス
DePrince, Elaine 343
DePrince, Michaela 343
デ・ブール
Boer, Erik-Jan De 153
De Boer, Frank 331
デフール
Defour, Steven 333
デブール
De Boer, Frank 331
デブルーイン
De Bruijn, Inge 331

デプルシャン
Desplechin, Arnaud 346
Desplechin, Marie 346
デ・フルトス
De Frutos, Javier 333
デブルム
Debrum, Tony 331
デブレ
De Broe, Marc E. 331
デプレ
Després, Jacques 346
Desprez, Michaël 346
デプレイスト
De Preist, James 343
デ・フレイタス
De Freitas, Juan 333
デプレシャン
Desplechin, Arnaud 346
デブレツィオン
Debretsion, Gebremichael 331
デフレル
Defrel, Gregoire 333
デブロック
De Block, Maggie 331
テブン
Tebben, Maryann Bates 1388
Tebboune, Abdelmadjid 1388
テーベ
Teewe, Natan 1388
デ・ヘア
De Gea, David 333
デヘウス
De Geus, Aart-Jan 333
De Geus, Lilian 333
デヘージア
Dehejia, Vidya 334
デベシュ
Debeche, Smail 330
テベス
Teves, Margarito 1393
Tévez, Carlos 1393
デヘスス
De Jesus, Edilberto 335
De Jesus, Ivan, Jr. 335
De Jesus, Jose 335
テヘダ
Tejeda, Gladys 1389
デベツィ
Devetzi, Hrysopiyi 347
テベッツ
Tebbetts, Chris 1388
デ・ペナ
De Pena, Carlos 343
デ・ベニート・セカデス
De Benito Secades, Gonzalo 330
デベネシア
De Venecia, Jose 347
デベベツ
Debevec, Rajmond 330
デベベッチ
Debevec, Rajmond 330
テペラ
Tepera, Ryan 1391
テヘラニアン
Tehranian, Majid 1388
デベリャスキー
Debeljački, Tatjana 330
デベリン
Develin, James 347
デベンスキー
Devenski, Chris 347
テポー
Thépaut, Nicole 1395
デボ
Degbo, Clément 333
デボイス
Debois, Patrick 331
デボーキン
DeVorkin, David H. 348
デボス
Devos, Betsy 348
Devos, Richard 348
デボスト
Debost, Michel 331
デ・ボック
De Bock, Laurens 331
デ・ボード
De Board, Robert 331
デボニッシュ
Devonish, Marlon 348
デ・ボーノ
De Bono, Edward 331
デボノ
De Bono, Edward 331
Debono, Giovanna 331
デホフ
DeHoff, Jessica Niles 334
デホープスヘッフェル
De Hoop Scheffer, Jaap 334
デポミエ
Despommier, Dickson D. 346
デ・ポーラ
de Paula, Julio 343
デポランコ
de Polanco, Jesús 343
デボリーニ
Debolini, Francesca 331
デーボル
Devold, Kristin Krohn 348
デボルド
Desbordes, Astrid 345
デポルト
Desportes, Francoise 346
デボワ
De Boer, Roelf 331
デボン
Devon, Georgina 348
デマイヤー
DeMyer, Marian K. 341
デマウロ
De Mauro, Tullio 340
デマーク
DeMark, Thomas R. 339
デマーコ
DeMarco, Kathleen 339
デマコワ
Demakova, Helēna 339
デ・マージ
De Masi, Francesco 339
デマズィエール
Desmazières, Sandra 346
デ・マッテオ
Matteo, Drea de 920
デマティーズ
Dematteis, J.M. 340
デマトス
De Matos, José Luís 339
De Matos, Rosa Pedro Pacavira 339
デマトーン
Dematons, Charlotte 339
デーマートンス
Dematons, Charlotte 339
デマノフ
Demanov, Andrey 339
デマフ
Demafouth, Jean-Jacques 339
テマリ
Temari, Mikarite 1390
デ・マーリ
De Mari, Silvana 339
デ・マリア
De Maria, Walter 339
デマリーニ
DeMarini, David M. 339
テマール
Temmar, Abdelhamid 1390
Temmar, Hamid 1390
デマルキ
De Marchi, Alessandro 339
デマルケ
Desmarquet, Michel 346
デ・マルコ
de Marco, Michael 339
デマルコ
Demarco, Chris 339
De Marco, Guido 339
De Marco, Mario 339
DeMarco, M.J. 339
DeMarco, Tom 339
デ・マルコス
De Marcos, Oscar 339
デ・マルチニス
De Martinis, Massimo 339
デマルト
Desmarteau, Claudine 346
デマレ
Desmarest, Thierry 345
デマレイス
Demarais, Ann 339
テマン
Temman, Michel 1390
デマンド
Demand, Thomas 339
デミ
Demi 340
Demme, Jonathan 340
Demme, Ted 340
デ・ミケーレ
De Michele, Girolamo 340
デミストゥラ
de Mistura, Staffan 340
テミストクレウス
Themistocleous, Kostas 1395
テミストクレス・モンタス
Temístocles Montás, Juan 1390
デミチェリス
Demichelis, Martin 340
デミック
Demick, Barbara 340
デミッコ
DeMicco, Kirk 340
デミトリオス
Démetrios, Eames 340
デミヤネンコ
Demyanenko, Valentin 341
デミヤン
Demian, Hany Kadry 340
デミル
DeMille, Nelson 340
Demir, Mustafa 340
テミルカーノフ
Temirkanov, Yurii 1390
テミルカノフ
Temirkanov, Yurii 1390
デミルタシュ
Demirtaş, Aslihan 340
デミルタス
Demirtas, Soner 340
デミルバイ
Demirbay, Kerem 340
デミレゼン
Demirezen, Ali Eren 340
デミレル
Demirel, Erol 340
Demirel, Süleyman 340
デミレワ
Demireva, Mirela 340
デミロヴィッチ
Demirović, Alex 340
テミン
Temin, Howard M. 1390
Temin, Peter 1390
デミング
Deming, A.G. 340
Deming, Richard 340
Deming, Rust 340
テーム
Tame, Lachlan 1379
テム
Temu, Puka 1390
デム
Demme, Jonathan 340
テムキン
Temkin, Owsei 1390
テムージン
Temuujin, Khishigdemberel 1390
テームズ
Thames, Eric 1394
Thames, Marcus 1394
テムズ
Temes, Roberta 1390
デームス
Demus, Jörg 341
デムース
DeMuth, Phil 341
デムス
Demus, Jörg 341
デムスキ
Demski, Joel S. 341
デムスキー
Demsky, Terry 341
デムスキィ
Demsky, Andrew 341
デムチシン
Demchyshyn, Volodymyr 340
デムチャック
Demchak, MaryAnn 340
デムチュク
Demchuk, Mikhail 340
デムツチェンコ
Demtschenko, Albert 341
テムニク
Temnyk, Hennady 1390
テムベヌ
Tembenu, Samuel

Batson 1390
デムベレル
Demberel, Sanj 340
デムラン
Desmoulins, Marthe 346
テムレゾフ
Temrezov, Nauruz 1390
デムーロ
Demuro, Mirco 341
デムワノー
Desmoinaux, Christel 346
テメ
Teme, Jorge 1390
デメ
Deme, Victor 340
デメイオ
DeMeo, Albert 340
デメケ
Demeke, Mekonnen 340
デメジエール
De Maizière, Thomas 339
デメゾン
Desmaison, René 345
デメター
Demeter, Ervin 340
デメテル
Demeter, Bence 340
デメトリュー
Demetriou, Cleo 340
テメニル
Temengil, Baklai 1390
デ・メネゼス
De Menezes, Fradique 340
デメネゼス
De Menezes, Fradique 340
De Menezes, Jean Charles 340
デメラシュ
Demelash, Yigrem 340
デメールスマン
Demeersman, Dirk 340
テメル・ルリア
Temer Lulia, Michel Miguel Elias 1390
デ・メロ
De Mello, Sergio Vieira 340
デメロ
De Mello, Sergio Vieira 340
デメンチェワ
Dementieva, Elena 340
デ・メンテ
De Mente, Boye 340
デメンティエフ
Dementiev, Eugeniy 340
デメント
Dement, William C. 340
テモク
Temoku, Tawita 1390
デモス
Demos, Gary 341
DeMoss, Nancy Leigh 341
デモステヌス
Demosthenous, Giorgos 341
デモット
Demotte, Rudy 341
デ・モラエス
De Moraes, Ron 341
デモラエス
De Moraes, Marcus Pratini 341
デモリ
Demolli, Haki 340
デモリーナ
De Molina, Ana Ordóñez 340
デモワ
Demois, Agathe 340
デモワノー
Desmoinaux, Christel 346
デーモン
Damon, Johnny 316
Damon, Matt 316
Demon, Franco Rudy 341
デモン
Demong, Bill 341
デモング
Demong, Bill 341
テモンチニ
Timoncini, Daigoro 1405
デモンテ
Demonte, Violeta 341
テヤ
Teya, Jean Eudes 1393
デヤガー
De Jager, Lodewyk 335
デヤーヘル
De Jager, Jan Kees 335
デヤルシン
Deyalsingh, Terrence 349
テュー
Tew, Jeffrey 1393
デュー
Due, Reidar 377
デュア
Dyhr, Pia 386
デュアー
Dewar, Andrew 348
Duerr, Johannes 378
デュアト
Duato, Nacho 376
デュアメル
Duhamel, Meagan 379
Duhamel, Ronald 379
デュアリング
During, Lloyd 384
テュアル
Tual, Natalie 1425
デュアルテ
Duarte, Anselmo 376
Duarte, Nancy 376
Duarte, Thomas 376
デュアン
Duane, William 376
デューイ
Dewe, Philip 348
Dewey, Ariane 349
Duey, Kathleen 378
デュイジット
Duisit, Bernard 379
テュイリエ
Thuillier, Jacques R. 1402
デューヴ
Duve, Thierry de 385
デュヴァリエ
Duvalier, Jean-Claude 385
デュヴァル
Duval, David 385
Duval, Loïc 385
Duval, Michelle 385
Duval, Thomas 385
Duvall, Daniel 385
Duvall, Robert 385
デュヴェルジェ
Duverger, Maurice 385
デュヴォール
Duvall, Robert 385
デュウシエー
Doucet, Julie 369
デュエイン
Duane, Diane 376
デュエナス
Duenas, Cremencio Manso 377
デュエネス
Duenez, Samir 378
デュエーム
Duhème, Jacqueline 379
デュエム
Duhem, Pierre 379
デュエル
Duell, Donna 377
デュエルダン
Duerden, Jean M. 378
デュガ
Dugas, Florence 378
デュカキス
Dukakis, Michael Stanley 379
デュカシー
Ducasse, Vladimir 377
デューカス
Dukas, Chuck 379
デュカス
Ducasse, Alain 377
デュガス
Dugasse, Jacquelin 378
デュカトー
Ducatteau, Florence 377
デュガード
Dugard, Jaycee Lee 378
Dugard, Martin 378
デュカルム
Ducarme, Alain 377
デューガン
Dugan, Dennis 378
Dugan, Marcia B. 378
デュカン
Dukan, Pierre 379
デュガン
Dugain, Marc 378
Dugan, David 378
デューク
Duke, Annie 379
Duke, Elizabeth 379
Duke, George 379
Duke, James 379
Duke, James A. 379
Duke, Mike 379
Duke, Patty 379
Duke, Sue 379
Duke, Zach 379
デュクードレ
Ducoudray, Aurélien 377
デュグラン
Dugrand, Alain 379
デュクリ
Ducre, Greg 377
デュクレ
Ducret, Diane 377
デュクレール
Duclert, Vincent 377
デュクロ
Duclos, Jean-Yves 377
Ducros, Michel 377
デュケット
Duquette, Anne Marie 383
Duquette, Dan 383
デュケノワ
Duquennoy, Jacque 383
デュケンヌ
Dequenne, Emilie 344
Duquesne, Antoine 383
デュコック
Duquoc, Christian 383
デュサトワール
Dusautoir, Thierry 384
デュサパン
Dusapin, Pascal 384
デュシェ
Duché, Didier Jacques 377
デュシコーヴァ
Dusíková, Maja 384
デューシック
Dusik, Jiri 384
デュシャーズ
Deuchars, Marion 347
デュシャトレ
Duchatelet, Bernard 377
デュジャリック
Dujarric, Robert 379
デュジャルダン
Dujardin, Jean 379
デュショーソワ
Duchaussoy, Michel 377
デュショソワ
Duchaussoy, Michel 377
デュース
Dewes, Kate 348
デュースバーグ
Duesberg, Peter H. 378
デューズバーグ
Duesberg, Peter H. 378
デュースバリー
Dewsbury, Ryan 349
テューズリー
Tewsley, Robert 1393
デューセ
Doucet, Michael 369
デュセンヌ
Dussenne, Noe 384
デューゼンバーグ
Duisenberg, Wim 379
デューゼンベリ
Duesenberry, James Stemble 378
デューゼンベリー
Duesenberry, James Stemble 378
Dusenbery, Susan M. 384
デューゼンベルク
Duisenberg, Wim 379
デュ・ソートイ
Du Sautoy, Marcus 384
テューダー
Tudor, Seth 1425
Tudor, Tasha 1425
Tudor, Winslow 1425
デューダ
Duda, Lucas 377
デューターマン
Deutermann, Peter T. 347
デュダメル
Dudamel, Gustavo 377
デュッケ
Duque, Francisco 383

テ

デュットー
Dutto, Giovanni 385
デュットマン
Düttmann, Alexander García 385
デュッフェル
Düffel, John von 378
デュティユー
Dutilleux, Henri 384
デュトア
Dutoit, Charles E. 384
デュトイ
Du Toit, Pieter-Steph 384
デュトイト
Du Toit, Natalie 384
デュトゥ
Duthu, François 384
デュトゥールトゥル
Duteurtre, Benoît 384
デュトゥルトル
Duteurtre, Benoît 384
デュドク・ドゥ・ヴィット
Dudok de Wit, Michael 377
Wit, Michael Dudok de 1518
デュードニー
Dewdney, A.K. 348
デュドネ
Dieudonné, Cléa 354
デュドヤ
Dyudya, Volodymyr 386
デュトルイユ
Dutrail, Renaud 384
デュトレイユ
Dutrail, Renaud 384
デュトワ
Dutoit, Charles E. 384
Du Toit, Natalie 384
デュナガン
Dunagan, Deanna 380
デュナント
Dunant, Sarah 380
テューニソン
Tunison, Joseph S. 1426
デューニング
Duening, Thomas N. 378
デュ・ノイヤー
Du Noyer, Paul 382
デューハスト
Dewhurst, Stephen C. 349
デュバテ
Dioubate, Elhadi Abdul Karim 357
デュバニー・ターディフ
Duvarnay-taidif, Laurent 385
デュバリ
D'Vari, Marisa 385
デュバリエ
Duvalier, Jean-Claude 385
デューバル
Duvall, Sylvanus Milne 385
デュバル
Dubal, David 376
Duval, Charles Gaëtan Xavier-Luc 385
Duval, David 385
Duval, Loïc 385
Duvall, Adam 385
Duvall, Paul M. 385
Duvall, Robert 385
デュバン
Duban, Nixon 376
デュパン
Dupin, Jacques 382
デュービー
Dubee, Rich 376
デュピィ
Dupuy, Philippe 383
デュヒッグ
Duhigg, Charles 379
デュヒティング
Düchting, Hajo 377
デュ・ピュイ
De Puy, Candace 343
デュピュイ
Dupuis, Mélanie 383
Dupuy, Jean-Pierre 383
Dupuy, Mario 383
デュビュニョン
Dubugnon, Richard 377
デュピュレ
Dupré, Dirk 383
デュビラール
Duvillard, Robin 385
デュビレ
Doubilet, David 369
デュービン
Dubin, Dale 376
デュビン
Dubin, Jon C. 376
デュプー
Dupoux, Emmanuel 382
テュフェンキチ
Tüfenkçi, Bülent 1425
デュフォー
Dufau, Guillaume 378
Dufaud, Marc 378
Dufour, Mathieu 378
デュ・ブーシェ
Du Bouchet, André 376
デュブーシェ
Du Bouchet, André 376
デュプラ
Duprat, Guillaume 382
デュプリー
Dupree, Bud 383
Dupree, Cornell 383
デュプリッツァー
Duplitzer, Imke 382
デュプリッツアー
Duplitzer, Imke 382
デュフール
Duffour, Michel 378
Dufour, Daniel 378
Dufour, Francois 378
Dufour, Jean-Frederic 378
Dufour, Mathieu 378
Dufour, Simon 378
デュフール・ラポワント
Dufour-Lapointe, Justine 378
デュフールラポワント
Dufour-lapointe, Chloe 378
デュ・プレ
Prez, John Du 1134
デュプレ
Dupré, Ben 383
Dupré, Judith 383
デュプレア
Du Preez, Fourie 383
デュ・ブーレイ
Du Boulay, Clair 376
デュ・プレシス
Du Plessis, Erik 382
デュ・プレシックス・グレイ
Du Plessix Gray, Francine 382
デュフレス
Dufraisse, Roger 378
デュ・プレッシー
Du Plessis, Tinus 382
デュプレッシー
Du Plessis, Bismarck 382
Du Plessis, Jannie 382
デュフレーヌ
Dufresne, Didier 378
Dufresne, Todd 378
デュフレーン
Dufresne, Didier 378
デュープロ
DuPrau, Jeanne 382
デュフロ
Duflo, Esther 378
Duflot, Cécile 378
デュブロ
Dubro, Alec 377
デュベ
Dube, Jessica 376
Dubet, François 376
デュペイロン
Dupeyron, François 382
デュベルジェ
Duverger, Maurice 385
デュベルダム
Dubbeldam, Jeroen 376
デュペルバル・ギヨーム
Duperval Guillaume, Florence 382
デュペレ
Duperey, Anny 382
デュペロン
Dupeyron, François 382
デュボ
Dubost, Michel 376
デュボー
Deveaux, Earl 347
デュボア
DeBlois, Dean 331
DuBois, Allison 376
Dubois, Bastien 376
Dubois, Jacques 376
Dubois, Marie 376
Dubois, Pierre 376
Du Bois, William Pène 376
デュボイス
DuBois, Brendan 376
DuBois, Ellen Carol 376
デュボイズ
DuBois, Brendan 376
デュボウスキー
Dubowski, Cathy East 377
デュボサルスキー
Dubosarsky, Ursula 376
デュボーズ
Dubose, Lou 376
デュボス
Duboscq, Hugues 376
デュボスト
Dubost, Paulette 376
デュボフ
Dubov, Vladimir 377
デュボール
Duvall, Robert 385
デュポール
DuPaul, George J. 382
デュ・ボワ
Du Bois, Francois 376
デュボワ
Dubois, Claude K. 376
Du Bois, Francois 376
Dubois, Gérard 376
Dubois, Jacques 376
Dubois, Jean-Paul 376
Dubois, Marie 376
DuBois, Paul 376
デュポン
Depondt, Luk 343
Dupond, Patrick 382
Dupont, Ambroise 382
Dupont, Aurélie 382
DuPont, Caroline M. 382
Dupont, Christian 382
Dupont, Jean-Michel 382
duPont, Margaret Osborne 382
DuPont, Robert L. 382
デュポン・ブリエ
Dupont-Beurier, Pierre-François 382
デュマ
Duma, William 379
Dumas, Axel 380
Dumas, Charlotte 380
Dumas, Lynne S. 380
Dumas, Philippe 380
Dumas-Hermés, Jean-Louis Robert Frédéric 380
デュマ・エルメス
Dumas-Hermés, Jean-Louis Robert Frédéric 380
デュマス
Dumas, Margaret 380
Dumas, Marlene 380
Dumas, Rennie 380
デュマービル
Dumervil, Elvis 380
デュムシェル
Dumouchel, Paul 380
デュムベ
Djoumbe, Maïtine 360
デュムラン
Dumoulin, Alexandre 380
Dumoulin, Franck 380
Dumoulin, Tom 380
デュメイ
Dumay, Augustin 380
デュメジル
Dumézil, Georges 380
デュメーズ
Dumais, Justin 380
Dumais, Troy 380
デュメニル
Duménil, Gérard 380
Dumenil, Lynn 380
デュメーヌ
Dumaine, Deborah 380
デュモヴィッツ
Dujmovits, Julia 379
デュモビッツ
Dujmovits, Julia 379
デユモビッツ
Dujmovits, Julia 379
デュモン
Dumont, Bruno 380
Dumont, François 380
Dumont, Guylaine 380
Dumont, Ivy 380

Dumont, Louis 380
デュモン・タック
Dumon Tak, Bibi 380
デュモン・ダヨ
Dumont d'Ayot, Catherine 380
デュモント
Dumont, Ivy 380
テュラノ
Turano, AnnaMaria 1427
デューラム
Durham, Leon 383
テュラール
Tulard, Jean 1426
デュラン
Dulin, Brice 379
Duran 383
Duran, Jacques 383
Durán, José Luis 383
Duran, Khalid 383
Duran, Meredith 383
Duran, Rosa Maria 383
Duran, Rudy 383
Durand, Delphine 383
Durand, Elodie 383
Durand, Jannic 383
Durand, Jean-Nicolas-Louis 383
Durand, Marc 383
Durand, Rodolphe 383
Durant, Sam 383
Durran, Jacqueline 384
デュランテ
Durante, Viviana 383
デュラーンド
Durand, Delphine 383
デュラント
Durant, Alan 383
Durant, David N. 383
Durant, Justin 383
Durant, Kevin 383
Durant, Stuart 383
Durrant, Joan E. 384
Durrant, S.E. 384
デュリー
Duly, Leila 379
デュリーゲル
Düriegl, Günter 383
デュリュアル
Durual, Christophe 384
デュリュック
Duluc, Vincent 379
デューリング
During, Elie 383
デュル
Duerr, Hans Peter 378
Dürr, Hans-Peter 384
Dürr, Walther 384
デュルカル
Durcal, Rocio 383
テュルク
Turk, Hikmet Sami 1427
テュルパン
Turpin, Dominique 1429
デュルビアーノ
Durbiano, Lucie 383
デュルーリー
Drury, Brandon 375
テュレ
Tullet, Hervé 1426
デュレ
Duret, Paul 383
テュレイ
Ciulei, Liviu 265
テューレック
Turek, Rosalyn 1427
デュレット
Delaet, Graham 335
Durrett, Richard 384
デュロヘリー
Dulohery, Shawn 379
デュ・ロンド
de Rond, Mark 344
デュワーティ
Duarte, Judy 376
デュワル
Dewael, Patrick 348
デューン
Dunn, Katherine 382
デュンガ・バイ
Durga Bai 383
デュンケル
Dunckel, Jean Benoit 381
Dunker, Elisabeth 381
デヨン
De Jong, Chase 335
デ・ヨング
De Jong, Frenkie 335
De Jong, Luuk 335
De Jong, Siem 335
デヨング
De Jong, Antoinette 335
De Jong, Bob 335
De Jong, Tonny 335
De Jonge, Mark 335
デヨンゲ
De Jonge, Mark 335
テーラー
Taylor, Angelo 1385
Taylor, Ann 1385
Taylor, Barbara 1385
Taylor, Billy 1385
Taylor, Brenda 1385
Taylor, Cecil 1385
Taylor, Charles 1385
Taylor, Charlotte 1385
Taylor, Christian 1385
Taylor, David E. 1385
Taylor, Elizabeth 1385
Taylor, Emmet 1385
Taylor, Gilbert 1385
Taylor, James B. 1385
Taylor, John 1386
Taylor, John B. 1386
Taylor, John Bernard 1386
Taylor, Jonathan 1386
Taylor, Katie 1386
Taylor, Ken 1386
Taylor, Koko 1386
Taylor, Leon 1386
Taylor, Marilyn 1386
Taylor, Paul Belville 1386
Taylor, Peter 1386
Taylor, Rachael 1386
Taylor, Richard Edward 1387
Taylor, Robert 1387
Taylor, Rod 1387
Taylor, Ron 1387
Taylor, Sean 1387
Taylor, Talus 1387
Taylor, W.L. 1387
テラ
Di Tella, Guido 358
Terra, Osmar Gasparini 1392
テラー
Teller, Astro 1389
Teller, Edward 1389
Teller, Janne 1389
デラー
Deller, Jeremy 338
Deller, Nicole 338
デ・ラ・イグレシア
De la Iglesia, Álex 336
デ・ライター
De Ruiter, John 344
テライユ
Terrail, Claude 1392
デライロマロマ
Delailomaloma, Nelson 336
デライン
Delaine, Alison 336
デラヴィ
Deravy, Echan 344
Gabriel, J.C. 470
デラヴェドバ
Dellavedova, Matthew 338
デラウライヤー
DeLauriers, Austin M. 337
デ・ラウレンティース
De Laurentiis, Dino 337
デ・ラウレンティス
De Laurentiis, Dino 337
De Laurentiis, Martha 337
デラエスプリエジャ
Noguera de la Espriella, Elsa 1030
テラオカ
Teraoka, Carlos B. 1391
デラ・カーサ
Della Casa, Lisa 338
デラ・カーザ
Della Casa, Lisa 338
デラカジェ
De La Calle, Humberto 335
デラカシャニ
Derakhshani, Dariush 344
デラグアルディア
De La Guardia, Dulcidio 336
デ・ラ・クルーズ
De la Cruz, Melissa 335
デラクロワ
Delacroix, Claire 335
デラコート
Delacorte, Shawna 335
テラサキ
Terasaki, Paul 1391
テラサキ・ミラ
Terasaki Miller, Mariko 1391
テラジマ
Terajima, Shinobu 1391
デラシュー
Delassus, Jean-Marie 336
テラス
Terras, Anthony 1392
Terras, Christian 1392
Terrasse, Antoine 1392
デ・ラス・クエバス
De Las Cuevas, Miguel 336
デラスサラス
De Las Salas, Habib 336
デラセガ
Dellasega, Cheryl 338
デラセルナ・エルナイス
De La Serna Hernáiz, Íñigo 336
テラダ
Terada, Alicia 1391
テラッツィーニ
Terrazzini, Daniela Jaglenka 1392
テラッツィーノ
Terrazzino, Marco 1392
テラップ
Terap, Hassan 1391
デラト・イ・フィガレド
De Rato y Figaredo, Rodrigo 344
デ・ラ・トゥーア
De la Tour, Frances 336
デ・ラ・トーレ
De La Torre, Robert 336
デラトレ
De La Torre, Teófilo 336
デラトレ・ヒメノ
De La Torre Gimeno, Sergio 336
デラニー
Delaney, Ashley 336
Delaney, Gayle M.V. 336
Delaney, John 336
Delaney, Kalen 336
Delaney, Luke 336
テラニシ
Teranishi, Dennis Yoshito 1391
デラヌエス・ラミレス
De La Nuez Ramírez, Raúl 336
デラノ
Delano, James Whitlow 336
デラバー
Delabar, Steve 335
デ・ラ・ハープ
De La Harpe, Darryl 336
デ・ラ・パーラ
de la Parra, Alondra 336
テラビ
Telavi, Willy 1389
デ・ラ・フエンテ
De La Fuente, Jeronimo 335
デラフエンテ
De La Fuente, Juan 335
デラフォッス
Delafosse, Claude 335
デ・ラ・ヘイ
De La Haye, Amy 336
デラベガ
De La Vega, María Teresa Fernández 337
デラ・ベドイエール
De la Bédoyère, Camilla 335
デ・ラ・ペーニャ
De La Peña, Matt 336
デラペニャ
De La Peña, Fortunato 336
デラ・ペルゴラ
Della Pergola, Massimo 338
デ・ラ・ホズ
De La Hoz, Cindy 336
デラポータス
Dellaportas, Steven 338
デ・ラ・ホーヤ
DeLaHoya, Oscar 336
デラ・ホーヤ
DeLaHoya, Oscar 336

テ

デラホーヤ
DeLaHoya, Oscar 336
デラマター
DeLaMater, Douglas Charles 336
デラ・マッジョーラ
Della Maggiora, Paul L. 338
デ・ラ・マドリ
De la Madrid Hurtado, Miguel 336
デ・ラ・マドリ・ウルタード
De la Madrid Hurtado, Miguel 336
デラマドリ・ウルタド
De la Madrid Hurtado, Miguel 336
デラマドリ・コルデロ
De La Madrid Cordero, Engique 336
デラマドリード・ウルタド
De la Madrid Hurtado, Miguel 336
デ・ラ・モッツ
de la Motte, Anders 336
デ・ララベッティ
De Larrabeiti, Michael 336
デラルア
De La Rúa, Fernando 336
De La Rúa, Jorge 336
デ・ラ・レンタ
de la Renta, Oscar 336
デ・ラ・ロサ
de la Rosa, Pedro 336
デラロサ
De La Rosa, Jorge 336
de la Rosa, Pedro 336
De La Rosa, Rubby 336
Delarosa, Siquio 336
デ・ラ・ロッチャ
de la Rocha, Zack 336
テラーン
Teheran, Julio 1388
テラン
Teran, Alejandra 1391
Teran, Boston 1391
Teran, Jose Manuel 1391
Terán, Pablo 1391
デランク
Delank, Claudia 336
デ・ランジュ
De Lange, Nicholas Robert Michael 336
テランス
Terence, Isabelle 1391
デランダ
De Landa, Manuel 336
デランティ
Delanty, Gerard 336
テリー
Terry, Beverly 1392
Terry, Clark 1392
Terry, Douglas A. 1392
Terry, Jason 1392
Terry, John 1392
Terry, Kimberly Kaye 1392
Terry, Michelle 1392
デーリ
Daehli, Mats Moller 312
デーリー
Daley, Kevin 314
Daley, Tom 314
Daley, William M. 314
Daly, Herman E. 315
Daly, John 315
Daly, Kate 315
デリ
Deri, Aryeh 344
デリー
Derry, Gregory Neil 344
Doerry, Martin 362
Dörrie, Doris 368
デリア
D'Elia, Toshiko 337
テリアオ
Teriao, Abdelkerim Souleymane 1391
テリアノ
Telliano, Jean Marc 1389
デリヴェラ
D'Rivera, Paquito 374
テリエ
Theillier, Patrick 1395
デリエ
Dörrie, Doris 368
テーリエセン
Terjesen, Siri 1391
テリエンテス
Terrientes, Javier 1392
テリオ
Terrio, Chris 1392
デーリー・カラベラ
Daley-Caravella, Laura 314
デリクソン
Derrickson, Bryan 344
Derrickson, Scott 344
デリグラゾワ
Deriglazova, Inna 344
デリ・コリ
Delli Colli, Tonino 338
デリコリ
Delli Colli, Tonino 338
デリーサ
DeLisa, Michael C. 337
デリシ
DeLisi, Lynn E. 337
DeRisi, William J. 344
テリーズ
Telis, Tomas 1389
テリス
Tellis, Gerard J. 1389
Terris, Susan 1392
デリス
Deris, Andi 344
デリソーラ
Dell'Isola, Alphonse J. 338
デリダ
Derrida, Jacques 344
デリック
Derrick, Colin 344
Derrick, Robin 344
デ・リッダー
de Ridder, Michael 344
デ・リデル
De Ridder, Dirk 344
テリト
Telito, Filoimea 1389
テリド
Terrid, Peter 1392
テリニ
Tellini, Gian 1389
デリパスカ
Deripaska, Oleg 344
デリーベス
Delibes, Miguel 337
デリベス
Delibes, Miguel 337
デ・リマ
de Lima, Lilia Bagaporo 337
デリマ
De Lima, Frank 337
De Lima, Leila 337
De Lima, Vanderlei 337
テリム
Terim, Fatih 1391
デリャエフ
Deryayev, Annaguly 345
デリュ
DeRue, D.Scott 344
デリューギン
Deriugin, V.A. 344
テリョーシキナ
Tereshkina, Viktoria 1391
テリル
Terrill, Marshall 1392
デリーロ
DeLillo, Don 337
テリン
Terrin, Peter 1392
デリンク
Delling, Gerhard 338
デリング
Dolling, Beate 364
デリンジャー
Dellinger, Susan 338
デリンスキー
Delinsky, Barbara 337
テリントン・ジョーンズ
Tellington-Jones, Linda 1389
デール
Dale, Anna 314
Dale, Jim 314
Dale, Kenneth J. 314
Dale, M.Maureen 314
Dale, Paulette 314
Dayre, Valérie 329
Deal, Terrence E. 329
デル
Dell, Christopher 338
Dell, Diana L. 338
Dell, Michael S. 338
Dell, Susan 338
デルー
Deru, Myriam 344
デルアギラ
Del Águila, Cynthia Carolina 336
デルイーズ
DeLuise, Dom 339
デルイゼムリャ
Deryzemlya, Andriy 345
デルイベル
De Ruyver, Dirk 344
デルヴァル
Delval, Marie-Hélène 339
デルヴィス
Delves, Peter J. 339
デルヴェッキオ
Del Vecchio, Leonardo 339
デルヴェール
Delvert, Jean 339
デル・ヴェント
Del Vento, Elena 339
デルヴォ
DeRuvo, Silvia L. 344
デルヴス
Delves, Peter J. 339
デ・ルカ
De Luca, Daniela 339
デルーカ
DeLuca, Fred 339
デルカ
De Luca, Riccardo 339
DeLuca, Steve Adrien 339
デルカスティージョ
Del Castillo, Jorge 337
デルカスティジョ
Del Castillo, Jorge 337
Del Castillo, José 337
デルカスティジョ・ガルベス
Del Castillo Gálvez, Jorge Alfonso 337
デル・カスティーリョ
Del Castillo, Jorge 337
デルカスティリョ・ベラ
Del Castillo Vera, Pilar 337
デルガディジョ
Delgadillo Terceros, Wálter 337
デルガディジョ・テルセロス
Delgadillo Terceros, Wálter 337
テルガト
Tergat, Paul 1391
デルガード
Delgado, Ricardo 337
デルガド
Delgado, Antonio Jorge 337
Delgado, Daniel 337
Delgado, Isabel 337
Delgado, Maria Filomena De Fátima Lobão Telo 337
Delgado, Maria.Filomena de Lobão Telo 337
Delgado, Matias 337
Delgado, Norberto 337
Delgado, Randall 337
デルカンブル
Delcambre, Anne-Marie 337
テルクリュク
Telukluk, Paul 1390
テルクルック
Telukluk, Paul 1390
デルケン
Dölken, Mechthild 364
テルジ
Terzi, Lorella 1392
テルジエフ
Terziev, Kiril 1392
テルジス
Terzis, Athanasios 1392
テルジッチ
Terzić, Adnan 1392
テルジディス
Terzidis, Kostas 1392
デルシド・ボニジャ
Del Cid Bonilla, Maria Antonieta 337
デルジャービン
Derzhavin, Gavriil Romanovich 345
デル・ジュディチェ
Del Giudice, Daniele 337
テルズ

Telles, Edward Eric 1389
デ・ルース
De Roos, Dolf 344
デルース
DeLuce, Daniel 339
テルセイロ
Terceiro, Jorge 1391
デルソー
Delsaux, Cédric 339
デルソラル
Del Solar, Matias 339
デルソラル・ラバルテ
Del Solar Labarthe, Salvador Alejandro Jorge 339
デルソン
Delson, Brad 339
テルチン
Telchin, Stan 1389
テルツァー
Toelzer, Andreas 1408
Tolzer, Andreas 1410
テルツァーニ
Terzani, Tiziano 1392
テルツィ
Terzi di Sant'Agata, Giulio 1392
デルッカ
De Lucca, Joao 339
デルデヴェ
Derdevet, Michel 344
デルトゥゾー
Dertouzos, Michael L. 344
デルドゥリ
Derdouri, Zohra 344
デルトゥルコ
Del Turco, Ottaviano 339
テルトレ
Tertrais, Bruno 1392
デル・トロ
Del Toro, Benicio 339
Del Toro, Guillermo 339
デルトロ
Del Toro 339
Del Toro, Guillermo 339
デルトン
Delton, Judy 339
デル・ネーリ
Del Neri, Luigi 338
デルネリ
Del Neri, Luigi 338
デルノボイ
Dernovoy, Anatoly 344
デルバイエ
Delvalle, Eric 339
デルバス
Derbas, Rashid 344
デルバル
Derbal, Abdelwahab 344
デルバンコ
Delbanco, Thomas L. 337
デルピー
Delpy, Julie 339
デルピアノ
Delpiano, Adriana 338
デル・ピエロ
Del Piero, Alessandro 338
デルピエーロ
Del Piero, Alessandro 338
デルピエロ
Del Piero, Alessandro 338
デルビシ
Dervishi, Besnik 345
テルビシダグワ
Terbishdagva, Dendev 1391
デルビシャイ
Dervishaj, Sokol 345
デルビシュ
Derviş, Kemal 345
デルピノ
Del Pino, Eulogio 338
デルピール
Delpire, Robert 338
デルフ
Delf, Brian 337
Delph, Fabian 338
デルプ
Delp, Brad 338
テルファー
Telfer, David J. 1389
Telfer, Randall 1389
デルフィニ
Delfini, Pablo 337
デルフォー
Delfour, Lucien 337
テルフォード
Telford, William R. 1389
デルフス
Delfs, Hans 337
テルプストラ
Terpstra, Mike 1392
デルフライン
Doerflein, Thomas 362
デル・ブラーヴォ
Del Bravo, Carlo 337
デルブリュック
Delbruck, Emmy 337
Delbrück, Matthias 337
テルベシュ
Terbèche, Mohamed 1391
デルペシュ
Delpech, Noe 338
Delpech, Thérèse 338
デルベス
Derbez, Luis Ernesto 344
デル・ベッキオ
Del Vecchio, Claudio 339
デルベッキオ
Del Vecchio, Janina 339
デルベニエフ
Derbenev, Vitaly 344
デル・ボスケ
Del Bosque, Vicente 337
デルボスケ
Del Bosque, Vicente 337
デルボスコ
Delbosco, Christopher 337
デルボーステレス
Delvaux-stehres, Mady 339
デル・ポトロ
Del Potro, Juan Martin 338
デルポトロ
Calderon Del Valle, Juan 215
Del Potro, Juan Martin 338
デルボニス
Delbonis, Federico 337
デルポポロ
Delpopolo, Nicholas 338
テルホルスト
Terhorst, Guusje 1391
デルポンテ
Delponte, Carla 338
デルマー
Del Mar, Chris 338
デルマ＝マルティ
Delmas-Marty, Mireille 338
デルマン
Dermane, Bamba Ould 344
テルモルス
Ter Mors, Jorien 1392
デルモンテ
Delmonte, Patti 338
デルリー
Delury, John 339
デルリオ
Delrio, Graziano 339
Del Rio, Jack 339
デルリコ
D'Errico, Camilla 344
デル・リット
Del Litto, Victor 338
デル・ルナール
Deru-Renard, Béatrice 344
デルレアル
Del Real, diego 339
デル・レイ
Del Rey, Lana 339
デ・ルー・レンヒフォ
De Roux Rengifo, Francisco Jose 344
テルローヴァ
Terloeva, Milana 1392
デルロサリオ
Delrosario, Albert 339
Del Rosario, María 339
テルンクヴィスト
Törnqvist, Marit 1413
デルングス
Derungs, Isabel 344
テレ
Théret, Bruno 1395
Tölle, Rainer 1409
デレ
Delle, Moana 338
デレアー
Delaire, Ryan 336
デ・レイナ
De Reyna, Rudy 344
デ・レーウ
De Leeuw, Jan 337
テレウォダ
Telewoda, Youngor Sevelee 1389
テレオー
Thereau, Cyril 1395
デレオ
De Leo, Maryann 337
デ・レオン
De León, Joanne 337
デレオン
De León, Eneida 337
De León, Joanne 337
De Leon, Jose 337
De León, Juan Alfonso 337
De Leon Carpio, Ramiro 337
デレオン・カルピオ
De Leon Carpio, Ramiro 337
デレカース
Delle Karth, Nico 338
デレグ
Deleg, Tumurbaatar 337
テレグアリオ
Teleguario, Aurora Leticia 1389
テレシ
Teresi, Dick 1391
テレシチュク
Tereshchuk, Tetyana 1391
Tereshchuk, Viktoriya Anatoliivna 1391
デレシュ
Deresz, Weronika 344
テレシュク
Tereshchuk, Viktoriya Anatoliivna 1391
テレス
Tellez, Rowdy 1389
デレズウィッツ
Deresiewicz, William 344
テレスチェンコ
Terestchenko, Ivan 1391
テレタ
Téréta, Bocary 1391
テレップ
Telep, Peter 1389
テレトビッチ
Teletovic, Mirza 1389
テレビシダグバ
Terbishdagva, Dendeviin 1391
テレヒン
Terekhin, Sergei 1391
デレフィンコ
Derefinko, Karen J. 344
テレヘン
Tellegen, Toon 1389
テーレホフ
Terekhov, Dmitry 1391
テレホフ
Terekhov, Alexandr A. 1391
テレム
Tellem, Nancy 1389
テレル
Terrell, Heather 1392
Terrell, Steven 1392
テレン
Tellen, Thoma Anna 1389
Terraine, John 1392
テレンバッハ
Tellenbach, Hubertus 1389
デロ
Dello, Jean 338
Delo, Jean 338
デロア - ベタンクール
Delloye-Betancourt, Lorenzo 338
Delloye-Betancourt, Mélanie 338
テロウ
Terro, Alaaeddine 1392
デローザン
Derozan, Demar 344
デロシェール
Derocher, Andrew E. 344
デローシュ＝ノブルクール
Desroches-Noblecourt, Christiane 346
デ・ロス・サントス
De Los Santos, Marisa 338
デロスレイエス
De Los Reyes, Virgilio 338

テ

デローチ
Deloach, Janay 338
デ・ロッシ
De Rossi, Daniele 344
デロッシュ
Déroche, François 344
テロッテ
Telotte, Jay P. 1390
テロデルガド
Telo Delgado, Maria Filomena de Lobão 1389
デロネ
Delaunay, Eric 337
デロペス・コントレラス
De Lopez Contreras, Armida Villela 338
デロベル
Delobel, Isabelle 338
デロリア
Deloria, Vine, Jr. 338
デロリアン
Delorean, John Z. 338
デロール
De Loor, Barbara 338
デロレンツィ
De Lorenzi, Christian 338
デロワ
Déloye, Yves 338
テロン
Theron, Charlize 1395
デ・ローン
De Roon, Marten 344
デロンギ
De'Longhi, Giuseppe 338
デロング
DeLong, G.Robert 338
Delong, Lisa 338
デワ
Dewa, Eri 348
デ・ワイス
De Wijs, Jordy 349
デーワーナンダ
Devananda, Douglas 347
テワリー
Tewarie, Bhoendradatt 1393
デワール
Dewael, Patrick 348
デ・ワールト
De Waart, Edo 348
テン
Ten, Denis 1390
Tenn, William 1390
デーン
Dean, Zoe Z. 330
Dern, Bruce 344
デン
Deng, Beda Machar 341
Deng, Galwak 341
Deng, Lin-lin 341
Deng, Li-qun 341
Deng, Lual 341
Deng, Luol 341
Deng, Nan 341
Deng, Pu-fang 341
Deng, Ya-ping 341
Deng, You-mei 341
デン・アジャク
Deng Ajak, Oyai 341
デン・アトルベイ
Deng Athorbei, David 342
デンアロール
Deng Alor, Kuol 341
デン・アロル・クオル
Deng Alor, Kuol 341
デン・アロル・コル
Deng Alor, Kuol 341
デンカー
Denker, Bradley M. 342
Denker, Henry 342
テン・カテ
Ten Cate, Arnold Richard 1390
テンカネン
Tenkanen, Tuula 1390
テンク・アドナン
Tengku Adnan, Tengku Mansor 1390
テンク・シャムスル・バリン
Shamsul Bahrin 1280
デンクタシュ
Denktas, Rauf 342
デンコ
Danko, Taras 318
デンコワ
Denkova, Albena 342
デーンジェロ
D'Angelo, Edward 316
デンジャーフィールド
Dangerfield, Jared 316
Dangerfield, Jordan 316
Dangerfield, Rodney 316
デンシャム
Densham, Erin 343
テンジュア
Tenjua, Edite Ramos Da Costa 1390
テンジン
Tenzing, Judy 1391
Tenzing, Tashi 1391
デンジン
Denzin, Norman K. 343
テンジン・デレク・リンポチェ
Tenzin Delek Rinpoche 1391
テンジン・デレック・リンポチェ
Tenzin Delek Rinpoche 1391
デーンズ
Danes, Claire 316
デンスウィル
Denswil, Stefano 343
デンスリー
Densley, Moriah 343
デンスロウ
Denselow, Robin 343
テンタ
Tenta, John 1391
テンダー
Tender, Priit 1390
デンチ
Dench, Judi 341
デンチフィールド
Denchfield, Nick 341
テンティ
Temte, Myrna 1390
デンディ
Dendy, Leslie A. 341
デンディアス
Dendias, Nikolaos 341
デンデッカー
Den Dekker, Matt 341
デンデビーン・プレブドルジ
Dendeviin PÜrevdorj 341
テンテリア
Renteria, Jackeline 1172
テンデン
Tendeng, Georges 1390
デンデンホッチ
Deng Deng Hoc, Yai 342
デント
Dent, Akeem 343
Dent, Fiona Elsa 343
Dent, Harry S., Jr. 343
Dent, Kyle D. 343
Dent, Taylor 343
テントア
Tentoa, Tewareka 1391
デントセレドン
Dent-zeledon, Alberto 343
デントン
Denton, Gregory A. 343
Denton, Jamie 343
Denton, Kady MacDonald 343
Denton, Terry 343
テンナクーン
Tennakoon, Janaka Bandara 1390
デン・ニアル
Deng Nhial, Nhial 342
テンネーペル
TenNapel, Douglas 1391
デンネマン
Denneman, Frank 342
デンバ
Demba, Ba Ibrahima 340
デンバー
Denver, Bob 343
テンバーケン
Tenberken, Sabriye 1390
デンハム
Denham, Anthony 342
Denham, Margery 342
テンパリー
Temperley, Alan 1390
デンビー
Demby, Albert Joe 340
Denby, Joolz 341
デンプ
Dempf, Peter 341
デンプシー
Dempsey, Clint 341
Dempsey, John V. 341
Dempsey, Martin E. 341
Dempsey, Nick 341
Dempsey, Noel 341
デンプス
Demps, Dell 341
Demps, Quintin 341
デンプスター
Dempster, Al 341
デンプフ
Dempf, Peter 341
テンプラー
Templar, Richard 1390
テンブランセル
Tenbrunsel, Ann E. 1390
テンプリン
Templin, Stephen 1390
テンプル
Temple, Christine M. 1390
Temple, Garrett 1390
Temple, Julien 1390
Temple, Peter 1390
Temple, Robert K.G. 1390
Temple, Wick 1390
テンプルスミス
Templesmith, Ben 1390
テンプルトン
Templeton, John Marks 1390
Templeton, Julia 1390
Templeton, Karen 1390
Templeton, Lauren C. 1390
Templeton, Suzie 1390
Templeton, Timothy L. 1390
テンプルマン
Templeman, Julian 1390
テン・ヘイブ
Ten Have, Andrew G. 1390
テンヘイブ
Ten Have, Andrew G. 1390
テンペスト
Temperley, Alan 1390
デンベック
Dembeck, Mary Grace 340
デンベレ
Dembelé, Manga 340
Dembele, Mousa 340
Dembele, Ousmane 340
テン・ベンセル
Ten Bensel, Robert W. 1390
テンボ
Tembo, Christon 1390
デンボ
Dembo, Tidjani Harouna 340
デンボー
Denbow, James Raymond 341
デン・ホック
Deng Hoc, Deng 342
デンホフ
Dönhoff, Marion 365
テンポラン
Temporão, José Gomes 1390
テンポリン
Temporin, Elena 1390
デンボロー
Denborough, Michael A. 341
デンボロウ
Denborough, David 341
デンマーク
Denmark, Leila 342
デンメ
Demme, Diego 340
デンレル
Denrell, Jerker 343

【ト】

トー
To, Johnnie 1407
To, Raymond 1407
Toh, Chin Chye 1408
トーア
Toua, Dika 1414
ドーア
Doerr, Anthony 362
Doerr, John 362
Dore, Ronard Philip 367

Dorr, Michael K. 368
ドア
Dorr, Robert F. 368
トアス
Toatu, Teuea 1407
ドーアティー
Daugherty, Leo J., Ⅲ 322
Doughty, Brandon 370
ドアティ
Daugherty, Michael 322
Doherty, William Joseph 363
Dougherty, James 370
トアネス
Tørnaes, Ulla 1413
トアファ
Toafa, Maatia 1407
トアン
Tran, le Quoc Toan 1417
ド・アントニオ
D'Antonio, Michael 318
トーイ
Toye, J.F.J. 1416
Toye, Nigel 1416
トイア
Toia, Patrizia 1408
ドイエ
Douillet, David 370
ドイグ
Doig, Ivan 363
ドイザー
Deusser, Daniel 347
ドイジ
Doidge, Geoffrey 363
Doidge, Norman 363
トイズ
Touyz, Stephen W. 1415
ドイセノワ
Duissenova, Tamara 379
ドイセンベルク
Duisenberg, Wim 379
トイチ
Teutsch, Betsy Platkin 1393
ドイチェ
Deutsch, Stacia 347
トイチェエフ
Toychiyev, Hojamuhammet 1416
トイチュ
Teutsch, Betsy 1393
ドイチュ
Deutsch, Erwin 347
ドイチュクローン
Deutschkron, Inge 347
ドイッチ
Deutsch, Morton 347
Doetsch, Richard 362
ドイッチェ
Deutsch, Stacia 347
ドイッチマン
Deutschmann, David 347
ドイッチャー
Deutscher, Guy 347
Deutscher, Penelope 347
ドイッチュ
Deutsch, Danica 347
Deutsch, David 347
Deutsch, Karl Wolfgang 347
トイテンベルク
Teutenberg, Ina-Yoko 1393
トイト
Teut, Michael 1393
ドイニン
Dhoinine, Ikililou 349
トイバッカ
Toivakka, Lenita 1409
トイバヤトイバ
Toiva Ya Toiva, Andimba 1409
トイブナー
Teubner, Gunther 1393
ドイブラーグメリン
Däubler-gmelin, Herta 321
トイボネン
Toivonen, Sami 1409
Toivonen, Tuukka Hannu Ilmari 1409
トイボヤトイボ
Toivo Ya Toivo, Andimba 1409
ドイムリンク
Deumling, Christoph 347
ドイヨル
Doyal, Len 372
ドイル
Doyle, Bob 372
Doyle, Brian 372
Doyle, Christopher 372
Doyle, Craig 372
Doyle, Debra 372
Doyle, Donal 372
Doyle, Eilidh 372
Doyle, Hilary Louis 372
Doyle, Jack 372
Doyle, John 372
Doyle, Laura 372
Doyle, Malachy 372
Doyle, Marilyn 372
Doyle, Michael 372
Doyle, Ming 372
Doyle, Paddy 372
Doyle, Peter 372
Doyle, Roddy 372
Doyle, Sandra 372
Doyle, Tom 372
Doyle, Ursula 372
Doyle, Virginia 372
Doyle, William 372
トイルイエフ
Toylyev, Sapardurdy 1416
トイロロ
Toilolo, Levine 1409
ドイロン
Doiron, Paul 363
トイン
Toyne, Brian 1416
Toyne, Simon 1416
トインビー
Toynbee, Jason 1416
Toynbee, Philip 1416
Toynbee, Polly 1416
トゥ
Thu, Le Thi 1402
To, Marcus 1407
Tou, Alain Ludovic 1414
Tou, Amar 1414
Tu, Anthony T. 1425
トゥー
To, Nelson 1407
Too, Lillian 1412
Tou, Amar 1414
Tu, Anthony T. 1425
Tu, You-you 1425
トウ
To, Chung 1407
Toe, Christopher 1408
ドゥー
Du, Qing-lin 376
Du, Run-sheng 376
ドウ
Doe, Jackson 362
Doe, Juan 362
Dohou, Frédèric 363
トゥーア
Thur, Daniel 1402
トウア
Toua, Dika 1414
ドーヴァー
Dover, Gabriel A. 371
Dover, Kenneth James 371
ドゥアー
Duah, Kwadwo 376
ドウア
Doerr, Harriet 362
トゥアキー
Tourky, Loudy 1415
ドヴァシュテール
Dewachter, Michel 348
ドゥアティ
Douati, Alphonse 369
トゥアデラ
Touadéra, Faustin-Archange 1414
ドゥアト
Duato, Nacho 376
ドーヴァーニュ
Dauvergne, Peter 322
トゥアパティ
Tuapati, Talemaitoga 1425
トゥアボイ
Touaboy, Bertrand 1414
ドゥアユア
Douayoua, Lia Bi 369
ドゥアラム
Doualamou, Germain 369
ドゥア・リー
Doua Lee 369
ド・ヴァール
de Waal, Frans B.M. 348
トーヴァルズ
Torvalds, Linus Benedict 1414
ドゥアルテ
Duarte, Cristina 376
Duarte, Emerson 376
Duarte, Isaias 376
Duarte, María de los Ángeles 376
Duarte, Vera 376
ドゥアルデ
Duhalde, Eduardo 379
トヴァルデツキ
Twardecki, Alojzy 1430
ドゥアルテ・ドゥラン
Duarte Durán, José Napoleón 376
ドゥアルテ・フルトス
Duarte Frutos, Nicanor 376
ド・ヴァロア
De Valois, Ninette 347
ドヴァロワ
De Valois, Ninette 347
トゥアン
Tuan, Tran Van 1425
Tuan, Truong Minh 1425
Tuan, Yi-fu 1425
ドゥーアン
Doohan, James 367
トゥアンゼベ
Tuanzebe, Axel 1425
ドゥアンチャイ
Douangchay, Phichit 369
Duoangchay, Phichit 382
ドゥアンドゥアン・ブンニャヴォン
Douangdeuane Bounyavong 369
ドゥアンヌ
Dehaene, Stanislas 334
トーヴィ
Tovey, Bramwell 1415
トゥーイ
Twohy, Robert 1430
トゥイ
Nguyen, Thi Thuy 1021
Thuy, Le Duc 1403
トゥイアフィトゥ
Tu'i'afitu 1426
トゥイオネトア
Tuionetoa, Pohiva 1426
トゥイギー
Twiggy 1430
トゥイクソー
Tuiksoo, Ester 1426
トゥイスト
Twist, Lynne 1430
ドゥイセノワ
Duissenova, Tamara 379
トゥイタ
Tuita, Siosaia Ma'Ulupekotofa 1426
ドヴィチ
Dovitch, Dana 371
トゥイッギー
Twiggy 1430
トゥイッグ
Twigg, Emma 1430
トゥイット
Tuitt, Stephon 1426
トゥイティ
Touiti, Ridha 1414
トウィーディー
Tweedie, David 1430
トゥイート
Tweet, Jonathan 1430
トゥィード
Tweed, Matt 1430
トゥイトゥンボウ
Tuitubou, Laisenia 1426
トゥイニアウ
Tuineau, Joe (Joseph) 1426
トゥイバカノ
Tu'ivakano 1426
トゥイマン
Twyman, Richard M. 1430
トゥイメバエフ
Tuymebayev, Zhanseit 1430
ドウィヨゴ
Dowiyogo, Bernard 371
Dowiyogo, Valdon 371
ドウイヨゴ
Dowiyogo, Bernard 371
トゥイラエパ・サイレレ・マリエレガオイ
Tuilaepa Sailele Malielegaoi 1426
トゥイランギ

ト

Tuilagi, Alesana 1426
Tuilagi, Vavae 1426
ドウイリ
Douiri, Adil 370
Douiri, Fouad 370
ド・ヴィリエ
De Villiers, Marq 348
ドヴィル
Deville, Nancy 348
Deville, Patrick 348
ド・ヴィルパン
De Villepin, Dominique 348
トゥイン
Twin, Colin 1430
トゥインズ・セブン・セブン
Twins Seven Seven 1430
ドゥヴァイヨン
Devoyon, Pascal 348
ドゥ・ヴァール
De Waal, Edmund 348
de Waal, Frans B.M. 348
ドゥヴァンク
Devynck, Thierry 348
ドゥヴィル
Deville, Patrick 348
トゥヴェ
Touvay, Monique 1415
ドゥヴェイニー
Devaney, Robert L. 347
トゥヴェーデ
Tvede, Lars 1430
ドゥヴェルネ
Duverney, Daniel 385
ドゥヴェーン
DeVane, C.Lindsay 347
ドゥヴォー
Devaux, Clément 347
ドゥウォーキン
Dworkin, Ronald Myles 385
ドゥヴォス
Devos, Emmanuelle 348
Devos, Jodie 348
トゥヴォルシュカ
Tworuschka, Udo 1430
ドゥウス
Duus, Peter 385
トウェイシ
Tweisi, Adel 1430
トウェイツ
Thwaites, Thomas 1403
ドウェイヒ
Dweihi, Haitham 385
ドウェイラ
al-Duwaila, Bader Fahad Ali 385
ドゥエック
Dweck, Carol S. 385
トウェドル
Tweddle, Elizabeth 1430
ドゥエニャス
Dueñas, Lola 378
Dueñas, María 378
Dueñas, Tomás 378
トゥエヤ
Tweya, Tjekero 1430
トヴェルト
Tvert, Mason 1430
トゥエルブトゥリーズ
Twelvetrees, Alan C. 1430
トゥエン
Tuyen, Truong Dinh 1430
トウェン・P.T.
Tuyen, Thi Phuong 1429
ドヴェンカー
Drvenkar, Zoran 375
トウェンギ
Twenge, Jean M. 1430
ドゥオーキン
Dworkin, Ronald Myles 385
Dworkin, Susan 385
ドウォーキン
Dworkin, Andrea 385
Dworkin, Ronald Myles 385
Dworkin, Susan 385
ド・ヴォージョリ
De Vosjoli, Philippe 348
ドゥオスキン
Dwoskin, Hale 385
ドゥオダ
Dhuoda 349
トゥオミオヤ
Tuomioja, Erkki 1427
トゥオメイ
Twomey, Nora 1430
ドヴォルコヴィッチ
Dvorkovich, Arkady Vladimirovich 385
ドヴォルザーク
Dvořák, Marta 385
ドゥオルスキー
Dworsky, Alan L. 385
ドヴォロヴェンコ
Dvorovenko, Irina 385
トゥオンブリ
Twombly, Cy 1430
トゥオンブリー
Twombly, Cy 1430
トゥーカー
Tooker, Marilyn 1412
ドゥカ
Duca, Gheorghe 377
Duka, Agron 379
ドゥガイル
al-Dugair, Jalal Yousef 378
ドゥカヴニー
Duchovny, David 377
トゥガデ
Tugade, Arthur 1425
トゥーガー＝デッカー
Touger-Decker, Riva 1414
ドゥカトバ
Dukatova, Jana 379
ドゥカブニー
Duchovny, David 377
トゥーカン
Toukan, Khalid 1414
Touqan, Khalid 1415
トゥカン
Touqan, Khalid 1415
トウカン
Toukan, Umayya 1414
ドゥーガン
Dougan, Andy 370
Dougan, Brady W. 370
Dougan, Terrell Harris 370
ドゥカンルチュマン
Dookunluchoomun, Leela Devi 367
ドゥギ
Deguy, Michel 334
ドゥギー
Deguy, Michel 334
ドゥギナ
Dugina, Olga 379
ドゥ・キャストゥル
de Castries, Henri 331
ドゥギン
Dugin, Andrej 379
ドウキンズ
Dawkins, Kristin 328
トゥーク
Tuke, Blair 1426
トゥク
Touq, Muhyddine 1415
ドゥク
Dâncu, Vasile 316
Janda Duku, James 662
トゥクタミシェワ
Tuktamisheva, Elizaveta 1426
ドゥグッド
Duguid, Paul 379
ドゥクパ
Dukpa, Mingbo 379
Dukpa, Zangley 379
ドゥクフレ
Decouflé Philippe 332
ドゥークラウス
Dūklavs, Jānis 379
ドゥクラウス
Dūklavs, Jānis 379
ドゥグラス
Douglas 370
ドゥグラス・コスタ
Douglas Costa 370
ドゥグラス・サントス
Douglas Santos 370
ドゥグラツィア
DeGrazia, David 334
ドゥークラン
Dookeran, Winston 367
ドゥクリィ
Dukuly, Morris 379
ドゥクール
Doucoure, Ladji 369
ドゥクルス
Dukurs, Martins 379
Dukurs, Tomass 379
トゥクレ
Tuculet, Joaquin 1425
ドゥクレ
Doucoure, Abdoulaye 369
Doucoure, Ladji 369
Doucoure, Mamadou 370
ドゥグレ
Degre, Alain 334
Degre, Tippi 334
ドゥ・クレシー
de Crécy, Hervé 332
ドゥケ
Duke, Edem 379
Duque, Gabriel 383
ドゥ・ゲイ
Du Gay, Paul 378
ドゥケ・エストラダ
Duque Estrada, Esteban 383
ドゥケット
Duquette, Donald N. 383
トゥーゲントハット
Tugendhat, Ernst 1425
ドゥケンヌ
Dequenne, Emilie 344
トゥーゲンハット
Tugendhat, Ernst 1425
ドゥコ
Duco, Natalia 377
ドゥコー
Decaux, Alain 331
Guillaume, Decaux 544
ドゥコーヴァン
Dekoven, Marianne 335
ドゥコトゥー
De Coteau, Clifton 332
トゥサ
Tusa, Tricia 1429
ドゥサ
Dhussa, Ramesh C. 349
ドゥサバ
Dusava, Gabriel John Klero 384
トゥザール
Tousart, Lucas 1415
ドゥ・サール
De Salle, Marie 345
ドゥサーレ
DeSalle, Robert 345
トゥーサン
Toussaint, Allen 1415
Toussaint, Eric 1415
Toussaint, Jean-Philippe 1415
Toussaint, John 1415
トゥサン
Toussaint, Jean-Paul 1415
トゥザン
Touzaint, Nicolas 1415
トゥーサン＝サマ
Toussaint-Samat, Maguelonne 1415
トゥサント
Toussaint, Fitzgerald 1415
ドゥジ
Dusi, Detlev 384
トゥシェク
Tušek, Alojz 1429
トゥーシェット
Touchette, Nancy 1414
ドゥシェバエフ
Dushebayev, Keneshbek 384
ドゥジェビエツキ
Drzewiecki, Mirosław 376
トゥシェブリャク
Tusevljak, Spasoe 1429
ドゥジェンコワ
Dudzenkova, Hanna 377
ドゥ・ジェンヌ
de Gennes, Pierre-Gilles 333
ドゥシコウワ
Dusíková, Maja 384
トゥシシビリ
Tushishvili, Otar 1429
ドゥシット
Douthitt, Robin 371
ドゥシミイマナ
Dushimiyimana, Abel 384
ドゥシャ
Duşa, Mircea 384
トゥジュ
Tuju, Raphael 1426
ドゥーシュ
Deutsch, Jean 347

ドゥ・ジュール
De Jour, Belle 335
ドゥジョブヌ・オルティス
Dujovne Ortiz, Alicia 379
ドゥジンスカヤ
Dudinskaya, Nataliya Mikhailovna 377
トゥーズ
Toews, Miriam 1408
トウズ
Toews, Barb 1408
ドウス
Duus, Peter 385
ドゥズィーナス
Douzinas, Costas 371
トゥースヴァルトナー
Thuswaldner, Werner 1403
ドゥ・スウザ
de Souza, Marcel Alain 346
トゥスク
Tusk, Donald 1429
トゥスプベコフ
Tusupbekov, Rashid 1429
ドゥスマトフ
Dusmatov, Hasanboy 384
ドゥスムロトフ
Dustmurotov, Sardorbek 384
トゥズメン
Tüzmen, Kürşad 1430
ドゥスユ
Dessus, Benjamin 346
ドゥ・スワーフ
De Swaef, Emma 346
ドゥーセ
Doucet, Dominique 369
ドゥセ
Dussey, Robert 384
ドウセット
Doucette, Paul 369
ドゥソーヴ
Desseauve, Thierry 346
ドゥゾン
Dzon, Mathias 386
ドゥダ
Duda 377
Duda, Andrzej 377
Duda, Ondrej 377
ドゥダシュ
Dudas, Miklos 377
トゥタッチコワ
Tutatchikova, Elena 1429
ドゥダメル
Dudamel, Gustavo 377
ドゥチェブヤニクシュ
Dusev-Janics, Natasa 384
ドゥチェフヤニツ
Douchev-janic, Natasa 369
ドゥチェミン
DuChemin, David 377
トゥチッチ
Tučić, Boris 1425
トゥッカーマン
Tuckermann, Anja 1425
トゥック
Took, Barry 1412
トゥッシュ
Tusch, Manuel 1429
トゥッチ
Tucci, Stanley 1425
ドゥッチ
Deutsch, Lorànt 347
トゥッチロ
Tuccillo, Dylan 1425
ドゥット
Dutt, Yogeshwar 384
ドゥットン
Dutton, Mary Ann 385
トゥッリーニ
Turrini, Leo 1429
ドゥデ
Doudet, Sophie 370
ドゥーディ
Doody, Margaret Anne 367
ドゥティ
Doty, James Robert 369
ドゥディ
Dudi, Nadia Arop 377
ドゥティエンヌ
Detienne, Marcel 347
ドゥデウ
Dudau, Nicolae 377
ドゥデッケール
Dedecker, Armand 332
ドゥテュランス
Dethurens, Pascal 347
トゥテリャン
Tutelyan, Victor A. 1429
ドゥテルテ
Duterte, Rodrigo 384
ドゥーデン
Duden, Barbara 377
トウド
Toldo, Guilherme 1409
ド・ウート
De Woot, Emma 349
トゥトゥ
Tootoo, Hunter 1412
ドゥドゥ
Dudou, Emile Boga 377
ドゥドゥ・ニジャエ・ローズ
Doudou Ndiaye Rose 370
トゥトゥム
Ntoutoume, Aurélien 1036
ドゥドゥ・ンジャイ・ローズ
Doudou Ndiaye Rose 370
ドゥートキナ
Dutkina, Galina 384
トゥドセ
Tudose, Mihai 1425
トゥトハラン
Tutkhalian, Seda 1429
ドゥトラ
Dutra, Olívio 384
トゥドラケ
Tudorache, Ioan-Dragos 1425
トゥドリン
Tudorin, Nikolaus 1425
ドゥートレ・ルーセル
Doutre-Roussel, Chloé 371
トゥドワ
Todua, Alexander 1408
トウナイ
Tonai, Minoru 1411
ドゥナイツェフ
Dunaytsev, Vitaly 380
ドゥナエフ
Dunayev, Arman 380
ドゥーナン
Doonan, Jane 367
Doonan, Simon 367
ドゥニ
Denis, Jean-Claude 342
Denis, Paul 342
ドウニー
Doney, Meryl 365
ドゥニア
Dounia, Sanjima 371
ドゥニチ - ニヴィンスカ
Dunicz-Niwińska, Helena 381
トゥニッソン
Tõnisson, Liina 1412
ドゥニミカ
Duminica, Valeriu 380
ドゥヌ
Deneux, Xavier 341
ドゥネス
Dnes, Antony W. 360
ドゥノー
Dhunnoo, Mayuri 349
ドゥノール
Denord, François 342
トゥバイララ
Tuivailala, Sam 1426
ドゥハチェク
Duhachek, Adam 379
ドゥハッス
Dehasse, Joel 334
ドゥバティ
Debaty, Vincent 330
ドゥハート
De Hart, Jane Sherron 334
ドゥパルドン
Depardon, Raymond 343
トゥーパン
Toupane, Axel 1415
ドゥーハン
Doohan, James 367
ドゥバン
Doubane, Charles Armel 369
Duban, Nixon 376
ドゥバンヌ
Doubane, Charles Armel 369
トゥーヒー
Toohey, Peter 1412
Twohy, David 1430
トゥービー
al-Toobi, Mohammed bin Salim bin Said 1412
トゥビアーナ
Tubiana, Raoul 1425
トゥビアナ
Toubiana, Serge 1414
トゥーヒグ
Twohig, Karl R. 1430
Twohig, Michael 1430
トゥビシャト
Tubishat, Ahmad 1425
ドゥビツカヤ
Dubitskaya, Aliona 376
ドゥビーニン
Dubinin, Yurii Vladimirovich 376
ドゥビニン
Dubinin, Yurii Vladimirovich 376
ドゥビュシー
Debuchy, Mathieu 331
ドゥ・ピュルフォール
De Pulford, Nicola 343
トゥヒライシヴィリ
Tkhilaishvili, Giorgi 1407
ドゥ・ビリー
De Billy, Bertrand 331
トゥービン
Toobin, Jeffrey 1412
トゥープ
Toop, David 1412
ドゥーブ
Doob, Joseph Leo 367
ドゥブ
Dub, Tomas 376
トゥフィク
Toufiq, Ahmed 1414
トゥフェザー
Two Feather, William 1430
ドゥ・フェル
De Fer, Thomas M. 333
トゥフェンク
Tufenk, Seref 1425
ドゥフォー
Dufuor, Kwabena 378
ドゥ・ブーケラー
De Beukelaer, Edward 330
ドゥブシッツ
Debschitz, Uta von 331
トゥープス
Toops, Diane 1412
Toups, Wayne 1415
ドゥブーズ
Debbouze, Jamel 330
トゥフテ
Tufte, Olaf 1425
トゥプテン・ジンパ
Geshe Thupten Jinpa 492
ドゥプラ
Duprat, Pierre 382
Duprat, Rogério 382
ドゥブランク
DeBlank, Ricco 331
ドゥ・フランス
De France, Cecile 333
ドゥ・フリース
De Vries, Brian 348
ドゥブリュ
Debru, Claude 331
トゥブルジーク
Tvrdík, Jaroslav 1430
ドゥフルニ
Defourny, Jacques 333
ドゥブレ
Debray, Régis 331
ドゥブレイ
Du Boulay, Shirley 376
ドゥブロ
Dubro, Peggy Phoenix 377
ドゥフロウ
Dhuhulow, Mustafa Sheikh Ali 349
ドゥプロスト
Deprost, Michel 343
ドゥーヘ
D'Hooge, R. 349
ドゥベ
Dube, Tshinga 376
トゥーヘイ
Tuhey, John 1426
ドゥベーキ
DeBakey, Michael Ellis 330
ドゥベッケール
Debecker, Benoit 330

トゥヘル
Tuchel, Thomas 1425
トゥポー
Tupou, Taani 1427
ドゥボイ
Duboy, Carlos 377
トゥポウ
Topou, Una 1412
Tupou, Tania Laumanulupe 'o Talafolika 1427
ドゥボヴィッツ
Dubowitz, Howard 377
ドゥボウスキ
Dubowski, Cathy East 377
トゥポウトア・ウルカララ
Tupouto'a Ulukalala 1427
ドゥ・ポゥム
De Paume, Jeu 343
ドウボバヤ
Dubovaya, N.F. 377
トゥボール
Teboul, James 1388
ドゥボルコビッチ
Dvorkovich, Arkady Vladimirovich 385
ドゥポワトル
Depoitre, Laurent 343
トゥーマー
Toomer, Korey 1412
トゥマ
Tuma, Kamal Eddin 1426
ドゥ・マイオ
De Maio, Sebastian 339
ドゥマス・ロドリゲス
Dumas Rodrígues, Edgardo 380
ドゥマニャン
Dumanyan, Derenik 380
ドゥマラ
Dumala, Piotr 380
トゥマラクディ
Thummarukudy, Muralee 1402
トゥマルキン
Toumarkin, Yakov 1414
トゥーミー
Toomey, David M. 1412
トゥミ
Toumi, Khalida 1414
ドゥミトル
Dumitru, Alina 380
ドゥミトレスク
Dumitrescu, Rares 380
ドゥムイ
Demouy, Patrick 341
トゥムウェシジェ
Tumwesigye, Elioda 1426
トゥムクンデ
Tumukunde, Henry 1426
ドゥムゴル
Doumgor, Hourmadji Moussa 371
ドゥムースティエ
Demoustier, Anäis 341
ドゥムチュス
Dumcius, Vytautas 380
トゥムバゼ
Tumwebaze, Frank 1426
トゥムルバートル
Tumurbaatar, Deleg 1426
トゥムルフー
Tumurkhuu, Namkhai 1426
ドゥムレル・クヤ
Dumler Cuya, Francisco 380
ドゥメ
Doumet, Christian 371
ドゥメズウェニ
Dumezweni, Noma 380
ドゥメニル
Duménil, Gérard 380
トゥメルテキン
Tümertekin, Han 1426
トゥーモア
Toomua, Matt 1412
ドゥモント
Du Mont, Rosemary Ruhig 380
ドゥ・モンブリアール
De Montbrial, Thierry 341
ドゥーヤ
Dououya, Sandjima 371
トゥヤガ
Tuyaga, Herman 1429
トゥラ・アウン・コー
Thura Aung Ko 1402
トゥライフィ
al-Turaifi, Adel bin Zaid 1427
ドゥライミ
al-Dulaimi, Sadun 379
ドゥラヴォー
Delavaux, Céline 337
ドゥ=ラ=ウーグ
de La Hougue, Catherine 336
ドゥラエ
Delahaye, Jean-Paul 336
トゥラ・エイ・ミン
Thura Aye Myint 1402
トゥラガノフ
Tulaganov, Rustam 1426
トゥラキ
Turaki, Kabiru Tanimu 1427
ドゥラク
Duraku, Sadula 383
ドゥラージュ=カルヴェ
Delage-Calvet, Agnès 335
トゥラシュビリ
Turashvili, Otar 1427
トゥラジョンゾダ
Turadzhonzoda, Akbar 1427
トゥラーティ
Turati, Valeria 1427
ドゥラトゥール
Delatour, Patrick 337
ドゥラーニ
Durrani, Akram Khan 384
ドゥラニ
Durrani, Akram Khan 384
Durrani, Muhammado Ali 384
Durrani, Nasir Ahmad 384
トゥラノ
Thurano, Konrad 1402
ドゥラノ
Durano, Joseph 383
Durano, Joseph Ace 383
ドゥラノエ
Delanoe, Bertrand 336
ドゥラブリエール
Delabruyère, Stéphane 335
トゥラ・ミン・マウン
Thura Myint Maung 1402
ドゥ・ラ・ルペル
De La Rupelle, Guy 336
トゥーラン
Toolan, John Aloysius, Jr. 1412
ドゥラン
Duran, Alejo 383
Duran, Oscar 383
Durán, Sylvie 383
Duran, Teresa 383
Durant, Isabelle 383
ドゥラント
Dulanto, Alfonso 379
トゥーリ
Taulli, Tom 1384
ドゥーリー
Dooley, Anne 367
Dooley, Dolores 367
Dooley, Jim 367
Dooley, Joseph F. 367
Dooley, Mike 367
Dooley, Roger 367
ドゥリア
Deriaz, Anne 344
ドゥーリエ
Duriez, Colin 383
トゥリク
Theurig, Karin 1395
トゥリジオリス
Trigeorgis, Lenos 1420
トゥリシニ
Turisini, Valentina 1427
ドヴリース
Devreese, Frederic 348
トゥリスベコフ
Turisbekov, Zautbek 1427
ドゥリッチ
Dulić, Oliver 379
ドゥーリトル
Doolittle, Sean 367
トゥリーニ
Turrini, Peter 1429
トウリニョ
Tourinho, Rodolfo 1415
トゥリノ
Turino, Thomas 1427
トゥリヒ
Thurig, Karin 1402
トゥリムンプニ
Tri Mumpuni 1420
ドゥリュル
Dulull, Mohammed Asraf Ally 379
ドゥリール
Delisle, Guy 337
ドウリル
Doreal, M. 367
トゥリン
Turin, Luca 1427
ドゥーリング
Dooling, Richard 367
トゥール
Toole, F.X. 1412
Tour, Geneviève 1415
Tuell, Steven Shawn 1425
Tur, Pramudya Ananta 1427
トゥルー
True, Everett 1422
True, Sarah 1422
トウル
Towle, Philip 1415
ドゥル
Dull, Ryan 379
ドゥルー
Drew, John 374
Drewe, Sheryle Bergmann 374
Dulloo, Madan Murlidhar 379
トゥルーアー
Treuer, Paul 1419
ドゥルヴェール
Druvert, Hélène 375
ドゥルヴォー
Delvaux, Catherine 339
トゥルオグ
Truog, Robert D. 1422
ドゥルカル
Durcal, Rocio 383
トゥルカン
Turcan, Vladimir 1427
トゥルガンバエフ
Turganbaev, Melis 1427
トゥルキ
Turki, Kasim 1427
トゥルク
Türk, Danilo 1427
Turk, Žiga 1427
トゥルクス
Turks, Viktoriia 1427
トゥルクマン
Turkman, Fakhri 1427
トゥルコ
Turco, Livia 1427
ドゥルコ
Dulko, Gisela 379
トゥルコヴィチ
Turkovič, Milan 1427
トゥルコヴィッチ
Turkovič, Milan 1427
トゥルコウスキィ
Turkowski, Einar 1427
トゥルコット
Turcotte, Mathieu 1427
トゥルコビッチ
Turković, Bisera 1427
ドゥルコビッチ
Durkovic, Bojan 384
トゥルシエ
Troussier, Philippe 1422
ドゥルシュミート
Durschmied, Erik 384
トゥールス
Thors, Astrid 1402
ドゥルーズ
Drewes, Athena A. 374
トゥルスノフ
Tursunov, Farrukh Islomdjonovich 1429
Tursunov, Khusan 1429
トゥルスンクロフ
Tursunkulov, Nurlan 1429
ドゥルソー
Durusau, Patrick 384
トゥールソン
Toulson, Lois 1414
ドゥルタイユ
Deletaille, Albertine 337
ドゥルタロ
Durutalo, Andrew 384

ト

トゥルチノフ
Turchynov, Oleksandr Valentynovych 1427
トゥルチンスカス
Turčinskas, Rimvydas 1427
ドゥルッケル
Drucker, Tomáš 375
ドゥルディネツ
Durdynets, Vasyl 383
ドゥルディルイエフ
Durdylyyev, Samuhammed 383
トゥルテルボーム
Turtelboom, Annemie 1429
ドゥルドイルイエフ
Durdylyyev, Samuhammed 383
トゥルドゥバエフ
Turdubaev, Kubanychbek 1427
トゥルナトゥーリ
Turnaturi, Gabriella 1428
トゥルナン
Tournant, Arnaud 1415
トゥルニェ
Tournier, Jacques 1415
トゥルニエ
Tournier, Michel 1415
トゥルネ
Tourné, Daisy 1415
トゥルネル
Turner, Rosario 1429
トゥルネンコフ
Trunenkov, Dmitry 1422
ドゥルビエテ
Druviete, Ina 375
トゥルヒーオ
Trujillo, Leigh Ann 1422
トゥルヒーリョ
Trujillo Villar, Rafael 1422
トゥルーブ
Troob, Peter 1421
トゥループ
Troupe, Quincy 1422
トゥルブ
Tulub, Serhiy 1426
トゥルファント
Trufant, Desmond 1422
トゥルブラム・サンダグドルジ
Turburam Sandagdorj 1427
ドゥルベッコ
Dulbecco, Renato 379
トゥルボヴィッツ
Tulbovitz, Ernesto 1426
トゥルマニゼ
Turmanidze, Irakli 1428
ドゥルミシ
Durmisi, Riza 384
トゥールミン
Toulmin, Stephen Edelston 1414
トゥルーミン
Toulmin, Stephen Edelston 1414
ドゥールム
Doerum, Odd Einar 362
ドゥルム
Durm, Erik 384
トゥルーラブ
Truelove, Emily 1422
Trulove, James Grayson 1422
ドゥルーリー
Drury, Susan 375
ドゥルレシチャヌ
Durlesteanu, Mariana 384
トゥルン
Thurn, Valentin 1403
Truong, Monique 1422
トゥルンパ
Trümper, Joachim 1422
Trungpa, Chogyam 1422
トゥーレ
Teulé, Jean 1393
Touray, Alhaji Yankuba 1415
Touray, Kebba 1415
Touré 1415
Toure, Ali Farka 1415
Toure, Almamy 1415
Touré, Amadou Toumani 1415
Touré, Aminata 1415
Touré, Bassari 1415
Touré, Boubacar Sidiki 1415
Toure, Fodeba 1415
Toure, Gaoussou 1415
Toure, Ibrahim Oumar 1415
Toure, Mahamane Elhadji Bania 1415
Toure, Oumar Ibrahima 1415
Toure, Sanoussi 1415
Touré, Saramady 1415
Toure, Sidi Tiémoko 1415
Toure, Yaya 1415
トゥレ
Touray, Omar 1415
Touray, Yankouba 1415
Toure, Ibrahima Sory 1415
Toure, Ndiawar 1415
ドゥレ
Delay, Florence 337
トゥレイ
Touray, Yankouba 1415
ドゥ・レイシー
De Lacey, Gerald 335
トゥレイズ
Terease, Amanda 1391
トゥレイン・タン・ズィン
Thurain Thant Zin 1402
トゥーレーヌ
Touraine, Alain 1415
Touraine, Marisol 1415
トゥレーヌ
Touraine, Alain 1415
トゥレプ
Turepu, Kiriau 1427
トゥレール
Teulere, Jean 1393
トゥロー
Turow, Scott F. 1429
ドゥーロー
Deurloo, Bart 347
ドゥロ
Duro, Anastas 384
トゥロウ
Tlou, Sheila 1407
トゥロウィツキ
Tulowitzki, Troy 1426
トゥロウィツキー
Tulowitzki, Troy 1426
トゥロクメ
Trocmé, Suzanne 1421
トゥロースル
Trostle, James A. 1421
トゥロック
Turok, Neil 1429
ドゥロッフル
Deloffre, Frederic 338
ドゥロルム
Delorme, Pierre-Gilles 338
ドゥロン
Delon, Michel 338
ドゥロング
DeLong, Thomas J. 338
ドゥ・ロンジェ
De Londjet, Liano 338
トゥワイマン
Twyman, James F. 1430
トゥワギラムング
Twagiramungu, Ascension 1430
トゥーン
Thun, Maria 1402
Toon, John D. 1412
トゥンウェバゼ
Tumwebaze, Frank 1426
ドゥンガ
Dunga 381
トゥンカット
Tuncat, Levent 1426
トゥンガムエセ
Tungamwese, Emmanuel 1426
トゥンカラ
Tounkara, Fatoumata 1415
Tounkara, Makan 1415
Tounkara, Mamadou 1415
トゥンガラ
Toungara, Adama 1414
トゥンギ
Toungui, Paul 1414
ドゥンク
Dîncu, Vasile 356
トゥングバラ
Toungouvara, Marie Joseph Songomali 1414
ドゥンケル
Dunkel, Arthur 381
ドゥンゲル
Dhungyel, D.N. 349
トゥン・サライ
Thun Saray 1402
ドゥンドゥーロ
Dunduro, Silva Armando 381
トゥントーンカム
Thoungthongkam, Saralee 1402
Thungthongkam, Saralee 1402
トゥンバ
Tumba, Gérard 1426
ドゥンバ
Doumba, Emile 370
ドゥンバゼ
Dumbadze, Gela 380
ドゥンビア
Doumbia, Seydou 370
Doumbia, Tiecoura 370
ドゥンブヤ
Doumbouya, Mohamed Dorval 371
Doumbouya, Mohamed Lamine 371
ドゥンブラヴァ
Dumbrava, Danut 380
トゥンベリ
Thunberg, Stefan 1402
ドエジェル
Deheeger, Jean-Sébastien 334
ドェルフラー
Dörfler, Herbert 367
トカー
Tokar, Brian 1409
ドガ
Doga, María Nélida 362
ドガー
Dogar, Sharon 363
ドカイル
al-Du-qayr, Jalal Yousif Mohamed 383
トカエフ
Tokayev, Kasymzhomart 1409
ドーカス
Dorcas, Phil 367
ドカストル
de Castries, Henri 331
ドカストレ
de Castries, Henri 331
ド・ガズマン
De Guzman, Michael 334
トーガスン
Thorgerson, Storm 1401
トーガーソン
Torgerson, Carole 1413
Torgerson, David John 1413
トカタアケ
Tokataake, Willie 1409
トカターケ
Tokataake, Willie 1409
ドーガーダス
Daugirdas, John T. 322
トカチ
Tkatch, Elena 1407
トカチェンコ
Tkachenko, Vadim 1407
Tkatchenko, Justin 1407
トカチオスタプチュク
Tkach Ostapchuk, Yuliia 1407
トカチョフ
Tkachev, Alexander N. 1407
Tkachov, Oleg 1407
ドカティ
Docherty, Bevan 361
Docherty, Helen 361
Docherty, Thomas 361
ドガーディン
Dogadin, Sergey 362
ドガトキン
Dugatkin, Lee Alan 378
ドガニス
Doganis, Rigas 362
ドガノフ
Doganov, Boyan 362
トカルチュク
Tokarczuk, Antoni 1409
Tokarczuk, Olga 1409
トカレフ
Tokarev, Nikolai 1409
トカレンコ

ト

Tkalenko, Ivan 1407
トカン
Tohtobvbv, Isak 1408
ドーガン
Dogan, Erdal 362
ドガン
Dogan, Mattei 362
ドーキー
Doky, Chris Minh 363
ドキアディス
Doxiadis, Apostolos 372
ドギオーム
Deguillaume, Martine 334
ドキス
Dekiss, Jean-Paul 335
ドキック
Dokic, Jelena 363
トキッチ
Tokic, Bojan 1409
ドキッチ
Dokić, Branko 363
Dokic, Jelena 363
ド・ギヨーム
De Guillaume, André 334
ドーキンス
Dawkins, Edward 328
Dawkins, Marian Stamp 328
Dawkins, Richard 328
ドーキンズ
Dawkins, Marian Stamp 328
トーキントン
Torkington, Nathan 1413
ドーク
Doak, Kevin Michael 360
ドク
Nguyen Duc 1021
ドグ
Dogou, Alain 363
ドクシアディス
Doxiadis, Apostolos 372
ドクジュンガー
Docdjengar, Ngarlenan 361
トークス
Talks, Audrey Sansbury 1378
ドークス
Dokes, Michael 363
トクスヴィグ
Toksvig, Sandi 1409
トクセン
Toxen, Bob 1416
ドクター
Docter, Pete 361
Doctor, Marcio 361
ドクター・ケイ
*Dr.*K 361
ドクター・ジョン
*Dr.*John 361
ドクター・ドット
*Dr.*Dot 361
ドクター・ドレー
*Dr.*Dre 361
ドクターマン
Dochterman, Joanne McCloskey 361
ドクター・リックス
*Dr.*Licks 362
ドクトゥリシビリ
Dokturishvili, Aleksandr 363
ドクトル
Doktor, Martin 363
ドクトロウ
Doctorow, Cory 362
Doctorow, Edgar Laurence 362
トグナジーニ
Tognazzini, Bruce 1408
トグネジーニ
Tognazzini, Bruce 1408
トグネッティ
Tognetti, Stefano 1408
トクパ
Tokpah, Henrique 1409
トグバ
Togba, Maurice Zogbélémou 1408
トクパクバエフ
Tokpakbayev, Sat 1409
ドグベ
Dogbe, Kokuvi 363
トクマン・ラモス
Tokman Ramos, Marcelo 1409
ドグラ
Dogra, Chander Suta 363
Dogra, Nisha 363
トグライ
Toghraie, Adrienne Laris 1408
ドグリー
Dogley, Didier 363
ドクリストフォロ
De Cristoforo, Violet Kazue 332
ドクール
Deaucourt, Jean-Louis 330
ドクールシェル
Decourchelle, Agnès 332
ドクレ
Dokle, Namik 363
ド・クレシー
De Crécy, Nicolas 332
ドグレール
Deglaire, Roselyne 334
ド・クレルク
De Clercq, Willy 332
ドクレルク
De Clercq, Willy 332
ドゲ
Dogue, Patrick 363
トーケイム
Tokheim, Roger L. 1409
トケイヤー
Tokayer, Marvin 1409
トケシェラシビリ
Tkeshelashvili, Davit 1407
Tkeshelashvili, Eka 1407
ドゲット
Doggett, Peter 363
ド・ゲネス
de Gennes, Pierre-Gilles 333
トーゲル
Toegel, Ginka 1408
ド・ケルシズ
de Quercize, Stanislas 344
トケーロ
Toquero, Gaizka 1412
トーゴ
Togo, Kénékouo Barthélémy 1408
Togo, Marie Madeleine 1408
ドコ
Doko, Dragan 363
Doko, Michel 363
ドコー
Decaux, Alain 331
トーゴヴニク
Torgovnik, Jonathan 1413
ドコス
Décosse, Lucie 332
ドゴース
Degos, Laurent 334
トコト
Tokoto, J.P. 1409
ドゴナゼ
Dogonadze, Anna 363
トーゴフ
Torgoff, Martin 1413
ドコマルモン
De Comarmond, Simone 332
ドゴヨ
Dogojo, Joan 363
ドコラ
Dokora, Lazarus 363
ド・ゴール
de Gaulle, Charles 333
ド・ゴール・アントニオズ
de Gaulle-Anthonioz, Genevieve 333
ドゴール・アントニオズ
de Gaulle-Anthonioz, Genevieve 333
ドコルモ
Do Carmo, Allan 361
ドーサ
Dosa, David 368
Dousa, Mohammed Bushara 371
ドーザー
Dauser, Lukas 322
ドサエフ
Dosayev, Erbolat 368
Dossayev, Yerbolat 369
トザカ
Tozaka, Milner 1416
ドーザブル
Douzable, Leger 371
ドサリ
al-Dousari, Hassan Dhabit 371
トサル
Tosul, David 1414
ドサール
Dossar, Mohamed Bacar 369
トーザン
Tauzin, Dora 1384
ドサンジュ
Dosanjh, Ujjal 368
ドサンセルナン
Saint-Sernin, Frédéric de 1228
トシ
Tosi, Piero 1414
ドーシ
Doshi, Balkrishna 368
ドーシー
Dorsey, David 368
Dorsey, Glenn 368
Dorsey, Jack 368
Dorsey, James 368
Dorsey, Pat 368
Dorsey, Thomas J. 368
ドシ
Doshi, Neel 368
ドシー
Dechy, Nathalie 332
ドージア
Dozier, Rush W., Jr. 372
ドジアー
Dozier, Dakota 372
トジアン
Tozian, Gregory 1416
ドジェ・ツェリン
Doje Cering 363
ドジェツェリン
Doje Cering 363
ド・ジェンヌ
de Gennes, Pierre-Gilles 333
トジク
Tozik, Anatoly A. 1416
ドジソン
Dodgson, Mark 362
トシッチ
Tosic, Dusko 1414
Tosic, Zoran 1414
トジバエフ
Tojibaev, Hurshid 1409
ドージャー
Dozier, Brian 372
Dozier, Hunter 372
ドジャスナバイユ
Djasnabaille, Abderamane 359
ド・ジャンヌ
de Gennes, Pierre-Gilles 333
トーシュ
Tosches, Nick 1414
トシュチャコフ
Toshchakov, Igor 1414
トシュテンソン
Torstensson, Åsa 1414
ドジュニアック
De Juniac, Alexandre 335
ドシルギ
De Silguy, Yves-Thibault 345
ドージン
Dodin, Lev 362
ドジンスカヤ
Dudinskaya, Nataliya Mikhailovna 377
トス
Tos, M. 1414
Toth, Alex 1414
Toth, Andre De 1414
Toth, Linda A. 1414
Toth, Pamela 1414
ドーズ
Doz, Yves L. 372
ドス
Doss, Lorenzo 369
Doss, Mohan 369
Dosse, François 369
ドス・アンジョス
Dos Anjos, Felipe 368
ドスアンジョス
Dos Anjos, Carlos Gustavo 368
トズゥン
Tozoun, Kokou Biossey 1416
トスカ

ト

Toska, Igli 1414
トスカーニ
Toscani, Oliviero 1414
ドスカリエフ
Doskaliyev, Zhakcylyk 368
トスカン・デュ・プランティエ
Toscan du Plantier, Daniel 1414
トスカン・デュ・プロンチエ
Toscan du Plantier, Daniel 1414
ドスキ
Doski, Dindar 369
ドスコチロヴァー
Doskochrová, Hana 369
ドスコツィル
Doskozil, Hans Peter 369
ドスザ
de Souza, Marcel Alain 346
ドス・サントス
Dos Santos, José Eduardo 369
Dos Santos, Mauro 369
Giovani 501
ドスサントス
Dos Santos, Alberto Manuel 369
Dos Santos, Daiane 369
Dos Santos, Fernando Da Piedade Dias 369
Dos Santos, José Eduardo 369
Dos Santos, Marilson 369
Dos Santos, Nicolau 369
Dos Santos, Norberto Fernando 369
トスタ
Tosta, Sheena 1414
ド・スタイガー
De Steiguer, Joseph Edward 346
ドスタム
Dostam, Abdul Rashid 369
Dostum, Abdul Rashid 369
ドスタール
Dostál, Pavel 369
ドスタル
Dostal, Josef 369
ドスタレール
Dostaler, Gilles 369
ドースチャー
Doescher, Ian 362
ドスト
Dost, Bas 369
ドストブラジ
Douste-blazy, Philippe 371
ドストベ
Dossou Togbe, Pascal 369
ドスナキ
Dossou Naki, Honorine 369
ドスフイ
Doussouhoui, Cossi Gaston 371
ドスプラゼレス
Dos Prazeres, Arzemiro 369
ドスプレゼレス
Dos Prezeres, Luis Alberto Carneiro 369
ドスムハンベトフ
Dosmukhanbetov, Temirkhan 369
トーズランド
Toseland, Ronald W. 1414
ドスレイスサントス
Dos Reis Santos, Rosane 369
トスン
Tosun, Buse 1414
ドーセ
Dausset, Jean 322
ドゼ
Dauzet, Dominique-Marie 322
ドセアニロン
Dossehanyron, Gabriel Sassouvi 369
ドセッター
Dossetor, John 369
ドーセット
Dorsett, Kenred 368
Dorsett, Phillip 368
トセリ
Toselli, Leigh 1414
ド・セルトー
De Certeau, Michel 331
トセンジョジョ
Tosendjojo, Don 1414
トゾーリ
Tozzoli, Guy F. 1416
トゾリーニ
Tosolini, Tiziano 1414
ドゾロ
Dzoro, Morris 386
ドゾワ
Dozois, Gardner 372
ドーソン
Dawson, Andre 328
Dawson, Ann 328
Dawson, Barry 328
Dawson, Branden 328
Dawson, Chester 328
Dawson, Craig 328
Dawson, Eric 328
Dawson, George 328
Dawson, Geraldine 328
Dawson, James 328
Dawson, Janet 328
Dawson, Jodi 328
Dawson, John A. 328
Dawson, John William, Jr. 328
Dawson, Jonathan 328
Dawson, Karl 328
Dawson, Luke 328
Dawson, Michael 328
Dawson, Mike 328
Dawson, Pamela 328
Dawson, Peter 328
Dawson, Phil 328
Dawson, P.J. 328
Dawson, Roger 328
Dawson, Shawn 328
Dawson, Terry 328
Dawson, Toby 328
Dawson-Saunders, Beth 328
Dowson, Nick 372
ドーソン－ヒューズ
Dawson-Hughes, Bess 328
ドダ
Doda, Viktor 362
トタニャナ
Thotanyana, Lebohang 1402
トダール
Todahl, Jeffrey 1408
トダロ
Todaro, Michael P. 1408
ドダンゴダ
Dodangoda, Amarasiri 362
ドーチ
Doczi, György 362
トツカ
Totka, Sandor 1414
トッカフォンド
Toccafondo, Gianluigi 1407
トツキー
Totsky, Konstantin V. 1414
ドック
Dock, Lennart 361
Nguyen Duc 1021
トックウィグニー
Tocquigny, Rick 1408
トックヴィル
Tocqueville, Aude de 1408
ドックソン
Doctson, Josh 362
ドックリル
Dockrill, Michael L. 361
ドックレー
Dockwray, Ruth 361
ドックレル
Dockrell, Hazel M. 361
ドッケンドルフ
Dockendorff, Eduardo 361
ドッシ
Dossi, Moses 369
ドッシー
Dossey, Barbara Montgomery 369
Dossey, Larry 369
ドッジ
Dodge, David A. 362
Dodge, Edwin Newton 362
Dodge, Mark 362
Dodge, Toby 362
ドッス
Dosse, François 369
ドッズ
Dodds, James 362
Dodds, Klaus 362
Dodds, Sarah 362
Dodds, Shauna 362
ドッソ
Dosso, Moussa 369
ドッターウィック
Dotterweich, Kass Perry 369
トッチ
Tocci, Giovanni 1407
トッツ
Todts, Herwig 1408
ドッツ
Dotz, Warren 369
トッツィ
Tozzi, Giorgio 1416
トッツォ
Tozzo, Andrea 1416
Tozzo, Pepe 1416
トッデ
Todde, Antonio 1408
トッティ
Totti, Francesco 1414
ドッティ
Dotti, Andrea 369
Dotti, Luca 369
ドッティーノ
Dottino, Tony 369
トッテン
Totten, Bill 1414
Totten, Christopher W. 1414
トッド
Todd, Anna 1408
Todd, Bryan 1408
Todd, Chad 1408
Todd, Charles 1408
Todd, Emmanuel 1408
Todd, Garfield 1408
Todd, Jacquelyne 1408
Todd, Janet 1408
Todd, Kim 1408
Todd, Mark 1408
Todd, Olivier 1408
Todd, Richard 1408
Todd, Richard Watson 1408
Todd, Selina 1408
Todde, Antonio 1408
Todt, Jean 1408
ドット
Dodd, Christina 362
Dutt, Yogeshwar 384
ドッド
Dodd, Annabel Z. 362
Dodd, Christopher 362
Dodd, Emma 362
Dodd, James L. 362
Dodd, Johnny 362
Dodd, Judith L. 362
Dodd, Kevin 362
Dodd, Lynley 362
Dodd, Philip 362
Dodd, Ray 362
Dodd, Sarah J. 362
Dodd, Stephen 362
ドットソン
Dodson, Terry 362
Dotson, Demar 369
Dotson, Jeff 369
ドッドソン
Dodson, Regilio 362
トッドハンター
Todhunter, Andrew 1408
トッドマン
Todman, Jordan 1408
ドッドマン
Dodman, Nicholas H. 362
ドッドラーズ
Doodlers, Artful 367
トッピ
Toppi, Sergio 1412
トッピン
Toppin, Ronald 1412
トッピング
Topping, Wayne W. 1412
トップ
T.O.P 1412
ドップ
Dobbs, Barbara 361
ドップス
Dobbs, Richard 361
トップフ
Topf, Jonathan 1412
ドップマン
Doppmann, Priska 367
ドップラー
Doppler, Clemens 367
トッリ
Tolli, Abbas 1409

ト

Tölli, Tapani 1409
トッリネン
Töllinen, Markku 1410
ドーデ
Daudet, Joris 322
ドテ
Doté, Elie 369
トデア
Todea, Alexandru 1408
トーディ
Torday, Paul 1412
トーデイ
Torday, Piers 1412
トティ
Toti, Andrew 1414
ドーティ
Doherty, Tom 363
Doty, Mark 369
Doughty, Caitlin 370
Doughty, Rebecca 370
ドティ
Doti, 'Matebatso 369
Doty, Gwen 369
ドディエ
Dodier, Alain 362
Dodier, Bernard 362
ドディグ
Dodig, Ivan 362
トーディチ
Tosić, Milanka 1414
トディノ
Todino, Grace 1408
ドディヤ
Dodiya, Atul 362
トーデス
Todes, Daniel Philip 1408
ドデュ
Dedieu, Virginie 332
ド・デューヴ
De Duve, Christian René 332
ド・デューブ
De Duve, Christian 332
De Duve, Christian René 332
ドーテン
Dauten, Dale 322
トーデンヘーファー
Todenhöfer, Jürgen 1408
トート
Toth, Krisztian 1414
Toth, Matej 1414
Toth, Tamas 1414
トド
Todd, Richard 1408
ドド
Dodo 362
トートゥー
Tautou, Audrey 1384
トトゥ
Tautou, Audrey 1384
ドートゥルメール
Dautremer, Rébecca 322
ド・トス・アンドレ
Toth, Andre De 1414
ドドソン
Dodson, Aidan 362
ド・トナック
De Tonnac, Jean-Philippe 347
トトフ
Toth, Matej 1414
ドドフスキ
Dodovski, Marjan 362
トトミアニナ
Totmianina, Tatiana 1414
トートラ
Tortora, Gerard J. 1414
ドトレス・マルティネス
Dotres Martínez, Carlos 369
トドロヴィッチ
Todorovitch, Marie-Ange 1408
トドログロ
Todoroglo, Dmitrii 1408
トドロバ
Todorova, Hristiana 1408
トトロフ
Totrov, Rustam 1414
トドロフ
Todorov, Nikola 1408
Todorov, Tzvetan 1408
トドロフスキー
Todorovskii, Pyotor 1408
トドロワ
Todorova, Anastasiia 1408
ドドン
Dodon, Igor 362
トーナー
Toner, Jacqueline B. 1411
トナー
Toner, Brenda B. 1411
Toner, Cole 1411
Toner, Devin 1411
Toner, Jerry 1411
ドナ
Dona, Klaus 365
ドナー
Doner, Richard F. 365
Donner, Clive 366
Donner, Fred McGraw 366
Donner, Irah H. 366
Donner, Richard 366
Donner, Robert 366
ドナシメント
Do Nascimento, Adão 365
ドナースマルク
Donnersmarck, Florian Henckel von 366
ドナーティ
Donati, Angela 365
Donati, Danilo 365
Donati, Giulio 365
Donati, Umberto 365
ドナティ
Donati, Danilo 365
ドナディウー
Donnadieu, Jean-Louis 366
トナト
Tonato, José Didier 1411
ドナート
Donato, Fabrizio 365
ドナドーニ
Donadoni, Roberto 365
ドナドニ
Donadoni, Roberto 365
トナーニ
Tonani, Dario 1411
ドナヒュー
Donahue, Ann 365
Donahue, Bill 365
Donahue, Claire 365
Donahue, Gary A. 365
Donahue, John D. 365
Donahue, Jonathan 365
Donahue, Mark 365
Donahue, Neal 365
Donahue, Troy 365
Donoghue, Daniel 366
Donoghue, Emma 366
Donoghue, John 366
Donoghue, Paul J. 366
ドナフー
Donohoe, Paschal 366
ドナール
Denard, Bob 341
ドナル
Donnal, Andrew 366
ドナールタイサ
Denard, Bob 341
ドナルド
Donald, Aaron 365
Donald, Anna 365
Donald, Graeme 365
Donald, Howard 365
Donald, Lisa 365
Donald, Luke 365
Donald, Robyn 365
Donard, Isabelle 365
ドナルド・オコナー
O'Connor, Donald 1043
ドナルドスン
Donaldson, Roger 365
ドナルドソン
Donaldson, Denis 365
Donaldson, Emma 365
Donaldson, Gordon 365
Donaldson, J.Ana 365
Donaldson, Jean 365
Donaldson, Josh 365
Donaldson, Julia 365
Donaldson, Julianne 365
Donaldson, Mary 365
Donaldson, Roger 365
Donaldson, Sue 365
Donaldson, Thomas 365
Donaldson, William H. 365
ドーナン
Dornan, Jim 368
Dornan, Tim 368
ドナン
Donnan, Kristin 366
トーニ
Toni, Luca 1412
トニ
Toni, Loujaya 1412
Toni, Luca 1412
トーニオ
Torneo, Erin 1413
ドニオ
Donnio, Sylviane 366
ド・ニース
de Niese, Danielle 342
ドニソーン
Donnithorne, Larry R. 366
トニー・タン・カクチョン
Tony Tan Cacktiong 1412
トニー・タン・カクティオン
Tony Tan Cacktiong 1412
トニツァ
Tonita, Ovidiu 1412
ドーニック
Doornik, Jurgen A. 367
トニ・ドバレ
Toni Dovale 1412
トニー・マクウェイ
Tony McQuay 1412
トーニョ・ラミレス
Tono Ramirez 1412
ドニヨロフ
Doniyorov, Tulashboy 366
ドーニン
Dornin, Laird 368
ドーニンク
Van Doninck, Sebastiaan 1443
トーニングシュミット
Thorning-Schmidt, Helle 1401
ドヌー
Deneux, Xavier 341
ドヌーヴ
Deneuve, Catherine 341
ドヌデュードバーブル
Donnedieu de Vabres, Renaud 366
ドヌーブ
Deneuve, Catherine 341
ドヌリアズ
Deneriaz, Antoine 341
ドーネ
Doane, Deborah 360
ドネ
Donnet, Jean-Luc 366
Donnet, Pierre-Antoine 366
ドネー
d'Aunay, Arnaud le Peletier 322
トネッティ
Tognetti, Stefano 1408
トネッリ
Tonelli, Lorenzo 1411
トネフ
Tonev, Aleksandar 1411
トネラ
Tonela, Ernesto Max Elias 1411
ドネラン
Donnellan, Michael A. 366
トネリ
Tonelli, Gilles 1411
ドネリ
Donnelly, Elfie 366
ドネリー
Donnelly, Anne Cohn 366
Donnelly, Jane 366
Donnelly, Jennifer 366
Donnelly, Judith K. 366
Donnelly, Michael 366
Donnelly, Peter 366
Donnelly, Steven Gerard 366
Donnelly, Thomas 366
ドネール
Donner, Christophe 366
ドネル
Donnell, Larry 366
Donner, Piet Hein 366
トネロ
Tonello, Michael 1411
ドネロン
Donnellon, Anne 366
ドノヴァン
Donovan, Dale 366
Donovan, Jim 366
Donovan, Mary 366
Donovan, Susan 366
トノーニ
Tononi, Giulio 1412
ドノバン

Donovan, Alan A.A. 366
Donovan, Anne 366
Donovan, Billy 366
Donovan, Dennis Michael 366
Donovan, Derec 366
Donovan, Eddie 366
Donovan, Jeremey 366
Donovan, John J. 366
Donovan, Kevin 366
Donovan, Landon 366
Donovan, Robert J. 366
Donovan, Shaun 366
Donovan, William J. 366

ドノヒュー
Donoghue, Emma 366
Donoghue, Susan 366
Donohue, Keith 366

ドノフリオ
Donofrio, Beverly 366

トーバー
Tober, Jan M. 1407

トバ
Toba, Andreas 1407
Tobă, Petre 1407

ドーバー
Dover, Kenneth James 371
Dover, Robert 371

トバァイアス
Tobias, Roy 1407

トバイアス
Tobias, Phillip Vallentine 1407
Tobias, Roy 1407
Tobias, Sheila 1407

トバイシケ
Tobai Sike, Renata 1407

ドバーグ
de Berg, Mark 330

トバック
Tobback, Bruno 1407

ドバッシュ
Dobadh, R.Emerson 361
Dobash, Russell P. 361

ドハーティ
Daugherty, Evan 322
Doherty, Berlie 363
Doherty, Gerard M. 363
Doherty, Gillian 363
Doherty, Jim 363
Doherty, Neil A. 363
Dougherty, Steve 370

ドハティ
Docherty, Iain 361
Doherty, Berlie 363
Doherty, P.C. 363
Doherty, Peter Charles 363
Doherty, William Joseph 363
Dougherty, Brandi 370
Dougherty, James 370
Dougherty, Kerrie 370
Dougherty, Martin J. 370
Dougherty, Ned 370

ドハティー
Doherty, P.C. 363
Dougherty, James 370

ドバート
Dobbert, Tim 361

ドバーム
Debeurme, Ludovic 330

ド・ハメル
De Hamel, Christopher 334

トバル
Tóvar, Roberto 1415

トーバルズ
Torvalds, Linus Benedict 1414

ドハルティ
Doherty, Glen 363

ドパルデュー
Depardieu, Gérard 343
Depardieu, Guillaume 343

ドパルドン
Depardon, Raymond 343

ド・バロア
De Valois, Ninette 347

ドバロワ
De Valois, Ninette 347

トパン
Topan, Sani Mohamed 1412

ド・パンス
De Pins, Arthur 343

トーピー
Torpey, John C. 1413
Torpey, Pat 1413

トビ
Toby, Ronald P. 1407

トビー
Tobey, Deborah D. 1407
Tobey, Kenneth 1407
Tobey, Mike 1407

トピ
Topi, Bamir 1412

ドービー
Doby, Larry 361

ドビー
Doby, Larry 361

トビアス
Tobias, Andrew P. 1407
Tobias, Nataliya 1407
Tobias, Roy 1407

ドビアス
Dobias, Frank 361

トピック
Topik, Steven 1412

ドビック
Dobic, Mina 361

ドビデニエネ
Dovydeniene, Roma 371

ドビニク
Dobinick, Susan 361

ドビニン
Dubinin, Yurii Vladimirovich 376

トビーマック
TobyMac 1407
Tobyn, Graeme 1407

トー・ヒュー
To Huu 1408

ド・ビュッシェ
De Busscher, Jacques F. 331

トビラ
Taubira, Christiane 1384

ド・ビリー
De Billy, Bertrand 331

トピリナ
Topilina, Gelena 1412

トピリン
Topilin, Maxim A. 1412

トビルクン
Tvircun, Victor 1430

ドビルパン
De Villepin, Dominique 348
Villepin, Dominique de 1457

トービン
Tobin, Brian 1407
Tobin, James 1407
Tobin, JP 1407
Tobin, Kristin M. 1407
Tobyn, Graeme 1407

トーピン
Taupin, Bernie 1384

トビーン
Toibin, Colm 1409

トビン
Tobin, Bob 1407
Tobin, Matt 1407
Tobin, Mike 1407

トピン
Toppin, Ronald 1412

ドビン
Dobbin, Shane 361

トピンコバクナプコバ
Topinkova Knapkova, Miroslava 1412

ドビンズ
Dobyns, Emery 361
Dobyns, Jay 361
Dobyns, Stephen 361

トー・フー
To Huu 1408

トーブ
Taub, Lawrence 1383

ドーフ
Dorf, Bob 367
Dorf, Richard C. 367

ドーファン
Dorfan, Jonathan 367

トフィギ
Tofigi, Jafar 1408

トフィールド
Tofield, Simon 1408

トフィンガ
Tofinga, Martin 1408

トー・フウ
To Huu 1408

ドフェイ
D'Offay, Tim 362

ドフォルク
de Valk, Jeroen 347

ドフォルジュ
Deforges, Régine 333

ドブガリュク
Dovgalyuk, Mikhail 371

ドブキン
Dobkin, Larry 361
Dobkin, Patricia L. 361

ドフグン
Dovgun, Olga 371

トブゲ
Tobgay, Tshering 1407

トブゲイ
Tobgay, Tshering 1407

ドブザンスキー
Dobzynski, Charles 361

ドブシー
Daubechies, Ingrid 321

トブシア
Tovosia, Bradley 1415

トフジェフスキ
Tchórzewski, Krzysztof 1387

トプジャン
Topuzian, Manook 1412

ドブジャン
Devedjian, Patrick 347

トプシュ
Topsch, Wilhelm 1412

ドブジンスキ
Dobrzyński, Roman 361

ドブス
Dobbs, Horace 361

ドブズ
Dobbs, Michael 361

ドーフスマン
Dorfsman, Louis 367

ドブスン
Dobson, Tamara 361

トプセル
Topsell, John 1412

ドブソン
Dobson, Aaron 361
Dobson, Andrew 361
Dobson, Annette J. 361
Dobson, Charlotte 361
Dobson, Christopher M. 361
Dobson, Hugo 361
Dobson, James C. 361
Dobson, Linda 361
Dobson, Pat 361
Dobson, Tamara 361

トプチック
Topchik, Gary S. 1412

トーフテ
Tofte, Sarah 1408

トフト
Toft, Anthony D. 1408

ドーブニー
Daubney, Kate 322

ドブハル
Dovhal, Yuliya 371

ドプファー
Dopfer, Fritz 367

トフーフト
't Hooft, Gerardus 1401

トブマシャン
Tovmasyan, Hrair 1415

トーブマン
Taubman, Alfred 1384

ドーフマン
Dorfman, Ariel 367
Dorfman, Lisa 367
Dorfman, Peter William 367

トフメ
Tohme, Nehmeh 1408

トフラー
Toffler, Alvin 1408
Toffler, Heidi 1408

ドブラー
Dobler, Tobias K. 361

トプラク
Toprak, Omer 1412

ドフラスン
Defrasne, Vincent 333

ド・フランス
De France, Cecile 333

ドブリギン
Dobrygin, Grigori 361

ド・フリース
De Vries, Jan 348

ドフリース
DeFries, Ruth S. 333

ドブリスキー
Dobriskey, Lisa 361

ドブリツォイユ
Dobritoiu, Corneliu 361
ドブリュー
Debreu, Gerard 331
ドブリン
Dobrin, Arthur 361
ドブリント
Dobrindt, Alexander 361
ドブルー
Debreu, Gerard 331
ドブルィニン
Dobrynin, Anatolii Fedorovich 361
ドブルイニン
Dobrynin, Anatolii Fedorovich 361
ドブルインスカ
Dobrynska, Natallia 361
ドブレ
Debray, Régis 331
Debré, Jean Louis 331
Dobre, Gheorghe 361
ドフレージ
De Freij, Nabil 333
ドブレス
Daubresse, Marc-Philippe 322
Dobles, Roberto 361
ドブレフ
Dobrev, Dellian 361
Dobrev, Milen 361
ド・ブロカ
De Broca, Philippe 331
ドブロスコク
Dobroskok, Alexander 361
Dobroskok, Dmitriy 361
ドブロビッチ
Dobrović, Slaven 361
ドブロボルスキス
Dobrovolskis, Konstantinas 361
トベ
Tobe, Glenn R. 1407
Tové, Jean-Lucien Savi de 1415
ドベイキー
DeBakey, Michael Ellis 330
トベイシャト
Tbeishat, Abdul-Razzaq 1387
ドヘイリ
al-Dekhairi, Ibrahim Adam Ahmed 335
ド・ベーキ
DeBakey, Michael Ellis 330
ドベーキ
DeBakey, Michael Ellis 330
ドベジャン
Devedjian, Patrick 347
ドベシュ
Dobeš, Josef 361
トーベス
Taubes, Gary 1384
ドベリ
Dobelli, Rolf 361
ドベリス
De Bellis, Jack 330
ドベール
d'Aubert, François 321
ドベルソン
Deverson, Martine 347
ドペルト
Doppert, Monika 367
ド・ベルニエール
De Bernieres, Louis 330
ドーベルニュ
d'Auvergne, Ausbert 322
トー・ホアイ
Tô Hoài 1408
ドー・ホアン・ジュウ
Do Hoang Dieu 363
ドーボイ
Dåvøy, Laila 327
トポエフ
Topoyev, Esen 1412
トボギャル
Tobgyel, Tashi 1407
ドボジャーク
Dvorak, Filip 385
ドボダール
Bodard, Aliette de 152
ド・ボトン
De Botton, Alain 331
ドホナーニ
Dohnányi, Christoph von 363
ドボヌ
Dovonou, Roger 371
ド・ボヌヴァル
Bonneval, Gwen de 160
ドボーブ
Debauve, Marine 330
ト・ホーフト
't Hooft, Gerardus 1401
トホーフト
Hooft, G.'t 621
トポラーネク
Topolánek, Mirek 1412
ドボルコビッチ
Dvorkovich, Arkady Vladimirovich 385
ドボロベンコ
Dvorovenko, Irina 385
ドー・ホン・ゴック
Do Hong Ngoc 363
トーマ
Thoma, Dieter 1396
Thoma, Erwin 1396
Thoma, Zdenek 1396
トーマー
Tomar, Narendra Singh 1410
トマ
Thomas, Chantal 1397
Thomas, Isabelle 1397
Thomas, Jean François 1397
Thomas, Jerome 1397
Thomas, Patrick 1398
Toma, Miguel 1410
Toma, Miguel Angel 1410
Toma, Sergiu 1410
ドーマ
Doma, Damir 364
トマイチク
Tomajczyk, Stephen F. 1410
トマージ
Tomasi, Dario 1410
Tomasi, Jacopo 1410
Tomasi, Peter J. 1410
トマシ
Tomasi, Massimiliano 1410
トマジ
Tomasi, Peter J. 1410
トマシェフスキ
Tomaszewski, Henryk 1410
ドマジエール
Demaziere, Didier 340
ドマシェンコ
Domashenko, Marina 364
トマシュ
Tomaš, Marko 1410
ドマージュリー
De Margerie, Christophe 339
トマショワ
Tomashova, Tatyana 1410
トーマス
Thomas, Abbator 1397
Thomas, Abigail 1397
Thomas, Alan Ken 1397
Thomas, Anne 1397
Thomas, Barry 1397
Thomas, Bernadette 1397
Thomas, Brandon 1397
Thomas, Cam 1397
Thomas, Carol 1397
Thomas, Chris 1397
Thomas, Craig 1397
Thomas, Dallas 1397
Thomas, Dana 1397
Thomas, Daniel 1397
Thomas, Dave 1397
Thomas, David 1397
Thomas, David Hugh 1397
Thomas, De'Anthony 1397
Thomas, Delma 1397
Thomas, Demaryius 1397
Thomas, Diane Coulter 1397
Thomas, Don 1397
Thomas, Donald 1397
Thomas, Duke 1397
Thomas, Earl 1397
Thomas, Edward Donnall 1397
Thomas, Edwin 1397
Thomas, Elizabeth Marshall 1397
Thomas, Emma 1397
Thomas, Eugene E. 1397
Thomas, Evan 1397
Thomas, Frank 1397
Thomas, Frank N. 1397
Thomas, George Banda 1397
Thomas, Geraint 1397
Thomas, Glyn V. 1397
Thomas, Gordon 1397
Thomas, Heinz 1397
Thomas, Helen 1397
Thomas, Hugh 1397
Thomas, Irma 1397
Thomas, Isabel 1397
Thomas, Isaiah 1397
Thomas, Jacquelyn S. 1397
Thomas, James 1397
Thomas, Janet 1397
Thomas, Jarret 1397
Thomas, J.C. 1397
Thomas, Jefferson 1397
Thomas, Jennifer 1397
Thomas, Jeremy 1397
Thomas, Jerry D. 1397
Thomas, Jim 1397
Thomas, Joe 1397
Thomas, John B. 1397
Thomas, John Meurig 1397
Thomas, Josh 1398
Thomas, Joshua R. 1398
Thomas, Joy 1398
Thomas, J.Philip 1398
Thomas, J.T. 1398
Thomas, Julia Adeney 1398
Thomas, Julian 1398
Thomas, Jullius 1398
Thomas, Karine 1398
Thomas, Kathy 1398
Thomas, Kristian 1398
Thomas, Kristin Scott 1398
Thomas, K.V. 1398
Thomas, Lance 1398
Thomas, Lawrence 1398
Thomas, Logan 1398
Thomas, Lorraine 1398
Thomas, Marion 1398
Thomas, Marlo 1398
Thomas, Michael 1398
Thomas, Mike 1398
Thomas, Nanette 1398
Thomas, Neil 1398
Thomas, Orin 1398
Thomas, Partey 1398
Thomas, Pat 1398
Thomas, Peter 1398
Thomas, Petria 1398
Thomas, Phil 1398
Thomas, Phillip 1398
Thomas, Rachael 1398
Thomas, Ralph 1398
Thomas, Rasta 1398
Thomas, Ray 1398
Thomas, Rhys 1398
Thomas, Richard 1398
Thomas, Rob 1398
Thomas, Robert 1398
Thomas, Robert, Jr. 1398
Thomas, Robert Joseph 1398
Thomas, Roy 1398
Thomas, R.Roosevelt, Jr. 1398
Thomas, Rufus 1398
Thomas, Sandra P. 1398
Thomas, Sara 1398
Thomas, Scarlett 1398
Thomas, Shamarko 1398
Thomas, Shelley Moore 1398
Thomas, S.Justin 1398
Thomas, Stephen A. 1398
Thomas, Taffy 1398
Thomas, Tessa 1398
Thomas, Thomas M., Ⅱ 1398
Thomas, Tillman 1398
Thomas, Todd M. 1398
Thomas, Valérie 1398
Thomas, Vinod 1398
Thomas, William H. 1398
Thomas, William Karl 1398
Thomas, Zach 1399
Tomas, Yasmany 1410
トマス
Thomas, Alma 1397
Thomas, Bob 1397
Thomas, Ceri Louise 1397
Thomas, Donald 1397
Thomas, Edward Donnall 1397
Thomas, George Banda 1397
Thomas, Helen 1397
Thomas, John Meurig 1397

Thomas, Julia Adeney 1398
Thomas, Keir 1398
Thomas, Keith Vivian 1398
Thomas, Lewis 1398
Thomas, Margaret Ann 1398
Thomas, Robert Paul 1398
Thomas, Scarlett 1398
Thomas, Sherry M. 1398
Tomás, August Da Silva 1410
Tomas, Jason 1410

トマスコ
Tomasko, Robert M. 1410

トマスホッフ
Thomashoff, Hans-Otto 1399

トーマスマ
Thomasma, David C. 1399

トーマス＝ミフネ
Thomas-Mifune, Werner 1399

トマスン
Thomason, Dustin 1399

ドマゼト
Domazet, Dragan 364

トマセビツ
Tomasevicz, Curtis 1410

トマセリ
Tomaselli, Keyan G. 1410
Tomaselli, Paige 1410

トマセロ
Tomasello, Michael 1410

トマセン
Thomassen, Theo 1399

トマソン
Thomasson, Chris 1399
Tomassone, Gian-Michele 1410

トマゾン
Tommasone, Cyril 1411

トーマタ
Toomata, Alapati Poese Toomata 1412

トマダ
Tomada, Carlos 1410

トマチェフスキー
Tomaševski, Katarina 1410

ドマッシュ
Domash, Harry 364

トマティート
Tomatito 1410

トマティト
Tomatito 1410

トマニ
Tomane, Joe 1410

トマノバー
Tomanová, Viera 1410

ドーマラパッリ
Domalpalli, Rajnesh 364

トマリン
Tomalin, Claire 1410

トーマル
Tomar, Narendra Singh 1410

トマール
Tomar, Sandeep 1410

ドマルジェリー
De Margerie, Christophe 339

ドマルジュリ
De Margerie, Christophe 339

ド・マレルブ
De Malherbe, Virginia Arraga 339

トーマン
Thoman, Nick 1397
Toman, Michael A. 1410

ドーマン
Doman, Alex 364
Doman, Douglas 364
Doman, Glenn 364
Doman, Glenn J. 364
Doman, Janet 364
Dorman, Brandon 368
Dorman, Colin Cresswell 368
Dorman, David W. 368
Dorman, Gary J. 368
Dorman, Sam 368

ドーマンズ
Dormans, Joris 368

ドマンスキー
Domanski, Don 364

トーミ
Thome, Jim 1399

トーミー
Thome, Jim 1399

ドミィトリエフ
Dmitriev, Nikolai 360

トミチェビッチ
Tomicevic, Marko 1411

トミック
Tomić, Tomislav 1411

トミッチ
Tomiq, Radojica 1411

ドミトラシュ
Dmytrash, Olena 360

ドミトリーヴ
Dmitriev, Valentine 360

ドミトリエフ
Dmitriev, Denis 360

ドミトリエワ
Dmitrieva, Liudmila 360

ドミトリエンコ
Dmitriyenko, Mariya 360

ドミトリューク
Dmitruk, Valeri 360

ドミニ
Domini, Amy L. 364

ドミニク・ブシェ
Bouchet, Dominique 166

トミネ
Tomine, Adrian 1411

ドミネリ
Dominelli, Lena 364

ドミノ
Domino, Fats 364

ドミル
DeMille, Nelson 340

ドミーン
Domin, Hilde 364

ドミンゲス
Domingues, Ernesto Horacio 364
Domingues, Leticia 364
Dominguez, Alvaro 364
Dominguez, Carlos 364
Dominguez, Julián 364
Domínguez, Marco 364
Dominguez, Matt 364
Dominguez Asensio, Nuria 364
Dominguez Lara, Monica Patricia 364

ドミンゲス・アリオサ
Domínguez Ariosa, Estela Marta 364

ドミンゲス・オルティス
Domínguez Ortiz, Antonio 364

ドミンゲス・ビゲラ
Domínguez Viguera, Carlos 364

ドミンゲス・ブリト
Domínguez Brito, Francisco 364

ドミンゴ
Domingo, Gregory 364
Domingo, Plácido 364
Santo-Domingo, Alejandro 1240

ドミンゴス
Domingos, Wagner 364

トム
Thom, Gertel 1396
Thom, Randy 1396
Thom, René 1396
Thom, Stephen R. 1396
Tom, James 1410
Tom, Jessica 1410
Tom, Peeping 1410
Tom, Peter 1410
Tom, Teri 1410
Tomb, David A. 1410

ドーム
Dohm, James M. 363

ド・ムオイ
Do Muoi 365

ドー・ムオイ
Do Muoi 365

トムキンス
Tomkins, James 1411

トムキンズ
Tomkins, Calvin 1411
Tomkins, James 1411
Tompkins, Heelan 1411

ドムク
Domke, Todd 365

ドムシャイト‐ベルク
Domscheit-Berg, Daniel 365

ドムシャイトベルク
Domscheit-Berg, Daniel 365

トムズ
Tomes, Susan 1411
Toms, David 1411

トムスコル
Tomscoll, Tommy 1411

トムスン
Thomson, Keith 1400
Tomsen, Mai-Lan 1411

トムセット
Thomsett, Michael C. 1400
Thomsett, Rob 1400

トムセン
Thomsen, Anne Lolk 1400
Thomsen, J. 1400
Thomsen, Kåre 1400
Thomsen, Mark H. 1400
Thomsen, Mark W. 1400
Thomsen, Steen 1400

トムセンフアタガ
Thomsen-fuataga, Kaino 1400

トムソン
Thomson, Anne 1400
Thomson, Colin E. 1400
Thomson, David 1400
Thomson, Dorothy Lampen 1400
Thomson, Eddie 1400
Thomson, Emma 1400
Thomson, Harry 1400
Thomson, Keith 1400
Thomson, Kenneth 1401
Thomson, Pat 1401
Thomson, Paul 1401
Thomson, R. 1401
Thomson, Rob 1401
Thomson, Robert James 1401
Thomson, Ruth 1401
Thomson, Sarah 1401
Thomson, Sarah L. 1401
Thomson, William 1401

ドムニナ
Domnina, Oksana 365

トムパート
Tompert, Ann 1411

トムプキンズ
Tompkins, Peter 1411

トムプスン
Thompson, Dorothy 1399

トムプソン
Thompson, Michael 1400

ドムブロフスキス
Dombrovskis, Valdis 364

ドムラチェワ
Domracheva, Darya 365

トムリエサ
Tomuriesa, Douglas 1411

トムリン
Tomblin, Gill 1410
Tomlin, Chris 1411
Tomlin, Jenny 1411
Tomlin, Josh 1411
Tomlin, Lily 1411
Tomlin, Mike 1411

トムリンソン
Tomlinson, Alan 1411
Tomlinson, Charles 1411
Tomlinson, Christopher 1411
Tomlinson, Eric 1411
Tomlinson, Jane 1411
Tomlinson, Janis A. 1411
Tomlinson, John 1411
Tomlinson, Kelby 1411
Tomlinson, LaDainian 1411
Tomlinson, Laken 1411
Tomlinson, Louis 1411
Tomlinson, Patrick 1411
Tomlinson, Paul 1411
Tomlinson, Raymond 1411
Tomlinson, Sally 1411

ド・ムーロン
De Meuron, Pierre 340

トーメ
Thome, Jim 1399

トメ
Tome, David 1410

ドメ
Demez, Colette 340

トーメイ
Thome, Jim 1399

トメイ
Tomei, Manuela 1410
Tomei, Marisa 1410

トメイン
Tomeing, Litokwa 1411

ドメイン
Demaine, Erik D. 339
トメガドグベ
Tomegah-dogbe, Victoire Sidemeho 1410
ドメシーヌ
Demessine, Michèle 340
トメスク
Tomescu, Constantina 1411
トメック
Tomek, Ellen 1411
ドメック・ガルシア
Domecq Garcia, Manuel 364
ド・メディロス
De Medeiros, Michael 340
ドメニチ
Domenici, Pete V. 364
ドメネク
Domenech, Jaume 364
Domenech, Raymond 364
トメノフ
Tmenov, Tamerlan 1407
トメンコ
Tomenko, Mikola 1411
トモヴィッチ
Tomovic, Nenad 1411
トモダ
Tomoda, Kiichiro 1411
ドモトリエワ
Dmitrieva, Daria 360
トモフスカ
Tomovska, Marta Arsovska 1411
ドモホフスキ
Dmochowski, Piotr 360
トモリ
Tomori, Fikayo 1411
ド・モンブリアル
De Montbrial, Thierry 341
ドモンブリアル
De Montbrial, Thierry 341
トヤド
Toyad, Leo Michael 1416
トー・ユエン
Toe Yuen 1408
ドュドイト
Dudoit, Sandrine 377
ドュリュ＝ベラ
Duru-Bellat, Marie 384
トュルコット
Turcotte, Mathieu 1427
ドュルセ
Durce, Maguy 383
トヨトシ
Toyotoshi, Naoyuki 1416
ドヨン
Doyon, Patrick 372
トラ
Tola, Betty 1409
Tola, Tamirat 1409
Tora, Apisai 1412
Tora, James 1412
トラー
Toler, Greg 1409
ドラ
Dora, Vontarrius 367
ドラー
Dolar, Mladen 363
トライ
Trye, Hindolo Sumanguru 1423
ドライ
Dry, Sarah 375
トライアー
Treier, Daniel J. 1419
ドライアー
Dreyer, Eileen 374
トライアス
Tieryas, Peter 1404
ドライヴァー
Driver, Janine 374
トライオン
Tryon, Amy 1423
ドライカース
Dreikurs, Rudolf 373
Dreikurs, Sadie 373
トライコビッチ
Trajkovic, Milan 1417
トライコフ
Traikov, Traicho 1417
トライコフスキ
Trajkovski, Aleksandar 1417
Trajkovski, Boris 1417
ドライスデイル
Drysdale, John 376
ドライスデール
Drysdale, Mahé 376
Drysdale, Peter 376
ドラーイスマ
Draaisma, Douwe 372
ドライゼク
Dryzek, John S. 376
トライツ
Trites, Roberta Seelinger 1420
ドライデン
Dryden, Delphine 375
Dryden, Ken 376
Dryden, Spencer 376
Dryden, Windy 376
トライドス
Trajdos, Martyna 1417
トライーニ
Traini, Agostino 1417
トライネン
Treinen, Blake 1419
ドライバー
Driver, Adam 374
Driver, Michael J. 374
ドライバーグ
Dryburgh, Alastair 375
トライブ
Tribe, John 1420
Tribe, Steve 1420
ドライフ
Drife, James Owen 374
ドライファス
Dreyfuss, Richard 374
ドライフス
Dreifuss, Ruth 373
ドライヤー
Dreyer, Danny 374
Dreyer, Katherine 374
ドライリング
Dreiling, Vicky 373
トライロン
Trairong, Suwannakhiri 1417
トライン
Trine, Greg 1420
トラウ
Traugh, Cecelia 1418
ドラヴィエ
Delavier, Frédéric 337
トラヴィス
Travis, Cecil Howell 1418
Travis, Daryl 1418
Travis, Randy 1418
Travis, Sarah 1418
トラヴィス - ビルダール
Travis-Bildahl, Sandra 1418
トラウィック
Trawick, Brynden 1418
トラヴェルソ
Traverso, Enzo 1418
トラヴォルタ
Travolta, John 1418
トラウゴット
Traugott, Elizabeth Closs 1418
トラウト
Traut, Dennis 1418
Trout, Jack 1422
Trout, Mike 1422
Trout, Nick 1422
Trout, Shirley K. 1422
トラウトマン
Trautman, Melissa 1418
トラヴニー
Trawny, Peter 1418
ドラウニンダロ
Draunidalo, Savenaca 373
トラウブ
Traub, Ellis 1418
トラウフラー
Trauffler, Gaston 1418
トラウンスタイン
Trounstine, Jean 1422
ドラオッタ
Drahotta, Felix 373
トラオーレ
Traoré, Lacina 1417
トラオレ
Traore, Abou-Bakar 1417
Traore, Adama 1417
Traore, Alain 1417
Traore, Ayouba 1417
Traore, Bertrand 1417
Traore, Clémence 1417
Traoré, Daouda 1417
Traoré, Demba 1417
Traoré, Dioncounda 1417
Traore, Ibrahima 1417
Traoré, Lacina 1417
Traoré, Lassana 1417
Traore, Maharafa 1417
Traore, Mamadou Lamine 1417
Traoré, Mamadou Namory 1417
Traore, Mohamed 1417
Traoré, Moussa 1417
Traoré, Salif 1418
Traoré, Sékou 1418
Traore, Seydou 1418
Traore, Toure Alima 1418
Traoré, Yacouba 1418
ドラガサキス
Dragasakis, Yannis 372
トラカス
Trakas, Sotirios 1417
トラガノフ
Tolaganov, Kozim 1409
ドラガンヤ
Draganja, Duje 372
ドラギ
Draghi, Mario 372
ドラギッチ
Dragic, Goran 372
トラキディス
Tsolakidis, Vasileios 1424
ドラギン
Dragin, Saša 372
トラク
Trakh, Maz 1417
ドラクザル
Draksal, Michael 373
ドラクシッチ
Draksic, Rok 373
トラクスラー
Traxler, Hans 1418
Traxler, Julie 1418
ドラクスラー
Draxler, Julian 373
ドラクスル
Draxl, Ernst 373
ドラクスレル
Draxler, Juraj 373
ドラグティノビッチ
Dragutinović, Diana 373
トラクテンバーグ
Trachtenberg, Robert 1416
ドラグネア
Dragnea, Liviu 372
ドラグネバ
Dragneva, Izabela 372
ドラグネフ
Dlagnev, Tervel 360
ドラグ・パリウ
Dragu Paliu, Anca Dana 373
ドラクール
Delacourt, Grégoire 335
ドラグレスク
Dragulescu, Marian 372
ドラーグン
Dragun, Andrew K. 372
ドラゴイ
Dragoi, Gabriela 372
ドラコヴァ
Drakova, Anastasiia 373
ドラゴヴィッチ
Dragovic, Aleksandar 372
ドラゴフスキ
Dragowski, Bartlomiej 372
ドラゴンワゴン
Dragonwagon, Crescent 372
トラサルディ
Trussardi, Francesco 1423
ドラジッチ
Draghici, Marina 372
ドラジャト
Drajat, Ben Perkasa 373
ドラジャン
Dragin, Dimitri 372
ドラシュコビッチ
Drašković, Vuk 373
Draskovics, Tibor 373
トラジュコワ
Trazhukova, Inna 1418
ドラジン
Drazhin, Vladimir N. 373
トラース
Tolaas, Sissel 1409

トラス
Torres, Xavier 1413
Truss, Elizabeth 1422
Truss, Lynne 1422
Truss, Warren 1423
トラスク
Trask, Haunani-Kay 1418
トラーゼ
Toradze, Aleksandr 1412
ドラツェフ
Drattsev, Evgeny 373
ドラッカー
Drucker, Doris 375
Drucker, Peter Ferdinand 375
Druker, Brian J. 375
ドラッカーマン
Druckerman, Pamela 375
トラックス
Trucks, Derek 1422
ドラッグセット
Dragset, Ingar 372
ドラックマン
Drachman, Virginia G. 372
トラックル
Truckle, Brian 1422
トラッサルディ
Trussardi, Francesco 1423
トラッソーニ
Trussoni, Danielle 1423
ドラッツィオ
D'Orazio, Costantino 367
トラットー
Trattou, Justin 1418
トラッドギル
Trudgill, Peter 1422
ドラットフィールド
Dratfield, Jim 373
トラットラー
Trattler, Bill 1418
トラッパー
Trepper, Terry S. 1419
トラップ
Trapp, Agathe 1418
Trapp, Kevin 1418
Trapp, Robert G. 1418
ドラップス
Draps, Pierre 373
ドラトゥール
Delatour, Calixte 336
ドラドリエール
Deladrière, Jean-Luc 335
トラニアン
Toranian, Valérie 1412
ドラニコフ
Dranikoff, Lee 373
ドラーネン
Draanen, Wendelin Van 372
ドラノア
Delannoy, Jean 336
ドラノエ
Delanoe, Bertrand 336
Delanoe, Pierre 336
ドラノブ
Dranove, David 373
ドラノワ
Delannoy, Jean 336
トラバシオ
Travascio, Victoria 1418
トラバース
Travers, Mary 1418
Travers, Paul 1418
トラバース＝スペンサー
Travers-Spencer, Simon 1418
トラパットーニ
Trapattoni, Giovanni 1418
トラーパニ
Trapani, Francesco 1418
トラパニ
Trapani, Gina 1418
トラバント
Trabant, Jurgen 1416
トラビ
Torabi, Nooruddin 1412
トラビエソ
Travieso, Nick 1418
トラビス
Travis, Cecil Howell 1418
Travis, Devon 1418
Travis, Mark W. 1418
Travis, Ross 1418
Travis, Sam 1418
ド・ラ・ビーニュ
De La Bigne, Antoine Lepetit 335
ドラファン
Draffan, George 372
トラフォード
Trafford, Jeremy 1417
ドラフォン
Delafon, Marie 335
トラブショー
Trubshaw, Brian 1422
ドラフト
Dragt, Tonke 372
トラーブリー
Torabli, Hamid 1412
ドラブル
Drabble, Margaret 372
ドラーベク
Drábek, Jaromír 372
ド・ラ・ベドワイエール
De la Bédoyère, Camilla 335
トラベルシ
Trabelsi, Mohamed 1416
トラベルソ
Traverso, Debra Koontz 1418
トラベル・トマス
Traver Tomás, Vicente 1418
ドラボ
Drabo, Gaoussou 372
ドラポウ
Drapeau, Anne Seibold 373
ドラホトバ
Drahotova, Anezka 373
ドラボラ
Dlabola, Otto 360
トラボルタ
Travolta, John 1418
ドラマニ
Dlamani, Lutfo 360
Dramani, Dama 373
ドラマネ
Dramane, Koné 373
Dramane, Sangare Abou 373
ドラマール
Delamare, François 336
ドラマン
Dramane, Koné 373
ドラミニ
Dlamini, Absalom 360
Dlamini, Barnabas Sibusiso 360
Dlamini, Bathabile 360
Dlamini, Bathabile Olive 360
Dlamini, Clement 360
Prince Dlamini, David 360
Dlamini, Gideon 360
Dlamini, Lindiwe 360
Dlamini, Lutfo 360
Dlamini, Mabili 360
Dlamini, Martin 360
Dlamini, Mathendele 360
Dlamini, Mduduzi 360
Dlamini, Mntonzima 360
Dlamini, Ntuthuko 360
Dlamini, Paul 360
Dlamini, Phetsile 360
Dlamini, Sibusiso 360
Dlamini, Themba 360
ドラミニ・ズマ
Dlamini-Zuma, Nkosazana 360
トラム
Tram Iv Tek 1417
Trm Iv Tek 1421
ドラム
Drum, Mary 375
Dulam, Sendenjav 379
トラムズ
Trahms, Creistine M. 1417
ドラメ
Drame, Boukary 373
Drame, Kandioura 373
トラメル
Trammell, Terrence 1417
ドラモット
Delamotte, Guibourg 336
ドラモンド
Drummond, Allan 375
Drummond, Andre 375
Drummond, Bill 375
Drummond, Kurtis 375
Drummond, Laurie Lynn 375
Drummond, Mary Jane 375
Drummond, Michael 375
Drummond, Michael F. 375
Drummond, Richard Henry 375
Drummond, Sarah 375
Drumonnd, Richard Henry 375
ド・ラ・ルペル
De La Rupelle, Guy 336
ドラレクス
Delalex, Hélène 336
ドラロジエール
Delarosiere, Jacques 336
トーラン
Tauran, Jean-Louis 1384
トラン
Toan, Tran Le Quoc 1407
Train, Michel 1417
Tran, Mariana 1417
Tran, Mervin 1417
Tran, Quoc Cuong 1417
Tran, Thi Ngoc Truc 1417
ドーラン
Dolan, Alan 363
Dolan, James 363
Dolan, John Lawrence 363
Dolan, Lawrence 363
Dolan, Paul 363
Dolan, Robert J. 363
Doran, Gregory 367
Doran, Jamie 367
ドラン
Dolan, Cam 363
Dolan, Xavier 363
Dolan, Yvonne M. 363
Doran, Rodney L. 367
Doran, Teresa 367
Dorin, Francoise 367
Dorin Habert, Marie 367
トラン・アン・ウング
Tran Anh Hung 1417
トラン・アン・ユン
Tran Anh Hung 1417
トラン・アン・ユング
Tran Anh Hung 1417
トラン・ヴァン・トゥ
Tran Van Tho 1417
トラン・ヴァン・トウ
Tran Van Tho 1417
トラン・クアン・ハイ
Tran Quang Hai 1417
ドランゴ
Drango, Spencer 373
トランコフ
Trankov, Maxim 1417
トランシャン
Tranchant, Géraldine 1417
トーランス
Torrance, James 1413
Torrance, Thomas Forsyth 1413
トランス
Torrance, George W. 1413
トラーンストレーメル
Tranströmer, Tomas 1417
トランストレーメル
Tranströmer, Tomas 1417
トランストレンメル
Tranströmer, Tomas 1417
トランストロンメル
Tranströmer, Tomas 1417
ドランテ
Dorantes 367
トランティ
Tranthi, Thuy 1417
トランティニャン
Trintignant, Jean-Louis 1420
Trintignant, Marie 1420
トラン・ティ・マイ・ホア
Tran Thi Mai Hoa 1417
トーランド
Toland, John 1409
トラン・ニュット
Tran-Nhut 1417
ドランノア
Delannoy, Jean 336
トランプ
Trump, Donald John 1422
Trump, Ivanka Marie 1422
トランブル
Trumbull, Douglas 1422
トランブレ
Tremblay, François-Louis 1419
トランボ
Trumbo, Mark 1422
トランボア

Trumbore, Cindy 1422
トランリー
Tranly, Guy 1417
トーリ
Torre, Frank 1413
Torre, Joe 1413
トーリー
Thole, Josh 1396
Torrey, Edwin Fuller 1413
トリー
Tolley, Anne 1409
Tolley, Justin 1409
ドーリー
Dawley, Evan N. 328
Dooley, Jim 367
Doorley, Scott 367
トリアー
Trier, Lars von 1420
トリアカ
Triaca, Jorge 1420
トリアス・デ・ベス
Trias de Bes, Fernando 1420
トリアーノ
Triano, Jay 1420
トリアン
Toljan, Jeremy 1409
ドリアン
Dorian, Jean Pierre 367
Dorian, Marguerite 367
ドリアンスキー
Dryansky, Gerry 375
Dryansky, Joanne 375
トリアンディス
Triandis, Harry Charalambos 1420
ドーリアント
Dorleant, Makinton 368
トリイフォッシュ
Tolgfors, Sten 1409
トリヴァー
Toliver, Raymond F. 1409
ドリーヴァー
Dreaver, Jim 373
トリヴェディ
Trivedi, Kirti 1421
ドリエージュ
Deliège, Robert 337
ドリエセン
Driessen, Paul 374
トリエル
Trier, Lars von 1420
トリエルヴェレール
Trierweiler, Valerie 1420
トリエンテ
Torriente, Idel 1413
トリオー
Triau, Christophe 1420
トリオラ
Toriola, Segun 1413
ドリオン
Dorion, Christiane 367
トリガノ
Trigano, Gilbert 1420
トリグボフ
Triguboff, Harry 1420
トリケット
Trickett, Libby 1420
トリゲロス
Trigueros, Jose Luis 1420
トリゴー
Tregoe, Benjamin B. 1419
ドリゴ
Drigo, Johnson 374
トリゴソ・アグド
Trigoso Agudo, José Gonzalo 1420
トリコ・ロハス
Torrico Rojas, Celima 1413
トリーザイズ
Trezise, Rhona 1420
トリジアーニ
Trigiani, Adriana 1420
トリシェ
Trichet, Jean-Claude 1420
Trichet, Pierrette 1420
トリシエ
Troussier, Philippe 1422
ドリーシャー
Drescher, Justin 374
トリース
Treece, Patricia 1418
ドリス
Dorais, M.A. 367
Doris, Troy 367
Dries, Luk van den 374
Drys, Georgios 376
ドリズィン
Drizin, Steven A. 374
ドリスケル
Driskel, Jeff 374
ドリスコール
Driscoll, Laura 374
Driscoll, Michael 374
ドリスコル
Driscoll, Amy 374
Driscoll, Dawn-Marie 374
Driscoll, Jon 374
Driscoll, Katherine 374
Driscoll, Marcy P. 374
Driscoll, M.J. 374
トリスター
Treaster, Joseph B. 1418
トリステム
Tristem, Ben 1420
ドリスデル
Drisdelle, Rosemary 374
トリストラム
Tristram, Claire 1420
トリスラー
Trissler, Brandon 1420
ドリスレン
Dorjsuren, Munkhbayar 368
ドリゼ
Dolidze, Victor 364
ドリーゼン
Driesen, Steffen 374
トリソ
Tolisso, Corentin 1409
トリソン
Tollison, Robert D. 1410
ドリチェンコ
Dorichenko, Sergeĭ Aleksandrovich 367
ドリツァス
Dritsas, Thodoris 374
トリッガー
Trigger, Bruce G. 1420
トリックス
Tricks, Henry 1420
トリッグス
Triggs, Andrew 1420
Triggs, Teal 1420
ドリッサー
deLisser, Peter 338
ドリッジャー
Driedger, Crystal 374
トリッチャー
Tritscher, Bernhard 1421
トリッツ
Tritz, Gerry 1421
トリッティン
Trittin, Jürgen 1421
トリッピ
Trippi, Peter 1420
トリッピアー
Trippier, Kieran 1420
トリップ
Tripp, Charles 1420
Tripp, Jordie 1420
Trippe, William 1420
トリート
Treat, John W. 1418
トリート・ジェイコブソン
Treat-Jacobson, Diane 1418
ドリドビッチ
Dolidovich, Sergei 364
ドリトル
Doolittle, Nancy D. 367
トリトン
Tritton, D.J. 1421
ドリナー
Doliner, Roy 364
ドリーニュ
Deligne, Pierre 337
ドリネンベルク
Drinnenberg, Julia 374
トリバー
Tolliver, Anthony 1410
Tolliver, Ashur 1410
トリバース
Trivers, Robert 1421
トリパティ
Tripathi, Hridayesh 1420
トリビー
Tribby, MaryEllen 1420
トリビオ
Toribio, César Pina 1413
トリビオン
Toribiong, Johnson 1413
トリビザス
Trivizas, Eugene 1421
トリブイヤール
Tribouillard, Daniel 1420
トリフォナス
Trifonas, Peter Pericles 1420
トリフォーニ
Trifoni, Jasmina 1420
トリフォノフ
Trifonov, Daniil 1420
トリフォノポウロス
Tryphonopoulos, Demetres P. 1423
トリフォン
Tryphon, Anastasia 1423
トリフソン
Tollifson, Joan 1410
ドリフテ
Drifte, Collette 374
Drifte, Reinhard 374
トリブル
Trible, Phyllis 1420
トリプルH
Triple H 1420
トリプレット
Triplett, William C., Ⅱ 1420
ドリベイララモス
D'oliveira Ramos, Américo 364
トリベット
Tribbett, Tye 1420
トリベニョ・チャン・ハン
Triveño Chan Jan, Gladys 1421
トリベリ
Trivelli, Carolina 1421
トリホス
Torrijos, Martin 1414
トリマー
Trimmer, Joseph F. 1420
ドリムレン
Drimmelen, J.van 374
トリメイン
Tremaine, Frank 1419
トリヤトノ
Triyatno, Triyatno 1421
ドリュー
Drew, David 374
Drew, Larry 374
Drew, Naomi 374
Drew, Ray 374
Drew, Robert Lincoln 374
Drew, Ronnie 374
Drew, Stephen 374
ドリュイエ
Druillet, Philippe 375
ドリュオン
Druon, Maurice 375
トリュオング
Truong, Nicolas 1422
ドリューケ
Drüke, Milda 375
ドリュケール
Drucker, Marie 375
ドリュスカット
Druskat, Vanessa Urch 375
トリュフォー
Truffaut, François 1422
ドリュモー
Delumeau, Jean 339
トリユルヴァイレール
Trierweiler, Valerie 1420
トリユルバイレール
Trierweiler, Valerie 1420
トリュンパー
Trümper, Joachim 1422
トリリーニ
Trillini, Giovanna 1420
トリリョ・フィゲロア・イ・マルティネス・コンデ
Trillo Figueroa y Martínez-Conde, Federico 1420
トリリン
Trillin, Calvin 1420
トリリング
Trilling, Bernie 1420
ドリール
Doreal, M. 367
ドリロン
Drilon, Alexander E. 374
Drilon, Franklin M. 374
トーリン
Tolin, David F. 1409

ト

トリン
Trinh, Thi Minh-Ha 1420
ドリン
Dolin, Eric Jay 364
Dolin, Tim 364
Doling, Tim 364
トリンカ
Trinca, Jasmine 1420
Trynka, Paul 1423
トリンカ・パサット
Trinca-pasat, Louis 1420
ドーリング
Dorling, Daniel 368
ドリンクウォーター
Drinkwater, Danny 374
ドリンクホール
Drinkhall, Paul 374
ドーリンジャー
Doeringer, Peter B. 362
トリンスキー
Tolinski, Brad 1409
トリンダデ
Trindade, José 1420
トリンダール
Trindall, Susan 1420
トリントン
Tollington, Tony 1410
トリンブル
Trimble, Chris 1420
Trimble, David 1420
Trimble, Irene 1420
Trimble, Melo 1420
トール
Thor, Annika 1401
Toll, Ian W. 1409
Tolle, Eckhart 1409
Tort, Patrick 1414
ドール
Dhoore, Jolien 349
Dole, Elizabeth Hanford 363
Dole, George F. 363
Doll, Beth 364
Doll, Richard 364
ドル
Doll, Richard 364
ドルー
Drew, Jennifer 374
ドルーアン
Drouin, Jean-Marc 375
ドルアン
Drouin, Derek 375
ドルーイン
Drouin, Derek 375
トールヴァルト
Thorwald, Jürgen 1402
トールヴァルド
Thorwald, Jürgen 1402
ドルウィック
Dolwick, William 364
トルヴィル
Trouville, Matthew 1422
ドルエ
Druet, Isabelle 375
ドルーエット
Drewett, Brad 374
トルエバ
Trueba, Fernando 1422
トルガ
Tolga, Zengin 1409
ドルーカー
Druker, Steven M. 375
トルカチェワ
Tolkacheva, Maria 1409
ドルギエル
Dolghieru, Vasile 363
ドルギフ
Dolgikh, Maria 363
トルキルセン
Thorkildsen, Inga Marte 1401
トルキルドセン
Thorkildsen, Andreas 1401
トールキン
Tolkien, Baillie 1409
Tolkien, Christopher 1409
Tolkien, Simon 1409
トルキン
Tolkin, Mike 1409
トルクノフ
Torkunov, Anatoliĭ Vasil'evich 1413
トルクマニ
Turkmani, Hassan 1427
トルグレン
Thorgren, Sven 1401
トルケシュ
Türkeş, Tuğrul 1427
トルケスタニ
Torkestani, Farahnaz 1413
トルケマーダ・シド
Torquemada Cid, Ricard 1413
ドルーゲンブルート
Droogenbroodt, Germain 375
ドルーゲンブロート
Droogenbroodt, Germain 375
トルコウスキー
Tolkowsky, Jean Paul 1409
ドルゴフ
Dolhov, Maksym 364
ドルゴリョフ
Dolgolev, Vasily B. 363
ドルゴル
Dolgor, Badraagiin 363
ドルゴルスレン・ダグワドルジ
Dolgorsürengiin Dagvadorj 363
ドルゴレフ
Dolgolev, Vasily B. 363
ドルゴワ
Dolgova, Irina 363
ドルサンビル
Dorsainvil, Daniel 368
ドルシー
Dorsey, Gary 368
ドルジ
Dorji, Chenkyab 368
Dorji, Damcho 368
Dorji, Kinzang 368
Dorji, Leki 368
Dorji, Minjur 368
Dorji, Namgay 368
Dorji, Nedup 368
Dorji, Rinzin 368
Dorji, Yeshey 368
Dorji, Yeshi 368
トルシエ
Troussier, Philippe 1422
トールシェーテル
Torseter, Oyvind 1414
トルシエール
Troussier, Philippe 1422
ドルジェ・ワンモ・ワンチュック
Ashi Dorji Wangmo Wangchuck 63
ドルジスレンスミヤ
Dorjsuren, Sumiya 368
トルシッチ
Tolušić, Tomislav 1410
ドルジニャンブオトゴンダライ
Dorjnyambuu, Otgondalai 368
ドルジャーク
Dolšak, Nives 364
トルジャーン
Torgyán, József 1413
ドルシュ
Dorsch, Niklas 368
トルジュマン
Tordjman, Nathalie 1412
トルシン
Trooshin, Igor' 1421
トルジーン
Tolzien, Scott 1410
トルジンカ
Trzynka, Penny 1423
ドルジーン・ガルマー
Dorjiin Garmaa 368
ドルジンツレン
Doljintseren, B.O. 364
トールズ
Toles, Andrew 1409
ドルース
DeLuce, Daniel 339
Druce, Duncan 375
Druce, Madeline 375
トルスタヤ
Tolstaia, Natalia Olegovna 1410
Tolstaya, Tatiyana Nikitichna 1410
トルステニャク
Trstenjak, Tina 1422
トルステンコ
Tolstenko, Petr 1410
ドルスト
Dorst, Tankred 368
トルストウホフ
Tolstoukhov, Anatoliy 1410
トールスドッティル
Thorsdottir, Eythora 1402
トールソン
Tolleson, Shawn 1409
トルダ
Torda, Ilona 1412
ドルタ
Dorta, Kristen Pollack 368
トルタハーダ
Tortajada, Ana 1414
トールダルソン
Þórðarson, Guðlaugur Þór 1401
トルチアック＝デュヴァル
Trzeciak-Duval, Alexandra 1423
ドルチェ
Dolce, Domenico 363
Dolce, Lucia 363
トールチーフ
Tallchief, Maria 1378
トルチュ
Tortu, Christian 1414
トルチンスキー
Tolchinsky, David E. 1409
トルツ
Toltz, Steve 1410
ドルツァス
Droutsas, Dimitris 375
トルテローロ
Torterolo, Anna 1414
トルドー
Trudeau, Justin 1422
Trudeau, Kevin 1422
ドルト
Dolto, Francoise 364
Dolto-Tolitch, Catherine 364
トルトーサカブレラ
Tortosa Cabrera, Jesus 1414
トルトネフ
Trutnev, Yury P. 1423
トルートマン
Troutman, Anne C. 1422
ドールトン
Dalton, David 315
Dalton, David J. 315
ドルトン
Dalton, Annie 315
Dalton, Pamela 315
Dalton, Peter 315
トルナトーレ
Tornatore, Giuseppe 1413
ドルニェイ
Dörnyei, Zoltán 368
ドルニチャヌ
Dolniceanu, Tiberiu 364
ドルニック
Dolnick, Edward 364
トルネウス
Torneus, Michel 1413
トールネケ
Törneke, Niklas 1413
トルネ・ベッテル
Thorne Vetter, Alfredo Eduardo 1401
トルネ・レオン
Thorne Leon, Jaime 1401
ドルネレス
Dornelles, Francisco 368
トルネンコフ
Trunenkov, Dmitry 1422
トルノ
Tolno, Pierrette 1410
ドルノウシェク
Drnovšek, Janez 374
トルハ
Tolchah, Hasan 1409
トルバ
Tolba, Mohamed Ould 1409
Toleba, Soumanou 1409
トルバイ
Turbay Ayala, Julio Cesar 1427
トルバイ・アヤラ
Turbay Ayala, Julio Cesar 1427
トルバート
Tolbert, Mike 1409
Torbert, William R. 1412
ドルバニ
Dorbani, Lakhdar 367

ドルバル
Delval, Marie-Hélène 339
トールバルズ
Torvalds, Linus Benedict 1414
トルバルズ
Torvalds, Linus Benedict 1414
ドルビー
Dalby, Andrew 313
Dolby, Ray M. 363
トルヒジョ・カルデナス
Trujillo Cárdenas, Carmen 1422
トルヒジョ・モリ
Trujillo Mori, Edmer 1422
トルーヒヨ
Trujillo, Sergio 1422
トルヒーリョ
Trujillo, María Antonia 1422
トルヒリョ
Trujillo, Rafael 1422
ドルービン
Drubin, Daniel T. 375
トループ
Troup, Gary 1422
Troupe, Quincy 1422
ドルフマイスター
Dorfmeister, Michaela 367
ドルフマン
Dorfman, Ariel 367
ドルベルグ
Dolberg, Kasper 363
トールボット
Talbott, Strobe 1378
ドルボワ
Delevoye, Jean-Paul 337
ドルマル
Dormal, Alexis 368
トールマン
Tollman, Peter 1410
トルーマン
Trueman, Terry 1422
Truman, Margaret 1422
トルマン
Tolman, Anton O. 1410
Tolman, Marije 1410
Tolman, Ronald 1410
ドルマン
Dolman, Everett Carl 364
Dormann, Jürgen 368
ドルミッチ
Drmic, Josip 374
トールミン
Toulmin, Camilla 1414
ドルムシュ
Durmus, Osman 384
トルモフ
Tolmoff, Kati 1410
ドルヨゴトフ
Tserenkhand, Dorjgotov 1423
ドルリー
Drury, Fritz 375
ドルリグジャブ
Dorligjav, Dambii 368
ドルリュ
Delerue, Paul-Henri 337
ドルリュー
Delerue, Paul-Henri 337
トル・ロア
Tol Lah 1409
トルロポワ
Torlopova, Nadezda 1413
トルン
Thorn, Gaston 1401
ドルン
Dorn, Ludwik 368
Dorn, Thea 368
ドルンダ
Durunda, Marina 384
トールン・ビューロ・ヒューベ
Tourun Bulow-Hube, Vivianna 1415
トーレ
Torre, Joe 1413
Touré, Amadou Toumani 1415
トレ
Trez, Alain 1419
Trez, Denise 1419
ドーレ
Dhoore, Jolien 349
ドレ
Doray, Malika 367
Dore, Domani 367
Doré, Durus Yalé 367
ドレー
Deray, Jacques 344
*Dr.*Dre 361
ドレーアー
Dreher, Walther 373
トーレアイズ
Torreyes, Ronald 1413
ドレアック
Doleac, Charles B. 363
トレアフォア
Toleafoa, Apulu Faafisi 1409
トレアルバ
Torrealba, Francisco 1413
トレイ
Trey, Torsten 1419
ドレイ
Delay, Florence 337
Dray, Jim 373
ドレイアー
Dreher, Henry 373
ドレイク
Drake 373
Drake, Dian 373
Drake, Hal 373
Drake, Kenyan 373
Drake, Marjorie 373
Drake, Oliver 373
Drake, Olivia 373
Drake, Robert E. 373
Drake, Salamanda 373
Drake, Shannon 373
トレイシー
Tracey, Doreen 1416
Tracy, Brian 1416
Tracy, Diane 1416
Tracy, Jack W. 1416
Tracy, Marilyn 1416
Tracy, Moira 1416
Tracy, Pat 1416
Tracy, Paul 1416
Tracy, P.J. 1416
トレイツ
Tracz, Will 1417
ドレイトン
Drayton, Bill 373
トレイナー
Trainor, Conor 1417
ドレイパー
Draper, Jennifer-Lynn 373
Draper, Robert 373
Draper, Sharon Mills 373
ドレイプ
Drape, Joe 373
ドレイファス
Dreyfus, Hubert L. 374
Dreyfus, Suelette 374
Dreyfuss, Richard 374
トレイマニス
Treimanis, Edzus 1419
ドレイミ
al-Dulaimi, Mezher 379
トレイラ
Torreira, Lucas 1413
トレイラー
Trailer, Barry 1417
Traylor, Austin 1418
トレイル
Trail, Lynden 1417
トレイン
Train, John 1417
ドレイン
Drane, John 373
トレヴァー
Trevor, William 1419
トレヴァス
Trevas, Chris 1419
トレヴァーセン
Trevarthen, Colwyn 1419
トレヴァ・ローパー
Trevor-Roper, Hugh Redwald 1419
トレヴァー・ローパー
Trevor-Roper, Hugh Redwald 1419
トレヴィット
Trevitt, Corinne 1419
トレヴィノ
Trevino, Lee 1419
ドレヴィヨン
Drévillon, Hervé 374
トレヴィラヌス
Treviranus, Ofisa 1419
ドレウェット
Drewett, Brad 374
トレヴェニアン
Trevanian 1419
トレェラー
Tröhler, Daniel 1421
トレオ
Toleo, El 1409
トレーガー
Traeger, Jörg 1417
Trager, James C. 1417
ドレーガー
Draeger, Heinz-Joachim 372
ドレガ
Dolega, Marcin 363
Dolega, Robert 363
ドレガー
Dreger, Alice Domurat 373
トレギボフ
Tregybov, Nikita 1419
ドレクスレ
Drexler, Jorge 374
ドレコール
Drecoll, Volker Henning 373
トレザイス
Trezise, Philip Harold 1420
トレーシー
Tracey, Karina 1416
Tracey, Monica W. 1416
Tracey, Ristananna 1416
Tracy, Diane 1416
Tracy, John A. 1416
Tracy, Kristina 1416
Tracy, Mary Fran 1416
Tracy, Paul 1416
Treacy, Michael 1418
Treacy, Sara Louise 1418
ドレーシー
De Lacy, Hugh 335
ドレシーノ
Dressino, Giulio 374
トレジャー
Treasure, Alyxandria 1418
Treasure, Janet 1418
Treasure, Julian 1418
トレーシュ
Trasch, Christiam 1418
トレシューイー
Trethewey, Natasha 1419
トーレス
Torres, Carlos 1413
Torres, Carlos Alberto 1413
Torres, Dara 1413
Torres, Diego 1413
Torres, El 1413
Torres, Fernando 1413
Torres, Gleyber 1413
Torres, J. 1413
Torres, Jose 1413
Torres, Juan Pablo 1413
Torres, Lolita 1413
Torres, Luis E. 1413
Torres, Ramon 1413
Torres, Tico 1413
トレス
Torres, Guillermo 1413
Torres, Maria Santos Tebus 1413
Torres, Mario 1413
Torrès, Olivier 1413
Torres, Oscar Orlando 1413
Torres, Robin Diller 1413
Torres, Rodolfo Marco 1413
Torres, Rosa 1413
ドレーズ
Drèze, Jean 374
ドレス
Dolles, Harald 364
Dress, Robert 374
トーレス＝アルピ
Torres-Arpi, Magdalena E. 1413
トレス・オブレアス
Torres Obleas, Jorge 1413
ドレスタイン
Dorrestein, Renate 368
トレストマン
Trestman, Marc 1419
ドレズナー
Drezner, Daniel W. 374
トレスニオウスキ
Tresniowski, Alex 1419
トレズニヤック
Tresnjak, Darko 1419
トーレスファルコ
Torres Falcó, Jordi 1413
トレスプシュ

ト

Trespeuch, Chloe 1419
トレス・ブリオネス
Torres Briones, Alba Luz 1413
トレスラー
Tressler, S.K. 1419
ドレスラー
Dressler, Joshua 374
Dressler, Larry 374
ドレスレル
Dressler, Stephan 374
トレゼゲ
Trezeguet, David 1420
ドレセル
Dressel, Caeleb 374
ドレーセン
Dreesen, Jaak 373
トレタ
Tréta, Bocary 1419
トレダウェイ
Treadaway, Chris 1418
トレダノ
Toledano, Éric 1409
Toledano, Sidney 1409
トレチオカス
Trečiokas, Kęstutis 1418
トレチャク
Tretiak, Vladislav 1419
Tretyak, Maksym 1419
トレチャコフ
Tretiakov, Alexander 1419
Tretiyakov, Vitalii 1419
Tretyakov, Sergei Olegovich 1419
ドレツキ
Dretske, Fred I. 374
トレッグス
Treggs, Bryce 1418
ドレッサー
Drösser, Christoph 375
ドレッシャー
Drescher, John M. 373
ドレッセル
Dressel, Holly Jewell 374
ドレッセルハウス
Dresselhaus, Mildred Spiewak 374
トレッター
Tretter, JC. 1419
トレッダウェイ
Treadaway, Luke 1418
トレッテル
Trettel, Lidia 1419
トレッドウェル
Treadwell, Laquon 1418
Treadwell, Ty 1418
トレッドウェル-オーウェン
Tredwell-Owen, Caspian 1418
トレド
Toledo, Alejandro 1409
Toledo, Braian 1409
Toledo, Hernan 1409
Toledo, Yasnier 1409
Toledo Lopez, Yasniel 1409
ドレート
Drate, Spencer 373
トレド・マンリケ
Toledo Manrique, Alejandro 1409
トレトーラ
Tretola, Sebastian 1419
トレトラ
Tretola, Rich 1419
トレトリ
Tletli, Slim 1407
トレナート
Trennert, Robert A., Jr. 1419
ドレーニ
Dregni, Michael 373
トレーニン
Trenin, Dmitri 1419
トレネ
Trénet, Charles 1419
トレバー
Trevor, William 1419
ドレーパー
Draper, Warwick 373
トレバサン
Trevathan, Danny 1419
トレバ・ローパー
Trevor-Roper, Hugh Redwald 1419
トレバー・ローパー
Trevor-Roper, Hugh Redwald 1419
トレバーローパー
Trevor-Roper, Hugh Redwald 1419
トレハーン
Treherne, J.E. 1419
トレビシック
Trevithick, Pamela 1419
トレビノ
Trevino, Lee 1419
トレフ
Träff, Åsa 1417
トレフィル
Trefil, James S. 1418
Trefil, Lukas 1418
ドレフュス
Dreifuss, Ruth 373
トレブル
Treboul, Jean-Baptiste 1418
トレベニアン
Trevanian 1419
トレーベン
Treben, Maria 1418
トレホス
Trejos, Alberto 1419
Trejos, Fernando 1419
トレボーラング
Treborlang, Robert 1418
トレホン
Torrejon, Mark 1413
トレマリャ
Tremaglia, Mirko 1419
ドレマン
Dreman, David N. 373
ドレムス
Dorémus, Gaëtan 367
トレムリナス
Tremoulinas, Benoit 1419
トレメイン
Tremain, Chris 1419
Tremain, Rose 1419
Tremayne, Peter 1419
Tremayne, S.K. 1419
トレメル
Trammell, Jeremiah 1417
トレメーン
Tremaine, Frank 1419
トレモリエール
Trémolières, Francois 1419
トレモン
Traimond, Jean-Manuel 1417
トレモンティ
Tremonti, Giulio 1419
ドレーヤー
Dreher, Anna Ursula 373
ドレーリ
Dorelli, Peter 367
ドレル
Drell, Sidney David 373
トレルス
Trelles, Miguel 1419
ドレルム
Delerm, Philippe 337
トレロア
Treloar, Debi 1419
ドーレン
Doolen, Gary D. 367
Doren, Dennis M. 367
ドレン
Doren, Kim 367
トレンク
Trenc, Milan 1419
ドレングソン
Drengson, Alan R. 373
トレンザーノ
Torrenzano, Richard 1413
トレンサム
Trentham, Laura 1419
トーレンス
Torrence, David 1413
Torrence, Phillip D. 1413
Torrens, Luis 1413
ドレンスキー
Dorensky, Sergey L. 367
トレンダフィロワ
Trendafilova, Milena 1419
トレンチノ
Tolentino, Arturo M. 1409
トレンチャード
Trenchard, Hugh (Viscount) 1419
トレンティノ
Tolentino, Arturo M. 1409
Tolentino, Jorge Homero 1409
トレンティノ・ディップ
Tolentino Dipp, Hugo 1409
トレント
Trent, D.D. 1419
Trent, John T. 1419
トレンド
Trend, Michael 1419
ドレント
Drenth, Jan 373
Drenth, Jelto 373
トレンドビッツ
Trendowicz, Adam 1419
トレントマン
Trentmann, Frank 1419
トレンパー
Tremper, Bruce 1419
トレンブレイ
Tremblay, Marie-Eve 1419
ドレンボス
Dorenbos, Jon 367
トレンメル
Tremmel, Gerhard 1419
トロ
Tolo, Bréhima 1410
Toro, Cristian 1413
トロー
Traa, Kari 1416
ドロ
Dolo, Lamine 364
ドロア
Dror, Yehezkel 375
トロアイア
Troyat, Henri 1422
トロアイヤ
Troyat, Henri 1422
トロイ
Toloi, Rafael 1410
Troy, Virginia Gardner 1422
トロイチュ
Troitzsch, Klaus G. 1421
トロイツキ
Troicki, Viktor 1421
トロイボ
Trojborg, Jan 1421
トロヴァヨーリ
Trovajoli, Armando 1422
トロウガー
Troeger, Thomas H. 1421
ドロウカー
Draucker, Claire Burke 373
ドロウヒ
Dlouhý, Vladimír 360
トロエル
Troel, Sarah 1421
トロエンコ
Troenco, Valeriu 1421
トロキー
Trokey, Christian 1421
ドローギン
Drogin, Bob 375
トロクスラー
Troxler, Peter 1422
ドログバ
Drogba, Didier 375
トロクメ
Trocmé, Étienne 1421
ドロゲル
Dologuele, Anicet Georges 364
トロサ
Tolosa, Shagui 1410
ド・ロザリオ
Do Rosario, Antonio Gualberto 368
ドロザリオ
Dorosário, Arlindo Nascimento 368
トロシディス
Torosidis, Vasilis 1413
トロジャー
Trojer, Thomas 1421
ドロジャトゥン・クンチョロヤクティ
Dorodjatun Kuntjoro-Jakti 368
ドロジャトン・クンチョロジャクティ
Dorodjatun Kuntjoro-Jakti 368
トロシャニ
Troshani, Arenca 1421
ドロス
Dorros, Arthur 368

ト

ドロステ
Droste, Magdalena 375
トロステン・ブルーム
Trosten-Bloom, Amanda 1421
トロステン＝ブルーム
Trosten-Bloom, Amanda 1421
トロスト
Trost, Alessia 1421
Trost, Melanie R. 1421
ドロズドフ
Drozdov, Maksim 375
ドロズドフスカヤ
Drozdovskaya, Tatiana 375
ドロズニン
Drosnin, Michael 375
トロスビー
Trosby, Finn 1421
トロスラー
Trostler, Mark Ethan 1421
トローチャーニ
Trócsányi, László 1421
トロツィグ
Trotzig, Birgitta 1421
トロックスラー
Troxler, Niklaus 1422
トロッケル
Trockel, Rosemarie 1421
トロッジェ
Trotzier, Jean-Bernard 1421
トロッタ
Trotta, Marcello 1421
トロッター
Trotter, Chris 1421
Trotter, David 1421
Trotter, DeeDee 1421
Trotter, Lloyd 1421
ドロッター
Drotter, Stephen J. 375
トロッツィグ
Trotzig, Birgitta 1421
トロッテン
Trottein, Gwendolyn 1421
トロット
Trott, Dave 1421
Trott, James 1421
Trott, James R. 1421
Trott, Laura 1421
Trott, Marion 1421
トロットマン
Trotman, Alexander J. 1421
Trotman, Raphael 1421
トロッパー
Tropper, Jonathan 1421
トロッレ
Trolle, Maria 1421
トロティエ
Trottier, Maxine 1421
ドロート
Drought, Theresa S. 375
トロニック
Tronick, Edward Z. 1421
トロハ
Torroja, Eduardo 1414
トロバヨーリ
Trovajoli, Armando 1422
ドローヒー
Dlouhý, Vladimír 360
ドロビアズコ
Drobiazko, Margarita 375
トロピアーノ
Tropeano, Nick 1421
ドロビアン
Robien, Gilles de 1190
トロビッシュ
Trobisch, Walter 1421
ドロビッチ
Dolovich, Jerry 364
トローピン
Tropin, Vladimir Ivanovich 1421
トロープ
Trope, Zoe 1421
ドロープ
Droop, Constanza 375
トロフアイバレレイ
Tolofuaivalelei, Falemoe Leiataua 1410
ドロフェエフ
Dorofeyev, Dmitry 368
トロフティー
Torokhtiy, Oleksiy 1413
ドロブニー
Drobny, Jaroslav 375
Drobny, Steven 375
ドロブニチ
Drobnič, Janez 375
トローブリッジ
Trowbridge, Robert L., Jr. 1422
トロペイ
Tropea, John 1421
トロペール
Troper, Michel 1421
トロボ
Trobo, Jaime 1421
トロボアダ
Trovoada, Miguel 1422
Trovoada, Patrice Emery 1422
トロポフ
Toropov, Brandon 1413
トロミー
Tromey, Tom 1421
ド・ロミーイ
de Romilly, Jacqueline 344
ド・ロミイ
de Romilly, Jacqueline 344
ドロムグール
Dromgoole, Glenn 375
トロヤノフ
Trojanow, Ilija 1421
トロヤノフスキー
Troyanovskii, Oleg Aleksandrovich 1422
ドロール
Delors, Jacque 338
Delors, Jacques Lucien Jean 338
Delort, Robert 338
Dolor, Ernesta 364
ドロレ
Drolet, Marie-Eve 375
トロロープ
Trollope, Joanna 1421
トローワー
Trower, Peter 1422
ドロワ
Droit, Roger-Pol 375
トロワイア
Troyat, Henri 1422
トロワイヤ
Troyat, Henri 1422
トロワグロ
Troisgros, Michel 1421
Troisgros, Pierre Emile René 1421
ドローン
Draughn, Shaun 373
ドロン
Delon, Alain 338
ドロンケ
Dronke, Peter 375
トロンコン
Troncon, Renato 1421
ドロンゼック
Dronzek, Laura 375
トロンダイム
Trondheim, Lewis 1421
トロンプ
Tromp, Johan 1421
ドロンフィールド
Dronfield, Jeremy 375
トロンペテラー
Trompeteler, Helen 1421
トロンペナールス
Trompenaars, Alfons 1421
ドロンベリ
Dromberg, Kaarina 375
ドワー
Dauer, Sheila 322
トワイクロス
Twycross, Robert G. 1430
トワイデル
Twidell, John 1430
ドワイフィ・ドワイフィ
al-Duwaihi al-Duwaihi, Shuwaish 385
ドワイヤー
Dwyer, Conor 385
Dwyer, Jim 385
Dwyer, Judith 385
ドワイヨン
Doillon, Jacques 363
トワクス
Toikeusse, Mabri 1409
トワルドフスキー
Tvardovskij, V. 1430
トワンバ
Twamba, Charlotte 1430
トン
Deng, Ya-ping 341
Deng, You-mei 341
Thon, Philip 1401
Ton, Svatoslav 1411
Tong, Anote 1411
Tong, Jian 1411
Tong, Jinquan 1411
Tong, Jong-ho 1412
Tong, Wen 1412
Tonge, Robert 1412
Tung, Chee-hwa 1426
ドーン
Doane, Darren 360
Doane, Dudley J. 360
Lemay Doan, Catriona 811
ドン
Don, Pramudwinai 365
Dong, Dong 365
Dong, Fu-reng 365
Dong, Joseph Malwal 365
Dong, Ming-zhu 365
Tung, Chee-hwa 1426
ドンウッド
Donwood, Stanley 366
トンガイ
Tongai, Bauro 1412
トンガウイハ
Tonga'uiha, Soane 1412
ドンカスター
Doncaster, Patrick 365
トンガベロ
Tongavelo, Athanase 1412
トンキン
Tonkin, Michael 1412
ドンキン
Donkin, Andrew 366
トング
Tong, Richard 1412
ドンク
Donk, Ryan 366
Donk, Wim B.H.J.van de 366
トーンクィスト
Tornquist, Elizabeth M. 1413
ドングザシビリ
Donguzashvili, Tea 365
ドングム
Dongmo, Auriole 365
ドンケル
Dunkel, Arthur 381
ドンケルス
Donckers, Karin 365
ドンゲン
Dongen, Ron van 365
ドンコフ
Donkov, Samuil 366
ドンコル
Donkor, Anton 366
ドンサー
Donsah, Godfred 366
ドンジェ
Dongier, Philippe 365
トーンシン
Thongsing Thammavong 1401
トンシン・タマウォン
Thongsing Thammavong 1401
トンシン・タンマヴォン
Thongsing Thammavong 1401
ドンスコイ
Donskoi, Sergei Ye. 366
ドンズロ
Donzelot, Jacques 367
ドンゼ
Donzé, Pierre-Yves 367
ドンゼッリ
Donzelli, Valerie 367
ドンゾ
Donzo, Luseni 367
トンダ
Tonda, Patrice 1411
トンダマン
Thondaman, Arumugan 1401
ドンチェフ
Donchev, Tomislav 365
トンチャイ・ウィニッチャクン
Thongchai Winitcakun 1401
ドンデ
Dondey, Marc 365
トンド
Tondo, Clovis L. 1411

ドント
Hondt, Jacques d' 619
ドンドゥコフ
Dondukov, Aleksandr N. 365
ドンナイ
Donnai, Dian 366
ドンナルンマ
Donnarumma, Gianluigi 366
トンネ
Tonne, Tore 1412
トンバイ・トンパオ
Thongbai Thongpao 1401
ドンバヴァンド
Donbavand, Tommy 365
ドーンバーグ
Doernberg, Richard L. 362
ドンババンド
Donbavand, Tommy 365
トンバン
Thongbanh, Sengaphon 1401
ドンビ
Dombi, Rudolf 364
トンビアノ
Thombiano, Justin Tieba 1399
トンビニ
Tombini, Alexandre 1410
ドンファック
Donfack, Lekene 365
ドーンフェスト
Dornfest, Rael 368
ドーンフォード=メイ
Dornford-May, Mark 368
トンプキンス
Thompkins, Kenbrell 1399
Tompkins, Douglas 1411
Tompkins, Douglas R. 1411
トンプキンズ
Tompkins, Chuck 1411
Tompkins, Dave 1411
Tompkins, Ptolemy 1411
トンプスン
Thompson, Julian F. 1400
Thompson, Steven L. 1400
トンプソン
Thompson, Andrea B. 1399
Thompson, Andy 1399
Thompson, Barbara Rose 1399
Thompson, Bonita S. 1399
Thompson, Brandon 1399
Thompson, Brett 1399
Thompson, Bronwyn 1399
Thompson, Bruce R. T. 1399
Thompson, Carlos 1399
Thompson, Caroline 1399
Thompson, Cedric 1399
Thompson, Chris 1399
Thompson, Claire 1399
Thompson, Craig 1399
Thompson, Cy 1399
Thompson, Damian 1399
Thompson, Darian 1399
Thompson, Dave 1399
Thompson, David 1399
Thompson, David C. 1399
Thompson, Deonte 1399
Thompson, Dick 1399
Thompson, Donald N. 1399
Thompson, Douglas Henry 1399
Thompson, Dylan 1399
Thompson, E.A. 1399
Thompson, Elaine 1399
Thompson, Elizabeth 1399
Thompson, Elspeth 1399
Thompson, Emma 1399
Thompson, Ernest 1399
Thompson, Evan 1399
Thompson, Frank 1399
Thompson, Frank T. 1399
Thompson, Fred Dalton 1399
Thompson, Geoff 1399
Thompson, Gregory 1399
Thompson, Hank 1399
Thompson, Harvey 1399
Thompson, Henrietta 1399
Thompson, Hollis 1399
Thompson, Hugh, Jr. 1399
Thompson, Hunter S. 1399
Thompson, J.A. 1399
Thompson, Jake 1399
Thompson, James 1399
Thompson, James R. 1399
Thompson, Jason 1399
Thompson, Jenny 1399
Thompson, Jerrol 1399
Thompson, J.Lee 1399
Thompson, John Griggs 1399
Thompson, Jon 1400
Thompson, Jordan 1400
Thompson, Joyce Beebe 1400
Thompson, Juwan 1400
Thompson, Kane 1400
Thompson, Kate 1400
Thompson, Ken 1400
Thompson, Kendal 1400
Thompson, Kim 1400
Thompson, Kimberly M. 1400
Thompson, Klay 1400
Thompson, Kristin 1400
Thompson, Larry W. 1400
Thompson, Lauren 1400
Thompson, Laurie Ann 1400
Thompson, Leonard Monteath 1400
Thompson, Lexi 1400
Thompson, Margot 1400
Thompson, Marielle 1400
Thompson, Mark 1400
Thompson, Mark C. 1400
Thompson, Michael 1400
Thompson, Mike 1400
Thompson, Molly 1400
Thompson, Mykkele 1400
Thompson, Nainoa 1400
Thompson, Neil 1400
Thompson, Nick 1400
Thompson, Obadele 1400
Thompson, Paul Richard 1400
Thompson, Peter 1400
Thompson, Peter M. 1400
Thompson, Peyton 1400
Thompson, Richard 1400
Thompson, Rodney 1400
Thompson, Ron 1400
Thompson, Soren 1400
Thompson, Tommy 1400
Thompson, Trayce 1400
Thompson, Tristan 1400
Thompson, Tyrus 1400
Thompson, Vicki Lewis 1400
Thompson, Warren E. 1400
Thompson, William Ladd 1400
Tompson, Amanda 1411
Tompson, Ken 1411
トンプソン‐カニーノ
Thompson-Cannino, Jennifer 1400
ドーンブッシュ
Dornbusch, Rudiger 368
ドンフリード
Donfried, Karl P. 365
ドンブレット
Dombret, Andreas 364
ドンブロウスキ
Dombrowski, Dave 364
ドンブロフスキ
Dąbrowski, Waldemar 311
ドンブロフスキー
Dombrovsky, Pavel 364
トンベ
Tombet, Andre 1410
ドーンヘルム
Dornhelm, Robert 368
ドンポック
Dompok, Bernard 365
ドンマラボ
Don Malabo, Estanislao 366
ドンラ
Dondra, Henri Marie 365
ドンラン
Donlan, Jane 366
トンルン
Thongloun, Sisoulith 1401
ドンワイ
Donwahi, Alain Richard 366

【ナ】

ナ
Na, An 1000
Na, Il Sung 1000
Na, Jin 1000
Ra, Jong-yil 1146
ナイ
Nigh, Douglas William 1025
Nighy, Bill 1025
Nye, Doug 1039
Nye, Jody Lynn 1039
Nye, Joseph Samuel, Jr. 1039
Nye, Naomi Shihab 1039
ナイア
Nair, V.P. 1003
ナイアー
Nayar, Vineet 1009
ナイアド
Nyad, Diana 1038
ナイエンフェイス
Nijenhuis, Ellert R.S. 1025
ナイカンプ
Nijkamp, Franciscus Petrus 1025
ナイク
Naek, Farooq Hamid 1001
Naik, Ram 1002
Naik, Shripad Yesso 1002
Naik, Zakir 1002
ナイサー
Neisser, Ulric 1013
ナイシュ
Naish, Ginny 1003
ナイス
Nice, Claudia 1022
Nice, Jill 1022
ナイゼ
Neise, Ludwig 1013
ナイセス
Neises, Charles P. 1013
ナイダ
Nida, Eugene Albert 1024
ナイダン
Naidan, Tuvshinbayar 1002
ナイチンゲール
Nightingale, Virginia 1025
ナイテ
Naite, Moustapha 1003
ナイディック
Neidich, Charles 1013
ナイデク
Najdek, Pawel 1003
ナイデノフ
Naydenov, Miroslav 1009
ナイデノワ
Naydenova, Tsvetelina 1009
ナイデル
Nydell, Margaret Kleffner 1039
ナイ・テ・ルウィン
Nai Thet Lwin 1003
ナイト
Knight, Alanna 747
Knight, Bianca 747
Knight, Bob G. 748
Knight, Brandon 748
Knight, Charles F. 748
Knight, Christopher 748
Knight, Clifford 748
Knight, Damon 748
Knight, E.E. 748
Knight, Frida 748
Knight, Gary A. 748
Knight, George R. 748
Knight, Gladys 748
Knight, Hilary 748
Knight, India 748
Knight, Jaquel 748
Knight, Joan 748
Knight, Judy Zebra 748
Knight, Jules 748
Knight, Kathryn Huang 748
Knight, Keith D. 748
Knight, Kenneth L. 748
Knight, Lucy 748
Knight, Martin 748
Knight, Natasha 748
Knight, Nicholas 748
Knight, Peter 748
Knight, Philip 748
Knight, Raymond A. 748
Knight, Renée 748
Knight, Stan 748
Knight, Stephen 748
Night, P.J. 1025
ナイドゥ
Naidu, Siddartha 1002
Naidu, Venkaiah 1002

ナイドゥー
Naidoo, Beverly 1002
Naidoo, Trevor 1002
ナイトフランク
Knight-Frank, Karen 748
ナイトリー
Knightley, Erin 748
Knightley, Phillip 748
ナイトレイ
Kightley, Rosalinda 731
Knightley, Keira 748
ナイトン
Knighton, Elaine 748
Knighton, Terrance 748
ナイハウグ
Nyhaug, Tory 1039
ナイバーグ
Naiburg, Eric J. 1002
Nyberg, Lars 1039
ナイハード
Neidhart, Christoph 1013
ナイバート
Nibert, David Alan 1022
ナイバル
Naivalu, Solomone 1003
ナイハルト
Neihardt, John Gneisenau 1013
ナイフ
al-Nayef, Sa'ad Abdul-Salam 1009
ナイポール
Naipaul, Vidiadhar Surajprasad 1003
ナイマーク
Naimark, Norman M. 1003
ナイマン
Naĭman, Anatoliĭ 1003
Najman, Dragoljub 1003
Nyman, Mark 1039
ナイーム
al-Naeem, Halima hassaballa 1001
ナイム
Naim, Asher 1002
Naim, Basem 1002
Naím, Moisés 1003
ナイヤル
Nair, Thottuvelil Krishna Pilla Aiyappankutty 1003
ナイラティカウ
Nailatikau, Ratu Epeli 1002
ナイランド
Nijland, Stern 1025
Niland, Kilmeny 1026
Nylund, David 1039
Nylund, Eric S. 1039
ナーイル
Nair, Mira 1003
ナイール
Nair, Mira 1003
Nair, Ramesh 1003
ナイル
Nair, Kanika 1003
Nile, Richard 1026
ナイルス
Niles, Angie 1026
ナイルズ
Niles, Meredith 1026
ナイレンバーグ
Nirenberg, Marshall Warren 1027
ナイワート
Neiwert, David A. 1013
ナーイン
Nahin, Paul J. 1002
ナインガム
Naiqamu, Osea 1003
ナインゴラン
Nainggolan, Radja 1003
ナウ
Nau, Heinz 1008
Nau, Henry R. 1008
ナウー
Nuhu, Kasim 1037
ナーヴァ
Nava, Michael 1008
ナヴァスキー
Navasky, Victor S. 1009
ナヴァセル
Navacelle, Marie-Christine de 1008
ナヴァーロ
Navarro, Morgan 1008
Navarro, Yvonne 1009
ナヴァロ
Navarro, Garcia 1008
Navarro, Guillermo 1008
Navarro, Joe 1008
Navarro, Morgan 1008
Navarro, Peter 1008
Navarro, Yvonne 1009
ナヴィア
Navia, Luis E. 1009
ナヴィーン
Naveen, Ron 1009
ナウィンナ
Nawinne, S.B. 1009
ナヴェー
Naveh, Joseph 1009
ナウェジ・ムンデレ
Nawej Mundele, Charles 1009
ナウェジムンデレ
Nawej Mundele, Charles 1009
ナウエル
Nahuel, Matias 1002
ナヴォン
Navon, Yitzhak 1009
ナウク
Nauck, Todd 1008
Nauk, Todd 1008
ナウセ・ペレス
Nauzet Perez 1008
ナウタ
Nauta, Yvonne 1008
ナウド
Naldo 1004
ナウバット
Nawbatt, Harrinarine 1009
ナウポト
Naupoto, Villiame 1008
ナウマワ
Naumava, Darya 1008
ナウマン
N., Ebi 1000
Nauman, Bruce 1008
Naumann, Bernd 1008
Naumann, Francis M. 1008
Naumann, G.O.H. 1008
Naumann, Klaus Dieter 1008
Naumann, Klaus Friedrich 1008
ナウーモフ
Naumov, Oleg V. 1008
ナウモフ
Naumov, Radomir 1008
Naumov, Vladimir V. 1008
ナウモブ
Naumov, Radomir 1008
ナウモブスキ
Naumovski, Vasko 1008
ナウヤマ
Naoueyama, François 1005
ナウラ
Nowra, Louis 1035
ナウル
Naul, Roland 1008
Naulu, Josateki 1008
ナエス
Naess, Arne 1001
ナエゾン
Naezon, Walton 1001
ナエフ・ビン・アブドルアジズ
Nayef bin Abdul-Aziz 1009
ナオウラ
Naoura, Salah 1005
ナカ
Naka, John Yoshio 1003
ナカイ
Nakai, Kate Wildman 1003
Nakai, Sardar Talib Husain 1003
ナガオ
Nagao, Haruka 1001
ナカザワ
Nakazawa, Donna Jackson 1003
ナカシュ
Nakache, Olivier 1003
ナカッチ
Nakkach, Silvia 1003
ナカノ
Nakano, Helen Michiyo 1003
Nakano, Lane 1003
Nakano, Russell 1003
ナガノ
Nagano, Kent 1001
ナガムートゥー
Nagamootoo, Moses 1001
ナカムラ
Nakamura, Masumi 1003
Nakamura, Robert M. 1003
Nakamura, Shuji 1003
Nakamura, Yuichi 1003
ナカモト
Nakamoto, Steve 1003
ナガモートー
Nagamootoo, Moses 1001
ナカヤマ
Nakayama, Tosiwo 1003
ナカラ
Nakara, Tetabo 1003
ナガラジュ
Nagaraju, Harsha 1001
ナガラートナ
Nagarathna, R. 1001
ナカラワ
Nakarawa, Leone 1003
ナカリャコフ
Nakariakov, Sergei 1003
ナギ
Nagy, Zsolt 1002
ナギー
Nagy, Charles 1002
Nagy, Krisztina Kállai 1002
ナーキウィズ
Narkiewicz, Jan D. 1006
ナギエフ
Nagiyev, Alib 1002
Nagiyev, Ali T. 1002
ナギザデ
Naghizadeh, Mohammad 1002
ナキスベンディ
Nakisbendi, Kara 1003
ナキッチ
Nakić, Dario 1003
ナキーブ
al-Naqeeb, Falah 1005
ナキルスキ
Nakielski, Kathleen P. 1003
ナグ
Nagou, Yves Mado 1002
Nagu, Mary 1002
ナグアモ
Ngauamo, Paula 1020
ナグダ
Nagda, Ann Whitehead 1001
ナクト
Nacht, Jonathan 1001
ナクトウェー
Nachtwey, James A. 1001
ナクトウェイ
Nachtwey, James A. 1001
ナグパル
Nagpal, Sarita 1002
ナクビ
Naqvi, Mukhtar Abbas 1005
ナグベ
Nagbe, Eugene 1001
ナグマノフ
Nagmanov, Kazhmurat 1002
ナグリエリ
Naglieri, Jack A. 1002
ナクルズ
Knuckles, Willis 749
ナーグル＝ドツェカル
Nagl-Docekal, Herta 1002
ナグワ
Naguwa, Stanley M. 1002
ナグワニ
Nagwani, Anoop 1002
ナゲイ
Nagay, Agnieszka 1001
ナゲイキナ
Nagejkina, Svetlana 1001
ナケシュバンディ
Nakeshbandi, Mohamad Nouraldin 1003
ナケタシ
Nakaitaci, Noa 1003
ナゲル
Nagel, Maggy 1001
ナーゲルスマン
Nagelsmann, Julian 1002
ナゲンドラ
Nagendra, H.R. 1002
ナコ
Nako, Sokol 1003
ナゴ

Nago, Mathurin 1002
ナコーネ
Nakone, Lanna 1004
ナコネチニー
Nakonechnyi, Vitalii 1004
ナゴルスキ
Nagorski, Andrew 1002
ナゴルニー
Nagornyy, Nikita 1002
ナサー
Nasar, Sylvia 1006
ナ・サインチョクト
Na Sainchogt 1006
ナサシラ
Nasasira, John 1006
Nasasira, John Mwoono 1006
ナザリ
Nazari, Dilbar 1009
Nazari, Enayatullah 1009
ナザリアン
Nazarian, Arthur 1009
ナサリク
Nasalyk, Ihor 1006
ナザリャン
Nazarian, Armen 1009
Nazaryan, Armen 1009
ナザル＝アガ
Nazare-Aga, Isabelle 1009
ナザルアーハリ
Nazarahari, Reza 1009
ナザルーク
Nazaruk, Viacheslav Mikhailovich 1009
ナザルバーエフ
Nazarbaev, Nursultan Abishuli 1009
ナザルバエフ
Nazarbaev, Nursultan Abishuli 1009
ナザルバエワ
Nazarbayeva, Dariga 1009
ナザロフ
Nazarov, Dilshod 1009
Nazarov, Talbak 1009
ナザロワ
Nazarova, Anna 1009
Nazarova, Olga 1009
ナーザン
Nathan, S.R. 1007
ナザン
Nathan, S.R. 1007
ナサンジャルガル
Nasanjargal, Darjaagiin 1006
ナサンソン
Nathanson, Paul 1007
ナサンチャムナ
Nasantchamna, Dinis Kadlon 1006
ナサンブルマー・オチルバト
Nasanburmaa Ochirbatyn 1006
ナージ
Naji, Jawad 1003
ナジ
Nagy, Adam 1002
Nagy, József 1002
Nagy, Margit Maria 1002
Nagy, Peter 1002
ナジエ
Najie, Reza 1003
ナシェフ
Nachev, Gencho 1000
ナシエフ
Nassief, Yvor 1007
ナジェル
Nagel, Christian 1001
ナジタ
Najita, Tetsuo 1003
ナシード
Nasheed, Mohamed 1006
ナシフ
Nassif, Michael 1007
ナジフ
Nazif, Ahmad Muhammad 1010
ナジブ
Nagib, Lúcia 1002
Najib, Razak 1003
ナジブ・アブドル・ラザク
Najib Abdul Razak, Mohamad 1003
ナジブ・ラザク
Najib Abdul Razak, Mohamad 1003
ナジマロシィ
Nagymarosy, András 1002
ナシム
Nasim, Mohammed 1007
ナジム
Nazim, Mohamed 1010
ナジムディノフ
Nadzhmuddinov, Safarali 1001
Nazhmuddinov, Safarali 1010
ナシメント
Nascimento, Adão Do 1006
Nascimento, Alfredo 1006
Nascimento, Milton 1006
ナシャ
Nasha, Margaret 1006
ナジャ
Nadja 1001
ナジャー
Najjar, Mohammed Al 1003
ナジャフィ
Najafi, Babak 1003
Najafi, Daoud Ali 1003
al-Nujayfi, Usama 1037
ナジャール
Najjar, Ibrahim 1003
Najjar, Raouf 1003
ナジャル
Najjar, Mohamed Raouf 1003
Najjar, Mohammad 1003
ナーシュ
Naish, Darren 1003
ナジュ
Nagy, Timea 1002
ナジュムディノフ
Najmuddinov, Safarali 1003
ナシリ
Naciri, Khalid 1001
Naciri, Mohamed 1001
ナシリニア
Nasirinia, Shahin 1007
ナシール
Naseer, Umar 1006
Nasir, Mohamad 1007
ナシル
Nashir, Abdallah Abd al-Wali 1006
Nasir, Amir Ibrahim 1007
Nasir, bin Muhammad al-Thani 1007
ナジール
Nazeer, Kamran 1009
ナシルシェラル
Nasirshelal, Navab 1007
ナジロフ
Nazirov, Abdukakhir 1010
Nazirov, Feruz 1010
ナシンベニ
Nascimbeni, Barbara 1006
ナース
Naes, Tormod 1001
Nourse, Alan Edward 1034
Nurse, Cristy 1038
Nurse, Nick 1038
Nurse, Paul Maxime 1038
ナス
Nas, Tevfik F. 1006
Nass, Clifford Ivar 1007
Nass, Herbert E. 1007
ナスコ
Nasko, Siegfried 1007
ナスター
Knaster, Scott 747
ナスタシ
Nastasi, Alison 1007
ナスタシッチ
Nastasic, Matija 1007
ナスターセ
Năstase, Adrian 1007
ナスターゼ
Năstase, Adrian 1007
ナスタセ
Năstase, Adrian 1007
Năstase, Adrian 1007
ナスタゼ
Năstase, Adrian 1007
ナスダーフト
Nothdurft, William E. 1034
ナスティオン
Nasution, Darmin 1007
ナスト
Nast, Jamie 1007
ナズバ
Nacuva, Pita 1001
ナズパ
Nacuva, Pita 1001
ナスバウム
Nussbaum, Jay 1038
Nussbaum, Robert L. 1038
ナスフィ
Nasufi, Dzevdet 1007
ナスララ
Nasrallah, Hassan 1007
ナスララ師
Nasrallah, Hassan 1007
ナスリ
Nasri, Samir 1007
ナズリ
Nazri, Abdul Aziz 1010
Nazri, Aziz 1010
ナズリン
Nazrin, Muizzuddin Shah 1010
ナスール
Naceur, Mohamed 1000
ナスル
Nasr, Farouk Seif El 1007
Nasr, Sahar 1007
ナスールマディ
Nassur Madi, Abdou 1007
ナスルラエフ
Nasrullayev, Namik N. 1007
ナズロー
Nazroo, James Y. 1010
ナーセ
Nasser, Vali 1007
ナセヒ
Nassehi, Armin 1007
ナセリ
Naceri, Samy 1000
ナセリヤル
Naseryar, Amin 1006
ナーセル
al-Nassir, Hala Muhammad 1007
ナーゼル
Nazer, Hisham 1010
Nazer, Mende 1010
ナセル
Nasser, Hazem al 1007
Nasser, Kamal 1007
Nasser, Sabah al-Ahmad al-Sabah 1007
ナセルディン
Naser Din, Safa 1006
ナセル・ムハンマド・アハマド・サバハ
Nasser Muhammad al-Ahmad al-Sabah 1007
ナソー
Nasaw, David 1006
Nasaw, Jonathan Lewis 1006
ナータ
Ngata, Haloti 1020
ナタ
Nata, Theophile 1007
ナター
Natter, Tobias Günter 1008
ナダ
Nada, Abbas Haffadh 1001
ナーダシュ
Nádas, Péter 1001
ナタノ
Natano, Kausea 1007
ナダーフ
Naddaf, Atef 1001
ナタペイ
Natapei, Edward 1007
ナタラジャン
Natarajan, Jayanthi 1007
ナタラヤン
Natarajan, Bharathi 1007
ナタリ
Natali, Vincenzo 1007
ナタリーニ
Natalini, Sandro 1007
ナダル
Nadal, Rafael 1001
Nadar, Shiv 1001
Nadeau, Rodney A. 1001
ナダル・ベルダ
Nadal Belda, Alvaro 1001
ナダレイシビリ
Nadareishvili, Revaz 1001
ナタン
Nathan, Tobie 1007
ナタンバ
Na Tamba, Adelina 1007
ナチオス

Natsios, Andrew S. 1008
ナチョ
Nacho, Fernandez 1000
Naço, Nasip 1001
ナチョ・カセス
Nacho Cases 1001
ナチンションホル
Nachinshonhor 1000
ナツァグドルジ
Natsagdorzh, Shagdarzhavyn 1008
ナッキー
Knuckey, Deborah 749
ナックウェイ
Nachtwey, James A. 1001
ナックスホール
Nuxhall, Joe 1038
ナックマン
Nachman, Patricia Ann 1000
ナッケン
Nakken, Craig 1003
ナッサー
Nasser, Jacques A. 1007
ナッシー
Naschy, Paul 1006
ナッシブ
Nassib, Carl 1007
Nassib, Ryan 1007
ナッジャル
Najjar, Mostafa Mohammad 1003
ナッシュ
Nash, Andrew 1006
Nash, Catherine 1006
Nash, Damien 1006
Nash, Douglas E. 1006
Nash, Fiona 1006
Nash, Graham 1006
Nash, Jay Robert 1006
Nash, John Forbes, Jr. 1006
Nash, Juliana C. 1006
Nash, Katerina 1006
Nash, Lewis 1006
Nash, Poppy 1006
Nash, Roderick Frazier 1006
Nash, Ronald H. 1006
Nash, Sophia 1006
Nash, Stephen 1006
Nash, Susan Smith 1006
ナッシンベンネ
Nascimbene, Yan 1006
ナッズ
Nudds, John R. 1036
ナッスル
Nussle, James Allen 1038
ナッセル
Nasser, José 1007
Nussle, James Allen 1038
ナッセン
Knussen, Oliver 749
ナッタ
Natta, Alessandro 1008
ナッダ
Nadda, Jagat Prakash 1001
ナッターマン
Nattermann, Peter 1008
ナッチー
Naschy, Paul 1006
ナッチル
Natsir, Liliyana 1008
Natsir, Lilyana 1008
ナッティング
Nutting, Bob 1038
ナット
Nutt, Amy Ellis 1038
Nutt, David J. 1038
Nutt, Gary J. 1038
Nutt, Roberta L. 1038
ナットビーム
Nutbeam, Donald 1038
ナットール
Nuttall, Jeff 1038
ナッパー
Napper, Lewis 1005
ナッハース
Nahhas, Nicolas 1002
ナップ
Knapp, Andrew 747
Knapp, Caroline 747
Knapp, Ruthie 747
Knapp, Sarah Edison 747
Napp, Daniel 1005
ナップマン
Knapman, Timothy 747
ナッペイ
Nappey, Grégoire 1005
ナッポ
Nappo, Donato 1005
ナツマン
Natuman, Joe 1008
ナテア
Natea, Daniel 1007
ナティ
Natti, Susanna 1008
ナティエ
Nattiez, Jean-Jacques 1008
ナティシン
Hnatyshyn, Ramon John 610
ナティッシン
Hnatyshyn, Ramon John 610
ナティビダッド
Natividad, Irene 1007
ナディラ
Nadir, Manzoor 1001
ナディラゼ
Nadiradze, Zaza 1001
ナディル
Nadir, Manzoor 1001
ナディンガー
Nadingar, Emmanuel 1001
ナディンガル
Nadingar, Emmanuel 1001
ナテラ
Natera, Francisco 1007
ナデラ
Nadella, Satya 1001
ナデリ
Naderi, Amir 1001
Naderi, Sadat Mansoor 1001
ナデル
Nadel, Barbara 1001
Nadel, Ira Bruce 1001
Nadel, Olivier 1001
ナート
Nath, Kamal 1007
ナード
Nardo, Anna K. 1005
ナドー
Nadaud, Stéphane 1001
Nadeau, Janice 1001
Nadeau, Jean-Benoît 1001
Nadeau, Kathleen G. 1001
Nadeau, Stepahane 1001
ナドア
Naddour, Alexander 1001
ナドイム
Nadhoim, Idi 1001
ナトゥバ
Natuva, Timoci Lesi 1008
ナトゥマン
Natuman, Joe 1008
ナトホ
Natcho, Bibras 1007
ナドラー
Nadler, David A. 1001
Nadler, Mark B. 1001
Nadler, Steven M. 1001
ナトラス
Nattrass, Sue 1008
ナトーリ
Natoli, Joseph P. 1007
ナトリ
Natoli, Louise 1007
ナトリー
Nutley, Sandra M. 1038
ナドルニー
Nadolny, Sten 1001
ナドロ
Nadolo, Nemani 1001
ナトンデ
Natonde, Aké 1007
ナナイ=ウィリアムズ
Nanai-williams, Tim 1004
ナナジム
Nana Djimou Ida, Antoinette 1004
ナナス
Nanus, Burt 1005
ナナヤッカラ
Nanayakkara, Vasudeva 1004
ナナン
Nanan, Adesh Curtis 1004
ナーニ
Nani 1005
ナニ
Nani 1005
Nani, Christel 1005
Nani, Mohamed Ould 1005
ナニエフ
Naniyev, Alan 1005
ナネスタッド
Nannestad, Katrina 1005
ナネッティ
Nanetti, Angela 1004
ナノ
Nano 1005
Nano, Fatos Thanas 1005
ナバ
Nava, Daniel 1008
Nava, Horacio 1008
ナーバイン
Nawijn, Hilbrand 1009
ナハヴァンディ
Nahavandi, Afsaneh 1002
ナバカウスカス
Navakauskas, Ignas 1008
ナバカモチェア
Navakamocea, Jone 1008
ナバグ
Nabagou, Bissoune 1000
ナバジオ
Navazio, Franco 1009
ナハス
Nahas, Charbel 1002
ナパステック
Naparstek, Belleruth 1005
ナバス・ベラ
Navas Vera, César 1009
ナパット
Napat, Jotham 1005
ナバッロ
Navarro, Garcia 1008
ナバッロ・ユデス
Navarro Yudes, David Fernando 1009
ナハテルゲーレ
Nachtergaele, F.O. 1001
ナバブキン
Nababkin, Kirill 1000
ナハマノヴィッチ
Nachmanovitch, Stephen 1000
ナハヤン
Nahayan, bin Mubarak al-Nahayan 1002
Nahyan, bin Mubarak al-Nahyan 1002
al-Nahyan, Hamdan bin Mubarak 1002
al-Nahyan, Mansour bin Zayed 1002
al-Nahyan, Saif bin Zayed 1002
ナハヨ
Nahayo, immaculée 1002
ナハリ
Nahari, Meshulam 1002
ナハル
Nahar, Ahmed Babiker 1002
ナーバルセーテ
Navarsete, Liv Signe 1009
ナバルダウスカス
Navardauskas, Ramunas 1008
ナバレ
Nabare, Bernard 1000
ナバレッテ・ザネッティ
Nabarrete Zanetti, Arthur 1000
ナバレテ・プリダ
Navarrete Prida, Jesús Alfonso 1008
ナバレマリ
Navarre-marie, Marie Arianne 1008
ナハーロ
Najarro, Antonio 1003
ナハロ
Najarro, Antonio 1003
ナバーロ
Navarro, Efren 1008
ナバロ
Navarro, Ann 1008
Navarro, Fernanda 1008
Navarro, Garcia 1008
Navarro, Héctor 1008
Navarro, José Augusto 1008
Navarro, Julia 1008
Navarro, Leopoldo 1008
Navarro, Leticia 1008
Navarro, Peter 1008
Navarro, Vicenç 1009
Navarro Valdez, Carlos Ruben 1009
ナバロ・カスタニェダ

Navarro Castañeda, Emilio 1009
ナバロ・ガルシア
Navarro García, Andrés 1009
ナバロ・ディアス
Navarro Díaz, Héctor Augusto 1009
ナバロ・ミランダ
Navarro Miranda, César 1009
ナーバーン
Nerburn, Kent 1015
ナハン
Nahan, Stu 1002
ナバーン
Nabhan, Gary Paul 1000
ナビ
Nabi, Heiki 1000
Nabi, Youcef 1000
ナピヴォツキー
Napiwotzky, Annedore 1005
ナビウリナ
Nabiullina, Elvira Sakhipzadovna 1000
ナビチータ
Na Bitchita, Sola Nquilin 1000
ナビツカス
Navickas, Vytas 1009
ナーヒード
Nahid, Kishvar 1002
ナヒド
Nahid, Nurul Islam 1002
ナビト
al-Nabit, Saleh Mohamed Salem 1000
ナビンナ
Nabinne, S.B. 1000
Navinne, S.B. 1009
Nawinne, S.B. 1009
Nvinne, S.B. 1038
ナフィーサ
al-Nafisah, Matlab bin Abdullah 1001
ナフィサ
al-Nafisah, Matlab bin Abdullah 1001
ナフィーシー
Nafisi, Azar 1001
ナフィル
Nafile, Nafile Ali 1001
ナプウォン
Napwon, Josephine 1005
ナフォ
Nafo, Traore Fatoumata 1001
ナフカ
Navka, Tatiana 1009
ナフシア
Nafsiah, Mboi 1001
ナフス
Nafus, Dawn 1001
ナブハン
Nabhan, Gary Paul 1000
Nabhan, Mohammed bin 1000
ナブラチッチ
Navracsics, Tibor 1009
ナブラチロワ
Navratilova, Martina 1009
ナフル
Nakhle, Carole 1003
ナブルシ
Nabulsi, Faris 1000
ナフルゾフ
Navruzov, Ikhtiyor 1009
ナベ
Naveh, Danny 1009
ナベリア
Navellier, Louis 1009
ナヘル
Nagel, Monica 1002
ナボ
Nabo, Clément 1000
ナボコフ
Nabokov, Dmitri 1000
ナホザ
Nahodha, Shamsi 1002
ナポリ
Napoli, Donna Jo 1005
Napoli, Mike 1005
ナポリオーニ
Napoleoni, Loretta 1005
ナポリターノ
Napolitano, Giorgio 1005
Napolitano, Janet 1005
Napolitano, Jim 1005
ナポレオン
Napoléon, Charles 1005
Napoleon, Nanette Naioma 1005
Napoleon, Ryan 1005
ナホロ
Naholo, Waisake 1002
ナボン
Navon, Yitzhak 1009
ナマ
Namah, Belden 1004
ナマジ
Namazi, Hosein 1004
ナマシュルア
Namashulua, Carmelita Rita 1004
ナマタ
Namata, Adamou 1004
ナマドゥク
Namaduk, Remy 1004
ナマヤンジャ
Namayanja, Rose 1004
ナマリュー
Namaliu, Rabbie 1004
ナマンガニ
Namangoniy, Juma 1004
ナマンゴニ
Namangoniy, Juma 1004
ナム
Naam, Ramez 1000
Nam, Duck-woo 1004
Nam, Gisèle Annie 1004
Nam, Jaeook 1004
Nam, Tae-hyun 1004
Nam, Vignaket 1004
Nam, Yong 1004
ナムカイ・ノルブ
Namkhai Norbu 1004
ナムガラ
Namugala, Catherine 1004
ナムジュー
Namjoo, Majid 1004
ナムセネイ
Namsénéï, Robert 1004
ナムダク
Namdak, Tenzin 1004
ナムナム
Namnam, Helmy 1004
ナムヤンバ
Namuyamba, Bates 1004
ナムラ
al-Namla, Ali bin Ibrahim 1004
ナムランベ
Namulambe, Gabriel 1004
ナムワンディ
Namwandi, David 1004
ナムワンバ
Namwamba, Ababu 1004
ナモロ
Namoloh, Charles 1004
ナヤ
Naja, Karolina 1003
ナヤク
Nayak, Ajaya Shankar 1009
ナヤザレヴ
Nayacalevu, Waisea 1009
ナヨ
Nayo Ketchanke, Gaelle Verlaine 1009
ナーラーシムハーン
Narasimhan, Sundar 1005
ナラデボー
Naradevo, Phra Yuki 1005
ナラニィ
Naranji, Corine 1005
ナラヤナン
Narayanan, Arvind 1005
Narayanan, Kocheril Raman 1005
Narayanan, M.P. 1005
ナーラーヤン
Narayan, R.K. 1005
Narayan, Uma 1005
ナラヤン
Narayan, Giddu 1005
Narayan, R.K. 1005
Narayen, Shantanu 1005
ナラン
Narang, Rishi K. 1005
ナランゲ
Narang, Gagan 1005
ナランツァツァラルト
Narantsatsralt, Janlav 1005
ナランツァツラルト
Narantsatsralt, Janlav 1005
ナランホ
Naranjo, Jose 1005
Naranjo, Sandra 1005
ナリ
Nali, Nestor Mamadou 1004
Nari, Tony 1006
ナリアシヴィリ
Nariashvili, Mikheil 1006
ナリス
Narace, Jerry 1005
ナリタ
Narita, Megumi 1006
Narita, Tatsuki 1006
ナリッツァーノ
Narizzano, Silvio 1006
ナリーニ
Nalini, Andrea 1004
ナリマニゼ
Narimanidze, Khatuna 1006
ナリワイコ
Nalivaiko, Sergey E. 1004
ナリン
Narine, Jarette 1006
Narine, Jarrette 1006
ナリンドラポン
Narindrapong, Norodom 1006
ナルアック
Naluak, Vesa Gomes 1004
ナルィシキン
Naryshkin, Sergei Yevgenyevich 1006
ナルイシキン
Naruishkin, Sergei E. 1006
Naryshkin, Sergei Yevgenyevich 1006
ナールガング
Nahrgang, Frauke 1002
ナルキェヴィッチ
Narkiewicz, Władysław 1006
ナルケドロゴ
Nalke Dorogo, André 1004
ナルシプル
Narsipur, Chandramouli 1006
ナルシン
Narsingh, Luciano 1006
ナルス
Narus, James A. 1006
ナルセブ
Naruseb, Alpheus 1006
ナルチェマシビリ
Narchemashvili, Koba 1005
ナルディーニ
Naldini, Nico 1004
ナルデリ
Nardelli, Robert L. 1005
ナルドーネ
Nardone, Giorgio 1005
ナルバエズ
Narvaez, Omar 1006
ナルバエス・オヘダ
Narváez Ojeda, Paula 1006
ナルバエワ
Narbaeva, Tanzila 1005
ナルバンジャン
Nalbandian, Edward 1004
ナルバンディアン
Nalbandyan, Aleksan 1004
ナルバントオウル
Nalbantoğlu, Hasan Ünal 1004
ナールビコヴァ
Narbikova, Valeriya Spartakovna 1005
ナールビコワ
Narbikova, Valeriya Spartakovna 1005
ナルボナ
Narbona, Cristina 1005
ナルボーン
Nalbone, John 1004
ナルマニア
Narmania, David 1006
ナルマン
Nulman, Andy 1037
ナルマンゴ
Nalumango, Mutale 1004
ナルラ
Narla, Francisco 1006

ナレ
Naret, Jean-Luc 1006
ナーレス
Nahles, Andrea 1002
ナーレンホア
Naren-hua 1006
ナロ・ロブレス
Narro Robles, José 1006
ナロン
Narong, Pipatanasai 1006
ナロンチャイ
Narongchai, Akrasanee 1006
ナワウィチット
Navavichit, Bhusdee 1009
ナワフ
Nawaf al-Ahmad al-Jabir al-Sabah 1009
Nawwaf, al-Ahmad al-Sabah 1009
ナワフ・アル・アハマド・アル・サバハ
Nawaf al-Ahmad al-Jabir al-Sabah 1009
ナワフ・アル・アハマド・アル・ジャビル・アル・サバハ
Nawaf al-Ahmad al-Jabir al-Sabah 1009
ナワリヌイ
Navalnyi, Aleksei Anatolievich 1008
ナワルニー
Navalnyi, Aleksei Anatolievich 1008
ナン
Nunn, John Francis 1037
Nunn, Kem 1037
ナンガ
Nanga, Mawapanga Mwana 1004
ナンクムワ
Nankhumwa, Kondwani 1005
ナンコセレナ
Namkosserena, Salomon 1004
ナンゴンベ
Nangombe, Sophia-Namupa 1004
ナンサヴォンドァンシイ
Nanthavongdouangsy, Viengkham 1005
ナンシー
Nancy, Jean-Luc 1004
Nancy, Ted L. 1004
ナンジー
Nanji, Azim 1005
ナンジャ
Nandja, Zakari 1004
ナンジャッパ
Nanjappa, Prakash 1005
ナンス
Nance, John J. 1004
Nance, Larry, Jr. 1004
ナンスノン
Nansounon, Rufin Orou Nan 1005
ナンセン
Nansen, Fridtjof 1005
ナンソン
Nanson, Bill 1005
ナンダ
Nanda, Ashish 1004
Nanda, Bal Ram 1004
Nanda, Ved P. 1004
Nanda, Vikram 1004
ナンツ
Nantz, Michael H. 1005
ナンディグナ
Nandigna, Adiato Diallo 1004
ナンディナ
Nandigna, Maria Adiato Djalo 1004
ナンディヌダイトワ
Nandi Ndaitwah, Netumbo 1004
ナンディンザヤ・ガンフヤグ
Nandinzayaa Gankhuyagiin 1004
ナンドラル
Nandlall, Anil 1004
ナンネリー
Nunneley, John 1037
ナーンバーガー
Nurnberger, John I. 1038
ナンバチャ
Nanbatcha, Boata 1004
ナンブ
Nambu, Yoichiro 1004
ナンブレーテ
Namburete, Salvador 1004
ナンブレテ
Namburete, Salvador 1004

【ニ】

ニ
Ni, Xia Lian 1022
ニー
Knee, Sam 747
Ni, Maoshing 1022
Ni, Zhi-fu 1022
ニーア
Neer, Robert M. 1012
ニアジ
Niazi, Sher Afghan Khan 1022
ニアセ
Niasse, Alamara 1022
Niasse, Moustapha 1022
ニアリー
Neary, David 1011
Neary, Ian 1011
Neary, Paul 1011
ニアル
Nhial, Abdalla Deng 1022
ニアレ
Niare, Haby 1022
ニアン
Nearne, Eileen 1011
Niang, Amadou 1022
Niang, Georges 1022
Niang, Madické 1022
Niang, Mamadou 1022
Niang, M'Baye 1022
ニアング
Niang, Assmaa 1022
Niang, Hamane 1022
ニアンクアラ
Niangkouara, Nery Mantey 1022
ニアンドゥ
Niandou, Barry Bibata 1022
ニィクル
Nickl, Hans 1023
ニィクル・ウェーラー
Nickl-Weller, Christine 1023
ニイベルゲルト
Nievergelt, Yves 1025
ニイミ
Nimi, Robert Koji 1026
ニイムラ
Niimura, J.M.Ken 1025
ニイラハビマナ
Nyirahabimana, Solina 1039
ニイラミリモ
Nyiramirimo, Odette 1039
ニィリエ
Nirje, Bengt 1027
ニィーレエンベルク
Nierenberg, Danielle 1025
ニウ
Niu, Chen-zer 1027
ニウア
Niua, Folau 1027
ニヴェル
Nivelle, Armand 1027
ニヴォラ
Nivola, Claire A. 1028
ニウ・シトン
Niv Sithong 1028
ニーヴス
Neves, Richard 1017
ニーヴン
Niven, Jennifer 1028
Niven, Larry 1028
ニヴン
Niven, Paul R. 1028
ニエウィアドマ
Niewiadoma, Katarzyna 1025
ニエタ
Nieta, Ana I.Sánchez de la 1025
ニェト
Gneto, Priscilla 506
ニエト
Nieto, Alejandro 1025
Nieto, Sonia 1025
ニエト・メネンデス
Nieto Menéndez, Jorge 1025
ニエト・モンテシノス
Nieto Montesinos, Jorge 1025
ニェト＝ロドリゲス
Nieto Rodrígues, Rigoberto 1025
ニェト＝ロペス
Nieto López, José de Jesús 1025
ニエベアロヨ
Nieve Arroyo, Oliba Seledina 1025
ニエベス
Nieves, Juan 1025
ニエポムニン
Nepomnin, V.Ya. 1015
ニエミ
Niemi, Hannele 1025
Niemi, Marjaana 1025
Niemi, Mikael 1025
ニエミネン
Nieminen, Kai 1025
Nieminen, Leo 1025
ニェムチッチ
Nemcsics, Robert 1014
ニェメツ
Němec, Pavel 1014
ニエン
Nien, Nguyen Dy 1025
ニェンゼ
Nyenze, Francis 1039
ニエンチク
Niemczyk, Leon 1025
ニオンビ
Nyombi, Peter 1039
ニカ
Nica, Dan 1022
ニカイドウ
Nikaidô, Fumi 1025
ニカウ
N!xau 1028
ニカシオ
Nicasio, Juan 1022
ニーガス
Negus, Keith 1012
ニカストロ
Nicastro, Nicholas 1022
ニキエマ
Nikiema, Frederic 1025
ニキシン
Nikishin, Bogdan 1025
ニキータス
Nikitas, Derek 1025
ニキチナ
Nikitina, Elena 1026
ニキチン
Nikitin, Gleb 1025
Nikitin, Vladimir 1025
Nikitin, Yuri 1025
ニキティン
Nikitin, Evgeny 1025
Nikitin, Gleb 1025
ニキフォロフ
Nikiforov, Nikolai A. 1025
Nikiforov, Toma 1025
ニグ
Nigg, Joe 1025
ニクヴィスト
Nykvist, Sven 1039
ニクザド
Nikzad, Ali 1026
ニクス
Nix, Garth 1028
ニクス＝ライス
Nix-Rice, Nancy 1028
ニクソン
Nickson, David 1023
Nixon, Cynthia 1028
Nixon, Paul G. 1028
Nixon, Rob 1028
Nixon, Robin 1028
Nixon, Taurean 1028
ニクツェック
Nyczek, Tadeusz 1039
ニクパ
Nikpai, Rohullah 1026
ニクパイ
Nikpai, Rohullah 1026
ニークビスト
Nykvist, Ann-Christin 1039
ニクビスト
Nykvist, Sven 1039
ニグラ

Gnigla, Venance 506
ニクラウス
Nicklaus, Jack 1023
Niklaus, Andre 1026
ニクラス
Nicklaus, Jack 1023
Niklas, Troy 1026
ニクリーナ
Nikulina, Anna 1026
ニクリナ
Nikulina, Ina 1026
ニクルズ
Nickles, Elizabeth 1023
ニクルチナ
Nikulchina, Irina 1026
ニクレスク
Niculescu, Monica 1024
ニグレン
Nygren, Lennart 1039
Nygren, Tord 1039
ニークロ
Niekro, Joe 1024
ニケ
Niquet, Hervé 1027
ニコ
Niko, D.J. 1026
Niko, Lee Hang 1026
ニコシア
Nicosia, Gerald 1024
ニコデマス
Nicodemus, Ryan 1023
ニーコノフ
Nikonov, Vyacheslav Alekseevich 1026
ニコノフ
Nikonov, Vyacheslav Alekseevich 1026
ニー・ゴーノル
Ní Dhomhnaill, Nuala 1024
ニゴーノル
Ní Dhomhnaill, Nuala 1024
ニコバミェ
Nikobamye, Gaetan 1026
ニコポウラス
Nichopoulos, George 1023
ニコラ
Nicola, Davide 1023
Nicola, Jill 1023
Nicolas, Alrich 1024
Nicolas, Astier 1024
Nikolla, Lindita 1026
Nikora, Amberoti 1026
ニコライ
Nicolaï, Atzo 1023
Nicolai, Paolo 1023
Nicolaj, Aldo 1023
ニコライエフ
Nikolaev, Andrian Grigorievich 1026
ニコライシビリ
Nikolaishvili, Ramaz 1026
ニコライセン
Nicholaisen, Ida 1022
ニコライディ
Nicolaidi, Mike 1023
ニコライディス
Nikolaidis, Alexandros 1026
Nikolaidis, Antonis 1026
ニコライデス
Nikolaides, Nicos 1026
ニコラウ
Nicolaou, Ionas 1023
Nikolaou, Ionas 1026
ニコラウス
Nicholaus, Bret 1022
ニコラウドウ
Nikolaidou, Aikaterini 1026
ニコラエヴァ
Nikolajeva, Maria 1026
ニコラエス
Nicolăescu, Eugen 1023
ニコラエバ
Nikolajeva, Maria 1026
ニコラーエフ
Nikolaev, Andrian Grigorievich 1026
ニコラエフ
Nikolaev, Andrian Grigorievich 1026
ニコラエンコ
Nikolayenko, Stanislav 1026
ニコラシカ
Nikolaschka, Jack 1026
ニコラス
Nicholas, Albert 1022
Nicholas, Alexander S. 1022
Nicholas, Brett 1022
Nicholas, Evan A. 1022
Nicholas, Fayard 1022
Nicholas, Jack D. 1022
Nicholas, Joseph G. 1022
Nicholas, Lynn H. 1022
Nicholas, Melford 1022
Nicholas, Ted 1022
Nicolas 1023
Nicolas, Adolfo 1023
Nicolas, Dadi 1024
Nicolas, Moritz 1024
ニコラ-リサ
Nicola-Lisa, W. 1023
ニコリッチ
Nikolic, Djordje 1026
Nikolić, Mišo 1026
Nikolić, Tomislav 1026
ニコリーノ
Nicolino, Justin 1024
ニコリン
Nicollin, Louis 1024
ニコール
Nicoll, Neil 1024
ニコル
Niccol, Andrew 1022
Nichol, David 1022
Nichol, James W. 1022
Nicholl, Charles 1022
Nicol, A.M. 1023
Nicol, C.W. 1023
Nicol, Janni 1023
Nicol, Maggie 1023
Nicol, Rachel 1023
Nicole 1024
Nicoll, Andrew 1024
Nicoll, Helen 1024
Nicoll, Mercedes 1024
Nicolle, David 1024
ニコルス
Nicholls, Bob 1022
Nichols, Austin 1023
Nichols, Jeff 1023
Nichols, John 1023
Nichols, Michael P. 1023
Nichols, Ralph G. 1023
Nichols, Robin 1023
Nichols, Sarah 1023
Nichols, Theo 1023
ニコルズ
Nicholls, Alex 1022
Nicholls, David 1022
Nicholls, Geoff 1022
Nicholls, Henry 1022
Nicholls, Jamie 1023
Nicholls, Peter 1023
Nicholls, Sally 1023
Nichols, Catherine 1023
Nichols, Linda 1023
Nichols, Lisa 1023
Nichols, Michael 1023
Nichols, Mike 1023
Nichols, Shana 1023
ニコルスン
Nicholson, Geoff 1023
Nicholson, Jack 1023
ニコルソン
Nicholson, Andrew 1023
Nicholson, Arnold 1023
Nicholson, Bill 1023
Nicholson, Ernest Wilson 1023
Nicholson, Geoff 1023
Nicholson, Heather Norris 1023
Nicholson, Helen 1023
Nicholson, Jack 1023
Nicholson, Jim 1023
Nicholson, Jon 1023
Nicholson, Joy 1023
Nicholson, Michael 1023
Nicholson, Nigel 1023
Nicholson, Peggy 1023
Nicholson, Robert 1023
Nicholson-Lord, David 1023
Nicolson, Iain 1024
Nicolson, Nigel 1024
ニコレ
Nicolet, Aurèle 1024
ニコレイ
Nicolay, Chris 1024
ニコレッティ
Nicoletti, Manuel 1024
ニコレリス
Nicolelis, Miguel 1024
ニコロー
Nicholaw, Casey 1022
ニコローゾ
Nicoloso, Paolo 1024
ニコロフ
Nickoloff, Edward L. 1023
Nikolov, Vladmir 1026
ニザミ
Nizami, Maulana M. Rahman 1028
Nizami, Rahman 1028
ニサラ
Nissala, Laoukissam 1027
ニーザーランド
Netherland, Wynn 1016
ニシ
Nish, Ian Hill 1027
Nishi, Setsuko Matsunaga 1027
Nishi, Tak Takehiro 1027
ニシエ
Nishié, Sarah Ann 1027
ニジェゴロゴフ
Nizhegorodov, Denis 1028
ニジェゴロドフ
Nizhegorodov, Denis 1028
ニシェック
Neshek, Pat 1015
ニシオ
Nishio, Alan Takeshi 1027
ニシオ・ニシオ
Nishio Nisio, Victor 1027
ニジガマ
Nizigama, Clotilde 1028
Nizigama, Gabriel 1028
ニジギビマナ
Nizigivimana, Marie Rose 1028
ニシクボ
Nishikubo, Mizuho 1027
ニシーザ
Nicieza, Fabian 1023
ニシザワ
Nishizawa, Luis 1027
Nishizawa, Ryue 1027
ニジジレ
Nizigire, Potame 1028
ニシチェク
Nyschuk, Yevhen 1039
ニシマ
Nisima, Maureen 1027
ニジムベレ
Nijimbere, Josiane 1025
ニシャニ
Nishani, Bujar Faik 1027
ニシャニアン
Nichanian, Veronique 1022
ニース
Neath, Ian 1011
Nies, Alan S. 1025
ニーズィー
Gneezy, Uri 506
ニスカ
Niska, Kathleen 1027
ニスカネン
Niskanen, Iivo 1027
Niskanen, Kerttu 1027
ニスキエル
Niskier, Arnaldo 1027
ニスタット
Nystad, Claudia 1039
ニーストランド
Nystrand, Stefan 1039
ニストル
Nistor, Steliana 1027
ニースバーガー
Nies-Berger, Edouard 1025
ニスベット
Nisbett, Patrice 1027
Nisbett, Richard E. 1027
ニズベット
Nisbett, Patrice 1027
ニース＝マズール
Nys-Mazure, Colette 1039
ニースマン
Neasman, Sharrod 1011
ニースリング
Neethling, Ryk 1012
ニースン
Neeson, Liam 1012
ニセゼラナ
Ntisezerana, Gabriel 1036
ニーセン
Niessen, Susan 1025
ニソール
Nesaule, Agate 1015

ニ

ニーソン
Neeson, Gael 1012
Neeson, Liam 1012
ニーダー
Neider, Jackie 1013
ニーダーベルガー
Niederberger, Andreas 1024
ニーダホッファ
Niederhoffer, Victor 1024
ニーダーマイアー
Niedermeier, Georg 1024
ニーダーマイヤー
Niedermeier, Michael 1024
ニーダーマン
Niederman, Derrick 1024
ニーダム
Needham, Hal 1012
Needham, Richard Francis 1012
Needham, Roger 1012
Needham, Tristan 1012
ニーダ＝リューメリン
Nida-Rümelin, Julian 1024
ニーダーレヒナー
Niederlechner, Florian 1024
ニーダン・ファイヒティンガー
Niedan-Feichtinger, Susana 1024
ニーダン＝ファイヒティンガー
Niedan-Feichtinger, Susana 1024
ニーチェ
Nice 1022
ニチカソフ
Nichkasov, Anatoly I. 1022
ニーチュ
Nitzsch, Rudiger Von 1027
ニツァ
Niţă, Constantin 1027
ニッカム
Niccum, Christian 1022
ニッキ
Nikki 1026
ニッキー
Nikki 1026
ニック
Nick 1023
Nick, Christophe 1023
ニックス
Nicks, Stevie 1023
Nix, Jonathan 1028
Nix, Louis 1028
Nix, Matt 1028
ニックリン
Nicklin, Flip 1023
Nicklin, Jane 1023
Nicklin, Linda 1023
ニッグル
Niggle, Christopher J. 1025
ニックレン
Nicklen, Paul 1023
ニッケル
Nickell, Joe 1023
ニッコリ
Niccoli, Riccardo 1022
ニッサン
Nisan, Noam 1027
ニッシム
Nissim, Doron 1027
ニッシュ
Nish, Ian Hill 1027
ニッスク
Nix, Roosevelt 1028
ニッセル
Nissel, John J. 1027
ニッセン
Nissen, George P. 1027
Nissen, Kyle 1027
ニッセンズ
Nyssens, Marthe 1039
ニッセンボーム
Nissenbaum, Stephen 1027
ニッチェ
Nitzsche, Dirk 1027
ニッチュ
Nitsch, Cornelia 1027
ニッツ
Nitz, Wolfgang R. 1027
Nitze, Paul Henry 1027
ニット
Nitya, Pibulsonggram 1027
ニッパー
Nipper, Zachary 1027
ニッパート
Nippert, Louise 1027
ニッフェネガー
Niffenegger, Audrey 1025
ニディ
Nidhi, Bimalendra 1024
ニティ・イーオシーウォン
Nithi Ieosiwong 1027
ニティ・イオシーウォン
Nithi Ieosiwong 1027
ニティリキナ
Ntilikina, Frank 1036
ニーデラー
Niederer, Armin 1024
ニーデルハウゼル
Niederhauser, Emil 1024
ニーデルンフーバー
Niedernhuber, Barbara 1024
ニーデンドルフ
Nierendorf, Karl 1025
ニート
Neate, Patrick 1011
Nieto, Jamie 1025
ニド
Nido, Tomas 1024
ニドゥップ
Ngedup, Sangay 1020
ニドゥプ
Nedup, Sangey 1012
ニードハム
Needham, Kate 1012
ニードラー
Needler, Matthew 1012
ニーナン
Neenan, Michael 1012
ニニー
Ninie 1027
ニニオ
Ninio, Jacques 1027
ニーニスト
Niinistö, Jussi 1025
Niinistö, Sauli Väinämö 1025
Niinistö, Ville 1025
ニニナハズウェ
Nininahazwe, Godelieve 1027
ニー・ニー・ミン
Ni Ni Mynt 1027
ニニンビ
Gnininvi, Léopold Messan 506
ニネ
Niney, Pierre 1026
ニノミヤ
Ninomiya, Joanne Miyako 1027
Ninomiya, Sonia Regina Longhi 1027
ニーバー
Niebuhr, Richard R. 1024
ニーハウス
Niehaus, Dave 1024
Niehaus, Greg R. 1024
ニパート
Nippert, Louise 1027
ニバリ
Nibali, Vincenzo 1022
ニハンガザ
Nihangaza, Charles 1025
ニビギラ
Nibigira, Concilie 1022
ニピット
Niphit, Intharasombat 1027
ニビャバンディ
Nivyabandi, Martin 1028
ニビラティジェ
Nibiratije, Jean-Marie 1022
ニーフ
Knief, Herman 747
ニフォントフ
Nifontov, Ivan 1025
ニーフース
Nyhus, Svein 1039
ニブス
Nibbs, Arthur 1022
ニブリー
Nibley, Lydia 1022
ニブレット
Niblett, Robin 1022
ニブロム
Nyblom, Haakan Erik 1039
ニーブン
Niven, David 1028
ニーベリ
Nyberg, Fredrik 1039
ニーベル
Niebel, Dirk 1024
ニベン
Niven, Steve 1028
ニーベンヒューゼン
Nieuwenhuysen, Andrée Van 1025
ニーボッド
Nievod, Abraham 1025
ニーポート
Nieporte, Grant 1025
ニーホフ
Niehoff, Debra 1024
Nyhoff, Larry R. 1039
ニーポルド
Niepold, Ruprecht 1025
ニマー
Nimmer, Melville B. 1026
ニーマイアー
Neimeyer, Robert A. 1013
Niemeyer, Oscar 1025
Niemeyer, Peter 1025
ニーマイヤー
Niemeyer, Oscar 1025
ニーマーク
Neimark, Jill 1013
ニマニ
Nimani, Fuad 1026
ニーマン
Ne'eman, Jacob 1012
Neeman, Yaakov 1012
Neiman, Carol 1013
Neiman, LeRoy 1013
Niemann, Linda 1025
Nyman, Marcus 1039
ニミ
Nimy, Romain 1026
ニミア
Neemia, Namoliki 1012
ニミエ
Nimier, Marie 1026
ニーム
Neame, Ronald 1011
Nghiem, Paul T. 1020
ニムケ
Nimke, Stefan 1026
ニームス
Nemeth, Maria 1015
ニムチェンコ
Nimchenko, Ievgeniia 1026
ニムボナ
Nimbona, Leon 1026
Nimubona, Julien 1026
ニムラ
Nimura, Janice P. 1026
ニムレ
Nimley, Thomas Yaya 1026
ニムロッド
Nimrod, Elvin 1026
ニムロド
Nimrod, Elvin 1026
ニーメシュ
Niemesch, Luisa 1025
ニーメヤー
Neimeyer, Robert A. 1013
ニーメラー
Niemöller, Martin 1025
ニモ
Nimmo, Brandon 1026
Nimmo, Harry 1026
Nimmo, Jenny 1026
ニモイ
Nimoy, Leonard 1026
ニャ
Nha, Chu Tuan 1021
Nha, Phung Xuan 1021
ニャオレ
Gnahope, Eddy 506
Gnahore, Dobet 506
ニャガ
Nyagha, Joseph 1038
ニャカイリマ
Nyakairima, Aronda 1038
ニャカジャ
Gnacadja, Luc 506
ニャカニ
Nyakane, Trevor 1038
ニャク
Nhek Bun Chhay 1022
ニャク・ブンチャイ
Nhek Bun Chhay 1022
ニャザリエワ
Niyazalieva, Damira 1028

ニ

ニャサンゴ
Nyasango, Cuthbert 1039
ニヤジムベトフ
Niyazymbetov, Adilbek 1028
ニャシンベ
Gnassinbé, Kpatcha 506
Gnassingbe, Amah 506
Gnassingbé, Faure 506
ニャス
Nhasse, Bilony 1022
ニヤズベコフ
Niyazbekov, Daulet 1028
ニヤゾフ
Niyazov, Saparmurat A. 1028
Niyazov, Shailoobek 1028
ニャチャエ
Nyachae, Simeon 1038
ニャッカ
Nhaca, Soares 1021
ニャット・ハイン
Thich Nhat Hanh 1396
ニャーナアムリターナンダ
Jnanamritananda Puri 674
ニャナスマナ
Gnanasumana, Delduwe 506
ニャナセカラン
Gnanasekaran, Linda 506
ニャニェス
Ñáñez, Freddy 1004
ニャノ
Nyanor, Charles Omar 1038
ニャバ
Nyaba, Peter Adowok 1038
ニャバリ
Nyabally, Lamin 1038
ニャブリ
Gnabry, Serge 506
ニヤマ
Niyama, Haruo 1028
ニャミアン
Gnamien, Konan 506
ニャミトウェ
Nyamitwe, Alain Aimé 1038
ニャム
Nyamu, Jesaya 1038
ニャムウィザ
Nyamwiza, Gerard 1038
ニャムウィシ
Nyamwisi, Antipas Mbusa 1038
ニャムガボ
Nyamugabo, Claude Bazibuhe 1038
ニャムダバー
Nyamdavaa, Pagvajavyn 1038
ニャムドルジ
Nyamdorj, Tsendiin 1038
ニャムラブ
Nyamugabo, Claude Bazibuhe 1038
ニャランドゥ
Nyalandu, Lazaro Samuel 1038
ニャルヒリラ
Nyaruhirira, Innocent 1039
ニャン
Nhan, Nguyen Thien 1022
Niane, Mary Teuw 1022
Niang, Mame Mbaye 1022
ニャン・ウィン
Nyan Win 1039
ニャンガ
Nyanga, Yannick 1038
ニャンガウ
Nyangau, Ruth Bisibori 1038
ニャング
Niang, Cheikh 1022
Niang, Mamadou 1022
ニャンドウィ
Nyandwi, Desire 1038
Nyandwi, Simon 1038
ニャン・トゥン
Nyan Tun 1039
ニャン・トゥン・アウン
Nyan Tun Aung 1039
ニャンバヤル
Nyambayar, Tugstsogt 1038
ニャンビウ
Nhambiu, Jorge Olívio Penicela 1022
ニャンブヤ
Nyambuya, Michael 1038
ニュー
New, W.H. 1017
ニューイッツ
Newitz, Annalee 1018
ニューイット
Newitt, Malyn 1018
ニュウ
Nyeu, Tao 1039
ニューウェル
Newell, Adam 1018
Newell, Gabe 1018
Newell, Mike 1018
Newell, Tricia 1018
ニュウエル
Newell, Patrick 1018
ニューウェンハイス
Nieuwenhuis, Kirk 1025
ニュウニュウ
NiuNiu 1027
ニューエル
Newell, Pete 1018
Newell, Ronald J. 1018
ニューエン
Nguyen, Marcel 1021
ニュエン
Nguyen, Thi Thiet 1021
Nuyen, Jenny-mai 1038
ニュエンヤマ
Ngwenyama, Ojelanki 1021
ニューオール
Newall, Diana 1017
ニューカーク
Newkirk, James 1018
ニューカム
Newcomb, Jacky 1017
Newcomb, Richard F. 1018
Newcomb, Sean 1018
ニューキー＝バーデン
Newkey-Burden, Chas 1018
ニュクリ
Gnoukouri, Assane Demoya 506
ニューコム
Neukom, Bill 1016
Newcomb, Jacky 1017
ニューサム
Newsom, Gavin Christopher 1019
Newsome, James D. 1019
ニュシ
Nyusi, Filipe Jacint 1039
ニューシェル
Neuschel, Robert Percy 1017
ニュージェント
Nugent, David 1037
Nugent, Mike 1037
Nugent, Richard 1037
Nugent, Stephen 1037
Nugent, Tom 1037
ニュースタット
Neustadt, Richard E. 1017
ニューストローム
Newstrom, John W. 1019
ニューズナー
Neusner, Jacob 1017
ニュスライン・フォルハルト
Nüsslein-Volhard, Christiane 1038
ニュスラインフォルハルト
Nüsslein-Volhard, Christiane 1038
ニューソン
Newson, Elizabeth 1019
Newson, John 1019
ニュッスリ
Nüssli, Rosmarie 1038
ニュッセル
Nüssel, Friederike 1038
ニューディック
Newdick, Thomas 1018
ニュート
Newth, Eirik 1019
ニュートン
Newton, Cam 1019
Newton, Chris 1019
Newton, Derek 1019
Newton, Eddie 1019
Newton, Grant W. 1019
Newton, Helmut 1019
Newton, Jill 1019
Newton, John 1019
Newton, Kristin 1019
Newton, Michael 1019
Newton, Richard 1019
Newton, Roger G. 1019
Newton, Teddy 1019
Newton, William Ritchey 1019
ニュートン・ジョン
Newton-John, Olivia 1019
ニューハウス
Newhouse, Donald 1018
Newhouse, John 1018
Newhouse, Joseph P. 1018
Newhouse, Marshall 1018
Newhouse, Samuel, Jr. 1018
ニューバーガー
Neuberger, Roy 1016
ニューバーグ
Neuburg, Matt 1016
Newberg, Andrew B. 1017
ニューハース
Neuharth, Allen H. 1016
Neuharth, Dan 1016
ニューハード
Newhard, Jamie 1018
ニューハム
Newham, Cameron 1018
ニュービー
Newby, David M. 1017
Newby, Eric 1017
ニュービッグ
Neubig, Graham 1016
ニューフェルツ
Neufeldt, Susan Allstetter 1016
ニューフェルド
Neufeld, Gordon 1016
Neufeld, Mace 1016
Neufeld, Peter 1016
ニュフェルド
Neufeld, Jacqueline Krause 1016
ニューベリー
Newberry, Deb 1017
Newberry, Giorgio 1017
Newbery (michell), Chantelle 1017
Newbery, Linda 1017
Newbery, Robert 1017
Newbury, John Ernest 1017
Newbury, Mickey 1017
ニューベル
Nubel, Alexander 1036
ニューポート
Newport, Cal 1018
Newport, Jerry 1018
Newport, Mary 1018
Newport, Mary T. 1018
ニューボルド
Newbold, Heather 1017
Newbold, Robert C. 1017
ニューマイヤー
Neumeier, Marty 1017
Newmyer, Robert F. 1018
ニューマーク
Newmark, Andy 1018
ニューマン
Neuman, M.Gary 1016
Neuman, Tom S. 1016
Neuman, W.Russell 1016
Neumann, Adam 1016
Newman, Arnold 1018
Newman, Barbara 1018
Newman, Brooke 1018
Newman, Cory Frank 1018
Newman, Danny 1018
Newman, David 1018
Newman, Frank 1018
Newman, Jack 1018
Newman, Jeff 1018
Newman, Joseph P. 1018
Newman, Katherine S. 1018
Newman, Kevin 1018
Newman, Kim 1018
Newman, Margaret A. 1018
Newman, Marjorie 1018
Newman, Mark 1018
Newman, Martin 1018
Newman, Michael G. 1018
Newman, Mildred 1018
Newman, Nanette 1018
Newman, Paul 1018
Newman, Phyllis 1018
Newman, Randy 1018
Newman, Robert G. 1018
Newman, Sally 1018
Newman, Sam 1018
Newman, Stuart A. 1018
Newman, Terence 1018
Newman, Thomas 1018

Newman, Victor 1018
Nyman, Anders 1039
ニューメイヤー
Newmyer, Robert F. 1018
ニューライタ
Neureiter, Norman P. 1017
ニューランド
Newland, Marv 1018
Newland, Samuel J. 1018
ニュランド
Nyland, Orjan 1039
ニュリ
Nury, Fabien 1038
ニューリン
Newlin, Keith 1018
ニュルンベルガー
Nürnberger, Christian 1038
ニューワース
Neuwirth, Robert 1017
ニューワーバー
Nieuwerburgh, Stijin Van 1025
ニュンガ
Nhunga, Marcos Alexandre 1022
ニユンゲコ
Niyungeko, Vincent 1028
ニューンズ
Nunes, Debra A. 1037
Nunes, Paul F. 1037
ニュン・ティン
Nyunt Tin 1039
ニーヨ
Ne-Yo 1019
ニヨット・コック
Niyot Kok, Peter 1028
ニョトゥン
Njaatun, Ida 1028
ニョニ
Nyoni, Sithembiso 1039
ニョファム
Gnofam, Ninsao 506
Gnofame, Zoumaro 506
ニョム
Nyom, Allan 1039
ニヨヤンカナ
Niyoyankana, Germain 1028
ニョーリ
Gnoli, Gherardo 506
ニョリ
Gnoli, Gherardo 506
ニヨンクル
Niyonkuru, Emmanuel 1028
Niyonkuru, Pélate 1028
ニョンゴ
Nyongo, Anyang 1039
Nyong'o, Lupita 1039
ニヨンサバ
Niyonsaba, Ambroise 1028
Niyonsaba, Francine 1028
ニョンロンフン
Gnonlonfoun, Isidore 506
Gnonlonfoun, Joseph 506
ニーラー
Nealer, Kevin G. 1011
ニラ
Nila, F. Moeloek 1026
ニラ・F.
Nila, F. Moeloek 1026
ニライガス
Ngiraingas, Jackson 1020
ニラサファリ
Nyirasafari, Esperance 1039
ニラジラ
Niragira, Clotilde 1027
ニラハビネザ
Nyirahabineza, Valerrie 1039
ニラハビマナ
Nyirahabimana, Solina 1039
ニーリー
Nealy, Quayshaun 1011
Neary, Aaron 1011
Neely, Andy D. 1012
ニール
Kneale, Matthew 747
Kneale, Nigel 747
Neal, Christopher Silas 1011
Neal, Durron 1011
Neal, Keanu 1011
Neal, Larry 1011
Neal, M.J. 1011
Neal, Patricia 1011
Neal, Penelope 1011
Neal, Rajion 1011
Neal, Virginia 1011
Neale, John M. 1011
Neel, Julien 1012
Neil, Fred 1013
Neil, Joanna 1013
Neil, Theresa 1013
Neil, Vince 1013
Neill, Andrew 1013
Neill, Michael 1013
Neill, Sam 1013
Niere, Mary 1025
ニル
Nil, Adam 1026
ニルア
Nirua, Jean-Pierre 1027
ニールギーン - ブジュン
Neergheen-Bhujun, Vidushi S. 1012
ニールズ
Neels, Betty 1012
ニールスン
Nielsen, Helen 1024
ニールセン
Nelsen, Robert 1013
Nelsen, Roger B. 1013
Nielsen, Christopher 1024
Nielsen, Elsebeth Gerner 1024
Nielsen, Gyda Skat 1024
Nielsen, Hanne Warming 1024
Nielsen, Hans Frede 1024
Nielsen, Havard 1024
Nielsen, Helen 1024
Nielsen, Holger 1024
Nielsen, Jaime 1024
Nielsen, Jakob 1024
Nielsen, Jakob Axel 1024
Nielsen, Jennifer A. 1024
Nielsen, Jerri 1024
Nielsen, Jorgen Erik 1024
Nielsen, Kim E. 1024
Nielsen, Kris R. 1024
Nielsen, Leslie 1024
Nielsen, Michael 1024
Nielsen, Michael A. 1024
Nielsen, Mie 1024
Nielsen, Niels Christian 1024
Nielsen, Peder Holk 1024
Nielsen, Rick 1025
Nielsen, Sofie Carsten 1025
Nielsen, Stine 1025
Nilsen, Anna 1026
ニールソン
Neilson, Gary L. 1013
Nielsen, Helen 1024
Nilsson, Pia 1026
ニルソン
Nilsson, Ann-Mari 1026
Nilsson, Birgit 1026
Nilsson, Henrik 1026
Nilsson, Lennart 1026
Nilsson, Mattias, Jr. 1026
Nilsson, Stefan 1026
Nilsson, Sten 1026
Nilsson, Ulf 1026
ニルソン・トーレ
Nilsson Thore, Maria 1026
ニルッコ
Nirkko, Tapio 1027
ニールド
Nield, Ted 1024
ニルマーラ
Nirmala 1027
ニルマラ尼
Nirmala 1027
ニルマン
Ngirmang, Gregorio 1020
ニールント
Nylund, Camilla 1039
ニールンド
Nylund, Camilla 1039
ニルンド
Nylund, Camilla 1039
ニレカニ
Nilekani, Nandan M. 1026
ニーレンダー
Nieländer, Peter 1024
ニレンダ
Nyirenda, Carol 1039
ニーレンドルフ
Nierendorf, Karl 1025
ニーレンバーグ
Nierenberg, Juliet 1025
Nirenberg, Jesse S. 1027
Nirenberg, Louis 1027
Nirenberg, Marshall Warren 1027
ニレンバーグ
Nirenberg, Marshall Warren 1027
ニロンゴ
Nyirongo, Gladys 1039
ニワットタムロン
Nivatthamrong, Boonsongpaisal 1027
ニン
Ning, Feng 1026
Ning, Tak H. 1026
Ninh, Vu Van 1027
ニンガトルム・サヨ
Ningatoloum Sayo, Armel 1027
ニンガトルムサヨ
Ningatoloum Sayo, Armel 1027
ニンコヴィッチ
Ninkovic, Nikola 1027
ニンコビッチ
Ninkovich, Rob 1027
ニンジャ
Ninja, Willi 1027
ニンドレラ
Nindorera, Eugene 1026
ニンノボア
Nin Novoa, Rodolfo 1027

【ヌ】

ヌー
Nuh, Mohammad 1037
ヌアイミ
al-Nuaimi, Abdullah Belhaif 1036
al-Nuaimi, Ali Ibrahim 1036
al-Nuaimi, Issa Saad al-Jafali 1036
al-Nuaimi, Majid bin Ali 1036
al-Nuaymi, Mohammed Yahya Awdah 1036
ヌアチューク
Nwachukwu, Uzoma 1038
ヌアラ
Noualhat, Laure 1034
ヌーイ
Nooyi, Indra K. 1031
ヌイ
Noui, Ahmed 1034
Noui, Tarik 1034
Nouy, Danièle 1034
ヌイスル
Nuissl, Ekkehard 1037
ヌヴィアン
Nouvian, Claire 1034
ヌウェケ
Nweke, Frank 1038
ヌーヴェル
Nouvel, Jean 1034
ヌウォス
Nwosu, Alphonsus 1038
ヌエイミ
Nueimi, Tayseer 1036
ヌエニミガボ
Nyenimigabo, Jean-Jacques 1039
ヌオン・チア
Nuon Chea 1037
ヌオン・チェア
Nuon Chea 1037
ヌカイセリー
Nkaissery, Joseph 1028
ヌカクラ
Nqakula, Charles 1035
ヌガコトムディオ
Ngako Tomdio, Michael 1019
ヌガソンガ
Ngasongwa, Juma 1019
ヌガソングワ
Ngasongwa, Juma 1019
ヌガチゼコ
Ngatjizeko, Immanuel 1020
ヌカテ
Nkate, Jacob 1028
ヌガヌジュメシ
Nganou Djoumessi, Emmanuel 1019
ヌカバデカ
Nkavadeka, Isabel

Manuel 1028
ヌガファン
Ngafuan, Augustine 1019
ヌガラレ
Ngalale, Precious 1019
ヌガランベ
Ngarambe, Francois 1019
ヌガリ
Ngari, Idriss 1019
ヌガリマデン
Ngarimaden, David Houdeingar 1019
ヌガルソ
Ngarso, Silvère 1019
ヌガルディギナ
Ngardiguina, Abdoulaye 1019
ヌガル・ビベ・マセナ
Ngalle Bibehe Massena, Jean Ernest 1019
ヌガロ
Ngaro, Alfred 1019
Nougaro, Claude 1034
ヌガワラ
N'gawara, Mamouth Nahor 1020
ヌカン
Nukan, Atinc 1037
ヌガンガ
Nouganga, Jean-Baptiste 1034
ヌカンギ
Nkangi, Mayanja 1028
ヌガンダジーナ
Ngandajina, João Baptista 1019
ヌガンパララ
Ngcamphalala, David 1020
ヌガンビア
Ngambia, Magloire 1019
ヌカンブレ
Nkambule, Mfomfo 1028
ヌギゲ
Ngige, Chris Nwabueze 1020
ヌギディンワ
Nghidinwa, Rosalia 1020
ヌギムティナ
Nghimtina, Erkki 1020
ヌキリ
Nkili, Robert 1028
ヌキリムナビシタ
Nquilim Nabitchita, Sola 1035
ヌギル
Ngilu, Charity 1020
ヌギンビ
Ngimbi, César Lubamba 1020
Nguimbi, Pierre Michel 1020
ヌギンブ
Ngimbu, Christabel 1020
ヌク
Nuku 1037
ヌグ
Ng, Josiah 1019
ヌクァクラ
Nqakula, Charles 1035
ヌグア・ヌフム
Ngua Nfumu, Santiago 1020
ヌグアヌム
Ngoua Neme, Pastor 1020
ヌグアンジカ
Ngouandjika, Fidéle 1020
ヌグインダ
Nguinda, Pierre-Daniel 1020
ヌグウィリジ
Ngwilizi, Hassan 1021
ヌクウィンティ
Nkwinti, Gugile 1029
ヌクエ
N'koue, Ange 1029
ヌクエテ
Nkuete, Jean 1029
ヌクェト
Nkuete, Jean 1029
ヌグエニャ
Nguhenha, Alcido 1020
ヌグオニンバ
Ngouonimba, Josué Rodrigue 1020
ヌグザ・カルルイボンド
Nguza Karl-I-Bond 1021
ヌクシ
Nkusi, Laurent 1029
Nkusi, Sam 1029
ヌクジ
Nkusi, Laurent 1029
ヌグトゥ
Ngute, Joseph Dion 1020
Ngutu, Joseph 1021
ヌクトゥムラ
Nkutumula, Alberto Hawa Januário 1029
ヌグニ
Nguni, Sylvester 1020
ヌグバネ
Ngubane, Ben 1020
ヌグブ
Ngoubou, Etienne 1020
ヌグベユ
Ngoubeyou, Françoins-Xavier 1020
ヌクル
Nkoulou, Nicolas 1029
ヌグル
N'goulou, Abraham Gotto 1020
Ngoulou, Gata 1020
Ngoulou, Ngata 1020
Nguele, Réné Ze 1020
ヌクルニザ
Nkurunziza, Pascal 1029
ヌクルンジザ
Nkurunziza, Pierre 1029
Nkurunziza, Triphonie 1029
ヌグワブブ
Ngwaboubou, Ernest 1021
ヌグワンドゥ
Mg'wandu, Pius 941
Ng'wandu, Pius 1021
ヌグワンメッシア
Ngwanmessia, Lucy 1021
ヌクンク
Nkunku, Christopher 1029
ヌクンジキエ
Nkundikije, Andre 1029
ヌケア
Nkea, Francis 1028
ヌゲアドゥーム
Ngueadoum, Assane 1020
ヌゲアドゥム
Ngueadoum, Assane 1020
ヌケカ
Nkeka, René Issekemanga 1028
ヌケザバヒジ
Nkezabahizi, Tharcisse 1028
ヌゲサン
N'guessan, Amani 1020
ヌゲシ
Nxesi, Thembelani Thulas 1038
ヌゲニ
Ng'eny, Kipng'eno arap 1020
ヌゲーニャ
Nguenha, Alcido 1020
ヌゲヌ・ケンデク
Nguene Kendeck, Pauline Iréne 1020
ヌゲマ
Nguema, Teodoro Obiang 1020
ヌゲマ・エソノ
Nguema Esono, Lucas 1020
ヌゲマエソノ
Nguema Esono, Lucas 1020
ヌゲマオビアンマング
Nguemaobiang Mangu, Teodoro 1020
ヌゲマオボノ
Nguema Obono, Salomón 1020
ヌゲマ・オングエン
Nguema Onguene, Marcelino 1020
ヌゲマ・オンゲネ
Nguema Onguene, Clemente Engonga 1020
Nguema Onguene, Marcelino 1020
ヌゲマムバ
Nguema Mba, Manuel 1020
ヌゲマ・ムバソゴ
Nguema Mbasogo, Teodoro Obiang 1020
ヌゲレ
Nguele, Réné Ze 1020
ヌゲレジャ
Ngeleja, William Mganga 1020
ヌゲレード
Nougayrède, Natalie 1034
ヌゲンダンガニャ
Ngendanganya, Casimir 1020
ヌコアナマシャバネ
Nkoana-mashabane, Maite 1028
ヌゴイ
Ngoy, Honorius 1020
ヌゴウェムボナ
Ngowembona, Dieudonne 1020
ヌゴグワヌブサ
Ngogwanubusa, Juvenal 1020
ヌコゲベカレ
Nkoghe Bekale, Julien 1028
ヌコゴ
Ncogo, Braulio 1010
ヌコゴ・ヌドン
Nkogo Ndong, Florentino 1028
ヌゴマ
Ngoma, Angelique 1020
Ngoma, Arthur 1020
ヌゴママドゥングウ
Ngoma Madoungou, Senturel 1020
ヌゴム
Ngom, Nafissatou Diouf 1020
Ngom, Ousmane 1020
ヌコムブラ
Nko-mbula, Juan 1028
ヌコモ
Nkomo, John 1028
Nkomo, Samuel 1028
ヌゴモムメノノ
Ngomo Mbengono, Francisco Javier 1020
ヌゴル
Ngor, Ngor Kolong 1020
ヌゴルヌゴル
Ngolle Ngolle, Elvis 1020
ヌゴレヌグウェセ
Ngole Ngwese, Philip 1020
ヌゴレヌグエセ
Ngole Ngwese, Philip 1020
ヌコロ
Nkolo, Balamage 1028
Nkolo, Cecile Bomba 1028
ヌコンゴ
Nkongo, Maxime N'Koue 1028
ヌゴンジェ
Ngaunje, Marjorie 1020
ヌゴンババ
N'gon Baba, Laurent 1020
ヌサイラト
Nsairat, Soud 1035
ヌサドゥ
Nsadhu, Basoga 1035
ヌサムプトゥエリマ
N'sa Mputu Elima, Bavon 1035
ヌサンザバガンワ
Nsanzabaganwa, Monique 1035
ヌサンゼ
Nsanze, Augustin 1035
ヌジー
Njie, Malick 1028
Njie, Nancy 1028
ヌジェイ
Ndiaye, Diakite Fatoumata 1010
ヌジェゼ
Njeze, Fidelia 1028
ヌジェムン
Njiemoun, Issac 1028
ヌジェル
Njeru, Peter 1028
ヌジェンダハヨ
Ngendahayo, Francoise 1020
ヌジェント
Nugent, Leah 1037
ヌジェンボ
Ndjengbot, Fernande 1011
ヌジーセイディ
Njiesaidy, Isatou 1028

ヌシバンゼ
Nsibandze, Macford 1036
ヌシバンビ
Nsibambi, Apolo 1036
ヌジマンデ
Nzimande, Blade 1039
ヌシミリマナ
Nshimirimana, Adolphe 1036
Nshimirimana, Denis 1036
ヌジャイ
Ndiaye, Aly Ngouille 1010
Ndiaye, Aminata Mbengue 1010
N'diaye, Bah 1010
N'diaye, Kéita Rokiatou 1010
Ndiaye, Mankeur 1010
Ndiaye, Mbagnick 1010
Ndiaye, Rachid 1010
Njie, Alhaji Bakary 1028
Njie, Mamburay 1028
ヌジャイセイディ
Njiesaidy, Isatou 1028
ヌージャイム
Noujaim, Jehane 1034
ヌシュティ
Nshuti, Manasseh 1036
ヌシュレコ
Nhleko, Nkosinathi 1022
ヌジョニ
Njoni, Philippe 1028
ヌジョマ
Nujoma, Sam 1037
Nujoma, Sam Daniel 1037
ヌジョムエル
Njoh Mouelle, Ebénézer 1028
ヌジラ
Nzila, Pierre 1039
ヌシル
Nsilou, Claude Alphonse 1036
ヌシルー
Nsilou, Clause Alphonse 1036
ヌシンゴ
Nsingo, Marina 1036
ヌシンバ
Nsimba, Charles Mwando 1036
ヌスエミチャ
Nsue Micha, Fidel 1036
ヌスエミラン
Nsue Milang, Diosdado Vicente 1036
ヌスエモクイ
Nsue Mokuy, Alfonso 1036
ヌズジ・ワムボンボ
Nzuzi Wa Mbombo, Catherine 1039
ヌースター
Knoester, Bob 748
ヌズバ
Nzouba, Léon 1039
ヌスバウム
Nussbaum, Martha Craven 1038
ヌズマロ
Nxumalo, Owen 1038
ヌズラマ・ティモテ
Nzulama Thimothe, Moleka 1039
ヌスール
Ensour, Abdullah 404
ヌゼイマナ
Nzeyimana, Léontine 1039
ヌゼソ
Nzesso, Madias 1039
ヌセ・ヌフマ
Nse Nfuma, Augusutin 1035
ヌセヌフム
Nse Nfumu, Agustin 1035
ヌゼビテゲ
Nzet Biteghe, Honorine 1039
ヌセンギマナ
Nsengimana, Jean Philbert 1035
ヌセンギユムバ
Nsengiyumva, Jean-Pacifique 1035
ヌセンギュンバ
Nsengiyumva, Albert 1035
ヌゼンギンズゥンドゥ
Nziengui Nzoundou, Flavien 1039
ヌソベヤ・エフマン
Nsobeya Efuman Nchama, Santiago 1036
ヌソベヤエフマンヌチャマ
Nsobeya Efuman Nchama, Santiago 1036
ヌーソン
Knudson, Mary Jane 749
ヌゾンド
Nzondo, Eloi 1039
ヌダ
N'dah, Eric Kouagou 1010
ヌダイシミイエ
Ndayishimye, Evaristre 1010
ヌダイゼイエ
Ndayizeye, Domitien 1010
ヌダイトワ
Ndaitwah, Netumbo 1010
ヌダイマナンジャラ
Ndahimananjara, Bénédicte Johanita 1010
ヌダイラギエ
Ndayiragije, Serges 1010
ヌダイラギジェ
Ndayiragije, Samuel 1010
ヌダイルキエ
Ndayirukiye, Cyrille 1010
ヌダウ
Ndau, Malison 1010
ヌタウクリリャヨ
Ntawukuriryayo, Damascéne 1036
ヌタカブリムボ
Ntakaburimvo, Ancilla 1036
ヌタカルチマナ
Ntakarutimana, Sabine 1036
ヌダキ
Ndaki, Barnabé 1010
ヌダコロ
Ndakolo, Penda Ya 1010
ヌダッカラ
N'dackala, Marie Solange Pagonendji 1010
ヌタップ
Ntap, Innocence 1036
ヌタニュング
Ntanyungu, Festus 1036
ヌダヌサ
Ndanusa, S.M. 1010
ヌタバ
Ntaba, Hetherwick 1036
ヌダヒマナジャラ
Ndahimananjara, Bénédicte Johanita 1010
ヌタフ
Ntafu, George 1036
ヌタホバリ
Ntahobari, Stanislas 1036
ヌタホムブキエ
Ntahomvukiye, Severin 1036
ヌタホメニエレイエ
Ntahomenyereye, Salvator 1036
ヌタホンビュキエ
Ntahomvukiye, Emmanuel 1036
ヌダムンジカム
N'dam N'jikam, Hassan 1010
ヌダラタ
Ndarata, Jean-Dominique 1010
ヌタン
Ntang, Ignacio Milam 1036
ヌダンガヌディンガ
Ndanga Ndinga, Badel 1010
ヌタントゥメイ
Ntantu-mey, Jean-Marie 1036
ヌダンブキ
Ndambuki, Gideon 1010
ヌタンヨトラ
Ntanyotora, Joseph 1036
ヌチェンバ
Nchemba, Mwingulu Lameck 1010
ヌチャマ
Ntchama, Antonio Suka 1036
N'tchama, Caetano 1036
ヌチャム
Ntcham, Olivier 1036
ヌチャンゴ
Ntchango, Gabriel 1036
ヌチラムペバ
Ntirampeba, Gaspard 1036
ヌチルフングワ
Ntiruhungwa, Jean de Dieu 1036
ヌチンビ
Nchimbi, Emmanuel John 1010
ヌツァガセ
Ntshagase, Abednego 1036
ヌツァンガセ
Ntshagase, Abednego 1036
ヌツィニ
Ntsinyi, Lebohang 1036
ヌツィバ
Ntsiba, Florent 1036
ヌツェベ
Ntshebe, Siphiwo 1036
ヌツォアオレ
Ntsoaole, Sekh'ulumi 1036
ヌッチ
Nucci, Leo 1036
ヌッツィ
Nuzzi, Gianluigi 1038
ヌツツム
Ntutumu, Juan Antonio Bibang 1036
ヌット
Nuth Sokhom 1038
ヌット・ソコム
Nuth Sokhom 1038
ヌッペナイ
Nuppeney, Burkhard 1037
ヌツンガムロンゴ
Ntungamulongo, Raymond Tshibanda 1036
ヌディアイ
Ndiaye, Youssoupha 1010
ヌディアイエ
Ndiaye, Kadiatou 1010
ヌディアエ
Ndiaye, Awa 1010
N'diaye, Ibrahima 1010
Ndiaye, Ousmane Masseck 1010
Ndiaye, Sada 1010
Ndiaye, Souleymane Ndéné 1010
Ndiaye, Youssoupha 1010
ヌディアエセク
Ndiaye-seck, Saoudatou 1010
ヌディアエバ
Ndiaye-ba, Soukeyna 1010
ヌディカ
N'dicka Matam, Samson 1010
ヌディクマゲンゲ
Ndikumagenge, Pierre 1010
ヌディクマナ
Ndikumana, Jean Bosco 1010
Ndikumana, Victoire 1010
ヌディクムゴニョ
Ndikumugongo, Severin 1010
ヌディクムゴンゴ
Ndikumugongo, Severin 1010
ヌディタビリエ
Nditabiriye, Dismas 1010
ヌティハボーズ
Ntihabose, Salvator 1036
ヌディホクブワヨ
Ndihokubwayo, Domitien 1010
ヌティママ
Ntimama, William Ole 1036
ヌディラシャ
Ndirahisha, Janviére 1010
ヌティルフングワ
Ntiruhungwa, Jean de Dieu 1036
ヌデグベシ
Noudegbessi, François Gbénoukpo 1034
ヌーテバーグ
Nöteberg, Staffan 1034
ヌデベシ
Noudegbessi, François Gbénoukpo 1034
ヌデベレ
Ndebele, Joel Sbusiso 1010
ヌデマンガ
Ndémanga, Jacques 1010
ヌデメゾオビアン

Ndemezoobiang, Rene 1010
ヌデラガクラ
Nderagakura, Ferdinand 1010
ヌーデル
Nuder, Pär 1036
ヌテルヌンビ
Ntelnoumbi, Faustin 1036
ヌーデルマン
Noudelmann, François 1034
ヌデレバ
Ndereba, Catherine 1010
ヌデンゲ
Ndenge, Tsiy William 1010
ヌート
Newth, Philip 1019
ヌドイ
Ndoye, Arame 1011
ヌトウ
Ntow, Saah 1036
ヌドゥアン
Ndouane, Lambert 1011
ヌドゥイガ
Ndwiga, Peter Njeru 1011
ヌドウィガ
Ndwiga, Peter 1011
ヌドゥイマナ
Nduwimana, Edouard 1011
Nduwimana, Martin 1011
ヌドゥウィマナ
Nduwimana, Marie-Goreth 1011
Nduwimana, Osesime 1011
ヌドゥグ
Ndougou, Raymond 1011
ヌトゥシャンガセ
Ntshangase, Wilson 1036
ヌトゥジャンガゼ
Ntshangase, Wilson 1036
ヌトゥトゥムエマヌ
Ntoutoume-émane, Jean-François 1036
ヌトゥトゥムエマネ
Ntoutoume-émane, Jean-François 1036
ヌトゥトゥムヌゲマ
Ntutumu Nguema, Filiberto 1036
ヌドゥバ
Ndouba, Florence Lydie 1011
ヌドウム
Nduom, Kwesi 1011
ヌトゥムケ
Ntumuke, Atanásio Salvador 1036
ヌドゥランガマンドラ
Ndlangamandla, Dumisani 1011
ヌドゥリヨマン
N'dri-yoman, Thérèse 1011
ヌドゥワヨ
Nduwayo, Jean-Claude 1011
ヌドウンジャイ
Ndownjie, Sira Wally 1011
ヌトゥンズウェニマナ
Ntunzwenimana, Jean Bosco 1036
ヌードセン
Knudsen, Keith 749
Knudsen, Michelle 749
ヌドティンガイ
N'doutingai, Sylvain 1011
ヌドマ
Ndoma, Ibrahim Françoise 1011
ヌドム
Nduom, Kwesi 1011
ヌドラム
Ndoram, Kevin 1011
ヌドリ
N'dori, Raymond Abouo 1011
ヌドリアナスル
Ndrianasolo 1011
ヌドリマナ
Ndorimana, Romaine 1011
ヌドル
Ndolou, Jacques Yvon 1011
ヌードルズ
Noodles 1031
ヌドレ
N'dré, Paul Yao 1011
ヌドレマンジャリ
Ndremanjary, Jean André 1011
ヌドロブ
Ndlovu, Hlobsile 1011
Ndlovu, Sikhanyiso 1011
ヌドン
Ndong, Joseph 1011
Ndong, Pierre Marie 1011
ヌドンエソノヤン
Ndong Esonoeyang, Fausto 1011
ヌドンガラ
Ndongala, Eugene 1011
ヌドング
Ndong, Demetrio Elo 1011
Ndongou, Jean François 1011
ヌドングヌトゥトゥム
Ndong Ntutumu, Antonio Martin 1011
ヌドンシマ
Ndongsima, Raymond 1011
ヌドンジャッタ
Ndong-jatta, Ann Therese 1011
ヌドンヌゲマ
Ndong Nguema, Juan 1011
Ndong-nguéma, Paul 1011
ヌドンバシ
Ndombasi, Abdoulaye 1011
ヌドン・ミフム
Ndong Mifumu, Miguel Oyono 1011
ヌドンミフム
Ndong Mifumu, Miguel Oyono 1011
ヌドン・ムバ
Ndong Mba, Anatolio 1011
ヌーナン
Noonan, David 1031
Noonan, Maryellen 1031
Noonan, Michael 1031
ヌーニェス
Núñez, Marisa 1037
Núñez, Rafael E. 1037
ヌニェス
Ñúñez, Aloha 1037
Núñez, Carlos 1037
Nunez, Eduardo 1037
Nuñez, Gabriela 1037
Nuñez, Marianela 1037
Nunez, Renato 1037
ヌニェス・コレイア
Nunes Correia, Francisco 1037
ヌニェスデオリベイラ
Nunes De Oliveira, Lais 1037
ヌニャブ
Nunyabu, Komlan 1037
ヌーニョ
Nuno, Vidal 1037
ヌニョ・マジェル
Nuño Mayer, Aurelio 1037
ヌヌ・クンバ
Nunu Kumba, Jemma 1037
ヌヌクンバ
Nunu Kumba, Jemma 1037
ヌーネス
Nunes, Paul F. 1037
Nunez, Sigrid 1037
ヌネス
Nunez, Mijain Lopez 1037
ヌネス・フェレイラ
Nunes Ferreira, Aloysio 1037
ヌーネス・ロークス
Nunez-roches, Rakeem 1037
ヌーネン
Nunen, Anton van 1037
ヌーノ
Nuno, Espirito Santo 1037
ヌーバー
Nuber, Ursula 1036
ヌハク・プームサワン
Nouhak Phoumsavanh 1034
ヌハマジョ
Nhamajo, Manuel Serifo 1021
ヌービュルジェ
Neuburger, Robert 1016
ヌビル
Neuville, Jerome 1017
ヌフ
Nouhou, Amadou 1034
ヌーブルジェ
Neuburger, Jean-Frederic 1016
ヌーベ
Ncube, Abednigo 1010
Ncube, Welshman 1010
ヌベ・ヌグ
Nve Ngu, Antonio Fernando 1038
ヌーベル
Nouvel, Jean 1034
ヌホ
Nouhou, Amadou 1034
ヌポク
Noupokou, Dammipi 1034
ヌボニヌパ
Mbonimpa, Barnabe 927
ヌマノビッチ
Numanović, Suad 1037
ヌメイリ
Numeiry, Gaafar Mohammed 1037
ヌメイリー
Numeiry, Gaafar Mohammed 1037
ヌメルドル
Nummerdor, Reinder 1037
ヌモンビ
Noumonvi, Melonin 1034
ヌヤム
Nyamu, Jesaya 1038
ヌヤルガボムイジ
Nyarugabomuhizi, Moïse 1039
ヌヨマ
Nujoma, Utoni 1037
ヌヨンゴロ
Nyongolo, Ami Ambatombe 1039
ヌラポ
Nhlapo, Sifiso 1022
ヌーランド
Nuland, Sherwin B. 1037
ヌーランラ
Nhlanhla, Joe 1022
ヌーリ
al-Nouri, Hassan 1034
Nuri, Said Abdullo 1037
ヌリ
Nouri, Abdelhak 1034
Nouri, Abdelouahab 1034
Nouri, Mahamat 1034
al-Nuri, Mahmud Abdul-Khalid 1037
Nuri, Said Abdullo 1037
ヌーリシエ
Nourissier, François 1034
ヌーリジュイニ
Nouri Jouini, Mohamed 1034
ヌリスタニ
Nuristani, Yusuf 1037
ヌール
Noor, Asaduzzaman 1031
Noor, Muhamad 1031
al-Nour, Abdel-safi 1034
Nour, Mariam Mahamat 1034
Noure, Moukadas 1034
Nur, Abdullahi Abyan 1037
al-Nur, Awad al-Hassan 1037
ヌル
Nur, Dahir Sheikh Muhammad 1037
Nur, Hassan Mohammed 1037
Nur, Mohamud Salaad 1037
Nur, Sheikh Adan Mohamed 1037
Nur, Uulu 1037
ヌルガリエフ
Nurgaliyev, Rashid Gumarovich 1037
ヌルキッチ
Nurkic, Jusuf 1037
ヌルコビッチ
Nurković, Amir 1037
ヌルザイ
Noorzai, Aref 1031
ヌルサヘドフ
Noursakhedov, Dovran 1034
ヌールサリム
Noersalim, Mohamed 1029

ヌル・シャティグドゥド
Nur Shatigudud, Hassan Mohamed 1038
ヌルディノフ
Nurudinov, Ruslan 1038
ヌルディン・トップ
Noordin Top 1031
ヌルディンヌ
Nourdine, Chabani 1034
ヌルブ
Norbu, Tenzin 1031
ヌルマトフ
Nurmatov, Shermat 1037
ヌルマフマトフ
Nurumakhmatov, Dzhurabek 1038
ヌルマフムディ
Nurmahmudi, Ismail 1037
ヌルマメドフ
Nurmammedov, Mammetniyaz 1037
ヌールマンド
Nourmand, Tony 1034
ヌルミネン
Nurminen, Marjo T. 1038
ヌルムイラドワ
Nurmyradova, Byagul 1038
ヌルムハンベトワ
Nurmukhambetova, Anna 1038
ヌルメスニエミ
Nurmesniemi, Antti 1037
Nurmesniemi, Vuokko Eskolin 1038
ヌルヤナ
Nuryana, Mu'man 1038
ヌレンド
Nlend, Henri Hogbe 1029
ヌワウェア
Nuwawea, Jacob 1038
ヌワクウィ
Nwakwi, Edith 1038
ヌワバ
Nwaba, Barbara 1038
ヌワンゼ
Nwanze, Kanayo F. 1038
ヌーン
Noon, Jeff 1031
Noon, Steve 1031
ヌーンズ
Nunes, Paul F. 1037
ヌンドゥ
Nundu, Omar Rashidi 1037
ヌンビ
Numbi, Denis Kalume 1037
Numbi, Félix Kabange 1037

【ネ】

ネーア
Neher, Erwin 1012
ネーアー
Naeher, Ulrich 1001
Neher, Erwin 1012
ネアン
Nairne, Sandy 1003
ネイ
Nay, Meagen 1009
Nye, David 1039
ネイヴィン
Navin, Jacqueline 1009
ネイギー
Nagy, Thomas F. 1002
ネイク
Knake, Robert K. 747
ネイクイン
Naquin, Tyler 1005
ネイゲル
Nagel, Thomas 1002
Nagle, Thomas T. 1002
ネイコバ
Neykova, Rumyana 1019
ネイコフ
Neikov, Ivan 1013
Neykov, Svilen 1019
ネイサン
Nathan, Andrew James 1007
Nathan, Debbie 1007
Nathan, Ian 1007
Nathan, Joe 1007
Nathan, Sarah 1007
ネイスタット
Neistat, Van 1013
ネイスワース
Neisworth, John T. 1013
ネイスン
Nathan, John 1007
ネイセ
Nijssen, Elfi 1025
ネイセン
Nijssen, Elfi 1025
ネイダー
Nader, George 1001
Nader, Ralph 1001
ネイダッチ
Nayduch, Donna 1009
ネイツ
Neyts, Annemie 1019
ネイック
Naick, Indran 1002
ネイディス
Nadis, Steven J. 1001
ネイテル
Natel, Jean-Marc 1007
ネイテンバーグ
Natenberg, Sheldon 1007
ネイドー
Naidoo, Trevor 1002
ネイドゥ
Naidoo, Rajani 1002
ネイニー
Neini, Ahmed Ould Mohamed 1013
ネイハム
Nahum, Lucien 1002
ネイピア
Napier, Bill 1005
Napier, Charles 1005
Napier, Susan Jolliffe 1005
ネイピアー
Napier, Shabazz 1005
ネイフ
Naifeh, Steven W. 1002
ネイブ
Nave, Yolanda 1009
ネイポール
Naipaul, Vidiadhar Surajprasad 1003
ネイマーク
Naimark, Michael 1003
Naimark, Norman M. 1003
ネイマール
Neymar 1019
ネイミ
Neimi, Salwa Al 1013
Nuaymi, Salwá 1036
ネイヤー
Nayar, Ritu 1009
Naylor, Sharon 1009
ネイラ
Nheira 1022
ネイラー
Nayler, Sarah 1009
Naylor, Craig 1009
Naylor, Grant 1009
Naylor, Lesley 1009
Naylor, Phyllis Reynolds 1009
Naylor, Thomas H. 1009
Naylor, William 1009
ネイル
Neil, Drew 1013
Neill, Jason 1013
ネイルソン
Neilson, Gary L. 1013
ネイルバフ
Nalebuff, Barry 1004
ネイロン
Neylon, Margaret 1019
ネヴァース
Nevers, Patricia 1017
ネウアニック
Néouanic, Lionel Le 1015
ネヴィル
Neville, Adam M. 1017
Neville, Barret 1017
Neville, Helen 1017
Neville, John 1017
Neville, Katherine 1017
Neville, Leigh 1017
Neville, Lesley 1017
Neville, Miranda 1017
Neville, Morgan 1017
Neville, Stuart 1017
ネヴィル - ニール
Neville-Neil, George V. 1017
ネ・ウィン
Ne Win 1018
ネー・ウィン
Ne Win 1018
ネウィン
Ne Win 1018
ネヴィンズ
Nevins, Francis M. 1017
ネーヴェリング
Neveling, Elmar 1017
ネウェル
Newell, Frederick 1018
ネヴェンズ
Nevens, T.Michael 1017
ネウォウナ
Nawowuna, Alice Aprot 1009
ネウストプニー
Neustupný, Jiři Václav 1017
ネウフビル
Neufville, Christian 1016
ネオパネ
Nuepane, Badri Prasad 1036
ネオフィトゥ
Neophytou, Averof 1015
ネガーズ
Neggers, Carla 1012
ネガソ
Negaso, Gidada 1012
ネギシ
Negishi, Ei-ichi 1012
ネギン
Negin, Oleg 1012
ネクシ
Nxesi, Thembelani Thulas 1038
ネクテル
Knechtel, Larry 747
ネクト
Knecht, G.Bruce 747
ネクトゥー
Nectoux, Jean Michel 1012
ネクラソワ
Nekrassova, Irina 1013
ネグラン
Negrão, Fernando 1012
ネグリ
Negri, Antonio 1012
ネクリオシウス
Nekriosius, Ricardas 1013
ネグリノ
Negrino, Tom 1012
ネグリン
Negrin, Fabian 1012
ネグルツァ
Negruta, Veaceslav 1012
ネグレド
Negredo, Alvaro 1012
ネグロポンテ
Negroponte, John Dimitri 1012
Negroponte, Nicholas P. 1012
ネグロモンテ
Negromonte, Mario 1012
ネーゲル
Nagel, Susan 1002
Nagel, Thomas 1002
ネゴダイロ
Negodaylo, Alexey 1012
ネシ
Nesi, Sioux 1015
ネシー
Nesse, Randolph M. 1016
ネジ
Nesi, Nerio 1015
ネシェトリル
Nesetril, Jaroslav 1015
ネシッジ・ブコビッチ
Nesic-Vuckovic, Tanja 1015
ネシブ
Necib, Hocine 1012
ネジプ
Necip, Uysal 1012
ネシャット
Neshat, Shirin 1015
ネジュマ
Nedjma 1012
ネーション
Nation, I.S.P. 1007
ネス
Naess, Arne 1001
Nes, Irene van 1015

Ness, Caro 1015
Ness, Patrick 1016
ネズ
Nez, Chester 1019
Nezu, Christine M. 1019
ネスィン
Nesin, Aziz 1015
ネスケンス
Nesquens, Daniel 1015
ネスタ
Nesta, Alessandro 1016
ネスター
Nestor, Daniel 1016
ネステレンコ
Nesterenko, Alexey V. 1016
Nesterenko, Vasiliĭ Borisovich 1016
Nestsiarenka, Yuliya 1016
ネストマン
Nestmann, Earle R. 1016
ネストリンガー
Nöstlinger, Christine 1034
Nöstlinger, Christine, Jr. 1034
ネストル
Nestor, Diaz 1016
Nestor, Eiki 1016
Nestor, Grigory 1016
ネストルエフ
Nestruev, Mikhail 1016
ネストロフスキ
Nestorovski, Ilija 1016
ネスビッツ
Naisbitt, John 1003
ネズビッツ
Naisbitt, John 1003
ネスビット
Nesbitt, Christine 1015
ネスボ
Nesbø, Jo 1015
ネスポリ
Nespoli, Mauro 1015
ネズム
Nesme, Alexis 1015
ネスラー
Nestler, Eric Jonathan 1016
ネスリシャー・スルタン
Neslisah Sultan 1015
ネスリシャ妃
Neslisah Sultan 1015
ネスル
Nestle, Marion 1016
ネースルンド
Näslund, Görel Kristina 1007
ネスルント
Naeslund, Sandra 1001
ネスレディン
Nesredin, Ali Bekit 1015
ネゼ・セガン
Nézet-Séguin, Yannick 1019
ネゾースキ
Nezworski, Mary Teresa 1019
ネーソン
Nason, John William 1007
ネゾン
Naezon, Walton 1001
ネーダー
Nader, George 1001
Nader, Ralph 1001
ネダゴー
Nedergaard, Tina 1012
ネタニヤウ
Netanyahu, Benjamin 1016
ネタニヤフ
Netanyahu, Benjamin 1016
ネダーペルト
Nederpelt, Travis 1012
ネタラ
Netara, Atarake 1016
ネチャーエヴァ
Nechaeva, Lyudmila Timofeevna 1012
ネチャエワ
Nechayeva, Yelena 1012
ネチャス
Nečas, Petr 1011
ネツィリ
Neziri, Bekim 1019
ネッカー
Necker, Tyl 1012
ネッスル
Nestle, Marion 1016
ネッセ
Nesse, Randolph M. 1016
ネッセル
Nesser, Håkan 1016
ネッツ
Netz, Reviel 1016
ネッツァー
Netzer, Calin Peter 1016
ネッテルホルスト
Nettelhorst, R.P. 1016
ネットルトン
Nettleton, Sarah 1016
ネッパー
Knepper, Jimmy 747
ネデアルコ
Nedealco, Evgheni 1012
ネディアルコフ
Nedialkov, Dimitar 1012
ネディモビッチ
Nedimović, Branislav 1012
ネディロフ
Nedirov, Bayramgeldi 1012
ネーデル
Nadel, Dan 1001
ネデルク
Nedelcu, Clément 1012
ネデルシェワ
Nedelcheva, Petya 1012
ネーデルフェーン・ピーテルス
Nederveen Pieterse, Jan 1012
ネーテレンボス
Netelenbos, Tineke 1016
ネト
Neto 1016
Neto, Antonio Burity Da Silva 1016
Neto, António Domingos Pitra Costa 1016
Neto, Ernesto 1016
Neto, Joao 1016
Neto, Manuel da Cruz 1016
Neto, Natália Pedro Da Costa Umbelina 1016
Neto, Pedro Hendrick Vaal 1016
Neto, Raul 1016
Neto, Vitória Francisco Lopes Cristovąo De Barros 1016
ネドヴェド
Nedvěd, Pavel 1012
ネドビェド
Nedvěd, Pavel 1012
ネドベド
Nedvěd, Pavel 1012
ネトル
Nettle, Daniel 1016
ネトルズ
Nettles, Jennifer 1016
ネトレプコ
Netrebko, Anna 1016
ネナ
Nena, Nena 1015
ネーネ
Nene, Bhushan 1015
ネネ
Nene 1015
Nene, Nhlanhla Musa 1015
ネネジッチ
Nenezić, Predrag 1015
ネネム
Nenem, Kourabi 1015
ネノラ
Nenola, Aili 1015
ネハマス
Nehamas, Alexander 1012
ネパール
Nepal, Madhav 1015
ネハンカイ
Niepanhui 1025
ネバンスー
Nevansuu, Mira 1017
ネハンハイ
Niepanhui 1025
ネーピア
Napier, Bill 1005
Napier, Susan 1005
ネビス
Neves, Andrea M.P. 1017
ネピリー
Nepilly, Ellen 1015
ネビル
Neville, Adam M. 1017
Neville, David 1017
Neville, John 1017
Neville, Stuart 1017
ネビン
Nevin, John Joe 1017
Nevin, Phil 1017
ネフ
Knef, Hildegard 747
Naef, Kurt 1001
Naef, Ralph 1001
Nef, Sonja 1012
Neff, Henry H. 1012
Neff, Jolanda 1012
Neff, Kristin 1012
Neff, Mindy 1012
Neff, Thomas J. 1012
ネファーティ
Neffati, Chadli 1012
ネファティ
Neffati, Chadli 1012
ネフィンジャー
Neffinger, John 1012
ネフェールインガニ
Neferingani, Inès Bertille 1012
ネフツィ
Neftci, Salih N. 1012
ネプトゥン
Neptune, Yvon 1015
ネプ・ブン・チン
Nhep Bun Chin 1022
ネーブン
Neven, Ruth Schmidt 1017
ネベス
Neves, Carlos da Costa 1017
Neves, Francisco Pedro 1017
Neves, Javier 1017
Neves, José Maria Pereira 1017
Neves, Madalena 1017
Neves, Vania 1017
ネベラスカス
Neverauskas, Dovydas 1017
ネベル
Knebel, Corey 747
ネベロビッチ
Neverovic, Jaroslav 1017
ネーベン
Neben, Amber 1011
ネベンザール
Nebenzahl, Kenneth 1011
ネボ
Nebo, Chinedu Ositadinma 1011
ネポ
Nepo, Mark 1015
ネボルスキー
Neborsky, Robert J. 1011
ネマ
Nhema, Francis 1022
ネマトザデ
Nematzadeh, Mohammad Reza 1014
ネマルク
Nemarq, Alain 1014
ネーマン
Neeman, Sylvie 1012
Neeman, Yuval 1012
ネマン
Neiman, Ophélie 1013
ネーミ
Nemi, Orsola 1015
ネミリャ
Nemyria, Hryhoriy 1015
ネミルスキ
Nemirschi, Nicolae 1015
ネムザー
Nemzer, Nickolay 1015
ネムサゲ
Nemsadze, Giorgi 1015
ネームスニック
Namesnik, Eric 1004
ネムチク
Nemcsik, Zsolt 1014
ネムチーノフ
Nemchinov, Anatolii 1014
ネムツォーフ
Nemtsov, Boris Yefimovich 1015
ネムツォフ
Nemtsov, Boris Yefimovich 1015
ネムバン
Nembang, Narendra Bikram 1014
ネメシェギ
Nemeshegyi, Peter 1015

ネメス
Nemes, László 1015
Nemes, Viktor 1015
Nemeth, Evi 1015
ネメセック
Nemecek, Larry 1014
ネメチェク
Němeček, Svatopluk 1014
Nemeczek, Alfred 1014
ネーメト
Németh, Imre 1015
Németh, Lászlóné 1015
Németh, Miklós 1015
ネメト
Nemeth, Zsanett 1015
ネメロフ
Nemeroff, Charles B. 1014
Nemerov, Bruce 1014
Nemerov, Howard 1015
ネモ
Nemo, Philippe 1015
ネモト
Nemoto, Rina 1015
ネモフ
Nemov, Alexei 1015
ネモヤト・ベゲポレ
Nemoyato Begepole, Jean-Paul 1015
ネモヤトベゲポレ
Nemoyato Begepole, Jean-Paul 1015
ネヤジ
Neyazi, Yousuf 1019
ネヤマ
Neyama, Ryo 1019
ネラー
Kneller, Scott 747
ネラン
Neyrand, Georges 1019
ネランク
Neirinck, Edmond 1013
ネリ
Neri, Kris 1015
Neri, Romulo 1015
ネリー
Nelly 1013
ネリウス
Nerius, Steffi 1015
ネリエール
Nerrière, Jean-Paul 1015
ネリース
Neris, Hector 1015
ネリス
Nellis, J.G. 1013
ネリナ
Nerina, Nadia 1015
ネル
Nel, Philip 1013
Nel, WP. 1013
Nell, Edward J. 1013
ネルガート
Nergard, Torger 1015
ネルキン
Nelkin, Dorothy 1013
ネルシーニョ
Nelsinho 1013
ネルスコット
Nelscott, Kris 1013
ネルスン
Nelson, Kent 1014
Nelson, Ray Faraday 1014
ネルセット
Norsett, Syvert Paul 1032
ネルソヴァ
Nelsova, Zara 1014
ネルソバ
Nelsova, Zara 1014
ネルソン
Nelson, Aaron P. 1013
Nelson, Adam 1013
Nelson, Allen 1013
Nelson, Andy 1013
Nelson, Anne 1013
Nelson, Audrey 1013
Nelson, Barbara 1013
Nelson, Barry 1013
Nelson, Blamo 1013
Nelson, Bob 1013
Nelson, Brendan 1013
Nelson, Bret 1013
Nelson, Bruce 1013
Nelson, Byron 1013
Nelson, Corey 1013
Nelson, David Lee 1013
Nelson, Donn 1013
Nelson, Dwight 1013
Nelson, Ed 1013
Nelson, Edward 1013
Nelson, Gaylord Anton 1013
Nelson, Gerald E. 1013
Nelson, G.Lynn 1013
Nelson, Gunnar 1013
Nelson, Hank 1013
Nelson, Jameer 1013
Nelson, Jamie 1014
Nelson, Jandy 1014
Nelson, Jessie 1014
Nelson, Jesy 1014
Nelson, Jimmy 1014
Nelson, J.J. 1014
Nelson, John D. 1014
Nelson, Jon 1014
Nelson, Jordy 1014
Nelson, Kadir 1014
Nelson, Kevin 1014
Nelson, Kyle 1014
Nelson, Larry 1014
Nelson, Lars 1014
Nelson, Lee 1014
Nelson, Mary 1014
Nelson, Mary Carroll 1014
Nelson, Matthew 1014
Nelson, Maureen 1014
Nelson, Mexico Mike 1014
Nelson, Michael J. 1014
Nelson, Noelle C. 1014
Nelson, Paula 1014
Nelson, Peter 1014
Nelson, Ralph Lowell 1014
Nelson, Ray Faraday 1014
Nelson, Reggie 1014
Nelson, Rhonda 1014
Nelson, Richard E. 1014
Nelson, Richard Hedeen 1014
Nelson, Richard R. 1014
Nelson, Robbie 1014
Nelson, Robert 1014
Nelson, Robert S. 1014
Nelson, Sioban 1014
Nelson, Stanley 1014
Nelson, Stephen L. 1014
Nelson, Steven 1014
Nelson, Sue 1014
Nelson, Suzanne Marie 1014
Nelson, Theodor Holm 1014
Nelson, Troy 1014
Nelson, Vaunda Micheaux 1014
Nelson, Waldo Emerson 1014
Nelson, Willie Hugh 1014
ネルソンス
Nelsons, Andris 1014
ネルソン=スピールマン
Nelson-Spielman, Lori 1014
ネルソン・セメド
Nelson Semedo 1014
ネルソン－ポールミヤー
Nelson-Pallmeyer, Jack 1014
ネルツ
Nerz, Ryan 1015
ネルディンガー
Nerdinger, Winfried 1015
ネルバーン
Nerburn, Kent 1015
ネレ
Néré, Jacques 1015
Néret, Gilles 1015
ネレル
Nerell, Ida-Theres 1015
ネワル
Nehwal, Saina 1012
ネン
Nen, Nguyen Van 1015
ネンチェフ
Nenchev, Nikolay 1015
ネンバガチンバンガ
Nengbaga Tshingbangba, Jean 1015
ネンボット
Nembot, Stephane 1014

【ノ】

ノ
Nau, Jean-Yves 1008
Noh, Jin-kyu 1030
Noh, Mu-hyun 1030
Noh, Seung-yul 1030
Ro, Myong-gun 1186
Roh, Jae-won 1198
Roh, Jun-hyong 1198
Roh, Moo-hyun 1198
Roh, Tae-woo 1198
ノー
Noh, Omar 1030
ノア
Noa 1029
Noah, Joakim 1029
Noah, Mohamed Abdullahi Hassan 1029
ノアウッド
Norwood, Ann E. 1033
ノアビュ
Nørby, Ellen Trane 1031
ノアンス
Noens, Nastasia 1029
ノーイ
Nooyi, Indra K. 1031
ノイアー
Neuer, Manuel 1016
ノイヴィルト
Neuwirth, Erich 1017
ノイシュツ
Neuschutz, Karin 1017
ノイシュテッター
Neustadter, Roman 1017
ノイス
Noyes, Deborah 1035
Noyes, Randi B. 1035
ノイズ
Noyes, John K. 1035
ノイト
Nuyt, Andrea 1038
ノイド
Noyd, Dale Edwin 1035
ノイドルファ
Neudorfer, Alfred 1016
ノイナー
Neuner, Angelika 1017
Neuner, Frank 1017
Neuner, Magdalena 1017
ノイハウス
Neuhaus, Nele 1016
ノイフェルト
Neufeld, Irvin 1016
Neufeldt, Victor A. 1016
ノイベルト
Neubert, Ehrhart 1016
ノイマイヤー
Neumayer, Michael 1017
Neumeier, John 1017
ノイマノバ
Neumannová, Katerina 1017
ノイマン
Neuman, Michael 1016
Neuman, Robert P. 1016
Neumann, Craig S. 1016
Neumann, Iver B. 1016
Neumann, Jennifer 1017
Neumann, Karl 1017
ノイラート
Neurath, Hans 1017
ノイロイター
Neureuther, Felix 1017
ノイロール
Neurohr, Jean Frederic 1017
ノウ
Noe, Barbara A. 1029
ノヴァク
Novac, Ana 1034
Novak, B.J. 1034
ノヴァクイエジョランスキ
Nowak-Jeziorański, Jan 1035
ノヴァコヴィチ
Novakovich, Josip 1035
ノヴァコヴィッチ
Novakovich, Josip 1035
ノヴァコフスキー
Nowakowski, Richard S. 1035
ノヴァチェック
Novacek, Michael J. 1034
ノヴァリナ
Novarina, Valère 1035
ノヴィク
Novik, Naomi 1035
ノーヴィコフ
Novikov, Sergei Petrovich 1035
ノヴィコフ
Novikov, Sergei Petrovich 1035
Novikov, Yury

Vasilievich 1035
ノウィツキ
Nowicki, Maciej 1035
ノヴィック
Novick, Ed 1035
ノーウィッチ
Norwich, Brahm 1033
Norwich, Grace 1033
Norwich, John Julius 1033
ノーヴィル
Norville, Deborah 1033
ノヴィンスキー
Nowinski, Joseph 1035
ノーヴェ
Nove, Aldo 1035
ノヴェッリ
Novelli, Luca 1035
ノーウェル
Norwell, Andrew 1033
ノーヴェル
Norvell, Anthony 1033
ノウェル
Nowell, Jack 1035
ノヴォグラッツ
Novogratz, Jacqueline 1035
ノヴォセリック
Novoselic, Krist 1035
ノヴォセル
Novosel, John 1035
ノヴォセルスキー
Novoselsky, Anguel 1035
ノヴォセロフ
Novoselov, Konstantin Sergeevich 1035
ノーウッド
Norwood, Ann E. 1033
Norwood, Jordan 1033
Norwood, Kevin 1033
Norwood, Levi 1033
Norwood, Mary Marcia 1033
Norwood, Melita 1033
ノウラ
Nowra, Louis 1035
ノウルズ
Knowles, Caroline 748
Knowles, Ronald 748
ノウルソン
Knowlson, Elizabeth 749
Knowlson, James 749
ノエ
Noë, Alva 1029
Noé, Gaspar 1029
ノエセル
Noessel, Christopher 1029
ノエフ
Noev, Boiko 1029
ノエル
Noël, Alyson 1029
Noël, Bernard 1029
Noel, Genevieve 1029
Noel, Gordon L. 1029
Noel, James L. 1029
Noel, Nerlens 1029
Noel, William 1029
Noel-Bardis, Melanie 1029
ノエルズ
Noels, Kimberly A. 1029
ノエルソン
Noelson, William 1029
ノエル・ノイマン
Noelle-Neumann, Elisabeth 1029
ノカ
Noka, Flamur 1030
ノガ
Noga, Artur 1030
ノガイデリ
Noghaideli, Zurab 1030
ノーガード
Norgaard, Richard B. 1031
ノークス
Nokes, Sebastian 1030
ノクタ
Nokta, Harripersaud 1030
ノグチ
Noguchi, Marcio 1030
ノーグラー
Knögler, Mario 748
ノーグレット
Naugrette, Jean-Pierre 1008
ノグレーディー
Nogrady, Bianca 1030
ノーグレン
Norgren, Christiana A. E. 1031
Norrgren, Flemming 1032
ノークロス
Norcross, John C. 1031
ノーケ
Norkeh, Frederick 1032
ノゲイラ
Nogueira, Antonio Rodorigo 1030
Nogueira, Antonio Rogerio 1030
Nogueira, Lucas 1030
Nogueira, Ronald 1030
Nogueira, Rui 1030
ノゲーズ
Noguez, Dominique 1030
ノゲス
Noguès, Jean-Côme 1030
ノケド
Noked, Orit 1030
ノゲーラ
Noguera, Lucas 1030
ノザキ
Nozaki, Albert 1035
ノザゼ
Nozadze, Ramaz 1035
ノーザリ
Nozari, Gholamhossein 1035
ノージ
Nój, Nahta 1030
ノシター
Nossiter, Anthony 1033
Nossiter, Jonathan 1034
ノージック
Nozick, Robert 1035
ノース
North, Adrian C. 1033
North, Chris 1033
North, Claire 1033
North, Darian 1033
North, Douglass Cecil 1033
North, George 1033
North, Marquez 1033
North, Robert C. 1033
North, Ryan 1033
North, Sheree 1033
North, Will 1033
ノースカット
Northcutt, Stephen 1033
Northcutt, Wendy 1033
ノスコ
Nosco, Peter 1033
ノースコット
Northcott, Deryl 1033
ノスター
Knoster, Tim 748
ノスティック
Nostitz, Nick 1034
ノースフィールド
Northfield, Sian 1033
ノースラップ
Northrup, Jim 1033
Northrup, Tony 1033
ノースロップ
Northrop, Suzane 1033
Northrup, Christiane 1033
ノセ
Nosé, Alberto 1033
ノセダ
Noseda, Gianandrea 1033
ノセラ
Nocera Pucet, Gwladys 1029
ノセンティ
Nocenti, Ann 1029
ノーソフ
Nothof, Anne 1034
ノソフ
Nossov, Dmitri 1034
ノタリ
Notari, Aldo 1034
ノーダン
Naudin, Jean-Bernard 1008
ノチェッラ
Nocella, Anthony J., Ⅱ 1029
ノック
Nauck, Todd 1008
Nock, Matthew 1029
Nock, Mike 1029
ノックス
Knox, David 749
Knox, Dean 749
Knox, Elizabeth 749
Knox, Garth 749
Knox, MacGregor 749
Knox, Melissa 749
Knox, Paul L. 749
Knox, Rob 749
Knox, Tom 749
ノックトン
Naughten, Denis 1008
ノッツ
Knotts, Don 748
ノッティンガム
Nottingham, Jacob 1034
ノッテージ
Nottage, Bernard J. 1034
Nottage, Lynn 1034
ノット
Knott, Frederick 748
Knott, Thomas 748
Not, Sara 1034
Nott, Andrea 1034
Nott, Jonathan 1034
ノットボム
Notbohm, Ellen 1034
ノップ
Knopp, Kelly 748
ノップラー
Knopfler, Mark 748
ノディア
Naude, Beyers 1008
ノーディング
Nordeng, Donald 1031
ノディングス
Noddings, Nel 1029
ノディングズ
Noddings, Nel 1029
ノテージ
Nottage, Bernard J. 1034
ノーテボーム
Nooteboom, Cees 1031
ノデル
Nodell, Martin 1029
ノーデルマン
Nodelman, Perry 1029
ノーデン
Norden, Lisa 1031
ノート
Note, Kessai H. 1034
ノード
Knode, Helen 748
Nord, Walter R. 1031
ノト
Noto, Phil 1034
ノードクイスト
Nordqvist, Anna 1031
ノードクヴィスト
Nordqvist, Sven 1031
ノードストリューム
Nordström, Jockum 1031
ノードストレム
Nordström, Kjell A. 1031
ノードハイム
Nordhielm, Christie L. 1031
ノートハウス
Northouse, Laurel Lindhout 1033
Northouse, Peter Guy 1033
ノードハウス
Nordhaus, William D. 1031
ノードフォース
Nordfors, Mikael 1031
ノードヘーゲン
Nordhagen, Christine 1031
ノートヘルファー
Notehelfer, Fred George 1034
ノートマン
Nortman, Brad 1033
ノートン
Naughton, Barry 1008
Naughton, Elisabeth 1008
Naughton, Gabriel 1008
Naughton, Kyle 1008
Norton, Andre 1033
Norton, Carla 1033
Norton, Cliff 1033
Norton, David L. 1033
Norton, David P. 1033
Norton, Edward 1033
Norton, Gale 1033
Norton, George 1033
Norton, George W. 1033
Norton, Jim 1033
Norton, Joseph Jude 1033
Norton, Ken 1033
Norton, Ken, Jr. 1033
Norton, Liss 1033

ノ

ノ

Norton, Marcellene 1033
Norton, Michael 1033
Norton, Mike 1033
Norton, Miriam 1033
Norton, Natalie 1033
Norton, O.Richard 1033
Norton, Richie 1033
Norton, Rob 1033
Norton, Steve 1033
Norton, Trevor 1033
Nothomb, Amélie 1034

ノトン
Nothomb, Amélie 1034

ノニ
Noni, Alda 1030

ノヌー
Nonu, Ma'a 1030

ノーネス
Nornes, Markus 1032

ノノー
Soudan Nonault, Arlette 1330

ノバ
Nova, Ivan 1034

ノバイス・リマ
Novais Lima, Pedro 1034

ノバク
Novak, Alexander V. 1034
Novak, B.J. 1034
Novak, Nick 1034
Novak, Robert 1034
Nowak, Sławomir 1035

ノーバーグ・ホッジ
Norberg-hodge, Helena 1031

ノバコビッチ
Novakovic, Marko 1034
Novakovic, Phebe 1034

ノバコフスカ
Nowakowska-ziemniak, Weronika 1035

ノバコフスカジェムニアク
Nowakowska-ziemniak, Weronika 1035

ノバチコフ
Novachkov, Borislav 1034

ノーバック
Novak, Steve 1034

ノバック
Novak, David 1034
Novak, Jeannie 1034
Novak, Ljudmila 1034
Novak, Miroslav Michal 1034
Novak, Robert 1034
Novak, Thomas P. 1034

ノバフト
Nobakht, Mohammad Baqer 1029

ノヒ
Knoch, Viktor 748

ノビカウ
Novikau, Mikalai 1035

ノビカワ
Novikava, Nastassia 1035

ノビク
Novik, Naomi 1035

ノビコフ
Novikov, Sergei Petrovich 1035
Novikov, Sergey 1035

ノビツキ
Nowicki, Wojciech 1035
Nowitzki, Dirk 1035

ノビツキー
Novitsky, Gennady V. 1035
Novitsky, Volodimir 1035
Nowitzki, Dirk 1035

ノビッチ
Nović, Sredoje 1035

ノーフ
Noh, Omar 1030

ノフィ
Nofi, Albert A. 1029

ノーフォーク
Norfolk, Lawrence 1031

ノフコフスキ
Novkovski, Nenad 1035

ノフジガー
Nofziger, Lyn 1029

ノフシンガー
Nofsinger, John R. 1029

ノフジンガー
Noffsinger, Jay E. 1029

ノブス
Nobbs, Jeffrey 1029
Nobs, Olivia 1029

ノブズ
Nobbs, David 1029

ノーブリー
Norbury, Paul Henri 1031

ノーフル
Norful, Smokie 1031

ノーブル
Noble, Adrian Keith 1029
Noble, Cate 1029
Noble, David F. 1029
Noble, Denis 1029
Noble, James 1029
Noble, Kate 1029
Noble, Mark 1029
Noble, Martha 1029
Noble, Paul 1029
Noble, Vicki E. 1029

ノーブルズ
Nobles, Ralph 1029

ノーブルマン
Nobleman, Marc Tyler 1029

ノブレガ
Nóbrega, Tobías 1029

ノブローチ
Knoblauch, Steven H. 748

ノブロック
Knoblauch, Steven H. 748

ノベスキー
Novesky, Amy 1035

ノベリン
Novelline, Robert A. 1035

ノベル
Novell, Cappi 1035

ノベルグ＝シュルツ
Norberg-Schulz, Christian 1031

ノーベン
Nowén, Ylva 1035

ノボア
Noboa, Gustavo 1029
Novoa, Rodolfo 1035
Novoa, Teresa 1035

ノボグラッツ
Novogratz, Jacqueline 1035

ノボスヨロフ
Novosjolov, Nikolai 1035

ノボセロフ
Novoselov, Konstantin Sergeevich 1035

ノボトナ
Novotna, Katerina 1035

ノボトニー
Novotny, Roman 1035
Nowotny, Ewald 1035

ノボビエイスカ
Nowowiejska, Kasia 1035

ノボビルスキ
Novobilski, Andrew J. 1035

ノポラ
Nopola, Sinikka 1031
Nopola, Tiina 1031

ノマオ
Nomao, Ibrahim 1030

ノーマン
Nauman, Bruce 1008
Naumann, Earl 1008
Noman, Abdullah Al 1030
Nomuan, Abdul-Hafez 1030
Norman, Al 1032
Norman, Colin 1032
Norman, David 1032
Norman, David James 1032
Norman, Donald Arthur 1032
Norman, Dwayne 1032
Norman, Edward 1032
Norman, Elizabeth M. 1032
Norman, Geoffrey R. 1032
Norman, Greg 1032
Norman, Howard A. 1032
Norman, Jessye 1032
Norman, Jill 1032
Norman, John Matthew 1032
Norman, Josh 1032
Norman, Marie K. 1032
Norman, Marsha 1032
Norman, Michael 1032
Norman, Peter 1032
Norman, Philip 1032
Norman, Remington 1032
Norman, Richard 1032
Norman, Richard J. 1032
Norman, Sam Hinga 1032
Norman, Trevor R. 1032

ノーマンド
Normand, Michelle 1032
Nourmand, Tony 1034

ノーマントン
Normanton, E.L. 1032

ノーム
Noam, Eli M. 1029

ノムトイバヤル
Nomtoibayar, Nyamtaishiryin 1030

ノムラ
Nomura, Carl 1030
Nomura, Catherine 1030

ノヨリ
Noyori, Ryoji 1035

ノーラー
Noller, Bill 1030

ノラ
Nola, Aaron 1030
Nola, Austin 1030
Nora, Pierre 1031

ノラス
Noras, Arto 1031

ノラスコ
Nolasco, Ricky 1030

ノラック
Norac, Carl 1031

ノラム
Noramou, Siba 1031

ノーラン
Nolan, Bernie 1030
Nolan, Christopher 1030
Nolan, Graham 1030
Nolan, Jonathan 1030
Nolan, Ken 1030
Nolan, Liam 1030
Nolan, Richard L. 1030
Nolan, Thomas E. 1030
Nolan, William F. 1030

ノラン
Nolan, Riall W. 1030

ノーランダー
Norlander, Linda 1032

ノーランド
Noland, Kenneth 1030
Noland, Marcus 1030
Noland, Mimi 1030
Norland, Erik 1032

ノーリ
Nori, Micah 1032

ノーリア
Nohria, Nitin 1030

ノリエガ
Noriega, Manuel Antonio 1032

ノリエド
Nolledo, Jose N. 1030

ノーリス
Norris, Rick 1032

ノリス
Norris, Bruce 1032
Norris, Bud 1032
Norris, Carina 1032
Norris, Chris 1032
Norris, Christopher 1032
Norris, Chuck 1032
Norris, Dan 1032
Norris, Daniel 1032
Norris, Derek 1032
Norris, Jared 1032
Norris, John 1032
Norris, Keith 1032
Norris, Patricia 1032
Norris, Pippa 1032
Norris, Robert F. 1032
Norris, Stephanie 1032
Norriss, Andrew 1032
Norrix, Linda 1032

ノリート
Nolito 1030

ノリリー
Norilee, Wizard 1032

ノーリング
Knorring, Laura von 748

ノリントン
Norrington, Roger 1032

ノール
Knoll, Andrew H. 748
Knoll, John 748
Knoll, Patricia 748
Nall, Tamara 1004
Noll, Mark A. 1030
Noll, Terrie 1030
Nool, Erki 1031
Noor, Fadzil 1031

ノル
Knoll, Glenn F. 748

Noll, Richard 1030
ノルガード
Norgaard, Mette 1031
ノルグ
Norguet, Jean-Pierre 1031
ノルケ
Norkeh, Frederick 1032
ノルゴー
Norgard, Jorgen Stig 1031
ノルサ
Norsa, Michele 1032
ノルジュ
Norge 1031
ノルシュタイン
Norshtein, Yurii 1033
ノルシュテイン
Norshtein, Yurii 1033
ノールズ
Knowles, James 748
Knowles, John 748
Knowles, Ronald 749
Knowles, Valerie 749
Knowles, William Standish 749
ノールストッケ
Nordstokke, Kjell 1031
ノールダム
Noordam, Bart 1031
ノルダル
Nordal, Ólöf 1031
ノルテ
Nolte, Ernst 1030
ノールティ
Nalty, Bernard C. 1004
ノルティ
Nolte, Nick 1030
ノルディーン
Nordeen, Lon O. 1031
ノルディン
Nordin, Margareta 1031
ノルディーン・ソピー
Noordin Sopiee 1031
ノルディン・ソピー
Noordin Sopiee 1031
ノルデン
Norden, Arthur van 1031
Norden, Lisa 1031
ノルデンスタム
Nordenstam, Sara 1031
ノルデンフェルト
Nordenfelt, Lennart 1031
ノルト
Nault, Robert 1008
Nolt, Steven M. 1030
Nolte, Dorothy Law 1030
North, Michael 1033
ノルドウィンド
Nordwind, Timothy 1031
ノルトヴェイト
Nordtveit, Havard 1031
ノールトゥグ
Northug, Petter 1033
ノルドクビスト
Nordqvist, Anna 1031
ノルドグレン
Nordgren, Pehr Henrik 1031
ノルトフ
Northoff, Georg 1033
ノルトマン
Nordmann, Ingeborg 1031
ノルドランダー
Nordlander, Lars 1031
ノルドリリョ
Nardolillo, Jo 1005
ノールトン
Knowlton, Dwight 749
ノルバート
Palanovics, Norbert 1071
ノルビ
Norrby, Erling 1032
ノルビー
Norrby, Erling 1032
ノルブ
Norbu, Wangdi 1031
ノルフェルト
Nordfeldt, Kristoffer 1031
ノルベリ
Norberg, Anette 1031
ノルベルグ＝シュルツ
Norberg-Schulz, Christian 1031
ノルマン
Nollmann, Gerd 1030
Norman, Victor 1032
ノルマンド
Normand, Charles E. M. 1032
ノルムラドフ
Normuradov, Mamarizo 1032
ノレゴール
Norregaard, Allan 1032
ノーレス
Knowles, William Standish 749
ノレット
Nolet, Carlos 1030
ノーレットランダーシュ
Norretranders, Tor 1032
ノレム
Norem, Julie K. 1031
ノレル
Norell, Mark 1031
ノーレン
Nolen, Stephanie 1030
ノレーン
Norén, Lars 1031
ノーレン・ホークセマ
Nolen-Hoeksema, Susan 1030
ノロゥバンザト
Norovbanzad, Namjilyn 1032
ノロヴバンザド
Norovbanzad, Namjilyn 1032
ノロオジ
Noroozi, Omid Haji 1032
ノロバンザド
Norovbanzad, Namjilyn 1032
ノロフ
Norov, Vladimir 1032
ノロブバンザド
Norovbanzad, Namjilyn 1032
ノワイエ
Noyer, Christian 1035
ノワヴィル
Noiville, Christine 1030
ノワク
Novak, Vasily A. 1034
Nowak, Drew 1035
ノワコフスキー
Nowakowski, Richard J. 1035
ノワツカ
Nowacka, Oktawia 1035
ノワリエル
Noiriel, Gérard 1030
ノワレ
Noiret, Philippe 1030
ノンコンテ
Gnonkonte, Désiré 506
ノンソア
Gnonsoa, Angèle 506
ノンデシムココ
Nonde-simukoko, Joyce 1030
ノン・ドゥク・マイン
Nong Duc Manh 1030
ノン・ドク・マイン
Nong Duc Manh 1030
ノンボ
Nombo, Louis-Marie 1030

【ハ】

ハ
Ha, Gene 550
Ha, Ji-won 550
Ha, Jung-woo 550
Han, Woon-sa 565
Jin, Ha 674
ハー
Ha, Gene 550
Ha, Pham Hong 550
Ha, Tran Hong 550
Harr, Jonathan 573
Herr, Edwin L. 599
Herr, Michael 599
Herr, Paul 599
バ
Ba, Amadou 75
Ba, Amadou Tidiane 75
Ba, Boubacar 75
Ba, Diallo Madeleine 75
Ba, Lamine 75
Ba, Matar 75
Ba, N'diaye 75
Ba, Salif 75
Ba, Sekou 75
Ba, Sulin 75
Bas, Philippe 101
Ma, Jingle 857
バー
Ba, Amadou 75
Ba, Amadou Hampate 75
Ba, Coumba 75
Bá, Gabriel 75
Ba, Housseynou Hamady 75
Ba, Ousmane 75
Bah, Abdoul Aziz 80
Bah, Ahmed Ould 80
Bah, Hadja Aicha 80
Bah, Mariam 80
Bah, Minkailu 80
Bah, Njogou 80
Bah, Oury Bailo 80
Bah, Ousmane 80
Bah, Ramatoulaye 80
Bah, Sangaré Oumou 80
Barr, Anthony 96
Barr, Charles 96
Barr, Davey 96
Barr, Ed 96
Barr, Jeff 96
Barr, Michael 96
Barr, Mike W. 96
Barr, N.A. 96
Barr, Nevada 96
Barr, Pat 96
Barr, Thomas 96
Barr, Tricia 96
Burr, Vivien 205
パ
Pas, Rob Ten 1083
パー
Paar, Jack 1067
Parr, Ben 1081
Parr, Jerry 1081
Parr, Martin 1081
Parr, Terence John 1082
バアアター
Baatar, Yadambat 76
パァイファー
Pfeiffer, Steven I. 1106
パァウ
Paauw, Douglas S. 1067
ハアネル
Haanel, Charles Francis 551
パァラバン・ダナパン
Paelabang Danapan 1069
バアル
Baalu, T.R. 75
ハイ
Hai, Hoang Trung 555
Hai, M.Jalalul 555
バーイー
Vyam, Durgabai 1465
バイ
Bai, Bing 80
Bai, Ke-ming 80
Bai, Shu-xian 80
Bai, Xian-yong 80
Baj, Enrico 82
Baye, Natharie 107
Pai, Yang 1070
Vai, Steve 1438
パイ
Bai, Xian-yong 80
Bai, Yun-feng 80
Pye, Ali 1141
Pye, Claire 1141
Pye, Jennifer 1141
Pye, Michael 1141
ハイアー
Hyer, Martha 641
バイアー
Baier, Daniel 80
Bayer, Oswald 107
Bayer, Sebastian 108
バイアシュ
Baias, Silviu 80
バイアース
Byers, Thomas H. 210
バイアーズ
Byars, Betsy 210
Byers, Stephen 210
バイアースタイン
Beyerstein, Barry L. 135
ハイアセン
Hiaasen, Carl 603
ハイアーチェク
Hyerczyk, James A. 641
ハイアッセン
Hiaasen, Carl 603

ハイアット
Hiatt, Howard H. 603
Hiatt, James L. 603
Hiatt, Kristina D. 603
Hyatt, Amy M. 640
Hyatt, Michael S. 640
Hyatt, Peter 640
Hyatt, Sandra 640
バイアット
Byatt, Antonia Susan 210
パイアット
Pyatt, David 1141
バイアード
Byard, Kevin 210
Byard, Roger W. 210
パイアーマ
Pahiama, Kundi 1070
パイアマ
Paihama, Kundi 1070
ハイアム
Higham, Charles 604
バイアム
Byam, Michele 210
Byham, Tacy M. 210
Byham, William C. 210
バイアム・ショー
Byam Shaw, Ros 210
ハイアムズ
Hyams, Edward 640
バイアラスキー
Bialaski, Tom 136
バイアリー
Bierley, Paul E. 137
Byerly, Kenny 210
バイアルディ
Baiardi, Ana 80
バイアルディ・ケスネル
Baiardi Quesnel, Ana María 80
バイイ
Bailly, Jean Christophe 81
Bailly, Séry 81
パイヴァ
Paiva, Marcella de 1070
Paiva, Tatiana 1070
パイヴァー
Piver, Susan 1116
ハイウェイ
Highway, Tomson 605
パイウェル
Pywell, Sharon L. 1142
ハイウォーター
Highwater, Jamake 605
バイエ
Baillet, Gilles 81
パイェ
Payet, Dimitri 1089
パイエ
Payet, Laetitia 1089
ハイエク
Hayek, Nicolas George 585
ハイエス
Heyes, Josef 602
バイェス
Bayés, Pilarín 108
バイエズ
Baez, Javier 79
Baez, Pedro 79
Baez, Sandy 79
パイエス
Pailles, Lionel 1070
ハイエック
Hayek, G.Nick, Jr. 585
Hayek, Nicolas George 585
バイエフ
Baiev, Khassan 80
バイエル
Bayerl, Cynthia Taft 108
パイエルス
Peierls, Tim 1092
バイエルツ
Bayertz, Kurt 108
パイオン
Pion, Joseph 1114
Pion, Paul D. 1114
パイオンニ
Paionni, Alessandra 1070
ハイカニ
al-Khaikani, Tariq 724
パイカリ
Peikari, Cyrus 1092
バイガンバ
Bayigamba, Robert 108
ハイキオ
Häikiö, Martti 555
パイク
Paik, Keun Wook 1070
Paik, Kun-woo 1070
Paik, Nam June 1070
Pike, Douglas 1111
Pike, Graham 1111
Pike, Robert W. 1111
Pike, Rosamund 1111
パイクスペース
Pikus-pace, Noelle 1111
バイクタル
Baichtal, John 80
ハイグル
Heigl, Katherine 589
バイグレイブ
Bygrave, William D. 210
パイケット
Pykett, Lyn 1141
バイケル
Bikel, Theodore 138
バイゲルト
Weigelt, Udo 1487
ハイケン
Hiken, Marti 605
バイコウスキー
Bykowski, Carter 210
バイゴット
Bygott, David 210
パイコフ
Peikoff, Lori 1092
ハイザー
Heiser, Gemma 590
バイザー
Beiser, Frederick C. 115
ハイサミ
al-Haisami, Khadijah Ahmad 555
ハイサム
Haitham, bin Tariq al-Said 555
バイサン
Hansawong, Phaisan 567
ハイジ
Heidi 589
ハイジー
Heisey, Chris 590
Hyzy, Julie 641
ハイジック
Heisig, James W. 590
パイシャー
Paischer, Ludwig 1070
パイシュ
Paes, Rui 1069
ハイシュール
Haichour, Boudjemaa 555
バイシンク
Buissink, Frans 200
ハイジンハ
Huizinga, Mark 634
ハイス
Hais, Michael D. 555
Heiss, Deborah Givens 590
バイス
Bais, Sander 82
Bajs, Damir 82
Weiss, Birthe 1490
Weiss, Hans 1490
Weiss, Oded 1490
パイス
Pais, Gabriel 1070
ハイスケル
Heiskell, Andrew 590
バイスコップ
Weisskopf, Victor Frederik 1490
ハイスター
Heister, Beate 590
バイスター
Byster, Mike 211
バイステック
Biestek, Felix Paul 137
ハイスト
Haist, Steven A. 555
ハイズマンズ
Huysmans, Greg 640
ハイスミス
Highsmith, Cyrus 604
Highsmith, James A. 604
ハイスロップ
Hyslop, Bruce 641
ハイセラー
Heisserer, Eric 590
バイセル
Bycel, Benjamin 210
バイゼル
Beisel, Elizabeth 115
パイゼル
Peisel, Thomas 1092
ハイゼルマン
Heiserman, Hewitt, Jr. 590
ハイセンフーバー
Heissenhuber, Alois 590
ハイダー
Haider, Jörg 555
Haider, Maximilian 555
Haider, Mian Shamin 555
Haider, Moinuddin 555
Hyder, Kerry 641
バイダ
Vaida, Cornelia 1438
Vajda, Attila Sandor 1438
パイダシ
Païdassi, Solenne 1070
ハイダシュドンチッチ
Hajdaš Dončić, Siniša 555
ハイダル
Haidar, Abdullatif 555
Haidar, El Ali 555
Haider, Mian Shamin 555
Haydar, Ali 584
ハイダロフ
Haydarov, Utkirbek 584
ハイタワー
Hightower, Dont'a 605
Hightower, Lee 605
Hightower, Lynn S. 605
Hightower, Rosella 605
Hightower, Tim 605
バイチチャク
Bajcicak, Martin 82
ハイツ
Heitz, Markus 590
Hite, Sid 610
バイツ
Beitz, Berthold 115
バイツァー
Bizer, Christian 142
バイツェル
Beitzel, Barry J. 115
ハイッス
Heiss, Hubert 590
パイッチ
Pajic, Dejan 1071
ハイデ
Haydée, Marcia 584
ハイディナガ
Hajdinaga, Gezim 555
ハイティンク
Haitink, Bernard 555
ハイティング
Heiting, Manfred 590
バイテクーナス
Vaitiek-unas, Petras 1438
ハイデマン
Heideman, Eugene P. 589
Heidemann, Britta 589
バイデヤ
Baidya, Sangina 80
ハイデュ
Hajdu, Patricia A. 556
ハイデル
Hidell, Al 604
ハイデルシャイト
Heiderscheit, Annie 589
ハイデルバッハ
Heidelbach, Nikolaus 589
ハイデン
Hayden, Dolores 584
Hayden, Elizabeth P. 584
Hayden, Tom 584
バイデン
Biden, Beau 137
Biden, Joseph, Jr. 137
バイデンス
Buydens, Hubert 210
ハイデンライク
Heidenreich, Barbara 589
Heidenreich, Jerry 589
ハイデンライヒ
Heidenreich, Elke 589
ハイト
Haidt, Jonathan 555
Haight, Barbara K. 555
Haight, Barrett S. 555
Height, Dorothy 589
Heyd, David 602
Hight, Elena 604
Hight, Julian 605
Hite, Robert 610
Hite, Shere 610
ハイド
Hayd, Mohamed Mahmud 584
Heide, Florence Parry 589

Hyde, Brandon 640
Hyde, Bubba 640
Hyde, Carlos 640
Hyde, Catherine Ryan 640
Hyde, Cordel 640
Hyde, Henry J. 640
Hyde, Jerry 640
Hyde, Karl 640
Hyde, Lewis 640
Hyde, Maggie 640
Hyde, Micah 640
Hyde, Michael 640
Hyde, Stella 641
Hyde, Unmani Liza 641

パイト
Pite, Crystal 1116

ハイドゥ
Hajdu, Jonatan 555

ハイドゥック＝フート
Heyduck-Huth, Hilde 602

パイトゥーン
Phaithoon, Kaeothong 1106

ハイドシェク
Heidsieck, Eric 589

ハイドシェック
Heidsieck, Eric 589

ハイドシュッター
Heidschötter, Uwe 589

ハイトナー
Hytner, Nicholas 641

バイトニオ
Bitonio, Joel 142

ハイトフ
Khaitov, Aktam 724

バイトマン
Weidmann, Jens 1487

ハイドラー
Heidler, Betty 589

ハイドリッヒ
Heidrich, Debra E. 589
Heidrich, Jens 589

ハイドリヒ
Heidrich, Joana 589

ハイナー
Hainer, Herbert 555

バィナイ
Bajnai, Gordon 82

バイナイ
Bajnai, Gordon 82

ハイナーヒルズ
Heiner Hills, Madeline 590

バイナム
Bynum, Helen 211
Bynum, Will 211
Bynum, William F. 211

ハイニッシュホーゼク
Heinisch-hosek, Gabriele 590

バイニマラマ
Bainimarama, Voreqe 82

ハイネ
Heine, Ernst W. 590
Heine, Helme 590
Heine, Hilda 590
Heine, Jan T. 590
Heine, Thomas 590
Heine, Wilbur 590

ハイネケ
Heinicke, Taylor 590

ハイネケン
Heineken, Alfred Henry 590
Heineken, Charlene 590

バイネス
Byrnes, Robert G. 211

ハイネマン
Heineman, George T. 590
Heinemann, Erich 590
Heinemann, Gundi 590
Heinemann, Klaus 590
Heinemann, Klaus W. 590
Hieneman, Meme 604

パイノ
Paino, Melinda 1070

バイノン
Beynon, Emily 135

バイバー
Biber, Douglas 136

パイパー
Piper, Adrian 1114
Piper, Carly 1114
Piper, Frederick Charles 1114
Piper, John 1114
Piper, Michael Collins 1114
Piper, Roddy 1114
Piper, Ross 1114
Piper, Sophie 1114
Piper, Watty 1115
Pyper, Andrew 1141
Pyper, Robert 1141

ハイバーガー
Heiberger, Richard M. 589

パイバ・サラス
Paiva Salas, Ernesto José 1071

パイバス
Pybus, Catherine 1141
Pybus, Meg 1141

パイパール
Peiperl, Maury A. 1092

バイビー
Bybee, Rodger W. 210

パイプ
Pipe, Jemima 1114

ハイフィ
al-Haifi, Mohammad 555

ハイフィールド
Highfield, Kathy 604
Highfield, Roger 604

ハイフェッツ
Heifetz, Ronald Abadian 589

バイブクイン
Vivequin, Wanda 1460

パイプス
Pipes, Richard 1115

ハイブラエフ
Khaibulaev, Tagir 724

ハイブリッジ
Highbridge, Dianne 604

バイプル
Vaipulu, Samiu Kuita 1438

パイブーン
Paiboon, Khumchaya 1070
Paiboon, Wattanasiritham 1070

ハイベク
Hayboeck, Michael 584

ハイベタ
Haiveta, Chris 555

ハイベルズ
Hybels, Bill 640

バイマガンベトフ
Baimaganbetov, Serik 81

ハイマス
Hymas, Johnny 641

ハイマン
Heimann, Jim 589
Heimann, Rolf 589
Heyman, Melvin B. 602
Heymann, Klaus 603
Hyman, Clarissa 641
Hyman, Ed 641
Hyman, Jane Wegscheider 641
Hyman, Jay 641
Hyman, Mark 641
Hyman, Steven E. 641

バイマン
Byman, Daniel L. 210

ハイマンズ
Heymans, Emilie 603

パイミドゥベ
Payimi Deubet, Kalzeubé 1089

パイミ・パダケ
Pahimi Padacke, Albert 1070

ハイム
Haim, Corey 555
Heim, Michael 589
Heim, Pat 589
Heim, Scott 589
Heim, Theresa Marie 589
Heym, Stefan 602
Hime, James L. 608

ハイムズ
Heims, Steve J. 590
Hymes, Dell Hathaway 641

ハイムズフィールド
Heymsfield, Steven B. 603

ハイムバーグ
Heimberg, Richard G. 589

ハイムブーヒャー
Heimbucher, Christoph 589

ハイムラー
Himler, Ronald 608

ハイメ
Jaime, Romero 659

バイメノフ
Baymenov, Alikhan 108

ハイメラン
Heimeran, Ernst 589

ハイメル
Heymel, Michael 603
Hymel, Glenn M. 641

ハイメロート
Heimeroth, Christofer 590

ハイモヴィッツ
Haimovitz, Matt 555

ハイモビッツ
Haimovitz, Matt 555

ハイヤー
Hyer, Martha 641

バイヤ
Beyer, Jannik 134

バイヤー
Beyer, Andreas 134
Beyer, Frank 134
Byer, Esther 210
Byer, Tom 210

ハイヤーズ
Hyers, Tim 641

バイヤース
Byers, Aruna Rea 210

バイヤーズ
Byers, Dremiel 210

バイヤースクー
Byer-suckoo, Esther 210

バイヤット
Byatt, Antonia Susan 210

ハイヤート
Khayyat, Yaseen 727

バイヤー＝フローレス
Beyer-Flores, Carlos 135

バイヤーライン
Bayerlein, Reinhard 108

バイヤリー
Byerly, Carolyn M. 210

バイヤール
Bayard, Pierre 107

パイヤール
Paillard, Jean-François 1070

バイヤン
Vaillant, Daniel 1438
Vaillant, John 1438

ハイラー
Hairer, Ernst 555
Hairer, Martin 555
Huyler, Frank 640
Huyler, LaDeana 640

バイラ
Bajrami, Hikmete 82

バイラー
Byler, Stephen Raleigh 210

バイラーク
Beirach, Richie 115

バイラクタル
Bayraktar, Erdoğan 108

パイラック・ノルテ
Pyrak-Nolte, Laura J. 1141

パイラト
Pilate, Pascal 1111

バイラミ
Bajrami, Arsim 82
Bajrami, Hikmete 82
Bajrami, Xhelal 82

バイラム
Byram, Michael 211
Byram, Sam 211

バイラムイラドフ
Bayrammyradov, Gapurberdi 108

バイラモフ
Bayramov, Afgan 108
Bayramov, Dovrangeldy 108
Bayramov, Dzhumageldi 108
Bayramov, Rovshan 108

バイラン
Baylan, Ibrahim 108

ハイランド
Highland, Chris 604
Hyland, Angus 641
Hyland, Henry Stanley 641
Hyland, Jason P. 641
Hyland, William G. 641

バイリー
Bailly, Eric 81

ハイリヒ
Heilig, Loren 589

バイリャコフ
Bayryakov, Nikolay 108

バイリン
Bylin, Gunnar 210

ハイル

Heil, Erik 589
Heil, Jennifer 589
Heill, Claudia 589
Heyl, Matthias 602
Hile, Lori 605
al-Khail, Suleiman bin Abdullah Aba 724
Kheir, Salah Wanasi Mohammed 727
バイル
Bayrou, François 108
Byl, Christine 210
バイルー
Bayrou, François 108
パイル
Pile, John F. 1112
Pyle, James O. 1141
Pyle, Kenneth B. 1141
Pyle, Rod 1141
バイルス
Biles, Simone 138
ハイルディーン
Kheir El-dine, Marwan 727
ハイルブラン
Heilbrun, Robert 589
ハイルブローナー
Heilbronor, Robert L. 589
ハイルブロン
Heilbron, J.L. 589
ハイルマイヤー
Heilmeier, George Harry 589
ハイルマン
Heilemann, John 589
Heilman, Anna 589
Heilman, Kenneth M. 589
Hileman, Betle 605
ハイルラエフ
Khayrulloyev, Sherali 727
ハイルロエフ
Khayrulloyev, Sherali 727
ハイレ
Haile, Asegidie 555
Haile, Weldensae 555
バイレ
Baylet, Jean-Michel 108
ハイレセラシエ
Haileselassie, Yemane 555
バイレッティ
Bailetti, Fabrizio 81
ハイレマリアム・デサレン
Hailemariam Desalegn 555
ハイロ
Jairo, Samperio 659
ハイロヴィッチ
Hajrovic, Izet 556
バイロジ
Bailodji, Barthelemy Natoingar 81
バイロック
Beilock, Sian 114
パイロット
Pilot, Sachin 1112
ハイロフ
Khairov, Ruslan 724
バイロン
Bryron, Tanya 196
Byrom, Jamie 211
Byron, John 211
Byron, Vincent 211
パイロン
Pilone, Dan 1112
Pyron, Tim 1142
ハイン
Hein, Christoph 590
Hein, George E. 590
Hein, James L. 590
Hein, Laura Elizabeth 590
Hein, Lutz 590
Hein, Rick 590
Hein, Sybille 590
Hein, Trent R. 590
Heine, Steven 590
Hine, David 608
Huynh, Carol 640
バイン
Baing, Andrew 82
パイン
Paine, Angela E. 1070
Pine, Arthur 1113
Pine, B.Joseph, Ⅱ 1113
Pine, Chris 1113
Pine, Daniel 1113
Pine, Fred 1113
Pine, Karen Jane 1113
Pine, Ray 1113
Pyne, Christopher 1141
Pyne, Stephen J. 1141
バインガム
Bingham, Neil 139
バイング
Baing, Andrew 82
ハインズ
Haines, Duane E. 555
Haynes, Jeffrey 585
Hinds, David M. 608
Hinds, Fitzgerald 608
Hinds, Samuel 608
Hines, Anna Grossnickle 608
Hines, Barry 608
Hines, Colin 608
Hines, Gregory 608
Hines, Jerome 608
Hines, Joanna 608
Hines, Sandra H. 608
Hines, Stephen W. 608
Hines, Terence 608
Hinze, Matt 609
バインズ
Bynes, Josh 210
パインズ
Pines, Ayala M. 1113
Pines, David 1113
Pines, Jesse M. 1113
ハインズ・スティーブンス
Hines-Stephens, Sarah 608
ハインソー
Heinsoo, Rob 590
ハインゾーン
Heinsohn, Gunnar 590
バインダー
Binder, Gordon M. 139
パインダー
Pinder, Eric 1113
バインダム
Byndom, Carrington 210
ハインツ
Heintz, Dominique 590
Heintz, Philip 590
ハインツァー
Heinzer, Max 590
ハインデル
Heindel, Robert 590
ハインド
Hind, Rebecca 608
Hinde, Thomas 608
バインドゥラシビリ
Baindurashvili, Kakha 82
ハインドゥル
Heindl, Gottfried 590
ハインドマーチ
Hindmarch, Anya 608
ハインドマン
Hyndman, Emerson 641
Hyndman, Noel 641
ハインドル
Haindl, K. 555
バイントン
Bainton, Rolnad H. 82
ハインバーグ
Heinberg, Richard 590
バインハート
Beinhart, Larry 115
ハインリッチ
Heinrich, Bernd 590
ハインリッヒ
Heinrich, Michael 590
Heinrich, Patrick 590
Heinrichs, H.C.Helmut 590
ハインリッヒス
Heinrichs, H.C.Helmut 590
Heinrichs, Maurus 590
ハインリヒ
Heinrich, Richard 590
ハウ
Howe, Daniel Walker 628
Howe, David 628
Howe, Eddie 628
Howe, Geoffrey 628
Howe, Gordie 628
Howe, James 628
Howe, Jeff 628
Howe, John 628
Howe, Kenneth Ross 628
Howe, Rufus 628
Howe, Stephen 628
Howe, Steve 628
バーウー
Ba-u'um, Masir 107
パーヴ
Parv, Valerie 1083
ハウア
Jaua, Elias 666
ハウアー
Hauer, Cheryl 581
Hauer, K.A. 581
Hauer, Rutger 581
バウアー
Bauer, Angeline 105
Bauer, Belinda 105
Bauer, Billy 105
Bauer, Brian S. 105
Bauer, Brigitte 105
Bauer, Christian 105
Bauer, Günther G. 105
Bauer, Hank 105
Bauer, Hans 105
Bauer, Hans-Joachim 105
Bauer, Heather 105
Bauer, Ina 105
Bauer, Joan 105
Bauer, Joy 106
Bauer, Jutta 106
Bauer, Klemen 106
Bauer, Lukas 106
Bauer, Marion Dane 106
Bauer, Pamela 106
Bauer, Robert 106
Bauer, Trevor 106
Bauer, Walter F. 106
Bower, Gordon Howard 170
Bower, Joseph L. 170
パウァ
Power, Rhoda 1130
パヴァオ
Pavao, Aaron 1088
バウアージーマ
Bauersima, Igor 106
ハヴァシュ
Havas, Kató 583
ハウアス
Howarth, Chris 628
バウアーズ
Bauers, Jake 106
Bowers, Barbara 170
Bowers, Brian 170
Bowers, C.A. 170
Bowers, Helen 170
Bowers, Jenny 170
Bowers, Kathryn 170
ハヴァースカ
Chawarska, Katarzyna 250
ハヴァーティ
Haverty, Ann 583
ハーヴァード
Harvard, Joe 578
パヴァネル
Pavanel, Jane 1088
バウアーライン
Bauerlein, Mark 106
バヴァロ
Bavaro, Jackie 107
パヴァロッティ
Pavarotti, Luciano 1088
ハーヴィ
Harvey, David 578
Harvie, Shane 578
ハーヴィー
Harvey, Giles 578
Harvey, Leslie Daryl Danny 578
ハウイ
Howey, M.Oldfield 628
Howie, George 628
ハウイー
Howey, Hugh C. 628
Howie, Betsy 628
Howie, Vicki 628
ハウィー・D
Howie D 628
ハーヴィオ - マンニラ
Haavio-Mannila, Elina 551
パーヴィス
Purvis, Christopher Thomas Bremner 1140
Purvis, Leland 1140
パヴィチ
Pavić, Milorad 1088
バーウィック
Berwick, Donald Mark 132
ハーウィックス
Hurwicz, Leonid 638
ハーヴィッコ
Haavikko, Paavo Juhani 551
ハーヴィッチ
Hurvich, Leo Maurice 638
パヴィッチ
Pavich, Frank 1088
ハーウィッツ
Hurwicz, Leonid 638
Hurwitz, Brian 638

Hurwitz, Gregg Andrew 638
Hurwitz, Johanna 638
Hurwitz, Matt 638
Hurwitz, Trevor A. 638
ハーヴィッツ
Hurwicz, Leonid 638
ハーウィット
Harwit, Eric 578
パウィナ
Pawina, Thongsuk 1088
ハーヴィル
Harville, David A. 578
ハヴィル
Havil, Julian 583
バーウィレドゥ
Baah-wiredu, Kwadwo 75
パウィロナディ
Pawironadi, Samuel 1088
ハーウィン
Hurwin, Davida 638
バーウィン
Barwin, Connor 101
バヴィン
Bavin, Carol 107
ハウヴェ
Hauwe, Walter van 582
ハウウェル
Howell, William 628
ハウウェレーウ
Gouweleeuw, Jeffrey 522
バヴウドリ
Bavuudorj, T.S. 107
ハーヴェ
Have, O.ten 583
ハーヴェー
Harvey, Allison G. 578
Harvey, Barbara F. 578
ハーウェイ
Harway, Michele 578
ハーヴェイ
Harvey, Allison G. 578
Harvey, Burton 578
Harvey, Clay 578
Harvey, David 578
Harvey, Eric Lee 578
Harvey, Joan C. 578
Harvey, John 578
Harvey, John H. 578
Harvey, John Robert 578
Harvey, Jonathan 578
Harvey, Jonathan Dear 578
Harvey, Kenneth J. 578
Harvey, Michael 578
Harvey, Pat 578
Harvey, Xen 578
パヴェウ
Pawel, Dybala 1088
バヴェラス
Bavelas, Janet Beavin 107
ハーヴェル
Harvell, Richard 578
ハウエル
Howell, Cate 628
Howell, Dara 628
Howell, David 628
Howell, David L. 628
Howell, David Luke 628
Howell, Frank Scott 628
Howell, Hannah 628
Howell, J.P. 628
Howell, Margaret 628
Howell, Rob 628
Howell, Steve N.G. 628
Howell, Tony 628
Howell, William G. 628
ハヴェル
Havel, Václav 583
バーウェル
Barwell, Fred 101
Barwell, Graham 101
Burwell, Sylvia 207
Burwell, Tyreek 207
パウェル
Powell, Jillian 1129
パウエル
Pawel, Rebecca 1088
Powell, Alonzo 1129
Powell, Andy 1129
Powell, Antoinette 1129
Powell, Asafa 1129
Powell, Aubrey 1129
Powell, Benjamin 1129
Powell, Benny 1129
Powell, Bilal 1129
Powell, Billy 1129
Powell, Boog 1129
Powell, Brian 1129
Powell, Colin Luther 1129
Powell, Douglas H. 1129
Powell, Dwight 1129
Powell, Ellen 1129
Powell, Gareth L. 1129
Powell, James 1129
Powell, James Lawrence 1129
Powell, James Newton 1129
Powell, Jennie 1129
Powell, Jillian 1129
Powell, Joe 1129
Powell, John 1129
Powell, John Wesley 1129
Powell, Joseph Michael 1129
Powell, Julie 1129
Powell, Ken 1129
Powell, Lane H. 1129
Powell, Michael 1129
Powell, Michael K. 1129
Powell, Mike 1129
Powell, Natalie 1129
Powell, Norman 1129
Powell, Richard 1129
Powell, Sandy 1129
Powell, Sophie 1129
Powell, Stacie 1129
Powell, Thomas A. 1129
Powell, Tim 1129
Powell, Tony 1129
Powell, Tyvis 1129
Powell, Vance 1129
Powell, Walt 1130
Powell, William Dylan 1130
Powell, William F. 1130
パヴェル
Pavel, Margaret Paloma 1088
パウエル＝ジョブズ
Powell Jobs, Laurene 1130
パウエル＝ジョーンズ
Powell-Jones, Mark 1130
ハウエルズ
Howells, Coral Ann 628
Howells, Debbie 628
Howells, Kevin 628
Howells, Lynn 628
Howells, Robert 628
パウェルスキー
Pawelski, Cheryl 1088
パヴォード
Pavord, Anna 1088
パヴォーニ
Pavoni, Verena 1088
パヴォーネ
Pavone, Chris 1088
ハウオファ
Hau'ofa, Epeli 582
パヴォレッティ
Pavoletti, Leonardo 1088
パウカ
Palka, Krystyna 1072
パウカー
Pauker, Benjamin 1086
ハウキニマ
Haukinima, Peauafi 582
ハウク
Houck, Herbert 625
ハウグ
Haug, Anne 582
Haug, Peder 582
バウク
Bauk, Arsen 106
パウク
Pauc, Robin 1086
ハウグラン
Haugland, Knut 582
Haugland, Valgerd Svarstad 582
ハウグリ
Haugilie, Anniken 582
Haugli, Maren 582
Haugli, Sverre 582
ハウゲ
Hauge, Jens Christian 582
ハウケネス
Haukenes, Havard 582
ハウゲン
Haugen, Robert A. 582
Haugen, Tormod 582
ハウゴーア
Haugaard, Jakob 582
ハウサー
Hausser, Romuald 582
Howsare, Julian 629
ハウザー
Hauser, Alan R. 582
Hauser, Frank 582
Hauser, Janet 582
Hauser, Julia 582
Hauser, Kitty 582
Hauser, Marc D. 582
Hauser, Peter C. 582
Hauser, Priscilla 582
Hauser, Stjepan 582
Hauser, Stuart T. 582
Hauser, Thomas 582
Hauser, Tim 582
Hauser, Ulrike 582
Houser, Adrian 626
Houser, Alan 626
ハウシク
Hausiku, Marco 582
パウジーニ
Pausini, Laura 1087
ハウシャビ
al-Hawshabi, Mansour Ahmad 584
バウシュ
Bağiş, Egemen 79
Bausch, François 106
Bausch, Pina 106
パウシュ
Pausch, Jai 1087
Pausch, Randy 1087
バウシュケ
Baushcke, Martin 107
バウジンガー
Bausinger, Hermann 107
ハウス
Haus, Illona 582
House, Allan 626
House, Alvin E. 626
House, Charles H. 626
House, Danuel 626
House, Davon 626
House, Freeman 626
House, John 626
House, Jonathan M. 626
House, Richard 626
House, Robert J. 626
House, Steve 626
House, Tom 626
Howse, Derek 629
Howse, Justin 629
Howse, Philip Edwin 629
ハウズ
Hawes, Jason 583
Howes, George E. 628
Howes, John Forman 628
Howes, Justin 628
Howes, Rupert 628
バウズ
Baus, Ursula 106
パーヴス
Purves, Barry J.C. 1140
ハウスクロフト
Housecroft, Catherine E. 626
ハウスケラー
Hauskeller, Michael 582
ハウスチャイルド
Hauschild, Mike 582
ハウスデン
Housden, Maria 626
Housden, Martyn 626
ハウストン
Houston, Kelli 626
ハウスナー
Hausner, Jessica 582
ハウスネル
Hausner, Jerzy 582
ハウスホールド
Household, Geoffrey 626
バウズマ
Bouwsma, William James 169
ハウスマン
Hausman, Jerry 582
Hausman, Kalani Kirk 582
Hausman, Robert E. 582
Houseman, Susan N. 626
バウスマン
Buisman, Jantien 200
バウズマン
Bousman, Darren Lynn 168
ハウスワルト
Hauswald, Simone 582
ハウゼ
Hause, Alfred 582
パウゼヴァング
Pausewang, Gudrun 1087
バウゼンヴァイン
Bausenwein,

Christoph 107
ハウゼンブラス
Hausenblas, Heather A. 582
パウター
Powter, Daniel 1130
ハウタッカー
Houthakker, Hendrik Samuel 627
ハウタマキ
Hautamaeki, Matti 582
ハウタラ
Hautala, Heidi 582
バウダルベック・コジャタエフ
Baudarbek-kozhatayev, Yerlan 105
バウチ
Bauch, Tom 105
バウチャー
Boucher, David 166
Britton, Dorothy 184
バウチャル
Bavčar, Igor 107
バウツ
Bauc, Jarosław 105
Bautts, Tony 107
ハウツァハー
Houtzager, Marc 627
ハウック
Houck, Colleen 625
ハーウッド
Harwood, Beth 578
Harwood, Jeremy 579
Harwood, Kerri 579
Harwood, Louise 579
Harwood, Robert J. 579
Harwood, Ronald 579
ハウツブロム
Goudsblom, Johan 521
ハウディー
Howdy, Buck 628
バウディス
Baudis, Ulrich 105
バウティスタ
Bautista, Jon 107
Bautista, Jose 107
Bautista Agut, Roberto 107
バウディッチ
Bowditch, Bruce 169
パウデル
Paudel, Bishnu Prasad 1086
パウデル
Paudel, Purshottam 1086
Poudel, Ramchandra 1128
ハウト
Hout, Mies van 627
ハウトマン
Hautman, Pete 582
パウナル＝グレイ
Pownall-Gray, Dickon 1130
ハウナレナ
Jaunarena, José Horacio 666
パウノフスキ
Paunovski, Ljuben 1087
バウハウス
Bauhaus, Ingrid 106
Bouhuys, Mies 167
パウビツキ
Pałubicki, Janusz 1073
ハウフ
Hauff, Michael von 581
ハウフィク
Haufiku, Bernhard 582
ハウフェ
Hauffe, Thomas 582
ハウプト
Haupt, Herbert 582
ハウプトマン
Hauptman, Herbert Aaron 582
パウフラー
Paufler, Alexander 1086
ハウブリッヒ
Haubrich, Julia 581
バウマー
Baumer, Franz 106
バウマイスター
Baumeister, Roy F. 106
バウマン
Bauman, Howard 106
Bauman, Janina 106
Bauman, Richard 106
Bauman, Yoram 106
Bauman, Zygmunt 106
Baumann, Chris 106
Baumann, Jürgen 106
Baumann, Kurt 106
Baumann, Oliver 106
Baumann, Reinhard 106
Baumann, Romed 106
Baumann, Stephan 106
Bowman, Alisa 170
Bowman, Noah 170
バーウーム
Ba-u'um, Masir 107
バウム
Baum, Friedemann 106
Baum, Louis 106
Baum, Michael S. 106
バウムガートナー
Baumgartner, Eric 106
バウムガルテン
Baumgarten, Eduard 106
バウムガルテン・ラバンド
Baumgarten Lavand, Dario 106
バウムガルト
Baumgart, Reinhard 106
バウムガルトナー
Baumgartner, Karl 106
バウムガルトリンガー
Baumgartlinger, Julian 106
バウムヨハン
Baumjohann, Alexander 106
パウラ
Paula, Paulo Roberto 1087
パヴラック
Pawlak, Paweł 1088
パヴラトヴァ
Pavlátová, Michaela 1088
ハウランド
Howland, Chris 628
Howland, Jason 628
ハウリー
Hawley, Joe 584
Howley, Marie 628
パウリ
Pauli, Gunter 1087
Pauli, Lorenz 1087
Pauli, Tatjana 1087
パウリカ
Paulica, Ion 1087
パヴリーシン
Pavlishin, G. 1088
パウリセン
Paulissen, Roel 1087
パウリニチュクレブス
Pavlinič-krebs, Irma 1088
パウリーニョ
Paulinho, Sergio 1087
パウリーノ
Paulino, David 1087
パウリノ
Paulino, Alberto 1087
パウリノ・セム
Paulino Sem, Rubén Darío 1087
ハウリハン
Hourihane, Ursula 626
ハウリン
Howlin, Brendan 629
Howlin, Patricia 629
バウリング
Bowring, Richard 171
Bowring, Richard John 171
パウル
Paul, Ayonika 1086
Paul, Stephan 1087
バウルクーム
Baulcombe, David 106
パウルス
Paulus, Diane 1087
Powles, Cyril 1130
パウルスマイアー
Paulsmeier, Karin 1087
ハウレギ・アトンド
Jáuregui Atondo, Ramón 666
パウレッジ
Powledge, Tabitha M. 1130
ハウレット
Howlett, Darryl 628
Howlett, Kevin 628
パヴレンカ
Pawlenka, Claudia 1088
パウロ
Paulo, Filo 1087
パヴロー
Pavlou, Stel 1088
パヴロヴィッチ
Pavlovic, Daniel 1088
パウロ・オリヴェイラ
Paulo Oliveira 1087
パウロス
Paulos, John Allen 1087
パウロ・ソウザ
Paulo Sousa 1087
ハヴロック
Havelock, Christine Mitchell 583
パウロバ
Pavlova, Lilyana 1088
パヴロフ
Pavloff, Franck 1088
Pavlov, Valentin S. 1088
パヴロフスキー
Pavlovsky, Bruno 1088
パウロ・ロペス
Pauro Lopes 1087
バウワー
Bauer, Laurie 106
Bauer, Wolfgang 106
Bouwer, Ton 169
Bower, Jeff 170
Bower, Marvin 170
Verwer, George 1454
バウワース
Bowers, Chris 170
Bowers, David 170
バウワーズ
Bowers, Bob 170
バウワー・ミュラー
Bauer Mueller, Pamela 106
バウン
Baun (rasmussen) , Tine 106
Bown, Stephen R. 170
パウンガ
Paunga, Giulio Masasso 1087
パウンガー
Paungger, Johanna 1087
パウンシー
Pouncey, Maurkice 1128
Pouncey, Mike 1128
ハウンズフィールド
Hounsfield, Godfrey Newbold 626
ハウンズロー
Hounslow, Richard 626
パウンダーズ
Pounders, Brooks 1128
バウンティー・キラー
Bounty Killer 167
パウンテン
Pountain, Dick 1128
パウンド
Pound, John 1128
Pound, Peter 1128
Pound, Richard 1128
パウンドストーン
Poundstone, William 1128
パウントニー
Pountney, David Willoughby 1128
バウンフォード
Bounford, Trevor 167
バエア
Vaea 1438
ハエク
Hajek, Antonin 556
バエクワ
Bahekwa, Esdras Kambale 80
バエサ
Baeza, Servulo 79
Fernández Baeza, Mario 430
バエザ
Baeza, Servulo 79
バエジ
Vaezi, Mahmoud 1438
バエショノイ
Vayeshnoi, Lekh Ram 1448
バエス
Báez, Sabino 79
バエズ
Baez, Joan Chandos 79
パエス
Paes, Leander 1069
バーエズザデ
Vaaezzadeh, Saadegh 1437
ハエック
Hayek, Salma 585

パエト
Paet, Urmas 1069
パエニ
Paeni, Stephen 1069
パエニウ
Paeniu, Bikenibeu 1069
バエベック
Bahebeck, Jean-Christophe 80
バーエワ
Baeva, Alena 79
ハオ
Hao, Ran 568
Hau, Lung-bin 581
バオ
Bao, Yuntuvi 90
Bao, Zun-xin 90
パオ
Pao, Basil 1075
Phao, Bounnaphonh 1106
バオ・ニン
Báo Ninh 90
ハオマエ
Haomae, William 568
ハオモリ
Ha'amori, Dickson 551
ハオラテ
Gaolathe, Baledzi 477
パオリット
Paolitto, Diana Pritchard 1075
パオリーニ
Paolini, Christopher 1075
パオルッチ
Paolucci, Antonio 1075
パオロッツィ
Paolozzi, Eduardo Luigi 1075
ハーガ
Haga, Åslaug Marie 553
ハーガー
Hager, Leopold 554
Hager, Nicky 554
ハガー
Hagger, Martin 554
バーカー
Barker, Alan 94
Barker, Chris 94
Barker, Clive 94
Barker, Cordell 94
Barker, David 94
Barker, Debi 94
Barker, Gord 94
Barker, Graham Richard 94
Barker, Joel Arthur 94
Barker, Jonathan 94
Barker, Juliet R.V. 94
Barker, Kathy 94
Barker, Margaret 94
Barker, Pat 94
Barker, Paul 94
Barker, Rick 94
Barker, Rob 94
Barker, Rodney 94
Barker, Roger A. 94
Barker, Ronnie 94
Barker, Sarah 94
Barker, Stephen 94
Barker, Tom 94
バーガー
Berger, Barbara W. 126
Berger, David 126
Berger, Fred W. 126
Berger, George 126
Berger, Glenn 126
Berger, Gordon Mark 126
Berger, Howard 126
Berger, Iris 126
Berger, Jennifer Garvey 126
Berger, Joe 126
Berger, Jonah 126
Berger, Lisa 126
Berger, M. 126
Berger, Nancy O. 126
Berger, Peter Ludwig 126
Berger, Samuel R. 126
Berger, Sandy 126
Berger, Sebastian 126
Berger, Suzanne 126
Berger, Teresa 126
Berger, Thomas 126
Berger, Todd R. 126
Berger, Warren 126
Bergere, Lee 126
Boerger, Andy 153
Burger, Corey 203
Burger, Edward B. 203
Burger, Jacques 203
Burger, Jeff 203
Burger, Schalk 203
バカ
Baca, Claudia 77
バガー
Bagger, Jonathan 79
パーカー
Paker, Henry 1071
Paker, Willie 1071
Parker, Alan 1079
Parker, Alan William 1079
Parker, Andrew 1079
Parker, Annise 1080
Parker, Ant 1080
Parker, Barry R. 1080
Parker, Brant 1080
Parker, Brian 1080
Parker, Candace 1080
Parker, David 1080
Parker, D.C. 1080
Parker, DeVante 1080
Parker, Eddie 1080
Parker, Edna 1080
Parker, Edward 1080
Parker, Eleanor 1080
Parker, Fess 1080
Parker, Franklin Calvin 1080
Parker, Frederick D. 1080
Parker, Geoffrey 1080
Parker, Ian 1080
Parker, Jabari 1080
Parker, Jake 1080
Parker, Jarrett 1080
Parker, Jason 1080
Parker, Jeff 1080
Parker, Jonathan 1080
Parker, Kenneth P. 1080
Parker, K.J. 1080
Parker, Marjorie Blain 1080
Parker, Mark G. 1080
Parker, Mary-Louise 1080
Parker, Michael D. 1080
Parker, Nathan 1080
Parker, Nathaniel 1080
Parker, Olivia 1080
Parker, Peter 1080
Parker, Philip 1080
Parker, Randall E. 1080
Parker, Richard 1080
Parker, Robert B. 1080
Parker, Robert Henry 1080
Parker, Robert McDowell, Jr. 1080
Parker, Ron 1080
Parker, Rosalie 1080
Parker, Sarah Jessica 1080
Parker, Sean 1080
Parker, Sonja 1080
Parker, Steve 1080
Parker, Suzy 1080
Parker, T.Jefferson 1080
Parker, Tony 1080
Parker, Trey 1080
Parker, Victoria 1080
Parker, Virginia Reynolds 1080
Parker, Walter 1080
バカア
al-Bakaa, Taher 82
パーカー・アロテ
Parker-allotey, Sylvester Jude Kpakpo 1080
バガイ
Baqaei, Hamid 91
バーカイク
Verkaik, Robert 1453
バガヴァン
Bhagavan, Kalki 135
ハーカウェイ
Harkaway, Nick 571
バガザ
Bagaza, Jean Baptiste 79
バカ・ジョーンズ
Vaca Jones, Cecilia 1437
バーカス
Burkus, David 204
バカス
Vacas, José Francisco 1437
バーカソン
Bercuson, David Jay 125
バカタ
Vakata, Fe'ao 1438
Vakata, Sosefo Fe'aomoeata 1438
バカチュク
Bakatyuk, Tatyana 82
ハーカップ
Harcup, John W. 569
Harkup, Kathryn 571
ハガティ
Hagerty, Barbara Bradley 554
ハガティー
Haggerty, Rosanne 554
バカティアル
Bakhtiar, Nilofar 84
ハーガデン
Hargaden, Helena 571
ハーカート
Herkert, Barbara 597
ハガード
Haggard, Merle 554
Haggard, Stephan 554
バーガード
Burgard, Wolfram 203
Burghardt, Renie Szilak 203
バガトル
Bagatur 79
パガネリ
Paganelli, Flavia 1069
パガーノ
Pagano, Joe 1069
パガノ
Pagano, Chuck 1069
Pagano, John 1069
Pagano, John O.A. 1069
バガバンディ
Bagabandi, Natsagiin 79
ハカビー
Hucaby, David 631
Huckabee, Mike 631
パカビラデマトス
De Matos, Rosa Pedro Pacavira 339
バーガフ
Berghof, Michael 127
バガプシ
Bagapsh, Sergei Uasyl-ipa 79
バガプシュ
Bagapsh, Sergei Uasyl-ipa 79
バカフワヌセンダ
Bakafwa Nsenda, Symphorien Mutombo 82
パーカー＝ポープ
Parker-Pope, Tara 1080
ハカマダ
Hakamada, Irina Mutsuovna 556
ハカミエス
Häkämies, Jyri 556
Hakamies, Kari 556
バーカム
Barcomb, Wayne 93
バーガム
Bergum, Vangie 127
バカヨコ
Bakayoko, Hamed 82
Bakayoko, Tiemoue 82
Bakayoko, Youssouf 82
ハガラ
Hagara, Lubomir 553
Hagara, Roman 553
バカラク
Bacharach, Jere L. 77
バカラック
Bacharach, Burt 77
Bacharach, Samuel B. 77
パカラック
Pakaluk, Michael 1071
バカリ
Bakari, Hassan Sylla 82
Bakary, Diabira 82
Bakkali, Zakaria 84
バガリー
Baggaley, Nathan 79
パカリ
Pacari, Nina 1067
バガリェフ
Begaliev, Kanatbek 114
パーカー＝リース
Parker-Rees, Guy 1080
バカール
Bacar, Harithi 77
バカル
Bakar, Muhammad Nurani 82
バカルドサール
Dossar, Mohamed Bacar 369
バカレアング
Bakale Angüe, Eucario 82

バカレオビアン
Bakale Obiang, Bonifacio 82
バカーロ
Vaccaro, Kenny 1437
バーカン
Barkun, Michael 94
バカン
Buchan, Elizabeth 197
Buchan, James 197
パガーン
Pagan, Angel 1069
パガン
Pagan, Jose 1069
バーカンキャンプ
Berkenkamp, Lauri 128
バーガンジィ
Bergonzi, Jerry 127
バカンデジャ
Bakandeja, Gregriore 82
バカンブ
Bakambu, Cedric 82
バカン・ムボク
Bakang Mbock, Catherine 82
バカンムボック
Bakang Mbock, Catherine 82
ハーキー
Harkey, Cory 571
Harkey, Mike 571
バーキー
Berkey, Jonathan Porter 128
Varkey, Sunny 1447
バーギー
Bergey, Jean Lindquist 127
バキ
Bakhit, Abdelkerim Ahmadaye 84
Baki, Ivonne 84
パーキー
Parkey, Cody 1080
パキアノ・アラマン
Pacchiano Alamán, Rafael 1067
バキエフ
Bakiyev, Kurmanbek Saliyevich 84
ハキジマナ
Hakizimana, Godefroy 556
ハギス
Haggis, Paul 554
パーギター
Pargiter, Russell 1078
バーギッソン
Birgisson, Jon Thor 140
パキート・デリヴェラ・クインテット
Quintet, Paquito D'Rivera 1145
バキナ
Vaquina, Alberto 1446
ハキミ
Hakimi, Eklil 556
ハキーム
Hakeem, Rauff 556
al-Hakim, Abdel Aziz 556
al-Hakim, Mohammad Baqil 556
ハキム
al-Hakim, Abdel Aziz 556
al-Hakim, Akram 556
Hakim, Alain 556
Hakim, Catherine 556
Hakim, Christine 556
al-Hakim, Mohammad Baqil 556
al-Hakim, Mohammed Ali 556
パキャット
Pacat, C.S. 1067
ハキール
al-Haqeel, Majid bin Abdullah 568
バキル
Bakir, Nancy 84
バギロフ
Baghirov, Parviz 79
Bagirov, Huseingulu 79
Bahgirov, Huseyn 80
ハーキン
Harken, Alden H. 571
Harkin, James 571
バーキン
Bakin, Dmitriĭ 84
Barkin, Ellen 94
Birkin, Jane 140
バーギン
Burgin, Clayton 203
パーキン
Parkin, Alan J. 1081
Parkin, D.Maxwell 1081
Parkin, John C. 1081
Parkin, Margaret 1081
Parkyn, Chetan 1081
パキン
Paquin, Anna 1077
バーキンショー
Birkinshaw, Julian M. 140
ハギンズ
Huggins, Bob 632
Huggins, Diana 632
Huggins, Hal A. 632
Huggins, James Byron 632
Huggins, Roy 632
パーキンス
Perkins, Edwin J. 1098
Perkins, Glen 1098
Perkins, Greg 1098
Perkins, Gwyn 1098
Perkins, John 1098
Perkins, Josh 1098
Perkins, Lynne Rae 1098
Perkins, Mike 1098
Perkins, Mitali 1099
Perkins, Paul 1099
Perkins, Ralph 1099
Perkins, Shane 1099
Perkins, Willie 1099
パーキンズ
Parkins, David 1081
Perkins, Anne 1098
Perkins, Christopher 1098
Perkins, Dwight H. 1098
Perkins, Franklin 1098
Perkins, Kenneth J. 1098
Perkins, Susan L. 1099
バギンスキー
Baginski, Bodo J. 79
ハギンズ=クーパー
Huggins-Cooper, Lynn 632
パーキンスン
Parkinson, Joy 1081
パーキンソン
Parkinson, Barry 1081
Parkinson, Brett T. 1081
Parkinson, Cecil 1081
Parkinson, Georgina 1081
Parkinson, Kathy 1081
Parkinson, Michael 1081
Parkinson, Siobhán 1081
Parkinson, Tessa 1081
バーキンヘッド
Birkinhead, Damien 140
ハーグ
Haag, Anna 551
Haag, Michael 551
Haeg, Joe 553
Hague, Albert 554
ハク
Bo, Yi-bo 151
Haq, Abdul 568
Haq, Khurshid Jahan 568
Haque, Aminul 569
Haque, Khurshid Jahan 569
Haque, Mohammed Sayedul 569
Haque, Promod 569
Huq, A.K. Faezul 637
Huq, Animul 637
Paek, Nam-sun 1069
バーク
Bach, Lauren 77
Bahrke, Shannon 80
Berk, Ari 127
Berk, Ariel 127
Berk, Jonathan B. 128
Berk, Laura E. 128
Berk, Lee Eliot 128
Berk, Terri 128
Bourke, Angela 168
Bourke, Anthony 168
Bourque, Susan C. 168
Burck, Charles 202
Burk, John R. 203
Burk, Kathleen 203
Burk, Kevin 203
Burke, Alafair 203
Burke, Alfred Michael 203
Burke, Anthony 203
Burke, Barbara 203
Burke, Bill 203
Burke, Brian 203
Burke, Dan 203
Burke, Edward 203
Burke, Evan 203
Burke, James Lee 203
Burke, Jan 203
Burke, Jason 203
Burke, Jim 203
Burke, Martha 203
Burke, Michael 203
Burke, Monte 203
Burke, Nazim 203
Burke, Oliver 203
Burke, Peggy 203
Burke, Peter 204
Burke, Raymond V. 204
Burke, Sarah 204
Burke, Solomon 204
Burke, Steven 204
Burke, Tony 204
Burke, Trey 204
バーグ
Bagh, Peter von 79
Berg, Adriane Gilda 125
Berg, A.Scott 125
Berg, Bill 125
Berg, Björn 125
Berg, Bob 125
Berg, Cynthia A. 125
Berg, Elizabeth 125
Berg, Gerben Van den 125
Berg, Gretchen J. 125
Berg, Howard Stephen 125
Berg, Insoo Kim 125
Berg, Kristian 125
Berg, Leila 126
Berg, Michael 126
Berg, Patty 126
Berg, Richard 126
Berg, Walter 126
Burg, Bob 203
Burge, Constance M. 203
Burge, Gary M. 203
バク
Bak, Jenny 82
バグ
Bugg, Jake 199
Bugg, Rachel 199
Bugg, Tim 199
パーク
Park, Barbara 1078
Park, Christine 1078
Park, Clara Claiborne 1078
Park, Denise C. 1078
Park, Gene 1078
Park, Jack 1079
Park, James 1079
Park, Linda Sue 1079
Park, Michael 1079
Park, Nick 1079
Park, Robert 1079
Park, Robert L. 1079
Park, Ruth 1079
Park, Sonya S. 1079
Park, Steven 1079
Park, Yong Kun 1079
Pugh, Kenneth 1139
パク
Bahk, Jae-wan 80
Bak, Sangmee 82
Bark, Tae-ho 94
Paik, Nam June 1070
Pak, Cheor-su 1071
Pak, Chol Min 1071
Pak, Chun-nam 1071
Pak, Hak-son 1071
Pak, Hyon Suk 1071
Pak, Kyong-ni 1071
Pak, Nam-chil 1071
Pak, Nam-gi 1071
Pak, Ok-Song 1071
Pak, Pong-ju 1071
Pak, Pyong-shik 1071
Pak, Se-ri 1071
Pak, Song-chol 1071
Pak, Song-nam 1071
Pak, Su-gil 1071
Pak, Thae-won 1071
Pak, Ui-chun 1071
Pak, Wan-so 1071
Pak, Yong-hui 1071
Pak, Yong-sik 1071
Pak, Yong-sok 1071
Paku 1071
Park, Byung Ho 1078
Park, Chang-o 1078
Park, Chan-ho 1078
Park, Chan-mo 1078
Park, Chan-wook 1078
Park, Cheol-hee 1078
Park, Chung-cha 1078
Park, Chu-young 1078
Park, Geun-hye 1078
Park, Hae-il 1078
Park, Hae-jin 1078
Park, Hee-tae 1078
Park, Ho-koon 1078

Park, Hong-soo 1078
Park, Hyesang 1078
Park, Hye-yoon 1078
Park, Hyuk-moon 1078
Park, Hyun-bin 1078
Park, Hyun-wook 1078
Park, In-bee 1078
Park, In-yong 1079
Park, Jae-Kyu 1079
Park, Janie Jaehyun 1079
Park, Jisoo 1079
Park, Ji-sung 1079
Park, Ji-won 1079
Park, Ji Yoon 1079
Park, Jong-ku 1079
Park, Jongmin 1079
Park, Jong-soo 1079
Park, Joo-bong 1079
Park, Joo-ho 1079
Park, Joong-hoon 1079
Park, Jung-bum 1079
Park, Junyoung 1079
Park, JuYoung 1079
Park, Kye-hyung 1079
Park, Min-gyu 1079
Park, Myong-chol 1079
Park, Myung-jae 1079
Park, Sae-Eun 1079
Park, Sae-jik 1079
Park, Sam 1079
Park, Sam-koo 1079
Park, Sejong 1079
Park, Seong-yowng 1079
Park, Seung-hi 1079
Park, Seung-ho 1079
Park, Shin-yang 1079
Park, So-hee 1079
Park, Sol-mi 1079
Park, Tae-hwan 1079
Park, Tae-joon 1079
Park, Tong-jin 1079
Park, Won-heung 1079
Park, Won-soon 1079
Park, Yang-shin 1079
Park, Ye-jin 1079
Park, Yong-ha 1079
Park, Yong-sung 1079
Park, Young-ok 1079
Park, Young-sook 1079
Park, Yu-ha 1079

バークウィッジ
Berkowits, Ruth 128

バークウィル
Barkwill, Ray 94

バグウェル
Bagwell, Philip Sidney 80
Bagwell, Stella 80

ハグウッド
Hagwood, Scott 554

バークガフニ
Burke-Gaffney, Brian 204
Burke-Gaffney, Taka 204

パクサス
Paksas, Rolandas 1071

バクサニ
Buxani, Ram 209

ハクサル
Khaksar, Mullah Abdul Samad 724

バクサンドール
Baxandall, Michael David Kighley 107

バクシ
Bakshi, Dwijendra Nath 84

バクーシュ
Baccouche, Taieb 77

バクシュ
Baccouche, Taieb 77
Baksh, Nizam 84
Baksh, Sadiq 84
Baksh, Shaik 84

バグシュカ
Baguška, Petras 80

バグショウ
Bagshawe, Louise 80

バークス
Barks, Carl 94
Birks, Tony 140
Burks, Alec 204
Burks, Brandon 204
Burks, Jewel 204

パークス
Parkes, Colin Murray 1080
Parks, Dennis 1081
Parks, Gordon 1081
Parks, Rosa 1081
Parks, Sharon Daloz 1081
Parks, Steve 1081
Parks, Tim 1081
Parks, Walter F. 1081
Parks, Will 1081
Perks, W.David 1099

バクスター
Backster, Cleve 77
Baxter, Alain 107
Baxter, Charles 107
Baxter, Claire 107
Baxter, Clifford 107
Baxter, Glen 107
Baxter, Ian 107
Baxter, John 107
Baxter, Kirk 107
Baxter, Mary Lynn 107
Baxter, Stephen 107
Baxter, Stuart W. 107
Baxter, Tom 107
Baxter, William Hubbard 107

ハクスタブル
Huxtable, Ada Louise 640

バークスデイル
Barksdale, Joe 94

バーグステン
Bergsten, C.Fred 127
Bergsten, Hans 127

バーグストーム
Bergstrom, Tony 127

ハグストローム
Hagstrom, Robert G. 554

バーグストローム
Bergstrom, Signe 127

バクストン
Buxton, Byron 209
Buxton, Ian 209
Buxton, James 209
Buxton, R.G.A. 209
Buxton, William A.S. 210

パクストン
Paxton, James 1089
Paxton, Robert O. 1089

パクスマン
Paxman, Jeremy 1088
Paxmann, Christine 1088

ハクスリ
Huxley, Andrew Fielding 640

ハクスリー
Huxley, Andrew Fielding 640
Huxley, Elspeth 640
Huxley, Francis 640
Huxley, Hugh Esmor 640
Huxley, Robert 640

ハクスレー
Huxley, Andrew Fielding 640
Huxley, Hugh Esmor 640
Huxley, Laura Archera 640

ハクソーゼン
Huchthausen, Peter A. 631

バークソン
Berkson, Burt 128

バーグソン
Bergson, Abram 127

パクソン
Paxson, Monica Rix 1088

パクター
Pachter, Barbara 1068

パグタカン
Pagtakhan, Rey 1070

バグダディ
al-Baghdadi, Abdulghadir Mohamed 79
Baghdadi, Abdulkadir Sheikh Ali 79

バグダディ師
Abu Bakr al-Baghdadi 9

パクダマン
Pakdaman, Ali 1071

バクタミャン
Bakhtamyan, Norayr 84

バクタミヤン
Bakhtamyan, Norayr 84

バークダル
Barkdull, Larry 94

パグダンガナン
Pagdanganan, Robert 1069

バグチ
Bagchi, Debasis 79

バクティアリ
Bakhtiari, David 84

バクティアル
Bachtiar, Chamsyah 77

パグデン
Pagden, Anthony 1069

バクト
Bakht, Sikander 84

バーグドルフ
Bergdorf, Greg 126

ハーグナー
Hagner, Viviane 554

バークナー
Buckner, Greg 198
Bürkner, Hans-Paul 204

バグナー
Bagner, Sarah 80
Wagner, Jaques 1467

ハクナザリャン
Hakhnazaryan, Narek 556

バグナル
Bagnall, Brian 79

バグナルディ
Bagnardi, Frankie 80

パグニーニ
Pagnini, Marta 1070

ハークネス
Harkness, Daniel 571
Harkness, Deborah E. 571

バグネル
Wagner, Ulla 1467

バグネル・ティソン
Wagner Tizón, Allan 1467

バグノーラ
Bagnola, Jim 80

バグハイ
Baghai, Mehrdad 79

バーグハウス
Berghuis, David J. 127

ハグバーグ
Hagberg, David 553

パークハースト
Parkhurst, Carolyn 1080

バークハート
Burkhart, John Ernest 204

バグビエゲ
Bagbiegue, El-hadj Tairou 79

バグビン
Bagbin, Alban Sumana 79

ハグブリンク
Hagbrink, Bodil 553

バークヘッド
Birkhead, Tim R. 140
Burkhead, Rex 204

バグボ
Gbagbo, Laurent 485

バークホーダリアン
Barkhordarian, Arnold 94

バークホルダー
Burkholder, Lisanne R. 204

バクマニヤ
Bakumanya, Gracin 84

ハーグマン
Hageman, Ra'Shede 554

ハグマン
Hagman, Larry 554

バークマン
Berkman, Lance 128
Burkeman, Oliver 204

バーグマン
Bergman, Anni 127
Bergman, Mara 127
Bergman, Ronen 127
Bergmann, Jonathan 127
Bergmann, Nicolai 127
Burgman, Mark A. 203

バグラー
Bugler, Caroline 199

バクラーズ
Baklarz, George 84

バクラゼ
Bakradze, David 84

バクラーノフ
Baklanov, Grigorii Yakovlevich 84

パグラヤン
Pagulayan, Carlos 1070

パクラル
Pacuraru, Ion 1068

ハグランド
Haglund, Pamela 554

バーグランド
Bergland, Anthony 127
Bergland, Suzan 127

バークリー
Barkley, Matt 94
Barkley, Ross 94

バクリ
al-Bakri, Abdullah bin Nasser bin Abdullah 84
Bakri, Ben Abdoulfatah Charif 84
Bakri, Hassan Salih 84

al-Bakri, Nayef 84
Bakrie, Aburizal 84
バクリー
Buckley, William Frank, Jr. 198
バグリー
Bagley, Jessixa 79
Baguley, David M. 80
Baguley, Elizabeth 80
パグリ
Pagli, John Michael, Jr. 1069
パグリアルーロ
Pagliarulo, Mike 1070
ハーグリーヴス
Hargreaves, Beryl Joyce 571
ハーグリーヴズ
Hargreaves, David J. 571
Hargreaves, David John 571
バグリオ
Baglio, Matt 79
バグリオーシ
Bugliosi, Vincent 199
パグリッシ
Puglisi, Becca 1139
ハーグリーブス
Hargreaves, Andy 571
バーグリン
Berggren, Eric G. 127
バクリン
Bakulin, Sergey 84
バークル
Barkl, Andy 94
Burckle, Clark 202
バクル
Baqr, Ahmad Yaqub 91
バクルー
Buckelew, Alan B. 198
ハグルンド
Haglund, Carl 554
バークレー
Barclay, Alex 92
Barclay, Eddie 92
Barclay, Eric 92
Barclay, Patrick 93
Barclay, Robert L. 93
Barclay, Ronald 93
Barkley, Russell A. 94
Berkley, Seth 128
バークレイ
Barclay, Don 92
Barclay, Linwood 92
Barkley, Brad 94
Barkley, Elizabeth F. 94
ハーグレイブ
Hargrave, Javon 571
ハークレス
Harkless, Maurice 571
バクレーヌ
Bacquelaine, Daniel 78
バークレム
Barklem, Jill 94
ハークレロード
Harclerode, Peter 569
バーグレン
Bergren, Lisa Tawn 127
パグレン
Paglen, Jack 1069
ハーグローヴ
Hargrove, Dean 571
パグロツキー
Pagrotsky, Leif 1070
ハーグローブ
Hargrove, Robert A. 571
ハーグローブス
Hargroves, Karlson 571
バグワティ
Bhagwati, Jagdish Notwarlal 135
バグワティー
Bhagwati, Jagdish Notwarlal 135
バグワン
Bhagwan, Rajesh Anand 135
バークン
Berkun, Scott 128
ハーケ
Haacke, Hans 551
Haake, Martin 551
Hake, Sabine 556
ハーゲ
Hage, Anike 553
バケー
Baquet, Dean Paul 91
パケ
Paquet, Marcel 1077
バーゲス
Burgess, Williams T. 203
ハケス・クルス
Jaquez Cruz, Eligio 665
バケダーノ
Baquedano, Elizabeth 91
バゲッタ
Baggetta, Marla 79
ハケット
Hackett, Buddy 552
Hackett, Chris 552
Hackett, Grant 552
Hackett, Jane 552
Hackett, Jeremy 552
Hackett, Kathleen 552
Hackett, Michael 552
Hackett, Pat 552
Hackett, Semoy 552
Hackett, Steve 552
バーケット
Birkett, Georgie 140
Burkett, Mary Parsons 204
バケット
Buckett, Chris 198
Burkett, Molly 204
パケット
Paquet, Catherine 1077
Paquette, Yanick 1077
Puckett, Kelley 1138
Puckett, Kirby 1138
Puckette, Madeline 1139
パケテ
Paquete, Helder 1077
パケナム
Pakenham, Thomas 1071
パケニテ
Pakenyte, Santa 1071
ハーゲネーダー
Hageneder, Fred 554
ハーゲネダー
Hageneder, Fred 554
バケビュムサヤ
Bakevyumusaya, Vénérand 84
パケ・ブレネール
Paquet-Brenner, Gilles 1077
ハーゲマン
Hagemann, Ludwig 554
Hagemann, Sigrid 554
バゲラ
Vaghela, Shankersinh 1438
バケリソマクミラン
Baquerizo McMillan, Elsa 91
バゲリモタメド
Bagheri Motamed, Mohammad 79
バゲリランキャラニ
Bagherilankarani, Kamran 79
バケル・アブドラ
Baqer al-Abdullah, Ahmad 91
ハーゲルップ
Hagerup, Klaus 554
バーゲルマン
Burgelman, Robert A. 203
バケロ
Vaquero, Tomás 1446
ハーケン
Haken, Hermann 556
ハーゲン
Hagen, Clemens 554
Hagen, Rainer 554
Hagen, Rose-Marie 554
Hagen, Silvia 554
Hagen, Uta 554
Hagen, Veronika 554
Hagen, William 554
バーケン
Baeken, Serge 79
バーゲン
Bergen, Candice 126
Bergen, Lara 126
Bergen, Lara Rice 126
Bergen, Peter L. 126
Bergen, Polly 126
Bergen, Sam 126
バーゲンソール
Buergenthal, Thomas 199
ハーゲンバーグ
Hagenberg, Roland 554
ハーゲンバック
Hagenbach, Keith 554
ハーケンワース
Hakenewerth, Quentin 556
バーゴ
Vargo, Stephen L. 1447
バコ
Bako, Nassirou Arifari 84
パゴー
Pagot, Tony 1070
パコ・アジェスタラン
Pako Ayestaran 1071
パコ・アルカセル
Paco Alcacer 1068
バーゴイン
Burgoyne, Patrick 203
Burgoyne, Robert 203
バゴーイン
Burgoyne, Bernard 203
バーコウ
Berkow, Robert 128
パーコウィツ
Perkowitz, Sidney 1099
バーコウィッツ
Berkowitz, Eric 128
Berkowitz, Eric N. 128
パーコウィッツ
Perkowitz, Sidney 1099
ハコエン
Hacohen, Dean 552
バコ・サアキャン
Sahakian, Bako S. 1226
バコシ
Bacosi, Diana 78
バーゴス
Burgos, Enrique 203
バゴット
Baggott, Jim E. 79
Baggott, Stella 79
パゴット
Pagot, Tony 1070
パコ・デ・ルシア
Paco de Lucía 1068
ハーコート
Harcourt, Geoffrey Colin 569
パコ・ドゥラン
Paco Durán, Marianela 1068
パゴネンジヌダカラ
Pagonendjindakara, Marie Solange 1070
バーコビチ
Bercovici, Mike 125
バーコビッツ
Berkowitz, Marvin W. 128
バーコフ
Berkoff, Steven 128
Berkov, Tamara 128
パコ・ヘメス
Paco Jemez 1068
ハーコムビー
Harcombe, Elnora 569
ハコメ
Jácome, Joaquín 658
バコヤンニ
Bakogiani, Ntora 84
Bakoyannis, Dora 84
パコラ
Pakola, Eija 1071
パゴラ
Pagola, José Antonio 1070
バーコール
Bahcall, John Noris 80
バコール
Bacall, Lauren 77
Bahcall, John Noris 80
バコル
Bakoru, Zoe Bakoko 84
バコレ
Bakore, Amit 84
バゴロ
Bagoro, Bessolé René 80
バコンガ
Bakonga, Willy 84
バコンスキ
Baconschi, Teodor 78
バーザ
Boese, Alex 153
バザー
Bazer, Fuller W. 108
Buser, Daniel 207
ハサイネ
al-Hasayneh, Mofeed 579
パサイライゲ
Passailaigue, Roberto 1083
ハザイール
Hazair, Abdullah 586
ハサウェイ

ハ

Hathaway, Anne 581
Hathaway, James C. 581
Hathaway, Lalah 581
Hathaway, Robin 581
Hathaway, Steve 581
Hathaway, Susan 581
Hathway, John 581
ハザウェイ
Hathaway, Lalah 581
Hathaway, Sandee E. 581
ハサウネ
al-Khasawneh, Awn Shawkat 727
Khasawneh, Bisher 727
バサエフ
Basayev, Shamil Salmanovich 101
パサコフ
Pasachoff, Naomi E. 1083
バサス
Busath, Isabelle 207
バザック
Bazac, Ion 108
ハサド
Hassad, Mohamed 580
ハザード
Hazard, David 586
Hazzard, Kevin 586
パサード
Persaud, Ganga 1101
Persaud, Robert 1101
Persaud, Robert Montgomery 1101
バサトジョンデ
Buassat Djonde, Bedopassa 197
パーサドビスサー
Persad-bissessar, Kamla 1101
パサードビセッサー
Persad-bissessar, Kamla 1101
バザーナ
Bazzana, Kevin 109
ハザナヴィシウス
Hazanavicius, Michel 586
ハサニ
al-Hasani, Abdulmunim bin Mansour bin Said 579
al-Hassani, Hachim 580
Hassani, Nemat 580
バサニニ
Bassanini, Franco 102
ハサニヤル
Hassanyar, Amir Shah 580
ハサネイン
Hassanein, Muhammad Medhat Abdel-Atti 580
バサネズ
Basáñez, Miguel 101
ハサノフ
Hasanov, Ali 579
Hasanov, Jabrayil 579
Hasanov, Sardar 579
Hasanov, Zakir 579
ハザーノフ
Khazanov, Dmitrii 727
ハサビ
Hasbi, Muhamad 579
バサビ
Bassabi, Safiatou 102
バーサミアン
Barsamian, David 99
ハザム
Khazam, Adnan 727
バサム
Ba Samb, Bineta 101
バサラーマ
Basalamah, Hussein 101
ハザリカ
Hazarika, Hemanta 586
パサリブ
Pasaribu, Linda 1083
バサルギン
Basargin, Viktor F. 101
バザルグレエフ
Bazarguruev, Bazar 108
バザルデュア
Bazaldua, Barbara 108
バサルドゥア
Bazaldua, Barbara 108
バザルバエフ
Bazarbaev, Kudaybergen 108
Bazarbayev, Umurbek 108
ハザレ
Hazare, Anna 586
Khaza'leh, Salem 727
バザロフ
Bazarov, Batyr 108
Bazarov, Rejep 108
バザロワ
Bazarova, Vera 108
ハサン
Hasan, Ali Kaldirim 579
Hasan, Asma Gull 579
Hasan, Hanif 579
Hasan, Malek 579
Hasan, Najwa Qassab 579
al-Hassan, Osama Abdalla Mohamed 580
al-Hassan, Salah Mohamed 580
ハザン
Hazan, Cindy 586
バーザン
Barzun, Jacques Martin 101
バサン
Bazan, Kaiser Baldonero 108
Vasan, G.K. 1447
バザン
Bazan, Rodrigo 108
Bazin, Henri 108
Bazin, Marc Louis 108
バザンジョ
Bizinjo, Hasil Khan 143
バーサンスレン・ボロルマー
Baasansuren Bolormaa 76
ハサンベゴビッチ
Hasanbegović, Zlatko 579
パーサンラル
Parsanlal, Neil 1082
ハーシ
Hirschi, Travis 609
ハーシー
Hersey, John 600
Hersey, Paul 600
Hershey, Robert L. 600
ハージ
Hage, Ghassan 553
Hage, Rawi 553
ハージー
Haji, Morteza 556
ハシ
al-Hassi, Kamal 580
al-Hassi, Omar Slaiman 580
ハジ
Hagi, Georghe 554
Hagi, Ianis 554
Haji, Morteza 556
Haji, Yusuf 556
Haji, Zakariya Mahmud 556
バージ
Bargh, John A. 93
Birge, Edward Asahel 140
バシ
Vaszi, Tünde 1448
バジ
Badji, Fatim 78
Badji, Ndiss Kaba 78
パーシー
Pacey, Arnold 1067
Percy, Benjamin 1096
Percy, Charles Harting 1096
Percy, David S. 1096
Percy, Iain 1096
Pursey, Ann 1140
パシ
Passy, Solomon 1084
バシアコス
Basiakos, Evangelos 102
ハジアホンドザデ
Haji Akhondzadeh, Masoud 556
ハジアリッチ
Hadzialic, Aida 553
ハーシィ
Hersey, Paul 600
パーシヴァル
Percival, Brian 1096
Percival, John 1096
バシェ
Bashe, Philip 102
バジェ
Badje, Halidou 78
Batlle, Jorge 104
Vallejo, Carlos 1440
バーシェイ
Barshay, Andrew E. 99
パシェコ
Pacheco, Alexander J. 1067
Pacheco, José Condungua António 1067
バージェス
Berges, Paul Mayeda 127
Burgess, Adrienne 203
Burgess, James 203
Burgess, Mark 203
Burgess, Melvin 203
Burgess, Sam 203
Burgis, Tom 203
バジェス
Batjes, N.H. 104
パジェス
Batjes, N.H. 104
Pagès, Alain 1069
ハジェスキー
Hajeski, Nancy J. 556
バシェスギオウル
Başesgioğlu, Murat 101
ハシェック
Hasek, Ivan 579
ハシェッド
Hached, Noureddine 552
ハジェット
Huggett, Monica 632
バージェット
Bardgett, Richard D. 93
バジェット
Badgett, Tom 78
パジェット
Padgett, Herman 1068
Padgett, Jason 1068
Paget, Lou 1069
バジェッホ・ガルシア・マウリーニョ
Vallejo Garcia-Maurinõ, Luis 1440
ハジェフ
Khadjiev, Zelimkhan 724
バーシェフスキ
Barshefsky, Charlene 99
バシェフスキ
Barshefsky, Charlene 99
バシェフスキー
Barshefsky, Charlene 99
バジェホ
Vallejo, Fernando 1440
Vallejo, Jesus 1440
Vallejo, Raúl 1440
バジェホス・ソログレン
Vallejos Sologuren, Carlos 1440
バジェホ・ロペス
Vallejo López, Gabriel 1440
ハシェミ
Hashemi, Ali 579
Hashemi, Hassan Qazizadeh 579
Hashemi, Mohammad 579
Hashemi, Ray H. 579
ハシェミアン
Hashemian, H.M. 579
ハシェミタバ
Hashemi-taba, Mostafa 579
バシェリ
Bascelli, Gabriella 101
バシェレ
Bachelet, Michelle 77
バシエレ
Bassiere, Batio 102
バージェロン
Bergeron, Bryan P. 126
Bergeron, David Moore 126
ハジェンス
Hudgens, Dave 631
ハジェンズ
Hudgens, Vanessa 631
ハーシェンソン
Hirshenson, Janet 610
ハジガキス
Hadjigakis, Sotiris 553
バシク
Basic, Zdenko 102
パーシグ
Pirsig, Robert M. 1115
パーシケッティ
Persichetti, Bob 1101
パーシコ
Persico, Joseph E. 1101
ハシコス
Hasikos, Socratis 579
ハージス
Haasis, Hellmut G. 551

パージター
Pargeter, Margaret 1078
ハジダキス
Chatzidakis, Kostantinos 249
Hadjidakis, Kostis 553
バシチェンコ
Vashchenko, Vladimir A. 1447
バシツカ
Barzycka, Paulina 101
ハジッチ
Hadžić, Damir 553
バシッチ
Vasic, Milos 1447
パシッチ
Pasic, Jelena 1083
バシット
Bassitt, Chris 103
ハージティ
Hargitay, Mariska 571
バシトハノワ
Basitkhanova, Elmira 102
ハシナ
Hasina, Sheikh 579
ハジナスト
Haxhinasto, Edmond 584
ハシナ・ワセド
Hasina, Sheikh 579
ハシナ・ワゼド
Hasina, Sheikh 579
バジーニ
Baggini, Julian 79
パジーニ
Pasini, Marilena 1083
Pasini, Willy 1083
バーシニック
Bersinic, Damir 131
パシネッティ
Pasinetti, Luigi Lodovico 1083
バジノビッチ
Vujnovich, Jeremy 1465
パシノビッチ
Pasinović, Milenko 1083
バジパイ
Vajpayee, Atal Bihari 1438
ハージババイ
Hajibabai, Hamid-Reza 556
バジバモ
Bazivamo, Christophe 108
パーシバル
Percival, Bernard 1096
バシブ
Bathib, Wa'ed Abdullah 104
ハジファキ
Hajifaqi, Abdihakim Mohamoud 556
ハジ・ブハドール
al-Hajji Bukhadhour, Faisal Muhammad 556
ハジベコフ
Khadjibekov, Artem 724
Khadzhibekov, Artem 724
ハシミ
al-Hashimi, Asad 579
al-Hashimi, Saad 579
al-Hashimi, Tariq 579
ハシーム
Hasheem, Kabir 579
ハシム
Hachimou, Saidou 552
Hashim, Ali 579
Hashim, Kabir 579
ハシモト
Hashimoto, Mitchell 579
ハージャー
Harger, Fern 571
バージャー
Barger, Ralph 93
Berger, John Peter 126
Berger, Thomas 126
バシャ
Basha, Lulzim 101
al-Basha, Sayed Abdel-Jaleel 102
バシャー
Basher, Simon 102
パシャ
Pasha, Mustapha Kamal 1083
パシャエフ
Pashayev, Nizami 1083
バシャク
Wasiak, Maria 1480
バジャック
Bajac, Quentin 82
パジャノ
Rayano, Felipe 1162
バーシャフスキー
Varshavsky, Alexander 1447
パシャリッチ
Pasalic, Mario 1083
バジャリノ
Vallarino, Alberto 1440
Vallarino, Arturo Ulises 1440
Vallarino, Carlos 1440
Vallarino, Joaquín José 1440
バーシャリーフ
Ba-shareef, Lutfy 102
バシャリ・モハメド
Bashari Mohamed, Eissa 102
ハジャル
Hadjar, Tahar 553
Hajar, Hajar bin Ahmad 555
バシャル
Assad, Bashar al 65
パーシャル
Parshall, Sandra 1082
Parshall, Steven 1082
Prchal, Josef T. 1132
パジャレス
Pallares, Galo 1072
ハシャーン
Khashaan, Ali 727
バジャンマル
al-Bajammal, Abdul-Qadir 82
ハーシュ
Hersh, Anita K. 600
Hersh, Richard H. 600
Hersh, Seymour M. 600
Hirsch, Amy B. 609
Hirsch, Barry T. 609
Hirsch, Elroy 609
Hirsch, Emile 609
Hirsch, Irl Bennett 609
Hirsch, Jeff 609
Hirsch, Jeffrey A. 609
Hirsch, Morris W. 609
Hirsh, Elizabeth 609
Hirsh, Katherine W. 609
Hirsh, Michael 609
Hirsh, Sandra Krebs 609
Hursh, Jason 637
ハジュー
Hajdu, David 555
バーシュ
Barsh, Joanna 99
バジュー
Bagieu, Pénélope 79
パージュ
Page, Martin 1069
バシュカ
Baška, Jaroslav 102
パシュキス
Paschkis, Julie 1083
パシュク
Paşcu, Ioan Mircea 1083
ハーシュコ
Hershko, Avram 600
ハーシュコップ
Hirschkop, Ken 609
ハーシュコプ
Hirschkop, Ken 609
バシュティクス
Baštiks, Ainars 103
パシュトゥン
Pashtun, Yousef 1083
バージュナイド
Ba-junaid, Khalid 82
バージュニ
Vážny, L'ubomír 1449
バシュニ
Basyuni, Muhammad Maftuh 103
ハーシュバーグ
Hirschberg, Lora 609
Hirshberg, Gary 610
ハーシュ＝パセック
Hirsh-Pasek, Kathy 610
ハーシュバック
Herschbach, Dudley Robert 600
バシュバニアイ
Vasbanyai, Henrik 1447
ハーシュフィールド
Hirshfield, Jane 610
ハーシュフェルダー
Hirschfelder, Arlene B. 609
ハーシュフェルド
Hirschfeld, Al 609
Hirschfeld, Julie 609
Hirschfeld, Tom 609
ハーシュホーン
Hirschhorn, Larry 609
ハーシュマン
Harshman, Marc 576
Hershman, Morris 600
Hershman, Seymour 600
Hirschman, Albert Otto 609
バシュメット
Bashmet, Yurii 102
ハジュラフ
al-Hajraf, Nayef Falah 556
ハジュリ
al-Hajri, Ibrahim Umar 556
バシュレ
Bachelet, Gilles 77
Bachelet, Pierre 77
ハシュレイ
Haseley, Dennis 579
バシュロッド
Bushrod, Jermon 207
バシュロナルカン
Bachelot-narquin, Roselyne 77
バジョ
Bajo, Lamine 82
Bajo, Lamin Kaba 82
ハーショック
Hershock, Peter D. 600
ハショティ
Haşotti, Puiu 580
バション
Vachon, Mad Dog 1437
パーション
Paerson, Anja 1069
Pehrsson, Cristina Husmark 1092
Persson, Kristina 1101
Persson, Nina 1101
パション
Pasion, Francis Xavier 1083
バジラチャーヤ
Bajracharya, Buddhi Raj 82
ハジラ＝リー
Hajra-Lee, Felicia 556
ハジリ
al-Hajiri, Falah Fahad Muhammad 556
Haziri, Lutfi 586
バシリ
al-Bashiri, Abdullah Hussein 102
Basili, Victor 102
Bathily, Abdoulaye 104
Vasili, Petrit 1447
バシリウ
Vassiliou, Antonis 1448
バシリオ
Basilio, Carmen 102
バジリハマネ
Vaziri Hamaneh, Kazem 1449
パジーリャ
Padilha, Jose 1068
パジリャ
Padilha, Alexandre 1068
Padilha, Eliseu 1068
パーシリンナ
Paasilinna, Arto 1067
ハシル
Jacir, Ana Evelyn 655
バージル
Bergel, Reinhard R. 126
バシール
Bachir, Ahmat Mahamat 77
Bachir, Mohamed Salem Ould 77
Basheer, Shamnad 102
Bashir, Ala 102
Bashir, Halima 102
al-Bashir, Omar Hassan Ahmed 102
Bashir, Salah 102
Bechir, Ahmed Salem Ould 111
バシル
al-Bashir, Isam Ahmed 102
al-Bashir, Omar Hassan Ahmed 102
Bashir, Salah 102

al-Bashir, Salaheddin 102
Bassil, Gebran 102
Bassil, Ray 103
バジル
Bazile, David 108
バシレ
Basile, Fabio 102
Vasile, Radu 1447
バシレバ
Vassileva, Ivelina 1448
バシレフ
Vasilev, Kristian 1447
Vassilev, Nikolay 1448
バシレフスキス
Vasilevskis, Vadims 1447
バーシン
Bersin, Brenton 131
Bersin, Josh 131
バージン
Ba-jin 82
Burgin, Clayton 203
バジン
Ba-jin 82
パジン
Pasin, Lucia 1083
Pažin, Zoran 1089
バシンスキー
Bacsinszky, Timea 78
パジンスキ
Pazinski, Piotr 1089
ハシント・サバラ
Jacinto Zavala, Agustín 655
バシンドワ
Basindwa, Mohammed Salem 102
ハース
Haas, Charles N. 551
Haas, Cornelia 551
Haas, Gary Van 551
Haas, Irene 551
Haas, Jacqui Greene 551
Haas, Jeffrey J. 551
Haas, Jens Oliver 551
Haas, Peter E. 551
Haas, Robert B. 551
Haas, Townley 551
Haas, Wolf 551
Haase, Kim 551
Hearth, Amy Hill 587
Heath, Chip 587
Heath, Dan 587
ハーズ
Herz, Robert Henry 600
ハス
Hass, Amira 580
Hass, Robert 580
Haz, Hamzah 586
Khasu, Tlali 727
ハズ
Haz, Hamzah 586
バース
Baars, Bernard J. 76
Baas, Thomas 76
Bars, Brad 99
Barth, Connor 99
Barth, Jack 100
Barth, John 100
Barth, John Simmons 100
Bass, Irina Isaevna 102
Bass, Laura Geringer 102
Bass, L.G. 102
Burse, Isaiah 206
バーズ
Baase, Sara 76
バス
Bass, Anthony 102
Bass, Brandon 102
Bass, Christopher 102
Bass, David 102
Bass, Ellen 102
Bass, Fontella 102
Bass, Lee 102
Bass, Len 102
Bass, Paul 102
Bass, Rick 102
Bass, Robert 102
Bass, Steve 102
Bass, Thomas A. 102
Bass, William M. 102
Basu, Anurag 103
Basu, Kaushik 103
Basu, Sanjay 103
Buss, David M. 208
Buss, Jeanie 208
Buss, Jerry 208
Vaz, Fernando 1449
バスー
Basu, Kaushik 103
バズ
Vaz, Fernando 1449
Vaz, José Mário 1449
Vaz, Lurdes 1449
Vaz, Marcelino 1449
Vaz, Mário 1449
パス
Pass, Ingrid 1083
Pass, John 1083
Paz, Abel 1089
Paz, Anton 1089
Paz, Jacobo 1089
Paz, Moira 1089
バスア
Basua, David 103
パースィ
Parse, Rosemarie Rizzo 1082
ハズィザランティス
Chatzisarantis, Nikos 249
パス・エステンソーロ
Paz Estenssoro, Victor 1089
パス・エステンソロ
Paz Estenssoro, Victor 1089
パスエステンソロ
Paz Estenssoro, Victor 1089
バーズオール
Birdsall, Jeanne 140
バスカー
Bhaskar, Roy 135
Bhasker, Jayaram 135
パスカリ
Pasquali, Elena 1083
パスカル
Pascal, Amy Beth 1083
Pascal, Dominique 1083
Pascal, Georges 1083
Pascal, Philippe 1083
Pascale, Richard T. 1083
Pascall, Robert 1083
パスカル・レオン
Pascual-Leone, Álvaro 1083
ハスカンプ
Haskamp, Steve 579
バースキー
Buirski, Peter 200
バスキ
Basuki, Hadimuljono 103
パースキー
Persky, Lester 1101
パスキエ
Pasquier, Eva 1083
バスギャング
Bussgang, Jeffrey 208
ハスキュー
Haskew, Michael E. 579
パスキュアル
Pascual, Amparo Serrano 1083
バスキン
Baskin, Diana 102
Baskin, Jonathan Barron 102
Baskin, Nora Raleigh 102
Baskin, Yvonne 102
ハスキンズ
Haskins, Jim 579
バスク
Bascou, Dimitri 101
パスク
Pask, Scott 1083
パスクア
Pascua, Marlon 1083
Pasqua, Charles Victor 1083
パスクアル
Pascual, Beatriz 1083
Pascual, Claudia 1083
Pascual, Gema 1083
Pasqual, Manuel 1083
パスクイーニ
Pasquini, Nello 1083
パスクワ
Pasqua, Charles Victor 1083
バスケス
Másquez, Rocío 915
Vásquez, Alcibiades 1448
Vásquez, Aldo 1448
Vásquez, Juan Gabriel 1448
Vasquez, Julio 1448
Vásquez, Ricaurte 1448
Vazquez, Christian 1449
Vazquez, Franco 1449
Vazquez, Luis Franco 1449
Vázquez, Norma 1449
Vazquez, Ramon 1449
Vázquez, Tabaré 1449
バスケス・ガルシア
Vázquez García, Francisco 1449
バスケス・トレス
Vasquez Torres, Wilmer Jose 1448
バスケス・ビジャモル
Vasquez Villamor, Luis 1448
バスケス・モタ
Vásquez Mota, Josefina 1448
Vázquez Mota, Josefina Eugenia 1449
バスケス・モンタルバン
Vázquez Montalbán, Manuel 1449
バスケス・ラーニャ
Vázquez Raña, Mario 1449
パスケービッチ
Paskevich, Sergeĭ 1083
ハスケル
Haskell, David George 579
Haskell, James 579
Haskell, John 579
バスコ
Basco, Monica Ramirez 101
Basko, Ihor John 102
Vasco, Maria 1447
Vasco, Pedro 1447
パスコー
Pascoe, Bear 1083
Pascoe, Judy 1083
バスコウ
Bascou, Fernando 101
ハズコック
Hathcock, John N. 581
バスコム
Bascomb, Neal 101
バスコンセロス
Vasconcelos, José Maria Botelho De 1447
パス・ソルダン
Paz Soldán, Edmundo 1089
バスタ
Basta, Dusan 103
パスター
Pastor, Robert A. 1084
Pastor, Terry 1084
パズダー
Puzder, Andy 1141
バースタイン
Burstein, Daniel 206
Burstein, Gabriel 206
ハスタート
Hastert, Dennis 580
バスタード
Bastardo, Antonio 103
パスターナック
Pasternack, Bruce A. 1084
Pasternak, Harley 1084
パスター・ボルニック
Pastor Bolnick, Jamie 1084
バスタルロー
Bastareaud, Mathieu 103
バスタン
Bastin, Christine 103
パースック・ポンパイチット
Pasuk Phongpaichit 1084
バスティ
el-Basti, Abderraouf 103
バスティアン
Bastian, Till 103
Bastien, Samuel 103
Bastien, Vincent 103
バスティアンス
Bastiaans, Christiaan 103
パスティオール
Pastior, Oskar 1084
バスティダス
Bastidas, Adina 103
ハスティード
Husted, Ted 639
バスティーユ
Bastille, Guillaume 103
バースティン
Burstyn, Ellen 206
バスティーン
Bastienne, Charles 103
バスティン
Bastien, James W. 103
Bastien, Jane Smisor 103

ハ

Bastien, Lisa 103
Bastien, Lori 103
Bastin, Marjolein 103
Vastine, Alexis 1448
バーステーゲン
Verstegen, Mark 1454
ハーステッド
Harstedt, Axel 576
ハステッド
Husted, Gladys L. 639
Husted, James H. 639
バスデバ
Vasudeva, Guru 1448
パステルナーク
Pasternak, Ken 1084
バーステン
Bursten, Bruce Edward 206
バスデン
Basden, Paul 101
ハースト
Hearst, George 587
Hirst, Damien 610
Hirst, Paul Q. 610
Hurst, Brandon 637
Hurst, Carol Otis 637
Hurst, Demontre 637
Hurst, Henry 637
Hurst, James 637
Hurst, Pat 637
Hurst, Philip Wiley 637
Hurst, Roy Edward 637
ハスト
Hast, Dorothea E. 580
パストア
Pastore, Frank 1084
バーストウ
Barstow, Anne Llewellyn 99
ハストヴェット
Hustvedt, Siri 639
パストウスキー
Pastowski, Andreas 1084
パストゥロー
Pastoureau, Michel 1084
バストス
Bastos 103
Bastos, Márcio Thomaz 103
ハーストハウス
Hursthouse, Rosalind 637
ハストベット
Hustvedt, Siri 639
バストラ
Bastola, Chakra Prasad 103
パストラス
Pastoras, Das 1084
ハストラップ
Hastrup, Jannik 581
パストラナ
Pastrana, Andrés 1084
パストール
Pastor, Ana 1084
Pastor, Anthony 1084
Pastor, Perico 1084
Pastor, Rodolfo 1084
パストル
Pastor, Ana 1084
Pastor, Miguel 1084
Pástor, Wilson 1084
パストル・ファスケル
Pastor Fasquelle, Rodolfo 1084
パストーレ
Pastore, Francesco 1084
Pastore, Javier 1084
ハーストレッチト
Haastrecht, Rob van 551
パストレリ
Pastorelli, Robert 1084
バーストン
Burstone, Charles J. 206
ハスナイン
Hasnain, Saleem Ul 579
ハスナウィ
al-Hasnawi, Saleh 580
ハスーネ
Hasouneh, Kamal 580
バスネット
Basnet, Badri Narayan 102
Basnet, Shakti Bahadur 102
バスネト
Basnet, Mahesh 102
バースパー
Verspoor, Rudi 1454
ハーズバーグ
Herzberg, Frederick 600
ハスバーニ
Hasbani, Ghassan 579
パスハリディス
Paschalidis, Georgios 1083
パスハリーデス
Paschalides, Antonis 1083
パスハリーデス
Paschalides, Antonis 1083
ハズバンズ
Husbands, Clifford 638
ハスバンド
Husband, James 638
ハズバンド
Husband, Rick Douglas 638
Husband, Ron 638
バスビー
Busby, Richard D. 207
バズビー
Busby, Ailie 207
Busby, Christopher 207
Busby, Thomas L. 207
Buzby, Jean C. 210
パスフェール
Pasveer, Remko 1084
バスフォード
Basford, Johanna 101
Bassford, Christopher 102
バスブース
Basbous, Antoine 101
パスプレ
Puspure, Sanita 1140
ハスブン・バラケ
Hasbún Barake, Franzi 579
バスベインズ
Basbanes, Nicholas A. 101
ハズペス
Hudspeth, Eric B. 632
パスマン
Passman, Donald S. 1084
ハスミ
Hassoumi, Massaoudou 580
パスミーニョ・ボルハ
Pazmiño Borja, Miguel 1089
バズム
Bazoum, Mohamed 108
パスモア
Passmore, John Arthur 1084
Passmore, Kevin 1084
ハースラー
Haasler, Sue 551
ハスラー
Hasler, Adrian 579
Hasler, Christopher V. A. 579
Hasler, Curt 579
Hasler, Eveline 579
Hasler, Otmar 579
Hassler, Jeff 580
バスラ
Basura, Saleh Ali 103
パスラック
Passlack, Felix 1084
ハスラム
Haslam, Chris 579
Haslam, Jonathan 579
ハズラム
Haslam, Bill 579
ハスラン・メンドサ
Haslam Mendoza, Pedro Antonio 579
バーズリー
Bardsley, Phil 93
パーズリー
Parsley, Lea Ann 1082
パスリー
Pasley, Malcolm 1083
パスリチャ
Pasricha, Neil 1083
バズール
Bazoer, Riechedly 108
ハスレム
Haslem, Udonis 579
パスロン
Passeron, René 1084
バスワニ
Vaswani, Neela 1448
パスワン
Paswan, Bishwendra 1084
Paswan, Ramvilas 1084
パースンズ
Parsons, Russ 1082
ハーセ
Haase, Robin 551
ハーゼ
Haase, Chet 551
Haase, Kim 551
Haase, Ulrike 551
ハーゼー
Hersey, Kathleen 600
パセカ
Paseka, Maria 1083
パセク
Pacek, Martin 1067
ハーセス
Herseth, Adolph 600
バセスク
Băsescu, Traian 101
バセッティ
Bassetti, W.H.C. 102
パセッティ
Pasetti, Alessandro 1083
ハセット
Hassett, Ann M. 580
Hassett, John 580
Hassett, Kevin A. 580
バセット
Bassett, Lucinda 102
Bassett, Michael J. 102
パセット
Passet, Joanne Ellen 1084
バゼッリ
Baselli, Daniele 101
バーゼドウ
Basedow, Jürgen 101
バセドウ
Basedow, Jürgen 101
バゼーヌ
Bazaine, Jean René 108
ハゼネイ
Haseney, Sebastian 579
バセバ
Vaseva, Elina 1447
ハゼラー
Hazelaar, Wim 586
バセラ
Vasella, Daniel 1447
バーセリ
Berceli, David 125
バーゼリッツ
Baselitz, Georg 101
バゼリッツ
Baselitz, Georg 101
バーセル
Burcell, Robin 202
バーゼル
Bardzell, Jeffrey 93
Bardzell, Shaowen 93
Barzel, Ronen 101
Barzel, Yoram 101
バゼル
Bazell, Josh 108
Bazell, Robert 108
パーセル
Pacelle, Mitchel 1067
Purcell, Deirdre 1140
Purcell, Mike 1140
Purcell, Rosemary 1140
Pursel, Jack 1140
パーセルズ
Parcells, Bill 1077
バーセルマ
Ba-salma, Bader 101
バーセルミ
Barthelme, Donald 100
バゼロン
Bazelon, Emily 108
ハーセン
Hersen, Michel 600
ハーゼン
Hazen, Thomas Lee 586
ハゼン
al-Khazen, Farid 727
バゼンゲジ
Basengezi, Norbert 101
ハセンスタブ
Hasenstab, Michael 579
ハーゼンヒュットル
Hasenhuttl, Ralph 579
ハソウ
Hassau, Lawal 580
バー・ゾウハー
Bar-Zohar, Michael 101
パソス
Passos, Paulo Sérgio 1084
パゾス
Pazos, James 1089

パソス・コエーリョ
Coelho, Pedro Passos 273
パソス・コエリョ
Coelho, Pedro Passos 273
パソード
Persaud, Reepu Daman 1101
パソ・トラド
Pazo Torrado, Carlos Manuel 1089
バソビッチ
Vasovic, Velibor 1448
ハーソフ
Hersov, L. 600
バーソープ
Barthorp, Michael 100
バーソフ
Basov, Nikolai Gennadievich 102
バソフ
Basov, Nikolai Gennadievich 102
バソム
Bassom, David 103
パゾリーニ
Pasolini, Uberto 1083
パソル
Pasols, Paul-Gérard 1083
バソレ
Bassolet, Yipènè 103
バーソロミュー
Bartholomew, Alick 100
バソワ
Basova, Liubov 102
バーソン
Berson, Dvera 131
Burson, Nancy 206
バソン
Basson, Jean 103
パーソン
Parson, Ann B. 1082
Person, Mike 1101
Persson, Anders 1101
Persson, Hans 1101
パーソンズ
Parsons, April 1082
Parsons, Caroline 1082
Parsons, Chandler 1082
Parsons, Charles 1082
Parsons, Craig 1082
Parsons, David 1082
Parsons, Garry 1082
Parsons, Jim 1082
Parsons, Joanne 1082
Parsons, Julie 1082
Parsons, Michael J. 1082
Parsons, Paul 1082
Parsons, Polly E. 1082
Parsons, Richard Dean 1082
Parsons, Scott 1082
Parsons, Thomas Sturges 1082
Parsons, Tina 1082
Parsons, Tom 1082
Parsons, Tony 1082
バゾンバンザ
Bazombanza, Prosper 108
バソンブリオ・イグレシアス
Basombrío Iglesias, Carlos Miguel 102
ハーター
Harter, James K. 577
Harter, Marc 577
ハダ
Hada, James 552
ハダー
Hadar, Dori 552
バータ
Bahta, Meraf 80
バーター
Barter, Christine 99
Barter, Peter 99
バーダー
Bader, Hillary 78
Bader, Wolfgang 78
バタ
Bhatta, Lekh Raj 135
バター
Butter, Andrea 209
バダ
Bada, Mahamat Zene 78
パタ
Pata, Levi 1084
ハダイ
El Hady, Ameen 396
バタイエ
Bataille, Sylvia 103
パダイガ
Padaiga, Žilvinas 1068
バタイネ
Batayneh, Alaa 103
バタイネハ
Batayneh, Muhammad 103
ハータイネン
Haatainen, Tuula 551
バタイユ
Bataille, Christophe 103
Bataille, Marion 103
Bataille, Nicolas 103
Bataille, Sylvia 103
バダイン
Bhadain, Sudarshan 135
バダウィ
Badawi, al-Tayeb Hassan 78
Badawy, M.K. 78
バタウィック
Butterwick, Richard 209
ハーダウェー
Hardaway, Hannah 569
ハーダウェイ
Hardaway, Tim 569
Hardaway, Tim, Jr. 569
パタキ
Pataki, George 1084
バータク
Bartak, Lawrence 99
バタグリア
Battaglia, Aurelius 104
パダケ
Padacke Albert, Pahimi 1068
バタゲーリ
Batagelj, Vladimir 103
パタコス
Pattakos, Alex 1085
バタシュ
Batash, Mohammadullah 103
ハータス
Hartas, Leo 577
ハタズリー
Hattersley, Michael E. 581
Hattersley, Roy 581
パタースン
Paterson, Ron 1085
Patterson, James 1086
Patterson, Richard North 1086
Patterson, Scott 1086
パタセ
Patassé, Ange-Félix 1084
ハダセビッチ
Khadasevich, Pavel 724
パターソン
Paterson, Barbara L. 1085
Paterson, Brian 1085
Paterson, Jeff 1085
Paterson, Katherine Womeldorf 1085
Paterson, Mark 1085
Paterson, Mike 1085
Paterson, Owen 1085
Patterson, Barbara J. 1086
Patterson, Carly 1086
Patterson, Casey 1086
Patterson, Charles 1086
Patterson, Colin 1086
Patterson, Cordarrelle 1086
Patterson, Danny 1086
Patterson, David 1086
Patterson, David A. 1086
Patterson, Ellie 1086
Patterson, Eric 1086
Patterson, Floyd 1086
Patterson, Francine 1086
Patterson, James 1086
Patterson, James T. 1086
Patterson, JoEllen 1086
Patterson, Jordan 1086
Patterson, Kerry 1086
Patterson, Lamar 1086
Patterson, Miles L. 1086
Patterson, Orlando 1086
Patterson, Patrick 1086
Patterson, Ray 1086
Patterson, W.Bruce 1086
Patterson, William Patrick 1086
Peterson, Eric T. 1102
パタソン
Patterson, Kay 1086
Patterson, Percival J. 1086
バタチャルヤ
Bhattacharya, Arundhati 135
ハータック
Hurtak, J.J. 638
バーダック
Bardach, Eugene 93
パダッケ・アルベール
Padacke Albert, Pahimi 1068
ハダッタン・サナディ
Hadattan Sanady, Tchimadem 552
ハダット
Jadad, Alejandro R. 658
ハダッド
Haddad, Amy Marie 552
Haddad, Demiye Zuher 552
Haddad, Wadi D. 552
ハダディ
Hadadi, Ehsan 552
ハダド
Hadad, Ibrahim 552
Haddad, Habib 552
Haddad, Ibrahim 552
Haddad, Soraya 552
Haddad, Tijani 552
パタニティ
Paterniti, Michael 1085
バタネン
Vatanen, Ari Pieti Uolevi 1448
ハタノ
Hatano, Lilian Terumi 581
バダノヴィッチ
Bahdanovich, Aliaksandr 80
Bahdanovich, Andrei 80
バダノビッチ
Bahdanovich, Aliaksandr 80
Bahdanovich, Andrei 80
パタビ・ジョイス
Pattabhi Jois, Sri K. 1085
パタビジョイス
Pattabhi Jois, Sri K. 1085
ハタブ
Hatabu, Hiroto 581
Khattab, Mokhtar Abdel-Moneim 727
パータプ
Partap, Harry 1083
バターフィールド
Butterfield, Brian 209
Butterfield, Moira 209
ハターヘト
Hatahet, Ayman 581
バーダマン
Vardaman, James M. 1446
Vardaman, Maya 1446
ハターミー
Khatami, Mohammad 727
ハタミ
Khatami, Mohammad 727
ハーダム
Khaddam, Abdul Halim 724
ハダーム
Khaddam, Abdul Halim 724
ハダム
Khaddam, Abdul Halim 724
バダム
Badham, John 78
パーダム
Purdum, Tanner 1140
バダムジュナイ
Badamjunai, Tunjingiin 78
パダヤチ
Padayachie, Radhakrishna 1068
バタライ
Bhattarai, Baburam 135
Bhattarai, Krishna Prasad 135
バダラッコ
Badaracco, Joseph L., Jr. 78
ハダリ
Hadary, Oumarou 552
ハダリィ
Hadary, Sharon 552
バタリック
Butterick, George F. 209
バータリーン・ガルサンスフ
Baataryn Galsansükh 76
バダル
Badal, Harsimrat Kaur 78
パダル

Padar, Ivari 1068
パタルカツィシビリ
Patarkatsishvili, Badri 1084
バータルスフ
Baatarsukh, Chinzorig 76
バダルディン
Badaruddin, Othman 78
パダレ
Padare, Jean Bernard 1068
バターロフ
Batalov, Aleksei 103
パタロン
Patalon, William, Ⅲ 1084
バターワース
Butterworth, Brian 209
Butterworth, Christine 209
Butterworth, Nick 209
バタワース
Butterworth, Alex 209
ハタン
Hatang, S.K. 581
バーダン
Bardhan, Pranab K. 93
パタン
Patang, Ghulam Mujtaba 1084
Patin, Cléa 1085
Pattern, Melvin A. 1086
パタンチュシュ
Pattantyus, Adam 1085
バダンテール
Badinter, Elisabeth 78
Badinter, Robert 78
バーチ
Bacsi, Peter 78
Birch, Alex 140
Birch, Charles 140
Birch, Hayley 140
Birch, Paul 140
Birch, Silver 140
Birch, Will 140
Burch, Geoff 202
Burch, Mary R. 202
Burch, Rebecca C. 202
Burch, Tory 202
バチ
Buatsi, Joshua 197
パーチ
Paci, Paolo 1068
バーチウッド
Birchwood, Max 140
Birchwood, M.J. 140
パーチェ
Pace, Alessandro 1067
パーチェイス
Purchase, Zac 1140
パチェーコ
Pacheco, José Emilio 1067
パチェコ
Pacheco, Abel 1067
Pacheco, Gabriel 1067
Pacheco, Jorge 1067
Pacheco, José Emilio 1067
Pacheco, Máximo 1067
Pacheco, Ovidio 1068
Pacheco, Peter S. 1068
Pacheco, Rommel 1068
Pacheco, Rubén 1068
Pachecoo, Julián 1068
バーチェット
Burchett, Jan 202
パチェット
Patchett, Ann 1084
バチェバロバ
Bachvarova, Rumiana 77
バチェビッチ
Bačević, Milan 77
バーチェフスキー
Barczewski, Stephanie L. 93
バチェラー
Batchelor, David 103
Batchelor, Doug 103
Batchelor, Stephen 103
ハチェリディ
Khacheridi, Yevhen 724
バーチェル
Burchell, Michael 202
パチエルピナク
Pacierpnik, Natalia 1068
パチエルプニク
Pacierpnik, Natalia 1068
バチェレ
Bachelet, Michelle 77
ハチェンス
Hutchens, David 639
バチカ
Batica, Pascoal Domingos 104
バチガルピ
Bacigalupi, Paolo 77
バチコフ
Bachkov, Hovhannes 77
バチスタ
Batista, Cergio 104
ハチゼ
Khachidze, Giorgi 724
Khachidze, Goga 724
ハチソン
Hutcheson, Peggy G. 639
バチッチ
Bačić, Branko 77
パチーノ
Pacino, Al 1068
パーチメント
Parchment, Hansle 1077
ハーチャー
Hartcher, Peter 577
パチャ
Pacha, David Day 1067
パチャウリ
Pachauri, Rajendra K. 1067
Pachauri, Rajendra Kumar 1067
バーチャック
Berczuk, Stephen P. 125
バーチャード
Burchard, Brendon 202
Burchard, Evan 202
ハチャトゥリアン
Khachaturyan, Sergei 724
ハチャトゥリヤン
Khachaturyan, Sergei 724
ハチャトリアン
Khachatryan, Ara 724
Khachatryan, Vardan 724
ハチャトリャン
Khachatrian, Vardan 724
Khachatryan, Gagik 724
パチャブト
Pachabut, Darya 1067
バーチャル
Birchall, Chris 140
Birchall, Mark 140
バチャロ
Bachalo, Chris 77
バーチュ
Virtue, Doreen L. 1459
バーチュー
Virtue, Charles 1459
Virtue, Doreen L. 1459
Virtue, Grant 1459
Virtue, Tessa 1459
バチュー
Bachoo, Anil Kumar 77
バチュアイ
Batshuayi, Michy 104
バチューシュカ
Batsiushka, Hanna 104
パチューリア
Pachulia, Zaza 1068
ハチョン
Hutcheon, Pat Duffy 639
バチリ
Bathily, Aly 104
バチロフ
Batirov, Mavlet 104
バーチン
Ba-jin 82
パチンスキー
Paczynski, Bohdan 1068
ハチンソン
Hutchinson, Alberta 639
Hutchinson, Bobby 639
Hutchinson, Stephan 639
ハーツ
Hartz, Paula 578
Hertz, Janice 600
Hertz, Noreena 600
Herz, Rachel Sarah 600
バーツ
Bartz, Carol Ann 101
Bartz, Gary 101
バツ
Batshu, Edwin Jenamiso 104
バツァラシュキナ
Batsarashkina, Vitalina 104
パツァリス
Patsalis, Philippos 1085
パツァリデス
Patsalides, Christos 1085
バツィウア
Batsiua, Mathew 104
ハーツィグ
Herzig, Edmund 600
パツィット
Pázsit, Imre 1089
パツィ・パコ
Patzi Paco, Félix 1086
バツィン・チョホフ
Batzín Chojoj, Carlos Enrique 105
ハーツェル
Harzer, Jens 579
ハーツェンバーグ
Herzenberg, Leonard Arthur 600
パツォウスカー
Pacovská, Kveta 1068
ハーツォグ
Herzog, Harold A. 600
パツォーリ
Pacolli, Behgjet 1068
ハッカー
Hacker, Marcel 552
Hacker, Peter Michael Stephan 552
バッカ
Bacca, Carlos 77
バッカー
Backer, Jos De 77
Backker, Vera de 77
Bakker, Arnold B. 84
Bakker, Frank 84
パッカー
Packer, Alex J. 1068
Packer, Ann 1068
Packer, Duane R. 1068
Packer, Frank 1068
Packer, George 1068
Packer, James 1068
Packer, James Innell 1068
Packer, Jane 1068
Packer, Kerry Francis Bullmore 1068
Packer, Lester 1068
Packer, Tracy 1068
ハッカウイ
Hakkaoui, Bassima 556
バッカス
Backus, John 77
ハーツガード
Hertsgaard, Mark 600
パッカード
Packard, George R. 1068
Packard, Jake 1068
Packard, Mary 1068
Packard, Vance 1068
ハッカニ
Haqqani, Jalaloddin 568
ハッカビー
Huckabee, Mike 631
ハッカーミュラー
Hackermüller, Rotraut 552
パッカラ
Pahkala, Riikka 1070
バッカラリオ
Baccalario, Pierdomenico 77
バッカール
Baccar, Taoufik 77
ハッカンソン
Hakansson, Joyce 556
バッキー
Bakke, Dennis 84
バツキ
Batki, Noemi 104
ハッキネン
Hakkinen, Henri 556
Häkkinen, Mika 556
パッキャオ
Pacquiao, Manny 1068
バッキン
Bacchin, Matteo 77
バッキンガム
Buckingham, Charlie 198
Buckingham, David 198
Buckingham, Jamie 198
Buckingham, Marcus 198
Buckingham, Will 198
ハッキング
Hacking, Ian 552
ハック
Hack, Alexander 552
Haque, Mohammed Sayedul 569
Haque, Ruhal 569

ハ

バック
Bach, Christian 77
Bach, David 77
Bach, Howard 77
Bach, Patricia A. 77
Bach, Richard 77
Bach, Steven 77
Back, Amanda 77
Back, Frederic 77
Back, Les 77
Buch, Eric F. 197
Buck, Alexy 198
Buck, Carole 198
Buck, Chris 198
Buck, Linda B. 198
Buck, Math 198
Buck, Peter 198
Buck, Philippa 198
Buck, Ross 198
パック
Pack, Charles A. 1068
Pack, Joe 1068
Pack, Robert 1068
Pak, Greg 1071
Puck, Wolfgang 1138
パッグ
Pogge, R.C. 1120
バックウィート・ザディコ
Zydeco, Buckwheat 1560
バックウォルド
Buchwald, Art 198
バック - エムデン
Buck-Emden, Rüdiger 198
バックサル
Buchthal, Stanley F. 198
バックシー
Bucksey, Colin 198
ハックス
Hax, Arnoldo C. 584
Hax, Herbert 584
バックス
Bachs, Ramon 77
Backes, Ernest 77
Bax, Johannes Gesinus 107
パックス
Pax, Salam 1088
パックスマン
Paxman, Jeremy 1088
ハックスリ
Huxley, Andrew Fielding 640
ハックスリー
Huxley, Andrew Fielding 640
バックター
Buchter, Ryan 198
バックナー
Buckner, DeForest 198
Buckner, M.M. 198
ハックニー
Hackney, Ki 552
バックハウス
Backhaus, Peter 77
Backhouse, Roger E. 77
ハックフォード
Hackford, Taylor 552
バックホルツ
Buchholz, Clay 197
Buchholz, Rachel 197
Buchholz, Todd G. 197
ハックマン
Hackman, Gene 552
Hackman, J.Richard 552
バックマン
Bachmann, Glenn 77
Bachmann, Michele Marie 77
Backman, Fredrik 77
Backman, Jouri 77
Backman, Kennard 77
Buchman, Peter 197
Buckman, Robert 198
Buckman, Robert H. 198
バック＝モース
Buck-Morss, Susan 198
バックラック
Bachrach, Arthur J. 77
バックランド
Buckland, Bruce Stoddart 198
Buckland, Ian 198
Buckland, Jonny 198
Buckland, Marc 198
Buckland, Raymond 198
Buckland, Rosina 198
Buckland, Stephane 198
Buckland, Warren 198
バックリー
Backley, Steve 77
Buckley, Bruce 198
Buckley, Callum 198
Buckley, Christopher 198
Buckley, David 198
Buckley, Markino 198
Buckley, Michael 198
Buckley, Susan Washburn 198
Buckley, William F. 198
Buckley, William Frank, Jr. 198
バックリー・アーチャー
Buckley-Archer, Linda 198
ハックル
Hackl, Georg 552
Huckle, John 631
バックル
Buckle, Jane 198
バックルー
Buckelew, Alan B. 198
バックルズ
Buckles, Frank 198
Buckles, Luke 198
バックレー
Buckley, Carol 198
Buckley, David 198
Buckley, William Frank, Jr. 198
バックレイ
Buckley, Belinda 198
Buckley, Julia 198
バックワルド
Buchwald, Art 198
ハッケ
Hacke, Axel 552
バッケ
Bacqué, Marie-Frédérique 78
バッケ・イェンセン
Bakke-jensen, Frank 84
パツケビッチ
Patskevich, Aleksandra 1085
ハッケル
Hackel, Sergei 552
バッケル
Buckell, Tobias S. 198
バッケン
Bakken, Jill 84
ハッケンバーグ
Hackenberg, Christian 552
バツコ
Baczko, Bernadett 78
バツコビッチ
Backović, Slobodan 77
バッコルツ
Buchholz, Steve 197
パッサー
Pusser, Brian 1141
ハッサナリ
Hassanali, Noor Mohammed 580
ハッサニ
Hassani, Djaffar Ahmed 580
ハッサネイン
Hassanein, Muhammad Medhat Abdel-Atti 580
パッサーマン
Passerman, Daniel S. 1084
パッサール
Passard, Alain 1083
パッサルゲ
Passarge, Eberhard 1083
パッサロ
Pássaro, Dulce 1083
ハッサン
al-Hajj Hassan, Hussein 556
Hasan, Wirajuda 579
Hassan, Abdella 580
Hassan, Abdiqassim Salad 580
Al-hassan, Aisha Jummai 580
Hassan, bin Abdulla Fakhroo 580
Hassan, Fred 580
Hassan, Hanif 580
Hassan, Hussein al-Hajj 580
Hassan, Jafar 580
Al-hassan, Khaliru 580
Hassan, Mahamat Ali 580
Hassan, Mahamat Nasser 580
Hassan, Mahamud Ahmed 580
al-Hassan, Malik Dohan 580
Hassan, Mohsen 580
Hassan, Moumina Houmed 580
Hassan, Moussa Ahmed 580
al-Hassan, Nabil 580
Hassan, Nouhou 580
al-Hassan, Raya 580
Hassan, Sifan 580
Hassan, Steven 580
Hassan, Wirajuda 580
Hassan, Yaël 580
Hassan, Zubeir Ahmed 580
Hassan, Zubeir Mohammed 580
Hassane, Kounou 580
Hassane, Souley 580
ハッサン・イブラヒム
Hassan Ibrahim, Houssein 580
ハッサン王子
Hassan bin Talal 580
ハッサンカーン
Hassankhan, Maurits 580
ハッサンヌ
Hassane, Come 580
ハッサン・ヌフ
Hassan Nuh, Mohamed Abdullahi 580
ハッサンバハドン
Bahdon, Ali Hassan 80
ハッサン・ビン・タラール
Hassan bin Talal 580
ハッシ
Hassi, Satu 580
バッシ
Bassi, Davide 102
バッシー
Bassey, E.Joan 102
バッジ
Badjie, Ousman 78
バッジェン
Budgen, Frank 199
バッジオ
Baggio, Roberto 79
バッジーニ
Baggini, Julian 79
パッシノ
Passineau, Joseph 1084
ハッジャ
Hajjeh, Tamir 556
バッシャー
Bashir, Layli Miller 102
バッシャム
Bassham, Gregory 102
ハッジャル
Hajjar, Bandar bin Muhammad 556
バッシャール
Assad, Bashar al 65
バッシュ
Basch, Ethan M. 101
Basch, Paul F. 101
Bash, Barbara 101
バッジョ
Baggio, Roberto 79
パッシン
Passin, Günther 1084
Passin, Herbert 1084
バッスィ
Bassi, Adriano 102
ハッセ
Haase, Tina 551
Hasse, Jeanette M. 580
Hasse, Peter 580
ハッセイ
Hussey, Edward 639
バッセイ
Bussey, Cathy 208
ハッセマー
Hassemer, Winfried 580
パッセラ
Passera, Corrado 1083
ハッセル
Hassell, Anthony 580
バッセル
Bussell, Darcey 208
ハッセンザール
Hassenzahl, David M. 580
ハッソ
Hasso, Signe 580
バッソ
Basso, Adrienne 103
Basso, Bill 103
Basso, Jorge 103
Basso, Thomas F. 103
バッソー
Boisseau, Christina L. 155

パッソー
Pat-sowe, Momodu Allieu 1085
バッソン
Bassom, David 103
ハッタ
Hatta, Kayo Matano 581
Hatta, Meutia 581
Hatta, Rajasa 581
Hutta, K.Emily 639
バッダギ
Baddaghi, Fatemeh 78
バッタチャヤ
Bhattacharjee, Debashish 135
Bhattacharjee, Sandip 135
Bhattacharya, Arindam K. 135
バッタッリア
Battaglia, Romano 104
ハッダーディ
Hadadi, Hoda 552
ハッダディン
Haddadin, Bassam 552
ハッダード
Haddad, Amy Marie 552
Haddad, Sami 552
ハッダド
Haddad, Lahcen 552
Haddad, Malek 552
ハッターブ
Khatab 727
Khattab, Mokhtar Abdel-Moneim 727
ハッタブ
Khatab 727
Khattab, Ahmad Al 727
ハッダミーン
Hademine, Yahya Ould 552
ハッダーム
Khaddam, Abdul Halim 724
バッタリア
Battaglia, Romano 104
ハッチ
Hatch, Annia 581
Hatch, Connie 581
Hatch, David K. 581
Hatch, Frank 581
Hatch, Mark 581
Hatch, Mary Cottam 581
Hatch, Mary Jo 581
パッチ・アダムス
Patch Adams 1084
バッチェラー
Batchelor, Rosemary 103
パッチェル
Patchell, Angela 1084
バッチェン
Batchen, Geoffrey 103
ハッチオン
Hutcheon, Linda 639
ハッチクラフト
Hutchcroft, Paul D. 639
ハッチソン
Hutchison, Barry 639
Hutchison, C.A., Ⅲ 639
Hutchison, Drew 639
Hutchison, Michael M. 639
バッチニ
Baccini, Mario 77
ハッチャー
Hatcher, Billy 581
Hatcher, Chris 581
Hatcher, Ruth 581
Hatcher, Teri 581
パッチャ
Pacha, David Day 1067
ハッチンス
Hutchins, Carleen 639
Hutchins, Chris 639
Hutchins, Hazel 639
Hutchins, Pat 639
ハッチンソン
Huchingson, James Edward 631
Huchinson, Tim 631
Hutchinson, Alex 639
Hutchinson, Atiba 639
Hutchinson, Mark Norman 639
Hutchinson, Peter 639
Hutchinson, Robert 639
Hutchinson, Sally A. 639
Hutchinson, Tom A. 639
Hutchinson, William M. 639
バッツ
Butts, Donna 209
Butts, Ellen 209
Butz, Norbert Leo 209
パッツ
Puts, Kevin 1141
パッツァー
Pasztor, Austin 1084
Patzer, Andrew 1086
ハッツフェルド
Hatzfeld, Jean 581
バッティ
Bhatti, Shahbaz 135
バッティー
Bhatti, Liaqat Abbas 135
バッティアート
Battiato, Giacomo 105
バッティスティーニ
Battistini, Matilde 105
バッティン
Battin, Patricia 105
ハッテスタ
Hattestad, Ola Vigen 581
ハッテスタット
Hattestad, Ola Vigen 581
ハッテスタート
Hattestad, Ola Vigen 581
バッテル
Battelle, John 105
バッテン
Batten, Don 105
バッデン
Budden, Julian 199
パッテン
Patten, Brian 1085
Patten, Cassandra 1085
Patten, Christine Taylor 1085
Patten, Christopher Franeis 1085
Patten, Edward 1085
Patten, Terry 1086
パッデン
Padden, Carol 1068
ハッテンドーフ
Hattendorf, Linda 581
ハット
Hatt, Anna-Karin 581
Hutt, Michael D. 639
ハットー
Hatto, Joyce 581
ハッド
al-Hadd, Mohammed Abdelkarim 552
バット
Bhatt, Ela Ramesh 135
バッド
Budd, Philip J. 199
Budd, Timothy 199
パット
Patt, Doug 1085
Patt, Hugo 1085
ハットウッド
Hatwood, Mark David 581
ハットシュタイン
Hattstein, Markus 581
バットストーン
Batstone, David 104
バットドーフ
Batdorff, John 103
パットナム
Phatlum, Pornanong 1106
Putnam, Lance 1141
Putnam, Robert D. 1141
Putnam, Zach 1141
Puttnam, David Terence 1141
バッドニュース・アレン
Bad News Allen 78
ハットフィールド
Hatfield, Bobby 581
Hatfield, James 581
Hatfield, Mark Odom 581
バッドマン
Badman, Keith 78
パットモン
Patmon, Tyler 1085
ハットリー
Hatley, Tim 581
バットロ
Battro, Antonio M. 105
ハットン
Hatton, Grady 581
Hutten, Joan 639
Hutton, Betty 639
Hutton, Brian G. 639
Hutton, David W. 639
Hutton, Jim 639
Hutton, John 639
Hutton, Shaaron 639
Hutton, Wendy 639
ハッドン
Haddon, Mark 552
パットン
Patton, Bruce M. 1086
Patton, Darvis 1086
Patton, Harvey 1086
Patton, Jeff 1086
Patton, Mark 1086
Patton, Michael Quinn 1086
Patton, Paul 1086
Patton, Quinton 1086
ハットン - イオ
Hatton-Yeo, Alan 581
バッハ
Bach, Dominique 77
Bach, Patricia A. 77
Bach, Thomas 77
バッハー
Bacher, Hans 77
パッハ
Pach, János 1067
ハーツバーグ
Hertzberg, Jeff 600
ハッバード
Hubbard, Ruth 631
パッパーノ
Pappano, Antonio 1076
バッハフィッシャー
Bachfischer, Margit 77
バッハマン
Bachmann, Daniel 77
パッハマン
Pachman, Luděk 1068
バッハラー
Bachler, Nikolaus 77
パッパラルド
Pappalardo, Marco 1076
Pappalardo, Umberto 1076
ハーツバンド
Hartzband, Pamela 578
ハップ
Happ, Ian 568
Happ, J.A. 568
バッブ
Babb, Michael 76
パップ
Papp, Laszlo A. 1076
Papp, Lisa 1076
Papp, Stefan 1076
バッファ
Buffa, Dudley W. 199
ハーツフィールド
Hartsfield, Henry W., Jr. 578
Hartsfield, Roy 578
Hertzfeld, Andy 600
ハーツフェルト
Hertzfeldt, Don 600
ハーツフェルド
Hertzfeld, Andy 600
ハッブズ
Hobbs, Christopher James 611
パップワース
Pappworth, Sara 1077
パッペ
Pappe, Ia.Sha. 1076
ハッベル
Hubbell, Stephen P. 631
ハッポネン
Happonen, Sirke 568
ハーツホーン
Hartshorne, Robin 578
ハッマーディ
Hammadi, Hamdi Ould 563
ハッマート
Hammat, Jub Abdoul 563
バツミケ
Batumike, Jean-Baptiste Ntahwa Kuderwa 105
パッラ
Parra, John 1082
ハッラーク
Hallaq, Wael B. 558
バッラーク
Barrak, Ahmad Younos S. Al 97
パッラディーノ
Palladino, Raffaele 1072
ハッラーフ
Khallaf, 'Abd al-Wahhab 725
パツラフ
Patzlaff, Rainer 1086

バッラルディーニ
Ballardini, Davide 87
パッランティ
Pallanti, Giuseppe 1072
バツリーク
Vaculík, Ludvík 1437
ハーツリッチ
Herzlich, Mark 600
バッレーカ
Barreca, Antonio 97
パッロッタ・デッラ・トッレ
Pallotta della Torre, Leopoldina 1072
ハーテ
Harte, Lawrence 577
ハーデ
Haarde, Geir H. 551
パテ
Pathé, Michele 1085
バデア
Carlescu-badea, Laura 226
ハーディ
Hardie, Bruce G.S. 569
Hardy, Blaine 570
Hardy, Chris E. 570
Hardy, Clarisa 570
Hardy, Darel W. 570
Hardy, David T. 570
Hardy, Edward 570
Hardy, Henry 570
Hardy, James D. 570
Hardy, Jeff 570
Hardy, Jessica 570
Hardy, J.J. 570
Hardy, Kate 570
Hardy, Kristin 570
Hardy, Lucy 570
Hardy, Matt 570
Hardy, Paula 570
Hardy, Phil 570
Hardy, Robin 570
ハーディー
Hardee, Trey 569
Hardie, Andrew 569
Hardie, John 569
Hardy, Chris 570
Hardy, David B. 570
Hardy, James D. 570
Hardy, Justin 570
Hardy, Vincent 570
Hrdy, Sarah Blaffer 629
ハディ
Hadi, Abd-Rabbo Mansur 553
Huddy, Delia 631
バーティー
Bartee, Kimera 99
バーディ
Burdi, Zack 202
バティ
Bati, Anwer 104
Battie, David 105
Batty, Emily 105
バディ
Badi, Sihem 78
al-Badi, Sultan bin Saeed 78
Badie, Bertrand 78
パーディ
Pardi, Charlotte 1077
Purdy, Gregor N. 1140
Purdy, James 1140
パティー
Pattie, Charles 1086
バティア
Bhatia, Rahul 135
バディア
Badia, Pedro Franco 78
バティアシュヴィリ
Batiashvili, Lisa 104
バディアシル
Badiashile, Loic 78
ハディアットモジョ
Hadiatmodjo, Carmen Carreon 553
パディアン
Padian, Kevin 1068
バディイ
Badii, R. 78
バディウ
Badiou, Alain 78
ハーティカ
Hertica, Michael 600
ハーティガン
Hartigan, Pamela 577
ハディザ
Hadiza, Maizama 553
ハディーシ
al-Hadithi, Mahir Ibrahim 553
バティースタ
Bautista, Jose 107
バティスタ
Baptista, Paulino Domingos 90
Batista, Cergio 104
Batista, Michel 104
Batiste, Mike 104
Bautista, Jose 107
Bautista, Rafael 107
バティスティ
Battisti, Romano 105
バティスト
Baptiste, Rene 90
パティスン
Pattison, Eliot 1086
ハディセ
Hadise 553
ハーディソン
Hardison, Marcus 570
パティソン
Pattison, James M. 1086
Pattison, Jim 1086
Pattison, Ted 1086
バーディック
Berdik, Chris 125
Brudick, Lydia 193
Burdick, Alan 202
Burdick, Eugene 202
Burdick, Robert 202
Verdick, Elizabeth 1452
ハディックス
Haddix, Margaret Peterson 552
バティッチ
Batić, Vladan 104
ハディッド
Hadid, Zaha 553
ハディディ
Hadidi, Amer 553
Hadidi, Niloufar Niakosari 553
ハーディド
Hadid, Zaha 553
ハディード
Hadeed, Gerald 552
ハディド
Hadeed, Aziz 552
Hadid, Jawad 553
Hadid, Nayef 553
Hadid, Zaha 553
バーディーニ
Bardini, Thierry 93
バディーニ
Badini, Carlo Maria 78
バディニ
Badini, Boureima 78
パティニョ
Patiño, Raúl 1085
Patiño, Ricardo 1085
パティニョ・アロカ
Patiño Aroca, Ricardo 1085
バーティネット
Bertinet, Richard 131
バディバンガ
Badibanga, Samy 78
ハティビ
Khatibi, Abdelkébir 727
ハーディープ
Hardeep, Hardeep 569
ハティーブ
Khatib, Abdul Ilaha 727
Khatib, Maha 727
al-Khatib, Tarek 727
Khatteb, Nabil 727
ハティブ
al-Khatib, Ahmed bin Aqeel 727
al-Khatib, Ghassan 727
バティーフ
Battikh, Othmane 105
バティフリエ
Batifoulier, Philippe 104
ハディペトロ
Hadzipetros, Emmanuel 553
ハーディーボーイズ
Hardie-boys, Michael 569
ハティボヴィッチ
Hatibovic, Dzemal 581
ハーディモン
Hardymon, G.Felda 570
バティヤ
Bathia, Diallo Mamadou 104
パディーヤ
Padilha, Janea 1068
Padilla, Cesar 1068
バティユティーン
Badhiutheen, Risad 78
Bathiudeen, Rishad 104
バティユディーン
Bathiudeen, Rishad 104
パディラ
Padilla, Mathew 1068
Padilla, Stan 1068
パディラック
Padirac, Commandant de 1068
パティラナ
Pathirana, Richard 1085
バティラリエフ
Batyraliev, Talantbek 105
パディーリャ
Padilla Castro, Nelson Fredy 1068
パディリャ
Padilha, Eliseu 1068
バディル
Badir, Sémir 78
パティル
Patil, Balasahib Vikhe 1085
Patil, Pratibha 1085
Patil, Shivraj V. 1085
バティロフ
Batirov, Adam 104
Batirov, Mavlet 104
Batyrov, Saparmyrat 105
ハーディン
Hardin, Chad 569
Hardin, Jeff 569
Hardin, Kimeron N. 569
Hardin, Milton Edward 569
バーディーン
Bardeen, Marjorie G. 93
ハディンガー
Hadinger, Boglarka 553
ハーディング
Harding, Christpher 569
Harding, Daniel 569
Harding, David 570
Harding, Deborah 570
Harding, Douglas Edison 570
Harding, Geoffrey 570
Harding, Georgina 570
Harding, Jennie 570
Harding, Justine 570
Harding, Kichener 570
Harding, Luke 570
Harding, Matt 570
Harding, Mona Lisa 570
Harding, Niall 570
Harding, Paul 570
Harding, Prince 570
Harding, R.R. 570
Harding, Sally 570
Harding, Sandra 570
Harding, Stephen 570
Harding, Vanessa 570
Harding, Vincent Gordon 570
Hardinge, Fred G. 570
ハーディング＝エッシュ
Harding-Esch, Edith 570
バディンジャー
Budinger, Chase 199
バーティンスキ
Bartynski, Julie M. 101
バーティンスキー
Burtynsky, Edward 207
バディンスキー
Budinsky, Frank 199
パティンソン
Pattinson, Robert 1086
パテヴ
Patteeuw, Veronique 1085
バデク
Bádescu, Ramona 78
バテス
Bates, Luis 104
パデスキー
Padesky, Christine A. 1068
バデスキュー
Bádescu, Ramona 78
ハーデスティ
Hardesty, Von 569
パーデック
Pardeck, John T. 1077
バーデット
Burdett, Lois 202

ハ

Burdette, Jonathan H. 202
パデッリ
Padelli, Daniele 1068
ハデニウス
Hadenius, Stig 552
バデニエル
Badenier, Pablo 78
バデノック
Badenoch, Alexander 78
Badenoch, Douglas 78
Badenoch, Nathan 78
バデノフ
Badenov, Bair 78
ハデミ
Khademi, Noureddine 724
バデモーシ
Bademosi, Johnson 78
バテュ
Battut, Eric 105
パーデュー
Pardew, Alan 1077
Perdue, Leo G. 1096
Perdue, Lewis 1096
Perdue, Sonny 1096
バーデュゴ
Bardugo, Leigh 93
Verdugo, Alex 1452
バテュム
Batum, Nicolas 105
バーテラ
Vahtera, Jussi 1438
パテラ
Patella, Vincent Michael 1084
パデランガ
Paderanga, Cayetano 1068
バデリ
Badelj, Milan 78
バデリー
Baddeley, Aaron 78
パテリ
Patelli, Alessandra 1084
バテリキ
Bateriki, Boutu 104
パデリナ
Paderina, Natalia 1068
ハーテルー
Heurtelou, Calvin 602
ハデル
Khader, Asma 724
バーテル
Bartel, Cori 99
Bartell, Susan S. 99
Bertell, Rosalie 131
バテル
Battel, Giovanni Umberto 105
Battelle, Ann 105
パテル
Patel, Burzin 1084
Patel, Dinsha 1084
Patel, Dipak 1084
Patel, Ebrahim 1084
Patel, Indraprasad Gordhanbhai 1084
Patel, Lilian 1084
Patel, Mukesh Mangalbhai 1084
Patel, Nipam H. 1084
Patel, P.R. 1084
Patel, Praful 1084
Patel, Priti 1084
Patel, Raj 1084
ハデルジョナイ
Hadergjonaj, Florent 552
バーテルス
Bartels, Kuwamena 99
バーテルスマン
Bartelsman, Jan 99
バーテルセン
Bertelsen, Cynthia D. 131
バーテルソン
Bartelson, Jens 99
バーテルニー
Vertelney, Scott 1454
パーテロ
Paatero, Sirpa 1067
ハーデン
Harden, Blaine 569
Harden, Elisabeth 569
Harden, James 569
Harden, Marcia Gay 569
Harden, Ronald M. 569
バーデン
Barden, Leonard 93
Burden, Chris 202
Burden, Gary 202
Burden, Matthew Currier 202
Vaden, Rory 1437
パテン
Patten, Christopher Franeis 1085
バーデンス
Bardens, Pete 93
バーデンズ
Bardens, Pete 93
ハーテンスタイン
Hartenstein, Isaiah 577
ハーテンステイン
Hertenstein, Matthew J. 600
パテント
Patent, Arnold M. 1085
ハート
Hardt, Michael 570
Hart, Allison 576
Hart, Annbel 576
Hart, Benjamin L. 576
Hart, Bobby 576
Hart, Carolyn G. 576
Hart, Caryl 576
Hart, Charles Anthony 576
Hart, Christopher 576
Hart, Colin 576
Hart, David J. 576
Hart, Diane 576
Hart, Donna 576
Hart, Donnie 576
Hart, Dorian 576
Hart, Erin 576
Hart, George 576
Hart, Graeme 576
Hart, Harold 576
Hart, Jessica 576
Hart, Jillian 576
Hart, Joe 576
Hart, John 576
Hart, John Fraser 577
Hart, Johnny 577
Hart, Jolene 577
Hart, Josephine 577
Hart, Kevin 577
Hart, Kitty Carlisle 577
Hart, Lizzie 577
Hart, Louise 577
Hart, Matthew 577
Hart, Megan 577
Hart, Mickey 577
Hart, Oliver D. 577
Hart, Onno van der 577
Hart, Penny 577
Hart, Stephen 577
Hart, Stephen D. 577
Hart, Stuart L. 577
Hart, Susan 577
Hart, Susan J. 577
Hart, Taylor 577
Hart, Thomas N. 577
Hart, Tina 577
Hart, Vaughan 577
Harte, John 577
Harte, Lawrence 577
Herdt, Gilbert H. 597
Hunter, Ian 636
Hurt, John 637
Hurt, Robert 637
Hurt, William 637
ハード
Heard, Christopher 587
Heard, Heidi L. 587
Heard, Neal 587
Hird, Thora 609
Hurd, Douglas Richard 637
Hurd, Mark 637
バート
Bart, Delano 99
Batt, Rosemary L. 104
Bert, Eddie 131
Burt, Donald Graham 206
Burt, George 206
Burt, Guy 206
Burt, Michael 206
Burt, Peter 206
Burt, Ronald S. 206
バード
Baird, Jacqueline 82
Bard, Allen J. 93
Bard, E.M. 93
Bard, Josh 93
Bard, Ron 93
Bird, Allan 140
Bird, Antonia 140
Bird, Beverly 140
Bird, Brad 140
Bird, Christopher 140
Bird, Graham R. 140
Bird, Greg 140
Bird, Jemima 140
Bird, Jo 140
Bird, John 140
Bird, Kai 140
Bird, Larry 140
Bird, Lester 140
Bird, Stephen 140
Bird, Timothy 140
Bird, Vere 140
Byrd, Damiere 211
Byrd, Donald 211
Byrd, Elizabeth 211
Byrd, Jairus 211
Byrd, James P. 211
Byrd, LaRon 211
Byrd, Michelle R. 211
Byrd, Nicole 211
Byrd, Patricia 211
Byrd, Robert Carlyle 211
Byrde, Penelope 211
バードー
Bardoe, Cheryl 93
バト
Batho, Delphine 104
バド
Budd, Matthew 199
パート
Part, Michael 1082
Peart, Sandra 1091
パト
Pato, Alexandre 1085
Pato, Rimbink 1085
パドア・スキオッパ
Padoa-Schioppa, Tommaso 1069
パドアスキオッパ
Padoa-Schioppa, Tommaso 1069
パドアン
Padoan, Pier Carlo 1068
パドイン
Padoin, Simone 1069
バートゥ
Bartu, Joplo 101
バトゥー
Battut, Eric 105
バドゥ
Badu, Emmanuel 79
Badu, Erykah 79
バドゥー
Baddou, Yasmina 78
パードウ
Pardoe, James 1077
Pardoe, Jon 1077
パドヴァニ
Padovani, Martin 1069
ハートヴィ
Hartvig, Kirsten 578
バートウィスル
Birtwistle, Harrison 141
ハードウィック
Hardwick, Elizabeth 570
Hardwicke, Edward 570
ハトウィック
Hattwick, La Berta Weiss 581
ハートウェル
Hartwell, David G. 578
Hartwell, Leland H. 578
バードウェル
Birdwell, Robyn L. 140
バドゥエル
Baduel, Raúl Isaías 79
バトゥーシャク
Bartusiak, Marcia 101
バドゥスキー
Badowski, Rosanne 78
ハドゥソン
Hudson, Winson 632
バトゥーツ
Battuz, Christine 105
パドゥームチャイ
Phadermchai, Sasomsab 1106
バトゥムビラ
Batumubwira, Antoinette 105
パドゥーラ
Padura, Leonardo 1069
バドゥーラ・スコダ
Badura-Skoda, Paul 79
バドゥーラ＝スコダ
Badura-Skoda, Paul 79
バドゥラ・スコダ
Badura-Skoda, Paul 79
パドゥラル
Paduraru, Simona 1069

ハ

ハドゥリ
Khaduri, Nodar 724
ハートゥング
Hartung, William D. 578
バトエルデネ
Baterdene, Badmaanyambuugiin 104
Baterdene, Dashidemberel 104
バトカー
Batker, David K. 104
ハートキ
Hartke, Stephen 577
バトキ
Batki, Noemi 104
ハドギンス
Hudgins, Patricia A. 631
バトコ
Batoko, Ousmane 104
ハトコフ
Hatkoff, Craig 581
Hatkoff, Isabella 581
Hatkoff, Juliana 581
バートシック
Bartosik, Alison 101
バトジャルガル
Batjargal, Zambyn 104
ハトシュ
Hatos, Gabor 581
バトシュトゥバー
Badstuber, Holger 79
バードスミス
Bird-smith, Dane 140
バトスーリ
Batsuuri, Jamiyansurengiin 104
ハトソン
Hutson, Don 639
Hutson, George 639
Hutson, Matthew 639
ハドソン
Hodson, Jennifer 612
Hudson, Annabel 631
Hudson, Brian James 631
Hudson, Chuck 631
Hudson, Daniel 631
Hudson, Diane 631
Hudson, Gabe 631
Hudson, Gail E. 631
Hudson, Jennifer 632
Hudson, Julie 632
Hudson, Kate 632
Hudson, Kim 632
Hudson, Kurt 632
Hudson, Lion 632
Hudson, Michael 632
Hudson, Pookie 632
Hudson, Richard L. 632
Hudson, Robert 632
Hudson, Rodney 632
Hudson, Russ 632
Hudson, Tim 632
バトソン
Batson, Charles Daniel 104
Batson, Susan 104
ハドソンスミス
Hudson-smith, Matthew 632
パトータ
Patota, Giuseppe 1085
バトツェツェグ・ソロンゾンボルド
Battsetseg Soronzonboldyn 105
バトツェレグ
Battsereg, Namdag 105
ハドック
Hudock, Ann 631
バードック
Burdock, George A. 202
パトック
Puttock, Simon 1141
バートット
Bertot, John Carlo 132
ハート＝デイヴィス
Hart-Davis, Adam 577
バトトルガ
Battulga, Haltmaagiin 105
Battulga, Khaltmaa 105
Battulga, Temuulen 105
ハドナジー
Hadnagy, Christopher 553
パトナム
Putnam, Frank W. 1141
Putnam, Hilary 1141
Putnam, James 1141
Putnam, Lawrence H. 1141
Puttnam, David Terence 1141
パトニー
Putney, Mary Jo 1141
Putney, William W. 1141
パドニー
Pudney, Warwick 1139
バドニッツ
Budnitz, Judy 199
ハートネット
Hartnett, Josh 578
Hartnett, Sonya 578
パトノー
Patnoe, Shelley 1085
パートノイ
Partnoy, Frank 1083
バトバヤル
Batbayar, Nyamjav 103
Batbayar, Shiilegiin 103
Batbayiar, Ts. 103
バートフ
Burtoft, Jeff 206
バトフー
Batkhuu, Gavaagiin 104
バートファイ
Bartfai, Tamas 99
ハドフィ
Hadfi, Daniel 553
ハートフィールド
Hartfield, Trevon 577
Heartfield, Marie 587
ハドフィールド
Hadfield, Chris 553
バートベック
Vertovec, Steven 1454
バトボルド
Batbold, Sükhbaataryn 103
Batbold, Sunduin 103
パトマワティ
Patmawa, Patmawati 1085
ハートマン
Hartman, Bob 577
Hartman, Cherry 577
Hartman, Kent 577
Hartman, Thomas 577
Hartmann, Annabelle 577
Hartmann, Eddo 577
Hartmann, Edmund L. 578
Hartmann, R.R.K. 578
Hartmann, Thom 578
ハードマン
Hardman, Graham Peter 570
Hardman, Kath 570
Herdman, Alan 597
Herdman, T.Heather 597
バートマン
Bertman, Stephen 131
バードマン
Birdman 140
バトマンゲリジ
Batmanghelidji, F. 104
ハドミン
Hademine, Yahya Ould 552
パードム
Purdom, Edmund 1140
パードモ
Perdomo, Carlos 1096
ハドラ
Khadra, Labib 724
ハドラー
Hudler, Ad 631
バトラ
Batra, Raveendra N. 104
バトラー
Batler, John 104
Butler, Alan 208
Butler, Billy 208
Butler, Brice 208
Butler, Charles 208
Butler, Chris 208
Butler, Christopher 208
Butler, Crezdon 208
Butler, Darius 208
Butler, David 208
Butler, Donald 208
Butler, Dori Hillestad 208
Butler, Dorothy 208
Butler, Drew 209
Butler, Eddie 209
Butler, Edgar W. 209
Butler, Erik 209
Butler, Gerard 209
Butler, Gillian 209
Butler, Jack 209
Butler, Jeremy 209
Butler, Jill 209
Butler, Jimmy 209
Butler, John 209
Butler, John Marshall 209
Butler, Judith 209
Butler, Katy 209
Butler, Keith 209
Butler, Malcolm 209
Butler, Mario 209
Butler, Mark 209
Butler, Penelope Johnson 209
Butler, Rasual 209
Butler, Richard 209
Butler, Robert Neil 209
Butler, Robert Olen 209
Butler, Rupart 209
Butler, Ruth 209
Butler, Stephen 209
Butler, Timothy 209
Butler, Vernon 209
バドラス
Budras, Klaus-Dieter 199
バトラー・ボードン
Butler-Bowdon, Eddie 209
バトラー＝ボードン
Butler-Bowdon, Tom 209
バートラム
Bartram, Pamela 101
Bertram, Holli 132
ハート＝ランズバーグ
Hart-Landsberg, Martin 577
ハートランド
Hartland, Jessie 577
Heartland, James 587
バートランド
Bertrand, Michael T. 132
Bertrand, Ryan 132
バトランド
Butland, Jack 208
ハートリー
Hartley, Blythe 577
Hartley, Bridgitte 577
Hartley, Gregory 577
Hartley, Hal 577
Hartley, Keef 577
Hartley, Sue 577
Hartley, William J. 577
ハトリ
Khattry, Mohamed Kaber Ould 727
ハトリー
Hatry, Harry P. 581
ハドリ
Hadhri, Taieb 553
ハドリー
Hadley, Constance N. 553
Hadley, Jerry 553
Hadley, Robert 553
Hadley, Stephen J. 553
バートリー
Bartley, Mel 100
Bartley, Robert LeRoy 100
Bartley, William Warren, Ⅲ 100
バドリ
al-Badri, Abdulsalam 78
バドリー
Baddeley, Alan D. 78
パトリア
Patriat, François 1085
パトリアリス
Patrialis, Akbar 1085
パトリアルカ
Patriarca, Camilla 1085
パトリオタ
Patriota, Antonio 1085
バドリカ
Badrika, I Wayan 78
パトリケフ
Patrikeev, Yuri 1085
パトリコフ
Patricof, Alan J. 1085
パトリシア
Patricia, Matt 1085
バドリス
Budrys, Algis 199
パトリセリ
Patricelli, Leslie 1085
ハドリチコヴァー
Hrdlickova, Venceslava 629
パトリック
Patric 1085
Patrick, Bethanne Kelly 1085
Patrick, Christopher J. 1085
Patrick, Danica 1085
Patrick, Graham L. 1085

Patrick, Hugh T. 1085
Patrick, John 1085
Patrick, Lucas 1085
Patrick, Natalie 1085
Patrick, Ronald 1085
Patrick, William 1085
Patrick, William B. 1085
パートリッジ
Partridge, Andy 1083
Partridge, Christopher Hugh 1083
Partridge, James 1083
パトリッシ
Patrissi, JAC 1085
パドリノ・ロペス
Padrino López, Vladimir 1069
ハドリン
Hudlin, Reginald 631
バートリング
Bertling, Thomas 131
ハートル
Hartl, Daniel L. 577
Hartl, Franz-Ulrich 577
Hartle, James B. 577
ハードル
Hurdle, Clint 637
ハドル
Huddle, David 631
Huddle, Molly 631
Huddle, Norie 631
バートル
Bartl, Reiner 100
Bartol, Anne M. 100
Bartol, Curt R. 100
バトル
Battle, Eric 105
Battle, Isaiah 105
Battle, Lucius Durham 105
Battle, Rebecca 105
Buttel, Frederick H. 209
Buttle, Jeffrey 209
バドル
Badr, Ahmed 78
Badr, al-Sherif Ahmed Omar 78
Badr, bin Saud al-Busaidi 78
Badr, Hisham Mohamed Mostafa 78
Badr, Yárub Sulayman 78
パトルシェフ
Patrushev, Nikolai P. 1085
バトルズ
Battles, Brett 105
Battles, Matthew 105
ハドルストーン
Huddlestone, Tom 631
ハドルストン
Huddleston, Jack 631
バートルディ
Bertoldi, Concetta 132
バドルディヌ
Badreddine, Delphine 78
バドルディン
Badreddine, Mustafa 78
バトルフ
Buttolph, Angela 209
ハートレー
Hartley, Celia Love 577
ハドレー
Hadley, Eleanor M. 553
Hadley, Stephen J. 553
バートレー
Bartley, Robert LeRoy 100
バドレー
Baddeley, Gavin 78
バドレイシン
Badrising, Niermala 78
バドレイフ
Vadlejch, Jakub 1437
バトレス
Batres, Mireya 104
Batres, Yolany 104
バートレッタ
Bartoletta, Tianna 100
バートレッティ
Bartoletti, Susan Campbell 100
バートレット
Bartlett, Alan 100
Bartlett, Alex 100
Bartlett, Alison 100
Bartlett, Allison Hoover 100
Bartlett, Atlanta 100
Bartlett, Christopher A. 100
Bartlett, Edmund 100
Bartlett, Jamie 100
Bartlett, Jane 100
Bartlett, John G. 100
Bartlett, Richard 100
Bartlett, Robert 100
Bartlett, Sarah 100
Bertolet, Taylor 132
パードロ
Pardlo, Gregory 1077
パドロー
Padró, Santi 1069
バートロメ
Bartolomé, Fernando 100
パトロン
Patron, Susan 1085
パドロン
Padrón, Justo-Jorge 1069
パトワ
Patwa, Sunder Lal 1086
バードワジ
Bhardwaj, Mohini 135
バトワース
Butterworth, Nick 209
バドワース
Budworth, Geoffrey 199
ハードン
Hardon, Anita 570
ハトン
Hutton, Betty 639
ハドン
Haddon, Chris 552
バートン
Barton, Beverly 100
Barton, Byron 100
Barton, Cheryl Johnson 100
Barton, Dominic 100
Barton, Doyle Rayburn, Jr. 100
Barton, Jill 100
Barton, John 100
Barton, John Bernard Adie 100
Barton, Karim 100
Barton, Keith C. 100
Barton, Len 100
Barton, Michael 100
Barton, Nicholas H. 100
Barton, Patrice 100
Barton, Susan 100
Barton, Suzanne 100
Barton, Tamsyn 100
Barton, Thomas L. 100
Barton, Will 100
Barton, William A. 100
Burton, Anthony 206
Burton, Anwar "Flii" 206
Burton, Brian 206
Burton, Christopher 206
Burton, Dennis R. 206
Burton, Euan 206
Burton, Gary 206
Burton, Jaci 206
Burton, James 206
Burton, Jessie 206
Burton, Joan 206
Burton, Jonathan 206
Burton, Jordan 206
Burton, Linda 206
Burton, Mark 206
Burton, Mary 206
Burton, Michael 206
Burton, Michael E. 206
Burton, Neel L. 206
Burton, Olive 206
Burton, Robert 206
Burton, Robert Alan 206
Burton, Robert Earl 206
Burton, Sandra 206
Burton, Sarah 206
Burton, Tim 206
Burton, Tom 206
Burton, Trey 206
Burton, Valorie 207
Burton, Willie D. 207
Verton, Dan 1454
バードン
Bahdon, Ali Hassan 80
バトン
Batten, John D. 105
Batton, Philippe 105
Button, Diane 209
Button, Gregory V. 209
Button, Jenson 209
Button, John 209
Button, Malk 209
パートン
Parton, Allen 1083
Parton, Dolly 1083
Parton, Sandra 1083
Purton, Campbell 1140
パドン
Padden, Carol 1068
バートン＝ジョーンズ
Burton-Jones, Alan 207
バトンズ
Buttons, Red 209
ハナ
Hanna, Heidi 566
Hanna, Roland 566
Hanna, William Denby 566
Hannah, Gail Greet 566
Hannah, Kristin 566
Hannah, Sophie 566
ハナー
Hannah, Daryl 566
バーナ
Barna, George 95
バーナー
Barner, Kenjon 95
Varner, Jacob Stephen 1447
Verner, Alterraun 1453
バナー
Banner, Sarah Louise 90
パーナー
Perner, Josef 1099
パナ
Pana, Gisèle 1074
パナイー
Panayi, Panikos 1074
ハナイアリイ
Hanaialii, Amy 565
パナイオトゥ
Panayioutou, Andreas 1074
ハナウ
Hanau, Peter 565
バーナウ
Barnouw, Erik 96
ハナウェイ
Hannaway, Jane 566
バナガス
Vanagas, Povilas 1441
ハナーコバー
Hanáková, Alena 565
バナージ
Banaji, Mahzarin R. 88
バナジ
Banaji, Mahzarin R. 88
バナジー
Banerjea, Subrata Kumar 89
Banerjee, Abhijit V. 89
Banerjee, Mamata 89
Banerji, Prasanta 89
Banerji, Pratip 89
バナス
Vanas, D.J. 1441
パナス
Panas, Jerold 1074
バーナーズ・リー
Berners-Lee, Tim 129
バーナーズリー
Berners-Lee, Tim 129
バーナーダ
Bernarda, Greg 129
パナダ
Panadda, Diskul 1074
バナタオ
Banatao, Dado P. 88
ハーナッキー
Hernacki, Michael C. 598
バナック
Banach, Daniel T. 88
バーナット
Barnatt, Christopher 95
ハナティ
Hanati, Silamu 565
バーナディン
Bernadine, Franca 128
バーナデュー
Bernadeau, Mackenzy 128
バーナード
Barnard, Alan 95
Barnard, Aneurin 95
Barnard, Christiaan Neethling 95
Barnard, Julian 95
Barnard, Lucy 95
Barnard, Malcolm 95
Barnard, Martine 95
Barnard, Robert 95
Bernard, Ali 129
Bernard, André 129
Bernard, Bill 129
Bernard, Bruno 129

Bernard, Carlos 129
Bernard, Cheryl 129
Bernard, Giovani 129
Bernard, Hannah 129
Bernard, Sheila Curran 129
Bernard, Susan 129
Bernard, Victor L. 129
Bernhard, Durga 129
Bernhard, Emery 129
Burnard, Lou 204
バナート
Bannert, Valerie 90
バナナ
Banana, Canaan Sodindo 88
バーナネン
Paananen, Ilkka 1067
バーナビー
Barnaby, Brenda 95
Barnaby, Wendy 95
パナヒ
Panahi, Jafar 1074
ハナフ
Khanafou, Abdallah 726
バーナーブ
Bernabe, David 128
ハナフィ
Hanafi, Khaled 565
パナフィユー
Panafieu, Jean-Baptiste de 1074
ハナフィン
Hanafin, Mary 565
Hannafin, Michael J. 566
パナフュー
Panafieu, Jean-Baptiste de 1074
パナマ
Panama, Norman 1074
バナーマン
Bannerman, Cecilia 90
Bannerman, James 90
バナミュエレバリエネ
Banamuhere Baliene, Salomon 88
バーナム
Barnum, Carol M. 96
Burnham, Chris 205
Burnham, David H. 205
Burnham, Erick 205
Burnham, I.W. 205
Burnham, June 205
Burnham, Kevin 205
Burnham, Nicole 205
Burnham, Robert 205
Burnham, Terry 205
バナムヘレ
Banamuhere Baliene, Salomon 88
パナヨトフ
Panayotov, Plamen 1074
パナヨトプル
Panayotopoulou, Penny 1074
パナヨトプロス
Panagiotopoulos, Panagiotis 1074
Panayiotopoulos, Panos 1074
パナラ・シリブット
Panara Sereyvuth, Sisovath 1074
パナリッティ
Panariti, Franco 1074
パナリティ
Panariti, Edmond 1074
パナリナ
Panarina, Olga 1074
バーナル
Bernall, Misty 129
バナール
Bernal, Martin 129
パーナル
Parnall, Peter 1081
バーナンキ
Bernanke, Ben S. 129
ハーニー
Harney, Alexandra 572
Harney, Mary 572
Harney, Michael 572
ハニー
Haney, Anne 566
Honey, John 620
バーニー
Barney, Darwin 96
Barney, Jay B. 96
Barney, Matthew 96
Barney, Tarow 96
Berney, Charlotte 129
Berney, Lou 129
Birney, Betty 141
Birnie, Patricia W. 141
Burney, Ian 205
Burnie, David 205
Verny, Thomas R. 1453
バニ
Bani, Arno 89
Bani, John 89
バニー
Banny, Charles 90
バーニアー
Bernier, Doug 129
パーニア
Parnia, Sam 1081
パニアグア
Paniagua, Valentín 1075
パニアグア・コラサオ
Paniagua Corazao, Valentín 1075
バニアード
Banyard, Philip 90
バニアン
Bunyan, Vashti 202
バーニィ
Birney, Betty 141
バニエ
Banier, François-marie 89
Vanier, Jean 1444
バニエー
Vanier, Melanie K. 1444
バニェス・ガルシア
Báñez García, María Fátima 89
バニエッテマード
Banietemad, Rakhshan 89
バニオニス
Banionis, Donatas 89
ハニガー
Hanin, Roger 566
ハニーカット
Honeycutt, Brad 620
ハニカット
Honeycutt, Jerry 620
Honeycutt, Kris 620
Honeycutt, Rick 620
ハニガン
Hanigan, Ryan 566
Hannigan, Ben 567
Hannigan, John A. 567
ハニグ
Hanig, Robert 566
バーニコウ
Bernikow, Louise 129
ハーニシュ
Harnish, Verne 572
バニスター
Banister, Jeff 89
Banister, Peter 89
Bannister, Brian 90
Bannister, Desmond 90
Bannister, Jarrod 90
Bannister, Jo 90
バニステンダール
Vanistendael, Judith 1444
バニスロバート
Bannis-roberts, Loreen 90
パニチェリ
Panichelli, Stéphanie 1075
バニチョイユ
Bănicioiu, Nicolae 89
パニツァ
Panizza, Oskar 1075
パーニック
Pernick, Ron 1099
パニック
Panik, Joe 1075
バーニッジ
Barnidge, Gary 96
ハーニッシュ
Hanisch, Ernst 566
Harnish, Verne 572
パニッチ
Panitch, Leo 1075
Panych, Morris 1075
ハニティ
Hannity, Sean 567
ハニフ
Hanif, Dhakiri 566
ハニーマン
Honeyman, George 620
ハニヤ
Haniya, Ismail 566
バニヤ
Banya, Sama S. 90
パーニャ
Pernia, Ernesto 1099
バニャレロ
Bagnarello, Erika 80
バニャン
Bagnan, Kémoko 80
バニュエロス
Banuelos, Manny 90
パニョッタ
Pagnotta, Antonio 1070
パニョーニ
Pagnoni, Roberta 1070
ハニン
Janín, Mikel 663
バーニンガム
Burningham, John 205
ハニング
Hanning, M. 567
バーニング
Berning, Jacqueline R. 129
バニンク
Bannink, Fredrike 90
バニング
Bunning, Jim 201
Bunning, Joan 201
ハニングトン
Hannington, Terry 567
ハニントン
Hanington, Bruce 566
パヌ
Panou, Themis 1075
パヌー
Panou, Koffi 1075
ハヌシェク
Hanuschek, Sven 568
ハーヌスタイン・スミス
Herrnstein Smith, Barbara 599
パヌラ
Panula, Jorma 1075
ハヌーン
Hanoune, Louisa 567
パネ
Panné, Jean-Louis 1075
ハネイ
Hannay, Barbara 567
バーネヴィク
Barnevik, Percy Nils 96
バネガ
Banega, Ever 89
パネク
Panek, Richard 1074
ハネグビ
Hanegbi, Tzachi 566
ハネグラフ
Hanegraaff, Hank 566
ハーネケ
Haneke, Michael 566
ハネケ
Haneke, Michael 566
ハネコム
Hanekom, Derek 566
ハーネス
Haanaes, Knut 551
パーネス
Parness, Michael 1081
ハーネッカー
Harnecker, Marta 572
バネッサ・メイ
Vanessa-Mae 1443
パネッタ
Panetta, Leon Edward 1074
パネッティーア
Panettiere, Hayden 1074
バーネット
Barnet, Sylvan 95
Barnett, Arthur G. 95
Barnett, Bill 95
Barnett, Cynthia 95
Barnett, Donald M. 96
Barnett, Jill 96
Barnett, Josh 96
Barnett, Kristine 96
Barnett, Mac 96
Barnett, Peter B. 96
Barnett, Richard 96
Barnett, R.Michael 96
Barnett, Sloan 96
Barnett, Steven 96
Barnett, Thomas P.M. 96
Barnett, Vincent 96
Barnette, Tony 96
Barnett-hinchley, Tamsin 96
Burnett, A.J. 204
Burnett, Alyce 204
Burnett, Bill 204
Burnett, Daniel C. 204

Burnett, D.Graham 204
Burnett, Jason 204
Burnett, Lindy 204
Burnett, Mark 204
Burnett, Morgan 204
Burnett, Peter 204
Burnett, Sean 204
Burnett, Simon 204
Burnett, Stephen 204
Burnett, T Bone 204
Burnette, Ed 205
バネット
Burnett, Richard T. 204
Vannett, Nick 1444
パーネット
Pernetta, John 1099
パネッラ
Pannella, Marco 1075
バネハム
Baneham, Richard 89
パーネビアンコ
Panebianco, Angelo 1074
バーネビク
Barnevik, Percy Nils 96
バーネビック
Barnevik, Percy Nils 96
ハーネボル
Hanevold, Halvard 566
パネラ
Panella, Vince 1074
バネリ
Vanelli, Federico 1443
バネリック
Vanourek, Gregg 1445
バーネル
Burnell, Cerrie 204
Burnell, Jack 204
Burnell, Mark 204
パーネル
Parnell, Bobby 1081
Parnell, Jermey 1081
Parnell, Mel 1081
Parnell, Peter 1081
Pournelle, Jerry E. 1129
Purnell, James 1140
バーネルソン
Wörnersson, Ingegerd 1526
パネンベルク
Pannenberg, Wolfhart Ulrich 1075
バノ
Bano, Arsenio 90
ハーノイ
Harnoy, Ofra 572
バーノウィン
Barnouin, Kim 96
バーノタス
Bernotas, Eric 130
ハノフ
Khanov, Nodirkhon 726
バーノフ
Bernoff, Josh 130
パノフ
Panoff, Michel 1075
Panov, Aleksandr Nikolaevich 1075
パノフスキー
Panofsky, Dora 1075
Panofsky, Wolfgang 1075
Panofsky, Wolfgang K. H. 1075
ハノーマンジー
Hanoomanjee, Santi Bai 567
ハーノン
Hernon, Peter 599
ハノン
Hannon, Frances 567
Hannon, Gregory J. 567
バーノン
Vernon, Michelle 1453
Vernon, Olivier 1453
Vernon, Sue 1453
バノン
Bannon, John A. 90
ハーバー
Haber, Eitan 551
Haber, Ludwig Fritz 551
Haber, Tino 551
Harbaugh, Karen 569
Harbor, Clay 569
Harbour, Elizabeth 569
Harbour, Ivan 569
Herber, Keith 596
ハーパー
Harper, Ben 572
Harper, Bryce 572
Harper, Chandler 572
Harper, Charise Mericle 572
Harper, Chris 572
Harper, Damian 572
Harper, Dawn 572
Harper, Elizabeth 572
Harper, Fiona 572
Harper, Harold Anthony 572
Harper, Jessica 572
Harper, Jo 572
Harper, John 572
Harper, John Lander 572
Harper, Karen 572
Harper, Kenn 572
Harper, Laureen 572
Harper, Peter S. 572
Harper, Piers 572
Harper, Richard H.R. 573
Harper, Roman 573
Harper, Ruth E. 573
Harper, Stephen 573
Harper, Steve 573
Harper, Timothy 573
Harpur, James 573
Harpur, Tom 573
バーバ
Barba, Rick 91
Bhabha, Homi K. 135
バーバー
Barber, Anthony 92
Barber, Antonia 92
Barber, Barrington 92
Barber, Benjamin R. 92
Barber, Dan 92
Barber, Jared 92
Barber, John 92
Barber, Lizzie 92
Barber, Luke 92
Barber, Nicholas 92
Barber, Nicola 92
Barber, Paul 92
Barber, Peyton 92
Barber, Shawnacy 92
Barber, Theodore Xenophon 92
Barber, Tom 92
Barber, William J. 92
Barbir, Frano 92
Barbour, Ian G. 92
Barbour, Ian Graeme 92
Barbour, Karen 92
Barbour, Nancy E. 92
ババ
Baha, Abdelilah 80
ババ
Baba, Abdul Rahman 76
Baba, Frank S. 76
Baba, Hamadou 76
Baba, Immanuel 76
Baba, Jaroslav 76
Vava 1448
馬場
Baba, Frank S. 76
バハアディン
Baha El-din, Muhammad 80
ババアハメド
Baba Ahmed, Abdelatif 76
ババ・アミ
Baba Ami, Hadji 76
ババ・アムテ
Amte, Murlidhar Devidas 42
パパイオアンヌ
Papaioannou, Virginia E. 1076
バハウィ
Bahawi, Nesar Ahmad 80
パパ・ウェンバ
Papa Wemba 1076
パパウェンバ
Papa Wemba 1076
パパヴラミ
Papavrami, Tedi 1076
ババエフ
Babayev, Heydar 76
ババエワ
Babaeva, Aynabat 76
バーバー・オブ・ウエントブリッジ
Lord Barber of Wentbridge 92
ババカル
Babacar, Khouma 76
ババキル
Babakir, Kheer 76
パパコスタス
Papacostas, Costas 1075
パパコンスタンティヌ
Papaconstantinou, Georgios 1075
パパサナシウ
Papathanasiou, Aimilios 1076
Papathanasiou, Joannis 1076
パパサナシュ
Vangelis 1443
パパザン
Papasan, Jay 1076
パパジアン
Papazian, Charlie 1076
ババジャン
Babacan, Ali 76
ババジャンザデ
Babajanzadeh Darzi, Bashir Asgari 76
ハバシュ
Habash, George 551
Habbash, Mahmoud 551
ハバシュネ
Habashneh, Samir 551
ハーバス
Harbus, Robert 569
パパス
Papas, Nikos 1076
Pappas, Chris H. 1076
Pappas, Theoni 1076
パパスタソプーロス
Papastathopoulos, Sokratis 1076
パパゾグル
Papazoglou, Evangelia 1076
ハーバーソン
Halvorson, Michael 560
パパダキス
Papadakis, Maxine A. 1075
パパダトス
Papadatos, Alecos 1075
バーバチー
Barbaccia, Lynda 91
ハーバーツ
Harberts, Aaron 569
ハーバック
Harbach, Chad 569
ハーバット
Harbutt, Juliet 569
パパディミトリウ
Papadimitriou, Christos H. 1076
Papadimitriou, Demetrio 1076
Paradimitriu, Dimitris 1077
パパディメトリュー
Papademetriou, Lisa 1075
パパディモス
Papademos, Lucas Demetrios 1076
バハティルクウェボ
Bahati Lukwebo, Modeste 80
パパデメトリュー
Papademetriou, Lisa 1075
パパデモス
Papademos, Lucas Demetrios 1076
バハデリ
al-Bahadeli, Ali 80
ハーバート
Herbert, Anne 596
Herbert, Brian 597
Herbert, Christian 597
Herbert, Cicely 597
Herbert, David T. 597
Herbert, James 597
Herbert, James D. 597
Herbert, Martha R. 597
Herbert, Martin 597
Herbert, Nick 597
Herbert, Rupert 597
Herbert, Trevor 597
Herbert, Wally 597
Herbert, Wray 597
ハーバード
Harberd, Nicholas 569
Herbert, Jake 597
ハバート
Hébert, Fred 587
ハバード
Habbard, Sherry K. 551
Hubbard, Barbara Burke 630
Hubbard, Barbara Marx 630
Hubbard, Chris 630
Hubbard, David 630

ハ

Hubbard, Freddie 630
Hubbard, Gill 630
Hubbard, Glenn 630
Hubbard, Kate 631
Hubbard, Kenneth 631
Hubbard, Nancy 631
Hubbard, R.Glenn 631
Hubbard, Thomas 631
ハパート
Huppert, Jonathan D. 637
バーバト
Barbato, Johnny 92
パハド
Pahad, Essop 1070
パパート
Papert, Seymour 1076
バハドゥール
Bahadur, Khadga 80
ハーバート＝チェザリー
Herbert-Caesari, Edgar F. 597
パパドプーロス
Papadopoulos, Kyriakos 1076
パパドプロス
Papadopoulos, Alekos 1076
Papadopoulos, Tassos 1076
ババトンデ
Babatounde, Jean-Pierre 76
ハバナ
Habana, Bryan 551
ババナ
Babana, Abdellahi Ould 76
Babana, Cheikh El Moctar Ould Horma Ould 76
ババ・ナカオ
Baba Nakao, Luis 76
ハーパニエミ
Haapaniemi, Klaus 551
パパニコラウ
Papanikolaou, Nikos A. 1076
パパーネック
Papanek, Ernst 1076
Papanek, Helene 1076
バーバネル
Barbanell, Maurice 91
Barbanell, Sylvia 91
パパーノ
Pappano, Marilyn 1076
ババノフ
Babanov, Omurbek 76
バハーハ
Bahah, Khaled Mahfoudh 80
パパバシロプル
Pappa-papavasilopoulou, Eftihia 1076
パパパブル
Papapavlou, Cleopatra Helen Claire 1076
パパーブオリ
Vapaavuori, Jan 1446
パパフリストゥ
Papahristou, Paraskevi 1076
バハベ
Bahawi, Nesar Ahmad 80
パパーボリ
Vapaavuori, Jan 1446
ハーバーマス
Habermas, Jürgen 551
ハーバマス
Habermas, Jürgen 551
ハーパム
Herpham, Geoffrey Galt 599
バハム
Baham, Messaouda Mint 80
パーハム
Parham, A.Philip 1078
バハムウィティ・ムケシャイラ
Vahamwiti Mukesyayira, Jean-Chrisostome 1438
ババムサ
Baba-moussa, Ramatou 76
バハムダン
Bahamdan, Kamal 80
ババムラトワ
Babamuratova, Gulbadam 76
ハバムレミ
Habumuremyi, Pierre Damien 552
ハバメンシ
Habamenshi, Patrick 551
バハモンデ
Bahamonde, Francisco Mba Olo 80
パパヤニス
Papagiannis, Georgios 1076
パパヨアヌ
Papaioannou, Miltiades 1076
バーバラ
Barbara, Agatha 92
Barber, Christine 92
Barbera, Robert J. 92
バーバリー
Barbaree, Howard 92
パハリア
Paharia, Rajat 1070
パパリグーラス
Papaligouras, Anastasis 1076
パパリグラス
Papaligouras, Anastasis 1076
パハリナ
Pakhalina, Julia 1071
ババル
Babar, Lalita Shivaji 76
Vaval, Jean-Robert 1448
パバル
Paval, Ana 1088
パバルキス
Pavalkis, Dainius 1088
ハバルギラ
Habarugira, Tharcisse 551
バハルナ
Baharna, Nizar 80
パハーレス
Pajares, Santiago 1071
パバロッティ
Pavarotti, Luciano 1088
ババロラ
Babalola, Aderemi 76
Babalola, Rilwan 76
パパローン
Paparone, Pamela 1076
バーハン
Bahan, Benjamin J. 80
ババン
Baban, Ali 76
Babin, Jean-Christophe 76
Babin, Jean-Sylvain 76
パバン
Pavan, Sarah 1088
バーバンク
Burbank, Patricia M. 202
Burbank, Ross 202
パパントニウ
Papantoniou, Yiannos 1076
パパンドレウ
Papandreou, Georgios A. 1076
Papandreou, Giōrgos A. 1076
Papandreou, Vasso 1076
ハービー
Harvey, Eleanor 578
Harvey, Matt 578
Harvey, Michael 578
Harvie, Michelle 578
バビ
Baby, Mahamane 76
バビー
Babbie, Earl R. 76
パピー
Puppy, Rain Forest 1140
Puppy, Snarky 1140
バービア
Barbier, Edward B. 92
パビア
Pavia, Automne 1088
パピアー
Papier, Hans-Jürgen 1076
バビアク
Babiak, Paul 76
バビアック
Babiuk, Andy 76
ハビ・アラモ
Javi Alamo 666
パピエフ
Papiev, Mykhailo 1076
Papiyev, Mykhaylo 1076
バービエリー
Barbieri, Elaine 92
ハビエル
Xavier, Anthony 1531
ハビエル・フラーニョ
Javier Flano 666
ハビ・カステジャーノ
Javi Castellano 666
バービーク
Verbeek, Tonya Lynn 1452
バビコフ
Babikov, Ivan 76
バービジ
Burbidge, Eleanor Margaret Peachey 202
バビシュ
Babiš, Andrej 76
パービス
Purvis, Christopher 1140
ハービソン
Harbison, Elizabeth 569
Harbison, Samuel P., Ⅲ 569
バビタ
Babita, Kumari 76
パビチ
Pavić, Milorad 1088
ハービック
Herbig, George Howard 597
バービック
Berbick, Trevor 125
ハービッコ
Haavikko, Paavo Juhani 551
バービッジ
Burbidge, Eleanor Margaret Peachey 202
Burbidge, Geoffrey 202
Burbidge, John B. 202
バビッチ
Babić, Milan 76
Babicz, Lionel 76
パビッチ
Pavich, Frank 1088
バビット
Babbitt, Luke 76
Babbitt, Milton Byron 76
Babbitt, Natalie 76
パビット
Pavitt, K.L.R. 1088
バヒディ
Vahidi, Ahmad 1438
バヒート
Bakhit, Marouf 84
バヒト
Bakhit, Marouf 84
バヒドダストジェルディ
Vahid-dastjerdi, Marzieh 1438
パピナシビリ
Papinashvili, Amiran 1076
パピーニ
Papini, Mauricio R. 1076
ハビネザ
Habineza, Joseph 551
バビノー
Babineaux, Jonathan 76
Babineaux, Ryan 76
ハビ・バラス
Javi Varas 667
ハビビ
Habibi, Hassan Ibrahim 551
Habibie, Bachruddin Jusuf 551
ハビーブ
Habeeb, Mocky 551
Habib, Fatma 551
ハビブ
Habib, Ali 551
ハビ・フエゴ
Javi Fuego 666
ハビ・マルケス
Javi Marquez 666
ハビ・マルティネス
Javi Martinez 666
パヒミ
Pahimi, Kalzeube 1070
パヒミパダッケ
Pahimi Padacke, Albert 1070
バーヒヤ
Bahia, Ahmed Ould 80
ハビャリマナ
Habyarimana, Emmanuel 552
パピョー
Papillault, Anne 1076
バーピラー
Varpilah, Tornolah 1447

ハ

バヒリ
Bhiri, Noureddine 135
ハビ・ロペス
Javi Lopez 666
ハービン
Harbin, Thomas J. 569
バビン
Babbin, Jed L. 76
Babin, Charles E. 76
パヒン・イラオラ
Pajín Iraola, Leire 1071
バービンスキー
Verbinski, Gore 1452
ハービンソン
Harbinson, Patrick 569
バビントン
Babington, Kevin 76
ハーフ
Herf, Jeffrey 597
ハーブ
Herb, Erika 596
ハフ
Hough, Richard Alexander 625
Huff, Josh 632
Huff, Justin 632
Huff, Marqueston 632
Huff, P.J. 632
Huff, Tanya 632
Huff, William S. 632
バフ
Buff, Joe 199
バブ
Babou, Abdoulaye 76
バブー
Baboo, Santaram 76
バプー
Bappou, Sheilabai 90
パーブ
Purves, Ian 1140
パプ
Papp, Mark 1076
バーファキーフ
Bafaqef, Alawi 79
パプアシビリ
Papuashvili, Georgi 1077
バファルコス
Bafaloukos, Ted 79
バーフィクト
Burfict, Vontaze 203
ハフィズ
al-Hafidh, Mahdi 553
パーフィット
Parfit, Derek 1078
Parfitt, Adam 1078
バーフィールド
Barfield, Thomas Jefferson 93
ハフィントン
Heffington, Ryan 588
Huffington, Arianna 632
パプウォース
Papworth, Michael 1077
ハーフェイカー
Halfacree, Gareth 557
ハーフェズ
Hafez, Suleiman 553
Hafiz, Amin 553
ハフェズ
Hafez, Suleiman 553
Hafez, Wael 553
Hafiz, Amin 553
バフェット
Buffet, Warren Edward 199
Buffett, Astrid 199
Buffett, Jimmy 199
Buffett, Mary 199
ハーフェナー
Havener, Thorsten 583
ハーフェル
Havel, Václav 583
ハーブオオタ
Ohta, Herb 1047
ハーフォート
Herford, Oliver 597
ハーフォード
Harford, David K. 571
Harford, Tim 571
Hurford, James R. 637
Hurford, William E. 637
バーフォード
Barfoed, Lars 93
Barford, Anna 93
Burford, Pamela 203
バフォン
Buffone, Gary W. 199
ハプカ
Hapka, Cathy 568
ハブカイネン
Havukainen, Aino 583
バブギンユンビラ
Bamvuginyumvira, Frederic 88
バブク
Babuc, Monica 76
パプク
Papuc, Gheorghe 1077
ハフケ
Haffke, Bernhard 553
バブコック
Babcock, Dorothy E. 76
Babcock, Linda 76
ハブサデ
Habsade, Mohamed Ibrahim Mohamed 551
ハーフーシュ
Harfoush, Rahaf 571
ハブズ
Hobbs, Valerie 611
ハフステトラー
Huffstertler, Lynn M. 632
ハーブスト
Herbst, Judith 597
パプスト
Pabst, Reinhard 1067
ハプスブルク
Habsburg-Lothringen, Otto von 552
ハプスブルク・ロートリンゲン
Habsburg-Lothringen, Otto von 552
バフチェリ
Bahceli, Devlet 80
パプチス
Papoutsis, Christos 1076
パプツィス
Papoutsis, Christos 1076
バフデ
Bahude, Marcel 80
ハプティー
Haptie, Charlotte 568
パプーディ
Papoudi, Despina 1076
バフティアリ
Bakhtiari, Seyed Morteza 84
Bakhtiari, Soraya Esfandiari 84
バプティスト
Baptiste, Alva 90
Baptiste, Hilson 90
Baptiste, Kelly-Ann 90
Baptiste, Moses 90
バプティストコーネリス
Baptiste-cornelis, Therese 90
バプティストプリマス
Baptiste-primus, Jennifer 90
ハプトマン
Hauptman, Andrej 582
ハフナー
Haffner, Herbert 553
Hafner, Katie 553
ハプナー
Hapner, Mark 568
ハフナゲル
Hufnagel, Lucas 632
バブナニ
Bhavnani, Vin 135
ハフバウアー
Hufbauer, Gary Clyde 632
ハーフペニー
Halfpenny, Jill 557
Halfpenny, Leigh 557
ハフマン
Huffman, Arthur 632
Huffman, Felicity 632
Huffman, Yale 632
バフマンヤール
Bahmanyar, Mir 80
バブラ
Vavra, Joe 1448
パブライ
Pabrai, Mohnish 1067
パブラク
Pawlak, Waldemar 1088
バーブリー
Barbre, Allen 92
パブリアシビリ
Pavliashvili, Solomon 1088
パプリアス
Papoulias, Karolos 1076
パブリクス
Pabriks, Artis 1067
パブリーシン
Pavlishin, G. 1088
パブリス
Pavlis, Pavol 1088
パブリセヴィッチ
Pavlicevic, Zeliko 1088
パブリセビッチ
Pavlicevic, Zeliko 1088
パブリチェヴィック
Pavlicevic, Mercédès 1088
パブリチェンコ
Pavlichenko, Semen 1088
パブリチッチ
Pavličić, Miodrag 1088
バーブリッジ
Burbridge, Aaron 202
パブリディス
Pavlidis, Aristotelis 1088
Pavlidis, Elias 1088
パブリデス
Pavlides, Merope 1088
ハーブリーブス
Hargreaves, Vernon 571
パブリャチェンコ
Pavlyatenko, Victor 1088
パブリャテンコ
Pavlyatenko, Victor 1088
パブリュチェンコワ
Pavlyuchenkova, Anastasia 1088
パブリュツ
Pavluts, Daniels 1088
ハブリュツェル
Habluetzel, David 551
バブリンカ
Wawrinka, Stan 1483
ハブル
Hubble, Mark A. 631
ハブルザニヤ
Khaburzaniya, Valery 724
バフルーシン
Bakhrushin, S.V. 84
ハブレ
Habré, Hissène 551
バフレダツルシ
Bachleda-curus, Katarzyna 77
ハープレヒト
Harpprecht, Klaus 573
パブレンコ
Pavlenko, Oleksii 1088
Pavlenko, Yuriy 1088
パブロ・エルナンデス
Pablo Hernandez 1067
パプロッタ
Paprotta, Astrid 1077
パブロバ
Pavlova, Lilyana 1088
パブロフ
Pavlov, Aleksandr 1088
Pavlov, Igor 1088
Pavlov, Valentin S. 1088
パブロ・フェルナンデス
Pablo Fernandez 1067
パブロフスキー
Pavlovsky, Bruno 1088
パブロプロス
Pavlopoulos, Prokopios 1088
バブロヤン
Babloian, R. 76
パブロワ
Pavlova, Anna 1088
バブン
Babún, Roberto 76
ハーベ
Hirbe, Angela 609
バーヘ
Berhe, Nat 127
パーペ
Pape, René 1076
Pape, Ulf 1076
パヘ
Paje, Ramon 1071
パペ
Pape, Baptist de 1076
Pape, Lygia 1076
Pape, Pascal 1076
Pappé, Ilan 1076
バヘーア
Bachér, Peter 77
ハーベイ
Harvey, Abner

McGehee 578
Harvey, Alison Phinney 578
Harvey, Charles 578
Harvey, David 578
Harvey, Derek 578
Harvey, Jonathan Dear 578
Harvey, Michael 578
Harvey, Miles 578
Harvey, Steve 578
Harvey, Wilson 578
Havey, Michael 583
Hervey, Cheston 600

バーヘイゲン
Verhagen, Drew 1452

バベシ
Bavasi, Buzzie 107

パペ・シェイク
Pape Cheikh 1076

パヘス
Pagés, Maria 1069

バベストック
Baveystock, Sacha 107

ハベック
Habeck, Fritz 551
Habeck, Reinhard 551

パベッツァ
Paveza, Gregory J. 1088

パベディンスキエネ
Pabedinskienė, Algimanta 1067

バペバペ
Bapès Bapès, Louis 90

ハベラー
Haberer, Janik 551

バーベラ
Barbera, Joseph 92

パーベリー
Parberry, Ian 1077

バーベリ・アナヤ
Barbery Anaya, Roberto 92

ハベル
Havel, Václav 583
Hubbell, Sue 631

ハペル
Happell, Charles 568

バヘル
Vaher, Ken-Marti 1438

バベルスバーグ・スタジオ
Babelsberg, Studio 76

パペルボン
Papelbon, Jonathan 1076

バベレル
Baverel, Myriam 107

バベレルロベール
Baverel-robert, Florence 107

ハーヘン
Hagen, Hans 554
Hagen, Monique 554

バベンコ
Babenco, Héctor 76
Babenko, Dmitry 76
Babenko, Marina 76
Babenko, Vladimir 76

ハーペンディング
Harpending, Henry 572

ハーボ
Harbo, Christopher L. 569

ハーボー
Harbaugh, Jim 569
Harbaugh, John 569

バーボー
Barbeau, Jeffrey W. 92

バーポ
Burpo, Sonja 205
Burpo, Todd 205

バホウィ
Bahoui, Nabil 80

バホエ
Vahoe, Partrick 1438

バボーギーン・ルハグバスレン
Bavuugiin Lkhagvasüren 107

バーボザ
Barboza, David 92

バボシュ
Babos, Timea 76

バボータ
Babauta, Leo 76

パボーネ
Pavone, Chris 1088

バーホフ
Verhoef, Marcel 1452

パポフ
Papov, Vadim 1076

バーホーベン
Verhoeven, Paul 1452

バホボフ
Vakhobov, Alisher 1438

バボラーク
Baborák, Radek 76

バボラク
Baborák, Radek 76

パホル
Pahor, Borut 1070

バホルン
Bahorun, Theeshan 80

パポロス
Papolos, Demitri F. 1076
Papolos, Janice 1076

パホン
Pajón, Mariana 1071

パポン
Papon, Maurice 1076

パボンカッパ
Phabongkhapa, Je 1106

パボン・カルドソ
Pavón Cardozo, Antolín 1088

バボン・ヌサ・ムプトゥ・エリマ
Bavon N'sa Mputu Elima, Bavon 107

ハーマー
Hamer-Monod de Froideville, Marguerite 561
Harmer, Jeremy 572
Harmer, Wendy 572
Hirmer, Oswald 609

ハマ
Hama, Baba 560
Hammah, Mike 563
Hammer Jacobsen, Lotte 563
Hammer Jacobsen, Søren 563

ハマー
Hagmar, Lars 554
Hammar, M. 563
Hammer, Armie 563
Hammer, Bjarne 563
Hammer, Bonnie 563
Hammer, Marc 563
Hammer, Martin 563
Hammer, Michael 563
Hammer, Sarah 563
Hammer, William 563
Hanmer, Jalna 566

バーマ
Varmah, Eddington 1447

バーマー
Balmer, Nigel 87

パーマー
Palmer, Alan Warwick 1072
Palmer, Alex 1072
Palmer, Amanda 1072
Palmer, Andy 1072
Palmer, Ann 1072
Palmer, Arnold 1072
Palmer, Bartlett Joshua 1072
Palmer, Betsy 1072
Palmer, Brandon 1072
Palmer, Brooks 1072
Palmer, Carl 1073
Palmer, Carson 1073
Palmer, Craig 1073
Palmer, Diana 1073
Palmer, Douglas 1073
Palmer, Earl 1073
Palmer, Gabrielle 1073
Palmer, Helen 1073
Palmer, Hugh 1073
Palmer, Jessica 1073
Palmer, John D. 1073
Palmer, John Milton 1073
Palmer, Joy A. 1073
Palmer, Kelvin 1073
Palmer, Kylie 1073
Palmer, Libbi 1073
Palmer, Lindsey J. 1073
Palmer, Louis 1073
Palmer, Mark 1073
Palmer, Martin 1073
Palmer, Michael 1073
Palmer, Michel 1073
Palmer, Nate 1073
Palmer, Nathan 1073
Palmer, Parker J. 1073
Palmer, Robert 1073
Palmer, Robert L. 1073
Palmer, Sarah 1073
Palmer, Stephen 1073
Palmer, Steven Paul 1073
Palmer, Sue 1073
Palmer, Svetlana 1073
Palmer, Tom 1073
Palmer, Tony 1073
Palmer, William J. 1073

バマイン
Vamain, Carlos Joaquim 1441

ハマークヴィスト
Hammarqvist, Sten-Erik 563

バマクラマ
Bamakhrama, Rifki Abdoulkader 88

ハマサキ
Hamasaki, Kengo 561

ハマーシュミット
Hammerschmid, Sonja 563

ハマジョダ
Hamadjoda, Adjoudi 560

バーマス
Varmus, Harold Eliot 1447

ハマースタイン
Hammerstein, William 563

ハマダ
Hamada, Abdallah 560
Hamada, Nadhir 560

ハマック
Hammack, Floyd M. 563
Hammack, Justin 563

ハーマッハー
Hamacher, Werner 560

ハマーデ
Hmadeh, Marwan 610

ハマデ
Hamadeh, Trad 560
Hmadeh, Marwan 610

ハマディ
Hamadi, Hamadi Ould Baba Ould 560
Hamadi, Hassani 560
Hamady, Maty Mint 560
Hamady, Sania 560
al-Hammadi, Hussain bin Ibrahim 563
Hammadi, Sa'adoun 563

ハマデハ
Hmadeh, Marwan 610

ハマド
Hamad, Abdul-Rahman 560
Hamad, Amat al-Razaq Ali 560
Hamad, bin Faisal bin Thani al-Thani 560
Hamad, Jiloan 560
al-Hamad, Rashid Hamad Muhammad 560
Hamad, Sherif 560
Hamad, Yahiya Abdallah Mohamed 560
Hamad, Zakaria 560
al-Hammaad, Rashed Abdul Mohsen 563

ハマドゥ
Hamadou, Barkat Gourad 560
Hamadou, Djida 560
Hamadou, Yakoubou 560

ハマド・ビン・イーサー・アール・ハリーファ
Hamad bin Isa al-Khalifa 560

ハマド・ビン・イサ・アル・ハリファ
Hamad bin Isa al-Khalifa 560

ハマド・ビン・ジャーシム
Hamad bin Jassim al-Thani 560

ハマド・ビン・ジャシム・アル・サーニ
Hamad bin Jassim al-Thani 560

ハマド・ビン・ジャシム・ビン・ジャブル・サーニ
Hamad bin Jassim al-Thani 560

ハマド・ビン・ハリファ・アル・サーニ
Hamad bin Khalifa al-Thani 560

ハマド・ビン・ハリファ・サーニ
Hamad bin Khalifa al-Thani 560

ハマーバッカー
Hammerbacher, Jeff 563

ハマーマ

ハ

Hamama, Faten 560
ハママ
Hamama, Faten 560
ハマミ
al-Hamami, Kadhim 560
ハマーメッシュ
Hamermesh, Daniel S. 561
ハマモト
Hamamoto, Howard Hiromi 560
ハマラゼ
Khmaladze, Lasha 728
ハマル
al-Hamar, Bassem bin Yacoub 560
al-Hammer, Faysal 563
ハマレーザー
Hammaleser, Lisl 563
ハーマン
Haarmann, Claudia 551
Haarmann, Dirk 551
Hamann, Brigitte 560
Harman, Bob 571
Harman, Gilbert 571
Harman, Harriet 571
Harman, Jay 571
Harman, Nigel 571
Harman, Oren Solomon 572
Harman, Patricia 572
Harman, Sidney 572
Herman, Amy 597
Herman, Arthur 597
Herman, Barbara 597
Herman, David 597
Herman, Edward S. 597
Herman, Eleanor 597
Herman, Gail 597
Herman, Jerry 597
Herman, Joan 597
Herman, Richard 597
Herman, Ronna 597
Hermann, Iselin C. 597
Hermann, Valerie 597
Herrmann, Chris 599
Herrmann, Edward 599
ハマン
Haman, Adji Abdoulaye 560
Hamman, Shane 563
バーマン
Behrman, Andy 114
Behrman, Jack N. 114
Berman, Carol W. 128
Berman, Claire 128
Berman, Gail 128
Berman, Harold J. 128
Berman, Jennifer 128
Berman, Laura 128
Berman, Laurence 128
Berman, Lisa 128
Berman, Peter A. 128
Berman, Shari J. 128
Berman, Ted 128
Briman, Joan S. 182
Burman, Barney 204
Burman, Ben Lucien 204
Burman, Erica 204
パーマン
Perman, Finley 1099
Perman, Stacy 1099
バマンイルエ
Bamanyirue, Boji Sangara 88
ハーマンス
Hermans, H.J.M. 598
ハーマンセン
Hermansen, Søren 598
ハーマンソン
Hermansson, Gary L. 598
ハーマン・ダン
Herman-Dunn, Ruth 597
パミー
Pammi, Tara 1074
ハミアニ
Hamiani, Réda 561
ハミス
Khamis, Ali Khamis 725
Khamis, bin Mubarak al-Alawi 725
Khamis, Imad Muhammad Deeb 725
ハミタッシュ
Hamitouche, Kamel 562
ハミッド
Hamid, Adam 561
Hamid, Mohsin 561
ハミディ
Hameedi, Ghulam Haidar 561
Hamidi, Abudul Quduus 561
ハミディー
al-Hamidi, Nasser bin Abdulla 561
ハミード
Hameed, Abdulla 561
Hameed, Hamdoon 561
Hameed, Syeda S. 561
ハミド
Hameed, Abdulla 561
Hamid, Abderahim Bureme 561
Hamid, Abdul 561
Hamid, Abdul-Mustapha 561
Hamid, Ibrahim Mahmoud 561
Hamid, Zahid 561
ハミードッ＝ラー
Hamidullah, Muhammad 561
ハミドフ
Khamidov, Khalifabobo 725
Khamidov, Masaid 725
ハミドホジャエフ
Khamidkhodjaev, Alisher 725
ハミミド
Hamimid, Mohamed Nadir 562
バーミューデッツ
Bermudez, Joseph S., Jr. 128
バーミューレン
Vermeulen, Al 1453
Vermeulen, Duane 1453
ハミリ
al-Hamli, Mohammed bin Dha'en 562
パーミリー
Parmelee, Arthur H. 1081
ハミル
Hamill, Joseph 561
Hamill, Pete 561
ハミルトン
Hamilton, Andy 561
Hamilton, Anthony 561
Hamilton, Antonio 562
Hamilton, Bernie 562
Hamilton, Bethany 562
Hamilton, Billy 562
Hamilton, Carrie 562
Hamilton, Celeste 562
Hamilton, Clive 562
Hamilton, Cobi 562
Hamilton, David 562
Hamilton, David R. 562
Hamilton, Denise 562
Hamilton, Diana 562
Hamilton, Doug 562
Hamilton, Emma Walton 562
Hamilton, Eugene 562
Hamilton, Geoffrey 562
Hamilton, G.R. 562
Hamilton, Ian 562
Hamilton, James 562
Hamilton, James Douglas 562
Hamilton, Jane 562
Hamilton, Janice 562
Hamilton, Jason 562
Hamilton, Josh 562
Hamilton, Judy 562
Hamilton, Justin 562
Hamilton, Kim 562
Hamilton, Laurell K. 562
Hamilton, Lewis 562
Hamilton, Libby 562
Hamilton, Mark 562
Hamilton, Maurice 562
Hamilton, Meredith 562
Hamilton, Michele V. 562
Hamilton, Mina 562
Hamilton, Pep 562
Hamilton, Peter F. 562
Hamilton, Rich 562
Hamilton, Richard 562
Hamilton, Roger 562
Hamilton, Steve 562
Hamilton, Tom 562
Hamilton, Tyler 562
Hamilton, Victoria 562
Hamilton, Virginia 562
Hamilton, Woodrow 562
Hamilton and Brandon, Jill Douglas-Hamilton 562
ハミルトン＝ギアクリトシス
Hamilton-Giachritsis, Catherine 562
バーミンガム
Birmingham, Christian 140
Birmingham, David 140
Birmingham, Kevin 140
Birmingham, Lucy 141
Birmingham, Simon 141
バーミングハム
Birmingham, Ruth 141
ハム
Ham, Anthony 560
Ham, C.J. 560
Ham, Darvin 560
Ham, Ken 560
Hamm, Bernd 562
Hamm, Harold 562
Hamm, Jack 562
Hamm, Je'Ron 562
Hamm, Jesse 562
Hamm, Jon 562
Hamm, Mia 562
Hamm, Morgan 563
Hamm, Paul 563
Hamm, Steve 563
ハムー
al-Hamo, Ahmad 564
Hamou, Ahamed 564
バーム
Baum, Herb 106
パム
Pamg, Pandelela Rinong 1074
Rinong, Pandelela 1183
バムガーナー
Bumgarner, Madison 201
パムク
Pamuk, Orhan 1074
ハムクヤ
Hamukuya, Albertina Julia 564
ハムザ
Hamza, Bedri 564
Hamza, Said 564
Hamza, Samar Amer Ibrahim 564
Hamzah, Haz 564
Hamzah, Isam 564
Hamzah, Khidr Abd al-Abbas 564
Hamzah, Zainuddin 564
Haz, Hamzah 586
ハムザ・アワン・アマット
Hamzah Awang Amat 564
ハムザーウィ
Hamzawy, Amr 564
ハムザタウ
Hamzatau, Javid 564
ハムザ・ハス
Haz, Hamzah 586
ハムザ・ハズ
Haz, Hamzah 586
ハムシーク
Hamsik, Marek 564
ハムシク
Hamsik, Marek 564
ハムジーク
Hamžík, Pavol 564
ハームス
Harms, Thelma 572
ハームズ
Harms, Daniel 572
パームス
Parms, Damian 1081
バムステッド
Bumstead, Henry 201
ハムゼ
Hamzeh, Wafaa 564
ハムダラ
Hamdallah, Rami 561
ハムダーン
Hamdan, Ma'moun 561
ハムダン
Hamdan, Akram Abu 561
Hamdan, bin Mubarak al-Nahyan 561
Hamdan, bin Rashid al-Maktoum 561
Hamdan, bin Zayed al-Nahyan 561
Hamdan, Muhammad 561
al-Hamdan, Sulaiman bin Abdullah 561
ハムディラ
Hamdillah, Abdul Wahab 561
ハムテニャ
Hamutenya, Hidipo 564
ハムデン・ターナー
Hampden-Turner, Charles 564

ハムデン＝ターナー
Hampden-Turner, Charles 564
ハムード
Hammoud, Ali 564
Hamood, bin Faisal al-Busaidi 564
Hamoud, bin Faisal al-Busaidi 564
al-Homoud, Moudhi Abdulaziz 619
al-Humoud, Moudhi Abdul Aziz 635
ハムト
Hamout, Mohamed 564
ハムド
Hamud, Mohamed Ali 564
ハムドゥニ
Hamdouni, Hichem 561
ハムナー
Hamner, Jesse 564
ハムネット
Hamnett, Brian R. 564
Hamnett, Katharine Eleanor 564
ハムバルドズミャン
Hambardzumyan, Arsen 561
バムビザ
Bambiza, Ivan M. 88
ハムピッケ
Hampicke, Ulrich 564
ハムフェリー
Humphrey, Craig R. 635
バムフォード
Bamford, James 88
ハムメス
Hammes, M. 563
ハムラ
Hamra, Khalil 564
ハムラリエフ
Hamraliev, Farrukh 564
バムランガキ
Bamulangaki, Vincent 88
ハムリスカ
Jamriska, Fernando 662
ハムリッシュ
Hamlish, Marvin 562
ハームリン
Hermelin, Beate 598
ハムリン
Hamlin, Erin 562
Hamlin, J.Scott 562
ハムル
Huml, Alison 635
ハムレ
Hamre, John J. 564
ハムレー
Hamley, Ian W. 562
ハムレット
Hamlett, Connor 562
ハムンク・ブウォノ
Hamengku Buwono X 561
ハメイダ
H'meyda, Zeidane Ould 610
ハメスファール
Hammesfahr, Petra 563
ハメッケン
Hammeken, Peggy A. 563
ハメッド
Hamed, Hamid 561
ハメド
Hamed, Mohammad 561
Hamed, Muhammad Mostafa 561
ハメド・フランコ
Hamed Franco, Alejandro 561
ハーメネイー
Khamenei, Ali Hossein 725
ハメネイ
Khamenei, Ali Hossein 725
パーメリー
Parmelee, Chris 1081
ハメリン
Hamelin, Tiffany T. 561
ハーメル
Hamer, Bent 561
ハメル
Hamel, Debra 561
Hamel, Gary 561
Hamel, Sylvain 561
Hammel, Jason 563
Hummel, Arthur William, Jr. 635
ハメル＝グリーン
Hamel Green, Michael 561
ハメルズ
Hamels, Cole 561
ハメルマン
Hamelman, Jeffrey 561
バメン
Wammen, Nicolai 1475
ハメンクブウォノ
Hamengku Buwono X 561
ハメンク・ブオノ10世
Hamengku Buwono X 561
ハメンクボウォノ
Hamengku Buwono X 561
パモツェ
Phamotse, Mahali 1106
バー・モーテ
Mbah A Moute, Luc 926
ハーモン
Harmon, Butch, Jr. 572
Harmon, Claude, Jr. 572
Harmon, Dick 572
Harmon, Dominic 572
Harmon, Duron 572
Harmon, Joseph 572
Harmon, Judith Smith 572
Harmon, Kathleen A. 572
Harmon, Paul 572
ハモン
Hammon, Becky 563
ハモンズ
Hammons, A.J. 564
パーモンティエ
Parmentier, Michael 1081
ハモンド
Hammond, Benjamin 563
Hammond, Chelsea 563
Hammond, Claudia 563
Hammond, Darell 563
Hammond, Francis 563
Hammond, Frankie 563
Hammond, Fred 563
Hammond, Jeffrey 563
Hammond, John 563
Hammond, John S. 563
Hammond, Karl 563
Hammond, Kathleen A. 563
Hammond, Michael P. 563
Hammond, Paul 563
Hammond, Paula 563
Hammond, Philip 563
Hammond, Richard 563
Hammond, Robert 563
Hammond, Roger 563
Hammond, Rosemary 563
Hammond, Tammy R. 563
Hammond, Wayne G. 563
バーモント
Bermont, Becky 128
バーモンド
Balmond, Cecil 87
バヤ
Baya, Raymond 107
パーヤー
Puryear, Herbert B. 1140
パヤ
Payá, Oswaldo 1089
パヤオ・プーンタラット
Payao Poontarat 1089
ハヤシ
Hayashi, Alden M. 584
Hayashi, Masumi 584
Hayashi, Shigeki 584
Hayashi, Shigeru 584
パヤジティ
Pajaziti, Zenun 1071
ハヤット
Hayat, Candice 584
Hyatt, James 640
バヤティ
al-Bayati, Muhammad 107
ハヤト
Hayat, Makhdoom Syed Faisal Saleh 584
ハヤトウ
Hayatou, Issa 584
バヤノ
Rayano, Felipe 1162
バヤフメトフ
Bayakhmetov, Darkhan 107
パヤマ
Paihama, Kundi 1070
Payama, Kundy 1089
Payhama, Kundy 1089
バヤモンデ
Mba Olo Bahamonde, Francisco 926
バヤル
Bayar, Sanjaagiin 107
バヤルサイハン
Bayarsaihan, Gardkhuu 107
Bayarsaihan, Tsevelmaagiin 107
Bayarsaikhan, Tsevelmaa 107
バヤルツォグト
Bayartsogt, Sangajav 107
バヤルツォグド
Bayartsogt, Sangajavyn 107
バヤルディ
Bayardi, José 107
バヤルトサイハン
Bayartsaihan, Nadmidiin 107
バヤンセレンゲ
Bayanselenge, Zangad 107
パユ
Pahud, Emmanuel 1070
バユク
Bajuk, Andrej 82
ハユス
Huijs, Jan 634
パユットー
Payutto, P.O. 1089
バユミ
Bayoumi, Tamer 108
バユリュネン
Väyrynen, Paavo 1449
バヨ
Bayo, Kalilou 108
Bayo, Momodou Aki 108
バヨウミ
Bayoumi, Tamer 108
バヨキサキスラ
Baayokisa Kisula, Gudianga 76
バヨナ
Bayona, Juan Antonio 108
バヨナピネダ
Bayona Pineda, Martha 108
バヨール
Bajohr, Frank 82
ハーラー
Harrar, George 573
ハラ
Hara, Catherine Gotani 569
Hara, Keiichi 569
Hara, Terry Saburo 569
Harrar, George 573
Jara, Ana 665
ハラー
Haller, Dorcas Woodbury 559
Haller, L.Michael 559
Haller, Lynn 559
Haller, Rebecca L. 559
Haller, Walter 559
Harrer, Heinrich 573
バーラ
Baala, Medhi 75
Barra, Mary T. 96
バーラー
Vaaler, Paul M. 1437
バラ
Bara, Dave 91
Bara, Michael 91
Bhalla, A.S. 135
Valat, Pierre-Marie 1438
パーラ
Pala, Giovanni Maria 1071
Parra, Derek 1082
Parra, Gerardo 1082
パーラー
Perler, Jeremy 1099
パラ
Pala, Ano 1071
Para, Jean-Baptiste 1077
Parra, Morgan 1082
Parra, Nicanor 1082
パラー
Paller, Kenneth Alan 1072
バラアシ
al-Barasi, Awad 91
バライ
Barai, Carlitos 91
ハライカ
Halaiqa, Mohammad 556
バライカ
Valaika, Pat 1438
パライティス
Palaitis, Raimundas 1071
パライデン

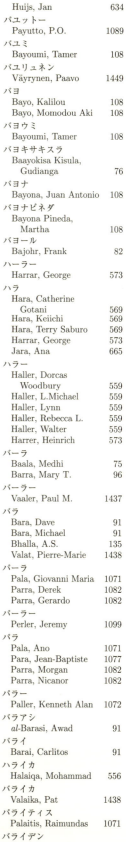

Valayden, Jayarama 1438
ハライフォヌア
Halaifonua, David 556
バライル
Balail, Makki Ali 84
ハラウィ
Hrawi, Elias 629
バラウィ
Balawi, Hakam 85
Barahowie, Karim 91
Brahoye, Mohammad Karim 175
ハラヴェ
Halavais, Alexander M. Campbell 556
ハラウェイ
Haraway, Donna Jeanne 569
ハラウビア
Harraoubia, Rachid 573
ハラウラウ
Halawlaw, Ateib Idriss 556
バラカ
Baraka, Amiri 91
Baraka, Nizar 91
バラガ
Balaga, Sonja 84
バラカウスカス
Barakauskas, Dailis Alfonsas 91
バラカエフ
Balakan Aleksej 84
バラカート
Barakāt, Halīm Isber 91
バラカト
Barakat, Ghayath 91
Barakat, Nisreen 91
バラガン
Barragan, Antonio 97
バラカン・アレクセイ
Balakan Aleksej 84
ハラキー
al-Halqi, Wael Nadir 560
バラキビ
Valakivi, Jakke 1438
バラク
Barak, Ehud 91
al-Barrak, Abdulrahman bin Abdullah 97
バラクシン
Balakshin, Georgy 84
バラクラフ
Barraclough, Jennifer 96
バラクリシュナン
Balakrishnan, Vivian 84
バラクロウ
Barraclough, Kyle 97
バラゲ
Balagué, Guillem 84
バラゲイ
Bala-gaye, Mousa 84
バラゲール
Balaguer, Joaquin 84
バラゲル
Balaguer, Joaquin 84
バラゲル・カブレラ
Balaguer Cabrera, José Ramón 84
バラサ
Barraza, Marcos 97
ハラジ
Kharrazi, Kamal 727
バラシ
Barasi, Stephen 91
バラジ
Balaji, T. 84
パラシオ
Palacio, Alfredo 1071
Palacio, Kache 1071
Palacio, R.J. 1071
Palacio, Rodrigo 1071
パラシオス
Palacios, Beatriz 1071
Palacios, Héctor 1071
Palacios, Julian 1071
Palacios, Rolando 1071
Ruizpalacios, Alonso 1216
パラシオス＝ウエルタ
Palacios-Huerta, Ignacio 1071
パラシオ・ベタンクール
Palacio Betancourt, Diego 1071
パラシオ・ベラタンクール
Palacio Betancourt, Diego 1071
パラシキブイユ
Paraschivoiu, Ion 1077
ハラシモヴィチ
Harasymowicz, Sława 569
ハラジャ
Harazha, Dzianis 569
パラシャー
Parashar, Fiona 1077
ハラシャマニ
Halasyamani, Lakshmi K. 556
バラージュ
Balázs, Anna 85
Balázs, Éva H. 85
バラシュ
Balazs, Artur 85
Barash, David P. 91
Barash, Susan Shapiro 91
バラシュキエビッチ
Baraszkiewicz, Pawel 91
パラジュリ
Parajuli, Hari Prasad 1077
バラージョ
Varallo, Francisco 1446
バラシンガム
Balasingham, Anton Stanislaus 85
ハラス
Hallas, James H. 558
バラス
Ballas, Dimitris 87
Barras, Romain 97
Bharath, Vasant 135
Burruss, James A. 206
パラス
Palas, Jaroslav 1071
パラスカ
Parasca, Vasile 1077
バラスカス
Balaskas, Janet 85
パラスケボプロス
Paraskevopoulos, Nikos 1077
パラスト
Palast, Greg 1072
ハラスノバ
Hrasnova, Martina 629
パラス・ビール・ビクラム・シャハ
Paras bir Bikram Shah 1077
バラスリヤ
Balasuriya, Jagath 85
ハラセ
Halaseh, Sami 556
バラゾバ
Balazova, Barbora 85
ハラダ
Harada, Tsuneo 569
パラタ
Parata, Hekia 1077
バラダイ
Elbaradei, Muhammad Mostafa 396
バラダランショラカ
Baradaranshoraka, Hamid-Reza 91
バラダン
Varadhan, Srinivasa S. R. 1446
ハラヅェツスキ
Haradzetski, Yury 569
バラッカー
Varadkar, Leo 1446
パラッキーニ
Paracchini, Gian Luigi 1077
バラック
Balak 84
Barac, Lilian 91
Barak, Ehud 91
バラッタ
Baratta, Anthony John 91
パラッチ
Palacci, Patrick 1071
パラッツァーニ
Palazzani, Guglielmo 1072
バラッツ‐スノーデン
Baratz-Snowden, Joan C. 91
バラッツ・ログステッド
Baratz-Logsted, Lauren 91
バラッティニ
Barattini, Claudia 91
ハラット
Kharrat, Muhammad Yahya 727
バラット
Barrat, James 97
Barratt, Bronte 97
パラット
Parratto, Jessica 1082
Parrott, Andrew Haden 1082
パラット＝ダヤン
Parrat-Dayan, Silvia 1082
ハラッハ
Harach, L'ubomír 569
ハラッホ
Harrach, Péter 573
ハラデー
Halladay, Roy 558
パラーデ
Palade, George Emil 1071
ハラデイ
Halladay, Roy 558
バラティ
Bharati, Uma 135
パラーディ
Palade, George Emil 1071
パラディ
Palade, George Emil 1071
Paradis, Annie 1077
Paradis, Vanessa 1077
パラディー
Palade, George Emil 1071
Paradis, Christian 1077
ハラーディアス
Jara-Díaz, Sergio 665
バラティエ
Baratier, Jacques 91
Barratier, Christophe 97
パラディス
Paradis, Matt 1077
Paradis, Nichole 1077
パラディーソ
Paradiso, Michael A. 1077
パラディーノ
Palladino, Lucy Jo 1072
ハラデツカ
Hradecka, Lucie 629
バラート
Baráth, Etele 91
Barath, Klara 91
バラード
Ballard, Carol 87
Ballard, Chris 87
Ballard, Glen 87
Ballard, Hank 87
Ballard, James Graham 87
Ballard, Jim 87
Ballard, Juliet Brooke 87
Ballard, Robert 87
Ballard, Robert D. 87
Ballard, Stan 87
Ballard, William Lewis 87
Bullard, Jonathan 200
パラード
Parrado, Nando 1082
パラド
Parad, Howard J. 1077
Parad, Libbie G. 1077
バラドゥーリン
Baradulin, Ryhor Ivanavich 91
ハラドビッチ
Khaladovich, Tatsiana 724
パラトワ
Paratova, Iuliia 1077
バラドワージ
Bharadwaj, Arya Bhushan 135
バラトン
Baraton, Alain 91
バラドン
Valladont, Jean-Charles 1440
パラーナ
Pallana, Kumar 1072
バラニフスキー
Baranivsky, Oleksandr 91
パラニベル
Palanivel, G. 1071
バラニャオ
Barañao, José Lino 91
パラニューク
Palahniuk, Chuck 1071
ハラネ
Halane, Hussein Abdi 556
バラノウスカ
Baranowska, Katarzyna 91
バラーノフ
Baranov, Andrey 91
Baranov, Yurii Evseevich 91

ハ

バラノフスキ
Baranowski, Zbigniew 91
バラノワ
Baranova-masolkina, Natalia 91
バラバシ
Barabási, Albert-László 91
バラバス
Barabas, Andras 91
パラバツ
Paravac, Borislav 1077
バラバノフ
Balabanov, Aleksei 84
ハラビ
Halabi, Bassam 556
Halabi, Warif 556
パーラビ
Pahlevi, Reza II 1070
ハラピオ
Halapio, Jon 556
パラビチニ
Parravicini, Giuseppe Pastori 1082
ハラビン
Harabin, Štefan 569
ハラフ
Khalaf, Essam bin Abdulla 724
バラフィ
Barahowie, Karim 91
パラフォクス・ガミル
Palafox Gamir, J. 1071
ハラブシェ
Khrabsheh, Saad 729
バラホノワ
Balakhonova, Anzhela 84
バラホバー
Valachová, Kateřina 1438
パラポロ
Parapolo, Bartholomew 1077
パラマートマーナンダ
Paramatmananda 1077
パラマリウ
Palamariu, George Alexandru 1071
パラマル
Palamar, Vita 1071
ハラミシュ
Halamish, Aviva 556
ハラミジョ
Jaramillo, Pedro 665
バラミゼ
Baramidze, Giorgi 91
ハラミロ
Jaramillo, Tony 665
ハラム
Halam, Ann 556
Hallam, Elizabeth M. 558
Hallam, Susan 558
Hallam, Tracey 558
パーラム
Parham, Peter 1078
バラムパマ
Barampama, Marina 91
パラメイカ
Palameika, Madara 1071
パラメーカ
Palameika, Madara 1071
パラーモ
Palermo, Tony 1072
パラモ
Palamo, Thretton 1071
パラモノヴァ
Paramonova, Irina M. 1077
バーラモフ
Varlamoff, Marie-Thérèse 1447
バラヨギ
Balayogi, Ganti Mohana Chandra 85
バララ
Balala, Mohamed Moussa Ibrahim 84
Balala, Najib 84
ハラランブス
Charalambous, Charis 247
Charalambous, Sotiroula 247
ハラランボス
Charalambous, Sotiroula 247
ハラーリ
Harari, Oren 569
ハラリ
Harari, Yuval Noah 569
バラリ
Barari, Mohammadreza 91
バラル
Barral, David 97
Barral, J.P. 97
Barral, Xavier 97
バラル・イ・アルテ
Barral i Altet, Xavier 97
ハラルデ
Khalaldeh, Khaled al 724
バラルディ
Baraldi, Claudio 91
パラルディ
Pallardy, Pierre 1072
ハラルド
Harald V 569
バラルト
Balart, Gustavo 85
ハラルド5世
Harald V 569
パラルナウ
Perarnau, Martí 1096
ハラワニ
Halawani, Hatem al 556
ハーラン
Harlan, Jan 571
Harlan, Patrick 571
バラン
Balan, Gheorghe 84
Balán, Jorge 84
Baran, Myriam 91
Baran, Paul 91
Baran, Radoslaw 91
Baran, Robert 91
Baran, Stanley J. 91
パラーン
Palán, Aleš 1071
パラン
Palan, Ronen 1071
Parent, Claude 1077
バランキエヴィッチ
Barankiewich, Filip 91
パランゴー
Paringaux, Roland-Pierre 1078
バランシラ
Barancira, Alphonse 91
バランジン
Balandin, Aleksandr 84
ハーランズ
Herlands, Tiffany 597
パランス
Palance, Jack 1071
バーランダー
Verlander, Justin 1453
バランタ
Balanta, Eder 84
バランタイン
Ballantine, Betty 87
Ballantine, Jeanne H. 87
Ballantyne, Andrew 87
Ballantyne, Frederick 87
Ballantyne, Lisa 87
バランダギエ
Barandagiye, Pascal 91
バランチャク
Barańczak, Stanisław 91
バーランディ
Bárándy, Péter 91
バランディエ
Balandier, Georges 84
バランディン
Balandin, Dmitriy 84
バランテス
Barrantes, Gilberto 97
バランデレカ
Barandereka, Bernard 91
ハーランド
Harland, Georgina 571
バーラント
Berlant, Lauren 128
ハーリ
Harley, Willard F. 571
ハーリー
Hurley, Courtney 637
Hurley, Dan 637
Hurley, Deborah 637
Hurley, Kelley 637
Hurley, Tonya 637
ハリ
Hali, Tamba 557
Hari, Badr 571
Hari, Daoud 571
Hari, Sabarno 571
ハリー
Halley, Ned B. 559
Halley, Peter 559
Harry, Debra 576
Harry, Jimmy 576
Harry, Rebecca 576
Harry, Robert Reese 576
Hulley, Stephen B. 634
Hurry, Helen 637
バーリー
Buehrle, Mark 199
Burleigh, Michael 204
Burleigh, Nina 204
Burley, Justine 204
Burley, Marcus 204
Varley, John 1447
Varley, John Silvester 1447
Varley, Nick 1447
Varley, Susan 1447
バリ
Balit, Christina 86
Bari, Abdul Majeed Abdul 93
Barry, Auguste-Denise 98
Barry, Boubacar 98
Barry, Catherine 98
Barry, Kaba Rougui 99
Barry, Yacouba 99
Valli, Alida 1440
バリー
Bailly, Séry 81
Barrie, Susie 98
Barry, Alpha 98
Barry, B.H. 98
Barry, Boubacar 98
Barry, Bruce 98
Barry, Brunonia 98
Barry, Camara Aminatou 98
Barry, Dana M. 98
Barry, Dave 99
Barry, Frances 99
Barry, Gareth 99
Barry, Gerard 99
Barry, Gerard Stephen 99
Barry, Joe 99
Barry, John 99
Barry, John M. 99
Barry, Kate 99
Barry, Kevin 99
Barry, Maggie 99
Barry, Mamadou Boye 99
Barry, Margaret Martin 99
Barry, Marion 99
Barry, Max 99
Barry, Nancy H. 99
Barry, Nancy Marie 99
Barry, Norman P. 99
Barry, Patricia D. 99
Barry, Peter 99
Barry, Raymond 99
Barry, Siaka 99
Barry, Steve 99
Barry, Susan R. 99
Barry, Tahirou 99
Barry, Trevor 99
Barry, Wendy E. 99
Burry, Pamela J. 206
Demet-barry, Deirdre 340
パリ
Bari, Abdul Majeed Abdul 93
パリー
Pally, Regina 1072
Parry, Alan 1082
Parry, David 1082
Parry, James 1082
Parry, Linda 1082
Parry, Mark E. 1082
Parry, Michael 1082
Parry, Richard Lloyd 1082
Parry, S.Jim 1082
Parry, Stephen 1082
Phaly, Nuon 1106
Pulley, Spencer 1139
バーリア
Balia, Mimma 86
バリア
Barría, María Soledad 98
バーリイ
Varley, John 1447
パリィ
Parry, Jo 1082
ハリウェル
Halliwell, Ed 559
Halliwell, Geri 559
Halliwell, Jonathan J. 559
バリエー
Vargö, Lars 1447
パリエ
Palier, Bruno 1072
バリェステロス
Ballesteros, Seve 87
バリエット

Balliett, Blue 87
バリエフ
Bariev, Enver R. 93
バリエール
Vallieres, Ingrid 1440
バリエワ
Baliyeva, Zagipa 86
バリエントス
Barrientos, Byron 98
Barrientos, Edin 98
バリオ
Barrio, Hilda 98
バリオス
Barrios, Antonio 98
Barrios, Carlos 98
Barrios, Enrique 98
Barrios, Juan Luis 98
Barrios, Yarelys 98
Barrios, Yhonathan 98
バリオス・イペンサ
Barrios Ipenza, Pio Fernando 98
バリオ・テラサス
Barrio Terrazas, Francisco Javier 98
バリオヌエーボ
Barrionuevo, Al 98
ハリカ
Harika, Haroye 571
バリーカ
Barrica, José Marcos 98
パリカル
Parrikar, Manohar 1082
ハリガン
Halligan, Brian 559
Halligan, Fionnuala 559
Halligan, Peter W. 559
Harrigan, Pat 573
ハリキミ
Halikimi, Mahamat Issa 557
ハリキャル
Khaliqyar, Fazal Haq 725
バリーク
Baleegh, Mahmood 86
パリクス
Palix, Flore 1072
ハリクヤル
Khaliqyar, Fazal Haq 725
パリサー
Palliser, Charles 1072
Pariser, Eli 1078
バリサカン
Balisacan, Arsenia 86
ハリシー
Hallisey, Caroline 559
パリージ
Parisi, Arturo 1078
Parisi, Giorgio 1078
Parisi, Paolo 1078
パリシ
Parisi, Hugo 1078
パリジ
Parrilli, Oscar 1082
バリシェワ
Barysheva, Varvara 101
バリシオ
Basilio, Carmen 102
バリシッチ
Barišić, Pavo 94
パリジーニ
Parigini, Vittorio 1078
バリシニコフ
Baryshnikov, Mikhail 101
バリシニコワ
Baryshnikova, Anastasia 101
バリジャス
Barillas, Natalia 94
バリシュニコフ
Barichnikoff, Catherine 93
パリー・ジョーンズ
Parry-Jones, Jemima 1082
ハリス
Harries, Keith D. 573
Harris, Amanda 573
Harris, Anne 573
Harris, Anthony 573
Harris, Bill 573
Harris, Bob 573
Harris, Bonnie 573
Harris, Brandon 573
Harris, Brian F. 573
Harris, Bryce 573
Harris, Calvin 573
Harris, Carla A. 573
Harris, Charlaine 573
Harris, Chloe 573
Harris, Chris 573
Harris, Christine 573
Harris, Clare 573
Harris, Clark 573
Harris, Damon 573
Harris, Dan 573
Harris, Darien 573
Harris, David 573
Harris, David Money 573
Harris, Demetrius 573
Harris, De'Vante 573
Harris, Devin 573
Harris, DuJuan 573
Harris, Dwayne 573
Harris, Ed 573
Harris, Eleanor L. 574
Harris, Elizabeth 574
Harris, Elmer Beseler 574
Harris, Emmylou 574
Harris, Erik 574
Harris, Eugene E. 574
Harris, Frances P. 574
Harris, Frederick 574
Harris, Gary 574
Harris, Gemma Elwin 574
Harris, Godfrey 574
Harris, Graham 574
Harris, Grant T. 574
Harris, Gregg 574
Harris, Henry 574
Harris, Howard S. 574
Harris, Ian 574
Harris, Ian S. 574
Harris, Jamie O. 574
Harris, Jason 574
Harris, Jeanne G. 574
Harris, Jeremy 574
Harris, Jet 574
Harris, Joanne 574
Harris, Jodie 574
Harris, Joe 574
Harris, John 574
Harris, Jonathan 574
Harris, Jose 574
Harris, Joseph 574
Harris, Josh 574
Harris, Joshua 574
Harris, Julie 574
Harris, Kim 574
Harris, Larry 574
Harris, Lynn Raye 574
Harris, Maria G. 574
Harris, Marvin 574
Harris, Maurice 574
Harris, Melodee 574
Harris, Michael 574
Harris, Michael David 574
Harris, Michelle R. 574
Harris, M.Key 574
Harris, Nancy G. 574
Harris, Nathaniel 574
Harris, Neil Patrick 574
Harris, Nicholas 574
Harris, Nick 574
Harris, Norm 574
Harris, Oliver 574
Harris, Otis 574
Harris, Patricia E. 574
Harris, Paul 574
Harris, Paul Arthur 574
Harris, Rachel 574
Harris, Richard 574
Harris, R.J. 575
Harris, Robert 575
Harris, Roberta L. 575
Harris, Robie H. 575
Harris, Ron 575
Harris, Rosemary 575
Harris, Russ 575
Harris, Ryan 575
Harris, Sandra L. 575
Harris, Sarah Gomes 575
Harris, Sarah L. 575
Harris, Seth 575
Harris, Shannon 575
Harris, Shelby 575
Harris, Sheldon H. 575
Harris, Simon 575
Harris, Sue 575
Harris, Tamara 575
Harris, Thomas 575
Harris, Timothy 575
Harris, Tobias 575
Harris, Tony 575
Harris, Vernon 575
Harris, Whitney 575
Harris, Will 575
Harriss, Edmund 576
Paris, Wendy 1078
バリス
Baris, Alcino 94
Barris, Chuck 98
Burris, Juston 205
Varis, Kaisa 1447
パリース
Parijs, Philippe van 1078
Paris, A. 1078
パリス
Pallis, Yuki 1072
Paris, Barry 1078
Paris, Erna 1078
Paris, Gilles 1078
Paris, Hernando 1078
Paris, Joel 1078
Paris, Reine-Marie 1078
Paris, Wendy 1078
パリスカ
Palisca, Claude V. 1072
ハリスカ＝ベイス
Huliska-Beith, Laura 634
ハリスン
Harrison, A.S.A. 575
Harrison, Colin 575
Harrison, George 575
Harrison, Harry 575
Harrison, Hazel 575
Harrison, Jim 575
Harrison, Kenneth 575
Harrison, Kim 576
Harrison, Mike John 576
Harrison, Noel 576
Harrison, Olivia 576
Harrison, Royden John 576
Harrison, William 576
バリセヴィック
Balicevic, Didier 86
パリゾ
Parizeau, Jacques 1078
パリゾー
Parizeau, Jacques 1078
ハリソン
Harrison, Aaron 575
Harrison, Alan 575
Harrison, Andrew 575
Harrison, Brian Howard 575
Harrison, Charles 575
Harrison, Christopher 575
Harrison, Claire 575
Harrison, Colin 575
Harrison, Damon 575
Harrison, Edward Robert 575
Harrison, Elaine 575
Harrison, Emma 575
Harrison, Erica 575
Harrison, George 575
Harrison, Graeme Thomas 575
Harrison, Guy P. 575
Harrison, Harry 575
Harrison, Harry H. 575
Harrison, Howard 575
Harrison, James 575
Harrison, Jane 575
Harrison, Jarvis 575
Harrison, Jean 575
Harrison, Jeffrey D. 575
Harrison, Jeffrey L. 575
Harrison, Jeffrey S. 575
Harrison, Jim 575
Harrison, Joanna 575
Harrison, John E. 575
Harrison, John R. 575
Harrison, Jonotthan 575
Harrison, Josh 575
Harrison, Kathryn 575
Harrison, Kathy 575
Harrison, Kayla 575
Harrison, K.David 575
Harrison, Kenneth 575
Harrison, Lindsay 576
Harrison, Lisi 576
Harrison, Lorraine 576
Harrison, Lou 576
Harrison, Mark 576
Harrison, Max 576
Harrison, Mike 576
Harrison, Neil B. 576
Harrison, Noel 576
Harrison, Oscar 576
Harrison, P. 576
Harrison, Paul 576
Harrison, Paula 576
Harrison, Richard 576
Harrison, Roland Kenneth 576
Harrison, Sam 576
Harrison, Selig S. 576
Harrison, Shaquille 576
Harrison, Shirley 576
Harrison, Suzanne S. 576
Harrison, Thomas 576
Harrison, Thomas L. 576
Harrison, Todd A. 576

Harrison, Tony 576
Harrison, Walter Ashley 576
Harrison, William Burwell, Jr. 576
Harrisson, Astrid 576
バリチ
Barić, Maija 93
バリチェロ
Barichello, Richard 93
ハリツキ
Halicki, Andrzej 557
バリツキ
Balicki, Marek 86
バリッキオ
Varricchio, Eda 1447
バリッコ
Baricco, Alessandro 93
バーリッジ
Berridge, David 130
バリッジ
Burridge, Richard A. 205
バリッシュ
Barish, Leora 94
パリッシュ
Parish, John Howard 1078
Parrish, P.J. 1082
Parrish, R.G. 1082
パリッセ
Parisse, Sergio 1078
バリッチ
Balic, Andrija 86
バーリット
Barritt, Brad 98
Burritt, Roger L. 205
パーリット
Perlitt, Lothar 1099
バリッラ
Barilla, Antonino 93
ハリデー
Halliday, Fred 559
Halliday, Michael Alexander Kirkwood 559
ハリディ
Halliday, David 559
Haridi, Seif 571
Haridy, Shaimaa Ahmed Khalaf 571
ハリデイ
Halliday, Fred 559
Halliday, Jon 559
Halliday, Tim 559
ハリディ＝サムナー
Halliday-Sumner, Linda 559
バリテック
Varitek, Jason 1447
ハリート
Khriit, Najim al-Din 729
ハリト
Harito, Milena 571
ハリド
Khalid, Assadullah 724
Khalid, bin Abdullah al-Khalifa 724
Khalid, bin Ahmed bin Mohammed al-Khalifa 725
Khalid, bin Ali al-Khalifa 725
Khalid, bin Hilal al-Busaidi 725
ハリド・イラニ
Khalid Irani 725
ハリド・ジャラハ
Khaled al-Jarrah, al-Sabah 724
ハリトーノフ
Kharitonov, Daniel 727
ハリトノワ
Kharitonova, Marta 727
バーリナー
Berliner, Lucy 128
ハリナン
Hallinan, Camilla 559
Hallinan, Joseph T. 559
パリーニ
Parini, Jay 1078
バーリニャ
Bālina, Signe 86
パリネロ
Parinello, Anthony 1078
ハリーハウゼン
Harryhausen, Ray 576
ハリハラン
Hariharan, P. 571
バリバール
Balibar, Étienne 86
Balibar, Jeanne 86
Balibar, Renee 86
ハリブ
Haribou, Ali 571
ハリーファ
Khalifa, Abdel Kawy 725
Khalifa bin Zayed al-Nahyan 725
ハリファ
al-Khalifa, Ahmed bin Ateyatala 725
Khalifa, bin Ahmed al-Khalifa 725
Khalifa, bin Salman al-Khalifa 725
al-Khalifa, Khalid bin Ahmed bin Mohammed 725
Khalifeh, Mohammed Jawad 725
ハリファックス
Halifax, Joan 557
ハリーファ・ビン・ザーイド・アール・ナヒヤーン
Khalifa bin Zayed al-Nahyan 725
ハリファ・ビン・ザイド・ナハヤン
Khalifa bin Zayed al-Nahyan 725
パリペトラリア
Palli-petralia, Fani 1072
ハリー・ベラフォンテ
Belafonte, Harry 115
ハリホズィク
Halilhodžić, Vahid 557
パリボディッチ
Parivodić, Milan 1078
バリー・ボンズ
Bonds, Barry 158
ハリーマ
Houleimeta, Sao 626
バリマ
Barimah, Yaw 94
ハリマン
Harimann, Sierra 571
Harriman, Richard 573
ハーリミ
Abdulhai, Murad Ali Mohammed 4
ハリミ
Halimi, Eduard 557
ハリーム
Haleem, Abdul 557
ハリム
Halim, Atef 557
バリモア
Barrymore, Drew 99
Barrymore, John, Jr. 99
ハリモフ
Khalimov, Danil 725
バリャダレス
Valladares, Jadier 1440
パリュ
Pallud, Jean-Paul 1072
パリュウカ
Pagliuca, Steve 1070
バリュケビッチ
Gurova, Viktoriya 547
パリョ
Pal'o, L'uboslav 1073
バリラ
Barilla, Jean 93
バリラック
Barylak, Lucy 101
ハリーリー
Hariri, Rafik Bahaa Edinburghe 571
ハリリ
Hariri, Bahia 571
al-Hariri, Fawzi 571
Hariri, Rafik Bahaa Edinburghe 571
Hariri, Saad 571
al-Khalili, Abdulmalik bin Abdullah bin Ali 725
Khalili, Mohammad Karim 725
al-Khalili, Salem bin Hilal 725
バリリ
Barylli, Walter 101
ハリリアン
Khalilian, Sadegh 725
バリリエ
Barilier, Étienne 93
ハリール
Khalil, Karam 725
Khalil, Nagwa 725
ハリル
Jalil, Osvaldo 660
Khalil, Ahmad Murtada Ahmad 725
Khalil, Ali Hassan 725
Khalil, Issam 725
Khalil, Safwan 725
Kh'lil, Mohamed 728
バリル
Burrill, G.Steven 205
ハリルザド
Khalilzad, Zalmay 725
ハリール・ビン・イブラヒーム・ハッサン
Khalil bin Ibrahim Hassan 725
ハリル・ビン・イブラヒム・ハッサン
Khalil bin Ibrahim Hassan 725
ハリルホジッチ
Halilhodžić, Vahid 557
パリレニャトワ
Parirenyatwa, David 1078
パーリロ
Parrillo, Lucio 1082
ハリロヴィッチ
Halilovic, Alen 557
ハリロジッチ
Halilhodžić, Vahid 557
ハリロビッチ
Halilović, Jasminko 557
Halilović, Safet 557
ハリロフ
Halylov, Muhammetnur 560
ハーリン
Harlin, Renny 571
ハリン
Hallin, Daniel C. 559
バーリン
Bahrin, Abdullah 80
Berlin, Brent 128
Berlin, Ira 128
Berlin, Irving N. 128
パリン
Palin, Michael 1072
バーリンガム
Burlingham, Bo 204
ハーリング
Herring, Darreon 599
バーリング
Burling, Peter 204
Burling, Robbins 204
パーリング
Parling, Geoff 1081
バーリンゲーム
Burlingame, Jeff 204
ハーリンゲン
Haeringen, Annemarie van 553
バリンジャー
Barringer, Janice 98
Bollinger, Gary 156
バーリンスキ
Berlinski, David 128
パリンストン
Pallingston, Jessica 1072
パリンダー
Parrinder, Edward Geoffrey 1082
バーリント
Bálint, Ágnes 86
バリント
Balint, Enid 86
ハリントン
Harrington, Adam 573
Harrington, Donna L. 573
Harrington, J.D. 573
Harrington, Joel Francis 573
Harrington, John 573
Harrington, Joyce 573
Harrington, Kent A. 573
Harrington, Lea 573
Harrington, Nina 573
Harrington, Padraig 573
Harrington, Paul 573
Harrington, Scott E. 573
Harrington, William 573
バーリントン
Barrington, Sam 98
バリントン
Barrington, Anne 98
Barrington, James 98
バーリンホースト
Baringhorst, Maria

Franziska 94
ハール
Haar, Gert ter 551
ハル
Gal, Edward 472
Hal, Andre 556
Hall, Katarzyna 558
Hull, Arthur 634
Hull, Charley 634
Hull, Derek 634
Hull, Edith Maude 634
Hull, Janet Starr 634
Hull, John 634
Hull, John M. 634
Hull, Linda Joffe 634
Hull, Mike 634
Hull, Suzanne W. 634
Hull, Thomas 634
Hulls, Michael 634
al-Khair, Abdul-Qadir Omar 724
バール
Bahr, Daniel 80
Bahr, Egon 80
Bar, Christian Von 91
Barre, Raymond 97
Bart, Patrice 99
Berle, Milton 128
Burl, Aubrey 204
Burr, Chandler 205
バル
Bal, Ahmedou Tidjane 84
Bal, Hartosh Singh 84
Bale, Débaba 85
Baru 101
Baru, Morea 101
Val, Elena 1438
Vall, Ely Ould Mohamed 1440
Vall, Taleb Ould Abdi 1440
バルー
Barouh, Pierre 96
Barroux 98
パール
Paal, Douglas 1067
Parr, Todd 1082
Pearl, Eric 1090
Pearl, Eve 1090
Pearl, Harold 1090
Pearl, Mariane 1090
Pearl, Matthew 1090
Pearl, Peggy S. 1090
Pearl, Phillip L. 1090
Perl, Arnold 1099
Perl, Lila 1099
Perl, Martin Lewis 1099
Perl, Susan 1099
Perle, Richard N. 1099
パールー
Palu, Wycliff 1073
パル
Pal, Vannarirak 1071
Parr, Maria 1081
バルア
Barua, Dilip 101
ハルイコフ
Khalykov, Khudaikuly 725
ハルヴァーソン
Halvorson, Heidi Grant 560
パル・ヴァンナリーレアク
Pal Vannarirak 1073
ハルウィ
Haloui, Hamza 559
ハルウエイル
Halweil, Brian 560
パルヴェラ
Parvela, Timo 1083
バルエコ
Barrueco, Manuel 98
バルエル
Barel, Sari 93
ハルカ
Harka, Haroye 571
バルカ
Barka, Koco 94
バルカー
Barkhah, Mohammad Hossein 94
バルガ
Varga, Erik 1446
Varga, Gabriella 1446
Varga, Mihály 1446
Varga, Richard 1446
Varga, Siniša 1446
Varga, Tibor 1446
Varga, Viktoria 1446
パルカ
Palca, Joe 1072
Palka, Daniel 1072
バルカカティ
Barkakati, Nabajyoti 94
バルガシ
al-Bargati, Mohammad Mahmoud 93
バルガーシム
Belqasem, Massoud Ahmed 118
バルガス
Valgas, Guillermo 1440
Valgas, Rafael 1440
Vargas, Antonio 1446
Vargas, Cesar 1446
Vargas, Devin 1446
Vargas, Eduardo 1446
Vargas, Georgina 1446
Vargas, Jason 1446
Vargas, Kennys 1446
Vargas, Oscar 1446
Vargas, Pepe 1446
Vargas, Victor 1446
Vargas Llosa, Mario 1447
バルガス・ゴメス
Vargas Gomez, Luis Andres 1446
バルガス・ジェラス
Vargas Lleras, Germán 1447
バルガス・ジョサ
Vargas Llosa, Mario 1447
バルガス・ディアス
Vargas Díaz, Marco 1446
バルガス・パディジャ
Vargas Padilla, Arlen Patricia 1447
バルガス・マルドナド
Vargas Maldonado, Miguel 1447
バルガス・リョサ
Vargas Llosa, Mario 1447
バルガス・ロドリゲス
Vargas Rodriguez, Luis Aristobulo 1447
バルカセル
Balcácer, Robiamny 85
バルカダウド
Barkat Daoud, Hasna 94
バルカット
Barkat, Said 94
バルカトアブディラヒ
Barkat Abdillahi, Mohamed 94
バルカドダウド
Barkad Daoud, Hasna 94
パルカノバー
Parkanová, Vlasta 1079
バルカノフ
Valkanov, Stanislav 1440
ハルカパー
Härkäpää, Maria 571
バルガバ
Bhargava, Manjul 135
Bhargava, Ravindra Chandra 135
Bhargava, R.C. 135
バルカレッジ
Valcareggi, Ferruccio 1438
バルガワ
Bhargava, Ravindra Chandra 135
バルカン
Bulkan, Ronald 200
バルガンボア
Mbarga Mboa, Philippe 926
ハルキ
Kharki, Farkhad 727
バルキ
Balci, Serhat 85
ハルキア
Khalkia, Fani 725
ハルキアス
Halkias, Georgios T. 557
ハルギッタイ
Hargittai, István 571
ハルキナ
Halkina, Katsiaryna 557
バルギムバエフ
Balgimbayev, Nurlan 86
ハルギン
Hargin, Mattias 571
バルキン
Barquín Sanz, Jesús 96
バルギンバエフ
Balgimbayev, Nurlan 86
ハルク
Jalkh, Gustavo 660
バルーク
Baruch, Janice 101
バルクウィル
Balkwill, Mike 86
バルグーティ
Barghouthi, Muhammed 93
Barghouti, Siham 93
Bargouthi, Siham 93
バルグナイム
Balghunaim, Fahd bin Abdulrahman bin Sulaiman 86
バルグハンセン
Berg-hansen, Lisbeth 127
バルクフレーデ
Bargfrede, Philipp 93
バルクマイヤー
Barkmeier, Julie 94
バルクリー
Bulkeley, Kelly 200
Bulkley, Patricia 200
バルクール
Valcourt, Bernard 1438
ハルケ
Jarque, Daniel 665
バルケネンデ
Balkenende, Jan Peter 86
バルケンホール
Balkenhol, Stephan 86
パルコ
Palko, Vladimír 1072
バルコ・イサクソン
Barco Isackson, Carolina 93
バルコウスキー
Bulkowski, Thomas N. 200
バールコバー
Válková, Helena 1440
バルコフスキ
Balkovski, Ljupco 86
ハルコベツ
Kharkovets, Andrei M. 727
バルコム
Balcombe, Jonathan P. 85
Balkom, Frans van 86
バルコワ
Valkova, Ekaterina 1440
ハルコン
Halcón, Linda L. 556
バルサ
Balsa, Gerardo 87
バルサー
Balcer, Marc J. 85
Balcer, Rene 85
バルザコフ
Barzakov, Serafim 101
バルザー・ライリー
Balzer-Riley, Julia W. 88
バルザーリ
Barzagli, Andrea 101
ハルサル
Halsall, Francesca 560
パルサルエ
Palusalue, Faapo II 1073
ハルザルドッティル
Harðardóttir, Eygló 569
ハルシ
Harouchi, Abderrahim 572
al-Harthy, Mohammed bin Abdullah 577
ハルジー
Halsey, Brad 560
バルジ
Barzi, Sajjad 101
パルーシ
Palusci, Vincent J. 1073
パルシアウスカス
Palciauskas, Victor 1072
ハルジェ
Khalje, Suzan 725
パルシテ
Palsyte, Airine 1073
バルシム
Barshim, Mutaz Essa 99
バルシャイ
Barshai, Rudolf Borisovich 99
バルジャス
Valjas, Kristina 1440
バルシュ
Barusch, Amanda Smith 101
パルシュ
Pars, Krisztián 1082
バルシロン
Barcilon, Marianne 92

ハルス
Hulse, Godwin 634
Hulse, Russel Alan 634
Hulse, Sarah M. 634
Hulse, Terra 634
バルス
Valls, Manuel 1440
バルスー
Barsoux, Jean-Louis 99
パールズ
Perls, Thomas T. 1099
バルス・イ・ソレ
Valls i Solé, Josep 1440
バルスキ
Barski, Conrad 99
バルスク
Barsouk, Dmitri 99
Barsuk, Tatiana 99
パールスタイン
Perlstein, Susan 1099
バールズディンシュ
Bārzdiņš, Juris 101
ハルステッド
Halstead, Lauro S. 560
Halsted, Laurence 560
ハルステンベルク
Halstenberg, Marcel 560
ハルスドルフ
Halsdorf, Jean-Marie 560
ハルストレム
Hallström Lasse 559
バルストロム
Wallström, Margot 1473
バルスボルド
Barsbold, Ulambayaryn 99
バルズリー
Balsley, Darren 88
ハルゼー
Halsey, A.H. 560
Halsey, Brad 560
Halsey, Simon 560
バルセカール
Balsekar, Ramesh S. 88
バルセルス
Balsells, Edgar 88
バルソニー
Barsony, Andre 99
バールソン
Burleson, Sieglien 204
バルソン
Balson, John B. 88
ハルダー
Halder, Veronika 556
Harder, Jens 569
バールタ
Bárta, Vít 99
バルタ
Balta, Ksenija 88
Barta, Jiří 99
バルター
Balter, Dan 88
Walter, Fritz 1473
バルダ
Barda, Henri 93
Varda, Agnès 1446
ハルダウ
Hărdău, Mihail 569
バルダサリ
Baldassari, Anne 85
バルタス
Baltas, Aristides 88
バルダチ
Bardach, Georgina 93
バルタック
Bartak, Lawrence 99
バルダッチ
Baldacci, David 85
Balducci, Rita 85
パルダニウス
Paldanius, Sofia 1072
バルダニャン
Vardanian, Aghvan 1446
バルタバス
Bartabas 99
バルダヒ
Bardaji, Ander 93
バル・タル
Bar-Tal, Daniel 99
バルダル
Bardal, Anders 93
ハルタルト
Hartarto, Airlangga 577
バルタン
Vartan, Sylvie 1447
バルダン
Vardhan, Harsh 1446
パルーダン
Paludan, Johan Peter 1073
バルタンズ
Bertans, Davis 131
バルチ
Baruch, Leonel 101
バルチェフ
Valtchev, Daniel 1440
ハルチェンコ
Kharchenko, Ihor 727
バルチティス
Balčytis, Zigmantas 85
ハルチャ
Harcsa, Zoltan 569
パルチュ
Partsch, Susanna 1083
バルチュカイテ
Valciukaite, Milda 1438
バルチュス
Balthus 88
ハルチュニャン
Harutyunian, Davit 578
Harutyunyan, Haik 578
バルツ
Balz, Rodolphe 88
パルツ
Parts, Juhan 1083
バルツァ
Baltsa, Agnes 88
バルツェル
Barzel, Rainer Candidus 101
バルツェロヴィチ
Balcerowicz, Leszek 85
バルツェロヴィッチ
Balcerowicz, Leszek 85
バルツェロビッチ
Balcerowicz, Leszek 85
パルッキネン
Parkkinen, Jukka 1081
バルッツィ
Baruzzi, Agnese 101
Baruzzi, Arno 101
パルッツィ
Paruzzi, Gabriella 1083
ハルツマン
Holzman, Gerard J. 619
バルデ
Balde, Abdoulaye 85
Balde, Abdoulaye Yéro 85
Baldé, Abubacar 85
Baldé, Carlos Mussa 85
Baldé, Hadja Mariama 85
Balde, Kazaliou 85
Baldé, Mamadu Saido 85
Balde, Mariama Deo 85
Balde, Tumane 85
Bardet, Solenn 93
ハルディ
Khaldi, Ahmed 724
Khaldi, El-Hadi 724
バルティ
Baruti, Théo 101
Bharti, Uma 135
バルディ
Bardi, Carla 93
パルディ
Pardi, Francesca 1077
バルティア
Bhartia, Shobhana 135
バルディガ
Baldyga, Scott 85
パルティカ
Partyka, Natalia 1083
ハルティニ
Hartini 577
バルディニ
Baldini, Andrea 85
Baldini, Stefano 85
バルディビア・バウティスタ
Valdivia Bautista, Lenny Tatiana 1439
バルディビア・ロメロ
Valdivia Romero, Juan Gualberto 1439
バルディビエソ
Valdivieso, Fabián 1439
パルディール
Paldiel, Mordecai 1072
ハルティング
Harting, Christoph 577
Harting, Robert 577
ハルディング
Harding, Arturo 569
ハルディング・ラカヨ
Harding Lacayo, Arturo 570
バルデゥーチ
Balducci, Alex 85
バルデサリーニ
Baldessarini, Ross J. 85
バール=テシューヴァ
Baal-Teshuva, Jacob 75
バルデス
Valdés, Bebo 1439
Valdés, Chucho 1439
Valdes Paris, Maria Fernanda 1439
Valdez, Lisa 1439
Valdéz, Rodrigo 1439
Valdez Fierro, Oscar 1439
Vargas, Ildemaro 1446
バルデストビエル
Valdes Tobier, Alejandro Enrique 1439
バルデスメサ
Valdés Mesa, Salvador 1439
バルデス・メネンデス
Valdés Menéndez, Ramiro 1439
バルデッサリ
Baldessari, John 85
バルデッティ
Baldetti, Ingrid Roxana 85
バルデッリ
Bardelli, Giorgio G. 93
バルデム
Bardem, Javier 93
Bardem, Juan Antonio 93
バルテュス
Balthus 88
Baltus, Martine 88
バルデラス
Balderas, Carlos Zenon, Jr. 85
バルデラモス
Balderamos, Dolores 85
バルデリ
Baldelli, Rocco 85
Bardeli, Marlies 93
ハルテル
Hartel, Marcel 577
Hartel, Stefan 577
バルテルス
Bartels, Fin 99
Bartels, Ralf 99
バルテレミ
Bartelem, Yan 99
ハルテロス
Harteros, Anja 577
パルデン・ギャツォ
Palden Gyatso 1072
バルテンシュタイン
Bartenstein, Martin 99
バルテンス
Bartens, Werner 99
ハルテンバッハ
Hartenbach, Walter 577
ハルデンベルグ
Hardenberg, F. 569
バールト
Barth, Hans-Martin 100
バルード
Baroud, Ziad 96
バルト
Barth, Fredrik 100
Barth, Helmut 100
Barth, Mario 100
Barth, Ulrich 100
バルド
Baroud, Aziza 96
バルドー
Bardo, Blayne 93
Bardot, Brigitte 93
パルド
Pardo, Laura S. 1077
Pardo, Mauricio 1077
Pardo, Robert 1077
Pardo, Rogelio 1077
Pardo, Ruben 1077
バルドゥツィ
Balduzzi, Renato 85
バルドゥッチ
Balducci, Rita 85
ハルトゥーニアン
Harootunian, Harry D. 572
ハルトゥング
Hartung, Max 578
Hartung, Wolfgang 578
ハルトグ
de Hartog, Jan 334
バルトーク

Bartok, Dennis 100
Bartók, Peter 100
バルトクス
Bartkus, Gintautas 100
パルド・クルス
Pardo Cruz, Salvador 1077
バルトコ
Bartko, Robert 100
バルトシェフスキ
Bartoszewski, Władysław 101
バルトシャイト
Baltscheit, M. 88
Baltscheit, Martin 88
バルトシュ
Bartoş, Daniela 101
バルトス
Bartos, Burghard 100
バルドス
Baldoz, Rosalinda 85
バルドーニ
Baldoni, John 85
ハルトノ
Hartono, A.Budi 578
Hartono, Michael 578
Hartono, Robert Budi 578
Hartono, Umar 578
バルドビッチ
Baldovici, Vladimir 85
ハルトフ
Haltof, Marek 560
ハルトマイヤー
Haltmayr, Petra 560
ハルトマン
Hartmann, Andy 577
Hartmann, Kerstin 578
Hartmann, Moritz 578
Hartmann, Sven 578
バルトラ
Bartra, Marc 101
バルトライティエネ
Baltraitienė, Virginija 88
バルトリ
Bartoli, Cecilia 100
Bartoli, Marco 100
Bartoli, Marion 100
パルトリニエリ
Paltrinieri, Gregorio 1073
ハルトル
Hartl, Alfred 577
Hartl, Gabrielle 577
パルド・ルエダ
Pardo Rueda, Rafael 1077
ハルドールスドッティル
Halldorsdottir, Kolbrun 558
バルトルッチ
Bartolucci, Marisa 100
バルトレッティ
Bartoletti, Bruno 100
バルトロ
Bartolo, Evarist 100
パルトロー
Paltrow, Gwyneth 1073
バルトロウ
Bartrow, Kay 101
パルトロウ
Paltrow, Bruce 1073
Paltrow, Gwyneth 1073
バルトローヌ
Bartolone, Claude 100
バルトロメイ
Bartolomey, Franz 100
バルトロメオ
Bartolomeo, Joey 100
バルドワジ
Bhardwaj, H.R. 135
ハルナ
Harna, István 572
Harouna, Hamani 572
Harouna, Lamido Moumouni 572
Haruna, Boni 578
バルナイ
Varnay, Astrid 1447
ハルーニ
Harouni, Karim 572
バルニエ
Barnier, Michel 96
バルニカ
Barnica, Víctor 96
バルニク
Värnik, Andrus 1447
ハルニッシュマッヒャー
Harnischmacher, Robert 572
バルニャーニ
Bargnani, Andrea 93
パルネ
Parnet, Claire 1081
バルネイ
Barnay, Sylvie 95
バルネッタ
Barnetta, Tranquillo 96
バールネト
Vaal-neto, Pedro Hendrik 1437
バルネル
Balner, Michal 87
パルノヤ
Parnoja, Mihkel 1081
ハルバ
Harbah, Muhammad 569
ハルパ
Chalupa, Tomáš 243
Chalupa, Vaclav 243
ハルパー
Halper, Barry 559
Halper, Stefan A. 559
バルハ
Baruja, Juan Carlos 101
バルバ
Barba, Andrés 91
Barba, Eric 91
Barba, Eugenio 91
Barba, Federico 91
バルハウス
Ballhaus, Michael 87
Ballhaus, Verena 87
バルバシャン
Barbachan, Ana Luiza Busato 91
ハルバーシュ
Kharbash, Muhammad Khalfan bin 726
ハルバーシュタット
Halberstadt, Hans 556
パルバース
Pulvers, Roger 1139
ハルバースタット
Halverstadt, Jonathan Scott 560
ハルバースタム
Halberstam, David 556
Halberstam, Joshua 556
Mandelbaum, Yitta Halberstam 893
ハルバスタム
Halberstam, David 556
ハルバーソン
Halverson, Richard 560
Halvorson, Heidi Grant 560
Halvorson, Michael 560
ハルバータル
Halbertal, Moshe 556
ハルパート
Halpert, Sam 560
バルハトヴァ
Barkhatova, Elena Valentinovna 94
パルバノフ
Parvanov, Georgi 1083
バルハフティク
Warhaftig, Zorach 1478
バルバラ
Barbara Seixas 92
ハルハリ
Khalkhali, Mohammed Sadeq 725
パルパリ
Parupalli, Kashyap 1083
バルバーリョ
Barbalho, Helder 91
バルバリョ
Barbalho, Helder 91
ハルパリン
Halperin, Charles J. 559
Halperin, Ian 559
Halperin, Morton H. 559
Halperin, Wendy Anderson 559
バルバロ
Barbaro, Paolo 92
ハルパーン
Halpern, Adena 559
Halpern, Howard Marvin 559
Halpern, Jeanne 559
Halpern, Justin 559
Halpern, Paul 560
Halpern, Sue 560
ハルパン
Halpern, Shari 560
ハルビ
Halbi, Mohammad Yusuf 556
ハルビー
Hruby, Raymond J. 629
バルヒ
Balkhi, Sayed Hussain Alemi 86
Balkhi, Sediqa 86
Balkhy, Assadullah Hanif 86
バルビエ
Barbier, Geneviève 92
Barbier, Jean-Claude 92
パルピエフ
Parpiyev, Azimzhon 1081
Parpiyev, Botir 1081
バルビエーリ
Barbieri, Fedora 92
バルビエリ
Barbieri, Fedora 92
Barbieri, Gato 92
ハルピン
Halpin, Brendan 560
ハルブ
Harb, Boutros 569
バルフ
Balfe, Kevin 86
バルブ
Barbe, André-Francois 92
Barbu, Gheorghe 92
Barbu, Sulfina 92
バルファキス
Varoufakis, Yanis 1447
ハルファーティ
Halferty, Mike 557
ハルフィ
Khalfi, Mustapha El 724
パールフィ
Palfi, Gyorgy 1072
パルフェ
Parfait, Françoise 1078
バルブエナ
Valbuena, Luis 1438
バルフォア
Balfour, Alex 86
Balfour, Ngconde 86
ハルフォード
Halford, Rob 557
ハルフォン
Halfon, Eduardo 557
バルブ・ガル
Barbe-Gall, Françoise 92
バルブーザ
Valbusa, Fulvio 1438
ハルブース
Khalbous, Slim 724
バルブッソ
Balbusso, Anna 85
Balbusso, Elena 85
ハルブートリー
Kharboutli, Muhammad Zuhair 726
バルブラン
Valbrun, Lyonel 1438
バルフール
Balfour, Ludmilla 86
バルブル
Balbul, Nafia 85
ハルフレイタグ
Charfreitag, Libor 247
ハルフレドソン
Hallfredsson, Emil 559
ハルブレント
Halbrendt, Catherine 556
バルベイロ
Barbeiro, Marciano Silva 92
ハルベ・バウアー
Halbe-Bauer, Ulrike 556
バルベーラ
Barbera, Carlo 92
バルベリ
Barbery, Muriel 92
バルベリー
Barberi, Carlo 92
バルベリス
Barberis, Andrea 92
Barberis, Jaime 92
Barberis, Juan Carlos 92
ハルペリン
Halperin, Bertrand I. 559
Halperin, James L. 559
Halperin, Mark 559
Halperin, Morton H. 559
Halperin, Richard W. 559
バルベルデ

ハ

Valverde, Ernesto 1441
Valverde Belmonte, Alejandro 1441

バルベーロ
Barbero, Alessandro 92

バルボウサ
Barbosa, Leandro 92

バルボーサ
Barbosa, Edson 92

バルボサ
Barbosa, Mariano 92
Barboza, Raul 92

バルボザ
Barbosa, Nelson 92
Barbosa, Tomás Gomes 92
Fernandes Barbosa, Jade 429

バルボザビセンテ
Barbosa Vicente, Abraão Aníval Fernandes 92

ハルボーシェン
Halvorsen, Krsistin 560

ハルボーセン
Halvorsen, Andreas 560

ハルホナク
Harchonak, Hanna 569

ハルボム
Hallbom, Tim 558

バルボラ・シェルジ
Valvola Scelsi, Raf 1441

バルマ
Varma, Yatindra Nath 1447
Verma, Sahib Singh 1453
Verma, Satya Bhushan 1453

バルマー
Ballmer, Connie 87
Ballmer, Steve 87
Balmer, Paul 87

パルマ
Palma, Félix J. 1072
Palma, Nivia 1072

パルマー
Palmer, Anna 1072
Palmer, Donald 1073
Palmer, Earl 1073
Palmer, Harry 1073
Palmer, Joy A. 1073
Palmer, Parker J. 1073
Palmer, Pat 1073
Palmer, Rebekka S. 1073
Palmer, Stephen Richard 1073
Parmar, Babubhai Chimanbhai 1081

バルマク
Barmak, Wais Ahmad 95

バルマセーダ
Balmaceda, Carlos 87

パールマター
Perlmutter, David 1099
Perlmutter, Saul 1099

パールマッター
Perlmutter, Saul 1099

パルマドッティル
Palmadottir, Ingibjorg 1072

バルマー＝トーマス
Bulmer-Thomas, V. 201

パルマノ
Palmano, Penny 1072

パルマル
Palmaru, Raivo 1072

ハルマン
Halman, Greg 559
Halman, Talât Sait 559

バルマン
Bulmahn, Jason M. 201
Bulman, Chris 201

パールマン
Paalman, Anthony 1067
Pearlman, Cindy 1090
Pearlman, Edith 1090
Pearlman, Leslie K. 1090
Perlman, Carol A. 1099
Perlman, Itzhak 1099
Perlman, Nicole 1099
Perlman, Radia 1099
Perlman, Steve 1099

バルミ
Balmy, Coralie 87

パルミエーリ
Palmieri, Franco 1073

パルミエリ
Palmieri, Eddie 1073

パルミオッティ
Palmiotti, Jimmy 1073

パルミサーノ
Palmisano, Samuel J. 1073

パルミザノ
Palmisano, Antonella 1073

バルミル・ビルドゥラン
Balmir Villedrouin, Stéphanie 87

パルム
Palm, Carl Magnus 1072
Palm, Jean-Pierre 1072

パールムッター
Perlmutter, Bruce 1099

パルムラン
Parmelin, Guy 1081

ハルムルザエフ
Khalmurzaev, Khasan 725

パルメジャーニ
Parmegiani, Francesco 1081

パルメタ
Palmetta, Alberto 1073

パルメッサー
Parmessar, Rabindre 1081

パルメル
Palmer, Cristiana Paşca 1073

パルモア
Palmore, Erdman Ballagh 1073

ハルモコ
Harmoko 572

バルモシ
Balmos, Galina 87

バルモンド
Balmond, Cecil 87

ハルラウト
Harlaut, Henrik 571

ハルラプ
Kharlap, Anatoly D. 727

ハルラプ
Kharlap, Anatoly D. 727

ハルラン
Kharlan, Olga 727

パルリ
Parly, Florence 1081

バルレス・バゲナ
Barlés Báguena, Elena 94

パルロー
Perlow, Leslie 1099

バルワリ
Barwari, Nasreen 101

ハルーン
al-Haroun, Ahmad Rashed 572
Haroun, Baradine 572
Haroun, Mahamat-saleh 572

パルン
Pärn, Olga 1081
Pärn, Priit 1081

バルンドルフーニールセン
Barndorff-Nielsen, Ole E. 95

パルンビ
Palumbi, Anthony R. 1073
Palumbi, Stephen R. 1073

ハーレー
Harley, David 571
Harley, Madeline M. 571
Hurley, Chad 637
Hurley, Elizabeth Jane 637
Hurley, Matthew M. 637
Hurley, Michael 637
Hurley, Tonya 637

ハレ
Harre, Laila 573
Harré, Rom 573

バーレ
Baare, Yahaya 76
Valle, Laura 1440

バーレー
Burley, John 204
Varley, Susan 1447

バレ
Bale, Qoriniasi 86
Ballé, Catherine 87
Ballé, Freddy 87
Ballé, Michael 87
Wäre, Mervi 1478

バレー
Barreh, Moumin Hassan 97
Valley, Kenneth 1440

パレ
Pare, Joseph 1077
Paré, P.D. 1077
Pared, Sigfrido 1077

バレア
Barea, Jose 93
Barea Tejeiro, José 93

ハーレイ
Haley, Amanda 557
Harley, Bill 571
Harley, Richard C. 571
Hurley, Catherine 637

バーレイ
Buley, Leah 200
Varley, Susan 1447

パーレイ
Parley, Winifred A. 1081

バーレイ・アレン
Burley-Allen, Madelyn 204

パレイエ
Palayer, Jean 1072

ハレイサト
Khreisat, Azmi 729

バレイジ
Burrage, Alfred McLelland 205

ハレイシム
Harasym, Sarah 569

ハーレイデ
Hareide, Knut Arild 570

パレイデス
Paredes, Eduardo 1077

バレイラ
Didi 353
Parreira, Carlos Alberto 1082

バレイロ・スパイニ
Bareiro Spaini, Luís Nicanor 93

バレイロ・ファハルド
Barreiro Fajardo, Georgina 97

バレウ
Balew, Birhanu 86

ハレヴィ
Halevi, Ilan 557
Halevi, Z'ev ben Shimon 557
Halevy, Efraim 557

パレオログ
Paleologu, Theodor 1072

バレカ
Valeca, Şerban Constantin 1439

ハレギ
Khaleqi, Naser 724

パレク
Parekh, Nikunj 1077

バレケット
Bareket, Rachael 93

バレサル
Balesar, Dewanand 86

バーレサン
Burreson, Jay 205

バレ・シヌシ
Barré-Sinoussi, François Claire 97

バレシヌシ
Barré-Sinoussi, François Claire 97

バレス
Valles, Hakeem 1440
Valles, Max 1440

パーレス
Paras bir Bikram Shah 1077

バレステロス
Ballesteros, Seve 87

バレストラッチ
Balestracci, Duccio 86

バレストリーニ
Balestrini, Nanni 86

バレストル
Balestre, Jean-Marie 86

ハレスレベン
Halleslevens, Moisés Omar 559

ハレスレベンス
Halleslevens, Moisés Omar 559

パレゾン
Paraison, Edwin 1077

パレチェク
Palecek, Josef 1072

パレチコヴァー
Palecková, Libuse 1072

バレッカ
Barreca, Christopher 97

パレツキー
Paretsky, Sara N. 1078

バーレッタ
Barletta, Martha 94

バレッタ

ハ

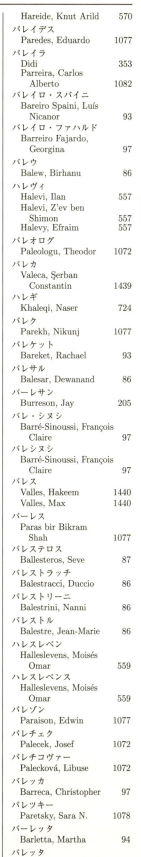

Barletta, Martha 94
パレッタ
Paletta, Gabriel 1072
バレッツ
Bareigts, Ericka 93
ハレット
Hallet, Bryce 559
Hallett, Christine E. 559
Hallett, Lisa 559
Hallett, Tom 559
バレット
Barreto, Ricardo 97
Barreto Rodriguez, Ysis 97
Barrett, Andrea 97
Barrett, Angela 97
Barrett, Beauden 97
Barrett, Brigetta 97
Barrett, Colleen C. 97
Barrett, Craig R. 97
Barrett, Daniel 97
Barrett, Daniel J. 97
Barrett, Danny 97
Barrett, Deirdre 97
Barrett, Diane 97
Barrett, Gary W. 97
Barrett, Jake 97
Barrett, James 97
Barrett, Judi 97
Barrett, Lorna 97
Barrett, Louise 97
Barrett, Margaret S. 97
Barrett, Neal, Jr. 97
Barrett, Neil 97
Barrett, Paul M. 97
Barrett, Peter 97
Barrett, Richard 97
Barrett, Rob 97
Barrett, Robert 97
Barrett, Ron 97
Barrett, Scott 97
Barrett, Shaquil 97
Barrett, Syd 97
Barrett, Tracy 97
Barrett, William C. 97
Barrette, Elizabeth 97
Barretto, Francisco Carlos, Jr. 97
Barretto, Ray 98
パレット
Pallett, Clare 1072
Paret, Peter 1078
バレット-ヒル
Barrett-Hill, Florence 97
バレッラ
Barella, Nicolo 93
バレデアルメイダ
Vale de Almeida, Joao 1439
パレーデス
Paredes, Carlos 1077
パレデス
Paredes, Juan Carlos 1077
Paredes, Leandro 1077
Paredes, Marcela 1077
Paredes, Melanio 1077
パレデス・ロドリゲス
Paredes Rodríguez, Carlos 1077
ハレド
Khaled, Abdo Razzaz Saleh 724
Khaled, Mohamed Sidya Ould Mohamed 724
バレート
Barreto, Edgar 97
バレト
Barreto, Alvaro 97
Barreto, Franklin 97
パレト
Pareto, Paula 1078
バレナ
Balena, Francesco 86
パレーニョ
Parreño, Earl G. 1082
バレネチェ
Barreneche, Raul A. 97
バレネチェア
Barrenetxea, Iban 97
パレハ
Pareja, Nicolas 1077
パレハ・ヤヌセリ
Pareja Yannuzzelli, Carlos 1077
ハレビ
Halevy, Efraim 557
パーレビ
Pahlavi, Ali-Reza 1070
Pahlevi, Reza II 1070
パレプ
Palepu, Krishna G. 1072
パレファウ
Palefau, Tevita 1072
ハレーブン
Hareven, Tamara K. 571
パレ・ペレス
Pared Pérez, Sigfrido 1077
パレホ
Parejo, Daniel 1077
ハーレマンス
Hallemans, Ina 558
ハーレム
Harlem, Hanne 571
パレム
Palem, Robert M. 1072
バレラ
Barrera, Hugo 97
Valera, Breyvic 1440
Valera y Alcala Galiano, Juan 1440
Varela, Afonso 1446
Varela, Guillermo 1446
Varela, Iris 1446
Varela, Juan Carlos 1446
Varela, María Iris 1446
バレラ・パーラ
Barrera Parra, Jaime 97
バレラ・ラディオ
Varela Radio, Alfonso 1446
バレリー
Barrely, Christine 97
Vallely, Paul 1440
バレリアン
Valérien, Jean 1440
パレリス
Parellis, Apostolos 1077
バレリーニ
Ballerini, Richard M. 87
ハレリマナ
Harerimana, Sheikh Mussa 571
ハーレル
Harrell, Wilson 573
ハレル
Harel, Elchanan S. 570
Harel, Isser 570
Harrell, Lynn 573
Harrell, Montrezl 573
Hurrell, Karen 637
バーレル
Burrell, Ty 205
バレル
Burrel, Duke 205
Burrell, Boz 205
Burrell, Brian 205
Burrell, Gibson 205
Burrell, Paul 205
Burrell, Roy Eric Charles 205
Burrell, Shelia 205
ハレル＝セスニアック
Harrell-Sesniak, Mary 573
ハレルソン
Harrellson, Josh 573
Harrelson, Woody 573
パレルモ
Palermo, Jeffrey 1072
バレロ
Valero, Edwin 1440
ハーレン
Harlan, Jean Durgin 571
ハレン
Hallen, Lexie 558
バーレン
Baaren, Rickert Bart van 76
ハレングレン
Hallengren, Bo 558
Hallengren, Lena 559
バレンシア
Valencia, Alejandra 1439
Valencia, Antonio 1439
Valencia, Danny 1439
Valencia, Enner 1439
Valencia Victoria, Ingrit Lorena 1439
バレンシア・アラナ
Valencia Arana, Ramón Arístides 1439
バレンシアガ
Balenziaga, Mikel 86
バレンシア・コシオ
Valencia Cossio, Fabio 1439
バレンジャー
Ballenger, James C. 87
バレンズエラ
Valenzuela, Arturo 1440
バレンスエラ・ゴンサレス
Valenzuela González, Abraham 1440
ハレンスレーベン
Hallensleben, Anne 559
Hallensleben, Georg 559
バレンタ
Valenta, Ales 1439
バレンタイン
Balentine, Samuel Eugene 86
Ballentine, Lonnie 87
Valentine, Alan D. 1439
Valentine, Bobby 1439
Valentine, Chelsea 1439
Valentine, Denzel 1439
Valentine, James 1439
Valentine, Jean 1439
Valentine, Jenny 1439
Valentine, Penny 1439
Valentine, Radleigh 1439
Valentine, R.James 1439
Valentine, Vincent 1439
バレンチ
Valenti, Jack 1439
パレンチ
Parente, Pedro 1078
バレンチッチ
Valencic, Mitja 1439
バレンチノス
Valentinis, Pia 1439
バレンチン
Valentim, Maria Gomes 1439
パレンツァン
Parenzan, Peter 1078
バレンテ
Valente, Catherynne M. 1439
Valente, Ivo 1439
Valente, Maria Idalina De Oliveira 1439
バレンティ
Valenti, Jack 1439
パレンティ
Parenti, Enrico 1078
バレンティーニ
Valentini, Giacomo 1439
Vanentini, Pasquale 1443
バレンティノ
Valentino 1439
Valentino, Domenico 1439
Valentino, Manon 1439
バレンティン
Valentim, Jorge Aliceres 1439
Valentim, Maria Gomes 1439
Valentin, Jesmuel 1439
Valentin, Lidia 1439
Valentin Perez, Lidia 1439
バーレント
Barendt, E.M. 93
バレント
Barend, Johnny 93
Barendt, E.M. 93
パレントー
Parenteau, Shirley 1078
バレントビッチ
Valentovič, Ivan 1439
バレンドレクト
Barendrecht, Wouter 93
バレンバウム
Berenbaum, David 125
バレンボイム
Barenboim, Daniel 93
ハロー
Hallo, William W. 559
バーロ
Barlow, Zenobia 95
バーロー
Barlow, Emilie-claire 94
Barlow, Gary 94
Barlow, Margaret Johnstone 94
Barlow, William 95
バロ
Baro 96
バロー
Barrault, Jean-Michel 97
Barrault, Marie-Christine 97
Barro, Robert J. 98
Barrow, Dean Oliver 98
Barrow, John David 98
Barrow, Martin 98
Barrow, Sarah 98
Barrow, Terence 98
Bullough, Max 201
Burrow, Thomas 206

ハ

パロ
Pallo, Jackie 1072
Palo, Urve 1073
Parot, Catalina 1081
Paroz, Jean-François 1081
Parrot, Maxence 1082
ハロアルドッティル
Haróardóttir, Eygló 572
バロイ
Balói, Oldemiro Júlio Marques 87
Baloyi, Richard Masenyani 87
ハーロウ
Harlow, Barbara 571
Harlow, Bill 571
Harlow, Joan Hiatt 571
Harlow, Joel 571
バーロウ
Barlow, David H. 94
Barlow, Emilie-claire 94
Barlow, Gary 94
Barlow, Julie 94
Barlow, Maude 95
Barlow, Rebecca 95
Barlow, Steve 95
Barlow, Tani E. 95
Barrow, Modou 98
Barrow, Tony 98
バロウ
Barough, Nina 96
Barrow, Adama 98
Barrow, John David 98
Barrow, Lamin 98
Barrow, Rosemary J. 98
Barrow, Steve 98
Barrow, William Hansel 98
Burrow, Colin 206
Burrow, John Wyon 206
Burrow, Rufus 206
バロヴァ
Barova, Todorka Mincheva 96
ハロウェイ
Halloway, Eke Ahmed 559
Halloway, Stuart Dabbs 559
Holloway, Susan D. 617
Holloway, Todd 617
ハロウェル
Hallowell, Edward M. 559
バロウクリフ
Barrowcliffe, Mark 98
バロウ＝グリーン
Barrow-Green, June 98
ハロウズ
Hallows, Richard 559
バロウズ
Barrows, Kate 98
Burroughs, Augusten 206
Burroughs, Jordan 206
Burrows, Annie 206
Burrows, Donald 206
Burrows, Gideon 206
Burrows, Graham D. 206
Burrows, John 206
Burrows, Mathew 206
パロウベク
Paroubek, Jiří 1081
バロエスクエスタ
Valoyes Cuesta, Ubaldina 1440
バロエフ
Baroev, Khasan 96
Valuev, Nikolay 1440
バロガ
Baloga, Viktor 87
バローグ
Balog, James 87
Balog, Kati 87
Balogh, Norbert 87
バログ
Balog, Zoltán 87
Balogh, Gabor 87
Balogh, Mary 87
バログン
Balogun, Leon 87
ハロシ
Haroche, Serge 572
パロシ
Palocci Filho, Antonio 1073
パロシ・フィリョ
Palocci Filho, Antonio 1073
バロシャンブリエ
Barro-chambrier, Alexandre 98
バロシュ
Baros, Milan 96
ハローズ
Hallows, Jolyon E. 559
バロース
Burroughs, John 206
バローズ
Barrows, Eddy 98
Burroughs, Franklin 206
Burroughs, Jordan 206
Burroughs, William James 206
Burrowes, Grace 206
Burrows, Eva 206
Burrows, Hal 206
Burrows, Peter 206
Burrows, Terry 206
バロス
Baros, Milan 96
Barros, Ricardo 98
Barros, Rui Duarte de 98
パロスキ
Paloschi, Alberto 1073
バローゾ
Barroso, José Manuel Durão 98
バロゾ
Barroso, José Manuel Durão 98
バロチ
Baloch, Abdul Qadir 87
Baroti, Lajos 96
バロック
Bullock, Alan Louis Charles 201
Bullock, Sandra 201
バロッソ
Barroso, Luiz André 98
パロッタ＝キアロッリ
Pallotta-Chiarolli, Maria 1072
パロッチャードクトレロ
Parrocha-Doctolero, Beth 1082
パロット
Parrot, Andrea 1082
Parrott, Andrew Haden 1082
Parrott, Leslie L. 1082
Parrott, Ryan 1082
ハロップ
Harrop, Loretta 576
バロティ
Baroti, Lajos 96
パロディ
Parodi, Claudia 1081
Parodi, John 1081
Parodi, Teresa 1081
バロディス
Balodis, L. 87
パロディ・デチェオナ
Parody d'Echeona, Gina María 1081
バロテッリ
Balotelli, Mario 87
バロテリ
Balotelli, Mario 87
バロトン
Vallotton, Kris 1440
バロニアン
Baronian, Jean Baptiste 96
バローネ
Vallone, Raf 1440
ハロネン
Halonen, Tarja 559
パロノー
Paronnaud, Vincent 1081
バロノヴァ
Baronova, Irina 96
バロノワ
Baronova, Irina 96
バローフ
Balogh, Suzanne 87
パーロフ
Parloff, Gloria H. 1081
バローベルカセム
Vallaud-Belkacem, Najat 1440
パロメケ
Palomeque, Mathias 1073
パロモ＝ロヴィンスキー
Palomo-Lovinski, Noël 1073
パロライン
Paroline, Shelli 1081
ハロラン
Halloran, Edward J. 559
Halloran, Richard 559
Raymond, Halloran 1162
バロリー
Valory, Ross 1440
パロリン
Parolin, Pietro 1081
バロルスキー
Barolsky, Paul 96
ハロルド
Harold, Eli 572
Harrold, A.F. 576
Harrold, Jess 576
Harrold, Ruby 576
パローロ
Parolo, Marco 1081
バロワフォルティエ
Valois-fortier, Antoine 1440
バロワン
Baroin, François 96
ハーロン
Herron, Dan 599
ハロン
Herron, Ronald W. 600
バーロン
Barron, Mark 98
バロン
Ballon, Robert J. 87
Baron, David 96
Baron, Francine 96
Baron, J.Steve 96
Baron, Peter P. 96
Bar-on, Roni 96
Baron, Steve 96
Baróon, Mercedes 96
Barron, Carla 98
Barron, Craig 98
Barron, Earl 98
Barron, James 98
Barron, Natania 98
Barron, Sean 98
Barron, T.A. 98
Barron-Tieger, Barbara 98
バロン・コーエン
Baron-Cohen, Simon 96
バロン・シクルナ
Baron Scicluna 96
バロンスキー
Baronsky, Eva 96
バロン-ティーガー
Barron-Tieger, Barbara 98
バロンド
Barrondo, Erick 98
パロンド
Parrondo, José 1082
パロンボ
Palombo, Angelo 1073
バロン-リード
Baron-Reid, Colette 96
バワー
Baur, Fredric J. 106
パワー
Power, Anne 1130
Power, Carla 1130
Power, Dermot 1130
Power, Elizabeth 1130
Power, James D., Ⅳ 1130
Power, Martin 1130
Power, Michael 1130
Power, Michael A. 1130
Power, Samantha 1130
Power, Sean 1130
Power, Simon 1130
Power, Ted 1130
Power, Thomas J. 1130
Power, Thomas M. 1130
Power, Vic 1130
パワシュ・ルトコフスカ
Palasz Rutkowska, Ewa 1072
ハワース
Howarth, Daniel 628
Howarth, David 628
Howarth, Glennys 628
Howarth, Peter 628
ハワス
Hawas, Zahi 583
パワーズ
Powers, Alan 1130
Powers, Becky J. 1130
Powers, Bruce R. 1130
Powers, Jerraud 1130
Powers, Joan 1130
Powers, Joseph 1130
Powers, Kevin 1130
Powers, Kimiko 1130
Powers, Richard 1130
Powers, Richard B. 1130
Powers, Ron 1130
Powers, Ross 1130
Powers, Shelley 1130

ハ

Powers, Tim 1130
Powers, William 1130
バワーソクス
Bowersox, Donald J. 170
ハワード
Howard, *Sir* Albert 627
Howard, Anita G. 627
Howard, Annabel 627
Howard, Anne 627
Howard, Austin 627
Howard, B. 627
Howard, Bart 627
Howard, Byron 627
Howard, Chris 627
Howard, Clark 627
Howard, David 627
Howard, David John 627
Howard, Dwight 627
Howard, Edward Lee 627
Howard, Gail 627
Howard, Gregory Allen 627
Howard, Harlan 627
Howard, James Newton 627
Howard, Jaye 627
Howard, John 627
Howard, Jonathan C. 627
Howard, Jordan 627
Howard, Jules 627
Howard, Juwan 627
Howard, Ken 627
Howard, Linda 627
Howard, Michael 627
Howard, Michael Eliot 627
Howard, Pam 627
Howard, Patricia A. 627
Howard, Paul 627
Howard, Ra'Zahn 627
Howard, Richard 627
Howard, Richard D. 627
Howard, Richard E. 627
Howard, Rick 627
Howard, Ron 627
Howard, Ryan 627
Howard, Stephanie 627
Howard, Stephen 627
Howard, Steven R. 627
Howard, Terry 628
Howard, Tim 628
Howard, Tracy 628
Howard, Xavien 628
ハワードウォロコリィ
Howardwolokollie, Jamesetta 628
バワトネ
Bawatneh, Jamal 107
ハワートメ
Hawatmeh, Nayef 583
ハワトメ
Hawatmeh, Nayef 583
バワラ
Bawara, Gilbert 107
パワル
Pawar, Sharad 1088
ハワールデ
Khawaldeh, Khleif al 727
ハワーワス
Hauerwas, Stanley 581
バーワンガー
Berwanger, Jay 132
ハーン
Haan, Amanda 551
Haan, Linda de 551
Hahn, Alexander 554
Hahn, Andre 554
Hahn, Carole L. 554
Hahn, Ferdinand 554
Hahn, Hilary 554
Hahn, Jesse 554
Hahn, Joe 554
Hahn, Johannes 554
Hahn, Kimberly 554
Hahn, Linaya 554
Hahn, Lothar 554
Hahn, Mary Downing 554
Hahn, R.A. 554
Hahn, Rick 554
Hahn, Robert W. 555
Hahn, Scott 555
Hahn, Ulla 555
Hamm, Steve 563
Hearn, Chick 587
Hearn, Ciaran 587
Hearn, David 587
Hearn, Diana 587
Hearn, Geoffrey 587
Hearn, Julie 587
Hearn, Lian 587
Hearn, Loyola 587
Hearn, Marcus 587
Hearn, Robert A. 587
Hearne, Kevin 587
Hern, Candice 598
Khan, Ismael 726
Khan, Mohammad Ismail 726
Mandel, Gabriel 893
ハン
Hahn, Seung-hun 555
Han, Byong-sam 564
Han, Chae-young 564
Han, Duck-soo 564
Han, Fook Kwang 564
Han, Hwa-kap 564
Han, Hye-jin 564
Han, Hyo-joo 564
Han, Hyo-yon 564
Han, Kap-soo 564
Han, Kook-young 564
Han, Kwang-bok 564
Han, Min-koo 564
Han, Myeong-sook 564
Han, Pong-chun 564
Han, Ryong-guk 564
Han, Seo Hye 564
Han, Seung-soo 564
Han, Soo-san 564
Han, Suk-kyu 564
Han, Sung-joo 564
Han, Sungpil 565
Han, Sun Woo 565
Han, Suyin 565
Han, Tok-su 565
Han, Wan-sang 565
Han, Woon-sa 565
Han, Xiao-peng 565
Han, Xing 565
Han, Yaya 565
Han, Ying 565
Han, Zheng 565
Hang, Nguyen Thi 566
Hang Chuon Naron 566
Hung, Erick K. 635
バーン
Bahn, Paul G. 80
Berne, Jennifer 129
Berne, Robert M. 129
Berne, Suzanne 129
Burn, Doris 204
Byrne, Alexandra 211
Byrne, David 211
Byrne, David S. 211
Byrne, Gabriel 211
Byrne, John 211
Byrne, John A. 211
Byrne, Julia 211
Byrne, Kerrigan 211
Byrne, Lorna 211
Byrne, Mike 211
Byrne, Paula 211
Byrne, Rhonda 211
Byrne, Richard 211
Byrne, Richard W. 211
Byrne, Robert 211
Byrne, Sarah 211
Byrne, Skye 211
Vaughn, Herschell Read 1448
バン
al-Ban, Huda Abdul-Latif 88
Ban, Ki-moon 88
Ban, Shigeru 88
Bann, Stephen 90
Bunn, Cullen 201
Bunn, Howard Franklin 201
Van, Ernest N.D. 1441
パン
Ban, Ki-moon 88
Bang, Yong-suk 89
Pamg, Pandelela Rinong 1074
Pan, Lynn 1074
Pan, Marta 1074
Pan, Philip P. 1074
Pan, Sutong 1074
Pan, Xiang-li 1074
Pang, Alex 1074
Pang, Chol Ram 1074
Pang, Danny 1074
Pang, Ho-cheung 1074
Pang, May 1074
Pang, Mei-che Samantha 1074
Pang, Oxide 1074
Pang, Qing 1074
Pan Sorasak 1075
Rinong, Pandelela 1183
パン・アウン
Pan Aung 1074
バンアッカー
Van Acker, Evi 1441
バンアルフェン
Van Alphen, Hans 1441
バン・アレン
Van Allen, James Alfred 1441
バンアンデル
Van Andel, Jay 1441
Van Andel, Steve 1441
パンウィチャイ
Punwichai, Lakkana 1140
ハンウィック
Hunwick, Heather Delancey 637
バンヴィル
Banville, John 90
バンカ
Bańka, Witold 89
バンカー
Banker, Ashok K. 89
Banker, Kyle 89
Bunker, Edward 201
バンガ
Banga, Ajay 89
バンカーク
Van Kirk, Theodore 1444
パーンカット
Parncutt, Richard 1081
バンガードナー
Bumgardner, Gregory 201
バンガーナー
Bumgarner, Madison 201
パンガニバン
Panganiban, Domingo 1075
パンカム
Phankham, Viphavanh 1106
バンカール
Bancquart, Marie-Claire 88
バンガル
Bhangal, Sham 135
バンガルテル
Bangalter, Thoma 89
パンガロス
Pangalos, Theodoros 1074
パンガンダマン
Pangandaman, Nasser 1074
ハンキ
Hanke, John 566
バンギ
Vangi, Venant Tshipasa 1443
ハンキソン
Hankison, Whitney 566
バンキーニ
Banchini, Chiara 88
パンギリナン
Pangilinan, Manuel Velez 1075
ハンキンス
Hankins, Johnathan 566
ハング
Hang, Ann 566
バンク
Bank, Melissa 89
Bank, Ondrej 89
Banke, Karl 89
バング
Bang, Derrick 89
Bang, Mary Jo 89
Bang, Molly 89
パンク
Punke, Michael 1140
バンクシー
Banksy 90
ハンクス
Hanks, Helga G.I. 566
Hanks, Tom 566
バンクス
Banks, Carolyn 89
Banks, Catherine 89
Banks, Cherry A. McGee 89
Banks, Dennis J. 89
Banks, Erik 89
Banks, Ernie 89
Banks, Iain 90
Banks, James A. 90
Banks, Johnthan 90
Banks, Kate 90
Banks, Leanne 90
Banks, Lynne Reid 90
Banks, Marcus 90
Banks, Maya 90
Banks, Melaine Josephin 90
Banks, Philip 90

Banks, Rosie 90
Banks, Russel 90
Banks, Sarah 90
Banks, Steven 90
Banks, Tyra 90
バンクストン
Bankston, John 90
バングスボ
Bangsbo, Jens 89
パンクハースト
Pankhurst, Andy 1075
パングボーン
Pangborn, Edgar 1075
バンクムクンジ
Bankumukunzi, Nestor 90
バングーラ
Bangura, Zainab Hawa 89
バングラ
Bangoura, Fode 89
Bangoura, Ibrahim 89
Bangoura, Kiridi 89
Bangoura, Mamadoub Max 89
Bangoura, Mathurin 89
Bangura, Alimamy Paolo 89
Bangura, Bai Mamoud 89
Bangura, M'mah Hawa 89
Bangura, Mohamed 89
パンクラトフ
Pankratov, Oleg 1075
バングリ
Banguli, Marco 89
パングリッツ
Pangritz, Walter 1075
バンクリーフ
Vanclief, Lyle 1441
バングル
Bangle, Christopher 89
バングレ
Bangre, Taïrou 89
パンクレチッチ
Pankretić, Božidar 1075
パンクレティッチ
Pankretić, Božidar 1075
バンクロフト
Bancroft, Anne 88
Bancroft, Lundy 88
Bancroft, Tom 88
ハンケ
Handke, Danny 565
パンケ
Panke, Helmut 1075
バンゲイ・スタニエ
Bungay Stanier, Michael 201
パンゲストゥ
Pangestu, Mari Elka 1075
バンゲリス
Vangelis 1443
パンゴ
Pango, Ylli 1075
パンゴー
Pingaud, Bernard 1113
ハンコック
Hancock, Graham 565
Hancock, Herbie 565
Hancock, Ian F. 565
Hancock, James Gulliver 565
Hancock, John Lee 565
Hancock, Jonathan 565
Hancock, Josh 565
Hancock, Marguerite Gong 565
Hancock, Sheila 565
Hancock, Vincent 565
ハンコックス
Hancox, Dan 565
バンコバーデン
Van Koeverden, Adam 1444
パンコール
Pancol, Katherine 1074
パンコル
Pancol, Katherine 1074
バンコン
Bancon, Francois 88
バーンサイド
Burnside, Julian 205
Burnside, Robert Lee 205
ハンサード
Hansard, Glen 567
バンサル
Bansal, Binny 90
Bansal, Pawan K. 90
Bansal, Sachin 90
バンサーン
Bansarn, Bunnag 90
バン・サント
Van Sant, Gus 1445
バンシ
Banchi, Roger 88
バンジ
Banzi, Massimo 90
ハンジェス
Hanges, Paul J. 566
バンジェナー
Bungener, Janet 201
バンシェルス
Banscherus, Jürgen 90
バンジオ
Banzio, Dagobert 90
パンジキゼ
Pandzhikidze, Maya 1074
バンシタート
Vansittart, Peter 1445
バンシッタート
Vansittart, Peter 1445
バンジャイ
Banjai, Barros Bacar 89
パンジャイタン
Panjaitan, Luhut Binsar 1075
パンジャビ
Panjabi, Archie 1075
ハンシュ
Hansch, Corwin 567
バンシュ
Bansch, Helga 90
ハンシュタイン
Hanstein, Mariana 568
バーンシュタイン
Bernstein, Jeremy 130
バンジョー
Banjo, Chris 89
BonJour, Laurence 159
バンジョーニ
Vangioni, Leonel 1443
バーン＝ジョーンズ
Burne-Jones 204
バンジョン・ピサンタナクーン
Banjong Pisanthanakun 89
バンジル
Van Zyl, L.J. 1446
パンジンスキー
Panzhinskiy, Alexander 1075
ハーンズ
Hurns, Allen 637
ハンス
Hans, Joachim 567
Hans, Manoj 567
Hans, Valerie P. 567
ハンズ
Hands, Guy 565
Hands, Marina 565
バーンズ
Barnes, Adairius 95
Barnes, Ashley 95
Barnes, Austin 95
Barnes, Barry 95
Barnes, Ben 95
Barnes, Brandon 95
Barnes, Brenda C. 95
Barnes, Colin 95
Barnes, Courtney M. 95
Barnes, Danny 95
Barnes, Deion 95
Barnes, Elinor 95
Barnes, Elizabeth 95
Barnes, Emm 95
Barnes, Gregg 95
Barnes, Harrison 95
Barnes, Ian 95
Barnes, Jacob 95
Barnes, Jacqueline 95
Barnes, James A. 95
Barnes, Jennifer Lynn 95
Barnes, John A. 95
Barnes, Jonathan 95
Barnes, Julian 95
Barnes, Kathleen H. 95
Barnes, Lesley 95
Barnes, Louis B. 95
Barnes, Matt 95
Barnes, Mike 95
Barnes, Nathaniel 95
Barnes, Patrick 95
Barnes, Simon 95
Barnes, Sophie 95
Barnes, Steven 95
Barnes, Tavaris 95
Barnes, Tim 95
Barnes, T.J. 95
Berns, Gregory 130
Burnes, Caroline 204
Burns, Artie 205
Burns, Billy 205
Burns, Bob 205
Burns, Chantal 205
Burns, Charles 205
Burns, Conrad 205
Burns, David D. 205
Burns, Ed 205
Burns, Glenn 205
Burns, Jim 205
Burns, Ken 205
Burns, Laura J. 205
Burns, Lawrence D. 205
Burns, Marc 205
Burns, Marilyn 205
Burns, Nancy 205
Burns, Nicholas 205
Burns, Pat 205
Burns, Ralph 205
Burns, Richard 205
Burns, Sarah 205
Burns, Scott 205
Burns, Steve 205
Burns, Tom 205
Burns, Ursula M. 205
Burns, William 205
Byrnes, James P. 211
Byrnes, Jonathan L.S. 211
Byrnes, Michael J. 211
Byrnes, Robert Francis 211
Byrnes, Tricia 211
バンス
Bunce, William K. 201
Vance, Ashlee 1441
Vance, Cyrus Roberts 1441
Vance, Jack 1441
Vance, Lee G. 1441
ハンス・アダム2世
Hans Adam II 567
バンスカ
Vänskä, Osmo 1445
ハンスキ
Hanski, Ilkka 568
パンスキー
Pansky, Ben 1075
バン・スコイック
Van Scoyck, Robert 1445
バンスコイック
Van Scoyck, Robert 1445
バーンスタイン
Bernstein, Abbie 130
Bernstein, Alan B. 130
Bernstein, Albert J. 130
Bernstein, Alvin 130
Bernstein, Bill 130
Bernstein, Carl 130
Bernstein, Elmer 130
Bernstein, Eytan 130
Bernstein, Henry 130
Bernstein, Jacob 130
Bernstein, Jake 130
Bernstein, J.B. 130
Bernstein, Joanne Scheff 130
Bernstein, Laurie 130
Bernstein, Leora 130
Bernstein, Paula 130
Bernstein, Peter L. 130
Bernstein, Peter W. 130
Bernstein, Richard J. 130
Bernstein, Richard K. 130
Bernstein, Seymour 130
Bernstein, Sid 130
Bernstein, William J. 130
バーンスティール
Birnsteel, Laurie 141
バーンスティン
Bernstein, Gabrielle 130
バーンステイン
Bernstein, Sid 130
バンステッド
Bumstead, Henry 201
ハンステン
Hansten, Philip D. 568
ハンスドター
Hansdotter, Frida 567
バン・ストラーテン
Van Straten, Michael 1445
バンストン
Vanstone, Amanda 1445
パンズナー
Panzner, Michael J. 1075
バンスニック
Van Snick, Charline 1445
ハーンズバーガー
Harnsberger, H.Ric 572
Harnsberger, Lindsey C. 572

ハンズフォード
Hansford, Susan J. 568
ハンスブロー
Hansbrough, Russell 567
バーンズマーフィー
Barnes-Murphy, Frances 95
Barnes-Murphy, Rowan 95
ハンスマン
Hansmann, Henry 568
Hansmann, Liselotte 568
バンスライク
Van Slyke, Scott 1445
ハンスリー
Hansley, Joe 568
Hunsley, John 635
バンスリー
Bansley, Heather 90
ハンスン
Hansson, Tomoko 568
バンセ
Vance, Carina 1441
ハンセ・イマルワ
Hanse-himarwa, Katrina 567
パンセラ
Pansera, Celso 1075
ハンゼリック
Hanzelik, Edward S. 568
ハンセル
Hansell, Michael Henry 567
Hanser, Anders 568
バンセル
Bancel, Nicolas 88
Bánzer Suárez, Hugo 90
バンセル・スアレス
Bánzer Suárez, Hugo 90
ハンセルマン
Hanselman, Eric 567
ハンセン
Hansen, Abby J. 567
Hansen, Are 567
Hansen, Brendan 567
Hansen, Brian 567
Hansen, Carla 567
Hansen, Carsten 567
Hansen, Dave 567
Hansen, Eric K. 567
Hansen, Erik Fosnes 567
Hansen, Eva Kjer 567
Hansen, Flemming 567
Hansen, Gaby 567
Hansen, Gus 567
Hansen, Henriette Engel 567
Hansen, James E. 567
Hansen, James R. 567
Hansen, Jesper 567
Hansen, Joan 567
Hansen, Joseph 567
Hansen, Krishan 567
Hansen, Larry 567
Hansen, Lars 567
Hansen, Lars Peter 567
Hansen, Lasse Norman 567
Hansen, Marc 567
Hansen, Mark Victor 567
Hansen, Martin 567
Hansen, Mary 567
Hansen, Morten T. 567
Hansen, Natasha 567
Hansen, Ron 567
Hansen, Rosanna 567
Hansen, Stan 567
Hansen, Steve 567
Hansen, Sunny Sundal 567
Hansen, Valerie 568
Hansen, Vilh. 568
Hansen, Wade 568
Hansen, Willy 568
Hanson, Victor Davis 568
Hanssen, Bjarne Hakon 568
Hanssen, Jan-Inge 568
Lundgaard Hansen, Martin 853
ハンゼン
Hansen, Conrad 567
Hansen, Walter 568
ハンセン・ラヴ
Hansen-Love, Mia 568
ハンソ
Hanso, Hannes 568
パンソナ
Pinsonnat, Paul 1114
バンソール
Bansal, Sachin 90
ハンソン
Hanson, Alen 568
Hanson, Brooke 568
Hanson, Carol 568
Hanson, Curtis 568
Hanson, James Edward 568
Hanson, Jason 568
Hanson, Jaydee 568
Hanson, Lars 568
Hanson, Lewis 568
Hanson, Maryann 568
Hanson, Mirja P. 568
Hanson, Muriel 568
Hanson, Neil 568
Hanson, Nils 568
Hanson, Pamela 568
Hanson, Peter 568
Hanson, Rick 568
Hanson, R.Karl 568
Hanson, Shirley May Harmon 568
Hanson, Susan 568
Hanson, Thor 568
Hanson, Tommy 568
Hanson, Ward A. 568
Hanson, Warren 568
Hansson, David Heinemeier 568
Hansson, Robert O. 568
Harrison, Rob 576
バーンソン
Bahnson, Paul R. 80
パンソン
Pinçon, Michel 1112
パンソン＝シャルロ
Pinçon-Charlot, Monique 1112
ハンター
Hunter, Anthony R. 636
Hunter, Bob 636
Hunter, Christine 636
Hunter, Dan 636
Hunter, Danielle 636
Hunter, Dave 636
Hunter, David 636
Hunter, Evan 636
Hunter, Evie 636
Hunter, Graham 636
Hunter, Holly 636
Hunter, James C. 636
Hunter, Janet 636
Hunter, Jesse 636
Hunter, Joe 636
Hunter, John 636
Hunter, John A. 636
Hunter, Justin 636
Hunter, Kathy 636
Hunter, Kim 636
Hunter, Lawrie 636
Hunter, Maddy 636
Hunter, Madeline 636
Hunter, Mark 636
Hunter, Mark Lee 636
Hunter, Michael 636
Hunter, Montario 636
Hunter, Nick 636
Hunter, Richard 636
Hunter, R.J. 636
Hunter, Robin 636
Hunter, Ryan Ann 636
Hunter, Sally 637
Hunter, Stephen 637
Hunter, Torii 637
Hunter, Vince 637
McBain, Ed 859
バンタ
Banta, Milt 90
Banta, Susan 90
バンダ
Banda, Aleke 88
Banda, Anthony 88
Banda, Charles 88
Banda, Etta 88
Banda, Grenenger Kidney Msulira 88
Banda, Henry 88
Banda, Henry Chimunthu 88
Banda, Joyce Hilda 88
Banda, Mary 88
Banda, Rupiah 88
パンター
Punter, David 1140
バンダイク
Van Dyk, Mitchell 1443
Van Dyke, DeMarcus 1443
バン・ダイクン
Van Dyken, Rachel 1443
バンダウェイ
Vandeweghe, Coco 1443
バンダーカーイ
Vanderkaay, Peter 1442
バンダク
al-Bandak, Ziad 89
バンダーケイ
Vanderkaay, Peter 1442
バンダー・ジー
Vander Zee, Ruth 1443
バンダジェフスキー
Bandazhevskiĭ, IUriĭ Ivanovich 89
バンダーソン
Bunderson, C.Victor 201
パンタツィス
Pantazis, Christina 1075
パンターニ
Pantani, Marco 1075
パンタニ
Pantani, Marco 1075
ハンダノヴィッチ
Handanovic, Samir 565
バンダービーク
Vanderbeek, Kelly 1442
バンダープールウォレス
Vanderpool-wallace, Arianna 1442
バンダープールワレス
Vanderpool-wallace, Vincent 1442
バンダマ
Bandaman, Maurice Kouakou 89
バンダマン
Bandaman, Maurice Kouakou 89
バン・ダー・ミアー
Van der Meer, Ron 1442
バンダミア
VanderMeer, Jeff 1442
バン・ダム
Van Damme, Jean-Claude 1441
バンダム
Van Damme, Jean-Claude 1441
バンダラ
Bandara, Chandrani 89
バンダラナイケ
Bandaranaike, Anura 89
バンダーラーン
Vander Laan, Jason 1442
バンダリ
Bhandari, Bidhya Devi 135
Bhandari, Shankar 135
ハンダル
Handal, Schafik Jorge 565
Hándal, William 565
Jandar, William 662
パンタル
Pantale, Chris 1075
パンタレオニ
Pantaleoni, Lucia 1075
パンタロン
Pantalon, Michael V. 1075
バンチ
Bunch, John L., Jr. 201
パンチ
Punch, Keith 1140
パンチェンコ
Panchenko, Aleksandr Mikhailovich 1074
バン・チエン・ズン
Van Tien Dung 1445
パンチェン・ラマ11世
Panchen Lama X I 1074
パンチッチ
Pančić, Ivica 1074
パンチャス
Pontzious, Richard 1124
ハンチャロウ
Hancharou, Uladzislau 565
ハン・チュウン・ナロン
Hang Chuon Naron 566
パンチュロー
Pinturault, Alexis 1114
パンチョホバ
Pancochova, Sarka 1074
パンチョン
Puncheon, Jason 1140
バンチング
Bunting, Eve 202
ハンチントン.サミュエル
Huntington, Samuel Phillips 637
パンツァー
Pantzer, Peter 1075
パンツィエーリ
Panzieri, Lucia 1075
パンツェッタ
Panzetta, Girolamo 1075

ハ

ハンツマン
Huntsman, Jon 637
Huntsman, Jon, Sr. 637
ハンツリク
Hanzlik, Steffi 568
バンデ
Bande, John 89
Bindé, Jérôme 139
パンテ
Pantè, Franca Antonietta 1075
パンデ
Panday, Bikram 1074
Panday, Hitraj 1074
Pande, Kabinga 1074
Pande, Mahendra Bahadur 1074
バンテアクススアレス
Banteaux Suarez, Carlos 90
ハンディ
Handy, Charles 566
Handy, Phil 566
バンディ
Bandy, Jett 89
Bundy, Dylan 201
Bundy, Lorenzo 201
Bundy, Mary Lee 201
Vandy, Peter 1443
バンディー
Bundy, Marquis 201
パンディ
Pande, Peter S. 1074
Pandey, Ramesh Nath 1074
Pandey, Som Prasad 1074
パンデイ
Panday, Basdeo 1074
バンディエラ
Bandeira, Andreia 89
バン・ティエン・ズン
Van Tien Dung 1445
バンディオンオルトナー
Bandion-ortner, Claudia 89
ハンディク
Handique, B.K. 565
バンティケルト
Van Tichelt, Dirk 1445
ハンディサイズ
Handysides, Allan 566
パンディック
Pundick, Michele 1140
パンティッチ
Pantic, Aleksandar 1075
バンディット
Bandit, Clean 89
パンディット
Pandit, Vikram S. 1074
パンディト
Pandit, Lal Babu 1074
パンディブイキ
Pendy-bouyiki, Jean-Rémy 1094
バンティヘルト
Van Tichelt, Dirk 1445
パーンディヤ
Pandya, Anand A. 1074
Pandya, Kamlesh 1074
パンティリモン
Pantilimon, Costel 1075
ハンティング
Hunting, Sam 637
バンティング
Bunting, Eve 202
Bunting, Fred 202
Bunting, Kara 202
Bunting, Peter 202
パンティング
Panting, Patricia 1075
ハンティントン
Huntington, Greg 637
Huntington, Neal 637
Huntington, Samuel Phillips 637
ハンティントンホワイトリー
Huntington-Whiteley, Rosie 637
パンデニ
Pandeni, John 1074
パンデフ
Pandev, Goran 1074
バンデベンター
Van Deventer, Juan 1443
パンデム
Pandemou, Desire 1074
パンデューク
Pundyk, Grace 1140
バンデューラ
Bandura, Albert 89
バンデュラ
Bandura, Albert 89
バンデラス
Banderas, Antonio 89
ハンデランド
Handeland, Lori 565
パンテリス
Pantelis, Christos 1075
パンテリモン
Pantelimon, Oana 1075
ハンデル
Handel, Ari 565
Handel, Michael I. 565
バンデルカンプ
Van der Kemp, Gerald 1442
バン・デル・スツール
van der Stoel, Max 1442
ハンデルスマン
Handelsman, J.B. 565
Handelsman, Leonard 565
Handelsman, Walt 565
バン・デル・ブリスト
Van der Vlist, Eric 1443
ハンデルマン
Handelman, Susan A. 565
バン・デール・ルグト
van der Lugt, Cornis 1442
パンテレイ
Pantelei, Nikolai P. 1075
パンデレラ・パム
Pandelela Rinong Anak Pamg 1074
バーンデン
Barnden, Betty 95
バン・デン・ボイナンツ
Van den Boeynants, Paul 1442
バンデンボッセ
Vandenbossche, Freya 1442
ハント
Hundt, Reed 635
Hundt, Reed E. 635
Hunt, Aaron 635
Hunt, Akeem 635
Hunt, Alan 635
Hunt, Alexa 635
Hunt, Andrew 635
Hunt, Angela Elwell 635
Hunt, Anna 635
Hunt, Cameron 635
Hunt, Caroline 635
Hunt, Craig 635
Hunt, David 636
Hunt, Elizabeth Singer 636
Hunt, Errol 636
Hunt, Gareth 636
Hunt, Gary 636
Hunt, Greg 636
Hunt, Helen 636
Hunt, Howard Everette 636
Hunt, Irmgard Albine 636
Hunt, Jackson 636
Hunt, Jan 636
Hunt, Jeremy 636
Hunt, Joey 636
Hunt, Laird 636
Hunt, Lamar 636
Hunt, Lynn 636
Hunt, Margus 636
Hunt, Melvin 636
Hunt, Peter 636
Hunt, Peter Roger 636
Hunt, Philip 636
Hunt, Ray Lee 636
Hunt, Stephen 636
Hunt, Susan 636
Hunt, Tara 636
Hunt, Terry 636
Hunt, Tim 636
Hunt, Tristram 636
Hunt, Van 636
ハンド
Hand, Brad 565
Hand, David J. 565
Hand, Elizabeth 565
Hand, John R.M. 565
Hand, Michael S. 565
Hand, Richard 565
Hand, Thomas G. 565
バーント
Berndt, Bruce C. 129
バント
Wand, Günter 1475
バンド
Band, Edward 88
バンドゥー
Bundhoo, Lormus 201
パンドゥアンチット
Phandouangchit, Vongsa 1106
バンドゥネム
Vandúnem, Osvaldo de Jesus Serra 1443
バン・ドゥーネン
Van Dunem, Francisca 1443
バンドゥーネン
Van-dúnem, Cândido Pereira Dos Santos 1443
Van-dúnem, José Vieira Dias 1443
Van-dúnem, Pedro José 1443
バンドゥネン
Van-dúnem, Cândido Pereira Dos Santos 1443
ハンドゥルディエワ
Handurdyeva, Gurbansoltan 566
バンドゥレスパー
Vanderspar, Elizabeth 1442
ハントケ
Handke, Peter 565
パントコート
Pentecôte, Philippe 1095
バーンドーフ
Birndorf, Catherine 141
ハンドフィールド
Handfield, Robert B. 565
ハンドフィールド=ジョーンズ
Handfield-Jones, Helen 565
ハンドフォード
Handford, Martin 565
バンドマン
Bandman, Bertram 89
Bandman, Elsie L. 89
ハンドラー
Handler, David 565
Handler, Elliot 565
Handler, Lowell 565
Handler, Ruth 565
バンドラー
Bandler, Richard 89
バンドラント
Bundrant, Mike 201
ハントリー
Huntly, Alyson C. 637
ハンドリー
Handley, Ann 565
Handley, Rima 565
Hundley, Brett 635
Hundley, Nick 635
パントリー
Pantley, Elizabeth 1075
パントリアーノ
Pantoliano, Joe 1075
バントリーズ
Vantrease, Brenda Rickman 1445
パンドール
Pandor, Naledi 1074
バンドルス
Vandross, Luther Ronzoni 1443
パンドルフィーニ
Pandolfini, Bruce 1074
ハンドレイ
Handley, Caro 565
Handley, David 565
Handley, Tim 565
バンドレイジ
Bundrage, Quenton 201
バンドロス
Vandross, Luther Ronzoni 1443
バンドワール
van de Walle, Bartel 1443
ハーンドン
Herndon, Javontee 599
Herndon, Nolan Anderson 599
バントン
Banton, Buju 90
ハンナ
Hanna, Arthur 566
Hanna, James 566
Hanna, Lisa 566
Hanna, Mark 566
Hanna, William Denby 566
Hannah 566
Hannah, Angela 566
Hannah, Daryl 566

ハ

Hannah, Kathryn J. 566
Hannah, Leslie 566
ハンナー
Hanna, Bassam 566
バンナ
Banna, Mamiya el 90
ハンナウィ
al-Hannawi, Abdul Muttaleb 566
ハンナシ
Hannachi, Salah 566
ハンナス
Hannas, William C. 566
バン・ナット
Vann Nath 1444
ハンナバルト
Hannawald, Sven 566
ハンナフォード
Hannaford, Carla 566
ハンナマーチン
Hanna-martin, Glenys 566
パンナー・リットグライ
Panna Rittikrai 1075
バンナント
Bamnante, Komikpime 88
バンニ
Vanni, Simone 1444
ハンニバル
Hannibal, James R. 567
バンニャイ
Banyai, Istvan 90
ハンネスソン
Hannesson, Gudbjartur 567
パンネッラ
Pannella, Marco 1075
ハンネマン
Hanneman, Jeff 567
Hannemann, Jacob 567
Hannemann, Robert E. 567
バンノ
Banno, Robert Tadashi 90
バンノイ
Van Noy, Kyle 1445
ハンバー
Humber, Ramon 634
バンバ
Bamba, Antonio 88
Bamba, Mamadou 88
バーンハイマー
Bernheimer, Kate 129
バーンバウム
Barnbaum, Deborah R. 95
Birnbaum, Molly 141
バン・パオ
Vang Pao 1444
バンバーガー
Bamberger, Jeanne 88
バンバークレオ
Van Burkleo, Ty 1441
バンパーズ
Bumpers, Dale 201
バーンバック
Birnbach, Lisa 141
バーンハート
Barnhart, Tucker 96
Bernhardt, Michele 129
Bernhardt, William 129
バンハネン
Vanhanen, Matti Taneli 1444
バンバハンザ
Bamba Hamza, Fatoumata 88
バーンハム
Burnham, Andy 205
パーンハム
Parnham, Michael J. 1081
バンバラ
Bambara, Linda M. 88
ハンハルト
Hanhart, Robert 566
バンバーレン
Bambaren, Sergio 88
バンバン
Bambang, Brodjonegoro 88
バンハーン・シンラパアーチャ
Banharn Silpaarcha 89
バンハーン・シンラパアーチャー
Banharn Silpaarcha 89
ハンビー
Hamby, Mark A. 561
Hanby, Jeannette 565
バンビ
Bambi, Luzolo 88
バンビー
Bun B 201
ハンビィ
Humby, Clive 634
バン・ビーバー
Van Bever, Derek 1441
バンビル
Banville, John 90
ハンプ
Hamp, Julie 564
パンフィーロフ
Panfilov, Evgenii 1074
Panfilov, Gleb 1074
バンフォード
Bamford, Julian 88
Bamford, Kathleen B. 88
Bamford, Patrick 88
ハンプシャー
Hampshire, Mark 564
Hampshire, Stuart 564
バンプス
Bamps, Benji 88
Bumpus, Cornelius 201
ハンプソン
Hampson, Anne 564
Hampson, Thomas 564
Hampson, Tim 564
ハンブッヘン
Hambuechen, Fabian 561
ハンプトン
Hampton, Dan 564
Hampton, Lionel 564
Hampton, Michael 564
Hampton, Mike 564
Hampton, Slide 564
バンプトン
Bampton, Claire 88
パンプファイル
Pamphile, Kevin 1074
バンブラ
Bhambra, Gurminder K. 135
ハンプラブ
Hanprab, Tawin 567
ハンフリー
Humfrey, Peter 635
Humphrey, John 635
Humphrey, Nicholas 635
Humphrey, Terin 635
Humphrey, Watts S. 635
ハンブリー
Hambrey, Michael J. 561
バンフリー
Boumphrey, Frank 167
ハンフリース
Humphrys, John 635
ハンフリーズ
Humphreys, Andrew 635
Humphreys, Colin J. 635
Humphreys, Glyn W. 635
Humphreys, Heather 635
Humphreys, Hilroy 635
Humphreys, Jessica Dee 635
Humphreys, Margaret 635
Humphreys, Patrick N. 635
Humphries, Adam 635
Humphries, D.J. 635
Humphries, Kaillie 635
Humphries, Kris 635
Humphries, Patrick 635
Humphries, Sam 635
Humphries, Stephen 635
Humphries, Tom L. 635
Humphries, Tudor 635
ハンブリン
Hamblin, Nikki 561
Hamblyn, Richard 561
ハンブル
Humble, Jez 634
Humble, Nicola 634
ハンブルガー
Hamburger, Franz 561
ハンフレー
Humphrey, Lisa 635
ハンフレィ
Humphrey, James H. 635
パンプロ
Pampuro, José 1074
ハンペ
Hampe, Michael 564
バン・ヘイガン
Von Hagen, William 1463
バン・ヘイレン
Van Halen, Edward 1444
ハンベリ - テニソン
Hanbury-Tenison, Robin 565
ハンベルイェル
Hamberger, Lars 561
バンベルトーベン
Van Velthooven, Simon 1445
バンベルトホーベン
Vanvelthoven, Peter 1445
パンボ
Pambo, Dieudonné 1073
バンホーフ
Vanhoof, Elke 1444
パンボリディス
Pamborides, George 1074
ハンマー
Hammer, Alexander 563
Hammer, Petra-Marina 563
バンマー
Bammer, Sybille 88
ハン=マゴメードフ
Khan-Magomedov, Selim Omarovich 726
ハンマースリー
Hammersley, Ben 563
ハンマーディ
al-Hammadi, Isa Abdulrahman 563
al-Hammadi, Isa bin Abdulrahman 563
al-Hammadi, Mohammed Abdul Wahed Ali 563
Hammadi, Sa'adoun 563
ハンマード
Hammad, Salamah 563
ハンマミ
Hammami, Imed 563
バンミールト
Van Miert, Karel 1444
バンミルロー
Van Mierlo, Hans 1444
ハンムード
Hammoud, Mahmoud 564
ハンメル
Hammer, Kristian 563
Hummel, John H. 635
ハンモ
Khammo, Iakiv 725
バンモアカーク
Van Moerkerke, Evan 1444
バン・モリバン
Vann Molyvann 1444
パンヤージャン
Panyachand, Preeda 1075
バンヤード
Banyard, Joe 90
バンヤン
Bunyan, Reem 202
ハンラッティ
Hanratty, Malachy 567
バンランデゲム
Van Landeghem, Chantal 1444
ハンリー
Hanley, Paul R.J. 566
Hanley, Victoria 566
バンリアー
Van Liere, Donna 1444
バンリール
Van Riel, Marten 1445
ハンレー
Hanley, Jesse 566
Hanley, Nick 566
Hanley, Susan B. 566
バン・レンテン
van Lenteren, J.C. 1444
ハンロン
Hanlon, James A. 566
Hanlon, Kevin 566
Hanlon, Thomas E. 566
バンローン
Van Loan, Peter 1444
バーンワート
Banwart, Travis 90

【ヒ】

ビー
Bee, J.Y. 113
Bee, Susan M. 113
Bee, William 113
Bie, Linne 137

ピ
Pi, Hongyan 1109
ピー
P., Melissa 1067
ビーア
Beer, Lawrence Ward 113
ビア
Beer, Gillian 113
Bia, Purna 136
Bier, Susanne 137
ビアー
Beer, Michael 113
Villar, Jonathan 1457
ピア
Pia, David 1109
ビアウ
Biaou, Rogatien 136
ビアウデ
Biaudet, Eva 136
ビーアオ
Vaeao, Destiny 1438
ヒアコボーネ
Giacobone, Nicolás 494
ピアサス
PierSath, Chath 1111
ヒアサート
Hiasat, Ali al 603
ヒアサト
Hiasat, Ali al 603
ピアサル
Pearsall, Thomas P. 1090
ビアージ
Biasi, Marco de 136
ビアシ
Biasi, Pieree-Marc de 136
ピアシー
Piercy, Rohase 1111
ピアジェ
Piaget, Yves G. 1109
ビアジーニ
Biagini, Joe 136
ビァーズ
Beers, Susan-Jane 114
ビアーズ
Beers, Mark H. 114
ビアス
Bias, Esperança 136
ピアース
Pearce, Craig L. 1090
Pearce, Guy 1090
Pearce, John A., II 1090
Pearce, Joseph 1090
Pearce, Kate 1090
Pearce, Russel G. 1090
Pearce, Steve 1090
Pearce, Virginia H. 1090
Pears, Erik 1090
Peirce, Penney 1092
Pierce, Billy 1110
Pierce, Casey 1110
Pierce, David Hyde 1110
Pierce, John Robinson 1110
Pierce, Lloyd 1110
Pierce, Michael 1110
Pierce, Paul 1110
Pierce, Valerie 1110
Pierce, William 1111
Pierse, Annamay 1111
ピアーズ
Pearce, Donn 1090
Peers, Bobbie 1092
Peers, John 1092
ピアス
Morris-Pierce, Elizabeth 978
Pearce, Ann Philippa 1090
Pearce, Chris 1090
Pearce, David William 1090
Pearce, Douglas G. 1090
Pearce, Fred 1090
Pearce, Marni 1090
Pearce, Philippa 1090
Pearce, Steven 1090
Peirce, Lincoln 1092
Pierce, Barbara 1110
Pierce, Meredith Ann 1110
Pierce, Patricia 1110
Pierce, Tamora 1110
ピアスキー
Piasecki, Bruce 1109
ビアズドルファー
Biersdorfer, J.D. 137
ビアスレイ
Beasley, William Gerald 109
ピアスン
Pierson, Christopher 1111
ピアセキ
Piasecki, Pierre Edmond 1109
ピアセツキ
Piasecki, Bartosz 1109
ピアソール
Pearsall, Paul 1090
ピアソル
Peirsol, Aaron 1092
ピアーソン
Pearson, Ryne Douglas 1090
Pierson, Matt 1111
ピアソン
Pearson, Allison 1090
Pearson, Anne 1090
Pearson, Carol Lynn 1090
Pearson, Carol S. 1090
Pearson, Christine 1090
Pearson, Christopher E. M. 1090
Pearson, David 1090
Pearson, Jason 1090
Pearson, Judy C. 1090
Pearson, Lea 1090
Pearson, Linda Joan 1090
Pearson, Mary E. 1090
Pearson, Matt 1090
Pearson, Michael 1090
Pearson, Neil D. 1090
Pearson, Nick 1090
Pearson, Pat 1090
Pearson, Ridley 1090
Pearson, Sally 1090
Pearson, Simon 1090
Pearson, Stuart 1091
Pearson, Sue 1091
Pearson, Thomas Reid 1091
Persson, Roland S. 1101
Pierson, Frank 1111
Pierson, Kate 1111
Pierson, Melissa Holbrook 1111
Pierson, Paul 1111
ピアツァ
Pjaca, Marco 1117
ピアッザ
Piazza, Giovanni 1109
ピアッツァ
Piazza, Marina 1109
ピアッティ
Piatti, Pablo 1109
ピアッティ＝ファーネル
Piatti-Farnell, Lorna 1109
ビアディラ
Biadillah, Mohammed 136
ビアード
Beard, Amanda 109
Beard, Henry 109
Beard, Richard 109
ピアート
Peart, Dean A. 1091
ビアードショー
Beardshaw, Rosalind 109
ピアトレニア
Piatrenia, Tatsiana 1109
ビアナ
Viana, Hugo 1455
ピアニッチ
Pjanic, Miralem 1117
ピアノ
Piano, Renzo 1109
ビアビアニー
Biabiany, Jonathan 136
ビアフラ
Biafra, Jello 136
ビーアマン
Biermann, Wolf 137
ビアーマン
Biermann, Kroy 137
ビアマン
Biermann, Franziska 137
ピーアマン
Peerman, Cedric 1092
ヒアムズ
Hyams, Nina M. 640
ピアモンテージ
Piemontesi, Francesco 1110
ピアラ
Pialat, Maurice 1109
ビアリック
Bialik, Maya 136
ビアリング
Beerling, David J. 113
ビアール
Biard, Philippe 136
ビアル・イエル
Biar Yel, Madut 136
ビアルドー
Biardeau, Madeleine 136
ビアレツカ
Bialecka, Malgorzata 136
ピアロッシ
Pialorsi, Paolo 1109
ビアロボス
Bialobos, Philippe 136
ヒアン
Hian, Eng 603
ビーアン
Behan, Kevin 114
ビアン
Gbian, Jonas Aliou 485
ビアンエメ
Bien-aimé, Paul Antoine 137
ビアンキ
Bianchi, Alessandro 136
Bianchi, David W. 136
Bianchi, Ilaria 136
Bianchi, Jules 136
Bianchi, Robert Steven 136
Bianchi, Simone 136
ビアンケシ
Bianchessi, Paolo 136
ビアンケッシ
Bianchessi, Peppo 136
ビアンケリ
Biancheri, Boris 136
ビアンコ
Bianco, Antoninho 136
Bianco, Enzo 136
ビアンチ
Bianchi, Carlos 136
ビアンチン
Bianchin, Helen 136
ピィ
Py, Olivier 1141
ピィオトゥロウスキー
Piotrowski, Maryann V. 1114
ビーヴァー
Beevor, Antony 114
ビーヴァーズ
Beevers, D.Gareth 114
ビヴァリッジ
Beveridge, Thomas H. J. 134
ビーヴァン
Beavan, Colin 110
ピーヴィー
Peavy, Jake 1091
ピヴェン
Piven, Jeremy 1116
Piven, Jerry S. 1116
ビヴェンズ-テイタム
Bivens-Tatum, Wayne 142
ビウォット
Biwott, Nicholas 142
ピウォワースキ
Piwowarski, Marcin 1116
ピウカラ
Piukala, Saia 1116
Piukala, Sione 1116
ピウタウ
Piutau, Siale 1116
ピウミーニ
Piumini, Roberto 1116
ビエ
Biet, Christian 137
Billet, Marie-France 138
ピエ
Pie, Luisito 1110
Pied, Jeremy 1110
ビェアグラウ
Bjerregrav, Henrik 143
ビエイラ
Vieira, Gastão Dias 1456
Vieira, João-Bernardo 1456
Vieira, Joazinho 1456
Vieira, Mauro 1456
Vieira, Meredith Louise 1456
Vieira, Thyago 1456
Vieira De Jesus, Robenilson 1456
ビエイラ・ダシルバ
Vieira Da Silva, José António 1456
ビエイラダシルバ
Vieira Da Silva, José António 1456
ビエガ

Viega, John 1456
ビエガス
Viegas, Jose Santiago 1456
Viegas, Justino Tavares 1456
Viegas, Orlando 1456
ピェシェヴィチ
Piesiewicz, Krzysztof 1111
ピエース
Pierce, William 1111
ヒエストゥッド
Hersted, Lone 600
ビエタ
Vieta, Eduard 1456
ヒエタニエミ
Hietaniemi, Rami Antero 604
ピエタリネン
Pietarinen, Pertti A. 1111
ビエッシュ
Bieshu, Maria 137
ビエッツ
Viets, Elaine 1456
ビエット
Vietto, Luciano 1456
ピエティレホルムナー
Pietilae-holmner, Maria 1111
ピエテルス
Pieters, Thomas 1111
ビエドゥー
Billetdoux, Marie 138
ピエトラガラ
Pietragalla, Marie-Claude 1111
ピエトリ
Pietri, Loic 1111
ピエトロ
Pietro, Mary Jo Cook Santo 1111
ピエヒ
Piëch, Ferdinand Karl 1110
ピエホチンスキ
Piechociński, Janusz 1110
ヒエム
Hiem, Phommachanh 604
ビエラガジョ・ケスネイ
Viera-gallo Quesney, José Antonio 1456
ピエラントッツィ
Pierantozzi, Sandra 1110
ピエリエシェンコ
Pielieshenko, Oleksandr 1110
ビェリツァ
Bjelica, Nemanja 143
ビエリッキー
Bielicki, John K. 137
ビエリト
Bieryt, Krzysztof 137
ピエリボン
Pieribone, Vincent 1111
ビエール
Bier, Susanne 137
ピエール
Pierre, Abbé 1111
Pierre, Dominique 1111
Pierre, Emmalin 1111
Pierre, Martina 1111
Pierre, Olsen 1111
Pierre, Philip 1111
Pierre, Roland 1111
Pierre, Vanneur 1111
Pierre, Webster 1111
ビェルウェスト
Verwest, Tijs Michiel 1454
ビエルクリー
Bjerklie, Steve 143
ビエルケ－ホルターマン
Bjelke-Holtermann, Claudia 143
ビエルサ
Bielsa, Marcelo 137
Bielsa, Rafael 137
ピエールサンティ
Piersanti, Silvio 1111
ピエルサンティ
Piersanti, Silvio 1111
ピエルス
Pierce, Mary 1110
ビエルダン
Vieilledent, Sebastien 1456
ビエルナツキ
Biernacki, Marek 137
ビエルナト
Biernat, Andrzej 137
ピエルフェデリチ
Pierfederici, Mirco 1111
ピエール・ポール
Pierre-paul, Jason 1111
ビエルマ
Bierma, Lyle D. 137
Vielma, Engelb 1456
ビエルマン
Vielman, Carlos 1456
ピエールルイ
Pierre-louis, Michèle Duvivier 1111
ピエール・ルイス
Pierre-louis, Kevin 1111
ピエレ
Pierret, Christian 1111
ピエロート
Pieroth, Bodo 1111
ピエローニ
Pieroni, Aldo 1111
ヒエロニムス
Hieronimus, Robert 604
ビエロフラーヴェク
Bělohlávek, Jiří 118
ビエロフラーベク
Bělohlávek, Jiří 118
ヒエン
Hien, Nguyen Minh 604
ビエン
Bien, Kejjo 137
ビエンエメ
Bien-aime, Gabriel 137
ビエンコウスキ
Bienkowski, Piotr 137
ビエンコフスカ
Bieńkowska, Elżbieta 137
ピエンコフスキー
Pieńkowski, Jan 1110
ビエンストック
Bienstock, Richard 137
ビオ
Bio, Ibrahim Isa 140
ピオッシュ
Pioche, Bonne 1114
ビオッティ
Viotti, Marcello 1459
ピオット
Piot, Peter 1114
ピオトロフスキー
Piotrovskii, Mikhail Borisovich 1114
ビオラ
Viola, Al 1459
ビオラン
Violan, Miquel Ángel 1459
ピオリ
Piore, Michael Joseph 1114
ピオレ
Piollet, Wilfried 1114
ビオレッティ
Bioletti, Alessandro 140
ビオン
Bion, Francesca 140
Biong, Luka 140
ビオンディ
Biondi, Fabio 140
ビオンディーニ
Biondini, Davide 140
ピオンテク
Piontek, Heinz 1114
Piontek, Zack 1114
ピオンテック
Piontek, Heinz 1114
ヒーガー
Heeger, Alan Jay 588
ヒガ
Higa, Santiago 604
ビガー
Biggar, Dan 137
Biggar, Trisha 137
ピーカー
Pekar, Harvey 1093
ピカ
Picat, Marie-Laure 1109
ヒガシ
Higashi, Sandra 604
ピカシオ
Picacio, John 1109
ヒガシオカ
Higashioka, Kyle 604
ビーガス
Bigus, Jennifer 138
Bigus, Joseph P. 138
ビカス
Vikas, Krishan 1456
ビガース
Biggers, E.J. 137
ビガス
Bigas, Pedro 137
ピカソ
Picasso, Marina 1109
Picasso, Paloma 1109
ピカディ
Picardie, Justine 1109
ヒーガード
Heegaard, Marge Eaton 588
ピカート
Pickart, Joan Elliott 1109
ピカード
Picado, Sonia 1109
Picard, Barbara Leonie 1109
Picard, Carol 1109
Picard, Liza 1109
Picard, Michaël 1109
Pickard, Nancy 1109
ヒカム
Hikam, Muhammad A. S. 605
ピカモル
Picamoles, Louis 1109
ビガライ
Vigaray, Carlos 1456
ピカリング
Pickering, Eric B. 1110
Pickering, Heydon 1110
Pickering, William Hayward 1110
Pickering, W.S.F. 1110
ピカール
Piccard, Bertrand 1109
Piccard, Jacques 1109
ピカルディ
Picardi, Vincenzo 1109
ピカレッラ
Picarella, Giuseppe 1109
ピキオウネ
Pikioune, Gaetan 1111
ビギリマナ
Bigirimana, Balthazar 138
Bigirimana, Euphrasie 138
Bigirimana, Jean 138
ヒギンス
Higgins, David R. 604
Higgins, Mary Clerkin 604
Higgins, Rashard 604
Higgins, Richard S. 604
ヒギンズ
Higgins, Billy 604
Higgins, Clare 604
Higgins, Jack 604
Higgins, Jane 604
Higgins, John 604
Higgins, J.Wally 604
Higgins, Kristan 604
Higgins, Kyle 604
Higgins, Michael D. 604
Higgins, Monica C. 604
Higgins, Peter M. 604
Higgins, Robert C. 604
Higgins, Robert N. 604
Higgins, Ronald 604
Higgins, Rosalyn 604
ヒギンセン
Higginsen, Vy 604
ヒギンボウサム
Higginbotham, Don 604
ビーク
Beeke, Tiphanie 113
ビグ
Vig, Butch 1456
ピーク
Peake, Charone 1090
Peake, Karolína 1090
Peake, Lilian 1090
Peake, Ryan 1090
Peek, Charles A. 1092
Peek, Dan 1092
Peek, Hammond 1092
Peek, Jerry D. 1092
Piek, Selena 1110
ヒークス
Heeks, Alan 588
ヒグズ
Higgs, Peter Ware 604
ビクストレム
Wikstroem, Emelie 1503
ビクスビー
Bixby, Donald E. 142
ピクスペース
Pikus-pace, Noelle 1111
ビクスラー

ヒ

Bixler, Dave 142
Bixler, Susan 142
ビクスレー
Bixley, Donovan 142
ビクセル
Bichsel, Peter 136
Wigzell, Hans 1503
ビグセル
Wigzell, Hans 1503
ヒクソン
Hickson, Andy 604
Hickson, David John 604
Hickson, J.J. 604
Hixon, Emily 610
Hixon, Lex 610
Hixon, Michael 610
ヒグソン
Higson, Charles 605
Higson, Séamus P.J. 605
ビクター
Victor, Cynthia 1455
ビクタシェフ
Biktashev, Val 138
ヒグチ
Higuchi, William I 605
ピクテ
Pictet, Jean S. 1110
ビクトゴ
Bictogo, Adama 137
ビクトリア王女
Victoria, HRH Crown Princess 1455
ビクトリーノ
Victorino, Shane 1455
ビクトリノ
Victorino, Shane 1455
ビクトール
Victor, Odete 1455
ビクトル・アルバレス
Victor Alvarez 1455
ビクトル・サンチェス
Victor Sanchez 1455
ビクトル・ディアス
Victor Diaz 1455
ビクトル・バルデス
Victor Valdes 1455
ビクトル・ルイス
Victor Ruiz 1455
ビクトル・ロドリゲス
Victor Rodriguez 1455
ヒグドン
Higdon, Jennifer 604
ピクトン
Picton, Margaret 1110
ビクーニャ
Vicuña, Ana María 1455
ビグニョリ
Bouzout Vignoli, Eduardo 169
Vignoli, Ana 1456
ピクネット
Picknett, Lynn 1110
ピクネル
Reyes-Picknell, James V. 1174
ヒクバニ
al-Haqbani, Mufrej bin Saad 568
ヒグビー
Higbee, Tyler 604
ヒクマトゥッロゾダ
Hikmatullozoda, Nematullo 605
ピクマル
Piquemal, Michel 1115
ビークマン
Beekman, Scott 113
ピークマン
Peakman, Julie 1090
ビークランド
Wikland, Ilon 1503
ピグリア
Piglia, Ricardo 1111
ビグリオン
Viglione, Donald J. 1456
ビーグル
Beagle, Peter Soyer 109
ピクルス
Pickles, Eric 1110
ビーグルンズソン
Víglundsson, Þorsteinn 1456
ビクレー
Biklé, Anne 138
ビグレー
Begley, Louis 114
ピクレム
Pickrem, Sydney 1110
ビクレン
Biklen, Douglas 138
ビグロー
Bigelow, Kathryn Ann 137
ビグロウ
Bigelow, Kathryn Ann 137
ビークロフト
Beecroft, Simon 113
Beecroft, Vanessa 113
ピケ
Picqué, Charles 1110
Pique, Gerard 1115
ピケ・イ・カンプス
Piqué i Camps, Josep 1115
ビーケズ
Bekes, Jr. 115
ビケット
Bicket, Zenas J. 136
ピケット
Pickett, George B. 1110
Pickett, John A. 1110
Pickett, Kate 1110
Pickett, Philip 1110
Pickett, Rex 1110
Pikett, Wilson 1111
ピケティ
Piketty, Thomas 1111
ビケフレイベルガ
Vīķe-freiberga, Vaira 1456
ビゲラ
Viguera, Borja 1456
ビゲライゼン
Bigeleisen, Jacob 137
ヒーゲル
Heeger, Alan Jay 588
ビケル
Bikel, Theodore 138
ビケルト
Bikert, Yekaterina 138
ビゲロー
Bigelow, Kathryn Ann 137
ビケン
Wikén, Emma 1503
ピケンズ
Pickens, Andrea 1109
Pickens, Thomas Boone 1109
ビーゴ
Bego, Mark 114
ビコ
Vicaut, Jimmy 1455
ビゴ
Bego, Mark 114
Bigot, Bernard 138
Bigot, Gigi 138
ピコー
Picot, Arnold 1110
Picoult, Jodi 1110
ヒコック
Hickok, J.T. 603
ピーコック
Peacock, Alison 1090
Peacock, Brad 1090
Peacock, Edward 1090
Peacock, Fletcher 1090
Peacock, Janet 1090
Peacock, John 1090
Peacock, Judith 1090
Peacock, Shane 1090
ヒコックス
Hickox, Richard 603
ピコット
Picot, Arnold 1110
ピゴット
Piggott, Arnold 1111
ピコッロ
Picollo, Franco 1110
ピコフスキー
Pikovsky, Arkady 1111
ピコリ
Piccoli, Michel 1109
ビゴーン
Begoun, Paula 114
ピコン
Picon, Charline 1110
ヒサイ
Hysaj, Elseid 641
ピザカーネ
Pisacane, Fabio 1115
ビザッツァ
Bisazza, Piero 141
ピザヌ
Pisanu, Giuseppe 1115
ピサノ
Pisano, Gary 1115
Pisano, Gary P. 1115
Pizano, Eduardo 1116
ピザム
Pizam, Abraham 1116
ビザーリ
Bizzarri, Albano 143
ピサリデス
Pissarides, Christopher 1115
Pissarides, Christopher A. 1115
ビーザルスキ
Biesalski, Hans Konrad 137
ピサレフスキー
Pisarevskiy, Gleb 1115
ピサーロ
Pizarro, Claudio 1116
ピサロ
Pizarro, Claudio 1116
ピサンタナクーン
Pisanthanakun, Banjong 1115
ビザンツ
Bisanz, Gero 141
ピシ
Pisi, George 1115
Pisi, Ken 1115
Pisi, Tusi 1115
ピシアニ
Picciani, Leonardo 1109
ピジェ
Pisier, Marie-France 1115
ピジエ
Pisier, Marie-France 1115
ビジェガス
Villegas, Camilo 1457
Villegas, Ernesto 1457
Villegas, Fernanda 1457
ビジェガス・エチェベリ
Villegas Echeverri, Luis Carlos 1457
ビジェガス・キロガ
Villegas Quiroga, Carlos 1457
ビジェガス・ポリアック
Villegas Poljak, Ernesto 1457
ピシェッツリーダー
Pischetsrieder, Bernd Peter 1115
ピシェツリーダー
Pischetsrieder, Bernd Peter 1115
ビジェンデル
Vijender 1456
ビシオ
Viscio, Albert J. 1459
ビジオ
Biggio, Craig 137
ピシオーニ
Piscione, Deborah Perry 1115
ビジク
Widzyk, Jerzy 1502
ピジクス
Piziks, Steven 1116
ピシチャルニコフ
Pishchalnikov, Bogdan 1115
ピシチャルニコワ
Pishchalnikova, Darya 1115
ビシネフスカヤ
Vishnevskaya, Galina Pavlovna 1459
ヒジノ
Hijino, Ken Victor Leonard 605
ビジマナ
Bizimana, Evariste 142
ビジムング
Bizimungu, Pasteur 143
ビジャ
Villa, David 1457
ヒジヤ－キルシェネライト
Hijiya-Kirschnereit, Irmela 605
ヒジヤ・キルシュネライト
Hijiya-Kirschnereit, Irmela 605
ビジャク
Bizjak, Ivan 143
Bizjak, Ivo 143
ビジャゴメス
Villagomez, David 1457
ビジャゴメス・ロイグ
Villa-Gómez Roig, Guido 1457

ビジャサンテ・アラニバル
Villasante Aranibar, Jorge 1457
ヒジャージ
Hijazi, Mohamed 605
ヒジャジ
Hijazi, Hassan 605
ビジャトーロ
Villatoro, Marcos M. 1457
ビジャヌエバ
Villanueva, Mikel 1457
ビジャビセンシオ・アルバレス
Villavicencio Álvarez, Jorge 1457
ヒシャムディン
Hishammuddin, Hussein 610
ビジャヤラガバン
Vijayaraghavan, Vineeta 1456
ビシャラ
Bishara, Issac 141
Bishara, Shukri 141
ビジャラニ
Bijarani, Mir Hazar Khan 138
ビジャラン
Villarán, Fernando 1457
ビジャラン・デラプエンテ
Villarán de la Puente, Susana 1457
ビジャル
Villar, Jose 1457
ビジャルタ・ビジェガス
Villalta Villegas, Carlos 1457
ビジャルバ
Villalba, Rodrigo 1457
ビジャレホ
Villarejo, Luis 1457
ビジャロボス
Villalobos, José Miguel 1457
Villalobos, Juan Pablo 1457
Villalobos, Vilma 1457
ビジュー
Bijou, Sidney William 138
Bijoux, Jousette 138
ビシュクピッチ
Biškupić, Božo 141
ビシュコフ
Bychkov, Semyon 210
ピシュチェク
Piszczek, Lukasz 1115
ビシュト
Bist, Vandana 142
ビシュネフスキ
Wischnewski, Anke 1518
ビシュル
Beshr, Muhammad Ali 132
ヒジュロス
Hijuelos, Oscar 605
ビシュワナータン
Viswanathan, Gauri 1460
ピショー
Pichot, Teri 1109
ビショック
Bishok, Dak Dob 141
ビショッフ
Bischoff, Cordula 141
Bischoff, Kendra 141
Bischoff, Ulrich 141
Bischoff, Winfried Franz Wilhelm 141
ビショップ
Bishop, Alan J. 141
Bishop, Anne 141
Bishop, Beata 141
Bishop, Bill 141
Bishop, Bronwyn 141
Bishop, Chris 141
Bishop, Christopher 141
Bishop, Claire 141
Bishop, Dorothy V.M. 141
Bishop, Farzad 141
Bishop, Freddie 141
Bishop, Gavin 141
Bishop, George 141
Bishop, Jim 141
Bishop, J.Michael 141
Bishop, Joey 141
Bishop, John Leslie 141
Bishop, Julie 141
Bishop, Melissa 141
Bishop, Michael 141
Bishop, Michael J. 141
Bishop, Nic 141
Bishop, Robert H. 141
Bishop, Russell 141
Bishop, Teina 141
Bishop, William John 141
ビショフ
Bischof, Ole 141
ビジョルド
Bujold, Lois McMaster 200
ピショワ
Pichois, Claude 1109
ピーション
Pichon, Liz 1109
ピション
Pichon, Frederic 1109
ピジョン
Pigeon, Sharon 1111
ビジラニ
Bijarani, Mir Hazar Khan 138
ビジル
Vigil, Nick 1456
Vigil, Zach 1456
ヒシントゥカ
Hicintuka, Cyrille 603
ヒース
Gies, Miep 496
Heath, Alan 587
Heath, Christopher 587
Heath, Craig 587
Heath, Dwight B. 587
Heath, Edward Richard George 587
Heath, Ian 587
Heath, Iona 587
Heath, Jeff 587
Heath, Joel 587
Heath, Joseph 587
Heath, J.R. 587
Heath, Liam 587
Heath, Lorraine 587
Heath, Percy 587
Heath, Robin 587
Heath, Tom 587
Heehs, Peter 588
Heese, Mark 588
ビス
Biss, Jonathan 142
Visse, Dominique 1459
ピース
Peace, David 1089
Peace, John 1089
Peace, Richard Arthur 1089
Pees, Dean 1092
ピーズ
Pease, Allan 1091
Pease, Barbara 1091
ピズ
Pisu, Silverio 1115
ビズエルヌ
Bizouerne, Gilles 143
ビズカイーノ
Vizcaino, Arodys 1460
ビスカラ・コルネホ
Vizcarra Cornejo, Martín Alberto 1460
ビスカルディ
Viscardi, Henry 1459
ピスキエヴィッチ
Piśkiewicz, Agnieszka 1115
ピスク
Piszk, Sandra 1115
ビスクシィ
Viscusi, W.Kip 1459
ピスクール
Piskur, Jure 1115
ピスケ
Pischke, Jörn-Steffen 1115
ビスケル
Vizquel, Omar 1460
ビスコ
Visco, Vincenzo 1459
ヒスコック
Hiscock, Geoff 610
ピスコッティ
Piscotty, Stephen 1115
ヒースコート・ジェームズ
Heathcote-James, Emma 587
ピスコロスキ
Piskorski, Mikołaj Jan 1115
ピスシェリナ
Pischelina, Valeriya 1115
ヒース・スタッブス
Heath-Stubbs, John Francis Alexander 587
ヒース・スタッブズ
Heath-Stubbs, John Francis Alexander 587
ビースタ
Biesta, Gert J.J. 137
ビスタ
Bista, Deepak 142
ビスタテイト
Vistartaite, Donata 1459
ビースティー
Biesty, Stephen 137
ビスディキアン
Bisdikian, Chatschik 141
ビステル
Bystoel, Lars 211
ピストリウス
Pistorius, Martin 1115
Pistorius, Oscar 1115
ピストレット
Pistoletto, Michelangelo 1115
ピストレッロ
Pistorello, Jacqueline 1115
ビスノース
Bisnauth, Dale 142
ビスバナサン
Visvanathan, Chettiyappan 1459
ビスバル
Bisbal, David 141
ビースヒューヘル
Biesheuvel, Barend Willem 137
ビースベルガー
Wiesberger, Bernd 1502
ビスマス
Bismuth, Pierre 142
ビスマルク
Bismarck, Beatrice von 142
ヒースマン
Heasman, Michael 587
ビスマン
Wissman, Johan 1518
ビスミュト
Bismuth, Pierre 142
ピスメンスカ
Pysmenska, Hanna 1142
ビズヤック
Vizjak, Andrej 1460
ビスランド
Bisaland, Elizabeth 141
ビースリー
Beasley, Cole 109
Beasley, Vic 109
ビーズリ
Beasley, William Gerald 109
ビーズリー
Beasley, David 109
Beasley, Malik 109
Beasley, Michael 109
Beasley, Sandra 109
Beasley, Tony 109
Beasley, William Gerald 109
Beazley, Kim 110
Beazley, Mitchell 110
ビズリー
Bisley, Nick 142
ピースリー
Peaslee, Robert L. 1091
ヒースリイ
Heasley, Brendan 587
ヒースリップ
Heaslip, Jamie 587
Heaslip, William 587
ピースリンガー
Piehslinger, Eva 1110
ビズレー
Bisley, Simon 142
ヒスロップ
Hislop, Malcolm 610
Hislop, Victoria 610
ビスロワ
Vislova, Nina 1459
ビスワス
Biswas, Abdul Latif 142
Biswas, Asit K. 142
Biswas, Pulak 142
ビスワス＝ディーナー
Biswas-Diener, Robert 142
ビセ
Bicet, Noraida 136
ビゼ
Bizet, François 142
ビセイラ
Viceira, Luis M. 1455

ヒ

ピゼック
Pyzdek, Thomas 1142
ピセット
Bisset, Fergus 142
Bisset, Jacqueline 142
Bisset, Sonia 142
Bissette, Stephen 142
ヒセニ
Hyseni, Skender 641
ビセネブスキー
Vishnevsky, Denis 1459
ヒセラ・ベルガラ
Gisela Vergara, Carmen 502
ビーゼル
Beisel, Elizabeth 115
Wiesel, Elie 1502
Wiesel, Torsten Nils 1502
ヒセン
Hissene, Mahamat 610
ビセンテ
Vicente, Manuel Domingos 1455
ビセンティ・バルガス
Vicenti Vargas, Fernando 1455
ビセンテ・ゴメス
Vicente Gomez 1455
ビセント
Vicent, Tania 1455
ビゾ
Bizot, Emmanuel 143
Bizot, Francois 143
Bizzo, Emmanuel 143
ピゾ
Pizzo, Christopher 1116
ビゾニー
Bizony, Piers 143
ビソネット
Bissonnette, Barbara A. 142
Bissonnette, Paul 142
ピゾラット
Pizzolatto, Nic 1117
ピゾルノ
Pizzorno, Joseph E., Jr. 1117
ビーソン
Beeson, Pelagie M. 114
ピー・ソン
Pyi Sone 1141
ヒーター
Heater, Derek Benjamin 587
ビーダー
Beder, Sharon 113
ビダー
Beder, Tanya Styblo 113
ピーター
Peter, Elizabeth 1102
Peter, John 1102
Peter, Yukio 1102
Petre, Peter 1103
ピタ
Pita, Elisala 1115
Pita, Matthieu 1115
ピタウ
Pittau, Joseph 1116
ピダエフ
Pidaev, Andriy 1110
Pidaev, Shakirdzhan Rasulovich 1110
ピタカカ
Pitakaka, Moses Puibangara 1115
ピーターキン
Peterkin, Mike 1102
ヒダシェリ
Khidasheli, Tinatin 728
ピータース
Peters, Andy 1102
Peters, Anne 1102
Peters, B.Guy 1102
Peters, Brian 1102
Peters, Brock 1102
Peters, Chris 1102
Peters, Corey 1102
Peters, Diane McFerrin 1102
Peters, Elizabeth Dipuo 1102
Peters, Hank 1102
Peters, Jason 1102
Peters, John 1102
Peters, Lana 1102
Peters, Marcus 1102
Peters, Michael 1102
Peters, Scott 1102
ピーターズ
Peters, Ann 1102
Peters, Anya 1102
Peters, Bernadette 1102
Peters, Charlie 1102
Peters, David 1102
Peters, Elizabeth 1102
Peters, James F. 1102
Peters, Lana 1102
Peters, Mary E. 1102
Peters, Steffen 1102
Peters, Steve 1102
Peters, Ted 1102
Peters, Tom 1102
Peters, William 1102
Peters, Winston 1102
ピータースン
Klavan, Andrew 743
Peterson, William S. 1103
ピーターセン
Petersen, David 1102
Petersen, James R. 1102
Petersen, Jenna 1102
Petersen, Sandy 1102
Petersen, Sara Slott 1102
Pietersen, JP. 1111
ピーダーセン
Pedersen, Peter David 1091
ピーターソン
Peterson, Adrian 1102
Peterson, Bob 1102
Peterson, Brandon 1102
Peterson, Bryan 1102
Peterson, Christopher 1102
Peterson, Darrin 1102
Peterson, D.J. 1102
Peterson, Eugene H. 1102
Peterson, Greg 1102
Peterson, Holly 1103
Peterson, Jace 1103
Peterson, Jeret 1103
Peterson, Jon A. 1103
Peterson, Ken M. 1103
Peterson, Kevin 1103
Peterson, Linda Mary 1103
Peterson, Linda Whitney 1103
Peterson, L.Mark 1103
Peterson, Lorne 1103
Peterson, Marilyn Strachan 1103
Peterson, Mark F. 1103
Peterson, Monique 1103
Peterson, Oscar Emmanuel 1103
Peterson, Patrick 1103
Peterson, Peter G. 1103
Peterson, Richard L. 1103
Peterson, Rudolph A. 1103
Peterson, Shane 1103
Peterson, Stacy 1103
Peterson, Theodore 1103
Peterson, Vicki 1103
Petersson, Tom 1103
ピーダーソン
Pederson, Doug 1091
Pederson, Joc 1091
ピターソン
Peterson, Kent D. 1103
ピタック
Pitak, Intravitayanun 1115
ビータネン
Viitanen, Jukka 1456
Viitanen, Pia 1456
ピーターフロインド
Peterfreund, Diana 1102
ビタマジレ
Bitamazire, Geraldine 142
Bitamazire, Namirembe 142
ビダーマン
Biderman, Charles 137
ピーターマン
Peterman, Michael 1102
ヒダヤット
Hidayat, Mohamad 604
Hidayat, Taufik 604
ヒダヤト
Hidayat, Taufik 604
ヒダラ
Hydara, Sheikh Tijan 640
ビータラフ
Bitaraf, Habibollah 142
ビターリ
Vitali, Andrea 1460
ヒタル
al-Hitar, Hamud Abdul-Hamid 610
ビタル
Bitar, Sergio 142
Vital, Albert Camille 1460
ビダール
Bidal, Jean 137
Vidal, Gore 1455
ビダル
Vidal, Arturo 1455
Vidal, Clara 1455
Vidal, Doriane 1455
Vidal, Francisco 1455
Vidal, Gore 1455
Vidal, Jean-Pierre 1455
Vidal, Laurent 1455
Vidal, Vanessa 1455
ビダル・イリングウォルス
Vidal Illingworth, Gloria 1455
ビダル・エレラ
Vidal Herrera, Antonio Ketín 1455
ヒダルゴ
Hidalgo, Pablo 604
ヒダルゴ=クライン
Hidalgo-clyne, Sam 604
ビダル・サリナス
Vidal Salinas, Francisco 1455
ピタルト
Pithart, Petr 1116
ビダル・ナケ
Vidal-Naquet, Pierre 1455
ビダルフ
Biddulph, Steve 137
ピタロ
Pitaro, Regina M. 1115
ビダン
Bident, Christophe 137
ピタンパリ
Pittampalli, Al 1116
ビーチ
Beach, Edward Latimer 109
Beach, Heather L. 109
Beach, Jerry 109
Beach, Nancy 109
Beech, Anthony 113
Beech, Beau 113
Beech, Charlotte 113
ビーチー
Beachy, Roger N. 109
ピーチ
Peach, Ceri 1089
ビーチウッド
Beechwood, Beth 113
ビーチェ
Beache, Glen 109
Beache, Vincent 109
ピチェート
Pichet, Durongkaveroj 1109
ピチェニック
Pieczenik, Steve R. 1110
ヒチェル
Hitcher, Alejandro 610
ビチェルマイヤー
Bichelmeyer, Barbara A. 136
ビーチェン
Beechen, Adam 113
ヒチコック
Hitchcock, Billy 610
ビチコフ
Bychkov, Semyon 210
ビチナシュビリ
Bichinashvili, Davyd 136
ヒチマナ
Hitimana, Jean Bosco 610
ビーチム
Beachem, V.J. 109
ビーチャー
Beecher, Henry Knowles 113
Beecher, Jonathan 113
Beecher, Marguerite 113
Beecher, Willard 113
ビチャ
Bitcha, Sola Nkilin Na 142
ピーチャー
Peecher, Mark E. 1092
ビチャクチッチ
Bicakcic, Ermin 136
ビーチャム
Beacham, Travis 109
Beachum, Kelvin 109
Beauchamp, Tom L. 110
ビチュイク
Bichyk, Yuliya 136
ピチョット
Picciotto, Concepcion 1109

ビーチング
Beeching, Angela Myles 113
ビーツ
Beetz, Andrea 114
ビツィンドゥ
Bitsindou, Gerard 142
ビーツェ
Vietze, Peter M. 1456
ビッカーズ
Bickers, Robert A. 136
Vickers, Jon 1455
ピッカースギル
Pickersgill, Robert 1110
ピッカーズギル
Pickersgill, Robert 1110
ビッカースタッフ
Bickerstapp, J.B. 136
ビッカートン
Bickerton, Derek 136
Bickerton, Ian J. 136
ヒッカム
Hickam, Homer H., Jr. 603
ピッカール
Piccard, Bertrand 1109
ピッカレラ
Piccarella, John 1109
ヒッキー
Hickey, G.Ivor 603
Hickey, Howard 603
Hickey, Jim 603
Hickey, Joanne V. 603
Hickey, John 603
Hickey, John Benjamin 603
Hickey, Mary Cassandra 603
Hickey, Sean 603
ヒッキィ
Hickey, Samuel 603
ヒック
Hick, John 603
Hick, John Harwood 603
ビック
Bick, Esther 136
Vick, Michael 1455
Witch, Juan Julio 1518
ピック
Pic, Anne-Sophie 1109
ピックオーバー
Pickover, Clifford A. 1110
ビッグ・ショー
Big Show 138
ヒックス
Hicks, Aaron 603
Hicks, Akiem 603
Hicks, Barbara Jean 603
Hicks, David 603
Hicks, Donald L. 603
Hicks, Esther 603
Hicks, Gary 603
Hicks, Greg 603
Hicks, Jerry 603
Hicks, John 603
Hicks, Jordan 603
Hicks, Michael R. 603
Hicks, Mike 603
Hicks, Neill D. 603
Hicks, Paul 603
Hicks, Peter 604
Hicks, Scott 604
Hicks, Tyler 604
ヒッグス
Higgs, Chris 604
Higgs, Peter Ware 604
ヒッグズ
Higgs, Tracy J. 604
ビックス
Biggs, Simon 138
Bix, Herbert P. 142
ビッグス
Biggs, Barton Michael 137
Biggs, Matthew 137
Biggs, Ranald 138
Biggs, Simon 138
ビッグズ
Biggs, Barbara 137
Biggs, Ranald 138
ビッグ・ダディV
Big Daddy V 137
ビッグバン・ベイダー
Big Bang Vader 137
ビッグバン・ベーダー
Big Bang Vader 137
ピックフォード
Pickford, Jordan 1110
Pickford, Louise 1110
ヒックマン
Hickman, Craig R. 603
Hickman, Jonathan 603
Hickman, Tracy 603
ビックリー
Bickley, Lynn S. 137
ヒックリング
Hickling, Meg 603
ビックル
Bickle, Mike 137
ピッケラル
Pickeral, Tamsin 1110
ヒッケル
Hickel, Hal T. 603
Hickel, Wally 603
ビッケル
Bickel, Gabriele 136
ピッケル
Pikkel, Ryan 1111
ピッケン
Picken, Stuart 1109
ピッケンズ
Pickens, Charles 1109
Pickens, James W. 1109
ビッケンバッハ
Bickenbach, Jörg 136
ヒッケンルーパー
Hickenlooper, George 603
ビッコ
Vickos, Jean-Bruno 1455
ピッコーネ
Picone, Giuseppe 1110
ビツコフ
Bitskoff, Aleksei 142
ピッコリ
Piccoli, Michel 1109
ビッザーリ
Bizzarri, Giulio 143
Bizzarri, Marco 143
ビッサロ
Bissaro, Vittorio 142
ビッスン
Bisson, Terry 142
ビッセル
Bissell, Sallie 142
ビッセルス
Biessels, Carli 137
ビッター
Bitter, Joshua 142
ピッタ
Pitta, Dennis 1116
ヒッタヴァイネン
Hittavainen 610
ビッタンテ
Bittante, Luca 142
ヒッチ
Hitch, Bryan 610
Hitch, Elizabeth J. 610
ビッチ
Vich, Vanna R. 1455
Witch, Juan Julio 1518
ピッチオーニ
Piccioni, Piero 1109
ヒッチコック
Hitchcock, Andrew Carrington 610
Hitchcock, Billy 610
Hitchcock, Laura 610
Hitchcock, Susan Tyler 610
ピッチーニ
Piccini, Cristiano 1109
ピッチニーニ
Piccinini, Patricia 1109
ピッチフォード
Pitchford, Liam 1116
ピッチャー
Pitcher, Annabel 1115
Pitcher, Caroline 1115
Pitcher, Frederick 1116
Pitcher, Wallace S. 1116
ピッチャウバー
Petschauer, Joni Webb 1104
ピッチョート
Picciotto, Richard 1109
ピッチョーニ
Piccionni, Giuseppe 1109
ヒッチョン
Hitchon, Sophie 610
ピッチョン
Pitchon, Patricia 1116
ヒッチングズ
Hitchings, Henry 610
ヒッチンス
Hitchens, Christopher 610
ヒッチンズ
Hitchens, Anthony 610
Hitchens, Christopher 610
Hitchens, Tim 610
ヒッツ
Hitz, Marwin 610
ビッツ
Bitz, Michael 142
ピッツ
Pitts, Brenda G. 1116
Pitts, David 1116
Pitts, Forrest Ralph 1116
Pitts, Lafayette 1116
ピッツィ
Pizzi 1116
ピッツォ
Pizzo, Paolo 1116
Pizzo, Philip A. 1117
ビッツォーニ
Vizzoni, Nicola 1460
ピッツォルノ
Pitzorno, Bianca 1116
ヒッツフェルト
Hitzfeld, Ottmar 610
ピッティポン
Pitipong, Pungbun Na Ayudhaya 1116
ピッティン
Pittin, Alessandro 1116
ヒッテル
Hyttel, Paul 641
Riter, Caio 1184
ビッテンコート
Bittencourt, Fernando 142
Bittencourt, Leonardo 142
ヒット
Hitt, Michael A. 610
ビット
Vitt, Elizabeth 1460
ピット
Pitt, Brad 1116
Pitt, Brice 1116
Pitt, Esmond 1116
Pitt, Harvey Lloyd 1116
Pitt, Michael 1116
Pitt, Steve 1116
Pitt, William Rivers 1116
Pitte, Jean-Robert 1116
ビットナー
Bittner, Kurt 142
ピットニー
Pitney, Gene 1116
ビットフェルト
Huitfeldt, Anniken 634
ビットブロート
Wittbrod, Edmund 1519
ピットマン
Pitman, Neil 1116
Pitman, Teresa 1116
Pitman, Walter C. 1116
Pittman, Jana 1116
ビットラー
Bittler, Corinne 142
ビットリッヒ
Bittrich, Dietmar 142
ビットリングメイヤー
Bittlingmayer, George 142
ピット・ワトソン
Pitt-Watson, David 1116
ヒットン
Higton, Bernard 605
ヒッバート
Hibbert, Christopher 603
ビッフェン
Biffen, John 137
ヒッペル
Hippel, Eric von 609
ヒッポライト
Hippolyte, Emma 609
ピッラ
Picula, Tonino 1110
ヒッレル
Hiller, István 607
ビデアヌ
Videanu, Adriean 1455
ビーティ
Beattie, David Stuart 110
Beattie, Douglas 110
Beattie, Melody 110
Beatty, David 110
Beatty, Jack 110
Beatty, Joy 110
Beatty, Scott 110
Beatty, Warren 110
ビーティー
Beattie, Ann 110
Beattie, David Stuart 110
Beattie, Michelle 110
Beaty, Daniel 110
ビティ

Biti, Tendai 142
ピーティ
Peaty, Adam 1091
ピーティー
Peattie, Mark R. 1091
ビディエラ
Vidiella, Álex Sánchez 1455
ピティオ
Pitiot, Sylvain 1116
ビティッチ
Bititci, Umit 142
ピティッチ
Pitić, Goran 1116
ピティーノ
Pitino, Rick 1116
ビーティービー
BTB 196
ビディヤマーヒー
Vidyamurthy, Ganapathy 1456
ビテイリ
Vitale, Dan 1460
ヒティロヴァ
Chytilová, Věra 264
ヒティロバ
Chytilová, Věra 264
ヒディンク
Hiddink, Guus 604
ヒディング
Hiddink, Guus 604
ビーディング
Beeding, Francis 113
ピディングトン
Piddington, Phyllis 1110
ビデガライ・カソ
Videgaray Caso, Luis 1455
ビーデキング
Wiedeking, Wendelin 1502
ヒデクチ
Hidegkuti, Nándor 604
ヒデグチ
Hidegkuti, Nándor 604
ビテズニック
Biteżnik, Bojan B. 142
ビデラ
Videla, Jorge Rafael 1455
ピテリス
Pitelis, Christos 1116
ビデルース
Wideroos, Ulla-Maj 1501
ピーテルス
Pieters, Danny 1111
Pieters, Erik 1111
ピーテルスマ
Pietersma, Paul 1111
ビーデルマン
Biedermann, Paul 137
ヒテン・アフホ
Hiteng Ofuho, Cirino 610
ビート
Vito, Elio 1460
ビートー
Vietor, Richard H.K. 1456
ビト
Vito, Louie 1460
ピート
Peat, Andrus 1091
Peat, F.David 1091
Peat, Malcolm 1091
Peet, Bill 1092
Peet, Mal 1092
Peet, M.M. 1092
Peet, Vincent 1092
Peete, Calvin 1092
ピード
Pead, Isaisah 1090
ピトー
Pittau, Francisco 1116
ピトイ
Pitoi, Falesa 1116
ピトイトゥア
Pitoitua, Ropati 1116
ビトゥガ
Bitougat, Chirstiane 142
ヒドゥベギ
Hidvegi, Vid 604
ビートゥン
Bethune, Zina 133
ビドゥンクプワット
Bidoung Kpwatt, Ismaël 137
ピトカマキ
Pitkamaki, Tero 1116
ビトコバ
Vitkova, Veronika 1460
ビトシェビッチ
Vitošević, Saša 1460
ビトズ
Vittoz, Vincent 1460
ビトーセク
Vitousek, Peter M. 1460
ビトナー
Bitner, Mary Jo 142
Bitner, Richard 142
Bittner, Mark 142
ピトニアック
Pitoniak, Scott 1116
ピトネル
Pittner, Ladislav 1116
ビドバイ
Widvey, Thorhid 1502
ピトハルト
Pithart, Petr 1116
ビトビッチ
Vidović, Rudo 1456
ビドビッチ
Vidović, Davorko 1456
ビートフ
Bitov, Andrei Georgievich 142
ピトフ
Pitof 1116
ピトフスキー
Pitofsky, Robert 1116
ビドベイ
Widvey, Thorhid 1502
ビドヘルツル
Widhölzl, Andreas 1501
ビドマーシュルンプフ
Widmer-schlumpf, Eveline 1502
ビードマルク
Widmark, Martin 1502
ヒート＝ムーン
Heat Moon, William Least 587
ピートライ
Petri, Thomas Evert 1104
ピトラネト
Pitra Neto, António Domingos 1116
ビトラン
Bitrán, Eduardo 142
ヒートリー
Heatley, Michael 587
Heatley, Phil 587
ビートリス
Beatrice, Chris 110
ビトリーノ
Vitorino, Ana Paula 1460
ビードル
Beedle, Mike 113
ビドル
Biddle, Jesse 137
Biddle, Stuart J.H. 137
Biddle, Wayne 137
ピトル
Pitol, Sergio 1116
ピドルシュナ
Pidhrushna, Olena 1110
ピドルシュナー
Pidhrushna, Olena 1110
ヒドルストン
Hiddleston, Tom 604
ビトルストン
Bittleston, Jennie 142
ビードレス
Beadles, Zane 109
ピトレニエネ
Pitrėnienė, Audronė 1116
ビトーロ
Vitolo 1460
ヒートン
Heaton, John 587
Heaton, Ken W. 587
Heaton, Patricia 587
Heaton, Tom 587
ビートン
Beaton, Clare 109
Beaton, M.C. 110
Beaton, Roderick W. 110
Beeton, Sue 114
ビードン
Beedon, Julie 113
ビーナー
Buehner, Caralyn 199
Buehner, Mark 199
ピナ
Pina, Filomeno de 1112
Pina, Francisco Conduto de 1112
Pina, Joao 1112
Pina, Jorge 1112
Pina, Tomas 1112
ヒナイ
al-Hinai, Mohammed bin Abdullah 608
ビナイ
Binay, Jejomar C. 139
Binay, Mete 139
ビナイサ
Binaisa, Godfrey 139
ビナグワホ
Binagwaho, Agnes 139
ピナス
Pinas, Falisie 1112
ビナティエリ
Vinatieri, Adam 1458
ビナード
Binard, Arthur 139
ピナード
Pinard, Ian 1112
ピーナール
Pienaar, Steven 1110
ピナール
Pienaar, Ruan 1110
ヒーニー
Heaney, Andrew 587
Heaney, Marie 587
Heaney, Seamus Justin 587
Heeney, Ben 588
ピニ
Pini, Ryan 1113
ピニェイロ
Piñeiro, Caridad 1113
Pinheiro, Miguel 1113
Pinheiro, Tenny 1113
ビニェス
Vines, Josep Barahona 1458
ビニエス
Biniez, Adrian 139
ピニェラ
Piñera, Sebastián 1113
ピニエラ
Piniella, Lou 1113
ピニェーロ
Piñeiro, Caridad 1113
ピニオン
Pinion, Bradley 1113
ビニジェ
Gbinije, Michael 485
ピニージャ
Pinilla, Mauricio 1113
ピニジャ・シスネロス
Pinilla Cisneros, Susana 1113
ピニット
Phinit, Charusombat 1108
Pinij, Jarusombat 1113
ピーニャ
Piña, Antonio Velasco 1112
Pina, Manny 1112
ピニャール
Pignarre, Philippe 1111
ピニュール
Pigneur, Yves 1111
ピニョ
Pinho, Manuel 1113
ピニョシンワット
Pinyosinwat, Jumpol 1114
ピニョニ
Pignoni, Maria Teresa 1111
ピニョル
Piňol, Emmanuel 1114
ビニョン
Bugnon, The-Vinh 199
ビニヨンスキ
Binunsky, Izik 140
ビニンガ
Bininga, Ange Aimé 139
ピニングトン
Pinnington, Noel John 1114
ピニンファリーナ
Pininfarina, Andrea 1113
Pininfarina, Sergio 1113
ビヌア
Binoua, Josué 140
ピヌール
Pineur, Catherine 1113
ビネ
Binet, Laurent 139
ピーネ
Piene, Otto 1110
ピネ
Pinet, Hélène 1113

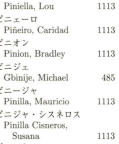

Pinet, Paul R. 1113
ピネイダ
Pineda, Michael 1113
ピネイロ
Pinheiro, José C. 1113
ビネガー
Vinegar, Ben 1458
ビネシュ
Vinesh, Vinesh 1458
ピネス
Pines, Ophir 1113
ピネダ
Pineda, Ana 1113
Pineda, Arnel 1113
Pineda, José Felipe 1113
Pineda, Pedro Alexander 1113
Pineda, Victor 1113
ピネダ・ポンセ
Pineda Ponce, Rafael 1113
ピネッリ
Pinelli, Tullio 1113
ピネラ
Piniella, Lou 1113
ピネル
Pinel, John P.J. 1113
Pinel, Sylvia 1113
ピネル - スティーブンズ
Pinnell-Stephens, June 1113
ピノー
Pinaud, Florence 1112
Pinault, François 1112
Pinault, François-Henri 1112
ビノグラド
Vinograd, Sonia 1458
ビノグラドフス
Vinogradovs, Dagnis 1458
ビノクロフ
Vinokurov, Alexandr 1458
ビノシュ
Binoche, Juliette 140
ピノチェト
Pinochet, Augusto 1114
ピノック
Pinnock, Anna 1114
Pinnock, Jonathan 1114
Pinnock, Leigh-Anne 1114
Pinnock, Trevor 1114
ビノッシュ
Binoche, Juliette 140
ピノッティ
Pinotti, Marco 1114
Pinotti, Roberta 1114
ピノトー
Pinoteau, Claude 1114
ピノ・トロ
Pino Toro, Manuel 1114
ビノパル
Vinopal, Ray 1459
ビノフラドフ
Vynohradov, Yevhen 1466
ヒーバー
Heber, David 587
ビーハー
Behar, Howard 114
ビーバ
Biba, Otto 136
ビーバー
Beaver, William H. 110
Beevor, Antony 114
Bieber, Janet 137
Bieber, Justin 137
ビバ
Viva, Frank 1460
ビバー
Biver, Jean-Claude 142
ピーパー
Pieper, Annemarie 1110
Pieper, Christiane 1110
Pieper, Martha Heineman 1110
Pieper, William J. 1110
Piper, Nikolaus 1114
ピバ
Piva, Alfio 1116
パイパー
Piper, Tom 1114
ビーバース
Beavers, Willie 110
ビーバーズ
Beavers, Keith 110
ビバス
Vivas, Julie 1460
ヒーバート
Hiebert, Helen 604
Hiebert, James 604
ヒバート
Hibbert, Adam 603
Hibbert, Christopher 603
Hibbert, Roy 603
ピパード
Pippard, A.B. 1115
ビバリー
Beverley, Patrick 134
ビバリッジ
Beveridge, Allison 134
ビバリネン
Hyvärinen, Aapo 641
ビバール
Bibard, Laurent 136
ビーハン
Behan, Beverly 114
Behan, Keith 114
ビーバン
Bevan, Brinn 134
ヒビー
Hiby, Lydia 603
ビービ
Beebe, Katy 113
ビービー
Beebe, Beatrice 113
ビビー
Bibby, Martin 136
Bibby, Reginald Wayne 136
ピービ
Peavy, Jake 1091
ピービー
Peavy, Jake 1091
ビビア
Bevere, John 134
ビビアニ
Viviani, Elia 1460
ビビアーノ
Bibiano, Bernadine 136
ビビアン
Vivian, Mititaiagimene Young 1460
B・B・キング
B.B.King 109
ビービージョン
Beebeejaun, Ahmed Rashid 113
ピピテ
Pipite, Marcellino 1115
ピヒト・アクセンフェルト
Picht-Axenfeld, Edith 1109
ピヒラー
Kirchgasser-pichler, Maria 740
Pichler, Günter 1109
Pichler, Roman 1109
ビヒレ
Bihire, Linda 138
ピピン
Pippin, Robert B. 1115
ヒープ
Heap, Imogen 587
Heap, Sue 587
ビーブ
Beebe, Catherine 113
Beebe, Dion 113
Beebe, Jonathan 113
ピフェイロ
Piffero, Benoit 1111
ピプキン
Pipkin, Bernard W. 1115
ヒープス
Heaps, Jake 587
ビブス
Bibbs, E.J. 136
Bibbs, Kapri 136
ピブニチェル
Pivniceru, Mona 1116
ピープマイヤー
Piepmeier, Alison 1110
ヒブラー
Hibler, Winston 603
ヒブル
Hybl, William Joseph 640
ピフル
Pihl, Jüri 1111
ピーブルス
Peebles, P.James E. 1092
ピーブルズ
Peebles, Curtis 1092
Peebles, Mary Jo 1092
Peebles, P.James E. 1092
ビブン
Biven, W.Carl 142
ビベスシシリア
Vives i Sicilia, Joan Enric 1460
ピベッタ
Pivetta, Nick 1116
ヒベット
Hibbett, Howard Scott 603
ビーヘル
Biegel, Paul 137
ビーベル
Bebelle, Carol 110
ビーベルシュテイン
Bieberstein, Norbert 137
ビボー
Bibeau, Marie-Claud 136
Bibeault, Bear 136
Viborg Andreasen, Anette 1455
ピーボディ
Peabody, Bo 1089
Peabody, Cora 1089
ピボバルスキー
Pyvovarskyi, Andrii 1142
ヒポリト
Hypólito, Diego 641
ビボル
Bivol, Victor 142
ビーマー
Beamer, Lisa 109
Beemer, Bob 113
ビマ
Bimha, Mike 139
ビマー
Bimmer, Andreas C. 139
ピマソン
Phimmasone, Leauangkhamma 1108
ヒマネン
Himanen, Pekka 608
ビーマン
Beaman, Brian 109
ヒミシュ
Himmich, Bensalem 608
ビミス
Bimis, Thomas 139
ピミス
Psimhis, Monthe Mauricette Joséphine 1138
ビーム
Beahm, George W. 109
Beame, Abraham David 109
ピム
Pim, Ralph L. 1112
Pym, Anthony 1141
Pym, Christine 1141
Pym, Francis 1141
ピムシリ
Sirikaew, Pimsiri 1307
ヒムチャン
Him-chan 608
ピムペア
Pimpare, Stephen 1112
ヒムラル
Himlal, Bhattarai 608
ヒムレイ
Himley, Margaret 608
ピムロット
Pimlott, John 1112
ヒメダ
Himeda, Manabu 608
ヒメネス
Gimenez, Jose 500
Gimenez, Juan 500
Jiménes, Alcidez 673
Jimenez, Eloy 673
Jiménez, Félix 673
Jiménez, Francisco 673
Jiménez, Miguel Ángel 673
Jimenez, Phil 673
Jiménez, Ramón 673
Jimenez, Ramon 673
Jimenez, Raul 673
Jiménez, Salvador 673
Jiménez, Soraya 673
Jimenez, Ubaldo 674
ヒメネスカイセド
Jimenez Caicedo, Andres Eduardo 674
ヒメネスガオナ
Jiménez Gaona, Ramón 674
ヒメネス・ガルシア・エレラ
Jiménez García-Herrera, Trinidad 674
ヒメネス・ガルシアエレーラ
Jiménez García-Herrera, Trinidad 674

ヒメネス・タラベラ
Jiménez Talavera, Mariano 674
ヒメネス・デラハラ
Jiménez de la Jara, Mónica 674
ヒメネス・プエルト
Jiménez Puerto, Milton 674
ヒメネス・ベルデホ
Jiménez Verdejo, Juan Ramón 674
ヒメネス・マジョル
Jiménez Mayor, Juan Federico 674
ヒメネス・マリン
Jiménez Marín, Melvin 674
ヒメノ
Gimeno, Gustavo 500
ヒメル
Hymel, Bryan 641
ピメンタ
Pimenta, Fernando 1112
ピメンテル
Pimentel, Fernando Damata 1112
Pimentel, José Antonio 1112
Pimentel, Josefina 1112
Pimentel, Miguel Jontel 1112
ピモン
Pimont, Marie-Renée 1112
ビヤ
Biya, Paul 142
ピヤサコン
Piyasakol, Sakolsatayadorn 1116
ピヤサワット
Piyasvasti, Amranand 1116
ピヤシェワ
Piyasheva, Larisa Ivanovna 1116
ビャシモワ
Byasimova, Maral 210
ビャチャニン
Vyatchanin, Arkady 1466
ピヤッチ
Piatti, Celestino 1109
ピャテツキー・シャピロ
Pyatetski-Shapiro, Ilya Iosifovich 1141
ピャテッツキイ・シャピロ
Pyatetski-Shapiro, Ilya Iosifovich 1141
ピャトイフ
Pyatykh, Anna 1141
ピャートニッツァ
Pyatnytsya, Oleksandr 1141
ビャバガンビ
Byabagambi, John 210
ビヤマ
Biyama, Roy 142
ビャムバツォグト
Byambatsogt, Sandagiin 210
ビヤモズ
Vuillermoz, Alexis 1465
ビャルケ
Bjerke, Siri 143
ビヤルスラノフ
Biyarslanov, Arthur 142
ビャルトゥマルツ
Bjartmarz, Jónína 143
ビャルナソン
Bjarnason, Birkir 143
Bjarnason, Bjorn 143
Bjarnason, Jon 143
Bjarnason, Rúnar 143
ビヤルハンガ
Byaruhanga, William 210
ヒャン
Hyun, Jane 641
ビヤンキ
Bianchi, Lino 136
ビャンダーラ
Byandaala, James 210
ピャント
Pyant, Paul 1141
ピャンヌコチョン
Peinnukrochon, Vichai 1092
ビャンバ
Byamba, Tuvshinbat 210
ビャンバジャビーン・ツェンドドー
Byambajavyn Tsenddoo 210
ヒュー
Few, Roger 432
Hew, Choy Khoun 602
Høegh, Henrik 612
Howe, Alan 628
Hsu, Albert Y. 630
ピーユ
Pille, Lolita 1112
ピュー
Pugh, Derek 1139
Pugh, Gareth 1139
Pugh, Justin 1139
Pugh, Marc 1139
ヒュアヴェーガー
Fürweger, Wolfgang 468
ビュアシャーパー
Buerschaper, Cornelius 199
ビューアメスター
Burmester, Moss 204
ピュアール
Puard, Bertrand 1138
ビュアン
Buin, Yves 200
ヒューイ
Huey, John 632
Huey, Michael 632
ヒュイゲン
Huygen, Wil 640
ピュイゼ
Puisais, Jacques 1139
ビュイダン
Buydens, Mireille 210
ヒューイッシュ
Hewish, Antony 602
ヒューイット
Hewitt, Andrea 602
Hewitt, Angela 602
Hewitt, Don 602
Hewitt, Eben 602
Hewitt, Jennifer Love 602
Hewitt, J.Joseph 602
Hewitt, Kate 602
Hewitt, Lleyton 602
Hewitt, Paolo 602
Hewitt, Patricia 602
Hewitt, Paul G. 602
Hewitt, Philip 602
Hewitt, Ryan 602
Hewitt, Sally 602
Hewitt, William W. 602
Huett, Leonora 632
Huitt, William G. 634
Huyett, Bill 640
ビュイトナー
Buettner, Dan 199
ピュイバレ
Puybaret, Éric 1141
ヒュイラー
Huwyler, Max 640
ビュウ
Bure, Gilles de 202
ヒューウィット＝テイラー
Hewitt-Taylor, Jaqui 602
ヒュウマー
Huemer, Dick 632
ピュエシュ
Puech, Michel 1139
ピュエット
Puett, Michael J. 1139
ビュエル
Buell, Hal 199
Buell, Lawrence 199
Buhl, Philipp 200
ピュエル
Puel, Claude 1139
ビュエル＝トンプソン
Buell-Thompson, Bonita S. 199
ビュオ
Buot, François 202
ヒューガー
Hüger, Johannes 632
ヒュカーデ
Hykade, Andreas 641
ヒューガート
Hughart, Barry 632
ヒューガム
Hygum, Ove 641
ヒューギル
Huegill, Geoff 632
ビュークス
Beukes, Lauren 134
ヒューゲル
Huegel, Kelly 632
ビューケルマン
Beukelman, David R. 134
ヒューゴー
Hugo, Lynne 633
ヒュコバ
Maruskova, Lenka 913
ヒュージ
Huge, Barbara Settles 632
ビュシーク
Busiek, Kurt 207
ピュシャラ
Puchala, Véronique 1138
ピュジャレープラー
Pujalet-Plaà, Éric 1139
ビュジョール
Bujor, Flavia 200
ピュジョル
Pujol, Laetitia 1139
ヒュース
Hughes, Barry O. 633
Hughes, Thomas J.R. 633
ヒューズ
Hughes, Adam 632
Hughes, Anthony 632
Hughes, Anthony J. 632
Hughes, Arthur 633
Hughes, Barnard 633
Hughes, Bettany 633
Hughes, Bob 633
Hughes, Carol 633
Hughes, Catherine 633
Hughes, Chris 633
Hughes, Clara 633
Hughes, Cynrig E. 633
Hughes, Damian 633
Hughes, David 633
Hughes, David Wolstenholme 633
Hughes, Doug 633
Hughes, Dustin 633
Hughes, Emily 633
Hughes, Emlyn 633
Hughes, Eric 633
Hughes, Gabe 633
Hughes, George 633
Hughes, Geraldine 633
Hughes, Gerard William 633
Hughes, Glenn 633
Hughes, Graham Atkins 633
Hughes, James E., Jr. 633
Hughes, Jared 633
Hughes, Jeffrey F. 633
Hughes, Jerry 633
Hughes, John 633
Hughes, Johnson Donald 633
Hughes, Jonathan 633
Hughes, Judith E. 633
Hughes, Karen 633
Hughes, Karen Parfitt 633
Hughes, Ken 633
Hughes, Kent H. 633
Hughes, Marcia M. 633
Hughes, Mark 633
Hughes, Martin 633
Hughes, Matthew 633
Hughes, Montori 633
Hughes, Natalie 633
Hughes, Neil C. 633
Hughes, Patrick Henry 633
Hughes, Patrick John 633
Hughes, Peter Carlisle 633
Hughes, Phil 633
Hughes, P.J. 633
Hughes, Robert 633
Hughes, Sally Smith 633
Hughes, Sarah 633
Hughes, Shirley 633
Hughes, Solomon 633
Hughes, Sterling 633
Hughes, Thomas 633
Hughes, Tom 633
Hughes, Wendy 633
Hughes, Will 633
ヒューズ＝ウイルソン
Hughes-Wilson, John 633
ヒュースティス
Huestis, Josh 632
ビュースト
Beust, Cedric 134
ヒューストン
Houston, Drew 626
Houston, Gregory 626
Houston, James 626
Houston, Jeanne Wakatsuki 626
Houston, Jordan 626
Houston, Julie 626
Houston, Justin 626
Houston, Lamarr 626

Houston, Pam 626
Houston, Philip 626
Houston, Stephen 626
Houston, Whitney 626
Huston, Anjelica 639
Huston, Darren 639
Huston, Nancy 639
Huston, Stephen D. 639
ヒューストン・カーソン
Housuton-carson, DeAndre 626
ヒューズ＝ハレット
Hughes-Hallett, Deborah 633
ヒュースマン
Huismann, Wilfried 634
ヒュスメノワ
Husmenova, Filiz 638
ヒュースラー
Housler, Rob 626
ピューズリー
Pughsley, Jarrod 1139
ビュスロー
Bussereau, Dominique 208
ピューセリック
Pucelik, R.Frank 1138
ビューソ
Biuso, Julie 142
ヒューソン
Hewson, David 602
Hewson, J.B. 602
Hewson, Marillyn A. 602
Hewson, Rob 602
ヒューター‐ベッカー
Hüter-Becker, Antje 639
ビューチュラー
Buechler, Sandra 199
ビュッカー
Bücker, Jutta 198
ヒュッサラ
Hyssälä, Liisa 641
ビュッシ
Bussi, Michel 208
ビュッセマ
Buscema, John 207
Buscema, Sal 207
Buscema, Stephanie 207
ヒュッター
Hutter, Adi 639
ピュッツナー
Pfützner, H. 1106
ヒュッテル
Huettel, Scott A. 632
ビュッテル
Butel, Lucile 208
ヒュッテンマイスター
Hüttenmeister, Frowald Gil 639
ヒュットナー
Hüttner, Hannes 639
ビュッヒァ
Bucher, Martin A. 197
ヒュッベ
Hübbe, Nikolaj 631
ヒュディス
Hudes, Quiara Alegría 631
ビューテラ
Butera, Drew 208
ビューテル
Beutel, Phillip 134
ビュテル
Butelle, Ludovic 208
ビュート
Butte, Atul J. 209
ビュートー
Butow, Robert Joseph Charles 209
ビュトナー
Büttner, Peter O. 209
ビュートリッヒ
Wüthrich, Kurt 1530
ビュートリヒ
Wüthrich, Kurt 1530
ビュトール
Butor, Michel 209
ヒュートン
Houghton, Edith 625
ビューナー
Buhner, Stephen Harrod 200
ヒューニッヒ
Hünig, Siegfried 635
ヒューネック
Huneck, Stephen 635
ヒューバー
Huber, Jack T. 631
Huber, Janice 631
Huber, Joan 631
Huber, Kevin 631
Huber, Marilyn 631
ヒューバート
Hubert, Chris 631
ヒューバマン
Huberman, Toni 631
ビュヒ
Büchi, Christophe 197
ビューヒェル
Buchel, Marco 197
ビュヒター＝レーマー
Büchter-Römer, Ute 198
ビューヒナー
Büchner, Barbara 198
ビューヒュル
Buchel, Marco 197
ビュフェ
Buffet, Marie-George 199
ヒューフェル
Heuvel, Eric 602
ビューフォイ
Beaufoy, Simon 110
ビュフォード
Buford, Bill 199
Buford, Bob 199
Buford, R.C. 199
ヒューブナー
Hübner, Maria 631
Hübner, Peter 631
Huebner, Dawn 632
Huebner, Fredrick D. 632
ヒュープナー
Hübner, Roger 631
ヒュフナー
Hüefner, Tatjana 632
ヒュブナー
Hubner, Benjamin 631
ヒューブナー＝ディミトリウス
Huebner-Dimitrius, Jo-Ellan 632
ビュフラー
Buchler, Nicole 197
ヒュー・ヘフナー
Hefner, Hugh 589
ヒューベル
Hubel, David Hunter 631
ビュヘル
Buchel, Marcel 197
ヒューマン
Human, Charlie 634
ヒューム
Hulme, Charles 634
Hume, John 635
Hume, John R. 635
Hume, Lachie 635
ヒュームズ
Humes, Edward 635
Humes, H.David 635
Humes, James C. 635
ヒュラー
Hüller, Sandra 634
ビューラー
Bühler, Dirk 200
Buhler, Matias 200
ビュラール＝コルドー
Bulard-Cordeau, Brigitte 200
ビュラン
Buren, Daniel 202
ビューリ
Beaulieu, Elise M. 110
ビュリ
Bury, Pol 207
ビュリー
Bury, Pol 207
ピューリス
Pulis, Tony 1139
ピュリツァー
Pulitzer, Lilly 1139
ピュリッジ
Pulizzi, Joe 1139
ピュリッツァー
Pulitzer, Lilly 1139
ビュリビュリ
Byul-byul, Polad 211
ピュリャグ
Purryag, Rajkeswur Kailash 1140
ビュリュス
Burrus, Christina 206
ヒューリン
Hewlin, Todd 602
ヒューリング
Huling, Jim 634
ビュール
Buhle, Paul 200
ビュルヴェニヒ
Brüvenich, Paul 195
ビュルキ
Burki, Roman 204
ビュルギ
Burgy, Nicolas 203
ビュルギエール
Burguière, André 203
ビュルグヒュラーヴ
Burggraeve, Roger 203
ビュールストロム
Bjurstrøm, Hanne 143
ビュルドー
Burdeau, Emmanuel 202
ヒュルネ
Huirne, Rund B.M. 634
ビュルネ
Buenet, Régis 199
ヒューレット
Hewlette, William 602
Hughlett, Charley 633
ヒューレン
Hew Len, Ihaleakala 602
ビューレン
Buren, Mark E.Van 202
ビュレン
Buren, Daniel 202
ビュレンヌ
Buren, Daniel 202
ビューロー
Bureau, Loïc 202
ピューワック
Puwak, Hildegard Carola 1141
ヒューワード
Heward, William L. 602
ヒュワード
Heward, Lyn 602
ヒューン
Huhne, Chris 634
ビュンテ
Bunte, Frank 201
ヒュンメル
Hummel, Robbie 635
ビヨー
Billaud, Ludivine 138
ヒョウ
Feng, Ji-cai 427
ビョーク
Björk 143
ビョークマン
Bjorkman, Stig 143
ビョークランド
Bjorklund, David F. 143
ビョークレン
Bjorkgren, Nate 143
ビヨゲンバ
Biyoghe Mba, Paul 142
ピヨット
Piot, Peter 1114
ヒョードル
Fedor, Emelianenko 424
ピョトロフスカ
Piotrowska, Teresa 1114
ヒョドロフ‐ダビドフ
Fedrov-Davidov, G.A. 425
ビョーネルード
Bjornerud, Marcia 143
ビョーム
Böhm, Michaela 154
ビョーリング
Björling, Ewa 143
ビョルク
Björk, Anita 143
Bjork, Samuel 143
Björk, Tomas 143
ビヨルク
Björk, Christina 143
ビヨルクルンド
Björklund, Jan 143
Björklund, Leni 143
Bojörklund, Jan 155
ビョルケン
Bjorken, James D. 143
ビョルゲン
Bjorgen, Marit 143
ビヨルソン
Bjørnson, Maria 143
ヒョルン
Hjörne, Eva 610
ビョルン
Bjorn 143
Björn, Michael 143

ヒ

ビヨルン
Bjorn 143
Björn, Lars Olof 143
ビョルンヴィ
Bjørnvig, Thorkild Strange 143
ビョルンオイ
Bjørnøy, Helen Oddveig 143
ビョルンシェーナ
Björnstjerna, Jonna 143
ビョルンソン
Bjornson, Craig 143
Bjørnson, Maria 143
ビョルンダーレン
Bjoerndalen, Ole Einar 143
ビョルンルンド
Bjoernlund, Jesper 143
ビョレンダル
Bjerendal, Christine 143
ヒョン
Hyon, Gi-yong 641
Hyon, Yong-chol 641
Hyun, Hong-choo 641
Hyun, Hwa-Jin 641
Hyun, In-taek 641
Hyun, Seung Tak 641
ビョーン
Bjoern, Frank 143
ビヨン
Billon, Béatrice 139
Billon, Jean-Louis 139
ピョン
Byun, Do-yoon 211
Kwang, Sun Pyon 777
Pyon, Yong-rip 1141
ビョーンヴィ
Bjørnvig, Thorkild Strange 143
ビョンジュン
Byeong-Joon, Hwang 210
ビヨンセ
Beyoncé 135
ヒョンビン
Hyun-bin 641
ビヨンボ
Biyombo, Bismack 142
ヒラ
Hira, Rezaul Karim 609
ヒラー
Hiller, Arthur 607
Hiller, Wilfried 607
ビーラー
Bealer, Bonnie K. 109
Bieler, Christoph 137
ビラ
Billah, Al-Muhtadee 138
Villa, Rene 1457
ピーラー
Piehler, G.Kurt 1110
Pierer, Heinrich von 1111
ピラー
Pillar, Kevin 1112
Piller, Gerina 1112
Piller, Ingrid 1112
ビライ
Viray, Erwin 1459
ヒライエル
Hilayel, Ahmad 605
ビラカティ
Vilakati, George 1456
Vilakati, Moses 1456
ビラーギ
Biraghi, Cristiano 140
ビラサウミ
Virahsawmy, Devanand 1459
ヒラサキ
Hirasaki, George J. 609
ヒラジ
Hiraj, Hamid Yar 609
Hiraj, Raza Hayat 609
ビラジョンガ
Vilallonga, Jose Luis de 1456
ビラスキ
Biraschi, Davide 140
ヒラスナ
Hirasuna, Delphine 609
ビラス・ボアス
Villas-Boas, Andre 1457
ビラセカ
Vilaseca, Andres 1457
Vilaseca, Santiago 1457
ヒラータ
Hirata, Helena Sumiko 609
ヒラタ
Hirata, Andrea 609
ビラック
Billac, Pete 138
ビラップス
Billups, Ayako 139
ピラーティ
Pilati, Stefano 1111
ピラーティー
Pilati, Stefano 1111
ピラード
Pierard, Richard V. 1110
ビラヌエバ
Villanueva, Alejandro 1457
ヒラノ
Hirano, Irene 609
Hirano, Sedi 609
Hirano, Thomas Toshio 609
Hirano, Toshio 609
ビラノバ
Vilanova, Tito 1456
ピラバッキ
Pilavachi, Costa 1111
ヒラバヤシ
Hirabayashi, George 609
Hirabayashi, Gordon K. 609
Hirabayashi, James A. 609
Hirabayashi, Lane Ryo 609
ヒラハラ
Hirahara, Naomi 609
ピラパン
Pirapan, Salirathavibhaga 1115
ビラ・マタス
Vila-Matas, Enrique 1456
ヒラーマン
Hillerman, Tony 607
ヒラヤマ
Hirayama, Nathan 609
ヒラリー
Hillary, Darius 607
Hillary, Edgar 607
Hillary, Edmund Percival 607
Hillary, Peter 607
Hillery, Patrick John 607
ピラリ
Pillari, Ross J. 1112
ヒラル
Helal, Hany Mahfouz 591
Hilal, Ali Eddin El Desuqi 605
Hilal, Hassan Abdel-Gader 605
ビラール
Bilal, Yousef Mohamed 138
ビラル
Bilal, Enki 138
Bilal, Mohammed Gharib 138
Bilal, Muhsin 138
Bilal, Salka Mint 138
ヒラルト
Girat, Arnie David 501
ヒラルド
Giraldo, Javier 501
ビラルド
Bilardo, Carlos 138
ビラロ
Vilaró, Ramón 1457
ビラロンガ
Vilallonga, Jose Luis de 1456
ビーラン
Veeran, Renuga 1449
ビラント
Virant, Gregor 1459
ヒーリー
Healey, Denis 586
Healey, Jeff 586
Healey, Patsy 586
Healy, Ann Marie 586
Healy, Christopher 586
Healy, Cian 586
Healy, David 586
Healy, Fran 586
Healy, Jeremiah Francis 586
Healy, Karen 586
Healy, Kent 586
Healy, Mary 587
Healy, Paul M. 587
Healy, Ryon 587
Heeley, Desmond 588
Hehre, Warren J. 589
ヒリー
Hilly, Francis Billy 607
ビーリー
Vealey, Robin S. 1449
ピリ
Phiri, John 1108
ピリー
Pirie, David 1115
ヒリアー
Hillier, Jennifer 607
Hillier, Jim 607
Hillier, Paul 607
Hillier, Scot 607
ビリア
Biglia, Lucas 138
ビリアーズ
Villiers, Theresa 1458
ピリアチェッリ
Pigliacelli, Mirko 1111
ヒリアード
Hilliard, Darrun 607
Hilliard, Kenny 607
ヒーリィ
Healy, Fran 586
ヒーリイ
Healy, Jeremiah 586
Healy, Jeremiah Francis 586
ビリウコワ
Biryukova, Vera 141
ヒリェマルク
Hiljemark, Oscar 605
ビリエリ
Biglieri, Ezio 138
ビリギッティ
Birighitti, Mark 140
ピリジャン
Piligian, Craig 1112
ピリシン
Pylyshyn, Zenon W. 1141
ヒリス
Hillis, David M. 607
Hillis, W.Daniel 607
ビリス
Bilis, Simonas 138
Willis, Helena 1511
ピリス
Pires, Maria João 1115
ビリッグ
Billig, Michael 138
ビリッチ
Bilic, Slaven 138
ビーリッツ
Bieritz, Karl-Heinrich 137
ビーリヒ
Wierig, Martin 1502
ビリビンゼ
Bilie By Nze, Alain Claude 138
ビリマーク
Birgmark, Daniel 140
ビリモント
Vil'mont, Ekaterina 1458
ビリャエシワ
Villaecija Garcia, Erika 1457
ヒリヤード
Hilliard, Nerina 607
ビリャムーサ
Villamuza, Noemí 1457
ビリヤール
Villar, Mark 1457
ビリャルバルボサ
Villar Barbosa, Rusmeris 1457
ビリャロボス・タレロ
Villalobos Talero, Celia 1457
ビリャーン
Villán, Óscar 1457
ビリリス
Bililis, Dini Abdallah 138
ビリン
Birren, James E. 141
ビリンガム
Billingham, Mark 138
ヒーリング
Herring, Papa John 599
ビリング
Billing, Jacob 138
ピーリング
Peeling, Nic 1092
ピリング
Pilling, David 1112
ビリングス
Billings, Andrew 138
Billings, J.Andrew 138

ヒ

ビリングズ
Billings, Lee 138
ビリングズリー
Billingsley, Barbara 138
Billingsley, Jace 138
ビリングスレイ
Billingsley, Randall S. 138
ビーリンスキー
Bielinsky, Claudia 137
Bielinsky, Fabian 137
ビリントン
Billington, David P. 138
Billington, James Hadley 138
ヒール
Heal, G.M. 586
Heal, M.R. 586
Heal, Robert 586
ヒル
Gil, Carmen 497
Gil, Federico 497
Gil, Jennifer 497
Gil, Jordi 497
Gil, Melisa 497
Gil, Rosalía 497
Hill, Aaron 605
Hill, Amber 605
Hill, Andrew 605
Hill, Anthony 605
Hill, Armond 605
Hill, Austin 605
Hill, Benjamin Mako 605
Hill, Bonnie Hearn 605
Hill, Brett 605
Hill, Bronson 605
Hill, Brooks 605
Hill, C. 605
Hill, Casey 605
Hill, Charles W.L. 605
Hill, Christopher 605
Hill, Christopher R. 606
Hill, Christopher T. 606
Hill, Clara E. 606
Hill, Clint 606
Hill, Cyndi 606
Hill, David 606
Hill, David, Rev 606
Hill, Debra 606
Hill, Declan 606
Hill, Douglas 606
Hill, Edward 606
Hill, Eric 606
Hill, Faith 606
Hill, Felicity 606
Hill, Fiona 606
Hill, Gary 606
Hill, Geoffrey 606
Hill, George 606
Hill, George Roy 606
Hill, Gina 606
Hill, G.Perry 606
Hill, Grant 606
Hill, Gregg 606
Hill, Heather 606
Hill, Helen 606
Hill, Jeremy 606
Hill, Joe 606
Hill, John 606
Hill, John R. 606
Hill, Jordan 606
Hill, Josh 606
Hill, Julia Butterfly 606
Hill, Kathleen M. 606
Hill, Kevin 606
Hill, Kirkpatrick 606
Hill, Laban Carrick 606
Hill, Linda A. 606
Hill, Lister 606
Hill, Lorna 606
Hill, Lundy 606
Hill, Lynda 606
Hill, Lynn 606
Hill, Michael 606
Hill, Michael James 606
Hill, Nellie 606
Hill, Perry 606
Hill, Peter B.E. 606
Hill, Philip 606
Hill, Rashod 606
Hill, Reginald 606
Hill, Rich 606
Hill, Richard P. 606
Hill, Robert 606
Hill, Rosanna 606
Hill, Sam 606
Hill, Sandra 606
Hill, Shaun 606
Hill, Shirley Ann 606
Hill, Solomon 606
Hill, Stephen 606
Hill, Stuart 606
Hill, Stuart B. 606
Hill, Susan 606
Hill, Susanna Leonard 606
Hill, Tatyana 606
Hill, Tim 607
Hill, Timothy 607
Hill, Toni 607
Hill, Troy 607
Hill, Tyreek 607
Hill, Walter 607
ビール
Beal, Andrew 109
Beal, Bradley 109
Beal, Gillian 109
Beale, Hugh 109
Beale, Kurtley 109
Biel, Alexander L. 137
Biel, Jessica 137
ビル
Bill 138
Bill, Helen E. 138
Birou, Anis 141
Will, Liane 1506
ピール
Peel, Andrée 1092
Peel, Ian 1092
Peel, John 1092
Peel, Laura 1092
Peele, Roger 1092
ピル
Pil, Frits K. 1111
ピルー
Pielou, E.C. 1110
ビルアドゥ
Billeaudeaux, Elizabeth Michelle 138
ピルヴェリ
Pirveli, Medea 1115
ヒルガー
Hilger, Matthew 605
ビルカイティス
Vilkaitis, Remigijus 1457
ヒルガース
Hilgers, R. 605
ヒルガード
Hilgard, Ernest Ropiequet 605
ビルキー
Bilkey, Tim 138
ピルキー
Pilkey, Dav 1112
ピルギエ
Parghie, Cristi-Ilie 1078
ヒル卿
Lord Hill 605
ビルギン
Bilgin, Erol 138
ピルキングトン
Pilkington, Doris 1112
Pilkington, J.D.H. 1112
ピルキントン
Pilkington, Brian 1112
ピルキントン＝スマイズ
Pilkington-Smythe 1112
ビルク
Bilk, Acker 138
ビルクス
Vilks, Andris 1457
ビルクマイヤー
Birkmayer, Walther 140
ビルクリフ
Billcliffe, Roger 138
ピルグリム
Pilgrim, Mark 1112
Pilgrim, Will Corona 1112
ビルクル
Vilkul, Oleksandr 1457
ヒルゲルトバ
Hilgertova, Stepanka 605
ビルケンマイヤー
Birkenmeier, Beat 140
ヒルコ
Khilko, Ekaterina 728
ピルゴス
Pyrgos, Henry 1142
ビル・コン
Kong, Bill 755
ビルサ
Birsa, Valter 141
ピールザダ
Pirzada, Riaz Hussain 1115
ビルサック
Vilsack, Tom 1458
ビルサラーゼ
Virsaladze, Elisso 1459
ヒルシ
Hirsi, Abdullahi Il-Mooge 610
Hirsi, Ali Abdirahman 610
Hirsi, Nur Farah 610
ヒルシ・アリ
Hirsi Ali, Ayaan 610
ヒルシェゾン
Hirchson, Abraham 609
ヒルシバリン
Hirsch Ballin, Ernst 609
ヒルシャー
Hirscher, Marcel 609
ピルジャー
Pilger, John 1112
ヒルシュ
Hirsch, Joachim 609
ヒルシュハウゼン
Hirschhausen, Eckart von 609
ヒルシュビーゲル
Hirschbiegel, Oliver 609
ヒルシュマン
Hirschmann, Jan V. 609
ビル・シューメーカー
Shoemaker, Willie 1292
ビルジョン
Viljoen, Annari 1457
ヒルズ
Gilds, Siegfried Franklin 498
Hills, Ben 607
Hills, Carla 607
Hills, Tad 607
Hills, Tony 607
ビールス
Beals, Jennifer 109
ビールズ
Beals, Sharon 109
ビルスタイン
Bilstein, Frank F. 139
ヒルスタッド
Hillestad, Steven G. 607
ビルストローム
Billström, Tobias 139
ビルストン
Bilston, Sarah 139
ピルズベリー
Pillsbury, Michael 1112
ビルスホイ
Hvilshøj, Rikke 640
ヒルズボロウ
Hillsborough, Romulus 607
ビルスマ
Bijlsma, Anner 138
ビルセル
Bilsel, Can 139
Birsel, Ismet 141
ビルゼール
Wiltzer, Pierre-André 1515
ビルセン
Bilsen, Rita Van 139
Wirsén, Carin 1518
Wirsén, Stina 1518
ヒルゼンラート
Hilsenrath, Edgar 607
ビルソン
Billson, Bruce 139
Billson, Mangala 139
ビルタ
Biruta, Vincent 141
ヒルタイ
Giltaij, Jeroen 500
ビルタジ
Biltaji, Aqel 139
ビルタネン
Virtanen, Marianna 1459
ビルチェス・ジュクラ
Vilchez Yucra, Nidia 1457
ピルチャー
Pilcher, Jane 1111
Pilcher, Jeffrey M. 1111
Pilcher, Rosamunde 1111
ヒルツ
Hilts, Elizabeth 608
ピルツァー
Pilzer, Paul Zane 1112
ヒルツィック
Hiltzik, Michael A. 608
ヒルツェビゲル
Hirschbiegel, Oliver 609
ヒルツェブルク
Hirzebruch, Friedrich Ernst Peter 610
ヒルツェブルッフ
Hirzebruch, Friedrich Ernst Peter 610
ヒルツェブルフ

Hirzebruch, Friedrich Ernst Peter 610
ヒルツェル
Hirzel, Andreas 610
ビルツェン
Biltgen, François 139
ビルックネン
Virkkunen, Henna 1459
ヒル・ディアス
Gil Díaz, Francisco 498
ビルティス
Birutis, Šarūnas 141
ヒルディック
Hildick, Edmund Wallace 605
ビルテック
Birbeck, Mark 140
ヒルデブラント
Hildebrandt, Dieter 605
Hildebrandt, Tim 605
ヒルデブランド
Hildebrand, Sara 605
ビルテール
Billeter, Jean François 138
ヒルデンブランド
Hildenbrand, Suzanne 605
ヒルデンベルグ
Hildenberg, Humphrey 605
ヒルデンベルフ
Hildenberg, Humphrey 605
ヒールド
Hield, Buddy 604
ヒルト
Hirt, Manfred A. 610
Hirut, Dilebo 610
Hirut, Waldemariam 610
ビルト
Bildt, Carl 138
Wild, Kirsten 1504
ビルドソ・チリノス
Vildoso Chirinos, Carmen 1457
ヒルドレッド
Hildred, Stafford 605
ヒルトン
Hilton, Anthony 607
Hilton, Christopher 607
Hilton, Dunstan 607
Hilton, Dyan 607
Hilton, Isabel 607
Hilton, Jonathan 607
Hilton, Margery 607
Hilton, Mike 607
Hilton, Nette 607
Hilton, Nicky 607
Hilton, Paris 608
Hilton, T.Y. 608
Hilton, William Barron 608
Hylton, Anthony 641
ビルトン
Bilton, Nick 139
ヒルトン・バーバー
Hilton-Barber, Miles 608
ビルナイ
Vilnai, Matan 1458
ビルヌーブ
Villeneuve, Jacques 1457
ヒルバーグ
Hilberg, Raul 605
ヒルバート
Hilbert, Ray 605
Hilbert, Roberto 605
ヒルビ
Hirvi, Juha 610
ビルビー
Bilby, Charlotte 138
ビルヒナ
Vilukhina, Olga 1458
ヒルビヒ
Hilbig, Wolfgang 605
ビルビリ
Birbili, Tina 140
ヒルフ
Gilb, Dagoberto 497
ヒルブ
Hilb, Martin 605
ヒルフィガー
Hilfiger, Tommy 605
ヒルブラント
Hillebrand, Friedhelm 607
ビルヘルムセン
Vilhelmsen, Annette 1457
ヒルホースト
Hilhorst, Max A. 605
ヒルボーン
Hilborn, Ray 605
Hilborn, Ulrike 605
ピルマー
Pillemer, Karl A. 1112
ビルマイヤー
Billmeier, Uschi 138
Billmeyer, Mick 138
ヒルマン
Hillman, Arye L. 607
Hillman, Bruce J. 607
Hillman, D.C.A. 607
Hillman, Henry 607
Hillman, James 607
Hillman, Robert S. 607
Hillman, Ronnie 607
Hillman, Saul 607
Hillman, Susan Kay 607
Hillman, Trey 607
Hillmann, Michael R. 607
ビールマン
Villemin, Christine Naumann 1457
ヒルミ
Helmi, Atef 592
ヒルミー
Hilmy, Hussain 607
Hilmy, Midhath 607
ビルムズ
Bilmes, Linda 139
ビルムセン
Villumsen, Linda 1458
ビルモッツ
Wilmots, Marc 1512
ヒルユ
Khilko, Volha 728
ビルラ
Birla, Kumar Mangalam 140
ビルレ
Villeret, Jacques 1457
ビルレス・ベルトラン
Birulés Bertrán, Ana 141
ピルロ
Pirlo, Andrea 1115
ピルログ
Pirlog, Vitalie 1115
ビルロワ
Birlova, Ekaterina 140
ビルンスティル
Birnstill, Francisco 141
ビルンバウム
Birnbaum, Immanuel 141
ビルンボーム
Birnbaum, Pierre 141
ヒーレー
Healey, John 586
ヒレ
Hille, Karoline 607
ビレ
Bile, Sheikh Hassann Ismail 138
ビレー
Villers, Françoise 1457
ピレ
Pillet, Jean 1112
Pillet, Julien 1112
ピレイ
Pillay, Navanethem 1112
Pillay, Patrick 1112
Pillay, Srinivasan S. 1112
ピレイ・チェダンブラム
Pillay Chedumbrum, Tassarajen 1112
ピレイチェダンブラム
Pillay Chedumbrum, Tassarajen 1112
ビレイラ
Virreira, Mario 1459
ピレインス
Piryns, E. 1115
ヒレオ
Hileo, Brahim Alkhalil 605
ヒレガス
Hillegass, Aaron 607
ピレク
Pyrek, Monika 1141
ビレグジャニン
Vylegzhanin, Maxim 1466
ピレシュ
Pires, Maria João 1115
ピレス
Pires, Alfredo 1115
Pires, Carmelita 1115
Pires, Emília 1115
Pires, Mamadú Dialó 1115
Pires, Mario 1115
Pires, Pedoro Verona Rodrigues 1115
Pires, Sandra 1115
Pires, Waldir 1115
ピーレスデリマ
Pires De Lima, António 1115
ピレス・デリマ
Pires de Lima, Isabel 1115
ヒレスハイム
Hillesheim, Jan 607
ビーレック
Viereck, Peter 1456
ビレッタ
Viletta, Sandro 1457
ヒレル
Hillel, Daniel 607
Hillel, Zak 607
Hiller, István 607
ビレル
Birrell, Anne 141
Birrell, Pamela J. 141
ヒレン
Hillen, Hans 607
ビレン
Vilén, Jari 1457
ビレンケン
Vilenkin, Alexander 1457
ビレンコ
Bilenko, Tetyana 138
ビーレンス
Bierens, Joost J.L.M. 137
ビレンドラ・ビル・ビクラム・シャー
Birendra Bir Bikram Shah 140
ビレンドラ・ビル・ビクラム・シャー・デブ
Birendra Bir Bikram Shah 140
ヒーレンバーグ
Hillenburg, Stephen 607
ヒレンブラント
Hillenbrand, Tom 607
ヒレンブランド
Hillenbrand, Carole 607
Hillenbrand, Laura 607
Hillenbrand, Will 607
ヒーロー
Hero, Monte 599
ヒロ
Hiro, Dilip 609
ピロ
Pillot, Giancarlo 1112
ピロー
Pillo, Cary 1112
Pillow, Michelle M. 1112
ピロイネン
Piiroinen, Peetu 1111
ビーロウ
Biro, Val 141
ビロウス
Bilous, Rudy W. 139
ビロウル
Bilour, Ghulam Ahmad 139
ピロゴフ
Pyrohov, Volodymyr Leonidovich 1142
ビロジル
Bilozir, Oksana 139
ピロズコフ
Pirozhkova, Elena 1115
ピロッタ
Pirotta, Saviour 1115
ビロディド
Bilodid, Gennadiy 139
ビロドー
Bilodeau, Alexandre 139
ビロドウ
Bilodeau, Alexandre 139
ヒロノ
Hirono, Mazie Keiko 609
ビロノク
Bilonog, Yuriy 139
ピロムパックディー
Bhirombhakdi, Chutinant 135
ビロル
Birol, Fatih 141
ピロロ
Pirollo, Nick 1115
ピロン
Piron Candelario, Beatriz Elizabeth 1115
ヒーン
Heen, Sheila 588
ビーン
Bean, Alan L. 109

ヒ

Bean, Henry 109
Bean, Jeff 109
Bean, John 109
Bean, Jonathan 109
Bean, Rachel 109
Bean, Sean 109
Beane, Allan L. 109
Beane, Billy 109
Beane, James A. 109
Beane, Odette 109
Beene, Geoffrey 113

ビン
Bin Chhin 139
Binh, Dao Dinh 139
Binh, Nguyen Thai 139
Binh, Nguyen Thi 139
Binh, Nguyen Van 139
Binh, Truong Hoa 139
Vinh, Bui Quang 1458

ピン
Pind, Søren 1112
Ping, Jean 1113

ピンカー
Pinker, Robert 1113
Pinker, Steven 1113
Pinker, Susan 1113

ピンカス
Pincus, Jonathan H. 1112
Pincus, Mark 1112
Pincus, P.A. 1112

ピンカートン
Pinkerton, Elizabeth 1113

ヒンカネン
Hinkkanen-Lievonen, Merja-Liisa 608

ビンガム
Bingham, Alpheus 139
Bingham, Benedict F. W. 139
Bingham, Clara 139
Bingham, Harry 139
Bingham, Lisa 139
Bingham, Ryan 139
Bingham, Tony 139

ピンカム
Pinkham, Mary Ellen 1113

ビンキー
Binchy, Maeve 139

ビンキェレ
Viņķele, Ilze 1458

ヒンギス
Hingis, Martina 608

ピンキンス
Pinkins, Eric 1113

ヒンク
Hink, Werner 608

ビング
Bing, Diana A. 139
Bing, Stanley 139
Byng, Edward J. 211
Byng, Georgia 211

ピンク
P!NK 1113
Pink, Daniel H. 1113
Pink, Sidney W. 1113
Pink, Steve 1113

ピング
Ping, Jean 1113

ヒンクス
Hincks, Gary 608

ヒングスト
Hingst, Carolin Tamara 608

ピンクナー
Pinkner, Jeff 1113

ピンクニー
Pinkney, Bill 1113
Pinkney, Jerry 1113

ビングハム
Bingham, Jane 139

ビンクリー
Binkley, Howell 139

ヒングル
Hingle, Metsy 608

ヒンクレー
Hinckley, Gordon Bitner 608

ビンクレー
Binkley, Marilyn 139

ビンゲイ
Bingea, Marian L. 139

ピンゲーオ
Prachya Pinkaew 1131

ピンゲル
Pingel, Falk 1113

ピンコット
Pincott, Jena 1112

ビンサラマ
Binsalama, Nabil Khalaf Saeed 140

ビンサント
Vinsant, Savannah 1459

ヒンシェルウッド
Hinshelwood, R.D. 608

ビンシャトワン
Shetwan, Fathi Omar Bin 1289

ビンシャーマン
Winschermann, Helmut 1516

ピンショー
Pinchot, Gifford 1112

ヒンシル
Hinshir, Al-Hadi Suleiman 608

ヒーンス
Geens, Koen 486

ヒーンズ
Heens, Caroline 588

ヒンス
Hince, Peter 608

ビンス
Vince, Ralph 1458

ビンズヴァンガー
Binswanger, Mathias 140

ピンスカー
Pinsker, Henry 1114

ヒンスキー
Hinske, Eric 608

ビンスキー
Vinsky, Iosif 1459

ピンスキー
Pinsky, Linda E. 1114
Pinsky, R.H. 1114
Pinsky, Robert Neal 1114

ピンスティック
Pincetich, Maria T. 1112

ピンストラップ - アンダーセン
Pinstrup-Andersen, Per 1114

ヒンスペテル
Hinzpeter, Rodrigo 609

ピンゼニク
Pinzenik, Viktor 1114

ピンゼル
Pinzel, Johann Georg 1114

ビンセント
Vincent, Alan 1458
Vincent, George 1458
Vincent, Nick 1458

ピンソン
Pinson, Joe 1114

ピンソン・ブエノ
Pinzón Bueno, Juan Carlos 1114

ビンダー
Binder, Alfred 139
Binder, Devin K. 139
Binder, Hans 139

ピンター
Pinter, Harold 1114
Pintér, Sándor 1114

ピンダ
Pinda, Mizengo Kayanza Peter 1112

ピンダー
Pinder, Andrew 1112
Pinder, Chad 1113
Pinder, Demetrius 1113
Pinder, Ryan 1113

ピンダイク
Pindyck, Robert S. 1113

ヒンダウィ
Hindawi, Ahmad 608
Hindawi, Orion 608

ビンダグル
Daghr, Ahmed Obaid bin 312

ピンタシルゴ
Pintasilgo, Maria 1114

ピンタド
Pintado, Enrique 1114

ヒンターベルガー
Hinterberger, Ernst 608

ヒンチ
Hinch, A.J. 608

ビンチ
Vinci, Roberta 1458

ビンチー
Binchy, Maeve 139

ピンチ
Pinch, Steven 1112
Pinch, Trevor J. 1112

ビンチェチ
Vincec, Gasper 1458

ヒンチマン
Hinchman, B.L. 608

ピンチョン
Pynchon, Thomas 1141

ヒンチリフ
Hinchliffe, Alan 608
Hinchliffe, Ben 608

ピンツェーシュ
Pinczés, István 1112

ヒンディ
Hindy, Steve 608

ピンディク
Pindyck, Robert S. 1113

ヒンデル
Hindle, Emma 608

ピンテール
Pintér, Sándor 1114

ヒンテルゼーア
Hinterseer, Lukas 608

ヒンテレッガー
Hinteregger, Martin 608

ピント
Pint, Helder 1114
Pinto, Alexandre Gonçalves 1114
Pinto, Alfonso 1114
Pinto, Armando Sevinate 1114
Pinto, Arthur R. 1114
Pinto, Elsa Teixeira de Barros 1114
Pinto, Freida 1114
Pinto, Inbal 1114
Pinto, Matthew 1114
Pinto, Pedro 1114
Pinto, Ricardo 1114
Pinto Perez, Andreina del Valle 1114

ビンドゥーミ
Bindoumi, Joseph 139

ピント・デデハルト
Pinto de De Hart, Martha Elena 1114

ピントフ
Pintoff, Ernest 1114
Pintoff, Stefanie 1114

ビンドラ
Bindra, Abhinav 139
Bindra, Guljit 139

ビントリー
Bintley, David 140

ビンドリヒ
Bindrich, Karsten 139

ピンドリング
Pindling, Marguerite 1113

ピーンドル
Piendl, Stefan 1110

ヒンドレー
Hindery, Leo Joseph Jr. 608

ビントレー
Bintley, David 140

ヒンドレイ
Hindley, Judy 608

ビンドロス
Bindloss, Joe 139

ヒントン
Hinton, Christina 608
Hinton, Christopher 609
Hinton, Joan 609
Hinton, Matthew 609
Hinton, Michael 609
Hinton, S.E. 609

ピンナ
Pinna, Nicola 1113

ヒンナーズ
Hinners, Noel W. 608

ヒンプ
Himpe, Tom 608

ビンフォード
Binford, Harvey 139
Binford, Lewis Roberts 139

ピンフォールド
Pinfold, Levi 1113

ビンフッタイス
Bin Futtais, Saif 139

ピンヘイロ
Pinheiro, Angela Dos Santos Ramos Jose Da Costa 1113

ビンベリ
Winberg, Margareta 1515

ビーンホベン
Veenhoven, Ruut 1449

ビンホール
Bynghall, Steve 211

ピンボロー
Pinborough, Jan 1112

ヒ

ヒンマン
Hinman, Rachel 608
ヒンメルファーブ
Himmelfarb, Martha 608
ヒンメルマン
Himmelman, John 608
ヒンメルワイト
Himmelweit, Hilde 608
ビンモア
Binmore, K.G. 140
ピン・ヤータイ
Pin Yathay 1114
ピンヤタロ
Pignataro, Anna 1111
ビン・ラーディン
Bin Laden, Osama 139
ビン・ラディン
Bin Laden, Osama 139, 140
ビンラーディン
Bin Laden, Osama 139
ビンラディン
Bin Laden, Osama 139
Bin Ladin, Carmen 140
ビン・ラーデン
Bin Laden, Osama 139
ヒンリッチセン
Hinrichsen, Don 608
ヒンリヒス
Henrichs, Benjamin 595

【フ】

フ
Fu, Hai-feng 466
Hu, Ji-wei 630
フー
Foo, Jixun 447
Fou, Ts'ong 452
Fu, Biao 466
Fu, Hai-feng 466
Fu, Hao 466
Fu, Quan-you 466
Fu, Tie-shan 466
He, Xiang-jian 586
Hoo, Kah Mun 620
Hu, An-gang 630
Hu, Bing 630
Hu, Chun 630
Hu, Chun-hua 630
Hu, De-ping 630
Hu, Frank B. 630
Hu, Jin-tao 630
Hu, Ji-wei 630
Hu, Jun 630
Hu, Melek 630
Hu, Shu-li 630
Hu Tsu Tau, Richard 639
Phu, Giang Seo 1109
ブー
Boo, Katherine 160
Bouh, Yacin Elmi 167
Bouh, Yacin Houssein 167
プー
Bu, Ping 196
ファー
Farr, Amanda 420
Farr, Diane 420
Farr, Michael 420
Fuhr, Arlan 466
Furr, Nathan R. 468
フア
Fua, Alani 466
ブア
Boer, Margot 153
Bua, Kevin 196
Buah, Emmanuel Armah-Kofi 197
プアー
Poor, H.Vincent 1124
ファアサヴァル
Fa'asavalu, Maurie 415
ファアッペル
Fa'apale, Patrick 415
ファアフヌア
Fa'afunua, Daniel 415
ファアモエタウロア
Faamoetauloa, Ulaitino Faale Tumaalii 415
ファーイ
Fay, Laurel E. 423
Fáy, Miklós 423
ファイ
Faÿ, Olivier 423
Faye, Fatou Lamin 423
Faye, Mansour 423
Faye, Sheikh Omar 423
Pih, Darren 1111
ブーアイ
Bouhail, Thomas 167
ファイア
Fire, Arcade 437
ファイアー
Fire, Andrew Z. 437
ファイアーズ
Fiers, Mike 434
ファイアスタイン
Firestein, Stuart 437
ファイアスティン
Firestien, Roger L. 437
ファイアストーン
Firestone, Andrew 437
ファイアブレイス
Jones, Francis Firebrace 683
ファイエ
Fahiye, Hussein Eelaabe 416
Fahiye, Hussein Elabe 416
Faye, El Hadj Daouda 423
ファイエラ
Faiella, Federica 416
ファイエル
Veiel, Andres 1450
ファイガー
Fieger, Doug 433
ファイグル
Feigl, Erich 425
ファイゲンバウム
Feigenbaum, Edward A. 425
ファイサル
Faisal, Ameen 417
Faisal, bin Abdullah bin Muhammad 417
Faysal, bin Ali al-Said 424
ファイジズ
Figes, Orlando 434
ファイーズ
Fayez, Eid 423
ファイズ
Fayez, Nayef al 424
ファイスナー
Feissner, Clinton 426
ファイズロエフ
Faizulloyev, Nusratullo 417
ファイソン
Fison, Josie 439
ファイチ
Faiti, David 417
ファイチュウ
Faitchou, Etienne 417
ファイッラ
Failla, Donatella 416
ファイト
Fight, Andrew 434
ファイド
Al Fayed, Mohamed 30
Fayed, Essam 423
ファイトゥーリ
Faitouri, Muftah M.H. 417
ファイナー
Feiner, Michael 425
ファイナル
Fainaru, Steve 416
ファイニク
Huainigg, Franz-Joseph 630
ファイヌマン
Fijneman, Rob 434
ブアイネーン
al-Buainain, Ghanim bin Fadhil 197
ファイヒター
Feichter, Walter 425
ファイヒティンガー
Feichtinger, Frederic 425
Feichtinger, Thomas 425
ファイフ
Fife, Bruce 434
ファイファー
Feiffer, Jules 425
Pfeifer, Melanie 1105
Pfeifer, Phillip E. 1105
Pfeiffer, Bruce Brooks 1106
Pfeiffer, Michelle 1106
Pfeiffer, Raymond S. 1106
ファイフィールド
Fifield, Mitch 434
Fyfield, Frances 469
ファイベルマン
Feibelman, Peter J. 425
ファイマン
Faymann, Werner 424
ファイヤード
Fayyad, Salam 424
ファイヤド
Fayyad, Salam 424
ファイユ
Faye, Jean-Pierre 423
ファイラー
Feiler, Bruce S. 425
Feiler, Matt 425
Feiler, Thomas 425
Feirer, Martina 426
ファイライス
Feireiss, Lukas 426
ファイル
Feil, Ernst 425
Feil, Naomi 425
ファイルシフター
Pfeilschifter, Sonja 1106
ファイルーズ
Fairouz 417
ファイロ
Filo, David 435
Philo, Phoebe 1108
ファイン
Fein, Ellen 425
Fein, G. 425
Fine, Anne 435
Fine, Aubrey H. 435
Fine, Charles H. 435
Fine, Cordelia 435
Fine, Gary Alan 435
Fine, Susan B. 435
ファインゴールド
Finegold, David 435
ファインズ
Fiennes, Joseph 434
Fiennes, Ranulph 434
Fienns, Ralph 434
ファインズ・クリントン
Fynes-Clinton, Christine 469
ファインスタイン
Feinstein, Andrew 425
Feinstein, Barry 426
Feinstein, David 426
Feinstein, John 426
Feinstein, Mark H. 426
Feinstein, Steve 426
ファインスティーン
Feinstein, C.H. 426
ファインタック
Feintuch, David 426
ファインバーグ
Feinberg, Jonathan 425
Feinberg, Kenneth R. 425
Feinberg, Margaret 425
Feinberg, Todd E. 425
Fienberg, Anna 434
Fineberg, Harvey V. 435
ファインマン
Feinman, Jay M. 425
Feinmann, Jane 425
Feynman, Michelle 432
Fineman, Martha Albertson 436
ファウ
Fau, Sebastian 422
Fau, Yamandu 422
ファウアー
Fawer, Adam 423
ファヴァッツァ
Favazza, Armando R. 423
ファヴァレット
Favaretto, Lara 423
ファヴァーロ
Favaro, Simone 423
ファヴィエ
Favier, Jean 423
ファーウェル
Farwell, Nick 421
ファヴォリン
Favorin, Yury 423
ファヴォルー
Favoreu, Louis 423
ファウジ
Fawzy, Samiha 423
ファウジー
Fowzie, A.H.M. 453
ファウジア
Fawzia, Hashim 423
Fouzia, Hashim 452
ファウジア・ファード王女
Princess Fawzia Fuād 423
ファウジア・ファド王女
Princess Fawzia Fuād 423
ファウス

フ

Faus, Francisco 423
ファウスティ
Fausti, Silvano 423
ファウスト
Faust, Anselm 423
Faust, Aushor 423
Faust, Drew Gilpin 423
Faust, Isabelle 423
Faust, Lou 423
Faust, Michael 423
Faust, Ron 423
Fausto, Boris 423
ファウスト・ティエンサ
Fausto Tienza 423
ファウチ
Fauci, Anthony S. 422
ファウヒ
Fouhy, Ben 452
ファウムイア
Faumuia, Liuga 422
ファウムイナ
Faumuina, Tiatia Liuga 422
ファウラー
Fowler, Adrian 452
Fowler, Antony 452
Fowler, Bennie 452
Fowler, Chad 452
Fowler, Christopher 452
Fowler, Connie May 452
Fowler, Dante 452
Fowler, David Robert 452
Fowler, Dexter 452
Fowler, Edward 452
Fowler, Eleri 452
Fowler, Ernest M. 452
Fowler, Frances C. 452
Fowler, Jalston 453
Fowler, James H. 453
Fowler, Karen Joy 453
Fowler, Katherine A. 453
Fowler, Marsha 453
Fowler, Martin 453
Fowler, Richard 453
Fowler, Rickie 453
Fowler, Ron 453
Fowler, Sally 453
Fowler, Simon 453
Fowler, Susan 453
Fowler, Theres Anne 453
Fowler, Tom 453
Fowler, Will 453
ファーヴル
Favre, Benoît 423
Favre, Henri 423
ファウルシュティッヒ＝ヴィーラント
Faulstich-Wieland, Hannelore 422
ファウルズ
Fowles, Don C. 453
Fowles, John 453
ファヴロー
Favreau, Julien 423
ファウンティン
Fountain, Jane E. 452
ファウンテン
Fountain, Hyleas 452
ファエズ
Faez, Sharif 416
Fayez, Eid 423
al-Fayez, Faisal 424
al-Fayez, Muhammad bin Ali 424
Fayez, Nayef Hmeidi 424
ファエミ
Fayemi, Federick Kayode 423
ファオシリヴァ
Faosiliva, Alafoti 419
ファオトゥシア
Fa'otusia, Vuna 419
ファーカー
Farquhar, Peter H. 420
ファーカス
Farkas, Bart 420
Farkas, Charles M. 420
ファーガス
Fergus, Maureen 428
ファーガストローム
Fagerstrom, Derek 416
ファーガスン
Ferguson, Ian 428
ファーカーソン
Farquharson, Vanessa 420
ファーガソン
Fargason, James Scott 419
Ferguson, Alex 428
Ferguson, Bill 428
Ferguson, Charles H. 428
Ferguson, Eamom 428
Ferguson, Ego 428
Ferguson, Eugene S. 428
Ferguson, Eva Dreikurs 428
Ferguson, Ian 428
Ferguson, Josh 428
Ferguson, Kitty 428
Ferguson, Kyle E. 428
Ferguson, Lee 428
Ferguson, Linda 428
Ferguson, Martin 428
Ferguson, Maynard 428
Ferguson, Niall 428
Ferguson, Reid 429
Ferguson, Richard 429
Ferguson, Sarah 429
Ferguson, Steven 429
Ferguson, Will 429
Ferguson-mckenzie, Debbie 429
Fergusson, Adam 429
Fergusson, David 429
ファーガソンマッケンジー
Ferguson-mckenzie, Debbie 429
ファカハウ
Fakahau, Semisi 417
ファカファヌア
Fakafanua, Tutoatasi 417
ファーギー
Fergie 428
ファキー
al-Faqih, Nabil Hasan 419
ファギー
al-Figi, Muftah Ali Muftah 434
ファーキオーニ
Farchione, Todd J. 419
ファキーフ
Fakeih, Adel 417
Faqih, Adel bin Mohammed 419
ファキフ
Faqikh, Osma Bin Jafar Bin Ibrahim 419
ファキーラ
Fakaira, Jalal Ibrahim 417
Fakirah, Jalal 417
ファク
Fak, Jakov 417
ファークアー
Farquhar, Danny 420
ファクゼ
Fakudze, Mtiti 417
ファーグソン
Ferguson, Fenton 428
ファクソン
Faxon, Brad 423
Faxon, Nat 423
ファクタ
Fakta, Bonnier 417
ファクッゼ
Fakodze, Mtiti 417
ファクリー
al-Fakhri, Abdul-Kabeer Mohamed 417
ファークワー
Farquhar, Scott 420
ファーケッチ
Ferketich, Sandra 429
ファケッティ
Facchetti, Giacinto 415
ファゴニー
Fagone, Jason 416
ファサッシ
Fassassi, Kamarou 422
ファザーナ
Fasana, Erika 421
ファサーノ
Fasano, Anthony 421
ファザリ
Fazzari, Michelle 424
ファーシ
el-Fassi, Abbas 422
ファシ
el-Fassi, Abbas 422
ファシアネ
Faciane, Isame 415
ファシアノス
Fasianos, Nicolaos 421
ファジア・ファード
Princess Fawzia Fuād 423
ファジェイリ
Bourjaily, Vance Nye 168
ブアジェイリー
Bourjaily, Vance Nye 168
ファジェット
Faget, Maxime 416
ファシオ
Fazio, Federico 424
ファジオ
Fazio, Robert 424
ファージカス
Fazekas, Nick 424
ファシナ
Fassina, Jean 422
ファシノ
Fassino, Piero 422
ファシフィフリ
Fassi-fihri, Taieb 422
ファーシャイン
Firshein, Richard 437
ファジャス
Fallas, Helio 418
ファジャス・ベネガス
Fallas Venegas, Helio 418
ファジャル
Fajar, Abdul Malik 417
ファーシュティ
Farshtey, Greg 421
ファーシュト
Fersht, Alan R. 432
ファショラ
Fashola, Babatunde Raji 421
ブアジラ
Bouajila, Sami 166
ファジル
Fajr, Faycal 417
ファジン
Fagin, Dan 416
ファージング
Farthing, Pen 421
Farthing, Stephen 421
ファース
Faas, Horst 415
Faas, Patrick 415
Firth, Barbara 437
Firth, Colin 437
Firth, Raymond William 437
Fuerth, Leon S. 466
Furse, Clara 468
Furth, Gregg M. 468
ファス
Fass, Paula S. 422
ファス
Houas, Mehdi 625
ファースター
Foerster, Paul 445
ファースタッド
Farstad, Arthur L. 421
ブーアスティン
Boorstin, Daniel Joseph 160
ブアスティン
Boorstin, Daniel Joseph 160
ファステンバーグ
Furstenberg, Diane von 468
Furstenberg, Harry 468
ファースト
Fast, Becky 422
Fast, Howard Melvin 422
First, Michael B. 437
Furst, Alan 468
Furst, Lilian R. 468
ファスト
Fast, Edward 422
Fast, Julie A. 422
ファストフスキー
Fastovsky, David E. 422
ファーストマン
Firstman, Richard 437
ファストリッヒ
Fastrich, Lorenz 422
ファスベンダー
Fassbender, Michael 422
ファスラー
Fassler, David 422
ファズリ
Fazli, Abdolreza Rahmani 424
ファースン
Farson, Richard Evans 421
ファゼカシュ
Fazekas, Robert 424
Fazekas, Sándor 424
ファゼーカス
Fazekas, Andrew 424
ファセラ
Facella, Paul 415

フ

ファゼル
Fazel, Mohammad 424
ファーソン
Farson, Richard 421
Farson, Richard Evans 421
ブアソン・ブパワン
Bouasone Bouphavanh 166
ファダ
Fada, Modou Diagne 415
ファタス
Fatus, Sophie 422
ファタック
Phatak, S.R. 1106
ファータド
Furtado, Peter 468
ファタードー
Furtado, Peter 468
ファターマン
Futerman, Samantha 469
ファチ
Fachi, Peter 415
ファチオ
Faccio, Leonardo 415
ファーチゴット
Furchgott, Robert Francis 468
ファツァーリ
Fazzari, Steven M. 424
ファツィ
Fazi, Thomas 424
ファツィオ
Fazio, Ferruccio 424
ファツィオリ
Fazioli, Paolo 424
ファーツィガー
Ferziger, Joel H. 432
ファッキ
Facci, Loris 415
ファックス
Fox, Harry Robert 453
ファックレル
Fackrell, Kyler 415
ファッシー
Fassie, Brenda 422
ファッセル
Fussell, Chris 469
Fussell, Paul 469
Fussell, Tif 469
ファッタフ
Fattah, Parviz 422
ファッチ
Futch, Eddie 469
ファッチネッティ
Facchinetti, Paolo 415
ファッツァーニ
Fazzani, Linda 424
ファッツィ
Fazzi, Nicolo 424
ファット
Phat, Cao Duc 1106
ファットゥシュ
Fattoush, Nicolas 422
ファットボーイ・スリム
Fatboy Slim 422
ファット・マン・スクープ
Fat Man Scoop 422
プファッフ
Pfaff, Tristan 1105
ファッブリ
Fabbri, Davidé 415
ファッラ
Falla, Maiken Caspersen 418
ファッラー
Faller, Adolf 418
ファッラーチ
Fallaci, Oriana 418
ファッルッジャ
Farrugia, Michael 421
ファーディー
Fardy, Scott 419
ファティ
Fathi, Sherif 422
Fathy, Safaa 422
Fati, Sandji 422
ファディア
Fadia, Ankit 415
Fadia, Joao 416
ファティカ
Fatica, Massimiliano 422
ファディグア
Fadigua, Elhadj Ibrahima Sory 416
ファーティック
Fertik, Michael 432
ファーディナンド
Ferdinand, Rio 428
ファティマ
Fatima, Mohammed al-Beloushi 422
Fatima, Rabab 422
Fatima, Trapsida 422
ファディマン
Fadiman, Anne 416
ファディラ
Fadillah, Yusof 416
ファディル・モハメド・アハメド
al-Fadil Mohamed Ahmed, Amira 416
ファデーエフ
Faddeev, Ludwig D. 415
Fadeyev, Gennady M. 415
ファテミ
Fatemi, Sayed Mohammad Amin 422
Fatimie, Sayed Mohammad Amin 422
ファーデル
Fardell, John 419
ファデル
Fadel, Charles 415
Fadel, Muhammad 415
al-Fadhel, Abdulaziz 415
ファトゥーフ
Fattouh, Hamdy Mohamed 422
ファドゥール
Fadoul, Abdoulaye Sabre 416
ファドゥル
Fadoul, Abdoulaye Sabre 416
Fadul, José Ramón 416
ファトクリナ
Fatkulina, Olga 422
ファトフ
Fath, Abdulrakib 422
ファトファト
Fatfat, Ahmad 422
ファートマン
Firtman, Maximiliano R. 437
ファドラッラー
Fadlallah, Mohammed Hussein 416
ファドラッラー師
Fadlallah, Mohammed Hussein 416
ファドララ
Fadlallah, Mohammed Hussein 416
ファドララ師
Fadlallah, Mohammed Hussein 416
ファドリ
al-Fadhli, Abdulrahman bin Abdulmohsen 415
al-Fadhli, Ahmed Obaid 415
ファード=ルーク
Fuad-Luke, Alastair 466
ファトルーソ
Fattoruso, Hugo 422
ブアトン
Bouathong, Vonglokham 166
ファナイカ
Fanaika, Jason 418
ファーナス
Furnas, Doug 468
ファーナム
Furnham, Adrian 468
ファナロ
Fanaro, Barry 418
ファナロフ
Fanaroff, Avroy A. 418
ファーナンド
Fernando, Iranganie H. 430
ファニ
Fani, Aliasqar 419
ファーニィ
Fernie, John 430
ファニカヨデ
Fani-kayode, Femi 419
ファーニク
Farnik, Thomas 420
ファーニス
Farnese, A. 420
ファニセロ
Funicello, Annette 468
ファニング
Fanning, Dakota 419
Fanning, Elle 419
Fanning, Jim 419
ファネゴ
Fanego, Julio Cesar 418
フアネス
Juanes 690
ファネトリ
Fanetri, Lindaweni 418
ファネリ
Fanelli, Sara 418
ファーネル
Farnell, Kim 420
ファネル
Funnell, Philippa 468
ファノラキス
Fanourakis, Roy 419
ファーバー
Faber, Anne 415
Faber, Gustav 415
Faber, Liz 415
Faber, Marc 415
Faber, Patrick 415
Farber, Norma 419
Farber, Steve 419
Ferber, Michael 428
ファバー
Faber, Patrick 415
ファハイエ
Fahiye, Hussein Elabe 416
ファーバーグ
Furberg, Bengt 468
Furberg, Curt 468
ファハダウィ
al-Fahdawi, Qasim 416
ファハド
Fahd, bin Jasim al-Thani 416
Fahd, bin Mahmoud al-Said 416
Fahd, Rashid Ahmed bin 416
ファハド・イブン・アブドルアジズ
Fahd bin Abdul-Aziz 416
ファハド国王
Fahd bin Abdul-Aziz 416
ファハド・ビン・アブドル・アジズ
Fahd bin Abdul-Aziz 416
ファハド・ビン・マハムード・アル・サイド
Fahad bin Mahmoud Al-Said 416
ファハド・ビン・マフムード・アール・サイード
Fahad bin Mahmoud Al-Said 416
ファハド・ブン・アブド・アル・アジーズ
Fahd bin Abdul-Aziz 416
ファハファハ
Fakhfakh, Elyes 417
ファハミ
Fahmi, Amin Sameh Samir 416
Fahmi, bin Ali Jowder 416
Fahmi, Raed 416
Fahmy, Amin Sameh 416
Fahmy, Khaled 416
ファハリ
al-Fakhari, Saleh 417
ファハロ
Fakhro, Hassan bin Abdullah 417
ファーヒー
Fahey, Frank 416
ファビアーノ
Fabiano 415
Fabiano, Anthony 415
ファビアノ
Fabiano, Emmanuel 415
ファビアン
Fabian, Alessandro 415
Fabian, Douglas 415
Fabian, Marco 415
Fabian, Ruiz 415
Fabian, Stephen 415
ファビアンスキ
Fabianski, Lukasz 415
ファビウス
Fabius, Laurent 415
ファビエン
Fabien, John 415
ファビオ
Fabio, Da Silva 415
ファビオラ王妃
Fabiola 415
ファビオルイス
Magalhaes, Fabio Luiz 882
ファビーニョ

フ

Fabinho 415
ファヒーム
Fahim, Mohammad Qassim 416
ファヒム
Fahim, Makhdoom Amin 416
Fahim, Mohammad Qassim 416
ファビラ
Favila, Peter B. 423
プアプア
Puapua, Tomasi 1138
ファー・ファンキー
Farr-Fahncke, Susan 421
ファフィ
Fafi 416
プアフィシ
Puafisi, Sila 1138
ファーフォー
Farfor, Susannah 419
ファフド
Fahd bin Abdul-Aziz 416
ファブヤン
Fabjan, Vesna 415
ファフリ
Fakhoury, Imad 417
Fakhri, Mohamed Madni 417
ファブリ
Fabri 415
ファブリキウス
Fabricius, Johannes 415
ファブリシアス
Fabricius, Julia 415
ファブリス
Fabris, Enrico 415
ファブリツィ
Fabbrizi, Massimo 415
ファブリッツィ
Fabbrizi, Massimo 415
ファーブル
Fabre, Jan 415
Fabre, Moumouni 415
Fabre, Paul-Henri 415
ブアブレ
Bouabré, Bohoun 166
ファブレガ
Fábrega, Jorge Ricardo 415
ファブレガス
Cesc 241
ファブレガス・イ・モラス
Fàbregas i Molas, Sílvia 415
ファブロー
Favreau, Jon 423
ファーブロウ
Farberow, Norman L. 419
ファベ
Favez, Isabelle 423
ファーヘイ
Fahey, Ciarán 416
Fahey, Trish 416
ファベリア
Fabella, Virginia 415
ファーベル
Ferbel, Thomas 428
ファベロン・パトリアウ
Faverón Patriau, Gustavo 423
ファーボス
Ferbos, Lionel 428
ファボック
Fabok, Jason 415
ファボッツィ
Fabozzi, Frank J. 415
ファーマ
Fama, Eugene F. 418
ファーマー
Farmar, Jordan 420
Farmer, Anne 420
Farmer, Buck 420
Farmer, David H. 420
Farmer, George 420
Farmer, Jerrilyn 420
Farmer, Kyle 420
Farmer, Nancy 420
Farmer, Paul 420
Farmer, Philip José 420
Fermor, Patrick Leigh 429
ファーマー＝ノウルズ
Farmer-Knowles, Helen 420
ファーマン
Farman, John 420
Farman, Joseph 420
Ferman, Edward L. 429
Firman, Dorothy 437
Firman, Ralph, Jr. 437
Fuhrman, Chris 466
Fuhrman, Joel 466
Fuhrmann, Matthew 466
Furman, Ben 468
Furman, Irv 468
Furman, Leola Dyrud 468
Furman, Simon 468
ブアマン
Boorman, Charley 160
Boorman, John 160
ファーミ
Fahmi, Idris 416
ファミ
Fahmi, Said Ibrahim 416
ファミリア
Familia, Jeurys 418
Familiar, Bob 418
ファーミン
Firmin, Josie 437
ファム
Pham, Dinh Son 1106
Pham, Duc Nam 1106
Pham, Khoi 1106
Pham, LeUyen 1106
Pham, Tommy 1106
ファム・ズイ
Pham Duy 1106
ファム・ヌドンゴ
Fame Ndongo, Jacques 418
ファメヌドンゴ
Fame Ndongo, Jacques 418
ファーメロ
Farmelo, Graham 420
ファーモー
Fermor, Patrick Leigh 429
ファーモア
Fermor, Patrick Leigh 429
ファーユ
Faye, Éric 423
ファーラー
Faller, Adolf 418
Farah, M.J. 419
Ferrer, Mel 431
Ferrer, Sean Hepburn 431
ファラ
Falla, Maiken Caspersen 418
Farah, Abdishakur Sheikh Hassan 419
Farah, Ali Abdi 419
Farah, Hassan Abshir 419
Farah, Mahmud Umar 419
Farah, Mohamed 419
Farah, Robert 419
Farah, Saalah Ali 419
Farrah, David Lee 421
ファラー
Farah, Douglas 419
Farah, Mohamed 419
Farrar, Jon 421
Ferrer, Mel 431
ファラーアソウェー
Farah Assoweh, Ali 419
ファラアソウェー
Farah Assoweh, Ali 419
ファラウ
Farau, Alfred 419
ファラウト
Faraut, Charisse 419
Faraut, Philippe 419
ファラオーニ
Faraoni, Davide 419
ファラオーネ
Faraone, Stephen V. 419
ファラオン
Pharaon, Michel 1106
ファラカーン
Farrakhan, Louis 421
ファラカン
Farrakhan, Louis 421
ファラゴ
Farago, Andrew 419
ファラージ
Farage, Nigel Paul 419
ファラシ
Farrachi, Armand 421
ファラーチ
Fallaci, Oriana 418
ファラネジャド
Farahnejad, Hamid 419
ファラハ
Falah, bin Jassim bin Jabral-Thani 417
ファラハニ
Farahani, Golshifteh 419
ファラビーニャ
Falavigna, Natalia 417
ファラベッリ
Faravelli, Carlo 419
ファラヘン
Falahen, Amir 417
ファラー・ホールズ
Farrer-Halls, Gill 421
ファラーミギル
Farah Miguil, Hassan 419
ファラルドー
Falardeau, Philippe 417
ファーランド
Farland, David 420
ファーリ
Farhi, Donna 420
ファーリー
Farley, Christopher John 420
Farley, David 420
Farley, Matthias 420
Farley, Reginald 420
ファリー
Faree, Waheeba 419
ファリア
Faría, Carlos 420
Faria, César 420
Faria, Jacob 420
Faría, Jesús 420
Faria, Rosana 420
ファリアス
Farías, Carolina 420
Farias, Diego 420
Farías, Erika 420
Farias, Juan 420
ファリアダコスタ
Faria Da Costa, Rui Alberto 420
ファリゴ
Faligot, Roger 417
ファーリス
Faris, Shihab 420
ファリーズ
Falise, Thierry 417
ファリス
Faris, Issam 420
Faris, Stephan 420
Farris, Chase 421
Farris, Kendrick 421
Farris, Mike 421
Farris, Pamela J. 421
Farris, Paul W. 421
Farris, Vickie 421
ファリズ
Fariz, Ziad 420
ファリッシュ
Farish, Terry 420
ファリード
Farid, Ahmed 420
Faried, Kenneth 420
ファリド
Farid, Hilmar 420
ファリーナ
Farina, Dennis 420
ファリネッティ
Farinetti, Oscar 420
ファリネッラ
Farinella, Matteo 420
ファリハ
al-Faleh, Khalid bin Abdulaziz 417
ファリン
Farin, Gerald E. 420
ファーリンゲッティ
Ferlinghetti, Lawrence 429
ファーリンゲティ
Ferlinghetti, Lawrence 429
ファーリントン
Farrington, Karen 421
ファリントン
Farrington, David P. 421
Farrington, Kaitlyn 421
Farrington, Karen 421
Farrington, Kent 421
Farrington, Martha 421
ファール
Fall, François Lounsény 418
ファル
Faal, Samba 415
Fall, Abdou 418
Fall, Ibrahima 418
Fall, Khady 418
Fall, Loncény 418
ファルー
Falú, Eduardo 418
ファルヴァイ
Falvai, Sandor 418

ファルウィルゲン
Verwilghen, Marc 1454
ファルカオ
Falcao, Radamel 417
ファルカス
Farkas, Marianne D. 420
ファルガス・イ・フェルナンデス
Fargas i Fernández, Josep 419
ファルガスコッホ
Vargas Koch, Laura 1447
ファルカム
Falcam, Leo 417
ファルカン
Falcão 417
Falcao, Paulo Roberto 417
ブアルキ
Buarque, Chico 197
ファルキンハム
Falkinham, J.O., Ⅲ 418
ファルーク
Farouk, El-Amry 420
Faruq, Osman 421
ファルク
Falk, Ulrich 418
Al-farouk, Oumar Idriss 420
Faruq, Osman 421
ファルーク・モハマッド
Faruque Mohammad, Mostafa 421
ブアルケ
Buarque, Crstovam 197
ファルケン
Falken, Linda 418
ファルケンハウゼン
Falkenhausen, Lothar von 418
ファルケンブルグ
Valkenburg, Ben 1440
ファルコ
Falco, Edie 417
Falco, Hubert 417
Falco, Mark 417
ファルコナー
Falconer, Daniel 417
Falconer, Ian 417
Falconer, K.J. 417
Falconer, Tom 417
ファルコナー卿
Lord Falconer 417
ファルコーニ
Falconi, Fabrizio 417
ファルコニ
Falconi, Fander 417
ファルコネス
Falcones, Ildefonso 417
ファルコン・パラディ
Falcón Paradí, Arístides 417
ファルザト
Farzat, Hussein 421
Farzat, Hussein Mahmoud 421
ファルシ
Farsi, Fuad bin Abdul-Salam Bin Muhammad 421
al-Farsy, Fouad bin Abdul-Salaam bin Muhammad 421
ファルシディ
Farshidi, Mahmoud 421
ファルージャ
Farrugia, Michael 421
ファルジュ
Farge, Arlette 419
ファルタク
Fartak, Sayed Ali Tamin 421
ファルチ
Pfoertsch, Waldemar 1106
ファルチネッリ
Falcinelli, Diego 417
ファルチャック
Falchuk, Brad 417
ファルチャーニ
Falciani, Hervé 417
ファルチャン
Falt'an, L'ubomír 418
ファルディ
Faludi, Robert 418
ファルド
Fuld, Richard S., Jr. 467
ファルニ
Fahrni, Linda 416
ファルニエフ
Farniev, Irbek 420
ファルヌー
Farnoux, Alexandre 420
ファルバッケン
Faldbakken, Knut 417
ファルハーディー
Farhadi, Asghar 419
ファルハディ
Farhadi, Asghar 419
Farhadi, Mohammad 419
ファルハン
Farhan, Amal 419
ファルハング
Farhang, Mohammad Amin 419
ファルビー
Falvey, Derek 418
ファルフトジーノフ
Farkhutdinov, Igor Pavlovich 420
ファルマン
Farman, J.C. 420
ファルリー
Farrelly, Liz 421
ファレ
Falay, Georges Buse 417
ファーレイ
Farley, Alan S. 420
Farley, David 420
Farley, Joshua C. 420
ファレイ
Farey, Pat 419
ファーレス
al-Fares, Mohammad Abdulatif 419
ファレス
Fares, Issam 419
Fares, Qadoura 419
フアレス
Juarez, Fernando 690
Juarez, Heidy 690
ファレタウ
Faletau, Taulupe (Toby) 417
ファレッティ
Faletti, Giorgio 417
ファレット
Faletto, Enzo 417
ファーレモ
Faremo, Grete 419
ファレリー
Farrelly, Bobby 421
Farrelly, Elizabeth 421
Farrelly, Peter 421
Farrelly, Ross 421
ファーレル
Farrell, Dillon 421
Farrell, John 421
Farrell, Shawn O. 421
ファレル
Faller, Régis 418
Farrell, Colin 421
Farrell, Diana 421
Farrell, Eileen 421
Farrell, Gilda 421
Farrell, Gordon 421
Farrell, J.G. 421
Farrell, Joan M. 421
Farrell, John 421
Farrell, John D. 421
Farrell, Michael 421
Farrell, Nicholas Burgess 421
Farrell, Owen 421
Farrell, Peter T. 421
Farrell, Roger 421
Farrell, Suzanne 421
Farrell, Terry 421
Farrell, Warren 421
Farrell, William R. 421
Pharrell 1106
ファレン
Farren, Mick 421
ファレンチノス
Farentinos, Robert C. 419
ファレンティーノ
Farentino, James 419
ファレンティノ
Farentino, James 419
ファーレンバッハ
Fahrenbach, Helmut 416
ファレンホルスト
Varenhorst, Christiaan 1446
ファロ
Pharo, Ingvild 1106
ファロー
Farrow, Mia 421
ファロウ
Farrow, Kenneth 421
ファローズ
Fallows, Dorothy 418
Fallows, Mike 418
ファロッキ
Farocki, Harun 420
ファーロン
Furlong, Lisa 468
ファロン
Fallon, Craig 418
Fallon, James H. 418
Fallon, Jane 418
Fallon, Jimmy 418
Fallon, Joe 418
Fallon, Michael 418
Fallon, Richard H., Jr. 418
Fallon, Steve 418
ブアロン
Bualong, Keerati 197
ファーロング
Furlong, Andy 468
Furlong, J. 468
Furlong, Jim 468
Furlong, Tadhg 468
ファワズ
Fawaz, bin Mohammed al-Khalifa 423
ファーン
Fearn, Nicholas 424
Fern, Tracey E. 429
ファン
Fan, Bing-bing 418
Fan, Gang 418
Fan, Rong-kang 418
Fan, You-chen 418
Fang, Leslie S.T. 419
Fang, Li-zhi 419
Fung, Khun Yee 468
Hawng, Kyo-ahn 584
Huang, Allen 630
Huang, George 630
Huang, Hua 630
Huang, Ju 630
Huang, Nellie S. 630
Huang, Qiang 630
Huang, Robert 630
Hwang, Byung-ki 640
Hwang, Dong-hyeuk 640
Hwang, Hak-won 640
Hwang, Hee-tae 640
Hwang, Hokyu 640
Hwang, In-sung 640
Hwang, Jae-gyun 640
Hwang, Jang-yop 640
Hwang, Jung-min 640
Hwang, Kyo-ahn 640
Hwang, Kyung-seon 640
Hwang, Min 640
Hwang, Pyong-so 640
Hwang, Sok-yong 640
Hwang, Sumi 640
Hwang, Woo-suk 640
Hwang, Woo-yea 640
Phan, Michelle 1106
Phan, Ngoc Liên 1106
Phan, Van Dop 1106
フアン
Huang, Gregory T. 630
Huang, Jensen 630
Juan, Ana 689
Juan, Jesus 689
プアン
Puan, Maharani 1138
ファンアケレ
Vanackere, Steven 1441
ファン・アットマール
van Agtmael, Antoine 1441
ファンアバマート
Van Avermaet, Greg 1441
ファンアールツェン
Van Aartsen, Jozias 1441
ファンアルデンヌ
Van Ardenne, Agnes 1441
ファンアルムジック
Van Almsick, Franziska 1441
ファンアンデルシッペル
Van Andel-Schipper, Hendrikje 1441
ファン・アーンホルト
Van Aanholt, Patrick 1441
ファンイエルセル
Van Iersel, Marleen 1444
ファン・ヴァイク
Van Wyk, Danie 1445
Van Wyk, Russell 1446
ファン・ヴァン・カイ

Phan Van Khai 1106
ファン・エック
Van Eck, Richard N. 1443
ファンエーペン
Van Eupen, Marit 1443
ファンエムデン
Van Emden, Anicka 1443
ファンオフェルトフェルト
Van Overtveldt, Johan 1445
フアン・カルロス
Juan Carlos 690
ファン・カルロス1世
Juan Carlos I 690
フアン・カルロス1世
Juan Carlos I 690
ファンキーニ
Fanchini, Nadia 418
ファンク
Funk, Dory, Jr. 468
Funk, McKenzie 468
Funk, Terry 468
ファング
Fung, Kaiser 468
Huang, Cliff J. 630
ファンクイッケンボルヌ
Van Quickenborne, Vincent 1445
ファン・ザーネン
van Zanen, Jan Hendrikus Cornelis 1446
ファンジェ
Fanget, Frédéric 419
ファンジオ
Fangio, Vic 419
ファンシルファウト
Van Silfhout, Diederik 1445
ファーンズ
Ferns, Lyndon 430
ファンスカルクビック
Van Schalkwyk, Martinus 1445
ファン・スシャーイク
van Schaaik, Erik 1445
ファンステン
Fansten, Maïa 419
ファン・ストックム
Van Stockum, Hilda 1445
ファンストラーレン
Van Straelen, Henry 1445
ファンスハールデンベルク
Van Schaardenburg, Rutger 1445
ファーンズワース
Farnsworth, Dee 420
Farnsworth, Edward Allan 420
ファンダー
Funder, Anna 468
ファン・ダイク
Van Dijk, Hans 1443
Van Dijk, Lutz 1443
Van Dijk, Virgil 1443
ファンタジア
Fantasia 419
ファンタズマ
Fantasma, Grupo 419
ファンダー・ニルセン
Funder-Nielsen, Jens 468
ファンチェス
Funchess, Devin 468
ファンチャー
Fancher, Lou 418
ファンテ
Fante, Dan 419
ファンデアベレン
Van Der Bellen, Alexander 1442
ファンデイク
Van Dijk, Ellen 1443
ファンティーニ
Fantini, Norma 419
ファンティノ
Fantino, Julian 419
ファンデプト
Vandeput, Steven 1442
ファン・デ・ベーク
Van De Beek, Donny 1441
ファンテラ
Fantela, Sime 419
ファンデラノッテ
Vandelanotte, Johan 1442
ファンデ・ラモス
Juande Ramos 690
ファン・デル・ヴィール
Van Der Wiel, Gregory 1443
ファン・デル・ウェストハイゼン
Van Der Westhuizen, Louis 1443
ファン・デル・ウォルプ
van der Worp, Jacco 1443
ファンデルコルク
Van Der Kolk, Kirsten 1442
ファン・デル・シュティーン
van der Steen, Jan-Pieter 1442
ファンデル・スコール
Van der Schoor, Roos 1442
ファン・デル・スツール
van der Stoel, Max 1442
ファンデルステュール
Van Der Steur, Ard 1442
ファン・デル・スロット
van der Slot, Arnoud 1442
ファンデルバイデン
Van Der Weijden, Annouk 1443
Van Der Weijden, Maarten 1443
ファンデルバーグ
Van der Burgh, Cameron 1442
ファンデルビゼン
Van Der Biezen, Raymon 1442
ファン・デル・ファールト
Van der Vaart, Rafael 1442
ファンデルファールト
Van der Vaart, Rafael 1442
ファンデルフェン
Van Der Ven, Rick 1443
ファンデルフーフェン
Van Der Hoeven, Maria 1442
ファンデルプレートセン
Van Der Plaetsen, Thomas 1442
ファンデルブレーヘン
Van Der Breggen, Anna 1442
ファンデルヘイデン
Vanderheyden, Thaïs 1442
ファンデルヘースト
Van Der Geest, Dennis 1442
Van Der Geest, Elco 1442
ファンデルヘルデン
Van Der Velden, Nicole 1443
ファン・デル・ホート
Van der Goot, Syne Jacob 1442
ファン・デル・ホールン
Van Der Hoorn, Mike 1442
ファン・デル・メール
Van der Meer, Ron 1442
ファンデルメルヴァ
Van Der Merwe, D.T.H. 1442
ファン・デル・メール・フィッシャー
Van Der Meer-Fischer, Cornelia Verena 1442
ファンデルラーン
Van Der Laan, Eberhard 1442
ファンデンビルデンベルフ
Van Den Wildenberg, Rob 1442
ファンデンブルック
Vandenbroucke, Frank 1442
ファンデンベルク
Vandenberg, Philipp 1442
Van Den Berg, Sjef 1442
ファン・デン・ボイナンツ
Van den Boeynants, Paul 1442
ファンデン・ボイナンツ
Van den Boeynants, Paul 1442
ファンデンボイナンツ
Van den Boeynants, Paul 1442
ファンデンボシュ
Van Den Bossche, Luc 1442
ファンデンボス
VandenBos, Gary R. 1442
ファンデンホーヘンバント
Van Den Hoogenband, Pieter 1442
ファント
Fant, George 419
ファントエント
Van T End, Noel 1445
ファンドラノット
Vandelanotte, Johan 1442
ファントリ
Fantoli, Annibale 419
ファンドレイ
Vandrey, Jan 1443
ファーンドン
Farndon, John 420
ファントン
Fanton, Jude 419
Fanton, Michel 419
ファンニーケルク
Van Niekerk, Wayde 1444
ファンネメル
Fannemel, Anders 419
ファンネル
Funnell, Martha Mitchell 468
Funnell, Philippa 468
ファンバ
Famba, Macaire Mwangu 418
ファンバイステルフェルト・フリーヘントハルト
Van Bijsterveldt Vliegenthart, Marja 1441
ファン・バステン
Van Basten, Marco 1441
ファンバステン
Van Basten, Marco 1441
ファンハーヘン・マース・ヘーステラヌス
Van Haegen Maas Geesteranus, Melanie Schultz 1444
ファン・ハール
Van Gaal, Louis 1443
ファン・ハルメレン
Van Harmelen, Frank 1444
ファン・バン・カイ
Phan Van Khai 1106
フアンピ
Juanpi 690
ファンビーク
Van Beek, Lotte 1441
ファン・ヒュレ
Van Hulle, Dirk 1444
ファンビリオン
Van Biljon, Suzaan 1441
ファン・ヒンケル
Van Ginkel, Hans 1443
ファンフェルデ
Van Velde, Gerard 1445
ファンフェン
Van Veen, Anneloes 1445
ファン フック
Hoek, Remko I.van 612
ファン・フフト
Van Vugt, Mark 1445
フアンフラン
Juanfran 690
ファンフリューテン
Van Vleuten, Annemiek 1445
ファン・フルンスフェン
Van Grunsven, Anky 1444
ファンフルンスフェン
Grunsven, Anky van 541
ファン・ヘイン
Van Gijn, Jan 1443
ファン・ベーク
Van Beek, Lotte 1441
ファンベーク
Van Beek, Lotte 1441
ファンベッケフォールト
Vanbeckevoort, Liebrecht 1441
ファン・ペルシ
Van Persie, Robin 1445
ファン・ペルシー
Van Persie, Robin 1445
ファン・ヘールデン
Van Heerden, Johannes 1444
ファンヘンゲル
Vanhengel, Guy 1444
ファン・ヘンスベルヘン
Van Hensbergen, Gijs 1444
ファンベンタム
Van Benthem, Merle 1441
ファンヘント
Van Gendt, Twan 1443
ファンホウテ
Vanhoutte, Edward 1444

ファンボクステル
Van Boxtel, Roger 1441
ファン・ボメル
Van Bommel, Mark 1441
ファンボメル
Van Bommel, Mark 1441
ファンホルコム
Van Gorkom, Jelle 1443
ファン・ボンメル
Van Bommel, Mark 1441
ファン・マルヴァイク
Van Marwijk, Bert 1444
ファンマルウェイク
Van Marwijk, Bert 1444
ファンマルバイク
Van Marwijk, Bert 1444
ファン・マルワイク
Van Marwijk, Bert 1444
ファンミ
Juanmi 690
ファン・ミエルト
Van Miert, Karel 1444
ファンミデルコープ
Van Middelkoop, Eimert 1444
ファン・ミルロー
Van Mierlo, Hans 1444
ファンモールセル
Zijlaard-van Moorsel, Leontien 1554
ファン・ヤースフェルト
Van Jaarsveld, Torsten 1444
ファン・ライン
Van Rhijn, Ricardo 1445
ファンラウエンダール
Van Rouwendaal, Sharon 1445
ファンラーフェンスワイ
Van Ravenswaay, Ricardo 1445
ファーンリー
Fearnley, Jan 424
ファンリエセルベルゲ
Van Rijsselberghe, Dorian 1445
ファンリーセン
Van Riessen, Laurine 1445
ファン・リル
Van Lill, PJ. 1444
ファンルッセル
Van Russel, Romeo 1445
ファンローイエン
Van Rooijen, Olivia 1445
ファンロイヤン
Van Rooyen, David 1445
ファン・ロッサム
van Rossum, Guido 1445
ファン・ロペス
Juan López, Mercedes 690
ファン・ローン
Glastra van Loon, Karel 504
ファン・ロンパイ
Van Rompuy, Herman 1445
ファン・ロンパウ
Van Rompuy, Herman 1445
フィー
Fee, Gordon D. 425
ブーイ
Bouy, Ouasim 169
ブイ
Boui, David 167
Bui, Kim 200
Buy, Margherita 210
Thanh, Tin 1394
プイ
Pouy, Jean-Bernard 1129
ブイアイ
V.I 1455
フィアスコ
Fiasco, Lupe 433
フィアット
Fait, Vigilio 417
Fiat, Christophe 433
フィアマン
Fiarman, Sarah Edith 433
フィアマンテ
Fiammante, Marc 433
フィアミンゴ
Fiamingo, Rossella 433
フィアメ
Fiame, Naomi Mataafa 433
フィアメンゴ
Fiamengo, Janice 433
フィアモッツィ
Fiamozzi, Riccardo 433
フィアラ
Fiala, Karel 433
Fiala, Václav 433
フィアリ
Fialli, Joseph 433
フィアリョ
Fialho, Fátima 433
フィアーリンジャー
Fierlinger, Paul 434
Fierlinger, Sandra 434
フィアロン
Fearon, Margaret 424
Fearon, Tim 424
フィアンリー
Fearnley, Jan 424
フィーヴァー
Feaver, William 424
フィウーザ
Fiuza, Guilherme 440
フィウラウア
Fiulaua, Jackson 440
フイエ
Feuillet, Michel 432
ブイエー
Buyea, Rob 210
プイエ
Pouhier, Frédéric 1128
フィエヴェ
Fiévet, Cyril 434
フィエナンド
Fjelland, Ragnar 440
フィエネナナ
Fienenana, Richard 434
フィエラケパ
Fielakepa 433
フィエロ
Fierro, Alfred 434
Fierro, Aurelio 434
フィエン
Fien, John 434
ブイエン
Boeijen, Annemiek van 153
フィオーコフ
Fialkov, Joshua 433
フィオドロフ
Fiodorov, Michael 437
Fiodorow, Joanna 437
フィオナ
Fiona, Melanie 437
フィオラゾ
Fioraso, Geneviève 437
フィオラート
Fiorato, Marina 437
フィオリ
Fiori, Christine 437
フィオリッロ
Fiorillo, Vincenzo 437
フィオリーナ
Fiorina, Carly 437
フィオリナ
Fiorina, Carly 437
フィオリノ
Fiorino, Gioacchino 437
フィオル
Fior, Manuele 437
フィオルッチ
Fiorucci, Elio 437
フィオーレ
Fiore, Mauro 437
Fiore, Neil A. 437
Fiore, Quentin 437
Fiore, Rob 437
フィオレンツァ
Fiorenza, Elisabeth Schussler 437
Fiorenza, Francis Schüssler 437
Fiorenza, Letizia 437
Fiorenza, Stephanie 437
フィオレンティーノ
Fiorentino, Fabrizio 437
Fiorentino, Marc 437
フィオロニ
Fioroni, Giuseppe 437
ブイガス
Bohigas, Oriol 154
フィカッチ
Ficacci, Luigi 433
フィカドゥ
Fekadu, Beyene 426
フィガール
Figal, Günter 434
フィガロ
Figallo, Daniel 434
フィーガン
Fegan, James Edward 425
フィキ
Fiqi, Abdihakin Mahamud 437
フィギス
Figgis, Mike 434
フィギュエイレド
Figueiredo, Cristina 434
フィーク
Feek, Joey 425
フィーグ
Figues, Solenne 434
フィクー
Fickou, Gaël 433
プイーグ
Puig, Yasiel 1139
プイグ
Puig, Max 1139
Puig, Monica 1139
フィクセル
Fixel, Lee 440
フィクテルバーグ
Fichtelberg, Grace 433
フィグレド
Fegredo, Duncan 425
フィゲイレド
Figueiredo, André 434
ブイケビッチ
Buikevich, Aliaksandr 200
フィケラ
Fichera, Marco 433
フィゲーラス
Figueras, Montserrat 434
フィゲラス
Figueras, Josep 434
Figueras, Montserrat 434
フィゲル
Figel', Ján 434
フィゲルスキー
Figlewski, Stephen 434
フィゲレス
Figueres, Christiana 434
Figueres, José Maria 434
フィゲロア
Figueroa, Julia 434
Figueroa, René 434
フィゲロア・デラパス
Figueroa De La Paz, Fidel Fernando 434
フィゲロアデラパス
Figueroa De La Paz, Fidel Fernando 434
フィゲロアモスケラ
Figueroa Mosquera, Oscar Albeiro 434
フィーゲン
Vygen, Jens 1466
フィーゴ
Figo, Luis 434
ブイコフ
Bykov, Vasilii Vladimirovich 210
ブイコフ
Bykov, Dmitriĭ Lvovich 210
Bykov, Vasilii Vladimirovich 210
ブィーコワ
Bykova, Stella Artemievna 210
ブイコワ
Bykova, Stella Artemievna 210
フィーザー
Vieser, Michaela 1456
フィサー
Visser, Tim 1459
ブーイサック
Bouissac, Paul 167
フィサック・バデル
Fisac Badell, Taciana 437
プイージ
Puglisi, Anna B. 1139
フィシェッティ
Fischetti, Mark 438
フィシェル
Fischer, Jan 438
フィシェルソン＝ホルスタイン
Fishelson-Holstine, Hollis 438
フィージデレム
Fejedelem, Clayton 426
フィシャク
Fisiak, Jacek 439

フ

フィシャニルセン
Fischer Nielsen, Joachim 438
フィジャル
Fijal, Jarrett 434
フィシュキン
Fishkin, James S. 439
フィシュナラー
Fischnaller, Dominik 438
Fischnaller, Roland 438
フィジュリッチ
Fižulić, Goranko 440
フィシラウ
Fisilau, Samisoni 439
フィージン
Whee Jine 1496
フィース
Vieth, Norbert 1456
フィス
Fiess, Jean-marc 434
Fiss, Mary S. 439
ブイスー
Bouissou, Sylvie 167
フィスク
Fisk, Arthur D. 439
Fisk, Pauline 439
Fisk, Raymond P. 439
Fiske, John 439
Fiske, Neil 439
Fiske, Susan T. 439
フィースター
Feaster, Sharon A. 424
フィスター
Fister, Doug 439
Pfister, Marcus 1106
Pfister, Wally 1106
フィスチェル
Fischel, Astrid 437
フィースティ
Feisty, Lillian 426
フィースト
Feast, Julia 424
Feist, Raymond E. 426
フィスバック
Fisbach, Frédéric 437
フィスマン
Fisman, Raymond 439
フィスリンガー
Fisslinger, Johannes R. 439
フィセル
Visser, Thijs 1459
フィーダー
Feder, Kenneth L. 424
フィダ
Fida, Cyrille 433
フィチェル
Fischel, Astrid 437
フィチキデス
Fitikides, T.J. 439
ブイチチ
Vujicic, Nick 1465
フィツェック
Fitzek, Sebastian 440
フィツォ
Fico, Robert 433
フィツォフスキ
Ficowski, Jerzy 433
フィックス
Fickes, Bob 433
Fix, James D. 440
フィッケン
Ficken, Sam 433
フィッサー
Visser, Carolien 1459
Visser, Eric J.W. 1459
Visser, Rian 1459
フィツジェラルド
Fitzgerald, Luke 440
フィッシェル
Fischer, Ádám 437
Fischer, Iván 438
Fishel, Catharine 438
フィッシャ
Fisher, Craig W. 438
フィッシャー
Fischer, Ádám 437
Fischer, Alain 437
Fischer, Bill 437
Fischer, Bobby 437
Fischer, Clare 437
Fischer, Claude S. 437
Fischer, David Hackett 437
Fischer, Edmond H. 437
Fischer, Eileen 437
Fischer, Ernst Otto 437
Fischer, Felice 438
Fischer, Gerhard 438
Fischer, Hank 438
Fischer, Heike 438
Fischer, Heinz 438
Fischer, Iván 438
Fischer, John F. 438
Fischer, Joschka 438
Fischer, Julia 438
Fischer, Kathleen R. 438
Fischer, Kurt W. 438
Fischer, Marcel 438
Fischer, Nancy 438
Fischer, Robert 438
Fischer, Rusty 438
Fischer, Simon 438
Fischer, Stanley 438
Fischer, Steven R. 438
Fischer, Sven 438
Fischer, Thierry 438
Fischer, Tibor 438
Fischer, Urs 438
Fischer, Uwe 438
Fischer, Viktor 438
Fischer, Wolfgang Georg 438
Fisher, Aaron 438
Fisher, Adrian 438
Fisher, Aileen Lucia 438
Fisher, Alec 438
Fisher, Anastasia 438
Fisher, Ann 438
Fisher, Antwone Quenton 438
Fisher, Carrie 438
Fisher, Catherine 438
Fisher, Catherine Jane 438
Fisher, Dalmar 438
Fisher, Danyel 438
Fisher, David 438
Fisher, Dawn 438
Fisher, Deborah C. 438
Fisher, Derek 438
Fisher, Donald George 438
Fisher, Doris 439
Fisher, Doris F. 439
Fisher, Eddie 439
Fisher, Elizabeth A. 439
Fisher, Eric 439
Fisher, Gary L. 439
Fisher, Helen E. 439
Fisher, Henry 439
Fisher, Jake 439
Fisher, Jane E. 439
Fisher, Jeff 439
Fisher, Jeffrey D. 439
Fisher, John 439
Fisher, Jude 439
Fisher, Judith 439
Fisher, Jules 439
Fisher, Kenneth L. 439
Fisher, Len 439
Fisher, M. 439
Fisher, Marc 439
Fisher, Mark 439
Fisher, Mark B. 439
Fisher, Mary Pat 439
Fisher, Murray 439
Fisher, Peter 439
Fisher, Philip A. 439
Fisher, Rick 439
Fisher, Robert 439
Fisher, Roger 439
Fisher, Ronald J. 439
Fisher, Ronald P. 439
Fisher, Ryan 439
Fisher, Sara E. 439
Fisher, Saul 439
Fisher, Scott 439
Fisher, Scott S. 439
Fisher, Sibyl 439
Fisher, Susan 439
Fisher, William F. 439
Vischer, Lukas 1459
フィッシャー・ディースカウ
Fischer-Dieskau, Dietrich 438
フィッシャー・デイビス
Fisher-davis, Matthew 439
フィッシャーニールセン
Fischer Nielsen, Joachim 438
フィッシャー＝ファビアン
Fischer-Fabian, S. 438
フィッシャー＝フーノルト
Fischer-Hunold, Alexandra 438
フィッシャー＝ライト
Fischer-Wright, Halee 438
フィッシャー＝リヒテ
Fischer-Lichte, Erika 438
フィッシュ
Fisch, Liam 437
Fisch, Richard 437
Fish, Mardy 438
Fish, Robert L. 438
Fish, Sharon 438
Fish, William 438
Physh, Alice 1109
フィッシュバイン
Fischbein, Nancy J. 437
フィッシュバハー
Fischbacher, Andrea 437
フィッシュバーン
Fishburne, Laurence 438
フィッシュホフ
Fischhoff, Baruch 438
フィッシュマン
Fishman, Charles 439
Fishman, Elliot K. 439
Fishman, Luis 439
Fishman, Scott 439
Fishman, Ted C. 439
フィッシュリ
Fischli, Peter 438
フィッセルス
Vissers, Greet 1459
フィッソロ
Fissolo, Maria Franca 439
フィッタリング
Fitterling, Thomas 439
フィッチ
Fitch, Val Logsdon 439
ブイッチ
Vujić, Antun 1465
フィッチェン
Fitschen, Jüergen 439
Fitschen, Keith 439
フィッチャー
Fisher, Simon 439
フィッツ
Fitts, Robert K. 440
フィッツアール
Fitz-Earle, Malcolm 440
フィッツィンジャー
Pfitzinger, Pete 1106
フィッツエンツ
Fitz-enz, Jac 440
フィッツギボン
Fitzgibbon, Dermot R. 440
Fitzgibbon, Joel 440
フィッツギボンズ
Fitzgibons, Mark 440
フィッツジェラルド
Fitzgerald, Catherine 440
Fitzgerald, Conor 440
Fitzgerald, Edmund Bacon 440
Fitzgerald, Frances 440
Fitzgerald, Garret 440
Fitzgerald, Geraldine 440
Fitzgerald, Helen 440
Fitzgerald, Jerome 440
Fitzgerald, Joan 440
Fitzgerald, Joanne 440
Fitzgerald, John 440
Fitzgerald, Judith 440
Fitzgerald, Karen 440
Fitzgerald, Larry 440
Fitzgerald, Laura Marx 440
FitzGerald, Mary 440
Fitzgerald, Maura 440
Fitzgerald, Michael 440
Fitzgerald, Michael Oren 440
Fitzgerald, M.J.T. 440
Fitzgerald, Randall 440
Fitzgerald, Rebecca 440
Fitzgerald, Robert 440
Fitzgerald, Sally 440
Fitzgerald, Sarah Moore 440
フィッツデール
Fizdale, David 440
フィッツパトリック
Fitzpatrick, Becca 440
Fitzpatrick, Brian W. 440
Fitzpatrick, Freya H. 440
Fitzpatrick, Jennifer 440
Fitzpatrick, Joyce J. 440
Fitzpatrick, Kylie 440
Fitzpatrick, Lisa 440
Fitzpatrick, Marie-Louise 440
Fitzpatrick, Mark 440
Fitzpatrick, Owen 440
Fitzpatrick, Peter 440
Fitzpatrick, Ryan 440
Fitzpatrick, Sonya 440
Fitzpatrick, Thomas Bernard 440
Fitzpatrick, Tony 440

フィッツモーリス
Fitzmaurice, Laura 440
フィッツランドルフ
Fitzrandolph, Casey 440
フィッツロイ
FitzRoy, Charles 440
フィッティング
Fitting, Elizabeth M. 440
フィット
Fitto, Raffaele 440
フィップス
Phipps, Nick 1108
Phipps, Simon 1108
ブイテンダーク
Buitendag, Eniell 200
フィード
Fede, Terrence 424
フィトゥシ
Fitoussi, Jean-Paul 439
フイ・ドゥック
Huy Duc 640
フイトフェルト
Huitfeldt, Claus 634
フィードラー
Fiedler, Irmi 433
Fiedler, Johanna 433
Fiedler, Jorg 433
Fiedler, Kurt 433
Fiedler, Leslie Aaron 433
フィドラー
Fidler, Gail S. 433
ブイトラゴ
Buitrago, Jairo 200
フィトリ
al-Fituri, Suleiman Ali Lteef 440
フィドリア
Fidelia, Bernice 433
フィードローウィックス
Fiedorowicz, C.J. 433
フィナーティ
Finnerty, John D. 436
フィナモア
Finnamore, Suzanne 436
フィナラン
Finneran, Katie 436
フィナルディ
Finaldi, Gabriele 435
フィナンダー
Finander, Lisa 435
フィナンド
Finando, Donna 435
フィーニ
Fini, Gianfranco 436
フィーニー
Feeney, Charles 425
Feeney, Chuck 425
Feeney, Floyd 425
Feeney, Ray 425
Feeney, Travis 425
Phinney, Taylor 1108
フィニ
Fini, Gianfranco 436
フィニー
Fini, Gianfranco 436
Finney, Albert 436
Finney, B.J. 436
Finney, Kathryn Kunz 436
Finney, Nikky 436
Finney, Patricia 436
Finney, Tom 436
フィニアノス
Fenianos, Yussef 427
フィーニィ
Feeney, Stephanie 425
フィニカソ
Finikaso, Taukelina 436
フィニステール
Finisterre, Felix 436
フィニー・スミス
Finney-smith, Dorian 436
フィーニフ
Fienieg, Annette 434
フィニョン
Fignon, Laurent 434
フィネガン
Finnegan, Brandon 436
Finnegan, Cortland 436
Finnegan, Michael 436
Finnegan, Ruth H. 436
Finnegan, William 436
フィネッシ
Finessi, Beppe 436
フィノ
Fino, Bashkim 436
Fino, Catherine 437
フィノグリオ
Fenoglio, Zach 428
フィノッキアロ
Finocchiaro, Anna 437
フィノル
Finol, Yoel Segundo 437
フィーバー
Feverman, Alexander 432
ブイバウ
Vuibau, Tevita 1465
フィーハン
Feehan, Christine 425
フィブ
Fives, Carole 440
フィファー
Fiffer, Sharon 434
フィフィタ
Fifita, Penisimani 434
50セント
50CENT 434
フィフナー
Pfiffner, Pamela S. 1106
フィフリ
Fihri, Taieb Fassi 434
フィーベ
Five, Kaci Kullmann 440
フィーベル
Feibel, Bruce J. 425
フィーマン
Feeman, Timothy G. 425
フィメイエ
Fiemeyer, Isabelle 434
フィヤウェク
Fijalek, Grzegorz 434
フィヤレク
Fijalek, Grzegorz 434
ブイヤン
Bhuiyan, Abdul Mannan 135
Bhuiyan, Momtazuddin 136
フィユー
Filloux, Jean Claude 435
プイヨー
Pouyaud, Dominique 1129
フィヨン
Fillon, François 435
ブイヨン
Bouillon, Eveline 167
プイヨン
Pouillon, Fernand 1128
フィラー
Filler, Aaron G. 435
フィラト
Filat, Vladimir 434
フィラートフ
Filatov, Leonid 434
フィラトフ
Filatov, Leonid 434
Filatov, Tarja 434
フィラトワ
Filatova, Elena Vladimirovna 434
フィラリ
Filali, Abdellatif 434
フィーラン
Phelan, Mike 1106
フィランサンユード
Fila Sainteudes, Nicephore Antoine Thomas 434
フィランダー
Philander, David 1107
フィーリー
Feeley, Nancy 425
Feely, Debbie 425
フィリ
Fili, Louise 434
Fili, Sunia Manu 434
フィーリィ
Farley, Jim 420
フィリォ
Filho, Esmir 434
フィリオ
Filho, Esmir 434
フィリオザ
Filliozat, Isabelle 435
Filliozat, Pierre-Sylvain 435
フィリオン
Filion, Roseline 434
Fillion, Kate 435
フィリガー
Villiger, Kaspar 1458
フィリケ
Filliquet, Etsuko 435
フィリス
Filis, Nikos 435
フィリソラ・セラ
Filizzola Serra, Rafael Augusto 435
フィリッピ
Filippi, Alessia 435
Filippi, Denis-Pierre 435
フィリッピー
Filippi, Adam 435
フィリッピーニ
Filippini, Carlo 435
フィリップ
Filip, Ota 434
Philip, Danny 1107
Philip, Neil 1107
Philipp, Lillie H. 1107
Philipp, Maximilian 1107
Philippe, Jacques 1107
Philippe, Jean 1107
Phillip, Glen 1107
Phillip, Njisane Nicholas 1107
Phillip, Rohan 1107
Phillippe, Ryan 1107
Phillips, Peg 1108
フィリップ1世
Philippe I 1107
フィリップ・グラス
Glass, Philip 504
フィリップス
Philipps, Carolin 1107
Philipps, Eugène 1107
Philips, Charles 1107
Philips, George K. 1107
Philips, Sabrina 1107
Philipsz, Susan 1107
Philliips, Matt 1107
Phillipps, Steve 1107
Phillips, Adam 1107
Phillips, Adrian 1107
Phillips, Andrew 1107
Phillips, Anne K. 1107
Phillips, Barty 1107
Phillips, Bob 1107
Phillips, Brandon 1107
Phillips, Brett 1107
Phillips, Carl 1107
Phillips, Carly 1107
Phillips, Carmen 1107
Phillips, Caryl 1107
Phillips, Cassandra 1107
Phillips, Charles 1107
Phillips, Christopher 1107
Phillips, Clare 1107
Phillips, Dashaun 1107
Phillips, David 1107
Phillips, David M.H. 1107
Phillips, D.C. 1107
Phillips, Dwayne 1107
Phillips, Dwight 1107
Phillips, Estelle 1107
Phillips, Flip 1107
Phillips, Fredelic J. 1107
Phillips, Graham 1107
Phillips, Hubert 1107
Phillips, Ian 1107
Phillips, Jack J. 1107
Phillips, Jo 1107
Phillips, John 1107
Phillips, Jonathan P. 1107
Phillips, Jordan 1107
Phillips, Judith E. 1107
Phillips, Julia 1107
Phillips, Kathy 1107
Phillips, Liam 1107
Phillips, Lou Diamond 1107
Phillips, Maggie 1108
Phillips, Marie 1108
Phillips, Melba 1108
Phillips, Michael W., Jr. 1108
Phillips, Neil 1108
Phillips, Nicholas 1108
Phillips, Patricia P. 1108
Phillips, Peg 1108
Phillips, Peter 1108
Phillips, Philip W. 1108
Phillips, Richard 1108
Phillips, Robert S. 1108
Phillips, Ronald L. 1108
Phillips, S. 1108
Phillips, Sam 1108
Phillips, Scott 1108
Phillips, Sean 1108
Phillips, Shakim 1108
Phillips, Susan Elizabeth 1108
Phillips, Susanna 1108
Phillips, Tim 1108
Phillips, Todd 1108
Phillips, Tony 1108

Phillips, Tori 1108
Phillips, Trish 1108
Phillips, Valerie 1108
Phillips, Wade 1108
Phillips, William Daniel 1108
Phillips, Zara Anne Elizabeth 1108
フィリップソン
Phillipson, Andy 1108
Phillipson, Chris 1108
Phillipson, Nicholas T. 1108
フィリッポ
Filippo, Eduardo De 435
Philippo, Witten 1107
Phillipo, Witten 1107
フィリッポウ
Filippou, Efthimis 435
フィリピディス
Filippidis, Konstadinos 435
フィリプ
Filip, Pavel 434
フィリーファボー
Fillie-faboe, Sahr Randolph 435
フィリプソン
Phillipson, Chris 1108
Phillipson, Robert 1108
フィリプチュク
Filipchuk, Heorhy 434
フィリペティ
Filippetti, Aurélie 435
フィリペ・ルイス
Filipe Luis 434
フィリポネ
Philiponet, Gabrielle 1107
フィリポフ
Filippov, Vladimir M. 435
Phillipov, Michelle 1107
フィリポフスキ
Filipovski, Ilija 435
フィリポーン
Philippon, Thomas 1107
フィリモノフ
Filimonov, Sergey 434
フィリューン
Viljoen, Marais 1457
フィーリョ
Filho, Esmir 434
フィリョ
Filho, Esmir 434
Filho, José Viegas 434
フィーリン
Filin, Sergei 434
フィリン
Flin, Rhona H. 443
フィリンガム
Fillingham, Lydia Alix 435
フィール
Fiell, Charlotte 433
Fiell, Peter 434
Viel, Julius 1456
フィル
Fill, Peter 435
フィルキンス
Filkins, Dexter 435
フィールズ
Fields, Carlos 433
Fields, Connor 433
Fields, Debbi 433
Fields, Freddie 433
Fields, George 433
Fields, Jeantet 433
Fields, Josh 433
Fields, Mark 433
フィルステンベルグ
Fyrstenberg, Mariusz 469
フィールズ・バビノ
Fields-Babineau, Miriam 433
フィルスマイヤー
Vilsmeier, Stefan 1458
フィールダー
Prince Fielder 433
Fielder, Cecil 433
フィルダー
Prince Fielder 433
Fielder, Cecil 433
フィルツモザー
Filzmoser, Sabrina 435
フィールディング
Fielding, Betty 433
Fielding, Helen 433
Fielding, Joy 433
Fielding, Liz 433
フィルデブラント
Fildebrandt, Christoph 434
フィールド
Field, Barry C. 433
Field, Colin Peter 433
Field, Eugene 433
Field, Jacob F. 433
Field, Jim 433
Field, John 433
Field, Lynda 433
Field, Mary Lee 433
Field, Norma 433
Field, Peggy-Anne 433
Field, Sally 433
Field, Sam 433
Field, Sandra 433
Field, Simon Quellen 433
Field, Syd 433
Field, Tiffany 433
フィールド=ルイス
Field-Lewis, Jane 433
フィルノウ
Fearnow, Matt 424
フィルビン
Filbin, Dan 434
Philbin, J.J. 1107
Philbin, John 1107
フィルプ
Philp, Janette 1108
Philp, Mark 1108
フィルブリック
Philbrick, Nathaniel 1107
フィルブリヒ
Filbrich, Jens 434
フィールヘフェル
Viergever, Nick 1456
フィルポッツ
Phillpotts, Beatrice 1108
フィルポット
Philpot, Terry 1108
Philpott, Jane 1108
Philpott, Tom 1108
フィルマー
Vilmar, Fritz 1458
フィルミーノ
Firmino, Roberto 437
フィルムス
Filmus, Daniel 435
フィルモ
Firmo, Dawidh di 437
フィルモア
Philmore, R. 1108
フィルユン
Viljoen, Sunette 1457
フィールライト
Wheelwright, Julie 1497
フィレモン
Philemon, Bart 1107
プイレワ
Pyleva, Olga 1141
フィロウ
Filloux, Catherine 435
フィロネンコ
Philonenko, Alexis 1108
Philonenko, Laurent 1108
Philonenko, Marc 1108
フィローバ
Firova, Dan 437
フィロワ
Firova, Tatiana 437
フィロン
Philon, Darius 1108
フィーン
Fien, Casey 434
フィン
Finn, Adharanand 436
Finn, Chester E., Jr. 436
Finn, Larry 436
Finn, Mickey 436
Finn, Stephen Edward 436
Phinn, Gervase 1108
フイン
Houin, Pierre 626
フィンガドー
Fingado, Monika 436
フィンク
Finck, August von, Jr. 435
Fink, Bruce 436
Fink, Galit 436
Fink, Laurence 436
Fink, L.Dee 436
Fink, Michael 436
Fink, Richard Paul 436
Fink, Sheri 436
Fink, Thomas 436
Van Rooy-vink, Elsbeth 1445
フィンクバイナー
Finkbeiner, Brad 436
フィングルトン
Fingleton, Eamonn 436
フィンケ
Finke, Volker 436
Vinke, Hermann 1458
フィンケラー
Finkelhor, David 436
フィンケル
Finkel, David 436
Finkel, Martin A. 436
フィンケルクロート
Finkielkraut, Alain 436
フィンケルシュタイン
Finkelstein, Israel 436
Finkelstein, Joanne 436
Finkelstein, Sydney 436
フィンケルスタイン
Finkelstein, David M. 436
Finkelstein, Michael O. 436
Finkelstein, Norman G. 436
フィンケルスティーン
Finkelstein, Maggie M. 436
Finkelstein, Sydney 436
フィンケルホー
Finkelhor, David 436
フィンコ
Finco, Antonio 435
フィンコフ
Finkov, Bojidar 436
フィンスターブッシュ
Finsterbusch, Monika 437
フィンセン
Findsen, Owen 435
フィンダー
Finder, Joseph 435
フィンチ
Finch, Brian 435
Finch, Carol 435
Finch, Chris 435
Finch, Christopher 435
Finch, David 435
Finch, Frederic E. 435
Finch, Keith 435
Finch, Paul 435
Finch, Peter 435
Finch, Steven R. 435
フィンチャー
Fincher, David 435
Fincher, Susanne F. 435
フィンチャム
Finchum, Thomas 435
フィンテルマン
Fintelmann, Volker 437
フィンドリー
Findley, Timothy 435
フィンドリング
Findling, Rhonda 435
Findling, Robert L. 435
フィンドレー
Findlay, Christopher Charles 435
Findlay, Michael 435
フィンドレイ
Findlay, John Malcolm 435
Findlay, Kathryn E. 435
Findlay, Susan 435
フィンドレン
Findlen, Paula 435
フィーンバーグ
Feenberg, Andrew 425
フィンボガソン
Finnbogason, Alfred 436
フィンボーガドゥッティル
Finnbogadóttir, Vigdís 436
フィンボガドチル
Finnbogadóttir, Vigdís 436
フィンボガドッティル
Finnbogadóttir, Vigdís 436
フィンボガドティル
Finnbogadóttir, Vigdís 436
フィンマーク
Finmark, Sharon 436
フィンリー
Finlay, Ian Hamilton 436
Finley, Diane 436
Finley, Guy 436
Finley, Mason 436
フィンリースン
Finlayson, James Gordon 436
フィンレー
Findlay, Kerry 435
Finlay, Ian Hamilton 436
Finlay, Janet 436

Finlay, Victoria 436
Finley, Gerald 436
Finley, Mark 436
フィンレイ
Finlay, Ian Hamilton 436
Finlay, Lizzie 436
フィンレイソン
Finlayson, Christopher 436
Finlayson, Clive 436
フウ
Feng, Ji-cai 427
フーヴァー
Hoover, Colleen 621
Hoover, Dave H. 621
Hoover, William Graham 621
フゥーヴェリンク
Heuvelink, Ep 602
ブーヴェ
Bouvet, Michel 169
フヴォロストフスキー
Khvorostovskii, Dmitrii 729
ブゥル
Bull, Peter 200
ブーヴレス
Bouveresse, Jacques 169
プウン
Phoeung Sakona 1108
フエ
Hue, Vuong Dinh 632
ブエ
Bouée, Charles-Edouard 166
フェア
Fehr, Donald 425
フェアクラフ
Fairclough, Norman 416
フェアクロー
Fairclough, Norman 416
フェアゴ
Fergo, Tove 428
フェアスタイン
Fairstein, Linda A. 417
フェアチャイルド
Fairechild, Diana 416
フェアバリン
Fairbairn, Ka'imi 416
フェアバーン
Fairbairn, Brett 416
Fairbairn, John 416
Fairburn, Christopher G. 416
フェアファクス
Fairfax, John 416
フェアフィールド
Fairfield, Julian 416
フェアブラザー
Fairbrother, Scott 416
フェアフール
Verheul, Ad 1452
フェアプレツェ
Verplaetse, Jan 1453
フェアベーン
Fairbairn, William Ronald Dodds 416
フェアホルム
Fairholme, Christopher P. 416
フェアマン
Fahrmann, Ralf 416
Fairman, Tarine K. 417
フェアリー
Fairley, Josephine 417
Fairley, Nick 417
フェイ
Fahey, John 416
Fahy, Christopher 416
Fahy, Warren 416
Fay, Brad 423
Fay, Gail 423
Fay, Jim 423
Fay, Martha 423
Faye, Jennifer 423
Faye, Lyndsay 423
Faye, Sabina 423
Fei, Xiao-tong 425
Fey, Tina 432
フェイガン
Fagan, Brian M. 416
Fagin, Claire M. 416
フェイゲン
Fagen, Donald 416
フェイゲンバウム
Feigenbaum, Aaron 425
フェイサ
Fejsa, Ljubomir 426
フェイジョ
Feijó, Carlos Maria Da Silva 425
フェイジン
Faigin, Gary 416
フェイス
Faeth, Stanley H. 416
Faiss, Robert D. 417
Faith, Curtis M. 417
フェイスト
Feist, Peter H. 426
フェイスフル
Faithfull, Marianne 417
フェイズラフ
Fejzulahu, Ernad 426
フェイズーレ
Feizoure, Honoré 426
フェイゼル
Fazel, Christopher 424
フェイト
Fate, John 422
Feight, Curtis 425
フェイドン
Faden, Ruth R. 415
フェイバ
Faber, Adele 415
フェイバー
Faber, Amanda 415
Faber, Lee 415
Faber, Michel 415
Faber, Polly 415
Faber, Toby 415
フェイバーズ
Favors, Derrick 423
フェイビング
Fabing, Robert 415
フェイファー
Feiffer, Jules 425
Pfeiffer, Michelle 1106
フェイム
Fame, George 418
フェイヤー
Fayer, Michael D. 423
フェイヤーズ
Fayers, Peter M. 423
フェイラ
Failla, Don 416
Failla, Nancy 416
フェイル
Pfeil, Ken 1106
フェイルーズ
Fairouz 417
フェイロン
Phalon, William 1106
フェオクチストフ
Feoktistov, Lev Petrovich 428
フェオファノワ
Feofanova, Svetlana 428
フェカ
Feka, Dren 426
フェガー
Feger, Hans 425
フェガール
Fegerl, Stefan 425
フェーガン
Fagan, Brian M. 416
Fagan, Robert 416
フェキ
Fekki, Anas Al 426
フェキセウス
Fexeus, Henrik 432
フェキトア
Fekitoa, Malakai 426
フェキル
Fekir, Nabil 426
フェク
Feck, Stephan 424
フェクサス
Feixas, Jean 426
フェクター
Fekter, Maria 426
フェグリ
Feghouli, Sofiane 425
フェグリー
Phegley, Josh 1106
フェケテ
Fekete, Thomas 426
フェーゲン
Fagen, Donald 416
フェザー
Feather, Jane 424
Feather, Robert 424
フェザーズ
Feathers, Michael C. 424
フェザーストーン
Featherstone, Carolyn 424
Featherstone, Charlotte 424
フェザーストン
Featherstone, Mike 424
フェザーリング
Fetherling, Dale S. 432
フェザリング
Fetherling, George 432
フェザント
Pheasant, Stephen 1106
フェシュネール
Fechner, Christian 424
プエスケル
Pueschel, Siegfried M. 1139
フェスタ
Festa, Marco 432
フェスト
Fest, Joachim 432
フェスラー
Fesler, Rene A. 432
フェゾン
Faison, Christian 417
フェター
Vetter, Johannes 1454
フェタイ
Fetai, Besnik 432
フェダク
Fedak, Jolanta 424
フェターズ
Fetters, Mike 432
フェダチンスキ
Fedaczynski, Rafal 424
フェターマン
Fetterman, David M. 432
フェダーマン
Federman, Rachel 424
フェダマン
Federman, Raymond 424
フェダル
Feddal, Zouhair 424
フェタロフ
Fetterolf, Monty L. 432
フェッカー
Fecker, Andreas 424
フェッカイ
Fekkai, Frédéric 426
フェッセル
Fessel, Karen-Susan 432
フェッター
Vetter, Anouk 1454
Vetter, Gabriela 1454
フェッター - ヴォーム
Fetter-Vorm, Jonathan 432
フェッチャー
Fetscher, Iring 432
フェッツァー
Fetzer, Amy J. 432
フェッテン
Whetten, Delon 1497
フェッド
Fedde, Erick 424
フエット
Huett, Annika 632
フエット・ニルソン
Huett Nilsson, Ulf 632
フェットマン
Fettmann, Eric 432
フェッファー
Feffer, John 425
フェッラーリ
Ferrari, Andrea 431
Ferrari, Antonella 431
Ferrari, Antongionata 431
フェッリ
Ferri, Francesca 431
フェッレギ
Fellegi, Tamás 427
フェッロ
Ferro, Laura 432
フェディ
Fedi, Peter F., Jr. 424
フェティータ
Fertitta, Lorenzo 432
フェディダ
Fédida, Pierre 424
ブエティロボニ
Vuetilovoni, Tomasi 1465
フェデ・カルタビア
Fede Cartabia 424
フェデツキー
Fedetskyy, Artem 424
フェデラー
Federer, Roger 424
フェデリ

Fedeli, Valeria 424
フェデリー
Federle, Michael P. 424
フェデリーギ
Federighi, Paolo 424
フェデリチ
Federici, Adam 424
フェテル
Vettel, Sebastian 1454
フェドー
Feydeau, Elisabeth de 432
フエト
Fet, Afanasii Afanasievich 432
フェドゥーシア
Feduccia, J.Alan 425
フェトゥーリ
Faitouri, Muftah M.H. 417
フェトジェンヌ
Fetjaine, Jean-Louis 432
フェドセイエフ
Fedoseev, Vladimir 425
フェドセーエフ
Fedoseev, Vladimir 425
フェートチャック
Feertchak, Helene 425
フェドートフ
Fedotov, Victor 425
フェドトフ
Fedotov, Victor 425
フェドトワ
Fedotova, Irina 425
フェドリーシン
Fedoryshyn, Myron Semenovych 425
フェドリワ
Fedoriva, Aleksandra 424
フェドルイシン
Fedoryshyn, Vasyl 425
フェドルチューク
Fedorchuk, Sergei 424
フェドルチュク
Fedorchuk, Valery 424
フェドレンコ
Fedorenko, Nikita 424
フェドロバ
Fedorova, Mariana 425
フェドロフ
Fedoroff, Nina Vsevolod 424
フェドロワ
Fedorova, Olena 425
フェナー
Fenner, Frank John 428
ブエナー
Buehner, Mark 199
フェナンド
Fennand, Bernadette 428
フェニック
Fenwick, Lex 428
フェニックス
Phoenix 1108
Phoenix, Joaquin 1108
Phoenix, Tom 1108
フェニート
Feneet, Salem Ahmed 427
フェニン
Fenin, Martin 427
フェニンガー
Fenninger, Anna 428
フェネク
Fenech, Tonio 427
フェネク・アダミ
Adami, Edward Fenech 11
フェネクアダミ
Fenech-adami, Edward 427
フェネチアン
Venetiaan, Runaldo Ronald 1451
フェネック
Fenech, Karen 427
フェネティアン
Venetiaan, Runaldo Ronald 1451
フェーネマンス
Venemans, Ab 1451
フェネール
Fehner, Léa 425
フェネル
Fennell, Frederick 428
Fennell, Jan 428
Fennell, Melanie J.V. 428
フェーネンダール
Veenendaal, Erik van 1449
フェノ
Faynot, Martin 424
ブエノ
Bueno, Alberto 199
Bueno, B.J. 199
ブエノ・デ・メスキータ
Bueno de Mesquita, Bruce 199
フェーバー
Faber, Patrick 415
フェハティ
Faherty, Catherine 416
フェビアン
Fabian, A.C. 415
フェビエン
Fabien, John 415
フェヒナー
Fechner, Carl A. 424
フェファー
Pfeffer, Jeffrey 1105
フェブラロ
Febbraro, Flavio 424
フェフリ
Fehri, Noomane 425
フェブリヤンティ
Febrianti, Citra 424
フェーブル
Faivre, Virginie 417
Fevre, R. 432
フェブレス
Febres Cordero, León 424
フェブレス・コルデロ
Febres Cordero, León 424
フェヘイラ
Ferreira, Paulo André 431
フェヘリ
Fehri, Noomane 425
フェーヘル
Feher, George 425
フェラ
Férat, Laurence 428
Ferrat, Jean 431
フェラー
Feller, Bob 427
Ferrer, Mel 431
Ferrer, Melchor G. 431
Ferrer, Sean Hepburn 431
フェライ
Felaj, Ermonela 426
フェライニ
Fellaini, Marouane 427
フェラウン
Feraoun, Iman Houda 428
フェラオン
Ferrão, Luis Jorge Manuel T.A. 431
フェラガモ
Ferragamo, Ferruccio 430
Ferragamo, Govanna Gentile 430
Ferragamo, James 430
Ferragamo, Leonardo 430
Ferragamo, Wanda Miletti 430
フェラーズ
Fellers, Richard 427
フェラダス・ガルシア
Ferradaz García, Ibrahim 430
フェラッジ
Ferrazzi, Keith 431
フェラテ
Ferraté, Luis 431
フェラーティ
Ferati, Sadri 428
フェラーラ
Ferrara, Abel 431
Ferrara, America 431
Ferrara, Napoleone 431
フェラーリ
Ferrari, Alessandro Q. 431
Ferrari, Alex 431
Ferrari, Federico 431
Ferrari, Giammarco 431
Ferrari, Jérôme 431
Ferrari, León 431
Ferrari, Luc 431
Ferrari, Vanessa 431
フェラリ
Ferrari, Bruno 431
Ferrari, Luc 431
フェラレーラ
Ferrarella, Marie 431
フェラーロ
Ferraro, Geraldine Anne 431
Ferraro, Pier Miranda 431
フェラロ
Ferraro, Fernando 431
Ferraro, Sandra 431
フェーラン
Whelan, Bride M. 1497
フェラン
Ferrand, Alain 430
Ferrand, Franck 430
Phelan, Jay 1106
Phelan, John Joseph, Jr. 1106
Phelan, Karen 1106
Phelan, Matt 1106
Phelan, Peggy 1106
Phelan, Thomas W. 1106
フェランテ
Ferrante, Louis 430
フェランド
Ferrando, Roseline 430
フェランプルボ
Ferrand Prevot, Pauline 430
フェリ
Feri, Attila 429
Ferri, Jordan 431
Ferry, Bjorn 432
Ferry, Mursyidan Baldan 432
フェリー
Ferri, Giuliano 431
Ferry, Bryan 432
Ferry, David 432
Ferry, David K. 432
Ferry, Georgina 432
Ferry, Luc 432
Ferry, Michelle 432
Ferry, Pasqual 432
フェリアル王女
HRH Princess Farial Farouk 420
フェリィニ
Ferrini, Armeda F. 432
Ferrini, Rebecca L. 432
フェリエ
Ferrier, Bertrand 431
Ferrier, Michaël 431
フェリエル
Ferriell, Jeffrey Thomas 431
ブエリク
Vuerich, Gaia 1465
フェリクス
Felíx, António Bagaão 427
Félix, Bagão 427
Felix, Heriberto 427
Félix, María 427
フェリジー
Felisie, Michel 427
フェリシアーノ
Feliciano, Cheo 426
Feliciano, Jon 426
Feliciano, José 426
フェリシアン
Felicien, Perdita 426
フェリシオ
Felicio, Cristiano 427
フェリシチンスキー
Fel'shtinskii, IUrii 427
フェリース
Feliz, Neftali 427
フェリーズ
Feliz, Neftali 427
フェリス
Feliz, Neftali 427
Ferris, Amy Schor 432
Ferris, Jean 432
Ferris, Joshua 432
Ferris, Julie 432
Ferris, Kenneth R. 432
Ferris, Michael 432
Ferris, Paul 432
Ferris, Timothy 432
Ferriss, Timothy 432
Vries, Leonard de 1465
フェリスベルタダシルバ
Felisberta da Silva, Juliana 427
フェリーチ
Felici, Emanuela 426
フェリチェッティ
Felicetti, Cinzia 426
フェリッカ
Fellke, Jens 427
フェリックス
Felix, Allyson 427
Felix, Ana Dulce 427
Felix, Antonia 427
Felix, Kurt 427
Félix, María 427
Félix, Marie Mimose 427
Felix, Stanley 427
フェリーニ

Ferrini, Paul 432
フェリーニョ
Ferrigno, Robert 432
Ferrigno, Vance 432
フェリペ
Felipe 427
Felipe Ⅵ 427
フェリペ6世
Felipe Ⅵ 427
フェリペ・アンデルソン
Felipe Anderson 427
フェリペ・グティエレス
Felipe Gutierrez 427
フェリペ・メロ
Felipe Melo 427
フーエル
Houel, Alan 625
フェール
Fehér, György 425
Fer, Émilie 428
Fert, Albert 432
Veul, Franciscus 1454
フェル
Fell, Heather 427
Fer, Émilie 428
Fer, Leory 428
フェルウィルヘン
Verwilghen, Marc 1454
フェルウェイレン
Verwijlen, Bas 1454
フェルカー
Völker, Sabine 1462
フェルキ
Ferroukhi, Sid Ahmed 432
フェルク
Fercu, Catalin 428
フェルケルク
Verkerk, Marhinde 1453
フェルゴワーズ
Felgoise, Stephanie H. 426
フェルシェリノ
Felscherinow, Christiane Vera 427
フェルジュク
Ferdjoukh, Malika 428
フェルシューレン
Verschuren, Sebastiaan 1454
フェルシング
Felsing, John M. 427
フェルス
Felce, David 426
フェルズ
Fells, Darren 427
フェルスター
Forester, Lutz 449
フェルスターリンク
Forsterling, H.D. 450
フェルステッド
Vejlsted, Morten 1450
フェルステハウセン
Felstehausen, Ginny 427
フェルステーヘ
Versteegh, C.H.M. 1454
フェルスハフェル
Verschaffel, Bart 1454
フェルズリ
Ferzli, Elie 432
フェルスレン
Verschuren, Sebastiaan 1454
フェルセリゼ
Pherselidze, Guram 1106
フェルソン
Felson, Marcus 427
フェルダー
Felder, Don 426
Felder, Kay 426
Felder, Leonard 426
Felder, Naoko 426
プエルタ
Puerta, Antonio 1139
フェルダウス
Feldhaus, Hans-Jürgen 426
プエルタサパタ
Puerta Zapata, Fabian Hernando 1139
フェールチャック
Feertchak, Sonia 425
フェルツマン
Feltsman, Vladimir 427
フェルテ
Ferté, Bruno 432
フェルディ
Földi, Mihály 446
フェルデール
Felder, Christophe 426
フェルテン
Felten, Edward 427
Felten, Eric 427
Felten, Franz J. 427
フェルデンクライス
Feldenkrais, Moshe 426
フェルト
Felt, Mark 427
フェルド
Feld, Eliot 426
フェルトカンプ
Veldkamp, Bart 1450
フェルドーシ
Ferdowsi, Arash 428
フェルドシュタイン
Feldstein, Martin Stuart 426
フェルドスタイン
Feldstein, Martin Stuart 426
フェルトハイス
Veldhuis, Marleen 1450
フェルトバウアー
Feldbauer, Peter 426
フェルトホイス
Veldhuis, Marleen 1450
フェルトマン
Veltman, Joel 1451
Veltman, Martinus J. G. 1451
フェルドマン
Feldman, Allan M. 426
Feldman, Bernard Frank 426
Feldman, David 426
Feldman, Eric A. 426
Feldman, Frayda 426
Feldman, Jack 426
Feldman, Jane 426
Feldman, Jon Harmon 426
Feldman, Kenneth Wayne 426
Feldman, Martha S. 426
Feldman, Michael 426
Feldman, Mitchell D. 426
Feldman, Richard 426
Feldman, Robert 426
Feldman, Robert Alan 426
Feldman, Robert Stephen 426
Feldman, Ronen 426
Feldman, Ron H. 426
Feldman, Scott 426
Feldman, Stephen M. 426
Feldman, Thea 426
Feldmann, Evelyn 426
Feldmann, Tobias 426
プエルトラス
Puértolas, Romain 1139
フェルトリネッリ
Feltrinelli, Carlo 427
フェルトン
Felton, Jerome 427
Felton, Raymond 427
フェルドンク
Verdonk, Rita 1452
フェルナー
Fellner, Eric 427
Fellner, Till 427
フェルナルス
Fornals, Pablo 449
フェルナルド
Fernald, Ivan 429
フェルナン・ゴメス
Fernán Gómes, Fernand 430
フェルナンジーニョ
Fernandinho 430
フェルナンデス
Fernandes, Agostinho Quaresma Dos Santos Afonso 429
Fernandes, Daniel 429
Fernandes, Desmond 429
Fernandes, Edimilson 429
Fernandes, George 429
Fernandes, Luis Anibal Vaz 429
Fernandes, Maria 429
Fernandes, Mario Gomes 429
Fernandes, Tony 429
Fernandes, Ulpio Napoleãn 429
Fernandes, Vanessa 429
Fernandes, Vicente 429
Fernandez, Alberto 429
Fernández, Alberto Angel 429
Fernandez, Alvaro 429
Fernández, Aníbal 429
Fernández, Aníbal Domingo 429
Fernandez, Antonio 429
Fernández, Carlos Rafael 429
Fernandez, Charles 429
Fernández, Damián J. 429
Fernandez, Dominique 429
Fernandez, Federico 429
Fernandez, Francisco Javier 429
Fernández, Gonzalo 429
Fernandez, Guillermo 429
Fernandez, Horacio 429
Fernandez, Hubert H. 429
Fernandez, Isabel 429
Fernández, Jaime David 429
Fernandez, Javier 429
Fernandez, Jordi 429
Fernández, José 429
Fernandez, Jose Antonio Diaz 429
Fernandez, Juan Antonio 429
Fernandez, Leandro 429
Fernández, Leonel 429
Fernandez, Lydia 429
Fernández, Manuel 429
Fernández, Mario 430
Fernandez, Miguel 430
Fernandez, Obie 430
Fernandez, Oscar Edward 430
Fernandez, Robert 430
Fernandez, Santiago 430
Fernandez, Silvio 430
Fernández, Tomas Mecheba 430
Fernández, Vicente 430
Fernandez, Victor 430
Fernandez, Xavier 430
Fernandez, Yolanda M. 430
Fernandez Briceno, Silvio 430
Fernández de Kirchner, Cristina Elisabet 430
Ferrandez-Castro, Pablo 430
フェルナンデズ
Fernandez, Enrique Fabian 429
フェルナンデス - アラオス
Fernandez Araoz, Claudio 430
フェルナンデス・アルバレス
Fernández Álvarez, José Ramón 430
フェルナンデス・アルメスト
Fernandez-Armesto, Felipe 430
フェルナンデス・エスティガリビア
Fernández Estigarribia, José Félix 430
フェルナンデス・カスタニエダ
Fernández-Castañeda, Alvarez-Ossorio Jaime 430
フェルナンデスシュタイナー
Fernandez Steiner, Liliana 430
フェルナンデス・ディアス
Fernández Díaz, Jorge 430
フェルナンデスディアス
Fernandesdias, Cristina Maria 429
フェルナンデス・デ・キルチネル
Fernández de Kirchner, Cristina Elisabet 430
フェルナンデスデラベガ
De La Vega, María Teresa Fernández 337
フェルナンデス＝ビダル
Fernández-Vidal, Sonia 430
フェルナンデス・ファガルデ
Fernández Fagalde, Luis 430
フェルナンデス・フィゲロア
Fernandez Figueroa, Rosario del Pilar 430
フェルナンデス・ロッベ
Fernandez Lobbe, Juan Martin 430
フェルナンド
Fernand, Bayani 429
Fernandinho 430
Fernando, António 430

Fernando, Chandrasiri 430
Fernando, Francisco Jose, Jr. 430
Fernando, Harin 430
Fernando, Johnston 430
Fernando, Milroy 430
Fernando, Tyronne 430
フェルナンド・トーレス
Fernando Torres 430
フェルナンド・ナバーロ
Fernando Navarro 430
フェルナンド・パチェコ
Fernando Pacheco 430
フェルナンドプッレ
Fernandopulle, Jeyaraj 430
フェルナンドプレ
Fernandopulle, Jeyaraj 430
フェルナンドン
Fernandão 429
フェルネ
Ferney, Alice 430
フェルネー
Ferney, Alice 430
フェルネクス
Fernex, Michel 430
Fernex, Solange 430
フェルバイ
Verweij, Koen 1454
フェルハイエン
Verheijen, Carl 1452
フェルハーヘン
Verhagen, Maxime 1452
フェルヒィーム
Verheem, Rob 1452
フェルビンガー
Felbinger, Helga 426
フェルフィノ
Ferrufino, Guillermo 432
フェルフォット
Vervotte, Inge 1454
フェルプス
Phelp, Michael 1106
Phelps, Bruce 1106
Phelps, David 1106
Phelps, Edmund Strother 1106
Phelps, Elizabeth A. 1106
Phelps, James R. 1106
Phelps, Marshall 1106
Phelps, Michael 1106
Phelps, Timothy H. 1106
フェルプランケ
Verplancke, Klaas 1453
フェルブルク
Verburg, Kees 1452
フェルブルグ
Verburg, Gerda 1452
フェルフルスト
Verhulst, Dimitri 1453
フェルベーク
Verbeek, Peter-Paul 1452
フェルヘーフ
Verhaegh, Paul 1452
フェルベール
Ferber, Christine 428
フェルホフスタット
Verhofstadt, Guy 1452
フェールマン
Veerman, Cees 1449
フェルマン
Fellman, Wilma 427
Fellmann, Emil Alfred 427
フェルミ
Fermi, Sarah 429
フェルミーヌ
Fermine, Maxence 429
フェルメリ
Felmerỳ, Lili 427
フェルメーント
Vermeend, Willem 1453
フェルラ
Ferla, Joe 429
フェルラーロ
Ferraro, Pier Miranda 431
フェルリーデ
Verliefde, Erik 1453
フェルリト
Ferlito, Carlotta 429
フェルリンデン
Verlinden, Joeri 1453
フェルルーン
Verroen, Dolf 1453
フェーレ
Veere, H.van der 1449
フェレ
Féret, René 428
Férey, Caryl 428
Ferré, Gianfranco 431
Ferré, Rosario 431
フェレイオロ
Ferraiolo, Jack D. 430
フェレイラ
Ferreira, Elisa 431
Ferreira, Jaqueline 431
Ferreira, Juca 431
Ferreira, Marcelo 431
Ferreira, Marina 431
Ferreira, Pedro G. 431
Ferreira, Silvio 431
フェレイラ・フスティニアノ
Ferreira Justiniano, Reymi 431
フェレイラ・ブルスケティ
Ferreira Brusquetti, Manuel 431
フェレイロ
Ferreiro, Alejandoro 431
フェレイロス・クーペルス
Ferreyros Küppers, Eduardo 431
フェレイロス・クペルス
Ferreyros Küppers, Eduardo 431
フェレオビオル
Ferrer Obiols, Maria Rosa 431
フェレス
Veres, Mariska 1452
フェレッソン
Fellesson, Markus 427
フェレッティ
Ferretti, Dante 431
フェレメレン
Vermeulen, John 1453
フェレーラ
Ferrera, America 431
フェレーラス
Ferreras, Francisco 431
フェレラス
Ferreras, Ignacio 431
フェレール
Ferrer, David 431
Ferrer, Ibrahim 431
フェレル
Ferrell, David 431
Ferrell, Will 431
Ferrell, Yogi 431
Ferrer, Alejandro 431
フェレルサラト
Ferrer-salat, Beatriz 431
フェレーロ
Ferrero, Elisabetta 431
Ferrero, Paolo 431
フェレロ
Ferrero, Alfredo 431
Ferrero, Carlos 431
Ferrero, Michele 431
Ferrero, Pietro 431
フェレロワルトナー
Ferrero-waldner, Benita 431
フェーレン
Veelen, Matthijs van 1449
フェレンツ
Ferentz, James 428
フェレンツィ
Ferenczi, Sándor 428
フェーレンバッハ
Fohrenbach, Jonas 446
フェロ
Ferro, Costanza 432
フェロー
Ferro, Marc 432
フェローズ
Fellowes, Jessica 427
フェロズ
Feroz, Ferozuddin 430
フェロナート
Feronato, Emanuele 430
フェロニエール
Ferronnière, Erlé 432
フェン
Feng, Mei 427
Feng, Tianwei 427
Fenn, Donna 428
Fenn, Elizabeth A. 428
Fenn, John B. 428
フェンウィック
Fenwick, Ian 428
Fenwick, Lex 428
フェンキノス
Foenkinos, David 445
フェンケル
Fenchel, Michael 427
フェンジェブス
Fenjves, Pablo F. 427
フェンスク
Fenske, Mark 428
フェンスター
Fenster, Julie M. 428
フェンスターヘイン
Fensterheim, Herbert 428
フェンター
Venter, Al J. 1451
Venter, Janco 1451
Venter, Sahm 1451
フェンダー
Fender, Freddy 427
フェンチェル
Fenchel, Tom 427
フェンツル
Fencl, Jan 427
フェンテ
Fuente, Alejandro de la 466
フエンテス
Fuentes, Andrea 466
Fuentes, Carlos 466
Fuentes, Gregorio 466
Fuentes, Juan 466
Fuentes, Juan Alberto 466
Fuentes Bustamante, Jose Luis 466
フェンテスピラ
Fuentes-pila, Iris 466
フェンドリック
Fendrick, Lauren 427
フェントン
Fenton 428
Fenton, Eileen Gifford 428
Fenton, Marcy 428
Fenton, Nicole 428
Fenton, Peter 428
Fenton, Steve 428
フェントン・オクリーヴィ
Fenton-O'Creevy, Mark 428
フェントン＝オクリービー
Fenton-O'Creevy, Mark 428
フェンリー
Fennelly, Tony 428
フェンリイ
Fennelly, Beth Ann 428
フェンレイ
Fenley, Molissa 428
フォ
Fo, Dario 445
Foh, Victor Bockarie 446
Hou, Jian-qi 625
フォー
Fo, Dario 445
フォア
Foa, Edna B. 445
Foer, Franklin 445
Foer, Jonathan Safran 445
Foer, Joshua 445
フォアグリムラー
Vorgrimler, Herbert 1464
フォアシイ
Foissy, Guy 446
フォアハンド
Forehand, Joe W., Jr. 449
Forehand, Rex Lloyd 449
フォアマン
Foreman, George Edward 449
Foreman, Jack 449
Foreman, Michael 449
Foreman, Nigel 449
Forman, Gayle 449
Forman, George E. 449
Forman, Milos 449
Voormann, Klaus 1464
フォーイ
Fouhy, Ben 452
フォイ
Foy, Barry 454
Foy, Brian D. 454
Foy, Mackenzie 454
Foye, Randy 454
フォイアー
Feuer, Cy 432
フォイクト
Voigt, Christopher 1462
Voigt, Thomas 1462
フォイス
Fois, Marcello 446
フォイファー
Pfeuffer, Martina 1106
フォイヤー
Feuer, Cy 432
フォイヤーシュタイン

Feuerstein, Georg 432
フォイヤヘアト
Feuerherd, Karl-Heinz 432
フォイルナー
Feulner, Markus 432
フォウアスタイン
Feuerstein, Steven 432
フオヴィ
Huovi, Hannele 637
フォーヴェ
Fauvet, Jacques 423
フォヴェ
Fauvet, Jacques 423
フォウナ
Fonua, Opeti 447
フォウルクス
Foulkes, Fred K. 452
フォエ
Foe, Marc-Vivien 445
フォカ
Phoca, Sophia 1108
フォカイディス
Fokaides, Christoforos 446
フォガシュ
Fogaš, L'ubomír 445
フォーガス
Fogus, Michael 446
Forgas, Joseph P. 449
フォーガッシュ
Forgash, Carol 449
フォーガッティー
Fogarty, Miko 445
フォガティ
Fogerty, John 445
フォキエフ
Fokeev, Vitaly 446
フォキン
Fokin, Anton 446
フォーク
Falk, Dan 418
Falk, Dean 418
Falk, Florence Arlene 418
Falk, Nick 418
Falk, Peter 418
Falk, Richard A. 418
Faulk, Marshall 422
Faulk, Martha 422
Faulk, Rick 422
Folk, Nick 446
フォグ
Vogg, Felix 1461
フォクサ
Focsa, Boris 445
フォクシーズ
Foxes 454
フォークス
Faulks, Keith 422
Faulks, Sebastian 422
Fawkes, L.T. 423
Fawkes, Sara 423
Foulkes, Arthur 452
Foulkes, Bill 452
Foulkes, Dion 452
Fowkes, Andrew 452
フォークスタッド
Folkestad, Göran 446
フォクスレイ
Foxley, Janet 454
フォクツ
Vogts, Berti 1462
フォグデン
Fogden, Michael 445
フォークト
Vogt, Carina 1462
Vogt, Klaus Florian 1462
フォクト
Vogt, Carina 1462
Vogt, Kevin 1462
Vogt, Stephanie 1462
フォークトマイヤー
Vogtmeier, Andreas 1462
フォークナー
Falkner, Brian 418
Falkner, Jayson 418
Faulkner, Andrew 422
Faulkner, Christine 422
Faulkner, John 422
Faulkner, Judith 422
Faulkner, Keith 422
Faulkner, Newton 422
Faulkner, Rebecca 422
フォークナー卿
Lord Falconer 417
フォークマン
Folkman, Judah 446
フォグラー
Fogler, Dan 445
フォグリア
Foglia Costa, Andrea 446
フォグリアコスタ
Foglia Costa, Alejandro 446
フォグリン
Fogelin, Robert J. 445
フォーグル
Fogle, Bruce 445
フォーゲイ
Forgey, Bill 449
フォゲリン
Fogelin, Adrian 445
フォーゲル
Fogel, Gary 445
Fogel, Robert William 445
Vogel, Florian 1461
Vogel, Friedemann 1461
Vogel, Friedrich 1461
Vogel, Jürgen 1461
Vogel, Jutta 1461
Vogel, Kristina 1461
Vogel, Winfried 1461
フォーゲルバーグ
Fogelberg, Dan 445
フォケン
Focken, Aline 445
フォゴー
Faugoo, Satya Veyash 422
フォーコウスキー
Falkowski, Paul G. 418
フォーコールト
Soucault, David 1330
フォコンプレ
Faucompré, Quentin 422
フォザ
Fozza, Jean-Claude 454
フォーサイス
Forsyth, Adam 450
Forsyth, Allison 450
Forsyth, Frederick 450
Forsyth, John P. 450
Forsyth, Kate 450
Forsyth, LeighAnn 450
Forsyth, Neil 450
Forsyth, Patrick 450
Forsyth, Robert 450
Forsythe, John 450
Forsythe, Logan 450
Forsythe, Michael 450
Forsythe, Patricia 450
Forsythe, William 450
フォサーギ
Fosshage, James L. 451
フォザギル
Fothergill, Alastair 452
フォーシ
Fouci, Anthony 452
フォージ
Forge, John 449
フォージア
Fozia, Hashim 454
フォーシェ
Faucher, Wayne 422
フォシェ
Foucher, Trevor 452
フォジエ
Fozie, Tuo 454
フォシェッル
Forsell, Jacob 450
フォシタ
Fosita, Latiume 451
フォーシャー
Forcier, Chad 448
フォシャール
Fauchard, Pierre 422
フォーシュ
Fors, Mats 449
Forsch, Bob 450
フォシュベリ
Forsberg, Hans G. 450
Forsberg (wallin), Magdalena 450
フォーシュロー
Fauchereau, Serge 422
フォーショー
Forshaw, Adam 450
Forshaw, Andy 450
Forshaw, Barry 450
Forshaw, Jeffrey Robert 450
フォーショウ
Forshaw, Louise 450
フォース
Force, Marie Sullivan 448
フォス
Foss, Craig 451
Foss, Joe 451
Foss, Lukas 451
Foss, Per-Kristian 451
Foss, Rene 451
Vos, Marianne 1464
ブオース
Buaas, Kjersti 196
フォースター
Forster, Fraser 450
Forster, Marc 450
Forster, Margaret 450
Forster, Mark 450
Forster, Suzanne 450
Foster, Karen 451
フォスター
Forster, Marc 450
Forster, Margaret 450
Foster, Adriance S. 451
Foster, Alan Dean 451
Foster, Alethea V.M. 451
Foster, Arian 451
Foster, Ben 451
Foster, Brad W. 451
Foster, Chris 451
Foster, Corey 451
Foster, Cynthia Ewell 451
Foster, Devid 451
Foster, D.J. 451
Foster, Donte 451
Foster, Greg 451
Foster, Hal 451
Foster, Harold D. 451
Foster, Jack 451
Foster, Jeff 451
Foster, Jodie 451
Foster, John 451
Foster, John Bellamy 451
Foster, Jonathan K. 451
Foster, Juliana 451
Foster, Kay 451
Foster, Ken 451
Foster, L.L. 451
Foster, Lori 451
Foster, Marilynne E. 451
Foster, Mason 451
Foster, Nancilea 451
Foster, Norman 451
Foster, Ramon 451
Foster, Richard J. 451
Foster, Richard N. 451
Foster, Rick 451
Foster, Russell G. 451
Foster, Sally 451
Foster, Shirley 452
Foster, Steve 452
Foster, Steven 452
Foster, Sutton 452
Foster, Terry 452
Foster, Thomas C. 452
フォスター＝コーエン
Foster-Cohen, Susan H. 452
フォスター・ジョンソン
Foster-Johnson, Eric 452
フォスターヒルトン
Foster-hylton, Brigitte 452
フォスターリング
Forsterling, Karsten 450
フォーステイター
Forstater, Mathew 450
フォステイター
Forstater, Mark 450
フォステル
Foster, Graça 451
フォズニアック
Wozniak, Curt 1527
フォースバーグ
Forsberg, Aaron 450
Forsberg, Ralph P. 450
Forsberg, Randall 450
フォス・メンサー
Fosu-mensah, Timothy 452
フォスル
Fosl, Peter S. 451
フォーセット
Fawcett, Don 423
Fawcett, Farrah 423
Fawcett, Jacqueline 423
Fawcett, Quinn 423
Fawcett, Tom 423
Forsett, Justin 450
フォセット
Fosset, Steve 451
フォーセット・タン
Fawcett-Tang, Roger 423
フォータ
Forta, Ben 450
フォーダー
Fowdar, Sangeet 452

フォーダイス
Fordice, Kirk, Jr. 449
Fordyce, W.D. 449
フォーチェック
Forczyk, Robert 448
フォーチュナティ
Fortunati, Leopoldina 451
フォック
Fock, Jeno 445
Phuoc, Ksor 1109
フォッグ
Fogg, B.J. 445
Fogg, Daniel 445
Fogg, John Milton 445
Fogg, Marnie 445
フォックス
Fox, Alan C. 453
Fox, Andrew Jay 453
Fox, Andy 453
Fox, Anthony Mark 453
Fox, Candice 453
Fox, Charles M. 453
Fox, Charlotte Kate 453
Fox, Chloe 453
Fox, Christyan 453
Fox, Claudine 453
Fox, Cynthia 453
Fox, De'Aaron 453
Fox, Diane 453
Fox, Dieter 453
Fox, Elaine 453
Fox, Erica Ariel 453
Fox, Helen 453
Fox, Howard 453
Fox, James Alan 453
Fox, Jeffrey J. 453
Fox, Jenifer 453
Fox, Jeremy 453
Fox, Jessica 453
Fox, John 453
Fox, John A. 453
Fox, John Edward 453
Fox, Josh 453
Fox, Justin 453
Fox, Kerry 453
Fox, Liam 453
Fox, Lyle 453
Fox, Matthew 453
Fox, Megan 453
Fox, Mem 453
Fox, Michael J. 453
Fox, Michael W. 453
Fox, Morgan 453
Fox, Natalie 453
Fox, Paula 453
Fox, Renée Claire 453
Fox, Robin 453
Fox, Roz Denny 453
Fox, Scott C. 453
Fox, Sherry W. 453
Fox, Steve 453
Fox, Susan 453
Fox, Tina 454
Fox, Vicente 454
Foxx, Anthony 454
Foxx, Deshon 454
Foxx, Jamie 454
フォックス・ケサダ
Fox Quesada, Vicente 454
フォックス・デイビス
Fox-Davies, Sarah 454
フォックス・デービス
Fox-Davies, Sarah 454
フォックスピット
Fox-pitt, William 454
フォックスレイ
Foxley, Alejandoro 454
フォックソール
Foxall, James 454
フォッケン
Focken, Ulrich 445
フォッシー
Fossey, Dian 451
フォッスム
Fossum, Karin 451
フォッスン
Fosten, Bryan 451
フォッセ
Fosse, Jon 451
Vosse, Wilhelm 1464
フォッセラ
Fossella, Frank V. 451
フォッピ
Foppe, John 447
フォーティ
Forte, Matt 450
Fortey, Richard A. 450
フォーティー
Forty, Adrian 451
フォディ
Fodi, Ibrahim Binta 445
フォーティア
Fortier, Anne 450
フォティウ
Fotiou, Fotis 452
フォティガ
Fotyga, Anna 452
フォティカーム
Photikarm, Elma D. 1108
フォーティッチ
Fortich, Antonio Y. 450
フォーティンブローチュ
Fortin, Ariane 450
フォーテネイス
Fortanasce, Vincent 450
フォーデン
Foden, Giles 445
Forden, Sara Gay 449
フォート
Fort, L.J. 450
Forte, Allen 450
Voth, Hans-Joachim 1464
フォード
Fforde, Jasper 432
Ford, A.G. 448
Ford, Amanda 448
Ford, Ann 448
Ford, Arielle 448
Ford, Ber 448
Ford, Bernette G. 448
Ford, Betty 448
Ford, Brent 448
Ford, Charles V. 448
Ford, David 448
Ford, Debbie 448
Ford, Dee 448
Ford, Edward R. 448
Ford, Eileen 448
Ford, George 448
Ford, Gerald Rudolph 448
Ford, Gina 448
Ford, Glenn 448
Ford, Glyn 448
Ford, G.M. 448
Ford, Harrison 448
Ford, Jaime José 448
Ford, Jamie 448
Ford, Jeffrey 448
Ford, Josephine Clay 448
Ford, Judy 448
Ford, Justin 448
Ford, Katie 448
Ford, Kenneth Willian 448
Ford, Laura 448
Ford, Marsha 448
Ford, Martin R. 448
Ford, Michael 448
Ford, Nancy 448
Ford, Neal 448
Ford, Quincy 448
Ford, Rachel 448
Ford, Richard 448
Ford, Richard B. 448
Ford, Rob 448
Ford, Robert Clayton 448
Ford, Roger 448
Ford, Ross 448
Ford, Tom 448
Ford, Warwick 448
Ford, Wendel Hampton 448
Ford, William Clay 448
Ford, William Cray, Jr. 448
Forde, Barry 448
Forde, Ralph Quinlan 449
フォトゥアリ
Fotuali'i, Kahn 452
フォートガング
Fortgang, Laura Berman 450
Fortgang, Ron S. 450
フォートシス
Fortosis, Stephen 451
フォート - トラメル
Forte-Trammell, Sheila 450
フォートナウ
Fortnow, Lance 450
フォートナム
Fortnum, Peggy 450
フォトリーノ
Fottorino, Eric 452
フォトリノ
Fottorino, Eric 452
フォドル
Fodor, Zoltan 445
ブーオドワ
Bouh Odowa, Moussa 167
フォーナー
Foner, Eric 447
フォナギー
Fonagy, Peter 447
フォナジ
Fonagy, János 447
フォーナス
Fornas, Bernard 449
ブオナッシージ
Buonassisi, Vincenzo 202
フォーニー
Forney, Ellen 449
フォーニア
Fournier, Steven 452
フォーニエ
Fournier, Evan 452
フォーニーズ
Fournies, Ferdinand F. 452
フォニーニ
Fognini, Fabio 446
フォーネル
Fournel, Emilie 452
フォノ
Fono, Fred 447
ブオノ
Buono, Vito 202
フォノトエ
Fonotoe, Nuafesili Pierre Lauofo 447
ブオノマーノ
Buonomano, Dean 202
フォーバス
Forbath, Kai 447
フォーハンド
Forehand, Joe W., Jr. 449
フォビ
Fobih, Dominic 445
フォビー
Fobih, Dominic 445
フオビ
Huovi, Hannele 637
フォービス
Forbis, Amanda 448
フオビネン
Huovinen, Susanna 637
フォファーナ
Fofana, Wesley 445
フォファナ
Fofana, Adama 445
Fofana, Bakalawa 445
Fofana, Gakou Salimata 445
Fofana, Gueida 445
Fofana, Mohamed Lamine 445
Fofana, Mohamed Saïd 445
Fofana, Seko 445
Fofana, Siandou 445
Fofanah, Abubakarr 445
フォファナー
Fofanah, Abubakarr 445
フォフォナ
Fofana, Bakalawa 445
フォーブス
Forbes, Bryan 448
Forbes, Bryn 448
Forbes, Damar 448
Forbes, Leslie 448
Forbes, Nancy 448
Forbes, Scott 448
Forbes, Steve 448
フォーブズ
Forbes, Peter 448
Forbes, Steve 448
フォーベ
Fauvet, Jacques 423
フォベ
Fauvet, Jacques 423
フォーベック
Forbeck, Matt 447
フォーベル
Fovel, J.Tyler 452
フォーペル
Faupel, Adrian 422
フォーヘルサング
Vogelsang, W.J. 1461
フォーマイーナ
Faumuina, Charlie 422
フォーマン
Forman, Gar 449
Forman, Janis 449
フォミチョフ
Fomičev, Valerij 446
フォミナ
Fomina, Nina Lutfalievna 447
フォミーン

Fomin, Dmitrii Vladimirovich 447
フォームイナ
Faumuina, Beatrice 422
フォメンコ
Fomenko, Pyotr Naumovich 446
フォヤ
Phoya, Henry 1109
フォーラー
Faller, Bryan A. 418
Forrer, Matthi 449
Fowler, Wyche, Jr. 453
フォラー
Forrer, Isabelle 449
Forrer, Matthi 449
フォラウ
Folau, Israel 446
Forau, Clay 447
フォラウホラ
Folauhola, Lynda 446
フォラツェン
Vollertsen, Norbert 1462
フォーラン
Foran, Bill 447
フォラン
Foran, Bill 447
フォラン＝カーラン
Folan-Curran, Jean 446
フォラント
Volland, Kevin 1462
フォーリー
Foley, Andrew 446
Foley, Bernard 446
Foley, Caroline 446
Foley, Charles 446
Foley, Duncan K. 446
Foley, Edward 446
Foley, James D. 446
Foley, Thomas A. 446
Foley, Thomas Stephen 446
Foley, Tom 446
フォリ
Folì, Gianluca 446
フォリー
Foley, Gaelen 446
Foley, Greg E. 446
Foley, Mary Jo 446
フォリアーノ
Fogliano, Julie 446
フォリエ
Folliet, Luc 446
フォリシエ
Forissier, Nicolas 449
フォリース
Follese, Ryan 446
フォリス
Follis, Arianna 446
フォリスタル
Forristal, Jeff 449
フォーリナッシュ
Forinash, Michele 449
フォリーニ
Follini, Marco 446
フォリバジ
Foli-bazi, Katari 446
フォリヤンティ＝ヨースト
Foljanty-Jost, Gesine 446
フォリヤンティ・ヨースト
Foljanty-Jost, Gesine 446
フォーリン
Fallin, Taylor 418
フォール
Falle, Sam 418
Faure, Bernard 422
Faure, Danny 422
Faure, Philippe 423
Fort, Patrick 450
フォールウェル
Falwell, Jerry L. 418
フォルウェル
Falwell, Jerry L. 418
フォルカー
Volker, Craig Alan 1462
フォルカーツ
Folkerts, Brian 446
フォルカード
Folkard, Claire 446
Folkard, Naomi 446
Fourcade, Martin 452
フォールクス
Foulkes, Dion 452
フォルクス
Ffoulkes, Fiona 433
Foulkes, Andrea S. 452
フォルクマン
Volckman, Christian 1462
フォールケス
Foulkes, Francis 452
フォルケンバーグ
Folkenberg, Judith 446
フォルサイト
Forsyth, Harold W. 450
フォールサム
Folsom, James P. 446
フォルサム
Folsom, Allan 446
フォルーザンデ
Forouzandeh, Lotfollah 449
フォルシェー
Folscheid, Dominique 446
フォルジャール
Forgeard, Noël 449
フォールズ
Falls, Caroline E. 418
Falls, Kat 418
Faulds, Richard 422
Foles, Nick 446
Foulds, Brooke 452
フォルス
Folse, Keith S. 446
フォルスガール
Folsgaard, Mikkel Boe 446
フォルスタイン
Folstein, Susan 446
フォルスティンガー
Forstinger, Monika 450
フォルステマン
Forstemann, Robert 450
フォルスベリ
Forsberg, Emil 450
フォルスマン
Forsman, Sven Erik 450
フォルソン
Folsom, Ralph Haughwout 446
フォルタ
Forta, Ben 450
フォルタイン
Fortuyn, Pim 451
フォルタン
Fortin, François 450
フォルチェ
Fortier, Natali 450
フォルチニティ
Forciniti, Rosalba 448
フォルツ
Foltz, Richard C. 446
Voltz, William 1463
フォルツァーニ
Forzani, Silvia 451
フォルテ
Forte, Antonino 450
Forte, Charles 450
Forte, Trudy M. 450
フォルディー
Foldy, Erica 446
フォルティエ
Fortier, Michael 450
フォルティチ
Fortich, Antonio Y. 450
フォルティッチ
Fortich, Antonio Y. 450
フォルティーニ＝キャンベル
Fortini-Campbell, Lisa 450
フォルティネビッチ
Foltynewicz, Mike 446
フォルテス
Fortes, Leonesa 450
Fortes, Márcio 450
フォルトゥイン
Fortuyn, Pim 451
フォルトゥナーティ
Fortunati, Taeko 451
フォルトゥナト
Fortunato, Artur Carlos Andrade 451
フォルトゥン
Fortún, Guillermo 451
フォルトナー
Fortner, John D. 450
フォルナシエール
Fornasier, Michele 449
フォルナーリ
Fornari, Giuliano 449
Fornari, Sonia 449
フォルナリス
Fornaris, Erick 449
フォルニ
Forni, Pier Massimo 449
フォルニエル
Fournier Rodriguez, Angel 452
フォルネフェルト
Fornefeld, Barbara 449
フォルネロ
Fornero, Elsa 449
フォルハジ
Foldhazi, Zsofia 446
フォールハーバー
Faulhaber, Gerald R. 422
フォルブス
Forbes, Fidélis 448
フォール＝ポワレ
Faure-Poirée, Colline 423
フォルマン
Folman, Ari 446
フォルミケッティ
Formichetti, Nicola 449
フォルミゲーラ
Formiguera, Pere 449
フォルミザーノ
Formisano, Roger A. 449
フォルム
Vorm, Michel 1464
フォルメル
Formell, Juan 449
Vormer, Ruud 1464
フォルモ
Formo, Ivar 449
フォルラン
Forlán, Diego 449
フォーレ
Faure, Gilbert C. 422
Faure, Maurice Henri 423
フォーレー
Foley, Mark D. 446
Foley, Thomas Stephen 446
フォーレス
Fales, David 417
フォレスター
Forester, Amanda 449
Forester, John 449
Forrester, Duncan B. 449
Forrester, Maureen 449
Forrester, Owen 449
Forrester, Paul 449
Forrester, Sandra 449
フォレスティエ
Forestier, Sara 449
Forestier, Sylvie 449
フォレステル
Forrester, Viviane 449
フォーレスト
Forrest, Steve 449
フォレスト
Forest, Philippe 449
Forrest, Andrew 449
Forrest, Brett 449
Forrest, Emma 449
Forrest, Josh 449
Forrest, Margot Silk 449
Forrest, Steve 449
フォレセー
Follese, Jamie 446
Follese, Ryan 446
フォレット
Follett, Ken 446
Follette, Victoria M. 446
フォレンゼティ
Fruzzetti, Alan E. 465
フォロタル
Folotalu, Walter 446
フォロフ
Forov, Denis 449
フォロモ
Foromo, Blaise 449
フォロロ
Phororo, Rakoro 1108
フォロン
Folon, Jean-Michel 446
フォワード
Forward, David C. 451
Forward, Robert L. 451
Forward, Simon A. 451
Forward, Susan 451
Forward, Toby 451
フォン
Feng, Cong-de 427
Feng, Ji-cai 427
Feng, Shanshan 427
Feng, Xiao-gang 427
Feng, Yan 427
Feng, Zheng-hu 427
Fong, Chan Onn 447
Fong, Kevin A. 447
Fong, Siu Yan 447
Huong, Le Minh 637

Phong, Hoang Van 1108
フオン
Phuong, Do Nguyen 1109
ブオン
Vuong, Thi Huyen 1465
フォン・アルメン
Von Allmen, Peter 1463
フォン・イーク
Von Oech, Roger V. 1463
フォン・ヴァイクス
Von Weichs, Marie-Caroline 1464
フォン・ヴィーゼ
Von Wiese, Johanna Inge 1464
フォン・ウリクト
von Wright, Georg Henrik 1464
フォン・ヴリグト
von Wright, Georg Henrik 1464
フォン・エールライシ
von Oelreich, Eva 1463
フォンク
Vonk, Hans 1463
フォンクベルタ
Fontcuberta, Joan 447
フォン・クライスト
Von Kleist, Ewald-Heinrich 1463
フォン・クライスラー
Von Kreisler, Kristin 1463
フォン・クロー
Von Krogh, George 1463
フォン・コーフ
von Korff, M. 1463
フォン・ジーゲザー
Von Ziegesar, Cecily 1464
フォンシードリッツクルツバッハ
Von Seydlitz-kurzbach, Antje 1463
フォン・ジーベンタール
von Siebenthal, Elsbeth 1463
フォンスタッド
Fonstad, Karen Wynn 447
フォンセカ
Fonseca, Clotilde 447
Fonseca, Elizabeth 447
Fonseca, Francis 447
Fonseca, Gautama 447
Fonseca, Jorge Carlos 447
Fonseca, Ralph 447
Fonseca, Roberto 447
Fonseka, Sarath 447
フォンソカ
Fonseca, Mabel 447
フォンダ
Fonda, Jane 447
Fonda, Peter 447
フォンタイネ
Fontaine, Juan Andrés 447
フォンタス
Fontas, Andreu 447
フォンターナ
Fontana, Micol 447
フォンタナ
Fontana, Antonia Ida 447
Fontana, Arianna 447
Fontana, Ellen 447
Fontana, Joseph Frank 447
Fontana, Marco Aurelio 447
Fontana, Nolan 447
Fontana, Tom 447
フォンタネ
Fontanet, Xavier 447
フォンタネル
Fontanel, Sophie 447
フォンテ
Fonte, Jose 447
フォン・デア・プフォルテン
von der Pfordten, Dietmar 1463
フォンデアライエン
Von der Leyen, Ursula 1463
フォンティーヌ
Fontaine, Jessica 447
フォンティーン
Fontaine, Joan 447
フォンティン
Fontijn, Nouchka 447
フォンテイン
Fontaine, Joan 447
フォンテス
Fontes, Cristina 447
Fontes, Justine 447
Fontes, Ron 447
フォンテス・リマ
Fontes Lima, Cristina 447
フォンテスリマ
Fontes Lima, Cristina 447
フォンテーヌ
Fontaine, André 447
Fontaine, Anne 447
Fontaine, Nicole 447
Fontaine, Pascal 447
フォンテーン
Fontaine, Joan 447
フォント
Font, Jordi 447
フォンドゥカヴ
Fondecave, Audrey 447
フォントネ
Fontenay, Elisabeth de 447
フォンドラン
Vondran, Ruprecht 1463
フォン・トリアー
Trier, Lars von 1420
フォン・トロッタ
Von Trotta, Margarethe 1463
フォントン
Fonton, Noël 447
フォン=バイヤー
Von Baeyer, Hans Christian 1463
フォーンビー
Formby, Bent 449
フォンヒッペル
Von Hippel, Frank 1463
フォン・ビューロー
von Bulow, Martha 1463
フォンビューロー
von Bulow, Martha 1463
フォン・ブラウンハイム
Praunheim, Rosa von 1132
フォンブラン
Fombrun, Charles J. 446
フォンヘッセ
Von Hesse, Milton 1463
フォンベル
Fombelle, Timothée de 446
フォン・ベルゲン
Von Bergen, Steven 1463
フォン・ベルタランフィ
Von Bertalanffy, Ludwig 1463
フォン・ミーゼス
Von Mises, Ludwig 1463
Von Mises, Margit 1463
フォン・ミューフリング
Von Mueffling, Dini 1463
フォン・ライン
von Rein, Antje 1463
フォン・ランツェナウアー
von Lanzenauer, Johann Haehling 1463
ブーカ
Bouka, Elie 167
ブカ
Bhuka, Flora 136
プカ
Puka, Temu 1139
ブカイ
Bucay, Jorge 197
ブガーイ
Bugai, Arkadii Sil'vestrovich 199
フガエフ
Khugaev, Alan 729
ブカエフ
Bukaev, Gennady I. 200
ブカサ
Bukasa, Clément Kanku 200
Bukasa, Martine Ntumba 200
プガチョワ
Pugacheva, Alla 1139
フーカート
Goedhart, Marc 507
フーガード
Fugard, Athol 466
フガード
Fugard, Athol 466
ブーカブーム
Beukeboom, Brett 134
ブカーリ
Bukhari, Emir 200
ブカリ
Boukari, Wassalké 167
ブーカル
Boukar, Oumar 167
ブカル
Boukar, Oumar 167
ブガルスキー
Bugarski, Katarina 199
ブーカールト
Bouckaert, Geert 166
ブカルド・ロチャ
Bucardo Rocha, Ariel 197
フーガン
Hougan, Claire Ayemona 625
ブキア
Bouquillat, Florence 167
ブキナ
Bukina, Ekaterina 200
ブキャナン
Buchanan, Brian 197
Buchanan, Caroline 197
Buchanan, Donald 197
Buchanan, Edna 197
Buchanan, Heather S. 197
Buchanan, Jake 197
Buchanan, James McGill, Jr. 197
Buchanan, Mark 197
Buchanan, Neil 197
Buchanan, Pat 197
Buchanan, Peter 197
Buchanan, Robert Angus 197
Buchanan, Sarah 197
ブキャナン・スミス
Buchanan-Smith, Peter 197
ブキャノン
Bucannon, Deone 197
フーク
Hooke, Wayne 621
フグ
Hug, Ilona 632
ブク
Vuc, Emilia Alina 1465
プーク
Pook, Jocelyn 1124
フクア
Fuqua, Harvey 468
フグイ
Fugui, John Moffat 466
フクサ
Fuksa, Ivan 467
Fuksa, Martin 467
フクサス
Fuksas, Massimiliano 467
ブクサノビッチ
Vuksanović, Danilo 1465
Vuksanović, Slobodan 1465
フクシマ
Fukushima, Glen S. 467
フクス
Fuchs, Christian 466
Fuchs, Ken 466
Fuchs, Mario 466
Fuchs, Michael 466
Fuchs, Radovan 466
ブクスティ
Buksti, Jacob 200
フクダ
Fukuda, keiji 467
ブクチェビッチ
Vukčević, Vojislav 1465
プークティ
Pookutty, Resul 1124
フクナガ
Fukunaga, Cary Joji 467
フクハラ
Fukuhara, Harry Katsuji 467
ブクビ
Boukoubi, Faustin 167
ブクペシ
Boukpessi, Payadowa 167
ブクペッシ
Boukpessi, Payadowa 167
ブグマ
Bougouma, Eric Wendmanegda 166
Bougouma, Jérôme 166
ブクミ
Bucumi, Moïse 198
フークーム
Hookoom, Balkissoon 621
フクモト
Fukumoto, Benjamin

フ

Iwao 467
フクヤマ
Fukuyama, Francis 467
フクライ
Fukurai, Hiroshi 467
フーグラント
Hoogland, Jeffrey 621
ブクル
Bucur, Ciprian 198
フグルサング
Fuglsang, Jakob 466
ブークルーハ
Boukrouh, Noureddine 167
ブクロー
Buchloh, Benjamin 197
フーケー
Fouquet, Gerhard 452
ブーケ
Boucke, Laurie 166
Bouquet, Carole 167
Bouquet, Michel 167
ブケー
Bouquet, Carole 167
ブーケイ
Bouquet, Tim 167
フーケス
Houkes, Ruben 626
ブケニヤ
Bukenya, Gilbert 200
Bukenya, Gilbert Balibaseka 200
フゲニン
Huguenin, Farrington 633
ブゲラ
Bouguerra, Soltani 167
ブケリッチ
Vukelić, Branko 1465
フゲール
Fougère, Martin 452
ブケルザザ
Boukerzaza, Abderrachid 167
フーゲワーフ
Hoogewerf, Rupert 621
ブーゲンタール
Bugental, James F.T. 199
ブケンヤ
Bukenya, Balibaseka 200
ブーコ
Phooko, Motloheloa 1108
ブコウィツキ
Bukowiecki, Konrad 200
ブー・ゴク・ニャ
Vu Ngoc Nha 1465
ブコサブリェビッチ
Vukosavljević, Vladan 1465
ブコシ
Bukoshi, Bujar 200
ブーゴンディエン
Bourgondien, Mary E. Van 168
ブーザー
Boozer, Carlos 161
Buser, Daniel 207
ブザ
Buza, Nedim 210
ブーサイド
Boussaid, Mohamed 169
フサイン
Fusein, Adilah 469
Hussain, Abdul Rasheed 638
Hussain, Mohamed 638
Hussain, Syed Shahnawaz 638
Hussein, Saddam 638
ブザカリニ
Buzacarini, Rafael 210
ブサコフ
Bvsakov, Batyr 210
フザノフ
Husanov, Sherzod 638
ブザノフスキ
Budzanowski, Mikołaj 199
プサパティ
Pusapati, Ashok Gajapathi Raju 1140
フサミ
al-Husami, Maher 638
プサラ
Psarra, Evangelia 1138
フサール
Huszar, Erika 639
ブサル
Bhusal, Pampha 136
ブサルキス
Buzarquis, Enrique Salyn 210
プサルラ
Pusarla, V.Sindhu 1140
フサロ
Fusaro, Peter C. 469
フサロフ
Husarov, Hryhorii 638
ブザン
Buzan, Barry 210
Buzan, Tony 210
ブザンスノ
Besancenot, Oliver 132
フージア
Fouzia, Hashim 452
ブーシェ
Boucher, Chris 166
ブシェ
Bouche, Salifou Labo 166
Bouchet, Dominique 166
プシエ
Poussier, Audrey 1129
プジェ
Pujeh, Momoh 1139
ブジェジナ
Brezina, Corona 181
ブジェジンスキ
Brzezinski, Marcin 196
ブシエネイ
Busienei, Janeth Jepkosgei 207
ブジェマ
Boudjemaa, Dalila 166
ブシェーミ
Buscemi, Steve 207
ブシェミ
Buscemi, Steve 207
ブージェムリン
Boudjemline, Adem 166
ブーシェル
Buechele, Steve 199
ブシェロン
Boucheron, Hugo 166
フジェンカ
Khudzenka, Volha 729
プジグ
Poudiougou, Abdoulaye 1128
プジ・クンタルソ
Koentarso, Poedji 751
プジコフ
Puzikov, Aleksandr 1141
フジタ
Fujita, Edmundo Sussumu 467
Fujita, Kazu 467
フジタニ
Fujitani, T. 467
Fujitani, Yoshiaki 467
プシッチ
Pusić, Vesna 1140
プジビテク
Przybytek, Lukasz 1138
フジモト
Fujimoto, Masakazu Jack 466
Fujimoto, Michi 467
フジモリ
Fujimori, Alberto 466
ブシャー
Bouchard, Patrice 166
プジャツ
Pujats, Pauls 1139
ブシャティ
Bushati, Ditmir 207
ブシャード
Bouchard, Constance Brittain 166
プジャード
Poujade, Pierre 1128
プジャド
Poujade, Pierre 1128
フシャール
Fouchard, Dominique 452
ブシャール
Bouchard, Antoine 166
Bouchard, Camille 166
Bouchard, Claude 166
Bouchard, Eugenie 166
Bouchard, Gérard 166
Bouchard, Michel Marc 166
フジャレ
Hujaleh, Hassan Farah 634
フシュ
Fuche, Karl 466
ブシュアレブ
Bouchouareb, Abdessalem 166
プシュカシュ
Puscas, Vasile 1140
ブシュキン
Bushkin, Joe 207
プシュコフ
Pushkov, Vladimir 1140
ブシュシュルテ
Buschschulte, Antje 207
フシュチャ
Huszcza, Romuald 639
ブシュック
Bushuk, Walter 207
フシュトフ
Khushtov, Aslanbek 729
ブシュネル
Bushnell, Candace 207
Bushnell, Laura 207
プシュパクマラ
Pushpakumara, Jagath 1140
ブシュラー
Buechler, Jud 199
フージュルー
Fougeroux, Nicolas de 452
ブショー
Bouchaud, Jean-Philippe 166
ブジョステク
Brzostek, Monika 196
ブジョストフスキ
Brzostowski, Edward 196
ブジョゾフスキ
Brzozowski, Krystian 196
プジョル
Poujol, Catherine 1128
Poujol, Geneviève 1128
Pujol, Jordi 1139
Pujol, Laetitia 1139
Puyol, Carles 1141
プジョル・サフォルカーダ
Puyol, Carles 1141
ブジョルド
Bujold, Mandy 200
フジラ
Hjira, Toufiq 610
フジーリ
Fusilli, Jim 469
ブシンゲ
Busingye, Johnston 207
ブジンゴ
Buzingo, Séverin 210
ブジンスカス
Bužinskas, Gintautas 210
フース
Hoose, Phillip 621
フス
Fusu, Corina 469
Huss, Chris 638
ブース
Booth, Anne 161
Booth, Brett 161
Booth, Charlotte 161
Booth, Cody 161
Booth, David 161
Booth, David Wallace 161
Booth, Eric 161
Booth, Ken 161
Booth, Lewis William Killcross 161
Booth, Louise 161
Booth, Lynne 161
Booth, Martin 161
Booth, Michael 161
Booth, Mike 161
Booth, Richard 161
Booth, Stephen 161
Booth, Tony 161
Booth, Wayne C. 161
プース
Pousse, André 1129
ブスカーク
Buskirk, Richard Hobart 207
プスカシュ
Puskas, Ferenc 1140
ブスクブンバ
Boussoukouboumba, Pierre Damien 169
ブスケー
Bousquet, Michele 169
ブスケツ
Busquests, Sergio 208
Busquets, Milena 208
ブースケット
Bousquet, Rufus George 169

プスケパリス
Puskepalis, Sergei 1140
フースコ
Huusko, Anna-Kaisa 640
フスコ
Fusco, Brandon 469
Fusco, John 469
ブスコバー
Buzková, Petra 210
ブースタニ
Boustany, Naji 169
ブスタマンテ
Bustamante, Fernando 208
Bustamante, Jayro 208
Bustamante, Paola 208
フスティニアノ
Justiniano, José Guillermo 693
ブスティンサ
Bustinza, Unai 208
プステヨフスキー
Pustejovsky, James 1141
プステルラ
Pusterla, Fabio 1141
フーズデン
Housden, Roger 626
ブスト
Wüst, Ireen 1530
フストヴェット
Hustvedt, Lloyd 639
ブストス
Bustos, David 208
Bustos, Natacha 208
ブストリヒ
Wustlich, Torsten 1530
ブストルフ
Bustorff, Maria João 208
フーストン
Houston, James Macintosh 626
ブスナリ
Busnari, Alberto 208
フスニ
Husni, Samir 638
Husni, Wafiqa 638
ブーズーバー
Bouzoubaa, Mohammed 169
プスパヨガ
Puspanyoga, Aagn 1140
ブースマ
Bouwsma, William James 169
ブースマン
Boothman, Nicholas 161
Bousmanne, Bernard 168
ブスマン
Bussmann, Gaetan 208
フーズモラー
Husemoller, Dale 638
ブスラー
Bussler, Patrick 208
ブースリ
Bhusri, Aneel 136
プースール
Pousseur, Henri 1129
プスール
Pousseur, Henri 1129
フスレ
Borjigin, Husel 162
ブズロフ
Buzlov, Alexander 210
フセイニ
Fuseini, Inusah 469
Husseini, Adnan 638
Husseini, Bello Kazaure 639
Husseini, Faisal 639
フセイノフ
Huseynov, Rovshan 638
Huseynov, Zelimkhan 638
ブセイリ
al-Busairi, Mohammed Mohsen 207
フセイン
Fussein, Qusay 469
Hossain, Akbar 625
Husain, Maqbool Fida 638
Husain, Masud 638
Husain, Mishal 638
al-Husayn, Hamud 638
Husayn, Husayn Mahmud Shaykh 638
al-Husayn, Muhammad 638
Hussain, Chaudhry Wajahat 638
Hussain, Mamnoon 638
Hussain, Mohamed Zahir 638
Hussain, Tanveer 638
Hussain, Zakaria 638
Hussain, Zakir 638
Hussein, Abdirahman Mohamed 638
Hussein, Abdullah Khalil 638
Hussein, Abdul-Rahim Mohammed 638
Hussein, Abdulwahab Mohamed 638
Hussein, Ahmad Musaed 638
Hussein, Ahmed 638
Hussein, Cabdirixman Mohamed 638
Hussein, Fowsiiya Mohamed Sheikh 638
Hussein, Hani Abdulaziz 638
Hussein, Hussein Mohamud Sheikh 638
Hussein, Saddam 638
Hussein, Saynab Aweys 638
Hussein, Tamer 638
Hussein, Uday 638
Hussein, Yusof 638
フセイン・カンデミール
Huseyin Kandemir 638
ブゼック
Buzek, Jerzy 210
フーセネッガー
Fussenegger, Gertrud 469
フーゼマン
Husemann, Armin J. 638
フセリド
Huselid, Mark A. 638
フーゼル
Fuser, Marco 469
ブーゼロー
Bouzereau, Laurent 169
ブーセン
Busen, Susan Jeffrey 207
ブゾー
Buzo, Adrian 210
フソビッチ
Husović, Rafet 638
ブゾヤ
Buzoya, Elie 210
フソング
Hussong, Christin 639
フーダ
Fawdah, Yusrī 423
フタ
Futa, André Philippe 469
フダ
Fouda, André Mama 452
Huda, Nazmul 631
ブダ
Bouda, Jean-Claude 166
Bouda, Seydou 166
Boudat, Thomas 166
フダイクリエフ
Khudaikuliev, Mukhammednazar 729
フタイシ
al-Futaisi, Ahmed bin Mohammed bin Salim 469
フダイビー
Hodaibi, Mamoun El- 612
フダイベルガノフ
Khudayberganov, Tursinkhon 729
フダイベルケノフ
Hudaibergenov, Tolkunbek 631
フダイベルディエフ
Khudaiberdyyev, Orazberdy 729
ブタヴァン
Boutavant, Marc 169
フダエダト
Khudaidad, General 729
プタカウスカス
Ptakauskas, Kestutis 1138
フダーク
Hudák, Vazil 631
プダコフ
Pudakov, Amangeldy 1139
プタシュネ
Ptashne, Mark 1138
プタチニコバ
Ptacnikova, Jirina 1138
フタチュニク
Ftáčnik, Milan 466
プタック
Ptak, Thomas 1138
ブダトキ
Budhathoki, Keshab Kumar 199
プタピパット
Puttapipat, Niroot 1141
フータモ
Huhtamo, Erkki 634
フダリ
Khudari, Jamal 729
ブターリア
Butalia, Urvashi 208
ブタリアー
Butalia, Subhadra 208
ブダリカ
Boudalika, Litsa 166
ブタレ
Butale, Chapson 208
ブタレブ
Boutaleb, Mohammed 169
ブタン
Boutin, Christine 169
ブタンバ
Boutamba, Alexis 169
ブーチ
Booch, Grady 160
ブチ
Buci, Antoniu 198
プチ
Petit, Jean-Pierre 1103
プチェルニク
Pchelnik, Darya 1089
ブーチキー
Bouchikhi, Hamid 166
プチコ
Pucko, Danijel 1139
ブチコフ
Vuchkov, Veselin 1465
プチコフ
Puchkov, Vladimir A. 1138
ブチコフスキ
Bučkovski, Vlado 198
プチコラン
Petitcollin, Christel 1103
ブーチス
Voutsis, Nikos 1464
ブチッチ
Vučić, Aleksandar 1465
フチート
Fucito, Salvatore 466
ブチニッチ
Vučinić, Boro 1465
ブチャツキ
Buceatchi, Pavel 197
Buczacki, S.T. 198
ブチャナヤンディ
Bucyanayandi, Tress 198
ブーチン
Bootzin, Richard R. 161
プーチン
Putin, Vladimir Vladimirovich 1141
プチン
Putin, Vladimir Vladimirovich 1141
ブツェンコ
Butsenko, Mykola 209
フー・ツォン
Fou, Ts'ong 452
フッカー
Hooker, John Lee 621
Hooker, Marshevet 621
Hooker, Neal H. 621
Hooker, Richard 621
Hooker, Steve 621
ブッカー
Booker, Cory 160
Booker, Devin 160
Booker, Devontae 160
Booker, Jean 160
Booker, Rob 160
Booker, Sue 160
Booker, Trevor 160
Bouckaert, Peter 166
Bücker, Jutta 198
フッキ
Hulk 634
フック
Hook, Glenn D. 621
Hook, John R. 621
Hook, Peter 621
Hook, Philip 621
Hook, Richard 621
Phuc, Nguyen Xuan 1109
Phuc, Vo Hong 1109
ブック
Book, Howard 160

Boucq, François 166
フックス
Fuchs, Catherine 466
Fuchs, Dmitry 466
Fuchs, Ernst 466
Fuchs, Ingrid 466
Fuchs, John 466
Fuchs, Michael 466
Fuchs, Sarah Katherine 466
Fuchs, Susan 466
Fuks, Abraham 467
hooks, bell 621
Hooks, Lavon 621
ブックス
Boeckx, Cedric 153
プックス
Pucks, Marianne 1139
ブックステーバー
Bookstaber, Richard M. 160
フックスベルガー
Fuchsberger, Joachim 466
ブックチン
Bookchin, Murray 160
ブックホルツ
Buchholz, Rogene A. 197
ブックマン
Bookman, Marc 160
ブッケ
Boeke, Jet 153
ブッサ
Bussa, Jean Lucien 208
ブッサディー・ナーワーウィチット
Bhusdee Navavichit 136
ブッシ
Bussi, Maria G. Bartolini 208
ブッシー
Bouchy, Anne 166
ブッシィ
Bouchy, Anne 166
ブッシイ
Bouchy, Anne 166
ブッシェ
Bouchet, Dominique 166
Busche, Laura 207
ブッシェル
Bushell, Mark 207
ブッシェンドルフ
Buschendorf, Christa 207
ブッシャ
Buscha, Joachim 207
ブッシュ
Boush, David M. 168
Busch, Andrew 207
Busch, Andrew M. 207
Busch, Eberhard 207
Busch, Fredric 207
Busch, Noel Fairchild 207
Busch, Petra 207
Busch, Werner 207
Bush, Angela Cassell 207
Bush, Barbara 207
Bush, Darren 207
Bush, Deon 207
Bush, George Herbert Walker 207
Bush, George Walker, Jr. 207
Bush, Helen 207
Bush, Jeb 207
Bush, Kate 207
Bush, Laura 207
Bush, Laura Welch 207
Bush, Lauren 207
Bush, Matt 207
Bush, Michael 207
Bush, M.L. 207
Bush, Rafael 207
Bush, Reggie 207
Bush, Richard C. 207
ブッシュナー
Buschner, Georg 207
ブッシュネル
Bushnell, Nolan 207
ブッシュマン
Buschman, John E. 207
プッジョーニ
Puggioni, Christian 1139
ブッセ
Busse, Gisela von 208
ブッセマーカー
Bussemaker, Jet 208
フッセン
Hussen, Ahmed D. 639
ブッソラーティ
Bussolati, Emanuela 208
フッソング
Hussong, Stefan 639
ブッダ
Bodha, Nandcoomar 153
ブッタタート
Buddhadasa, Bhikkhu 199
フッタリー
Huttary, Karin 639
プッチ
Pucci, Aldo R. 1138
Pucci, Lou Taylor 1138
ブッチェラート
Buccellato, Brian 197
プッチ・オルトネーダ
Puig Ortoneda, Albert 1139
プッチーニ
Puccini, Simonetta 1138
ブッチャー
Butchart, Alexander 208
Butcher, A.J. 208
Butcher, Andy 208
Butcher, Christina 208
Butcher, Eugene C. 208
Butcher, Howard Karl 208
Butcher, Jim 208
Butcher, Mike 208
Butcher, Nancy 208
Butcher, Shannon K. 208
Butcher, Susan 208
Butcher, Tim 208
ブッチャート
Butchart, Andrew 208
ブッチャレッリ
Bucciarelli, Fabio 197
Bucciarelli, Marina 197
プッチャレッリ
Pucciarelli, Manuel 1138
プッツァー
Putzer, Karen 1141
プッツェ
Putze, Martin 1141
ブッツェッティ
Buzzetti, Dino 210
プッツガー
Putzger, F.W. 1141
ブッツ - ヨルゲンセン
Budtz-Jørgensen, Ejvind 199
フッテ
Foote, Horton 447
ブッテ
Boutte, Phillip, Jr. 169
ブッデ
Budde, Nadia 199
プッディーヌ
Puddinu, Paolo 1139
ブッテルスカヤ
Butyrskaya, Maria 209
ブッデンベルク
Buddenberg, Susanne 199
フット
Foot, Michael Mackintosh 447
Foot, Philippa Ruth 447
Foot, Robert 447
Foote, Daniel H. 447
Foote, Judy M. 447
Foote, Kenneth E. 447
Foote, Nathaniel 447
フッド
Hood, Ann 620
Hood, Brenda 620
Hood, Bruce M. 620
Hood, Joshua 620
Hood, Karl 620
Hood, Leroy E. 620
Hood, Philip 620
Hood, Rodney 620
Hood, Ziggy 620
al-Hudd, Mohamed Abdelkarim 631
ブット
Bhutto, Benazir 136
Bhutto, Shahid Hussain 136
Bhutto Zardari, Bilawal 136
But, Franc 208
Butt, Hans-Jürgen 209
ブットー
Bhutto, Benazir 136
ブット・ザルダリ
Bhutto Zardari, Bilawal 136
フッド・スチュアート
Hood-Stewart, Fiona 620
ブットディー
Butdee, Chatchai 208
プットナム
Putnam, Joe Billy, Jr. 1141
フッドボーイ
Hoodbhoy, Pervez Amirali 620
フットマン
Footman, Tim 447
ブットマン
Butman, John 209
Buttmann, Günther 209
プットマン
Putman, Andrée 1141
プットリー
Puedpong, Buttree 1139
フットレル
Futrelle, Jacques 469
ブッハー
Bucher, Philip 197
Bucher, Reto 197
ブッパー
Boupha, Phongsavath 167
ブッヒャー
Bucher, Ursula 197
ブッフ
Buch, Esteban 197
ブッフォーニ
Buffoni, Franco 199
ブッフォン
Buffon, Gianluigi 199
ブッフハイム
Buchheim, Lothar-Günther 197
Buchheim, Ralf 197
ブッフバウアー
Buchbauer, Robert 197
ブッフバルト
Buchwald, Guido 198
ブッフビンダー
Buchbinder, Rudolf 197
ブッフホルツ
Buchholz, Horst 197
ブッフマン
Buchmann, Rudolf 198
プッリチーノ
Pullicino, George 1139
ブテ
Buthe, Britta 208
ブデ
Boudet, Jean-Patrice 166
ブディ
Budi, Karya Sumadi 199
プティ
Petit, Philippe 1103
Petit, Roland 1103
Petit, Xavier-Laurent 1103
Petitt, Barbara S. Pécherot 1103
フティーア
Futia, Carl 469
ブティア
Bhutia, Topgay 136
プティアイネン
Poutiainen, Tanja 1129
ブディアフ
Boudiaf, Abdelmalek 166
ブディアルジョ
Budiardjo, Carmel 199
ブディアンスキー
Budiansky, Stephen 199
ブディウ
Budiu, Raluca 199
ブティエ
Bouthier, Daniel 169
ブーティエット
Boutiette, KC 169
ブディオノ
Boediono 153
ブディコ
Budyko, Mikhail Ivanovich 199
プディコム
Puddicombe, Andy 1139
ブティッチ
Vtic, Maja 1465
プティット
Pettitt, Charles William 1105
プティパ
Petitpas, Albert J. 1103
プティフィス
Petitfils, Jean Christian 1103
プティボン
Petibon, Patricia 1103
ブディミル
Budimir, Ante 199

フ

ブティメ
Butime, Tom 208
ブティリオーネ
Buttiglione, Rocco 209
ブティリョネ
Buttiglione, Rocco 209
フデインガル
Houdeingar, David 625
ブーテェ
Büthe, Tim 208
フデック
Hudec, Jan 631
ブーテフリカ
Bouteflika, Abdelaziz 169
ブデュ
Bedu, Jean-Jacques 113
ブーデリ
Buderi, Robert 199
ブーテルファ
Boutarfa, Noureddine 169
フデルブルガ・ドルジハンド
Khuderbulga Dorjkhandyn 729
ブーデルマン
Budelmann, Kevin 199
ブテレジ
Buthelezi, Mangosuthu 208
Buthelezi, Mangosuthu Gatsha 208
Buthelizi, Mangosuthu 208
ブデン
Bouden, Chiheb 166
ブテンカラム
Puthenkalam, John Joseph 1141
ブーテンコ
Boutenko, Victoria 169
ブデンホルツァー
Budenholzer, Mike 199
フート
Foot, Michael Mackintosh 447
Foot, Philippa Ruth 447
Foote, Horton 447
Foote, Nathaniel 447
Hoet, Jan 613
al-Hout, Shafig 627
Huth, Jannik 639
Huth, Joe, Ⅳ 639
Huth, Robert 639
Huth, Werner 639
フード
Hood, Amy 620
Hood, Bruce M. 620
Hood, Destin 620
ブトー
Buteau, Pierre 208
ブトイ
Butoyi, Antoine 209
フドイナザーロフ
Khudoinazarov, Bakhtijar 729
ブードゥー
Boedhoe, Wonnie 153
ブドゥ
Boudou, Amado 166
ブトヴァン
Bouttevin, Frank 169
ブトゥザザ
Botozaza, Pierrot 165
ブトゥマヌバツアラ
Botomanovatsara 165
ブトカ
Bîtca, Vasile 142
ブトケビチュス
Butkevičius, Algirdas 208
ブトコビッチ
Butković, Oleg 208
ブドスコウ
Bødskov, Morten 153
ブトト
Putoto, Giovanni 1141
ブートナー
Buettner, Robert 199
ブトネ
Boutonnet, Mathilde 169
ブドビナ
Vdovina, Daria 1449
ブドラ
Bdolak, Levanah Shell 109
ブドラス
Budras, Klaus-Dieter 199
フドリ
Khoudri, Mahmoud 728
ブートル
Bootle, Roger 161
Bootle, R.P. 161
ブトレ
Butore, Joseph 209
ブードロー
Boudreau, Lou 166
ブドロー
Boudreau, J.Donald 166
Boudreault, Gabriel 166
ブドローガニョン
Boudreau Gagnon, Marie-Pier 166
ブートン
Bouton, Katherine 169
フーナ
Khouna, Mohamed Ould 729
Khouna, Seyidna Ali Ould Mohamed 729
プナ
Puna, Henry 1140
ブーナウ
Boonow, Mohamud Mohamed 160
フナキ
Funaki, Fineasi 468
ブナキスタ
Benacquista, Tonino 119
ブナバンディカニャミヒゴ
Vunabandikanyamihigo, Célestin 1465
プナワラ
Poonawalla, Cyrus S. 1124
ブナンタ
Bunanta, Murti 201
ブーニ
Bououni, Lazhar 167
ブニエ
Bunye, Ignacio 202
Buyne, Ignacio 210
フニエフ
Huniehu, Edward 635
ブニャキ
Bunjaki, Enis 201
ブーニュー
Bougnoux, Daniel 166
ブニョニ
Bunyoni, Alain Guillaume 202
ブニョン
Bugnion, François 199
ブニワンガ
Vuniwaqa, Merseini 1465
ブーニン
Bunin, Stanislav 201
フヌエフ
Hunu'ehu, Edward 637
ブーネ
Bune, Poseci 201
フネイシュ
Fneish, Mohammed 445
フネイファート
Huneifat, Khaled 635
ブーネクラフ
Bounekraf, Abdelkader 167
フネス
Funes, Mauricio 468
フネス・モリ
Funes Mori, Ramiro 468
フネリウ
Funeriu, Daniel 468
ブネル
Bunnell, David 201
ブーネン
Boonen, Harry 160
プノ
Puno, Ronald 1140
プノー
Penot, Christophe 1095
ブノア
Benoir, Victor 123
フノル
Hunor, Kelemen 635
ブノワ
Benoist, Luc 123
Benoît, Guy 123
Benoit, Marcelle 123
ブノワ＝ブロウエズ
Benoit-Browaeys, Dorothée 123
プノンバヤン
Punongbayan, Raymundo S. 1140
フーバー
Furber, Stephen Bo 468
Hoover, Colleen 621
Hoover, J.J. 621
Hoover, John 621
Hoover, Ryan 621
Huber, Anja 631
Huber, Gerd 631
Huber, Joseph 631
Huber, Karin 631
Huber (horn), Liezel 631
Huber, Robert 631
Huber, Wolfgang 631
フーパー
Hooper, Anne 621
Hooper, Austin 621
Hooper, Charles L. 621
Hooper, Dan 621
Hooper, Geoffrey 621
Hooper, Jeff 621
Hooper, Kay 621
Hooper, Mary 621
Hooper, Meredith 621
Hooper, Michael 621
Hooper, N.M. 621
Hooper, Rowan 621
Hooper, Tom 621
ブバ
Bouba, Maigari Bello 166
Buba, Ismail Mahmud Hurre 197
ブーバカル
Boubacar, Kane 166
ブバカール
Boubacar, Sidi Mohamed Ould 166
フーパー - キリアキディス
Hooper-Kyriakidis, Patricia Lee 621
ブバクリ
Boubakri, Ines 166
ブパシ
Bhupathi, Mahesh 136
ブパチョフ
Pykhachov, Artem 1141
ブパティラジュ
Bhupathiraju, Kiran 136
プハラツ
Puhalac, Slobodan 1139
ブハリ
Buhari, Muhammadu 199
ブバル
Boubal, Christophe 166
プハルス
Pujals, Bernadette 1139
ブバロ
Bubalo, Predrag 197
フーヒェル
Huchel, Uwe 631
フビーニ
Fubini, David 466
ブヒンガー
Buchinger, Erwin 197
ブブ
Boubou, Camara Moussa Seydi 166
プファー
Pfarr, Bernd 1105
プファイファ
Pfeiffer, Boris 1105
プファイファー
Pfeifer, Erik 1105
Pfeiffer, Gabriele 1106
フファネ
Houffaneh, Hassan Darar 625
ブファル
Boufal, Sofiane 166
プファルツ
Pfaltz, Kay 1105
プファンド
Pfund, Arthur 1106
プファンメラー
Pfannmoller, Stefan 1105
プフィスター
Pfister, Daniel 1106
プフェンドザック
Pfendsack, Werner 1106
プフォーゲル
Puvogel, Renate 1141
ブフォネス
Bujones, Fernando 200
プーフォロ
Phoofolo, Haae Edward 1108
ブフォン
Buffon, Gianluigi 199
ブブカ
Boubka, Sergei 166
フープス
Hoopes, James 621
フープト

Houpt, Simon 626
ブフト
Bucht, Sven-Erik 198
ブフナー
Buchner, Hartmut 198
ブブナー
Bubner, Rüdiger 197
フーフナーゲル
Hufnagl, J.Michael 632
ブブノビッチ
Bubnovich, Vitali 197
ブーフハイム
Buchheim, Lothar-Günther 197
ブーフビンダー
Buchbinder, Rudolf 197
ブフビンダー
Buchbinder, Rudolf 197
ブーフフォルツ
Buchholz, Andreas 197
ブフペ
Buhpe, Atimeng 200
ブーフホルツ
Buchholz, Horst 197
フープマン
Hoopmann, Kathy 621
ブーフマン
Buchmann, Johannes 197
フーブラー
Hoobler, Dorothy 620
Hoobler, Thomas 620
ブフラル
Bouhlal, Mohammed Rachad 167
ブブラン
Bublan, František 197
ブフリ
Buchli, Matthijs 197
ブーブリエム
Boubryemm, Vanessa 166
フーブリヒト
Hubricht, Manfred 631
フーフル
al-Hoofr, Ahmed Mohammed 620
プフルークバイル
Pflugbeil, Sebastian 1106
プフルグバイル
Pflugbeil, Sebastian 1106
ブーブレ
Buble, Michael 197
ブブンバ
Bbumba, Sydda 109
ブベ
Bouvet, Sofian 169
プーペット
Phouphet, Khamphounvong 1108
ブベニチェク
Bubeníček, Jiří 197
プーペル
Poupel, Antoine 1128
フーヘルフォルスト
Hoogervorst, Hans 621
プポ
Pupo, Leuris 1140
プポー
Poupeau, Franck 1128
フボステンコ
Khvostenko, Oksana 729
フボストフ
Khvostov, Mikhail M. 729
プホル
Pujol, Rosendo 1139
プーホルズ
Pujols, Albert 1139
プホルス
Pujols, Albert 1139
フマイディ
al-Humaidi, Ahmed Amer Mohamed 634
al-Humaydi, Badr Mishari 634
al-Humaydi, Badr Naser 634
フマイディー
al-Humaydi, Nasir 634
フマガッリ
Fumagalli, Andrea 468
フマガッリ＝ベオニオ＝ブロッキエーリ
Fumagalli Beonio Brocchieri, Mariateresa 468
フマコイ
Foumakoye, Nana Aicha 452
ブマコフ
Bumacov, Vasile 201
フマディ
Hummadi, Hamed Yousif 635
フマド
Humado, Clement Kofi 634
Hummad, Amat al-Razzaq 635
フマフィ
Phumaphi, Joy 1109
ブマヤ
Bumaya, André 201
プマリエガ
Pumariega, Andres J. 1139
プーミー
Phoumy, Thippavone 1108
フミェレフスカ
Chmielewska, Iwona 257
フミエレフスカ
Chmielewska, Iwona 257
フミッチ
Fumic, Manuel 468
プーミポン
Bhumibol Adulyadej 136
プミポン・アドゥンヤデート
Bhumibol Adulyadej 136
プミポンアドゥンヤデート
Bhumibol Adulyadej 136
プミポン・アドンヤデート
Bhumibol Adulyadej 136
プミポン国王
Bhumibol Adulyadej 136
フーミンネ
Goeminne, Siska 507
フム
Him Chhem 608
ブムチ
Bumçi, Aldo 201
フメイダ
H'meyda, Zeidane Ould 610
フメイダン
Humaidan, Jameel bin Mohammed Ali 634
フーメイド
Houmeid, Boydiel Ould 626
フメド
Houmed, Ismael Ibrahim 626
フメル
Chmel, Rudolf 257
プーモン
Peuhmond, Jeanne 1105
ブヤ
Bouya, Jean-Jacques 169
Buja, Ramë 200
ブーヤクーブ
Bouyacoub, Lyes 169
ブヤチッチ
Vujacic, Sasha 1465
ブヤノヴィッチ
Vujanović, Filip 1465
ブヤノビッチ
Vujanović, Filip 1465
フヤル
Khyar, Walide 729
ブヤルスキー
Buialskyi, Vitaliy 200
プヤンネ
Pouyanné, Patrick 1129
ブヤンヤフ
Buyanjav, Batzorig 210
フュ
Fu, Peter P. 466
フューアー
Feuer, Cy 432
フュアリー
Fury, Dalton 468
フユウメ
Fuyuume, John 469
フユエンテス
Fuentes, Nick 466
ブユカクジャイ
Buyukakcay, Cagla 210
フュガード
Fugard, Athol 466
フューク
Fyk, Jannina 469
フュークス
Fuchs, Bernie 466
フュージ
Fuge, Charles 466
フュージェ
Fouére, Barbara 452
フュジェッタ
Fuggetta, Rob 466
フュースター
Fewster, Mark 432
フュステンベルク
Furstenberg, Egon von 468
フュースト
Fuest, Robert 466
フュマロリ
Fumaroli, Marc 468
フュミーサ
Phumisa, Kaliyoma 1109
フュミーサー
Phumisa, Samuel 1109
フュラー
Fuller, DicQie 467
フューリク
Furyk, Jim 469
フューリック
Furick, Jack 468
Furyk, Jim 469
フュール
Fuhr, Ute 466
フュルスト
Fürst, Walther 468
フュルニス
Fürniss, Tilman 468
ブュールマン
Bühlmann, Philippe 200
フューレイ
Furey, John 468
フュロップ
Fülop, C.V.Ralph 467
フューン
Fuehne, Adam 466
フョードロフ
Fedorov, Boris Grigorievich 425
Fyodorov, Nikolai V. 469
ブーヨビッチ
Vujović, Dušan 1465
ブヨヤ
Buyoya, Pierre 210
フーラー
Fuhrer, Marcus J. 466
Fuller, Bryan 467
フラー
Fuller, Christa 467
Fuller, Corey 467
Fuller, Devin 467
Fuller, Edwin D. 467
Fuller, Elizabeth A. 467
Fuller, H.W.C. 467
Fuller, Keith 467
Fuller, Kendall 467
Fuller, Kyle 467
Fuller, Millard 467
Fuller, Ray 467
Fuller, Steve 467
Fuller, Thomas 467
Fuller, Timothy 467
Fuller, Will 467
ブーラー
Buhler, Urs 200
ブラ
Boula, Rhissa Ag 167
Bras, Michel 177
Bulla, Clyde Robert 200
ブラー
Blah, Moses 145
フライ
Frei, Fabian 460
Frei, Kerim 460
Frei, Norbert 460
Frei, Pierre 460
Frey, Bruno S. 462
Frey, Friedrich 462
Frey, Glenn 462
Frey, Jana 462
Frey, Jörg 462
Frey, Michael 462
Frey, Walter J. 462
Fry, Andrew C. 465
Fry, Ben 465
Fry, Carolyn 465
Fry, Christopher 465
Fry, Colin 465
Fry, Eric 465
Fry, Gareth 465
Fry, Graham 465
Fry, Jason 465
Fry, Paul 465
Fry, Sara T. 465
Frye, Barbara 466
Frye, Channing 466
Frye, Curt 466
Frye, Curtis 466
Frye, Don 466

Frye, Mary Elizabeth 466
Frye, Richard Nelson 466
ブライ
Bley, Anette 148
Bligh, Anna 148
Bly, Karen M. 151
Bly, Robert Elwood 151
Bly, Robert W. 151
Bray, Adam 178
ブライアー
Blair, R.J.R. 145
Brier, Bob 182
Pryor, Terrelle 1138
プライア
Prior, Mary 1136
Prior, Vivien 1136
Priore, Domenic 1136
Pryor, Karen 1138
Pryor, Richard 1138
プライアー
Prior, James Michael Leathes 1136
Prior, Katherine 1136
Prior, Mary 1136
Prior, Natalie Jane 1136
Pryor, Calvin 1138
Pryor, Richard 1138
フライアイゼン
Freyeisen, Astrid 462
フライアーズ
Fryers, Zeki 466
ブライアーズ
Briers, Richard 182
フライアリ
Friary, Ned 462
ブライアリー
Brierley, Saroo 182
ブライアン
Brian 181
Brian, Janeen 181
Brian, Kate 181
Brian, Mary 181
Brian, William L. 181
Bryan, Ashley 195
Bryan, Bob 195
Bryan, Courtlandt Dixon Barnes 195
Bryan, David 195
Bryan, Denver 195
Bryan, Dora 195
Bryan, Elizabeth M. 195
Bryan, Emily 195
Bryan, Jenny 195
Bryan, Kim 195
Bryan, Lowell L. 195
Bryan, Luke 195
Bryan, Mike 195
Bryan, Wayne 195
Bryant, Nick 196
Bryant, Russ 196
ブライアント
Bryant, Ann 195
Bryant, Armonty 195
Bryant, Brandin 195
Bryant, Christian 196
Bryant, Corbin 196
Bryant, C.R. 196
Bryant, Dez 196
Bryant, Donna M. 196
Bryant, Felice 196
Bryant, Geoff 196
Bryant, Gyude 196
Bryant, Joe 196
Bryant, John E. 196
Bryant, Johnnie 196
Bryant, Karina 196
Bryant, Kelci 196
Bryant, Kobe 196
Bryant, Kris 196
Bryant, Laura J. 196
Bryant, Mark 196
Bryant, Martavis 196
Bryant, Matt 196
Bryant, Ray 196
Bryant, Red 196
Bryant, Rick 196
Bryant, Tamera 196
Bryant, Thomas 196
ブライアント＝モール
Bryant-Mole, Karen 196
ブライアン＝ブラウン
Bryan-Brown, Adrian 195
プライク
Pryke, Richard 1138
フライ・ゲアラッハ
Frei Gerlach, Franziska 461
ブライジ
Blige, Mary Jane 148
フライシャー
Fleischer, Richard.O 442
Fleischer, Sebastian 442
Fleisher, Leon 442
フライシュ
Fleisch, Daniel A. 442
ブライシュ
Bleich, Erik 148
フライシュハウアー
Fleischhauer, Wolfram 442
フライシュマン
Fleischman, Paul 442
Fleischman, Sid 442
Fleischman, Tom 442
Fleischmann, Martin 442
Fleischmann, Wim 442
フライス
Fleiss, Joseph L. 442
ブライス
Blais, Etienne 145
Blyth, Mark 151
Blythe, Austin 151
Brice, Austin 181
Brice, Kentrell 181
Bryce, D.L. 196
Bryce, Quentin 196
Bryce, Robert 196
Bryce, Sheradon 196
Bryce, Trevor 196
ブライズ
Blythe, Gary 151
プライス
Preis, Michael W. 1132
Price, Alan 1134
Price, Alfred 1134
Price, Bill 1134
Price, Bob 1134
Price, Brian 1134
Price, Bryan 1134
Price, Charlie 1134
Price, Chase 1134
Price, Colin 1134
Price, Daniel 1134
Price, David 1134
Price, Deanna 1134
Price, Deborah L. 1134
Price, Elizabeth 1134
Price, George Cadle 1134
Price, Givens 1134
Price, Glanville 1134
Price, Huw 1134
Price, Jabari 1134
Price, Jill 1134
Price, Joan 1134
Price, Joe D. 1134
Price, John Randolph 1134
Price, John Scott 1134
Price, Len 1134
Price, Lissa 1134
Price, Lonny 1134
Price, Maggie 1134
Price, Margaret 1134
Price, Mary V. 1134
Price, Mathew 1134
Price, Matthew Arlen 1134
Price, Nick 1134
Price, Norman 1134
Price, Penny 1134
Price, Ray 1134
Price, Raymond Lewis 1134
Price, Reynolds 1134
Price, Richard 1134
Price, Robert M. 1134
Price, Roger 1134
Price, Ronnie 1134
Price, Sheldon 1134
Price, Shirley 1134
Price, Steven 1134
Price, Susan 1134
Price, Tom 1135
Pryce, Evelyn 1138
Pryce, Nat 1138
Pryce, Vicky 1138
Pryce, Will 1138
ブライス・エチェニケ
Bryce Echenique, Alfredo 196
フライスナー
Friesner, Esther M. 464
プライス・ホッセル
Price Hossell, Karen 1135
プライスマン
Priceman, Marjorie 1135
ブライソン
Brayson, Oscar 178
Brison, Scott 183
Brison, Stuart 183
Bryson, Bill 196
Bryson, Norman 196
Bryson, Peabo 196
Bryson, Tina Payne 196
Bryson, Valerie 196
フライターグ
Freitag, Eberhard 461
フライタク
Freitag, Uschi 461
プライット
Pruitt, Jimmy 1138
Pruitt, MyCole 1138
ブライデイヴスキー
Bridavsky, Mike 181
ブライディッチ
Bridich, Jeff 182
ブライディング
Breiding, R.James 179
ブライデン
Blyden, Sylvia 151
Bryden, Christine 196
フライデンバーグ
Frydenberg, Josh 465
フライト
Hurajt, Pavol 637
ブライト
Blight, James G. 149
Bright, Charles 182
Bright, Dennis 182
Bright, J.E. 182
Bright, Laurey 182
Bright, Mark 182
Bright, Michael 182
Bright, Paul 182
Bright, Richard 182
Bright, Ruth 182
Bright, Susie 182
Bright, Torah 182
Brite, Poppy Z. 183
ブライトウェル
Brightwell, Emily 182
ブライドット
Braidot, Luca 175
ブライトナー
Breitner, Leslie Pearlman 179
Breitner, Paul 179
Pearlman, Leslie K. 1090
ブライトハウプト
Breithaupt, Don 179
ブライトバルト
Breitbarth, Andre 179
ブライトマン
Brightman, Alan J. 182
Brightman, Sarah 182
ブライトリング
Brightling, Geoff 182
フライドルフス
Fridolfs, Derek 462
ブライトン
Breitung, Joan Carson 179
Brighton, Catherine 182
ブライナー
Briner, Rob B. 183
ブライナースドルファー
Breinersdorfer, Fred 179
フライバーグ
Freiberg, H.Jerome 460
Freiberg, Jackie 460
Freiberg, Kevin 460
ブライハーゲン
Breiehagen, Per 179
フライハティ
Flaherty, Ryan 441
フライフィ
al-Khulaifi, Abdullah Saleh Mubarak 729
ブライブトロイ
Bleibtreu, Moritz 148
フライヘア・フォン・ヴェアテルン
Freiherr Von Werthern, Hans Carl 461
ブライヘル
Bliecher, Bella 148
フライ・ボルヒャース
Frei-Borchers, Martin 460
ブライマー
Brimah, Amida 182
Brymer, Chuck 196
フライマーク
Frymark, Sue Lynne 466
ブライマディアバクテ
Bouraïmadiabacte, Hamadou Brim 168
フライマン
Freymann, Saxton 462
Fryman, Woody 466
ブライマン
Bryman, Alan 196
フライマン・ウェア
Freymann-Weyr,

Garret 462
フライム
Frahim, Erum 454
プライム
Prime, George 1135
フライムート
Freimuth, Rico 461
フライヤー
Freyer, Greg A. 462
Fryer, Bronwyn 466
Fryer, Eric 466
Fryer, Peter 466
ブライヤー
Breyer, Jim 181
Breyer, Stephen G. 181
Bryer, Estelle 196
プライヤー
Pryor, Alton 1138
Pryor, Mark 1138
Pryor, Richard 1138
ブライラー
Bleiler, Gretchen 148
ブライリィ
Breidlid, Anders 179
フライリッチ
Freirich, Roy 461
ブライル
Bleyl, Steven B. 148
ブライルズ
Briles, Nellie 182
ブライン
Blain, Malika 145
プライン
Prine, John 1135
ブラインダー
Blinder, Alan Stuart 149
ブラウ
Blau, Andreas 148
Blau, Melinda 148
Blau, Peter Michael 148
Braw, Monica 178
ブラウァー
Brauer, Jerald C. 177
ブラウアー
Brauer, Michael H. 177
Brauer, Philip R. 177
Braugher, Andre 177
Brower, Howard 188
フラウィ
Hrawi, Elias 629
ブーラウイ
Bouraoui, Abdelhakim 168
ブラヴィ
Bravi, Soledad 178
プラヴィ
Prawy, Marcel 1132
プラウィット
Prawit, Wongsuwan 1132
プラウェッキ
Plawecki, Kevin 1117
ブラウエン
Brauen, Martin 177
フラウエンフェルダー
Frauenfelder, Mark 458
ブラヴォ
Bravo, Émile 178
Bravo, Manuel Alvarez 178
ブラヴォー
Bravo, Rose Marie 178
プラウガー
Plauger, P.J. 1117
ブラウグ
Blaug, Mark 148
プラウゴ
Plawgo, Marek 1117
ブラウコップフ
Blaukopf, Herta 148
ブラウシリ
Brauchli, Yannick 177
ブラウス
Brauss, Helmut 177
プラウス
Plous, Scott 1118
Prauss, Gerold 1132
プラウズ
Prouse, Lynda 1137
ブラウダー
Browder, Bill 188
プラウチャン
Plavčan, Peter 1117
プラゥティ
Prouty, Garry 1137
プラウティ
Prouty, IlaSahai 1137
Prouty, Leroy Fletcher 1137
フラウド
Floud, Jean Esther 444
Froud, Brian 465
Froud, Wendy 465
プラウト
Praught, Aisha 1132
プラウド
Proud, Ben 1137
Proud, Linda 1137
ブラウナー
Browner, Brandon 192
Browner, Keith 192
Browner, Warren S. 192
ブラウニー
Browne, Benson 192
ブラウニング
Breuning, Walter 181
Browning, Amanda 192
Browning, David M. 192
Browning, Dixie 192
Browning, Geil 192
Browning, Guy 192
Browning, John 192
Browning, Mary Grace 192
Browning, Michael 192
Browning, Pamela 192
Browning, Tyias 192
Browning, Tyson R. 192
ブラウネル
Brownell, Patricia J. 192
ブラウバー
Brouwer, Alexander 188
フラウヒガー
Frauchiger, Urs 458
フラウマーネ＝ヤッヘンス
Flaumane-Jachens, Anda 441
プラウメン
Ploumen, Lilianne 1118
ブラウリー
Brawley, John 178
フラウリー＝ホラー
Frawley-Holler, Janis 458
ブラウワー
Brawer, James R. 178
Brower, Kate Andersen 188
Brower, Kenneth 188
ブラウワーズ
Brouwers, Jeroen 188
ブラウン
Braun, Adam 177
Braun, Betsy Brown 177
Braun, Carie A. 177
Braun, Eldon M. 177
Braun, Jackie 177
Braun, Lilian J. 177
Braun, Markus Sebastian 177
Braun, Martin 177
Braun, Ryan 177
Braun, Sebastien 177
Braun, Stephen 177
Braun, Volker 177
Brown, Aaron 188
Brown, Adrian 188
Brown, Adrienne 188
Brown, Adrienne Maree 188
Brown, Alan 188
Brown, Albert 188
Brown, Alexandra 188
Brown, Alison 188
Brown, Alyson 188
Brown, Amanda 188
Brown, Andrew 188
Brown, Ann L. 188
Brown, Anthony 188
Brown, Antonio 188
Brown, Archie 188
Brown, Arthur 188
Brown, Ashley 188
Brown, Augustus 188
Brown, Beniquez 188
Brown, Bill 188
Brown, Blain 188
Brown, Bobbi 188
Brown, Bobby 188
Brown, Brendan 188
Brown, Brené 188
Brown, Brett 188
Brown, Brooks 188
Brown, Carrie 188
Brown, Carter 188
Brown, Catana 188
Brown, Charles C. 188
Brown, Charles L. 188
Brown, Chester M. 188
Brown, Chris 188
Brown, Christina 188
Brown, Chuck 188
Brown, Chykie 188
Brown, Claire Waite 188
Brown, Clarence 188
Brown, Clive 188
Brown, Corey 188
Brown, Cynthia Stokes 188
Brown, Dale 188
Brown, Dale S. 189
Brown, Dale W. 189
Brown, Dan 189
Brown, Daniel 189
Brown, Da'Ron 189
Brown, David 189
Brown, David Blayney 189
Brown, David F.M. 189
Brown, Debra Lee 189
Brown, Dee 189
Brown, Delmer Myers 189
Brown, Denise Wichello 189
Brown, Derren 189
Brown, DeSoto 189
Brown, Don 189
Brown, Donald 189
Brown, Donald Edward 189
Brown, Doug 189
Brown, Douglas 189
Brown, Douglas J. 189
Brown, Duane 189
Brown, Dustin 189
Brown, Dwayne 189
Brown, Ellen F. 189
Brown, E.R. 189
Brown, Eric R. 189
Brown, Errol 189
Brown, Fraser 189
Brown, Georgina 189
Brown, Gordon 189
Brown, Graeme 189
Brown, Graham 189
Brown, Helen 189
Brown, Helen Gurley 189
Brown, Herbert Charles 189
Brown, Hilary 189
Brown, H.Jackson, Jr. 189
Brown, Iona 189
Brown, Jabari 189
Brown, Jack 189
Brown, Jake 189
Brown, Jalil 189
Brown, James 189
Brown, James Robert 189
Brown, James Ward 189
Brown, Jamon 189
Brown, Janet L. 189
Brown, Jaron 189
Brown, Jason Ira 189
Brown, Jason Robert 189
Brown, Jatavis 189
Brown, Jaylen 189
Brown, Jeff 189
Brown, Jeff M. 189
Brown, Jeffrey 189
Brown, Jerry 189
Brown, Jesse 189
Brown, Jim 189
Brown, John 189
Brown, John Michael 189
Brown, John Seely 189
Brown, Jon 189, 190
Brown, Josh 190
Brown, Juanita 190
Brown, Judith Belle 190
Brown, Julie 190
Brown, Kate 190
Brown, Kathryn 190
Brown, Katie 190
Brown, Keith 190
Brown, Kelly Williams 190
Brown, Kenneth Francis 190
Brown, Kim 190
Brown, Kourtnei 190
Brown, Kyle 190
Brown, Larry 190
Brown, Lascelles 190
Brown, Laurene Krasny 190
Brown, Laurie M. 190
Brown, L.David 190
Brown, Lee E. 190
Brown, Les 190
Brown, Lesley 190
Brown, Lester Russell 190
Brown, Lewis 190
Brown, Lindsay 190
Brown, Lorenzo 190
Brown, Lynda 190
Brown, Lynette 190
Brown, Lynne 190
Brown, Mack 190
Brown, Mackenzie 190

Brown, Malcolm 190
Brown, Malcom 190
Brown, Marc 190
Brown, Marcia 190
Brown, Marc Tolon 190
Brown, Margot 190
Brown, Mark 190
Brown, Markel 190
Brown, Mark Graham 190
Brown, Marlene 190
Brown, Martin C. 190
Brown, Marty 190
Brown, Mason 190
Brown, Melissa K. 190
Brown, Michael 190
Brown, Michael Barratt 190
Brown, Michael E. 190
Brown, Michael Stuart 190
Brown, Mike 190
Brown, Milly 190
Brown, Monica 190
Brown, Morris Jonathan 190
Brown, Myra Berry 190
Brown, Nancy Marie 190
Brown, Naomi 190
Brown, Nick 190
Brown, Nicolas 190
Brown, Norman O. 190
Brown, Ogden, Jr. 190
Brown, Oscar, Jr. 190
Brown, Pat 191
Brown, Paul 191
Brown, Paul B. 191
Brown, Penelope 191
Brown, Peter 191
Brown, Peter C. 191
Brown, Peter Robert Lamont 191
Brown, Petra 191
Brown, Phil 191
Brown, Phillip 191
Brown, Pierce 191
Brown, Preston 191
Brown, Ralph 191
Brown, Randy 191
Brown, Ray 191
Brown, Rebecca 191
Brown, Reilly 191
Brown, Richard 191
Brown, Rita Mae 191
Brown, Robert Hanbury 191
Brown, Ronald T. 191
Brown, Rosemary 191
Brown, Rosie 191
Brown, Roy I. 191
Brown, Russell 191
Brown, Ruth 191
Brown, Ryan 191
Brown, Sam 191
Brown, Sandra 191
Brown, Sandra L. 191
Brown, S.Azby 191
Brown, Scott 191
Brown, Sergio 191
Brown, Shona L. 191
Brown, Simon 191
Brown, Sinai 191
Brown, Sneaky Pie 191
Brown, Stacy 191
Brown, Stanley A. 191
Brown, Stanley H. 191
Brown, Stephen 191
Brown, Stephen F. 191
Brown, Stephen J. 191
Brown, Steven 191
Brown, Stevie 191
Brown, Stuart L. 191
Brown, Sunni 191
Brown, Sylvia G. 191
Brown, Terea 191
Brown, Terence A. 191
Brown, Theodore Lawrence 191
Brown, Thomas E. 191
Brown, Thomas L. 191
Brown, Tim 191
Brown, Timothy A. 191
Brown, Tina 191
Brown, Tom 191
Brown, Tom, Jr. 191
Brown, Tony 191
Brown, Tracy 192
Brown, Trent 192
Brown, Trevor 192
Brown, Trisha 192
Brown, Tudor 192
Brown, Valerie B. 192
Brown, Vitto 192
Brown, Warren S. 192
Brown, Wendy 192
Brown, Will 192
Brown, William Henry 192
Brown, William J. 192
Brown, William P. 192
Brown, William S. 192
Brown, W.Steven 192
Brown, Zach 192
Browne, Amery 192
Browne, Anthony 192
Browne, Christopher H. 192
Browne, Des 192
Browne, Eileen 192
Browne, E.Janet 192
Browne, Gaston 192
Browne, Hester 192
Browne, Ian 192
Browne, Jackson 192
Browne, Jill Conner 192
Browne, John 192
Browne, Kevin 192
Browne, Kevin D. 192
Browne, Kingsley 192
Browne, Luke 192
Browne, Malcolm Wilde 192
Browne, Marcus 192
Browne, Michael 192
Browne, M.Neil 192
Browne, Robert 192
Browne, Roscoe Lee 192
Browne, Scott G. 192
Browne, S.G. 192
Browne, Sylvia 192
Browne, Thom 192
Browne, Thomas R. 192

ブラウンガート
Braungart, Michael 177

ブラウンシュヴァイク
Braunschweig, Ruth von 177

ブラウンシュヴァイグ
Braunschweig, Philippe 177

ブラウンシュタイン
Braunstein, Guy 177

ブラウンシュバイグ
Braunschweig, Philippe 177

ブラウンス
Brouns, Berund 188

ブラウンズ
Brauns, Axel 177

ブラウンスタイン
Brownstein, David 193

ブラウン・デュークス
Brown-dukes, Brandon 192

ブラウント
Blount, Roy, Jr. 150

ブラウン・トラフトン
Brown-Trafton, Stephanie 193

ブラウンベック
Braunbeck, Gary A. 177

ブラウンリー
Brownlee, Alistair 192
Brownlee, Gerry 192
Brownlee, Jonathan 192
Brownlee, Shannon 192

ブラウンル
Bräunl, Thomas 177

ブラウンレス
Brownless, Peter 192

ブラウンロー
Brownlow, Kevin 193

ブラウンワルド
Braunwald, Eugene 177

フラオー
Flahault, Jean-Francois 441
Flahaut, Andre 441

ブラオビック・ブラタノビック
Brajovic Bratanovic, Sonja 175

フラガ
Fraga, Manuel 454
Fraga Adrio Gonzalez Maquieira Valcarce de Lis, Cesar Adolfo 454

ブラガ
Blaga, Vasile 145
Braga, Eduarudo 174
Braga, Teo 174
Bulaga, Bryan 200

プラガー
Plager, Karen A. 1117

プラカーシュ
Prakash, G.K.Surya 1131

プラカシュ
Prakash, Madhu Suri 1131

フラガパネ
Fragapane, Claudia 454

ブラガンサ
Braganca, Rui 174

ブラガンザ
Braganza, Hernani 174

ブラギシュ
Braghis, Dumitru 175

ブラキシル
Blaxill, Mark 148

プラキン
Praquin, Marc 1131

ブラーク
Burak, Jacob 202

ブラク
Bulag, Uradyn Erden 200

プラーグ
Praag, Menna van 1130

プラク
Prak Sokhonn 1131

プラグ
Plug, Cornelis 1118

ブラク・エッグ
Brack Egg, Antonio 173

フラクション
Fraction, Matt 454

フラークス
Flerx, Vicki Crocker 442

ブラクス
Brax, Tuija 178

ブラクストン
Braxton, Toni 178

フラクスマン
Flaxman, Larry 441

ブラグドン
Bragdon, Allen D. 174

プラクネット
Plucknett, Benn 1118

ブラグマン
Brugman, Jaycob 193

ブラケ
Blake, Ian F. 146

ブラケット
Blackett, Steven 144

フラゴー
Flagor, Robin 441

プラコサ
Prakosa, M. 1131

フラゴソ
Fragoso, Margaux 454

ブラゴダーロワ
Blagodarova, Faina 145

ブラコニエ
Braconnier, Céline 173

ブラゴボリン
Blagovolin, Sergei Evgenievich 145

プラサ
Plaza, José María 1117

プラザー
Prather, Richard S. 1132
Prather, Richard Scott 1132

ブラザウスカス
Brazauskas, Algirdas Mykolas 178

ブラザーズ
Brothers, Kentrell 187

プラサーダム・ホールズ
Prasadam-Halls, Smriti 1131

プラサダム・ホールズ
Prasadam-Halls, Smriti 1131

プラサッド
Prasad, V.S.Skanda 1131

ブラサード
Brassard, Marla R. 177

プラサド
Prasad, Arnold 1131
Prasad, Lalu 1131
Prasad, Mahavir 1131
Prasad, Ravi Shankar 1131

ブラザートン
Brotherton, Mike 187

ブラサナツ
Brasanac, Darko 177

プラサヤボン
Phraxayavong, Viliam 1109

ブラシウ
Vraciu, Alexander 1465

ブラジェク
Blažek, Pavel 148

ブラシッチ

フ

Vlasic, Blanka 1461
フラシーノ
Frascino, Edward 457
プラシノス
Prassinos, Gisèle 1131
プラシャスタパーダ
Prasastapādācārya 1131
プラシャド
Prashad, Manniram 1131
Prashad, Vijay 1131
ブラシュー
Vraciu, Alexander 1465
ブラシュカ
Blaszka, Jessica 148
ブラジョーン
Blazon, Nina 148
ブラジル
Brazile, Donna 178
プーラシロカ
Pula-shiroka, Justina 1139
プラジン
Prajin, Jantong 1131
フラス
Fluss, Donna 445
ブラース
Braas, Roel 173
ブラス
Blass, Bill 147
Blass, Thomas 147
Bras, Michel 177
Brass, Peter 177
Brass, Tinto 177
Bruss, Deborah 195
ブラズ
Braz, Félix 178
プラース
Place, Adélaïde de 1117
プラス
Place, François 1117
ブラズウィック
Blazwick, Iwona 148
ブラスウェイト
Blathwayt, Benedict 148
Brathwaite, Adriel 177
Brathwaite, Ryan 177
フラスカ
Frasca, Erminio 457
Frasca, Gabriele 457
ブラスカ
Brusca, Robert 195
プラスカー
Plasker, Eric 1117
ブラスコ
Blasko, John C. 147
ブラスコ・ガビラン
Blasco Gavilan, Humberto 147
フラスティッチ
Hrastic, Drazen 629
プラステルク
Plasterk, Ronald 1117
ブラスト
Brust, Andrew J. 195
プラスート
Prasert, Boonchaisuk 1131
フラストニク
Hrastnik, Rok 629
フラストラ・ファン・ローン
Glastra van Loon, Karel 504
ブラストランド
Blastland, Michael 147
プラストリック
Plastrik, Peter 1117
プラスニク
Plassnik, Ursula 1117
フラスネリ
Frasnelli, Loris 458
ブラスバーグ
Blasberg, Erica 147
フラスベック
Flassbeck, Heiner 441
プラスマン
Plassmann, Engelbert 1117
ブラスム
Brasme, Anne-Sophie 177
ブラスール
Brasseur, Anne 177
ブラゼー
Brasey, Édouard 177
ブラゼルトン
Brazelton, T.Berry 178
フラーセン
Fraassen, Bas C.van 454
プラセンシア
Plascencia, Salvador 1117
プラセンジット・ドゥアラ
Prasenjit Duara 1131
ブラソフ
Vlasov, Roman 1461
フラソプロス
Vlassopoulos, Kōstas 1461
プラソロフ
Prasolov, Ihor 1131
フラーター
Frater, Michael 458
ブーラダ
Bourrada, Larbi 168
ブラーター
Brater, Jürgen 177
ブラダー
Vladar, Stefan 1460
プラタ
Prata, Guilhermina Contreiras Da Costa 1131
プラター
Prater, Kyle 1132
Prater, Matt 1132
Prater, Shaun 1132
プラダ
Prada, Joaquin 1131
Prada, Miuccia 1131
プラタス
Platas, Fernando 1117
ブラダック
Bradach, Jeffrey L. 173
プラタニオティ
Platanioti, Evangelia 1117
プラタ・パエス
Plata Páez, Luis Guillermo 1117
ブラタン
Bratan, Alexandru 177
Bratun, Katy 177
プラダン
Pradhan, Dharmendra 1131
Pradhan, Mahesh Lal 1131
Pradhan, Sahana Devi 1131
プラチェット
Prachett, Terry 1131
Pratchett, Terry 1131
フラチェフ
Khrachev, Murat 729
ブラチガルシア
Brachi Garcia, Josue 173
プラチコフ
Plachkov, Ivan 1117
ブラチチュ
Vlačič, Patrick 1460
プラチャー
Pracha, Promnok 1131
プラチャイ
Purachai, Piumsombun 1140
プラチャイ・リアオパイラット
Prachai Leophairatana 1131
プラチャイ・レオパイラタナ
Prachai Leophairatana 1131
ブラーチョ
Bracho, Silvino 173
プラツェク
Platzeck, Matthias 1117
ブラッカー
Blackah, Paul 144
Blacker, Carmen Elizabeth 144
Brucker, Gene A. 193
ブラッカイマー
Bruckheimer, Jerry 193
Bruckheimer, Linda 193
ブラッカード
Blackard, Sandra R. 144
ブラッカビー
Blackaby, Henry T. 144
フラッカーロ
Fraccaro, Walter 454
ブラック
Blach, Ty 143
Black, Alistair 143
Black, Anastasia 143
Black, Becky 143
Black, Benjamin 143
Black, Birdie 143
Black, Bob 143
Black, Bud 143
Black, Campbell 143
Black, Cara 143
Black, Cathie 143
Black, Christopher F. 143
Black, Claudia A. 143
Black, C.S. 143
Black, Dave 143
Black, David William 143
Black, Donald W. 143
Black, Dustin Lance 144
Black, Edwin 144
Black, Elsabeth 144
Black, Ervin L. 144
Black, Ethan 144
Black, George 144
Black, Holly 144
Black, Ira B. 144
Black, Jack 144
Black, Jacquelyn G. 144
Black, James Whyte 144
Black, Jeremy 144
Black, Joe 144
Black, Jonah 144
Black, Jonathan 144
Black, J.Stewart 144
Black, J.W. 144
Black, Karen 144
Black, Kathy 144
Black, Leon 144
Black, Lewis 144
Black, Lisa 144
Black, Maggie 144
Black, Mary 144
Black, Michael Ian 144
Black, Noel 144
Black, Paula 144
Black, Ray 144
Black, Rex 144
Black, Sandy 144
Black, Shayla 144
Black, Shirley Temple 144
Black, Silla 144
Black, Stanley 144
Black, Tabitha 144
Black, Tarik 144
Black, Uyless D. 144
Black, Wayne 144
Black, William 144
Brac, Guillaume 173
Brac, Virginie 173
Brach, Brad 173
ブラッグ
Blagg, Alicia 145
Bragg, Georgia 174
Bragg, Melvyn 174
Bragg, Rick 174
Bragg, Roberta 175
ブラックウィル
Blackwill, Robert D. 145
ブラックウェル
Blackwell 145
Blackwell, David 145
Blackwell, Otis 145
Blackwell, Roger D. 145
ブラックウッド
Blackwood, Alan 145
Blackwood, Brad 145
Blackwood, Dean 145
Blackwood, Freya 145
Blackwood, Gary L. 145
Blackwood, Grant 145
Blackwood, James 145
Blackwood, Michael 145
ブラックオール
Blackall, Sophie 144
ブラック・キャット
Black Cat 144
ブラックショー
Blackshaw, Anne 145
ブラックス
Brax, Tuija 178
ブラックストーン
Blackstone, Jerry 145
Blackstone, Stella 145
フラックスマン
Flaxman, Paul Edward 441
ブラックソン
Blackson, Angelo 145
ブラックハイマー
Bruckheimer, Jerry 193
ブラックハースト
Blackhurst, Jennifer 144
ブラックバーン
Blackbum, Paul 144
Blackburn, Clayton 144
Blackburn, Elizabeth Helen 144
Blackburn, jean-Pierre 144
Blackburn, Julia 144
Blackburn, Robin 144
Blackburn, Ronald 144

Blackburn, Simon 144
Blackburn, Thomas Henry 144
Blackburn, Vivienne 144
ブラックマン
Blackman, Cally 144
Blackman, Malorie 144
Brackman, Levi 173
ブラックムーア
Blackmoore, Rayburn 145
ブラックモア
Blackmoore, Rayburn 145
Blackmore, Ritchie 145
Blackmore, Stephen 145
Blackmore, Susan 145
ブラックモン
Blackmon, Charlie 144
Blackmon, Douglas A. 144
Blackmon, Justin 144
Blackmon, Kate 144
Blackmon, Will 145
ブラックリッジ
Blackledge, Catherine 144
フラッケ
Flacke, Uschi 440
ブラツケ
Bratzke, Mike 177
フラッケイ
Fluckey, Eugene 444
ブラッケージ
Brakhage, Stan 175
ブラッケビィ
Blackeby, Kathy 144
ブラッケン
Bracken, Beth 173
Bracken, Bruce A. 173
Bracken, Sam 173
フラッコ
Flacco, Joe 440
プラッコ
Plutko, Adam 1119
ブラッコリ
Bruccoli, Matthew Joseph 193
ブラッコール
Blackall, Sophie 144
ブラッシー
Blassie, Fred 147
ブラッシェアーズ
Brashares, Ann 177
フラッシュ
Flasch, Kurt 441
ブラッシュ
Blash, Jabari 147
Blush, Steven 151
Brasch, Thomas 177
Brash, Alan A. 177
Brash, Scott 177
Brush, Stephen G. 195
ブラッシュワイラー - スターン
Bruschweiler-Stern, Nadia 195
プラッソン
Plasson, Michel 1117
ブラッター
Blatter, Sepp 148
プラッター
Platter, Günther 1117
ブラッチアリ
Bracciali, Daniele 173
ブラッチフォード
Blatchford, Christie 148
プラッチャヤー
Prachya Pinkaew 1131
フラッツ
Flatts, Rascal 441
プラッツ
Platz, Thomas 1117
プラッツァー
Platzer, Werner 1117
プラッテ
Platte, Felix 1117
ブラッティ
Blatty, William Peter 148
フラッティーニ
Frattini, Franco 458
Frattini, Stéphane 458
プラッテンハルト
Plattenhardt, Marvin 1117
フラット
Flatt, Rachael 441
フラッド
Flood, David 443
Flood, Elizabeth Clair 443
Flood, Kellie 443
Flood, Naomi 443
Flood-beaubrun, Sarah 443
ブラッド
Blood, Rebecca 150
プラット
Plat, Nico 1117
Platt, Charles 1117
Platt, Cynthia 1117
Platt, Lewis E. 1117
Platt, Polly 1117
Platt, Richard 1117
Pratt, Andrew J. 1132
Pratt, Anna L. 1132
Pratt, Cynthia 1132
Pratt, Denise 1132
Pratt, Gill A. 1132
Pratt, Kathryn Ann 1132
Pratt, Ken 1132
Pratt, Larry 1132
Pratt, Oswald T. 1132
Pratt, Scott 1132
Pratt, Tim 1132
ブラッドウェイ
Bradway, Pat A. 174
プラットガイ
Prat Gay, Alfonso 1132
ブラッドシャー
Bradsher, Keith 174
ブラッドショー
Bleasdale, Holly 148
Bradshaw, Claudette 174
Bradshaw, John 174
Bradshaw, Martha J. 174
Bradshaw, Paul F. 174
ブラッドショウ
Bradshaw, Clair 174
Bradshaw, John 174
ブラッドスキー
Bradski, Gary 174
ブラットナー
Blatner, David 148
プラットナー
Plattner, Hasso 1117
Plattner, Marc F. 1117
ブラットバーグ
Blattberg, Robert C. 148
ブラッドハム
Bradham, Nigel 173
ブラッドバリー
Bradbury, Andrew 173
Bradbury, Steven 173
ブラッドビー
Bradby, Marie 173
ブラッドフィールド
Bradfield, Cameron 173
Bradfield, James Dean 173
Bradfield, Nancy Margetts 173
Bradfield, Ron 173
ブラッドフィールド・ムーディ
Bradfield Moody, James 173
ブラッドフォード
Bradford, Arthur 173
Bradford, Barbara Taylor 173
Bradford, Carl 173
Bradford, David Frantz 173
Bradford, David L. 173
Bradford, Isabella 173
Bradford, Nikki 173
Bradford, Rosalie 173
Bradford, Sam 173
ブラッドフォルド
Bratvold, Gretchen 177
ブラッドベリ
Bradberry, Travis 173
Bradbury, Glenys 173
Bradbury, Jennifer 173
Bradbury, Malcolm 173
Bradbury, Ray Douglas 173
ブラッドベリー
Bradberry, James 173
Bradberry, Travis 173
Bradbury, Dominic 173
Bradbury, Jim 173
Bradbury, John 173
Bradbury, Ray Douglas 173
フラッドボーブラン
Flood-beaubrun, Sarah 443
ブラットマン
Bratman, Michael 177
ブラッドマン
Bradman, Donald George 174
フラットラン
Flatland, Ann Kristin Aafedt 441
ブラッドリー
Bradlee, Benjamin 173
Bradley, Alan 173
Bradley, Alex 173
Bradley, Archie 173
Bradley, Avery 173
Bradley, Bill 174
Bradley, Celeste 174
Bradley, C.Randall 174
Bradley, Ed 174
Bradley, Eden 174
Bradley, Greta 174
Bradley, Gus 174
Bradley, Ian C. 174
Bradley, Ian G. 174
Bradley, Jackie, Jr. 174
Bradley, James 174
Bradley, Jonathan 174
Bradley, Karen 174
Bradley, Keegan 174
Bradley, Kimberly Brubaker 174
Bradley, Lloyd 174
Bradley, Michael 174
Bradley, Michael J. 174
Bradley, Michael John 174
Bradley, Neil 174
Bradley, Shelley 174
Bradley, Simon 174
Bradley, Tamdin Sither 174
Bradley, William G., Jr. 174
フラットレー
Flatley, Jay 441
ブラッドレー
Bradley, Arthur T. 173
Bradley, Beverly J. 173
Bradley, Bill 174
Bradley, Raymond S. 174
Bradley, Susan J. 174
Bradley, William Warren 174
ブラッドワース
Bloodworth, Venice J. 150
ブラットン
Bratton, John 177
Bratton, Sue C. 177
ブラットン＝ジェフリー
Bratton-Jeffery, Mary F. (Frankie) 177
ブラッハー
Blacher, Kolja 143
Bracher, Karl Dietrich 173
プラップ
Prap, Lila 1131
ブラッフォード
Bruford, Bill 193
プラデ
Prades, Valentin 1131
フラーティ
Flaherty, James 441
フラディ
Hlady, Mykhaylo 610
ブラディ
Brady, Christopher 174
Brady, Ed 174
Brady, Joseph A. 174
Brady, William 174
プラティクノ
Pratikno 1132
ブラディッチ
Bradić, Nebojša 173
プラディット
Pradit, Sintavanarong 1131
フラティニ
Frattini, Franco 458
プラティーニ
Platini, Michel 1117
プラティニ
Platini, Michel 1117
ブラディノバ
Vladinova, Neviana 1460
プラディープ
Pradeep, A.K. 1131
プラティープ・ウンソンタム
Prateep Ungsongtham 1132
フラディレク
Hradilek, Vavřinec 629
フラーデク
Chládek, Marcel 257
ブラデス
Blades, Rubén 145

フ

フラデツキー
Hradecky, Lukas 629
プラテル
Platel, Richard 1117
プラデル
Pradel, Jacques 1131
プラデーレ
Pradères, Jean-Pierre 1131
ブラーテン
Braaten, Carl E. 173
フラード
Jurado, Rocio 692
フラトー
Flatow, Ido 441
フラド
Jurado, Jose Manuel 692
Jurado, Katy 692
ブラード
Bullard, Roger Aubrey 200
Bullard, Steven 201
ブラドー
Brodow, Ed 185
プラート
Praet, Dennis 1131
Praet, Peter 1131
プラード
Prado Edgar 1131
Pullard, Hayes 1139
プラド
Prado, Joe 1131
Prado, Martin 1131
ブラトゥ
Bratu, Tudorel 177
ブラトヴィッチ
Bulatović, Momir 200
ブラトゥシェク
Bratušek, Alenka 177
フラトゥス
Fratus, Bruno 458
フラ・トゥン
Hla Tun 610
プラトキン
Platkin, Charles Stuart 1117
フラトコーフ
Fradkov, Mikhail Yefimovich 454
フラトコフ
Fradkov, Mikhail Yefimovich 454
Ye.fradkov, Mikhail 1537
プラドス
Prados, Emilio 1131
ブラドナー
Bradner, Leicester 174
ブラトビッチ
Bulatović, Momir 200
ブラドベリ
Bradbury, Malcolm 173
ブラドリー
Bradley, Bill 174
Bradley, Dickie 174
Bradley, Ed 174
Bradley, Keegan 174
Bradley, Richard 174
ブラドレー
Bradley, Pamela 174
フラドロペス
Jurado Lopez, Severo Jesus 692
フラートン
Fullerton, Carol S. 467
Fullerton, Judith 467
Fullerton, R.Donald 467
ブラナー
Branagh, Kenneth 175
Brunner, David 194
ブラナウカ
Bulanauca, Mitieli 200
フラナガン
Flanagan, Bill 441
Flanagan, Cara 441
Flanagan, Catherine 441
Flanagan, Charles 441
Flanagan, Damian 441
Flanagan, David 441
Flanagan, Dawn P. 441
Flanagan, John 441
Flanagan, Jon 441
Flanagan, Liz 441
Flanagan, Mike 441
Flanagan, Richard 441
Flanagan, Richard Miller 441
Flanagan, Shalane 441
Flanagan, Thomas 441
Flanagan, Tommy Lee 441
ブラナガン
Brannagan, Cameron 176
ブラナシルピン
Buranasilpin, Chongchetn 202
プラナス
Planas, Carles 1117
ブラナプラサラッス
Buranaprasertsuk, Porntip 202
ブラナマン
Brannaman, Buck 176
フラナリー
Flannery, David 441
Flannery, Sarah 441
Flannery, Tim Fridtjof 441
ブラナン
Brannan, J.T. 176
プラナント
Prananto, Jujur 1131
ブラニー
Blaney, John 147
フラニガン
Flanigan, Bob 441
ブラニガン
Branigan, Laura 176
Brannigan, Augustine 176
ブラニク
Blanik, Leszek 147
フラニッキ
Hulanicki, Barbara 634
フラニツキ
Vranitzky, Franz 1465
フラニツキー
Vranitzky, Franz 1465
プラニョル
Plagnol, Henri 1117
ブラニング
Blanning, T.C.W. 147
ブラネ
Bulane, Vova 200
フラネリー
Flannelly, John 441
Flannery, Daniele D. 441
プラネル
Planel, Niels 1117
ブラネン
Brannen, Mary Yoko 176
フラノイ
Flournoy, Don M. 444
プラノ・クラーク
Plano Clark, Vicki L. 1117
プラノール
Planhol, Xavier de 1117
ブラーハ
Bracha, Gilad 173
ブラハ
Blaha, Michael 145
プラーハ
Praag, Anna van 1130
プラパカモル
Prapakamol, Sudket 1131
プラバカラン
Prabhakaran, Velupillai 1131
フラバーチコバ
Hlavackova, Andrea 610
プラバッカー
Prabhakar, Arati 1131
プラパット
Prapat, Panyachatraksa 1131
フラハティ
Flaherty, Alice 441
Flaherty, Jack 441
ブラバトニック
Blavatnik, Len 148
ブラバム
Brabham, David 173
Brabham, Jack 173
プラハラード
Prahalad, C.K. 1131
ブラハルツ
Bracharz, Kurt 173
ブラバン
Brabban, Alison 173
ブラバンツ
Brabants, Tim 173
ブラバンデール
Brabandere, Luc De 173
フラビ
Churavy, Pavel 263
プラビ
Prawy, Marcel 1132
フラビエ
Flavier, Juan M. 441
フラピエ
Frapié, Léon 457
ブラビエ
Vrabie, Vitalie 1465
プラビニス
Plavins, Martins 1117
ブラヒミ
Brahimi, Lakhdar 175
Brahimi, Yacine 175
ブラヒム
Brahim, Ahmed 175
ブラフ
Braff, Zach 174
Brough, Mal 187
プラフ
Praff, Giora A. 1131
プラブ
Prabhu, Jaideep C. 1131
Prabhu, Suresh 1131
フラフェンステイン
Gravenstijn, Deborah 527
ブラフォード
Bruford, Bill 193
ブラフシッチ
Vlahušić, Andro 1461
プラブシッチ
Plavsic, Zac 1117
プラーブダー・ユン
Prabda Yoon 1131
ブラブツォバニーブルトバ
Vrabcova-Nyvltova, Eva 1465
フラプノフ
Khrapunov, Biktor 729
ブラフマン
Brafman, Ori 174
Brafman, Rom 174
フラブラーリス
Flabouraris, Alekos 440
フラーフラント
Graafland, Johan J. 522
フラフンスドッティル
Hrafnsdóttir, Steinunn 629
ブラベツ
Brabec, Richard 173
フラベンステイン
Gravenstijn, Deborah 527
ブラボ
Bravo, Angela 178
Bravo, Claudio 178
Bravo, Manuel Alvarez 178
ブラボー
Bravo, Eddie 178
Bravo, Rose Marie 178
プラボウォ・スビアント
Prabowo Subianto 1131
プラボカー
Prabhakar, Arati 1131
ブラホビッチ
Vlahović, Aleksandar 1461
Vlahović, Miodrag 1461
Vlahović, Sanja 1461
フラマー
Flammer, Josef 441
ブラマ
Boulama, Kané Aïchatou 167
Bulama, Abdu 200
ブラマー
Brammer, Lawrence M. 175
プラマー
Plummer, Andy 1118
Plummer, Christopher 1119
Plummer, David 1119
Plummer, Deborah 1119
Plummer, Henry 1119
Plummer, Terrance 1119
プラマス
Pramas, Chris 1131
プラマタルスキ
Pramatarski, Alexander 1131
ブラマーニ
Bramani, Lidia 175
プラマニク
Pramanik, Emaz Uddin 1131
フラマン
Flamant, Ludovic 441
Vlaemminck, Joseph H. 1460
ブラマン
Braman, Bryan 175
プラマーン・アディレークサーン
Pramarn Adireksarn 1131

プラマーン・アディレクサーン
Pramarn Adireksarn 1131
ブラミ
Brami, Elisabeth 175
ブラミス
Vlamis, Anthony S. 1461
フラミニ
Flamini, Mathieu 441
フラ・ミン・スエ
Hla Mint Swe 610
フラム
Flamm, Michael W. 441
Fullam, Scott 467
ブラーム
Brahm, Laurence J. 175
ブラム
Blum, Danny 150
Blum, Deborah 150
Blum, Howard 150
Blum, Ralph 150
Bram, Ben 175
Brame, Geneviève 175
プラム
Plum, Emily Lupita 1118
Plum, Fred 1118
Pullum, Geoffrey K. 1139
ブラムウェル
Bramwell, Martyn 175
フラムキン
Frumkin, Peter 465
ブラムス
Brams, Steven J. 175
ブラムソン
Bramson, Robert M. 175
プラムディア・アナンタ・トゥル
Pramoedya Ananta Toer 1131
プラムディヤ・アナンタ・トゥール
Pramoedya Ananta Toer 1131
プラムディヤ・アナンタ・トゥル
Pramoedya Ananta Toer 1131
ブラムバーグ
Blumberg, Baruch Samuel 150
ブラムフィット
Brumfitt, J.H. 194
ブラムブス
Brambs, Hans-Juergen 175
フラムホルツ
Flamholtz, Eric 441
プラムラン
Pflimlin, Édouard 1106
ブラムリー
Bramley, Tessa 175
Bramley, William 175
Bramly, Sophie 175
プラムリー
Plumlee, Marshall 1118
Plumlee, Mason 1118
Plumlee, Miles 1118
ブラムレット
Bramlett, Delaney 175
プラモン・スティウォン
Pramon Sutivong 1131
プラモンドン
Plamondon, Pascal 1117
プラヤシ
Pulayasi, Brian 1139
プラユキ・ナラテボー
Phrayuki Naradevo 1109
プラユット
Prayuth, Chan-ocha 1132
プラユット・ジャンオーチャー
Prayuth Chan-o-cha 1132
プラユット・チャンオーチャー
Prayuth Chan-o-cha 1132
ブラヨビッチ
Brajović, Ivan 175
フラリー
Frary, Carol D. 457
プラール
Prahl, Hans-Werner 1131
フラルチク
Fularczyk-kozlowska, Magdalena 467
ブラルドネ
Blardone, Massimiliano 147
ブラレ
Burale, Muhammad Meydane 202
ブラレィ
Braley, Frank 175
ブラレイ
Braley, Frank 175
フラワー
Flower, Derek Adie 444
Flower, R.J. 444
フラワーズ
Flowers, Betty Sue 444
Flowers, Brandon 444
Flowers, Ereck 444
Flowers, Marquis 444
Flowers, Trey 444
Flowers, Tyler 444
Flowers, Vonetta 444
ブラワヨ
Bulawayo, NoViolet 200
フラン
Fullan, Michael 467
ブーラン
Bouran, Alia 168
Bourin, Jeanne 168
ブラン
Blain, Christophe 145
Blain, Willy 145
Blanc, Christian 146
Blanc, Dominique 146
Blanc, François Paul 146
Blanc, Hélène 146
Blanc, Isabelle 146
Blanc, Laurent 146
Blanc, Leandro 146
Blanc, Myriam 146
Blanc, Olivier 146
Blin, Georges 149
Brand, Solange 175
Buran, Jon 202
プーラン
Poulain, Jean-Pierre 1128
プラン
Dith Pran 358
Poulain, Benoit 1128
ブラン・アシェメ
Brun Hacheme, Véronique 194
フラン・エスクリバ
Fran Escriba 456
ブランカース・クーン
Blankers-Koen, Francina 147
ブランカース・クン
Blankers-Koen, Francina 147
ブランカート
Brancato, John 175
ブランカトー
Brancato, John 175
フランカビラ
Francavilla, Francesco 454
フランカール
Flanquart, Alexandre 441
ブランカン
Blancan, Bernard 146
フランキ
Franqui, Carlos 457
ブランキ
Blanke, Gail 147
フランキスクス
Francis I 455
ブランキッチ
Vrankić, Dragan 1465
フランキッティ
Franchitti, Dario 454
フランキーナ
Franchina, Basilio 454
フランキナ
Franchina, Basilio 454
フランキニー
Frankeny, Frankie 456
ブランキーニ
Branchini, Giovanni 175
ブランキング
Blanking, Jonas 147
フランク
Franck, Didier 455
Franck, Egon 455
Franck, Julia 455
Franck, Martine 455
Franck, Mikko 455
Franck, Sebastian 455
Franckh, Pierre 455
Francq, Isabelle 456
Frank, Adam 456
Frank, Adrian 456
Frank, Arthur W. 456
Frank, Barney 456
Frank, Betsy 456
Frank, Chuck 456
Frank, Dorothea Benton 456
Frank, Ellen 456
Frank, E.R. 456
Frank, Gary 456
Frank, Jacquelyn 456
Frank, Jerome David 456
Frank, John P. 456
Frank, Julia B. 456
Frank, Kim Tip 456
Frank, Lawrence K. 456
Frank, Milo O. 456
Frank, Mitch 456
Frank, Pamera 456
Frank, Robert 456
Frank, Robert H. 456
Frank, Sergei O. 456
Frank, Suso 456
Franke, John R. 456
フラング
Frang, Vilde 456
ブランク
Blanc, Sébastien 146
Blanck, Gertrude 147
Blanck, Horst 147
Blanck, Sarah 147
Blanck, Ulf 147
Blank, Hanne 147
Blank, Martin 147
Blank, Rebecca 147
Blank, Steven Gary 147
Blank, Susanne 147
Blunck, Aaron 151
プランク
Plank, David N. 1117
Plank, Robert 1117
フランクス
Francks, Penelope 455
Franks, Andrew 457
Franks, Ben 457
Franks, Bill 457
Franks, Felix 457
Franks, Lynne 457
Franks, Owen 457
ブランクファイン
Blankfein, Lloyd 147
フランクファート
Frankfurt, Harry G. 456
ブランクフェイン
Blankfein, Lloyd 147
フランクフォート
Frankfort, Lew 456
フランク - マクニール
Frank-McNeil, Julia 457
フランクランド
Frankland, E.Gene 456
フランクリン
Franklin, Anna 456
Franklin, Aretha 456
Franklin, Ariana 456
Franklin, Bob 456
Franklin, Bonnie 457
Franklin, Caryn 457
Franklin, Colin 457
Franklin, Cynthia 457
Franklin, Derek 457
Franklin, Eric N. 457
Franklin, Howard Bruce 457
Franklin, Jeff 457
Franklin, John Hope 457
Franklin, Jon 457
Franklin, Jonathan 457
Franklin, Kirk 457
Franklin, Melissa 457
Franklin, Nick 457
Franklin, Orlando 457
Franklin, Paul 457
Franklin, Stephen T. 457
Franklin, Tom 457
Franklin, William E. 457
フランクル
Frankel, Fred H. 456
Frankel, Glenn 456
Frankel, Martha 456
Frankl, Peter 456
フランケ
Franke, Reiner 456
Franke, Rolf 456
ブランケ
Blanquet, S. 147
プランゲ
Prange, Heike 1131
フランケチエンヌ
Frankétienne 456
フランケッティ
Franchetti, Raymond 454
ブランケット
Blunkett, David 151

フ

プランケット
Plunkett, Kilian 1119
Plunkett, Kim 1119
Plunkett, Richar 1119
Plunkett, Signe J. 1119
フランケト
Franquet, Sonia 457
フランケビッチ
Frankiewicz, Wioletta 456
フランケモント
Franquemont, Sharon 457
フランケル
Frankel, Alexandra 456
Frankel, Alona 456
Frankel, Arthur J. 456
Frankel, David 456
Frankel, Ellen 456
Frankel, Jeffrey Alexander 456
Frankel, Laurie 456
Frankel, Lois P. 456
Frankel, Max 456
Frankel, Susannah 456
Frankel, Tamar 456
Frankel, Valerie Estelle 456
ブランケルス・クーン
Blankers-Koen, Francina 147
フランケン
Franken, Al 456
Vrancken, Kaat 1465
フランケンサーラー
Frankenthaler, Helen 456
ブランケンシップ
Blankenship, Ben 147
Blankenship, William D. 147
プランケンシュタイナー
Plankensteiner, Gerhard 1117
フランケンハイマー
Frankenheimer, John Michael 456
フランケンバーガー
Frankenberger, Karolin 456
フランケンバーグ
Frankenberg, Ronald 456
ブランケンビューラー
Blankenbuehler, Andy 147
ブランケンブルク
Blankenburg, Wolfgang 147
フランコ
Franco, Itamar 455
Franco, Jess 455
Franco, Jorge 455
Franco, Julio 455
Franco, Julio Cesar 455
Franco, Maikel 455
Franco, Michel 455
Franco, Peter 455
Franco, Sammy 455
Franco Gómez, Luis Federico 455
Franco Ramos, Jorge 456
ブランコ
Blanco, Alfonso 147
Blanco, Andres 147
Blanco, Billy 147
Blanco, Carlos 147
Blanco, Cecilia 147
Blanco, Giovanna 147
Blanco, Guillermo 147
Blanco, Ignacio Jiménez 147
Blanco, Javiera 147
Blanco, Jodee 147
Blanco, Salvador Jorge 147
Branco, Joaquim Rafael 175
フランコイス
Francois, Ricky Jean 455
フランコ・ゴメス
Franco Gómez, Luis Federico 455
フランコ・コレッリ
Corelli, Franco 290
フランコーナ
Francona, Terry 456
フランコーナー
Francona, Terry 456
フランコナ
Francona, Terry 456
フランコ・バディア
Franco Badia, Pedro 455
フランコマーノ
Francomano, Clair A. 455
ブラン・コム
Brun-Cosme, Nadine 194
フランコ・モジリアニ
Modigliani, Franco 959
ブランコ・ロペス
Blanco López, José 147
フランコン
Francon, Mellie 455
フランサ
Franca, Eliardo 454
Franca, Felipe 454
Franca, Mary 454
ブランザ
Branza, Ana Maria 177
ブランジ
Branzi, Andrea 177
フランジィーリ
Frangilli, Michele 456
Frangilli, Vittorio 456
フランジエ
Franjieh, Suleiman 456
ブーランジェ
Boulanger, Daniel 167
Boulanger, Philippe 167
Boulenger, Gilles 167
ブランシェ
Blanchet, Baptiste 147
ブランシェット
Blanchett, Cate 147
Blanchette, Jasmin 147
フランシオサ
Franciosa, Anthony 454
フランシク
Francique, Alleyne 455
フランシス
Frances, Craig 454
Francis, A.J. 455
Francis, Anne 455
Francis, Arlene 455
Francis, Brian 455
Francis, Charlie 455
Francis, Cindy 455
Francis, Colin 455
Francis, David A. 455
Francis, Dick 455
Francis, D.W. 455
Francis, Felix 455
Francis, Frank 455
Francis, George K. 455
Francis, Graham 455
Francis, Hermangild 455
Francis, H.G. 455
Francis, James 455
Francis, Javon 455
Francis, John 455
Francis, Julian 455
Francis, Kirk 455
Francis, Leslie J. 455
Francis, Lorenzo 455
Francis, Lowell 455
Francis, Mickey 455
Francis, Phyllis 455
Francis, Richard C. 455
Francis, Simon 455
Francis, Suzanne 455
Francis, Tomas 455
フランシス-ウェスト
Francis-West, Philippa H. 455
フランシスコ
Francisco, Ruth 455
フランシスコ1世
Francis I 455
フランシス＝ブライデン
Francis-Bryden, Selena 455
ブランシャール
Blanchard, Anne 146
Blanchard, Eugénie 146
Blanchard, Francis 146
Blanchard, Olivier 146
Blanchard, Pascal 146
ブランシャン
Blanchin, Matthieu 147
ブランショ
Blanchot, Maurice 147
Blanchot, Philippe 147
フランション
Fransson, Alexander 457
プランション
Planchon, Roger 1117
フランス
France, Anthony 454
France, Dan 454
France, Melissa Dorfman 454
France, Michael 454
France, R.T. 454
Frans, Hendrickx 457
フランズ
Franz, Raymond 457
ブランズ
Brands, H.W. 176
Bruns, Bill 195
Bruns, Roger 195
プランス
Prance, *Sir* Ghillean T. 1131
Prance, Ghillean Tolmie 1131
フランスコービアック
Franscoviak, Chad 457
ブランスタッド
Branstad, Terry Edward 176
ブランストロム
Brännström, Victor 176
ブランスフォード
Bransford, John 176
Bransford, John D. 176
ブランスマン
Brunsman, James 195
ブランゼイ
Branzei, Sylvia 177
フランセス
Frances, Allen 454
フランゼーゼ
Franzese, Michael 457
フランセーン
Franzén, Torkel 457
フランセン
Franssen, Emile 457
フランゼン
Franzen, Jonathan 457
フランソア・ポンセ
François-Poncet, Jean André 455
フランソワ
François, Déborah 455
François, Rotchild, Jr. 455
François, Walter 455
François, Zoë 455
フランソワーズ
Francoise 455
フランソワ・ポンセ
François-Poncet, Jean André 455
フランソン
Fransson, Anna Jenny 457
ブランソン
Branson, Douglas M. 176
Branson, Jeff 176
Branson, Richard 176
Branson, Robert K. 176
Brunson, Rick 195
フランダース
Flanders, Julia 441
Flanders, Rebecca 441
ブランダム
Brandom, Robert 176
プランタムラ
Plantamura, Carol 1117
ブランダン
Brandão, André Luís 175
ブランダンロドリゲス
Brandão Rodrigues, Tiago 175
ブランチ
Blanche, Tony 147
Branch, Alan 175
Branch, Andre 175
Branch, Gigi 175
Branch, Michelle 175
Branch, Robert M. 175
Branch, Tyvon 175
フランチェスカート
Francescato, Donata 454
フランチェスキーニ
Franceschini, Dario 454
フランチェスコ
Francesco, Bellissimo 454
フランチェスチェッリ
Franceschelli, Christopher 454
フランチシス
Franciscis, Alfonso de 455
ブランチャード
Blanchard, Frank 146
Blanchard, Ken 146
Blanchard, Madeleine Homan 146
Blanchard, Miriam 146
Blanchard, Tammy 146
Blanchard, Terence 147
フランチョーネ
Francione, Gianni 454
フランツ
Frantz, Douglas 457
Frantz, Mike 457
Franz, Christian 457

フ

Franz, James K. 457
Franz, Marion J. 457
Franz, Max 457
Franz, Rudolf 457
Franz, Stephen 457
Franz, Steve 457
プランツ
Plunz, Richard 1119
フランツキー
Franzki, Harald 457
フランデ
Flinde, Albert 443
ブランティ
Bulanti, Francisco 200
ブランディ
Brandy, Othello 176
プランティ
Prunty, Joe 1138
Prunty, Morag 1138
プランディ
Prandi, Kyle 1131
プランティエ
Plantier, Laurent 1117
ブランデイジ
Brundage, Anthony 194
ブランディス
Brandis, George 176
Brandis, Jonathan 176
プランティリア
Plantilla, Jefferson R. 1117
プランティンガ
Plantinga, Adam 1117
ブランディング
Blanding, Michael 147
ブランデス
Brandes, Oliver M. 176
Brandes, Stuart Dean 176
フランデル
Flander, Rok 441
ブランデル
Blundell, Barry 151
Blundell, Judy 151
Blundell, Kim 151
ブランデル・ジョーンズ
Blundell Jones, Peter 151
ブランデン
Blunden, Caroline 151
Branden, Nathaniel 175
ブランデンバーガー
Brandenburger, Adam 176
ブランデンバーグ
Brandenberg, Aliki 176
Brandenburg, Jim 176
Brandenburg, John 176
Brandenburg, Judy 176
ブランデンブルグ
Brandenburg, Sieghard 176
ブランデンベルク
Brandenberg, René 176
ブラント
Blunt, Emily 151
Blunt, Giles 151
Blunt, James 151
Brandt, Aage 176
Brandt, Jennifur 176
Brandt, Julian 176
Brandt, Katrin 176
Brandt, M.IU. 176
Brandt, Nat 176
Brandt, Peter L. 176
Brandt, Reinhard 176
Brandt, Richard L. 176
Brandt, R.L. 176
Brandt, Sherry 176
Brandt, Thomas 176
Brant, James 176
Brant, Kylie 176
Brunt, Chris 195
Brunt, Stephen 195
ブランド
Bland, Bobby 147
Bland, Martin 147
Bland, Nick 147
Brand, Clare 175
Brand, Elton 175
Brand, Fiona 175
Brand, Joyce B. 175
Brand, Koen 175
Brand, Stewart 175
Brando, Marlon 176
ブランドー
Brandeau, Greg 175
プラント
Plant, Jane A. 1117
Plant, Robert 1117
Plante, Elena 1117
ブランドウ
Brandow, Todd 176
フラントヴァー
Frantová, Eva 457
ブラント・エリッセン
Brandt-Erichsen, Martha 176
ブラントシュテッター
Brandstetter, Wolfgang 176
ブランドナー
Brandner, Judith 176
ブランドフォード
Blandford, Steven 147
ブランドフォンブレナー
Brandfonbrener, Alice G. 176
ブランド・ミラー
Brand-Miller, Jennie 176
フランドラン
Flandrin, Jean Louis 441
ブラントリー
Brantley, Jeffrey 176
Brantley, Mark 176
Brantley, Michael 176
Brantly, Rob 176
Brantly, Susan 176
ブランドリーニ
Brandolini, Andreas 176
ブラントリー＝ニュートン
Brantley-Newton, Vanessa 176
ブランドル
Brandl, Karin 176
ブランドルップ
Brandrup, Monika 176
ブランドレイ
Brandley, Gunilla 176
ブランドレス
Brandreth, Gyles Daubeney 176
フランドロワ
Flandrois, Isabelle 441
ブランドワイン
Brandewyne, Rebecca 176
ブラントン
Blanton, Joe 147
Blanton, Robert 147
Branton, Matthew 177
Brunton, Finn 195
Brunton, John 195
ブランドン
Brandon, Ali 176
ブランナー
Brunner, Conrad 194
ブランニング
Blanning, T.C.W. 147
ブランヌ
Bourhane, Nourdine 168
ブランネン
Brannen, Nathan 176
ブランバーグ
Blumberg, Baruch Samuel 150
Blumberg, Mark Samuel 150
ブランハム
Bramham, Jessica 175
ブランパン
Blanpain, Roger 147
ブランビラ
Brambilla, Michela Vittoria 175
フランプトン
Frampton, Kenneth 454
Frampton, Megan 454
Frampton, Peter 454
Frampton, Susan B. 454
フランベール
Flambert, Mathilde 441
フランベルガー
Framberger, Raphael 454
プランマー
Plummer, Michael G. 1119
フラン・メリダ
Fran Merida 457
ブラン＝モンマイユール
Blanc-Montmayeur, Martine 147
ブラン＝ランベール
Brun-Lambert, David 194
ブランリー
Branley, Franklyn Mansfield 176
フラン・リコ
Fran Rico 457
ブランロト
Blanlot, Vivianne 147
フリー
Flea 441
Free, Doug 459
Free, Duncan 459
Freeh, Louis J. 459
ブリ
Burri, René 205
ブリー
Bury, Aliaksandr 207
プーリー
Pooley, Emma 1124
プリ
Puri, Amrish 1140
Puri, Kamal 1140
フリアー
Friaa, Ahmed 462
ブリア
Bhuria, Kantilal 136
Breer, William T. 179
Briere, John 182
ブリアー
Boullier, Dianna 167
Breer, William T. 179
プリアー
Preer, Jean L. 1132
フリアオ
Juliao, Victor 690
フリアカ
Friaca 462
フリアサ
Friaca 462
フリアーズ
Frears, Stephen 458
フリアス
Frias, Carlos 462
ブリアーズ
Blears, Hazel 148
プリアニシュニコフ
Prianishnikov, Vladyslav 1134
ブリアリ
Brialy, Jean Claude 181
ブリアン
Brian, Marcus 181
Briant, Pierre 181
Burian, Peter K. 203
プリアンバムルン
Plienbamrung, Preeprem 1118
ブリーヴィオ
Brivio, Davide 184
プリヴェス
Prywes, Yaron 1138
フーリエ
Fourie, Lehann 452
ブリエ
Blie, Bertrand 148
プリエージ
Pugliesi, Maurizio 1139
フリエット
Vliet, Jurg van 1461
プリエト
Prieto, José Luis 1135
プリエト
Prieto, Rodrigo 1135
プリエト・ヒメネス
Prieto Jiménez, Abel 1135
ブリェビッチ
Buljević, Josip 200
フリエフナスキダエワ
Friev Naskidaeva, Taimuraz 464
フリエル
Friel, Brian 463
Frier, Raphaële 464
ブリエール
Briere, John 182
フリエロス
Frieros, Toni 464
ブリオディ
Briody, Dan 183
ブリオニ
Vryoni, Maria 1465
ブリオネス
Briones, Leonor 183
プリオロ
Priolo, Lou 1136
ブリオン
Brion, Alain 183
Brion, Arturo 183
プリオン
Plihon, Dominique 1118
フリガ
Friga, Paul N. 464
ブリーカー
Bleker, Maria-M. 148
ブリガ

Buliga, Valentina 200
ブリーガー
Pfleeger, Shari Lawrence 1106
フリーガオフ
Fliegauf, Bence 443
ブリガジン
Brigadin, Pyotr I. 182
プリガターノ
Prigatano, George P. 1135
ブリーキー
Breakey, Annabelle 178
ブリキ
Briki, Abid 182
ブーリキネ
Bourykine, Anatoli 168
フリギン・ラルセン
Flygind-Larsen, Mikael 445
フリーク
Freke, Timothy 461
プリーグ
Preeg, Steve 1132
フリークス
Fleecs, Tony 442
ブリクス
Blix, Hans Martin 149
Brix, Herman 184
ブリクモン
Bricmont, Jean 181
フリケット
Flicket, Roland 443
ブリゲリ
Brighelli, Jean-Paul 182
ブリケル
Briquel, Dominique 183
プリゴジーン
Prigogine, Ilya 1135
プリゴジン
Prigogine, Ilya 1135
プリゴロフ
Pryhorov, Oleksiy 1138
フリーザー
Frieser, Karl-Heinz 464
フリーザイラー
Freezailah, Che Yeom 460
フリサル
Flisar, Filip 443
ブリザール
Brisard, Jean-Charles 183
Brisard, Jean-Christophe 183
プリーサント
Pleasant, Eddie 1118
プリザント
Prizant, Barry M. 1136
フリーシー
Freethy, Barbara 460
フリシ
Flissi, Mohamed 443
プリージ
Puglisi, Gianni 1139
フリシイク
Hricik, Donald E. 629
フリジェリオ
Frigerio, Luciana 464
プリジオーニ
Prigioni, Pablo 1135
フリージケ
Friesike, Sascha 464
フリシチェンコ
Hryschenko, Kostyantyn 629
プリシッチ
Pulisic, Christian 1139
プリジナー
Prusiner, Stanley Ben 1138
プリシマ
Purisima, Cesar 1140
プリシャジニュク
Prysyazhnyuk, Mykola 1138
フリシャル
Flisar, Filip 443
フリシュクネヒト
Frischknecht, Thomas 464
フリショー
Frichot, Sylvette 462
ブリジョ
Burillo, Giselle 203
プリショタ
Plichota, Anne 1118
フリージンガー
Friesinger, Anni 464
フリース
Freese, Katherine 460
Frese, Nolan 461
Friis, Agnete 464
Friis, Lotte 464
Friis, Lykke 464
Vries, Anke de 1465
フリーズ
Freese, David 460
Fries, Brant E. 464
Friese, Kurt Michael 464
Frieze, Jennifer 464
フリス
Fris, Kristijan 464
Frith, Alex 464
Frith, Christopher D. 464
Frith, Simon 464
Frith, Uta 464
ブリーズ
Brees, Drew 179
Brize, Laurence 184
ブリス
Bliss, E.Veronica (Vicky) 149
Bliss, Harry 149
Bliss, Michael 149
Briz, Jorge 184
ブリスヴィル
Brisville, Jean-Claude Gabriel 183
ブリスエラ
Brizuela, Dario 184
Brizuela, Mariá Eugenia 184
ブリスキン
Briskin, Alan 183
ブリスコ
Brisco, Jack 183
Brisco, Meredith A. 183
ブリスコー
Briscoe, Barrie 183
プリースター
Priester, Gary 1135
フリースタッド
Friestad, Marian 464
プリスターフキン
Pristavkin, Anatolii Ignatievich 1136
フリスチェンコ
Khristenko, Viktor Borisovich 729
ブリーズデール
Bleasdale, Holly 148
Bleasdale, Julia 148
フリステンコ
Khristenko, Stanislav 729
Khristenko, Viktor Borisovich 729
フリスト
Frist, Thomas, Jr. 464
プリースト
Priest, Cherie 1135
Priest, Christopher 1135
Priest, Dana 1135
Priest, Graham 1135
Priest, Keith 1135
フリストゥ
Christou, Andreas 262
Khristou, Jeanne 729
フリストウ
Christou, Andreas 262
ブリストウ
Bristow, M.J. 183
Bristow, Robert G. 183
フリストヴァ
Hristova, Ljudmila 629
Hristova, Svetla 629
フリストドゥロス
Christodoulos 261
フリストバ
Hristova, Mimi 629
フリストフ
Hristov, Valentin 629
フリストフィアス
Christofias, Demetris 261
プリーストランド
Priestland, Andreas 1135
プリーストリー
Priestley, Chris 1135
Priestley, Mark 1135
Priestley, Mary 1135
ブリストル
Bristol, Jimmy 183
フリーストーン
Freestone, Peter 460
フリーズナー
Friesner, Esther M. 464
ブリズナコフ
Bliznakov, Vesslin 149
ブリズニュク
Bliznyuk, Anastasia 149
ブリズビン
Brisbin, Terri 183
フリスボールド
Frisvold, Melissa H. 464
プリスメンスカ
Pysmenska, Anna 1142
ブリスランド
Bilsland, Greg 139
プリースランド
Priestland, Rhys 1135
ブリスリー
Brisley, Joyce L. 183
フリズレイフスドッティル
Fridleifsdottir, Siv 462
プリズレニ
Prizreni, Sahit 1136
ブリセ
Brisset, Claire-akiko 183
プリーセ
Pugliese, Ella 1139
プリセーツカヤ
Plisetskaya, Maiya 1118
プリセツカヤ
Plisetskaya, Maiya 1118
ブリセット
Blissett, Luther 149
Brissett, Jacoby 183
ブリセニョ
Briceño, John 181
フリゼール
Frisell, Bill 464
フリーゼン
Friesen, Jeff 464
ブリゼンディーン
Brizendine, Louann 184
フリゾ
Frizot, Michel 464
フリソストミデス
Chrysostomides, Kypros 262
フリソフォイディス
Chrisochoidis, Michalis 260
ブリゾラ
Brizola, Carlos Daudt 184
プリソン
Plisson, Philip 1118
フリーダ
Frida 462
プリータ
Purita, Marcela 1140
フリーダン
Friedan, Betty Naomi Goldstein 462
ブリタン
Brittan, Leon 184
フリダンソン
Fridenson, Patrick 462
ブリーチ
Bleach, Fiona 148
プリチェット
Pritchett, Price 1136
プリチェリ
Puricelli, Arturo 1140
ブリチス
Bricis, Ilmars 181
プリチネージョ
Prichinello, Michael 1135
プリチャー
Pricha, Rengsomboonsuk 1135
プリチャード
Pritchard, Alexis 1136
Pritchard, Anthony 1136
Pritchard, Dorian J. 1136
Pritchard, John 1136
Pritchard, Michael 1136
プリチャニッチ
Pličanič, Senko 1118
プリーチャー・ヌンスック
Prichā Nunsuk 1135
フリッカー
Flicker, Barry 443
Fricker, Janet 462
ブリッカー
Bricker, Diane D. 181
プリツカー
Pritzker, J.B. 1136
Pritzker, M.K. 1136
Pritzker, Penny S. 1136
Pritzker, Thomas J. 1136
フリッキオーネ
Fricchione, Gregory 462

フリッキンガー
Flickinger, Hali 443
フリック
Flick, Uwe 443
Frick, Aurelia 462
Frick, Paul J. 462
Fullick, Ann 467
ブリック
Bricq, Nicole 181
ブリッグ
Brigg, Cathy 182
ブリックス
Blix, Hans Martin 149
Brix, Michael 184
ブリッグス
Briggs, Andy 182
Briggs, David 182
Briggs, D.E.G. 182
Briggs, Jason R. 182
Briggs, John 182
Briggs, Julie K. 182
Briggs, Mary 182
Briggs, Rex 182
ブリッグズ
Briggs, Anita 182
Briggs, Asa 182
Briggs, Patricia 182
Briggs, Raymond Redvers 182
プリックス
Prix, Wolf D. 1136
ブリックナー
Brickner, Szabolcs 181
ブリッグハウス
Brighouse, Tim 182
フリックヒンガー
Frickhinger, Karl Albert 462
ブリッグマン
Brigman, Greg 182
ブリッケル
Brickell, Christopher 181
Brickell, Edie 181
ブリッケン
Blickhan, Daniela 148
フリッケンガー
Flickenger, Rob 443
フリッシー
Flichy, Patrice 443
ブリッジ
Bridges, David 181
Burridge, Rich 205
ブリッジウォーター
Bridgewater, Dee Dee 182
Bridgewater, George 182
Bridgewater, Teddy 182
ブリッジス
Bridges, Jeff 181
Bridges, Mark 181
Bridges, Miles 182
ブリッジズ
Bridges, Beau 181
Bridges, Edwin Michael 181
Bridges, Jeff 181
Bridges, Linda 181
Bridges, Michael W. 182
Bridges, Shirin Yim 182
Bridges, Simon 182
Bridges, William 182
ブリッジマン
Bridgman, Roger 182
ブリッジャー
Bridger, Darren 181
フリッシュ
Frisch, Aaron 464
Frisch, Bertha 464
Frisch, Otto Robert 464
Frisch, Wolfgang 464
ブリッシュ
Blish, James 149
Brisch, Karl Heinz 183
フリッシュマン
Frishman, Austin M. 464
ブリッセ
Brisset, Claire-akiko 183
フリッセン
Frissen, Jerry 464
プリッソン
Plisson, Pascal 1118
フリッター
Fliter, Ingrid 443
フリッタマン＝ルイス
Flitterman-Lewis, Sandy 443
フリッチ
Fritsch, Thierry 464
Fritsch, Toni 464
ブリッチ
Brycz, Pavel 196
プリッチン
Pritchin, Aylen 1136
フリッツ
Fritz, Clemens 464
Fritz, Harry 464
Fritz, Jean 464
Fritz, John 464
Fritz, Robert 464
Fritz, Sandy 464
Fritz, Wolfgang 464
ブリッツ
Blitz, Jeff 149
Brits, Schalk 183
Britz, Travis 184
ブリッツァー
Blitzer, Barbara 149
Blitzer, David M. 149
プリッツァーリ
Plizzari, Alessandro 1118
フリッツェ
Fritze, Ronald H. 464
フリッツォン
Fritzon, Thorbiörn 464
プリッツカー
Pritzker, Thomas J. 1136
フリット
Gullit, Ruud 545
フリッド
Frid, Martin J. 462
ブリット
Britt, Fanny 183
Britt, Justin 183
Britt, Kenny 183
Britt, Rosmarie 183
ブリッドウェル
Bridwell, Norman 182
Bridwell, Parker 182
フリットクロフト
Flitcroft, Ian 443
フリットフム
Fritthum, Karl Michael 464
プリットマン
Plitmann, Hila 1118
フリットリ
Frittoli, Barbara 464
Frittoli, Mario 464
ブリットン
Britton, Leon 184
Britton, Zach 184
フリップ
Fripp, Robert 464
プリディ
Priddy, Eunice F. 1135
ブリディガム
Bridigum, Todd 182
ブリーディティス
Brieditis, Katarina 182
プリティフロンザック
Pretti-Frontczak, Kristie 1133
プリティマン
Prettyman, Tristan 1133
プリディヤトーン
Pridiyathorn Devakula 1135
プリディヤトン・デバクラ
Pridiyathorn Devakula 1135
プリディヤトン・テワクン
Pridiyathorn Devakula 1135
ブリテェインーキャトリン
Brittain-Catlin, William 184
ブリテナム
Brittenham, Dean 184
Brittenham, Greg 184
フリーデン
Frieden, Luc 462
Frieden, Tanja 462
ブリーデン
Breeden, Elaine 178
Breeden, Jake 178
ブリテン
Britain, Kristen 183
Brittain, Bill 183
Brittain, Jason 183
Brittain, William 184
Britten, Rhonda 184
フリデンソン
Fridenson, Patrick 462
フリーデンタール
Friedenthal, Sanford 463
フリーデンバーグ
Friedenberg, Jay 462
フリート
Fleet, Bruce 442
Fleet, Jon “Apestyles” van 442
Vliet, Jacques van der 1461
フリード
Freed, James Ingo 459
Freed, Jan 459
Freed, Stanley A. 459
Fried, Bradley 462
Fried, Dinah 462
Fried, Jason 462
Fried, Max 462
Fried, Seth 462
ブリト
Brito, Humberto Santos 183
Brito, José 183
Brito, Lidia 183
Brito, Pedro 183
Britto, Boniface 184
ブリトー
Brito, Casimiro de 183
Brito, Socrates 183
プリード
Pulido, Javier 1139
プリドー
Prideaux, Sue 1135
フリートウッド
Fleetwood, Steve 442
フリードゥル
Fliedl, Gottfried 443
フリードキン
Friedkin, William 463
ブリトス
Britos, Miguel 183
フリドーノ
Fridono, Judy 462
フリードハイム
Freedheim, Donald K. 459
フリードバーグ
Friedberg, Aaron L. 462
Friedberg, Anne 462
Friedberg, Barbara A. 462
Friedberg, Errol C. 462
Friedberg, Rebecca J. 462
Friedberg, Robert D. 462
フリードビヒレル
Friedbichler, Ingrid 462
Friedbichler, Michael 462
フリードベルグ
Friedberg, Erhard 462
フリードマン
Freedman, Claire 459
Freedman, David H. 459
Freedman, Estelle B. 459
Freedman, Ezra 459
Freedman, Françoise Barbira 459
Freedman, Lawrence David 459
Freedman, Lisa 459
Freedman, Marc 459
Freedman, Mike 459
Freedman, Paul H. 459
Freedman, Ralph 459
Freedman, Robert 459
Freedman, Robert L. 459
Freedman, Rory 459
Fridman, Gal 462
Fridman, Mikhail Maratovich 462
Fridmann, Dave 462
Friedman, Abigail 463
Friedman, Adena 463
Friedman, Andrew 463
Friedman, Art 463
Friedman, Benjamin M. 463
Friedman, Bill 463
Friedman, Daniel 463
Friedman, David M. 463
Friedman, Ellen 463
Friedman, Eric 463
Friedman, George 463
Friedman, Grant 463
Friedman, Howard S. 463
Friedman, Jeffrey M. 463
Friedman, Jerome Isaac 463
Friedman, Kinky 463
Friedman, Laurie B. 463
Friedman, Lawrence 463
Friedman, Lawrence Jacob 463
Friedman, Lawrence Meir 463
Friedman, Marty 463
Friedman, Matthew J. 463
Friedman, Meyer 463
Friedman, Michael 463
Friedman, Michael Jan 463

Friedman, Mildred S. 463
Friedman, Milton 463
Friedman, Neil 463
Friedman, Nelson 463
Friedman, Philip 463
Friedman, Robert I. 463
Friedman, Robert Lawrence 463
Friedman, Robert S. 463
Friedman, Ron 463
Friedman, Ron J. 463
Friedman, Rose D. 463
Friedman, Russell P. 463
Friedman, Stephen 463
Friedman, Steve 463
Friedman, Stewart D. 463
Friedman, Thomas 463
Friedman, Thomas Lauren 463
Friedmann, Daniel 463
Friedmann, Harriet 463
Friedmann, John 463
Friedmann, Theodore 463
Frydman, Monique 465
フリードランダー
Friedländer, Saul 463
フリードランド
Freedland, Jonathan 459
Friedland, Jerold A. 463
フリードリック
Friedrich, Christian 463
Friedrich, Otto 463
フリードリヒ
Friedrich, Ariane 463
Friedrich, Hans-Peter 463
Friedrich, Joachim 463
Friedrich, Jörg 463
Friedrich, Marvin 463
Friedrich, Mike 463
フリドリヒ
Frydrych, Petr 466
フリドリン
Fridolin, Gustav 462
フリドレイフスドッティル
Fridleifsdottir, Siv 462
フリードレンダー
Friedländer, Saul 463
ブリトン
Britton, Andrew 184
Britton, Catherine 184
Britton, Chris 184
Britton, Dorothy 184
Britton, Esmeralda 184
Britton, Lesley 184
Britton, Paul 184
Britton, Ronald 184
Britton, Ronald S. 184
Britton, Terry 184
フリーナー
Fleener, Coby 442
ブリナ
Vrinat, Jean-Claude 1465
プリーナ
Prina, Francesca 1135
フリーニー
Freeney, Dwight 460
Freeny, Jonathan 460
ブリニ
Brini, al-Ugili Abdel-Salam 183
プリニース
Prineas, Sarah 1135
ブリニャック
Brignac, Reid 182
フリニャーティ
Fulignati, Andrea 467
ブリニョーリ
Brignoli, Alberto 182
ブリニョルフソン
Brynjolfsson, Erik 196
ブリヌル
Brignull, Irena 182
フリネビチ
Hrynevych, Lilia 629
プリノ
Prenot, Josh 1132
ブリノフ
Blinov, Alexander 149
Blinov, Vladimir M. 149
ブリノワ
Blinova, Mila 149
フリーバーガー
Freiberger, Fred 460
プリバーセック
Plibersek, Tanya 1118
フーリハン
Houlihan, Brian 626
Houlihan, Declan 626
Hourihan, Gary 626
プリビテラ
Privitera, James R. 1136
プリビル
Pribyl, Bill 1134
ブリファ
Briffa, John 182
プリフィテラ
Prifitera, Aurelio 1135
プリーブケ
Priebke, Erich 1135
プリブケ
Priebke, Erich 1135
フリプケンス
Flipkens, Kirsten 443
プリープスト
Priebst, Christin 1135
プリブル
Pribyl, Charles B. 1134
プリプレム・プリアンバムルン
Preeprem Plienbamrung 1132
フリーベリ
Friberg, Anders 462
フリヘリオ
Frigerio, Rogelio 464
プリベール
Privert, Jocelerme 1136
プリホチコ
Prikhodko, Sergei E. 1135
プリホドチェンコ
Prikhodtchenko, Konstantin 1135
ブリマ
Brima, Sidikie 182
ブリマー
Brimmer, Rebecca J. 182
Brimner, Larry Dane 182
プリマー
Plimmer, Martin 1118
プリマコーフ
Primakov, Evgenii Maksimovich 1135
プリマコフ
Primakov, Evgenii Maksimovich 1135
プリマック
Primack, Richard B. 1135
フリーマン
Feeman, Mary E. Wilkins 425
Freeman, Adam 459
Freeman, Al, Jr. 459
Freeman, Alan 459
Freeman, Allyn 459
Freeman, Angela Beasley 460
Freeman, Arthur 460
Freeman, Barbara K. 460
Freeman, B.J. 460
Freeman, Brian 460
Freeman, Charles 460
Freeman, Dalton 460
Freeman, Dena 460
Freeman, Devonta 460
Freeman, Elisabeth 460
Freeman, Eric T. 460
Freeman, Freddie 460
Freeman, Houghton 460
Freeman, Jane 460
Freeman, Jerrell 460
Freeman, Kathleen 460
Freeman, Laurie Anne 460
Freeman, Linton C. 460
Freeman, Lydia 460
Freeman, Mark Philip 460
Freeman, Martha 460
Freeman, Martin 460
Freeman, Mason W. 460
Freeman, Michael 460
Freeman, Mike 460
Freeman, Mona 460
Freeman, Morgan 460
Freeman, Orville Lothrop 460
Freeman, Paul K. 460
Freeman, Ray 460
Freeman, R.Edward 460
Freeman, Roy 460
Freeman, Russ 460
Freeman, Sam 460
Freeman, Samuel Richard 460
Freeman, Steve 460
Freeman, Tor 460
Freeman, Trey 460
Freeman, Walter J. 460
Frieman, Wendy 464
ブリーマン
Vreeman, Rachel C. 1465
フリマンソン
Frimansson, Inger 464
フリーマントル
Freemantle, Brian 460
Freemantle, Glenn 460
ブリーム
Bream, Jon 178
プリムローズ
Primrose, Neil Maxwell 1135
ブリモア
Bullimore, David W. 201
プリモラツ
Primorac, Dragan 1135
Primorac, Zoran 1135
フリーモント
Fremont, Eleanor 461
ブリャ
Burya, Viktor P. 207
プーリヤ
Pouria, Soroor 1128
プリヤダルサナ
Priyadharsana, Anura 1136
プリヤディ
Prijadi, Prapto Suhardjo 1135
プリャーヒン
Priakhn, Georgii 1134
ブリュー
Brew, Bruce 181
プリュー
Plewe, Brandon 1118
フリューア
Flur, Wolfgang 445
ブリューア
Brewer, John 181
Brewer, Leo 181
ブリュア
Brewer, John 181
ブリュエル
Bruel, Nick 193
フリュゲン
Fluggen, Lars 444
プリューゴープト
Pflughaupt, Laurent 1106
フリューザン
Flusin, Bernard 445
プリュザン
Pruzan, Todd 1138
ブリュージェ
Bruges, James 193
ブリュジーズ
Bruzzese, Anita 195
Bruzzese, J.Peter 195
フリューシュトゥック
Frühstück, Sabine 465
ブリュソロ
Brussolo, Serge 195
ブリュチ
Blutch 151
フリュック
Flueck, Martin 444
ブリュックゲマイアー
Brüggemeier, Franz-Josef 193
ブリュックナー
Brueckner, Keith Allan 193
ブリュックネール
Bruckner, Pascal 193
ブリュッグマン
Brüggemann, Anna 193
Brüggemann, Dietrich 193
ブリュッセイ
Blussé, Leonard 151
ブリュッヘン
Brüggen, Frans 193
ブリュテュス
Brutus, Duly 195
ブリューデレ
Brüderle, Rainer 193
プリュドム
Prudhomme, David 1138
ブリュナメール
Brunhammer, Yvonne 194
ブリュニール
Bruyneel, Johan 195
ブリュネ
Brunet, Michel 194
ブリュネル
Brunel, Charlotte 194
Brunel, Henri 194
Brunel, Jacques 194
Brunel, Patrick 194
Brunel, Pierre 194

ブリュノー
Brunot, Patrick 195
ブリュノフ
Brunhoff, Cécile de 194
Brunhoff, Laurant de 194
ブリュハンコフ
Bryukhankov, Alexander 196
ブリュフォード
Bruford, Walter Horace 193
フリューベック・デ・ブルゴス
Frühbeck de Burgos, Rafael 465
ブリューム
Blühm, Andreas 150
プリュム
Prüm, André 1138
ブリュモン
Brumont, Maryse 194
ブリュール
Brühl, Daniel 193
Brühl, P. 193
ブリューレ
Brûlé, Michel 194
ブリュレ
Brûlé, Tyler 194
Bruley, Yves 194
ブリューワ
Brewer, John 181
ブリューワー
Brewer, Corey 181
Brewer, Heather 181
Brewer, Noel T. 181
Brewer, Sarah 181
Brewer, Zac 181
ブリュワー
Brewer, Aaron 181
Brewer, Gay 181
Brewer, Leo 181
Brewer, Rosalind 181
Brewer, Sarah 181
ブリュワー＝カリアス
Brewer-Carías, Charles 181
ブリュワード
Breward, Christopher 181
プリョイセン
Prøysen, Alf 1137
プリョードル
Prodl, Sebastian 1136
ブリヨン
Brion, Fabienne 183
プリラツキー
Prelutsky, Jack 1132
フリーランド
Freeland, Alison 459
Freeland, Chrystia 459
Freeland, Claire A.B. 459
Freeland, Cynthia A. 459
Freeland, Kyle 459
ブリーランド
Breeland, Bashaud 179
Vreeland, Shannon 1465
フリーリ
Freely, John 459
ブリーリー
Brealey, Richard A. 178
ブリリアント
Brilliant, Jennifer 182
フリーリング
Freeling, Nicolas 459
ブリリンスキー
Brylinsky, Cynthia M. 196
フリール
Freel, Ryan 459
Friel, Brian 463
Friel, Howard 463
Friel, John C. 463
Friel, Linda D. 463
Friel, Thomas J. 463
ブリル
Brill, Howard 182
Brill, Marlene Targ 182
ブリルアン
Brillouin, Léon 182
プリルコフ
Prilukov, Yuri 1135
ブリルメイアー
Brielmaier, Bret 182
プリレポフ
Prilepov, Anton 1135
プリワロワ
Privalova, Alexandra 1136
フリン
Flindt, Flemming 443
Flinn, Alex 443
Flinn, Kathleen 443
Flynn, Anthony 445
Flynn, Brian 445
Flynn, Brian J. 445
Flynn, Christine 445
Flynn, Dennis Owen 445
Flynn, Don 445
Flynn, Gillian 445
Flynn, Hal 445
Flynn, James Robert 445
Flynn, Kevin 445
Flynn, Laura 445
Flynn, Matt 445
Flynn, Michael F. 445
Flynn, Nick 445
Flynn, Noriko 445
Flynn, Robert M. 445
Flynn, Vince 445
ブーリン
Boulin, Jean-Yves 167
ブリーン
Breen, Bill 179
Breen, John 179
Breen, Jon L. 179
ブリン
Blinn, Bruce 149
Brin, David 182
Brin, Sergey 183
Bryhn, Ole Kristian 196
Vulin, Aleksandar 1465
プリーン
Prien, Gunther 1135
プリン
Pullin, Jorge 1139
フリンカ
Hlinka, Ivan 610
ブリンカー
Brinker (wenzel), Christine 183
Brinker, Wade O. 183
ブリンカット
Brincat, Leo 183
ブリンク
Brink, André Philippus 183
Brink, Derek 183
Brink, Gerrit Jan van den 183
Brink, H.M.van den 183
Brink, Jan 183
Brink, Julius 183
Brink, Satya 183
プリング
Pring, Linda 1135
Pring, Roger 1135
プリングスハイム
Pringsheim, Klaus H. 1136
ブリンクボイマー
Brinkbäumer, Klaus 183
ブリンクホルスト
Brinkhorst, Laurens-Jan 183
ブリンクマン
Brinckmann, Hans 183
Brinkman, Rick 183
ブリンクリ
Brinkley, Alan 183
ブリンクリー
Brinkley, Beau 183
Brinkley, Dannion 183
Brinkley, David 183
Brinkley, Douglas 183
Brinkley, Jasper 183
Brinkley, Joel 183
Brinkley, Kathryn 183
プリングル
Pringle, Colombe 1135
Pringle, David 1135
Pringle, Heather Anne 1135
ブリンケビチウテ
Blinkevičiūtė, Vilija 149
ブリンケーホフ
Brinkerhoff, Ron L. 183
ブリンコウ
Blincoe, Nicholas 149
プリンシピ
Principi, Anthony 1135
プリンジャー
Pullinger, Kate 1139
プリンス
Prince 1135
Prince, Alan 1135
Prince, Alison 1135
Prince, Charles O. Ⅲ 1135
Prince, Clive 1135
Prince, George M. 1135
Prince, Gerald 1135
Prince, Harold 1135
Prince, Jane 1135
Prince, Jefferson 1135
Prince, Jonathan 1135
Prince, Russ Alan 1135
Prince, St.Clair 1135
Prince, Taurean 1135
Prince, Tom 1135
Prins, Nomi 1136
ブリンスター
Brinster, Ralph L. 183
プリンス・ロベール
Prince Robert 1187
ブリンソン
Brinson, Lewis 183
フリンタム
Flintham, Thomas 443
プリンチペ
Principe, Lawrence M. 1135
プリンツ
Prinz, Alfred 1136
Prinz, Jesse J. 1136
Prinz, Peter 1136
Prinz, Steven M. 1136
プリンツラー
Prinzler, Hans Helmut 1136
フリント
Flindt, Flemming 443
Flindt, Rainer 443
Flint, Anthony 443
Flint, Colin 443
Flint, Garry A. 443
ブリント
Blind, Daley 149
プリント
Print, Bobbie 1136
フリントワ
Frintova, Vendula 464
フリントン
Fullington, John 467
ブリントン
Brinton, Laurel J. 183
Brinton, Mary C. 183
ブリンナー
Brynner, Rock 196
プリンプトン
Plimpton, George 1118
Plympton, Bill 1119
ブリンブルコーム
Brimblecombe, Nicola 182
ブリンブルコム
Brimblecombe, Peter 182
ブリンヨルフソン
Brynjolfsson, John B. 196
フールー
Fouroux, Jacques 452
フル
Hure, Ismail Mohamed 637
フルー
Flew, Terry 443
Flu, Melvin Brand 444
Fouroux, Jacques 452
ブール
Boer, Diederik 153
Boer, Esther de 153
Bour, Danièle 167
Bour, Laura 168
Bourg, Dominique 168
Bourre, Martine 168
Buhr, Manfred 200
ブールー
Beaulieu, Alan 110
ブル
Brou, Jean-Claude 187
Bull, Adam 200
Bull, Alyssa 200
Bull, Andy 200
Bull, David 200
Bull, George Anthony 200
Bull, Jane 200
Bull, Ray 200
ブルー
BLU 150
Blue, Alfred 150
Blue, Anthony Dias 150
Blue, Lucy 150
Blue, Sarah 150
Brew, Derrick 181
Brout, Robert 188
プール
Pool, Jackie 1124
Pool, Mic 1124
Pool, Robert 1124
Pool, Sylvette 1124
Poole, Brian 1124
Poole, Hilary 1124
Poole, Jack 1124

フ

Poole, Josephine 1124
Poole, Regan 1124
Poole, Richard A. 1124
Poole, Sara 1124
Poole, Terry 1124
プル
Pull, C. 1139
Pulu, Isileli 1139
プルー
Proulx, Annie 1137
ブルーアー
Brewer, Derek 181
Brewer, John 181
ブルア
Bloor, Michael 150
プルアイッチ
Pruaitch, Patrick 1138
ブルイギナ
Bulygina, Anna 201
プルイザー
Pruyser, Paul W. 1138
プルィス
Plewis, Ian 1118
プルイゼ
Pruidze, Giorgi 1138
プルーイット
Pruitt, Austin 1138
ブルーイット
Pruitt, Gary 1138
Pruitt, John 1138
Pruitt, William Obadiah 1138
プルイット
Pruitt, Gary 1138
フルーイン
Fruin, W.Mark 465
ブルーイン
Bruhin, Ursula 193
ブルウ
Bleou, Martin 148
プルーヴ
Proeve, Michael 1136
プルーヴォ
Prouvost, Laure 1137
ブルーウン
Bruen, Ken 193
プルエ
Pruett, M.K. 1138
フルエリン
Flewelling, Lynn 443
フルーカー
Fluker, D.J. 444
ブルカ
Bulka, Dov 200
Burka, Gelete 203
Burka, Jane B. 203
ブルガー
Boulger, Carolyn 167
Brugger, Nathalie 193
Burger, Adolf 203
ブルガダ
Brugada, Josep 193
Brugada, Pedro 193
Brugada, Ramón 193
フールカデ
Fourcade, Martin 452
フルカネリ
Fulcanelli 467
フルガム
Fulghum, Hunter Samuel 467
Fulghum, Robert 467
ブルガラキス
Voulgarakis, Georgios 1464
ブルガリ
Bulgari, Nicola 200
Bulgari, Paolo 200
プルガル
Pulgar, Erick 1139
ブルカルテール
Burkhalter, Didier 204
ブルカルテル
Burkhalter, Didier 204
ブルカルト
Burkart, Erika 203
プルガルビダル
Pulgar-vidal, Manuel 1139
ブルガン
Bourgain, Catherine 168
Bourgain, Jean 168
Bourgain, Mickael 168
ブルギ
Burgui 203
フルキエ
Foulquier, Dimitri 452
ブルキッチ
Brkic, Courtney Angela 184
ブルギニョン
Bourguignon, François 168
Bourguignon, Jean-Pierre 168
Bourguignon, Laurence 168
ブールキン
Bourquin, Tim 168
フルーク
Fluke, Joanne 444
ブルーク
Brooke, Elisabeth 186
ブルグ
Burg, Sarah Emmanuelle 203
ブルークス
Broocks, Rice 186
Brooks, John C. 187
Brooks, Lynne M. 187
プルークス
Proulx, Gregory A. 1137
プルグチエワ
Plugtschieva, Meglena 1118
ブルクネル
Brukner, Josef 194
ブルクハルト
Burkhard, Gudrun 204
Burkhardt, Franziska 204
プルーグフェルダー
Pflugfelder, Gregory 1106
ブルーグマン
Brueggeman, William B. 193
Brueggemann, William G. 193
ブルグマン
Brugman, Gaston 193
フルケ
Fourquet, Francois 452
ブルケ
Bourque, Francois 168
Bulcke, Paul 200
ブルゲ
Bürge, Elisabeth 203
ブルケニヤ
Burkenya, Daniil Sergeyevich 204
ブルケルト
Burkert, Walter 204
ブルゴ
Burgo, Andrés 203
Burgo, Carlos Augusto Duarte 203
ブルゴアン
Bourgoing, Pascale de 168
ブルゴス
Burgos, Ana 203
Burgos, Jorge 203
Burgos Ortiz, Lely Berlitt 203
フルゴタ
Hrgota, Branimir 629
フルゴーニ
Frugoni, Chiara 465
ブルコフ
Vâlcov, Darius 1438
ブルゴワン
Bourgoin, Louise 168
Bourgoing, Jacqueline 168
フルザ
Flouzat, Denise 444
ブルザ
Bourzat, Fabian 168
プルサック
Prusak, Laurence 1138
ブルサット
Brusatte, Stephen 195
ブルサール
Broussard, Philippe 188
ブルザン
Burzan, Dragisa 207
ブルシ
Blushi, Ben 151
ブルシア
Bruscia, Kenneth E. 195
フルシアンテ
Frusciante, John 465
ブルジェール
Brugère, Fabienne 193
ブルジェーワ
Brzechwa, Christina 196
プルシェンコ
Plushenko, Evgenii 1119
Plyushchenko, Evgeny 1119
ブルシーク
Brusík, Martin 195
フルシチョフ
Khrushchev, Sergei 729
プルシナー
Prusiner, Stanley Ben 1138
プルジナー
Prusiner, Stanley Ben 1138
フルシャ
Hrusa, Jakub 629
ブルジャ
Bourgeat, Pierrick 168
ブルジャイレ
Buryaile, Ricardo 207
ブルジャナゼ
Burjanadze, Nino 203
ブールジャン
Bourgin, Thomas 168
フルシュカ
Hruschka, Peter 629
フルシュデヤン
Khurshudyan, Hripsime 729
ブルジョ
Bourgeau, Vincent 168
ブルジョア
Bourgeois, L.J., Ⅲ 168
Bourgeois, Louise 168
ブルジョワ
Bourgeois, Louise 168
ブルジョン・ド・ラヴェルニェ
Brejon de Lavergnee, Arnauld 179
ブルジン
Bourgin, Thomas 168
フルス
Hulse, Melvin 634
ブールス
Bource, Ludovic 168
ブルース
Bluth, Toby 151
Breus, Michael 181
Bruce, Alex 193
Bruce, Alexandra 193
Bruce, Anne 193
Bruce, Colin 193
Bruce, Jack 193
Bruce, Jay 193
Bruce, Robert Bowman 193
Bruice, Paula Yurkanis 193
Bruse, Claudius 195
ブルス
Brousse, Michel 188
Brus, Erik 195
ブルスィヒ
Brussig, Thomas 195
プルスカベツ
Prskavec, Jiri 1138
ブルスカンティーニ
Bruscantini, Sesto 195
ブルスキ
Bruschi, Arnaldo 195
ブルースタ
Brustad, Sylvia 195
Brustad, Sylvia Kristin 195
ブルースター
Brewster, Bill 181
Brewster, Jean 181
Brewster, Mike 181
Brewster, Susan 181
ブルースタイン
Blustein, Paul 151
フルスタレワ
Khrustaleva, Elena 729
フルスト
Fulst, Guido 467
Hurst, Paul J. 637
ブルースト
Brust, Steven 195
ブルース＝ミットフォード
Bruce-Mitford, Miranda 193
ブルセ
Bresset, Julie 180
Bruce, Carlos 193
プルセ
Prce, Franjo 1132
ブルセイエ
Bourseiller, Philippe 168
ブルーセヴィッツ
Brusewitz, Gunnar 195
フルゼッティ

Fruzzetti, Alan E. 465
フルセッヘ
Hulsegge, Jan 634
フルセン
Hulsen, Esther van 634
フルセンコ
Fursenko, Andrei A. 468
ブルーソー
Brousseau, Kenneth R. 188
Brusaw, Charles T. 195
プールソン
Poulsson, Tina Grette 1128
フルダ
Fulda, Hans Friedrich 467
ブルーダー
Bruder, Melissa 193
ブルータス
Brutus, Dennis 195
Brutus, Lamarcus 195
ブルタン
Broutin, Christian 188
フルチェ
Furche, Carlos 468
プルーチェク
Pluchek, Valentin Nikolaevich 1118
プルチェク
Pluchek, Valentin Nikolaevich 1118
ブルチエリ
Burchielli, Riccardo 202
ブルチカ
Burcica, Constanta 202
ブルチス
Broutsis, Giannis 188
フルーチト
Fruechte, Isaac 465
ブルチャ
Burcea, Stelian 202
ブルチャン
Bručan, Andrej 193
プルチョウ
Plutschow, Herbert E. 1119
プルチョワ
Plutschow, Herbert E. 1119
フルツ
Fultz, Markelle 468
ブルツ
Wurz, Alex 1530
プルツェル・トーマス
Pruetzel-Thomas, Anna 1138
ブルツォシュテク
Brzostek, Tomasz 196
ブルッカー
Brooker, Christine 186
Brooker, Dawn 186
Brooker, Gary 186
Brooker, Peter 186
フルッキガー
Fluckiger, Mathias 444
Flueckiger, Peter 444
ブルッキンズ
Brookins, Dana 186
フルック
Flook, Richard 443
Fluck, Gabi 444
ブルック
Brook, George J. 186
Brook, Jennifer H. 186
Brook, Judy 186
Brook, Peter 186
Brook, Stephen 186
Brook, Timothy 186
Brook, Tony 186
Brooke, Christina 186
Brooke, Christopher 186
Brooke, Edward William 186
Brooke, John Hedley 186
Brooke, Lauren 186
Brooke, Paul 186
Brooke, Thomas Sears 186
Bruch, Heike 193
Bruch, Michael 193
Bruck, Anthony 193
プルックサコーン
Prucksakorn, Tanyaporn 1138
ブルックス
Brookes, Adam 186
Brookes, John 186
Brookes, Jon 186
Brookes, Kieran 186
Brookes, Olivia 186
Brooks, Aaron 186
Brooks, Adam 186
Brooks, Ahmad 186
Brooks, Al 186
Brooks, Albert 186
Brooks, Brandon 186
Brooks, Cariel 186
Brooks, Chris 186
Brooks, Christopher 186
Brooks, Cyrus Harry 186
Brooks, David 187
Brooks, David B. 187
Brooks, Derrick 187
Brooks, Dillon 187
Brooks, Douglas 187
Brooks, Felicity 187
Brooks, Frederick Phillips, Jr. 187
Brooks, Garth 187
Brooks, Geraldine 187
Brooks, Greg 187
Brooks, Hadda 187
Brooks, Helen 187
Brooks, Herb 187
Brooks, James L. 187
Brooks, Jerome Edmund 187
Brooks, John 187
Brooks, Joseph 187
Brooks, Kevin 187
Brooks, Martha 187
Brooks, Max 187
Brooks, Mel 187
Brooks, Michael 187
Brooks, Nick 187
Brooks, Peter 187
Brooks, Rand 187
Brooks, Robert B. 187
Brooks, Rodney Allen 187
Brooks, Ron 187
Brooks, Scott 187
Brooks, Stephen G. 187
Brooks, Susie 187
Brooks, Terrence 187
Brooks, Terry 187
Brooks, Zac 187
ブルックスビー
Brooksby, Carl 187
ブルックナー
Brookner, Anita 186
ブルックフィールド
Brookfield, Karen 186
ブルックマイア
Brookmyre, Christopher 186
ブルック＝マルシニアック
Brook, Beth 186
ブルック・ローズ
Brooke-Rose, Christine 186
ブルック＝ローズ
Brooke-Rose, Christine 186
ブルッゲマン
Brueggemann, Walter 193
ブルッゲル
Brøgger, Fredrik Christian 185
ブルッコリ
Bruccoli, Matthew Joseph 193
フルッサー
Flusser, David 445
ブルッサール
Broussard, Robert 188
ブルッシーノ
Brussino, Nicolas 195
プルッセ
Prusse, Daniela 1138
ブルッツェーゼ
Bruzzese, Sebastien 195
プルット
Pruett, Michael H. 1138
ブルッフフェルド
Bruchfeld, Stephane 193
フルティ
Huszti, Szabolcs 639
ブルディ
Bourdy, Gregory 168
フルティガー
Frutiger, Adrian 465
ブルディッソ
Burdisso, Nicolas 202
ブルディナツ
Bouloudinats, Chouaib 167
ブルデュー
Bourdieu, Pierre 168
プルデル
Prudel, Mariusz 1138
プルーデルマッハー
Pludermacher, Georges 1118
ブルテン
Brittain, William 184
ブルデンコ
Burdenko, Roman 202
プルデンシオ
Prudencio, Claudine 1138
フルート
Fruth, Eduard 465
フルド
Fuld, Richard S., Jr. 467
ブルト
Blute, Vicent 151
Bulut, Gamze 201
Bulut, Onur 201
Woerth, Eric 1520
プルート
Pruitt, George 1138
フルトゥ
Fourtou, Jean-René 452
プルドゥニコバス
Prudnikovas, Vladimiras 1138
フルトゥル
Flutur, Cristina 445
Flutur, Gheorghe 445
フルトクビスト
Hultqvist, Peter 634
ブルートマン
Bluttman, Ken 151
プルドーム
Prud'homme, Alex 1138
プルドム
Purdom, Vivianne 1140
プルードラ
Pludra, Benno 1118
ブルドリャク
Vrdoljak, Ivan 1465
フルトン
Fulton, Charlie 467
Fulton, Hal Edwin 467
Fulton, Jay 467
Fulton, Jeff 467
Fulton, Steve 467
Fulton, Zach 468
ブルートン
Brueton, Diana 193
Bruton, David 195
Bruton, John Gerard 195
Bruton, Richard 195
Bruton, Stephen 195
ブルトン
Breton, Auguste le 180
Breton, Thierry 180
Burton, Mark 206
プルードン
Prudon, Theodore H. M. 1138
ブルーナ
Bruna, Dick 194
ブルーナー
Bruner, Edward M. 194
Bruner, Jerome 194
Bruner, Kurt D. 194
Bruner, Olivia 194
ブルナー
Bruner, Robert F. 194
Brunner, David J. 194
プルナ
Prună, Raluca Alexandra 1138
ブルナビッチ
Brnabić, Ana 184
ブルーニ
Bruni, Carla 194
Bruni, Sergio 194
ブルニ
Bruni, Rachele 194
プルニー
Plný, Luboš 1118
ブルニアス
Brunious, John 194
フルニエ
Fournier, Helene 452
Fournier, Jean-Louis 452
ブルニエ
Burnier, Arno 205
ブルニェッティ
Brugnetti, Ivano 193
プルニエール
Prunier, James 1138
フルニエ＝ロッセ
Fournier-Rosset, Jany 452
フルニーク
Hurník, Ilja 637

フ

ブルニッチ
Burnic, Dzenis 205
ブルニフィエ
Brenifier, Oscar 180
ブルーニング
Breuning, Walter 181
Bruning, John R. 194
ブルヌティアン
Bournoutian, George A. 168
ブールヌトン
Bourneton, Dorine 168
フルネ
Fournet, Jean 452
ブルネ
Brunet, Manon 194
Brunet, Marie Laure 194
プルネ
Purne, Iveta 1140
フルーネウォルト
Groenewold, Renate 538
ブルネーズ
Brenez, Nicole 179
ブルネス
Bulnes, Felipe 201
ブルネッタ
Brunetta, Gian Piero 194
Brunetta, Leslie 194
Brunetta, Renato 194
ブルネッティ
Brunetti, Argentina 194
ブルネット
Brunet, Caroline 194
ブルネティ
Brunetti, Argentina 194
ブルネリ
Brunelli, Roberto 194
ブルネロ
Brunello, Mario 194
フルネロン
Fourneyron, Valérie 452
プールネン
Puurunen, Paavo 1141
フルノ
Furno, Joshua 468
ブルーノ
Bruno, A.Anthony 194
Bruno, Alessandro 194
Bruno, Dave 194
Bruno, Ferrero 194
Bruno, Gonzalez 194
Bruno, Josh 194
Bruno, Kimberley M. 194
Bruno, Luca 194
Bruno, Marco 194
Bruno, Soriano 194
ブルーノ・アルヴェス
Bruno Alves 194
ブルーノ・エンリケ
Bruno Henrique 194
ブルーノ・ガマ
Bruno Gama 194
ブルーノ・セーザル
Bruno Cesar 194
ブルーノ・パウリスタ
Bruno Paulista 194
ブルーノ・フェルナンデス
Bruno Fernandes 194
ブルーノ・ペレス
Bruno Peres 194
プルノモ
Purnomo, Yusgiantoro 1140
ブルノン
Brenon, Anne 180
ブルバキ
Bourbaki, Nicolas 168
ブルバノフ
Vurbanov, Ventsislav 1465
ブルハン
Bourhan, Hassan Omar Mohamed 168
ブルハンフセイン
Boulhan Houssein, Nimo 167
フルービー
Hrubý, Pavel 629
フルビマーリ
Fulvimari, Jeffrey 468
ブルヒャルト
Burchard, Doris 202
フルヒュルスト
Verhulst, Adriaan E. 1452
プルーフ
Plouffe, Trevor 1118
Proof 1137
ブルフィー
Bruffy, Charles 193
フルフォード
Fulford, Benjamin 467
Fulford, K.W.M. 467
ブルーフォード
Bruford, Bill 193
フルーフト
Vlugt, Ron van der 1461
ブルブリス
Burbulis, Gennadii Eduardovich 202
フルブルック
Fulbrook, Mary 467
フルブロック
Fulbrook, Mary 467
ブルーベイカー
Brubaker, Rogers 193
ブルベイカー
Brubaker, Ed 193
ブルペスク
Vulpescu, Ioan 1465
ブルーベック
Brubeck, Dave 193
フルベット
Chrbet, Ján 260
ブールペープ
Boulpaep, Emile L. 167
ブルボー
Bourbeau, Lise 168
フルマー
Fulmer, Carson 467
Fulmer, David 467
Fulmer, Michael 467
Fulmer, Terry T. 467
ブルマ
Bruma, Jeffrey 194
Buruma, Ian 207
フルマナビチウス
Furmanavičius, Gintaras 468
フールマン
Fuhrmann, Geri S.W. 466
フルマン
Fullman, Joe 467
ブールマン
Buhlman, William L. 200
Bühlmann, Walbert 200
ブルマーン
Bulmahn, Edelgard 201
プルマン
Pullman, Philip 1139
ブルミッヒ
Brummig, Volker 194
フールム
Hurum, Jørn H. 638
フルーム
Froom, Richard 465
Froome, Christopher 465
フルム
Flum, Johannes 444
ブルーム
Bloom, Alexander 150
Bloom, Alfred 150
Bloom, Amy 150
Bloom, Barbara 150
Bloom, Cameron 150
Bloom, Claire 150
Bloom, Floyd E. 150
Bloom, Harold 150
Bloom, Jeremy 150
Bloom, Jerry 150
Bloom, Jonathan M. 150
Bloom, Lary 150
Bloom, Mark 150
Bloom, Orlando 150
Bloom, Paul 150
Bloom, Paul N. 150
Bloom, Steve 150
Bloom, Valerie 150
Bloom, William 150
Bloome, Indigo 150
Bluhm, Christian 150
Blum, Andrew 150
Blum, Ulrich 150
Blume, Arthur W. 150
Blume, Judy 150
Blume, Lesley M.M. 151
Broohm, Octave Nicoué 186
Broom, Glen M. 187
Broom, Jenny 187
Broom, Neil 187
Broome, Lissa Lamkin 187
Vroom, Victor 1465
ブルム
Bbum, Jon 109
Blum, Richard 150
Blum, William 150
プルーム
Plume, Ilse 1118
ブルムクビスト
Blomkvist, Johan 149
ブルムズ
Broms, Anders 186
ブルームバーグ
Bloomberg, Michael Rubens 150
ブルームフィールド
Bloomfield, Barbara 150
Bloomfield, Harold H. 150
Bloomfield, Paul 150
Bloomfield, Paula 150
Bloomfield, Steve 150
ブルムラー
Blumler, Jay G. 151
ブルーメ
Brume, Ese 194
ブルメ
Blume, Pernille 151
ブルメー
Broomé, Per 187
ブルメスター
Burmester, Geld-Rüdiger 204
ブルメリ
Brumel, Valery Nikolaevich 194
ブルメル
Brumel, Valery Nikolaevich 194
フルーメン
Vroemen, Simon 1465
ブルーメンクローン
Blumencron, Maria 151
ブルーメンシュタイン
Blumenstein, Lars 151
ブルーメンソール
Blumenthal, Brett 151
ブルーメンタール
Blumenthal, Karen 151
ブルメンタール
Blumenthal, Neil 151
ブルーメンフィールド
Blumenfield, Michael 151
ブルーメンフェルト
Blumenfeld, Hal 151
ブルメンフェルド
Blumenfeld, Laura 151
ブルモア
Bullmore, Jeremy 201
プルモハンマディ
Pour-mohammadi, Mostafa 1128
フルラ
Frulla, Liza 465
ブルラツキー
Burlatsky, Fedor Mikhailovich 204
ブルラーツキイ
Burlatsky, Fedor Mikhailovich 204
フルラネット
Furlanetto, Ferruccio 468
Furlanetto, Giovanna 468
ブル・ラモス
Bull Ramos 201
フルラン
Furlan, Luiz Fernando 468
フルーリ
Fluri, Philipp 445
フルーリー
Floury, Marie-France 444
Flury, Dieter 445
ブルリッチ
Bullrich, Esteban 201
Bullrich, Patricia 201
プルリッチ
Prlić, Jadranko 1136
ブルリューク・ホルト
Burliuk Holt, Mary Clare 204
フルール
Fluhr, Joachim 444
ブルールセン
Broersen, Nadine 185
ブールレス
Bourlès, Jean-Claude 168
ブルレネ
Bleu-lainé, Gilbert 148
フルーレン
Fluellen, David 444
フルレンゾス
Flourentzos, Efthymios 444
ブルロック
Bullock, Reggie 201
ブルーワ

フ

Brewer, Derek 181
ブルーワー
Brewer, Duncan 181
Brewer, Gay 181
Brewer, Gene 181
Brewer, Jeannie 181
Brewer, John 181
Brewer, Leo 181
Brewer, Sarah 181
ブルワー
Brewer, Derek 181
Brewer, Gay 181
ブルーン
Bruun, Bertel 195
Bruun, Erik 195
Bruun, Frank Jarle 195
Bruun, Ruth Dowling 195
Bruun, Staffan 195
ブルン
Brun, Kristoffer 194
ブルンクホルスト
Brunkhorst, Hauke 194
ブルンケット
Brunkert, Ola 194
フルンザベルデ
Frunzăverde, Sorin 465
ブルンシュ
Bruns, Adela 195
ブルーンス
Bruhns, Nina 193
Bruhns, Wibke 193
ブルンスウィック
Brunswic, Étienne 195
プルンスキエネ
Prunskienė, Kazimira 1138
ブルンツェル
Brunzel, Nancy A. 195
ブルントラン
Brundtland, Gro Harlem 194
ブルントラント
Brundtland, Gro Harlem 194
ブルンナー
Brunner, Bernd 194
Brunner, Henri 194
プルンブ
Plumb, Rovana 1118
ブルンリー
Brun-lie, Celine 194
ブーレ
Beuret, Michel 134
Boere, Jeroen 153
Boulet, Benoit 167
ブーレー
Boulay, Jacques 167
ブレ
Blais, Marie-Claire 145
Boulet, Gwenaëlle 167
Bule, James 200
Bure, Pavel 202
プーレ
Poulet, Gerard 1128
プレ
Pre, Sinfeitcheou 1132
Pule, Dina Deliwe 1139
フレア
Flea 441
Frare, Michela 457
Freer, Amelia 460
フレアー
Flair, Reid 441
Flair, Ric 441
ブレア
Blair, Aaron 145
Blair, Annette 145
Blair, Cherie 145
Blair, DeJuan 145
Blair, Dennis 145
Blair, Faye A. 145
Blair, Forbes Robbins 145
Blair, Gary Ryan 145
Blair, James 145
Blair, James P. 145
Blair, Janet 145
Blair, Karina 145
Blair, Linda 145
Blair, Mark 145
Blair, Paul L.D. 145
Blair, Richard 145
Blair, Sara 145
Blair, Sheila 145
Blair, Tony 145
ブレアー
Blair, Margaret M. 145
Blair, Ronald 145
プレア
Pleah, Natié 1118
ブレアース
Lord Blears 148
フレアティ
Flaherty, James Michael 441
フレアリー
Frary, Mark 457
ブレアリー
Brealey, Erica 178
フレイ
Frei, David 460
Frei, Eduardo 460
Frei, Frances 460
Frey, Bruce 462
Frey, Charles H. 462
Frey, Darcy 462
Frey, Isaiah 462
Frey, James 462
Frey, Karl-Richard 462
Frey, Lonny 462
Frey, Nicolas 462
ブーレイ
Boulay, Olivier 167
ブレイ
Blay, Charlotte 148
Bley, Paul 148
Blij, Harm de 149
Bray, Adam 178
Bray, Alan 178
Bray, Dennis 178
Bray, Francesca 178
Bray, Ken 178
Bray, Mark 178
Bray, Quan 178
Bray, Tyler 178
ブレイヴァー
Braver, Adam 178
フレイヴィン
Flavin, Christopher 441
フレイカー
Fraker, William Ashman 454
ブレイカー
Braiker, Harriet B. 175
フレイグ
Fleig, Dieter 442
ブレイク
Blake, Ally 145
Blake, Andrea 145
Blake, Andrew 145
Blake, Antwon 145
Blake, David 145
Blake, Donal S. 146
Blake, James 146
Blake, James Carlos 146
Blake, Jennifer 146
Blake, Jenny 146
Blake, Jillian 146
Blake, John 146
Blake, Jon 146
Blake, Joy 146
Blake, Lily 146
Blake, Mark 146
Blake, Maya 146
Blake, Melissa 146
Blake, Michael 146
Blake, Peter 146
Blake, Peter G. 146
Blake, Quentin Saxby 146
Blake, Rich 146
Blake, Robert R. 146
Blake, Russell 146
Blake, Stephanie 146
Blake, Stephen 146
Blake, Stephen P. 146
Blake, Susannah 146
Blake, Tchad 146
Blake, Toni 146
Blake, Yohan 146
ブレイク卿
Blake, Peter 146
フレイクス
Frakes, Mary H. 454
ブレイクスリー
Blakeslee, Matthew 146
Blakeslee, Sandra 146
ブレイクナム
Blakenham, Michael 146
ブレイクニー
Blakeney, Issac 146
ブレイクモー
Blakemore, Michael 146
ブレイクモア
Blakemore, Sarah-Jayne 146
ブレイクリー
Blakely, Sara 146
ブレイクリー・カートライト
Blakley-Cartwright, Sarah 146
フレイザー
Fraizer, Colin 454
Fraser, Alison 457
Fraser, Andy 457
Fraser, Antonia Pakenham 457
Fraser, Arvonne S. 457
Fraser, Brendan 457
Fraser, Bruce 457
Fraser, Campbell 458
Fraser, Douglas Andrew 458
Fraser, Evan D.G. 458
Fraser, Flora 458
Fraser, Jill Andresky 458
Fraser, Karen Riese 458
Fraser, Malcolm 458
Fraser, Mark W. 458
Fraser, Mary Ann 458
Fraser, Nancy 458
Fraser, Richard S. 458
Fraser, Romy 458
Fraser, Ryan 458
Frasier, Lori D. 458
Frazer, Dan 458
Frazer, Ian 458
Frazier, Joe 458
Frazier, John 458
ブレイザー
Blaser, Don 147
Blaser, Martin J. 147
Blaser, Susan I. 147
プレイサー
Prather, Hugh 1132
フレイジ
al-Freij, Fahd Jassem 461
フレイジー
Frazee, Marla 458
フレイジアー
Frazier, Kavon 458
Frazier, Mose 458
プレイジア
Plazier, Mark 1118
フレイジェル
Fragel, Reid 454
フレイジャー
Frasier, Anne 458
Frasier, Debra 458
Frazier, Adam 458
Frazier, Amy 458
Frazier, Charles 458
Frazier, Clint 458
Frazier, Joe 458
Frazier, Tim 458
Frazier, Todd 458
ブレイシャー
Brashear, Jean 177
Brasher, Chris 177
ブレイジャ
Brazier, Chris 178
ブレイジャー
Brashear, Jean 177
Brasier, M.D. 177
Brazier, Caroline 178
Brazier, David 178
フレイズ
Frase, H.Michael 457
ブレイズ
Blades, Rubén 145
ブレイスウェイト
Braithwaite, Doug 175
Braithwaite, Dougie 175
Braithwaite, Jeffrey 175
Braithwaite, John 175
Braithwaite, Kent 175
Braithwaite, Victoria 175
フレイスタット
Fraistat, Neil 454
フレイスネロバ
Fleissnerova, Kristyna 442
フレイセ
Vrijsen, Ellen 1465
ブレイゼック
Blazek, Michael 148
ブレイゼル
Brazell, Bennie 178
フレイター
Frater, Joel 458
ブレイター
Breiter, Paul 179
プレイター
Prater, John 1132
フレイタス
Freitas, Acelino 461
Freitas, Bendito 461
Freitas, Marcos 461
Freitas, Patricia 461
フレイタスダシルバ
Freitas Da Silva, Edson

フ

Isaias 461
プレイター＝ピニー
Pretor-Pinney, Gavin 1133
フレイディ
Frady, Marshall 454
ブレイディ
Brady, Henry E. 174
Brady, James S. 174
Brady, Shelly 174
Brady, Tom 174
Brady, William J. 174
ブレイディー
Brady, Frank 174
Brady, Tom 174
フレイテス
Fréitez, Lorena 461
ブレイデン
Braden, Dallas 173
Braden, Gregg 173
Braden, Vic 173
フレイド
Flade, Becky 440
Freyd, Jennifer J. 462
ブレイト
Brate, Cameron 177
ブレイド
Braid, Connor 175
Braid, Kate 175
プレイト
Plait, Philip C. 1117
プレイトー
Prato, Rodica 1132
ブレイトマン
Breitman, Patti 179
フレイドント
Freydont, Shelley 462
ブレイナ
Branagh, Nicole 175
ブレイナー
Breiner, Mark A. 179
ブレイナード
Brainard, Lael 175
ブレイニー
Blaney, Steven 147
ブレイバーマン
Braverman, Daniel 178
Braverman, Eric R. 178
フレイバルス
Freivalds, Laila 461
フレイハン
Fleihan, Basel 442
フレイビン
Flavin, Christopher 441
ブレイベン
Brayben, Katie 178
ブレイホバ
Brejchová (tomeckova), Nikola 179
フレイマン・ウェア
Freymann-Weyr, Garret 462
フレイマン＝ウェア
Weyr, Garret 1496
フレイム
Flaim, Denise 441
Frame, Janet 454
ブレイム
Braim, Joly 175
ブレイモファット
Bray-Moffat, Naia 178
フレイヤー
Frayer, David W. 458
Freyer, John D. 462
ブレイヤー
Breyer, Jim 181
プレイヤー
Player, Gary 1117
フレイリー
Frailey, Dennis J. 454
フレイリング
Frayling, Christopher 458
フレイレ
Freire, Nelson 461
Freire, Roberto 461
ブレイロック
Blaylock, James P. 148
フレイン
Frayn, Michael 458
Frayn, Rebecca 458
Frayne, Henry 458
ブレイン
Blane, Davis 147
Brain, Archie I.J. 175
Brain, C.K. 175
Brain, Marshall 175
ブレインホルスト
Breinholst, Willy 179
プレーヴァ
Plewa, Martin 1118
ブレヴァートン
Breverton, Terry 181
プレヴァル
Préval, René Garcia 1134
プレヴィット
Previto, Robert 1134
プレヴィン
Previn, André George 1134
プレーヴェ
Pleve, I.R. 1118
Pröve, Ralf 1137
プレヴォ
Prévot, Franck 1134
プレヴォー
Prévost, Guillaume 1134
プレヴォスト
Prevost, Greg 1134
プレヴォタ
Prévotat, Jacques 1134
プレヴネリエフ
Plevneliev, Rosen Asenov 1118
ブレオー
Breault, William 178
プレオ
Puleo, Joe 1139
プレオブラジェンスカヤ
Preobrazhenskaya, Natalya E. 1133
フレーカー
Fraker, Benn 454
Fraker, William Ashman 454
フレガ
Frega, Muriel 460
ブレーガー
Braegger, Pablo 174
Breger, Louis 179
Breger, Rosemary Anne 179
ブレガ
Brega, Gheorghe 179
プレガー
Prager, Dennis 1131
プレカス
Plecas, Jennifer 1118
プレガルディエン
Prégardien, Christoph 1132
ブレカロ
Brekalo, Josip 179
ブレキリアン
Brékilien, Yann 179
ブレーク
Blake, James 146
Blake, James Carlos 146
Blake, James F. 146
Blake, Jose Francisco 146
Blake, Michael 146
Blake, Peter 146
Blake, Quentin Saxby 146
Blake, Robert Norman William 146
Blake, Yohan 146
ブレグ
Bregu, Majlinda 179
ブレグヴァゼ
Bregvadze, Jaba 179
ブレーク卿
Blake, Peter 146
プレクシャー王女
Princess Preksha 1132
ブレークスリー
Blakeslee, Thomas R. 146
フレクセン
Flexen, Chris 443
プレクター
Prechter, Robert Rougelot, Jr. 1132
ブレークナム
Blakenham, Michael 146
ブレクネ
Brekne, Odd Arne 179
ブレグバッド
Blegvad, Erik 148
ブレグマン
Bregman, Alex 179
Bregman, Peter 179
ブレークリー
Blakely, Edward James 146
ブーレグレーン
Buregren, Sassa 202
ブレーケンリッジ
Breakenridge, Deirdre 178
フレゴ
Flego, Gvozden 442
フレゴシ
Fregosi, Jim 460
プレコップ
Prekop, Jirina 1132
プレコート
Precourt, Geoffrey 1132
フレゴレント
Fregolent, Alessandra 460
フレーザー
Fraser, Andy 457
Fraser, Angus M. 457
Fraser, Brendan 457
Fraser, Douglas Andrew 458
Fraser, George MacDonald 458
Fraser, Gordon 458
Fraser, Lindsey 458
Fraser, Malcolm 458
Fraser, Marcus 458
Fraser, Max 458
Fraser, Robin 458
Fraser, Roderick D. 458
Fraser, Ronald 458
Fraser, Tara 458
Fraser-pryce, Shelly-Ann 458
Frazer, Dan 458
Frazer, Ian 458
フレサー
Fraser, Clare 458
ブレーザー
Blaser, Don 147
フレーザー・プライス
Fraser-pryce, Shelly-Ann 458
フレーザープライス
Fraser-pryce, Shelly-Ann 458
フレーザーホームズ
Fraser-holmes, Thomas 458
フレーザーモレケティ
Fraser-moleketi, Geraldine 458
フレサンジュ
Fressange, Ines de la 461
プレザンス
Pleasence, Pascoe 1118
プレサント
Presant, Seth 1133
ブレシア
Brescia, George 180
プレシアド
Preciado, Antonio 1132
フレシィエ
Fréchet, Jean M.J. 459
フレジェ
Fréger, Charles 460
フレシェット
Fréchette, Louise 459
Freschet, Berniece 461
プレシェット
Pleshette, Suzanne 1118
ブレジェリー
Bregerie, Romain 179
プレジオーシ
Preziosi, Alessandra 1134
ブレジナ
Brezina, Karel 181
フレージャー
Frazier, Joe 458
ブレシャー
Brecher, Paul 178
プレジャー
Pledger, Maurice 1118
プレシャコフ
Pleshakov, Konstantin 1118
フレーシュ
Frèches, Claire 459
Frèches, José 459
ブレーシュ
Brache, Alan P. 173
ブレシュ
Bureš, Jaroslav 203
プレシュ
Pretsch, Ernö 1133
ブレジンスキー
Brzezinski, Matthew 196
Brzezinski, Richard 196
Brzezinski, Zbigniew Kazimierz 196
Brzinski, Matthew 196
ブーレーズ
Boulez, Pierre 167

フ

ブレーズ
Blaise, Zoana 145
Boulez, Pierre 167
Brase, Michael 177
ブレス
Bures, Doris 202
プレス
Pless, Claudia 1118
Press, Frank 1133
Press, Hans Jürgen 1133
Press, Irina 1133
Press, James E. 1133
Press, Julian 1133
プレスイール
Pressouyre, Léon 1133
ブレースウェート
Braithwaite, Rodric 175
プレスカ
Plesca, Valeriu 1118
ブレスク
Bresc-Bautier, Geneviève 180
フレスコ
Fresco, Nadine 461
プレスコット
Prescott, Dak 1133
Prescott, David S. 1133
Prescott, Edward C. 1133
Prescott, John 1133
プレスコッド
Prescod, Nzingha 1133
Prescod, Trevor 1133
フレズティ
Fredsti, Dana 459
プレスティ
Presti, Sam 1133
プレスティジャコモ
Prestigiacomo, Stefania 1133
ブレスデール
Bleasdale, Marcus 148
プレステル
Prestel, Alexander 1133
プレストウィッツ
Prestowitz, Clyde V., Jr. 1133
フレストン
Freston, Tom 461
プレストン
Preston, Billy 1133
Preston, Brian 1133
Preston, Douglas J. 1133
Preston, Fayrene 1133
Preston, Gary A. 1133
Preston, Janice 1133
Preston, John D. 1133
Preston, Katherine 1133
Preston, Marcia K. 1133
Preston, Neal 1133
Preston, Paul 1133
Preston, Paul M. 1133
Preston, Peter 1133
Preston, Richard 1133
プレストン‐サビン
Preston-Sabin, Jennie 1133
プレストン・マフハム
Preston-Mafham, Ken 1133
プレストン＝ワーナー
Preston-werner, Tom 1133
ブレズナ
Brzezna, Paulina 196
ブレスナック
Breathnach, Teresa 178
プレスニエクス
Plesnieks, Arturs 1118
フレズネ
Fresney, Catherine Duboys 461
フレスネダ
Fresneda, Pilar Martinez 461
プレスネル
Pressnell, Forest Charles 1133
フレスノ
Fresno, Juan Francisco 461
プレスフィールド
Pressfield, Steven 1133
プレスブルゲル
Pressburger, Chava 1133
プレスヘジ
Pries-Heje, Jan 1135
ブレスマン
Bleathman, Graham 148
Bresman, Henrik 180
プレスマン
Pressman, Norman 1133
Pressman, Roger S. 1133
ブレスラー
Bresler, Liora 180
Bresler, Siegfried 180
プレスラー
Pressler, Menahem 1133
Pressler, Mirjam 1133
Pressler, Paul S. 1133
プレスランド
Presland, Gary 1133
プレスリー
Presley, Alex 1133
Presley, Cora Ann 1133
Presley, Lisa-Marie 1133
Pressley, Jhurrell 1133
Pressly, Jaime 1133
Pressly, Ryan 1133
ブレスリン
Breslin, Herbert H. 180
Breslin, Theresa 180
ブレスロー
Breslau, Alan Jeffry 180
ブレズロウ
Breslow, Craig 180
フレーゼ
Frese, Erich 461
ブレセ
Bresset, Julie 180
プレセチュニク
Presečnik, Jakob 1133
フレーゼル
Frazelle, Edward 458
フレセル
Flessel-Colovic, Laura 442
プレセル
Pressel, Morgan 1133
フレセル・コロビク
Flessel-Colovic, Laura 442
ブレダウ
Bredau, Ivanhoe 178
フレータス
Freitas, Robert A., Jr. 461
ブレチェク
Bulechek, Gloria M. 200
フレチェット
Fréchette, Carole 459
フレチェロウ
Freccero, Carla 458
ブレチェン
Blechen, Brian 148
プレチコシツ
Pletikosic, Stevan 1118
フレチャー
Fletcher, Susan 443
ブレチャージク
Blecharczyk, Nathan 148
ブレツィナ
Brezina, Thomas 181
ブレツィンカ
Brezinka, Wolfgang 181
ブレツェリ
Brecely, Roman 178
ブレッカー
Brecher, Jeremy 178
Brecher, Max 178
Brecker, Michael 178
Brecker, Randy 178
Broecker, Wallace 185
フレック
Fleck, Béla 441
ブレック
Blech, Benjamin 148
Breck, Peter 178
Brekk, Lars Peder 179
ブレックナー
Brechner, Eric 178
ブレックマン
Blechman, Hardy 148
Blechman, Nicholas 148
Braeckman, Johan 174
ブレッケ
Brekke, Asgeir 179
フレッケンシュタイン
Fleckenstein, William A. 441
プレッサー
Presser, Helmut 1133
ブレッサン
Bressan, Walter 180
プレッシー
Pressey, Phil 1133
プレッジ
Pledge, Robert 1118
ブレッシャン
Breschan, Matthias 180
フレッシュ
Fresh, Bankroll 461
ブレッシュ
Bresch, Heather 180
Buresh, Bernice 203
ブレッシン
Blethyn, Brenda 148
ブレッシング
Vlessing, Monett 1461
プレッセル
Pressel, Morgan 1133
ブレッソ
Brezzo, Luis 181
ブレッソード
Bressoud, David M. 180
フレッソン
Fresson, Bernard 461
ブレッソン
Bredeson, Lenore 178
ブレッチアロリ
Brecciaroli, Stefano 178
フレッチャー
Fletcher, Adlene 442
Fletcher, Ashley 442
Fletcher, Benjamin 442
Fletcher, Brenden 442
Fletcher, Brian 442
Fletcher, Charlie 442
Fletcher, Chris 442
Fletcher, Claire 442
Fletcher, Colin 442
Fletcher, Corina 442
Fletcher, Daisy 442
Fletcher, Darren 442
Fletcher, David 442
Fletcher, Geoffrey 442
Fletcher, Gordon A. 442
Fletcher, Grant S. 442
Fletcher, Hugh L. 442
Fletcher, James 442
Fletcher, James J. 442
Fletcher, Joann 443
Fletcher, Joseph Francis 443
Fletcher, Kate 443
Fletcher, Kingsley A. 443
Fletcher, Lynne 443
Fletcher, Martin 443
Fletcher, Meredith 443
Fletcher, Neville Horner 443
Fletcher, Nichola 443
Fletcher, Ralph 443
Fletcher, Robert H. 443
Fletcher, Ron A. 443
Fletcher, Rosey 443
Fletcher, Seth 443
Fletcher, Susan 443
Fletcher, Suzanne W. 443
Fletcher, Tony 443
Fletcher, William Miles 443
ブレッチャー
Brecher, John 178
ブレッチャッハー
Bletschacher, Richard 148
ブーレッツ
Bouretz, Pierre 168
プレッツェル
Plaetzer, Kjersti 1117
フレット
Flett, Christopher V. 443
ブレット
Barrett, Daniel J. 97
Brett, Jan 180
Brett, Jeanne M. 180
Brett, Ken 180
Brett, Peter V. 180
Brett, Rachel 180
Brett, Regina 180
Brett, Simon 180
ブレット＝サーマン
Brett-Surman, M.K. 180
ブレッドソー
Bledsoe, Eric 148
Bledsoe, Jerry 148
フレッドバーグ
Fredberg, Tobias 459
ブレットン
Bretton, Barbara 180
フレデ
Frode, Lukas 464
フレディ
Freddy, Numberi 459
ブレーディ
Brady, James S. 174
Brady, Tom 174
プレティ
Pretty, Jules N. 1133
プレティヒャ

フ

Pleticha, Heinrich 1118
ブレディン
Bredin, Kathleen 178
フレディンバーグ
Fredinburg, Dan 459
ブレーデカンプ
Bredekamp, Horst 178
ブレデカンプ
Bredekamp, Horst 178
ブレデス
Vlădescu, Sebastian 1460
フレデッテ
Fredette, Jimmer 459
ブレデラ
Bredella, Miriam A. 178
フレデリク皇太子
Prince Frederik 459
フレデリクス
Fredericks, Clayton 459
Fredericks, Frank 459
Fredericks, Neal L. 459
フレデリクセン
Frederiksen, Claus Hjort 459
Frederiksen, Mette 459
フレデリクソン
Eriksson, Peter 406
フレデリック
Frederick, Jim 459
Frederick, Matthew 459
Frederick, Nicholas 459
Frederick, Richard 459
Frederick, Travis 459
Fredericq, Simon 459
Frederik, Karen 459
フレデリック皇太子
Prince Frederik 459
フレデリックス
Fredericks, Matthew M. 459
Fredericks, Neal L. 459
フレデル
Freidel, Louis Henri Jean Raymond 461
ブレーデル
Blaedel, Sara 145
プレテル・サラテ
Pretell Zárate, Eduardo 1133
プレテル・デラベガ
Pretelt Dela Vega, Sabas 1133
フレーデン
Friden, Bertil 462
ブレーデン
Braden, Dallas 173
Braden, Gregg 173
ブレード
Blade, Adam 145
ペレド・エルハナン
Peled-Elhanan, Nurit 1093
プレドコ
Predko, Michael 1132
ブレトシュナイダー
Bretschneider, Andreas 180
ブレドソー
Bledsoe, Lucy Jane 148
プレトニェフ
Pletnëv, Mikhail 1118
ブレードニヒ
Brednich, Rolf Wilhelm 178
プレトニョフ
Pletnëv, Mikhail 1118
ブレードホルン
Bloedhorn, Hanswulf 149
ブレドマン
Bledman, Keston 148
プレドユ
Predoiu, Catalin 1132
ブレトラウ
Bretlau, P. 180
プレトリウス
Pretorius, E.Scott 1133
フレドリクソン
Fredrickson, Barbara L. 459
Fredrickson, George M. 459
Fredricson, Peder 459
Fredriksson, Gert 459
Fredriksson, Thobias 459
フレドリック
Fredrick, Richard 459
プレトリック
Pretrick, Eliuel 1133
フレードリヒ
Friedrich, Walter Ludwig 463
プレートル
Prêtre, Georges 1133
ブレナー
Brenner, Joël Glenn 180
Brenner, Menachem 180
Brenner, Michael 180
Brenner, Robert 180
Brenner, Sam 180
Brenner, Sydney 180
Brenner, Veronica 180
Brönner, Till 186
プレーナー
Planer, Christian 1117
ブレナウアー
Brennauer, Lisa 180
ブレナン
Brenan, Fran 179
Brennan, Allison 180
Brennan, Bridget 180
Brennan, Edward A. 180
Brennan, Eileen 180
Brennan, Fionnuala 180
Brennan, J.H. 180
Brennan, John Owen 180
Brennan, Kimberley 180
Brennan, M.Carol 180
Brennan, Richard 180
Brennan, Sarah Rees 180
Brennan, Scott 180
Brennan, Séamus 180
Brennan, Troyen A. 180
フレーニ
Freni, Mirella 461
ブレーニー
Blaney, Steven 147
ブレーヌ
Boulaine, Jean 167
フレネ
Freney, Jean 461
ブレネ
Brenet, Joshua 179
プレネ
Pleynet, Marcelin 1118
ブレネス・イカバルセタ
Brenes Icabalceta, Horacio Manuel 179
ブレネッケ
Brennecke, Hanns Christof 180
ブレネマン
Breneman, David W. 179
プレネル
Plenel, Edwy 1118
プレパー
Propper, Davy 1137
ブレハッチ
Blechacz, Rafał 148
プレハノフ
Plekhanov, Sergeĭ 1118
ブレーバーマン
Braverman, Eric R. 178
プレバル
Préval, René Garcia 1134
プレヒト
Precht, Richard David 1132
ブレヒビュール
Brechbühl, Beat 178
フレ＝ビュルネ
Fraix-Burnet, Thibaut 454
フレービン
Flavin, Christopher 441
プレビン
Previn, André George 1134
ブレビンス
Blevins, Jerry 148
Blevins, Nathan 148
Blevins, Nick 148
プレフ
Pulev, Tervel 1139
プレーフェア
Playfair, J.H.L. 1117
フレーフェル
Frevel, Christian 462
プレプク
Prepuk, Anikó 1133
プレブジャビーン・バヤルサイハン
Pürevjavyn Bayarsaikhan 1140
プレブジャルガル
Purevjargal, Lkhamdegd 1140
プレブスレン
Purevsuren, Lundeg 1140
プレブツ
Prevc, Peter 1134
プレブドルジ
Purevdorj, Serdamba 1140
プレブネリエフ
Plevneliev, Rosen Asenov 1118
プレブル
Preble, Adam 1132
ブレベ・トラビエソ
Brevé Travieso, Federico 181
ブレベ・レジェス
Brevé Reyes, Marlon 181
プレボララキ
Prevolaraki, Maria 1134
プレボワ
Prébois, Sigolène 1132
ブレマ
Boureima, Takoubakoye Aminata 168
ブレマー
Bremer, Martina 179
Bremer, Paul 179
Bremmer, Ian 179
プレマジャヤンタ
Premajayantha, Susil 1132
フレマス
Flem-Ath, Rand 442
プレマダサ
Premadasa, Sajith 1132
プレマック
Premack, Ann J. 1132
Premack, David 1132
フレミング
Fleming, Alejandro 442
Fleming, Anne Taylor 442
Fleming, Cameron 442
Fleming, Candace 442
Fleming, Carolyn 442
Fleming, Charles 442
Fleming, Chris 442
Fleming, Colin 442
Fleming, Denise 442
Fleming, Fergus 442
Fleming, Garry 442
Fleming, Graham Lewis 442
Fleming, Jack W. 442
Fleming, Jamell 442
Fleming, James Rodger 442
Fleming, John 442
Fleming, John Howland 442
Fleming, Mark 442
Fleming, Peter 442
Fleming, Quentin W. 442
Fleming, Runée 442
フレーム
Frame, Janet 454
Frame, J.Davidson 454
Frame, Roddy 454
フレム
Flem, Lydia 442
ブレーム
Brehm, Matthew T. 179
Brême, Abderahim 179
ブレム
Brem, Eva-Maria 179
Breme, Ousman Matar 179
ブレム＝グレーザー
Brem-Gräser, Luitgard 179
プレムジ
Premji, Azim 1132
プレムジッチ
Premužić, Jagoda 1132
プレム・チンスラノン
Prem Tinsulanonda 1132
プレーム・ティンスーラーノン
Prem Tinsulanonda 1132
プレム・ティンスラノン
Prem Tinsulanonda 1132
ブレムナー
Bremner, Brian 179
Bremner, J.Douglas 179
Bremner, Robert H. 179
ブレムネス
Bremness, Lesley 179
フレムリン
Fremlin, Celia 461
ブレメ
Vreme, Valerian 1465
ブレモー
Brémaud, Pierre 179
プレモリ＝ドルーレ
Premoli-Droulers, Francesca 1132

プレモン
Premont, Marie-Helene 1132
フレモント
Fremont, Eleanor 461
プレーヤー
Player, Gary 1117
プレラー
Preller, A.J. 1132
Preller, James 1132
フレーラッジ
Flerlage, Raeburn 442
ブレーリー
Brayley, Martin 178
フレリック
Frelich, Phyllis 461
フレリッチ
Frerichs, Courtney 461
フレーリッヒ
Froehlich, Susanne 464
フレーリヒ
Fröhlich, Uwe 465
フレール
Frère, Paul 461
ブーレル
Boolell, Arvin 160
ブレル
Bourel, Guillaume 168
プレル
Pröll, Josef 1137
ブレルク
Blerk, René van 148
プレルジョカージュ
Preljocaj, Angelin 1132
フレルスフ
Hurelsuh, Uhnaagiin 637
Khurelsukh, Uhnaagiin 729
Kurelsukh, Ukhnaa 774
フレルバータル
Khurelbaatar, Sodovjamts 729
フレルバートル
Khurelbaatar, Chimediin 729
ブレーン
Braein, Ane 174
Brehm, Ulrich 179
ブレン
Bren, Donald 179
Brenn, Bruce M. 180
プレン
Prehn, Kristin 1132
ブレンカス
Brenkus, John 180
フレンク・モラ
Frenk Mora, Julio 461
フレンケル
Fränkel, Rolf 456
Frenkel, Edward 461
Frenkel, Jacob Aharon 461
ブレンコウ
Blencowe, Andrew 148
プレンコビッチ
Plenković, Andrej 1118
ブレンゴラ
Brengola, Riccardo 180
プレンスキー
Prensky, Marc 1132
ブレンストレム
Brännström, Mats 176
ブレンタ
Brenta, Eduardo 180
ブレンダー
Brender, Alan S. 179
プレンダー
Plender, John 1118
プレンダギャスト
Prendergast, Grace 1132
ブレンダン
Brendan, Mary 179
フレンチ
French, Christy Tillery 461
French, Emily 461
French, Gina 461
French, Howard W. 461
French, Jackie 461
French, Karl 461
French, Kate 461
French, Marilyn 461
French, Nicci 461
French, Paul 461
French, Philip 461
French, Sally 461
French, Sean 461
French, Simon 461
French, Tana 461
French, Vivian 461
ブレンチッチ
Brenčič, Maja Makovec 179
ブレンツ
Brentz, Bryce 180
フレンツェル
Frenzel, Eric 461
プレンツドルフ
Plenzdorf, Ulrich 1118
ブレンデ
Brende, Boerge 179
Brende, Børge 179
プレンティス
Prentice, Jim 1132
ブレンデル
Brendel, Alfred 179
Brendel, Jake 179
Brendel, Sebastian 179
ブレンデンゲンイエンセン
Brendengen Jensen, Julie 179
フレンド
Frendo, Michael 461
Friend, George 464
Friend, Kyle 464
Friend, Trudy 464
ブレント
Brendt, Peter 179
Brent, David A. 180
Brent, Joseph 180
Brent, K.J. 180
Brent, Mike 180
ブレントエンス
Brentjens, Bart 180
フレンドル
Frendl, Gyorgy 461
ブレントン
Brenton, Chris 180
ブレンナー
Bremner, John 179
Brenner, Barry M. 180
Brenner, Bernhard 180
Brenner, Lenni 180
Brenner, Michael 180
Brenner, Sydney 180
フレーンニコフ
Khrennikov, Tikhon 729
フレンニコフ
Khrennikov, Tikhon 729
ブレンネック
Brennecke, Carsten 180
ブレンヒオ
Blengio, Manuel 148
ブレンビラ
Brembilla, Emiliano 179
ブレンフルト
Burenhult, Göran 202
フーレンワイダー
Fulenwider, David 467
ブロ
Burro, Jose Angel 206
ブロー
Blau, Evelyne 148
Blau, Marthe 148
Blow, David 150
Brault, Jacques 177
Brault, Michel 177
Breaux, Delvin 178
プーロ
Poulot, Dominique 1128
プロ
Prot, Baudouin 1137
Puro, Jukka-Pekka 1140
プロー
Peraud, Jean-Christophe 1096
プロアキス
Proakis, John G. 1136
フロアラック
Floirac, Charles Andre 443
プロイ
Pourroy, Janine 1129
ブロイアー
Breuer, Christoph 181
Breuer, Rolf-Ernst 181
Breuer, William B. 181
ブロイシュ
Breusch, Steffen J. 181
プロイス
Preus, Margi 1134
プロイスラー
Preussler, Otfried 1134
フロイデンバーガー
Freudenberger, Herbert J. 461
フロイト
Freud, Lucian 461
Freud, Martin 461
フロイド
Floyd, Bill 444
Floyd, Chris 444
Floyd, Donald W. 444
Floyd, Gavin 444
Floyd, Leonard 444
Floyd, Madeleine 444
Floyd, Michael 444
Floyd, Sharrif 444
Floyd, Susan 444
Freud, Lucian 461
ブロイド
Broyd, Richard 193
プロイハー
Ployhar, James D. 1118
フロイモビッチ
Froymovich, Riva 465
ブロイヤー
Breuer, Rolf-Ernst 181
プローイユ
Plooij, Frans X. 1118
フロイリシェ
Froyliche, Dan 465
ブロイル・ヨナサンズ
Bruil-jonathans, Lotte 194
フロイレル
Freuler, Remo 461
ブロインガー
Broinger, Kurt 185
フローインスティン
Vroeijenstijn, A.I. 1465
フロイント
Freund, Ken 461
Freund, Peter 461
Freund, Severin 462
Freund, Werner 462
Freund, Winfried 462
ブロウ
Blow, David Mervyn 150
Blow, Isabella 150
プロヴァイン
Provine, Robert R. 1137
ブローウィ
Blowey, Roger William 150
プロヴォースト
Provoost, Anne 1137
プロヴォスト
Provost, Foster 1137
ブロウカリング
Brokering, Jon 185
ブロウサード
Broussard, Ella 188
ブロウツマン
Brotzman, S.Brent 187
フロウド
Floud, Jean Esther 444
ブロウド
Broad, Eli 184
ブロウヤー
Brallier, Jess M. 175
ブロウンリー
Brownlee, Nick 192
プロエセル
Ploßel, Thomas 1118
ブロエット
Brouette, Thomas E. 187
フローエンフェルダー
Frauenfelder, Mark 458
フロガット
Froggatt, Joanne 464
フロガート
Froggatt, Cynthia C. 464
ブローガン
Brogan, Tracy 185
ブロキャビチュス
Burokevičius, Mykolas 205
ブローグ
Blaug, Mark 148
ブロークス
Broackes, Victoria 184
ブロクス
Broks, Normunds 185
Broks, Rolands 185
ブロクストン
Broxton, Jarell 193
Broxton, Jonathan 193
Broxton, Keon 193
プロクター
Procter, Garry 1136
Procter, James 1136
Proctor, Bob 1136
Proctor, Peter 1136
Proctor, Robert N. 1136
Proctor, Sue 1136
Proctor, William 1136

ブログドン
Brogdon, Malcolm 185
フロクハイゼン
Blokhuijsen, Jan 149
ブロークンシャー
Brokenshire, James 185
ブロケイル
Brocail, Doug 184
ブロケヴィチュス
Burokevičius, Mykolas 205
ブロコー
Brokaw, Tom 185
ブロコウ
Brokaw, Tom 185
プロコツォフ
Prokopcov, Dmitrij 1137
プロコップ
Prokop, Liese 1137
プロコーフィエフ
Prokof'ev, M.M. 1136
プロコフィエフ
Prokofieff, Sergei O. 1137
プロコフィエワ
Prokofyeva, Elena 1137
Prokofyeva, Maryna 1137
プロコフスキー
Prokovsky, André 1137
プロコプチュク
Prokopchuk, Iuliia 1137
プロコプツカ
Prokopcuka, Jelena 1137
プロコペンコ
Prokopenko, Anastasiya 1137
プロコポビッチ
Prokopovič, Pavol 1137
ブロコリ
Brocoli, Steffie 185
プロサイス
Prosise, C.J. 1137
Prosise, Jeff 1137
フロジェ
Froger, Jae 464
Froger, Stéphane 464
ブロジェット
Blodgett, E.D. 149
フローシェルズ
Froeschels, Emil 464
ブロシェンコ
Bloshenko, Artem 150
プロシネチキ
Prosinečki, Robert 1137
プロシネツキ
Prosinečki, Robert 1137
ブロシャール・ヴィアール
Brochard-Wyart, Françoise 184
ブロシュー
Brochu, André 184
プロシュ
Prosch, Jay 1137
プロシュキン
Proshkin, Andrei 1137
ブロジンスキ
Brosinski, Daniel 187
プロシンスキー
Prosinski, Chris 1137
ブーロス
Boolos, George 160
ブローズ
Burroughs, Jordan 206
ブロス
Bross, Donald C. 187
Brosse, Jacques 187
プローズ
Prose, Francine 1137
プロスクリャコフ
Proskuriakov, Oleh 1137
フロスティッグ
Frostig, Marianne 465
フロスト
Frost, Alfred John 465
Frost, David 465
Frost, Frank J. 465
Frost, Jack 465
Frost, Jo 465
Frost, Julie 465
Frost, Katie 465
Frost, Kenneth D. 465
Frost, Lori 465
Frost, Mark 465
Frost, Nick 465
Frost, Orcutt William 465
Frost, Peter 465
Frost, Randy O. 465
Frost, Scott 465
ブロスナン
Brosnan, Peter 187
Brosnan, Pierce Brendan 187
ブロスボル
Brosbøl, Kirsten 187
ブロズマン
Brozman, Bob 193
フローゼ
Froese, Edogar 464
ブロゼック
Brozek, Gary 193
プロセック
Prosek, James 1137
プロセロ
Prothero, Donald R. 1137
Prothero, Stephen R. 1137
ブロゾヴィッチ
Brozovic, Marcelo 193
ブロソレ
Brossollet, Jacqueline 187
ブローダー
Broder, David Salzer 185
Brodeur, Paul 185
Browder, Sue Ellin 188
Browder, Walter 188
ブロダー
Broder, Jamie 185
フロータイシュ
Groothuis, Stefan 538
プロダン
Prodan, Yuriy 1136
ブローチ
Broach, Elise 184
プロチャスカ
Prochaska, James O. 1136
プロチョロウ
Prochorow, Alexej 1136
プロツェンコ
Protsenko, Andriy 1137
フロッカ
Floca, Brian 443
フロッカー
Flocker, Michael 443
ブロッカー
Broecker, Wallace Smith 185
ブロッカーズ
Brockers, Michael 184
フロッカリ
Floccari, Sergio 443
ブロッキー
Brocquy, Louis le 185
ブロツキ
Blocki, Adrian 149
フロック
Flock, Agneta 443
ブロック
Bloch, Abby S. 149
Bloch, Arthur 149
Bloch, Douglas 149
Bloch, Joshua 149
Bloch, Michael 149
Bloch, Muriel 149
Bloch, Olivier 149
Bloch, Patrick Harry 149
Bloch, Robert L. 149
Bloch, Sidney 149
Bloch, Susan 149
Block, Etienne 149
Block, Francesca Lia 149
Block, Herbert Lawrence 149
Block, Joel D. 149
Block, Lawrence 149
Block, Paula M. 149
Block, Peter 149
Block, Ralph L. 149
Block, Thomas 149
Block, Thomas R. 149
Block, Walter 149
Blok, Stef 149
Brock, Andie 184
Brock, Ann Graham 184
Brock, Betty 184
Brock, Carolyn 184
Brock, Dan 184
Brock, David 184
Brock, James W. 184
Brock, Jeremy 184
Brock, Napoleon Murphy 184
Brock, Peter 184
Brock, Sabra E. 184
Brock, Stephen E. 184
Brock, Tramaine 184
Brock, William Hodson 184
Bullock, Alan Louis Charles 201
Bullock, Darryl W. 201
Bullock, Hiram 201
Bullock, Ian 201
Bullock, Sandra 201
プロック
Prock, Markus 1136
ブロックウェイ
Brockway, Connie 185
ブロックウェル
Brockwell, Peter J. 185
ブロックシュミット
Brockschmidt, Kraig 185
ブロックス
Broks, Paul 185
ブロックスミス
Brocksmith, Roy 185
ブロックハウス
Brockhouse, Bertram Neville 184
フロックハート
Flockhart, Calista 443
ブロックバンク
Brockbank, Wayne 184
ブロックホーベン
Broeckhoven, Diane 185
ブロックマイヤー
Brockmeier, Kevin 185
ブロックマン
Brockman, John 185
Brockmann, Suzanne 185
ブロック＝ラーナー
Block-Lerner, Jennifer 149
ブロックランド
Blokland, Michel 149
ブロックリー
Blockley, John 149
ブロックルハースト
Brocklehurst, Ruth 185
ブロッコフ
Brockhoff, Belle 184
プロッサー
Prosser, Julien 1137
Prosser, Peggy Lin 1137
ブロッサムゲーム
Blossomgame, Jaron 150
フロッサール
Frossard, Claire 465
Frossard, Etienne 465
ブロッシュ
Bloch, Serge 149
ブロッズマン
Brozman, Bob 193
プロッター
Protter, Eric 1137
ブロッダドッティル
Broddadóttir, Ingibjörg 185
プロッツ
Plotz, David 1118
プロッツマン
Protzman, Ferdinand 1137
ブロッド
Brod, Ruth Hagy 185
ブロッドスキー
Brodsky, Paul 185
ブロットナー
Blottner, Dieter 150
ブロッドベック
Brodbeck, Harald 185
ブロットマン
Brotman, Eric 187
ブロットン
Brotton, Jerry 187
プロッパー
Plopper, George 1118
プロッペ
Proppé, Óttarr 1137
ブロッホ
Bloch, Joseph 149
Bloch, Wilhelm 149
フローデ
Frohde, Liv 464
プロテ
Prothée, Claude 1137
ブローディ
Broadie, Mark Nathan 184
Brody, Howard 185
Bródy, Vera 185
ブローディー
Brodie, Renee 185
ブロディ
Braude, Eric J. 177
Brodie, Richard 185
Brody, Adrien 185
Brody, Howard 185

Brody, Hugh 185
Brody, Neville 185
ブロディー
Brody, Evelyn 185
ブローディ
Prodi, Romano 1136
ブロディ
Prodi, Romano 1136
ブロデック
Brodek, Ayako 185
フロデノ
Frodeno, Jan 464
ブロデューア
Brodeur, Martin 185
ブロデュール
Brodeur, Adrienne 185
ブロデリック
Broderick, Matthew 185
ブローデル
Braudel, Paule 177
ブローデン
Brogden, William B. 185
フロード
Flood, Jorgen Kornelius 443
ブロート
Brault, Steven 177
ブロード
Broad, Edythe 184
Broad, Eli 184
Broad, Peter 184
Broad, Robin 184
Broad, William 184
ブロト
Broto, Carles 187
ブロードウェイ
Broadway, Michael J. 184
ブロドカ
Bródka, Zbigniew 185
プロトキン
Plotkin, Mark J. 1118
ブロドスキー
Brodsky, Archie 185
Brodsky, Beth S. 185
Brodsky, Jack 185
Brodsky, Norm 185
プロトセヴィッチ
Protosevich, Mark 1137
プロトニコフ
Plotnikoff, Gregory A. 1118
ブロードハースト
Broadhurst, Michael 184
プロトパパス
Protopapas, Christos 1137
ブロドビン
Brodbin, Kevin 185
プロートプラソップ
Plodprasop, Suraswadi 1118
ブロードベント
Broadbent, Jim 184
Broadbent, John Michael 184
Broadbent, Marianne 184
ブロドマイヤー
Brodmeier, Daniel 185
プロドーム
Preud'homme, Michel 1133
ブロードリック
Broadrick, Annette 184
ブロドリック
Broderick, Reymond 185
Brodrick, William 185
フロドン
Frodon, Jean-Michel 464
ブロートン
Broughton, Frank 187
Broughton, Philip Delves 188
ブロトン
Brotton, Jerry 187
ブローナー
Blauner, Peter 148
ブロナー
Bronaugh, Robert L. 186
ブロナス
Bronäs, Ulf G. 186
ブローネカー
Braunecker, Ben 177
ブローネマルク
Brånemark, Per-Ingvar 176
フロノイ
Flournoy, Michele 444
フロノフスキ
Chronowski, Andrzej 262
ブロハー
Blocher, Christoph 149
プロパー
Proper, Darcy 1137
ブロバーグ
Broberg, Catherine 184
プロハスカ
Prohaska, Wolfgang 1136
プロハースコヴァー
Prochazkova, Iva 1136
フロパーチェフ
Khlopachev, Gennadiĭ Adol'fovich 728
ブロハマー
Brohamer, Tom 185
プロバンス
Provance, Patricia Geise 1137
プロバンチャ
Provancha, Briana 1137
プロヒューモ
Profumo, John 1136
ブロヒン
Blokhin, Aleksandr V. 149
Blokhin, Oleg 149
フローブ
Froeb, Lori C. 464
プロフ
Prokh, Andy 1136
プロファー
Profar, Jurickson 1136
ブロフィ
Brophy, Jere E. 187
Brophy, Philip 187
プロフィト
Proffit, William R. 1136
プロブスト
Probst, Jeff 1136
Probst, Jennifer 1136
Probst, Pierre 1136
プロフモ
Profumo, Francesco 1136
プロフューモ
Profumo, John 1136
フロブラー
Grobler, Piet 537
ブロプレ
Bropleh, Lawrence 187
フロペツキー
Khlopetskiĭ, Anatoliĭ 728
ブロベト
Brovetto, Jorge 188
ブローベル
Blobel, Günter 149
ブロベン
Broben, Brittany 184
プロベンセン
Provensen, Alice 1137
プロボステ
Provoste, Yasna 1137
プロボステジョ
Probosutedjo 1136
プロボスト
Provost, Ronald H. 1137
フロポニン
Khloponin, Alexander G. 728
ブロボル
Brovold, Tore 188
プローホロフ
Prokhorov, Aleksandr Mikhailovich 1136
Prokhorov, Mikhail Dmitriyevich 1136
プロホロフ
Prokhorov, Aleksandr Mikhailovich 1136
Prokhorov, A.V. 1136
Prokhorov, Mikhail Dmitriyevich 1136
プロホロワ
Prokhorova, Yelena 1136
ブロマー
Bromer, Viktor 185
ブロマーズ
Blommers, John 149
フローマン
Froman, Robert 465
フロマン
Froman, Michael 465
Froment, Pascale 465
Frommann, Holger 465
フロマンタル
Fromental, Jean-Luc 465
プローミン
Plomin, Robert 1118
フローム
Flaum, Jonathon A. 441
Flaum, Mechele 441
Flaum, Sander A. 441
フロム
Fromm, Helena 465
ブローム
Broohm, Octave Nicoué 186
ブロム
Blom, Gunnar 149
プロム
Plum, Claus Munk 1118
Plum, Ingrid 1118
ブロムウィッチ
Bromwich, Michael 186
ブロムカンプ
Blomkamp, Neill 149
フロムキン
Fromkin, David 465
ブロムクヴィスト
Blomquist, Hans 149
ブロムシュテット
Blomstedt, Herbert Thorson 149
ブロムステット
Blomstedt, Herbert Thorson 149
ブロムフィールド
Bromfield, John 185
ブロムホール
Bromhall, Clive 185
ブロムリー
Bromley, David G. 185
Bromley, Jay 186
Bromley, Kristan 186
プロムレック
Promlek, Kasem 1137
ブローメ
Blome, Götz 149
プロメガー
Prommegger, Andreas 1137
ブロメージ
Bromage, Philip Raikes 185
ブロメット
Bromet, Hugo Guilherme 185
ブロメル
Bromell, Trayvon 185
フロメンボーム
Flaumenbaum, Danièle 441
フロモ
Flomo, Richard 443
フロモワ
Khromova, Tatyana 729
フローラ
Flora, Carlin 443
フロー・ライダー
Flo Rida 444
フローラン
Florent, Guillaume 444
フローランド
Florand, Laura 443
フローリー
Flory, Denis 444
Frawley, David 458
フロリアン
Florian, Douglas 444
ブローリイ
Brawley, Elizabeth C. 178
フローリー＝オーディ
Frawley-O'Dea, Mary Gail 458
フロリダ
Florida, Richard 444
フローリッヒ
Frolich, Cornelia 465
フロリモン
Florimon, Pedro 444
フロル
Grol, Henk 538
ブロル
Brol, Enrique 185
プロール
Prole, Helen 1137
Proulx, Jean 1137
フロルシュッツ
Florschuetz, Andre 444
フロレア
Florea, Razvan Ionut 443
Florea, Sandu 443
フローレス
Flores, Francisco 444
Flores, Ignacio 444

フ

Flores, Jacob 444
Flores, Wilmer 444
Flórez, Juan Diego 444
フロレス
Flores, Carlos 444
Flores, Carmelo 444
Flores, Eugenia 444
Flores, Fernando 444
Flores, Francisco 444
Flores, Roberto 444
Flores, Sylvia 444
フロレスアラオス
Flores-aráos, Ántero 444
フロレス・アレマン
Flores Alemán, José Armando 444
フロレス・ガラルサ
Flores Galarza, Javier 444
プロレスコフスキー
Proleskovsky, Oleg V. 1137
フロレス・バレリアノ
Flores Valeriano, Enrique 444
フロレス・モジャ
Flores Moya, Allan 444
フロレス・ランサ
Flores Lanza, Enrique 444
ブロレニウス
Brolenius, Johan 185
フロレンザーノ
Florenzano, Eric 444
フローレンス
Florence, David 443
フロレンセ
Florence, Afonso Bandeira 443
フロレンツィ
Florenzi, Alessandro 444
フロレンティノ
Falcao Florentino, Esquiva 417
Falcao Florentino, Yamaguchi 417
フローレント - トレーシー
Florent-Treacy, Elizabeth 444
フローロス
Floros, Constantin 444
フロロバ
Frolova, Olga 465
フローロ・フローレス
Floro Flores, Antonio 444
プロロンジョ
Prolongeau, Hubert 1137
フロワサール
Froissart, Lionel 465
フロン
Flon, Suzanne 443
ブローン
Braun, Edward 177
Braun, Ryan 177
ブロン
Blanc, Christian 146
Bron, Zachar 186
Bullon, Alejandro 201
Burlon, Marcelo 204
Buron, Kari Dunn 205
プロン
Pron, Nick 1137
プロンガー
Pronger, Chris 1137
ブロンカンプ
Blomkamp, Neill 149
プロンク
Pronk, Jan 1137
フロングワネ
Hlongwane, Makhosini 610
プロンコ
Pronko, Michael 1137
ブロンジット
Bronzit, Konstantin 186
ブロンジーニ
Bronzini, Giorgia 186
プロンジーニ
Pronzini, Bill 1137
ブロンスカヤ
Vronskaya, Anna 1465
ブロンスキ
Błoński, Jan Kidawa 150
プロンスキー
Pronsky, Zaneta M. 1137
ブロンスタイン
Bronstein, Catalina 186
ブロンゼッティ
Bronzetti, Ernesto 186
ブロンソン
Bronson, Charles 186
Bronson, Eric 186
Bronson, Fred 186
Bronson, Howard F. 186
Bronson, Po 186
Bronson, Rachel 186
フロンツ
Fronc, Martin 465
Frontera, Walter R. 465
フロンティ
Fronty, Aurélia 465
フロンテラ
Frontera, Walter R. 465
ブロンデル
Blondel, Jean 150
Blondel, Rachelle 150
Blondelle, Thomas 150
ブローント
Blount, Akil 150
Blount, LeGarrette 150
ブロンド
Blondeau, Sylvie 150
フロントニ
Frontoni, Angelo 465
ブーロンニュ - ガルサン
Boulongne-Garcin, Maryse 167
ブロンバーグ
Bromberg, Philip M. 185
ブロンフマン
Bronfman, Edgar Miles 186
Bronfman, Edgar Miles, Jr. 186
Bronfman, Yefim 186
プロンミン
Prommin, Lertsuridej 1137
フロンメル
Frommel, Christoph Luitpold 465
ブーワ
Bhuva, Kumud Narendra 136
フワイジ
Houej, Mohamed Ali 625
フワイシュ
Huwaish, Abdul-Tawwab al-Mulla 640
フワイティル
al-Khuwaiter, Abdul-Aziz bin Abdullh 729
ブワシュチク
Blaszczyk, Lucjan 148
ブワシュチコフスキ
Blaszczykowski, Jakub 148
ブワシュチャク
Błaszczak, Mariusz 148
ブワナカワ
Bwana Kawa, Nionyi 210
フーン
Hoon, Geoff 621
フン
Hung, Le Minh 635
Hung, Nguyen Sinh 635
ブーン
Boon, Dany 160
Boon, Mario 160
Boon, Maureen 160
Boone, Alex 160
Boone, Ezekiel 160
Boone, Kadron 160
Boone, Ray 160
プーン
Poon, Christine A. 1124
Poon, Thomas 1124
プン
Pun, Barshaman 1140
Pun, Ganesh Man 1140
Pun, Narayan Singh 1140
フンカ
Junca, David 691
プンカ
Punka, György 1140
ブンカセン
Bunkasem, Thavrith J. 201
ブンガート
Bungert, Niko 201
フンギト・ボネット
Junuguito Bonnet, Roberto 692
フンク
Funck, Carolin 468
ブンクート
Bounkeut, Sangsomsak 167
プングラ
Pungura, Vicente 1140
フンケ
Funcke, Liselotte 468
Funke, Cornelia Caroline 468
ブーンゲ
Bunge, Mario Augusto 201
ブンゲイ
Bungei, Wilfred 201
ブンゴー
Bundegaard, Anita Bay 201
Bundsgaard, Lotte 201
フンコデルピノ
Junco Del Pino, Juan Mario 691
フンゴン
Fung-on, George 468
ブンコーン
Bounkong, Sihavong 167
ブンサック
Bunsuk, Tairat 201
プンジェア
Pungea, Horatiu 1140
ブンスアイ
Bounxouei, Alexandra 167
ブンステル・ベットリー
Bunster Betteley, Jorge 201
フンズトルファー
Hundstorfer, Rudolf 635
ブンスン
Bunson, Matthew 201
プンセット
Punset, Elsa 1140
フン・セン
Hun Sen 635
ブンソン
Boonsong, Teriyapirom 160
フンダートプフント
Hundertpfund, Jörg 635
プンダリ
Pundari, John 1140
ブンチ
Bumçi, Aldo 201
プンチ・バンダ
Punchi Banda, Sabhapathi Mudiyanselage 1140
ブンチャン
Bounchanh, Sinthavong 167
プンツィ
Punzi, Andrea 1140
フンツィカー
Hunziker, Nicolas 637
プンツェル
Punzel, Tina 1140
プンツォク・ワンギェル
Phun-tshogs-dbaṅ-rgyal, Sgo-ra-naṅ-pa 1109
ブンティアム
Bountiem, Phitsamay 167
プンティシュ
Pontes, Leonel Pinto d'Assunção 1124
ブンティッチ
Buntic, Fabijan 202
ブンティング
Bunting, Peter 202
フンテラール
Huntelaar, Klaas-Jan 636
フント
Hundt, Martin 635
Hunte, Julian 636
ブンドゥ
Bundhoo, Lormesh 201
ブンドノシマンゴイ
Boundono Simangoye, Egide 167
フンドラ
Fundora, Ivan 468
ブントーン
Bounthong, Chitmany 167
ブンナーク
Bunnag, Tej 201
ブンニ
Bounni, Adnan 167
al-Bunni, Nadir 201
ブンニャン
Boungnang, Vorachith 167
Bounyang, Vorachit 167
ブンニャン・ウォラチット
Bounnhang Vorachith 167
ブンバ
Bumba, Syda 201
ブーンペーン

Bounpheng, Mounphosay 167
フンボ
Houngbo, Albert Ségbégnon 626
ブンホン
Boon Heong, Tan 160
ブンポン
Bounpone, Bouttanavong 167
フンメル
Hummel, Arthur William, Jr. 635
フンメルス
Hummels, Mats 635
ブンヤシット・チョクワタナ
Boonsithi, Chokwatana 160
ブンヤシット・チョクワタナー
Boonsithi, Chokwatana 160
ブンヤシット・チョークワッタナー
Boonsithi, Chokwatana 160
ブンロート
Boonrawd, Somtat 160
ブンワリ
Bunwaree, Vasant Kumar 202

【へ】

へー
Hee, Otto 588
ベ
Bae, Doo-na 79
Bae, Sang-moon 79
Bae, Yong-joon 79
ベー
B., David 75
Bae, Jae-chul 79
Boe, Johannes Thingnes 153
Boe, Tarjei 153
ペ
Bae, Doo-na 79
Bae, Tae Soo 79
Bae, Yong-joon 79
Pae, Hak 1069
Pae, Tal-jun 1069
Pez, Catherine 1105
ヘア
Hare, Brian 570
Hare, David 570
Hare, Richard Mervyn 570
Hare, Robert D. 570
Hehr, Kent 589
ヘアー
Hare, David 570
ベーア
Baer, Alexander B. 79
Bähr, Karl 80
Behr, Edward 114
Behr, Hans-Georg 114
ペァ
Bair, Deirdre 82
ベア
Baer, Gregory 79
Baer, Jean L. 79
Baer, Lee 79
Baer, Richard K. 79
Baer, Robert 79
Beah, Ishmael 109
Bear, Elizabeth 109
Bear, George G. 109
Bear, Greg 109
Behr, Edward 114
Behr, Kevin 114
ベアー
Baehr, Evan 79
Baer, Lee 79
Baer, Michael A. 79
Bear, Mark F. 109
Behr, Edward 114
ペア
Paire, Benoit 1070
Pare, Richard 1077
ベアイヌ
Veainu, Telusa 1449
ベアジャイナ
Behajaina, Petera 114
ヘアシン
Hairsine, Trevor 555
ベアーズ
Beres, Samantha 125
ベアス
Béasse, Anne-Marie 109
ベアストー
Bairstow, Cameron 82
ヘアーストン
Hairston, Chris 555
ヘアストン
Hairston, P.J. 555
ヘアツォーク
Herzog, Annette 600
ヘアツォグ
Herzog, Werner 600
ペア・デイビス
Paire Davis, Lavone 1070
ペア・デービス
Paire Davis, Lavone 1070
ベアデン
Bearden, Milt 109
ベアード
Baird, Davis 82
Baird, John 82
Baird, Lloyd 82
Baird, Vanessa 82
Beard, Christine H. 109
Beard, Jim 109
ベアトリ
Beatrix, Jean Guillaume 110
ベアトリクス王女
Princess Beatrix 110
ベアトリックス
Princess Beatrix 110
ベアドン
Beardon, Luke 109
ヘアマン
Herrmann, Patrick 599
ペアマン
Pearman, Roger R. 1090
ベアラー
Barer, Burl 93
ベアリング
Baring, Anne 94
Beerling, David J. 113
ベアリンググールド
Baring-Gould, Ceil 94
Baring-Gould, William S. 94
ベアール
Béart, Emmanuelle 109
Behar, Adriana 114
ベアルツォット
Bearzot, Enzo 109
ペアレント
Parent, Joseph 1078
Parent, Marc 1078
ベァワルド
Baerwald, Hans Herman 79
ベアワルト
Baerwald, Hans Herman 79
ベアワルド
Baerwald, Hans Herman 79
ヘイ
Hay, Colin 584
Hay, Elizabeth 584
Hay, James 584
Hay, Louise L. 584
Hay, Phil 584
Hay, Phillipa 584
Hey, Anthony J.G. 602
ベイ
Bay, Damon 107
Bay, Jason 107
Bay, Michael 107
Bei, Ta 114
Bey, Arfin 134
ペイ
Paye, Burrall 1089
Paye, Won-Ldy 1089
Pei, Ieoh Ming 1092
Pei, Minxin 1092
ベイアー
Baer, Ann 79
ペイア
Paea, Stephen 1069
ベイアード
Baird, David Carr 82
ペイヴァー
Paver, Michelle 1088
ヘイヴァーズ
Havers, Richard 583
ヘイヴァン
Haven, Anne 583
ヘイウッド
Haywood, Dan 586
Haywood, Dave 586
Haywood, Gar Anthony 586
Haywood, John 586
Haywood, Trevor 586
Heywood, Derek 603
Heywood, Rosie 603
Heywood, Vernon Hilton 603
ヘイヴンズ
Havens, Leston L. 583
ペイエ
Payet, Rolph 1089
ヘイエダール
Heyerdahl, Thor 602
ペイエット
Payette, Bruce 1089
ベイエルガンス
Weyergans, François 1496
ヘイエルダール
Heyerdahl, Thor 602
ベイエル・ブルゴス
Beyer Burgos, Harald 135
ベイエレ
Beyle, Nur Idow 135
ヘイガー
Hagar, Sammy 553
Hager, M.G. 554
Hager, Thomas 554
ベイカー
Baicker, Karen 80
Baker, A. 82
Baker, Alan 82
Baker, Alan R.H. 82
Baker, Annie 82
Baker, Bob 82
Baker, Bruce L. 82
Baker, Buddy 82
Baker, Chris 83
Baker, Christopher 83
Baker, Darrell 83
Baker, David 83
Baker, Doris M. 83
Baker, Dusty 83
Baker, Dylan 83
Baker, E.D. 83
Baker, Emma 83
Baker, Ginger 83
Baker, Glenn A. 83
Baker, Houston A., Jr. 83
Baker, James Addison Ⅲ 83
Baker, James Ireland 83
Baker, Jeannie 83
Baker, Jed 83
Baker, Joanne 83
Baker, John Austin 83
Baker, John Hamilton 83
Baker, Kage 83
Baker, Kate 83
Baker, Keith 83
Baker, Kyle 83
Baker, Linda L. 83
Baker, Liza 83
Baker, L.M., Jr. 83
Baker, Lorian 83
Baker, Marina 83
Baker, Mark 83
Baker, Mark C. 83
Baker, Mona 83
Baker, Nicholson 83
Baker, Ray 83
Baker, Richard 83
Baker, Rick 83
Baker, Ron 83
Baker, Roy Ward 83
Baker, Sean 83
Baker, Simon 83
Baker, Stephen 83
Baker, Trevor 83
Baker, William F. 83
ベイガ
Veiga, Emanuel Antero 1450
Veiga, Fatima Lima 1450
Veiga, José Maria 1450
Veiga, Justino 1450
Veiga, Manuel 1450
ベイカー・スミス
Baker-Smith, Grahame 84
ベイカー＝スミス
Baker-Smith, Grahame 84
ヘイガーマン
Hagerman, Eric 554
ヘイカル
Heikal, Muhammad Hassanein 589
ヘイガン
Hagan, Kenneth J. 553
Hagan, Patricia 553
ベイカン

Bakan, Joel 82
ベイギハルチェガニ
Beigi Harchegani, Milad 114
ヘイグ
Hague, Gill 554
Hague, William Jefferson 554
Haig, Alexander Meigs, Jr. 555
Haig, Brian 555
Haig, Francesca 555
Haig, Matt 555
Haig, Milton 555
Haigh, John 555
Haigh, Thomas 555
ペイク
Paik, Nam June 1070
ヘイグッド
Haygood, Wil 585
ヘイゲル
Hagel, Chuck 554
ペイゲルス
Pagels, Elaine H. 1069
ヘイゲン
Hagen, Earle H. 554
Hagen, Erica 554
Hagen, Uta 554
ベイコソ
Veikoso, Viliame 1450
ベイコン
Bacon, Tony 77
ヘイザー
Heiser, Bryan 590
Heyzer, Noeleen 603
ペイサー
Peyser, John 1105
ペイザー
Peyser, John 1105
ベイサット
Beissat, Mohamed 115
ベイザーマン
Bazerman, Max H. 108
ベイサム
Betham, Stephen 133
ペイザント
Payzant, Geoffrey 1089
ヘイジー
Hagy, Jessica 554
ペイジ
Page, Andrew 1069
Page, Anita 1069
Page, Ann E.K. 1069
Page, Betty 1069
Page, Christine R. 1069
Page, Elen 1069
Page, Janet Blair 1069
Page, Jason 1069
Page, Jimmy 1069
Page, Katherine Hall 1069
Page, Larry 1069
Page, Nick 1069
Page, Patti 1069
Page, Raymond Ian 1069
Page, Robin 1069
Page, Scott E. 1069
Page, Sharon 1069
Page, Tim 1069
Page, Willis 1069
Paige, Alison 1070
Paige, Laurie 1070
Paige, Marcus 1070
Paige, Rudy 1070
ベイシェナリエワ
Beishenaliyeva, Nelya 115
ペイシェンス
Patience, Allan 1085
Patience, Luke 1085
ベイジェント
Baigent, Michael 81
ペイジ＝ジョーンズ
Page-Jones, Meilir 1069
ヘイジャー
Hager, Bryce 554
ヘイジャーマン
Hagerman, Jennifer 554
ヘイジャン
Hagen, Jacob 554
ベイジョー
Bajo, David 82
ベイシンガー
Basinger, Kim 102
ペイシンガー
Paysinger, Spencer 1089
ヘイス
Haythe, Justin 585
ヘイズ
Hayes, Al 585
Hayes, Bill 585
Hayes, Bob 585
Hayes, Brian 585
Hayes, David K. 585
Hayes, Deborah 585
Hayes, Declan 585
Hayes, Dermot J. 585
Hayes, Elisabeth 585
Hayes, Isaac 585
Hayes, Joanna 585
Hayes, John 585
Hayes, John Michael 585
Hayes, John Phillip 585
Hayes, Linda J. 585
Hayes, Louise 585
Hayes, Nicky 585
Hayes, Patricia 585
Hayes, Patrick 585
Hayes, Peter 585
Hayes, Philip 585
Hayes, Randall 585
Hayes, Richard E. 585
Hayes, Rob 585
Hayes, Rosemary 585
Hayes, Samantha 585
Hayes, Samuel L. 585
Hayes, Sharon 585
Hayes, Simon 585
Hayes, Sophie 585
Hayes, Steven C. 585
Hayes, Terrance 585
Hayes, Terry 585
Hayes, Thomas Joseph 585
Hayes, William 585
Hays, Daniel 585
Hays, R.D. 585
Hays, Richard B. 585
Hays, Samuel P. 585
Heyes, Jane 602
Heyes, Terry 602
ベイス
Base, Graeme 101
Beys, Kostas E. 135
ベイズ
Bays, Brandon 108
Bays, Jan Chozen 108
ペイス
Paeth, Scott R. 1069
Peijs, Karla 1092
ヘイスターバング
Heisterberg, Rasmus 590
ヘイスティ
Hastie, Reid 580
Hastie, Trevor 580
ヘイスティングス
Hastings, Reed 581
Hastings, Robert L. 581
Hastings, Thomas John 581
ヘイスティングズ
Hastings, Natasha 580
Hastings, Reed 581
ヘイステッド
Hasted, Nick 580
ヘイスト
Haist, Steven A. 555
ペイズナー
Paisner, Daniel 1070
ベイズモア
Bazemore, Kent 108
ヘイスリー
Heisley, Michael 590
ペイズリー
Paisley, Brad 1070
Paisley, Ian Richard Kyle 1070
ヘイズリット
Haslett, Adam 579
ヘイズルウッド
Hazlewood, Lee 586
ヘイズレット
Hazlett, Thomas W. 586
ヘイスロップ
Hyslop, Jonathan 641
ベイセヴィッチ
Bacevich, A.J. 77
ヘイセック・リバロラ
Heisecke Rivarola, Ricardo Martin 590
ヘイゼル
Hazel, Matt 586
ペイセル
Peyceré, David 1105
ヘイゼルグローブ
Hazelgrove, William Elliott 586
ヘイゼルベイカー
Hazelbaker, Jeremy 586
ヘイゼン
Hazen, Mike 586
Hazen, Robert M. 586
ベイソロー
Beysolow, Miata 135
ベイソン
Bateson, Margaret 104
ヘイソーンスウェイト
Haythornthwaite, Philip J. 585
ヘイター
Hayter, Sparkle 585
ヘイダー
Hader, Josh 552
Hayder, Mo 584
ベイタ
Bejta, Nevzat 115
ベイダ
Vayda, Thomas P. 1448
ベイダー
Bader, Christine 78
Bader, Harrison 78
Bader, Thomas J. 78
ベイタイ
Bejtaj, Engjell 115
Vaitai, Halapoulivaati 1438
ベイダオ
Bei-dao 114
ペイタオ
Bei-dao 114
ベイダーギー
Beidaghi, Hamid Reza 114
ヘイダリ
Heidari, Alireza 589
ヘイダロフ
Heydarov, Kemaleddin 602
ペイチェバ
Peycheva, Simona 1105
ベイチェル
Bachel, Beverly K. 77
ペイチッチ
Pejcic, Snjezana 1093
ベイツ
Baitz, Jon Robin 82
Bates, A.D. 104
Bates, Alan 104
Bates, Amy Barrett 104
Bates, Amy June 104
Bates, Bert 104
Bates, Bob 104
Bates, Daren 104
Bates, Douglas M. 104
Bates, Elena 104
Bates, Houston 104
Bates, Ivan 104
Bates, J.Leonard 104
Bates, Katherine 104
Bates, Kathy 104
Bates, Marilyn M. 104
Bates, Trevor 104
ヘイッキラ
Heikkilä, Petra 589
ベイティ
Batey, Colleen E. 104
Beatty, Brian J. 110
Beatty, John Lee 110
Beatty, Warren 110
ベイティー
Batey, Rick 104
Beaty, Andrea 110
ベイティア
Beitia, Ruth 115
Veitia, Yosbany 1450
ヘイデン
Haden, Charlie 552
Haden, Christen 552
Haden, Joe 552
Hayden (walden), Ashley 584
Hayden, Brent 584
Hayden, Christopher 584
Hayden, D.J. 584
Hayden, Gary 584
Hayden, G.Miki 584
Hayden, Laura 584
Hayden, Lucy 584
Hayden, Michael Vincent 584
Hayden, Nick 584
Hayden, Patrick Nielsen 584
Hayden, Tom 584
Hayden, Torey L. 584
ベイデン
Baden, Michael M. 78
ヘイト
Heidt, Adam 589
ヘイド
Heide, Florence Parry 589
ベイト
Bate, David 103

Bate, Jonathan 103
Bate, Lucy 103
Bate, Richard 103
ベイド
Bade, Patrick 78
ペイド
Pade, Victoria 1068
ベイドゥーン
Baydoun, Mohammed Abdel-Hamid 107
ヘイトコッター
Heitkoetter, Markus 590
ベイトソン
Bateson, Anna 104
Bateson, Gregory 104
Bateson, Margaret 104
Bateson, Paul Patrick Gordon 104
ベイトマン
Bateman, Anthony W. 103
Bateman, Bradley W. 103
Bateman, Chris 103
Bateman, Colin 103
Bateman, Donald 103
Bateman, Ian 103
Bateman, Jason 103
Bateman, John 103
Bateman, Robert McLellan 104
ペイトマン
Pateman, Carole 1084
ペイトレス
Paytress, Mark 1089
ヘイトン
Hayton, Bill 585
Hayton, Darren 585
Hayton, Mike 586
ヘイドン
Hayden, Melissa 584
Hayden, Tom 584
Haydon, Elizabeth 585
ペイトン
Paton, Carol 1085
Paton, John 1085
Payton, Elfrid 1089
Payton, Gary, II 1089
Payton, Jordan 1089
Payton, Sean 1089
Payton, Stephen 1089
Peyton, Kathleen M. 1105
ペイトン・ウォルシュ
Paton Walsh, Jill 1085
ヘイナー
Hayner, Priscilla B. 585
ベイナー
Beiner, Ronald 115
Boehner, John 153
ペイナード
Peinado, Javier 1092
ヘイナルオマ
Heinäluoma, Eero 590
ヘイニ
Haney, Eric L. 566
ヘイニー
Haney, Tyler 566
ヘイニング
Haining, Peter 555
ベイヌク
Vainuku, Soma 1438
ベイノ
Bayno, Bill 108
ヘイノネン
Heinonen, Olli-Pekka 590
ヘイノバ
Hejnova, Zuzana 590
ベイノン
Beynon, Emily 135
ヘイバー
Haber, Karen 551
ベイバー
Baver, Allison 107
ペイバー
Paver, Michelle 1088
ヘイバーグ
Heiberg, Morten 589
ペイビン
Piven, Joshua 1116
ペイファー
Peiffer, Vera 1092
ベイファス
Beyfus, Drusilla 135
ヘイフェリー
Haefele, Fred 553
ヘイフマン
Hafemann, Scott J. 553
ヘイブンズ
Havens, Richie 583
ペイベイ
Paye-baye, Mewaseh 1089
ヘイヘナール
Hijgenaar, Yvonne 605
ヘイベル
Habel, Robert E. 551
ヘイマー
Hamer, Ben 561
Hamer, Dean H. 561
Hamer, Martin 561
Hamer, Mary 561
Hamer, Susan 561
ペイマー
Paymar, Michael 1089
ペイマニ
Peymani, Christine 1105
ヘイマン
Hayman, Dawn E. 585
Heyman, David 602
Heyman, Richard D. 603
ベイマン
Bijman, Jos 138
ヘイミソン
Heimisson, Hannes 590
ベイム
Baim, Donald S. 81
Baime, Albert J. 81
Baym, Gordon 108
ヘイムズ
Hames, B.D. 561
ヘイモア
Haymore, Jennifer 585
ベイヤー
Bayer, Ronald 108
Bayer, Samuel 108
Bayer, William 108
Beyer, Andrew 134
Beyer, Bob 134
Beyer, Brennen 134
Beyer, Damon 134
Beyer, Peter L. 134
Beyer, Rick 134
Beyer, Roberta 135
Beyer, Thomas R., Jr. 135
ベイヤード
Bayard, Louis 107
ベイヤー・フォン・モルゲンスターン
Beyer von Morgenstern, Ingo 135
ヘイヤール
Heyer, C.J.den 602
ベイユ
Veil, Simone 1450
ペイヨン
Peillon, Vincent 1092
ヘイラー
Hayler, Damon 585
ベイラー
Bailor, Jonathan 81
Baylor, Byrd 108
ペイラーノ
Peirano, Louis 1092
ペイラノ
Peirano, Louis 1092
ペイラノ・ファルコニ
Peirano Falconí, Luis Alberto 1092
ヘイララ
Heilala, Katariina 589
ヘイリー
Hailey, Arthur 555
Haley, Gail E. 557
Haley, Guy 557
Haley, Jack, Jr. 557
Haley, Jay 557
Haley, Jocelyn 557
Haley, John O. 557
Haley, Justin 557
Haley, Todd 557
Hayley 585
ベイリー
Bailey, Aleen 81
Bailey, Alice A. 81
Bailey, Allen 81
Bailey, Alvin 81
Bailey, Andrew 81
Bailey, Ann 81
Bailey, Anthony 81
Bailey, Arthur 81
Bailey, Champ 81
Bailey, Christopher 81
Bailey, Clive 81
Bailey, Dan 81
Bailey, Derek 81
Bailey, Dion 81
Bailey, Elisabeth Tova 81
Bailey, Elizabeth 81
Bailey, Gerry 81
Bailey, Gwen 81
Bailey, Helen 81
Bailey, Herbert Smith, Jr. 81
Bailey, Homer 81
Bailey, Jill 81
Bailey, Jon S. 81
Bailey, Joseph V. 81
Bailey, Kenneth E. 81
Bailey, Martin 81
Bailey, Michael Reeves 81
Bailey, Patricia 81
Bailey, Peter 81
Bailey, Philip 81
Bailey, Philip M. 81
Bailey, Rachel 81
Bailey, Rasheed 81
Bailey, Rosemary 81
Bailey, Royston 81
Bailey, Ryan 81
Bailey, Sean 81
Bailey, Sterling 81
Bailey, Sydney Dawson 81
Bailie, Ryan 81
Baillie, Marilyn 81
Baillie, Tim 81
Baillieu, Amanda 81
Bairy, Maurice 82
Bayley, Anne 108
Bayley, Barrington J. 108
Bayley, David H. 108
Bayley, John 108
Bayley, John Oliver 108
Bayley, Nicola 108
Bayley, Ryan 108
Bayley, Stephen 108
Bayly, Christopher 108
ペイリー
Paley, Grace 1072
Paley, Maggie 1072
Paley, Nina 1072
ベイリス
Baylis, John 108
ペイリス
Peiris, Gamini L. 1092
ベイリン
Bailin, Sharon 81
Bailyn, Bernard 81
Bailyn, Lotte 81
ペイリン
Palin, Michael 1072
Palin, Sarah 1072
ヘイル
Hale, Bob 556
Hale, Chip 556
Hale, Deborah 557
Hale, DeMarlo 557
Hale, Ginn 557
Hale, Irina 557
Hale, James Graham 557
Hale, Joel 557
Hale, J.R. 557
Hale, Lori Brandt 557
Hale, Rachael 557
Hale, Sandra Beatriz 557
Hale, Shannon 557
Hale, Steve 557
Hale, Tony 557
ベイル
Bail, Murray 81
Bale, Christian 85
Bale, Gareth 85
Vale, Jason 1439
Vale, Lawrence J. 1439
Veil, Simone 1450
ペイル
Peile, Ed 1092
ヘイルシャム卿
Lord Hailsham 555
ヘイルス
Hales, Robert E. 557
ヘイルズ
Hails, Rosemary 555
Hales, Dianne R. 557
Hales, Jonathan 557
Hayles, Rob 585
ベイルズ
Bales, Kevin 86
Bayles, David 108
ペイルス
Peyrous, Bernard 1105
ヘイルベク
Kheir Bek, Ghazwan 727
ペイルポイ
Palepoi, Tenny 1072
ペイルルヴァッド
Peyrelevade, Jean 1105
ベイレス
Bayless, Jerryd 108
ペイレフィッテ

ヘ

Peyrefitte, Michael 1105
ヘイレン
Heylen, Ilse 602
ベイレンソン
Beilenson, Susanne 114
ペイロ・ゴンサレス
Peyrot González, Marco Antonio 1105
ペイロト・ゴンサレス
Peyrot González, Marco Antonio 1105
ヘイワース
Hayworth, Ray 586
ヘイワード
Hayward, Casey 586
Hayward, Francesca 586
Hayward, Gordon 586
Hayward, Jennifer 586
Hayward, Peter 586
Hayward, Susan 586
Hayward, Tony 586
Heyward, Cameron 603
Heyward, Craig 603
Heyward, Jason 603
Heyward, Louis M. 603
ヘイワード・ベイ
Heyward-bey, Darrius 603
ヘイン
Hain, Peter 555
ベイン
Bain, Barbara J. 81
Bain, Carolyn 81
Bain, Conrad 81
Bain, James A. 81
Bain, Julie 81
Bain, Ken 81
Bain, Neville 81
Bain, Terry 81
Vane, John Robert 1443
Veng Sakhon 1451
ペイン
Pain, Clare 1070
Pain, Jeff 1070
Pain, Roger H. 1070
Paine, Caleb 1070
Paine, Lynn Sharp 1070
Paine, Robert 1070
Paine, Robert Treat 1070
Paine, Sheila 1070
Paine, Sheperd 1070
Paine, Stephen 1070
Payne, Adreian 1089
Payne, Alex 1089
Payne, Alexander 1089
Payne, Binet 1089
Payne, Cameron 1089
Payne, Chris 1089
Payne, David 1089
Payne, Don 1089
Payne, Douglas William 1089
Payne, Frederick 1089
Payne, Geoffrey K. 1089
Payne, Jared 1089
Payne, Judy 1089
Payne, Katharine 1089
Payne, Keri-Anne 1089
Payne, Kim John 1089
Payne, Liam 1089
Payne, Marise 1089
Payne, Michael 1089
Payne, Roger 1089
Payne, Stuart 1089
ペインコファー
Peinkofer, Jim 1092
ペイン・ジェームズ
Payne-James, Jason 1089
ヘインズ
Haines, Annette M. 555
Haines, Carolyn 555
Haines, Duane E. 555
Haines, George 555
Haines, Michael 555
Haines, Mike 555
Haines, Staci 555
Haines, Tim 555
Hanes, Jeffrey E. 566
Hanes, Mari 566
Haynes, Christopher D. 585
Haynes, Cyndi 585
Haynes, Dana 585
Haynes, Elizabeth 585
Haynes, Jasmine 585
Haynes, John Earl 585
Haynes, John Harold 585
Haynes, Johnny 585
Haynes, Roslynn Doris 585
Haynes, Stephen R. 585
Haynes, Todd 585
ベインズ
Baines, Gertrude 82
Baines, John 82
Baines, Leighton 82
Baines, Nigel 82
Baines, Oliver 82
Baines, Phil 82
Baines, Rebecca 82
Bains, Navdeep Singh 82
Baynes, Aron 108
Baynes, Pauline 108
ペインター
Painter, Anthony 1070
Painter, Melissa 1070
Painter, Nell Irvin 1070
Painter, Vinsten 1070
ベイントン
Baynton, Douglas C. 108
ヘインバーグ
Haneberg, Lisa 566
ベインブリッジ
Bainbridge, Beryl 81
Bainbridge, David 82
ベインホースフォード
Bain-horsford, Yolande 82
ベインホッカー
Beinhocker, Eric D. 115
ヘインリック
Heinrich, Elmer G. 590
ヘウアー
Heuer, Meredith 601
ベヴァリー
Bevarly, Elizabeth 134
Beverley, Jo 134
ベヴァリッジ
Beveridge, Bruce 134
ヘヴィ・D
Heavy D 587
ヘウィット
Hewitt, Les 602
Hewitt, Neville 602
Hewitt, Terry 602
ベヴィラックァ
Bevilacqua, Alberto 134
ベヴィラックワ
Bevilacqua, Piero 134
ヘウェット
Hewett, Richard 602
ヘーヴェデス
Höwedes, Benedikt 628
ヘヴェデス
Höwedes, Benedikt 628
ヘヴェトソン
Hewetson, Tom 602
ヘウス
Geus, Mireille 492
ペヴニー
Pevney, Joseph 1105
Pevný, Pavol 1105
ベェトゲ
Baetge, Jörg 79
ペエトコヴィッチ
Petković, Dušan 1103
ヘオ
Heo, Jenice 596
ヘーガー
Hoger, Marco 614
ベーカー
Baker, Brian 82
Baker, Buddy 82
Baker, Christopher John 83
Baker, David Weston 83
Baker, Delmon 83
Baker, Dusty 83
Baker, Ginger 83
Baker, Heidi 83
Baker, Howard Henry, Jr. 83
Baker, James Addison Ⅲ 83
Baker, James E. 83
Baker, J.I. 83
Baker, Joanne 83
Baker, John 83
Baker, John Austin 83
Baker, Kage 83
Baker, Kathleen 83
Baker, Kim 83
Baker, Nicholson 83
Baker, Nick 83
Baker, Ox 83
Baker, Randal 83
Baker, Robin 83
Baker, Rolland 83
Baker, Roy Ward 83
Baker, Sandra L. 83
Baker, Stephen 83
Baker, Steve 83
Baker, Sunny 83
Baker, Victor R. 83
Baker, Wayne E. 83
Baker, William Oliver 84
Barker, Richard 94
Barker, Thomas M. 94
ベガ
Vega, Gaspar 1449
Vega, Phyllis 1449
ベガイ
Begaj, Romela 114
ベガ・エレラ
Vega Herrera, Patricia 1449
ベガ・カシジャス
Vega Casillas, Salvador 1449
ベガ・ガルシア
Vega García, Gerardo Clemente Ricardo 1449
ベガグ
Begag, Azouz 114
ヘガジ
Hegazy, El-Morsi 589
ベガス
Vegas, Jhonattan 1449
ベーカー・スミス
Baker-Smith, Dominic 84
ベカゼ
Begadze, Giorgi 114
ヘガーティ
Hegarty, Patricia 589
ヘガティ
Hegarty, Jean 589
Hegarty, Paul 589
ベガ・デ・ラ・ファジャ
Vega de la Falla, Jesus 1449
ヘガート
Haegert, Sandy 553
ベカトル
Bekatorou, Sofia 115
ベガ・パスキエル
Vega Pasquier, Julio 1449
ベーカー＝ブライアン
Baker-Brian, Nicholas J. 84
ペカリーク
Pekarik, Peter 1093
ヘーガン
Hagan, John 553
Hagen, Joshua 554
Hagen, Uta 554
ヘガン
Heggan, Christiane 589
ペガーン
Pagan, Jeoffrey 1069
ヘギ
Hegi, Ashley 589
Hegi, Lori 589
ベーキー
Bekey, George A. 115
ベギーチ
Begich, Nick 114
ベキュ
Bécue, Benjamin 113
ベキリ
Bekiri, Ilirijan 115
ベキロワ
Vekilova, Bibitach 1450
ヘーグ
Hague, William Jefferson 554
Haig, Alexander Meigs, Jr. 555
ベーグ
Baig, Mirza E. 81
ベク
Baek, Matthew J. 79
ベグ
Begu, Irina-Camelia 114
ベグー
Bégou, Georges 114
ペク
Paek, Chang-ryong 1069
Paek, Hak-rim 1069
Paek, Nam-sun 1069
Paik, Hee-young 1070
Pek, Ryong-chon 1093
ペグ
Pegg, Simon 1092
ヘクサム
Hexum, Angela L. 602
ベクシー
Vecsey, George 1449
ベクシガス
Bexigas, Joao Quaresma Viegas 134
ヘクシャー

Heckscher, Melissa 588
ベクシンスキ
Beksiński, Zdzisław 115
ベグズィーン・ヤボーホラン
Begziin Yavuukhulan 114
ヘクスター
Hexter, Eric 602
ヘクター
Hechter, Michael 588
Hector, Jonas 588
Hector, Michael 588
ベクター
Waechter, Katja 1467
ベクターシュ
Bektas, Cengiz 115
ベクダル
Bechdel, Alison 111
ベクツルガノフ
Bekturganov, Nuraly 115
ヘクデ
Hegde, Ramakrishna Mahabaleshwar 589
ベクテル
Bechtel, Carol M. 111
Bechtel, Stephen, Jr. 111
ヘクト
Hecht, Ann 588
Hecht, Ben 588
Hecht, Eugene 588
ベクトルシェイマー
Bechtolsheimer, Laura 111
ベクドルト
Bechdolt, Jack 111
ヘグナー
Hegnor, Hans-Dieter 589
ベグニ
Begheni, Ndeh John 114
ペクニョ
Pequegnot, Laure 1096
ベグベデ
Beigbeder, Frederic 114
ベクボエフ
Bekboev, Turdunazir 115
ベクマン
Beckmann, Jana 112
ベクマンベトフ
Bekmambetov, Timur 115
ベグムイラドフ
Begmuradov, Orazmurat 114
ベグムラドフ
Begmuradov, Orazmurat 114
ヘクラー
Hächler, Bruno 552
ペグラー
Pegler, Martin 1092
ペグラム
Pegrum, Juliet 1092
ベグラリャン
Beglaryan, Gagik 114
ベグリー
Begley, Adam 114
Begley, Ann 114
Begley, Sharon 114
ペクリ
Pekli, Maria 1093
ヘグルンド
Hägglund, Göran 554
Höglund, Anna 615
Hoglund, Greg 615
ベグレイ
Begley, Sharon 114
ペクレス
Pécresse, Valérie 1091
ペゲ
Pege, Aladar 1092
ベケシュ
Bekes, Andrej 115
ヘーゲス
Höges, Clemens 614
ベケタエフ
Beketayev, Marat 115
ヘゲダス
Hegedus, Louis S. 589
ベケット
Beckett, Bernard 112
Beckett, John D. 112
Beckett, Josh 112
Beckett, Lori 112
Beckett, Margaret Mary 112
Beckett, Neil 112
Beckett, Ray 112
Beckett, Simon 112
Beckett, Wendy 112
ペケノ
Pequeno, Ovidio 1096
ヘゲマン
Hegeman, Jamin 589
ヘゲラー
Hegeler, Jens 589
ペゲラー
Pöggeler, Otto 1120
ヘーゲル
Hagel, Chuck 554
Hagel, John, Ⅲ 554
ヘゲル
Heger, Leoš 589
ペケルマン
Pekerman, José 1093
ベケレ
Bekele, Alemitu 115
Bekele, Gulado 115
Bekele, Kenenisa 115
Bekele, Tariku 115
ヘーケレン
Heekeren, Hauke R. 588
ヘケロップ
Hækkerup, Karen 553
Hækkerup, Nick 553
ヘーゲン
Hagen, Earle H. 554
ヘーケンス
Heerkens, Gary 588
ベコー
Bécaud, Gilbert 111
ベゴ
Bego, Mark 114
ペコ
Peko, Domata 1093
Peko, Kyle 1093
ベゴヴィッチ
Begovic, Asmir 114
ベゴス
Begos, Kevin 114
ペコティック
Pecotic, Branka 1091
ベコート
Bacote, Vincent 78
ベゴドー
Bégaudeau, François 114
ペコビッチ
Pekovic, Nikola 1093
ベコフ
Bekoff, Marc 115
Bekov, Torogul 115
ペゴラノ
Pegoraro, Renzo 1092
ペコラロ・スカニオ
Pecoraro Scanio, Alfonso 1091
ペコラロスカーニオ
Pecoraro Scanio, Alfonso 1091
ペコリーノ
Pecorino, Lauren 1091
ペーゴロ
Pegolo, Gianluca 1092
ベーコン
Bacon, John U. 77
Bacon, Jono 77
Bacon, Kevin 77
Bacon, Tony 77
Bacon, Ursula 77
ベゴン
Begon, Michael 114
ヘザー
Heather, Teariki 587
ベサイテ
Vėsaitė, Birutė 1454
ベサーズ
Bethards, Betty 133
ベサニス
Bethanis, Susan J. 133
ベサニーリャ
Bezanilla, Clara 135
ペサベント
Pesavento, Larry 1101
ペサホビッチ
Peisakhovitch, Larissa 1092
ベサラブ
Bessarab, Maiia IAkovlevna 132
ベザリー
Bezaly, Sharon 135
ベサレル
Besalel, Victoria A. 132
ペサロッシ・ガルシア
Pezzarossi García, Dwight Antony 1105
ベサンコ
Besanko, David 132
ペサンテス・ベニテス
Pesántez Benítez, Johana 1101
ベサント
Bessant, Claire 132
Bessant, J.R. 132
ページ
Page, Anita 1069
Page, Betty 1069
Page, Bryony 1069
Page, Elen 1069
Page, Jeffrey 1069
Page, Jimmy 1069
Page, Larry 1069
Page, Lesley 1069
Page, Malcolm 1069
Page, Patti 1069
Page, Stephen 1069
Page, Willis 1069
Paige, Rod 1070
ペシ
Pesce, Mark 1101
Pesci, Joe 1101
ベシア
Bethea, Antoine 133
ペシィック
Pethick, Christopher 1103
ペシェ
Peche, Matthieu 1091
ペシエ
Peschier, Benoit 1101
ペジェグリーノ
Pellegrino, Mauricio 1093
ベジェティ
Bexheti, Blerim 134
ペシェフスキ
Peshevski, Vladimir 1101
ベジェリン
Bellerin, Hector 117
ページェン
Padjen, Robert 1068
ヘーシク
Hasik, James M. 579
ヘシコ
Heshko, Ivan 600
ペジック
Pesic, Peter 1101
ベシッチ
Besic, Muhamed 132
ペシッチ
Pesic, Aleksandar 1101
Pešić, Dragiša 1101
ペシーナ
Pessina, Massimo 1101
ベシーノ
Vecino, Matias 1449
ベジノ
Bésineau, Jacques M. 132
ベジノー
Bésineau, Jacques M. 132
ベシノ・アレグレ
Vecino Alegret, Fernando 1449
ベジ・ビアオ
Gbedji Vyaho, Christine 485
ベシミ
Besimi, Fatmir 132
ページャー
Pajor, Jeffrey J. 1071
ベジャウィ
Bedjaoui, Mohamed 113
ベジャク
Bezjak, Roman 135
ペシャラ
Pechalat, Nathalie 1091
ベジャール
Béjart, Maurice 115
ペシャロフ
Peshalov, Nikolai 1101
ベジャン
Bejan, Adrian 115
ペジュ
Péju, Pierre 1093
ベジューズ
Bezduz, Bulent 135
ベシュテル
Bechtel, Guy 111
ペシュレ
Paicheler, Pénélope 1070
ベシューン
Bethune, Zina 133
ベジョ
Bejo, Bérénice 115
Bello, Yván 117

ペーション
Persson, Göran 1101
Persson, Johanna 1101
Persson, Jörgen 1101
ベシリンド
Vesilind, Priit 1454
ベシール
Bethel, Marcus 133
ベーシンガー
Basinger, Kim 102
ヘーシンク
Geesink, Anton 486
ヘジンボサム
Heginbotham, Eric 589
ヘス
Hess, Barbara 601
Hess, Dean 601
Hess, Dick 601
Hess, Don 601
Hess, Frederick M. 601
Hess, Joan 601
Hess, Patricia A. 601
Hess, Paul 601
Hess, Richard S. 601
Hess, Tom 601
Hesse, Karen 601
Hessou, Félix 601
ベス
Bès, Daniel R. 132
Bess, Clayton 132
Bess, Georges 132
Besse, Francoise 132
ペース
Pace, Jim 1067
Pace, Peter 1067
Paese, Matthew J. 1069
ベズアシビリ
Bezhuashvili, Gela 135
ペー・ズィン・トゥン
Re Zin Tun 1175
ベスウィック
Beswick, Bill 133
ベスガ
Vesga, Mikel 1454
ベスカン
Vescan, Cynthia Vanessa 1454
ペスキー
Pesky, Johnny 1101
ベスキマギ
Veskimägi, Taavi 1454
ペスキーモ
Peskimo 1101
ペスケ
Peske, Nancy K. 1101
ヘスケス
Hesketh, Karne 601
ヘスケット
Heskett, James L. 601
Heskett, John 601
ペスコ
Pesko, Manuela Laura 1101
ベスコフ
Beskov, Konstantin 132
ベスコン
Bescond, Anais 132
ヘスス・ナバス
Jesus Navas 672
ベススメルトヌイ
Bezsmertny, Roman 135
ベススメルトノワ
Bessmertnova, Natalia 132
ヘスター
Hester, Beth Landis 601
Hester, Carl 601
Hester, Devin 601
Hester, D.Micah 601
Hester, Elliott Neal 601
Hester, James 601
Hester, Paul 601
Hester, Stephen 601
ベスター
Bestor, Theodore C. 133
ベスタエワ
Bestaeva, Zinaida 133
ヘースタース
Heesters, Johannes 588
ベスターダイン
Westerduin, Anne 1495
ベスタルド
Bestard, Jaime 133
ベステアー
Vestager, Margrethe 1454
ヘステネス
Hestenes, Roberta 601
ペステル
Paster, Maxim 1084
ヘスト
Hest, Amy 601
ベスト
Best, Antony 133
Best, Aprille 133
Best, Cari 133
Best, Eve 133
Best, George 133
Best, Isabel 133
Best, Joel 133
Best, Kathryn 133
Best, Pete 133
Best, Richard 133
Best, Rory 133
Best, Rupert 133
Best, Thomas M. 133
Vest, Charles Marstiller 1454
West, Franz 1494
ペストカ
Pestka, Elizabeth L. 1101
ペーストフ
Pestov, Pyotr 1101
ペストフ
Pestoff, Victor Alexis 1101
ベスド・リオン
Bessudo Lion, Sandra 133
ヘストン
Heston, Charlton 601
Heston, Chris 601
Heston, Steven 601
ベズニエ
Besnier, Emmanuel 132
ベスニナ
Vesnina, Elena 1454
ヘス＝バイバー
Hesse-Biber, Sharlene Nagy 601
ヘスバーグ
Hesburgh, Theodore Martin 600
ベスパーマン
Vesperman, Jennifer 1454
ベスフルグ
Boespflug, Francois 153
ベスベス
Besbes, Azza 132
Besbes, Sarra 132
ベズボロードワ
Bezborodova, Irina Vradimirovna 135
ヘスマン
Hessman, Mike 601
Hethmon, Robert H. 601
ヘスミラー
Hessmiller, Joanne M. 601
ベスメルトニフ
Bessmertnykh, Alexander 133
ベスメルトノワ
Bessmertnova, Natalia 132
ベースメント・ジャックス
Jaxx, Basement 667
ベズモーズギス
Bezmozgis, David 135
ヘスラー
Hessler, Keith 601
Hessler, Peter 601
ヘスラム
Heslam, Peter S. 601
ヘスリップ
Heslip, Brady 601
ペスル
Pessl, Marisha 1101
ヘスロヴ
Heslov, Grant 601
ヘスロフ
Heslov, Grant 601
ヘスロプ
Heslop, Pauline 601
ヘセ
Jese, Rodriguez 672
ベセ
Besse, Albert 132
ペゼシュキア
Pezeshkian, Masoud 1105
ペゼシュキアン
Pezeshkian, Masoud 1105
ベセーソ
Bessaiso, Ehab 132
ペセック
Pesek, John 1101
Pesek, William 1101
ベセベス
Besebes, Otoichi 132
ベセラ
Becerra, Elson 111
Becerra, Wuilmer 111
ベゼラ
Bezerra, Fernando 135
ペーゼラ
Peizerat, Gwendal 1093
ベーゼラガー
Boeselager, Philipp Freiherr von 153
ベゼラ・コエリョ
Bezerra Coelho, Fernando 135
ベセリー
Vesely, Vitezslav 1454
ベゼリデス
Bezzerides, Albert 135
ベセリノフ
Veselinov, Doragan 1454
ベセル
Besser, Jiří 132
Bethel, Carl 133
Bethel, Justin 133
Bethel, Marcus 133
ヘセルデン
Heselden, Jimi 600
ヘゼルデン
Heselden, Jimi 600
ベセル・トンプソン
Bethel-thompson, McLeod 133
ヘーゼルリーダー
Haselrieder, Oswald 579
ベセン
Besen, Ellen 132
ペソア
Pessoa, Anna 1101
Pessoa, Regina 1101
Pessoa, Rodrigo 1101
ベゾス
Bezos, Jeff 135
ヘゾニャ
Hezonja, Mario 603
ベゾブラゾヴァ
Besobrasova, Marika 132
ベソム
Besom, Mae 132
ペゾルド
Petzold, Charles 1105
ベソロ
Veloso, Paulina 1451
ベゾロフスキ
Wesołowski, Józef 1494
ヘソン
Hyesung 641
ヘダー
Heder, Stephen R. 588
ベーダー
Bader, Jeffrey A. 78
Bader, Sara 78
ベター
Bettah, Mohfoudh Ould 133
ペーター
Peter, Niklaus 1102
Peter, Ralf 1102
Petre, Tracy 1103
ヘダーウィック
Hedderwick, Mairi 588
ヘタグリ
Khetaguri, Aleksandre 727
ペタション
Petersson, Olof 1103
ペータース
Peeters, Benoît 1092
Peeters, Frederik 1092
Peters, Artuur 1102
Peters, Ulrich 1102
ペーターセン
Petersen, Rasmus 1102
Petersen, Sue 1102
ペーターゼン
Petersen, Nils 1102
Petersen, Rudolf 1102
Petersen, Wolfgang 1102
ペーダーセン
Pedersen, Rikke 1091
Pedersen, Thor 1091
ペターセン
Petersen, Jan 1102
Pettersen, Suzann 1105
ペダーセン
Pedersen, Olof 1091
ベターソン
Betterson, Stanley 134
ペダーソン
Pedersen, Lasse H. 1091

ヘ

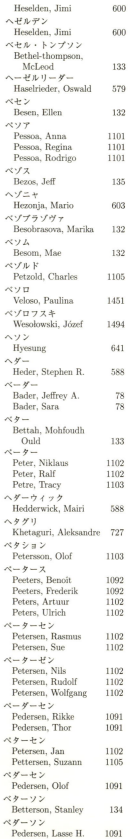

ベダード
Bedard, Michael 113
Bedard, Tony 113
ペターニャ
Petagna, Andrea 1101
ベダール
Bédard, Éric 113
ベダン
Bédan, Gisèle 113
Bedin, Frédéric 113
Vedin, Bengt-Arne 1449
ペタン
Peten, Chantal 1101
ベタンクール
Betancourt, Edmée 133
Betancourt, Ingrid 133
Betancourt, Jorge 133
Bethancourt, Alexis 133
Bettencourt, Liliane 134
ベタンコート
Bethancourt, Christian 133
ベタンコート＝スアレス
Betancourt Suárez, María del Socorro 133
ベタンセス
Betances, Dellin 133
ベタンソス
Betanzos, Yoandri 133
ベタンゾスモロ
Betanzos, Berta 133
ベタンヌ
Bettane, Michel 133
ベーチ
Beci, Veronika 111
ペチ
Peci, Spiro 1091
ペチェフスキー
Pechefsky, Rebecca 1091
ヘチカシビリ
Khechikashvili, Tariel 727
ベチック
Becík, Stanislav 111
ベチテル
Bechtel, Stefan 111
ベチミフィラ
Betsimifira, Fredo 133
ベチャ
Beqaj, Ilir 124
ベチャイ
Beqaj, Besim 124
ペチャノバ
Pechanova, Jana 1091
ペチャルニコス
Petsalnikos, Philippos 1104
ベチャワ
Beczala, Piotr 113
ペチュ
Pötzsch, Oliver 1128
ペチョンキナ
Pechonkina (nosova), Yuliya 1091
ベチリ
Beqiri, Valton 124
ベーツ
Bates, Alan 104
Bates, Evan 104
Bates, Kathy 104
ベツァーリ
Vezzali, Valentina 1454
ベツィグ
Betzig, Eric 134
ペツェク
Pecek, Željko 1091
ペツォス
Petsos, Thanos 1105
ペツォールト
Petzold, Christian 1105
ペツォルド
Petzold, Linda Ruth 1105
ヘッカー
Haecker, Katharina 553
Hecker, Hans-Ulrich 588
Hekker, Johnny 591
ベッカ
Baecker, Dirk 79
ベッカー
Baecker, Dirk 79
Baecker, Ronald 79
Becker, Aaron 111
Becker, Bonny 111
Becker, Boris 111
Becker, Brian E. 112
Becker, Carl B. 112
Becker, Catherine Kalama 112
Becker, Charlotte 112
Becker, Deborah R. 112
Becker, Donald J. 112
Becker, Gary Stanley 112
Becker, Gay 112
Becker, Gretchen E. 112
Becker, Hal B. 112
Becker, Hartmuth 112
Becker, Helaine 112
Becker, Holly 112
Becker, Howard Saul 112
Becker, Irving S. 112
Becker, James 112
Becker, Jasper 112
Becker, John D. 112
Becker, Joshua 112
Becker, Jürgen 112
Becker, Marty 112
Becker, Siegfried 112
Becker, Suzy 112
Becker, Wayne M. 112
Becker, Wolfgang 112
Bekker, Cajus 115
ベッカーズ
Beckers, Dominiek 112
ヘッカート
Heckart, Eileen 588
ベッカート
Beckert, Stephanie 112
ペッカネン
Pekkanen, Robert 1093
ベッカーマン
Beckerman, Joel 112
ベッカム
Beckham, David 112
Beckham, Odell 112
Beckham, Tim 112
Beckham, Victoria 112
ペッカム
Peckham, Morse 1091
ペッカリネン
Pekkarinen, Mauri 1093
ベッカーリンク
Bekkering, Annemiek 115
ヘツキ
Hedtke, Lorraine 588
ベッキ
Becchi, Matteo 111
Vecchi, Irene 1449
ベッキー
Betsky, Aaron 133
ベツキー
Betsky, Aaron 133
ヘッキング
Hecking, Dieter 588
Hekking, Brock 591
ベッキンセイル
Beckinsale, Kate 112
ベッキンセール
Beckinsale, Kate 112
ヘック
Heck, Howard L. 588
Heck, Peter J. 588
Heck, Richard Fred 588
Heck, Stefan 588
Hek, Youp van't 591
ベック
Baecque, Antoine de 79
Bech, Per 111
Beck 111
Beck, Aaron T. 111
Beck, Alan M. 111
Beck, Andreas 111
Beck, Annika 111
Beck, Bruce 111
Beck, Charlotte Joko 111
Beck, Cheryl Tatano 111
Beck, Chris 111
Beck, Clive 111
Beck, Elizabeth 111
Beck, Françoise 111
Beck, Glenn 111
Beck, Hans 111
Beck, Hans Georg 111
Beck, Ian 111
Beck, Jackson 111
Beck, Jean 111
Beck, Jeff 111
Beck, Jerry 111
Beck, Jessica 111
Beck, John C. 111
Beck, Judith S. 111
Beck, Kent 111
Beck, Knut 111
Beck, Kurt George 111
Beck, Martha Nibley 111
Beck, Martine 111
Beck, Matthias 111
Beck, Paul 111
Beck, Raymond W. 111
Beck, Samanthe 111
Beck, Ulrich 111
Böck, Johannes 152
Boeck, Karin 153
ベッグ
Begg, George 114
ペック
Paik, Karen 1070
Peck, Gregory 1091
Peck, Jamie 1091
Peck, M.Scott 1091
Peck, Richard 1091
Peck, Robert Newton 1091
Peck, Robert S. 1091
ペッグ
Pegg, Simon 1092
ベックウィス
Beckwith, Harry 113
ベックウィズ
Beckwith, Michael Bernard 113
Beckwith, Tobias 113
ベック＝ゲルンスハイム
Beck-Gernsheim, Elisabeth 112
ベックストローム
Beckström, Rod A. 112
ベックス＝マローニー
Becks-Malorny, Ulrike 112
ベッグ・スミス
Begg-Smith, Dale 114
ベッグスミス
Begg-Smith, Dale 114
ベック＝ダニエルセン
Bech-Danielsen, Claus 111
ベックナー
Beckner, Michael Frost 112
Beckner, Rebecca 112
ベックフォード
Beckford, James 112
Beckford, Sam 112
ベック・フリス
Beck-Friis, Barbro 112
ベック＝フリス
Beck-Friis, Barbro 112
ヘックマイヤー
Heckmair, Anderl 588
ヘックマン
Heckman, James Joseph 588
ベックマン
Beckman, Adam 112
Beckman, Thea 112
Beckmann, Jan Peter 112
Beckmann, Regine 112
ベックマン＝ウェルズ
Beckmann-Wells, Patricia 112
ベックラー
Bechler, Steve 111
ベックリー
Beckley, Timothy Green 112
ベックルズ
Beckles, Pennelope 112
ベックレ
Böckle, Günter 152
ベックレー
Baechle, Thomas R. 79
ベックレイク
Becklake, Sue 112
ベックロフ
Beckloff, Mark 112
ベッケ
Bethge, Lutz 133
ベッケメレム
Bekkemellem, Karita 115
ヘッケル
Haeckael, Stephen H. 553
ベッケール
Becker, Jean Jacques 112
ベッケル
Beckel, Heather 111
ベッケルス
Bekkers, Dennis 115
ベッケルト
Beckert, Patrick 112
Beckert, Stephanie 112
ベッケル＝ホー
Becker-Ho, Alice 112
ヘッケルマン
Hoekelman, Robert A. 612
ベッケン
Bekken, Jon 115
Bekken, Nancy 115
ベッケンシュタイン

Bekenstein, Jacob D. 115
ベッケンバウアー
Beckenbauer, Franz 111
ベッケンフェルデ
Bockenforde, Ernst Wolfgang 152
ベッコ
Bokko, Havard 155
ペツコ
Petsko, Gregory A. 1104
ベッコン
Beckon, Madge 112
ヘッサ
Hessa, Sultan al-Jaber 601
ヘッサー
Hesser, Amanda 601
Hesser, Leon F. 601
ベッサ
Bessa, Julio 132
ベッサラー
Bessallah, Hamid 132
ヘッジス
Hedges, Kristi 588
Hedges, Michael 588
ヘッジズ
Hedges, Austin 588
Hedges, Chris 588
ペッシュ
Pech, Benjamin 1091
ペッショ
Pescio, Claudio 1101
ヘッセ
Hesse, Christian 601
Hesse, Helge 601
Hesse, Konrad 601
Hesse, Reinhard 601
Hesse, Wolfgang 601
ベッセ
Besse, Albert 132
ヘッセキエル
Hessekiel, David 601
ペッセージャ
Pezzella, German 1105
ヘッセ・ブコフスカ
Hesse-Bukowska, Barbara 601
ヘッセ・リヒテンベルガー
Hesse-Lichtenberger, Ulrich 601
ヘッセリンク
Hesselink, I.John 601
ベッセル
Bessel, Richard 132
ヘッセルバイン
Hesselbein, Frances 601
ベッセン
Bessen, James 132
ベッソノワ
Bessonova, Anna 133
ベッソン
Besson, Billy 133
Besson, Eric 133
Besson, Jean-Louis 133
Besson, Louis 133
Besson, Luc 133
Besson, Philippe 133
ベッタ
Vetah, Mohamed Abdel 1454
ペッター
Petter, Frank Arjava 1105
ベッタイエブ
Bettaieb, Riadh 133
ベッチ
Veatch, Chauncey 1449
ベッチウ
Becciu, Giovanni Angelo 111
ベッチェル
Bechtel, Stefan 111
ベッチグ
Betzig, Eric 134
ベッチャー
Bettcher, James 133
ヘッチャー - ローゼンバウアー
Hatcher-Rosenbauer, Wolfgang 581
ベッツ
Betts, Dion Emile 134
Betts, Heidi 134
Betts, Julian R. 134
Betts, Mookie 134
Betts, Raymond F. 134
Betts, Stacey Waldman 134
Betz, Cecily Lynn 134
Betz, Frederick 134
Betz, Pauline 134
ヘッツァー
Hetzer, Nicole 601
ベッツァリ
Vezzali, Valentina 1454
ペッツェッラ
Pezzella, Giuseppe 1105
ヘッツェル
Hetzel, Steve 601
ペッツェル
Petzel, Todd E. 1105
ベッツォージ
Vezzosi, Al'essandro 1454
ペッツォルト
Petzold, Christian 1105
Petzoldt, Martin 1105
ペッツート
Pezzutto, Antonio 1105
ペッツワン
Petchsuwan, Kosol 1101
ベッテ
Bette, Karl-Heinrich 133
ベッティ
Betti, Laura 134
ペッティナート
Pettinato, Tuono 1105
ペッティナーリ
Pettinari, Stefano 1105
ベッティーニ
Bettini, Paolo 134
ペッティ・パガディサバル
Petti Pagadizabal, Guido 1105
ベッテス
Bettes, Hannah 134
ベッテッティーニ
Bettetini, Maria 134
ベッテル
Bettel, Xavier 133
Vettel, Sebastian 1454
ペッテルソン
Petterson, Per 1105
ベッテルハイム
Bettelheim, Charles 133
ベッテンコート
Bettencourt, Matt 134
ヘッド
Head, Jenny 586
Head, Maaike 586
ベット
Bett, David 133
Bett, Franklin 133
Bett, Willy 133
ペット
Phet, Phomphiphak 1106
ペットウェイ
Petteway, Shaq 1105
Pettway, D.J. 1105
ヘットガーシュ
Hetto-gaasch, Françoise 601
ヘットカンプ
Hetcamp, Ruth 601
ベッドグッド
Bedggood, Domonic 113
ベッドソン
Bedson, Günther 113
ヘットナー
Hettner, Alfred 601
ベットヒャー
Böttcher, Jürgen 165
ヘットフィールド
Hetfield, James 601
ベッドフォード
Bedford, Carol 113
Bedford, David 113
Bedford, Deborah Jackson 113
Bedford, Neal 113
Bedford, T. 113
ベットホイザー
Betthäuser, Andreas 134
ペットマン
Pettman, Ralph 1105
Pettman, Simon 1105
ヘッドリー
Headley, Chase 586
Headley, Heather 586
Headley, Victor 586
Hedley, Timothy P. 588
ヘッドリク
Headrick, Daniel R. 586
ベットレーム
Bettelheim, Charles 133
ペッパー
Pepper, Barry 1096
Pepper, Hamish 1096
Pepper, John Ennis, Jr. 1096
Pepper, Terence 1096
ペッパーコーン
Peppercorn, David 1096
ペッパーズ
Peppers, Julius 1096
ベッヒャー
Becher, Bernd 111
Becher, Will 111
ペップ
Pep, Willie 1096
ペッファー
Pfeffer, Jeffrey 1105
ヘッファメール
Heffermehl, Fredrik S. 588
ヘッフェ
Höffe, Otfried 613
ヘップナー
Heppner, Ben 596
ヘップバーン
Hepburn, Brandon 596
Hepburn, Katharine 596
ヘッフルバウアー
Heffelbower, Holly A. 588
ヘッフル・リーシュ
Höfl-Riesch, Maria 614
ヘッペル
Heppell, Michael 596
ベッラ
Vella, George 1451
ペッリコ
Pellico, Silvio 1093
ベッルッシ
Bellusci, Giuseppe 118
ペッレグリーニ
Pellegrini, Lorenzo 1093
ヘッレラン
Helleland, Linda 591
ヘーデ
Heede, Sylvia Vanden 588
ベーテ
Bethe, Hans Albrecht 133
ベティ
Béti, Mongo 133
ペティ
Petit, Laurence 1103
Petty, Kate 1105
Petty, Will 1105
ペティー
Petty, Bryce 1105
ペディー
Peddi, Parvin F. 1091
ベティアソモ
Beti Assomo, Joseph 133
ペティヴィッチ
Petievich, Gerald 1103
ベディエ
Bédier, Pierre 113
ベディエント
Bedient, Timothy J. 113
ベティカー
Boetticher, Budd 153
ベディク
Bedik, Nenad 113
ペティグリー
Pettegree, Andrew 1105
ペティグリュー
Pettigrew, Antonio 1105
ペティグルー
Pettigrew, Antonio 1105
Pettigrew, Brandon 1105
Pettigrew, Jim, Jr. 1105
Pettigrew, Pierre 1105
ペティス
Bettis, Chad 134
Bettis, Jerome 134
Pettis, Gary 1105
ペティット
Pettitt, Sabina 1105
Pettitt, Stephen 1105
Pettitte, Andy 1105
ヘティッヒ
Hettich, Georg 601
ヘデイド
Hedeid, Mintana Mint 588
ペティート
Petit, Yusmeiro 1103
Pettit, Justin 1105
Pettitte, Andy 1105
ペティナート
Pettinato, Dan 1105
ヘティヒ
Hettich, Georg 601
ベティマラス
Beti-marace, Martial 133

ペティヨン
Pétillon, René 1103
ペティリア
Petilla, Carlos Jericho 1103
ベティン
Bettin, Jorn 134
ベティング
Beting, Mauro 133
ベディントン
Beddington, John 113
ベーデカー
Bödeker, Anke 152
ベデカー
Böddeker, Günter 152
ペー・テ・キン
Pe Thet Khin 1103
ヘデゴー
Hedegaard, Connie 588
ペデシェン
Pedersen, Helga 1091
Pedersen, Sverre Lunde 1091
ペーテション
Peterson, Ingela 1103
ペテション
Peterson, Teodor 1103
ベテスニク
Vetesnik, Jan 1454
Vetesnik, Ondrej 1454
ベテタ
Beteta, Hugo 133
ヘテマイ
Hetemaj, PerParim 601
ペデリアーリ
Pederiali, Giuseppe 1091
ベテリッジ
Betteridge, Keith 134
ヘデル
Kheder, Hassan Ali Ali 727
ペーテルス
Peeters, Elvis 1092
Peeters, Kris 1092
Peters, W.J.Th. 1102
ペテルス
Peters, Dimitri 1102
ペテルセン
Pettersen, Oeystein 1105
Pettersen, Suzann 1105
ペデルセン
Pedersen, Anders 1091
Pedersen, Christinna 1091
Pedersen, Hilde G 1091
Pedersen, Maya 1091
Pedersen, Niels-Henning Orsted 1091
Pedersen, Rikke Moller 1091
ペーテルソヌス
Pētersons, Reinis 1103
ペテルソネ
Petersone, Karina 1103
ペテルソン
Petersson, Havard Vad 1103
ペテルノッリ
Peternolli, Giovanni 1102
ペテルバリモリナル
Petervari-molnar, Bendeguz 1103
ベテルビエフ
Beterbiev, Artur 133
ペデロッツォリ
Pederzolli, Nicola 1091
ベーテン
Baeten, Yolande 79
ベード
Bade, Lance 78
Bade, Patrick 78
ベト
Beto 133
Nguyen Viet 1021
ベド
Gbedo, Marie-Elise 485
ペト
Pheto, Moeng 1107
ベドゥイ
Bedoui, Nouredine 113
ペドゥッツィ
Peduzzi, Antono 1092
ペドゥッラ
Pedullà, Alfredo 1092
ペトゥホフ
Petukhov, Alexey 1105
ヘドゥル
Kheder, Hassan Ali Ali 727
ベートゥレーム
Bettelheim, Charles 133
ペトカノフ
Petkanov, Georgi 1103
ヘドクヴィスト
Hedqvist, Olle 588
ベートゲ
Bethge, Renate 133
ベトゲ
Batge, Leon 104
ペトコバ
Petkova, Temenuzhka 1103
ペトコビッチ
Petkovic, Andrea 1103
Petković, Bratislav 1103
ペトコフ
Petkov, Rumen 1103
ペトコブセク
Petkovšek, Mitja 1103
ベドーズ
Beddoes, Zanny Minton 113
ヘードストレム
Hedström, Per 588
ペドッティ
Pedotti, Christine 1091
ベトヒー
Vetchý, Vladimír 1454
ベドフォード - ターナ
Bedford-Turner, Shelagh 113
ベトベーズ
Betbèze, Jean-Paul 133
ベドベリ
Bedbury, Scott 113
ヘドマティ
Khedmati, Najmeh 727
ヘードマン
Hedman, Annalena 588
ベートマン
Bateman, Robert McLellan 104
ベードム
Vedum, Trygve Slagsvold 1449
ペトヤ
Petaja-siren, Tuuli 1101
ペトラー
Pettler, Pamela 1105
ペドラー
Pedler, Caroline 1091
ペトラウスカス
Petrauskas, Evaldas 1103
ペドラサ
Pedraza, Gustavo 1091
ペドラサ・シエラ
Pedraza Sierra, Wilfredo 1091
ペドラサ・ロドリゲス
Pedraza Rodríguez, Lina 1091
ペトラス
Petras, James F. 1103
Petras, Kathryn 1103
Petras, L. 1103
Petrus, Hugo 1104
ペトラーチェ
Petrache, Mihai 1103
ペトラッシ
Petrassi, Goffredo 1103
ペドラッツィーニ
Pedrazzini, Mauro 1091
ペトラフ
Peteraf, Margaret A. 1102
ヘトラン
Hetland, Tor Arne 601
ヘドリ
Khedri, Mahmoud 727
ヘドリー
Hedly, Carol 588
ペトリ
Petri, Bernhard 1104
Petri, Carl-Johan 1104
Petri, Michala 1104
Petri, Mike 1104
ペトリー
Petrie, Aviva 1104
Petrie, Geoff 1104
ペトリアシビリ
Petriashvili, Aleksi 1104
Petriashvili, Geno 1104
ペトリコフ
Petrikov, Pavel 1104
ペトリス
Petris, Giovanni 1104
ペトリソン
Petorison, Lisa A. 1103
ペトリチカ
Petricka, Jake 1104
ヘドリック
Hedrick, Chad 588
ペトリック
Petrick, Joseph A. 1104
ベトリッジ
Bettridge, Andrea 134
ペトリッチ
Petrich, Mike 1104
ペトリーナ
Petryna, Adriana 1104
ペトリーニ
Petrini, Carlo 1104
ベドリーヌ
Védrine, Hubert 1449
ベドリヌ
Védrine, Hubert 1449
ペトリフ
Petriv, Oleksandr 1104
ペトリラ
Petrila, John 1104
ベドリン
Védrine, Hubert 1449
ペトリン
Petrin, Tea 1104
ヘドル
Heddle, Iris E. 588
ペトルシェフスカヤ
Petrushevskaya, Liudmila Stefanovna 1104
ペトルシャーンスカヤ
Petrushanskaia, Rèma 1104
ペトルスドッティル
Petursdottir, Solveig 1105
ペトルソン
Petursson, Pall 1105
ペトルニアス
Petrounias, Eleftherios 1104
ペトルニク
Petrunek, Viktor Petrovich 1104
ペトルリック・フセイノヴィッチ
Petrlik-Huseinović, Andrea 1104
ペトレアス
Petraeus, David 1103
ペトレスク
Petrescu, Dan 1104
ペドレッティ
Pedretti, Carlo 1091
ペトレーティ
Petrétei, József 1104
ペトレーテイ
Petrétei, József 1104
ペトレニア
Piatrenia, Tatsiana 1109
ベトレーム
Bettelheim, Charles 133
ペトレリ
Petreley, Nick 1103
ヘドレン
Hedren, Tippi 588
ペトレンコ
Petrenko, Kirill 1103
Petrenko, Pavlo 1103
Petrenko, Vasilii 1104
ベトロ
Betro, Maria C. 133
ペトロ
Petro, Louis W. 1104
Petro, Robert J. 1104
ペドロ
Pedro, Diaz 1091
Pedro, Jimmy 1091
ペドロイア
Pedroia, Dustin 1091
ペトロヴァ
Petrova, Olesya 1104
ペドロヴィック
Petrovic, Svetlana 1104
ペトロヴィッチ
Petrovic, Mihailo 1104
Petrovic, Radosav 1104
ペドロ - キャロル
Pedro-Carroll, JoAnne L. 1091
ペトロ・コニ・ゼゼ
Petro-koni-zeze, Marguerite 1104
ペドロサ
Pedrosa, Cyril 1092

Pedrosa, Dani 1092
ペドロージアン
Bedrosian, Cam 113
ペトロシャン
Petrosian, Karlos 1104
Petrosyan, Artur 1104
ペトロス
Petros, Matheus 1104
Petros, Peter 1104
Petros, Solomon 1104
ペトロスキー
Petroski, Henry 1104
ペドロソ
Pedroso, Giovanna 1092
Pedroso, Ivan 1092
Pedroso, Joao Pedro 1092
Pedroso, Yadier 1092
ペトロッシアン
Petrossian, Michel 1104
ペドロ・デ・ラ・ロサ
de la Rosa, Pedro 336
ペトローネ
Petrone, Sonia 1104
Petrone, Valeria 1104
ペトロバ
Petrova, Stanimira 1104
ペトロビッチ
Petrovic, Mihailo 1104
Petroviq, Slobodan 1104
ペトロフ
Peterov, Aleksandr Mikhailovich 1102
Petroff, N. 1104
Petrov, Alexandre 1104
Petrov, Andrei Pavlovich 1104
Petrov, Anton 1104
Petrov, Ivan Ivanovich 1104
Petrov, Leonid A. 1104
Petrov, Nikolai 1104
Petrov, Plamen 1104
Petrov, Slavko 1104
Petrov, Vasilii Alekseevich 1104
Petrov, Vasilii Ivanovich 1104
Tjukin, Eduard 1407
ペトロブ
Petrov, Božo 1104
ペトロフスキー
Petrovskii, Vladimir Fedorovich 1104
ペドロラポソ
Pedro Raposo, Roberto 1091
ペート・ロールフス
Paeth Rohlfs, Bettina 1069
ペドロ・レオン
Pedro Leon 1091
ペドロ・ロドリゲス
Pedro Rodriguez 1091
ペトロワ
Petrova, Galina 1104
Petrova, Lyudmila 1104
Petrova, Maria 1104
Petrova, Nadia 1104
Petrova, Stoyka 1104
Petrova Arkhipova, Tatyana 1104
ヘードン
Hayden, Melissa 584
ペートン
Paton, John Glenn 1085
ベーナー
Bener, Peter Christian 120
Boehner, John 153
ベナー
Benner, Patricia E. 122
ペナ
Pena, Paul 1094
ペナー
Penner, Elvin 1095
Penner, Erdman 1095
ベナイサ
Benaissa, Mohammed 119
Benaissa, Rachid 119
Benaissa, Tarek 119
ベナヴィデス・ベドジャ
Benavidez Bedoya, Alfredo 119
ペナウベル
Penalber, Victor 1094
ヘナガン
Hennagan, Monique 594
ベナキスタ
Benacquista, Tonino 119
ペナク
Pennak, Sara 1095
ベナグリア
Bénaglia, Frédéric 119
ベナサジャグ
Benasayag, Miguel 119
ベナサール
Bennassar, Bartolomé 122
ペナシュー
Penashue, Peter 1094
ベナシュヌー
Benachenhou, Abdellatif 119
ベナーズ
Venners, Bill 1451
ペナス
Penas, Oscar 1094
ベナセラフ
Benacerraf, Baruj 119
ベナゼラフ
Bénazéraf, José 119
ベナター
Benatar, Solomon R. 119
ペナック
Pennac, Daniel 1095
ベナッシ
Benassi, Benny 119
Benassi, Marco 119
ベナティア
Benatia, Medhi 119
ヘナティオス
Genatios, Carlos 488
ベナビディス
Benavides, Freddie 119
ベナビデス
Benavides, Carlos Ricardo 119
Benavides Lopez De Ayala, Alfonso 119
Benavidez Lopes De Ayala, Alfonso 119
ベナベンテ
Benavente y Martinez, Jacinto 119
ベナーリ
Benali, Ahmad 119
ベナリオ
Benaglio, Diego 119
ペナリオ
Pennario, Leonard 1095
ペナール
Pennart, Geoffroy de 1095
ベナルアン
Benalouane, Yohan 119
ベナルド
Bennardo, Matthew 122
ヘナレ
Henare, Mānuka 593
ベナン
Benan, Umit 119
ベナンティ
Benanti, Laura 119
ペナンリー
Pennant-Rea, Rupert 1095
ヘニー
Henne, Chad 594
Henney, Kevlin 595
ベニ
Beny, Pierre Yves 124
ベニー
Benny 123
Benny, Mike 123
ペニ
Peni, Istvan 1095
ペニー
Penney, Alexandra 1095
Penney, Dixianne 1095
Penney, Stef 1095
Pennie, Fiona 1095
Penny, Elijhaa 1095
Penny, Louise 1095
Penny, Nicholas 1095
ベニア
Bennia, Catherine Juan 123
ベニアト
Beniato, Kouraiti 121
ベニアミナ
Beniamina, Rimeta 121
ベニオフ
Benioff, David 121
Benioff, Marc 121
ヘニカン
Henican, Ellis 594
ヘニガン
Hennigan, Rob 595
ヘニグ
Henig, Robin Marantz 594
ベニシュ
Bonisch, Yvonne 159
ベニシュー
Bénichou, Paul 121
ベニス
Bennis, Phyllis 123
Bennis, Warren Gameliel 123
ヘニス・プラスハルト
Hennis Plasschaert, Jeanine 595
ベニスン
Benison, C.C. 121
ベニゼロス
Venizelos, Evangelos 1451
ヘニッグ
Hennig, Benjamin 595
ペニック
Pennick, Nigel 1095
ヘニッケ
Hennicke, Peter 595
ヘニッシュ
Henisch, Bridget Ann 594
ベーニッシュ
Behnisch, Günter 114
ヘニディ
al-Henedi, Ibrahim 594
ベニテス
Benites, Juan Manuel 121
Benitez, Cristian 121
Benítez, Maria Ignacia 121
Benítez, Pánfilo 121
Benitez, Rafael 121
Benitez, Rogelio 121
ベニテズ
Benitez, M.Joaguim 121
ベニテス・パラダ
Benítez Parada, José Atilio 121
ベニート
Benito, Loris 121
ベニーニ
Benigni, Roberto Remigio 121
ベニノック
Benenoch, Caleb 120
ペニーパッカー
Pennypacker, Sara 1095
ベニハレフ
Benikhlef, Amar 121
ベニ・ムルダニ
Murdani, Benny 993
ベニャ
Benat, Etxebarria 119
ペーニャ
Peña, Elizabeth 1094
Pena, Felix 1094
Pena, Francisco 1094
Pena, Tony 1094
Pena, William 1094
ペニャ
Pena, Ernesto 1094
Peña, Javier López 1094
Peña, Marcos 1094
Peña, Maritza Rosabal 1094
Peña, Pedro 1094
Peña, Roberto 1094
Peña, Santiago 1094
ペニャアブレウ
Pena Abreu, Yamilet 1094
ペニャイリジョ
Peñailillo, Rodrigo 1094
ペニャエレラ
Peñaherrera, Estuardo 1094
ペニャ・グアバ
Peña Guaba, Antonio 1094
Peña Guaba, Francisco 1094
ペニャ・クラロス
Peña Claros, Claudia 1094
ペニャニエト
Peña Nieto, Enrique 1094
ペニャフィエル・ラレア
Peeñafiel Larrea, Freddy 1092
ペニャ・ペントン
Peña Pentón, Damodar 1094
ペニャランダ
Penaranda, Adalberto 1094
ベニュク
Beniuc, Valentin 121
ベニュシュ
Benus, Matej 124
ベニュス
Benyus, Janine M. 124

ベニンガ
Benninga, Simon 123
ベニンガー
Weninger, Brigitte 1493
ベニンカーサ
Benincasa, Joseph P. 121
ヘニング
Hennig, Curt 595
Henning, Alex 595
Henning, Bob 595
Henning, Joseph M. 595
Henning, Rasmus 595
ベーニング
Behning, Ute 114
ベニング
Bening, Annette 121
Benning, Stephen D. 123
ペニンクス
Penninx, Kees 1095
ヘニングセン
Henningsen, Eckart 595
ベニンテンディ
Benintendi, Andrew 121
ベニントン
Bennington, Chester 123
ペニントン
Pennington, Bill 1095
Pennington, Cliff 1095
Pennington, Kate 1095
Pennington, Matthew 1095
ベヌ
Bennu, Pierre 123
ペヌティエ
Pennetier, Jean-Claude 1095
ヘーネ
Hoehne, Andre 612
Hohne, Heinz 615
ベネ
Benét, Stephen Vincent 120
ペネ
Pennes, Gregoire 1095
ベネヴェリ
Benevelli, Alberto 120
ベネヴォロ
Benevolo, Leonardo 120
ベネガス
Venegas, Jorge 1451
Venegas, Julieta 1451
ヘネガン
Heneghan, Carl 594
Heneghan, James 594
Heneghan, Tom 594
ヘネシー
Hennessey, Meagan 594
Hennessey, Sarah 595
Hennessey, Wayne 595
Hennessy, Barbara G. 595
Hennessy, Catherine Hagan 595
Hennessy, John L. 595
Hennessy, Killian 595
ベネシュ
Benes, Nicholas E. 120
ベネショヴァー
Benešová, Marie 120
ヘネス
Henes, Donna 594
ベーネス
Benes, Laszlo 120
ペネス
Penev, Luboslav Mladenov 1094
ベネックス
Beineix, Jean-Jacques 115
ヘネッケ
Hennecke, Susanne 594
ベネッケン
Benecken, Sascha 120
ベネッディネ
Beneddine, Mehdi 120
ベネット
Bennet, Nancy 122
Bennet, Robert John 122
Bennett, Adrienne L. 122
Bennett, Alan 122
Bennett, Amanda 122
Bennett, Andrew 122
Bennett, Andrew E. 122
Bennett, Anthony 122
Bennett, Bob 122
Bennett, Caroline 122
Bennett, Carolyn 122
Bennett, Charles Henry 122
Bennett, Cherie 122
Bennett, Clay 122
Bennett, David 122
Bennett, Deborah J. 122
Bennett, Edgar 122
Bennett, Elizabeth 122
Bennett, Frances 122
Bennett, Greg 122
Bennett, Harve 122
Bennett, Hugh Hammond 122
Bennett, Jay 122
Bennett, Jeffrey W. 122
Bennett, Jill 122
Bennett, Joe 122
Bennett, John E. 122
Bennett, Jules 122
Bennett, Kelly 122
Bennett, Laura 122
Bennett, Marisa 122
Bennett, Mark 122
Bennett, Martellus 122
Bennett, Mary D.M. 122
Bennett, Matthew 122
Bennett, Michael 122
Bennett, M.R. 122
Bennett, Naftali 122
Bennett, Nathan 122
Bennett, Paul 122
Bennett, Paula 122
Bennett, P.N. 122
Bennett, R. 122
Bennett, Richard 122
Bennett, Richard Rodney 122
Bennett, Robert Jackson 122
Bennett, Robert Russell 122
Bennett, Ronan 122
Bennett, Sara 122
Bennett, Sophia 122
Bennett, Steve 122
Bennett, Tara 122
Bennett, Tony 122
Bennett, Vicki 122
Bennett, William M. 123
Bennett, W.Lance 123
ベネット・ギデンズ
Bennett Giddens, Rebecca 123
ベネディクタス
Benedictus, David 120
ベネディクト
Benedict, Alexandra 120
Benedict, Barbara 120
Benedict, Pinckney 120
ベネディクト16世
Benedict XVI 120
ベネディクトゥス16世
Benedict XVI 120
ベネディクトソン
Benediktsson, Bjarni 120
ベネディティ
Benedetti, Jean 120
ベネデェック
Benedek, Wolfgang 120
ベネデッティ
Benedetti, Gaetano 120
Benedetti, Jean 120
Benedetti, Mario 120
Benedetti, Michele 120
Benedetti, Ryan 120
ベネデュース
Beneduce, Ann Keay 120
ベネトー
Benneteau, Julien 122
ベネトン
Benetton, Alessandro 120
Benetton, Giuliana 120
Benetton, Luciano 120
ペネニッチ
Panenić, Tomislav 1074
ベネネイト
Benenate, Becky 120
ベネビデス・フェレイロス
Benavides Ferreyros, Ismael Alberto 119
ヘネヒテン
Genechten, Guido van 488
ペネフ
Penev, Luboslav Mladenov 1094
ペネベイカー
Pennebaker, D.A. 1095
ペネベーカー
Pennebaker, James W. 1095
ベネマ
Venema, Theodore H. 1451
ベネマン
Veneman, Ann Margaret 1451
ベネリ
Benelli, Andrea 120
ヘーネル
Haehnel, Stefan 553
Hänel, Wolfram 566
ヘネル
Hänel, Wolfram 566
ベネール
Venner, Dominique 1451
ベネル
Bennell, Sheila J. 122
ペネル
Pennell, Joan 1095
ベネンソン
Benenson, Peter 120
ベネンティ
Benenti, Giuliano 120
ペネンバーグ
Penenberg, Adam L. 1094
ベノー
Benaud, Richie 119
Benoit, Charles 123
ペノー
Peneux, Robert 1094
ベノイ
Benoit, Chris 123
ペノーネ
Penone, Giuseppe 1095
ベノワ
Benoit, Chris 123
Benoit, Joaquin 123
ペパー
Pepper, Daisy 1096
Pepper, John Ennis, Jr. 1096
ベハジャイナ
Behajaina, Petera 114
ペパーズ
Peppers, Don 1096
ヘバート
Hebert, Ben 587
ペーパーナウ
Papernow, Patricia L. 1076
ペハノバ
Pechanova, Jana 1091
ペパーバーグ
Pepperberg, Irene M. 1096
ベハピ
Vehapi, Idriz 1450
ベハーム
Beham, Maria 114
ペパン
Pépin, Charles 1096
Pépin, Jacques 1096
ベバンダ
Bevanda, Vjekoslav 134
ペービー
Pavey, Joanne 1088
ベビア
Bevir, Mark 134
ヘビアシビリ
Kheviashvili, Georgi 727
ペピアット
Peppiatt, Michael 1096
ペヒシュタイン
Pechstein, Claudia 1091
ベヒター
Waechter, Philip 1467
ベヒトラー
Bechtler, Hildegard 111
ペピトン
Pepitone, James S. 1096
ベビーフェイス
Babyface 76
ヘヒラー
Hächler, Bruno 552
ベヒラー
Bächler, Wolfgang 77
ベビル
Beville, Hugh Malcom 134
ヘブ
Hebb, Bobby 587
ベーブ
Beebe, Nelson H.F. 113
ベフ
Bekh, Maryna 115
ベブ
Bebb, Mike 110
Bebb, Peter 110
ペフ
Pech, Stanley Z. 1091
Pef 1092
ペプ
Pep, Melchior 1096

ヘファーナン
Heffernan, John 588
Heffernan, Margaret 588
Heffernan, Richard 588
Heffernan, Robert 588
ヘファナン
Heffernan, John 588
ヘフェリン
Haefelin, Sandra 553
ベフェルグアニパ
Weffer Guanipa, Jarimit 1487
ベフェルス
Wevers, Lieke 1496
Wevers, Sanne 1496
ベフォルト
Weffort, Francisco 1487
ヘプカー
Hoepker, Thomas 613
ペプキン
Pipkin, Donald L. 1115
ペフクル
Pevkur, Hanno 1105
ペブクル
Pevkur, Hanno 1105
ヘブゲン
Hebgen, Eric 588
ヘフス
Hoefs, Jochen 612
ペフツォフ
Pevtsov, Rostyslav 1105
ヘフト
Heft, Robert 589
ヘプトゥラー
Heptulla, Najma A. 596
ヘフナー
Häfner, Peter 553
Heffner, John E. 588
Hefner, Christie 589
Hefner, Hugh 589
ヘプナー
Heppner, Mary J. 596
Heppner, Vaughn 596
ペブニー
Pevney, Joseph 1105
ベフバハニ
Behbahani, Hamid 114
ベフバヤル・エルデネバト
Bekhbayar Erdenebatyn 115
ヘプバーン
Hepburn, Audrey 596
Hepburn, Claire 596
Hepburn, Katharine 596
Hepburn, Michael 596
ヘフラー
Hofler, Nicolas 614
ヘプラー
Hopler, Brigitta 622
ペプラー
Pepler, Tina 1096
ベブラウィ
Beblawi, Hazem 111
ヘブラング
Hebrang, Andrija 588
ペブリー
Pebley, Jacob 1091
ヘフリガー
Haefliger, Ernst 553
Haefliger, Michael 553
ペフリワン
Pehlivan, Ferhat 1092
ヘブル
Hebl, James R. 588
ペプル
Pepple, Ama 1096
ヘフルリーシュ
Höfl-Riesch, Maria 614
Riesch, Maria 1181
ヘブロン
Hebron, Sandra 588
ヘプワース
Hepworth, Dean H. 596
Hepworth, Jeri 596
ヘブンス
Havens, Richie 583
ヘブンスタイン
Havenstein, Rob 583
ベベ
Bebe 110
ペペ
Pepe 1096
Pepe, Osman 1096
Pepe, Phil 1096
Pepe, Simone 1096
ベヘアーマン
Bhaerman, Steve 135
ベベアール
Bébéar, Claude 110
ベヘイダ
Beheida, Saadna Ould 114
ベベット
Bebeto 111
ヘベデス
Höwedes, Benedikt 628
ベベート
Bebeto 111
ベベト
Bebeto 111
ベヘビライネン
Vehviläinen, Anu 1450
ベヘラノ・ポルテラ
Bejerano Portela, Gladys 115
ベベル
Bevell, Darrell 134
Veber, Janko 1449
ベヘールマン
Beherman, Jacques Paul 114
ヘーベルレ
Häberle, Peter 551
ペーボ
Pääbo, Svante 1067
ベボアリミサ
Beboarimisa, Ralava 111
ヘホメ
Hehomey, Hervé 589
ヘマー
Hemmer, Nina 592
ベーマイヤー
Wehmeyer, Michael L. 1487
ペマ・ギャルポ
Pema Gyalpo 1094
ペマ・ツェテン
Pema Tseden 1094
ヘマリング
Hemerling, James W. 592
ヘミオ
Jemio, Luis Carlos 669
ヘミオン
Hemion, Timothy 592
ヘミラ
Hemila, Hanna 592
Hemila, Kalevi 592
ペー・ミン
Pe Myint 1094
ヘミング
Hemming, Fujiko 592
Hemming, James 592
Hemming, John 592
ヘミングウェー
Hemingway, Gregory 592
Hemingway, Matt 592
ヘミングウェイ
Hemingway, Gregory 592
Hemingway, Temarrick 592
ヘミングス
Hemmings, David 592
Hemmings, Kaui Hart 593
ヘミングズ
Hemmings, David 592
ベーム
Boehm, Annett 153
Boehm, Barry W. 153
Boehm, Gottfried 153
Bohm, Annett 154
Böhm, Bartholomäus 154
Böhm, Karl-Heinz 154
Böhm, Winfried 154
ベム
Bem, Daryl J. 118
ペーム
Pohm, Matthias 1120
ベムーサ
Benmoussa, Chakib 121
ヘムサス
Hemsath, Dave 593
ヘームスケルク
Heemskerk, Femke 588
ヘムステッヘ
Hemstege, Anne 593
ヘムズリイ
Hemsley, David R. 593
ヘムズレイ
Hemsley, David R. 593
ヘムスワース
Hemsworth, Chris 593
ベームドルファー
Böhmdorfer, Dieter 155
ベーメ
Böhme, Gernot 155
Böhme, Hartmut 155
ヘメウェイ
Hemenway, Kevin 592
ヘメリー
Hemery, David 592
ヘーメル
Hämel, Beate-Irene 561
ヘメル
Hamel, Wouter 561
ヘモン
Hemon, Aleksandar 593
ベヤ
Beja, Fatos 115
ペヤ
Peya, Alexander 1105
ベヤジバ
Vejjajiva, Jane 1450
ペヤノビッチジュリシッチ
Pejanović-Đurišić, Milica 1093
ベヤール
Beyerle, Jamie 135
ベヤールガンス
Weyergans, François 1496
ベーヨニス
Vējonis, Raimonds 1450
ヘラー
Heller, Ben 591
Heller, H.Craig 591
Heller, Jane 591
Heller, Marcel 591
Heller, Peter 591
Heller, Philip 591
Heller, Rachel S.F. 591
Heller, Richard Ferdinand 591
Heller, Robert 591
Heller, Sarah E. 591
Heller, Steven 591
Heller, Ted 591
Heller, Zoë 591
Herer, Jack 597
Holler, Jurgen 617
ベーラ
Béla, Tarr 115
ベーラー
Behler, Ernst 114
Boehler, Stefanie 153
ベラ
Bela, Marko 115
Berra, Yogi 130
Vela, Carlos 1450
Vela, Sandra 1450
Vella, Adam 1450
Vera, Billy 1451
Vera, Oswaldo 1451
ベラー
Bellah, Robert Neelly 117
Beller, Ken 117
Beller, Steven 117
ペラ
Pera, Robert 1096
ペラー
Peller, Jane E. 1093
Perer, Adam 1097
ベライ
Belay, Ejigu 115
ベライー
Belyea, Barbara 118
ペライ
Perrey, Hans-Jürgen 1099
ペライア
Perahia, Murray 1096
ベライズ
Belaiz, Tayeb 115
ベライード
Belaïd, Chokri 115
ベライド
Belaid, Slaheddine 115
ヘライナー
Helleiner, Eric 591
ベライブ
Belaib, Bakhti 115
ベライル
Belisle, Lisette 116
Belisle, Matt 116
ベーラウ
Bohlau, Hermann 154
ヘラウィ
Hrawi, Elias 629
ベラウンデ
Belaúnde Terry, Fernando 115
ベラウンデ・テリ
Belaúnde Terry, Fernando 115
ベラウンデ・テリー
Belaúnde Terry,

Fernando 115
ベラ・オルモ
Vela Olmo, Carmen 1450
ベラキ
Beraki, Gebreselassie 124
ベラク
Belak, Wade 115
ペラゴッティ
Pelagotti, Alberto 1093
ヘラーコリン
Heller Korin, Ellen S. 591
ベラザ
Belaza, Nacera 115
ペラーザ
Peraza, Jose 1096
ベラジック
Velagic, Almir 1450
ヘラシメニア
Herasimenia, Aliaksandra 596
ペラジョ・カスタニョン
Pelayo Castañón, José 1093
ベラスケス
Velasquez, Alfonso 1450
Velásquez, David 1450
Velásquez, Ramón 1450
Velasquez, Vince 1450
Velázquez, Consuelo 1450
Velázquez, Julio César 1450
ベラズケズ
Velázquez, Celso R. 1450
ベラスケス・ガステル・ルイス
Velázquez-Gáztelu Ruiz, Cándido 1450
ベラスケス・コビエジャ
Velázquez Cobiella, Ena Elsa 1450
ベラスケス・バルディビア
Velásquez Valdivia, Aníbal 1450
ベラスケス＝マノフ
Velasquez-Manoff, Moises 1450
ベラスコ
Velasco, Andrés 1450
Velasco, Belisario 1450
Velasco, Fernando 1450
ベラスコ・コンドリ
Velasco Condori, Virginia 1450
ペラゼラ
Perazella, Mark A. 1096
ペラタ
Pélata, Patrick 1093
ベラック
Bellack, Alan S. 117
ペラッツ
Perutz, Max 1101
ベラッティ
Verratti, Marco 1453
ベラディ
Berardy, Lloyd 124
ヘラード
Hellard, Susan 591
ヘラト
Herath, Vijitha 596
ベラトリス
Beratlis, Greg 124
ペラトン
Perraton, Jonathan 1099
ベラニー
Bellany, John 117
ベラネク
Beranek, Leo Leroy 124
ベラネスガルシア
Veranes Garcia, Haislan 1451
ベラーノ
Vellano, Joe 1451
ペラハイヤ
Perahia, Murray 1096
ベラ・バルデス
Vela Valdés, Juan 1450
ベラバンス
Bellavance, Scott 117
ベラヒーノ
Berahino, Saido 124
ベラフィオーレ
Bellafiore, Mike 117
ペラフィネ
Pellat-finet, Lucien 1093
ベラフォンテ
Belafonte, Harry 115
ベラ・ベハラノ
Vera Bejarano, Candido Carmelo 1451
ヘラベール
Gelabert, María José 487
ベラマッジ
Vela Maggi, Pau 1450
ベーラミ
Behrami, Valon 114
ベラミー
Bellamy, Carol 117
Bellamy, David J. 117
Bellamy, Josh 117
Bellamy, Matthew 117
Bellamy, Olivier 117
Bellamy, Richard Paul 117
Bellamy, Rufus 117
ペラム
Pelham, Erik 1093
ベララビ
Bellarabi, Karim 117
ベラル
Bellal, Mohamed Vall Ould 117
ペラルタ
Peralta, David 1096
Peralta, Jhonny 1096
Peralta, José Ramón 1096
Peralta, Patrick 1096
Peralta, Wandy 1096
Peralta, Wily 1096
Peralta, Yamil Alberto 1096
Peralta Gascon, Juan 1096
Peralta Jara, Yamil 1096
ベラルディ
Berardi, Alexander J. 124
Berardi, Domenico 124
Berardi, Fabio 124
ベラルディ（ビフォ）
Berardi (Bifo), Franco 124
ベラルデスカ
Berardesca, Enzo 124
ヘラルド
Herald, Justin 596
ペラルナウ
Perarnau, Martí 1096
ベラン
Berran, Robert L. 130
ペラン
Pelenc, Arielle 1093
Perrin, Gaetan 1100
Perrin, Georgette 1100
Perrin, Jacques 1100
Perrin, Josyane 1100
Perrin, Martine 1100
ベランコバ
Berankova, Katerina 124
ベランジェ
Bélanger, Lynda 115
Bérenger, Paul Raymond 125
ヘランダー
Helander, Bernhard 591
ヘランデル
Herander, Filip 596
ヘランド
Roy Helland, J. 1212
ベラントーニ
Bellantoni, Jeff 117
ヘーリー
Haley, Jack, Jr. 557
Haley, Jay 557
Haley, John O. 557
ヘリー
Heley, Veronica 591
ベーリー
Bailey, Lowell 81
Bayley, Nicola 108
ベリ
Berri, Claude 130
Berri, Nabih 130
Berry, Richard 131
Veli, Evagjelia 1450
ベリー
Bailly, Sandrine 81
Belly, Chuck 118
Berrie, Phill 130
Berry, Andrew 130
Berry, Bill 130
Berry, Brian Joe Lobley 130
Berry, Craig A. 130
Berry, Eric 130
Berry, Francis 130
Berry, Gaynor 130
Berry, Halle 130
Berry, Holly 130
Berry, James 130
Berry, Jan 131
Berry, Jedediah 131
Berry, Jeffrey M. 131
Berry, Jordan 131
Berry, Leonard L. 131
Berry, Lynne 131
Berry, Michael J.A. 131
Berry, Mike 131
Berry, Orna 131
Berry, Patricia H. 131
Berry, Ron 131
Berry, Siân 131
Berry, Steve 131
Berry, Thomas 131
Berry, Wendell 131
ペーリー
Paley, Nicholas 1072
ペリ
Péry, Nicole 1101
ペリー
Pelley, Kathleen T. 1093
Perrie, Maureen 1099
Perry, Abigayl 1100
Perry, Alycia 1100
Perry, Anne 1100
Perry, Anne Griffin 1100
Perry, Brian 1100
Perry, Bruce.D. 1100
Perry, Bruce W. 1100
Perry, Dave 1100
Perry, Galen P. 1100
Perry, Grayson 1100
Perry, Greg M. 1100
Perry, Helen Swick 1100
Perry, Jacquelin 1100
Perry, Jan 1100
Perry, Joe 1100
Perry, John 1100
Perry, John D. 1100
Perry, Joshua 1100
Perry, Katy 1100
Perry, Kenny 1100
Perry, Ludlow 1100
Perry, Matthew Galbraith 1100
Perry, Michael R. 1100
Perry, Nick 1100
Perry, Paul 1100
Perry, Philippa 1100
Perry, Phyllis J. 1100
Perry, Rick 1100
Perry, Rupert 1100
Perry, Senorise 1100
Perry, Stephani Danelle 1100
Perry, Steve 1100
Perry, Thomas 1100
Perry, Tyler 1100
Perry, William E. 1100
Perry, William James 1100
ベリアイ
Veliaj, Erion 1450
ベリアコワ
Beliakova, Anastasiia 116
ベリアス
Veliath, Deepak 1450
ベリアニゼ
Berianidze, Levan 127
ベリアーノ
Bereano, Philip 125
ベリアン
Berian, Boris 127
ベリイ
Berg, Björn 125
ペリィ
Perry, George C. 1100
ベリィグレン
Berggren, Christian 127
ベリィマン
Bergman, Ingmar 127
ベリィリンド
Berglind, Kajsa Larsson 127
ベリヴィエ
Bellivier, Florence 117
ヘリウェル
Helliwell, Thomas M. 591
ベリエ
Verrier, Steven 1453
ペリエ
Périer, François 1098
Peslier, Olivier 1101
ペリエロ
Pellielo, Giovanni 1093
ベリオ
Berio, Luciano 127
ベリオス
Berrios, Jose 130
ヘリオット
Herriott, Alain 599
Herriott, Luke 599

へ

Herriott, Nikole 599
ベリカヤ
Velikaya, Sofya 1450
ベリガン
Berrigan, Daniel 130
Berrigan, Frances J. 130
Berrigan, Philip Francis 130
ベリカーン
Pilikán, Robert 1112
ペリカン
Pelikan, Jaroslav 1093
ペリキャック
Pericak, Will 1098
ヘリクソン
Hellickson, Jeremy 591
ペリグロ
Peligro, Kid 1093
ペリコーネ
Pellicone, Mateo 1093
ベリコフ
Velikov, Radoslav Marinov 1450
ベリコワ
Belikova, Marina 116
ペリコーン
Perricone, Nicholas 1099
ベリサリオ・マルティネス
Belisario Martínez, Ángel 116
ペリサン
Perisan, Samuele 1098
Perrissin, Christian 1100
ペリシェ
Pellissier, Caroline 1093
ペリシエ
Pellisier, Jérôme 1093
Pellissier, Sergio 1093
ベリジキ
Beriziky, Jean Omer 127
ペリシッチ
Perisic, Ivan 1098
ベリシャ
Berisha, Etrit 127
Berisha, Sali 127
ヘリス
Herries, Anne 599
ペリス
Peris, Luisa 1098
Perris, Andrew 1100
ベリストレーム
Bergström, Sune Karl 127
ベリストローム
Bergstrom, Fredrik 127
ベリストロム
Bergstrom, Fredrik 127
ヘリスン
Hellison, Donald R. 591
ベリゼール
Belizaire, Fritz 116
ベリチック
Bellchick, Bill 117
ペリツァ
Perica, Stipe 1098
ヘリック
Herrick, Elizabeth 599
ベリツコビッチ
Velickovic, Bobana 1450
ペリッシノット
Perissinotto, Alessandro 1098
ベリッソ
Berizzo, Eduardo 127
ペリッソロ
Pélissolo, Antoine 1093
ベリッチ
Belich, James 116
ペリッチ
Perić, Milovan 1098
ヘリッツェン
Gerritsen, Paula 491
ペリッロ
Perillo, Giuseppe 1098
ヘリテイジ
Heritage, Andrew 597
ヘリテッジ
Heritage, John 597
ベリド
Berido, Avery Allan 127
ベリーニ
Bellini, Hilderaldo Luiz 117
ベリネッリ
Belinelli, Marco 116
ベリネリ
Belineli, Josè 116
ベリーノ
Bellino, Ricardo 117
ペリーノ
Perino, Dana Marie 1098
ベリホフ
Velikhov, Evgenii Pavlovich 1450
ベリーマン
Berryman, Guy 131
Berryman, Jerome 131
ベリマン
Bergman, Ingmar 127
Berryman, Julia C. 131
ペリーマン
Perryman, Denzel 1101
ペリマン
Perriman, Breshad 1100
ベリャコーヴィッチ
Belyakovich, Valery 118
ベリャコービッチ
Belyakovich, Valery 118
ベリャコフ
Belyakov, Rostislav Apollosovich 118
ベリヤコフ
Belyakov, Rostislav Apollosovich 118
ベリヤード
Veryard, Richard 1454
ベリャフスキー
Belyavskiy, David 118
ベリョ
Bello, Silvestre 117
ペリーリ
Perilli, Alessandra 1098
ペリリ
Perilli, Alessandra 1098
Perilli, Arianna 1098
ヘリル
Khelil, Chakib 727
ベリルンド
Berglund, Paavo 127
ベリロ
Bellillo, Katia 117
ペリロ
Perillo, Justin 1098
ヘリン
Herrin, Judith 599
ベリーン
Vereen, Brock 1452
Vereen, Shane 1452
ベリン
Bellin, David 117
ペリン
Perin, Mattia 1098
Perine, Denzell 1098
Perrin, David 1100
Perrin, Ignacio 1100
Perrin, Robin D. 1100
Perrin, Sean 1100
ヘリンガ
Hellinga, Lotte 591
ヘリンガー
Hellinger, Bert 591
ベーリンガー
Behringer, Wolfgang 114
ベリンガー
Wellinger, Andreas 1491
ベリンガム
Berrigan, Frida 130
ヘーリンク
Häring, Bernhard 571
ヘーリング
Häring, Norbert 571
ヘリング
Hering, Sabrina 597
Herring, Ann King 599
Herring, James E. 599
Herring, Jonathan 599
Herring, Mary 599
Herring, Peter J. 599
Herring, William 599
ベリング
Balling, Derek J. 87
Bering, Jesse 127
ヘリングス
Hellings, Paul 591
ベリンコ
Belinco, Ariel 116
ベーリンジャー
Behringer, Richard R. 114
ベリンジャー
Bellinger, Cody 117
ベリンチェク
Berinchyk, Denys 127
ヘリントン
Herrington, Jack D. 599
Herrington, Terri 599
ヘール
Hale, Fred 557
Hale, Ginn 557
Heel, Werner 588
Khair, Abidine Ould 724
ヘル
Hell, Richard 591
Hell, Rudolf 591
Hell, Stefan W. 591
Helu, William 592
Herr, Robert 599
Höll Hartmut 617
ヘルー
Hélou, Charles 592
ベール
Baer, Nils 79
Bale, Christian 85
Bale, Gareth 85
Beer, Matias 113
Berre, André-Dieudonné 130
Berre, Madeleine 130
Vaile, Mark 1438
ベル
Bell, Alexei 116
Bell, Andy 116
Bell, Anthea 116
Bell, Art 116
Bell, Arthur H. 116
Bell, Blake 116
Bell, Byron 116
Bell, C.Gordon 116
Bell, Chad 116
Bell, Charlie 116
Bell, Chip R. 116
Bell, Daniel 116
Bell, Daniel A. 116
Bell, David 116
Bell, Derek 116
Bell, Devon 116
Bell, Graham A. 116
Bell, Gustavo 116
Bell, James S., Jr. 116
Bell, Jan 116
Bell, Janice M. 116
Bell, Jennifer 116
Bell, Jered 116
Bell, Jim 116
Bell, Jonathan 116
Bell, Josh 116
Bell, Joshua 116
Bell, Kenny 116
Bell, Kristen Leigh 116
Bell, Lenora 116
Bell, Le'Veon 116
Bell, Lorraine 116
Bell, Louis M. 116
Bell, Michael 117
Bell, Mitchell 117
Bell, Neal 117
Bell, O'Neil 117
Bell, Reggie 117
Bell, Robin 117
Bell, Sandy 117
Bell, Serena 117
Bell, Shannon 117
Bell, S.J. 117
Bell, Stefan 117
Bell, Sylvia 117
Bell, Ted 117
Bell, Timothy B. 117
Bell, Vonn 117
Bell, Wally 117
Bell, William 117
Bell, Zachary 117
Belle, Logan 117
ベルー
Belew, Bill 116
ペール
Pöhl, Karl Otto 1120
ペル
Pell, Arthur R. 1093
Pell, Claiborne de Borda 1093
ペルー
Peyroux, Madeleine 1105
ベールイ
Bely, Mikhail Mikhailovich 118
Belyi, Yurii Aleksandrovich 118
ベルイストレーム
Bergström, Sune Karl 127
ベルイストレム
Bergström, Sune Karl 127
ベルイストローム
Bergström, Sune Karl 127
ベルイード
Belaïd, Chokri 115
ベルイマン

Bergman, Ingmar 127
ヘルヴァジュオウル
Helvacioğlu, Banu 592
ペルヴィエ
Pervillé, Guy 1101
ベルヴィソ
Belviso, Meg 118
ヘルウィッグ
Hellwig, Friedemann 592
Hellwig, Monika 592
ベルウッド
Bellwood, Peter 118
ベルカ
Belka, Marek Marian 116
ベルカー
Belker, Loren B. 116
ベルガー
Berger, Ida 126
Berger, Jens 126
Berger, Maria 126
Berger, Michael 126
Berger, Richard 126
Berger, Roland 126
Berger, Thomas 126
ペルカ
Pelka, Fred 1093
ベルガーハウゼン
Bergerhausen, Johannes 126
ベルガマスコ
Bergamasco, Mauro 126
ペルガメンシコフ
Pergamenschchikov, Boris 1098
ペルガメンシチコフ
Pergamenschchikov, Boris 1098
ベルカヤト
Belkayat, Moncef 116
ベルガラ
Bergala, Alain 126
Bergara, Mario 126
Bergara, Markel 126
Vergara, Franklin 1452
Vergara Vergara, Sofía Margarita 1452
ベルカン
Berkane, Nadia 128
ベルガンサ
Berganza, Teresa 126
ベルガンティ
Verganti, Roberto 1452
ベルカンプ
Bergkamp, Dennis 127
ベルキ
Berki, Krisztián 128
ヘルギアニ
Khergiani, Nestor 727
ベルキオル
Belchior, Miriam 116
ヘルキスト
Helquist, Brett 592
ベルキムバエワ
Berkimbaeva, Shamsha 128
ベルキン
Belkin, Boris 116
Belkin, Kristin Lohse 116
ベルク
Belk, Russell W. 116
Berg, Christian 125
Berque, Augustin 130
ベルグ
Berg, Vebjoern 126
ベルグストレーム
BergStröm, Jan 127
ベルクストローム
Bergström, Sune Karl 127
ベルグスマ
Bergsma, Jorrit 127
ペルクゼン
Pörksen, Uwe 1125
ベルクハーン
Berghahn, Volker Rolf 127
ベルクハン
Berckhan, Barbara 125
ベルグマニス
Bergmanis, Raimonds 127
ベルクマン
Bergemann, Carsten 126
Bergmann, Arnfinn 127
Bergmann, Christine 127
Bergmann, Monika 127
ベルグマン
Bergman, Nir 127
Bergman, Sergio 127
Bergman, Tamar 127
ペルクマンス
Pelkmans, Jacques 1093
ベルグラン
Berggruen, Heinz 127
ヘルグリ
Hergli, Moncef 597
ベルグルンド
Berglund, Paavo 127
ベルグレーブ
Belgrave, Elliott 116
ベルグレーン
Berggreen, Emil 127
ベルケ
Berke, Hendrik 128
Berquet, Gilles 130
ベルゲ
Berge, Stig-Andre 126
ヘルゲーセン
Helgesen, Sally 591
ヘルゲセン
Helgesen, Barbro 591
Helgesen, Sally 591
Helgesen, Vidar 591
ベルゲソン
Bergethon, Peter R. 127
ベルゲデプレ
Verge-depre, Anouk 1452
ヘルゲランド
Helgeland, Brian 591
ベルケリエフ
Berkeliev, Serdar 128
ベルゲリンク
Boergeling, Lars 153
ベルゲル
Berger, Janine 126
Berger, Tora 126
ベルゲン
Bergen, David 126
ヘルゴー
Helgoe, Laurie A. 591
ベルコ
Bercot, Emmanuelle 125
ペルコ
Perko, Sandra J. 1099
ペルコヴィッチ
Perković, Sandra 1099
ヘルコヴィッツ
Hercovicz, Anna 597
ペルコビッチ
Perković, Sandra 1099
ベルコビッツ
Berkowitz, Bernard 128
ベルゴンツィ
Bergonzi, Carlo 127
ペルザー
Pelzer, Dave 1094
Pelzer, Richard B. 1094
ベルサーチ
Versace, Donatella 1454
ベルサナウ
Bersanau, Aliaksandr 131
ベルサーニ
Bersani, Leo 131
Bersani, Pier Luigi 131
Bersani, Shennen 131
ベルサニ
Bersani, Pier Luigi 131
ベルザー・メスト
Welser-Möst, Franz 1492
ペルサン
Percin, Laurence de 1096
ヘルシ
Hersi, Nur Farah 600
ヘルジ
Herzi, Hafsia 600
ベルシー
Belsey, Catherine 118
ベルジー
Belsey, Catherine 118
ペルシ
Persse, Lee-Ann 1101
ベルジェ
Bergé, Pierre 126
Berger, Cécile 126
Berger, Yves 126
Bergier, Jacques 127
Bergier, Jean-Francois 127
ベルジェス
Vergès, Jacques 1452
Vergés, Pedro 1452
ベルシェ・ペルドモ
Berger Perdomo, Oscar 127
ベルジツァ
Berzicza, Tamas 132
ベルシニ
Versini, Dominique 1454
ペルシャク
Peršak, Anton 1101
ペルシャーニ
Persányi, Miklós 1101
ヘールシャム卿
Lord Hailsham 555
ベルジュ
Berge, Claude 126
Vergès, Jacques 1452
ベルジュイス
Velthuijs, Max 1451
ヘルシュコ
Hershko, Avram 600
ヘルシュコビッチ
Hershkowitz, Daniel 600
ヘルシュコビッツ
Hershkowitz, Daniel 600
ヘルシュタット
Herstatt, Cornelius 600
ヘルシュトレーム
Hellström, Anders 592
ベルジュラック
Bergerac, Jacques 126
ベルジュロン
Bergeron, Alain M. 126
Bergeron, Nathalie 126
ペルシン
Pershin, Ivan 1101
ベルシンガー
Belsinger, Susan 118
ヘルシング
Hellsing, Lennart 592
ベルジンシ
Bērziņš, Andris 132
Berziņš, Indulis 132
ベルジンシュ
Bērziņš, Andris 132
Bērziņš, Gaidis 132
Bērziņš, Gundars 132
ベールズ
Bales, Robert Freed 86
ベルズ
Bells, Antonio 117
ペルス
Peltz, Lois 1094
Perrus, Leonore 1100
ベルスヴォルト＝ヴァルラーベ
Berswordt-Wallrabe, Silke von 131
ベルスキ
Belsky, Scott 118
ベルスキー
Belsky, Gary 118
Belsky, Jay 118
ヘルスコビッチ
Herskovic, William 600
ヘルスターン
Hellstern, Melissa 592
ヘルストスキー
Helstosky, Carol 592
ペルーズ・ド・モンクロ
Pérouse de Montclos, Jean-Marie 1099
ベルストルフ
Bellstorf, Arne 117
ヘルストレム
Hellström, Anders 592
Hellström, Börge 592
ベルストレーム
Bergström, Sune Karl 127
ヘルストローム＝ケネディ
Hellstrom-Kennedy, Marika 592
ヘルスビー
Helsby, Gill 592
ヘルスベルク
Hellsberg, Clemens 592
ベルスマ
Bersma, René 131
ベルセ
Bercé, Yves Marie 125
Berset, Alain 131
ベルゼ
Berse, Andreas A. 131
ヘルセン
Helsen, Kristiaan 592
ペルーゾ
Peluso, Federico 1094
ベルゾイーニ
Berzoini, Ricardo 132
ペルソナ
Personnaz, Raphaël 1101
ベルソン
Bellson, Louis Paul 117

Belson, Ken 118
Berthon, Laurie 131
ペルソン
Persson, Gunilla Linn 1101
Persson, Markus 1101
Persson, Stefan 1101
ペルゾーンス
Persoons, Jan 1101
ベルタ
Berta, Annalisa 131
ベルダー
Verdad, S.T. 1452
ベルタイナ
Bertaina, Norberto Antonio 131
ベルターギ
al-Beltagy, Adel 118
ベルタギ
Beltagi, Muhammad Mamdouh Ahmad El 118
ベルターニャ
Bertagna, Julie 131
Bertagna, Silvia 131
ベルタレリ
Bertarelli, Dona 131
Bertarelli, Ernesto 131
ペルチヴァーレ
Percivale, Tommaso 1096
ベルチェアヌ
Berceanu, Radu 125
ベルチェシ
Berchesi, Felipe 125
ベルチェフ
Velchev, Milen 1450
ベルチャー
Belcher, Jovan 115
Belcher, Lani 115
Belcher, Mathew 115
ベルチャシビリ
Beruchashvili, Tamar 132
ベルチリ
Verchili, Carlos Álvaro 1452
ヘルツ
Herz, Shirley 600
ベルツ
Belz, Carl 118
ペルーツ
Perutz, Max 1101
ペルツ
Peltz, Nicola 1094
Perutz, Max 1101
ヘルツェル
Hölzel, Petra 619
Hölzel, Wolfgang 619
ヘルツェン
Holzen, Edmund 619
ヘルツォーク
Herzog, Dagmar 600
Herzog, Jacques 600
Herzog, Werner 600
Herzog, Wolfgang 600
ヘルツォグ
Herzog, Isaac 600
ヘルツカ
Hertzka, Gottfried 600
ベルッシ
Bellucci, Thomaz 118
ヘルツゾマー
Herz-Sommer, Alice 600
ベルッチ
Bellucci, Monica 117
ベルッツィ
Belluzzi, Iro 118
ペルッツィ
Peruzzi, Britt 1101
ヘルツニヤン
Harutyunyan, Artem 578
ヘルツベリ
Hertzberg, Ludvig 600
ヘルツベルハー
Hertzberger, Herman 600
ヘルツ・マネロ
Gertz Manero, Alejandro 492
ヘルツム
Herzum, Peter 600
ヘルツリンガー
Herzlinger, Regina E. 600
ヘルツル
Hoelzl, Kathrin 613
Hölzl, Bernhard 619
Hölzle, Urs 619
ヘルデ
Herde, Ariane 597
ベルテ
Berthe, Abudoul Wahab 131
Berthé, Baba 131
Welte, Miriam 1492
ベルデ
Berder, Cecilia 125
Verde, Elio 1452
Verde, Susan 1452
Verdet, Jean-Pierre 1452
ベルティ
Berrutti, Azucena 130
Berti, Eduardo 131
Berti, Giordano 131
ベルディ
Verdy, Violette 1452
ベルディーア
Veldheer, Jared 1450
ベルティエ
Berthier, Philippe 131
ペルティエ
Pelletier, David 1093
Pelletier, Louis-Thomas 1093
Pelletier, Paul 1093
Peltier, Melissa Jo 1094
ベルディエフ
Berdiev, Kabul 125
Berdiyev, Yaylym 125
Berdyev, Atamurad 125
Berdyev, Atamyrat 125
Berdyyev, Atamyrat 125
ヘルティッヒ
Hertig, Gerard 600
ベルティーニ
Bertini, Gary 131
Bertini, Maria Barbara 131
ベルディハ
Berdych, Tomas 125
ベルディムハメドフ
Berdimuhamedov, Gurbanguly 125
ヘルディンク
Herding, Klaus 597
ベルティンク
Belting, Hans 118
ベルティング
Belting, Hans 118
ペルテガス
Pertegaz, Manuel 1101
ヘルデーゲン
Herdegen, Matthias 597
ベルテコバ
Bartekova, Danka 99
ベルデツ
Verdet, Ilie 1452
ベルテッリ
Bertelli, Patrizio 131
Bertelli, Sergio 131
ベルデニック
Verdenik, Zdenko 1452
ベルテネ
Berthenet, Angelique 131
ベルデホ
Verdejo Sanchez, Felix 1452
ベルテュッセリ
Bertuccelli, Jean-Louis 132
ベルデュッチ
Verducci, Tom 1452
ベルテルセン
Bertelsen, A. 131
ペルテルソン
Pertelson, Indrek 1101
ベルデン
Belden, Bob 116
ベルテンス
Bertens, Johannes Willem 131
Bertens, Kiki 131
ヘルテンフーバー
Hortenhuber, Kurt 624
ヘルト
Held, Jutta 591
Held, Klaus 591
Heldt, Gustav 591
Hert, Marc De 600
ヘルド
Held, David 591
Held, Michael 591
Held, Ryan 591
Held, Vera 591
ベルト
Belt, Brandon 118
Bertaud, Jean Paul 131
Berto, Andre 131
Veldt, Tim 1450
Wert, José Ignacio 1494
ベルトー
Bertaux, Daniel 131
Berthault, Jean-Yves 131
ペールト
Pärt, Arvo 1082
ペルト
Pärt, Arvo 1082
ベルトイア
Bertoia, Judi 132
ベルドイエフ
Berdyev, Batyr 125
Berdyev, Poran 125
ベルドイムハメドフ
Berdimuhamedov, Gurbanguly 125
Berdymukhammedov, Gurbanguly 125
ベルドゥーゴ
Berdugo, Ignacio Gomez de la Torre 125
ペルトゥージ
Pertusi, Michele 1101
ベルトゥチェリ
Bertuccelli, Jean-Louis 132
Bertucelli, Julie 132
ベルトゥロ
Berthelot, Jean-Michel 131
ペルトゥン
Pelton, Fred L. 1094
ベルトグリオ
Bertoglio, Edo 132
ヘルトゲン
Höltgen, Karl Josef 619
ベルトッチ
Bertocci, Vittorio 132
ベルトート
Berthod, Marc 131
Berthod, Sylviane 131
ペルトナー
Pöltner, Günther 1122
ペルトニエミ
Peltoniemi, Sari 1094
ベルトーネ
Bertone, Leonardo 132
ヘルドブラー
Hölldobler, Bert 616
ヘルドマン
Heldman, Kim 591
ペルドモ
Perdomo, Antonio 1096
Perdomo, Luis 1096
ベルトーラ
Bertola, Giuseppe 132
Bertola, Juan Luis 132
ペルトラ
Peltola, Markku 1094
ベルトラシ
Bertolasi, Sara 132
ベルトラッチ
Bertolacci, Andrea 132
ベルトラッティ
Beltratti, Andrea 118
ベルトラミ
Beltrami, Edward J. 118
ベルトラミーニ
Beltramini, Micol Arianna 118
ベルトラメ
Beltrame, Francisco 118
ベルトラン
Beltran, Carlos 118
Beltran, Daima 118
Beltrán, Francisco López 118
Beltran, Fred 118
Beltrão, Marx 118
Bertrand, Claude Jean 132
Bertrand, Frédérique 132
Bertrand, Julie Winnifred 132
Bertrand, Léon 132
Bertrand, Xavier 132
ベルトラン・オシオ
Beltran Osio, Raul Armando 118
ベルトランド
Bertrando, Francisco 132
ベルトーリ
Bertoli, Marco 132
ベルトリッチ
Bertolucci, Bernardo 132
ヘルドリヒ
Heldrich, Andreas 591
ヘルトリング
Härtling, Peter 577
ベルトルッチ
Bertolucci, Bernardo 132

ベルトルト
Berthold, Will 131
ベルトレ
Beltre, Adrian 118
Bertholet, Denis 131
ベルトレー
Beltre, Adrian 118
ベルドレ
Veldre, Vinets 1450
ベルトレイ
Beltre, Adrian 118
ベルトローテ
Bertolote, Jose M. 132
ベルトローニ
Veltroni, Walter 1451
ベルトワーズ
Beltoise, Jean-Pierre 118
ベルトン
Belton, Christopher 118
Belton, Robyn 118
ペルトン
Pelton, Jeremy 1094
Pelton, Leroy H. 1094
Pelton, Robert Young 1094
ヘルナー
Hellner, Marcus 592
ベルナ
Berna, Carlos 128
ベルナー
Berner, Rotraut Susanne 129
Werner, Klaus 1493
ペルナー
Perner, Wolfgang 1099
ベルナウ
Bernau, Anke 129
ベルナウアー
Bernauer, Ursula 129
ベルナズ
Bernaz, Jean Baptiste 129
ベルナート
Bernat, Enrique 129
ベルナード
Bernád, Dénes 128
Bernard, Renee 129
ベルナト
Bernat, Juan 129
ベルナドッテ
Bernadotte, Lennart 128
Bernadotte, Sigvard 129
ベルナドット
Bernadotte, Sigvard 129
ベルナトーニス
Bernatonis, Juozas 129
ベルナベウ
Bernabeu, Maria 128
ベルナボ
Bernabó, Valerio 128
ベルナール
Bernard, Alain 129
Bernard, Fred 129
Bernard, Hipolito 129
Bernard, Marcel 129
ベルナル・アレマニ
Bernal Alemany, Rafael 129
ベルナルダキス
Vernardakis, Christoforos 1453
ベルナルディ
Bernardi, Bruno 129
ベルナルデスキ
Bernardeschi, Federico 129
ベルナルト
Bernard, Andreas 129
ベルナルド
Bernardo 129
Bernardo, Barbara 129
Bernardo, Espinosa 129
Bernardo, Mike 129
Bernardo, Paulo 129
ベルナルド・シルヴァ
Bernardo Silva 129
ベルナルド・シルバ
Bernardo Silva, Paulo 129
ヘルナンデス
Hernandez, Ariel 598
Hernandez, Cesar 598
Hernandez, Chuck 598
Hernandez, David 598
Hernández, Diego E. 598
Hernandez, Enrique 598
Hernández, Enzo 598
Hernandez, Felix 598
Hernandez, Gorkys 598
Hernandez, Jaime 598
Hernandez, Jay 598
Hernandez, Lauren 598
Hernandez, Marco 598
Hernandez, Nico Miguel 598
Hernandez, Oscar 598
Hernandez, Rudy 598
Hernandez, Teoscar 598
ベルニ
Berni, Tommaso 129
ベルニエ
Bernier, Maxime 129
ベルニエ＝パリエス
Vernier-Palliez, Claudine 1453
ペルニオーラ
Perniola, Mario 1099
ベルニケ
Wernicke, Herbert 1493
ベルニック
Bernicke, Shadlog 129
ベルニャエフ
Verniaiev, Oleg 1453
ベルニュ
Vergne, Jean-Philippe 1452
ベルヌイユ
Verneuil, Henri 1453
ベルネール
Verner, Josee 1453
ベルネル
Berner, Anne 129
Verner, Tomáš 1453
ベルノルド
Bernold, André 130
ヘルパー
Helper, Susan 592
ベルバー
Belber, Stephen 115
ベルハイド
Verheyde, Mieke 1452
ベールバウム
Beerbaum, Ludger 113
ベルハジ
Belhaj, Hisham 116
ベルバシ
Belbase, Kumar 115
ベルハージ・ヤヒヤ
Belhaj Yahia, Emna 116
ベルハジュ
Belhaj, Samira Khayach 116
ヘルバース
Herbers, Klaus 596
ヘルバス
Relvas, Miguel 1171
ベルハッセン
Belhasen, Naṭali 116
ペルパット
Perrupato, Mariangela 1100
ベルハデム
Belkhadem, Abdelaziz 116
ペルパト
Perrupato, Mariangela 1100
ベルバトフ
Berbatov, Dimitar 124
ベルハヌ
Berhanu, Adelo 127
Berhanu, Dejene 127
Berhanu, Yoseph Woldemichael 127
ベルハネ
Berhane, Abrehe 127
Berhane, Habtemariam 127
Berhane, Hailu 127
ペルハム
Pelham, David 1093
Pelham, Sophie 1093
ベールパル
Veerpalu, Andrus 1449
ベルハン
Berhan, Hailu 127
ヘルビグ
Hellvig, Eduard 592
ペルビス
Pervis, Francois 1101
ベルビッチ
Verbić, Srđan 1452
ヘルビッヒ
Hellwig, Martin F. 592
Herbig, Günter 597
ヘルビヒ
Helbig, Gerhard 591
Herbig, Günter 597
ベルヒャー
Belcher, Daniel 115
ベルビン
Belbin, Tanith 115
ヘルファ
Helfer, Mary Edna 591
Helfer, Ray E. 591
ヘルファウイ
Khelfaoui, Anissa 727
ヘルファット
Helfat, Constance E. 591
ヘルファート
Helfert, Erich A. 591
ベルフィールド
Belfield, Clive R. 116
Belfield, Richard 116
ペルフェクト
Perfecto, Ivette 1098
ペルフェッティ
Perfetti, Carlo 1098
ベルフォート
Belfort, Edward 116
Belfort, Jordan 116
ヘルフケンス
Herfkens, Eveline 597
ヘルフゴット
Helfgott, David 591
ヘルブスト
Herbst, Jaya 597
Herbst, Reinfried 597
ベルフスマ
Bergsma, Jorrit 127
ペルフヒン
Pervukhin, Ilya 1101
ヘルプマン
Helpman, Elhanan 592
ヘルブラフ
Helbrough, Emma 591
ベルプリ
Velpuri, Rama 1451
ペルフリー
Pelfrey, Mike 1093
ヘルプリン
Helprin, Mark 592
ベルブルーノ
Belbruno, Edward 115
ベルフレージ
Belfrage, Nicolas 116
ペルフロム
Pelgrom, Els 1093
ベルフワイン
Bergwijn, Steven 127
ベルーベ
Berube, David M. 132
ベルベオーク
Belbéoch, Bella 115
Belbéoch, Roger 115
ベルベリアン
Berberian, Charles 124
ヘルベル
Gelber, Bruno-Leonardo 487
ヘルペル
Herpell, Gabriela 599
ベルベル
Berber, Ibrahim 124
ベルヘン
Bergen, Ernst 126
ペルベン
Perben, Dominique 1096
ペルホ
Perho, Maija 1098
ヘルボイ・コチャール
Herboly Kocsár, Ildikó 597
ベルホウリアド
Verkhogliad, Daryna 1453
ベルポリーティ
Belpoliti, Marco 118
ベルマ
Verma, Beni Prasad 1453
Verma, Vikram 1453
ヘルマッシ
Hermassi, Abdelbaki 598
ヘルマリング
Helmering, Doris Wild 592
ヘルマン
Gelman, Juan 488
Germán, Alejandrina 491
German, Domingo 491
Hellman, Hal 591
Hellman, Lillian Florence 591
Hellman, Monte 591
Hellmann, Kai-Uwe 592
Hellmann, Thomas F. 592
Helman, Zofia 592

Herman, Daniel 597
Herman, Gail 597
Herman, Yaron 597
Hermann, Judith 597
Herrman, Siegfried 599
Herrmann, Cornelia 599
Herrmann, Denise 599
Herrmann, Joachim 599
Herrmann, Ulrike 599
ベルマン
Bellman, Steven 117
Berman, Boris 128
Berman, Gennady P. 128
Berman, Lazar 128
Velleman, Daniel J. 1451
ペールマン
Pöhlmann, Horst Georg 1120
ヘルマンス
Hermanns, William 597
Hermans, Jo 598
Hermans, Loek 598
ヘルマンソン
Hermannsson, Steingrimur 597
Hermansson, Mia 598
ヘルマンダー
Hörmander, Lars Valter 622
ヘルマント
Hermand, Jost 597
ヘルマントーラー
Helmantoler, Bill 592
ヘルミス
Hellmiss, Margot 592
ヘルミック
Helmig, Rainer 592
ヘルミナ
Hermina, Szecsei 598
ヘルム
Helm, Leslie 592
Helm, Levon 592
Helm, Mathew 592
Helm, Paul 592
ベルム
Beloum, Cécile 118
ベルムウエドラオゴ
Beloumouedraogo, Cecilia 118
ヘルムス
Helms, Antje 592
Helms, Siegmund 592
Helms, Tobias 592
ヘルムズ
Helms, Clyde A. 592
Helms, Jesse 592
Helms, Richard Mcgarrah 592
ヘルムステッター
Helmstetter, Richard C. 592
Helmstetter, Shad 592
ベルムデス
Bermúdez, Francisco 128
Bermudez, Patricia Alejandra 128
ベルムデス・メリサルデ
Bermúdez Merizalde, Jaime 128
ヘルムート
Hellmuth, Jerome 592
ヘルムト
Rahn, Helmut 1150
ヘルムート・ラーン
Rahn, Helmut 1150
ヘルムライク
Helmreich, William B. 592
ヘルムンド
Hellmund, Carlos Eduardo 592
ペルメー
Permeh, Ryan 1099
ベルメーカー
Belmaker, Robert H. 118
ベルメシ
Vermes, Geza 1453
ベルメシュ
Vermes, Geza 1453
ヘルメス
Hermes, Edward 598
Hermes, Hans 598
ベルメホ
Bermejo, Lee 128
Bermejo, Mariano Fernández 128
ベルモ
Vermot, Marie-Sophie 1453
ベルモイ
Bermoy Acosta, Yanet 128
ベルモフタール
Belmokhtar, Mokhtar 118
Belmokhtar, Rachid 118
ベルモフタル
Belmokhtar, Mokhtar 118
ベルモン
Belmont, Joseph 118
ベルモンテガルシア
Belmonte Garcia, Mireia 118
ベルモント
Belmont, Alejandro Rafael 118
ベルモンド
Belmondo, Jean-Paul 118
Belmondo, Stefania 118
ペルラ
Perla, Victoria 1099
ベルラコビッチ
Berlakovich, Nikolaus 128
ペルラン
Pellerin, Fleur 1093
ペルリス
Perlis, Michael L. 1099
ヘルリツィウス
Herlitzius, Evelyn 597
ヘルリッツ
Herlitz, Gillis 597
ベルリッツ
Berlitz, Charles 128
ベルリーブ
Bellerive, Jean-Max 117
ペルリンジェイロ
Perlingeiro, Marlene 1099
ベルリンスキ
Berlinski, David 128
ベルール
Bellour, Raymond 117
ベルルスコーニ
Berlusconi, Silvio 128
ベルルッティ
Berluti, Olga 128
ペルルミュテール
Perlemuter, Vlado 1099
ヘルレ
Harle, Isabelle 571
ベルレユング
Berlejung, Angelika 128
ベルローニ
Berloni, William 128
ヘルンガ
Herunga, Uahekua 600
ベルンシュタイン
Bernstein, Michel 130
ベルンデス
Berndes, Göran 129
ベルント
Bernd, Schacht 129
Berndt, Ernst R. 129
Berndt, Jaqueline 129
ベルントセン
Berntsen, Hedda 130
ベルンドル
Berndl, Klaus 129
ヘルンドルフ
Herrndorf, Wolfgang 599
ベルンハイム
Bernheim, Nicole Lise 129
ベルンハルト殿下
Bernhard Leopold 129
ベルンハルト・レオポルト
Bernhard Leopold 129
ヘレ
Helle, Helle 591
Herre, Johnny 599
Hölle, Erich 617
ベレ
Bere, Jason 125
ペレ
Pelé 1093
Perez, John 1097
Pérez, Joseph 1097
ベレア
Bellaire, Jordie 117
ペレイラ
Didi 353
Pereira, Agio 1096
Pereira, Alexander 1096
Pereira, Andy 1096
Pereira, Aristides Maria 1096
Pereira, Camilo Simoes 1096
Pereira, Carla Soares 1096
Pereira, Domingos Simões 1096
Pereira, Florentino 1096
Pereira, Heitor 1097
Pereira, Joao 1097
Pereira, João Aníbal 1097
Pereira, Luís Filipe 1097
Pereira, Luís Miguel 1097
Pereira, Marcos Antônio 1097
Pereira, Matheus 1097
Pereira, Pedro 1097
Pereira, Rui 1097
Pereira, Teliana 1097
Pereira, Teresinka 1097
Pereira, Thiago 1097
Pereira, Virgílio Ferreira De Fontes 1097
Pereyra, Roberto 1097
Perreira, Marcelino 1099
Perreira, Raimundo 1099
ペレイロ
Pereiro, Gaston 1097
ベレイロ・ファハルド
Berreiro Fajardo, Georgina 130
ペレーヴィン
Pelevin, Viktor Olegovich 1093
ヘレヴェ
Helleve, Torstein 591
ヘレヴェッヘ
Herreweghe, Philippe 599
ペレヴォースチコフ
Perevozchikov, Aleksandr 1097
ベレオケン
Beleoken, Jean-Baptiste 116
ヘレガー
Heregger, Selina 597
ペレ=クリスタン
Péré-Christin, Evelyne 1096
ペレグリーニ
Pellegrini, Anthony D. 1093
Pellegrini, Peter 1093
ペレグリニ
Pellegrini, Federica 1093
Pellegrini, Peter 1093
ペレグリーノ
Pellegrino, Charles R. 1093
ペレグリン
Pelegrín, Javier 1093
Pellegrin, Paolo 1093
ベレケ
Bereket, Simon 125
ベレケイ
Vereckei, Akos 1452
ペレケーノス
Pelecanos, George P. 1093
ペレサグア
Perezagua, Marina 1098
ペレサダ
Peresada, Anatolii 1097
ペレサラ
Pelesala, Leti 1093
ペレシ
Peleshi, Niko 1093
ペレジカ
Perezchica, Tony 1098
ベレシュ
Veres, János 1452
Voros, Zsuzsanna 1464
ヘレス
Jerez, Nelly 671
ベレス
Velez, Oliver L. 1450
Veres, Ruth C. 1452
ペレーズ
Peláez, Martha 1093
Pérèz, Vincent 1098
ペレス
Botella Perez, Isaac 165
Peres, Asher 1097
Peres, Shimon 1097
Pérez, Asier 1097
Perez, Carlos 1097
Perez, Cecilia 1097
Pérez, Cecilia 1097
Perez, Darley 1097
Perez, Eddie 1097
Perez, Eury 1097
Perez, Felipe 1097
Pérez, Florentino Rodriguez 1097
Pérez, George 1097
Perez, Guillermo 1097
Perez, Hernan 1097
Perez, Hernani 1097

Perez, Irving 1097
Perez, Jefferson 1097
Peréz, Jesus Arnoldo 1097
Perez, Juan J. 1097
Pérez, Manuel de Jesús 1097
Perez, Martin 1097
Perez, Monica 1097
Pérez, Nancy 1097
Perez, Oliver 1097
Perez, Paola 1097
Perez, Pascual 1097
Pérez, Patricia 1098
Perez, Paul 1098
Perez, Pere 1098
Perez, Roberto 1098
Pérez, Rodrigo 1098
Pérez, Rodulfo 1098
Perez, Salvador 1098
Perez, Santiago 1098
Perez, Thomas 1098
Perez, Vincent 1098
Pérez, Walter Fernando 1098
Perez, William 1098
Perez, Yaime 1098
Perez, Yefri 1098
Perez Mora, Luillys Jose 1098
Pérez Rodríguez, Carlos Andrés 1098
Perez Tigrero, Mercedes Isabel 1098

ペレズ
Pérez, Christophe-Alexis 1097
Perez, Jessica 1097

ペレス・アバド
Pérez Abad, Miguel 1098

ペレス・アリアス
Pérez Arias, Guillermo 1098

ペレス・エスキベル
Pérez Esquivel, Adolfo 1098

ベレスエタ
Berrezueta, Leonardo 130

ペレス・オトン
Pérez Othón, Jesús 1098

ペレス・グアダルペ
Pérez Guadalupe, José 1098

ペレスコ
Pelesko, John A. 1093

ペレス・シエラ
Pérez Sierra, Nancy 1098

ペレス・ジョマ
Pérez Yoma, Edmundo 1098

ベレズツキ
Berezutski, Aleksei 125
Berezutski, Vasili 125

ペレス・テジョ
Pérez Tello, María Soledad 1098

ペレスデルカスティジョ
Pérez Del Castillo, Santiago 1098

ベレスト
Berest, Anne 125

ベレストフ
Berestov, Dmitry 125

ベレズナヤ
Berezhnaya, Elena 125

ベレスニエワ
Beresnyeva, Olga 125

ペレス・ハラ
Pérez Jara, Cecilia 1098

ペレス・ヒメネス
Pérez Jiménez, Marcos 1098

ペレス・フェリス
Pérez Féliz, Joaquín 1098

ベレスフォード
Beresford, Bonnie 125
Berresford, Susan Vail 130

ベレス・ホワイト
Vélez White, Cecilia María 1450
Vérez White, Cecilia María 1452

ペレス・モラレス
Pélez Morales, Alvaro 1093

ペレス・モリーナ
Pérez Molina, Otto Fernando 1098

ペレス・モリナ
Pérez Molina, Otto Fernando 1098

ペレスモリナ
Pérez Molina, Otto Fernando 1098

ペレス・モンテーロ
Pérez Montero, José 1098

ペレス・モントヤ
Pérez Montoya, Elba Rosa 1098

ペレス・レベルテ
Pérez-Reverte, Arturo 1098

ペレス＝レベルテ
Perez-Reverte, Arturo 1098

ペレス・ロケ
Pérez Roque, Felipe Ramón 1098

ベレゾフスキ
Berezovsky, Igor 125

ベレゾフスキー
Beresovskii, Boris 125
Berezovskii, Boris Abramovich 125

ペレチャギン
Peretyagin, Aleksander 1097

ベレツ
Berecz, Zsombor 125

ペレツ
Peretz, Amir 1097

ベレツキー
Beletsky, Les 116

ベレッタ
Beretta, Lia 125

ベレッティ
Belletti, Adriana 117

ベレット
Verrett, Jason 1453
Verrett, Logan 1453

ペレット
Perret, Geoffrey 1099
Perrett, Bryan 1099

ベレテ
Belete, Tefera 116

ペレティ
Peretti, Frank E. 1097

ヘレディア
Heredia, Guillermo 597
Heredia, Manuel 597

ペレティエ
Pelletier, Michel 1093
Pelletière, Stephen C. 1093

ペレーニ
Perényi, Miklós 1097

ペレニセ
Perenise, Anthony 1097

ベレニュク
Beleniuk, Zhan 116

ペレネラ
Perenara, TJ. 1097

ベレビー
Berreby, Patricia 130

ベレービッチ
Belēvičs, Guntis 116

ペレービン
Pelevin, Viktor Olegovich 1093

ベレブ
Vereb, Istvan 1452

ベレブールトセ
Willeboordse, Elisabeth 1506

ペレベ
Pérévet, Zacharie 1097

ペレペチェノフ
Perepetchenov, Oleg 1097

ヘレベッヘ
Herreweghe, Philippe 599

ヘレム
Helem, Mohamed Abdoulkader Moussa 591

ヘレーラ
Harrera, Rosell 573
Herrera, Dilson 599
Herrera, Francisco 599
Herrera, Josè 599
Herrera, Kelvin 599
Herrera, Odubel 599
Herrera, Paloma 599
Herrera, Ronald 599
Herrerra, Amarlo 599

ヘレラー
Höllerer, Walter Friedrich 617

ベレラ
Verela, Frantz 1452

ペレラ
Perera, Dilan 1097
Perera, Felix 1097
Perera, Gamini Jayawickrema 1097
Perera, Joseph Michael 1097
Perera, Sylvia Brinton 1097

ベレリス
Verelis, Christos 1452

ヘレリマナ
Hererimana, Mussa Sheikh 597

ペレリン
Pellerin, Charles James 1093
Pellerin, David 1093

ペレル
Perel, Daniel 1097
Perel, Esther 1097

ペレルマン
Perelman, Grigori 1097
Perelman, Ronald 1097

ベレワ
Berewa, Solomon 125

ヘレーン
Hären, Fredrik 570
Hären, Teo 570

ペレン
Perren, Irina 1099

ベレンゲル
Berenguer, Alex 125

ベレンジャー
Berenger, Tom 125

ベーレンス
Behrens, Hildegard 114
Behrens, Katja 114
Behrens, Peter 114

ベレンズ
Berens, Ricky 125

ベーレンス＝アブーセイフ
Behrens-Abouseif, Doris 114

ベレンスティン
Berenstain, Jan 125
Berenstain, Stan 125

ベレンスン
Berenson, Alex 125

ベレンセク
Velensek, Anamari 1450

ベレンソン
Berenson, Mark L. 125
Berenson, Robert A. 125

ベーレンツ
Behrends, Ehrhard 114
Behrends, Okko 114

ベーレント
Behrendt, Amiira 114
Behrendt, Greg 114

ベレント
Berendt, Eric 125
Berendt, John 125

ペーレント
Parent, Nancy 1078

ベーレンバウム
Berenbaum, May 125

ヘレンバルト
Hellenbart, Gyula 591

ヘレンブラント
Hellenbrand, Peter 591

ペレンベ
Pelembe, Luis 1093

ベロ
Belaud, Valentin 115
Bello, Adamu 117
Bello, Antoine 117
Bello, Marko 117
Bello, Muhammed Musa 117
Bello, Mustapha 117
Bellot, Francois 117
Belo, Ademir Nelson 118
Belo, Carlos Felipe Ximenes 118
Verrot, Pascal 1454

ベロー
Bello, Walden F. 117
Bellow, Saul 117
Belot, Anne-Marie 118
Beraud, Alan Claudio 124

ペロ
Pero, Lenier Eunice 1099
Perrot, Charles 1100
Perrot, Jean-Yves 1100

ペロー
Pelot, Pierre 1094
Perot, Ross 1099
Perraud, Marie-Aurore Marie-Joyce 1099
Perrault, Dominique 1099
Perrault, Gilles 1099

Perraut, Laetitia 1099
Perro, Bryan 1100
Perrot, Michelle 1100
Perrow, Mike 1100
Perrow, Susan 1100
ベロアー
Bellore, Nick 117
ヘロイーズ
Heloise 592
ベロウ
Bellow, Saul 117
ベロウソフ
Belousov, Andrei R. 118
ヘロウド
Heraud, Conrad 596
ペロウフ
Pelouch, Jan 1094
ベロカル
Berrocal, Fernando 130
ペローシ
Pelosi, Nancy 1093
ペロシ
Pelosi, Nancy 1093
ベローズ
Bellows, Keith 117
ベロス
Bellos, Alex 117
Bellos, David 117
ベロスト
Belhoste, Bruno 116
ベロセルスキー
Beloselskiy, Dmitriy 118
ベローゾ
Veloso, Miguel 1451
Veloso, Sebastião Sapuile 1451
ベロソ
Veloso, Juliana 1451
ベロッキオ
Bellocchio, Marco 117
ペロッタ
Perrotta, Lucilla 1100
Perrotta, Paolo 1100
ベロッティ
Belotti, Andrea 118
ペロッティ
Perotti, Diego 1099
ペロテット
Perrottet, Tony 1100
ベロテラン
Berroterán, José Luis 130
ベローナ
Verona, Edelyn 1453
ペローナ
Perona, Elizabeth 1099
ベローニ
Belloni, Valentina 117
ペロニ
Peroni, Carlo 1099
ベロニカ
Veronika, Marék 1453
ベロニーズ
Veronese, Keith 1453
ペローネ
Perrone, Paul 1100
ベロネージ
Veronesi, Sandro 1453
ベロネジ
Veronesi, Umberto 1453
ペロネ＝モイセス
Perrone-Moisés, Leyla 1100
ベロノゴフ
Belonogoff, Alexander 118
ベローフ
Belov, Vasilii Ivanovich 118
ベロフ
Belov, Vasilii Ivanovich 118
Béroff, Michel 130
Berov, Lyuben 130
Bialou, Yury 136
ベロフウォストフ
Belokhvostov, Vladimir M. 118
ベロフスキー
Belofsky, Nathan 118
ベロブーバ
Bello Bouba, Maïgari 117
ベロ・ブーバ・マイガリ
Bello Bouba, Maïgari 117
ベロフボストフ
Belokhvostov, Vladimir M. 118
ベロブラーデク
Bělobrádek, Pavel 118
ベローブル
Belaubre, Frederic 115
ベロモイナ
Belomoina, Yana 118
ペロル
Perol, Huguette 1099
Pérols, Sylvaine 1099
ペロワ
Perova, Ksenia 1099
ヘロン
Heron, Timothy E. 599
Herron, Abigail J. 599
Herron, David E. 599
Herron, Mick 600
ベロン
Verón, Juan Sebastián 1453
ペローン
Perowne, Stewart 1099
ペロン
Pelon, Claude 1093
Perón, María Estela Martínez de 1099
ペロンズ
Perrons, Diane 1100
ヘーン
Hoehn, John P. 612
Hohn, Immanuel 615
ヘン
Heng, Swee Keat 594
Henn, Günter 594
Henn, Sophy 594
ベーン
Boehn, Max von 153
Vane, John Robert 1443
ベン
Benn, Andy 121
Benn, Anthony Neil Wedgwood 121
Benn, Arrelious 122
Benn, Brindley 122
Benn, Haynesley 122
Benn, Hilary 122
Benn, Robeson 122
Benne, Haynesley 122
ペーン
Payne, Frederick 1089
ペン
Peng, Lucy 1095
Peng, Scott Y. 1095
Peng, T.K. 1095
Peng, Zhaoqian 1095
Penn, Arthur 1095
Penn, Audrey 1095
Penn, Chris 1095
Penn, David L. 1095
Penn, Donald 1095
Penn, Irving 1095
Penn, Mark J. 1095
Penn, Robert 1095
Penn, Sean 1095
Penn, Thomas 1095
ベンアイサ
Ben Aïssa, Mohamed Salah 119
ベンアシュール
Ben Achour, Mohammed Aziz 119
ベンアブダラ
Ben Abdallah, Moncef 119
ベンアブドラ
Benabdellah, Nabil 119
ベン＝アミ
Ben-Ami, Uzi 119
ベン・アリ
Ben Ali, Zine el-Abidine 119
ベンアリ
Ben Ali, Rahma 119
Ben Ali, Zine el-Abidine 119
ベン・アルー
Ben Arous, Eddy 119
ベンアルツィ・ペロソフ
Ben Artzi-Pelossof, Noa 119
ベン・アルファ
Ben Arfa, Hatem 119
ベン・イェデル
Ben Yedder, Wissam 124
ベンイエデル
Ben Yedder, Neziha 124
ベン・イジー
Ben Izzy, Joel 121
ベンイズリ
Ben Yizri, Jacob 124
ベンヴェヌーティ
Benvenuti, Jurgen 124
Benvenuti, Tommaso 124
ヘンウッド
Henwood, Suzanne 596
ペンエク
Karaket, Pen-Ek 704
ベンエリエザー
Ben-Eliezer, Benjamin 120
ベンエリエゼル
Ben-Eliezer, Benjamin 120
ペンカー
Penker, Magnus 1095
ベンカイティス
Venckaitis, Edgaras 1451
ベンカタラマン
Venkataraman, Ramaswamy Iyer 1451
ベンカトラマン
Venkatraman, Padma 1451
ベンカブラ
Benchabla, Abdelhafid 119
ベンガリ
Bengaly, Berthe Aissata 120
ベンガルビーヤ
Bengarbia, Mehdi 120
ベンキラー
Benkirane, Abdelilah 121
ベンキラン
Benkirane, Abdelilah 121
ペンギリー
Pengilly, Adam 1095
ヘング
Heng, Anne 594
ベング
Weng, Heidi 1493
ペンク
Penck, Stefanie 1094
Penque, Sue 1095
ヘンクス
Henkes, Kevin 594
ベングトション
Bengtsson, Eva-Lena 120
ベングトソン
Bengtsson, Anna 120
Bengtsson, Jonas T. 120
ヘンクマン
Henckmann, Wolfhart 593
ベンクラー
Benkler, Yochai 121
ヘンケ
Henke, James 594
Henke, Jana 594
Henke, Jim 594
ヘンゲ
Hengge, Paul 594
ベンケ
Benke, Britta 121
ペンケ
Penke, Normans 1095
ベンゲブリ
Benghebrit, Nouria 120
ペンゲリー
Pengelly, Andrew 1095
ヘンケル
Henkel, Andrea 594
Henkel, Hans-Olaf 594
Henkel, Manuela 594
ヘンゲル
Hengel, Martin 594
ベンゲル
Wenger, Arsène 1493
ペンゲル
Pengel, Patrick 1095
ベンケルファ
Benkhelfa, Abderrahmane 121
ヘンゲルブロック
Hengelbrock, Thomas 594
ベンゲーロフ
Vengerov, Maxim 1451
ヘンケン
Henkin, Nancy 594
ベンコ
Benko, Attila 121
Benko, Fabian 121
Benko, Laura B. 121
ベンゴア
Bengoa, Vicente 120
ベンコスキー
Benkoski, Stan 121
ベンザー
Benzer, Seymour 124
ベンサイード
Bensaïd, Daniel 123
ベンサイド
Bensaïd, Daniel 123
ベンサム

Bentham, Susan 123
ヘン・サムリン
Heng Samrin 594
ベン・サレム
Ben Salem, Hatem 123
ベンサレム
Ben Salem, Mohamed 123
Ben Salem, Moncef 123
ベンジ
Benge, Sophie 120
ペンジアス
Penzias, Arno Allan 1096
ベン・ジェッルーン
Ben-Jelloun, Tahar 121
ベンシェリフ
Bencherif, Mohamed El Amine 119
ヘンシェル
Henschel, Jane 596
Henschell, Dietrich 596
ベンジェルール
Bendjelloul, Malik 120
ベン・ジェルーン
Ben-Jelloun, Tahar 121
ベンジオ
Bengio, Ofra 120
ベンジオール
Benjor, Jorge 121
ベンシオン
Bension, Alberto 123
ベンシニョール
Bensignor, Rick 123
ベン・シャハー
Ben-Shahar, Tal 123
ベンジャバラー
Bendjaballah, Souad 120
ベンシャブラ
Benchabla, Abdelhafid 119
ベンジャミン
Benjamin, Alfred 121
Benjamin, Arthur 121
Benjamin, Barnaba Marial 121
Benjamin, Carol Lea 121
Benjamin, Craig 121
Benjamin, Daniel 121
Benjamin, Daniel K. 121
Benjamin, David 121
Benjamin, Elizabeth 121
Benjamin, Henry 121
Benjamin, John 121
Benjamin, Kelvin 121
Benjamin, Leanne 121
Benjamin, Lorna Smith 121
Benjamin, Ludy T., Jr. 121
Benjamin, Marina 121
Benjamin, Medea 121
Benjamin, Nikki 121
Benjamin, Robert I. 121
Benjamin, Ryan 121
Benjamin, Steadroy 121
Benjamin, Stuart 121
Benjamin, Travis 121
ベンシャラル
Benchallal, Nadia 119
ヘンシュ
Hänsch, Theodor 567
ベンシューフ
Benshoof, Tony 123
ヘンショー
Henshaw, George B. 596
Henshaw, Katherine 596
Henshaw, Robbie 596
Henshaw, Russell 596
ヘンショウ
Henshaw, Mark 596
ベンショップ
Benschop, Ronni 123
ベンジョール
Benjor, Jorge 121
ペンシリ
Laosirikul, Pensiri 790
ヘーンズ
Geens, Jelle 486
ベンス
Bence, Evelyn 119
ペンス
Pence, Alan 1094
Pence, Ellen 1094
Pence, Gregory E. 1094
Pence, Hunter 1094
Pence, Mike 1094
ベンスイラ
Bensouilah, Janetta 123
ベンズキッゼ
Bendukidze, Kakha 120
ベンスサン
Bensoussan, Georges 123
ベンステッド
Benstead, Christopher 123
ベンストロング
Benstrong, Michael 123
ベンストン
Benston, George J. 123
ヘンスラー
Henssler, Martin 596
Henssler, Ortwin 596
ペンズラー
Penzler, Otto 1096
ヘンズリー
Hensley, Joe L. 596
ヘンスレー
Hensley, Frederick A. 596
ヘンズレー
Hensley, Laura 596
ベンズレー
Bensley, Graham 123
ベンスン
Benson, Raymond 123
ペン・セタリン
Penn Setharin 1095
ベンゼマ
Benzema, Karim 124
ヘンゼラー
Henseler, Thomas 596
ヘンゼル
Hänsel, Lutz 567
ベンセン
Bemdtsen, Bendt 119
Bendtsen, Bendt 120
ペン・ソヴァン
Pen Sovan 1095
ベンソーダ
Bensouda, Fatou B. 123
ペン・ソバン
Pen Sovan 1095
ヘンソン
Henson, Heather 596
Henson, John 596
Henson, William 596
ベンソン
Benson, Beverly 123
Benson, Donald C. 123
Benson, Elizabeth P. 123
Benson, George 123
Benson, Gerard 123
Benson, Gordon 123
Benson, Harry 123
Benson, Herbert 123
Benson, Jessica 123
Benson, Keith 123
Benson, M.Christina 123
Benson, Michael 123
Benson, Mike 123
Benson, Mildred Wirt 123
Benson, Nigel C. 123
Benson, Patrick 123
Benson, Raymond 123
Benson, Renaldo 123
Benson, Sara'Sam' 123
Benson, Sonja 123
Benson, Stella 123
Benson, Sue 123
Benson, Tom 123
ベンゾン
Benzon, William 124
ベンソンポープ
Benson-pope, David 123
ベンソンモイトイ
Venson-moitoi, Pelonomi 1451
ベンター
Venter, J.Craig 1451
ベンダー
Bender, Aimee 119
Bender, Arnold E. 119
Bender, Bob 119
Bender, Donna S. 119
Bender, Dragan 119
Bender, Lars 119
Bender, Lionel 119
Bender, Sven 119
Bender, Walter 119
ペンダーグラス
Pendergrass, Teddy 1094
ペンダーグラスト
Pendergrast, Mark 1094
ベンダース
Wenders, Wim 1492
ベンダースキー
Bendersky, Joseph W. 119
ヘンダースン
Henderson, Anne 593
Henderson, Lauren 593
ヘンダーソン
Henderson, Amy 593
Henderson, Anne 593
Henderson, Benson 593
Henderson, Beth 593
Henderson, Bill 593
Henderson, Bobby 593
Henderson, Brooke 593
Henderson, Bruce 593
Henderson, Bruce B. 593
Henderson, Bruce E. 593
Henderson, Cal 593
Henderson, Caspar 593
Henderson, Dave 593
Henderson, David 593
Henderson, David R. 593
Henderson, David Wilson 593
Henderson, Deborah A. 593
Henderson, Denys 593
Henderson, Denys Hartley 593
Henderson, Donald Ainslie 593
Henderson, Elizabeth 593
Henderson, Erin 593
Henderson, Frederick A. 593
Henderson, Gerald 593
Henderson, Greg 593
Henderson, Hazel 593
Henderson, Iain 593
Henderson, Jeff 593
Henderson, Jim 593
Henderson, Joe 593
Henderson, Jordan 593
Henderson, Laura 593
Henderson, Mark 593
Henderson, Mark C. 593
Henderson, Monique 593
Henderson, Paula 593
Henderson, Rickey Nelson Henley 593
Henderson, Seantrel 593
Henderson, Theodore A. 593
Henderson, Tracey R. 593
Henderson, Valerie Land 593
Henderson, Vince 593
Henderson, Virginia A. 593
Henderson, Wayne 593
Henderson, William 593
ヘンダソン
Henderson, Kathy 593
ペンタック
Pentak, Stephen 1095
Pentak, William 1095
ベンダニャ
Bendaña, Arturo 119
ベンタレブ
Bentaleb, Nabil 123
ヘンチ
Hench, John 593
Hench, Thomas J. 593
ベンチェラ
Ventura, Judy 1451
ベンチック
Bencich, Steve 119
ベンチュラ
Ventura, Jesse 1451
Ventura, Robin Mark 1451
Ventura, Steve 1451
ベンチュリー
Benchley, Peter 119
ベンチョリーニ
Benciolini, Paolo 119
ベンチリー
Benchley, Peter 119
ベンツ
Benz, Chris 124
Benz, Wilhelm 124
Benz, Wolfgang 124
ベンツァイン
Benzien, Jan 124
ヘンツィ
Henzi, Petra 596
ヘンツェ
Henze, Hans Werner 596
ベンツェン
Bentsen, Lloyd Millard, Jr. 124
ベンツェンヘーファー
Benzenhöfer, Udo 124
ペンツォ
Penzo, Jeanine A. 1096
ヘンデ
Hende, Csaba 593

ヘンディ
Hendy, Alastair 594
ヘンディー
Hendy, A.J. 594
ベンディア
Ben Dhia, Abdelaziz 120
Ben Dhiaa, Maher 120
ベンティヴェーニャ
Bentivegna, Accursio 124
ベンティヴォリオ
Bentivoglio, Leonetta 124
ペンティエ
Pennetier, Jean-Claude 1095
ベンディス
Bendis, Brian Michael 120
ベンディックス＝バルグリー
Bendix-Balgley, Noah 120
ヘンティッヒ
Hentig, Hartmut von 596
ベンディティ
Venditte, Pat 1451
ヘンティレッティ
Gentiletti, Santiago 489
ヘンディン
Hendin, Herbert 593
ベンティーン
Benthien, Claudia 123
Bentyne, Cheryl 124
ベンティン
Bentin, Mohammed Saleh bin Taher 124
ベンテケ
Benteke, Christian 123
ペンデシュ
Pendeš, Marina 1094
ベンデビッド
Bendavid, Naftali 119
ベンデビットーバル
Bendavid-Val, Leah 119
ベンデビッド・バル
Bendavid-Val, Leah 119
ベンテューラ
Ventura, Jesse 1451
ヘンデル
Haendel, Ida 553
ペンデレッキー
Penderecki, Krzysztof 1094
ペンデレツキ
Penderecki, Krzysztof 1094
ペンデレツキー
Penderecki, Krzysztof 1094
ベント
Bent, Ian 123
Bent, Stephen 123
Vendt, Erik 1451
Wendt, Henry 1493
ベントー
Bentow, Max 124
ヘントヴァ
Khentova, Sof'ia Mikhailovna 727
ペントゥスロシマヌス
Pentus-rosimannus, Keit 1095
ベントゥネス
Bentounès, Khaled 124
ベントゥーラ
Ventura, Jesse 1451
Ventura, Piero 1451
Ventura, Rey 1451
ベントゥラ
Ventura, José Alejandro 1451
Ventura, Mauricio 1451
ベントゥラ・カメホ
Ventura Camejo, Ramón 1451
ベントゥリーニ
Venturini, Gian Carlo 1451
ベンドゥル
Bendure, Glenda 120
ペントス
Pentus-rosimannus, Keit 1095
ベントソン
Bengtsson, Anna 120
Bengtsson, Jonas T. 120
Bengtsson, Rolf-Goran 120
ベントナー
Bendtner, Nicklas 120
ベンドヒア
Ben Dhia, Abdelaziz 120
ヘントフ
Hentoff, Nat 596
ペンドラゴン
Pendragon, Paul 1094
ペントランド
Pentland, Alex 1095
ヘンドリー
Hendry, David F. 594
Hendry, Diana 594
Hendry, Joy 594
Hendry, Leo B. 594
ベントリー
Bentley, Dawn 124
Bentley, D.M.R. 124
Bentley, Eilean 124
Bentley, Jon Louis 124
Bentley, Judy K.C. 124
Bentley, Katrin 124
Bentley, Pauline 124
Bentley, Peter J. 124
Bentley, V'Angelo 124
Bentley, Vicci 124
Bently, Peter 124
ヘンドリクス
Hendricks, Barbara 594
Hendricks, Elrod Jerome 594
Hendricks, Kyle 594
Hendriks, Liam 594
Hendrix, Harville 594
Hendrix, Jorrit 594
Hendryx, James B. 594
ヘンドリクセン
Hendriksen, Coenraad F. M. 594
ヘンドリクソン
Hendrickson, Chet 594
Hendrickson, Halva 594
Hendrickson, Sarah 594
Hendrickson, Thomas 594
ヘンドリック
Hendrick, George 594
Hendrick, Hal W. 594
Hendrick, Jeff 594
Hendrick, Willene 594
ヘンドリックス
Hendricks, Barbara 594
Hendricks, Elrod Jerome 594
Hendricks, Gay 594
Hendricks, Lindiwe Benedicta 594
Hendricks, Shellee 594
Hendricks, Vicki 594
Hendrickx, Sarah 594
Hendrix, C.Terry 594
Hendrix, Janie 594
ヘンドリックソン
Hendrickson, Janis 594
ベントル
Bentil, Ben 123
ベンドル
Bendl, Petr 120
Bendle, Neil J. 120
ペンドルトン
Pendleton, Don 1094
Pendleton, Terry 1094
Pendleton, Victoria 1094
Pendleton, William Frederic 1094
ベン＝ドル・ベニテ
Ben-Dor Benite, Zvi 120
ペンドルベリー
Pendlebury, Sarah T. 1094
ベントレー
Bentley, Dawn 124
Bentley, Jonathan 124
Bentley, Rachel 124
Bentley, Sue 124
Bentley, Tom 124
Bentley, Toni 124
ベントレイ
Bentley, Ian 124
ペンドレル
Pendrel, Catharine 1094
ヘンドレン
Hendren, Robert L. 593
ヘントン
Henton, Doug 596
Henton, Douglas C. 596
ベントン
Benton, Caroline F. 124
Benton, Christine M. 124
Benton, Debra 124
Benton, Jim 124
Benton, Michael 124
ベンナー
Benner, Dietrich 122
ベン＝ナイム
Ben-Naim, Arieh 122
ベンニ
Benni, Stefano 123
ベンニア
Ben Hnia, Karem 120
ペンネッタ
Pennetta, Flavia 1095
ベンネマルス
Wennemars, Erben 1493
ペンネル
Pennel, Mike 1095
ベンハー
Ben-Hur, Shlomo 121
ベンバ
Bemba, Jean-Pierre 118
ペンパー
Pemper, Mieczysław 1094
ベンハシ
Benhassi, Hasna 120
ペンバーシー
Penberthy, John 1094
ベンバジズ
Benbaziz, Reda 119
ベンバダ
Benbada, Mustapha 119
ベン・ハティラ
Ben-hatira, Anis 120
ベンハドラ
Benkhadra, Amina 121
ペンバートン
Pemberton, Delia 1094
ベンハビブ
Benhabib, Seyla 120
ベンハビレス
Benhabyles, Abdelmalek 120
ベンハマディ
Benhamadi, Moussa 120
ベンハムザ
Ben Hamza, Khaoula 120
ペンハロウ
Penhallow, David 1095
ベンバンバ
Bembamba, Lucien 119
ベンビイ
Benbihy, Emmanuel 119
ベンフィー
Benfey, Christopher 120
ベンフィート
Benfeito, Meaghan 120
ベンフィールド
Banfield, Richard 89
ベンフォード
Benford, Gregory 120
ペンフォールド
Penfold, Brent 1094
ベンブジット
Benbouzid, Boubekeur 119
ベンブジド
Benbouzid, Boubekeur 119
ヘンプフリンク
Hempfling, Klaus Ferdinand 593
ベンフミダン
Ben Hmidane, Slim 120
ヘンブリー
Hembree, Elizabeth Ann 592
Hembree, Heath 592
ベンブリー
Bembry, DeAndre 119
ベンフリス
Benflis, Ali 120
ペンブローク
Pembroke, Greg 1094
Pembroke, Sophie 1094
ベンベ
Bembe, António Bento 119
ヘンベスト
Henbest, Nigel 593
ベンベニスト
Benveniste, Jacques 124
ベン・ベラ
Ben Bella, Ahmed 119
ベンベラ
Ben Bella, Ahmed 119
ヘンペル
Hempel, Sandra 593
ペンペル
Pempel, T.J. 1094
ベンマスンディ
Ben Massoundi, Rachid 121
ベンマソンディ
Ben Massoundi, Rachid 121
ヘンマート
Hemmert, Martin 592
ペンマン
Penman, Danny 1095

ヘ

Penman, Stephen H. 1095
ベンムーバンバ
Ben Moubamba, Bruno 121
ベンメラディ
Benmeradi, Mohamed 121
ヘンメル
Hemmer, Mari 592
ベンモシェ
Benmosche, Robert H. 121
ベンモハジ
Ben Mohadji, Fouad 121
ベンヤヒア
Ben Yahia, Amor 124
ベンヤヒヤ
Ben Yahia, Habib 124
ベンユネス
Benyounes, Amara 124
ヘンリー
Henle, James M. 594
Henley, Bob 594
Henley, Claire 594
Henley, Don 594
Henley, Russell 594
Henry, Alan 595
Henry, Amy 595
Henry, Anne 595
Henry, April 595
Henry, Beverly 595
Henry, Charlie 595
Henry, Chris 595
Henry, Derrick 595
Henry, Desiree 595
Henry, Doug 595
Henry, Gianna 595
Henry, Guy 595
Henry, Hunter 595
Henry, Jed 595
Henry, Jodie 595
Henry, Joe 595
Henry, John 595
Henry, John W. 595
Henry, Kevin 595
Henry, Larry 595
Henry, Marcus 595
Henry, Marie-Adeline 595
Henry, Marion 595
Henry, Mark 596
Henry, Michael 596
Henry, Mike 596
Henry, Mitchell 596
Henry, Nancy 596
Henry, Nicole 596
Henry, Patrick 596
Henry, Rohan 596
Henry, Sara J. 596
Henry, Todd 596
Henry, Tom 596
Henry, Willie 596
ヘンリーウィルソン
Henry-wilson, Maxine 596
ヘンリー王子
Prince Henry 595
ヘンリクス
Henriques, Adrian 595
ヘンリクセン
Henriksen, Markus 595
ヘンリクソン
Henriksson, Anna-Maja 595
ヘンリク・バシュバニアイ
Henrik Vasbanyai 595
ヘンリー＝ストッカー
Henry-Stocker, Sandra 596
ヘンリック
Henrich, Tommy 595
ヘンリックセン
Henrichsen, Colleen 595
ヘンリッヒ
Henrich, Dieter 595
ベーンリード
Wernlid, Eva 1493
ヘンリー・バン・ティオ
Henry Van Thio 596
ヘンリヒ
Henrich, Dieter 595
ヘンリヒス
Henrichs, Bertina 595
ペンローズ
Penrose, Andrea 1095
Penrose, Antony 1095
Penrose, Roger 1095
ベンロムダーネ
Ben Romdhane, Mahmoud 123
ベンロムダン
Ben Romdhane, Mahmoud 123
ベンワー
Benoit, Chris 123
ベンワイケレ
Benwikere, Bene' 124

【ホ】

ホ
Heo, Jin-ho 596
Ho, Thaek 611
Huh, Joon-ho 633
Huh, Jung-moo 633
Huh, Moon-doh 634
Huh, Nam Jung 634
ホー
Haw, Brian 583
He, Guo-qiang 586
He, Ke-xin 586
He, Xiang-jian 586
He, Yan-xin 586
He, Zhen-liang 586
He, Zuo-xiu 586
Ho, Ching 610
Ho, Daniel 611
Ho, Don 611
Ho, Jannie 611
Ho, Kai Hang 611
Ho, Kwon-ping 611
Ho, Minfong 611
Ho, Peter 611
Ho, Tracey 611
Ho, Y.-J. 611
Hoh, Erling 615
Howe, Julia Ward 628
Ko, Chun-hsiung 749
ボー
Baud, Jean-Pierre 105
Baugh, Kenneth 106
Baugh, Leon 106
Beaud, Michel 110
Bo, Armando 151
Bo, Xi-lai 151
Bo, Yi-bo 151
Boe, Mathias 153
Pai, Yang 1070
Vaux, Joe 1448
Vieaux, Jason 1456
ポー
Pai, Yang 1070
Poe, Curtis Ovid 1119
Poe, Dontari 1119
Poe, Fernando, Jr. 1119
Poe, Grace 1119
*Dr.*Poe, Harry Lee 1119
Poe, Maxwell 1119
Poe, Richard 1119
ホーア
Hoare, Antony 611
Hoare, Katharine 611
ホア
Hawe, Celia 583
Hoa, Nguyen Thi Hoang 611
Hoa, Truong My 611
Hoare, Joanna 611
Hoare, Katharine 611
Hore, Kerry 622
ホアー
Hoare, Ben 611
Hoare, Stephen 611
ボーア
Bohr, Aage Niels 155
Bour, Justin 168
ボア
BoA 151
Bor, Robert 161
ボアカイ
Boakai, Joseph 151
ボアカマラ
Boie-kamara, Usman 155
ホアキン
Joaquin, Nick 674
Joaquin, Sanchez 674
ボアジウ
Boagiu, Anca-Daniela 151
ボアジェイリー
Bourjaily, Vance Nye 168
ボアズ
Boaz, Noel Thomas 151
ボアティン
Boateng, Asamoah 151
ボアデッフル
Boisdeffre, Pierre de 155
ボアデフル
Boisdeffre, Pierre de 155
ボアテング
Boateng, Jerome 151
Boateng, Kevin-Prince 151
ボアーニョ
Boagno, Marina 151
ボアビダ
Boavida, Madalena 151
Boavida, Maria 151
ボアマ
Boamah, Omane 151
ポアランガン
Poarangan, Siri 1119
ボアール
Boal, Augusto 151
ボアル
Boal, Augusto 151
ボアロー
Boileau, Myriam 155
ホァン
Huang, Jim 630
Huang, Xiao-ming 630
ホアン
Hoan, Le Ngoc 611
Hoàng, Minh Tuong 611
Hoang, Tan Tai 611
Hoang, Vu Huy 611
Hoang, Xuan Vinh 611
Huang, Chao-tang 630
Huang, Hua 630
Huang, Ju 630
Huang, Mengla 630
Huang, Shan-shan 630
Huang, Shi-ming 630
Huang, Shung-xing 630
Huang, Vincent 630
Huang, Ying 630
Huang, Yunte 630
ホアング
Hoang, Anh Tuan 611
ホアン・バン・チャウ
Hoang Van Chau 611
ホーイ
Hoeye, Michael 613
ホイ
Hoj, Frank 615
Hooi, Den Huan 621
Hoy, Chris 629
Hui, Ann 634
Hui, K. 634
Hui, Liang-yu 634
Hui, Michael 634
Hui, Ricky 634
Hui, Wing Mau 634
ボーイ
Bowie, David 170
ボイ
Boy, Armelle 171
ボイアー
Boer, F.Peter 153
Boyer, Joan 171
ホイアマン
Heuerman, Jeff 602
ポイアレスマドゥーロ
Poiares Maduro, Miguel 1120
ホイヴェルス
Heuvers, Hermann 602
ホイエ
Høie, Bent 615
ボイエ
Boie, Kirsten 155
ボイエス
Boyes, Christopher 172
ボイエット
Boyett, Jimmie T. 172
Boyett, Joseph H. 172
ボイカー
Beuker, Ralf 134
ポイカー
Peuker, Elmar T. 1105
ホーイカース
Hooykaas, R. 621
ボイキン
Boykin, Brandon 172
Boykin, Jarrett 172
Boykin, Trevone 172
ボイク
Boik, John 155
Voicu, Mihai 1462
ボイケルス
Beukers, Harmen 134
ボイコ
Boiko, Bob 155
Boyko, Brett 172
Boyko, Denys 172
Boyko, Yuriy 172
ホイザー
Heuser, Uwe Jean 602
ボイザーリー

ホ

Boisserée, Wolfgang 155
ホイシャー
Heuscher, Patrick 602
ボイシャー
Beuscher, Armin 134
ボーイ・ジョージ
Boy George 172
ホイジンガ
Huizenga, John Robert 634
ホイス
Hojs, Aleš 615
ボイス
Boyce, Brandon 171
Boyce, Frank Cottrell 171
Boyce, Jim 171
Boyce, John 171
Boyce, Martin 171
Boyce, Mary 171
Boyce, Natalie Pope 171
ボイスヴァート
Boisvert, Raymond D. 155
ボイスター
Boister, Neil 155
ホイスディンク
Hausding, Patrick 582
ポイストゴワ
Poistogova, Ekaterina 1120
ホイスラー
Häusler, Thomas 582
ポイスレス
Poythress, Norman G. 1130
ホイセンスタム
Heussenstamm, Paul 602
ボイゼンベ
Boyssembe, Daniel Nditifei 172
ボイタ
Vojta, Vaclav 1462
ボイチェホフスカ
Wojciechowska, Maia 1520
ボイチツカ
Bachleda-curus, Katarzyna 77
ホイッタム
Whitham, Gerald Beresford 1500
ホイッツマン
Whitzman, Carolyn 1501
ホイッティントン
Whittington, Harry Blackmore 1500
ホイット
Howitt, Mary 628
ホイットテイカー
Whittaker, Terry 1500
ホイットニー
Whitney, Diana Kaplin 1500
Whitney, Phillis A. 1500
ホイットビー
Whitby, Evan R. 1497
Whitby, Nancy L. 1497
ホイットフィールド
Whitfield, John 1500
Whitfield, Philip 1500
Whitfield, Raoul 1500
Whitfield, Simon 1500
ホイットマイア
Whitmire, Susan J. 1500
ホイットマーシュ
Whitmarsh, Mike 1500
ホイットマン
Whitman, Barbara Y. 1500
Whitman, Christine Todd 1500
Whitman, Drew Eric 1500
Whitman, John 1500
Whitman, Meg 1500
Whitman, Michael E. 1500
Whitman, Robert A. 1500
Whitman, Slim 1500
ホイットモア
Whitmore, Ed 1500
Whitmore, James 1500
ホイットラム
Whitlam, Edward Gough 1500
ホイットル
Whittle, Jeremy 1500
ホイットルトン
Whittleton, Alex 1500
ホィットロック
Whitlock, Flint 1500
ホイップル
Whipple, Fred L. 1497
Whipple, Mark B. 1497
ホイテ
Hoyte, Hugh Desmond 629
ボイデ
Boyde, Cissé Mint Cheikh Ould 171
ホイテカー
Whitaker, Forest 1497
ホイテーマ
Hoijtema, T.van 615
ボイテル
Beutel, Albrecht 134
Beutel, Manfred E. 134
ボイテルスパッハー
Beutelspacher, Albrecht 134
ボイテルスパッヒャー
Beutelspacher, Albrecht 134
ホイト
Hoyt, Dick 629
Hoyt, Edwin Palmer 629
Hoyt, Elizabeth 629
Hoyt, James 629
Hoyt, Kenneth B. 629
Hoyt, Sarah A. 629
Hoyte, Doug 629
ボイト
Voight, Jon 1462
ボイド
Boyd, Alan 171
Boyd, Alana 171
Boyd, Brandon 171
Boyd, Brenda 171
Boyd, Brian 171
Boyd, Charles 171
Boyd, Danah 171
Boyd, Donna 171
Boyd, Drew 171
Boyd, Eric L. 171
Boyd, George 171
Boyd, Gerald M. 171
Boyd, Hilary 171
Boyd, Jimmy 171
Boyd, John 171
Boyd, John Dixon Iklé 171
Boyd, Lizi 171
Boyd, Matt 171
Boyd, Michael 171
Boyd, Michael A., Jr. 171
Boyd, Noah 171
Boyd, Pattie 171
Boyd, Robert 171
Boyd, Sheryl Thalman 171
Boyd, Terrence 171
Boyd, Tyler 171
Boyd, William 171
ホイトマン
Whiteman, Burchell 1499
ボイトラー
Beutler, Bruce Alan 134
Beutler, Ernest 134
ポイトレス
Poythress, Alex 1130
ポイナー
Poyner, Barry 1130
ホイニケ
Heunicke, Magnus 602
ホイニシュ
Hojnisz, Monika 615
ボイノワ
Voinova, Anastasiia 1462
ホイバーグ
Hoiberg, Fred 615
ホイビュルク
Højberg, Simon 615
Hojbjerg, Pierre-Emile 615
ホイブローテン
Hoeybraaten, Dagfinn 613
Høybråten, Dagfinn 629
ホイベルガー
Heuberger, Valeria 601
ボイマ
Boima, Caiser 155
ホイマン
Heumann, Theodor 602
ボイム
Boim, Ze'ev 155
Boime, Albert 155
ホイヤー
Hoyer, Andrea 629
Hoyer, Brian 629
Hoyer, Steny Hamilton 629
Hoyer-Larsen, Poul-Erik 629
ボイヤー
Boyer, Blaine 171
Boyer, Clete 171
Boyer, M.Christine 171
Boyer, Pascal 171
Boyer, Paul Delos 171
Boyer, Paul S. 171
Boyer, Rick 172
ポイヤー
Poyer, Jordan 1130
ボイヤーズ
Boyers, Peter James 172
Boyers, Robert 172
ホイヤー・フェルナンデス
Heuer-fernandes, Daniel 602
ホイヤー・ラーセン
Hoyer-Larsen, Poul-Erik 629
ポイユラ
Poijula, Soili 1120
ホィーラー
Wheeler, Lisa 1497
ホイーラー
Wheeler, Charles 1496
Wheeler, Joe 1497
Wheeler, John Archibald 1497
Wheeler, Patricia 1497
Wheeler, Thomas Hutchin 1497
ボイラン
Boylan, Bob 172
Boylan, Clare 172
Boylan, Jim 172
Boylan, Patrick 172
ボイリール
Boilil, Mohamed Ould 155
ホイル
Hoyle, Fred 629
ボイル
Boyle, Alan 172
Boyle, Alan E. 172
Boyle, Cailin 172
Boyle, Danny 172
Boyle, David 172
Boyle, Elizabeth 172
Boyle, Feidhlim 172
Boyle, Francis Anthony 172
Boyle, Kevin 172
Boyle, Lauren 172
Boyle, Mark 172
Boyle, Michael 172
Boyle, Nick 172
Boyle, Patricia A. 172
Boyle, Peter 172
Boyle, Phelim P. 172
Boyle, Rob 172
Boyle, Robert 172
Boyle, Stephen M. 172
Boyle, Susan 172
Boyle, T.Coraghessan 172
Boyle, Willard S. 172
Boyle, Willard Sterling 172
ポイル
Poile, David 1120
ボイルス
Boyles, Denis 172
ボイレン
Boylen, Jim 172
ボイン
Boyne, John 172
ホーイング
Hoying, Scott 629
ホイング
Heung, Tyson 602
ボインス
Boynes, Roger 172
ポインセット
Poinsett, Brenda 1120
ポインター
Pointer, June 1120
Poynter, Dan 1130
Poynter, Ray 1130
Poynter, Toni Sciarra 1130
ボイントン
Boynton, Andrew C. 172
Boynton, Andy 172
ホゥ
Hoeg, Peter 612
Hu, Chih-Wei 630
ホウ
Haw, Brenda 583
Haw, Mark 583
Hou, Hsiao-hsien 625
Hua, Guo-feng 630
ボウ
Bou, Louis 166
Bowe, Brittany 169
Bowe, Tommy 169
ボウアー
Bower, Joseph L. 170

ホーヴァス
Horvath, David 624
Horvath, Polly 624
ホーヴァット
Horvat, Erin McNamara 624
ホーヴァート
Horvath, Polly 624
ボーヴァル
Bauval, Robert 107
ボヴァレ
Beauvallet, Cathy 110
ホウイ
Hoye, Bob 629
ボウィ
Gbowee, Leymah Roberta 485
ボウイ
Bouye, A.J. 169
Bowie, David 170
Bowie, Norman E. 170
Bowie, Tori 170
ボウイー
Bowie, David 170
Gbowee, Leymah Roberta 485
ポウィー
Powe, Darius 1129
Powe, Jerrell 1129
ポウイス
Powys, John Cowper 1130
ホーウィッチ
Horwich, Arthur L. 624
ホーウィッツ
Horwitz, Allan V. 624
Horwitz, Debra 624
Horwitz, Ethan 624
Horwitz, Morton J. 624
ホーヴィッツ
Horvitz, Leslie Alan 624
ホウィトモア
Whitmore, James 1500
ボーヴィン
Bovin, Aleksandr Evgenievich 169
ホーヴィング
Hoving, Thomas 627
ボウヴ
Bove, Cheryl Browning 169
ホーヴェ
Hove, Chenjerai 627
ボウエー
Bauer, Alain 105
ボヴェ
Bové, José 169
ポヴェイ
Povey, Jeff 1129
ホヴェイダ
Hoveyda, Mandana 627
ポヴェダ
Poveda, Christian 1129
ホウエニプエラ
Houenipwela, Ricky 625
ホーヴェル
Heuvel, Joan Vanden 602
ボウェル
Bower, Walter 170
ポーヴェール
Pauvert, Jean Jacques 1088
ポウエル
Powell, Anthony 1129
Powell, Josh C. 1129
ボーウェン
Bauwen, Patrick 107
Bowen, Anne 169
Bowen, Chris 169
Bowen, Gregory 169
Bowen, Hezekia 169
Bowen, Jarrod 170
Bowen, Julie 170
Bowen, Kevin 170
ボウエン
Bowen, Chris 169
Bowen, Edward L. 169
Bowen, Gregory 169
Bowen, Judith 170
Bowen, Rhys 170
Bowen, Ryan 170
Bowen, Sarah 170
Bowen, Will 170
Boyens, Philippa 171
Boyens, Phillipa 171
ボーヴェンシェン
Bovenschen, Silvia 169
ボヴォ
Bovo, Cesare 169
ボーヴォワ
Beauvois, Jean-Léon 110
Beauvois, Xavier 110
ボウカー
Bowker, John Westerdale 170
ボウガエバ
Bougaeva, Sonja 166
ボウカム
Bauckham, Richard 105
ホウグ
Hoag, Tami 611
ホウグランド
Hougland, Damon 626
ボウケット
Bowkett, Steve 170
ボウコット
Bowcott, Nick 169
ホウジョウ
Hojo, Masaaki 615
ボウシンスキー
Boshinski, Blanche 164
ボウズ
Boase, Susan 151
Bowes, Richard 170
ポウスト
Post, Willard Ellwood 1127
ボウスビブ
Bousbib, Gabriel 168
ボウズロフ
Bouzlov, Alexander 169
ボウソ
Bouso, Raquel 168
ポウタラ
Poutala, Mika 1129
ボウチー
Bochy, Bruce 152
ボウディア
Boudia, David 166
ボウティラ
Voutila, Ritva 1464
ポウデル
Powdyel, Thakur Singh 1129
ボウデン
Bowden, David 169
Bowden, John Stephen 169
Bowden, Mark 169
Bowden, Mike 169
Bowden, Tripp 169
ボウドウ
Bodo, G. 153
ボウネス
Bowness, Alan 170
ホウバン
Hoban, Russell 611
ホウマン
Hovmand, Mette 627
Hovmand, Svend Erik 627
ボウマン
Baumann, Buddy 106
Beauman, Sally 110
Bouman, Tom 167
Bowman, Barbara A. 170
Bowman, Bob 170
Bowman, Braedon 170
Bowman, Christopher 170
Bowman, Judith S. 170
Bowman, Kim 170
Bowman, Matt 170
Bowman, NaVorro 170
Bowman, Robert Maxwell James 170
Bowman, Stephen 170
Bowman, Valerie 170
ボウメスター
Bouwmeester, Hans 169
ボウモル
Baumol, William J. 106
ボウモント
Beaumont, Nina 110
ボーヴュ
Beauvue, Claudio 110
ボウラー
Bowler, G.Q. 170
Bowler, Peter J. 170
Bowler, Tim 170
ホウラハン
Houlahan, Greta 626
ホウリハン
Houlihan, Shelby 626
ボゥルズ
Bowles, Esther Joy 170
ボウルズ
Bolles, Edmund Blair 156
Bolles, Richard Nelson 156
Bolls, Paul David 157
Bowles, Esther Joy 170
Bowles, Paula 170
Bowles, Samuel 170
Bowles, Sheldon M. 170
Bowles, Todd 170
ポウルセン
Poulsen, Rene Holten 1128
Poulsen, Simon 1128
Poulsen, Yussuf 1128
ポウルソン
Poulsson, Emilie 1128
ボウルター
Boulter, Michael Charles 167
ホゥルト
Holt, James Clarke 618
ホウルト
Holt, James Clarke 618
ボウン
Bohoun, Paul-Antoine Bouabré 155
Bone, Robert G. 158
ボウンブアブレ
Bohoun, Paul-Antoine Bouabré 155
ボウンメスター
Bouwmeester, Marit 169
ボエ
Boye, Mohamed Mahmoud Abdallahi Ould 171
ホエイ
Khoei, Abdul Majid Al 728
ボエスフルグ
Boespflug, Barbara 153
ボエチウス
Boetius, Jean-Paul 153
ポエット
Poet, Bruno 1119
ボエティウス
Boëtius, Henning 153
ボエドロ
Boedoro, Philip 153
ボエニシュ
Boenisz, Paulina 153
ポェヒハッカー
Pöchhacker, Franz 1119
ボエボドスキー
Voevodsky, Vladimir 1461
ボーエム
Bohem, Leslie 154
ホエーリー
Whalley, Lawrence J. 1496
ホエーリング
Whaling, Carol 1496
ボエル
Boel, Mariann Fischer 153
ボーエン
Bowen, Helen 169
Bowen, James 170
Bowen, John R. 170
Bowen, Kelly 170
Bowen, Murray 170
Bowen, Rex 170
Bowen, Rhys 170
Bowen, Richard Cooper 170
ポー・オー・パユットー
Phra Thēpwēthī Prayut 1109
ホーカー
Hawker, Deborah M. 583
Hawker, Mark D. 583
ボカ
Boka, Angele 155
ボガ
Boga, Jeremie 153
ボガー
Bogar, Tim 154
ボガエヴィッチ
Bogayevicz, Yurek 154
ボカサ
Bokassa, Jean Serge 155
ホガース
Hogarth, Emily 614
Hogarth, Jimmy 614
Hogarth, Stuart 614
Hogarth, William 614
ボーカス
Baucus, Max S. 105
ポカスキ
Pokaski, Joe 1120
ポガチュニク
Pogačnik, Milan 1119
ボガーツ
Bogaerts, Xander 154

ボガツカ
Bogacka, Sylwia 153
ボガツキ
Bogacki, Tomek 154
ホカット
Hocutt, Robert J. 612
ボーガット
Bogut, Andrew 154
ホガーティ
Hogarty, Rio 614
ボガティ
Bogati, Posta Bahadur 154
Bogaty, William J. 154
ボガティリョワ
Bohatyriova, Raisa 154
ボガティン
Bogatin, Eric 154
ホガート
Hoggart, Richard 615
ボガート
Bogart, Leo 154
Bogart, Paul 154
Bogart, Tim 154
ボガード
Bogard, Jimmy 154
Bogard, Paul 154
ポガニー
Pogany, Elaine 1119
ボガノワ
Boganova, Valentina 154
ポーガム
Paugam, Serge 1086
ボガリ
Bogaliy, Anna 154
ポカレル
Pokharel, Aananda Prasad 1120
Pokharel, Girirajmani 1120
ポーカロ
Porcaro, Mike 1125
ホーガン
Hagan, Keith 553
Haugan, Gregory T. 582
Hogan, Barbara 614
Hogan, Brian P. 614
Hogan, Brooke 614
Hogan, Chris 614
Hogan, Chuck 614
Hogan, Edward 614
Hogan, Elizabeth R. 614
Hogan, Hulk 614
Hogan, James Patrick 614
Hogan, Jamie 614
Hogan, Julie 614
Hogan, Kelly A. 614
Hogan, Kevin 614
Hogan, Lara Callender 614
Hogan, Linda 614
Hogan, Mark T. 614
Hogan, Michael J. 614
Hogan, Paul 614
Hogan, Phil 614
Hogan, P.J. 614
Hogan, Thomas P. 614
Horgan, John 622
Hougan, Carolyn 625
ボーガン
Baughan, Michael Gray 106
Vaughan, Norman 1448
ホーキー
Hawkey, Ian 583
ポギ
Poggi, Bruno 1120
ボキエフ
Boqiev, Rasul 161
ポギシオ
Poghisio, Samuel 1120
ホキッシュ
Jokisch, José Walter Ernesto 681
ボキューズ
Bocuse, Paul 152
ポーキン
Bhokin, Bhalakula 135
ホーキング
Hawking, Lucy 583
Hawking, Stephen William 583
ポーキングホーン
Polkinghorn, Bette 1121
Polkinghorne, J.C. 1121
Polkinghorne, John 1121
ホーキンス
Hawkins, Alexandra 583
Hawkins, Bill 583
Hawkins, Brian L. 583
Hawkins, Callum 583
Hawkins, Colin 583
Hawkins, Edwin Preston, Jr. 583
Hawkins, Emily 583
Hawkins, Gary E. 583
Hawkins, George 583
Hawkins, Jeff 583
Hawkins, John N. 583
Hawkins, Karen 583
Hawkins, Laurence 584
Hawkins, Lawrence E. 584
Hawkins, Ronnie 584
Hawkins, Sally 584
Hawkins, Walter 584
ホーキンズ
Hawkins, Andrew 583
Hawkins, Bradley K. 583
Hawkins, Colin 583
Hawkins, David R. 583
Hawkins, Donald 583
Hawkins, Gail 583
Hawkins, Jacqui 583
Hawkins, Jerald 583
Hawkins, Jimmy 583
Hawkins, Josh 583
Hawkins, Paula 584
Hawkins, Peter 584
ホーク
Hauck, Paul A. 581
Hawk, David 583
Hawk, Rip 583
Hawke, Brett 583
Hawke, Ethan 583
Hawke, Harry 583
Hawke, Richard 583
Hawke, Robert 583
Hook, Jason 621
Hook, Richard 621
Houck, Herbert 625
ホーグ
Hoag, John D. 611
Hoegh, Daniel 612
Hogue, Joe 615
ホク
Hok, Jim 615
Hoque, Mohammed Sayedul 622
Hoque, Mozibul 622
Huq, Anisul 637
Huq, Mozammel 637
ホグ
Hogg, Christine 614
ボーク
Balk, Malcolm 86
ボーグ
Borg, James 162
Borg, Marcus J. 162
Borg, Simon 162
Bourg, David M. 168
Bourg, Wendy 168
ボク
Bok, Derek C. 155
Bok, Sissela 155
ポーク
Polk, Laray 1121
ポーグ
Pogue, David 1120
ポク
Pok, Fabian 1120
ボークウィル
Balkwill, Frances R. 86
ホーク・ウォリアー
Hawk Warrior 584
ホグウッド
Hogwood, Christopher 615
ボー・グエン・ザップ
Vo Nguyen Giap 1463
ホグクリステンセン
Hogh-christensen, Jonas 615
ボクシル
Boxhill, Edith Hillman 171
ホークス
Hawkes, John 583
Hawkes, Kevin 583
Hawkes, Rob 583
Hawkes, Terence 583
Hawks, John Twelve 584
ボクスオール
Boxall, Peter 171
ホクスター
Hoxter, Shirley 629
ホクスブロ
Høxbro, Vivian 629
ホークスリー
Hawksley, Humphrey 584
Hawksley, Lucinda 584
ボグセビッグ
Bogusevic, Brian 154
ボクセル
Boxsel, Matthijs van 171
ボクソール
Boxall, Ed 171
ポクソン
Poxon, David 1130
ボグダナー
Bogdanor, Vernon 154
ボグダニッチ
Bogdanich, Walt 154
ボグダノーヴィチ
Bogdanovich, Peter 154
ボグダノヴィッチ
Bogdanovich, Peter 154
ボグダノス
Bogdanos, Matthew 154
ボグダノビッチ
Bogdanovic, Bojan 154
Bogdanović, Goran 154
Bogdanovic, Tijana 154
ボグダノフ
Bogdanov, Michael 154
ボグダノワ
Bogdanova, Anna 154
Bogdanova, Lyudmila 154
ボグツキー
Bohutsky, Yuriy 155
ボグト
Vogt, Kyle 1462
ボグナー
Bogner, Norman 154
ボーグナイン
Borgnine, Ernest 162
ボグナル
Bognar, Richard 154
ボグネス
Bogsnes, Bjarte 154
ポクバ
Pogba, Paul 1119
ボクペティ
Boukpeti, Benjamin 167
ボグラー
Vogler, Christopher 1462
ホーグランド
Hoagland, Edward 611
Hoagland, Mahlon Bush 611
Hoagland, Richard C. 611
ホクリー
Hockley, Dick 612
ポグリアニ
Pogliani, Giuliano 1120
ホクリシビリ
Khokrishvili, Elguja 728
ボクリス
Bockris, John O'M. 152
Bockris, Victor 152
ボーグル
Bogle, Bob 154
Bogle, John C. 154
ボーグルソン
Vogelsong, Ryan Andrew 1461
ポグレバン
Pogreban, Vasily 1120
ポグレブ
Pogreb, Sofya 1120
ホグロギアン
Hogrogian, Nonny 615
ポクローフスキー
Pokrovskii, Boris Aleksandrovich 1121
ポクロフスキー
Pokrovskii, Boris Aleksandrovich 1121
ボクングアスム
Bokung Asumu, Mauricio 155
ポグントケ
Poguntke, Thomas 1120
ホーゲ
Hoghe, Raimund 615
ホゲット
Hoggett, Steven 615
ボゲナ
Boguena, Toufta 154
ボーゲニクト
Borgenichit, Louis 162
Borgenicht, David 162
Borgenicht, Joe 162
ボーゲル
Vogel, Craig M. 1461
Vogel, David 1461
Vogel, David A. 1461
Vogel, Ezra Feivel 1461
Vogel, Fernanda 1461

Vogel, Joseph 1461
Vogel, Steven K. 1461
Vogel, Susan 1461
ボケール
Vaucaire, Cora 1448
ボケル
Boquel, Anne 161
ボーゲルスタイン
Vogelstein, Fred 1461
ボーゲルソン
Vogelsong, Ryan Andrew 1461
ボーゲルバック
Vogelbach, Daniel 1461
ホーケン
Hawken, Paul 583
ボコ
Boco, Major Akira-Esso 152
Boko, Akila-Esso 155
ボゴイヤビッチ・ナラス
Bogojević-Narath, Simon 154
ボコヴァ
Bokova, Irina 155
ボコーヴン
Bockoven, Georgia 152
ボゴエフ
Bogoev, Slavcho 154
ボゴシアン
Pogossian, Garegin 1120
ボゴジェレツ
Pogorzelec, Daria 1120
ボゴシャン
Poghosyan, Hasmik 1120
Poghosyan, Sona 1120
Pogosian, David 1120
Pogosyan, Grant 1120
ボーコス
Voulkos, Peter 1464
ホーコック
Hawcock, David 583
ポーコック
Pocock, Barbara 1119
Pocock, David 1119
Pocock, John Greville Agard 1119
ポゴーニイ
Pogonii, Ya.F. 1120
ポコーニク
Pokornik, Brigitte 1121
ボコバ
Bokova, Irina 155
ボゴビチ
Bogovič, Franc 154
ボゴモーロフ
Bogomolov, Vladimir Osipovich 154
ボゴモロフ
Bogomolov, Oleg 154
Bogomolov, Vladimir Osipovich 154
ボゴラガマ
Bogollagama, Rohitha 154
ボゴリ
Vongoli, Aikaterini 1463
ポコルニ
Pokorni, Zoltán 1120
ポゴレリチ
Pogorelich, Ivo 1120
ポゴレリッチ
Pogorelich, Ivo 1120
ポゴレロフ
Pogorelov, Aleksandr 1120
ホーコン皇太子
Prince Haakon, Crown 551
ホーコンセン
Haakonssen, Knud 551
ホーザ
Hoza, Volodymyr 629
ボーサ
Bosa, Joey 163
ボサ
Botha, Roelof 165
Botha, Ted 165
ボザ
Bozza, Anthony 173
ホザイ
al-Khozai, Khodayir 729
ボーサイカム
Bosaikham, Vongdala 163
ホサイン
al-Hosain, Abdullah bin Abdulrahman 624
Hossain, Anwar 625
Hossain, Khandker Mosharraf 625
Hossain, Mohammad Nazir 625
Hossain, Mosharraf 625
Hossain, Syed Abur 625
ポサヴェツ
Posavec, Josip 1126
ポザコフ
Podsakoff, Philip M. 1119
ポサス
Pozas, Claudio 1130
ポサダ
Posada, Jennifer 1126
Posada, Joachim de 1126
Posada, Jorge 1126
Posada, Mia 1126
ポサダ・モレノ
Posada Moreno, Jesús 1126
ホサック
Hossack, Michael 625
ボサック
Bossak, Jan Wincenty 164
ボサート
Bossert, Gregory Norman 164
Bossert, Karen W. 164
ボサニンボラ
Vosanibola, Josefa 1464
ボサビ
Bossavit, Alain 164
ポザマンティエ
Posamentier, Alfred S. 1126
ポサメ
Possamai, Stephanie 1127
ポサラック
Pošarac, Aleksandra 1126
ボーザルー
Bouzereau, Laurent 169
ホー・サン
Ho Sang, Franchesca 624
ボーサン
Baussan, Olivier 107
Bosan, Sikandar Hayat Khan 163
ボサン
Bosan, Sikandar Hayat 163
ポージー
Posey, Buster 1126
Posey, DeVier 1127
Posey, James 1127
ポジィ
Poggi, Matthew Adam 1120
ボジウカ
Vougiouka, Vassiliki 1464
ボシエ
Baussier, Sylvie 107
ボジェ
Boye, Lucas 171
ポジェ
Poje, Andrew 1120
Poyet, Gustavo 1130
ポジェア
Pogea, Gheorghe 1120
ホージェイゴ
Howgego, Raymond John 628
ホジェッツ
Hodgetts, Geoffrey 612
ボーシェーヌ
Beauchesne, Hervé 110
ボシェマンピナール
Beauchemin-pinard, Catherine 110
ホーシェル
Horschel, Billy 624
ボシオ
Bosio, Chris 164
ボジオ
Bozzio, Terry 173
ホジキン
Hodgkin, Luke Howard 612
ホジキンソン
Hodgkinson, Leigh 612
Hodgkinson, Mark 612
Hodgkinson, Peter 612
Hodgkinson, Tom 612
Hodgkinson, Virginia A. 612
ボジク
Bozic, Luka 172
ボシコ
Bozhko, Vladimir 172
ホジス
Hodges, John R. 612
ポージス
Porges, Arthur 1125
ボジゼ
Bozizé, François 172
ボジゼ・ヤングヴォンダ
Bozizé, François 172
ホジソン
Hodgson, Antonia 612
Hodgson, Geoffrey Martin 612
Hodgson, James D. 612
Hodgson, Pete 612
ボジダル
Boyadzhiev, Bozhidar 171
ホジダン
Hodgdon, Linda A. 612
ホジッチ
Božič, Janez 172
ボジッチ
Božič, Janez 172
ボシディ
Bossidy, Larry 164
ボジート
Bozeat, Matt 172
ボジノビッチ
Božinović, Davor 172
ボジモ
Bozimo, Broderick 172
ホージャ
Khoujah, Abdul-Aziz 728
ホジャ
Hoxha, Dhurata 629
ボーシャー
Bosher, Matt 164
ボージャ
Borgia, Anthony 162
ボージャー
Bojar, Robert M. 155
ホジャイ
Hoxhaj, Enver 629
ホジャエフ
Khodjayev, Batir 728
ホジャクルバノフ
Khodzhagurbanov, Resulberdy 728
ホジャグルバノフ
Khodzhagurbanov, Resulberdy 728
ボージャス
Bourjos, Peter 168
ボシャーズ
Boshers, Buddy 164
ボジャック
Vojak, Bruce A. 1462
ボジャット
Boggiatto, Alessio 154
ホジャティ
Hojjati, Mahmoud 615
ボージャ・ド・モゾタ
Borja de Mozota, Brigitte 162
ボジャノウスキ
Bojanowski, Marc 155
ボジャノフ
Bozhanov, Evgeni 172
ボシャブ・マブジューマービレンゲ
Boshab Mabujaa-bilenge, Evariste 164
ホジャマメドフ
Hojamammedov, Byashimmyrat 615
Khodzhamammedov, Byashimmyrat 728
ホジャムハメドフ
Hojamuhammedov, Baymyrad 615
ボジャリアン
Bohjalian, Christopher A. 154
ポーシャルト
Poschardt, Ulf 1126
ポジャルノフス
Pozarnovs, Andrejs 1130
ボージャン
Bojan, Krkić 155
ボジャン
Bojang, Lamin 155
Bojang, Sheriff 155
ポジャン
Pollán, Laura 1122
ボーシュ
Bausch, Richard 107
ボージュ
Bauge, Gregory 106
ボシュ
Bausch, Paul 106
Bosch, Juan 164

ホーシュカ
Hauschka, Steven 582
ボシュコビッチ
Bošković, Predrag 164
Bošković, Snežana Bogosavljević 164
ボシュナー
Bochner, Arthur Berg 152
ボシュニャコヴ
Boshniakov, Stephan 164
ボシュニャコビッチ
Bošnjaković, Dražen 164
ボシュネク
Bochenek, Valérie 152
ポシュピシル
Pospisil, Vasek 1127
ボーシュマンナドー
Beauchemin-nadeau, Marie-Eve 110
ボシュミンナドー
Beauchemin-nadeau, Marie-Eve 110
ボシュロン
Baucheron, Éléa 105
ボーショー
Bauchau, Henry 105
ボジョナ
Bodjona, Pascal Akousoulèlou 153
ボショフ
Boshoff, Carel 164
ボジョワルド
Bojowald, Martin 155
ボーション
Beauchamp, Doris 110
ホシルド
Khorshid, Dalia 728
ボジロフ
Bozhilov, Georgi 172
ボージンク
Bosing, Walter 164
ホース
Hauss, David 582
Horse, Harry 624
ホーズ
Hawes, Colin S.C. 583
Hawes, Spencer 583
ホス
Hoss, Nina 625
ボース
Bose, Partha Sarathi 164
Bose, Rash Behari 164
Bose, Ruma 164
Bose, Shonali 164
ボーズ
Bose, Amar G. 164
Bose, Sanjay K. 164
ボス
Bass, Tom 102
Boos, André 160
Bos, Ben 163
Bos, Burny 163
Bos, Elly 163
Bos, Jan 163
Bos, Saskia 163
Bos, Theo 163
Bos, Wouter 163
Bosch, Edith 164
Boss, Alan 164
Boss, Medard 164
Boss, Pauline 164
Bosse, Pierre-Ambroise 164
Bosz, Peter 165
Voss, Brian 1464
Voss, Tage 1464
Voth, Austin 1464
ボースウィック
Borthwick, Sophia 163
ボスウイック
Borthwick, Mark 163
ボスウェル
Boswell, Chris 165
Boswell, Dave 165
ボズウェル
Boswell, Barbara 165
Boswell, Dave 165
Boswell, Dustin 165
Boswell, John 165
Boswell, Mark 165
Boswell, Sophie 165
ボスカ
Bosca, Francesca 163
ボスガニア
Vosganian, Varujan 1464
ボスキ
Boschi, Maria Elena 164
ホスキソン
Hoskisson, Robert E. 625
ポスキット
Poskitt, Kjartan 1127
ボスキリア
Boschilia, Gabriel 164
ホスキン
Hoskin, Michael A. 625
ボスキン
Boskin, Joseph 164
Boskin, Michael Jay 164
ホスキング
Hosking, Antony 625
Hosking, Sophie 625
ホスキンス
Hoskins, Bob 625
Hoskins, Johnny D. 625
Hoskyns, Barney 625
ホスキンズ
Hoskins, Bob 625
Hoskyns, Barney 625
ボズクル
Bozkir, Volkan 172
ボスケ
Bosque, Ignacio 164
ポースケ
Paaske, Lars 1067
ボスコ
Bosco, Don 164
Bosco, Juan 164
Bosco, Ronald A. 164
Bosco, Teresio 164
ボスコフ
Boškov, Vujadin 164
ボスコボワ
Voskoboeva, Galina 1464
ボズダー
Bozdağ, Bekir 172
ポスター
Poster, Mark 1127
Poster, Randall 1127
ボスタン
Bostan, Marius-Raul 165
ボスタンジオール
Bostancioglu, Metin 165
ポスツマ
Posthuma, Sieb 1127
ボスティック
Bostic, Jon 165
Bostic, Keith 165
Bostick, Brandon 165
Bostick, Chris 165
ホスティン
Horsting, Viktor 624
ホーステッド
Husted, Ted 639
ホステトラー
Hostetler, Bob 625
ポステル
Postel, Sandra 1127
ポステルスウェイト
Postlethwaite, Pete 1127
ボーステン
Boesten, Ludwig 153
ホースト
Hoost, Ernesto 621
ボスト
Bost, Brent W. 165
Bost, Roger-Yves 165
ポースト
Poast, Paul D. 1119
ポスト
Post, Alise 1127
Post, James E. 1127
Post, Jeffrey Edward 1127
Post, Peggy 1127
Post, Peter 1127
Post, Robert M. 1127
Post, Stephen Garrard 1127
Post, Ted 1127
ポストウ
Postow, Michael A. 1127
ボストウィック
Bostwick, Janet Gwenett 165
ポストゲイト
Postgate, John Raymond 1127
ポストゲート
Postgate, John Raymond 1127
ボストック
Bostock, Mike 165
ポズドニアコワ
Pozdnyakova, Anastasia 1130
ポストマ
Postma, Ids 1127
Postma, Lidia 1127
Postma, Pieter-Jan 1127
ポストマン
Postman, Leo Joseph 1127
Postman, Neil 1127
ポストメス
Postmes, Theo 1127
ポストヤルコ
Postoyalko, Ludmila A. 1127
ポストリガイ
Postrigay, Yury 1127
ボストリッジ
Bostridge, Ian 165
ボーストロプ
Bostrup, Eva 165
ボストロム
Bostrom, Allen B. 165
ボストン
Boston, Arthure 165
Boston, Bernard 165
Boston, Daryl 165
Boston, Jonathan 165
Boston, Mary 165
Boston, Peter 165
Boston, Tre 165
ポストン
Postone, Moishe 1127
ボスナー
Bosner, Leo 164
ポスナー
Posner, Barry Z. 1127
Posner, Donn 1127
Posner, Jerome B. 1127
Posner, John 1127
ポズナー
Posener, Alan 1126
Posner, Eric A. 1127
Posner, Kenneth 1127
Posner, Kenneth A. 1127
Posner, Michael I. 1127
Posner, Richard Allen 1127
ボスナク
Bosnak, Robert 164
ポズナー・サンチェス
Posner-Sanchez, Andrea 1127
ボスナック
Bosnak, Karyn 164
Bosnak, Robert 164
ホスニ
Hosni, Farouk Abdel-Aziz 625
ボズニツキ
Voznitski, Borys 1465
ボズネセンスキー
Voznesenskii, Andrei 1464
ボスハウベェルス
Boshouwers, Suzan 164
ボズバルソン
Bodvarsson, Sturla 153
ボースビー
Bausby, DeVante 106
ポスピーシル
Pospíšil, Jiří 1127
ポスピシロバ
Pospisilova-cechlova, Vera 1127
ホスピタル
Hospital, Janette Turner 625
ホスプ
Hosp, David 625
Hosp, Nicole 625
ポスポス
Pospos, P. 1127
ボスポート
Bospoort, Maarten van de 164
ホスマー
Hosmer, David W. 625
ホズマー
Hosmer, Eric 625
ボスマ
Bosma, Javier 164
Bothma, Renaldo 165
ボスマンス
Bosmans, Phil 164
ボズムバエフ
Bozumbayev, Kanat 172
ホスラー
Hosler, Jay 625
ボスラク
Boslak, Vanessa 164
ポスラズニー
Posluszny, Paul 1127

ホ

ボスラフ
Boslaugh, Sarah 164
ホースリー
Horsley, Andy 624
ホーズリー
Horsley, Mary 624
ボズリ
Bosley, Tom 164
ボズリー
Bosley, Tom 164
ボスール
Bosseur, Jean-Yves 164
ポスルスウェイト
Postlethwaite, Pete 1127
ボスレー
Bosley, Katrine 164
ボズレー
Bosley, L.Lee 164
ボスレット
Boßlet, Joashim 164
ホスロハヴァル
Khosrokhavar, Farhad 728
ボスワース
Bosworth, Michael T. 165
Bosworth, Stephen Warren 165
Bosworth, Tom 165
ボズワース
Bosworth, Patricia 165
Bosworth, Stephen Warren 165
ホセ
Jose 687
José, Ruy 687
ホゼ
Jose 687
ホセ・アンヘル
Jose Angel 687
ポセイ
Posey, Buster 1126
ホセイニ
Hoseini, Safdar 624
Hosseini, Seyed Mohammad 625
Hosseini, Seyed Shamsedin 625
ホセイン
Hossain, Md.Zakaria 625
Hossain, Moazzem 625
ホセウス
Hoseus, Michael 625
ホセ・カルロス
Jose Carlos 687
ポセケリ
Pothecary, Andrew 1127
ボゼツキー
Bosetzky, Horst 164
ポゼッサー
Pozzessere, Heather Graham 1130
ボセッティ
Bosetti, Giancarlo 164
ボゼット
Bozzetto, Mathieu 173
ボセト
Boseto, Leslie 164
ボゼト
Bozzetto, Mathieu 173
ボーセニュー
Beauseigneur, James 110
ホセル
Joselu 687
ポーセル
Peaucelle, Jean Louis 1091
ポセル・ダコスタ
Posser Da Costa, Guilherme 1127
ポーセロ
Porcello, Rick 1125
ホセ・ロドリゲス
Jose Rodriguez 688
ポーゼン
Posen, Adam S. 1126
Pozen, Robert C. 1130
ポゼーン
Posehn, Brian 1126
ポゼン
Posen, Willie 1126
ボーセンカム
Bosengkham, Vondara 164
ホーセンス
Goossens, Philippe 517
ポソ
Pozo, Mauricio 1130
ポソ・ガルサ
Pozo Garza, Luz 1130
ホソカワ
Hosokawa, Bill 625
ホーソーン
Hawthorne, David 584
Hawthorne, Mike 584
Hawthorne, Nigel 584
Hawthorne, Steven C. 584
ホーソン
Hawthorne, Fran 584
Hawthorne, Nigel 584
ボソン
Bosson, Lydia 164
ポーソン
Pawson, Anthony James 1088
Pawson, John 1088
Pawson, T. 1088
ホーター
Hauter, Wenonah 582
ホーダー
Haarder, Bertel 551
ホタ
Jota 688
ホダー
Hodder, Mark 612
ボータ
Botha, Johan 165
ボーダー
Boeder, Lukas 153
Bouder, Ashley 166
ボタ
Botha, Chrysander 165
Botha, Johan 165
Botha, Pieter Willem 165
ボダ
Bodha, Nandcoomar 153
ポータ
Pota, Georgina 1127
ポーター
Porter, Andrew N. 1125
Porter, Angela 1125
Porter, Billy 1125
Porter, Bruce 1125
Porter, Christian 1125
Porter, Darrell Ray 1125
Porter, Donald 1125
Porter, Don E. 1126
Porter, Edgar A. 1126
Porter, Eduardo 1126
Porter, George 1126
Porter, George A. 1126
Porter, George Albert 1126
Porter, Glenn 1126
Porter, Gregory 1126
Porter, Henry 1126
Porter, Howard 1126
Porter, Jane 1126
Porter, Lindsay 1126
Porter, Louise 1126
Porter, Lynnette R. 1126
Porter, Michael E. 1126
Porter, Oliver W. 1126
Porter, Otto 1126
Porter, Pamela 1126
Porter, Peter 1126
Porter, Philip 1126
Porter, Richard C. 1126
Porter, Roy 1126
Porter, Sanford D. 1126
Porter, Sarah 1126
Porter, Sean 1126
Porter, Stephen 1126
Porter, Theodore M. 1126
Porter, Tiffany 1126
Porter, Tracey 1126
Porter, Tracy 1126
ポター
Potter, Andrew 1128
Potter, Giselle 1128
Potter, Robert F. 1128
ポダ
Poda, Jean-Noel 1119
ポータヴィー
Powdthavee, Nattavudh 1129
Powdthavee, Nick 1129
ホダエイ
Khodaei, Majid 728
ホタカイネン
Hotakainen, Kari 625
ボダケン
Bodaken, Bruce 152
ポータシ
Poutasi, Jeremiah 1129
ボタシュ
Botash, Ann S. 165
ボダージュ
Bordage, Georges 161
ボータース
Vaughters, James 1448
ボーターセ
Bouterse, Desi 169
ボーダッシュ
Bourdaghs, Michael K. 168
ボダニス
Bodanis, David 152
ポターニン
Potanin, Vladimir 1127
ポーターフィールド
Porterfield, Kay Marie 1126
ポタペ
Potape, Francis 1127
ボーダベリー
Bordaberry, Pedro 161
ポダルコ
Podalko, Petr 1119
ボダルト＝ベイリー
Bodart-Bailey, Beatrice M. 152
ポータルピ
Portalupi, JoAnn 1125
ポーター・ロス
Porter-Roth, Bud 1126
ボーダン
Baudin, Gabrielle Prévilon 105
ボダン
Baudin, Ronald 105
Bodin, Dominique 153
ボダンスキー
Bodansky, Yossef 152
ボー・チー
Bo Kyi 155
ボーチー
Bochy, Bruce 152
Bo Kyi 155
ポチ
Poci, Spartak 1119
ポチアテク
Počiatek, Ján 1119
ポチエ
Pottier, Johan 1128
ポチェッティーノ
Pochettino, Mauricio 1119
ボチェッリ
Bocelli, Andrea 152
ホチェバル
Hocevar, Simon 611
ポチェヒナ
Potyekhina, Viktoriya 1128
ホチキス
Hotchkiss, Lee 625
Hotchkiss, Sandy 625
ボチコ
Bochco, Steven 152
ボー・チ・コン
Vo Chi Cong 1461
ボー・チー・コン
Vo Chi Cong 1461
ボチトラー
Bochtler, Doug 152
ポチノク
Pochinok, Aleksandr P. 1119
ポチバルシェク
Počivalšek, Zdravko 1119
ポチョムキン
Potemkin, Aleksandr 1127
Potyomkin, Aleksandr 1128
ボーツ
Bots, Hans 165
ポーツ
Ports, Suki Terada 1126
ボツァキス
Botzakis, Stergios 166
ボーツウェイン
Boatswain, Anthony 151
ボツェフスキ
Bocevski, Ivica 152
ホッカー
Hocker, Zach 612
ボッカシーニ
Boccassini, Ilda 152
ボッカチーニ
Boccacini, Corinna 152
ボッカーマン
Bockermann, Markus 152
ホッキー
Hockey, Joe 612
ボッキーノ
Bocchino, Anthony J. 152
ホッキング

Hocking, Amanda 612
Hocking, Belinda 612
ホック
Hoch, Edward Dentinger 611
Hock, Roger R. 612
Huq, Anisul 637
Huq, Mozammel 637
ホッグ
Hogg, D.J. 614
Hogg, John Mervyn 614
Hogg, Stuart 614
Hogg, Tracy 614
ボック
Boc, Emil 152
Boc, Victor 152
Bock, David 152
Bock, Dennis 152
Bock, Janna 152
Bock, Jason 152
Bock, Jerry 152
Bock, Laszlo 152
Bock, William Sauts 152
Bok, Derek C. 155
ボックウィンクル
Bockwinkel, Nick 152
ホックシールド
Hochschild, Arlie Russell 612
ホックス
Fox, Howard 453
ボックス
Box, C.J. 171
Box, Don 171
Box, John 171
Box, Steve 171
Box, Su 171
ボッグス
Boggs, John 154
Boggs, Taylor 154
ボッグズ
Boggs, Mathew 154
ホックステイター
Hochstatter, Daniel J. 612
ボックスバーガー
Boxberger, Brad 171
ホッグスヘッド
Hogshead, Sally 615
ホックニー
Hockney, David 612
ホックマン
Hochman, Larry 612
Hochman, Michael E. 612
Hochman, S.D. 612
ボックリス
Bockris, John O'M. 152
ホッケ
Hocke, Patrick 612
Hocke, Roman 612
Hocke, Stephan 612
ポッゲ
Pogge, Thomas Winfried Menko 1120
ボッケミュール
Bockemühl, Michael 152
ホッケンスミス
Hockensmith, Steve 612
ボッコ
Bocco, Vicentia 152
Guarneri, Andrea Bocco 541
ボツコ
Boczko, Gabor 152
ボッサート
Bosshart, Dominique 164
ホッシ
Rossi, Marcelo 1207
ホッジ
Hodge, Alison 612
Hodge, Bonnie M. 612
Hodge, Brian 612
Hodge, Douglas 612
Hodge, Geoff 612
Hodges, Jill 612
Hoge, Robert D. 614
ボッシ
Bossi, Umberto 164
ボッシー
Bossi, Umberto 164
Bossy, John 164
ボッジオ
Boggio, Philippe 154
ポッジオ
Poggio, Tomaso A. 1120
ホッジス
Hodges, Andrew 612
Hodges, Gerald 612
Hodges, Zack 612
Hodgetts, William H. 612
ホッジズ
Hodges, C.Walter 612
Hodges, Michael 612
ボッジス
Boggess, K.A. 154
ボッシーニ
Bossini, Paolo 164
ポッジャー
Podger, Rachel 1119
ボッシュ
Bosch, David Jacobus 164
Bosch, Juan 164
Bosh, Chris 164
Bosh, Marcelo 164
ポッシュ
Posch, Waltraud 1126
ホッシンガー
Hoessinger, Enid 613
ホッスー
Hosszu, Katinka 625
ポッスルウェイト
Postlethwaite, T. Neville 1127
ホッス・レゴツキ
Hosszu-Legocky, Geza 625
ボッセ
Bosse, Gerhard 164
ホッセイニ
Hosseini, Khaled 625
ホッター
Hotter, Hans 625
ポッター
Potter, Beverly A. 1128
Potter, Ellen 1128
Potter, Frank 1128
Potter, Grace 1128
Potter, Heidi Caroline 1128
Potter, Henry 1128
Potter, Jeff 1128
Potter, John Deane 1128
Potter, Keith 1128
Potter, Lawrence 1128
Potter, Melody Milam 1128
Potter, Mick 1128
Potter, Patricia 1128
Potter, Patricia Ann 1128
Potter, Patrick 1128
Potter, Pitman B. 1128
Potter, Sally 1128
Potters, Marc 1128
ポッターエフロン
Potter-Efron, Patricia S. 1128
Potter-Efron, Ronald T. 1128
ホッチ
Hoch, Stephen James 611
ボッチ
Bocci, Velio 152
ボッチェリ
Bocelli, Andrea 152
ホッツ
Hotz, Robert Lee 625
ポッツ
Potts, Debby 1128
Potts, Paul 1128
Potts, Rolf 1128
Potts, Stephen 1128
ポッツォ・ディ・ボルゴ
Pozzo di Borgo, Philippe 1130
ボッツマン
Botsman, Rachel 165
ボッテ
Bottet, Nicole 166
ボッティ
Botti, Chris 166
ボッディ
Boddie, John 152
ポッティンガー
Pottinger, Stanley 1128
ボッティング
Botting, Douglas 166
ポッテージ
Pottage, Hazel D.L. 1127
ホッテズ
Hotez, Peter J. 625
ボッテン
Borten, Per 163
ボット
Bot, Ben 165
Bott, Danièle 165
Bott, Ed 165
Votto, Joey 1464
ボットー
Votto, Joey 1464
ポット
Pot, Chimney 1127
ホッドソン
Hodgson, James D. 612
ボットナー
Bottner, Barbara 166
ポットハスト
Potthast, Thomas 1128
ポットマン
Potman, George 1127
ポツナンスキ
Poznanski, Ursula 1130
ポツニャコフ
Pozdnyakov, Stanislav 1130
ホッパー
Hopper, Dennis 622
Hopper, Elizabeth 622
Hopper, Paul J. 622
ポッパー
Popper, Nathaniel 1125
ボッビオ
Bobbio, Norberto 151
ホッフ
Hoff, Moa 613
ホップ
Hop, Le Doan 621
Hoppe, Felicitas 622
Hoppe, Geoffrey 622
Hoppe, Linda 622
ボップ
Bopp, Mary Ann 161
ポッフ
Povh, Bogdan 1129
ポップ
Pop, Iggy 1124
Popp, Eduard 1125
Popp, Walter 1125
ホッファ
Hoffa, Reese 613
Hoffer, Bates L. 613
ホッファー
Hoffer, Abram 613
ボッファ
Boffa, Alessandro 153
ホップウッド
Hopwood, Anthony G. 622
Hopwood, V. 622
ホッフェカー
Hoffecker, John 613
ホップカーク
Hopkirk, Peter 622
ホップクロフト
Hopcroft, John E. 621
ポップコーン
Popcorn, Faith 1124
ホッブス
Hobbes, Nicholas 611
Hobbs, Christopher 611
Hobbs, Christopher James 611
Hobbs, Jeremy 611
Hobbs, Marian 611
Hobbs, Nancy 611
Hobbs, Renee 611
ホッブズ
Hobbs, Alan 611
Hobbs, Jeremy 611
Hobbs, Roger 611
ホッフバウアー
Hofbauer, Josef 613
ポップルストーン
Popplestone, John A. 1125
ホッヘ
Hoche, Alfred Erich 611
ホッペ
Hoppe, A. 622
Hoppe, Rene 622
ポッペ
Pobbe, Marcella 1119
ポッペ
Poppe, K.J. 1125
Poppe, Thomas 1125
ポッペル
Poppel, Peter 1125
ポッペン
Poppen, Christoph 1125
ポッペンディーク
Poppendieck, Mary 1125
Poppendieck, Thomas David 1125
ホッペンフェルド
Hoppenfeld, Stanley 622
ホッホシールド
Hochschild, Jutta 612
ホッホスタイン
Hochstein, Lorin 612

ホ

ボツマン
Botsman, Dani 165
ポツラ
Kpotsra, Yao Roland 762
ボッラドリ
Borradori, Giovanna 163
ポッリーニ
Pollini, Maurizio 1122
ボッレ
Bolle, Roberto 156
ホッロ
Hollo, Anselm 617
ボーデ
Bode, Ingo 152
ボデ
Bode, Ridvan 152
ボテアック
Boteach, Shmuel 165
ホティ
Hoti, Avdullah 625
Hoti, Khan 625
ボティ
Boti, Jacques 165
ボディ
Boddy, Kasia 152
Bodie, Zvi 153
ポティ
Pottie, Marjolein 1128
ボティア
Botia, Lepani 165
ボディアス
Bodias, Michel Botoro 153
ボディアン
Bodian, Stephan 153
ポティエ
Pothier, Eric 1127
Pothier, Gilles 1127
Pottier, Magalie 1128
ホディエフ
Khodiyev, Bakhodir 728
ボティオ
Bottieau, Joachim 166
ボディー・カルホーン
Boddy-calhoun, Briean 152
ボティシュ
Botiş, Ioan Nelu 165
ボディシュチャヌ
Bodisteanu, Octavian 153
ポーティス
Portis, Antoinette 1126
Portis, Bobby 1126
Portis, Charles 1126
ボ・ディドリー
Bo Diddley 153
ホディビ
Hodaibi, Mamoun El- 612
ホデイビ
Hodaibi, Mamoun El- 612
ポティリツィナ
Potylitsina, Olga 1128
ポーティロ
Portillo, Michael Denzil Xavier 1126
ボーディン
Bodin, Art 153
Bodine, Sherrill 153
ボーデイン
Bourdain, Anthony 168
ボティン
Botín, Ana Patricia 165
ボディン
Bodin, Issara 153
Bodine, Russell 153
Botín, Ana Patricia 165
ポティング
Poting, Tatiana 1127
ボーデウィヒ
Bodewig, Kurt 153
ポテク
Potec, Camelia 1127
ボテザトゥ
Botezatu, Ionut 165
ポデスキ
Podeschi, Marco 1119
ポデスタ
Podesta, Connie 1119
Podesta, John David 1119
Podestà, Rossana 1119
ポーテラ
Portela, Francis 1125
ボテーリョ
Botelho, Emiliano Pereira 165
ホーデル
Hodel, Jan 612
ホデル
Hodel, Steve 612
ボデル
Bodell, Lisa 152
ポーデル
Paudel, Bishnu Prasad 1086
Paudel, Dhaniram 1086
ボテロ
Botero, Fernando 165
Botero, Jorge Humberto 165
Botero, Santiago 165
Botero Villegas, Jhonnatan 165
Bottéro, Jean 165
ボテロ・アングロ
Botero Angulo, Jorge Humberto 165
ボーデン
Bawden, Louise 107
Bawden, Nina 107
Boden, Christine 152
Boden, Fernand 152
Boden, Jens 152
Borden, Iain 161
Borden, Louise 161
Bowden, Oliver 169
Bowden, S. 169
Vodden, Lucy 1461
Vousden, Neil 1464
ポテン
Pothain, Jordan 1127
ボーテング
Boateng, Ozwald 151
ポテント
Potent, Warren 1127
ボーデンハマー
Bodenhamer, Bob G. 152
ホート
Haught, John F. 582
ホード
Hoedt, Wesley 612
ボート
Boot, Willem Jan 160
Vogt, Stephen 1462
ボード
Beaude, Pierre Marie 110
Board, Ken 151
Bode, N.E. 152
ボト
Boto, Ahmed 165
ボトー
Votto, Joey 1464
ポート
Poort, Jarrod 1124
Port, Michael 1125
Porte, Richie 1125
ポドイニコバ
Podoinikova, Irina 1119
ポトィリチャク
Potil'chak, Oleksandr 1127
ボードイン
Beaudoin, Steven Maurice 110
ボドゥ
Baudou, Jacques 105
ボドゥー
Baudoux, Dominique 105
ボードウィッツ
Bordowitz, Hank 161
ボドウィン
Boddewyn, Jean J. 152
ボードウェイ
Boadway, Robin W. 151
ボードウェル
Bordwell, David 161
ポトゥプチク
Potupchik, Vladimir N. 1128
ボトゥラライ
Botralahy, Gérard 165
ボトカー
Bodker, Cecil 153
ポトカー
Potokar, John 1127
ポドガイヌイ
Podgainy, Mikhail V. 1119
ボトキン
Botkin, James W. 165
ホドキンソン
Hodkinson, Paul 612
ポトク
Potok, Chaim 1127
ポトクニック
Potocnik, Felix 1127
ポトコネン
Potkonen, Mira 1127
ポトコワツ・エンドリゲッティ
Potkovac-Endrighetti, Mirna 1127
ボトストレーム
Bodström, Thomas 153
ポトチュニク
Potočnik, Janez 1127
ボドック
Bodoc, Liliana 153
ポトック
Potok, Chaim 1127
ポトーティ
Potorti, David 1127
ポートナー
Portner, Paul 1126
ボトナリ
Botnari, Vasile 165
ボドナル
Bodnar, Maciej 153
ポドニークス
Podnieks, Elizabeth 1119
ボトビノフ
Botvinov, Mikhail 166
ボドフ
Bodoff, Stephanie 153
ポートフ
Portoff, Michael 1126
ポドブニク
Podobnik, Janez 1119
ポドフラースキー
Podhrasky, Martin 1119
ホートベイト
Haatveit, Andreas 551
ポドベドワ
Podobedova, Svetlana 1119
ホードマン
Hoedeman, Olivier 612
ボードマン
Boardman, Anthony E. 151
Boardman, Donnell W. 151
Boardman, John 151
Boardman, Paul Harris 151
Boardman, Thomas Gray 151
ボドマン
Bodman, Samuel Wright Ⅲ 153
ポートマン
Portman, Natalie 1126
ボトム
Bottom, Norman R. 166
Bottome, Phyllis 166
ボトムス
Bottoms, Sam 166
ボトムズ
Bottoms, Sam 166
ボトムリー
Bottomley, Jennifer M. 166
ホドラー
Hodler, Marc 612
ボトラー
Boteler, Alison 165
ボートライト
Boatwright, Bennie 151
Boatwright, Peter 151
ポドラドチコフ
Podladtchikov, Iouri 1119
ボートラン
Vautrin, Catherine 1448
ボトラン
Vautrin, Catherine 1448
ホートリー
Hawtree, Christopher 584
ホードリー
Hoadley, Graham 611
Hoadley, James E. 611
ポドリスキイ
Podol'skii, Nal' 1119
ボードリック
Bauderlique, Mathieu Albert Daniel 105
ボードリヤール
Baudrillard, Jean 105
ボートリン
Bortolin, Matthew 163
ポートル
Poeltl, Jakob 1119
ホドルコフスキー
Khodorkovskii, Mikhail Borisovich 728
ボートルズ

Bortles, Blake 163
Bortles, JoAnn 163
ポドルスキ
Podolski, Lukas 1119
ポドルスキー
Podolski, Lukas 1119
ポドルニー
Podolny, Joel Marc 1119
ボトルバ
Votruba, Jiří 1464
ホードレイ
Hoadley, Christopher 611
ポドレス
Podres, Johnny 1119
ボートレル
Bottrell, Melissa M. 166
ボードロ
Baudelot, Christian 105
ボドロフ
Bodrov, Sergei 153
Bodrov, Sergei, Jr. 153
ホドロフスキー
Jodorowsky, Alexandro 675
ボードワン
Baudoin, Edmond 105
Beaudoin, Réjean 110
ホートン
Haughton, Brian 582
Haughton, Chris 582
Haughton, Laurence 582
Hawton, Keith 584
Horton, Cole 624
Horton, Genevieve 624
Horton, Gladys 624
Horton, H.Robert 624
Horton, John 624
Horton, Jonathan 624
Horton, Mack 624
Horton, Naomi 624
Horton, Patrick 624
Horton, Ray 624
Horton, Robert 624
Horton, Robert Baynes 624
Horton, Sarah 624
Horton, Tom 624
Horton, Wes 624
Horton, William 624
Horton, William Kendall 624
Houghton, Andrew R. 625
Houghton, David 625
Houghton, Frances 625
Houghton, Israel 625
Houghton, James Richardson 626
Houghton, John 626
Houghton, Peter 626
ボートン
Boateng, Paul 151
ボードン
Bourdon, Rob 168
ホーナー
Horner, James 623
Horner, John R. 623
Horner, Miranda 623
Horner, Richard 623
Horner, Robert H. 623
ボナ
Bona, Dominique 157
Bona, Richard 157
Bona, Septano 157
ボナー
Bonner, John Tyler 159
Bonner, Logan 159
Bonner, Sarah E. 159
Bonner, Sebastian 159
Bonner, William 159
ボナイ
Boni, William C. 159
ボナイティ
Bonaiti, Paolo 157
ボナヴェントゥーラ
Bonaventura, Giacomo 158
ホナヴォグト
Honervogt, Tanmaya 620
ボーナス
Bownas, Geoffrey 170
ボナーズ
Bonners, Susan 159
ホーナセク
Hornacek, Jeff 623
ホーナーセック
Hornacek, Jeff 623
ホーナセック
Hornacek, Jeff 623
ボーナッカー
Bohnacker, Hartmut 155
ボナッティ
Bonatti, Walter 158
ボナーティ
Bonati, Angelo 157
ボナネ
Bonanet, Maurice Dieudonné 157
ボナーノ
Bonanno, Antonio C. 157
Bonanno, Bill 157
Bonanno, George A. 157
Bonanno, Joseph 157
ボナノ
Bonanno, José 157
ボナノス
Bonanos, Christopher 157
ボナノッテ
Bonanotte, Cecco 157
ボナーバーグ
Vonarburg, Andre 1463
ボナパルト
Bonaparte, Felicia 157
ボナフー
Bonafoux, Pascal 157
ボナファシオ
Bonifacio, Emilio 159
ボナボー
Bonabeau, Eric 157
ボナボロンタ
Bonavolontà, Giuseppe 158
ボナーミ
Bonami, Francesco 157
ボナム
Bonham, Margaret H. 159
ボナム・カーター
Bonham-Carter, Helena 159
ホー・ナムホン
Hor Namhong 623
ボナモー
Bonameau, Isabelle 157
ボナール
Bonnard, Marc 159
ホーナング
Hornung, Alfred 623
Hornung, David 623
ボナンジンガ
Bonansinga, Jay R. 157
ボナンノ
Bonanno, Joseph 157
ホニー
Jonny 686
Jony 686
ボーニ
Boni, Valerio 159
ボニ
Boni, Mariam Aladji 159
Boni, Michał 159
ボニー
Bonney, Barbara 160
Bonney, Grace 160
Bonney, Sean 160
Bonnie, Richard J. 160
Bonny, Ed 160
Bony, Wilfried 160
ポーニア
Poonia, Krishna 1124
ポニア
Ponniah, Thomas 1123
ポニアチク
Poniachik, Karen 1123
ポニアトウスカ
Poniatowska, Elena 1123
ポニアトウスキ
Poniatowski, Michel Casimir 1123
ボニウェル
Boniwell, Ilona 159
ボーニエ
Baugniet, Rebecca 106
ホニェク
Honyek, Gyula 620
ホーニグ
Honig, Donald 620
ボニージャ
Bonilla, Jose 159
Bonilla, Juan 159
ボニジャ
Bonilla, Conrado 159
Bonilla, Miguel Ángel 159
ボニジャ・レジェス
Bonilla Reyes, Pompeyo 159
ボニゼール
Bonitzer, Pascal 159
ボニゾッリ
Bonisolli, Franco 159
ボニゾルリ
Bonisolli, Franco 159
ボニチ
Bonnici, Josef 160
ボニツェール
Bonitzer, Pascal 159
ホーニッグ
Honig, Bonnie 620
ボーニッシュ
Borniche, Laurent 163
ボニッチ
Bonnici, Peter 160
ボニーニ
Bongini, Barbara 159
Bonini, Sandrine 159
ボニーノ
Bonino, Emma 159
Bonino, Luigi 159
ボニファシオ
Bonifacio, Avelino 159
Bonifacio, Jorge 159
ボニファス
Boniface, Pascal 159
Boniface, Sauguelni 159
ボニーヤ
Bonilla, Lisalverto 159
ポニャトスキー
Poniatowski, Martin 1123
ポニョムー
Kpoghomou, Togba Césaire 762
ボニーリャ・パラシオス
Bonilla Palacios, Juan José 159
ポニ・ロクドゥ
Poni Lokudu, Agnes 1123
ホーニング
Hornig, George 623
Horning, Sandra 623
ボニング
Bonning, Tony 160
ボーヌ
Beaune, Colette 110
ボヌ
Bonou, Alphonse 160
ボヌッチ
Bonucci, Leonardo 160
ボヌフォワ
Bonnefoy, Yves 159
ボーネ
Boone, Marc 160
ボネ
Bonnet, Charlotte 160
Bonnet, Gérard 160
ボネウィッツ
Bonewitz, Ronald Louis 158
ボネヴィル
Bonneville, Hugh 160
ホーネガー
Hohenegger, Beatrice 615
ボネガット
Vonnegut, Kurt, Jr. 1463
Vonnegut, Norb 1463
ホーネス
Honess, Paul 620
ホーネッカー
Honecker, Margot 620
ホネッカー
Honecker, Margot 620
ホーネック
Honeck, Manfred 619
Honeck, Rainer 619
ホネック
Honeck, Rainer 619
ボネッティ
Bonetti, Luis Manuel 158
ホネット
Honneth, Axel 620
ボネット
Bonnet, Andrew 160
Bonnet, James 160
Bonnett, Alastair 160
ボネテ・マルティーニョ
Bonete Martiho, Carlos 158
ボネバ
Boneva, Antoaneta 158
ボネビル
Bonneville, Hugh 160
ホネフ
Honnef, Klaus 620
ボネーラ
Bonera, Daniele 158

ボーネル
Bonnell, Gary 159
ボネール
Bonnaire, Sandrine 159
ポーネル
Poehnell, Gray R. 1119
ボネロドリゲス
Bonne Rodriguez, Yowlys 159
ホーネン
Hönen, Nicole 620
ボーネン
Boonen, Stefan 160
ボーノ
Bono 160
ボノ
Bono 160
Bono, José 160
ボノー
Bonneau, Joseph 159
ボノアン
Bonoan, Manuel 160
ホノヴィッチ
Honovich, Nancy 620
ポノオパペ
Pono Opape, Jöel 1123
ボノーニュ
Bononge, José Endundo 160
ホノハン
Honohan, Patrick 620
ポノマレンコヤニッチ
Ponomarenko Janic, Spela 1123
ボノミ
Bonomi, Eduardo 160
ボノム
Bonhomme, Matthieu 159
ボノーリ
Bonoli, Giuliano 160
ポノル
Ponor, Cătălina 1123
Ponor, Catalina 1123
ボノンゲ
Bononge, José Endundo 160
ボノンム
Bonhomme, Annie 159
ホーバ
Hoeber, Mark 612
ボーバ
Borba, Michele 161
ボーバー
Bowbeer, Joseph 169
ホーバス
Horvath, David B. 624
ボパット
Vopat, James 1464
ボバディジャ
Bobadilla, Raul 151
ボパ・デビ
Bopha Devi, Norodom 161
ホバート
Hobart, Alice Tisdale (Nourse) 611
ホバニシャン
Hovhannisyan, Artur 627
ホバネツ
Chovanec, Milan 260
ボハノン
Bohanon, Tommy 154
ホバマン
Hoberman, John Milton 611
ポパム
Popham, Peter 1124
ボハラ
Bohara, Deepak 154
ポパルラン
Popirlan, Valentin 1124
ホーバン
Hoban, Lillian 611
Hoban, Russell 611
Hoban, Tana 611
ボバン
Bobin, Christian 152
ポハン
Pohan, Saur Maruli 1120
ボー・バン・キエット
Vo Van Kiet 1464
ボー・バン・キエト
Vo Van Kiet 1464
ボパンナ
Bopanna, Rohan 161
ポハンバ
Pohamba, Hifikepunye 1120
ホーヒー
Haughey, Charles James 582
ホビー
Hobbie, Holly 611
Hobbie, Wendy 611
ボビ
Bobi, Emilienne 152
ポピヴァノフ
Popivanov, Peter R. 1124
ポピエラ
Popiela, Dariusz 1124
ボービエンカム
Boviengkham, Vongdara 169
ポピック
Popik, Emma 1124
ホービッツ
Horvitz, Louis J. 624
ボビット
Bobbitt, Malcolm 151
ポヒバ
Pohiva, Akilisi 1120
ボビー・ハットフィールド
Hatfield, Bobby 581
ポピヤッツ
Popijać, Duro 1124
ポヒワラ
Pochwala, Marcin 1119
ボービン
Bovin, Aleksandr Evgenievich 169
ボビン
Bobin, James 152
Vovin, Alexander 1464
ホービング
Hoving, Erik 627
Hoving, Thomas 627
ボビンスキー
Bobinski, George Sylvan 152
ボヒンツ
Bohinc, Rado 154
ホーブ
Haub, Erivan 581
ホープ
Hope, Annette 621
Hope, Bob 621
Hope, Dale 621
Hope, Daniel 621
Hope, Jeremy 621
Hope, Lesa Nitcy 621
Hope, Murry 621
Hope, Saskia 621
Hope, Terry 621
Hope, Tim 621
Hope, Tony 621
ホフ
Hof, Marjolijn 613
Hoff, Christian 613
Hoff, Ferdinand 613
Hoff, Frans van der 613
Hoff, Max 613
Hoff, Nils Jakob 613
Hoff, Sydney 613
ホブ
Hobb, Robin 611
ポープ
Pope, Catherine 1124
Pope, Jeff 1124
Pope, Nick 1124
Pope, Rob 1124
Pope, Troymaine 1124
ポフ
Povkh, Mariya 1129
ポプ
Pop, Mihail 1124
ホーファー
Hofer, Myron A. 613
Hofer, Paul 613
Hofer, Tom 613
ポファラ
Pofalla, Ronald 1119
ホーフィンガー
Hofinger, Gesine 614
ボーフィンガー
Bofinger, Peter 153
ホーフィング
Hoving, Isabel 627
ホープウェル
Hopewell, Chris 621
ホーフォード
Horford, Al 622
ポプキン
Popkin, Barry M. 1124
Popkin, Michael 1124
Popkin, Samuel L. 1124
ホプキンス
Hopkins, Anthony 622
Hopkins, Bernard 622
Hopkins, Cathy 622
Hopkins, DeAndre 622
Hopkins, Dustin 622
Hopkins, Emmet 622
Hopkins, Jane 622
Hopkins, Jeffrey 622
Hopkins, John 622
Hopkins, Juliet 622
Hopkins, Marilyn 622
Hopkins, Michael 622
Hopkins, Michael John 622
Hopkins, Nigel 622
Hopkins, Owen 622
Hopkins, Paul Henry 622
Hopkins, Stephen 622
Hopkins, Terence K. 622
Hopkins, Todd 622
Hopkins, Tom 622
Hopkins, Trey 622
ホプキンズ
Hopkins, Andrea 622
Hopkins, Anthony 622
Hopkins, Antony 622
Hopkins, Edward J. 622
Hopkins, H.Joseph 622
Hopkins, Keith 622
Hopkins, Michael Francis 622
Hopkins, Nancy H. 622
ホプキンスン
Hopkinson, Nalo 622
ホプキンソン
Hopkinson, Deborah 622
ホプグッド
Hopgood, Mei-Ling 621
Hopgood, Tim 622
ホプクラフト
Hopcraft, Carol Cawthra 621
Hopcraft, Xan 621
ポプコフ
Popkov, Alexander A. 1124
Popkov, Sergei P. 1124
ポプシェンツカ
Poprzecka, Maria 1125
ホフショルネル
Hochschorner, Pavol 612
Hochschorner, Peter 612
ボプジョン
Beop Jeong 124
ホブズ
Hobbs, Mike 611
ホフスタッター
Hofstadter, Douglas R. 614
ホフステード
Hofstede, Gert Jan 614
ホブズボウム
Hobsbawm, Eric John Ernest 611
ホブズボーム
Hobsbawm, Eric John Ernest 611
ホブスン
Hobson, M.K. 611
ホブソン
Hobson, J.Allan 611
Hobson, Sally 611
ポプチェンコ
Popchanka, Alena 1124
ボプチョン
Beop Jeong 124
ボフツキー
Bohutsky, Yuriy 155
ホブデイ
Hobday, Richard 611
ホプト
Hopt, Klaus J. 622
ボブドナールタイサ
Denard, Bob 341
ホフナニアン
Hovnanian, Sebouh 627
ホブハウス
Hobhouse, Penelope 611
ポープ＝ヘネシー
Pope-Hennessy, John Wyndham 1124
ボブ・ホープ
Hope, Bob 621
ホフマイアー
Hofmeyr, Dianne 614
ホフマイスター
Hoffmeister, David 614
ホフマイヤー
Hoffmeyer, Jesper 614
ホーフマン

ホ

Hofmann, Michael 614
ホフマン
Hoffman, Alice 613
Hoffman, Bob 613
Hoffman, Carl 613
Hoffman, David 613
Hoffman, David E. 613
Hoffman, Donald D. 613
Hoffman, Donna L. 613
Hoffman, Dustin 613
Hoffman, Edward 613
Hoffman, Ellen 613
Hoffman, Eva 613
Hoffman, Glenn 613
Hoffman, Howard S. 613
Hoffman, Jay R. 613
Hoffman, Jeff 613
Hoffman, Jilliane 613
Hoffman, Lynn 613
Hoffman, Mark 613
Hoffman, Martin L. 613
Hoffman, Mary 613
Hoffman, Michael A. 613
Hoffman, Nina Kiriki 613
Hoffman, Paul 613
Hoffman, Perry D. 613
Hoffman, Philip Seymour 613
Hoffman, Reid 613
Hoffman, Susannah M. 613
Hoffman, W.Michael 613
Hoffmann, Ambrosi 613
Hoffmann, Bernhard 613
Hoffmann, Christian 613
Hoffmann, David 613
Hoffmann, Franz 613
Hoffmann, Freia 613
Hoffmann, Georg Friedrich 613
Hoffmann, Gleisi Helena 613
Hoffmann, Gudrun 613
Hoffmann, Helmut 613
Hoffmann, James 613
Hoffmann, Jules A. 613
Hoffmann, Jürgen 613
Hoffmann, Karol 614
Hoffmann, Kate 614
Hoffmann, Klaus 614
Hoffmann, Peter 614
Hoffmann, Rainer 614
Hoffmann, Reiner 614
Hoffmann, Roald 614
Hoffmann, Stanley 614
Hoffmann, Stefan-Ludwig 614
Hoffmann, Steve 614
Hofmann, Albert 614
Hofmann, Corinne 614
Hofmann, Jonas 614
Hofmann, Olivia 614
Hofmann, Paul 614
Hofmann, Peter 614
Hofmann, Sabine 614
Hofmann, Stefan G. 614
Hohmann, Luke 615
ホプマン
Hopman, Philip 622
ボフマン
Bochmann, Annika 152
ホフマン・ヴェレンホーフ
Hofmann-Wellenhof, B. 614
ホフマン - ウェレンホフ
Hofmann-Wellenhof, B. 614
ホフマンズ
Hoffmans, Lara 614
ボーフム
Boehm, Paul 153
ホフメクラー
Hofmekler, Ori 614
ポプラウスキー
Poplawski, Paul 1124
ホフラント
Hofland, H.J.A. 614
ホプリー
Hopley, Hannes 622
ボブリック
Bobrick, Benson 152
ボブリッジ
Bobridge, Jack 152
ポープル
Pople, John Anthony 1124
Pople, Nicolas 1124
ポプルトン
Poppleton, Marjorie 1125
ホープレス
Hopeless, Dennis 621
ポブレテ
Poblete, Patricia 1119
ホフロワ
Khokhlova, Iryna 728
ボブロワ
Bobrova, Ekaterina 152
ホーベ
Hove, Chenjerai 627
ボベ
Bové, José 169
ポーベ
Poewe, Sarah 1119
ホーヘイ
Jorge, Felix 687
ポベイ
Povey, Thomas 1129
ポペイ
Popay, Jennie 1124
ホベイカ
Hobeika, Elie 611
ポペスク
Popescu, Adela 1124
Popescu, Ana Maria 1124
Popescu, Dan-Ioan 1124
Popescu, Georgian 1124
Popescu, Ionel 1124
ポペスクタリチェアヌ
Popescu-tăriceanu, Călin 1124
ボベダ
Boveda, Eneko 169
ポベダ
Poveda, Christian 1129
ポベダ・ボニジャ
Poveda Bonilla, Rafael 1129
ポベダ・リカウルテ
Poveda Ricaurte, Walter 1129
ボベット
Bovet, Daniel Pierre 169
ポベトキン
Povetkin, Alexander 1129
ホベナゲール
Houvenaghel, Wendy 627
ホベヤン
Hoveian, Hovik 627
ボベール
Bovaird, Tony 169
ボベル
Bovell, George Richard 169
ボーヘルト
Boogerd, Dominic van den 160
ボベロ
Baubérot, Jean 105
ホーベンカンプ
Hovenkamp, Herbert 627
ホベンカンプ
Hovenkamp, Herbert 627
ポボア
Povoa, Pedro 1129
ポポーヴァ
Popova, Tatiyana 1125
ポポヴィッチ
Popović, Dragana 1125
Popovic, Ranko 1125
Popović, Veljko 1125
ボボエフ
Boboev, Gulomdzhon 152
Boboev, Olimjon 152
Bobozoda, Gulomjon 152
ボホ・カモ
Boho Camo, Gregorio 155
ボボカロノフ
Bobokalonov, Rahmat 152
ポポスキ
Poposki, Nikola 1124
ボボゾダ
Bobozoda, Gulomjon 152
Bobozoda, Shavkat 152
ボボト
Boboto, Jeanne Ebamba 152
ポポナワ
Poponawa, Benjamin 1124
ボホノン
Bohonnon, Mac 155
ポポバ
Popova, Margarita 1125
ポポビッチ
Popović, Aleksandar 1125
Popovic, Branimir 1125
Popovich, Gregg 1125
ポポフ
Popov, Aleksandr 1124
PoPov, Alexander N. 1124
Popov, Dan 1124
Popov, Dimitar 1125
Popov, Ivan 1125
Popov, Linda Kavelin 1125
ポポフスキ
Popovski, Nikola 1125
Popovski, Vlado 1125
ホーホフート
Hochhuth, Rolf 611
ホーホルト
Høholdt, Tom 615
ボボレンタ
Bovolenta, Arnaud 169
ホホロフ
Khokhlov, A.R. 728
ポポーワ
Popova, Lidiya 1125
ポポワ
Popova, Valentina 1125
Popova, Veronika 1125
ボーボン
Borbon, Pedro 161
ホーマ
Houma, Sione 626
ホーマー
Homer, Alex 619
Homer, Daryl 619
ボーマー
Bohmer, Richard 155
ボマー
Bomer, Matt 157
ポマ
Poma, Ruben 1123
ホマイラ・シャー
Homaira Shah 619
ポマガルスキ
Pomagalski, Julie 1123
ホーマッツ
Hormats, Robert D. 623
ポマト
Pomat, Job 1123
ホーマナワヌイ
Hoomanawanui, Michael 621
ポマレ
Pommaret-Imaeda, Francoise 1123
ホーマン
Hormann, Mark 622
ボーマン
Baughman, Matthew 106
Baumann, Anne-Sophie 106
Bohman, Berndt 154
Bohman, James 154
Bowman, Alisa 170
Bowman, Carol 170
Bowman, Christopher 170
Bowman, John 170
Bowman, Lucy 170
Bowman, Maddie 170
Bowman, Martin W. 170
Bowman, Pete 170
ボマン
Baumann, Anne-Sophie 106
ホーマンズ
Homans, John 619
ポーミア
Paumier, Cy 1087
ポミアン
Pomian, Krzysztof 1123
ボミエ
Baumier, Jean-Claude 106
ポミエ
Pommier, Maurice 1123
ボミチアデ
Vomitiadé, Romaric 1463
ホミドフ
Khomidov, Masaid 728
ポミーニ
Pomini, Alberto 1123
ボ・ミヤ
Bo Mya 157
ボー・ミャ
Bo Mya 157
ポミャノフスキ
Pomianowski, Jerzy 1123
ホーム
Holme, Dan 617
Holme, Michelle 617
Home, Robert K. 619
Hougham, Paul 625
ボーム
Baum, David 106
Baum, Sandy 106
Baum, William M. 106
Baume, Sara 106

ホ

Boehm, Christopher 153
Boehm, Evan 153
Boom, Maike van den 160
ボム
Baum, Gilles 106
ホームウッド
Homewood, Stephen 619
ホームズ
Holmes, Andre 617
Holmes, Andrew 617
Holmes, Caroline 618
Holmes, Chet 618
Holmes, Chris 618
Holmes, Clay 618
Holmes, Dale 618
Holmes, Danielle 618
Holmes, Darren 618
Holmes, David 618
Holmes, Elizabeth 618
Holmes, Eva 618
Holmes, Gabe 618
Holmes, Greg 618
Holmes, Gregory L. 618
Holmes, Hannah 618
Holmes, James 618
Holmes, James R. 618
Holmes, Janet 618
Holmes, Jenny 618
Holmes, Jeremy 618
Holmes, John 618
Holmes, Jonathan 618
Holmes, Jordan 618
Holmes, Katie 618
Holmes, Kelly 618
Holmes, Lyman 618
Holmes, Margaret M. 618
Holmes, Nigel 618
Holmes, Paul 618
Holmes, Philip 618
Holmes, Richard 618
Holmes, Richaun 618
Holmes, Ronald M. 618
Holmes, Santonio 618
Holmes, Stephen T. 618
Holmes, Steve 618
Holmes, Tommy 618
Holmes, Tony 618
Holmes, Tyrone 618
Homes, A.M. 619
Homes, Khaled 619
ボーム＝デュシェン
Bohm-Duchen, Monica 155
ポムピュイ
Pommepuy, Marie 1123
ホーム・プロムォン
Hon Phrom-on 620
ポムラ
Pommerat, Joël 1123
ポムロール
Pomerol, Charles 1123
ホムロワ
Khomrova, Olena 728
ホメイディ
al-Himedi, Nuri Daw 608
ホメキ
Homeky, Oswald 619
ポメランツ
Pomerants, Marko 1123
Pomerantz, Charlotte 1123
Pomeranz, Drew 1123
Pomeranz, Kenneth 1123
ポメロイ
Pomeroy, Charles 1123
ポモー
Pommaux, Yvan 1123
ホモキ
Homoki, Andreas 619
ポモドーロ
Pomodoro, Arnaldo 1123
ボーモル
Baumol, William J. 106
ボーモン
Beaumont, Emilie 110
Beaumont, Jean de 110
Beaumont, Maxime 110
Beaumont, Pierre de 110
ボーモント
Beaumont, Hunter 110
Beaumont, J.Graham 110
Beaumont, Matt 110
Beaumont, Matthew 110
Beaumont, Mike 110
Beaumont, Ralph H. 110
ポーヤ
Pólya, George 1122
ポヤ
Phoya, Henry 1109
ボヤジェフ
Boyadzhiev, Mario 171
ボヤツィス
Boyatzis, Richard E. 171
ボヤーニ
Bojani, Gian Carlo 155
ボヤーリン
Boyarin, Daniel 171
Boyarin, Jonathan 171
ボヤルチコフ
Boyarchikov, Nicolai Nikolayevich 171
ボヤン
Bojan, Krkić 155
ボヤンZ
Zulfikarpasic, Bojan 1559
ポーヤンパロ
Pohjanpalo, Joel 1120
ボヨティ
Boyoti, Sayo 172
ホーラー
Horler, Terry 622
ホラー
Holler, Wolfgang 617
ボーラー
Bohrer, Karl Heinz 155
Vogler, Sara 1462
ボラ
Bhola, Roland 135
ボラー
Bholah, Soomilduth 135
Boller, Paul F. 156
ポーラー
Poehler, Amy 1119
ボーライ
Bohley, Barbel 154
ホライス
Horeis, Heinz 622
ボライソー
Bolitho, Janie 156
ポライテス
Polites, Geoff 1121
ホライン
Hollein, Hans 617
ポラウデル
Polavder, Lucija 1121
ホラーク
Horák, Jan 622
ポーラジ
Paulraj, Arogyaswami 1087
ボラシエ
Bolasie, Yannick 156
ボラージオ
Borasio, Gian Domenico 161
ホラーズ
Hollars, B.J. 616
ホラス
Horace, Gatien 622
ボラス
Bollas, Christopher 156
Boras, Rob 161
Boras, Scott 161
ポラス
Porath, Christine 1125
Porras, Jerry I. 1125
ポラスキ
Polaski, Deborah 1121
ポラタイコ
Polatajko, Helene J. 1121
ポラタイバオ
Polataivao, Fosi 1121
ポラーチェク
Poláček, Karel 1121
ポラチェク
Polaczek, Jerzy 1121
ホラチェック
Horáček, Petr 622
ポラチク
Polaczyk, Grzegorz 1121
Polaczyk, Mateusz 1121
ポラック
Polak, Christian Philippe 1121
Polak, Paul 1121
Pollack, Golan 1121
Pollack, Henry 1121
Pollack, Judah 1121
Pollack, Kay 1122
Pollack, Kenneth Michael 1122
Pollack, Mark H. 1122
Pollack, Nathaniel 1122
Pollack, Olaf 1122
Pollack, Pam 1122
Pollack, Rachel 1122
Pollack, Sydney 1122
Pollack, William S. 1122
Pollak, Avshalom 1122
Pollak, David 1122
Pollock, Allyson 1122
ボラックス
Borax, Mark 161
ポラッコ
Polacco, Patricia 1121
ポーラッド
Pohlad, Carl 1120
Pohlad, Jim 1120
ポラット
Porat, Ruth M. 1125
ホラディ
Holladay, Tom 616
ボラート
Wollert, Heide 1522
ポラード
Pollard, C.William 1122
Pollard, Handré 1122
Pollard, Justin 1122
Pollard, Nigel 1122
ポラト
Porat, Hanan 1125
Porath, Finn 1125
ポラトジ
Polatci, Aydin 1121
ボラ・トレド
Borra Toledo, Dora Virginia 163
ポラナー
Polaner, David M. 1121
ボラニ
al-Bolani, Jawad 155
ポラーニ
Polanyi, John Charles 1121
ポラニ
Polanyi, John Charles 1121
ポラニー
Polanyi, John Charles 1121
ボラーニョ
Bolaño, Roberto 156
ボラニョス
Bolaños, Enrique 156
Bolaños, Jorge Wálter 156
Bolaños, Juan Miguel 156
Bolaños, Manuel Antonio 156
Bolaños, Mario 156
ボラニョス・ゲイエル
Bolaños Geyer, Enrique 156
ホラバード
Holabird, Katharine 615
ホーラボウ
Hollabaugh, Craig 616
ホラム
Khoram, Abdul Karim 728
Khoram, Ahmad 728
ボーラム
Bolam, Emily 155
ボーラム・スミス
Bolam-Smith, David 155
ポラリス
Polaris, Michelle 1121
ボラレーヴィ
Boralevi, Antonella 161
ホーラン
Horan, Niall 622
ホラン
Horan, Eileen C. 622
Horan, Jane 622
ポーラン
Pawlan, Monica 1088
Pollan, Michael 1122
Pollan, Stephen M. 1122
ボーランガー
Boulanger, Jennifer L. 167
ポランコ
Polanco, Gregory 1121
Polanco, Jorge 1121
ポーランジュバン
Pau-langevin, George 1087
ポランスキ
Polanski, Andrzej 1121
Polanski, Eugen 1121
Polanski, Roman 1121
ポランスキー
Polanski, Roman 1121
ホランダー
Hollander, Carl 616
Hollander, Dory 616
Hollander, Eric 616
Hollander, John 616
Hollander, Maria 616

Hollander, Michael 616
ポランチェツ
Polančec, Damir 1121
ホーランド
Holland, Agnieszka 616
Holland, Dexter 616
Holland, Jennifer S. 616
Holland, John 616
Holland, Sarah 616
Holland, Tanya 616
Holland, Todd 616
Hollands, Arthur 616
ホラント
Holland, Agnieszka 616
Holland, Carola 616
Holland, Fabian 616
ホランド
Holland, Agnieszka 616
Holland, Angus 616
Holland, Barbara A. 616
Holland, Bart K. 616
Holland, Charles Hepworth 616
Holland, Dave 616
Holland, Derek 616
Holland, Earle 616
Holland, Greg 616
Holland, Henry Scott 616
Holland, Jennifer S. 616
Holland, Jimmie C. 616
Holland, John 616
Holland, John L. 616
Holland, Julian 616
Holland, Karen 616
Holland, Mina 616
Holland, Nate 616
Holland, Patricia M. 616
Holland, Peter W.H. 616
Holland, Tom 616
Holland, Vicky 616
ボーランド
Boland, Eavan 155
Boland, Yasmin 155
Borland, John M. 162
ボランド
Bolland, Brian 156
ポーランド
Poland, Marguerite 1121
ホランド・エリオット
Holland-Elliott, Kevin 616
ポランニー
Polanyi, John Charles 1121
ポランボア
Porumboiu, Corneliu 1126
ホーリ
Hohri, William Minoru 615
ホーリー
Hawley, Elizabeth 584
Holley, Anna 617
Khoury, Ghattas 729
Khoury, Nazim 729
Khoury, Raed 729
ホリ
Hori, Masahiro 622
ホリー
Holley, Kevin 617
Holly, Emma 617
Holy, Petr 619
ボリ
Boly, Koumba 157
Boly, Willy 157
Boly, Yéro 157
Borg, Anders 162
ポーリ
Poli, Andrea 1121
ポーリー
Pauly, Daniel 1087
Pawley, Christine 1088
Pohly, Michael 1120
Polley, Sarah 1122
Powrie, Olivia 1130
Powrie, Polly 1130
ポリ
Fusar-poli, Barbara 469
Pólit, Carlos 1121
ポリー
Polii, Greysia 1121
Pulley, Kelly 1139
ポリアコフ
Poliakov, Sergei 1121
Polyakov, Vladislav 1122
ポリアルシュ
Polyarush, Dmitry 1122
ホリアン
Holian, Gary 616
ポリヴィ
Polivy, Janet 1121
ポーリウ＝フライ
Pawliw-Fry, J.P. 1088
ボーリエー
Bouiller, Claire 167
ポリエ
Polye, Don 1123
ボリエッロ
Borriello, Marco 163
ボリオ
Vollio, Alfredo 1462
ポリオ
Pollio, Howard R. 1122
ホリガー
Holliger, Heinz 617
ボリガー
Bolliger, Max 156
ボーリガード
Beauregard, Mario 110
ホリガン
Horrigan, Leo 624
ボリコ
Borico, Miguel Abia Biteo 162
ボリコモイセス
Borico Moisés, Ángel 162
ホリサワ
Horisawa, Yuko 622
ボリシャデ
Borishade, Babalola 162
ボリシャド
Borishade, Babalola 162
ボーリシュ
Borish, Steven M. 162
ポリシュク
Polishuk, Mikola 1121
ホリス
Hollis, Billy S. 617
Hollis, Christina 617
Hollis, James 617
Hollis, Jennifer L. 617
ボーリス
Bouris, Karen 168
ボリス
Boris, Elizabeth T. 162
Boris, Jean-Pierre 162
Karaev, Boris 704
ポーリス
Paulis, Ilse 1087
ポリス
Polis, Ben 1121
Pollice, Gary 1122
ボリスキー
Volskii, Arkadii Ivanovich 1463
ポリスキー
Poritsky, Ray 1125
ホリス・ジェファーソン
Hollis-jefferson, Rondae 617
ボリス＝ダンチュンスタン
Borris-Dunchunstang, Eileen 163
ボリソグレフスキー
Borisoglebsky, Nikita 162
ボリソフ
Borisov, Boyko 162
Borisov, IUrii A. 162
Borissov, Boyko 162
ポリターノ
Politano, Anthony 1121
Politano, Matteo 1121
ボリツァー
Boritzer, Etan 162
ポリツァー
Politzer, H.David 1121
ポリツィン
Polzin, David J. 1123
ホリック
Holick, Michael F. 616
ボーリック
Bolick, Teresa 156
ポーリック
Paulick, Ray 1087
Powlik, James 1130
ホーリッジ
Horwich, Paul 624
ホリッシナ
Horishna, Olha Vasilivna 622
ボリット
Boritt, Beowulf 162
ポーリット
Polit-O'Hara, Denise 1121
ポリット
Pollitt, J.J. 1122
Pollitt, Michael 1122
Porrit, Jonathon 1125
ホリデー
Holiday, Jrue 616
Holiday, Justin 616
Holliday, Charles, O. Jr. 617
ホリデイ
Holiday, Ryan 616
Holliday, Charles, O. Jr. 617
Holliday, Ian 617
Holliday, John 617
Holliday, Matt 617
Holliday, Melanie 617
ポリティ
Politi, A. 1121
ポリティキ
Politycki, Matthias 1121
ホリデー＝ウィリー
Holliday-Willy, Liane 617
ポリトコフスカヤ
Politkovskaya, Anna 1121
ポリドラス
Polidoras, Byron 1121
ボリーニ
Borini, Fabio 162
ポリーニ
Pollini, Maurizio 1122
ポリニキス
Polynikis, Michalis 1123
ポリーノ
Paulino, David 1087
Pollino, David 1122
ホリフィールド
Holyfield, Evander 619
ホリマン
Holliman, Jonathan 617
ボリムラドフ
Volmuradov, Gurbangeldy 1462
ポリメニ
Polimeni, Albert D. 1121
ポリャク
Polyák, Imre 1122
ポリャコフ
Polyakov, Viktor 1122
ポリャコワ
Polyakova, Evgeniya 1122
ポリャチェンコ
Polyachenko, Yuriy 1122
ポリャーン
Polian, P.M. 1121
ポリャンスキー
Polyanskiy, Dmitry 1122
Polyanskiy, Igor 1122
ボーリュー
Beaulieu, Baptiste 110
Beaulieu, Elizabeth Ann 110
ボリュクバシ
Bolukbasi, Ibrahim 157
ボリュシク
Borysik, Igor 163
ボリリンド
Börjlind, Cecilia 162
Börjlind, Rolf 162
ボリロン
Vorilhon, Claude 1464
ホーリン
Horin, Niki 622
Howlin, Patricia 629
ボーリン
Bohlin, Karen E. 154
Bohlin, Nils 154
Bolin, Jane 156
Bolin, M.C. 156
ボリン
Bolin, Bert 156
ポーリーン
Paulien, Jon 1087
ポーリン
Polin, Richard A. 1121
Pollin, Robert 1122
ホリンガー
Hollinger, David A. 617
ボーリンガー
Boehringer, Moritz 153
ホリンガム
Hollingham, Richard 617
ホリング
Holling, Jen 617
ボーリング
Bauling, Jayne 106
Boling, Elizabeth 156
Boring, Mel 162
ボリング
Boling, Clint 156
ポーリング

Poling, Harold Arthur 1121
Powling, Chris 1130

ポリング
Poling, Kimberly D. 1121
Polling, Kim 1122

ホリングスヘッド
Hollingshead, Mike 617

ホリングスワース
Hollingsworth, Joseph Rogers 617
Hollingsworth, Mellisa 617

ホリングワース
Hollingsworth, Cliff 617
Hollingworth, Peter 617

ボリンゴリ・ムボンボ
Bolingoli-mbombo, Boli 156

ボリンジャー
Bollinger, John 156
Bollinger, Lee Carroll 156
Bollinger, Simone 156

ポリンスキー
Polinsky, Maria 1121

ボリンチェス
Bolinches, Antonio 156

ホリンデイル
Hollindale, Peter 617

ホール
Hall, Allen 557
Hall, Alvin 557
Hall, Amanda 557
Hall, Arman 557
Hall, Benjamin 557
Hall, Brian 557
Hall, Brian Keith 557
Hall, Bruce Edward 557
Hall, Christina 557
Hall, Conrad L. 557
Hall, Constance Margaret 557
Hall, Daryl 557
Hall, David D. 557
Hall, DeAngelo 557
Hall, Deiondre' 558
Hall, Donald 558
Hall, Douglas 558
Hall, Douglas T. 558
Hall, Edward Twitchell 558
Hall, Edwin 558
Hall, Gary, Jr. 558
Hall, Gary McLean 558
Hall, George Martin 558
Hall, Grady 558
Hall, Henry Edgar 558
Hall, Jacqueline 558
Hall, James 558
Hall, James W. 558
Hall, Jason R. 558
Hall, Jim 558
Hall, Jimmy 558
Hall, John 558
Hall, John Lewis 558
Hall, John R. 558
Hall, Joseph N. 558
Hall, J.Storrs 558
Hall, Judy 558
Hall, Kenneth 558
Hall, Klay 558
Hall, Lee 558
Hall, Lena 558
Hall, Leon 558
Hall, L.Michael 558
Hall, Margaret 558
Hall, Margaret Ann 558
Hall, Marie-Louise 558
Hall, Mark A. 558
Hall, Marty 558
Hall, Marvin 558
Hall, Michael C. 558
Hall, Mindy 558
Hall, Nicola 558
Hall, Parnell 558
Hall, Peter A. 558
Hall, Phil 558
Hall, Rannel 558
Hall, Richard 558
Hall, Sean 558
Hall, Simon W. 558
Hall, Stacey 558
Hall, Steven 558
Hall, Stuart 558
Hall, Thomas 558
Hall, Trish 558
Hohl, Joan 615
Hol, Coby 615
Hole, Abigail 616
Holl, Steven 616

ボール
Ball, Alan 86
Ball, Alan James 86
Ball, Barbara L. 86
Ball, Bill 86
Ball, Christopher M. 86
Ball, David A. 86
Ball, David Warren 86
Ball, Desmond 86
Ball, Doug 86
Ball, Eric R. 86
Ball, Ernie 86
Ball, Errie 86
Ball, Jacqueline A. 86
Ball, Jake 86
Ball, James 86
Ball, Jessica 86
Ball, Johnny 86
Ball, Keith M. 86
Ball, Lonzo 86
Ball, Marcus 86
Ball, Marion J. 86
Ball, Michael 86
Ball, Neiron 86
Ball, Pamela 86
Ball, Phil 87
Ball, Philip 87
Ball, Richard A. 87
Ball, Stefan 87
Ball, Stephen J. 87
Boal, Mark 151
Bohl, Willi 154
Bole, William 156
Borle, Christian 162
Vohor, Serge 1462

ボル
Bol, Manute 155
Boll, Thomas 156
Boll, Timo 156
Boll, Uwe 156
Bor, Barna 161
Bor, Hillary 161

ポール
Pall, Ellen 1072
Paul, Aaron 1086
Paul, Alan 1086
Paul, Ann Whitford 1086
Paul, Barbara 1086
Paul, Bill 1086
Paul, Billy 1086
Paul, Brandon 1086
Paul, Chris 1086
Paul, Christian 1086
Paul, David 1086
Paul, Evans 1086
Paul, Gill 1086
Paul, Graham Sharp 1087
Paul, Harry 1087
Paul, Henry A. 1087
Paul, John 1087
Paul, Korky 1087
Paul, Les 1087
Paul, Marilyn 1087
Paul, Maruthanakuzhiyil 1087
Paul, Nigel 1087
Paul, Niles 1087
Paul, Pamela 1087
Paul, Rand 1087
Paul, Richard W. 1087
Paul, Romain 1087
Paul, Ron 1087
Paul, Roselyn 1087
Paul, Sandra 1087
Paul, Susan Spencer 1087
Paull, Jennifer 1087
Paull, Marion 1087
Paurd, Clément 1087
Pohl, Dieter 1120
Pohl, Frederik 1120
Pohl, Ira 1120
Pohl, Klaus 1120
Pohl, Manfred 1120
Pohl, Stephanie 1120
Poole, Charles P. 1124

ポル
Pol, Anne-Marie 1121
Pol, Lotte van de 1121
Pol, Marek 1121

ポール・アリヴィサトス
Paul Alivisatos, A. 1087

ポル・アルファロ
Pohl Alfaro, Lina Dolores 1120

ホールアンデル
Hörmander, Lars Valter 622

ボルイストレム
Borgström, Camilla 162

ホルヴァート
Horváth, Juraj 624
Horvath, Michael 624

ホルヴァートヴァー
Horváthová, Tereza 624

ホルヴィッツ
Horwitz, Joshua 624
Horwitz, Tony 624

ポルヴィーノ
Polvino, Lynne 1122

ホルウェグ
Holweg, Matthias 619

ボールウェル
Bolwell, Laurence Henry 157

ポールウェル
Paulwell, Phillip 1087

ポルヴェロージ
Polverosi, Alberto 1122

ボルカー
Volcker, Paul Adolph 1462

ボルガー
Borger, Karla 162

ボルカキス
Volikakis, Christos 1462

ボルカート
Volkaert, Redd 1462

ポルカノワ
Polcanova, Sofia 1121

ボールガール
Beauregard, Éric 110
Beauregard, Paul 110

ホルカン
Horkhang, Jampa Tendar 622

ボルギ
Borghi, Catherine 162

ボルキア
Bolkiah, Hassanal 156
Bolkiah, Muda Mohammed 156

ボルキア国王
Bolkiah, Hassanal 156

ホルキナ
Khorkina, Svetlana 728

ホールギン
Holguin, Jeff 616

ボルク
Borc, Costin 161
Borch, Kjetil 161

ボルグ
Borg, Björn 162
Borg, James 162
Borg, Joseph 162

ボルクス
Bolks, Shane 156

ボルクバシ
Bolukbasi, Ibrahim 157

ボルクバゼ
Bolkvadze, Shmagi 156

ボルグマン
Borgman, Peter 162

ボルゲ
Borge, Dan 162

ポルケ
Polke, Christian 1121
Polke, Sigmar 1121

ボルゲイ
Bourqeie, Amir Mansour 168

ホールゲイト
Holgate, Mason 616

ホルゲイト
Holgate, Alan 616

ボルゲージ
Borghesi, Silvia 162

ボルケス
Volquez, Edinson 1463

ボルゲス
Borges, Antonio 162

ボルゲーゼ
Borgese, Elisabeth Mann 162
Borghese, Alessandra 162

ホルゲート
Holgate, Sharon Anne 616

ホルケリ
Holkeri, Harri Hermanni 616

ボルコーヴァー
Bolchover, David 156

ボルコフ
Volkov, Alexey 1462

ホルコム
Holcomb, Rod 615
Holcomb, Steven 615
Holcombe, Larry 615

ボルコム
Bolcom, William 156

ホルザー
Hoelzer, Margaret 613

ボルザガ

Borzaga, Calro 163
ボルザコフスキー
Borzakovskiy, Yuriy 163
ボルサレロ－エルマン
Borsarello-Herrmann, Mathilde 163
ボルザンパルク
Portzamparc, Christian de 1126
ホルシー
Holsey, Ron 618
ボルジ
Borg, Tonio 162
ボルシェ
Porcher, Louis 1125
Porsche, Ferdinand Alexander 1125
ボルジェス
Borges, João Baptista 162
Borges, Jorge Abalbero da Silva 162
Borges, Michel 162
Borges, Victor 162
ボルジギン・ブレンサイン
Borjigin Burensain 162
ホルジク
Khoruzhik, Leonty I. 728
ホルシド
Khorshid, Salah Abdel-Reda 728
ボルジャー
Bolger, Dermot 156
Bolger, James Brendan 156
ボルシャコフ
Bolshakov, Sergey 157
ホルシャニ
Horchani, Farhat 622
ホルシュ
Horsch, Andreas 624
ボルジュク
Bordjug, Sergej 161
ホルシュタイン
Hollstein, Martin 617
ボルジュロワ
Boldzhurova, Ishengul 156
ボルシル
Porcile, François 1125
ボルシン
Polcyn, Kenneth A. 1121
ボルシンガー
Bolsinger, Mike 157
ボルジンギス
Porzingis, Kristaps 1126
ホルス
Holthe, Tess Uriza 619
ボールズ
Balls, Ed 87
Bohls, Elizabeth A. 154
Bowles, Samuel 170
ポールズ
Poehls, William 1119
ボルスス
Borsus, Willy 163
ボルスター
Polster, Burkard 1122
ホルスタイン
Holstein, James A. 618
Holstein, William J. 618
ボルスタッド
Bolstad, Francesco 157
Bolstad, Richard 157
Volstad, Ron 1463
ホルスティン
Horsting, Viktor 624
ホルステージ
Holstege, Christopher P. 618
ホルスト
Holst, Lars 618
Holst, Spencer 618
Horst, Alexander 624
Horst, Jørn Lier 624
ボルスト
Borst, Arno 163
Borst, Els 163
ボルストフ
Bolstorff, Peter 157
ホルストマン
Horstmann, Bernhard 624
ホルストン
Halston, Carole 560
ボルセン
Borssen, Therese 163
ポールセン
Paulsen, Gary 1087
Paulsen, Logan 1087
Paulsen, Norman 1087
Paulsen, Sandra 1087
Poulsen, Jens Aage 1128
Poulsen, Keila 1128
Poulsen, Kevin 1128
Poulsen, Troels Lund 1128
ホルゼンターラー
Holzenthaler, Jean 619
ポールソン
Paulson, Henry 1087
Paulson, Henry Merritt, Jr. 1087
Paulson, John 1087
Paulson, Steven D. 1087
ホールダー
Holder, Geoffrey 615
ホルタ
Horta, José Ramos 624
ホルダー
Holder, Alex 615
Holder, Donald 615
Holder, Eric Himpton Jr. 615
Holder, Geoffrey 615
Holder, Jay M. 615
Holder, Jonathan 615
Holder, Nancy 615
Holder, Noel 615
ボールダー
Baldor, Robert A. 85
ボルター
Bolter, J.David 157
ボルダ
Borda, Dionisio 161
ボルダー
Bolder, Linda 156
ホルダウ
Holdau, Felicitas 615
ボルダス
Bordas, Ramon Alfredo 161
ポルタス
Portas, Paulo 1125
ボルダック
Bolduc, Michael 156
ホルダネス・ロダン
Holderness-Roddam, Jane 616
ホルダネス＝ロダン
Holderness-Roddam, Jane 616
ポルタベツ
Poltavets, Viktor 1122
ボルダベリ
Bordaberry, Juan María 161
ボルダベリー
Bordaberry, Juan María 161
ポルタラニン
Poltoranin, Alexey 1122
ポルタル・レオン
Portal León, Marcos 1125
ボルダンス
Bordans, Janis 161
ボルタンスキー
Boltanski, Christian 157
Boltanski, Luc 157
ホルダン・モラレス
Jordán Morales, Alfredo 687
ボルチ
Bolch, Ben W. 156
ボルチモア
Baltimore, David 88
ボルチャコフ
Bolchakov, Nikolaj 156
ボルチン
Borchin, Valeriy 161
ポルチンスキー
Polchinski, Joseph Gerard 1121
ホルツ
Holtz, Geoffrey T. 619
Holtz, J.P. 619
Holtz, Shel 619
Holtz, Thomas R., Jr. 619
ボルツ
Boelts, Maribeth 153
Bolz, Norbert 157
Boruc, Artur 163
ホルツァー
Holzer, Jenny 619
ポルツァー
Polzer, Miroslav 1123
ポルツァー‐スリエンツ
Polzer-Srienz, Mirjam 1123
ボルツィ＝ヴレナ
Borzillo-Vrenna, Carrie 163
ボルツィロ
Borzillo-Vrenna, Carrie 163
ホルツヴァルト
Holzwarth, Werner 619
ホルツェン
Holzen, Heinz von 619
ボルツォーニ
Bolzoni, Lina 157
ボルッキ
Borucki, Ryan 163
ホルツグレーフェ
Holtgrefe, Karen 619
ホルツシュラグ
Holzschlag, Molly E. 619
ホルツデッペ
Holzdeppe, Raphael 619
ホルツナー
Holzner, Steven 619
ホルツハウス
Holtshouse, Dan 619
ホルツマン
Holtzman, Jerome 619
Holzman, Lois 619
Holzman, Robert S. 619
Holzman, Todd F. 619
ホルデ
Haarde, Geir H. 551
ボルティエ
Vaultier, Pierre 1448
ボルディエ
Bordier, Anaïs 161
ボルディコワ
Boldykova, Svetlana 156
ポルティージョ
Portillo, Blanca 1126
ポルティジョ
Portillo, Alfonso 1126
ボルディック
Baldick, Chris 85
ボルディニョン
Bordignon, Giorgia 161
ボールティモア
Baltimore, David 88
ボルティモア
Baltimore, David 88
ボールディン
Balldin, Bo 87
ボルディン
Boldin, Anquan 156
ホールディング
Holding, Rob 616
ボールティング
Boulting, Roy 167
ボールディング
Bolding, Per Olof 156
Boulding, Elise 167
Boulding, Kenneth E. 167
ポルテス
Portes, Alejandro 1126
ポルテッリ
Portelli, Alessandro 1125
ボルデマン
Wordemann, Wolfram 1526
ポールデュリス
Poledouris, Basil 1121
ポルテラ
Portela, Maria 1125
Portela, Teresa 1125
ポルテラリバス
Portela Rivas, Teresa 1125
ボルテール
Voltaire, Henri-Claude 1463
Voltaire, Leslie 1463
ホールデン
Holden, Cathie 615
Holden, Craig 615
Holden, Kritina 615
Holden, Paul 615
Holden, Reed K. 615
Holden, Robert 615
Holden, Terri 615
Holden, Todd 615
Holden, Wendy 615
ホルテン
Holten, Rene 619
ボールデン
Bolden, Brandon 156
Bolden, Elizabeth 156
Boulden, Kay 167
ボルテン
Bolten, Joshua B. 157
Borten, Per 163
Borten, Sylvie 163

ボルデン
Bolden, Elizabeth 156
ホールト
Holt, James Clarke 618
ホルト
Holt, Anne 618
Holt, Barbara J. 618
Holt, Bradley P. 618
Holt, Brock 618
Holt, Cheryl 618
Holt, Douglas B. 618
Holt, Ian 618
Holt, James Clarke 618
Holt, Jim 618
Holt, John Caldwell 619
Holt, Jonathan 619
Holt, Kimberly Willis 619
Holt, Linda 619
Holt, Lyssa Royal 619
Holt, Nathalia 619
Holt, Peter 619
Hort, Barbara E. 624
Hoult, Nicholas 626
ボールド
Bald, Margaret 85
ボルト
Boldt, Harry 156
Boldt, Rosemarie 156
Bolt, Carol 157
Bolt, Nancy M. 157
Bolt, Usain 157
ボルド
Bold, Luvsanvandan 156
Bordo, Susan 161
ホルドヴィック
Hordvik, Stein 622
ボールドウィン
Baldwin, Alec 85
Baldwin, Carey 85
Baldwin, Carliss Young 85
Baldwin, Christina 85
Baldwin, Danny 85
Baldwin, Darryl 85
Baldwin, Doug 85
Baldwin, Gabrielle 85
Baldwin, J. 85
Baldwin, Jan 85
Baldwin, Janice I. 85
Baldwin, John D. 85
Baldwin, John Templeton 85
Baldwin, Joyce G. 85
Baldwin, Scott 85
Baldwin, Wade 85
Boldwin, Carliss Y. 156
ボルドウィン
Baldwin, John 85
ポルトゥオンド
Portuondo, Omara 1126
ポールドゥリス
Poledouris, Basil 1121
ホルトエフ
Kholtoyev, Torup 728
ポルトカレロ
Portocarrero, Blancanieve 1126
ホールドーソン
Halldorson, Phyllis 558
ポルトナール
Portenart, Victor 1125
ポルトヌーブ
Porteneuve, Christophe 1125
ボルトーネ
Bortone, Cristiano 163
ポルトノイ
Portenoy, Russell K. 1125
ホルトビー
Holtby, Lewis 619
ポルトフ
Polutov, Andrei Vadimovich 1122
ボルドベリ
Bordaberry, Juan María 161
ホールドマン
Haldeman, Joe 556
ホルトマン
Holtmann, Gerrit 619
ポルドミンスキイ
Porudominskiĭ, Vladimir 1126
ポルトラク
Poltorak, Stepan 1122
ポルトラーニ
Portolani, Maurizio 1126
ボルドリー
Baldry, Long John 85
ボルドリッジ
Baldrige, Letitia 85
ボルドリーニ
Boldorini, Maria Grazia 156
Boldrini, Stefano 156
ボルドリニ
Boldrini, Laura 156
ボルドリン
Boldrin, Michele 156
ホールドレン
Holdren, Dax 616
ホルトン
Holton, Johnny 619
Holton, Wendy M. 619
ボールトン
Boulton, James T. 167
ボルトン
Bolton, Anthony 157
Bolton, Bill 157
Bolton, Gillie 157
Bolton, Ivor 157
Bolton, José 157
Bolton, Richard M. 157
Bolton, Robert 157
Bolton, Sharon 157
ボルドン
Bordon, Willer 161
ポルナー
Pollner, John D. 1122
ホルナゲル
Hollnagel, Erik 617
ボルニー
Volney, Herbert 1462
ポルニン
Polunin, Sergiy 1122
ホルネ
Horne, Solveig 623
ホルネス
Holness, Andrew 618
ボルノワ
Volnova, Marina 1462
ボルハ
Borja, Francisco 162
ボルハ・イグレシアス
Borja Iglesias 162
ボールハイマー
Ballheimer, David 87
ホールバイン
Hohlbein, Heike 615
Hohlbein, Wolfgang 615
ホールバーグ
Hallberg, David 558
Hallberg, Per 558
ボールハチェット
Ballhatchet, Helen 87
ホルバット
Horvat, Darko 624
ホルバート
Holbert, Keith E. 615
Horvat, Andrew 624
ボルハ・バジェ
Borja Valle 162
ボルハ・バストン
Borja Baston 162
ボルハ・バレーロ
Borja Valero 162
ボルハ・フェルナンデス
Borja Fernandez 162
ボルハルト
Vollhardt, K.Peter C. 1462
ホルバーン
Holburn, Steve 615
ボルバーン
Bollwahn, Barbara 157
ボルピ
Volpi, Jorge 1463
Volpi, Mike 1463
ボルビエフ
Borbiyev, Bolotbek 161
ホルビッツ
Horvitz, Robert 624
ホルブ
Holub, Joan 619
ホルプ
Holpp, Lawrence 618
ボルフ
Borch, Christian 161
Wolf, Markus 1521
ボルプ
Volpe, Joseph 1463
ポルブー
Poorvu, William J. 1124
ポルファー
Polfer, Lydie 1121
ホルフォード
Holford, Jeremy 616
Holford, T.R. 616
ホルフォード-ストレブンズ
Holford-Strevens, Leofranc 616
ポールフリー
Palfrey, John Gorham 1072
ホルブルック
Holbrook, D. 615
Holbrook, Teri 615
Holbrooke, Richard Charles 615
ボルヘ
Borge, Tomás 162
ホルヘ・アレバロ・マテウス
Jorge Arévalo Mateus 917
ボルヘス
Borges, Celso 162
Borges, Guilherme 162
ホルベック
Holbek, Jonny 615
Holubec, Edythe Johnson 619
ホルヘ・メレ
Jorge Mere 687
ボルベリ
Borbely, Laszlo 161
ボルペール
Beaurepaire, Pierre-Yves 110
ホルボロー
Holborow, Barbara 615
ホルボーン
Holborn, Mark 615
ポルボンゾダ
Polvonzoda, Abdusamad 1122
ボルマー
Bormaa, Radnaa 162
Vollmer, Dana 1462
Vollmer, Sebastian 1462
ポルマー
Pollmer, Udo 1122
Polmear, Caroline 1122
ホールマン
Hallman, Patsy Spurrier 559
Hallman, Tom, Jr. 559
Holman, Halsted 617
Holman, Sheri 617
ホルマン
Holman, Bob 617
Holman, Brad 617
Holman, Robert 617
ボールマン
Bohlman, Philip Vilas 154
ボルマン
Bollmann, Ralph 157
Borrmann, Mechtild 163
Volman, Bob 1462
ポールマン
Paulman, Audrey A. 1087
Paulman, Paul M. 1087
Pohlman, Jennifer 1120
Pohlmann, Petra 1120
ポルマン
Polman, Linda 1122
ボルマンス
Bormans, Leo 162
ホルム
Holm, Celeste 617
Holm, Chris F. 617
Holm, Georg 617
Holm, Jennifer L. 617
Holm, Monica 617
Holm, Soren 617
Holm, Stefan 617
Holmes, Oliver Wendell 618
ボルム
Bolum, Nestor 157
ホルムグレン
Holmgren, David 618
ホールムス
Holmes, Efner Tudor 618
ホルムス
Holmes, Lee 618
ホルムズ
Holmes, Besby Frank 618
Holmes, Katie 618
ホルムナー
Pietilae-holmner, Maria 1111
ホルムバリ
Holmberg, Barbro 617
ホルムベルイ
Holmberg, Bo R. 617
ホルムルンド
Holmlund, Anna 618

Holmlund, Anne 618
ホルメル
Hollmer, Lars 617
ホルモス
Holmas, Heikki 617
ポルヤン
Poluyan, Vladimir M. 1122
Poluyan, Vladimir N. 1122
ポール・ラウターバー
Lauterbur, Paul C. 796
ポルリーニ
Pollini, Maurizio 1122
ボルレー
Borlee, Jonathan 162
Borlee, Kevin 162
ボルロー
Borloo, Jean-Louis 162
ボール＝ロキーチ
Ball-Rokeach, S.J. 87
ホルワード
Hallward, Peter 559
ホルン
Horm, Jannes 622
Horn, Günther 623
Horn, Gyula 623
Horn, Rebecca 623
Horn, Stefanie 623
Horn, Timo 623
ボルン
Bourne, Mike 168
ホルンガハー
Horngacher, Stefan 623
ボルンシュタイン
Bornstein, Izyk Mendel 163
ボルンド
Bolund, Per 157
ホーレー
Hawley, David 584
Hawley, Raina 584
ボーレ
Bohle, Jason 154
ボレ
Bole, Filipe 156
ボレー
Borré, Caroline 163
ポーレ
Pohle, Rita 1120
ポレ
Polet, François 1121
Pollet, Cédric 1122
ポーレイ
Pollay, David J. 1122
ホレイティ
al-Huraiti, Hussein Nasser 637
ホレイハート
Khleifat, Awad 728
ボレイン
Boraine, Alex 161
ボレガラ
Bollegala, Danushka 156
ボーレゴ
Borrego, James 163
ポレシュ
Pollesch, René 1122
ホレス
Horres, Robert 624
ポレスカ
Poleska, Anne 1121
ボレツ
Borec, Tomáš 161
ポレッティ
Poletti, Giuliano 1121
Poletti, Rosette 1121
ポレット
Polet, Robert 1121
Poletto, Eraldo 1121
ホレバス
Holebas, Jose 616
ボレハム
Boreham, Puakena 161
ホレーベン
Holleben, Jan von 617
ボレムンゲテンゲバレラ
Bolengetenge Balela, Dieudonné 156
ボレリ
Borrelli, Daniel 163
Borrelli, Laird 163
ボレル
Borel, Cleopatra 161
Borel, Jacques 161
Borel, Petrus 161
Borel, Yannick 161
Borrel, Marie 163
ボレーロ
Borrero, Yordanis 163
ボレロモリナ
Borrero Molina, Ismael 163
ホレワ
Khoreva, Natalia 728
ホーレン
Foren, Robert 449
ボーレン
Bohren, Rudolf 155
Bolen, Jean Shinoda 156
Boren, Mike 161
ボレン
Bolen, Cheryl 156
ポーレン
Pohren, D.E. 1120
ボレンガ
Bolenga, Maguy Kiala 156
ホーレンシュタイン
Holenstein, Elmar 616
ボレンスタイン
Borenstein, Greg 162
ホーレンダー
Hollender, Ioan 617
ホレンダー
Holländer, Karen 616
ボレンダー
Bolender, Todd 156
ボレン・ニヤミ
Boreng Niyami, George 161
ポロ
Pollo, Genc 1122
Polo, Sela 1122
ボロヴィアック
Borowiak, Mateusz 163
ホロウィッツ
Horowitz, Alexandra 623
Horowitz, Anthony 623
Horowitz, Ben 623
Horowitz, Eliot 624
Horowitz, Leonard G. 624
Horowitz, Norman Harold 624
Horowitz, Seth S. 624
ホロウイッツ
Horowitz, Shel 624
ホロヴィッツ
Horowitz, Amy 623
Horowitz, Anthony 623
Horowitz, Joseph 624
ホロウェイ
Holloway, Charles A. 617
Holloway, Gillian 617
Holloway, Immy 617
Holloway, Jacky 617
Holloway, John 617
Holloway, Ron 617
ホロウェイチャック
Holowaychuk, T.J. 618
ボロウォイ
Borovoy, Mikhail I. 163
ホロエンコ
Holowenko, Henryk 618
ボーローグ
Borlaug, Norman Ernest 162
ボロシェンコ
Voloshchenko, Mariya 1463
ポロシェンコ
Poroshenko, Petro Oleksiyovych 1125
ホロシコフスキー
Horoshkovskyi, Valeriy 623
ボロシナ
Voloshyna, Anna 1463
ホロシビ
Holosivi, David 618
ポロジャニ
Pollzhani, Aziz 1122
ボロシュ
Boros, Imre 163
Boros, Tamara 163
バローズ
Burroughs, John 206
ボロスキー
Boroski, Stan 163
ホロストフスキー
Khvorostovskii, Dmitrii 729
ポロゼニ
Polozeni, Aziz 1122
ボロソジャル
Volosozhar, Tatiana 1463
ボロソワ
Volosova, Lubov 1463
ボロソン
Boroson, Marttin 163
ポロタ＝ナウ
Polota-nau, Tatafu 1122
ボロダフキン
Borodavkin, Aleksei N. 163
ボロダフコ
Borodavko, Jevgenijs 163
ポロック
Pollock, A.J. 1122
Pollock, David C. 1122
Pollock, John Charles 1122
ポロック・エルワンド
Pollock-Ellwand, Nancy 1122
ホロックス
Horrocks, Chris 624
ボロディナ
Borodina, Olga 163
ボロディーン
Borodin, Aleksei Ivanovich 163
ボロディン
Boroden, Carolyn 163
ボロテリ
Bollettieri, Nick 156
ボロテリー
Bollettieri, Nick 156
ホロデンコ
Kholodenko, Vadym 728
ボロドゥリナ
Borodulina, Tatiana 163
ボロドコフ
Volod'kov, Roman 1462
ボロニナ
Voronina, Victoria 1464
ボローニ＝バード
Borroni-Bird, Christopher E. 163
ボローニン
Voronin, Vladimir Nikoraevich 1464
ボロノフ
Boronov, Kubatbek 163
ボロバッツ
Boravac, Semiha 161
ボロビエワ
Vorobieva, Natalia 1464
ボロビック
Borovik, Alexandre 163
Borovik, Anna 163
ホロビッツ
Horowitz, Anthony 623
ボロビョフ
Vorobiov, Oleksandr 1464
ホロビン
Horrobin, David F. 624
Horrobin, Peter James 624
ボロフィー
Brophy, David J. 187
ホロフコ
Holovko, Anatoliy 618
ボロベワ
Vorobieva, Natalia 1464
ボロボイ
Borovoy, Mikhail I. 163
ホロホルディン
Khorokhordin, Sergey 728
ホロミア
Horomia, Parekura 623
ホロムコヴィッチ
Hromkovic, Juraj 629
ホロラン
Holloran, Peter 617
ボロル
Bolor, Bayarbaatar 157
ボロルマー
Bolormaa, A. 157
Bolormaa, B. 157
ポロロ
Phororo, Rakoro 1108
ホロン
Hollon, Frank Turner 617
ボロン
Bollon, Patrice 157
Boron, Robert de 163
Boron, Walter F. 163
ボロンゴ
Bolongo, Norbert Likulia 157
ホロンスキー
Polonsky, Gill 1122
ポロンスキー
Polonskii, Yakov Petrovich 1122

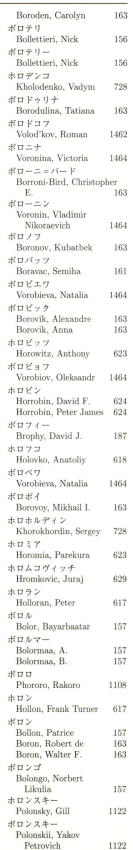

Polonsky, Gennady 1122
ボロンツォフ
Vorontsov, Nikolai Nikolaevich 1464
ボロンボイ
Bolomboy, Joel 157
ホワ
Hua, Guo-feng 630
ボーワ
Bowa, Larry 169
ボワ
Bois, Yve Alain 155
ホワイ
Howai, Larry 627
ボワイエ
Boyer, Marc 171
Boyer, Marine 171
Boyer, Regis 172
Boyer, Robert 172
ホワイティング
Whiting, Robert 1500
Whiting, Steven Moore 1500
Whiting, Sue 1500
ホワイテントン
Whitenton, James B. 1499
ホワイト
Whight, Patrick David 1497
White, Abbie Leigh 1497
White, Adam 1497
White, Alex 1498
White, Andrew J. 1498
White, Andy 1498
White, Barry 1498
White, Benedict 1498
White, Betty 1498
White, B.Joseph 1498
White, Bruce 1498
White, Byron Raymond 1498
White, Caroline McCoy 1498
White, Charlie 1498
White, Clifton 1498
White, Colin 1498
White, Corey 1498
White, Dan 1498
White, Danny 1498
White, Darius 1498
White, David 1498
White, David A. 1498
White, David Gordon 1498
White, DeAndrew 1498
White, D.J. 1498
White, D.Lynn 1498
White, Edmund 1498
White, E.Frances 1498
White, Gloria 1498
White, Graham 1498
White, Hal 1498
White, Hayden V. 1498
White, Hugh 1498
White, Ian 1498
White, Jack 1498
White, James 1498
White, James F. 1498
White, Jan V. 1498
White, Jennifer 1498
White, Jerald R. 1498
White, Jim 1498
White, JoAnna 1498
White, John 1498
White, John Myles 1498
White, John Paul 1498
White, Julie 1498
White, Kate 1498
White, Kathryn 1498
White, Kevin 1498
White, Kiersten 1498
White, Kit 1498
White, Lauren 1498
White, Laurie 1498
White, Lawrence J. 1498
White, Lee 1498
White, Lenny 1498
White, Loreth Anne 1498
White, Mary 1498
White, Mary Jo 1498
White, Matthew 1498
White, Maurice 1498
White, Melvin 1498
White, Merry 1498
White, Michael 1498, 1499
White, Michael C. 1499
White, M.R.H. 1499
White, Myles 1499
White, Nathan 1499
White, Okaro 1499
White, Paul A. 1499
White, Peter 1499
White, Reggie 1499
White, Roberto 1499
White, Robert Winthrop 1499
White, Robin A. 1499
White, Ron 1499
White, Ruth 1499
White, Ruth C. 1499
White, Ryan 1499
White, Sailor 1499
White, Shaun 1499
White, Susan Williams 1499
White, Tarnee 1499
White, Teri 1499
White, T.H. 1499
White, Tiffany 1499
White, Timothy 1499
White, Tom 1499
White, Tony L. 1499
White, Tyler 1499
White, Valerie 1499
White, Verdine 1499
Whyte, Abe 1501
Whyte, Angela 1501
Whyte, Annsert 1501
Whyte, Douglas 1501
Whyte, Mary 1501
Whyte, Rob 1501
Whyte, Rosemarie 1501
Whyte, Susan Reynolds 1501
ホワイトウェイ
Whiteway, Michael 1499
ホワイトゥン
Whiten, Andrew 1499
ホワイトクロス
Whitecross, Mat 1499
Whitecross, Roy H. 1499
ホワイトサイズ
Whitesides, George M. 1499
ホワイトサイド
Whiteside, Bates H. 1499
Whiteside, Hassan 1499
Whiteside, Kerry H. 1499
ホワイトハウス
Whitehouse, David 1499
Whitehouse, Éliane 1499
Whitehouse, Mary 1499
Whitehouse, Peter J. 1499
ホワイトハースト
Whitehurst, Jim 1499
ホワイトフェザー
WhiteFeather, Sheri 1499
ホワイトフォード
Whiteford, Frank 1499
ホワイトヘアー
Whitehair, Cody 1499
ホワイトヘッド
Whitehead, Isaish 1499
Whitehead, Jermaine 1499
Whitehead, John 1499
Whitehead, John Stainton 1499
Whitehead, Lorne A. 1499
Whitehead, Lucky 1499
Whitehead, Paul 1499
Whitehead, Robert 1499
Whitehead, Stephen M. 1499
Whitehead, Tahir 1499
ホワイトホース
Whitehorse, Johnny 1499
ホワイトマン
Whiteman, Burchell 1499
Whiteman, Philip 1499
Whiteman, Robin 1499
ホワイトモア
Whitemore, Hugh 1499
ホワイトリー
Whiteley, Philip 1499
Whitley, A.Stewart 1500
ホワイトロー
Whitelaw, Billie 1499
Whitelaw, Ian 1499
Whitelaw, Stella 1499
ホワイトロウ
Whitlow, Steve 1500
ホワイトロック
Whitelock, Derek A. 1499
Whitelock, Sam 1499
ホワイブラウ
Whybrow, Ian 1501
ホワイマン
Whyman, Robin 1501
ボワオ
Bowao, Charles Zacharie 169
ボワシエ
Boissier, Jean-Louis 155
ホーワース
Haworth, Cheryl 584
ボワーズ
Bowers, Clint A. 170
ボワス
Boisse, Erik 155
ボワスリエ
Boisselier, Jean 155
ボワソー
Boisseau, Marie-Thérèse 155
ボワソン
Poisson, David 1120
ボワソン=バルディ
Boysson-Bardies, Bénédicte de 172
ボワチエ
Poitier, Sidney 1120
ボワヂフル
Boisdeffre, Pierre de 155
ホワット
Howat, Roy 628
ホワットリー
Whatley, Bruce 1496
ボワティエ
Poitier, Anton 1120
Poitier, Sidney 1120
ボワデフル
Boisdeffre, Pierre de 155
ホワード
Howard, Rob 627
ボワナール
Boisnard, Fabienne 155
ボワニョ
Poignault, Rémy 1120
ボワネ
Voynet, Dominique 1464
ボワノ
Boinot, Isabelle 155
ボワラーヌ
Poilâne, Lionel 1120
ボワリ
Boiry, Véronique 155
ボワリエ
Poirier, Jacques 1120
ボワルヴェ
Poilvet, Laurent 1120
ボワルドン
Boisredon, Christian de 155
ボワレ
Boilet, Frédéric 155
ボワレ
Poiree (skjelbreid) , Liv Grete 1120
Pöirée, Raphael 1120
Skjelbreid-poiree, Liv Grete 1310
ボワレヴェ
Poillevé, Sylvie 1120
ボワロ
Boillot, Laurent 155
ボワロ=シェリフ
Poirot-Cherif, Sandra 1120
ボワロー・デルペッシュ
Poirot-Delpech, Bertrand 1120
ボワロベール
Boisrobert, Anouck 155
ボワロン
Boisrond, Michel 155
ホワン
Huang, Hua 630
Huang, Ju 630
Huang, ling chih 630
Hwang, In-sung 640
Hwang, Jason 640
ボワンコ
Bowanko, Luke 169
ホーン
Haun, Jeremy 582
Hawn, Goldie 584
Horn, C.Steven 623
Horn, David 623
Horn, Ellen 623
Horn, Emily 623
Horn, Greg 623
Horn, Jeffrey 623
Horn, Michael B. 623
Horn, Miriam 623
Horn, Pamela 623
Horn, Paul 623
Horn, Paul M. 623
Horn, Rebecca 623
Horn, Reece 623
Horn, Sandra Ann 623
Horn, Shirley 623

Horn, Stacy 623
Horn, Stephen 623
Horn, Trevor 623
Horn, Zoia 623
Horne, Andrew 623
Horne, Ann 623
Horne, Donald 623
Horne, Gerald 623
Horne, Howard 623
Horne, James A. 623
Horne, John 623
Horne, Lena 623
Horne, Peter 623
Horne, Richard 623
Horne, Rob 623
Horne, Sarah 623
Whone, Herbert 1501

ホン
Hoang, Quy Tinh 611
Hon, David 619
Hong, Eun-ju 620
Hong, Haeran 620
Hong, Hyang Gee 620
Hong, Hyung 620
Hong, Jung-eun 620
Hong, Jung Sum 620
Hong, Jun-pyo 620
Hong, Kuk Hyon 620
Hong, Kwang-sun 620
Hong, Lily Toy 620
Hong, Mi-ran 620
Hong, Myung-bo 620
Hong, Myungpyo 620
Hong, Ok-song 620
Hong, Ra-hee 620
Hong, Sang-soo 620
Hong, Seok-hyun 620
Hong, Song-nam 620
Hong, Suk-woo 620
Hong, Sung-yop 620
Hong, Un Jong 620
Hong, Xue-zhi 620
Hong, Yong-pyo 620
Hong, Yun-sik 620
Hung, Sin-nui 635

ボーン
Bone, Emily 158
Bone, Eugenia 158
Bone, Robert G. 158
Born, Hans 162
Born, Klaus 162
Born, Richard 162
Borne, Matt 162
Bourn, Michael 168
Bourne, Edmund J. 168
Bourne, Joanna 168
Bourne, Matthew 168
Bourne, Possum 168
Bourne, Sam 168
Bourne, Shae-Lynn 168
Bourne, Stanford 168
Vaughan, Dustin 1448
Vaughn, Terran 1448

ボン
Bon, François 157
Bong, Jun-ho 159
Vong Soth 1463
Vonn, Lindsey 1463
Vorng Saut 1464

ポン
Bong, Jun-ho 159
Peng, Chong 1095
Peng, Eddie 1095
Peng, Li-yuan 1095
Peng, Lucy 1095

ボンヴィシニ
Bonvicini, Stéphanie 160

ボンガ
Bonga, Timothy 159

ボンガード
Bongard, Josh 159

ホンカネン
Honkanen, Jenni 620
Honkanen, Tarja 620

ボンク
Bonk, Bartlomiej 159

ホーングレン
Horngren, Charles T. 623

ボンクングバリマ
Bonkoungou-balima, Marie Odile 159

ホンゴー
Hongo, Garrett Kaoru 620

ボンゴ
Bongo, Ali 159
Bongo, Omar 159
Bongo Ondimba, Omar 159

ボンゴ・オンディンバ
Bongo Ondimba, Ali 159
Bongo Ondimba, Omar 159

ボンコディン
Boncodin, Emilia 158

ホンコポヴァー
Honcoopova, Helena 619

ホーンコール・ベネガス
Hornkohl Venegas, Marigen 623

ボンゴンダ
Bongonda, Theo 159

ポンサクレック・ウォンジョンカム
Pongsaklek Wonjongkam 1123

ポンサクレック・ワンジョンカム
Pongsaklek Wonjongkam 1123

ポンサック
Pongsak, Ruktapongpisal 1123

ポンサナ
Ponsana, Boonsak 1123

ボンジェリ
Bongeli, Emile 159

ボンジャ
Bonja, Ed 159

ボンジャース
Bongers, Sally 159

ボンジャン
Bonjean, Helene 159

ポンジュ
Ponge, Francis 1123

ボーンシュタイン
Bornstein, Roni Aaron 163

ポンショー
Ponchaud, François 1123

ボン・ジョヴィ
Bon Jovi, Jon 159

ボンジョビ
Bon Jovi, Jon 159

ボンジョルニ
Bongiorni, Sara 159

ボーンズ
Bones, Ricky 158

ボンズ
Bonds, Barry 158
Bonds, Bobby Lee 158
Bonds, Ray 158

ポンス
Pons, Philippe 1123
Pons Ramon, Joan Lluis 1123

ポンズ
Pons, Peter T. 1123

ボーンスタイン
Bornstein, Kate 163
Bornstein, Niel M. 163
Bornstein, Ruth 163

ボーンステイン
Bornstein, David 163

ホーンズビー
Hornsby, Keith 623
Hornsby, Richard 623

ホーンズフィールド
Hounsfield, Godfrey Newbold 626

ポンスミス
Pondsmith, Michael 1123

ホン・スン・フォット
Hong Sun Huot 620

ポンセ
Ponce, Charles 1123
Ponce, Ezequiel 1123
Ponce, Javier 1123
Poncet, Christophe 1123

ホーンゼイ
Hornsey, Chris 623

ポンセ・デ・レオン・パイヴァ
Ponce de León Paiva, Antón 1123

ポンセ・レオン
Ponce León, Ximena 1123

ボン・ソート
Vong Sauth 1463

ボンソン
Bonson, Richard 160

ホンダ
Honda, Mike 619

ボンダ
Bonda, Ted 158

ポンタ
Ponta, Victor 1123

ポンダー
Ponder, Catherine 1123
Ponder, Christian 1123

ポンタリス
Pontalis, J.B. 1123

ボンダル
Bondar, Oleksandr 158

ボンダルク
Bondaruk, Roman 158

ボンダレンコ
Bondarenko, Aleksandr 158
Bondarenko, Alexei 158
Bondarenko, Alona 158
Bondarenko, Bohdan 158
Bondarenko, Ivan Petrovych 158
Bondarenko, Kateryna 158
Bondarenko, Svitlana 158
Bondarenko, Yaroslava 158

ボンタン
Bontemps, Julien 160

ボーンチェ
Boontje, Tord 160

ポンチャイ
Pornchai, Rujiprapa 1125

ポンツァ
Ponza, Michela 1124

ボンデ
Bonde, Emmanuel 158

ボンディ
Bondi, Hermann 158
Bondi, Sandro 158
Bondy, Andy 158

ポンティ
Ponti, Carlo 1124
Ponti, Claude 1124
Ponti, James 1124

ポンティセリ
Ponticelli, Lazare 1124

ポンティッジャ
Pontiggia, Giuseppe 1124

ポーンティワ
Pornthiva, Nakasai 1125

ポンティング
Ponting, Clive 1124

ボンデヴィック
Bondevik, Kjell Magne 158

ポンデクスター
Pondexter, Quincy 1123

ポンテコルヴォ
Pontecorvo, Gillo 1123

ポンテコルボ
Pontecorvo, Gillo 1123

ボンデソン
Bondeson, Jan 158

ボンデビック
Bondevik, Kjell Magne 158

ポンテープ
Phongthep, Thepkanjana 1108
Pongthep, Thepkanjana 1123

ボンデュラント
Bondurant, Matt 158

ボーン＝デリアン
Bohn-Derrien, Laetitia 155

ホンデリック
Honderich, Ted 619

ホント
Hont, Istvan 620

ボント
Bonto, Hassane Souley Dit 160

ボンド
Bond, Al 158
Bond, Alan 158
Bond, Bradley 158
Bond, Brian 158
Bond, Christine 158
Bond, Devante 158
Bond, Edward 158
Bond, Felicia 158
Bond, Frank W. 158
Bond, Hamish 158
Bond, Henry 158
Bond, John 158
Bond, Jonathan 158
Bond, Julian 158
Bond, Larry 158
Bond, Lloyd 158
Bond, Martin 158
Bond, Mary 158
Bond, Michael 158
Bond, Michael Harris 158
Bond, Nelson 158
Bond, Peter 158
Bond, Rebecca 158
Bond, Ruskin 158
Bond, Stephanie 158

ポンド
Pond, David 1123

Pond, Graham 1123
ボンドゥ
Bondoux, Anne-Laure 158
ボンドゥー
Bondoux, Anne-Laure 158
ホンドゥル
Hondru, Angela Varvara 619
ボンドック
Bondoc, Elmo 158
ボンドラ
Vondra, Alexandr 1463
ポントルモ
Pontormo, Jacopo Carucci 1124
ホンドロス
Hondros, Chris 619
ポントン
Ponton, Lynn E. 1124
ボンニーチ
Bonnici, Owen 160
ポンニミット
Ponnimit, Wisut 1123
ボンヌフォワ
Bonnefoy, Yves 159
ボンヌフォン
Bonnefond, Cecile 159
ボンネヴィーク
Bondevik, Kjell Magne 158
ボンネル
Bonner, Elena Georgievna 159
ボンパ
Bompa, Tudor O. 157
ボンバエル
Von Baer, Ena 1463
ボンハーゲ
Bonhage, Barbara 159
ボンバック
Bomback, Mark 157
Bomback, Suzanne 157
ボンバール
Bombard, Alain 157
ボンバルディエーリ
Bombardieri, Simone 157
ホーンビー
Hornby, Jane 623
Hornby, Kirstin.R. 623
Hornby, Nick 623
Hornby, Simon Michael 623
ホーンビィ
Hornby, Nick 623
ボンビエーリ
Bombieri, Enrico 157
ボンビエリ
Bombieri, Enrico 157
ボーンビッチ
Baumbich, Charlene Ann 106
ポンピドー
Pompidou, Claude 1123
ポンピドゥー
Pompidou, Claude 1123
ポンピリオ
Pompilio, Pedro 1123
ボンファ
Bonfa, Luiz Floriano 158
ボンフィス - マビヨン
Bonfils-Mabilon, Béatrice 159
ボンフィム
Bonfim, Caio 159
Bonfim, Fernanda Pontifece 159
ボンフィリオ
Bonfiglio, Giuseppe 158
ボンフィールド
Bonfield, Peter Leahy 158
ボンフォード
Bomford, David 157
ホンブルク
Homburg, Cornelia 619
ホンブルフ
Homburg, Cornelia 619
ボンブレイマン・バルケロ
Vonbreymann Barquero, Wilhelm 1463
ポンフレット
Pomfret, Richard 1123
ポンペイ
Pompey, Dalton 1123
ホーンベック
Hornbech, Birthe Rønn 623
ボンヘッセ・ラセルナ
Von Hesse la Serna, Milton 1463
ボン・ペッツィンガー
Von Petzinger, Genevieve 1463
ポンボ
Pombo, Guy Mikulu 1123
ポンボシルバ
Pombo Silva, Alex William 1123
ポンポン
Pongpol, Adirekusarn 1123
ホンマ
Homma, Akira 619
ホンマドフ
Hommadov, Yazmyrat 619
ボンマリー
Von-mally, Louis Joseph 1463
ボンマン
Bonmann, Hendrik 159
ポーンメク
Phonemek, Dalaloy 1108
Ponemek, Dalaloy 1123
ポンメーク
Ponmek, Dalaloi 1123
ホンメル
Hommel, Scott 619
ボンヤスキー
Bonjasky, Remy 159
ボンレム
Bonnelame, Jérémie 159

【マ】

マ
Ma, Chih-hsiang 857
Ma, Eric Kit-Wai 857
Ma, Jennifer Wen 857
Ma, Jingle 857
Ma, Yo-Yo 857
Ma, Zhao-xu 857
マー
Ma, Chih-hsiang 857
Ma, Dewen 857
Ma, Feng 857
Ma, Hong 857
Ma, Hua-teng 857
Ma, Jack 857
Ma, Jeffrey 857
Ma, Ji 857
Ma, Kai 857
Ma, Long 857
Ma, Shu-li 857
Ma, Ying-jeou 857
Mah, Bow Tan 883
Mah, Siew Keong 883
Marr, Andrew 905
Marr, Bernard 905
マア
Ma, Ronald 857
マアー
Meagher, Janet 928
マアケ
Ma'ake, Sosefo 858
マアスアシ
Mahazoasy, Roger 884
マアスーミヤーン
Masoomiyan, Mehrnoosh 915
マアタル
Maatar, Abdelwaheb 858
マアーニ
Maani, Fauoa 858
マアフ
Ma'afu 857
Ma'afu, Campese 857
Ma'afu, Viliami 857
マアーヤア
Maa'yaa, Rula 858
マアルーフ
Maalouf, Amin 858
Maârouf, Anouar 858
マアルフ
Ma'ruf, Muhammad 912
マーイー
Mahy, Margaret 885
マイ
Mai, Lý Quang 885
Mai, Manfred 885
May, Ekkehard 923
マイア
Maia, Armindo 885
Mayr, Ernst Walter 925
Mya 999
マイアー
Maier, Hans 885
Maier, Paul L. 885
Mair, Avil 886
Mayer, Kevin 924
Mayr, Ernst Walter 925
Meier, Alexander 930
Meier, Heinrich 930
Meier, Sarah 930
Meier, Waltraud 930
Meyer, Cameron 940
Meyer, Heiko 940
Muir, Blake 987
マイアシンシー
Maesincee, Suvit 881
マイアーズ
Myers, Michael F. 999
Myers, Norman 999
Myers, Walter Dean 999
マイアーズコフ
Myerscough, Morag 999
マイアソン
Myerson, George 999
Myerson, Joel 1000
マイアミ
Miami, Rita 942
マイアル
Miall, Hugh 942
Miall, Lawrence 942
マイウェン
Maïwenn 886
マイエ
Maillet, Antonine 886
マイエッタ
Maietta, Domenico 885
Maietta, Lenny 885
マイエッロ
Maiello, Raffaele 885
マイエ・ヌスエ
Maye Nsue, Ruben 924
マイエ・ヌセ
Maye Nsue, Ruben 924
マイエール
Maier, Corinne 885
マイエル
Meyer, Morten Andreas 940
マイエレ
Mayel, Jason 924
マーイェンス
Maeyens, Tim 881
マイエンス
Maeyens, Tim 881
マイエンブルク
Mayenburg, Marius von 924
マイオルカ
Maiorca, Enzo 886
マイカ
Majka, Rafal 887
Micah, Ben 942
マイガ
Maïga, Abdoulaye Idrissa 885
Maiga, Bruno 886
Maïga, Choguel Kokalla 886
Maiga, Mahamane Kalil 886
Maiga, Ousmane Issoufi 886
Maiga, Sadou 886
Maiga, Sina Damba 886
Maiga, Soumeylou Boubeye 886
Maiga, Touré Aminatou 886
マイガリ
Maïgari, Bello Bouba 886
マイカル
Maykall, Laura Alfaro 924
マイカン
Mikan, George Lawrence 945
マイ・キエウ・リエン
Mai Kieu Lien 886
マイーク
Mayiik, Ayii Deng 924
マイクル
Michl, Thomas R. 943
マイクルザック
Majchrzak, Ann 887
マイクルズ
Michaels, Anne 942
Peters, Elizabeth 1102
マイクロジアナキス
Mikrogianakis, Angelo 946
マイグロフ
Maigourov, Victor 886
マイゲ
Maige, Ezekiel

マ

Magolyo 886
マイケル
Michael 942
Michael, Albert 942
Michael, Asot 942
Michael, Christine 942
Michael, David 942
Michael, George 942
Michael, Jan 942
Michael, Kamran 942
Michael, Livi 942
Michael, T.S. 942
Michel, Mario 943
Michel, Rodolphe 943
マイケルズ
Michaels, Anne 942
Michaels, Ed 942
Michaels, Fern 942
Michaels, Helga 942
Michaels, J.C. 942
Michaels, Jeff 942
Michaels, Jess 942
Michaels, Jillian 942
Michaels, Kasey 942
Michaels, Leigh 942
Michaels, Leonard 942
Michaels, Walter Benn 942
Michels, Barry 943
Mikels, Jennifer 945
マイケルセン
Michelsen, Neil F. 943
Mikaelsen, Ben 945
マイケルソン
Michaelson, Gerald A. 942
Michaelson, Steven 942
Michelson, G.G. 943
Michelson, Patricia 943
Mikalson, Jon D. 945
マイケロン
Michelon, Pascale 943
マイコ
Majko, Pandeli Sotir 887
マイゴシ
Maïgochi, Sani 886
マイコラス
Mikolas, Lauren 945
マイコン
Maicon 885
マイサ
Maitha, Karisa 886
マイザー
Meiser, Annette 931
Meiser, Gernot 931
マイサリ
al-Maisari, Ahmad 886
マイシオ
Mycio, Mary 999
マイシュ
Meisch, Claude 931
マイスキー
Maisky, Mischa 886
マイスター
Maister, David H. 886
マイズナー
Meissner, Kimmie 931
Misner, Ivan R. 955
マイスニッツァー
Meissnitzer, Alexandra 931
マイスラーゼ
Maisuradze, Simon 886
マイセル
Meisel, Klaus 931
マイゼル
Meisel, Paul 931
マイゼルス
Maizels, Stanley D. 886
マイゼルズ
Maizels, Jennie 886
マーイタ
Maaytah, Musa 858
Maayteh, Sameeh 858
マイダ
Maida, Luisa 885
マイタミ
al-Maytami, Mohammed 925
マイダンス
Mydans, Carl 999
Mydans, Shelley 999
マイツェン
Majcen, Irena 887
マイティ・ファイン
Mighty Fine 944
マイデル
Maydell, Bernd von 924
マイト
Meid, Karl-Heinz 930
マイトランド
Maitland, Sean 886
マイトルーヤ
Maitreya, Sananda 886
マイトン
Mighton, John 944
マイナ
Maina, Michael 886
Maina, Solomon Karanja 886
Maina, Zainab 886
マイナー
Miner, Al 952
Miner, Earl 953
Miner, Robert C. 953
Minor, Halsey 953
Minor, Marian 953
Minor, Mike 953
Minor, Vernon Hyde 953
Minor, Wendell 953
マイナサラ
Maïnassara, Idi Illiasou 886
マイナーズ - ウォリス
Mynors-Wallis, Laurence 1000
マイナリ
Mainali, Chandra Prakash 886
Mainali, Govinda Prasad 886
Mainali, Radha Krishna 886
マイニ
Miani, Marcello 942
マイニー
Meinig, George 931
マイニエリ
Mainieri, Ronnie 886
マイノット
Minot, Susan 953
マイパカイ
Maipakai, Mark 886
マイバーグ
Myburgh, Alwyn 999
マイヒトリ
Meichtry, Dominik 930
マイヒル
Myhill, Boaz 1000
Myhill, Debra 1000
マイホーファー
Maihofer, Andra 886
マイマンガ
Mai Manga, Oumara 886
マイミ
Mahinmi, Ian 884
マイミン
Maymin, Senia 925
マイメツ
Maimets, Toivo 886
マイヤー
Maier, Bernhard 885
Maier, Hermann 885
Maier, Simon 885
Maier, Tomas 885
Mayer, Claudia 924
Mayer, Hans 924
Mayer, Johannes G. 924
Mayer, Matthias 924
Mayer, Robert 924
Mayer, Sabine 924
Mayr, Ernst Walter 925
Meier, August 930
Meier, David 930
Meier, Deborah 930
Meier, Dieter 930
Meier, Eduard 930
Meier, Gerald Marvin 930
Meier, Joan S. 930
Meier, Norbert 930
Meier, Richard Alan 930
Meyer, Albrecht 940
Meyer, Andreas K. 940
Meyer, Armin H. 940
Meyer, Birgit 940
Meyer, Cameron 940
Meyer, Cheryl L. 940
Meyer, Christopher 940
Meyer, Clemens 940
Meyer, Danny 940
Meyer, Deon 940
Meyer, Dominique 940
Meyer, Eduard 940
Meyer, Hilbert 940
Meyer, James Sampson 940
Meyer, Joyce 940
Meyer, Kai 940
Meyer, Karl-Heinz 940
Meyer, Kerstin 940
Meyer, Lothar B. 940
Meyer, Marshall W. 940
Meyer, Martin 940
Meyer, Marvin W. 940
Meyer, Max 940
Meyer, Michael 940
Meyer, Michael J. 940
Meyer, Paul J. 940
Meyer, Roy 940
Meyer, Urs A. 941
Myers, Arnold 999
Myers, Jean 999
Myhre, John 1000
マイヤー＝アービッヒ
Meyer-Abich, Klaus Michael 941
マイヤーウィッツ
Meyerowitz, Joel 941
マイヤー・クラーマー
Meyer-Krahmer, Frieder 941
マイヤー＝グレーヴェ
Meier-Gräwe, Uta 930
マイヤシェーンバーガー
Mayer-Schönberger, Viktor 924
マイヤー＝ショーンベルガー
Mayer-Schönberger, Viktor 924
マイヤース
Meyers, Anne Akiko 941
Myers, Sonny 999
Myers, Thomas W. 999
マイヤーズ
Mayers, Mike 924
Meyers, Anne Akiko 941
Meyers, Jean-Victor 941
Meyers, Joe 941
Meyers, Jonathan Rhys 941
Meyers, Morton A. 941
Meyers, Nancy 941
Meyers, Randy 941
Myers, Bob 999
Myers, Brandon 999
Myers, Cindi 999
Myers, David G. 999
Myers, Ehren 999
Myers, Eleanor W. 999
Myers, Glenford J. 999
Myers, Helen R. 999
Myers, Isabel Briggs 999
Myers, Jason 999
Myers, John E.B. 999
Myers, John Peterson 999
Myers, Katharine D. 999
Myers, Lorna 999
Myers, Marc 999
Myers, Mike 999
Myers, Norman 999
Myers, Paul 999
Myers, Pete 999
Myers, Richard B. 999
Myers, Robert 999
Myers, Stewart C. 999
Myers, Tony 999
Myers, Walter Dean 999
Myers, Ware 999
Myers, Wil 999
Myers, William 999
マイヤー・スクマンツ
Mayer-Skumanz, Lene 924
マイヤスコウ
Myerscough, Marie 999
マイヤースン
Myerson, Joel 1000
マイヤーソン
Myerson, Roger B. 1000
マイヤーブレーカー
Meyerbröer, Helga 941
マイヤーラ
Mayyaleh, Adib 925
マイヤーロホ
Meyer-Rochow, V.B. 941
マイヨー
Maillot, Jean-Christophe 886
Maillot, Pierre 886
マイヨール
Mayol, Jacques 925
Mayol, Pierre 925
Mayor, Michel G.E. 925
マイラ
Mayila, Louis Gaston 924
マイラウ
Mailau, Tevita 886
マイラファ
Mailafa, Hadiza 886
マイランダー
Mylander, Maureen 1000
マイランド
Myland, Jan C. 1000

マイリ
Meili, Katie 931
Miley, Hannah 946
マイリー
Miley, Arthur 946
Miley, Linda 946
Miley, Marissa 946
Miley, Wade 946
マイリック
Myrick, Leland 1000
マイル
Mailu, Cleopa 886
Mayr, Juan 925
マイルス
Miles, Russell 946
Mills, Mike 951
マイルズ
Mails, Thomas E. 886
Miles, Al 946
Miles, Ava 946
Miles, Barry 946
Miles, C.J. 946
Miles, Derek 946
Miles, Gina 946
Miles, Hugh 946
Miles, Ian 946
Miles, Jack 946
Miles, Linda 946
Miles, Lisa 946
Miles, Louella 946
Miles, Michelle 946
Miles, Robert P. 946
Miles, Rontez 946
Miles, Rosalind 946
Miles, Ruthie Ann 946
Miles, Stephen A. 946
Miles, Thom 946
Miles, Wyman 946
Mills, Alan 950
Myles, Brenda 1000
Myles, Bruce 1000
マイレッカー
Mayröcker, Friederike 925
マイロウィッツ
Meyerowitz, Joel 941
マイロン
Milon, J.Walter 951
Myron, Vicki 1000
マインケ
Meinke, Katrin 931
マインチェス
Meintjes, Louis 931
マインツァー
Mainzer, Klaus 886
マインハート
Meinhardt, Gerek 931
マインヘーヴェル
Meinhövel, Harald 931
マインベルク
Meinberg, Eckhard 931
マウ
Mau, Bruce 921
Mouw, Richard J. 983
マウア
Mower, Thomas W. 984
マウアー
Mauer, Joe 921
マウアルーガ
Maualuga, Rey 921
マーウィ
Maaoui, Slaheddine 858
マヴィッサカリアン
Mavissakalian, M.R. 922
マーウイヤ
Maaouya, Mohamed Ould 858
マーウィン
Merwin, William Stanley 937
Merwin, W.S. 937
マーヴィン
Marvin, Carolyn 913
Marvin, Garry 913
マヴィンクルヴェ
Mavinkurve, Brahmanand 922
マウエル
Mauel, Hildegard M. 921
マウガ
Mauga, Josh 921
マウクス
Mauch, Gene William 921
マウサー
Mouser, David B. 983
マウス
Maus, Ingeborg 922
Mouse, Danger 983
マーウッド
Marwood, Alex 913
Marwood, Michael 913
マウテ
Maute, Christiane 922
マウデ
Maoudé, Koroné 898
マウニー
Mauny, Fabienne 922
マウハー
Maucher, Helmut Oswald 921
マウラ
Maura, Carmen 922
マウラー
Maurer, Brandon 922
Maurer, Gaylyn Gaddy 922
Maurer, Kevin 922
Maurer, Konrad 922
Maurer, Leopold 922
Maurer, Michael 922
Maurer, Peter 922
Maurer, Robert 922
Maurer, Ueli 922
Maurer, Ulrike 922
Mowrer, O.Hobart 984
マヴーラ
Mvula, Laura 998
マヴライ
Mavraj, Mergim 923
マウラテ
Maurate, Daniel 922
マウラナ
Moulana, Alavi 982
マウリ
Mauri, Carolina 922
Mauri, Jose 922
マウリー
Maury, Marianne 922
マウリシオ
Maurício, Armindo Cipriano 922
Mauricio, Rufino 922
マウリチ
Maurizi, Stefania 922
マウリッリ
Maurilli, Franco 922
マウリディ
Maulidi, Paul 922
マウリャ
Maurya, Ash 922
マウル
Maul, Heinz Eberhard 922
Maull, Hanns Walter 922
マウルード
Mauloud, Amal Mint 922
マウレッリ
Maurelli, Alessia 922
マウロ
Mauro 922
Mauro, Alessandra 922
Mauro, Josh 922
Mauro, Vincent F. 922
マウン
Maung, Cynthia 922
マウン・ウ
Maung Oo 922
マウン・エイ
Maung Aye 922
マウン・ティン・アウン
Maung Htin Aung 922
マウンテン
Mountain, Fiona 982
Mountain, Ross Stewart 982
マウンテン・ドリーマー
Mountain Dreamer, Oriah 982
マウント
Mount, A.R. 982
Mount, Balfour M. 982
Mount, David W. 982
Mount, Deiontrez 982
マウントカッスル
Mountcastle, Vernon 982
マウントキャッスル
Mountcastle, Robert 982
マウン・フティン・アウン
Maung Htin Aung 922
マウン・マウン・キン
Maung Maung Khin 922
マウン・マウン・スエ
Maung Maung Swe 922
マウン・マウン・テイン
Maung Maung Thein 922
マウン・ミン
Maung Myint 922
マウン・ミン・ニョウ
Maung Min Nyo 922
マーエ
Mahé, Louis-Pascal 884
マエ
Mae, Epp 881
Mae, Jaak 881
マエグリ
Maegli, Juan Ignacio 881
マエシュ
Mahesh, Shri 884
マエストリ
Maestri, Yoann 881
マエストリピエリ
Maestripieri, Dario 881
マエストレ
Maestre, Gabriel 881
Maestre Perez, Gabriel 881
マエゾノ・ヤマシタ
Maezono Yamashita, Luis Katsumi 881
マエダ
Maeda, Sae 881
マエヌウ
Maenu'u, Paul 881
マエフスカ
Maevska-velichkova, Mihaela 881
マエフスキ
Majewski, Tomasz 887
マエムラ
Maemura, Héctor Solares 881
マエムラ・ウルタード
Maemura Hurtado, Mary 881
マエモフ
Mahemoff, Michael 884
マエラン
Maelanga, Manasseh 881
マエランガ
Maelanga, Manasseh 881
マエリッケ
Maelicke, Alfred 881
マエル・C.
Maëlle C. 881
マエルス
Majerus, Christine 887
マエレ
Prince Maele 881
マオ
Mao, An-qing 898
Mao, Xin-yu 898
Mao, Yong 898
Maoh, Alfred 898
マオア
Mouer, Ross E. 982
マオコラマジョゴ
Maokola-majogo, Edgar 898
マオシェルジ
al-Maosherji, Sharida 898
マオズ
Maoz, Samuel 898
マオペ
Maope, Kelebone 898
マオマ
Mahoma, Moussa 885
マオラー
Maurer, Reinhart Klemens 922
マオール
Maor, Eli 898
マーカー
Marker, Gary 903
Marker, Steve 903
Merker, Björn 936
マーガー
Mager, Craig 882
マカー
Macur, Juliet 879
マガ
Magga, Martin 882
マガー
McGerr, Patricia 868
マカーイ
McKay, Sandy 872
マカイヴァー
McIver, Meredith 871
マカイナイ
Makainai, Mailani 887
マカイバー
McIvor, Ashleigh 871
マガイヤー
Maguire, Jack 883
マカイユ
Marcaillou, Agnès 899

マ

マカウ
McCaw, Patrick 862
Makau, Patrick 887
マガウアン
McGowan, Richard A. 869
McGowan, Shane 869
マカヴォイ
McAvoy, James 859
マカウチ
McCouch, Hanna 863
マガウワン
McGowan, Christopher 869
マーカーキス
Markakis, Nick 903
マガグラ
Magagula, Phineas 882
Magagula, Winnie 882
マカーゴウ
McKergow, Mark 873
マカーシー
Mccarthy, Mike 861
マカジ
Makadji, Soumana 887
マーカス
Marcus, Alan J. 900
Marcus, Ben 900
Marcus, Bernard 900
Marcus, Bess 900
Marcus, Cindy 900
Marcus, Dawn A. 900
Marcus, Eric 900
Marcus, Eric Colton 900
Marcus, Erik 900
Marcus, Gary Fred 900
Marcus, George E. 900
Marcus, Greil 900
Marcus, James 900
Marcus, Joan 900
Marcus, Leonard S. 900
Marcus, Richard 900
Marcus, Richard L. 900
Marcus, Robert 900
Marcus, Rudolph Arthur 901
Marcus, Stanley 901
Markus, Donalee 904
Markus, Lindsey 904
マカス
Macas, Luis 859
マカスキー
McCaskey, Virginia Halas 861
マカスキル
McCaskill, Mary K. 861
マガスバ
Magassouba, Abdoulaye 882
マーカーソン
Epatha Merkerson, S. 404
マカーター
McArtor, Mike 859
マカダム
Macadam, Heather Dune 858
マカダムス
McAdams, Frank 858
McAdams, Joshua A. 858
McAdams, Michael Andrew 858
マガダン
Magadan, Dave 882
マカッチャン
McCutcheon, Marc 864
マーカット
Murcutt, Glenn 993
マーカティ
Mercati, Maria 935
マカーティ
McCarty, Cara 861
McCarty, Nick 861
マカーディ
McCurdy, Michael 864
マーカート
Markert, Tom 903
Marquardt, Michael J. 905
マーカード
Marquard, William H. 905
Marquardt, Luke 905
マカト
Makgato, Dorcus 888
マガト
Magath, Felix 882
マカドゥー
Mcadoo, Ben 858
Mcadoo, Mike 858
マカートニ
Macartney, Lady 859
マカートニー
Mccartney, Eliza 861
マカートニ夫人
Macartney, Lady 859
マガナウェ
Maganawe, Yao Florent Badjam 882
マカーニー
McCarney, Rosemary A. 860
マカニコ
Maccanico, Antonio 860
マガニャ
Magana, Alvaro 882
マカヌフォ
Macanufo, James 859
マカネラ
Makanera, Alhoussein Kaké 887
マガノ
Magano, Lisa 882
マカビンズ
McCubbins, Mathew Daniel 864
マカファーティ
MaCafferty, Catherine 859
McCafferty, Megan 860
マカファティ
McCafferty, Daniel 860
マカフィー
McAfee, Andrew 858
McAfee, Jeanette L. 858
McAfee, Pat 859
マカボイ
McAvoy, Gary 859
McAvoy, James 859
マーカム
Marcum, Dave 900
Marcum, David 900
Markham, Dewey, Jr. 903
マカモア
Muchamore, Robert 985
マカラー
McCullough, Joseph A. 864
マカラウ
Makarau, Ihar 887
マカラシビリ
Makarashvili, Jakob 887
マカランカ
Makaranka, Viachaslau 887
マカリー
McCully, Murray 864
マガリエフ
al-Magariaf, Mohammad Yusuf 882
マガリカエス
Magalhaes, Roberto Roleta 882
マーガリス
Margalis, Melanie 901
Murgallis, Robert R. 993
マカリース
McAleese, Mary Patricia 859
マカリスター
MacAlister, Katie 859
McAllister, Angela 859
McAllister, Anne 859
MacAllister, Heather 859
McAllister, Maggi 859
McAllister, Pam 859
McAllister, Tim 859
Mcallister, Zach 859
Mccalister, Alex 860
マガリャエス
Magalhaes, Vinicius Draculino 882
マカリン
McCallin, Margaret 860
マーカル
Mácal, Zdenek 859
マカール
Mácal, Zdenek 859
マカル
Macalou, Badra Alou 859
マカルー
McCullough, David, Jr. 864
マガール
Magerl, Caroline 882
マガル
Magal, Jiri 882
マカルビー
McKelvie, Jamie 872
マカルマン
McCalman, Iain 860
マカレー
Macauley, Henry 859
マーガレット王女
Margaret 901
マーガレット・ミーク
Spencer, Margaret Meek 1335
マカレンコ
Makarenko, Evgeny 887
Makarenko, Yevhen 887
マカロ
Macalou, Badra Alou 859
マカロウ
McCullough, James P. 864
マカロック
MacCulloch, Diarmaid 864
McCullough, Colleen 864
McCullough, Henry 864
マカロフ
Makarov, Oleg Grigorievich 887
Makarov, Sergey 887
Makarov, Vitaliy 887
マカロフス
Makarovs, Vladimirs 887
マカロル
Macarol, Veronika 859
マカロワ
Makarova, Ekaterina 887
Makarova, Natalia 887
Makarova, Veronika 887
マカロン
McCarron, Al 860
マカン
McCann, A.L. 860
McCann, Andrew Lachlan 860
McCann, Richard 860
マガンガムサブ
Maganga Moussavou, Biendi 882
Maganga Moussavou, Pierre Claver 882
マカンガラ
Makangala, Eunice 887
マガンデ
Magande, Ngandu Peter 882
マカンバ
Makamba, January Yusuf 887
マーキー
Markey, Rob 903
マキ
Maki, John McGilvrey 888
マギ
Maggi, Maurren Higa 882
Magi, Rasmus 882
マギー
McGee, Gerry 868
McGee, Harold 868
Mcgee, Jake 868
McGee, Jake 868
McGee, JaVale 868
McGee, J.Brad 868
McGee, Paul 868
McGee, Robert 868
McGee, Stacy 868
McGhee, Alison 868
Magee, Bryan 882
Magee, Chloe 882
Magee, Christopher L. 882
Magee, David 882
Magee, John 882
Magee, Sean 882
Magee, Susan 882
Magee, Terrence 882
Magee, Wendy 882
マギー・Q
Maggie Q 882
マキアシ
Makiashi, Willy 888
マキァーネル
MacCannell, Dean 860
マキヴェイ
Mcquivey, James 879
マギエラ
Magiera, Holly M. 882
マキエンゴ
Maquengo, Fernando 898
マキオン
McKeon, David 873
McKeon, Emma 873
McKeon, James 873
Mckeown, Taylor 873
マキサック
McKissack, Patricia C. 874
マキシック
Mckissic, J.D. 874

マキシ・ペレイラ
Maxi Pereira 923
マキシム
Maksim 888
マキシモワ
Maksimova, Anastasia 888
マキシ・ロペス
Maxi Lopez 923
マーキス
Marquez, Bradley 905
Marquis, Vincent 905
マーキソン
Markison, Robert E. 903
マキタリック
Mckitterick, Rosamond 874
マギット
Maggitt, Curt 882
マキナニー
McInerney, Francis 871
MacInerney, Karen 871
McInerny, Dennis Q. 871
McInerny, Ralph 871
マキニー
McKinney, Meagan 874
マキニス
McInnis, Craig 871
McInnis, Melvin G. 871
McInnis, William P. 871
マキーヌ
Makine, Andreï 888
マキネス
MacInnes, Elaine 871
McInnes, Roderick R. 871
マキネン
Mäkinen, Kirsti 888
マキノン
MacKinnon, Roderick 874
マキーバー
McKeever, Brian 872
マキパー
Mäkipää, Heikki 888
マギャヴィン
McGavin, Darren 868
マキャフリー
McCaffrey, Max 860
マキャフリィ
McCaffery, Larry 860
マキャフリイ
McCaffrey, Anne 860
マキャベロ
Machiavello, José 870
マキャモン
McCammon, Robert R. 860
マキャリオン
McCallion, Hazel 860
マキャン
McCann, Brian 860
Mccann, James 860
Mccann, Kirsten 860
Mccann, Melanie 860
マキュー
McHugh, Collin 870
マキューアン
McEwan, Geraldine 867
McEwan, Ian 867
McEwan, Patrick J. 867
McEwen, Bruce S. 867
マキューエン
McEwen, Dorothy 867
McEwen, Scott 867
マキューシック
McKusick, James C. 874
マキュージック
McKusick, Marshall Kirk 874
マーキュリー
Mercury, Michael 936
マーギュリス
Margulis, Lynn 902
マキューン
McCune, Grant 864
McKeown, Greg 873
Mckeown, Max 873
McKuen, Rod 874
マキラ
Makila, José 888
マキリップ
McKillip, Patricia Ann 874
マキロイ
Mcilroy, Rory 871
マギロウェイ
McGilloway, Brian 868
マキロップ
McKillop, Tom 874
マーキン
Murkin, Henry R. 993
マキン
Makine, Andreï 888
マギン
McGinn, Richard A. 868
マーキンズ
Makens, James C. 888
マギンティ
McGinty, Frank 868
マキンドー
McIndoe, Andrew 871
マキントッシュ
McIntosh, Jason 871
マギンリ
Maginley, John Herbert 882
マギンリー
Maginley, John 882
マーク
Maag, Peter 857
Mark, Dave 903
Mark, David 903
Mark, Jan 903
Mark, Joan T. 903
Mark, Jonathan 903
Mark, Lauryn 903
Mark, Mary Ellen 903
Mark, Maxey Walter 903
Mark, Robert 903
Mark, Russell 903
Mark, Thomas 903
マク
Maku, Labaran 888
マグァイア
McGuire, Dorothy 870
Maguire, Peter 883
マグアイア
Maguire, Tobey 883
マクアイヴァー
McIver, Joel 871
マークァドゥー
McAdoo, Wm George 858
マクイーウェン
McEwen, Scott 867
マクイオワン
MacEoin, Beth 867
マクイストン
McQuiston, Jennifer 879
マクイーワン
McEwan, Geraldine 867
マクィーン
McQeen, Alexander 878
マクイーン
McQeen, Alexander 878
マクヴィカー
McVicar, John 879
マクヴィティ
McVittie, Andy 879
マクウィニー
MacWhinney, Brian 879
マクウィリアム
McWilliam, Fergus 880
マクウィリアムス
McWilliams, Brian S. 880
McWilliams, Chandler 880
マクウィリアムズ
McWilliams, Judith 880
マクウェイグ
McQuaig, Linda 879
マクウェール
McQuail, Denis 879
マクウォーリー
Macquarrie, John 879
McQuarrie, Ralph 879
マクエイド
Mcquaide, Jake 879
マークエステル
Marcestel 899
マクガイア
McGuire, Barbara 870
McGuire, Christine 870
McGuire, Dennis Eugene 870
McGuire, Dorothy 870
McGuire, Hugh 870
McGuire, Jamie 870
McGuire, Meredith B. 870
Mcguire, Reese 870
マクガイアー
McGuire, William 870
マグガイア
McGwire, Mark 870
マクガイヤー
McGuire, Benny 870
マクガヴァン
McGavin, George 868
McGovern, George Stanley 869
マクガヴィン
McGavin, Darren 868
マクガキン
McGuckin, John Anthony 870
マクカーター
McCarter, R.Harris G. 861
マクガーティ
McGarty, Craig 868
マクガーハン
McGahan, Anita Marie 867
マクガハン
McGahern, John 868
マクガバン
McGovern, Ann 869
McGovern, George Stanley 869
McGovern, Janett Blair Montgomery 869
Mcgovern, Matt 869
マクガビン
McGavin, Darren 868
マクガフィン
McGuffin, Michael 870
McGuffin, Peter 870
マクガレル
McGarrell, Lawrence Michael 868
マクガン
McGann, Eileen 868
マクギー
McGee, Greg 868
McGhee, Karen 868
マクギガン
McGuigan, Paul 870
マクギナス＝ケリー
McGuinness-Kelly, Tracy-Lee 870
マクギニス
McGinnis, Alan Loy 868
McGinnis, Patrick J. 868
McGinnis, Reginald 868
マクギネス
McGinness, Ryan 868
McGuinness, Brian 870
McGuinness, Deborah L. 870
McGuinness, Ed 870
McGuinness, Frank 870
McGuinness, Lisa 870
McGuinness, Martin 870
McGuinness, Michael 870
マクギャヴィン
McGavin, Darren 868
マクギャバン
McGavin, Barbara 868
マクギャレイ
McGarey, Gladys 868
マクキャンツ
McCants, Matt 860
マクギリヴレイ
MacGillivray, Deborah 868
マクギリブレー
MacGillivray, Alex 868
マクギル
McGill, Craig 868
Mcgill, Tyler 868
マクキーン
McKean, Alan 872
マクギン
McGinn, Noel F. 868
マクギンティ
Macginty, AJ. 868
McGinty, Alice B. 868
マクギンティー
Mac Ginty, Roger 868
マクグアーク
McGuirk, Terry 870
マクグーガン
McGugan, Will 870
マクグラス
McGrath, Alister E. 869
McGrath, Constance 869
McGrath, James 869
McGrath, Jinks 869
McGrath, Joanna Collicutt 869
McGrath, Judy 869
McGrath, Michael 869
McGrath, Michael E. 869
McGrath, Roland 869
マクグルー
McGrew, William Clement 869
マクグレイス
McGrath, Judy 869

マクグレイド
McGrade, Arthur Stephen 869
マククレラン
McClellan, Keith 862
マクグロー
McGraw, Laura 869
マクゲイリー
McGary, Mitch 868
マクゲーリィ
McGary, Norman 868
マクケルビー
McKelvie, Jamie 872
マクゴー
McGaw, Barry 868
マクゴニガル
McGonigal, David 868
McGonigal, Jane 868
McGonigal, Kelly 868
McGonigal, Mike 868
マクゴフ
McGough, Roger 869
マクコラム
McCollum, Eric E. 862
マクゴーリ
McGorry, Patrick D. 869
マクゴールドリック
McGoldrick, Monica 868
マクゴーワン
McGowan, Bill 869
マクザ
Makuza, Bernard 888
マクザンバ
Mackouzangba, Gaston 874
マークシー
Marqusee, Mike 905
マクシー
Maxey, Johnny 923
マクシェーン
McShane, Ian 879
McShane, Mark 879
McShane, Megan 879
マクシミー
Maximy, Hubert De 923
マクシムス
Maximus, Ongkili 923
マクシムチャック
Maksimchuck, Robert A. 888
マクシメンコ
Maksymenko, Alina 888
マクシモヴァ
Maksimova, Ekaterina 888
Maksimova, Natalia Aleksandrovna 888
マクシモヴィッチ
Maksimovic, Nikola 888
マクシモバ
Maksimova, Ekaterina 888
マクシモビッチ
Maksimovic, Ivana 888
マクシーモワ
Maksimova, Ekaterina 888
マクシモワ
Maksimova, Ekaterina 888
マクシャ
Makusha, Ngonidzashe 888
マクジャニ
Makhijani, Arjun 888
マクシャフリー
McShaffry, Mike 879
マグジャルチク
Magdziarczyk, Roman 882
マクシャン
McShann, Jay Hootie 879
マクジョーンズ
McJones, Paul 871
マクジルトン
McJilton, Charles E. 871
マークス
Maex, Dimitri 881
Malks, Dan 890
Marks, Alan 904
Marks, David 904
Marks, Edith S. 904
Marks, Evan R. 904
Marks, Howard 904
Marks, Jonathan 904
Marks, Lara 904
Marks, Paul Alan 904
Marks, R.Austin 904
Marks, Robert W. 904
Marks, Sean 904
Marks, Sen'Derrick 904
Marks, Suzanne 904
Marx, Anthony W. 913
Marx, Edward 913
Marx, Jonny 913
Marx, Morris L. 913
Marx, Robert F. 913
Marx, Steven 913
Merks, Ed 936
マクスウィーニー
McSweeney, Leah 879
マクスウェル
Maxwell 923
Maxwell, Cathy 923
Maxwell, Duane 923
Maxwell, Fredric Alan 923
Maxwell, Hamish 923
Maxwell, Jimmy 923
Maxwell, John C. 923
Maxwell, Lois 923
Maxwell, Mel 923
Maxwell, Willaim 923
マクスウェル - ハドソン
Maxwell-Hudson, Clare 923
マクスウド
Maqsood, Ruqaiyyah Waris 898
マクスキミング
McSkimming, Geoffrey 879
マクスティーン
McSteen, Kerstin 879
マクストフ
Maksutov, Altynbek 888
マクスフィールド
Maxfield, David 923
マクスミス
Smith, Jason McColm 1317
マクズラック
Maczulak, Anne Elizabeth 880
マクセル
Maksel, Krzysztof 888
マークソン
Markson, David 904
Markson, Larry 904
マーグソン
Margeson, Susan M. 901
マクタイ
McTighe, Jay 879
マクダイアミッド
MacDiarmid, Alan G. 865
マクダウェル
McDowell, Bart 866
McDowell, Gayle Laakmann 866
McDowell, John Henry 866
Mcdowell, Roger 866
マクダエニルズ
McDaniels, Josh 864
マクタガート
McTaggart, David 879
McTaggart, Lynne 879
マクダナー
McDonough, William 866
McDonough, Yona Zeldis 866
マクダニエル
McDaniel, Boyce 864
McDaniel, Lurlene 864
McDaniel, Mark A. 864
McDaniel, Mildred 864
McDaniel, Scott 864
McDaniel, Susan H. 864
Mcdaniel, Tony 864
McDaniel, Wahoo 864
マクダニエルズ
McDaniels, Eugene 864
McDaniels, K.J. 864
マグダニス
Magdanis, Panagiotis 882
マクダネル
McDonell, Nick 866
マクダフ
McDuff, Jack 866
マクダフィ
MacDuffie, John Paul 866
マクダフィー
McDuffie, Glenn 866
マクダーミッド
MacDiarmid, Hugh 865
マクダーミド
McDermid, Val 864
マクダーモット
McDermott, Andy 864
McDermott, Bridget 864
Mcdermott, Doug 864
McDermott, Gerald 864
McDermott, James Adelbert 864
McDermott, John 865
Mcdermott, Kevin 865
McDermott, Michael T. 865
McDermott, Paul 865
McDermott, Richard Arnold 865
Mcdermott, Sean 865
Mcdermott, Shane 865
マクーチ
Makuch, William M. 888
マクチャーグ
McChargue, Dennis 862
マクティア
McTeer, Janet 879
Mactier, Katie 879
マクディアミッド
McDiarmid, Ian 865
マクデヴィット
MacDevitt, Brian 865
McDevitt, Jack 865
マクデッド
McDaid, Jim 864
マクデード
McDade, Travis 864
マクドゥアルゲイ
Mocdouall-gaye, Neneh 959
マクドーウェル
McDowell, Michael 866
マクドウェル
McDowell, Josh 866
McDowell, Marta 866
マクドウォール
McDowall, Anne 866
マクドゥーガル
MacDougal, Bonnie 866
McDougall, Charles 866
McDougall, Christopher 866
MacDougall, Lee 866
McDougall, Lorna 866
McDougall, Richard 866
マクドゥガル
MacDougall, Kathy 866
MacDougall, Tom 866
マクドゥーガルド
Mcdougald, Bradley 866
マクドゥーグル
McDougle, Dexter 866
マクトゥーム
Almaktoum, Shaikh Ahmed 35
Al-maktoum, Maitha 888
マクドナー
McDonagh, John 865
McDonagh, Martin 865
McDonagh, Theresa A. 865
McDonough, William Joseph 866
マクドナルド
McDonald, Adrian 865
MacDonald, Amy 865
McDonald, Andrew 865
Macdonald, Andy 865
MacDonald, Angus W., Ⅲ 865
McDonald, Ann 865
McDonald, Anne 865
Macdonald, Arlyn J. 865
McDonald, Arthur B. 865
McDonald, Atholl 865
McDonald, Audra 865
McDonald, Bob 865
MacDonald, Brian 865
MacDonald, Bruno 865
McDonald, Christopher W. 865
Mcdonald, Clinton 865
McDonald, Colm 865
McDonald, Craig 865
McDonald, Daniel 865
Macdonald, David Whyte 865
Mcdonald, Deborah 865
McDonald, Dewey 865
McDonald, Dexter 865
McDonald, Dora Edith 865
McDonald, Duff 865
Macdonald, Fiona 865
MacDonald, Ginger 865
Macdonald, Glynn 865
McDonald, Gregory 865
Macdonald, Guy 865
Mac Donald, Heather 865
Macdonald, Helen 865
Macdonald, Helen Z. 865
Macdonald, Holly 865
Macdonald, Hugh 865
McDonald, Ian 865
McDonald, Jacquie 865

McDonald, James 865
Macdonald, James D. 865
McDonald, James Ian Hamilton 865
MacDonald, James M. 865
McDonald, John 865
MacDonald, John D. 865
Macdonald, Kelly 865
Macdonald, Kevin 865
McDonald, Kim 865
MacDonald, Kyle 865
MacDonald, Laurence 865
McDonald, Lawrence G. 865
McDonald, L.L. 865
McDonald, Lynn 865
MacDonald, Margaret Read 865
McDonald, Marie A. 866
McDonald, Mark 866
McDonald, Marlene 866
McDonald, Megan 866
Macdonald, Pam 866
MacDonald, Patricia 866
McDonald, Peter 866
MacDonald, Phil 866
MacDonald, Raymond A. R. 866
Macdonald, Richard 866
McDonald, Robert 866
McDonald, Robert A. 866
Macdonald, Roderick 866
McDonald, Roger B. 866
Macdonald, Rose 866
Macdonald, Steven C. 866
MacDonald, Suse 866
Mcdonald, T.J. 866
Mcdonald, Vance 866
MacDonald, William 866

マクドネル
McDonnell, Evelyn 866
McDonnell, Hector 866
McDonnell, Janet 866
McDonnell, Patrick 866

マクドネル・スミス
MacDonell Smith, Nancy 866

マクドノー
McDonough, Denis R. 866
Mcdonough, Ryan 866
McDonough, Yona Zeldis 866

マクドノフ
McDonough, Denis R. 866

マグドフ
Magdoff, Fred 882

マクドーマンド
McDormand, Frances 866

マクトム・ビン・ラシド・アル・マクトム
Maktoum bin Rashid al-Maktoum 888

マクトム・ビン・ラシド・マクトム
Maktoum bin Rashid al-Maktoum 888

マクナイト
McKnight, Jenna 874
McKnight, Rosalind A. 874
McKnight, Scot 874

マクナージル
McGonagill, Grady 868

マグナス
Magnus, Sharon Maxwell 883

マクナーズニー
McNerthney, Casey 878

マグナセン
Magnusen, Christy 883

マグナソン
Magnason, Andri 883
Magnuson, Christine 883

マクナット
McNutt, Jennifer Powell 878

マクナニー
McNerney, Jim 878

マクナブ
McNab, Andy 877
McNab, Chris 877
McNab, Tom 877
McNabb, Donovan 877

マクナマス
McManus, Brandon 876

マクナマラ
McNamara, Ashamarae 877
Macnamara, Ashlyn 877
McNamara, Denis Robert 877
McNamara, Heather 877
McNamara, Helen 877
McNamara, James O. 877
McNamara, Kenneth J. 877
McNamara, Margaret 877
Macnamara, Niall 877
McNamara, Robert S. 877
McNamara, Robert Strange 877
McNamara, Timothy Francis 877

マクナミー
McNamee, Graham 877
McNamee, Roger 877
McNamee, Sheila 877
McNamee, Thomas 877

マクナリー
McNally, Christie 877
McNally, Dave 877
McNally, David 877
McNally, Joe 877
McNally, Raymond T. 877
McNally, Robert Aquinas 877
McNary, Josh 877

マクナル
McNall, M.Chris Cadelinia 877

マクナルティ
MacNulty, W.Kirk 878

マグナン
Magnan, Morris A. 883

マクニー
Macnee, Carol Leslie 878
MacNee, Patrick 878

マクニコル
MacNicol, Peter 878
McNicoll, Colin I.R. 878

マクニック
Macknik, Stephen L. 874

マクニッシュ
McNish, Cliff 878
MacNish, Tracy 878

マクニフ
McNiff, Shaun 878

マグニフィコ
Magnifico, Damien 883

マクニーブン
McNiven, Steve 878

マクニーリ
McNealy, Scott Glenn 878

マクニーリー
McNealy, Scott Glenn 878
McNeely, Ian F. 878
McNeilly, Kevin 878
McNeilly, Michael A. 878

マクニーリィ
McNeely, Scott 878
McNeilly, Mark 878

マクニール
MacNeal, Susan Elia 877
McNeil, Beth 878
McNeil, David 878
Mcneil, Douglas 878
McNeil, Gil 878
Macneil, Ian 878
MacNeil, Ian 878
McNeil, John 878
McNeil, Legs 878
McNeil, Lyndon 878
MacNeil, Robert 878
McNeill, David 878
McNeill, John Robert 878
McNeill, Sandra 878
McNeill, William Hardy 878
McNeill, Wykeham 878

マグヌスソン
Magnusson, Gylfi 883

マグヌスドッティル
Magnúsdóttir, Sigrún 883

マグヌスン
Magnusson, Kris 883

マグヌセン
Magnussen, James 883

マグヌソン
Magnusson, Arni 883
Magnusson, Lars 883

マグヌッセン
Magnussen, James 883

マグヌッソン
Magnusson, Conny 883

マクネー
Mcnay, Stuart 877

マクネア
McNair, Barbara Joan 877
McNair, Brian 877
McNair, Paddy 877
Macnair, Patricia Ann 877
McNair, Steve 877
Macnair, Trisha 877

マクネアー
McNair, Sylvia 877

マクネリー
McNealy, Scott Glenn 878

マクネール
McNair, Brian 877

マグネロ
Magnello, Eileen 883

マクノート
McNaught, Jenny 877
McNaught, Jon 877
McNaught, Judith 877

マクノートン
McNaughton, Colin 877
MacNaughton, Ian 877
Macnaughton, Jane 877
McNaughton, Phoebe 877
MacNaughton, Robin 877
Macnaughton, Tina 877

マクハ
Makukha, Volodymyr 888

マクバ
Makuba, Aaron 888

マクハーグ
McHarg, Ian Lennox 870

マグバシ
Magvaši, Peter 883

マクパーソン
Mcpherson, Stephenie Ann 878

マクバード
MacBird, Bonnie 859

マクパートランド
McPartland, Marian 878

マクバーニー
McBurney, Simon 859
McBurnie, Oliver 859

マクビカー
McVicar, Jekka 879

マクピーク
Mcpeak, Holly 878

マクビッカー
Mcvicker, Helen 879

マクビーティ
McVety, Kenneth G. 879

マクビティ
McVittie, Rosaleen 879

マクヒュー
McHugh, Andrea 870
McHugh, Donald E. 870
McHugh, Rhonda 870

マクファイル
MacPhail, Lee 878

マクファーカー
MacFarquhar, Roderick 867

マクファーゼン
Mcfadzean, Elspeth 867

マクファーソン
MacPherson, Dougal 878
McPherson, Gary E. 878
McPherson, Inika 878
MacPherson, Malcolm 878
McPherson, Marion White 878
Mcpherson, Paige 878
McPherson, Stephanie Sammartino 878

マクファッデン
Mcfadden, Darren 867
Mcfadden, Kimario 867
Mcfadden, Leon 867

マクファディン
McFadyen, Cody 867

マクファーデン
McFadden, Daniel Little 867

マクファデン
McFadden, Daniel Little 867
McFadden, Johnjoe 867

マクファーラン
McFarlan, Bill 867

マクファーランド
McFarland, Alastair 867
McFarland, Gerald W. 867
McFarland, Jim 867
McFarland, John Robert 867
Mcfarland, Keith R. 867
McFarland, Lyn Rossiter 867
McFarland, Mike 867
Mcfarland, M.J. 867
Mcfarland, T.J. 867

マクファーリン
Mcferlin, Bobby 867
McFerrin, Samantha 867

マクファーリング
Mcfarling, Usha Lee 867
マクファーレイン
McFarlane, Judith M. 867
マクファーレン
Macfarlane, Alan 867
McFarlane, Alexander C. 867
Macfarlane, Alison 867
Macfarlane, Allison 867
Mcfarlane, Danny 867
Macfarlane, Eve 867
McFarlane, Fiona 867
Macfarlane, Ian 867
Macfarlane, Iris 867
McFarlane, Nigel 867
Macfarlane, Seth 867
マクフィー
McPhee, Isaac 878
MacPhee, John 878
McPhee, John 878
Mcphee, Pernell 878
マクフィーリー
McFeely, Stephen 867
マクフェイル
Macphail, Andy 878
McPhail, David M. 878
Mcphail, Michael 878
マクフェリン
McFerrin, Bobby 867
マグフォード
Mugford, Simon 986
マクブヤ
Makubuya, Khiddu 888
マクブライト
McBright, Henry F. 859
マクブライド
McBride, Christian 859
McBride, James 859
McBride, Jule 859
McBride, Karyl 859
McBride, Marc 859
McBride, Margret 859
McBride, Mary 859
McBride, Michael Joseph 859
McBride, Reo H. 859
MacBride, Stuart 859
McBride, Tre 859
Mcbryde, B.J. 859
マクブラットニィ
McBratney, Sam 859
マグフリ
Magufuli, John Pombe Joseph 883
マクブリーン
McBreen, Pete 859
マクブール
Maqboul, bin Ali bin Sultan 898
マクベイ
Mcvay, Sean 879
Mcveigh, Timothy 879
マクヘイル
MacHale, D.J. 870
McHale, Jean Vanessa 870
McHale, Kevin 870
マクベイン
McBain, Ed 859
McBain, Laura-Lynne 859
McBain, Laurie 859
マグヘンベ
Maghembe, Jumanne 882
マクホルム
McHolm, Angela E. 870
マクマキン
McMackin, Leila 876
マクマスター
McMaster, Juliet 876
マクマスターズ
McMasters, Eric 876
マクマートリー
McMurtry, John 877
McMurtry, Larry 877
マクマナーズ
McManners, Hugh 876
マクマナス
McManus, Freda 876
McManus, I.C. 876
McManus, James 876
McManus, Jamie 876
McManus, Patty 876
MacManus, Sean 876
Ross-mcmanus, Heather 1208
マクマナマン
McManaman, Callum 876
マクマニス
Mcmanis, Sherrick 876
Mcmanis, Wynton 876
マクマーホン
McMahon, David 876
マクマホン
McMahon, Ed 876
MacMahon, Kathleen 876
McMahon, Richard Alan 876
McMahon, Vince 876
マクマラン
McMullan, Jim 877
McMullan, Kate 877
マクマリー
McMurry, John 877
マクマーレイ
McMurray, Rick 877
マクマロウ
McMorrow, Des 877
マークマン
Markman, Arthur B. 903
Markman, Howard 903
Markman, Jon D. 903
マクマーン
McMahon, Barbara 876
Mcmahon, Ryan 876
McMahon, Sean 876
マクマン
Mcmann, Sara 876
マクミーキン
McMeekin, Gail 876
マクミュラン
McMullan, Kate 877
マクミラン
McMillan, Beverly 876
MacMillan, Ian C. 876
McMillan, John 876
MacMillan, Margaret 876
Mcmillan, Nate 876
McMillan, Ron 877
MacMillan, Terri 877
McMillan, Terry 877
Mcmillan, Trevor 877
McMillen, Alison 877
マクミリン
McMillin, Scott 877
マクミロン
Mcmillon, Doug 877
マクミン
McMinn, Derek 877
McMinn, Suzanne 877
マクメナミン
McMenamin, Steve 876
マクメネミー
McMenemy, Sarah 876
マクモニーグル
McMoneagle, Joseph 877
マクモリス
Mcmorris, Mark 877
マクモロー
McMorrough, Julia 877
マクユーイング
Mcewing, Joe 867
マグラア
McGrath, Patrick 869
マグラウィ
Maghlaoui, Mohamed 882
マグラウイ
Maghlaoui, Mohamed 882
マクラウド
McCloud, Andrea 862
McCloud, Kevin 862
MacLeod, Alexander D. 876
MacLeod, Alistair 876
McLeod, Alistair 876
MacLeod, Carla 876
MacLeod, Charlotte 876
Macleod, Donald 876
McLeod, Errol 876
MacLeod, G. 876
MacLeod, Glen 876
MacLeod, Ian R. 876
MacLeod, Jay 876
MacLeod, Jilly 876
McLeod, Judyth A. 876
MacLeod, Ken 876
マクラーガン
McLagan, Patricia A. 875
マクラガン
Maclagan, David 875
マクラーキン
McClurkin, Donnie 862
マクラクラン
McLachlan, Craig 874
MacLachlan, Emily 874
MacLachlan, James H. 874
MacLachlan, Patricia 874
McLachlin, Beverley 874
マクラグレン
McLaglen, Andrew V. 875
マクラケン
McCracken, Stanley Glenn 863
McCracken, Thomas 863
マグラス
McGrath, Alister E. 869
McGrath, Jack 869
マクラスター
McCluster, Dexter 862
マクラッケン
McCracken, Craig 863
McCracken, G.M. 863
McCracken, Grant 863
McCracken, Paul Winston 863
マクラッチ
McLatchie, Greg R. 875
マクラッチー
Mcclatchey, Caitlin 862
McClatchy, Steve 862
マクラーティ
MacLarty, Jay 875
McLarty, Ron 875
マクラナハン
McClanahan, Rue 862
McClannahan, Lynn E. 862
マグラビ
Al-maghrabi, Ahmed 882
El-maghraby, Ahmed Amin 882
マーグラフ
Margraff, Ruth 901
マクラーフリン
MacLaughlin, Don 875
マクラフリン
McLaughlin, Brett 875
McLaughlin, Chris 875
McLaughlin, John 875
McLaughlin, R.M. 875
McLaughlin, Thomas 875
マクラム
McCrum, Robert 864
McCrumb, Sharyn 864
Makram, Nabila 888
マクラルティー
McClaugherty, Charles 862
マクラーレン
McLaren, Anne 875
Mclaren, John 875
McLaren, John 875
Mclaren, Malcolm 875
McLarren, Steve 875
マクラレン
McLaren, Angus 875
マグラン
McGauran, Hugh 868
マクリ
Macri, Mauricio 879
マグリ
Magri, Mayara 883
マグリオ
Maglio, Paul P. 882
マグリシオ
Maglischo, Ernest W. 882
マクリーシュ
McLeish, Todd 875
マーグリス
Margulis, Lynn 902
マグリス
Magris, Claudio 883
マクリスタル
McChrystal, Stanley A. 862
マクリービー
McCreevy, Charlie 864
マクリーランド
McClelland, Susan 862
マクリーリ
McCleery, David 862
マクリーリー
McCreery, Crash 864
マクリーン
McCleen, Grace 862
MacLean, Alex S. 875
Maclean, Anna 875
Maclean, Brittany 875
MacLean, Charles 875
Maclean, Craig 875
Maclean, Dorothy 875
McLean, Ian 875
McLean, Jackie Lenwood 875
McLean, Jim 875
MacLean, Julianne 875
MacLean, Kerry Lee 875
McLean, Richard 875

Mclean, Robert J. 875
Maclean, Ronald 875
MacLean, Rory 875
MacLean, Sarah 875
Maclean, Siobhan 875
McLean, William F. 875
マクリン
Macklin, Jenny 874
Maclin, Jeremy 876
McLinn, Patricia 876
Mclynn, Frank 876
マクリントック
McClintock, Barbara 862
マグルー
McGrew, Anthony G. 869
マクルーア
Mcclure, Bob 862
McClure, Stefan 862
マクルアー
McClure, Vimala Schneider 862
マクルキン
McQuilkin, J. Robertson 879
マグルーダー
Mcgruder, Rodney 870
マクルーハン
McLuhan, Eric 876
マクルラス
McLlrath, Paul 876
マクルーン
McLoone, Margo 876
マークルンド
Marklund, Liza 903
マークレー
Marclay, Christian 900
マクレー
McClay, Todd 862
McCrae, Christina S. 863
McRae, Anne 879
McRae, Colin 879
Macrae, Janet A. 879
McRae, John 879
McRae, John R. 879
Mcrae, Jordan 879
McRae, Steven 879
McRae, Tony 879
マクレア
Maclear, Kyo 875
Mcrae, James 879
マクレアリー
McCreary, Elizabeth Kendall 864
マクレイ
McCray, Demetrius 864
Mccray, Kelcie 864
Mccray, Lerentee 864
Mccray, L.J. 864
Maclay, Charlotte 875
Mcrae, Kimberley 879
McRae, Steven 879
マグレイス
McGrath, Judy 869
McGrath, Rita Gunther 869
マクレイト
McCreight, Tim 864
マクレイニー
McRaney, David 879
マクレイノルズ
McReynolds, Louise 879
マクレイン
Mcclain, Antoine 862
McClain, Johnny 862
Mcclain, Robert 862
Mcclain, Terrell 862
McLain, Paula 875
McLaine, Lachlan 875
MacLaine, Shirley 875
マグレイン
McGrayne, Sharon Bertsch 869
マクレオッド
McLeod, John 876
マクレオド
McLeod, Norman 876
Mcleod, Omar 876
マクレガー
McGregor, Allan 869
McGregor, Ewan Gordon 869
MacGregor, Kinley 869
McGregor, Lana 869
McGregor, Lindsay 869
MacGregor, Neil 869
マグレガー
MacGregor, Alastàir 869
MacGregor, Anne 869
McGregor, James 869
Macgregor, Jerry 869
McGregor, Jon 869
McGregor, Keli S. 869
McGregor, Ken 869
MacGregor, Neil 869
McGregor, Richard 869
MacGregor, Rob 869
MacGregor, T.J. 869
MacGregor, Trish 869
マクレガン
McLagan, Ian 875
マグレス
Magoulès, Frédéric 883
マークレスク
Marculescu, Gail L. 900
マグレッタ
Magretta, Joan 883
マグレッリ
Magrelli, Valerio 883
マクレディ
McCreadie, Karen 864
MacCready, Paul 864
マグレディ
McGrady, Mike 869
McGrady, Tracy 869
マクレナン
McLennan, A.G. 875
Mclennan, Ivan 876
Maclennan, Rosannagh 876
マクレモア
McLemore, Ben 875
マクレラン
McClellan, Albert 862
McClellan, Barr 862
McClellan, Edwin 862
McClellan, Scott 862
Mcclellan, Sheldon 862
McClelland, Alison 862
Maclellan, Alec 875
McLellan, Anne 875
McLellan, Janet 875
McLellan, Todd 875
Pearson-mclellan, Sally 1091
マクレランド
McClelland, David C. 862
McClelland, Deke 862
McClelland, Robert 862
マクレリー
McCrery, Nigel 864
マクレーリン
McClellin, Shea 862
マクレーン
McClain, David 862
McClean, James 862
McLain, Paula 875
MacLaine, Shirley 875
McLane, Derek 875
McLane, Gerard D. 875
McLane, Kathryn J. 875
McLean, Alistair Murray 875
McLean, Andrew 875
Maclean, Dorothy 875
マクレンドン
McClendon, Jaques 862
Mcclendon, Lloyd 862
McClendon, Sarah 862
McLendon, Steve 875
マグロー
Mcgraw, *Dr.*Phil 869
McGraw, Gary 869
McGraw, James R. 869
McGraw, Jay 869
McGraw, Phillip C. 869
McGraw, Tim 869
McGraw, Tug 869
マグロアール
Magloire, Paul 882
マクロイ
McElroy, Ken 867
マグロイン
McGloin, Matt 868
マクロウ
McCraw, Thomas K. 864
McCullough, Colleen 864
Mucklow, Lacy 985
マグロウ
McGraw, Harold Whittlesey Ⅲ 869
McGraw, Peter 869
マクロスキー
McCloskey, Deirdre N. 862
McCloskey, Joanne Comi 862
McCroskey, James C. 864
マクロード
McLeod, Ian 876
Mcleod, Kembrew 876
Mcleod, Ken 876
Mcleod, Rodney 876
マクロバーツ
Mcroberts, Josh 879
Mcroberts, Paul 879
マクロビー
McRobbie, Linda Rodriguez 879
マクロフリン
Mcloughlin, Patrick 876
マクローリー
McClorey, Josh 862
Mccrory, Nicholas 864
McRorie, Gordon 879
マクローリン
McLaughlin, Emma 875
McLoughlin, John C. 876
マクローリン＝レンペニング
McLaughlin Renpenning, Kathie E. 875
マグロワール
Magloire, Paul 882
Magloire, René 882
マクローン
McClone, Melissa 862
マクロン
Macron, Emmanuel 879
マクワイア
McGwire, Mark 870
マグワイア
McGuire, Richard 870
McGwire, Mark 870
Maguire, Charles H. 883
Maguire, Darcy 883
Maguire, George 883
Maguire, Gregory 883
Maguire, Harry 883
Maguire, Kay 883
Maguire, Margo 883
Maguire, Nick 883
Maguire, Peter 883
Maguire, Tobey 883
Maguire, Toni 883
マグワイアー
Mcguire, Bill 870
Maguire, Charles H. 883
マグワイヤ
Corrigan-Maguire, Mairead 292
マクワーター
McWhirter, Cameron 880
McWhirter, Norris Dewar 880
マクワラ
Makwala, Isaac 888
マグーン
Magoon, Scott 883
マケイ
Makey, Vladimir V. 888
マーケイキス
Markakis, Nick 903
マゲイジョ
Magueijo, Joao 883
マケイド
McQuaid, Matilda 879
マケイブ
McCabe, J.Terrence 860
マケイン
McCain, Charles 860
McCain, Donald V. 860
McCain, John Sidney Ⅲ 860
McKain, Kelly 872
マーケーゼイ
Marchese, John 900
マーケッタ
Marchetta, Melina 900
マケナリー
McEnally, Stephen 867
McEnery, Tony 867
マケバ
Makeba, Miriam 887
マケベニュ
McEvenue, Kevin 867
マケボイ
Mcevoy, Cameron 867
マケミッシュ
McKemmish, Sue 872
マケラ
Mäkelä, Hannu 887
Makela, Kristiina 887
マケラヌメラ
Makela-nummela, Satu 887
マケリゴット
McElligott, Matthew 867
マーケル

Markel, Michelle 903
Markel, Rita J. 903
Markel, Susan Gale 903
マケルダウニー
McEldowney, John 867
マゲレ
Magele, Mauiliu Magele 882
マケレレ
Makelele, Claude 887
マーケン
Maken, Ajay 888
Marken, James 903
マゲンベ
Maghembe, Jumanne 882
マーコー
Markoe, Merrill 903
マーゴ
Margot, Manuel 901
マコーイ
McCoy, Judi 863
マコ・イワマツ
Mako Iwamatsu 888
マコ岩松
Mako Iwamatsu 888
マーコウ
Markoe, Glenn E. 903
マコウ
McCaw, Richie 862
マコウィアク
Mackowiak, Philip A. 874
マーコウィッツ
Markowitz, Harry Max 904
Markowitz, John C. 904
マコヴェイ
Macovei, Mihai 878
マコヴェツ
Makovecz, Imre 888
マコヴェッツ
Makovecz, Imre 888
マコウスキー
Makowsky, Lucas 888
マコーヴチック
Markovchick, Vincent J. 904
マーゴシス
Margosis, Aaron 901
マーコスキー
Merkoski, Jason 936
マコソ
Makosso, Anatole Colinet 888
マコックラン
McCaughrean, Geraldine 861
マゴッチ
Magocsi, Oscar 883
マコッリ
Makolli, Ibrahim 888
マコーティー
McCourty, Devin 863
McCourty, Jason 863
マーコーデス
Marcordes, Tyler 900
マーコード
Marquardt, Michael J. 905
マコート
McCourt, Frank 863
マゴナ
Magona, Sindiwe 883
マコナキー
Maconachie, Don 878
マコナヘイ
McConnaughey, Matthew 863
マコニ
Makoni, Simba 888
マゴニーグル
McGonigle, Chris 868
マコネ
Makone, Theresa 888
マゴネット
Magonet, Jonathan 883
マコーネル
Mcconnell, Daniel 863
McConnell, Mike 863
McConnell, Mitch 863
マコネル
McConnell, Mike 863
McConnell, Mitch 863
McConnell, Steve 863
マコネルーグ
McConneloug, Mary 863
マコノヒー
McConaughey, Matthew 862
McConnaughey, Matthew 863
マゴバーン
McGovern, Connor 869
マコビー
Maccoby, Michael 862
マコービイ
Maccoby, Hyam 862
マーコビッツ
Markowitz, Harry Max 904
マーコフ
Murkoff, Heidi Eisenberg 993
マコフ
Makhov, Bilyal 888
マコベイ
Macovei, Monica 878
マコベツ
Makovecz, Imre 888
マコーマック
McCormac, Pip 863
McCormack, Dennis K. 863
McCormack, Eric 863
McCormack, Gavan Patrick 863
McCormack, Kevin 863
McCormack, Mark Hume 863
McCormack, Moira 863
McCormack, Pete 863
MacCormack, Sabine 863
McCormack, Timothy L. H. 863
マコーミック
McCormick, Blaine 863
McCormick, Brian 863
McCormick, Carlo 863
McCormick, Christopher 863
McCormick, Elizabeth Wilde 863
MacCormick, John 863
McCormick, Malcolm 863
MacCormick, Neil 863
McCormick, Patricia 863
マコームズ
McCombs, Maxwell E. 862
マゴメドフ
Magomedov, Islam 883
Magomedov, Jamaladdin 883
マゴーラン
McGauran, Peter 868
マコーリ
Macaulay, Lawrence 859
マコーリー
McAuley, Gareth 859
マコーリアン
McCaughrean, Geraldine 861
マコーリィ
McCauley, Barbara 861
マコーリイ
McAuley, Paul J. 859
マーゴリス
Margolis, Char 901
Margolis, Jonathan 901
Margolis, Leslie 901
Margolis, Sue 901
マーゴリック
Margolick, David 901
マーゴリン
Margolin, Leslie 901
Margolin, Malcolm 901
Margolin, Phillip 901
マコーリン
McCaughrean, Geraldine 861
マコール
McCall, Dinah 860
McCool, William C. 863
Mackall, Dandi Daley 872
マコルガン
Mccolgan, Eilish 862
マコール・スミス
McCall Smith, Alexander 860
マコーレー
Macaulay, Lawrence 859
Macaulay, Thomas 859
マコーレイ
Macaulay, David A. 859
マコロリー
Mccorory, Francena 863
マコーワー
Makower, Josh 888
マゴーワン
McGowan, Anthony 869
McGowan, Kathleen 869
マゴワン
Mcgowan, Dustin 869
マゴーン
McGown, Jill 869
マゴン
Magone, Claire 883
マゴンゴ
Magongo, Charles 883
マコンビー
McCombie, Karen 862
マーサ
Murtha, John 995
マーサー
Mercer, Geoffrey 935
Mercer, Jeremy 935
Mercer, John 935
Mercer, Jordy 935
Mercer, Judy 935
Mercer, Michelle 935
Mercer, Sienna 935
Murcer, Bobby 992
マーザー
Merzer, Glen 937
マサ
Masa 913
Massa, Sergio 915
Maza, José 925
マザ
Maza 925
マザー
Mather, John Cromwell 918
Mather, Nancy 918
Mather, Tim 918
Mazarr, Michael J. 925
マサイ
Masai, Linet Chepkwemoi 913
Masai, Moses Ndiema 913
マザイ
Maathai, Wangari 858
マサイアス
Mathias, Peter 918
マサイディエ
M'saidie, Houmed 985
マザウィ
Mazawi, André Elias 925
マサ・カステジャノス
Maza Castellanos, Manuel 925
マ・サガプリヤ
Ma Sagarpriya 913
マサクワ
Massaquoi, Francois 915
Massaquoi, Roland 915
マサゲ
Massagué, Joan 915
マサーコイ
Mssaquoi, Jonathan 985
マサゴス
Masagos, Zulkifli 913
マサシ
Mathathi, Martin Irungu 917
マザーシル
Mothersill, Cydonie 981
マザーズ
Mathers, Petra 918
マザースキー
Mazursky, Paul 926
マサデ
Masaadeh, Ahmad 913
Masadeh, Daifallah Salem 913
マサト
Masato, Rika 913
マザネス
Masanès, Fabrice 913
マザネック
Masannek, Joachim 913
マザノーブル
Mazzanoble, Shelly 926
マサハリア
Masakhalia, Francis 913
マザヘリ
Mazaheri, Tahmasb 925
マザーラ
Mazara, Nomar 925
マサーリ
Masali, Luca 913
マサリ
Mazali, Gustavo 925
マザリ
Mazali, Gustavo 925
マーサリス
Marsalis, Wynton 906
マサール

マ

Massar, Hisseine 915
マザール
Mazar, Amihay 925
マザルト
Mazalto, Avi 925
マザレイ
Mazarei, Adam 925
マサロ
Masaro, Anastasia 913
マーサン
Marshan, Eddie 907
マーシー
Masi, Dale A. 914
マージ
Majd, Kam 887
Masi, Andrea 914
マシー
Massy, Kevin 916
マジ
Maj, Kisimba Ngoy 886
マーシア
Mercier, Patricia 936
マシア
Massiah, Joanne 916
マシアス
Macias, Patrick 871
マシアッセン
Mathiassen, Lars 918
マシアーニ
Masiani, Elisa 914
マジアーノ
Maggiano, David 882
マシアラス
Massialas, Alexander 916
マシウス
DeMatteis, Bob 340
マシウリス
Masiulis, Eligijus 914
Masiulis, Rokas 914
マジェイチュク
Madejczyk, Barbara 880
マシェケ
Masheke, Sylvain Maurice 914
マシェッテ
Machete, Rui 870
マジエッロ
Masiello, Andrea 914
マシエ・ミブイ
Mesie Mibuy, Ángel 938
マシエミブイ
Mesie Mibuy, Ángel 938
マシェラン
Masschelein, W. 915
マシエル
Maciel, Marco 871
マシェンベラ
Matchembera, Patrick Sulubika 917
マシオス
Mathios, Alan D. 918
マジガイヤ
Majgaiya, Baldev Sharma 887
マジキン
Masikin, Aleksey 914
マシシ
Masisi, Mokgweetsi 914
Masisi, Mokgweetsi Eric Keabetse 914
マシス
Mathis, Evan 918
Mathis, Jeff 918
Mathis, Robert 918
マジストリス
Magistris, Rosalba de 882
マジストレッティ
Magistretti, Pierre Julius 882
マシスン
Matheson, Richard 918
Mathison, Melissa 918
マシーセン
Matthiessen, Peter 921
マシソン
Matheson, Christie 918
マシチェワ
Masycheva, Maria 917
マジッチ
Majdic, Petra 887
マジッド
Majid, Nurcholis 887
Majid, Shahn 887
マシップ
Masip, Jordi 914
マジディ
Majidi, Majid 887
マシード
Macedo, Stephen 866
マジド
Majeed, bin Muhsin al-Alawi 887
al-Majid, Ali Hassan 887
Majid, bin Ali al-Nuaimi 887
Majid, Nurcholis 887
el-Majid, Reda Hafiz 887
マジドゥーブ
Majdoub, Hédi 887
マジドフ
Majidov, Mahammadrasul 887
マジドフブ
al-Majdhub, Mubarek Mohamed Ali 887
マジーナ
Masina, Adam 914
マシーニー
Matheny, Mike 917
マジーニ
Masini, Beatrice 914
マジニ
al-Mazini, Kamila Khamis 925
マーシニアック
Marciniak, Barbara 900
マシフィーロ
Masifilo, Matthew 914
マジブコ
Mazibuko, Solani Mirriam 925
マジブリ
al-Majbri, Fatthi 887
al-Majibri, Fatthi Abdulhamid 887
マシマ
Mashima, Ted Y. 914
Massima, Jean 916
マシミラ
Massimilla, Edna 916
マジメル
Magimel, Benoit 882
マシモフ
Masimov, Karim 914
Massimov, Karim 916
マシャ
Masha, Lawrence 914
マジャ
Maya, Mario 924
マシャイ
Mashaei, Esfandiar Rahim 914
マシャカダ
Mashakada, Tapiwa 914
マーシャーク
Marschark, Marc 906
マシャクベ
Mashagbeh, Awad 914
マーシャック
Marschark, Marc 906
マシャティレ
Mashatile, Paul 914
マシャード
Machado, Jean Jacques 870
Machardo, Mario 870
マシャド
Machado, Ana Maria 870
Machado, Nelson 870
マジャドレ
Majadele, Raleb 886
マジャノビッチ
Marjanovic, Boban 903
マシャベラ
Machavela, Esperança Alfred 870
マーシャム
Marsham, Liz 907
マジャリ
Majali, Amjad 887
Majali, Hussein al 887
Majali, Qaftan 887
Majali, Sahl 887
マジャリチ
Mad'ariČ, Marek 880
マジャリワ
Majaliwa, Majaliwa Kassim 887
マーシャル
Marchal, Benoit 899
Marschall, Christoph von 906
Marshall, Andrew G. 906
Marshall, Barry 906
Marshall, Brandon 906
Marshall, Byron 906
Marshall, Chester 906
Marshall, Chris 906
Marshall, Colin Marsh 906
Marshall, Dale 906
Marshall, David 906
Marshall, Donis 906
Marshall, Evan 906
Marshall, Frank 906
Marshall, Garry 906
Marshall, Hallie 906
Marshall, I.Howard 906
Marshall, I.N. 906
Marshall, Jalin 906
Marshall, Jason 906
Marshall, Jayne E. 907
Marshall, Jim 907
Marshall, John C. 907
Marshall, Kathleen 907
Marshall, Keith 907
Marshall, Liam E. 907
Marshall, Lisa B. 907
Marshall, Mary 907
Marshall, Megan 907
Marshall, Michael 907
Marshall, Nick 907
Marshall, Paula 907
Marshall, Paul A. 907
Marshall, P.David 907
Marshall, Penny 907
Marshall, Perry S. 907
Marshall, Richard M. 907
Marshall, Rob 907
Marshall, Robert 907
Marshall, Rommell 907
Marshall, Ruth Ann 907
Marshall, Samantha 907
Marshall, Sarah C. 907
Marshall, Savannah 907
Marshall, Stephanie Pace 907
Marshall, Susan 907
Marshall, Tim 907
Marshall, William L. 907
マシャル
Mashaal, Khaled 914
Mashaal, Maurice 914
マジャル
Magyar, Bálint 883
マシャルカ
Masharkha, Mohamad Zuheir 914
マシャール・テニー
Machar Teny, Riak 870
マーシャン
Marchant, Katy 900
マーシュ
Marsh, Ann C. 906
Marsh, Cassius 906
Marsh, David 906
Marsh, Dilleen 906
Marsh, Ed.W. 906
Marsh, Geoffrey D. 906
Marsh, George P. 906
Marsh, Graham 906
Marsh, Henry 906
Marsh, Jhonasan 906
Marsh, Jonathan 906
Marsh, June 906
Marsh, Katherine 906
Marsh, Nicola 906
Marsh, Paul R. 906
Marsh, Peter 906
Marsh, Stanley 906
マシュ
Massu, Jacques 916
マシュー
Massu, Jacques 916
Mathieu, Christine 918
Mathieu, Michael 918
Mathieu, Tyrann 918
Matthew, Amenta 920
Matthew, Catriona 920
Matthew, Donald 920
Matthew, Neil 920
Matthew, Norman 920
Matthew, Sidney L. 920
マジュ
Maj, Kisimba Ngoy 886
マシュイカ
Maciuika, John V. 871
マシュウ
Matthews, Alex 920
マシュウズ
Mathews, Andrew 918
Matthews, Caitlín 920
Matthews, John 920
マシュキン
Mashkin, Oleg 914
マシュース
Matthews, Rupert 920

マシューズ
Mathews, Christopher K. 918
Mathews, Craig 918
Mathews, Derrick 918
Mathews, Eddie 918
Mathews, Francine 918
Mathews, Gordon 918
Mathews, Harry 918
Mathews, Jay 918
Mathews, Jessica Tuchman 918
Mathews, Jonathan 918
Mathews, Mitch 918
Mathews, Ricardo 918
Mathews, Robin 918
Mathews, Ryan 918
Mathews, Temple 918
Matthews, Andrew 920
Matthews, Arlene Modica 920
Matthews, Bonnie 920
Matthews, Caitlín 920
Matthews, Chris 920
Matthews, Christine 920
Matthews, Claire 920
Matthews, Clay 920
Matthews, Cliff 920
Matthews, David 920
Matthews, Delia 920
Matthews, Derek 920
Matthews, D.H. 920
Matthews, Elizabeth 920
Matthews, Francis 920
Matthews, Gerald 920
Matthews, Gordon 920
Matthews, Jake 920
Matthews, Jana B. 920
Matthews, Jason 920
Matthews, Jeff 920
Matthews, J.Jennifer 920
Matthews, John 920
Matthews, John A. 920
Matthews, John Frederick 920
Matthews, Jordan 920
Matthews, Julie 920
Matthews, Kathy 920
Matthews, L.S. 920
Matthews, Mike 920
Matthews, Owen 920
Matthews, Patrick 920
Matthews, Penny 920
Matthews, Rishard 920
Matthews, Robert 920
Matthews, Rupert 920
Matthews, Sadie 920
Matthews, Stephen 921
Matthews, Wesley 921
マジュダラーニ
Majdalani, Ahmad 887
マシュチュク
Maszczyk, Lukasz 917
マシュナー
Maschner, Herbert D. G. 914
マシュヌク
Mashnouq, Mohammad 914
Mashnouq, Nuhad 914
マジューブ
Mahjoub, Hamdi Ould 884
マジュプリア
Majupuria, Trilok Chandra 887
マシュフール
Mashhour, Houriah Ahmed 914
Mashhur, Mustafa 914
マシュラー
Maschler, Tom 914
マシュラケング
Mahlakeng, Thulo 884
マシュラングヌカビンデ
Mahlangu-nkabinde, Gwen 884
マジュレル
Masurel, Claire 917
マシュロボ
Mahlobo, David 884
マシュワマ
Mashwama, Jabulile 914
マジュンダ
Majumdar, Basanti 887
マジョ・ディベジョ
Mayo di Bello, Miguel 925
マジョーニ
Maggioni, Romeo 882
マジョブ
Mahjoub, Javad 884
マジョラル
Mayoral, Borja 925
マジョール
Major, Fouad.G. 887
マジョルガ・カスタニェダ
Mayorga Castañeda, Francisco Javier 925
マジョル・ボウチョン
Mayol Bouchon, Luis 925
マジョロ
Majoro, Moeketsi 887
マーシラス
Mercilus, Whitney 936
マーシリイ
Marsilii, Bill 907
マシリンギ
Masilingi, Wilson 914
マジル
Mahdzir, Khalid 884
マシン
Masisi, Mokgweetsi 914
マシンゲ
Massingue, Venâncio 916
マース
Maas, Heiko 858
Maas, James B. 858
Maas, Meridean L. 858
Maas, Peter 858
Maas, Sarah J. 858
Maas, Winy 858
Maes, Francis 881
Marrs, Jim 906
Marz, Tyler 913
マーズ
Marrs, Jason 906
Marrs, Texe W. 906
Mars, Bruno 906
Mars, Forrest, Jr. 906
Mars, Jacqueline 906
Mars, John 906
Mars, Mick 906
Marz, Bruno 913
Marz, Marcos 913
Marz, Nathan 913
マス
Mas, Nicolas 913
Mas, Sophie 913
Mass, Wendy 915
Massu, Nicolas 916
Muss, David 997
マズーア
Masur, Kurt 916
マズア
Masur, Kurt 916
マスアク
Masuaku, Arthur 916
マスカー
Musker, John 996
マスカエフ
Maskaev, Oleg 914
マスカラ
Muscala, Mike 996
マスカレナス
Mascarenhas, Fio 913
マスカレル
Mascarell, Omar 913
マスカレンハス
Mascarenhas, Fio 913
マスカワ
Maskawa, Toshihide 914
マスキノ
Maschino, Maurice T. 914
マスキン
Maskin, Eric S. 914
マスク
Masuk, Wuttichai 916
Masuku, Themba 916
Musk, Elon 996
マスクビナー
Moskvina, Marina 980
マスグボジ
Massougboji, Marina 916
マスグレイヴス
Musgraves, Kacey 996
マスグレイブ
Musgrave, Bill 996
Musgrave, James 996
Musgrave, Richard Abel 996
マスグレーヴ
Musgrave, Richard Abel 996
マスグローブ
Musgrove, Joe 996
マスケビッチ
Maskevich, Sergei A. 914
マスケラーノ
Mascherano, Javier 913
マスケル
Maskell, Hazel 914
マスコ
Masco, Joseph 914
マスコトーバ
Masgutova, Svetlana 914
マスコリーノ
Muscolino, Joseph E. 996
マスサ
Masutha, Michael 917
マスジドジャメイ
Masjid Jamei, Ahmad 914
マーズーズ
Maâzouz, Abdellatif 858
マスター
Master, Farokh J. 916
Master, Irfan 916
マスター "K"
Master K 916
マスターズ
Masters, Alexander 916
Masters, Blake 916
Masters, Christopher 916
Masters, Marshall 916
Masters, Priscilla 916
Masters, Tom 916
Masters, Willam A. 916
Masters, William Howell 916
マスターソン
Masterson, James F. 916
Masterson, Julie J. 916
Masterson, Michael 916
マスタートン
Masterton, Graham 916
マスターマン
Masterman, Becky 916
Masterman, Len 916
マスタロフ
Masteroff, Joe 916
マスチェラーノ
Mascherano, Javier 913
マスーディ
Masodi, Omara Khan 914
マスディ
Masodi, Omara Khan 914
Masudi, Ngele 916
マースティン
Marsten, Richard 907
マステパノフ
Mastepanov, Aleksei Mikhailovich 916
マステラ
Mastella, Clemente 916
マースデン
Marsden, Carolyn 906
Marsden, David 906
Marsden, Jane Doughty 906
Marsden, Simon 906
マーズデン
Marsden, John 906
マステンブルーク
Mastenbroek, Rie 916
マスード
Masood, Ahmad Shah 915
Massoud, Ahmad Shah 916
Massoud, Ahmad Zia 916
マストロ
Mastro, Michael 916
Mastro, Robin 916
マストローコラ
Mastrocola, Paola 916
マストロマリーノ
Mastromarino, Diane 916
マストロヤンニ
Mastroianni, Marcello 916
マストロロレンゾ
Mastrolorenzo, Hugo 916
マーストン
Marston, J.D. 907
Marston, Joshua 907
マスナゲッティ
Masnaghetti, Alessandro 914
マズノフ
Mazunov, Dmitry 926
マスハドフ
Maskhadov, Aslan 914
マスビェア
Madsbjerg, Christian 881
マスーム
Masoum, Fuad 915
マスラック
Maslach, Christina 914
マーズラフ

Marzluff, John M. 913
マスラロワ
Maslarova, Emilia 914
マスランスキー
Maslansky, Michael 914
マスリ
al-Masri, Maher 915
al-Masri, Majda 915
al-Masri, Mutahar Rashad 915
Masri, Walid al 915
マスリー
Masry, Edward L. 915
マズリッシュ
Mazlish, Elaine 925
マスリベツ
Maslivets, Olha 914
マスリュコフ
Maslyukov, Yurii Dmitrievich 914
マスリン
Maslin, Mark 914
マズルイ
Mazrui, Ali A. 926
マズルケビッチ
Mazurkiewicz, Ladislao 926
マスレ
Masseret, Jean-Pierre 915
マスレエフ
Masleev, Dmitry 914
マスレンニコフ
Maslennikov, Vladimir 914
マスロウ
Maslow, Katy 914
マスロウスキー
Maslowski, Peter 914
マズロナク
Mazuronak, Volha 926
マズローニス
Mazuronis, Valentinas 926
マズロバ
Mazurova, Nikola 926
マスロフスカ
Maslovska, Vanda 914
マズロン
Maslon, Laurence 914
マスン
Madsen, Birgit 881
マズンガ
Mazunga, Kimbembe 926
マズング
Mazoungou, Sylvie Annick 926
マスンディ
Massoundi, Bahiat 916
マセ
Macé, François 866
Macé, François Yves Robert 866
Mace, Lilou 866
Maze, Michael 925
マゼ
Maze, Tina 925
マセイ
Massey, Jeanne 916
Masthay, Tim 916
マセイラ・デ・ローゼン
Maceira de Rosen, Sagra 867
マセオ・クルス
Maceo Cruz, Damar 867
マセコ
Maseko, Grace Zinenani 914
マゼッテ
Mazette, Jacquesson 925
マセッティ
Mascetti, Daniela 913
Mazzetti, Pilar 926
マゼッティ
Mazzetti, Annamaria 926
Mazzetti, Mark 926
Mazzetti, Riccardo 926
マセッティ・ソレル
Mazzetti Soler, Pilar 926
マゼット
Mazette, Jacquesson 925
マセード
Macedo, Miguel 866
Macedo, Paulo 866
マセド・デラコンチャ
Macedo de la Concha, Rafael Marcial 866
マセドニオ
Macedonio, Mike 867
マセニー
Matheny, Samuel C. 917
マセボ
Masebo, Sylvia 914
マーセラ
Marsella, Anthony J. 906
マゼラ
Mazzella, Neil 926
マーセラス
Marcellas, Diana 899
マセリバネ
'Maseribane, Thesele 914
マーセル
Marcel, Kelly 899
Mursell, Gordon 995
マーゼル
Maazel, Lorin 858
マゼール
Maazel, Lorin 858
マゼル
Maazel, Lorin 858
Mazel, Judy 925
マセロ
Masello, David 914
Masello, Robert 914
マーセン
Maassen, Norbert 858
マセン
Madsen, Mark Overgaard 881
マソー
Massaud, Jean-Marie 915
マゾヴィエツキ
Mazowiecki, Tadeusz 926
マソウミ
Masoumi, Fardin 915
マゾーニー
Mazzone, Leo 926
マゾネット
Mathonet, Pierre-Yves 918
マゾビエツキ
Mazowiecki, Tadeusz 926
マソプスト
Masopust, Josef 915
マソル
Massol, Vincent 916
マゾレラ
Madzorera, Henry 881
マゾワー
Mazower, Mark 926
マゾワイエ
Mazoyer, Claire 926
マーソン
Marson, Jacqui 907
Merson, Sarah 937
マソン
Masson, Caroline 916
マタ
Mata, Gustavo 917
Mata, Juan 917
Mata, Victoria 917
Mata Perez, Andres Eduardo 917
Matha, Lambert 917
マータイ
Maathai, Wangari 858
Maathai, Wanjira 858
マタイ
Mathai, Kimberly 917
マダイ
Madaj, Natalia 880
マタイス
Mataix, Anselmo 917
マタイトガ
Mataitoga, Isikeli Uluinairai 917
マタイラブラ
Matairavula, Irami 917
マーダウィ
el-Maadawy, Wael 857
マタヴェシ
Matavesi, Josh 917
マダウ・ディアツ
Madau Diaz, Antonello 880
マータ王女
Princess Märtha 908
マタケビッチ
Matakevich, Tyler 917
マタス
Matas, Carol 917
Matas, David 917
マタス・イ・パロウ
Matas i Palou, Jaume 917
マタスケレケレ
Mataskelekele, Kalkot 917
マタソン
Matterson, Stephen 920
マタタ・ポニョ・マポン
Matata Ponyo Mapon, Augustin 917
マダックス
Maddux, Dave 880
Maddux, Greg 880
Maddux, Mike 880
マタディゴ
Matadigo, Masi 917
マタディ・ネンガ・ムガマンダ
Matadi Nenga Ngamanda, Jeannot 917
マダドハ
Madadha, Maher 880
マダニ
Madani, Iyad bin Ameen 880
Medany, Aya 928
マターニュ
Matagne, Patrick 917
マタネ
Matane, Paulias 917
マタノビッチ
Matanović, Slavko 917
マタバ
Mathaba, Kimetso 917
マタ・フィゲロア
Mata Figueroa, Carlos 917
マダヘ
Madahe, Abd-al-Qadir Muhammad Abdulle 880
マタベーレ
Matabele, Virgilia 917
マタベレ
Matabele, Virgilia 917
マダミノフ
Madaminov, Voris 880
マタヨシ
Matayoshi, Mary Y. 917
マタラタ
Mattalata, Andi 919
マタール
Matar, Hisham 917
マータ・ルイーセ
Princess Märtha 908
マ・ダルマ・ジョティ
Ma Dharm Jyoti 880
マタレーズ
Matarese, Laura E. 917
マタレラ
Mattarella, Sergio 919
マタワル
Matawalu, Nikola 917
マターン
Mattern, Frank 920
Mattern, Thomas 920
マダン
Madan, Veaceslav 880
マタングル
Matungulu, Helva 921
マタンボ
Matambo, Kenneth 917
Matambo, Ontefetse Kenneth 917
マーチ
March, Ashley 899
March, Ava 899
March, Catherine 899
March, James G. 899
March, Jason 899
March, Jerry 899
March, John S. 899
Murch, Walter 993
マーチー
Murchie, David Neil 993
マチ
Machi, Jean 870
マチウ＝リーデル
Mathieu-Riedel, Elisabeth 918
マチェク
Macek, Bostjan 867
マチェズニー
McChesney, Chris 862
マチエヨフスキー
Maciejowski, Jan Marian 871
マチェレウィチ
Macierewicz, Antoni 871
マチカオ・バンコビッチ
Machicao Bankovic, Marko Marcelo 870
マチス
Machis, Darwin 870
Matisse, M. 919
マチソン

マ

Mattison, Chris 921
マチニック
Muchnick, Marc 985
マチネア
Machinea, José 870
マチャケラ
Machakela, Clement 870
マチャゼウスキー
Matyjaszewski, Krzysztof 921
マチャード
Machado, Angel 870
マチャド
Machado, Adam 870
Machado, Dixon 870
Machado, Manny 870
マチャド・カナレス
Machado Canales, María Antonieta 870
マチャド・ベントゥラ
Machado Ventura, José Ramón 870
マチャリア
Macharia, James 870
マチャレロ
Maciariello, Joseph A. 871
マチャワリアニ
Machavariani, Mikheil 870
マーチャント
Marchant, Jo 900
Marchant, Sally 900
Merchant, Dennis 935
Merchant, Ismail 935
マチュー
Mathieu, Bertrand 918
Mathieu, Caroline 918
Mathieu, Georges Victor Adolphe 918
Mathieu, Jeremy 918
Mathieu, Marc-Antoine 918
Mathieu, Nonie 918
Mathieu, Paul-Henri 918
Mathieu, Philippe 918
マチュウ
Mathieu, Georges Victor Adolphe 918
マチュシェフスキー
Matyushevsky, Vasily S. 921
マチュラット
Matschullat, Dale 919
マチュンワ
Machungwa, Peter 871
マーチ・リラード
March-lillard, Justin 900
マーチン
Martin, Bill 908
Martin, Bob 908
Martin, Chuck 908
Martin, Curly 908
Martin, Deborah L. 908
Martin, Emily 908
Martin, George Henry 908
Martin, Iain 909
Martin, James 909
Martin, John 909
Martin, Katherine 909
Martin, Lawrence 909
Martin, Marcos 909
Martin, Michael 909
Martín, Raul 909
Martin, Richard M. 910
Martin, Robert C. 910
Martin, Russell 910
Martin, Ruth 910
Martin, Sieglinde 910
Martin, Stephen 910
Martin, Steve 910
Martin, Terry Dean 910
Martin, William F. 910
Martyn, John 912
マーツ
Martz, Paul 912
Mertz, C.J. 937
マーツァル
Mácal, Zdenek 859
マーツィ
Marzi, Christoph 913
マツイ
Matsui, Robert T. 919
Matsui, Saburo 919
マツィコ
Matsiko, Kabakumba 919
マツィリア
Marzillier, John S. 913
マツウラミューラー
Matsuura Mueller, Kumiko 919
マツェイコ
Macejko, Josef 867
マツェイチュク
Matseichuk, Oleg 919
マツーエフ
Matsuev, Denis 919
マツェペカサブリ
Matsepe-casaburri, Ivy 919
マツェラ
Mazzella, Luigi 926
マツォウカス
Matsoukas, William 919
マッカイ
McKaie, Andy 871
Mckay, Hilary 872
Mackay, Paul 872
Mackay, Roger 872
マッカウ
MacCaw, Alex 861
マッガウ
McGaugh, James L. 868
マッガヴァン
McGovern, George Stanley 869
マッカーサー
MacArthur, Brian 859
McArthur, Fiona 859
MacArthur, Hugh 859
McArthur, James 859
MacArthur, John F., Jr. 859
McArthur, Neil C. 859
McArthur, Sarah 859
McArthur, Tomas Burns 859
McArthur, Victoria 859
マッカーシー
McCarthy, Alex 861
Mccarthy, Brandon 861
McCarthy, Cameron 861
McCarthy, Clifford Thomas 861
McCarthy, Cormac 861
McCarthy, Courtney Watson 861
McCarthy, Dennis 861
McCarthy, Erin 861
McCarthy, Eugene Joseph 861
McCarthy, Gregory 861
McCarthy, Helen 861
McCarthy, James 861
McCarthy, Jenny 861
McCarthy, Joan 861
McCarthy, John 861
McCarthy, John Philip 861
McCarthy, Kevin 861
Mccarthy, Kevin 861
McCarthy, Kevin W. 861
McCarthy, Melissa 861
McCarthy, Michelle 861
McCarthy, Nobu 861
McCarthy, Pat 861
McCarthy, Patrick D. 861
McCarthy, Susan 861
McCarthy, Susanne 861
McCarthy, Thomas R. 861
McCarthy, Tim 861
McCarthy, Tom 861
McCarthy, Trevor 861
マッカージー
Mukherjee, Paul 988
マッカーシイ
McCarthy, Wil 861
マッカスキー
McCaskey, Michael B. 861
マッカッチェン
Mccutchen, Andrew 864
マッカーティ
McCarty, Bill 861
McCarty, James Allen 861
McCarty, Lambert Blanchard 861
McCarty, Marilu Hurt 861
McCarty, Monica 861
McCarty, Nick 861
McCarty, Peter 861
マッカーティー
McCarty, Peter 861
Mccarty, Walter 861
マッカドゥー
Michael McAdoo, James 942
マッカートニー
Macartney, Scott 859
McCartney, Ian 861
McCartney, Jennifer 861
McCartney, Linda 861
McCartney, Paul 861
McCartney, Sarah 861
McCartney, Scott 861
McCartney, Stella 861
マッカードル
McArdle, Neil 859
マッカニン
Mackanin, Pete 872
マッカヒル
McCahill, Leonard J. 860
マッカビン
McCubbin, Lisa 864
マッカラ
McCullough, Colleen 864
McCullough, Dennis M. 864
マッカラー
McCullough, Chris 864
McCullough, Colleen 864
マッカラーズ
McCullers, Lance 864
マッカラム
McCallum, David 860
McCallum, Graham Leslie 860
Mccallum, John 860
McCallum, Q.Ethan 860
Mccallum, Ray 860
McCallum, William Gordon 860
McCollum, C.J. 862
マッカラン
McClung, Gordon W. 862
McCullin, Don 864
マッカーリ
McQuarrie, Donald Allan 879
マッカーリー
McCurley, T.Mark 864
マッカリー
McCully, Emily Arnold 864
McCurry, Steve 864
McCurry, Susan M. 864
マッカリース
McAleese, Mary Patricia 859
マッカルマン
McCalman, Ben 860
マッカロー
McCullough, John 864
McCullough, Keith 864
McCullough, Leigh 864
マッカローネ
Maccarone, Massimo 860
マッカーン
McKern, Leo 873
マッカン
McCann, Jesse Leon 860
McCann, Philip 860
マッキ
Macki, Ahmad bin Abdul-Nabi 874
マッキー
Mckay, Dave 872
McKee, Annie 872
McKee, David 872
McKee, Elsie Anne 872
McKee, James Robert 872
McKee, John 872
McKee, Kathryn 872
McKee, Laurel 872
McKee, Lucky 872
McKee, Robert 872
McKee, Tim 872
McKee, Trudy 872
Mackey, John 873
Mackey, Nathaniel 873
Mackey, Steven 874
McKie, Cecil 874
McKie, Robin 874
Mackie, Vera C. 874
Macky, Ian 874
Macky, Sarah 874
Makie, Vivien 888
マッギ
McGee, Nikita 868
マッギー
Mcgee, Brad 868
McGee, Garry 868
McGee, Matt 868
McGee, W.J. 868
マッキア
Macchia, Maria 862
マッキース
McKeith, Gillian 872
マッキナリー
McInally, Stuart 871
マッキニー
McKinney, Benardrick 874
McKinney, Cynthia 874
McKinney, Phil 874
マッギニス

McGinnis, Robert E. 868
マッキネス
McInnes, Angus 871
McInnes, Mike 871
McInnes, Stuart 871
マッキノン
MacKinnon, Amy 874
MacKinnon, Catharine A. 874
Mckinnon, Jeremiah 874
Mckinnon, Jerick 874
Mackinnon, Mairi 874
MacKinnon, Pam 874
MacKinnon, Roderick 874
マッキーバー
McKeever, Brian 872
McKeever, Ed 872
マッキーハン
McKeehan, Valerie 872
マッキベン
McKibben, Bill 874
マッキム
McKim, Donald K. 874
マッキャリー
McCarry, Charles 861
マッキャロン
McCarron, Anthony 861
マッキャン
McCann, A.L. 860
McCann, Brian 860
McCann, Colum 860
McCann, Ian 860
McCann, Jim 860
McCann, Joseph T. 860
McCann, Renetta 860
McCann, Robert M. 860
マッギャン
McGann, Jerome 868
McGann, Oisín 868
マッキャント
McCants, Glynis 860
マッキャンリーズ
McCanlies, Tim 860
マッキューアン
McEwan, Ian 867
マッキュアン
McEwan, Ian 867
マッキューン
McCune, Grant 864
McCune, Lorraine 864
マッキラン
McQuillan, Mary 879
マッギル
McGill, Keith 868
McGill, T.Y. 868
マッキルヴァニー
McIlvanney, William 871
マッキルウェーン
McIlwain, John 871
マッギルヴレイ
McGilvray, James Alasdair 868
マッキルバニー
McIlvanney, William 871
マッキルロイ
McIlroy, Richard 871
マッキロイ
Mcilroy, Rory 871
マッキロップ
MacKillop, James 874
マッキーン
MacEoin, Beth 867
McKean, Dave 872
McKean, Sylvia C. 872
McKean, Thomas A. 872
McKeen, Claudia 872
Macqueen, James G. 879
マッキン
Machin, David 870
Mackin, J.C. 874
Mackin, Mary Ann 874
マッギン
McGinn, Anne Platt 868
McGinn, Colin 868
McGinn, Richard A. 868
マツキン
Matzkin, Jorge 921
マッキンジー
McKinzie, Clinton 874
マッキンストリー
McKinstry, Nancy 874
マッキンタイア
MacIntyre, Alasdair 871
McIntyre, Anne 871
MacIntyre, Peter 871
マッキンタイアー
MacIntyre, Alasdair 871
Macintyre, Ben 871
マッキンタイヤ
McIntyre, Sarah 871
マッキンタイヤー
MacIntyre, Andrew 871
Mcintyre, John Collin 871
マッギンティ
McGinty, Sarah Myers 868
マッキントーシュ
Mackintosh, Cameron Anthony 874
マッキントッシュ
McIntosh, Christopher 871
McIntosh, D.J. 871
McIntosh, Gary L. 871
McIntosh, Jane 871
Mcintosh, Stuart 871
Mcintosh, Toga 871
Mackintosh, Cameron Anthony 874
Mackintosh, Michelle 874
McKintosh, Peter 874
Mclntosh, John 876
マッキンネル
McKinnell, Hank 874
McKinnell, Henry A., Jr. 874
マッキンリ
McKinley, Michael P. 874
マッキンリー
McKinlay, Deborah 874
McKinlay, Jenn 874
McKinley, Deborah 874
マッキンリイ
Mckinley, Robin 874
マッキンレー
MacKinlay, Elizabeth 874
マック
Mac, Bernie 858
Mack, Alex 871
Mack, Burton L. 871
Mack, Carol K. 871
Mack, David 871
Mack, Donny 871
Mack, Jeff 871
Mack, John J. 871
Mack, Khalil 871
Mack, Lorrie 871
Mack, Noelle 871
Mack, Phil 871
Mack, Ryan 871
Mack, Shelvin 871
Mack, T. 871
Mack, Theresa B. 871
Mack, Timothy 871
Mack, Wayne A. 871
Mak, Alan 887
Mak, Cheung Ping 887
Mak, Geert 887
Mak, James 887
Mak, Juno 887
Mauck, Joe 921
マックアイザック
MacIsaac, Bruce 871
マックアリスター
McAllister, Hester 859
マックィラン
McQuillan, Martin 879
マックィーン
McQeen, Alexander 878
McQueen, Glenn 879
McQueen, Steve 879
マックィン
McQuinn, Anna 879
McQuinn, Colm 879
マックイーン
McQeen, Alexander 878
McQueen, Barbara 879
McQueen, Brian 879
McQueen, Craig 879
McQueen, Glenn 879
Mcqueen, Mike 879
McQueen, Sam 879
McQueen, Steve 879
マックウィリアム
McWilliam, Rohan 880
マックウィリアムズ
McWilliams, Nancy 880
マックウェイ・ジョーンズ
Mackway-Jones, Kevin 874
マックウェイド
McQuade, Pamela 878
マックエルマリー
McElmurry, Jill 867
マックエルロイ
McElroy, Paul 867
マックォーリ
McQuarrie, Donald Allan 879
マックガイア
McGuire, Christine 870
マックガーク
McGuirk, Leslie 870
マックギネス
McGuinness, Mary C. 870
マックキャファティ
McCafferty, Catherine 860
マックギャレイ
McGarey, Gladys 868
McGarey, William A. 868
マックギル＝キャラハン
MacGill-Callahan, Sheila 868
マックギルブレイ
McGilvray, Jill 868
マッククライスター
McClister, M.T. 862
マッククラウド
McCloud, Andrea 862
マックグラース
McGrath, Tom 869
マックグレイス
McGrath, Judy 869
マック＝グレゴル
Mac-Gregor, Eduardo Ferrer 869
マックグロウ
McGraw, Tim 869
マックザンバ
Mackouzangba, Gaston 874
マックジャネット
McJannet, Linda 871
マックス
Max, Daniel T. 923
Max, Peter 923
Max, Philipp 923
マックスウェル
Maxwell 923
Maxwell, Bruce 923
Maxwell, Byron 923
Maxwell, Hamish 923
Maxwell, Lois 923
Maxwell, Robin 923
Maxwell, William Delbert 923
マックストゥーラー
Max-theurer, Victoria 923
マックス・ローチ
Roach, Max 1186
マッククック
McCook, Kathleen de la Peña 863
マックデイド
McDade, Moira 864
マックドナルド
NicDhòmhnaill, Flòraidh 1022
マックナイト
McKnight, Lee W. 874
マックナーニ
McNerney, Jim 878
マックナリー
McNally, Peter R. 877
マックニーズ
McNeese, Vicki 878
マックパートランド
McPartland, James 878
マッグーハン
McGoohan, Patrick 869
マックフィー
Mcphee, Charles 878
マックフェラン
McPherran, Mark L. 878
マックフォーター
McWhorter, Ladelle 880
マックブライド
McBride, Alex 859
McBride, Angus 859
マックペイク
McPake, Barbara 878
マックマス
McMath, Robert M. 876
マックミラン
McMillan, Peter 877
マックミーンズ
MacMeans, Donna 876
マックヤング
MacYoung, Marc 880
マックラー
Mackler, Carolyn 874
マックラウド
McCloud, Carol 862
マックラーカン
McClurkan, Rob 862
マックラース

McCullers, Dan 864
マッグラス
McGrath, Sean 869
マックラム
McCrum, Robert 864
マックラング
McClung, David 862
マックリーン
Mcclean, Maxine 862
MacLean, Andrew Okpeaha 875
McLean, Kathleen 875
McLean, Luke 875
マッグリン
McGlynn, Sue 868
マックリントン
McClinton, Delbert 862
マックール
McCool, Michael D. 863
McCool, Stephen F. 863
McCool, William C. 863
マックル
Mackle, Marisa 874
マッグルー
McGrew, Anthony G. 869
マックルア
McClure, Wallace B. 862
マックルストーン
Mucklestone, Mary Jane 985
マッグルーダー
McGruder, Aaron 869
マックルモア
Macklemore 874
マックルーリック
MacLulich, Carolyn 876
マックレー
Mccray, Ross 864
Macrae, Finlay 879
McRae, Steven 879
マックレイ
McCray, Cheyenne 864
MacRae, Tom 879
マックレオド
McLeod, Peter 876
マックレディ
MacCready, Paul 864
マックレディー
MacCready, Robin Merrow 864
マックレラン
McClellan, Edwin 862
McLellan, Betty 875
マックレル
Mackrell, Judith 874
マックレーン
McLane, Daisann 875
MacLane, Saunders 875
マッグロー
McGraw, Tim 869
マックロウ
McCullough, Jack 864
マッグロウ
McGraw, Tim 869
マックロスキー
McCloskey, Joanne Comi 862
McCloskey, Robert 862
McCloskey, William W. 862
マックロッホ
McCulloch, Gary 864
マックーン
McKune, Carolyn M. 874
マッケイ
McCay, Bill 862
McCay, William 862
Mackay, Alan L. 872
McKay, Andy 872
MacKay, David J.C. 872
McKay, Dean 872
McKay, Derek 872
Mackay, Donald 872
McKay, Emily 872
McKay, George 872
Mackay, Harvey 872
Mackay, Hugh 872
Mackay, Iain 872
McKay, John 872
McKay, Judith 872
MacKay, Julian 872
McKay, Matthew 872
McKay, Mekale 872
Mackay, Peter Gordon 872
McKay, Rena 872
McKay, Rhian 872
Mackay, Richard 872
Mackay, Roger 872
Mackaye, Benton 872
Mackey, Chris 873
Mckey, James E. 873
Mackey, Sandra 873
マッケイグ
McCaig, Donald 860
マッケイド
McKade, Mackenzie 871
McQuaid, John 878
McQuaid, Matilda 879
マッケイバリー
MacAvery, Tristan 859
マッケイブ
McCabe, Bob 859
MacCabe, Colin 859
McCabe, Dorothy 860
McCabe, George P. 860
McCabe, Janet 860
McCabe, Pete 860
McCabe, Randi E. 860
McCabe, Richard 860
マッケイル
MacKail, Davina 871
マッケイン
McCain, Bobby 860
McCain, Brice 860
McCain, Chris 860
McCain, Gillian 860
McCain, John Sidney Ⅲ 860
マッケヴォイ
McEvoy, Sean 867
マッケカーン
MacEachern, Robyn 866
マッケシー
Mackesy, Serena 873
マッケナ
Mckenna, Catherine 872
Mckenna, David 872
Mckenna, Juliet E. 872
McKenna, Patrick J. 872
McKenna, Rachael Hale 873
McKenna, Shannon 873
McKenna, Shannon S. 873
McKenna, Terence 873
マッケニー
Mckenney, Michael 873
マッケーブ
McCabe, John 860
McCabe, Kirwan 860
McCabe, Laura 860
Mccabe, Martha 860
マッケボイ
McEvoy, Joseph P. 867
Mcevoy, Tanner 867
マッケラー
McKellar, Don 872
マッケラス
Mackerras, Charles 873
マッケラン
McKellen, Ian 872
McKellen, *Sir* Ian 872
McKellen, Ian Murray 872
マッケリー
McQuerry, Steve 879
マツケリー
Mazzucchelli, David 926
マッケルビン
Mckelvin, Leodis 872
マッケルロイ
McElroy, Susan Chernak 867
マッケレン
McKellen, Ian Murray 872
マッケロイ
McElroy, Laurie 867
マッケン
Macken, JoAnn Early 872
McKuen, Rod 874
マッケンジー
Mackenzie, Alexander 873
Mackenzie, Alice 873
McKenzie, Alyce M. 873
Mckenzie, Ashley 873
McKenzie, Bret 873
MacKenzie, Bruce 873
McKenzie, C.B. 873
McKenzie, Chuck 873
MacKenzie, Cindy 873
McKenzie, Colin 873
McKenzie, Dan 873
Mackenzie, Dana 873
McKenzie, Dan P. 873
Mackenzie, David 873
Mckenzie, Desmond 873
MacKenzie, Donald A. 873
McKenzie, Eleanor 873
Mckenzie, Evan 873
MacKenzie, George 873
McKenzie, Hamish 873
Mackenzie, Jamie 873
MacKenzie, John M. 873
McKenzie, Kevin 873
MacKenzie, K.Roy 873
McKenzie, Kwame 873
Mackenzie, Linda 873
McKenzie, Lionel Wilfred 873
McKenzie, Margaret 873
Mackenzie, Myrna 873
Mackenzie, Norman 873
Mackenzie, Phil 873
Mackenzie, Richard 873
Mac Kenzie, Robert J. 873
McKenzie, Robin 873
MacKenzie, Sally 873
McKenzie, Scott 873
MacKenzie, Scott Bradley 873
McKenzie, Shawn 873
Mackenzie, Sophie 873
McKenzie, Susan 873
Mackenzie, W.S. 873
マッケンゼン
Mackensen, Ina von 873
マッケンドリー
Mckendry, Sam 872
マッケンナ
McKenna, Aline Brosh 872
Mckenna, James R. 872
McKenna, Lindsay 872
McKenna, Paul 873
McKenna, Regis 873
McKenna, Tim 873
マッケンハウプト
Muckenhoupt, Margaret 985
マッケンブリッジ
McCambridge, Mercedes 860
マッケンリー
McKenley, Herb 872
マッケンロー
McEnroe, John Patrick 867
マッコイ
McCoy, Angel Leigh 863
McCoy, Charles W., Jr. 863
Mccoy, Colt 863
McCoy, Elin 863
Mccoy, Gerald 863
McCoy, Karen 863
Mccoy, Kerry 863
McCoy, LeSean 863
McCoy, Mike 863
McCoy, Mimi 863
マッコイル
McCoil, Dexter 862
マッコウン
McCown, Josh 863
Mccown, Luke 863
マッコーネル
McConnell, Carmel 863
McConnell, Denise 863
McConnell, Harry 863
マッコネル
McConnel, Patricia 863
McConnell, Malcolm 863
McConnell, Steve 863
McConnell, T.J. 863
マッコノーヒー
McConnaughey, Matthew 863
マッコーマー
Macomber, Debbie 878
マッコーマック
MacCormack, Kim 863
McCormack, Mark Hume 863
マッコーリー
MacAuley, Domhnall 859
McCauley, Kirby 861
Macquarrie, John 879
マッコリー
McCoury, Del 863
マッコーリーン
McCaughrean, Geraldine 861
マッコール
McCall, Lauren 860
McCall, Morgan W. 860
McCall, Randy 860
McCall, Timothy 860
MacColl, Michaela 862
McColl, Peggy 862
マッコーレイ
McCauley, Cynthia D. 861
マッゴーワン

マ

McGowan, Michael 869
マッコーン
McKone, Mike 874
マッコンキー
McConkie, Mark 863
マッコンネル
McConnell, Mike 863
McConnell, Mitch 863
マッサ
Massa, Anthony J. 915
Massa, Felipe 915
マッサー
Musser, Charles 997
Musser, David R. 997
マッサーリ
Massari, Alida 915
マッサールカビンダマカガ
Massard Kabinda Makaga, Etienne 915
マッシ
Massi, Charles 916
マッシー
Massey, Anna 916
Massey, Doreen B. 916
Massey, Guy 916
Massey, Jane 916
Massey, Sujata 916
Massey, Walter E. 916
Massie, Bobby 916
Massie, Matt 916
Massie, Robert K. 916
マッジ
Maggi, Blairo 882
マッジェ
Matje, Martin 919
マッジオ
Maggio, Carole 882
Maggio, Rosalie 882
マッシーニ
Massini, Luca 916
Massini, Sarah 916
マッシメッロ
Massimello, Giovanni 916
マッシュ
Mash, Robert 914
マッジョ
Maggio, Christian 882
マッジョーリ
Maggiori, Robert 882
マツシラ
Matusila, Pierre Anatole 921
マッシローニ
Massironi, Daniela 916
マッスイミーニ
Massimini, Marcello 916
マッズケリ
Mazzucchelli, David 926
マッスルホワイト
Musselwhite, Charlie 997
マッセ
Masse, Gerard 915
Masse, Kylie 915
マッセイ
Massei, Stefano 915
Massey, Anna 916
Massey, Howard 916
Massey, Robert 916
マッセラ
Massera, Emilio 915
マッセロ
Masello, Robert 914
マッソマ
Massoma, David Siegfreid 916
マッソン
Masson, Jeffrey Moussaieff 916
Masson, Terrence 916
マッタ
Matta, Nadim F. 919
Matta, Roberto Sebastiano 919
マツダ
Matsuda, Ethan Khiem 919
Matsuda, Michael 919
マッタ・エチャウレン
Matta, Roberto Sebastiano 919
マッタレッラ
Mattarella, Sergio 919
マツタロウ
Matsutaro, Francis 919
マッダーン
Maddern, Eric 880
マッチ
Mutch, Jordon 997
マッチニック
Muchnick, Marc 985
マッチャー
Matchar, Emily 917
マッチュー
Mattu, Amal 921
マッツ
Matz, Peter 921
Matz, Steven 921
Matz, Tim 921
Mazzù, Domenica 926
マッツァ
Mazza, Viviana 926
マッツァーリ
Mazzarri, Walter 926
マッツァンティーニ
Mazzantini, Margaret 926
Mazzantini, Mirko 926
マッツィテッリ
Mazzitelli, Luca 926
マッツィーニ
Mazzini, Stefano 926
マッツェ
Mathse, David 918
マッツェイ
Mazzei, Franco 926
マッツェオ
Mazzeo, Michael 926
マッツエオ
Mazzeo, Tilar J. 926
マッツェッティ
Mazzetti, Lorenza 926
マッツォ
Mazzo, Mauro 926
マッツォーラ
Mazzola, Mario 926
マッツォレーニ
Mazzoleni, Donatella 926
マッツカート
Mazzucato, Mariana 926
マッツッコ
Mazzucco, Melania G. 926
マッディ
Maddi, Salvatore R. 880
マッティエセン
Mathiesen, Arni M. 918
マッティラ
Mattila, Karita 921
Mattila, Pirkko 921
マッティングリー
Mattingly, Don 921
マッティンソン
Mattinson, Pippa 921
マッテウッチ
Matteuzzi, William 920
マッテウッツィ
Matteuzzi, William 920
マッテオ
Matteo, Steve 920
マッテオッティ
Matteotti, Luca 920
マッテオーリ
Matteoli, Altero 920
マッデン
Madden, Beezie 880
Madden, John 880
マット
Matt, Andreas 919
Matt, Mario 919
マットゥ
Mattu, Sasha.K. 921
マットシェロト
Mattscherodt, Katrin 921
マッドセン
Madsen, Chris 881
Madsen, Leif 881
マットソン
Matteson, Mark 920
Matteson, S. 920
Mattsson, Malin Johanna 921
Mattsson, Sofia 921
マットフィールド
Matfield, Victor 917
マットリ
Mattli, Walter 921
マッド・ルース
Mudd-Ruth, Maria 985
マッドン
Maddon, Joe 880
マツナガ
Matsunaga, Tatsuo 919
マツバラ・オダ
Matsubara Oda, Amelia Kayo 919
マッピン
Mappin, Jennifer 898
マップ
Mapp, Wayne 898
マッフェイ
Maffei, Giorgio 881
マッフル
Maffre, Jean-Jacques 882
マツモト
Matsumoto, David Ricky 919
Matsumoto, Tak 919
マツモト・タナカ
Matsumoto Tanaka, Lino Toshio 919
マツヤマ
Matsuyama, Saeka 919
マッリ
Malli, Yunus 890
マッリア
Mallia, Emanuel 890
マテ
Mate, Dragutin 917
Maté, Gabor 917
Matte, Magdalena 919
マデ
Made, Joseph 880
マーティ
Marte, Ketel 907
Marte, Starling 907
Marty, Martin E. 912
マーテイ
Marte, Jefry 907
マティ
Matti, Truus 921
マテイ
Matteí, Jean-François 919
Mattéi, Jean-François 919
Matthei, Evelyn 920
マディ
Madi, Ahamada 880
Madi, Nabil 880
Mmadi, Djaffar 958
マティア
Matje, Martin 919
マディア
Madia, Maria Anna 880
マティアス
Maltias, Josue 891
Mathias, Bob 918
Matyas, Steve 921
マティアスコ
Matiasko, Marek 918
マティアス・スミス
Matias-smith, Geno 918
マティアス・フェルナンデス
Matias Fernandez 918
マーディアン
Mardian, Robert 901
マティアンギ
Matiangi, Fred 918
マティヴェ
Mathivet, Éric 918
マティオリ
Mattioli, Gianni Francesco 921
マディオル・ボイエ
Madior Boye, Mame 881
マディガン
Madigan, Carol Orsag 880
Madigan, Charles 880
Madigan, Ian 881
Madigan, Stephen 881
マディキゼラ・マンデラ
Madikizela-Mandela, Winnie 881
マテイケン
Matheiken, Sheena 917
マティザック
Matyszak, Philip 921
マティシク
Matysik, Larry 921
マティース
Matīss, Anrijs 919
マティス
Mathes, Rainer 918
Mathies, Lukas 918
Mathis, Brandon 918
Mathis, Lukas 918
Mathis, Robert L. 918
Mathis, Thomas 918
Mathys, Adidjatou 918
Matisse, M. 919
Matthies, Holger 921
Mattis, James 921
マティスヤフ
Matisyahu 919
マティソン

Mattison, Chris 921
マディソン
Maddison, Angus 880
Maddison, Jill E. 880
Madison, Susan 881
Madison, Tianna 881
マティック
Mattick, Lindsay 921
マティッチ
Matic, Barbara 918
Matić, Jasna 918
Matic, Nemanja 918
Matić, Predrag 918
マティーニ
Martini, Frederic 912
マティニョン
Matignon, Karine Lou 918
マーティヌー
Martineau, Jason 910
Martineau, John 910
マーティネス
Martinez, Elizabeth A. 911
Martinez, Michele 911
マティネンガ
Matinenga, Eric 919
マディーハ
Madeeha, bint Ahmed bin Nassir al-Shibaniyah 880
マティプ
Matip, Joel 919
Matip, Marvin 919
マディヘレ
Madigele, Alfred 881
マティベンガ
Matibenga, Lucia 918
マディマン
Muddiman, Dave 985
マティヤシェク
Matyjaszek, Przemyslaw 921
マティヤス
Matijass, Julia 918
マデイラ
Madeira, Francisco Caetano 880
マデイラス
Medeiros, Teresa 928
マーティン
Martin, Agnes 908
Martin, Andrea 908
Martin, Andrew 908
Martin, Angela 908
Martin, Anne 908
Martin, Annie 908
Martin, Ann M. 908
Martin, Archer John Porter 908
Martin, Arthurton 908
Martin, Barbara 908
Martin, Barbara Y. 908
Martin, Bella 908
Martin, Bob 908
Martin, Boyd 908
Martin, Bradley K. 908
Martin, Brian 908
Martin, Brian M. 908
Martin, Carole Hurd 908
Martin, Catherine 908
Martin, Chris 908
Martin, Christina 908
Martin, Cody 908
Martin, Colin 908
Martin, Cory 908
Martin, Daniel 908
Martin, Daniella 908
Martin, David 908
Martin, David E. 908
Martin, David S. 908
Martin, Deborah L. 908
Martin, Deirdre 908
Martin, Didier 908
Martin, Donald E. 908
Martin, Doug 908
Martin, Douglas A. 908
Martin, E.A. 908
Martin, Earl 908
Martin, Earl Asim 908
Martin, Eric 908
Martin, Felix 908
Martin, Gabe 908
Martin, Gail 908
Martin, George Henry 908
Martin, George R.R. 909
Martin, Giles 909
Martin, Glenys Hanna 909
Martin, Grady 909
Martin, Harvey 909
Martin, Henry 909
Martin, Jacqueline Briggs 909
Martin, James 909
Martin, James A. 909
Martin, James P. 909
Martin, James Robert 909
Martin, Jane 909
Martin, Jane Roland 909
Martin, Janis 909
Martin, Jarell 909
Martin, John Harry 909
Martin, Jonathan E. 909
Martin, Josh 909
Martin, Judy 909
Martin, Kareem 909
Martin, Kat 909
Martin, Katherine L. 909
Martin, Keshawn 909
Martin, Kevin 909
Martin, Kyle 909
Martin, Leonys 909
Martin, Les 909
Martin, Leslie R. 909
Martin, Lucy 909
Martin, Madeline 909
Martin, Marcos 909
Martin, Marcus 909
Martin, Max 909
Martin, Michael Robert 909
Martin, Micheal 909
Martin, Mike 909
Martin, Nadine 909
Martin, Nancy 909
Martin, Neale 909
Martin, Nick 909
Martin, Paul 909
Martin, Paul R. 909
Martin, Peter 909
Martin, Philip 909
Martin, Rafael 909
Martin, Ralph P. 909
Martin, R.E. 910
Martin, Rex 910
Martin, Richard 910
Martin, Richard P. 910
Martin, Ricky 910
Martin, Robert D. 910
Martin, Robert S. 910
Martin, Rod A. 910
Martin, Roger L. 910
Martin, Ronald 910
Martin, Rosemary 910
Martin, Ross 910
Martin, Russell 910
Martin, Ruth 910
Martin, Sam 910
Martin, Seamus J. 910
Martin, Simon 910
Martin, Steve 910
Martin, Steve J. 910
Martin, Stuart 910
Martin, Sven 910
Martin, Terry E. 910
Martin, Thomas 910
Martin, Tony 910
Martin, Wednesday 910
Martin, William 910
Martin, William C. 910
Martin, William F. 910
Martin, Zack 910
Martyn, Christopher N. 912
Martyn, John 912
Martyn, Tim 912
マーディン
Mardin, Arif 901
Murdin, Paul 993
マーティン・アセニャ
Martín Aceña, Pablo 910
マーティンス
Martins, Peter 912
マーティンズ
Martins, Benedict 912
Martins, Peter 912
マーティンデイル
Martindale, Margo 910
マーティンデール
Martindale, Jennifer L. 910
マディンバ・カロンジ
Madimba Kalonji, Daniel 881
マーティン・ララナーガ
Martín Larrañaga, Ana 912
マテウシャク
Mateusiak, Robert 917
マテウス
Matthäus, Lother 920
マテウス・ペレイラ
Matheus Pereira 918
マテウッツィ
Matteuzzi, William 920
マテウ＝メストレ
Mateu-Mestre, Marcos 917
マテオ
Mateo, Garcia 917
Mateo, Ibarra C. 917
Mateo, Jorge 917
Mateo, Wander 917
マテオプーロス
Matheopoulos, Helena 917
マテオリ
Matteoli, Altero 920
マテジ
Mattesi, Michael D. 920
マテシアス
Muthesius, Stefan 998
マテシッツ
Mateschitz, Dietrich 917
マーテス
Martes, Francis 908
マテス
Mattes, Kate 920
マテソン
Matteson, John 920
Matteson, Priscilla 920
マテチナー
Matečná, Gabriela 917
マテック
Mattheck, Claus 920
マテックサンズ
Mattek-sands, Bethanie Lynn 919
マデックス
Maddex, Robert L. 880
マテナ
Matena, Vlada 917
マテニア
Mathenia, Christian 917
マテパラエ
Mateparae, Jeremiah 917
マテ・ブランコ
Matte Blanco, Ignacio 919
マテュー
Mathieu, Georges Victor Adolphe 918
マデュ
Madhur, Jas 880
マテュイディ
Matuidi, Blaise 921
マテーラ
Matera, Pablo 917
マデラ
Madera, Paul 880
マデライン
Madelaine 880
マテラッツィ
Materazzi, Marco 917
マーテリ
Martelli, Alex 907
マーテリー
Martelly, Michel 907
マテリ
Martelly, Michel 907
マーテル
Martel, Yann 907
Martell, Christopher R. 907
Martell, Hazel 907
Martell, Nevin 907
マテル
Mater, Zeyad 917
Mattel, Coline 920
マデル
Madeer, Sheikh Adan 880
マデロ
Madero, Carlos Alberto 880
マテロバ
Matelova, Hana 917
マテーロング
Mateelong, Richard Kipkemboi 917
マーテン
Marten, Gerald G. 907
マーデン
Maden, Pim van der 880
マデン
Madden, Bartley J. 880
Madden, Mickey 880
Madden, Paul 880
Madden, Tre 880
マーテンス
Mertens, Krista 937
マーテンズ
Martens, Brian K. 907
マーテンセン
Martensen, Anne 907

マト
Mato, Ana 919
マドア
Madore, Nancy 881
マトゥー
Mattu, Amal 921
マドゥ
Madet, Bechir 880
マトヴィエフスカヤ
Matvievskaia, Galina Pavlovna 921
マトヴィエンコ
Matvienko, Denis 921
Matvienko, Valentina Ivanovna 921
マドゥイケ
Maduekwe, Ojo 881
マトゥウ
Matu'u, Motu 921
マトヴェーエフ
Matveev, Lev Pavlovich 921
マドゥエケ
Maduekwe, Ojo 881
マトゥク
al-Matuq, Abdullah 921
Ma'tuq, Ma'tuq Muhammad 921
マドゥグ
Madougou, Reckya 881
マトウシェク
Matoušek, Jiří 919
マトゥシャック
Matusiak, Wojtek 921
マトゥス
Matus, Lujan 921
マトゥーテ
Matute, Ana María 921
マトゥテ
Matute, Ana María 921
Matute, Brenie Liliana 921
マドゥナ
Maduna, Penuel 881
マドゥマバンダラ
Maddumabandara, Ranjith 880
マトゥーラ
Matura, Thaddée 921
マトゥラ
Matla, Khotso 919
マトゥーロ
Matturro, Claire Hamner 921
マドゥロ
Maduro, Nicolás 881
Maduro, Ricardo 881
マトゥロビッチドロプリッチ
Matulović-dropulić, Marina 921
マドゥロ・モロス
Maduro Moros, Nicolás 881
マトゥロン
Matheron, François 918
マトゥーン
Mattoon, Ashley 921
マトウーン
Mattoon, John S. 921
マドエンクク
Madyenkuku, Sycheye 881
マドカ
Madoka, Marsden 881
マトーク
Ma'atoug, Ma'atoug Mohamed 858
Matouq, Matouq Mohamed 919
マトコウスキー
Matkowski, Marcin 919
マトコビッチ
Matković, Gordana 919
マトコフスカ
Matkowska, Iwona 919
マトコフスキ
Matkowski, Marcin 919
マトシアン
Matossian, Mary Allerton Kilbourne 919
マトス
Matos, Angel 919
Matos, Ian 919
Matos, Michaelangelo 919
Matos, Ryder 919
マトスフェルナンデス
Matos Fernandes, João Pedro 919
マドセン
Madsen, Charles H., Jr. 881
Madsen, Clifford K. 881
Madsen, David 881
Madsen, Mark 881
Madsen, Mark Overgaard 881
Madsen, Michael 881
Madsen, Richard 881
マトソウカス
Matsoukas, Melina 919
マトソン
Mattson, Gregory Louis 921
マドソン
Madson, Patricia Ryan 881
Madson, Ryan 881
マトチキナ
Matochkina, Yulia 919
マードック
Murdoch, Andrew 993
Murdoch, David Hamilton 993
Murdoch, Elisabeth 993
Murdoch, Elizabeth 993
Murdoch, Iris 993
Murdoch, James 993
Murdoch, John 993
Murdoch, Julian 993
Murdoch, Lachlan 993
Murdoch, Rupert 993
Murdoch, Tom 993
マトック
Mahtook, Mikie 885
マドックス
Maddocks, Ian 880
Maddox, John 880
マトード
Mattord, Herbert J. 921
マトト
Matoto, Afualo 919
マドニック
Madnick, Stuart E. 881
マトニヤゾワ
Matniyazova, Gulnoza 919
マドハヴァン
Madhavan, Guruprasad 880
マトビエンコ
Matvienko, Valentina I. 921
Matvienko, Valentina Ivanovna 921
マドファ
al-Madfa, Hamad Abdul-Rahman 880
マドブリ
Madbouli, Moustafa 880
マトベイチュク
Matveichuk, Vladimir F. 921
マトム
Matom, Victor 919
マドモアゼル・イヴ
Mademoiselle Ève 880
マトラス
Matras, John 919
マトリ
Matori, Abdul Djalil 919
Matri, Alessandro 919
マトリコン
Matricon, Jean 919
マトリック
Mattrick, Don 921
マドリック
Madrick, Jeffrey G. 881
マドリード
Madrid, Africo 881
Madrid, Marcos 881
マトリュボフ
Matlubov, Bahodir 919
マトリン
Matlin, Marlee 919
マトリンズ
Matlins, Antoinette Leonard 919
マードル
Mádl, Ferenc 881
マドル
Mádl, Ferenc 881
マトルチ
Matolcsy, Gyögy 919
マドレーヌ
Madelaine, Frédéric 880
マトロソワ
Matrosova, Anastasiia 919
マトロフ
Matloff, Norman 919
マドロン
Maddron, Tom 880
マートン
Martens, Rainer 907
Marton, Anna 912
Marton, Carmen 912
Marton, Dana 912
Marton, Renee 912
Marton, Sandra 912
Martone, Elaine L. 912
Merton, Robert Cox 937
Merton, Robert King 937
Murton, Matt 995
マードン
Mardon, Daniel 901
Mardon, Steven 901
マドン
Madden, Matt 880
Maddon, Joe 880
マトンド
Matondo, Rosalie 919
マドンナ
Madonna 881
マトンバ
Matomba, Teobaldo Nchaso 919
マーナ
Mahner, Martin 885
マナ
al-Mana', Mohammed bin Abdulatif bin Abdulrahman 892
マナア
Mana'a, Ibrahim 892
マナイ
Manaj, Ramë 892
Manaj, Rey 893
マナシエフスキ
Manasievski, Jovan 893
マナスター
Manaster, Guy J. 893
マナセロ
Manassero, Matteo 893
マナッセロ
Manassero, Matteo 893
マナドゥ
Manaudou, Florent 893
Manaudou, Laure 893
マナナエラ
Manana Ela, Cristobal 893
マナニ
Manani, Ahmat Rakhis 893
Manany, Rakhis 893
Mannany, Ahmat Rakhis 896
マナニ・マガヤ
Manani Magaya, Alison 893
マナビ
Manavi, Shanta 893
マナプル
Manapul, Francis 893
マナモレラ
Manamolela, Pinkie 893
マナラ
Manara, Cédric 893
Manara, Milo 893
マナリノ
Mannarino, Anthony P. 896
マナーリン
Munnerlyn, Captain 991
マナン
Mannan, M.A. 896
マナンダル
Manandhar, Mangal Siddhi 893
マナンツア
Manantsoa, Victor 893
マーニ
Maani, Walid 858
マーニー
Marney, Dean 905
マニ
Maani, Fauoa 858
Mani, Abdou 894
Mani, Inderjeet 895
マニアー
Munyer, Daniel 992
マニアッチ
Maniacci, Michael 895
マニウ
al-Maniu, Hamad bin Abdullah 895
マニウロワ
Maniourova, Gouzel 895

マニエ
Magnier, Thierry 883
マニェット
Magnette, Paul 883
マニエル
Manuel, Charlie 897
マニェンジ
Manhenje, Almerino 894
マニオン
Mannion, Sean 896
マニカ
Manicka, Rani 895
Manyika, Elliot 898
マニガ
Manigat, Charles 895
Manigat, Leslie François 895
Manigat, Mirlande H. 895
Manigat, Nesmy 895
マニカス
Manikas, Stefanos 895
マニク
Maniku, Ibrahim Hussain 895
マニクチャンド
Manickchand, Priya 895
マニケ
Manniche, Lise 896
マニタキス
Manitakis, Antonios 895
マニタス・デ・プラタ
Manitas de Plata 895
マニーチ
Manici, Andrea 895
マニチャンド
Manichand, Priya 895
マニーニ
Magnini, Filippo 883
マニフィカ
Manificat, Maurice 895
マニーペニー
Moneypenny, *Mrs.* 966
マニベ・ヌガイ
Manibe Ngai, Kosti 895
マニャーゴ・ランプニャーニ
Magnago Lampugnani, Vittorio 882
マニャーニ
Magnani, Stefano 883
マニャニャ
Magnagna, Christian 882
マニャネッリ
Magnanelli, Francesco 883
マニャリク
Mañalich, Jaime 893
マニャリチ
Mañalich, Jaime 893
マニャン・ジュック
Manyang Juuk, Kuol 898
マーニュ
Magne, Henri 883
マニュエラ
Manuella, Satini 898
マニュエル
Manuel, Charlie 897
Manuel, EJ. 897
Manuel, Frank E. 897
Manuel, Simone 897
Manuel, Trevor Andrew 898
マニュエル・ビラ・ノバ
Manuel Vila Nova, Carlos 898
マニュロワ
Manyurova, Guzel 898
マニョ
Magno, Diego 883
マニョンガ
Manyonga, Luvo 898
マニラキザ
Manirakiza, Côme 895
Manirakiza, Tabu Abdallah 895
マニロウ
Manilow, Barry 895
マニン
Manin, Yuri Ivanovich 895
マニンガー
Manninger, Alex 896
マニンガム＝ブラー
Manningham-buller, Eliza 896
マニング
Manning, Drew 896
Manning, Eli 896
Manning, Frankie 896
Manning, Greg 896
Manning, Hazel 896
Manning, Jackie 896
Manning, Janice 896
Manning, John T. 896
Manning, Matthew K. 896
Manning, Maureen A. 896
Manning, Mick 896
Manning, Molly Guptill 896
Manning, Nick 896
Manning, Patrick 896
Manning, Peyton Williams 896
Manning, Phillip Lars 896
Manning, Richard 896
Manning, Robert A. 896
Manning, Shari Y. 896
マヌ・アットリ
Manu Attri 897
マヌアレサガララ
Manualesagalala, Enokati Posala 897
マヌイラ
Manuila, Alexandre 898
マヌエル
Manuel, Armando 897
マヌ・エレーラ
Manu Herrera 898
マヌ・ガルシア
Manu Garcia, Alonso 898
Manu Garcia, Sanchez 898
マヌキャン
Manukian, Andranik 898
Manukyan, Ashot 898
Manukyan, Hovhannes 898
Manukyan, Maksim 898
Manukyan, Mkhitar 898
マヌーチェッリ
Manoochehri, Michael 896
マヌ・チャオ
Mánu Chao 897
マヌー・チャオ
Mánu Chao 897
マヌト
Boonjumnong, Manus 160
Manus, Boonjumnong 898
マヌ・トリゲロス
Manu Trigueros 898
マヌ・バレイロ
Manu Barreiro 897
マヌル
Manoro, Régis 896
マネ
Mane, Abdú 894
Mané, Malam 894
Mane, Sadio 894
Monnet, Léon-Emmanuel 966
マネー
Money, Nicholas P. 966
マネイア
Manaea, Sean 892
マネカ
Maneka, Samson 894
マネガッティ
Menegatti, Marta 934
マネクショウ
Manekshaw, Sam Hormuzji Framji Jamshedji 894
マネザ
Maneza, Maiya 894
マネス
Mannes, Elena 896
マネトアリ
Manetoali, Samuel 894
マネニアル
Maneniaru, John 894
マネバ
Maneva, Milka 894
マネフスキ
Manevski, Mihajlo 894
マネポラ
Manepora'a, Andrew 894
マネポン
Maneepong, Jongjit 894
マネル
Munnell, Alicia Haydock 991
マネワ
Maneva, Evdokiya 894
マノア
Manoa, Samu 896
マノヴィッチ
Manovich, Lev 896
マノキャン
Manoukian, Don 896
マノッキア
Manocchia, Pat 896
マノック
Mannock, John 896
マノッティ
Manotti, Dominique 896
マノニ
Mannoni, Gérard 896
マノラケ
Tirlea-manolache, Ionela 1406
マノラス
Manolas, Kostas 896
マノリ
Manoli, Mihai 896
マノリキ
Manoriky, Sylvain 896
マノロハンタ
Manorohanta, Cecile 896
マーハ
Maher, John Christopher 884
マーバー
Marber, Patrick 899
マバイレ
Mavhaire, Dzikamai 922
マハグーブ
Mahgoub, Abdel Salam Al 884
マハ・コーサナンダ
Ghosananda 494
マハ・ゴサナンダ
Ghosananda 494
マハゴサナンダ
Ghosananda 494
マハザカ
Mahazaka, Clermont Gervais 884
マハジャン
Mahajan, Pramodo 883
Mahajan, Rahul 883
Mahajan, Sanjoy 883
Mahajan, Vijay 883
マハースウェーラチャイ
Mahasuverrachai, Lers 884
マハスーリ
Mahsouli, Sadeq 885
マハセ
Mahase-moiloa, Mpeo 884
マハセモイロア
Mahase-moiloa, Mpeo 884
マハゾアジ
Mahazoasy, Freddie 884
マハダビキャニ
Mahadavi Kani, Mohammadreza 883
マハタン
Machtan, Lothar 870
マハチ
Mahachi, Moven 883
マハディ
al-Mahdi, al-Sadil al-Hadi Abdul-Rahman 884
マハティール・モハマド
Mahathir Mohamad 884
マハティール・モハメド
Mahathir Mohamad 884
マハト
Mahat, Prakash Sharan 884
Mahat, Ram Sharan 884
Mahato, Rajendra 884
マハノ
Majano, Ana Maria 887
マハファリ
Mahafaly, Solonandrasana Olivier 883
マハフーズ
Mahfūz, Najīb 884
マハマ
Mahama, Alima 883
Mahama, Aliu 883
Mahama, John Dramani 883
マハマト
Mahamat, Abderamane Mouctar 883
Mahamat, Brahi 883
Mahamat, Moussa Faki 883
マハマドゥ
Mahamadou, Boukari Zila 883
Mahamadou, Karidjo 883
マハムーディ
al-Mahmoudi, al-Baghdadi Ali 885
Mahmudi, Baghdadi Ali 885
マハムード
Mahamoud, Dirir 884

al-Mahmoud, Ahmad bin Abdullah bin Zayed 884
Mahmoud, Ahmed Sharifo 884
Mahmoud, Amin 884
al-Mahmoud, Faisal bin Abdullah 884
Mahmoud, Fatin 884
Mahmoud, Haidar 884
Mahmoud, Ishraga Sayed 884
Mahmoud, Lemrabott Sidi 885
Mahmoud, Mohamed 885
Mahmoud, Nagi Ould Mohamed 885
Mahmud, Anisul Islam 885
Mohamud, Hassan Sheikh 962

マハムド
Mahamoud, Ali Yacoub 884
Mahamoud, Moustapha Mohamed 884
Mahmud, Ali Hussein Mohamed 885
Mahmud, Hasan 885
Mahmud, Mowlid Ma'ane 885

マハメダウ
Mahamedau, Amarhajy 884

マハラ
Mahara, Krishna Bahadur 884

マバラ
Mabala, Martin 858

マハラジ
Maharaj, Devant 884
Maharaj, Ramesh Lawrence 884

マハラブ
Mahlab, Ibrahim 884

マハラレラ
Mahlalela, Jama 884

マハランテ
Maharante, Jean de Dieu 884

マハラント
Maharante, Jean de Dieu 884

マハリー
Maharey, Steve 884

マハリッジ
Maharidge, Dale 884

マハリナ
Makhalina, Yulia Victorovna 888

マハル
Mahar, Ghaus Bakhsh Khan 884
Mahr, Ghaus 885

マハルコ
Michalko, Michael 942

マハルーフ
Makhlouf, Anisa 888

マハルマダン
Mahalmadane, Hameye Founé 883

マハレー
Maharey, Steve 884

マバレ・ムバ・ヌノモ
Mabale Mba Nnomo, Fernando 858

マハン
Magang, David 882
Mahan, L.Kathleen 884

マパング
Mapangou, Guy Bertrand 898

マバンドラ
Mabandla, Brigette Sylvia 858

マバンロ
Mabanglo, Elynia S. 858

マーヒー
Mahy, Margaret 885

マヒ
Mahi, Khelil 884

マビアラ
Mabiala, Pierre 858

マヒガ
Mahiga, Augustine Philip 884

マビカ
Mabika, Alfred 858

マビカムヤマ
Mabika, Alfred 858

マピサヌカクラ
Mapisanqakula, Nosiviwe Noluthando 898

マビティ
Mavity, Roger 922

マビトレ
Mabitle, Mopshatla 858

マビラ
Mabilat, Jean-Jacques 858

マビール
Mabire, Gregoire 858

マヒンドラ
Mahindra, Anand G. 884

マーフィ
Murphy, Bill 993
Murphy, Brittany 993
Murphy, Catherine J. 993
Murphy, Cillian 993
Murphy, Colleen 993
Murphy, Eddie 993
Murphy, Gillian 993
Murphy, Graeme 993
Murphy, James E. 994
Murphy, Jana 994
Murphy, Jill 994
Murphy, Margaret 994
Murphy, Mark L. 994
Murphy, Mary 994
Murphy, Paul 994
Murphy, Sean 994
Murphy, Tab 994
Murphy, Thomas A. 994
Murphy, Warren 994

マーフィー
Murphy, Alan 993
Murphy, Annalise 993
Murphy, Bill, Jr. 993
Murphy, Bobby 993
Murphy, Brittany 993
Murphy, Cathy 993
Murphy, Cecil John, Jr. 993
Murphy, Chris 993
Murphy, Chuck 993
Murphy, Cillian 993
Murphy, Clayton 993
Murphy, Craig 993
Murphy, Dallas 993
Murphy, Daniel 993
Murphy, Dean E. 993
Murphy, Eddie 993
Murphy, Gael 993
Murphy, Gillian 993
Murphy, Glenn 993
Murphy, Graeme 993
Murphy, James T. 994
Murphy, Jean 994
Murphy, Jim 994
Murphy, Jobi 994
Murphy, John 994
Murphy, John J. 994
Murphy, John Joseph 994
Murphy, John Ryan 994
Murphy, Jordi 994
Murphy, Kelly 994
Murphy, Kevin 994
Murphy, Kyle 994
Murphy, Laurence 994
Murphy, Liam B. 994
Murphy, Louis 994
Murphy, Marcus 994
Murphy, Mary 994
Murphy, Michael 994
Murphy, Michael Patrick 994
Murphy, Pace 994
Murphy, Pat 994
Murphy, Raymond 994
Murphy, Richard 994
Murphy, Rita 994
Murphy, Robert Patrick 994
Murphy, R.Taggart 994
Murphy, Ryan 994
Murphy, Scott 994
Murphy, Shane 994
Murphy, Terry Weible 994
Murphy, Thomas A. 994
Murphy, Tom 994
Murphy, Trent 994
Murphy, Warren 994

マフィ
Mafi, Steve 882
Mafi, Tahereh 882

マーフィー・オコナー
Murphy-O'Connor, Jerome 994

マーフィ・シゲマツ
Murphy-Shigematsu, Stephen 994

マフィーユ
Mafille, Emmanuelle 882

マーフィン
Murfin, Teresa 993

マフェオ
Maffeo, Pablo 881

マフェゾリ
Maffesoli, Michel 881

マブサ
Mabuza, Jabulani 858
Mabuza, Phiwayinkhosi 858

マブザ
Mabuza, Njyabulo 858

マフソン
Mufson, Laura 986

マフタ
Mahuta, Nanaia 885

マーフード
Mahfood, Jim 884

マフネワ
Makhneva, Marharyta 888

マブバニ
Mahbubani, Kishore 884

マフフーズ
Mahfūz, Najīb 884

マフフド
Mahfud, Mahmodin 884

マフマダミノフ
Mahmadaminov, Mahmadamin 884

マフマルバフ
Makhmalbaf, Mohsen 888
Makhmalbaf, Muhsin 888
Makhmalbaf, Samira 888

マフムード
Mahmoud, Izidbih Ould Mohamed 885
al-Mahmoud, Shaykha bint Ahmad 885
Mahmoud, Yusri Ismail 885

マフムド
Mahmud, Abd-al-Wahab Maalin 885
Mahmud, Ahmad Shaykh 885
Mahmud, Ahmed Sherifo 885
Makhmudov, Eldar 888

マフムード・ダルウィーシュ
Darwīsh, Mahmūd 320

マフムドフ
Makhmudov, Eldar 888

マフムノフ
Mahmudov, Dilshod 885

マフラ
Mafura, Kabelo 882

マブーラ
Mvula, Laura 998

マフラヒ
al-Maflahi, Mohammed Abu-Bakr 882

マブリ
Mabri, Albert Toikeusse 858
Mabri, Toikeusse 858

マプリ
Mapuri, Omar Ramadhani 898

マブリャノワ
Mavlonova, Khairinisso 923

マブル
Mavrou, Eleni 923

マブルーク
Mabrouk, Mehdi 858
al-Mabrouk, Mohamed Abu Ujayl 858

マフルーフ
Makhlouf, Hussein 888

マフレズ
Mahrez, Riyad 885

マブロニコラス
Mavronicolas, Kyriakos 923

マブロノワ
Mavlonova, Khairinisso 923

マフロフィ
Makhloufi, Taoufik 888

マブンドゥ
Maboundou, Rigobert 858

マブンバ
Mabumba, David 858

マヘ
Mahe, Jean 884

マベオ
Mabeo, Tshenolo 858

マヘシュ
Mahesh, Mahadevappa 884

マヘシュヴァラナンダ
Maheshvarananda, Dada 884

マヘスワリ
Maheswari, Nitya Krishinda 884
マーペット
Marpet, Ali 905
マペラ
Mapera, Jeannette Kavira 898
マーヘル
Maher, Ahmad 884
マヘル
Maher, Thomas Francis 884
マベルリー
Mabberley, David 858
マベンガ
Mabenga, Michael 858
マホエ
Māhoe, Noelani 885
マボテ
Mabote, Tefo 858
マホーニー
Mahoney, Anne 885
Mahoney, David J. 885
Mahoney, Michael J. 885
マホニ
Mahoney, Basirou 885
マホニー
Mahoney, Daniel J. 885
Mahoney, James 885
Mahoney, Travis 885
マホーニィ
Mahoney, Michael Sean 885
マホバ
Machová, Mária 870
マホフ
Makhov, Bilyal 888
マホーン
Mahone, Austin 885
マポン
Mapon, Matata Ponyo 898
マポンガ
Maponga, Stansly 898
マボンゾ
Mabonzo, Emile 858
マーマー
Marmer, Mike 904
Marmor, Theodore 904
ママー
Momah, Ifeanyi 965
マーマウ
Maamau, Taneti 858
ママサリエフ
Mamasaliyev, Duishonali 892
ママシュク
Mamashuk, Maryia 892
ママス
Mamas, Michael 892
ママタリエフ
Mamataliev, Abdyrakhman 892
ママチェク
Momatiuk, Yva 965
ママドゥ
Mamadou, Bello 892
Mamadou, Dagra 892
Mamadou, Ousmane 892
Mamadou, Tanja 892
Mamadou, Zakaria 892
ママドゥファディア
Mamadu Fadia, João Alage 892
ママドフ
Mammadov, Fikret 892
Mammadov, Teymur 892
Mammadov, Ziya 892
ママドリ
Mammadli, Elnur 892
ママトワ
Mamatova, Natalya 892
マーマニス
Marmanis, Haralambos 904
ママニ・マルカ
Mamani Marca, Abel 892
ママ・フダ
Mama Fouda, André 892
マーマリ
al-Ma'amari, Ali bin Majid 858
ママン
Maman, Abdou 892
ママンディウラ・ファギマタ
Maman Dioula Fadjimata, Sidibe 892
マーミ
el-Mami, Mohamed Lemine Ould 892
マミザラ
Mamizara, Jules 892
マミシュザダ
Mamishzada, Elvin 892
マーミーズ
Mermuys, Jesse 936
マーミン
Mermin, N.David 936
マミン
Mamin, Askar 892
マム
Mam, Antonio Sedja 891
Mam, Somaly 892
Mumm, Dean 990
マムー
Mamou, Jacky 892
マムイトフ
Mamytov, Mitalip 892
マムイトベコフ
Mamytbekov, Asylzhan 892
マムカシヴィリ
Mamukashvili, Shalva 892
マムケグ
Mamkegh, Lana 892
マムダーニ
Mamdani, Mahmood 892
マームード
Mahmud, Abdul Ghffar 885
マームド
Mahmud, Al 885
マムドク
Mamdhouq, Abdullah Aubal 892
マムフォード
Mumford 990
マムベタリエワ
Mambetalieva, Zhyldyz 892
マムベトフ
Mambetov, Marat 892
マームラ
Marmura, Michael James 904
マームリ
al-Maamri, Mohammed 858
マムル・メテ
Mamur Mete, Obote 892
マームーン
Maumoon, Dunya 922
マムン
Mamun, Margarita 892
マメダリエフ
Mamedaliyev, Geidar 892
マメディヤロフ
Mamedyarov, Elmar 892
マメドゲリディエフ
Mamedgeldiyyev, Agageldy 892
マメトゲルドイエフ
Mammetgeldyyev, Agageldy 892
マメドフ
Mamedov, Fazil 892
Mamedov, Fikret 892
Mamedov, Ziya 892
Mammadov, Aghasi 892
Mammadov, Ziya 892
マメドワ
Mammedova, Gulshat 892
マーメル
Marmell, Ari 904
マメン
Mammen, David 892
マーモット
Marmot, Michael 904
マモナ
Mamona, Patricia 892
マーモル
Marmol, Oliver 904
マヤ
Maya, Mario 924
Maya, Mofazzal Hossain Chowdhury 924
マヤコフスキー
Maiakovskii, Vladimir Vladimirovich 885
マヤルオマ
Majaluoma, Markus 887
マヤワティ
Mayawati 924
マヤングサリ
Mayangsari, Sekar 924
マユ
Mahut, Nicolas 885
Mahut, Sandra 885
マヨラ
Mayora, Yolanda 925
マヨーリ
Majoli, Alex 887
マヨール
Mayor, Michel G.E. 925
マヨール・オレハ
Mayor Oreja, Jaime 925
マヨルガ・アルバ
Mayorga Alba, Eleodoro 925
マヨロシュ
Majoros, Istvan 887
マヨロワ
Mayorova, Albina 925
マーラ
Mara, Rooney 898
Mara, Thalia 898
Mara, Wellington 898
Marra, Thomas 905
マーラー
Mahler, Margaret S. 884
Mala, Matthias 888
Marler, Joe 904
Marler, Peter 904
マラ
Mara, Barbara A. 898
Mara, Kamisese Kapaiwai Tuimacilai 898
マラー
Marah, Kaifala 899
Muller, Marcia 989
Muller, René J. 989
Muller, Robert J. 989
Mullur, Rashmi S. 990
マライ
Malaj, Arben 888
マライス
Marais, Conrad 899
マライーニ
Maraini, Dacia 899
Maraini, Fosco 899
マライニ
Maraini, Dacia 899
Maraini, Fosco 899
マラウ
Marau, William Bradford 899
マラヴァル
Maraval, Pierre 899
マラヴィア
Malavia, Jignesh 889
マラガンバ
Malagamba, Marcelo 888
マラーキー
Mularkey, Mike 988
マラグラゼ
Malaghuradze, Lasha 888
マラゴス
Maragos, Chris 899
マラザリボ
Malazarivo, Félix 889
マラシ
Marashi, Hossein 899
マラジ
Maraj, Ralph 899
マラシコ
Malashko, Valery A. 889
マラシンスキー
Malacinski, George M. 888
マラス
Maras, Gordan 899
マラスコ
Marasco, Joe 899
マラゾーグ
Malazogu, Leon 889
マラチ
Marach, Oliver 898
マラック
Marrack, Philippa 905
マラッケ
Maracke, Catharina 898
マラッツィ
Marazzi, Christian 899
マーラット
Marlatt, G.Alan 904
マラット
Marat, Allan 899
マラディアガ
Maradiaga, Olga 898
マラディナ
Maladina, Moses 888
マラティンスキー

マ

Malatinský, Tomáš 889
マラテール
Malaterre, Christophe 889
マラード
Mallard, Trevor 890
マラドーナ
Maradona, Diego 898
マラーニ
Malani, Laufitu 889
Marani, Diego 899
マラニ
Malani, Nalini 889
マラニー
Mullaney, James 989
Mullaney, Richard 989
マラーノ
Marano, Tony 899
マラバエフ
Malabaev, Argynbek 888
マラバグ
Malabag, Michael 888
マーラパネ
Marapane, Thilak 899
マラビー
Mallaby, Sebastian 890
マラヒモフ
Marahimov, Avazjon 899
マラフ
Mallah, Ababar 890
マラブー
Malabou, Catherine 888
マラファ
Marafa, Hamidou Yaya 899
マラブル
Marable, Manning 898
マラペ
Marape, James 899
マラボ
Malabo, Estanislao Don 888
マラホビッチ
Malajovich, Gustavo 889
マラーホフ
Malakhov, Vladimir 889
マラホフスキ
Malachowski, Piotr 888
マラミ
Malami, Abubakar 889
マラム
Malam, John 889
Mallam, Abdoulkarim Dan 890
Mallam, Laurentia Laraba 890
マラムフィー
Malamphy, Timothy J. 889
マラモッティ
Maramotti, Achille 899
Maramotti, Luigi 899
マラーリー
Mulally, Alan 988
マラル
Malal, Dia Moktar 889
Maral, Alexandre 899
マラルド
Maraldo, John C. 899
マーラワナ
Malawana, Rupa 889
マラン
Malan, David 889
Malan, Pedro 889
Maran, Dayanidhi 899
Maran, Murasoli 899
Maran, Roland 899
Marant, Isabel 899
Marin, Claire 902
Marin, Maguy 902
マランヴォー
Malinvaud, Edmond 890
マランゴン
Marangon, Lucas 899
マランソン
Malençon, Gilles 889
Melancon, Mark 931
マランディ
Marrandi, Jaanus 905
マラント
Maranto, April Gresham 899
Maranto, Robert 899
マランド
Maland, Nick 889
マランドラ
Malandra, Mieke C. 889
マランパチー
Mallampati, Seshagiri Rao 890
マランボ
Malambo, Vincent 889
マランボー
Malinvaud, Edmond 890
マーリ
Maali, Othmane Ould Cheikh Ahmed Aboul 858
Mari, Enzo 902
マーリー
Mahle, Greg 884
Marley, Rita 904
Marley, Ziggy 904
マリ
Mali, Andreja 889
Mally, Komlan 891
Mari, Enzo 902
Mari, Iela 902
Marie, Michel 902
al-Marri, Ahmad bin Abdullah 905
Mary, Donatien 913
マリー
Maile, Luke 886
Maley, Kynan 889
Mallee, John 890
Malley, Gemma 890
Mally, Komlan 891
Marie, Teena 902
Murray, Albert 994
Murray, Alex 994
Murray, Andy 994
Murray, Charles Shaar 994
Murray, Glenn 995
Murray, Jamie 995
Murray, John 995
Murray, Lynne 995
Murray, Margo 995
Murray, Richard 995
Murray, Samantha 995
Murry, Toure 995
マリアヴァン
Malliavin, Paul 890
マリアス
Marías, Javier 902
マリアッパ
Mariappa, Adrian 902
マリアテギ
Mariategui, Jose Carlos 902
マリアナッチ
Marianacci, Dante 902
マリアーニ
Mariani, Marc 902
Mariani, Scott 902
マリアニ
Mariani, Gael 902
マリアーニ・ビテンクール
Mariani Bittencourt, Carlos 902
マリアネッリ
Marianelli, Dario 902
マリアーノ
Mariano, Diaz 902
Mariano, Ferreira 902
Mariano, Rafael 902
Oyakawa Mariano, Arthur 1066
マーリーイ
Maareeye, Mohamed Hayir 858
マーリィ
Marley, Ziggy 904
マリイ
Mary, Baby 913
マリエ
Malie, Mpho 889
Mariez, Jérémy 902
マリエット
Malliet, G.M. 890
マリエトア・タヌマフィリ2世
Malietoa Tanumafili II 890
マリオ
Mario, Fernandez 903
Mario, Gaspar 903
Mario, Gonzalez 903
マリオ・スアレス
Mario Suarez 903
マリオータ
Mariota, Marcus 903
マリオッコ
Magliocco, Karlha 882
マリオット
Marriott, David 905
Marriott, J.W., Jr. 906
Marriott, Lynn 906
Marriott, Susannah 906
マリオネット
Marionnet, Michel 903
マリオ・フェルナンデス
Mario Fernandes 903
マリオ・ルイ
Mario Rui 903
マリオン
Marion, Isaac 903
Marion, Jean-Claude 903
Marion, Jean-Luc 903
Marion, Robert 903
マリカ
Marica, Clifford Paul 902
マリガン
Mulligan, Andy 990
Mulligan, Blackjack 990
Mulligan, Carey 990
Mulligan, John P. 990
Mulligan, Matthew 990
Mulligan, Robert 990
Mulligan, Timothy Patrick 990
マリキ
al-Maliki, Adil 890
Maliki, Baroumi 890
al-Maliki, Nouri 890
al-Maliki, Nouri Kamel 890
マリク
Malek, Zahawi Ibrahim 889
Malik, Rehman 890
Malik, Sakshi 890
Malik, Sayed al-Zahawi Ibrahim 890
Malik, Sumaira 890
Malik, Zayn 890
Mariq, Lubomir 903
マリコ
Maliko, Sylvain 890
マリコヴァ
Marikova, Anna 902
マリゴールド
Marigold, Lys 902
マリジー
Maligie, Momodu 890
マリシク
Malyshik, Hanna 891
マリシュ
Malysz, Adam 891
マリシュコ
Malyshko, Dmitry 891
マーリーズ
Mirrlees, James Alexander 955
マリス
Mullis, Kary B. 990
マリスカル
Mariscal, Javier 903
マリスコ
Malyszko, Michael 891
マリズニック
Marisnick, Jake 903
マリダリン
Contreras, Yuderqui Maridalia 285
マリチェバ
Mal'tseva, Ol'ga 891
マリツィア
Malizia, Andrea L. 890
マリツェフ
Maltsev, Leonid S. 891
マリック
Malick, Terrence 889
Malik, Waqar 890
マリッサ
Marissa, Vita 903
マリッチ
Marić, Alisa 902
Maric, Borislav 902
Marić, Ljerka 902
Marić, Zdravko 902
マリーナ
Malina, Bruce J. 890
Malina, Robert M. 890
Marina, José Antonio 902
マリナー
Marriner, Neville 905
マリナー・トメイ
Marriner-Tomey, Ann 905
マリナンジェリ
Marinangeli, Luciana 902
マリーニナ
Marinina, Aleksandra 902
マリーニョ
Marino, Diego 902
マリニョ

Marinho, Luiz 902
マリニョ・フェロ
Mariño Ferro, Xosé Ramón 902
マリニン
Marinin, Maxim 902
マリヌツァ
Marinuta, Vitalie 903
マリネス
Marinez, Jhan 902
マリネスキュー
Marinescu, Floyd 902
マリネッリ
Marinelli, Carol 902
マリネリ
Marinelli, Rod 902
マリネン
Malinen, Pauliina 890
Malinen, Tapio 890
マリーノ
Marino, Carolyn 902
Marino, Susan 902
マリノ
Marino, Dorothy 902
Marino, Gianna 902
Marino, Paul L. 902
マリノー
Malineau, Jean-Hugues 890
マリノビッチ
Antičevič-marinović, Ingrid 51
マリノフ
Marinoff, Lou 902
マリーブ
Maleev, Alex 889
Marieb, Elaine Nicpon 902
マリプー
Maripuu, Maret 903
マリファント
Maliphant, Russell 890
マリポール
Maripol 903
マリマ
Malima, Philemon 890
マリャイェ
Mallaye, Mahamat Nour 890
マーリヤ大公女
Mariia, Grand Duchess of Russia 902
マリャノビッチ
Marjanovic, Marko 903
マリヤンスキー
Maryanski, Alexandra 913
マリユール
Mariur, Kerai 903
マリラ
Malila, Sami 890
マリー・リリアン
Mary Liliane 913
マリルンゴ
Marilungo, Guido 902
マーリン
Maalin, Abdi-al-Aziz Muqtar 858
Maalin, Yusuf 858
Marlin, Debra 904
マリーン
Marine, Linda 902
マリン
Malin, Shimon 890
Malin, Suzi 890
Marin, Amy J. 902
Marin, Carlos 902
Marin, Carolina 902
Marín, Fernando 902
Marin, Florencio 902
Marin, Ion 902
Marin, José Maria 902
Marín, Juan 902
Marin, Luca 902
Marin, Marino 902
Marin, Pablo 902
Marin, Philippe 902
Marín, Rolando Ernesto 902
Marin, Vildo 902
Marrin, West 905
マーリンガー
Mahringer, Marita 885
マリンカー
Marinker, Marshall 902
マリンガ
Mallinga, Stephen 890
マーリング
Marling, Karal Ann 904
マリングス
Mullings, Clive 990
マリングズ
Mullings, Seymour 990
マリンズ
Mullins, Debra 990
Mullins, Eustace 990
Mullins, John Walker 990
Mullins, Mark 990
マリンソン
Mallinson, John C. 890
マール
Mahr, Kurt 885
Mall, Ram Adhar 890
Marr, Bernard 905
Marr, Melissa 905
マル
Malu, Jorge 891
Maru, Richard 912
マルー
Maloux, Maurice 891
Marrou, Henri Irénée 906
マルアーン
Marouane, Fatema 905
マルイー
Marei, Mamdouh 901
マルヴィー
Mulvey, Lisa 990
マルヴィノン
Mulvenon, James C. 990
マルヴィーロバーツ
Mulvey Roberts, Marie 990
マルエホル
Maruejol, Florence 912
マルカ
Malka, Eric 890
Malka, Salomon 890
Maruca, Regina Fazio 912
マルガニ
Margani, Salah Bashir 901
マルカーノ
Marcano, Cristina 899
マルカノ
Marcano, Ivan 899
Marcano, Luis José 899
マルガリオ
Margaglio, Maurizio 901
マルガリート
Margalit, Avishai 901
マルガリャン
Margarian, Andranik 901
Margaryan, Vladimir 901
マルカル
Markale, Jean 903
マルカル・リマ
Marcal Lima, Manuel 899
マルキ
Malki, Habib 890
al-Malki, Riyad 890
マルキ！
Malki!, David 890
マルギ
Margi, Jacob 901
マルギエバ
Marghieva, Zalina 901
マルギエフ
Marghiev, Serghei 901
マルギエワ
Marghieva, Zalina 901
マルキオディ
Malchiodi, Cathy A. 889
マルキオーネ
Marchionne, Sergio 900
マルキオンネ
Marchionne, Sergio 900
マルキージオ
Marchisio, Claudio 900
マルキデス
Markides, Constantinos C. 903
Markides, Kyriacos C. 903
マルキナ・バリオ
Marquina Barrio, Antonio 905
マルキーニョス
Marquinhos 905
マルキール
Malkiel, Burton G. 890
マルキン
Malkin, Lawrence 890
Malkin, Peter Z. 890
マルクシース
Markschies, Christoph 904
マルクス
Markus, Christopher 904
Marx, Brian P. 913
Marx, György 913
Marx, Hans-Jürgen 913
Marx, Jeffrey A. 913
Marx, Patricia 913
Marx, Thierry 913
マルクソバー
Marksová, Michaela 904
マルクッゾ
Marcuzzo, Maria Cristina 901
マルクッチ
Marcucci, Catherine 900
Marcucci, Lisa 900
マルグッチ
Marguc, Rok 901
マルクッツォ
Marcuzzo, Maria Cristina 901
マルクッツオ
Marcuzzo, Maria Cristina 901
マルグベラシビリ
Margbelashvili, Giorgi 901
Margvelashvili, Giorgi 902
Margvelashvili, Vazha 902
マルクム
Malkum, José 890
マルク＝ユングクヴィスト
Mark-Jungkvist, Anna 903
マルクラス
Markoulas, Georgios 903
マルクリス
Marcoullis, Erato Kozakou 900
マルグリース
Margulies, Julianna 901
マルグリーズ
Margulies, Julianna 901
マルグリス
Margulis, Gregory A. 901
Margulis, Vitaly 902
マルグレイ
Mulgray, Helen 988
Mulgray, Morna 988
マルグレーテ2世
Margrethe II 901
マルク・ロカ
Marc Roca 900
マルクワット
Marquardt, Hanne 905
マルケ
Marcke, Leen van 900
Marquet, Christophe 905
Marquet, L.David 905
マルゲ
Margai, Charles Francis 901
マルケイヒー
Mulcahy, Anne Marie 988
マルケシ
Marchesi, Michele 900
マルケス
Marques, Antonio Henrique R.de Oliveira 905
Marques, Fernanda 905
Marques, Maria Antónia 905
Marques, Pedro 905
Marques, Yane 905
Márquez, Arnoldo 905
Marquez, German 905
Márquez, Herón 905
Márquez, Marc 905
Márquez, Rafael 905
Marquez, Roberta 905
マルケスゲーデス
Marques Guedes, Luís 905
マルケス・ダ・シルバ
Marques da Silva, Ernani 905
マルケッティ
Marchetti, Federico 900
マルケット
Marchetto, Ennio 900
マルゲーヌ
Margaine, Clémentine 901
マルケビチウス
Markevičius, Vytautas 903
マルゲム
Marghem, Marie-Christine 901
マルゲラズ
Margairaz, Michel 901
マルゲリータ
Margherita, Lesli 901
マルケル
Markell, Bruce A. 903
Marker, Chris 903

マ

マルケロフ
Markelov, Stanislav 903
マルゲン
Margain, Ismaël 901
マルコ
De Marco, Guido 339
Marco, Patrizio di 900
Marko, Bela 903
マルコウ
Malchau, Henrik 889
マルコヴァ
Markova, Alicia 904
マルコヴィチ
Marković, Ante 904
マルコヴィッチ
Malkovich, John 890
Marković, Ante 904
Markovic, Danica Jankovic 904
Markovic, Lazar 904
マルコヴィッツ
Marcovitz, Hal 900
Markovits, Francine 904
マルゴシビリ
Margoshvili, David 901
マルコーズ
Marcousé, Ian 900
マルコス
Marcos, Imelda Romualdez 900
Marcos, Juan Manuel 900
Marcos, subcomandante 900
Marcos, Susan 900
Markos 903
マルコス・アロンソ
Marcos Alonso 900
マルコス・ジョレンテ
Marcos Llorente 900
マルコッティ
Marcotti, Gabriele 900
マルコテ
Marcotte, Elise 900
マルコ・トレス
Marco Torres, Rodolfo 900
マルコバ
Markova, Alicia 904
マルコビチ
Marković, Ante 904
マルコビッチ
Malkovich, John 890
Marković, Ante 904
Marković, Duško 904
Marković, Milan 904
マルコビッツ
Markowitz, Harry Max 904
Markowitz, John S. 904
マルコフ
Markoff, John 903
Markov, Aleksandr 903
Markov, Alexey 903
Markov, Ivan 904
マルコプロス
Markopoulos, Konstantinos 903
マルコム
Malcolm, Christian 889
Malcolm, Elizabeth 889
Malcom, Shirley M. 889
マルコラ
Malcorra, Susana 889
マルゴラン
Margolin, Jean-Louis 901
マルコリーニ
Marcolini, Pierre 900
マルコルム
Malcolm, Martin 889
マルコーワ
Markova, Alicia 904
マルコワ
Markova, Alicia 904
マルコン
Marcon, Andrea 900
マルコンチーニ
Marconcini, Matteo 900
マルザ
Maluza, Monjeza 891
マルサギシビリ
Marsagishvili, Dato 906
マルザーノ
Marzano, Robert J. 913
マルサリス
Marsalis, Ellis 906
Marsalis, Wynton 906
マルザリュク
Marzaliuk, Vasilisa 913
マルザン
Malzahn, Luise 891
マルシ
Marsee, Monica A. 906
マルシー
Malsy, Victor 891
マルシアーノ
Marciano, John Bemelmans 900
マルシェ
Marchais, Pierre 899
Marché, Gary E. 900
マルシェル
Marshall, Diana 906
マルジェル
Margel, Serge 901
マルシカノ
Marsicano, Trevor 907
マルシッチ
Marušič, Dorijan 913
マルシード
Malseed, Mark 891
マルシニアック
Brook, Beth 186
マルシャル
Marchal, Olivier 899
Marshall, Dennis 906
Martial, Anthony 908
マルシャン
Marchand, Bernard 899
Marchand, Colette 900
Marchand, Dominique 900
Marchand, Jean 900
Marchand, Stephane 900
マルシャンアルビエ
Marchand-arvier, Marie 900
マルーシュ
Malouche, Slaheddine 891
マルシュコバ
Maruskova, Lenka 913
マルジョン
Margeon, Gérard 901
マルス
Marus, Francis 913
マルズーキ
Marzouki, Moncef 913
マルズキ
Tan Sri Marzuki, bin Mohd Noor 1381
マルズーク
Marzouk, Mohamed Salem Ould 913
Marzouk, Mongi 913
al-Marzouq, Essam Abdulmohsen 913
マルセー
Marsé, Juan 906
マルセロ
Marcello 899
Marcello, Peter W. 899
Marcelo 899
マルセロ・ディアス
Marcello Diaz 899
マルソー
Marceau, Alma 899
Marceau, Fani 899
Marceau, Félicien 899
Marceau, Jane 899
Marceau, Marcel 899
Marceau, Olivier 899
Marceau, Sophie 899
マルゾッキ
Marsocci, Joey 907
マルソーリ
Marsoli, Lisa Ann 907
マルソリ
Marsoli, Lisa Ann 907
マルソル
Marsol, Manuel 907
マルゾーロ
Marzollo, Jean 913
マルソン
Marson, Leonardo 907
マルゾーン
Malzone, Frank 891
マルタ
Maltais, Dominique 891
Marta 907
マルタ王女
Princess Märtha 908
マルダニ
Mardani, Sajjad 901
マルダノフ
Mardanov, Misir 901
マルタン
Martin, Boris 908
Martin, Claude 908
Martin, Daniel 908
Martin, David 908
Martin, Guy 909
Martin, Henri-Jean 909
Martin, Herve 909
Martin, Jacques 909
Martin, Jean-Clet 909
Martin, Marcel 909
Martin, Paul 909
Martin, René 910
Martin, Thérèse 910
Martins, Jennifer 912
マルタンゲ
Martingay, Claude 911
マルタン＝フュジエ
Martin-Fugier, Anne 911
マルチ
March, Aleida 899
マルチェガリア
Marcegaglia, Emma 899
マルチェリーノ
Marcellino, Fred 899
マルチェンコ
Marchenko, Igor 900
Marchenko, Illya 900
Marchenko, Veronika 900
Martchenko, Michael 907
マルチヌ
Martineau, David 910
マルチネス
Martinez, Blake 910
Martinez, Julio 911
Martinez, Linda P. 911
Martinez, Pedro 911
Martinez, Rocio 911
Martinez, Tino 911
マルチネズ
Martinez, Claude 910
マルチネスールイス
Martinez-Ruiz, Ricardo 911
マルチノフ
Martynov, Sergei 912
マルチノワ
Martynova, Iana 912
マルチューク
Marchuk, Guri Ivanovich 900
マルチュケ
Marutschke, Hans Peter 913
マルチュワイティス
Marczulajtis-walczak, Jagna 901
マルチョー
Malchow, Tom 889
マルチロシャン
Martirosian, Razmik 912
Martirosyan, Vahan 912
マルチンクス
Marcinkus, Paul 900
マルチンス
Martins, Alberto 912
Martins, Guilherme De Olibeira 912
Martins, Isabel Minhós 912
マルツァノ
Marzano, Antonio 913
マルツィーノ
Marzino, Dario 913
マルツェフ
Maltsev, Leonid S. 891
マルツォ・マーニョ
Marzo Magno, Alessandro 913
マルツバーグ
Malzberg, Barry N. 891
マルテ
Maltais, Dominique 891
Maltais, Valerie 891
Martet, Richard 908
Marthé, Daouda 908
マルデ
Malde, Melissa 889
マルティ
Martí, David 908
Marty, Éric 912
Marty, Natalegawa 912
Marty, Olivier 912
マルディ
Mardi, Khadija 901
al-Mardi, Mohammed Ali 901
マルティカン
Martikan, Michal 908
マルデイキス
Maldeikis, Eugenijus 889
マルティーナ
Martina, Maurizio 910

マルティナ
Martina, Churandy 910
Martina, Cuco 910
マルティーニ
Martini, Carlo Maria 911
Martini, Christiane 912
Martini, Malgorzata 912
マルティニ
Martini, Carlo Maria 911
Martini, Mohamad Radwan 912
Martini, Radwan 912
Martini, Steve 912
Martini, Steven Paul 912
マルディーニ
Maldini, Cesare 889
マルディニ
Mardini, Muhammad Amer 901
マルティニエア
Martiniere, Stephan 912
マルティニエッロ
Martiniello, Marco 912
マルティネ
Martinet, Jeanne 910
マルティネス
Martinez, Alberto A. 910
Martinez, Aleix 910
Martinez, Anthony 910
Martinez, Arthur C. 910
Martinez, Bernard 910
Martinez, Carlos 910
Martinez, Conchita 911
Martínez, Daniel 911
Martinez, Dave 911
Martínez, Diógeneos 911
Martinez, Eden 911
Martinez, Edgar 911
Martinez, Emiliano 911
Martínez, Esperanza 911
Martínez, Ever 911
Martinez, Fernando Daniel 911
Martinez, Gabriel 911
Martínez, Gerson 911
Martínez, Guillermo 911
Martínez, Hernán 911
Martinez, Iker 911
Martinez, J.D. 911
Martínez, Jesús 911
Martinez, Joan Lino 911
Martinez, Jose 911
Martinez, Josef 911
Martínez, Juan Antonio 911
Martínez, Julio 911
Martinez, Lazaro 911
Martinez, Luis 911
Martinez, Magdelin 911
Martinez, Manuel 911
Martínez, Matías 911
Martinez, Mel 911
Martinez, Michael 911
Martínez, Nelson 911
Martinez, Nick 911
Martinez, Nicole 911
Martinez, Pedro 911
Martinez, Rafael 911
Martínez, Ricardo 911
Martinez, Richard 911
Martínez, Rogelio 911
Martinez, Sergio 911
Martinez, Sigrid 911
Martinez, Sylvia Libow 911
Martinez, Tino 911
Martínez, Tomás Eloy 911
Martinez, Victor 911
Martinez, Wilfredo 911
Martinez, Yurberjen Herney 911
マルティネズ
Martinez, Claude 910
Martínez, Josè Carlos 911
マルティネス・イ・マルティネス
Martínez y Martínez, Enrique 911
マルティネス・エスピノサ
Martínez Espinoza, Pablo Fernando 911
マルティネス・カサレス
Martínez Cázares, German 911
マルティネス・ケリー
Martinez Kelly, Michelle 911
マルティネス＝コンデ
Martinez-Conde, Susana 911
マルティネス・ドルダン
Martínez Doldán, Oscar 911
マルティネス・トレス
Martínez Torres, Hernán 911
マルティネスパラシオ
Martinez Palacio, Miguel 911
マルティネス・ボニジャ
Martínez Bonilla, Hugo Roger 911
マルティネス＝メンチェン
Martínez-Menchén, Antonio 911
マルティネッティ
Martinetti, Anne 910
Martinetti, Guido 910
Martinetti, John 910
マルティネッリ
Martinelli, Ricardo 910
マルティネリ
Martinelli, Ricardo 910
Martinelli, Russ J. 910
マルティネル
Martinell, Emma 910
Martinell, Francisco 910
マルティーノ
Martino, Al 912
Martino, Fabio 912
Martino, Freddie 912
マルティノ
Martino, Antonio 912
Martino, Wayne 912
Martinod, Marie 912
マルティノー
Martineau, John 910
マルティノフ
Martynov, Sergei 912
Martynov, Sergei N. 912
マルティノラガルド
Martinot-lagarde, Pascal 912
マルティ・プティ
Martí Petit, Antoni 912
マルディヤント
Mardiyanto 901
マルティロシャン
Martirosyan, Simon 912
マルティン
Maltin, Leonard 891
Martin, Alex 908
Martin, Andrej 908
Martin, Damir 908
Martín, Esteban 908
Martin, Leo 909
Martin, Luis Miguel 909
Martín, Lydia 909
Martin, Razvan Constantin 909
Martin, Tony 910
Martín i Roig, Gabriel 912
マルティン・ウエルタ
Martín Huerta, Ramón 911
マルティン＝ガルソ
Martín Garzo, Gustavo 911
マルティン＝コルピ
Martin Korpi, Barbara 912
マルティンス
Martins, Alberto 912
Martins, Cidalia 912
Martins, Filomena 912
Martins, Geraldo João 912
Martins, Luis 912
Martins, Nelson 912
Martins, Sebastião José António 912
Martins, Zeferino 912
マルティンス・インディ
Martins Indi, Bruno 912
マルティーンセン
Martienssen, Rob 908
マルテッラ
Martella, Bruno 907
マルテリー
Martelly, Michel 907
マルテル
Martel, Frédéric C. 907
マルデン
Malden, Karl 889
マルテンス
Martens, Burkhard 907
Martens, Ekkehart 907
Martens, Ernesto 907
Martens, Wilfried 907
マルテンス・レボジェド
Martens Rebolledo, Ernest 907
マルト
Marto, Michael 912
マルトゥシエッロ
Martusciello, Giovanni 912
マルドナード
Maldonado, Kirstin 889
Maldonado, Martin 889
マルドナド
Maldonado, Erwin 889
Maldonado, Mervin 889
Maldonado, Nicia 889
Maldonado, Salvador 889
Vargas Maldonado, Miguel 1447
マルドナド・クルティ
Maldonado Curti, Carlos 889
マルトニ
Martonyi, János 912
マルトニー
Martonyi, János 912
マルトーネ
Martone, Mario 912
マルトバイ
Maltby, J.Roger 891
マルトハウス
Malthouse, Edward C. 891
マルトラーナ
Martorana, Marina 912
マルトワルドヨ
Martowardojo, Agus 912
マルトン
Marton, Anita 912
Marton, Anna 912
マルナ
Maruna, Shadd 913
マルーニ
Mrouni, Elie 985
マルーニー
Marooney, Kimberly 905
マルネ
Marnay, Eddy 904
マルハス
Malhas, Omar 889
マールバック
Muhlbach, Don 987
マルハーン
Mulhern, Francis J. 988
マルバーン
Malvern, Gladys 891
マルヒ
March, Aaron 899
マルーフ
Maloof, Joe 891
Malouf, David 891
Malouf, David George Joseph 891
Malouf, Doug 891
Maruf, Taha Muhieddin 912
マルフォード
Mulford, Charles W. 988
マルブラー
Marbler, Margarita 899
マルブリ
Marvulli, Franco 913
マルフーン
al-Marhoon, Khalid bin Omar bin Said 902
マルホトラ
Malhotra, Arvind 889
Malhotra, Deepak 889
Malhotra, Naresh K. 889
Malhotra, Shriya 889
マルホール
Mulhall, Douglas 988
マルミエルカ
Malmierca, Isidoro 891
マルミエルカ・ディアス
Malmierca Díaz, Rodrigo 891
マルーム
Malloum, Yakoura 890
マルムース
Malmuth, Bruce 891
マルムスティーン
Malmsteen, Yngwie 891
マルムステン
Malmsten, Ernst 891
マルムストローム
Malmström, Cecilia 891
マルモ
Marmo, Costantino 904
マルモッタン
Marmottan, Anemone 904
マルモレホス
Marmolejos, Jose 904

マルヤマ
Maruyama, Paul Kuniaki 913
マルヨマキ
Marjomäki, Heikki 903
マルラ
Marra, Michael F. 905
マルライ
Marurai, Jim 913
マルランダ
Marulanda, Manuel 912
マルラン・ミリテロ
Marland-Militello, Muriel 904
マルーリス
Maroulis, Helen 905
Maroulis, William 905
マルルーニー
Mulroney, Martin Brian 990
マルロー
Malraux, Madeleine 891
マルロス・モレノ
Marlos Moreno 904
マルワル
Malwal, Josef 891
マルワン
Marwan, Jafar 913
マルン
Marún, Jorge 913
マルンガ
Malunga, Grain 891
マーレー
Marley, Christopher 904
Marley, Damian 904
Marley, Stephen 904
Murray, Bill 994
Murray, Williamson 995
マレ
Mallé, Sanogo Aminate 890
Mallet, Marie-Louise 890
Marais, Pia 899
Maret, Cyrille 901
Maret, Pascale 901
Murray, Dain H. 994
マレー
Mallet, Corinne 890
Marée, Marcel 901
Murray, Aaron 994
Murray, Alan S. 994
Murray, Albert 994
Murray, Alison 994
Murray, Andy 994
Murray, Bill 994
Murray, Bruce 994
Murray, Charles A. 994
Murray, Conor 994
Murray, Dejounte 994
Murray, DeMarco 994
Murray, Donald Morison 995
Murray, Eric 995
Murray, Gordon S. 995
Murray, Jamal 995
Murray, James Dickson 995
Murray, Joseph Edward 995
Murray, Justin 995
Murray, Kiel 995
Murray, Latavius 995
Murray, Liz 995
Murray, Nicholas 995
Murray, Patrick 995
Murray, Paul 995
Murray, Raymond L. 995
Murray, Robert Emmett 995
Murray, Robert K. 995
Murray, Robin 995
Murray, Sarah Elizabeth 995
Murray, Simon 995
Murray, Stuart 995
Murray, Stuart A.P. 995
Murray, T.Scott 995
Murray, Virginia 995
Murrey, Jeneth 995
マレア
Marea, Tauanei 901
マーレイ
Marley, Jo 904
Murray, Alan Robert 994
Murray, Alan S. 994
Murray, Bill 994
Murray, Jocelyn 995
Murray, Katherine 995
Murray, Peter J. 995
マレイ
Murray, Bill 994
Murray, David 994
Murray, David Kord 994
Murray, Joseph Edward 995
Murray, Linda 995
Murray, Martine 995
Murray, Michael T. 995
Murray, Scott 995
Murray, William H. 995
マレイアーネ
Maleiane, Adriano Afonso 889
マレーヴィチ
Malevich, Kazimir Severinovich 889
マレウェジ
Malewezi, Justin 889
マレーク
Marék, Veronika 901
マレク
Malek, Doreen Owens 889
Malek, William A. 889
マレクザデ
Malekzadeh, Mohammad -Sharif 889
マレシュ
Mareš, Petr 901
Maresch, Sven 901
マレシュカ
Maleszka, Andrzej 889
マレスギア
Mares Guia, Walfrido 901
マレスコッティ
Marescotti, Rosette 901
マレー＝スミス
Murray-Smith, Joannna 995
マレースミス
Murray-Smith, Joannna 995
マレック
Malec 889
Málek, Jaromir 889
Malek, Kamal M. 889
Malleck, Ryan 890
Marek, Norma Cornett 901
マレット
Mallet, David 890
Mallett, Richard 890
Mallett, Ronald L. 890
Mallett, Ryan 890
マレッロ
Marrero, David G. 905
マレニッチ
Marenic, Igor 901
マレボ
Malebo, Moeketse 889
マレヨンボ
Maleyombo, Thierry 889
マレリー
Mallery, Susan 890
マレル
Morrell, David 976
Murrell, Amy R. 995
Murrell, John 995
Murrell, Kenneth L. 995
マレルブ
Malherbe, Frans 889
マレーロ
Marrero, Conrado 905
Marrero, Deven 905
マレロ・クルス
Marrero Cruz, Manuel 905
マレン
Mullen, Brendan 989
Mullen, Larry 989
Mullen, Michael 989
Mullen, Tony 989
マレンカ
Malenka, Robert C. 889
マレンガ
Malenga, Ernest 889
マレンコ
Marenco, Jose 901
マレンザパ
Malénzapa, Dorothée Aimée 889
マレンダー
Mullender, Audrey 989
マレント
Marent, Thomas 901
マレンボン
Marenbon, John 901
マーロー
Marleau, Marie-Eve 904
マロ
Maroh, Julie 905
マロー
Maroh, Julie 905
マロイ
Malloy, Emmett 891
Malloy, Marti 891
Maloi, Lebesa 891
Maloy, Joe 891
Mulloy, Peggy 990
マーロウ
Marlow, Layn 904
Marlow, Simon 904
Marlowe, Mia 904
Marlowe, Stephen 904
マーロウィー
Marlowe, Dean 904
マロヴィッチ
Marović, Svetozor 905
マロウィッツ
Marowitz, Charles 905
Marowitz, Gail 905
Marowitz, Richard 905
マロウチック
Murowchick, Robert E. 993
マロク
Maloku, Leonardo 891
マロクィン
Marroquin, Manny 906
マロザ
Maloza, Mangeza 891
マロシ
Marosi, Adam 905
マロス
Malos, Ellen 891
マーロック
Marok 905
マロック・ブラウン
Malloch Brown, Mark 890
マロッタ
Marotta, Millie 905
マロット
Malott, John R. 891
Marotte, Maxime 905
マローニ
Maroni, Roberto 905
マローニー
Maloney, Chris 891
Maloney, Shane 891
Mulroney, Louise 990
マロニ
Maroni, Roberto 905
マロニー
Maloney, Mike 891
Maloney, Shaun 891
Maroney, McKayla 905
マロニィ
Maloney, David C. 891
マロビッチ
Malović, Snežana 891
Marović, Svetozor 905
マーロフ
Malov, Sergey 891
マロフ
Maroh, Dominic 905
マロマト
Malomat, Ali 891
マロヤ
Maloya, Thengo 891
マロヤン・キシダ
Maloyan-Kishida, Ana 891
マロユ
Maroiu, Anca 905
マロリー
Mallory, Anne 890
Mallory, Margaret 890
マローン
Mallon, Meg 890
Malone, Ainsley M. 891
Malone, Brendan 891
Malone, Casey 891
Malone, David M. 891
Malone, Gareth 891
Malone, John C. 891
Malone, John Williams 891
Malone, Marianne 891
Malone, Michael 891
Malone, Michael Shawn 891
Malone, Peter 891
Malone, Robert 891
Malone, Thomas W. 891
Maron, Hermann 905
Maron, Monika 905
Marone, Mark D. 905
マロン
Mallon, Brenda 890
Mallon, Gerald P. 890
Maron, Jordan 905
Maron, Margaret 905

マワイ
Mawae, Kevin 923
マワジュデ
Mawajdeh, Salah 923
マワホフスキ
Malachowski, Piotr 888
マワリ
al-Mawali, Hilal bin Khalid bin Nasser 923
マワレ
Mawere, Moses 923
マーン
Marn, Michael V. 904
マン
Man, John 892
Man, Paul de 892
Mang, Paul Y. 894
Mann, Abby 895
Mann, Aimee 895
Mann, Antony 895
Mann, Bethany 895
Mann, Catherine 895
Mann, Charles C. 895
Mann, Chris 895
Mann, Craig 895
Mann, David 895
Mann, Delbert 895
Mann, Elise 895
Mann, George 895
Mann, Gurinder Singh 895
Mann, Heinrich 895
Mann, Herbie 895
Mann, Holly 895
Mann, J. 895
Mann, Jim 895
Mann, John David 895
Mann, Joy Hewitt 895
Mann, Michael 895
Mann, Michael E. 895
Mann, Nick 895
Mann, Ruth E. 895
Mann, Susan 895
Mann, Ted 895
Mann, William 895
Mun, Jonathan 990
Munn, Pamela 991
マンヴィル
Manville, Lesley 898
マンカ
Manca, Joseph 893
マンガー
Munger, Katy 991
マンカスター
Muncaster, Harriet 991
マンカッド
Mankad, Mehul V. 895
マンガーノ
Mangano, Joseph J. 894
Mangano, Sal 894
マンガベイラ
Mangabeira, Gabriel 894
マンガラ
Mangala, Eliaquim 894
マンガル
Mangal, Mohammad Gulab 894
マンカレ
Mönkäre, Sinikka 966
マンガレリ
Mingarelli, Hubert 953
マンガン
Mangan, Anne 894
マーンキ
Mahnke, Doug 885
マンキーウィッツ
Mankiewicz, Tom 895
マンキェヴィチ
Mankiewicz, Richard 895
マンキエフ
Mankiev, Nazyr 895
マンキージョ
Manquillo, Javier 896
マンキュー
Mankiw, N.Gregory 895
マンキューソ
Mancuso, Gail 893
マンキュソ
Mancuso, Thomas J. 893
マンギンダアン
Mangindaan, E.E. 894
マンク
Munck, Ronaldo 991
マングウェンデ
Mangwende, Witness 894
マングェル
Manguel, Alberto 894
マンクーシ
Mancusi, Mari 893
マンクーゾ
Mancuso, Julia 893
Mancuso, Stefano 893
マングテ
Komm, Mary 754
マンクテロウ
Manktelow, K.I. 895
マングラマ
Mangulama, Leonard 894
マングワナ
Mangwana, Paul 894
マンゲアインゴノ
Mamgue Ayingono, Salvador 892
マンゲイラ
Mangueira, Augusto Archer de Sousa 894
Mangueira, Rui Jorge Carneiro 894
マンゲ・オバマ・ヌフベ
Mangueobama Nfubea, Ricardo 894
マンゲ・オバマ・ヌフベア
Mangueobama Nfubea, Ricardo 894
マンゲオバマヌフベア
Mangueobama Nfubea, Ricardo 894
マンゲナ
Mangena, Mosibudi 894
マンケル
Mankell, Henning 895
Munkel, Wayne I. 991
マンゲル
Manguel, Alberto 894
マンゲルスドルフ
Mangelsdorff, Albert 894
マンゲーレ
Manguele, Alexandre 894
マンケン
Mahnken, Thomas G. 885
マンゲンス
Mangenz, Richard Muyej 894
マンゴー
Mango, Nicholas 894
Mango, Spenser 894
Mingau, Muriel 953
マンゴヴァ
Mangova, Plamena 894
マンゴマ
Mangoma, Elton 894
マンゴールド
Mangold, James 894
Mangold, Nick 894
マンサー
Mensha, Spéro 935
マンサニリャ
Manzanilla, Hector 898
マンザノ
Manzano, Leonel 898
マンサライ
Mansaray, Minkailu 896
マンサレー
Mansaray, Minkailu 896
マンザレク
Manzarek, Ray 898
マンザレック
Manzarek, Ray 898
マンシ
Mancz, Greg 893
マンシー
Manthey, Marie 897
Munchy, Max 991
マンジォーネ
Mangione, Salvatore 894
マンシジャ
Mansilla, Claudio 896
マンシジャ・フェルナンデス
Mansilla Fernández, Williams 896
マンシズ
Mansiz, Ilhan 897
マンシーニ
Mancini, Fabrizio 893
マンジャカプレ
Mangiacapre, Vincenzo 894
マンジャニ
Maniani, Mirela 895
マンジャロッティ
Mangiarotti, Angelo 894
マンジヤン
Manjian, Panos 895
マンシュ
Manche, Matthieu 893
マンジュ
Manju, Anwar Hossain 895
マンジュキッチ
Mandzukic, Mario 894
マンジュコヴ
Mandjukov, Petko 894
マンジョ
Mandjo, Yérima Youssoufa 894
Mangeot, Sylvain 894
マンシル
Mancill, Tony 893
マンス
Mans, Elizabeth 896
Manzur, Juan Luis 898
マンズ
Manns, Mary Lynn 896
Manns, William 896
Munz, Diana 992
マンスキー
Manski, Samuil 897
マンスズ
Mansiz, Ilhan 897
マンズバック
Mansbach, Adam 896
マンスフィールド
Mansfield, Andy 896
Mansfield, Michael Joseph 896
Mansfield, Peter 896
Mansfield, Stephen 896
マンスーリ
Mansoori, Deyarullah 897
al-Mansouri, Abubaker Mabrouk 897
Mansouri, Mustapha 897
al-Mansouri, Sultan bin Saeed 897
マンスール
Manseur, Nadjim 896
Mansoor, Edmond 897
Mansour, Abdessalem 897
Mansour, Adly 897
Mansour, Adnan 897
Mansour, Ahmad 897
Mansour, Akhtar Mohammad 897
Mansour, Albert 897
Mansour, bin Mutuib 897
Mansour, bin Zayed al-Nahyan 897
Mansour, Muhammad Loutfy 897
Mansour, Omar 897
Mansur, Abdol Latif 897
Mansur, Akhtar Mohammad 897
Mansur, Yusuf 897
マンスル
Mansur, Abd al-Malik 897
Manzur, Juan Luis 898
マンスロフ
Mansurov, Dilshod 897
Mansurov, Farid 897
マンスロン
Manceron, Gilles 893
マンセリ
Mansaray, Minkailu 896
マンセル
Mansel, Philip 896
Mansell, Dom 896
マンセル・カストリジョ
Mansell Castrillo, Salvador 896
マンソ
Mansot, Frédérick 897
マンゾ
Manzo, Mahamane 898
マンソー・ソーセダ
Manseau Sanceda, James 896
マンゾーニ
Manzoni, Jean-François 898
マンソン
Manson, Ainslie 897
Manson, Cynthia 897
Manson, Leigh 897
Manson, Marilyn 897
Manson, Robert 897
Manson, Shirley 897
マンダー
Mander, Jerry 893
マンダイン
Mundine, Jimmay 991
マンダバ
Mandaba, Jean-Michel 893
マンダル
Mandal, Badri Prasad 893
Mandal, Shatya

Narayan 893
マンダンダ
Mandanda, Steve 893
マンダンディ
Mandandi, Godden 893
マンチ
Munsch, Robert N. 992
マンチェスター
Manchester, William 893
マンチェフ
Mantchev, Lisa 897
マンチーニ
Mancini, Roberto 893
Mancini, Trey 893
マンチネッリ
Mancinelli, Antonio 893
マンチャム
Mancham, James Richard Marie 893
マンチョン
Manchon, Blanca 893
マンツ
Manz, Charles C. 898
Manz, Daniel 898
マンツィオス
Mantsios, Gregory 897
マンツィック
Manzuik, Steve W. 898
マンツェンライター
Manzenreiter, Sonja 898
Manzenreiter, Wolfram 898
マンテ
Mante, Enid 897
Manthe, Ulrich 897
マンデ
Mande, Bala 893
マンディ
Mandi, Aissa 893
Mundy, Jon 991
Mundy, Linus 991
Mundy, Liza 991
マンデイ
Monday, Will 965
Munday, Jeremy 991
マンディア
Mandia, Kevin 893
マンディギ
Mandigui, Yokabdjim 893
マンディーサ
Mandisa 894
マンティジャ
Mantilla, Felipe 897
Mantilla, Jesús 897
マンティス
Mantis, Panagiotis 897
マンディチ
Mandić, Milica 893
マンディッチ
Mandić, Milica 893
マンティラ
Mantila, Jari 897
マンディワンジラ
Mandiwanzira, Supa 894
マンディンガ
Mandinga, Victor Luís Pinto Fernandes 893
マンテガ
Mantega, Guido 897
マンテガッツァ
Mantegazza, Giovanna 897
マンデッリ
Mandelli, Mariuccia 893
マンデハツァラ
Mandehatsara, Georget 893
マンテュラ
Mäntylä, Hanna 897
マンデラ
Mandela, Nelson Rolihlahla 893
マンデリ
Mandelli, Mariuccia 893
マンテル
Mantel, Gerhard 897
Mantel, Hilary 897
Mantell, Paul 897
マンデル
Mandel, Brett H. 893
Mandel, Emily St. John 893
Mandel, Michael J. 893
Mandell, Muriel 893
Mandell, Sibyl 893
Minder, Robert 952
Mundell, David 991
Mundell, Robert Alexander 991
マンデルカー
Mandelker, Scott 893
マンデルソン
Mandelson, Peter Benjamin 893
マンデルソン卿
Lord Mandelson 893
マンデルバウム
Mandelbaum, Lily 893
Mandelbaum, Michael 893
Mandelbaum, W. Adam 893
マンデルブロー
Mandelbrot, Benoît B. 893
マンデルブロート
Mandelbrot, Benoît B. 893
マンデルボウム
Mandelbaum, Alexandra 893
マントゥロフ
Manturov, Denis V. 897
マントバーニ
Mantovani, Martin 897
マンドラゴラ
Mandragora, Rolando 894
マンドラーテ
Mandlate, Tomas 894
マントリー
Mantley, John 897
マントル
Mantle, Anthony Dod 897
Mantle, Ben 897
マンドル
Mandl, Franz 894
マントレ
Mentré, Pascale 935
マントロ
Mantlo, Bill 897
マントン
Manton, Steve 897
Munton, Don 992
マンナ
Manna, Giovanni 896
マンニーナ
Mannina, Calogero 896
マンニネン
Manninen, Hannes 896
Manninen, Hannu 896
マンニーノ
Mannino, Franco 896
マンヌッチ
Mannucci, Umberto 896
マンネル
Mannell, Roger C. 896
マンノ
Manno, Bruno V. 896
マンノーネ
Mannone, Vito 896
マンバ
Mamba, Mashako 892
Mamba, Ndumiso 892
Mamba, Patrick Magobetane 892
Mamba, Rogers 892
マンバー
Manber, Rachel 893
マンハイマー
Mannheimer, Max 896
マンハーツ
Manhertz, Chris 894
マンハート
Manhart, Cole 894
マンハレス
Manjarrez Bastidas, Itzel Adilene 895
マンビー
Manby, Chris 893
Munby, Zoë 991
マンビル
Manville, Brook 898
マーンフィー
Marneffe, Catherine 905
マンフェルト・デ・ファビアニス
Manferto, Valeria 894
マンフォード
Mountford, S.Joy 982
Mumford, David Bryant 990
Mumford, Susan 990
Munford, William Arthur 991
Munford, Xavier 991
マンブニャリ
Mambou Gnali, Aimee 892
マンプヤ
Mampouya, Hellot Matson 892
Mampouya, Michel 892
マンプヤ・マトソン
Mampouya Matson, Hellot 892
マンプヤマンツォネ
Mampouya Mantsone, Elo 892
マンフリー
Mumphery, Keith 990
マンフレッド
Manfred, Rob 894
マンフレーディ
Manfredi, John Frederick 894
マンフレディ
Manfredi, Matt 894
Manfredi, Nino 894
Manfredi, Valerio Massimo 894
マンフレド
Manfrédo, Stéphane 894
マンフンビ
Manfoumbi, Yves Fernand 894
マンベトフ
Mambetov, Asset 892
マンホランド
Munholland, John Kim 991
マンマ
Mamma, Lemina Mint Kotob Ould 892
Momma, Lemina Mint Kotob Ould 965
マンマナ
Mammana, Emanuel 892
マンメドワ
Mammedova, Gulshat 892
マンヤニ
Manjani, Ylli 895
マンリー
Manley, Bill 895
Manley, John 895
Manley, Lissa 895
Manley, Melanie 895
Manly, Steven L. 895
マンリケ
Manrique, Jaime 896
Manrique, Juan 896
マンレー
Manley, John 895
マンレイ
Manley, Bill 895
マンロ
Munro, Roxie 992
マンロー
Munro, Alice 991
Munro, Christiaan 991
Munro, Moira 991
Munroe, Randall 992
マンワニ
Manwani, Harish 898

【ミ】

ミー
Mee, Ben 929
Mee, Benjamin 929
Mee, Bob 929
ミーア
Mear, Stephen 928
Meer, Fatima 929
ミア
Meer, Cor van der 929
Mia, Sidik 941
ミアー
Mier, Martha 944
ミアイユ
Miailhe, Florence 941
ミアシャイマー
Mearsheimer, John J. 928
ミアーズ
Meares, Anna 928
Mears, Chris 928
ミアッツォ
Miazzo, Francesca 942
ミアルス
Mearls, Mike 928
ミアルチンスキ
Miarczynski, Przemyslaw 942
ミアレ
Mialet, Hélène 942
ミアロム
Miarom, Betel 942

ミアン
Mian, Atif 942
Mian, Jasmine 942
Mian, Marcellina 942
ミアング
Miangue, Senna 942
ミアンコワ
Miankova, Aksana 942
ミアンボ
Mihambo, Malaika 945
ミーヴィル
Miéville, China 944
ミウォシュ
Miłosz, Czesław 952
ミウ・ミウ
Miou-Miou 954
ミウラ
Mihura, Joni L. 945
Miura, Mieko 957
ミエ
Millet, Catherine 950
ミエヴィル
Miéville, China 944
ミエシュコフスカ
Mieszkowska, Krystyna Zabojszcz 944
ミエッティネン
Miettinen, Reijo 944
Miettinen, Satu 944
ミエール
Miele, Lino 944
ミエル
Miell, Dorothy 944
ミエレス
Mieres, Gaston 944
ミーオドヴニク
Miodownik, Mark 954
ミオン
Mion, Jeremie 954
ミーカ
Mika 945
ミーカー
Meaker, Marijane 928
Meeker, Mary 929
ミカイル
Mikha'il, Murad 945
ミカウタゼ
Mikautadze, Kote 945
ミカエル
Michael 942
Michaels, Alan C. 942
ミカーティ
Mikati, Najib 945
ミカティ
Mikati, Mohammed Najib 945
Mikati, Najib 945
ミカライティス
Mikalaitis, Marcella Ann 945
ミカルスカ
Michalska, Julia 942
ミカルスキ
Michalski, Brent 942
ミカロウィッツ
Michalowicz, Mike 942
ミガン
Migan, Assétou Founè Samaké 944
ミキ
Miki, Arthur Kazumi 945
Miki, Danny 945
Miki, Toshio 945
Miky, Fuji Roy 946
ミキエレット
Michieletto, Damiano 943
ミキーシン
Mikishin, Yury 945
ミキテンコ
Mikitenko, Irina 945
ミキナ
Mikina, Sabina 945
ミギル
Miguil, Abdallah Abdillahi 944
ミキレナ
Miquilena, Luis 954
ミギロ
Migiro, Asha-rose 944
ミーク
Meek, James 929
Meek, Paul 929
Meeke, Kieran 929
ミクサル
Mikser, Sven 946
ミークス
Meeks, Jodie 929
Meeks, Jonathan 929
ミクセル
Mikser, Sven 946
ミクダド
Miqdad, Kassem 954
ミクナース
Mouknass, Naha Mint Hamdy Ould 982
ミクラウチ
Miklautsch, Karin 945
ミクラウチチュ
Miklavčič, Borut 945
ミクラク
Mikulak, Samuel 946
ミグラニ
Miglani, Bob 944
ミグリオリ
Migliore, Daniel L. 944
ミクリーノワ
Miklínová, Galina 945
ミークル
Meikle, Denis 931
ミクルスウェイト
Micklethwait, John 943
ミクルライトナー
Miklleitner, Johanna 945
ミクレア
Miclea, Mircea 943
ミクロシ
Miklósi, Adam 945
ミクローシュ
Miklóš, László 945
ミクロシュ
Miklos, Edit 945
Mikloš, Ivan 945
ミクロス
Micklos, David A. 943
Miklóš, László 945
Mikos 946
ミケシュ
Mikesh, Robert C. 945
ミゲス・ボニーノ
Míguez-Bonino, José 944
ミケッチ
Mikec, Damir 945
ミケッツ
Mikec, Damir 945
ミケティ
Michetti, Gabriela 943
ミケーリ
Michelli, Joseph A. 943
ミケリ
Micheli, Enrico 943
ミケリーニ
Michelini, Carlo Alberto 943
ミケル
Mickel, Tom 943
Mikel, John Obi 945
Miquel, Pierre Gabriel Roger 954
ミゲル
Miguel, Edward 944
Miguel, Girlyn 944
Miguel, Luis 944
ミケル・ゴンサレス
Mikel Gonzalez 945
ミケルス
Michels, Rinus 943
ミケルセン
Mikkelsen, Brian 945
Mikkelsen, Mads 945
ミケルソン
Mickelson, Phil 943
Mikhelson, Leonid 945
ミケルッツィ
Micheluzzi, Attilo 943
ミゲル・トーレス
Miguel Torres 944
ミゲル・フラーニョ
Miguel Flano 944
ミケル・リコ
Mikel Rico 945
ミゲレコ
Migereko, Daudi 944
ミケレッティ
Micheletti, Andrea 943
ミケロッティ
Michelotti, Augusto 943
ミケロット
Michelotto, Gabriella 943
Michelotto, Paolo 943
ミケンズ
Mickens, Jaydon 943
ミコウスキー
Mikowski, Michael S. 946
ミコシュ
Mikosch, Thomas 946
ミコフ
Mikov, Mihail 946
ミコライ
Mikolaj, Ján 945
ミコライチェフスキ
Mikolajczewski, Artur 945
ミコライチュク
Mikolajczyk, Beata 945
ミコロ
Micolo, Rosa Luís De Sousa 943
Mikolo, Jacqueline Lydia 945
ミサ
Misa, Telefoni Retzlaff 955
ミザーヴ
Meserve, Jessica 938
ミサカ
Misaka, Jeanette M. 955
ミサク
Mysak, Denis 1000
ミザーズ
Mithers, Carol Lynn 957
ミザーニ
Misani, Nicola 955
ミサヤロフスキ
Misajlovski, Vlado 955
ミザン・ザイナル・アビディン
Mizan Zainal Abidin 958
ミサンチャク
Misanchuk, Melanie 955
ミサンボ
Missambo, Paulette 955
ミシ
Misi, Koa 955
ミジ
Midzi, Amos 944
ミシアノ
Misiano, Christopher 955
ミジェット
Midgette, Anne 944
ミジェリンスカ
Mizielińska, Aleksandra 958
ミジェリンスキ
Mizieliński, Daniel 958
ミシェル
Michel, Cécile 943
Michel, Charles 943
Michel, Gilles 943
Michel, Henri 943
Michel, James 943
Michel, James Alix 943
Michel, Jean-Baptiste 943
Michel, Louis 943
Michel, Macedo 943
Michel, Marjory 943
Michel, Marken 943
Michel, Smark 943
Michel, Sylvio 943
Mischel, Walter 955
ミシェルズ
Michels, Elizabeth 943
Michiels, Githa 943
ミシェル＝チリエ
Michel-Thiriet, Philippe 943
ミジオ
Mizio, Francis 958
ミシジャン
Miesiedjan, Martin 944
ミシチュク
Mishchuk, Taras 955
ミシーノ
Misino, Dominick J. 955
ミシハイラブウィムションガ
Misihairabwimushonga, Priscilla 955
ミシャネック
Michanek, Christina 942
ミシャバエ
Mishabae 955
ミシャラク
Michalak, Frédéric 942
ミシャル
Mishal, Nissim 955
ミジャル・バルエコ
Miyar Barrueco, José Miguel 958
ミジャレス・ロドリゲス
Millares Rodríguez, José Manuel 947
ミジヤワ
Mijiyawa, Moustafa 945

ミシャン
Mishan, E.J. 955
ミシュカ
Myszka, Piotr 1000
ミシュコフ
Miškov, Juraj 955
ミシュニク
Mischnick, Wolfgang 955
ミシュラ
Mishra, Kalraj 955
Mishra, Pankaj 955
ミシュラン
Michelin, Edouard 943
Michelin, François 943
ミシュロ
Michelot, Pierre 943
Michelot, Vincent 943
ミショー
Michaud, Andrée A. 942
Michaud, Ellen 942
Michaud, Stephen G. 942
ミジョン
Migeon, Mary B. 944
ミシリエ
Missillier, Steve 955
ミシローリ
Missiroli, Massimo 955
ミズエ
Mizue, Mirai 958
ミズガイティス
Mizgaitis, Mindaugas 958
ミスキナ
Myskina, Anastasia 1000
ミスキン
Miskin, Michael 955
ミスキンド
Mischkind, Louis A. 955
ミズシリ
Mizushiri, Yoriko 958
ミスタキドウ
Mystakidou, Elisavet 1000
ミースターズ
Meesters, Erik H.W.G. 929
ミズタニ
Mizutani, Miki 958
Mizutani, Satoshi 958
ミスターペッツ
*Mr.*Pets 985
ミズダル
Mizdal, Ewa 958
ミスターローディ
*Mr.*Lordi 985
ミステリー
Mystery 1000
ミストゥル
Mistoul, Flore 956
ミストリー
Mistry, Cyrus Pallonji 956
Mistry, Dilaawar 956
Mistry, Neville F. 956
ミズナー
Misner, Stacia 955
ミズノ
Mizuno, Reina 958
ミスフェルト
Misfeldt, Trevor 955
ミスマリ
al-Mismari, Saleh Rajab 955
ミースラー
Miessler, Gary L. 944
ミズラヒ
Mizrahi, Isaac 958
ミズーリ
Mizouri, Laroussi 958
ミス・リード
Miss Read 956
ミスルカニェ
Missouloukagne, Marie 956
ミズレー
Miserey, Yves 955
ミスワコフスキ
Mysłakowski, Piotr 1000
ミズン
Mithen, Steven J. 957
ミセジニコフ
Misejnikov, Stas 955
Misezhnikov, Stas 955
ミセリ
Miceli, Joe 942
ミセレンディーノ
Miserendino, Leo J. 955
ミゼロッキ
Miserocchi, H.Kevin 955
ミソンゴ
Missongo, Pascal Désiŕe 956
ミーダー
Meador, Clifton K. 928
ミタキス
Mitakis, Ioannis 956
ミタス
Mitas, Efthimios 956
ミーダナー
Miedaner, Talane 944
ミダナ
Midana, Augusto 943
ミタリ
Mitali, Protais 956
ミタル
Mittal, Lakshmi Niwas 957
ミーチ
Meech, Molly 929
Meech, Sam 929
ミチー
Michie, David 943
ミチェリ
Miceli, Felisa 942
ミチェルスカ
Mycielska, Małgorzata 999
ミチェレッティ
Micheletti, Roberto 943
ミチャイ・ヴィラヴァイディア
Mechai Viravaidya 928
ミーチャイ・ウィラワイタヤ
Mechai Viravaidya 928
ミチャイ・ビラバイディア
Mechai Viravaidya 928
ミーチャイ・ビラワイタヤー
Mechai Viravaidya 928
ミチャイル
Michail, Ashraf 942
ミチャエル・サントス
Michael Santos 942
ミチャード
Mitchard, Jacquelyn 956
ミチャビリャ
Michavilla, José María 942
ミーチャム
Meacham, Jon 927
ミチャンアルビンゲル
Michan, Alberto 942
ミチュキ
Michuki, John 943
ミチュコフ
Mityukov, Ihor A. 957
ミチュノビッチ
Mićunović, Branislav 943
ミチョビッチ
Micovic, Zarko 943
ミチン
Michine, Alexei 943
Mishin, Aleksey 955
ミツカハリッチ
Mickaharic, Draja 943
ミッキー
Michie, Christine 943
Mickey, Jordan 943
ミックフィ
McPhee, Stephen J. 878
ミックミラン
McMillan, Robert 877
ミツコ
Mitsuko 957
ミッコネン
Mikkonen, Suvi 945
ミッシェル
Michel, Dominique 943
Michel, Donald E. 943
Michel, James Alix 943
Michel, Serge 943
Michele, Chrisette 943
ミッシュ
Misch, Rochus 955
ミッジリー
Midgley, Mary 944
Midgley, Nick 944
ミッジリィ
Midgley, James 944
ミッジレー
Midgely, Amy 944
ミッシローリ
Missiroli, Simone 956
ミッソーニ
Missoni, Angera 956
Missoni, Ottavio 956
Missoni, Vittorio 956
ミッター
Mitter, Matt 957
Mitter, Rana 957
ミッターマイヤー
Mittermeier, Russell 957
ミッタル
Mittal, Banwari 957
Mittal, Lakshmi Niwas 957
Mittal, Suneet 957
ミッチアンチオ
Micciancio, Daniele 942
ミッチェル
Mitchel, Doug 956
Mitchel, Tevin 956
Mitchell, Adrian 956
Mitchell, Alex 956
Mitchell, Andrew 956
Mitchell, Billy 956
Mitchell, Brian R. 956
Mitchell, Bryan 956
Mitchell, Chris 956
Mitchell, Colin 956
Mitchell, Craig 956
Mitchell, David 956
Mitchell, David R. 956
Mitchell, Derek Robert 956
Mitchell, Dreda Say 956
Mitchell, Drew 956
Mitchell, Earl 956
Mitchell, Ed 956
Mitchell, Edgar D. 956
Mitchell, Emma 956
Mitchell, Ethan 956
Mitchell, Fred 956
Mitchell, Frederick 956
Mitchell, George John 956
Mitchell, George P. 956
Mitchell, Greg 956
Mitchell, Jack 956
Mitchell, James A. 956
Mitchell, James K. 956
Mitchell, Jann 956
Mitchell, Jeffrey T. 956
Mitchell, Jerry 956
Mitchell, John Cameron 956
Mitchell, John G. 956
Mitchell, Jon 956
Mitchell, Joni 956
Mitchell, Kathryn 956
Mitchell, Keith 956
Mitchell, Lauren 956
Mitchell, Lawrence E. 956
Mitchell, Lisa 956
Mitchell, Malcolm 956
Mitchell, Marc 956
Mitchell, Margaree King 956
Mitchell, Mark 956
Mitchell, Mary 956
Mitchell, Melanie 957
Mitchell, Mike 957
Mitchell, Mitch 957
Mitchell, Neil James 957
Mitchell, Olivia S. 957
Mitchell, Peter R. 957
Mitchell, Randall 957
Mitchell, Robert Cameron 957
Mitchell, Ryan 957
Mitchell, Scott 957
Mitchell, Sirah 957
Mitchell, Stephen 957
Mitchell, Terrance 957
Mitchell, Timothy 957
Mitchell, Tyler 957
Mitchell, William John 957
Mitchell, W.J.Thomas 957
ミッチエル
Mitchell, Jeffrey T. 956
ミッチャード
Mitchard, Jacquelyn 956
ミッチャム
Mitcham, Matthew 956
Mitcham, Samuel W. 956
Mitchum, John 957
ミッチャーリッヒ
Mitscherlich, Alexander 957
ミッチャーリヒ
Mitscherlich, Margarete 957
ミッチンソン
Mitchinson, John 957
ミッツィ
Mizzi, Joe 958
Mizzi, Konrad 958
ミッティカ
Mittica, Pierpaolo 957
ミッテラン
Mitterrand, Danielle 957
Mitterrand, Frédéric 957
ミッテルシュタット

Mittelstadt, Maximilian 957
ミッテルスタッド
Mittelstaedt, Ted 957
ミッテルバーグ
Mittelberg, Mark 957
ミッデルホフ
Middelhoff, Thomas 943
ミッテルマン
Mittelman, James H. 957
ミッテルレーナー
Mitterlehner, Reinhold 957
ミッテン
Mitten, Andy 957
ミッドグレイ
Midgley, John 944
ミットラー
Mittler, Peter J. 957
ミットン
Mitton, Jacqueline 957
Mytton, Jill 1000
ミッハル
Michal, Kristen 942
ミーディエート
Mediate, Rocco 928
ミテワ
Miteva, Silviya 957
ミーデン
Meaden, Alan 928
ミーテンビュラー
Mitenbuler, Reid 957
ミード
Mead, Alice 927
Mead, Chris 927
Mead, Eric 927
Mead, Hassan 927
Mead, Margaret 927
Mead, Marianne 927
Mead, Richelle 927
Mead, Syd 927
Mead, Virginia Hoge 927
Mead, Walter Russell 927
Meade, Glenn 928
Meade, Holly 928
Meade, Starr 928
Mede, Charlotte 928
Meed, Benjamin 929
ミードウ
Meadow, Merrill 928
ミトゥ
Mitu, Andreea 957
ミトゥーリチ
Miturich, Mai 957
Miturich, Mai Petrovich 957
ミトゥーリチ・フレブニコフ
Miturich-Khlebnikov, Mai 957
ミトゥーリチ＝フレーブニコフ
Miturich-Khlebnikov, Mai 957
ミード・クリブレニャ
Meade Kuribreña, José Antonio 928
ミートケ
Miethke, Wolfgang 944
ミトゴ
Mitogo, Alfredo Mitogo 957
ミトコーワ
Mitkova, Tatyana 957
ミトコワ
Mitkova, Tatyana 957
ミトニック
Mitnic, Kevin 957
ミトフ
Mitov, Daniel 957
ミトラ
Mitra, Amit 957
Mitra, Siddhartha 957
ミドラー
Midler, Bette 944
Midler, Paul 944
ミトリ
Metri, Tareq 939
ミトリタ
Mitrita, Alexandru 957
ミトル
Mitrou, Viktor 957
ミドル
Midol, Jonathan 944
ミドルズ
Middles, Mick 943
ミドルトン
Middleton, Charlotte 943
Middleton, Doug 944
Middleton, John 944
Middleton, Keynan 944
Middleton, Khris 944
Middleton, Nick 944
Middleton, Robin 944
Middleton, Susan 944
Middleton, Timothy 944
Middleton, William D. 944
ミドルバーグ
Middleberg, Don 943
ミドルブルックス
Middlebrooks, Will 943
ミトレア
Mitrea, Miron Tudor 957
ミトレワ
Mitreva, Ilinka 957
ミトログル
Mitroglou, Konstantinos 957
ミトロフ
Mitroff, Ian 957
ミトワ
Mittwer, Henry 957
ミトン
Mitton, Tony 957
ミドン
Midon, Raul 944
ミナ
Mina, Carlos Andres 952
Miná, Gianni 952
Minah, Vandi Chidi 952
ミナー
Minnaar, Hannes 953
ミナキル
Minakir, Pavel Aleksandrovich 952
ミナシ
Minasi, Mark 952
ミナシャン
Minasyan, Artsvik 952
Minasyan, Gor 952
ミナージュ
Minaj, Nicki 952
ミナース
Minirth, Frank B. 953
ミナハン
Minahan, Brian 952
ミナミ
Minami, Shion 952
Minami, Thomas 952
ミナヤ
Minaya, Jorge 952
Minaya, Juan 952
ミナラ
Minala, Joseph 952
Minallah, Fauzia Aziz 952
ミーナ・ラグナータン
Meena Raghunathan 929
ミナリッチ
Mlinarić, Marijan 958
ミニー
Minney, Safia 953
ミニエ
Minier, Bernard 953
ミニグ
Minning, Michel 953
ミニス
Minnis, Hubert 953
Minnis, Ivan 953
ミニスター
Minister, Peter 953
ミニター
Miniter, Richard 953
Miniter, Richard F. 953
ミニック
Minnick, Chris 953
Minnick, Mary E. 953
ミニバエフ
Minibaev, Viktor 953
ミニバニ
Mineebani, Abdul-Nasser 952
ミニヒマイヤー
Minichmayr, Birgit 953
ミニューチン
Minuchin, Salvador 954
ミニョソ
Miñoso, Minnie 953
ミニョーラ
Mignola, Michael 944
ミニョレ
Mignolet, Simon 944
ミニョン
Mignon, Patrick 944
Mignon, Philippe 944
ミニヨン
Mignon, Jean-Marie 944
ミニング
Minning, Michel 953
ミヌ
Minwoo 954
ミヌイ
Minoui, Delphine 953
ミヌッチ
Minucci, Daria 954
ミヌートコ
Minutko, Vitaliĭ Leonidovich 954
ミネタ
Mineta, Norman 953
ミネリ
Minelli, Laura Laurencich 952
Minnelli, Liza 953
ミネリー
Mignerey, Sharon 944
Minnery, John 953
ミネルヴィニ
Minervini, Mark 953
ミノウ
Minow, Martha 953
ミノヴスキー
Menovsky, Tomas 935
ミノーグ
Minogue, Kylie 953
ミノスキ
Minoski, Kiril 953
ミノーソ
Miñoso, Minnie 953
ミノソ
Miñoso, Minnie 953
ミノーレ
Minore, Renato 953
ミノワ
Minois, Georges 953
ミハイ
Michael 942
ミハイチャック
Mihychuk, MaryAnn 945
ミハイリディス
Michaelides, Antonis 942
ミハイリン
Mikhaylin, Alexandre 945
ミハイル
Mikhail, Jessica 945
ミハイレスク
Mihailescu, Constantin 944
Mihăilescu, Petru Şerban 944
ミハイロヴィッチ
Mihailovic, Dragoslav 945
Mihajlovic, Sinisa 945
ミハイロビッチ
Mihajlivić, Dušan 945
Mihajlovic, Lidija 945
Mihajlovic, Sinisa 945
Mihajlović, Zorana 945
ミハイロフ
Mikhailov, Boris 945
ミハイロフスカヤ
Mikhailovsky, Katya 945
ミハイロフスキ
Mihajlovski, Ljubomir 945
ミハイロワ
Mihailova, Nadezhda 944
ミハウ
Michal, Ptaszynski 942
ミハエル
Mikhael, Wijdan 945
ミハエル1世
Michael 942
ミハリク
Michalik, Michal 942
Michalik, Monika 942
ミハール
Mihál, Jozef 945
ミハル
Mihal, Dzianis 945
ミハルコーフ
Mikhalkov, Sergei Vladimirovich 945
ミハルコフ
Mikhalkov, Nikita 945
Mikhalkov, Sergei Vladimirovich 945
ミハルコフ・コンチャロフスキー
Mikhalkov-Konchalovskii, Andrei Sergeevich 945
ミハルジェビック
Mihaljevic, John 945
ミハルスキ
Michalski, Arkadiusz 942
ミハルチェンコ

ミ

Mykhal'chenko, Iryna 1000
ミハロビッチ
Mikhalovich, Aleh 945
ミーハン
Meehan, Bernard 929
Meehan, John David 929
Meehan, Thomas 929
Meehan, Tony 929
ミハンゴス
Mijangos, José Luis 945
ミヒェルス
Michels, Volker 943
ミヒェルス＝ヴェンツ
Michels-Wenz, Ursula 943
ミヒャエルスビールバウム
Michaels-beerbaum, Meredith 942
ミヒャルスキィ
Michalski, Tilman 942
Michalski, Ute 942
ミービル
Miéville, China 944
ミブイ
Mibuy, Angel Masie 942
ミフスッド
Mifsud, Hubert Charles 944
ミフスッドボンニチ
Mifsud-bonnici, Carmelo 944
ミフナーシェフ
Mikhnushev, Alexander 945
ミフネビッチ
Mikhnevich, Andrei Anatolyevich 945
Mikhnevich, Natallia 945
ミフビ
Mihoubi, Azzedine 945
ミフベク
Mihbek, Muhammad Zafer 945
ミフラーフ
al-Mikhlafi, Mohammed 945
ミフラーフィ
al-Mikhlafi, Abdul-Malek 945
ミフラーフィー
al-Mikhlafi, Mohammed 945
ミヘイレアニュ
Mihaileanu, Radu 944
ミヘリッチ
Mihelic, Tina 945
ミヘルス
Michels, Birgit 943
ミボト
Myboto, Zacharie 999
ミミコ
Mimiko, Rahman 952
ミミツァ
Mimica, Neven 952
ミーム
Mihm, Stephen 945
ミムス
Mims, Cedric A. 952
ミムーン
Mimoune, Smail 952
ミモーニ
Mimouni, Gilles 952
ミヤ
Mia, Mohammed Sidik 941
Mia, Sidik 941
ミャ・エイ
Mya Aye 999
ミヤオウ
Miyao, Richard Takaomi 958
ミヤギシマ
Miyagishima, Tak 958
ミャクシュコ
Miakushko, Serhiy 941
ミャグマルジャヴ・ガンバータル
Miagmarzhavyn Ganbaatar 941
ミヤケ
Miyake, Issey 958
ミヤサカ・マチダ
Miyasaka Machida, Francisco Shinichi 958
ミヤザキ
Miyazaki, Hayao 958
ミャスニコビッチ
Myasnikovich, Mikhail V. 999
ミヤタキ
Miyataki, Glenn Katsuichi 958
ミャト・ヘイン
Myat Hein 999
ミヤハラ
Miyahara, Maki Hiroyuki 958
ミヤヒラ
Miyahira, Wayne Tadashi 958
ミャ・ヘイン
Myat Hein 999
ミャ・ミャ・オン・キン
Myat Myat Ohn Khin 999
ミャリツァ
Myalytsya, Anatoliy 999
ミャルチンスキ
Miarczynski, Przemyslaw 942
ミヤンダ
Miyanda, Godfrey 958
Miyanda, Samuel 958
ミュー
Mew, Darren 940
ミューア
Muir, Robin 987
ミュア
Muir, Laura 987
Muir, Tom 987
ミュアンバ
Muamba, Henoc 985
ミュウ・ミュウ
Miou-Miou 954
ミューエ
Mühe, Ulrich 987
ミュエック
Mueck, Ron 986
ミュオロ
Muolo, Paul 992
ミュゲ
Mügge, Andreas 986
ミューザー
Mueser, Kim Tornvall 986
ミュージアル
Musial, Stan 996
ミュジカ
Muzyka, Zhena 998
ミュージグ
Musig, Todd 996
ミュージック
Music, Graham 996
Musick, John A. 996
ミュジック
Muzik, Katherine 998
ミュース
Muhs, William 987
Muth, Jon J. 997
ミューズ
Meeus, Cathy 929
Muse, Charlie 996
ミュスナー
Müssner, Renate 997
ミュズリエ
Muselier, Renaud 996
ミューダール
Myrdal, Jan 1000
ミュッカネン
Mykkänen, Kai 1000
ミュッシャンブレ
Muchembled, Robert 985
ミュッソ
Musso, Guillaume 997
ミュデジ
Müjdeci, Kaan 987
ミューバーン
Mewburn, Kyle 940
ミューヘイム
Muheim, Harry 987
ミューホート
Mewhort, Jack 940
ミューラー
Mueller, Charles 986
Mueller, Dennis C. 986
Mueller, Don 986
Mueller, Donna H. 986
Mueller, Jessie 986
Mueller, M. 986
Mueller, Tom 986
Muller, Eddie 989
Muller, Eric L. 989
Muller, Gerda 989
Müller, Jan-Werner 989
Muller, Jerry Z. 989
Müller, Lars 989
Müller, Michael 989
ミュラ
Murat, Laure 992
ミュラー
Mueller, Dagmar H. 986
Mueller, Felice 986
Mueller, Manuela 986
Mueller, Martin 986
Mueller, Pamela Bauer 986
Müller, Bernhard 989
Müller, Birte 989
Muller, Bobby 989
Müller, Christian Philipp 989
Müller, Florence 989
Muller, Florian 989
Müller, George 989
Müller, Gerd 989
Müller, Hans-Harald 989
Müller, Herta 989
Müller, Hildegard 989
Müller, Jörg 989
Müller, Jost 989
Müller, Jürgen 989
Müller, Leos 989
Müller, Lothar 989
Muller, Marie 989
Muller, Marius 989
Müller, Matthias 989
Muller, Nadine 989
Müller, Nestor Luiz 989
Muller, Nicolai 989
Müller, Peter 989
Muller, Sven 989
Müller, Thomas 989
Müller, Werner 989
ミュライユ
Murail, Elvire 992
Murail, Lorris 992
Murail, Marie-Aude 992
ミュラー‐ヴォールファート
Müller-Wohlfahrt, Hans-Wilhelm 990
ミュラシオル
Muracciole, Jean-François 992
ミュラー・ショット
Müller-Schott, Daniel 990
ミューラー・スタール
Mueller-Stahl, Armin 986
ミュラティアン
Muratyan, Vahram 992
ミュラー＝ドーム
Müller-Doohm, Stefan 989
ミュラー・プライス
Müller-Preis, Ellen 989
ミュラー‐マデイ
Müller-Madej, Stella 989
ミューラー・ロンメル
Müller-Rommel, Ferdinand 990
ミューラン
Mullane, Brendan 989
Murrain, Paul 994
ミュランバ
Mulumba, Andy 990
ミューリー
Mühry, Henry 987
ミュリエル
Muriel, Oscar de 993
ミュリス
Mulisch, Harry 988
Mullis, Darrell 990
ミュリン
Murrin, Jack 995
ミューリンク
Mühling, Markus 987
ミュール
Muir, Julia 987
Mulle, Karen 989
ミュルケ
Mulkey, Marthe 988
ミュルシュタイン
Muhlstein, Anka 987
ミュールダール
Myrdal, Jan 1000
ミュルダール
Myrdal, Jan 1000
ミュルデル
Mulder, Harm 988
Mulder, M.J. 988
ミュールホイザー
Mühlhäuser, Regina 987
ミューレ
Mühle, Jörg 987
ミュレ
Muller, Aurelie 989
ミュレイ
Murray, Marti P. 995
ミュレイン
Mullane, R.Mike 989

ミューレッカー
Muhlocker, Friedrich 987
ミューレック
Mühlegg, Johann 987
ミュレヘーヴェ
Møllehave, Johannes 964
ミューレマン
Mühlemann, Lukas 987
ミューレル
Murrell, Kathleen Berton 995
ミュレロヴァ
Müllerovà, Lucie 989
ミュレロバー
Müllerová, Ludmila 989
ミューレン
Meulens, Hensley 939
Mullen, Larry 989
Mullen, Paul E. 989
Mullen, Rodney 989
ミュレンハイム＝レッヒベルク
Mullenheim-Rechberg, Burkard 989
ミューレンベルク
Mullenberg, Peter 989
ミュンケル
Münkel, Andreas 991
ミュンテフェーリング
Müntefering, Franz 992
ミュンテフェリンク
Müntefering, Franz 992
ミュンテフェリング
Müntefering, Franz 992
ミュンヒ
Münch, Karlheinz 991
ミュンヒハウゼン
Münchhausen, Marco von 991
ミヨ
Millot, Laurent 950
ミヨシ
Miyoshi, Masao 958
ミョー・テイン・ジー
Myo Thein Gyi 1000
ミョルス
Moers, Walter 960
ミョンヒョク
Kim, Myong Hyok 734
ミーラー
Mealer, Bryan 928
ミラ
Milla, Roger 947
ミラー
Millar, David 947
Millar, Mark 947
Millar, Martin 947
Millar, Miles 947
Millar, Peter 947
Millard, Glenda 947
Miller, A.D. 947
Miller, Alan S. 947
Miller, Alec L. 947
Miller, Alex 947
Miller, Alice 947
Miller, Allisha A. 947
Miller, Andrea Wells 947
Miller, Andrew 947
Miller, Ann 947
Miller, Arthur 947
Miller, Arthur I. 947
Miller, Arthur Raphael 947
Miller, Ashley Edward 947
Miller, Bennett 947
Miller, Bill 947
Miller, Billie 947
Miller, Blair 947
Miller, Bode 947
Miller, Brad 947
Miller, Braxton 947
Miller, Brent A. 948
Miller, Brian Cole 948
Miller, Bruce 948
Miller, Bryan 948
Miller, Bryan Q. 948
Miller, Carolin 948
Miller, Carolyn 948
Miller, Christopher 948
Miller, Clark 948
Miller, Cody 948
Miller, Craig 948
Miller, Dan 948
Miller, Danny 948
Miller, David 948
Miller, David A. 948
Miller, David Alan 948
Miller, David Cameron 948
Miller, David M.O. 948
Miller, Deanna 948
Miller, Derek B. 948
Miller, Diane Disney 948
Miller, Don 948
Miller, Donalyn 948
Miller, Douglas 948
Miller, Edgar 948
Miller, Edward 948
Miller, Edward S. 948
Miller, Edwin Haviland 948
Miller, Elisa 948
Miller, Elise Abrams 948
Miller, Emma 948
Miller, Erica T. 948
Miller, Ezra 948
Miller, Frank 948
Miller, Franklin G. 948
Miller, Fred L. 948
Miller, Gail 948
Miller, Geoffrey F. 948
Miller, George 948
Miller, George Armitage 948
Miller, Gerhard 948
Miller, Gloria J. 948
Miller, Granville 948
Miller, Greg 948
Miller, Gustavus Hindman 948
Miller, G.Wayne 948
Miller, G.William 948
Miller, Harlan 948
Miller, Harland 948
Miller, Ian 948
Miller, James 948
Miller, James D. 948
Miller, Jane 948
Miller, Jason 948
Miller, Jason Alan 948
Miller, Jay 948
Miller, J.David 948
Miller, J.Elizabeth 948
Miller, Jeremie 948
Miller, Jeremy C. 948
Miller, Joe 948
Miller, John 949
Miller, John Donald Bruce 949
Miller, John E. 949
Miller, John G. 949
Miller, John Jackson 949
Miller, John P. 949
Miller, John Parr 949
Miller, Jonathan Wolfe 949
Miller, Jonny Lee 949
Miller, Joseph Hillis 949
Miller, Judith 949
Miller, Julie 949
Miller, Justin 949
Miller, K.C. 949
Miller, Keith 949
Miller, Kim 949
Miller, Kirsten 949
Miller, Lamar 949
Miller, Laura 949
Miller, Lennox 949
Miller, Leslie 949
Miller, Light 949
Miller, Linda 949
Miller, Linda Lael 949
Miller, Lisa 949
Miller, Lyle H. 949
Miller, Madeline 949
Miller, Marcus 949
Miller, Marc W. 949
Miller, Maria 949
Miller, Mark 949
Miller, Mark Crispin 949
Miller, Mark D. 949
Miller, Mark J. 949
Miller, Marshall V. 949
Miller, Martin 949
Miller, Marvin Julian 949
Miller, Mary 949
Miller, Mary Alice 949
Miller, Melissa 949
Miller, Merle 949
Miller, Michael 949
Miller, Michael Vincent 949
Miller, Mike 949
Miller, Mitch 949
Miller, Mitchell 949
Miller, Nancy E. 949
Miller, Nicole 949
Miller, Norman G. 949
Miller, Paddy 949
Miller, Patina 949
Miller, Paul B.W. 949
Miller, Paul D. 949
Miller, Paul Steven 949
Miller, Peter 949
Miller, Ramon 949
Miller, Randi 949
Miller, Rebecca 949
Miller, Rex 949
Miller, Richard 949
Miller, Riel 949
Miller, Robert Bruce 949
Miller, Robert S. 949
Miller, Robert Stevens 949
Miller, Robert Warwick 949
Miller, Roger LeRoy 949
Miller, Ron 949
Miller, Ronald D. 950
Miller, Ross M. 950
Miller, Rowland S. 950
Miller, Roy 950
Miller, Roy W. 950
Miller, R.Tyler 950
Miller, Sara 950
Miller, Sara Swan 950
Miller, Scott 950
Miller, Scott D. 950
Miller, Shaunae 950
Miller, Shelby 950
Miller, Sienna 950
Miller, Stephan 950
Miller, Sue 950
Miller, Thoms C. 950
Miller, Von 950
Miller, Wayne F. 950
Miller, W.David 950
Miller, Wentworth 950
Miller, William 950
Miller, William F. 950
Miller, William P., II 950
Miller, William Richard 950
Miller, Zach 950
Mueller, Bill 986
Mueller, Don 986
ミラクル
Miracle, Donna Jo 954
ミラージェス
Miralles, Francesc 954
ミラー・ゼルニケ
Miller-Zarneke, Tracey 950
ミラーチ
Mirarchi, Adam J. 954
ミラード
Millard, Anne 947
Millard, Candice 947
Millard, Trey 947
ミラーニ
Milani, Milena 946
Milani, Mino 946
Milani, Raffaele 946
ミラノ
Milano, Brett 946
ミラノヴィッチ
Milanović, Branko 946
Milanović, Zoran 946
ミラノビッチ
Milanović, Zoran 946
ミラノフ
Milanov, Georgi 946
Milanov, Philip 946
ミラバイ
Mirabai, Chanu Saikhom 954
ミラバル
Mirabal, Jaime David 954
ミラバル・アコスタ
Mirabal Acosta, Roberto Ignacio 954
ミラー・フランク
Miller Frank, Felicia 950
ミラベラ
Mirabella, Erin 954
ミラー - ペリン
Miller-Perrin, Cindy Lou 950
ミラム
Milam, Erin E. 946
ミラム・タン
Milam Tang, Ignacio 946
ミラムタン
Milam Tang, Ignacio 946
ミラムタング
Milam Tang, Ignacio 946
ミララス
Mirallas, Kevin 954
ミラリエフ
Miraliyev, Movlud 954
ミラーリッチ
Miller-Ricci, May 950
ミラン
Mielants, Eric 944
Milan, Courtney 946
Millan, Bruce 947
Millan, Cesar 947

Millan, Gordon 947
Millan, Scott 947
ミランスキー
Milunsky, Aubrey 952
ミランダ
Miranda 954
Miranda, Ariel 954
Miranda, Arturo 954
Miranda, Claudio 954
Miranda, Erika 954
Miranda, João Bernardo de 954
Miranda, Lin-Manuel 954
Miranda, Patricia 954
Miranda, Rosa America 954
ミランダ・ナバ
Miranda Nava, Luis Enrique 954
ミランテ
Mirante, Antonio 954
ミランティ
Miranti, Paul J., Jr. 954
ミランファシャンディ
Miran Fashandi, Mahmoud Reza 954
ミランボ
Mirambo, Prosper Kibuey 954
ミリアス
Milius, John 947
ミリアッチョ
Migliaccio, Giulio 944
ミリエズ
Milliez, Jacques 950
ミリェニッチ
Miljenić, Orsat 947
ミリオティ
Milioti, Cristin 947
ミリカン
Millikan, Ruth Garrett 950
ミリガン
Milligan, Andy 950
Milligan, Douglas John 950
Milligan, J. 950
Milligan, John 950
Milligan, Peter 950
Milligan, Spike 950
ミリキタニ
Mirikitani, Jimmy 954
ミリク
Milik, Arkadiusz 947
ミリス
Milis, Ludovicus 947
ミリッジ
Millidge, Judith 950
ミリッシュ
Mirisch, Marvin 954
ミリッチ
Milic, Hrvoje 947
ミリナー
Milliner, Dee 950
ミリノビッチ
Milinović, Darko 947
ミリバンド
Miliband, David 947
Miliband, Ed 947
ミリ・フセイン
Milli Hussein, Michael 950
ミリマノフ
Mirimanov, Vil' Borisovich 954
ミリャニッチ
Miljanic, Miljan 947
ミリャン
Millán, José Antonio 947
ミリュコフ
Milyukov, Pavel 952
ミリヨ
Milliot, Sylvette 950
ミリングトロ
Miringtoro, Jimmy 954
ミリンコヴィッチ・サヴィッチ
Milinkovic-savic, Sergej 947
ミリントン
Millington, Barry 950
Millington, Mil 950
ミール
Miell, Dorothy 944
Mir, Amir 954
ミル
Mil, José van 946
Mille, Richard 947
Milous, Sofiane 952
Mir, Amidou 954
ミルウォード
Millward, Gwen 951
ミルウッド
Millwood, Kevin 951
ミルカゼミ
Mirkazemi, Masoud 955
ミルガニ
Mirghani, Ahamad Al 954
ミルガニ・フセイン
Mirghani Hussein, Ammar 954
ミルグリム
Milgrim, David 946
ミルグレン
Myrgren, Rasmus 1000
ミルグロム
Milgrom, Paul R. 946
ミールケ
Mielke, Fred 944
Mielke, Thomas R.P. 944
ミルケ
Milquet, Joëlle 952
ミルコウスキー
Milkowski, Bill 947
ミルコ・クロコップ
Milko CroCop 947
ミルコタ
Milkota, Aleksandr A. 947
ミルザ
Mirza, Abdulhussain bin Ali 955
Mirza, Haroon 955
Mirza, Jill 955
Mirza, Sania 955
ミルザエフ
Mirzaev, Zoyir 955
Mirzayev, Ruslan 955
ミルザエワ
Mirzaeva, Yodgoroy 955
ミルサタエフ
Myrsatayev, Ruslan 1000
ミルザッカニアン
Mirzakhanian, Emil 955
ミルサップ
Millsap, Paul 951
ミルザハニ
Mirzakhani, Maryam 955
ミルザヒドフ
Mirzakhidov, Khurshid 955
ミルシュタイン
Milstein, César 952
ミルジヨエフ
Mirziyoyev, Shavkat M. 955
ミルス
Mills, David 951
ミルズ
Mills, Alden M. 950
Mills, Alec 950
Mills, Alice 950
Mills, Andrea 950
Mills, Billy 950
Mills, Brad 950
Mills, Christopher 950
Mills, Claudia 950
Mills, Crispian 951
Mills, Daniel 951
Mills, Daniel Quinn 951
Mills, D.L. 951
Mills, Hannah 951
Mills, Harry 951
Mills, Jalen 951
Mills, Janet 951
Mills, Jeff 951
Mills, Jenna 951
Mills, John Atta 951
Mills, John Lewis Ernest Watts 951
Mills, Jordan 951
Mills, Kyle 951
Mills, Magnus 951
Mills, Marie 951
Mills, Mark 951
Mills, Mike 951
Mills, Nii Osah 951
Mills, Patty (Patrick) 951
Mills, Roger W. 951
Mills, Sara 951
Mills, Steve 951
Mills, William J. 951
ミルスタイン
Millstein, Seth 951
Millstine, Wendy 951
Milstein, César 952
Milstein, Cindy 952
Milstein, Sarah 952
ミルステイン
Milstein, César 952
ミルストーン
Millstone, Erik 951
ミルゾ
Mirzo, Sherali 955
ミルゾエフ
Mirzayev, Turan 955
ミルソム
Milsom, Clare 952
Milsom, Jeffrey W. 952
Milsom, Lauren 952
ミルダー
Milder, Edmund A. 946
Milder, Eugene 946
ミルタジェッディニ
Mir-tajeddini, Mohammad-Reza 955
ミルチェフ
Milchev, Mikola 946
ミルチノビッチ
Milutinovic, Bora 952
ミルチャンダニ
Mirchandani, Bharati 954
ミルツフラワ
Mirtskhulava, David 955
ミルティテ
Meilutyte, Ruta 931
ミルティノヴィッチ
Milutinovic, Bora 952
Milutinović, Milan 952
ミルティノビッチ
Milutinović, Milan 952
ミルディンホール
Mildinhall, John 946
ミルテンバーガー
Miltenberger, Raymond G. 952
ミルト
Mildt, Christina 946
ミルトン
Milton, Chris 952
Milton, Giles 952
Milton, Jane 952
Milton, Keavon 952
Milton, Michael 952
Milton, Nick J. 952
Milton, Stephanie 952
ミルナー
Millner, Denene 950
Milner, A.David 951
Milner, Angela C. 951
Milner, Chris 951
Milner, Hoby 951
Milner, James 951
Milner, Judith 951
Milner, Rebecca 951
Milner, Yuri 951
Milnor, J. 951
Milnor, John 951
Milnor, John Willard 951
ミルナー - ガランド
Milner-Gulland, Robin R. 951
ミルナー＝スカッダー
Milner-skudder, Nehe 951
ミルヌイ
Mirnyi, Max 955
ミルハウザー
Millhauser, Steven 950
ミルハウス
Milhouse, Greg 947
ミルバーグ
Milberg, William S. 946
ミルハム
Milham, Allan 946
ミルバーン
Milburn, Alan 946
Milburn, Gerard J. 946
Milburn, Ken 946
Milburn, Michael A. 946
Milburne, Melanie 946
Millburn, Joshua Fields 947
ミルフォード
Milford, Kate 946
ミールヘイダール
Mirheydar, Dorreh 954
ミルベコフ
Mirbekov, Serik 954
ミール＝ホセイニー
Mir-Hosseini, Ziba 954
ミルホロン
Millhollon, Mary 950
ミルボーン
Milbourne, Anna 946
ミル・マスカラス
Mil Mascaras 951
ミルマン
Millman, Cynthia R. 950

Millman, Dan 950
Millman, John 950
Millman, Marcia 950
Mirman, Anne 955
ミルラン
Millerand, Helene 950
ミルロイ
Milroy, Patrick 952
Mylroie, Laurie 1000
ミルロッド
Milrod, Barbara 952
ミルワード
Millward, Gwen 951
Milward, Peter 952
ミルン
Milne, Derek L. 951
Milne, Hugh 951
Milne, Jo 951
Milne, Kevin Alan 951
Milne, Markus 951
Milne, Rebecca 951
Milne, Simon 951
Milne, Stephen 951
ミーレ
Miele, Markus 944
ミレー
Millay, Edna St. Vincent 947
Millet, Damien 950
ミレイユ
Mireille, Ossey 954
ミレイユ・マルタン
Mireille Martin, Maria Francesca 954
ミレガン
Millegan, Kris 947
ミレット
Millet, Lydia 950
Millett, Allan Reed 950
Millett, Kate 950
ミレド
Miled, Houda 946
ミレブ
Milev, Emil 946
ミレ・プリエト
Miret Prieto, Pedro 954
ミレール
Miller, Claude 948
Miller, Jacques-Alain 948
ミレル
Miler, Katerina Lovis 946
Miler, Zdenek 946
Miller, Aleksei Borisovich 947
Miller, Jerzy 948
Miller, Leszek 949
Myhrer, Andre 1000
ミレン
Millen, Joyce V. 947
Mirren, Helen 955
ミレンダーマクドナルド
Millender-McDonald, Juanita 947
ミロ
Milo, Paskal 951
Milo, Roni 951
Miro, Mohamad Mustafa 955
ミロヴァノヴィチ
Milovanovic, Nicolas 952
ミロサブリェビッチ
Milosavlević, Tomica 951
Milosavljević, Slobodan 951
Milosavljević, Tomica 951
ミロシェヴィッチ
Milošević, Slobodan 951
ミロシェビッチ
Milosevic, Alexander 951
Milošević, Domagoj Ivan 951
Milošević, Slobodan 951
Milošević, Tarzan 952
ミロシュ
Miloš 951
Miłosz, Czesław 952
ミロショスキ
Milososki, Antonio 952
ミロセビッチ
Milošević, Dragan 951
Milošević, Slobodan 951
ミロティッチ
Mirotic, Nikola 955
ミローノフ
Mironov, Evgenii 955
Mironov, Sergei Mikhailovich 955
ミロノフ
Mironov, Evgenii 955
Mironov, Gennady 955
Mironov, Sergei Mikhailovich 955
ミロノワ
Mironova, Ekaterina 955
ミロバノビッチ
Milovanović, Dragan 952
Milovanović, Vojislav 952
ミローン
Milone, Tommy 951
ミロン
Millon, Marc 950
Millon, Theodore 950
ミロンチイッチ
Mironcic, Florin Georgian 955
ミロンチュクイワノワ
Mironchyk-Ivanova, Nastassia 955
ミワ
Miwa, Masahiro 957
ミン
Min, Kyung Ji 952
Min, Willemien 952
Ming 953
Minh, Pham Binh 953
Min Khin 953
ミン・アウン
Myint Aung 1000
ミンガー
Minger, Elda 953
ミンガース
Mingers, John 953
ミンカラ
Minkara, Ahmad Sami 953
ミンギンズ
Mingins, Christine 953
ミンク
Minc, Carlos 952
Mink, Janis 953
Mink, Nicolaas 953
Mink, Patsy Takemoto 953
ミングス
Mings, Tyrone 953
ミンクッツィ
Mincuzzi, Angelo 952
ミングッツィ
Minguzzi, Andrea 953
ミンクヤン
Minkjan, Mark 953
ミンクラー
Minkler, Michael 953
ミンケ
Minke, Gernot 953
ミンゲラ
Minghella, Anthony 953
ミンケル
Minkel, Jean 953
ミンゴ
Mingo, Barkevious 953
ミンコフ
Minkoff, Eli C. 953
Minkoff, Rebecca 953
Minkoff, Rob 953
Minkov, Michael 953
ミンコフスキ
Minkowski, Marc 953
ミンコフスキー
Minkowski, Eugène 953
ミーンズ
Means, David 928
Means, Grady 928
Means, Howard B. 928
Means, Russell 928
Means, Steven 928
Means, W.Scott 928
ミン・スエ
Myint Swe 1000
ミンスキー
Minsky, Marvin Lee 954
ミンゼンバーグ
Minzenberg, Michael J. 954
ミンター
Minter, J. 954
Minter, Kevin 954
ミンダウドゥ
Mindaoudou, Aichatou 952
ミンチン
Minchin, Nick 952
ミンチントン
Minchinton, Jerry 952
ミンツ
Mintz, Elliot 954
Mintz, Shlomo 954
Mintz, Sidney W. 954
ミンツァ
Mincza-nébald, Ildikó 952
ミンツァナバルド
Mincza-nébald, Ildikó 952
ミンツァー＝マクマホン
Mintzer-McMahon, Barbara 954
ミンツィ
Mintzi, Vali 954
ミンツバーグ
Mintzberg, Henry 954
ミン・テイン
Min Thein 954
ミンテインカ
Min Thein Kha 954
ミンテコエ
Mintekoé, Thierry Marie 954
ミンデル
Mindell, Amy 952
Mindell, Arnold 952
Mindell, Earl 952
ミンデルフート
Minderhoud, Hans Peter 952
ミント
Minto, Barbara 954
Minto, Francesco 954
ミン・トゥエ
Myint Htwe 1000
ミントフ
Mintoff, Dominic 954
ミンドラシビリ
Mindorashvili, Revazi 952
ミントン
Minton, Kekuni 954
Minton, Stephen James 954
Minton, T.D. 954
ミンナ
Minna, Maria 953
ミンニーティ
Minniti, Marco 953
ミンヌ
Minne 953
ミンネ
Minne, Brigitte 953
ミンハ
Minh-ha, Trinh T. 953
ミンバエフ
Mynbayev, Sauat 1000
ミン・ハン
Minh Hanh 953
ミン・フライン
Myint Hlaing 1000
ミン・マウン
Myint Maung 1000
ミンムーン
Mingmoon, Witoon 953
ミンヤナ
Minyana, Philippe 954

【ム】

ム
Mu, Qing 985
ムー
Moo, Barbara E. 969
Moo, Douglas J. 969
Mu, Guo-guang 985
Mu, Qing 985
ムーア
Moore, Alan 969
Moore, Ann S. 970
Moore, Arden 970
Moore, A.W. 970
Moore, Basil J. 970
Moore, Beth 970
Moore, Betty 970
Moore, Caleb 970
Moore, Carlos 970
Moore, Charlotte 970
Moore, Chris 970
Moore, Christlyn 970
Moore, Christopher 970
Moore, Corey 970
Moore, David Cooper 970
Moore, David S. 970
Moore, David Scott 970
Moore, Dawn 970
Moore, Dayton 970
Moore, Demi 970
Moore, Don A. 970
Moore, Dudley 970
Moore, Ernest Eugene 970
Moore, Eva 970
Moore, Francis Charles Timothy 970
Moore, Gary 970

ム

Moore, Geoffrey A. 970
Moore, Gordon Earle 970
Moore, Graham 970
Moore, Harold G. 970
Moore, Heidi 970
Moore, Inga 970
Moore, James 970
Moore, James Richard 970
Moore, Jane 970
Moore, Jo 970
Moore, Joel David 970
Moore, John 970
Moore, John Alexander 970
Moore, John T. 970
Moore, Julianne 970
Moore, Kashif 970
Moore, Katherine A. 970
Moore, Keith L. 970
Moore, Kellen 970
Moore, LeRoi 970
Moore, Lilian 970
Moore, Lorrie 970
Moore, Lynne 970
Moore, Margaret 970
Moore, Mark H. 970
Moore, Marlon 970
Moore, Mary-Margaret 970
Moore, Matt 970
Moore, Melodie 970
Moore, Michael 970
Moore, Michael G. 970
Moore, Michael Kenneth 970
Moore, Pat 970
Moore, Patrick 970
Moore, Pauline 971
Moore, Pete 971
Moore, Peter D. 971
Moore, Puala Hotston 971
Moore, Rahim 971
Moore, Ray A. 971
Moore, Ray Arvil 971
Moore, Rich 971
Moore, Robin 971
Moore, Rodney J. 971
Moore, Roger 971
Moore, Ryan 971
Moore, Scotty 971
Moore, Sean 971
Moore, Sharon 971
Moore, Sio 971
Moore, Spencer 971
Moore, Stephen 971
Moore, Stephen Fred 971
Moore, Sterling 971
Moore, Steve 971
Moore, Stuart 971
Moore, Susanna 971
Moore, Susan Thompson 971
Moore, Suzi 971
Moore, Thomas 971
Moore, Thurston 971
Moore, Timothy E. 971
Moore, Tomm 971
Moore, Tony 971
Moore, Tyler 971
Moore, Wendy 971
Moore, William Gyude 971
Moore, Zach 971

ムア
Moore, James 970
Mua, Dickson 985

ムーアクラフト
Moorcraft, Paul.L. 969

ムアコック
Moorcock, Michael 969

ムアシェル
Muasher, Marwan 985

ムアジャーニ
Moorjani, Anita 971

ムーアズ
Moores, Donald F. 971

ムーアタワーズ
Moore-towers, Kirsten 971

ムアッハル
Mouakher, Riadh 982

ムアッラ
Mu'alla, Muhammad Yahya 985

ムーアハウス
Moorhouse, Roger 971

ムアフムア
Muafumua, Joaquim Ekuma 985

ムアヘッド
Moorhead, Sue 971

ムアラ
Muala, Elijah Doro 985

ムアリア
Muaria, Carvalho 985

ムアリミ
al-Mualimi, Abdul-Malik 985

ムアレム
al-Muallem, Walid 985

ムアワッド
Mouawad, Wajdi 982

ムアンドゥンバ
Muandumba, Gonçalves Manuel 985

ムアンバ
Mouamba, Clément 982

ムアンボ
Muambo, Rebecca 985

ムアンマル
Muammar, Abdullah Bin Abdul-Aziz Bin 985

ムーイ
Mooi, Raymond 969

ムイ
Mui, Anita 987
Mui, Chunka 987

ムイエジ・マンゲズ
Muyej Mangez, Richard 998

ムイエジマンゲズ
Muyej Mangez, Richard 998

ムイジネクス
Muižnieks, Nils 987

ムイズ
Muizzu, Mohamed 987

ムイゼンバーグ
Muyzenberg, Laurenz van den 998

ムイッズ
Muizzu, Mohamed 987

ムイーヌッディーン
Mueenuddin, Daniyal 986

ムイベルガー
Muhlberger, Joseph B. 987

ムイヤールト
Moeyaert, Bart 960

ムイラドフ
Myradov, Gulmyrad 1000

ムイルザフメトフ
Myrzakhmetov, Askar 1000

ムインバイ
Mynbay, Darkhan 1000

ムインバエフ
Mynbayev, Sauat 1000

ムーヴァーマン
Moverman, Oren 983

ムウイ
Moüy, Iris de 983

ムウィジャゲ
Mwijjage, Charles 999

ムウィニ
Mwinyi, Hussein 999

ムウィラ
Mwila, Davis 999

ムウィラリア
Mwiraria, Daudi 999
Mwiraria, David 999

ムウェジ
Muhwezi, Jim 987
Muhwezi, Katugugu 987

ムウェシジェ
Mwesige, Adolf 999
Mwesigye, Hope 999

ムウェニエ・ハディシ
Mwenye Hadithi 999

ムウェンダ・バンビンガニラ
Mwenda Bambinganila, Raphael 999

ムヴォゴ
Mvogo, Yvon 998

ムゥラー
Müller, Birte 989

ムエジンオール
Müezzinoğlu, Mehmet 986

ムエルコンビ
Mouelle Kombi, Jean Narcisse 982

ムエンザー
Muenzer, Lori-Ann 986

ムカイマ
Mkaima, Miguel 958

ムカサ
Mukasa, Muruli 987
Mukasa, Wilson 987

ムカジー
Mukherjee, Bharati 988
Mukherjee, Pranab 988
Mukherjee, Siddhartha 988

ムガジー
Moghazy, Hossam 960

ムガニ
Mougany, Yvonne Adélaïde 982

ムカパ
Mkapa, Benjamin William 958

ムカバグウィザ
Mukabagwiza, Edda 987

ムガベ
Mugabe, Robert 986

ムガボ
Mguabo, Stella Ford 941
Mugabo, Stella Ford 986

ムカライ・ヌスング
Mukalayi Nsungu, Banza 987

ムカライヌスング
Mukalayi Nsungu, Banza 987

ムカルリザ
Mukaruriza, Monique 987

ムカンガ
Mukanga, Yamfwa 987

ムカンガラ
Mukangara, Fenella 987

ムガンザ
Muganza, Angelina 986
Muganza, Angeline 986

ムカンタバナ
Mukantabana, Marie 987
Mukantabana, Séraphine 987

ムキ
Muki, Sagi 988

ムキア
Mukhia, Harish C. 988

ムギムワ
Mgimwa, William 941

ムーク
Moock, Colin 969

ムクアム
Muqam, Amir 992

ムクゥエジ
Mukwege, Denis 988

ムクタル
Mukhtar, Abdiaziz Sheikh 988
Mukhtar, Kedir 988

ムクチカ
Mkuchika, George 958

ムクナ
Mukuna, Tshiakatumba 988

ムクナス
Mouknass, Naha Mint Hamdy Ould 982

ムグニ
Mougouni, Ahmat Hissein 982

ムグニエ
Mughnieh, Imad 986

ムクパット
Mkpatt, Bidoung 958

ムクビル
Muqbil, Samir 992
Muqbil, Zarar Ahmad 992

ムクベル
al-Muqbel, Abdullah bin Abdulrahman 992

ムクマ
Mukuma, Ronald 988

ムクリンアブドルアジズ
Muqrin bin Abdul Aziz al-Saud 992

ムクリン皇太子
Muqrin bin Abdul Aziz al-Saud 992

ムクリン・ビン・アブドルアジズ・アル・サウド
Muqrin bin Abdul Aziz al-Saud 992

ムグルサ
Muguruza, Garbine 986

ムクルチャン
Mkrtchian, Ararat 958
Mkrtchian, Levon 958
Mkrtchyan, Levon 958
Mkrtchyan, Margarita 958

ムクルトチャン
Mkrtchian, Levon 958

ムクルマニア
Mukulumanya, Auguste Mopipi 988

ムクルング
Mukulungu, Benjamin 988

ム

ムグレ
Mugliett, Jesmond 986
ムクロ
Mkulo, Mustafa Haidi 958
ムクワヤ
Mukwaya, Janat 988
ムクンガ
Mukunga, Yamfwa 988
ムーゲイヤー
Mougayar, William 982
ムケシマナ
Mukeshimana, Geraldine 987
ムケナ
Mukena, Aimé Ngoy 987
ムケバ
Mukeba, Timothée 987
ムゲブリシビリ
Mghebrishvili, Giorgi 941
ムケルジー
Mukherjee, Pranab 988
ムゲルワ
Mugerwa, Kisamba 986
ムケンディ
Mukendi, Philémon 987
ムゴ
Mugo, Beth 986
ムココ・サンバ
Mukoko Samba, Daniel 988
ムココサンバ
Mukoko Samba, Daniel 988
ムココボンジョ
Moukoko Mbonjo, Pierre 982
ムココムボンジョ
Moukoko Mbonjo, Pierre 982
ムコッパダエ
Mukhopadhyay, Subhash 988
ムコノウェシューロ
Mukonoweshuro, Eliphas 988
ムゴレウェラ
Mugorewera, Drocella 986
ムーサ
Moosa, Ali bin Muhammad bin 971
Mousa, Allam 983
Mousa, Issam Suleiman 983
Moussa, Abderahman 983
Moussa, Abdoulaye 983
Moussa, Ahmed Gamal Eddin 983
Moussa, Amr Mahmoud 983
Moussa, Mohktar 983
Moussa, Noureddine 983
Moussa, Osman Ahmed 983
Moussa, Otban Goita 983
Moussa, Oumar Ben 983
Moussa, Pierre 983
Musa, Michel 996
Musa, Musa Tibin 996
ムサ
Moosa, Mohammed Valli 971
Moussa, Abary Maï 983
Moussa, Hassane Barazé 983
Moussa, Labo 983
Moussa, Mahaman 983
Moussa, Mati Elhadj 983
Moussa, Osman Ahmed 983
Musa, Ahmed 996
Musa, Ali bin Muhammad bin 996
Musa, Mohamad 996
Musa, Mutaz 996
Musa, Said 996
ムザ
Mouzat, Virginie 983
ムサイディエ
M'saidie, Houmed 985
ムーサウイ
Moussaoui, Ahmed 983
ムーサヴィー
Mousavi, Sayed Askar 983
ムサウイ
Moussaoui, Abd Samad 983
ムザヴィザドゥ
Mousavizadeh, Nader 983
ムサエフ
Musaev, Magomed 996
ムサカ
Msaka, Bright 985
ムサガラ
Musagala, Ronald 996
ムサッキオ
Musacchio, Mateo 996
ムザッティ
Musatti, Claire 996
ムサバハ
Msabaha, Ibrahim 985
ムサビ
Mousavi, Ahmad 983
Mousavi, Mirhossein 983
ムサビラリ
Mousavilari, Abdol-wahed 983
ムサブ
Moussavou, Florentin 983
Moussavou, Rufin 983
Moussavou, Rufin Martial 983
ムサフィリ
Musafiri, Papias Malimba 996
ムザラス
Mouzalas, Yannis 983
ムザリ
Mzali, Mohamed 1000
ムサンテ
Musante, Tony 996
ムージ
Mooji 969
ムシウタス
Moushioutas, Andreas 983
ムシェジャ
Musheja, Amanya 996
ムシェテスク
Muşetescu, Ovidiu Tiberiu 996
ムシェロヴィチ
Musierowicz, Małgorzata 996
ムシカ
Msika, Joseph 985
ムシキワボ
Mushikiwabo, Louise 996
ムジチ
Mujić, Nazif 987
ムシディ
Mushidi, Kostja 996
ムジト
Muzito, Adolphe 998
ムシビ
Msibi, Themba 985
ムシマング
Msimang, Mantombazana Tshabalala- 985
ムシャウィフ
Mushaweh, Lubanah 996
ムシャッラフ
Musharraf, Pervez 996
ムジャッワル
Mujawar, Farid Ahmed 987
ムジャヒド
Mujahid, Ali Ahsan Mohammad 987
ムシャラフ
Musharraf, Pervez 996
ムジャワマリヤ
Mujawamariya, Jeanned'Arc 987
ムジャワル
Mujawar, Ali Muhammad 987
Mujawar, Farid Ahmed 987
ムシャンタト
Mushantat, Nihad 996
ムシュク
Muschg, Adolf 996
Mushyk, Anatoliy 996
ムシュタス
Moushioutas, Andreas 983
ムジュラニ
al-Mjdlani, Ahmed 958
ムジュル
Mujur, Ali Mohammed 987
Mujuru, Joice 987
ムショウェ
Mushowe, Christpher 996
ムショカ
Musyoka, Kalonzo 997
ムショブエカ
Mushobueka, Marie Ange 996
ムシン
Musin, Aslan 996
ムシンバ
Mushimba, Brian 996
ムース
Muthu, Rajendran 998
ムス
Muss, Angela 997
ムスアド
Mosad, Mostafa 979
ムスカ
Muscă, Monica 996
ムスカット
Muscat, Joseph 996
ムスケンス
Muskens, Eefje 996
ムスタカス
Moustakas, Mike 983
ムスタキ
Moustaki, Georges 983
Moustaki, Nikki 983
ムスタパ
Mustapa, Fatehah 997
Mustapa, Mohamed 997
Mustappha, Sirat 997
ムスタファ
Moustapha, Imad 983
Moustapha, Kane 983
Moustpha, Isselmou Ould Sidi El 983
Mustafa, Abu Ali 997
Mustafa, Assad 997
Mustafa, Faizer 997
Mustafa, Isa 997
Mustafa, Mohammed Abu-Zaid 997
Mustafa, Muhammad 997
Mustafa, Shakir 997
Mustafa, Susan D. 997
Mustapha, Shettima 997
ムスタファイ
Mustafaj, Besnik 997
ムスタファヴィ
Mostafavi, Farid 981
Mostafavi, Mohsen 981
ムスタファエフ
Mustafayev, Shahin 997
ムスタフィ
Mustafi, Shkodran 997
ムスタフィナ
Mustafina, Aliya 997
ムステイン
Mustaine, Dave 997
ムスト
Must, Raul 997
Musto, David F. 997
ムストネン
Mustonen, Olli 997
ムストプロス
Moustopoulos, Roman 983
ムースハルト
Moeshart, Herman J. 960
ムースブラガー
Moosbrugger, Patty 971
ムズメキ
Musumeci, Gian-Paolo D. 997
ムスラスリク
Musrasrik, Emilio 996
ムスリモフ
Muslimov, Salim 996
ムスルベス
Moussoulbes, David 983
ムスルリス
Moussouroulis, Konstantinos 983
ムスレラ
Muslera, Graciela 996
ムスワティ3世
Mswati Ⅲ 985
ムスンガイ・バンパレ
Musungayi Bampale, Remy 997
ムスンガイバンパレ
Musungayi Bampale, Remy 997
ムズング
Muzungu, Christophe 998
ムセ
Mousset, Lys 983
Museh, Abdullahi Boqor 996
ムセヴェニ
Museveni, Yoweri Kaguta 996
ムセベニ
Museveni, Janet 996
Museveni, Yoweri Kaguta 996

ム

ムセボ
Musebo, Etienne Kitanga Eshima 996
ムセマ
Musema, Gaston 996
ムセミナリ
Museminari, Rosemary 996
ムゼンダ
Muzenda, Simon 998
ムゼンビ
Muzembi, Walter 998
ムーセンブロック
Muszenbrook, Anne 997
ムソエワ
Musoyeva, Rafiqa 996
ムー・ソクフア
Mu Sochua 996
ムー・ソク・フォー
Mu Sok Huor 996
ムソコトワネ
Musokotwane, Situmbeko 996
ムソニ
Musoni, James 996
Musoni, Protais 996
ムソラ
Msolla, Peter 985
ムソリーニ
Mussolini, Romano 997
ムゾレワ
Muzorewa, Abel Tendekayi 998
ムソング
Musonge, Peter Mafany 996
ムソンゲ
Musonge, Peter Mafany 996
ムソンダ
Musonda, Charly 996
ムータ
Moota, Yuma 971
ムター
Mutter, Anne-Sophie 998
ムタイ
Mutai, Abel Kiprop 997
Mutai, Geoffrey 997
Mutai, Munyo Solomon 997
ムタイエ
Moutaye, Anzoumana 983
ムタイブ
Mutaib, Ibn Abdul-Aziz 997
ムタガンバ
Mutagamba, Maria 997
ムタサ
Mutasa, Didymus 997
ムタッシム
Mutassim, bin Hamoud al-Busaidi 997
ムタッハル
Muttahar, Muhammad 998
ムタティ
Mutati, Felix 997
ムダディー
al-Mudadi, Abdullah bin Barak 985
ムダバディ
Mudavadi, Musalia 985
ムタハミ
al-Mutahami, Saud bin Saeed bin Abdul-Aziz abu Nuqtah 997
ムタハル
Muttahar, Muhammad 998
ムタフ
Mtafu, George 985
ムダファル
al-Mudhafar, Sami 985
ムータフィ
al-Mutaafi, Abdul-Halim Ismail 997
ムターフィ
al-Mutaafi, Abdul-Halim Ismail 997
ムタフチエフ
Mutafchiev, Petar 997
ムタボバ
Mutaboba, Joseph 997
ムタラム
Mutalamu, Laurent Muzangisa 997
ムタリ
Moutari, Kalla 983
ムタリカ
Mutharika, Arthur Peter 998
Mutharika, Bingu 998
Mutharika, Callista 998
ムタリモフ
Mutalimov, Marid 997
ムタワ
al-Mutawa, Abdulrahman Abdulkareem 997
al-Mutawa, Mohammed bin Ibrahim 997
Muttawa, Hamad Abdulla Al 998
ムタワキ
el-Moutawakil, Nawal 983
ムータワキル
Moutawakel, Nawal El 983
ムタワキル
al-Mutawakel, Yahya 997
Mutawakil, Abdul Wakil 997
ムタワリラ
Mtawarira, Tendai 985
ムタンギジ
Mutangiji, Anicet Kuzunda 997
ムタンバラ
Mutambara, Arthur 997
ムタンビ
Muthambi, Faith 998
ムチ
Muci, Mustafa 985
ムチェドリーゼ
Mchedlidze, Levan 870
ムチェドリゼ
Mchedlidze, Tamaz 870
ムチェナ
Muchena, Olivia 985
ムチェル
Mucheru, Joe 985
ムチュラー
Mutschler, Hans-Dieter 998
ムチョ
Mucyo, Jean de Dieu 985
ムチリ
Muchiri, Bedan Karoki 985
ムチングリ
Muchinguri, Oppah 985
ムツァングワ
Mutsvangwa, Christopher 998
ムツェクワ
Mutsekwa, Giles 998
ムッゲンターラ
Muggenthaler, Eva 986
ムッサ
Mussa, Henry Amon Robin 997
Mussa, Jaffali 997
Mussa, Uladi 997
Mussa, Yunus 997
ムッシ
Mussi, Fabio 997
ムッソーニ
Mussoni, Francesco 997
ムッソリーニ
Mussolini, Romano 997
ムッター
Mutter, Anne-Sophie 998
ムッチーノ
Muccino, Gabriele 985
ムッチュ
Mutsch, Lydia 998
ムッツァレッリ
Muzzarelli, Maria Giuseppina 998
ムッティ
Mutti, Andrea 998
ムッテルゼー
Muttelsee, Willy 998
ムッラ
Mulla, Muhammad bin Jameel bin Ahmad 988
ムッライナタン
Mullainathan, Sendhil 989
ムツリ
Mutrie, Nanette 998
ムッル
Murru, Nicola 995
ムッルーン
Merroun, Driss 937
ムーティ
Mootee, Idris 971
Muti, Riccardo 998
ムーディ
Moody, Anne 969
Moody, David 969
Moody, James 969
Moody, Raymond A. 969
Moody, Richard 969
Moody, Rick 969
Moody, Ron 969
Moody, Winfield 969
ムーディー
Moody, James 969
Moody, Patricia E. 969
ムーデイ
Muudey, Abdiweli Ibrahim Ali Sheikh 998
ムデイ
Mudey, Hassan Ahmed 985
ムティア
Moutia, Sutyadeo 983
ムテイア
Muteia, Helder dos Santos 997
ムーティエ
Moutier, Marie 983
ムディエイ
Mudiay, Emmanuel 985
ムーディソン
Moodysson, Lukas 969
ムティティ
Mutiti, Ndiyoi Muliwana 998
ムディディ
Mudidi, Emmanuel 985
ムティニリ
Mutinhiri, Ambrose 998
ムディヤンセラーゲー・スニル
Mudiyanselage Sunil, Lansakara Herath 985
ムティンデ
Mutinde, Pedro 998
ムティンディ
Mutinde, Pedro 998
ムテカ
Muteka, Fernando Faustino 997
ムテゾ
Mutezo, Munacho 997
ムテトワ
Mthethwa, Nathi 985
ムテラギラヌワ
Muteragiranwa, Barnabe 997
ムデンゲ
Mudenge, Stan 985
Mudenge, Stanislaus 985
ムテンバ
Muthemba, Cadmiel 998
ムテンビマハニェレ
Mthembi-mahanyele, Sankie 985
ムート
Moote, Margaret A. 971
Muth, Jörg 997
ムドイジュ
al-Medeij, Abdulmohsen 928
ムトイブ
Mutuib, bin Abdullah bin Abdul-Aziz 998
ムトゥ
Mutu, Adrian 998
ムトゥイブ
Mutuib, bin Abdul-Aziz 998
ムトゥムケ
Mtumuke, Atanásio Salvador 985
ムドゥルリ
Mdluli, Magwagwa 927
ムドゥンビ
Mudumbi, Joseph 985
ムトコ
Mutko, Vitaly L. 998
ムトラ
Mutola, Maria 998
ムトラク
al-Mutlaq, Saleh 998
ムドラドラナ
Mdladlana, Shepheerd 927
ムドラノフ
Mudranov, Beslan 985
ムトル
Mutlu, Halil 998
ムドルリ
Mdluli, Magwagwa 927
ムトルワ
Mutorwa, John 998
ムトワ

ム

Mutorwa, John 998
ムートン
Mouton, Alex 983
Mouton, Jane S. 983
Mouton, Patrick 983
ムトンボ
Mutombo, Patrick 998
ムナ
Muna, Ama Tutu 990
Muna, Noor Addin 990
ムナジド
al-Munajjid, Bashir 990
ムナツァカニャン
Mnatsakanyan, Garnik 959
ムナットサカニアン
Mnatsakanian, Mamikon A. 958
ムナッワル
Munawar, Ahmed 991
ムナバル
Munavvar, Mohamed 990
ムナフォ
Munafò, Marcus 990
ムナーリ
Munari, Gianni 990
ムナリ
Mounari, Claudine 982
Munari, Claudine 990
ムナンガ
Munanga, Kaliba 990
ムナンガグワ
Mnangagwa, Emmerson 958
ムーニー
Mooney, Bel 969
Mooney, Chris 969
Mooney, Edward, Jr. 969
Mooney, Harold Alfred 969
Mooney, Michael J. 969
Mooney, Stephen 969
ムニアイン
Muniain, Iker 991
ムーニイ
Mooney, Brian 969
Mooney, Stephen 969
Mooney, Ted 969
ムニエ
Meunier, Christiane 939
Meunier, Paul 939
Meunier, Thomas 939
Mounier, Anthony 982
Mounier, Fabienne 982
Mounier, Germaine 982
ムニエサ
Muniesa, Marc 991
ムニェス
Munyes, John 992
ムニェニェエンベ
Munyenyembe, Rodwel 992
ムニオン
Munion, W.Michael 991
ムニス
Muñiz, Susana 991
ムーニハム
Mooneyham, Mike 969
ムニポラ
Mulipola, Logovi'i 988
ムニャオ
Munyao, Joseph 992
Munyao, Jpseph Kanzolo 992
ムニャカヤンザ
Munyakayanza, Eugene 992
ムニヤッパ
Muniyappa, K.H. 991
ムニャンガニジ
Munyanganizi, Bikoro 992
ムニューシン
Mnuchin, Steven 959
ムニューチン
Mnuchin, Steve 959
ムニョース
Muñoz, José 991
ムニョス
Mugnos, Sabrina 986
Muños, Heraldo 991
Muñoz, Alexander 991
Munoz, Azahara 991
Muñoz, Cristina 991
Muñoz, David 991
Munoz, Ezequiel 991
Muñoz, Gema Martín 991
Muñoz, Gustavo Cano 991
Muñoz, María 991
Muñoz, Maria Isabel 991
Muñoz, María Julia 991
Munoz, Yairo 991
Munoz Oviedo, Oscar 991
ムニョス・アラ
Muñoz Alá, Alicia 991
ムニョス・デルガド
Muñoz Delgado, Maximiliano William 991
ムニョスハラミジョ
Munoz Jaramillo, Carlos Andres 991
ムニョス・ラミレス
Munoz Ramírez, Francesc 991
ムーニラル
Moonilal, Roodal 969
ムニール
Munir 991
ムニル
Nunir, El Haddadi 1037
ムヌーシュキン
Mnouchkine, Ariane 959
ムヌス
Munuz, Erol 992
ムヌナ・フツゥ
Mounouna Foutsou 982
ムネイムネ
Mneimneh, Hassan 959
ムネンブウェ
Munembwe, Elysee 991
ムハ
Mucha, Joanna 985
ムバ・アチャ・フォンダン
Mbah Acha Fomundam, Rose 926
ムバアバソレ
Mba Abessole, Paul 926
ムバアブソル
Mba Abessole, Paul 926
ムバイ
M'bay, Anicet-Parfait 927
Mbaye, Abdoul 927
Mbaye, Abdoul Aziz 927
Mbaye, Khoudia 927
M'baye, Parfait 927
Mbayi, Babi 927
ムバイエ
Mbaye, Keba 927
ムバイエサム
Mbaye Samb, Issa 927
ムバイクア
M'baïkoua, Timoléon 926
Mbaikoua, Virginie 926
ムハイシン
Muhaisin, Muzahim 986
ムバイタジム
Mbaïtadjim, Jacob 926
ムハイミン
Muhaimin, Iskandar 986
Muhaimin, Yahya 986
ムバイヤド
Moubayed, Sami M. 982
ムハイリク
Muhairiq, Ali Mohammad 986
ムハイルビ
al-Mhailbi, Abdullah Saud 941
ムパウェナヨ
Mpawenayo, Prosper 984
ムバオバム
Mba Obame, André 926
ムバオバメ
Mba Obame, André 926
ムハガマ
Mhagama, Jenista Joakim 941
ムバケ
Mbacké, Seynabou Ly 926
ムハジ
Mhadji, Naïlane 941
ムパシェーレ
Mphahlele, Es'kia 984
ムハジル
Muhajir, Effendy 986
ムバソゴ
Nguema, Teodoro Obiang 1020
ムバタ
Mbata, Flavien 927
ムバッザア
Mbazaa, Fouad 927
ムバディンガ
Mbadinga, Josué 926
ムバニ
Mbani, Marcel 926
ムバヌゲマ
Mba Nguema, Antonio 926
ムババジ
Mbabazi, Amama 926
ムバヒョ
Mbayo, Eya 927
ムバフ
Mbafou, Claude Joseph 926
ムバブ
Mbabu, Kevin 926
ムバペ
Mbappe, Kylian 926
Mbappe, Robert Mbella 926
ムバマ
Mbama, Alphonse 926
ムハマド
Hasabi, Muhamad 579
Muhammad, Abdi Gouled 986
Muhammad, Abdiguled 986
Muhammad, Abdiqadir Yussuf 986
Muhammad, Ali Mursale 986
Muhammad, bin Khalifa al-Thani 986
Muhammad, bin Khalifa bin Hamad al-Khalifa 986
Muhammad, bin Mubarak al-Khalifa 986
Muhammad, Faris Petra 986
Muhammad, Lutalo 986
Muhammad, Muhammad Dayfallah 986
Muhammad, Muhammad Taib 986
ムハマド5世
Muhammad V 987
ムハマド・ビン・ラシド・アル・マクトム
Muhammad bin Rashid al-Maktoum 987
ムバミ
Mbani, Marcel 926
ムハムディ
Mhamdi, Bilel 941
ムハムド
Muhammad, bin Khalifa al-Thani 986
ムハメジャノフ
Mukhamedzhanov, Abylai 988
ムハメディウリ
Mukhamediuly, Arystanbek 987
ムハメディウルイ
Mukhamediuly, Arystanbek 987
ムハメド
Muhammed, Bala 987
Muhammed, Bello 987
ムハメドジャノフ
Mukhamedjanov, Baurzhan 987
ムハメドフ
Muhammedov, Begmyrat 987
Muhammedov, Hojamuhammet 987
Muhammedov, Muhammetguly 987
Mukhamedov, Irek 988
Mukhammedov, Khodzhammukhamet 988
ムバーラク
Mubarak, Muhammad Hosni 985
ムバラク
al-Mubarak, Maasouma Saleh 985
Mubarak, Muhammad Hosni 985
Mubarak, Umid Midhat 985
ムバラワ
Mbarawa, Makame 926
Mbarawa, Makame Mnyaa 926
ムパリワグワニャニャ
Mpariwa-gwanyanya, Paurina 984
ムバルガアタンガナ
Mbarga Atangana, Luc Magloire 926
ムバルラ
Mbalula, Fikile 926
ムパルワ
Mpahlwa, Mandisi 984

ムバレ
M'baré, Ba Mamadou 926
ムバレク
M'barek, Habib 926
M'barek, Sghair Ould 926
M'barek, Sonia 926
ムハンゴ
Mhango, Bazuka 941
Mhango, Jappie 941
ムバンゴ
Mbango Etone, Francoise 926
ムパンゴ
Mpango, Philip 984
ムパンデ
Mphande, David 984
ムハンナ
Muhanna, Ali 987
ムハンナディ
al-Mohannadi, Hassan Lahdan Saqr 962
ムパンバ
Mpamba, David 984
ムハンマド
Mohamed, bin Abdurrahman al-Thani 961
Mohammad, Abdullah al-Mubarak al-Sabah 961
Mohammad, Abubaker al-Hadi 961
Mohammed, bin Ali al-Alawi 962
Mohammed, bin Mubarak al-Khalifa 962
Mohammed, bin Rashid al-Maktoum 962
Mohammed, bin Sultan bin Hamood al-Busaidi 962
Mohammed, Kamal Ahmed 962
Muhammad, Abd al-Zahra Uthman 986
Muhammad, al-Sabah al-Salem al-Sabah 986
Muhammad, bin Ali al-Alawi 986
Muhammad, bin Nayef 986
Muhammad, bin Salman 986
Muhammad, Dalilah 986
Muhammad, Ibtihaj 986
Muhammad, Lutalo 986
Muhammad, Samila 986
Muhammad, Shine 987
ムハンマド6世
Mohammed Ⅵ 962
ムハンマド・エッザド
Mohamed Ezzat A. Mostafa 961
ムハンマド・ハレド
Mohammad al-Khaled, al-Hamad al-Sabah 961
ムハンマド・ビン・ナエフ
Mohammad bin Naif 961
ムハンマド・ビン・ラシド・アル・マクトム
Muhammad bin Rashid al-Maktoum 987
ムハンマド・マクトム
Muhammad bin Rashid al-Maktoum 987
ムヒーカ
Mujica, Edward 987
ムヒカ
Mujica, José 987
ムビカイ
Mbikayi, Steve 927
ムヒタリアン
Mkhitaryan, Henrikh 958
ムヒディノフ
Muhiddinov, Farrukh 987
Mukhiddinov, Azimjan 988
ムヒディン
Muhyiddin, Yassin 987
ムヒトディノフ
Mukhitdinov, Ravshan 988
ムヒナ
Mukhina, Elena 988
ムヒャディン
Muhyadin, Abdirisak Sheikh 987
ムビュー
Mbu, Joey 927
ムビュンバ
Mbumba, John 927
ムピラ
Mupira, Pierre 992
ムビリ
Mbilli, Christian 927
ムビリニ
Mbilinyi, Marjorie J. 927
ムフ
Mouffe, Chantal 982
ムファ
Muffat, Camille 986
ムファフィ
Mphafi, Nyane 984
ムファマディ
Mufamadi, Sydney 986
ムファレレ
Mphahlele, Es'kia 984
ムファンコロ
Mufwankolo, Marie-Ange Lukiana 986
ムブウィンガ・ビラ
Mbwinga Bila, Robert 927
ムブウィンガビラ
Mbwinga Bila, Robert 927
ムフウェジ
Muhwezi, Jim 987
ムフェリハット
Muferihat, Kamil 986
ムブオ
Mvouo, Philippe 998
ムプオ
Mpouho, Ernest 984
ムフォンコロ
Mufonkolo, Marie-Ange Lukiana 986
ムフタル
Muhtar, Mansur 987
Mukhtar, Chaudhry Ahmed 988
ムフタール・マーイー
Mukhtar 988
ムフティ
al-Mufti, Turhan Mudhir 986
ムフトゥ
Mfoutou, Simon 941
ムフトゥー
Mfoutou, Simon 941
ムブナバンディ
Mvunabandi, Celestin 998
ムブバ
Mvouba, Isidore 998
ムプミラ
Mupfumira, Priscah 992
ムフム
Mfoumou, Edouard Akame 941
ムフムオンド
Mfoumou Ondo, Flavienne 941
ムブムブミヤク
Mboumbou Miyakou, Antoine de Padoue 927
ムブユ
Mbuyu, Célestin 927
Mbuyu, Jean 927
ムブラクブザ
Mbulakubuza, Esther 927
ムフラバ
Mhlaba, Raymond 941
ムブル
Mboulou, Raymond 927
ムフワンコル
Mufwankolo, Marie-Ange Lukiana 986
ムブンバ
Mbumba, Nangolo 927
ムブンバンゼンギ
Mboumba Nziengui, Mathieu 927
ムブンブミヤク
Mboumbou Miyakou, Antoine de Padoue 927
ムベガオビアンリマ
Mbega Obiang Lima, Gabriel 927
ムベキ
Mbeki, Govan 927
Mbeki, Thabo Mvuyelwa 927
ムベテ
Mbete, Baleka 927
ムヘヤ
Muheya, Richie 987
Muheya, Ritchie Bizwick 987
ムベラ・ムベラ
Mbella Mbella, Lejeune 927
ムベレ
Mbelle, Jacques Yves 927
ムベレブベヤ
Moubelet Boubeya, Pacôme 982
ムベング
Mbengue, Marie Lucienne Tissa 927
ムベンゴオ
Mebe Ngo'o, Edgar Alain 928
ムベンゴノ
Mbengono, Heriberto Meco 927
ムベンチュ
Mbwentchou, Jean Claude 927
ムヘンニ
M'henni, Hédi 941
ムベンバ
Mbemba, Jean-Martin 927
Mbemba, Theophile 927
ムベンバフンドゥ
Mbemba Fundu, Théophile 927
ムボ
Mbot, Paul 927
ムボウ
Mbow, Khady 927
ムボウェ
Mbowe, Tamsir 927
ムボカニ
Mbokani, Dieumerci 927
ムポコ
Mphoko, Phelekezela 984
ムポコマンジ
M'pokomandji, Sonny 984
ムボジ
Mbodj, Aida 927
ムボジ・セネ
M'bodji Sene, Diallo 927
ムボジセン
M'bodji Sene, Diallo 927
ムポゼリニガ
Mpozeriniga, Félix 984
ムボッジ
Mboge, Francis Liti 927
ムボト
Mbot, Paul 927
ムボドゥ
Mbodou, Gabriel Faustin 927
ムボネラネ
Mbonerane, Albert 927
ムポフ
Mpofu, Obert 984
ムボミオ・ヌセム・アブ
Mbomio Nsem Abu, Andrés Jorge 927
ムボリアエダス
Mboliaedas, Jacques Médard 927
ムボリ・ファトラン
Mboli Fatran, Léopold 927
ムホルトワ
Mukhortova, Maria 988
ムボワソナ
M'boïssona, Yvonne 927
ムボンガバ
Mbon'gaba, Cyprien 927
ムホンゴ
Muhongo, Sospeter 987
ムポンダ
Mponda, Haji Hussein 984
ムボンバック
Mbomback, Suzanne 927
ムボンボ
Mbombo, Catherine 927
ムポンボ
Mpombo, George 984
ムマディシディ
Mhoumadi Sidi, Ibrahima 941
ムマンガ
Mmanga, Dereck Lawrence 958
ムーミン
Moumin, Mashqatt 982
ムムジュ
Mumcu, Erkan 990
ムムニ
Moumouni, Amina 982
Mumuni, Muhammad 990
ムヤ
Muya, Generose Lushiku 998
ムヨ
Mucyo, Jean de Dieu 985
ムヨタ
Mujota, Fehmi 987

ムラ
Mura, David 992
ムラー
Møller, Per Stig 964
Muller, Frederick 989
Muller, Phillip 989
Muller, Richard A. 989
Muller, Tony 989
ムライ・コボリ
Muray Kobory, Alfonso 992
ムラウジ
Mulaudzi, Mbulaeni 988
ムラウスキー
Murawski, Bob 992
ムラウタ
Morauta, Mekere 972
ムラオカ
Muraoka, Joel T. 992
Muraoka, Roy 992
ムラカミ
Murakami, Asayo 992
Murakami, Haruki 992
Murakami, Jimmy Teruaki 992
Murakami, Raymond Shoji 992
Murakami, Sheryl 992
ムラカル
Mlakar, Davorin 958
Mlakar, Julijana Bizjak 958
ムラギルディン
Mullagildin, Rishat 989
ムラク
Mrak, Anja Kopač 984
ムラクタリタシュ
Mrak-taritaš, Anka 984
ムラシェフ
Murashev, Nurbek 992
ムラジッチ
Mladić, Ratko 958
ムラジャン
Muradyan, Armen 992
ムラーズ
Mraz, Jason 984
ムラースコヴァー
Mrázková, Daisy 984
ムラソ
Murazzo, Felix 992
ムラタジ
Murataj, Andamion 992
ムラック
Mrak, Tina 984
ムラッツァーニ
Mulazzani, Simona 988
ムラティ
Murati, Valon 992
ムラディッチ
Mladić, Ratko 958
ムラディヤン
Muradyan, Murad 992
ムラーデク
Mládek, Jan 958
ムラデノヴィッチ
Mladenovic, Filip 958
ムラデノビッチ
Mladenovic, Kristina 958
ムラデノフ
Mladenov, Ivan 958
Mladenov, Nickolay 958
Mladenov, Philip V. 958
Mladenov, Totyu 958
ムラデノフスカ＝ジョルジェフスカ
Mladenovska-djordjevska, Meri 958
ムラト
Mourad, Kenizé 982
ムラド
Murad, Abdel-Raheem 992
Murad, Abdul Satar 992
Murad, Ferid 992
Murad, Samir 992
ムラトゥ・テショメ
Mulatu Teshome 988
ムラトビッチ
Mratovic, Luka 984
ムラドフ
Muradov, Shirvani 992
ムラトリ
Muratori, Fred 992
ムラニー
Mullany, Janet 989
ムラネ
Moulinet, Bertrand 982
Mullane, Laura Ann 989
ムラベ
Mrabet, Mohamed Ali 984
ムラモル
Mramor, Dušan 984
ムラーリー
Mulally, Alan 988
ムラリー
Mullally, Megan 989
ムラリエフ
Muraliyev, Amangeldy 992
ムラリダール
Muralidhar, Arun S. 992
ムラルチク
Mularczyk, Andrzej 988
ムラローニ
Mularoni, Antonella 988
ムーラン
Moulin, Jean-Luc 982
Mourrain, Sébastien 983
Mullan, Cecil Brooke 989
ムランガ
Mlanga, Lee 958
ムランギブコス
Moulenguiboukossou, Vincent 982
ムランゲニ
Mlangeni, Titus 958
ムランバ
Mramba, Basil 984
ムランボヌクカ
Mlambo-Ngcuka, Phumzile 958
ムーリ
Meuris, Jacques 939
ムーリー
Moorey, Stirling 971
Moorey, Teresa 971
ムリ
Meuli, Daniela 939
ムリイラ
Muliira, Hamu 988
ムリエタ
Murrieta, Ed 995
ムリエル
Muriel, Luis 993
Murillo, John 993
ムリオケラ
Kuliokela, Wamundia 772
ムリオム・ロザレム
Mouliom Roosalem, Marlyn 982
ムリガン
Mulligan, Andy 990
ムリガンデ
Murigande, Charles 993
ムリコフ
Mulikov, Isgender 988
ムリシュ
Mulisch, Harry 988
ムリージョ
Murillo, Jeison 993
ムリジョ
Murillo, Luis Gilberto 993
Murillo, Miguel 993
ムリジョ・カラム
Murillo Karam, Jesús 993
ムリジョ・サンブラーナ
Murillo Zambrana, Rosario Maria 993
ムリジョ・デラロチャ
Murillo de la Rocha, Javier 993
ムリジョ・ホルヘ
Murillo Jorge, Marino Alberto 993
ムリス
Mouris, Jens 983
Mulisch, Harry 988
Mullis, Fran 990
ムリタロ
Mulitalo, Siafausa 988
ムリッチ
Muric, Robert 993
ムリナージ
Mlynář, Vladimír 958
ムリノ
Mulino, José Raúl 988
ムリノフスキ
Mlynowski, Sarah 958
ムリムリヴァル
Murimurivalu, Kini 993
ムリラ
Mulira, Hamu 988
ムリン
Mullin, Glenn H. 990
Mullin, Nancy 990
ムリンズ
Mullins, John Walker 990
ムル
Mul, Jos de 988
Murr, Elias 994
ムルア
Murua, Ainhoa 996
ムールヴァ
Mourlevat, Thérèse 983
ムルヴァル
Mrvar, Andrej 985
ムルヴィル
Meurville, Elizabeth de 939
ムルガニッチ
Murganič, Nada 993
ムルキ
Mulki, Hani 988
ムルギ
Murugi, Esther 996
ムルキッチ
Mrkić, Ivan 984
ムルク
Murk, Jöri 993
ムルケア
Mulcare, Mike 988
ムルゲイティオ
Murgueytio, Nelson 993
ムルコニッチ
Mrkonjić, Milutin 984
ムルサリエフ
Mursaliyev, Elvin 995
ムルシ
Morsi, Muhammad 978
ムルジ
Muluzi, Atupele 990
Muluzi, Bakili 990
ムルシェツ
Murschetz, Luis 995
ムルシッチ
Mrsić, Mirando 985
ムルジャ
Murgia, Alessandro 993
ムルタ
Murtagh, Johnny 995
ムルター
Murtagh, Niall 995
ムルダー
Mulder, Bertus 988
Mulder, Mandy 988
Mulder, Michel 988
Mulder, Ronald 988
Mulder, Teun 988
ムルタザリエフ
Murtazaliev, Makhach 995
ムルタダ
Murtada, Hani 995
ムルダニ
Murdani, Benny 993
ムルタラ
Multala, Sari 990
ムールティ
Murthy, B.N. Narashimha 995
ムールティー
Murthy, Narayana 995
ムルティ
Murthy, Narayana 995
Murthy, Vasudev 995
ムルティー
Murthy, Narayana 995
ムルデル
Mulder, Elisabeth 988
ムルトハウプ
Multhaup, Maurice 990
ムルドロー
Muldrow, Diane 988
ムルニエツェ
Mūrniece, Linda 993
ムルバ
Mulbah, Joe 988
Mulva, Jim 990
ムルバリエビッチ
Mrvaljevic, Srdjan 985
ムルホール
Mulhall, Stephen 988
ムールマンパシオ
Moolman-pasio, Ashleigh 969
ムルヤニ・インドラワティ
Mulyani Indrawati, Sri 990
ムルルヴァ
Mourlevat, Jean-Claude 983
ムルロヴァ
Mullova, Viktoria 990

ムルロワ
Mullova, Viktoria 990
ムルロン・ベールルネール
Mourlon Beernaert, Pierre 983
ムルンガル
Murungaru, Christopher 996
ムルンギ
Mouloungui, Jean Felix 982
Murungi, Kiraitu 996
ムルングラオディギエラ
Mulungulaodigiera, Elias 990
ムルンバ
Mulumba, Chantal Ngalula 990
ムレ
Mouret, Philippe 982
ムレー
Moulay, Zeinabou 982
ムーレイ
Murray, Elspeth 995
ムレケジ
Murekezi, Anastase 993
ムレタ
Mureta, Chad 993
ムレール
Muller, Mélanie 989
ムレルワ
Murerwa, Herbert 993
ムレンガ
Mulenga, Andrew 988
ムレンジ
Murenzi, Romain 993
ムレンスエレラ
Mulens Herrera, Pedro Isaac 988
ムーロ
Muro, Paco 993
ムロ
Murro, Ernesto 995
ムロイ
Mulloy, Phil 990
ムローヴァ
Mullova, Viktoria 990
ムロウスキー
Murawski, Darlyne 992
ムロージェク
Mrożek, Sławomir 985
ムロジェク
Mrożek, Sławomir 985
ムロディナウ
Mlodinow, Leonard 958
ムロートク
Mlotok, Natalia 958
ムロニ
Muloni, Irene 990
ムローバ
Mullova, Viktoria 990
ムローワ
Mullova, Viktoria 990
ムロンゲ
Moulonguet, Thierry 982
ムロンゴティ
Mulongoti, Mike 990
ムワアンガ
Mwaanga, Vernon 998
ムワウ
Mwau, Adelina Ndeto 999
ムワカサ
Mwakasa, Eva 998
ムワキェンベ
Mwakyembe, Harrison 998
ムワキエンベ
Mwakywmbe, Harrison 998
ムワキュサ
Mwakyusa, David 998
ムワクウェレ
Mwakwere, Chirau 998
ムワゾ
Mwazo, Danson 999
ムワナカトゥエ
Mwanakatwe, Margaret 998
ムワナムベカ
Mwanamveka, Joseph 998
ムワナワサ
Mwanawasa, Levy Patrick 998
ムワパチュ
Mwapachu, Bakari 999
Mwapachu, Harith Bakari 999
ムワリム
Mwalimu, Ummy 998
ムワレ
Mwale, Maxwell 998
Mwale, Theresa 998
Mwale, Vincent 998
ムワワ
Mwawa, Yusef 999
ムワングファンバ
Mwangu Famba, Maker 998
ムワングンガ
Mwangunga, Shamsa Selengia 998
ムワンケ
Mwanke, Augustin Katumba 999
ムワンゲ
Mwange, Marie Louise 998
ムワンサ
Mwansa, Kalombo 999
ムワンザ
Mwansa, Kalombo 999
Mwanza, Peter 999
Mwanza, Rachel 999
Mwanza, Thoto 999
ムワンドシャ
Mwandosha, Mark 998
ムワンバ
Mwamba, François 998
Mwanba, Godfrey 998
ムーン
Moon, Brian 969
Moon, Elizabeth 969
Moon, Fábio 969
Moon, Jo 969
Moon, Lilith 969
Moon, Marianne 969
Moon, Modean 969
Moon, Pat 969
Moon, Rev.S. 969
Moon, Sarah 969
ムン
Moon, Chae-won 969
Moon, Chung-in 969
Moon, Dae-sung 969
Moon, Daniel 969
Moon, Geun-young 969
Moon, Hee-sang 969
Moon, Hyung-pyo 969
Moon, Jae-in 969
Moon, kook-hyun 969
Moon, Kum Sook 969
Moon, So-ri 969
Moon, Sung-hyun 969
Moon, Sun-myung 969
Moon, Youngme 969
Mun, Il-bong 990
Mun, Jae-dok 990
Mun, Myong-hak 990
Mun, Ung-jo 990
ムンイー
Mun Yee, Leong 992
ムンエス
Munyes, John 992
ムンエンエンベ
Munyenyembe, Rodwel 992
ムンガイ
Mungai, Joseph 991
ムンガメソンジ
Munga Mesonzi, Louise 991
ムンガラ
Moungalla, Thierry 982
ムンガンバ
Reina, Francisco Mungamba 1170
ムンギア・パジェス
Munguía Payés, David Victoriano 991
ムンギウ
Mungiu, Cristian 991
ムンク
Munk, Walter 991
ムングアンベ
Mungwambe, Antonio Francisco 991
ムングンダ
Mungunda, Marlene 991
ムンケオ
Mounkeo, Olaboun 982
ムンシ
Munshi, Aaftab 992
ムンジウ
Mungiu, Cristian 991
ムーンジーン
Moonjean, Hank 969
ムンスキ
Munski, Maximilian 992
ムンター
Munter, Mary 992
ムンダ
Munda, Kariya 991
ムンタギーロフ
Muntagirov, Vadim 992
ムンタギロフ
Muntagirov, Vadim 992
ムンタサル
Muntasar, Omar Mustafa al 992
ムンチャヌ
Munteanu, Valeriu 992
ムンテアヌ
Munteanu, Marioara 992
ムンテアン
Muntean, Andrei 992
ムンティアヌ
Munteanu, Francisc 992
ムンティリ・ワ・バシャラ
Mutiri Wa Bashara, Elvis 998
ムンディンガー
Mundinger, Peter 991
ムンデレヌゴロ
Moundele-ngollo, Adélaïde 982
ムンド
Mundo, Mike Del 991
ムンドゥンガ
Moundounga, Séraphin 982
ムントン
Munton, Gill 992
ムンバ
Mumba, Nevers 990
ムンバ・マティパ
Mumba Matipa, Wivine 990
ムンバマティパ
Mumba Matipa, Wivine 990
ムンビオコ
Mumbioko, Patrick Mayombe 990
ムンフオリギル
Munkhorgil, Tsendiin 991
ムンフツェツェグ
Munkhtsetseg, T. 991
ムンフバト
Munkhbat, Jamiyangiin 991
ムンフバヤル
Munkhbayar, Gombosurengiin 991
ムンベンゲグウィ
Mumbengegwi, Samuel 990
Mumbengegwi, Simbarashe 990
Munbengegwi, Simbarashe 991
ムーンライト
Moonlight, John 969
ムンロ
Munro, Chris 991

【メ】

メア
Maher, Kevin 884
Mair, Victor H. 886
メアー
Mer, Francis Paul 935
メアーズ
Mares, Benny 901
Mares, Justin 901
Mears, Chris 928
メアス
Moers, Walter 960
メアダディー
al-Meadadi, Abdullah bin Barak 928
メアニー
Meany, Carlos 928
メアラ
Meara, Anne 928
メアラム
Mealamu, Keven 928
メアリー
Mary, Mary 913
メイ
Mai, bint Mohammed al-Khalifa 885

Mai, Robert P. 885
May, Antoinette 923
May, Brian 923
May, Dave 923
May, Elizabeth 923
May, Ernest R. 923
May, Hazel 923
May, Irenee duP., Jr. 923
May, Jacob 923
May, John 923
May, Jonny 923
May, Kara 923
May, Katie 923
May, Matthew E. 923
May, Misty 923
May, Mitchell 923
May, Mitchell Moses 923
May, Paul 923
May, Peter 923
May, Richard George 923
May, Robert McCredie 923
May, Simon 923
May, Susanne 923
May, Theresa 923
May, Tim 923
May, Trevor 923
Maye, K.J. 924
Mei, Bao-jiu 930
Mei, Eva 930
Mey, Jacob 940

メイアー
Meier, Susan 930

メイアスガルシア
Mejias Garcia, Marlies 931

メイ＝アンドリュース
Meigh-Andrews, Chris 930

メイイェル
Meijer, Marie 930

メイウェザー
Mayweather, Floyd 925
Mayweather, Garrick 925

メイヴェン
Maven, Max 922

メイエ
Maier, Corinne 885
Meier, Ursula 930
Meyer, Paul 940

メイエー
Meyer, Paul 940

メイエール
Meyer, Éric 940

メイエル
Meyer, Enrique 940

メイエル・コルネホ
Meier Cornejo, Ludwig 930

メイオー
Mayo, Lulu 925

メイカー
Makar, Jobe 887
Maker, Thon 888

メイク
Meike, G.Blake 931

メイコウ
Makow, Henry 888

メイコック
Maycock, Dianne 924

メイザー
Mather, Anne 918
Mather, Cynthia Lynn 918
Mazer, Anne 925
Mazur, Barry 926
Mazur, James E. 926
Mazur, Joseph 926

メイサミ
Meisami, Esmail 931

メイシー
Macy, Joanna 880
Macy, William H. 880

メイジャー
Major, Ann 887
Major, John 887

メイショア
Mashore, Justin 914

メイス
Mace, Virginia 866
Maze, Michael 925
Myss, Caroline 1000

メイズ
Maizes, Victoria 886
Mayes, Chris 924
Mayes, David G. 924
Mayes, Frances 924
Mayes, Peter A. 924
Mays, Freda Elizabeth 925
Mays, Nicholas 925
Mays, Nick 925

メイスト
Maisto, Stephen A. 886

メイスルズ
Maysles, Albert 925

メイズルス
Maysles, Albert 925

メイズロール
Mazerolle, Lorraine Green 925

メイスン
Mason, Connie 915
Mason, Conrad 915
Mason, Daniel Philippe 915
Mason, Jamie 915
Mason, Monica 915
Mason, Nick 915
Mason, Zachary 915

メイゼル
Maisel, Eric 886
Maisel, Natalya 886

メイソン
Mason, Andrew 914
Mason, Andrew G. 914
Mason, Antony 914
Mason, Beverley 915
Mason, Bill 915
Mason, Bobbie Ann 915
Mason, Brent 915
Mason, Chilembwe 915
Mason, Danny 915
Mason, David C. 915
Mason, Diana J. 915
Mason, Douglas J. 915
Mason, Germaine 915
Mason, Heidi 915
Mason, Jonathan 915
Mason, Linda 915
Mason, Margaret H. 915
Mason, Mark 915
Mason, Matt James 915
Mason, *Dame* Monica 915
Mason, Nick 915
Mason, Paul 915
Mason, Paul T. 915
Mason, Pip 915
Mason, Richard 915
Mason, Roy 915
Mason, Ryan 915
Mason, Shaq 915
Mason, Steve 915
Mason, Sue 915
Mason, Tony 915

メイダー
Mader, C.Roger 880
Mader, Sylvia S. 880

メイダニ
Meidani, Rexhep Qemal 930

メイツ
Mates, Barbara T. 917
Mates, Seth 917

メイッサー
Meisser, Simona 931

メイテ
Meite, Ben Youssef 931

メイデン
Maden, Anthony 880
Maden, Mike 880

メイト
Mate, C.Mathew 917

メイトランド
Maitland, Geoffrey Douglas 886
Maitland, Joanna 886
Maitland, Theresa L. 886

メイドリー
Madeley, John 880

メイトレイナー
May-Treanor, Misty 925

メイ・トレーナー
May-Treanor, Misty 925

メイナイロ
Mainiero, Lisa A. 886

メイナード
Maynard, Alan 925
Maynard, Charles 925
Maynard, Chris 925
Maynard, Douglas W. 925
Maynard, Janice 925
Maynard, Joyce 925
Maynard, Mary 925
Maynard, Micheline 925

メイナード・ギブソン
Maynard-gibson, Allyson 925

メイナードギブソン
Maynard-gibson, Allyson 925

メイナード・スミス
Maynard Smith, John 925

メイナルディ
Mainardi, Cesare 886

メイニー
Maney, Kevin 894

メイネル
Meinel, Carolyn P. 931

メイネロ
Mainairo, Lisa A. 886

メイハー
Maher, Barry 884
Maher, Paul 884

メイバーダック
Maybarduk, Linda 924

メイバック
Maibach, Howard I. 885

メイハール
Mahar, Dennis J. 884

メイバンク
Maybank, Alexis 924

メイビー
Mabey, Bill 858
Mabey, Richard 858

メイヒデ
Meijide, Graciela Fernandez 931

メイヒュー
Mayhew, Bradley 924
Mayhew, David R. 924
Mayhew, James 924
Mayhew, Mike 924
Mayhue, Melissa 924

メイビン
Maybin, Cameron 924

メイフィールド
Mayfield, Katherine 924
Mayfield, Mark 924

メイプス
Mapes, Mary 898

メイブリー
Mabry, Ashaad 858
Mabry, John 858

メイブリン
Mayblin, Bill 924

メイプルス
Maples, Wendy 898

メイプルズ
Maples, Mike 898

メイホン
Mahon, Basil 885

メイマナリエフ
Meymanaliyev, Tilekbek 941

メイマラキス
Meimarakis, Evangelos 931

メイマン
Maiman, T.H. 886

メイム
Maimes, Steven 886
Meimou, Hamadi Ould 931

メイヤー
Mayer, Bob 924
Mayer, Bruce 924
Mayer, Colin P. 924
Mayer, David R. 924
Mayer, Elizabeth Lloyd 924
Mayer, Gloria Gilbert 924
Mayer, Helena 924
Mayer, Jeffrey J. 924
Mayer, John 924
Mayer, John D. 924
Mayer, Marianna 924
Mayer, Marissa Ann 924
Mayer, Mercer 924
Mayer, Michael 924
Mayer, Mikaela Joslin 924
Mayer, Richard E. 924
Mayer, Roger 924
Mayer, Stephan A. 924
Mayer, Steven E. 924
Mayer, Thomas 924
Mayer, Thomas F. 924
Mayer, Travis 924
Mayor, Adrienne 925
Mayr, Diane 925
Meier, Leslie 930
Meier, Paul D. 930
Meijer, Maarten 930
Meyer, Alex 940
Meyer, Armin H. 940
Meyer, Bertrand 940
Meyer, Charlotte 940
Meyer, Chris 940
Meyer, Christopher 940
Meyer, Claude 940
Meyer, Cynthia 940
Meyer, Deon 940
Meyer, Edgar 940
Meyer, Eric A. 940
Meyer, Erin 940

Meyer, Gregory J. 940
Meyer, Heyneke 940
Meyer, Jürgen 940
Meyer, Marissa 940
Meyer, Marshall W. 940
Meyer, Pamela 940
Meyer, Paul J. 940
Meyer, Robert G. 940
Meyer, Roger N. 940
Meyer, Russ 940
Meyer, Stephenie 940
Meyer, Susan 940
Meyer, Thomas 940
Meyer, Trish 941
メイヤーズ
Mayers, George 924
Meyers, Andrew W. 941
Meyers, Charles 941
Meyers, Dave 941
Meyers, Nancy 941
Meyers, Robert J. 941
Meyers, Scott Douglas 941
Meyers, Steven N. 941
Meyers, Susan 941
メイヤスー
Meillassoux, Quentin 931
メイヤーソン
Meyerson, Daniel 941
Meyerson, Debra E. 941
メイヤー・ホール
Mayer-Hall, Val 924
メイヨ
Mayo, David 925
Mayo, Virginia 925
メイヨー
Mayo, Margaret 925
Mayo, Peter 925
メイヨム・アケック
Mayom Akec, Paul 925
メイヨール
Mayall, James 924
メイヨワ
Mayowa, Benson 925
メイラー
Mailer, Norman 886
Meyler, David 941
メイラン
Meylan, Thomas 941
メイリー
Maley, Alan 889
メイル
Mael, Ron 881
Mael, Russell 881
Mayle, David 924
Mayle, Peter 924
Mayle, Vince 925
メイルティーテ
Meilutyte, Ruta 931
メイルティテ
Meilutyte, Ruta 931
メイルーナス
Meilunas, Egidijus 931
メイルマン
Mailman, Deborah 886
メイレ
Meile, Víctor Grange 931
メイレーレス
Meireles, Maria de Jesus 931
メイレレス
Meirelles, Fernando Ferreira 931
Meirelles, Henrique 931
メイロー
Mailloux, Robert 886
メイロウィッツ
Meyrowitz, Carol 941
Meyrowitz, Joshua 941
メイワン
Maione, Dennis 886
メイン
Maine, David 886
Mane, Sherrill 894
Mayne, Elizabeth 925
Mayne, Thom 925
Mayne, William 925
メインズ
Maines, Rachel 886
Manes, Chridtopher 894
Manes, Stephen 894
メーウ
Meeuw, Helge 929
メオーニ
Meoni, Fabrizio 935
メガグ・サマター
Maygaag Samatar, Ibrahim 924
メカシェラ
Mékachéra, Hamlaoui 931
メカス
Mekas, Jonas 931
メガース
Meggers, Niels 929
メカム
Mekamne, Denise 931
メカムネ
Mekamne, Denise 931
メガリ
Maïgari, Bello Bouba 886
メガワティ・スカルノプトリ
Megawati Sukarnoputri 929
メキ
Mekki, Mustapha 931
メキシベナバ
Mekhissi, Mahiedine 931
Mekhissi-benabbad, Mahiedine 931
メギンソン
Megginson, David 929
メクシ
Meksi, Ermelinda 931
メグジ
Meghji, Zakia 929
メクティッチ
Mektić, Dragan 931
メクリア
Mekuria, Haile 931
メグレ
Maigret, Caroline de 886
Megre, Vladimir Nikolaevich 929
メクレンバーグ
Mecklenburg, Robert William 928
メゲ
Mège, Annabelle 929
メケレイネン
Makarainen, Kaisa 887
メコアベメ
Meko Aveme, Maximiliano 931
メゴット
Megot, Justin 929
メコンネン
Mekonnen, Manyzewal 931
メーザ
Mesa, Giuliano 938
メーザー
Mazur, Laura 926
メサ
Mesa, Carlos 937
Meza, Darlyn 941
Meza, Jenny 941
メザ
Meza, James P. 941
メサイア
Massiah, Joanne 916
メサウーディ
Messaoudi, Khalida 938
メサジェ
Messager, Annette 938
メサーディア
Messaadia, Mohamed Cherif 938
メサデロペス・コントレラス
Meza De Lopez Contreras, Armida Villela 941
メサ・バルガス
Meza Vargas, Ángela Yadira 941
メサ・ビジャファニャ
Mesa Villafaña, René 938
メサ・ヒスベルト
Mesa Gisbert, Carlos 938
メザーブ
Meserve, Jess 938
Meserve, Richard Andrew 938
メサヘル
Messahel, Abdelkader 938
メサ・ラモス
Mesa Ramos, Maimir 938
メサロヴィッチ
Messarovitch, Yves 938
メーサロシュ
Mészáros, István 939
メサーロシュ
Mészáros, Márta 939
メサロシュ
Meszaros, Anett 939
メサ・ロペス
Meza López, Víctor Orlando 941
メサンゲアボム
Messengue Avom, Bernard 938
メーシー
Macey, Dean 867
Macy, William H. 880
メシエ
Messier, Jean-Marie Raymond Pierre 938
Messier, Matt 938
メジェ
Metzger, Chantal 939
メジェシ
Medgyessy, Péter 928
メーシェル
Möschel, Wernhard 979
メシェル
Mechele, Brandon 928
メジェル
Meyer, Enrique 940
メジェレン
Meggelen, Jim Van 929
メシク
Meschik, Ina 938
メシック
Messick, Dale 938
Messick, W.Joseph 938
メシッチ
Mesić, Jasen 938
Mesić, Stipe 938
Mesić, Stjepan 938
メシティ
Mesiti, Pat 938
メジドフ
Medzhidov, Magomedrasul 929
メシーナ
Messina, Lynn 938
メシバ
Misbah, Hesham 955
メジボブ
Mesibov, Gary B. 938
メージャー
Major, Drew 887
Major, John 887
メジャー
Major, Claire Howell 887
Major, John 887
メシャウリ
Mechahouri, Mustapha 928
メジャニ
Medjani, Carl 929
メシャフリ
Mechahouri, Mustapha 928
メシャール
Mashaal, Khaled 914
Meshaal, Sayed Abdou Moustafa 938
メジューエワ
Mejoueva, Irina 931
メシュカティ
Meshkati, Najmedin 938
メジュドゥーブ
Mejdoub, Noureddine 931
メシュベルガー
Moeschberger, Melvin L. 960
メシュレフ
Meshref, Dina 938
メショニック
Meschonnic, Henri 938
メジリ
Mejri, Salah 931
メジル
Mezile, Yanick 941
メジロー
Mezirow, Jack 941
メジロフ
Mezilov, Gurbanmyrat 941
メジンスキ
Mejinschi, Valentin 931
メジンスキー
Medinsky, Vladimir R. 929
メス
Mes, Marcial 937
Messou, Malan 938
メズーアル
Mezouar, Salaheddine 941
メズアール
Mezouar, Salaheddine 941
メスキ
Mesqui, Jean 938
メスキータ
Mesquita, Bruce Bueno de 938
Mesquita, Carlos Alberto

Fortes 938
メスコフ
Meskov, Ljupco 938
メスタ
Mesta, Emily 939
メスター
Meystre, Pierre 941
メスーディ
Mesoudi, Alex 938
メステッキー
Mestecky, Jili M. 939
メステルス
Mesters, Carlos 939
メスード
Mehsud, Baitullah 930
Mehsud, Hakimullah 930
Messud, Claire 939
メストメッカー
Mestmäcker, Ernst-Joachim 939
メストラレ
Mestrallet, Gérard 939
メストレ
Maistre, Xavier de 886
Mestre, Dayaris 939
メストン
Meston, Cindy M. 939
メスナー
Messner, Kate 938
Messner, Reinhold 938
Messner, Tammy Faye 938
メスナリック
Mesnaric, Christa 938
メスバウアー
Mössbauer, Rudolf Ludwig 981
メスマール
Mesmar, Majida 938
メスメル
Messmer, Pierre 938
メスラー
Mesler, Steve 938
メスリ
Mesri, Abdulreza 938
メズリック
Mezrich, Ben 941
メスレー
Meslay, Olivier 938
メスレム
Meslem, Mounia 938
メーセイ
Mészöly, Miklós 939
メゼイ
Mezey, Mathy Doval 941
メセゲ
Mességué, Maurice 938
メセニー
Metheny, Norma A. 939
Metheny, Pat 939
メセルヒ
Messelhi, Ali 938
メゾジ
Mesozi, Louise Munga 938
メゾティチュ
Mesotitsch, Daniel 938
メソヌ
Messone, Nelson 938
メゾラコ
Mesoraco, Devin 938
メーソン
Mason, Andrew 914
Mason, Jamie 915
Mason, Jane B. 915
Mason, Mike 915
Mason, Monica 915
Mason, Nick 915
Mason, Roy 915
Mason, Zachary 915
メソンゲアボム
Messengue Avom, Bernard 938
メータ
Mehta, Apoorva 930
Mehta, Gita 930
Mehta, Lyla 930
Mehta, Mehli 930
Mehta, Mira 930
Mehta, Narendra 930
Mehta, Pavithra K. 930
Mehta, Samir 930
Mehta, Ved Parkash 930
Mehta, Zubin 930
メーター
Mehta, Samir 930
メーダー
Maeder, Roman 881
Möedder, Ulrich 960
メタ
Meta, Ilir Rexhep 939
メダー
Meder, Jamie 928
メダアディー
al-Meadadi, Abdullah bin Barak 928
メーダサーナンダ
Medhasananda 928
メダード
Medard, Laokein 928
メダリア
Medalia, Alice 928
メダワー
Medawar, Charles 928
メタワリ
Metwalli, Sulayman 939
メツ
Metsu, Bruno 939
メーツィッヒ
Maetzig, Kurt 881
メーツィヒ
Maetzig, Kurt 881
メツィン
Metsing, Mothetjoa 939
メツカー
Metsker, Steven John 939
メツガー
Metzgar, Jayme Farris 939
Metzger, Steve 939
メッキ
Mecchi, Irene 928
Mekki, Abdellatif 931
Mekky, Ahmed 931
メッキン
Meckin, David 928
メッケル
Meckel, Christoph 928
メッサー
Messer, Sam 938
メッザードラ
Mezzadra, Sandro 941
メッサーヘル
Messahel, Abdelkader 938
メッサム
Messam, Liam 938
メッシ
Messi, Lione 938
メッジェシ
Medgyessy, Péter 928
メッシェンモーザー
Meschenmoser, Sebastian 938
メッシーナ
Messina, Ettore 938
Messina, Maria 938
メッジョリーニ
Meggiorini, Riccardo 929
メッシング
Messing, David 938
Messing, Debra 938
Messing, Joachim 938
Messing, Ulrica 938
メッズィーニ
Medzini, Meron 929
メッセレル
Messerer, Sulamith 938
メッセンジャー
Messenger, Charles 938
Messenger, Norman 938
メッツ
Mets, Alan 939
Metz, Claudia 939
Metz, Eldon 939
Metz, Melinda 939
Metz, Sandi 939
メッツィンガー
Metzinger, Thomas 939
メッツェラー
Metselaar, Menno 939
メッツェルダー
Metzelder, Christoph 939
メッツォ
Mezzo 941
メッツォジョルノ
Mezzogiorno, Giovanna 941
メッツォラ
Metsola, Aino-Maija 939
メッツガー
Metzger, Barbara 939
Metzger, Philip William 939
Metzger, Phillippe Léopold 939
Metzger, Rainer 939
Metzger, Stein 939
メッツマッハー
Metzmacher, Ingo 939
メッテルニヒ
Metternich, Josef 939
メッテンバーガー
Mettenberger, Zach 939
メッドウェイ
Medway, Frederic J. 929
メッペリンク
Meppelink, Madelein 935
メッラー
Möller, Anne 964
メツラー
Metzler, Ruth 939
メツル
Metzl, Jonathan 939
メッレル
Möller, Cannie 964
メッロ
Mello, Rubens Ometto Silveira 932
Mero, Vittorio 936
メティア
Metia, Lotoala 939
メディアルデア
Medialdea, Salvador 928
メディウ
Mediu, Fatmir 929
メディエート
Mediate, Rocco 928
メディクス
Medicus, Thomas 928
メディナ
Medina, Danilo 928
Medina, João Baptista 928
Medina, John 928
Medina, Raquel 928
Medina, Rodolfo 929
Medina, Tulia Angela 929
メディナガリゲス
Medina Garrigues, Anabel 929
メディナ・ゲラ
Medina Guerra, Efraín 929
メディナモラ
Medina-mora, Eduardo 929
メデイロス
Medeiros, Etiene 928
メデスキ
Medeski, John 928
メテファラ
Metefara, Marcel 939
メテラ
Metella, Malia 939
Metella, Medhy 939
メデル
Medel, Gary 928
Medel, Joe 928
メデルシ
Medelci, Mourad 928
メデルチ
Medelci, Mourad 928
メーデンドルプ
Meedendorp, Teio 929
メドー
Meddaugh, Susan 928
メドイェヴィッチ
Medojevic, Slobodan 929
メドヴェイ
Medvei, Cornelius 929
メドヴェージェフ
Medvedev, Dmitrii 929
Medvedev, Roi Aleksandrovich 929
Medvedev, Zhores Aleksandrovish 929
メドヴェージェワ
Medvedeva, Svetlana 929
メドヴェーデフ
Medvedev, Roi Aleksandrovich 929
Medvedev, Zhores Aleksandrovish 929
メドウェド
Medwed, Mameve 929
メドヴェドコヴァ
Medvedkova, Olga 929
メドヴェドツェワ
Medvedtseva, Olga 929
メドウズ
Meadows, Austin 928
Meadows, Daisy 928
Meadows, Dennis L. 928
Meadows, Donella H. 928
メトカーフ
Metcalf, Barbara Daly 939
Metcalf, Dan 939

Metcalf, Paula 939
Metcalf, Thomas R. 939
Metcalfe, John 939
Metcalfe, Josie 939
Metcalfe, J.Stanley 939
メトカルフ
Metcalf, Franz 939
メトカルフェ
Metcalfe, Janet 939
メドース
Meadows, Linzi 928
メドニクス
Mednieks, Zigurd R. 929
メドニック
Mednick, Sara C. 929
メドヒン
Medhin, Teklemariam 928
メドベイ
Medvei, Cornelius 929
メドベシェク
Medvesek, Blaz 929
メドベージェフ
Medvedev, Dmitrii 929
Medvedev, Roi Aleksandrovich 929
Medvedev, Zhores Aleksandrovish 929
メドベージェワ
Medvedeva, Svetlana 929
メドベーデフ
Medvedev, Roi Aleksandrovich 929
Medvedev, Zhores Aleksandrovish 929
メドベデワ
Medvedeva-abruzova, Evgenia 929
Medvedeva-arbuzova, Yevgeniya 929
メドベド
Medved, Tomo 929
メドベドツェワ
Medvedtseva, Olga 929
メドモワゼル
Mesdemoiselles 938
メトラ
Mettra, Claude 939
メドラー
Medler, Alex 929
メドラン
Medran, Alvaro 929
メードル
Mödl, Martha 959
メトル
Methol, Javier 939
メトレ
Mettler, René 939
メドレー
Medoley, Linda 929
メドレス
Medress, Hank 929
メトロ
Metro, David G. 939
メナ
Mena, Belén 933
Mena, Paul David 933
メナカヤ
Menakaya, Tim 933
メナガリシビリ
Menagharishvili, Irakli 933
メナシェ
Menasche, David 933
メナズ
Menaz, Posai 933
メナスラ
Menasra, Abdelmadjid 933
メナセ
Ménasé, Stéphanie 933
メナード
Menard, Michelle 933
メナードギブソン
Maynard-gibson, Allyson 925
メナナ・エラ
Menana Ela, Cristobal 933
メナナエラ
Menana Ela, Cristobal 933
メナフロー
Menafro, Roberto 933
メナ・マルケス
Mena Marqués, Manuela B. 933
メナール
Mainard, Dominique 886
Menard, Jean-Francois 933
Ménard, Joël 933
Ménard, Robert 933
メナンド
Menand, Louis 933
メニ
Men, Mikhail A. 933
メニイ
Mény, Yves 935
メニーノ
Menino, H.M. 934
メニャン
Mégnin, Jean-Philippe 929
メニューイン
Menuhin, Yaltah 935
メニューク
Menyuk, Paula 935
メニューズ
Menuez, Doug 935
メニューヒン
Menuhin, Yaltah 935
メニンガー
Menninger, Karl 935
メニング
Menning, Petter 935
メニングハウス
Menninghaus, Winfried 935
メネガッチ
Menegatti, Marta 934
メネキーネ
Menechino, Frank 934
メネズ
Menuez, Doug 935
メネセス
Meneses, Antonio 934
メネゼス
Menezes, Mano 934
Menezes, Sarah 934
メネフィー
Menefee, Lynette Alice 934
メネム
Menem, Carlos Saúl 934
メネロコズ
Moenne Loccoz, Nelly 960
メネンデス
Menéndez, Jorge 934
Menéndez, Osleidys 934
Menéndez, Ricardo 934
メノカル
Menocal, Carlos 935
Menocal, Maria Rosa 935
メノッティ
Menotti, Gian Carlo 935
Menotti, Victor 935
メノン
Menon, Rashed Khan 935
メバザア
Mbazaa, Fouad 927
Mebazaa, Fouad 928
メハジ
Mehazi, Xemail 930
メハル
Mehal, Nacer 929
メバルキ
Mebarki, Mohamed 928
メヒーア
Mejia, Adalberto 931
Mejia, Francisco 931
Mejía, Rafael Hipólito 931
メヒア
Mejía, Arístides 931
Mejía, Miguel 931
Mejía, Rafael Hipólito 931
Mexia, António 940
メヒア・カストロ
Mejía Castro, Luis Ernesto 931
メヒアス
Mejias, Tomas 931
メヒアスガルシア
Mejias Garcia, Marlies 931
メヒア・デルシド
Mejía del Cid, Mayra 931
メヒア・ドミンゲス
Mejía Domínguez, Rafael Hipólito 931
メビアネ
Meviane, Francine 940
メビウス
Moebius 960
メヒディザデ
Mehdizadeh, Soleiman 930
メファート
Meffert, Jonas 929
メブス
Mebs, Gudrun 928
メーブセン
Meeuwsen, Robert 929
メフタヘジノワ
Meftakhetdinova, Zemfira 929
メフディエフ
Mehdiyev, Mammadali 930
メフディザヘディ
Mehdi Zahedi, Mohammad 930
メフト
Mejuto, Eva 931
メブトゥ
Meboutou, Michel Mava'a 928
メフメト・トパル
Mehmet Topal 930
メフルアリザーデ
Mehr-alizadeh, Mohsen 930
メフルジ
al-Mehrzi, Ahmed bin Nasser bin Hamad 930
メープルソン
Mapleson, William Wellesley 898
メベイン
Mebane, Brandon 928
メヘター
Mehta, Zubin 930
メヘラビアン
Mehrabian, Ali-Akbar 930
メヘラーン
Mehran, Marsha 930
メヘラン
Mehran, Alfred 930
メヘルバ
Mehelba, Azmy 930
メヘロトラ
Mehrotra, Vinaya 930
メホンツェフ
Mekhontcev, Egor 931
メムシ
Memushi, Luan 933
メムシャイ
Memushaj, Ledian 933
メーメディ
Mehmedi, Admir 930
メメニカラワ
Mwemwenikarawa, Nabuti 999
メメヌ
Memene, Seyi 933
メモリー
Memory, Thara 933
メヤ - スタブレ
Meyer-Stabley, Bertrand 941
メーラ
Meara, Anne 928
メーラー
Mailer, Norman 886
Mehler, Irving M. 930
Mehrer, Helmut 930
Möller, Torsten B. 964
メラ
Mella, Dorothee L. 932
Mella, Keury 932
Mera, Rosalia 935
メラー
Mellor, C.Michael 932
Mellor, Jodie 932
Mellor, Stephen J. 932
Moeller, David 960
Moeller, Felix 960
Moeller, Robert R. 960
Möller, Christian 964
Möller, Lennart 964
メライ
Merai, Samira 935
メライレイ
Melairei, Marcelino 931
メラク
Melaku, Fenta 931
メラース
Möllers, Christoph 964
メラート
Melato, Mariangela 932
メラニーB
Melanie B 931
メラニーC
Melanie C 931
メラビシビリ
Merabishvili, Ivane 935
メラフェ
Merafhe, Mompati 935
メラメド
Melamed, Daniel R. 931
Melamed, Leo 931
メラリソング

Malaythong, Bob 889
メーラン
Maeland, Monica 881
メラン
Mélin, Angéline 932
Mellan, Olivia 932
メランギ
Melingui, Roger 932
メランション
Melenchon, Jean-Luc 932
メランソン
Melanson, Luc 932
メランダー
Mellander, Klas 932
メランドリ
Melandri, Giovanna 931
メリ
Meli, Marcelo 932
Meli, Mark 932
Meri, Lennart 936
メリー
Melly, George 932
Merry, Sally Engle 937
Merry, Tony 937
メリアフ
Meliakh, Dzmitry 932
メリアム
Merriam, Sharan B. 936
メリアン
Melian, Alberto Ezequiel 932
Merrien, Francois-Xavier 937
メリアンヌ
Méliane, Loubna 932
メリカリオ
Merikallio, Katri 936
メリクジエフ
Melikuziev, Bektemir 932
メリゲッティ
Merighetti, Daniela 936
メリサルデ
Merizalde, Pedro 936
メリス
Meliz, Luis 932
メリチ
Meriç, Ahmet Bülent 936
メリック
Mellick, Jill 932
Merrick, Monte 937
メリックス
Merricks, Trenton 937
メリット
Merrit, Richard A. 937
Merritt, Aries 937
Merritt, Guy M. 937
Merritt, Jackie 937
Merritt, LaShawn 937
Merritt, Richard 937
Merritt, Rob 937
Merritt, Ryan 937
メリデール
Merridale, Catherine 937
メリデン
Merriden, Trevor 937
メリドール
Meridor, Dan 936
メリトン
Meriton, Vincent 936
メリニク
Melnik, Yuriy 932
メリニチェンコ
Mel'nichenko, Vladimir Efimovich 932
メリニューク
Maryniuk, Melinda D. 913
メリーノ
Merino, Mikel 936
Merlino, Joseph P. 936
メリノ
Merino, Camila 936
Merino, Jesús 936
Merino, Nuno 936
メリノ・タフル
Merino Tafur, Jorge Humberto 936
メリフ
Melich, Lukas 932
メリフィールド
Merrifield, Jeff 937
Merrifield, Robert Bruce 937
Merrifield, Whit 937
メリーマン
Merryman, Ashley 937
Meryman, Richard 937
メリマン
Merriman, Philippa 937
Merriman, Raymond Allen 937
メリュ
Meirieu, Philippe 931
メリル
Merril, Judith 937
Merrill, Adam 937
Merrill, A.Roger 937
Merrill, Cade 937
Merrill, Christine 937
Merrill, Christopher 937
Merrill, Dean 937
Merrill, Deborah J. 937
Merrill, Douglas Clark 937
Merrill, Helen 937
Merrill, Jean 937
Merrill, Lynn L. 937
Merrill, M.David 937
Merrill, Rebecca R. 937
Merrill, Robert 937
メリルス
Merrills, J.G. 937
メーリン
Melin, Else 932
メリン
Melin, Arthur 932
Melin, Leif 932
メリンガー
Mellinger, George 932
メーリング
Mehrling, Perry 930
メリング
Melling, David 932
Melling, O.R. 932
メール
Mehl, Richard 930
Mer, Francis Paul 935
メル
Mel, H.X. 931
メルC
Melanie C 931
メルア
Melua, Katie 933
メルウィッシュ
Melhuish, Edward C. 932
メルヴィン
Melvin, Bob 933
Melvin, Jermy 933
Melvin, Mungo 933
メルエグ
Mel Eg, Théodre 932
メルガ
Merga, Deriba 936
メルカダンテ・オリバ
Mercadante Oliva, Aloizio 935
メルカデル
Mercader, Antonio 935
メルカデルコスタ
Mercader Costa, Enrique 935
メルカード
Mercado, Gustavo 935
メルカド
Mercado, Gabriel 935
Mercado del Toro, Emiliano 935
メルカド・デル・トロ
Mercado del Toro, Emiliano 935
メルカム
Melkamu, Meselech 932
メルガル・エンリケス
Melgar Henríquez, José Manuel 932
メルカールス
Melchers, Mirjam 932
メルキオ
Melquiot, Fabrice 933
メルキオー
Melchior, Ib 932
メルキオッリ
Melchiorri, Federico 932
メルキオール
Merquior, Jose Guilherme 936
メルキゼデク
Melchizedek, Drunvalo 932
メルグ
Moelgg, Manfred 960
メルクス
Merckx, Axel 936
メルクリ
Märkli, Peter 903
メルクル
Märkl, Gottfried 903
Märkl, Jun 903
Merckle, Adolf 936
メルクレ
Merckle, Adolf 936
メルクロワ
Merkulova, Inessa 936
メルケル
Merkel, Angela 936
メルコ
Melko, Paul 932
メルコゥ
Morkov, Michael 976
メルザック
Melzack, Ronald 933
メルシ
Melzi, Gigliana 933
メルシー
Mercy, Dominique 936
メルシェ
Mercier, Isabelle 935
メルシエ
Mercier, Michel 935
Mercier, Pascal 936
メルジェ
Mergea, Florin 936
Merger, Marc 936
メルシオール=ボネ
Melchior-Bonnet, Sabine 932
メルジャーノフ
Merzhanov, Victor 937
メルジャノフ
Merzhanov, Victor 937
メルシュ
Melhuish, Edward C. 932
Mersch, Yves 937
メルショワール=デュラン
Melchior-Durand, Stéphane 932
メルズキ
Merzouki, Mourad 937
メルスン
Melson, Gail F. 933
メルセデス
Mercedes, Gabriel 935
メルセン
Melsen, Birte 933
メルダシ
Merdassi, Fethi 936
メルチャー
Melcher, Terry 932
メルツ
Mertz, Mechtild 937
Merz, Bruno 937
Merz, Christine 937
Merz, Hans-Rudolf 937
Merz, Mario 937
Merz, Marisa 937
Merz, Ulla 937
メルツァー
Meltzer, Allan H. 933
Meltzer, Bernard David 933
Meltzer, Brad 933
Meltzer, Donald 933
Meltzer, Kevin 933
Meltzer, Michael Irwin 933
Melzer, Jurgen 933
メルツィガー
Merziger, Gerhard 937
メルツォフ
Meltzoff, Andrew N. 933
Meltzoff, Julian 933
メルッチ
Melucci, Alberto 933
メルディニャン
Merdinyan, Harutyun 936
メルティン
Martin, Doris 908
Märtin, Ralf-Peter 909
メルテザッカー
Mertesacker, Per 937
メルテンス
Mertens, Dries 937
メルドー
Mehldau, Brad 930
メルドラム
Meldrum, Christina 932
メルトリク
Mertlík, Pavel 937
メルトル
Mertl, Monika 937
メルトン
Melton, Harold Keith 933
Melton, Jim 933
Melton, Patrick 933
メルニク
Melnyk (merleni),

メ

Irini 933
メルニコフ
Melnikov, Alexander 932
メルニーシー
Mernissi, Fatima 936
メルニック
Melnick, Daniel 932
メール・ハミス
Mer Khamis, Juliano 936
メルバールデ
Melbārde, Dace 932
メルバーン
Melvern, Linda 933
メルビー
Melby, Caleb 932
メルビル
Melville, John 933
メルビン
Melvin, Bob 933
Melvin, Rashaan 933
メルベイユ
Merveille, Christian 937
メールホルツ
Mehrholz, Jan 930
メールホルン
Mehlhorn, Kurt 930
メールホーン
Mehlhorn, Rolf J. 930
メルメッド
Melmed, Laura Krauss 932
メルモン
Miermont, Stephane 944
メルヨシン
Melyoshin, Roman 933
メルラン
Merlin, Christian 936
Merlin, Christophe 936
メルーリ
Mellouli, Oussama 932
メルリエ
Merlier, Frankie 936
メルリーノ
Merlino, Benito 936
メルル
Merle, Robert 936
メルレニ
Merleni, Irini 936
メルロ
Merlo, Claudio 936
Merlo, Gianni 936
メルローズ
Melrose, Richard B. 933
メルロッコ
Merlocco, Anthony 936
メーレ
Maehle, Gregor 881
メレ
Mele, Nicco 932
Merret, Faustine 936
メレケエフ
Melekeyev, Gurbangeldy 932
メレゲッティ
Mereghetti, Paolo 936
メレス
Melles, Carlos 932
メレス・ゼナウィ
Meles Zenawi 932
メレチンスキー
Meletinskii, Eleazar Moiseevich 932
メレット
Merrett, Alicia 936
Merrett, Christopher D. 936
メレップ
Merep, Alexander 936
メレティス
Meletis, Chris D. 932
メレディス
Meredith, Anthony 936
Meredith, Cameron 936
Meredith, Kevin 936
Meredith, Laurence 936
Meredith, Mimi 936
Meredith, Robyn 936
Meredith, Scott 936
Meredith, Spencer Barrett 936
メレトグル
Meletoglou, Hristos 932
メレドフ
Meredov, Rashid 936
メレトプロス
Meletopoulos, Tasos 932
メレニク
Merenik, Lidija 936
メレプ
Merep, Alexander 936
メレマン
Möllemann, Jürgen W. 964
メレール
Mehler, Jacques 930
メレル
Merrell, James 936
Moeller, Heinz 960
Moller, Kristjan 964
メーレン
Mehren, Elizabeth 930
メレンキャンプ
Mellencamp, John 932
メレンティン
Mellentin, Julian 932
メレンテス
Merentes, Nelson 936
メレンデス
Melendez, Bill 932
Meléndez, Carmen 932
メレンデス・デマニリア
Meléndez de Maniglia, Carmen Teresa 932
メーロ
Melo, Dias de 933
Merlo, Larry 936
メロ
Mello, Roger 932
Melo, Joanna 933
Melo, Ligia Amada 933
Melo, Luisana 933
Melo, Marcelo 933
Melo, Patrícia 933
Mero, Vittorio 936
メロー
Mello, Craig 932
メロタキス
Melotakis, Mason 933
メローチェ
Meloche, Tom 933
メロディ
Mellody, Pia 932
メロード
Mérode, Alexandre de 936
メロト
Meloto, Antonio 933
メーロトラ
Mehrotra, Rahul 930
メロートラ
Mehrotra, Rajiv 930
Mehrotra, Sanjay 930
メローニ
Meloni, Giorgia 933
Meloni, Julie C. 933
メワ
Mewa, Commins Aston 940
メン
Maeng, Hyung-kyu 881
Meng, Jin 934
Menn, Joseph 935
Men Sam An 935
メンイ
Menye, Essimi 935
メンガ
Menga, Justin 934
Menga, Michel 934
メンギスツ
Mengistu, Huluka 934
メング
Meng 934
メングアル
Mengual, Gemma 934
メンクス
Menkes, Justin 935
メンケ
Menke, Christoph 935
Menke, Sally 935
メンゲメングアン
Mengue M'engouang, Fidele 934
メンゲモウォノ
Mengue M'owono, Paulette 934
メンケン
Menken, Alan 935
メンコ
Manco, Tristan 893
メンコフ
Menkov, Vadim 935
メンサ
Mensah, E.T. 935
Mensah, J.H. 935
Mensah, Juliana Azumah 935
メンサー
Mensah, J.H. 935
Mensah, Joseph Henry 935
メンザ
Menza, Nick 935
メンサ・ズゲレ
Mensah Zoguelet, Alain 935
メン・サム・オン
Men Sam An 935
メンシコフ
Menshikov, Oleg 935
メンジーズ
Menzies, Gavin 935
メンジャー
Menger, Connie 934
Menger, Howard 934
メンシャーウィ
al-Menshawi, Reda 935
メンシンク
Mensink, Ron 935
メーンス
Meens, Estelle 929
メンスキー
Menski, Werner 935
メンズブルグ
Mensbrugghe, Dominique Van der 935
メンゼル
Menzel, Idina 935
メンチュ
Menchú, Rigoberta 933
メンチュウ
Menchú, Rigoberta 933
メンツィ
Menzi, Renate 935
メンツェル
Menzel, Albrecht 935
Menzel, Jiří 935
Menzel, Peter 935
Menzel, Phillip 935
メンデ
Mende, Lambert 933
メンディ
Mendy, Benjamin 934
Mendy, Nampalys 934
メンディウス
Mendius, Richard 934
メンディエッタ
Mendieta, Eduardo 934
メンディット
Menditto, Anthony A. 934
メンディリバル
Mendilibar, Jose Luis 934
メンティル
Menzel, Jiří 935
メンデ・オマランガ
Mende Omalanga, Lambert 934
メンデオマランガ
Mende Omalanga, Lambert 934
メンデス
Mendes, Degol 934
Mendes, Jose Luis Xavier 934
Mendes, Luís Marques 934
Mendes, Sam 934
Mendes, Sergio 934
Mendes, Valentina 934
Mendez, Antonio J. 934
Mendez, César 934
Mendez, Rodolfo 934
Méndez, Roxana 934
Mendez, Yohander 934
メンデス・コバル
Mendéz Cóbar, Mario Estuardo 934
メンデスデビゴ
Méndez De Vigo, Íñigo 934
メンデス・デビゴ・イ・モントホ
Méndez De Vigo y Montojo, Íñigo 934
メンデス・ピント
Mendes Pinto, Maria Helena Caleia Serra 934
メンデスペレイラ
Mendes Pereira, Florentino 934
メンデス・モンテネグロ
Mendéz Montenegro, Mario 934
メンデル
Mendel, Nate 933
Mendell, Pierre 933
メンデルサンド
Mendelsund, Peter 934
メンデルスゾーン

Mendelssohn, Kurt 934
メンデルソン
Mendelson, Anne 934
メンデル＝ハートヴィッグ
Mendel-Hartvig, Åsa 933
メンデルブラット
Mendelblatt, Mark 933
メンデン
Mengden, Daniel 934
メンデンホール
Mendenhall, Mark E. 934
メンドーサ
Mendosa, Herminio A. Blanco 934
Mendosa, Leandro 934
Mendoza, Brillante 934
Mendoza, Leandro 934
Mendoza, Plinio Apuleyo 934
Mendoza, Ronald U. 934
Mendoza, Tony 934
Mendoza, Vince 934
Mendoza, Vincent 934
メンドサ
Mendoza, Eduardo 934
メンドサ・デルソラル
Mendoza del Solar, Zoila Lourdes Carmen Sandra 934
メンドサ・トバル
Mendoza Tovar, Carlos Onan 934
メンドーヨー
Mend-Ooyo, G. 934
メンドンサ
Mendonça, António 934
メンドンサ・フィリョ
Mendonça Filho, José 934
メンナン
Mennan, Zeynep 935
メンネア
Mennea, Pietro 935
メンヒバル・エスカランテ
Menjívar Escalante, Elvia Violeta 934
メンベ
Membe, Bernard Kamillius 933
メンミ
Memmi, Albert 933

【モ】

モ
Mo, Tae-bum 959
モー
Mo, Tianquan 959
Mo, Timothy 959
Mo, Yan 959
Moe, Jorgen 960
Moe, Michael 960
Moe, Ola Borten 960
Moe, Terry M. 960
モーア
Mohr, Bärbel 962
Mohr, Tim 962
モア
Moeur, Kelly 960
Mohr, Franz 962
Mohr, Jean 962
Mohr, Magni 962
Mohr, Stephen 962
Mohr, Tara 962
Mooa, Baraniko 969
Moore, Charles 970
Moore, E'Twaun 970
Moore, Stephen 971
Moore, William Gyude 971
モアー
Mohr, Gerold 962
モアイヤド
Moayyad, Muhammad Mutia 959
モアカニン
Moacanin, Radmila 959
モーアキ
Moeaki, Tony 960
モアコット
Morkot, Robert 976
モアノ
Moignot, Daniel 962
モアノー
Morneau, Justin 976
モアハウス
Morehouse, Lyda 973
Morehouse, Timothy 973
Morehouse, Ward, Ⅲ 973
モアビーク
Moerbeek, Kees 960
モアランド
Moreland, Eric 973
Moreland, Mitch 973
Moreland, Peggy 973
モアレム
Moalem, Sharon 959
モアワド
Moawad, Nayla 959
モアン
Moan, Magnus 959
Moan, Magnus Hovdal 959
モーイ
Mooij, Marieke K.de 969
モイ
Moi, Daniel T. arap 962
Moi, Toril 962
Moy, John T. 984
モイア
Moir, Scott 963
モイオリ
Moioli, Michela 962
モイ・ゴメス
Moi Gomez 962
モイザー
Meuser, Bernhard 940
モイサンデル
Moisander, Niklas 963
モイジ
Moïsi, Dominique 963
モイシウ
Moisiu, Alfred 963
モイーズ
Moïse, Jovenel 963
Moyes, David 984
Moyes, Jojo 984
モイズ
Moyes, Rebecca Ann 984
Moyse, Heather 984
モイスブルガー
Meusburger, Peter 940
モイセーエフ
Moiseyev, Igor Aleksandrovich 963
モイセエフ
Moiseev, Andrey 963
モイソフ
Mojsov, Lazar 963
モイゾフ
Mojsov, Lazar 963
モイトランド
Moitland, Kristopher 963
モイナハン
Moynahan, Molly 984
モイニハン
Moynihan, Brian 984
Moynihan, Daniel Patrick 984
Moynihan, Lauren E. 984
Moynihan, Michael 984
Moynihan, Ray 984
モイヤー
Moir, Scott 963
Moyer, Edward W. 984
Moyer, Jack T. 984
Moyer, Jamie 984
モイヤーズ
Moyers, Bill D. 984
モイラー
Maurer, Angela 922
Meurer, Michael James 939
モイリー
Moily, M. Veerappa 962
モイル
Moyle, Franny 984
モイーン
Moin, Mostafa 962
モイン
Moine, Mohamed Ould Mohamed Abderrahmane Ould 962
モウ
Mowe, Ken 984
モウアー
Mauer, Joe 921
モウアット
Mouat, Adrian 982
モウィンケル
Mowinckel, Ragnhild 984
モウェット
Mowat, Farley McGill 983
モウギー
Mougey, Midge Odermann 982
モヴシュク
Movshuk, Oleksandr 983
モウツ
Moates, Marianne Merrill 959
モーウッド
Morwood, James 979
Morwood, Mike J. 979
モウブレイ
Mowbray, Miranda 983
モウミニ
Moumini, Ali 982
モウラ
Moura, Ann 982
モウラン
Mourao, Ronaldo 982
モウリッツェン
Mouritzen, Hans 983
モウリーニョ
Mourinho, Jose 982
モウル
Mowll, Joshua 984
モウワット
Mowat, Farley McGill 983
モエアキオラ
Moeakiola, Matekitonga 960
モエスタジャ
Moestadja, Soewarto 960
モエダノ
Mohedano, Lourdes 962
モエダン
Modan, Rutu 959
モエラネ
Moerane, Mofelehetsi 960
モエルアウゼン
Moellhausen, Nathalie 960
モーエン
Moen, Anita 960
Moen, Bruce 960
モエン
Moeng, Sophearith 960
モオ
Mo, Yan 959
モカ
Moka, Alain 963
モガー
Moggach, Deborah 960
Moggach, Lottie 960
モカイラ
Mokaila, Kitso 963
Mokaila, Onkokame Kitso 963
モカマネデ
Mokamanede, Godefroy 963
モガミ
Mogami, Thebe 960
モカラケ
Mokalake, Lebonamang 963
モーガン
Morgan, Adam 974
Morgan, Alex 974
Morgan, Alice 974
Morgan, Ben 974
Morgan, Bill 974
Morgan, Brian 974
Morgan, Brian Edward 974
Morgan, Chris 974
Morgan, Darin 974
Morgan, David 974
Morgan, David H.J. 974
Morgan, David Owen 974
Morgan, Derrick 974
Morgan, Edmund S. 974
Morgan, Edwin 974
Morgan, Edwin George 974
Morgan, Elaine 974
Morgan, Gareth 974
Morgan, Glen 974
Morgan, Glenn 974
Morgan, Harry 974
Morgan, Helen 974
Morgan, Howard 974
Morgan, Howard Lee 974
Morgan, James 974
Morgan, James M. 974
Morgan, Jerry L. 974
Morgan, Joël 974
Morgan, Johnny 974
Morgan, Judith 974
Morgan, Julie 974
Morgan, Karl Ziegler 974
Morgan, Kevin 974
Morgan, Lacey 974
Morgan, Lisa 974

モ

Morgan, Marcia K. 974
Morgan, Mark 974
Morgan, Matthew 974
Morgan, Michaela 974
Morgan, Michael Hamilton 974
Morgan, Michael John 974
Morgan, Mike 974
Morgan, Neil Bowen 974
Morgan, Nick 974
Morgan, Nicky 974
Morgan, Nicola 974
Morgan, Paul 974
Morgan, Peter 974
Morgan, Raye 974
Morgan, Rhea Volk 974
Morgan, Richard K. 974
Morgan, Robert 974
Morgan, Sally 975
Morgan, Sarah 975
Morgan, Shirley 975
Morgan, Steve 975
Morgan, Tesni 975
Morgan, Tina 975
Morgan, Victoria 975
Morgan, Wes 975

モーガン＝ジョーンズ
Morgan-Jones, David 975

モギリョフ
Mohylov, Anatoliy 962

モーギル
Mogil, H.Michael 960

モーク
Mauch, Gene William 921
Moog, Helmut 969

モーグ
Moog, Robert 969

モク
Mok, Heidi 963
Mok, Karen 963
Mok Mareth 963

モクイ
Mokuy, Agapito Mba 963
Mokuy, Alfonso Nsue 963

モクイムバオボノ
Mekuy Mbaobono, Guillermina 931

モクォトゥ
Mokgothu, Boometswe 963

モクシーイングラハム
Moxey-ingraham, Theresa 984

モクスレイ
Moxley, Russ S. 984

モクタール
el-Moctar, Brahim Ould M'Bareck Ould Mohamed 959
Moctar, Brahim Ould M'bareck Ould Mohamed El 959
Moctar, Isselmou Ould Sid'el 959
el-Moctar, Moulaty Mint 959
Moctar, Moulaty Mint El 959

モクベル
Maqbel, Zarar Ahmad 898
Moqbel, Zarar Ahmad 971

モク・マレット
Mok Mareth 963

モークリー
Moakley, Joe 959

モグリッジ
Moggridge, Donald Edward 960
Moggridge, William 960

モクンビ
Mocumbi, Pascoal Manuel 959

モケット
Mockett, Marie Mutsuki 959

モゲナラ
Moguenara, Sosthene 960

モゲリーニ
Mogherini, Federica 960

モケレトラ
Mokeretla, Tšoeu 963

モーゲン
Morgen, Brett 975

モーゲンサル
Morgenthal, Jeffrey P. 975

モーゲンスターン
Morgenstern, Dan 975
Morgenstern, Erin 975
Morgenstern, Joe 975
Morgenstern, Julie 975

モゲンセン
Mogensen, Carsten 960

モーゲンソーラー
Morgensoror, Jyon 975

モーゲンタール
Morgenthal, Deborah 975

モコ
Moko, Démole Issa 963

モコエナ
Mokoena, Godfrey Khotso 963

モコキ
Mokoki, Gilbert 963

モコシ
Mokhosi, Tšeliso 963

モコセ
Mokose, Lincon Ralechate 963
Mokose, Ralechate 963

モコトゥ
Mokgothu, Boometswe 963
Mokhothu, Mathibeli 963

モコペテ
Mokopete, Guy Marc 963

モコマ
Mokoma, Lesole 963

モコンヤネ
Mokonyane, Nomvula 963

モーザー
Moser, Alfred 979
Moser, Barry 979
Moser, Edvard Ingjald 979
Moser, Maximilian 979
Moser, May-Britt 979
Moser, Mike 980
Moser, W.O.J. 980

モーサー＝ウェルマン
Moser-Wellman, Annette 980

モサコフスキー
Mosakowski, Elaine 979

モサック
Mosak, Harold H. 979

モザファル
Mozafar, Hosein 984

モージー
Mauzy, Jeff 922

モシアロス
Mossialos, Elias 981

モシオ
Mocio, Lucas 959

モシク・ストレルコースカス
Moszyk-Strelkauskas, Danielle 981

モシシリ
Mosisili, Pakalitha 980

モジニェー
Mosionier, Beatrice 980

モージャー
Moger, Peter 960

モシャー
Mosher, Steven 980

モシャイ
Mashaei, Esfandiar Rahim 914
Moshaei, Rahim 980

モシャラフ
Mosharaf, Alhaj Rashed 980

モジャーン
Morjane, Kamel 976

モジュムダル
Majumdar, Binoy 887

モーション
Motion, Andrew 981

モジリアニ
Modigliani, Franco 959

モシン
Mosin, Vasily 980

モース
Morse, Janice M. 978
Morse, Jeremy 978
Morse, John J. 978
Morse, Mike 978
Morse, Mitch 978
Morse, Ronald A. 978
Morse, Samuel C. 978
Morse, Stephen J. 978

モス
Moos, Moritz 971
Moss, Alexandra 980
Moss, Brandon 980
Moss, David A. 980
Moss, Dena Simone 980
Moss, Eliot 980
Moss, Elisabeth 980
Moss, Frank 980
Moss, Helen 980
Moss, Jane 980
Moss, Jason 980
Moss, Jeff 980
Moss, Joanne 980
Moss, Joel W. 980
Moss, Kate 980
Moss, Lenny 980
Moss, Margaret P. 980
Moss, Michael 980
Moss, Michael S. 980
Moss, Miriam 980
Moss, Randy 980
Moss, Robert 981
Moss, Sarah 981
Moss, Steve 981
Moss, Tara 981
Moss, Todd 981
Mosse, Kate 981

モスカ
Mosca, Paolo 979

モスカット
Moscatt, Valentina 979

モスカビチャス
Mockevicius, Egidijus 959

モスカレンコ
Moskalenko, Alexander 980
Moskalenko, Svetlana 980
Moskalenko, Vitaly 980

モズガロワ
Mozgalova, Kira 984

モスケイオ
Moscheo, Joe 979

モスケーダ
Mosqueda, Olga T. 980

モスケラ
Mosquera, Alecksey 980
Mosquera, Mabel 980
Mosquera, Pedro 980
Mosquera Lozano, Luis Javier 980

モスコー
Moscow, Alvin 979

モスコヴィッチ
Moscovich, Rotem 979
Moscovitch, Hannah 979

モスコウィッツ
Moskowitz, Howard R. 980
Moskowitz, Tobias Jacob 980

モスコヴィッツ
Moskovitz, Dustin 980

モスコソ
Moscoso, Mireya Elisa 979

モスコビシ
Moscovici, Pierre 979

モスコビッチ
Moscovich, Ivan 979
Moscovitch, Dylan 979

モスコフ
Moskov, Petre 980

モズゴフ
Mozgov, Timofey 984

モスコフスキ
Moskovski, Ivaylo 980

モスコワ
Moskova, Emma 980

モースタッド
Morstad, Julie 978

モスタート
Mostert, Raheem 981

モスタファ
Mostafa, Atef 981

モスティン
Mostyn, David 981

モズデル
Mosdell, Chris 979

モースト
Moost, Nele 971

モストウ
Mostow, George 981
Mostow, Joshua S. 981

モスバカー
Mosbacher, Robert Adam 979

モスバッカー
Mosbacher, Robert Adam 979

モスビー
Mosby, Steve 979

モズマナシビリ
Modzmanashvili, Davit 960

モースラッド
Morstead, Thomas 978

モーズリー
Mawdsley, Emma 923
Moseley, Michael E. 979
Moseley, Rachel 979
Mosley, Jamahl 980

モ

Mosley, Michael 980
Mousley, Kevin 983
モスリ
Mossely, Estelle 981
モスリー
Mosley, C.J. 980
Mosley, Michael 980
モズリー
Moseley, Jonny 979
Mosley, Shane 980
Mosley, Walter 980
モズリイ
Mosley, Walter 980
モズリー・スミス
Mosley-smith, Khaynin 980
モズレー
Mosley, Shane 980
モスレヒ
Moslehi, Heydar 980
モーセズ
Moses, Brian 980
モーゼス
Moses, Brian 980
Moses, Dennis 980
Moses, Dezman 980
Moses, Donna 980
Moses, Elissa 980
Moses, Kate 980
Moses, Kim 980
Moses, Morgan 980
Mosès, Stéphane 980
Moses, Victor 980
Moses, Will 980
モーゼズ
Morzez, Philip Ninj@ 979
モーセラ
Morsella, Ezequiel 978
モゼラック
Mozeliak, John 984
モーセル
Moser, Edvard Ingjald 979
Moser, May-Britt 979
モーゼル
Moser, Benjamin 979
モゼール
Moser, Edvard Ingjald 979
モセルヒ
Al-moselhi, Ali El-Sayed 979
モソツォアネ
Mosothoane, 'Makabelo Priscilla 980
モソプ
Mosop, Moses 980
モーソン
Mawson, Alfie 923
Mawson, Robert 923
モタ
Mota, Rosa 981
モタキ
Motaqi, Khan 981
モタゼ
Motaze, Louis Paul 981
モタセム
Motasem, Abdol Wasay Aghajan 981
モタソアレス
Mota Soares, Pedro 981
モーダック
Morduch, Jonathan 973
モダック
Modak, Prasad 959
モタニャネ
Motanyane, Sephiri 981
モタメディ
Motamedi, Ahmad 981
モタング
Motang, Hlalele 981
モチアン
Motian, Paul 981
モチェハ
Motshekga, Angelina 981
モチズキ
Mochizuki, Ken 959
Mochizuki, Mike Masato 959
モチヅキ
Mochizuki, Ken 959
Mochizuki, Mike Masato 959
モチョボロアネ
Mochoboroane, Selibe 959
モーツ
Moats, Arthur 959
モツェカ
Motshekga, Angelina 981
モツェンヤネ
Motsuenyane, Samuel 981
モツォアレディ
Motsoaledi, Pakishe Aaron 981
モック
Mock, Ray 959
モックフォード
Mockford, Caroline 959
モックラー
Mockler, Marcus 959
モッコ
Mocco, Steven 959
モツザス
Motuzas, Remigijus 981
モッシ
Mossi, Hafsa 981
モッシャー
Mosher, Steven W. 980
モッセ
Mossé, Philippe 981
モッタ
Motta, Thiago 981
モッター
Motter, Taylor 981
モッタキ
Mottaki, Manouchehr 981
モッタ・ドミンゲス
Motta Domínguez, Luis 981
モッツ
Motz, Bill 982
モッツィ
Mozzi, Giulio 984
モッツェッティ
Mozzetti, Francesco 984
モッティーニ
Mottini, Roger 981
モッテルリーニ
Motterlini, Matteo 981
モット
Mott, Edith 981
Mott, Jason 981
Mott, Tony 981
Motte, Jason 981
モットラム
Mottram, Craig 981
モッフォ
Moffo, Anna 960
モツミ
Motsumi, Lesego 981
モッラ
Molla, Tareq el 964
モツワハエ
Motswagae, Oscar Naledi 981
モデ
Maudet, Matthieu 921
モーティ
Mauti, Michael 922
モティ
Motee, Ahmmadollah 981
モディ
Modi, Monkaila 959
Modi, Narendra 959
モティア
Motyer, J.A. 982
Motyer, S. 982
モディアーノ
Modiano, Patrick 959
モディアノ
Modiano, Patrick 959
モディカ
Modica, Guy 959
Modica, Joe 959
モディボウマル
Modibbo Umar, Aliyu 959
モーティマー
Mortimer, Anne 979
Mortimer, Carole 979
Mortimer, Charlie 979
Mortimer, Emily 979
Mortimer, John 979
Mortimer, Sean 979
Mortimer, Vicki 979
モディリアーニ
Modigliani, Franco 959
モディーン
Modine, Matthew 959
モディン
Modine, Matthew 959
モデステ
Modeste, Dennoth 959
モデスト
Modeste, Anthony 959
Modeste, Clarice 959
モデストカーウェン
Modestecurwen, Clarice 959
モテット
Mottet, Maxime 981
モデーノ
Modderno, Craig 959
モーテル
Mortell, Peter 978
モデル
Modell, Art 959
モデルト
Modert, Octavie 959
モデルモグ
Moddelmog, Debra A. 959
モデレ
Modéré, Armelle 959
モーテンセン
Mortensen, Dale T. 978
Mortensen, Kurt W. 978
Mortensen, Viggo 978
モーテンソン
Mortenson, Greg 979
モド
Mod, Craig 959
モトイリ
Motyl, Vladimir 982
モドゥアクセビンダン
Modu Acuse Bindang, Carmelo 960
モドゥアクゼビンダン
Modu Acuse Bindang, Carmelo 960
モドキンス
Modkins, Curtis 959
モトク
Motoc, Mihnea Ioan 981
モトコ
Mothokho, Mapalesa 981
モドシュ
Modos, Peter 960
モトボリ
Motoboli, Maphoka 981
モトマ
Motum, Mekasa 981
モートマン
Mortman, Doris 979
モトムマモニ
Mottommamoni, Leonidas Carel 981
モトーラ
Mottola, Chad 981
モトラナ
Motlana, Nthato Harrison 981
モトランテ
Motlanthe, Kgalema 981
モトリー
Motley, Constance Baker 981
Mottley, Barnice Williams 981
Mottley, Mia 981
モドリッチ
Modrić, Luka 960
Modrich, Paul 960
モトルスキー
Motulsky, Arno G. 981
Motulsky, Harvey 981
モトレアヌ
Motreanu, Dan 981
モドレイ
Modley, Rudolf 959
モトロ
Motro, Joseph Michel Georges 981
モトワニ
Motwani, Prem 981
Motwani, Rajeev 981
モートン
Moreton, David C. 973
Morton, A.L. 979
Morton, Alan R. 979
Morton, Andrew 979
Morton, Brian 979
Morton, Charlie 979
Morton, Chris 979
Morton, Danelle 979
Morton, David B. 979
Morton, Frederic 979
Morton, James 979
Morton, John 979
Morton, Kate 979
Morton, Lisa 979
Morton, Samantha 979
Morton, Stephanie 979
Morton, Stephen 979
モートン＝クーパー

Morton-Cooper, Alison 979
モートン＝ショー
Morton-Shaw, Christine 979
モーナー
Moerner, William Esco 960
モナ
Mona, Erik 965
モナキノ
Monachino, Ted 965
モナク
Monaque, Mathilde 965
モナコ
Monaco, Juan 965
Monaco, Octavia 965
モナシュ
Monash, Paul 965
モナスティルスキー
Monastyrskiĭ, Mikhail Il'ich 965
モナストラ
Monastra, Vincent J. 965
モナハン
Monaghan, Paul 965
Monahan, John 965
Monahan, William 965
モナレ
Monare, Phallang 965
モニ
Moni, Dipu 966
モニエ
Monnier, Gerard 966
Monnier, Jeremy 966
Monnier, Mathilde 966
モニーク
Mo'nique 966
モニズ
Moniz, Ernest 966
モニチェッリ
Monicelli, Mario 966
モニチェリ
Monicelli, Mario 966
モーニック
Maunick, Jean-Paul 922
モニャマネ
Monyamane, Molotsi 969
モニング
Moning, Karen Marie 966
モネ
Monet, Nicole 966
モネイ
Monáe, Janelle 965
モネイロン
Monneyron, Frédéric 966
モネスティエ
Monestier, Alain 966
Monestier, Martin 966
モネッチ
Monetti, David M. 966
モネネムボ
Monénembo, Tierno 966
モーネメント
Mornement, Adam 976
モーノー
Morneau, Justin 976
モーノウ
Morneau, Justin 976
モノリ
Monory, Jacques 966
Monory, René 966
モハー
Moher, Frank 962
モハイ
Mohay, Miklos 962
モハエ
Mogae, Festus 960
モハキ
Mohaqqeq, Mohammad 962
モバーグ
Moberg, Gary P. 959
モーパーゴ
Morpurgo, Michael 976
モバサカニャ
Movasakanya, Henri 983
モハジ
Mohadi, Kembo 960
モハダム
Moghaddam, Fathali M. 960
モハッケク
Mohaqqeq, Mohammad 962
モハッシェタ・デビ
Mahasweta Devi 884
モハディ
Mohadi, Kembo 960
モハマディ
Mohammadi, Bismillah 961
Mohammadi, Juma Mohammad 961
モハマディザデ
Mohammadizadeh, Mohammad-Javad 961
モハマド
Mohamad, Khairul Anuar 960
Mohamad, M.H. 960
Mohammad, Abdul Rahman 961
Mohammad, Qari Din 961
Mohammad, Yar 961
Mohmod, Abdul Latif 962
モハマド・オスマニ
Mohammad Osmani, Faiz 961
モハマドポウルカルカラグ
Mohammadpour Karkaragh, Saeid 961
モハマド・ユソフ・ビン・イスマイル
Mohd.Yusof Bin Ismail 962
モハムド
Mohamud, Abdinur Moallim 962
Mohamud, Hassan Sheikh 962
モハムド・フィリッシュ
Mohamud Filish, Omar Mohamed 962
モハメッド
Mohamed, Ahmed 961
Mohamed, Said Ahmed 961
Mohammed, Khadra 962
Mohammed Ⅵ 962
モハメッド・ディレイタ
Mohamed Dileita, Dileita 961
モハメド
Mohamed, Abdi 960
Mohamed, Abdinur Sheikh 961
Mohamed, Abdirisak Omar 961
Mohamed, Abdoulkarim 961
Mohamed, Abdullahi Yussuf 961
Mohamed, Ahmed 961
Mohamed, Ahmed Jamseed 961
Mohamed, Aida 961
Mohamed, Amina C. 961
Mohamed, Daud 961
Mohamed, Dini Farah 961
Mohamed, Dirir 961
Mohamed, Gaber 961
Mohamed, Hassan Shatigadud 961
Mohamed, Hawo Hassan 961
Mohamed, Hussein Bantu 961
Mohamed, Ibrahim 961
Mohamed, Issa Bushura 961
Mohamed, Mohamed Ali 961
Mohamed, Mohamed Ibrahim 961
Mohamed, Mohamed Moallim Hassan 961
Mohamed, Musa 961
Mohamed, Omer 961
Mohamed, Samiyah Ahmad 961
Mohamed, Shakeel Ahmed Yousuf Abdul Razack 961
Mohamed, Shifa 961
Mohamed, Suad Abdelrazig 961
Mohamed, Zahabi Ould Sidi 961
Mohammed, Abdi 961
Mohammed, Abubakar Sadiq 961
Mohammed, Adan 961
Mohammed, Ali bin al-Shaikh Mansoor al-Sitri 961
Mohammed, Amina 961, 962
Mohammed, Bala 962
Mohammed, bin Abdul-Ghaffar 962
Mohammed, bin Abdullah al-Khalifa 962
Mohammed, bin Ahmed bin Jassim al-Thani 962
Mohammed, bin Khalifa al-Khalifa 962
Mohammed, Dirir 962
Mohammed, Jamal 962
Mohammed, Kamal Ahmed 962
Mohammed, Kamal Ali 962
Mohammed, Khaled al-Hamad al-Sabah 962
Mohammed, Lai 962
Mohammed, Maalim 962
Mohammed, Magaji 962
Mohammed, Muntaka 962
Mohammed, Nurudeen 962
Mohammed, Rafi 962
Mohammed, Sabah al-Salem al-Sabah 962
Mohammed, Salah bin Ali 962
Mohammed, Samiya Ahmad 962
Mohammed Ⅵ 962
Muhammad, Shabazz 987
モハメド6世
Mohammed Ⅵ 962
モハメド・アウジ
Mohamed Auzi, Bin Daud 961
モハメドアフメドマンソイブ
Mohamed Ahmed Mansoib, Djaffar 961
モハメド・アリ・ウルド・シディ・モハメド
Mohamed Aly Ould Sidi Mohamed 961
モハメド・イドリス
S.M.Mohamed Idris 1320
モハメドゥ
Mohamedou, Mohamed Mahmoud Ould 961
モハメドザイン
Mohamed Zain, Serudin 961
モハメド・ジン
Mohd Zin, Mohamed 962
モハメド・ソイ
Mohamedo Soilihi, Ali 961
モハメドディディ
Mohamed Didi, Aishath 961
モハメド・ムスタファ・イスハック
Mohamed Mustafa Ishak 961
モハメドレミン
Mohamed-lemine, Mohamed Mahmoud Ould 961
モハン
Mohan, Giles 962
Mohan, Mohan 962
モーハンティー
Mohanty, Chandra Talpade 962
モハンマディ
Mohammadi, Mohammad Hosein 961
Mohammadi, Seyedmorad 961
モービー
Moby 959
Morby, John E. 973
モヒェルディン
Mohyeldin, Mohamed 962
モヒカ
Mojica, Beatriz Pardiñas 963
Mojica, Melissa 963
モービーク
Moerbeek, Kees 960
モービル
Morville, Peter 979
モヒンドラ
Mohindra, Dhruv 962
モファズ
Mofaz, Shaul 960
モファット
Moffat, Chris 960
Moffat, David Burns 960
Moffat, Ivan 960
Moffat, John W. 960
Moffat, Mike 960
Moffat, Sarah 960
Moffat, Steven 960
Moffatt, Emma 960
モーフィ
Morphy, Howard 976
モフィット
Moffitt, John 960

モ

モフィッド
Mofid, Kamran 960
モフェット
Moffett, Mark W. 960
Moffett, Michael H. 960
Moffett, Sebastian 960
Moffett, Shannon 960
モブシシャン
Movsissyan, Armen 983
モフチャン
Movchan, Olena 983
モブツ
Mobutu, François Nzanga 959
モーブッシン
Mauboussin, Michael J. 921
モフラ
Maufras, Jérôme 921
モーブリー
Mobley, Mary Ann 959
モペス
Moppès, Catherine van 971
モヘディン
Mohieddin, Mahmoud 962
モベリ
Moberg, Kerstin Uvnäs 959
モヘレ
Mokhehle, Shakhane 963
モホセニエジェイ
Mohseni Ezhei, Gholamhossein 962
モボルニュ
Mauborgne, Renée 921
モホンビ
Mohombi 962
モマート‐ヤオホ
Mommert-Jauch, Petra 965
モマニ
Momani, Mohammad al 965
モマンド
Momand, Farida 965
モム
Mam Bun Heng 892
モムジャン
Momjian, Bruce 965
モムゼン
Mommsen, Hans 965
Mommsen, Wolfgang J. 965
モムナリエフ
Momunaliev, Nurkhanbek 965
モメカ
Moemeka, Jerod 960
モモ
Momo 965
Momoh, Joseph Saidu 965
モモタロウ
Momotaro, Dennis 965
モヤ
Moya, Carlos 984
Moya, María 984
Moya, Miguel Angel 984
Moya, Sergio Alvarez 984
Moya, Steven 984
モヤ・ポンス
Moya Pons, Frank 984
モヨ
Moyo, Dambisa 984
Moyo, Gorden 984
Moyo, Jonathan 984
Moyo, July 984
Moyo, Nkosana 984
モーラ
Moala, David 959
Mora, Pat 971
Moura, Joaquim Pina 982
モーラー
Mohler, Diana 962
モラ
Mola, Mario 963
Molla, Jean 964
Mora, Alexander 971
Mora, Galo 971
Mora, Gilles 971
Mora, Gladys 971
Mora, Nelson 971
Mora, Sonia Marta 971
モラー
Mueller, Robert Swan Ⅲ 986
モライス
Dos Santos Morais, Davilson 369
Morais, Eduardo Leopoldo Severim De 971
Morais, Isaltino 971
Morais, José Maria da Silva Vieira de 971
Morais, José Pedro de 972
Morais, Marisa Helena 972
モライン
Molijn, Radboud L.J. Maria 964
モラウィエツキ
Morawiecki, Mateusz 972
モラヴィック
Moravcik, Eva 972
モラヴェク
Moravek, Jan 972
モラヴェツ
Moravec, Ivan 972
モラヴェッツ
Moravec, Ivan 972
モラウタ
Morauta, Mekere 972
モラヴチク
Moravcik, Gina Marie 972
モラエイ
Mollaei, Saeid 964
モラエス
Moraes, Alexandre 971
Moraes, Junior 971
モラゴダ
Moragoda, Milinda 971
モラース
Morath, Inge 972
モラス
Morath, Inge 972
Morath, Kurt 972
モラスキー
Molasky, Michael S. 963
モラタ
Morata, Alvaro 972
Morata, Ginés 972
モラーツ
Moraz, Patrick 973
モラッティ
Moratti, Letizia 972
モラディ
Moradi, Behrooz 971
Moradi, Sohrab 971
モラティノス
Moratinos, Miguel Ángel 972
モラート
Morath, Inge 972
モーラヌ
Mowlam, Marjorie 984
モラーヌ
Maurane, Camille 922
モラノ・ベガ
Molano Vega, Diego 963
モラフコバ
Moravcova, Martina 972
モラベツ
Moravec, Ondrej 972
モラベック
Moravec, Hans P. 972
モラベルディ
Molaverdi, Shahindokht 963
モラポ
Molapo, Joang 963
モーラム
Mowlam, Marjorie 984
モラ・モラ
Mora Mora, Alejandra 972
モラール
Mollard, Claude 964
Mollard, Michel 964
Morar, Sandra 972
モラル
Moral, Rafael del 972
Morrall, John B. 976
モラレ
Molale, Eric Mothusi 963
Mollaret, Henri H. 964
モラーレス
Morales, José F. 972
Morales, Kendrys 972
Morales, Manuel, Jr. 972
Morales, Roberta A. 972
モラレス
Morales, Alfredo 972
Morales, Ana Teresa 972
Morales, Carlos 972
Morales, Erik 972
Morales, Evo 972
Morales, Francisco 972
Morales, Gil 972
Morales, Jimmy 972
Morales, Kendrys 972
Morales, Michael 972
Morales, Rags 972
Morales, Sebastian 972
Morales, Victor 972
モラレス・アイマ
Morales Ayma, Juan Evo 972
モラレス・オヘダ
Morales Ojeda, Roberto 972
モラレス・カラソ
Morales Carazo, Jaime 972
モラレス・カルタヤ
Morales Cartaya, Alfredo 972
モラレス・マスン
Morales Mazún, Ana Isabel 972
モラレス・モスコソ
Morales Moscoso, Carlos Raúl 972
モラレス・モラ
Morales Mora, Victor 972
モラレスモンロイ
Morales Monroy, Rubén Estuardo 972
モラレス・ランディバル
Morales Landívar, Carlos 972
モーラン
Maurin, Christelle 922
Moran, Jim 972
モラーン
Moran, Colin 972
モラン
Molan, Peter C. 963
Moran, Daniel 972
Moran, Daniel J. 972
Moran, Elizabeth 972
Moran, Lindsay 972
Moran, Paul 972
Moran, Peter 972
Moran, Richard 972
Moran, Robin Macloni 972
Moran, Thomas 972
Moran, Timothy 972
Moran, Victoria 972
Morant, Bénédicte 972
Morin, Edgar 975
Morin, Hervé 975
モランヴィル
Moranville, Sharelle Byars 972
モランタ
Moronta, Reyes 976
モランダー
Molander, Roger 963
モランデ
Morandé, Felipe 972
モランディ
Morandi, Matteo 972
モランディーニ
Morandini, Mickey 972
モーランド
Moland, Lydia L. 963
モランビル
Moranville, Sharelle Byars 972
モーリ
Maury, Jean-Pierre 922
Morey, Trish 974
Mori, Gioia 975
モーリー
Morey, Daryl 974
Morley, Isla 976
Morley, Karen 976
Morley, Simon 976
Morrey, Bernard F. 976
Mourey, Risa Lavizzo 982
モリ
Moli, Kalfau 964
Mori, Emmanuel 975
Mori, Kazuhiro 975
Mori, Kyoko 975
Mori, Masako 975
Mori, Shino 975
Mori, Shiro Floyd 975
モリー
Morey, Tomeu 974
モーリア
Mauriat, Paul 922
モリア
Morias, Marisa Helena 975
モリアス
Morias, Dan 975
モリアーティ
Moriarty, Kieran J. 975

Moriarty, Liane 975
Moriarty, Michael 975
モリウチ
Moriuchi, Mique 976
モリエス
Mauriès, Patrick 922
モリオオ
Molio'o, Teofilo 964
モリオン
Morion, Pierre 975
モリカワ
Morikawa, Dennis J. 975
モリク
Molik, Alicia 964
モリグチ
Moriguchi, Ignácio Tadayoshi 975
Moriguchi, Tomio 975
モリコ
Morico, Lucia 975
モリコーネ
Morricone, Ennio 976
モリサ
Molisa, Sela 964
モリザ
Molisa, Sela 964
モリサレ
Molisale, Havo 964
モリージ
Morisi, Luca 975
モリシタ
Morishita, Yoko 975
モーリス
Morris, Broderick 976
Morris, Tom 977
Morris, Wayne 977
モリス
Morrice, Norman 976
Morris 976
Morris, Akeel 976
Morris, Alfred 976
Morris, Amanda 976
Morris, Annie 976
Morris, Aubrey 976
Morris, Ben 976
Morris, Bob 976
Morris, Bryan 976
Morris, Charles R. 976
Morris, Darryl 976
Morris, David 976, 977
Morris, Derek John 977
Morris, Desmond 977
Morris, Dick 977
Morris, Doug 977
Morris, Elizabeth A. 977
Morris, Errol 977
Morris, George H. 977
Morris, Gilbert 977
Morris, Henry Madison 977
Morris, Howard J. 977
Morris, Ian 977
Morris, Jackie 977
Morris, James 977
Morris, James T. 977
Morris, Jan 977
Morris, Jasper 977
Morris, Jay Hunter 977
Morris, Jim 977
Morris, John 977
Morris, John David 977
Morris, John E. 977
Morris, Julianna 977
Morris, Julie 977
Morris, Justin 977
Morris, Kenneth M. 977
Morris, Kimberly 977
Morris, Langdon 977
Morris, Leon 977
Morris, Lisa Rappaport 977
Morris, Marcus 977
Morris, Mark 977
Morris, Markieff 977
Morris, Mary 977
Morris, Meaghan 977
Morris, Melvyn 977
Morris, Monte 977
Morris, Neil 977
Morris, Oswald 977
Morris, Peter 977
Morris, Ramona 977
Morris, Richard 977
Morris, Rien 977
Morris, Robin 977
Morris, Romar 977
Morris, Sandi 977
Morris, S.Brent 977
Morris, Stephen 977
Morris, Virginia 977
Morris, Virginia B. 977
Morriss, Anne 978
モーリス＝ジョーンズ
Maurice-Jones, Tim 922
モーリス・スズキ
Morris Suzuki, Tessa I. J. 978
モーリス・鈴木
Morris Suzuki, Tessa I. J. 978
モーリスモ
Mauresmo, Amélie 922
モリズロー
Morrisroe, Patricia 978
モリスン
Morrison, Judith H. 978
Morrison, Martha A. 978
Morrison, Slade 978
Morrison, Toni 978
モーリセイ
Morrissey, Muriel 978
モリセイ
Morrissey, Kevin 978
モリセット
Morissette, Alanis 975
Morrissette, Rob 978
モリゾー
Morizot, Raymonde 976
モリソン
Morison, David 975
Morison, Robert 975
Morison, Slade 975
Morison, Toby 975
Morrison, Alex 977
Morrison, Anthony P. 977
Morrison, Antonio 977
Morrison, Blake 977
Morrison, Boyd 977
Morrison, Delcy Schram 977
Morrison, Denny 977
Morrison, Elizabeth 977
Morrison, Frank 977
Morrison, Gary 977
Morrison, Gary R. 977
Morrison, Gordon 977
Morrison, Grant 977
Morrison, Greg 977
Morrison, Helen 977
Morrison, James 978
Morrison, Jasper 978
Morrison, J.B. 978
Morrison, Jenean 978
Morrison, Karin 978
Morrison, Logan 978
Morrison, Malcolm 978
Morrison, Melissa 978
Morrison, Michael L. 978
Morrison, Phillip 978
Morrison, Phylis 978
Morrison, Ravel 978
Morrison, Scott 978
Morrison, Steven J. 978
Morrison, Taylor 978
Morrison, Todd A. 978
Morrison, Tommy 978
Morrison, Toni 978
Morrison, Walter 978
モリタ
Morita, Noriyuki Pat 975
Morita, Richard H. 975
モリター
Molitor, Katharina 964
Molitor, Paul 964
モリツグ
Moritsugu, Frank 975
モリッシー
Morrissey 978
Morrissey, Donna 978
Morrissey, Thomas 978
モーリッツ
Moritz, Helmut 976
モリッツ
Moritz, Dorothea 975
モリテルノ
Moliterno, James E. 964
モリトル
Molitor, Katharina 964
モリーナ
Molina, Marcos 964
Molina, Mario José 964
Molina, Rocío 964
Molina, Terese 964
Molina, Yadier 964
Molina Jiménez, Iván 964
モリナ
Molina, Alfred 964
Molina, César Antonio 964
Molina, Jorge Alberto 964
Molina, Juan Manuel 964
Molina, Luisa T. 964
Molina, Mario José 964
Molina, Ricardo 964
Molina, Yadier 964
モリナーリ
Molinari, Marco Paolo 964
モリナリ
Molinari, Federico 964
モリナル
Molinar, Lucy 964
モリナル・オルカシタス
Molinar Horcasitas, Juan Francisco 964
モリナーロ
Molinaro, Albert 964
Molinaro, Cristian 964
モリナロ
Molinaro, Anthony 964
Molinaro, Edouard 964
Molinaro, Frank 964
モリーナ・ロペス
Molina Lopez, T. 964
モーリーニョ
Mourinho, Jose 982
モリネロ
Molinero, Cecilio Mar 964
モリノ
Molino, Jean 964
モリノー
Molyneaux, Brian Leigh 965
Morineau, Michel 975
モリビアティス
Molyviatis, Petros 965
モリペ
Molipe, Jean-Claude 964
モリマンド
Morimando, Shawn 975
モリヤマ
Moriyama, Raymond 976
モリヤ・マシエル
Moriya Maciel, Zunilda 976
モリュー
Moreau, Donna 973
Morieux, Yves 975
モリワ
Moliwa, Athanasie 964
Moliwa, Moleko 964
モーリン
Maurine, Camille 922
Morin, Amy 975
Morin, Jack 975
モリーン
Moline, Georganne 964
Moline, Karen 964
モリン
Morin, Charles M. 975
Morin, Mike 975
モーリング
Moring, Wim 975
モール
Maul, Dianna 921
Mohr, Klaus 962
Moll, Sam 964
モル
Mol, Annemarie 963
Moll, James 964
Moll, Jorge 964
Moll, Stephen 964
Mor, Emre 971
モルア
Moloua, Félix 965
モルヴァン
Morvan, Lydwine 979
Morvan, Stéphanie 979
Morvan, Véronique 979
モルガチェワ
Morgachyov, Nikita 974
モルガド
Morgado, Carlos 974
モルガネッラ
Morganella, Michel 975
モルガーノ
Morgano, Michael 975
モルガン
Morgan, Joël 974
Morgan, Juan David 974
Morgan, Michèle 974
Morgan, Nina 974
モルガンティ
Morganti, Giuseppe Maria 975
モルク
Moerk, Christian 960
Molkhou, Jean-Michel 964
Mørk, Christian 976
Mørk, Truls 976

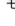

モルグロフ
Morgulov, Igor V. 975
モルグン
Morgun, Zoya Fyodorovna 975
モルケット
Morquette, Yves Rose 976
モルゲンシュテルン
Morgenstern, Thomas 975
モルゲンステルヌ
Morgenstern, Susie 975
モルゲンロート
Morgenroth, Hartmut 975
モルコス
Morqos, Joudeh 976
モルシ
Morsi, Muhammad 978
Morsi, Pamela 978
モルジャン
Morjane, Kamel 976
モルシュバッハ
Morsbach, Helmut 978
モルシュホイザー
Morschheuser, Klaus 978
モールズワース
Molesworth, Carl 963
モルダノフ
Moldanov, Timofei 963
モルタラー
Molterer, Wilhelm 965
モルチエ
Mortier, Roland F.J. 979
モルツ
Molz, Redmond Kathleen 965
モルツバーガー
Maltsberger, John T. 891
モルティ
Morte, Albertino Francisco Boa 978
モルティエ
Mortier, Gérard 979
Mortier, Roland F.J. 979
モルディス・メルカド
Moldiz Mercado, Hugo 963
モルティモア
Mortimore, Denise 979
モルティール
Mortier, Tine 979
モールディン
Maulden, John 922
Mauldin, Bill 922
Mauldin, John 922
Mauldin, Lorenzo 922
モルディン
Mauldin, Bill 922
モルテーニ
Molteni, Sonia 965
モルテラー
Molterer, Wilhelm 965
モルテレト
Mortelette, Dorian 978
モールデン
Moulden, Heather M. 982
モルデンケ
Moldenke, Alma Lance 963
モルテンセン
Mortensen, Dale T. 978
モールド
Mould, Richard Francis 982
モルド
Mould, Chris 982
モルドヴァア
Moldvaer, Anette 963
モルトケ
Moltke, Freya von 965
モルドナーシュミット
Moldner-schmidt, Antje 963
モルドバヌ
Moldovanu, Mihai 963
モルドバン
Moldovan, Nikolina 963
Moldovan, Olivera 963
モルドベアヌ
Moldoveanu, Alin George 963
モルトマン
Moltmann, Jürgen 965
モールトン
Moulton, Alexander Eric 982
Moulton, Brent R. 982
Moulton, Gary 982
モルトン
Morton, Patricia A. 979
モルナー
Molnár, Ilona 965
Molnar, Peter 965
モルナール
Molnár, Csaba 965
Molnár, Lajos 965
Molnar, Michael 965
モルナル
Molnar, Peter 965
Mornar, Vedran 976
モルノー
Morneau, Justin 976
Morneau, William Francis 976
モルノス
Molnos, Angela 965
モールバッハ
Morbach, Bernhard 973
モルフェッタ
Molfetta, Carlo 964
モルホ
Molho, Renata 964
モルポワ
Maulpoix, Jean-Michel 922
モルマンド
Mormando, Franco 976
モルメンティ
Molmenti, Daniele 965
Molmenti, Ernesto P. 965
モルレオ
Morleo, Archimede 976
モルロー
Morlot, Frédéric 976
モーレー
Moorey, Teresa 971
モレ
Mollé, Roland Le 964
Moret, Roger 973
モレー
Moré, Ivan 973
Morrey, Matthew C. 976
モレア
Morea, Valentina 973
モーレイ
Morley, Eileen D. 976
モレイ
Molay, Bruce 963
Molay, Frédérique 963
Morei, Ion 973
モレイコ
Mureiko, Sergei 993
モレイス
Morais, Richard C. 972
モレイティス
Moraitis, Dimitri 972
モレイラ
Moreira, Andre 973
Moreira, Inacio 973
Moreira, João 973
Moreira, Telmo 973
Moreira, Yanick 973
モレイラダシルバ
Moreira Da Silva, Jorge 973
モレイラ・ロペス
Moreira Lopéz, María Alexandra 973
モレジーニ
Molesini, Andrea 963
モレス
Morais, Marisa Helena 972
Moreti, Martin 973
モレスキー
Molesky, Joanne 963
モレスコ
Moresco, Robert 973
モレスモ
Mauresmo, Amélie 922
モレスモー
Mauresmo, Amélie 922
モレゾン
Molaison, Henry 963
モレツァネ
Moletsane, Maboee 963
モレッツ
Moretz, Chloe Grace 974
モレッティ
Moretti, Emiliano 973
Moretti, Enrico 973
Moretti, Franco 974
Moretti, Nanni 974
モレッロ
Morello, Paolo 973
モレティ
Moreti, Martin 973
モレネス
Morenés, Pedro 973
モレーノ
Moreno, Joyce 973
モレノ
Moreno, Alfredo 973
Moreno, Arte 973
Moreno, Hector 973
Moreno, Jonathan D. 973
Moreno, José Guillermo 973
Moreno, Lenín 973
Moreno, Maria José 973
Moreno, Michael R. 973
Moreno, Mike 973
Moreno, Patricia 973
Moreno, Paula Marcela 973
Moreno, Rodrigo 973
Moreno, Yipsi 973
モレノオカンポ
Moreno-Ocampo, Luis 973
モレーノ・メンヒバル
Moreno Mengíbal, Andrés 973
モレフィ
Molefhi, Nonofo 963
モレホン
Morejón, Pedro 973
モレマ
Molema, Leloba Sefetogi 963
Mollema, Bauke 964
モレラ
Morella, Constance Albanese 973
モレリ
Morelli, Anne 973
Morelli, Marco 973
モレリオ
Molerio, Pedro Antonio Valle 963
モーレル
Morrell, Maureen F. 976
モレール
Møller, Claus 964
モレル
Moller, N. 964
Morel, Alex 973
Morel, Anaïk 973
Morel, Christian 973
Morel, Françoise 973
Morel, Jeremy 973
Morel, Tanja 973
Morell, Michael J. 973
Morell, Virginia 973
Morrell, Jon 976
Morrell, Margot 976
Morrell, Peter S. 976
Morrell, Steve 976
モレル・サミュエルズ
Morrel-Samuels, Palmer 976
モレレキ
Moleleki, Monyane 963
モレロ
Merello, Tom 936
モレロ・ベジャビア
Molero Bellavia, Diego Alfredo 963
モレワ
Molewa, Bomo Edna 963
モーレン
Mooren, Jeroen 971
Moreń, Peter 973
モレンコフ
Mollenkopf, Steve 964
モーロ
Mauro, Jim 922
モロ
Moro, Abba 976
Moro, Javier 976
モロー
Moreau, Daniel 973
Moreau, Edgar 973
Moreau, Hervé 973
Moreau, Jeanne 973
Moreau, Laurent 973
Moreau, Marc-Andre 973
Moreau, Pauline 973
Moreau, Pierre-François 973
Moreau, Yolande 973
Morrow, Anthony 978
Morrow, Bill 978
Morrow, Bradford 978
Morrow, Brandon 978
Morrow, Chris 978
Morrow, Cousin Brucie 978
Morrow, James D. 978
Morrow, Lance 978

モロア
Mauroy, Pierre 922
モロイ
Molloy, John T. 965
Molloy, Michael 965
モロウ
Morrow, Carol Ann 978
Morrow, Keith 978
モロカ
Moroka, Daniel 976
Moroka, Neo 976
モロクマ
Morokuma, Keiji 976
モロゴ
Morogo, William 976
モロジェン
Molojen, Vladimir 965
モロジーニ
Morosini, Piermario 976
モロジャコフ
Molodiakov, Vasiliĭ 965
モロジュク
Moroziuk, Mykola 976
モローゾフ
Morozov, Valeriĭ Ėdgartovich 976
モロゾフ
Morozov, Nikolai 976
Morozov, Stanislav 976
Morozov, Vladimir 976
モロドガジエフ
Moldogaziev, Rysbek 963
モローニ
Moloney, Paddy 965
Moroni, Lisa 976
Moroni, Matias 976
モローニー
Moroney, Tracey 976
モロニー
Moloney, Kate 965
モロフ
Mollov, Nezhdet 964
Moroff, Max 976
モロポ
Molopo, Notsi 965
モーロワ
Mauroy, Pierre 922
モロワ
Mauroy, Pierre 922
Morova, Antonina P. 976
モロン
Mollon, Phil 964
モーワー
Mower, Liam 984
モワイアン
Moyen, Georges 984
モワッセフ
Moisseeff, Michaël 963
モーワット
Mowat, Farley McGill 983
モワット
Mowat, Farley McGill 983
モワヤン
Moyen, Georges 984
モンヴァロン
Montvalon, Dominique de 969
モンカダ
Moncada, Riccy 965
Moncada, Yoan 965
モンカダ・コリンドレス
Moncada Colindres, Denis Ronald 965
モンカレ
Mönkäre, Sinikka 966
モンク
Monk, Ellen F. 966
Monk, Gerald 966
Monk, Jane 966
Monk, Karyn 966
Monk, Malik 966
Monk, Ray 966
Monk, Simon 966
Monk, Thelonious 966
モンクス
Monks, Jonathan 966
Monks, Judith 966
Monks, Julie 966
Monks, Lydia 966
モンクリーフ
Moncrief, Donte 965
モンクリフ
Moncrief, William 965
モングレディエン
Mongolian Stomper 966
モンケビチウス
Monkevičius, Algirdas 966
モンケン
Monken, Todd 966
モンゴメリ
Montgomery, Scott L. 968
Montgomery, Toccara 968
モンゴメリー
Montgomerie, Colin 968
Montgomery, Alex 968
Montgomery, Alice 968
Montgomery, Cynthia A. 968
Montgomery, David 968
Montgomery, David R. 968
Montgomery, Jon 968
Montgomery, Lee 968
Montgomery, Mike 968
Montgomery, Ruth 968
Montgomery, Sy 968
Montgomery, Ty 968
Montgomery Hunter, Kathryn 968
モンゴリアン・ストンパー
Mongolian Stomper 966
モンコン
Mongkol, Na Songkhla 966
モンサルバーチェ
Montsalvatge, Xavier 968
モンサルバチェ
Montsalvatge, Xavier 968
モンサンジョン
Monsaingeon, Bruno 967
モンジェル
Mongel, Aurore 966
モンシャン
Monchamp, Marie-Anne 965
モンジャン
Mongin, Jean Paul 966
Mongin, Pierre 966
モンジュ
Monge, Jean-Baptiste 966
モンジョ
Mondjo, Charles Richard 966
モンスター
Monster 967
モンズマン
Monsman, Gerald Cornelius 967
モンセフ
Monsef, Maryam 967
モンセラット・モンセラット
Montserrat Montserrat, Dolors 968
モンソン
Monzon, Roberto 969
Monzón Campos, José Luis 969
モンダ
Monda, Antonio 965
Monda, Lorena 965
モンダヴィ
Mondavi, Robert G. 965
モンタギュー
Montague, John 967
Montague, Lisa 967
Montague, Ty 967
モンタス
Montas, Frankie 967
Montás, Temístocles 967
モンタゼリ
Montazeri, Hussein Ali 967
モンタゼリー
Montazeri, Hussein Ali 967
モンタゼリ師
Montazeri, Hussein Ali 967
モンタナ
Montana, Claude 967
Montana, LeRoy 967
モンタナーリ
Montanari, Eva 967
Montanari, Massimo 967
モンタナリ
Montanari, Eva 967
Montanari, Richard 967
モンタナーロ
Montanaro, Silvana Quattrocchi 967
モンタニー
Montagny, Franck 967
モンタニエ
Montagnier, Luc Antoine 967
モンタニェス
Montañes, Polo 967
モンタニョ・リベラ
Montaño Rivera, Tito Rolando 967
モンタネリ
Montanelli, Indro 967
モンターノ
Montano, Judith 967
モンタノ
Montano, Aldo 967
Montano, Danny 967
モンタノアロヨ
Montano Arroyo, Andres Roberto 967
モンダビ
Mondavi, Robert G. 965
モンダビー
Mondavi, Robert G. 965
モンタランベール
Montalembert, Anne de 967
モンタルバン
Montalban, Ricardo 967
Montalván, Luis Carlos 967
モンタルボ
Montalvo, Gustavo 967
モンタン
Montan, Chris 967
モンチ
Monte, Marisa 967
モンチョ
Montcho, Théophile 967
モンツォ
Montsho, Sejo 968
モンツチ
Montuschi, Olivia 969
モンツローズ
Montrose, Sharon 968
モンテ
Monte, Tom 967
モンデ
Monde, Greyford 965
モンデー
Mondeh, Sama Sahr 966
モンテアグド
Monteagudo, Lourdes 967
モンテアレグレ
Montealegre, Eduardo 967
モンティ
Montgomerie, Colin 968
Monti, Mario 968
モンティア
Montier, James 968
モンティアス
Montias, John Michael 968
モンティエ・カルレ
Montillet-Carles, Carole 968
モンティエル
Montiel, Eduardo 968
Montiel, Fernando 968
モンディエール
Mondiere, Anne-Sophie 966
モンティジアニ
Montigiani, Nicolas 968
モンティス
Monteith, Cory 967
モンティーリャ
Montilla, José 968
モンデイル
Mondale, Walter Fritz 965
モンティロ
Monteiro, Longuinhos 967
モンテイロ
Monteiro, Alexandre Dias 967
Monteiro, Antonio Isaac 967
Monteiro, Antonio Mascarenhas 967
Monteiro, Armando 967
Monteiro, Helder 967
Monteiro, Jaime Basílio 967
Monteiro, Joao Jose Silva 967
Monteiro, José Antonio Pinto 967
Monteiro, Longuinhos 967
Monteiro, Roberto Leal 967
Monteiro, Sidónio 967
Monteiro, Telma 967
Monteiro, Walcyr 967
モンテイロドデアン
Monteiro Dodean, Daniela 967
モンテオレーネ
Monteleone, Claudio 967
モンテギュー
Montague, Robert 967

モンデサー
Mondesir, Keith 966
モンデシー
Mondesi, Raul 966
モンデジー
Mondesir, Keith 966
モンテース
Monteith, Cory 967
モンテス
Montes, Cristina 968
Montes, Juan Carlos 968
Montes, Julio 968
モンテスゴンゴラ
Montes Gongora, Jose Lino 968
モンテス・デ・オカ
Montes de Oca, Wendy 968
モンテゼモーロ
Montezemolo, Luca Cordero di 968
モンテッラ
Montella, Vincenzo 968
モンテーニュ
Montaigne, Marion 967
モンテネグロ
Montenegro, Diego 968
Montenegro, Mario 968
モンテフィオーリ
Montefiore, Simon Sebag 967
モンテフィオーレ
Montefiore, Simon Sebag 967
モンテホ
Montejo, Daynellis 967
Montejo, Mario 967
モンテマヨール
Montemayor, Leonard 968
モンテラ
Montella, Vincenzo 968
モンテリオン
Monteleone, James A. 967
モンデール
Mondale, Eleanor 965
Mondale, Joan Adams 965
Mondale, Walter Fritz 965
モンテルオーニ
Monteleone, Thomas F. 968
モンテーロ
Montero, Jefferson 968
Montero, Luis 968
モンテロ
Montero, Fernando 968
Montero, Miguel 968
Montero, Rafael 968
Montero, Rene 968
モンテロソ
Monterroso, Augusto 968
モンテロッソ
Monterroso, Augusto 968
Monterroso, Luis Enrique 968
モントゥート
Montoute, Lenard 968
モントゴメリー
Montgomerie, Colin 968
Montgomery, David R. 968
Montgomery, Michael 968
Montgomery, Ruth 968
モントショー
Montsho, Amantle 968
モントート
Montoute, Lenard 968
モントフォード
Montford, A.W. 968
モントブラン
Montebrun, Manuela 967
モントブール
Montebourg, Arnaud 967
モントミニー
Montminy, Zelana 968
モントーヤ
Montoya, Antonio Nunez 968
Montoya, Juan 968
Montoya, Julian 968
Montoya, Martin 968
Montoyo, Charlie 968
モントヤ
Montoya, Peter 968
モンドラーネ
Mondlane, Agostinho Salvador 966
モンドラネ
Mondlane, Alberto 966
モントリーヴォ
Montolivo, Riccardo 968
モントレソール
Montresor, Beni 968
モントロ
Montoro, Angel 968
Montoro, Cristóbal 968
モントローズ
Montrose, Kenneth A. 968
モントロス
Montross, David H. 968
モントロ・ロメロ
Montoro Romero, Cristóbal 968
モンドン
Mondon, Macsuzy 966
モンノ
Monno, Harunur Rashid Khan 966
モンハイト
Monheit, Jane 966
モンパーカー
Montparker, Carol 968
モンバロン
Monbaron, Simon 965
モンビオ
Monbiot, George 965
モンビオット
Monbiot, George 965
モンフィス
Monfils, Gael 966
モンフェリー
Monféry, Dominique 966
モンフォート
Monfort, Charles K. 966
モンフオリギル
Monkhorgil, Tsendiin 966
モンブーケット
Monbouquette, Bill 965
モンブケット
Monbouquette, Bill 965
モンフバット
Munkhbat, Urantsetseg 991
モンブルケット
Monbourquette, Jean 965
モンフレッド
Monfreid, Dorothée de 966
モンヘ
Monge, Guido Alberto 966
モンベショラ
Mombeshora, Douglas 965
Mombeshoro, Swithun 965
モンベショロ
Mombeshoro, Swithun 965
モンヘス
Monges, Juan Darío 966
モンマルシェ
Monmarche, Carole 966
モンル
Monrou, Rafiatou 967
モンルブ
Monloubou, Laure 966
モンレアル
Monreal, Nacho 966
モンロ
Munro, Nell 992
モンロー
Monro, Robin 966
Monroe, Aly 966
Monroe, Chris 966
Monroe, Donald 966
Monroe, Greg 966
Monroe, Keith 966
Monroe, Lucy 967
Monroe, Mary Alice 967
Monroe, Robert A. 967
Monroe, Steve 967
モンローズ
Mountrose, Jane 982
Mountrose, Phillip 982
モンワイエ
Monnoyer, Eric 966

【ヤ】

ヤアロン
Ya'alon, Moshe 1532
ヤイ
Yayi, Boni 1536
ヤイスマン
Jeismann, Michael 669
ヤイタネス
Yaitanes, Greg 1532
ヤイリ
Yairi, Ehud 1532
ヤウ
Yau, Herman 1536
Yau, Shing-Tung 1536
Yow, Valerie Raleigh 1542
ヤヴァーバウム
Yaverbaum, Eric 1536
ヤウギッツ
Jaugitz, Markus 666
ヤウク
Yauch, Adam 1536
ヤウス
Jauss, Hans Robert 666
ヤウチ
Yauch, Adam 1536
ヤーウッド
Yarwood, Vaughan 1536
ヤウヒ
Jauch, Ursula Pia 666
ヤウフ
Jauch, Herbert 666
ヤウホヤルヴィ
Jauhojärvi, Sami 666
ヤウマン
Jaumann, Bernhard 666
ヤヴリンスキー
Yavlinskii, Grigorii Alekseevich 1536
ヤウンゼメグレンデ
Jaunzemegrende, Žaneta 666
ヤオ
Yao, Caroline 1535
Yao, Chen 1535
Yao, Feila 1535
Yao, Guang 1535
Yao, Ming 1535
Yao, Wen-yuan 1535
Yau, Shing-Tung 1536
ヤオワパ
Yaowapa, Boorapolchai 1535
ヤーガー
Jager, Evan 659
Jágr, Jaromír 659
ヤガチャク
Jagaciak, Anna 659
ヤカボシュ
Jakabos, Zsuzsanna 660
ヤーガン
Yeargan, Michael 1537
ヤーキズ
Yerkes, Leslie 1538
ヤキメンコ
Yakimenko, Alexey 1533
ヤキモフスキ
Jakimovski, Stevče 660
ヤーギン
Yergin, Daniel A. 1538
ヤグエ
Yague Enrique, Brigitte 1532
ヤクシュ
Yakis, Yasar 1533
ヤグジラー
Yağcilar, Mahir 1532
ヤークス
Yerkes, Leslie 1538
ヤクスト
Jaksto, Jaroslav 660
ヤグディン
Yagudin, Alexei 1532
ヤクトーヴィチ
Jakutovich, Olga 660
ヤクバ
Yacoubou, Ibrahim 1532
ヤクピ
Yakupi, Nexhati 1533
ヤクブ
Yacoubou, Ibrahim 1532
Yakubu, Hawa 1533
ヤクブチャク
Jakubczak-pawelec, Anna 660
ヤクポヴィッチ
Jakupovic, Eldin 660
ヤーグラン
Jagland, Thorbjørn 659
ヤーグラント
Jagland, Thorbjørn 659
ヤーグランド
Jagland, Thorbjørn 659
ヤゲ
Yague, Brigitte 1532
ヤケテ
Yakete, Joseph 1532

ヤ

ヤーゲルフェルト
Jägerfeld, Jenny 659
ヤーゴ
Yago, Glenn 1532
ヤゴ
Yago, Glenn 1532
ヤコヴレフ
Yakovlev, Aleksandr Nikolaevich 1533
Yakovlev, Egor Vladimirovich 1533
Yakovlev, Yuri 1533
ヤコカ
Iacocca, Liliana 641
Iacocca, Michele 641
ヤコシッツ
Jakosits, Michael 660
ヤコスト
Jaksto, Jaroslav 660
ヤコッビ
Jacobbi, Paola 657
ヤコバシビリ
Yakobashvili, Temur 1533
ヤコービ
Jacoby, Mario 658
ヤコビ
Jacobi, Aart 657
Yakob, Yala 1533
ヤコビナ
Jakovina, Tihomir 660
ヤーコブ
Yaacob, Ibrahim 1532
ヤコブ
Iacovou, Georgios 641
Jacob, Gitta 657
Jacobs, René 657
Yaqoob, Salma 1535
ヤコプ
Jacob, Klaus 657
ヤーコブス
Jacobs, René 657
ヤーコプス
Jacobs, René 657
ヤコブス
Jacobs, Marie-Josée 657
Jakobs, Günther 660
ヤコブスドッティル
Jakobsdottir, Katrin 660
ヤコブスン
Jakobsen, Sander 660
ヤコブセン
Jacobsen, Astrid Uhrenholdt 658
Jacobsen, Mette 658
Jacobsen, Michael Hviid 658
Jacobsen, Steffen 658
Jakobsen, Lisbet 660
Jakobsen, Liselotte 660
ヤーコブソン
Jakobson, Kristin M. 660
Jakobson, Linda 660
ヤコブソン
Jacobson, Alan M. 658
Jacobson, Howard 658
Jacobson, Ivar 658
Jacobson, James L. 658
Jacobson, Robert E. 658
Jacobsson, Erin E. 658
Jakobosson, Joel 660
Jakobson, Max 660
ヤコブチッチ
Jakovčić, Ivan 660
ヤコブリジ
Iacob-ridzi, Monica 641
ヤーコブレフ
Yakovlev, Aleksandr Nikolaevich 1533
ヤコブレフ
Yakovlev, Aleksandr Nikolaevich 1533
Yakovlev, Egor Vladimirovich 1533
Yakovlev, Vasyl 1533
Yakovlev, Vladimir A. 1533
ヤコペッティ
Jacopetti, Gualtiero 658
ヤコボビッチ
Jacobovici, Simcha 657
ヤサイ
Yasay, Perfecto 1536
ヤサル
Yasar, Selim 1536
ヤサント
Hyacinthe, Gabrielle 640
ヤジジ
Yazigi, Besher Riyad 1536
Yazigi, Nizar Wehbe 1536
ヤジディ
al-Yazidi, Ali Mohamed 1536
ヤージニク
Yajnik, Birad Rajaram 1532
ヤジマ
Yajima, Lillian Emiko Noda 1532
ヤシャリ
Jashari, Adnan 666
ヤシャル・ケマル
Yaşar Kemal 1536
ヤーシル・アブダッラ・アブデルサラーム・アフマド
Yasir Abdalla Abdelsalam Ahmed 1536
ヤシン
Yassin, Ahmed 1536
Yassin, Ali Mohamed Osman 1536
Yassin, Osama 1536
ヤシン師
Yassin, Ahmed 1536
ヤシンスキ
Jasinski, Daniel 666
Jasiński, Wojciech 666
ヤズガン
Yazgan, Kerem 1536
ヤズギ
el-Yazghi, Mohammed 1536
ヤスケビッチ
Yaskevich, Liubov 1536
ヤスコ
Yasko, Amy 1536
ヤズジュ
Yazici, Hayati 1536
ヤズダニ
Yazdani, Reza 1536
ヤズダニチャラティ
Yazdani Cherati, Hassan 1536
ヤーステイン
Jarstein, Rune 665
ヤーストレボヴァ
IAstrebova, Lidiia 642
ヤスハラ
Yasuhara, Denny 1536
ヤスミン・アハマド
Yasmin Ahmad 1536
ヤスミン・ウマール
Yasmin Umar, Mohammad 1536
ヤズムイラドフ
Yazmyradov, Annageldi 1536
ヤズムハメドワ
Yazmuhammedova, Maysa 1536
ヤセル
Yasser, Mohammed Ali 1536
Yasser, Ramadan 1536
ヤセン
Yasen, Yunus 1536
ヤソンナ
Yasonna, Laoly 1536
ヤーダヴ
Yadav, Rajendra 1532
ヤタバレ
Yatabare, Sambou 1536
ヤダフ
Yadav, Ram Baran 1532
ヤダブ
Yadav, Mahendra Prasad 1532
Yadav, Narsingh Pancham 1532
Yadav, Raj Kishor 1532
Yadav, Ram Baran 1532
Yadav, Renu Kumari 1532
Yadav, Sharad 1532
Yadav, Sitadev 1532
Yadav, Umesh 1532
Yadav, Upendra 1532
Yadhav, Chitralekha 1532
ヤチェンコ
Yatchenko, Iryna 1536
ヤツェニュク
Yatsenyuk, Arseniy 1536
ヤツェンコ
Yatsenko, Borys Pavlovych 1536
ヤッカリーノ
Yaccarino, Dan 1532
ヤツキエウィチ
Jackiewicz, Dawid 655
ヤックーシーヴォネン
Jakku-Sihvonen, Ritva 660
ヤツコ
Yatsko, Pamela 1536
ヤップ
Yap, Arthur 1535
Yap, Lynn 1535
Yapp, Nicholas 1535
ヤッファ
Yaffe, Risa Sacks 1532
ヤッフェ
Jaffe, Eric 659
Yaffe, James 1532
ヤッヘンス
Jachens, Lueder 655
ヤティルマン
Yatilman, Andrew 1536
ヤーデンフォシュ
Gärdenfors, Peter 479
ヤーテーンマキ
Jäätteenmäki, Anneli Tuulikki 655
ヤト
Yato, Peceli 1536
ヤド
Yade, Rama 1532
ヤトコフスカ
Jatkowska, Ag 666
ヤドランカ
Jadranka 658
ヤードリー
Yardley, Cathy 1535
Yardley, Joanna 1535
ヤナ
Yanah 1534
ヤナイ
Yanai, Itai 1534
ヤナーエフ
Yanaev, Gennadii Ivanovich 1534
ヤナキエスキ
Janakieski, Mile 662
ヤナキエフ
Yanakiev, Ivo 1534
Yanakiev, Yavor 1534
ヤナギハラ
Yanagihara, Hanya 1534
ヤナク
Yiannakou, Marietta 1538
ヤナツイネン
Janatuinen, Mailis 662
ヤニオティス
Gianniotis, Spyridon 494
ヤニク
Janik, Krzystof 663
Yanik, Viola 1535
ヤニコヴスキー
Janikovszky, Éva 663
ヤニコフスキ
Janikovszky, Éva 663
Janikowski, Damian 663
ヤニツ
Janics, Natasa 663
ヤニツィス
Yiannitsis, Athanasios 1538
ヤーニッシュ
Janisch, Heinz 663
ヤニッチ
Janic, Stjepan 663
ヤニッヒ
Janich, Peter 663
ヤニロブ
Yanilov, Eyal 1535
ヤーニン
Yanin, V.L. 1535
ヤーニン・ジージャー・ウィサミタナン
Jija 673
ヤヌコーヴィチ
Yanukovych, Viktor Fedorovych 1535
ヤヌコヴィッチ
Yanukovych, Viktor Fedorovych 1535
ヤヌコビッチ
Yanukovych, Viktor Fedorovych 1535
ヤヌザイ
Januzaj, Adnan 664
ヤヌサイティス
Janusaitis, Vytautas 664
ヤヌシェヴスキ
Januszewski, Tadeusz 664
ヤヌシェック
Janušek, Marian 664

ヤヌソニス
Janusonis, Vincas 664
ヤヌト
Yanit, Nevin 1535
ヤネス
Jänes, Laine 662
Jannes, Kim-Anne 663
ヤネフ
Janev, Ljubomir 662
Yanev, Bojidar 1534
Yanev, Filip 1534
ヤノ
Yano, Christine Reiko 1535
Yano, Ryoko 1535
Yano, Victor 1535
ヤノヴィッツ
Janovitz, Bill 664
ヤノウィン
Yenawine, Philip 1537
ヤーノシ
Jánosi, György 663
ヤーノシュ
Janosch 663
ヤノハ
Janocha, Peter 663
ヤノビチ
Janowicz, Jerzy 664
ヤノービッチ
Janovich, Andy 664
ヤノーフスカヤ
Ianovskaia, V.E. 642
ヤノフスキ
Janowski, Marek 664
ヤノフスキー
Janowski, Marek 664
Nikki 1026
ヤーノルド
Yarnold, Elizabeth 1535
Yarnold, Paul R. 1535
ヤパ
Yapa, Anura Priyadharshana 1535
ヤハウイ
Yahyaoui, Insaf 1532
ヤハテンベルフ
Jagtenberg, Yvonne 659
ヤーハム
Yarham, Robert 1535
ヤハヤ
Yahaya, Mamane Bachir 1532
ヤハンソン
Jahnsson, Kai 659
ヤパンデ
Yapande, Bruno 1535
ヤヒヤ
al-Yahia, Abdul Razzaq 1532
Yahya, Pehin 1532
ヤヒヤガ
Jahjaga, Atifete 659
ヤヒヤ・バカル
Yahya Bakar, Pehin 1532
ヤファイ
Yafai, Galal 1532
ヤファイー
Yafaee, Saeed 1532
ヤファロフ
Jafarov, Galib 659
ヤブウォニスキ
Jaboński, Henryk 655
ヤブウォンスキ
Jaboński, Henryk 655
ヤブオニスキ
Jaboński, Henryk 655
ヤブキ
Yabuki, Nanae 1532
ヤフケ
Jaffke, Freya 659
ヤフナーテク
Jahnátek, L'ubomír 659
ヤフマー
Yaghmour, Karim 1532
ヤブムラン
Yav Muland, Henri 1536
ヤブムランド
Yav Muland, Henri 1536
ヤブラノビッチ
Jabllanoviq, Aleksandër 655
ヤブリャン
Jaburyan, Mihran 655
ヤブリンスキー
Yavlinskii, Grigorii Alekseevich 1536
ヤフルフ
Yakhluf, Yahiya 1533
ヤーブロ
Yarbro, Chelsea Quinn 1535
ヤーブロー
Yarborough, Emmanuel 1535
Yarbrough, Eddie 1535
ヤブロコフ
IAblokov, Alekseĭ Vladimirovich 641
ヤブロンスキー
Jablonski, Peter 655
ヤホドバ
Jahodova, Libuse 659
ヤマイチ
Yamaichi, Jimi 1533
ヤマウチ
Yamauchi, Edwin M. 1533
Yamauchi, Gary 1533
Yamauchi, Mara 1533
ヤマグチ
Yamaguchi, Hiroshi 1533
Yamaguchi, Nobuyuki 1533
ヤマサキ
Yamasaki, Sakura 1533
ヤマザキ
Yamazaki, Michele 1533
ヤマシタ
Yamashita, Karen Tei 1533
Yamashita, Keith 1533
Yamashita, Michael S. 1533
ヤマスム
Yamassoum, Nagoum 1533
ヤマゾエ
Yamazoe, Guenji 1533
ヤマダ
Yamada, Haru 1533
Yamada, Kobi 1533
Yamada, Mike 1533
Yamada, Mitsuye 1533
Yamada, Yoji 1533
Yamada David, T. 1533
ヤマナカ
Yamanaka, Shinya 1533
ヤマーニー
Yamani, Ahmed Zaki 1533
ヤマニ
Yamani, Ahmed Zaki 1533
al-Yamani, Hashim bin Abdullah bin Hashim 1533
ヤマニー
Yamani, Ahmed Zaki 1533
ヤマネ
Yemane, Gebremeskel 1537
ヤマムラ
Yamamura, Hiroshi 1533
Yamamura, Kôzô 1533
ヤマモト
Yamamoto, Hisaye 1533
Yamamoto, Lani 1533
Yamamoto, Loren 1533
Yamamoto, Luci 1533
Yamamoto, Masaya 1533
Yamamoto, Mindy 1533
Yamamoto, Takashi 1533
ヤマモト・ミヤカワ
Yamamoto Miyakawa, Victor 1533
ヤマワキ
Yamawaki, Jorge 1533
ヤーマン
Yalman, Nur 1533
ヤミ
Yami, Hisila 1533
ヤーミン
Yaameen, Abdulla 1532
ヤミーン
Yameen, Abdullah 1533
ヤミン
Jamin, Ermansyah 662
Yamin, Elliott 1534
ヤム
Yam, Philip M. 1533
ヤメオゴ
Yameogo, Salvador 1533
ヤメチ
Yamechi, Madeleine 1533
ヤヤ
Yaya, Aboubacar 1536
Yaya, Marafa Hamidou 1536
ヤヤロ
Jajalo, Mato 660
ヤヤン・ルヒアン
Yayan Ruhian 1536
ヤラ
Yalá, Kumba 1533
ヤーライ
Járai, Zsigmond 665
ヤライ
Járai, Zsigmond 665
ヤラス
Jarass, Hans D. 665
ヤラドゥア
Yar'Adua, Umaru 1535
ヤラファ
Yarafa, Eugénie 1535
ヤリ
Yari, Rabiou Hassane 1535
ヤリーヴ
Yariv, Amnon 1535
ヤーリング
Jarring, Gunnar Valfrid 665
ヤリング
Jarring, Gunnar Valfrid 665
ヤル
Yarou, Théophile 1536
ヤルアドゥア
Yar'Adua, Umaru 1535
ヤルヴィ
Järvi, Kristjan 665
Järvi, Neeme 665
Järvi Paavo 665
ヤルヴェラ
Jarvela, Jonne 665
ヤルヴェンパー
Järvenpää, Leena 665
ヤルカ
Yarka, Kappa 1535
ヤルガノワツカ
Jaruga-nowacka, Izabela 665
ヤルク
Yark, Damehane 1535
ヤルゴスキー
Jargodzki, Christopher 665
ヤルジンカヤ
Yalcinkaya, Atagun 1533
ヤルゼルスキ
Jaruzelski, Wojciech Witold 665
ヤルチュンバユル
Yalcinbayir, Ertgrul 1533
ヤルドレイ＝マトヴェイチュク
Yardley-Matwiejczuk, Krysia M. 1535
ヤルビ
Järvi, Neeme 665
ヤルビネン
Järvinen, Katariina 665
ヤールブソヴァ
Yarbusova, Francheska 1535
ヤールブソワ
Yarbusova, Francheska 1535
ヤルベラ
Jarvela, Jonne 665
Jarvela, Sanna 665
ヤルベンパー
Jarvenpaa, Tero 665
ヤルホフスキー
Jarchovsky, Petr 665
ヤルマ
Yaluma, Christopher 1533
ヤルマン
Yalman, Nur 1533
ヤルモリンスカ
Jarmolinska, Aleksandra 665
ヤルモレンコ
Yarmolenko, Andriy 1535
ヤレスコ
Jaresko, Natalia 665
Yaresko, Natalia 1535
ヤーレット
Yarlett, Emma 1535
ヤロ
Yaro, Nebila Amadou 1535
ヤロー
Yalow, Rosalyn Sussman 1533
Yarrow, Peter 1536
ヤーロウ
Yalow, Rosalyn Sussman 1533

ヤ

Yarrow, Peter 1536
ヤロウ
Yalow, Rosalyn Sussman 1533
Yarrow, Alexandra 1536
ヤロウィッツ
Yalowitz, Paul 1533
ヤロシェンコ
Yaroshenko, Fedir 1535
ヤロシュ
Jarosz, Maria 665
ヤロシンスカヤ
Yaroshinska, Alla 1535
ヤロスラーバ
Yaroslava, pseud 1535
ヤロツカ
Yarotska, Irina 1536
ヤロネン
Jalonen, Riitta 660
ヤロミチアヌ
Ialomitianu, Gheorghe 642
ヤーロム
Yalom, Irvin D. 1533
Yalom, Marilyn 1533
ヤローン
Yalon, Dafna 1533
ヤロン
Yaron, Hadas 1535
ヤワキャン
Javakhyan, Hrachik 666
ヤワル
Yawar, Ghazi 1536
ヤーン
Jahn, Martin 659
Jahn, Ryan David 659
ヤン
Jess, Weng 672
Yan, Ik-jun 1534
Yan, Vasilii G. 1534
Yan, Xue-tong 1534
Yan, Yunxiang 1534
Yan, Zheng 1534
Yang, Bai-bing 1534
Yang, Bo-jiang 1534
Yang, Charles J. 1534
Yang, Chein-Ming 1534
Yang, Cheng-wu 1534
Yang, Chen-ning 1534
Yang, Chuan-kuang 1534
Yang, Dai-kang 1534
Yang, Edward 1534
Yang, Erche Namu 1534
Yang, Fu-dong 1534
Yang, Hak-seon 1534
Yang, Huan 1534
Yang, Huiyan 1534
Yang, Hyong-sop 1534
Yang, In Mo 1534
Yang, James 1534
Yang, Jerry C. 1534
Yang, Jiang 1534
Yang, Jie-chi 1534
Yang, Jing-ren 1534
Yang, Jung-mo 1534
Yang, Jung-ung 1534
Yang, Kyong-il 1534
Yang, Lan 1534
Yang, Li-gong 1534
Yang, Li-ping 1534
Yang, Mu 1534
Yang, Philémon 1534
Yang, Sung Hoo 1534
Yang, Tony 1534
Yang, Vivian 1534
Yang, X. Jie 1534
Yang, Yang 1534
Yang, Yao-hsun 1535
Yang, Y.E. 1535
Yang, Yuan-qing 1535
Yang, Yun-ho 1535
Yann 1535
Yeung, Charlie 1538
Yeung, Rob 1538
ヤン・イエン
Yang Ying 1535
ヤンカ
Janka, Carlo 663
Yanca, Stephen J. 1534
ヤンカー
Janker, Christoph 663
ヤンガー
Younger, George Kenneth Hotson 1542
Younger, Jon 1542
ヤンカウスカス
Jankauskas, Donatas 663
ヤンガ・エムビワ
Yanga-mbiwa, Mapou 1535
ヤンカリク
Jancarik, Lubomir 662
ヤンキー
Yankey, David 1535
ヤンギャ
Yangya, Philippe Undji 1535
ヤンク
Janku, Tomas 663
ヤング
Yang, Jerry C. 1534
Yang, Yaling 1534
Yong, Eric, Jr. 1539
Young, Al 1540
Young, Alison 1540
Young, Allan 1540
Young, Andrew R. 1540
Young, Angus 1540
Young, Ashley 1540
Young, Barbara 1541
Young, Beverley 1541
Young, Brittany 1541
Young, Caroline 1541
Young, Chris 1541
Young, Christopher E. 1541
Young, Colville 1541
Young, Curt 1541
Young, Cybèle 1541
Young, Darrel 1541
Young, David Earl 1541
Young, David W. 1541
Young, Dennis R. 1541
Young, Ed 1541
Young, Emma 1541
Young, Frances Margaret 1541
Young, Hugo John Smelter 1541
Young, Indi 1541
Young, Iris Marion 1541
Young, James 1541
Young, Jamie 1541
Young, Jeffrey E. 1541
Young, Jeffrey S. 1541
Young, Jimmy 1541
Young, Jock 1541
Young, Joe 1541
Young, John Lloyd 1541
Young, Joshua D. 1541
Young, Karen 1541
Young, Karen Romano 1541
Young, Katherine K. 1541
Young, Katrina 1541
Young, Kelsey 1541
Young, Larry J. 1541
Young, Lou 1541
Young, Louisa 1541
Young, Louise 1541
Young, Malcolm 1541
Young, Marilyn Blatt 1541
Young, Mark A. 1541
Young, Mary O'keefe 1541
Young, Maurus 1541
Young, Michael 1541
Young, Michael F.D. 1541
Young, Michael J. 1541
Young, Michèle Ann 1541
Young, Moira 1541
Young, Neil 1541
Young, Nick 1541
Young, Nicole S. 1541
Young, Noela 1541
Young, Paloma 1541
Young, Peter 1541
Young, Peter C. 1541
Young, Rebecca 1541
Young, Robert J.C. 1541
Young, Robert R. 1541
Young, Rosaleen 1541
Young, Roxanne K. 1541
Young, Sam 1541
Young, Samantha 1541
Young, Sarah 1541
Young, S.David 1541
Young, Selina 1541
Young, Simone 1541
Young, Skottie 1541
Young, Stephen 1541
Young, Stephen T. 1542
Young, Steven 1542
Young, Stuart 1542
Young, Sue Fostaty 1542
Young, Susan 1542
Young, Tavon 1542
Young, Thaddeus 1542
Young, Thomas W. 1542
Young, Tim 1542
Young, Tony 1542
Young, Victor Leyland 1542
Young, William Paul 1542
Young, Willie 1542
ヤング＝エイゼンドラス
Young-Eisendrath, Polly 1542
ヤングス
Youngs, Ben 1542
Youngs, Chris 1542
Youngs, Tom 1542
ヤングズ
Youngs, Elaine 1542
ヤングスト
Juengst, Sara Covin 690
ヤンクト
Jankto, Jakub 663
ヤングハズバンド
Younghusband, Bill 1542
ヤングバード
Martin, Marilyn Youngbird 909
ヤング・バルデス
Young Valdez, Ivonne 1542
ヤングブラッド
Youngblood, Mary 1542
ヤング・ブルーエル
Young-Bruehl, Elisabeth 1542
ヤングマン
Jungmann, Taylor 691
ヤング - メイスン
Young-Mason, Jeanine 1542
ヤンクロフスカ
Jankulovska, Gordana 663
ヤンクロフスキ
Jankulovski, Zivko 663
ヤーンケ
Jahnke, Christine K. 659
ヤンケ
Janke, Yuki Manuela 663
ヤンケイ
Yankey, George 1535
ヤンケロビッチ
Yankelovich, Daniel 1535
ヤンコ
Janko, Marc 663
ヤンコヴィッチ
Jankovic, Jelena 663
ヤンコウスキー
Jankowsky, Kurt Robert 663
ヤンコスキー
Jankowsky, Kurt Robert 663
ヤンコバ
Yankova, Elitsa 1535
ヤンコビック
Yankovic, "Weird Al" 1535
ヤンコビッチ
Jankovic, Jelena 663
Jankovic, Stefan 663
ヤンコフスキ
Jankowski, Henryk 663
Jankowski, Milosz 663
Jankowski, Timo 663
ヤンコフスキー
Jankovský, Kamil 663
Yankovskii, Oleg 1535
ヤンサネ
Yansane, Kerfalla 1535
ヤン・サン
Yang Xang 1535
ヤンシー
Yancey, Philip D. 1534
Yancey, Rick 1534
ヤンシャ
Janša, Janez 664
ヤンシュ
Jansch, Bert 664
ヤンス
Jans-ignacik, Klaudia 664
ヤンスドッター
Jansdotter, Lotta 664
ヤンスルッド
Jansrud, Kjetil 664
ヤンスルード
Jansrud, Kjetil 664
ヤンセ
Janse, Herman 664
ヤンセン
Jansen, Henri V. 664
Jansen, Janine 664
Jansen, Marcell 664
Jansen, Theo 664
Janssen, Daniel 664
Janssen, Roel 664
Janssen, Ulrich 664
Janssen, Vincent 664
Janssen, Werner 664

ヤ

ヤンゼン
Jansen, Marcell 664
ヤン・セン・コマ
Yang Saing Koma 1535
ヤーンソン
Jaanson, Juri 655
ヤンソン
Janson, P.O. 664
Jansson, Anna 664
Jansson, Per Olov 664
Jansson, Tove 664
ヤンソンス
Jansons, Mariss 664
ヤンダ
Yanda, Marshal 1534
ヤンダルビエフ
Yandarbiev, Zelimkhan 1534
ヤンチェン・ガロ
dbyans can dga'blo 329
ヤンチース
Jantjies, Eugene 664
ヤンチュケ
Jantschke, Tony 664
ヤンチョー
Jancsó, Miklós 662
ヤンツ
Jantsch, John 664
ヤンッティ
Jäntti, Riikka 664
ヤンデル
Yandel 1534
ヤンドゥル
Jandl, Ernst 662
ヤンドル
Jandl, Ernst 662
ヤンドロコビッチ
Jandroković, Gordan 662
ヤンヌ
Yanne, Jean 1535
ヤンバイ
Younbaii, Ahmed Ammar 1540
ヤンバキ
Yabaki, Konisi 1532
ヤーンベリ
Jernberg, Ann-Christine 671
ヤンポリスキー
IAmpol'skii, M.B. 642
ヤンボン
Jambon, Jan 661
ヤンマー
Jammer, Max 662
ヤンマート
Janmaat, Daryl 663
ヤンヤン
Janjan, Nora A. 663
ヤン・ロン
Yang Long 1535

【ユ】

ユ
Rhyu, Si-min 1176
Ryu, Eun-kyu 1222
Ryu, So-yeon 1222
Yoo, Chang Keun 1539
Yoo, Chang-soon 1539
Yoo, Heung-soo 1539
Yoo, Il-ho 1539
Yoo, Jeong-bok 1539
Yoo, Taeeun 1539
Yoo, Young-sook 1539
You, Hong-june 1540
Yu, Fu 1542
Yu, Ha 1542
Yu, Hye-jin 1542
Yu, Hyeon-mok 1542
Yu, In-chon 1542
Yu, Ji-tae 1543
Yu, Mengyu 1543
Yu, Myung-hwan 1543
Yu, Seung-min 1543
Yu, Woo-ik 1543
ユー
Hue, Robert 632
Ye, Shi-wen 1537
Yoo, Esther 1539
Yoo, Hansung 1539
Yoo, Michael 1539
Yu, Joseph 1543
Yu, Leinil Francis 1543
Yu, Lik-wai 1543
Yu, Nan 1543
Yue, Shawn 1543
ユーア
Ure, Jean 1435
ユアグロー
Yourgrau, Barry 1542
Yourgrau, Palle 1542
ユアット
Youatt, June Pierce 1540
ユアート
Ewart, Gavin 414
ユアン
Yuan, Long-ping 1543
Yuan, Ruixi 1543
Yuan, Xue-fen 1543
ユアンズ
Ewans, Martin 414
ユイ
U-ie 1432
Yu, Guang-yuan 1542
Yu, Hua 1542
Yu, Jie 1543
Yu, Shi-zhi 1543
Yu, Zheng-sheng 1543
ユイグ
Huyghe, François-Bernard 640
ユイスー
Huissoud, Jean-Marc 634
ユイレ
Huillet, Danièle 634
Huillet, Danièlle 634
ユーイング
Ewing, Alexander Crum 414
Ewing, Heather 414
Ewing, Jim Path Finder 414
Ewing, Patrick 414
Ewing, William A. 414
ユウ
Yu, Charles 1542
Yu, Ovidia 1543
ユヴァクラン
Yuvakuran, Utku 1544
ユーウィラー
Yuwiler, Arthur 1544
ユーウィン
Ewin, Dabney M. 414
ユーウェン
Ewen, Stuart 414
ユエリュート
Jõerüüt, Jaak 675
ユエン
Yuen, Lenora M. 1543
ユガル・パラガ
Yugar Párraga, Zulma 1543
ユグ
Jug, Azbe 690
ユグダ
Yuguda, Isa 1543
ユークナ
Yukna, Raymond A. 1543
ユクナ
Jukna, Vigilijus 690
ユクネビチエネ
Juknevičienė, Rasa 690
ユークレスタ
Juklestad, Olaug 690
ユーグロウ
Uglow, Jennifer S. 1432
ユゲ
Hugue, Coraline 633
ユーケス
Joekes, Willem 675
ユーケッター
Uekötter, Frank 1432
ユケッター
Uekötter, Frank 1432
ユーゴー
Hugo, Pierre de 633
ユゴー
Hugault, Romain 632
ユコフ
Ukhov, Ivan 1432
ユコン
Yukol, Limlamthong 1543
ユーザス
Yuthas, Kristi 1544
ユサフ
Yousaf, Muhammad 1542
ユージー
Ug, Philippe 1432
ユージェニデス
Eugenides, Jeffrey 411
ユジェーヌ
Eugene, Tabe 411
ユジェル・ギュレチ
Yücel Güleç, Selim 1543
ユーシェンコ
Yushchenko, Viktor Andriyovich 1544
ユシェンコフ
Yushenkov, Sergei Nikolaevich 1544
ユシコ
Iushko, Daria 653
ユシチェンコ
Yushchenko, Viktor Andriyovich 1544
ユージック
IUzik, Iuliia 653
ユージニー
Youzhny, Mikhail 1542
ユージニウスキー
Zauszniewski, Jaclene A. 1548
ユシーム
Useem, Michael 1436
ユジャノフ
Yuzhanov, Iliya A. 1544
ユージン
Yudin, Georgii 1543
ユジン
Yudin, Andrey 1543
ユスコ
Jusko, Ismir 692
ユスコフ
Yuskov, Denis 1544
ユスタス
Eustace, Arnhim Ulric 411
Justus, Julian 693
ユーズチェック
Juszczyk, Kyle 693
ユスチノフ
Ustinov, Peter 1437
ユスティノフ
Ustinov, Peter 1437
ユステセン
Justesen, Jørn 692
ユスヌー
Husnoo, Mohammad Anwar 638
ユースフ
Yoosuf, Raasida 1540
Yousif, al-Haj Adam 1542
Yousif, Mohammed Yousif Ali 1542
Yusuf, Shahid 1544
ユスフ
Youssouf, Mahamoud Ali 1542
Yussuf, Abdiaziz Sheikh 1544
Yusuf, Abdullahi 1544
Yusuf, Andi Mohamad 1544
Yusuf, Chowdhury 1544
Yusuf, Kalla 1544
Yusuf, Kamal Ibne 1544
ユスフ・アディジャ
Youssouf Adidja, Alim 1542
ユースーフィ
Youssoufi, Abderrahmane 1542
ユースフィー
Yousfi, Youcef 1542
ユスフォフ
Kh.yusufov, Igor 729
ユスフザイ
Yousafzai, Malala 1542
ユスポフ
Yusupov, Nosirjon 1544
ユスポワ
Yussupova, Aliya 1544
ユスリル
Yusron Ihza Mahendra 1544
ユスロン
Yusron Ihza Mahendra 1544
ユスロン・イフザ・マヘンドラ
Yusron Ihza Mahendra 1544
ユセイン
Yusein, Taybe Mustafa 1544
ユーセフ
Yousef, Mosab Hassan 1542
ユセフ
Yousef, Kareem Sayed 1542
ユーセフソン
Josephson, Erland 688

ユ

ユーソフ
Uthoff, Jarrod 1437
Yusov, Vadim 1544
ユソフ
Yusof, Eddy 1544
Yusof, Pengiran 1544
Yusov, Vadim 1544
ユーチャス
Jučas, Jonas 690
ユチョン
Yuchun 1543
ユッカー
Jucker, Sita 690
Uecker, Gerd 1432
Uecker, Günther 1432
ユッスー・ウンドゥール
Youssou N'dour 1542
ユッスー・ンドゥール
Youssou N'dour 1542
ユッセラー
Uesseler, Rolf 1432
ユッセン
Jussen, Arthur 692
Jussen, Lucas 692
ユッテ
Jutte, Jan 693
ユディ
Yuddy, Chrisnandi 1543
ユテウン
Yoo, Taeeun 1539
ユーデル
Youdell, Deborah 1540
ユード
Uhde, Thomas W. 1432
ユドゥリジエ
Hudrisier, Cécile 631
ユドフスキー
Yudofsky, Stuart C. 1543
ユドヨノ
Yudhoyono, Susilo Bambang 1543
ユードリー
Udry, Janice May 1432
ユドール
Udall, Brady 1431
ユドン
Hudon, Cecile 631
ユナイタス
Unitas, Johnny 1434
ユナコビッチ
Junaković, Svjetlan 691
ユニ
U;Nee 1434
ユニアント
Junianto, Gustar 691
ユニス
Younes, Mohaned Saied Ahmed 1540
Younis, Ibrahim 1542
Yunis, Abd al-Karim 1543
ユヌス
Younous, Abderahim 1542
Younous, Adoum 1542
Younous, Djibert 1542
Younous, Kedellah 1542
Yunus, Muhammad 1543
ユヌスミ
Younousmi, Adoum 1542
ユヌスメトフ
Yunusmetov, Rashid 1543
ユヌゾヴィッチ
Junuzovic, Zlatko 692
ユヌソフ
Yunusov, Anvar 1543
Yunusov, Rustam 1543
ユネシ
Yunesi, Ali 1543
ユーネス
Younes, Hassan Ahmed 1540
Younes, Karim 1540
Youness, Ahmad 1540
ユネス
Younes, Amin 1540
ユバ
Youba, Maiga Zeinab Mint 1540
ユーバーシェア
Ueberschär, Gerd R. 1432
ユハース
Juhász, Ferenc 690
ユバック
Ubac, Claire 1431
ユバール
Huwart, François 640
ユハレワ
Yukhareva, Natalia 1543
ユーバンク
Ewbank, Tim 414
ユビ
Youbi, Zine Eddine 1540
ユフ
Juch, Harald 690
ユフェルマンス
Juffermans, Cees 690
ユフス
Youssouf, Mahamoud Ali 1542
ユーベ
Uebe, Ingrid 1432
ユペダール
Djupedal, Øystein Kåre 360
ユベール
Hebert, Yvonne 587
Hubert, Etienne 631
ユペール
Huppert, Isabelle 637
ユーベルアッカー
Ueblacker, Peter 1432
ユベロス
Ueberroth, Peter 1432
ユー・ホセ
Yu-Jose, Lydia N. 1543
ユー・ホックリー
You Hockry 1540
ユマーシェフ
Yumashev, Valentin Borisovich 1543
ユマシェフ
Yumashev, Valentin Borisovich 1543
ユミ・ズハニス・ハスユン・ハシム
Yumi Zuhanis Has-Yun Hashim 1543
ユム
Youm, Oumar 1540
ユムティティ
Umtiti, Samuel 1433
ユメニオーラ
Umenyiora, Osi 1433
ユメンヨラ
Umenyiora, Osi 1433
ユラ
Youla, Mamady 1540
ユーラック
Ulak, James Thomas 1433
ユラック
Jurack, Michael 692
ユーランダー
Uhlaender, Katie 1432
ユーリ
Yuri, Berchiche 1543
ユーリー
Ury, William 1436
ユリ
Juri, Hugo Oscar 692
ユリアナ
Juliana 690
ユリアナ女王
Juliana 690
ユリアーンス
Jurriaanse, Aart 692
ユリアンティ
Yulianti, Maria Kristin 1543
ユリウス
Jurjus, Hidde 692
ユリウスドッティル
Juliusdottir, Katrin 691
ユーリウソン
Júlíusson, Kristján Þór 691
ユーリス
Uris, Leon Marcus 1435
ユリス
Ulis, Tyler 1433
Uris, Leon Marcus 1435
ユーリック
Urich, Robert 1435
Urick, Robert J. 1435
Yurick, Sol 1543
ユーリッチ
Ulrich, Katherine 1433
ユリッチ
Juric, Ivan 692
ユリナッチ
Jurinać, Sena 692
ユリナッツ
Jurinać, Sena 692
ユリーネク
Julínek, Tomáš 690
ユーリン
Uehling, Mark 1432
Ulin, David L. 1433
ユーリングス
Eurlings, Camiel 411
ユール
Juul, Jesper 693
Youell, Biddy 1540
Yule, Andrew 1543
Yule, William 1543
ユールウィリアムズ
Yuille-williams, Joan 1543
ユルギエル
Jurgiel, Krzysztof 692
ユルゲンス
Jurgens, S. 692
Jürgens, Udo 692
ユルゲンスマイヤー
Juergensmeyer, Mark 690
ユルゲンソン
Jurgenson, Toivo 692
ユルコフ
Yurkov, Yuriy 1544
ユルシェウスカ
Jurševska, Ilona 692
ユルジツァ
Jurzyca, Eugen 692
ユールズ
Eulls, Kaleb 411
ユルダシェフ
Yuldoshev, Nigmatilla 1543
ユルチェク
Vlcek, Erik 1461
ユルチェンコ
Yurchenko, Denys 1543
Yurchenko, Vladlen 1543
ユルチッチ
Jurčić, Ljubo 692
ユルチョク
Jurczok, Victoria 692
ユルドゥズ
Yildiz, Taner 1538
ユルドゥルム
Yildirim, Binali 1538
Yildirim, Yusuf Ersoy 1538
ユルドシェフ
Yuldoshev, Nigmatilla 1543
ユルファラキャン
Julfalakyan, Arsen 690
ユールベリ
Djurberg, Nathalie 360
ユルマズ
Yilmaz, Cevdet 1538
Yilmaz, İsmet 1538
Yilmaz, Mesut 1538
ユレ
Huré, Jean 637
ユーレケ
Uehleke, Bernhard 1432
ユレチカ
Jurečka, Marian 692
ユレティッチ
Juretić, Bernardica 692
ユレニア
Yurenia, Aleh 1543
ユレニャ
Jureňa, Miroslav 692
ユーレン
U'Ren, Andrea 1435
ユーロ
Eulo, Ken 411
ユーロー
Eulau, Heinz 411
ユロー
Hureau, Simon 637
ユロウスキ
Jurowski, Vladimir 692
ユロウスキー
Jurowski, Vladimir 692
ユーン
Yoon, Paul 1539
Yoon, Salina 1539
ユン
Jung 691
Jung, Andrea 691
Yon, Moo-byong 1539
Yoon, Eun-hye 1539
Yoon, Je-kyun 1539
Yoon, Jeong-min 1539
Yoon, Jeung-hyun 1539
Yoon, Jong-hwan 1539
Yoon, Kwang-ung 1539
Yoon, Kyung-shin 1539
Yoon, Myung-kil 1539
Yoon, Prabda 1539

Yoon, Salina 1539
Yoon, Sang-hyeon 1539
Yoon, Sang-jick 1539
Yoon, Seong-kyu 1540
Yoon, Si-yoon 1540
Yoon, Sok-ho 1540
Yoon, Son-ha 1540
Yoon, Soyoung 1540
Youn, Samuel 1540
Yuen, Biao 1543
Yum, Hyewon 1543
Yun, Brother 1543
Yun, Byung-se 1543
Yun, Duk-min 1543
Yun, Gi-bok 1543
Yun, Hak-jun 1543
Yun, Ho-jin 1543
Yun, Won-chol 1543
Yung, Dany 1543

ユンカー
Juncker, Jean-Claude 691

ユンガー
Junger, M. 691
Junger, Sebastian 691

ユンガーネル
Junghaenel, Henri 691

ユンカーマン
Junkerman, John 692

ユンク
Jung, Gideon 691

ユング
Jung, Anthony 691
Jung, Emma 691
Jung, Franz Josef 691
Jung, Kwanghee 691
Jung, Martin H. 691
Jung, Michael 691
Jung, Sebastian 691

ユンクィアン
Uncuyan, Jacques 1434

ユンクヴィスト
Ljungkvist, Laura 836

ユングヴィルト
Jungwirth, Florian 691

ユンググレーン
Ljunggren, Kerstin 836

ユング=ヒュッテル
Jung-Hüttl, Angelika 691

ユングフライシュ
Jungfleisch, Marie-Laurence 691

ユングブルート
Jungbluth, Rüdiger 691

ユングベリ
Ljungberg, Mikael 836

ユンゲ
Junge, Norman 691
Junge, Traudl 691
Jüngel, Eberhard 691

ユンケラ
Yumkella, Foday 1543

ユンケル
Juncker, Jean-Claude 691

ユンゲル
Jüngel, Eberhard 691

ユンケルマン
Junkelmann, Marcus 692

ユン・シク・ユアン
Yeung Sik Yuen, Michael Tzoun Sao 1538

ユンシクユアン
Yeung Sik Yuen, Michael Tzoun Sao 1538

ユンソナ
Yoon, Son-ha 1540

ユンソン
Eunson, Baden 411

ユンティラ
Junttila, Henri 692

ユンバーグ
Ljungberg, Gay 836

ユンホ
Yunho 1543

【ヨ】

ヨ
Yeo, Woon-kay 1537

ヨー
Joo, Abigel 686
Yeo, Cheow Tong 1537
Yeo, Eileen 1537
Yeo, Geoffrey 1537
Yeo, George Yong-Boon 1537
Yeoh, Michelle 1537

ヨアウェンセン
Jørgensen, Anker Henrik 687

ヨアディムナジ
Yoadimnadji, Pascal 1539

ヨアニディ
Ioannidi, Christina 648

ヨアニデス
Ioannides, Ouranios 648

ヨアヒムスターラー
Joachimsthaler, Erich 674

ヨアンソン
Johansson, Håkan 675

ヨイアク
Jozwiak, Bogna 689

ヨイッチ
Jojic, Milos 681

ヨーヴァイシャ
Jovaiša, Marius 689

ヨヴィッチ
Jovic, Luka 689

ヨーヴィル
Yeovil, Jack 1537

ヨウヴィル
Yeovil, Jack 1537

ヨヴェティッチ
Jovetic, Stevan 689

ヨウコココ
Yokococo 1539

ヨーエル
Youell, Biddy 1540

ヨカ
Yoka, Aimé Emmanuel 1539
Yoka, Tony Victor James 1539

ヨーカム
Yoakum, James D. 1539
Yocum, Lewis A. 1539

ヨーキー
Yorkey, Brian 1540

ヨーギー
Yogi, Maharishi Mahesh 1539

ヨギ
Yogi, Maharishi Mahesh 1539

ヨキッチ
Jokic, Bojan 681
Jokic, Nikola 681

ヨキレット
Jokilehto, Jukka 681

ヨーキン
Yorkin, Bud 1540

ヨーク
York, Andrew 1540
York, Dan 1540
York, Jerome Bailey 1540
York, Rebecca 1540
York, Ritchie 1540
York, Susannah 1540
Yorke, James A. 1540
Yorke, Thom 1540
Yorke, Trevor 1540

ヨクシモビッチ
Joksimović, Jadranka 681

ヨゲヴ
Yogev, Ram 1539

ヨケルソイ
Ljøkelsøy, Roar 836

ヨーゲンセン
Jørgensen, Anker Henrik 687

ヨコタ
Yokota, Rio 1539

ヨコヤマ
Yokoyama, John 1539

ヨーコランド
Yokoland 1539

ヨシ
Joshi, S.T. 688

ヨシオカ
Yoshioka, Reimei 1540

ヨシダ=クラフト
Yoshida-Krafft, Barbara 1540

ヨシナガ
Yoshinaga, George 1540

ヨシハラ
Yoshihara, Susan 1540
Yoshihara, Toshi 1540

ヨシペル
Iosiper, Svetlana Tatiana 648

ヨシペンコ
Yosypenko, Lyudmyla 1540

ヨシポヴィッチ
Josipović, Ivo 688

ヨシポビッチ
Josipović, Ivo 688

ヨシヤス
Yoshiyasu, Sonoko 1540

ヨシヤマ
Yoshiyama, Charles Lewis 1540

ヨース
Hjorth, Maria 610
Joos, Klemens 686
Joosse, Barbara M. 686

ヨス
Joss, Sven 688

ヨスコビッツ
Yoskovitz, Benjamin 1540

ヨースト
Jost, Wolfram 688
Yost, Ned 1540

ヨスト
Jost, Eugen 688
Jost, Jürgen 688
Jost, Wolfgang H. 688
Yost, Christopher 1540
Yost, Paul 1540
Yost, Paul R. 1540

ヨズビク
Jozwik, Joanna 689

ヨセフ
Yosef, Moni 1540
Yosef, Ovadia 1540
Youssef, Michael 1542

ヨセフソン
Josephson, Erland 688

ヨゼフゾーン
Jozefzoon, Florian 689

ヨーダー
Yoder, Andy 1539
Yoder, Bo 1539
Yoder, Millie 1539

ヨダ
Yoda, Bédouma Alain 1539
Yoda, Celine M. 1539

ヨダー
Yoder, Dave 1539

ヨダコンコボ
Yoda-konkobo, Celine M. 1539

ヨーダン
Yordan, Philip 1540

ヨチッチ
Jočić, Dragan 674

ヨック
Yock, Paul G. 1539

ヨックス
Jocks, Heinz-Norbert 674

ヨッセル
Iossel, Mikhail 648

ヨッツォ
Jotzo, Markus 688

ヨッフィー
Yoffie, David B. 1539

ヨッフェ
Joffe, Dina 675
Joffe, Ellis 675
Yoffe, Emily 1539

ヨーデル
Youdell, Deborah 1540

ヨート
Hjorth, Michael 610

ヨトバ
Iotova, Iliana 648

ヨトフ
Yotov, Boris 1540

ヨートン
Yorton, Tom 1540

ヨードン
Yourdon, Ed 1542
Yourdon, Edward 1542

ヨナ
Yona, Daniel 1539

ヨナス
Yonath, Ada E. 1539

ヨーナスソン
Jonasson, Ogmundur 681

ヨナソン
Jonasson, Jonas 681

ヨナット
Yonath, Ada E. 1539

ヨナル
Önal, Ayşe 1053

ヨーネン
Johnen, Wilhelm 676

ヨーバ
Youba, Maiga Zeinab

ヨ

Mint 1540
ヨーハウグ
Johaug, Therese 675
ヨハナ
Yohana, Yambise 1539
ヨハニス
Iohannis, Klaus 648
ヨハネスドッティル
Johannesdottir, Asta 675
ヨハネス・パウルス
Johannes Paulus Ⅱ 675
ヨハネソン
Jóhannesson, Benedikt 675
Jóhannesson, Guðni 675
ヨハネ・パウロ
Johannes Paulus Ⅱ 675
ヨハネ・パウロ2世
Johannes Paulus Ⅱ 675
ヨバノビッチ
Jovanovic, Nikola 689
Jovanović, Željko 689
ヨハン
Johann, Lang 675
ヨハンセン
Johansen, Christian 675
Johansen, Robert 675
Johansen, Tarje Riis 675
ヨーハンソン
Johannsson, Aron 675
ヨハンソン
Jóhannsson, Jóhann 675
Jóhannsson, Kristinn G. 675
Jóhannsson, Sigurður 675
Johanson, Gregory J. 675
Johanson, Karl J. 675
Johansson, Anna 675
Johansson, B.B. 675
Johansson, Bjørn 675
Johansson, Caroline 675
Johansson, Elin 675
Johansson, Emma 675
Johansson, Frans 675
Johansson, Gunn 675
Johansson, Henna 675
Johansson, Ingemar 675
Johansson, Jonatan 675
Johansson, Karin 675
Johansson, K.M. 675
Johansson, Morgan 675
Johansson, Scarlett 675
Johansson, Thomas 675
Johansson, Ylva 675
ヨビチェビッチ
Jovicevic, Andrija 689
ヨピッヒ
Joppich, Peter 686
ヨーブ
Joob, Marton 686
ヨフィー
Yoffie, David B. 1539
ヨプケ
Joppke, Christian 686
ヨープスト
Jobst, Christlieb Yuho 674
Jobst, K. 674
ヨプチェフ
Iovtchev, Iordan 648
Yovchev, Yordan 1542
ヨブレギャット
Llobregat, Jordi 837
ヨベル
Yovel, Yirmiahu 1542
ヨーマンズ
Yeomans, Donald K. 1537
Yeomans, Matthew 1537
ヨム
Yom, Sang-uk 1539
ヨリッセン
Jorissen, Engelbert 687
ヨリツマ
Jorritsma, Annemarie 687
ヨーリンクス
Yorinks, Arthur 1540
ヨル
Yorou, Guécadou Bawa 1540
ヨルガトゥ
Georgatou, Diamantina 489
ヨルギアデス
Georgiades, Pefkios 490
ヨルゲンス
Jörgens, Viktor 687
ヨルゲンセン
Jørgensen, Anker Henrik 687
Jorgensen, Ann-Lou 687
Jörgensen, Christer 687
Jørgensen, Dan 687
Jorgensen, Emma 687
Jorgensen, Jan O. 687
Jorgensen, Martin 687
Jorgensen, Morten 687
ヨルダノバ
Yordanova, Daniela 1540
ヨルダノフ
Jordanov, Minco 687
Yordanov, Emanuil 1540
ヨルダン
Jordan, Peter 687
ヨルヤディス
Georgiades, Harris 490
ヨーレウスカヤ
Yauhleuskaya, Lalita 1536
ヨレフスキ
Jolevski, Zoran 681
ヨーレン
Yolen, Jane 1539
ヨロ
Yoro, Bernard 1540
ヨロフ
Yorov, Abdullo 1540
ヨワンソン
Johansson, Nette 675
ヨーン
John, Radek 676
Yoon, Carol Kaesuk 1539
Yoon, Salina 1539
ヨン
Yon, Hyong-muk 1539
ヨンク
Jong, Cees de 685
ヨング
Jong, Dola de 686
Jong, Elaine C. 686
Jongh, E.de 686
ヨングク
Yong-guk 1539
ヨングスマ
Jongsma, Arthur E., Jr. 686
ヨング・バルデス
Young Valdez, Ivonne 1542
ヨンジェ
Young-jae 1542
ヨーンセン
Johnsen, N.J. 676
ヨンセン
Johnsen 676
Johnsen, Åge 676
Johnsen, Åshild Kanstad 676
Johnsen, Christian 676
Johnsen, Sigbjørn 676
ヨーンソン
Johnsson, Anders B. 680
ヨンソン
Johnson, Hilde Frafjord 678
Jönsson, Maria 686
Jonsson, Pirkko 686
Jonsson, Runer 686
ヨンチンファ
Jong Tjien Fa, Michael 686
ヨンパルト
Llompart, José 837
ヨンブノ
Yombouno, Marck 1539
ヨンボ
Yombo, Thomas 1539
ヨンボウノ
Yombouno, Emile 1539
ヨンユット
Yongyuth, Yuthawong 1539
ヨンユット・ユッタウォン
Yongyuth Yuthavong 1539
ヨンユート・チャラムウォン
Yongyuth Chalamwong 1539
ヨンリ
Yonli, Ernest Paramanga 1539
Yonli, Paramanga Ernest 1539

【ラ】

ラ
Ra, Jong-yil 1146
Ra, Tong-hui 1146
Ra, Un-sim 1146
ラー
Lah, Thomas E. 782
Lahr, John 782
Lal, Lakshmi 783
ラアジャソン
Rahajason, Harry Laurent 1149
ラアダリ
Laadhari, Zied 779
ラアビディ
Laabidi, Neziha 779
ラアリー
Laharie, Muriel 782
ライ
Lai, Eileen 782
Lai, Jennie 782
Lai, Jimmy 782
Lai, Leon 782
Lai, Pak-Sang 782
Lai, Thanhha 782
Lay, Francisco Kalbuadi 799
Lay, Pedro 799
Lay Prohas 799
Rai, Arisha 1150
Rai, Bali 1150
Rai, Dhanpat 1150
Rai, Jitu 1150
Rai, Milan 1150
Rai, Nandalal 1150
Rai, Sherdhan 1150
Rai, Yash 1150
Ray, Mo 1162
Wrye, Donald 1529
ライアー
Reiher, Tinian 1169
Reyher, Becky 1174
ライアダン
Riordan, Rick 1184
ライアニエミ
Rajaniemi, Hannu 1151
ライアル
Lyall, Gavin 855
Lyall, John 855
ライアルズ
Ryalls, John H. 1220
ライアン
Lyon, David 857
Lyon, James 857
Lyon, Todd 857
Ryan, Alan 1220
Ryan, Anthony 1220
Ryan, Bill 1220
Ryan, Brendan 1220
Ryan, Brittney 1220
Ryan, Cathy 1220
Ryan, Charles 1220
Ryan, Chris 1220
Ryan, Christopher 1220
Ryan, David 1220
Ryan, Donal 1220
Ryan, Donnacha 1220
Ryan, Eamon 1220
Ryan, Eric 1220
Ryan, Frank 1220
Ryan, Gail 1220
Ryan, Hank Phillippi 1220
Ryan, Jaime 1220
Ryan, Jake 1220
Ryan, James R. 1220
Ryan, Jeff 1220
Ryan, Jo 1220
Ryan, Jon 1220
Ryan, Kay 1220
Ryan, Kevin 1220
Ryan, Kyle 1220
Ryan, Logan 1220
Ryan, Marie-Laure 1220
Ryan, Mary Jane 1220
Ryan, Mathew 1220
Ryan, Matt 1220
Ryan, Meg 1220
Ryan, Mia 1220
Ryan, Michael 1220
Ryan, Mike 1220
Ryan, Nan 1220
Ryan, Nolan 1220
Ryan, Pam Muñoz 1220
Ryan, Patricia 1220
Ryan, Patrick G. 1220
Ryan, Paul 1221
Ryan, Raymund 1221
Ryan, Rex 1221
Ryan, Rob 1221
Ryan, Robbie 1221
Ryan, Robert L. 1221
Ryan, Sean 1221
Ryan, Stephen G. 1221
Ryan, Terry 1221
Ryan, Tony 1221

Ryan, William B.F. 1221
ライアンズ
Lyons, John 857
Lyons, Judith 857
Lyons, Laurence S. 857
Lyons, Martyn 857
Lyons, Mary 857
Lyons, Nathan 857
Lyons, Nick 857
Lyons, Phyllis I. 857
ライヴ
Ryave, Alan 1221
ライヴリー
Lively, Blake 836
ライエンダイク
Luyendijk, Joris 855
ライオネット
Lionnet, Annie 832
ライオラ
Raiola, Joe 1151
ライオール
Ryall, Tony 1220
ライオンズ
Lyons, Albert S. 857
Lyons, Caushaud 857
Lyons, Michelle 857
Lyons, Rebecca 857
Lyons, Tyler 857
ライカー
Liker, Jeffrey K. 827
ライガ
Lyga, Barry 855
ライガー
Reiger, John F. 1169
ライカート
Reichert, Susan K. 1168
ライカールト
Rijkaard, Frank 1182
ライカン
Lycan, William G. 855
ライク
Reich, Christopher 1168
Reich, Steve 1168
ライクス
Reichs, Kathy 1168
ライクヘルド
Reichheld, Frederick F. 1168
ライクマン
Rajchman, John 1152
ライクラー
Reichler, Robert J. 1168
ライグラフ
Leygraf, Hans 823
ライクリー
Raichle, Marcus E. 1150
Reichle, Joe 1168
ライクル
Reichl, Ruth 1168
ライクレン
Raichlen, Steven 1150
ライ・ゲバラ
Ray Guevara, Milton 1162
ライケマン
Ryckeman, Brian 1221
ライゲルース
Reigeluth, Charles M. 1169
ライケンズ
Likens, Gene E. 827
ライゴ
Lygo, Raymond Derek 855
ライコヴィッチ
Rajkovic, Slobodan 1152
ライコネン
Räikkönen, Kimi 1151
ライザ
Ryza, Sandy 1222
ライザー
Leiser, Ernest 810
Lithur, Nana Oye 834
Raiser, Thomas 1151
Reiser, Jesse 1170
Reiser, Paul 1170
ライザーソン
Leiserson, Charles Eric 810
ライサチェク
Lysacek, Evan 857
ライザチェク
Lysacek, Evan 857
ライザート
Reisert, Rebecca 1170
ライシ
Reich, Russell 1168
ライシャワー
Reischauer, Haru Matsukata 1170
ライシュ
Reich, Michael 1168
Reich, Robert Bernard 1168
Reich, Steve 1168
Reisch, Lisa 1170
Reisch, Lucia 1170
ライシュラム
Laishram, Devendro Singh 783
ライシュリン
Reichlin, Bruno 1168
ライジンガー
Leisinger, Urlich 810
Reisinger, Dan 1170
ライジング
Rising, Linda 1184
ラーイス
Raiss, Sid'Ahmed Ould 1151
ライス
Lyth, Peter J. 857
Rais, Yatim 1151
Reiss, Eric L. 1170
Reiss, R.Scott 1170
Reiss, Sidonia 1170
Reisz, Karel 1171
Reisz, Tiffany 1171
Rice, Anne 1177
Rice, Anthony 1177
Rice, Ashley 1177
Rice, Ben 1177
Rice, Christopher 1177
Rice, Condoleezza 1177
Rice, David 1177
Rice, Denzel 1177
Rice, Dorothy P. 1177
Rice, Eve 1177
Rice, Heidi 1177
Rice, Jeff 1177
Rice, Jerry 1177
Rice, Laura North 1177
Rice, Lisa Marie 1177
Rice, Luanne 1177
Rice, Mark P. 1177
Rice, Marnie E. 1177
Rice, Patricia 1177
Rice, Patrick 1177
Rice, Randall W. 1178
Rice, Robert 1178
Rice, Rob S. 1178
Rice, Stephanie 1178
Rice, Stuart A. 1178
Rice, Susan 1178
Rice, Tim Miles Bindon 1178
Rice, William H., Ⅳ 1178
ライズ
Ries, Al 1181
Ries, Eric 1181
Ries, Laura 1181
ライズィ
Leisi, Ernst 810
ライスター
Leister, Karl 810
ライスナー
Raisner, Kim 1151
Reisner, Howard M. 1170
ライズナー
Riesner, Dean 1181
ライスマン
Reisman, Michael 1170
ライゼナール
Ruizenar, Theo 1216
ライゼン
Raizen, Senta 1151
Risen, James 1184
ライゾ
Laiso, Emilio 783
ライソン
Lyson, Thomas A. 857
ライタ
Raita, Henna 1151
ライター
Leiter, Michael P. 810
Reiter, Austin 1171
Reiter, Mark 1171
ライダー
Leider, Richard J. 809
Reider, Katja 1169
Ryder, Alex 1221
Ryder, Julian 1221
Ryder, Mads 1221
Ryder, Peter 1221
Ryder, Rowland 1221
Ryder, Samuel 1221
Ryder, Winona 1221
ライダル
Rydahl, Malene 1221
ライタン
Litan, Robert E. 834
ライチ
Leitch, Donovan 810
ライチェア
Raicea, Iulian 1150
ライチェビッチ
Raicevic, Ivan 1150
ライチェル
Raichle, Bernadette 1150
ライチェン
Rychen, Dominique Simone 1221
ライチャーク
Lajčák, Miroslav 783
ライツ
Reitz, Christian 1171
Reitz, Joe 1171
ライッコネン
Räikkönen, Kimi 1151
ラーイディ
Laïdi, Adila 782
ライティ
Laity, Paul 783
ライティック・スミス
Leitich Smith, Greg 810
ライディング
Riding, Alan 1181
Ryding, Erik S. 1221
ライデスドルフ
Leydesdorff, L.A. 823
ライテマイヤー
Reitemeier, Lutz 1171
ライデル
Rydell, Patrick J. 1221
ライデン
Layden, Joseph 799
Lyden, Jacki 855
Ryden, Barbara Sue 1221
Ryden, Mark 1221
Ryden, Vassula 1221
ライデンバーグ
Reidenberg, Joy 1169
ライト
Light, Alan 827
Light, Janice Catherine 827
Light, Judith 827
Light, Michael 827
Light, Pat 827
Light, Richard W. 827
Lite, Lori 834
Reit, Seymour V. 1171
Wright, Angus Lindsay 1527
Wright, Annabel 1527
Wright, Bob 1527
Wright, Brandan 1527
Wright, Byron 1527
Wright, Camron Steve 1527
Wright, Carol S. 1527
Wright, Chris 1527
Wright, Christopher J. H. 1527
Wright, Cliff 1527
Wright, Crispin 1527
Wright, Daniel 1527
Wright, Daniel B. 1527
Wright, Dare 1527
Wright, David 1527
Wright, David James 1527
Wright, David John 1527
Wright, Delon 1527
Wright, Derrick 1527
Wright, Dorell 1527
Wright, Ed 1527
Wright, Edgar 1527
Wright, Edward Maitland 1527
Wright, Eric 1528
Wright, Erik Olin 1528
Wright, Gabe 1528
Wright, Gary R. 1528
Wright, George 1528
Wright, Harry Cory 1528
Wright, Helen 1528
Wright, James 1528
Wright, James Claude, Jr. 1528
Wright, Janet 1528
Wright, Jarius 1528
Wright, Jason 1528
Wright, Jason F. 1528
Wright, Jeffrey 1528
Wright, Jeremy 1528
Wright, Joe 1528
Wright, John 1528
Wright, John Barry Debenham 1528
Wright, John Charles 1528

Wright, Jonathan V. 1528
Wright, Kendall 1528
Wright, Kenneth Weston 1528
Wright, Kit 1528
Wright, K.J. 1528
Wright, Laura 1528
Wright, Lauren 1528
Wright, Lawrence 1528
Wright, Liz 1528
Wright, Lorraine M. 1528
Wright, Machaelle Small 1528
Wright, Major 1528
Wright, Margaret Nickelson 1528
Wright, Mary Ann 1528
Wright, Micah Ian 1528
Wright, Mike 1528
Wright, Nicholas Thomas 1528
Wright, Pádraig 1528
Wright, Pamela Darr 1528
Wright, Peter 1528
Wright, Peter Robert 1528
Wright, Peter W.D. 1528
Wright, Ralph 1528
Wright, Randall 1528
Wright, Rebecca 1528
Wright, Richard 1528
Wright, Richard Bruce 1528
Wright, Rick A., Jr. 1528
Wright, Robert 1528
Wright, Robert Eric 1528
Wright, Robin 1528
Wright, Ronald 1528
Wright, Sally Ann 1528
Wright, Sally S. 1528
Wright, Scooby 1528
Wright, Scott 1528
Wright, Shareece 1528
Wright, Stephen Francis 1528
Wright, Steve 1528
Wright, Steven 1528
Wright, Terence R. 1528
Wright, Teresa 1528
Wright, Timothy 1528
Wright, Will 1528
Wright, William 1528

ライド
Reid, Theresa A. 1169
Ride, Sally 1180

ライドアウト
Rideout, Patricia L. 1180
Rideout, Philip 1180

ライトストーン
Lightstone, Sam 827

ライトソン
Wrightson, Patricia 1529

ライトナー
Leitner, Moritz 810
Leitner, Patric 810
Leitner, Patric-Fritz 810

ライトバウン
Lightbown, Patsy 827

ライトバーガー
Ritberger, Carol 1184

ライトバーン
Lightburn, Ron 827

ライトフット
Lightfoot, Elizabeth 827

ライトブールン
Lightbourne, Muriel 827

ライト・ペン
Wright, Robin 1528

ライトボーン
Lightbourne, Drothy 827

ライドマ
Raidma, Mati 1150

ライトマイヤー
Reithmayer, Nina 1171

ライトマン
Lightman, Alan P. 827
Lightman, Alex 827
Reitman, Ivan 1171
Reitman, Jason 1171

ライトル
Lytle, Hugh 857

ライドル
Leidl, Werner 809
Lidle, Cory 826

ライトン
Righton, Caroline 1182
Wrighton, Tony 1528

ライドン
Lydon, John 855
Lydon, Michael 855
Lydon, Nicholas B. 855
Lydon, Tyler 855

ライナー
Rainer, Ingomar 1151
Rainer, Luise 1151
Rainer, Reinhold 1151
Reiner, Jonathan 1170
Reiner, Rob 1170

ライナス
Lynas, Mark 856

ライナソン
Rynearson, Edward K. 1221

ライナード
Rinard, Martin 1183

ライナム
Lynam, Donald R. 856

ライニッヒ
Reinig, Patricia 1170

ライニンガー
Leininger, Andrea 810
Leininger, Bruce 810

ライネ
Laine, Matti 782

ライネス
Lainez, Francisco 782

ライネッケ
Reinecke, Mark A. 1170

ライネリ
Raineri, Ricardo 1151

ライネルト
Reinert, Dietmar 1170

ライバー
Reiber, Erhard 1168

ライバス
Rivas, Robert F. 1185

ライバック
Ryback, David 1221
Ryback, Timothy W. 1221

ライバード
Liburd, Cedric 825
Liburd, Ian 825
Liburd, Marcella 825

ライヒ
Raich, Benjamin 1150
Reich, Steve 1168
Righi, Carol 1182

ライヒェ
Reiche, Dietlof 1168

ライヒェル
Reichel, Peter 1168

ライヒェルト
Reichert, Folker 1168

ライヒシュタイン
Reichstein, Alexander 1168

ライビッチ
Reivich, Karen 1171

ライヒトフリード
Leichtfried, Jörg 809

ライヒマン
Reichman, Henry 1168
Reichmann, Paul 1168

ライヒャルト
Reichert, Bernhard 1168

ライヒラー
Reichler, Robert J. 1168

ライヒ・ラニツキ
Reich-Ranicki, Marcel 1168

ライヒ・ラニツキー
Reich-Ranicki, Marcel 1168

ライビンガー
Leibinger, Berthold 809

ライフ
Reif, F. 1169

ライプ
Laib, Wolfgang 782

ライファ
Raiffa, Howard 1150

ライファイマー
Leipheimer, Levi 810

ライフェルド
Liefeld, Rob 826

ライブソン
Liveson, Jay Allan 836

ライプブラント
Leibbrand, Werner 809
Leibbrand-Wettley, Annemarie 809

ライブリー
Lively, Ben 836
Lively, Blake 836
Lively, Emma 836
Lively, Lynn 836

ライ・プロハ
Lay Prohas 799

ライベウルン
Laybourn, Thomas 799

ライベル
Rivele, Stephen J. 1185

ライペルツ
Leipertz, Robert 810

ライヘルン・メルデッジ
Reichlin-meldegg, Hanni 1168

ライベングッド
Libengood, Jeff 825

ライヘンバッハ
Reichenbach, Harald 1168

ライポルト
Leipold, Dieter 810
Leipold, Gerd 810

ライポルド
Leipold, Dieter 810

ライマ
Rima, Samuel D. 1183

ライマー
Reimer, Joseph 1170
Riemer, Edith 1181
Rimer, Danny 1183

ライマン
Lyman, Arthur 856
Lyman, Edwin Stuart 856
Lyman, Howard F. 856
Reiman, Jeffrey H. 1169
Reiman, Tonya 1169
Reimann, Aribert 1169
Reimann, Matthias 1170
Reimann, Monika 1170
Reimann, Renate 1170
Reimann, Stefan 1170
Reimann, Wolfgang 1170
Ryman, Geoff 1221
Ryman, Robert 1221

ライミ
Rahimi, Atiq 1150
Raimi, Ivan 1151
Raimi, Sam 1151

ライミス
Ramis, Harold 1154

ライムズ
Rhimes, Shonda 1175

ライモ
Laimo, Michael 782

ライモンディ
Raimondi, Cristian 1151
Raimondi, Gianni 1151
Raimondi, Pablo 1151
Raimondi, Ruggero 1151

ライヤー
Ryer, Mat 1221

ライラ
Lira, Gonzalo 833

ライランス
Rylance, Mark 1221

ライラント
Rylant, Cynthia 1221

ライリ
Reilly, Robert F., Jr. 1169

ライリー
Reilly, Charles Nelson 1169
Reilly, Edward T. 1169
Reilly, James 1169
Reilly, John C. 1169
Reilly, Mark 1169
Reilly, Matthew 1169
Reilly, Mike 1169
Reilly, Patrick M. 1169
Reilly, Rick 1169
Reilly, Trevor 1169
Riley, Andy 1182
Riley, Bridget 1182
Riley, Curtis 1182
Riley, Dick 1182
Riley, Elizabeth 1182
Riley, Gillian 1182
Riley, Gregory John 1182
Riley, James C. 1182
Riley, James Whitcomb 1182
Riley, Joe 1182
Riley, Michael 1182
Riley, Mike 1182
Riley, Olive 1182
Riley, Pat 1182
Riley, Patrick G. 1182
Riley, Perry 1182
Riley, Peter D. 1182
Riley, Philip 1182
Riley, Richard Wilson 1183
Riley, Sam 1183
Riley, Shirley 1183
Riley, Steve 1183
Riley, Talulah 1183

Riley, Terence 1183
Ryrie, Charlie 1221
ライリー・スポング
Reilly-Spong, Maryanne 1169
ライリヒ
Rajlich, Jirí 1152
ライール
Lahire, Bernard 782
ライル
Lisle, Janet Taylor 834
Lisle, Rebecca 834
Lyle, John 855
Lyle, Sue 856
ライルズ
Lyles, Jordan 856
Lyles, Kevin 856
Lyles, Richard I. 856
Lyles, Trey 856
ライルド
Laird, Linda M. 782
ライレアヌ
Raileanu, Ion 1151
ライン
Line, Zach 831
Lyne, Patricia M. 856
Lyne, Roderic 856
Rhyne, Teresa J. 1176
ラインアルター
Reinalter, Helmut 1170
ライング
Laing, Cleyon 782
Laing, Gordon 782
ラインコ
Rainko, Marcin 1151
ラインゴールド
Rheingold, Howard 1175
ラインシュミット
Reinschmidt, Joerg 1170
ラインス
Lainz, Lluís 782
ラインズ
Lines, Clifford John 831
Lines, Malcolm E. 831
Lines, Mark 831
Lines, Thomas 831
Lynes, Barbara Buhler 856
Rines, Robert 1183
ラインスタイン
Reinstein, Mara 1170
ラインズドルフ
Reinsdorf, Jerry 1170
ラインデル
Raindl, Marco 1151
ラインバーガー
Rheinberger, Marguerite M. 1175
ラインバーグ
Reinberg, Danny 1170
Rineberg, Dave 1183
ラインバック
Lineback, Kent 831
ラインハート
Reinhardt, Burt 1170
Reinhart, Carmen M. 1170
Reinhart, Matthew 1170
Rinehart, Georgina Hope 1183
ラインハルト
Reinhard, Johan 1170
Reinhard, Rebekka 1170
Reinhardt, Robert 1170
Reinhardt, Stephan 1170
ラインフィエスタ・デモラレス
Lainfiesta De Morales, Lucy 782
ラインフェルト
Reinfeldt, Fredrik 1170
ラインホルト
Reinhold, Caroline 1170
ラウ
Lau, Alan Chong 794
Lau, Andrew 794
Lau, Andy 794
Lau, Carina 794
Lau, Ching-wan 794
Lau, Emily 794
Lau, Joseph 794
Lau, Kar-leung 794
Lau, Poh Yok 795
Lau, Teck-Chai 795
Lau, Theodora 795
La'u, Yiśra'el Me'ir 795
Law, Hieng Ding 797
Low, Thia-khiang 848
Rau, Dana Meachen 1160
Rau, Gretchen 1160
Rau, Johannes 1160
Rau, Okka 1160
ラヴ
Love, Dennis 847
Love, Donald 847
Love, Kathy 847
Love, Mike 847
Love, Patrick 847
Love, Roger 847
Love, Valerie L. 847
ラウアー
Lauer, Bernhard 795
ラヴァージ
Ravasi, Gianfranco 1161
ラヴァッキオーリ
Ravacchioli, Maria Rosaria 1161
ラヴァーティ
Laverty, Paul 796
ラヴァニーノ
Lavagnino, John 796
ラヴァリイ
Lavallee, David 796
ラヴァール
Ravard, François 1161
ラヴァル
Laval, Christian 796
Laval, Marie-Édith 796
Laval, Thierry 796
ラウアン
Laouan, Magagi 790
Laouan, Waziri Maman 790
ラヴァン
Lavant, Denis 796
ラヴィシャンカ
Ravishankar, Anushka 1161
ラヴィス
Lavis, Chris 797
ラウイッツ
Rawicz, Slavomir 1161
ラヴィーニュ
Lavigne, Marie 796
ラウィヤ
Rawiya, bint Saud al-Busaidiyah 1162
Rawiya, bint Saud bin Ahmed al-Busaidi 1162
ラヴィル
Laville, Jean-Louis 796
ラヴィレオン
Lavilleon, Artus De 796
ラヴィーン
Lavigne, Avril 796
Lavigne, Dru 796
Levine, Peter A. 819
ラヴィントン
Lavington, Frederick 797
ラヴェ
Ravet, Yoric 1161
ラヴェッチ
Ravetch, Irving 1161
Ravetch, Jeffrey 1161
ラヴェッツ
Ravetz, Jerome Raymond 1161
Ravetz, Jerry 1161
ラヴェット
Lovett, Charlie 847
Lovett, Sarah Poland 847
ラヴェーニュ
Lavergne, Didier 796
ラウェハ
Raweh, Abdul-Wahhab 1161
ラヴェル
Lovell, Bernard 847
ラヴェルダン
Laverdunt, Damien 796
ラヴェル=ピント
Ravell-Pinto, Thelma 1161
ラヴェンヌ
Ravenne, Jacques 1161
ラヴォア
Lavoie, Johanne 797
Lavoie, Marc 797
Lavoix, Cédric 797
ラヴォイ
Lavoie, Richard D. 797
ラヴォーダン
Lavaudant, Georges 796
ラウク
Lauck, Jennifer 795
ラウクホースト
Rauckhorst, Louise Hartnett 1160
ラヴグローヴ
Lovegrove, Keith 847
ラウゲルー
Laugerud, Kjell 795
ラウゲルー・ガルシア
Laugerud, Kjell 795
ラウジ
Lawzi, Ahmed 798
al-Lawzi, Hasan Ahmad 798
ラウジー
Rousey, Ronda 1210
ラウシェンバーグ
Rauschenberg, Robert 1161
ラウシェンブッシュ
Raushenbush, Paul B. 1161
ラウシャー
Rauscher, Sibylle 1161
ラウシュ
Rausch, Konstantin 1161
ラウシュター
Lauster, Peter 796
ラウス
Rouse, Allan 1210
Rouse, Irving 1210
Rouse, Pete 1210
Routh, Brandon 1211
Routh, Lisa C. 1211
ラウズ
Rouse, Christopher 1210
ラウスティアラ
Raustiala, Kal 1161
ラウスベルク
Lausberg, Heinrich 796
ラヴゼイ
Lovesey, Peter 847
Lovesey, Phil 847
ラウソン
Lawson, Cina 798
ラウダ
Lauda, Niki 795
ラウターヴァッサー
Lauterwasser, Alexander 796
ラウタヴァーラ
Rautavaara, Einojuhani 1161
ラウダーデール
Lauderdale, Jim 795
ラウターバー
Lauterbur, Paul C. 796
ラウタバーラ
Rautavaara, Einojuhani 1161
ラウタフィ
Lautafi, Fio Selafi Purcell 796
ラウターベルグ
Rauterberg, Hanno 1161
ラウダレス
Raudales, Julio 1160
ラウダン
Laudan, Larry 795
ラウチ
Louch, Jan 846
ラウツェン
Luitzen, Jan 852
ラウッピ
Raupp, Marco Antonio 1160
ラウティアイネン
Rautiainen, Pirjo 1161
ラウディシナ
Laudicina, Paul A. 795
ラウデス・ロドリゲス
Ráudez Rodríguez, Miriam Soledad 1160
ラウト
Lauth, Reinhard 796
ラウド
Raud, Piret 1160
Raud, Rein 1160
ラウドシク
Raudsik, Riina 1160
ラウトリッジ
Routledge, Wayne 1211
ラウドルップ
Laudrup, Michael 795
ラウニス
Launis, Mika 795
ラウバー
Lauber, David 795
Lauber, Kurt 795
ラウハウス
Rauhaus, Alfred 1160
ラウハラ

ラ

Rauhala, Pirkko-Liisa 1160
ラウヒ
Rauhi, Samih 1160
ラウブ
Laub, Julia 795
ラウファー
Laufer, Peter 795
ラウフン
Ruyven, Kees van 1220
ラウベ
Laube, Sigrid 795
ラウヘルド・ガルシア
Laugerud, Kjell 795
ラウベンタール
Laubenthal, Klaus 795
ラウラ
Laoura, Sandra 790
ラウラヤイネン
Laulajainen, Leena 795
ラウリ
Lauri, Maris 796
ラウリー
Lowery, B.J. 848
Lowery, Dwight 848
Lowrie, Jed 848
Lowry, Dean 848
Lowry, Kyle 848
Rowly, Janet Davison 1212
ラウリセンス
Lauryssens, Stan 796
ラウリッセン
Lauridsen, Irma 796
ラウリツセン
Lauritzen, Karsten 796
ラウリーン
Laurin, Anna-Lena 796
ラウリング
Rowling, J.K. 1212
ラウル
Laourou, Grégoire 790
Raoul, Élisabeth 1157
Raoul, Émilienne 1157
ラウール・ガルシア
Raul Garcia 1160
ラウール・ゴンサーレス
Raúl Gonzáles 1160
ラウル・ゴンサレス
Raúl Gonzáles 1160
ラウルセン
Laurijssen, Manuel 796
ラウール・ナバス
Raul Navas 1160
ラウール・リソアイン
Raul Lizoain 1160
ラウレ
Laure 795
ラヴレイス
Lovelace, Earl 847
Lovelace, Linda 847
ラウレナウ
Laurenau, Siarhei 795
ラウレル
Laurel, Francis C. 795
Laurel, Jose C., V 795
Laurel, Salvador Hidalgo 795
Laurell, Anna 795
Laurell Nash, Anna 795
ラヴレンチェフ
Lavrentiev, Boris 797
Lavrentiev, Evgeny 797
ラウレンツァ
Laurenza, Domenico 796
ラウロ
Lauro, German 796
ラヴロック
Lovelock, James Ephraim 847
ラヴロネンコ
Lavronenko, Konstantin 797
ラヴローフ
Lavrov, Sergei Viktorovich 797
ラヴロフ
Lavrov, Sergei Viktorovich 797
ラウンズ・ガニンラウ
Rounds Ganilau, Bernadette 1210
ラウンスレー
Rawnsley, Vivienne 1162
ラウンデス
Lowndes, Leil 848
ラウントリー
Rowntree, Kate 1212
ラエフ
Raeff, Marc 1148
Rayev, Sultan 1162
ラエル
Vorilhon, Claude 1464
ラーオ
Rao, C.N.R. 1157
ラオ
Rao, Calyampudi Radhakrishna 1157
Rao, Chandra Sekhar 1157
Rao, Chintamani Nagesa Ramachandra 1157
Rao, C.N.R. 1157
Rao, Inderjit Singh 1157
Rao, Kotamraju Ashu 1157
Rao, Kotamraju Narayana 1157
Rao, Narasimha 1157
Rao, Shanta Rameshwar 1157
Rao, Sirish 1157
Rao, Srikumar S. 1157
Rau, Johannes 1160
ラオス
Raos, Andrea 1157
ラオス・カセレス
Laos Cáceres, Teresa Nancy 790
ラーオーテ
Raote, Komilla 1157
ラオニッチ
Raonic, Milos 1157
ラオペアム
Laopeam, Peamwilai 790
ラオホカラト
Rauch-kallat, Maria 1160
ラオレ
Laore, Christopher 790
ラカー
Laqueur, Walter Ze'ev 791
ラガス
Ragas, Matthew W. 1149
ラカゼ
Lacaze, Genevieve 779
ラカゼット
Lacazette, Alexandre 779
ラガッセ
Lagasse, Emeril John 781
ラガッタ
Lagatta, Florian 781
ラガッツィ
Lagazzi, Paolo 781
ラカッラ
Lacarra, Lucia 779
ラガト
Lagat, Bernard 781
ラカトシュ
Lakatos, Imre 783
Lakatos, Roby 783
ラカトン
Lacaton, Anne 779
ラガバニ
al-Ragabani, Saeed Muhammad 1149
ラガブ
Ragab, Abdelhay Saad Abdelrazek 1149
ラガーフィールド
Lagerfeld, Karl-Otto 781
ラガーフェルト
Lagerfeld, Karl-Otto 781
ラガーフェルド
Lagerfeld, Karl-Otto 781
ラガフェルド
Lagerfeld, Karl-Otto 781
ラカモイレ
Lacamoire, Alex 779
ラカヨ
Lacayo, Miguel 779
ラガリア
Ragalia, A.L. 1149
ラガルド
Lagarde, Christine 781
Lagarde, Jean de 781
ラガレス
Lagares, Juan 781
ラカン
Lacão, Jorge 779
ラガン
Ragan, Anthony 1149
Raguin, Virginia Chieffo 1149
ラーキー
Larkey, Pat 791
ラギー
Ruggie, John Gerard 1215
ラキティッチ
Rakitic, Ivan 1152
ラキブ
Raqib, Abdol 1158
ラギモフ
Ragimov, Azad 1149
ラーキン
Lakein, Alan 783
Larkin, Emily 791
Larkin, Emma 791
Larkin, Maurice 791
Larkin, Mitch 791
Larkin, Sandar 791
Larkin, Shane 791
Larkin, T.J. 791
ラーキンス
Larkins, Ellis Lane 791
ラーク
Lalk, Jamison 783
Lark, Liz 791
Lark, Michael 791
ラク
Lak, Daniel 783
ラグ
Lagou, Henriette 782
ラクーア
Lacour, Lawrence L. 780
ラクアトラ
Laquatra, Idamarie 791
ラグアルディア
Laguardia, Victor 782
ラクヴァ
Laqua, Carsten 791
ラクオアネ
Rakuoane, Lekhetho 1152
ラクーザ
Rakusa, Iluma 1152
ラグーザ
Ragusa, Antonino 1149
ラクサマナ
Laksamana, Sukardi 783
ラクサール
Laxalt, Diego 799
ラグーシス
Ragoussis, Yiannis 1149
ラクシモヴ
Raczymow, Henri 1147
ラクシュマン
Lakshman, Bulusu 783
ラクシュミー・ナラス
Lakshmi Narasu, Pokala 783
ラクース
Lakhous, Amara 783
ラグス
Rags, Eriks 1149
ラグズ
Raguz, Martin 1149
ラグスデール
Ragsdale, Grady, Jr. 1149
ラークソ
Laakso, Seija-Riitta 779
ラクソノ
Laksono, Agung 783
ラグダフ
Laghdhaf, Moulaye Ould Mohamed 781
ラクチェビッチ
Rakcevic, Zarko 1152
ラクチュール
Lacouture, Jean 780
ラグチン
Lagutin, Sergey 782
ラクトゥアリスア
Rakotoarisoa, Florent 1152
ラクトゥニライニ
Rakotonirainy, Soalahy Georges 1152
ラクトゥマモンジ
Rakotomamonjy, Jean Max 1152
ラクトゥンドラスア
Rakotondrasoa 1152
ラクトンドラザカ
Rakotondrazaka, Arsène 1152
ラグノー
Ragueneau, Philippe 1149
ラクハニ
Lakhani, Dave 783
ラグバルシン
Raghoebarsing, Kermechend 1149
ラクマン
Lachmann, Frank M. 780
Rahman, Hasim 1150
ラグマン

Rugman, Alan M. 1215
ラグムジヤ
Lagumdžija, Zlatko 782
ラクラウ
Laclau, Ernesto 780
ラグラヴェネーズ
Lagravenese, Richard 782
ラクー・ラバルト
Lacoue-Labarthe, Philippe 780
ラグランジュ
Lagrange, Pierre 782
ラグランド
Ragland, Reggie 1149
Ragland, Robert Oliver 1149
ラクリン
Laughlin, Terry 795
Rachlin, Julian 1147
ラクール
Lacourt, Camille 780
ラクルス
La Cruz, Julio Cesar 780
La Cruz Peraza, Julio 780
ラグルス
Ruggles, Lucy 1215
Ruggles, Rudy L. 1215
ラクレア
Leclaire, Day 802
ラグレインジ
La Grange, Zelda 782
ラグレナード
La Grenade, Cécile 782
ラクロア
Lacroix, Christian 780
ラ・クロワ
La Croix, Arnaud de 780
la Croix, Isobyl 780
ラクロワ
Lacroix, Christian 780
LaCroix, Darren 780
Lacroix, Delphine 780
Lacroix, Jean Paul 780
Lacroix, Karl 780
ラケヴィルツ
Rachewiltz, Boris de 1147
ラゲス
Lages, Andrea 781
ラケット
Luckett, Cavellis 850
Luckett, Roy 850
ラゲット
Ragette, Friedrich 1149
Raggett, Dave 1149
Raggett, Isobel 1149
Raggett, Jenny 1149
ラーゲルクランツ
Lagercrantz, David 781
Lagercrantz, Rose 781
ラーゲ・ロイ
Lage-Roy, Carola 781
ラケン
Laken, Thomas 783
ラーコ
Rahko, Peter S. 1150
ラーゴ
Lago, Andre Aranha Correa do 781
Lago, Umberto 781
Rago, Stephen A. 1149
ラコ
Lakoe, Richard 783
ラゴ
Lago, Mário 781
Lago, Pilar 781
Lago, Raul 781
Lago, Scott 781
ラゴウスキー
Lagowski, Barbara 782
ラコグニャタ・サラゴサ
Lacogñata Zaragoza, Hector Ricardo 780
ラコシー
Lacosse, Matt 780
ラコス
Lakos, John 783
ラゴス・ウェベル
Lagos Weber, Ricardo 782
ラゴス・エスコバル
Lagos Escobar, Ricardo 782
ラゴスタ
Ragosta, Michael 1149
ラコステ
Lacoste, Anne 780
Lacoste, Bernard 780
ラコスト
Lacoste, Bruno 780
Lacoste, Jean 780
Lacoste, Yves 780
ラ・コタルディエール
La Cotardière, Philippe de 780
ラコトアリマシ
Rakotoarimasy, Lucien 1152
ラコトアリマナナ
Rakotoarimanana, François Marie Maurice Gervais 1152
ラコトゥリピス
Lakkotrypis, Georgios 783
ラコトゥール
Lacouture, María Claudia 780
ラコトザフィ
Rakotozafy, Dominique Jean Olivier 1152
ラコトバオ
Rakotovao, Rivo 1152
ラコトバヒニー
Rakotovahiny, Emmanuel 1152
ラコトマモンジ
Rakotomamonjy, André Neypatraiky 1152
ラコトマララ
Rakotomalala, Mireille Mialy 1152
ラコトミハンタリザカ
Rakotomihantarizaka, Rémy Sylvain Organès 1152
ラゴネグロ
Lagonegro, Melissa 781
ラコービニエー
Lacorbiniere, Victor 780
ラコビニエール
Lacobiniere, Victor Phillip 780
ラコフ
Rakoff, Joanna 1152
Rakov, Maxim 1152
ラコフスキ
Rakowski, Mieczysław Franciszek 1152
ラコーム
Lacombe, Michel 780
ラゴン
Ragon, Michel 1149
ラゴンデ
Ragondet, Nathalie 1149
ラコンブ
Lacombe, Clément 780
ラサ
Lasa, Emiliano 793
ラサー
Rasaw, Humayoon 1158
ラザ
Raza, Werner G. 1163
ラザー
Lazar, Jerry 799
Rather, Dan 1160
ラザイ
Rezaei, Alireza 1175
ラサイク
Lasike, Paul 793
ラサウリス
Lathouris, Nico 794
ラザカ
Razaka, Elise 1163
ラザク
Razaq, Abdol 1163
ラサクエロ
Lasaquero, Purificatión Buari 793
ラサクリシュナン
Rathakrishnan, Ethirajan 1159
ラザコフ
Razakov, Zhenish 1163
ラサス
al-Rasas, Rashad Ahmad 1158
al-Rasas, Rashad Ahmad Yahya 1158
al-Rassas, Rashad Ahmad 1159
ラザースフェルド
Lazarsfeld, Sofie 799
ラサーソン
Laserson, Uri 793
ラサター
Lasater, Judith Hanson 793
ラザック
Razzaque, Muhammad Abdur 1163
ラサート
Russert, Tim 1219
ラザナマハソア
Razanamahasoa, Chiristine 1163
ラサネン
Räsänen, Päivi 1158
ラザビ
Razavi, Amir H. 1163
ラザファード
Rutherfurd, Edward 1219
ラザフィトンブ
Razafitombo, Elisa 1163
ラザフィナカンガ
Razafinakanga, Alice 1163
ラザフィマエファ
Razafimahefa, Ivohasina 1163
ラザフィマナザト
Razafimanazato, Julien 1163
ラザフィマンジャート
Razafimanjato, Blandin 1163
ラザフィマンディンビ
Razafimandimby, Eric 1163
ラザフィミハリ
Razafimihary, Mejamirado 1163
ラザフィンジャチアマニリ
Razafindrandriatsimaniry, Dieudonne Michel 1163
ラザフィンジャトゥブ
Razafinjatovo, Haja 1163
ラザフィンジャトボ
Razafinjatovo, Haja Nirina 1163
ラザフィンデイベ
Razafindehibe, Etienne Hilaire 1163
ラザフィンドロリアカ
Razafindroriaka, Nestor 1163
ラザフォード
Rutherford, Adam 1219
Rutherford, Ann 1219
Rutherford, Edmund J. 1219
Rutherford, Greg 1219
Rutherford, James 1219
Rutherford, Kevin 1219
Rutherford, Stuart 1219
ラザフンジャランブ
Razafindramiandra, Vola Dieudonne 1163
ラサミンジャクツカ
Rasamindrakotrokotra, Andry 1158
ラサモエリ
Rasamoely, Brigitte 1158
ラザラス
Lazarus, Shelly 799
ラザリ・イスマイル
Razali Ismail 1163
ラザリデス
Lazarides, Linda 799
ラーザール
Lázár, János 799
ラサール
LaSalle, Diana 793
ラザール
Lazar, Veronica 799
Lazard, Madeleine 799
ラザル
Lazar, Mihai 799
Lazar, Valeriu 799
ラザルス
Lazarus, Arnold A. 799
Lazarus, Richard S. 799
Lazarus, Tom 799
ラザーレ
Lazare, Carol 799
ラーザレフ
Lazarev, Aleksandr 799
ラザレフ
Lazarev, Aiaal 799
Lazarev, Aleksandr 799
Lazarev, Sergey N. 799
ラザレワ
Lazareva, Tetyana 799
ラザーロ
Lazzaro, Joseph J. 799
ラザロヴァ
Lazarova, Rouja 799
ラザローニ

Lazaroni, Sebastião Barroso 799
ラザロニ
Lazaroni, Sebastião Barroso 799
ラサーン
Lassahn, Rudolf 793
ラザン
Lazan, Marion Blumenthal 799
ラージ
Large, David Clay 791
ラシ
Hashi, Abdirashid 579
Rasi, Abdul-Kareem 1159
ラジ
Raj, George Shiu 1151
Raj, Kapil 1151
ラジー
Razee, Mahmood 1163
ラシアノフ
Russianoff, Penelope 1219
ラシィ
Lathi, Bhagwandas Pannalal 794
ラジウィウ
Radziwiłł, Konstanty 1148
ラシヴェール
Lachiver, Marcel 780
ラーシェ
Larcher, Bertrand 791
ラシェーヴァー
Laschever, Sara 793
ラジェス
Lages, Vincius Nobre 781
ラシェタ・ブコサブリェビッチ
Rašeta Vukosavlević, Marija 1158
ラーシェド
Rashed, Roshdi 1158
ラジェービチ
Radevich, Alexander M. 1147
ラジェリナ
Rajoelina, Andry Nirina 1152
ラジェル
Rajel, Ishagh Ould 1152
ラジエル
Rasiel, Ethan M. 1159
ラシエルダ
Lacierda, Edwin 780
ラーシェン
Larsen, Eirik Veraas 792
Larsen, Marit 792
ラジェンダー
Gendre, Esther Le 488
ラージェント
Largent, David L. 791
ラシガ
Laciga, Martin 780
Laciga, Paul 780
ラジコフ
Radkov, Aleksandr M. 1148
ラシザーデ
Rasi-Zade, Artur Tair Oglu 1159
ラシター
Lassiter, Rhiannon 793
Lassiter, Timothy 793
ラジチョヴァー
Radičová, Iveta 1148
ラシツキ
Lasicki, Igor 793
ラシッチ
Rašić, Nenad 1159
Rasič, Saša 1159
ラジッチ
Lazic, Dejan 799
ラシッド
Rashid, Ahmed 1158
Rashid, Seif Seleman 1158
ラシーディ
al-Rasheedi, Thekra 1158
ラシティ
Raciti, Travis 1147
ラシディ
Alrashidi, Abdullah 36
Rashidi, Syed Sadaruddin Shah 1159
Rushdie, Salman 1217
ラシード
Rasheed, Mohamed 1158
al-Rasheed, Muhammad bin Ahmad 1158
Rasheed, Raid 1158
Rashid, Abdul-Latif 1158
al-Rashid, Kazim 1158
Rashid, Pervaiz 1158
Rashid, Rashid Muhammad 1158
ラシド
Rachid 1147
Rashed, bin Abdulla al-Khalifa 1158
Rashed, Muhammad Yehia 1158
Rashid, Abdullah al-Nuaimi 1158
Rashid, Mohamed Abu Ujaylah 1158
ラシド・アル・ウバイディ
Rashid al-Ubaydi, Amir Muhammad 1159
ラシードケシシュ
Rachid Kechiche, Mohamed 1147
ラシドフ
Rashidov, Vezhdi 1159
ラシーナ
Racina, Thom 1147
ラシナック
Lacinak, Thad 780
ラジニカーント
Rajinikanth 1152
ラシーヌ
Racine, Magalie 1147
ラジハ
Rajiha, bint Abdul Amir bin Ali 1152
Rajiha, Dawoud 1152
ラシヒ
Lashkhi, Revaz 793
ラジビル
Radzivil, Svetlana 1148
ラジミ
Lajimi, Khelil 783
Lajmi, Rajiv 783
ラージメイカーズ
Raijmakers, Bas 1151
ラジャ
Raja, A. 1151
Raja, Ali S. 1151
Raja, Andimuthu 1151
Raja, Farzana 1151
ラジャ・イーサ・アル・ガルグ
Raja Easa Al Gurg 1151
ラジャウナ
Rajaonah, Alice 1152
ラジャオナリソン
Rajaonarison, Pascal Jacques 1152
ラジャオナリベロ
Rajaonarivelo, Pierrot 1152
ラジャオナリマンピアニナ
Rajaonarimampianina, Hery 1152
ラジャコビッチ
Rajakovic, Darko 1151
ラシャッド
Rashad, Shakeel 1158
ラジャ・ノン・チク
Raja Nong Chik, Raja Zainal Abidin 1152
ラージャパクサ
Rajapaksa, Lalitha 1152
ラジャパクサ
Rajapaksa, Basil 1152
Rajapaksa, Mahinda 1152
Rajapaksa, Wijeyadasa 1152
ラジャパクセ
Rajapaksa, Mahinda 1152
Rajapakse, Mahinda 1152
ラジャブ
Rajab, Mansoor bin Hassan bin 1151
ラジャブザーデ
Rajabzadeh, Hashem 1151
ラシャペル
LaChapelle, David 779
ラジャボフ
Radzhabov, Safarali 1148
ラジャポフ
Rajabov, Safarali 1151
Rajapov, Matkarim 1152
ラジャマニ
Rajamani, Lavanya 1151
ラシャムジャ
Iha byams rgyal 644
ラジャラム
Rajaram, Dhiraj 1152
ラジャル
Rajar, Haji Khuda Bukhsh 1152
Rajar, Haji Khuda Bux 1152
ラジャン
Rajan, Kaushik Sunder 1151
Rajan, Raghuram G. 1151
Rajan, S.Ravi 1151
Rajan, Yagnaswami Sundara 1151
ラシャンズ
LaChanze 779
ラジュ
Radjou, Navi 1148
Raju, B.Ramalinga 1152
Raju, Pallam 1152
ラジュー
Raju, Jagmohan 1152
ラシュカ
Raschka, Christopher 1158
Raschka, Sebastian 1158
Rashka, Jeff 1159
ラシュガリ
Lashgari, Ehsan Naser 793
ラシュガル
Lachgar, Driss 780
Lachgar, Hasnaa 780
ラシュキ
Raschke, Linda Bradford 1158
ラシュコ
Lashko, Irina 793
ラシュコフスキー
Rashkovskiy, Ilya 1159
ラシュディ
Rachedi, Mabrouck 1147
al-Rashdi, Hamad bin Mohammed 1158
Rushdie, Salman 1217
ラシュトン
Rushton, Rosie 1217
ラシュナー
Lashner, William 793
ラシュナウアー
Lachenauer, Rob 780
ラシュビー
Rushby, Kevin 1217
ラジュヒ
Rajhi, Farhat 1152
ラジューブ
Rajoub, Nayef 1152
ラシュマノワ
Lashmanova, Elena 793
ラシュリー
Lashley, Hamilton 793
Lashley, Michael 793
Lashley, Stephen 793
ラシュルト
Rahschulte, Tim J. 1150
ラシュレイ
Lashley, Michael 793
ラシュワン
Rashwan, Mohamed Ali 1159
ラジュン
Layun, Miguel 799
ラジョイ
Lajoie, Bill 783
ラジョエリナ
Rajoelina, Andry Nirina 1152
ラショーム
Lachaume, Virginie 779
ラジョワ
Lajoie, Josée 783
ラーショーン
Larsson, Ulf 793
ラーション
Larson, Lisa 792
Larsson, Arne 792
Larsson, Gustav 792
Larsson, Henrik 792
Larsson, Johanna 792
Larsson, Kjell 792
Larsson, Linus 792
Larsson, Maria 792
Larsson, Markus 792
Larsson, Mats G. 793
Larsson, Nathalie 793
Larsson, Sebastian 793
ラジョンソン
Rajohnson, Rija 1152
ラシラ
Lassila, Lydia 793
ラジリック
Rajlich, Nathan 1152
ラージン

ラ

Razin, Aharon 1163
ラシーン
Rasseen, Ba Emdo 1159
ラシン
Rusin, Chris 1217
ラシンスキー
Lashinsky, Adam 793
ラジンスキー
Radzinskii, Edvard 1148
Radzinskii, Edvard Stanislavovich 1148
ラス
Lass, Roger 793
Rath, Tom 1159
Russ, Joanna 1218
ラズ
Raz, Jakob 1163
Raz, Joseph 1163
Raz, Tahl 1163
ラスアニ
Lassouani, Leila Francoise 793
ラースイ
Raši, Richard 1159
ラーズィ
Radhi, Ahmed Ould Idey Ould Mohamed 1148
ラズウェル
Laswell, Bill 794
ラスカー
Lasker, Alex 793
ラズガイティス
Razgaitis, Richard 1163
ラスカー＝ウォルフィッシュ
Lasker-Wallfisch, Anita 793
ラスカス
Laskas, Jeanne Marie 793
ラースガード
Larsgaard, Chris 792
ラスカム
Luscombe, David Edward 854
ラスカル
Rascal 1158
ラスキー
Laskey, Zach 793
Lasky, Kathryn 793
Lasky, Melvin Jonah 793
Lasky, Sue 793
ラスキン
Luskin, Frederic 854
Raskin, Jef 1159
ラスク
Lask, Bryan 793
Lusk, Ewing 854
Lusk, Linda 854
Rask, Maija 1159
Rask, Märt 1159
ラスゲバー
Rathgeber, Holger 1160
ラスコ
Lasco, Daniel 793
ラスコー
Rasco, Jermauria 1158
ラ・スコーラ
La Scola, Vincenzo 793
ラスザラ
Ruszala, Sue 1219
ラスジャ
Rasoja, Charles 1159
ラスター
Raster, Michael J. 1159
ラスタミ
Rastami, Mouhidine 1159
ラスダン
Lasdun, James 793
ラスディ
Rusdi, Prima 1217
ラスティグ
Lustig, Theodore 854
ラズティナ
Lazutina, Larissa 799
ラスティン
Rustin, Judice 1219
Rustin, Margaret 1219
ラステッリ
Rastelli, Massimo 1159
ラステラ
La Stella, Tommy 794
ラスト
Last, Annie 793
Last, Shari 793
Rast, Gregory 1159
Rust, Dan 1219
Rust, Graham 1219
Rust, Roland T. 1219
ラストヴォロフ
Rastvorov, Yurii A. 1159
ラストガーテン
Lustgarten, Abrahm 854
ラストナー
Rastner, Patrick 1159
ラストバーグ
Lustberg, Arch 854
ラストベーダー
Lustbader, Eric Van 854
Lustbader, Wendy 854
ラストボロフ
Rastvorov, Yurii A. 1159
ラストマイアー
Rustemier, Sharon 1219
ラストマン
Rustmann, F.W. 1219
ラスナッチ
Rasnačs, Dzintars 1159
ラスニック
Lassnig, Maria 793
ラズバルト
Rusbult, Caryl E. 1217
ラスバーン
Rathburn, Cliff 1160
ラ・スピーナ
La Spina, Emma 793
ラスプーチン
Rasputin, Valentin Grigorievich 1159
ラスブリッジャー
Rusbridger, Alan 1217
ラスボーン
Rathbone, Jackson 1160
ラズボーン
Rathbone, Dominic 1160
Rathbone, Julian 1160
ラスマス
Rasmus, Colby 1159
ラスマセン
Rasmusson, Jonathan 1159
ラスマン
Rathmann, Peggy 1160
ラズム
Razem, Alam 1163
ラスムセン
Rasmusen, Eric 1159
Rasmussen, Alex Nicki 1159
Rasmussen, Anders Fogh 1159
Rasmussen, Hedvig 1159
Rasmussen, Jonas 1159
Rasmussen, Juliane 1159
Rasmussen, Lars Løkke 1159
Rasmussen, Mads 1159
Rasmussen, Mikkel B. 1159
Rasmussen, Poul Nyrup 1159
Rasmussen, Robert 1159
ラスムッセン
Rasmussen, Eric 1159
Rasmussen, Inger Johanne 1159
Rasmussen, Mads 1159
Rasmussen, Patricia 1159
Rasmussen, Steven A. 1159
ラズリー
Lasley, Elizabeth Norton 793
Lasry, Marc 793
ラスリンガー
Luthringer, Mélisande 854
ラスール
Rasoul, Ali Mahmoud Abdel 1159
Rassoul, Zalmai 1159
ラスルゾダ
Rasulzoda, Qohir 1159
ラスルナイ
Rasolonahy, Charles Angelo 1159
ラスルフニリナ
Rasolofonirina, Beni Xavier 1159
ラスルンドライベ
Rasolondraibe, Jean-Jacques 1159
ラズレグ
Lazreg, Hacene 799
ラースロ
László, Tőkés 794
ラースロー
László, Csaba 794
László, Tőkés 794
ラスロー
Laszlo, Pierre 794
ラズロ
Laszlo, Andrew 794
Laszlo, Ervin 794
Laszlo, Hana 794
Laszlo, Pierre 794
László, Tony 794
ラズロー
Laszlo, Ervin 794
ラスロップ
Lathrop, Laura 794
Lathrop, Tad 794
ラスロフ
Rasulov, Elshod 1159
Rasulov, Hojiakbar Abdurahimovich 1159
ラースン
Larsen, Andrew 792
Larsen, Jonas 792
Larson, Neal L. 792
Lasn, Kalle 793
ラセーグ
Lassègue, Marie Laurence Jocelyn 793
ラセグ
Lassègue, Marie Laurence Jocelyn 793
ラセター
Lasseter, John 793
ラセッター
Lasseter, John 793
ラセッティ
Laccetti, Margaret Saul 779
ラセット
Russett, Bruce M. 1219
ラゼブニック
LaZebnik, Claire Scovell 799
ラセル
Russell, Harold 1218
ラゼール
Lazere, Cathy A. 799
ラーセン
Larsen, Carolyn 792
Larsen, Eirik Veraas 792
Larsen, Esben Lunde 792
Larsen, Gaylord 792
Larsen, Henning 792
Larsen, Henrik 792
Larsen, Janet 792
Larsen, Jørn Neergaard 792
Larsen, Kirsten 792
Larsen, Matt 792
Larsen, Nicole Broch 792
Larsen, Pamala D. 792
Larsen, Peter Gorm 792
Larsen, Ralph 792
Larsen, Reif 792
Larsen, Stine 792
Larsen, Ted 792
Larsen, Tyler 792
Larssen, Erik Bertrand 792
ラソアザナネラ
Rasoazananera, Marie Monique 1159
ラソアマナリヴォ
Rasoamanarivo, Rosette Lalatiana 1159
ラゾヴィッチ
Lazovic, Darko 799
ラソ・エルナンデス
Lazo Hernández, Juan Esteban 799
ラソーダ
Lasorda, Thomas Charles 793
Lasorda, Tommy 793
ラソッガ
Lasogga, Pierre-Michel 793
ラゾッタ
Lassotta, Arnold 793
ラゾビッチ
Lazović, Vujica 799
ラゾロノフ
Razoronov, Igor 1163
ラーソン
Larson, Beverly 792
Larson, Breeja 792
Larson, B.V. 792
Larson, Erik 792
Larson, Frances 792
Larson, Jean Russell 792
Larson, Jeffry H. 792
Larson, Johanna 792
Larson, Kirby 792
Larson, Lisa 792
Larson, Loren C. 792

Larson, M.A. 792
Larson, Olaf F. 792
Larson, Peter L. 792
Larson, Raoul 792
Larsson, Asa 792
Larsson, Henrik 792
Larsson, Rikard 793
Larsson, Stieg 793
Mathews Larson, Joan 918

ラゾン
Razon, Enrique K. 1163

ラター
Rutter, Michael 1219

ラダー
Rudder, Christian 1214

ラーダークリシュナン
Radhakrishnan, Sarvepalli 1148

ラダクリシュナン
Radhakrishnan, Neelakanta 1148
Rādhākrshnana, Mimi 1148

ラタケレ
Ratakele, Talemo 1159

ラタス
Ratas, Juri 1159

ラタッシュ
Latash, Mark L. 794

ラダニュー
Ladagnous, Matthieu 780

ラダノワ
Radanova, Evgenia 1147
Radanova, Evgeniya 1147

ラダビドソン
Radavidson, Andriamparany Benjamin 1147

ラダ・ベレス
Rada Vélez, Alfred Octavio 1147

ラダーマン
Laderman, Ezra 780

ラダロドリゲス
Rada Rodriguez, Sergio Armando 1147

ラタン
Ruttan, Sandra 1219

ラタンゼ
Lattanze, Anthony J. 794

ラチアルバラ
Ratsiarovala, Lala 1160
Ratsiharovala, Lala Henriette 1160

ラ・チェクラ
La Cecla, Franco 779

ラチェッキ
Lachecki, Marina 779

ラチェデリ
Lacedelli, Lino 779

ラチチュラー
Ratschiller, Tobias 1160

ラチド
Rachid, Leila 1147

ラチナウ
Lachinau, Asadulla 780

ラチバ
Rachyba, Vasyl 1147

ラチファンドリアマナナ
Ratsifandrihamanana, Lila 1160

ラチャン
Račan, Ivica 1147

ラチラカ
Ratsiraka, Didier 1160
Ratsiraka, Roland 1160

ラチーン
Lacheen, Steve 780

ラーツ
Rácz, Jenö 1147
Rahtz, Sebastian 1150

ラーツィス
Latsis, Otto Rudolifovich 794

ラツィス
Latsis, Otto Rudolifovich 794

ラツィック
Lazic, Dejan 799

ラツィラカ
Ratsiraka, Larovana Roland 1160

ラッカ
Lakha, Pia Kryger 783

ラッカー
Rucker, Darius 1214
Rucker, Frostee 1214
Rucker, Rudy von Bitter 1214

ラッカーバーマー
Racherbaumer, Jon 1147

ラッカム
Rackham, David W. 1147
Rackham, Neil 1147
Rackham, Oliver 1147

ラッガム
Raggam, August 1149

ラッキ
Lucke, Deb 850

ラッキー
Lackey, John 780
Lackey, Mercedes R. 780
Luckey, Palmer 851
Luckey, Thomas D. 851

ラツギ
Razeghi, Andrew J. 1163

ラッキン
Lackin, Winston 780

ラック
Lack, Andrew J. 780
Lack, John Alastair 780
Lack, Leon 780
Luck, Andrew 850

ラッグ
Wragg, Ted 1527

ラックス
Laks, Simon 783
Lax, David A. 798
Lax, Eric 798
Lax, Peter David 798
Lux, Loretta 855

ラックストン
Ruxton, Ian C. 1220

ラックスマン
Lakshman, C. 783

ラックナー
Lackner, Jeffrey M. 780

ラックマン
Lachmann, Frank M. 780
Lachmann, Henri 780
Rachman, Carla 1147
Rachman, Stanley 1147
Rachman, Stephen 1147
Rachman, Tom 1147
Ruckman, William P. 1214

ラッグルズ
Ruggles, Dede Fairchild 1215

ラッケンメイヤー
Lachenmeyer, Nathaniel 780

ラッサート
Russert, Tim 1219

ラッサーノ
Rasano, Eva 1158

ラッサム
Rassam, Suha 1159

ラッジ
Raggi, Andrea 1149

ラッジェン
Luggen, Martin 851

ラッシオ
Ruscio, John 1217

ラッジカク
Rajcak, Hélène 1152

ラッシュ
Lash, Marilyn 793
Lash, Scott 793
Lusch, Robert F. 854
Rash, Jim 1158
Rash, Ron 1158
Rusch, Gloria 1217
Rusch, Kristine Kathryn 1217
Rusch, Laura C. 1217
Rush, A.John 1217
Rush, Alexander 1217
Rush, Brandon 1217
Rush, Geoffrey 1217
Rush, Mallory 1217
Rush, Marcus 1217
Rush, Xavier 1217

ラッシュネル
Rushnell, Squire D. 1217

ラッシュビー
Rushby, Nick 1217

ラッシュフォード
Rashford, Marcus 1158

ラッシング
Rushing, Brad 1217

ラッセル
Russel, Charlie 1218
Russel, Colin 1218
Russel, Daniel R. 1218
Russel, George 1218
Russel, Ken 1218
Russell, Addison 1218
Russell, Alan 1218
Russell, Allan 1218
Russell, Alonzo 1218
Russell, Bob 1218
Russell, Colin A. 1218
Russell, Craig 1218
Russell, Cristine 1218
Russell, D'Angelo 1218
Russell, Daniel C. 1218
Russell, David 1218
Russell, David E. 1218
Russell, David O. 1218
Russell, Diana E.H. 1218
Russell, Eric Frank 1218
Russell, Ethan A. 1218
Russell, Finn 1218
Russell, Gary 1218
Russell, Gordon 1218
Russell, Harold 1218
Russell, Henry 1218
Russell, Jane 1218
Russell, Janieve 1218
Russell, Jeffrey Burton 1218
Russell, Jeffrey Lee 1218
Russell, Jenna 1218
Russell, John 1218
Russell, Karen 1218
Russell, KeiVarae 1218
Russell, Ken 1218
Russell, Kenneth 1218
Russell, Kenneth A. 1218
Russell, Kurt 1218
Russell, Leon 1218
Russell, Letty M. 1218
Russell, Linda 1218
Russell, Matthew A. 1218
Russell, Natalie 1218
Russell, Peter 1218
Russell, Rachel Renee 1218
Russell, Raymond 1218
Russell, Rebecca 1218
Russell, Roberta 1218
Russell, Robert J. 1218
Russell, Robert M. 1218
Russell, Robyn 1218
Russell, Ronald 1218
Russell, Ruth 1218
Russell, Ryan 1218, 1219
Russell, Shona 1219
Russell, Sinead 1219
Russell, Stuart Jonathan 1219
Russell, Vivian 1219
Russell, Willard 1219

ラッセル＝ウォリング
Russell-Walling, Edward 1219

ラッセルズ
Lascelles, Christopher 793

ラッセン
Lassen, Catherine 793
lassen, Christian Riese 793
Lassen, Jeane 793

ラッソ
Lasso, Gloria 793

ラッタ
Latta, Jan 794

ラッタウット・ラープチャルーンサップ
Lapcharoensap, Rattawut 790

ラッタンシ
Rattansi, Piyo 1160

ラッチェ
Rathje, Annette 1160

ラッチカ
Raczka, Bob 1147

ラッチマン
Latchman, David S. 794

ラッチャタ
Rajata, Rajatanavin 1152

ラッツ
Lutz, John 855
Lutz, Lisa 855
Lutz, Robert A. 855
Lutz, Will 855

ラッツァ
Latza, Danny 794

ラッツアーダ
Lattuada, Alberto 794

ラッツァラート
Lazzarato, Maurizio 799

ラッツィ
Razzi, Manuela 1163

ラッツェローニ
Lazzeroni, Claudius 799

ラッツォーリ
Razzoli, Giuliano 1163

ラ

ラッティカン
Gulnoi, Rattikan 545
ラッティモア
Lattimore, Jamari 794
ラッテルミュラー
Rattelmüller, Paul Ernst 1160
ラット
Lat 794
ラッド
Ladd, Diane 780
Ladd, Ernie 780
Ladd, Fred 780
Ladd, Paddy 780
Rad, Parviz F. 1147
Rudd, Amber 1214
Rudd, Kevin 1214
ラットゥアーダ
Lattuada, Alberto 794
ラッドビル
Radbill, Samuel X. 1147
ラットマン
Luttman, Robert J. 854
ラッドマン
Rudman, Shelley 1215
Rudman, Warren Bruce 1215
ラットル
Rattle, Simon 1160
ラッバディア
Labbadia, Bruno 779
ラッハム
Lahham, Ghassan 782
ラップ
Lapp, Charles W. 790
Lapp, Ralph Eugene 790
Rapp, Adam 1158
Rapp, Bernard André 1158
Rapp, Birgitta 1158
Rapp, Burt 1158
Rapp, Charles Anthony 1158
Rapp, Clemens 1158
Rapp, Richard T. 1158
Rapp, William V. 1158
Rupp, Cameron 1217
Rupp, Deborah E. 1217
Rupp, Galen 1217
Rupp, Rebecca 1217
ラッファー
Laffer, Arthur 781
ラッファイ
Raffay, Ágnes 1149
ラッファン
Lapham, David 790
ラップマンド
Rapmund, Norm 1158
ラッフル
Raffle, Angela E. 1149
Ruffle, Mark 1215
ラッペ
Lappé, Anna 790
Lappé, Marc 790
Rappé, Tamara 1158
ラッヘンマン
Lachenmann, Helmut 780
ラッワス
al-Rowas, Abdullah bin Salim 1211
ラーティー
Lahti, Torbjörn 782
ラーディ
Radi, Ahmed 1148
ラティ
Laty, Dominique 794
Ratih, Ayu 1160
ラテイ
Ratej, Martinka 1159
ラディ
Lady, Messa Ould Mohamed 781
Radi, Abdelwahed 1148
al-Radi, Mahmoud 1148
ラテイエ
Latteier, Amos 794
ラティク
Latyk, Olivier 794
ラティシェフ
Latyshev, Igor Aleksandrobits 794
ラディシッチ
Radišić, Živko 1148
ラディツォヴァー
Radičová, Iveta 1148
ラディツォバー
Radičová, Iveta 1148
ラディック
Hladik, Jean 610
Radic, Smiljan 1148
ラディッシュ
Radish, Kris 1148
ラディッチ
Radić, Darja 1148
Radic, Smiljan 1148
ラディティス
Ruditis, Paul 1215
ラディビロフ
Radivilov, Igor 1148
ラティーフ
Latheef, Hassan 794
Latheef, Mohamed 794
Latif, Adrees 794
ラティファ
Latifa 794
Latifah, Queen 794
ラティマー
Latimer, Cody 794
Latimer, Richard 794
ラティモア
Lattimore, Ralph 794
ラディン
Radin, Dean I. 1148
Rudin, Donald O. 1214
ラティンジャー
Luttinger, Nina 854
ラディンスキー
Radinsky, Scott 1148
ラデカン
Ladekan, Elénore 780
ラデゴー
Ladegaard, Jette 780
ラテック
Lattek, Udo 794
ラデッケ
Radecke, Gabriele 1147
ラデビチャ
Radevica, Ineta 1147
ラデフ
Radev, Mouravei 1147
Radev, Rumen 1147
ラデベ
Radebe, Jeff 1147
Radebe, Jeffrey 1147
Radebe, Mamahele 1147
ラデボー
Radebaugh, Lee H. 1147
ラーデマッハ
Rademacher, Christoph 1147
ラデメーカーズ
Rademakers, Fons 1147
ラテュ
Räty, Laura 1160
ラデュサー
Ladusaw, William A. 781
ラテュリッペ
Latulippe, Denis 794
ラテリエー
Latelier, Maria Flores 794
ラテル
Latell, Brian 794
Ratelle, Will 1159
ラーデン
Lardon, Michael 791
ラデン
Rudden, Marie 1214
ラート
Rath, Claudia 1159
ラード
Raad, Khaled 1146
ラト
Lato 794
Rato, Rodrigo 1160
ラドイ
Radoi, Andrei 1148
ラトゥ
Latou, Andre 794
Latu, Nili 794
Latu, Viliami 794
ラトゥー
Latour, Lamuré 794
ラドゥ
Radu, Ionut 1148
Radu, Stefan 1148
ラトゥアーダ
Lattuada, Alberto 794
ラドヴァノヴィッチ
Radovanovic, Ivan 1148
ラドウィック
Rudwick, Martin J.S. 1215
ラドウィッグ
Ludwig, Joe 851
Ludwig, Trudy 851
ラドゥカン
Răducan, Marcel 1148
Raducan, Marcel 1148
ラドゥク
Răducu, Aura Carmen 1148
ラドゥ・ゴレ
Ladu Gore, Alfred 781
ラトゥジェベール
Rathgeber, David 1160
ラトゥーシュ
Latouche, Serge 794
ラトゥシュコ
Latushko, Pavel P. 794
ラドゥスキー
Ladowsky, Ellen 781
ラトゥニャラワ
Ratuniyarawa, Api 1160
ラドゥノビッチ
Radunović, Miodrag 1148
ラトゥーフ
Lattouf, Hala 794
ラトゥール
Latour, Bruno 794
Latour, Jason 794
Latour, Jose 794
ラドゥロヴィッチ
Radulovic, Nemanja 1148
ラトゥンジ
Latoundji, Massiyatou 794
ラドゥンスキー
Radunsky, Vladimir 1148
ラドエビッチ
Radojević, Velimir 1148
ラートカウ
Radkau, Joachim 1148
ラドキー
Radtke, Autumn 1148
ラトキン
Lutkin, Tim 854
ラトクリフ
Ratcliff, Todd 1159
Ratcliffe, Spurgeon Vaughn 1159
ラドクリフ
Radcliffe, Daniel 1147
Radcliffe, James Christopher 1147
Radcliffe, Paula 1147
Radcliffe, Steve 1147
Radcliffe, Ted 1147
Radcliffe, Timothy 1147
ラトケ
Radke, Robert 1148
ラドケ
Radtke, Matt 1148
Radtke, Philipp 1148
ラトケビッチ
Ratkevich, Yuliya 1160
ラド・ゴア
Lado Gore, Alfred 780
ラトコフスキス
Latkovskis, Ainars 794
ラドーサー
Ladouceur, L.P. 781
ラドジ
Radzi, Sheikh Ahmad 1148
ラドシュ
Radoš, Jozo 1148
ラドセヴィッチ
Radosevich, Jennifer 1148
ラドソン＝ビリング
Ladson-Billings, Gloria 781
ラドチェンコ
Radchenko, Volodymyr 1147
ラドック
Ruddock, Philip 1214
ラトナー
Ratner, David L. 1160
Ratner, Vaddey 1160
ラトナヤケ
Rathnayake, C.B. 1160
Ratnayake, Amara P. 1160
Ratnayake, Sagala 1160
ラトニック
Lutnick, Howard 854
ラドニック
Rudnick, Elizabeth 1215
ラドネッジ
Radnedge, Keir 1148
ラドビッチ
Radović, Miraš 1148
ラトフィ
Lutfi, Mustafa 854

ラトフェン
Ruthven, Orlanda 1219
ラドフォード
Radford, Andrew 1147
Radford, Eric 1148
Radford, Jill 1148
Radford, John 1148
Radford, Lorraine 1148
Radford, Michael 1148
Radford, Robert 1148
ラートブルフ
Radbruch, Gustav 1147
ラトボマララ
Ratovomalala, Mamy 1160
ラドマノヴィッチ
Radmanović, Nebojša 1148
ラドマノビッチ
Radmanović, Nebojša 1148
ラドマン
Rudman, Peter Strom 1215
Rudman, Warren Bruce 1215
ラトマンスキー
Ratmansky, Alexei 1160
ラドヤ
Radoja, Nemanja 1148
ラドラム
Ludlum, Robert 851
ラドランスキー
Radlanski, Ralf Johannes 1148
ラトランド
Rutland, Eva 1219
ラドリー
Radley, Chris 1148
Radley, Tessa 1148
ラトリッジ
Rutledge, Cynthia 1219
Rutledge, Leigh W. 1219
ラトリフ
Ratliff, Ben 1160
ラドリン
Rudlin, Pernille 1215
ラトール
Rathore, Rajyavardhan Singh 1160
ラトル
Rattle, Simon 1160
ラトルチュ
Latortue, Gérard 794
ラドルフ
Lerdorf, Rasmus 815
ラトレイ
Rattray, Ben 1160
ラトレッジ
Rutledge, Josh 1219
ラトレル
Luttrell, Marcus 854
ラトロ・ジャナハリ
Ratolojanahary, Marius 1160
ラドロビッチ
Radulović, Milan 1148
ラドロン
Ladrönn, José 781
ラトワッテ
Ratwatte, Anuruddha 1160
ラドワン
Radwan, Samir 1148
ラドワンスカ
Radwanska, Agnieszka 1148
ラードン
Lardon, Michael 791
ラトン
Raton, Dithny Joan 1160
ラドン
Hladon, Paul R. 610
Ladon, Rogen 781
Radon, Jaroslav 1148
ラドンチッチ
Radončić, Fahrudin 1148
ラーナ
Rana, Kashiram Chabildas 1156
ラーナー
Larner, John 791
Lerner, Alexander 815
Lerner, Bernice 815
Lerner, Daniel 815
Lerner, Gerda 815
Lerner, Isha 815
Lerner, Josh 815
Lerner, Paul M. 815
Lerner, Theodore N. 815
ラナ
Rana, Dal Bahadur 1156
Rana, Ivan 1156
Rana, Kashiram 1156
Rana, Madhukar Shumsher 1156
ラナー
Renner, Barbara Rochen 1172
ラナイバアリボ
Ranaivoharivony, Bakolalao 1156
ラナイボ
Ranaivo, Serge 1156
ラナイボソア
Ranaivosoa, Roilya 1156
ラナガン
Lanagan, Margo 786
ラナシンハ
Ranasinghe, Thusitha 1156
ラナーデ
Ranade, Subhash 1156
ラナディヴェ
Ranadivé, Vivek 1156
ラナトゥンガ
Ranatunga, Arjuna 1156
ラナリット
Ranariddh, Norodom 1156
ラナリット殿下
Ranariddh, Norodom 1156
ラナルド
Ranaldo, Lee 1156
ラナワカ
Ranawaka, Patali Champika 1156
ラーナン
Ra'anan, Uri 1146
ラニー
Lunney, Margaret 853
Ranney, Karen 1157
ラニア
Lanier, Shannon 789
ラニアー
Lanier, Anthony 789
Lanier, Jaron 789
ラニア王妃
Rania 1157
ラニアン
Runyon, Brent 1217
ラニエリ
Ranieri, Claudio 1157
ラニオン
Runion, Meryl 1217
ラニガンオキーフ
Lanigan-okeeffe, Arthur 789
ラニクルズ
Runnicles, Donald 1217
ラニース
La Niece, Susan 789
ラニッチ
Lanicci, Rachael 789
ラーニド
Learned, Andrea 800
ラニャード
Lanyado, Monica 790
ラニヨン
Lanyon, Josh 790
Runyon, Melissa K. 1217
ラニング
Lanning, Andy 789
ラヌー
Lanoue, David G. 789
ラヌッチ
Ranucci, Claudia 1157
ラネカー
Langacker, Ronald W. 788
ラーネッド
Larned, William Trowbridge 791
ラーネト
Laanet, Kalle 779
ラーネヤク
Ratnayake, Rakhitha Nimesh 1160
ラネルズ
Rannells, Andrew 1157
Runnells, Treesha 1217
ラノッキア
Ranocchia, Andrea 1157
ラノッテ
Lanotte, Luca 789
ラノワ
Lanois, Daniel 789
ラノンラック
Ranongruk, Suwunchwee 1157
ラーハ
Laher, Ludwig 782
ラハ
Laha, Robert R., Jr. 782
ラバア
Raba'a, Rasheed Ba 1146
ラバイ
Ravai, Peni 1161
ラーパイ・センロー
Lahpai Seng Raw 782
ラバイン
Labine, Clem 779
ラハイングスア
Rahaingosoa, Odette 1149
ラパヴィツァス
Lapavitsas, Costas 790
ラハエル
Rahael, John 1149
ラバク
Labak, Alexander 779
ラバグリアティ
Rabagliati, Michel 1146
ラバゴ
Rábago, Karl R. 1146
ラバサ・ディアス
Rabasa Díaz, Enrique 1146
ラバージ
LaBerge, Stephen 779
ラパージュ
Lappage, Danielle 790
ラバース
Lubbers, Peter 849
ラパス
Lapuss, Stéphane 791
Rapace, Noomi 1157
ラパチオリ・バルトダノ
Rappaccioli Baltodano, Emilio de Jesús 1158
ラバッティ
Rabatti, Alerrandro 1146
ラバット
Labatt, Mary 779
ラバテ
Rabaté, Dominique 1146
Rabaté, Pascal 1146
ラハティ
Lahti, Louna 782
ラハテラ
Lahtela, Janne 782
Lahtela, Juuso 782
ラバード
al-Labad, Al-Mahdi Hassan 779
ラパドゥーラ
Lapadula, Gianluca 790
ラバドス・モンテス
Lavados Montes, Hugo 796
ラバトマンガ
Ravatomanga, Rolland 1161
ラバニ
Rabbani, Burhanuddin 1146
Rabbani, Muhammad 1146
Rabbani, Raza 1146
Rabbani, Salahuddin 1146
ラバニーニ
Lavanini, Tomas 796
ラバニャ
Lavagna, Roberto 796
ラバネリ
Ravanelli, Terry 1161
ラハバ
Rahbar, M.Reza 1150
ラバハ
Rabah, Sadok 1146
Rabbah, Aziz 1146
ラパポート
Rapaport, Era 1157
Rapaport, Herman 1157
Rappaport, Alfred 1158
Rappaport, Doreen 1158
Rappaport, Ivan 1158
Rappaport, Laury 1158
Rappaport, Stephen D. 1158
Rappaport, Theodore S. 1158
Rappoport, Paul N. 1158
ラパポルト
Rappoport, Xenia 1158
ラハマニ
Rahamani, Cherif 1149
Rahmani, Chérif 1150
ラハマニファズリ
Rahmani Fazli, Abdolreza 1150
ラハーマン

ラ

Rahaman, Vashanti 1149
ラハマン
Rahman, Matior 1150
Rahman, Mostafizur 1150
ラハムゥ
Rahamou, Gazobi 1150
ラハヤ
Rahaya, Hassan 1150
ラハリ
Rahali, Maroua 1149
ラバリ
Rabary, Andrianiaina Paul 1146
ラバリー
Ravelli, Louise 1161
ラバリスア
Rabarisoa, Jacky 1146
ラバリスン
Rabarison, Jacquis 1146
ラバリソン
Rabarison, Philémon 1146
ラハリマララ
Raharimalala, Marie Lydia Toto 1150
ラハリミ・アラミ
Lahlimi Alami, Ahamed 782
ラハリン
Rachlin, Julian 1147
ラハール
Rahal, Mohammed 1149
ラバール
LaBarre, Polly G. 779
ラバル
Rabal, Francisco 1146
ラーバレスティア
Larbalestier, Justine 791
ラバロマナナ
Ravalomanana, Marc 1161
ラバーン
Lauvergne, Joffrey 796
ラバン
Labben, Saloua Ayachi 779
ラバーンウェイ
Lavarnway, Ryan 796
ラハンタララウ
Rahantalalao, Henriette 1150
ラービ
Raabe, Peter B. 1146
ラビ
Rabhi, Pierre 1146
Rabii, Mohammed 1146
Ravi, Vayalar 1161
ラビー
Labie, Marc 779
Rabii, Abdessadek 1146
ラピ
Lapi, Giulia 790
ラビーア
Rabiah, Abdessadek 1146
al-Rabiah, Abdullah 1146
ラビア
al-Rabiah, Tawfeeq bin Fawzan 1146
ラビイー
Rabiei, Ali 1146
ラヒエル
Rahiel, Mustapha Karim 1150
ラピエール
Lapierre, David P. 790
Lapierre, Dominique 790
Lapierre, Fabrice 790
Lapierre, Jean-C. 790
ラビオ
Rabiot, Adrien 1147
ラピコフ
Lapikov, Dmitry 790
ラビシエ
Labissiere, Skal 779
ラビ・シャンカール
Ravi Shankar, Sri Sri 1161
ラビシャンカル
Ravishankar 1161
ラビッチ
Ravitch, Diane 1161
ラビット
Rabbitte, Pat 1146
ラピッド
Lapid, Efrayim 790
ラビディ
Laabidi, Lilia 779
Labidi, Nadia 779
Labidi, Samir 779
ラピド
Lapido, Paula Coll 790
ラピドゥス
Lapidus, Jens 790
ラピドス
Lapidus, Ted 790
ラビナ
Ravina, Mark 1161
ラビーニュ
Lavigne, Ariane 796
ラビネ
Ravinet, Jaime 1161
ラビノヴィッツ
Rabinowitz, Alan 1146
ラビノビッチ
Rabinovich, Abraham 1146
Rabinovitch, Isaac 1146
ラビブ
Labib, Adel 779
ラヒーミー
Rahimi, Atiq 1150
ラヒミ
Rahimi, Hassan 1150
Rahimi, Mohammad Asif 1150
Rahimi, Mohammad Reza 1150
ラヒム
Rahim, Tahar 1150
ラヒムゾダ
Rahimzoda, Hamro 1150
Rahimzoda, Ramazon 1150
Rahimzoda, Sharif 1150
ラヒモフ
Rahimov, Abdurahim 1150
Rahimov, Azad 1150
Rahimov, Nijat 1150
Rahimov, Rustamhodza 1150
Rahimov, Vitaliy 1150
Rakhimov, Ramazan 1152
Rakhimov, Saidakhmad 1152
ラヒモワ
Rakhimova, Regina 1152
ラビユニ
Lavillenie, Renaud 796
ラヒリ
Lahiri, Anirban 782
Lahiri, Jhumpa 782
ラピリオ
Lapilio, Joseph W., Ⅲ 790
ラビリンス
Labyrinth, Matthew 779
ラビロ
Labilo, Martin Kabwelulu 779
ラヒーン
Raheen, Sayed Makhdoom 1150
ラビーン
Lavigne, Avril 796
Lavigne, Gilles J. 796
Lavine, Zach 797
ラビン
Lavín, Joaquín 796
Lavin, Richard 797
Rabin, Susan 1146
Rabin, Trevor 1146
Ravin, Josh 1161
ラピン
Lappin, Roderick 790
ラビング
Loving, Mildred 847
ラビンドラン
Ravindran, Karthik 1161
ラフ
Raff, Gideon 1149
Raff, Murray 1149
Ruff, Matt 1215
ラブ
Cusimano, Maryann K. 310
Lab, Steven P. 779
Love, Courtney 847
Love, John E. 847
Love, Kevin 847
Love, Kyle 847
Love, Mike 847
Love, Robert W., Jr. 847
Love, Russell J. 847
Love, Scott 847
Love, Susan M. 847
Rabb, Ivan 1146
Rabb, M.E. 1146
ラーファー
Laufer, Niel 795
ラファ
Rafa, Silva 1148
ラーファイ
Laafai, Monise 779
ラファイ
Laafai, Monise 779
ラファイロフスカ
Rafajlovska, Vera 1149
ラファウ
Rafal, Rzepka 1149
ラファエウ
Rafael 1148
Rafael, Da Silva 1148
Raffael 1149
ラファエル
Lafell, Brandon 781
Rafael, Vicente L. 1149
Raphael, Beverley 1158
Raphael, Frederic Michael 1158
Raphael, John 1158
Raphael, Lev 1158
Raphael, Serge 1158
Raphael, Taffy E. 1158
Raphaell, Katrina 1158
ラファエル・ミル
Rafael Mir 1149
ラファエル・ランティグア
Rafael Lantigua, José 1149
ラファエル - レフ
Raphael-Leff, Joan 1158
ラファエロヴィッチ
Rafaelovich, Kamaile 1149
ラファエロフ
Rafaelov, Lior 1149
ラファザニス
Lafazanis, Panagiotis 781
ラファージ
La Farge, Paul 781
ラファージュ
LaFarge, Lucy 781
ラファティ
Lafferty, Raphael Aloysius 781
Rafferty, Laura 1149
ラファ・ナバーロ
Rafa Navarro 1149
ラファラン
Raffarin, Jean-Pierre 1149
ラファルグ
Lafargue, François 781
ラファルスカ
Rafalska, Elżbieta 1149
ラファロ
Ruffalo, Mark 1215
ラファロビッチ
Rafalovich, Nikita 1149
ラファロ・フェルナンデス
LaFaro-Fernandez, Helene 781
ラフィア
Lafia, Sacca 781
ラフィーヴァー
LeFever, Lee 807
ラフィーク
Rafeeq, Hamza 1149
Rafeeq, Ibrahim 1149
Rafique, Saad 1149
ラフイス
Labouisse, Eve Curie 779
ラフィダ
Rafidah, Aziz 1149
ラフィタエルナンデス
Laffita Hernandez, Andris 781
ラフィット
Laffitte, Sophie 781
Lafitte, Jacques 781
ラフィディマナナ
Rafidimanana, Narson 1149
ラフィニ
Rafini, Brigi 1149
ラフィーニャ
Rafinha 1149
ラフィーバー
LaFeber, Walter 781
ラフィーバース
LaFevers, R.L. 781
ラフィル
Raphael, D.D. 1158
ラフィン
Laffin, Christina 781
Ruffin, Jimmy 1215
ラ・フェイブ
LaFave, Kim 781
ラフェス
Rhafes, Mohammed 1175
ラフェリエール

Laferrière, Dany 781
ラフェル
Lafer, Celso 781
ラフエンテ
Lafuente, Marta 781
Pastor Lafuente, Ivan 1084
ラフォーニ
Raffoni, Melissa 1149
ラフォルグ
Lafforgue, Laurent 781
ラフォレ
Laforet, Marc 781
ラフォン
Laffont, Jean-Jacques 781
Lafont, Bernadette 781
ラ・フォンテイン
La Fontaine, Jean. Sybil 781
ラフォンテーヌ
LaFontaine, Donald 781
Lafontaine, Oskar 781
ラブガーデン
Lovegarden, Leela 847
ラブカン
Ruvkun, Gary 1220
ラブキン
Lubkin, Ilene Morof 849
Rabkin, Yakov M. 1147
ラブグロウブ
Lovegrove, Ross 847
ラブグローブ
Lovegrove, Ross 847
ラブケス
Lapkes, Dmitry 790
ラフコフ
Ravkov, Andrei A. 1161
ラフサンジャーニー
Rafsanjani, Ali Akbar Hashemi 1149
ラフサンジャニ
Rafsanjani, Ali Akbar Hashemi 1149
ラフサンジャニー
Rafsanjani, Ali Akbar Hashemi 1149
ラプジャード
Lapoujade, David 790
ラブジョイ
Lovejoy, Asara 847
Lovejoy, Thomas Eugene Ⅲ 847
ラブシン
Lovsin, Polona 847
ラブス
Labus, Miroljub 779
ラプス
Lapus, Jesli 791
ラプスリー
Lapsley, Hilary 791
Lapsley, Irvine 791
ラプスレー
Lapsley, Michael 791
ラブソン
Labson, Erick 779
ラフダル
Lakhdhar, Latifa 783
ラブチェニュク
Rabchenyuk, Anastasiya 1146
ラープチャルーンサップ
Lapcharoensap, Rattawut 790
ラプチャルンサプ
Lapcharoensap, Rattawut 790
ラブツカ
Labucka, Ingrida 779
ラブティア
Ravutia, Albert 1161
ラフード
Lahood, Ray 782
Lahoud, Emile 782
ラブトゥアリスン
Rabotoarison, Charles Sylvain 1147
ラフトス
Raftos, Peter 1149
ラプトン
Lupton, Ellen 854
Lupton, Rosamund 854
Lupton, Simon 854
ラフニト
Lachnit, Petr 780
ラブニャク
Ravnjak, Tim-Kevin 1161
ラプノー
Rappeneau, Jean-Paul 1158
ラブーフ
Labeouf, Shia 779
ラブフェッティ
Rabuffetti, Clementina 1147
ラフーマ
Rahoma, Masood 1150
ラフマット
Rahmat, Gobel 1150
ラフマティ
Rahmati, Mohammad 1150
ラフマトフ
Rahmatov, Tursun 1150
ラフマナリエフ
Rakhmanaliev, Rustan 1152
ラブマナンジャラ
Rabémananjara, Jacques 1146
ラフマノフ
Rakhmanov, Akmamed 1152
ラフマン
Rahman, Abdul 1150
ラフモノフ
Rahmonov, Uktamjon 1150
Rakhmonov, Abbos 1152
Rakhmonov, Abdujabbor 1152
ラフモン
Rakhmon, Emomali 1152
ラフューズ
Rafuse, Erin 1149
ラフラー
Löffler, Elke 839
ラブラダ
Labrada, Yanelis 779
ラブラブ
Lavulavu, Etuate 797
ラブランク
LaBlanc, Tom 779
ラフランス
LaFrance, Marianne 781
LaFrance, Mary 781
ラプランテ
LaPlante, Debi A. 790
ラプラント
LaPlante, Alice 790
ラフーリ
Rahouli, Baya 1150
ラフリー
Lafley, Alan G. 781
LaFree, Gary 781
Loughery, John 846
ラブリー
Lovely, Deborah 847
ラプリ
Lapli, John Ini 790
ラブリノビッチ
Lavrinovich, Oleksandr 797
Lavrynovych, Oleksandr 797
ラフリン
Laughlin, Greg 795
Laughlin, Richard 795
Laughlin, Robert B. 795
Loughlin, Martin 846
Rakhlin, Anatolii 1152
ラフル
Raful, Tony 1149
ラブル
Rabl, Walter 1147
ラフルーア
LaFleur, Suzanne 781
LaFleur, William R. 781
ラーブル・シュタットラー
Rabl-stadler, Helga 1147
ラブルース
Labrousse, Alain 779
ラブルス
Labrousse, Robert 779
ラブレイス
Lovelace, Linda 847
ラプレヴォット
Laprevotte, Charles-Elie 791
ラブレク
LaBrecque, Jennifer 779
ラブレース
Lovelace, Linda 847
Lovelace, Merline 847
ラブレス
Loveless, Avril 847
Loveless, Cheri 847
Loveless, Patty 847
ラブロ
Labro, Philippe 779
Ravulo, Malakai 1161
ラブロック
Lovelock, Christopher H. 847
Lovelock, James Ephraim 847
ラプロビットラ
Laprovittola, Nicolas 791
ラブロフ
Lavrov, Sergei Viktorovich 797
ラブロワ
Lavrova, Olga 797
ラーベ
Rabbe, Max 1146
Rabe, Hubertus 1146
ラヘ
Lage, Carlos 781
ラベ
Labbé, Brigitte 779
Labé, Louise 779
Rabbe, Luis 1146
ラペー
Rapee, Ronald M. 1157
ラヘイ
LaHaye, Tim 782
ラベイ
Rabei, Carolina 1146
ラペイル
Lapeyre, Patrick 790
ラペサ
Lapesa, Rafael 790
ラベサハラ
Rabesahala, Henri 1146
ラヘ・ダビラ
Lage, Carlos 781
ラベッチ
Ravetch, Irving 1161
ラベッツ
Ravetz, Jerome Raymond 1161
ラベッツァリ
Lavezzari, Fabrizio 796
ラベット
Lovett, Charlie 847
Lovett, Joan 847
Lovett, Marsha C. 847
ラペッリ
Rapelli, Paola 1157
ラベド
Labed, Ariane 779
ラベニリナ
Rabenirina, Jean Jacques 1146
ラヘブ
Raheb, Mitri 1150
ラベフ
Rabeh, Sadok 1146
ラベマアウ
Lavemaau, Tevita 796
ラベマナンジャラ
Rabemananjara, Charles 1146
Rabémananjara, Jacques 1146
ラベライス
Rabelais, Manuel António 1146
ラベラスカラモジーノ
Ravera-scaramozzino, Elodie 1161
ラベール
Labère, Nelly 779
ラベル
Lovell, Bernard 847
Lovell, Harold 847
Lovell, Mary S. 847
Lovell, Winifred 847
ラペール
Lapeyre, Emilie 790
Lapeyre, Frédéric 790
ラベルアリジョナ
Raveloarijaona, Marcel 1161
ラペレ
Lapeyre, Walter 790
ラベロナリボ
Ravelonarivo, Jean 1161
Ravelonarivo, Julien Laporte 1161
ラベロハリソン
Raveloharison, Herilanto 1161
ラベロマナナ
Ravalomanana, Marc 1161

ラ

ラベロマナンツア
Ravelomanantsoa, Elia 1161
ラベンスクロフト
Ravenscroft, Linda 1161
ラボ
Labo, Abdou 779
ラボーア
Laboa, Juan María 779
ラホイ
Rajoy Brey, Mariano 1152
ラホイブレイ
Rajoy Brey, Mariano 1152
ラホウニク
Lahovnik, Matej 782
ラホウル
Lahouel, Ridha 782
ラボーダン
Lavaudant, Georges 796
ラボート
Labourt, Jairo 779
ラボード
Laborde, Genie Z. 779
ラボフ
LaBouff, Jackie 779
ラボフスキー
Hrabovsky, George 629
ラポフスキー
Lapovsky, Lucie 790
ラポポート
Rapoport, Amos 1158
ラボリ
Laborie, Francoise 779
ラポルタ
La Porta, Sandra 790
ラボルデ
Laborde, Yurisel 779
ラポルテ
Laporte, Aymeric 790
Laporte, Julien Ravelonarivo 790
ラポルト
Laporte, Pierre 790
Laporte, Roger 790
ラホルム
Raholm, Maj-Britt 1150
ラポワント
Lapointe, Eugène 790
ラボーン
Labone, Brian 779
ラポンシュ
Laponche, Bernard 790
ラマ
Lama, Edouard Gnankoye 784
Lama, Teófilo 784
Lamah, Edouard Gnankoye 784
Lamah, Rémy 784
Rama, Edi 1153
Rama, Luan 1153
ラマー
Lamar, Kendrick 784
Lamarre, Daniel 784
Lammer, Kerstin 785
ラマ・S.
Lama S., R.Eduardo 784
ラマイリ
Ramaili, Mannete 1153
ラーマイル
Rameil, Udo 1154
ラマクリシュナ
Ramkrishna, Chitra 1154
ラーマクリシュナン
Ramakrishnan, P.S. 1153
ラマクリシュナン
Ramakrishnan, Niranjan 1153
Ramakrishnan, Venkatraman 1153
ラマザニ
Ramazani, Emmanuel 1153
ラマザニ・バヤ
Ramazani Baya, Raymond 1153
ラマザノグル
Ramazanoglu, Caroline 1153
ラマザノフ
Ramazanov, Murad 1153
ラマザン
Ramazan, Ayvalli 1153
ラマザンオール
Ramazanoğlu, Sema 1153
ラマ・スールヤ・ダス
Surya Das 1368
ラマスワミ
Ramaswamy, Venkatram 1153
Ramaswamy, Vivek 1153
ラマダー
Ramadhar, Prakash 1153
ラマダーシン
Ramadharsingh, Glenn 1153
ラマダネ
Ramadane, Abakar 1153
ラマダン
Ramadan, Fatime Issa 1153
Ramadan, Noël 1153
Ramadan, Samah 1153
Ramadan, Taha Yassin 1153
Ramadane, Fatime Issa 1153
ラマダンイブラヒム
Ramadan Ibrahim, Ibrahim 1153
ラマダンモハメド
Ramadan Mohamed, Nahla 1153
ラマーチ
LaMarche, Jeff 784
ラマチャンドラン
Ramachandran, A. 1153
Ramachandran, Rama 1153
Ramachandran, Vilayanur S. 1153
ラマディエ
Ramadier, Cédric 1153
ラマート
Lammert, Norbert 785
ラマトフ
Ramatov, Achilbay 1153
ラマトラペン
Ramatlapeng, Mphu 1153
ラマトロディ
Ramatlhodi, Ngoako 1153
ラマナ
Lamanna, Franco 784
Ramanna, Raja 1153
ラマナウスカス
Ramanauskas, Edvinas 1153
ラマナンツァ
Ramanantsoa, Herivelona 1153
ラマナンツア
Ramanantsoa, Benjamina Ramarcel 1153
ラマナンツォア
Ramanantsoa, Ramarcel Benjamina 1153
ラマナンテナソア
Ramanantenasoa, Noëline 1153
ラマナントソア
Ramanantsoa, Jean Rodolphe 1153
ラーマニ
Rrahmani, Imet 1213
ラマポーザ
Ramaphosa, Cyril 1153
ラマムラ
Lamamra, Ramtane 784
ラマモンジソア
Ramamonjisoa, Virapin 1153
ラマラソン
Ramalason, Olga 1153
ラマーリョ
Ramalho, Andre 1153
ラマール
Lamarre, Kim 784
Lamarre, Ryan 784
Lamarre, Thomas 784
ラマルシェ
LaMarche, Jim 784
ラマルソン
Ramaroson, Olga 1153
ラマレイ
Ramaley, Judith A. 1153
ラマ・ロサン・ガンワン
Lobsang Ngawang 838
ラマロソン
Ramaroson, Nadine 1153
ラーマン
Larman, Craig 791
Lerman, Rory S. 815
Lerman, Stewart 815
Luhrmann, Baz 851
Rahman, Abdul 1150
Rahman, A.R. 1150
Rahman, Hasim 1150
Rahman, Mustafizur 1150
Rahman, Najeeb. Abdur 1150
Rahman, Saifur M. 1150
Rahman, Salifur M. 1150
Rahman, Shamsur 1150
Rahman, Zillur 1150
Raman, Sengadu Abbu Pattabi 1153
ラマン
Raman, Anand P. 1153
ラマンディンビアリスン
Ramandimbiarison, Zaza Manitranja 1153
ラマンナ
Lamanna, Eugenio 784
LaManna, Ross 784
Ramanna, Raja 1153
ラミ
Rami, Adil 1154
ラミー
Lamy, Pascal 786
ラミアラマナナ
Ramiaramanana, Patrick 1154
ラミィ
Lamy, Matthew 786
ラミザナ
Lamizana, Mariam 785
ラミー・シャプイ
Lamy Chappuis, Jason 786
ラミーシャプイ
Lamy Chappuis, Jason 786
ラミス
Lummis, Douglas 852
Ramis, Ivan 1154
ラミッド
Ramid, Mustafa 1154
ラミド
Lamido, Sule 785
ラミニー
Larminie, James 791
ラミネ・ゼイン
Lamine Zeine, Ali Mahamane 785
ラミレス
Ramírez, Augusto 1154
Ramirez, Bruno 1154
Ramirez, Cristina 1154
Ramírez, Edgardo 1154
Ramirez, Erasmo 1154
Ramirez, Gaston 1154
Ramirez, Hanley 1154
Ramirez, Harold 1154
Ramirez, J.C. 1154
Ramirez, Jose 1154
Ramírez, Luis 1154
Ramirez, Manny 1154
Ramírez, Marta 1154
Ramirez, Noe 1154
Ramírez, Patricia 1154
Ramírez, Rafael 1154
Ramirez, Robeisy 1154
Ramirez, Sara 1154
Ramirez, Yefrey 1154
Ramírez Mercado, Sergio 1154
ラミレズ
Ramirez, Matthew 1154
ラミレス・アクニャ
Ramírez Acuña, Francisco Javier 1154
ラミレスジェペス
Ramirez Yepes, Carlos Alberto 1154
ラミレス・デリンコン
Ramírez de Rincón, Martha Lucía 1154
ラミレス・ノゲラ
Ramírez Noguera, Glenda Auxiliadora 1154
ラミレス・マリン
Ramírez Marín, Jorge Carlos 1154
ラミレス・メルカド
Ramírez Mercado, Marcia Petrona 1154
ラミレス・ランダベルデ
Ramírez Landaverde, Mauricio Ernesto 1154
ラミレス・レスカノ
Ramírez Lezcano, Rubén 1154
ラミン
Lamin, Make 785
Lamine, Issa 785
Ramin, Cathryn Jakobson 1154
Ramin, Obaidullah 1154

ラミン・ゼイン
Lamine Zeine, Ali Mahamane 785
ラミンヌ
Lamine, Affoussiata Bamba 785
ラーム
Lahm, Philipp 782
ラム
Lam, Akol 784
Lam, Aubrey 784
Lam, Carrie 784
Lam, Dante 784
Lam, Debra 784
Lam, Dominic H. 784
Lam, Gabriel Duop 784
Lam, Gladys S.W. 784
Lam, Jack 784
Lam, James 784
Lam, Kai Shue 784
Lam, Kam Chuen 784
Lam, Monica S. 784
Lam, N.Mark 784
Lam, Paul 784
Lam, Sandy 784
Lam, Sui-Lun 784
Lam, Thi My Da 784
Lam, Tin Yu 784
Lam, To 784
Lam, Vanessa 784
Lam, Vincent 784
Lam, Willy Wo-Lap 784
Lamb, Albert 784
Lamb, Braden 784
Lamb, Christina 784
Lamb, Christopher 784
Lamb, Gillian 784
Lamb, Jake 784
Lamb, Jeremy 784
Lamb, John 784
Lamb, John J. 784
Lamb, Linda 784
Lamb, Marjorie 784
Lamb, Roberta 784
Lamb, Roger 784
Lamb, Sandra 784
Lamb, Simon 785
Lamb, Wally 785
Lamb, Willis Eugene, Jr. 785
Lamm, Gina 785
Lamm, Kendall 785
Lamou, Alice 786
Lum, Kate 852
Ram, Andi 1153
Ram, Jack 1153
Ram, Rajeev 1153
Ramm, Alexander 1154
ラムーア
Lamur, Emmanuel 786
ラムゥニ・ベンヒーダ
Rahmouni Benhida, Bouchra 1150
ラムグーラム
Ramgoolam, Navinchandra 1154
Ramgoolam, Rudrawatee 1154
ラムグラーム
Ramgoolam, Navinchandra 1154
ラムサ
Ramtha 1155
ラムザイヤー
Ramseyer, J.Mark 1155
ラムザウアー
Ramsauer, Peter 1155
ラムサミー
Ramsammy, Leslie 1155
ラムサラン
Ramsaran, Bheri 1155
Ramsaran, Manohar 1155
ラムサン
Ramthun, Bonnie 1155
ラムジ
Ramzi, Rashid 1155
ラムジー
Ramsey, Aaron 1155
Ramsey, Benjamin 1155
Ramsey, Dave 1155
Ramsey, Norman Foster 1155
ラムジャッタン
Ramjattan, Khemraj 1154
ラムスタイン
Ramstein, Anne-Margot 1155
ラムステッター
Ramstetter, Eric D. 1155
ラムスデン
Ramsden, Frank 1155
ラムズデン
Ramsden, Paul 1155
ラムスドルフ
Lambsdorff, Otto Graf 785
ラムズドン
Lumsdon, Les 853
ラムズフェルド
Rumsfeld, Donald 1217
ラムズボサム
Ramsbotham, Oliver 1155
ラムゼー
Ramsey, Norman Foster 1155
ラムゼイ
Ramsay, Anna 1155
Ramsay, Ansil 1155
Ramsay, Gordon 1155
Ramsay, J.Russell 1155
Ramsey, Jalen 1155
Ramsey, Norman Foster 1155
ラムゼス
Ramzes, Vadim 1155
ラムセラール
Ramselaar, Bart 1155
ラムソン
Ramson, Charles 1155
ラム・ダス
Ram Dass 1154
ラムダス
Ramdass, Motee 1154
ラムディン
Lambdin, Dewey 785
ラムドス
Ramdoss, Anbumani 1154
ラムナライン
Ramnarine, Kevin 1154
ラムバー
Lambaa, Sambuugiin 785
ラムバート
Lambert, Margaret Bergman 785
ラムバリー
Rambally, Menissa 1153
ラムビー
Lambie, Rosemary 785
ラムファルシー
Lamfalussy, Alexandre 785
ラムボ
Lambo, Eyitayo 785
ラムマラ
Lamamra, Ramtane 784
ラムラー
Ramler, Siegfried 1154
ラムラス
Lamlas, Abdullah Salem 785
ラムラル
Ramlall, Vishva 1154
ラムリ
Ramli, Rizal 1154
ラムール
Lammle, Todd 785
Lamour, Catherine 786
Lamour, Jean-François 786
ラムル
Rummel, Rudolph J. 1216
ラムルー
Lamoureux, Justin 786
ラムール＝クロッシェ
Lamour-Crochet, Céline 786
ラムルム
Lamloum, Olfa 785
ラムレイ
Lumley, Brian 852
ラムローガン
Ramlogan, Anand 1154
ラーメ
Rame, Franca 1154
ラメ
Lame, Ibrahim 785
ラメイヒュー
Lemahieu, DJ. 811
ラメシュ
Ramesh, Jairam 1154
ラメーズ
Lamaze, Eric 784
ラメゾン
Lamaison, Pierre 784
ラメラ
Lamela, Erik 785
ラメル
Ramel, Charlotte 1154
ラメルティンク
Lammertink, Ilona 785
ラメンクーサ
Lamancusa, Kathy 784
ラモ
Rammo, Karl-Martin 1154
Ramo, Joshua Cooper 1154
Ramo, Simon 1154
Ramos, Mario 1155
ラモー
Ramo, Simon 1154
ラーモア
Larmore, Jennifer 791
ラモシテル
Lamositele, Titi 786
ラモス
Ramos, Adrian 1155
Ramos, A.J. 1155
Ramos, Americo d'Oliveira Dos 1155
Ramos, Arlindo 1155
Ramos, Basílio Mosso 1155
Ramos, Edubray 1155
Ramos, Fidel Valdez 1155
Ramos, Humberto 1155
Ramos, Joana 1155
Ramos, José Reis da Silva 1155
Ramos, Juan Antonio 1155
Ramos, Manuel Salvador Dos 1155
Ramos, Pablo Marcial Ortiz 1155
Ramos, Rogelio 1155
Ramos, Tommy 1155
Ramos, Vitorino 1155
Ramos, Wilmer 1155
Ramos, Wilson 1155
Ramos-vinolas, Albert 1155
ラモスポーキ
Ramos-Poqui, Guillem 1155
ラモス・ホルタ
Ramos-Horta, José 1155
ラモス・マルティネス
Ramos Martínez, Rogelio 1155
ラモス・モラレス
Ramos Morales, Ana Verónica 1155
ラモター
Ramotar, Donald 1155
ラモット
Lamothe, Laurent Salvador 786
Lamott, Anne 786
Lamotte, E. 786
ラモトケ
Lamotke, Klaus 786
ラモネ
Ramonet, Ignacio 1155
ラモネダ
Ramoneda, Arturo M. 1155
ラモノフ
Ramonov, Murat 1155
Ramonov, Soslan 1155
ラモノワ
Lamonova, Evgeniya 786
ラモリナラ
LaMolinara, Anthony 785
ラモワン
Ramoin, Tony 1154
ラモーン
Ramone, Dee Dee 1155
Ramone, Joey 1155
Ramone, Johnny 1155
Ramone, Phil 1155
Ramone, Tommy 1155
ラモン
Ramon, Elisa 1154
Ramon, Haim 1154
Ramon, Ilan 1154
ラモン・コルテス
Ramon-Cortés, Ferran 1155
ラモンターニュ
Lamontagne, André 786
LaMontange, Ray 786
ラモント
Lamont, Alexandra 786
Lamont, Ann 786
Lamont, Gene 786
Lamont, Priscilla 786
Lamont, Sean 786
ラヤ
Raja, Allar 1151
ラヤトン
Rajaton 1152
ラヤマキ
Rajamäki, Kari 1151

ラヤマジ
Rayamajhi, Top Bahadur 1162
ラヤラ
Rajala, Kari 1151
ラユネン
Lajunen, Samppa 783
ラーラ
Lara, Adair 791
ララ
Lara, Saúl Octavio 791
Lara, Willian 791
Rare, Mohamed Ould Ahmed Salem Ould Mohamed 1158
ララ・アイシャ
Princess Lalla Aicha 783
ララィア
Laraia, Michele T. 791
ララィズ
Laaraidh, Ali 779
ラライン
Larraín, Felipe 791
Larraín, Pablo 791
ララキ
Laraki, Azeddine 791
ララサバル・コルドバ
Larrazabal Córdova, Hernando 792
ララズ
Larraz, Pepe 792
ララーナ
Lallana, Adam 783
ララナーガ
Larranaga, Jay 792
ララニ
Lalani, Amina 783
ララニャガ
Larrañaga, Ignacio 792
Martín Larrañaga, Ana 912
ララネーガ
Larranaga, Jim 792
ララハリサイナ
Lalaharisaina, Joéli Valérien 783
ララビー
Larrabee, Michael 791
ララ・フェルナンデス
Lara Fernández, Benito Antonio 791
ララ・ボナムナ
Lalah Bonamna, Bernard 783
ラランバラブ
Lalabalavu, Ratu Naiqama 783
ラーリ
Lari, Emilio 791
ラリー
Lally, Tom 784
Lari, S.Mujtaba Musavi 791
Larry, H.I. 792
ラリアー
Larrier, Terry 792
ラリエフ
Laliyev, Gennadiy 783
ラリオティス
Laliotis, Konstantinos 783
ラリオノフ
Larionov, Dmitry 791
Larionov, Yuri 791
ラリオノワ
Larionova, Yekaterina 791
ラリーサ・フランカ
Larissa Franca 791
ラリジャニ
Larijani, Ali 791
ラリス
Rallis, Georgios 1153
ラリソン
Ralison, Alphonse 1153
ラリソンラマロソン
Rarison Ramaroson, Hyppolite 1158
ラーリッグ
Rahrig, Collin 1150
ラリック
Lalich, Janja 783
Lalique, Marie-Claude 783
ラリバ
Lariba, Ian 791
ラリバテ
Laliberté, Guy 783
ラリベルテ
Laliberté, Guy 783
ラ・ルー
Roux, La 1211
ラール
Laar, Mart 779
Lahr, Gerhard 782
Rahl, Leslie 1150
ラル
Lal, Vikram 783
Lall, Kellawan 783
Lalle, Tankpadja 784
ラルー
Laloux, René 784
Larue, Mitcy 793
ラルヴォヴァー
Larvore, Emilie 793
ラルエル
Laruelle, Sabine 793
ラルガエスパダ・フレデルスドルフ
Largaespada Fredersdorff, Carmen 791
ラルカカ
Lalkaka, Rustam 783
ラルコ
Larco Cox, Guillermo 791
ラルゴ
Largo, Michael 791
ラルコ・コックス
Larco Cox, Guillermo 791
ラ・ルーサ
La Russa, Tony 793
ラルーサ
La Russa, Tony 793
ラルーシ
Laroussi, Chadli 791
ラルシェ
Larcher, Gérard 791
ラルーシュ
LaRouche, Lyndon H. 791
ラルストン
Ralston, Aron 1153
ラルセン
Larsen, Alex 792
Larsen, Christian 792
Larsen, Eirik Veraas 792
Larsen, Timothy 792
ラールソン
Larsson, Asa 792
Larsson, Stieg 793
ラルソン
Larsson, Asa 792
Larsson, Stieg 793
ラルッサ
La Russa, Ignazio 793
La Russa, Tony 793
ラルテギー
Lartéguy, Jean 793
ラールテ・ヘール
Raalte-Geel, Henriette van 1146
ラルデユエト
Larduet Gomez, Jose 791
ラルドゥエト
Larduet, Manrique 791
ラルドロ
Lardreau, Suzanne 791
ラルフ
Ralph, Derry 1153
Ralph, LeAnn 1153
ラルベス
Rahlves, Daron 1150
ラルヘル
Larcher, W. 791
ラルレット
Larroulet, Cristián 792
ラレ
Lalle, Tankpadja 784
ラレア
Larrea, Gustavo 792
Larrea, Lídice 792
Larrea, Pablo 792
ラレイン
Larrain, Sara 792
ラレカ
Laleka, Abdul Sattar 783
ラレンコフ
Lalenkov, Yevgeny 783
ラロ
Laleau, Wilson 783
ラロー
Lareau, Annette 791
ラロウレ
Larroulet, Cristián 792
ラロクエット
Larroquette, John 792
ラローサ
Larosa, Lewis 791
ラロシェル
LaRochelle, David 791
ラロジャ
Laloggia, Enrico 784
ラロシュ
Laroche, Robert de 791
ラロース
Larose, Peter 791
ラローチャ
Larrocha, Alicia de 792
ラロツィア
Ralotsia, Patrick Pule 1153
ラロッカ
Larroca, Salvador 792
ラロック
LaRoche, Catherine 791
Laroque, François 791
ラロッシュ
Laroche, Agnès 791
Laroche, Giles 791
ラロバ
Lalova, Ivet 784
ラロバッツ
Lalovac, Boris 784
ラロビッチ
Lalović, Slobodan 784
ラロワコリオ
Lalova-collio, Ivet 784
ラロンデ
Lalonde, Genevieve 784
ラロンド
Laronde, André 791
ラワット
Rawat, Harish 1161
Rawat, Prem 1161
ラワト
Rawat, Harish 1161
ラワニ
Lawani, Soule Mana 797
ラワル
Lawal, Amadou 797
Lawal, Hassan M. 797
Lawal, Lukeman 797
Rawal, Bhim Bahadur 1161
ラワンドゥジ
Rawanduzi, Firyad 1161
ラーン
Rahn, Helmut 1150
ラン
Laeng, Danielle 781
l'Ain, Alix Girod de 782
Lam, Peter 784
Lang, Lang 788
Lang, Ping 788
Lun, Desmond Sui 853
Lunn, Martin 853
ランヴィル
Rainville, Claudia 1151
ランガ
Langa, Andrew 788
Langa, Castigo 788
ランガー
Langer, Bernhard 789
Langer, Ellen J. 789
Langer, Helmut 789
Langer, Robert Samuel 789
Langr, Jeff 789
ランカス
Lankas, Aurimas 789
ランカスター
Lancaster, Stuart 786
Lancaster, Tony 786
ランガット
Langat, Nancy Jebet 788
ランガート
Rangert, Bo 1157
ランカトーレ
Rancatore, Désirée 1156
ランガネー
Langaney, André 788
ランガム
Wrangham, Richard W. 1527
ランガー＝ローザ
Langer-Rosa, Marina 789
ランガン
Langan, Ruth 788
Rangan, V.Kasturi 1157
ラーンキ
Ránki, Dezsö 1157
ランギエリ
Ranghieri, Alex 1157
ランキャラニ
Lankarani, Kamran

Bagheri 789
ランキン
Rankin, Arthur, Jr. 1157
Rankin, Casey 1157
Rankin, Ian 1157
Rankin, Kenny 1157
Rankin, Kyle 1157
Rankin, Laura 1157
Rankin, Lissa 1157
Rankin, Marianne 1157
Rankin, Nicholas 1157
Rankin, Robert 1157
Rankin, Robert A. 1157
ランギンギア
Ragiagia, Mataiasi Vave 1149
ランキンズ
Rankins, Sheldon 1157
ラング
Laing, Dave 782
Laing, Jennifer 782
Laing, Lloyd Robert 782
Lang, Alan R. 788
Lang, Antonio 788
Lang, Bernhard 788
Lang, David 788
Lang, Florian 788
Lang, Gladys E. 788
Lang, Glenna 788
Lang, Gregory E. 788
Lang, Jack 788
Lang, Jochen von 788
Lang, Jonny 788
Lang, J.Stephen 788
Lang, Kimberly 788
Lang, Klaus 788
Lang, Kurt 788
Lang, Meagan 788
Lang, Michael 788
Lang, Noël 788
Lang, Norma M. 788
Lang, Paul 788
Lang, Reg 788
Lang, Rein 788
Lang, Robert J. 788
Lang, Serge 788
Lang, Susan S. 788
Lang, Thomas Allen 788
Lang, Tim 788
Lang, T.J. 788
Lang, Wes 788
Lange, Gerry 788
Lange, Hope 788
Lange, Jessica Phyllis 788
Lange, Larry 788
Lange, Paul 788
Rang, H.P. 1157
ラングカンプ
Langkamp, Sebastian 789
ランクシア
Lankshear, Colin 789
ラングース
Langguth, Berthold 789
ラングスタッフ
Langstaff, John 789
ラングストン
Langston, Laura 789
ラングデル
Langdell, Joseph 788
ラングドリッジ
Langdridge, Darren 788
ランクトン
Lankton, Stephen R. 789
ラングトン
Langton, Calvin 789
Langton, Cleve 789
Langton, Jane 789
ラングナー
Langner, Tilman 789
Langner, Wolfgang Klein 789
ラングバド
Langvad, Annika 789
ランクフォード
Lankford, Raye 789
Lankford, Terrill 789
ラングフォード
Langford, Carol Mae 789
Langford, David 789
Langford, Jeremy 789
Langford, Joseph 789
Langford, Kendall 789
Langford, Paul 789
Langford, Ryan 789
ラングマイヤー
Langemeier, Loral 788
ラングミューアー
Langmuir, Charles Herbert 789
ラングミュア
Langmuir, Erika 789
ラングーラム
Ramgoolam, Navinchandra 1154
ラングリー
Langley, Andrew 789
Langley, Myrtle 789
Langley, Winston 789
ラングリッジ
Langridge, Matt 789
Langridge, Roger 789
ラングリッシュ
Langrish, Katherine 789
ランクル
Rankle, Theadora Van 1157
ラングレー
Langley, Bob 789
Langley, Donna 789
Langley, J.L. 789
Langley, Jonathan 789
ラングレィ
Langley, Ann 789
ラングレイ
Langley, Noel 789
ラングレン
Lundgren, Dolph 853
Rundgren, Todd 1217
ランクロ
Lenclos, Jean-Philippe 812
ラングロワ
Langlois, Richard Normand 789
ランゲ
Lange, Andre 788
Lange, Klaus 788
Lange, Matthias 788
Lange, Santiago 788
Lange, Sten 788
Lange, Yago 788
Runge, Val M. 1217
ランゲーアンエンベルク
Langehanenberg, Helen 788
ランゲビーシュ
Langewiesche, Wolfgang 789
ランゲベック
Langebaek, Rikke 788
ランゲラ
Langella, Frank 788
ランゲル
Langer, Ivan 789
ランゲン
Langen, Annette 788
Langen, Christoph 789
ランゲンハン
Langenhan, Andi 789
ランコフ
Lankov, Andrei 789
ランサ
Lanza, A.Stephen 790
ランザ
Lanza, Robert Paul 790
ランザック
Lanzac, Abel 790
ランサム
Ransom, David 1157
Ransom, Stephen 1157
Ransome, James E. 1157
ランジアナザリ
Randrianazary 1156
ランジアフェノ
Randriafeno, Tolotrandry Rajo Daniella 1156
ランジアマナンツア
Randriamanantsoa, Tabera 1156
ランジアマンドラント
Randriamandranto, Ihanta 1156
ランジアリマナナ
Randriarimanana, Harison Edmond 1156
ランジアンジャトボ
Randrianjatovo, Henri François Victor 1156
ランシェ
Lanchais, Aurelie 786
ランシエ
Lanssiers, Hubert 790
ランジェ
Lange, Billy 788
ランジェバ
Ranjeva, Marcel 1157
ランジェラ
Langella, Frank 788
ランシェール
Lanssiers, Hubert 790
ランシエール
Lanssiers, Hubert 790
Rancière, Jacques 1156
ランジェル
Rangel, Doris 1157
ランシナ
Lancina, Michèle 786
ランシーニ
Lanzini, Manuel 790
ランジバー
Ranjbar, Amir S. 1157
ランジバスン
Ranjivason, Théodore 1157
ランジバソン
Ranjivason, Jean Theodore 1157
ランジャトエリナ
Ranjatoelina, Rolland 1157
ランジュニュー＝ヴィヤール
Langenieux-Villard, Philippe 789
ランジュバン
Langevin, Mary 789
ランシュブルグ
Ranschburg, Jenó 1157
ランシング
Lansing, Margaret D. 789
Lansing, Sherry 790
ランス
Lance, Steve 786
Rance, Joseph 1156
Rheims, Bettina 1175
ランスキー
Lansky, Bruce 790
Lansky, Vicki 790
ランズデール
Lansdale, Joe R. 789
ランストーム
Ranstrom, Gail 1157
ランズバーグ
Landsberg, Max 787
Landsburg, Steven E. 787
ランスフォード
Lunsford, John 853
Lunsford, Seleste E. 853
ランズベリー
Lansbury, Angela 789
ランズベルギス
Landsbergis, Vytautas 787
ランズマン
Lanzmann, Claude 790
ランズリー
Lansley, Andrew 790
ランズレイ
Ransley, Joan K. 1157
ランスロ
Lancelot, Jacques 786
ランセリオ
Lancerio, Jerónimo 786
ランセル
Laenser, Mohand 781
ランソン
Lançon, Bertrand 786
Ransom, Jeanie Franz 1157
ランダ
Landa, Alfredo 786
Landa, Norbert 786
ランダー
Lander, Christian 786
Lander, Guy P. 786
Lander, Jared P. 786
Lander, Suzanne 786
ランダイト
Landuyt, Renaat 787
ランダウ
Landau, Rudolf 786
Landau, Sigalit 786
Landau, Uzi 786
ランダース
Landers, Ann 786
Landers, Karen Baker 786
Landers, Kirk 787
Landers, Rick 787
Randers, Jorgen 1156
ランダーズ
Landers, Ann 786
ランダソ
Randazzo, Aníbal Florencio 1156
ランダホ
Landajo, Martin 786
ランダル
Randall, Lisa 1156
Randall, Mac 1156

ラ

ランチェスター
Lanchester, John 786
ランチェッティ
Lancetti, Pino 786
ランチベリー
Lanchbery, John Arthur 786
ランチョン
Luncheon, Roger 853
ランツ
Lentz, Thierry 813
Luntz, Frank I. 853
ランツァ
Lanza, Fabrizia 790
ランツェッタ
Lanzetta, Maria Carmela 790
ランツォ
Rantšo, Keketso 1157
ランツベルギス
Landsbergis, Vytautas 787
ランディ
Landi, Teri 787
Landy, Derek 787
Landy, Marcia 787
Lunde, Ken 853
Lunde, Paul 853
Lundy, Miranda 853
ランデイ
Landay, William 786
ランティグア
Lantigua, José Rafael 790
ランティシ
al-Rantissi, Abdel Aziz 1157
ランディージ
Randisi, Robert J. 1156
ランティス
Lantis, Jeffrey S. 790
ランディス
Landis, Geoffrey A. 787
Landis, Jill Marie 787
Landis, John 787
ランティモス
Lanthimos, Yorgos 790
ランディン
Lundin, Stephen C. 853
ランティング
Lanting, Frans 790
ランディンビソア
Randimbisoa, Blaise Richard 1156
ランデス
Landes, David S. 787
Landes, Jimmy 787
ランデルティンガー
Landertinger, Dominik 787
ランデルマン
Randleman, Kevin 1156
ラント
Land, Haus 786
ランド
Land, Brad 786
Land, Fiona 786
Land, Harold 786
Land, Jonathan 786
Lando, Amir 787
Lund, John 853
Lund, Nick 853
Lund, Zachary 853
Rand, Ann 1156
Rand, Casey 1156
Rand, Harry 1156
Rand, Mailis 1156
Rand, Nicholas Thomas 1156
Rando, Caterina 1156
ランドー
Landau, Elaine 786
Landau, Jennifer 786
Landau, Jon 786
Landau, Martin 786
Landau, Neil 786
Lando, Ole 787
ランドウ
Landau, Sidney I. 786
Landow, George P. 787
ランドガーテン
Landgarten, Helen B. 787
ランドクウィスト
Landquist, Kristine 787
ランドグレン
Lundgren, Dolph 853
Lundgren, Tobias 853
ラントス
Lantos, Tom 790
ランドストローム
Landström, Olof 787
ランドバーグ
Lundberg, Paul 853
Lundburg, Leila 853
ランドバール
Randver, Rein 1156
ランド・ブルックス
Brooks, Rand 187
ランドベル
Landver, Sofa 787
ランド＝ポランコ
Land-Polanco, Sharli 787
ランドホルム
Lundholm, Russell James 853
ランドマン
Landman, Tanya 787
Landmann, Bimba 787
ラントラートフ
Lantrotov, Vladislav 790
ランドラム
Landrum, Chris 787
ラントリー
Lantry, Eileen E. 790
ランドリー
Landry, Charles 787
Landry, Dave S. 787
Landry, Jarvis 787
ランドリアナンビニナ
Randrianambinina, Alfonse 1156
ランドリアマンピオノナ
Randriamampionona, Rolland 1156
ランドリアリマナナ
Randriarimanana, Harison 1156
ランドリュー
Landrieu, François 787
ランドール
Randall, Connor 1156
Randall, Damarious 1156
Randall, Kikkan 1156
Randall, Lisa 1156
Randall, Ronne 1156
Randall, Tony 1156
Randall, William T. 1156
ランドル
Randal, Jude 1156
Randall, Peter 1156
Randle, Chasson 1156
Randle, John H. 1156
Randle, Julius 1156
Randle, Michael 1156
Randle, Rueben 1156
Randle, Yvonne 1156
ランドルス
Landrus, Matthew Hayden 787
ランドルズ
Randles, Jenny 1156
ランドルフ
Randolph, Boots 1156
Randolph, Brian 1156
Randolph, Darren 1156
Randolph, Elizabeth 1156
Randolph, Shakiel 1156
Randolph, Zach 1156
ランドレス
Landless, Peter N. 787
Landreth, Chris 787
Landreth, Garry L. 787
ラントン
Langton, Roger 789
ランドン
Landon, Howard Chandler Robbins 787
Landon, Juliet 787
Landon, Laura 787
Landon Matthews, Leslie 787
Lindon, Vincent 831
ランナート
Lannert, Stacey Ann 789
ランヌ
Lasne, Laurent 793
ランネルズ
Runnels, Rachel 1217
ランバ
Rangba, Samuel 1157
ランバーグ
Lamberg, Lynne 785
Ramberg, Jan 1153
ランパサッド
Rampersad, Hubert K. 1155
ランバチャン
Rambachan, Surujrattan 1153
ランバック
Rambach, Anne 1153
ランバート
Lamberd, Haralambos 785
Lamberd, Mariko 785
Lambert, Adam 785
Lambert, Bo 785
Lambert, Christopher 785
Lambert, David 785
Lambert, Davonte 785
Lambert, Gavin 785
Lambert, Jonathan 785
Lambert, Keenan 785
Lambert, Kelly 785
Lambert, Lisa 785
Lambert, Margaret Bergman 785
Lambert, Mary 785
Lambert, Mercedes 785
Lambert, Miranda 785
Lambert, Patricia L. 785
Lambert, Phyllis 785
Lambert, Sally Anne 785
Lambert, Stephen 785
ランパード
Lampard, Frank 786
ランバラット
Rambharat, Clarence 1153
ランパラニ
Ramparany, Anthelme 1155
ランバルディ
Rambaldi, Carlo 1153
ランビ
Rambi, Sani 1153
ランビー
Lambie, Pat 785
ランビエール
Lambiel, Stéphane 785
ランビエル
Lambiel, Stéphane 785
ランビス
Rambis, Kurt 1153
ランビリー
Lambilly-Bresson, Élisabeth de 785
ランブ
Lambe, Claire 785
ランプ
Lampe, Lisa 786
ランフォード
Rumford, James 1216
ランプキン
Lumpkin, Peggy 852
Lumpkin, Ricky 852
Lumpkin, Susan 852
ランブクウェラ
Rambukwella, Keheliya 1154
ランプソス
Lampsos, Parisoula 786
ランプティ
Lampty, Jake Obetsebi 786
ランフト
Ranft, Joe 1156
ランプトン
Lampton, David M. 786
Rampton, Sheldon 1155
ランプマン
Lampman, Jake 786
ランブラン
Lamblin, Christian 785
ランプリング
Rampling, Charlotte 1155
Rampling, Isabelle 1155
ランブル
Rumble, Mike 1216
ランプルゥ
Lempereur, Alain 812
ランプレアベ
Lampreave, Chus 786
ランブレクト
Lambrecht, Bill 785
ランプレヒト
Lamprecht, Barbara Mac 786
ランヘル
Rangel, Angel 1157
Rangel, José 1157
Rangel, José Vicente 1157
ランベール
Lambert, Alain 785
Lambert, Gilles 785
Lambert, Jérôme 785
Lambert, Nicole 785
Lambert, P.J. 785
Rambert, Pascal 1153
Runberg, Sylvain 1217
ランペル
Lampel, Joseph 786

ランベルアリゾンヌ
Rambeloalijaona, Jean Seth 1153
ランベルト
Lamperth, Mónika 786
ランペルト
Lamperth, Mónika 786
ランヘル・ブリセニョ
Rangel Briceño, Gustavo 1157
ランベーン
Langbehn, Jenny 788
ランボー
Lambo, Andrew 785
Lambo, Josh 785
Rambo, Joyce 1154
Rambo, Lewis Ray 1154
Rumbaugh, James 1216
ランボ・グンビワ
Lambo Gondiwa, Eusébio 785
ランボ・ゴンディワ
Lambo Gondiwa, Eusébio 785
ランボット
Lambot, Ian 785
ランボルギーニ
Lamborghini, Tonino 785
ランメロ
Ramnerö, Jonas 1154
ランヤン
Runyan, Marla 1217
ランリッジ
Langridge, Chris 789

【リ】

リ
I, Yong-hui 641
Lee, Seung-chul 806
Lee, Shang-Chia 806
Lee, Tsung-dao 806
Lee, Ufan 806
Lee, Won-soon 806
Li, Chung-gil 823
Li, Du-Ik 823
Li, Fen 823
Li, Jian-rou 823
Li, Jiao 823
Li, Jiawei 823
Li, Ka-shing 824
Li, Michelle 824
Li, Narangoa 824
Li, Thomas S.C. 824
Li, Vl.F. 824
Li, Wentao 824
Li, Xue-rui 824
Li, Yi-yun 824
Li, Yong-ho 824
Li, Yundi 824
Ri, Chol-man 1176
Ri, Chun-hi 1176
Ri, Chun-sam 1176
Ri, Hak-chol 1176
Ri, Ha-sop 1176
Ri, Hyok 1176
Ri, Hyon-ok 1176
Ri, Ja-bang 1176
Ri, Je-son 1176
Ri, Jong-guk 1176
Ri, Jong-mu 1176
Ri, Jong Myong 1176
Ri, Ju-o 1176
Ri, Kum-bom 1176
Ri, Kwang-gon 1176
Ri, Kwang-gun 1176
Ri, Kwang-ho 1176
Ri, Kwang-nam 1176
Ri, Kyong-sik 1176
Ri, Mu-yong 1176
Ri, Myong-su 1176
Ri, Myong Sun 1176
Ri, Ryong-nam 1176
Ri, Sang-mu 1176
Ri, Se Gwang 1176
Ri, Sol-ju 1176
Ri, Song-ho 1176
Ri, Song Hui 1176
Ri, Song-ung 1176
Ri, Sung-ho 1176
Ri, Su-yong 1176
Ri, Thae-nam 1176
Ri, Won-il 1176
Ri, Yong-gil 1176
Ri, Yong-ho 1176
Ri, Yong-mu 1176
Ri, Yong-son 1176
Ri, Yong-su 1176
Rin, Sang-mu 1183
リー
Le, Nam 799
Lea, Dale Halsey 799
Lea, Douglas 799
Lea, Per 799
Lea, Sandie 799
Leahy, Monica Mendez 800
Lee, Abby 803
Lee, Adruitha 803
Lee, Alan 803
Lee, Albert 803
Lee, Alvin 803
Lee, Amos 803
Lee, Amy 803
Lee, Andy 803
Lee, Ang 803
Lee, Angelica 803
Lee, Anthony 803
Lee, A.Robert 803
Lee, Arthur 803
Lee, Barbara 803
Lee, Bill 803
Lee, Bob 803
Lee, Boo-Jin 803
Lee, Boon Thong 803
Lee, Boon Yang 803
Lee, Brian 803
Lee, Brittney 803
Lee, Carol Ann 803
Lee, Catherine M. 803
Lee, C.C. 803
Lee, Chang-rae 803
Lee, Chiao 803
Lee, Chinlun 803
Lee, Chong-Moon 803
Lee, Chong Wei 803
Lee, Chris 803
Lee, Christopher 803
Lee, Chu-ming 803
Lee, Cliff 803
Lee, Courtney 803
Lee, Damion 803
Lee, Danny 803
Lee, Darron 803
Lee, David 803
Lee, David Morris 804
Lee, Derrek 804
Lee, Diane G. 804
Lee, Dick 804
Lee, Dillon 804
Lee, Dom 804
Lee, Don 804
Lee, Edward 804
Lee, Ee Hoe 804
Lee, Eric 804
Lee, Eva 804
Lee, Frazer 804
Lee, Gentry 804
Lee, Geok Boi 804
Lee, Grace 804
Lee, Gregory W. 804
Lee, Gwen 804
Lee, Harper 804
Lee, Harrison 804
Lee, Helene 804
Lee, Hsien Loong 804
Lee, Hyong Joo 804
Lee, Ilhyung 804
Lee, Jack 804
Lee, Jade 804
Lee, Jae 804
Lee, James 804
Lee, Jay 804
Lee, Jennifer 804
Lee, Jenny 804
Lee, J.H. 804
Lee, Jim 804
Lee, Jisun 804
Lee, John 804
Lee, Johnny 805
Lee, John R. 805
Lee, Jordan 805
Lee, Joseph 805
Lee, Julie Anne 805
Lee, Ka-Ling Colleen 805
Lee, Kang-sheng 805
Lee, Kate 805
Lee, Kate Kiefer 805
Lee, Khari 805
Lee, Kuan Yew 805
Lee, Laurie 805
Lee, Leon 805
Lee, Linda-Eling 805
Lee, Linda Francis 805
Lee, Manning de Villeneuve 805
Lee, Marqise 805
Lee, Maurice 805
Lee, Meng 805
Lee, Michelle 805
Lee, Ming Cho 805
Lee, Minjee 805
Lee, Miranda 805
Lee, Mo Yee 805
Lee, Muna 805
Lee, Nancy 805
Lee, Patrick 805
Lee, Patty 805
Lee, Paul 805
Lee, Paul C. 805
Lee, Peggy 805
Lee, Peter 805
Lee, Rachel 806
Lee, Rebecca Hagan 806
Lee, Rensselaer W., Ⅲ 806
Lee, Robbie 806
Lee, Robert 806
Lee, Robert Ellis 806
Lee, Robert Ernest 806
Lee, Robert G. 806
Lee, Ronald 806
Lee, Sam 806
Lee, Samson 806
Lee, Sandra 806
Lee, Sean 806
Lee, Seen 806
Lee, Shau-kee 806
Lee, Shin Cheng 806
Lee, Spike 806
Lee, Stan 806
Lee, Suzy 806
Lee, Tanith 806
Lee, Teng-hui 806
Lee, Tommy 806
Lee, Tsung-dao 806
Lee, Vinny 806
Lee, Wai-Yung 806
Lee, Wan Wah 806
Lee, Warren T. 806
Lee, Will 806
Lee, William W. 806
Lee, Yock Suan 806
Lee, Yuan-tseh 807
Lee, Zach 807
Leigh, Allison 810
Leigh, Barbara 810
Leigh, David 810
Leigh, Eva 810
Leigh, James 810
Leigh, Janet 810
Leigh, Jannifer Jason 810
Leigh, Jo 810
Leigh, Lora 810
Leigh, Marion 810
Leigh, Mike 810
Leigh, Mitch 810
Leigh, Morgan 810
Leigh, Richard 810
Leigh, Wendy 810
Ley, Sussan 823
Li, Amanda 823
Li, Chang-chun 823
Li, Charlene 823
Li, Cunxin 823
Li, David Daokui 823
Li, De-sheng 823
Li, Dong-sheng 823
Li, Fang-ping 823
Li, George 823
Li, Guo-hao 823
Li, Hejun 823
Li, Huan 823
Li, Jet 823
Li, Jian-rou 823
Li, Jiao 823
Li, Jie 823
Li, Ji-nai 824
Li, Jiu-long 824
Li, Ka-shing 824
Li, Ke-qiang 824
Li, Kuo-ting 824
Li, Meng-hua 824
Li, Na 824
Li, Ni-na 824
Li, Patrick 824
Li, Pei-lin 824
Li, Peng 824
Li, Ping 824
Li, Qian 824
Li, Qian-kuan 824
Li, Qing 824
Li, Qun 824
Li, Richard 824
Li, Robin 824
Li, Shen-Zhi 824
Li, Sing 824
Li, Tie-ying 824
Li, Wang-yang 824
Li, Weiwei 824
Li, Xiaojun 824
Li, Xiao-xia 824
Li, Xi-ming 824
Li, Xue 824
Li, Xue-ying 824
Li, Yan-hong 824
Li, Yi-yun 824
Li, Yong-tai 824

リ

Li, Yuan-chao 824
Li, Yujia 824
Li, Yundi 824
Li, Zhao-xing 824
Li, Zi-jun 824
Li, Zi-song 824
Lih, Andrew 827
Lu, Yuan-ming 849
Rees, Gareth J.G. 1166
Rhee, Soo Hyun 1175
リーア
Lea, Gil 799
Rhea, James T. 1175
リア
Lear, Amanda 800
Lear, Evelyn 800
Lear, Jonathan 800
Lear, Linda J. 800
Lear, Martha Weinman 800
Lia, Simone 824
リアー
Lear, Evelyn 800
Liehr, Günter 826
Lier, Julia 827
リアク
Riak, Awan Guol 1176
リアーシ
Riachi, Melham 1176
リアシェンコ
Liaschenko, Joan 825
リア＝シャフリー
Leir-Shuffrey, Sandi 810
リアーズ
Lears, T.J.Jackson 800
リアダン
Riordan, Jim 1183
リーアック
Riach, P.A. 1176
リアディ
Riady, Mochtar 1176
リアト
Liato, Austin 825
リアドン
Reardon, Betty 1164
Reardon, Jim 1164
Reardon, Lisa 1164
Reardon-Reeves, Nina 1164
リアーナ
Rihanna 1182
リアノシェク
Rianoshek, Richard 1176
リアビ
Riabi, Hela 1176
リアピス
Liapis, Michalis 825
リアブコ
Riabko, Alexandre 1176
リアマ・エルハジ・イブラヒム
Mariama Elhadj Ibrahim, Ali 902
リアミン
Liamin, Nikita 824
リアリー
Leary, Mark R. 800
Leary, Ronald 800
リアリー＝ジョイス
Leary-Joyce, Judith 800
リアリン
Lialin, Vadzim 824
リアル
Ryall, Chris 1220
リアル・クレージー・マン
Real Crazy Man 1163
リアルト・モンタネル
Riart Montaner, Luis Alberto 1176
リアルミュート
Realmuto, J.T. 1163
リーアン
Leanne, Shelly 800
リアン
Leanne, Shelly 800
Liang, Bo-qi 824
Liang, Cong-jie 824
Liang, Dave 824
Liang, Mindy 824
Liang, Wen-gen 824
Liang, Xiao-sheng 824
Ryan, Margaret O'Loghlin 1220
リイ
Leigh, Mitch 810
リィアムプットーン
Liamputtong, Pranee 824
リィウ
Liu, Xiao-qing 835
Liu, Ye 835
リーヴ
Raeve, Louise de 1148
Reeve, Christpher 1167
Reeve, Philip 1167
Reeve, Rosie 1167
リウ
Liow, Tiong Lai 832
Liu, Bin-yan 835
Liu, Chao-shiuan 835
Liu, Hua-qing 835
Liu, Jin-biao 835
Liu, Pei-qi 835
Liu, Qi 835
Liu, Qi-bao 835
Liu, Xiao-bo 835
Liu, Xiao-qing 835
Liu, Yan-dong 835
Liu, Ye 835
Liu, Yun-shan 835
Riou, Marie 1184
リウー
Rieu, Alain-Marc 1181
Rihoux, Benoît 1182
Riou, Marc 1184
リーヴァー
Leaver, Robin A. 800
リヴァ
Riva, Emmanuelle 1185
Riva, Giovanni 1185
リーヴァイ
Levay, Sylvester 817
リヴァイン
Levine, Peter A. 819
リヴァース
Rivers, Joan 1186
リヴァーズ
Rivers, Christian 1186
Rivers, Joan 1186
リーヴァスミクー
Rivas-Micoud, Miguel 1185
リヴァモア
Livermore, Jake 836
リヴァヤ
Livaja, Marko 836
リヴァール
Rivard, Yvon 1185
リヴァンス
Rivans, Stuart 1185
リーヴィ
Leavy, Calvin 800
Levey, Richard H. 818
リーヴィー
Levi, Erik 818
リヴィー
Levy, Thomas E. 820
リヴィア
Revere, Paul 1174
リヴィエール
Riviere, Emmanuel 1186
Rivière, François 1186
リヴィオ
Livio, Mario 836
リーヴィット
Leavitt, Martine 800
リヴィ - バッチ
Livi Bacci, Massimo 836
リヴィングストーン
Livingston, Jay 836
リヴィングストン
Livingston, Alan 836
Livingston, Gordon 836
Livingston, Isabella 836
Livingstone, Alistair 836
Livingstone, David N. 836
Livingston-Stuart, Carole 836
リヴェット
Rivett, Rachel 1186
Rivette, Jacques 1186
リヴェラ
Rivera, Jessica 1185
Rivera, Lupillo 1185
Rivera, Mariano 1185
リーヴェル
Leavel, Beth 800
Leavell, Chuck 800
リヴェール
Rivere, Isabelle 1185
リーウェンバーグ
Leeuwenburgh, Erica 807
リウカス
Liukas, Linda 836
リヴキン
Rivkin, Steve 1186
リウゲット
Liuget, Corey 835
リーヴス
Reaves, Michael 1164
Reeves, Carl Nicholas 1167
Reeves, Dianne 1167
Reeves, Keanu 1167
Reeves, Marjorie 1167
Reeves, Paul 1167
Reeves, Paul Alfred 1167
Reeves, Tony 1167
リーヴズ
Reeves, Hubert 1167
Reeves, Paul Alfred 1167
リウス
Rius, Edwardo 1185
Rius Espinosa, Adrián 1185
リウスカ
Liwska, Renata 836
リーヴセイ
Lievsay, Skip 827
リウッコ＝スンドストロム
Liukko-Sundström, Heljä 836
リウッツィ
Liuzzi, Vitantonio 836
リヴニ
Livni, Tzipi 836
リウマナ
Riumana, Selwyn 1185
リヴレン
Rivlin, Reuven 1186
リエヴォーレ
Lievore, Carlo 827
リエクスティンシュ
Riekstiņš, Maris 1181
リエス
Riès, Philippe 1181
リエスゴ
Riesgo, Asier 1181
リエター
Lietaer, Bernard A. 827
リエナール
Liénard, Laurent 826
Lienard, Pierre 826
リエベルス・バルディビエソ
Liebers Baldivieso, Arturo 826
リエミエン
Ryemyen, Mariya 1221
リエラ
Riera, Enrique 1181
Riera, Joan 1181
リーエン
Lien, Kathy 826
リェン
Lien, Chan 826
リエン
Lien, Chan 826
Lien, Thikeo 826
Lien, Tord 826
リエンナール
Lienhard, Marc 827
リオ
Rio, Joao do 1183
Rio, Michel 1183
リオウ
Liow, Tiong Lai 832
リオコ
Lioko, Jeannine Mabunda 832
リオーダン
Riordan, Jim 1183
Riordan, Rick 1184
リオット
Riot, Richard 1184
リオトー
Liautaud, Bernard 825
リオネ
Lionnet, Christian 832
リオネッティ
Lionetti, Pia Carmen 832
リオネル＝マリー
Lionel-Marie, Annick 832
リオペール
Riopelle, Jean-Paul 1183
リオペル
Riopelle, Jean-Paul 1183
リオム
Ryom, Heidi 1221
リオン
Leon, Kenny 813
Leon, Sandy 813
Leone, Dominic 814
Liohn, André 832
Lion, Brigitte 832
Lions, Bernard 832
Lyon, Alice 856

リオンギナス
Lionginas, Jonas 832
リオンス
Lions, Jacques-Louis 832
リオンズ
Lyons, Fergus 857
リーカ
Liedtke, Michael 826
リーガー
Reger, Rob 1167
Rieger, Berndt 1181
リカー
Ricker, Maëlle 1180
リカイゼン
Rickayzen, Alan 1180
リガウド
Rigaudo, Elisa 1182
リガジオ - ディジリオ
Rigazio-DiGilio, Sandra A. 1182
リカーズ
Rickards, James 1180
Rickards, John 1180
Rickards, Lynne 1180
リカタ
Licata, Arturo 825
Licata, Joe 825
リカーディ
Riccardi, Theodore 1177
リカティー
Rickerty, Simon 1180
リガティ
Ligety, Ted 827
リカード
Rickard, Brenton 1180
Rickard, Joey 1180
リカードソン
Rikardsson, Richard 1182
リカフィカ
Lykawka, Patryk Sofia 855
リカーマン
Likierman, Meira 827
リカラ
Rikala, Anne 1182
リカール
Ricard, Matthieu 1177
リカルジーニョ
Ricardinho 1177
リカルツィ
Licalzi, Lorenzo 825
リガルディー
Regardie, Israel 1167
リカルド
Ricardo Santos 1177
リカルド・ゲラ
Ricardo Guerra, José Amado 1177
リーガン
Reagan, Steven J. 1163
Regan, Donald Thomas 1167
Regan, Geoff 1167
Regan, Geoffrey 1167
Regan, Lisa 1167
Regan, Patrick 1167
Regan, Sally 1167
リーキー
Leakey, Richard Erskine Frere 800
リギ
Ligi, Jürgen 827
リキエル
Rykiel, Sonia 1221
リキクエ
Likikouet, Odette 827
リギンス
Liggins, DeAndre 827
リギンズ
Riggins, Lloyd 1182
リーク
Leak, Nancy M. 800
Leake, Kate 800
Leake, Mike 800
リーグ
League, Brandon 800
リク
Liku, Maria 827
リグ
Rigg, Diana 1182
リー・クアン・ユー
Lee, Kuan Yew 805
リクエア
Ricquier, William J. M. 1180
リクス
Rix, Megan 1186
リグズ
Riggs, Paula Detmar 1182
Riggs, Ransom 1182
リクソン
Wrixon, Fred B. 1529
リクター
Richter, Brian D. 1180
Richter, Burton 1180
Richter, Sandra L. 1180
Richter, W.D. 1180
リクターマン
Lichterman, Gabrielle 825
リグダン
Rigdon, Susan M. 1182
リグット
Rigutto, Bruno 1182
リクテン
Lichten, William 825
リグデン
Rigden, John S. 1182
リクテンスタイン
Lichtenstein, Nelson 825
リクト
Licht, Alan 825
リクトマン
Lichtman, Flora 825
Lichtman, Marshall A. 825
リグビー
Rigbey, Liz 1182
Rigby, Eleanor 1182
Rigby, Robert 1182
Rigby, Susan 1182
リークマン
Riekeman, Guy 1181
リーグラー
Riegler, Claudia 1181
リクラー
Richler, Mordecai 1179
リクリス
Riklis, Eran 1182
リクール
Ricoeur, Paul 1180
リグルマン
Riggleman, Jim 1182
リクレンジョス
Likourentzos, Andreas 827
リグロ
Rigoulot, Pierre 1182
リグロン
Ligron, Inés 827
リー・クワン・ユー
Lee, Kuan Yew 805
リーゲ
Lighe, Neto Zarzar 827
リゲス
Ligges, Uwe 827
リケッツ
Ricketts, Tom 1180
リケッティ
Ricchetti, Alberto 1177
リゲッティ
Righetti, Dave 1182
リケット
Liquette, Kolja Raven 833
リゲット
Leggett, Phillippa 808
リゲティ
Ligeti, Daniel 827
Ligeti, György Sándor 827
Ligety, Ted 827
リゲトバリ
Ligetvári, Ferenc 827
リケーナ
Riqueña, La 1184
リケルメ
Riquelme, Hernán 1184
Riquelme, Juan Román 1184
リケレツ
Likerecz, Gyongyi 827
リゲンバヌ
Regenvanu, Ralph 1167
リーゴ
Rigo, Laura 1182
リコ
Rico, David F. 1180
リゴ
Rigault, Robert 1182
Rigo, Laura 1182
リゴー
Rigaud, Louis 1182
Rigaux, Jacky 1182
リゴッキ
Ligocki, Kathleen 827
リーコック
Leacock, Elspeth 800
Leacock, Stephen 800
リコッサ
Ricossa, Sergio 1180
リコップ
Licoppe, Christian 825
リコーナ
Lickona, Thomas 825
リゴーニ
Rigoni, Luca 1182
Rigoni, Nicola 1182
リゴーニ・ステルン
Rigoni Stern, Mario 1182
リゴバート
Rigobert, Gale T.C. 1182
リコーマン
Liquorman, Wayne 833
リゴンドー
Rigondeaux, Guillermo 1182
リゴンドウ
Rigondeaux, Guillermo 1182
リーサ
Risser, Thomas 1184
リーサー
Reaser, Keith 1164
Reiser, Robert A. 1170
リサ
Rhissa, Ousmane Ag 1175
リーサック
Lissack, Michael 834
リサック
Hricak, Hedvig 629
リザディノワ
Rizatdinova, Ganna 1186
リーサム
Leatham, Victoria 800
Letham, Robert 816
リザラガ
Lizarraga, Armida 836
リザーランド
Litherland, Jay 834
リサール
Rizal y Alonso, Jose 1186
リザル
Rifzal, Rivai 1182
Rizal, Ramli 1186
リサルド
Lizardo, Elías 836
Lizardo, Simón 836
リサンチ
Lisanti, Christopher J. 834
リサンドロ・ロペス
Lisandro Lopez 834
リージ
Lisi, Virna 834
Risi, Dino 1184
リシ
Ritchie, Catherine 1184
リジ
Risi, Bruno 1184
リジー
Lidzey, John 826
リシアック
Lysiak, Matthew 857
リシェ
Riché, Pierre 1179
Richet, Jean-Francois 1179
リジェ
Ligier, Guy 827
リジェイ
Lidzey, John 826
リシエツキ
Lisiecki, Jan 834
リジェ＝ベレール
Liger-Belair, Gérard 827
リシェル
Rischel, Anna-Grethe 1184
リー・シェンロン
Lee, Hsien Loong 804
リシキ
Lisicki, Sabine 834
リシチアン
Lisitsian, Pavel 834
リシチンスカ
Lishchynska, Iryna 834
リシツキー
Lysytsky, Viktor 857
リシッコ
Risikko, Paula 1184
リシャー
Lischer, Richard 834
リジャ
Ryzih, Lisa 1222
リシャース
Reishus, Sandra 1170

リシャック
Lishak, Antony 834
リシャール
Richard, Alain 1178
Richard, Guy 1178
Richard, Jean 1178
Richard, Jean-Pierre 1178
Richard, Pierre 1178
Rischard, J.F. 1184
リジャル
Rijal, Minendra 1182
リシャレ
Richalet, Jacques 1178
リシュカ
Liška, Juraj 834
Liška, Ondrej 834
リジュク
Ryzhuk, Serhiy 1222
リシュチュン
Hryshchun, Inna 629
リシュナー
Lischner, Ray 834
リージョ
Lillo 828
リシール
Richir, Marc 1179
リシン
Rischin, Rebecca 1184
リース
Leas, Connie 800
Leece, Sharon 807
Leith, John B. 810
Leith, Sam 810
Reas, Casey 1164
Reece, Jane B. 1165
Reece, Marcel 1165
Reece, Robert M. 1165
Rees, Chris 1166
Rees, Fran 1166
Rees, G. 1166
Rees, Gordon Jackson 1166
Rees, Libby 1166
Rees, Martin John 1166
Rees, Matt Beynon 1166
Rees, Matthew J. 1166
Rees, Paul 1166
Rees, P.John 1166
Rees, Roger 1166
Rees, Stephen 1166
Rees, Teresa 1166
Rees, William E. 1166
Reese, Brittney 1166
Reese, George 1166
Reese, Mark 1166
Reese, Samuel J. 1166
Reese, Tracy 1166
Reese, William J. 1167
Reis, Ivan 1170
Reiss, Bob 1170
Reiss, Gary 1170
Reiss, Mike 1170
Reiss, Steven 1171
Reiss, Tom 1171
Reith, Peter 1171
Ries, Eric 1181
Riese, Jane 1181
Riess, Adam G. 1181
Riess, Stefan 1181
リーズ
Leeds, Alan 807
Leeds, Dorothy 807
Leeds, Michael Allen 807
Lees, Graham V. 807
Lees, James 807
Lees, John 807
Lees, Martin 807
Lies, Brian 827
Rees, A.L. 1166
Rees, Andrew 1166
Rees, Celia 1166
Rees, Judy 1166
Rees, Roy 1166
Reese, Fabian 1166
Reese, Laura 1166
リス
Lis, Halina 834
Liss, David 834
Liss, Jerome 834
Liss, Peter S. 834
リズカ
Rizqa, Yousef 1186
リスキン
Riskin, Daniel K. 1184
リズク
Rizk, Charles 1186
Rizq, Hassan Osman 1186
リスケス・コルベーリャ
Risques Corbella, M. 1184
リスコ
Risco, Elle D. 1184
リスゴー
Lithgow, John 834
リースター
Riester, Walter 1181
リスター
Lister, Carolyn 834
Lister, Jenny 834
Lister, Jim 834
Lister, Pamela 834
Lister, Ruth 834
Lister, Tim 834
Lister, Timothy R. 834
リステ
Riste, O. 1184
リスティク
Ristic, Ivan 1184
リズデイル
Ridsdale, Colin 1181
Ridsdale, Julian Errington 1181
リズデール
Ridsdale, Julian Errington 1181
リスト
List, John A. 834
Rist, Pipilotti 1184
リストゥ
Hiristu, Yirdaw 609
リストハウグ
Listhaug, Sylvi 834
リストフ
Risztov, Éva 1184
リストフスキ
Ristovski, Spiro 1184
リーストマー
Leestma, Sanford 807
リストム
Ristom, Bassam Mohamad 1184
リストン
Wriston, Walter 1529
リースナー
Riesner, Frank 1181
リーズナー
Reasoner, James 1164
Riesner, Dean 1181
リスナー
Lissner, Stéphane Michael 834
リースハウト
Lieshout, Elle van 827
リスバーグ
Lythberg, Billie 857
リースバッケン
Lysbakken, Audun 857
リースパッサー
Riess-Passer, Susanne 1181
リス・バルチン
Lis-Balchin, Maria 834
リスベドス
Rissveds, Jenny 1184
リスポリ
Rispoli, Andrea 1184
Rispoli, Umberto 1184
リースマラー
Riethmuller, Paul 1181
リースマン
Reisman, William Michael 1170
Riesman, David 1181
Riessman, Catherine Kohler 1181
リスマン
Lisman, Stephen A. 834
Lithman, Jerry 834
リスモア
Lissemore, Sean 834
リース・モッグ
Rees-Mogg, William 1167
リースヨハンセン
Riisjohansen, Terje 1182
リスラー
Rissler, Albrecht 1184
リースレ
Riessle, Fabian 1181
リースン
Leeson, Christine 807
Leeson, Tiffany 807
リーズン
Reason, Ben 1164
Reason, James 1164
リズン
Ruthven, Malise 1219
リーセ
Reese, Rebecca 1166
Reese, Vibeke Sch 1166
リセ
Rise 1184
リセク
Lisek, Piotr 834
リゼック
Lysek, Gernot 857
リーゼン
Riessen, Reimer 1181
リセンコ
Lysenko, Anastasiya 857
Lysenko, Tatyana 857
リーゼンフェルト
Liesenfeld, Stefan 827
リーゼンフーバー
Riesenhuber, Karl 1181
Riesenhuber, Klaus 1181
リソ
Riso, Don Richard 1184
リゾ
Rizzo, Joe 1186
リゾー
Rizzo, Anthony 1186
Rizzo, Mike 1186
リソ・カステジョン
Rizo Castellón, José 1186
リソゴール
Lisogor, Oleg 834
リゾフ
Rizov, Anton 1186
リソム
Risom, Ole 1184
リゾラッティ
Rizzolatti, Giacomo 1186
リソワスキー
Lisowski, Crusher 834
リーソン
Leeson, Marianne 807
Leeson, Peter T. 807
Leeson, Sharon 807
リーター
Riether, Sascha 1181
リーダ
Lyda, Kevin 855
リーダー
Leader, Darian 800
Leader, Imre 800
Lieder, Johannes 826
Reader, D.J. 1163
Reader, Eddi 1163
Reeder, Clare 1166
Rieder, Anton 1181
Rieder, Ludwig 1181
Rieder, Tim 1181
リタ
Rita, Mateus Meira 1184
リター
Lithur, Nana Oye 834
リーダス
Reedus, Norman 1166
リーダーバッハ
Liederbach, Hans Peter 826
リーダーマン
Leiderman, P.Herbert 809
リターマン
Litterman, Robert B. 834
リターユヒル
Rytter Juhl, Kamilla 1222
リーチ
Leach, Andrew 799
Leach, Barry A. 799
Leach, Garry 800
Leach, Julia 800
Leach, Larry 800
Leach, Neil 800
Leach, Richard M. 800
Leech, Geoffrey N. 807
Leech, Kenneth 807
Leech, Stewart A. 807
Leitch, Kellie 810
Reach, Andrew R. 1163
リチー
Richie, Donald 1179
Ritchie, Elspeth Cameron 1184
Ritchie, Guy 1184
リーチェル
Rietschel, Ernst Theodor 1181
リチェルソン
Richelson, Jeffrey 1179
リチティンヘル
Lichtinger, Víctor 825
リチートラ
Licitra, Salvatore 825
リチャーズ
Richards, Ann 1178
Richards, Anne Willis 1178

Richards, Charles L. 1178
Richards, Christina 1178
Richards, Cliff 1178
Richards, David 1178
Richards, Emilie 1178
Richards, Frederic Middlebrook 1178
Richards, Garrett 1178
Richards, George Maxwell 1178
Richards, Jack C. 1178
Richards, Janet Radcliffe 1178
Richards, Jordan 1178
Richards, Joscelyn 1178
Richards, Justin 1178
Richards, Keith 1178
Richards, Keith N. 1178
Richards, Kitty 1178
Richards, Kristi 1178
Richards, Lloyd 1178
Richards, Lucy 1178
Richards, Lyn 1178
Richards, Mose 1178
Richards, Norman 1178
Richards, Odayne 1178
Richards, Paul G. 1178
Richards, Penny 1178
Richards, Shawn 1178
Richards, Stephen 1178
Richards, Theodora 1178
リチャーズ・ロス
Richards-Ross, Sanya 1179
リチャート
Richert, Willi 1179
Richert, William 1179
Ritchhart, Ron 1184
リチャード
Reichard, Kevin 1168
Richard, Clayton 1178
Richard, Cliff 1178
Richard, Jalen 1178
Richard, John 1178
Richard, Kris 1178
Richard, Sophie 1178
リチャードスン
Richardson, Hazel 1179
Richardson, Miranda 1179
リチャドスン
Richardson, Natasha 1179
リチャードソン
Richardson, Arleta 1178
Richardson, Bill 1178
Richardson, Bobby 1178
Richardson, Bradley M. 1178
Richardson, Cheryl 1179
Richardson, C.S. 1179
Richardson, Cyril 1179
Richardson, Daryl 1179
Richardson, David 1179
Richardson, Don 1179
Richardson, Doug 1179
Richardson, Ellen 1179
Richardson, Hazel 1179
Richardson, Heather 1179
Richardson, Hugh 1179
Richardson, Ian William 1179
Richardson, Jack 1179
Richardson, Jared 1179
Richardson, Jason 1179
Richardson, Jerry 1179
Richardson, John 1179
Richardson, John E. 1179
Richardson, John T. E. 1179
Richardson, John W. 1179
Richardson, Josh 1179
Richardson, Julie 1179
Richardson, Justin 1179
Richardson, Kate 1179
Richardson, Keith 1179
Richardson, Leonard 1179
Richardson, Louise 1179
Richardson, Malachi 1179
Richardson, Matt 1179
Richardson, Matthew 1179
Richardson, Miranda 1179
Richardson, Natasha 1179
Richardson, Paul 1179
Richardson, Peter 1179
Richardson, Phyllis 1179
Richardson, Rico 1179
Richardson, Robert 1179
Richardson, Robert Coleman 1179
Richardson, Robin 1179
Richardson, Rosamond 1179
Richardson, Ruth 1179
Richardson, Scott 1179
Richardson, Sheldon 1179
Richardson, Terry 1179
Richardson, Virginia E. 1179
Richardson, Wallace G. 1179
Richardson, Wendy 1179
Richardsson, Daniel 1179
リチョウ
Lichaw, Donna 825
リーツ
Rith, Klaus 1184
リツァ
Rizza, Manfredi 1186
リツィ
Ryzih, Lisa 1222
リツィバ
Litsiba, Thabiso 834
リツォアネ
Lits'oane, Lits'oane Simon 834
リッカ
Ricca, Federico 1177
リッカー
Ricker, Audrey 1180
リッカート
Rickert, M. 1180
リッカートセン
Rickertsen, Rick 1180
リッカルディ
Riccardi, Andrea 1177
Riccardi, Marino 1177
リッカルド
Riccardo, John J. 1177
リッキー
Lidsky, Mikhail 826
Ricky, George 1180
リツキー
Lidsky, Mikhail 826
リッキー・Kej
Ricky Kej 1180
リック
Lich, Ngo Xuan 825
リッグ
Rigg, Bryan Mark 1182
リックス
Ricks, Christopher B. 1180
Ricks, Thomas E. 1180
Rix, Jamie 1186
Rix, Martyn 1186
リッグス
Riggs, Cody 1182
Riggs, Roger 1182
リックスティン
Lichstein, Kenneth L. 825
リッグスビー
Rigsbee, Jordan 1182
リックフォード
Rickford, Greg 1180
リックマン
Rickman, Alan 1180
リック・リエラ
Ric Riera, Salvador 1180
リッケ
Ricke, Kai-Uwe 1180
リッケル
Rickel, Annette U. 1180
リッケン
Lykken, David T. 855
リッケンバッハー
Rickenbacher, Karl Anton 1180
リッケンバッヒャー
Rickenbacher, Karl Anton 1180
リッジ
Ridge, Tess 1180
Ridge, Tom 1180
リッジウェイ
Ridgeway, Andrei 1180
Ridgeway, Hassan 1180
Ridgway, Christie 1180
Ridgway, Judy 1180
リッシュ
Richer, Néron 1179
リッズデール
Ridsdale, Leone 1181
リッスンビー
Listenbee, Kolby 834
リッセ
Risse, Marcel 1184
リッソ
Risso, Eduardo 1184
リッター
Ritter, Gerhard A. 1185
Ritter, J.M. 1185
Ritter, John 1185
Ritter, Scott 1185
リッターズハウゼン
Rittershausen, Brian 1185
Rittershausen, Wilma 1185
リッターマン
Litterman, Robert B. 834
リッチ
Ricci, Barbara 1177
Ricci, Christina 1177
Ricci, Federico 1177
Ricci, Nino 1177
Ricci, Ron 1177
Ricci, Ruggiero 1177
Ricci, Stefania 1177
Rich, Adrienne 1178
Rich, Alexander 1178
Rich, David A. 1178
Rich, Frank Hart, Jr. 1178
Rich, Mike 1178
Rich, Phil 1178
リッチー
Ricci, Lawrence 1177
Richie, Donald 1179
Richie, Lionel 1179
Richie, Nicole 1179
Ritchie, Dennis 1184
Ritchie, Guy 1184
Ritchie, Michael 1184
リッチェソン
Richeson, David Scott 1179
リッチズ
Riches, John Kenneth 1179
リッチバーグ
Richburg, Weston 1179
リッチフィールド
Lichfield, Patric 825
Litchfield, Brenda C. 834
Litchfield, Max 834
リッチフィールドハクシャク
Lichfield, Patric 825
リッチマン
Reichman, Nancy 1168
Richman, Jason 1179
Richman, Josh 1179
Richman, Linda 1180
Richman, Lucas 1180
Richman, Shira 1180
Richman, William M. 1180
リッチモント
Richemont, Enid 1179
リッチモンド
Richmond, Emma 1180
Richmond, Howard 1180
Richmond, Joshua 1180
Richmond, Virginia P. 1180
リッチャー
Richer, John 1179
Ritcher, Nick 1184
リッチャルディ
Ricciardi, Antonio 1177
リッチョーニ
Riccioni, Francesca 1177
リッチラー
Richler, Mordecai 1179
リッツ
Ritts, Herb 1185
Ritz, Charles C. 1185
Ritz, David 1185
Ritz, Gerry 1185
リッツア
Ritzer, George 1185
リッツァーニ
Lizzani, Carlo 836
リッツィ
Rizzi, Luigi 1186
Rizzi, Renato 1186
リッツォ
Rizzo, Gary A. 1186
Rizzo, Luca 1186
Rizzo, Michele 1186
Rizzo, Paula 1186
リッツォーリ
Rizzoli, Paul 1186
リッツト
Rizzuto, Ron 1186
リッツマン
Litzman, Yakov 835
リッデルストラレ
Ridderstrale, Jonas 1180
リッテルトン
Lyttelton, Celia 857
リッテルマイヤー
Rittelmeyer, Christian 1184
リッテンハウス
Rittenhouse, Ariel 1185
Rittenhouse, L.J. 1185

リ

リッテンバーグ
Rittenberg, Larry E. 1185
リット
Litt, Steve 834
Litt, Toby 834
Ritt, Michael J., Jr. 1184
リットマン
Litman, Mike 834
Littman, Ellen 835
Littman, Jonathan 835
リットリン
Littorin, Sven Otto 835
リットン
Litton, Jonathan 835
リッパート
Lippert, Margaret H. 833
Lippert, Mark 833
リッヒ
Rich, Michael 1178
リッピ
Lippi, Donatella 833
Lippi, Marcello 833
Rippe, James M. 1184
リッヒェベッヒャー
Richebächer, Sabine 1179
リップ
Lip, Gregory Y.H. 833
Lipp, Douglas 833
Rip, Michael Russell 1184
リツフィンコ
Licwinko, Kamila 825
リッフォ
Riffo, Natalia 1182
リップコウスキー
Ripkowski, Aaron 1184
リップシアス
Lipsius, Fred 833
リップス
Lips, Ferdinand 833
Lips, The Flaming 833
Rips, Michael 1184
リップスコーム
Lipscomb, Scott D. 833
リップナック
Lipnack, Jessica 833
リップマン
Lipman, Laura 833
Lipman, Matthew 833
Lippman, Laura 833
Lippman, Peter J. 833
Lippman, Stanley B. 833
Lippmann, Julie 833
リップマンブルーメン
Lipman-Bluman, Jean 833
リップルウッド
Ripplewood, Dean 1184
リッポネン
Lipponen, Paavo Tapio 833
リッレヴィーク
Lillevik, Linda 828
リーデ
Wrede, Patricia C. 1527
リーディ
Leedy, Loreen 807
リーディー
Reedie, Craig 1166
Reedy, Bernard 1166
リティ
Littbarski, Pierre 834
リディアード
Lydiard, Arthur 855
Lydiard, R.Bruce 855
リディエイト
Lydiate, Dan 855
リディック
Riddick, Shaquille 1180
Riddick, Theo 1180
リティ・パニュ
Rithy Panh 1184
リティ・パン
Rithy Panh 1184
リディング
Ridding, John 1180
リディントン
Lidington, David 826
リーデヴァルト
Riedewald, Jairo 1181
リデゴー
Lidegaard, Martin 826
リーデラー
Riederer, Sven 1181
リーデル
Riedel, Ingrid 1181
Riedel, Lars 1181
Riedel, Manfred 1181
リテル
Littell, Jonathan 834
Littell, Robert 834
Ritter, Saulius 1185
リデル
Lidell, Lucy 826
Riddell, Chris 1180
リーデン
Lidén, Klara 826
リート
Leto, Julie Elizabeth 817
Vanderijt, Hetty 1442
リード
Read, Andrew P. 1163
Read, Anthony 1163
Read, Cedric 1163
Read, Edna Eguchi 1163
Read, Kieran 1163
Read, Miss 1163
Read, N.W. 1163
Read, Piers Paul 1163
Read, Raudy 1163
Reade, Julian 1163
Reade, Shanaze 1163
Reed, Addison 1165
Reed, A.J. 1165
Reed, Alfred 1165
Reed, Allison 1165
Reed, Barry 1165
Reed, Ben 1165
Reed, Benjamin 1165
Reed, Beverly 1165
Reed, Brooks 1165
Reed, Cathy 1165
Reed, Cedric 1165
Reed, Chris 1165
Reed, Christopher 1165
Reed, Cody 1165
Reed, Douglas S. 1165
Reed, Fred A. 1165
Reed, Gary 1166
Reed, Hannah 1166
Reed, Harrison 1166
Reed, Henry 1166
Reed, Jan 1166
Reed, Jarran 1166
Reed, Jennie 1166
Reed, Jeremy 1166
Reed, Jerry 1166
Reed, John Roland 1166
Reed, John Shepard 1166
Reed, Jordan 1166
Reed, Kalan 1166
Reed, Kit 1166
Reed, Lou 1166
Reed, Mandy 1166
Reed, Marty 1166
Reed, Michael 1166
Reed, Patrick 1166
Reed, Paul R., Jr. 1166
Reed, Pete 1166
Reed, Peyton 1166
Reed, Robert 1166
Reed, Rondi 1166
Reed, Roy M. 1166
Reed, Trovon 1166
Reed, Walter 1166
Reed, Warren 1166
Reed, William 1166
Reed, William S. 1166
Reed, Willie 1166
Reid, Aileen 1168
Reid, Alastair 1168
Reid, Anthony 1168
Reid, Brendan 1168
Reid, Brian J. 1168
Reid, Brigid 1168
Reid, Camilla 1168
Reid, Caraun 1168
Reid, Constance 1168
Reid, Cornelius L. 1168
Reid, Eric 1168
Reid, Francis 1168
Reid, Gordon 1168
Reid, Grace 1168
Reid, Greg S. 1168
Reid, Harry 1169
Reid, Howard 1169
Reid, Jah 1169
Reid, John 1169
Reid, Jon 1169
Reid, L.A. 1169
Reid, Lori 1169
Reid, Martine 1169
Reid, Mary Graham 1169
Reid, Michelle 1169
Reid, Morris L. 1169
Reid, Pamela J. 1169
Reid, Robert 1169
Reid, Ruel 1169
Reid, Ryan 1169
Reid, Sarah 1169
Reid, Stacy 1169
Reid, Stella 1169
Reid, Steven 1169
Reid, Susan 1169
Reid, Tom R. 1169
Reid, Winston 1169
Reld, Andy 1171
Wrede, Patricia C. 1527
リドー
Lidow, Derek 826
リトゥ
Ritoo, Satyaprakash 1184
リトゥー
Ritoo, Satyaprakash 1184
リトヴァク
Litvak, Alex 835
リトヴァーン
Litván, György 835
リトヴィネンコ
Litvinenko, Alexander 835
Litvinenko, Marina 835
リトヴィーノフ
Litvinoff, Miles 835
リトウィン
Litwin, Eric 835
リドウェル
Lidwell, William 826
リトヴォ
Ritvo, Harriet 1185
リトヴォー
Ritvo, Edward R. 1185
リ・トゥチ
Ly Thuch 857
リトガー
Littger, Klaus Walter 834
リートケ
Liedtke, Dieter 826
Liedtke, Hatsuhi 826
リドストロム
Lidström, Nicklas Erik 826
リドック
Riddoch, M.Jane 1180
リトナー
Ritenour, Lee Mack 1184
リドパス
Ridpath, Ian 1181
リトバルスキ
Littbarski, Pierre 834
リトバルスキー
Littbarski, Pierre 834
リードビーター
Leadbeater, Charles 800
リードビター
Leadbitter, Grant 800
リトビネンコ
Litvinenko, Alexander 835
Litvinenko, Marina 835
リトビンチュク
Litvinchuk, Maryna 835
リドフ
Lidoff, Lorraine 826
リードベック
Lidbeck, Petter 825
リドベリ
Lidberg, Jimmy 825
リードホルム
Liedholm, Nils 826
リードマン
Lidman, Sara 826
リドマン
Lidman, Sara 826
リドリー
Ridley, Glynis 1181
Ridley, John 1181
Ridley, Mark 1181
Ridley, Stevan 1181
リトリージ
Retreage, Vanessa 1173
リトル
Little, Adrian 834
Little, Brian R. 834
Little, Claire 834
Little, Clark 834
Little, Conyth 834
Little, Denise 834
Little, Doric 834
Little, Eddie 834
Little, Greg 834
Little, Ian Malcolm David 835
Little, Jean 835
Little, John 835
Little, John R. 835
Little, Kate 835
Little, Margaret I. 835
Little, Mike 835
Little, Peter 835
Little, Reg 835
Little, Stephen 835

Little, William 835
リドル
Liddell, Helen 825
Liddle, Elizabeth 826
Riddle, A.G. 1180
Riddle, J.T. 1180
Riddle, Mike 1180
リトルウッド
Littlewood, Joan 835
Littlewood, William C. 835
リトル・エバ
Little Eva 835
リトル・ジョー
Little Joe 835
リドルストーン
Riddlestone, Sue 1180
リトルチャイルド
Littlechild, Michael 835
リトルトン
Littleton, Cory 835
Lyttelton, Humphrey 857
Lyttleton, Ben 857
リトルフィールド
Littlefield, Sophie 835
リドレー
Ridley, Mark 1181
Ridley, Matt 1181
リドレイ
Ridley, Jane 1181
リトワク
Litwak, Robert 835
リナ
Lina, Jose 829
リナー
Rinner, Louann 1183
リーナメン
Linamen, Karen Scalf 829
リナルディ
Rinaldi, Joe 1183
リナレス
Linares, Jorge 829
リナーレス・フェルナンデス
Linares Fernandez, Alfonso 829
リニ
Lini, Ham 832
Rini, Snyder 1183
Rini, Soemarno 1183
Rini, Soewandi 1183
リニー
Linney, Laura 832
リーニッシュ
Rheinisch, Eoin 1175
リニッチ
Linić, Slavko 832
リニバヌアロロア
Lini Vanuaroroa, Ham 832
リネア
Linnea, Ann 832
リネカー
Lineker, Gary 831
リネッテ
Linette, Magda 831
リネッティ
Linetty, Karol 831
リネット
Linett, Mark 831
Lynette, Rachel 856
リネハン
Linehan, Marsha 831
Linehan, Patrick J. 831
Linehan, Scott 831
リネール
Riner, Teddy 1183
リネンジャー
Linenger, Jerry M. 831
リノ
Lino, Genoveva Da Conceição 832
Lino, Mário 832
Reno, Hilary 1172
Reno, Janet 1172
リノー
Reynaud, Florence 1174
リノース
Linowes, Jonathan 832
リノーフ
Renouf, Eloise 1172
リノフ
Linoff, Gordon S. 832
リーハ
Riha, Karl 1182
リーバ
Riba, Michelle B. 1176
Riva, Pam 1185
リーバー
Leiber, Jerry 809
Lieber, Arnold L. 826
Lieber, Charles M. 826
Lieber, Jeffrey 826
Lieber, Larry 826
Lieber, Steve 826
Rieber, Lloyd P. 1181
リーパー
Leaper, Steven 800
リバ
Riva, Emmanuelle 1185
Ryba, Alexander J. 1221
リパ
Lipă, Elisabeta 833
リーバイ
Levay, Sylvester 817
リバウド
Ribaudo, Julie 1177
Rivaldo 1185
リ・バカヨコ
Ly-bakayoko, Ramata 855
リバコ
Rybakou, Andrei 1221
リーバサール
Lieberthal, Kenneth 826
リバシー
Livesey, Jeff 836
リバージャ
Rivža, Baiba 1186
リーバス
Ribas, Rosa 1177
リバース
Rivers, Austin 1186
Rivers, Charlotte 1186
Rivers, Doc 1186
Rivers, Gerald 1186
Rivers, Joan 1186
Rivers, Natalie 1186
Rivers, Philip 1186
リバーズ
Rivers, Joan 1186
リバス
Rivas, Candido Muatetema 1185
Rivas, Claudia 1185
Rivas, Delia 1185
Rivas, Ivonne 1185
Rivas, Jon 1185
Rivas, Lazaro 1185
Rivas, Manuel 1185
Rivas, Oscar 1185
Rivas Ordonez, Lina Marcela 1185
リバスアルテアガ
Rivas Arteaga, Betsi Gabriela 1185
リバス・アルマダ
Rivas Almada, Francisco José 1185
リバス・フランチニ
Rivas Franchini, Eda Adriana 1185
リバス・ララ
Rivas Lara, Francisco 1185
リバソール
Lieberthal, Kenneth 826
リーバーソン
Lieberson, Lorraine Hunt 826
リバット
Ribbat, Ernst 1177
リバティ
Liberty, Jesse 825
リバデネイラ
Rivadeneira, Francisco 1185
リバート
Levert, Gerald 818
Libert, Barry 825
リパート
Lippert, Lynn 833
リハーノフ
Likhanov, Al'bert Anatol'evich 827
リバプール
Liverpool, Nicholas 836
リバーベンド
Riverbend 1185
リーバーマン
Lieberman, Adrienne B. 826
Lieberman, Anne R. 826
Lieberman, Avigdor 826
Lieberman, Daniel E. 826
Lieberman, David J. 826
Lieberman, Fredric 826
Lieberman, Joseph Aloysius, Ⅲ 826
Lieberman, Joseph I. 826
Lieberman, Matthew D. 826
Lieberman, Moshe 826
Lieberman, Paul 826
Lieberman, Shari 826
リーバマン
Lieberman, Alicia F. 826
リバーマン
Liberman, Nancy 825
Liberman, Robert Paul 825
リバモア
Livermore, Ann 836
リパモンティ
Ripamonti, Nicola 1184
リバリス
Liveris, Andrew N. 836
リバルカ
Rybalka, Serhiy 1221
リパルテリアニ
Liparteliani, Varlam 833
リーハング
Lee Hang, Niko 807
リーヒ
Leahy, Robert L. 800
リーヒー
Leahy, Terry 800
リービ
Levy, Indra 820
Levy, Rick 820
リービー
Leavy, Calvin 800
Levey, Stan 818
Levy, Mark 820
リビ
al-Libi, Abu Laith 825
リビア
Revere, Ben 1174
Revere, Paul 1174
リーヒイ
Leahy, Robert L. 800
リビエア
Riviere, Osborne 1186
リピェツ
Lipiec, Tomasz 833
リヒェツキー
Rychetský, Pavel 1221
リピエッツ
Lipietz, Alain 833
リビエラトス
Livieratos, Evangelos 836
リビェルグ
Livbjerg, Signe 836
リビエールリュバン
Rivière Lubin, Ginette 1186
リビオ
Livio, Mario 836
リビシ
Ribisi, Giovanni 1177
リヒター
Richter, Ansgar 1180
Richter, Burton 1180
Richter, Falk 1180
Richter, Gerhard 1180
Richter, Jeffrey 1180
Richter, Jutta 1180
Richter, Peter-Cornell 1180
Richter, Philipp 1180
Rihter, Andreja 1182
リヒター - ゲバート
Richter-Gebert, Jürgen 1180
リビック
Ribic, Esad 1177
リビッチ
Ribic, Esad 1177
リービット
Leavitt, Craig 800
リピット
Lippit, Akira Mizuta 833
Lippitt, Lawrence L. 833
Lippitt, Mary Burner 833
リピット水田尭
Lippit, Akira Mizuta 833
リービッヒ
Liebich, Hans-Georg 826
リヒテネガー
Lichtenegger, Herbert 825
リヒテル
Richtel, Matt 1180
Rikhter, Elena Roudolfovna 1182
リヒテンエッガ
Lichtenegger, Herbert 825
リヒテンシュタイン
Lichtenstein, R. 825

リ

Lichtenstein, Warren 825
リヒテンスタイジャー
Lichtensteiger, Kory 825
リヒテンターラー
Lichtenthaler, Eckhard 825
リヒテンバーガー
Lichtenberger, Elizabeth O. 825
リヒテンバーグ
Lichtenberg, Joseph D. 825
Lichtenberg, Ronna 825
リヒテンベルク
Lichtenberg, Bernd 825
リヒテンヘルド
Lichtenheld, Tom 825
リヒトシュタイナー
Lichtsteiner, Stephan 825
リヒトブラウ
Lichtblau, Eric 825
リヒトリー
Ligtlee, Elis 827
リヒャルト
Richert, Stefanie 1179
リーヒュス
Rehfuess, Eva 1168
リピューマ
LiPuma, Joseph A. 833
LiPuma, Tommy 833
リービン
Libin, Phil 825
リビン
Libin, Paul 825
Rybin, Viktor Viktorovich 1221
リビングストン
Livingston, Cindy 836
Livingston, Jay 836
Livingston, Jessica 836
Livingston, J.Sterling 836
Livingston, Katy 836
Livingston, Larned W. 836
Livingston, Shaun 836
Livingstone, Ian 836
Livingstone, Ken 836
リピンコット
Lippincott, Charles 833
リビンビ
Liwimbi, Daniel 836
リーフ
Leaf, David 800
Lief, Michael S. 826
Reiff, Chris 1169
Relf, Adam 1171
Rieff, David 1181
リーブ
Leeb, Donna 807
Leeb, Stephen 807
Lieb, Rebecca 826
Lieb, Robert P. 826
Reeve, Christpher 1167
Reeve, Dana 1167
Reeve, Philip 1167
Riebe, Deborah 1181
リープ
Leape, Lucian L. 800
リフ
Liff, Samuel (Biff) 827
Riff, Hélène 1182
Ryf, Daniela 1221
リブ
Ribes, Guy 1177
リブー
Riboud, Antoine Amédée Paul 1177
Riboud, Franck 1177
Riboud, Marc 1177
リーファー
Leaffer, Marshall A. 800
リファイ
Rifai, Samir 1181
Rifai, Taleb 1181
リフィ
Rifi, Ashraf 1182
リフィチウ
Lificiu, Petru 827
リーフェルス
Liefers, Gert-Jan 826
リーフェンシュタール
Riefenstahl, Leni 1181
リーフェンス
Levens, Maria Elisabeth 817
リフォー
Lefor, Alan T. 808
リーフォード
Wreford, Polly 1527
リブカ
Rybka, Olexandr 1221
リフキン
Rifkin, Benjamin A. 1182
Rifkin, Glenn 1182
Rifkin, Jeremy 1182
リブキン
Rivkin, Neta 1186
リプキン
Rivkin, Mary S. 1186
リフキンド
Rifkind, Malcolm Leslie 1182
リプキンド
Lipkind, William 833
リプケン
Ripken, Cal, Jr. 1184
リプコーウィッツ
Lipkowitz, Daniel 833
リブゴーシュ
Rivgauche, Michel 1186
リープゴット
Liebgott, Bernard 826
リプシー
Lipsey, Jeanne 833
リプシアス
Lipsius, Fred 833
リフシツ
Livshits, Aleksandr Yakovlevich 836
リプシツ
Lipšic, Daniel 833
リプシッチ
Lipšic, Daniel 833
リフシッツ
Lifschitz, Konstantin 827
Lifshitz, Felice 827
リーブシャー
Liebscher, Tom 826
リプシュルツ
Lipschultz, Jeremy Harris 833
リーブス
Liebs, Chester H. 826
Reaves, Darrin 1164
Reaves, DeAndre 1164
Reeves, Byron 1167
Reeves, David 1167
Reeves, Dianne 1167
Reeves, Keanu 1167
Reeves, Martin 1167
Reeves, Paul Alfred 1167
Reeves, Richard 1167
Reeves, Robert 1167
Reeves, Ron 1167
Reeves, Rosser 1167
Rives 1186
リーブズ
Reeves, Helen 1167
Reeves, Martin 1167
Reeves, Matthew 1167
リブス
Riggs, Paula Detmar 1182
Rybus, Maciej 1221
リプスキ
Lipski, Alexander 833
Lipski, John M. 833
リプスキー
Lipsky, John 833
リプスコム
Lipscomb, William Nunn, Jr. 833
リーブス - スティーブンス
Reeves-Stevens, Garfield 1167
Reeves-Stevens, Judith 1167
リープスター
Liebster, Max 826
Liebster, Simone Arnold 826
リプステイン
Ripstein, Gabriel 1184
リプセイ
Lipsey, Mark W. 833
リプセット
Lipset, Seymour Martin 833
リプセンタール
Lipsenthal, Lee 833
リフソン
Lifson, Lawrence E. 827
リプソン
Lipson, Hod 833
リプチック
Lipchik, Eve 833
リプチンスキ
Lipczynski, John 833
Rybczynski, Witold 1221
リフティン
Liftin, Hilary 827
リフテル
Richter, Ján 1180
リフトン
Lifton, Robert Jay 827
リプトン
Lipton, Bruce H. 833
Lipton, Eric 833
Lipton, James 833
Lipton, Judith Eve 833
Lipton, Lenny 833
リブナット
Livnat, Limor 836
リブニ
Livni, Tzipi 836
リプニツカヤ
Lipnitskaya, Yulia 833
リブハイム
Livheim, Fredrik 836
リプハーヘ
Riphagen, Loes 1184
リブハーベル
Libkhaber, IUrii 825
リープヘン
Liebchen, Kay 826
リーブマン
Liebman, Henry G. 826
リープマン
Liebmann, Susanne 826
リプマン＝ブルーメン
Lipman-Bluman, Jean 833
リーブラ
Lebra, Joyce C. 801
リプリー
Ripley, Alexandra 1184
Ripley, Alice 1184
Ripley, Amanda 1184
Ripley, Brian D. 1184
Ripley, Martin 1184
Ripley, Warren L. 1184
リプリイ
Ripley, Kimberly 1184
リブリン
Rivlin, Alice Mitchell 1186
Rivlin, Reuven 1186
リーブリング
Leibling, Mike 809
リーブル
Livre, Hachette 836
リブレクト
Libbrecht, Kenneth George 825
リブレスク
Librescu, Liviu 825
リブレン
Rivlin, Reuven 1186
リベ
Ribé, Montse 1177
リベイロ
Ribeiro, Aguinaldo 1177
Ribeiro, André 1177
Ribeiro, Joao 1177
Ribeiro, Jonas 1177
Ribeiro, José António Pinto 1177
Ribeiro, Licínio Tavares 1177
Ribeiro, Marcus Venício 1177
Ribeiro, Mendes 1177
リーベク
Libaek, Ivar 825
リベス
Ribes, Emilio 1177
リベスキンド
Libeskind, Daniel 825
リベスト
Rivest, Ronald L. 1186
リヘツキー
Pychetský, Pavel 1141
リベット
Libet, Benjamin 825
Rivette, Jacques 1186
リペット
Lippett, Tony 833
リベナ
Rībena, Inguna 1177
リベーラ
Rivera, Jose 1185
リベラ
Libera, Alain de 825
Rivera, Alba Marina 1185
Rivera, Arden 1185
Rivera, Christian 1185
Rivera, Luis 1185
Rivera, Mariano 1185
Rivera, Mychal 1185

Rivera, Paolo 1185
Rivera, Patricio 1185
Rivera, Rene 1185
Rivera, Reynaldo 1185
Rivera, Ron 1185
Rivera, T.J. 1185
Rivera, Yadiel 1185
リベラー
Reveler, Norma 1174
リベラ・サラサル
Rivela Salazar, Rodrigo 1185
リベラトーレ
Liberatore, Adam 825
リベリ
Ribery, Frank 1177
リベリー
Ribery, Frank 1177
リーベルス
Liebers, Peter 826
リーベルマン
Liberman, Avigdor 825
Lieberman, Avigdor 826
リベルマン
Liberman, Luis 825
Liverman, Luis 836
リベロ
Rivero, Armando 1185
Rivero, Felipe 1185
Rivero, José Ramón 1185
Rivero, Mary Antoinette 1185
Rivero, Oswaldo de 1185
Rivero, Wigberto 1185
リベロ・グスマン
Rivero Guzman, Susana 1186
リベロス
Riveros, Blas 1186
Riveros Diaz, Barbara 1186
リベロ・トレス
Rivero Torres, Otto 1186
リーベン
Liben, Stephen 825
Lieven, D.C.B. 827
リペンガ
Lipenga, Ken 833
Lipenga, Kenneth 833
リーベンソン
Liebenson, Craig 826
リーベンボイム
Ribenboim, Paulo 1177
リーボ
Lebo, Harlan 801
リボー
Ribault, Nadine 1177
Ribault, Thierry 1177
Ribaut, Jean-Claude 1177
リポ
Lipo, T.A. 833
リーボウ
Liebow, Elliot 826
リポヴァチャ
Lipovača, Miran 833
リーボヴィッツ
Leibovitz, Annie 809
Liebowitz, Michael R. 826
リポヴェツキー
Lipovetsky, Gilles 833
リボウスキー
Ribowsky, Mark 1177
リホビツキー
Likhovitskiy, Andrey 827
リーボビッツ
Leibovitz, Annie 809
リボム・リ・リケン・メンドモ
Libom Li Likeng Mendomo, Minette 825
リボリ
Rivoli, Pietra 1186
リボルグ
Leborg, Christian 801
リボンボ
Libombo, Joel 825
リーマー
Reamer, Frederic G. 1164
Riemer, Robert Joseph 1181
リマ
Lima, Adriana Francesca 828
Lima, Cristina Fontes 828
Lima, Geddel Vieira 828
Lima, Gustavo 828
Lima, Jorge 828
Lima, José 828
Lima, Luciano 828
Lima, Manuel 828
Lima, Paula 828
Lima, Taciana 829
リマー
Rimmer, Christine 1183
リマイ
Limaj, Fatmir 829
リマジタ
Rimadjita, Ngariera 1183
リマス
Remus, Timothy 1171
Rimas, Andrew 1183
リマズイスキー
Rymaszewski, Michael 1221
リマッサ
Rimassa, Alessandro 1183
リマ=デ=ファリア
Lima-de-Faria, Antonio 829
リマルド
Limardo, Francisco 829
Limardo Gascón, Rubén 829
リマルド・ガスコン
Limardo Gascón, Rubén 829
リマルドガスコン
Limardo Gascón, Rubén 829
リーマン
Leaman, Oliver 800
Lehman, Carolyn 809
Lehmann, Tim 809
Leman, Brady 811
Reeman, Douglas 1166
Riemann, Bernhard 1181
リミナ
Limina, Dave 829
リミントン
Rimington, Stella 1183
リーム
Liem, Torsten 826
リム
Lim, Alberto 828
Lim, Boon Heng 828
Lim, Cher Ping 828
Lim, Evelyn 828
Lim, Goh-tong 828
Lim, Guat Imm 828
Lim, H.J. 828
Lim, Hng Kiang 828
Lim, Hwee Hua 828
Lim, Hyeshin 828
Lim, Jes T.Y. 828
Lim, Jock Seng 828
Lim, Kee Heen 828
Lim, Keng Yaik 828
Lim, Lydia 828
Lim, Max 828
Lim, Phillip 828
Lim, Swee Say 828
Lim, Wendell 828
Lim, William Siew Wai 828
Limb, Sue 829
Lim Kean Hor 829
Lim Siang Keat, Raymond 829
Lim Tik En, David 829
Rim, Jong-sim 1183
Rim, Kyong-man 1183
Rim, Nam-su 1183
リム・キエン・ホー
Lim Kean Hor 829
リム・シウ・リオン
Salim, Sudono 1231
リームシュナイダー
Riemschneider, Burkhard 1181
リム・スゥリョン
Salim, Sudono 1231
リムランド
Rimland, Bernard 1183
リーメスタ
Rimestad, Erling 1183
リーメン
Remen, Rachel Naomi 1171
リーメンシュナイダー
Remensnyder, Amy G. 1171
リャイッチ
Ljajic, Adem 836
Ljajić, Rasim 836
リャオ
Liao, Carol 824
Liao, Fan 824
Liao, Han-sheng 824
Liao, Jimmy 825
Liao, Xi-long 825
リャザノフ
Ryazanov, Yury 1221
リヤディ
Riady, Mochtar 1176
リャドワ
Lyadova, Yelena 855
リヤナゲー
Liyanage, Hemakeerthi 836
リャネラス
Llaneras, Joan 836
リャフ
Lyakh, Ivan A. 855
リャペシュカ
Liapeshka, Nadzeya 825
リャホビッチ
Lyakhovych, Tetyana 855
リャホフ
Ryahov, Anton 1220
リャマサーレス
Llamazares, Julio 836
リャミザルド
Ryamizard, Ryacudu 1220
リャル
Lyall, John 855
リヤルド
Richard, Jean-Louis Robinson 1178
リャン
Leung, Amy S.P. 817
Liang, Cong-jie 824
Liang, Diane Wei 824
Liang, Su-jung 824
Liang, Xiao-sheng 824
Ryan, Rocky 1221
Ryang, Sonia 1221
Ryang, Ui-kyong 1221
Ryang, Yong-gi 1221
リャンカ
Leancă, Iurie 800
リャンババイエ
Lyambabaje, Alexandre 855
リャンババジェ
Lyambabaje, Alexandre 855
リュ
Liu, Bai-yu 835
Liu, Bing-sen 835
Liu, Bin-yan 835
Liu, Chao-shiuan 835
Liu, Hua-qing 835
Liu, Qi-bao 835
Liu, Tai-ying 835
Liu, Tsun-yan 835
Liu, Xiao-bo 835
Liu, Xiao-qing 835
Liu, Yan-dong 835
Liu, Yong-hao 835
Liu, Youg-xing 835
Liu, Yun-shan 835
Ryoo, Kihl-jae 1221
Ryoo, Seung-bum 1221
Ryu, Eun-kyu 1222
Ryu, Hyun-Jin 1222
Ryu, Seung-wan 1222
Ryu, Si-won 1222
Ryu, Yong-sop 1222
Yu, Woo-ik 1543
リュー
Liu, Cricket 835
Liu, Lucy 835
Rew, Quentin 1174
Ryu, So-yeon 1222
リュアノ=ボルバラン
Ruano-Borbalan, Jean-Claude 1213
リュイ
Ro, Ming-soo 1186
リュイエ
Ruillier, Jérôme 1216
リュイス
Lewis, Jerry 822
リュイテリ
Rüütel, Arnold 1220
リューイン
Lewin, Alex 821
Lewin, Benjamin 821
Lewin, J.G. 821
Lewin, Michael Z. 821
リュウ
Lau, Andy 794
Liu, Chuan-zhi 835
Liu, Fang 835
Liu, Ken 835
Liu, Marjorie M. 835
Liu, Qiangdong 835
Liu, Xiang 835
Liu, Xiao-qing 835

リ

Liu, Yong-hao 835
Liu, Yongxing 835
Liu, Youg-xing 835
Liu, Yun-shan 835
Luu, Uong Chu 855
Rieu, André 1181
Ryu 1222
リュウイス
Lewis, Fobes D. 821
リューウェリン
Llewhellin, Gareth 837
リュウジャ
Liu, Jia 835
リュエ
Luyet, Claude 855
リュエット
Luyet, Ronald J. 855
リュカ
Luca, Nathalie 849
リュカ・エルナンデス
Lucas Hernandez 850
リュカノ
Lucano, Frédéric 850
Lucano, Sonia 850
リュカン
Lucan, Jacques 849
リューキン
Liukin, Nastia 836
リュークマン
Lukeman, Josh 852
Lukeman, Noah 852
リュグラン
Lugrin, Lisa 851
リュケトフト
Lykketoft, Mogens 855
リュケン
Lucken, Micael 850
リューゲンベルク
Ruegenberg, Lukas 1215
リューシュ
Ruesch, Hans 1215
リュース
Luce, R.D. 850
リュスター
Rüster, Detlef 1219
リュスト
Lust, Ulli 854
リュダクリス
Ludacris 851
リュチュミーナライド
Lutchmeenaraidoo, Seetanah 854
リュチュミーンアライドゥ
Lutchmeenaraidoo, Seetanah 854
リュツェラー
Lützeler, Paul Michael 855
リュッカート
Rückert, Sabine 1214
リュックス
Lux, Lucien 855
リュッターマン
Rüttermann, Markus 1219
リュッチエン - ドゥレコール
Lütjen-Drecoll, Elke 854
リュッファー
Rüffer, Anne 1215
リュッフェル
Ruffel, Denis 1215
リュッベン
Lubben, Kristen 849
リューティ
Luthi, Max 854
リューティエン＝ドレコール
Lütjen-Drecoll, Elke 854
リュディガー
Rudiger, Antonio 1214
リューデマン
Ludeman, Gerd 851
リューデリッツ
Lüderitz, Berndt 851
リュデル
Rudel, Jean 1214
リュート
Lüth, Hans 854
リュド
Ludot, Emmanuel 851
リュトバク
Luttwak, Edward Nicolae 854
リュードベリ
Rydberg, Jan 1221
リュパノ
Lupano, Wilfrid 853
リュビ
Ruby, Karine 1214
リュビチッチ
Ljubicic, Ivan 836
Ljubičić, Neven 836
リュービッチ
Ljubić, Damir 836
リュビッチ
Ljubić, Božo 836
リュビーモフ
Lubimov, Alexei 849
Lyubimov, Yurii Petrovich 857
リュビモフ
Lubimov, Alexei 849
リュープ
Leupp, Gary P. 817
リュファン
Rufin, Jean Christophe 1215
リュフォ
Rufo, Marcel 1215
リュープザーメン＝ヴァイクマン
Rübsamen-Waigmann, Helga 1214
リュプシャンスキー
Lubtchansky, William 849
リュブリナ
Lubrina, Jean-Jacques 849
リュボミアスキー
Lyubomirsky, Sonja 857
リューマン
Lewman, David 823
リュレル
Lurel, Victorin 854
リョ
Yeo, Woon-kay 1537
リョウ
Liao, I Chiu 825
リョウワーリン
Lyovarin, Win 857
リョサ
Llosa, Claudia 837
リヨタジョリ
Liyota Ndjolii, Bienvenu 836
リヨネ
Lyonnet, Monique 857
リョム
Ryom, Chol-su 1221
リョン
Leong, Stephen 814
Leung, Gigi 817
リヨン
Lyon, George Ella 857
リョング
Leong, Stephen 814
リラ
Lilla, Mark 828
リラ・オリバレス
Lira-Olivares, Joaquin-Alberto 833
リラード
Lillard, Damian 828
リランゾ
Liranzo, Jesus 833
リーランド
Leland, David 811
Leland, John 811
Leyland, Jim 823
リリー
Lilley, Jake 828
Lilley, James Roderick 828
Lilly, J.Robert 828
Lilly, Leonard S. 828
Lilly, Simon 828
Lilly, Sue 828
リリアーノ
Liriano, Francisco 833
Liriano, Rymer 833
リリアン王女
Princess Lilian 827
リリィ
Lilly, John C. 828
リリェロート
Liljeroth, Lena Adelsohn 828
リリエンサール
Lilienthal, Sally 827
リリエンソール
Lilienthal, David E. 827
Lilienthal, Sally 827
リリエンフェルト
Lilienfeld, Scott O. 827
リリエンフェルド
Lilienfeld, Scott O. 827
リリカー
Lilleker, Darren G. 828
リリカス
Lillikas, Yiorgos 828
リリクイスト
Lilliquist, Derek 828
リリス
Lillis, John 828
リリーフック
Lilliehöök, Catarina 828
リリーホワイト
Lillywhite, Alison 828
Lillywhite, Steve 828
リリー・ユー
Lily Yu, E. 828
リリン
Lilin, Nicolai 827
リリング
Rilling, Helmuth 1183
リール
Reil, Steve 1169
Riel, Cees B.M.Van 1181
リル・キム
Lil'Kim 828
リルゼンツィン
Liljenzin, Jan-Olov 827
リルハーゲ
Lillhage, Josefin 828
リレサ
Lilesa, Feyisa 827
リレスフォード
Relethford, John 1171
リーレフェルト
Relyveld, Steven 1171
リレホルト
Lilleholt, Lars Christian 828
リレロン・ベック
Lillelund Beck, Gitte 828
リーロー
Lee-lo, Rey 807
リロ
Lilo, Gordon Darcy 828
Lilo, Vungakoto 828
リロイ
LeRoy, J.T. 815
リーロウ
Lierow, Bernie 827
Lierow, Diane 827
リロフ
Lilov, Alexander Vassilev 828
Rylov, Evgeny 1221
リロラ
Lirola, Pol 834
リロンデル
L'hirondel, Jean 823
L'hirondel, Jean-Louis 823
リワノフ
Livanov, Dmitry V. 836
リワン
Lewan, Taylor 821
リーン
Lean, Sarah 800
リン
Lin, Alfred 829
Lin, Bai 829
Lin, Cheng-sheng 829
Lin, Chi-ling 829
Lin, Chin-ching 829
Lin, Cho-Liang 829
Lin, C.-T.Jordan 829
Lin, Dan 829
Lin, Elly 829
Lin, Francie 829
Lin, Grace A. 829
Lin, Hurst 829
Lin, Hwai-min 829
Lin, Jeremy 829
Lin, Jimmy 829
Lin, Joseph 829
Lin, Justin 829
Lin, Lin 829
Lin, Mego 829
Lin, Mun-lee 829
Lin, Nan 829
Lin, Pi-shoung 829
Lin, Pi-Xiong 829
Lin, Ruo 829
Lin, Shao-hua 829
Lin, Shen 829
Lin, Tao 829
Lin, Tom 829
Lin, Wen-yueh 829
Lin, Yang-kang 829
Lin, Yi-fu 829
Lin, Ying-Tzu 829
Lin, Yu-chun 829
Lin, Yu-fang 829
Lin, Yu-lin 829
Lin, Zhao-hua 829

Ling, Hao 831
Ling, Liong Sik 831
Ling, Richard 831
Linn, Denise 832
Linn, Dennis 832
Linn, Matthew 832
Linn, Sheila Fabricant 832
Lyn, Michelle A. 856
Lynn, Barry C. 856
Lynn, Cari 856
Lynn, Greg 856
Lynn, Lance 856
Lynn, Lonnie 856
Lynn, Loretta 856
Lynn, Matt 856
Lynn, Pamela 856
Lynn, Rebecca 856
Lynn, Steven J. 856
Lynn, W. 856
Lynne, Gillian 856
Ryn, Aude van 1221

リンカ
Linka, Tibor 832

リンカー
Rinker, Sherri Duskey 1183

リンガー
Linger, Andreas 832
Linger, Wolfgang 832
Ringer, Jenifer 1183
Ringer, Robert J. 1183

リンガード
Lingard, Jesse 831
Lingard, Joan 832

リンガニ
Lingani, Hippolite 831

リンカーン
Lincoln, Abbey 829
Lincoln, Edward J. 830

リンカン
Lincoln, Nan 830
Lincoln, Tim 830
Lincoln, Yvonna S. 830

リンギ
Ringi, Kjell 1183

リンキーズ
Linkies, Mario 832

リンギス
Lingis, Alphonso 832

リンキン・パーク
Park, Linkin 1079

リンク
Link, Andre 832
Link, Charlotte 832
Link, Eugene Perry 832
Link, Gail 832
Link, Greg 832
Link, Kelly 832
Link, Marcel 832
Link, William 832
Rynck, Patrick De 1221

リング
Ling, Edward 831
Ling, Roger 831
Ring, Peter 1183
Ring, Reinhard 1183
Ring, Wallace Harold 1183

リンクイスト
Lindquist, Ruth 831

リングダール
Ringdahl, Debbie 1183

リングトゥヴィズ
Ringtved, Glenn 1183

リンクナー
Linkner, Josh 832

リングフォード
Lingford, Ruth 832

リングボム
Ringbom, Antonia 1183

リングホルム
Ringholm, Bosse 1183

リングメルト
Lingmerth, David 832

リングル
Lingle, Linda 832

リンクレイター
Linklater, Magnus 832
Linklater, Richard 832

リンクレーター
Linklater, Richard 832

リンクレター
Linkletter, Arthur Gordon 832
Linkletter, Karen E. 832

リングレン
Lindgren, Jacob 830
Lindgren, Joonas 830
Lindgren, Niklas 830

リンケ
Linke, Christopher 832
Rinke, Claudia 1183

リンゲ
Ringe, Dagmar 1183

リンケビチュス
Linkevičiūtė, Linas 832

リンケービッチ
Rinkēvičs, Edgars 1183

リンケンバック
Linkenbach, Jeffrey 832

リンゲンフェルター
Lingenfelter, Mike 832

リンゴ
Ringo, Christian 1183

リンゴー
Ringo, John 1183

リンコン
Rincon, Lucas 1183
Rincon, Tomas 1183
Rincón, Ximena 1183

リンザー
Rinser, Luise 1183

リンジ
Ringe, Donald A. 1183

リンジー
Lindsay, Elizabeth 831
Lindsay, Jeff 831
Lindsay, Marion 831
Lindsay, Robert 831
Lindsey, Crawford 831
Lindsey, David L. 831
Lindsey, Dennis 831
Lindsey, Johanna 831
Lyndsey, Anna 856

リンシカム
Lincicome, Brittany 829

リンシコム
Lincicome, Brittany 829

リンス
Lins, Euripedes Ferreira 832
Lins, Gustavo 832
Lins, Ivan 832
Linz, Juan José 832
Linz Storch de Gracia, Juan Jose 832

リンズ
Lynds, Gayle 856

リンズィー
Lindsay, Dhugal J. 831

リンズイー
Lindsay, Dhugal J. 831

リンスカム
Lincecum, Tim 829

リンスキー
Linskey, Patrick 832
Linsky, Martin 832

リンスコット
Linscott, Gillian 832

リンストローム
Lindström, Anne-Marie 831
Lindström, Elisabet 831
Lindström, Martin 831

リンズラー
Rinzler, Jonathan W. 1183

リンスリー
Linsley, Corey 832

リンセ
Lynce, Pedro 856

リンゼー
Lindsay, William 831
Lindsey, Lawrence B. 831

リンゼイ
Lindsay, Alexander Dunlop Lindsay, baron 831
Lindsay, Bill 831
Lindsay, David Michael 831
Lindsay, Katrina 831
Lindsay, Paul 831
Lindsay, Rachel 831
Lindsay, Ryan K. 831
Lindsay, Sarah 831
Lindsay, Yvonne 831
Lindsey, Lawrence B. 831
Lindsey, Lee 831
Linsey, Robin 832
Linzey, Andrew 832

リンゼイ・アベイア
Lindsay-Abaire, David 831

リンゼイ＝ホッグ
Lindsay-Hogg, Michel 831

リンダー
Linder, Brandon 830
Linder, Joselin 830
Linder, Laura R. 830
Linder, Robert Dean 830

リンタ＝アホ
Rinta-Aho, Harri 1183

リンダース
Lindars, Barnabas 830

リンダール
Lindahl, Cathrine 830
Lindahl, Tomas 830

リンチ
Lynch, Aaron 856
Lynch, Anthony W. 856
Lynch, Arthur 856
Lynch, Brian 856
Lynch, Caitrin 856
Lynch, Cameron 856
Lynch, David 856
Lynch, Eric “Rizen” 856
Lynch, F.William 856
Lynch, Gerald 856
Lynch, Jane 856
Lynch, Jerry 856
Lynch, John 856
Lynch, Kermit 856
Lynch, Loretta Elizabeth 856
Lynch, Michael 856
Lynch, Noel 856
Lynch, Patricia 856
Lynch, Patrick 856
Lynch, Patrick J. 856
Lynch, Patrick James 856
Lynch, Paxton 856
Lynch, Peter S. 856
Lynch, Richard 856
Lynch, Ross 856
Lynch, Sarah 856
Lynch, Scott 856
Lynch, Thomas 856
Lynch, Wayne 856
Lynch, Zack 856

リンチ・エラリントン
Lynch-Ellerington, Mary 856

リンツ
Linz, Cathie 832
Linz, Juan José 832
Linz, Manfred 832

リンツメイヤー
Linzmayer, Owen W. 832

リンデ
Linde, Andrei 830
Linde, Ann 830
Lindhe, Jan 830

リンティカム
Linthicum, David S. 832

リンデグレーン
Lindgreen, Edo Roos 830

リンデマン
Lindemann, Laura 830

リンデル
Rindell, Suzanne 1183

リンデルクネヒト
Rinderknecht, Nico 1183

リンデルス
Linders, Joke 830

リンデル・ビカルビー
Lindell-vikarby, Jessica 830

リンデルフ
Lindelof, Victor 830

リンデロフ
Lindelof, Damon 830

リンデン
Linden, Caroline 830
Linden, David J. 830
Linden, Desiree 830
Linden, Eugene 830
Linden, Frank van der 830
Linden, Frans P.G.M.van der 830
Linden, Martijn van der 830
Linden, Roger W.A. 830
Lindén, Suvi 830

リンデンシュトラウス
Lindenstrauss, Elon 830

リンデンハウゼン
Lindenhuizen, Eline van 830

リンデンバウム
Lindenbaum, Pija 830

リンデンフィールド
Lindenfield, Gael 830

リンド
Lind, Adam 830
Lind, Björn 830
Lind, Hailey 830
Lind, Jens 830
Lind, Michael 830
Lindh, Anna 830

Lindhout, P. 830
Lindo, Elvira 831
Rind, Sardar Yar Muhammad 1183
リンドーア
Lindor, Francisco 831
リンドクィスト
Lindqvist, Cecilia 831
リンドクヴィスト
Lindquist, Hans 831
Lindqvist, John Ajvide 831
Lindqvist, Svante 831
リンドグレーン
Lindgren, Astrid Anna Emilia 830
Lindgren, Barbro 830
リンドグレン
Lindgren, Astrid Anna Emilia 830
Lindgren, Barbro 830
リンドスコーグ
Lindskoog, Kathryn Ann 831
リンドストレム
Lindstroem, Fredrik 831
Lindstroem, Veli-Matti 831
リンドストロム
Lindström, Jari 831
Lindström, Kati 831
リンドスミス
Lindsmith, Beth 831
リントット
Lintott, Chris 832
リントナー
Lindner, Mag.Alexia 830
Lindner, Simone 831
Lindner, Ulrich 831
リンドナー
Lindner, Carl, Jr. 830
Lindner, Heinz 830
Lindner, Robert 831
リンドハウト
Lindhout, Amanda 830
リンドバーグ
Lindberg, Carter 830
Lindberg, Charles 830
Lindberg, David C. 830
Lindbergh, Anne Morrow 830
Lindbergh, Reeve 830
リンドフィールド
Lindfield, Helen 830
リンドブラッド
Lindblad, Paul Aaron 830
リンドブルーム
Lindblom, Josh 830
リンドブロム
Lindblom, Charles Edward 830
リンドベック
Lindbeck, George A. 830
リンドベリ
Lindberg, Anna 830
リンドベルイ
Lindberg, Christian 830
リンドホルム
Lindholm, Andreas 830
Lindholm, Tim 830
リントラー
Lindlar, Angela 830
リンドリー
Lindley, David 830
リンドレー
Lindley, Cody 830
リンドン
Lyndon, Donlyn 856
Rindom, Anne-Marie 1183
リンネ
Rinne, Antti 1183
Rinne, Leena 1183
リンネマン
Linneman, Peter 832
リンバー
Limber, Sue 829
リンバッハ
Limbach, Jutta 829
Limbach, Nicolas 829
リーンハード
Lienhard, John H. 827
リンパニー
Lympany, Moura 856
リンビオ
Limbio, Florence 829
リンフォード
Linford, Lloyd 831
リンベリー
Lymbery, Philip 856
リンペレ
Limpele, Flandy 829
リンボー
Limbaugh, Rush 829
リンボウ
Limbaugh, Rush 829
リンポチェ
Rinpoche, Tenzin Wangyal 1183
Rinpoche, Yongey Mingyur 1183
リンボンベ
Limbombe, Anthony 829
リンリー
Linley, P.Alex 832

【ル】

ルー
Leu, Evelyne 817
Lew, Darren 820
Lew, Jack 820
Lew, Jacob 821
Loe, Meika 839
Loue, Sana 846
Louh, Tayeb 846
Lu, Chu-an 849
Lu, David John 849
Lu, Guan-qiu 849
Lu, Hanchao 849
Lu, Jia-xi 849
Lu, Keng 849
Lu, Marie 849
Lu, Teresa 849
Lu, Wen-fu 849
Lu, Xue-chang 849
Lu, Zhiqiang 849
Lue, Tyron 851
Rhue, Morton 1176
Roux, Emmanuel de 1211
Roux, François-Xavier 1211
Roux, Jean-Luc 1211
Roux, Jean-Paul 1211
Roux, Marie-Genevieve 1211
Roux, Simone 1211
Roux, Stephane 1211
Ruhe, Dick 1216
ルーアー
Lauer, David A. 795
ルア
Loua, Alexandre Cece 846
Loua, André 846
Rua, Ryan 1213
Rua, To Huy 1213
ルアー
Leuer, Jon 817
Luer, Greg 851
ルアイビ
al-Luaibi, Abdul Karim 849
al-Luaibi, Jabbar 849
ルアカロセンジョラ
Luhaka, Thomas 851
ルアク
Ruak, Taur Matan 1213
ルーアズ
Luhrs, Janet 851
ルアーズ
Ruurs, Margriet 1220
ルアニ
Louani, Mahamat 846
ルアーノ
Ruano, Alfonso 1213
ルアノパスクアル
Ruano Pascual, Virginia 1213
ルアノ＝ボルバラン
Ruano-Borbalan, Jean-Claude 1213
ルアバ
Luaba, Ntumba 849
ルアール
Louart, Carina 846
ルアル
Lual, Haroon Ron 849
ルアル・アクイル
Lual Achuil, Joseph 849
ルアル・アチュイル
Lual Achuil, Joseph 849
ルアレン
Luallen, Matthew 849
ルアン
Luan, Pham Vu 849
ルアンバ
Rouamba, Jean-Paul 1210
ルーイ
Looi, Mun keat 842
ルイ
Louis, Alain 846
Louis, Édouard 846
Lui, Tuck Yew 851
Luis, Vincent 851
Rui, Paolo 1216
Rui, Xing-wen 1216
ルイア
Ruia, Ravi 1216
Ruia, Shashi 1216
ルイアラモ
Luialamo, George 851
ルイ・ヴィトーリア
Rui Vitoria 1216
ルイエ
Rouyer, Philippe 1211
ルイカート
Luikart, T.S. 851
ルイキン
Lykin, Dmitri 855
ルイク
Luik, Juri 851
ルイサダ
Luisada, Jean-Marc 851
ルイサリエフ
Rysaliyev, Zarylbek 1221
ルイ・サンチェス
Ruy Sánchez, Alberto 1220
ルーイシ
Rouissi, Moncer 1210
ルイージ
Luisi, Fabio 852
Luisi, Pier Luigi 852
ルイシ
Rouissi, Moncer 1210
ルイジ
Louisy, Pearlette 846
Luisi, Fabio 852
ルイジーニョ
Luisinho 852
ルイジン
Lyzhyn, Pavel 857
ルーイス
Lewis, D.F. 821
Lewis, Michael J. 822
ルイース
Ruiz, Pedro 1216
ルイーズ
Louise, T.P. 846
Ruiz, Carlos 1216
Ruiz, Jose 1216
Ruiz, Rio 1216
ルイス
Joe Lewis, W. 675
Leuis, Jerry Lee 817
Lewis, Alan 821
Lewis, Alex 821
Lewis, Alison M. 821
Lewis, Anthony 821
Lewis, Bernard 821
Lewis, Brad Alan 821
Lewis, Brenda Ralph 821
Lewis, Byron A. 821
Lewis, Carl 821
Lewis, Carole Bernstein 821
Lewis, Catherine 821
Lewis, Cathleen 821
Lewis, Charles A. 821
Lewis, Cherry 821
Lewis, Claudia A. 821
Lewis, Colby 821
Lewis, Damian 821
Lewis, Daniel 821
Lewis, Daniel Jason 821
Lewis, Dave 821
Lewis, David 821
Lewis, David B. 821
Lewis, David E. 821
Lewis, David J. 821
Lewis, David Kellogg 821
Lewis, Deborah Shaw 821
Lewis, Dezmin 821
Lewis, Dion 821
Lewis, Earl B. 821
Lewis, Edward B. 821
Lewis, Edward Zammit 821
Lewis, Emanuel 821
Lewis, Eric 821
Lewis, Evan 821
Lewis, Evelyn L. 821
Lewis, Flora 821
Lewis, Gaspar J. 821
Lewis, Geoffrey 821
Lewis, Gill 822
Lewis, Gordon 822

Lewis, Gregg 822
Lewis, Harriet R. 822
Lewis, James R. 822
Lewis, Jan 822
Lewis, Jane 822
Lewis, Jennifer 822
Lewis, Jerry 822
Lewis, Jesse 822
Lewis, Jim 822
Lewis, Joél P. 822
Lewis, John 822
Lewis, John Aaron 822
Lewis, Jonathan Robert 822
Lewis, J.Patrick 822
Lewis, Julia M. 822
Lewis, Juno 822
Lewis, Karen R. 822
Lewis, Keith 822
Lewis, Kendrick 822
Lewis, Kenneth D. 822
Lewis, Kevin 822
Lewis, Kim 822
Lewis, Kyle 822
Lewis, Lange 822
Lewis, Leona 822
Lewis, Lisa 822
Lewis, Marc 822
Lewis, Marcedes 822
Lewis, Marvin 822
Lewis, Mary Tompkins 822
Lewis, Michael 822
Lewis, Michael C. 822
Lewis, Michael D. 822
Lewis, Michael M. 822
Lewis, Naomi 822
Lewis, Norman 822
Lewis, Patrick 822
Lewis, Paul 822
Lewis, Penelope A. 822
Lewis, Rachel 822
Lewis, Ray 822
Lewis, Richard D. 822
Lewis, Richard Warrington Baldwin 822
Lewis, Ricki 822
Lewis, Rob 822
Lewis, Robert 822
Lewis, Robert M. 822
Lewis, Robin Baird 822
Lewis, Roger 822
Lewis, Ruth M. 822
Lewis, Ryan 822
Lewis, Sally 822
Lewis, Samuel 822
Lewis, Scott M. 822
Lewis, Sharon C. 822
Lewis, Sheldon 822
Lewis, Simon 822
Lewis, Stacy 822
Lewis, Steven 822
Lewis, Ted 822
Lewis, Thad 822
Lewis, Timothy J. 822
Lewis, Tommylee 822
Lewis, Wayne 823
Lewis, William Arthur 823
Louis, Claudell 846
Louis, Lamar 846
Louis, Ricardo 846
Louis, Ron 846
Luis, Jone 851
Luiz, Fernando 852
Ruess, Nate 1215
Ruiz, Alan 1216
Ruiz, Bryan 1216
Ruiz, Carlos 1216
Ruiz, Don Jose 1216
Ruiz, Flor 1216
Ruiz, Hilton 1216
Ruiz, Laureano 1216
Ruiz, Lazaro 1216
Ruiz, Marco Vinicio 1216
Ruiz, Mari-Jo P. 1216
Ruiz, Mark 1216
Ruiz, Miguel 1216
Ruiz, Miguel, Jr. 1216
Ruiz, Raoul 1216

ルイズ
Ruiz, Hector de Jesus 1216

ルイス・C.K.
Louis C.K. 846

ルイス・アドリアーノ
Luiz Adriano 852

ルイス・アルベルト
Luis Alberto 851

ルイス＝ウィリアムズ
Lewis-Williams, J. David 823

ルイス・エスパルサ
Ruiz Esparza, Gerardo 1216

ルイスエスパルサ
Ruiz Esparza, Gerardo 1216

ルイス・エルナンデス
Luis Hernandez 852

ルイス・エンリケ
Luis Enrique 852

ルイス・グスタヴォ
Luiz Gustavo 852

ルイス・サフォン
Ruiz Zafón, Carlos 1216

ルイス・ジーン
Louis-jean, Al 846

ルイス・セビジャ
Ruíz Sevilla, Marta Elena 1216

ルイス＝ドレイファス
Louis-Dreyfus, Julia 846

ルイス・ドレイフス
Louis-Dreyfus, Robert 846

ルイス＝ドレイフュス
Louis-dreyfus, William 846

ルイストロ
Luistro, Armin 852

ルイス・ナバロ
Lewis Navarro, Samuel 823

ルイス・ハリス
Lewis-harris, Chris 823

ルイス・ファビアーノ
Luis Fabiano 852

ルイス・フィーゴ
Figo, Luis 434

ルイスフランシス
Lewis-francis, Mark 823

ルイスマシエウ・サリナス
Ruiz Massieu Salinas, Claudia 1216

ルイスマシュー・サリナス
Ruiz Massieu Salinas, Claudia 1216

ルイス・マテオス
Ruiz Mateos, Gerardo 1216

ルイス・ムーア
Lewis-moore, Kapron 823

ルイセリー
Luiselli, James K. 851

ルイセンコ
Lysenko, Tatyana 857

ルイゾッティ
Luisotti, Nicola 852

ルイソン
Lewisohn, Mark 823

ルイゾン
Luisao 851

ルーイット
Lewitt, Sol 823

ルイテン
Luiten, Joost 852
Luyten, Joseph Maria 855

ルィトヘウ
Rytkheu, Yurii 1222

ルイトヘウ
Rytkheu, Yurii 1222

ルイバク
Rybak, Volodymyr 1221

ルイバコウ
Rybakou, Andrei 1221

ルイバコフ
Rybakov, Yaroslav 1221

ルイパコワ
Rypakova, Olga 1221

ルイバチュク
Rybachuk, Oleh 1221

ルイ・パトリシオ
Rui Patricio 1216

ルイビン
Rybin, Volodymyr 1221

ルイヤール
Rouillard, Pierre 1210

ルーイン
Lewin, Benjamin 821
Lewin, Frank 821
Lewin, Harris A. 821
Lewin, Patricia 821

ルイン
Lewin, Joan L. 821
Lewine, Frances 821

ルゥ
Loo, Marie 842

ルウ
Lu, Cindy 849
Lu, Karen H. 849
Roux, Christian 1211

ルヴァ
Rêvah, Frédéric 1173

ルヴァスール
Levasseur, Claire 817

ルヴァンソン
Levenson, Claude B. 817

ルヴィア
Levere, Trevor H. 818

ルヴィヴィエ
Levivier, Juliette 820

ルヴィエ
Rouvier, Jaques 1211

ルウィッキー
Lewicki, Christine 821

ルウィット
Lewitt, Sol 823

ルヴィロワ
Rouvillois, Frédéric 1211

ルーウィン
Lewin, Roger 821
Lewin, Walter 821

ルウィン
Lewin, Ted 821

ルーヴェ
Louve, Rhiannon 846

ルヴェ
Lever, Evelyne 818

ル・ウェラー
Le Houelleur, Kaidin Monique 809

ル・ウエラー
Le Houelleur, Kaidin Monique 809

ルウェリン
Llewellyn, Grace 836
Llewellyn, Sam 837

ルヴェル
Revel, Jean-François 1174

ルウェンゲ
Lwenge, Gerson 855

ルーヴェンホルスト
Rouwenhorst, K. Geert 1211

ルヴォー
Leveaux, David 817

ルヴォー・ダロンヌ
Revault d'Allonnes, Myriam 1173

ルヴォーニス
Levounis, Petros 820

ルヴォワル
Revoyr, Nina 1174

ルエス
Lueth, Michael Makuei 851

ルエダ
Rueda, Claudia 1215

ルエダ・デ・レオン
Rueda de Leon, Hector 1215

ルエット
Louette, Jean-François 846

ルエノ
le Héno, Hélène 808

ルエール
Ruelle, David Pierre 1215

ルエル
Ruelle, Karen Gray 1215

ルーエンバーガー
Luenberger, David G. 851

ルエンベ
Louembe, Blaise 846

ルエンロング
Ruenroeng, Amnat 1215

ルオ
Lo, Fu-cheng 837
Luo, Nkandu 853
Luo, Ying 853

ルオー
Rouaud, Jean 1210

ルオ・ジャバオ
Law, Kar Po 797

ル・オデ
le Hodey, Dominique 809

ルオフ
Ruoff, Kenneth J. 1217

ルオマ
Luoma, Jayson 853

ル・オロ
Lú Olo 853

ルオロ
Lú Olo 853

ルオン
Luong, Hy V. 853
Luong, Tran Due 853

ルオンゴ
Luongo, Roberto 853

ルーカ
Louca, Loucas 846

ルーガー
Lugar, Richard Green 851

ルカ
Luka, Faimalaga 852
Ruka, Ethem 1216
ルカイユ
Lecaye, Olga 802
ルカヴィシニコフ
Rukavishnikov, Nikolai Nikolayevich 1216
ルカヴィナ
Rukavina, Antonio 1216
ルカウフ
Ruckauf, Carlos Federico 1214
ルカク
Lukaku, Jordan 852
Lukaku, Romelu 852
ルカサー
Lukther, Steve 852
ルカシ
Lucaci, Viorel 849
ルカシェンコ
Lukashenko, Aleksandr 852
Lukashenko, Alexander G. 852
Lukashenko, Volodymyr 852
ルカシュ
Lukash, Olena 852
ルカショフ
Lukashov, Sleksandr V. 852
ルーカス
Loukas, Christina 846
Lucas, Albert James 850
Lucas, Betty L. 850
Lucas, Bill 850
Lucas, Caroline 850
Lucas, Cornelius 850
Lucas, Daryl 850
Lucas, David 850
Lucas, David W. 850
Lucas, Gareth 850
Lucas, Gavin 850
Lucas, George 850
Lucas, Geralyn 850
Lucas, Jennie 850
Lucas, John 850
Lucas, John Ⅲ 850
Lucas, Jon 850
Lucas, Jordan 850
Lucas, Katherine 850
Lucas, Leiva 850
Lucas, Marcus 850
Lucas, Marquis 850
Lucas, Michael 850
Lucas, Moura 850
Lucas, Norman 850
Lucas, Robert Emerson 850
Lucas, Stephen 850
Lukas, Patryk 852
ルカス
Lucas, Timothy 850
Lukas, Jan 852
Lukas, Tõnis 852
ルーカス・シウヴァ
Lucas Silva 850
ルーカス・バスケス
Lucas Vazquez 850
ルーカス・ペレス
Lucas Perez 850
ルカーチ
Lukács, Ervin 852
Lukacs, John 852
ルカチッチ
Lukačič, Marija 852
ルカート
Rueckert, Carla 1215
ルカード
Rookard, Jilleanne 1201
ルカド
Lucado, Max 849
ルガーニ
Rugani, Daniele 1215
ルカビシニコフ
Rukavishnikov, Nikolai Nikolayevich 1216
ルカヤルビ
Rukajarvi, Enni 1216
ル・ガル
Le Gall, Jean-Yves 808
ルーカル
Lucal, Betsy 849
ル＝ガル
Le Gall, Pierre 808
ルカルスキ
Loukarsky, Bojidar 846
ルカルディ
Lucardie, Paul 850
ル・カレ
Le Carré, John 802
ルカレッリ
Lucarelli, Carlo 850
ルガンスキー
Luganskii, Nikolai 851
ルカンツォフ
Lukantsov, Evgenii 852
ル・カントレック
Le Quintrec, Guillaume 815
ルキタ
Lukita, Enggartiasto 852
ルキダス
Loukides, Michael Kosta 846
ルキッチ
Lukic, Sasa 852
ルキーニ
Luchini, Fabrice 850
ルキャネンコ
Lukyanenko, Evgeniy 852
ルキヤネンコ
Lukyanenko, Sergey 852
ルギラ
Lugira, Aloysius Muzzanganda 851
ルーキン
Lukin, Vladimir Petrovich 852
ルキン
Lukin, Vladimir Petrovich 852
ルキンガマ
Rukingama, Luc 1216
ルーク
Leuck, Laura 817
Rooke, David 1201
Rooke, Steve 1201
ルク
Luc, Jeff 849
ルクー
Lequeu, Jean 815
ルクィエ
Lecuyer, Christophe 802
ル・グイック＝プリエト
Le Gouic-Prieto, Claudine 808
ル・グィン
Le Guin, Ursula Kroeber 808
ル・グイン
Le Guin, Ursula Kroeber 808
ルクヴィ
Lukuvi, William 852
ル・グウィン
Le Guin, Ursula Kroeber 808
ル・グエン
Le Guen, Paul 808
ルグエン
Le Guen, Paul 808
ルクシチュ
Lukšić, Igor 852
ルクシッチ
Lukšić, Igor 852
ルクジムバルキ
Legzimbalouki, Bernadette Essossimna 808
ルグジムバルキ
Leguezim-balouki, Bernadette Essozimna 808
Legzimbalouki, Bernadette Essossimna 808
ルークス
Roux, Rómulo 1211
Roux, Rómulo Alberto 1211
ルクス
Lux, Amelie 855
Lux, German 855
Lux, Otilia 855
ルクセンバーグ
Luxenberg, Jay 855
ルクーター
Le Couteur, Penny 802
ルクテンバーグ
Leuchtenburg, William Edward 817
ルグマヨ
Rugumayo, Edward 1216
ルクマン
Lukman, Hakim Saifudin 852
Lukman, Rilwanu 852
ル・グラン
Le Grange, Daniel 808
ルグラン
Golliot-legrand, Lise 512
Legrand, Benjamin 808
Legrand, Catherine 808
Le Grand, Julian 808
Legrand, Michel 808
Legrand, Ugo 808
ルグリ
Legris, Manuel 808
ルクリュビユ
Lecrubier, Yves 802
ルークル
Rükl, Antonín 1216
ルクール
Lecourt, Dominique 802
ル・グルヴァン
Le Goulven, Katell 808
ルクレーア
Leclaire, Jacques 802
ルクレア
LeClaire, Anne D. 802
ル・クレジオ
Le Clézio, J.M.G. 802
ルクレール
Lecler, Yveline Michelle 802
Leclerc, Edouard 802
Leclerc, Eloi 802
Leclercq, Patrick 802
Leclerre, Daniel 802
ルクロイ
Lucroy, Jonathan 851
ルクロス
Le Clos, Chad 802
ルークロフト
Roocroft, Amanda 1201
ルグワビザ
Rugwabiza, Valentine 1216
ルグンダ
Rugunda, Ruhakana 1216
ルクンド
Rukundo, Sam 1216
ル・ゲ
Le Guay, Marie-Claire 808
ルゲ
Lougué, Kouamé 846
ル・ゲイ
Le Guay, Marie-Claire 808
ルケシーニ
Lucchesini, Andrea 850
ルケシュ
Lukeš, Milan 852
ルケード
Lucado, Max 849
ル・ケマン
Le Quement, Patrick 815
ル・ケモン
Le Quement, Patrick 815
ルケーレ
Lukhele, Stella 852
ルケレ
Lukhele, Stella 852
ルゲレ
Leguellec, Jean Philippe 808
ルゲレク
Leguellec, Jean Philippe 808
ルゲン
Luggen, Ann Schmidt 851
ルケンカニャ
Rukenkanya, Adolphe 1216
ルケンヌ
Lequesne, Christian 815
ルーゴ
Lugo, Dawel 851
Lugo, Seth 851
ルゴ
Lugo, Fernando 851
ル・ゴアジウ
Le Goaziou, Marie 808
ル＝ゴアズィウ
Le Goaziou, Marie 808
ルーコヴィッチ
Luckevich, Michael 851
ル・ゴエデック
Le Goëdec, Benoît 808
ルゴカブレラ
Lugo Cabrera, Yasmany Daniel 851
ルコック
Le Coq, Pierre 802

ル

ル・ゴッフ
Le Goff, Jacques Louis 808
ルゴネッサ
Regonessa, Maurice 1167
ルゴバ
Rugova, Ibrahim 1215
ルコバツ
Lukovac, Branko 852
ル・ゴフ
Le Goff, Herve 808
Le Goff, Jacques Louis 808
ルゴフ
Le Goff, Jean-Pierre 808
ル・ゴフィック
Le Goff, Jean-Pierre 808
ルコフスキ
Lukowski, Jerzy 852
ルコムスキー
Lukomski, Judith 852
ルコムニク
Lukomnik, Jon 852
ルゴ・メンデス
Lugo Méndez, Fernando 851
ル・コール
Le Corre, Pascal 802
ルコルギーユ
Le Corguille, Laetitia 802
ルコレ
Le Corre, Pierre 802
ルコワントル
Lecointre, Camille 802
ルコンデ・キエンゲ
Lukonde Kyenge, Sam 852
ルコント
Lecomte, Bernard 802
Leconte, Ounie 802
Leconte, Patrice 802
ルーサ
Roosa, Mark 1202
ルザイミ・マット・ラニ
Ruzaimi Mat Rani 1220
ルサク
Rusak, Leonid V. 1217
ルーサーグレン
Rutherglen, Jason 1219
ルサケビッチ
Rusakevich, Vladimir V. 1217
ルサコフ
Rusakov, Alexander 1217
ル・サージュ
Le Sage, Éric 815
ルサッフル
Lesaffre, Patrick 815
ルサート
Russert, Tim 1219
ルーサン
Roussan, Bassem 1210
ルーシー
Lucy, Niall 851
ルージー
Lougy, Richard A. 846
ルシー
Russie, Alice 1219
ルジ
Rulli, Geronimo 1216
ルシア
Lucia, Anntoinette D. 850
ルシアーノ
Luciano 850
ルシアン・マリー
Lucien Marie de Saint Joseph 850
ルーシェ
Ruscha, Edward 1217
ルージェ
Rougé, Jean 1210
ルシエ
Lussier, David 854
ルジェ
Rougé, Jean-Luc 1210
ルジェヴィチ
Różewicz, Tadeusz 1213
ルジェウィッチ
Różewicz, Tadeusz 1213
ルジェヴィッチ
Różewicz, Tadeusz 1213
ルジェービチ
Różewicz, Tadeusz 1213
ルジェビチ
Różewicz, Tadeusz 1213
ルジェビッチ
Różewicz, Tadeusz 1213
ルジエフ
Ruziev, Zafar 1220
ルジェフスカヤ
Rzhevskaya, Elena 1222
ルシェルメイエル
Lechermeier, Philippe 802
ルジェーロ
Ruggiero, Murray A. 1215
ルジェロ
Ruggiero, Renato 1215
ルジエロ
Ruggiero, Renato 1215
ルシエン
Lucien, Devin 850
ルシオ
Lúcio 850
ルシコフ
Luzhkov, Yurii Mikhailovich 855
ルジコフスキー
Rudkovsky, Mykola 1215
ルーシー＝スミス
Lucie-Smith, Edward 850
ルジチッチベネデク
Ruzicic Benedek, Dalma 1220
ルージチュカ
Růžička, Oldřich 1220
ルシティ
Rushiti, Sulejman 1217
ルシーナ
Rusiná, Enrica 1217
ルーシニグ
Loeschnig, Louis V. 839
ルシーノ
Luceno, James 850
ルシノバ
Roussinova, Zornitsa 1211
ルシノビッチ
Russinovich, Mark E. 1219
ルシバエア
Lusibaea, Jimmy 854
ルジマートフ
Ruzimatov, Farukh 1220
ルジマトフ
Ruzimatov, Farukh 1220
ルシャイロ
Rushailo, Vladimir Borisovich 1217
ル・ジャン
Le Jan, Régine 811
ルシャン
Le Shan, Eda J. 816
LeShan, Lawrence L. 816
ルジャンティ
Legentil, Christianne 808
ルジャンドル
Legendre, Pierre 808
ルーシュ
Rouch, Jean 1210
Routh, Marvin L. 1211
Ruch, Barbara 1214
ルージュ
Logue, Mary 840
Rouge, Corentin 1210
Rouge, Élodie 1210
ルシュ
Lusch, Christian 854
ルーシュV
Roosh V 1202
ルシュヴァリエ
Lechevalier, Bernard 802
Lechevalier, Sébastien 802
ルシュコフ
Luzhkov, Yurii Mikhailovich 855
ルシューズ
Rouchouse, Jacques 1210
ルシュディ
Rushdie, Salman 1217
ルジューヌ
Lejeune, Florian 811
ルジュヌ
Lejeune, Chad 811
ルシュノク
Rušnok, Jiří 1218
ルジュモン
Rougemont, Charlotte 1210
ルシュール
Lesieur, Jennifer 816
Lesueur, Eloyse 816
Lesure, Francois 816
ルシール
Lucille, Francis 850
ルジンスカ
Ruzhinska, Slaveyka 1220
ルシンチ
Lusinchi, Jaime 854
ルース
Loos, Bruno G. 842
Luce, Edward 850
Luce, Stephen C. 850
Lueth, Michael Makuei 851
Luz, Jucelino Nobrega da 855
Roos, Daniel 1201
Roos, Don 1201
Roos, Göran 1201
Roos, Johan 1202
Roos, John 1202
Rousse, Georges 1210
Ruse, Michael 1217
ルースー
Rusu, Meredith 1219
ルーズ
Rudes, Jerome 1214
ルス
Luz, Nuno 855
Rus, Ioan 1217
Russ, Marco 1218
ルースア
Luusua, Tapio 855
ルスイ
Rusyi, Mikhail I. 1219
ルスィノヴァー
Rusinová, Zora 1217
ルーズヴェルト
Roosevelt, Kermit Ⅲ 1202
ルースヴェン
Ruthven, Malise 1219
ルスカ
Ruska, Willem 1218
ルースカネン
Ruuskanen, Antti 1220
ルスコ
Rusko, Pavol 1218
ルスコーニ
Rusconi, Arturo Jahn 1217
ルスコビッチ
Rusković, Pave Župan 1218
ルスタン
Restayn, Jean 1173
ルスティオーニ
Rustioni, Daniele 1219
ルスティク
Lustig, Arnost 854
ルスティジェ
Lustiger, Jean-Marie 854
ルステンベコフ
Rustenbekov, Dzhanysh 1219
ルステンベルガー
Lustenberger, Fabian 854
ルーズバハニ
Rouzbahani, Ehsan 1211
ルズバハニ
Rouzbahani, Ehsan 1211
ルーズベルト
Roosevelt, Kermit Ⅲ 1202
ルスマイリ
Rusmajli, Ilir 1218
ルースラーティ
Ruoslahti, Erkki 1217
ルースランド
Rusland, Andojo 1218
Rusland, Gregory 1218
ルースルンド
Roslund, Anders 1206
ルーセ
Rousset, Christophe 1211
ルセ
Rousset, Christophe 1211
ルセサバギナ
Rusesabagina, Paul 1217
ルセツキー
Rusetsky, Anatoly M. 1217
ルゼック
Rydzek, Johannes 1221
ルセット・イ・ジュベット
Rosset i Llobet, Jaume 1207
ルセナ
Lucena, Nick 850
ルセフ
Rousseff, Dilma Vana 1211
ルーセル
Roussel, Eric 1211
Roussel, Joseph 1211
ルセルクル
Lecercle, Jean-Jacques 802
ルセングワミヒゴ

Rusengwamihigo, Deogratias 1217
ルーゼンスキー
Ruszcynski, Stanley 1219
ルセンティ
Lucenti, Emmanuel 850
ルーソー
Russo, Patricia F. 1219
ルソー
Rousseau, Jacques 1210
Rousseau, Jean-Charles 1210
Rousseau, Nina 1210
Rousseau, Pierre-Alexandre 1211
ルソナ
Lusona, Kalema 854
ルソン・バトレ
Lussón Batlle, Antonio Enrique 854
ルタ
Ruta, Pietro 1219
ルタイーフ
al-Lutayyif, Ammar Mabruk 854
ル・タコン
Le Tacon, François 816
ルーダーズ
Lueders, Pierre Fritz 851
ルダーマン
Ruderman, Marian N. 1214
Ruderman, Rachel 1214
ルダレビチウス
Rudalevicius, Jonas 1214
ル・タン
Le-Tan, Olympia 816
ルダン
Ludan, Lilia 851
ルタンス
Lutens, Serge 854
ル・タンドル
Le Tendre, Serge 816
ルチアーニ
Luciani, Domenica 850
Luciani, Joseph J. 850
Luciani, Roberto 850
ルチェスク
Lucescu, Mircea 850
ルチョウ・ストンポロウスキー
Rutschow-stomporowski, Katrin 1219
ルチン
Lučin, Šime 850
ルチンスキー
Lucinschi, Petru 850
ルーツ
Lutz, Joe 855
Roets, Jo 1196
ルツ
Luz, Ulrich 855
ルーツィ
Luzi, Mario 855
ルツィ
Luzi, Mario 855
ルツイ
Lutui, Aleki 855
ルツェンコ
Lutsenko, Yuriy 854
ルツェンベルガー
Lutzenberger, Jose 855
ルッカ
Rucka, Greg 1214
ルッカー
Looker, Terry 842
ルッキ
Rucki, Eva 1214
ルック
Luck, Frank 850
ルックス
Lux, Lucien 855
ルックスバーカー
Luxbacher, Irene 855
ルックスビー
Rooksby, Rikky 1201
ルックマン
Luckmann, Thomas 851
ルッケ
Lucke, Bernd 850
ルツコスキ
Rutkoski, Marie 1219
ルーッコネン
Luukkonen, Monika 855
ルッサール
Rosell, Quim 1203
ルッジウ
Ruggiu, François-Joseph 1215
ルッジェーロ
Ruggiero, Renato 1215
ルッジェロ
Ruggiero, Renato 1215
ルッシオ
Lúcio 850
ルッス
Russu, Ion 1219
ルッセ
Russet, Pierre 1219
ルッソ
Russo, Anthony 1219
Russo, Clemente 1219
Russo, J.Edward 1219
Russo, Joe 1219
Russo, Kristin 1219
Russo, Marisabina 1219
Russo, Nancy Felipe 1219
Russo, Patricia F. 1219
Russo, Rene 1219
ルッター
Rutter, Virginia 1219
ルッチオ
Ruccio, David F. 1214
ルッツ
Ludz, Ursula 851
Lutz, Christel 855
Lutz, Mark 855
Lutz, Robert A. 855
Lutz, Tom 855
Rutz, Wolfgang 1219
ルッツァット
Luzzatto, Sergio 855
ルッツィア
Ruzzier, Sergio 1220
ルッツェン
Rutzen, Allan Richard 1220
ルッツ＝バッハマン
Lutz-Bachmann, Matthias 855
ルッテ
Rutte, Mark 1219
ルップ
Rupp, Hans Karl 1217
Rupp, Lukas 1217
ルップレヒター
Rupprechter, Andrä 1217
ルップレヒト
Rupprecht, Gerhard 1217
ルッモ
Rummo, Paul-Eerik 1217
ルーテ
Luthe, Andreas 854
ルーティ
Lewty, Marjorie 823
ルーティー
Luty, Tadeusz Michal 855
ルーディー
Loudiyi, Abdellatif 846
ルティ
Luti, Claudio 854
ルディ
Rudy, Matthew 1215
Rudy, Rajiv Pratap 1215
Rudy, Sebastian 1215
ルディー
Rudy, Kazuko 1215
ルディアンタラ
Rudiantara 1214
ルディエール
Loudières, Monique 846
ルディー和子
Rudy, Kazuko 1215
ルディシャ
Rudisha, David 1215
ルティチャウ
Lüttichau, Chris 854
ルディティス
Ruditis, Paul 1215
ルディテイス
Ruditis, Paul 1215
ルディニ
Rudini 1214
ルディネスコ
Roudinesco, Elisabeth 1210
ルティマン
Reutimann, Romuald 1173
ルティリアーノ
Rutigliano, Tony 1219
ルーディン
Ludin, Marine 851
ルディン
Rudin, Walter 1214
ルデオ
Le Déaut, Jean-Yves 802
ルーテクス
Routex, Diane 1211
ルデジ
Rudez, Damjan 1214
ルテステュ
Letestu, Agnès 816
ルテッリ
Rutelli, Francesco 1219
ルテムル
Leterme, Yves 816
ルデュック
Leduc, Albert 803
Leduc, Olivier 803
ルテリ
Rutelli, Francesco 1219
ルーデル
Rudel, Anthony J. 1214
ルデル
Ruddell, Peter 1214
ルテルスドティル
Luthersdottir, Hrafnhildur 854
ルテルム
Leterme, Yves 816
ルーデンスタイン
Rudenstine, Neil Leon 1214
ルーテンベルグ
Rutenberg, Peter 1219
ルート
Lute, Jane Holl 854
Root, Barry 1202
Root, Jeff 1202
Root, Kimberly Bulcken 1202
Root, Phyllis 1202
Root, Sue C. 1202
Root, Wayne Allyn 1202
ルード
Rood, Brian 1201
Rude, Steve 1214
ルト
Ruto, William 1219
ルドアラン
Le Douarin, Nicole 803
ル＝ドアレ
Le Doaré, Hélène 802
ルドゥー
Ledoux, Joseph E. 803
ルドウィグ
Ludwig, Gail 851
ルドヴィクセン
Ludvigsen, Karl E. 851
ルドヴィシ
Ludovisi, Livio 851
ルドウィック
Ludwig, Ken 851
ルートヴィヒ
Ludwig, Bob 851
Ludwigm, Bob 851
ルー・ドゥ・ウー・ラ
Ludu U Hla 851
ルトヴェラーゼ
Rtveladze, Edvard Vasilévich 1213
ルトヴェラゼ
Rtveladze, Edvard Vasilévich 1213
ルトゥクタ
Lutukuta, Gilberto Buta 855
ルードゥス
Loodus, Tarmo 842
ルトゥフィー
Luthfee, Musthafa 854
ルトゥルノー
Letourneau, Fanny 817
ルトクヴィスト
Rutqvist, Jakob 1219
ルトケ
Luttke, Gerhard 854
ルドコ
Rudko, Artur 1215
ルドック
Rudock, Jake 1215
ルドニェフス
Rudnevs, Artjoms 1215
ルドニック
Rudnick, Elizabeth 1215
ルドニャンスカ
Rudniańska, Joanna 1215
ルトノ
Retno, Marsudi 1173
ルトビガー
Ludwiger, Illobrand

ル

von 851
ルドビク
Ludwig, Laura 851
ルードビクセン
Ludvigsen, Svein 851
ルートビヒ
Ludwig, Laura 851
ルトフィ
Lutfi, Amir Husni 854
ルトフィウ
Lutfiu, Pishtar 854
ルードマン
Ludeman, Kate 851
ルドリアン
Le Drian, Jean-Yves 803
ルートリッジ
Routledge, Victoria 1211
ル・トール
Le Tord, Bijou 817
ルドルフ
Rudolf, Mary 1215
Rudolph, Frederick 1215
Rudolph, Jenny 1215
Rudolph, K. 1215
Rudolph, Kurt 1215
Rudolph, Kyle 1215
ルートレッジ
Rutledge, Thom 1219
ルドレール
Roederer, Charlotte 1196
ルドロワ
Ledroit, Olivier 803
ルトワク
Luttwak, Edward Nicolae 854
ルトワック
Luttwak, Edward Nicolae 854
ルドン
Redon, Juan 1165
ルナ
Luna, Antonio 853
Luna, Audrey 853
Luna, Bigas 853
Luna, Bigasu 853
Luna, Diego 853
Luna, Ian 853
Luna, Jashia 853
Luna, J.J. 853
Luna, Julio 853
ルナウシ
Lounaouci, Hamid 846
ルナ・サンチェス
Luna Sánchez, David 853
ルナ・フェルナンデス
Luna Fernández, Juan José 853
ルナ・メンドサ
Luna Mendoza, Licardo 853
ルナルディ
Lunardi, Pietro 853
Renardy, Lisbeth 1171
ルナン
Lenain, Thierry 812
ルーニー
Looney, Joe 842
Looney, Kevon 842
Rooney, Andy 1201
Rooney, Anne 1201
Rooney, Gerald P. 1201
Rooney, Giaan 1201
Rooney, Glenda Dewberry 1201
Rooney, Martyn 1201
Rooney, Michael 1201
Rooney, Mickey 1201
Rooney, Natalie 1201
Rooney, Ronald H. 1201
Rooney, Wayne 1201
ル・ヌウアニック
Le Neouanic, Lionel 812
ルネ
René, France Albert 1172
ルネソン
Runeson, Bo 1217
ルネプブー
Le Nepvou, Marie 812
ルーノー
Luhnow, Jeff 851
ルノー
Luhnow, Jeff 851
Renauld, Lener 1171
Renault, Emmanuel 1172
Renault, Michel 1172
Renaut, Alain 1172
ルノード
Renaude, Noëlle 1171
ルノートル
Lenôtre, Gaston 813
ル・ノルマン
Le Normand, Véronique M. 813
ルノワール
Lenoir, Frédéric 813
Lenoir, Noëlle 813
Lenoir, Yves 813
ルーハ
Louh, Tayeb 846
ルバイ
Le Bail, Hélène 800
al-Rubai, Nasir 1213
ルバイン
Levine, Brett 818
Levine, Paul J. 819
ルハカ
Luhaka, Thomas 851
ルパキヨティス
Roupakiotis, Antonis 1210
ルハグバスレン
Lkhagvasuren, Otgonbaatar 836
ルパージュ
Lepage, Claudie 814
Lepage, Corinne 814
Lepage, Emmanuel 814
Lepage, Robert 814
ルバート
LeBert, Margo A. 801
LeVert, Suzanne 818
ルバ・ヌタンボ
Luba Ntambo, Alexandre 849
ルバヌタンボ
Luba Ntambo, Alexandre 849
ルバノビック
Lubanovic, Bill 849
ルパプ
Lepape, Sebastien 814
ルバルカーバ
Rubalcaba, Jill 1213
ルバルカバ
Rubalcaba, Alfredo Pérez 1213
Rubalcaba, Gonzalo 1213
ルバルスキー
Lubarsky, David A. 849
ルーバン
Luban, David 849
ルーパン
Roopun, Prithvirajsing 1201
ルハン
Luján, Jorge 852
ルバン
Ruban, Viktor 1213
ルパンネ
Lepennec, Emilie 814
ルハンビオ・イラサバル
Lujambio Irazábal, Alonso 852
ルーピ
Lupi, Maurizio 854
ルビ
Ruby, Karine 1214
ルビー
Luby, Frank 849
Ruby, Sam 1214
ルピ
Lupi, Carlos 854
ルピア
Lupia, Arthur 854
ル・ビアン
Le Bihan, Frèdèric 801
ルーピィ
Loupy, Christophe 846
ルビエア
Reviere, Osborne 1174
ルビオ
Rubio, Gabriela 1214
Rubio, Israel Jose 1214
Rubio, Marco 1214
Rubio, Ricky 1214
ルビオ・コレア
Rubio Correa, Marcial 1214
ルビオ・バロー
Rubio-Barreau, Vanessa 1214
ルビオロドリゲス
Rubio Rodriguez, Eduardo 1214
ルビオ・ロペス・デ・ラ・ジャベ
Rubio López de la Llave, Carlos 1214
ルピカ
Lupica, Mike 854
ルピカール
Lepicard, Louise 814
ルヒテンベルク
Luchtenberg, Sigrid 850
ルヒト
Rucht, Dieter 1214
ルービニ
Roubini, Nouriel 1210
ルビーニ
Rubini, Alessandro 1214
ルビーノ
Rubino, Guido P. 1214
Rubino, Joe 1214
ルビノ
Rubino, John A. 1214
ルビモフ
Lyubimov, Yurii Petrovich 857
ルビャンツェフ
Lubjantsev, Alexander 849
ル・ビロン
Le Billon, Karen 801
ルービン
Lubin, Albert J. 849
Rubin, Ahtyba 1213
Rubin, Barry R. 1213
Rubin, Charles 1213
Rubin, Emanuel 1213
Rubin, Emily 1213
Rubin, Gretchen 1213
Rubin, James Henry 1213
Rubin, Jay 1214
Rubin, Judith Aron 1214
Rubin, Ken 1214
Rubin, Kenneth S. 1214
Rubin, Richard 1214
Rubin, Rick 1214
Rubin, Robert Edward 1214
Rubin, Ron 1214
Rubin, Theodore Isaac 1214
ルビーン
Levine, David M. 818
ルビン
Rubin, Kenneth S. 1214
Rubin, Louis, Jr. 1214
Rubin, Sergio 1214
ルビンジャー
Rubinger, Andrew Lee 1214
Rubinger, Richard 1214
ルービンシュタイン
Rubinstein, Ariel 1214
ルビンシュタイン
Rubinstein, Ariel 1214
ルビンダ
Lubinda, Given 849
ルビンチク
Rubinchik, IUrii Aronovich 1214
ルヒンディ
Ruhindi, Fredrick 1216
ルービン・ドランゲル
Rubin Dranger, Joanna 1214
ルビンフェルド
Rubinfeld, Daniel L. 1214
ルーブ
Louv, Richard 846
ループ
Loup, Aaron 846
ルフ
Ruff, Anne 1215
ルプ
Lupu, Marian Ilie 854
ルプー
Lupu, Radu 854
ルファ
Leffa, Gaby Francky 807
ルファイ
El-rufai, Nasir 1215
Rufai, Ruqayyatu 1215
ルファート
Ruffato, Luca 1215
ルファー - バック
Rufer-Bach, Kimberly 1215
ルフイキリ
Rufyikiri, Gervais 1215
ルフィーニ
Ruffini, Remo 1215
ルフィニ
Ruffini, Simone 1215
ルフィネリ

ル

Ruffinelli, Antonio Moreno 1215
ルフィーノ
Ruffino, Marco 1215
ルフィン
Zomahoun Rufin 1557
ルーフェ
Rufe, Philip D. 1215
ルフェーヴル
Lefebvre, Sandrine 807
Lefèvre, Brigitte 807
Lefèvre, Christian 807
Lefèvre, Didier 807
Lefèvre, Raymond 807
ルフェーブル
Lefebvre, Gabriel 807
Lefebvre, Jean 807
Lefebvre, Michel 807
Lefevre, Fabien 807
Lefèvre, Raymond 807
ルフェブル
Lefebvre, Gabriel 807
ルフェール
Lefert, Clement 807
ルーフォー
Ruffo, Armand Garnet 1215
ルフォール
Lefort, Claude 808
Lefort, Enzo 808
ルフォル
Lefoll, Stéphane 807
ルブシェ
Leboucher, Laurence 801
ルーフス
Rúfus, Milan 1215
ルフタネン
Luhtanen, Leena 851
ルブチェンコ
Lubchenco, Jane 849
ルフット
Luhut, Panjaitan 851
ルブティリエ
Lebouthillier, Diane 801
ルフト
Lucht, Irmgard 850
ルフトナー‐ナーゲル
Luftner-Nagel, Susanne 851
ルブナ
Lubna, bint Khalid al-Qasimi 849
ルブナー
Lubner, Sam J. 849
ループナライン
Roopnaraine, Rupert 1201
ル＝ブラ
Le Bras, Yann 801
ル・ブラーズ
Le Bras, Hervé 801
ルプラト
Rupprath, Thomas 1217
ル・ブラン
Le Brun, Annie 801
ルフラン
Lefranc, Jean 808
ルブラン
LeBlanc, David 801
Leblanc, Dominic 801
LeBlanc, Janet 801
LeBlanc, Matt 801
LeBlanc, Robin M. 801
Leblanc, Sophie 801
LeBlanc, Sydney 801
Leblanc, Wade 801
Leblang, Camille 801
Lebrun, Bernard 801
Lebrun, Celine 801
Lebrun, Francois 801
Lebrun, Marc 801
ルブランシュ
Lebranchu, Marylise 801
ルブランブシェ
Leblanc-boucher, Anouk 801
ルブリン
Lublin, Nancy 849
ルブルク
Le Blouch, Kilian 801
ル・ブレトン＝ミラー
Le Breton-Miller, Isabelle 801
ルブレフスカ
Rublevska, Elena 1214
ルプレボス
Leprevost, Penelope 814
ル・フロッシュ・ソワ
Le Floćh Soye, Yves 807
ルブロン
Leblond, Joëlle 801
ルプンガ
Lupunga, Dawson 854
ルベ
Lebet, Jean-Paul 801
ルベイ
LeVay, Simon 817
ルベイロ
Rebeyrol, Antoine 1164
ルヘイン
Lehane, Dennis 808
Lehane, John Robert 808
ルベオ
Rubeo, Bruno 1213
ルペシュー
Le Pechoux, Erwann 814
ル・ベスコ
Besco, Isild Le 132
ルベスコ
Lebesco, Kathleen 801
ルベツキ
Lubezki, Emmanuel 849
ル・ベック
Le Bec, Gwendal 801
ルベッソン
Lebesson, Emmanuel 801
ルベット
Lubet, Steven 849
ルペテイ
Lupetey, Yurisleydis 854
ルベニ
Luveni, Jiko 855
ルベニス
Rubenis, Martins 1213
ルベマジエル
Le Bemadjiel, Djerassem 801
ルヘマン
Ruhemann, Andrew 1216
ルーベル
Rubel, David 1213
Rubel, Nicole 1213
Rubel, William 1213
ルベル
Revel, Jean-François 1174
ルペル
Rupel, Dimitrij 1217
ルペルティエ
Lepeltier, Serge 814
ルベルワ
Ruberwa, Azarias 1213
ルーベン
Reuben, Jacklyn 1173
Reuben, Susan 1173
Ruben, Nicholas E. 1213
Rueben, Hannah Amuchechi 1215
ルベン
Ruben 1213
Ruben, Blanco 1213
ルペン
Le Pen, Jean-Marie 814
Le Pen, Marine 814
ルベン・ヴェソ
Ruben Vezo 1213
ルベン・カストロ
Ruben Castro 1213
ルベン・ジャニェス
Ruben Yanez 1213
ルーベンシュタイン
Rubenstein, David M. 1213
ルーベンス
Rubens, Bernice Ruth 1213
ルーベンスタイン
Rubenstein, David M. 1213
Rubenstein, Richard E. 1213
ルベン・セメド
Ruben Semedo 1213
ルベン・ソブリーノ
Ruben Sobrino 1213
ルベン・ドゥアルテ
Ruben Duarte 1213
ルベン・ネヴェス
Ruben Neves 1213
ルヘンバ
Ruhemba, Kweronda 1216
ルーベンフェルド
Rubenfeld, Jed 1213
ルベン・ペーニャ
Ruben Pena 1213
ルベン・ペレス
Ruben Perez 1213
ル・ボ
Lebot, Yvon 801
ルーボー
Roubaud, Jacques 1210
ルボー
LeBeau, Charles 801
Lebeau, Dick 801
Leveaux, Amaury 817
Leveaux, David 817
Rebaud, Denis 1164
ルポ
Lupo, Daniele 854
Lupo, Jośe Luis 854
ルーボディ
Roubaudi, Ludovic 1210
ルボーフ
LeBoeuf, Michael 801
ルポフ
Lupoff, Richard A. 854
ルボーム
Lebeaume, Clément 801
Lebeaume, Joël 801
ル・ボン
Le Bon, Simon 801
ルポーン
LuPone, Patti 854
ルーマー
Rumer 1216
ルマ
Ruma 1216
Ruma, S. Abba 1216
ルマス
Rumas, Sergei N. 1216
ル・マスヌ
Le Masne, Christophe 811
ルマセ・マンディア
Lemasset Mandya, Charles Paul 811
ルマニー
Lemagny, Jean-Claude 811
ルマーニエール
Rousmaniere, Nicole Coolidge 1210
ルマニエール
Rousmaniere, Nicole Coolidge 1210
ルマヌ
Lumanu, Adolphe 852
ルマル
Lemar, Thomas 811
ルマルク
Lemarque, Francis 811
ルーマン
Lewman, David 823
ルーミー
al-Roumi, Maryam Mohammaed Khalfan 1210
ルミエール
Lemierre, Jean 812
ルーミス
Loomis, Carol 842
Loomis, Christine 842
Loomis, Evan 842
Loomis, Jake 842
Loomis, Mary 842
Loomis, Randy 842
ルミス
Lummis, Adair T. 852
ルミナティ
Luminati, Michele 852
ルミャンツェフ
Rumyantsev, Aleksandr Y. 1217
ルミヤンツェフ
Rumianzev, Evgeniy 1216
ル・ミュエ
LeMuet, Pierre 812
ルムスデン
Lumsden, Thomas 853
ルムヒ
al-Rumhy, Mohammed bin Hamad 1216
ルムヤンチェフス
Rumjancevs, Aleksejs 1216
ルムンバ
Lumumba, Juliana 853
ルメー
Rummé, Daigaku 1216
ル・メアー
Le Merrer, David 812
ルメイ
LeMay, Harold Eugene, Jr. 811
ルメイヒ
al-Rumaihi, Mohamed bin Abdullah 1216

ルメジュラー
Lemesurier, Peter 812
ルメット
Lumet, Sidney 852
ルメートル
Lemaitre, Christophe 811
Lemaître, Pascal 811
Lemaitre, Pierre 811
ルーメル
Luhmer, Klaus S.J. 851
ルメール
Le Maire, Bruno 811
Lemaire, Christophe 811
Lemaire, Gérard-Georges 811
Lemaire, Ghislain 811
Lemaire, Thomas 811
ルメルシエ
Lemercier, Frédéric 811
ルメルト
Rumelt, Richard P. 1216
ルメルル
Lemerle, Paul 811
ルメン
Le Men, Ségolène 811
ルモアンヌ
Lemoine, Bertrand 812
Lemoine, Patrick 812
ルモワン
Lemoine, Serge 812
ルモワンヌ
Lemoine, Patrick 812
Lemoine, Serge 812
ルヤール
Rouillard, Pierre 1210
ルヤンス
Lujās, Juris 852
ルーラ
Lula da Silva, Luiz Inácio 852
ルラ
Lula da Silva, Luiz Inácio 852
ル・ライ・スレーン
Lu Lay Sreng 852
ル・ライスレーン
Leu Laysreng 817
Lu Lay Sreng 852
ルラギ
Luraghi, Silvia 854
ルーラ・ダ・シルヴァ
Lula da Silva, Luiz Inácio 852
ルラ・ダ・シルバ
Lula da Silva, Luiz Inácio 852
ルラ・ダシルバ
Lula da Silva, Luiz Inácio 852
ルラングァ
Rurangwa, Révérien 1217
ルランジス
Lerangis, Peter 815
ルーランド
Reuland, Rob 1173
ルーリー
Lurie, Alan J. 854
Lurie, Alison 854
Lurie, Morris 854
Lury, Giles 854
Rury, John L. 1217
ルリ
Ruli, Genc 1216
ルリアス
Ruelius, Joseph 1215
ルリエーヴル
Lelièvre, Marie-Dominique 811
ルーリオ
Luglio, Radha C. 851
ル・リッシュ
Le Riche, Nicolas 815
ルリッチ
Lulic, Senad 852
ル・リデー
Le Rider, Jacques 815
ル・ル
Le Roux, Patrick 815
ル・ルー
Le Roux, Bernard 815
Le Roux, François 815
ルール
Luhr, James F. 851
Rule, Ann 1216
Rule, James B. 1216
ルルー
Leleux, François 811
Le Roux, Bruno 815
Leroux, Christian 815
Leroux, Georges 815
Leroux, Janette 815
Le Roux, Mathieu 815
Leroux, Nicole 815
Leroux, Philippe 815
Le Roux, Willie 815
ルルア
Rurua, Nikoloz 1217
ルルエ
Lerouet, Michel 815
ルル・ガトクオス
Lul Gatkuoth, Ezekiel 852
ルルーシュ
Lelouch, Claude 811
ルルージュ
Lerouge, Jacques 815
Lerouge, Stéphane 815
ルールストン
Roulston, Hayden 1210
ルールズマ
Roelfzema, Erik Hazelhoff 1196
ルルツ
Lurz, Thomas 854
ルールティオズ
Lourtioz, Jean-Michel 846
ルールマン
Lüllmann, Heinz 852
Ruhlman, Michael 1216
ルレマ
Rurema, Déo Guide 1217
ルロア
Leroi, John 815
Leroi, Rita 815
ルロール
Lelord, François 811
ル・ロワ
Le Roy, Maximilien 815
ルロワ
Leroi, Armand Marie 815
Le Roy, Alain 815
Leroy, Francoise 815
Leroy, Gilles 815
Leroy, Jean 815
Leroy, Maurice 815
ル・ロワ・ラデュリ
Le-Roy-Ladurie, Emmanuel 815
ルワイシャン
al-Rawishan, Jalal 1161
al-Ruwayshan, Khalid Abdullah Saleh 1220
ルワウ
Luwawu, Timothe 855
ルワカイカラ
Rwakaikara, Kamara 1220
ルワカバンバ
Lwakabamba, Silas 855
ルワブヒヒ
Rwabuhihi, Ezekias 1220
ルワンゴムブワ
Rwangombwa, John 1220
ルワンヒ
Lwanghy, Celestin 855
ルーン
Luhn, Achim 851
ルン
Lunn, Gayry 853
ルンガ - ラーセン
Lunge-Larsen, Lise 853
ルンガルディエル
Runggaldier, Lukas 1217
ルンキナ
Lunkina, Svetlana 853
ルング
Lungu, Edgar 853
Lungu, Mkhondo 853
ルングワングワ
Lungwangwa, Geoffrey 853
ルンシン
Leung Shing, Emmanuel Jean 817
ルンス
Luns, Joseph Marie Antoine Hubert 853
ルンデ
Lunde, Ken 853
Lunde, Per Halvor 853
Runde, Jochen 1217
ルン・ティ
Lun Thi 853
ルンデスタッド
Lundestad, Geir 853
ルンド
Lund, Eva 853
Lund, Gunnar 853
Lund, James P. 853
Lund, Kristin 853
Lund, Sardar Khalid Ahmed Khan 853
ルンドゥウェ
Lundwe, Gradys 853
ルンドクゥイスト
Lundquist, Matthew 853
ルンドクビスト
Lundqvist, Therese 853
ルンドグレーン
Lundgren, Gunilla 853
ルーンバ
Loomba, Ania 842
ルンバウト
Rumbaut, Rubén G. 1216
ルンバック
Lembach, Charlotte 811
ルンバラ
Lumbala, Roger 852
ルンビ
Lumbi, Pierre 852
ルンビー
Lundby, Maren 853
ルンベワス
Rumbewas, Raema Lisa 1216
ルン・マウン
Lun Maung 853
ルンメニゲ
Rummenigge, Karl-Heinz 1217

【レ】

レ
Lê, Phạm Lê 799
Lê, Văn Dịnh 799
Rey, Marie Michèle 1174
レー
Lê, Khac Cuong 799
Ree, Jonathan 1165
Reh, Rusalka 1167
レア
Löer, Martin 839
Rehr, Henrik 1168
レアー
Lehr, William 809
レアテギ
Reátegui, Jabier Edmundo 1164
レアード
Laird, Elizabeth 782
Laird, Melvin Robert 783
レアマー
Laermer, Richard 781
レアリ
Réaly, Onitiana Voahariniaina 1163
レアリー
Leary, Joyce 800
Leary, Mark R. 800
レアル
Leal, Linda 800
Real, Ubaldino 1163
レアルサンチェス
Leal Sanches, Marcelino 800
レアル・スペングラー
Leal Spengler, Eusebio 800
レアンドロ・カスタン
Leandro Castan 800
レイ
Lai, David 782
Lai, Dilys 782
Lai, Leon 782
Lay, Kenneth Lee 799
Lay, Thorne 799
Lei, Jie-qiong 809
Lei, Jun 809
Leigh, Andrew 810
Leigh, Roberta 810
Leigh, Susannah 810
Lèye, Mamadou Bousso 823
Li, Zi-song 824
Rae, Andrew 1148
Rae, Corinne bailey 1148
Rae, Ian 1148
Rae, Michael 1148
Ray, Angie 1162
Ray, Billy 1162
Ray, Erik T. 1162
Ray, James A. 1162
Ray, Jane 1162
Ray, Jenny 1162
Ray, John 1162

Ray, Joseph 1162
Ray, Mary 1162
Ray, Mary Lyn 1162
Ray, Meg 1162
Ray, Michael L. 1162
Ray, Nicholas 1162
Ray, Nick 1162
Ray, Rachael Domenica 1162
Ray, Rebbecca 1162
Ray, Robbie 1162
Ray, Shane 1162
Ray, Sondra 1162
Ray, Susan 1162
Ray, Wendel A. 1162
Ray, William 1162
Ray, William J. 1162
Raye, Kimberly 1162
Rea, Colin 1163
Reah, Danuta 1163
Reay, Dave 1164
Reay, Diane 1164
Rej, Bent 1171
Rey, Jean-François 1174
Rey, Jean-Michel 1174
Rey, Luis V. 1174
Rey, Patrick 1174
Rey, Vincent 1174
Wray, Alyson 1527
Wray, Carlos 1527
Wray, David 1527
Wray, Fay 1527
Wray, Harry 1527
Wray, William 1527

レイア
Lehr, Dick 809

レイアタウア
Leiataua, Manu 809

レイアロハ
Leialoha, Steve 809

レイイェン
Reijen, Willem van 1169

レイヴ
Lave, Jean 796

レイヴァーズ
Lavers, Chris 796

レイヴァリ
Lavery, Brian 796

レイヴィン
Lavin, Sylvia 797

レイヴェン
Leeuwen, Mattheis Lars van 807

レイヴェンズクロフト
Ravenscroft, Helena 1161

レイエ
Leye, Jean-Marie 823

レイエス
Reyes, Alex 1174
Reyes, Alina 1174
Reyes, Angelo 1174
Reyes, Erick 1174
Reyes, Fabiola 1174
Reyes, Francisco 1174
Reyes, Jose 1174
Reyes, José Adolfo 1174
Reyes, José Manuel 1174
Reyes, Kendall 1174
Reyes, Sonia 1174

レイカー
Laker, Freddie 783
Laker, Mike 783
Laker, Tim 783

レイガダス
Reygadas, Carlos 1174

レイガン
Ragan, Sandra L. 1149
Ragin, Charles C. 1149

レイキー
Lakey, Andy 783

レイキン
Lakin, Christine 783

レイク
Lake, Charles D. Ⅱ 783
Lake, Darren 783
Lake, Gina 783
Lake, Greg 783
Lake, Jon 783
Lake, Patricia 783
Lake, Sam 783
Lake, Selina 783
Rake, Katherine 1152
Wrake, Run 1527

レイ・クウォ・ポ
Li Kwok-Po, David 827

レイクス
Reichs, Kathy 1168

レイグラーフ
Leygraf, Hans 823

レイグラフ
Leijgraaf, Deborah van de 810

レイコフ
Lakoff, George 783

レイコブ
Lacob, Joe 780

レイサー
Reiser, Robert P. 1170

レイサス
Rathus, Jill H. 1160

レイサム
Latham, Darius 794
Latham, Gary P. 794
Latham, Julia 794

レイサン
Lathen, Emma 794

レイシー
Lacey, Anne 779
Lacey, Meg 779
Lacey, Richard Westgarth 779
Lacey, Stephen 779
Lacey, Sue 779
Lacy, Eddie 780
Lacy, Kyle 780
Lacy, Peter 780
Lacy, Shirley 780
Lacy, Steve 780
Laithi, Ahmed Al 783

レイジ
Reij, Chris 1169

レイシェ
Reisheh, Hassan 1170

レイシェル
Reichel, Kealii 1168

レイション
Leyshon, Cressida 823

レイジン
Reizin, Paul 1171

レイス
Leys, Simon 823
Race, Harley 1147
Raysse, Martial 1163
Reis, Maria Edileuza Fontenelle 1170

レイズ
Leys, Colin 823
Raize, Jason 1151
Reyes, Kyle 1174

レイステン
Leisten, Jay 810

レイズニエツェオゾラ
Reizniece-ozola, Dana 1171

レイズマン
Raisman, Alexandra 1151

レイスロップ
Lathrop, Gordon 794

レイセルベルヘ
Van Rijsselberghe, Dorian 1445

レイセン
Leysen, Thomas André 823

レイゼンビー
Lazenby, Roland 799

レイソン
Dyrason, Orri 386
Leyson, Leon 823

レイダー
Leider, Richard J. 809
Rader, Cheryl 1147
Rader, Kae 1147
Reder, Peter 1165

レイタォン
Leitao, Joao Luis da Silva Guerreiro 810

レイタンマルケス
Leitão Marques, Maria Manuel 810

レイチ
Leitch, Donovan Philips 810
Reich, Frank 1168

レイチェル
Reichel Verlag, G. 1168

レイチェルズ
Rachels, James 1147
Rachels, Stuart 1147

レイチャート＝アンダーソン
Reichert-Anderson, Pamela 1168

レイツェラル
Leitzelar, German 810

レイット
Raitt, Bonnie Lynn 1151
Raitt, John Emmett 1151

レイテ
Leite, Arcângelo 810
Leite, Gustavo 810
Leite, Manuela Ferreira 810

レイティ
Ratey, John J. 1159
Ratey, Nancy A. 1159

レイディ
Reidy, Jamie 1169

レイデン
Layden, Joseph 799
Layden, Scott 799

レイデンバッハ
Reidenbach, R.Eric 1169

レイデンフロスト
Leydenfrost, Robert 823

レイト
Raitt, Bonnie Lynn 1151
Raitt, Lisa 1151

レイド
Reid, Anita 1168
Reid, Dennis H. 1168
Reid, Elizabeth J. 1168
Reid, Grant 1168
Reid, Jan 1169
Reid, Neil P. 1169

レイトス
Latos, Mat 794

レイトナー
Leitner, Bernhard 810

レイドメイカーズ
Rademakers, Fons 1147

レイドラー
Laidler, David E.W. 782
Laidler, Keith James 782

レイトリフ
Rateliff, John D. 1159

レイドロー
Laidlaw, Anne 782
Laidlaw, Greig 782
Laidlaw, Rob 782

レイトン
Layton, Eddie 799
Layton, Neal 799
Leighton, Paul 810
Leighton, Ralph 810
Leighton, Robert B. 810

レイトン・ムニョス
Leyton Muñoz, Carlos 823

レイナ
Reina, Carlos Roberto 1170
Reina, Jorge Arturo 1170
Reina, Jose Manuel 1170

レイナー
Leyner, Mark 823
Rainer, Luise 1151
Rayner, Catherine 1162
Rayner, Harvey 1162
Rayner, John L. 1162
Rayner, Olivia 1162
Rayner, Richard 1162
Rayner, Sarah 1162
Raynor, Michael E. 1163
Raynor, Nigel 1163

レイナード
Reynard, Sylvain 1174

レイナルディ
Raynaldy, Romain 1162

レイニー
Laney, Marti Olsen 788
Laney, William R. 788
Rainey, Bobby 1151
Rainey, Lawrence 1151
Raney, Richard. Beverly 1156
Raney-norman, Catherine 1156
Rhaney, Demetrius 1175

レイニウス
Reinius, Kaj 1170

レイノ
Leino, Marko 810

レイノー
Raynaud, Alexis 1162
Raynaud, Jean Pierre 1162
Raynor, Maureen D. 1162

レイノルズ
Reynolds, Adrian 1174
Reynolds, Albert 1174
Reynolds, Alvina 1174
Reynolds, Andre' 1174
Reynolds, Anna 1174
Reynolds, Ann E. 1174
Reynolds, Anthony 1174
Reynolds, Betty 1174
Reynolds, Bonnie Jones 1174
Reynolds, Brett 1174
Reynolds, Burt 1174

Reynolds, Chase 1175
Reynolds, David K. 1175
Reynolds, David West 1175
Reynolds, Debbie 1175
Reynolds, Ed 1175
Reynolds, Garr 1175
Reynolds, Garrett 1175
Reynolds, Helen 1175
Reynolds, John 1175
Reynolds, John Lawrence 1175
Reynolds, Keenan 1175
Reynolds, LaRoy 1175
Reynolds, Lauren 1175
Reynolds, Mark 1175
Reynolds, Matt 1175
Reynolds, Matthew 1175
Reynolds, Nancy 1175
Reynolds, Patrick 1175
Reynolds, Paul 1175
Reynolds, Paula Rosput 1175
Reynolds, Peter H. 1175
Reynolds, Rashaad 1175
Reynolds, Robert Hugh 1175
Reynolds, Ross 1175
Reynolds, Ryan 1175
Reynolds, Sean K. 1175
Reynolds, Shirley 1175
Reynolds, Siimon 1175
Reynolds, Simon 1175
Reynolds, Stanley 1175
Reynolds, Toby 1175
Reynolds, William L. 1175
レイノルド
Reynolds, Frances 1175
レイバ
Leyba, Domingo 823
Leyva, Danell 823
Leyva, Pío 823
Leyva Yepez, Alfonso Antonio 823
レイバー
Leiber, Vivian 809
Raber, Douglas 1146
レイパー
Leiper, Tim 810
レイバス
Leivas, Leandro 810
レイバーン
Raburn, Ryan 1147
Raeburn, Paul 1148
Reyburn, Wallace 1174
レイヒー
Lahey, Lisa Laskow 782
レイビー
Rabe, Tish 1146
Raby, Fiona 1147
Raby, Julian 1147
Raby, Peter 1147
レイフ
Reif, Emil 1169
Reĭf, Igor' 1169
Reiff, Riley 1169
レイフィール
Rayfiel, David 1162
レイフィールド
Layfield, Rhonda 799
レイフェルクス
Leiferkus, Sergei Petrovich 810
レイブシュタイン
Reibstein, David J. 1168
レイプハルト
Lijphart, Arend 827
レイブブラント
Leibbrandt, Kees 809
レイフル
Raphael, Frederic Michael 1158
レイブロック
Leibrock, Cynthia 809
レイブン
Raven, Hazel 1161
Raven, Simon Arthur Noël 1161
レイブンズクロフト
Ravenscroft, Thurl 1161
レイヘルド
Reiherd, Dmitriy 1169
レイベン
Raven, Floyd 1161
レイボ
Leivo, Margus 810
レイボヴィッチ
Leibovici, Martine 809
レイポート
Rayport, Jeffrey F. 1163
レイボーン
Laybourn, Thomas 799
レイマー
Raymer, Beth 1162
Reimer, Stan 1170
レイマン
Laman, Tim 784
Layman, Andrew 799
Layman, Jake 799
Layman, John 799
Reiman, Leonid D. 1169
Reimann, Robert 1170
レイミス
Ramis, Harold 1154
レイム
Rehm, Patrice K. 1168
Rhame, Jacob 1175
レイモ
Raymo, Chet 1162
レイモン
Laymon, Richard 799
Raimond, Jean Bernard 1151
レイモンド
Raymond, Eric S. 1162
Raymond, Janice L. 1162
Raymond, Kalif 1162
Raymond, Lee R. 1162
Raymond, Lisa 1162
Raymond, Scott 1162
レイヨン
Lejon, Britta 811
レイヨンボリ
Leijonborg, Lars 810
レイヨンボリー
Leijonborg, Lars 810
レイラー
Lalor, Liz 784
レイラ・アリグッド
Raile Alligood, Martha 1151
レイランド
Leyland, Jim 823
Reiland, Rachel 1169
レイリー
Railey, Paige 1151
Railey, Zach 1151
Reilly, Charles Nelson 1169
Reilly, Harold J. 1169
Reilly, Jack 1169
Reilly, Peter 1169
Reilly, Philip 1169
レイリアン
Reiljan, Villu 1169
レイリス
Leilis, Edmund 810
Reirs, Jānis 1170
レイリング
Reiling, J. 1169
レイルー
Raylu, Namrata 1162
レイルス
Reirs, Jānis 1170
レイルズバック
Railsback, Brian E. 1151
レイ・レイ
Rey Rey, Rafael 1175
レイローサ
Rey Rosa, Rodrigo 1175
レイン
Laine, Christine 782
Laine, Frankie 782
Laing, Dave 782
Laing, R.D. 782
Laing, Robert 782
Lane, Bernard 787
Lane, Charles 787
Lane, Diane 787
Lane, Elizabeth 787
Lane, Harlan L. 787
Lane, Jani 787
Lane, Jeremy 787
Lane, John 787
Lane, Nathan 787
Lane, Richard J. 787
Lane, Roderick 788
Lane, Tami 788
Layne, Christopher 799
Layne, Tommy 799
Rain 1151
Raine, Adrian 1151
Raine, Craig 1151
Raine, Derek J. 1151
Raine, Jerry 1151
Raine, Kathleen Jessie 1151
Raine, Sue 1151
Rayne, Mark 1162
レインコネ
Leingkone, Bruno 810
レインゴールド
Reingold, Dan 1170
Reingold, Jennifer 1170
レインサル
Rainsalu, Urmas 1151
Reinsalu, Urmas 1170
レインズ
Lanes, Selma G. 788
Raines, Martin 1151
Rains, Rob 1151
レインダース
Reinders, James 1170
レインデルス
Reynders, Didier 1174
レインハンマー
Reinheimer, Jack 1170
レイン・フォックス
Lane Fox, Robin 788
レインワンド
Leinwand, Allan 810
Leinwand, Paul 810
レーウ
Leeuw, Richard de 807
Löw, Joachim 848
レーヴ
Loew, Franklin M. 839
Löw, Joachim 848
レヴァイン
Levine, Alison 818
Levine, Amy-Jill 818
Levine, David D. 818
Levine, David K. 818
Levine, Ellen 818
Levine, James 819
Levine, Judith 819
Levine, Margie 819
Levine, Robert 819
Levine, Robert A. 819
Levine, Stephen 819
レヴァル
Réval, Annie 1173
Réval, Bernard 1173
レヴァンソン
Levenson, Michael H. 817
レヴァンドフスキ
Lewandowski, Robert 821
Lewandowski, Sascha 821
レーヴィ
Levi, Peter 818
レヴィ
Leavy, Hannelore R. 800
Levi, Aaron 818
Levi, David 818
Levi, Lennart 818
Levi, Mark 818
Levi, Michael 818
Levi, Natalie 818
Levi, Yannets 818
Levy, Adrian 820
Levy, Alain M. 820
Lévy, Andre 820
Levy, Barbara 820
Lévy, Bernard-Henri 820
Lévy, Catherine 820
Lévy, Christine 820
Levy, Clifford J. 820
Levy, Daniel Saul 820
Lévy, Didier 820
Lévy, Dominique 820
Levy, Howard 820
Levy, Jaime 820
Levy, Janice 820
Levy, Joe 820
Lévy, Justine 820
Lévy, Lorraine 820
Levy, Marc 820
Levy, Matthew N. 820
Levy, Matthys 820
Levy, Peter 820
Lévy, Pierre 820
Levy, Raymond A. 820
Levy, R.S. 820
Levy, Shawn 820
Levy, Udi 820
Löwy, Michael 849
Revy, Shawn 1174
レヴィー
Levy, Barry L. 820
Levy, Joel 820
Levy, Leonard Williams 820
Levy, Luis 820
レヴィサン
Levithan, David 819
レヴィ・ストロース
Lévi-Strauss, Claude 819

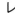

レヴィタン
Levitan, Steven 819
レヴィツカ
Lewycka, Marina 823
レヴィツキ
Levitzki, Alexander 820
レヴィツキー
Levitsky, Aleksey 820
レヴィック
Levick, J.Rodney 818
レーヴィット
Leavitt, David 800
レヴィット
Leavitt, David 800
Leavitt, Harold J. 800
Leavitt, Mike 800
Leavitt, Sarah A. 800
Levit, Alexandra 819
Levitt, John 820
Levitt, Leonard 820
Levitt, Michael 820
Levitt, Steven D. 820
Levitt, Theresa 820
レヴィティン
Levitin, Anany 819
Levitin, Daniel J. 819
Levitin, Maria 820
レヴィトン
Leviton, Alex 820
レーヴィ・モンタルチーニ
Levi-Montalcini, Rita 818
レヴィ・モンタルチーニ
Levi-Montalcini, Rita 818
レヴィラ
Revilla, Beatriz Pineda 1174
レ・ウイルソン
Wreh-wilson, Blidi 1527
レヴィ＝ルボワイエ
Lévy-Leboyer, Maurice 820
レーヴィン
Lavin, Marilyn Aronberg 797
Lewin, Waldtraut 821
レヴィーン
Levene, Malcolm 817
Levine, Adam 818
Levine, Darren 818
Levine, Janice Ruth 819
Levine, Jeremy 819
Levine, Lawrence W. 819
Levine, Leslie 819
Levine, Melvin D. 819
Levine, Paul Ansel 819
Levine, Peter 819
Levine, Rhoda 819
Levine, Robert 819
Levine, Suzanne 819
レヴィン
Levin, Al S. 818
Levin, Carl 818
Levin, Caroline D. 818
Levin, Christoph 818
Levin, Freddie 818
Levin, Gail 818
Levin, Gerald Manuel 818
Levin, Henry M. 818
Levin, Ira 818
Levin, Janna 818
Levin, Kim 818
Levin, Mark Reed 818
Levin, Neal 818
Levin, Simon Asher 818
Levin, Thunder 818
Levin, Tony 818
Levine, James A. 819
Levine, Jeremy 819
Levine, John R. 819
Levine, Ken 819
Levine, Madeline 819
Levine, Mark 819
Levine, Michael 819
Levine, Raphael D. 819
LeVine, Steve 819
レヴィンサール
Leventhal, Judith 817
レヴィンスン
Levinson, Robert S. 819
レヴィンソン
Levinson, Arthur D. 819
Levinson, Barry 819
Levinson, Cynthia 819
Levinson, David 819
Levinson, Mark 819
Levinson, Stephen C. 819
Levinson, Steve 819
レウィントン
Lewington, Anna 821
レウヴァン
Reouven, René 1172
レヴェスク
Levesque, Allen H. 818
Levesque, Roger J.R. 818
レヴェック
Lévêque, Claude 817
レヴェッリ
Revelli, Nuto 1174
レウェニンギラ
Leweniqila, Isireli 821
レウェリン
Llewellyn, Claire 836
レウエルマルック
Rehuher-marugg, Faustina 1168
レーウェン
Leeuwen, Cornelis van 807
Leeuwen, Joke van 807
Leeuwen, Thomas A.P. van 807
レヴェン
Leven, Jeremy 817
レーヴェンスウェーイ
Ravenswaay, Eileen O. van 1161
レヴェンソン
Levenson, Bill 817
Levenson, Thomas 817
レウォンティン
Lewontin, Richard 823
レヴキン
Revkin, Andrew C. 1174
レウス
Reus, Katie 1173
レウス・ゴンサレス
Reus González, María Esther 1173
レヴスティク
Levstik, Linda S. 820
レヴハイム
Revheim, Nadine 1174
レウルス
Leurs, Bernard 817
レヴンズクロフト
Ravenscroft, Trevor 1161
レエ
Rey, Anne 1174
レオ
Léaud, Jean-Pierre 800
Leo, Albert 813
Leo, Melissa 813
Leo, Richard A. 813
Leo, Veronica 813
レオクム
Leokum, Arkady 813
レオタ
Leota, Johnny 814
レオタール
Léotard, Philippe 814
レオナード
Leonard, Barbara 813
Leonard, Herman B. 813
Leonard, Tina 814
Leonard, Victoria 814
レオナール
Leonard, Yves 814
レオナルト
Leonhard, Gerd 814
レオナルド
Leonard, Dorothy 813
Leonard, Isabel 813
Leonard, Kelly 813
Leonard, Max 813
Leonard, Pamela Blume 814
Leonardo 814
レオナルド・スアレス
Leonardo Suarez 814
レオナルド＝バートン
Leonard-Barton, Dorothy 814
レオーニ
Leoni, Giulio 814
レオニダス・ダ・シルバ
Leonidas da Silva 814
レオニードブナ
Leonidovna, Klavdija 814
レオーネ
Leone, Dan 814
Leone, Giovanni 814
レオネ
Leone, Giovanni 814
レオーノフ
Leonov, Aleksei Arkhipovich 814
レオ・バチストン
Leo Baptistao 813
レオポルド
Leopold, Aldo 814
Leopold, Allison Kyle 814
Leopold, David 814
Leopold, Estella 814
Leopold, Günter 814
Leopold, Jason 814
レオモギー
Leo Moggie, Anak Irok 813
レオン
Layyoun, Gaby 799
Lean, Rob 800
Leao, Emerson 800
Leon, Donna M. 813
León, Vicki 813
Leone, Douglas 814
Leong, Stephen 814
Leong Mun Yoon, Stephen 814
Leung, Ka-fai 817
Leung, Tony 817
Rheon, Iwan 1175
レオン・アバド
León Abad, Santiago 813
レオンアラルコン
Leon Alarcon, Yankiel 813
レオン・カーファイ
Leung, Ka-fai 817
レオン・カーフェイ
Leung, Ka-fai 817
レオンシス
Leonsis, Ted 814
レオンチェヴァ
Leontyeva, Elena Livovna 814
レオン＝デュフール
Léon-Dufour, Xavier 814
レーオンハルト
Leonhardt, Gustav 814
レオンハルト
Leonhard, Kurt Ernst Albert 814
Leonhardt, Gustav 814
レオンフォルト
Léonforte, Pierre 814
レオン・リー
Lee, Leon 805
レーカー
Laker, Freddie 783
レーガー
Reger, Steven I. 1167
レ・カオ・ダイ
Le Cao Dai 801
レカク
Lekhak, Ramesh 811
レガス
Regás, Lluis 1167
レガツォーニ
Regazzoni, Clay 1167
レガッツォ
Regazzo, Lorenzo 1167
レガート
Legat, Dieter 808
レガト
Legato, Marianne J. 808
Legato, Rob 808
レカナティ
Recanati, Francois 1164
レー・カー・フィエウ
Le Kha Phieu 811
レ・カ・フュー
Le Kha Phieu 811
レガラ
Regalla, Agnelo 1167
レガラード
Regalado, Antonio 1167
レガラド
Regalado, Jacobo 1167
レガリ
Leghari, Awais Ahmed Khan 808
Leghari, Farooq Ahmed Khan 808
レガーリア
Regalia, Ida 1167
レガーレ
Legare, Martha 808
レーガン
Ragan, Philip 1149
Ragins, Mark 1149
Reagan, Maureen 1163
Reagan, Nancy Davis 1163
Reagan, Ronald Wilson 1163
Reagan, Susan 1163
Reagan, Timothy G. 1163
Regan, Lara Jo 1167
Regan, Sally 1167
レキーク
Rekik, Selma 1171

レキク
Rekik, Selma 1171
レギサモン
Leguizamon, Juan Manuel 808
レキット
Reckitt, Helena 1164
レキーナ
Lekhina, Ekaterina 811
レギナルド
Reginald, Stanley 1167
レキャン
Recean, Dorin 1164
レーク
Lake, Charles D. II 783
Lake, Eustace 783
Lake, Greg 783
Lake, Morgan 783
Reek, Harriët van 1166
Reek, Wouter van 1166
レクエ
Lekue, Inigo 811
レグコフ
Legkov, Alexander 808
レクスロート
Rexrodt, Günter 1174
レクター
Lechter, Sharon L. 802
Rector, Edward 1164
レークタック
Lake-tack, Louise 783
レクトシャッフェン
Rechtschaffen, Stephan 1164
レクトン
Lekuton, Joseph 811
レークナー
Rögner, Heinz 1197
レーグナー
Rögner, Heinz 1197
レグナー
Rögner, Heinz 1197
レグネール
Regnér, Åsa 1167
レクフレール
Lescouflair, Evans 816
レクラー
Lechler, Shane 802
レグラ
Röggla, Kathrin 1197
レクラーク
Leclerc, Jose 802
レクレー
Lecrae 802
レグレ
Legre, Phillippe 808
レクロー
Le Clos, Chad 802
レゲァスティ
Legerstee, Maria Theresia 808
レゲヴィー
Leggewie, Claus 808
レゲセ
Legese, Adisu 808
レゲゼル
Regasel, Yanni 1167
レゲット
Leggett, Anthony James 808
Leggett, Jeremy K. 808
Leggett, Trevor Pryce 808
レケーナ
Requena, Osvaldo 1173
レケナ
Requena, Gladys 1173
レゲブ
Regev, Miri 1167
レーケン
Löhken, Sylvia C. 840
レゲンバヌ
Regenvanu, Ralph 1167
レコ
Leko, Jonathan 811
レゴ
Legaut, Charlotte 808
Rego, Emanuel 1167
レコタ
Lekota, Mosiuoa 811
Lekota, Patrick 811
レコード
Record, Jeffrey 1164
レゴネッサ
Regonessa, Maurice 1167
レコルヴィッツ
Recorvits, Helen 1164
レゴレッタ
Legorreta, Ricardo 808
レコンバルムトゥポンボ
Lekomba Loumetou-pombo, Jeanne Françoise 811
レコンバルムトポンボ
Leckombaloumeto-pombo, Jeanne Françoise 802
レーサー
Loeser, John David 839
レーザー
Loeser, John David 839
レサ
Lessa, Luzolo Bambi 816
レサー
Lesser, Erik 816
レザ
Reza, Ovais 1175
RZA 1222
レザー
Lazar, Ralph 799
Leather, Stephen 800
レザーイー
Rezaei, Ghasem 1175
レザエ
Rezaei, Ghasem 1175
レザエイ
Rezaei, Ghasem 1175
レザク
Lezak, Jason 823
レザザデ
Reza Zadeh, Hossein 1175
レザーシッチ
Leathersich, Jack 800
レザビー
Lethaby, Jo 816
レザーランド
Letherland, Lucy 817
レサール
Laissard, Vincent 783
レザレン
Letheren, Tim 816
レーシー
Lacey, Minna 779
Lacey, Richard Westgarth 779
レシ
Lleshi, Ismail 836
レジ
Regy, Claude 1167
レジアニ
Reggiani, Serge 1167
レジェ
Léger, Charles 808
レジエ
Légier, Gérard 808
Regier, Darrel A. 1167
レジェス
Reyes, Jose 1174
Reyes, Jose Antonio 1174
Reyes, Melba Falck 1174
Reyes, Samuel Armando 1174
レジェス・アルバラド
Reyes Alvarado, Yesid 1174
レジェノ
Legeno, Dave 808
レジェピ
Rexhepi, Bajram 1174
レジェポフ
Rejepov, Berdimirat 1171
Rejepov, Dovranmammet 1171
レジェンド
Legend, John 808
レシオ
Recio 1164
レシオフ
Leschiov, Vladimir 815
レシグ
Resig, John 1173
レジシ
Legizi, Ndre 808
レジス
Regis, Edward 1167
レシック
Resick, Patricia A. 1173
レジーニ
Regini, Marino 1167
Regini, Vasco 1167
レージネヴァ
Lezhneva, Julia 823
レシノス
Recinos, Julio 1164
レシーノス・デ・マルティネス
Recinos de Martínez, María Emma 1164
レジミ
Redjimi, Mourad 1165
レージャー
Leisure, Mary Jo 810
レジャ
Leja, Darryl L. 810
レジャー
Ladger, Heath 780
Ledger, Heath 802
レシャソー
Lechasseur, Eric 802
レシャード
Reshad, Khaled 1173
レジャーニ
Reggiani, Serge 1167
レシャヌ
Lesanu, Ion 815
レシュ
Laissus, Marie 783
Loesch, Uwe 839
Resch, Nikolaus 1173
レジュロン
Légeron, Patrick 808
レジューン
Lejeune, Anthony 811
レジョリー
Le Joly, Edward 811
レジョンガー
Lesjongard, Georges Pierre 816
レーシン
Lesin, Mikhail Y. 816
レス
Ress, Georg 1173
レスウィック
Leswick, Tony 816
レスウイック
Leswick, Tony 816
レスカイ
Leskaj, Bujar 816
Leskaj, Valentina 816
レスカーノ
Lezcano, Dario 823
レスカノ
Lescano, Héctor 815
レスキン
Leskin, Barry 816
レスク
Lesk, Arthur M. 816
レスコ
Lescot, David 816
レスコヴァル
Leskovar, Simona 816
レスター
Leicester, Henry Marshall 809
Leicester, Mal 809
Lester, Adrian 816
Lester, Alison 816
Lester, Buddy 816
Lester, Eva P. 816
Lester, Jon 816
Lester, Julius 816
Lester, Justin Dashaun 816
Lester, Linda B. 816
Lester, Paul 816
Lester, Richard 816
Lester, Richard Keith 816
Lester, Toby 816
レスタック
Restak, Richard M. 1173
レスタニー
Restany, Pierre 1173
レスタリ
Lestari, Noortje 816
レステリーニ
Restellini, Marc 1173
レストレーポ
Restrepo, Laura 1173
レストレポ・サラサル
Restrepo Salazar, Juan Camilo 1173
レストレポ・リベラ
Restrepo Rivera, Jairo 1173
レスナー
Lesnar, Brock 816
レズナー
Reznor, Trent 1175
レスニー
Lesnie, Andrew 816
レズニク
Resnik, Regina 1173

レ

Reznik, Boris L'vovich 1175
レスニック
Resnick, Mitchel 1173
Resnick, Robert 1173
レズニック
Resnick, Lynda 1173
Resnick, Mike 1173
Resnick, Robert J. 1173
Resnick, Steve 1173
Resnick, Stewart 1173
Resnik, Regina 1173
Reznick, David N. 1175
レスブリッジ
Lethbridge, Lucy 816
レスブロ
Lesbros, Dominique 815
レスマン
Lessmann, C.B. 816
レスラー
Resler, Bill 1173
Ressler, Robert K. 1173
Ressler, Tony 1173
Rösler, Philipp 1206
Rössler, Almut 1208
Rossler, Otto E. 1208
Rössler, Roman 1208
レスリー
Lesley, Taylor 816
Leslie, Ainslie 816
Leslie, Jordan 816
Leslie, Keith 816
Leslie, Mark 816
レズリー
Leslie, Ian 816
レスロー
Leslau, Wolf 816
レスン
Lesun, Alexander 816
レゼピ
Redzepi, René 1165
レセム
Lethem, Jonathan 816
レーゼル
Rösel, Peter 1203
レゼンジ
Rezende, Sérgio 1175
レゼンデ
Resende, Nuno 1173
Rezende, Antonio Claret de 1175
レゼンテス
Rezentes, William C., Ⅲ 1175
レソェ
Laessøe, Thomas 781
レーダー
Rader, Laura 1147
Rehder, Ben 1168
レダ
Réda, Jacques 1164
レーダーバーグ
Lederberg, Joshua 802
Lederberg, Marguerite S. 802
レダーバーグ
Lederberg, Joshua 802
レダーハンドラー
Lederhandler, Marty 802
レタベック
Letavec, Craig 816
レーダーマン
Lederman, Leon M. 802
Lederman, Michelle Tillis 802
Lederman, Norman G. 802
レターマン
Leterman, Elmer G. 816
Letterman, David Michael 817
レタラック
Retallack, Simon 1173
レタリック
Retallick, Brodie 1173
レダン
Reddan, Eoin 1164
レチキン
Redkin, Sergey 1165
レチッチ
Lečić, Branisrav 802
Rechichi, Elise 1164
レツァツィ
Letsatsi, Khotso 817
レツィエ3世
Letsie Ⅲ 817
レツォサ
Letsosa, Motlalentoa 817
レッカー
Recker, Anthony 1164
Recker, Keith 1164
レッキー
Leckey, Mark 802
Leckie, Ann 802
Leckie, Gloria J. 802
Leckie, Mathew 802
Leckie, Robert 802
レッキア
Recchia, Lucia 1164
レック
Reck, Ross R. 1164
Roeck, Bernd 1196
レックス
Lex, Stefan 823
Rex, John Arderne 1174
レックスフォード
Rexford, Jennifer 1174
レックスロート
Rexrodt, Günter 1174
レックバリ
Läckberg, Camilla 780
レッケ
Luecke, Richard A. 851
レッケルマン
Reckermann, Jonas 1164
レッサ
Lessa, Espólio Luis Carlos Barbosa 816
Lesser, Rose 816
レッサー
Lesser, Elizabeth 816
Lesser, Jeffery 816
Lesser, Michael 816
Lesser, Milton 816
Lesser, Richard 816
レッシグ
Lessig, Lawrence 816
レッシャー
Löscher, Peter 845
レッジャーニ
Reggiani, Serge 1167
レッシュ
Resch, Alexander 1173
レッシング
Lessing, Doris May 816
Pomarède, Vincent 1123
レッスル
Lossl, Jonas 845
レッセル
Lessell, Colin B. 816
レッソン
Raisson, Virginie 1151
レッタ
Letta, Corrado G.M. 817
Letta, Enrico 817
Letta, Gianni 817
レッチュ
Rätsch, Christian 1160
レッツ
Letts, Billie 817
Letts, Tracy 817
レッツェリーニ
Lezzerini, Luca 823
レッテリ
Letteri, Joe 817
レッテルブッシュ
Rettelbusch, Ernst 1173
レッデン
Redden, Jim 1164
レット
Leth, Nina 816
Lett, Michael Denis 817
Lett, Travis 817
Lette, Kathy 817
Rhett, Alicia 1175
レッド
Redd, Silas 1164
レッドウィン
Redwin, Eleanor 1165
レッドグレイヴ
Redgrave, Corin 1165
Redgrave, Lynn 1165
Redgrave, Vanessa 1165
レッドグレーヴ
Redgrave, Corin 1165
Redgrave, Lynn 1165
Redgrave, Vanessa 1165
レッドグレーブ
Redgrave, Corin 1165
Redgrave, Lynn 1165
Redgrave, Vanessa 1165
レッドストーン
Redstone, Sumner Murray 1165
レッドソム
Leadsom, Andrea 800
レッドパス
Redpath, Ophelia 1165
レッドバンク
Redbank, Tennant 1164
レッドファーン
Redfern, Elizabeth 1165
Redfern, Ioteba 1165
Redfern, Kasey 1165
Redfern, Martin 1165
Redfern, Nicholas 1165
レッドフィールド
Redfield, James 1165
レッドフォード
Redford, Dorothy Spruill 1165
Redford, Robert 1165
レッドベター
Leadbetter, David 800
Leadbetter, Tom 800
Ledbetter, Lilly M. 802
Ledbetter, Mark 802
Ledbetter, Steven 802
レッドマン
Redman, Dewey 1165
Redman, Joshua 1165
Redman, Matt 1165
Redman, Peter 1165
Redman, Rich 1165
レッドメイン
Redmayne, Eddie 1165
レッヒ
Rech, Benno 1164
Rech, Irmgard 1164
レッピン
Leppin, Volker 814
レップ
Lepp, Mati 814
レッベ
Rebbe, Peter 1164
レッペル
Lepper, Andrzej 814
レツヘルト
Letschert, Timo 817
レッペン
Reppen, Randi 1173
レツヤクス
Lecjaks, Jan 802
レーテ
Reete, Tangariki 1167
レテ
Lété, Nathalie 816
レディ
Reddy, Dabbala Raj 1164
Reddy, Linda A. 1164
Reddy, Mahendra 1164
Reddy, Martin 1164
Reddy, Patsy 1165
Reddy, S. Jaipal 1165
Reddy, Vasudevi 1165
レディー
Ready, Dee 1163
レディカー
Rediker, Marcus 1165
レディー・ガガ
Lady Gaga 471
レディスミス・ブラック・マンバゾ
Mambazo, Ladysmith Black 892
レディック
Reddick, Josh 1164
Redick, J.J. 1165
レディッシュ
Redish, Edward F. 1165
レ・ティ・ニャム・トゥエット
Le Thi Nham Tuyet 817
レティネン
Lehtinen, Jere 809
Lyytinen, Kalle 857
レディング
Reading, Mario 1163
Redding, Noel 1164
Redding, Stan 1164
Reding, Jamie 1165
レテギス
Reteguiz, Jo-Ann 1173
レデスマ
Ledesma, Xavier 802
レデスマ・コルネホ
Ledezma Cornejo, Jorge 802
レデスマ・レバサ
Ledesma Rebaza, Walter 802
レデツカ
Ledecka, Ester 802

レデッキー
Ledecky, Katie 802
レテノアソヌエ
Reteno Assonouet, Ida 1173
レデラック
Lederach, John Paul 802
レテリエ
Leterrier, Louis 816
レデリンハイス
Redelinghuys, Johnny 1165
レーデル
Redel, Kurt 1165
レテン
Letén, Mats 816
レト
Reto, Paula 1173
レトー
Leto, Jared 817
レドウィズ
Ledwith, Míceál 803
レトウィン
Letwin, Oliver 817
レドウォン
Ledwon, Adam 803
レー・ドゥク・アイン
Le Duc Anh 803
レ・ドク・アイン
Le Duc Anh 803
レトゲン
Röttgen, Norbert 1210
レドチャウスキー
Ledochowski, Igor 802
レドナー
Ledner, Catherine 802
レドニス
Redniss, Lauren 1165
レドフスカヤ
Ledovskaya, Nataliya 803
レートヘイ
Réthelyi, Miklós 1173
レドマン
Redman, Thomas C. 1165
レドモンド
Redmond, Adam 1165
Redmond, Alex 1165
Redmond, Eric 1165
Redmond, Michael 1165
Redmond, Mike 1165
Redmond, Nathan 1165
Redmond, Patrick 1165
Redmond, Will 1165
レドラー
Lederer, Chris 802
Lederer, Richard 802
レドリ
Redli, Andras 1165
レドリー
Ledley, Deborah Roth 802
Ledley, Joe 802
レトリア
Letria, André 817
レトル
Rettl, Martin 1173
レトレ＝メラン
Réthoret-Mélin, Marie-Anne 1173
レトロトロ
Letlotlo, Molahlehi 817
レドワン
Redwan, Hussein 1165
レドンド
Redondo, Dolores 1165
レーナー
Lehner, Mark 809
Lehner, Ulrich 809
Lerner, Betsy 815
Lerner, Harriet Goldhor 815
Lerner, Preston 815
レナ
Renna, Tony 1172
レナー
Renner, Bryn 1172
Renner, Diana 1172
Renner, Jack 1172
Renner, James 1172
Renner, Jeremy 1172
Renner, Michael 1172
Renner, Sara 1172
レナタ
Ribeiro, Renata 1177
レナード
Lennard, Erica 812
Leonard, Adam 813
Leonard, Elmore 813
Leonard, Herman 813
Leonard, Kawhi 813
Leonard, Mark 813
Leonard, Meyers 813
Leonard, M.G. 814
Leonard, Peter 814
Leonard, Queenie 814
Leonard, Susan 814
Leonard, Thomas J. 814
Leonard, Victoria 814
Leonard-Barton, Dorothy 814
Leonhardt, Brian 814
Renard, David 1171
Renard, Gary R. 1171
レナト
Renato, Stefani 1171
レナト・サンチェス
Renato Sanches 1171
レーナ・マリア
Klingvall, Lena Maria 746
Lena Maria 812
レナル
Reynard, Denise 1174
レナルズ
Reynolds, Alastair 1174
レーナルト
Lehnert, Felicitas A. 809
Lehnert, Volker A. 809
レーニ
Laney, Dennis H. 788
レーニー
Laney, James T. 788
レニ
Leni, Nollen 812
レニー
Rennie, Drummond 1172
レニウ
Leniu, Tofaeono Avamagalo 812
レーニエ
Rainier Ⅲ 1151
Regnier, Victor 1167
Regniers, Beatrice Schenk de 1167
レニエ
Regniers, Beatrice Schenk de 1167
レーニエ3世
Rainier Ⅲ 1151
レニソン
Rennison, Louise 1172
レニック
Renik, Owen 1172
Resnick, Evelyne 1173
レニハン
Lenihan, Brian 812
Lenihan, Edmund 812
レニ・リーフェンシュタール
Riefenstahl, Leni 1181
レニール
LeNir, Philip 812
レーニンジャー
Lehninger, Albert L. 809
レーヌ
Lesne, Annick 816
レネ
Lenné, Michael G. 812
Resnais, Alain 1173
レーネ・アデレード
Reine-adelaide, Jeff 1170
レネキー
Roenicke, Ron 1196
レネベルク
Roenneberg, Till 1196
レーネルト
Lehnert, Gertrud 809
レーネルト・シュロス
Lehnert-Schroth, Christa 809
レーネン
Rainen, William 1151
レノ
Leno, Bernd 813
Leno, Charles 813
Leno, Jay 813
Reno, Janet 1172
Reno, Jean 1172
レノー
Raineau, Guillaume 1151
レノス
Lenos, Melissa 813
レノックス
Lennox, Annie 813
Lennox, Catriona 813
Lennox, Graham 813
Lennox, Kara 813
Lennox, Marion 813
Lenox, Adriane 813
レノード
Renaud, Blake 1171
レーノルズ
Reynolds, Burt 1174
Reynolds, Debbie 1175
レノルズ
Reynolds, Anna 1174
レノルド
Renold, Emma 1172
レノレ
L'Henoret, Andre 823
L'Hénoret, Yann 823
レノン
Lennon, Aaron 813
Lennon, Cynthia 813
Lennon, Julian 813
Lennon, Robert L. 813
Lennon, Sean 813
Lennon, Sharron J. 813
レバ
Reva, Andrii 1173
レバイン
Levin, Carl 818
Levine, Amir 818
Levine, James 819
Levine, Jonathan 819
Levine, Laura 819
Levine, Mark 819
Levine, Richie F. 819
Levine, Rick 819
レーバーガー
Rehberger, Tobias 1168
レーハーゲル
Rehhagel, Otto 1168
レバス
Lebas, Michel 801
レパス
Reppas, Dimitris 1173
レハタ
Lehata, Mokone 808
Lehata, Rammotsi 808
レハチ
Lehaci, Ionela-Livia 808
レパチョリ
Repacholi, Daniel 1172
レハック
Rehak, Melanie 1168
レバート
Levert, Caris 818
Levert, Gerald 818
レバニゼ
Lebanidze, Tamar 801
レバーラー
Leberer, Sigrid 801
レバリアーティ
Rebagliati, Gabriele 1164
レハレタ
Lejarreta Errasti, Inaki 811
レバンジー
Levangie, Dana 817
レバンドフスキ
Lewandowski, Marcin 821
Lewandowski, Robert 821
Lewandowski, Sascha 821
レ・バンナ
Le Banner, Jerome 801
レビ
Levi, Aaron 818
Levi, Antonia J. 818
Levi, Marcel M. 818
Levi, Maria Benvinda 818
Lévy, Bernard-Henri 820
Levy, Joaquim 820
Levy, Peter 820
Levy, Steven 820
Levy, Yitzhak 820
Revy, Shawn 1174
レビー
Levi, Nick 818
Levy, Alain M. 820
Levy, DeAndre 820
Levy, Elinor 820
Levy, Paul F. 820
Levy, Steven 820
Levy, Thomas E. 820
レヒアイス
Recheis, Käthe 1164
レビィ
Levy, Barrie 820
Levy, Joaquim 820
レビィ・ストロース
Lévi-Strauss, Claude 819
レヒコイネン
Lehikoinen, Petri 809
レビサン
Levithan, Steven 819

レ

レビス
Lewis, Stephen H. 822
Revis, Darrelle 1174
レビスキー
Lewicki, Roy J. 821
レピスト
Lepisto, Laura 814
レビ・ストロース
Lévi-Strauss, Claude 819
レビソン
Levison, Julie H. 819
Levison, Sandra P. 819
レビチン
Levitin, Igor E. 819
Ye.levitin, Igor 1537
レビツカ
Lewycka, Marina 823
レビッチ
Rebic, Ante 1164
レビッツ
Levitz, Paul 820
レピッツ
Lippitz, Michael J. 833
レビット
Leavitt, Harold J. 800
Leavitt, Mike 800
Levit, Michael 819
Levit, Vassiliy 819
Levitt, Arthur 820
Levitt, Peter 820
Levitt, Raymond E. 820
Levitt, Theodore 820
Levitte, Jean D. 820
Lipman-Bluman, Jean 833
レヒトネン
Lehtonen, Olli 809
レビトレイ
Levitre, Andy 820
レヒナー
Lechner, Eva 802
レピーヌ
Lépine, Jean-Pierre 814
レビ・モンタルチーニ
Levi-Montalcini, Rita 818
レビモンタルチーニ
Levi-Montalcini, Rita 818
レビル
Revill, Jo 1174
レービン
Levin, Gerald Manuel 818
レーピン
Repin, Vadim 1172
レビーン
Leveen, Lindsay 817
Levien, Roy 818
Levine, Adam 818
Levine, Gene 819
レビン
Lavin, Christine 796
Levin, Bernard 818
Levin, Carl 818
Levin, Gerald Manuel 818
Levin, Ira 818
Levin, Lawrence S. 818
Levin, Michal 818
Levin, Simon Asher 818
Levin, Tomer T. 818
Levin, Tony 818
Levin, Yariv 818
Levin, Ze'ev 818
Levine, Anthony 818
Levine, Barbara G. 818
Levine, Donald 818
Levine, Gail Carson 819
Levine, Hillel 819
Levine, Joseph 819
Levine, Karen 819
Levine, Peter G. 819
レピンスキー
Repinski, Martin 1173
レビンスン
Levinson, Robert S. 819
レビンソン
Levinson, Arthur D. 819
Levinson, Barry 819
Levinson, Boris Mayer 819
Levinson, Edward 819
Levinson, Harry 819
Levinson, Jay 819
Levinson, Jay Conrad 819
Levinson, Marc 819
Levinson, Martin H. 819
Levinson, Robert S. 819
レーブ
Löw, Joachim 848
レフ
Lehu, Marcel Ilunga 809
レブ
Lev, Baruch 817
レファロ
Refalo, Anton 1167
Refalo, Michael 1167
レフイ
Levy, Maximilian 820
レフィスゾーン
Levijssohn, Joseph Henry 818
レフィングウェル
Leffingwell, Dean 807
レフェビュア
Lefebure, Molly 807
レフェーブル
Lefebvre, Helene 807
レフェルス
Levels, Tobas 817
レブエルタ
Revuelta, Pilar 1174
レフキ
Loeffke, Bernard 839
レプコ
Repko, Allen F. 1173
レフコウィッツ
Lefkowitz, Robert J. 807
レフコート
Lefcourt, Peter 807
レフコビッチ
Lefkovitz, Dan 807
レフコビッツ
Lefkowitz, Robert J. 807
レブザ
Reboza, Julien 1164
レブサマン
Rebsamen, François 1164
レプシウス
Lepsius, Oliver 815
レプシェ
Repše, Einars 1173
レプシンガー
Lepsinger, Richard 815
レプス
Reps, Mailis 1173
レフスナイダー
Refsnyder, Rob 1167
レプセ
Repše, Einars 1173
レブソン
Leveson, Nancy 818
レプチェック
Repcheck, Jack 1172
レフチェンコワ
Levtchenkova, Natalia 820
レフティマキ
Lehtimäki, Juhani 809
レフテリ
Lefteri, Chris 808
レフトアイ
LEFT EYE 808
レフラ
Rehula, Juha 1168
レフラー
Leffler, Karen 807
Leflar, Robert B. 807
Loeffler, Bruce 839
Löffler, Rainer 839
レプラ
Lepra, Jorge 814
レブランク
Leblanc, Cre'von 801
レフリー
Lifley, Harriet P. 827
レプリ
Lepri, Laura 814
レープリンク
Lehbrink, Hartmut 808
レブル
Levolo, Boniface 820
レブレヒト
Lebrecht, Norman 801
レブロフ
Rebrov, Serhiy 1164
レブロン
Leblond, Michaël 801
レーブン
Raven, Simon Arthur Noël 1161
レフン
Refn, Nicolas Winding 1167
レベ
Levet, Thomas 818
レーヘイン
Leyhane, Vici 823
レヘイン
Lehane, Dennis 808
レベサ
Lebesa, Popane 801
レベジ
Lebed', Aleksander Ivanovich 801
レーベシェフ
Lebeshev, Pavel 801
レベシェフ
Lebeshev, Pavel 801
レベジェフ
Lebedev, Alexsander 801
Lebedev, Pavlo 801
Lebedev, Sergei N. 801
レベシス
Lebesis, Spiridon 801
レベージャ
Rebella, Juan Pablo 1164
レペシンスカヤ
Lepeshinskaya, Oliga 814
レペタ
Repeta, Lawrence 1172
レベヂェフ
Lebedev, Larion Aleksandrovich 801
レベック
Lebech, Johannes 801
Rebeck, Theresa 1164
レベーテ
Levete, Sarah 818
レヘティネン
Lehtinen, Tuija 809
レベディンスキー
Lebedynsky, Iaroslav 801
レベデフ
Lebedev, Viktor 801
Lebedev, Vladimir 801
レベデワ
Lebedeva, Tatyana 801
レ・ペドヴィン
Le Poidevin, Robin 814
レペトゥーヒン
Lepetukhin, A.P. 814
レヘトマキ
Lehtomäki, Paula 809
レヘトライネン
Lehtolainen, Leena 809
レベナ
Rébéna, Frédéric 1164
レペニース
Lepenies, Wolf 814
レベネ
Levene, Gustavo Gabriel 817
レベリン
Rebellin, Davide 1164
レーベル
Réber, László 1164
レベル
Lebel, Denis 801
Rebell, Walter 1164
Reibel, Emmanuel 1168
レベレ
Rey-Bellet, Corinne 1174
レベレンズ
Leverenz, Caitlin 818
レベロ
Rebello, Stephen 1164
Rebelo, Aldo 1164
レベロデソウザ
Rebelo De Sousa, Marcelo 1164
レベロ・フィゲイレド
Rebelo Figueiredo, José Aldo 1164
レベロル
Reverol, Néstor 1174
レーベン
Levene, Malcolm I. 817
Raven, Peter Hamilton 1161
レベンクロン
Levenkron, Steven 817
レベンコ
Revenco, Valerian 1174
レーベンシュテイン
Lebensztejn, Jean Claude 801
レベンスクロフト
Ravenscroft, Anna Martelli 1161
レーベンスブルク
Rebensburg, Viktoria 1164
レベンソン
Levenson, Mark 817
Revenson, Jody 1174
レボー

LeBor, Adam 801
レボウ
Lebow, Grace 801
レボウィッツ
Lebowitz, Fran 801
レボヴィッツ
Leibowitz, Marvin 809
レボネト
Rebonato, Riccardo 1164
レポノ
Lepono, Mathabiso 814
レーホーファー
Lehofer, Michael 809
レホラ
Lehohla, Lesao 809
レポール
Lepore, Domenico 814
レポーレ
Lepore, Stephen J. 814
レボン
Lebbon, Tim 801
レーマ
Lerma, John 815
レーマー
Roemer, Lizabeth 1196
Römer, Thomas 1200
レマース
Remmers, Mike 1171
レマート
Lemert, Charles 812
レマニ
Lemani, Dumbo 811
レマメア
Lemamea, Ropati Mualia 811
レマル
Lemalu, Fa'atiga 811
Lemalu, Jonathan 811
レマレンコ
Remarenco, Ivan 1171
レーマン
Lehman, Barbara 809
Lehman, Ernest 809
Lehmann, Albrecht 809
Lehmann, André 809
Lehmann, Andreas C. 809
Lehmann, Christine 809
Lehmann, Donald R. 809
Lehmann, E.L. 809
Lehmann, Hans-Peter 809
Lehmann, Hans-Thies 809
Lehmann, Ingmar 809
Lehmann, Johannes 809
Lehmann, Klaus-Dieter 809
Lehmann, Matthias 809
Leman, Kevin 811
Leman, Martin 811
Rahman, Abdul 1150
Rehman, Sherry 1168
レマン
Lemann, Jorge Paulo 811
Lemann, Nicholas 811
レマンスキー
Lemanski, Mike 811
レミ
Remy, Pascal 1171
レミー
Raemy, Marianne de 1148
Remy, Loic 1171
レミィ
Rémy, Bernard 1171
レミグ
Remig, Valentina M. 1171
レミナ
Lemina, Mario 812
レミュズ
Remus, Timothy 1171
レミラード
Remillard, Kemp 1171
レミン
Lemine, Mohamed Ahmed Ould Mohamed 812
レーム
Röhm, Klaus-Heinrich 1198
レム
Lem, Stanisław 811
レムケ
Lembcke, Marjaleena 811
レムケス
Remkes, Johan 1171
レムス
Lemus, Jorge 812
レムナル
Lemnaru, Madalin 812
レムニック
Remnick, David J. 1171
レームブルッフ
Lehmbruch, Gerhard 809
レムラボット
Lemrabott, Selama Mint Cheikhna Ould 812
レメイン
Remijn, Gerard B. 1171
レメショウ
Lemeshow, Stanley 812
レメニイ
Remenyi, Dan 1171
レメリー
Lemery, Francis P. 812
レーメル
Römer, Thomas 1200
レメル
Remmel, Kerri S. 1171
レメルメ
Rey-Mermet, Théodule 1174
レメンゲサウ
Remengesau, Tommy 1171
レメンスキ
Remenski, Frosina Tashevska 1171
レーモー
Ramo, Simon 1154
レモイネ
Le Moine, Anna 812
Lemoine, Pablo 812
レモス
Lemos, Alvaro 812
Lemos, Maria Tereza 812
Lemos, Mauricio 812
Lemos, Vladir 812
レモニアー
Lemonier, Corey 812
レモニック
Lemonick, Michael D. 812
レモフ
Lemov, Doug 812
レモン
Lemmon, Gayle Tzemach 812
Lemmon, Jack 812
Lemon, Cyril 812
Lemon, Jim 812
Lemon, Katherine Newell 812
Raimond, Jean Bernard 1151
Remond, Rene 1171
Reymond, Bernard 1174
Reymond, William 1174
レーヤ
Leja, Magda 811
レーヤー
Loehr, James E. 839
レーラー
Lehrer, Jim 809
Lehrer, Jonah 809
Lehrer, Scott 809
Rohler, Thomas 1198
レラ
Lera, Joe 815
レラーニョ
Relaño, Alfredo 1171
レランツ
Roelandts, Jurgen 1196
レリガ
Religa, Zbigniew 1171
レリス
Leiris, Antoine 810
レーリッヒ
Röhig, Bernard 1198
レリト
Lelito, Tim 811
レーリヒト
Roericht, Hans (Nick) 1196
レリベウス
Leribeus, Josh 815
レリーベルド
Relyveld, Steven 1171
レリベルド
Lelyveld, Joseph Salem 811
レ・リベレンド
Le Riverend, Julio 815
レリュー
Lerew, Jenny 815
レーリン
Relin, David Oliver 1171
レーリンツ
Lorincz, Tamas 845
Lorincz, Viktor 845
レール
Lehl, Jurgen 809
レル
Lel, Martin 811
Röll, Iris 1199
レ・ルオン・ミン
Le Luong Minh 811
レルケ
Roelcke, Eckhard 1196
レールス
Leers, Gerd 807
レルナー
Lerner, Natan 815
レルヌー
Lernoud, Frédéric 815
レルネル
Lerner, Jaime 815
レルヒェ
Lerche, Wolfgang 815
レルヒャー
Lercher, Martin 815
レルフ
Relph, Edward C. 1171
レルン
Sundvall, Viveca 1366
レーレ
Lele, Avinash 811
レレイ・マフィ
Lelei Mafi, Amanaki 811
レーレルト
Raelert, Andreas 1148
レレンバーグ
Lellenberg, Jon L. 811
レロ
Lello, Jose 811
レワ
Reva, Grygoriy 1173
レーン
Laine, Frankie 782
Lane, Andrew 787
Lane, Bill 787
Lane, Brandie 787
Lane, Charles 787
Lane, Christopher 787
Lane, David Stuart 787
Lane, Dean 787
Lane, Diane 787
Lane, Eric 787
Lane, Joel 787
Lane, Katie 787
Lane, Mark 787
Lane, Nathan 787
Lane, Neal 787
Lane, Nick 787
Lane, Patrick T. 787
Lane, Rachel 787
Lane, Robert Wheeler 787
Lane, Steve 788
Lehn, Marty 809
Rehn, Olli 1168
レン
Len, Alex 812
Len, Christopher 812
Leng, Qin 812
Ren, Hui-ying 1171
Ren, Ji-yu 1171
Ren, Zheng-fei 1171
Ren, Zhuoling 1171
Wren, Brian A. 1527
Wren, Christopher Sale 1527
Wren, Daniel A. 1527
レンウィック
Renwick, Robbie 1172
レンヴォール
Renvall, Johan 1172
レンガチェリー
Rengachary, Dave A. 1172
レンキスト
Rehnquist, William H. 1168
レンク
Lenk, Hans Albert Paul 812
Lenk, Krzysztof 812
Lenku, Joseph Ole 812
レーンクイスト
Rehnquist, William H. 1168
レンケ
Lemke, Robert J. 812
Rennke, Helmut G. 1172
レンゲル
Lengel, Matt 812
レンコフ
Lenkov, Peter M. 812
レンゴモ
Lengomo, Barthélemy Botswali 812

レンシオーニ
Lencioni, Patrick 812
レンシック
Rencic, Joseph J. 1172
レンシナ
Lencina, Jorge 812
レンジャー
Ranger, Terence 1157
レンショー
Renshaw, Amanda 1172
Renshaw, Mark 1172
Renshaw, Molly 1172
レンス
Lens, Jeremain 813
Rönns, Christel 1201
レンズ
Lenz, Elinor 813
レンズコールド
Lenskold, James 813
レーンストラ
Leenstra, Marrit 807
レンズメント
Lensment, Jaak 813
レンズーリ
Renzulli, Joseph S. 1172
レンゼン
Lenzen, J.D. 813
レンタ
Rentta, Sharon 1172
レンダ
Renda, Tony 1172
レンダー
Lender, Mark E. 812
レンダース
Lenders, Andrea 812
レンダル
Rendall, John 1172
レンチ
Wrench, Katie 1527
Wrensch, Tom 1527
レンチニー・チョイノム
Renchinii Choinom 1172
レンツ
Ertl-renz, Martina 407
Lentz, Arjen 813
Lentz, Martha J. 813
Lentz, Michael 813
Lenz, Josh 813
Lenz, Patrick 813
Lenz, Siegfried 813
Lenz, Vickie 813
レンツィ
Renzi, Matteo 1172
レンツェン
Lenzen, Dieter 813
レンツナー
Lenzner, Terry 813
レンテ
Lente, Fred Van 813
レンテリーア
Renteria, Edgar 1172
Renteria, Rick 1172
レンテリア
Renteria, Edgar 1172
Renteria Castillo, Jackeline 1172
レンテリーヤ
Renteria, Edgar 1172
レンデル
Rendell, Ruth 1172
レンデル‐ベーカー
Rendell-Baker, Leslie 1172
レント
Lendt, C.K. 812
Lent, Blair 813
Lent, Robin 813
レンドヴァイ
Lendvai, Ernő 812
Lendvai, Paul 812
レントシュミット
Rendschmidt, Max 1172
レンドラ
Rendra 1172
レンドリー
Rendely, Ruth 1172
レントリッキア
Lentricchia, Frank 813
レンドル
Lendl, Ivan 812
Rendle, Steve 1172
レントン
Lenton, Lisbeth 813
Renton, Julia C. 1172
レンドーン
Rendon, Anthony 1172
レンドン
Rendon, Ana Maria 1172
Rendon, Rebecca 1172
Rendon, Rodolfo 1172
レンナー
Renner, Rolf Gunter 1172
レンネバーグ
Renneberg, Reinhard 1172
レンパー
Lemper, Ute 812
レンバーグ
Lemberg, Paul 811
レンハード
Lenhard, Elizabeth 812
Lenhardt, Carol 812
レンバート
Rembert, Virginia Pitts 1171
Renvert, Stefan 1172
レンバレンバ
Lembalemba, Kaunda 811
レンビ
Rembi, Lauren 1171
レンピネン
Lempinen, Erja 812
レンヒフォ・ベレス
Renjifo Vélez, Federico 1172
レンプ
Lempp, Reinhart 812
レンプト
Rempt, Fiona 1171
レンフリー
Renfree, Sean 1172
レンフリュー
Renfrew, Glen 1172
レンフルー
Renfrew, Colin 1172
Renfrew, Glen 1172
Renfrew, Mary 1172
レンフロ
Renfro, Brad 1172
レンフロー
Renfroe, Hunter 1172
レンフロウ
Renfrow, Justin 1172
レンベリ
Lemberg, Ulla 811
レンベール
Reinberg, Alain 1170
レンホフ
Lennhoff, F.G. 813
レンボール
Renvall, Johan 1172
レンボン
Lembong, Thomas 811
レンメルト
Remmert, Reinhold 1171

【ロ】

ロ
Lo, Aminata 837
Lo, Thierno 837
Ro, Tu-chol 1186
ロー
Laur, Joe 795
Law, Alex 797
Law, David Stephen 797
Law, Debbie 797
Law, Derek 797
Law, Felicia 797
Law, Jane Marie 797
Law, John Philip 797
Law, Jude 797
Law, Leslie 797
Law, Stephanie Pui-Mun 797
Law, Stephen 797
Law, Ty 797
Lo, Fu-cheng 837
Lo, Lieh 837
Lo, Ming-cheng Miriam 837
Loe, Erlend 839
Loë, Stefano von 839
Loh, Wan Inn 840
Lohr, Jeffrey M. 840
Lohr, Steve 840
Loo, Sanne te 842
Loo, Tessa de 842
Louw, Francois 846
Low, Thian Seng 848
Lowe, Chaunte 848
Lowe, Derek 848
Lowe, Jemma 848
Lu, Chien-hui 849
Racinet, Delphine 1147
Rault, Lucie 1160
Roe, Chaz 1196
Roe, Preacher 1196
Rowe, Mary 1211
ローアー
Loher, Dea 840
ロア
Loehr, Patrick 839
Lore, Pittacus 844
Roa, Hugbel 1186
ロアー
Laugher, Jack 795
Loehr, Anne 839
ロアイサ
Loaiza, Marcela 837
ロアーク
Roark, Tanner 1187
ロアット
Roitt, Ivan M. 1198
Roitt, Ivan Maurice 1198
ロア・バストス
Roa Bastos, Augusto Antonio 1186
ロアバック
Rohrbach, Peter-Thomas 1198
ロアボー
Rohrbaugh, Richard 1198
ローアーマン
Lauerman, John F. 795
ロアレット
Loyrette, Henri 849
ローイ
Looy, Bart Van 842
ロイ
Loy, David 849
Loy, Jessica 849
Loy, John 849
Loy, Marc 849
Lui, Che-woo 851
Roy, Arundhati 1212
Roy, Ashok 1212
Roy, Callista 1212
Roy, Geoffrey 1212
Roy, Indrapramit 1212
Roy, Jan 1212
Roy, Jim 1212
Roy, Kenny 1212
Roy, Lori 1212
Roy, Ravi 1212
Roy, Roberto 1212
Roy, Ron 1212
Roy, Sander 1212
Roy, Sara M. 1212
Roy, Sofie 1212
Roy, Stapleton 1212
ロイ・アンダーソン
Anderson, Roy 45
ロィエ
Loje, Neno 840
ロイエ
Rauhe, Ronald 1160
ロイエロ
Loiero, Agazio 840
ロイエンベルガー
Leuenberger, Moritz 817
Leuenberger, Robert 817
ロイサガ
Loizaga, Eladio 840
ロイジディス
Loizidis, Lazaros 840
ロイス
Lois, George 840
Reus, Marco 1173
Reuss, Norman H. 1173
Royce, Amara 1212
Royce, Catherine 1212
Royce, Walker 1212
Røys, Heidi Grande 1213
ロイズ
Loizou, Andreas 840
ロイストン
Royston, Angela 1213
ロイゼン
Roizen, Michael F. 1198
ロイター
Reuter, Andreas 1173
Reuter, Bjarne B. 1173
Reuter, Hans-Richard 1173
Reutter, Katherine 1173
ロイッター
Reutter, Angelika U. 1173
ロイット
Rohit, Swami Antar 1198
ロイツル
Loitzl, Wolfgang 840
ロイテラー

Reuteler, Fabienne 1173
ロイテンエッガー
Leutenegger, Gertrud 817
ローイド
Lloyd, Margaret 837
ロイト
Royte, Elizabeth 1213
ロイド
Lloyd, Alan B. 837
Lloyd, Charles 837
Lloyd, Christopher 837
Lloyd, Dan Edward 837
Lloyd, David 837
Lloyd, Earl 837
Lloyd, Erna Athanasius 837
Lloyd, Geoffrey Ernest Richard 837
Lloyd, John 837
Lloyd, Kenneth L. 837
Lloyd, Kristina 837
Lloyd, Marie-Pierre 837
Lloyd, Paul 837
Lloyd, Peter E. 837
Lloyd, Petter 837
Lloyd, Robbin 837
Lloyd, Sam 837
Lloyd, Seth 837
Loyd, Alexander 849
ロイトヴィラー
Leutwiler, Anita 817
ロイド＝ウィリアムズ
Lloyd-Williams, Mari 837
ロイド・ウェッバー
Lloyd Webber, Andrew 837
ロイド・ウェバー
Lloyd Webber, Andrew 837
ロイド＝ジョーンズ
Lloyd-Jones, Sally 837
ロイド・デイヴィス
Lloyd-Davies, Megan 837
ロイトハウザー
Leuthäuser, Gabriele 817
ロイトハルト
Leuthard, Doris 817
ロイド・ヒューズ
Lloyd-Hughes, Sarah 837
ロイトホイサーシュナレンベルガー
Leutheusser-schnarrenberger, Sabine 817
ロイトマン
Roitman, Zoya Pavlovna 1198
ロイトメ
Loitme, Tiia-Ester 840
ロイトリンガー
Reutlinger, Raanon 1173
ロイバス
Rõivas, Taavi 1198
ロイブ
Roibu, Alexei 1198
ロイフェ
Roiphe, Katie 1198
ロイブル
Loibl, Torsten 840
ロイヤー
Rojer, Jean-Julien 1198
Royer, Paul S. 1212
ロイヤル
Royal, Eddie 1212
Royal, Jacob 1212
Royal, Lyssa 1212
Royal, Mark 1212
ロイヤル卿
Royall, Baroness 1212
ロイランド
Reuland, Konrad 1173
ロイル
Royle, Aaron 1213
Royle, Nicholas 1213
Royle, Trevor 1213
ロウ
Law, Alex 797
Law, Andrew 797
Law, Andy 797
Law, Ingrid 797
Law, Jude 797
Lo, Bernard 837
Lou, Ye 846
Lou, Zheng-gang 846
Low, Dan 847
Low, Deborah 848
Low, Guat Tin 848
Low, Ignatius 848
Lowe, Andy 848
Lowe, Chris 848
Lowe, Denis 848
Lowe, Derek 848
Lowe, Jacques 848
Lowe, James Steven 848
Lowe, Janet 848
Lowe, Jemma 848
Lowe, Kathy 848
Lowe, Keith 848
Lowe, Mark 848
Lowe, Martin 848
Lowe, Nicholas J. 848
Lowe, Nick 848
Lowe, Rob 848
Lowe, Roy 848
Lowe, Sid 848
Lowe, Sidney 848
Lowe, Stuart 848
Lowe, Tamara 848
Roe, Paula 1196
Rowe, David C. 1211
Rowe, Eric 1211
Rowe, Eriko 1211
Rowe, Jeannette 1211
Rowe, Leonard 1211
Rowe, Michael 1211
Rowe, Michele 1211
Rowe, Thomas D., Jr. 1211
ロヴァース
Lovaas, O.I. 847
Lovász, László 847
ロヴァス
Lovaas, Ole Ivar 847
ロヴァッティ
Rovatti, Pier Aldo 1211
ロヴァート
Lovato, Demi 847
ローウィ
Lowe, Scott 848
ローウィー
Lowy, Frank 848
ローヴィック
Rorvik, David M. 1202
ロヴィック
Lovick, John 847
ロウイッツ
Lowitz, Leza 848
ロウィラ
Lowilla, Emmanuel 848
ロヴィローザ＝マドラーゾ
Rovirosa-Madrazo, Citlali 1211
ロヴィーン
Lövin, Isabella 847
ロヴィン
Rovin, Jeff 1211
ローウィング
Lowing, Matthew 848
ロヴェッリ
Rovelli, Carlo 1211
ローヴェーデル
Rohweder, Liisa 1198
ローウェル
Lowell, Elizabeth 848
Lowell, Heather 848
Lowell, Nathan 848
Lowell, Sophia 848
Lowell, Virginia 848
Rowell, Rainbow 1211
ロヴェルシ
Roversi, Tiziana 1211
ローヴェルジョン
Lauvergeon, Anne Alice Marie 796
ロヴェロ・カレズ
Rovéro-Carrez, Julie 1211
ローウェン
Loewen, James W. 839
Rowen, Ben 1211
Rowen, Michelle 1211
ローヴェン
Roven, Charles 1211
ローウェンスタイン
Loewenstein, Dora 839
Loewenstein, Rupert 839
Lowenstein, Alison 848
Lowenstein, Arlene 848
Lowenstein, Roger 848
Lowenstein, Stephen 848
ローウェンハーツ
Lowenherz, David H. 848
ロヴォンバラ
Lovobalavu, Gabby 847
ロゥキマ
Roukema, Richard W. 1210
ロウザー
Rother, Steve 1209
ロウズ
Laws, D.Richard 798
ロウチャー
Locher, F.A. 838
ロウ・ドッグ
Low Dog, Tieraona 848
ロウパー
Roper, Jon 1202
ロウハニ
Rouhani, Hassan 1210
ロウヒ
Louhi, Kristiina 846
ロウヒミエス
Louhimies, Aku 846
ロウベルジォン
Lauvergeon, Anne Alice Marie 796
ロウマン
Roman, Sanaya 1199
ロウラー
Lawler, Andrew 797
Lawler, Edward E., Ⅲ 797
Lawlor, Krista 797
ロウランズ
Rowlands, Graham 1212
ロウリー
Lawrie, Brett 798
Lowry, Joe Dan 848
Lowry, Joe P. 848
Lowry, Lois 848
Rowly, Janet Davison 1212
ロヴリー
Løvlie, Lavrans 847
ロヴリック
Lovric, Michelle 847
ロウルズ
Rawls, Lou 1162
ロウレス
Lawless, Clive 797
ロヴレン
Lovren, Dejan 847
ロウレンソ
Lourenço, Ana Afonso Dias 846
Lourenço, João Manuel Gonçalves 846
ロウントリー
Rowntree, Derek 1212
ローエ
Lowe, James Steven 848
Roehe, Stephanie 1196
ロエウ
Loew, Andreas 839
ロエク
Loaëc, Marie-Hélène 837
ローエル
Rowell, Patricia Frances 1211
ロエルズ
Roels, Marc James 1196
ローエン
Lowen, Alexander 848
Rohen, Johannes Wilhelm 1198
Rowen, Henry S. 1211
ローエンサル
Lowenthal, Barbara 848
ローエンタール
Lowenthal, Mark M. 848
ロエンバ
Loemba, André Raphaël 839
ロオジエ
Losier, Michael J. 845
ロカ
Roca, François 1192
Roca, Núria 1192
ロカ・イグレシアス
Roca Iglesias, Alejandro 1192
ロガチョフ
Rogachev, Igor Alekseevich 1196
ロガック
Rogak, Lisa 1196
ロカディア
Locadia, Jurgen 838
ロカティス
Locatis, Craig 838
ロカテッリ
Locatelli, Manuel 838
ロカトモザー
Rochat-Moser, Franzisca 1193
ロカフォート
Rocafort, Kenneth 1192
ローカム

ロ

Rohkamm, Reinhard 1198
ロガラ
Rogala, Jozef 1196
ローカル
Rocard, Michel Louis Léon 1192
ロカール
Rocard, Michel Louis Léon 1192
ロガルスキー
Rogalski, Kelly M. 1196
ローガン
Logan, Bennie 839
Logan, Boone 839
Logan, Chuck 839
Logan, Dan 839
Logan, David Coleman 839
Logan, Devin 839
Logan, Elle 840
Logan, Jessica 840
Logan, John 840
Logan, Kimberly 840
Logan, Leandra 840
Logan, Scott 840
Logan, Todd 840
Logan, William Bryant 840
Logan, Winifred W. 840
Rogan, Charlotte 1196
Rogan, Eugene L. 1196
Rogan, Markus 1196
ロガーン
Rogán, Antal 1196
ロキャン
Lokyan, Davit 840
ローク
Lauck, Joanne Elizabeth 795
Roach, Melanie 1186
Roques, Dominique 1202
Rourke, Mickey 1210
ローグ
Logue, Mark 840
ロク
Loc, Nguyen Dinh 838
ログ
Lougué, Kouamé 846
Rog, Marko 1196
ロクヴィグ
Lokvig, Jytte 840
ロクゲ
Lokuge, Gamini 840
ロクシン
Roxin, Claus 1212
ロクストン
Loxton, Daniel 849
Loxton, Howard 849
ログスドン
Logsdon, John M. 840
Logsdon, Veronica 840
ログズドン
Logsdon, John M. 840
ロクスバーグ
Roxburgh, Peter 1212
ロクソン
Roxon, Nicola 1212
ロクテ
Lochte, Ryan 838
ロクティ
Lochte, Dick 838
ログナー
Roegner, Eric V. 1196
ロクナン
Loughnane, Olive 846
ログノワ
Logunova, Tatiana 840
ロクバンダラ
Lokubandara, W.J.M. 840
ロクベール
Roquebert, Michel 1202
ログボール
Logevall, Fredrik 840
ロクマワティ
Rochmawati, Ika Yuliana 1193
ロクマン
Lokman, Adriaan 840
ロクマンヘキム
Lokmanhekim, Dilara 840
ロクミン
Rokhmin, Dahuri 1198
ロケ
Rocquet, Claude Henri 1193
Roque, Marianito 1202
Roqué, Miki 1202
Roque Mendoza, Bredni 1202
ロゲ
Rogge, Jacques 1197
ロゲインズ
Loggains, Dowell 840
ロケット
Lockett, Tyler 838
Lockett, Walker 838
Rockett, Paul 1193
ロケベルト
Roquebert, María 1202
ロケ・メサ
Roque Mesa 1202
ロゲリン
Logelin, Matthew 840
ロコ
Roco, Raul 1193
ロゴイスカ
Rogoyska, Jane 1198
ロコヴィッチ
Luckovich, Mike 851
ロゴヴィン
Rogovin, Milton 1198
ロゴシュ
Logosz, Michal 840
ロゴジン
Rogozin, Dmitry O. 1198
ロゴジンスキー
Rogoziński, Marek 1198
ロコツイ
Lokotui, Lua (Tukulua) 840
ロゴビン
Rogovin, Milton 1198
ロコフ
Rokoff, June 1199
ロゴフ
Rogoff, Barbara 1197
Rogoff, Kenneth S. 1197
Rogov, Igor 1197
ロゴフスカ
Rogowska, Anna 1198
ロゴフスキー
Rogowski, Michael 1198
ローサ
Roosa, John 1202
ローサー
Lawther, James 798
Lowther, Deborah 848
ローザ
Losa, Valérie 845
Rosa, Emilton Moreira 1202
Rosa, Gilberto Santa 1202
Rozsa, Ameni 1213
ローザー
Rother, Mike 1209
ロサ
de la Rosa, Pedro 336
Rosa, Draco 1202
Rosa, Henrique Pereira 1202
ロサー
Rosser, Alvin 1207
ロザ
Rosa, Henrique Pereira 1202
ロザー
Rother, Franklyn M. 1209
ローザク
Roszak, Theodore 1208
ロサス
Rosas, Aldrick 1202
ロサス・デマタ
Rosas De Mata, Doris 1202
ロサーダ
Losada, Isabel 845
ロサチャベス
Rosa Chávez, Herman Humberto 1202
ローザック
Roszak, Theodore 1208
ロサティ
Rosati, Dariusz Kajetan 1202
Rosatti, Horacio 1202
ロザーティ
Rosati, Ivo 1202
Rosati, Simon 1202
ロサディジャ
Rosadilla, Luis 1202
ロサート
Rothert, Gene 1209
ロサード
Rosado, Marlow 1202
ロザーナ
Rosanas, Ramon 1202
ロザナス
Rosanas, Ramon 1202
ロサノ
Losano, Tomas 845
Lozano, Juan 849
Lozano, Luciano 849
ロサノ・アラルコン
Lozano Alarcón, Javier 849
ロサノ・ラミレス
Lozano Ramírez, Juan Francisco 849
ロサ・バウティスタ
Rosa Bautista, Leonidas 1202
ロザフォート
Rosaforte, Tim 1202
ローザム
Rozum, John 1213
ロザーリオ
Rosário, Carlos Agostinho do 1202
ロザリオ
Rosario, Alberto 1202
Rosario, Amed 1202
Rosario, Eddie 1202
Rosario, Jose 1202
Rosario, Randy 1202
ロサーレス
Rosales, Emili 1202
ロサレス
Rosales, Ramon 1202
Rosales, Roberto 1202
ロザレス
Rosales, Adam 1202
ロサレス・デルトロ
Rosales del Toro, Ulises 1202
ローザン
Rozan, S.J. 1213
ロザンヴァロン
Rosanvallon, Pierre 1202
ロザーンス
Rosanes, Kerby 1202
ロザンスキ
Rozanski, Nick 1213
ロザンタール
Rosenthal, Manuel 1205
ロザンタル
Rosenthal, Manuel 1205
ロサント
Rossant, Cyrille 1207
ロサントス
Losantos, Àgata 845
ロサン・トンデン
Blo-bzan-don-ldan 149
ローザンフェルド
Rosenfeld, Alexis 1205
ローザンベール
Rosenberg, Pierre 1204
ロサンヘレス
Los Angeles, Victoria De 845
ロザンボ
Rosanbo, Loïc de 1202
ローシー
Losey, Meg Blackburn 845
ロージ
Lorge, Peter Allan 845
Rosei, Federico 1203
Rosi, Aleandro 1206
Rosi, Francesco 1206
Rosi, Gianfranco 1206
ロジアー
Rozier, Terry 1213
ロシアク
Losiak, Bartosz 845
ロシェ
Roche, Mary Alice 1193
Rocher, Yves 1193
ロシエ
Rochier, Gilles 1193
ロジェ
Rauger, Jean-François 1160
Rogé 1196
Rogé, Pascal 1196
Roger, frère 1196
Roger, Michel 1196
Roger, Philippe 1196
Rosier, Andree 1206
ロジエ
Rozier, Jacques 1213
ロジェク
Rojek, Chris 1198
ロジェストヴェンスキー
Rozhdestvenskii, Gennadii 1213

ロ

ロジェストベンスキー
Rozhdestvenskii, Gennadii 1213
ロジェーツキン
Rozhetskin, A.M. 1213
ロシェット
Rochette, Joannie 1193
ロシェル
Rochell, Hannah 1193
ロジェール
Roger 1196
ロシェロン
Rocheron, Guillaume 1193
ローシェンバーグ
Rauschenberg, Robert 1161
ロジオノフ
Rodionov, Igor Nikolayevich 1194
Rodionov, Valentin 1194
ロジキン
Rodkin, Denis 1194
ロシコーワ
Rozhkova, Ekaterina 1213
ロジスキー
Rozycki, John J. 1213
ロシター
Rossiter, John R. 1208
Rossiter, Marsha 1208
ロシツキ
Rosicky, Tomás 1206
ロシツキー
Rosicky, Tomás 1206
ロシト
Rossit, Desiree 1208
ロシニョル
Rossignol, Laurence 1208
ロシミアン
Lossimian, Mbailaou Naïmbaye 845
ローシャ
Rocha, Luís Miguel 1192
Rocha, Paulo 1193
ロシャ
Rocha, José Carvalho Da 1192
Rocha, Paulo 1193
Rocha, Paulo Augusto Costa 1193
Rochat, Alain 1193
Rochat, Philippe 1193
ロジャー
Roger, Elena 1196
Rogers, Gabriele 1197
ロジャース
Rodgers, Aaron 1194
Rodgers, Brady 1194
Rodgers, Frank 1194
Rodgers, Jacquizz 1194
Rodgers, Jake 1194
Rodgers, Kacy 1194
Rodgers, Nile 1194
Rodgers, Paul 1194
Rodgers, Richard 1194
Rogers, Adam 1196
Rogers, Anthony 1197
Rogers, Brittany 1197
Rogers, Chester 1197
Rogers, Edward 1197
Rogers, Eli 1197
Rogers, Emma 1197
Rogers, Eric 1197
Rogers, Helene 1197
Rogers, James Beeland, Jr. 1197
Rogers, Jason 1197
Rogers, John 1197
Rogers, Kazuko 1197
Rogers, Mary M. 1197
Rogers, Michael 1197
Rogers, Michael E. 1197
Rogers, Nicole L. 1197
Rogers, Paul 1197
Rogers, P.Clint 1197
Rogers, Richard 1197
Rogers, Richard A. 1197
Rogers, Richard George 1197
Rogers, Robert D. 1197
Rogers, Roo 1197
Rogers, Simon 1197
Rogers, Steven 1197
Rogers, Taylor 1197
Rogers, Tommy 1197
Rogers, Wendy A. 1197
ロジャーズ
Rodgers, Aaron 1194
Rodgers, David 1194
Rodgers, Ilona 1194
Rodgers, Joann Ellison 1194
Rodgers, Mary 1194
Rodgers, Nigel 1194
Rodgers, Theodore Stephen 1194
Rogers, Alan 1196
Rogers, Ann E. 1196
Rogers, Benedict 1197
Rogers, Bernard William 1197
Rogers, Bruce Holland 1197
Rogers, C. 1197
Rogers, Colin 1197
Rogers, David J. 1197
Rogers, Donald W. 1197
Rogers, Elizabeth Kendall 1197
Rogers, Everett M. 1197
Rogers, James Beeland, Jr. 1197
Rogers, James Steven 1197
Rogers, Jane 1197
Rogers, Jim 1197
Rogers, Julia 1197
Rogers, Katharine M. 1197
Rogers, Kirsteen 1197
Rogers, Martha 1197
Rogers, Matt 1197
Rogers, Michael 1197
Rogers, Paul 1197
Rogers, Peter Denny 1197
Rogers, Richard George 1197
Rogers, Rita 1197
Rogers, Roo 1197
Rogers, Rosemary 1197
Rogers, Scott 1197
Rogers, Selwyn O., Jr. 1197
Rogers, Shirley 1197
Rogers, Todd 1197
Rogers, William Pierce 1197
ロジャース・クロマティ
Rodgers-Cromartie, Dominique 1194
ロジャース・クロマティー
Rodgers-Cromartie, Dominique 1194
ロジャーズ・クロマティ
Rodgers-Cromartie, Dominique 1194
ロジャーソン
Rogerson, Barnaby 1197
Rogerson, John William 1197
ロシャ・モザー
Rochat-Moser, Franzisca 1193
ローシュ
Roche, Charlotte 1193
Roš, Hana 1202
ロシュ
Losch, Brian 845
Roche, Daniel 1193
Roche, Nicolas 1193
ロジュマナ
Rojumana, Clement 1198
ロジョ
Loyo, Juan Carlos 849
ローシン
Losin, Veniamin 845
ロージング
Rosing, Norbert 1206
ロジンスキー
Rosinski, Philippe 1206
ロシンヌ
Rosine, Baiwong Djibergui Aman 1206
ロー・シンハン
Lo Hsing Han 840
ローシンハン
Lo Hsing Han 840
ロース
Loos, François 842
Rose, Oren H. 1203
Roth, Kurt 1209
ローズ
Lawes, Courtney 797
Laws, Bill 798
Laws, D.Richard 798
Laws, Emma 798
Laws, John Muir 798
Laws, Kenneth 798
Laws, Robin D. 798
Lords, Traci 844
Rause, Vince 1161
Rhoades, Gary 1175
Rhodes, Antony 1176
Rhodes, Arthur 1176
Rhodes, Dan 1176
Rhodes, David 1176
Rhodes, Jordan 1176
Rhodes, Luke 1176
Rhodes, Neil 1176
Rhodes, Nick 1176
Rhodes, R.A.W. 1176
Rhodes, Richard 1176
Rhodes, William R. 1176
Rhodes, Xavier 1176
Roads, Michael J. 1187
Roese, Neal J. 1196
Rose, Andrea 1203
Rose, Axl 1203
Rose, Carol 1203
Rose, Colin 1203
Rose, Daniel E. 1203
Rose, Danny 1203
Rose, David 1203
Rose, Deborah Bird 1203
Rose, Derrick 1203
Rose, Eilidh 1203
Rose, Elizabeth 1203
Rose, Emilie 1203
Rose, Frank 1203
Rose, Gerald 1203
Rose, Gideon 1203
Rose, Gillian 1203
Rose, Harald 1203
Rose, Irwin 1203
Rose, Jack 1203
Rose, Jacqueline 1203
Rose, Jeanne 1203
Rose, Joan B. 1203
Rose, Joel 1203
Rose, June 1203
Rose, Justin 1203
Rose, Karen 1203
Rose, Kay 1203
Rose, Kimberly 1203
Rose, Leo E. 1203
Rose, Linda Joy 1203
Rose, Lionel 1203
Rose, Louis F. 1203
Rose, Malcolm 1203
Rose, Matthew 1203
Rose, Michael Robertson 1203
Rose, Mike 1203
Rose, M.J. 1203
Rose, Morris E. 1203
Rose, Murray 1203
Rose, Nancy Patricia 1203
Rose, Nikolas S. 1203
Rose, Pauline 1203
Rose, Pete 1203
Rose, Resinald 1203
Rose, Richard 1203
Rose, Robert 1203
Rose, Samantha 1203
Rose, Sarah 1203
Rose, Shane 1203
Rose, Sonya O. 1203
Rose, Tara 1203
Rose, Tom 1203
Rose, Tricia 1203
Rose, Winston 1203
ロス
Ros, Carolyn 1202
Ros, Elisabet 1202
Rose, David 1203
Ross, A.B. 1206
Ross, Adam 1206
Ross, Alec 1206
Ross, Alex 1206
Ross, Alistair 1206
Ross, Andrew 1206
Ross, Andy 1206
Ross, Ann B. 1206
Ross, April 1206
Ross, Atticus 1206
Ross, Brandian 1206
Ross, Brandon 1206
Ross, Cameron 1206
Ross, Carne 1206
Ross, Catherine 1206
Ross, Catherine Sheldrick 1206
Ross, Colin A. 1206
Ross, David 1206
Ross, David Robertson 1206
Ross, David Southerland 1206
Ross, Dennis B. 1206
Ross, Diana 1206
Ross, Emily 1206
Ross, Erin 1206
Ross, Finn 1206
Ross, Gary 1206
Ross, Gary Earl 1206
Ross, Helen Elizabeth 1206
Ross, Herbert 1206

Ross, Irene S. 1206
Ross, Irwin 1206
Ross, James 1206
Ross, Jenny 1206
Ross, Jeremy 1206
Ross, Jerilyn 1206
Ross, Jim 1206
Ross, JoAnn 1206
Ross, Joe 1207
Ross, Joel 1207
Ross, John F. 1207
Ross, Joseph 1207
Ross, Josephine 1207
Ross, Julie A. 1207
Ross, Karen 1207
Ross, Kathryn 1207
Ross, Keith W. 1207
Ross, Kenneth 1207
Ross, Kevin 1207
Ross, Kristin 1207
Ross, Lisa M. 1207
Ross, Luke 1207
Ross, Marilyn 1207
Ross, Michael Lewin 1207
Ross, Mike 1207
Ross, Nikki 1207
Ross, Paul 1207
Ross, Rashad 1207
Ross, Reuben 1207
Ross, Richard 1207
Ross, Robbie, Jr. 1207
Ross, Robert 1207
Ross, Robert J. 1207
Ross, Ronald G. 1207
Ross, Ruth 1207
Ross, Sara 1207
Ross, Shane 1207
Ross, Sheldon M. 1207
Ross, Stephen A. 1207
Ross, Steven M. 1207
Ross, Stewart 1207
Ross, Suzanne 1207
Ross, Ted 1207
Ross, Terrence 1207
Ross, Tony 1207
Ross, Tyson 1207
Ross, Werner 1207
Ross, Wilbur L., Jr. 1207
Ross, William C. 1207
Rosu, Monica 1208
Roth, Alvin 1208
Roth, Andrew 1208
Roth, Ann 1208
Roth, Ariel Adrean 1208
Roth, Bennett E. 1208
Roth, Bernard 1208
Roth, Carolyn Kaut 1208
Roth, David 1208
Roth, Eric 1208
Roth, Erik A. 1209
Roth, Geneen 1209
Roth, George 1209
Roth, Joe 1209
Roth, John 1209
Roth, John K. 1209
Roth, Klaus Friedrich 1209
Roth, Lauren 1209
Roth, Megan 1209
Roth, Melinda 1209
Roth, Pamela 1209
Roth, Philip 1209
Roth, Robert H. 1209
Roth, Sanford 1209
Roth, Susan L. 1209
Roth, Sydney 1209
Roth, Tim 1209
Roth, Veronica 1209
Roth, Werner 1209
Roth, William V., Jr. 1209
Wros, Peggy L. 1529
ロス・アンヘレス
Los Angeles, Victoria De 845
ロズイエフ
Rozyev, Kurbanmurad 1213
ロスウィリアムズ
Ross-williams, Tiffany 1208
ロスウェル
Rothwell, Timothy 1210
Rothwell, William J. 1210
ロズウェル
Rothwell, Peter M. 1210
ローズウォーン
Rosewarne, Graham 1206
ローズウッド
Rosewood, Theresa 1206
ロ・スキアーヴォ
Lo Schiavo, Francesca 845
ロスクートフ
Loskutov, Igor G. 845
ローズクランス
Rosecrance, Richard N. 1203
ロスクロウ
Roskrow, Dominic 1206
ロズクロフ
Rozukulov, Ulugbek 1213
ロスケ
Loske, Reinhard 845
ロスコ
Rothko, Christopher 1209
ロスコウ
Roscoe, Lily 1203
ロスコス
Loscos, Bruno 845
ロスコフ
Rothkopf, David Jochanan 1209
ロスジェン
Loesgen, Brian 839
ロスシュタイン
Rothstein, Larry 1210
ローススタイン
Rothstein, Barry 1210
Rothstein, Betsy 1210
ロススタイン
Rothstein, Lawrence R. 1210
ロスステイン
Rothstein, Dan 1210
ロスタイン
Rostain, Anthony L. 1208
ロスタミ
Rostami, Kianoush 1208
ロースタム
Råstam, Hannes 1159
ロスタン
Rostain, Michel 1208
ロスチャイルド
Rothchild, John 1209
Rothschild, Babette 1209
Rothschild, David de 1209
Rothschild, Edmund Leopold de 1209
Rothschild, Erica 1209
Rothschild, Frank D. 1209
Rothschild, Guy de 1209
Rothschild, Joel 1210
Rothschild, Larry 1210
Rothschild, Nadine de 1210
Rothschild, William E. 1210
ロスティーラ
Rostila, Mikael 1208
ローズデール
Rosedale, Philip 1203
ロスト
Rost, Andrea 1208
Rost, Gottfried 1208
Rost, Peter 1208
Rost, Richard 1208
ロストー
Rostow, Walt Whitman 1208
ロストウ
Rostow, Eugene V. 1208
Rostow, Walt Whitman 1208
ロストーヴァ
Rostova, Natasha 1208
ロストウォロフスキ・デ・ディエス・カンセコ
Rostworowski de Diez Canseco, María 1208
ローズトゥリー
Rosetree, Rose 1206
ロストツキー
Rostotskii, Stanislav 1208
ロストーノフ
Rostunov, Ivan Ivanovich 1208
ロストフスキ
Rostowski, Jan Vincent 1208
ロストフツェフ
Rostovtsev, Pavel 1208
ロストミャン
Rostomyan, Hrachya 1208
ロストロポーヴィチ
Rostropovich, Mstislav Leopoldovich 1208
ロストロポーヴィッチ
Rostropovich, Mstislav Leopoldovich 1208
ロストロポービチ
Rostropovich, Mstislav Leopoldovich 1208
ロストロポービッチ
Rostropovich, Mstislav Leopoldovich 1208
ロスナー
Roessner, Jane 1196
Roessner, Michaela 1196
Rossner, Judith 1208
Rothner, A.David 1209
ロズナー
Rosner, Bob 1206
Rosner, Elizabeth 1206
ローズナウ
Rosenau, James N. 1204
ロズノー
Rosnau, Wendy 1206
ローズノウ
Rosenau, James N. 1204
ロスノウ
Rosnow, Mimi 1206
Rosnow, Ralph L. 1206
ロスバウアー
Rothbauer, Paulette M. 1209
ロスバウム
Rothbaum, Barbara O. 1209
ロスバート
Rothbart, Mary Klevjord 1209
ロスファス
Rothfuss, Patrick 1209
ロスフィーダー
Rothfeder, Jeffrey 1209
ロスフィールド
Rothfield, Lawrence 1209
ローズブーム
Roseboom, David 1203
ローズベリー
Roseberry, Monica 1203
ロズベルグ
Rosberg, Nico 1202
ロズボッテン
Rødbotten, Marit 1193
ロスマン
Rothman, Carole R. 1209
Rothman, Ellen Lerner 1209
Rothman, James E. 1209
Rothman, Johanna 1209
Rothman, Tony 1209
ローズムーア
Rosemoor, Patricia 1204
ロスモ
Rossmo, D.Kim 1208
ローズモンド
Rosemond, John K. 1204
ロズモンド
Rosemond, John K. 1204
ロースラー
Roessler, Pat 1196
ローズラン
Lozerand, Emmanuel 849
ロズラン
Lozerand, Emmanuel 849
ロスリスバーガー
Roethlisberger, Ben 1196
ロスリン
Rothlin, Viktor 1209
ロズールド
Losurdo, Domenico 845
ロスロック
Rothrock, Jane C. 1209
ロースン
Lawson, John 798
Lawson, M.A. 798
ローゼ
Lohse, Eduard 840
Lohse, Rene 840
Rose, Romani 1203
ロゼ
Rose, Mārtiņš 1203
ロゼー
Losee, John Price 845
ロゼアヌ
Rozeanu, Angelica 1213
ロセー・イ・リョベー
Rosset i Llobet, Jaume 1207
ロゼタ
Roseta, Pedro 1206
ロセット
Rosset, Barney 1207
Rossett, Allison 1207
Rossetto, Miguel 1207
ローゼナウ
Rosenau, Henning 1204

ローセフ
Losev, Aleksei Fedrovich 845
ローゼマン
Roozeman, Jonathan 1202
ローゼル
Roszel, Renee 1208
ロセルウビアル
Rosellubial, Paulyn Jean 1203
ロセーロ
Rosero, Evelio 1206
Rosero Diago, Evelio 1206
ロセロ
Rosero, Gabriela 1206
ローゼン
Rosen, Alan 1204
Rosen, Alan D. 1204
Rosen, Andrew 1204
Rosen, Brenda 1204
Rosen, Charles 1204
Rosen, David H. 1204
Rosen, Emanuel 1204
Rosen, Gerald M. 1204
Rosen, Harris 1204
Rosen, Jeremy 1204
Rosen, John 1204
Rosen, Larry D. 1204
Rosen, Lawrence 1204
Rosen, Leonard 1204
Rosen, Marion 1204
Rosen, Michael 1204
Rosen, Michael J. 1204
Rosen, Mike 1204
Rosen, Paul M. 1204
Rosen, Rebecca 1204
Rosen, Robert H. 1204
Rosén, Staffan 1204
ローゼンガーテン
Rosengarten, Jacob 1205
Rosengarten, Theodore 1205
ローゼンクィスト
Rosenquist, James 1205
ローゼンクイスト
Rosenquist, James 1205
ローセングレン
Rosengren, Björn 1205
ローゼングレン
Rosengren, David B. 1205
ロゼンコ
Rozenko, Pavlo 1213
ローゼンサール
Rosenthal, Amy Krouse 1205
ローゼンスタイン
Rosenstein, Donald L. 1205
ローゼンスティール
Rosenstiel, Tom 1205
ロゼンスティール
Rosenstiehl, Agnès 1205
ローゼンステイン
Rosenstein, Bruce 1205
ローゼンストック
Rosenstock, Aron 1205
Rosenstock, Barb 1205
Rosenstock, Gabriel 1205
ローセンストレーム＝ベンハーゲン
Rosenström-Bennhagen, Susann 1205
ローゼンスワイグ
Rosensweig, Larry 1205
ローゼンソール
Rosenthal, Abraham Michael 1205
Rosenthal, Joe 1205
Rosenthal, Sandra B. 1205
ローゼンタール
Rosenthal, Abraham Michael 1205
Rosenthal, Amy Krouse 1205
Rosenthal, David K. 1205
Rosenthal, Donna 1205
Rosenthal, Eileen 1205
Rosenthal, Jan 1205
Rosenthal, Jeffrey Seth 1205
Rosenthal, Joe 1205
Rosenthal, Marc 1205
Rosenthal, Michael 1205
Rosenthal, Norman E. 1205
Rosenthal, Pam 1205
Rosenthal, Philip 1205
Rosenthal, Richard N. 1205
Rosenthal, Saul H. 1205
Rosenthal, Steve 1205
Rosenthal, Todd 1205
Rosenthal, Trevor 1205
ローゼンタル
Rosenthal, Sean 1205
Rosenthal, Uri 1205
ロセンタル
Rosenthal, Yani 1205
ロゼンタル
Rosenthal, Manuel 1205
ロセンタル・ケニスベルゲル
Rosenthal Koeningsberger, Gert 1205
ローゼンツァイク
Rosenzweig, Saul 1205
ローゼンツヴァイク
Rosenzweig, Paul 1205
ローゼンツヴァイグ
Rosenzweig, Miriam 1205
ローゼンツワイグ
Rosenzweig, Philip M. 1205
ローゼンドルフ
Rosendorf, Neal M. 1205
ローゼンハイム
Rosenheim, Stephanie 1205
ローゼンハウス
Rosenhouse, Jason 1205
ローゼンバウム
Rosenbaum, Art 1204
Rosenbaum, Deborah 1204
Rosenbaum, Jerrold F. 1204
Rosenbaum, Marcus 1204
Rosenbaum, Robert G. 1204
Rosenbaum, Stephen 1204
Rosenbaum, Steven C. 1204
ローゼンバーグ
Rosenberg, Aaron 1204
Rosenberg, Alexander 1204
Rosenberg, Bob 1204
Rosenberg, Donna Andrea 1204
Rosenberg, Doug 1204
Rosenberg, Emily S. 1204
Rosenberg, Frank P. 1204
Rosenberg, Joel C. 1204
Rosenberg, Jonathan 1204
Rosenberg, Justin 1204
Rosenberg, Larry 1204
Rosenberg, Marc J. 1204
Rosenberg, Mario Z. 1204
Rosenberg, Marshall B. 1204
Rosenberg, Nancy Taylor 1204
Rosenberg, Neil V. 1204
Rosenberg, Scott 1204
Rosenberg, Scott Mitchell 1204
Rosenberg, Steven A. 1204
Rosenberg, Stuart 1204
Rosenberg, Tina 1204
Rosenberg, Viqui 1204
Rosenberg, William 1204
Rothenberg, Lawrence S. 1209
Rothenberg, Leon 1209
ローゼンバッハ
Rosenbach, Marcel 1204
ローゼンバラット
Rosenblatt, Bill 1204
ローゼンハン
Rosenhan, David L. 1205
ローセンフェルト
Rosenfeldt, Hans 1205
ローゼンフェルト
Rosenfeld, Hellmut 1205
Rosenfeld, Herbert A. 1205
Rosenfelt, David 1205
ローゼンフェルド
Rosenfeld, Alvin A. 1205
Rosenfeld, Irene B. 1205
Rosenfeld, Isadore 1205
ローゼンブラット
Rosenblatt, Bill 1204
Rosenblatt, David S. 1204
Rosenblatt, Julia Carlson 1205
Rosenblatt, Roger 1205
ローゼンブラム
Rosenblum, Lawrence D. 1205
Rosenblum, Michael 1205
Rosenblum, Mort 1205
Rosenblum, Richard 1205
ローゼンブルース
Rosenbluth, Frances McCall 1205
Rosenbluth, Hal F. 1205
ローゼンブルーム
Rosenbloom, Alfred A., Jr. 1205
ローゼンベルク
Rosenberg, Shalom 1204
ローゼンベルグ
Rosenberg, Raben 1204
Rozenberg, Jacques J. 1213
ローゼンボーム
Rosenboom, Hilke 1205
ローゼンマン
Rosenman, Leonard 1205
ロソス
Losos, Jonathan B. 845
ロソッティ
Rossotti, Charles O. 1208
ローゾフ
Rosoff, Meg 1206
Rozov, Viktor Sergeevich 1213
ロソリーノ
Rosolino, Massimiliano 1206
ロソロバ
Rosolova, Denisa 1206
ローソーン
Rawsthorn, Alice 1162
ローソン
Lawson, Andrew 798
Lawson, Anthea 798
Lawson, Bruce 798
Lawson, Christine Ann 798
Lawson, Colin 798
Lawson, Corrina 798
Lawson, Dorie McCullough 798
Lawson, Edward H. 798
Lawson, Jacqueline 798
Lawson, Jarrion 798
Lawson, Joan 798
Lawson, JonArno 798
Lawson, Juah 798
Lawson, Karen 798
Lawson, Kristan 798
Lawson, Manny 798
Lawson, Nevin 798
Lawson, Ricky 798
Lawson, Sarah 798
Lawson, Shaq 798
Lawson, Sue 798
Lawson, Tony 798
Lawson, Ty 798
Lawson, Wendy 798
Lowson, Iain 848
Rawson, Hugh 1162
Rawson, Jane 1162
Rawson, Martyn 1162
Rawson, Nancy E. 1162
Rawson, Richard A. 1162
Rowson, James 1212
Rowthorn, Robert 1212
ローター
Lauter, Ed 796
Lothar, Susanne 845
Rother, Rainer 1209
ローダ
Lodha, Suresh K. 839
ローダー
Lauder, Estee 795
Lauder, Evelyn 795
Lauder, Hugh 795
Lauder, Judy Glickman 795
Lauder, Leonard 795
Loader, Brian D. 837
Loder, Elizabeth 839
Roder, Heinrich 1194
ロター
Lothar, Susanne 845
ロダー
Lodder, Gerrit 839
ローター・エメリッヒ
Emmerich, Lothar 401
ロダオ
Rodao García, Florentino 1193
ロダキ
Rodaki, Mohammad Reza 1193
ローダス
Rodas, João Grandino 1193
ロダス
Rodas, Haroldo 1193
ロダス・ガメロ
Rodas Gamero, Jorge

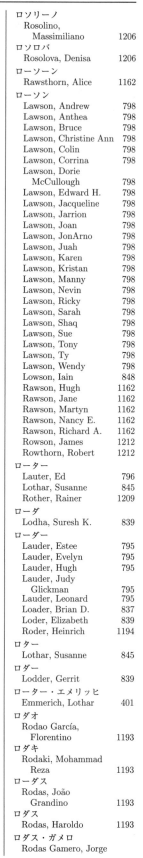

Alberto 1193
ロータースタイン
Lauterstein, Andrew 796
ロダス・バカ
Rodas Baca, Patricia 1193
ロダット
Rodat, Robert 1193
ロダート
Lodato, Victor 839
ロダド・ノリエガ
Rodado Noriega, Carlos Enrique 1193
ローダーバーグ
Roderbourg, Makiko 1194
ローダラー
Roederer, Juan G. 1196
ロダール
Lodahl, Michael E. 839
ロダーレス
Lodares, Juan R. 839
ロダレス
Lodares, Juan R. 839
ロータン
Lauthan, Samioullah 796
ローダーン
al-Roudan, Khaled Nasser Abdullah 1210
ローダン
Laudan, Rachel 795
Roden, Steve 1194
ロダン
al-Roudhan, Roudhan Abdulaziz 1210
ロタンダ
Rotunda, Ronald D. 1210
ローチ
Loach, Jim 837
Loach, Ken 837
Rauch, Scott L. 1160
Roach, Chris 1186
Roach, Geshe Michael 1186
Roach, Jay 1186
Roach, Marion 1186
Roach, Mary 1186
Roach, Max 1186
Roach, Pat 1186
Roach, Stephen S. 1186
Roach, Trevor 1187
Roche, Dick 1193
Roche, James M. 1193
ロチ
Rochi, José Rubén 1193
ローチェ
Locche, Nicolino 838
ロチェフ
Rotchev, Vasily 1208
ロチェン
Roćen, Milan 1192
ロチマ
Lotsima, Chelo 846
ローチュレレイ
Lotulelei, John 846
Lotulelei, Star 846
ローツェン
Roozen, Nico 1202
ロツェンベルク
Rozenberg, Pavlo 1213
ロッカ
Rocca, Alessandro 1192
Rocca, Giorgio 1192
ロッカー
Locker, Sari 838
ロッキー
Locke, Jeff 838
Lockey, Andrew 838
Lockie, Andrew 838
Lockie, Mark 838
ロック
Lock, Andy 838
Lock, James 838
Lock, Margaret 838
Lock, Margaret M. 838
Lock, Norman 838
Lock, Timothy 838
Locke, Attica 838
Locke, Christopher 838
Locke, Gary F. 838
Locke, Jeff 838
Locke, Vince 838
Rock 1193
Rock, Allan 1193
Rock, Andrea 1193
Rock, Chris 1193
Rock, Edward B. 1193
Rock, Joanne 1193
Rock, Lois 1193
Rock, Michael T. 1193
Rock, Mick 1193
Rock, Robert M. 1193
ロックウェル
Rockwell, Anne 1193
Rockwell, David B. 1193
Rockwell, Robert 1193
Rockwell, Thomas 1193
ロックウッド
Lockwood, David 838
Lockwood, Lewis 838
Lockwood, Lucy 838
Lockwood, Robert, Jr. 838
Rockwood, Charles A. 1193
ロックシュタイン
Rockstein, Margitta 1193
ロックストローム
Rockström, Johan 1193
ロックスリー
Locksley, Richard M. 838
ロックバウム
Lochbaum, David A. 838
ロックバーグ
Rochberg, George 1193
ロックバーグ＝ハルトン
Rochberg-Halton, Eugene 1193
ロックハート
Lockhart, Alexander 838
Lockhart, Andrew 838
Lockhart, Calvin 838
Lockhart, Christy 838
Lockhart, Paul 838
Lockheart, Susanna 838
ロックフェラー
Rockefeller, David 1193
Rockefeller, James Stillman 1193
Rockefeller, John Davison Ⅳ 1193
Rockefeller, Laurance Spelman 1193
Rockefeller, Richard 1193
Rockfeller, Steven C. 1193
ロックマン
Lockman, Whitey 838
ロックモア
Rockmore, Tom 1193
ロックリー
Lockley, Andrew 838
ロックワード
Lockward, Angel 838
ロッケンバウアー
Rockenbauer, Zoltán 1193
ロッコ
Rocco, Alex 1192
Rocco, John 1192
Rocco, Marc 1192
ロッサー
Rosser, Zevan 1207
ロッサー＝オーエン
Rosser-Owen, Mariam 1207
ロッサーニ
Lossani, Chiara 845
ロッサビ
Rossabi, Morris 1207
ロッサム
Rossum, Emmy 1208
ロッシ
Losse, Katherine 845
Rochi, José Rubén 1193
Rosi, Mauro 1206
Rossi, Agustín 1207
Rossi, Allegra 1207
Rossi, Armand 1207
Rossi, Berardo 1207
Rossi, Ernest Lawrence 1207
Rossi, Franco 1207
Rossi, Giuseppe 1207
Rossi, Jacques 1207
Rossi, Jessica 1207
Rossi, Paolo 1208
Rossi, Peter Henry 1208
Rossi, Rossana 1208
Rossi, Sheila I. 1208
Rossi, Tiziano 1208
Rossi, Valentino 1208
Rossi, Víctor 1208
Rossi, Wagner 1208
ロッジ
Lodge, David John 839
Lodge, Henry S. 839
Lodge, Jo 839
Lodge, Katherine 839
ロッシオ
Rossio, Terry 1208
ロッシター
Rossiter, David 1208
ロッシーニ
Rossini, Stéphane 1208
ロッジャー
Rodger, Iain 1194
ロッシュ
Lorsch, Jay William 845
Roche, Alex F. 1193
Roche, Eileen 1193
Roche, Maïte 1193
Roesch, Jacob 1196
Roesch, Roberta 1196
Rosch, Eleanor 1202
Rosch, Michael 1202
ロッシング
Rossing, Thomas D. 1208
ロッスマン
Rossmann, Irmgard 1208
ロッスム
Rossum, Wouter van 1208
ロッセッティーニ
Rossettini, Luca 1207
ロッセティ
Rossetti, Gabriele 1207
ロッセリーニ
Rossellini, Gil 1207
Rossellini, Isabella 1207
ロッセル
Rossell, Judith 1207
ロッセンスウィート
Rosensweet, Jesse 1205
ロッソ
Rosso, Brian 1208
Rosso, Lionel 1208
Rosso, Renzo 1208
Russo, Marco 1219
ロッター
Lotter, Konrad 846
Lotter, V. 846
Rotter, Ariel 1210
ロッダ
Rodda, Emily 1193
ロッダー
Lodder, Steve 839
ロッダム
Roddam, George 1194
ロッツ
Lotz, Sarah 846
ロッデ
Lodde, Luigi 839
ロッディス
Roddis, Miles 1194
ロッテスリー
Wrottesley, Clifton 1529
ロッテラー
Lotterer, Alexander 846
Lotterer, Andre 846
ロッデンベリー
Roddenberry, Eugene W., Jr. 1194
Roddenberry, Majel 1194
ロット
Lott, Derrick 846
Lott, Felicity 846
Lott, Joey 846
Lott, Pixie 846
Lott, Tim 846
Lott, Trent 846
ロッド
Rodd, Jillian 1193
Rodd, Laurel Rasplica 1193
ロッドウェル
Rodwell, Victor W. 1196
ロッドナイト
Rodnight, R. 1194
ロットマン
Lottman, Herbert R. 846
Rotman, Joseph 1210
Rottman, Gordon L. 1210
Rottmann, Wolfgang 1210
ロッドマン
Rodman, Dennis 1194
Rodman, Francis Robert 1194
Rodman, Robert 1194
ロッパー
Ropper, Allan H. 1202
ロップ
Lopp, Michael 844
Rop, Albert Kibichii 1202
Rop, Anton 1202
ロッベン
Robben, Arjen 1187
ロッホ
Loch, Felix 838
ロッホマン
Lochman, Jan Milic 838

ローデ
Løhde, Sophie 840
Rode, Herbert 1194
Rode, Sebastian 1194
Rohde, Julia 1198
ロデ
Lodde, Luigi 839
Rodet, Alain-Pierre 1194
ローティ
Rorty, Richard Mckay 1202
ローディ
Lodi, Francesco 839
Lordi, Susan L. 844
Roedy, Bill 1196
ロディ
Lodi, Sofia 839
Roddie, Shen 1194
Rodi, Robert 1194
ロディオノワ
Rodionova, Alexandra 1194
ローディガー
Roediger, David R. 1196
Roediger, Henry L. 1196
ロディガリ
Rodigari, Nicola 1194
ロティチ
Rotich, Henry 1210
ロディック
Roddick, Anita Lucia 1194
Rodic, Yvan 1194
ローディッシュ
Lodish, Leonard M. 839
ロディッシュ
Lodish, Harvey F. 839
Lodish, Leonard M. 839
ロティッチ
Rotich, Ferguson Cheruiyot 1210
Rotich, Lydia Chebet 1210
ロディノ
Rodino, Peter Wallace, Jr. 1194
ロティリャ
Rotilla, Rafael 1210
ローデイル
Rodale, Maya 1193
ロデイロ
Lodeiro, Nicolás 839
ロディン
Rodin, Gail 1194
ローデス
Rhodes, Dusty 1176
Rhodes, Linda 1176
ローテムンド
Rothemund, Marc 1209
ロデリス
Rodelys, Maharavo 1194
ロデリック
Roderick, John 1194
ローテルト
Roetert, Paul 1196
ロデロ
Rodero, Paz 1194
ローテン
Wroten, Tony 1529
ローデン
Lorden, Gary 844
Lowden, Jack 848
Roden, Barbara 1194
Roden, Christopher 1194
Rohden, Marcus 1198
ローテンガッター
Rothengatter, Werner 1209
ローテンスレーガー
Lautenslager, Al 796
ローテンバーグ
Lautenberg, Frank R. 796
Rotenberg, Robert 1208
ローデンバーグ
Rodenburg, Patsy 1194
ローデンベック
Rodenbeck, Christina 1194
ローテンベルガー
Rothenberger, Anneliese 1209
ロート
Loth, Sebastian 845
Roth, Brigitta 1208
Roth, François-Xavier 1209
Roth, Hans-Dieter 1209
Roth, Susanne 1209
ロード
Load, Walter 837
Lord, Bob 844
Lord, Catherine 844
Lord, Cynthia 844
Lord, Evelyn 844
Lord, James 844
Lord, Jon 844
Lord, Richard 844
Lord, Tony 844
Lord, Walter 844
Lord, Winston 844
Lorde 844
Rhode, Deborah L. 1175
Rhode, Kim 1175
Rhode, Maria 1175
Rhode, Robin 1175
Rhode, Will 1175
ロト
Roth, François-Xavier 1209
ロトゥイガ
Lotu-iiga, Peseta Sam 846
ロドヴィチ・チェホフスカ
Rodowicz-Czechowska, Jadwiga Maria 1194
ロドウィック
Lodwick, Todd 839
ロドウェル
Rodwell, Jack 1196
ロドウフォ
Rhodolfo 1176
ロートエルメル
Rothärmel, Sonja 1209
ロトカ
Lhotka, Rockford 823
ロトキルヒ
Rotkirch, Anna 1210
ロートシルト
Rothschild, Elie de 1209
Rothschild, Guy de 1209
ロート＝ツィマーマン
Roth, Marie-Louise 1209
ロトド
Lotodo, Francis 845
ロートナー
Lautner, Taylor 796
ロドニー
Rodney, Fernando 1194
ロートネル
Lautner, Georges 796
ロドハム
Rodham, Karen 1194
ロートフェルト
Rotfeld, Adam Daniel 1208
ロートブラット
Rotblat, Joseph 1208
ロード・ブレアース
Lord Blears 148
ロドマン
Rodman, Dennis 1194
ロドラ
Llodra, Michael 837
ロドリ
Lodoli, Marco 839
ロドリー
Rodley, Chris 1194
ロドリギュー
Rodriguez, Sophie 1195
ロドリグ
Pinheiro Rodrigues, Danny 1113
ロドリゲス
Dominguez Rodriguez, Hector Paulino 364
Rodorigues, Roque 1194
Rodrigues, Anabela 1194
Rodrigues, Antonio Carlos 1194
Rodrigues, Arinda 1194
Rodrigues, Carolyn 1194
Rodrigues, Eduardo Ferro 1194
Rodrigues, Joao 1195
Rodrigues, Maria de Lurdes 1195
Rodrigues, Roberto 1195
Rodriguez, Alex 1195
Rodriguez, Alexis 1195
Rodríguez, Alí 1195
Rodríguez, Carlos Manuel 1195
Rodríguez, Carolina 1195
Rodriguez, Deborah 1195
Rodríguez, Delcy 1195
Rodriguez, Disney 1195
Rodriguez, Edel 1195
Rodríguez, Edgar Leonel 1195
Rodriguez, Eduardo 1195
Rodríguez, Erick 1195
Rodriguez, Fernando 1195
Rodriguez, Francisco 1195
Rodríguez, Franklin 1195
Rodríguez, Gabriel 1195
Rodríguez, Gilberto 1195
Rodriguez, Gina 1195
Rodríguez, Héctor 1195
Rodriguez, Ismael 1195
Rodriguez, Ivan 1195
Rodríguez, James 1195
Rodriguez, Jay 1195
Rodriguez, Jennifer 1195
Rodriguez, Joely 1195
Rodríguez, Jorge 1195
Rodríguez, José Antonio 1195
Rodriguez, Juan Miguel 1195
Rodríguez, Luis Ramón 1195
Rodríguez, Manuel 1195
Rodríguez, María Cecilia 1195
Rodríguez, María Isabel 1195
Rodríguez, Mauricio 1195
Rodríguez, Maxi 1195
Rodriguez, Miguel Angel 1195
Rodriguez, Misael Uziel 1195
Rodriguez, Natalia 1195
Rodriguez, Noelie 1195
Rodriguez, Paco 1195
Rodríguez, Rachel 1195
Rodriguez, Raiber 1195
Rodriguez, Ramon L. 1195
Rodriguez, Ricardo 1195
Rodriguez, Richard 1195
Rodriguez, Robbi 1195
Rodriguez, Robert 1195
Rodríguez, Salvador 1195
Rodriguez, Sean 1195
Rodriguez, Sergio 1195
Rodriguez, Sophie 1195
Rodriguez, Victor 1195
Rodriguez, Yorgelis 1195
Rodriguez Mitjan, Marina de la Caridad 1195
Rodriguez Pargas, Rosa Andreina 1196
ロドリゲスアギアル
Rodriguesaguiar, Armindo Vaz 1195
ロドリゲスオリバー
Rodriguez Oliver, Joaquin 1196
ロドリゲス・ガイリ
Rodríguez Gairí, Sique 1195
ロドリゲス・ガルシア
Rodríguez García, José Luis 1195
ロドリゲス・ゴンサレス
Rodriguez Gonzalez, Manuel 1195
ロドリゲス・ゴンザレス・ルビオ
Rodríguez González-Rubio, Cecilia 1195
ロドリゲス・サパテーロ
Rodríguez Zapatero, José Luis 1196
ロドリゲス・サパテロ
Rodríguez Zapatero, José Luis 1196
ロドリゲズシオス
Rodriguez Sios, Vicente 1196
ロドリゲス・ソルデビジャ
Rodríguez soldevilla, José 1196
ロドリゲス・ソルデビラ
Rodríguez soldevilla, José 1196
ロドリゲス＝チャムシー
Rodriguez-Chamussy, Lourdes 1195
ロドリゲス・デル・アリサル
Rodriguez del Alisal, Maria Dolores 1195
ロドリゲス・トレス
Rodoríguez Torres, Miguel 1194
ロドリゲスバーケット
Rodrigues-birkett, Carolyn 1195
ロドリゲス・パリジャ
Rodríguez Parrilla, Bruno 1196
ロドリゲス・ペレイラ
Rodrigues Pereira, Maria Celeste 1195
ロドリゲス・マカル
Rodriguez Macal,

Virgilio 1195
ロドリゲス・メドラノ
Rodriguez Medrano, Antonia 1195
ロドリゲス・メネンデス
Rodriguez Menéndez, Romeo Augusto 1195
ロドリゲス・ロジェロ
Rodríguez Rollero, Gustavo 1196
ロドリゲス・ロマイ
Rodríguez Romay, Orlando Felipe 1196
ロドリゲス・ロメロ
Rodríguez Romero, Casimira 1196
ロドリゴ
Rodrigo 1194
Rodrigo, Hernandez 1194
Rodrigo, Miguel 1194
ロドリック
Roderick, John 1194
Rodrik, Dani 1196
ロートリン
Rothlin, Philippe 1209
ロトロ
Rotolo, Suze 1210
ロートン
Lawton, Mary 798
Lawton, Thomas 798
Loton, Brian Thorley 846
Lowton, Matthew 848
ロードン
Loudon, Kyle 846
Rawdon, Alexina 1161
ロドン
Rodon, Carlos 1194
ロトンディ
Rotondi, Gianfranco 1210
ローナー
Launer, John 795
Röhner, Thomas 1198
Rohner, Tim 1198
ロナ
Wrona, Robert J. 1529
ロナウジーニョ
Ronaldinho 1200
ロナウド
Ronaldo 1200
ロナーガン
Lonergan, Tom 841
ロナメイ
Lonamei, Varian 841
ロナルド
Cristiano Ronaldo 302
Ronald, Pamela C. 1200
Ronald, Pamera C. 1200
ロナルドソン
Ronaldson, Jake 1201
ローナン
Ronan, Brian 1201
Ronan, Saoirse 1201
ロナン
Ronan, Mark 1201
ローニー
Roney, J.Matthew 1201
ロニー
Loney, Kevin 841
Roney, Carley 1201
Roney, Christopher R. J. 1201
ロニス
Ronis, Aivis 1201
Ronis, Willy 1201
ローニッツ
Lonitz, Henri 842
ロニングスタム
Ronningstam, Elsa F. 1201
ロネ
Launet, Édouard 795
Rosnay, Tatiana de 1206
ロネー
Rosnay, Joël de 1206
ロネット
Lonette, Reisie 841
ロノフ
Lonoff de Cuevas, Sue 842
ロー・ノルト
L.Nolte, Dorothy 837
ローバー
Lauber, Patricia 795
Lorber, Robert 844
ローパー
Lauper, Cyndi 795
Loper, Edward 843
Loper, Whitly 843
Roper, Miryam 1202
Roper, Nancy 1202
ロパ
Lopa, Alhadj Abakaka Moustapha 842
Lopa, Baharuddin 842
ロハーイ
Rohály, Gábor 1198
ロバイナ
Robaina, Alejandro 1187
ローハイム
Róheim, Geza 1198
ローバオ
Lauvao, Shawn 796
ロバーグ
Loberg, Kristin 838
ロバシュ
Lovas, Petra 847
ロハス
Rojas, Álvaro 1198
Rojas, Euclides 1198
Rojas, Germán 1198
Rojas, Gonzalo 1198
Rojas, José 1198
Rojas, Miguel 1198
Rojas, Roberto 1198
Rojas, Yulimar 1198
Roxas, Manuel Ⅱ 1212
ロバース
Lovász, László 847
ロバーズ
Robards, Karen 1187
ロハス・ゴメス
Rojas Gómez, Bautista 1198
ロハス・ヒラルド
Rojas Giraldo, Jorge Eduardo 1198
ロハス・メサ
Rojas Mesa, Miguel Tadeo 1198
ロハスリベラ
Rojas Rivera, Julian Alberto 1198
ロバーソン
Roberson, Andre 1187
Roberson, Bruce 1187
Roberson, Marcus 1187
Roberson, Tre 1187
Roberson, Tyler 1187
ロバチェワ
Lobacheva, Irina 837
ロバーツ
Michael Roberts, R. 942
Roberts, Alice M. 1188
Roberts, Alison 1188
Roberts, Andre 1188
Roberts, Andrew 1188
Roberts, Anil 1188
Roberts, Anita 1188
Roberts, Anthony 1188
Roberts, Barbara 1188
Roberts, Ben 1188
Roberts, Benjamin 1188
Roberts, Bernadette 1188
Roberts, Bernard 1188
Roberts, Bradley 1188
Roberts, Brian 1188
Roberts, Bryan 1188
Roberts, Buddy 1188
Roberts, Caroline 1188
Roberts, Chalmers McGeagh 1188
Roberts, Charlotte 1188
Roberts, Chris 1188
Roberts, Clare 1188
Roberts, Darryl 1188
Roberts, Dave 1188
Roberts, David 1188
Roberts, David L. 1188
Roberts, Donna H. 1188
Roberts, Doreen 1188
Roberts, Doris 1188
Roberts, Dorothy 1188
Roberts, Dustyn 1188
Roberts, Earl 1188
Roberts, Ed 1188
Roberts, Elandon 1188
Roberts, Elisabeth 1188
Roberts, Gene 1188
Roberts, Geoffrey 1188
Roberts, Gerrylynn 1188
Roberts, Gil 1188
Roberts, Gillian 1188
Roberts, Glyn 1188
Roberts, Glynis 1188
Roberts, Gregory David 1188
Roberts, Jacqueline 1189
Roberts, Jaleel 1189
Roberts, James 1189
Roberts, James Deotis 1189
Roberts, Jamie 1189
Roberts, Jeffrey W. 1189
Roberts, Jimmy 1189
Roberts, John 1189
Roberts, John Glover, Jr. 1189
Roberts, John Morris 1189
Roberts, John Peter Lee 1189
Roberts, Julia 1189
Roberts, Justin 1189
Roberts, Katherine 1189
Roberts, Keith 1189
Roberts, Ken 1189
Roberts, Kenny Sr. 1189
Roberts, Kevin 1189
Roberts, Kyle 1189
Roberts, Luke 1189
Roberts, Marc J. 1189
Roberts, Mary Louise 1189
Roberts, Michael 1189
Roberts, Michael C. 1189
Roberts, Monty 1189
Roberts, M.Susan 1189
Roberts, Nancy L. 1189
Roberts, Nora 1189
Roberts, Paul 1189
Roberts, Pernell Elvin 1189
Roberts, Peter 1189
Roberts, Ralph 1189
Roberts, Richard John 1189
Roberts, Robin Evan 1189
Roberts, Russell D. 1189
Roberts, S.C. 1189
Roberts, Seth 1189
Roberts, Seth Douglass 1189
Roberts, Siobhan 1189
Roberts, Susan 1189
Roberts, Susan Barbara 1189
Roberts, Tanya 1189
Roberts, Vaughan 1189
Roberts, Vega Zagier 1189
Roberts, Victoria 1189
Roberts, Walter B., Jr. 1189
Roberts, Wayne 1189
Roberts, Wess 1189
Roberts, Willo Davis 1189
ローバック
Robach, Nils Magnus 1187
Roebuck, John Arthur, Jr. 1196
Roorbach, Bill 1201
ロバーティ
Roberty, Marc 1190
ロハティン
Rohatyn, Felix G. 1198
ロバート
Lobato, Arcadio 837
Robert, Caroline 1187
Robert, Christian P. 1188
Robert, Lorin 1188
Robert, Maketo 1188
Robert, Na'íma bint 1188
Robert, Pierre 1188
ロバト
Lobato, Lúcia 837
Lobato, Rogerio 837
Lovato, Rick 847
ロバートキナ
Lopatkina, Ulyana 843
ロバートショー
Robertshaw, Angela 1189
ロバートスン
Robertson, Cliff 1189
Robertson, Imogen 1190
ロバートソン
Robertson, Andrea 1189
Robertson, Andrew 1189
Robertson, Bryon 1189
Robertson, Chad 1189
Robertson, Cliff 1189
Robertson, Craig 1189
Robertson, Daniel 1189
Robertson, David 1189
Robertson, David Chandler 1189
Robertson, D.Gordon E. 1189
Robertson, Douglas L. 1190
Robertson, Edwin 1190
Robertson, George Islay MacNeill 1190
Robertson, Ian H. 1190
Robertson, Imogen 1190
Robertson, James 1190
Robertson, Jason 1190
Robertson, Jin Kyu 1190

Robertson, John 1190
Robertson, Julian, Jr. 1190
Robertson, Malcolm 1190
Robertson, Mary M. 1190
Robertson, Michael 1190
Robertson, Michelle M. 1190
Robertson, Mike 1190
Robertson, Miranda 1190
Robertson, M.P. 1190
Robertson, Nathan 1190
Robertson, Pat 1190
Robertson, Paul D. 1190
Robertson, Paul L. 1190
Robertson, Pete 1190
Robertson, Ritchie 1190
Robertson, Robert Ireland 1190
Robertson, Scott 1190
Robertson, Scott A. 1190
Robertson, S.D. 1190
Robertson, Sheila 1190
Robertson, Shirley 1190
Robertson, Suzanne 1190
Robertson, Terence 1190
Robertson, Theo 1190
Robertson, William H. P. 1190

ロバートソン・ハリス
Robertson-harris, Roy 1190

ロバトン
Lobaton, Jose 837

ロハニ
Rohani, Abdul Karim 1198
Rouhani, Hassan 1210

ロバノフスキー
Lobanovsky, Valery 837

ローバリー
Rowbury, Shannon 1211

ロバロ
Lovallo, Dan 847

ローハン
Lohan, Lindsay 840

ロバン
Lobão, Edison 837
Robin, Marie-Monique 1190

ロバンソン
Robinson, Jean-Louis 1191

ローヒー
Rohee, Clement 1198

ロビー
Robey, Nickell 1190
Roby, Bradley 1192
Roby, Steven 1192

ロヒア
Lohia, Sri Prakash 840

ロビシェワ
Lobysheva, Yekaterina 838

ロビショー
Robichaud, Audrey 1190

ロビスキー
Robiskie, Terry 1192

ロビソン
Robison, Arch D. 1192
Robison, John Elder 1192

ロビット
Rovit, Sam 1211

ロビドー
Robideaux, Sharon 1190

ロビニヒ
Lobnig, Magdalena 838

ロビーニョ
Robinho 1190

ロビネッティ
Robinette, Scott 1190

ロビノヴィッツ
Robinovitz, Karen 1190

ロビヤール
Robillard, Lucienne 1190

ロビュション
Robuchon, Joël 1192

ロビラ
Rovira, Alex 1211
Rovira, Guiomar 1211

ロビラ・カロル
Rovira Carol, Francisca 1211

ロビリャール
Robillard, Lucienne 1190

ロビーン
Lovén, John 847

ロビン
Robin, Jennifer 1190

ロビンコーカー
Robbin-coker, Oluniyi 1187

ロビンス
Lovins, Amory B. 847
Lovins, L.Hunter 847
Robbins, Alexandra 1187
Robbins, Arnold 1187
Robbins, Clarence R. 1187
Robbins, Dianne 1187
Robbins, Harold 1187
Robbins, Irvine 1187
Robbins, James 1187
Robbins, Jesse 1187
Robbins, Jim 1187
Robbins, John B. 1187
Robbins, Kathleen A. 1187
Robbins, Keith 1187
Robbins, Matthew 1187
Robbins, Richard 1187
Robbins, Stephen P. 1187
Robbins, Tim 1187
Robins, Arthur 1190
Robins, Kevin 1190
Robins, Sari 1190
Robins, Sinai 1190

ロビンズ
Lovins, Amory B. 847
Robbins, Anthony 1187
Robbins, Carol 1187
Robbins, Clive 1187
Robbins, David L. 1187
Robbins, Frederick Chapman 1187
Robbins, Herbert 1187
Robbins, John 1187
Robbins, Keith 1187
Robbins, Ken 1187
Robbins, Lisa A. 1187
Robbins, Louise E. 1187
Robbins, Louise S. 1187
Robbins, Maurice 1187
Robbins, Mike 1187
Robbins, Richard 1187
Robbins, Tim 1187
Robins, David 1190
Robins, Kevin 1190

ロビンスン
Robinson, Francis 1191
Robinson, Jeremy 1191
Robinson, Kim Stanley 1191
Robinson, Peter 1191
Robinson, Roxana 1192

ロビンソン
Robinson, Adam 1190
Robinson, Alan G. 1190
Robinson, Aldrick 1190
Robinson, Allen 1190
Robinson, Aminah Brenda Lynn 1190
Robinson, Andrew 1190
Robinson, Andrew C. 1190
Robinson, A.N. Raymond 1190
Robinson, Arthur Howard 1190
Robinson, A'Shawn 1190
Robinson, Bill 1191
Robinson, Brett 1191
Robinson, Chris 1191
Robinson, Christian 1191
Robinson, Clark 1191
Robinson, Clint 1191
Robinson, Corey 1191
Robinson, D.A. 1191
Robinson, Dana Gaines 1191
Robinson, David 1191
Robinson, David J. 1191
Robinson, David Ryan 1191
Robinson, Demarcus 1191
Robinson, Denard 1191
Robinson, Donny 1191
Robinson, Drew 1191
Robinson, Edmond 1191
Robinson, Elisabeth 1191
Robinson, Fay 1191
Robinson, Francis 1191
Robinson, Frank 1191
Robinson, Frank M. 1191
Robinson, Fred Miller 1191
Robinson, Gertrude J. 1191
Robinson, Glenn, Ⅲ 1191
Robinson, Greg 1191
Robinson, Gwen 1191
Robinson, Hilary 1191
Robinson, Jamal 1191
Robinson, James A. 1191
Robinson, James C. 1191
Robinson, James McConkey 1191
Robinson, Jancis 1191
Robinson, Janet L. 1191
Robinson, Jeffrey 1191
Robinson, Jennifer 1191
Robinson, Jeremy 1191
Robinson, Jonathan 1191
Robinson, Josh 1191
Robinson, Julian 1191
Robinson, Kara 1191
Robinson, Keenan 1191
Robinson, Ken 1191
Robinson, Khiry 1191
Robinson, Kim Stanley 1191
Robinson, Lauri 1191
Robinson, Leah Ruth 1191
Robinson, Lynn A. 1191
Robinson, Lynne 1191
Robinson, Lytle W. 1191
Robinson, Maggie 1191
Robinson, Marilynne 1191
Robinson, Martin 1191
Robinson, Mary 1191
Robinson, Michael J. T. 1191
Robinson, Mike 1191
Robinson, Nicola 1191
Robinson, Patricia 1191
Robinson, Patrick 1191
Robinson, Paul 1191
Robinson, Peter 1191, 1192
Robinson, Phil Alden 1192
Robinson, Rashard 1192
Robinson, Ray 1192
Robinson, Raymond 1192
Robinson, Richard 1192
Robinson, Robert G. 1192
Robinson, Roger 1192
Robinson, Russ 1192
Robinson, Ryan 1192
Robinson, Scott 1192
Robinson, Shahine 1192
Robinson, Simon 1192
Robinson, Thelma M. 1192
Robinson, Thomas 1192
Robinson, Timothy M. 1192
Robinson, Tony 1192
Robinson, Trenton 1192
Robinson, Wendy 1192
Robison, Brian 1192

ロビンソンベーカー
Robinson-baker, Nicholas 1192

ロビンソンレジス
Robinson-regis, Camille 1192

ロビンツェフ
Lobintsev, Nikita 838

ローフ
Lööf, Fredrik 842
Roaf, Michael 1187

ローブ
Lobe, Lisa 837
Loeb, Daniel 839
Loeb, Gerald M. 839
Loeb, Jeph 839
Loeb, Sebastian 839
Lööf, Anni 842
Roob, Alexander 1201
Rove, Karl 1211

ロープ
Lop, Willie 842
Rope, Crispin 1202

ロブ
Lob, Jacques 837
Rob, A.S.M. Abdur 1187
Robb, Andrew 1187
Robb, Brian J. 1187
Robb, Douglas 1187
Robb, J.D. 1187
Robb, John 1187

ロファ
Roffat, Sébastien 1196

ロ・ファソ
Lo Faso, Simone 839

ロフィー
Roffey, Maureen 1196

ローフィンク
Lohfink, Norbert 840

ロフェ
Roffe, Marcelo 1196
Roffe, Thomas J. 1196

ローフェン
Loeffen, Peter 839

ローフォード
Lawford, Patricia Kennedy 797

ロブ・グリエ
Robbe-Grillet, Alain 1187

ロフグレン
Lofgren, Nils 839

ロ

ロブサンドルジーン・ウルズィートゥグス
Luvsandorzhiĭn Ölziĭtógs 855
ロブサン・ランパ
Lobsang Rampa, T. 838
ロブショウ
Robshaw, Chris 1192
ロブション
Robuchon, Joël 1192
ロープス
Lopes, Davey 843
ロブスティーン
Lobstein, Kyle 838
ロブズハニゼ
Lobzhanidze, Vasil 838
ロブスン
Robson, William Wallace 1192
ロブソン
Rabson, Arthur 1147
Robson, Bobby 1192
Robson, Eleanor 1192
Robson, Ethan 1192
Robson, John E. 1192
Robson, Josh 1192
Robson, Justina 1192
Robson, Keith 1192
Robson, Kirsteen 1192
Robson, Laura 1192
Robson, Matt 1192
Robson, Tom 1192
ロブソン・カヌ
Robson-kanu, Hal 1192
ロフタス
Loftus, Elizabeth F. 839
Loftus, Geoffey R. 839
Loftus, Paul 839
ロフタス・チーク
Loftus-cheek, Ruben 839
ロブテル
Lobdell, Scott 837
ロブデル
Lobdell, Scott 837
ロブデン
Lovden, Lars-Erik 847
ローフート
Rouvoet, André 1211
ロフトハウス
Lofthouse, Nat 839
ロフバル
Rohbar, Qosim 1198
ロフマン
Roffman, Roger A. 1196
ロブマン
Lobman, Carrie 838
ロブラン
Robelin, Cécile 1187
Robelin, Jean 1187
ロフランド
Lofland, Donald J. 839
ローブリアヤオ
Lobriayao, Somthone 838
ロブリン
Lovrin, Ana 847
ロブレ
Robleh, Bodeh Ahmed 1192
ロブレス
Robles, Dayron 1192
Robles, Hansel 1192
Robles, Joel 1192
Robles, Sarah 1192
ロブレスキー
Wroblewski, David 1529
ロプレスティ
Lopresti, Aaron 844
ロブレス・ベルランガ
Robles Berlanga, Rosario 1192
ロブレト
Robleto, David 1192
Robleto, Fernando 1192
ロブレド
Robredo, Jesse 1192
Robredo, Maria Leonor 1192
ロブレヒト
Robberecht, Thierry 1187
ロブロ
Lovullo, Torey 847
ロブロット
LoBrutto, Vincent 838
ローベ
Rowe, Mary 1211
ロベヴァ
Robeva, Neshka Stefanova 1190
ロペス
Lopes, Anthony 843
Lopes, António Figueiredo 843
Lopes, Carlos Alberto 843
Lopes, Emanuela Afonso Vieira 843
Lopes, Filomena 843
Lopes, Lívio Fernandes 843
Lopes, Sara 843
Lopes-schliep, Priscilla 843
Lopez, Al 843
López, Alfonso 843
Lopez, Arlen 843
Lopez, Ben 843
Lopez, Brook 843
López, Celso 843
Lopez, Cesar 843
López, Daniel 843
Lopez, Delano 843
Lopez, Diana 843
López, Eduardo 843
Lopez, Elena 843
Lopez, Feliciano 843
Lopez, Gaby 843
Lopez, Gerry 843
López, Guillermo 843
Lopez, Helder Vaz 843
Lopez, Israel 843
Lopez, Javier 843
Lopez, Jennifer 843
Lopez, Jorge 843
López, José 843
Lopez, Jose 843
López, Juan Torres 843
Lopez, Judy 843
Lopez, Livan 843
Lopez, Marc 843
López, María Elena 843
Lopez, Mark 843
Lopez, Miguel Angel 843
Lopez, Mijain 843
Lopez, Nicolas 843
López, Orlando 843
Lopez, Paul 843
Lopez, Peter 843
Lopez, Ramon 843
López, Ramón E. 843
Lopez, Regina Paz 843
Lopez, Reynaldo 843
Lopez, Robert 843
Lopez, Robin 843
Lopez, Rosa Argentina 843
Lopez, Shane J. 843
Lopez, Steve 843
Lopez, Steven 843
López, Tenky 843
Lopez, Yeimer 843
López Arellano, Oswaldo 843
Lopez Azcuy, Livan 844
López-García, Antonio 844
Lopez Laguna, Maria Luisa 844
Lopez Nunez, Michel 844
López Portillo, José 844
Lopez Rivera, Teofimo Andres 844
Vidiaux Lopez, Katerina 1455
ロペス＝アウスティン
López-Austin, Alfredo 844
ロペス・アギラル
López Aguilar, Juan Fernando 843
ロペスアギラル
López Aguilar, Juan Fernando 843
ロペスアセア
López Acea, Lázara Mercedes 843
ロペス・アレヤノ
López Arellano, Oswaldo 843
ロペス・アレリャノ
López Arellano, Oswaldo 843
ロペスアロチャ
Lopez Arocha, Jessica Brizeida 843
ロペス・アンブロシオ
López Ambrosio, Manuel 843
ロペス - オーティン
López-Otín, Carlos 844
ロペス・オブレゴン
López Obregón, Clara 844
ロペス "カチャーオ"
López"Cachao", Israel 844
ロペス＝カルバ
Lopez-Calva, Luis Felipe 844
ロペス・キュルヴァル
Lopes-Curval, Julie 843
ロペス・キュルバル
Lopes-Curval, Julie 843
ロペス・グスマン
López Guzmán, Tharsis Salomón 844
ロペス・コボス
López-Cobos, Jesús 844
ロペス - コルヴォ
López Corvo, Rafael E. 844
ロペスサライバ
Lopes Saraiva, Flavia 843
ロペス・サントス
López Santos, Antonio 844
ロペス・スアレス
López Suárez, José Guillermo 844
ロペス＝ソリア
López Soria, Marisa 844
ロペストルヒッリョ
López Trujillo, Alfonso 844
ロペス・ナルバエス
Lopez Narvaez, Concha 844
ロペスヌネス
Lopez Nunez, Mijain 844
ロペス・バルデス
López Valdés, Alfredo 844
ロペス・ビジャファニェ
López Villafañe, Victor Manuel 844
ロペス・ビヒル
López Vigil, José Ignacio 844
López Vigil, María 844
ロペス・フィゲロア
López Figueroa, Bernardo 844
ロペスボニジャ
López Bonilla, Mauricio 844
ロペス・ポルティジョ
López Portillo, José 844
ロペス・ポルティーヨ
López Portillo, José 844
ロペス・ムルフィ
López Murphy, Ricardo 844
ロペスモレイラ
López Moreira, Juan Carlos 844
ロペス・リバス
López Rivas, Óscar Hugo 844
ロペス＝ルイス
López Ruiz, José Luis 844
ロペス・ロドリゲス
López Rodriguez, Dolores 844
López Rodríguez, Elmer 844
López Rodríguez, Wilfredo 844
ローベック
Robeck, Sylvia 1187
ロベット
Lovett, David 847
ローベル
Lobel, Adrianne 837
Lobel, Anita 837
Lobel, Gillian 837
Lobel, Leonard 838
Lobel, Thalma 838
ロベール
Lobert, Jonathan 838
Robert, Alain 1187
Robert, Denis 1188
Robert, Frederic 1188
Robert, Jean-Noël 1188
Robert, Julien 1188
Robèrt, Karl-Henrik 1188
Robert, Nadine 1188
Robert, Philippe 1188
Robert, Véronique 1188
Robert, Yves 1188
ロベル
Lobell, John 838
Lovell, Harold 847
Rovell, Darren 1211
ロベール皇太子
Prince Robert 1187
ロベルジェ
Roberge, Kalyna 1187
ロベルジュ
Roberge, Claude 1187
ローベルジョン
Lauvergeon, Anne Alice

Marie 796
ロベルジョン
Lauvergeon, Anne Alice Marie 796
ロベルティ
Roberti, Alessio 1188
ロベール殿下
Prince Robert 1187
ロベルト
Roberto, Jimenez 1188
Roberto, Michael A. 1188
ロベルト・イバニェス
Robert Ibanez 1188
ロベルト・カルロス
Roberto Carlos 1188
ロベルドス
Loverdos, Andreas 847
ロベルト・トーレス
Roberto Torres 1188
ロベルト・ミケ
Robert Mike 1188
ロベールミション
Robert-michon, Melina 1188
ロベーン
Löfven, Stefan 839
ロベンディ
Lobendi, Bamboka 838
ローベンハイム
Lovenheim, Peter 847
ローホー
Loreau, Dominique 844
ロホ
Rojo, Marcos 1198
Rojo, Tamara 1198
ロボ
Lobo, Démis 838
Lobo, Porfirio 838
Lobo, Ramon 838
Lobo, Sérgio 838
ロボサム
Robotham, Michael 1192
ロボ・ソサ
Lobo Sosa, Porfirio 838
ローボトム
Rowbottom, David G. 1211
Rowbottom, Mike 1211
ロボニョン
Lobognon, Alain Michel 838
ロポネン
Roponen, Riitta-Liisa 1202
ロホビイ
Rohovy, Vasyl 1198
ロホマン
Rahman, Sheikh Mujibur 1150
ロボリク
Loborik, Jason 838
ロボリック
Loborik, Jason 838
ローボルト
Raubolt, Richard Raleigh 1160
ロボワ
Lobova, Natalia 838
ロボンツ
Lobont, Bogdan 838
ローマ
Rome, Adi 1200
ローマー
Laumer, Keith 795
Roemer, John E. 1196
Roemer, Kenneth M. 1196
Romer, Alfred Sherwood 1200
Romer, David 1200
ロマイア
Lomaia, Alexander 840
Lomaia, Kakha 840
ロマイケ
Romeike, Hinrich 1200
ローマイヤー
Lohmeyer, Dan 840
ロマイン
Romine, Andrew 1200
Romine, Austin 1200
ローマクス
Lomax, Eric 840
ロマクス
Lomax, Alan 840
ロマシナ
Romashina, Svetlana 1200
ローマス
Lomas, James 840
ロマス
Lomas, Bryan 840
Lomas, Robert 840
ロマス・モラレス
Lomas Morales, Martha 840
ロマゾウ
Lomazow, Steven 841
ロマチェンコ
Lomachenko, Vasyl 840
ローマックス
Lomax, Alan 840
Lomax, William 840
ロマックス
Lomax, Jordan 840
ロマーニ
Romani, Paolo 1199
ロマニ
Romani, Darlan 1199
ロマニョーリ
Romagnoli, Alessio 1199
ロマニリョス
Romanillos, José L. 1199
ロマネク
Romanek, Mark 1199
ロマネリ
Romanelli, Serena 1199
ロマーノ
Romano, Luciano 1199
Romano, Phil 1199
Romano, Ruggiero 1199
Romano, Sal 1199
ロマノ
Romano, Luke 1199
Romano, Ray 1199
Romano, Richard Michael 1199
ロマーノフ
Romanov, Andrey 1199
ロマノフ
Romanov, Alexander 1199
Romanov, Grigorii Vasilievich 1199
ロマノフスキー
Romanovsky, Alexander 1200
ロマノワ
Romanova, Elena 1200
Romanova, Leonida 1200
Romanova, Vera Konstantinovna 1200
ロマーリオ
Romário 1200
ロマリオ
Romário 1200
ローマン
Lohman, Timothy G. 840
Lohmann, Roger A. 840
Loughman, Bob 846
Rohmann, Eric 1198
Rohmann, Teresa 1198
Roman, Ed 1199
Roman, Kenneth 1199
Roman, Sela 1199
ロマーン
Roman, Christine 1199
ロマン
Roman, Aida 1199
Roman, Alberto 1199
Roman, Gil 1199
Roman, Greg 1199
Roman, Orlando 1199
ロマンジーク
Romanczyk, Raymond G. 1199
ロマンス
Romance, Trisha 1199
ロミゼ
Lomidze, Lasha 841
ロミゾウスキー
Romiszowski, Alexander 1200
ロミータ
Romita, John, Jr. 1200
Romita, John, Sr. 1200
ロミッチ
Romić, Davor 1200
ローム
Roam, Dan 1187
Rome, David I. 1200
Rome, Esther R. 1200
Rome, Margaret 1200
Romme, Marius A.J. 1200
ロム
Lom, Herbert 840
Lomb, Niklas 841
Rom, Paul 1199
Romm, James S. 1200
ロムー
Lomu, Jonah 841
ロムソン
Romson, Åsa 1200
ロムダン
Romdhane, Habiba Zéhi Ben 1200
ロムニー
Romney, Mitt 1200
ロムニツキ
Lomnicky, Marcel 841
ロムパル
Lompar, Andrija 841
ロムロ
Lomuro, Martin Elia 841
Romulo, Alberto 1200
ロメ
Romme, Gianni 1200
ロメイ
Lomey, Gomdigue Baidi 841
ロメイエ＝デルベ
Romeyer-Dherbey, Gilbert 1200
ロメイン
Romain, Trevor 1199
Romaine, Deborah S. 1199
Romaine, Suzanne 1199
ロメウ
Romeu, Oriol 1200
ロメオ
Lomeo, Angelo 841
ロメッティ
Rometty, Virginia M. 1200
ロメト
Lometo, Tadashi 841
ロメリ
Lomelí, Kyle 841
ロメリル
Romeril, John 1200
ロメール
Rohmer, Eric 1198
ロメル
Romer, Andrzej 1200
ロメレン
Romoeren, Bjoern Einar 1200
ロメーロ
Romero, Manueru Peresu 1200
ロメロ
Romerc, Cecilia 1200
Romero, Alvaro 1200
Romero, Amilcar 1200
Romero, Ana María 1200
Romero, Carlos 1200
Romero, Diego Emilio 1200
Romero, Enny 1200
Romero, Fernando 1200
Romero, George A. 1200
Romero, Jordan 1200
Romero, Luisa 1200
Romero, Otto 1200
Romero, Rebecca 1200
Romero, Ricky 1200
Romero, Sergio 1200
Romero, Yoel 1200
ロメロ・ボニファス
Romero Bonifaz, Carlos Gustavo 1200
ロメロ・ラウエサリ
Romerolozada Lauezzari, Ana María 1200
ロメロ・ラモス
Romero Ramos, Eduardo 1200
ロメロロサダ・ラウエサリ
Romerolozada Lauezzari, Ana María 1200
ロモ
Romo, Sergio 1200
Romo, Tony 1200
ロ・モナコ
Lo Monaco, Gérard 841
ロモンド
Lomond, Britt 841
ロヤック
Loeak, Christopher Jorebon 839
ロヨ
Loyo, Juan Carlos 849
ローラー
Laurer, Joanie 796
Lawler, Edward E., Ⅲ 797
Lawler, Janet 797
Lawler, Kenny 797
Lawlor, Robert 797
Rohrer, Heinrich 1198
ロラ
Lora, Alberto 844

ロラク
Lorak, Nidel 844
ローラック
Rolak, Loren A. 1199
ロラック
Lorak, Nidel 844
ローラン
Laulan, Sarah 795
Laurent, Éloi 795
Laurent, Éric 795
Laurent, Lucien 795
Laurent, Samuel 795
Loughran, P.J. 846
Rollin, Jean 1199
ロラン
Laurens, Alain 795
Laurent, Eric 795
Lorand, Jean-Marie 844
Roland, Claudine 1199
Rolland, Kevin 1199
ローランズ
Rowlands, Caroline 1212
Rowlands, Gena 1212
Rowlands, J.Craig 1212
Rowlands, Mark 1212
Rowlands, Penelope 1212
Rowlands, Tom 1212
ロランス
Laurens, Camille 795
ロランディス
Rolandis, Nicos 1199
ローランド
Roland, David 1199
Roland, Paul 1199
Rowland, Frank Sherwood 1212
Rowland, Ian 1212
Rowland, William C. 1212
ローランド＝ワーン
Rowland-Warne, L. 1212
ロラン‐レヴィ
Roland-Lévy, Christine 1199
ローリ
Laurie, Peter 796
ローリー
Laurie, Donald L. 796
Laurie, Hugh 796
Laurie, Victoria 796
Lawrie, J.Michael 798
Lawrie, Paul 798
Lawry, Kalyani 798
Lorey, Dean 845
Lorie, Peter 845
Lowrie, Paul 848
Lowry, Adam 848
Lowry, Clara 848
Lowry, Dave 848
Lowry, Lois 848
Raleigh, Lori E. 1152
Rolle, Jumal 1199
Rowley, Anna 1212
Rowley, Arthur 1212
Rowley, Chris 1212
Rowley, G.G. 1212
Rowley, Keith 1212
Rowley, Laura 1212
Rowley, Londi L. 1212
Rowley, Nic 1212
ロリ
Laury, Pierre 796
Lolli, Matteo 840
ローリア
Lauria, Frank 796
Loria, Jeffrey 845
ローリィ
Lory, Hillis 845
ロリウー
Laurioux, Bruno 796
ロリウス
Lorius, Claude 845
ロリオ
Loriod, Yvonne 845
ロリオ・アラナ
Lorío Arana, Amanda del Rosario 845
ロリオ＝メシアン
Loriod, Yvonne 845
ロリガ
Loeliger, Jon 839
ロリグ
Lorig, Khatuna 845
ロリス
Lloris, Hugo 837
ローリセラ
Lauricella, Michel 796
ローリッグ
Lorig, Kate 845
ローリナイティス
Laurinaitis, James 796
ローリーニ
Laurini, Vincent 796
ロリビエ＝ラオラ
Lolivier-Rahola, Gloria 840
ローリヘト
Rolighed, Arne 1199
ロリマー
Lorimer, Sally 845
ローリン
Rollin, Bernard E. 1199
Rollin, Jean 1199
ロリン
Rollin, Catherine 1199
ローリング
Roehling, Mark V. 1196
Röling, Niels 1199
Rowling, J.K. 1212
Rowling, Marye 1212
ローリングズ‐アンダーソン
Rawlings-Anderson, Karen 1162
ローリングホーフェン
Loringhoven, Baron Freytag von 845
ローリンズ
Rawlins, Debbi 1162
Rollins, Catherine E. 1199
ロリンズ
Rollins, Billy J. 1199
Rollins, Brianna 1199
Rollins, James 1199
Rollins, Jimmy 1199
Rollins, Kevin B. 1199
Rollins, Quinten 1199
Rollins, Sonny 1199
ローリンソン
Rawlinson, Julia 1162
Rowlinson, Michael 1212
ロール
Rol, Ruud van der 1199
ロル
Roll, Paul 1199
ロルヴァケル
Rohrwacher, Alba 1198
Rohrwacher, Alice 1198
ロルジュリル
Lorgeril, Michel de 845
ロールス
Rohls, Jan 1198
ロールズ
Rawls, John 1162
Rawls, Lou 1162
Rawls, Thomas 1162
Rawls, Wilson 1162
Rholes, William Steven 1176
Rolls, Edmund T. 1199
Rolls, Elizabeth 1199
ロールダー
Roleder, Cindy 1199
ロルタンギ
Rol-Tanguy, Henri 1199
ロ・ルッソ
Lo Russo, Rosaria 845
ロルドン
Lordon, Frédéric 844
ロルニック
Rollnick, Stephen 1199
ロールバッハ
Rohrbach, Gunter 1198
ロルビエッキ
Lorbiecki, Marybeth 844
ロルフ
Rolf, Robert 1199
Rolfe, John 1199
Rolph, Mic 1199
ロルフス
Rohlfs, Jeffrey H. 1198
ロルモー
Lormeau, Jean-Yves 845
ローレ
Rowley, Neville 1212
ロレイン
Lorraine, Walter H. 845
ローレス
Lawless, Annie 797
Lawless, Jade 797
Lawless, Julia 797
ロレタガリン
Loreta-garin, Janette 845
ロレデモラ・ボメ
Loret De Mola Bohme, Aurelio 845
ローレル
Laurel, Alicia Bay 795
Laurel, Brenda 795
Laurel, Lisa Kaye 795
ローレン
Lauren, Paul Gordon 795
Lauren, Ralph 795
Loren, Dennis 844
Loren, Roni 844
Loren, Sophia 844
Rolen, Scott 1199
ロレン
Loren, Halie 844
ロレンザーナ
Lorenzana, Delfin 845
ロレンシノ
Lorenzino, Hernán 845
ロレンジャー
Loranger, Hoa 844
ローレンス
Laurence, Andrea 795
Laurence, Ray 795
Laurens, Stephanie 795
Lawrence, Alfred 797
Lawrence, Alistair 797
Lawrence, Anne T. 797
Lawrence, Bruce 797
Lawrence, Carl 797
Lawrence, Caroline 797
Lawrence, Chris 797
Lawrence, Demarcus 797
Lawrence, Denis 797
Lawrence, Edmund 797
Lawrence, Eleanor 797
Lawrence, Eric 797
Lawrence, Felicity 797
Lawrence, Francis 797
Lawrence, Iain 797
Lawrence, Jacqueline 797
Lawrence, Jamie 797
Lawrence, Jennifer 797
Lawrence, Jennifer B. 798
Lawrence, John 798
Lawrence, Ken 798
Lawrence, Kim 798
Lawrence, Lawrence D. H. 798
Lawrence, Marc 798
Lawrence, Micah 798
Lawrence, Michael C. 798
Lawrence, Paul R. 798
Lawrence, Peter 798
Lawrence, Randee Lipson 798
Lawrence, Rashad 798
Lawrence, Richard 798
Lawrence, Robb 798
Lawrence, Sandra 798
Lawrence, Sihne 798
Lawrence, Tayna 798
Lawrence, Theodore S. 798
Lawrence, Tim 798
Lawrence, Volda 798
Lorenc, Z.Paul 844
Lourenço, Luís 846
ロレンス
Lawrence, Lyndsey 798
Lowrence, Claudia 848
ロレンズ
Lorenz, Jandira 845
ローレンス・スタンプル
Lawrence-stample, Nile 798
ローレンストン
Laurenston, Shelly 795
ローレンゼン
Lorenzen, Michael 845
ロレンソ
Lorenzo, Fernando 845
Lorenzo, Isidro 845
ロレンゾ
Lorenzo, Guy Madjé 845
Lorenzo, Luis, Jr. 845
ロレンチン
Lorencin, Darko 844
ローレンツ
Laurents, Arthur 796
Lorenz, Bettina 845
Lorenz, Edward N. 845
Lorenz, Jutta 845
ロレンツ
Lorenz, Alan 845
Lorenz, Anika 845
Lorenz, Robert 845
Lorenz, Sylvana 845
ロレンツァ
Laurenza, Domenico 796
ロレンツィ
Lorentzi, Hild 845
Lorenzi, Paolo 845
ロレンツィン
Lorenzin, Beatrice 845

ローレンツェン
Lorenzen, Melvyn 845
ロレンツェン
Lorentzen, Lois Ann 845
ロレンテ
Lorente, Joaquín 844
Lorente, José 845
ローレント
Laurent, Amy C. 795
Laurent, Diana 795
ロロ
Rollo, Gord 1199
ロロ・ピアーナ
Loro Piana, Pier Luigi 845
Loro Piana, Sergio 845
ロロフ
Roloff, Helmut 1199
Roloff, Jürgen 1199
ロロフソン
Rolofson, Kristine 1199
ローワー
Loewer, Barry 839
ロワ
Rowa, Karen A. 1211
Roy, Jean 1212
Roy, Jean-Philippe 1212
Roy, Olivier 1212
ロワー
Lower, Wendy 848
ロワイエ
Royer, Isabelle 1212
ロワイヤル
Royal, Ségolène 1212
ロワグ
Roig, Marie-Josée 1198
ロワサ
Lowassa, Edward 848
ロワゾー
Loiseau, Bernard 840
ロワダ
Loada, Augustin 837
ロワチー
Lowachee, Karin 848
ロワトフェルド
Roitfeld, Carine 1198
ロワヤル
Royal, Ségolène 1212
ロワラン
Loirand, Maurice 840
ロワリー
Lowery, Lynda Blackmon 848
ロワレット
Loyrette, Henri 849
ローワン
Roughan, Howard 1210
Rowan, Nina 1211
Rowan, Tiddy 1211
Rowan, Tim 1211
ローン
Loon, Paul van 842
Rohn, E.James 1198
Roon, T. 1201
ロン
Leong, James 814
Leong, Siu Hung Edwin 814
Lone, Abdul Ghani 841
Long, Hei 841
Long, Le Thanh 841
Lönn, Birgit 842
Lung, Kong 853
Rong, Gao-tang 1201
Rong, Yap Kun 1201
Rong, Yi-ren 1201
Rong, Yu 1201
ロンカ
Rönkä, Matti 1201
ロンガ
Longa, Marianna 842
Longa, Steve 842
ロンカイネン
Ronkainen, Mikko 1201
ロンカグリオロ・オルベゴソ
Roncagliolo Orbegoso, Rafael 1201
ロンガーステイ
Longerstaey, Jacques 842
ロンカッリア
Roncaglia, Alessandro 1201
ロンガバディ
Longabardi, Mike 842
ロンガメイ
Longamei, Varian 842
ロンカーリァ
Roncaglia, Silvia 1201
ロンカーリア
Roncaglia, Silvia 1201
ロンカリア
Roncaglia, Facundo 1201
ロンキ
Ronchi, Andrea 1201
ロンギ
Lange, David 788
ロング
Leung, Albert Y. 817
Long, A.A. 841
Long, Aljoscha A. 841
Long, Brian 841
Long, Chris 841
Long, Daniel 841
Long, David 841
Long, Don 841
Long, Elizabeth 841
Long, Eric 841
Long, Frederick W. 841
Long, Guillaume 841
Long, Jeannie 841
Long, Jeff 841
Long, Jeffrey 841
Long, John A. 841
Long, John H. 841
Long, Julie-Anne 841
Long, Kevin 841
Long, Kyle 841
Long, Larry 841
Long, Loren 841
Long, Melinda 841
Long, Nicholas 841
Long, Nicholas James 841
Long, Richard 842
Long, Shane 842
Long, Shawn 842
Long, Spencer 842
Long, Stephen 842
Long, Stephen Daniel 842
Long, Sylvia 842
Long, Terri 842
Long, Thomas G. 842
Long, William Ivey 842
ロングクロフト
Longcroft, Sean 842
ロングショー
Longshaw, Andy 842
ロングスウォース
Longsworth, Herman 842
ロングスタッフ
Longstaff, Alan 842
Longstff, Joshua 842
ロングストリート
Longstreet, Roy W. 842
ロングマン
Longman, Jere 842
ロングリー
Longley, Barbara 842
ロングール
Longour, Michèle 842
ロングレン
Lonegren, Sig 841
ロンゲア
Longair, Malcolm 842
ロンゲイカー
Longacre, Matt 842
ロンゲイラ
Longueira, Pablo 842
ロンゲーナ
Longhena, María 842
ロンゲネッカー
Longenecker, Clinton O. 842
ロンゲンバック
Longenbach, James 842
ロンゴ
Longo, Dan Louis 842
ロンゴ・シプレリ
Longo-ciprelli, Jeannie 842
ロンゴシワ
Longosiwa, Thomas Pkemei 842
ロンコーニ
Ronconi, Luca 1201
ロンゴボルギーニ
Longo Borghini, Elisa 842
ロンゴリア
Longoria, Evan 842
ロンジネリ
Rondinelli, Jackson 1201
ロンシャン
Longchamps, Fritz 842
ロンシュタット
Ronstadt, Frank 1201
ロンズデール
Lonsdale, Baldwin Jacobson 842
Lonsdale, Joe 842
ロンスン
Ronson, Jon 1201
ロンソン
Ronson, Jon 1201
Ronson, Mark 1201
ロンソンベーカー
Robinson-baker, Nicholas 1192
ロンダー
Londer, Olga 841
ロンチ
Ronchi, Susanna 1201
ロンチェビッチ
Rončević, Berislav 1201
ローンチベリー
Launchbury, Joe 795
ロンチャル
Lončar, Zlatibor 841
Lončar, Zoran 841
ロンディナ
Rondina, Catherine 1201
ロンド
Rondo, Rajon 1201
ロンドウ
Rondeau, Silas 1201
ロンドニョ
Londoño, Jorge Eduardo 841
ロンドニョ・オジョス
Londoño Hoyos, Fernando 841
ロンドバーグ
Rondberg, Terry A. 1201
ロンドン
Ennis-london, Delloreen 404
London, Cait 841
London, C.Alexander 841
London, Jeanie 841
London, Julia 841
London, Olivia 841
London, Robert E. 841
London, Ted 841
Rondon, Bruce 1201
Rondon, Hector 1201
Rondón, Isidro 1201
Rondon, Jose 1201
Rondon, Salomon 1201
ロンバック
Rombach, H.Dieter 1200
ロンバート
Lombard, George 841
ロンバード
Lombardo, C.Todd 841
ロンパル
Lompar, Andrija 841
ロンバルディ
Lombardi, Cristiano 841
Lombardi, Donald N. 841
Lombardi, Kristine 841
ロンバルド
Lombardo, Elizabeth 841
Lombardo, Héctor 841
ロンバン
Lomban, David 841
ロンプ
Romp, Graham 1200
ロンフェデル・アミット
Ron-Feder-Amit, Galilah 1201
ロンフェルニーニ
Lonfernini, Teodoro 841
ロンフォ
Ronfaut, Aurélie 1201
ロンブロム
Ronnblom, Anders F. 1201
ロンペッシュ
Lompech, Alain 841
ロンポ
Lompo, Francois 841
ロンボサム
Longbotham, Lori 842
ロンメル
Rommel, Frank 1200
Rommel, Manfred 1200
ロンメルスパッハー
Rommelspacher, Thomas 1200
ロンリー
Lonely, Jean M. 841
ロンロン
Rong Rong 1201

【ワ】

ワァーン
Juan, Stephen 690
ワイ
Wai, Ka-fai 1468
Wye, Trevor 1530
ワイアー
Wire, Nicky 1517
ワイアット
Wyatt, David 1530
Wyatt, James 1530
Wyatt, Jane 1530
Wyatt, Robert 1530
Wyatt, Rupert 1530
Wyatt, Stuart 1530
ワイアト
Wyatt, Jane 1530
ワイエス
Wyeth, Andrew 1530
ワイカー
Wiker, Benjamin 1503
ワイカート
Weikart, David P. 1487
ワイク
Wyke, R.Allen 1530
ワイクス
Wykes, Til 1530
ワイグル
Waiguru, Anne 1468
ワイグレ
Weigle, Sebastian 1487
ワイコフ
Wyckoff, H. 1530
Wycoff, Joyce 1530
ワイサー
Weiser, Matt 1489
ワイザー
Weiser, Philip J. 1489
ワイシック
Weissich, Paul R. 1490
ワイシャンペル
Weishampel, David B. 1489
ワイショーズ
Weisshaus, Melissa 1490
ワイス
Wais, Elmi Obsieh 1468
Waiss, Abdoulkader Doualeh 1468
Waiss, Elmi Obsieh 1468
Weis, Judith S. 1489
Weis, Margaret 1489
Weiss, Amy E. 1489
Weiss, Antonio E. 1490
Weiss, Bob 1490
Weiss, Brian Leslie 1490
Weiss, Carol H. 1490
Weiss, David J. 1490
Weiss, D.B. 1490
Weiss, Ellen 1490
Weiss, Gabriela 1490
Weiss, Gary R. 1490
Weiss, George David 1490
Weiss, Harvey 1490
Weiss, Jeff 1490
Weiss, Joshua N. 1490
Weiss, Laura B. 1490
Weiss, Lawrence G. 1490
Weiss, Lynn 1490
Weiss, Martin D. 1490
Weiss, Michael 1490
Weiss, Peter 1490
Weiss, Robin A. 1490
Weiss, Stephen L. 1490
Weiss, Steven M. 1490
Wice, Betsy 1501
ワイズ
Weisz, Rachel 1490
Wise, David 1518
Wise, David A. 1518
Wise, Dorothy 1518
Wise, Jeff 1518
Wise, Mark Ronald 1518
Wise, Michael G. 1518
Wise, Nicole 1518
Wise, Phyllis M. 1518
Wise, Richard 1518
Wise, Robert 1518
Wise, Steven M. 1518
Wise, Terence 1518
Wise, Thormas N. 1518
Wise, Tim J. 1518
Wyse, Liz 1531
ワイスコッター
Wieskotter, Tim 1503
ワイスコップ
Weisskopf, Victor Frederik 1490
ワイスコフ
Weisskopf, Victor Frederik 1490
ワイスチェクコルダス
Wieszczek-kordus, Agnieszka Jadwiga 1503
ワイズナー
Wisner, Benjamin 1518
Wisner, Erik R. 1518
ワイスハー
Weishaar, Marjorie E. 1489
ワイスハイディンガー
Weisshaidinger, Lukas 1490
ワイズバーガー
Weisberger, Lauren 1489
ワイスバーグ
Weisberg, Harold 1489
ワイズバーグ
Weisberg, Jacob 1489
ワイスバード
Weisburd, Richard Scott Jurick 1489
ワイス‐ファーナン
Weiss-Farnan, Pamela 1490
ワイスフェルド
Weisfeld, Matt A. 1489
ワイズベッカー
Weisbecker, Philippe 1489
ワイスボード
Weisbord, Marvin Ross 1489
ワイスマン
Waisman, David 1468
Weisman, Arinna 1489
Weisman, David 1489
Weissman, Myrna M. 1490
Weissman, Samuel Isaac 1490
Wuissman, David 1530
ワイズマン
Weisman, Andrew B. 1489
Weisman, Ben 1489
Weisman, Francesca 1489
Weisman, Jordan 1489
Weissman, Dick 1490
Weissman, Fabrice 1490
Weissman, Jerry 1490
Weizman, Abraham 1490
Wiseman, Alan 1518
Wiseman, Alan E. 1518
Wiseman, Donald John 1518
Wiseman, Frederick 1518
Wiseman, John 1518
Wiseman, Joseph 1518
Wiseman, Liz 1518
Wiseman, Richard 1518
Wiseman, Rosalind 1518
ワイゼンバウム
Weizenbaum, Nathan 1490
ワイゼンフェルド
Weisenfeld, Gennifer Stacy 1489
ワイセンベルク
Weissenberg, Alexis 1490
ワイセンベルグ
Weissenberg, Alexis 1490
ワイター
Whiter, Elizabeth 1499
ワイダ
Wajda, Andrzej 1468
ワイタ・アレグレ
Huaita Alegre, Marcela 630
ワイツ
Waitz, Grete 1468
Weits, John 1490
Weitz, Chris 1490
Weitz, Paul 1490
ワイツァー
Weitzer, Ronald John 1490
ワイツェル
Weitzeil, Abbey 1490
ワイツゼッカー
Weizsäcker, Carl-Friedrich von 1491
Weizsäcker, Ernst Ulrich von 1491
Weizsäcker, Richard von 1491
ワイット
Wyatt, Solange 1530
ワイツマン
Waitzman, Mimi S. 1468
Weitzman, Mark 1490
Weitzman, Martin L. 1490
Weitzman, Stuart 1490
Weizman, Ezer 1490
ワイデナー
Weidenaar, John 1487
ワイデンバウム
Weidenbaum, Murray Lew 1487
ワイデンボーム
Weidenbaum, Murray Lew 1487
ワイト
Wight, Jim 1503
ワイドナー
Weidner, Teri 1487
Widener, Chris 1501
ワイトマン
Wightman, Arthur Strong 1503
Wightman, Rob 1503
ワイドマン
Wideman, Graham 1501
ワイドリッヒ
Weidlich, Wolfgang 1487
ワイナ
Waena, Nathaniel 1467
ワイナー
Weiner, Alan M. 1488
Weiner, Bernard 1488
Weiner, David Avraham 1488
Weiner, Ellen 1488
Weiner, Eric 1488
Weiner, Irving B. 1488
Weiner, Jonathan 1488
Weiner, Kayla Miriyam 1488
Weiner, Marcella Bakur 1488
Weiner, Russ 1488
Weiner, Tim 1488
Wyner, Yehudi 1531
ワイナイナ
Wainaina, Binyavanga 1468
Wainaina, Erick 1468
ワイナンズ
Winans, BeBe 1515
Winans, CeCe 1515
ワイニンガー
Weininger, Elliot B. 1488
ワイニング
Weining, Frederick 1488
ワイブラウ
Whybrow, Alison 1501
ワイブル
Wible, Adrian 1501
ワイブレイ
Whybray, Roger Norman 1501
ワイポラ
Waipora, Japhet 1468
ワイマー
Weimer, David L. 1488
ワイマン
Whyman, Matt 1501
Wieman, Carl Edwin 1502
Wyman, Bill 1531
Wyman, Jane 1531
Wyman, Lance 1531
ワイマント
Whymant, Robert 1501
ワイモア
Wymore, Patrice 1531
ワイヤ
Wire, Antoinette Clark 1517
ワイヤー
Weir, Jamie 1489
ワイラー
Weiler, Edward John 1488
Weiler, Paul C. 1488
Wyler, Gretchen 1530
ワイランド
Weiland, K.M. 1488
ワイリ
Vail, Petr 1438
al-Waili, Shirwan 1468
ワイリー
Wiley, David A. 1505
Wiley, John, II 1505
Wiley, Luke L. 1505
Wiley, T.S. 1505
Wylie, Laura 1530
Wylie, Philip 1530
Wylie, Trish 1530
Wyllie, Timothy 1531
ワイル

ワ

Weil, Andrew 1487
Weil, Bruno 1487
Weil, David N. 1487
Weill, Sandy 1488
Weill, Sanford I. 1488
Wile, Matt 1505
Wyle, Dirk 1530
Wyle, George 1530
ワイルキエンス
Weilkiens, Tim 1488
ワイルズ
Wildes, Emma 1504
Wilds, Brandon 1504
Wiles, Deborah 1505
Wyles, Chris 1530
ワイルダー
Wilder, Billy 1504
Wilder, Clint 1504
Wilder, David A. 1504
Wilder, Deontay 1504
Wilder, Gene 1504
Wilder, James, Jr. 1504
Wilder, J.Welles, Jr. 1504
Wilder, Kris 1504
Wilder, Robert P. 1504
ワイルダマス
Wildermuth, Shawn 1504
ワイルディッシュ
Wildish, Lee 1504
ワイルディング
Wilding, Jo 1504
Wilding, Michael 1504
Wilding, Paul 1504
ワイルド
Wild, Antony 1504
Wild, David 1504
Wild, Jack 1504
Wild, John Julian 1504
Wild, Margaret 1504
Wild, Vic 1504
Wilde, Cindy 1504
Wilde, Clare 1504
Wilde, Darcie 1504
Wilde, Dean L., Ⅱ 1504
Wilde, Gerald J.S. 1504
Wilde, Jerry 1504
Wilde, Lori 1504
Wilde, Stuart 1504
ワイルドウッド
Wildwood, Christine 1505
ワイルドスミス
Wildsmith, Brian 1505
ワイルドホーン
Wildhorn, Frank 1504
ワイルドマン
Wildman, Frank 1504
Wildman-tobriner, Ben 1504
ワイルマン
Wileman, Andrew 1505
Wileman, Ralph E. 1505
ワイン
Wijn, Joop 1503
Wine, Mary 1515
ワインガーズ
Wijngaards, John 1503
ワインガードナー
Winegardner, Mark 1515
ワインガルトナー
Weingartner, Amy 1488
ワイングラス
Weinglass, Leonard 1488
ワインシュタイン
Weinstein, David E. 1489
Weinstein, Lawrence 1489
ワインズ
Wines, Jacquie 1515
ワインスタイン
Weinstein, Allen 1489
Weinstein, Amy 1489
Weinstein, Bruce D. 1489
Weinstein, David E. 1489
Weinstein, Harvey 1489
Weinstein, James N. 1489
Weinstein, Lissa 1489
ワインスティーン
Weinstein, Ellen 1489
Weinstein, Muriel Harris 1489
ワインストック
Weinstock, Arnold 1489
Weinstock, Bob 1489
Weinstock, David 1489
ワインチェンク
Weinschenk, Susan 1489
ワイントラウブ
Weintraub, Stanley 1489
ワイントラーブ
Weintraub, Bonnie S. 1489
ワイントローブ
Weintraub, Jerry 1489
Winetrobe, Boris 1515
ワインハウス
Winehouse, Amy 1515
ワインバーガー
Weinberger, Casper Willard 1488
Weinberger, David 1488
Weinberger, Peter J. 1488
Weinberger, Richard 1488
ワインバーグ
Weinberg, Alvin Martin 1488
Weinberg, Andrew David 1488
Weinberg, Bennett Alan 1488
Weinberg, Dana Beth 1488
Weinberg, Gabriel 1488
Weinberg, George H. 1488
Weinberg, Gerald M. 1488
Weinberg, Gerhard L. 1488
Weinberg, John.L 1488
Weinberg, Robert A. 1488
Weinberg, Robert E. 1488
Weinberg, Samantha 1488
Weinberg, Steven 1488
Wineberg, Mary 1515
ワインバック
Weinbach, Lawrence A. 1488
ワインバーン
Weinbren, Henrietta 1488
ワインマン
Weinman, Rosalind 1488
ワインメーカー
Winemaker, Susan 1515
ワインランド
Wineland, David 1515
ワインリッヒ
Weinrich, Wolfgang 1489
ワウ
Wau, Guma 1483
ワーウィッカー
Warwicker, John 1480
ワーウィック
Warwick, Dee Dee 1480
Warwick, Dionne 1480
Warwick, Mal 1480
ワーウィック・スミス
Warwick-Smith, Simon 1480
ワーウッド
Worwood, Valerie Ann 1527
ワウデ
Woude, A.M.van der 1527
ワウリンカ
Wawrinka, Stan 1483
Wawrinka, Stanislas 1483
ワエリ
Waeli, Ayman 1467
ワカ
Wacha, Michael 1466
ワガ
Waqa, Baron 1477
ワカナ
Wakana, Seraphine 1468
Wakana, Setsu 1468
ワガナー
Waggoner, Michael 1467
ワカマツ
Wakamatsu, Don 1468
ワカルチュク
Vakarchuk, Ivan 1438
ワーク
Wark, McKenzie 1479
ワグスタッフ
Wagstaffe, James 1468
ワクスベルク
Vaksberg, Arkadiĭ 1438
ワクター
Wachter, Robert M. 1466
ワグディ
Wagdy, Mahmoud 1467
ワクテル
Wachtel, Ellen F. 1466
Wachtel, Paul L. 1466
Wachtel, Ted 1466
ワーグナー
Wagenaar, Willem A. 1467
Wagner, Brigitte 1467
Wagner, Christoph 1467
Wagner, Clarence H., Jr. 1467
Wagner, Gudrun 1467
Wagner, Katharina 1467
Wagner, Katrin 1467
Wagner, Marsden 1467
Wagner, Siegfried 1467
Wagner, Wolfgang 1467
Wegner, Fritz 1487
ワグナー
Wagner, Andreas 1467
Wagner, Annette 1467
Wagner, Ashley 1467
Wagner, Bill 1467
Wagner, Bobby 1467
Wagner, Bret J. 1467
Wagner, Carlo 1467
Wagner, David 1467
Wagner, Dick 1467
Wagner, E.J. 1467
Wagner, Gernot 1467
Wagner, Heather Lehr 1467
Wagner, Jasmin A. 1467
Wagner, Karl 1467
Wagner, Karl Edward 1467
Wagner, Matt 1467
Wagner, Nicky 1467
Wagner, Richard E. 1467
Wagner, Richard S. 1467
Wagner, Ricky 1467
Wagner, Tony 1467
Wagner, Tyler 1467
Wagner, Ulla 1467
Wegner, Steven P. 1487
ワーグナーアウグスティン
Wagner-augustin, Katrin 1467
ワグネル
Wagner, Jaques 1467
ワグホーン
Waghorn, Terry 1467
ワークマン
Workman, Brandon 1526
ワーグマン
Wageman, Ruth 1467
ワクレンコ
Vakulenko, Oleksiy 1438
ワクング
Wakhungu, Judy 1469
ワケ
Waké, Victor 1469
ワゲ
Wague, Molla 1468
ワケナゲル
Wackernagel, Mathis 1466
ワーゲンホファー
Wagenhofer, Alfred 1467
ワコ
Wako, Amos 1469
ワコソン
Wakoson, Elias Nyammlel 1469
ワーゴナー
Wagoner, G.Richard, Jr. 1468
ワゴナー
Waggoner, Paul 1467
Waggoner, Tim 1467
Wagoner, G.Richard, Jr. 1468
Wagoner, Porter 1468
ワゴン
Wagon, S. 1467
ワーサイム
Wertheim, L.Jon 1494
ワサーマン
Wasserman, Dale 1481
ワーサル
Warsal, Ronald 1480
ワシアク
Wujciak, Connor 1530
ワジェニナ
Vazhenina, Alla 1449
ワジーエフ
Vaziev, Makharbek 1449
ワジエフ
Vaziev, Makharbek 1449
ワシコウスカ
Wasikowska, Mia 1480
ワシチェンコ
Vashchenko, Vladimir A. 1447
ワシチコフスキ
Waszczykowski, Witold 1481
ワシック
Wasik, Barbara Hanna 1480
Wasik, John F. 1480
ワジナー
Wojner, Anne W. 1520
ワジハ

al-Wajih, Sakhr Ahmed 1468
ワシャキゼ
Vashakidze, Valerian 1447
ワシャゼ
Vashadze, Grigol 1447
ワーシュ
Warsh, Sylvia Maultash 1480
ワシュカ
Waschka, Larry 1480
ワシュテル
Wachtel, Nathan 1466
ワシュニク
Vasyunik, Ivan 1448
ワシュバーガー
Andreas Waschburger 47
ワシュムート
Wassmuth, Conny 1481
ワシラ
Wassira, Stephen 1481
ワジリ
Waziri, Adamu Maina 1484
Waziri, Alhaji Idris 1484
ワシリエバ
Vassilieva, Anna 1448
ワシーリエフ
Vasil'ev, Valerii 1447
Vasiliev, Ivan 1447
Vasiliev, Vladimir Viktorovich 1447
Vassilyev, Vladimir 1448
ワシリエフ
Vasiliev, Ivan 1447
Vasiliev, Vladimir Viktorovich 1447
Vassiliev, Dimitry 1448
ワシリエワ
Vasilyeva, Olga Y. 1447
ワジル
al-Wazir, Intissar 1484
al-Wazir, Khalid Ibrahim 1484
ワジロフ
Vazirov, Zokir 1449
ワーシントン
Worthington, Sam 1527
ワージントン
Worthington, Charles 1527
Worthington, Janet Farrar 1527
ワシントン
Washington, Adolphus 1480
Washington, Charles 1480
Washington, Corey 1480
Washington, Cornelius 1480
Washington, David 1480
Washington, DeAndre 1480
Washington, Dennis 1480
Washington, Denzel 1480
Washington, Donald 1480
Washington, Dwayne 1480
Washington, Jabriel 1480
Washington, Johnny 1480
Washington, Kerry 1480
Washington, Nate 1480
Washington, Ron 1480
Washington, Tony 1480
Washington, Walter Edward 1480
ワース
Werth, Barry 1494
Werth, Jacques 1494
Werth, Jayson 1494
Wirth, Timothy Endicott 1518
Worth, Irene 1526
Worth, Taylor 1527
ワースター
Wurster, Christian 1530
ワーズディン
Wasdin, Howard E. 1480
ワスデーヴァ・ナイア・アイアンカー
Vasudeva Nair Ayyangar 1448
ワスニク
Wasnik, Mukul 1480
ワースリー
Worsley, Lucy 1526
ワーズリー
Worsley, Richard 1526
ワースレイ
Worsley, Peter 1526
ワズワース
Wadsworth, Ginger 1467
ワスン
Wathen, Dan 1481
ワセ
Wase, Brenson 1480
ワセイラ
al-Waseilah, al-Sammani al-Sheikh 1480
ワゼム
Wazem, Pierre 1484
ワーゼン
Warthen, Dan 1480
Worthen, John 1527
ワソー
Wasow, Mona 1481
Wasow, Thomas 1481
ワダ
Wada, Fred Isamu 1466
Wada, Minoru 1466
ワータイム
Wertime, Kent 1494
ワターソン
Watterson, Bill 1483
ワタナー
Watana, Muangsook 1481
ワタナベ
Watanabe, Issa 1481
Watanabe, José 1481
Watanabe, Kazuyoshi 1481
Watanabe, Masahiko 1481
Watanabe, Yoshiyuki Bill 1481
ワダニ
Wadagni, Romuald 1466
ワタヌキ
Watanuki, Shigeaki 1481
ワタラ
Ouattara, Alassane Dramane 1063
Ouattara, Bénoît 1063
Ouattara, Moussa 1063
Ouattara, Soungalo 1063
ワタンダル
Watndal, Erik 1482
ワーチ
Wertsch, James V. 1494
ワチェスバーガー
Wachsberger, Ken 1466
ワチック
Wacik, Jero 1466
ワチラロンコン
Vajiralongkorn, Maha 1438
ワチラロンコンコウタイシ
Vajiralongkorn, Maha 1438
ワチンガ
Wachinga, Dennis 1466
ワーツ
Waarts, Stephen 1466
Wirtz, Willard 1518
ワーツェル
Wortzel, Larry M. 1527
Wurtzel, Elizabeth 1530
ワッキー・エイステン
Wackie Eysten, P.A. 1466
ワックス
Wachs, Harry 1466
Wacks, Raymond 1466
Wax, Trace 1483
Wax, Wendy 1484
ワックスマン
Waxman, Sharon 1484
ワックバック
Waschbusch, Daniel A. 1480
ワックワック
Oak Oak 1040
ワッサー
Wasser, Thierry 1481
ワッサースタイン
Wasserstein, Bruce 1481
Wasserstein, Wendy 1481
ワッサーマン
Wasserman, Dale 1481
Wasserman, Lew R. 1481
Wasserman, Noam 1481
Wasserman, Tony 1481
ワッズ
al-Wazz, Hazwan 1484
ワッセルマン
Wasserman, Michel 1481
Wassermann, Zbigniew 1481
ワッソン
Wasson, Sam 1481
ワッタナ王女
Galyani Vadhana 474
ワッツ
Watts, André 1483
Watts, Barry D. 1483
Watts, Bernadette 1483
Watts, Brandon 1483
Watts, Charlie 1483
Watts, Claire 1483
Watts, Craig 1483
Watts, David V. 1483
Watts, Duncan J. 1483
Watts, Isaac 1483
Watts, Jonathan 1483
Watts, Margit Misangyi 1483
Watts, Naomi 1483
Watts, Peter 1483
Watts, Philip Beverley 1483
Watts, Shelley Marie 1483
Watts, Steven 1483
ワッデル
Waddell, Martin 1466
Waddell, Sonia 1466
ワッテンバーグ
Wattenberg, Martin 1483
ワット
Watt, Alan 1483
Watt, Chris 1483
Watt, Derek 1483
Watt, Fiona 1483
Watt, James 1483
Watt, J.J. 1483
Watt, Judith 1483
Watt, Mélanie 1483
Watt, Mitchell 1483
Watt, Ronald Stewart 1483
Watt, Sarah 1483
Watt, Tom 1483
Watt, William Montgomery 1483
ワットー
Wattoo, Mian Manzoor Ahmad 1483
ワッド
Wade, Abdoulaye 1466
Wade, Karim 1466
ワットフォード
Watford, David 1481
Watford, Earl 1481
ワットモア
Whatmore, Candice 1496
ワットン
Watton, Nick 1483
ワッハ
Wacha, Przemyslaw 1466
ワッハーブ
Wahab, Wi'am 1468
ワッブ
Wabbes, Marie 1466
ワッファオゴー
Waffa-ogoo, Susan 1467
ワツラウィック
Watzlawick, Paul 1483
ワツラヴィック
Watzlawick, Paul 1483
ワッリン
Wallin, Stefan 1472
ワディ
Waddy, Heather 1466
ワディントン
Waddington, Jeremy 1466
ワデキ
Wadecki, Adam A. 1466
ワテリー
Whateley, Jason Eric 1496
ワテル
Wachtel, Paul 1466
ワデル
Waddell, James M. 1466
Waddell, Norman 1466
Waddell, Patricia 1466
ワーテルベルグ
Waterberg, Celsius 1481
ワーテンベイカー
Wertenbaker, Timberlake 1494
ワート
Weart, Spencer R. 1484
ワード
Ward, Adam 1477
Ward, Amelia 1477
Ward, Andre 1477
Ward, Anthony 1477
Ward, Becca 1477
Ward, Beck 1477
Ward, Calvin Herbert 1477
Ward, Ivan 1477

Ward, Jared 1477
Ward, Jay 1478
Ward, Jesmyn 1478
Ward, Jessica 1478
Ward, John L. 1478
Ward, Joseph 1478
Ward, Lisa-Jane 1478
Ward, McLain 1478
Ward, O.Conor 1478
Ward, Ralph D. 1478
Ward, Simon 1478
Ward, Susan 1478
Ward, Suzanne 1478

ワドゥワ
Wadhwa, Deepa Gopalan 1466

ワトキン
Watkin, David 1481
Watkin, Henry 1481

ワトキンス
Watkins, Anna 1481
Watkins, Anne C. 1481
Watkins, D.D. 1481
Watkins, Derek 1481
Watkins, Jaylen 1481
Watkins, Jimmy 1481
Watkins, John Goodrich 1481
Watkins, Matthew 1481
Watkins, Michael 1481
Watkins, Michael D. 1481
Watkins, Richard 1481
Watkins, Sammy 1482
Watkins, Samuel Craig 1482
Watkins, Sherron 1482
Watkins, Susan M. 1482

ワトキンズ
Watkins, Claire Vaye 1481
Watkins, Evan 1481
Watkins, Graham 1481
Watkins, Jack 1481
Watkins, Tionne 1482
Watkins, Yoko Kawashima 1482

ワトキンスン
Watkinson, David 1482

ワトキンソン
Watkinson, Jeff 1482
Watkinson, Mike 1482

ワトシュタイン
Watstein, Sarah 1483

ワードスミス
Wordsmith, A.N. 1526

ワトスン
Watson, Ian 1482
Watson, John 1482
Watson, Larry 1482
Watson, Margaret 1482

ワトソン
Watson, Alan 1482
Watson, Alberta 1482
Watson, Aldren Auld 1482
Watson, Annesley J. 1482
Watson, Anthony 1482
Watson, Ben 1482
Watson, Benjamin 1482
Watson, Bubba 1482
Watson, Burton 1482
Watson, Camilla E. 1482
Watson, Christine 1482
Watson, C.J. 1482
Watson, Dekoda 1482
Watson, Devin 1482
Watson, Doc 1482
Watson, Edward 1482
Watson, Emily 1482
Watson, Emma 1482
Watson, Eral 1482
Watson, Frank Howard 1482
Watson, Fred 1482
Watson, Grant 1482
Watson, Heather 1482
Watson, Ian 1482
Watson, James Dewey 1482
Watson, James L. 1482
Watson, Jane Werner 1482
Watson, Jean 1482
Watson, Jeff 1482
Watson, Jessica 1482
Watson, Jude 1482
Watson, Karli 1482
Watson, Linda 1482
Watson, Lucy Rebecca 1482
Watson, Lyall 1482
Watson, Malcolm David 1482
Watson, Mark W. 1482
Watson, Menelik 1482
Watson, Michael 1482
Watson, Patricia J. 1482
Watson, Patrick 1482
Watson, Rachel 1482
Watson, Richard 1482
Watson, Robert 1482
Watson, Rosa Lee 1482
Watson, R.T. 1482
Watson, Russell 1483
Watson, Steven J. 1483
Watson, Terrell 1483
Watson, Tom 1483
Watson, Tony 1483
Watson, Victor 1483
Watson, Wendy 1483
Watson, Wendy L. 1483

ワード・トンプソン
Ward-Thompson, Derek 1478

ワートハイマー
Wertheimer, Alfred 1494

ワトビッツ
Wojtowycz, David 1520

ワートマン
Wortmann, Craig 1527

ワトモア
Watmore, Duncan 1482

ワドラウ
Vadlau, Lara 1437

ワトリング
Watling, Rob 1482
Watling, Roy 1482

ワードル
Wardle, David A. 1478
Wardle, Peter 1478

ワドル
Waddle, LaAdrian 1466

ワドワ
Wadhwa, Deepa Gopalan 1466

ワートン
Wharton, David A. 1496

ワーナー
Warner, Carl 1479
Warner, Chris 1479
Warner, Damian 1479
Warner, Elizabeth 1479
Warner, Jennifer 1479
Warner, Joel 1479
Warner, Malcolm-Jamal 1479
Warner, Penny 1479
Warner, Richard 1479
Warner, Sally 1479
Werner, Alex 1493
Werner, Bjoern 1493
Werner, David 1493
Werner, Emmy E. 1493
Werner, George 1493
Werner, Kirk 1493
Werner, Ruth A. 1493

ワナー
Wanner, Florian 1477

ワナウィラ・オナンゴ
Wanawilla Onango, Paulino 1475

ワナシ
Wanasi, Salah-eddin 1475

ワナビー
Warnaby, Gary 1479

ワナ・マウン・ルウィン
Wunna Maunga Lwin 1530

ワナラット
Wannarat, Channukul 1477

ワナルドゥム
Wijnaldum, Georginio 1503

ワナンディ
Wanandi, Jusuf 1475
Wanandi, Sofjan 1475

ワーニー
Warney, Jameel 1479

ワニアマ
Wanyama, Victor 1477

ワニーヴィ
Uanivi, Tjiuee 1431

ワネル
Whannell, Leigh 1496

ワーノック
Warnock, John E. 1479
Warnock, Mary 1479

ワパカブロ
Wapakhabulo, Wambogo 1477

ワーバック
Werbach, Kevin 1493

ワヒッド
Wahid, Abdurrahman 1468

ワヒディ
Vahidi, Abdul Razaq 1438

ワヒード
Waheed, Mohamed 1468
Waheed Hassan, Mohamed 1468

ワヒド
Wahid, Abdurrahman 1468
Wahid, Karim 1468

ワヒード・ハッサン
Waheed Hassan, Mohamed 1468

ワファオグ
Waffa-ogoo, Susan 1467

ワファオゴ
Waffa-ogoo, Susan 1467

ワファオゴー
Waffa-ogoo, Susan 1467

ワフィオ
Wafio, Jean Serge 1467

ワフィク
Wafiq, Tarek 1467

ワプショット
Wapshott, Nicholas 1477

ワーフスブラック
Wirfs-Brock, Rebecca 1518

ワブデヤ
Wabudeya, Beatrice 1466

ワプナー
Wapner, Jessica 1477
Wapner, Leonard M. 1477

ワプニック
Wapnick, Gloria 1477
Wapnick, Kenneth 1477

ワフバ
Wahba, Hedaya 1468

ワフワナ
Wafwana, Ngalula 1467

ワーヘナール
Wagenaar, Robert 1467

ワベリ
Waberi, Abdourahman A. 1466

ワベルズ
Wubbels, Lance 1529

ワポル
Wapol, Upio Kakura 1477

ワマルワ
Wamalwa, Eugene 1475
Wamalwa, Michael 1475

ワーマン
Werman, Robert 1493
Wurman, Richard Saul 1530

ワームズ
Worms, Penny 1526

ワムズリー
Wamsley, Keith 1475

ワームスレイ
Walmsley, A.Damien 1473

ワーラー
Warrer, Jonas 1480

ワラ
Walla, Bernard 1471
Walla, Sising Akawilou 1471

ワライチ
Warraich, Habibullah 1479

ワラウェンダー
Walawender, Richard A. 1469

ワラク
Wallach, Lori 1472

ワラシ
Wallace 1471

ワラス
Wallace, Amy 1471
Wallace, Walter L. 1472

ワラチ
Wallach, Lori 1472

ワラック
Walach, Harald 1469

ワラディ
Waradi, Taito 1477

ワラテープ
Warathep, Rattanakorn 1477

ワラドアリ
Ould Ali, El-Hadi 1064

ワーリ
Wahli, Ueli 1468

ワリ
Wali, Aminu Bashir 1469
Wali, Youssef Amin 1469

ワリー
Waly, Ghada 1475

ワ

ワリア
Walia, Hardeep 1469
Walia, Shelley 1469
ワリアッチ
Warriach, Habibullah 1480
ワリオ
Wario, Hassan 1478
ワリオニス
Valionis, Antanas 1440
ワーリック
Worick, Jennifer 1526
ワーリッチャ
Waricha, Jean 1478
ワリドゥ
Walidou, Modibo Bachir 1469
ワリナー
Wariner, Jeremy 1478
ワーリン
Werlin, Nancy 1493
ワリーン
Oualline, Steve 1063
Wallin, Stefan 1472
ワーリング
Waring, Adrian 1478
Waring, Claire 1478
ワリントン
Wallington, Aury 1472
ワルイ
Warui, Peter Mungai 1480
ワルーエフ
Valuev, Nikolay 1440
ワルグラーヴ
Walgrave, Jan 1469
ワルケンホルスト
Walkenhorst, Kira 1470
ワルゴツキ
Wargocki, Pawel 1478
ワルサー
Walser, David 1473
Walther, Steve 1474
ワルザー
Walser, Martin 1473
ワルサメ
Warsameh, Abdiweli Jama 1480
ワルシャウスキー
Warschawski, Michel 1480
ワルス
Walz, Marcus 1475
ワルゼラシビリ
Vardzelashvili, Vladimir 1446
ワルター
Walter, Fritz 1473
Walther, Eric 1474
ワルダ
Warda, Pascal 1478
ワルダク
Wardak, Abdullah 1478
Wardak, Abdul Rahim 1478
Wardak, Ghulam Farooq 1478
ワルタース
Walters, Gae 1474
ワルタニャン
Vartanian, Gevork 1447
ワルダニャン
Vardanian, Davit 1446
Vardanyan, Armen 1446
Vardanyan, Manuk 1446
Vardanyan, Vardan 1446
ワルチケビッチ
Walczykiewicz, Marta 1469
ワルチンスキー
Wallechinsky, David 1472
ワルツ
Waltz, Tom 1475
Walz, A. 1475
ワルツァー
Walzer, Norman 1475
ワルツマン
Wartzman, Rick 1480
ワルデ
Wardeh, Salim 1478
ワルテール
Walter, François 1473
ワルデン
Walden, Dana 1469
ワルド
Warde, Ibrahim 1478
ワルドナー
Waldner, Jan-Ove 1469
ワルトハイム
Waldheim, Kurt 1469
ワルドバウアー
Waldbauer, Gilbert 1469
ワールドピース
World Peace, Metta 1526
ワルドロン
Waldron, Linda 1469
ワルトン
Walton, Tracy 1475
ワルナース
Warners, Chiel 1479
ワールバーグ
Wahlberg, Mark 1468
ワルビタ
Walubita, Sipakeli 1475
ワルヒホファー
Walchhofer, Michael 1469
ワルベルク
Wallberg, Heinz 1472
ワールマン
Warman, Julieta V. 1479
ワーレ
Waare, Abdirahman Abdi 1466
Werle, Donyale 1493
ワレイ
Whalley, Oscar 1496
ワレサ
Walesa, Lech 1469
ワレス
Wallace, Amy 1471
ワレック
Walleck, A.Stephen 1472
ワレフスカ
Walevska, Christina 1469
ワーレン
Warren, Gretchen Ward 1479
ワレン
Walen, Susan R. 1469
Warren, Arnie 1479
Warren, Cat 1479
Warren, James Francis 1479
Whalen, Griff 1496
ワレンニコフ
Varennikov, Valentin Ivanovich 1446
ワロー
Wallot, Jean-Pierre 1473
ワロン
Wallon, Philippe 1473
ワン
Wan, James 1475
Wan, Li 1475
Wan, Long 1475
Wan, Michelle 1475
Wan, Samuel 1475
Wan, Zhong-cheng 1475
Wane, Ibrahima Lamine 1475
Wang, Alexander 1475
Wang, Bei-xing 1475
Wang, Bing 1475
Wang, Chen 1475
Wang, Chien-ming 1475
Wang, Chuanfu 1475
Wang, Chuanyue 1475
Wang, Dan 1475
Wang, Dao-han 1475
Wang, Dong-xing 1475
Wang, Dorothea DePrisco 1475
Wang, En-mao 1475
Wang, Eugene 1475
Wang, Fang 1475
Wang, Feng Ying 1475
Wang, Frank 1475
Wang, Gangwu 1476
Wang, Guang-mei 1476
Wang, Guang-ya 1476
Wang, Haiyan 1476
Wang, Hao 1476
Wang, Heinrich 1476
Wang, Hui 1476
Wang, Jian 1476
Wang, Jian-lin 1476
Wang, Kevin D. 1476
Wang, Le 1476
Wang, Lee-hom 1476
Wang, Le-quan 1476
Wang, Li-qin 1476
Wang, Lulu 1476
Wang, Meng 1476
Wang, Min 1476
Wang, Mingxuan 1476
Wang, Nina 1476
Wang, Paul 1476
Wang, Q.Edward 1476
Wang, Qi-min 1476
Wang, Qi-ren 1476
Wang, Qi-shan 1476
Wang, Quan-an 1476
Wang, Rung-nan 1476
Wang, Ruo-shui 1476
Wang, Ruo-wang 1476
Wang, Sam 1476
Wang, Shih-chang 1476
Wang, Shu 1476
Wang, Wayne 1476
Wang, Wei 1476
Wang, Xiang-rong 1476
Wang, Xiao-shuai 1476
Wang, Xuan 1476
Wang, Xue-zhong 1476
Wang, Yan 1476
Wang, Yang 1476
Wang, Yi 1476
Wang, Ying Wen 1476
Wang, Yng-Yuh Richard 1476
Wang, Yue 1476
Wang, Yuegu 1476
Wang, Yuja 1476
Wang, Yung 1476
Wang, Yung-ching 1476
Wang, Zengyi 1476
Wang, Zhao-guo 1476
Wang, Zhijiong 1476
Wang, Zhong-shu 1476
Wann, David 1477
Wong, Janet S. 1522
ワンカ
Wanka, Johanna 1477
ワンガオ・キジマル
Wangao-kizimale, Denis 1476
ワンガニンブロトゥ
Waqaniburotu, Dominiko 1477
ワンカール
Wankar 1477
ワンク
Wank, Andreas 1477
Wank, David L. 1477
ワング
Wang, David 1475
Wang, Huimin 1476
Wang, John X. 1476
Wang, Meg 1476
Wangu, Madhu Bazaz 1477
ワングイ
Kabuu, Lucy Wangui 694
ワンケ
Wanke, Christine A. 1477
Wanke, Daouda Mallam 1477
ワンゲ
Wangue, Didier 1477
ワンゲリン
Wangerin, Walter 1477
ワンジュナイディ
Wan Junaidi, Jaafar 1477
ワンジル
Wanjiru, Samuel 1477
ワンシンク
Wansink, Brian 1477
ワーンズ
Warnes, Tim 1479
ワンズ
Wanz 1477
ワンストラス
Wanstrath, Chris 1477
ワンダー
Wonder, Stevie 1522
ワンダーズマン
Wandersman, Abraham 1475
ワンダーマン
Wunderman, Lester 1530
ワンダーリ
Wunderle, Victor 1530
ワンチューク
Wangchuck, Jigme Khesar Namgyel 1476
Wangchuck, Jigme Singye 1477
ワンチュク
Wangchuck, Jigme Khesar Namgyel 1476
Wangchuck, Jigme Singye 1477
Wangchuck, Khandu 1477
Wangchuk, Norbu 1477
Wangchuk, Tandin 1477
Wangchuk, T.Sangay 1477
ワンデ
Ouande, Jules Bernard 1063
ワンディ
Wangdi, Dorji 1477

ワンディー
Kameaim, Wandee 699
ワンディー・シンワンチャー
Wandee Singwancha 1475
ワント
Wand, Günter 1475
ワントケ
Wandtke, Igor 1475
ワンドレス
Wandres, Alvina 1475
Wandres, Prasad David 1475
ワンナ
Wanna, John 1477
ワンニアラッチ
Wanniarachchi, Pavithra 1477
ワン・パオ
Vang Pao 1444
ワンバック
Wambach, Abby 1475
ワンブイ
Wambui, Margaret Nyairera 1475
ワンプラー
Wampler, Dean 1475
Wampler, Robert A. 1475
ワンムハマド
Wan Muhamad, Noor Matha 1477
ワンムハマトノー
Wan Muhamad, Noor Matha 1477

ン

【ン】

ン
Ng, Franees 1019
Ng, Philip 1019
Ng, Robert 1019
Ng, Sandra 1019
ンヴォヴォ
Mvovo, Lwazi 998
ンガム
Ngam, Yahya 1019
ング
Ng, Andrew 1019
Ng, Pan-Wei 1019
ングイ
Nguy, Thomson 1021
ングウェニア
Ngwenya, Takudzwa 1021
ンクルンジザ
Nkurunziza, Pierre 1029
ンゲッサン
N'guessan, Joel 1020
ンケムディック
Nkemdiche, Robert 1028
ンゲラ
Qera, Akapusi 1142
ンゴエペ
Ngoepe, Gift 1020
ンジェンゲ
Ndzengue, Pierre 1011
ンシミリマナ
Nshimirimana, Adolphe 1036
ンジャイ・ローズ
Ndiaye Rose, Doudou 1010
ンジャミ
Njami, Simon 1028
ンシンゴ
Nsingo, Marina 1036
ンダリチャコ
Ndalichako, Joyce 1010
ンチェンバ
Nchemba, Mwingulu Lameck 1010
ンディアイ
NDiaye, Marie 1010
Ndiaye, Pap 1010
ンドゥジ
Ndudi, Zherlin 1011
ントゥトゥムエマヌ
Ntoutoume Emane, Simon 1036
ンドゥール
Ndour, Maurice 1011
ンナウエ
Nnauye, Nape Moses 1029

21世紀 世界人名典拠録 欧文名
3 索 引

2017年7月25日 第1刷発行

発 行 者／大高利夫
編集・発行／日外アソシエーツ株式会社
〒140-0013 東京都品川区南大井6-16-16鈴中ビル大森アネックス
電話 (03)3763-5241(代表) FAX(03)3764-0845
URL http://www.nichigai.co.jp/
発 売 元／株式会社紀伊國屋書店
〒163-8636 東京都新宿区新宿 3-17-7
電話 (03)3354-0131(代表)
ホールセール部(営業) 電話 (03)6910-0519

電算漢字処理／日外アソシエーツ株式会社
印刷・製本／株式会社平河工業社

不許複製・禁無断転載 《中性紙H-三菱書籍用紙イエロー使用》
<落丁・乱丁本はお取り替えいたします>
ISBN978-4-8169-2671-6　　Printed in Japan,2017

本書はディジタルデータでご利用いただくことができます。詳細はお問い合わせください。